THE WEEKLY LAW REPORTS
1980

VOLUME 1

London

THE INCORPORATED COUNCIL OF LAW REPORTING
FOR ENGLAND AND WALES

3 STONE BUILDINGS, LINCOLN'S INN, LONDON, WC2A 3XN

Published by the Incorporated
Council of Law Reporting for
England and Wales · 3 Stone
Buildings, Lincoln's Inn, London,
WC2A 3XN, and printed by The
Eastern Press Ltd., London and
Reading

THE INCORPORATED COUNCIL OF LAW REPORTING FOR ENGLAND AND WALES

EDITORS AND REPORTERS

*

Editor—Carol Ellis Q.C.

Assistant Editor—Hilary Jellie, *Barrister-at-Law*

*

REPORTERS

House of Lords

F. H. Cowper   J. A. Griffiths

Privy Council

T. J. Moeran

Court of Appeal, Queen's Bench Division and Courts-Martial Appeal Court

M. M. Hill	E. M. Wellwood	A. H. Bray
L. Norman Williams	M. Gardner	H. Jellie
C. Noon	J. Winch	L. G. Stott
B. O. Agyeman	R. Davies	R. C. Williams

Chancery Division

Akhtar Razi   T. C. C. Barkworth   K. N. Busfield

Family Division

M. Bryn Davies

Employment Appeal Tribunal

J. Winch

Barristers-at-Law

HOUSE OF LORDS

Lord Chancellor: LORD HAILSHAM OF ST. MARYLEBONE

LORDS OF APPEAL IN ORDINARY

LORD WILBERFORCE
LORD DIPLOCK
VISCOUNT DILHORNE (retired August 1;
        died September 7, 1980)
LORD SALMON
      (retired September 30, 1980)
LORD EDMUND-DAVIES

LORD FRASER OF TULLYBELTON
LORD RUSSELL OF KILLOWEN
LORD KEITH OF KINKEL
LORD SCARMAN
LORD ROSKILL (appointed April 15, 1980)
LORD BRIDGE OF HARWICH
      (appointed September 29, 1980)

COURT OF APPEAL

Lord Chancellor: LORD HAILSHAM OF ST. MARYLEBONE

Lord Chief Justice of England: LORD WIDGERY (retired April 14, 1980)
LORD LANE (appointed April 15, 1980)

Master of the Rolls: LORD DENNING

President of the Family Division: Sir JOHN LEWIS ARNOLD

Sir JOHN MEGAW
      (retired September 29, 1980)
Sir DENYS BURTON BUCKLEY
Sir JOHN FREDERICK EUSTACE STEPHENSON
Sir ALAN STEWART ORR
      (retired February 1, 1980)
Sir EUSTACE WENTWORTH ROSKILL
Sir FREDERICK HORACE LAWTON
Sir ROGER FRAY GREENWOOD ORMROD
Sir PATRICK REGINALD EVELYN BROWNE
      (retired January 10, 1980)
Sir REGINALD WILLIAM GOFF
      (died January 17, 1980)
Sir NIGEL CYPRIAN BRIDGE
Sir SEBAG SHAW
Sir GEORGE STANLEY WALLER
The Hon. Sir JAMES ROUALEYN-HOVELL-
    THURLOW CUMMING-BRUCE

Sir EDWARD WALTER EVELEIGH
Sir HENRY VIVIAN BRANDON, M.C.
Sir SYDNEY WILLIAM TEMPLEMAN
Sir JOHN FRANCIS DONALDSON
Sir JOHN ANSON BRIGHTMAN
Sir DESMOND JAMES CONRAD ACKNER
      (appointed January 11, 1980)
Sir ROBIN HORACE WALFORD DUNN, M.C.
      (appointed February 29, 1980)
Sir PETER RAYMOND OLIVER
      (appointed February 29, 1980)
Sir TASKER WATKINS, V.C.
      (appointed April 15, 1980)
Sir PATRICK MCCARTHY O'CONNOR
      (appointed September 30, 1980)
Sir WILLIAM HUGH GRIFFITHS
      (appointed September 30, 1980)

CHANCERY DIVISION

Lord Chancellor: LORD HAILSHAM OF ST. MARYLEBONE

Vice-Chancellor: Sir ROBERT EDGAR MEGARRY

Sir JOHN PATRICK GRAHAM
Sir PETER HARRY BATSON WOODROFFE
    FOSTER
Sir JOHN NORMAN KEATES WHITFORD
Sir ERNEST IRVINE GOULDING
Sir RAYMOND HENRY WALTON
Sir PETER RAYMOND OLIVER
Sir MICHAEL JOHN FOX

Sir CHRISTOPHER JOHN SLADE
Sir NICOLAS CHRISTOPHER HENRY
    BROWNE-WILKINSON
Sir JOHN EVELYN VINELOTT
Sir GEORGE BRIAN HUGH DILLON
Sir MARTIN CHARLES NOURSE
      (appointed April 14, 1980)

QUEEN'S BENCH DIVISION

Lord Chief Justice of England: LORD WIDGERY (retired April 14, 1980)
LORD LANE (appointed April 15, 1980)

Sir ALAN ABRAHAM MOCATTA
Sir JOHN THOMPSON
Sir HELENUS PATRICK JOSEPH MILMO
Sir JOSEPH DONALDSON CANTLEY
Sir HUGH EAMES PARK
Sir STEPHEN CHAPMAN
Sir JOHN RAMSAY WILLIS
        (retired April 17, 1980)
Sir GRAHAM RUSSELL SWANWICK
        (retired January 9, 1980)
Sir PATRICK MCCARTHY O'CONNOR
Sir BERNARD CAULFIELD
Sir HILARY GWYNNE TALBOT
Sir WILLIAM LLOYD MARS-JONES
Sir RALPH KILNER BROWN
Sir PHILLIP WIEN
Sir PETER HENRY ROWLEY BRISTOW
Sir HUGH HARRY VALENTINE FORBES
Sir WILLIAM HUGH GRIFFITHS
Sir ROBERT HUGH MAIS
Sir NEIL LAWSON
Sir DAVID POWELL CROOM-JOHNSON
Sir TASKER WATKINS, V.C.
Sir JOHN RAYMOND PHILLIPS
Sir LESLIE KENNETH EDWARD BOREHAM
Sir JOHN DOUGLAS MAY
Sir MICHAEL ROBERT EMANUEL KERR
Sir ALFRED WILLIAM MICHAEL DAVIES
Sir JOHN DEXTER STOCKER
Sir KENNETH GEORGE ILLTYD JONES

Sir HAYDN TUDOR EVANS
Sir PETER RICHARD PAIN
Sir KENNETH GRAHAM JUPP
Sir STEPHEN BROWN
Sir ROBERT LIONEL ARCHIBALD GOFF
Sir GORDON SLYNN
Sir ROGER JOCELYN PARKER
Sir RALPH BRIAN GIBSON
Sir WALTER DEREK THORNLEY HODGSON
Sir JAMES PETER COMYN
Sir ANTHONY JOHN LESLIE LLOYD
Sir FREDERICK MAURICE DRAKE, D.F.C.
Sir BRIAN THOMAS NEILL
Sir RODERICK PHILIP SMITH
Sir MICHAEL JOHN MUSTILL
Sir BARRY CROSS SHEEN
Sir DAVID BRUCE MCNEILL
Sir HARRY KENNETH WOOLF
Sir THOMAS PATRICK RUSSELL
        (appointed January 10, 1980)
Sir PETER EDLIN WEBSTER
        (appointed April 14, 1980)
Sir THOMAS HENRY BINGHAM
        (appointed April 14, 1980)
Sir IAIN DEREK LAING GLIDEWELL
        (appointed June 3, 1980)
Sir HENRY ALBERT SKINNER
        (appointed September 30, 1980)
Sir PETER MURRAY TAYLOR
        (appointed September 30, 1980)

FAMILY DIVISION

President: Sir JOHN LEWIS ARNOLD

Sir JOHN BRINSMEAD LATEY
Sir ROBIN HORACE WALFORD DUNN, M.C.
Sir ALFRED KENNETH HOLLINGS
Sir CHARLES TREVOR REEVE
Sir FRANCIS BROOKS PURCHAS
Dame ROSE HEILBRON
Sir BRIAN DREX BUSH
Sir ALFRED JOHN BALCOMBE
Sir JOHN KEMBER WOOD

Sir RONALD GOUGH WATERHOUSE
Sir JOHN GERVASSE KENSINGTON SHELDON
Sir THOMAS MICHAEL EASTHAM
Dame MARGARET MYFANWY WOOD BOOTH
Sir CHRISTOPHER JAMES SAUNDERS FRENCH
Sir ANTHONY LESLIE JULIAN LINCOLN
Dame ANN ELIZABETH OLDFIELD
        BUTLER-SLOSS
Sir ANTHONY BRUCE EWBANK
        (appointed March 7, 1980)

Attorney-General

Sir MICHAEL HAVERS Q.C.

Solicitor-General

Sir IAN PERCIVAL Q.C.

CASES REPORTED

(Vol. 1)

HIGHWAY
Public path
Diversion order
Housing development obstructing footpath begun before diversion order published —Whether Secretary of State empowered to confirm order—Town and Country Planning Act 1971, ss. 209 (1), 210 (1)
Ashby v. Secretary of State for the Environment, C.A. **673**

Right of way
Protection of
Member of public claiming right of way over footpath—Highway authority not satisfied that public using path as of right—Whether highway authority under duty to assert right of public over path—Highways Act 1959, s. 116 (1) (as amended by Highways Act 1971, s. 70 and Local Government Act 1972, ss. 188 (2), 272 (1), Sch. 21, para. 34, Sch. 30)
Reg. v. Lancashire County Council, *Ex parte* **Guyer,** C.A. **1024**

HUSBAND AND WIFE
Divorce
Children
Practice
Joint custody order—Procedure to secure uniformity of practice in making order —Matrimonial Causes Act 1973, s. 41
Practice Direction (Child: Joint Custody Order), Fam.D. **301**

Financial provision
Agreement
Jurisdiction of court
Deed of separation negotiated by parties' legal advisers—Wife agreeing against legal advice and without duress not to seek capital payment other than provided by deed—Whether wife entitled to lump sum award on divorce— Matrimonial Causes Act 1973, ss. 23, 25 (1)
Edgar v. Edgar, C.A. **1410**

Conduct of parties
After decree absolute
Harassment of ex-husband after financial and property rights determined— Variation of periodical payments order—Whether subsequent conduct to be taken into account—Matrimonial Causes Act 1973, s. 31 (7)
J. (H. D.) v. J. (A. M.) (Financial Provision: Variation), Sheldon J. **124**

Dismissal of claim
Absence of consent
Wife claiming periodical payments for self and children—Dismissal of claim without consent—Whether court having jurisdiction to dismiss claim for children or for wife—Matrimonial Causes Act 1973, s. 23 (1)
Carter v. Carter, C.A. **390**

Divorce proceedings
" Clean break " order
Whether nominal periodical payments order desirable
Dunford v. Dunford, C.A. **5**
Provision for children
School fees—Order for fees to be paid direct to school—Tax relief—Form of order
Practice Direction (Minor: School Fees), Fam.D. **1441**

Pre-trial review
Procedure
Property adjustment and lump sum applications—Consideration of settlement of claim or clarification of issues—Applicant's affidavit—Matters to be set out —Need for attendance by counsel or solicitors—Matrimonial Causes Act 1973, ss. 23 (1), 24 (1)
Practice Direction (Pre-trial Review: Financial Provisions), Fam.D. **245**

Justices
Evidence
Witness present in court
No order excluding witnesses from court—Admissibility of evidence—Practice in matrimonial proceedings
Tomlinson v. Tomlinson, D.C. **322**

Maintenance
Quantum
Young unqualified wife without experience of employment—Jurisdiction to make order limited in time—Matrimonial Proceedings (Magistrates' Courts) Act 1960, s. 2 (1) (*b*)
Khan (Sajid) v. Khan (Sajid), D.C. **355**

PRACTICE
Chancery Division
Bespeaking order
Duty to bespeak judgment or order within seven days—Undue delay—Applications for leave to draw up order where excessive delay—Costs of application—R.S.C., Ord. 42, r. 7 (2) (3) **Practice Direction (Chancery: Bespeaking Orders),** Sir Robert Megarry V.-C. **754**

Costs
Assessment in chambers—Monetary limit of costs assessed or settled in chambers **Practice Direction (Costs: Assessment in Chambers) (No. 2), Ch.D. 1386**

Motion
Revised procedure for listing and hearing motions **Practice Direction (Chancery Division: Motions Procedure),** Ch.D. **751**

Discontinuance of action
Interim payments, effect of
Portuguese plaintiff injured on American ship in English port—English personal injuries action—Defendants making interim payments—Notice of discontinuance without leave—Injunction to restrain proceedings for higher damages in United States—Whether notice of discontinuance and injunction valid—R.S.C., Ord. 21, r. 2 (1) (2); Ord. 29, r. 9 **Castanho v. Brown and Root (U.K.) Ltd.,** Parker J. and C.A. **833**

Discovery
Motion for
Bank's customers obtaining moneys by forgery—Injured party's action seeking reimbursement—Interlocutory claim for bank to disclose confidential information concerning customers—Customers neither within jurisdiction nor served with notice of motion—Whether obligation on bank to assist in tracing action **Bankers Trust Co. v. Shapira, C.A. 1274**
Ex parte application for order to enter premises and remove documents—Plaintiff fearing destruction of documents in defendant's custody—Whether relief to be granted **Yousif v. Salama, C.A. 1540**

Privilege
Confidentiality—Child care records—Personal injuries' claim for breach of duty while child in local authority's care—Whether confidentiality of documents to be preserved—Whether court to inspect documents—Administration of Justice Act 1970, s. 31—R.S.C., Ord. 24, r. 7A (1) **Gaskin v. Liverpool City Council, C.A. 1549**

Judgment in default of appearance
Mareva injunction
Claim for liquidated damages and Mareva injunction—Mareva injunction granted—Application for leave to sign judgment in default of appearance—Court's jurisdiction to grant leave and continue Mareva injunction—R.S.C., Ord. 13, r. 6 **Stewart Chartering Ltd. v. C. & O. Managements S.A. (Practice Note),** Robert Goff J. **460**

Parties
Joinder
Joinder of defendant to action after claim against him statute-barred—Unconditional appearance to amended writ—Whether waiver of irregularity—Whether properly joined as party to action—R.S.C., Ord. 15, r. 6 (2) (a) **Liff v. Peasley, C.A. 781**

Payment into court
Payment out
Interest—Leave to defend on condition sum paid into court—Defendant serving notice of appropriation—Plaintiff not accepting moneys appropriated in settlement of claim—Order for money to be paid out to defendant—Whether payment out to include interest accrued on sum—Supreme Court Funds Rules 1975, r. 27 (1) (3) **Schroeder v. Accountant General, Woolf J. 1314**

Pleadings
Counterclaim
Writ issued in respect of dishonoured cheque—No defence—Summary judgment for plaintiffs—Judgment debt satisfied—Defendants purporting to serve counterclaim—Whether service valid—R.S.C., Ord. 15, r. 2 (1) **C.S.I. International Co. Ltd. v. Archway Personnel (Middle East) Ltd.,** C.A. **1069**

Possession of land
Order for possession
Students occupying part of university premises—Summary proceedings for possession of land—Whether order for possession to be limited to area occupied by students—R.S.C., Ord. 113, rr. 1, 2 **University of Essex v. Djemal, C.A. 1301**

REVENUE

Capital gains tax

Computation of gain

Allowable deductions—Repairs and improvements to cottage by taxpayer—Capital gain on sale of cottage—Whether notional value of taxpayer's labour deductible from gain as "amount of any expenditure" incurred on asset—Finance Act 1965, s. 22 (9), Sch. 6, para. 4 (1) **Oram v. Johnson, Walton J. 558**

Disposal of assets

Agreement establishing trust to hold shares in family company—Power of shareholders to dispose of shares to outsiders restricted by transfer to trustees—Whether shareholder transferring shares under agreement absolutely entitled as against trustees—Whether disposal of assets giving rise to chargeable gain—Finance Act 1965, s. 22 (5) **Booth v. Ellard, C.A. 1443**

Sale of shares for fixed price immediately payable plus deferred consideration in undetermined amount—Gain accruing on receipt of deferred consideration—Whether initial value of right to deferred consideration chargeable to tax at time of sale—Whether taxable as deemed disposal of assets on entitlement to deferred consideration matured—Whether right to deferred consideration within exemption from chargeable gains for "debts"—Finance Act 1965, s. 22 (1) (3), Sch. 7, para. 11 (1) (as amended by Finance Act 1968, Sch. 12, para. 8 (1)) **Marren v. Ingles, H.L.(E.) 983**

Capital transfer tax

Settled property

Capital distributions—Exemption for government securities held by non-resident trustees—Non-resident beneficiaries becoming entitled to interests in possession—Whether status as "excluded property" determined immediately before taxable event—Whether charities beneficially entitled to interest in possession—Finance Act 1975, Sch. 5, para. 6 (2) (4), Sch. 7, para. 3 (1) (2) **Von Ernst & Cie S.A. v. Inland Revenue Comrs., C.A. 468**

Corporation tax

Capital allowances

Industrial building—Security area for wage-packeting and cash storage by security company—Whether expenditure on construction expenditure on "industrial building" to qualify for allowance—Whether coins and notes of currency "goods"—Whether wage-packeting activity subjection of "goods" to "any process"—Capital Allowances Act 1968, ss. 1 (1), 7 (1) (e) **Buckingham v. Securitas Properties Ltd., Slade J. 380**

Chargeable gains

Allowable deductions—Investment company acquiring securities in exchange for issue of its own shares—Conditional agreement stipulating price of securities and number of shares to be issued in exchange—Market value of shares falling before completion of agreement—Value of consideration given for securities—Finance Act 1965, Sch. 6, para. 4 (1) (a) **Stanton v. Drayton Commercial Investment Co. Ltd. Vinelott J. 1162**

Expenses of trade

Parent company seconding employee to work for overseas subsidiary—Expenditure incurred by parent company in its own interest—Subsidiary benefiting from expenditure—Whether expenditure wholly and exclusively for purposes of parent company's trade—Income and Corporation Taxes Act 1970, s. 130 (a) **Robinson v. Scott Bader Co. Ltd., Walton J. 755**

Profits of trade

Acquisition and development of properties—Portfolio of investments—Object to float public company—Adverse business prospects—Sale of properties—Whether proceeds trading profits—Finance Act 1965, ss. 53, 77 **Simmons (as liquidator of Lionel Simmons Properties Ltd.) v. Inland Revenue Comrs., H.L.(E.) 1196**

Customs and excise

Duty chargeable

Rebate on heavy oil duty for certain uses—Specific penalties for misuse and provision entitling commissioners to recover amount equal to rebate—Pecuniary penalties recoverable in magistrates' court—Whether jurisdiction in civil courts to entertain commissioners' action to recover unpaid amount of rebate—Hydrocarbon Oil (Customs & Excise) Act 1971, s. 11 (1) **Customs and Excise Comrs. v. George Wimpey & Co. Ltd., C.A. 1003**

REVENUE—*continued*
Income tax
Appeal to commissioners
Construction company failing to make proper deductions from payments to sub-contractors—Collector of taxes refusing to exonerate company—Whether commissioners empowered to review exercise of discretion conferred on collector of taxes —Finance Act 1971, ss. 29 (4), 30 (1)—Income Tax (Payments to Sub-Contractors in the Construction Industry) Regulations 1971, reg. 6 (3)—Taxes Management Act 1970, s. 50 (6)   **Slater v. Richardson & Bottoms Ltd.,** Oliver J. **563**

Discretionary trusts, income of
Charge at additional rate—Settled property held on discretionary trust—Non-resident trustee—Trust income including distributions from United Kingdom companies— Distributions not chargeable to basic rate tax in hands of non-resident trustee— Whether chargeable at additional rate—Finance Act 1973, s. 16 (1)
Inland Revenue Comrs. v. Regent Trust Co. Ltd., Slade J. **688**

Employment
Payment on termination of employment—Award by industrial tribunal for unfair dismissal—Employee incurring expenditure on seeking new employment and on legal representation before tribunal—Whether expenditure deductible in computing liability to tax—Income and Corporation Taxes Act 1970, s. 187 (1) (2)
Warnett v. Jones, Slade J. **413**

Overseas earnings
United Kingdom resident's earnings abroad—Tax avoidance scheme—Taxpayer's overseas activities carried out on behalf of partnership between taxpayer and foreign company—Taxpayer's share of profits not remitted to United Kingdom— Whether company entitled to enter into partnership—Whether income from overseas activities partnership income—Whether taxpayer's unremitted share of partnership profits subject to United Kingdom tax—Income and Corporation Taxes Act 1970, ss. 109 (1) (2), 122, 153 (1)   **Newstead v. Frost,** H.L.(E.) **135**

Schedule D, Case VI
Agreement made in United Kingdom—Non-resident wife of criminal selling life story to newspaper—Whether money received by her capital or income—Whether profits or gains arising or accruing from property in United Kingdom—Income and Corporation Taxes Act 1970, s. 108   **Alloway v. Phillips,** C.A. **888**

Settlement
Annual payments to parents under deeds of covenant—Payments made out of covenantor's earned income—Whether investment income chargeable to tax at additional rates—Income and Corporation Taxes Act 1970, ss. 454 (1) (3), 457 (as amended by Finance Act 1971, Sch. 6, para. 67)   **Ang v. Parrish,** Walton J. **940**

Tax avoidance
Artificial transactions in land—Scheme designed and carried out whereby gains arising on sale of land in United Kingdom realised by non-resident companies— Taxpayer director of United Kingdom companies through which scheme implemented—Whether " opportunity of realising a gain, provided directly or indirectly " by taxpayer—Whether taxpayer liable to tax on part of gains still unrealised— Income and Corporation Taxes Act 1970, ss. 488 (2) (3) (6) (8), 489 (13)
Yuill v. Wilson, H.L.(E.) **910**

Value added tax
Gift of goods under £10
Company operating special retail schemes—Associated mail order company supplying goods without charge to agents under incentive scheme—Assessment by commissioners including tax on open market value of incentive supplies—Whether company accountable to tax on such supplies—Whether such supplies exempt as gifts —Finance Act 1972, Sch. 3, para. 6
G.U.S. Merchandise Corpn. Ltd. v. Customs and Excise Comrs.,
Woolf J. **1508**
Receiver's liability
Company in hands of receiver and manager—Company trading and charging tax —No personal liability on receiver to account for tax—Whether having discretion concerning payment of tax—Law of Property Act 1925, s. 109 (8)
In re John Willment (Ashford) Ltd., Brightman J. **73**

Return
Daily penalty imposed for failure to make return—Period of default—Whether terminating at date of information or to be calculated at date of hearing— Finance Act 1972, s. 38 (7)   **Grice v. Needs,** D.C. **45**

TRUSTS
Trustee
Breach of trust
Trustees dissipating trust funds—Solicitor assisting trustees in contravening terms of trust—Liability of solicitor's partner for breaches of trust—Trustees' liability to replace assets dissipated—Whether estate duty saving to be deducted in assessing compensation—Partnership Act 1890, ss. 10, 11
In re **Bell's Indenture,** Vinelott J. **1217**

WILL
Construction
Gift to non-charitable association
Gift to " Labour Party property committee " for benefit of constituency labour party —Rules of association alterable by outside body—Whether legacy valid
In re **Grant's Will Trusts,** Vinelott J. **360**

Substitutionary gift
Gift of capital to three named persons after termination of life interests " or their heirs and surviving issue "—Meaning of " surviving issue " and " heirs " in context —Whether reversionary interests vesting in heirs of those predeceasing last life tenant—Whether beneficiaries taking as joint tenants or tenants in common—Law of Property Act 1925, s. 132   *In re* **Bourke's Will Trusts,** Slade J. **539**

WORDS AND PHRASES
" *Agreement . . . on reasonable terms* "—Towns Ordinance (Laws of Fiji, 1967 rev., c. 106), s. 136 (1)   **Mukta Ben v. Suva City Council,** P.C. **767**
" *Agriculture* "—Rent (Agriculture) Act 1976, s. 1 (1) (*a*)
Earl of Normanton v. Giles, H.L.(E.) **28**
" *Amount of any expenditure* "—Finance Act 1965, Sch. 6, para. 4 (1) (*b*)
Oram v. Johnson, Walton J. **558**
" *Any process* "—Capital Allowances Act 1968, s. 7 (1) (*e*)
Buckingham v. Securitas Properties Ltd., Slade J. **380**
" *Banker's book* "—Bankers' Books Evidence Act 1879, s. 9   **Barker v. Wilson,** D.C. **884**
" *By reference to this Act* "—Race Relations Act 1976, s. 2 (1) (*c*)
Kirby v. Manpower Services Commission, E.A.T. **725**
" *Charges and expenses* "—Companies Act 1948, s. 267
In re **Mesco Properties Ltd.,** C.A. **96**
" *Claims* "—Arbitration Act 1950, s. 27
Sioux Inc. v. China Salvage Co., Kwangchow Branch, C.A. **996**
" *Contention* "—General Rate Act 1967, s. 76 (5)
Ellesmere Port and Neston Borough Council v. Shell U.K. Ltd., C.A. **205**
" *Debts* "—Finance Act 1965, s. 22 (1) (*a*)   **Marren v. Ingles,** H.L.(E.) **983**
" *Decision . . . on an appeal* "—Town and Country Planning Act 1971, s. 242 (3) (*b*)
Co-operative Retail Services Ltd. v. Secretary of State for the Environment, C.A. **271**
" *Discharged* "—Insolvency Act 1976, s. 7 (4) (*a*)
In re **A Debtor (No. 13 of 1964),** *Ex parte* **The Official Receiver v. The Debtor,** D.C. **263**
" *Disturbance* "—Finance Act 1969, Sch. 19, para. 11 (1)
Stoke-on-Trent City Council v. Wood Mitchell & Co. Ltd., C.A. **254**
" *Domestic sewage* "—Public Health (Drainage of Trade Premises) Act 1937, s. 14 (1)
Thames Water Authority v. Blue and White Launderettes Ltd., C.A. **700**
" *Excluded property* "—Finance Act 1975, Sch. 7, para. 3 (1)
Von Ernst & Cie S.A. v. Inland Revenue Comrs., C.A. **468**
" *Facilities . . . to the public* "—Sex Discrimination Act 1975, s. 29 (1)
Reg. v. Immigration Appeal Tribunal, *Ex parte* **Kassam,** C.A. **1037**
" *Firearm* "—Licensing Act 1872, s. 12   **Seamark v. Prouse,** D.C. **698**
" *Full-time course of study* "—Statement of Changes in Immigration Rules (1980), para. 22
Reg. v. Chief Immigration Officer, Gatwick Airport, *Ex parte* **Kharrazi,** C.A. **1396**
" *Furtherance of a trade dispute* "—Trade Union and Labour Relations Act 1974, s. 13 (1) (as amended)
Duport Steels Ltd. v. Sirs, Kenneth Jones J., C.A. and H.L.(E.) **142**
" *Goods* "—Capital Allowances Act 1968, s. 7 (1) (*e*)
Buckingham v. Securitas Properties Ltd., Slade J. **380**
" *Heard* "—Bankruptcy Rules 1952, r. 179
In re **A Debtor (No. 44 of 1978),** *Ex parte* **The Debtor v. Chantry Mount and Hawthorns Ltd.,** D.C. **665**
" *Heir* "—Law of Property Act 1925, s. 132 (1)   *In re* **Bourke's Will Trusts,** Slade J. **539**
" *Homeless intentionally* "—Housing (Homeless Persons) Act 1977, s. 17 (1)
Dyson v. Kerrier District Council, C.A. **1205**
" *Industrial building* "—Capital Allowances Act 1968, s. 1 (1)
Buckingham v. Securitas Properties Ltd., Slade J. **380**

WORDS AND PHRASES—*continued*

ERRATA

[1980] 1 W.L.R.

Page 2ʙ, line 14; *for* " February 17," *read* " January 23,"

Page 13ᴅ, line 22: *for* " March 15, 1974 " *read* " March 25, 1974."

Page 174ᴀ, lines 4–5: *for* the appearances for the Secretary of State
read
   Sir Michael Havers Q.C., A.-G., Simon D. Brown and *John Laws*
(of the English Bar) and *John Martin* (of the Northern Ireland and
English Bars) for the Secretary of State.

Page 227ɢ, line 42: *for* " the resolution as passed be the same "
         read " the resolution as passed had to be the same."

Page 246ᴅ, line 18: for " *allegations ' in support of '* "
      read " *allegations ' relevant in support of.'* "

Page 278ᴅ, line 32: *for* " vendors " *read* " purchasers "

Page 614ᴄ, line 12: The dates of hearing should read " 1979 Dec. 3, 4 "

Page 1102ʙ, line 15: for " October " *read* " October 1977."

Page 1175ʜ, lines 43 and 44 should read:
   " *Held,* allowing the appeal, that *Clarke* v. *Winchurch* laid down no
principle of law but was a decision on its own facts "

A

The Weekly Law Reports

B

Volume 1

Containing those cases of value to practitioners which are not intended to be included in The Law Reports, together with practice notes and directions.

C

[COURT OF APPEAL]

* REGINA *v.* FOLAN

D

1979 Feb. 13   Waller L.J., Lawson and Jupp JJ.

Crime—Sentence—Suspended sentence—Offence during currency of suspended sentence—Sentence in respect of offence—No order in respect of suspended sentence—Whether matter determined —Powers of Criminal Courts Act 1973 (c. 62), ss. 23 (1) (d), 25 [1]

E

The defendant was sentenced at the Crown Court to 18 months' imprisonment suspended for two years for burglary. During the currency of the suspended sentence he committed a further offence of burglary in respect of which the Crown Court made a community service order for 120 hours. He admitted before that court that a suspended sentence had been imposed in respect of a previous offence but no order was made in respect of that suspended sentence. He failed to comply with the community service order and was committed to the Crown Court to be dealt with. The judge revoked the community service order and sentenced the defendant to 12 months' imprisonment. He also ordered that the suspended sentence should take effect with the substitution of a term of six months' for the original term, to run consecutively.

On appeal against the sentence of six months' in respect of the suspended sentence:—

Held, allowing the appeal, that where a defendant was convicted of an offence punishable with imprisonment during the currency of a suspended sentence and the court before whom he was appearing had power to deal with that suspended sentence it was under a duty under section 23 (1) of the Powers

F

G

[Reported by MISS KATE O'HANLON, Barrister-at-Law]

H

[1] Powers of Criminal Courts Act 1973, s. 23: " (1) Where an offender is convicted of an offence punishable with imprisonment committed during the operational period of a suspended sentence and either he is so convicted by or before a court having power under section 24 of this Act to deal with him in respect of the suspended sentence or he subsequently appears or is brought before such a court, then, unless the sentence has already taken effect, that court shall consider his case and deal with him by one of the following methods:—. . . (d) it may make no order with respect to the suspended sentence; "

S. 25: " (1) If it appears to the Crown Court, . . . that an offender has been convicted . . . of an offence punishable with imprisonment committed during the operational period of a suspended sentence and that he has not been dealt with in respect of the suspended sentence, that court . . . may . . . issue a summons . . . "

2

The Weekly Law Reports, January 11, 1980

Reg. v. Folan (C.A.) [1980]

of Criminal Courts Act 1973 to consider the case and deal A
with the matter in one of the ways prescribed in paragraphs
(*a*) to (*d*) of the subsection; that since subsection (*d*) provided
for the court to make no order with respect to the suspended
sentence, it must have dealt with the matter under that paragraph when making the community service order and,
accordingly, the court had no jurisdiction when dealing with
the offence for which the community service order was imposed
to reconsider the defendant's suspended sentence. B
Per curiam. If a further offence were committed during the
currency of the suspended sentence the court would have power
to deal with it afresh under section 23 (1).

APPEAL against sentence.

On February 17, 1976, the defendant, Peter Paul Folan, was sentenced
at Huddersfield Crown Court to 18 months' imprisonment suspended for C
two years for burglary, with six offences taken into consideration. On
February 7, 1978, a community service order for 120 hours was made by
the same court in respect of a burglary committed on September 12,
1977. Before that court he admitted that he was subject to a suspended
sentence. On June 12, 1978, he was brought before the Huddersfield
Magistrates' Court and committed to Huddersfield Crown Court to be
dealt with under section 16 (3) (*b*) of the Powers of Criminal Courts Act D
1973 for breach of that community service order. On July 20, 1978, Judge
Randolph revoked the community service order and substituted a sentence
of 12 months' imprisonment. He also put six months of the suspended
sentence into effect, to run consecutively.

The defendant appealed against sentence.

E
Gordon Lakin for the defendant.

JUPP J. gave the judgment of the court. This is an application for leave
to appeal against an order made on July 20, 1978, in the Huddersfield
Crown Court. The defendant had been brought there, committed by the
justices, for failing to comply with a community service order made on an
earlier occasion. Little need be said about the offence in respect of which F
the community service order was passed. It had taken place on September
12, 1977. A drinking club had been broken into and the defendant was
charged with burglary. He was with another man. Together they took a
total of £260 from the cash box and the till. There was something of a
scene when police officers with a police dog went into the club to arrest
them.

G
The judge dealt with the matter under section 16 of the Powers of
Criminal Courts Act 1973. He revoked the community service order, and
sentenced the defendant to 12 months' imprisonment for that offence.

It has not been suggested before this court that there is anything wrong
with that sentence; nor could it be, considering the defendant's record.
He had been before a court no less than nine times as a juvenile for various
offences of dishonesty. Following that he went to borstal training for H
burglary in 1973, and three months' imprisonment for burglary and wounding in 1974. There were fines for further burglary offences after that, and
he was also in trouble for drug offences and a small matter of disorderly
conduct before the community service order was made against him.

The matter for appeal arises out of a further order made on July 20,
1978, at Huddersfield. It was made to appear to the judge that on
January 23, 1976, also for burglary and with six other offences taken into

A consideration, the defendant had been sentenced to 18 months' imprisonment suspended for two years. It followed that the commission of the burglary at the sports club in September 1977 was committed during the currency of the suspended sentence, some 17 months after it was passed. The judge ordered six months of the suspended sentence to come into effect to be served consecutively to the 12 months he had already passed. The question is whether the judge had jurisdiction to deal with the

B suspended sentence when dealing with the offence in respect of which the community service order had been made. The answer depends upon whether or not the court which made the community service order dealt at the same time with the suspended sentence. It is clear from the Powers of Criminal Courts Act 1973 that the matter might fall within one of two categories. Under section 23 of the Act the court before whom

C an offender is convicted of an offence punishable with imprisonment committed during the operational period of a suspended sentence " shall consider his case and deal with him by one of the following methods . . ." The four methods are set out in paragraphs (a) to (d). Paragraph (d) reads: " it may make no order with respect to the suspended sentence." On the other hand it is clear that the Act does contemplate circumstances, under section 25, where the court just does not deal with a suspended sentence at

D all. The sidenote to that section is: " Procedure where court convicting of further offence does not deal with suspended sentence." In this case it is unfortunate that counsel for the prosecution informed the judge that no action had been taken in respect of the suspended sentence by the court which made the community service order. It is true that later the matter is referred to by saying no order was made and it is also true that in a copy of the antecedents which counsel has shown this court the matter is entered

E as " no action re breach." This must have been misleading for it uses words which are quite unsuited to what in fact happened.

　　Counsel, Mr. Lakin, who appears before us was present in court on the earlier occasion when the community service order was made, and he tells us that on that occasion his client was asked whether he admitted that a suspended sentence had been passed on him earlier. He did so. The court

F therefore had before it the question of the suspended sentence and was, under section 23, bound to deal with the matter. Accordingly it must follow that, when the court made no order, it was making a decision under section 23 (1) (d) to make no order, which is one of the methods by which the court may deal with the offender. That being so, undoubtedly there was no power in any subsequent court to deal again with the same breach of suspended

G sentence. The suspended sentence of course continued and if there was a further breach it may well have been dealt with, but that breach had been considered and dealt with under section 23 of the Powers of Criminal Courts Act 1973 by the court deciding that no further action should be taken. Accordingly the judge at the Huddersfield Crown Court, on July 20, 1978, had no power to order the suspended sentence to come into operation.

　　In effect this is a point of law and no leave is, in the event, required for

H the submission that has been made to us. The appeal will be allowed by quashing the sentence of six months' imprisonment consecutive. The sentence of 12 months' imprisonment stands.

Appeal allowed.

Solicitor: *Registrar of Criminal Appeals.*

A

* PRACTICE NOTE
(MATRIMONIAL PROPERTY: ORDER FOR SALE)

Husband and Wife—Property—Practice—Sale of property—Court's B
jurisdiction to make order without specific application under
Acts of 1882 or 1925—Married Women's Property Act 1882
(45 & 46 Vict., c. 75), s. 17—Law of Property Act 1925 (15 & 16
Geo. 5, c. 20), s. 30—Matrimonial Causes Act 1973 (c. 18), s. 24

On May 1, 1979, in an unreported case of *Ward* v. *Ward and Greene,*
post, p. 4, the Court of Appeal held that judges and registrars have power
to order sale of property under section 24 of the Matrimonial Causes Act C
1973 and without specific application under section 17 of the Married
Women's Property Act 1882 or section 30 of the Law of Property Act 1925.

This decision is of considerable importance to practitioners but is not
generally known. The President considers that it should be given wide
publicity.

R. L. BAYNE-POWELL,
Senior Registrar. D
December 4, 1979.

NOTE E

* WARD v. WARD AND GREENE

1979 May 1 Ormrod L.J. and Sir David Cairns F

Husband and Wife—Property—Practice—Sale of property—Court's
jurisdiction to make order without specific application under
Acts of 1882 or 1925—Married Women's Property Act 1882
(45 & 46 Vict., c. 75), s. 17—Law of Property Act 1925 (15 & 16
Geo. 5, c. 20), s. 30—Matrimonial Causes Act 1973 (c. 18),
ss. 23, 24

G

APPEAL from Dunn J.

S. A. *Ritchie Q.C.* and David *Wurtzel* for the appellant.
Anthony *Ewbank Q.C.* and N. R. *Warren* for the respondent.

ORMROD L.J. gave a judgment, which does not call for report, in favour H
of dismissing the appeal, and continued: Before leaving it finally, however,
there is one point with which I want to deal. At the outset of his judgment Dunn J. referred to the fact that he had suggested that the husband
should issue a pro forma summons under section 17 of the Married
Women's Property Act 1882 asking for the sale of the former matrimonial

---

[Reported by ROBERT WILLIAMS, ESQ., Barrister-at-Law]

A home. This is a point which has been raised from time to time, which I know is concerning the Law Commission at the moment. I have heard it suggested on a number of occasions that in order for the court to make an order for a sale under the Matrimonial Causes Act 1973, sections 23 and 24, it is necessary to issue proceedings under either section 17 of the Married Women's Property Act 1882 or, in appropriate cases, under section 30 of the Law of Property Act 1925.

B   For my part, I have never understood the advantages of multiplying pieces of paper intituled in particular statutes named at the head of the summons. It seems to me to be quite clear that section 17 of the Act of 1882 gives the court power to order a sale—certainly as clarified by the Matrimonial Causes (Property and Maintenance) Act 1958—in proceedings between husband and wife in connection with property. Section 30 of the

C Law of Property Act 1925 gives the court power to order a sale where there is a trust for sale, and to my mind it cannot matter what the nature of the proceedings is; what matters is whether the circumstances are such as to bring the case within one or another of those Acts which give the necessary power to the court to order the sale. So I think it may be helpful if we were to say that it is not necessary to intitule proceedings as being under the Married Women's Property Act 1882 or the Law of Property Act 1925, or

D to issue pro forma summonses to enable the court to exercise its powers to order a sale where the circumstances justify it under one or other of those Acts. I hope that may be a helpful observation.

    SIR DAVID CAIRNS gave his reasons for dismissing the appeal and continued: I respectfully agree with what Ormrod L.J. has added to his

E judgment about the absence of any need for such a pro forma summons under section 17 of the Married Women's Property Act 1882 as the judge thought necessary.

Appeal dismissed.

Solicitors: *Abbott Thomas & Co.; Max A. Adler.*

F

———————

[COURT OF APPEAL]

* DUNFORD v. DUNFORD

G
1979 June 28   Lord Denning M.R. and Eveleigh L.J.

Husband and Wife—Matrimonial home—Divorce—Ownership of house—Wife living with children in matrimonial home—Order for transfer of husband's interest to wife—Husband's quarter charge on proceeds of sale when sold or death of wife

Husband and Wife—Financial provision—Divorce proceedings—

H *"Clean break" order—Whether nominal periodical payments order desirable*

    The parties were married in 1962. In 1971 they bought a council house in their joint names for £3,950 with a 100 per cent. mortgage. After a decree nisi of divorce in December 1978 the wife stayed in the matrimonial home with the three children of the family, aged 15, 13 and 11, and the husband moved into lodgings. His gross income was £93 a week. The wife earned £37 a week gross from part-time work and received

A for the children maintenance from the husband and social security benefit. About £3,600 remained outstanding on the mortgage.

The county court registrar ordered that the house was not to be sold until the youngest child had finished full-time education and that the husband should pay £5 a week maintenance for the wife and £7.50 a week for each child. On appeal Judge Galpin ordered the husband to transfer his interest in the house to the wife within three months and the house to B be charged with payment to the husband of one quarter of the net proceeds of sale when sold or on the death of the wife without regard to any future mortgage taken out by her. The judge reduced the order for periodical payments for the wife to 5p per annum and maintained the weekly payments order for the children.

On appeal by the husband, who contended inter alia that the judge failed to make any provision for the petitioner's C remarriage or cohabitation with another man, and cross appeal by the wife:—

Held, that the judge's order transferring the house to the wife within three months subject to the husband's quarter charge on sale or death of the wife fairly crystallised the interests of the parties, so that they knew where they stood with regard to the future, and was in accordance with the principle of the " clean break "; but that in accordance with that principle D the nominal order for periodical payments to the wife of 5p per annum should be struck out of the order.

Dicta of Lord Scarman in *Minton* v. *Minton* [1979] A.C. 593, 608, H.L.(E.) and Ormrod L.J. in *Hanlon* v. *Hanlon* [1978] 1 W.L.R. 592, 599, C.A. applied.

The following cases are referred to in the judgments:

Hanlon v. *Hanlon* [1978] 1 W.L.R. 592; [1978] 2 All E.R. 889, C.A.   E

Jessel v. *Jessel* [1979] 1 W.L.R. 1148; [1979] 3 All E.R. 645, C.A.

Mesher v. *Mesher,* The Times, February 13, 1973; Court of Appeal (Civil Division) Transcript No. 59 of 1973, C.A.

Minton v. *Minton* [1979] A.C. 593; [1979] 2 W.L.R. 31; [1979] 1 All E.R. 65, H.L.(E.).

The following additional cases were cited in argument: F

Cawkwell v. *Cawkwell* (1979) 9 Fam.Law 25, C.A.

Smith (P.S.) v. *Smith (A.J.),* April 27, 1977; Court of Appeal (Civil Division) Transcript No. 194 of 1977, C.A.

APPEAL from Judge Galpin sitting at Portsmouth County Court.

Following a decree nisi of divorce of the marriage between the wife G and the husband, Mr. Registrar Wroath in the Portsmouth County Court ordered that no order be made on the property adjustment application save that the house, which was the former matrimonial home, be not sold until the youngest child had completed her full-time education, that the husband pay the wife maintenance pending suit at the rate of £5 per week; and that he make periodical payments of £7.50 per week to each of the three children of the family.   H

Following the decree absolute on April 2, 1979, Judge Galpin, on May 21, allowed the wife's appeal and ordered the husband to transfer his interest in the house to the wife within three months of the order, that the house be charged with payment to the husband of 25 per cent. of the net proceeds of sale when sold or on the death of the wife such sum to be calculated without regard to any future mortgage taken out by the wife; and that the order for periodical payments for the wife be varied to

A 5p per annum, the periodical payments in respect of the children to remain the same.

The husband appealed on the grounds that (1) evidence on behalf of the wife was given at the hearing by a surveyor valuer and estate agents of 15 years experience in the locality who stated that the wife would need on current values about £12,000 to provide herself with a property suitable for her needs and agreed that on the wife's present income she could raise
B about £4,800; the wife's interest in the equity was agreed to be in the region of £6,000: the judge was wrong in not making a small adjustment in the equity of the house and then ordering the sale of the house on the youngest child of the family completing her full time education; (2) the judge was wrong in concluding that to satisfy her future requirements the wife should have the husband's interest transferred to her subject to the charge and that
C the charge would be unable to be enforced until the wife's death or sale of the property; (3) in making the order the judge failed to make any provision for the contingency of the wife's remarriage or cohabitation with another man; (4) in postponing the enforcement of the charge or any order for sale of the house until the wife's death or her own wish to sell the house thereby securing her future requirements for housing the judge was wrong to transfer any of the husband's interest in the said house to the wife.

D The wife cross appealed on the grounds that (1) the husband having been relieved of all responsibility for repayment of the mortgage of £3,950, which still stood at £3,594 on March 8, 1979, should not be granted 25 per cent. of the eventual net proceeds of sale of the house; (2) the charge of 25 per cent. in favour of the husband on the net proceeds of sale was an unnecessary and unfair restriction on the wife's ability to sell the house at
E any time should it become necessary or desirable in the interests of the family or of herself.

The facts are stated in the judgment of Lord Denning M.R.

Keith Cutler for the husband.
F. R. N. Massey for the wife.

F LORD DENNING M.R. This is an interesting case about a matrimonial home. The husband and wife were married on July 14, 1962, when he was 21 and she was 19. They have three children: boys of 15 and 13 and a girl of 11. They separated after 16 years of marriage in August 1978. Divorce proceedings have gone through very expeditiously. The wife took out a petition for divorce in September 1978 on the ground that the
G husband had behaved in such a way that she could not be expected to live with him any more and that the marriage had broken down irretrievably. The husband did not dispute it. He submitted to an order by consent. That can often be done nowadays just on an affidavit without going to court at all. The wife alleged that from 1974 onwards the husband drank to excess despite her repeated pleadings and became an alcoholic. She gave details of events in the August before the final breakdown of the
H marriage: how he went out drinking and when he returned home he behaved abominably to her. So much so that he struck her and the like. At all events, she said that owing to his conduct the marriage had broken down. The husband did not oppose it. The decree nisi was made in December 1978.

There arose the question of the arrangements for the children. The wife stayed with the children in the matrimonial home. She looked after them there, seeing them off to school, and working part-time while they were

at school. The question then arose as to what should be done with the   A
matrimonial home. Under the new legislation the court has a very wide
power to transfer the interest in the home from one spouse to the other.

In this case the matrimonial home had been a council house. The
husband and wife had bought it in 1971. They did not have to put down
a deposit. They obtained a 100 per cent. mortgage from the local authority.
The total price for that three-bedroomed house in 1971 was £3,950. But   B
during the last eight years the value of the house has gone up to £14,000 or
£15,000. The question is : what is to be done about the house? The wife
wants to stay there—and ought to be able to stay there—to bring up the
family. The house is still on mortgage : and over the years, when the
husband and wife were both living there, they paid off the interest and a
little off the capital. At the present time there is on the mortgage a sum of
about £3,600 outstanding.   C

The position of the parties is this. The husband is a press room
assistant. That is a good position. His gross income is £93 a week. The
wife now has part-time work concerned with school meals. She earns £37 a
week gross. He has to pay maintenance of £7.50 a week for each of the
three children, which totals £22.50. She receives family allowance, one-
parent benefit, and so forth. The husband, of course, has had to move   D
into lodgings elsewhere.

The matter first came before the registrar of the Portsmouth County
Court. He went by a decision which was made some years ago and which
was only reported in " The Times " newspaper. It is *Mesher* v. *Mesher,*
The Times, February 13, 1973. In our present case the house was in joint
names and belonged to the husband and wife in equal proportions. The
registrar ordered that the house was not to be sold until the youngest child   E
had finished her schooling, which would be when she is 17 or 18 years of
age. Presumably, after that time, it could be sold and the proceeds divided
equally between the parties. Meanwhile the registrar ordered the husband
to pay maintenance of £5 a week for the wife together with the sums of
£7.50 a week for each of the children.

That order left the parties in complete uncertainty as to the future.   F
After six or seven years the house would have to be sold and the husband
would take a half-share of the proceeds, and the wife would be left with
insufficient money to buy another house. The wife's solicitors appealed.
The judge made a different order. He ordered that the whole of the
interest in the house should be transferred to the wife within three months.
He realised that if it were transferred, the wife would have to pay the
mortgage instalments, the rates, and all the other outgoings on the house.   G
But the judge realised that the wife might die or might sell the house some
time in the future. If that should happen, the judge ordered that the
husband should then have 25 per cent. of the equity. His actual order
was :

> " The matrimonial home to be charged with the payment to the
> husband of 25 per cent. of the net proceeds of sale when sold or on   H
> the death of the wife, such sum to be calculated without regard to any
> future mortgage taken out by the wife."

By making that order, the parties would know exactly where they
stood with regard to the future. In so ordering, the judge applied the
principle which is now flowing through these cases. It was indicated in
the recent case of *Hanlon* v. *Hanlon* [1978] 1 W.L.R. 592, 599, *per*

A   Ormrod L.J. When it was suggested that there should be a postponement of the sale and then a distribution on a 50-50 basis, he said:

"... I do not think that that in this case would be in the least satisfactory; it would leave the wife in a state of perpetual uncertainty and neither party would know where ultimately they were going to be. It seems to me far better that the parties' interests should be crystallised now, once and for all, so that the wife can know what she is going to do about the property and the husband can make up his mind about what he is going to do about rehousing."

B

That principle was expressed again in the recent case of *Minton* v. *Minton* [1979] A.C. 593, 608, *per* Lord Scarman. He drew attention to the principle of the "clean break." He said:

C   "The law now encourages spouses to avoid bitterness after family break-down and to settle their money and property problems. An object of the modern law is to encourage each to put the past behind them and to begin a new life which is not over-shadowed by the relationship which has broken down."

There is only one variation which I think should be made to the order
D of the judge. He ordered that the order for periodical payments for the wife should be 5p per annum—a nominal sum. That should not be included in an order when you want a clean break. We recently had *Jessel* v. *Jessel* [1979] 1 W.L.R. 1148 in this court. We said that if an order for periodical payments were included, it kept the position fluid and the wife could come back later on for more and more maintenance. In order to avoid any such renewal of the past, the right thing is to have no
E order for periodical payments inserted at all—as in *Minton* v. *Minton* [1979] A.C. 593. So I think in this case the order of the judge should be varied by striking out the order for periodical payments of 5p a year. In that way we have the "clean break." The wife knows exactly where she stands. The house is vested in her. She has the property in it, and she can keep the family together. She can keep it as a home for the family as
F they grow up. She can keep it going indefinitely, knowing exactly where she stands. But if it should happen that she should sell the house (or should die) then the husband is to have one-quarter of the net proceeds.

It has to be remembered that she has to bear the expense of the outstanding mortgage of nearly £4,000. This is a legal aid case, so there may be a charge on the house in respect of costs. But, subject to the charge, if the house is sold, the husband will receive 25 per cent. and
G the wife will receive 75 per cent. of the net proceeds.

It seems to me that the judge made his order in accordance with the modern principle of the "clean break" so that both parties will know hereafter exactly where they stand. At all events, subject to the variation which I have indicated, it seems to me that the order of the judge was right, and I would dismiss the appeal and, incidentally, the cross appeal.
H I do not think the wife should have this house vested in her completely as she wanted.

So I would dismiss the appeal and the cross appeal subject to the variation that the order for periodical payments should be struck out.

EVELEIGH L.J. I agree. It is true that the husband is losing his share in the equity of the house, but it is a house where the mortgage is still at the original figure and the wife has the obligation of paying that off. The

husband's capital prospects are very much greater than those of the A
wife. He has a superior earning capacity; and, in the not-too-distant
future when the children's payments come to an end, the difference
between their earning capacity or their income will be even more
pronounced.

In those circumstances, I think that his prospects of acquiring a house
in due course are really quite good.

I agree with the order proposed by Lord Denning M.R.   B

> *Appeal and cross appeal dismissed
> subject to variation.
> Periodical payments order struck out.*

Solicitors: *Lovell, Son & Pitfield for Warner Goodman & Co.,* C
Portsmouth; Innes, Patassi & Co., Portsmouth.

A. H. B.

[CHANCERY DIVISION]   D

* BRADSHAW AND ANOTHER *v.* PAWLEY

[1978 B. No. 2797]

1979 April 5, 9   Sir Robert Megarry V.-C.   E

*Landlord and Tenant—Rent—When payable—Term expressed to
run from date prior to execution of lease—Covenant to pay
rent at stated rates during specified periods " of the said term "
—Whether rates stated apply to periods prior to execution of
lease*

A tenant held business premises at a rent of £312 a year
under a 21-year lease which terminated on March 24, 1974. F
Following the tenant's application to the county court under
the Landlord and Tenant Act 1954, negotiations with the
landlords resulted in an agreement for a new lease for ten
years from March 25, 1974, at a rent of £1,750 a year. The
consent order for the grant of the new lease was dated January
11, 1977, and a further order dated May 16, 1977, authorised
an agreement by the parties to exclude, in respect of the new
lease, sections 24 to 28 of the Act of 1954. On May 23, 1977, G
the old tenancy as extended by the Act came to an end. The
new lease was not executed until March 10, 1978, owing to
dissension between the parties as to whether the rent under
the new lease was payable from March 25, 1974.

In the landlords' action for a declaration that the new
rent was so payable: —

Held, that on ordinary principles of construction, the
consent order, combined with the agreed terms of the new H
lease, meant that the tenant had bound himself to pay rent
at £1,750 a year from March 25, 1974, irrespective of the
date when the lease was actually executed, for although at
common law the term created by a lease could not begin
before the lease was executed, there was nothing to prevent
the parties from defining the duration of the term by
reference to a date earlier than that of the lease, nor were
they prevented from creating obligations under the lease in
respect of some prior period; and that accordingly the land-

A   lords' claim for rent at the new rate from March 25, 1974,
     succeeded.
          Shaw v. *Kay* (1847) 1 Exch. 412; 17 L.J.Ex. 17; *Earl
     Cadogan* v. *Guinness* [1936] Ch. 515 and *M'Leish* v. *Tate*
     (1778) 2 Cowp. 781 considered.

     The following cases are referred to in the judgment:

B   *Bird* v. *Baker* (1858) 1 E. & E. 12.
     Cadogan (Earl) v. *Guinness* [1936] Ch. 515; [1936] 2 All E.R. 29.
     M'Leish v. *Tate* (1778) 2 Cowp. 781.
     Roberts v. *Church Commissioners for England* [1972] 1 Q.B. 278;
          [1971] 3 W.L.R. 566; [1971] 3 All E.R. 703, C.A.
     Shaw v. *Kay* (1847) 1 Exch. 412; 17 L.J.Ex. 17.
     Wyburd v. *Tuck* (1799) 1 Bos. & P. 458.

C   The following additional cases were cited in argument:

     Colton v. *Becollda Property Investments Ltd.* [1950] 1 K.B. 216, C.A.
     Kilburn, High Road, (No. 88), In re [1959] 1 W.L.R. 279; [1959] 1
          All E.R. 527.
     Tottenham Hotspur Football & Athletic Co. Ltd. v. *Princegrove Publishers
          Ltd.* [1974] 1 W.L.R. 113; [1974] 1 All E.R. 17.

D   ACTION
          By writ dated June 29, 1978, the plaintiff landlords, John Richard
     Bradshaw and Norman Richard Bradshaw, freeholders of 18, Berrylands
     Road, Surbiton, Surrey, claimed against the defendant tenant, Alexander
     Christopher Pawley, a declaration that on the true construction of a new
     lease made between the landlords and the tenant and executed on March
E   10, 1978, the tenant was obliged to pay rent to the landlords at the rate
     of £1,750 per annum from March 25, 1974, the day following the expira-
     tion of the term under the old lease. By his defence the tenant contended
     that, by virtue of sections 24 and 64 of the Landlord and Tenant Act
     1954, the tenancy under the old lease continued until March 10, 1978,
     when the new lease was executed, and that he was liable to pay only the
F   rent reserved by the old lease, i.e. £312 per annum, until that date.
          The facts are stated in the judgment.

          David Hands for the landlords.
          R. Moxon-Browne for the tenant.

                                                          Cur. adv. vult.

G
          April 9. SIR ROBERT MEGARRY V.-C. read the following judgment.
     This case raises a short point of principle on the law of landlord and
     tenant. The basic question is whether on the grant of a new lease to
     an existing lessee a covenant to pay rent at a certain rate from a date
     anterior to the date when the lease was executed can make the lessee
     liable for rent at that rate from that anterior date or only from the date
H   when the lease was executed. The question arises in an action brought by
     the landlords against the tenant claiming rent at the agreed rate from the
     anterior date; and a striking feature is that the two dates are nearly four
     years apart.
          The relevant facts may be briefly stated. The premises in question are
     business premises which the tenant formerly held under a lease for 21
     years less a day from March 25, 1953. The natural expiration of the
     term was thus on March 24, 1974, but of course the Landlord and Tenant

Bradshaw v. Pawley (Ch.D.) [1980]

Act 1954, Part II, applied to the tenancy. The landlords accordingly gave   A
a statutory notice on February 13, 1974, to determine the tenancy on
August 14, 1974; and on June 12, 1974, the tenant applied to the county
court for the grant of a new tenancy under the Act.

Prolonged negotiations then took place between those advising the
parties. From early on these were on the basis of a new term for ten
years, and after a while this emerged as being ten years from March 25,
1974. Finally, on January 11, 1977, a consent order was made in the   B
county court for the grant of a new lease of most of the premises for a
term of " ten years from March 25, 1974, at a rent of £1,750 " a year,
with provision for " upward reviews " during the term. The rent payable
under the previous lease, I may say, was £312 a year, with no provision
for rent revision. In each case there was in addition an insurance rent
which does not affect what I have to decide. It is regrettable that the   C
order does not state on the face of it that it was a consent order, as every
consent order ought to do; but it is common ground that in fact it was a
consent order. The order also provided that the parties should jointly
apply to the court under section 38 (4) of the Act of 1954 for an order
authorising an agreement to exclude sections 24 to 28 of the Act in respect
of the new lease; and it was agreed that this agreement should be included   D
in the lease. This, of course, would prevent the new lease from conferring
any right to a new tenancy under the Act when it expired. On May 16,
1977, the court made the requisite order to this effect.

A week later, on May 23, 1977, the tenancy flowing from the combined
effect of the old lease and the Act came to an end. Section 24 (1), when
read with section 64, had prolonged the tenancy until the expiration of
three months after the end of the period of six weeks allowed for an   E
appeal from the order of January 11, 1977. The Supreme Court of
Judicature (Consolidation) Act 1925, section 31 (1) (h), does not prohibit
appeals from consent orders, though it does require leave for such an
appeal. The new lease, however, still had not been executed, for dissension arose on the point now before me for decision. Finally, on March 10,
1978, the lease was duly executed; and on June 29, 1978, the writ was   F
issued.

It will be seen that there are thus four main periods with which I am
concerned. (1) Until March 24, 1974, the old lease was running at a rent
of £312 a year; and this period is not in issue. (2) From March 24, 1974,
until May 23, 1977, the tenancy created by the old lease was being
continued by force of the Act. This second period is very much in issue.
The tenant contends that his liability for this period is at the rate of £312   G
a year, whereas the landlords contend that it is at the rate of £1,750.
(3) From May 24, 1977, until March 10, 1978, the old lease was at
an end and the new lease had yet to be granted. This third period
is also in issue. There is the same dispute about the amount of the rent,
and Mr. Moxon-Browne, who appeared for the tenant, was forced to
contend that either the tenant was holding over during that period, without   H
any lease or tenancy, or else that he was there by virtue of the agreement
for a lease evidenced by the consent order, on the terms of that order.
(4) From March 10, 1978, onwards the new lease was in force, and there
is no dispute that thereafter the tenant was liable for rent at the rate of
£1,750 a year. Accordingly, what I have to decide is the liability of
the tenant during the second and third periods.

The Weekly Law Reports, January 11, 1980

13

1 W.L.R.   **Bradshaw v. Pawley (Ch.D.)**   Sir Robert
                                                          Megarry V.-C.

A   With that, I turn to the provisions of the new lease, which is expressed
in terms of "the lessor" and "the lessee." By the habendum, the
premises are demised to the lessee to hold the same unto the lessee

> "from March 25, 1974, for the term of ten years but determinable
> as hereinafter provided Yielding and paying therefor during the said
> term yearly and proportionately for any fraction of a year the rents
> hereunder set out."

B

There are then specified "for the first four and three-quarter years of the
said term" the rent of £1,750 a year, and "for the next three years of
the said term" a rent determined in accordance with clause 3, which
contains provisions for rent review. There is then a similar provision "for
the remainder of the said term"; and all the rents are to be paid quarterly
in advance on the usual quarter days. The lessee's covenants are made
C   "to the intent that the obligations may continue throughout the said
term"; and the first of these is "to pay during the said term the said
reserved rents at the times and in manner aforesaid," and so on.
    In considering the rival contentions, I think that the starting point
is to construe the lease in the ordinary way, before considering whether
there is anything in the law to modify that construction or to prevent its
D   being effectuated. In seems perfectly clear that the obligation to pay
a rent of £1,750 a year is an obligation to pay that rent for the period
of ten years from March 15, 1974. The reddendum is in terms of paying
rent at that rate "during the said term," and so is the covenant to pay
rent: and there is no term in the document that can be called the "said"
term except the "term of ten years" running "from March 25, 1974."
    That construction seems to me to be supported (if support be needed)
E   by the consequences of an answer which Mr. Moxon-Browne for the
tenant gave to a question from the bench. He was constrained to accept
that the time-table for increases of rent for the specified periods "of the
said term" was to operate during the ten years from March 25, 1974,
and not the six years and a few days running from the execution of the
lease on March 10, 1978. Accordingly, the revised rent was to run from
F   the expiration of "the first four and three-quarter years of the said term,"
and so would commence at Christmas 1978, and so on. Mr. Hands, for
the landlords, said that on this footing it was impossible to see how it
could be said that "the said term" meant one thing for the purpose of
laying down a rent of £1,750 a year and another for the purpose of the
time-table of rent increases, especially when the first $4\frac{3}{4}$ years of that time-
table provides for the rent to be £1,750 a year. The "said term" must
G   mean the same term, whether the phrase is "during the said term" or "of
the said term."
    That contention seems to me to be unanswerable. Mr. Moxon-
Browne's contentions reduced him to contending that the obligation to pay
at least £1,750 a year "during the said term" really meant not "during the
said term of ten years from March 25, 1974," but "during so much of the
H   said term of ten years from March 25, 1974, as subsists while the parties
are in the relationship of landlord and tenant under this demise," and so
when the lease was executed meant during the next six years and a few
days. Similarly, the provision in the consent order for the grant of a new
lease "for a term of ten years from March 25, 1974, at a rent of £1,750"
was really an agreement to pay a rent of £1,750 not for ten years but for
so much of the then unexpired period of approximately seven years and
two months out of that ten years as still remained unexpired when the

14

lease was finally executed. As the difference between the two rents   A
is nearly £4 a day, each day's delay in executing the lease would save
the tenant some £4. As a matter of construction I cannot accept these
contentions. I feel no doubt that on ordinary principles of construction
the true meaning of the consent order and the lease is that a rent of
£1,750 a year or more was to be paid throughout the period of ten years
from March 25, 1974, irrespective of the date on which the lease was
actually executed.   B

The question, then, is whether there is anything in the law to require
the lease to be construed differently, or to prevent effect being given to
the natural construction of its language. When asked, Mr. Moxon-
Browne agreed that on this he relied not on any provisions of the Act
but on the general principles of the law. The only qualification to this
was that he relied to some extent on the provisions of the Act which   C
prevented the old tenancy from determining when the old lease expired;
and he also contended that section 24A, when read with section 64,
would be pointless if the landlords were right. This latter point, however,
did not withstand investigation, and I need not pursue it further. In the
main, Mr. Moxon-Browne relied on authorities which for the most part
are conveniently collected in *Roberts* v. *Church Commissioners for
England* [1972] 1 Q.B. 278. As he contended, there are indeed some   D
limitations on the effect that can be given to a term expressed to run from
a date prior to the execution of the lease, and I must consider these.

First, it is well settled that a lease cannot retrospectively vest an estate
in the lessee. If today a lease is granted for seven years from this day
a year ago, no term of seven years is brought into being, but only a term
of six years from today. A lease, of course, is more than a mere contract,   E
for it operates by way of grant to create an estate or interest in the land;
and you cannot grant today that X shall have had a term of years vested
in him a year ago. Whatever contractual obligations there may be
between the parties, no actual term of years can be created until the lease
has been executed and so the grant has been made. Thus where the
question is what term has actually been created, as where a statute refers
to terms of a particular length, the commencement of the term cannot be   F
earlier than the date of the grant of the lease. There is, of course, no
objection to a lease defining the term by reference to some past date, as
in the grant of a term of seven years from this day a year ago; but this
merely creates a term of six years from today.

Second, a lease for a term from some past date will not, at any rate
normally, make into a breach of covenant that which was not a breach   G
when it was committed. An act or omission by a prospective lessee
which would be a contravention of the proposed lease is not turned into a
breach of covenant by him merely because he subsequently accepts the
grant of the lease for a term which is expressed to run from some date
anterior to the act or omission. That, I think, follows from *Shaw* v. *Kay*
(1847) 1 Exch. 412. There, the landlord sued on a repairing covenant in   H
respect of acts done by the tenant before the lease was executed, basing
the claim on the lease having been expressed to run from an earlier date.
The claim failed, though no reasoned judgments were delivered.

It may be tempting to infer from these two propositions that when
a term is expressed to run from some date prior to the actual grant of
the lease, that prior date can have no function save as a unit of calculation
in ascertaining the date on which the term will expire; and in *Shaw* v.

The Weekly Law Reports, January 11, 1980

15

1 W.L.R.   Bradshaw v. Pawley (Ch.D.)   Sir Robert
                                                             Megarry V.-C.

A *Kay* at p. 413 there is a dictum of Parke B. which can be read as indicating this. Whatever the temptation, I think that it would be wrong to draw any such inference. The dictum on which Parke B. relied, uttered by Eyre C.J. in *Wyburd* v. *Tuck* (1799) 1 Bos. & P. 458, 464, must be understood in relation to the facts of the case: and what the court was concerned with there was a lease of tithes as giving the plaintiff a title to sue for the tithes. As the lease did not vest the term in the tenant before it B was executed, he could not sue for tithes due before the date of execution. However, when what is in issue is not title but obligation or liability, I do not see why the parties should not, if they choose, make the obligation or liability enforceable in respect of such anterior date as they wish. Thus if a lease is granted for a term of 21 years from a date two years prior to the grant of the lease, with a provision for determination at the end C of the seventh or fourteenth years of the term, then, in the words of Clauson J. in *Earl Cadogan* v. *Guinness* [1936] Ch. 515, 518,

> " it is perfectly easy as a matter of construction of such a document to say that the seven years according to the obvious intention of the parties is not to run as from the date of the execution of the lease but from the moment spoken of, though inaccurately, as the D beginning of the term in the document."

Bird v. *Baker* (1858) 1 E. & E. 12 provides an example of this. There, the lease was granted in July 1851 for 14 years from Christmas 1849, with power to break " at the expiration of the first seven years thereof ": and the Court of Queen's Bench held that the break came at Christmas 1856 and not in July 1858.

E   I cannot see what there is to stultify an agreement in a lease to make payments in respect of past periods, or to require the court to construe a lease so as to prevent any agreement from relating to past periods unless compelled to it. It is by no means unknown for a lease not to be executed until after the prospective lessee has entered (usually with safeguards for the lessor), and for the lessee then to pay rent and observe the terms of the lease as from a date prior to the execution of the lease. F If as a matter of construction the obligation is to pay rent at a specified rate from some date earlier than that of the execution of the lease, why should that not be enforceable?

I think that some support for this view is provided by a dictum of Pollock C.B. in *Shaw* v. *Kay*. The report in 1 Exch. that was cited to me omits this, but it is to be found in the report of the case in 17 L.J.Ex. G 17 where Pollock C.B. said at p. 18:

> " A party may covenant to indemnify another from what has passed. I may demise premises today, and covenant to save my tenant harmless from what has happened six months before."

On the same footing I do not see why, by suitable wording, a lease should not impose on one of the parties some liability for things past.

H   Mr. Moxon-Browne stressed that rent was something that had to be paid periodically, and so an obligation to pay nearly four years' rent at a blow indicated that what was being paid could not truly be called rent. However, I do not think that rent becomes denatured when a sufficiency of gales remains unpaid. Nor do I see why an obligation to pay rent in respect of periods of occupation by the tenant prior to the grant of the lease should not be regarded as rent. What must matter, surely, is what the payments are due for, rather than how and when the payments

are in fact made. I would follow *Foa's General Law of Landlord and* A
Tenant, 8th ed. (1957), p. 101 in regarding rent as being prima facie
" the monetary compensation payable by the tenant in consideration for
the grant, however it be described or allocated," though I think that I
would insert the word " periodical " before the word " monetary." I
would also pay more attention to modern than mediaeval concepts in
considering the nature of rent. If the parties to a lease choose to agree
that the lessee shall pay rent to the lessor in respect of a period prior to B
the grant of the lease, I do not see why this should not be valid and
enforceable. So far as it goes, I think that *M'Leish* v. *Tate* (1778) 2
Cowp. 781, 784, supports the view that rent may still be rent even though
it is reserved in respect of the occupation by a tenant at some time prior
to the execution of the instrument which reserves the rent. Even if this
is wrong, and the payments in dispute, though described as " rent," are C
not in law " rent," strictly so called, I cannot see why the lessors should
not enforce payment. There is nothing to stop a man from being liable
on a covenant to pay a sum of money in respect of some past period.

Mr. Moxon-Browne relied to some extent on the tenant holding on
the terms of the old lease, as extended by the Act, from March 24, 1974,
until May 23, 1977; this is the second period that I mentioned earlier.
As during this period the tenant held at a rent of £312 a year, why should D
he now pay more? The answer, I think, is that he would be under no
obligation to pay more unless he had bound himself to do so; and on
the true construction of the new lease that is just what he has done. The
fact that he need not have paid more if he had not entered into a new
lease, or if instead he had entered into a differently worded lease, cannot
alter the consequences of what he did do. I know of nothing at common E
law to prevent a tenant under an existing tenancy from agreeing to pay a
higher rent, or from entering into a new tenancy at a higher rent, in place
of his existing tenancy. Nor can I see any magic in the Act which would
make the terms of the extended tenancy prevail over those of the new
lease. The position of the tenant during the third period is a fortiori; for
his old tenancy had ended and until the new lease was executed the tenant's
only right of occupation was by virtue of the agreement evidenced by the F
consent order of January 11, 1977. That agreement, of course, was for
the same rent as the initial rent under the new lease, namely, £1,750 a year,
and so whatever the road, the terminus is £1,750 a year.

I do not think that any difficulty arises from the payment and
acceptance of rent at the rate of £312 a year after March 25, 1974; and,
indeed, no difficulty has been suggested. Obviously credit must be given G
for the payments made against the payments due at the rate of £1,750 a
year, and the landlords' claim is, of course, properly made on that basis.
Nor, I think, is there any difficulty in the fact that the payments at the
higher rate have not been made punctually each quarter day since March
25, 1974. No obligation under the new lease to make these payments
could arise until the lease had been executed, and so the omission to make
those payments at any earlier date could not constitute a breach of H
covenant.

In the result, I think that where a lease creates a term of years which
is expressed to run from some date earlier than that of the execution of
the lease, the relevant law may be summarised as follows. (1) The term
created will be a term which commences on the date when the lease is
executed, and not the earlier date. (2) No act or omission prior to the
date on which the lease is executed will normally constitute a breach of

A the obligations of the lease. (3) These principles do not prevent the
parties from defining the expiration of the term by reference to a date
prior to that of the execution of the lease, or from making contractual
provisions which take effect by reference to such a date, as by defining
the period for the operation of a break clause or an increase of rent. (4)
There is nothing in these principles to prevent the lease from creating
obligations in respect of any period prior to the execution of the lease.
B (5) Whether in fact any such obligations have been created depends on the
construction of the lease; and there is nothing which requires the lease
to be construed in such a way as to avoid, if possible, the creation of such
obligations.

On the facts of the case before me, these principles and the other
matters that I have discussed point to only one conclusion, namely, that
C the landlords' claim succeeds. The precise terms of the order are for
discussion.

> Declaration that tenant obliged to pay
> rent to landlords at rate of £1,750 a
> year from March 25, 1974.

D Solicitors: *Kingsley, Napley & Co.; C. A. Maddin & Co.,* Surbiton,
Surrey.

K. N. B.

E [COURT OF APPEAL]

* BOCARDO S.A. *v.* S. & M. HOTELS LTD. AND ANOTHER

[1977 B. No. 4225]

1979 July 9, 10, 11; 31   Megaw, Lawton and Browne L.JJ.
F

*Landlord and Tenant — Assignment of lease or underletting —
Consent—Covenant not to assign or underlet without consent,
consent not to be unreasonably withheld—Proviso that tenant
desiring to assign should first offer surrender of lease to landlords—Whether valid—Landlord and Tenant Act* 1927 (17 &
18 *Geo.* 5, *c.* 36), *s.* 19 (1) (*a*)

G Section 19 (1) of the Landlord and Tenant Act 1927
provides:
"In all leases . . . containing a covenant condition or
agreement against assigning . . . demised premises . . .
without licence or consent, such covenant condition or
agreement shall, notwithstanding any express provision to
the contrary, be deemed to be subject—(*a*) to a proviso to
the effect that such licence or consent is not to be unreason-
H ably withheld, . . ."
By clause 2 (j) of a lease of a flat, the tenants, a limited
company, covenanted not to assign the flat without the previous
consent in writing of the landlords, such consent not to be
unreasonably withheld in the case of a respectable and responsible assignee. The clause further provided that, if the tenants
desired to assign, they should first by irrevocable notice in
writing to the landlords offer to surrender the lease to the
landlords by deed absolutely without any consideration. The
lease also contained a covenant entitling the landlords to

Bocardo S.A. v. S. & M. Hotels (C.A.)   **[1980]**

A re-enter and determine the lease if the tenants should enter into liquidation. On May 16, 1977, a winding up order was made in respect of the tenants, and the landlords issued a writ against them claiming possession. The tenants applied for relief against forfeiture and, with a view to assigning the lease to a director of theirs, sought a declaration that the provision in clause 2 (j) of the lease providing for the offer of surrender to the landlords was void by virtue of the provisions of section 19 (1) of the Act of 1927. It was accepted that, if they failed B in that claim, they could not obtain relief against forfeiture. Chapman J. in chambers held that the provision in clause 2 (j) of the lease was valid and affirmed an order of Master Waldman dismissing the tenants' application and refusing them relief against forfeiture.

On appeal by the tenants: —

Held, dismissing the appeal, that section 19 (1) of the Landlord and Tenant Act 1927 had had the limited objective C of providing that, where a lease provided for assignment by the tenant with the consent of the landlord, such consent should not be unreasonably withheld; that it did not purport to prevent the parties from agreeing that assignment should be prohibited altogether, nor did it prevent them from agreeing that the tenant should first offer to surrender the lease to the landlord; and that, accordingly, the proviso to that effect in clause 2 (j) of the lease in the instant case was valid (post, pp. 21H—22A, C–E, D 24D–H, 25D–E, 26D, 27B–C).

Adler v. *Upper Grosvenor Street Investment Ltd.* [1957] 1 W.L.R. 227 approved.

Creer v. *P. & O. Lines of Australia Pty. Ltd* (1971) 125 C.L.R. 84; 45 A.L.J.R. 697 followed.

In re Smith's Lease [1951] 1 All E.R. 346 considered.

Dicta of Lord Denning M.R. and Sir Eric Sachs in *Greene* v. *Church Commissioners for England* [1974] Ch. 467, 477, E 479–480 not applied.

Decision of Chapman J. affirmed.

The following cases are referred to in the judgments:

Adler v. *Upper Grosvenor Street Investment Ltd.* [1957] 1 W.L.R. 227; [1957] 1 All E.R. 229.

Bates v. *Donaldson* [1896] 2 Q.B. 241, C.A.   F

Creer v. *P. & O. Lines of Australia Pty. Ltd.* (1971) 125 C.L.R. 84; 45 A.L.J.R. 697.

Greene v. *Church Commissioners for England* [1974] Ch. 467; [1974] 3 W.L.R. 349; [1974] 3 All E.R. 609, C.A.

Houlder Brothers & Co. Ltd. v. *Gibbs* [1925] Ch. 575, C.A.

Kirkness v. *John Hudson & Co. Ltd.* [1955] A.C. 696; [1955] 2 W.L.R. 1135; [1955] 2 All E.R. 345, H.L.(E.).   G

Property & Bloodstock Ltd. v. *Emerton* [1968] Ch. 94; [1967] 3 W.L.R. 973; [1967] 3 All E.R. 321, C.A.

Smith's Lease, In re [1951] 1 All E.R. 346.

Woolworth (F. W.) & Co. Ltd. v. *Lambert* [1937] 1 Ch. 37; [1936] 2 All E.R. 1523, C.A.

The following additional cases were cited in argument: H

Balfour v. *Kensington Gardens Mansions Ltd.* (1932) 49 T.L.R. 29.

Creery v. *Summersell and Flowerdew & Co. Ltd.* [1949] Ch. 751.

Joseph v. *Joseph* [1967] Ch. 78; [1966] 3 W.L.R. 631; [1966] 3 All E.R. 486, C.A.

Plymouth Corporation v. *Harvey* [1971] 1 W.L.R. 549; [1971] 1 All E.R. 623.

West Layton Ltd. v. *Ford* [1979] Q.B. 593; [1979] 3 W.L.R. 14; [1979] 2 All E.R. 657, C.A.

A   INTERLOCUTORY APPEAL from Chapman J.

By specially indorsed writ dated July 18, 1977, the plaintiffs, Bocardo
S.A., claimed against the defendants, S. & M. Hotels Ltd. and Sidney
Winton, possession of premises, flat no. 48, 60, Park Lane, Mayfair,
London, W.1, on the ground of forfeiture. The first defendants, S. & M.
Hotels Ltd., applied by summons in the action for an order that they be
relieved from forfeiture and for a declaration that the proviso to clause
B   2 (j) of the lease of the premises was void and of no effect. Master
Waldman dismissed the application, and his order was affirmed by
Chapman J.

The first defendants appealed, contending that Chapman J. had been
wrong in law in following *Adler* v. *Upper Grosvenor Street Investment Ltd.*
[1957] 1 W.L.R. 227, in holding (by inference) that the proviso to clause
C   2 (j) of the lease was a valid provision and in refusing to hold that the
proviso was a contravention of the provisions of section 19 of the Landlord and Tenant Act 1927.

The facts are stated in the judgment of Megaw L.J.

Benjamin Levy for the first defendants.
Derek Wood Q.C. and *Jonathan Gaunt* for the plaintiffs.

D
Cur. adv. vult.

July 31. The following judgments were read.

MEGAW L.J. This is an appeal from an order of Chapman J. in
E   chambers, dismissing an appeal from an order of Master Waldman. The
master and the judge refused to order that the first defendants, S. & M.
Hotels Ltd., the tenants, should be relieved against forfeiture of a lease,
which forfeiture the plaintiffs, Bocardo S.A., the landlords, who are a
Liechtenstein company, were seeking to enforce. The judge, as I understand it—and this is not a criticism of him—gave no reasons except that he
regarded the case as indistinguishable from *Adler* v. *Upper Grosvenor*
F   *Street Investment Ltd.* [1957] 1 W.L.R. 227 (for brevity I shall call that
case "*Adler*"). That was a decision of Hilbery J. Chapman J. saw no
reason why he should not follow that decision. Of course, the decision was
not binding on him nor on us. But its persuasive authority has been
greatly increased by the fact that it has been approved and followed by the
High Court of Australia, in a case arising on a New South Wales enactment
G   which, so far as is relevant for this purpose, is in identical terms with
section 19 (1) of the Landlord and Tenant Act 1927. Hilbery J.'s
decision was concerned with section 19 (1). The present case depends
upon section 19 (1).

The facts, so far as they are relevant for this appeal, are short and
simple and not in dispute. The issue of law, once one has perused section
19 (1) of the Act of 1927 and struggled through the verbosity of clause 2 (j)
H   of the lease in the present case, is also capable of being very shortly stated.
The answer is not simple, because each of the two answers, contradictory
of one another, suggested respectively by the opposing parties, can be
criticised, and has been criticised by counsel, as being inconsistent with
common sense or the reasoning of decided cases. Yet we have to choose
between the two suggested answers.

First, the facts. The landlords were the owners of flat no. 48, 60, Park
Lane, Mayfair (I dare say they own other property as well). They are

assignees from the original lessors of the relevant lease. The tenants are A
(subject to the forfeiture now in question) tenants of flat no. 48, under a
lease for a a term of six years from December 25, 1973. The lease
included a covenant entitling the landlords to re-enter, thus determining
the lease, if the tenants should enter into liquidation. On May 16, 1977,
an order for the winding up of the tenant company was made. A notice
under section 146 of the Law of Property Act 1925 was served on the
tenants on June 25, 1977. On July 18 the landlords issued a writ claiming B
possession. On August 5, 1977, the tenants made application for relief
against forfeiture. They also, by a later amendment suggested by Master
Waldman, asked, both in their application and in a counterclaim, for a
declaration that a certain portion of the lease, contained in clause 2 (j)
thereof, was void. It is the issue raised as to that declaration which is the
issue in this appeal.
                                                                          C
     Mr. Sidney Winton, who was named as the second defendant in the
action, is, in theory, not concerned in this appeal. In reality, he is intimately
concerned; for if this appeal is decided against the tenants, Mr. Winton will
lose any right to continue in occupation of flat no. 48, where he has been
living for many years. He was a director of the tenant company and
occupied the flat as their subtenant or licensee. The lease is not within
the Rent Acts. Mr. Winton was made a defendant because he was a D
guarantor of the tenant company's obligations under the lease. No question,
however, arises in this appeal as to any failure or inability to pay the
proper rent, whatever it may be. (There are other proceedings, of no
relevance to the issue in this appeal, as to the proper amount of the rent).

     It is agreed between the parties that, if the tenants fail in their attack
on the legal validity of certain of the provisions of clause 2 (j) of the lease, E
then they cannot obtain relief against forfeiture. If, on the other hand,
they are right in their submission that those provisions are invalid because
of section 19 (1) of the Act of 1927, and cases decided with regard thereto,
then the landlords would still be entitled to consider whether it would be
reasonable for them to refuse consent to the assignment by the tenants of
the remainder of the lease to Mr. Winton. If the landlords were to refuse
consent, the tenants could then have the question of reasonableness F
determined by the courts. So, in one sense, this appeal is on a preliminary
issue; but there seems to me to be no good reason why we should refuse
to decide the preliminary issue. It is, I think, wrongly listed as a final appeal.
But that does not now matter. The issue, as I say, depends on the provisions
of section 19 (1) of the Act of 1927, and their application to the terms set
out in clause 2 (j) of the lease.
                                                                          G
     I shall set out the relevant words of section 19 (1). I should however
mention that, while the present case is concerned with assignment, the
subsection applies also to " underletting, charging or parting with . . .
possession." Section 19 (1):

     " In all leases . . . containing a covenant condition or agreeement
     against assigning . . . demised premises . . . without licence or con- H
     sent, such covenant condition or agreement shall, notwithstanding any
     express provision to the contrary, be deemed to be subject—(a) to a
     proviso to the effect that such licence or consent is not to be un-
     reasonably withheld, . . ."

     It is better that, despite its length, I should set out clause 2 (j) of the
lease in full. It reads:

A   " (i) Not to assign part only of the flat or charge or underlet or take in
     paying guests or share or (subject to the provisions of paragraph (ii)
     of this sub-clause) part with possession of the whole or any part of
     the flat (ii) Not to assign the whole of the flat without the previous
     consent in writing of the landlord such consent not to be unreasonably
     withheld in the case of a respectable and responsible assignee but the
     landlord shall not be required to consent to an assignment to a limited
B   company unless two directors thereof (being persons acceptable to the
     landlord in its absolute discretion) join in the licence or the assignment
     as sureties for the company and jointly and severally covenant with
     the landlord to pay the rents reserved by and other sums of money made
     payable by this lease and any damages accruing to the landlord by
     reason of the failure of the company to observe and perform the
     tenant's covenants and conditions herein contained Provided always
C   that every licence for an assignment relating to the flat shall if
     required by the landlord contain a covenant by the assignee directly
     with the landlord to observe and perform the covenants and conditions
     in this lease contained And further provided always that if the
     tenant desires to assign the whole of the flat as aforesaid he shall first
     by irrevocable notice in writing to the landlord offer to surrender
D   this lease by deed absolutely without any consideration on the next
     subsequent quarter-day or if that be within 28 days of the said notice
     then upon the second subsequent quarter-day (such surrender to be
     prepared by the landlord's solicitors at the tenant's expense) and the
     landlord may within 21 days of the service of such notice upon it
     accept such offer such acceptance to be in writing and without prejudice
     to all rights and remedies of the landlord in respect of rent or breach
E   of covenants If the said offer is not accepted by the landlord or on
     its behalf within the said 21 days it shall be deemed to have been
     rejected and if the tenant assigns or parts with possession of the flat
     without first making the said offer to surrender he shall be deemed to
     have made it and the landlord shall be entitled to accept it within
     seven days of becoming aware of the said assignment or parting with
F   possession in breach of this covenant."

     The only other provision of the lease to which I need refer is clause 6,
which entitles the tenants, on one month's notice, to terminate the lease on
December 24, 1976: that is, half-way through the term provided in the
habendum. No corresponding right of shortening the habendum term at
their will is given to the landlords.

G   We have had interesting and elaborate argument by counsel on either
side, analysing section 19 (1), with cross-references to subsections (2) and (3)
and to other statutory provisions including section 127 of the Rent Act
1977; analysing in detail the words of clause 2 (j); and discussing numerous
decided cases, before and after 1927.

     I hope that it will not be regarded as being in any way disrespectful of
H   those powerfully reasoned submissions if I do not specifically set them all
out in expressing my conclusion.

     What was section 19 (1) of the Act of 1927 intended to achieve? I
think, in the end, that it must be taken to have had a very limited
objective. Apart from legislation, a landlord and a tenant had freedom
of contract, in agreeing the terms of their lease, to permit or to limit or to
abrogate the right of either or both of them to assign their respective
interests. Section 19 (1) did not purport to destroy that freedom of contract

of the parties to agree to forbid assignment by the tenant. That proposition A is accepted by both parties before us, though counsel were unable to identify any decided case to that effect, such as Hilbery J. appears to have had in mind in his judgment in *Adler* [1957] 1 W.L.R. 227, 230, when he says, " It is clear and has been decided . . ." Neither of the parties before us asks us to give effect to the doubts on that point expressed by Danckwerts L.J. in *Property & Bloodstock Ltd.* v. *Emerton* [1968] Ch. 94, 119–120. It is hard to see how the words of sections 19 (1), " In all leases B . . . containing a covenant . . . against assigning . . . demised premises . . . without licence or consent, . . . " could fairly be construed as applying to leases which contain a simple covenant against assigning, with no reference whatever to " without licence or consent." I do not pursue that question because it is accepted before us that clause 19 (1) has no application where there is a prohibition of assignment. C

It follows that the deemed proviso, " such . . . consent is not to be unreasonably withheld," applies only if and to the extent that the covenant or agreement in the lease, by its terms, provides for assignment with consent. Such a provision would, in strict law, be meaningless or ineffective, unless it were to have implied in it some such term as " such . . . consent is not to be unreasonably withheld." For if the landlord was entitled to refuse consent at his own entirely unrestricted D discretion, the provision for assignment with consent would add nothing to, and subtract nothing from, the effect in law of the contract as it would be without those words being included. For a contracting party is entirely free to agree to a variation of the contract at the request of the other party. That applies equally where, as here, the variation of the contract would constitute a novation. It seems to me to follow E that the effect of section 19 (1) of the Act of 1927, on its true analysis, was merely to make statutory an implied term which must already have been implied, if the express words were to have any sensible purpose.

The nature of the implied term has in some degree been expounded by decisions of the courts subsequent to the Act of 1927. Such cases as *In re Smith's Lease* [1951] 1 All E.R. 346, a decision of Roxburgh J., hold that as a result of section 19 (1) the parties cannot by the terms of their contract F abrogate the right and duty of the court, in the event of a dispute as to the reasonableness of the withholding of consent where consent is required by the terms of the lease, to decide by an objective standard whether or not the refusal is reasonable. Thus, if the parties by their contract purport to say that in such and such circumstances the landlord may withhold his consent, that term of the contract is invalid and is to be disregarded. The G court itself decides whether in the circumstances which actually exist the refusal of consent is reasonable.

In *In re Smith's Lease* the provision of the contract which Roxburgh J. held to be invalid in the light of section 19 (1) was a term which provided expressly that a refusal of consent ". . . shall not be deemed to be an unreasonable withholding of consent . . .": and then the clause went on to provide, as not being unreasonable, an elaborate formulation of a trans- H action in which the landlord, when he gave his refusal, offered to the tenant to accept surrender of the tenancy. If that decision be right, the distinction between it and the present case depends, not in any way on the realities of what would be achieved by the respective provisions of the leases, but simply on the fact that a different verbal formula is used. That is not a satisfactory distinction.

After the decision in *In re Smith's Lease* [1951] 1 All E.R. 346, a

A different formula was evolved which it was hoped, at least by those who evolved it, would produce a different legal result. That new formula was tested in *Adler* [1957] 1 W.L.R. 227, and Hilbery J. held, distinguishing *In re Smith's Lease*, that the new formula achieved its object. Although the wording is in various respects different, there is, in my view no material difference from the point of view of legal effect between the *Adler* formula and the formula used in the present lease, in clause 2 (j) (ii) and the second

B of the two provisos. If anything, the *Adler* formula was more vulnerable than the present formula, because, after the words " such consent," it contained the parentheses which the opening words of clause 2 (j) (ii) do not contain, " (subject as hereinafter provided)." The *Adler* formula avoided the inclusion of any provision as to deeming anything not to be unreasonable. It stipulated, by a proviso, that before the tenant applied for consent

C to assign (literally, it said before he " desired " to assign), he should make an offer to the landlord to surrender the lease. If the offer of surrender were accepted, the question of consent to assignment would not arise. If it were refused, then the tenant would, if he wished, make his application to assign; and, if the landlord were to refuse consent, the tenant could invite the court to apply the objective test of reasonableness under section 19 (1) of the Act of 1927.

D   As I have said, the distinction between the *Adler* formula and the *In re Smith's Lease* formula is semantic. The practical result is the same. If the latter is not permissible or effective in the light of section 19 (1), why should the former escape the ban?

      On the other hand, if one is to assume, as for the reasons which I have given it seems to me right for us to assume, that section 19 (1) does not

E prevent or limit freedom of contract to ban assignments altogether by agreement in the lease, why should the subsection be treated as having the effect of preventing or limiting freedom of contract to ban assignments during a part of the lease? Counsel for the landlords, I think rightly, submitted that the courts could not treat section 19 (1) as invalidating a contractual proviso that no assignment should be made—that no question of assignment by consent should arise—during, say, the first, or the last, seven

F years of a 14-year lease. Why, then, as a matter of policy or practical sense or logic should the courts hold that section 19 (1) invalidates a proviso that, before the tenant's right of assignment with consent shall arise, a condition precedent shall be fulfilled: namely, the tenant's obligation first to offer a surrender? If by agreement an assignment by consent can be precluded altogether, what logical reason or policy can be invoked to

G preclude a limited right of the tenant to assign with consent; the limitation being that the landlord, if he wishes, can insist on a surrender?

      In *Adler* [1957] 1 W.L.R. 227, as I have said, Hilbery J. upheld the new formula. Thereafter, so far as counsel's researches go, there was no criticism or adverse comment on that decision or its reasoning in any reported, or, so far as is known, any unreported, case until 1974. The decision has been cited by text-book writers, almost without criticism. The

H *Adler* formula, no doubt with variation, has been set out in widely used books of forms and precedents. It has, we are told, I have no doubt correctly, been used in thousands of leases agreed between landlords and tenants. So far as is known this present case is one of only two cases in which the *Adler* decision and reasoning have been challenged in courts of this country. The other challenge was in *Greene* v. *Church Commissioners for England* [1974] Ch. 467. Although the section 19 (1) question had been raised in the county court from which that appeal was brought, it had not

been there decided, because another issue under the Land Charges Act A
1972, decided in favour of the tenant, rendered a decision on the section
19 (1) issue unnecessary. So, also, when the appeal in *Greene's* case came
to this court, the decision of Judge Leslie in the county court was upheld
by this court. (Counsel for the landlords in this case relies on the decision
in that case on that issue as supporting his submissions in the present case.
He may be right, but I do not find it necessary to go into that submission.
That particular point clearly cannot have been argued in *Greene's* case.) B
However, in *Greene's* case, there were observations by members of the
court, obiter, expressing doubt as to the correctness of *Adler* [1957]
1 W.L.R. 227: see *per* Lord Denning M.R., at p. 477, and Sir Eric Sachs,
at pp. 479–480.

What does seem clear is that the members of the court who expressed
those dicta of doubt as to *Adler* in *Greene's* case did not have the advantage, C
which we have had, of having had cited the judgments given in the High
Court of Australia in *Creer* v. *P. & O. Lines of Australia Pty. Ltd.* (1971)
125 C.L.R. 84. That case involved, directly and indistinguishably, the
correctness of Hilbery J.'s decision in *Adler.* The case arose on section
133B (1) of the Conveyancing Act 1919–1969 (New South Wales). The
statutory terms are identical with section 19 (1). The High Court, with
closely reasoned judgments by Sir Garfield Barwick C.J., Menzies J. and D
Windeyer J., approved and followed *Adler.*

I would do the same. In the balance of conflicting arguments, I reach
that conclusion substantially for three reasons. First, the respect due to the
decision of the High Court of Australia, and to the reasoning of the judgments therein; secondly (as is, indeed, a ground which clearly strongly
influenced Menzies J. in that case), the fact that the *Adler* decision has E
stood, and has been acted on, for so many years; and thirdly (a ground
which makes me feel able to place much greater reliance on the second
ground than I should otherwise have done), the fact that I cannot see
any good argument of policy for interfering, more than is essentially
required by the words of the statute or by binding authority, with freedom
of contract in respect of an agreement between the parties that the landlord should be entitled to the option of requiring a surrender of the lease, F
where the tenant desires to be freed from his obligation under the lease;
bearing in mind that the legislature did not in 1927 consider, and has not
since considered, that policy requires infringement of freedom of contract
between a potential landlord and a potential tenant validly and effectively
to agree that there shall be no right of assignment at all, however reasonable the tenant's subsequent desire to assign may be.

It is contended further for the tenants that, even if *Adler* [1957] G
1 W.L.R. 227 be right, clause 2 (j) is materially different from the *Adler*
clause. The chief ground for that submission is that the last few lines of
the second proviso to clause 2 (j) (ii) do not make provision for anything
that could be called a condition precedent to the tenant's right to such
consent for an assignment, but make provision for what is to happen after
the stage to which the preceding provisions of the proviso relate. I do not H
know what the effect, if any, in law of these last few lines of the proviso
would be. I doubt if they would have any effect. But if and in so far as
they might be thought to be inconsistent with what is required by section
19 (1), they would, as I understand the authorities, simply fall to be ignored.
They would not, as it were, carry through their infection into the rest of
the clause, so as to invalidate the rest of the proviso.

I would dismiss the appeal.

A   LAWTON L.J. At common law there were no fetters on what a landlord could put in a lease, if his tenant agreed, to restrain or control its assignment. He might insert a covenant prohibiting assignment; or he might give the tenant a right to assign with his consent; or he might allow the tenant to assign with his consent, undertaking that his consent would not be unreasonably withheld; or he might omit any covenant against assignment.

B   In 1927 Parliament by the Landlord and Tenant Act of that year provided for the payment of compensation for improvements and goodwill to the tenants of premises used for business purposes, or the grant of new leases, and for the amendment of the law of landlord and tenant : see the long title to that Act. Part I dealt with compensation for improvements and goodwill, Part II with amendments of the law. Three topics were dealt with in Part II : provisions as to covenants to repair; " provisions as to

C covenants not to assign, etc. without licence or consent " (I quote from the marginal note to section 19); and apportionment of rents.

What was the intention of Parliament in enacting section 19 in the terms it did? Was it intended to confer a jurisdiction upon courts to relieve lessees from covenants or to modify them? In *F. W. Woolworth & Co. Ltd.* v. *Lambert* [1937] 1 Ch. 37, Greene L.J. referred to this question in relation to section 19 (2) which was concerned with covenants against the

D making of improvements without licence or consent and answered it in these terms, at p. 60: " It is a statutory addition to the terms of a particular type of covenant, and the proviso which the subsection mentions is to be read into the covenant." The same can be said about the proviso mentioned in subsection (1) with which this appeal is concerned. This being so, the landlords submit that there is nothing in section 19 (1) which fetters

E a landlord's right, save in the terms of the proviso, to insert in a lease a covenant requiring his tenant to act in a specified way before asking for consent to assign and making his acting in that way a condition precedent to his acquiring any right to assign. This is what the landlords say they have done in the second proviso to covenant 2 (j) (ii) of the lease under consideration in this appeal. They rely on the decision of Hilbery J. in *Adler* v. *Upper Grosvenor Street Investment Ltd.* [1957] 1 W.L.R. 227, a

F case in which there was a proviso in broadly similar terms to the one with which we are concerned. The judge decided that a tenant's right to assign under this kind of proviso only arises where his landlord refuses the proffered surrender : see p. 230.

The decision in *Adler's* case does not seem to have surprised conveyancers, and although, as counsel informed us, it was discussed in articles in specialist legal journals, there was virtually no criticism of it. This form of

G covenant found its way into a number of precedent books; see for example *Prideaux Precedents in Conveyancing*, 25th ed., vol. 2 (1959), p. 28; *Encyclopaedia of Forms and Precedents*, 4th ed. vol. 11 (1965), p. 321. The probabilities are, as Mr. Levy accepted, that this kind of proviso is now to be found in many leases.

The decision of the High Court of Australia in *Creer* v. *P. & O. Lines*

H *of Australia Pty. Ltd.*, 125 C.L.R. 84 shows that this form of proviso was in use in the Commonwealth. That distinguished court had to consider its effect having regard to Australian legislation in much the same terms as section 19 (1) of the Act of 1927. Two members of that court, Barwick C.J. and Windeyer J. decided that *Adler's* case [1957] 1 W.L.R. 227 had been rightly decided. Menzies J. was not as certain about the correctness of that decision as his brethren, but decided in the end to accept it. For my part I found the reasoning of Barwick C.J. and Windeyer J. most convincing.

As Megaw L.J. has pointed out in his judgment, the *Adler* form of A proviso was queried obiter in *Greene* v. *Church Commissioners for England* [1974] Ch. 467. I adopt his comments on that case.

The history of the *Adler* form of proviso has had an odd twist which was made by the Rent Act 1977. Section 127 (1) of that Act excluded the statutory prohibition on premiums on grants of protected tenancies when a tenancy was both a long-term tenancy within the meaning of Part I of the Landlord and Tenant Act 1954 and a protected tenancy provided the B conditions specified in subsection (2) were fulfilled. The third of those conditions, which is set out in paragraph (c), was that assignment or underletting was precluded by the terms of the tenancy.

" and, if it is subject to any consent, there is neither a term excluding section 144 of the Law of Property Act 1925 " (I omit the words which are not necessary for this purpose) " nor a term requiring in connection C with a request for consent the making of an offer to surrender the tenancy."

Parliament in 1977 seems to have assumed that the *Adler* form of covenant was valid. This assumption does not make it valid; but it is a statutory reflection of what is in the precedent books.

I am satisfied that the judgment of Hilbery J. in *Adler's* case [1957] D 1 W.L.R. 227 was correct, for the reasons given by Barwick C.J. and Windeyer J. in *Creer* v. *P. & O. Lines of Australia Pty. Ltd.*, 125 C.L.R. 84. As I can find no significant difference between the *Adler* form of proviso and that under consideration in this case, I would dismiss the appeal.

E

BROWNE L.J. (judgment read by Lawton L.J.). I have found this a very difficult case, but in the end I agree that the appeal should be dismissed.

According to the law as it stood immediately before the passing of the Act of 1927 (which the draftsmen must be assumed to have had in mind), a lease could validly contain a covenant absolutely prohibiting assignment or subletting; on the other hand, if there was a covenant not to assign or sublet without the landlord's consent, such consent not to be unreasonably F withheld, the wish of the landlord to regain possession for himself was not a reasonable ground for refusing consent: see *Bates* v. *Donaldson* [1896] 2 Q.B. 241 and *Houlder Brothers & Co. Ltd.* v. *Gibbs* [1925] Ch. 575. As Megaw L.J. has said, neither party asked us to give effect to the doubts of Danckwerts L.J. in *Property & Bloodstock Ltd.* v. *Emerton* [1968] Ch. 94, 119–120 to which he has referred, and I accept that section 19 (1) of the G Act of 1927 does not affect an absolute covenant against assignment. The primary purpose of section 19 (1) seems to be to add a statutory proviso to a covenant not to assign without consent. The problem in this case is its application where there is already in the lease a contractual proviso that consent is not to be unreasonably withheld in the case of a respectable and responsible assignee, followed by further provisions which, if valid, limit the tenant's liberty to assign. I think that a possible view of the effect of H section 19 (1) is that the lease must be read as if it simply contained the statutory proviso " such licence or consent is not to be unreasonably withheld " and no more, and what follows must be disregarded. If so on the law as it stood in 1927 a refusal of consent on the ground that the landlord wanted possession for himself would be unreasonable. Further, as Megaw L.J. has said, the practical object and effect of the clause which was held invalid in *In re Smith's Lease* [1951] 1 All E.R. 346 and the clause which

A was held valid in *Adler* v. *Upper Grosvenor Street Investment Ltd.* [1957] 1 W.L.R. 227 and by the High Court of Australia in *Creer* v. *P. & O. Lines of Australia Pty Ltd.,* 125 C.L.R. 84 was the same (that is, to give the benefit of any increase in the value of the lease to the landlord and not the tenant), and the difference between the clauses was simply that the object and purpose was wrapped up in a different verbal formula. For these reasons I have shared the doubts expressed (obiter) by Lord Denning M.R.
B and Sir Eric Sachs in *Greene* v. *Church Commissioners for England* [1974] Ch. 467, 477, 479–480 and by Menzies J. in *Creer* v. *P. & O. Lines of Australia Pty. Ltd.,* at p. 90.

But after a good deal of hesitation I have come to the conclusion that this appeal should be dismissed, for the three reasons given by Megaw L.J. I will not try to paraphrase them or repeat them at length. In substance
C they are:

1. The respect due to the decision of the High Court of Australia.

2. The fact that *Adler* has stood for more than 20 years and has, we are told by Mr. Wood, been acted on in thousands of leases, without criticism except in *Greene's* case (which was followed by a guarded note in (1975) 91 L.Q.R. 3) and by Menzies J. As Windeyer J. pointed out in *Creer's* case,
D at p. 91, it had previously been noted, with apparent approval, by Mr. Megarry in (1957) 73 L.Q.R. 157, and Mr. Wood provided us with a number of extracts from text-books and precedent books which generally treat it as good law.

3. Since Parliament has not thought it necessary or desirable to prohibit or limit absolute covenants against assignment, I cannot discern any policy reason for invalidating a covenant which in effect prohibits assignment
E unless a condition precedent has been fulfilled—namely, the offer and refusal of a surrender. I was impressed by the analogy of an absolute covenant against assignment during (say) the first seven years or the last seven years of a 14-year lease.

I would only add that I cannot myself rely on the argument based on section 127 of the Rent Act 1977—see *Kirkness* v. *John Hudson & Co.*
F *Ltd.* [1955] A.C. 696, especially *per* Lord Reid, at p. 735.

Appeal dismissed with costs,
to include costs of motion
for security for costs.

G Solicitors: *Davidson, Doughty & Co.; Freshfields.*

M. G.

H

[1980]

A

[HOUSE OF LORDS]

* EARL OF NORMANTON . . . . . RESPONDENT

AND

GILES AND ANOTHER . . . . . . APPELLANTS

B

1979 Nov. 1;   Lord Wilberforce, Viscount Dilhorne,
     Dec. 13   Lord Diplock, Lord Salmon and
                                          Lord Russell of Killowen

*Agriculture—Security of tenure—Agricultural worker—Gamekeeper
employed to rear pheasants for sport—Whether employed in
" agriculture "—Rent (Agriculture) Act 1976 (c. 80), s. (1) (a) (2)*   C

By section 1 of the Rent (Agriculture) Act 1976:
    " (1) In this Act—(a) ' agriculture ' includes—(i) . . . live-
    stock keeping and breeding . . . (2) For the purposes of
    the definition in subsection (1) (a) above— . . . ' livestock '
    includes any animal which is kept for the production of
    food . . ."
        The appellant, as gamekeeper employed by the respondent,   D
    reared pheasants for shoots, catching birds for laying, clipping
    their wings, putting them into pens and, after the incubation
    of the eggs, putting the poults into release pens which they
    left, becoming wild and available for shooting. Most of the
    birds killed were sold to game dealers and butchers the
    proceeds being used to maintain the shoots. All the birds
    killed and retrieved were consumed as food. After the
    termination of the appellant's employment he was required   E
    to give up possession of the cottage he occupied with his
    wife on the respondent's estate but he refused to do so on
    the ground that he was a protected occupier by virtue of
    section 2 (1) [1] of the Act of 1976. The respondent brought
    an action in the county court to recover possession.
        The judge found as a fact that the purpose for which the
    birds were reared was not the production of food but sport,   F
    shooting and enjoyment and he therefore held that the appel-
    lant was not " employed in agriculture " within paragraph 3 (1)
    of Schedule 3 to the Act so as to be a " qualifying worker "
    within section 2 (1) whose occupation of the cottage was
    protected. The Court of Appeal affirmed his decision.
        On appeal by the appellant: —
        Held, dismissing the appeal, that on the facts found the
    pheasants were neither " kept for the production of food "
    within section 1 (2) of the Act nor was the keeping and   G
    rearing of them for sport an agricultural occupation so as to
    come within the scope of " agriculture " in section 1 (1) (a) (i)
    of the Act and accordingly the appellant was not " employed
    in agriculture " so as to be a " qualifying worker " within
    section 2 (1) (a) (post, pp. 30F–H, 33F–H, 36A–D, H, 38D, 39E–F).
        Lord Glendyne v. *Rapley* [1978] 1 W.L.R. 601, C.A.
    approved.
        Decision of the Court of Appeal affirmed.   H

The following cases are referred to in their Lordships' opinions:

Belmont Farm Ltd. v. *Minister of Housing and Local Government* (1962)
    60 L.G.R. 319, D.C.

[1] Rent (Agriculture) Act 1976, s. 2 (1): see post, p. 37C.
Sch. 3, para. 3: see post, p. 37D.

1 W.L.R.   Normanton v. Giles (H.L.(E.))

A   Glendyne (Lord) v. Rapley [1978] 1 W.L.R. 601; [1978] 2 All E.R. 110,
        C.A.
      Hardwick Game Farm v. Suffolk Agricultural Poultry Producers Associa-
        tion [1969] 2 A.C. 31; [1968] 3 W.L.R. 110; [1968] 2 All E.R.
        444, H.L.(E.).
      Minister of Agriculture, Fisheries and Food v. Appleton [1970] 1 Q.B.
        221; [1969] 3 W.L.R. 755; [1969] 3 All E.R. 1051, D.C.
B   Peterborough Royal Foxhound Show Society v. Inland Revenue Com-
        missioners [1936] 2 K.B. 497; [1936] 1 All E.R. 813.
      Smith v. Coles [1905] 2 K.B. 827, C.A.
      Stephens' Application, In re [1938] 2 K.B. 675; [1938] 3 All E.R. 311.
      Vellacott's Application, In re [1922] 1 K.B. 466.
      Walters v. Wright (1938) 159 L.T. 555; [1938] 4 All E.R. 116, D.C.

C   The following additional cases were cited in argument:
      Customs and Excise Commissioners v. Savoy Hotel Ltd. [1966] 1 W.L.R.
        948; [1966] 2 All E.R. 299.
      Inland Revenue Commissioners v. Joiner [1975] 1 W.L.R. 1701; [1975]
        3 All E.R. 1050, H.L.(E.).
      Lanarkshire Assessor v. Smith, 1933 S.C. 366.
      Lean v. Ball, 1926 S.C. 15.
D   Portsmouth Corporation v. Smith (1883) 13 Q.B.D. 184, C.A.
      Smithers v. Wallis [1903] 1 K.B. 200, C.A.

      APPEAL from the Court of Appeal.
      This was an appeal by Stanley Giles and Diana Mary Giles, the
first and second appellants, by leave of the House of Lords from an
order of the Court of Appeal (Stephenson and Lawton L.JJ.) dated
E July 25, 1978, dismissing their appeal from an order of Judge Lee
made on February 18, 1977, in the Salisbury County Court whereby
it was adjudged that the Earl of Normanton, the respondent, should
recover possession of the cottage premises known as Old Somerley,
Somerley Park, Ringwood, Hampshire.

F   The appellant, Stanley Giles, appeared in person.
      Robert Johnson Q.C. and Hugh Bennett for the respondent.

      Their Lordships took time for consideration.

      December 13, 1979. LORD WILBERFORCE. My Lords, is a gamekeeper
    a person working wholetime in agriculture? If so, he is, as a qualifying
G
    worker, entitled to the protection conferred by the Rent (Agriculture)
Act 1976 as regards occupation of his cottage.
      This is partly a question of impression—partly a question of statutory
interpretation. It is no easier to discard deep-seated preconceptions as
to the former than it is to unravel the confusions of the latter. There
is no doubt that the apparent simplicity of the case is deceptive.
H   Mr. Giles was gamekeeper to the Earl of Normanton, and as such,
until he was given notice to quit, he occupied Old Somerley, a cottage
on the estate. There was detailed evidence as to his duties and the case
must be decided upon it, but it is probably true to say that they were
fairly typical. He had the normal task of producing pheasants during
shoots and of preventing poaching: he cleared vermin and controlled
deer. Also (and this was what he relied on) he was responsible for
rearing pheasants. In the spring he would catch birds for laying, clip

their wings and put them in pens. These were in a walled garden adjoin- A
ing his cottage. After laying, and incubation of the eggs, the poults
were put into release pens and as they grew they walked out and in due
course, it was hoped, became wild and available for shooting. Some
figures were provided as to the number of birds reared and shot in several
seasons, interesting to the sportsman but not legally significant. The
one relevant point was that the great majority of the birds shot were
sold to butchers and game dealers, and no doubt ultimately to individuals B
by whom they were consumed as food. The proceeds went to maintain
the shoot.

I must now refer to the relevant provisions in the Act of 1976. These
are the following:

> " 1 (1) In this Act—(*a*) ' agriculture ' includes—(i) dairy-farming
> and livestock keeping and breeding (whether those activities involve C
> the use of land or not); . . . (2) For the purposes of the definition
> in subsection (1) (*a*) above—' consumable produce ' means produce
> grown for consumption or other use after severance or separation
> from the land or other growing medium on or in which it is grown;
> ' livestock ' includes any animal which is kept for the production
> of food, wool, skins or fur, or for the purpose of its use in the D
> carrying on of any agricultural activity, and for the purposes of
> this definition ' animal ' includes bird but does not include fish."

On these facts and this law the case was tried in Salisbury County
Court by Judge Lee who, it can safely be assumed, was not blind or
oblivious to the realities of country life. Before him, and subsequently,
the main reliance was placed on subsection (2) above. Mr. Giles con- E
tended that pheasants, or at any rate his pheasants, were animals kept
for the production of food; therefore were " livestock." This made
them livestock kept and bred within section 1 (1) (*a*) (i), therefore
keeping and breeding of them was " agriculture."

My Lords, I think that there are two good reasons why this argument
does not succeed. First, it was found by the judge that

> " the production of food is not the purpose for which birds are F
> reared or for which the defendant " (Mr. Giles) " was employed.
> The job of the gamekeeper is to get as many pheasants into the
> woods (sic) so that they become wild . . . A gamekeeper is there to
> keep game, for the purpose of shooting and enjoyment. The purpose
> of shooting pheasants is sport. It is no part of food production or
> the keeping of livestock."   G

There was clearly evidence to support these findings and they are
fatal to the argument. It may be the case that unless people in general
were willing to eat pheasants and to pay for that pleasure, shooting would
become uneconomic, but it does not follow from this that pheasants are
produced for food. If they were to be so produced many easier ways of
rearing and killing them could be found.   H

But, secondly, the argument fails, in my opinion, on another ground.
The section does not say " produced for food " but " kept for the
production of food." This seems to me to be a different thing altogether
and to be directed towards animals such as bees, or (as to skins or fur)
mink or silver foxes. Animals kept and bred for food—i.e., to be eaten,
such as cattle or chickens, come under subsection (1). The presence of
" wool " in subsection (2) is puzzling, but I cannot believe that sheep,

A kept as prospective mutton or lamb, do not come under subsection (1)—there could scarcely be anything which more obviously does. Subsection (2) is not needed to bring them in under " agriculture." If this is right, it is clear that pheasants do not come within subsection (2) at all. Whatever they do, they do not produce food: on the contrary they consume it.

B This conclusion however does not, as seems to have been thought, conclude the matter. It only leads to the real point as I see it: i.e., whether pheasants are livestock and whether Mr. Giles kept and bred livestock. Section 1 (1) (a) is quite independent of section 1 (2): the latter says what is *included* in livestock, not what " livestock " *means*. That " includes " here signifies " includes " is shown by the preceding definition of " consumable produce " which takes the form " means . . .".

C So we still have to consider whether apart from the special inclusions, pheasants can be described as " livestock." Though many people would instinctively deny this, it does, on the authorities, seem to be a puzzling question.

We were shown a number of other definitions in other Acts which are remarkable for their variety. In the Animals Act 1971 (section 11) " livestock " is said to mean cattle etc., and, in certain sections " while in

D captivity, pheasants, partridges and grouse." But I think this is a special provision designed to give their keepers protection from dogs. In the Diseases of Animals Act 1950 (section 84) pheasants and partridges are classified as poultry, but this does not necessarily mean they are livestock: they are not, in that Act, regarded as " animals." For V.A.T. purposes " game birds " are zero rated together with other edible animals which

E undoubtedly are " livestock " as contrasted with horses and racing pigeons, on the basis that they are held to be food for human consumption. But this does not mean that before the stage of consumption they are necessarily " livestock." So these statutes in the end are inconclusive.

Mr. Giles, with exemplary relevance and economy, referred us to a number of cases. In *Smith* v. *Coles* [1905] 2 K.B. 827 it was held that a man employed three months in the year as a gamekeeper and who

F assisted at hay and corn harvests, rick-making, and mangel-carting, who also acted as farm carpenter, was employed in agriculture for the purpose of workmen's compensation, but the question was whether the county court judge could so find in spite of his work as farm carpenter. It was not necessary to decide, and the court did not decide, whether as gamekeeper he was employed in agriculture. Indeed, Romer L.J.

G at p. 831 was careful to leave this question open.

" Sometimes he was engaged in what are admittedly agricultural pursuits, at other times he did work essential to the proper conduct of the farm such as the repair of fences, and for part of his time he acted as gamekeeper."

On this total picture he could be said to be employed in agriculture.

H In *Walters* v. *Wright* (1938) 159 L.T. 555, 557 Lord Hewart C.J. said that there was much to be said for a definition of " agriculture " as including " any use of land in connection with breeding or keeping any animal ordinarily found on a farm." The animals there in question were poultry and two Scottish cases had decided that poultry farms could be husbandry or agriculture—it seems that rent was sometimes paid by farmers in " kain hens." But even if " pheasants " are for some purposes " poultry " that does not mean that the keeping of them is agriculture:

the question remains whether they are animals " ordinarily kept on a A
farm "—a question to which I shall have to return. In *Peterborough
Royal Foxhound Show Society* v. *Inland Revenue Commissioners* [1936]
2 K.B. 497—a case concerned with foxhound breeding—Lawrence J. said,
" The words ' live stock ' are ordinarily and properly used in contrast
with dead stock and include all live animals and birds the breeding of
which is regulated by man " (p. 500). This is helpful to Mr. Giles but
later the judge makes it clear that he has in mind animals bred in the B
ordinary course of agriculture and shown throughout the country, for
example, hackneys, hunters, racehorses, dogs and fur-bearing animals.
The question still remains whether pheasants bred for shooting would
come within this conception. In *In re Stephens' Application* [1938] 2
K.B. 675, it was held that a man employed on a farm for breeding silver
foxes, nutria, etc., for their pelts, and having general duties on the farm C
was " employed in agriculture." Branson J. took the view, as a matter
of impression, that since breeding sheep for wool rather than for food
must clearly be an agricultural pursuit, so must breeding animals for
pelts, particularly when the breeding and feeding of them was integrated
with the farm as a whole. This view of the matter (on which there was
contrary opinion in Scotland) was evidently endorsed by Parliament in
various Acts preceding and in section 1 (2) of the Act of 1976, and D
may explain the appearance of " wool " in subsection (2).

Mr. Johnson for Lord Normanton contributed his share to the
learning on this subject. In *In re Vellacott's Application* [1922] 1 K.B.
466, questions arose whether a list of persons of various occupations
were (a) employed in agriculture or (b) employed in domestic service;
in either of which cases they were exempt from insurance against E
unemployment. A gamekeeper was held to be exempt but on the—some
may think curious—ground that he was employed in domestic service,
as were a huntsman of a pack of foxhounds and the whippers-in. A
river keeper was similarly treated and Roche J. said of him, at p. 473:

> " He is engaged by a private employer for the purpose of looking
> after the fishing, which is one of the interests and amusements in life F
> of his employer. Sport has universally been held to be one of the
> wants and needs of the average ordinary Englishman."

This is not conclusive that the gamekeeper was not, also, employed in
agriculture but certainly does not support the contention that he is.

An interesting citation was produced from the unlikely source of
Hardwick Game Farm v. *Suffolk Agricultural Poultry Producers Asso-* G
ciation [1969] 2 A.C. 31. Lord Reid said, at p. 85:

> " I do not think that these pheasants were poultry. They were
> reared for the purpose of being released to serve as targets for
> sportsmen, and pheasants which have never been in captivity are
> clearly not poultry. It may well be that, if it should prove profitable
> to rear and keep pheasants in captivity until killed for human con- H
> sumption, such pheasants should be regarded as poultry. But the
> mere fact that these pheasants like other game will come to the table
> after they have been shot seems to me to be immaterial. It would
> not in my view be in accordance with the ordinary use of language
> to say that they were poultry until released and then became game.
> They were game throughout and the farm where they were reared
> was properly called a game farm."

A   Some similar observations appear in the speeches of Lord Guest (p. 111) and myself (p. 126). I think that these reinforce the common impression that the rearing of pheasants for sport is sui generis and is not to be equated with the rearing of other livestock.

In *Minister of Agriculture, Fisheries and Food* v. *Appleton* [1970] 1 Q.B. 221, the court had to decide whether the breeding of cats and dogs was livestock breeding and keeping. The relevant Act (the Selective

B   Employment Payments Act 1966) contained definitions of " agriculture " and of " livestock " very similar to those in section 1 (1) and (2) of the Act of 1976. It was held that it was not. The definition of " livestock " showed that the word was not intended to refer to the breeding and keeping of animals of any sort, but only to those either within the separate definition (as in our subsection (2)) or in the course of an activity

C   which could properly be brought within the meaning of agriculture. In his judgment Lord Parker C.J. quoted at p. 226 from an earlier decision of his (*Belmont Farm Ltd.* v. *Minister of Housing and Local Government* (1962) 60 L.G.R. 319, 322) in which, referring to the definition of livestock (as in our subsection (2)) he had said, " that is clearly an extension to cover, no doubt, an argument that, for instance, bees, *possibly pheasants* and fish are not livestock." I do not think that this

D   helps Mr. Giles, if I am right in thinking that pheasants are not within the extension. On the definition of " agriculture " which we are now considering this case decidedly favours Lord Normanton.

Finally, I come to the recent decision of the Court of Appeal in *Lord Glendyne* v. *Rapley* [1978] 1 W.L.R. 601 which raised exactly the same question as that now before us and which was followed by the

E   Court of Appeal in the present case. Lord Scarman gave a short judgment in which he held, at pp. 603–604:

"... not every rural or country activity is intended to be included in the definition of agriculture. Fishing, for example, is clearly excluded. The definition is really directed towards including all operations involved in farming land for commercial purposes of which the one relevant to this appeal is the production of food. The

F   finding that these pheasants were kept for sport, though 80 per cent. of those killed and retrieved were in fact sold, is, in our judgment, conclusive. Mr. Rapley's employment was to promote not agriculture but a field sport. This is a country activity but not an agricultural one."

G   Apart from the reference to the " production of food," which to my mind is not the critical issue in this case, I agree with this passage. I think that it is in line with the tenor of the cases I have referred to, and in particular with the judgment of Lord Parker C.J. just mentioned. Agriculture, however wide that activity has become, does not include everything that goes on in the country. Rearing and keeping pheasants for sport is not thought of as, and there is no statutory or case authority

H   for holding it to be, an agricultural occupation: pheasants so kept and reared are not " livestock " in an agricultural context: only such " livestock " is designated in section 1 of the Act of 1976.

I cannot therefore, in the end, accept Mr. Giles' argument and his appeal must be dismissed.

VISCOUNT DILHORNE. My Lords, the appellant, Mr. Giles, who appeared in person, was employed by the respondent as head gamekeeper

on his estate, Somerley Park, Ringwood, Hampshire. His employment A
began on March 7, 1973, and throughout it he and his wife, the second
appellant, lived in a cottage on the estate called Old Somerley. The
respondent gave him notice terminating his employment on March 27,
1976, and sought to recover possession of the cottage through the county
court. On July 16, 1976, Judge Lee held that it was a term of the first
appellant's employment that it was only terminable by notice given on or
before December 1 in any year to expire on February 1 following. B

So on July 27, 1976, the respondent gave the appellant a fresh notice
terminating his employment with effect from February 1, 1977, and
requiring him to give up possession of the cottage. The first appellant
did not do so and so a summons for possession was issued and on
February 18, 1977, Judge Lee made an order for possession.

The Rent (Agriculture) Act 1976 came into force on January 1, 1977, C
and it was contended on behalf of Mr. Giles in the county court and in
the Court of Appeal, and by him in this House, that by virtue of the
Act, he was a protected occupier and entitled to continue to occupy the
cottage.

Section 2 (1) of the Act provides:

"Where a person has, in relation to a dwelling-house, a relevant D
licence or tenancy and the dwelling-house is in qualifying ownership . . . at any time during the subsistence of the licence or
tenancy . . . he shall be a protected occupier of the dwelling-house
if—(a) he is a qualifying worker, or (b) he has been a qualifying
worker at any time during the subsistence of the licence or
tenancy . . ."

E
So to establish that he was a protected occupier, Mr. Giles had to show
that the cottage was in qualifying ownership and that he was or had
been a qualifying worker.

Schedule 3, paragraph 3, the Act states that a dwelling-house is in
qualifying ownership at any time if, at that time, the occupier is employed
in agriculture and the occupier's employer is the owner of the dwelling-
house; and paragraph 1 of the Schedule provides that a person is a F
qualifying worker at any time if, at that time, he has worked whole time
in agriculture.

There was no dispute that if Mr. Giles had been employed in
agriculture and had worked in agriculture, the cottage was in qualifying
ownership and he was or had been a qualifying worker. The only
question for decision in this litigation is whether he had been employed G
and had worked in agriculture.

The Act does not attempt to define " agriculture " but by section 1
(1) (a) it states that " agriculture " includes: " (i) dairy-farming and
livestock keeping and breeding (whether those activities involve the use
of land or not) " and section 1 (2) states that " livestock " includes

"any animal which is kept for the production of food, wool, skins H
or fur, or for the purpose of its use in the carrying on of any
agricultural activity, and for the purposes of this definition ' animal '
includes bird but does not include fish."

So as these definitions are not exhaustive, one must first consider whether
if they were not in the Act, Mr. Giles should be held to have been
engaged in agriculture; and secondly, taking these definitions into account,
he should be held to have been so employed.

A   " Agriculture " is defined in the *Oxford English Dictionary* (1933)
vol. 1, p. 191 as: " The science and art of cultivating the soil; including
the allied pursuits of gathering in the crops and rearing live stock." And
" live stock " is defined in the dictionary vol. 6, p. 364 as: " Domestic
animals generally; animals of any kind kept or dealt in for use or profit."

Mr. Giles, who had two keepers under him, was employed in looking
after the respondent's pheasant shoot and he did the usual work of a
B   gamekeeper so employed, catching up cocks and hens after the shooting
season was over, putting them in a walled-in garden by his cottage,
collecting the eggs, putting them in incubators looking after the incubators and the hatched out chicks, and then when the time was right,
putting the pheasant poults in release pens in the woods. No doubt on
shooting days he supervised the beaters and saw that the drives were
C   properly conducted.

The pheasants which were shot, a number far less than the number
reared, were for the most part sold to dealers. Some were given to the
guns and some to the beaters at Christmas. However disposed of, there
is no doubt that they were consumed as food. The receipts from the sale
of the dead pheasants went to meet some of the expense of the shoot.

D   Mr. Giles stated that the pheasants were reared and kept for shooting.
They were not reared and kept for eating. This use for food was
consequently a by-product of the shooting.

I do not think that pheasants kept and reared for shooting, and which
when sufficiently grown are released from captivity, can properly be
regarded as " domestic animals " or as being kept for use or profit. They
cease to be kept when they are let to go free. I do not therefore consider
E   that the pheasants looked after by Mr. Giles were within the definition
of livestock in the dictionary and consequently the rearing and keeping
of them does not come within the definition in the dictionary of agriculture.

I do not think that the decision of Lawrence J. in *Peterborough Royal
Foxhound Show Society* v. *Inland Revenue Commissioners* [1936] 2 K.B.
F   497 that foxhound breeding was livestock breeding, is of any assistance
to Mr. Giles, for I do not think it follows from that decision that the
rearing of pheasants which are to be freed and which is for shooting is
to be similarly regarded. " Livestock " was contrasted by Lawrence J.
with " deadstock " and he did not have to deal with a definition of
agriculture which included livestock (see *Minister of Agriculture,
Fisheries and Food* v. *Appleton* [1970] 1 Q.B. 221, 225 *per* Lord Parker
G   C.J.) In my view the word " livestock " is usually used to cover all forms
of stock found on farms in the course of farming.

In *In re Vellacott's Application* [1922] 1 K.B. 466, Roche J. had to
decide whether a variety of persons were excepted from the provisions
of that Act as to insurance against unemployment. They were excepted
if employed in agriculture or in domestic services. He held that a
H   gamekeeper was exempt not because he was employed in agriculture
but because he was a domestic servant. He also held that a river keeper
was a domestic servant saying, at p. 473:

" He is engaged by a private employer for the purpose of looking
after the fishing, which is one of the interests and amusements in life
of his employer. Sport has universally been held to be one of the
wants and needs of the average ordinary Englishman."

If one replaces the word " fishing " by the word " shooting " this passage A
would be apt in its application to Mr. Giles.

I cannot regard any of his activities which I have described as agricultural activities. They were all directed to one end, to provide good sport
for the respondent and those who came to shoot with him.

In my opinion, ignoring the definitions in the Act, it is not right to
say that Mr. Giles when working for the respondent was employed in or
worked in agriculture.   B

I now turn to the second question. Is he to be regarded as having
been engaged in agriculture by virtue of the definitions in the Act? This
appears to me to depend on whether the pheasants were livestock as
defined. If they were kept for the production of food, they were but
not otherwise.

As I have said Mr. Giles said they were kept and reared for shooting, C
and Judge Lee held, in my opinion rightly, that: " The production of
food is not the purpose for which the birds are reared or for which the
defendant " (Mr. Giles) " was employed." To say that the pheasants
were kept for the production of food when they were reared for shooting
because the shot pheasants were eaten is in my opinion to confuse an
incidental result of the shooting with the purpose for which the pheasants
were reared.   D

In *Hardwick Game Farm* v. *Suffolk Agricultural Poultry Producers
Association* [1969] 2 A.C. 31 Lord Reid had to consider whether
pheasants were poultry and he said, at p. 85:

" I do not think that these pheasants were poultry. They were
reared for the purposes of being released to serve as targets for
sportsmen, and pheasants which have never been in captivity are E
clearly not poultry. It may well be that, if it should prove profitable
to rear and keep pheasants in captivity until killed for human consumption, such pheasants should be regarded as poultry. But the
mere fact that these pheasants like other game will come to the
table after they have been shot seems to me to be immaterial. It
would not in my view be in accordance with the ordinary use of
language to say that they were poultry until released and then F
became game. They were game throughout. . . ."

In my opinion the definitions in the Act do not help Mr. Giles and
I am fortified in this conclusion by the decision of the Court of Appeal
on the same question in *Lord Glendyne* v. *Rapley* [1978] 1 W.L.R. 601
when the judgment of the court was given by my noble and learned
friend, Lord Scarman.   G

In my opinion definitions in other Acts are of no assistance in
construing this Act and I do not therefore refer to them.

In my opinion the Court of Appeal in the present case and Judge
Lee came to the right conclusion and for the reasons stated, I would
dismiss this appeal with costs.

H

LORD DIPLOCK. My Lords, I have had the advantage of reading in
draft the opinion of my noble and learned friend, Viscount Dilhorne,
with which I agree, and would therefore dismiss the appeal.

LORD SALMON. My Lords, this appeal turns upon a short but, in my
view, not a very easy point of construction of the Rent (Agriculture) Act
1976. The question to be decided is whether Mr. Giles, who was the

A Earl of Normanton's head gamekeeper and occupied one of his cottages, was entitled to security of tenure.

The relevant facts are all set out in the speech of my noble and learned friend, Lord Wilberforce, which I gratefully adopt. The dictionary definition of agriculture and many interesting authorities (none of which related to the Act with which this appeal is concerned) and a number of other Acts dealing with agriculture were cited both by
B Mr. Giles (who conducted his case extremely well) and by counsel for Lord Normanton. No doubt that to describe a gamekeeper as an agricultural worker sounds somewhat incongruous, but no more so than to describe him as a domestic servant. All the learning relied upon by both parties was of considerable interest but in my view shed little light on the point which this House has to decide.

C I will now set out the relevant parts of the Act of 1976. Section 2 (1):

"Where a person has, in relation to a dwelling-house, a relevant licence or tenancy . . . he shall be a protected occupier . . . if—(a) he is a qualifying worker . . ."

Schedule 3:

D "1. A person is a qualifying worker for the purposes of this Act at any time if, at that time, he has worked whole time in agriculture . . . 3.—(1) A dwelling-house in relation to which a person ('the occupier') has a licence or tenancy is in qualifying ownership for the purposes of this Act at any time if, at that time, the occupier is employed in agriculture and the occupier's employer . . . (a) is the owner of the dwelling-house . . ."

E I now come to the interpretation section of the Act, parts of which are of great importance. Section 1:

"(1) In this Act (a) 'agriculture' includes (i) dairy farming and livestock keeping and breeding . . . (2) For the purposes of the definition in subsection (1) (a) above—. . . 'livestock' includes any animal which is kept for the production of food, wool, skins or fur,
F or for the purpose of its use in the carrying on of any agricultural activity, and for the purposes of this definition 'animal' includes bird but does not include fish."

This appeal, in my opinion, turns entirely upon whether the pheasants kept by Lord Normanton were kept by him for the production of food.

G The dictionary's definition of "live stock" is: "Domestic animals generally; animals of any kind kept or dealt in for use or profit." That definition covers a wide range of animals including dogs and horses. This may be why the Act set out in section 1 (2) the meaning of "livestock" in the sense in which it is used in section 1 (1). I cannot accept that the word "food" in the phrase "any animal which is kept for the production of food" is confined to milk and honey. Nor do I think
H that that phrase is in any way inept when applied to beef cattle, sheep or poultry, for, in my view, all these are kept for the production of food. The only question is—does the phrase apply to Lord Normanton's pheasants? None of these birds were wild birds but they were bred and reared by the head gamekeeper in a walled garden behind the cottage in which he lived. Well before the shooting season began, the keeper put the birds out into his employer's woods and with the help of the two junior gamekeepers protected them by keeping down vermin and poachers.

Lord Salmon   Normanton v. Giles (H.L.(E.))   **[1980]**

There is no doubt that the primary object of breeding, rearing and   A
keeping the pheasants was for the sport of shooting: indeed it is obvious
that no gamekeepers would have been employed nor any pheasants bred
and reared but for the shooting. There is, however, no doubt that all
the pheasants which are shot down and retrieved, whether given to the
guns and, as they sometimes were, to the gamekeepers and to some of
the beaters, or sold, as the bulk of them were, to butchers and merchants,
every bird brought down and retrieved at a shoot would eventually   B
become food on someone's table. If pheasants were not edible but only
decorative and rare, I wonder if pheasant shooting would continue to be
in vogue. I think not: indeed it would probably be illegal. It is perhaps
obvious that everyone who keeps pheasants must know that those which
are shot and retrieved will become food which will be eaten. Accordingly, there is, in my view, a good deal to be said for the proposition that   C
if you keep pheasants for shooting, it necessarily follows that you must
also keep them for the production of food. I have no doubt, however
(as I have already indicated), that the main purpose for which pheasants
are kept is shooting and, indeed, that, but for the shooting, they would
not be kept at all.

My Lords, although I have considerable doubt about the point at
issue, I am not prepared to dissent from the view that since the principal   D
reason for keeping the pheasants was the sport of shooting them, the
appeal should be dismissed.

LORD RUSSELL OF KILLOWEN. My Lords, the question in this appeal
is a short one. The appellant was employed by the respondent on his
estate as head gamekeeper. As such he was provided with a cottage on   E
the respondent's estate. The respondent, having by notice determined
that employment, obtained from the judge in the county court an order
for possession, which was upheld in the Court of Appeal. Whether that
order was correctly made depends upon whether the appellant was entitled
to the protection of the Rent (Agriculture) Act 1976. In order to assert
that protection the appellant must show that he was " employed to work   F
in agriculture." The short question is—was he?

I pause to say that in fact during the litigation the appellant vacated
the cottage and his successor in his employment has been installed in
the cottage. If the appellant is correct in his contentions, presumably
his successor would be entitled to the same protection, and the outcome
of success in this appeal would be, to say the least, obscure.

Returning to the short question, the Act of 1976 provides in section 1:   G

" (1) In this Act—(a) ' agriculture' includes—(i) dairy-farming and
livestock keeping and breeding (whether those activities involve the
use of land or not); (ii) the production of any consumable produce
which is grown for sale or for consumption or other use for the
purposes of a trade or business or of any other undertaking (whether
carried on for profit or not); (iii) the use of land as grazing, meadow   H
or pasture land or orchard or osier land; (iv) the use of land for
market gardens or nursery grounds; and (v) forestry; (b) ' forestry'
includes—(i) the use of land for nursery grounds for trees, and
(ii) the use of land for woodlands where that use is ancillary to
the use of land for other agricultural purposes. (2) For the purposes
of the definition in subsection (1) (a) above—' consumable produce'
means produce grown for consumption for other use after severance

A   or separation from the land or other growing medium on or in which it is grown; ' livestock ' includes any animal which is kept for the production of food, wool, skins or fur, or for the purpose of its use in the carrying on of any agricultural activity, and for the purposes of this definition ' animal ' includes bird but does not include fish."

B   I observe that subsection (2) refers to subsection (1) (*a*) as a " definition ": and section 1 (3) says that the expressions listed in column 1 of Schedule 1 to the Act have for the purposes of the Act " the meanings " given by the provisions shown in column 2 of that Schedule. " Agriculture " is one such expression, and against it is a reference to section 1 (1). Schedule 1 is headed " Index of General Definitions." Nevertheless it cannot be ignored that " includes " is not ordinarily to be regarded as
C   the same as " means."

      The respondent preserves and breeds pheasants on his estate for the sport of shooting. Others of your Lordships have described the activities involved, and the part played in those activities by the appellant in the course of his employment as head gamekeeper, which were those to be expected from that designation. I need not enlarge further upon them.

D   In my opinion " agriculture " per se is not a word appropriate to the preservation and breeding of pheasants for sporting purposes. Further the fact that in the Act " agriculture " includes " livestock keeping and breeding " cannot in my opinion per se be regarded in the context as embracing within the word " livestock " pheasants bred and kept for that purpose. I consider that the provisions of section 1 (2) reinforce that last conclusion. These pheasants are in no sense birds " kept for the
E   production of food." In so far as both home-bred pheasants and others are " preserved " in the woods on the estate this is done so that they may by way of sport be in due season shot at. The fact that those which are successfully shot at are for the most part sold and eaten is not the reason for their keeping, they are not " kept for " that. Accordingly in my opinion the provisions of subsection (2) do not extend " livestock
F   keeping and breeding " in subsection (1) (*a*) to cover this case. If anything the stress in subsection (2) on " kept for the production of food " tends to confirm the view that the language of subsection (1) (*a*) does not embrace a case such as the present.

      In my opinion the decision of the Court of Appeal, and the earlier decision of the Court of Appeal which it followed, that of *Lord Glendyne* v. *Rapley* [1978] 1 W.L.R. 601, were correct, and this appeal should be
G   dismissed.

      Mr. Giles, the appellant, conducted his case with relevance and courtesy. I wish only to add that he raised a point of complaint in that the judge in the county court, in consultation with *both* counsel, approved several alterations to counsel's original draft of his reasons for judgment. He is to be assured that there was nothing unusual (let alone improper)
H   in this, and that there is no cause for suspicion in the fact that the alterations in the copy signed as approved by the judge were in the handwriting of his opponent's counsel.

                                    Appeal dismissed.

Solicitors: *Payne, Hicks Beach & Co.*

                                                    F. C.

A

[PRIVY COUNCIL]

* WILFRED ISAAC . . . . APPELLANT

AND

ALFRED FRANCIS . . . . RESPONDENT

B

[ON APPEAL FROM THE COURT OF APPEAL OF TRINIDAD AND TOBAGO]

1979 July 24;   Lord Fraser of Tullybelton, Lord Scarman
      Oct. 2   and Sir Clifford Richmond

Trinidad and Tobago—Landlord and tenant—Summary proceedings
for possession—Summons issued against occupier—Whether C
tenant not in occupation necessary party to proceedings—
Summary Ejectment Ordinance (c. 27, No. 17), ss. 3, 4, 5

A tenant lived with the respondent on the demised land
until her death. After her death, the tenancy devolved on the
administrator of her estate, the Administrator General, and
the respondent remained in occupation of the land. The
appellant, the owner of the land, served notices to quit on the
Administrator General, who took no action, and on the res- D
pondent, who did not give up possession. The appellant then
made a complaint to the magistrate, under section 3 of
the Summary Ejectment Ordinance,[1] that the respondent had
failed to quit and deliver up possession of the land. The
magistrate issued a summons directed to the respondent, under
section 4 of the Ordinance, and at the hearing made an order
that a warrant for possession should issue against the respondent. On the respondent's appeal, the Court of Appeal of E
Trinidad and Tobago held that the conjoint effect of sections 3
and 5 of the Ordinance was that the summons had to be issued
against the tenant as well as the occupier and, therefore, since
it had not been issued against the Administrator General, the
magistrate had lacked jurisdiction to hear the complaint.

On appeal by the appellant to the Judicial Committee: —
Held, allowing the appeal, that, although the opening words F
of section 5, " If the tenant shall not appear in obedience to
such summons . . . ," implied that the tenant was a necessary
party thereto, sections 3 to 5 as a whole and the form of the
summons set out in Schedule 1 to the Ordinance showed that
the procedure was intended to be used against a person in actual
occupation; that, accordingly, it was not necessary that either
the complaint or the summons should be directed against a
non-occupying tenant and, therefore, the magistrate had had G
jurisdiction to make the order for possession.

Decision of the Court of Appeal of Trinidad and Tobago
reversed.

The following cases are referred to in the judgment of their Lordships:
Lewis v. *Gunter-Jones* [1949] W.N. 119, C.A.
Ramsbottom v. *Snelson* [1948] 1 K.B. 473; [1948] 1 All E.R. 201, D.C.

H

No additional cases were cited in argument.

APPEAL (No 23 of 1977) by Wilfred Isaac, the owner of a parcel of
land in Port of Spain, Trinidad, from a judgment dated November 16,

[1] Summary Ejectment Ordinance, s. 3: see post, pp. 41G—42A.
S. 4: see post, p. 42A–B.
S. 5: see post, p. 42B–F.

A 1976, of the Court of Appeal of Trinidad and Tobago (Corbin and
Rees JJ.A.) allowing an appeal by the respondent, Alfred Francis, from
a decision of the magistrate, Mr. Anthony Gapoor, given on January 17,
1975, granting a warrant of possession against the respondent who was in
occupation of the land.

The facts are stated in the judgment of their Lordships.

B
Fenton Ramsahoye S.C. (of the Bar of Trinidad and Tobago) and
David Guy for the appellant.

The respondent did not appear and was not represented.

Cur adv. vult.

C   October 2. The judgment of their Lordships were delivered by
LORD FRASER OF TULLYBELTON.

This appeal raises a short but not altogether easy point of construction
of the Summary Ejectment Ordinance of Trinidad and Tobago (c. 27,
No. 17). The appellant is the owner of a parcel of land in Port of Spain.
He let the land to a tenant named Myra Smith (also known as Edrina
D   Smith and as Admira Smith) who was the tenant at the date of her death
on November 25, 1966. Myra Smith was married and was survived by
her husband but at the date of her death she was not living with him
but was living with the respondent in her chattel house on the land which
is the subject of this appeal. The respondent has continued to live there
since her death. Before the magistrate the respondent contended that
he had paid rent to the appellant after Myra Smith's death but the
E   magistrate found that in fact he had paid no rent and had not been
accepted by the appellant as tenant. As Myra Smith was survived by her
husband, the respondent acquired no rights as tenant from her.

The appellant wished to obtain possession of the land and on August
14, 1972, he served a notice to quit on the Administrator General, who
was administering Myra Smith's estate under the Administration of
F   Estates Ordinance (c. 8, No. 1) and upon whom the tenancy had devolved
on her death. The Administrator General raised no question about the
notice to quit and took no action upon it, as neither he nor anyone
authorised or represented by him was in occupation of the land. On
September 21, 1972, the appellant served a notice to quit on the respondent informing him that the tenancy had been determined by the notice
of August 14, 1972. Notwithstanding the notice to him the respondent
G   remained in occupation and the appellant therefore had resort to the
procedure laid down by the Summary Ejectment Ordinance. The question is whether that procedure has been properly followed out.

The relevant sections of the Ordinance are as follows:

     " 3. When and so soon as the term or interest of the tenant of any
     premises held by him at will or for any term not exceeding two
H   years, either without being liable to the payment of any rent or at a
     rent not exceeding the rate of 240 dollars per annum, shall have ended
     or shall have been determined by a legal notice to quit or otherwise,
     and such tenant, or (if such tenant do not actually occupy the
     premises or only occupy a part thereof) any person by whom the same
     or any part thereof shall be then actually occupied, shall neglect or
     refuse to quit and deliver up possession of the premises or of such part
     thereof respectively, it shall be lawful for the landlord of the said

premises or his agent to make complaint on oath before the A
magistrate for the district in which such premises or any part thereof
is situate. Such complaint may be in the form contained in Schedule
1 hereto or such other form as the circumstances of the case may
require.

" 4. The magistrate shall, upon such complaint, issue a summons in
the form contained in Schedule 2 hereto or such other form as the
circumstances of the case may require, directed to such tenant or B
occupier, and requiring him to appear before such magistrate at such
place and time, being not less than three days after the service of
such summons, as may be mentioned therein.

" 5. If the tenant shall not appear in obedience to such summons
and show to the satisfaction of the magistrate reasonable cause why
possession should not be given up, and shall still neglect or refuse C
to deliver up possession of the premises, or of such part thereof as
he is then in possession of, to the landlord or his agent, it shall be
lawful for such landlord or agent to give to the magistrate proof of the
holding and of the end or other determination of the tenancy with
the time and manner thereof, and, where the title of the landlord
has accrued since the letting of the premises, the right by which he
claims the possession, and upon proof of the service of the summons D
and of the neglect or refusal of the tenant or occupier, as the case
may be, it shall be lawful for such magistrate to order such tenant
or occupier to pay a fine not exceeding 24 dollars and the costs
incurred by such landlord or agent, and such magistrate shall within
30 days of the making of the order issue a warrant under his hand
to any constable of the district within which such premises or any E
part thereof is situate commanding him, within a period to be named
therein, being not less than three nor more than seven clear days
from the date of such warrant, to enter, by force if needful into the
premises and give possession of the same to such landlord or agent:
provided that entry upon any such warrant shall not be made on
a Sunday, Good Friday, Corpus Christi, or Christmas Day. Such
warrant may be in the form set forth in Schedule 3 hereto or such F
other form as the circumstances of the case may require."

There is no doubt that section 3 applied in the circumstances of this
case and the contrary has not been suggested. The rent paid by Myra
Smith was $1.50 per month which is less than $240 per annum. When
Myra Smith's interest in the premises was terminated by the notice of
August 14, 1972, she of course did not actually occupy the premises. The G
person by whom they were then actually occupied was the respondent,
who refused to quit, and it therefore became lawful for the appellant to
make a complaint to a magistrate in accordance with section 3. That
he did on October 13, 1972. The complaint concluded with the statement that the respondent " being a person actually occupying the said
parcel of land has refused to deliver up possession thereof." The H
magistrate, in accordance with section 4, issued a summons directed to the
respondent. The respondent appeared before the magistrate and defended
the action on grounds with which this appeal is not concerned, but the
magistrate rejected his defence and made an order for possession in
favour of the appellant.

The respondent appealed to the Court of Appeal on several grounds,
of which the only one that appears to have been argued, and the only

A one now material, was that the magistrate had no jurisdiction to hear the complaint. The Court of Appeal (Corbin and Rees JJ.A.) upheld the respondent's contention to that effect, holding that the complaint which had been directed only against the respondent ought also to have been directed against the tenant. The judges said:

> " The conjoint effect of these two sections [section 3 and section 5]
B > of the Ordinance clearly is that the tenant must be made a party to the complaint."

The words in section 5 which the Court of Appeal quoted, and on which their decision was largely based, were the opening words: " If the tenant shall not appear in obedience to such summons. . . " Their Lordships are unable to agree that these words, even conjointly with section 3,
C could have the effect that the tenant must be made a party to *the complaint*. The Administrator General, upon whom the tenant's rights had devolved, had acquiesced in the notice to quit and he was not occupying the premises either himself or by anyone deriving right from him. There was therefore nothing to complain of against him. The form of the complaint in Schedule 1 to the Ordinance is to the effect that the person against whom complaint is made " refused or neglected to deliver
D up possession " of the premises " and still detains the same, although he has been required to deliver up the possession thereof." That form shows that the complaint is intended to be (as might be expected) against the person who is in occupation and, while section 3 provides for a complaint to be in " such other form as the circumstances of the case may require," it is difficult to see how it could be adapted to apply to a tenant who was not continuing to occupy the premises or doing anything
E else to which the landlord could reasonably object.

But the opening words of section 5 quoted above do create a difficulty in respect that they seem to imply that the *summons* ought to be addressed to the tenant, either alone or in addition to the occupier; otherwise he could not appear " in obedience to " it. But their Lordships are of opinion that any implication to that effect cannot prevail against
F the express provision in section 4 that the magistrate shall issue a summons " directed to such tenant *or occupier*." Clearly it is not necessary for the tenant to be a party.

That conclusion is confirmed by more general considerations. One of these is that, in a case such as the present, service of the summons upon the Administrator General representing the tenant would have been
G merely a formality because, as already mentioned, there was no ground of complaint against him. The position would have been the same if Myra Smith herself had been alive and had acquiesced in a notice to quit served upon her as tenant. The summons is directed only to the question of possession and does not raise any question of title, so that there appears to be no reason why formal service on the tenant should be necessary.

H A further consideration is that the three sections of the Ordinance quoted above clearly contemplate that the party against whom the whole procedure is directed may be either the tenant or the person actually occupying the premises. Section 3 refers to the tenant " or . . . any person by whom the [premises] . . . shall be then actually occupied," neglecting or refusing to quit. That is followed by the provision already mentioned in section 4. Finally section 5 provides that after proof of certain relevant matters, including:

" proof of the service of the summons and of the neglect or refusal   A
of the tenant *or occupier,* as the case may be, it shall be lawful for
such magistrate to order such tenant *or occupier* to pay a fine "

and the magistrate shall issue a warrant to any constable to enter the
premises and give possession to the landlord. In all these provisions the
alternative between the tenant or the occupier is preserved.

In the (English) Small Tenements Recovery Act 1838, from which no   B
doubt the Trinidad and Tobago Ordinance is derived, the provision
which corresponds to the opening words of section 5 of the Ordinance
is (in section 1) " and if the tenant *or occupier* shall not thereupon
appear " (emphasis added). The words " or occupier " in the English Act
do not give rise to the implication suggested by the Ordinance and their
Lordships are uncertain as to why similar words were not included in
section 5 of the Ordinance. For the reasons already given, however,   C
their Lordships are in no doubt that when sections 3, 4 and 5 are read
together, it is manifest that the Ordinance does not require the complaint
or the summons to be directed to the tenant in a case where the landlord
seeks to recover possession not from the tenant but from some other
person. The opening words of section 5 apply only in cases where the
landlord's complaint and the subsequent summons are directed against   D
the tenant.

The judges of the Court of Appeal in their judgment, after pointing
out (rightly) that the Summary Ejectment Ordinance is similar in terms
to the (English) Small Tenements Recovery Act 1838, went on to say:
" It is now well established that that Act applies only when the relationship of landlord and tenant exists between the parties."

With respect their Lordships do not regard that as an accurate state-   E
ment of the effect of the English Act. The Act, now repealed by the
Rent Act 1965, applied only where there was, or had been, a tenancy,
and it therefore did not apply in the case cited in the judgment of
Ramsbottom v. *Snelson* [1948] 1 K.B. 473 where there had been a
service occupancy and not a tenancy. But it was not necessary for the
relationship of landlord and tenant to have existed *between the parties*:   F
see *Lewis* v. *Gunter-Jones* [1949] W.N. 119. Indeed that relationship
could not exist between the landlord and the person described in the Act
as the person by whom the premises were " actually occupied." All that
was necessary was that the occupation to be terminated by the procedure
of the Act should have originated in a tenancy.

For these reasons their Lordships are of opinion that sections 3 to 5   G
of the Ordinance do not require that the tenant be made a party to either
the complaint or the summons, and that the Court of Appeal were wrong
in the view that they took as to the effect of these sections. Their
Lordships will therefore allow the appeal with costs of the appeal and of
the proceedings in the Court of Appeal, and will remit to the magistrate
to make an order that warrant of ejectment be issued.

                                                                        H
                                            Appeal allowed with costs.

Solicitors: *A. L. Bryden & Williams.*

[Reported by MICHAEL HAWKINGS, ESQ., Barrister-at-Law]

1 W.L.R.

A

[QUEEN'S BENCH DIVISION]

* GRICE v. NEEDS AND ANOTHER

1979 June 19   Lord Widgery C.J. and Lloyd J.

B *Revenue—Value added tax—Return—Daily penalty imposed for*
   failure to make return—Period of default—Whether terminat-
   ing at date of information or to be calculated at date of
   hearing—Finance Act 1972 (c. 41), s. 38 (7)

The defendants carried on a business in partnership and
were registered under the Finance Act 1972 for the purposes
of value added tax. They failed to furnish a return for the
C period June 1, 1976, to August 31, 1976. An information
was preferred against them on March 9, 1977, alleging that
they had failed to comply with regulation 51 of the Value
Added Tax (General) Regulations 1975 as amended by regulation 6 of the Value Added Tax (General) (Amendment)
Regulations 1976 by failing to furnish the return by January
31, 1977, contrary to section 38 (7) of the Finance Act 1972.[1]
The justices heard the information on April 18, 1977, when
D both defendants pleaded guilty. The justices were of opinion
that an information ought not to relate to a continuing failure
which had not taken place and, in imposing a daily penalty
in accordance with section 38 (7) of the Act, they limited the
period to between January 31, 1977, and March 9, 1977, the
date the information was laid.

On appeal by the prosecutor:—

Held, allowing the appeal, that the information defined the
E offence and not the period of default; that section 38 (7) of the
Finance Act 1972 imposed a penalty for each day of default
and the period of default was to be ascertained at the date of
the hearing of the information when it was known whether the
defendants had continued in default or had terminated the
period by compliance with the Regulations and the case would
be remitted to the justices for reconsideration (post, p. 47E–H).

F
No cases are referred to in the judgment.

The following case was cited in argument:
Airey v. *Smith* [1907] 2 K.B. 273.

CASE STATED by Warwickshire justices sitting at Nuneaton.
G   On March 9, 1977, an information was preferred by the prosecutor,
Michael John Grice, against the defendants, Peter John Needs and Alfred
George Davies Hale, that they, carrying on business at Anvil Precision
Engineering Co., Nuneaton, being registered under the Finance Act 1972
for the purposes of value added tax as persons carrying on a business in
partnership, failed to comply with regulation 51 of the Value Added Tax
H (General) Regulations 1975 as amended by regulation 6 of the Value
Added Tax (General) (Amendment) Regulations 1976, by failing to
furnish to the Controller, Customs and Excise, Value Added Tax Central
Unit, Southend-on-Sea, not later than January 31, 1977, a return for the
period from June 1, 1976, until August 31, 1976, in the form prescribed
by the regulations, contrary to section 38 (7) of the Finance Act 1972.

---

[1] Finance Act 1972, s. 38 (7): see post, p. 47A.

4

Grice v. Needs (D.C.)   [1980]

The justices heard the information on April 18, 1977. Both defendants A
attended at the hearing and pleaded guilty.

It was contended by the prosecutor that the failure to render a return
had continued from January 31, 1977, to March 18, 1977, and thus was
punishable by a maximum penalty of £100 plus a daily penalty of £10 in
respect of each of the continuing days. He did not quote any authority
in support of that argument.

 B

The defendants were not legally represented and made no representations to the justices.

The justices were of the opinion that they should limit any such daily
penalty to the period between January 31, 1977, and the date on which
the information was laid, namely, March 9, 1977, and that they should
not impose any penalty in respect of any period after March 9, 1977,
because they felt that an information should not relate to a continuing C
failure which had not then taken place. Accordingly, they imposed fines
against each defendant of £25 and in addition ordered each defendant to
pay a daily penalty of £3 for the relevant period of 36 days.

The prosecutor appealed. The question for the opinion of the High
Court was whether the justices were right in law in limiting the period
for the calculation of the daily penalty to the date on which the D
information was laid.

David Latham and *Valerie Pearlman* for the prosecutor.
The defendants were not represented and did not appear.

LORD WIDGERY C.J. This is an appeal by case stated by Warwickshire E
justices acting in and for the petty sessional division of Nuneaton in
respect of their adjudication as a magistrates' court sitting at the Law
Courts, Nuneaton on April 18, 1977.

On that date the justices had before them an information preferred
by the appellant, who is an officer of Customs and Excise, alleging that
the defendants, who were Anvil Precision Engineering Co., being
registered under the Finance Act 1972 for the purposes of value added F
tax as persons carrying on a business in partnership failed to comply with
regulation 51 of the Value Added Tax (General) Regulations 1975 as
amended by regulation 6 of the Value Added Tax (General) (Amendment) Regulations 1976 by failing to furnish to the Controller of Customs
and Excise, Value Added Tax Central Unit, Southend-on-Sea not later
than January 31, 1977, a return for the period from June 1, 1976, until G
August 31, 1976, in the form prescribed by the Regulations.

What all that amounted to was that the defendants were carrying on
business in circumstances which made them responsible for accounting
for value added tax in certain circumstances, and as part of that operation
they were required to make a return disclosing how much they were
prepared to account for. They committed the offence of failing to make H
the return as required, and they were prosecuted and perfectly properly
convicted because they had broken the terms of the law in that regard.

When the question arose as to what the penalty might be and how
much they might be fined in respect of this offence, one had to go and
look at the terms of the statute under which the obligation to make the
return is created. It is the Finance Act 1972 and the relevant part is to be
found in section 38 (7). It says:

A   " If any person fails to comply with any requirement imposed under section 34 or 35 of this Act or any regulations or rules made under this Part of this Act, he shall be liable to a penalty of £100, together with a penalty of £10 for each day on which the failure continues."

It became necessary to work out what the maximum fine might be according to that formula because this is the subsection under which the present defendants were prosecuted. There is no great difficulty about
B the penalty of £100. That can be put into the scale easily enough. When one comes to the second element of the penalty, which is a maximum of £10 for each day on which the failure continues, there again it was not too difficult to specify the initial date, the date upon which the initial failure to produce the return was committed.

C   But what gave rise to some problem was, having ascertained the date on which the £10 a day fine began to accrue, one had to find another date on which it was to stop, in other words, a date beyond which the justices could not impose a penalty. A difference of opinion arose here because the Customs and Excise said that the last day of the £10 a day was the date of the hearing, whereas it was contended by the defendants that the
D last day should be the date of the information.

We have got to decide which of those contentions is right. We have been taken by Mr. Latham into the legislation which lies behind this section, and we came out of it again as fast as we could because it was quite clear we were not going to gain any advantage by further researches there and the language is very uncomfortable and complicated.

E   I am quite satisfied that one has to go back to the section itself imposing the penalty. It is section 38 of the Act of 1972. Having done that, I think we must ask ourselves what the words of the subsection mean, given their ordinary meaning.

I do not think that is could possibly be right that the period over which the £10 a day accrues stops at the date of the information, because there
F is no link, as Mr. Latham submits, between the information and penalty. By the time the matter comes before the justices everybody knows at least that the default has continued up to that date, or, alternatively, knows an earlier date when it ceased, and the obligation up to the date of the hearing can be assessed with precision. That seems to me to be the intention of Parliament in this case.

G   I would, therefore, hold that in calculating the £10 a day penalty under section 38 (7) the period ends with the date of the hearing, if it has not been terminated earlier with a compliance with the regulations.

LLOYD J. I agree. Mr. Latham put the matter, if I may say so, very clearly when he said that the purpose of the information in a case such
H as this is to define the offence and not the penalty.

The language of section 38 (7) of the Finance Act 1972 is, in my judgment, clear and the justices were wrong to confine their view to the period up to the date of the information.

The matter, therefore, will have to be remitted to the justices for reconsideration of the sentence. But I, for my part, would emphasise that they are not obliged to impose a penalty for the balance of the period at

48

the same rate or indeed at any rate at all. The matter will be entirely A
for them.

Appeal allowed and case remitted
to justices for reconsideration.

Solicitor: *Solicitor, Customs and Excise.*

B

[*Reported by* MRS. CLARE BARSBY, *Barrister-at-Law*]

C

[QUEEN'S BENCH DIVISION]

* MONTEDISON S.p.A. *v.* ICROMA S.p.A.

1979　June 14; 21　　　　　　　　　　　　　　　　Donaldson J.　D

Shipping—Charterparty—Freight—Freight payable upon delivery of
cargo—Cargo of oil valuable as free of paraffin—Contamina-
tion by paraffin on voyage—Shipowners claiming payment of
freight—Cargo owners counterclaiming for breach of contract
—Whether cargo delivered
Ships' Names—Caspian Sea

E

　　　A clause in a charterparty provided for the payment of
freight upon delivery of the cargo. The cargo shipped was
Bachaquero crude, an oil whose value lay in the fact that it
was free of paraffin. It was alleged, and assumed for the
purpose of the present proceedings, that the oil, on delivery,
contained paraffin products from the residue of a previous
cargo. Arbitration proceedings were commenced in which the
shipowners claimed payment of the freight and the charterers
counterclaimed damages for breach of contract. On January F
9, 1979, the arbitrators stated an award in the form of a
consultative case asking whether the owners were entitled to
the payment of freight in full, without deductions, on the
assumption that the cargo delivered was unmerchantable as
Bachaquero crude or was not commercially identical with the
cargo loaded. The award was set down within four weeks, but
owing to various delays it did not come on for hearing until G
June 14, 1979.
　　　On the question posed by the arbitrators: —
　　　Held, that the mere fact that the oil as delivered was not
identical commercially with the cargo as loaded did not deprive
the shipowners of their right to freight; and that they were
entitled to the freight if what they delivered could, in commercial terms, bear a description which sensibly and accurately
included the words " Bachaquero crude " (post, pp. 53G–H, 54A); H
accordingly, the case would be remitted to the arbitrators for
them to consider what was meant by the description " Bachaquero crude," and whether the oil had been so contaminated
that it had ceased to be even contaminated Bachaquero crude
(post, p. 54E–F).
　　　Asfar & Co. v. *Blundell* [1896] 1 Q.B. 123, C.A. applied.
　　　Per curiam. The attractions of the consultative case or of
an application under section 2 (1) of the Arbitration Act 1979
are often more apparent than real. Before resorting to either

A   procedure, serious consideration should be given, in the words
of section 2 (2) of the Act of 1979, to whether "the determination of the application might produce substantial savings
in costs to the parties " (post, p. 51D).

The following cases are referred to in the judgment:

Aries Tanker Corporation v. *Total Transport Ltd.* [1977] 1 W.L.R. 185;
B   [1977] 1 All E.R. 398, H.L.(E.).

Asfar & Co. v. *Blundell* [1896] 1 Q.B. 123, C.A.

Dakin v. *Oxley* (1864) 15 C.B.N.S. 646.

Dickson v. *Buchanan* (1876) 13 Sc.L.R. 401.

Duthie v. *Hilton* (1868) L.R. 4 C.P. 138.

Garrett v. *Melhuish* (1858) 4 Jur.N.S. 943.

Shields v. *Davis* (1815) 6 Taunt. 65.

C
The following additional cases were cited in argument:

Berger v. *Pollock* [1973] 2 Lloyd's Rep. 442.

Henriksens Rederi A/S v. *T.H.Z. Rolimpex* [1974] Q.B. 233; [1973] 3
W.L.R. 556; [1973] 3 All E.R. 589, C.A.

St. John Shipping Corporation v. *Joseph Rank Ltd.* [1957] 1 Q.B. 267;
[1956] 3 W.L.R. 870; [1956] 3 All E.R. 683.

D
CONSULTATIVE CASE

By a voyage charterparty in the tank vessel form dated November 21,
1974, the shipowners, Montedison S.p.A. of Milan, chartered the *Caspian
Sea* to Icroma S.p.A. of Busalla, the charterers, for a voyage from Punta
Cardon to Genoa, on terms and conditions as set out therein. Clause 2
E   of the charterparty provided: " The freight to be payable upon delivery
of the cargo . . .." Disputes arose between the parties as a consequence of
which the shipowners appointed Mr. Donald Davies of 49 Queen Victoria
Street, London E.C.4, and the charterers appointed Mr. Cedric Barclay of
139 Sloane Street, London S.W.1, as arbitrators on their behalf respectively.
The matters referred to adjudication were a claim by the shipowners for
freight in the sum of Italian Lire 58,046,030, and a counterclaim by the
F   charterers for contamination of cargo in the sum of Italian Lire 172,380,294.

The shipowners' request that a speedy award be made in respect of their
claim for freight was opposed by the charterers who contended that the
goods were unmerchantable on delivery thus denying the shipowners any
immediate right to freight. It was decided that the most expedient way
of dealing with the matters in dispute was to obtain the court's ruling by
G   way of a consultative case pursuant to section 21 of the Arbitration Act
1950, on a preliminary point as to whether or not the shipowners were
entitled to payment of freight on the assumption that the goods were
delivered in an unmerchantable state, leaving over an award in respect of
the matters in dispute until the result of the court's decision.

The arbitrators found the following facts. The vessel proceeded to
Punta Cardon and there loaded a quantity of Bachaquero Crude. A bill of
H   lading was issued for a quantity of 16,459.31 L.T. Nett Bachaquero crude,
dated December 8, 1974. Being so loaded, the vessel proceeded via Puerto
La Cruz to Genoa, where she arrived on or about December 25, 1974. The
charterers there took delivery of the cargo discharged and consigned it to
the Iplom Refinery with whom they had a processing agreement. The
shipowners issued a freight invoice based on the bill of lading quantity
in the sum of Italian Lire 58,046,030, dated January 2, 1975. The
Caspian Sea was a British flag vessel, registered in Bermuda.

The charterers alleged that the cargo which was delivered in Genoa A was contaminated by the presence of paraffinic products by reason of the fact that residues of a previous cargo of low sulphur fuel oil remained in the vessel's tanks before loading the charterers' cargo at Punta Cardon. They contended that the cargo which was delivered was unmerchantable as Bachaquero crude, or alternatively was not identical commercially with the cargo loaded, and that accordingly no freight was payable under the charterparty. They further alleged that Bachaquero crude was unusual B in that it contained no paraffin and was therefore highly suitable for production of high quality/high value lubricating oils and that as a result of the contamination with paraffin products the oil could not be so used.

The shipowners did not accept the charterers' arguments as to the cause, extent or effect of the alleged contamination, but submitted that even if the cargo delivered was unmerchantable as Bachaquero crude or alterna- C tively not commercially identical with the cargo loaded, they would nevertheless be entitled to payment of freight in full without deduction, they having performed the carriage and having delivered the cargo. For the purposes of the consultative case, it was assumed that the cargo which was delivered was in the condition alleged by the charterers.

The question of law for the decision of the court was:

> "Whether the shipowners are entitled to payment of freight in full D without deductions on the assumption that the goods carried were delivered in a state which was unmerchantable as Bachaquero crude and/or was not identical commercially with the cargo loaded."

Jonathan Sumption for the shipowners.
Bernard Rix for the charterers.

Cur. adv. vult.   E

June 21. DONALDSON J. read the following judgment. The *Caspian Sea* was chartered to carry a part cargo of crude oil and/or dirty petroleum products from Punta Cardon to Genoa. Freight was payable "upon delivery of the cargo." The oil shipped was "Bachaquero crude," a Venezuelan crude whose special value lies in the fact that it is free of F paraffin and is therefore suitable for the production of lubricating oils of high quality and value. The charterers took delivery of the oil on discharge, but allege that what was discharged contained paraffinic products derived from the residues of a previous cargo of low sulphur fuel oil which had not been removed from the vessel's tanks before loading. I am asked to assume that the charterers' allegations are correct.

In arbitration proceedings the shipowners claimed payment of the G freight and the charterers counterclaimed damages for breach of contract. However, the shipowners contended that they were entitled to an immediate interim award covering the full amount of the freight, because a claim for damage to cargo cannot be set off against a claim for freight: *Aries Tanker Corporation* v. *Total Transport Ltd.* [1977] 1 W.L.R. 185. The charterers retorted that there was no *immediate* right to freight, because what was H delivered was not merchantable as "Bachaquero crude" or alternatively was not identical commercially with the cargo loaded. This contention was unarguable and has rightly been abandoned by Mr. Rix who has appeared for the charterers. The charterers' current contention is different. It is that in these circumstances there is no right to freight now or at any other time, because there was no "delivery of the cargo" and accordingly no freight was ever earned.

The Weekly Law Reports, February 1, 1980

51

1 W.L.R.   Montedison S.p.A. v. Icroma S.p.A. (Q.B.D.)   Donaldson J.

A   In these circumstances, Mr. Donald Davies and Mr. Cedric Barclay, the arbitrators appointed by the parties, decided to state an award in the form of a consultative case asking the court to decide as a matter of law:

> "Whether the shipowners are entitled to payment of freight in full without deductions on the assumption that the goods carried were delivered in a state which was unmerchantable as Bachaquero crude
B   and/or was not identical commercially with the cargo loaded."

The object of this exercise was to obtain a speedy decision on the shipowners' right to freight. In this I fear that it has failed. The award was published on January 9, 1979, and the parties were given six weeks in which to set it down for argument. A period of 14 days might have been more appropriate and this is the period prescribed for equivalent
C   proceedings under section 2 (1) of the Arbitration Act 1979. In fact the award was set down within about four weeks, but another month elapsed before it was transferred to the commercial list. A date for hearing was fixed for April, but the parties asked that the date be vacated. Owing to unforeseen circumstances a new date could not be given until June 14 and even now the award has to go back to the arbitrators for further consideration.
D   I mention these matters solely in order that arbitrators may be aware that the attractions of the consultative case or of an application under section 2 (1) of the Arbitration Act 1979 are often more apparent than real. Before resorting to either procedure, serious consideration should be given, in the words of section 2 (2) of the Act of 1979, to whether "the determination of the application might produce substantial savings
E   in costs to the parties." I fear that that has not been the result in the present case.

Mr. Sumption for the shipowners submits that the shipowner will be entitled to full freight unless the goods are a total or constructive total loss in insurance terms and that their identity must not only be changed, they must be worthless to the consignee. He also submits that whatever the
F   state of the goods at the port of discharge, the consignee is obliged to pay the freight if he takes delivery of those goods.

Scrutton on Charterparties, 18th ed. (1974), art. 163, p. 339 states the law as follows:

> "The shipowner will be entitled to full freight: (1) If he is ready to deliver in substance at the port of destination the goods loaded, though in a damaged condition. The freighter will not be entitled to make a
G   deduction from the freight for the damage, but will have a separate cause of action or counterclaim for the damage, unless caused solely by excepted perils or by the vice of the goods themselves. The question is whether the substance delivered is identical commercially with the substance loaded, though it may have deteriorated in quality."

H   This statement of the law seems to me to be fully supported by the authorities and indeed to be the obvious conclusion apart from authority. The freight clause specifies the circumstances in which freight becomes payable, namely, "upon delivery of the cargo." If there is no delivery of anything or if what is delivered is not "the cargo," no freight is payable. But the mere fact that goods are delivered in a damaged state does not necessarily, or even usually, involve the proposition that they are not "the cargo." The real problem is to determine the point at which the damage

to, or transformation of, the goods which were shipped is such as to   A
render them incapable of being any longer so described.

The earliest case to which I have been referred is *Shields* v. *Davis*
(1815) 6 Taunt. 65. Heath J. in argument said, at p. 66: ". . . the
principle is, that if he "—the cargo owner—" has received any benefit
whatever by the carriage, he cannot set up this defence." However the
point at issue was whether the mere fact that the goods had been
damaged was a bar to the claim for freight and I think that this   B
comment has to be read in that context.

A similar case was *Garrett* v. *Melhuish* (1858) 4 Jur.N.S. 943, in which
payment of freight on a cargo of bricks was resisted on the ground that
they were not delivered or alternatively were delivered damaged. It was
certainly open to the cargo owner to have argued that the bricks were so
damaged as no longer to be bricks, but this does not appear to have been   C
done.

Next came *Dakin* v. *Oxley* (1864) 15 C.B.N.S. 646, in which the goods
owner refused to take delivery of a cargo of damaged coal or to pay the
freight. He adopted this attitude because the coal was worth less than the
freight. But he did not deny that the substance tendered was still coal,
albeit damaged coal. Willes C.J., holding that the shipowners were entitled
to the freight, said at p. 667:   D

"In both classes of cases, whether of loss of quantity or change in
quality, the proper course seems to be the same, viz. to ascertain from
the terms of the contract, construed by mercantile usage, if any, what
was the thing for the carriage of which freight was to be paid, and by
the aid of a jury to determine whether that thing, or any and how
much of it, has substantially arrived."   E

Mr. Sumption seeks to support his argument by reference to a remark
by Mr. Brett Q.C. as counsel, at p. 655, that if any part of the cargo is
accepted, any claim for damage must be the subject matter of a cross-
action. This may well be a correct statement of the law in the context
of that case because what was tendered for delivery was admittedly " coal "
or " the cargo." But it does not help in a case such as the present where   F
that point is in issue and I see no reason in principle why a shipowner
should be entitled to freight if he delivers something to the consignee
which, although the latter's property, is not " the cargo." In such
circumstances the shipowner has not performed the act for, and upon the
occasion of which, the freight was payable, namely, delivery of " the
cargo."

Four years later *Duthie* v. *Hilton* (1868) L.R. 4 C.P. 138 was decided.   G
There a cargo of cement in bags was submerged when the ship was
scuttled to put out a fire. The cement solidified and was held no longer
to be cement. It was not merely a case of the shipowners offering to
deliver damaged cement. They could not deliver cement at all. Accordingly, the condition precedent to the right to receive the freight was not
satisfied.   H

This decision was followed in *Dickson* v. *Buchanan* (1876) 13 Sc.L.R.
401. The cargo consisted of bundles of wire which became so damaged
that two thirds were reduced to scrap iron and could no longer be
considered as wire. The remaining one third could, at great expense, be
restored to a condition in which it could be described as wire, but even
then could only be used for making small articles whereas the cargo as
loaded was intended to be used for fencing. Lord Shand in the Court

The Weekly Law Reports, February 1, 1980

53

1 W.L.R.   Montedison S.p.A. v. Icroma S.p.A. (Q.B.D.)   Donaldson J.

A   of Session held that the wire was actually or constructively totally lost. I
do not think that this decision is authority for the proposition that the
test of when freight is payable depends upon considerations of insurance
law. It is simply a decision that none of the goods could still be described
as wire and that although part could be put in a state in which it could
be so described, this was not a practical proposition from a commercial
point of view.

B   The most recent, and in my view the most helpful, authority is *Asfar
& Co.* v. *Blundell* [1896] 1 Q.B. 123. There a vessel carrying a cargo of
dates was sunk during the voyage. She was raised, but the dates were
" affected," to use a neutral term, by seawater and sewage. Although the
dates were unmerchantable as dates, and were not allowed to be landed
in London, a large proportion retained the appearance of dates and they
C   had considerable value abroad as the raw material for distillation into
spirit. They were in fact trans-shipped and sold for this purpose. The
claim was brought upon a policy insuring the freight and it was held that
the right to the freight had been lost. Lord Esher M.R. put the matter
in this way, at p. 127:

D   " There is a perfectly well known test which has for many years
        been applied to such cases as the present—that test is whether, as a
        matter of business, the nature of the thing has been altered. The
        nature of a thing is not necessarily altered because the thing itself has
        been damaged; wheat or rice may be damaged, but may still remain
        the things dealt with as wheat or rice in business. But if the nature
        of the thing is altered, and it becomes for business purposes something
        else, so that it is not dealt with by business people as the thing which
E   it originally was, the question for determination is whether the thing
        insured, the original article of commerce, has become a total loss. If
        it is so changed in its nature by the perils of the sea as to become an
        unmerchantable thing, which no buyer would buy and no honest
        seller would sell, then there is a total loss."

F   Lopes L.J., at p. 130, held that the dates were totally lost and Kay L.J.
at p. 132 held that whilst the substance of the dates still remained, it was
sufficient that there had been a total destruction of their mercantile
character.

    The editors of *Scrutton* have expressed doubt as to the correctness of
this decision, because the consignees took the cargo and sold it. With the
greatest respect, I do not share this doubt. The consignees took what was
their property, but it had been so damaged as to cease to be " the cargo "
G   and there was a total failure by the shipowners to perform the contract for
which the freight was payable, namely, the carriage and delivery of the
cargo at the port of destination. But however that may be, the decision is
binding upon me.

    I therefore turn to the question of law posed in the award. The mere
fact that the oil as delivered was not identical commercially with the cargo
H   loaded does not, in my judgment, deprive the shipowners of their right to
freight. Undamaged or uncontaminated goods can rarely be considered
to be identical commercially with damaged or contaminated goods, but
it is well settled that damage or contamination is not, as such, a bar to the
right to freight. Nor do I accept the argument that the test is to be found
in the amended definition of " merchantable quality " in section 62 (1A)
of the Sale of Goods Act 1893. Again I get no assistance by considering
the law of insurance and the concept of a constructive total loss of goods.

I also reject the argument that the consignee having accepted goods   A
tendered by the shipowner, the shipowners necessarily are entitled to be paid
the freight.

The shipowners will be entitled to the freight if what they delivered
could, in commercial terms, bear a description which sensibly and
accurately included the words "Bachaquero crude," e.g., "Bachaquero
crude contaminated with paraffin or low sulphur oil residues." The
question is whether an honest merchant would be forced to qualify the   B
description applicable to the goods on shipment to such an extent as to
destroy it. If the qualification destroys the description, no freight has been
earned because "the cargo" has not been delivered. If the description
is merely qualified, "the cargo" has been delivered, albeit damaged or,
as the case may be, contaminated. This, in my judgment, is what Lord
Esher M.R. meant by the test of merchantability or of the nature of the   C
goods being so altered as to become for business purposes something else:
Asfar & Co. v. *Blundell* [1896] 1 Q.B. 123, 127.

I can best illustrate this by examples. If one takes a carboy of
sulphuric acid and adds a limited quantity of water—an experiment which
should only be conducted with extreme care and with knowledge of the
likely consequences—the resulting liquid will still be sulphuric acid, albeit,
dilute sulphuric acid. But if one adds enough water, the point will be   D
reached at which the liquid is more properly described as water contaminated with acid than as dilute acid. This is the dividing line. Of course,
some descriptions of goods are such that any damage or contamination
contradicts the description, e.g., "pure water" or "sterile dressings."

The arbitrators will have to consider what is meant by the description
"Bachaquero crude." Does it mean a paraffin free crude? If it does,   E
"Bachaquero crude contaminated by paraffin" is a contradiction in terms
and the owners will not be entitled to freight. Or does it mean "a crude
from the Bachaquero region which in its natural state contains no paraffin?"
If so, there is no necessary contradiction in "Bachaquero crude contaminated by paraffin." In that event, the fact of contamination will not of itself
deprive the shipowners of their right to freight. However, the arbitrators
would have to consider the degree of contamination. They would have to   F
ask themselves the question: "is the oil so contaminated that it has ceased
to be even contaminated Bachaquero crude?" If so, the right to freight
has gone. No doubt a relevant factor will be the cost and practicability of
extracting the paraffin, but there may well be other criteria. These are
matters of fact which are for the arbitrators as the tribunal of fact.

The award will be remitted to the arbitrators in order that they may   G
make such further award or awards as is appropriate in the light of this
judgment.

Judgment accordingly.

Solicitors: *Ince & Co.; Middleton, Potts & Co.*

  H

[Reported by MICHAEL HAWKINGS, ESQ., Barrister-at-Law]

A

[COURT OF APPEAL]

* POLYVIOU v. SEELEY

1979   July 13   Megaw and Browne L.JJ.

B   *Landlord and Tenant—Business premises (security of tenure)—
Application for new tenancy—Request for new tenancy
beginning on specified date—Tenant failing to apply to court
within time limited by Act—Second request for new tenancy
specifying same date for commencement—Application to court
for new tenancy based on second request—Whether valid—
Landlord and Tenant Act* 1954 (2 & 3 Eliz. 2, c. 56), ss. 26 (5),
29 (3) [1]

C
        On August 11, 1978, a tenant of business premises under a
lease for three years from July 16, 1976, made a request pursuant
to section 26 of the Landlord and Tenant Act 1954 for a new
tenancy for three years commencing on July 16, 1979.   On
September 5, 1978, the landlord served a counter-notice on
the tenant stating that he would oppose any application to the
court for the grant of a new tenancy and giving his grounds.
D   The tenant made no application to the court within the time
limited by the Act, i.e. between October 11 and December 11,
1978.   On January 12, 1979, he purported to make a further
request for a new tenancy, again for a term of three years
commencing on July 16, 1979.   He applied to the county court
for a new tenancy, and the landlord took the preliminary point
that his request was invalid because of the previous request
and that, accordingly, his application was invalid as being out
E   of time following the original request.   The judge so held.
        On appeal by the tenant: —
        Held, dismissing the appeal, that, if a tenant who made a
request for a new tenancy did not make an application to the
court within the time specified by section 29 (3) of the Landlord and Tenant Act 1954, by virtue of section 26 (5) his existing
tenancy automatically came to an end on the date specified in
his request as being the date for the commencement of the
F   proposed new tenancy; and that he could not withdraw the
request and make another.
        Stile Hall Properties Ltd. v. *Gooch (Note),* post, p. 62,
C.A. applied.

The following case is referred to in the judgments:

Stile Hall Properties Ltd. v. *Gooch (Note),* post, p. 62; [1979] 3 All E.R.
G   848; 207 E.G. 715, C.A.

No additional cases were cited in argument.

APPEAL from Judge Hutton sitting at Bristol County Court.
        The tenant, Polyvios Polyviou, applied for a new tenancy under the
Landlord and Tenant Act 1954 of the premises known as Le Chalut
H   Restaurant, St. Paul's Road, Clifton, Bristol.   On May 1, 1979, Judge
Hutton gave judgment for the landlord, George Andrew Seeley, on a
preliminary point, viz. that the tenant's application was out of time and
invalid and that the tenant's request for a new tenancy made to the
landlord pursuant to the Act of 1954 was not a valid request.   The
tenant appealed on the grounds that the judge had been wrong in law

[1] Landlord and Tenant Act 1954, ss. 26 (5), 29 (3): see post, p. 57E–F.

in holding that the tenant's request for a new tenancy dated January 12,   A
1979, pursuant to section 26 of the Act of 1954 was not a valid request
for a new tenancy of the premises; that because the tenant had not made
an application to the court for a new tenancy of the premises pursuant to
his request for a new tenancy dated August 11, 1978, he was thereby
prevented from making a subsequent request for a new tenancy even
though the date specified in the second request as being the proposed
commencement date for the new tenancy was the same as that specified in   B
the first request and that the landlord did not need to show that he had
been prejudiced in any way by the tenant's failure to make an application
to the court for a new tenancy pursuant to his first request for a new
tenancy.

The facts are stated in the judgment of Browne L.J.

  C

Roderick Denyer for the tenant.
James Wigmore for the landlord.

MEGAW L.J. I shall ask Browne L.J. to deliver the first judgment.

BROWNE L.J. This is an appeal from a decision of Judge Hutton given
at the Bristol County Court on May 1, 1979. He gave judgment for the   D
respondent landlord on a preliminary point arising under the Landlord and
Tenant Act 1954. The appellant is the tenant (and I shall so call him),
and the landlord is the respondent in this court. Judge Hutton held that
the tenant's application for a new tenancy under the Act was out of time
and invalid and that his request for a new tenancy on which the application
to the court was based was not a valid request. The result of that decision   E
on the preliminary point is that the tenant has lost his right to apply for a
new tenancy under the Act.

The history of this case is as follows. By a lease dated March 4, 1977,
for three years from July 16, 1976, the present landlord granted to a Mr.
Serrat a lease for three years of the premises with which we are concerned,
which are premises in St. Paul's Road, Bristol, which were and are used
as a restaurant. By an assignment and other operations that lease became   F
vested first in the present tenant and his brother and later in the tenant
himself alone. In those premises the tenant carried on, and carries on, the
business of a restaurant. That tenancy, being for three years from July 16,
1976, would expire on July 15, 1979.

On August 11, 1978, the tenant made a request for a new tenancy
pursuant to the Act of 1954. That request asks for a new tenancy com-   G
mencing on July 16, 1979, and it asks for a new tenancy of, again, three
years.

On September 5, 1978, the landlord served a counter-notice to that,
setting out various grounds on which he stated that he proposed to oppose
any application to the court for the grant of that new tenancy.

Nothing more happened about that request. No application was made
to the court within the time limited by the Act, which would have been   H
between October 11, 1978, and December 11, 1978. However, on January
12, 1979, the tenant made, or purported to make, a further request for a
new tenancy. It relates to these premises, the Le Chalut Restaurant, St.
Paul's Road, and it again asks for a new tenancy beginning on the same day
as that specified in the first request, that is, July 16, 1979. It again asks for
a fresh term of three years.

In reply to that, by letter dated January 26, the landlord took the point

A that this request was invalid because of the previous request, and also repeated in the alternative the same grounds as those set out in his previous counter-notice, saying that he would object to the grant for a new tenancy.

The application to the court for a new tenancy, based on that request, was dated March 15, 1979, and it was a preliminary point in respect of that application which came before Judge Hutton on May 1. The application sets out the history as I have stated it. It does not refer to the first request
B for a new tenancy and is based on the request of January 12, 1979.

The relevant provisions of the Act of 1954 are as follows. Section 24:

"(1) A tenancy to which this Part of this Act applies shall not come to an end unless terminated in accordance with the provisions of this Part of this Act; and, subject to the provisions of section 29 of this Act, the tenant under such a tenancy may apply to the court for a new
C tenancy— . . . (b) if the tenant has made a request for a new tenancy in accordance with section 26 of this Act . . ."

Section 26:

"(2) A tenant's request for a new tenancy shall be for a tenancy beginning with such date, not more than 12 nor less than 6 months after the making of the request, as may be specified therein: . . .
D (3) A tenant's request for a new tenancy shall not have effect unless it is made by notice in the prescribed form given to the landlord and sets out the tenant's proposals . . ."

It is accepted, I think, that in this case both the requests which were made were made in the prescribed form.

E "(5) Where the tenant makes a request for a new tenancy in accordance with the foregoing provisions of this section, the current tenancy shall" (subject to certain other provisions as to the interim continuation of tenancies) "terminate immediately before the date specified in the request for the beginning of the new tenancy."

Then subsection (6) provides for a counter-notice by the landlord.
F Section 29:

"(3) No application under subsection (1) of section 24 of this Act shall be entertained unless it is made not less than two nor more than four months after the giving of the landlord's notice under section 25 of this Act or, as the case may be, after the making of the tenant's request for a new tenancy."

G It was because of that section that, as I have said, the application to the court, if it had been made as a result of the first request of August 11, 1978, would have had to be made between October 11 and December 11, 1978.

The judge based his decision on the view that this case was indistinguishable from an earlier decision of this court in *Stile Hall Properties Ltd.* v. *Gooch* (*Note*), post, p. 62. That case apparently is only reported in the Estates Gazette (1968) 207 E.G. 715, but the judge was supplied, and we
H have been supplied, with a transcript of the judgment of this court, which consisted of Danckwerts L.J., Davies L.J. and Edmund Davies L.J. The facts in that case, as they appear from the judgment, were these. The appellant, Mrs. Gooch, was the tenant of property in Brentford under a lease dated March 21, 1960, for seven years from January 7, 1960, so that that lease would have expired on January 6, 1967. The tenant first gave a notice on September 9, 1966, but that notice was invalid because the date specified for the commencement of the new lease was more than 12 months

after the date of the notice and was therefore invalid under the provisions of A
the Act that I have read. Then a second notice was served, dated March 20,
1967. That proposed that the date of commencement of the new tenancy
should be September 29, 1967, and that the lease should be for 14 years.
Nothing was done under that notice by way of making an application to the
court. On September 8, 1967, the landlords wrote: " As proceedings have
not been commenced within the statutory four months, we therefore assume
that your client will be vacating on the due date . . ." As a result of that, B
on September 26, 1967, that being only two or three days before the
termination of the tenancy by virtue of the previous notice, the tenant's
solicitors wrote to the landlord's solicitors:

> " We enclose tenant's request for a new tenancy of the above property.
> This is in place of our client's earlier request dated March 20, 1967,
> which was withdrawn by our letter . . . dated April 21, 1967." C

That enclosed a notice which was in the statutory form and which specified
June 24, 1968, as the date for the commencement of the new tenancy, that
being, of course, about nine months later than the date that had been
specified in the previous request for a new tenancy.

Danckwerts L.J. said, post, p. 63E:

> " Therefore there was an attempt by the tenant to withdraw her second D
> notice, which was perfectly valid, and substitute a fresh one after the
> period of four months mentioned in section 29 had expired."

He then went through the relevant provisions of the Act of 1954 and
said, post, p. 64C–F:

> " The only other thing to which I need refer is the passage in *Woodfall
> on Landlord and Tenant,* 26th ed. (1960), vol. 1, p. 1410, in which it E
> is observed: ' It is important to observe that if the tenant fails to make
> this application to the court, irrespective of whether the landlord has
> served a notice of intention to oppose, the current tenancy ends
> immediately before the date specified by the tenant in his request for
> the commencement of the new tenancy and the tenant loses his right to
> a new tenancy and indeed all his rights under the Act.' Apparently F
> there is no case which deals with the observations in *Woodfall,* and
> so far as we have been informed no text-book or other book of that kind
> has commented on it in any way. It seems to me that the observations
> are plainly right. The effect of what the tenant did was that, by her
> request, she fixed the date of the termination of the continued tenancy
> that the Act conferred upon her by section 24 by reference to the date
> when she was asking for a new lease, and accordingly automatically G
> under the provisions of section 26 the continued tenancy came to an
> end. That was the end of the matter, unless she had followed it up
> within two or four months as required by section 29 by an application
> to the appropriate court. She made no such application and accord-
> ingly the tenancy determined on September 28, 1967, and that is the
> end of the matter."
> H

Davies L.J. referred to the request of March 20, 1967, and said, post,
pp. 64G—65B:

> " The effect of that request would be, under section 26 (5) of the Act
> of 1954, to terminate the current tenancy on September 28, 1967. Of
> course, if the tenant had applied within the statutory period of four
> months the interim provisions for the continuation of the tenancy
> would have come into effect. But she did not. And therefore once

A the four months had expired the tenancy was due to come to an end on September 28. Speaking for myself, I agree with the observations by the editor of *Woodfall on Landlord and Tenant*, 26th ed., vol. 1, p. 1410, which have been read by Danckwerts L.J. It would seem to me, as Mr. Avgherinos suggests, to cut right across the intent of the Act if a tenant, such as the present defendant, having given a perfectly valid notice and having failed to take the necessary follow-up step to

B apply to the court for a new lease, could a couple of days before the statutory expiration of the tenancy serve (as was attempted to be done in the present case) another notice for June 24, 1968, which would, under the statute, continue the tenancy to June 23, 1968, and then, I suppose, on June 21 serve another one, and so on and on and on ad infinitum."

C Pausing there, it is that last sentence on which Mr. Denyer particularly relies, and I will come back to that later.

"The landlord would never know where he stood. The statute, as we all know, is an invasion of the landlord's right, for perfectly proper and sound reasons; but it must be construed strictly in accordance with its terms, and I can see nothing whatsoever in it

D that would permit the procedure that was adopted by the tenant in the present case. I entirely agree with Danckwerts L.J. that this appeal, bravely as it is sought to be supported by Mr. Beaumont on behalf of the tenant, is quite hopeless and should be dismissed."

Edmund Davies L.J. said, post, p. 65D–G:

E "In the present case Mr. Beaumont has had to struggle with a really impossible task and he has failed, despite his efforts, to discharge it. The suggestion put forward that it is open to the tenant, without the concurrence of the landlord, to withdraw his request for a new tenancy is one which would cut entirely across the statutory scheme. The Act vests radical rights in the tenant of business premises. It also recognises that the landlord also has certain rights and must be

F protected against exploitation and against harassment. If what is suggested here were indeed the position and the tenant could go on indefinitely serving the landlord with fresh requests, it appears to me that a quite impossible situation would result. The tenant having served an entirely valid request on March 20, 1967, it had certain legal consequences. If she did nothing more, section 26 (5) came into operation and would operate to terminate that tenancy immediately

G before the date specified in the request for the beginning of the new tenancy, in this case on September 28, 1967. In order that the tenant should prevent that event occurring it was up to her, pursuant to section 29 (3), to make an application to the court for a new tenancy, that application being made not less than two nor more than four months after the making of the tenant's request to her landlord for a

H new tenancy. This tenant never proceeded under section 29 (3), and accordingly the landlords perfectly properly sent her a letter of September 8, 1967, in which they said " what I have already quoted: that they assumed that as no application had been made the tenant would be giving up possession. " The result of that was, very belatedly, to evoke from the tenant the purported further request of September 26, to which reference has already been made. In my judgment that clearly will not do. The whole scheme would be frustrated were such

a request to have any validity. I have no doubt, any more than   A
Danckwerts and Davies L.JJ. have, that the editor of *Woodfall on
Landlord and Tenant*, 26th ed., vol. 1, has perfectly correctly
expounded the effect of the Act, and particularly of the operation of
section 26 (5) and section 29 (3), in the passage at p. 1410, which
has already been cited."

All three of their Lordships, accordingly, had no hesitation in dismissing   B
the appeal.

When this matter came before Judge Hutton, he set out the facts in his
judgment and referred to the relevant provisions of the Act and to the
applications. He went on:

" Mr. Wigmore "—who appeared for the landlord there, as he has
here—" has submitted that it was only possible for the tenant to make   C
one request. That once a request is made the procedure starts working.
The clock starts running and cannot be stopped and started again by
a further request."

He then referred to *Stile Hall Properties Ltd.* v. *Gooch* (*Note*), post,
p. 62, and said: " That case is similar to this one in all respects except
one." Then he referred to the judgments of Danckwerts L.J. and   D
Edmund Davies L.J. and quoted the passages that I have already quoted,
including the quotation from *Woodfall on Landlord and Tenant*, 26th
ed., vol. 1, p. 1410. He went on:

" That case is distinguished by Mr. Denyer on behalf of the tenant.
In the *Stile Hall* case, he says, the final request used a different
date for the start of a new tenancy, a later date. So there was
there a complete lack of merit on behalf of the tenant who was   E
simply stalling for more time. Mr. Denyer submits that here the
same date is requested, so no hardship could be alleged and the
landlord is being purely technical and lacking in merit. He further
says that the Act in itself does not provide that no further request
can be made. I reject the submissions by the tenant. The *Stile
Hall* case sets out the law not only on the facts of that case but   F
generally, and the findings in that case apply equally here. Merit
has no relevance to the decisions. The landlord is entitled to
rely upon the provisions of the Act, as set out by the court in *Stile
Hall*. Therefore the tenant's application is invalid as being out of time
following the original request."

Mr. Denyer in this court has sought valiantly to distinguish *Stile Hall*   G
Properties Ltd. v. *Gooch* (*Note*), post, p. 62, on the same ground as
that on which he relied before the judge: that is, that the ground of
the decision in the *Stile Hall* case was that the second request specified
a date for the commencement of the new tenancy which was different
from and later than that specified in the first request, whereas here
the second request specified the same date.

It seems to me that the ratio of the *Stile Hall* case was this. By virtue   H
of section 26 (5) the existing tenancy terminates immediately before the
date specified in the request for a new tenancy, unless the tenant within
the time specified by section 29 (3) makes an application to the court. If he
does make an application, the tenancy continues till three months after the
final disposal of the proceedings: see section 64. If, however, the tenant
does not make such an application, the tenancy automatically comes to an
end on that date. If the tenant fails to make an application within the

A proper time, he cannot withdraw the first request and make another. In the *Stile Hall* case the court was obviously impressed by the hardship to the landlord if the tenant could go on serving successive notices and so continuing the tenancy ad infinitum. Here, of course, the tenant is not trying to do any such thing. It is true that the particular hardship to the landlord that impressed this court in the *Stile Hall* case would not arise in this case, but I find it impossible to distinguish this case from the *Stile Hall* case on

B the ground put forward by Mr. Denyer.

I have already read section 29 (3) and I need not read it in full again, but it provides that no application under section 24 (1) of the Act " shall be entertained " unless it is made within the specified time. Mr. Denyer accepts that the first request was a valid request and that it had one of the consequences laid down: that is, the consequence of terminating the tenancy

C on July 15, 1979. He does not explicitly ask to withdraw that request, but in substance I think that that is really what he does ask: that is, that the request should be treated as withdrawn so as to allow the application based on the second request to be made. In the *Stile Hall* case this court held that the first notice could not be withdrawn. If Mr. Denyer's submission were right, I can see no reason why a tenant should not specify a later date in his second request than the date specified in his first request. It

D seems to me that in principle this case is indistinguishable from the *Stile Hall* case. It seems to me that it is exactly covered by the passage from the judgment of Danckwerts L.J. which I have already read. I do not think that I need read it again; it is the passage which begins " The effect of what the tenant did was that, by her request, she fixed the date of the termination of the continued tenancy . . ." and ends with the words

E " . . . and that is the end of the matter."

In spite of Mr. Denyer's very brave attempt to distinguish the *Stile Hall* case, it seems to me that it is quite impossible to distinguish that case from this; that decision is binding on this court, and accordingly this appeal must, in my judgment, be dismissed.

MEGAW L.J. I agree with the order proposed by Browne L.J., for

F the reasons given by him. Mr. Denyer, with, if I may say so, proper and admirable economy of words, has put forward his submission that there is a material distinction between the ratio decidendi of the decision of this court in *Stile Hall Properties Ltd.* v. *Gooch* (*Note*), post, p. 62, and the present case. In my judgment there is no such material distinction.

The only other thing that I should add, in case it might be of relevance in certain other contexts, is that the solicitors who have represented the

G tenant on the hearing of the preliminary issue in the county court and again on the appeal in this court are not the same as the solicitors who apparently, as agents for the appellant in this appeal, put forward the notices of August 11, 1978, and January 12, 1979, and the formal application for a new tenancy of March 15, 1979.

H   *Appeal dismissed with costs.*
                                        Leave to appeal refused.

Solicitors: *Leaman Sparks & Co., Bristol; Donald Bennett & Legat, Bristol.*

                                                            M. G.

A

NOTE

[COURT OF APPEAL]

* STILE HALL PROPERTIES LTD. *v.* GOOCH

1968   July 4   Danckwerts, Davies and Edmund Davies L.JJ.

B

Landlord and Tenant—Business premises (security of tenure)—
Application for new tenancy—Request for new tenancy begin-
ning on specified date—Tenant failing to apply to court within
time limited by Act—Second request for new tenancy specify-
ing later date for commencement—Application to court for
new tenancy based on second request—Whether valid—Hard-
ship on landlord—Landlord and Tenant Act 1954 (2 & 3 Eliz.
2, c. 56), ss. 26 (5), 29 (3) [1]

C

APPEAL from Judge Sir Shirley Worthington-Evans sitting at Brentford
County Court.

The defendant, Mrs. Mary Elizabeth Gooch, appealed from the judgment
of Judge Sir Shirley Worthington-Evans, on January 10, 1968, holding that the
plaintiffs, Stile Hall Properties Ltd., were entitled to possession of business
premises, 1a, Stile Hall Parade, Chiswick, London, W.4, against the defendant.

The facts are stated in the judgments.

D

Christopher Beaumont for the defendant.
George Avgherinos for the plaintiffs.

DANCKWERTS L.J.   This is an appeal from a judgment of Sir Shirley
Worthington-Evans, the county court judge at Brentford, on January 10, 1968.
The appellant was a tenant of the respondents under a lease dated March 21,
1960, for seven years from January 7, 1960. She had herself been there in this
lock-up shop and basement since 1956. The rent was £225 a year, rising to
£250 a year for the last four years.

E

I will refer to the first notice, which is in the form required for an
application under the Landlord and Tenant Act 1954. It was by the tenant in
respect of 1a, Stile Hall Parade, Chiswick, the shop where she carries on
business. It requests the landlords to grant a new tenancy commencing on
September 29, 1967:

F

"I propose that the property to be comprised in the new tenancy should
be the lock-up shop known as No. 1 Stile Hall Parade, Chiswick . . . My
proposals as to the rent to be payable under the new tenancy and as to the
other terms of the new tenancy are £250 per annum and otherwise upon
the terms of the present lease dated March 21, 1960."

Then there is a reference to section 26 of the Act of 1954. The date of that
is September 9, 1966.

G

That was invalid, because the period for the commencement of the tenancy
was more than 12 months ahead.

Then a second notice in the statutory form was served by the tenant, dated
March 20, 1967. That was in respect of the same premises, proposing that
the date for commencement of the new tenancy be September 29, 1967. The
terms were again the same: £250 per annum for rent on the terms of the
present lease dated March 21, 1960, for a period of 14 years from September
29, 1967.

H

Then the landlord suggested £400 a year. The result of that was a letter
of April 21, 1967, on behalf of the tenant:

"With reference to your client's offer of a new lease for seven years from
March 25 at £400 per annum subject to their paying your costs of

[1] Landlord and Tenant Act 1954, ss. 26 (5), 29 (3): see post, pp. 63F, 64B.

A   approximately £22, Mrs. Gooch feels that the rent is excessive and considers a rental of £300 per annum at most as advised by her surveyor and also that any new lease should not commence before September 29 next."

The next letter is on September 8, 1967, from the landlords:

B   " We refer to the notice served by your client under the Landlord and Tenant Act 1954 dated March 20, 1967, and expiring on September 29, 1967. As proceedings have not been commenced within the statutory four months, we therefore assume that your client will be vacating on the due date and will you please take your client's instructions in regard to her vacation and for arrangements to be made for our clients' surveyor to attend the premises and prepare a schedule of dilapidations."

Subsequently the landlords' solicitors wrote:

C   " We are in receipt of your letter of September 13, upon which we have taken our clients' instructions. In view of the subsequent correspondence that occurred since our clients' offer, they inform us that they are not agreeable to reopening negotiations and wish your client to vacate on September 29 in accordance with the notice which you served on her behalf."

On September 26, 1967, the tenant's solicitors wrote to the landlords'
D solicitors:

" We enclose tenant's request for a new tenancy of the above property. This is in place of our client's earlier request dated March 20, 1967, which was withdrawn by our letter to Messrs. Palmer, Paletz & Mark dated April 21, 1967."

The date of that letter is September 26, two days before the expiration of the
E period ending on September 28, 1967. That proposed notice is in the statutory form and it appears to accept the landlords' proposed £400 per annum for the rent, for the terms of the present lease and for a period of 14 years.

Therefore there was an attempt by the tenant to withdraw her second notice, which was perfectly valid, and substitute a fresh one after the period of four months mentioned in section 29 had expired.

Section 29 provides:

F   " . . . (3) No application under subsection (1) of section 24 of this Act shall be entertained unless it is made not less than two nor more than four months after the giving of the landlord's notice under section 25 of this Act or, as the case may be, after the making of the tenant's request for a new tenancy."

That period had, of course, expired by the time of the last request, and it is necessary to look at other provisions of the Act to see what is the effect of that.
G Section 24 provides:

" (1) A tenancy to which this Part of this Act applies shall not come to an end unless terminated in accordance with the provisions of this Part of this Act; and, subject to the provisions of section 29 of this Act "—we will have to refer to that—" the tenant under such a tenancy may apply to the court for a new tenancy— . . ."

H The result of that is that after the expiration of the old lease, which expired in January 1968, the tenant's lease continued by section 24, subject to the provisions of the Act. There is a provision in section 25 for the termination of the tenancy by the landlord, with which I need not trouble further, because the landlord did nothing in respect of that provision. The material provisions are found in section 26:

" (3) A tenant's request for a new tenancy shall not have effect unless it is made by notice in the prescribed form given to the landlord and sets out the tenant's proposals as to the property to be comprised in the new

Danckwerts L.J.   **Stile Hall Properties Ltd. v. Gooch (C.A.)**   **[1980]**

tenancy (being either the whole or part of the property comprised in the   A
current tenancy), as to the rent to be payable under the new tenancy and as
to the other terms of the new tenancy. (4) A tenant's request for a new
tenancy shall not be made if the landlord has already given notice under
the last foregoing section to terminate the current tenancy, or if the tenant
has already given notice to quit or notice under the next following section;
and no such notice shall be given by the landlord or the tenant after the
making by the tenant of a request for a new tenancy. (5) Where the   B
tenant makes a request for a new tenancy in accordance with the foregoing provisions of this section, the current tenancy shall, subject to the
provisions of subsection (2) of section 36 of this Act "—which are not
material for the present purpose—" and the provisions of Part IV of this
Act as to the interim continuation of tenancies, terminate immediately
before the date specified in the request for the beginning of the new
tenancy . . ."
                                                                              C
    Therefore the effect of that was that when the tenant served her second
notice it had the effect of determining the tenancy continued under section 24 on
September 28, 1967—that is to say, the day immediately before the date from
which she was asking for a new lease.
    The only other thing to which I need refer is the passage in *Woodfall on
Landlord and Tenant,* 26th ed. (1960), vol. 1, p. 1410, in which it is observed:

> " It is important to observe that if the tenant fails to make this application   D
> to the court, irrespective of whether the landlord has served a notice of
> intention to oppose, the current tenancy ends immediately before the date
> specified by the tenant in his request for the commencement of the new
> tenancy and the tenant loses his right to a new tenancy and indeed all his
> rights under the Act."

    Apparently there is no case that deals with the observation in *Woodfall,*   E
and so far as we have been informed no text-book or other book of that kind
has commented on it in any way. It seems to me that the observations are
plainly right. The effect of what the tenant did was that, by her request, she
fixed the date of the termination of the continued tenancy that the Act conferred
upon her by section 24 by reference to the date when she was asking for a new
lease, and accordingly automatically under the provisions of section 26 the
continued tenancy came to an end. That was the end of the matter, unless
she had followed it up within two or four months as required by section 29   F
by an application to the appropriate court. She made no such application and
accordingly the tenancy determined on September 28, 1967, and that is the end
of the matter.
    It seems to me that the county court judge plainly reached the right
conclusion, and this appeal must fail.

    DAVIES L.J. I agree. After the first abortive attempt in September 1966   G
to make a request under the Act for a new tenancy—an attempt which was
abortive because it proposed a date for the commencement of the new tenancy
more than 12 months ahead—a perfectly valid request was made on March 20,
1967, for a tenancy commencing on September 29. The effect of that request
would be, under section 26 (5) of the Act of 1954, to terminate the current
tenancy on September 28, 1967. Of course, if the tenant had applied within
the statutory period of four months the interim provisions for the continuation   H
of the tenancy would have come into effect. But she did not. And therefore
once the four months had expired the tenancy was due to come to an end on
September 28.
    Speaking for myself, I agree with the observations by the editor of *Woodfall
on Landlord and Tenant,* 26th ed., vol. 1, p. 1410, which have been read by
Danckwerts L.J. It would seem to me, as Mr. Avgherinos suggests, to cut right
across the intent of the Act if a tenant, such as the present defendant, having
given a perfectly valid notice and having failed to take the necessary follow-

The Weekly Law Reports, February 1, 1980

65

1 W.L.R.   Stile Hall Properties Ltd. v. Gooch (C.A.)   Davies L.J.

A up step to apply to the court for a new lease, could a couple of days before the statutory expiration of the tenancy serve (as was attempted to be done in the present case) another notice for June 24, 1968, which would, under the statute, continue the tenancy to June 23, 1968, and then, I suppose, on June 21 serve another one, and so on and on and on ad infinitum. The landlord would never know where he stood. The statute, as we all know, is an invasion of the landlord's right, for perfectly proper and sound reasons; but
B it must be construed strictly in accordance with its terms, and I can see nothing whatsoever in it that would permit the procedure that was adopted by the tenant in the present case.

I entirely agree with Danckwerts L.J. that this appeal, bravely as it is sought to be supported by Mr. Beaumont on behalf of the tenant, is quite hopeless and should be dismissed.

C EDMUND DAVIES L.J. Mr. Avgherinos has rightly said that when one has a statute of this kind which, albeit not a codification of the law, sets out to provide a comprehensive scheme dealing with the position of landlords and tenants of premises coming within the Act, those who assert that either the landlord or the tenant has rights over and above and independent of that statutory scheme are confronted by a formidable task.

In the present case Mr. Beaumont has had to struggle with a really impossible task and he has failed, despite his efforts to discharge it. The suggestion put
D forward that it is open to the tenant, without the concurrence of the landlord, to withdraw his request for a new tenancy is one that would cut entirely across the statutory scheme. The Act vests radical rights in the tenant of business premises. It also recognises that the landlord also has certain rights and must be protected against exploitation and against harassment. If what is suggested here were indeed the position and the tenant could go on indefinitely serving the landlord with fresh requests, it appears to me that a quite impossible
E situation would result. The tenant having served an entirely valid request on March 20, 1967, it had certain legal consequences. If she did nothing more, section 26 (5) came into operation and would operate to terminate that tenancy immediately before the date specified in the request for the beginning of the new tenancy, in this case on September 28, 1967. In order that the tenant should prevent that event occurring it was up to her, pursuant to section 29 (3), to make an application to the court for a new tenancy, that application being
F made not less than two nor more than four months after the making of the tenant's request to her landlord for a new tenancy. This tenant never proceeded under section 29 (3), and accordingly the landlords perfectly properly sent her a letter of September 8, 1967, in which they said: " As proceedings have not been commenced within the statutory four months, we therefore assume that your client will be vacating on the due date . . ." The result of that was, very belatedly, to evoke from the tenant the purported further request of September 26, to which reference has already been made.
G In my judgment that clearly will not do. The whole scheme would be frustrated were such a request to have any validity. I have no doubt, any more than Danckwerts and Davies L.JJ. have, that the editor of *Woodfall on Landlord and Tenant*, 26th ed., vol. 1, has perfectly correctly expounded the effect of the Act, and particularly of the operation of section 26 (5) and section 29 (3), in the passage at p. 1410, which has already been cited.

For those reasons I have no hesitation, with respect, in agreeing with
H Danckwerts and Davies L.JJ. that this appeal should be dismissed.

Appeal dismissed with costs.
Order for possession within 28 days.

Solicitors: *Bond & Banbury; Palmer, Paletz & Mark.*

M. G.

[1980]

[COURT OF APPEAL]   A

* ST. CATHERINE'S COLLEGE *v.* DORLING

1979 May 23, 24, 25   Megaw, Eveleigh and Brandon L.JJ.

*Landlord and Tenant—Rent restriction—Premises within the Acts—
House let to college for occupation by undergraduates—Each*   B
*undergraduate occupying study bedroom—Whether premises let
as single dwelling—Whether protected tenancy—Rent Act 1977
(c. 42), s. 1*

Under a scheme for providing residential accommodation
for university undergraduates, a college entered into a tenancy
agreement with the owner of a furnished house to be occupied
by five undergraduates. Each undergraduate had the exclusive   C
use of one room as a study bedroom and shared the kitchen and
bathroom. The college covenanted in clause 2 (1) of the
agreement " Not to use the demised premises otherwise than for
occupation by a person or persons . . . pursuing or intending
to pursue a course of study provided by " the college and, in
sub-clause (m) " to use or permit the same to be used as private
residence only in the occupation of one person per room. . . ."
The college applied to the county court for a declaration that
it had a protected tenancy under section 1 of the Rent Act   D
1977.[1] The judge found that the house had not been let as a
dwelling house but as a building for multiple occupation of a
number of sub-units and he refused to grant the declaration.
On appeal by the college: —
Held, dismissing the appeal, that, in determining whether
there was a letting of a separate dwelling for the purposes of a
joint occupation by a number of undergraduates, consideration   E
had to be given to the contemplated use of the premises, the
tenancy agreement and the surrounding circumstances at the
time the parties entered into the agreement; that the words " as
private residence only " in the context of clause 2 (m) of the
agreement could not be construed as meaning a letting as a
private residence but as referring to the user of the premises
being for residential purposes; and that, since the terms of the
agreement and the surrounding circumstances showed that there   F
had been a letting of premises containing a number of units of
habitation each to be occupied by an undergraduate, the house
had not been let as a separate dwelling and, therefore, the
college was not a protected tenant within the meaning of
section 1 of the Rent Act 1977 (post, pp. 68F, H, 70A–C, E–F,
72B).
Horford Investments Ltd. v. *Lambert* [1976] Ch. 39, C.A.
applied.
G

The following cases are referred to in the judgments:
Horford Investments Ltd. v. *Lambert* [1976] Ch. 39; [1973] 3 W.L.R.
872; [1974] 1 All E.R. 131, C.A.
Ponder v. *Hillman* [1969] 1 W.L.R. 1261; [1969] 3 All E.R. 694.
Whitty v. *Scott-Russell* [1950] 2 K.B. 32; [1950] 1 All E.R. 884, C.A.
Wolfe v. *Hogan* [1949] 2 K.B. 194; [1949] 1 All E.R. 570, C.A.
Wright v. *Howell* (1947) 204 L.T.J. 299.
H

The following additional cases were cited in argument:
Cole v. *Harris* [1945] K.B. 474; [1945] 2 All E.R. 146, C.A.
Curl v. *Angelo* [1948] 2 All E.R. 189, C.A.

[1] Rent Act 1977, s. 1: ". . . a tenancy under which a dwelling-house (which may
be a house or part of a house) is let as a separate dwelling is a protected tenancy for
the purposes of this Act."

A   *Feather Supplies Ltd.* v. *Ingham* [1971] 2 Q.B. 348; [1971] 3 W.L.R. 362;
          [1971] 3 All E.R. 556, C.A.
       Goodrich v. *Paisner* [1957] A.C. 65; [1956] 2 W.L.R. 1053; [1956]
          2 All E.R. 176, H.L.(E.).
       Langford Property Co. Ltd. v. *Goldrich* [1949] 1 K.B. 511; [1949] 1 All
          E.R. 402, C.A.
       Neale v. *Del Soto* [1945] K.B. 144; [1945] 1 All E.R. 191, C.A.

B

APPEAL from Judge Clover sitting at Oxford County Court.

By a written agreement dated July 8, 1978, the landlord, James Anthony
Dorling, let a house, 208, Headington Road, Oxford, to St. Catherine's
College, Oxford, for one year less seven days at the rent of £224·25 per
calendar month. The agreement contained a term permitting the house " to
be used as private residence only in the occupation of one person per
C   room. . . ." By an order of March 14, 1979, Judge Clover refused the
application of the college for a declaration that the tenancy was a protected
tenancy.

The college appealed against the order on the grounds, inter alia, that
the judge misdirected himself and erred in law in holding that the tenancy
was not a protected tenancy and that the house was let as a number of
D   dwellings.

The facts are stated in the judgment of Eveleigh L.J.

Alan Boyle for the college.
Terence Etherton for the landlord.

E   MEGAW L.J. I shall ask Eveleigh L.J. to deliver the first judgment.

EVELEIGH L.J. On March 14, 1979, in the Oxford County Court, Judge
Clover refused to grant a declaration, on the application of St. Catherine's
College, that the premises, 208, Headington Road, Oxford, of which the
college was the tenant, were the subject of a protected tenancy under section
1 of the Rent Act 1977. That section reads:
F
" Subject to this Part of this Act, a tenancy under which a dwelling-
house (which may be a house or part of a house) is let as a separate
dwelling is a protected tenancy for the purposes of this Act."

As a result of the reluctance of house-owners to provide rented accommodation for students, Parliament introduced section 8 of the Rent Act
G   1977, subsection (1) of which reads:

" A tenancy is not a protected tenancy if it is granted to a person who
is pursuing, or intends to pursue, a course of study provided by a
specified educational institution and is so granted either by that institution or by another specified institution or body of persons."

A firm of estate agents in Oxford, Messrs. Runyards, with the coopera-
H   tion of a large number of Oxford colleges, introduced a scheme by which
it was envisaged that accommodation would more readily be made available
to undergraduates. They published a booklet giving details of that scheme.
The general idea was that the owner of the house would let premises to the
college, which would then make the accommodation available to undergraduates. A £50 deposit was taken from the undergraduates who had made
an application for the accommodation, and that deposit was treated as an
application fee unless the arrangements were finally completed, when it was

treated as part-payment of rent. Messrs. Runyards orally guaranteed to the **A**
colleges concerned that every undergraduate would have a separate room.

In so far as 208, Headington Road is concerned, there were four
undergraduates of the college who applied to Messrs. Runyards for accommodation. They found a suitable house, namely, 208, Headington Road.
The college was willing to take those premises under a lease. On June 12,
1978, the undergraduates signed a document entitled " Agreement and
Indemnity," which stated: **B**

> " In consideration of the college, through the domestic bursar, entering
> on my behalf into a lease of 208, Headington Road, Oxford, from July
> 8, 1978, for one year less seven days at a rent of £224·25 per month . . .
> I hereby agree with the college to fulfil and observe all conditions and
> covenants contained in their lease and to indemnify the college against
> all liabilities which it may incur thereunder." **C**

That document bears five signatures, for, on discovering that the house would
accommodate five, one further undergraduate was found to live there.

It is not alleged in this case that the college took a lease as agent for the
undergraduates who signed that indemnity or for any other undergraduate.
Indeed, the landlord clearly would not have made a contract with the
undergraduates themselves. Nor is it shown that the landlord was aware of **D**
the terms of that agreement.

The premises consisted of three rooms upstairs and two rooms downstairs. There was a small kitchen, a bathroom, and two W.C.s, one inside
and one outside. One of the two downstairs rooms had a dining table and
four chairs. There were no locks on the doors of the rooms. Each room
was equipped with sufficient furniture for its use as a bedroom, a study and **E**
a sitting-room. The premises were occupied by the five undergraduates.
Each took a room. Each gave a cheque for his share of the total rent; and
generally speaking one of them would take all the cheques to Runyards.
The dining-table was taken from the room where it was when they first
occupied the premises and set up in the kitchen. The general practice was
for these occupants to cook in relays, providing their own individual food,
although on occasions, at weekends in particular, they might eat together **F**
around that table.

The question in this case is whether the premises were let as a separate
dwelling within the meaning of section 1. The important point in answering
that question is to determine the contemplated use of the premises. In
Ponder v. *Hillman* [1969] 1 W.L.R. 1261, 1263, Goff J. referred to *Wolfe*
v. *Hogan* [1949] 2 K.B. 194 and to a particular passage in the judgment of **G**
Evershed L.J. and then continued:

> " . . . [Evershed L.J.] approved the following passage in *Megarry on*
> *The Rent Acts* (1967) 4th ed., p. 19: ' Where the terms of the tenancy
> provide for or contemplate the use of the premises for some particular
> purpose, that purpose is the essential factor, not the nature of the
> premises or the actual use made of them. Thus, if the premises are let **H**
> for business purposes, the tenant cannot claim that they have been
> converted into a dwelling-house merely because somebody lives on the
> premises."

So it follows that one has to consider the terms of the lease and the
surrounding circumstances at the time that the lease was granted. It may
be that in some cases assistance can be obtained from the subsequent user

The Weekly Law Reports, February 1, 1980

69

1 W.L.R.   St. Catherine's College v. Dorling (C.A.)   Eveleigh L.J.

A of the premises. In my opinion generally speaking such assistance will be found to be a matter of last resort.

I turn to consider the terms of the tenancy agreement in this case. There is the usual habendum and reddendum, and then I turn to clause 2 (l), in which the tenant covenants:

B " (i) Not to use the demised premises otherwise than for occupation by a person or persons who are as specified by section 8 of the Rent Act 1977 pursuing or intending to pursue a course of study provided by the tenant whether the said person or persons occupy the demised premises as sub-tenants or licensees. (ii) Not to assign sub-let with possession or share possession or occupation of all or part of the demised premises furniture fixtures fittings or effects or any part thereof provided that there shall be no breach of this clause if the tenant shall be a specified educational institution as defined by section 8 of the Rent Act 1977 and either the tenant sub-lets only to a person who is pursuing or intending to pursue a course of study provided by the tenant or the tenant grants a licence for the use of the demised premises to such person."

C

D Then clause 2 (m), the user clause, reads:

" Not to carry on or permit to be carried on upon the demised premises any profession trade or business whatsoever or let apartments or receive paying guests in the demised premises but to use or permit the same to be used as private residence only in the occupation of one person per room and not in any way to contravene the Town and Country Planning Acts and not to exhibit any notice or poster on any portion of the demised premises."

E

Mr. Boyle has submitted that here a group of students, or under-graduates, intended to occupy the premises as joint occupants of the whole, and that this was the object and purport of the tenancy granted to the college. He particularly relied upon sub-clause (m) and invited the court to say that the words " to be used as private residence only " should

F be read to include the indefinite article: that is to say, " to be used as *a* private residence only."

Mr. Boyle then referred the court to *Whitty* v. *Scott-Russell* [1950] 2 K.B. 32. There, a house and cottage which were semi-detached were the subject of the letting. There was no internal intercommunication. The tenant covenanted " to use the premises as and for a private dwelling-house

G only." It was held in that case:

" that, notwithstanding that the tenant did not and had never intended to occupy the cottage himself, the house and cottage were, having regard to the terms of the lease and, in particular, the covenant by the tenant to use the demised property as a dwelling-house only, let as a single dwelling and therefore constituted a dwelling-house within the

H definition in section 16 (1) of the Act of 1933."

Mr. Boyle has argued, by analogy, that if these premises were to be used as *a* private residence—the emphasis being upon the indefinite article—it meant that they were not to be used as a number of different private residences: therefore they were let as a whole, with the object of their being inhabited jointly by the students. He also placed some reliance upon the words of sub-clause (l) (ii) " either the tenant sublets only to a person who is pursuing . . . a course of study." He said it was therefore contemplated that no more than one person would take, or that persons A could take jointly being responsible for the whole.

On the other hand, Mr. Etherton, for the landlord respondent, has contended that clause 2 (m) comes to his aid. He has invited the court to construe the phrase " as private residence " as meaning: for residential purposes. I would myself accept that submission. One cannot read the words " as private residence " without reading the words that follow, namely, " in the occupation of one person per room." In my opinion it B is no accidental omission of the indefinite article. There is an intentional omission and the phrase " as private residence " is used similarly to the expression " as business premises." It is descriptive of the user and not of the premises themselves.

When one then sees that what is envisaged is the occupation of one person per room, using that for private purposes, and then turns to the C other provision in sub-clause (l) which I have read, one sees that subletting or a licence to use is contemplated, and the words used are " sub-lets only to a person." The importance, to my mind, of the words in that sub-clause is that they show that a subletting is envisaged. That envisages, as I see it—for one must read this as a whole—that the college is permitted to sublet to a person who is to occupy a single room as a private residence. If the college is to be allowed to " sublet to a person " (to use the words D of the sub-clause) any part of the building, it would follow that it should be allowed to let to more than one person, or the building would otherwise have another part unused. Quite clearly it was never contemplated that the college itself should occupy or make any particular use of the premises —other, that is to say, than as accommodation for undergraduates. Furthermore, of course, the plural is used in sub-clause (l) (i), where we E see the words " for occupation by a person or persons."

I therefore read these two sub-clauses as saying that the college shall be in a position to sublet, and shall be in a position to sublet to " persons "; but they must be persons " pursuing or intending to pursue a course of study." The use of the singular in sub-paragraph (ii) is simply because it is describing the type of person who may be a sub-tenant; and, as the college may sublet to a particular type of sub-tenant and must do so only for F occupation of one person per room, it follows, in my opinion, that the purpose of this letting was that the college should be in a position to do just that. In other words, what was being granted to the college here was a tenancy of a building which contained a number of units of habitation, as they have been called. From that interpretation of this lease I would conclude that the premises were not let as separate dwellings.

In *Horford Investments Ltd.* v. *Lambert* [1976] Ch. 39, a landlord let G to a tenant two houses. Those houses had been converted into a number of " units of accommodation," and at the time of the lease those units were in fact occupied. The question arose in that case as to whether this was a letting of a dwelling-house, and indeed a separate dwelling-house, so as to attract the protection of the Rent Act 1968. Russell L.J. said, at p. 48:

> " Accordingly, in my judgment the tenancy of each of the two houses H
> in this case is not within the definition of a protected tenancy because
> of the plurality of dwellings, or, as I have labelled them, units of habita-
> tion, comprised in the premises when let and obliged by the terms of
> the letting to be so maintained."

In that case the covenant in regard to one of the two flats—the user clause in the lease—was in these terms:

The Weekly Law Reports, February 1, 1980

71

1 W.L.R.   St. Catherine's College v. Dorling (C.A.)   Eveleigh L.J.

A   " The lessee will not use . . . the . . . premises or any part thereof for
      the purposes of any trade or business nor for any purpose other than
      residential in multiple occupation."

In my opinion, clause 2 (m) of the lease which this court has to consider is
to the same effect: it is not to use for any purpose other than residential
in multiple occupation.

B   Mr. Boyle, however, has argued that the rooms in this house were not
dwellings and, consequently, *Horford Investments Ltd.* v. *Lambert* [1976]
Ch. 39 has no application.   He further submitted that there is a distinction
in that the individual units were already let in that case. I cannot accept
that those arguments prevent, or in any way militate against, the construction of the lease which I have just stated.

         He referred the court to *Wright* v. *Howell* (1947) 204 L.T.J. 299, where
C the appellant was the tenant of an unfurnished room in a flat of the respondent landlord. He used as toilet and other facilities those that existed
in another flat in the same building which was occupied by the parents-in-
law. It was held that, in those circumstances:

         " . . . as the room, when let to the tenant, was devoid of cooking
         arrangements and water supply, and as the word ' dwelling ' on its
D   true construction included all the major activities of life, particularly
         sleeping, cooking and feeding, and as one of those activities, sleeping,
         was at all relevant times no longer being carried on there, the room
         was not a dwelling and the tenancy was not protected."

I do not myself see a parallel, on the facts of that case. In the present case
the undergraduates were sleeping on the premises; there were facilities
E provided. It is not necessary, as the many cases under the Rent Acts show,
for those facilities to exist in the room itself. Mr. Boyle argued that these
rooms did not themselves attract the protection of the Rent Acts: as some
accommodation was shared they would be outside that protection, and from
this he inferred—in what I regard as a non sequitur—that, as they were not
themselves protected dwellings, the whole of the house was itself let as a
separate individual dwelling As I say, that to my mind is a non sequitur. The
F fact (and I would not concede this) that the rooms might not be protected
by the Rent Act 1977 does not mean that they were not let. There are
many cases where accommodation has been let but by virtue of the sharing
of other accommodation—essential accommodation—has been held not to
come within the terms of the Rent Act because of the words " let as a
separate dwelling." But that does not in any way deny the finding of the
G judge in this case—on ample evidence to support it—that the undergraduates in fact had the exclusive use of their own particular rooms.
Furthermore, on the facts of this case, in my judgment, the judge was
justified in concluding that it was the intention of the landlord and the
tenant college that that should be so.

         Mr. Etherton has submitted, and I agree with the submission, that such
an arrangement is not consistent, generally speaking anyway, with the
H conception of " a dwelling-house . . . let as a separate dwelling." Generally
speaking, " a dwelling-house . . . let as a separate dwelling " envisages
that at least someone—that someone being in most cases the tenant in
occupation—will have the right to go to any part of the premises he chooses.
It may well be that a tenant who takes a separate dwelling-house will sublet
so as to preclude himself, vis-à-vis the sub-lessee, from entering another
part of the premises for the period of the subletting; but that is something
which occurs after the lease has been entered into and in no way detracts

Eveleigh L.J.   St. Catherine's College v. Dorling (C.A.)   **[1980]**

from the right of the tenant vis-à-vis the landlord to go to another room. A
The existence of someone able to go of his own right to all the rooms of
the premises is one of the hallmarks of a dwelling-house. That is completely
absent on the findings in this case. That being so, I would agree with
Mr. Etherton's submission that the arrangement envisaged in this case was
inconsistent with the concept of a building which itself could be described
as a separate dwelling.

For those reasons I would dismiss this appeal.   B

BRANDON L.J.   I agree that the appeal should be dismissed, for the
reasons given by Eveleigh L.J. in his judgment.

MEGAW L.J.   I also agree with the conclusion reached by Eveleigh L.J.
and with the reasons given by him. The agreement in this case was made on C
July 8, 1978. On the face of it, it was agreed on that day by St. Catherine's
College that certain rent should be payable.   Five days later, on July 13,
1978, St. Catherine's College, being a party to that agreement, applied to
the rent officer for registration of a fair rent. That is to say, the college
sought to challenge that the rent which they appeared to have agreed five
days earlier was a fair rent, or the rent which in law could be insisted upon.
There is no doubt that the other party to that agreement of July 8, 1978, D
Mr. Dorling, through his authorised agents, was firmly of the opinion that
the form of the agreement was such as to take it outside the scope of the
provisions of law which would have enabled the rent to be referred for an
assessment of any rent different from the rent which had been, apparently,
agreed. It is difficult to think that the college, in entering into the agreement
on July 8, 1978, was not aware that that was the view held by the other E
party to the agreement. But as Mr. Boyle, in my opinion rightly, submits,
whatever view might be taken of that conduct in other respects, no such view
can properly influence the decision as to the legal effect of the agreement.
All that I would say about it, then, is this: it seems to me that the decision
at which this court has arrived is more likely to help the continuance of
schemes of this sort, if schemes of this sort are desirable, than would have
been the result if we had arrived at the contrary conclusion. But, once again, F
that is not a matter that can rightly affect our judgment in this matter. If
indeed it was the view of St. Catherine's College, when it made this agreement on July 8, 1978, that the figure of rent contained in that agreement
was higher than a fair rent and that therefore the rent which it itself
thereafter required the five undergraduates to pay was higher than the
college thought to be a fair rent, it might be a matter of hope and expecta- G
tion that the college, now that it has been established that its view of the
legal effect of that agreement is not justified, would feel that it would not
be appropriate that the undergraduates should bear the consequences of the
college having seen fit to agree a rent which it believed (if indeed it did
so believe) was a rent higher than the fair rent.

I agree that the appeal falls to be dismissed.
                                                                             H
                                    Appeal dismissed with costs.
                                    Leave to appeal refused.

Solicitors: *Linnell & Murphy, Oxford*; *Outred & Co., Weybridge.*

                                                                   B. O. A.

A

[FAMILY DIVISION]

* PRACTICE DIRECTION (CHILD: AIRPORT ARRIVAL)

Minor—Custody—Removal from jurisdiction—Order for return of child—Arrangements for meeting child at airport

B

Where a person seeks an order for the return to him of children about to arrive in England by air and desires to have information to enable him to meet the aeroplane, the judge should be asked to include in his order a direction that the airline operating the flight and, if he has the information, the immigration officer at the appropriate airport, should supply such information to that person.

C

To obtain such information in such circumstances in a case where a person already has an order for the return to him of children, that person should apply to a judge ex parte for such a direction.

Issued with the concurrence of the Lord Chancellor.

SIR JOHN ARNOLD P.

D *January* 18, 1980.

[CHANCERY DIVISION]

E

* *In re* JOHN WILLMENT (ASHFORD) LTD.

1978 Nov. 29, 30;   Brightman J.
        Dec. 1; 19

F

Revenue — Value added tax — Receiver's liability — Company in hands of receiver and manager—Company trading and charging tax—No personal liability on receiver to account for tax —Whether having discretion concerning payment of tax—Law of Property Act 1925 (15 & 16 Geo. 5, c. 20), s. 109 (8)

Section 109 (8) of the Law of Property Act 1925 provides:

" Subject to the provisions of this Act as to the application of insurance money, the receiver shall apply all money received by him as follows, namely: (i) In discharge of all rents, taxes, rates, and outgoings whatever affecting the mortgaged property; . . ."

G

The company ran a garage business. In 1974 a debenture holder exercised a power to appoint a receiver and manager. The company continued to trade and the receiver charged value added tax on taxable supplies and services as the company had done hitherto. He duly accounted for the tax to

H

the Customs and Excise Commissioners. In 1975 the receiver, acting on advice, deferred payment of future tax to the commissioners. At the invitation of the commissioners, who conceded that the tax was not recoverable from the receiver as a Crown debt, that they could not demand payment of it from the receiver under section 109 (8) of the Law of Property Act 1925 and that he was acting throughout only in his capacity as an agent of the company, the receiver issued an originating summons seeking the directions of the court as to the disposal of the value added tax received by him.

74

In re John Willment (Ashford) (Ch.D)   **[1980]**

On the question whether the receiver, so long as the com- A
pany was lawfully trading, was entitled as between himself and
the commissioners to demand and receive value added tax on
taxable supplies and to pay such tax to the debenture holder,
notwithstanding that such payment might cause an offence to
be committed under section 38 of the Finance Act 1972: —

Held, that the receiver and manager had no valid alternative
to paying the value added tax to the commissioners for, although in many circumstances it might be correct in theory to B
say that he had a discretion under section 109 (8) of the
Law of Property Act 1925 whether or not to pay the
money to the commissioners, there was only one way in which
that discretion could properly be exercised without making the
company liable for a criminal offence (post, pp. 77H—78A–D).

Liverpool Corporation v. *Hope* [1938] 1 K.B. 751, C.A.
applied.

Quaere. (1) Whether the receiver would be guilty of fradu- C
lent trading if he caused the company to trade and incur a liability for value added tax as a Crown debt which (owing to the
debenture) it would not have any possibility of discharging
(post, p. 78E–F).

(2) Whether a receiver who demanded payment of value
added tax from a customer of the company would impliedly
be representing that he was liable to account for it to the
commissioners (post, p. 78F–G).   D

The following cases are referred to in the judgment:

Attorney-General v. *Antoine* [1949] 2 All E.R. 1000; 31 T.C. 213.
Liverpool Corporation v. *Hope* [1938] 1 K.B. 751; [1938] 1 All E.R. 492,
    C.A.

The following additional cases were cited in argument: E

Beni-Felkai Mining Co. Ltd., In re [1934] Ch. 406.
British Fuller's Earth Co. Ltd., In re (1901) 17 T.L.R. 232.
Clark (A Bankrupt), In re, Ex parte The Trustee v. *Texaco Ltd.* [1975] 1
    W.L.R. 559; [1955] 1 All E.R. 453.
Condon, In re, Ex parte James (1874) L.R. 9 Ch.App. 609.
Glyncorrwg Colliery Co. Ltd., In re [1926] Ch. 951.
Gosling v. *Gaskell* [1897] A.C. 575, H.L.(E.).   F
Griffiths v. *Secretary of State for Social Services* [1974] Q.B. 468; [1973]
    3 W.L.R. 831; [1973] 3 All E.R. 1184.
Hand v. *Blow* [1901] 2 Ch. 721, C.A.
Inland Revenue Commissioners v. *Goldblatt* [1972] Ch. 498; [1972]
    2 W.L.R. 953; [1972] 2 All E.R. 202.
Johnson (B.) & Co. (Builders) Ltd., In re [1955] Ch. 634; [1955] 3 W.L.R.
    269; [1955] 2 All E.R. 775, C.A.   G
Mayfair and General Property Trust Ltd., In re [1945] 2 All E.R. 523.
Mesco Properties Ltd., In re [1979] 1 W.L.R. 558; [1979] 1 All E.R. 302.
Roundwood Colliery Co., In re [1897] 1 Ch. 373.
Sowman v. *David Samuel Trust Ltd.* [1978] 1 W.L.R. 22; [1978] 1 All
    E.R. 616.
Yourell v. *Hibernian Bank Ltd.* [1918] A.C. 372, H.L.(I.).

H

ORIGINATING SUMMONS

The applicant, Maurice Charles Withall, who had been appointed
the receiver and manager of the property of John Willment (Ashford)
Ltd. under an instrument made by the company and Williams & Glyn's
Bank Ltd., the debenture holder, at the invitation of the Customs and
Excise Commissioners applied to the court under section 369 (1) of the
Companies Act 1948 for directions.

A   The questions posed in the originating summons were (a) whether the liability on the part of the company for value added tax on taxable supplies made by the company after the appointment of the receiver and manager of its property was an expense properly payable to the commissioners by the receiver out of the assets of the company within his control and, if so, with what priority in relation to (i) the receiver's costs and expenses, (ii) his remuneration, (iii) the company's

B   preferential debts, and (iv) the company's secured debts; and (b) (without prejudice to the generality of head (a)) whether, after the coming into force of regulation 55A of the Value Added Tax (General) Regulations 1975 on September 6, 1976, the receiver had been under a duty to comply with the requirements of the commissioners under Part VII of those regulations. A third question was added to the summons by way

C   of amendment: (c) whether the receiver, so long as the company was lawfully trading, was entitled as between himself and the commissioners to demand and receive value added tax on taxable supplies and to pay such tax to the debenture holder notwithstanding that such payment might cause an offence to be committed under section 38 of the Finance Act 1972.

D   *David Graham Q.C.* and *Michael Crystal* for the receiver and manager.
Patrick Howell for the commissioners.
The debenture holder was not represented.

Cur. adv. vult.

E   December 19. BRIGHTMAN J. read the following judgment. This is a summons by a receiver and manager appointed by a debenture holder to decide what he should do with value added tax charged and received by him in the course of trading on behalf of the company. The obvious answer is that he should account to the Customs and Excise Commissioners. But an answer is not quite so simply given and it has been necessary to consider the apparently absurd alternative that he is entitled

F   to collect the tax and apply the money in discharge of the principal, interest and other moneys due under the debenture.

The company was incorporated in 1947 to carry on a garage business. On December 14, 1972, the company issued a debenture to secure its indebtedness to its bankers. The debenture included a fixed charge on certain land and also a floating charge over the whole undertaking. On

G   December 18, 1972, the company was registered for purposes of value added tax. As from April 1973, it became liable to charge those who purchased taxable goods and services with value added tax and also to account for such tax to the commissioners after deducting therefrom tax on its own relevant purchases.

On December 6, 1974, the debenture holder appointed Mr. Withall, a chartered accountant, to be the receiver and manager of all the pro-

H   perty comprised in the debenture. The company continued to trade and therefore to charge value added tax on taxable supplies and services. Invoices issued by the company would specify the cost to the customer of the supplies or services together with a sum in respect of value added tax. The total would be paid to the receiver. The receiver, on behalf of the company, duly made returns each quarter to the commissioners, stating the net output tax due or net input tax repayable. The receiver paid the amounts shown to be due to the quarter ending April 30, 1975.

At that stage the receiver took advice and as a result of the advice given A
to him he deferred payment of future tax pending discussions with the
commissioners. The financial position of the company is such that there
is no possibility of any surplus for unsecured creditors, or of course for
shareholders.

In order to resolve the position the receiver, at the invitation of the
commissioners, issued an originating summons seeking the following
directions: in paragraph (1) (a), whether the liability on the part of the B
company for value added tax on taxable supplies and services provided
by the company after the appointment of the applicant as receiver and
manager, is an expense properly payable to the commissioners by the
applicant as receiver and manager; if so, in what order of priority (i) the
receiver's costs and expenses, (ii) his remuneration, (iii) the preferential
debts of the company, and (iv) the secured debts of the company should C
rank. I can ignore the question raised in paragraph (1) (b) of the summons because this is covered by paragraph (2) of those matters which I
shall later describe as common ground between the parties. Paragraph
(1) (c) of the summons asks whether the receiver, so long as the company is lawfully trading, is entitled as between himself and the commissioners to demand and receive value added tax on taxable supplies and
to pay such tax to the debenture holder notwithstanding that such D
payment may cause an offence to be committed under section 38 of the
Finance Act 1972; this question was raised by amendment in the circumstances mentioned later.

The respondents to the summons are the commissioners and the
bank. The debenture holder has not appeared before me in order to
argue this case and is content to leave matters to the receiver. It goes E
without saying that the debenture holder has no desire that the receiver
should act improperly.

Under section 33 of the Finance Act 1972, value added tax due from
any person is recoverable as a Crown debt. This does not answer the
question before me, because it is conceded by the commissioners that
value added tax is not directly recoverable from the receiver either personally or to the extent of the assets which come to his hands. There is F
a large area of common ground between the parties which I shall outline.

(1) Despite the appointment of the receiver and manager, the company
continues to be a taxable person within the meaning of section 4 of the
Act. The tax cannot be recovered from the receiver or from the
debenture holder as a Crown debt. Supplies and services provided by
the receiver are provided by him only in his capacity as agent for the G
company and value added tax invoices are correctly treated as issued by
the company and not the receiver.

(2) The present case is not affected by regulation 55A which was added
to the Value Added Tax (General) Regulations 1975 (S.I. 1975 No. 2204)
by regulation 9 of the Value Added Tax (General) (Amendment) Regulations 1976 (S.I. 1976 No. 1234). This enables the commissioners in
certain circumstances to require a " receiver " to comply with value H
added tax regulations and to account for the tax. No such requirement
has been made by the commissioners. Furthermore, it is open to
argument whether a receiver appointed by a debenture holder is within
that regulation.

(3) There is no personal liability attaching to the receiver under
section 369 (2) of the Companies Act 1948, which provides that the
receiver of the property of a company appointed out of court shall be

A personally liable on contracts to the same extent as if appointed by the court.

(4) Money collected as value added tax, though expressly added to the invoice as value added tax, is not thereby impressed with any trust in favour of the commissioners: see *Attorney-General* v. *Antoine* [1949] 2 All E.R. 1000 in relation to P.A.Y.E.

(5) The commissioners have no right to demand the tax by virtue of
B section 109 of the Law of Property Act 1925. Section 109 (8) reads:

"Subject to the provisions of this Act as to the application of insurance money, the receiver shall apply all money received by him as follows, namely: (i) In discharge of all rents, taxes, rates, and outgoings whatever affecting the mortgaged property; . . ."

C The section means that if the receiver applies money received by him in discharge of taxes affecting the mortgaged property he cannot be charged by the debenture holder or by the person entitled to the property subject to the debenture, with having made an improper payment: see *Liverpool Corporation* v. *Hope* [1938] 1 K.B. 751. The section does not give the taxing authority a right to sue.

As I have indicated, the first question in the summons seeks guidance
D as to the respective priorities of the various liabilities, including value added tax if that is due. Section 94 (1) of the Companies Act 1948 provides that where a receiver is appointed pursuant to a floating charge, the debts of the company which would be preferential in a winding up shall be paid out of the assets coming to the hands of the receiver in priority to the claims of the debenture holder. This question of the
E summons has, however, little or no relevance; first, because all the preferential debts have been paid; secondly, because there is no one to argue the case of the preferential creditors, were it material to do so; thirdly, because no point has been raised in regard to the receiver's costs and remuneration. For this reason question (c) was added to the summons by amendment, in order to define the true issue between the commissioners and the receiver; in essence, can the receiver, without breaking
F the law, collect money as and for value added tax, but hand it over to the debenture holder towards discharge of the moneys due under the debenture? To a question so expressed, the answer seems obvious; either the receiver must stop collecting the value added tax because neither he nor the company intends to pay it to the commissioners, or alternatively, if the tax is in fact collected, it must be accounted for to the commissioners. But I must ask myself, what is the true legal analysis of the
G position if, as one hopes, the law points in the same direction as common sense?

Counsel for the receiver submits that under section 109 (8) of the Law of Property Act 1925 the receiver has a discretion, as between himself and the debenture holder, whether he does or does not pay the value added tax to the commissioners for the period of the receivership.
H If he does do so, he cannot be challenged by the debenture holder. If he does not do so, he cannot be sued by the commissioners. If I decide that such a discretion exists, it is the intention of the receiver to consider the position and determine for himself in what way he will exercise that discretion.

In many circumstances it may be correct in theory to say that a receiver has a discretion under section 109 (8). But in the instant case there is only one way in which that discretion can properly be exercised

in relation to value added tax, so perhaps it is not correct to describe it A
as a discretion at all. The reason for this conclusion is that if the receiver
does not pay the tax he will cause the company to commit a criminal
offence. In the present circumstances, and I would think in most if not
all circumstances, it cannot possibly be right for the holder of a discretion
to exercise it in such a way as to bring about a criminal result. Section
2 (2) of the Finance Act 1972 provides that tax on the supply of goods or B
services shall be payable by the person supplying the goods or services.
The person supplying the goods or services is the company, and it does so
by the direction of the receiver. The receiver, therefore, causes the
company to be liable to pay tax. Regulations 51 and 53 of the Value
Added Tax (General) Regulations 1975, made under Part I of the Act,
require a registered person, i.e. the company, to make each quarter a
return of the value added tax payable and to pay the amount of tax C
due according to such return. Section 38 (7) imposes a penalty on a
person who fails to comply with any regulations made under Part I of
the Act. Section 38 (8) provides that any act or omission in respect of
which a penalty is imposed shall be an offence within sections 281 to 291
of the Customs and Excise Act 1952. Non-compliance with the regulations is therefore a criminal offence.

Accordingly, if the receiver does not make value added tax returns and D
pay the tax, he will be causing the company to commit a criminal offence.
In the result the receiver, who is entitled as between himself and the
debenture holder to pay taxes, has no option but to make value added tax
returns and to pay the tax due. I do not need to consider whether the
receiver himself might be aiding and abetting the commission of a criminal offence if he were to cause the company to trade without paying E
value added tax to the commissioners.

There are alternative approaches to the problem which have not been
argued before me and upon which it is not necessary for me to express
any conclusion. For example, if the receiver caused the company to
trade and to incur a liability for value added tax as a Crown debt, which
(owing to the debenture) it would not have any possibility of discharging,
it might be argued that the receiver was guilty of fraudulent trading F
under section 332 of the Companies Act 1948. Furthermore, would a
receiver be entitled to demand payment of value added tax from a
customer of the company if it were the intention of the receiver to put
the money in the pocket of the debenture holder instead of accounting to
the commissioners? A member of the public is only liable to pay value
added tax on a supply or a service because he obtains it from a person G
who is liable to pay the tax. A demand for the tax might amount to an
implied representation that the recipient would be so liable. I leave such
questions unresolved. The answer to the question in paragraph 1 (c) of
the summons is, No.

Order accordingly.

                                                           H

Solicitors: *Clintons; Solicitor, Customs and Excise.*

[Reported by Paul Niekirk, Barrister-at-Law]

A

[CHANCERY DIVISION]

* *In re* TRANSATLANTIC LIFE ASSURANCE CO. LTD.

[No. 001164 of 1979]

B
1979   June 11; 13   Slade J.

*Company — Register — Rectification — Shares issued to American
parent company in contravention of exchange control legislation — Validity of issue — Whether parent company's name
entered in register without sufficient cause — Rectification in
respect of part of shareholding—Exchange Control Act 1947
(10 & 11 Geo. 6, c. 14), s. 8 (1)* [1]*—Companies Act 1948 (11*
C
& 12 Geo. 6, c. 38), s. 116 [2]

Following the company's incorporation in the United
Kingdom on March 21, 1966, to carry on long-term insurance
business, 50,000 ordinary shares of £1 each were issued to the
American company of which it was the wholly owned subsidiary.   The issue of such shares was made pursuant to
permission obtained from the Bank of England under the
Exchange Control Act 1947.   On March 12, 1974, the com-
D
pany purported to issue a further 200,000 shares to the
American company in consideration of a payment of £200,000
from the American company.   By an oversight the permission
of the Bank of England for the second issue was not obtained.
In 1977, the company having discovered that it had not
obtained the required permission for the 1974 issue applied
for retrospective permission.   Before any permission was
E
granted, however, the company decided to seek rectification
of the register and then by a new issue of shares with the
appropriate permission to provide the company with such
capital as was then required for its business.   Accordingly,
the application for retrospective permission was withdrawn,
and permission was obtained for a new issue of 50,000 ordinary
shares of £1 each to the American company.

On the company's application for rectification of its register
by striking out the name of the American company as the
F
holder of the 200,000 shares purportedly issued in 1974, there
was affidavit evidence that the American company was prepared
to subscribe for the new 50,000 shares, and that the company
intended, if rectification were ordered, to repay £150,000 to
the American company: —

Held, (1) that the issue of 200,000 shares to the American
company in 1974 was wholly invalid and void by reason of
G
section 8 (1) of the Exchange Control Act 1947 and the
name of the American company had been entered in the
company's register of members " without sufficient cause "
within the meaning of section 116 of the Companies Act 1948;
that, further, section 116 of the Companies Act 1948 was in
terms wide enough to empower the court to order rectification
of the register in relation to some only of a shareholder's
shares and, therefore, gave the court jurisdiction to order
H
rectification in the present case.

In re Fry, decd. [1946] Ch. 312 considered.

(2) That since the 200,000 shares were never validly issued,
no reduction of capital was involved, and rectification would
be ordered, as sought, subject to production of evidence on
affidavit confirming that no transfers of the shares, purportedly
issued in 1974, had been executed by the American company.

[1] Exchange Control Act 1947, s. 8 (1): see post, p. 81F–H.
[2] Companies Act 1948, s. 116: see post, p. 84C–D.

In re Transatlantic Life Assurance (Ch.D.)   **[1980]**

The following case is referred to in the judgment:

Fry, decd., In re [1946] Ch. 312.

The following additional case was cited in argument:

Portuguese Consolidated Copper Mines Ltd., In re (1889) 42 Ch.D. 160, C.A.

MOTION

By a notice of motion dated April 25, 1979, Transatlantic Life Assurance Co. Ltd. (" the company ") sought an order, pursuant to section 116 of the Companies Act 1948, that its register of members might be rectified by striking out the name of the respondent, Life Assurance Co. of Pennsylvania, as the holder of 200,000 ordinary shares of £1 each in the capital of the company, numbered 50,001 to 250,000 inclusive, and that the company be authorised to effect the necessary alterations in its register for carrying such order into effect, and that notice of such rectification might be ordered to be given to the Registrar of Companies, or that such other order might be made in the premises as to the court should seem meet.

The facts are stated in the judgment.

Richard Sykes for the company.
The respondent was not represented.

Cur. adv. vult.

June 13. SLADE J. read the following judgment. This is a motion seeking relief under section 116 of the Companies Act 1948 in somewhat unusual circumstances. By the terms of the notice of motion, Transatlantic Life Assurance Co. Ltd. (" the company ") seeks:

" An order pursuant to section 116 of the Companies Act 1948 that the register of members of the applicant may be rectified by striking out the name of Life Assurance Co. of Pennsylvania as the holder of the 200,000 ordinary shares of £1 each in the capital of the applicant numbered 50,001 to 250,000 inclusive. And that the applicant may be authorised to effect the necessary alterations in the said register for carrying such order into effect. And that notice of such rectification may be ordered to be given to the Registrar of Companies or that such other order may be made in the premises as to the court shall seem meet."

Life Assurance Co. of Pennsylvania (" L.A.C.O.P.") is sole respondent to the motion, but is not represented before me. It is a company resident outside the scheduled territories.

The motion is supported by an affidavit sworn by Mr. Robert James Beard, a director of the company. From this affidavit, and the exhibits thereto, the following facts appear. The company is a wholly owned subsidiary of L.A.C.O.P. It has an authorised capital of £250,000. Its objects include those of carrying on insurance business and it is authorised by the Department of Trade to carry on ordinary long-term insurance business. It was incorporated on March 21, 1966, as a company limited by shares. Following its incorporation, 50,000 ordinary shares of £1 each were issued for cash at par to L.A.C.O.P. This issue was made

The Weekly Law Reports, February 8, 1980

81

1 W.L.R.   In re Transatlantic Life Assurance (Ch.D.)   Slade J.

A on April 26, 1966, pursuant to a permission granted prior to the incorporation of the company, under the Exchange Control Act 1947, by the Bank of England on September 6, 1965. The shares were numbered 1 to 50,000. On March 5, 1974, the board of the company resolved that a further issue of 200,000 ordinary shares be made in favour of L.A.C.O.P. Pursuant to this resolution the issue was made on March 12, 1974, at par, and the shares were numbered 50,001 to 250,000. The

B consideration was satisfied by the transfer from L.A.C.O.P. to the company of sterling investments having a value of £200,000. It did not occur to any of the persons concerned that any permission under the Act of 1947 was required for this last-mentioned issue and no such permission was sought. In these circumstances, it is submitted that the issue, constituting—as it did—an infringement of the Act of 1947, was accordingly

C wholly void.

The company discovered early in 1977 that the requisite exchange control permission had not been obtained for the issue of shares in 1974. An application to the Bank of England for a retrospective permission was then made. Before it was granted, and while the company was still dealing with queries raised by the bank, it was decided by the company

D and L.A.C.O.P. that, instead of seeking to validate the issue, they would prefer to have the matter set right by rectification of the register of members of the company and then, by means of a new issue of shares with the appropriate permission, to provide the company with the capital required for its business. Accordingly the application for retrospective permission was withdrawn and application for a new permission was made. Permission has in fact been granted to the company to make a

E new issue of 50,000 ordinary shares of £1 each.

These are the circumstances in which the company makes the application before me. Mr. Beard states in his affidavit that L.A.C.O.P. consents to it and that it has agreed, upon the register of members of the company being rectified, forthwith to subscribe for 50,000 new ordinary shares of £1 each at par. If the order for rectification is made

F as sought, the company would intend immediately to repay £150,000 to L.A.C.O.P., which it would apparently regard as being due to L.A.C.O.P.

The first question that falls to be considered is whether, as Mr. Sykes submits, the further issue of 200,000 ordinary shares by the company in March 1974 was wholly void. Section 8 (1) of the Act of 1947 provides:

G "Except with the permission of the Treasury, no person shall in the United Kingdom issue any security or, whether in the United Kingdom or elsewhere, issue any security which is registered or to be registered in the United Kingdom, unless the following requirements are fulfilled, that is to say—(a) neither the person to whom the security is to be issued nor the person, if any, for whom he is to be a nominee is resident outside the scheduled territories; and (b) the prescribed evidence is produced to the person issuing the security as

H to the residence of the person to whom it is to be issued and that of the person, if any, for whom he is to be a nominee."

L.A.C.O.P. was a person resident outside the scheduled territories at the relevant time, and the permission of the Treasury was not obtained in respect of the issue of the 200,000 shares. Accordingly, it is clear that this issue did involve a breach of the provisions of section 8 (1). Though Schedule 5 to the Act of 1947 renders certain breaches of the provisions

of the Act a punishable offence, the Act appears to contain no further   A
explicit guidance as to the effect in law of issuing securities without
Treasury permission in breach of section 8 (1). Section 8 (2), so far as
material for present purposes, provides:

> " The subscription of the memorandum of association of a company
> to be formed under the Companies Act 1929 . . . by a person resident
> outside the scheduled territories . . . shall, unless he subscribes the   B
> memorandum with the permission of the Treasury, be invalid in so
> far as it would on registration of the memorandum have the effect
> of making him a member of or shareholder in the company, . . ."

This subsection therefore expressly provides for the invalidity of the
subscription to this extent, and in these circumstances. I do not, however, think it throws much light, one way or the other, on the construction   C
of section 8 (1).

Far greater assistance, in my judgment, is to be derived from section
18 (1), on which Mr. Sykes principally relied. Section 18 reads:

> " (1) The title of any person to a security for which he has given
> value on a transfer thereof, and the title of all persons claiming
> through or under him, shall, notwithstanding that the transfer, or   D
> any previous transfer, or the issue of the security, was by reason of
> the residence of any person concerned other than the first-mentioned
> person prohibited by the provisions of this Act relating to the transfer
> or issue of securities, be valid unless the first-mentioned person had
> notice of the facts by reason of which it was prohibited. (2) Without
> prejudice to the provisions of subsection (1) of this section, the
> Treasury may issue a certificate declaring, in relation to a security,   E
> that any acts done before the issue of the certificate purporting to
> effect the issue or transfer of the security, being acts which were
> prohibited by this Act, are to be, and are always to have been, as
> valid as if they had been done with the permission of the Treasury,
> and the said acts shall have effect accordingly. (3) Nothing in this
> section shall affect the liability of any person to prosecution for any   F
> offence against this Act."

In my judgment Mr. Sykes is correct in submitting that this section, by
necessary inference, presupposes that the purported issue of a security in
manner prohibited by the Act is wholly invalid. Were this not so, I
could see no point in the provisions of subsection (1) which, when
applicable, by their terms operate to validate the title to such a security   G
of a person who has given value on taking a transfer thereof. Were
this not so, I could likewise see no point in the provisions of subsection
(2), which empower the Treasury to issue a certificate, inter alia, retrospectively validating acts purporting to effect the issue of a security in
manner prohibited by the Act of 1947. The very use by the legislature
of the phrase " purporting to effect," in subsection (2), in my judgment
further illustrates that the acts which purport to effect the issue in a   H
prohibited manner do not in fact operate to effect that issue ab initio.
In these circumstances, on a bare reading of the Act, I would conclude
that the purported issue of 200,000 ordinary shares by the company in
March 1974 was wholly invalid and void.

Mr. Sykes has been unable to refer me to any decided case which
touches directly on the construction of section 8 of the Act of 1947, but
he has referred me to one decision which, I think, provides some indirect

The Weekly Law Reports, February 8, 1980

83

1 W.L.R.   In re Transatlantic Life Assurance (Ch.D.)   Slade J.

A   assistance. In *In re Fry, decd.* [1946] Ch. 312, Romer J. had to consider
the effect of a transfer of shares by a father in favour of a son, effected
in breach of the restrictions imposed on the transfer of securities by
sub-clause (1) of regulation 3A of the Defence (Finance) Regulations
1939 (S.R. & O. 1940 No. 1254). Sub-clause (1), so far as material for
present purposes and omitting immaterial words, provided:

B   " (1) Subject to any exemptions which may be granted by order of
the Treasury no person shall . . . transfer . . . otherwise than by
operation of law or by inheritance, any securities or any interest
in securities, unless the Treasury or persons authorized by or on
behalf of the Treasury are satisfied that no person resident outside
the sterling area has, immediately before the transfer . . . any interest
C   in the securities: Provided that nothing in this paragraph shall
prohibit any . . . transfer . . . which is effected with permission
granted by the Treasury or by a person authorized by them or on
their behalf."

Sub-clause (4) of that regulation provided:

        " (4) Subject to any exemptions which may be granted by order of
D   the Treasury no person shall, except with permission granted by the
Treasury or by a person authorized by them or on their behalf,
enter any transfer of securities in any register or book in which
those securities are registered or inscribed unless there has been
produced to him such evidence that the transfer does not involve a
contravention of this regulation as may be prescribed by instructions
E   issued by or on behalf of the Treasury."

This latter provision was to much the same effect as section 13 (a) of
the Act of 1947 which provides:

        " 13. Except with the permission of the Treasury, no person con-
cerned with the keeping of any register in the United Kingdom
shall—(a) enter in the register the name of any person in relation to
F   any security unless there has been produced to him the prescribed
evidence that the entry does not form part of a transaction which
involves the doing of anything prohibited by this Act; . . ."

The regulations in that case, like the present, did not expressly state
what was to be the effect in law of a purported transfer effected in
breach of them. Romer J., in his judgment, first considered the question
G   whether the purported transferees were in a position which entitled them,
as against the company, to be put on the register of members and
whether everything had been done that was necessary to put them in to
the position of the transferor. In this context he said, [1946] Ch. 312,
316:

        "Having regard, however, to the Defence (Finance) Regulations it
H   is impossible, in my judgment, to answer the questions other than
in the negative. The requisite consent of the Treasury to the
transactions had not been obtained, and, in the absence of it, the
company was prohibited from registering the transfers. In my
opinion, accordingly, it is not possible to hold that, at the date of
the testator's death, the transferees had either acquired a legal title
to the shares in question, or the right, as against all other persons
. . . to be clothed with such legal title."

Romer J. then proceeded to consider an argument that at the relevant
time a complete equitable assignment had been effected. He rejected
this argument on, inter alia, the following grounds, at p. 318:

> "The interest in the shares so acquired by the assignees would
> indubitably be an 'interest in securities' within the meaning of
> reg. 3A; and, inasmuch as they are prohibited from acquiring
> such an interest except with permission granted by the Treasury,
> this court cannot recognize a claim to such an interest where the
> consent of the Treasury was never given to its acquisition."

The reasoning of Romer J. in the *Fry* case, mutatis mutandis, in my
judgment, supports the conclusions which I would have reached in its
absence, that the relevant issue of the 200,000 shares to L.A.C.O.P. was
wholly invalid and void and that it operated to confer on L.A.C.O.P. no
title whatever to any such shares either at law or in equity.

Section 116 of the Companies Act 1948 provides:

> "(1) If—(*a*) the name of any person is, without sufficient cause,
> entered in or omitted from the register of members of a company;
> or (*b*) default is made or unnecessary delay takes place in entering
> on the register the fact of any person having ceased to be a member;
> the person aggrieved, or any member of the company, or the com-
> pany, may apply to the court for rectification of the register. (2)
> Where an application is made under this section, the court may
> either refuse the application or may order rectification of the register
> and payment by the company of any damages sustained by any party
> aggrieved."

In the circumstances, it seems to me clear that the name of L.A.C.O.P.
was entered in the register of members of the company, as the holder
of the relevant 200,000 shares, "without sufficient cause" within the
meaning of the last-mentioned section. Indeed by virtue of section
13 (*a*) of the Act of 1947 the company was, I think, actually prohibited
from making such entry in the absence of the prescribed evidence that
the entry did not form part of a transaction which involved the doing
of anything prohibited by that Act. In my judgment the wording of
section 116 of the Companies Act 1948 is wide enough in its terms to
empower the court to order the rectification of a company's register by
deleting a reference to some only of a registered shareholder's shares.
The section can, in my judgment, still operate, even though the proposed
rectification does not involve the entire deletion of the name of the
registered holder concerned as a member of the company concerned,
inasmuch as he, or it, is still properly shown as the holder of other shares,
to which the rectification does not relate. I therefore conclude that the
court has jurisdiction to order the rectification sought in the present case.

Are there then any reasons why the court should, in the exercise of
its discretion, decline to make the order sought? Mr. Beard's affidavit
contains evidence to the effect that the company no longer writes new
insurance business and its insurance liabilities would be amply covered
by its available assets, without the net amount of £150,000 which it
intends to repay to L.A.C.O.P. in the event of the order for rectification
sought being made. This evidence, however, is not very full and is not
directed at all to such liabilities of the company (if any) as are not
insurance liabilities; in theory, I suppose, these liabilities might be substantial. In these circumstances, the point which has principally troubled

The Weekly Law Reports, February 8, 1980

85

1 W.L.R.   In re Transatlantic Life Assurance (Ch.D.)   Slade J.

A me is the position of creditors of the company, none of whom are represented before me—particularly in the light of the announced intention of the company to repay the £150,000 to L.A.C.O.P. in the event of the proposed order being made. The transaction, viewed as a whole, has some flavour of a reduction of capital, carried through without the protection of the machinery provided for by sections 66 and 67 of the Companies Act 1948, which is designed in particular to safeguard the

B interests of creditors of the company.

I think, however, that there are two answers to any misgivings which may be felt on this account. First, if I am right in concluding that the issue of the 200,000 shares was wholly void then the position must, in my judgment, be that, though the issued capital of the company was, from March 1974, until at least 1977, thought by all concerned to be

C £250,000, it has in truth, at all material times, been only £50,000, so that in truth no reduction at all is involved by the order which the court is now asked to make. Secondly, an order in the terms sought would in any event be of only limited scope, inasmuch at it would embody no more than an order for rectification of the register of members and relief strictly ancillary to the making of such an order. It would not include express approval of the company's announced intention of repay-

D ing the £150,000 to L.A.C.O.P. after the order had been made and I do not, as at present minded, propose to give such express approval. The company has apparently been advised that, if and when the order has been made, it will be entitled, and indeed bound, to repay to L.A.C.O.P. the sum of £150,000, representing the consideration which was paid to the company under the unlawful transaction of March 1974. While not

E intending to cast any doubt on the correctness of this advice, I express no opinion as to whether it is correct. This is a question which has been canvassed only very briefly before me. I would merely observe that, if the advice should happen to be incorrect, and were acted upon, any remedies which creditors of the company might seek to pursue would, as I see the position, be unaffected by the order which I now propose to

F make.

The same comment applies to any remedies which creditors of the company might hereafter seek to pursue arising from the fact that, over a number of years, the company and its directors, albeit apparently quite innocently, have—for example in the company's latest audited accounts as at December 31, 1977—represented to the world that it had an issued share capital of £250,000, while its true issued share capital, according

G to my judgment, was only £50,000.

In all the circumstances I can see no good reason for declining to make the order sought. The effect of the order will merely be to direct that the register be rectified in such a manner as to reflect what I think has throughout been the true position according to law.

I propose therefore to grant relief in the terms of the notice of

H motion. This, however, will be subject to an undertaking, which I understand Mr. Sykes will be prepared to give on behalf of the company, that an affidavit will be sworn on its behalf, by someone who can properly speak to this matter, confirming that L.A.C.O.P. has not executed transfers of any of the 200,000 shares purportedly issued to it in March 1974. I require this undertaking in view of the provisions of section 18 (1) of the Act of 1947. My order will also be made subject to an undertaking hereafter being given to the court, on behalf of

L.A.C.O.P., to the effect that it will forthwith subscribe for 50,000 new   A
ordinary shares of £1 each, in the company, at par. This undertaking
will be required in order to ensure that the company will hereafter
comply with the requirements as to paid up share capital imposed by
the Insurance Companies Act 1974.

Order accordingly.
                                                                            B

Solicitors: *Lovell, White & King.*

                                                                   T. C. C. B.

                                                                            C

[CHANCERY DIVISION]

* *In re* CAMBURN PETROLEUM PRODUCTS LTD.

[No. 00839 of 1979]

1979   June 11, 12, 14   Slade J.   D

Company—Winding up—Petition—Creditor's petition—Contribu-
tory opposing petition seeking adjournment—Company unable
to pay its debts—Court's discretion to adjourn proceedings—
Companies Act 1948 (11 & 12 Geo. 6, c. 38), ss. 225, 346

In 1978 a private company with a capital of £100 was in-   E
corporated to buy and sell large quantities of petrol. The only
shares issued were two shares of £1 each issued to the only two
directors, K and C. Later in the same year a dispute arose
between K and C as to the way in which the company was
managed. On January 17, 1979, a debenture by way of floating
charge over the company's undertaking and assets was issued to
a creditor company to secure present and future indebtedness.
On January 17 and 22, cheques totalling £349,051·55 were   F
drawn by C and the company's secretary, in favour of the
creditor, in respect of petrol supplied. K countermanded payment of such cheques without, as was alleged, the authority or
consent of C. It was common ground that there were insufficient funds in the company's bank account to cover the full
amount of the cheques. Certain payments were made to reduce
the debt but over £300,000 remained outstanding. On February
14, K presented a contributory's petition in the Manchester District Registry seeking a compulsory winding up substantially on   G
the grounds of deadlock and C's alleged misconduct. On
March 19, 1979, the creditor presented a petition for compulsory
winding up on the grounds of insolvency. Progress with the
petition pending in the Manchester District Registry was
delayed owing to industrial troubles and on April 30 Slade J.
made an order under section 231 of the Companies Act 1948
giving leave for the creditor's petition to proceed. At the date   H
of the presentation of the creditor's petition the company was,
for the purposes of sections 222 (*e*) and 223 (*d*), unable to pay
its debts. The petition was supported by K and opposed by C
who alleged that the company's inability to pay its debts was
substantially due to the fault of K and that if the company were
allowed to continue operating it could quickly become solvent
again.
    On C seeking an adjournment of the hearing of the
creditor's petition:—

A   *Held,* that a creditor whose debt was established was prima
facie entitled to a winding up order even though the petition
was opposed by a contributory of the company, for although,
under sections 225 and 346 of the Companies Act 1948, the
court had a discretion to consider the wishes of a contributory,
it would ordinarily attach little weight to such wishes in comparison with the weight it attached to the wishes of any
creditor who proved both that he was unpaid and that the
B   company was " unable to pay its debts "; that while, therefore,
the court had jurisdiction to adjourn the creditor's petition, it
would only do so in exceptional circumstances which justified
that course, and since any injustice caused to the contributory,
C, would be far outweighed by the injustice which an adjournment would cause to the petitioning creditor, the court would
make an immediate winding up order (post, pp. 93H—94D,
95E–F).

C   *In re Brighton Hotel Co.* (1868) L.R. 6 Eq. 339 distinguished.

The following cases are referred to in the judgment:

Bowes v. *Hope Life Insurance and Guarantee Co.* (1865) 11 H.L.Cas. 389,
H.L.(E.).
Brighton Hotel Co., In re (1868) L.R. 6 Eq. 339.

D
The following additional case was cited in argument:

Bathampton Properties Ltd., In re [1976] 1 W.L.R. 168; [1976] 3 All
E.R. 200.

PETITION
On March 19, 1979, Chevron Oil (U.K.) Ltd. presented a creditor's
E   petition for the winding up of Camburn Petroleum Products Ltd. (" the
company ") in respect of a debt of £368,821·78 alleged to be due on
account of petroleum products sold and delivered to the company. The
petition was supported by Aubrey Kreike, a contributory and one of the
two directors of the company, but was opposed by Eric Cooper, also a
contributory and the other director of the company.

F   The facts are stated in the judgment.

Mary Arden for Chevron Oil (U.K.) Ltd.
John Cone for Mr. Kreike.
G. A. Mann for Mr. Cooper.

SLADE J. This is a creditor's petition presented by Chevron Oil (U.K.)
G   Ltd. (" Chevron "). It seeks the usual compulsory winding up order in
respect of Camburn Petroleum Products Ltd. (" the company "). The
petition is supported by one contributory, Mr. Aubrey Kreike, but is
opposed by another contributory, Mr. Eric Cooper.

Before the company's incorporation, Mr. Kreike had, since 1964, been
a director and shareholder of an oil company called Keburn Oil Distribu-
H   tors Ltd. (" Keburn "). Mr. Cooper for several years had had an interest
in a number of oil companies, in particular two named Baxenden Autopoint
Ltd. (" Baxenden ") and Eccles Autopoint Ltd. (" Eccles "), which were
not associated or connected with Keburn.

Mr. Cooper and Mr. Kreike had done business together on behalf of
their respective companies. In or about 1977 they decided, after some
discussion, to form a company which would fill what they regarded as a
gap in the oil distribution market, by buying large quantities of petrol from

the larger petrol companies and selling on smaller quantities of petrol to A
retail garages.   Accordingly the company was incorporated on March 16,
1978, as a private company limited by shares, with a registered office in
Manchester.   Shortly after its incorporation, one £1 share was issued and
allotted to Mr. Kreike, and one £1 share was issued and allotted to Mr.
Cooper.   These remain the only two issued shares.   Mr. Kreike and Mr.
Cooper were appointed and still remain the two sole directors of the company.   They appointed Mr. Stewart Last, an accountant, to be secretary   B
but he has since resigned.

The company began trading in April 1978.   The arrangement appears
to have been that the day to day administration should be left to Messrs.
Cooper and Last.   The company was initially quite successful; Mr. Kreike
has sworn an affidavit in which he states that from April 3, 1978, until
January 31, 1979, the total turnover of the company was about £500,000,   C
and he estimates that the profit after payment of costs and expenses was
£100,000.   These figures have not, I think, been challenged by
Mr. Cooper.

Unfortunately, however, from about August 1978 onwards disputes
began to arise between Mr. Kreike and Mr. Cooper as to the manner in
which the company was being and should be run.   There is a considerable   D
volume of affidavit evidence before me in which the disputes are ventilated
and in which charges and counter-charges are made by each of them
against the other.   There has, however, been no cross-examination on any
of the affidavits before me.   On the hearing of this creditor's petition by
Chevron, I think it is neither necessary nor appropriate to express even
a provisional view as to the rights and wrongs of the various matters in
dispute between Mr. Kreike and Mr. Cooper.   E

The further facts material for present purposes, in my judgment, are
the following, which I think are either common ground between the
parties or are sufficiently proved by the affidavit evidence before me.   For
some time prior to January 1979 Chevron had been supplying and delivering to the company petroleum products of very substantial value, which
had resulted in corresponding substantial indebtedness of the company to F
Chevron from time to time.   On January 17, 1979, the company executed
a debenture by way of floating charge on its undertaking and assets in
favour of Chevron, to secure the company's present and future indebtedness.   This was signed by Mr. Kreike and Mr. Cooper on behalf of the
company.   Also on January 17, 1979, Mr. Cooper and Mr. Last drew a
company's cheque for £93,330·41 in favour of Chevron.   On January 22,   G
1979, Mr. Cooper and Mr. Last drew two company's cheques respectively
for £142,786·84 and £112,934·30 in favour of Chevron.   These three
cheques, totalling £349,051·55, were drawn in respect of moneys due for
payment from the company to Chevron on January 20, 1979.   Payment
of the cheques was, however, countermanded on behalf of the company
and none of them was met on presentation.   Mr. Kreike was the director
who effected this countermanding; Mr. Cooper's evidence is that it was   H
done without his authority or consent and he suggests that Mr. Kreike
acted wrongly in doing it.   It is, however, common ground between Mr.
Kreike and Mr. Cooper that, at the time, the funds in the bank account
of the company would not nearly have sufficed to cover the full amount
of the three cheques drawn.

In or about the last week of January 1979 an arrangement was made
between Chevron and the company that the overnight balances standing

A to the credit of the company's account at its bank should be transferred direct to the credit of Chevron. Mr. Cooper's evidence is that five transfers totalling £211,964 were made in this manner between January 30, 1979, and February 7, 1979, which would or should have reduced the indebtedness of the company to Chevron accordingly.

B Chevron's evidence, contained in an affidavit sworn on its behalf by Mr. P. O. Marshall on June 8, 1979, is that the credits actually received by Chevron under this arrangement amounted to only £148,074·06, because an aggregate sum of £63,889·94 paid to Chevron by the company on January 31 was duly directed by the company to be applied in satisfaction of an account of a company named Koil Oil Products Ltd. with Chevron.

C There appears on the evidence to be some doubt as to the position in regard to the £63,889·94. Mr. Cooper suggests that the direction given by the company to Chevron in this respect was given by Mr. Kreike wrongly and without Mr. Cooper's knowledge or consent. But I do not think that this is really material for present purposes; for three points are, I think, common ground. First, no further payments have been made in reduction of the company's indebtedness to Chevron since February 7, 1979. Secondly, additional invoices became due for payment by the D company on February 20, 1979. Thirdly, at very least the aggregate amount of the debt owed by the company to Chevron on the latter date was £304,931·84—representing the difference between £368,821·78 and £63,889·94—and this sum still remains outstanding. If the sum of £63,889·94 is added to £304,931·84 the resulting outstanding aggregate debt is £368,821·78, and this is the debt on which Chevron's petition is E now based.

Though this fact has not been admitted by Mr. Cooper in his evidence, I think that the affidavit of Mr. Marshall, to which I have referred, establishes that demands had in fact been delivered to the company, seeking payment of all the debts relied on in the petition by January 31, 1979, though it has not been asserted that these demands entitle the petitioner to rely on section 223 (a) of the Companies Act 1948.

F Reverting to the history of the matter, on January 24, 1979, Mr. Last resigned as secretary of the company. On February 14, 1979, Mr. Kreike presented a contributory's petition to the Manchester District Registry seeking a compulsory winding up order in respect of the company, substantially on the grounds of deadlock and Mr. Cooper's alleged misconduct. The company and Mr. Cooper were and are respondents to this petition.

G On February 22, 1979, on Mr. Kreike's application, an order was made in the Manchester District Registry appointing one of the official receivers attached to the court to be provisional liquidator of the company until the conclusion of the hearing of the Manchester petition or further order. The court limited and restricted the powers of the provisional liquidator to taking possession of, collecting and protecting the assets of the company, H instituting proceedings for the recovery of its assets, including the collecting of debts and the paying of creditors where appropriate. The official receiver thus appointed has been present in court before me, and has told me that, by a further direction of the court, the only creditors of the company whom he has been authorised to pay are its employees.

On March 19, 1979, Chevron presented the petition which is now before me. I should read paragraphs 5 to 10 of this petition which summarise its essential case:

" 5. The company is indebted to your petitioner in the sum of A
£368,821·78 being the sum due to your petitioner in respect of
petroleum products sold and delivered by your petitioner to the
company.

6. On January 17 and 22, 1979, the company drew cheques in favour
of your petitioner for sums amounting to £349,052·55 in the aggregate
in respect of part of the moneys due to your petitioner as aforesaid. B
Payment of the said cheques was thereafter countermanded on behalf
of the company and the said cheques were accordingly not met on
presentation.

7. All moneys and liabilities by the company to your petitioner are
secured by a debenture created by the company in favour of your
petitioner and dated January 17, 1979. The said debenture created a C
floating charge in favour of your petitioner over the undertaking assets
and property whatsoever and wheresoever both present and future of
the company including its uncalled capital for the time being.

8. Your petitioner has made application to the company for payment
of the said sum of £368,821·78, but the company has failed and
neglected to pay the said sum or any part thereof.

9. The company is insolvent and unable to pay its debts. D

10. In the circumstances it is just and equitable that the company
should be wound up."

On April 30, 1979, Chevron's petition came before me for first hearing.
I was then told of the petition pending in the Manchester District Registry,
but was told that for practical purposes proceedings under that petition E
were frozen, owing to industrial troubles in the Manchester District
Registry. Counsel for Chevron asked for an order under section 231 of
the Companies Act 1948 giving leave to Chevron, so far as leave might
be necessary, to proceed with its petition, and also for an appropriate
adjournment for the purpose of dealing with evidence. Counsel for Mr.
Cooper asked for leave to be added to the list out of time and on the usual F
undertaking and opposed the making of any order under section 231.

After hearing argument I decided, contrary to the submissions made
on behalf of Mr. Cooper, that there was a sufficient allegation of insolvency
in the petition, and that in all the circumstances it was right that Chevron's
petition should be allowed to continue. I therefore made the order sought
under section 231 and gave certain further directions, to which I need not
refer. The Manchester petition has, I understand, now been set down for G
hearing on September 3 to 7 next.

In regard to the evidence before me I need only refer to the following
further points. Mr. Kreike has sworn an affidavit on April 27, 1979,
exhibiting a statement of affairs of the company as at February 22, 1979.
This statement shows assets of £432,652, comprising:

" Balance at bank	£ 53,613	H
Trade debtors	£347,718
Loans and advances	£ 26,971
Furniture, fittings and utensils	£ 4,250
Other property	£ 100 "

It shows as liabilities:

" Preferential creditors	£ 26,845

A	Owed to debenture holder	£368,965
	Owed to other creditors	£ 19,439
	Outstanding expenses	£ 2,289 "

This results in liabilities of £417,538 and would produce an estimated surplus of £15,114. This surplus, however, would fall to be reduced by the costs of the provisional liquidation, and could on the figures be reduced
B to nil, if 5 per cent. or more of the trade debts proved to be bad ones.

Mr. Cooper has not yet produced a statement of affairs. In his evidence before this court, however, he has given reasons for suggesting that Mr. Kreike has underestimated the value of the company's assets by at least £73,723. Thus, at least on the basis of Mr. Cooper's evidence, the company's assets, when all its book debts were collected, would be likely
C quite comfortably to exceed its liabilities. The fact remains, however, that Chevron has not been paid any part of the debt exceeding £300,000, which it is admitted on all sides has been owed to it by the company since January or February 1979. Furthermore, there is no immediate prospect of Chevron being paid this large outstanding debt. The official receiver has told me that all the tangible assets of the company have been realised;
D that he has so far collected £161,565 and is in the process of collecting the outstanding book debts which exceed £200,000. He has told me, however, that some of these book debts are due from companies which are controlled by Mr. Kreike or by Mr. Cooper, and have so far paid nothing. I understand from the affidavit evidence that these companies include Keburn, Baxenden and Eccles, and that the sums involved are substantial.
E The official receiver has informed me that some other small book debts are disputed, and that since April 30, 1979, only about £19,000 has been collected. The process of collection thus appears at present to be a somewhat slow one.

Against this background Miss Arden, on behalf of Chevron, has submitted that the position is a simple one. Chevron has been proved to be a creditor for a debt exceeding £300,000 which has not been paid; its
F demands for payments have not been complied with; cheques given to it in purported payment of debts have been countermanded on presentation; and the evidence, she submits, shows that the company is not presently able to pay what is owed to Chevron. Accordingly, in her submission, the only proper course can be for the court to make the usual compulsory winding up order.

G Section 224 of the Companies Act 1948 confers on any creditor such as Chevron the right to petition the court for a winding up order. Under section 222 (e) the court has jurisdiction to wind up the company if "the company is unable to pay its debts." Under paragraphs (a) and (d) of section 223 a company is deemed to be unable to pay its debts:

"... (a) if a creditor, by assignment or otherwise, to whom the
H company is indebted in a sum exceeding £50 then due has served on the company, by leaving it at the registered office of the company, a demand under his hand requiring the company to pay the sum so due and the company has for three weeks thereafter neglected to pay the sum or to secure or compound for it to the reasonable satisfaction of the creditor; or ... (d) if it is proved to the satisfaction of the court that the company is unable to pay its debts, and, in determining whether a company is unable to pay its debts, the court shall take

into account the contingent and prospective liabilities of the   **A**
company."

As I have already said no statutory notice under paragraph (*a*) is relied
on in the present case. As paragraph (*d*), however, indicates, neglect
on the part of a company to comply with a statutory notice is only one of
several methods of proving insolvency. Insolvency may be shown in any
way. The law, in my judgment, is correctly stated in two passages in   **B**
Buckley on the Companies Acts, 13th ed. (1957), p. 460:

> "Thus dishonour of the company's acceptance, or the fact that the
> company have informed him being a judgment creditor that he had
> better not levy, for they have no assets, is enough . . . The particular
> indications of insolvency mentioned in paras. (*a*) (*b*) and (*c*) are all
> instances of commercial insolvency, that is of the company being   **C**
> unable to meet current demands upon it. In such a case it is useless
> to say that if its assets are realised there will be ample to pay 20
> shillings in the pound: this is not the test. A company may be at
> the same time insolvent and wealthy. It may have wealth locked up
> in investments not presently realizable; but although this be so, yet if
> it have not assets available to meet its current liabilities it is com-
> mercially insolvent and may be wound up."   **D**

In my judgment, on the facts which I have summarised, the company
was, at the date of presentation of Chevron's petition, and is at the present
date, manifestly unable to pay its debts within the meaning of section 222
(*e*) and section 223 (*d*), inasmuch as it did not and does not have assets
available for the discharge of all its current liabilities.

Miss Arden, on behalf of Chevron, and Mr. Cone, on behalf of Mr.   **E**
Kreike, who supports Chevron's petition, thus affirm and rely on the present
inability of the company to pay its debts. Mr. Mann, who opposes the
petition on behalf of Mr. Cooper, does not dispute such inability, though
he suggests that it is substantially due to the fault of Mr. Kreike and could
be relatively quickly cured if the company were allowed to go into active
operation again.   **F**

Faced with these difficulties, Mr. Mann, in his excellent argument on
behalf of Mr. Cooper, has invited me neither to allow nor to dismiss
Chevron's petition, but to stand it over until the first petition day of next
term, by which time it appears that the Manchester petition would have
been heard and disposed of. He has referred me to section 225 of the
Companies Act 1948 which gives the court general jurisdiction, on hearing   **G**
a winding up petition, to " . . . dismiss it, or adjourn the hearing con-
ditionally or unconditionally, . . ." He has also referred me to section
346 (1) which, so far as material, provides:

> "The court may, as to all matters relating to the winding up of a
> company, have regard to the wishes of the creditors or contributories
> of the company, as proved to it by any sufficient evidence . . ."   **H**

He has also referred me to the decision of Malins V.-C. in *In re
Brighton Hotel Co.* (1868) L.R. 6 Eq. 339. In that case the petitioner was
a creditor of the company in respect of a debenture for £250 and a contributory inasmuch as he held 20 shares in it. He was the only person
before the court who wished to wind up the company and his petition
was opposed by a number of other contributories, together holding 1,450
shares. Malins V.-C. stood over the petition for some four weeks because

A he took the view that there was a hope of some " reasonable arrangement " being made to enable the company to pay its debts, and he considered that those who desired to make the effort should be given an opportunity of doing so: see p. 343. Mr. Mann naturally relied strongly on this decision because it was a case where the court granted an adjournment of a petition of a creditor at the request of persons who were no more than contributories, and in the face of opposition from the petitioning creditor.

B It appears, however, from Malin V.-C.'s judgment that, though he recognised that the petitioner was in fact a creditor, he paid far more regard to his other capacity as a contributory, and treated the petition, on the facts, as being for practical purposes a contributory's petition. He said, at p. 343:

C "Although it is very true this gentleman's debenture fell due in April, and no doubt he ought to have had his money, yet I do not think the money is of any very great importance to him, and it is not on account of that that he presses for the order. If I made an order for the immediate winding up of the company that would not give to him his £250. Therefore regarding the interest of everyone, except this petitioner, I feel bound to give the time asked for, and I

D am equally clear that it is to the interest of this petitioner himself that I should give the time asked for."

Thus I think that the *Brighton Hotel Co.* decision throws little light on the attitude which the court should generally adopt if faced with a request to make a winding up order in respect of a company shown to be unable to pay its debts, when that request is made by an undisputed

E unpaid creditor but opposing contributories seek an adjournment. Though there are a number of authorities which give guidance as to the attitude of the court where some creditors support the making of an immediate winding up order and other creditors oppose it, counsel have been unable to find any other authority which gives guidance as to such attitude where the contest is between a petitioning creditor on the one hand and contributories on the other hand.

F I do not, however, feel much doubt in principle as to what that attitude should be. In the case of a creditor's petition not opposed by other creditors, the general approach of the court was expressed by Lord Cranworth in *Bowes* v. *Hope Life Insurance and Guarantee Co.* (1865) 11 H.L.Cas. 389, 402:

G ". . . I agree with what has been said, that it is not a discretionary matter with the court when a debt is established, and not satisfied, to say whether the company shall be wound up or not; that is to say, if there be a valid debt established, valid both at law and in equity. One does not like to say positively that no case could occur in which it would be right to refuse it; but, ordinarily speaking, it is the duty of the court to direct the winding up."

H In other words a creditor in the circumstances mentioned is prima facie entitled to his order and is prima facie not bound to give time to enable the debtor to pay. In my judgment, subject to the discretion given to it by sections 225 and 346 of the Companies Act 1948, to which I have already referred, the attitude of the court should be, and is, essentially unchanged today. While I recognise that it would have the right under those two sections to pay regard to the wishes of contributories, in deciding whether or not to make a winding up order on a creditor's

petition, or to adjourn the hearing, in my judgment it can, and should, A
ordinarily attach little weight to the wishes of contributories, in comparison with the weight it attaches to the wishes of any creditor, who
proves both that he is unpaid and that the company is "unable to pay its
debts." A creditor giving credit to the company, after all, cannot ordinarily be expected to know of or ascertain the potential difficulties which
may face the company in regard to the discharge of its debts on account
of internal disputes between the directors or between the contributories   B
or on account of other internal matters. He is, I think, ordinarily entitled
to assume that his debt will be punctually paid by the company as and
when it falls due, and to exercise the remedies given to him by section
224 and the following sections of the Companies Act 1948 if it does not.
The exercise of such remedies may perhaps in some cases cause a
degree of hardship to a contributory, particularly if the failure of the   C
company to pay its debts has arisen on account of neglects or defaults
by other contributories or directors, to which the contributory in question
has not been a party. This, however, is a type of risk which a contributory
inevitably assumes when he first becomes a contributory of a company.
In my judgment, a creditor, in advancing money to a company, at least
in the absence of notice to the contrary, is ordinarily entitled to assume
that its affairs are being run in such a manner as will enable it promptly   D
to discharge its debts when they fall due, and to say to the court and to
other persons that internal disputes between directors and/or contributories of the company are no concern of his.

For these reasons, while I accept that the court would have jurisdiction to adjourn Chevron's petition, as asked by Mr. Mann, I think it
should only do so if it were satisfied that there were exceptional circum-   E
stances that justified this course.

There are some passages in the affidavits filed on behalf of Mr.
Cooper which imply that Chevron's petition may have been presented in
bad faith and in collusion with Mr. Kreike. If this suggestion had been
supported by any firm evidence, this might well have constituted an
exceptional circumstance sufficient to justify the court in acceding to Mr.
Cooper's request for an adjournment. The suggestion, however, is not   F
supported by any such firm evidence, and very properly, if I may say so,
Mr. Mann, during the course of his address, expressly disclaimed it for the
purpose of his argument.

The points upon which he relied in support of his application for an
adjournment were essentially as follows. He referred to the Manchester
petition and pointed out the close links between the events which gave   G
rise to that petition and those which gave rise to Chevron's petition. On
the hearing of the Manchester petition, it would be contended that Mr.
Kreike's unjustified acts were the cause of the company's failure hitherto
to discharge the debt due to Chevron. On this petition Mr. Mann told
me—though this is not formally in evidence—that Mr. Cooper would
now intend to seek relief under section 210 of the Companies Act 1948
with the object of both preventing a winding up order and enabling him   H
to resume the company's trading without interference from Mr. Kreike.
If this relief were granted to Mr. Cooper on the Manchester petition, it
would be his hope, I was told, that he would be in a position to pay off
the company's creditors sooner than they could ever be paid off by the
official receiver. Little would be gained, it was submitted, by making an
immediate winding up order; the company is not trading; its assets are
not in jeopardy because of the provisional liquidation; it could be that

A its creditors would in the event be paid off even more quickly if the adjournment sought were granted, than if a winding up order were made today. The making of such an order today would, in Mr. Mann's submission, do a substantial injustice to Mr. Cooper because it would deprive him of the opportunity of airing his grievances against Mr. Kreike on the Manchester petition.

B If this application for an adjournment were not opposed by Chevron, I might well accede to it. It is, however, strongly opposed by Chevron, and in my judgment there are no sufficient reasons why the wishes of Chevron, as the sole creditor appearing before me and an unpaid creditor for a very large sum, should not prevail. It has been owed over £300,000 by the company since at least February 1979. By October 1979 the debt will have been outstanding for over nine months. Chevron takes the

C view that the adjournment now sought would be likely to result in at least several further weeks' delay before its debt was discharged. Its prediction cannot, in my view, be regarded as an unreasonable one. Any such delay would be a serious matter in view of the size of the sum involved, and the fact that, in the winding up of an insolvent company, debts carry no interest after presentation of the petition. Every day that passes by, therefore, Chevron runs the risk of being deprived of the

D further use of its money without compensation.

The situation in the present case seems to be very far removed from that in In re Brighton Hotel Co., L.R. 6 Eq. 339, since, unlike Malins V.-C. in that case, I have no confidence that an adjournment would ultimately benefit the petitioning creditor. I think that an adjournment could well do it substantial injury; and Chevron, it must be remembered,

E is not at fault in any way and cannot, in my view, be reasonably expected to suffer because of the unhappy domestic disputes that have arisen between Mr. Cooper and Mr. Kreike in the running of this company.

In all the circumstances I think that any injustice that might be caused to Mr. Cooper by the making of an immediate winding up order would be far outweighed by the injustice to Chevron that would be caused by the grant of the adjournment sought, in opposition to its wishes. I

F should point out that if Mr. Cooper be right in suggesting that there has been misfeasance on the part of Mr. Kreike, remedies will be available to Mr. Cooper in the winding up, just as remedies will be available to Mr. Kreike himself, in so far as there may have been misfeasance on the part of Mr. Cooper. Chevron has, in my judgment, established its right to a winding up order in respect of this company and, subject to the question

G of costs, I propose to make the usual compulsory winding up order.

Order accordingly.

Solicitors: *Addleshaw, Sons & Latham, Manchester; Betesh & Co., Manchester; Pricketts, Stockport.*

T. C. C. B.

H

A

[COURT OF APPEAL]

* *In re* MESCO PROPERTIES LTD.

In re MESCO LABORATORIES LTD.

1979 July 11, 12   Buckley, Bridge and Templeman L.JJ. B

Company—*Winding up—Liquidator—Costs, charges and expenses
incurred — Sale of assets by liquidator — Liability to corporation tax on chargeable gains—Priority of tax—Whether tax
"charges and expenses" incurred in winding up — Whether
"necessary disbursements"* — Companies (Winding-up) Rules
1949 (S.I. 1949 No. 330), r. 195 (1) — Companies Act 1948
(11 & 12 Geo. 6, c. 38), s. 267   C

The liquidator of two companies which had been compulsorily wound up sold some of their properties at a profit
and as a result the companies became liable to corporation tax
under section 238 of the Income and Corporation Taxes Act
1970. The liquidator had a balance in hand of a sum which
was less than the corporation tax due, his remuneration as
liquidator being as yet unpaid. By summonses, the liquidator D
sought determination of the questions (1) whether the corporation tax was part of " the fees and expenses properly incurred
in preserving, realising or getting in the assets " within the
meaning of the opening words of rule 195 (1) of the Companies
(Winding-up) Rules 1949 [1] or was part of the necessary disbursements of any liquidator appointed in the winding up by
the court other than " expenses properly incurred in preserving, realising or getting in the assets heretofore provided E
for " within the fifth paragraph of the sub-rule and (2) whether
the corporation tax came within the expression " the costs,
charges and expenses incurred in the winding-up " within
section 267 of the Companies Act 1948.[2] Brightman J. held
on question (1) that the corporation tax was one of the
necessary disbursements which fell within the fifth paragraph
of rule 195 (1) and on question (2) that the tax, like Schedule D
income tax, was a charge or expense incurred by the liquidator F
in the winding up within the meaning of section 267 of the
Act of 1948.

On appeal by the liquidator : —
Held, dismissing the appeals, (1) that the corporation tax
liability was not a fee or expense incurred in realising the
assets but arose as a consequence of the sale of the assets by
the liquidator in the course of the winding up of the companies and, therefore, the tax was " necessary disbursements " G
falling within the fifth paragraph of rule 195 (1) of the Companies (Winding-up) Rules 1949, which the liquidator was under
a duty to pay in priority to the unsecured creditors (post,
pp. 97A–B, 101A–B, C–D).

[1] Companies (Winding-up) Rules 1949, r. 195: " (1) The assets of a company
in a winding up by the court remaining after payment of the fees and expenses
properly incurred in preserving, realising or getting in the assets, . . . shall, subject H
to any order of the court, . . . be liable to the following payments, which shall be
made in the following order of priority, namely: — . . . First—The taxed costs of
the petition. . . . Next [' the fifth paragraph '] the necessary disbursements of any
liquidator appointed in the winding up by the court, other than expenses properly incurred in preserving realising or getting in the assets heretofore provided
for. . . ."

[2] Companies Act 1948, s. 267: " The court may, in the event of the assets being
insufficient to satisfy the liabilities, make an order as to the payment out of the
assets of the costs, charges and expenses incurred in the winding up in such order
of priority as the court thinks just."

A   (2) That the liability to tax constituted " charges and
       expenses " within the meaning of section 267 of the Companies
       Act 1948 and, accordingly, since the companies' assets were
       insufficient to satisfy their liabilities, the court could make an
       order in accordance with the section as to the priority to be
       given to the payment of the tax among the other costs and
       charges incurred in the winding up (post, pp. 100D–E, 101C–D).
             Decision of Brightman J. [1979] 1 W.L.R. 558; [1979] 1
B   All E.R. 302 affirmed.

       The following cases were referred to in the judgment:
       Beni-Felkai Mining Co. Ltd., In re [1934] Ch. 406.
       Sadd v. *Griffin* [1908] 2 K.B. 510.

       The following additional cases were cited in argument:
C   *General Rolling Stock Co., In re* (1872) L.R. 7 Ch.App. 646.
       Lundy Granite Co., In re; Ex parte Heavan (1871) L.R. 6 Ch.App. 462.
       Sale Continuation Ltd. v. *Austin Taylor & Co. Ltd.* [1968] 2 Q.B. 849;
           [1967] 3 W.L.R. 1427; [1967] 2 All E.R. 1092.
       Webb v. *Whiffin* (1872) L.R. 5 H.L. 711, H.L.(E.).
       Whitney v. *Inland Revenue Commissioners* [1924] 2 K.B. 602, C.A.; [1926]
           A.C. 37, H.L.(E.).
D

       APPEALS from Brightman J.
           In December 1970, two companies, Mesco Properties Ltd. and Mesco
       Laboratories Ltd., were compulsorily wound up and, in February 1971,
       the court appointed a liquidator. The liquidator sold certain properties
       owned by the companies at a profit and, as a result, the companies became
E   liable to the payment of corporation tax under the Finance Act 1970 to
       the amount of £634,440, his balance in hand being £520,000. The Inland
       Revenue Commissioners claimed that the liability to tax ranked in priority
       over the costs of the winding up including the liquidator's remuneration.
           The liquidator issued a summons seeking determination of the priority
       to be given to the tax liability in discharging the debts of the companies.
       On November 7, 1978, Brightman J. held that the corporation tax was
F   one of the necessary disbursements within the fifth paragraph of rule 195
       (1) and ranked after the taxed costs of the petition but before the liquida-
       tor's fees; and that the corporation tax was a charge or expense within
       the meaning of section 267 of the Companies Act 1948 and that the court
       could order its payment out of the assets in such priority as seemed to
       it to be just. A similar order was made in the case of Mesco Labora-
G   tories Ltd.
           The liquidator appealed on the grounds that (1) the judge erred in law
       in holding that the liability was a charge which the liquidator was bound
       to discharge by payment to the extent that assets were available; (2) in
       holding that the liability had to be either a fee or expense incurred in pre-
       serving, realising or getting in the assets of the company within the
       meaning of the Companies (Winding-up) Rules 1949 or a necessary dis-
H   bursement of the liquidator within the meaning of the rule; (3) the
       liability arose as a necessary disbursement of the liquidator within the
       meaning of the rule; and (4) in not holding that the liability arose as a
       liability postponed to the claims of the ordinary unsecured creditors of
       the company.
           By a respondents' notice the Inland Revenue Commissioners gave
       notice that they intended on the hearing of the appeal to contend that
       the decision of Brightman J. should be varied in the event of the appeal

being allowed to the extent of the discharge of the declaration made by A
the judge that the liability of the company to account to the commissioners
in respect of the corporation tax on chargeable gains upon disposals
during the winding up by the court of assets vested in the company was a
necessary disbursement of the liquidator of the company within the
meaning of rule 195 (1) of the Companies (Winding-up) Rules 1949 and
that in lieu thereof it might be declared (1) that the liability arose as an
expense properly incurred in realising or getting in the assets of the B
company within the meaning of rule 195 (1); (2) alternatively that the
liability ranked after the matters provided for in rule 195 (1) but before
the claims of creditors with provable debts on the grounds (i) that the
liability was one properly incurred by the company but arising as it did
after the winding up could not be provided for; (ii) that the liability was
a cost, charge or expense of the winding up and rule 195 (1) provided for C
the making inter se of all such costs, charges and expenses; (iii) on the
disposal of each asset giving rise to a chargeable gain, a liability to
corporation tax arose (though the quantification of the liability attributable to that disposal depended on subsequent assessment); accordingly
the liability to account to the commissioners in respect of the corporation
tax was an expense properly incurred in realising or getting in the assets
of the company; and (iv) the scheme of the Companies Act 1948 was that D
the costs, charges and expenses of the winding up of a company were
payable in priority to all provable debts of the company.

G. B. H. Dillon Q.C. and *James Munby* for the liquidator.
Peter Gibson for the Inland Revenue Commissioners.

E

BUCKLEY L.J. We have before us two appeals from decisions of
Brightman J.; one in the matter of Mesco Properties Ltd., and the other,
notwithstanding the way in which the case is listed, in the matter of
Mesco Laboratories Ltd. The appeals arise on decisions of the judge on
two summonses, each issued in the compulsory liquidation of the company in question. The facts of the two cases are in all significant respects F
the same, so that the fate of one appeal must dictate the fate of the
other. I can confine myself to the appeal in *In re Mesco Properties Ltd.*

The facts are set out in the report of the judge's decision, which is to
be found in [1979] 1 W.L.R. 558; I need not repeat them at any length.

After the commencement of the winding up of the company, certain
immovable properties of the company were sold, some of them by
receivers appointed by mortgagees, some by mortgagees and some by the G
liquidator, at prices which realised profits over the cost of those properties to the company. Consequently the company became liable to
corporation tax in the considerable sum of £634,440, in respect of
chargeable gains so realised. The liquidator has a balance in hand in
the winding up of no more than about £520,000. In these circumstances
the liquidator, by the summons, asks (1) whether the corporation tax is H
(a) a fee or other expense properly incurred in preserving, realising or
getting in the assets of the company within the meaning of rule 195 (1) of
the Companies (Winding-up) Rules 1949; or (b) a necessary disbursement of the liquidator within the meaning of that rule. I need not read
paragraphs (c) and (d) of paragraph (1) of the summons: (c) has been
abandoned and (d) does not in fact arise.

The liquidator also asks, by paragraph (2) of the summons, whether

A in any event the liability for the tax is a cost, charge or expense of the winding up within the meaning of section 267 of the Companies Act 1948. The summons also raised a further question about how the liquidator's own remuneration should rank, but we are not now concerned with that.

Brightman J. answered paragraph (1) (a) of the summons in the negative, paragraph (1) (b) in the affirmative and paragraph (2) in the affirmative. The liquidator appeals against that decision.

B It is common ground that the Crown cannot prove in the winding up for tax the liability for which arose after the commencement of the winding up. It is also common ground that neither the liquidator, nor any mortgagee or receiver is liable for any of the tax: the company alone is liable.

In the events which have happened the liquidator is the proper officer C of the company to pay the tax: Taxes Management Act 1970, section 108 (1) and (3) (a). Under section 238 (1) of the Income and Corporation Taxes Act 1970, corporation tax is charged on a company's profits which, by virtue of subsection (4), means income and chargeable gains. Chargeable gains for this purpose are to be computed in accordance with capital gains tax principles (see section 265 (2) of that Act) and the amount to be included in respect of chargeable gains in a company's total profits D for any accounting period are the total amount of chargeable gains accruing to the company in that period after deducting allowable losses. Corporation tax assessed for an accounting period is in general payable within nine months from the end of that period or, if later, within one month from assessment: see section 243 (4).

Mr. Dillon, appearing for the liquidator, submits that the judge was E wrong to hold that the tax is a disbursement within rule 195 of the Winding-up Rules, because the liquidator has not paid the tax and does not wish to pay it unless, in accordance with the proper priority in which the company's liabilities should be discharged, he is bound to do so; and because the payment of the tax will not advance the liquidation in the sense of making the liquidator more able to distribute the company's assets among its creditors.

F Mr. Gibson, appearing on behalf of the Inland Revenue Commissioners, submits that the judge was right in holding that the tax constitutes a disbursement within the meaning of rule 195. He says that all liabilities which properly fall within the description of costs, charges and expenses of a winding up rank in front of the general body of creditors at the commencement of the winding up having provable debts, and that G they are, inter se, to be satisfied in the order of priority laid down in rule 195, subject to any order of the court under section 267 of the Companies Act 1948, and he submits that the tax ranks as a necessary disbursement of the liquidator and so falls within the fifth of the paragraphs set out in paragraph (1) of rule 195.

The commissioners have by a respondents' notice asserted that in the event of the liquidator's appeal being allowed, the judge's order should be H varied so as to declare that the liability for the tax is an expense properly incurred in realising or getting in the assets of the company within the opening words of rule 195.

The first question for consideration is, I think, whether Brightman J. was right in holding that the tax constitutes a necessary disbursement within the meaning of the rule. It would, in my view, be a very remarkable thing if the proper priority of a liability under rule 195 were to depend upon whether the liquidator decided to pay it or not, which seems to

be the effect of Mr. Dillon's argument, for he says that if the liquidator   A
had paid the tax it could properly be described as a disbursement, but
that until he pays it, it cannot be so described.

He referred us in this connection to *Sadd* v. *Griffin* [1908] 2 K.B. 510,
where it was held that a solicitor could not charge his client, as disbursements, for counsel's fees which he had not yet paid. That case is so far
from the present case on the facts and the considerations involved, that
I do not think it of any assistance in construing rule 195. It must, in my   B
view, be open to a liquidator to apply to the court for guidance upon the
question whether, if he discharges a certain liability of the company in
liquidation, the payment will be a necessary disbursement within the
meaning of rule 195. That is what the liquidator is doing in this case.
The company is liable for the tax which is due. The tax ought to be paid.
The liquidator is the proper officer to pay it. When he pays it, he will   C
clearly make a disbursement. In my judgment it will be a necessary disbursement within the meaning of the rule. Moreover, common sense and
justice seem to me to require that it should be discharged in full in
priority to the unsecured creditors, and to any expenses which rank lower
in priority under rule 195. The tax is a consequence of the realisation
of the assets in the course of the winding up of the company. That
realisation was a necessary step in the liquidation; that is to say, in the   D
administration of the insolvent estate. The fact that in the event there
may be nothing available for the unsecured creditors does not, in my view,
mean that the realisation was not a step taken in the interests of all who
have claims against the company. Those claims must necessarily be met
out of the available assets in due order of priority. Superior claims may
baulk inferior ones, but the liquidator's duty is to realise the assets for   E
the benefit of all in accordance with their rights. If in consequence of
the realisation, the company incurs a liability, the discharge of such
liability must, in my judgment, constitute a charge or expense incurred
in the winding up within section 267 of the Companies Act 1948 and must
also, in my view, fall within rule 195.

Brightman J. pointed out that, under section 243 (2) of the Income
and Corporation Taxes Act 1970, a company is expressly made charge-   F
able to corporation tax on a capital gain arising in a winding up. He
said [1979] 1 W.L.R. 558, 561:

"It follows that the tax is a charge which the liquidator is bound to
discharge by payment, to the extent that assets are available. It is,
therefore, to my mind, beyond argument that the payment of the
tax is a 'necessary disbursement' of the liquidator and must come   G
within the fifth paragraph of rule 195 (1) of the Companies (Winding-
up) Rules unless it is 'an expense properly incurred in preserving,
realising or getting in the assets,' in which case it is excepted from
the fifth paragraph because it falls within the opening words of the
sub-rule."

I agree. He went on to refer to certain dicta of Maugham J. in *In re*   H
Beni-Felkai Mining Co. Ltd. [1934] Ch. 406. That case was concerned
with a voluntary winding up and with income tax which had become due
in respect of profits earned after the commencement of the winding up.
Maugham J. expressed the view, at p. 417, that the tax could not be
properly described as "fees and actual expenses incurred in realising or
getting in the assets," but said that he was more doubtful whether it might
come within "the liquidator's necessary disbursements."

A   Brightman J. expressed the opinion that corporation tax on a capital gain, made when a liquidator sells an asset, is not an " expense incurred in realising that asset." I agree with this. The liability to tax is a consequence of, amongst other things, the realisation, but it is not a direct consequence of the realisation. It depends upon the amount of the company's " profits " as defined in section 238 of the Income and Corporation Taxes Act 1970 (if any) for the entire relevant accounting period.

B   It is, as the judge said, merely a possible consequence of a sale at a profit. He consequently reached the conclusion that the tax did not fall within the expression " fees and expenses . . . incurred in . . . realising . . . the assets " in the opening words of rule 195, but did fall within the words " the necessary disbursements of any liquidator appointed in the winding up by the court " in the fifth sub-paragraph of paragraph (1) of the rule.

C   On the question raised by paragraph (2) of the summons, he held that the corporation tax was a charge or expense incurred in the winding up, within section 267.

In my judgment the judge's conclusions were correct and I would dismiss both appeals.

D   BRIDGE L.J. I agree, both with the judgment just delivered by Buckley L.J. and with that of Brightman J. which is under appeal.

There is nothing of my own that I can usefully add. I too would dismiss the appeals.

TEMPLEMAN L.J. I agree.

E   *Appeals dismissed.*
                             Liquidator to be at liberty to retain
                                  his costs taxed on trustee basis out
                                  of assets.
                             Leave to appeal refused.

F   Solicitors: *Herbert Smith & Co.; Solicitor of Inland Revenue.*

L. G. S.

A

[QUEEN'S BENCH DIVISION]

* AIR-INDIA v. WIGGINS

1979   Oct. 15   Lord Widgery C.J., Eveleigh L.J. and
                                                      Kilner Brown J.

B

*Animal—Transit of animal—Carrier's duty—Birds carried by Indian
airline from Bombay to England—Failure to ventilate aircraft causing unnecessary suffering—Failure occurring outside
English airspace—Whether English courts having jurisdiction
—Transit of Animals (General) Order 1973 (S.I. 1973 No.
1377), art. 3 (3)*

C

Article 3 (3) of the Transit of Animals (General) Order
1973 provides:

"In relation to carriage by sea or air, the provisions
of this Order shall apply to animals carried on any vessel
or aircraft to or from a port or airport in Great Britain,
whether or not such animals are loaded or unloaded at
such port or airport."

The defendant airline carried a cargo of birds from Bom-   D
bay to London Heathrow Airport. Owing to lack of ventilation during a stop at Kuwait, many of the birds died, and it
was highly probable that the majority of the birds were dead
before the aircraft carrying them ever entered English airspace. The defendants were charged, inter alia, with contravening article 5 (2) of the Transit of Animals (General) Order
1973,[1] by carrying the birds in such a way as was likely to
cause them injury or unnecessary suffering. The justices held   E
that proceedings under the Order could, by virtue of article
3 (3), be brought in England against foreign nationals for acts
committed abroad, and convicted the defendants. An appeal
against conviction was dismissed by the Crown Court.

On the defendants' appeal: —

Held, dismissing the appeal, that article 3 (3) on its true
construction, and giving the words their natural meaning,
applied to the carriage of animals outside English territorial   F
limits and, therefore, the provisions of the Order of 1973
applied where animals were carried on a journey from abroad
and the aircraft landed at an airport in Great Britain; accordingly, the defendants were properly convicted in respect of
the summonses under article 5 (2).

No cases are referred to in the judgment.

G

The following cases were cited in argument:

Cox v. *Army Council* [1963] A.C. 48; [1962] 2 W.L.R. 950; [1962] 1 All
E.R. 880, H.L.(E.).
Philipson-Stow v. *Inland Revenue Commissioners* [1961] A.C. 727; [1960]
3 W.L.R. 1008; [1960] 3 All E.R. 814, H.L.(E.).
Reg. v. *Jameson* [1896] 2 Q.B. 425.   H
Reg. v. *Martin* [1956] 2 Q.B. 272; [1956] 2 W.L.R. 975; [1956] 2 All
E.R. 86.
Theophile v. *Solicitor-General* [1950] A.C. 186; [1950] 1 All E.R. 405,
H.L.(E.).

---

[1] Transit of Animals (General) Order 1973, art. 5: "(2) No person shall carry
any animal by sea, air, road or rail, or cause or permit any animal to be so carried,
in a way which is likely to cause injury or unnecessary suffering to the said animal."

Air-India v. Wiggins (D.C.)

A   CASE STATED by Middlesex Crown Court.

On June 17, 1976, the justices for the metropolitan commission area of Greater London, petty sessional division of Uxbridge, heard 36 summonses preferred by the prosecutor, Geoffrey Stuart Wiggins, against the defendants, Air-India, under the Transit of Animals (General) Order 1973 and the Diseases of Animals Act 1950.

B   The offences alleged against the defendants were: under article 5 (2), that they had carried the birds in such a way as was likely to cause them injury or unnecessary suffering; under article 6 (1) (a), that they had failed to ensure that the birds were adequately fed and watered at suitable intervals during carriage; under article 6 (1) (b), that they had failed to ensure that adequate supplies of food and water appropriate to the species of birds were available in the aircraft in which the birds were C   carried. The justices convicted on all 36 summonses and fined the defendants.

The defendants appealed to the Middlesex Crown Court by notice dated June 23, 1976, and amended on July 2, 1976, against conviction and sentence in respect of all the summonses on the grounds that the convictions were unsound in law and upon the facts and that the D   sentences were harsh and excessive in all the circumstances.

The Crown Court heard the appeal and found the following facts. On September 30, 1975, 2,120 birds were consigned from Bombay to London Heathrow Airport via Kuwait aboard one of the defendants' flights. The aircraft carrying the birds developed a technical fault at Kuwait and remained on the tarmac at Kuwait for 31 hours. During the delay at Kuwait the birds remained in the hold of the aircraft without the hold E   being opened or otherwise ventilated. On arrival at the R.S.P.C.A. hostel at Heathrow Airport on October 1, 1975, 89 of the birds were alive and 2,031 were dead. The overwhelming probability was that the birds which had died did so as a result of the heat and lack of ventilation during the period that they spent in Kuwait, and in consequence it was highly probable that the great majority of the birds were dead before F   ever the aircraft entered British airspace. By reason of the lack of ventilation at Kuwait all the birds had been carried in a way which was likely to cause them injury or unnecessary suffering. The court did not find that the boxes in which the birds had travelled had been over-crowded. The defendants were and at all material times had been a foreign national corporation.

At the close of the case for the prosecution it was contended by the G   defendants that (a) the Act and Order applied only to live animals because dead animals were incapable of suffering. The Crown Court agreed that that was so. (b) Accordingly an offence under section 78 of the Act and the Order could only be committed in relation to live animals. The Crown Court agreed that that too was so. (c) Since only 89 birds were alive at London Heathrow Airport and there was no way in H   which it could be established that more than 89 birds were alive during the time that the aircraft had been in British airspace, it followed that except in relation to 89 birds any offence which might have been committed against British law had been committed (i) by a foreign national and (ii) outside British territory. (d) That such offences as might have been committed were accordingly outside the jurisdiction of the British courts unless it was established as a matter of law that the Act and the Order which together created the offences had extra-territorial effect.

Since the defendants admitted that they were by their agents respon-   A
sible for the failure to ventilate the birds at Kuwait and likewise admitted
that such a failure would be caught by the words of article 5 (2) of the
Order if the Act and Order had extra-territorial effect, the question upon
which the appeal before the Crown Court largely turned was whether the
Act and the Order did have extra-territorial effect.

It was contended by the prosecutor that the Diseases of Animals
Act 1950, having particular regard to sections 20, 23 and 83 of the Act,   B
had extra-territorial effect; that by article 3 (3) of the Transit of Animals
(General) Order 1973 the provisions of the Order were applied with
extra-territorial effect.

For the prosecutor, who contended that the Act and the Order *did*
have extra-territorial effect, it was submitted (a) that by article 3 (3) of
the Transit of Animals (General) Order 1973, the provisions of the Order   C
applied to " animals carried on any vessel or aircraft to or from a port
or airport in Great Britain, whether or not such animals [were] loaded
or unloaded at such port or airport." (b) That section 83 (3) of the
Diseases of Animals Act 1950 gave to the Act extra-territorial effect.

For the defendants, who contended that the Act and Order did *not*
have extra territorial effect, it was submitted (a) that by reason of the   D
comity of nations and by analogy with other Acts of Parliament, no
statute of the British Parliament could have extra-territorial effect unless
it said as much in the clearest terms; (b) that section 83 (3) of the
Diseases of Animals Act 1950 was procedural only and provided for
venue rather than extending the provisions of the Act world-wide; and
(c) that article 3 (3) of the Order could not assume greater powers than
were originally provided for in the Act by the authority of which the   E
Order was made.

The court concluded that the Diseases of Animals Act 1950 and the
Transit of Animals (General) Order 1973 had extra-territorial effect and
were to be applied throughout the carriage from the point of loading,
whether or not that was within the jurisdiction, where the animals were
carried to or from a port or airport in Great Britain, applying article   F
3 (3) of the Order. After the court's ruling on the defendants' submission, the defendants called no evidence.

The court was of the opinion that in the light of the facts which it
had found and its ruling on the law the justices had been correct in finding
the 12 summonses under article 5 (2) proved but that there was insufficient
evidence to support convictions on the 24 summonses under articles
6 (1) (a) and 6 (1) (b). Accordingly, the court dismissed the appeals   G
against conviction in respect of the 12 summonses under article 5 (2) and
allowed the appeals against conviction in respect of the 24 summonses
under articles 6 (1) (a) and 6 (1) (b).

Keith Evans and *Frank Panford* for the defendants.
Roger Cox for the prosecutor.   H

LORD WIDGERY C.J. This is a case stated by Judge Martin and
justices for the Middlesex commission area in respect of their adjudication at the Middlesex Crown Court, on appeal from the Uxbridge
Magistrates' Court.

On June 17, 1976, which was the day the summonses were presented,
there was a total of 36 summonses issued against the defendants, Air-India,

A   alleging in broad terms cruel treatment of or insufficient attention paid to a cargo of birds which Air-India were at that time transporting.

What had happened was that 2,120 birds left Bombay destined to go to London. The aircraft was due to touch down at Kuwait en route. It did touch down at Kuwait. Some fault developed in the engine and it had to remain there for very much longer than was intended, and during that period the birds obviously suffered great privation, and of the 2,120 consigned from Bombay only 89 were alive when the aircraft reached Heathrow. The consequence of that was that it was almost clear beyond doubt that the death of the birds in question had occurred before the aeroplane entered English airspace.

At a very early stage in the proceedings the point was taken that, given the background facts which I have described, no proceedings could be brought in this country against Air-India because Air-India were a foreign national and the offence had been committed outside English airspace, somewhere in the Gulf of Kuwait.

The case raises a very short and very interesting, and no doubt very important point as to how far these days, when animals are carried by air in such large quantities, the carrier is responsible for looking after them and how far that obligation falls upon the consignor.

The view taken by the justices was that the answer to this problem had to be found in the relevant regulations which presently apply to the carriage of animals by air. The justices seem to have been properly advised at all times that, as a general principle, the law of England is a domestic law in so far as the criminal law is concerned, and consequently there are very powerful authorities that require the justices in the first instance, and us later on, to recognise that fact and not to create or be party to the creation of criminal offences which are extra-territorial in the sense that they can be committed outside the country.

Coming immediately to the situation affecting animals carried by air, one has to look first of all under the relevant authorities at the Diseases of Animals Act 1950. Section 20 of that Act is headed "Regulation of movement of animals, etc." It provides:

"The Minister may make such orders as he thinks fit, subject and according to the provisions of this Act, for all or any of the following purposes— . . . (x) for protecting animals from unnecessary suffering during inland transit . . ."

That is a clear power to the Minister to make orders to protect the birds against unnecessary suffering, but it is confined, and was confined at that stage, to inland transit.

The matter has been supplemented since, as developments occurred in air transport. An Order has been made, which we shall shortly see, under section 23 of the Act, which is in these terms:

"The Minister may make such orders as he thinks fit— . . . (b) for ensuring for animals carried by sea a proper supply of food and water and proper ventilation during the passage and on landing; (c) for protecting them from unnecessary suffering during the passage and on landing."

There again one has comprehensive power in the Minister to make orders for the welfare of animals in the circumstances, but it will be observed that section 23 as originally enacted was confined to passage by sea.

The final reference is made now to the Agriculture (Miscellaneous A
Provisions) Act 1954, section 11 of which applies the provisions of section
23 to travel by air as it had formerly applied to travel by sea.

The stage is set for the making of orders upon which the protection
of animals is to depend, and for this we go to the Transit of Animals
(General) Order 1973. Article 1 applies the Order to Great Britain,
and article 3 contains extensive definitive provisions about the words
used in the Order. I do not find it necessary specifically to refer to B
article 3 (1) and (2), but article 3 (3) is, in my judgment, the core and
heart of this case. Under article 3 (3) it is provided:

> " In relation to carriage by sea or air, the provisions of this Order
> shall apply to animals carried on any vessel or aircraft to or from a
> port or airport in Great Britain, whether or not such animals are
> loaded or unloaded at such port or airport." C

It seems to me (and I do not think it will be disputed) that that sub-
paragraph, if the words it contains are given their ordinary meaning in
the English language, will be wide enough to enable the Secretary of
State to make orders extending beyond the territorial limits of this
country and including such animal-carrying flights as the one with which D
we are concerned here.

The Crown Court judge and the justices on the appeal to the Crown
Court took the view that the power was thus extensive and had thus
been exercised and therefore, in the cases where there was no other
defence, the Crown Court upheld the convictions.

It is said today that the Crown Court were wrong, and there is just the
one point, because they failed to construe article 3 (3) correctly and they E
were wrong in allowing it to extend to flights outside the territorial limits
of this country. One can say at once that it is a very short point, and
so far as I can judge the only point for consideration is whether the
Crown Court erred in the construction which they were minded to give
to article 3 (3).

It seems to me, and has seemed to me throughout the case, that, if F
one excluded extra-territorial activities because they should be excluded
from the Order, there was nothing left in article 3 (3) at all. I took
the liberty of pressing Mr. Evans at one stage to show us what the
effect of the Order would be under any other approach to the construction of article 3 (3). It seems to me, with respect to him, that he
did not ever answer my question, and it certainly seems to me now that
the only alternative in regard to construction is that article 3 (3) operates G
fully in giving the words their natural meaning, or for all practical
purposes it is a dead provision with no life left in it at all. Those are
the alternatives before us, and I have no hesitation, speaking for myself,
in saying that we should give this article its full meaning.

There are many pointers in it which indicate that the draftsmen and
the Secretary of State had that in mind. Indeed one must remember that H
we are now in the jet age and all sorts of regulations about transit and
transit of animals have to be revised in the modern setting. As was
pointed out in argument, another pointer to the construction of article
3 (3) being the one which I have favoured is that in it there is a
reference to animals being carried on a vessel or aircraft to or from a
port in Great Britain. That seems to me to be an expression properly
related to international transport, and, as I say, it seems to me that in the

A year 1979 one has to have considerable international agreement on matters which are strictly of a criminal nature because it is nowadays impossible to say which country's domestic law should remain entirely domestic.

I think that the Crown Court reached a proper conclusion, and I turn to the question which they have asked us in the case:

B 　"Were we correct in holding that the provisions of the Transit of Animals (General) Order 1973 apply to acts done by foreign nationals in foreign territory provided that the vessel or aircraft in which such acts are done lands or docks in Great Britain during or at the conclusion of the same voyage."

The Crown Court thought the answer to that question would be yes. I think so too, and I would dismiss the appeal.

C
　　EVELEIGH L.J. I agree.

　　KILNER BROWN J. I also agree

Appeal dismissed with costs.

D 　November 2. Their Lordships certified the following to be a point of law of general public importance, namely, " Is there an offence punishable in England under the Diseases of Animals Act 1950 and Regulations made thereunder, if an airline carries animals from India to London Airport in conditions which constitute a breach of such Regulations, but the animals are dead before the aircraft enters English airspace? "

E
Leave to appeal refused.
Costs of application reserved to the
House of Lords.

　　Solicitors: *Bulcraig & Davis; Comptroller and City Solicitor, Corporation of London.*

B. O. A.

F

_____

[COURT OF APPEAL]

G
* CHARTERED BANK v. DAKLOUCHE AND ANOTHER

[1979 C. No. 1106]

1979　March 15, 16　　　　　　Lord Denning M.R., Eveleigh L.J.
　　　　　　　　　　　　　　　　　　and Sir Stanley Rees

H *Injunction—Interlocutory—Mareva injunction—Wrongful dispositions of moneys abroad by foreign defendants—Moneys traced to second defendant's London bank account—Second defendant served and having assets within jurisdiction—First defendant out of jurisdiction—Whether jurisdiction to grant Mareva injunction*

　　The defendants, who were Lebanese and husband and wife, traded under a business name in Abu Dhabi. In January 1979, when the husband's business account with the plaintiff bank was heavily overdrawn, three cheques made out to the business

Chartered Bank v. Daklouche (C.A.) [1980]

were cashed at another bank by the husband and the money   A
transferred by the wife to her account with a bank in London.
The plaintiff bank brought an action against the defendants
seeking, inter alia, an order setting aside the dispositions made
by the defendants, an injunction restraining the defendants
from disposing of any assets within the jurisdiction and
damages for conspiracy and/or breach of trust and/or fraud.
The writ was served on the wife, who was living at a house
owned by her in this country, but the husband's whereabouts   B
were unknown. An ex parte *Mareva* injunction, obtained by
the plaintiff bank, restraining the defendants from disposing of
moneys within the jurisdiction standing to the credit of the
wife, was ordered to be discharged as against the wife by
Donaldson J. on the wife's application on the ground that the
matter should be dealt with by the courts of Abu Dhabi.

On appeal by the plaintiff bank : —

Held, allowing the appeal, that a *Mareva* injunction could   C
be granted against a defendant such as the wife who, though
served within the jurisdiction and having assets here, was
likely to leave and withdraw the assets at short notice (post,
pp. 113D–E, 114D–E); that the plaintiff bank had a justiciable
cause of action in England in conspiracy and/or fraud to
which the husband was a proper party capable of being served
out of the jurisdiction under the rules of court (post, pp.
113B–C, 115D); and that, on the facts alleged, it was right that a   D
Mareva injunction should be granted against both defendants.

Observations of Lord Denning M.R. in *Rasu Maritima
S.A.* v. *Perusahaan Pertambangan Minyak Dan Gas Bumi
Negara* (*Government of Republic of Indonesia intervening*)
(*Pertamina*) [1978] Q.B. 644, 659, C.A. and of Lord Hailsham
of St. Marylebone in *Siskina* (*Owners of cargo lately laden
on board*) v. *Distos Compania Naviera S.A.* [1979] A.C. 210,
261, H.L.(E.) explained.   E

Decision of Donaldson J. reversed.

The following cases are referred to in the judgments:

Cadogan v. *Cadogan* [1977] 1 W.L.R. 1041; [1977] 3 All E.R. 831, C.A.
Midland Bank Trust Co. Ltd. v. *Green* (*No. 3*) [1979] 2 W.L.R. 594;
    [1979] 2 All E.R. 193.
Rasu Maritima S.A. v. *Perusahaan Pertambangan Minyak Dan Gas*   F
    Bumi Negara (*Government of Republic of Indonesia intervening*)
    (*Pertamina*) [1978] Q.B. 644; [1977] 3 W.L.R. 518; [1977] 3 All
    E.R. 324, C.A.
Siskina (*Owners of cargo lately laden on board*) v. *Distos Compania
    Naviera S.A.* [1979] A.C. 210; [1977] 3 W.L.R. 818; [1977] 3 All E.R.
    803, H.L.(E.).

                                                                G

The following additional cases were cited in argument:

Lister & Co. v. *Stubbs* (1890) 45 Ch.D. 1, C.A.
McCormick v. *Grogan* (1869) L.R. 4 H.L. 82, H.L.(I.).
Metropolitan Bank v. *Heiron* (1880) L.R. 5 Ex.D. 319, C.A.
Mawji v. *The Queen* [1957] A.C. 126; [1957] 2 W.L.R. 277; [1957] 1 All
    E.R. 385, P.C.
Rye v. *Rye* [1962] A.C. 496; [1962] 2 W.L.R. 361; [1962] 1 All E.R. 611,   H
    H.L.(E.).

APPEAL from Donaldson J.

On February 7, 1979, on the plaintiff, the Chartered Bank, undertaking to abide by any order the court might make as to damages and to
issue a writ, Mocatta J. made an order ex parte restraining the first and
second defendants, Suhail Daklouche and Salwa Daklouche, from re-

A   moving or otherwise disposing of any of their assets, and in particular
moneys standing to the credit of the second defendant in any bank
account, from within the jurisdiction of the court until trial or further
order. By writ dated February 8, 1979, and subsequently amended, the
plaintiff claimed, against the first defendant, for moneys lent and damages
for fraud and, against both defendants, (a) a declaration that dispositions
by the first and/or second defendant of moneys from the first defend-
B   ant's account at the First National Bank of Chicago, Abu Dhabi,
whereby the moneys were converted into cash and then transferred to
two deposit accounts of the second defendant with the First National
Bank of Chicago in London were voidable pursuant to section 172 of
the Law of Property Act 1925 and/or the inherent jurisdiction of the
court and/or were void or voidable pursuant to the law of Abu Dhabi;
C   (b) a declaration that the dispositions had been avoided and/or were null
and void and/or an order that the dispositions be set aside; (c) an injunction restraining the defendants from removing any of their assets from
within the jurisdiction or otherwise disposing of them and in particular
restraining them from so removing or disposing of the moneys presently
standing to the credit of the second defendant in any bank account
within the jurisdiction; (d) an injunction restraining the second defendant
D   from removing, disposing of or otherwise dealing with the moneys
standing to the credit of accounts in her name with the First National
Bank of Chicago, London; (e) a declaration that the moneys presently
standing to the credit of those accounts were held by the defendants as
trustees for the plaintiff as creditor of the first defendant and an order
that the defendants do everything necessary to make those moneys
E   available to the plaintiff for the purpose of satisfying the plaintiff's claim
as creditor of the first defendant; and (f) damages for conspiracy and/or
breach of trust and/or fraud.

On March 6, 1979, on the second defendant's application, Donaldson J.
ordered that the injunction granted on February 7 be discharged as
against the second defendant but ordered that the second defendant be
restrained from receiving, disposing or otherwise dealing with the
F   moneys standing to the credit of her account with the First National Bank
of Chicago until March 9, 1979, subsequently extended to March 16,
1979.

By notice of appeal dated March 9, 1979, the plaintiff appealed on
the grounds (1) that the judge was wrong in holding that he had no
jurisdiction to make any order restraining the second defendant from
dealing with the moneys in her accounts; and (2) that the judge ought to
G   have held that he had such jurisdiction by virtue of the fact that the
moneys in her accounts were transferred thereto pursuant to a conspiracy between the defendants to defraud the first defendant's creditors
such as the plaintiff and/or that the moneys were impressed with a trust
for the benefit of the plaintiff as creditor of the first defendant.

The facts are stated in the judgment of Lord Denning M.R.

H
Roger Buckley for the plaintiff bank.
Anthony Boswood for the second defendant.

LORD DENNING M.R. The Lebanese are born traders. They set up
businesses far and wide. Two of them are husband and wife, Suhail and
Salwa Daklouche. They did well in Abu Dhabi in the Persian Gulf.
That is a place grown rich on oil. The husband traded there under the

Lord Denning M.R.   **Chartered Bank v. Daklouche (C.A.)**   **[1980]**

business name of Gulf Trading and Cold Storage Co. He supplied food A
and drink wholesale to caterers at the airport and at clubs. Some of his
business was retail. He set up a supermarket and supplied goods retail
to the public. His wife helped him a good deal in both businesses. At
all events, on her own admission, she helped him quite a lot in managing
the supermarket.

The business was very successful. So much so that they were
attracted to England. They—or at least the wife—purchased a large B
house at Beech, which is near Alton in Hampshire. It was conveyed
into the wife's name. In 1977 it cost £50,000. The money seems to
have been available without any need to raise anything on mortgage. It
is now worth £80,000. The wife is having building work done on it to a
value, she says, of more than £34,000. Mr. and Mrs. Daklouche have
two daughters aged 15 and 13 who are at boarding school in England. C
They hope to go on to a university here.

Meanwhile, the husband has been carrying on the business in Abu
Dhabi. From January 1976 he has had an account with the branch of
the Chartered Bank there. That account is in the firm's name of Gulf
Trading and Cold Storage Co. But both husband and wife have power
to operate it individually on their sole signature. Each gave specimen
signatures to the bank in regard to the operation of that account. D

All seems to have gone reasonably well until January 1979. Then
the husband ran into financial difficulties. The account with the
Chartered Bank became very much overdrawn. The husband told the
manager of the branch at Abu Dhabi that he had many trade debts
owing to him and that he would pay off the overdraft with the proceeds
of these trade debts which he would get in by January 20, 1979. Other E
creditors were also pressing for payment of unpaid bills. We are told
that one of them called in the local police to help recover his debt.

During January 1979 three cheques were received by Gulf Trading
and Cold Storage Co. Two of them were from the Abu Dhabi International
Airport Caterers and one was from the Abu Dhabi Club. They were
all marked " Account payee." They were given in local currency, but F
in sterling they came to about £70,000. The husband, however, did not
pay these cheques into the Chartered Bank to clear the overdraft. He
paid them into his own account which he had in Abu Dhabi with the
First National Bank of Chicago there. Soon afterwards he drew out
the amount in cash and closed his account with the First National Bank
in Abu Dhabi. Although there is some conflict, it appears very likely
from the evidence that on the very next day, having drawn out the cash G
from the First National Bank, he handed it to his wife. Then she paid
it into two banks in Abu Dhabi, the City Bank and Barclays Bank
(International). She then asked those two banks to transfer the money
by telegraph to her personal account in London with the First National
Bank of Chicago. This was done. So the £70,000 stood in the wife's
name in the bank in London.
H
Soon afterwards the wife came back to England. But we do not
know what happened to the husband. He seems to have disappeared
without trace. The court officials in Abu Dhabi have taken possession
of his premises. They have sealed them up, and have put up a notice
calling on creditors to put in their claim.

The Chartered Bank seems to have got wind of some of these
happenings. At first they had very little knowledge about it. They found

A out that there was quite a large sum of money to the credit of the wife in the First National Bank of Chicago in London. So they issued a writ trying to stop it being dealt with. The writ was issued against both husband and wife here. The Chartered Bank moved the court for a *Mareva* injunction so as to stop any disposal of that £70,000 in the First National Bank which stood in the wife's name. Mocatta J. granted the injunction to stop the money being dealt with: and he

B further gave leave to serve the husband out of the jurisdiction. As for the wife, she was here in England. So she was duly served, I suppose at her house at Alton. At all events, the judge granted a *Mareva* injunction to stop any dealings with the money. The bank was told. Everything was held up.

Thereupon the wife moved the court to discharge the injunction.

C The matter came before Donaldson J. He did discharge the injunction. He gave his reasons quite shortly. He said:

"This matter should be dealt with by order of the court in whose jurisdiction the transaction took effect and, in my view, this is Abu Dhabi since orders of English courts do not have extra territorial effect."

D So Donaldson J. refused the injunction because he said this matter could not be dealt with in England. He would not even restrain the moneys from going out of England. The only course open to the Chartered Bank was to go to Abu Dhabi, sue the husband there, get judgment there and put the husband in bankruptcy there. It was only after all that was done that the Chartered Bank might stop any dealings with the

E money in London.

By that time I doubt whether there would be any money in the London bank. It is very easy to transfer money from one bank to another bank at a moment's notice. It could be transferred to Switzerland or Chicago, or wherever it may be.

Donaldson J., realising it is a difficult point, extended the injunction

F pending the appeal to this court until today. So we have heard it, and now have to give our decision.

There has been additional evidence filed on both sides, so we know a good deal more about the case. Earlier on the wife had said that this money was not given to her by her husband. She said it was never her husband's money at all. She said she was an entrepreneur on her own account. She said in her affidavit: "I am a Lebanese citizen and I am

G not a resident of the United Kingdom." She explained that she purchased the house in order to provide a base for herself and her husband because her two daughters were being educated at school here. She said:

"Since I purchased the house here and before that date, I have transferred sums of money to my accounts with the First National

H Bank of Chicago in London. The money transferred has always been my own money, owned by me in my own right. I own money which has come to me through my own family, from transactions entered into by me in Abu Dhabi on the gold market there, from land transactions entered into by me in Sharjah and from other business interests. Furthermore, my relatives often give me money to transfer for them to London. During the year 1978 I remitted over £60,000 to London."

Lord Denning M.R.   Chartered Bank v. Daklouche (C.A.)   [1980]

Then she deals with these specific items—the cheques which I have **A** mentioned which were in favour of the Gulf Trading and Cold Storage Co.—which were traced here. As to those, she said they were not her husband's at all. She said that they were sent to her by a family friend in Jordan and also from an uncle in Beirut, and she remitted those moneys to London.

That is what the wife said at first. But later the bank were able to get further evidence. They got the cheques and traced them all through. **B** As a result it appears that her story was altogether wrong. She had previously said that they were her moneys, given to her by her uncle and other friends and relatives. Now the evidence goes to show that they were the firm's moneys, drawn out by the husband in Abu Dhabi, handed to her, and she then put them in her name into the London bank. The reason is pretty plain. He wanted to get the moneys out **C** of the reach of his creditors. So, as often happens, the moneys were put into the wife's name. It appears on the evidence that she was the agent or nominee of the husband—whatever you like to call it—and they were his moneys still or the firm's moneys.

That being the case, the question became one of law. Has this court any jurisdiction to grant an injunction restraining the defendants from removing these moneys out of the jurisdiction? In this regard, it is as **D** well to take the wife and husband separately: because she is in this country, and he is not.

Counsel for the wife said: " She has these large assets here. You cannot get an injunction against her in regard to these moneys." He referred to what I myself said in *Rasu Maritima S.A.* v. *Perusahaan Pertambangan Minyak Dan Gas Bumi Negara* (*Government of Republic* **E** *of Indonesia intervening*) (*Pertamina*) [1978] Q.B. 644, 659:

> " So far as concerns defendants who are within the jurisdiction of the court and have assets here, it is well-established that the court should not, in advance of any order or judgment, allow the creditor to seize any of the money or goods of the debtor or to use any legal process to do so."
>
> **F**

In making that statement I had only in mind the cases where defendants were permanently settled here and had their assets here. I would not extend that statement so as to cover a case such as this. The wife declared at the beginning that she was a Lebanese citizen. Then, at a very late stage, she altered that and said that she intended to live here permanently. If a defendant is likely to leave England at short notice, **G** a *Mareva* injunction may well be granted.

Then, as regards the husband, counsel suggested that *Siskina* (*Owners of cargo lately laden on board*) v. *Distos Compania Naviera S.A.* [1979] A.C. 210 in the House of Lords precluded a *Mareva* injunction against him. But that was a case where there was no ground for serving the writ out of the jurisdiction. Here there is a cause of action on **H** which the husband could be served out. An amended writ has been issued with amended pleadings. There is a claim for a declaration that the moneys, although standing in the wife's name, are the husband's moneys, and there is a claim for an injunction. There is also a claim for damages for conspiracy and/or breach of trust and/or fraud. That is a claim against both the husband and wife. It has recently been held by Oliver J. that a husband and wife can be liable in a civil action

The Weekly Law Reports, February 15, 1980

113

1 W.L.R.   Chartered Bank v. Daklouche (C.A.)   Lord Denning M.R.

A against them for conspiracy: see *Midland Bank Trust Co. Ltd.* v. *Green* *(No. 3)* [1979] 2 W.L.R. 594. The husband is a proper party to those causes of action and comes within the provisions of R.S.C., Ord. 11, r. 1:

" (1) . . . service of a writ . . . out of the jurisdiction is permissible with the leave of the court . . . (*j*) if the action begun by the writ being properly brought against a person duly served within the B   jurisdiction, a person out of the jurisdiction is a necessary or proper party thereto . . ."

So it seems to me that the husband is brought within the *Mareva* principle of a person who is out of the jurisdiction—and can be served out of the jurisdiction—and has assets here which may disappear unless the injunction is ordered.

C   But I would not limit the *Mareva* principle. It seems to me, as Lord Hailsham of St. Marylebone indicated, that the law is developing in this field. Even when a defendant may be present in this country and is served here, it is quite possible that a *Mareva* injunction can be granted. Mr. Buckley told us that it has already been done from time to time in the commercial court. Eveleigh L.J. made this suggestion: suppose a person was able to be served here because he was on a short visit for a D weekend, or had dropped in for an hour or two, and was served, would that make all the difference as to whether a *Mareva* injunction could be granted or not? That cannot be. The law should be that there is jurisdiction to grant a *Mareva* injunction, even though the defendant may be served here. If he makes a fleeting visit, or if there is a danger that he may abscond or that the assets or moneys may disappear and be E taken out of the reach of the creditors, a *Mareva* injunction can be granted. That seems to me to be this very case. Here is this £70,000 lying in a bank in England which can be removed at the stroke of a pen from England outside the reach of the creditors.

For this reason it seems to me that the right thing would be to continue the injunction granted by Mocatta J., and to grant an injunction preventing the disposition of these moneys until further order of the F court. Notice will be given to the First National Bank, accordingly.

I would allow the appeal accordingly.

EVELEIGH L.J. The *Mareva* injunction is now established in my opinion so far as this court is concerned. I take that also to be the view of Lord Diplock in *Siskina (Owners of cargo lately laden on board)* v. G *Distos Compania Naviera S.A.* [1979] A.C. 210, 254:

" In the view that I take of the instant appeal, however, it can be disposed of on the grounds adopted by Kerr J. and Bridge L.J. They distinguished it from *The Mareva* and *The Pertamina* by which decisions they were bound."

What is required for such an injunction? First, that there should H be assets here, and, secondly, that there should be a substantial cause of action to which the injunction will be ancillary. So far as assets here are concerned, the affidavits, in my view, establish this. It may be argued that one cannot ascertain whether they are the husband's or the wife's or whether they belong to both. In a situation like this, I do not think that is a difficulty which should stand in the way of the court. They were assets of the husband. They were transferred fraudulently (as is claimed) to avoid the husband's liability to the bank. I, therefore,

regard them from the point of view of the husband and the point of   A
view of the wife as assets which could be made the subject of an injunction.

Furthermore, as this case is presented to the court, the money is the
subject matter of the action. I am aware of the difficulties of tracing
money, but it seems to me in the present case that the moneys which
the husband diverted in order to defraud the bank are moneys which
rest in the account which is in the name of the wife in London. That   B
being so, what are the objections to this injunction? It is said that
the wife has been served here, and reliance has been placed on the words
of Lord Hailsham of St. Marylebone in the *Siskina* case [1979] A.C. 210;
and counsel has argued that in the case of a person who is served an
injunction is not appropriate. But Lord Hailsham has not used the word
" served." He says, at p. 261:   C

> " Either the position of a plaintiff making a claim against an English
> based defendant will have to be altered or the principle of the
> *Mareva* cases will have to be modified."

In the first affidavit before this court the wife said:

> " I am a Lebanese citizen and I am not a resident of the United   D
> Kingdom. However, in September 1977 I purchased the house at
> the aforesaid address in Alton, Hampshire, so as to provide a base
> for myself and my husband when we periodically came to England
> to visit our two children, who are being educated at schools here."

That is not the kind of base that I regard Lord Hailsham as referring
to in his speech in the *Siskina* case. According to that affidavit, the wife   E
is certainly not based in this country. It is true that a subsequent
affidavit sought to claim that she was resident here, but I would not
place any reliance upon that. That being so, I take the view that a
Mareva injunction is possible in the case of a person such as the wife
who was served in this country. Were it otherwise the situation would
be ridiculous for, as counsel has pointed out, a person who anticipates
that he is going to be served with notice of a writ will come to this   F
country and accept actual service and thus defeat a *Mareva* injunction.
I do not believe that the law could be so futile.

So one is then concerned to see what causes of action there are.
Fraud is alleged in this case; and, if the money is to be regarded as
strictly speaking the money of the husband, it is pertinent to consider
what part in the fraud he has played which is justiciable in this country.   G
In *Cadogan* v. *Cadogan* [1977] 1 W.L.R. 1041, 1057 Buckley L.J. said:

> " If the voluntary conveyance was tainted with a fraudulent inten-
> tion on the part of the husband to defeat a legitimate claim upon
> him by the plaintiff, can the plaintiff seek to have it set aside to
> such extent as may be necessary to recompense her for any damage
> she may have suffered in consequence of the conveyance, notwith-   H
> standing that that damage has not taken the form of her being
> deprived of a particular claim which the conveyance was actually
> directed to defeating? The position can perhaps be made clearer
> in this way: there were two possibilities at the time of the voluntary
> conveyance: either the husband would succeed in obtaining a decree
> absolute or he would not. If he had survived and had obtained a
> decree absolute, the plaintiff would have been entitled to pursue her

A   claim against him under the Matrimonial Causes Act 1973 for financial provision."

Buckley L.J. went on to say that the wife's claim as pleaded disclosed a cause of action known to law. Goff L.J., concurring, referred to a passage from *Kerr on Fraud and Mistake,* 7th ed. (1952), p. 6 and quoted, at p. 1061:

B   " ' Civil courts have an original, independent, and inherent jurisdiction to relieve against every species of fraud not being relief of a penal nature. Every transfer or conveyance of property, by whatever means it be done, is vitiated by fraud. Deeds, obligations, contracts, awards, judgments, or decrees may be the instruments to which parties may resort to cover fraud, and through which they
C   may obtain the most unrighteous advantages, but none of such devices or instruments will be permitted by a court of equity to obstruct the requirements of justice.' "

Those words are apt to cover the facts alleged in the present case.

It is also alleged that there was a conspiracy by the husband and the wife. I do not regard it as necessary to determine the question whether
D   a husband and wife can conspire together. The fact is that they were acting jointly and acting wrongly in committing a fraud—whether one calls it " conspiracy " or not, to my mind, is not important.

It was also urged in argument that the husband could not be served with notice under R.S.C., Ord. 11 in this case. For the reasons stated by Lord Denning M.R., I am of the opinion that he can. I think that he is a proper party whether or not he is said to be a necessary party as well.
E   I further take the view that on the facts alleged in this case both the husband and wife are perpetuating their fraud here in this country by secreting the money in the bank out of the reach of the bank in Abu Dhabi. By their fraud they are depriving the plaintiffs of their full lawful right to bring an action. That right which they undoubtedly have, be it in Abu Dhabi or be it here, has in effect, if the fraud is successful,
F   been rendered worthless.

For these reasons, I agree that this appeal should be allowed.

SIR STANLEY REES. I agree that this appeal should be allowed and I agree with both judgments which have been delivered.

G   *Appeal allowed.*
                                    Plaintiffs' costs costs in cause.

Solicitors: *Coward Chance; Pothecary & Barratt.*

                                    C. N.

H

A

[COURT OF APPEAL]

* B. (A.) *v.* B. (L.) (MENTAL HEALTH : PATIENT)

1979   July 26   Megaw, Lawton and Browne L.JJ.

B

Mental Disorder—Application for admission to hospital—Nearest relative's objection—Mother refusing to consent to application for daughter's admission—Application for proper person to act as patient's nearest relative—Medical evidence in support —Mental Health Act 1959 (7 & 8 Eliz. 2, c. 72), s. 52 (1)— County Court Rules 1936 (S.R. & O. 1936 No. 626 (L. 17)) (as amended 1960), Ord. 46, r. 18 (5)

A mother, as the nearest relative of a patient in hospital   C
suffering from a mental illness, indicated that she would not
consent to a mental welfare officer applying, under section 26
of the Mental Health Act 1959,[1] as recommended by two
doctors after examining the patient, for the patient's compulsory admission and detention in a hospital for treatment.
The doctors, contrary to the requirements of section 28 (1),
had not carried out separate examinations of the patient
within seven days of each other.   The mental welfare officer   D
made an application to the county court for an order, under
section 52 of the Act, that the area health authority be
authorised to exercise the functions of the patient's nearest
relative on the ground that the mother was unreasonably
objecting to an application being made under section 26.   The
solicitor for the mother was handed copies of the medical
reports during the hearing and there was a short adjournment
for him to consider them.   He did not show the reports to   E
the mother but merely told her that the two doctors had
advised that the patient should be kept in hospital.   The judge
made the order sought.

On an appeal by the mother on the grounds that the
medical evidence in support of the application failed to fulfil
the requirements of the Act and that the failure to show to
the mother the medical reports or to disclose the substance
or any part of the reports bearing on her fitness or conduct   F
material to the application was contrary to the requirements
of the proviso to Ord. 46, r. 18 (5) of the County Court Rules
1936[2] : —

Held, dismissing the appeal, (1) that, on an application
under section 52 of the Act, the question for the court was
whether the nearest relative's objection was unreasonable and,
in determining that question, it was necessary to show that the   G
patient needed to be detained in a hospital; that the section
did not require that the medical evidence strictly complied
with the requirements for an application made under section
26 and it was sufficient, in accordance with Ord. 46, r. 18 (5)
of the County Court Rules, to submit medical evidence to
show that there was a prima facie case for the admission and
detention of the patient (post, pp. 121H—122A, D–E, H).

(2) That, since the mother's legal adviser had had an   H
opportunity to consider the evidence and advise her, there
had been a sufficient compliance with the proviso to Ord. 46,
r. 18 (5) of the rules (post, pp. 121C–D, 122E–F); and that,
therefore, since there was evidence that the patient needed to

[1] Mental Health Act 1959, s. 26: see post, p. 118C.
S. 27: see post, pp. 118H—119B.
S. 52: see post, p. 118E–F.
[2] County Court Rules 1936, Ord. 46, r. 18 (5), as amended: see post, p. 119F–G.

A   be detained in hospital and that the mother was unreasonably
objecting to the order being made, the judge had correctly
made the order under section 52 of the Act.

No cases are referred to in the judgment or were cited in argument.

APPEAL from Judge Forrester-Paton at the Whitby County Court.

B   On May 21, 1979, the mental welfare officer of the area health
authority applied to the court for an order that the area health authority
be appointed to exercise on behalf of the patient the functions under
Part IV of the Mental Health Act 1959 of the nearest relative of the
patient in place of her mother, the respondent to the application. The
main ground of the application was that the mother, despite the advice
of the doctors attending the patient, unreasonably objected to the making
C   of an application for the admission of the patient to hospital for treatment for mental illness. The judge in the county court made the order
sought.

By a notice of appeal dated July 24, 1979, the mother appealed on
the grounds, inter alia, that (i) the judge wrongly admitted in evidence
two documents purporting to be written recommendations in the pre-
D   scribed form of two medical practitioners recommending the admission
of the patient for treatment pursuant to section 26 of the Act of 1959
when those documents were inadmissible because (a) they were not in
the prescribed form, (b) the respective medical examinations of the
patient were more than seven days apart and (c) the substance of the
recommendations, in so far as they constituted reports for the purposes
of Ord. 46, r. 18 of the County Court Rules 1936, as amended, and in
E   so far as they bore on the medical fitness or conduct of the mother to
exercise the functions of the patient's nearest relative, had not been
communicated to the mother; and (ii) the judge erred in law in finding
that the mother's objections to an application for treatment under section
26 of the Act were and had been unreasonable.

F   *Peter Duckworth* for the mother.
William Gage for the mental welfare officer.

MEGAW L.J. I shall ask Lawton L.J. to deliver the first judgment.

LAWTON L.J. This is an appeal by the patient's mother against an
order made in the Whitby County Court, during a sitting at Teesside
G   County Court, by Judge Forrester-Paton, whereby he ordered that the
function of the nearest relative of the patient should, during the
continuance in force of the order, be exercisable by the area health
authority. The mother has submitted for a number of reasons that the
order was improperly made. The substance of her complaints, put
before the court by her counsel, really comes to this: before the area
H   health authority could apply to the judge in the county court for an
order in the terms which he granted, that authority should have had " all
its tackle in order " (to adopt counsel's phrase) for the making of an
application under section 26 of the Mental Health Act 1959.

It will be convenient if I start this judgment by referring to the
relevant provisions of the Act of 1959. That Act deals with mental
disorders. The statutory definition of " mental disorder " is such as to
include mental illness. Under Part IV of the Act provision is made for

Lawton L.J.   B. (A.) v. B. (L.) (C.A.)   [1980]

the " compulsory admission to hospital and guardianship " (this case is   **A**
not concerned with guardianship) of persons who are suffering from
" mental disorder " as defined by the Act. Section 25 of the Act makes
provision for the admission of patients for observation. No question
arises in this case about the legality of an order made under section 25
for the admission of the patient for observation.

Section 26 of the Act is concerned with compulsory admission for   **B**
treatment. Before a patient may be admitted to hospital and detained
for treatment, certain statutory provisions have to be complied with. It
has to be shown that the patient is suffering from mental disorder. It
also has to be shown that the admission to and detention in hospital for
treatment is necessary in the interests of the patient's health or safety
or for the protection of other persons. The section goes on in these
terms: **C**

> " (3) An application for admission for treatment shall be founded
> on the written recommendations in the prescribed form of two
> medical practitioners, including in each case a statement that in the
> opinion of the practitioner the conditions set out in paragraphs
> (a) and (b) of subsection (2) of this section are complied with; . . ."

Then the section goes on to provide what the recommendation " shall   **D**
include." I do not think it necessary to deal with what the recommendation should include.

The powers under section 26 depend upon an application being made
for the patient's admission to and detention in hospital for treatment.
Section 27 of the Act says who can make an application. It provides: **E**

> " (1) Subject to the provisions of this section, an application for the
> admission of a patient for observation or for treatment may be made
> either by the nearest relative of the patient or by a mental welfare officer;
> and every such application shall be addressed to the managers of the
> hospital to which admission is sought and shall specify the qualification
> of the applicant to make the application. (2) An application for   **F**
> admission for treatment shall not be made by a mental welfare officer
> if the nearest relative of the patient has notified that officer, or the
> local health authority by whom that officer is appointed, that he objects
> to the application being made . . ."

In this case the mother notified the mental welfare officer that she
objected to the application being made. It follows, therefore, that section   **G**
52 of the Act has to be considered, because section 52 gives jurisdiction to
the county court to dispense with the consent of the nearest relative who is
objecting to compulsory admission and detention for treatment. Section 52
provides:

> " (1) The county court may, upon application made in accordance with
> the provisions of this section in respect of a patient, by order direct   **H**
> that the functions under this Part of this Act of the nearest relative
> of the patient shall, during the continuance in force of the order, be
> exercisable by the applicant, or by any other person specified in the
> application, being a person who, in the opinion of the court, is a
> proper person to act as the patient's nearest relative and is willing
> to do so."

A Subsection (2) sets out who may make an application under section 52, and those who may make such an application include a mental welfare officer. Subsection (3) provides:

> " An application for an order under this section may be made upon any of the following grounds, that is to say . . . (c) that the nearest relative of the patient unreasonably objects to the making of an application for admission for treatment . . . in respect of the patient; . . ."

As I understand the structure of the Act of 1959 in relation to the compulsory admission and detention for treatment of patients, it is this: once it becomes apparent that a particular person may require compulsory admission to and treatment in hospital, either the mental welfare officer or the nearest relative can consent to the making of an application. When an application is made, that application must comply with the provisions of section 26 of the Act of 1959. But before any question of complying with section 26 arises, the problem of consent has to be dealt with; and where, as in this case, the nearest relative objects, then the county court is empowered to make an order dispensing with the consent of the nearest relative.

D That being the structure of the Act, the question now arises: upon what evidence should the county court act when deciding whether the consent of the nearest relative should be dispensed with. The county court is not concerned with the making of an application under section 26: that is a matter for the appropriate authority. The judge in the county court is concerned with the question of dispensing with the consent of the nearest relative. The judge must have some evidence that compulsory admission to hospital and detention for treatment is necessary. What is that evidence to be?

The rules committee of the county courts made provision for this problem. In 1960 a new rule was added to the County Court Rules 1936, namely, Ord. 46, r. 18. This rule was intended to settle the procedure for making applications to the county court under section 52 of the Act of 1959. Paragraph (5) of the rule provides:

> " On the hearing of the application the court may accept as prima facie evidence of the facts stated therein any report made by a medical practitioner and any report made in the course of his official duties by —(a) a probation officer, or (b) an officer of a local authority or of a voluntary organisation exercising statutory functions on behalf of a local authority, or (c) an officer of a hospital authority: provided that the respondent shall be told the substance of any part of the report bearing on his fitness or conduct which the judge considers to be material to the manner in which the application should be dealt with."

The following points arise with regard to that paragraph. First, the evidence is to be " prima facie evidence ": the party opposing the application for dispensing with consent can call evidence in rebuttal. There is nothing conclusive about the evidence which is tendered in support of the application. Secondly, it is " any report " which may be put in evidence, provided it is made by " a medical practitioner " or is a report made by any other person specified in the rule. Paragraph (5) does not say that the report must be in any prescribed form. It does not say, as section 26 of the Act of 1959 says, that the medical practitioner must be one who, in the words of section 28, is " approved . . . by a local health authority ", or, by a

subsequent amendment, by the Secretary of State. It follows, therefore, A
that any evidence in a report made by a doctor can be looked at by the
judge in the county court for the purposes of making an order dispensing
with consent.

It is clear now, after we have had the benefit of Mr. Gage's submissions,
why this is so. Applications for compulsory admission to and detention
in hospital for treatment often have to be made in an emergency. It is not
always possible to obtain the opinions of medical practitioners approved by B
the Secretary of State or a local health authority. Therefore, *any* doctor
can be called upon for the purposes of supporting an application to dispense
with consent in order to provide the necessary evidence for the county
court. That is what happened in this case.

It is now necessary to set out the relevant facts. At the end of
December 1978 the patient became mentally ill. She had to be admitted C
to hospital. In February 1979 those in charge of her in the hospital (she
was there as a voluntary patient) seem to have been of the opinion that
she was well enough to be discharged to the care of her sister. On April 4,
1979, it was necessary to admit her to hospital again, still as a voluntary
patient. For various reasons, which it is not necessary to go into for the
purposes of this judgment, the mental welfare officer employed by the area D
health authority, on April 10, 1979, thought it right to make an application
for the patient's compulsory admission to hospital and detention there for
observation. Whether he obtained the consent of the mother we do not
know; but no question arises with regard to the section 25 application.
On May 8, 1979, the patient's detention in hospital for observation came to
an end, in the sense that she could no longer be kept there compulsorily.
But in the opinion of the doctor in charge of her, Dr. Seymour-Shove, it E
was necessary to detain her in hospital for treatment. A few days before
May 8 he had made out a report on a hospital statutory form known as
Form 5A, setting out his reasons for thinking that the patient should remain
in hospital. It was clear to those in charge of the patient in the hospital
that there was going to be difficulty about getting the mother's consent to
the patient being detained—the mother being her nearest relative. The
mental welfare officer was authorised to make an application for compul- F
sory admission and detention for treatment under section 26. As I have
already recounted, for the purposes of section 26 examination by two
doctors was necessary; and for the purposes of an application under section
26 the examination either had to be made by the doctors at the same time
or within seven days of each other. A new doctor was called in and he
examined the patient on May 13, which was more than seven days after G
Dr. Seymour-Shove had examined her. The mental welfare officer, on or
about May 15, saw the mother; and it was clear to him that she was
not going to consent to the patient being kept in hospital. As a result the
mental welfare officer thought it necessary to apply to the county court for
an order under section 52. The appropriate county court was Whitby
County Court, but as Whitby County Court only sits infrequently the H
application was in fact heard initially on June 5, 1979, at Scarborough
County Court. At that time the mother was not legally represented.
The judge seems to have thought that she should be given an opportunity of being legally represented, and he adjourned the application
for hearing at a sitting of the Teesside County Court on June 7, 1979.
On June 7 the mother was legally represented; her solicitor was in court to
advise her and to conduct the proceedings on her behalf. Up to June 7 the

A mother had not been shown either of the medical reports upon which the mental welfare officer was basing his application for a section 26 order; but at the hearing on June 7 before Judge Forrester-Paton the solicitor acting for the welfare officer produced the two reports made by Dr. Seymour-Shove and the other psychiatrist and handed them to the solicitor representing the mother. Something seems to have been said to the judge, who suggested that the solicitor representing the mother should have an opportunity of considering what was in the reports, and he adjourned the application for a
B short time. We have been told that the adjournment was for about five minutes. During that time, as appears from an affidavit which was produced today and which was put in with the consent of Mr. Gage appearing for the mental welfare officer, the solicitor acting for the mother did not show her the reports but told her that two doctors had recommended that the patient
C should be kept in hospital. Complaint has been made to this court today that that way of dealing with the reports did not comply with the proviso to Ord. 46, r. 18 (5) of the County Court Rules 1936. In my judgment it did comply with rule 18 (5), and for this reason: it is clear that the object of paragraph (5) is to give the respondent to a section 52 application an opportunity of knowing what is being alleged against him. The paragraph refers specifically to the " part of the report bearing on his fitness or conduct
D which the judge considers to be material to the manner in which the application should be dealt with." If a report is handed to the legal adviser of the respondent to an application in circumstances where the legal adviser can give advice and take instructions, that seems to me to be enough to comply with the proviso to rule 18 (5).

It follows that there is no substance in any complaint made about the way
E the reports were dealt with at the county court hearing.

I turn now to the way in which the mother, through Mr. Duckworth, has put her case. Mr. Duckworth's submission was that before an application could be made to the county court under section 52 the applicant, in this case the mental welfare officer, had to have evidence which complied with the statutory provisions in section 26. He submitted that the evidence which was tendered to the judge did not comply with either section 26 or other
F statutory provisions. He gave a number of reasons. One was that the medical examinations had been more than seven days apart; that sufficient clinical detail was not set out in the reports; that the reports did not specify, as section 26 (3) says they should, why alternative methods were not suitable for the patient. He also complained that, contrary to a provision in the statutory rules governing the prescribed form of report, which are the Mental
G Health (Hospital and Guardianship) Regulations 1960, section 4 of the Act of 1959 had not been printed on the Forms 5A used by the two psychiatrists. He said that these defects in the medical reports before the judge vitiated the whole of the proceedings, because it was reasonable for the mother to say that the provisions of the Act of 1959 and in particular of section 26 had not been complied with. Indeed at one stage of his argument Mr. Duckworth went
H so far as to suggest that if the reports put before the judge did not comply with section 26 no valid application had been made to the county court. In my judgment, that puts the cart before the horse. The object of an application under section 52 is to enable the provisions of section 26 to be brought into operation, and until an application has been dealt with under section 52 the mental welfare officer is not in a position to make an application under section 26. It follows, so it seems to me, that if there were any defects for the purposes of section 26 in the form of the reports tendered to the judge in the

county court they were irrelevant for the purposes of the section 52 applica-   A
tion. The judge had to look at the reports for their medical content : he was
not concerned with their statutory form. The medical content of the two
reports made it clear, in my judgment, that the patient did require
compulsory admission to and detention for treatment in hospital, and therefore the grounds put forward by the mother, through Mr. Duckworth, for
objecting to the making of the section 52 application had no substance in
them and, on the evidence before the judge, she was unreasonable in   B
objecting to the making of an application under section 26.

  Accordingly, I would dismiss the appeal.

  BROWNE L.J. I agree that this appeal should be dismissed, for the
reasons given by Lawton L.J. The crucial issue between the parties in
this case seems to me to be this. Mr. Duckworth, for the appellant mother,   C
has said that for the purposes of section 52 an objection by a nearest relative
cannot be unreasonable unless at the time of the objection or at the time
of the hearing the mental welfare officer is in a position to make an
immediate application under section 26. That is, as counsel put it, that his
tackle is in order for making such an application and, in particular, that
the medical recommendations are in the form which is proper for a section
26 application. Mr. Gage, on the other hand, says that what the court has   D
to decide in a section 52 application is whether or not the nearest relative is
objecting unreasonably to the making of an application under section 26.
The stage of making a section 26 application has not yet been reached, and,
he submits, whether or not the medical reports are in the correct form to
support a section 26 application if and when made is irrelevant.

  In my judgment there is no doubt that Mr. Gage is right in his   E
submission. Lawton L.J. has already stated the arguments in favour of
this view and I need not repeat them. I am bound to say that it seems to
me that, as a matter of construction of the statute, Mr. Gage's submission is
clearly right.

  I agree also with Lawton L.J. in what he said about the effect of
Ord. 46, r. 18 (5) of the County Court Rules 1936. The reports which were   F
used in this case, even if they could be criticised on a section 26 application,
were, on the section 52 application, " prima facie evidence of the facts stated
therein." I also agree with Lawton L.J. that the proviso to that rule was
in this case complied with.

  I express no opinion at all about the points raised by Mr. Duckworth as
to the form of these reports and whether or not they complied with the
statutory requirements applicable to a section 26 application. That question,   G
it seems to me, is not before us in this appeal, though Mr. Gage concedes
that if this was a section 26 application these particular reports would not
be in order because the examinations by the two doctors were more than
seven days apart, contrary to section 28 (1) of the Act of 1959.

  For the reasons given by Lawton L.J., and the reasons I have tried to
express myself, I entirely agree that this appeal should be dismissed.   H

  MEGAW L.J. I agree with the conclusions expressed by Lawton L.J.
and Browne L.J. and with the reasons given by them for those conclusions.
I would add a word about the history of this matter before this court. It
came before this court originally on Monday, July 16, 1979, when the
mother appeared in person on a motion asking for leave to appeal out of
time from the order made by Judge Forrester-Paton in the Whitby County

A Court on June 7. We did not on that occasion have the assistance of
counsel instructed on behalf of the mental welfare officer of the area health
authority. It would be wrong for me to make criticism of that, because
we have not ascertained whether or not there may have been good reasons
for their non-appearance on the first hearing of that motion. On the hearing
of the motion, the mother tried to put before us what were her complaints
about the order that had been made. At her request, we looked at the
B bundle of correspondence which she had, including some of the documents
which have been before us subsequently. We thought it right in the
circumstances to adjourn the hearing of the application for leave to appeal
out of time, and it was accordingly adjourned until the following Monday,
July 23. On that occasion the mother had obtained legal representation.
Mr. Duckworth of counsel appeared on her behalf, instructed by solicitors
C who are not the solicitors who had represented her at the hearing in the
county court. We also had the advantage on that occasion of Mr. Gage
appearing instructed on behalf of the area health authority. All that we
were concerned to deal with on that occasion was the question of leave to
appeal. It was suggested then that it might well be that leave to appeal
out of time was not required because it may be the matter was to be treated
as being a final and not an interlocutory appeal. We granted leave to
D appeal if leave were necessary; and as it was obviously in the interests of
all concerned that the appeal for which leave was thus given should be
heard as soon as possible we directed that it should be expedited, with the
idea that it should be brought on in this court if possible today. I would
like to pay tribute to Mr. Duckworth and the solicitors instructing him for
the steps that they have taken urgently in that short period of time to
E enable the matter to be brought on today, and for the assistance that has
been given to this court. Mr. Duckworth, in my view, has said clearly and
well everything that could possibly be said in support of this appeal. It
is not through any fault of his or of his present instructing solicitors that the
appeal in fact does not succeed.

I agree, as I say, with Lawton and Browne L.JJ. and with the reasons
they have given why this appeal must be dismissed.
F

Appeal dismissed.
No order as to costs.

Solicitors: *Kenyon & Co., Whitby; Colin Brown & Kidson, Whitby.*

G   A. R.

H

A

* J. (H. D.) v. J. (A. M.)

(FINANCIAL PROVISION: VARIATION)

1979 July 5, 6, 9; 30   Sheldon J.

B

*Husband and Wife—Financial provision—Conduct of parties—After
decree absolute — Harassment of ex-husband after financial
and property rights determined—Variation of periodical payments order—Whether subsequent conduct to be taken into
account—Matrimonial Causes Act 1973 (c. 18), s. 31 (7)* [1]

C

The parties, who married in 1960, had two children. They
separated in 1967 and the petitioner was granted a decree nisi
of divorce on the ground of the husband's adultery. The
decree was made absolute in 1970 and, in ancillary proceedings
in 1972, the wife was awarded periodical payments of £1,000
a year less tax and £480 a year for each child. The husband
was also ordered to transfer to the wife his beneficial interest
in the former matrimonial home.

D

After the husband's remarriage in December 1972, the
petitioner, who suffered from schizophrenia, continually
pestered the husband and his second wife by frequent telephone
calls, letters and attempts to see the husband both at his home
and place of work. In 1976 the petitioner gained entry to the
husband's home and attacked the wife with the result that,
on a complaint to the justices, she was found guilty of assault
and was given a three year conditional discharge. She con-

E

tinued to harass the husband and the wife and that harassment
continued notwithstanding that, in 1978, an injunction was
made restraining her from molesting them. The husband, who
had ceased to make periodical payments to the petitioner
under the order of 1972, applied for a variation of that order.
The petitioner was given leave to apply for an increase in
the order and it was not seriously contested that, apart from
her conduct, she would be entitled to a substantial increase in

F

the amount.

On the question whether the petitioner's conduct was a
factor affecting the amount of the order: —

Held, (1) that, on an application to vary or discharge an
order under section 31 of the Matrimonial Causes Act 1973,
conduct after the marriage had been dissolved and after the
right to financial provision and property had been determined
was part of " all the circumstances of the case " within the

G

meaning of subsection (7) if it affected the other party's way
of life and standard of living to such a degree that it would
be repugnant to justice if the court made a full award (post,
p. 131C–G).

Jones (*M. A.*) v. *Jones* (*W.*) [1976] Fam. 8, C.A. applied.
W. v. *W.* (*Financial Provision: Lump Sum*) [1976] Fam.
107 distinguished.

H

(2) That, although the petitioner's behaviour was partly
due to her illness, she had deliberately harassed the husband
and his wife to such a degree that it would be repugnant to
justice to ignore that behaviour and increase the periodical
payments to the full amount; that, although it might become
repugnant to justice to award the petitioner any sum if she
continued in her conduct, the circumstances at the present

[1] Matrimonial Causes Act 1973, s. 31 (7): see post, p. 128F.

A　　time were such that it would be fair to the parties to continue the order for periodical payments at £1,000 a year and, since that sum was now a small maintenance order, the payments should be made without deduction of tax (post, p. 133A–H).

The following cases are referred to in the judgment:

Hadkinson v. *Hadkinson* [1952] P. 285; [1952] 2 All E.R. 567, C.A.

B　　*Jones (M. A.)* v. *Jones (W.)* [1976] Fam. 8; [1975] 2 W.L.R. 606; [1975] 2 All E.R. 12, C.A.

Katz v. *Katz* [1972] 1 W.L.R. 955; [1972] 3 All E.R. 219.

W. v. *W. (Financial Provision: Lump Sum)* [1976] Fam. 107; [1975] 3 W.L.R. 752; [1975] 3 All E.R. 970.

Wachtel v. *Wachtel* [1973] Fam. 72; [1973] 2 W.L.R. 366; [1973] 1 All E.R. 829, C.A.

C　　*West* v. *West* [1978] Fam. 1; [1977] 2 W.L.R. 933; [1977] 2 All E.R. 705, C.A.

Williams v. *Williams* [1964] A.C. 698; [1963] 3 W.L.R. 215; [1963] 2 All E.R. 994, H.L.(E.).

The following additional case, supplied by the courtesy of counsel, was cited in argument:

D　　*Bateman* v. *Bateman* [1979] Fam. 25; [1979] 2 W.L.R. 377.

SUMMONS

On March 5, 1969, the wife was granted a decree nisi on the ground of the husband's adultery. The decree was made absolute on March 13, 1970. Custody of the two children of the marriage was granted to the wife. On December 18, 1972, by consent, Mr. Registrar Stranger-Jones

E　　ordered the husband to make periodical payments of £1,000 a year, less tax, to the wife; £430 a year for each child and that on or before December 31, 1973, he would transfer to the wife the whole of his beneficial interest in the matrimonial home and in the assurance policy with the mortgagees upon the wife undertaking to assume responsibility for the mortgage repayments and premiums from June 1, 1973. On

F　　February 28, 1978, the husband filed a notice of his intention to apply for a variation of the periodical payments order of December 18, 1972. At the hearing which was in chambers Sheldon J. gave leave to the wife to apply for an increase in the periodical payments order. On July 30, 1979, Sheldon J. delivered judgment in open court.

The facts are stated in the judgment.

G　　*Michael Connell* for the respondent husband.
Quintin Iwi for the petitioner wife.

Cur. adv. vult.

July 30. SHELDON J. read the following judgment. The parties to

H　　these proceedings were married on June 25, 1960, when the petitioner was 32 and the respondent (the husband) was 27 years of age. They have two children—a son, born on February 5, 1961, and a daughter born on August 18, 1963. In general terms, however, the marriage was never happy—and in 1967 the husband left home, the children (who were then only 6 and 4) remaining with the petitioner.

In the same year, 1967, the husband commenced his association with his present wife—and on November 17, 1967, relying on their adultery,

the petitioner presented her petition for divorce. The petition was not   A
defended; and in due course their marriage was dissolved by a decree
nisi of March 5, 1969, which was made absolute on March 13, 1970.

On December 18, 1972, on the petitioner's application for ancillary
relief, including variation of settlement and periodical payments, orders
were made, by consent, first that the husband would make periodical
payments to the petitioner of £1,000 per annum less tax for herself and   B
of £480 per annum for each child; and second that, on or before
December 31, 1973, he would transfer to her the whole of his beneficial
interest in the matrimonial home and in the assurance policy with the
mortgagees, the Equitable Life Assurance Society, upon the petitioner's
undertaking, with effect from June 1, 1973, to assume responsibility for
all further mortgage repayments and premiums.

In fact, although all further payments after that date (June 1, 1973)   C
in connection with the mortgage and assurance policy have been paid by
the petitioner wife, the property itself has not yet been transferred to her
—a delay which has been due in part to the unwillingness of the mortgagees to concur in the transaction and partly to other factors for none of
which, as I am satisfied, was the husband in any way to blame. Nor,
indeed, in my opinion, has that delay had any effect whatever upon the   D
events which have led to the application now before me. I also accept
that the husband is prepared to take whatever steps may be required of
him to give effect to the order.

On the same day as that on which the order was made (December 18,
1972) the husband and his present wife were married; and on November
20, 1974, their child, C, was born. Regrettably, however, from the date of
their marriage the petitioner has conducted against them what, in my   E
view, the husband, with some justification, has described in an affidavit
of September 7, 1977, as " a sustained campaign of malice and persecution," subjecting them to relentless and unwelcome streams of letters and
telephone calls, ranging " from the irrational to the violently abusive "
and in some instances containing false reports of some serious accident
to their (the petitioner's and the husband's) daughter. In addition she   F
has repeatedly made attempts to see him or to speak to him at his place
of work. The telephone calls to his home, indeed, became so disturbing
—on one occasion in July 1974 amounting to some 20 or more in the
course of the evening—that in 1975 the husband was obliged to go " ex-
directory " and to have his telephone number changed.

The petitioner also became an unwelcome caller at the husband's
home, and, on one such visit, on August 28, 1976, gained admittance   G
and violently attacked the husband's present wife, punching her in the
face and stamping on her foot. Her violence, indeed, was so extreme that
it was only with difficulty that she was prevented from going upstairs to
the child C and was evicted. It was an incident which led, after a contested hearing, to her conviction on February 8, 1977, at Horseferry Rd.
Magistrates' Court of assault and to her then being given a three-year   H
conditional discharge and being ordered to pay £25 towards the complainant's costs. It is difficult, moreover, not to believe that in considering that order for costs the justices were not aware that the incident
had so incensed the husband that from its date and until the date of the
hearing he had paid little or nothing under the periodical payments order
of December 18, 1972—an accumulation of arrears, still outstanding, of
some £814·98. Nor, to date, has the petitioner taken any steps to enforce

A those arrears or to apply for the leave to do so which, by reason of the lapse of time, has now become necessary by virtue of section 32 (1) of the Matrimonial Causes Act 1973 nor, somewhat surprisingly, did Mr. Iwi on her behalf accede to the invitation to make such an application at this hearing before me.

Unfortunately that conviction seems to have had little effect in stemming the petitioner's harassment of the husband and his wife. The
B flow of letters still continued, she continued to call at or to telephone his place of work and she was unable to keep away from his home. On one such occasion, June 18, 1977, indeed, as I accept, she seriously alarmed the husband's wife (who, for protection, had put the door on a chain) by hammering at it for an appreciable time after she had been refused admittance.

C In these circumstances, on February 28, 1978, the husband issued his present summons for variation of the periodical payments order of December 18, 1972, asking in effect that, because of her conduct, the periodical payments for the petitioner herself should be reduced to a nominal amount. Even that, however, failed to curb her activities— with the result that on May 11, 1978, application was made by the
D husband for an injunction to restrain her from molesting him or his wife, from communicating with them save through solicitors and from calling at or loitering in the vicinity of their home. At three successive hearings, moreover, on May 23, June 20 and July 4, 1978, orders were made to such effect. Even so, the petitioner would not leave them alone. As soon as August 18, 1978, she was back at their house, pounding on the door to gain admittance. She was again at the house at 9.40 in the
E evening on September 2, 1978; again during the evening of December 5, 1978; and again during the early evening of March 10, 1979, when by ringing the bell and by hammering on the door she made repeated efforts to gain admission. In the meanwhile, on several occasions, she has attempted to communicate with the husband through his office.

In the event and perhaps not surprisingly, application was made for
F the petitioner's committal for breaches of the injunction. It was heard on May 25, 1979, before Judge Callman when the judge, although adjourning the application generally with liberty to restore, made it plain that, if the matter were restored before him, any further breach would result in an immediate custodial sentence. Fortunately, perhaps, for all concerned, for the greater part of the time since then the husband and his wife have been on holiday—though it is some reflection on the
G state of affairs that they have gone out of their way to keep the petitioner in ignorance of their movements.

Thus it is that I now have to adjudicate upon the husband's application for variation of the order of December 18, 1972, by the reduction to no more than a nominal amount of the order for periodical payments to be made for the petitioner.

H Before doing so, however, I should give brief details of their present incomes and of the situations of their two children. As to their incomes it is sufficient to say that the husband, after some 20 years with the same employers, is currently in receipt of a gross salary of £9,941 per annum— his only source of income and one that is precarious to this extent that he is on sick leave and not expected back to work until September 1979 after an orchidectomy (involving the removal of a malignant tumour) on October 25, 1978. Happily the prognosis is good, although he is still

128

suffering from the after-effects of the operation and of the radiotherapy   A
which followed it, and still has to undergo regular checks to ensure that
there is no sign of any recurrent disease.

The petitioner, however, is not employed—so that her only present
income is whatever may be provided by the husband, together with a
disability allowance from the Department of Health and Social Security
currently amounting to some £25·45 per week, and a further £5 per week   B
by way of child benefit.

In general terms, their only significant assets are the homes in which
they live—the petitioner's home (hers or to be hers by virtue of the
order of December 18, 1972) representing (apart from its contents, most
of which she also appears to enjoy) the sole asset of the parties at the
end of their marriage, of a present value of some £30,000, subject to a
mortgage of £4,000 upon which she has to pay by way of premiums and   C
mortgage repayments some £32 per month—and the husband's house,
one that he bought in 1975 for about £19,000 on which there is outstanding a mortgage of £15,460 repayable at the monthly rate of £181·77.

As regards the children—for some years after the husband left home
both children lived with the petitioner. In about 1974, however, the boy
(then 13) left home to live first with an aunt and then with his maternal   D
grandmother in Surrey, where he also went to school. It also appears
likely that, as he is now 18 and has been offered work in that neighbourhood, this summer term at school has been his last. The girl, however,
still lives with the petitioner and, at the age of almost 16, still has at
least two more years of education before her. It has also been agreed
between the parties that the order of December 18, 1972, should be
varied by increasing the periodical payments for her to the rate of £624   E
per annum.

As to the relationship between the husband and his children, as it
has not been the subject of any detailed investigation, I will say no more
than that it has clearly been subjected to great strain by the bitterness
of feeling between their parents.

Section 31 (7) of the Matrimonial Causes Act 1973 provides that in   F
exercising its power to vary an order (in this instance for periodical payments) previously made by it:

"... the court shall have regard to all the circumstances of the
case, including any change in any of the matters to which the court
was required to have regard when making the order to which the
application [to vary] relates ..."   G

Some of the particular matters to which the court was required to have
regard when making the original order are specified in section 25 (1) of the
Act of 1973 which concludes by enjoining the court:

"... to place the parties, so far as it is practicable and, having regard
to their conduct, just to do so, in the financial position in which
they would have been if the marriage had not broken down ..."   H

In these circumstances, in general terms, the husband's contention is
that, notwithstanding that the original order was an order made by consent, the conduct of the petitioner since the dissolution of their marriage
is a matter to which the court should now have regard in deciding
whether or to what extent it is just that the periodical payments should
continue.

A   It is a contention which has been opposed by Mr. Iwi on behalf of the petitioner on several grounds which may be tabulated: (i) that as the husband is himself in contempt of the order in question (in having failed to pay the arrears of £814·98 or to transfer to the petitioner his share in their previous matrimonial home) it is not open to him, or the court should not permit him, to seek to have it amended; (ii) that

B   the conduct of a party, after dissolution of their marriage, as it could no longer be described as " matrimonial conduct," cannot be taken into account; (iii) that, in any event, such conduct could be considered only if it was " both gross and obvious " in the sense in which that expression is used in *Wachtel* v. *Wachtel* [1973] Fam. 72 and that, on the facts, the petitioner's behaviour falls well below that standard; (iv) that even if conduct after divorce can be considered at all, it cannot be brought into

C   account after the party's right to financial relief (whether by way of lump sum, variation of settlement or periodical payments) has finally been established—as, in this case, they were by the order of December 18, 1972; (v) that, having regard to the parallel proceedings taken by the husband for an injunction and for the petitioner's committal, now also to reduce her entitlement to periodical payments would impose a double penalty upon her for the same behaviour; (vi) that, in all the

D   circumstances, the petitioner's conduct was not such as warranted her being deprived of more than a relatively small proportion of the periodical payments to which she would otherwise have been entitled.

In conclusion, turning defence into attack, Mr. Iwi at the outset of the hearing, asked for (and was given by me) leave to the petitioner herself to apply for an increase in the periodical payments ordered on

E   December 18, 1972. As to that, he submitted (nor did I understand this seriously to be challenged by Mr. Connell on the husband's behalf) that, on financial considerations alone, a proper rate would be that of £2,500 per annum.

It will be convenient to deal with these propositions seriatim. In my opinion, it is clear from the authorities, as in the event Mr. Iwi conceded,

F   that the court always has a discretion whether or not to permit a party in contempt to be heard on some further application by him in the same suit—balancing

   " the plain and unqualified obligation of every person against, or in respect of whom, an order is made by a court of competent jurisdiction, to obey it unless and until that order is discharged . . ."

G   against the need to do justice between the parties in the particular circumstances of the case: see *Hadkinson* v. *Hadkinson* [1952] P. 285 in which Romer L.J. gives examples of what he describes as exceptions from the general rule which would debar a party in contempt from being heard by the courts whose order he has disobeyed. In my view, the court's discretion in such a case is unfettered; but if guidelines are required, they are

H   to be found in the judgment in *Hadkinson's* case of Denning L.J., which after a review of the history of the general rule, contains the passages at p. 298:

   " It is a strong thing for a court to refuse to hear a party to a cause and it is only to be justified by grave considerations of public policy. It is a step which a court will only take when the contempt itself impedes the course of justice and there is no other effective means of securing his compliance. . . . Applying this principle I am

of the opinion that the fact that a party to a cause has disobeyed A
an order of the court is not of itself a bar to his being heard, but
if his disobedience is such that, so long as it continues, it impedes
the course of justice in the cause, by making it more difficult for the
court to ascertain the truth or to enforce the orders which it may
make, then the court may in its discretion refuse to hear him until
the impediment is removed or good reason is shown why it should   B
not be removed."

I have stated already that I do not regard the husband as having
been in contempt in one of the respects suggested by Mr. Iwi—that he
was not in any way to blame for the failure to date to transfer to the
petitioner his interest in their previous matrimonial home. On the other
hand he was clearly in contempt of the order of December 18, 1972, C
in discontinuing for a time after the incident of August 26, 1976, the
periodical payments to which she was prima facie entitled, although the
reason for his action is not difficult to understand. However that may
be, in the exercise of my discretion in accordance with the principles to
which I have referred, I have no doubt that I should not, because of
that contempt, now refuse to hear the husband's application for the
variation of the order in question.   D

I would add that, for similar reasons, I am satisfied that I should not
refuse to hear the petitioner's cross-application for an increase in the
periodical payments—notwithstanding that, on her own admission, she
had committed several " serious breaches " of the injunction made on
July 4, 1978.

I also reject Mr. Iwi's second submission—that, on an application to E
vary an order for periodical payments, the court cannot take into account
a party's conduct after the dissolution of the marriage. In my judgment,
indeed, not only is *Jones* v. *Jones* [1976] Fam. 8 clear authority to
the contrary, but to accede to such a proposition would be to ignore
the provisions of section 31 (7) of the Matrimonial Causes Act 1973 and
to act contrary to plain justice and common sense. Mr. Iwi has argued
that that decision is obiter because, although the point was raised in F
argument, as stated by Orr L.J., it was " certainly not pressed "—possibly
because its lack of merit had soon become apparent. I am not prepared
so to treat the judgment. In that case the conduct in question was
that of a husband who, two months after the decree absolute, had
violently attacked the wife with a razor. It was conduct which it was
held could be applied to increase the wife's claim for financial relief. G
Orr L.J. said, at p. 15:

"a case in which the conduct of the husband had been of such
a gross kind that it would be offensive to a sense of justice that
it should not be taken into account."

As was stressed by Megaw L.J., moreover, the word " conduct " in the
context of section 25 (1) of the Matrimonial Causes Act 1973 (and so, H
in my view, by reference in the context of a review within section 37 (7)):
" is not to be treated as being confined to matrimonial misconduct."

I also reject Mr. Iwi's further submission that if a party's conduct
after divorce is relevant at all to a claim for financial relief, it is to be
limited to conduct between the divorce and the date upon which that
claim is finally adjudicated. Certainly that was not a question which
arose for decision in *Jones* v. *Jones* [1976] Fam. 8 as the husband's

A conduct in that case occurred during that interval and the court was concerned merely to decide whether it could be taken into account in determining the parties' appropriate shares in the family assets. Clearly also, in the present context, a party's conduct after the making of a financial provision or property adjustment order is relevant only to those cases to which section 31 of the Act of 1973 applies—that is, to those cases in which the court has power to vary or even to discharge the

B original order. It cannot, therefore, affect orders already made for a lump sum or for the adjustment or settlement of property save in the limited respects provided by section 31 (2) (d) and (e) and section 31 (4). Thus, in general terms, in regard to orders made in divorce proceedings or on or after the grant of a decree of divorce, the only cases to which section 31 applies, and accordingly to which conduct after the making

C of the order could be relevant, are those which provide for periodical payments or payments of maintenance or of lump sum instalments. In my judgment, however, a party's conduct between the making of the original order and the hearing of the application for its discharge or variation may be as much a part of "all the circumstances of the case" and as material to the court's consideration as his conduct (between the decree absolute and the making of the orders for financial provision)

D was held to be in *Jones* v. *Jones* [1976] Fam. 8.

Clearly, in this context, any conduct might be relevant to the extent that it effectively reduced the other party's means, income or ability to earn his living—where, to adopt the words of Sir George Baker P. in *W.* v. *W.* (*Financial Provision: Lump Sum*) [1976] Fam. 107: "it directly affects the (other party's) finances." In that case, however, Sir George

E Baker P. was concerned to exclude from consideration behaviour on the part of the wife which, after the dissolution of their marriage, was of "no concern to her ex-husband." I do not understand him as having intended to deal with the wider question now before me.

In my judgment, indeed, any conduct by a party may be relevant in the present context which, whether or not it directly affects the other's finances, is such as to interfere with his or her life and standard

F of living and which is covered by the well-known passage in the judgment of Lord Denning M.R. in *Wachtel* v. *Wachtel* [1973] Fam. 72, 90 —that is conduct which is:

"'both obvious and gross' so much so that to order one party to support another whose conduct falls into this category is repugnant to anyone's sense of justice."

G
Or to put the question into other words, as used by Sir George Baker P. in *W.* v. *W.* (*Financial Provision: Lump Sum*) [1976] Fam. 107, 110, is the conduct:

"of the kind that would cause the ordinary mortal to throw up his hands and say, 'Surely, that woman is not going to be given any money,' or 'is not going to get a full award.'"

H
In Mr. Iwi's submission, however, the petitioner's conduct since the order of December 18, 1972, however reprehensible, falls far short of any such standard. I disagree.

Two important features in this case are the medical histories of the two parties. According to the medical reports placed before me the petitioner suffers from chronic schizophrenia in respect of which she has been "a very longstanding" hospital patient, both as an in-patient and

A

out-patient, " almost continuously since her first admission in 1950."
It is an illness in which rational intervals have been punctuated by bouts
of depression, outbursts of physical violence, threats of suicide and other
irrational manifestations. Unfortunately, moreover, she has only
allowed herself to be treated sporadically with medication, so that,
although she has shown some signs of improvement over the years, this
has not been as great as might otherwise have been achieved. Thus on
August 28, 1978, the consultant psychiatrist whose patient she is was
able to say only that there was a " reasonable chance " that she would
obey the injunction that was then in force and that was renewed on
July 4, 1978. In fact, she did not obey its terms—and in a later report
of May 18, 1979, he recorded that " her willingness or ability to co-
operate with treatment had been just as sporadic " and that, in the
interval, there had been several occasions upon which she had behaved
" very aggressively "—conduct which was manifested usually by " hair-
pulling or smashing furniture."

B

C

The husband, too, has a psychiatric history and, indeed, it was in
consequence of that that on an admission to hospital for treatment he
first met the petitioner. His condition, from which he has suffered for
several years, is described as one of " nervous depression," as to which,
in a report of May 1978, the consultant psychiatrist who had been
treating him wrote:

D

"Although he has, with the aid of treatment, been enabled to remain at work during most of this time, his capacity is seriously
impaired by exacerbations of the symptoms of his illness, particularly
by inability to concentrate, headaches, insomnia, morbid anxiety
and feelings of depression."

E

He also added:

"An important factor in bringing about these exacerbations and,
indeed, in perpetuating the illness, has been the anxiety induced by
the vagaries of [the petitioner's] behaviour " and that " continuation of this strain entails a real risk . . . of further breakdown and
loss of earning capacity."

F

So also, in a further report of March 28, 1979, he wrote that the
petitioner's behaviour was continuing to adversely affect his health and
added:

"The continued apprehension about the possibility of a recurrence
of an assault on, or other harm to his (present) wife, as well as
her own anxiety in this connection, contributes significantly to
his state of anxiety and to the consequent morbid depression."

G

I would add also that, having seen both the husband and his present
wife (in addition to the petitioner), I have no doubt as to the genuineness of their fears: nor am I prepared to say they are without justification. Clearly also these fears have significantly affected their way and
enjoyment of life, even to the extent of having made them consider
leaving England (and the husband's employment) for permanent residence
abroad.

H

In my judgment, indeed, as I have already stated, the husband has
cause for saying, as in his affidavit of September 7, 1977, that the
petitioner has been making his life and that of his present wife " a

A burden and a misery " and for describing her conduct as " a sustained campaign of malice and persecution."

I accept, of course, that the petitioner's behaviour is due to some—may be to a considerable—extent to her illness, although I cannot escape the conclusion that it has also contained a significant intentional element in the sense that she has deliberately set out to harass the husband and his present wife. I am also of the opinion that, in assessing the

B gravity of a party's conduct on the financial provision, the test to be applied is similar to that propounded by Lord Reid in *Williams* v. *Williams* [1964] A.C. 698 in regard to " cruelty," as applied by Sir George Baker P. in *Katz* v. *Katz* [1972] 1 W.L.R. 955 in connection with " behaviour " in the context of section 2 (1) (b) of the Divorce Reform Act 1969: that is to say that a party's conduct would be of

C sufficient gravity to affect the issue if the facts are such that, after making all allowances for his disabilities and for the temperaments of both parties, the character and gravity of his behaviour was of such a nature that it would be repugnant to anyone's sense of justice to ignore it in deciding the provision to be made by one for the other or what should be their appropriate shares in the family assets. In *West* v. *West* [1978] Fam. 1, indeed, it was emphasised that no moral judgment is necessarily

D to be inferred from a finding that a party's conduct was of such a nature. In all the circumstances, moreover, as I have already indicated, I am satisfied that the petitioner's conduct since December 18, 1972, has fallen within that category.

In deciding how that finding is to be reflected in financial terms, it will be convenient to consider together the cross-applications of both

E parties. In all the circumstances, moreover, bearing in mind particularly that the wife still has a contribution to make by bringing up their daughter until her education is completed, I am of the opinion that although it would not be doing justice between the parties to give her what might be described as a full award of periodical payments, she should by no means be deprived of all financial provision in that respect.

F I bear in mind also (a) that the husband has abandoned all claim to a share in their previous matrimonial home, substantially their only family asset; and (b) that, in the circumstances I have described, the periodical payments due under the order of December 18, 1972, are £814·98 in arrear—arrears which, as it seems to me, she is unlikely ever to be able to recover. Indeed, as she ignored the opportunity offered to her to apply in these proceedings for leave to enforce them, I consider it unlikely

G that some later application under section 32 (1) of the Matrimonial Causes Act 1973 would be regarded with favour. I have regard also to the figures suggested by Mr. Iwi as appropriate to a full order—although I am not persuaded that, if she were to make a real effort, the petitioner could not obtain at least some part-time employment to supplement her income. In the event, taking a broad view of the matter, I have come

H to the conclusion that a fair result would be, in this context, to dismiss both applications and to leave the periodical payments to the petitioner at the present rate of £1,000 per annum—although in such an event, as that is now a small maintenance order, the payments would be made without deduction of tax.

Nor do I accept Mr. Iwi's final submission—that, having regard to the previous proceedings initiated by the husband for an injunction and for the committal of the petitioner to deprive her now of a right

to a full award would be to penalise her twice. Apart from the fact **A**
that no order was made and no penalty was imposed on the committal
application, a restraint on future behaviour does not amount automatically to forgiveness for the past and for a court to punish a party
for contempt of its order cannot preclude the victim from claiming any
other relief to which he may be entitled.

I would add also this by way of warning to the petitioner—that, in **B**
my opinion, if she were to persist in her harassment of the husband or his
present family, the stage might well be reached at which a court would
say that it would be repugnant to anyone's sense of justice that the
husband should continue to maintain her at all.

There is one further matter I would mention. In the course of the
hearing the husband, by counsel, made an open offer to the petitioner
to compound her entitlement to periodical payments for herself by the **C**
immediate payment to her of £6,000—the most that he said he could
obtain on a further mortgage of his house—the only condition being
that £4,000 of that sum should be used to discharge the mortgage on
their previous matrimonial home. It was an offer which the petitioner
rejected. It would, however, have been one further step to the clean
break which, in my view, would be likely to benefit both parties; nor, **D**
having regard to all the circumstances and to their respective states of
health, is it, in my view, without merit. As it was not a solution, however, which I had any jurisdiction to impose, I will say no more about
it.

In conclusion—dealing with both applications together—there will be
no order on either application save that (1) the order of December 18,
1972, of Mr. Registrar Stranger-Jones will be varied to provide (a) that, **E**
with effect from July 9, 1979, the periodical payments to be made by
the husband to the petitioner for herself shall be at the rate of £1,000
per annum, payable monthly without deduction of tax; (b) that, with
effect from July 9, 1979, the periodical payments to be made to the
daughter shall be at the rate of £624 per annum payable monthly; (2)
that there be no order as to costs, save legal aid taxation of the **F**
petitioner's costs.

> *Order accordingly.*
> *Legal aid taxation.*
> *Leave to appeal refused.*

October 17, 1979. The Court of Appeal (Ormrod, Browne and
Donaldson L.JJ.) refused the petitioner's application for leave to appeal. **G**

Solicitors: *Charles Russell and Co*; *Lambert, Hale & Procter.*

                 M. B. D.

                    H

A

[HOUSE OF LORDS]

* NEWSTEAD (INSPECTOR OF TAXES) . . . APPELLANT

AND

FROST . . . . RESPONDENT

B

1979 Dec. 17, 18;   Lord Diplock, Viscount Dilhorne,
1980 Jan. 31   Lord Salmon, Lord Fraser of Tullybelton
and Lord Keith of Kinkel

Revenue—Income tax—Overseas earnings—United Kingdom resident's earnings abroad — Tax avoidance scheme — Taxpayer's
C   *overseas activities carried out on behalf of partnership between taxpayer and foreign company — Taxpayer's share of profits not remitted to United Kingdom—Whether company entitled to enter into partnership — Whether income from overseas activities partnership income—Whether taxpayer's unremitted share of partnership profits subject to United Kingdom tax— Income and Corporation Taxes Act 1970 (c. 10), ss. 109 (1) (2), 122, 153 (1)* [1]

D

The taxpayer, who was a successful television entertainer and performer in the United Kingdom, decided to exploit his talents in the United States while retaining residence in the United Kingdom. A scheme was devised under which he was to carry out all his overseas activities as a partner in a partnership between himself and a company incorporated in the Bahamas. The objects of the Bahamian company were, inter
E   alia: " To carry on business as bankers, capitalists, financiers, concessionaires and merchants and to undertake and carry on and execute all kinds of financial commercial trading or other operations . . ." and to enter into partnership with any company or person carrying on any business which the company was authorised to carry on. The partnership was to carry on the business of " exploiting copyrights and interests in copyrights and in the businesses of television and film consultants and advisers, publicity agents and providers of publicity services
F   and facilities throughout the world outside the United Kingdom . . ." No money was remitted to the United Kingdom from the taxpayer's share of the profits from the partnership. All the partnership activities took place abroad. The taxpayer was assessed to income tax under Case II of Schedule D in respect of profits of the trade, business or profession of entertainer for the year 1969–70 in the sum of £30,000; 1970–
G   71 an additional assessment of £29,256 and for 1971–72 of

[1] Income and Corporation Taxes Act 1970, s. 109: " (1) Tax under Schedule D shall be charged under the Cases set out in subsection (2) below, and subject to and in accordance with the provisions of the Tax Acts applicable to those Cases respectively. (2) The Cases are—. . . Case V—tax in respect of income arising from possessions out of the United Kingdom, not being income consisting of emoluments of any office or employment; . . ."
   S. 122: " (1) Subject to the provisions of this section and sections 123 and 124
H   below, income tax chargeable under Case IV or Case V of Schedule D shall be computed on the full amount of the income arising in the year preceding the year of assessment, whether the income has been or will be received in the United Kingdom or not . . . (2) Subsection (1) above shall not apply—. . . (b) to any income which is immediately derived by a person from the carrying on by him of any trade, profession or vocation, either solely or in partnership, . . . (3) In the cases mentioned in subsection (2) above, the tax shall, subject to sections 123 and 124 below, be computed—. . . (b) in the case of tax chargeable under Case V, on the full amount of the actual sums received in the United Kingdom in the year preceding the year of assessment from remittances payable in the United Kingdom, . . ."
   S. 153 (1): see post, p. 138D–E.

Newstead v. Frost (H.L.(E.))   **[1980]**

£115,398. On the taxpayer's appeal against those assessments   A
the general commissioners decided that the partnership income
was income arising from " possessions out of the United
Kingdom " within section 109 (2) of the Income and Corporation Taxes Act 1970 and that no tax was payable on that
income under sections 122 and 153 of the Act as no remittances to the United Kingdom were made. The decision was
upheld by Browne-Wilkinson J. and the Court of Appeal.

On appeal by the Crown: —   B

Held, dismissing the appeal, (1) that on its true construction
the partnership agreement bound the partners, not to act as
entertainers but to procure engagements for entertainers, not
excluding the taxpayer, and to that extent they were entitled
to exploit his skills as well as theirs, so that the agreement
was not invalid on the ground that he bound himself to do
either what the company could not do or what he could not
do himself; that the receipts from taxpayer's activities were   C
in those circumstances receipts of the partnership and, accordingly, the taxpayer was not liable to be taxed under Case II
of Schedule D (post, pp. 139H—140c, 141H).

(2) That in the objects clause of the memorandum of
association of the company the words " all kinds of financial
commercial trading or other operations " were wide enough
to empower the company to carry on the business of the
partnership (post, p. 141F).   D

Decision of the Court of Appeal [1978] 1 W.L.R. 1441;
[1979] 2 All E.R. 129 affirmed.

The following case is referred to in their Lordships' opinions:

De Beers Consolidated Mines Ltd. v. *Howe* [1906] A.C. 455, H.L.(E.).

The following additional cases were cited in argument: E

Brighton College v. *Marriott* [1926] A.C. 192, H.L.(E.).
Christophers v. *White* (1847) 10 Beav. 523.
Collins v. *Carey* (1839) 2 Beav. 128.
Colquhoun v. *Brooks* (1889) 14 App.Cas. 493, H.L.(E.).
Cotman v. *Brougham* [1918] A.C. 514, H.L.(E.).
Cox v. *Hickman* (1860) 8 H.L.Cas. 268, H.L.(E.).
Davies v. *Braithwaite* [1931] 2 K.B. 628.   F
Fenston v. *Johnstone* (1940) 23 T.C. 29.
Finsbury Securities Ltd. v. *Inland Revenue Commissioners* [1966] 1
    W.L.R. 1402; [1966] 3 All E.R. 105, H.L.(E.).
Gardner and Bowring, Hardy & Co. Ltd. v. *Inland Revenue Commis-
sioners* (1930) 15 T.C. 602.
Hall (George) & Son v. *Platt* (1954) 35 T.C. 440.
Inland Revenue Commissioners v. *Maxse* [1919] 1 K.B. 647, C.A.   G
Lupton v. *F.A. and A.B. Ltd.* [1972] A.C. 634; [1971] 3 W.L.R. 670;
    [1971] 3 All E.R. 948, H.L.(E.).
Poulton v. *London & South Western Railway Co.* (1867) L.R. 2 Q.B. 534.
Rolloswin Investments Ltd. v. *Chromolit Portugal Cutelarias e Produtos
Metalicos S.A.R.L.* [1970] 1 W.L.R. 912; [1970] 2 All E.R. 673.
San Paulo Brazilian Railway Co. Ltd. v. *Carter* [1896] A.C. 31, H.L.(E.).

       H

APPEAL from the Court of Appeal.

This case arose from assessments to income tax made under Case II
of Schedule D (" profession or vocation ") for three years of assessment 1969–70, 1970–71 and 1971–72 on the present respondent, David
Paradine Frost, a television entertainer. It was at all times common
ground that those assessments covered a profession or vocation of
entertainer carried on by him in the United Kingdom. However, the

A appellant, Michael David Eric Newstead (Inspector of Taxes), claimed
that the assessments extended to and included the respondent's share
of the profits of a business carried on outside the United Kingdom by
a Bahamian partnership of which he was a member. He appealed
against the assessments, contending that his share of the partnership
profits was chargeable to United Kingdom tax, not under Case II of
Schedule D, but under Case V (" possessions out of the United King-
B dom "). It followed from that contention that, because no part of those
profits was received in the United Kingdom, the charge under Case V
was nil. The appeal was heard by the Commissioners for the General
Purposes of the Income Tax Acts for the Division of Kensington in
February 1975, who determined the appeal in favour of the present
respondent. The inspector appealed from that determination by way of
C case stated to the High Court. The appeal was heard in November
1977 by Browne-Wilkinson J. who dismissed it with costs. The inspector
further appealed to the Court of Appeal (Buckley, Roskill and Goff
L.JJ.) who in June 1978 unanimously dismissed the appeal with costs.
The Court of Appeal granted the inspector leave to appeal to the House
of Lords on condition that he did not seek to disturb the orders for
D costs made in the High Court and the Court of Appeal.

The facts are stated in the opinion of Viscount Dilhorne.

Conrad Dehn Q.C., J. E. Holroyd Pearce Q.C. and A. G. Wilson for
the appellant.

D. C. Potter Q.C., Andrew Park Q.C. and R. Mathew for the
respondent.

E

Their Lordships took time for consideration.

January 31, 1980. LORD DIPLOCK. My Lords, I have had the
advantage of reading in draft the speech prepared by my noble and
learned friend, Viscount Dilhorne, and I agree with it. For the reasons
F given by him I would dismiss this appeal.

VISCOUNT DILHORNE. My Lords, Mr. Frost, who had by 1966
established himself as a very successful entertainer on television in this
country, in that year considered using his talents overseas and, in
particular, in the United States. He wished to continue to reside in
the United Kingdom and to avoid or reduce his liability to United
G Kingdom income tax on his earnings abroad. Under Schedule D Case
II tax is chargeable on the annual profits or gains arising or accruing
to a person residing in the United Kingdom from a profession, whether
carried on in the United Kingdom or elsewhere.

With this object in view his solicitors sent to the Trust Corporation
of Bahamas Ltd. a draft of a partnership agreement to be entered into
H between Mr. Frost and a Bahamian company. On February 8, 1967,
the Pembina Investment Co. Ltd., a 'shell' company held by the Trust
Corporation, changed its name to Leander Productions Ltd. and on
February 17 an " Indenture of Partnership " was entered into between
Mr. Frost and Leander Productions Ltd. The business of the partnership was to be carried on under the name Leander Enterprises and the
agreement provided that 99 per cent. of the capital assets of the partnership should belong to Mr. Frost and 1 per cent. to the company; and

that Mr. Frost should be entitled to 95 per cent. of the annual profits A
of the partnership and the company to 5 per cent.

The source of all the income of the partnership was Mr. Frost's
activities in the United States. In March 1969 Leander Enterprises
entered into a contract with Hellespont N.V., a company situate in
Curacao, under which that company acquired the sole and exclusive
benefit of the exploitation of the assets of Leander Enterprises. The
Hellespont company was owned by Tamarisk Investments Ltd., a B
Bahamian company. After this date moneys earned by Mr. Frost's
activities were channelled through the Hellespont company and through
the Tamarisk company to the partnership which received substantially
the whole benefit of the moneys earned by Mr. Frost. These two
companies were created on the advice of the Trust Corporation and
Mr. Frost's earnings were paid to these companies with a view to C
avoiding United States tax.

Mr. Frost was assessed to income tax under Case II for the year
1969–70 in the sum of £30,000, for the year 1970–71 in the sum of
£29,256 and for the year 1971–72 in the sum of £115,398, each assessment being made on the basis that his earnings in the United States in
those years were liable to tax under Case II.

It is convenient to refer to the provisions of the Income and D
Corporation Taxes Act 1970 rather than to the relevant provisions of
the earlier Acts which were replaced by that Act.

Section 153 (1) of the Act reads as follows:

"Where any trade or business is carried on by two or more persons
in partnership, and the control and management of the trade or
business is situated abroad, the trade or business shall be deemed E
to be carried on by persons resident outside the United Kingdom,
and the partnership shall be deemed to reside outside the United
Kingdom, notwithstanding the fact that some of the members of
the partnership are resident in the United Kingdom and that some
of its trading operations are conducted within the United Kingdom."

Mr. Frost claims that as the control and management of the business F
of the partnership was situated abroad—that was a term of the partnership agreement—its business is to be deemed to have been carried on
by persons resident outside the United Kingdom with the consequence
that his profits from his activities are not to be regarded as having
accrued to a person residing in the United Kingdom and so are not
assessable under Case II.

Further it is contended on his behalf that Case V of Schedule D is G
the case applicable. Under that Case tax is to be charged

". . . in respect of income arising from possessions out of the United
Kingdom, not being income consisting of emoluments of any office
or employment."

Section 122 of the Income and Corporation Taxes Act 1970 provides H
by subsection (1) that income tax chargeable under Case V is to be
computed on the income arising in the year preceding the year of
assessment ". . . whether the income has been or will be received in the
United Kingdom or not, . . ." Subsection (2) states that subsection (1) is
not to apply to "any income which is immediately derived by a person
from the carrying on by him of any trade, profession or vocation, either
solely or in partnership, . . ." In the case of such income subsection (3)

A   provides that tax shall be charged only on the full amount of the actual sums received in the United Kingdom in the year preceding the year of assessment from remittances payable in the United Kingdom.

Mr. Frost contended that as no part of his earnings in the United States were remitted to the United Kingdom in the years in respect of which he was assessed to tax on his earnings in the United States, he
B   should not have been assessed to tax in any sum in respect thereof.

The revenue did not contend that Mr. Frost's income from the carrying on of his profession in the United States was not immediately derived by him from the carrying on of his profession, either solely or in partnership, though the payments for his activities were received first by the Hellespont company and then from that company by the Tamarisk company and then from that company by the partnership. So for the
C   purposes of this appeal, one must assume that subsection (2) of section 122 applies.

The revenue challenged the conclusions of the commissioners which were upheld by Browne-Wilkinson J. and by the Court of Appeal (Buckley, Roskill and Goff L.JJ.) on a number of grounds.

Their main contention was that the commissioners' findings that
D   during the relevant years there was a partnership between the appellant and the company was erroneous in law. It was said acts done by one partner which another partner could not perform could not be regarded as acts done for the partnership. Reliance was placed on the following passage in *Lindley on Partnership*, 14th ed. (1979), p. 48:

"Speaking generally, no person can do by his agent what he cannot do himself; and although each member of a firm is a principal as
E   regards his own conduct, he is the agent of his co-partners; and he cannot therefore do for the firm what they cannot do. In other words, the disability of one of the partners affects the whole firm, so that the legal capacity of the firm is no greater than that of the partner with the least legal capacity."

F   As Lord Loreburn L.C. said in *De Beers Consolidated Mines Ltd.* v. *Howe* [1906] A.C. 455, 458 "A company cannot eat or sleep, . . ." Neither can it be a television entertainer or author and so it was said that there could not be in law a partnership between Mr. Frost and the company which covered their appearances as television entertainers or their being authors. But the partnership agreement was not an agreement between them that they should entertain on television or
G   write books. Clause 1 of the agreement as amended provided that they should become and remain partners

"in the business of exploiting copyright and interests in copyright and in the businesses of television and film consultants and advisers publicity agents and providers of publicity services and facilities and in the business of producing television programmes, films, stageplays and
H   other entertainments and using and exploiting the services of producers, actors, directors, writers and artistes, and material and facilities which may be used for the production of television programmes, films, stageplays and other entertainments, and in the business of television, films and stage advisers and agents throughout the world outside the United Kingdom."

Under this clause the partnership could procure engagements for artistes and enter into contracts undertaking that they would appear and perform

but it was said on behalf of the revenue that a man cannot exploit his A
own skills and that he consequently cannot enter into a valid partnership
agreement to exploit his own skills.   There is a difference, it was said,
between A exploiting his own skills and A exploiting the skills of others.
While recognising that there is a difference between the persons whose
skills are to be exploited, I am in agreement with Buckley L.J. in being
unable to see any reason why Mr. Frost and the company could not agree
to join in exploiting Mr. Frost's skills.   Just as they could procure engage- B
ments for other artistes and contract that they would appear and perform,
so could they procure engagements for Mr. Frost and undertake that he
would appear to fulfil them.   I see nothing to prevent such an agreement
being made and I cannot construe this clause as only covering the exploitation of the activities of artistes other than Mr. Frost.

   I cannot regard the partnership agreement as invalid either on the C
ground that Mr. Frost bound himself to do what the company could not
do or on the ground that under it he undertook to do what he could not
do and so I conclude that the receipts from his activities were receipts of
the partnership.

   The commissioners, after referring to the definition of a partnership in
section 1 of the Partnership Act 1890, held that during the relevant years
there was a partnership between Mr. Frost and the company.   This con- D
clusion can only mean that they were satisfied that Mr. Frost and the
company were carrying on business in common with a view of profit.   The
revenue challenged this conclusion, contending that the business carried
on in common was with a view to avoiding tax.   While it is clear that the
partnership was formed with that object, it must also have been formed
with a view of profit.   It was intended that profits should be made for if E
they were not made as a result of Mr. Frost's activities, there would have
been no tax to be avoided.   I therefore reject this contention.

   Before Browne-Wilkinson J. but not before the commissioners, the
revenue contended that it was not within the power of the company to
enter into the partnership agreement.   Whether this was so, depends on the
objects of the company as stated in its memorandum of association.
Clause 3 of the memorandum sets out the objects of the company and F
clause 3 (6) reads as follows:

   " To carry on business as bankers, capitalists, financiers, concessionaires and merchants and to undertake and carry on and execute
   all kinds of financial commercial trading or other operations and
   generally to undertake and carry out all such obligations and transactions as an individual capitalist may lawfully undertake and carry G
   out."

The paragraph ends with the following statement:

   " And it is hereby declared that the objects of the company as
   specified in each of the foregoing paragraphs of this clause . . . shall
   be separate and distinct objects of the company and shall not be in
   anywise limited by reference to any other paragraph or the order H
   in which the same occur as the name of the company."

That name was, as I have said, when the company was formed the
Pembina Investment Co. Ltd., and while no doubt the objects are entirely
suitable for an investment company, it was submitted for the revenue that
they were not wide enough to empower the company to carry on the business of the partnership.   This contention, which did not appear to be the

A one on which most reliance was placed, perhaps because it had not been advanced before the commissioners, is to my mind the most formidable of those put forward on behalf of the revenue. Whether or not it is well founded, depends on the construction to be placed on clause 3 (6) of the memorandum. It was submitted that the words " other operations " should be construed ejusdem generis with " financial commercial trading." The difficulty I feel about accepting this argument is that I am unable to find

B a genus in the clause. Carrying on the partnership business was not carrying on the business of bankers or of capitalists, financiers, concessionaires or merchants nor was it an activity which one would normally associate with the activities of an individual capitalist. So whether or not the carrying on of the partnership business was ultra vires the company appears to depend on the meaning to be given to the words " all kinds of financial

C commercial trading or other operations."

Reading clause 3 (6) as a whole, it gives me the impression that it was intended to cover every kind of activity that an investment company might want to carry on and that the words " other operations " were inserted ex abundanti cautela to cover any kind of such activity if any, not covered by the words " financial commercial trading." Noscitur a sociis.

In one sense the business of the partnership was financial. The clause

D covered all kinds of financial operations. " Commercial " has a very wide meaning. It is not infrequently contrasted with " industrial." I doubt if the business of the partnership which included the exploitation of the talents of artistes is properly to be described as a commercial operation, but if it is not a financial or commercial operation it certainly is covered by the word " all kinds of . . . other operations." It is true that if they

E are given an unlimited meaning, it is hard to see the purpose of the other words in clause 3 (6) or indeed the object of including the other paragraphs of clause 3 for a statement that the object of the company was to carry on and execute all kinds of operations would cover all the other stated objects.

This question has now been considered by four learned judges, all very experienced in construing the memorandum and articles of association of

F companies and they have all rejected the revenue's contention and have held that it was not ultra vires of the company to enter into the partnership agreement to carry on the business stated in that agreement. Having read and studied their judgments carefully, I am not prepared to dissent from their conclusion for with some hesitation I think that the business of the partnership can be regarded as a kind of financial operation, and if not,

G as covered by the words " all kinds of . . . other operations."

It follows that in my opinion Mr. Frost, by entering into the partnership agreement, which the revenue did not allege was a sham, with a " shell " Bahamian company of which the directors were repeatedly changed and were nominated by the Trust Corporation to give them training and experience and which provided only " financial, administrative, secretarial

H and fiscal services and an advisory contribution," Mr. Frost providing the " profit earning contribution," with Mr. Frost being entitled to 95 per cent. of the profits and 99 per cent. of the assets of the partnership, is not liable to be taxed under Case II and has successfully avoided liability to United Kingdom income tax on his earnings in the years in question in the United States.

In my opinion this appeal should be dismissed with costs.

Newstead v. Frost (H.L.(E.)) [1980]

A

LORD SALMON. My Lords, for the reasons set out in the speech of my noble and learned friend, Viscount Dilhorne, with which I agree. I also would dismiss this appeal.

LORD FRASER OF TULLYBELTON. My Lords, I have had the advantage of reading in draft the speech prepared by my noble and learned friend, Viscount Dilhorne, and I agree with it. For the reasons given by him I would dismiss this appeal.

B

LORD KEITH OF KINKEL. My Lords, I also would dismiss this appeal for the reasons set out in the speech of my noble and learned friend, Viscount Dilhorne, with which I agree entirely.

Appeal dismissed.

C

Solicitors: *Solicitor of Inland Revenue; Harbottle & Lewis.*

F. C.

D

[HOUSE OF LORDS]

* DUPORT STEELS LTD. AND OTHERS . . . RESPONDENTS

AND

SIRS AND OTHERS . . . . APPELLANTS

E

[1980 D. No. 222]

1980 Jan. 25 Kenneth Jones J.

Jan. 26 Lord Denning M.R., Lawton and Ackner L.JJ.

Feb. 1; 7 Lord Diplock, Lord Edmund-Davies, Lord Fraser of Tullybelton, Lord Keith of Kinkel and Lord Scarman

F

Trade Dispute—Act in furtherance of—Procuring breach of contract—Trade union involved in trade dispute with nationalised steel corporation—Strike of members employed by corporation—Members in private sector of steel industry also called out—Whether action in " furtherance of a trade dispute "—Whether test subjective—Trade union in political dispute with government—Whether preventing action from being in furtherance of trade dispute—Trade Union and Labour Relations Act 1974 (c. 52), ss. 13 (1) (2), 17 (2) (as amended by Employment Protection Act 1975 (c. 71), s. 125 (1), Sch. 16, Pt. III, para. 6 and Trade Union and Labour Relations (Amendment) Act 1976 (c. 7), s. 3 (2))

G

Section 13 of the Trade Union and Labour Relations Acts 1974 and 1976 provides:

H

" (1) An act done by a person in contemplation or furtherance of a trade dispute shall not be actionable in tort on the ground only—(*a*) that it induces another person to break a contract or interferes or induces any other person to interfere with its performance; . . . (2) . . . an act done by a person in contemplation or furtherance of a trade dispute is not actionable in tort on the ground only that

A   it is an interference with the trade, business or employment of another person . . ."

The British Steel Corporation (" B.S.C.") was a public
authority established under the Iron and Steel Act 1975 to
run the nationalised sector of the steel industry, which
produced about 50 per cent. of home-produced steel. It
employed a workforce of some 150,000, of whom about 95,000
were members of the defendant trade union, the Iron and
B   Steel Trades Confederation (" I.S.T.C."). Under the Act of
1975, the Secretary of State was entitled to exercise a relatively
close control over the finances of B.S.C., which for some time
prior to the present dispute had been operating at a loss.
Before the commencement of the dispute, the government had
announced its decision that no further public funds would be
provided to enable B.S.C. to meet its operating losses after
March 31, 1980; thereafter, it had to pay its own way and
C   meet its operating costs, including its current wages bill, out
of its current earnings. In the latter part of 1979, negotiations
began between I.S.T.C. and B.S.C. on increased wage rates
for 1980. Owing to B.S.C.'s expected financial stringency in
1980, little progress was made. On January 2, 1980, the
executive council of I.S.T.C. called a strike of its members
employed by B.S.C. By January 17, 1980, they were growing
dissatisfied at the progress that the strike was making, and
D   they accordingly resolved to call out on strike their members
employed in the private sector of the steel industry, which
consisted of some 100 companies producing some $17\frac{1}{2}$ per
cent. of home-produced steel and employing as part of their
total workforce some 15,000 members of I.S.T.C. There was
no existing trade dispute within the meaning of the Trade
Union and Labour Relations Acts 1974 and 1976 [1] between
those workers and any of their employers in the private sector.
E   The extension of the dispute to the private sector was intended
to put pressure on the government to find the money that
would enable B.S.C. to make an offer acceptable to I.S.T.C.
and so to put an end to the trade dispute between them.

The plaintiffs, 16 companies in the private sector, on January
24, 1980, issued a writ claiming injunctions against the general
secretary, the president and the vice-president of I.S.T.C. on
behalf of themselves and all other members of the executive
F   council against inducing the plaintiffs' employees to break their
contracts of employment by coming out on strike and against
inducing any members of I.S.T.C. to interfere with the supply
of steel to or from the plaintiffs' works or to picket their
premises. They applied to the judge in chambers for interlocutory injunctions in terms of the writ, and Kenneth Jones J.
refused the injunctions. In exercising his discretion under
section 17 (2) of the Acts of 1974 and 1976,[2] he held that the
G   case was indistinguishable from *Express Newspapers Ltd.* v.
McShane [1980] 2 W.L.R. 89 and that it was highly probable
that the defence that the defendants had acted in furtherance
of a trade dispute would succeed at trial. The plaintiffs
appealed to the Court of Appeal, who allowed the appeal.
The court took the view that the original trade dispute between
I.S.T.C. and B.S.C. had by January 17, 1980, generated a

H

[1] Trade Union and Labour Relations Acts 1974 and 1976, s. 29: " (1) . . . ' trade
dispute ' means a dispute between employers and workers . . . connected with one
or more of the following . . . (*a*) terms and conditions of employment, . . ."

[2] S. 17: " (2) It is hereby declared for the avoidance of doubt that where an
application is made to a court, pending the trial of an action, for an interlocutory
injunction and the party against whom the injunction is sought claims that he acted
in contemplation or furtherance of a trade dispute, the court shall, in exercising its
discretion whether or not to grant the injunction, have regard to the likelihood of
that party's succeeding at the trial of the action in establishing the matter or matters
which would, under any provision of section 13 . . . afford a defence to the action "

Duport Steels Ltd. v. Sirs (Q.B.D.)   **[1980]**

second dispute in which the parties were I.S.T.C. and the   A
government; that that second dispute did not fall within the
definition of " trade dispute " because the government were
not the employers; and that the calling out of workers in the
private sector was an act done in furtherance of that second
dispute. They held that, having regard to the injustice involved
in subjecting the employers and workers in the private sector,
who had no concern with the dispute between I.S.T.C. and
B.S.C., to serious economic loss, inconvenience and distress,   B
and to the potentially disastrous economic consequences to
the country as a whole of the action taken by the defendants,
the discretion under section 17 (2) of the Acts of 1974 and
1976 should be exercised in favour of granting the injunctions.
    On appeal by the defendants by leave of the House of
Lords: —
    Held, allowing the appeal, that *Express Newspapers Ltd.*
v. *McShane* had bindingly established that, on the true inter-   C
pretation of section 13 (1) of the Trade Union and Labour
Relations Acts 1974 and 1976, the test whether an act was
done by a person in contemplation or furtherance of a trade
dispute was subjective, i.e., provided that that person honestly
believed at the time when he did the act that it might help
one of the parties to a trade dispute to achieve its objectives,
and did it for that reason, he was entitled to the immunity
in tort granted by section 13; that *McShane's* case had also   D
rejected the view that, on a proper construction of the Acts
of 1974 and 1976, it was permissible to have regard to the
remoteness of the act done from the immediate source of
the dispute, or the extent to which it had reasonable prospects
of furthering the dispute, save in connection with testing the
genuineness, on the evidence as a whole, of the purpose professed by the defendants; that there was no justification for
implying into section 13 any limitation that an act relied on   E
as an act in furtherance of a trade dispute must be designed
to operate through a sequence of cause and effect of an
industrial character, and the fact, if it were a fact, that a
second dispute existed between I.S.T.C. and the government
did not prevent the defendants from honestly believing that
the extension of the strike to the private sector of the steel
industry would further their cause in the trade dispute with
B.S.C.; that, on the facts, it could not be said with any   F
plausibility that the defendants' actions had not been taken in
furtherance of that existing trade dispute; and that the Court
of Appeal had not been entitled to interfere with the judge's
exercise of his discretion in refusing the injunctions sought
by the plaintiffs (post, pp. 156F–G, 161B–F, H–162C, 163A–B, E–G,
164D—165A, G, 166F—167A, 170E—171B, 171H).
    Express Newspapers Ltd. v. *McShane* [1980] 2 W.L.R.
89, H.L.(E.) and *N.W.L. Ltd.* v. *Woods* [1979] 1 W.L.R.   G
1294, H.L.(E.) applied.
    Per curiam. The discretion whether to grant or withhold
an interlocutory injunction is the discretion of the judge alone,
not that of the Court of Appeal (post, pp. 160H—161B, 165E–F,
166F—167A, 171G). Parliament may not have expected, when
it passed the Acts of 1974 and 1976, that trade union leadership
would use the immunity granted to them by section 13 in such
a way as to produce consequences so injurious to the nation as   H
those that have in fact resulted, but if there is some legal limit
on the immunities under the existing legislation if must be
found as a matter of construction of the words of the legislation. It endangers continued public confidence in the political
impartiality of the judiciary, which is essential to the continuance of the rule of law, if judges, under the guise of
interpretation, provide their own preferred amendments to
statutes which experience of their operation has shown to have

A   had consequences that they consider to be injurious to the
    public interest (post, pp. 157D–H, 162F, 165F, 167G—168B, D, G,
    169C, G).
        Decision of the Court of Appeal, post, p. 148H, reversed.

    The following cases are referred to in their Lordships' opinions:
    British Broadcasting Corporation v. *Hearn* [1977] 1 W.L.R. 1004; [1977]
B   I.C.R. 685; [1978] 1 All E.R. 111, C.A.
    City of London v. *Wood* (1701) 12 Mod.Rep. 669.
    Express Newspapers Ltd. v. *McShane* [1979] 1 W.L.R. 390; [1979]
        I.C.R. 210; [1979] 2 All E.R. 360, C.A.; [1980] 2 W.L.R. 89; [1980]
        1 All E.R. 65, H.L.(E.).
    Inland Revenue Commissioners v. *Hinchy* [1960] A.C. 748; [1960] 2
        W.L.R. 448; [1960] 1 All E.R. 505, H.L.(E.).
C   *Midland Silicones Ltd.* v. *Scruttons Ltd.* [1962] A.C. 446; [1962] 2
        W.L.R. 186; [1962] 1 All E.R. 1, H.L.(E.).
    N.W.L. Ltd. v. *Woods* [1979] 1 W.L.R. 1294; [1979] I.C.R. 867; [1979]
        3 All E.R. 614, H.L.(E.).
    Practice Statement (Judicial Precedent) [1966] 1 W.L.R. 1234; [1966] 3
        All E.R. 77, H.L.(E.).

D   The following additional case was cited in argument in the House of
    Lords:
    Associated Newspapers Group Ltd. v. *Wade* [1979] 1 W.L.R. 697; [1979]
        I.C.R. 664, C.A.

    The following cases are referred to in the judgments in the Court of
        Appeal:
E   *Associated Newspapers Group Ltd.* v. *Wade* [1979] 1 W.L.R. 697; [1979]
        I.C.R. 664, C.A.
    Beaverbrook Newspapers Ltd. v. *Keys* [1978] I.C.R. 582, C.A.
    Express Newspapers Ltd. v. *McShane* [1980] 2 W.L.R. 89; [1980] 1 All
        E.R. 65, H.L.(E.).
    N.W.L. Ltd. v. *Woods* [1979] 1 W.L.R. 1294; [1979] I.C.R. 867; [1979]
        3 All E.R. 614, H.L.(E.).
F   *United Biscuits (U.K.) Ltd.* v. *Fall* [1979] I.R.L.R. 110.

    The following additional case was cited in argument in the Court of
        Appeal:
    Sherard v. *AUEW* [1973] I.C.R. 421, C.A.

    The following cases are referred to in the judgment of Kenneth Jones J.:
G   *Express Newspapers Ltd.* v. *McShane* [1980] 2 W.L.R. 89; [1980] 1 All
        E.R. 65, H.L.(E.).
    N.W.L. Ltd. v. *Woods* [1979] 1 W.L.R. 1294; [1979] I.C.R. 867; [1979]
        3 All E.R. 614, H.L.(E.).

    No additional cases were cited in argument before Kenneth Jones J.

H   SUMMONS
        By writ dated January 24, 1980, the plaintiffs, Duport Steels Ltd.,
    Ductile Steels Ltd., British Rolling Mills Ltd., Brymbo Steel Works Ltd.,
    Glynwed Steels Ltd., Sheerness Steel Co. Ltd., G.K.N. (South Wales)
    Ltd., G.K.N. Wire Products Ltd., G.K.N. Reinforcements Ltd., Firth
    Brown Ltd., Lee Steel Strip Ltd., Hadfields Ltd., Osborn Steels Ltd., Osborn
    Steel Extrusion Ltd., Edgar Allen Balfour Steels Ltd. and William Oxley
    & Co. Ltd., claimed against the defendants, William Sirs (general secre-

Duport Steels Ltd. v. Sirs (Q.B.D.)   **[1980]**

tary), Leslie Bramley (president) and Edward Makepiece (vice-president), A
on their own behalf and on behalf of all members of the executive council
of the Iron and Steel Trades Confederation, an injunction restraining the
defendants and each of them, by themselves, their officers, servants or
agents or otherwise, from instructing members of the Iron and Steel Trades
Confederation to break their contracts of employment with the plaintiffs
or any of them or from inducing or procuring such members to break their
said contracts of employment by striking or interfering with the supply or B
delivery of steel or steel products to, from or on behalf of the plaintiffs or
any of them or by taking any other industrial action; an injunction restraining the defendants and each of them, by themselves, their officers, servants
or agents or otherwise, from interfering with the business of the plaintiffs
of any of them by instructing or inducing or procuring members of the
Iron and Steel Trades Confederation to break their contracts of employ- C
ment with the plaintiffs or any of them by striking or interfering with the
supply or delivery of steel or steel products to, from or on behalf of the
plaintiffs or any of them or by taking any other industrial action; an injunction restraining the defendants and each of them, by themselves, their officers,
servants or agents or otherwise, from instructing members of the Iron
and Steel Trades Confederation to interfere with the business of the
plaintiffs or any of them by picketing at or adjacent to the premises of the D
plaintiffs or any of them; an injunction ordering the defendants and each
of them to withdraw and revoke any instruction or advice to members of
the Iron and Steel Trades Confederation to engage in any strike or picketing or to interfere with the supply or delivery of steel or steel products to,
from or on behalf of the plaintiffs or any of them or to take any other
industrial action in breach of their contracts of employment or in any way E
that would interfere with the business of the plaintiffs or any of them;
damages; further or other relief; and costs.

On January 25, 1980, the plaintiffs applied by summons to the judge
in chambers for an order until trial or further order for injunctions in the
terms of the writ.

The summons was heard by Kenneth Jones J. in chambers. A note
of his judgment was agreed by counsel and has been approved by the F
judge.

Alexander Irvine Q.C. and *Christopher Carr* for the plaintiffs.
J. Melville Williams Q.C. and *John Hendy* for the defendants.

KENNETH JONES J. In this case the defendants are sued as officers of G
the Iron and Steel Trades Confederation on behalf of all members of that
union. They are in dispute with the British Steel Corporation (" B.S.C.")
and since January 2 have been on strike. Steps have now been taken by
the defendants to bring about a strike in the private sector. The plaintiffs
are a number of steel-producing companies in that private sector. They
seek from me a interim injunction, having as its purpose the prevention
of the strike which is called to start at 6 a.m. on Sunday, January 27. H

I have come to the conclusion that I am unable in the proper administration of the law to grant that injunction. I come to that conclusion
solely because I am constrained from doing so, in my judgment, by the
decision of the House of Lords in *Express Newspapers Ltd.* v. *McShane*
[1980] 2 W.L.R. 89.

I am told by Mr. Irvine on behalf of the plaintiffs that the immediate
sequel of a refusal to grant an injunction will be an appeal to the Court

The Weekly Law Reports, February 22, 1980

147

1 W.L.R.   Duport Steels Ltd. v. Sirs (Q.B.D.)   Kenneth Jones J.

A of Appeal. Bearing that in mind, it seems unnecessary for me to give a lengthy judgment here or to do more than express in outline my reasons for arriving at the decision at which I have arrived.

These proceedings are subject to section 17 of the Trade Union and Labour Relations Act 1974, as amended. It is not necessary for me to read the subsection applicable, subsection (2), but what I have to concern myself with is the likelihood of the defendants succeeding at the trial of the action in establishing that the acts in calling this strike are done in contemplation or furtherance of a trade dispute. It is clear from the speeches of the majority of the House of Lords in *Express Newspapers Ltd.* v. *McShane* that the test is a subjective one. If the defendants say that they are acting in contemplation or in furtherance of a trade dispute, I can only examine that statement in two respects: first, to decide whether

C or not there is a trade dispute; secondly, to decide whether or not that belief is honestly held.

There is no dispute here but that there is a trade dispute between the defendants and B.S.C. Mr. Irvine would have me say that there is no honest belief that the defendants are acting in contemplation or in furtherance of that trade dispute because no person in their situation could reasonably think that calling a strike in the private sector is in furtherance

D of the dispute with B.S.C. This is a somewhat fine argument, as I am sure Mr. Irvine will concede, although not conceding that it is lacking in legal merit for that reason. As I understand it, what he contends is that an act can only be in furtherance of a trade dispute, in so far as it is directed to a party who is a stranger to the dispute, if it is designed to cause that party to bring pressure to bear upon the other party to the

E dispute within the industrial or commercial relationship which exists between that stranger and the party to the dispute. Mr. Irvine, while making that contention, for the moment confines himself to submitting that his contention or argument is sufficient to make it less than highly probable that the defendants would succeed in due course in showing that their act was in furtherance of this trade dispute. He advances that argument because in *Express Newspapers Ltd.* v. *McShane* [1980] 2 W.L.R.

F 89, 104–105 Lord Scarman particularly contemplated that in granting an interlocutory injunction the court may well be entitled to have regard to the consequences of allowing the strike to proceed, that is, not granting an injunction, and he quoted, at p. 105, the words of Lord Diplock in *N.W.L. Ltd.* v. *Woods* [1979] 1 W.L.R. 1294, 1307:

G " . . . this does not mean that there may not be cases where the consequences to the employer or to third parties or the public and perhaps the nation itself, may be so disastrous that the injunction ought to be refused, unless there is a high degree of probability that the defence will succeed."

I am persuaded that the words should read " that the injunction ought not to be refused." *

H Mr. Irvine says this strike would be disastrous; and although there may be a probability that the defendants will succeed, because of the argument to which I have just referred, there is no high degree of probability.

Dealing with that argument, it appears to me that it involves putting a gloss on the words in section 13 and section 17 of the Act of 1974. The

* *Reporter's note.* The correction of the phrase in the citation to read " the injunction ought not to be refused, . . . " has now been approved by Lord Diplock.

only question is whether the act contemplated is to be done in contem- **A**
plation or furtherance of a trade dispute. I see no warrant within the
Act for the importing of any further words indicating that the act should
be effective only within the commercial relationship existing here between
the private sector and the B.S.C. In my view Mr. Irvine's argument fails.

There is a probability that this defence will succeed. Indeed I would
go so far as to say that there is a high degree of probability that the **B**
defence will succeed here.

The other limb of Mr. Irvine's argument is that the disaster which
would be consequent on a strike, and which is to be put in the scale in
favour of granting an injunction, is so tremendous that that should certainly
outweigh any degree of probability of success in the defence. There is
ample evidence that this strike will bring in its train disaster or, without
using any emotive word, considerable and heavy loss. It may well be that **C**
it is designed to do precisely that. It is not surprising that such would be
the consequence. In any event, if and in so far as Mr. Irvine is availing
himself only of this escape route suggested by Lord Scarman in *Express
Newspapers* v. *McShane* [1980] 2 W.L.R. 89, 104–105, for my part I
would, with great respect, agree with the views expressed by Lord Wilberforce in that case, at p. 96, as to whether, if a subjective test is right, any **D**
such escape route does exist. Lord Salmon also had well in mind the
consequence that the decision of the House might inadvertently result
in danger to human life. His view, at p. 100, was that, to remove that
possibility, the time had come for the law—if that was its effect—to be
altered.

Be that as it may, I feel myself constrained to hold that, Mr. Bramley
having stated clearly that this act complained of, although tortious, he **E**
honestly believes to be done in furtherance of the dispute with B.S.C.,
the law makes Mr. Bramley really the judge of that, not I, and that, he
having so stated and there really being no sufficient evidence to the contrary, nor any sufficient weight that I can attach to Mr. Irvine's argument
to which I have already referred, it is highly probable that the defendants
will establish their defence.

In these circumstances, despite the forbidding consequences, I find **F**
myself unable to grant this injunction.

> *Application refused.*
> *Costs in cause.*

Solicitors: *Allen & Overy; Russell, Jones & Walker.*
G

M. G.

INTERLOCUTORY APPEAL from Kenneth Jones J. in chambers.
The plaintiffs appealed.

Alexander Irvine Q.C. and *Christopher Carr* for the plaintiffs. **H**
J. Melville Williams Q.C. and *John Hendy* for the defendants.

LORD DENNING M.R. It is important to distinguish between the public
sector and the private sector of the steel industry. The public sector is
under the control of the British Steel Corporation. It accounts for 40 to
50 per cent. of the production of crude steel and the processing of it. But
there is an important private sector which covers about 20 per cent. of the

The Weekly Law Reports, February 22, 1980

149

1 W.L.R.   Duport Steels Ltd. v. Sirs (C.A.)   Lord Denning M.R.

A rest of the industry. It is run by many private companies. The turnover is something in the region of £1,500,000,000 a year in the private sector.

At the beginning of this year there was a dispute between the workers in the British Steel Corporation (" B.S.C. ") and their employers, B.S.C. itself in regard to wages. Through their union, the Iron and Steel Trades Confederation (" I.S.T.C.") the workers in the public sector demanded higher wages. As they did not achieve what they desired, they called a
B strike (I think the first for many, many years in the industry) on January 2, 1980. They called out all the workers in the public sector: and brought the whole of that great sector to a standstill.

The strike does not seem to have achieved the objective which the union desired. So, on Wednesday, January 16, an important decision was made by the union or its representatives. They made the decision that they
C would call out the members of the union who were employed in the private sector.

Let it be said at once that those workers in the private sector had no dispute whatever with their employers. All was peaceful and contented. They were ready to go on, and wanted to go on, with their work—processing the steel, making it, supplying it, and so forth. When the union suggested—indeed ordered—that those in the private sector should come
D out, ballots were taken in some cases. These showed that the workers in the private sector did not want to come out. We know that the majority in a secret ballot did not. There is other evidence to show that many others of them did not want to come out. Nevertheless, if ordered to do so by their union, they would have no option: because, if they did not obey the union call, they would lose their union card and in due course
E their employment.

On January 16, 1980, there was a meeting of the executive council of the union. They came to a decision to extend the dispute into the private sector. They decided to call out all those men: and the date they chose for this action was January 27, 1980, at 6.00 a.m.

Meanwhile the movement of all steel throughout the United Kingdom was to cease from 6.00 a.m. on Thursday, January 17, 1980.
F

So there was a most important decision. The I.S.T.C. decided to call out the men, who had no quarrel whatever with their own employers—or between the employers and the men. They decided to call them out in regard to a dispute with which they were not in any way concerned. So the question must be asked, and is asked: Why did the trade union extend the strike to the private sector?

G It is amply shown by a letter which was written by Mr. William Sirs on January 17, 1980, and by instructions which were given to all the branches. I will read a sentence or two from the letter: because it is quite plain to my mind that by this time the trade union had determined that the one way in which they could achieve their ends—or might hope to achieve their ends—was by bringing pressure to bear on the government. They knew—as is indeed so by an Act of Parliament—that the B.S.C. is in
H many respects under the general direction and control of the Secretary of State. That appears in the Iron and Steel Act 1975, section 4, which provides:

" The Secretary of State may, after consultation with the Corporation, give to the Corporation directions of a general character as to the exercise and performance by the Corporation of their functions (including the exercise of rights conferred by the holding of interests in com-

panies) in relation to matters which appear to him to affect the A
national interest; and the Corporation shall give effect to any directions
so given."

They knew that the government had declined to print any more money for
the purpose of increasing the wages of the workers. In these circumstances,
the trade union seems to have directed its attack on the government.

On January 17, 1980, Mr. Sirs wrote to the Independent Steel Employers B
Association. He said:

"... whilst agreeing that there is no dispute with any independent
steel employer," they " were firmly of the opinion that this dispute is
becoming politically stage-managed by the Conservative Government.
We feel that with not being made an offer of any new money, that we
are being singled out for a direct government and B.S.C. attack. It C
is because of the political intervention that my executive council feel
that we should now take the action of involving the private sector in
the public battle against the government attitude."

They knew that they were going against all the industrial agreements which
had been made: because the letter goes on to say:

" I recognise the fact that our procedure agreements do exist and we D
do not have a dispute with you, nevertheless these points have been
made to our executive, who have ultimately taken this decision."

That letter was sent by Mr. Sirs to the independent employers. Then
on January 21 Mr. Sirs sent out a general direction to the union branches.

" It was apparent," he said, " that the strike was developing into a E
confrontation between the government and the trade unions. It was
also apparent that the continued operation of the private sector was
not only having the effect of prolonging the present dispute but was
creating a feeling of injustice with other trade unions. . . ."

There was further evidence, such as a statement broadcast on the
B.B.C. on January 16. The trade unions " decided to step up their pres- F
sure this afternoon: and they left no doubt that their aim was to force
government intervention." Passage after passage in the newspapers, and
on the evidence, show that the action taken against the private sector was
in order to bring pressure to bear on the government: so as to make the
government alter its policy and increase the payments to B.S.C.—out of
the taxpayer's money, I suppose.

That action taken was ratified, we are told, unanimously by all the 21 G
members of the executive council on January 24, which was last Wednesday. This action is timed to take place at six o'clock tomorrow morning.

There is evidence of the disastrous effect which this action will have, not
only on all the companies in the private sector, but on much of British
industry itself. The private sector, as I have said, has a turnover—if it
continues to work—of £1,500,000,000 a year. The turnover in the private H
sector is about £30,000,000 a week. If the men are called out in the
private sector, all these companies would have to shut down at enormous
loss. Not only will they have to shut down, but all the firms which they
supply will not be able to carry on with their work. They will not be able
to make their steel. British Leyland, who depend on 80 per cent. of their
supplies from the private sector, will have to shut down much of their
works too. Not only that: we will lose trade here in this country, and our

The Weekly Law Reports, February 22, 1980

151

1 W.L.R.   Duport Steels Ltd. v. Sirs (C.A.)   Lord Denning M.R.

A competitors abroad will clap their hands in anticipation of being able to send their products into England: because our industry is at a standstill.

In these circumstances, it is not surprising that 16 of the big private steel companies in this country have come to the courts—hoping they can get here in time—to restrain the three principal members of this union (Mr. Sirs, Mr. Bramley and Mr. Makepiece) calling this disastrous strike, which is going to injure British industry so much.

B The judge below heard the application yesterday afternoon. He felt that he had to refuse it because of the recent case in the House of Lords of *Express Newspapers Ltd.* v. *McShane* [1980] 2 W.L.R. 89. He inferred from that case that the majority of the House held that the test was purely subjective; that if the trade union leaders honestly believed that what they were doing was in furtherance of a trade dispute, they would have com-

C plete immunity; and the courts can do nothing, because they would be exempt from judicial review.

We have gone through that case, and have read the judgments. They are not nearly so clear on the point as some would believe; but I will deal with them as we come to consider the case. But, first, there is a preliminary point to be considered: What was the dispute here? Was

D it a trade dispute? Section 29 (1) of the Trade Union and Labour Relations Act 1974 defines a "trade dispute." It is quite plain that the dispute between the workers and the employers of B.S.C. was certainly a trade dispute. It was "a dispute between employers and workers . . . connected with . . . terms and conditions of employment." Beyond all doubt, it was a trade dispute. In regard to any acts done in contemplation or furtherance of that dispute, they were entitled to

E immunity under section 13 of the Act of 1974.

But was that the only dispute in this case? On the evidence which I have read, it seems to me that there is good ground at least for thinking that, besides that initial dispute, there was a second dispute: not between the unions and the private steel companies, because they were all in agreement and were happy working together: but a dispute

F between the union and the government of this country. I have read enough already to show that the union leaders were complaining of "political stage management" by the Conservative Government. They were engaged "in a public battle against the government's attitude." There was "a confrontation between the union and the government." All this goes to show that there is evidence that there was a second dispute here: a dispute between the union and the government, in

G which the union were seeking to bring pressure to bear on the government to make them change their attitude and provide more money, or take other steps in relation to B.S.C., so as to bring them to heel.

It seems to me that that second dispute cannot be regarded as a trade dispute within section 29 at all. In so far as the acts done—or the calling out of these workers—was in furtherance of that second

H dispute, they are entitled to no immunity whatsoever. It is not a trade dispute. It is not a dispute between employers and workers. It is a dispute between the union and the government.

Then it was suggested by Mr. Melville Williams that in any event it was in furtherance of that earlier dispute with B.S.C. That may be a question on the facts. It does not depend on a state of mind, or any-thing of that kind. I must say that it seems to me arguable that this step taken of calling out all the employees in the private sector—stopping

all the movement of steel into and out of the country—was taken in A
furtherance of a dispute with the government. To try and bring the
government to heel—and not in furtherance of the original dispute. If
that be so, then they are not protected: because they are only protected
for acts done in contemplation or furtherance of the original trade
dispute.

That is the first part of the case. But I would say at this point that
there is a question on remoteness. Some acts may be too remote to B
be in furtherance of a trade dispute. There was only one member of
the House of Lords in *Express Newspapers Ltd.* v. *McShane* [1980] 2
W.L.R. 89 who dealt with the question of remoteness. That was Lord
Wilberforce: and he certainly expressed the law as I have always
understood it to be. He said, at pp. 94–95 :

> " . . . it is always open to the courts—indeed their duty—with C
> open-ended expressions such as those involving cause, or effect, or
> remoteness, or in the context of this very Act, connection with "
> —or, I would add, " in furtherance of "—" to draw a line beyond
> which the expression ceases to operate. This is simply the common
> law in action. It does not involve the judges in cutting down what
> Parliament has given: it does involve them in interpretation in D
> order to ascertain how far Parliament intended to go."

In the cases which we have had very recently in this court, particularly
in *Associated Newspapers Group Ltd.* v. *Wade* [1979] 1 W.L.R. 697, we
granted an injunction especially because the act was too remote to be
considered in furtherance of it. It is significant that that case was not
overruled by the House of Lords nor was it said to be erroneous. I E
need only repeat what I said in *Associated Newspapers* v. *Wade*, at
p. 713 :

> " Some acts are so remote from the trade dispute that they cannot
> properly be said to be ' in furtherance ' of it. When conduct
> causes direct loss or damage to the employer himself (as by with-
> drawing labour from him or stopping his supplies) it is plainly ' in
> furtherance ' of the dispute with him. But when trade unions F
> choose not to cause damage or loss to the employer himself, but
> only to innocent third persons—who are not parties to the dispute
> —it is very different. The act done may then be so remote from the
> dispute itself that it cannot reasonably be regarded as being done
> ' in furtherance ' of it."—I cited two which have not been over-
> ruled, *Beaverbrook Newspapers Ltd.* v. *Keys* [1978] I.C.R. 582 and G
> *United Biscuits (U.K.) Ltd.* v. *Fall* [1979] I.R.L.R. 110—" Thus
> when strikers choose to picket, not their employers' premises, but
> the premises of innocent third persons not parties to the dispute—
> it is unlawful. ' Secondary picketing ' it is called. It is unlawful
> at common law and is so remote from the dispute that there is
> no immunity in regard to it."

H

The House did not say that that case was wrongly decided.

Apart from that point, it seems to me, as I have said, that it is
arguable in this case that there is no immunity for these acts done in
calling out the private sector, because those acts were done in furtherance
of the dispute with the government. It was not a trade dispute at all.
It is arguable that they were not done in furtherance of the original
trade dispute with B.S.C.

The Weekly Law Reports, February 22, 1980

153

1 W.L.R.   **Duport Steels Ltd. v. Sirs (C.A.)**   Lord Denning M.R.

A   Seeing that it is arguable, I come to the other point in this case. It arises out of the amended section 17 (2) of the Trade Union and Labour Relations Act 1974, which is in paragraph 6 of Part III of Schedule 16 to the Employment Protection Act 1975. That section says, in respect to an interlocutory injunction, that

B   ". . . the court shall, in exercising its discretion whether or not to grant the injunction, have regard to the likelihood of that party's succeeding at the trial of the action. . . ."

That section was much considered by the House of Lords in two recent cases: *N.W.L. Ltd.* v. *Woods* [1979] 1 W.L.R. 1294; and the recent case of *Express Newspapers Ltd.* v. *McShane* [1980] 2 W.L.R. 89. It is very interesting to see how the House of Lords have been dealing with C   section 17. They point out that it does not mean that the likelihood of success is to be the paramount or sole consideration in granting or refusing an injunction: there are other matters to be considered. In particular, damage to the employers, or to the public, or even to the nation can be considered in considering whether to grant or refuse an injunction. Although he put it in the form of a double negative, I would quote what Lord Diplock said (removing the double negative D   and putting it into the affirmative) in *N.W.L. Ltd.* v. *Woods*, at p. 1307:

". . . there may be cases where the consequences to the employer or to third parties or the public and perhaps the nation itself, may be so disastrous that the injunction ought to be granted, unless there is a high degree of probability that the defence will succeed."

E   Then Lord Fraser of Tullybelton speaks to the same effect at p. 1309. He said that the likelihood is not to be regarded as overriding or of paramount importance. And Lord Scarman, on that point, said, at p. 1315:

". . . I do not rule out the possibility that the consequences to the plaintiff (or others) may be so serious that the court feels it necessary to grant the injunction; for the subsection does leave a residual discretion with the court."

F

That seems to me to be the view of the majority of the House in *N.W.L. Ltd.* v. *Woods* [1979] 1 W.L.R. 1294. It was taken up by Lord Scarman in particular in *Express Newspapers Ltd.* v. *McShane* [1980] 2 W.L.R. 89. It had not been raised by counsel in the court, but he thought it so important that he brought it up himself. He referred to G   that passage, which I have quoted from Lord Diplock, and went on to say, at p. 105:

". . . in a case where action alleged to be in contemplation or furtherance of a trade dispute endangers the nation "—that is the point here, " endangers the nation "—" or puts at risk such fundamental rights as the right of the public to be informed and the H   freedom of the press, it could well be a proper exercise of the court's discretion to restrain the industrial action pending trial of the action. It would, of course, depend upon the circumstances of the case: but the law does not preclude the possibility of the court exercising its discretion in that way."

Those passages which I have read from the judgments of the House of Lords do show that there is a residual discretion in the courts to grant an injunction restraining such action as in this case, where it is

such as to cause grave danger to the economy and the life of the A
country, and puts the whole nation and its welfare at risk. In those
circumstances, the courts have a residual discretion to grant an injunction: unless it is clear—or in the highest degree probable—that there is
a defence which is likely to succeed.

I have said enough in this case to show that there is a very good
ground for argument that the so-called defence—the immunity—is not
likely to succeed. To call out these private steel workers, who have B
no dispute at all with their employers, would have such a disastrous
effect on the economy and well-being of the country that it seems to
me only right that the court should grant an injunction to stop these
people being called out tomorrow morning: to stop all this picketing:
and to stop all these people who are preventing the movement of steel
up and down the country.   C

It seems to me that this is a case where, in our residual discretion,
we should grant the injunction in the terms asked. I would allow
the appeal.

LAWTON L.J. On January 2, 1980, the I.S.T.C. called out on strike
its members employed by B.S.C. No doubt when they did so they
hoped that the strike would be a short one and that victory would D
come to them. The history of the last two decades tends to show that,
when there have been disputes between unions and nationalised industries,
there has usually been government intervention, followed fairly quickly
by a settlement to the advantage of the strikers.

Unfortunately for the I.S.T.C., on this occasion there was no government intervention of this kind; and by January 16, 1980, it became clear E
that there was not going, in the foreseeable future, to be any. There
was going to be no quick victory. The dispute was likely to go on
for a long time. What was to be done? The members of the I.S.T.C.
were likely to suffer hardship if the strike went on for too long. It is
clear from a letter which was sent out by Mr. Sirs, the general secretary
of the I.S.T.C. to all branch secretaries, what the decision was and why
a decision was made in the terms it was. I will read from the opening F
paragraph of the letter:

"Dear Colleagues . . . I wish to inform you that at the joint I.S.T.C.
and N.U.B. Executive Council meeting held on Wednesday January
16, 1980, a progress report was submitted on the strike of our
members employed by B.S.C. Arising from that report and subsequent discussion it was apparent that the strike was developing into G
a confrontation between the government and the trade unions."

That was what the situation was; and, as a result of finding that that
was the situation, it was decided (to use Mr. Sirs' words) " to involve
the private sector." The union had no dispute with the private sector
at all. Why did they want to involve the private sector? The answer
from the evidence which has been filed is clear, namely, by involving H
the private sector, pressure could be brought to bear upon the government. There would be a stoppage of steel going from the private sector
to industry; and industry would in consequence grind to a halt. There
would be mass unemployment, and then both workers and employers
would start beseeching the government to intervene. The whole purpose
of the decision of January 16 was by starting a strike in the private
sector to bring pressure to bear upon the government.

A   Trade unions are entitled to bring pressure to bear upon the government provided they do it in lawful ways. But one of the privileges they are not entitled to have when doing so is the immunity given by section 13 of the Trade Union and Labour Relations Act 1974, as amended, if what they are doing is done otherwise than in contemplation or furtherance of a trade dispute. So the question arises at once as to whether what happened after January 16 in relation to the private sector was in

B contemplation or furtherance of a trade dispute. It is arguable—indeed, strongly arguable—that a strike, the object of which is to coerce the government to change its policies, is not a trade dispute at all within the meaning of section 29 of the Act.

    In those circumstances, the question at once arises: Was there one dispute here, namely a trade dispute with B.S.C. which would attract

C the immunity given by section 13, or were there two disputes, the one with the private sector not attracting the immunity given by the Act? This is a matter of some complexity, as Mr. Melville Williams pointed out. The information before the court at the moment is scanty; and, before any firm decision could be reached as to what led the union to behave as it did would have to be the subject of much more evidence

D than the court has at the present time. Suffice for this purpose to say that prima facie it looks as if the decision to involve the private sector was made not for any purpose connected with terms and conditions of employment in that sector but for the purpose of coercing the government.

    If that is so, the courts have jurisdiction to decide whether what was done was a trade dispute within the meaning of the Act of 1974 as

E amended: see *Express Newspapers Ltd.* v. *McShane* [1980] 2 W.L.R. 89, 97, *per* Lord Diplock. It follows, therefore, that the courts are entitled to look at the evidence to see whether what was done in relation to the private sector was a trade dispute. It is only if they decide that there was a trade dispute that the tests in *Express Newspapers Ltd.* v. *McShane* come into operation. If there was a trade dispute with the private sector,

F then on the evidence what the defendants did was in furtherance of that dispute. But they have first to satisfy the court that there was a trade dispute with the private sector.

    In my judgment, on the evidence, it is strongly arguable that what was happening after January 16, 1980, was not in furtherance of a trade dispute with the private sector. It follows, so it seems to me, that section 17 (2) of the Act of 1974 as amended has little significance because, once there is

G a strong case for thinking that the union has behaved in a way which does not confer the immunity given by the Act of 1974, as amended, then an injunction should be granted.

    I too would grant the relief which is requested.

    ACKNER L.J. We are, of course, not deciding this action. We have

H only to consider whether in the exercise of our discretion we should give the pre-trial relief of an injunction. I agree with Lord Denning M.R. and Lawton L.J. that there is a seriously arguable question which involves deciding whether or not there are two disputes, one with the B.S.C. and the other with the government. If there was a second dispute, then it appears to be common ground that that in itself could not be a trade dispute because the government are not the employers of the defendants. Accordingly, if the acts sought to be restrained are to be done in further-

ance of *that second dispute,* they could not be " in furtherance of a trade   A
dispute."

Mr. Irvine has raised yet another point, which I think is arguable as
well, and that is this. Can action aimed at the government, who are not
the employers, to coerce the government to change its policy by visiting
disastrous consequences on the community at large, be action in furtherance
of a trade dispute within the meaning of the section? That Parliament
should have intended immunity in such circumstances is, to say the least,   B
surprising. " Stark " as the effect of the subjective interpretation may be,
this still remains in my judgment an arguable question. Having considered,
as required by section 17 (2) of the Act of 1974, the likelihood of the
defendants establishing a defence under section 13 of the Act and generally
the balance of convenience, I too agree that the relief should be granted
and the appeal allowed.   C

> *Appeal allowed with costs in*
> *Court of Appeal.*
> *Leave to appeal refused.*

Solicitors: *Allen & Overy; Russell, Jones & Walker.*

A. H. B.   D

January 31. The Appeal Committee of the House of Lords (Lord
Diplock, Lord Fraser of Tullybelton and Lord Scarman) allowed a petition
by the defendants for leave to appeal.

INTERLOCUTORY APPEAL from the Court of Appeal.
The defendants appealed.   E

J. Melville Williams Q.C. and *John Hendy* for the defendants.
Alexander Irvine Q.C. and *Christopher Carr* for the plaintiffs.

The appeal was heard on February 1, and at the conclusion of the
hearing the appeal was allowed for reasons to be given in writing later.   F

February 7. LORD DIPLOCK. My Lords, as recently as December 13,
1979, this House decided in *Express Newspapers Ltd.* v. *McShane* [1980]
2 W.L.R. 89 that upon the true interpretation of section 13 (1) of the Trade
Union and Labour Relations Acts 1974 and 1976 the test whether an act
was " done by a person in contemplation or furtherance of a trade dispute " and so entitled him to immunity from a part of the common law   G
of tort is purely subjective: i.e., provided that the doer of the act honestly
thinks at the time he does it that it may help one of the parties to a trade
dispute to achieve their objectives and does it for that reason, he is
protected by the section.

That conclusion as to the meaning of words that have been used by
successive parliaments since the Trade Disputes Act 1906, to describe acts   H
for which the doer is entitled to immunity from the law of tort over an
area that has been much extended by the Acts of 1974 and 1976, is (as I
pointed out in the *McShane* case) one which is intrinsically repugnant to
anyone who has spent his life in the practice of the law or the administration
of justice. Sharing those instincts it was a conclusion that I myself reached
with considerable reluctance, for given the existence of a trade dispute it
involves granting to trade unions a power, which has no other limits than

A their own self-restraint, to inflict by means which are contrary to the general law untold harm to industrial enterprises unconcerned with the particular dispute, to the employees of such enterprises, to members of the public and to the nation itself, so long as those in whom the control of the trade union is vested honestly believe that to do so may assist it, albeit in a minor way, in achieving its objectives in the dispute.

B My Lords, at a time when more and more cases involve the application of legislation which gives effect to policies that are the subject of bitter public and parliamentary controversy, it cannot be too strongly emphasised that the British constitution, though largely unwritten, is firmly based upon the separation of powers; Parliament makes the laws, the judiciary interpret them. When Parliament legislates to remedy what the majority of its members at the time perceive to be a defect or a lacuna in the existing law C (whether it be the written law enacted by existing statutes or the unwritten common law as it has been expounded by the judges in decided cases), the role of the judiciary is confined to ascertaining from the words that Parliament has approved as expressing its intention what that intention was, and to giving effect to it. Where the meaning of the statutory words is plain and unambiguous it is not for the judges to invent fancied ambiguities as an excuse for failing to give effect to its plain meaning because they them-D selves consider that the consequences of doing so would be inexpedient, or even unjust or immoral. In controversial matters such as are involved in industrial relations there is room for differences of opinion as to what is expedient, what is just and what is morally justifiable. Under our constitution it is Parliament's opinion on these matters that is paramount.

A statute passed to remedy what is perceived by Parliament to be a E defect in the existing law may in actual operation turn out to have injurious consequences that Parliament did not anticipate at the time the statute was passed; if it had, it would have made some provision in the Act in order to prevent them. It is at least possible that Parliament when the Acts of 1974 and 1976 were passed did not anticipate that so widespread and crippling use as has in fact occurred would be made of sympathetic with-drawals of labour and of secondary blacking and picketing in support of F sectional interests able to exercise " industrial muscle." But if this be the case it is for Parliament, not for the judiciary, to decide whether any changes should be made to the law as stated in the Acts, and, if so, what are the precise limits that ought to be imposed upon the immunity from liability for torts committed in the course of taking industrial action. These are matters on which there is a wide legislative choice the exercise of which G is likely to be influenced by the political complexion of the government and the state of public opinion at the time amending legislation is under consideration.

It endangers continued public confidence in the political impartiality of the judiciary, which is essential to the continuance of the rule of law, if judges, under the guise of interpretation, provide their own preferred H amendments to statutes which experience of their operation has shown to have had consequences that members of the court before whom the matter comes consider to be injurious to the public interest. The frequency with which controversial legislation is amended by Parliament itself (as witness the Act of 1974 which was amended in 1975 as well as in 1976) indicates that legislation, after it has come into operation, may fail to have the beneficial effects which Parliament expected or may produce injurious results that Parliament did not anticipate. But, except by private or

hybrid Bills, Parliament does not legislate for individual cases. Public Acts A
of Parliament are general in their application; they govern all cases falling
within categories of which the definitions are to be found in the wording
of the statute. So in relation to section 13 (1) of the Acts of 1974 and
1976, for a judge (who is always dealing with an individual case) to pose
himself the question: " Can Parliament really have intended that the acts
that were done in this particular case should have the benefit of the
immunity? " is to risk straying beyond his constitutional role as interpreter B
of the enacted law and assuming a power to decide at his own discretion
whether or not to apply the general law to a particular case. The legitimate
questions for a judge in his role as interpreter of the enacted law are:
" How has Parliament, by the words that it has used in the statute to
express its intentions, defined the category of acts that are entitled to the
immunity?   Do the acts done in this particular case fall within that C
description? "

The first of these questions was answered by this House in the *Express
Newspapers Ltd.* v. *McShane* [1980] 2 W.L.R. 89 in the way I have
already mentioned. The principal question in this appeal is whether the
Court of Appeal were right in overruling the High Court judge's finding
that it was highly probable that the acts complained of in the instant case
did fall within the category of acts entitled to the immunity. D

The relevant facts that were in evidence before the judge and the Court
of Appeal are to be found set out with customary clarity and simplicity
in the judgment of Lord Denning M.R. Except that I think it necessary
to transcribe in full one letter upon which the argument has mainly turned,
I need do no more than restate them here in summary form.

The British Steel Corporation (" B.S.C.") is a public authority estab- E
lished under the Iron and Steel Act 1975 to run the nationalised sector of
the steel industry. It produces some 50 per cent. of home produced steel
in the United Kingdom and for that purpose employs a workforce number-
ing some 150,000, of whom about 95,000 are members of the trade union,
the Iron and Steel Trades Confederation (" I.S.T.C."). Under the Act the
Secretary of State is empowered by section 4 to give to B.S.C. general F
directions as to the exercise and performance of its functions, and under
Part II of the Act, sections 14 to 24, he is entitled to exercise a relatively
close control over the finances of the corporation and in particular over its
borrowings. In effect, if B.S.C. is operating at a loss, as it notoriously has
been doing for some time past, the Secretary of State holds the purse-
strings. It is also in evidence, what is in any event a matter of public
knowledge, that before the commencement of the strike by I.S.T.C. mem- G
bers which has given rise to the events with which this appeal is concerned,
the government had announced its decision not to provide any public funds
to enable B.S.C. to meet its operating losses after March 31, 1980. Thereafter it must pay its own way and meet its operating costs, including its
current wages bill, out of its current earnings.

In the latter part of 1979 negotiations between I.S.T.C. and B.S.C. H
on wage rates for 1980 began. Owing to the financial stringency which
B.S.C. would experience in 1980, little progress was made; and on
January 2, 1980, the executive council of I.S.T.C. called a strike of its
members employed by B.S.C. This is the trade dispute in furtherance
of which the union claims the subsequent steps that are the subject of
the instant appeal were taken.

Alongside the nationalised sector of the iron and steel industry

A there is a private sector. It consists of about 100 companies producing some 17½ per cent. of the steel produced in the United Kingdom and employing as part of their total workforce some 15,000 who are members of I.S.T.C. It is common ground that there was no existing trade dispute between these workers and any of their employers in the private sector.

B By January 17, 1980, the executive council of I.S.T.C. were growing dissatisfied at the progress that the strike was making even with the aid of some sporadic secondary picketing and sympathetic blacking of movements of steel by members of other trade unions. Accordingly they resolved to call out on strike their members employed in the private sector on January 26 unless a wage settlement with B.S.C. had been reached by then.

C On the same date notice of this resolution was sent to the Independent Steel Employers' Association which represents employers in the private sector. It is convenient to set out this letter in full because it contains a contemporary explanation by the general secretary of I.S.T.C. of the purpose of the executive council in resolving upon this extension of the strike:

D "Dear Mr. Hale, I refer to your telegram and that of Mr. Alec Mortimer received yesterday. These telegrams were read to the members of my executive council who, after a full and detailed discussion on the position of the steel strike with the corporation, and whilst agreeing that there is no dispute with any independent steel employer, were firmly of the opinion that this dispute is becoming politically stage-managed by the Conservative government. We
E feel that with not being made an offer of any new money, that we are being singled out for a direct government and British Steel Corporation attack. It is because of the political intervention that my executive council feel that we should now take the action of involving the private sector in the public battle against the government attitude. Therefore a recommendation will be confirmed next
F which states as follows: ' That in the event of the dispute with the British Steel Corporation not being settled by Saturday, January 26, 1980, instructions are being given to all of our members in the private steel industry to withdraw their labour.' I recognise the fact that our procedure agreements do exist and we do not have a dispute with you, nevertheless these points have been made to our executive, who have ultimately taken this decision. I did manage
G to extend the period of time before the action will be taken. This will give us the opportunity to try and resolve the dispute. I would suggest that it could be very helpful if you and all of your affiliated organisations could write to the government complaining about their role in this matter which leaves a lot to be desired. Perhaps also pressures upon the corporation to settle the issue would be helpful
H now not only to the B.S.C. but to the private sector."

An affidavit of Mr. Bramley, the president of I.S.T.C., that was filed in these proceedings stated that there were other purposes too, concerned with maintaining the morale of the B.S.C. strikers, retaining the sympathy of members of other trade unions at home and abroad who were adversely affected by the strike and avoiding confusion between steel that was to be " blacked " and steel that was not. I regard these, however, as subsidiary to the main purpose as disclosed in the letter. That was to speed up the

time when the shortage of steel for manufacturing industry would really   A
begin to bite so that those manufacturers whose businesses would sustain
serious losses, those workers who would lose their jobs and members of the
public who would suffer hardship would be induced to put the maximum
pressure upon the government to revoke its previous decision and to loosen
the purse-strings to B.S.C. to an extent that would provide it with a subsidy
from public moneys sufficient to enable it to pay to its workforce wages
higher than it would be commercially possible for it to pay out of operating   B
earnings.

Faced with this threat the 16 companies operating in the private sector
who are respondents to this appeal (" the private sector companies ") issued
a writ on January 24 claiming injunctions against the three appellants who
are sued in a representative capacity on behalf of themselves and all other
members of the executive council of I.S.T.C. The injunctions sought were   C
against inducing the companies' employees to break their contracts of
employment by coming out on strike, and against inducing any members
of I.S.T.C. to interfere with the supply of steel to or from the companies'
works or to picket the companies' premises.

Having given the requisite notice to I.S.T.C. under section 17 (1) of the
Acts of 1974 and 1976 the private sector companies applied to the judge
in chambers for interlocutory injunctions in terms of the writ. The appli-   D
cation was heard in chambers on the afternoon of Friday, January 25, by
Kenneth Jones J. In a brief oral judgment the learned judge held that the
case was indistinguishable from *Express Newspapers Ltd.* v. *McShane*
[1980] 2 W.L.R. 89 the report of which had just been published. He
rejected the only argument addressed to him on behalf of the companies on
which it was sought to draw a distinction between that case and the instant   E
case. He held that it was highly probable that the defence that the executive council of I.S.T.C. had acted in furtherance of a trade dispute would
succeed. In the exercise of his discretion, he accordingly refused to grant
any of the injunctions.

An appeal against this decision was heard by the Court of Appeal (Lord
Denning M.R., Lawton and Ackner L.JJ.) at a special sitting held on
Saturday, January 26, 1980. They reversed the judge's decision, granted   F
the private sector companies the injunctions that they sought and, some-
what surprisingly, refused the executive council leave to appeal to your
Lordships' House.

The decision of the Court of Appeal was unanimous. The reasons
given by the individual members of the court were not identical, but in oral
judgments delivered extempore with little time for mutual consultation   G
this is neither surprising nor illegitimate, since the task before the court
was to consider the degree of likelihood that the executive council of
I.S.T.C. would establish that the act of calling upon their members in the
private sector to join the strike was done in furtherance of the trade dispute between the union and B.S.C. One possible argument that could be
advanced against the executive council's immunity might carry weight with
one member of the court, an alternative argument might be preferred by   H
another. The court acting collectively might legitimately take into account
the cumulative merits of the various arguments which commended themselves to one or other of its members.

A feature of the judgments which appears to me to be less legitimate
is the absence of any recognition that the task upon which the Court of
Appeal was engaged was not one of exercising an original discretion of its
own to grant or to withhold an interlocutory injunction but of reviewing

A   the exercise by a High Court judge of an original discretion which was his alone and which he had exercised in favour of withholding an injunction. Apart from a passing observation in the judgment of Lord Denning M.R. that the speeches of the majority of this House in the *McShane* case as to the purely subjective nature of the relevant test of entitlement to immunity under section 13 (1) of the Act was not nearly as clear as the learned judge had thought, no deference was paid to his exercise of a discretion which

B   the law had entrusted to him; there was no examination of his reasons for exercising it in the way he did. Indeed, both Lord Denning M.R. and Ackner L.J. in their judgments refer to the exercise of " *our* " discretion by the Court of Appeal.

    All three members of the Court of Appeal took the view that the original trade dispute between I.S.T.C. and B.S.C. about wages had by

C   January 17, 1980, generated a second dispute in which the parties were I.S.T.C. and the government; that this second dispute did not fall within the definition of " trade dispute " because the government were not the employers; and that the calling out of workers in the private sector was an act done in furtherance of that second dispute. It will be convenient to refer to this as the " two-disputes " argument.

    My Lords, if all this be accepted as an accurate description of the

D   situation on January 17, 1980, how does this prevent the act of calling out the workers in the private sector from being an act done in furtherance of the trade dispute between I.S.T.C. and B.S.C. which was still subsisting? If the executive council honestly believed that a principal reason why B.S.C. would not agree to raise wages to the level that I.S.T.C. was demanding was that the government was adhering to a policy of refusing to provide B.S.C. with the money to do so out of public funds, what could be better

E   calculated to promote the success of I.S.T.C.'s demands in its trade dispute with B.S.C. than to take steps to create a nationwide shortage of steel which would induce the victims of the shortage to put pressure on the government to change its policy? There may be some who would deplore this conduct; harsh words descriptive of it may come readily to the tongue; but it seems to me that, whatever else may be fairly said about it, it cannot

F   be said with any plausibility that it was not done in furtherance of the existing trade dispute with B.S.C.

    The " two-disputes " argument had not been advanced before the learned judge. Counsel for the private sector companies had relied upon a different argument to which I shall be adverting later. The " two-disputes " argument orginated from a suggestion proffered from the bench

G   during the hearing in the Court of Appeal; not unnaturally in the haste of a Saturday morning hearing counsel for the private sector companies was reluctant at that stage to reject it. Further reflection, however, prior to the hearing in this House had led him to the conclusion that the " two-disputes " argument cannot rationally be supported; he has not sought to uphold the judgments of the Court of Appeal upon this ground. In the circumstances I do not find it necessary to analyse those judgments in order

H   to pinpoint what I believe to be the fallacies in the trains of reasoning which led individual members of the court to accept the " two-disputes " argument as plausible. Suffice it to say that, for the reason I have already indicated briefly, I do not think it is.

    Lord Denning M.R. advanced an alternative reason for allowing the appeal which is not echoed in either of the other judgments. He was unwilling to accept that the majority speeches in this House in *Express Newspapers Ltd.* v. *McShane* [1980] 2 W.L.R. 89 had expressed a clear opinion that the test of whether an act was done in furtherance of a A trade dispute was purely subjective. This led him to conclude that this House had not rejected a test based on remoteness that he himself had adumbrated and adopted in three earlier cases. These cases, he said, had not been specifically singled out by name in the *McShane* case as being overruled. He inferred from this that it was arguable that they still remained good authority. In the *McShane* case this House B was not concerned to decide whether the actual decisions in any of a series of previous cases in the Court of Appeal were wrong. What was considered was whether any of three different tests which had been adumbrated in those cases as applicable to determine whether an act was done by a person in contemplation or furtherance of a trade dispute was right in law or not. Among the three tests rejected as wrong in law was the test of remoteness the authorship of which was specifically C ascribed in my own speech to Lord Denning. Recognising this, counsel for the respondents has not felt able to support the judgment of the Court of Appeal on this ground either.

The remains the argument for distinguishing the instant case from the *McShane* case that counsel for the companies had addressed to Kenneth Jones J. at first instance. He had been diverted by the "two-disputes" argument from developing it in the Court of Appeal. It formed the D only ground upon which he felt able to rely in inviting this House to overrule the exercise of his discretion by that learned judge. It receives no mention in the judgments of Lord Denning M.R. or Lawton L.J., but it attracts what may have been intended as a brief reference in the judgment of Ackner L.J. who treats it as arguable.

I do not however find the argument easy to formulate with precision. E It starts with a question in a form which I have suggested presents the court with an insidious temptation to cross the boundary between interpretation and legislation: "Can Parliament in passing the Acts of 1974 and 1976 have intended the immunity conferred by it to extend to acts the object of which was to coerce governments by the infliction of great damage on an innocent public?"

Parliament may not have expected when it passed the Acts of 1974 F and 1976 that trade union leadership would use the immunity granted to them by section 13 (1) in such a way as to produce consequences so injurious to the nation; but if there is some legal limit upon the immunities under the existing legislation it must be found as a matter of construction of the simple words to be found in the section "An act done by a person in contemplation or furtherance of a trade dispute...." That G Parliament contemplated that such an act might be directed at putting pressure upon (or, if you prefer the word, coercing) a minister to alter government policy where that policy relates to terms and conditions of employment is evident from section 29 (2) (*b*) which brings within the definition of a trade dispute a dispute between workers and a minister of the Crown if the dispute relates "to matters which cannot be settled without that minister exercising a power conferred on him by or under H an enactment." It is not necessary for present purposes to consider whether the dispute between the I.S.T.C. and the Secretary of State comes within this description by reason of his statutory powers of control over the finances of B.S.C.: but the existence of the provision disposes of the suggestion that Parliament intended that the mere fact that an act is done with the purpose of coercing government is sufficient in itself to take the act outside the immunity.

A   Faced by this difficulty counsel submitted that as a matter of construction the expression " an act done . . . in . . . furtherance of a trade dispute " is confined to acts which are intended to have an immediate adverse trade or industrial effect on the opposite party to the trade dispute or to set up a train of trade or industrial causes and effects which will have an adverse consequence of that kind on the opposite party. Like the learned judge I find elusive the concept of a train of causes and effects which

B   is confined to causes and effects that can be described as " trade or industrial," and is presumably supposed to be broken by the interposition of a cause and its effect which cannot be so described. There is clearly no principle of construction which would justify reading into the plain and simple words of section 13 (1) additional words (and counsel was quite unable to suggest what they would be) to give effect to so elusive

C   a concept.

        I turn last to the question of discretion. The effect of section 17 (2) of the Acts of 1974 and 1976 on the judge's discretion whether or not to grant an interlocutory injunction was discussed by this House in *N.W.L. Ltd.* v. *Woods* [1979] 1 W.L.R. 1294. The learned judge, before whom the only argument against the executive council's claim to immunity was that to which I have just referred, took the view that

D   there was a high degree of probability that the claim to immunity would succeed. He took account of the evidence that if the threatened strike in the private sector were to continue for any considerable length of time it would bring in its train consequences of crippling gravity to the manufacturing industries of this country, to workers employed in them and to the nation as a whole. In refusing to grant the injunction he

E   followed by the guidance given in my own speech in *N.W.L. Ltd.* v. *Woods,* at p. 1307G.

        My Lords, it is the exercise by the judge of a discretion vested in him, not in the Court of Appeal itself, that your Lordships are required to review. It has not been asserted before your Lordships that there is any real possibility that the executive council's claim to immunity will fail on either of the grounds referred to in the judgments of the Court of

F   Appeal. As to the only remaining ground on which it was argued in this House, as it was before the learned judge, that the executive council's claim to immunity for their action in extending the strike to the private sector might fail, I agree with his assessment of the likelihood of this argument ever succeeding. In my view, there is so high a degree of probability that it falls little short of certainty that it would not. I can

G   see no ground on which this House would be entitled to interfere with the judge's exercise of his discretion.

        The nature and gravity of the damage which would be caused if the strike as extended to the private sector continues for any length of time is not in itself exceptional. Comparatively recent experience has shown that almost any major strike in one of the larger manufacturing or service industries, if it is sufficiently prolonged, may have the effect

H   (figuratively) of bringing the nation to its knees. It is the ability in the last resort to carry out a threat to do this without involving any breach of the civil or criminal law as it now stands that gives to trade unions, individually and collectively, their " industrial muscle." In practice, one side or the other to the dispute gives way and a settlement is arrived at, either with or without government intervention, before this point is reached.

If the national interest requires that some limits should be put upon A
the use of industrial muscle, the law as it now stands must be changed
and this, effectively as well as constitutionally, can only be done by
Parliament—not by the judges.

As a means of controlling abuse of industrial muscle, injunctions
granted in civil actions depend for their efficacy upon the respect which
the majority of those taking part in industrial action pay to the law
as laid down by the judges. Civil actions cannot be brought against trade B
unions, but against individual defendants only; and only those individuals
are bound to observe the injunction. Everyone else involved in the
industrial action can carry on with impunity doing that from which the
individual defendants have been restrained.

If judges were to grant injunctions notwithstanding that they know
that it is highly probable that the acts that they are enjoining are C
perfectly lawful, it is unlikely that voluntary respect for the law as laid
down and applied by courts of justice will continue to have any influence
in controlling industrial action.

It was for these reasons that I expressed myself in favour of allowing
this appeal.

LORD EDMUND-DAVIES. My Lords, a judge's sworn duty to " do D
right by all manner of people after the laws and usages of this realm "
sometimes puts him in difficulty, for certain of those laws and usages
may be repugnant to him. When that situation arises, he may meet
it in one of two ways. First, where the law appears clear, he can shrug
his shoulders, bow to what he regards as the inevitable, and apply it.
If he has moral, intellectual, social or other twinges in doing so, he can E
always invoke Viscount Simonds, who once said (Midland Silicones Ltd.
v. Scruttons Ltd. [1962] A.C. 446, 467–468):

"... to me heterodoxy, or, as some might say, heresy, is not the
more attractive because it is dignified by the name of reform. Nor
will I easily be led by an undiscerning zeal for some abstract kind
of justice to ignore our first duty, which is to administer justice F
according to law, the law which is established for us by Act of
Parliament or the binding authority of precedent."

Alternatively, a judge may be bold and deliberately set out to make
new law if he thinks the existing legal situation unsatisfactory. But he
risks trouble if he goes about it too blatantly, and if the law has been
declared in statutory form it may prove too much for him, dislike it G
though he may. For, as Holt C.J. said in the first year of the 18th
century, "... an Act of Parliament can do no wrong, though it may do
several things that look pretty odd; ..." (City of London v. Wood (1701)
12 Mod.Rep. 669, 687–688). From time to time some judges have been
chafed by this supremacy of Parliament, whose enactments, however
questionable, must be applied. In Inland Revenue Commissioners v.
Hinchy [1960] A.C. 748, Lord Reid said, at p. 767: H

" What we must look for is the intention of Parliament, and I also
find it difficult to believe that Parliament ever really intended the
consequences which flow from the [commissioners'] contention.
But we can only take the intention of Parliament from the words
which they have used in the Act, and therefore the question is
whether these words are capable of a more limited construction.

A   If not, then we must apply them as they stand, however unreasonable or unjust the consequences, and however strongly we may suspect that this was not the real intention of Parliament. . . . One is entitled and indeed bound to assume that Parliament intends to act reasonably, and therefore to prefer a reasonable interpretation of a statutory provision if there is any choice. But I regret that I am unable to agree that this case leaves me with any choice."

B

My Lords, the principal task in this case at all its stages has been that of considering the meaning and ambit of the words, " An act done by a person in contemplation or furtherance of a trade dispute . . ." in section 13 (1) of the Trade Union and Labour Relations Act 1974. Similar words have appeared in United Kingdom statutes for over 100 years (see, for example, section 3 of the Conspiracy, and Protection of Property Act 1875) and they have many times been judicially considered.

C

Doubtless, they have sometimes been more favourably regarded from the Bench than at other times. They were considered by this House as recently as last December in *Express Newspapers Ltd.* v. *McShane* [1980] 2 W.L.R. 89. That decision was naturally binding upon Kenneth Jones J., and upon the members of the Court of Appeal who have had to deal with this case. In reality, though not in strict law, it is also presently binding upon this House. At first instance it was applied without qualification. But in the appellate court it was restrictively applied and held to have no operation upon certain grave and recent developments from what indubitably was in origin a trade dispute.

D

E   The proper impact of the decision in *McShane* upon the instant appeal, and particularly in relation to the restrictive approach of the Court of Appeal, has been considered with, if I may say so, admirable clarity in the speech of my noble and learned friend, Lord Diplock. This I have had the advantage of reading in draft. I respectfully agree with what he has written, and I feel that, particularly at this *interlocutory* stage, I cannot usefully add to it. Suffice it to say that, for the reasons he gives, I too would allow this appeal and discharge the injunctions granted below. This I regard as the inevitable outcome of the statutory provision. That this outcome is unpalatable to many has already been made clear. What should be equally clear is that the provision is not the work of the judges but of Parliament, and it is to Parliament alone that those who find this state of the law insupportable may now appeal.

F

G

LORD FRASER OF TULLYBELTON. My Lords, I respectfully agree with my noble and learned friends, Lord Diplock and Lord Scarman, that the acts of the appellants in calling out members of I.S.T.C. who are employed by firms in the private sector of the steel industry were acts done in furtherance of a trade dispute that was already in existence between I.S.T.C. and B.S.C. That conclusion is inevitable in light of the decision of this House in *Express Newspapers Ltd.* v. *McShane* [1980] 2 W.L.R. 89. In that case, my noble and learned friend Lord Wilberforce did not agree with the majority who held that the test whether an act was " in . . . furtherance of a trade dispute " was subjective. He considered that the test was whether the act was reasonably capable of furthering a trade dispute but he nevertheless agreed with the majority decision that the act of extending the strike in that case to the Press Association was in furtherance of the existing trade dispute. In my

H

A opinion, it is abundantly clear that if the " reasonably capable " test had been applicable in this case, its application would have led to the same result as application of the subjective test; the act of calling out the members of I.S.T.C. in the private sector would still have been held to be in furtherance of the trade dispute with B.S.C.

I come now to consider the discretion under section 17 (2) of the Act of 1974, as amended by the Act of 1975. I wish to explain in my B own words the kind of matters which in my opinion a judge ought to have in mind when exercising his discretion. For the reason that I stated in *N.W.L. Ltd.* v. *Woods* [1979] 1 W.L.R. 1294, I consider that the duty of the court, both in England and in Scotland, is to " have regard to " the likelihood that the party against whom an interlocutory injunction is sought will succeed in establishing the defence that his threatened action would be in contemplation or furtherance of a trade dis- C pute, but without giving overriding effect to that matter. It follows that in a case where the court considers that the defence is highly likely to be established it will be slow to grant an interlocutory injunction against acts which would be protected by the defence. But even in such a case the court has the duty to have regard also to the probable effects of the threatened act. If the court considers, on the available evidence, that the threatened act would probably have an immediate and devastating effect D upon the applicant's person or property—for example by ruining plant which could not be replaced without large expenditure and long delay— the court ought to take that into account. Similarly, if the probable result of the threatened act would be to cause immediate serious danger to public safety or health, and if no other means seemed to be available for averting the danger in time, the court would in my opinion not E be exercising its discretion wrongly if it were to grant an interim injunction. But the kinds of instance which I have suggested do not embrace the facts of the present case where the probable injury to the respondents, although undoubtedly very serious, is not so immediate as to tip the scale in favour of granting an injunction.

I would allow this appeal.

F LORD KEITH OF KINKEL. My Lords, I agree with the reasons for allowing this appeal which have been stated by my noble and learned friend Lord Diplock, and which I have had the opportunity of reading in draft.

In *Express Newspapers Ltd.* v. *McShane* [1980] 2 W.L.R. 89 this House authoritatively decided that, in considering whether an act was G done " in . . . furtherance of " a trade dispute within the meaning of section 13 (1) of the Trade Union and Labour Relations Act 1974, it was necessary for the court to examine the state of mind of the person doing the act in order to ascertain whether his honest purpose was to promote the success of his side in the dispute. It rejected the view that on a proper construction of the enactment it was permissible to have regard to the remoteness of the act done from the immediate source of H the dispute, or the extent to which it had reasonable prospects of furthering the dispute, otherwise than in connection with testing the genuineness, on the evidence as a whole, of the purpose professed by the defendant.

In the present case there are no reasonable grounds, on the evidence available at this interlocutory stage, for doubting that the action taken by the defendants was taken with the genuine purpose of promoting

A their union's side of its trade dispute with the British Steel Corporation.
That dispute is over wages. It is apparent that there is little or no
prospect of the British Steel Corporation being able to pay higher wages
to its workers, upon conditions acceptable to them, unless the government, which has power to do so, makes available to the corporation,
in sufficient quantity to allow of increased wages, money levied from
the general body of taxpayers. So action on the part of the defendants
B designed to result in pressure being applied to the government to make
such money available is plainly directed to improving the prospects of
the union's wages claim being met. Even if the quality of the action
properly fell to be tested objectively, which is not the position, the
test would in my opinion be satisfied.

The Court of Appeal took the view that the action designed to bring
C pressure to bear on the government was taken in pursuance of a
political dispute which was something separate and distinct from the
trade dispute with the British Steel Corporation. Having regard to the
considerations which I have mentioned, that was not, in my opinion,
a tenable view. Further, it was not a view which was urged upon the
Court of Appeal by counsel for the private sector. His argument, as he
made plain in his most attractively presented address to this House,
D was to quite a different effect. It was that in order to qualify as an act
in furtherance of a trade dispute, the act relied upon must be designed
to operate through a sequence of cause and effect of an industrial
character. An act designed to operate otherwise than by interfering in
some way with the processes of manufacturing and marketing of the
employer's product, so it was maintained, did not qualify. This argument
E was considered and rejected by Kenneth Jones J. at first instance. It
was barely noticed in the judgments of the Court of Appeal. In my
opinion it is unsound. However desirable its outcome might be thought
to be, I can find no warrant in the terms of section 13 (1) for implying
into the width of the language there used a limitation such as is contended
for.

F Perusal of the judgments in the Court of Appeal makes it clear that
their conclusion was strongly influenced by consideration of the injustice
involved, in their view, in subjecting to serious economic loss, inconvenience and distress employers and workers in the private sector of the
steel industry, who had no concern at all with the dispute between the
union and the British Steel Corporation, and also of the disastrous
economic consequences to the country as a whole of the action taken
G by the defendants. Such considerations cannot properly distract the
court from its duty of faithfully interpreting a statutory provision
according to its true intent, notwithstanding that events have shown the
provision to be capable of being relied on to enable privileged persons
to bring about disastrous consequences with legal impunity. There
is nothing in the apparent policy of the Act, or the amending Act of
1976, which might warrant a restrictive interpretation of section 13 (1)
H of the Act of 1974. Indeed, that policy seems to have been to enlarge,
not to abridge, the privileges by way of immunity conferred upon trade
unions, their officials and members. If these privileges should prove
to have been exercised, with insufficient sense of responsibility, to the
serious detriment of the national interest, then it is for the force of
public opinion to seek their curtailment through democratic processes
available to it. The considerations for and against such curtailment can

Duport Steels Ltd. v. Sirs (H.L.(E.)) **[1980]**

be properly and definitely debated only in Parliament. It is no part of A
the function of a court of law to form conclusions about the merits
of the issue. The one public interest which courts of law are properly
entitled to treat as their concern is the standing of and the degree of
respect commanded by the judicial system. Involvement in political
controversy, particularly in the legislatively governed field of industrial
relations, is calculated to damage that interest. In the interpretation of
statutes the courts must faithfully endeavour to give effect to the B
expressed intention of Parliament as gathered from the language used and
the apparent policy of the enactment under consideration.

I have therefore concluded that the appeal must be allowed.

LORD SCARMAN. My Lords, this appeal raises two specific questions
as to the interpretation of a statute, the Trade Union and Labour Rela- C
tions Act 1974, as amended. But below the surface of the legal argument lurk some profound questions as to the proper relationship in our
society between the courts, the government, and Parliament. The technical questions of law pose (or should pose) no problems. The more
fundamental questions are, however, very disturbing; nevertheless it is
upon my answer to them that I would allow the appeal. My basic
criticism of all three judgments in the Court of Appeal is that in their D
desire to do justice the court failed to do justice according to law. When
one is considering law in the hands of the judges, law means the body
of rules and guidelines within which society requires its judges to
administer justice. Legal systems differ in the width of the discretionary
power granted to judges: but in developed societies limits are invariably
set, beyond which the judges may not go. Justice in such societies is not E
left to the unguided, even if experienced, sage sitting under the spreading
oak tree.

In our society the judges have in some aspects of their work a discretionary power to do justice so wide that they may be regarded as
law-makers. The common law and equity, both of them in essence
systems of private law, are fields where, subject to the increasing intrusion
of statute law, society has been content to allow the judges to formulate F
and develop the law. The judges, even in this, their very own field of
creative endeavour, have accepted, in the interests of certainty, the
self-denying ordinance of " stare decisis," the doctrine of binding
precedent: and no doubt this judicially imposed limitation on judicial
law-making has helped to maintain confidence in the certainty and
evenhandedness of the law. G

But in the field of statute law the judge must be obedient to the will
of Parliament as expressed in its enactments. In this field Parliament
makes, and un-makes, the law: the judge's duty is to interpret and to
apply the law, not to change it to meet the judge's idea of what justice
requires. Interpretation does, of course, imply in the interpreter a power
of choice where differing constructions are possible. But our law requires H
the judge to choose the construction which in his judgment best meets
the legislative purpose of the enactment. If the result be unjust but
inevitable, the judge may say so and invite Parliament to reconsider its
provision. But he must not deny the statute. Unpalatable statute law
may not be disregarded or rejected, merely because it is unpalatable.
Only if a just result can be achieved without violating the legislative
purpose of the statute may the judge select the construction which best

A suits his idea of what justice requires. Further, in our system the rule "stare decisis" applies as firmly to statute law as it does to the formulation of common law and equitable principles. And the keystone of "stare decisis" is loyalty throughout the system to the decisions of the Court of Appeal and this House. The Court of Appeal may not overrule a House of Lords decision: and only in the exceptional circumstances set out in the Practice Statement of July 1, 1966 (*Practice Statement (Judicial*
B *Precedent)* [1966] 1 W.L.R. 1234), will this House refuse to follow its own previous decisions.

Within these limits, which cannot be said in a free society possessing elective legislative institutions to be narrow or constrained, judges, as the remarkable judicial career of Lord Denning himself shows, have a genuine creative role. Great judges are in their different ways judicial activists.
C But the constitution's separation of powers, or more accurately functions, must be observed if judicial independence is not to be put at risk. For, if people and Parliament come to think that the judicial power is to be confined by nothing other than the judge's sense of what is right (or, as Selden put it, by the length of the Chancellor's foot), confidence in the judicial system will be replaced by fear of it becoming uncertain and
D arbitrary in its application. Society will then be ready for Parliament to cut the power of the judges. Their power to do justice will become more restricted by law than it need be, or is today.

In the present case the Court of Appeal failed to construe or apply the statute in the way in which this House had plainly said it was to be construed and applied. This failure was recognised, significantly and courageously, by counsel for the respondents who at the outset of his
E argument in this House said he would not be relying upon the reasoning of the Court of Appeal. It was, he recognised, contrary to the ruling of the majority of this House in the recent case of *Express Newspapers Ltd.* v. *McShane* [1980] 2 W.L.R. 89. Instead of relying upon the grounds selected by the Court of Appeal for reversing the judge's decision to refuse the respondents the injunctions they were seeking, counsel
F advanced a skilful and serious argument upon the construction of the statute, which could plausibly be said to be open to him notwithstanding the decision in *McShane's* case. He had advanced it before the judge in chambers, who considered and rejected it. He advanced it before the Court of Appeal, who, so far as one can gather from the terms of their judgments, did not think it merited even consideration: for not one of the three judges dealt with it, though Ackner L.J. did refer to it. My
G Lords, I regret to have to say it, but in my opinion the Court of Appeal in this case, for the most laudable of motives, their desire to achieve a just result, strayed beyond the limits set by judicial precedent and by our (largely unwritten) constitution. Their decision was contrary to the statute as authoritatively interpreted by your Lordships' House.

The two questions which arise upon the statute are: first, the true
H construction of the words "An act done by a person in contemplation or furtherance of a trade dispute . . ." in section 13 of the Act of 1974, the section which confers upon persons contemplating or already engaged in a trade dispute certain immunities from tortious liability: secondly, the extent of the discretion possessed by the court where section 17 (2) of the Act of 1974 as amended applies.

There are two sectors in the British steel industry: the public in which the British Steel Corporation is the employer, and a much smaller private

Lord Scarman   **Duport Steels Ltd. v. Sirs (H.L.(E.))**   **[1980]**

sector which includes a number of private employers, among them the   A
16 plaintiffs in this action.   It is common ground that there exists in the
present case a trade dispute between the union and the B.S.C.   It is a
dispute about wages.   The union wants " more money on the table."   The
B.S.C. say that they cannot provide it: nor is the government, who
under the Iron and Steel Act 1975 retain ultimate financial control of
the corporation, willing to provide it.   In these circumstances, as Lord
Denning M.R. said in his judgment (ante, p. 149E), the union " came to a   B
decision to extend the dispute into the private sector."   It was apparent
to the union, as Mr. Sirs said in a letter written to union branches and
quoted in his judgment by the Master of the Rolls, " that the continued
operation of the private sector was not only having the effect of prolonging the present dispute but was creating a feeling of injustice with other
trade unions, . . ."   The extension of the dispute was intended to put   C
pressure upon the government to find the money which would enable the
B.S.C. to make an offer acceptable to the union and so to put an end to
the trade dispute.   Whether or not this extension brought into existence
a second and separate dispute with the government (as the Court of
Appeal thought), it was certainly an act done in furtherance of the wages
dispute with B.S.C. in the sense in which this House interpreted the
section in *Express Newspapers Ltd.* v. *McShane* [1980] 2 W.L.R. 89.   D
The executive council of the union honestly and sincerely believed that
by extending the strike into the private sector they were advancing, or
furthering, their cause in the wages dispute.

This analysis of the situation, which the respondents in this House
have not suggested is false, disposes of the reasons given by the Court
of Appeal for considering it " arguable " that what was done was not   E
in furtherance of the trade dispute.   And counsel did not contend to the
contrary.

His argument assumed that the acts of the appellants were done in
furtherance of the trade dispute.   But he argued that upon a true
construction of the section the acts which attract immunity must be acts
having industrial or commercial consequences and designed to bring
pressure upon a person or persons who could themselves bring industrial   F
or commercial pressure upon the employer who was in dispute with the
union.   Applying this criterion to the facts of this case, he submitted
that the private sector had no power to coerce, or exert industrial or
commercial pressure upon, the B.S.C.   It was neither a customer nor a
supplier of B.S.C., but a competitor.   The purpose of extending the strike
to the private sector was, therefore, political in character, i.e. to induce   G
the private sector to bring pressure upon the government to provide the
money needed to satisfy the union.

The plausibility of the submission derives from the fact that it is
directed to the quality of the act required for immunity and not to the
question whether or not it is in contemplation or furtherance of a trade
dispute.   Nevertheless, it must be rejected.   First, the Act imposes no   H
express limitation upon the character of the act which attracts immunity
other than that it must be done in contemplation or furtherance of a
trade dispute.   Secondly, an analysis of the submission reveals that it is
an attempt to define acts qualifying for immunity by reference to their
purpose.   But the only purpose mentioned by the statute is the advancement of a trade dispute.

In brief, the statute is not expressly limited in the way counsel

A suggests: and, in the light of Parliament's legislative purpose as analysed in *N.W.L. Ltd.* v. *Woods* [1979] 1 W.L.R. 1294 and *Express Newspapers Ltd.* v. *McShane* [1980] 2 W.L.R. 89, it cannot be said that Parliament intended that it should be. To the question—could Parliament have conceivably intended that any act which a trade disputant honestly believed would further his side of the dispute should attract the immunity provided by the section?—the answer is simply " Yes: and this House

B in its judicial examination of the legislative purpose of the statutory provisions has already so answered the question."

Section 17 (2), *as amended.*

This subsection requires that, where an application is made for an interlocutory injunction against a party claiming that he acted in con-

C templation or furtherance of a trade dispute, the court shall have regard to the likelihood of his succeeding at trial in establishing that he so acted. The subsection does not deprive the court of its discretion: and in both *N.W.L. Ltd.* v. *Woods* and *McShane's* case are to be found dicta recognising that the court has a residual discretion to grant an injunction notwithstanding the likelihood of such a defence succeeding at trial—for

D instance, where the consequences to the employer or to third parties or the public and perhaps the nation itself might be disastrous if it were refused (*per* Lord Diplock in *N.W.L. Ltd.* v. *Woods,* at p. 1307, and myself, at p. 1315), or where the action sought to be enjoined endangered a fundamental right of the public such as the freedom of the press (myself in *McShane's* case, at p. 105). But it would require an altogether exceptional case—some examples of which my noble and learned friend Lord

E Fraser of Tullybelton has given in his speech.

In the instant case the high probability is that the defence would succeed at trial. Indeed, my Lords, I think it " a virtual certainty " (to borrow Lord Diplock's words in *N.W.L. Ltd.* v. *Woods,* at p. 1307H). The economic damage threatened by the extension of the strike to the private sector, though very serious, is not so immediate as to justify

F intervention by the court granting relief to which it is probable that the plaintiffs are not entitled. There is time for the parties to come to terms or for the government to act either by intervention or by taking emergency powers or by some other executive or legislative action. When disaster threatens, it is ordinarily for the government, not the courts, to act to avert it.

G But, my Lords, there is a further ground for holding the Court of Appeal to have been in error in granting the injunctions. Injunctive relief is discretionary: and the discretion is the judge's. An appellate court may intervene if the judge misdirected himself in law, took into account irrelevant matters or failed to take into account relevant matters. The judge exercised his discretion in this case by refusing the injunc-tions: and there is no indication in his short and admirable judgment

H that he fell into any of these errors of law.

My Lords, for these reasons as well as for those set forth in the speech of my noble and learned friend, Lord Diplock, I would allow the appeal and discharge the injunctions.

If the law is unacceptable, the remedy lies with Parliament, not the judges. And if Parliament is minded to amend the statute, I would suggest that, instead of seeking to close what my noble and learned friend Lord Wilberforce has aptly called " open-ended expressions "

(*Express Newspapers Ltd.* v. *McShane* [1980] 2 W.L.R. 89, 94) such A
as those which have now given rise to bitter and damaging litigation
(e.g. *British Broadcasting Corporation* v. *Hearn* [1977] 1 W.L.R. 1004,
N.W.L. Ltd. v. *Woods* [1979] 1 W.L.R. 1294, *Express Newspapers Ltd.*
v. *McShane*), the draftsman should be bold and tackle his problems head-
on. If he is to put a limitation on the immunities in section 13, let
him do so by limiting the heads of tortious liability where immunity
is conferred: if he is to strengthen the availability of interlocutory relief B
in industrial relations, let him include clear guidelines in the statute.
And, if he is to limit secondary or tertiary " blacking " or picketing, the
statute must declare whose premises may, or may not, be picketed and
how far the " blacking " or picketing may extend. " Open-ended expressions " will bring the judges inevitably into the industrial arena
exercising a discretion, which may well be misunderstood by many and C
which can damage confidence in the administration of justice.

Appeal allowed with costs.

Solicitors: *Russell, Jones & Walker; Allen & Overy.*

M. G.   D

_____

[HOUSE OF LORDS]

* FARRELL (FORMERLY McLAUGHLIN)   .   .   RESPONDENT E

AND

SECRETARY OF STATE FOR DEFENCE .   .   .   APPELLANT

1979 Nov. 5, 6;   Viscount Dilhorne, Lord Edmund-Davies,
      Dec. 19   Lord Fraser of Tullybelton,
                           Lord Russell of Killowen and Lord Lane F

*Northern Ireland—Crime—Prevention of—Suspected bomb attack
    on bank—Soldiers shooting and killing man acting suspiciously
    —Action by widow alleging negligence and assault and battery
    by soldiers—Whether force used by soldiers "reasonable in
    the circumstances"—Whether negligence by others in planning
    of operation, if proved, depriving soldiers of defence—Criminal
    Law Act (Northern Ireland) 1967 (c. 18), s. 3 (1)*   G

By section 3 of the Criminal Law Act (Northern Ireland)
1967:
        "(1) A person may use such force as is reasonable in
    the circumstances in the prevention of crime, or in
    effecting or assisting in the lawful arrest of offenders or
    suspected offenders or of persons unlawfully at large . . ."

Soldier " X," serving in Northern Ireland, received infor-   H
mation that a bomb attack was likely to be made on a bank
that night, and he accordingly instructed soldier " A " to take
three others and take up position on a rooftop opposite the
bank. Later, three men were seen acting suspiciously, and,
after challenging them, the soldiers fired and the three men
were killed. It turned out that none of them was armed or
carrying a bomb. The plaintiff, the widow of one of the
three men, brought an action against the Secretary of State
for damages on the ground that his death had been caused

A   by the negligence of the Ministry, its servants and agents, and
by assaults and batteries committed by them. There was no
allegation in her pleadings that there had been negligence on
the part of anyone other than the four soldiers who had fired
the shots or in the planning of the operation to protect the
bank. The Secretary of State in his defence relied on section 3
(1) of the Act of 1967. At the trial, before Gibson L.J. and a
jury, no allegations of negligence on the part of persons other
B   than the four soldiers or in the planning of the operation were
advanced by the plaintiff. Gibson L.J. decided not to leave
the question of negligence to the jury. Following answers
given by the jury to questions put to them by him, he gave
judgment for the Secretary of State. The plaintiff appealed
and contended on the appeal that Gibson L.J. should have
left to the jury the question whether there had been negligence
on the part of any other servant or agent of the Ministry.
C   The Court of Appeal allowed the appeal and ordered a new
trial, Lowry L.C.J. holding that " in the circumstances " in
section 3 (1) of 1967 meant the circumstances in which an
operation was conceived and planned and in which the preparatory steps were taken as well as those in which the final
decisive act was performed; that, alternatively, the question
of negligence should have been left to the jury in order to
ensure that the reasonableness of the planning and preparatory
D   actions was considered by the jury; and that Gibson L.J. had
erred because he had omitted a question on negligence and
charged the jury in a manner that had invited their attention
only to the immediate conduct of soldier " A " and his detachment at the precise time and place of the shooting.
        On appeal by the Secretary of State: —
        Held, allowing the appeal, that, if negligence on the part
of persons other than the soldiers who had fired the shots had
E   been pleaded or alleged at the trial, the trial would have
taken a very different course; that information elicited by the
plaintiff in cross-examination of the soldiers at the trial had
not raised a prima facie case of such negligence; that, further,
" in the circumstances " in section 3 (1) of the Criminal Law
Act (Northern Ireland) 1967 meant that the question to be
determined when such a defence was put forward in a civil or
criminal action was whether the person sued or accused had
F   used such force as had been reasonable in the circumstances in
which he had been placed in the prevention of crime or in
bringing about a lawful arrest of an offender or suspected
offender, and, accordingly, defects in the planning of an operation by others would not deprive him of that defence; and
that accordingly, the Court of Appeal ought not to have
ordered a new trial (*post,* pp. 178D–E, G—179B, E—180C, 181H—
182B).
G   *Per curiam.* The primary purpose of pleadings, which is to
define the issues and thereby to inform the parties in advance
of the case that they have to meet and so enable them to take
steps to deal with it, still remains and can still prove of vital
importance (*post,* pp. 180B, 181H—182B).
        Decision of the Court of Appeal in Northern Ireland
reversed.

H   No cases are referred to in their Lordships' opinions and none were cited
in argument.

APPEAL from the Court of Appeal in Northern Ireland.
    This was an appeal by the defendant, the Secretary of State for Defence,
by leave of the Court of Appeal in Northern Ireland from their decision
on December 20, 1978, whereby they allowed an appeal by the plaintiff,
Olive Farrell (formerly McLaughlin), from the verdict and judgment given

on February 25, 1977, on the trial of the plaintiff's action before Gibson L.J.   A
and a jury and ordered a new trial.

The facts are set out in the opinion of Viscount Dilhorne.

Sir Michael Havers Q.C., A.-G. and *Simon Brown* for the Secretary of
State.
Richard Ferguson Q.C. and *Declan Morgan* (both of the Bar of Northern   B
Ireland) for the plaintiff.

Their Lordships took time for consideration.

December 19. VISCOUNT DILHORNE. My Lords, the respondent was
the widow of one of three men shot and killed in Newry in Northern
Ireland during the night of October 23, 1971. During that day soldier   C
" X," the officer in command of a detachment of troops in the town,
received information that it was highly likely that a bomb attack would
be made that night by three men on the National Provincial Bank in
Hill Street in that town.

Soldier " X " told soldier " A " this and told him to go with three
other soldiers " B," " C," " D," and take up a position on the roof of a   D
building in Hill Street opposite the National Provincial Bank. The four
soldiers did so at about 10.30 p.m. Soldier " A " told the soldiers with
him that on no account were they to open fire until he did. The street
was well lit and the soldiers on the roof were above the street lights and
so difficult, if not impossible, to see from the ground.

At a moment when soldier " B " was alone on the front of the roof,
he saw two men walking up Hill Street towards the National Provincial   E
Bank. He saw them cross the road and go to the night safe of the bank.
They appeared to be trying to open it. He then saw three men cross
the road to the night safe and then there was a scuffle with the two
already there. Soldier " B " called soldier " A " who saw the three men
close to the night safe, with their backs towards him. He did not see
the two who had got there first. After about 10 to 15 seconds soldier " A "   F
shouted " Halt." He saw the three men stop what they were doing and
look up and down the street. One of them shouted " Run " and the
three of them took to their heels. Soldier " A " cocked his rifle and
shouted " Halt, I am ready to fire." The men did not stop. He fired and
the three soldiers with him also fired, with the result that the three men
were killed. It turned out that none of them was armed or carrying a
bomb. One was found to be carrying a bag which had been in the   G
possession of one of the men who went first to the night safe. That bag
contained a coat. The other of the two men had a bag containing cash
which presumably he had intended to put in the night safe. That autumn
there had been about 35 bomb explosions in Newry and two days before
a bomb had been put outside the local savings bank.

On April 19, 1973, about 18 months later, the respondent issued a   H
writ claiming as widow and administratrix of McLaughlin, one of the three
men killed, damages from the Ministry of Defence on the ground that his
death was caused by the negligence of the Ministry, its servants and agents,
and by assaults and batteries committed by them. It was not until
January 23, 1974, that the statement of claim was delivered. Paragraph 2
thereof, so far as material, reads as follows:

A   " 2. . . . by reason of the negligence of the servants and agents of the
defendants, and further and in the alternative by reason of the assaults
on and batteries to the deceased by the said servants and agents of the
defendants, the deceased was struck by a bullet of bullets which had
been discharged from a firearm by one or more of the said servants
or agents, whereby the deceased sustained such severe personal injuries
B   that he died as a result thereof on October 23, 1971. *Particulars of
negligence.* (i) Failing and omitting to give any or adequate warning to the plaintiff. (ii) Causing and permitting a firearm to be
discharged at the deceased in the circumstances. (iii) Discharging a
firearm at the deceased with intent to kill him or cause him grievous
bodily harm. (iv) Failing and omitting to fire a warning shot. (v)
Failing and omitting to fire at the deceased in a fashion which
C   would have minimised the risk of causing him serious injury or death.
(vi) Striking a blow which was out of proportion to the occasion.
(vii) Using excessive force to effect an arrest. (viii) Causing and
permitting a firearm to be discharged at the deceased at all. *Particulars of assaults and batteries.* The plaintiff repeats the above
particulars of negligence and says that the circumstances in which
D   the deceased was killed by the servants or agents of the defendants
were such that they constituted in law an assault and battery upon
his person. In particular the plaintiff complains that the force used
in executing an arrest of the deceased was excessive and unnecessary
and unreasonable in the circumstances and was, therefore, out of
proportion to the occasion."

E   It is apparent from this paragraph that the case the respondent sought
to establish and the case that the Ministry had to meet was that it was
negligence on the part of the four soldiers who fired the shots and, alternatively, assaults and batteries committed by them that brought about
the death of McLaughlin.

There was no allegation in the statement of claim that there had been
any negligence on the part of anyone else or in the planning of the operation
F   to protect the bank.

In their amended defence, the Ministry, inter alia, pleaded:

" If any servant or agents of the defendants discharged any bullet
from any firearm and the deceased was struck thereby, which is denied,
such person in doing so was using such force as was reasonable in the
circumstances in the prevention of crime and/or the effecting or
G   assisting in the lawful arrest of the deceased, who (a) was attempting
to escape after the commission or attempted commission of offences
of robbery, assault and battery, and was unlawfully at large; (b) was
reasonably thought by such person to have been attempting to destroy
or damage bank premises in the town of Newry by the use of a bomb
or incendiary device at a time when in the recent past there had been
H   many attacks by bombs and incendiary devices upon premises in
Newry; . . ."

The trial of this action took place before Gibson L.J. and a Belfast
jury. After the evidence was heard, counsel made a number of submissions to the learned Lord Justice. In the course of the discussion,
Mr. Ferguson for the respondent suggested that a question should be left
to the jury along the lines " did the soldiers shoot the deceased without
lawful cause or excuse? " and that the second question left to them should

be "were the soldiers guilty of negligence causing the death of the A
deceased?" It is clear that both these questions were directed to the
conduct of the soldiers who had been on the roof in Hill Street and who had
fired and were not directed to any question of anyone else being guilty of
negligence. After the discussion, the learned Lord Justice decided not to
leave the question of negligence to the jury. In my opinion he was right
not to do so, for if the soldiers had an answer to the claim based on assault
and battery, that would also be an answer to the claim against them based B
on negligence and to leave both questions to them would only confuse. In
this House Mr. Ferguson did not contend that there should be a new trial
on account of negligence not being left to the jury.

The learned Lord Justice invited the jury to answer the following eight
questions and I append to them the answers that they gave:

"1. Did the soldiers fire because soldier 'A' suspected with reason- C
able cause—(a) that the husband of the plaintiff and two other men
had attempted to place an explosive bomb or an incendiary device in
or at the Provincial Bank and (b) that such explosive bomb or incendiary device would endanger life? Answer: (a) yes (b) yes. 2. If
the answers to questions 1 (a) and 1 (b) or to question 1 (a) is 'yes,'
was it reasonable in the circumstances (including the reasonable D
suspicion of soldier 'A') in the prevention of crime for the soldiers
to fire to kill? Answer: yes. 3. If the answers to questions 1 (a) and
1 (b) or to question 1 (a) is 'yes,' was it reasonable in the circumstances (including the reasonable suspicion of soldier 'A') in effecting
the lawful arrest of the three men for the soldiers to fire to kill?
Answer: yes. 4. Did the soldiers fire after soldier 'A' had twice
shouted at the three men to halt? Answer: yes. 5. When the bar- E
man Mr. O'Neill was at the night safe in the front wall of the Provincial
Bank did the husband of the plaintiff and two other men attempt to
rob him of the money he was going to place in the night safe?
Answer: yes. 6. Was the shooting entirely out of proportion to the
occasion? Answer: no. 7. Was there fault on the part of the husband of the plaintiff which contributed to his death? Answer: yes. F
8. If answers to questions 2 and 3 are 'no' and answer to question
7 is 'yes' what percentage reduction should be made in the damages
having regard to the responsibility of the plaintiff's husband for his
own death? Not answered."

The learned Lord Justice accordingly gave judgment for the Ministry.
The respondent appealed to the Court of Appeal on the following grounds: G

"1. That the learned trial judge was wrong in law in withdrawing
the issue of negligence from the jury. 2. That the learned trial judge
was wrong in law in directing the jury that the test to be applied to
the conduct of the soldiers was a subjective test. 3. That the learned
trial judge was wrong in law in failing to direct the jury that the test
to be applied to the conduct of the soldiers was an objective test. H
4. That the learned trial judge wrongly admitted evidence of acts of
terrorism in Newry and the surrounding district. 5. That the questions
put to the jury were of such a nature and couched in such a form as
to deprive the appellant of a fair trial. 6. That the learned trial judge
failed to put the case for the appellant adequately to the jury. 7. That
the finding that the appellant was not entitled to damages was perverse
and unreasonable."

A   It was not suggested in the course of the trial that there had been negligence on the part of anyone other than the four soldiers and failure to leave to the jury the question of negligence on the part of anyone else was not a ground of appeal. Mr. Ferguson nevertheless, in the Court of Appeal, on behalf of the respondent contended that the learned Lord Justice should have left to the jury the question whether there had been negligence on the part of any other servant or agent of the Ministry. In the course

B   of the cross-examination of the soldiers who gave evidence, it was elicited that soldier " X " had only selected and instructed one soldier; that he had given no instructions about summoning help; that there was no agreed procedure for the four soldiers reporting back to their base; that only four soldiers out of 80 under soldier " X's " command were selected for this operation; that all four were ordered to go on the roof; that they did not

C   have with them a loudhailer; and that they were left in a situation in which the only way they could stop or apprehend a terrorist or suspected terrorist if he refused to stop was by firing at him.

In this House Mr. Ferguson contended that these matters were circumstances which the jury should have been directed to take into account in relation to the use of force by the four soldiers.

D   Section 3 of the Criminal Law Act (Northern Ireland) 1967 reads as follows:

" (1) A person may use such force as is reasonable in the circumstances in the prevention of crime, or in effecting or assisting in the lawful arrest of offenders or suspected offenders or of persons unlawfully at large. (2) Subsection (1) shall replace the rules of the common law

E   as to the matters dealt with by that subsection."

In the Court of Appeal Lowry L.C.J. said:

" When the cause of action is framed in trespass and the assault in fact is proved, the defendants must then prove the defence of justification and, when debating that issue, it is not only the conduct of the soldiers on the ground which must be looked at but all the circum-

F   stances which led to the commission of the act complained of."

He thought that it was in order to leave only the issues of assault and battery and the alleged justification thereof to the jury where there was no separate issue of negligence. But in his opinion that depended on the proper direction being given as to the phrase " in the circumstances " in

G   section 3 (1). This meant, he said: " the circumstances in which an operation is conceived and planned and in which the preparatory steps are taken as well as those in which the final decisive act is performed."

If he was wrong as to this, then in his opinion the question of negligence should have been left to the jury " in order to ensure that the reasonableness of the planning and preparatory actions is considered by the jury."

H   He considered that the learned Lord Justice had erred because he omitted a question on negligence and

" charged the jury in a manner which invited their attention only to the immediate conduct of soldier ' A ' and his detachment at the precise time and place of the shooting. Liability was made to depend solely on the liability of the men on the spot viewed at the time of the shooting."

Jones L.J. said: A

"... there was more to the case, as it seems to me, than merely the shooting by the soldiers. That was the central incident and the one which led directly to the bringing of this action. Indeed that was what the action was about. But it by no means exhausted the relevant matters because the scene was set by the Ministry or at any rate by its officers. They laid on the operation, chose the location of the post and positioned the soldiers. They made the plan and provided the men and the equipment with which to carry out the plan."   B

McGonigal L.J. said that the claim in negligence was based on:

"a failure to take reasonable care for the safety of the men engaged in that robbery in that (1) the scene for the counter-action was set by soldier 'X' regardless of the fact that the likely result would be what   C did occur, and (2) no regard was had to any attempt to reduce the risk of serious injury to the robbers by, for example, establishing fixed ground positions or back-up ground patrols which might have enabled an arrest rather than a killing to result, or by the use of a loudhailer coupled with a clearer indication of who was challenging and where the challenge came from to enhance the possibility that   D the men challenged would stop instead of trying to escape by running away."

My Lords, I have already made it clear that no such allegations of negligence were contained in the statement of claim and that at the trial no such allegations of negligence were advanced. If in the statement of claim any such allegations had been put forward, the defence would have been notified of the fact that evidence might be required to meet them and   E the trial would then have taken a very different course.

Soldier " X " envisaged that persons challenged would stop, not that the likely result would be that they would be shot. He considered that a soldier at ground level at a static position would have been at considerable risk from a terrorist gunman. There were mobile patrols in Newry. They were diverted to the area after the shooting. One arrived in about five   F minutes. If the four soldiers had waited for their arrival, there can be no doubt that the three men would have made good their escape. As there was no doubt that the three men heard the challenges, the provision of a loudhailer would have made no difference. The use of a loudhailer would not have indicated who was challenging or where the challenge came from, nor can I see any reason for thinking that the use of one would   G have enhanced the possibility that the men challenged would stop.

My Lords, I do not consider that the information elicited in the course of cross-examination, to which I have referred, amounted to prima facie evidence of negligence on the part of anyone in the planning of this operation. Indeed, if on this evidence the learned judge had been invited to hold that there was a prima facie case of such negligence, he would, in my opinion, have been right, indeed obliged, to rule that there was not.   H

Further, my Lords, I am unable to agree that the phrase " in the circumstances " in section 3 (1) should be given the wide interpretation given to it in the Court of Appeal. That section is contained in a statute dealing with the criminal law. It may provide a defence for a person accused of a crime. It also may provide a defence for a person sued. In each case when such a defence is put forward the question to be determined is whether the person who is accused or sued used such force as

A   was reasonable in the circumstances in which he was placed in the prevention of crime or in bringing about a lawful arrest of an offender or suspected offender.

Section 3 (1) would provide no defence to soldier " X " in respect of a claim for negligence in the planning of the operation. It can only provide a defence for those who used force and if the force the four soldiers used

B   was reasonable in the circumstances in which they used it, the defects, if there were any, in the planning of the operation would not deprive them of that defence and render the force used unreasonable.

Further, I am unable to agree with the learned Lord Chief Justice that the questions put to the jury were of such a nature and couched in such a form as to deprive the respondent of a fair trial. The questions must not be considered in isolation, but with the charge of the learned Lord

C   Justice in regard to them. And reading them with the charge to the jury, I do not consider them to have deprived the respondent of a fair trial. It is true the learned trial judge did say that he thought one would still be preventing a crime if one saw a man trying to commit a crime and chased after him and shot him while trying to catch him. Soldier " A " said that he suspected that the three men were trying to put a bomb

D   or incendiary device in the night safe. His challenge stopped their actions. If they had gone to the bank with a bomb or incendiary device, he could not say whether they had succeeded in placing it in the night safe. If they had not, then it might be said that the force used was used in the prevention of crime, for it could not be assumed that the bomb or device would not be used elsewhere. However this may be, this observation in the course of a long charge to the jury did not, in my opinion, suffice to

E   render the trial unfair.

The Court of Appeal ordered a new trial. In my opinion they should not have done so. If, following upon their order, there was a trial conducted on the lines they suggest the original trial should have been, it would have been a trial of a very different case from that pleaded and presented to the jury in the trial before Gibson L.J.

F   It could have been pleaded that there was negligence on the part of persons other than the four soldiers. Any such allegations would have to have been properly formulated, and if such a case had been pleaded and presented, then the question whether any and if so what duty of care was owed to persons reasonably suspected of attempting to commit or of committing a serious crime would have arisen for consideration. Although debated in the Court of Appeal, no useful purpose would, in my opinion,

G   be served by considering that question in this appeal, for determination of it would in no way affect the question whether or not the order of the Court of Appeal that there should be a new trial was correct. I do not propose to comment on the views expressed on this question by the Court of Appeal, but it is not to be assumed that I agree with them.

In my opinion, for the reasons stated, this appeal should be allowed.

H

LORD EDMUND-DAVIES. My Lords, I am in respectful agreement with the speech prepared by my noble and learned friend, Viscount Dilhorne, which I have had the advantage of seeing in draft, and I desire to add no more than a few observations.

It has become fashionable in these days to attach decreasing importance to pleadings, and it is beyond doubt that there have been times when an insistence on complete compliance with their technicalities put justice at

risk, and, indeed, may on occasion have led to its being defeated. But A
pleadings continue to play an essential part in civil actions, and although
there has been since the Civil Procedure Act 1833 a wide power to permit
amendments, circumstances may arise when the grant of permission would
work injustice or, at least, necessitate an adjournment which may prove
particularly unfortunate in trials with a jury. To shrug off a criticism as
" a mere pleading point " is therefore bad law and bad practice. For the B
primary purpose of pleadings remains, and it can still prove of vital
importance. That purpose is to define the issues and thereby to inform the
parties in advance of the case they have to meet and so enable them to
take steps to deal with it.

I have regretfully to say that in my judgment this basic requirement
received insufficient consideration by the Court of Appeal in Northern
Ireland. The relevant parts of the statement of claim have already been C
set out in the speech of my noble and learned friend, Viscount Dilhorne,
and I need only point out that, in support of the allegation in paragraph 2
thereof of " the negligence of the servants and agents of the defendants,"
the only particulars pleaded related solely to alleged acts or omissions
by the soldiers stationed on the roof-top opposite the National Provincial
Bank premises. Indeed, after observing critically that, in the trial judge's D
direction to the jury, " liability was made to depend solely on the liability
of the men on the spot . . . at the time of the shooting," the learned
Lord Chief Justice of Northern Ireland correctly commented : " It must
in fairness be said that the particulars of negligence in the statement of
claim appear to look solely to the alleged acts and omissions of the men on
the spot; . . ." He continued: " . . . but Mr. Ferguson, for the plaintiff,
briefly cross-examined soldiers ' X ' and ' A ' on broader grounds without E
objection."

My Lords, I have studied with care the short cross-examination of
soldier " X " and I have been unable to find in it any accusation levelled
against him that he failed in his duty in any respect, and certainly no
admission by him of any neglect. Nor was the cross-examination of
soldier " A " directed to establishing negligence by soldier " X " or any F
other officer or N.C.O. It is therefore unnecessary to consider what
should have been done had useful admissions been elicited, save to say that
latitude extended by a trial judge in relation to cross-examination does not
per se broaden the pleaded issues, though it may give rise to a successful
application for leave to amend if such cross-examination proves fruitful.
In the present case no such application was made, and that for the good
reason that nothing useful to the plaintiff's case emerged. G

So the case in negligence remained at all times restricted to the conduct
of the soldiers on the roof-top. Yet Jones L.J. stressed that :

" . . . the Ministry of Defence . . . was, of course, the defendant and
ultimately responsible not only for the acts and omissions of the
soldiers on the ground but also for the lay-out of the operation—
the setting in which the soldiers found themselves." H

McGonigal L.J. said :

" The claim in negligence is based on a failure to take reasonable
care for the safety of the men engaged in that robbery in that (1) the
scene for the counter-action was set by soldier ' X ' regardless of
the fact that the likely result would be what did occur, and (2) no
regard was had to any attempt to reduce the risk of serious injury

A   to the robbers by, for example, establishing fixed ground positions or back-up ground patrols which might have enabled an arrest rather than a killing to result, or by the use of a loudhailer coupled with a clearer indication of who was challenging and where the challenge came from to enhance the possibility that the men challenged would stop instead of trying to escape by running away."

B   Now, not only were these matters ever pleaded, but, as I have already pointed out, no opportunity appears to have been given to soldier " X " to deal with them. Had they been, the proper course would have been to insist on the statement of claim being amended to meet the entirely new case which for the first time was being developed. For my part I cannot accept that the failure in this respect was attributable solely to the

C   trial judge's ruling that the issue of negligence was not to go to the jury, as to the rightness of which I need only recall that learned counsel for the respondent plaintiff told your Lordships, " If soldiers alone had been sued, I agree that they could not have been found liable." Despite that ruling, the view of McGonigal L.J. was that:

        ". . . the learned trial judge should have worded the questions or
D   so directed the jury as to lead them to consider the reasonableness of the force in relation not only to the immediate circumstances but to events prior to the patrol getting into position and, in particular, to soldier ' X's ' actions and preparations which set the scene in which the actual force used possibly was made necessary . . . the jury should have had an opportunity when dealing with questions 2 and 3 to consider all the relevant circumstances, not only those at the time

E   the urgency of the incident took over control but those prevailing at the earlier stage when there was time for planning and consideration that could have dictated the amount of force which might be required to be used later."

        My Lords, such allegations of negligence in preparation as were thus canvassed by the Court of Appeal were of gravity and importance. Had
F   they been made timeously, that is to say, in the statement of claim, they would have demanded careful consideration by the defendant Ministry before the case came to trial. But they found no place there, and the most that can be said of the trial is that, during the cross-examination of soldiers " X ' and " A," there was slight skirmishing which led nowhere.

        In the result, not only was the trial judge right in withdrawing negligence
G   from the jury but he was both correct and fair in omitting from his direction to them any suggestion that they were entitled to have regard to the adequacy or otherwise of the preparation for which soldier " X " appears to have been responsible. Indeed, I consider that justice would have been denied to the defendant Ministry had he followed a difference course.

        I therefore concur in holding that no new trial should have been ordered and that the appeal should be allowed.
H

        LORD FRASER OF TULLYBELTON. My Lords, I have had the advantage of reading in draft the speeches prepared by my noble and learned friends Viscount Dilhorne and Lord Edmund-Davies. I agree with both of them, and I would particularly associate myself with Lord Edmund-Davies' emphatic reminder of the importance of pleadings in defining the issue before the court in actions of this sort.

        I would allow the appeal.

LORD RUSSELL OF KILLOWEN. My Lords, I have had the advantage   A
of reading the speeches prepared by my noble and learned friends Viscount
Dilhorne and Lord Edmund-Davies. I agree with them and I also would
allow this appeal.

LORD LANE. My Lords, for the reasons expressed in the speeches of
my noble and learned friends Viscount Dilhorne and Lord Edmund-Davies,
I would allow this appeal.   B

> Appeal allowed.
> No order as to costs in House of
> Lords save that plaintiff's costs be
> taxed in accordance with provisions
> of Schedule 3 to Legal Aid and
> Advice Act (Northern Ireland) 1965.   C

Solicitors: *Treasury Solicitor; Ingledew, Brown, Bennison & Garrett.*

M. G.

D

[HOUSE OF LORDS]

* LONDON & CLYDESIDE ESTATES LTD. . . APPELLANTS

AND

ABERDEEN DISTRICT COUNCIL AND ANOTHER . RESPONDENTS   E

1979 Oct. 2, 3;   Lord Hailsham of St. Marylebone L.C.,
      Nov. 8   Lord Wilberforce, Lord Fraser of Tullybelton,
                                      Lord Russell of Killowen and
                                      Lord Keith of Kinkel

F

*Compulsory Purchase — Compensation — Certificate of alternative
development—No reference to right of appeal—Validity of
certificate—Right to new certificate—Land Compensation (Scotland) Act 1963 (c. 51), ss. 25, 26—Town and Country Planning
(General Development) (Scotland) Order 1959 (S.I. 1959 No.
1361), arts. 3, 4*

By virtue of section 25 of the Land Compensation (Scot-   G
land) Act 1963 a person whose interest in land was proposed
to be acquired by an authority with powers of compulsory
purchase might apply to the local planning authority for a
certificate of alternative development as to the nature of the
development for which planning permission might reasonably
have been expected to be granted if the land was not to be
compulsorily acquired for another purpose. A certificate was
relevant to the amount of compensation.

By article 3 (2) of the Town and Country Planning (General   H
Purposes) (Scotland) Order 1959 the time prescribed for the
issue of a certificate was two months. By article 3 (3), if the
local planning authority issued such a certificate
  " they shall in that certificate include a statement in
  writing . . . of the rights of appeal to the Secretary of
  State given by section 6 [section 26 of the Act of 1963]
  and this Order."
By article 4 (1) the time prescribed for appeal was one month.

A   The appellant company owning land which the respondent council proposed to acquire compulsorily for educational purposes applied for a certificate of alternative development, submitting that an appropriate class of redevelopment would be residential. The certificate issued stated that planning permission could not reasonably be expected for purposes other than educational. It did not mention the right of appeal. The company having appealed more than one month after the

B   date of the certificate, its appeal was rejected as incompetent.

The company raised an action for (a) reduction of the certificate and (b) declaration that the council was bound to issue a new certificate. The Lord Ordinary granted both. The Second Division of the Court of Session granted the reduction but refused the declaration.

On appeal by the company and cross-appeal by the council : —

C   *Held*, allowing the appeal and dismissing the cross-appeal, (1) that the requirement that the certificate should include information as to the rights of appeal was mandatory and the omission of it vitiated the certificate, giving the company ground for seeking the appropriate remedy of reduction for striking it down, and, further, that, since the issue of a vitiated certificate was not the same thing as a failure to issue any certificate at all, the company was not deprived of the

D   right to appeal by the statutory provisions as to appeals (post, pp. 186E–G, 187F, H—188A, 194B–D, 196A, 201D–E, 202D, 203C).

(2) That, since the duty under section 25 of the Act to issue a certificate was a continuing duty which was not terminated by the council's failure to comply with article 3 (2) of the Order in time, the court was not debarred from ordering the issue of a new certificate (post, pp. 190D–E, 197B–E, 203D–E, 204D–F).

E   *Per* Lord Hailsham of St. Marylebone L.C. When considering the effect of non-compliance by a statutory authority with statutory requirements affecting the discharge of its functions, the use of expressions such as " mandatory," " directory," " void," " voidable," a " nullity " and " purely regulatory " should not be regarded as requiring a particular case to be fitted into one or other of mutually exclusive compartments borrowed from other branches of law, since what

F   is to be considered is the legal consequence of non-compliance on the rights of the subject viewed in the light of the concrete state of facts and a continuing chain of events, which may present, not a stark choice of alternatives, but a spectrum of possibilities in which one compartment or description fades gradually into another (post, p. 189C–F).

Decision of the Second Division of the Court of Session, 1979 S.L.T. 221 affirmed in part and reversed in part.

G

The following cases were referred to in their Lordships' opinions:

Agricultural, Horticultural and Forestry Industry Training Board v. *Kent* [1970] 2 Q.B. 19; [1970] 2 W.L.R. 426; [1970] 1 All E.R. 304, C.A.

Brayhead (Ascot) Ltd. v. *Berkshire County Council* [1964] 2 Q.B. 303; [1964] 2 W.L.R. 507; [1964] 1 All E.R. 149, D.C.

H   *Calvin* v. *Carr* [1979] 2 W.L.R. 755; [1979] 2 All E.R. 440, P.C.

Edwick v. *Sunbury-on-Thames Urban District Council* [1962] 1 Q.B. 229; [1961] 3 W.L.R. 553; [1961] 2 All E.R. 10.

James v. *Minister of Housing and Local Government* [1966] 1 W.L.R. 135; [1965] 3 All E.R. 602, C.A.; [1968] A.C. 409; [1967] 1 W.L.R. 171; [1966] 3 All E.R. 964, H.L.(E.).

London Ballast Co. Ltd. v. *Buckinghamshire County Council* (1966) 65 L.G.R. 227.

Maitland, Petitioner, 1961 S.C. 291.   A
Rae v. *Davidson*, 1954 S.C. 361.
Rayner v. *Stepney Corporation* [1911] 2 Ch. 312.

The following additional cases were cited in argument:

Ferguson and Another, Petitioners, 1965 S.C. 16.
Howard v. *Bodington* (1877) 2 P.D. 203.
Howard v. *Secretary of State for the Environment* [1975] Q.B. 235;   B
    [1974] 2 W.L.R. 459; [1974] 1 All E.R. 644, C.A.
National Commercial Bank of Scotland v. *Fife Assessors*, 1963 S.C. 197.
Reg. v. *Woodbury Licensing Justices, Ex parte Rouse* [1960] 1 W.L.R.
    461; [1960] 2 All E.R. 205, D.C.
Rex v. *Hanley Borough Revising Barrister* [1912] 3 K.B. 518, D.C.
Train & M'Intyre Ltd., Petitioners, 1923 S.C. 291.

    C

APPEAL and CROSS-APPEAL from the Second Division of the Court of
Session.

This was an appeal against an interlocutor of the Second Division
of the Court of Session in Scotland dated January 26, 1979, in terms
of which the court granted decree of reduction in terms of the first
conclusion of the pursuers, London and Clydeside Estates Ltd. (the   D
appellants and cross-respondents), but refused the pursuers' second
conclusion as incompetent. The pursuers appealed as regarding the
second conclusion and the first defenders, the Aberdeen City Council
(the respondents and cross-appellants), cross-appealed as regarding the
decree of reduction. The second defender, the Secretary of State for
Scotland, had entered appearance and lodged defences and was joined
in this appeal as respondent and cross-appellant for any interest he might   E
have, but he took no part in the proceedings.

The facts are stated in their Lordships' opinions.

A. M. Morison Q.C. and *A. G. C. McGregor* (both of the Scottish
Bar) for the appellants.
M. S. R. Bruce Q.C. and *J. A. Cameron* (both of the Scottish Bar)   F
for the respondents.

Their Lordships took time for consideration.

November 3, 1979. LORD HAILSHAM OF ST. MARYLEBONE L.C. My
Lords, my task in this case is rendered considerably lighter by reason
of the fact that I have had the advantage of reading in draft the opinions
prepared by my noble and learned friends, Lord Fraser of Tullybelton   G
and Lord Keith of Kinkel. With them I agree, and accordingly I am
of the opinion that this appeal should succeed, the cross-appeal be
dismissed, and that the appellants should be allowed their expenses
throughout these proceedings, including those of the proceedings before
your Lordships' House, other than the expenses relating to the joinder
of the second defender as to which it is not now sought to disturb the   H
order of the Second Division of the Court of Session. Nevertheless
I wish to frame my own reasons for coming to this conclusion.

It will be logical to deal first with the cross-appeal which seeks to
reverse the interlocutors to the extent to which the pursuers succeeded
below. These interlocutors were in the terms of the first conclusion of
the pursuers' summons in these proceedings, which sought the reduction
of a purported certificate by the respondents. The appeal itself is

A   confined to the contention that the Second Division of the Court of Session were wrong to refuse the second conclusion in the appellants' summons after sustaining their contention that they were entitled to succeed on the first (which is the subject of the cross-appeal).

The proceedings relate to three areas of ground at Scotstoun, Bridge of Don, which the respondents or their predecessors desire to acquire for educational purposes.

B

On September 9, 1974, the appellants applied through their architects to the respondents' predecessor authority for a certificate of alternative development pursuant to section 25 of the Land Compensation (Scotland) Act 1963. The form of this certificate necessarily affects the amount of compensation payable for the acquisition, and, although this does not appear directly from the record, we were told that, independently of these proceedings, a reference to the Lands Tribunal following an agreement for sale has duly taken place and has resulted in an award in an alternative form on each of two alternative bases.

C

On October 22, 1974, and in response to the appellants' application, the respondents' predecessors issued what purported to be the appropriate certificate, described in the record as production No. 1. But this purported certificate was admittedly defective (to use a neutral word) because, contrary to the terms of article 3 (3) of the Town and Country Planning (General Development) (Scotland) Order 1959 (S.I. 1959 No. 1361), which is admitted to apply to the case, it did not " include a statement in writing . . . of the rights of appeal to the Secretary of State. . . ." These rights under the relevant terms of article 4 (1) of the Order, provided for notice of appeal to be given within one month from the date of receipt of the certificate.

D

E

In the events which happened, the appellants purported after the expiry of the time limit of one month to intimate an appeal to the Secretary of State. This they did by letter dated January 9, 1975 (production No. 3 in the record). But by letter dated January 15, 1975, the Secretary of State declined to accept this letter as a valid appeal on the grounds that it was out of time, and adhered to this decision despite a further letter on behalf of the appellants complaining in effect of the defective character of the respondents' certificate.

F

The outcome was the raising on April 11, 1975, of the present proceedings in which the appellants concluded (1) for a reduction of the purported certificate of October 22, 1974, and (2) for a declarator that the respondents were bound to issue an amended, or, more properly, a fresh, certificate complying with article 3 (1) of the Order, and a decree ordaining the respondents to issue such a certificate within two months of the decree. These are the only two conclusions still alive in the proceedings before your Lordships. There was a third and alternative conclusion, now no longer effective, which resulted from a provisional view framed by the Lord Ordinary in the course of the proceedings before him. The Lord Ordinary had at first been disposed to consider that the Secretary of State was wrong to decline jurisdiction to hear the attempted appeal, but changed his mind on hearing argument for the Secretary of State who had been joined by amendment for the purposes. No point on this abortive solution remains to be decided on this appeal, the appellants expressly refraining from pursuing the argument as to expenses raised in their case to your Lordships' House.

G

H

In the event, the appellants succeeded in their first conclusion (for

the reduction of the purported certificate) both before the Lord Ordinary   A
and the Second Division, and this result forms the subject of the
respondents' cross-appeal.   But before the Second Division the appellants
failed in their claim to the decree concluded for in their second claim
for relief (the subject of the appeal itself) on the ground, as the Second
Division held, that to ordain in accordance with the second conclusion
would be "flying in the face" of article 3 (2) of the development   B
Order.   This provided that the time within which the relevant certificate
was to be issued by the respondents was to be "the period of two
months from the date of receipt" of the relevant application, and from
this the Second Division were of opinion that the respondents had no
remaining power to issue a certificate in the form required by the
second conclusion of the appellants' summons.   In passing, I should
remark that the point was a novel one before the Second Division, the   C
respondents having conceded before the Lord Ordinary that the two
conclusions stood or fell together, and having withdrawn this concession
on the reclaiming motion in the Second Division.

It will be convenient to deal with the points raised in what I conceive
to be their logical order rather than the order in which they were
argued by the respective counsel.   D

On this basis, the first question for consideration is the consequence of what was admitted to be a defect in the purported certificate
of October 22, 1974, namely the failure by the predecessors of the
respondents to include in the certificate information in writing as to the
appellants' rights of appeal to the Secretary of State.   Was this requirement, which has the authority of Parliament behind it, mandatory or
was it in some sense directory only?   I have no doubt that it was   E
mandatory, and that the failure to include this information was fatal
to the certificate.   In the course of argument counsel for the respondents
candidly conceded that the only purpose of the requirement was to
inform the applicant of his rights of appeal, including the time limit
within which they should be exercised.   The present appellants aver
that they were misled by this defect and that it was as a result of this   F
that their appeal was out of time.   The averment has never been put
to the proof, and one of the respondents' alternative arguments was
that, in the event of otherwise total failure, the appellants should be
put to the proof of this.   But in my view this argument is without
foundation.   The validity of the certificate itself is in question, and if,
as I believe, the requirement is mandatory, the certificate falls independently of whether the appellants were in fact misled.   I find it   G
impossible to accept that a requirement by an instrument of statutory
force designed for the very purpose of compelling a public authority
to inform the subject of his legal rights can be treated as simply regulatory if the requirement is not complied with.   If I required authority
for this proposition I would refer to *Agricultural, Horticultural and
Forestry Industry Training Board* v. *Kent* [1970] 2 Q.B. 19, *Rayner* v.   H
Stepney Corporation [1911] 2 Ch. 312, and *Brayhead (Ascot) Ltd.* v.
Berkshire County Council [1964] 2 Q.B. 303, notwithstanding that it
relied on *Edwick* v. *Sunbury-on-Thames Urban District Council* [1962]
1 Q.B. 229 which was disapproved in *James* v. *Minister of Housing and
Local Government* [1968] A.C. 409, which was decided on an argument
irrelevant to the present appeal.   However I am content to assert a
general principle to the effect that where Parliament prescribes that an

A authority with compulsory powers should inform the subject of his right to question those powers, prima facie the requirement must be treated as mandatory. For the reasons which follow, however, this does not dispose the matter in the appellants' favour.

If the requirement that the subject should be informed of his legal rights was mandatory, what follows? The respondents attempted, as

B I thought, at one time, to argue that it thereupon became a nullity, and that therefore a decree of reduction was inappropriate because there was nothing upon which it could operate. But I do not accept this argument. The certificate was effective until it was struck down by a competent authority (cf. *Brayhead (Ascot) Ltd.* v. *Berkshire County Council* [1962] 1 Q.B. 229; *James* v. *Minister of Housing and Local Government* [1968] A.C. 409. In the course of argument I ventured to

C draw attention to the passage at p. 763 of the opinion of the Judicial Committee in *Calvin* v. *Carr* [1979] 2 W.L.R. 755, in which Lord Wilberforce says of a contention that a decision of the stewards of the Australian Jockey Club was void for breach of natural justice:

    " This argument led necessarily into the difficult area of what is
    void and what is voidable, as to which some confusion exists in
D   the authorities. Their Lordships' opinion would be, if it became
    necessary to fix on one or other of these expressions, that a decision
    made contrary to natural justice is void, but that, until it is so
    declared by a competent body or court, it may have some effect,
    or existence, in law. This condition might be better expressed by
    saying that the decision is invalid or vitiated. In the present context,
E   where the question is whether an appeal lies, the impugned decision
    cannot be considered as totally void, in the sense of being legally
    non-existent. So to hold would be wholly unreal."

The subject matter of that case was wholly different from the present, but my opinion is that the thinking behind it is applicable. The certificate was vitiated in the sense that it failed to comply with a mandatory

F requirement. But the subject could not safely disregard it as not having been issued. Had he done so, he might well have fallen into the very trap of losing his right to complain of the vitiating factor which has caught other subjects in the reported decisions, and, in my view, he was not only wise but bound to seek a decree of reduction or some other appropriate remedy striking down the offending certificate.

G A similar line of reasoning disposes of the next contention of the respondents, also rejected in the Second Division, to the effect that, if the certificate is vitiated, the position is the same as if no certificate had been issued and that section 26 (4) of the Land Compensation (Scotland) Act 1963 then operates in such a way that, no certificate having been issued under section 25, the preceding provisions of the section as to appeals should apply at the expiry of the prescribed period

H " as if " the local planning authority had issued a certificate " containing such a statement as is mentioned in " section 25 (4) (b) of the Act. The effect of this read with articles 3 and 4 of the Order would have put the appellants out of time for appeal on the expiry of one month after the expiry of the prescribed (2 months) for the due issue of the certificate by the respondents. The fallacy in this argument lies in the assumption (for it is no more) that the issue by an authority of a certificate vitiated by failure to comply with a mandatory requirement

188

is the same thing as the failure by that authority to issue any purported   A
certificate at all.

The respondents were at pains to argue that the issue by the authority
of a certificate vitiated for want of compliance with a mandatory
requirement was a casus omissus from the Act and that, in this context,
the law of Scotland (unlike the law of England) afforded no remedy at
all unless it be by the invocation of the jurisdiction peculiar to Scottish   B
law, which goes by the imposing name of " nobile officium." I was
utterly unpersuaded by this argument or that there was any difference
between Scottish and English law in this respect, and my want of belief
is reinforced by what my two learned and noble friends, Lord Fraser
of Tullybelton and Lord Keith of Kinkel, have to say about the more
arcane aspects of " nobile officium." In my opinion, in both jurisdictions
the law is the same. The first task is to construe the statute, and ask   C
the question whether the duty in question is mandatory or directory.
If it be mandatory, the second task is to ask what remedy is available
for non-compliance. If the statute specifies the remedy, well and good.
If it is silent, the ordinary remedies available in each jurisdiction, e.g.
proceedings for declaration or prerogative order in England, summons
for declarator or reduction in Scotland, should be pursued as appropriate.
There is no room for a casus omissus in either case. Counsel for the   D
appellants called in aid of this part of the case the authority of *Maitland,
Petitioner,* 1961 S.C. 291, but I do not think authority is required for a
proposition to my mind so evident on general principle.

More persuasive, in some ways, was the argument for the respondents
that it was an odd sort of statute which first provided that an applicant
should look at the Act in order to ascertain his right under section 25   E
(now amended and printed as a Keeling schedule in Schedule 9 to the
Community Land Act 1975) to make an application and then, if no
certificate were forthcoming, look at section 26 (4) of the Act and the
Order in order to note and exercise his right of appeal, but, as regards
a purported certificate failing to apprise him of his rights of appeal
(which by that time one would have supposed him to know) that he   F
should be in the position to rely on the invalidity of the certificate in
the way he now seeks to do. That there is a certain paradox in this
I do not deny. But I do not think we are entitled to play fast and
loose with statutory requirements designed to inform the subject as to
his legal rights against an authority possessed of compulsory powers.
There would be an even greater paradox in allowing an acquiring or
planning authority first to flout such a requirement and then be heard   G
to say that its non-compliance had no effect on the validity of its legal
documents. I do not think that prescriptions for the benefit of the
subject are so to be disregarded.

At this stage I should notice a contention on the part of the
respondents, which, though, as will be seen, I partly agree with it, does
not seem to me to be relevant to the disposal of the cross-appeal.   H

The contention was that in the categorisation of statutory requirements into " mandatory " and " directory," there was a subdivision of
the category " directory " into two classes composed (i) of those directory
requirements " substantial compliance " with which satisfied the requirement to the point at which a minor defect of trivial irregularity could
be ignored by the court and (ii) those requirements so purely regulatory
in character that failure to comply could in no circumstances affect the

A validity of what was done. The contention of the respondents was that, even on the assumption against themselves that the requirement of the Order that the certificate should include a notification of the appellants' rights to appeal to the Secretary of State, the rest of the certificate was so exactly in accordance with the provisions of the Order that the remaining defect could be safely ignored.

B I do not consider that this argument assists the respondents in the present appeal. I have already held that the requirement relating to notification of the appellants' rights of appeal was mandatory and not directory in either sense contended for by the respondents. But on the assumption that I am wrong about this, a total failure to comply with a significant part of a requirement cannot in any circumstances be regarded as " substantial compliance " with the total requirement in such a way C as to bring the respondents' contention into effect.

Nevertheless I wish to examine the contention itself. In this appeal we are in the field of the rapidly developing jurisprudence of administrative law, and we are considering the effect of non-compliance by a statutory authority with the statutory requirements affecting the discharge of one of its functions. In the reported decisions there is much D language presupposing the existence of stark categories such as " mandatory " and " directory," " void " and " voidable," a " nullity," and " purely regulatory."

Such language is useful; indeed, in the course of this opinion I have used some of it myself. But I wish to say that I am not at all clear that the language itself may not be misleading in so far as it may be supposed to present a court with the necessity of fitting a particular E case into one or other of mutually exclusive and starkly contrasted compartments, compartments which in some cases (e.g. " void " and " voidable ") are borrowed from the language of contract or status, and are not easily fitted to the requirements of administrative law.

When Parliament lays down a statutory requirement for the exercise of legal authority it expects its authority to be obeyed down to the F minutest detail. But what the courts have to decide in a particular case is the legal consequence of non-compliance on the rights of the subject viewed in the light of a concrete state of facts and a continuing chain of events. It may be that what the courts are faced with is not so much a stark choice of alternatives but a spectrum of possibilities in which one compartment or description fades gradually into another. At one end of this spectrum there may be cases in which a fundamental G obligation may have been so outrageously and flagrantly ignored or defied that the subject may safely ignore what has been done and treat it as having no legal consequences upon himself. In such a case if the defaulting authority seeks to rely on its action it may be that the subject is entitled to use the defect in procedure simply as a shield or defence without having taken any positive action of his own. At the other end H of the spectrum the defect in procedure may be so nugatory or trivial that the authority can safely proceed without remedial action, confident that, if the subject is so misguided as to rely on the fault, the courts will decline to listen to his complaint. But in a very great number of cases, it may be in a majority of them, it may be necessary for a subject, in order to safeguard himself, to go to the court for declaration of his rights, the grant of which may well be discretionary, and by the like token it may be wise for an authority (as it certainly would have been

here) to do everything in its power to remedy the fault in its procedure   A
so as not to deprive the subject of his due or themselves of their power
to act.   In such cases, though language like " mandatory," " directory,"
" void," " voidable," " nullity " and so forth may be helpful in argument,
it may be misleading in effect if relied on to show that the courts, in
deciding the consequences of a defect in the exercise of power, are
necessarily bound to fit the facts of a particular case and a developing
chain of events into rigid legal categories or to stretch or cramp them   B
on a bed of Procrustes invented by lawyers for the purposes of convenient exposition.   As I have said, the case does not really arise here,
since we are in the presence of total non-compliance with a requirement
which I have held to be mandatory.   Nevertheless I do not wish to be
understood in the field of administrative law and in the domain where
the courts apply a supervisory jurisdiction over the acts of subordinate   C
authority purporting to exercise statutory powers, to encourage the use
of rigid legal classifications.   The jurisdiction is inherently discretionary
and the court is frequently in the presence of differences of degree
which merge almost imperceptibly into differences of kind.

There was only one other argument for the respondents on their
cross-appeal that I need notice.   This was that the requirement not   D
complied with was separable from the rest of the requirements as to the
certificate.   I do not read it as such.   It was an integral part of the
requirement that the certificate should " include " a written notification
of the rights of appeal.

Once the cross-appeal is disposed of, I do not find much difficulty
in stating my reasons for allowing the appeal.   In my view the Second
Division only refused the second conclusion of the summons because in   E
their view of article 3 (2) of the Order the respondents had no power
to issue the new certificate demanded.   Again, I do not so read the
Order.   The duty under section 25 is a continuing duty.   The fact that
article 3 (2) of the Order is not complied with in time does not put an
end to the obligation of the authority to comply.   That this is so is
apparent from a construction of section 25 (as amended) in the light   F
of section 26 which expressly allows the parties to agree an extension of
time, which would not be possible if an extension of time was ultra vires
the authority.

In my view, therefore, the appeal succeeds, and the cross-appeal fails
with the results indicated in the first paragraphs of this opinion.

LORD WILBERFORCE.   My Lords, I have had the benefit of reading   G
in advance the opinions of the noble and learned Lord on the Woolsack
and my noble and learned friend, Lord Keith of Kinkel.   I agree with
them and with the conclusions proposed.

LORD FRASER OF TULLYBELTON.   My Lords, this appeal raises the
question whether a certificate of alternative development issued by a   H
local planning authority which was defective in form is valid or invalid
and, if invalid, what remedy is available to the party who applied for
it.   The defect was that the certificate did not include a statement of the
applicants' rights of appeal to the Secretary of State as required by the
relevant statutory instrument.   The appellants (pursuers in the action),
on whose behalf the certificate was applied for by their architects,
maintain that the defective certificate is invalid.   The respondents, who

A are the local planning authority, maintain that the requirement that the
certificate shall include a statement on the rights of appeal is not
mandatory but only directory, and that the failure to comply with it does
not affect the validity of the certificate that was issued. The action has
two conclusions still alive, apart from one for expenses. The first conclusion is for reduction of the defective certificate. The second is for
B decree of declarator that the respondents are bound to issue a fresh
certificate (sc. in proper form) and for decree ordaining the respondents
to issue such a certificate within two months after the date of decree.
The Lord Ordinary, Lord Dunpark, granted decree in terms of both
conclusions. The Second Division granted decree of reduction, but
refused decree in terms of the second conclusion. The respondents have
cross-appealed against the interlocutor of the Second Division, in so far
C as it granted decree of reduction, and their cross-appeal is opposed by
the appellants.

All the facts, which, in my opinion, are relevant are agreed. There
is a dispute on one matter of fact but, for reasons to be mentioned
later, I do not consider that the matter is material. The appellants are
the owners of three areas of ground at Scotstoun, Bridge of Don,
D Aberdeenshire, which Aberdeen County Council, who were then the
education authority, proposed to acquire compulsorily for educational
purposes. On September 9, 1974, a firm of chartered architects applied
on behalf of the appellants to Aberdeen County Council (in their capacity
as local planning authority) for a certificate of alternative development
under section 25 of the Land Compensation (Scotland) Act 1963. The
respondents are the statutory successors of the Aberdeen County Council
E as local planning authority. A certificate of alternative development
governs the amount of compensation payable to the appellants for the
compulsory acquisition of their land. The application specified "residential with associated commercial purposes" as a class of development
which appeared to the appellants to be appropriate for these areas of
land. If the local planning authority had issued a certificate that
F planning permission for that purpose might reasonably have been expected to be granted, compensation would have been assessed on the
assumption that it would have been granted: section 23 (5). (The
assumption has been changed by the Community Land Act 1975,
Schedule 10, paragraph 5, but the change does not affect this appeal).
On October 22, 1974, Aberdeen County Council issued a certificate
stating that "in the opinion of the local planning authority . . . planning
G permission could not reasonably be expected to be granted for any
development other than that proposed to be carried out by the acquiring
authority" (which may conveniently be called a "negative certificate")
and stating the reason for that opinion. But the certificate did not
include any statement of the rights of appeal to the Secretary of State
as it should have done in order to comply with the Town and Country
H Planning (General Development) (Scotland) Order 1959 (S.I. 1959 No.
1361), article 3 (3) of which provides as follows:

> "If a local planning authority issue a certificate otherwise than for
> the class or classes of development specified in the application made
> to them, or contrary to representations in writing made to them by
> a party directly concerned, they shall in that certificate include a
> statement in writing of their reasons for so doing and of the rights of
> appeal to the Secretary of State given by section 6 and this Order."

The reference to "section 6" is to a section of the Town and Country A
Planning (Scotland) Act 1959 which was repealed and superseded by
section 26 of the Land Compensation (Scotland) Act 1963. The Order
was continued in force under section 47 (1) of the Act of 1963.

The certificate was received by the appellants' architects on October
24, 1974. On January 9, 1975, the appellants' solicitors wrote to the
Scottish Development Department intimating an appeal against the B
certificate on its merits, on grounds stated in the letter. The intimation
was of course more than one month (actually about two and a half
months) after the receipt of the certificate and was therefore out of
time under article 4 (1) of the regulations which provides: "The time
for giving notice of an appeal under section 6 shall be the period of one
month from the date of receipt of the certificate . . ." On January 15,
1975, the Scottish Development Department replied stating that notice C
of appeal had to be given within one month and that the Secretary of
State had no power to extend the period. They added: "As the
certificate against which you wish to appeal was issued on October 22,
1974, the Secretary of State regrets that he is unable to accept your
letter as a valid appeal." On February 10, 1975, the appellants' solicitors
wrote again to the Scottish Development Department saying that the D
purported certificate had omitted to advise their clients of their rights
of appeal to the Secretary of State and that it was therefore defective
as a certificate. They requested that, rather than adopting the cumber-
some and expensive procedure of insisting on a fresh certificate, to be
followed by an appeal, the Secretary of State should allow the notice of
appeal in their letter of January 9 to stand. On March 6, 1975, the
Scottish Development Department replied that "the Secretary of State E
has no power to accept a late appeal" and suggested that the appellants
take up the matter with the county council. The solicitors then wrote
to the county clerk on March 14, 1975, pointing out the defect in the
certificate and asking for a "certificate in proper form" to be issued as
soon as possible. The county council refused to issue a fresh certificate
and on April 16, 1975, the appellants raised this action concluding for F
reduction and declarator. Aberdeen County Council were called as the
first defenders (now succeeded by the present appellants). The Secretary
of State for Scotland was called as second defender for any interest he
might have.

The action came before Lord Dunpark as Lord Ordinary in procedure
roll for the first time in January 1977 and by interlocutor dated February
24, 1977 (not January 24, 1977, as stated in the interlocutor sheet in G
appendix 1) he found in favour of the appellants. His Lordship, in a
laudable attempt to short circuit procedure, made a finding that: "The
notice of appeal given by letter dated January 9, 1975" (from the
[appellants] solicitors to the second named defender) "was a valid notice
of appeal." In his opinion the Lord Ordinary expressed the hope that
the Secretary of State would take his finding as equivalent to a decree H
of declarator that the appellants' notice of appeal was timeous and
valid in the circumstances and stated that he would certainly have
granted decree to that effect if there had been a conclusion for it. At
that stage the Secretary of State had not lodged defences. Aberdeen
County Council reclaimed against the Lord Ordinary's interlocutor of
February 24, 1977, and the appellants amended the closed record by
adding a conclusion for declarator in the terms which the Lord Ordinary

A   had said he would have upheld. The Secretary of State then lodged
defences and the case was remitted by the Second Division to the Lord
Ordinary to consider it further.

At a further hearing the Lord Ordinary was persuaded by counsel
for the Secretary of State that his finding made on February 24, 1977,
was wrong and on January 15, 1978, he refused to grant decree of
B   declarator in terms of the third conclusion (the one that had been
added by amendment) and dismissed the action so far as directed against
the Secretary of State. That part of his decision has been accepted by
all parties and his original finding was not supported by any party before
the Second Division. The Lord Ordinary granted decree of reduction
in terms of the first conclusion. He also granted decree of declarator
and ordaining the defenders to issue an amended certificate in terms
C   of the second conclusion; in this part of his interlocutor the Lord
Ordinary proceeded upon a concession made by senior counsel then
appearing for the respondents to the effect that if decree in terms of
the first conclusion was granted then decree in terms of the second
conclusion should follow. That concession was withdrawn when the
case came before the Second Division. The question of whether or not
D   the concession was rightly made is now in substance the question raised
in this appeal. The Second Division upheld the Lord Ordinary's interlocutor in granting decree of reduction, but they recalled the interlocutor in so far as it granted decree in terms of the second conclusion.
They held that the time limit for issuing a certificate of alternative
development had expired and that decree in terms of the second conclusion would be incompetent. The result is that matters are left in a
E   state which is clearly unsatisfactory. The defective certificate has been
reduced, but nothing has been put in its place, and no order has been
pronounced requiring the respondents to issue a fresh or amended
certificate. Their Lordships of the Second Division evidently recognised
that the position was unsatisfactory and in their opinion they said, 1979
S.L.T. 221, 227: " It may be, and on this we express no view, that the
F   pursuers have some other remedy against the first defenders for issuing
the certificate which has now to be reduced." But they gave no indication of what other remedy there might be.

It will be convenient to consider first the cross-appeal—that is, the
respondents' appeal against the decree reducing the certificate of October
22, 1974. Logically the first point to consider is whether the provision
in article 3 (3) of the Order of 1959 to the effect that the local planning
G   authority " shall in that certificate include a statement in writing
of . . . the rights of appeal " is mandatory or not. I do not think that
literal compliance with the provision is mandatory; for example, if a
statement of the rights of appeal had not been " included " in the
certificate but had been sent with it in a separate sheet, that would in
my opinion have been substantial compliance and would have been
H   sufficient. But here there was no compliance at all with the provision.
The purpose of the statement required by article 3 (3) clearly is to
inform the applicant first that he has a right of appeal and secondly of
the time in which the right has to be exercised. These are matters of
importance to an applicant and Parliament, acting through the Secretary
of State, has considered their importance to be such that they ought to
be expressly brought to the notice of an applicant. Failure to do so
cannot in my opinion be treated as if it were a mere technicality or a

procedural irregularity which might be overlooked. The omission in   A
this case was similar to, but more serious than, the omission of the
address for the service of a notice of appeal which was held by the
Court of Appeal to invalidate an assessment notice in *Agricultural,
Horticultural and Forestry Industry Training Board* v. *Kent* [1970] 2
Q.B. 19. It was much more serious than the omission in *Rae* v.
Davidson, 1954 S.C. 361, 369, which was described by Lord Justice-Clerk
Thomson as "the merest technicality," but which was held nevertheless   B
to invalidate a notice to remove from a farm because the statutory
requirements for such a notice had not been exactly complied with. I agree
with both those decisions, and I have no doubt that the effect of the
omission in this case was to make the certificate invalid in the sense
that it cannot stand, if challenged by the appellants. It is not a complete
nullity—for example it could have been appealed against by an appeal   C
taken timeously—and it exists until it is reduced, or set aside in some
way. I do not think it is possible to treat the certificate as consisting
of two parts, capable of being severed from one another, one part being
the actual certificate and the other being the statement of the rights of
appeal. Both parts are required by the order and both are of substantial
importance. The omission of either part is therefore fatal to the validity   D
of the whole.

Counsel for the respondents argued that there were three reasons
why the inclusion of a statement of rights of appeal to the Secretary
of State was not mandatory. The first was that the notice was not of
great assistance to the applicant, because receipt of the certificate would
not be the first he knew of the matter. He must have applied for the
certificate, and therefore he must already have read the Order of 1959.   E
I agree that he must have read the order, but in my opinion that does
not mean that a statement of these rights of appeal, even if it is only
a reminder of what he had already read, is not of value to him. The
second reason was that the obligation to include the statement was
imposed only by the Order of 1959 and not by the statute itself, whereas
the scheme of the legislation was for all the essential requirements of   F
the certificate to be laid down in the Act itself. In my opinion it is not
possible to distinguish in this way between essential and non-essential
requirements; any such distinction must depend on the importance of
the particular requirements and not upon the machinery by which they
are specified. The third reason was the only one that is in my opinion
entitled to some weight. It was based on the provisions of section 26 (4)
of the Act to the effect that if, at the expiry of the period of two months   G
within which the certificate is to be issued, no certificate has in fact
been issued, the provisions for appeal shall apply as if a negative certificate had been issued—i.e. the applicant can appeal within one further
month. In circumstances where that provision has to be applied, the
applicant ex hypothesi would not have the benefit of a statement of his
rights of appeal but he would have to discover them for himself. How   H
then, it was asked rhetorically, could the inclusion of such a statement
in a certificate, when one was issued, be essential? I see the force of
the argument but in my opinion it cannot prevail against the express
provision in the Order made under the authority of Parliament.

The appellants have averred that as a result of the failure of the
county council to comply with article 3 (3), they did not appreciate
that notice of appeal required to be given within one month of receipt

A   of the certificate and that that was the reason for the appeal being out of time. These averments are denied by the respondents and their counsel argued that in the event of the appeal succeeding otherwise they should be remitted for proof before the Lord Ordinary. In my opinion that is unnecessary and the averments themselves are irrelevant. The validity of a certificate is not in my opinion dependent on whether the appellants were actually prejudiced by it or not. This is the single

B   disputed matter of fact to which I referred above.

The next question is whether reduction of the certificate is the appropriate remedy in the circumstances. Counsel for the respondents argued that, whatever the appropriate remedy might be, it certainly was not reduction, because, he said, the nobile officium of the Court of Session was available to provide for what was a casus improvisus. The

C   argument as I understood it was that a casus improvisus arose in this way. It is now too late for the appellants to make a fresh or amended application for a certificate because a reference has been made to the Lands Tribunal for Scotland (which has replaced the Official Arbiter) to assess compensation: see section 25 (2) of the Act of 1963. We were told that the Lands Tribunal had, at the request of both parties, made alternative assessments on different assumptions. I agree that it is too

D   late for a fresh application. It is also too late, so it is said, for the respondents to issue a fresh or amended certificate because a certificate has to be issued within two months from the date of application (unless the period is extended by agreement) and after the expiry of the two months' period the local planning authority is functus and cannot issue a certificate. A complete impasse therefore arises comparable to that

E   which existed in the case of Maitland, Petitioner, 1961 S.C. 291 when a licensing court could not be reconvened to pronounce an order that it had omitted to make per incuriam. The Court of Session resolved the impasse by an exercise of its nobile officium. For reasons that I shall explain, I do not agree that it is too late for the respondents to issue a proper certificate, but, even assuming that it is, I am of opinion that the

F   argument is misconceived. The fact that Parliament has not provided for the legal consequences to follow from a failure to carry out the statutory procedure does not give rise to a casus improvisus. The consequences of such failure have to be ascertained according to the general rules of law. They may include a right to recover damages, or to have a document reduced, or to obtain a decree of declarator or some other redress but there is no impasse of the kind that has hitherto been

G   regarded as suitable for solution by an exercise of the nobile officium. That is an exceptional power and the court " does not view with favour its indefinite extension." See Maclaren, Court of Session Practice (1916), p. 101. Its proper use as the Lord President pointed out in Maitland, at p. 293, is " to enable justice to be done where, per incuriam, some formal step [my italics] has been omitted " but it cannot be invoked " even by

H   agreement of all parties interested, to enable the court to supplement the statutory procedure by what would, in effect, be an amendment of a statute." The proposal that the nobile officium should be invoked in the present case to extend the period either for issuing the certificate or for appealing against the certificate assumes that whichever period is to be extended is one which has been fixed by the statute or the Order and which has expired. Otherwise no extension would be necessary. But an exercise of the power for such a purpose would be in order to

get round the Act or the Order and thus in effect to amend it. That   A
would not be a proper exercise of the power.

I am therefore of opinion that the Lord Ordinary and the Second
Division were well founded in granting decree of reduction of the defective certificate, and I would dismiss the cross-appeal.

Turning now to the original appeal, the question is whether the issue
of a fresh or amended certificate of alternative development now, more   B
than five years after the application made on September 9, 1974, would
be contrary to the provisions of the Act of 1963 and the Order of 1959.
The second conclusion in its original form was for a " fresh " conclusion,
but for some reason it was amended while the case was before the
Second Division by substituting " amended " for " fresh." I do not
regard the difference as important, but I consider that " fresh " is the
more appropriate word and I would allow an amendment to restore it   C
to the second conclusion. The provision of the Act which is directly
relevant to this question is in subsection (4) of section 25, as follows:

> " Where an application is made to the local planning authority for a
> certificate under this section in respect of an interest in land, the
> local planning authority shall, not earlier than 21 days after the
> date [on which a copy of the application has been or will be served   D
> upon the other party] issue to the applicant a certificate stating
> that, in the opinion of the local planning authority in respect of the
> land in question, either . . ."

(Then follow two alternatives, the second of which is a negative certificate
such as the purported certificate issued in this case.)

Two points in subsection (4) are important for the present purpose.   E
First, it imposes a duty upon the local planning authority to issue a
certificate under the section when application is made for one. Second,
it prescribes a date " not earlier " on which a certificate is to be issued.
The reason, no doubt, is to allow time for the opposing party to make
representations to the authority. But neither in section 25 (4) nor
elsewhere in the Act itself is any date prescribed after which a certificate
may not be issued. The Act does provide for a time to be prescribed by   F
a " development Order " within which a certificate is to be issued, see
section 28: " (b) for prescribing the manner in which notices of appeals
under section 26 of this Act are to be given, and the time for giving
any such notice." A " development Order " is defined by section 45 (1)
to mean an Order under section 11 (1) of the Town and Country Planning (Scotland) Act 1947 and it therefore includes the Order of 1959.   G

The time for the issue of a certificate of alternative development is
prescribed by article 3 (2) of the order of 1959, which is as follows:

> " The time within which a certificate is to be issued by a local
> planning authority shall, subject to the provisions of subsection 4 of
> [section 26 of the Act of 1963] be the period of two months from the
> date of receipt of such an application by them."   H

It was argued for the respondents that the effect of article 3 (2) was to
fix a maximum period of two months (subject to extension by agreement
under section 26 (4) of the Act) for issuing a certificate and that after the
end of that period no certificate could lawfully be issued. The issue of a
certificate after that would be, in the words of the Second Division, 1929
S.L.T. 221, 227, " in the teeth of the statutory provisions." I am unable to
accept that submission. One starts with the fact that the local planning

A authority is under a duty to issue a certificate: section 25 (4). The purpose of article 3 (2) is in my opinion to direct the local planning authority to perform its duty within the period of two months (unless extended by agreement) and that is a provision primarily in the interests of the party who has applied for the certificate. But it seems to me wrong and, if I may say so without disrespect to those who think otherwise, almost perverse, to read article 3 (2) as implying that if the local
B planning authority can stall and avoid performing its duty for two months, the duty is then to fly off altogether. Yet that would be the result of the respondents' argument. On the contrary, I am of opinion that the local planning authority remains under a continuing duty to issue a valid certificate even though it may have failed to do so within two months. Mere delay cannot absolve it from its duty. The expiry
C of the two months' period from receipt of the application is not, on any view, an absolute bar to issue of a certificate because the period can be extended by agreement: see section 26 (4). Moreover, and this is a point of importance, an extension can be agreed upon " at any time." In my opinion those words mean at any time either during the period of two months or after the end of the period, and they are a positive
D indication that the power and duty of the local planning authority to issue a certificate do not cease at the end of the period. The subsequent provision of section 26 (4) to the effect that if no certificate has been issued by the local planning authority within the two-month period the provisions relating to appeal shall apply " as if " a negative certificate had been issued gives the applicant a right of appeal, but it does not include or imply a provision that if the applicant does not avail himself
E of his right of appeal, the certificate cannot be issued after the end of the two-month period. In my opinion, therefore, the Second Division was in error in thinking that it would be incompetent for them now to ordain the respondents to issue a fresh or amended certificate; but for their having taken that view, I think they would have pronounced decree in terms of the second conclusion.

F I would allow the appeal, recall the interlocutor of the Second Division dated January 20, 1979, so far as it refused to grant decree in terms of the second conclusion of the summons; sustain the second and third pleas in law for the appellants, and refuse the respondents' cross-appeal. The appellants should have the costs of the appeal in this House and their expenses in the Court of Session except that, as Mr. Morison conceded, they are not entitled to relief against the res-
G pondents for the expenses for which the appellants have been found liable to the second defender.

LORD RUSSELL OF KILLOWEN. My Lords, I have had the advantage of reading in draft the opinion to be delivered by my noble and learned friend, Lord Keith of Kinkel. I agree with it and with the order proposed by him.
H

LORD KEITH OF KINKEL. My Lords, in 1974 Aberdeen County Council, the respondents' predecessors as local authority for the area in question, were proposing to acquire for educational purposes three sites owned by the appellants at Scotstoun, Bridge of Don. Aberdeen County Council were an authority possessing powers of compulsory purchase. On September 9, 1974, a firm of architects acting for the appellants

A

applied to the council in its capacity as local planning authority for a
certificate of alternative development under the provisions of section 25
of the Land Compensation (Scotland) Act 1963. It is unnecessary to go
into the details of these provisions. Their effect, in outline, is that where
an authority possessing compulsory purchase powers proposes to acquire
an interest in land, either the authority or the owner of the interest may
(except in certain cases which do not include the present one) apply to
the local planning authority for what may conveniently be called a certificate of appropriate alternative development. The application is to be
served upon the other party, and (by subsection (4)), the local planning
authority is required, not earlier than 21 days after the date of
service, to issue to the applicant a certificate stating that, in the opinion
of that authority, either (a) planning permission for development of one
or more classes therein specified might reasonably be expected to be
granted, or (b) planning permission could not reasonably be expected
to be granted for any development other than that proposed to be carried
out by the acquiring authority.

B

C

By virtue of sections 22 (4) and 23 (5) of the Act, the terms of a
certificate issued under section 25 may affect very materially the amount
of compensation to be paid for acquisition of the relevant interest in
land. So section 26 provides for an appeal to the Secretary of State for
Scotland against such a certificate by the person entitled to the relevant
interest in land or by the acquiring authority. The Secretary of State
is required on appeal to him to consider the matter de novo, and, if
either party so desires, to afford the parties and also the local planning
authority an opportunity of appearing and being heard before a person
appointed by him. Subsection (4) is of some materiality and must be
quoted in full:

D

E

" Where an application is made for a certificate under section 25 of
this Act, and at the expiry of the time prescribed by a development
order for the issue thereof (or, if an extended period is at any time
agreed upon in writing by the parties directly concerned and the
local planning authority, at the end of that period) no certificate
has been issued by the local planning authority in accordance with
that section, the preceding provisions of this section shall apply as
if the local planning authority had issued such a certificate containing such a statement as is mentioned in subsection (4) (b) of that
section."

F

Section 28 of the Act deals with the making by development Order of
provisions regulating inter alia the making of applications under section 25
and appeals under section 26, in particular prescribing the time within
which a certificate is required to be issued under the former section and
the time for giving notice of appeal under the latter. Prior to the
coming into force of the Act of 1963, the Secretary of State for Scotland
had made, under the corresponding powers contained in the Town and
Country Planning (Scotland) Act 1959, the Town and Country Planning
(General Development) (Scotland) Order 1959. It was common ground
that this fell to be treated at the material time as having been made by
virtue of the powers of the Act of 1963. The provision of the Order
relevant for present purposes, read with the substitution of appropriate
references to the Act of 1963 for references to the Act of 1959, are as
follows:

G

H

A   " 3 (2) The time within which a certificate is to be issued by a
      local planning authority shall, subject to the provisions of sub-
      section (4) of [section 25], be the period of two months from the date
      of receipt of such an application by them. (3) If a local planning
      authority issue a certificate otherwise than for the class or classes
      of development specified in the application made to them, or con-
      trary to representations in writing made to them by a party directly
B   concerned, they shall in that certificate include a statement in writing
      of their reasons for so doing and of the rights of appeal to the
      Secretary of State given by [section 26] and this Order . . ."
           " 4 (1) The time for giving notice of an appeal under [section 26]
      shall be the period of one month from the date of receipt of the
      certificate or of the expiry of the time or extended period men-
C   tioned in subsection (4) of that section, as the case may be."

           To resume the factual narrative, it is to be observed that in the
      appellants' application of September 9, 1974, it was represented that an
      appropriate class of development for the land in question would be
      residential with associated commercial purposes. On October 22, 1974,
      the respondents issued to the appellants a certificate, in effect under
D   section 25 (4) (b) of the Act of 1963, stating that, in their opinion as local
      planning authority, planning permission could not reasonably be expected
      to be granted in respect of the land for any development other than that
      proposed to be carried out by themselves as acquiring authority, i.e.
      development for school purposes. The certificate was contained in a
      letter from the deputy town clerk, which went on to give the reasons for
E   which the respondents' planning committee took that view, but which
      omitted to comply with the requirement of article 3 (3) of the Order of 1959
      that a certificate under section 25 (4) (b) of the Act of 1963 should include
      also a statement in writing of the rights of appeal given by section 26
      of the Act and by the Order. On January 9, 1975, the appellants by
      letter to the Secretary of State for Scotland, sought to appeal to him
      against the certificate. This was, of course, outside the time limit of
F   one month prescribed by article 4 (1) of the Order of 1959. The
      appellants in their pleadings aver that they did not appreciate that notice
      of appeal had to be given within that period by reason that the certificate
      omitted the requisite statement of their rights of appeal, but the res-
      pondents dispute this. In the result, the Secretary of State refused to
      entertain any appeal on the ground that it was out of time and he there-
G   fore had no power to do so. The appellants' solicitors on March 14,
      1975, called on the respondents to issue a certificate in proper form, but
      they refused to do so.
           Accordingly the appellants, on April 16, 1975, raised the present
      action against the respondents concluding, first, for reduction of the
      purported certificate dated October 22, 1974, and second (as the con-
      clusion was amended in the Inner House) for declarator that the res-
H   pondents were bound, on the appellants' application of September 9, 1974,
      to issue an amended certificate in respect of the land in question and
      decree ordaining them to do so within two months of such decree. The
      Secretary of State was called as second defender for any interest which
      he might have.
           The case came before the Lord Ordinary (Lord Dunpark) on pro-
      cedure roll, and on February 24, 1977, he delivered an opinion in which
      he expressed the view that the certificate of October 22, 1974, was

invalid by reason that it contained no statement in writing of the   A
appellants' rights of appeal such as was required by article 3 (3) of the
Order of 1959. Instead, however, of granting decree of reduction and
declarator as concluded for, he made a finding that the appellants' letter
to the Secretary of State dated January 9, 1975, was a valid notice of
appeal against the certificate " in the belief," as he put it, " that the
Secretary of State will now accept it as such and arrange to hear the
appeal." The respondents reclaimed, and in the course of the pro-   B
ceedings before the Inner House the appellants proposed to amend their
pleadings by adding a conclusion for declarator that their letter of
January 9, 1975, was a timeous and valid notice of appeal with which
the Secretary of State was bound to deal. This amendment was allowed
and the Secretary of State thereupon lodged defences. The Lord
Ordinary's interlocutor of February 24, 1977, was then recalled and the   C
case was remitted back to him to proceed as accords. In due course
there was a further procedure roll debate before Lord Dunpark, as a
result of which he was persuaded, having heard argument for the
Secretary of State, to depart from his earlier finding that the appellants
had given valid notice of appeal. Accordingly he issued an interlocutor
dated June 15, 1978, granting decree of reduction of the certificate in
terms of the appellants' first conclusion and also, on the basis of a   D
concession by counsel for the respondents that this must necessarily
follow, decree of declarator in terms of the second conclusion, that the
respondents were bound to issue a fresh certificate within two months
of the date of decree. The action so far as directed against the Secretary
of State was dismissed as irrelevant, and that matter has since been
allowed to rest, the Secretary of State taking no further part in the   E
proceedings.

The respondents reclaimed, and the reclaiming motion was heard
by the Second Division (the Lord Justice-Clerk (Lord Wheatley), Lord
Kissen and Lord Robertson). Counsel for the respondents withdrew
the concession that decree in terms of the second conclusion must
necessarily follow from decree in terms of the first, and also argued
for the validity of the certificate dated October 22, 1974, on the ground   F
that the provisions of article 3 (3) of the Order of 1959 were not
mandatory but only directory. By interlocutor dated January 26, 1979,
which is that now appealed from, the Second Division affirmed the
Lord Ordinary's decision that the certificate was invalid and should be
reduced, but refused as incompetent decree in terms of the second
conclusion ordaining the respondents to issue an amended certificate.   G
Their ground for so refusing was thus stated in the opinion of the
court, 1979 S.L.T. 221, 227:

" The procedure called for in the second conclusion would involve
ignoring the specific statutory requirements regulating the issue of a
certificate, and issuing an order of court ordaining the first defenders
contrary to their wishes to do something for which there is not only
no statutory authority but which would be directly in the teeth of   H
the statutory provisions."

The appellants by their appeal to this House seek reversal of that
part of the Second Division's interlocutor which refused decree in terms
of the second conclusion. The respondents not only resist that but by
their cross-appeal attack that part of the interlocutor which granted
decree in terms of the first conclusion.

A   It is logical in the circumstances to consider first whether the Lord
Ordinary and their Lordships of the Second Division were right in
granting decree of reduction of the certificate dated October 22, 1974.
It was argued for the respondents initially that the notice as to rights
of appeal required by article 3 (3) of the Order of 1959 was something
severable from the certificate itself. The certificate, so it was main-
B tained, constituted a decision of the local planning authority which had
a force and validity of its own unaffected by any failure to give the
statutorily required notice about rights of appeal. Reference was made
to the decision of the Court of Appeal in *Brayhead (Ascot) Ltd.* v.
Berkshire County Council [1964] 2 Q.B. 303, where it was held that the
failure of a local planning authority, when granting planning permission
subject to a condition, to give reasons in writing for the imposition of
C the condition as required by article 5 (9) of the Town and Country
Planning (General Development) Order 1950 did not render the condition
void. This was upon the ground, as stated by Winn J. at pp. 313–314,
that while the requirement was mandatory in the sense that compliance
with it could be enforced by mandamus, non-compliance did not render
the condition void because that result was not required for the effective
achievement of the purposes of the statute under which the requirement
D was imposed, and not intended by Parliament on a proper construction
of that statute. In my opinion the argument is not assisted by the case
referred to and is unsound. Article 3 (3) of the Order of 1959 specifically
states that any certificate issued under section 25 (4) (*b*) of the Act
" shall include " a statement in writing of rights of appeal. This is
entirely contrary to any idea of severability, and the provision is clearly
E necessary for effectively achieving the obvious purpose that the applicant
receiving the certificate should know what his rights are. The consequences of failure to inform him of these rights may be irretrievable,
unlike the consequences of failure to state reasons in writing, which can
always be put right at a later date without anything more serious than
some inconvenience.

Then it was contended that article 3 (3) was not intended to be
F mandatory or imperative, but merely directory and procedural in effect.
It was said that any applicant for a certificate of appropriate alternative
development must have read the Order of 1959 for the purpose of finding
out how to make application. Reliance was also placed upon the circumstance that, in cases where section 26 (5) of the Act of 1963 operated so
as to give the applicant a right of appeal by reason of the planning
authority's failure to issue a certificate timeously, no machinery was
G provided whereby the applicant might have notice of that right of
appeal. It was pointed out that such machinery was provided in
Schedule 2 to the Town and Country Planning (General Development)
Order 1950 (S.I. 1950 No. 728) in relation to the analogous statutory
provisions regarding appeals against deemed refusal of planning permission (though curiously enough not in the corresponding Scottish
H Order (S.I. 1950 No. 942)), by way of the form there prescribed for
acknowledgment by local planning authorities of applications for planning
permission.

The word " shall " used in article 3 (3) is normally to be interpreted
as connoting a mandatory provision, meaning that what is thereby
enjoined is not merely desired to be done but must be done. In many
instances failure to obtemper a mandatory provision has the consequence
that the proceedings with which the failure is connected are rendered

invalid. But that is not necessarily so. As is shown by the case of A
Brayhead (Ascot) Ltd. v. *Berkshire County Council* [1964] 2 Q.B. 303
something may turn upon the importance of the provision in relation to
the statutory purpose which the provision is directed to achieving, and
whether any opportunity exists of later putting right the failure. I have
no doubt that in the present case the provision under consideration is
intended to be mandatory and is of such a character that failure to
comply with it renders the certificate invalid. Where Parliament, albeit B
through subordinate legislation, has enacted that a person is to be
informed of the rights of appeal conferred upon him by statute in
relation to a particular subject matter whereby his rights may be very
materially affected, it will not do to say that failure to comply with
the enactment has no legal result whatever. The matter is of great
importance and has been shown to have been so regarded by Parliament. C
Failure to comply may deprive the person concerned of his rights of
appeal with no opportunity of rectifying the situation. While it is indeed
curious that no provision is made for acquainting an applicant for a
certificate with his rights of appeal where no certificate is issued within
the prescribed time, I regard that omission as inadvertent, and not serving
in any way to indicate an intention that the provisions of article 3 (3)
about notification of rights of appeal should be merely directory. I D
note that authority in favour of the view that a provision of this nature
is mandatory in the sense that failure to comply renders the proceedings
invalid is to be found in *Agricultural, Horticultural and Forestry Industry
Training Board* v. *Kent* [1970] 2 Q.B. 19. That was a decision of the
Court of Appeal upon article 4 (3) of the Industrial Training Levy (Agricultural, Horticultural and Forestry) Order 1967 (S.I. 1967 No. 1747), E
whereby any notice of assessment to a levy made under section 4 of the
Industrial Training Act 1964 was required to state the appropriate address
for service of notice of appeal against the levy. Failure to comply with
this requirement was held to invalidate the notice of assessment.

The final argument for the respondents on this branch of the case
turned on the terms of section 26 (4) of the Act of 1963, which I have
quoted above. That enactment gives a right of appeal where the local F
authority fails to issue a certificate within the prescribed time, upon the
basis that a certificate in terms of section 25 (4) (*b*) is deemed to have
been issued. In the event, so the argument ran, that the certificate
actually issued in this case is held to have been invalid, the situation is
the same as if no certificate had been issued. Therefore section 26 (4)
applies, under which no question of notification of rights of appeal arises. G
The appellants should have appealed to the Secretary of State within
one month of the expiry of the period of two months from the receipt
by the respondents of the appellants' application for a certificate. They
did not do so, and therefore they have lost any right of appeal. In
my opinion this argument also is unsound. In the first place it is to
be observed that the argument is elided if decree is to be granted not
only reducing the certificate actually issued but also ordaining the res- H
pondents to issue a new certificate in proper form. It is not an argument in favour of the validity of the certificate issued. Indeed, it
requires that the certificate should have been totally void ab initio and
that the respondents should be treated as having done nothing at all
in response to the appellants' application. That would, in my opinion, be
totally unrealistic. The respondents did issue a certificate, but it contained a defect enabling it to be successfully attacked as invalid. I do

A not consider that section 26 (4) applies to that situation. It applies where
after the expiry of the time prescribed " no certificate has been issued."
Here a certificate was issued which, though defective, was not a complete nullity. In this context use of the expressions " void " and " voidable," which have a recognised significance and importance in certain
fields of the law of contract, is to be avoided as inappropriate and apt to
B confuse. A decision or other act of a more or less formal character may
be invalid and subject to being so declared in court of law and yet have
some legal effect or existence prior to such declaration. In particular,
it may be capable of being submitted to an appeal (cf. *Calvin* v. *Carr*
[1979] 2 W.L.R. 755, 763, *per* Lord Wilberforce). In my opinion the
certificate issued in the present case was of that character. It had some
legal effect unless and until reduced, and in particular it might, in my
C view, have been the proper subject of a timeous appeal to the Secretary
of State.

It follows that in my opinion the Lord Ordinary and the Second
Division were right in granting decree of reduction of the certificate,
and it is necessary to consider next whether the Second Division was
right to refuse decree in terms of the second conclusion.

D   The view taken in the Second Division was, as I have already mentioned, that the respondents had no power to issue a certificate after the
expiry of two months from the date of receipt of the appellants' application, that it would be " in the teeth of the statutory provisions " to
ordain them to do so, and that the second conclusion was therefore
incompetent. But article 3 (2) of the Order of 1959, while laying down
that the time within which a certificate is to be issued shall be the
E two months period, does not expressly forbid the issue of a certificate
after the expiry of that period. Nor, in my opinion, does it do so by
necessary implication. It cannot reasonably be considered necessary for
the achievement of the purposes of the Act of 1963 that the two months
time limit should be strictly adhered to, nor that failure to do so might
have irretrievable consequences. Therefore I would regard this provision
F as clearly having not a mandatory but a directory character, designed
to secure reasonable expedition on the part of the local planning authority. It is easy to envisage that an application for a certificate might
call for elucidation or further information than was at first available,
with the result that strict adherence to the time limit was impossible or
at least not conducive to the satisfactory disposal of the application,
G and might be departed from without any prejudice to anyone. Such
considerations make it quite unreasonable to regard the provision as
mandatory. I think that further support for the view that it is not
is to be gathered from that part of section 26 (4) of the Act which
indicates that the parties concerned and the planning authority may
" at any time " agree upon an extended period, of whatever duration,
H for the issue of a certificate. This also serves to show that the obligation to issue a certificate which is laid upon the local planning authority by section 25 (4) is a continuing one. I see no sound grounds for
supposing that this obligation is not to be capable of enforcement by
appropriate legal proceedings, where these are necessary in order to
vindicate the rights of an applicant. It is true that section 26 (4) provides a means whereby, if the local planning authority is guilty of delay
in issuing a certificate, the applicant can in effect short-circuit the

authority and go straight to the Secretary of State. But this remedy A
appears to be an optional one, and its existence does not, in my view,
lead properly to the inference that the authority's statutory duty to
issue a certificate can in no circumstances be enforced by legal proceedings.

In support of the proposition that the issue of a certificate outside the
statutorily prescribed periods is not ultra vires the local planning authority, counsel for the appellants founded on *James* v. *Minister of Housing* B
and Local Government [1966] 1 W.L.R. 135; [1968] A.C. 409 and
London Ballast Co. Ltd. v. *Buckinghamshire County Council* (1966) 65
L.G.R. 227. In each of these cases a point arose regarding the validity of
a conditional planning permission granted after the expiry of the period
statutorily prescribed for doing so. It is unnecessary to examine the
cases in detail. It is sufficient to say that in each of them opinions were C
expressed to the effect that a planning permission so granted was not
necessarily voidable, but that it might be so in certain circumstances.
That appears to me to be an unexceptionable statement of the law.

The argument for the respondents on this branch of the case, in
its main thrust, was concerned with the contention that the remedy
sought by the appellants was inappropriate. It was suggested that re- D
course might be had to the nobile officium of the court. I regard that
suggestion as entirely misplaced. The nobile officium does not exist to
deal with matters of disputed right. Its chief object is to provide a
means of rectifying obvious errors or omissions, principally of an
administrative character, which cannot be dealt with in any other way.
The present case is concerned with the appellants' right, disputed by E
the respondents, to require the latter to issue to them a certificate under
section 25 (4) of the Act of 1963 which is in proper form. That is a
matter appropriate to be dealt with by the ordinary processes of law,
and which does not in any respect concern the nobile officiam. The
argument for the respondents did not, in my opinion, come to grips
at all with the appellants' contentions upon this matter of disputed
right, let alone counter them successfully. These contentions must F
therefore prevail.

It remains to notice a submission for the respondents that the
appellants should be put to proof of their averment that they were
unaware of the time limit for appealing to the Secretary of State and
this was the reason why their appeal was late. I reject that submission.
The invalidity of the certificate derives from a defect of general applica- G
tion, and nothing turns on the state of the appellants' knowledge.

My Lords, for these reasons I would allow the appeal and dismiss
the cross-appeal. Counsel for the appellants asked leave to further
amend the second conclusion of the summons by substituting the word
" fresh " for the word " amended " before the word " certificate " in the
fourth line, and such leave should be granted. Subject to that, the H
appropriate order would be to recall the interlocutor of the Second
Division dated January 26, 1979, in so far as it refused decree in terms
of the second conclusion of the summons, and quoad that conclusion
as amended to sustain the second and third pleas in law for the pursuer
and to grant decree in terms thereof. The respondents will be liable
to the appellants for costs in this House and also for all expenses in the
Court of Session, apart from those for which the appellants were found

A liable to the second respondent by interlocutor of the Lord Ordinary
dated June 15, 1978.

Appeal allowed.
Cross-appeal dismissed.

Solicitors: *Stephenson, Harwood* for *Biggart, Baillie & Gifford W.S.,*
B *Edinburgh; Martin & Co.* for *Shepherd & Wedderburn W.S., Edinburgh.*

F. C.

[COURT OF APPEAL]

C * ELLESMERE PORT AND NESTON BOROUGH COUNCIL *v.*
SHELL U.K. LTD. AND ANOTHER

SAME *v.* U.K.F. FERTILIZERS LTD. AND ANOTHER

CHESTER CITY COUNCIL *v.* SHELL U.K. LTD. AND ANOTHER

D ELLESMERE PORT AND NESTON BOROUGH COUNCIL *v.*
BURMAH OIL TRADING LTD. AND ANOTHER

CHESTER CITY COUNCIL *v.* SAME AND ANOTHER

1979 Oct. 10, 11, 15;   Megaw, Shaw and Waller L.JJ.
E   Nov. 9

Rating—Local valuation court—Jurisdiction—Proposals for alter-
ations to valuation list—Agreement by ratepayers and valuation
officer—Agreed figures accepted by local valuation court—
Rating authority's appeal to Lands Tribunal—" Contention "
to be considered—Whether agreed figures or original proposals
F *— Rating authority's right to be heard — Whether Lands*
Tribunal entitled to increase assessments—General Rate Act
1967 (c. 9), ss. 76 (4) (5), 77 [1]

Three ratepayers, all companies owning oil pipelines and
refineries, negotiated with the valuation officer with regard to
the rating of certain hereditaments which came within the
districts of two rating authorities. Proposals for alterations in
the valuation list were made both by the ratepayers and by the
G valuation officer in relation to new entries. The valuation
officer objected to the ratepayers' proposals and the ratepayers
objected to the valuation officer's proposals but no objections

[1] General Rate Act 1967, s. 76: " (4) On the hearing of an appeal to a local
valuation court—. . . (d) the rating authority for the rating area in which the
hereditament in question is situated, when that authority are not the appellant . . .
shall be entitled to appear and be heard as parties to the appeal and examine any
H witness before the court and to call witnesses. (5) . . . after hearing the persons
mentioned in subsection (4) of this section, or such of them as desire to be heard,
the local valuation court shall give such directions with respect to the manner in
which the hereditament in question is to be treated in the valuation list as appear
to them to be necessary to give effect to the contention of the appellant if and so
far as that contention appears to the court to be well founded; . . ."
S. 77: " Any person who . . . appears before a local valuation court on the
hearing of an appeal and is aggrieved by the decision of the court thereon may
. . . appeal to the Lands Tribunal, and that tribunal, after hearing such of the
persons as appeared as aforesaid as desire to be heard, may give any direction which
the local valuation court might have given; . . ."

Ellesmere Port Council v. Shell U.K. Ltd. (C.A.) [1980]

A were made by the rating authorities. The ratepayers and the valuation officer eventually came to an agreement and the matter was referred to the local valuation court, where the valuation officer and the ratepayers put forward their agreed figures. The rating authorities, which had not been parties to the agreement, exercised their right to appear under section 76 (4) of the General Rate Act 1967 and claimed the right to call evidence. The local valuation court, however, accepted

B the agreed figures and directed that the valuation list be altered accordingly. The rating authorities appealed to the Lands Tribunal whereupon the ratepayers asked to have the preliminary issue decided that the Lands Tribunal had no jurisdiction to increase the figures found by the local valuation court. They submitted that the " contention " to be considered within the meaning of section 76 (5) of the Act of 1967 was the agreed figures which had been put forward and,

C further, that, in the light of that agreement, the rating authorities now had no right to be heard. The Lands Tribunal rejected those submissions, holding that it was entitled to consider the proposal and that it had jurisdiction to increase the assessments.

On appeal by the ratepayers: —

Held, dismissing the appeal, (1) that the " contention of the appellant " to be considered under section 76 (5) of the General Rate Act 1967 was the proposal put forward by the appel-

D lant for alteration of the valuation list and it was the function of the local valuation court or the Lands Tribunal to assess the impact of that contention upon the force of the objections; and that no agreement between two parties could affect the court's jurisdiction to allow the appeal in whole or in part and by rejecting or upholding the objections in whole or in part to uphold the proposal in its entirety or partially (post, pp. 213H, 215C–E, G–H, 218C–D).

E (2) That it was implicit in the scheme of Part V of the Act that the rating authority must be involved at all stages of the proceedings and that no concluded agreement could be reached without their co-operation; that there was no ambiguity in section 76 (4) of the Act and thereunder the rating authority had a right to appear as a party to an appeal and to require the ratepayer to prove his case; and that the Lands Tribunal could make a higher assessment than that determined

F by the valuation court so long as its assessment was not greater than that contained in the proposal (post, pp. 214C–F, 216A–D, 217F—218B).

Per Megaw L.J. Since an appeal to this court from the Lands Tribunal is only on questions of law, and since questions of fact are for the tribunal itself, it is in the highest degree undesirable that, in the absence of very exceptional circumstances, this court should admit evidence not given before the

G tribunal. The court has jurisdiction to do so; but it should be very sparingly exercised (post, pp. 216H—217A).

The following cases are referred to in the judgments:

Ellerby v. *March* [1954] 2 Q.B. 357; [1954] 3 W.L.R. 53; [1954] 2 All E.R. 375, C.A.

Morecambe and Heysham Corporation v. *Robinson* [1961] 1 W.L.R. 373; [1961] 1 All E.R. 721, C.A.

H

The following additional cases were cited in argument:

Brixham Urban District Council, In re [1955] 1 W.L.R. 5, 426; [1954] 3 All E.R. 561n.

City of Sheffield v. *Meadow Dairy Co. Ltd.* (1958) 2 R.R.C. 395.

Rex v. *East Norfolk Local Valuation Court, Ex parte Martin* [1951] W.N. 181; [1951] 1 All E.R. 743, D.C.

River Wear Commissioners v. *Adamson* (1877) 2 App.Cas. 743, H.L.(E.).

A   CASE STATED by the Lands Tribunal (Sir Douglas Frank Q.C., President).

These were determinations on a preliminary point of law on appeals by two rating authorities, Ellesmere Port and Neston Borough Council and Chester City Council, from decisions of a local valuation court for Cheshire given on April 27, 1977, reducing the assessments of various hereditaments.

B

Applications for a determination of the preliminary point of law were made by the ratepayers, Shell U.K. Ltd., U.K.F. Fertilizers Ltd. and Burmah Oil Trading Ltd., on the ground: " that the Lands Tribunal has no jurisdiction to increase the assessments which are the subject of the appeals."

The facts proved and admitted and the contentions of the parties are C   taken from the decision of the Lands Tribunal in relation to *Shell U.K. Ltd.* v. *Ellesmere Port and Neston Borough Council.* The other decisions were identical save for the names of the applicants. The point of law was the same in each case.

In his decision the President said that the material facts were that proposals were made both by the valuation officer, Mr. P. K. Brennan, D   and by the ratepayers for the assessment of various hereditaments connected with oil pipe lines and oil refineries, there were objections by the valuation officer and the ratepayers and the matter came before the local valuation court. At the hearing before the local valuation court it was asserted by counsel for the ratepayers and the solicitor appearing for the valuation officer that agreement had been reached on figures which were put before the court.

E

Lord Colville, appearing for the appellants, the rating authorities, submitted that there was no evidence on which the local valuation court could give effect to the agreed figures and further submitted that either it was open to the court or that they were compelled to confirm the figures in the proposals. However, the court in their decision, having recited section 76 (5) of the General Rate Act 1967, said that as there was F   no evidence before them they would accept the agreed figures as correct and would confirm them and directed that the valuation list be altered accordingly. The submission of counsel for the ratepayers before the Lands Tribunal was that the tribunal could only give directions which the local valuation court could give and that the local valuation court's power to give directions was limited to section 76 (5).

G   Counsel for the ratepayers said that the word " contention " in that subsection meant the figures as restricted by the appellant, that was to say, in the context of the present case, it meant the agreed assessment and that there was no issue for the local valuation court to determine. Mr. Fay (for Burmah Oil) said that an appellant might limit his contention and in particular where the two contending parties agreed that the proper figure was £x, that limited the contention and the jurisdiction of H   the court. He also said that as the agreements in the present case limited the appellants' contention within the meaning of section 76 (5) the ratepayers and the valuation officers were bound by what they said and he further submitted that the rating authority, not having served a proposal or objection, were not a party until the day of the hearing and as by that time an agreement had been reached, the contention was then dead and it would be contrary to good sense to revive it; and

that the agreement as to the figures was tantamount to partial withdrawal   A
of the proposals and the objections.

The President said that it was common ground that the question to
be determined was whether the word " contention " in subsection (5) of
section 76 meant the proposal or on the other hand the figure " aimed
at " under the agreements, in other words, the agreed figures. In
his judgment the word " contention " had to be construed noscitur a   B
sociis. Foremost in his mind was subsection (4) of section 76 which
gave the persons named not only the right to be heard but also the right
to be heard as parties. The effect of the submissions for the ratepayers
was that by agreement between two parties the third party could be
ousted unless he happened to be an objector. Indeed if the proposal
had been made by the rating authority and agreement had been reached
with the valuation officer, even the ratepayer could be ousted unless he   C
had taken the precaution of making his own objection. In his judgment
the effect of ousting persons expressed in the statute to be parties was a
fatal flaw in the ratepayers' proposition. It involved the consequences
that in tripartite litigation agreement by two parties bound the third and
it seemed to him that that proposition had only to be stated to expose its
incongruity. Further Mr. Fay had conceded that his proposition involved   D
this: Assume a proposal by the valuation officer for an entry of £1,000
gross value. By the time of the hearing before the local valuation court
he had changed his mind and by then was of the firm opinion that the
correct figure was £750 and that was what he contended for and led
evidence to. Mr. Fay had said that if he was right then the local
valuation court could not direct an entry in excess of £750, even though
the rating authority, relying on the proposal, abstained from making   E
their own proposal, and even if the evidence led inescapably to a gross
value of not less than £1,000. But there were other indicia that the
word " contention " meant the contention set out in the proposal.

There was no express provision for amending the proposal. In effect
Mr. Fay's submission, which he called a " partial withdrawal," would
have the effect of amending the proposal. Then there was section 72   F
which was designed to meet the situation where there was agreement,
but under that section no agreement was effective unless the persons
described in subsection (2) concurred in it. The effect of the ratepayers' submissions would be to escape or sidestep the precautions taken
in section 72 to ensure that there was no agreement other than with the
concurrence of those who were affected by it. Furthermore, one practical   G
consequence of the ratepayers' submission was that the Lands Tribunal
would be required to ascertain what were the issues before the local
valuation court, and if that were right he, the President, would expect
some machinery in the Act for ascertaining those issues. In his judgment
the contention in subsection (5) of section 76 meant the contention in
the proposal. He thought that the proposal, like a writ, contained the   H
contention which was and remained the foundation of the proceedings
and prescribed the ambit of them. There was support for that in the
judgment of Somervell L.J. in *Ellerby* v. *March* [1954] 2 Q.B. 357, 363,
where he was dealing with a Lands Tribunal appeal. Ex hypothesi it
would have taken clear words to satisfy him that it could have been
intended that the Lands Tribunal could not deal with all the issues
raised by the proposal. Under the circumstances he held that the Lands

A   Tribunal had jurisdiction to increase the assessments which were the subject of the appeals.

The ratepayers appealed and the question for the court was whether the Lands Tribunal had come to a correct decision in law holding that it had jurisdiction to increase the assessments which were the subject of the appeals.

B   The grounds of appeal were, inter alia, (1) that the tribunal had wrongly held that it had jurisdiction to increase the assessments; (2) that the tribunal had misconstrued the meaning of " contention " in section 76 (5) of the General Rate Act 1967; (3) that the tribunal had wrongly concluded that the effect of the ratepayers' argument would be to deprive the rating authority of their rights under section 76 of the Act of 1967; (4) that the tribunal had misconstrued the purpose and

C   ambit of section 72 of the Act and had wrongly held that the effect of the ratepayers' argument was to circumvent the section; (5) further, or in the alternative, that the tribunal had wrongly rejected the ratepayers' alternative argument that where the valuation officer and the ratepayers had reached agreement in respect of a proposal made by either of them prior to it coming to court and where no other party had objected to the proposal, either there was no issue for the court to determine or

D   there was no issue with regard to value for the court to determine.

David Widdicombe Q.C. and Matthew Horton for Shell U.K. Ltd.
Matthew Horton for U.K.F. Fertilizers Ltd.
Charles Fay for Burmah Oil Trading Ltd.
W. J. Glover Q.C. and Susan Hamilton for Ellesmere Port and Neston

E   Borough Council.
Viscount Colville of Culross Q.C. and Susan Hamilton for Chester City Council.
Alan Fletcher for the valuation officer.

Cur. adv. vult.

F   November 9.   The following judgments were read.

MEGAW L.J.   I shall ask Waller L.J. to deliver the first judgment.

WALLER L.J.   These are five appeals against decisions of the Lands Tribunal called on and heard together at the request of all parties.   The

G   case stated by the Lands Tribunal is in identical terms in each case and raises the same point for the decision of this court.   In each case it is the ratepayer who is appealing and the rating authority and the valuation officer who are supporting the decision of the Lands Tribunal.   The ratepayers own pipelines and oil refineries and, in the case of U.K.F. Fertilizers Ltd., manufacturing plant and, although in reality in each case there is only one hereditament, each is divided into a number of

H   items which are divided between two rating authorities.   The sums involved are very great; in the case of Shell U.K. Ltd., for instance, a total sum amounting to some £2,600,000 odd.   Some of the proposals were by the ratepayer for reductions and some were by the valuation officer for new items with a stated valuation.

We were told that, over a period of three years, the ratepayers and the valuation officer were in negotiation and that, at the end of that time, agreement was reached between them at figures which, in the case

of Shell, produced a total of some £2,150,000. Since in each case there A
had been an objection to the proposal by the valuation officer, or the
ratepayer as the case might be, it was necessary to go to the local
valuation court to effect any alteration to the valuation list. Before the
local valuation court neither the valuation officer nor the ratepayer
called evidence, but each put forward their agreed figures. The rating
authority, however, appeared and claimed the right to ask questions and
call evidence. The local valuation court, having heard argument, decided B
that the figures were agreed and that the rating authority had no further
right to be heard. The rating authority appealed to the Lands Tribunal
and the ratepayers took the preliminary point that the Lands Tribunal
had no jurisdiction to increase the figures found by the local valuation
court.

    Counsel on behalf of each of the ratepayers submit that it is unfair C
and contrary to the spirit of rating legislation since 1948 that the rating
authority should stand by for three years without even objecting to the
proposals and then be allowed to go before the local valuation court and
seek to argue and prove that the figures should be higher than that which
had been agreed.

    I do not propose to refer at this stage to the earlier legislation, namely, D
the Local Government Act 1948 and the Rating and Valuation (Miscellaneous Provisions) Act 1955, because they can only be relevant if there
is an ambiguity in the current statute, namely, the General Rate Act
1967, and, in particular, Part V. Section 67 deals with the publication of
a new valuation list and then there follow a number of sections dealing
with alterations to the current valuation list. Section 69 deals with
proposals for alteration of the current valuation and enables anyone E
aggrieved to make a proposal for amendment either by adding a hereditament or altering its description or value. Section 69 reads:

    " (1) Subject to subsection (6) of this section, any person (including
    a rating authority) who is aggrieved—(a) by the inclusion of any
    hereditament in the valuation list; or (b) by any value ascribed in
    the list to a hereditament or by any other statement made or omitted F
    to be made in the list with respect to a hereditament; or (c) in the
    case of a building or portion of a building occupied in parts, by the
    valuation in the list of that building or portion of a building as a
    single hereditament, may at any time make a proposal for the altera-
    tion of the list so far as it relates to that hereditament. (2) Subject
    to subsection (6) of this section, the valuation officer may at any
    time make a proposal for any alteration of a valuation list and in G
    particular, in addition to the proposals authorised or required by, or
    by virtue of, the following provisions of this Act, namely, paragraph
    6 (1) of Schedule 1, paragraph 4 (1) of Schedule 4, paragraph 8 (4)
    of Schedule 5, paragraph 13 of Schedule 6 and paragraph 15 of
    Schedule 7, shall from time to time make such proposals as may be
    requisite—(a) for deleting from the list any premises exempted from H
    rating by virtue of section 33 (1) (b) of this Act; (b) for excluding
    from the list any premises which form part of a hereditament shown
    in the list and which, by virtue of section 33 (1) (a) or (b) of this
    Act, are not liable to be rated, and for including in the list, as one
    or more separate hereditaments, so much of any such hereditament
    as remains liable to be rated; (c) for altering the list in consequence
    of any event whereby premises cease to be within the exemption from

The Weekly Law Reports, February 29, 1980

211

1 W.L.R.   Ellesmere Port Council v. Shell U.K. Ltd. (C.A.)   Waller L.J.

A   rating conferred by section 32 (3), 33 (1) or 34 (1) of this Act. (3) Without prejudice to any right exercisable by rating authorities by virtue of subsection (1) of this section, where—(a) it appears to a rating authority that a hereditament in their rating area which is not included in the list ought to be included therein; and (b) the valuation officer gives notice in writing to the rating authority that he does not intend to make a proposal for inserting that hereditament in the list, B   the rating authority, at any time within 28 days after the date on which that notice was given, may make a proposal for the alteration of the list by the insertion of that hereditament therein. . . . (5) Every proposal under this section must—(a) be made in writing; and (b) specify the grounds on which the proposed alteration is supported, and, (c) comply with any requirements of any regulations made by C   the Minister with respect to the form of such proposals and otherwise with respect to the making thereof, and every such proposal made otherwise than by the valuation officer must be served on the valuation officer."

Section 70 makes provision for objections to proposals:

D   " (1) The valuation officer shall, within 28 days after the date on which a proposal under section 69 of this Act is served on him, or within seven days after the date on which such a proposal is made by him, as the case may be, transmit a copy thereof, together with a statement in writing of the right of objection conferred by subsection (2) of this section, to each of the following persons, not being the maker of the proposal, that is to say—(a) the occupier of the hereditament to which E   the proposal relates; and (b) the rating authority for the area in which the hereditament in question is situated."

By section 70 (2) the owner or occupier or the rating authority may within 28 days of service serve notice of objection on the valuation officer. Where the proposal was made by the ratepayer the valuation officer must give him notice of objection by the rating authority. The valuation officer's F   duty is under section 74 (1) and he has to object within three months. In this case the proposals for alterations were made by both the ratepayer (in all cases) and the valuation officer in the cases of proposed new entries in the valuation list. The ratepayer objected to the valuation officer's proposals and the valuation officer in due course objected to the ratepayer's proposals but no objection was made by the rating authority. Section 71 G   deals with unopposed proposals:

" (1) Where in the case of any proposal under section 69 of this Act— (a) no notice of objection is served within the time limited by section 70 (2) of this Act, or every such notice is unconditionally withdrawn; and (b) either—(i) the proposal was made by the valuation officer; or (ii) the valuation officer is satisfied that the proposal is well-founded; H   or (iii) at the end of the period of four months beginning with the date on which the proposal was served on the valuation officer, that officer has not given a notice under section 74 (1) of this Act, the valuation officer shall cause the valuation list to be altered so as to give effect to the proposal.

There then comes section 72 which deals with agreed alterations after proposals but before determination by the local valuation court. If the

requirements of the section are fulfilled it becomes the duty of the valuation   A
officer to cause the alteration to be made in the valuation list.   Section 72
provides:

" (1) Where, in the case of any proposal under section 69 of this Act,
the requirements of section 71 of this Act are not satisfied, but—(a)
all the persons referred to in subsection (2) of this section agree on an
alteration of the valuation list (whether the alteration is that specified   B
in the proposal or another alteration); and (b) the agreement is
reached without, or before the determination of, any appeal to a
local valuation court, or reference to arbitration, with respect to
an objection to the proposal, the valuation officer shall cause that
alteration to be made in the valuation list. (2) The persons referred
to in subsection (1) (a) of this section are—(a) the valuation officer;   C
(b) the person who made the proposal, where the proposal was not
made by the valuation officer; (c) any person who has served and
who has not unconditionally withdrawn a notice of objection to the
proposal; (d) the occupier of the hereditament to which the proposal
relates, if he is not included by virtue of paragraph (b) or (c) of this
subsection; (e) the rating authority (if not included by virtue of
paragraph (b), (c), or (d) of this subsection), unless they have notified   D
the valuation officer that they do not desire to be included by virtue
of this paragraph either generally or as respects a class of hereditament which includes the hereditament to which the proposal relates."

It is not suggested that in this case section 72 had been complied with.
Under section 73 the valuation officer is under a duty to transmit proposals
to which there has been an objection to the clerk to the local valuation   E
court and section 74 makes provision for proposals to which the valuation
officer objects to be so transmitted.   Under either section the transmission
has effect as an appeal to the local valuation court by virtue of section
76 (1), which provides:

" (1) Where a copy of a proposal is transmitted to the clerk to a local
valuation panel and by virtue of section 73 (2), 74 (3) or 75 of this Act   F
that transmission has effect as an appeal to a local valuation court
against an objection to the proposal, it shall be the duty of the chairman or a deputy chairman of that panel to arrange for the convening
of such a court. (2) The procedure of a local valuation court shall,
subject to any regulations made in that behalf by the Minister, and
subject to subsection (3) of this section, be such as the court may
determine; and the court—(a) shall sit in public, unless the court other-   G
wise order on the application of any party to the appeal and upon
being satisfied that the interests of one or more parties to the appeal
would be prejudicially affected; and (b) may take evidence on oath and
shall have power for that purpose to administer oaths. . . . (4) On the
hearing of an appeal to a local valuation court—(a) the appellant; and
(b) the valuation officer, when he is not the appellant; and (c) the   H
owner or occupier of the hereditament to which the appeal relates,
when he is not the appellant; and (d) the rating authority for the
rating area in which the hereditament in question is situated, when that
authority are not the appellant; and (e) the objector, where he is not
one of the persons aforesaid, shall be entitled to appear and be heard
as parties to the appeal and examine any witness before the court and
to call witnesses. (5) Subject to the provisions of this Act, after

The Weekly Law Reports, February 29, 1980

213

1 W.L.R.   Ellesmere Port Council v. Shell U.K. Ltd. (C.A.)   Waller L.J.

A   hearing the persons mentioned in subsection (4) of this section, or such of them as desire to be heard, the local valuation court shall give such directions with respect to the manner in which the hereditament in question is to be treated in the valuation list as appear to them to be necessary to give effect to the contention of the appellant if and so far as that contention appears to the court to be well founded; and

B   the valuation officer shall cause the valuation list to be altered accordingly."

As I have already indicated, the rating authority exercised their right to appear and be heard as parties to the appeal but the local valuation court, having heard argument, decided that the figures were agreed. In effect, the question which is posed for the opinion of this court is: were

C   the local valuation court right in deciding that the agreed figures stood?

The case for the ratepayers is put in two ways. (1) In the case of proposals for new entries and valuations made by the valuation officer the "contention" of the valuation officer was not the proposal figure but was the agreed figure or some lower figure. This argument is based on the wording of section 76 (5) where it says:

D   ". . . the local valuation court shall give such directions with respect to the manner in which the hereditament in question is to be treated in the valuation list as appear to them to be necessary to give effect to the contention of the appellant if and so far as that contention appears to the court to be well founded; . . ."

It was submitted that, once the valuation officer reduced his own figure,

E   his "contention" was the new figure was a maximum; and it was not open to the local valuation court to go above the new figure because its jurisdiction was limited to "so far as that contention appears to the court to be well founded." (2) It was submitted that, in the case of proposals by the occupiers for a lower figure than in the valuation list, once there was agreement with the valuation officer there was no justiciable issue, i.e., no dispute. This argument did not depend on the

F   meaning of the word "contention," but on the simple submission that there was no issue for the local valuation court to try.

On the meaning of "contention" it was submitted that, once the valuation officer agreed a lower figure than that in the valuation list or in his proposal, as the case might be, this lower figure would be the limit of his contention and it would not be possible to say that the higher

G   figure in the proposal was his contention. _Morecambe and Heysham Corporation_ v. _Robinson_ [1961] 1 W.L.R. 373, when carefully considered, does not support this limited view of contention. Furthermore, the decision is really on the question of whether contention refers to the figures or refers to the arguments. I do not find any help from other authorities cited to us. In this case the valuation officer published a valuation list with valuations in it. These valuations were communicated

H   to all concerned including the rating authority. The occupier made a proposal of a nominal figure. In my judgment, the limits of contention were contained in the valuation list figure on the one hand and the figure in the proposal on the other and, unless all parties agreed, no agreement between the two parties could alter that. In other instances, where the valuation officer made proposals, the limits of contention would be that figure on the one hand and that made in any objection on the other.

We were referred also to *Ellerby* v. *March* [1954] 2 Q.B. 357, a **A** decision which was concerned with appearances before the Lands Tribunal. There the argument is on appeal from the local valuation court which is the court of first instance. In my opinion the decision does not apply to proceedings before the local valuation court.

Subsidiary arguments by the ratepayers that the words of section 76 (4) entitling the rating authority to be present at the local valuation court **B** do not give the rating authority the right to attack and overrule an agreement between the valuation officer and the ratepayer were to the effect that there were other possible ways of achieving an alteration without the rating authority's concurrence. One argument was based on making a number of proposals for one hereditament and then withdrawing all but one. Another was founded on section 81 (1) where there could be a partial withdrawal of the proposal. In my opinion these arguments do **C** not assist the ratepayers. The fact that it is possible to point to one anomaly is no argument for ignoring or restricting the meaning of plain words in the statute. It is implicit throughout the part of the Act that I have set out above that no conclusion can be reached without the co-operation of the rating authority. The rating authority could adopt one of three possible courses of action: first, they could object in accordance **D** with the provisions of section 70 and thereafter they would be an active party to the dispute; secondly, they could notify the valuation officer that they did not desire to be included: see 72 (2) (*e*); thirdly, they could do nothing until they could see whether things were going wrong, i.e., whether their rateable values were to be reduced to figures which they regarded as being too low. If they were, then the rating authority could attack the figure and call evidence before the local valuation court. **E** The sections I have mentioned above require that at every stage the rating authority must be involved unless they have notified the valuation officer that they do not desire to be included: see section 72 (2) (*e*).

I said earlier that I was not looking at the statutes which preceded the Act of 1967 unless there was an ambiguity about the General Rate Act 1967. Although there may be some anomalies I do not find any **F** ambiguity about the words of section 76 (4) which state that the rating authority " shall be entitled to appear and be heard as parties to the appeal and examine any witness before the court and to call witnesses " and I therefore do not need to examine these earlier statutes.

I am of opinion that the President of the Lands Tribunal came to a correct decision in law and that the Lands Tribunal has jurisdiction to increase the assessments which are the subject of these appeals. **G**

Since preparing this judgment I have had the advantage of reading in draft the judgments which Megaw L.J. and Shaw L.J. are about to deliver and I agree with them both.

SHAW L.J. I agree.

The scheme embodied in Part V of the General Rate Act 1967 for **H** the maintenance and alteration of valuation lists, recognises that, apart from other possible parties, the valuation officer, the ratepayer and the rating authority must always have an interest in the compilation and alteration of a valuation list which relates to the area of that authority and is a hereditament for which the ratepayer has a liability. This concurrence of interest is made clear from a cursory examination of the relevant provisions of the Act beginning with section 69.

The Weekly Law Reports, February 29, 1980

215

1 W.L.R.   Ellesmere Port Council v. Shell U.K. Ltd. (C.A.)   Shaw L.J.

A   Where a proposal has been made and has been met with a notice of objection which is persisted in, the valuation officer is required within the limits of time prescribed by section 73 to transmit a copy of the proposal and of every notice of objection to the local valuation panel, and by section 76 (1) this step in the procedure prescribed under the Act shall " take effect as an appeal to a local valuation court against an objection to the proposal."

B   By section 76 (5) after due hearing (a matter which gives rise to one aspect of this appeal and to which I shall later refer):

"the local valuation court shall give such directions . . . as appear to them to be necessary to give effect to the contention of the appellant if and so far as that contention appears to the court to be well founded."

C

As I understand these provisions they not only determine and delimit the function and jurisdiction of the valuation court but they also define the role of the party responsible for the proposal.   That role is to challenge and refute the objections and as a necessary corollary to support the proposal.   The function of the valuation court is to assess the impact of the contentions of the appellant (and in particular where D the appellant is the valuation officer) upon the force of the objections. The court may reject the objections or accept them in whole or in part with the consequence that the proposal may be left intact or may be reduced or obliterated.   Even if the appellant does not seek to support his proposal in its entirety it is still for the court to decide to what extent the objections to it have been refuted by facts proved before E them.   The appellant cannot modify his proposal (unless he withdraws it altogether) save as provided by section 72; and the court cannot determine upon a more onerous proposal than that which was objected to since it is the objections to that proposal which constitute the matter in contention rather than the primary validity of the proposal itself.

Thus the jurisdiction of the court is measured by the area of controversy lying between the proposal and the matters of objection.   The F court will refuse to give effect to these last to the extent that the appellant's contentions appear to the court to be well founded.   Prima facie the contention of the appellant must be that the objections are ill-founded.   Otherwise he is virtually putting forward a new proposal and must follow the procedural requirements appertaining to a fresh proposal unless there is an agreement to which all interested bodies or persons G are parties in accordance with the requirements of section 72 (2) of the Act.   It is pertinent to observe that section 72 (1) (b) provides that such an agreement may be reached without or before the determination of any appeal to a local valuation court with respect to an objection to the proposal.

No such agreement to which the rating authority was a party was made in the present case.   The agreement between the valuation officer H and the ratepayer could be no more than persuasive before the valuation court.   Their jurisdiction remained what it had been from the outset, namely, to allow the appeal in whole or in part and by rejecting or upholding the objections in whole or in part correspondingly to uphold the proposal in its entirety or partially.

As to the operation of subsection (4) of section 76 it seems to me plain that any of the persons or bodies enumerated in paragraphs (a), (b), (c), (d) and (e) are entitled to intervene in the appeal and to be heard as parties. Whether they support or oppose the objections will A depend on their interest; but the valuation court will take account of the results of their intervention in deciding whether and in what measure the contention of the appellant that the objections are untenable is well founded.

I see no substance in the suggestion made by the ratepayers that it is unfair on the part of the rating authority to come in as a party to the appeal when they have taken no earlier action. There B was neither need nor obligation to do so. When the proposal has been made and met with an objection the issue is defined and all parties whose interests may be affected have a status to intervene at the hearing.

When the matter is taken to the Lands Tribunal its jurisdiction corresponds to that which the valuation court had when the appeal before it was constituted; this may be stated shortly in the formula that it C is to decide the outcome by consideration of the validity of the objections rather than by addressing itself to the propriety of the proposal. It may therefore, in the result, arrive where the amount is in issue at a higher figure than that determined by the valuation court. What it cannot do is to find a figure higher than the proposal itself for it, like the valuation court, has no jurisdiction to entertain a different proposal D from that to which objection has been made.

It follows that the answer to the question posed by the case in each of the appeals is in the affirmative and that the Lands Tribunal can make a higher assessment than that determined by the valuation court so long as their assessment so found is not greater than that contained in the proposal.

I would accordingly dismiss these appeals.   E

MEGAW L.J. I agree with the conclusions and with the reasons expressed in the judgment of Waller L.J. on each of the points raised by the ratepayers in these appeals. I agree that the decision of the President of the Lands Tribunal was correct in law.

There are two procedural matters to which I should refer. The F responsibility of formulating, for consideration by the President of the Lands Tribunal, the question or questions of law on which they sought to contend before this court that the decisions were wrong rested with the respective ratepayers. It is unfortunate that the ratepayers formulated one general question, instead of formulating two separate questions. This is particularly to be regretted since the ratepayers put in the forefront of their criticism of the President's decision the submission that he G failed to recognise that there were two separate points of law. Before us it emerged that the ratepayers' submissions involved that if we were to decide one of the two points of law against them, but were to uphold their submission on the other point of law, it would be impossible for the court to answer the question asked other than by some such formula as " The Lands Tribunal has jurisdiction unless . . .", or " The Lands H Tribunal does not have jurisdiction except if and in so far as . . .".

We were asked on behalf of one of the ratepayers, Shell U.K. Ltd., by original motion, for leave to adduce additional evidence in the form of a lengthy affidavit and exhibits. Since an appeal to this court from the Lands Tribunal is only on questions of law, and since questions of fact are for the tribunal itself, it is obviously in the highest degree undesirable that, in the absence of very exceptional circumstances, this court should

The Weekly Law Reports, February 29, 1980

217

1 W.L.R.   Ellesmere Port Council v. Shell U.K. Ltd. (C.A.)   Megaw L.J.

A admit evidence not given before the tribunal. The court has jurisdiction to do so; but it should be very sparingly exercised. If evidence tendered in the Lands Tribunal has been rejected, and it is desired to contend that the rejection was wrong, that should be dealt with as a question of law: not as a ground for simply re-submitting the evidence in this court.

B We decided that the only course open to us was to look at the proposed evidence provisionally. Two of the parties to these appeals, the valuation officer and one of the rating authorities, said that, if the evidence were to be admitted, they would wish to put in affidavits in reply on certain matters of fact. In the end, they did not do so, perhaps because it became evident that the evidence was, at best, of little real significance to the issues of law which we had to decide.

C The proposed evidence turned out to be, to a considerable extent, argument which, if relevant, should not have been put forward in an affidavit. The affidavit dealt also with facts and figures concerned with the particular assessment. Such facts and figures, it was, I think, accepted on behalf of the party seeking to adduce the evidence, could not directly affect a decision of general principle to be reached on the construction of statutory provisions: which principle, when ascertained,
D must be equally applicable to all assessments, large or small, complex or simple. It was contended that some of the facts set out in the affidavit would be helpful to the court as what was called "background" in reaching its decision on the issues of law. In the end, I think it is right to say that the affidavit was used only for the purpose of drawing illustrations, or examples, from an exhibit thereto.

E We were not asked to give a definite ruling, following our decision to look at the evidence provisionally. I think we ought now to give such a ruling. In all the circumstances, it seems to me to be better to treat the evidence as admitted. But if I had thought that anything in it was material to the decision of this court, as putting in evidence facts which were not before the Lands Tribunal, I should have regarded it as neces-
F sary to consider further, with the assistance of counsel, whether the proper course would not have been to remit the relevant appeal to the Lands Tribunal for further consideration on the basis of the evidence now adduced.

The point which, logically I should have thought, was the ratepayers' first point was dealt with second in the arguments for the ratepayers and has thus been dealt with as the second point in the judgment of
G Waller L.J. If it were right, the answer to the question of law posed would be that the Lands Tribunal have no jurisdiction to increase any of the figures found by the local valuation court in any of the appeals. I have been unable to understand how, in the absence of some express provision in section 76 (4) of the General Rate Act 1967, affecting the position in cases such as those with which we are concerned, it can be
H said that the words of that subsection are consistent with the ratepayers' contention that the rating authority is precluded from being heard as parties to the appeal: that is, from saying, if they see fit, "we require the appellant ratepayer to prove his case on this appeal." It was suggested, if I understood the submission correctly, that the rating authority could, indeed, "be heard as parties to the appeal," to the extent of challenging the validity of the agreement as to figures between the ratepayer and the valuation officer. I do not understand either what

sort of "invalidity" is here contemplated, or why the words of the A
statute should be treated as being so limited in effect.   In substance, also,
as I see it, the ratepayers' argument on this point cannot stand in
the light of the provisions of section 72 of the Act of 1967.   They are
intended to provide for agreed alterations of the proposals, and not to
leave it open for the rights of a rating authority under section 76 (4) to
be circumvented by a purported "agreed alteration of the proposals"
which does not comply with the requirements of section 72 as to such   B
agreement.

As regards the ratepayers' other point, it would, if right, as I have
already said, not require or entitle this court to say that the Lands Tribunal had no jurisdiction to increase the values accepted by the local
valuation court.   The court would have to answer the question with a
qualification.   If I understood correctly, it was accepted at the end of   C
the argument before us that the question was whether "the contention"
of the appellant in section 76 (5) is to be treated as being the proposal
for the alteration of the list as set out in what I may call the relevant
"pleading," or is the figure (where it is an appeal as to the proper figure)
which the appellant is putting forward before the local valuation court
at the final moment before the local valuation court has to consider its
decision.   I think that both reason and convenience support the view   D
that it is the former.

Appeals dismissed with costs.
Valuation officer to have his costs of
  appeals against respective rate-
  payers.
Application of valuation officer for   E
  costs before the Lands Tribunal
  refused.
Leave to appeal refused.
Motion to adduce additional evidence
  by Shell U.K. Ltd. granted.

Solicitors: *J. D. Montgomery; F. Duffield, Liverpool; Allen & Overy;*   F
J. B. Bickerton, Ellesmere Port and Neston Borough Council; D. M.
Kermonde, Chester City Council; Solicitor of Inland Revenue.

E. M. W.

G

H

A

[CHANCERY DIVISION]

* *In re* SHARPE (A BANKRUPT), *Ex parte* TRUSTEE OF THE
BANKRUPT'S PROPERTY *v.* THE BANKRUPT AND ANOTHER

B

[No. 262 of 1978]

1979   July 23, 24; 30   Browne-Wilkinson J.

*Licence or Tenancy—Possession—Family arrangement—Bankrupt's
property partly purchased with loan from relative—Relative
living in premises in belief that she could stay as long as she
wished—Trustee in bankruptcy seeking vacant possession—*
C   *Relative's right of occupation as against trustee*

On April 27, 1978, a receiving order was made against a
bankrupt. He and his wife and his aunt J, aged 82,
were living together in a maisonette, which with a shop
formed leasehold premises purchased by the bankrupt in
1975 for £17,000. J had provided £12,000 of the purchase
price, the remainder having been raised on mortgage. In
D   providing the money, J had been told according to her
affidavit evidence, that she would be able to stay in the premises for as long as she liked, and that she would be looked
after by the bankrupt and his wife. J also paid some £2,271·16
for decorations and fittings for the property. She also paid
some £9,000 in an attempt to stave off the bankrupt's bankruptcy. In September 1975 on the advice of her solicitor, J
got from the bankrupt a promissory note for £15,700, the
E   reason being that by her will she had left her estate to her
three nephews equally, and she felt that it would be unfair
if the bankrupt were to take one third of what remained without bringing into account what he had already received. The
trustee in bankruptcy took steps to find out what rights, if
any, J claimed arising out of the provision by her of £12,000
towards the purchase price but J did not reply to his letters.
On April 30, 1979, the trustee in bankruptcy contracted to sell
F   the premises to a purchaser for £17,000 with vacant possession,
completion being fixed for May 29, 1979. After the date of
the contract J for the first time put forward a claim to an
interest in the premises.
On the trustee in bankruptcy's motion for an order that
the bankrupt and J give vacant possession of the premises:—
Held, dismissing the application, (1) that J had provided
the £12,000 by way of loan and not as a gift and, accordingly,
G   no interest in her favour was created under a resulting trust
but since it was an essential feature of the loan that J was to
make her home in the premises to be acquired with the
money lent, she had, as against the bankrupt, the right to
occupy the premises for as long as she liked while the loan
remained unrepaid (post, pp. 222E–F, 223A–B, H—224A).
Ramsden v. *Dyson* (1866) L.R. 1 H.L. 129, H.L.(E.) and
Hardwick v. *Johnson* [1978] 1 W.L.R. 683, C.A. applied.
H   (2) That J's right of occupation did confer some interest
in the property under a constructive trust and that, since in
the circumstances she was not barred from asserting her right
by reason of any laches or acquiescence on her part, the
trustee in bankruptcy took the property subject to her right
and, accordingly, he was not entitled to an order for possession
(post, pp. 225C–D, E—226D).
Binions v. *Evans* [1972] Ch. 359, C.A. and *D. H. N. Food
Distributors Ltd.* v. *Tower Hamlets London Borough Council*
[1976] 1 W.L.R. 852, C.A. applied.

The following cases are referred to in the judgment: A

Binions v. *Evans* [1972] Ch. 359; [1972] 2 W.L.R. 729; [1972] 2 All E.R.
 70, C.A.
D. H. N. Food Distributors Ltd. v. *Tower Hamlets London Borough
 Council* [1976] 1 W.L.R. 852; [1976] 3 All E.R. 462, C.A.
Dodsworth v. *Dodsworth* (1973) 228 E.G. 1115, C.A.
Errington v. *Errington and Woods* [1952] 1 K.B. 290; [1952] 1 All E.R.
 149, C.A.   B
Hardwick v. *Johnson* [1978] 1 W.L.R. 683; [1978] 2 All E.R. 935, C.A.
Hussey v. *Palmer* [1972] 1 W.L.R. 1286; [1972] 3 All E.R. 744, C.A.
Ramsden v. *Dyson* (1866) L.R. 1 H.L. 129, H.L.(E.).
Tanner v. *Tanner* [1975] 1 W.L.R. 1346; [1975] 3 All E.R. 776, C.A.

The following additional cases were cited in argument:

Bailey (A Bankrupt) (No. 25 of 1975), In re [1977] 1 W.L.R. 278; [1977] C
 2 All E.R. 26, D.C.
Bendall v. *McWhirter* [1952] 2 Q.B. 466; [1952] 1 All E.R. 1307, C.A.
Chandler v. *Kerley* [1978] 1 W.L.R. 693; [1978] 2 All E.R. 942, C.A.
Cowcher v. *Cowcher* [1972] 1 W.L.R. 425; [1972] 1 All E.R. 943.
Crabb v. *Arun District Council* [1976] Ch. 179; [1975] 3 W.L.R. 847;
 [1975] 3 All E.R. 865, C.A.
Debtor (No. 24 of 1971) A, In re, Ex parte Marley v. *Trustee of the Pro-* D
 perty of the Debtor [1976] 1 W.L.R. 952; [1976] 2 All E.R. 1010, D.C.
*Densham (A Bankrupt) In re, Ex parte Trustee of the Property of the
 Bankrupt* v. *The Bankrupt* [1975] 1 W.L.R. 1519; [1975] 3 All E.R.
 726.
Inwards v. *Baker* [1965] 2 Q.B. 29; [1965] 2 W.L.R. 212; [1965] 1 All E.R.
 446, C.A.
National Provincial Bank Ltd. v. *Hastings Car Mart Ltd.* [1965] A.C. E
 1175; [1965] 3 W.L.R. 1; [1965] 2 All E.R. 472, H.L.(E.).
Williams v. *Staite* [1979] Ch. 291; [1978] 2 W.L.R. 825; [1978] 2 All E.R.
 928, C.A.
Willmott v. *Barber* (1880) 15 Ch.D. 96; (1881) 17 Ch.D. 772, C.A.

MOTION

By a notice of motion dated May 31, 1979, the plaintiff, Vernon F
Charles Murrell, trustee in bankruptcy of the property of Thomas
Anthony Sharpe, against whom a receiving order in bankruptcy was
made on April 27, 1978, sought (1) an order that the respondents, the
bankrupt and Dorothy Annie Johnson, do give vacant possession of
certain leasehold property known as 30, Englands Lane, London N.W.3,
save such parts thereof as had been let to Mr. Blades and Mrs. Davey,
to the applicant as trustee in bankruptcy (2) an order that the second G
respondent, Mrs. Johnson, do pay the costs of and incidental to the
motion, and (3) such further or other relief as to the court should
seem just.

The facts are stated in the judgment.

G. S. Moss for the trustee in bankruptcy.   H
J. H. Vallat for the second respondent, Mrs. Johnson.

                                                    Cur. adv. vult.

July 30. BROWNE-WILKINSON J. read the following judgment. This
case arises out of the bankruptcy of Thomas Anthony Sharpe, against
whom a receiving order was made on April 27, 1978. The applicant, who

A is his trustee in bankruptcy, claims against the debtor and his aunt, Dorothy Annie Johnson, possession of certain premises, 30, Englands Lane, London N.W.3. That is a leasehold property which was purchased by the debtor for £17,000 in January 1975. It consists of a shop with a maisonette above, which is at present occupied by the debtor, his wife and Mrs. Johnson. There are also two other tenants on the premises.

B On April 30, 1979, the trustee contracted to sell the premises to a Mr. Promitzer for £17,000 with vacant possession of the shop and maisonette. Completion was to be on May 29, 1979. After the date of that contract, Mrs. Johnson for the first time put forward a claim to an interest in the premises. I have to decide whether she has such an interest and, if so, whether it is binding on the trustee in bankruptcy. The purchaser from the trustee in bankruptcy is not a party to this

C application and I cannot decide any question of priorities as between him and Mrs. Johnson.

Mrs. Johnson is a widow and is now 82 years old. She suffers from Parkinson's disease and senile arteriosclerosis. She is being looked after by the debtor and his wife. When her husband died in 1960 she inherited a property, 11, Chalcot Gardens, parts of which were let out as flatlets.

D The debtor is a nephew of Mrs. Johnson and he and his wife occupied one of those flatlets. In 1972, Mrs. Johnson's health declined. She decided to sell 11, Chalcot Gardens and agreed with the debtor and his wife that they would live together and look for somewhere else permanent to live. She sold 11, Chalcot Gardens in March 1972 for about £38,000 and they all went to live in a rented flat at 92, Fellowes Road. Mrs. Johnson lived there with the debtor and his wife, the rent, rates and

E telephone bills being shared.

Eventually, the debtor, who had apparently been carrying on a newsagent business at another shop in Englands Lane, found the shop and maisonette at 30, Englands Lane. He told Mrs. Johnson that it would cost some £17,000 and she agreed to provide £12,000 the rest being raised on mortgage. She made three payments totalling £12,000 in November and December 1974. In her affidavit she says:

F
"I made these payments to the bankrupt in order that he could buy the said premises. I cannot remember much about the circumstances now. However, I knew that I would be able to stay at the said premises as long as I wanted and that I would be looked after by the bankrupt and his wife. I am told that at his public examination the bankrupt stated that the £12,000 was a gift. This is not

G right. It represented a very substantial part of my wealth and I hoped that if the bankrupt's business prospered he might be able to repay me. I do not think that anything was said about the terms of repayment, but I knew that he could not hope to pay me back so long as we lived at the said premises."

Mrs. Johnson, the debtor and his wife moved into the maisonette in
H the autumn of 1975 and she made certain further payments in 1975 for decorations and fittings to the property, the cost of which to her totalled some £2,271·16.

Before the trustee in bankruptcy offered the property for sale steps were taken to find out from Mrs. Johnson what rights, if any, she claimed arising out of the provision of the £12,000. On June 1, 1978, the official receiver wrote to Mrs. Johnson a letter addressed to her at 30, Englands Lane. The letter is headed:

"Re: Thomas Anthony Sharpe" and, after a reference to the   A
making of the order receiving, continues: "The debtor has informed
me that you gave him a sum of money in order that he could
purchase the property 30, Englands Lane, London NW3. I would
be assisted therefore if you will let me know: (1) whether the sum
involved was a gift or a loan; (2) the amount and the date given;
(3) whether any security or consideration was given if the sum   B
involved was a loan. A franked addressed label is enclosed for your
reply."

It is to be noted that that letter does not in terms refer to her claiming
any equitable or other interest in the property, otherwise than by way
of secured loan.

No reply was received to that letter and on August 1, 1978, the   C
trustee in bankruptcy again wrote to Mrs. Johnson, referring back to the
official receiver's letter and asking for any comment. There was again
no reply to that letter. Mrs. Johnson in her affidavit states that she
never received those letters. That seems to me improbable. I think she
probably received them, but, in view of her age, took no steps about
them and has since forgotten their receipt.

On these facts Mrs. Johnson claims to have either a beneficial interest   D
in the property and its proceeds of sale or alternatively a right to stay in
the property by virtue of an irrevocable licence or equitable right.
I should mention that in addition to the substantial sums she provided
to acquire and decorate the property, she paid debts of the debtor
amounting to more than £9,000 in order to try to stave off his bankruptcy.

I will first consider whether she has established an equitable interest   E
in the property and its proceeds of sale by virtue of having provided the
bulk of the purchase money, that is to say, has she an interest under a
resulting trust? I have no doubt that she has not established any such
interest. It is clear that the parties never worked out in any detail
what was the legal relationship between them, but no one has suggested
that Mrs. Johnson advanced the money to the debtor otherwise than by
way of gift or loan. In his public examination the debtor suggested that   F
the moneys were a gift, but I find as a fact that the moneys were
advanced by way of loan.

In September 1975, on the advice of her solicitor, Mrs. Johnson got
the debtor to sign a promissory note for £15,700. The reason for the
promissory note was that by her will Mrs. Johnson had left her estate to
her three nephews equally and she felt it would be unfair if the debtor   G
were to take one third of what remained without bringing into account
what he had received already. The parties having, by the promissory
note, expressed the moneys to be repayable, the result must, in my
judgment, be that the moneys were paid by way of loan, not gift. I do
not think it matters which for the purposes of this aspect of the argument. In either case it is clear that Mrs. Johnson and her estate were
not to have a beneficial share in the value of the property, which was   H
to belong solely to the debtor. Mr. Vallat, who appeared for Mrs.
Johnson, on this aspect of the case relied on *Hussey* v. *Palmer* [1972] 1
W.L.R. 1286, where the Court of Appeal by a majority held that, even
though the plaintiff in that case described moneys used to improve a
property as having been paid by way of loan to the owner of the property, she was entitled to an equitable interest in the property. However,
her equitable interest was not apparently a share of the proceeds of sale,

A but something akin to a lien for the moneys advanced. The facts in that case were very special and I think the clue to the decision may be that the court reached the view that, although described in evidence as a loan, the parties did not in fact intend a loan since there was never any discussion of repayment: see *per* Lord Denning M.R. at p. 1288.

B In my judgment, if, as in this case, moneys are advanced by way of loan there can be no question of the lender being entitled to an interest in the property under a resulting trust. If he were to take such an interest, he would get his money twice: once on repayment of the loan and once on taking his share of the proceeds of sale of the property.

I turn then to the alternative claim that Mrs. Johnson is entitled to something less than an aliquot share of the equity in the premises, namely, the right to stay on the premises until the money she provided C indirectly to acquire them has been repaid. This right is based upon the line of recent Court of Appeal decisions which has spelt out irrevocable licences from informal family arrangements, and in some cases characterised such licences as conferring some equity or equitable interest under a constructive trust. I do not think that the principles lying behind these decisions have yet been fully explored and on occasion it seems D that such rights are found to exist simply on the ground that to hold otherwise would be a hardship to the plaintiff. It appears that the principle is one akin to or an extension of a proprietary estoppel stemming from Lord Kingsdown's well-known statement of the law in *Ramsden* v. *Dyson* (1866) L.R. 1 H.L. 129, 170. In a strict case of proprietary estoppel the plaintiff has expended his own money on the defendant's property in an expectation encouraged by or known to the defendant E that the plaintiff either owns the property or is to have some interest conferred on him. Recent authorities have extended this doctrine and, in my judgment, it is now established that, if the parties have proceeded on a common assumption that the plaintiff is to enjoy a right to reside in a particular property and in reliance on that assumption the plaintiff has expended money or otherwise acted to his detriment, the defendant F will not be allowed to go back on that common assumption and the court will imply an irrevocable licence or trust which will give effect to that common assumption. Thus in *Errington* v. *Errington and Woods* [1952] 1 K.B. 290, Denning L.J. held that the son, who had paid the instalments under the mortgage in the expectation that the property would eventually become his, had an equitable right to stay in occupation until the mortgage was paid off. In *Tanner* v. *Tanner* [1975] 1 W.L.R. 1346, G the plaintiff was held entitled to a licence to occupy a house bought in contemplation of it being a home for herself and her children, there being no express contract to that effect. In *Hardwick* v. *Johnson* [1978] 1 W.L.R. 683, where the plaintiff's house had been occupied by the plaintiff's son and his first wife under an informal family arrangement, the Court of Appeal imputed an intention to grant an irrevocable licence H to the wife on payment by her of a weekly sum.

Applying those principles to the present case, I have little doubt that as between the debtor on the one hand and Mrs. Johnson on the other, the circumstances in which she provided the money by way of loan in order to enable the premises to be bought do give rise to some right in Mrs. Johnson. It is clear that she only loaned the money as part of a wider scheme, an essential feature of which was that she was to make her home in the property to be acquired with the money loaned.

Say that immediately after the property had been bought the debtor had A
tried to evict Mrs. Johnson without repaying the loan; can it be supposed
that the court would have made an order for possession against her?
In my judgment, whether it be called a contractual licence or an equitable licence or an interest under a constructive trust, Mrs. Johnson
would be entitled as against the debtor to stay in the house. *Dodsworth*
v *Dodsworth* (1973) 228 E.G. 1115 shows that there are great practical
difficulties in finding that she is entitled to a full life interest: but B
there is no reason why one should not imply an intention that she should
have the right to live there until her loan is repaid, which was the result
reached in *Dodsworth* v. *Dodsworth*.

Unfortunately, this case does not arise for decision simply between
Mrs. Johnson on the one hand and the debtor on the other. She has to
show some right good against the trustee in bankruptcy and the purchaser C
from the trustee in bankruptcy. Due to an unfortunate procedural position, the purchaser is not a party to this application and nothing I can
say can, or is intended to, bind him. As an antidote to the over-indul-
gence of sympathy which everyone must feel for Mrs. Johnson, I put
on record that the purchaser's plight is little better. He apparently had
no reason to suspect that there was any flaw in the trustee's right to sell
with vacant possession. As a result of the trustee's inability to complete D
the sale he cannot open the business he intended and he and his wife and
two children are being forced to live in a small motorized caravan parked
in various places on or near Hampstead Heath.

Is then Mrs. Johnson's right against the debtor binding on the trustee
in bankruptcy? This is an important and difficult point and, were it not
for the urgency of the matter and the late stage of the term, I would like E
to have given it longer consideration. In general the trustee in bankruptcy steps into the shoes of the debtor and takes the debtor's property
subject to all rights and equities affecting it: see *Halsbury's Laws of
England,* 4th ed., vol. 3 (1973), para. 594. However, the trustee in
bankruptcy is free to break any merely contractual obligation of the
debtor, leaving the other party to his remedy in damages, which damages
will only give rise to a right to prove in the bankruptcy. F

Are rights of the kind spelt out in the cases I have referred to merely
contractual licences or do they fetter the property and create some right
over it? On the authorities as they stand, I think I am bound to hold that
the rights under such an irrevocable licence bind the property itself in
the hands of the trustee in bankruptcy. Lord Denning M.R. has, on a
number of occasions, said that these licences arise under a constructive G
trust and are binding on the third party's acquiring with notice. These
statements are for the most part obiter dicta with which other members
of the court have not associated themselves, preferring to rest their
decision on there being a contractual licence. But in *Binions* v. *Evans*
[1972] Ch. 359, a third party taking with notice of, and expressly subject
to, such a licence was held bound by it. In that case the liability could H
not have depended merely on contract. Closer to the present case is a
decision which was not referred to in argument and therefore my
comments on it must be treated with some reserve. In *D. H. N. Food
Distributors Ltd.* v. *Tower Hamlets London Borough Council* [1976] 1
W.L.R. 852 certain premises were legally owned by one company
(Bronze) but occupied by an associated company (D. H. N.) under an
informal arrangement between them. The premises were compulsorily

A acquired and the question was whether any compensation for disturbance was payable, it being said that Bronze had not been disturbed. The Court of Appeal held that D. H. N. had an irrevocable licence to remain in the premises indefinitely and this gave D. H. N. a compensatable interest in the land. Lord Denning M.R. said, at p. 859:

B " It was equivalent to a contract between the two companies whereby Bronze granted an irrevocable licence to D. H. N. to carry on their business on the premises. In this situation Mr. Dobry cited to us *Binions* v. *Evans* [1972] Ch. 359, to which I would add *Bannister* v. *Bannister* [1948] 2 All E.R. 133 and *Siew Soon Wah* v. *Yong Tong Hong* [1973] A.C. 836. Those cases show that a contractual licence (under which a person has the right to occupy premises indefinitely) gives rise to a constructive trust, under which the
C legal owner is not allowed to turn out the licensee. So, here. This irrevocable licence gave to D. H. N. a sufficient interest in the land to qualify them for compensation for disturbance."

Goff L.J. also made this a ground of his decision: see pp. 860 to 861.

It seems to me that this is a decision that such contractual or equitable licence does confer some interest in the property under a construc-
D tive trust. Accordingly, in my judgment, it follows that the trustee in bankruptcy takes the property subject to Mrs. Johnson's right to live there until she is repaid the moneys she provided to acquire it.

Mr. Moss, for the trustee in bankruptcy, argued that this was the wrong approach. He said that the species of constructive trust which Lord Denning M.R. was considering in the cases was different from the
E traditional constructive trust known to equity lawyers. It is not, Mr. Moss says, a substantive right but an equitable remedy: see *per* Lord Denning M.R. in *Hussey* v. *Palmer* [1972] 1 W.L.R. 1286, 1290 and in *Binions* v. *Evans* [1972] Ch. 359, 368. Then, says Mr. Moss, the time to decide whether to grant such a remedy is when the matter comes before the court in the light of the then known circumstances. In the present case those circumstances are that the debtor is a bankrupt and
F Mrs. Johnson has failed to put forward her claim until after the trustee has contracted to sell the property to an innocent third party, notwithstanding two inquiries as to whether she had a claim. Accordingly, he says, it would not be equitable to grant her an interest under a constructive trust at this time.

I cannot accept that argument in that form. Even if it be right to
G say that the courts can impose a constructive trust as a remedy in certain cases—which to my mind is a novel concept in English law—in order to provide a remedy the court must first find a right which has been infringed. So far as land is concerned an oral agreement to create any interest in it must be evidenced in writing: see section 40 of the Law of Property Act 1925. Therefore if these irrevocable licences create an interest in land, the rights cannot rest simply on an oral contract. The
H introduction of an interest under a constructive trust is an essential ingredient if the plaintiff has any right at all. Therefore in cases such as this, it cannot be that the interest in property arises for the first time when the court declares it to exist. The right must have arisen at the time of the transaction in order for the plaintiff to have any right the breach of which can be remedied. Again, I think the *D. H. N. Food Distributors Ltd.* case [1976] 1 W.L.R. 852 shows that the equity pre-dates any order of the court. The right to compensation in that case

depended on substantive rights at the date of compulsory acquisition, **A**
not on what remedy the court subsequently chose to grant in the subsequent litigation.

Accordingly, if I am right in holding that as between the debtor and
Mrs. Johnson she had an irrevocable licence to remain in the property,
authority compels me to hold that that gave her an interest in the property before the bankruptcy and the trustee takes the property subject
to that interest. In my judgment the mere intervention of the bank- **B**
ruptcy by itself cannot alter Mrs. Johnson's property interest. If she is
to be deprived of her interest as against the trustee in bankruptcy, it must
be because of some conduct of hers which precludes her from enforcing
her rights, that is to say, the ordinary principles of acquiescence and
laches which apply to all beneficiaries seeking to enforce their rights
apply to this case.   **C**

I am in no way criticising the trustee in bankruptcy's conduct; he
tried to find out if she made any claim relating to the £12,000 before
he contracted to sell the property. But I do not think that on ordinary
equitable principles Mrs. Johnson should be prevented from asserting her
rights even at this late stage. She is very old and in bad health. No one
had ever advised her that she might have rights to live in the property.
As soon as she appreciated that she was to be evicted she at once took **D**
legal advice and asserted her claim. This, in my judgment, is far removed
from conduct which precludes enforcement by a beneficiary of his rights
due to his acquiescence, the first requirement of acquiescence being that
the beneficiary knows his or her rights and does not assert them.

Accordingly, I hold that Mrs. Johnson is entitled as against the trustee
in bankruptcy to remain in the property until she is repaid the sums she **E**
advanced. I reach this conclusion with some hesitation since I find the
present state of the law very confused and difficult to fit in with established equitable principles. I express the hope that in the near future
the whole question can receive full consideration in the Court of
Appeal, so that, in order to do justice to the many thousands of people
who never come into court at all but who wish to know with certainty
what their proprietary rights are, the extent to which these irrevocable **F**
licences bind third parties may be defined with certainty. Doing justice
to the litigant who actually appears in the court by the invention of
new principles of law ought not to involve injustice to the other persons
who are not litigants before the court but whose rights are fundamentally
affected by the new principles.

Finally, I must reiterate that I am in no way deciding what are the **G**
rights of the purchaser from the trustee as against Mrs. Johnson. It
may be that as a purchaser without express notice in an action for
specific performance of the contract his rights will prevail over Mrs.
Johnson's. As to that, I have heard no argument and express no view.
I do, however, express my sympathy for him in the predicament in which
he finds himself.

I therefore dismiss the trustee's application for possession against **H**
Mrs. Johnson.

Motion dismissed.

Solicitors: *Peard, Son & Webster; Edwin Coe & Calder Woods.*

T. C. C. B.

A

[CHANCERY DIVISION]

* *In re* MOORGATE MERCANTILE HOLDINGS LTD.

[No. 001170 of 1979]

B   1979   June 18, 19, 20; 26   Slade J.

*Company—Meeting—Special resolution—Notice given of intention
to reduce share premium account by cancelling share premium
entirely—Purported amendment at extraordinary general meeting to reduce premium from £1,356,900·48 to £321·17—Whether
special resolution validly passed—Whether jurisdiction in court
to confirm reduction—Companies Act 1948 (11 & 12 Geo. 6,*
C   *c. 38), s. 141 (2).*[1]

Until March 12, 1979, the company's share premium account
had stood at £1,356,579·31, reflecting premiums received on
the issue of shares as consideration for the acquisition of
subsidiaries prior to 1973, less a scrip issue in 1973 and certain
issues expenses.   On March 12, 1979, a small issue of shares
was made upon the acquisition of the outstanding minority
D   interests in a subsidiary, which resulted in increasing the
amount of the share premium account by £321·17.   The
company's articles of association empowered the company to
reduce its share premium account and, on the basis that the
share premium account had been lost, notices, accompanied by
an explanatory circular, were sent out to members, convening
an extraordinary meeting for April 26, 1979, at which a special
resolution was to be proposed: "that the share premium
E   account of the company amounting to £1,356,900·48 be
cancelled."   The draftsman of the resolution was unaware of
the recent issue which had resulted in the share premium of
£321·17.   At the extraordinary general meeting, the chairman
of the company, having received advice that the £321·17 from
the recent share issue could not be regarded as having been
lost, proposed "that the share premium account of the company
amounting to £1,356,900·48 be reduced to £321·17."   That
F   amended version of the resolution was passed on a show of
hands and no poll was demanded.

On the company's petition for an order confirming the
reduction of the share premium account: —

Held, that for a special resolution to be valid under section
141 (2) of the Companies Act 1948, the notice of the meeting
had to specify either the entire text or the entire substance of
the resolution which was intended to be proposed as a special
G   resolution; that the resolution as passed be the same resolution as that identified in the notice circulated to members,
although grammatical or clerical errors might be corrected
provided that there was no departure from the substance of
the proposed resolution; that the resolution passed at the extraordinary general meeting of April 26, 1979, was not the same
either in form or in substance as the text that had been
circulated to shareholders and, accordingly, it was not validly
H   passed and the court had no jurisdiction to confirm the
reduction of the share premium account (post, pp. 231E—232A,
241H—242G, 244B—C, F).

In re Bridport Old Brewery Co. (1867) L.R. 2 Ch.App. 191;
Henderson v. *Bank of Australasia* (1890) 45 Ch.D. 330, C.A.;
In re Teede & Bishop Ltd. (1901) 84 L.T. 561; *Torbock* v. *Lord
Westbury* [1902] 2 Ch. 871 and *MacConnell* v. *E. Prill & Co.
Ltd.* [1916] 2 Ch. 57 considered.

[1] Companies Act 1948, s. 141 (2): see post, p. 230H.

In re Moorgate Holdings Ltd. (Ch.D.)   **[1980]**

The following cases are referred to in the judgment: A

Betts & Co. Ltd. v. *Macnaghten* [1910] 1 Ch. 430.

Bridport Old Brewery Co., In re, Ex parte Collis (1867) L.R. 2 Ch.App. 191.

Caldwell v. *Caldwell & Co. (Papermakers) Ltd.* [1916] W.N. 70, H.L. (Sc).

Duomatic Ltd., In re [1969] 2 Ch. 365; [1969] 2 W.L.R. 114; [1969] 1 All E.R. 161.

Henderson v. *Bank of Australasia* (1890) 45 Ch.D. 330, C.A.

Hoare & Co. Ltd. & Reduced, In re [1904] 2 Ch. 208, C.A.   B

MacConnell v. *E. Prill & Co. Ltd.* [1916] 2 Ch. 57.

Pearce Duff & Co. Ltd., In re [1960] 1 W.L.R. 1014; [1960] 3 All E.R. 222.

Picturesque Atlas and Publishing Co. Ltd., In re (1892) 13 N.S.W. Eq. 44.

Teede & Bishop Ltd., In re (1901) 84 L.T. 561.

Tiessen v. *Henderson* [1899] 1 Ch. 861.

Torbock v. *Lord Westbury* [1902] 2 Ch. 871.   C

The following additional cases were cited in argument:

Boschoek Proprietary Co. Ltd. v. *Fuke* [1906] 1 Ch. 148.

Cheshire v. *Gordon Hotels Ltd.,* The Times, February 14, 1953.

Clinch v. *Financial Corporation* (1868) L.R. 5 Eq. 450; (1868) 4 Ch.App. 117.   D

Floating Dock Co. of St. Thomas Ltd., In re [1895] 1 Ch. 691.

Foster v. *New Trinidad Lake Asphalt Co. Ltd.* [1901] 1 Ch. 208.

London & Mediterranean Bank, In re (Wright's case) (1868) L.R. 12 Eq. 334, note.

Welsbach Incandescent Gas Light Co. Ltd., In re (1903) 89 L.T. 645; [1904] 1 Ch. 87, C.A.

     E

PETITION

The company, Moorgate Mercantile Holdings Ltd., was incorporated in September 1969 as an investment company. Prior to March 12, 1979, the company's share premium account had stood at £1,356,579·31, but on that date it was increased to £1,356,900·48 by the addition of a premium of £321·17 on an issue of shares made on the acquisition of   F minority interests in a subsidiary. By a petition dated April 26, 1979, the company sought an order that the reduction of the share premium expressed to have been effected by a resolution passed that day should be confirmed. The petition was unopposed but the judge asked for assistance from an amicus curiae.

The facts are stated in the judgment.

     G

Ralph Instone for the company.

Mary Arden as amicus curiae.

                         Cur. adv. vult.

June 26. SLADE J. read the following judgment. This is a petition of Moorgate Mercantile Holdings Ltd. (" the company ") asking for the   H confirmation of the reduction of its share premium account. The company was incorporated in September 1969 under the Companies Acts, its objects being to acquire and hold shares and other investments, and other objects specified in its memorandum of association.

The share capital of the company was originally 14s. divided into seven shares of 2s. each. By virtue of subsequent increases, it is now £3,500,000, divided into 35 million ordinary shares of 10p each, of which

A 15,294,293 shares have been issued and are fully paid up. The remainder are unissued.

There is standing to the credit of the share premium account of the company the sum of £1,356,900·48, which represents the aggregate amount of premiums received in cash or otherwise by the company on the issue of shares at a premium, less the aggregate amount applied thereout in accordance with the provisions of section 56 (2) of the Companies Act 1948.

B

Article 9 of the company's articles of association empowers it, inter alia, by special resolution to reduce its share premium account. The share premium account of the company, which reflected premiums received on the issue of shares as consideration for the acquisition of subsidiaries prior to 1973, less a scrip issue in 1973 and certain issue expenses, stood from then onwards until March 12, 1979, at £1,356,579·31. On March 12, 1979, a small issue of shares was made upon the acquisition of the outstanding minority interests in a subsidiary. This resulted in the increase in the share premium account by £321·17, so that it has since then stood at £1,356,900·48.

C

On April 2, 1979, the secretary of the company sent a notice to the company's members, which was signed by him and accompanied by an explanatory circular letter from the company's chairman convening an extraordinary general meeting of the company. The notice was in the following terms:

D

" Notice is hereby given that an extraordinary general meeting of the company will be held at Moorgate House, 312 High Road, Tottenham, London, N.15, on Thursday April 26, 1979, at 11 a.m. when the following resolution will be proposed as a special resolution: ' That the share premium account of the company amounting to £1,356,900·48 be cancelled '."

E

There was added to the notice the usual note stating that a member entitled to attend and vote at the meeting was entitled to appoint a proxy or proxies, who need not be members, to attend and, on a poll, to vote on his behalf.

F

Before the holding of the meeting, valid instruments of proxy had been received, under which a total of 7,278,460 shares were voted in favour of the resolution as circulated and 7,212 against it. The figure specified as the amount of the share premium account, in the form of special resolution printed and circulated in the notice of the meeting, was accurately stated as being £1,356,900·48. This figure, however, included the sum of £321·17 credited to the share premium account on March 12, 1979, by virtue of the issue of shares made on that day. The draftsman of the notice was unaware that this issue either had taken place or was about to take place.

G

Before the members' meeting was held on April 26, 1979, the company was advised of a consequent legal difficulty. The court was to be asked to approve the proposed cancellation of the company's entire share premium account on the basis that the amount credited to the share premium account had all been lost. The amount of £321·17, however, resulting from the recent issue of shares, could not on any footing be regarded as having been lost. Accordingly, the company was advised there was no basis on which the cancellation of this sum could be justified.

H

In these circumstances, when the extraordinary general meeting of the

company came to be held on April 26, 1979, the chairman of the company, **A**
Mr. Julius Silman, in accordance with legal advice received by him,
proposed that the special resolution be passed in an amended form as
follows: " That the share premium account of the company amounting
to £1,356,900·48p be reduced to £321·17." The chairman had been advised
that the amendment could not affect the validity of the resolution, on
the ground that no shareholder, who had made up his mind how to vote
on the resolution in its original form, could reasonably adopt a different **B**
attitude to the amended form. He explained the reason for the amendment to the meeting, which was attended by seven members in person—a
sufficient quorum under the company's articles. The amended version
of the resolution was passed unanimously on a show of hands and a poll
was not demanded.

The company, by this petition, asks that the reduction of the share **C**
premium account of the company from £1,356,900·48 to £321·17,
expressed to be effected by the special resolution passed on April 26,
1979, may be confirmed by the court. The petition alleges that, before
the passing of the resolution, the entire share premium account had been
lost, with the exception of £321·17 credited thereto in March 1979. The
registrar has dispensed with an inquiry as to creditors.

No member or creditor has appeared before me to oppose the petition. **D**
Since, however, the case seemed to me to raise an important question of
principle, namely, as to the extent, if any, to which the form of a special
resolution may be validly amended, I asked for the assistance of an
amicus curiae. Miss Arden, instructed by the Treasury Solicitor, has
appeared in this capacity. She, and Mr. Instone, who has appeared for
the company, have both given me valuable assistance, for which I am **E**
grateful. Since there seemed to be possible doubts as to the sufficiency
of the evidence of loss of the share premium account, I requested Miss
Arden to address submissions to me on this point also.

In the event, therefore, two quite separate questions have fallen to be
argued. First, was the special resolution of April 26, 1979, validly passed?
Secondly, if the answer to the first question is " Yes," has the alleged loss
been sufficiently proved, and how should the court's discretion be **F**
exercised? I will begin by dealing with the first question.

Was the resolution of April 26, 1979, validly passed?

Section 141 (1) of the Companies Act 1948 defines an extraordinary
resolution as follows:

G
" A resolution shall be an extraordinary resolution when it has been
passed by a majority of not less than three fourths of such members
as, being entitled so to do, vote in person or, where proxies are
allowed, by proxy, at a general meeting of which notice specifying
the intention to propose the resolution as an extraordinary resolution
has been duly given."

H
Section 141 (2) of that Act, omitting an immaterial proviso, defines a
" special resolution " as follows:

" A resolution shall be a special resolution when it has been passed
by such a majority as is required for the passing of an extraordinary
resolution and at a general meeting of which not less than 21 days'
notice, specifying the intention to propose the resolution as a special
resolution, has been duly given: . . ."

A   Section 141 (5) provides that for the purposes of the section:

"... notice of a meeting shall be deemed to be duly given and the meeting to be duly held when the notice is given and the meeting held in manner provided by this Act or the articles."

B   The company's articles, so far as I am aware, contain no provisions which are relevant to the question which I have to decide. The doubts as to the validity of the special resolution of April 26, 1979, arise solely from the provisions of section 141 (2).

It will be seen that, under the terms of section 141 (2), one of the conditions precedent to the validity of any special resolution is that "... not less than 21 days' notice, specifying the intention to propose the resolution as a special resolution, has been duly given." As Miss Arden

C   has submitted, the phrase " the resolution " in this context in my judgment manifestly means " the aforesaid resolution," that is to say, the resolution which has been actually passed. This is a point of crucial importance in the present case.

The problem which now arises may be briefly summarised as follows. The notices dated April 2, 1979, specified the intention to propose as a

D   special resolution the resolution that "... the share premium account of the company amounting to £1,356,900·48 be cancelled." However, the resolution which was actually passed at the meeting of April 26, 1979, was a resolution that " the share premium account of the company amounting to £1,356,900·48 be reduced to £321·17." In these circumstances, did the notices of April 2, 1979, give notice within the meaning of section 141 (2), specifying the intention to propose the resolution which

E   was in the event actually passed?

In the absence of authority, I would have thought that the answer to this short question of statutory construction was manifestly " No." The notices of April 2, 1979, specified the intention to propose one resolution; the resolution actually passed at the meeting of April 26, 1979, was another, different resolution. Furthermore, the difference was not one

F   merely of form but also of substance, albeit of slight substance, in as much as one resolution provided for the entire cancellation of the company's share premium account, while the other provided merely for its reduction, albeit by almost the entirety thereof.

The terms of section 141 (2), at least if read in isolation and in the absence of authority, would seem to me to require that, if a special resolution passed at a meeting of members is to be valid, it must be the

G   same resolution as that which the requisite notice has specified the intention to propose. As I have already indicated, the phrase " the resolution " appearing in the later words of the subsection clearly refers back to and echoes the phrase " a resolution " appearing at the beginning of the subsection. I can see strong argument for contending that a resolution passed at a meeting of members may properly be regarded as

H   *the* resolution (that is the same resolution as that referred to in the preceding notice), if the only differences between the two are merely clerical or grammatical; I will revert to this point later. If, however, there is any difference whatsoever of substance between the two, I would not, in the absence of authority, have regarded the later resolution, which was actually passed, as having been preceded by proper notice for the purpose of section 141 (2).

Do the authorities lead me to a different conclusion? Mr. Instone

232

submitted that they imperatively should. He referred me in this context A
to a number of authorities in relation to statutes preceding the Companies
Act 1929 and the Companies Act 1948, though neither he nor Miss Arden
was able to produce any later authority directly relevant to the present
question. I shall now refer chronologically to the relevant earlier
statutory provisions mentioned by Mr. Instone and the authorities relied
on by him in the present context.   B

Section 51 of the Companies Act 1862 contained a definition of a
special resolution which, so far as material for present purposes, read:

" A resolution passed by a company under this Act shall be deemed
to be special whenever a resolution has been passed by a majority
of not less than three fourths of such members of the company for
the time being entitled, according to the regulations of the company,
to vote as may be present, in person or by proxy (in cases where   C
by the regulations of the company proxies are allowed), at any
general meeting of which notice specifying the intention to propose
such resolution has been duly given, and such resolution has been
confirmed by a majority of such members for the time being entitled,
according to the regulations of the company, to vote as may be
present, in person or by proxy, at a subsequent general meeting, of D
which notice has been duly given, and held at an interval of not less
than 14 days, nor more than one month from the date of the meeting
at which such resolution was first passed: . . ."

The procedure for the passing of special resolutions, embodied in the
Act of 1862, unlike that of the Act of 1948, thus contemplated that, if
a resolution was to be validly passed as a special resolution, it not only E
had to be passed by the requisite majority at a meeting of members of
the company, but also had to be confirmed at a subsequent general
meeting of which proper notice had been given.

Section 129 (3) of the Companies Act 1862 introduced the concept of
an " extraordinary resolution." That section, so far as material for
present purposes, read: F

" A company under this Act may be wound up voluntarily . . . (2)
whenever the company has passed a special resolution requiring the
company to be wound up voluntarily: (3) whenever the company
has passed an extraordinary resolution to the effect that it has been
proved to their satisfaction that the company cannot by reason of its
liabilities continue its business, and that it is advisable to wind up
the same: For the purpose of this Act any resolution shall be deemed G
to be extraordinary which is passed in such manner as would, if
it had been confirmed by a subsequent meeting, have constituted
a special resolution, as herein-before defined."

In *In re Bridport Old Brewery Co.* (1867) L.R. 2 Ch.App. 191, notice
had been given to shareholders of a company that an extraordinary meeting
of the shareholders would be held at a stated place, date and time ". . . for H
the purpose of considering and, if so determined on, of passing, a
resolution to wind up the company voluntarily . . ." The meeting passed,
inter alia, a resolution that it had been proved to the satisfaction of
the company that it could not by reason of its liabilities continue its
business and it was advisable to wind it up. No meeting was ever called
to confirm this resolution, so that it could not be treated as a special
resolution; it could only have been valid, if at all, as an extraordinary

A resolution. The Court of Appeal held that it was not valid as such.
Turner L.J. said, at p. 194 :

    " The first part of this resolution is, that it had been proved to the
    satisfaction of the company, that the company could not, by reason
    of its liabilities, continue its business. But the notice did not state
    that an extraordinary resolution to wind up the company would be
B   proposed; nor did it give any intimation that it was proposed to
    consider at the meeting the question whether the company was able
    to continue its business. Now it is evidently of great importance to
    shareholders that they should have proper notice what subjects are
    proposed to be considered at a meeting, and I do not think that in
    the present case they had such notice. I do not say that it was
    necessary to follow in the notice the precise terms of the Companies
C   Act, section 129, clause 2 [sic]; but it appears to me that the share-
    holders were entitled to have a notice which would give them to
    understand that it was proposed to pass an extraordinary resolution
    to wind up the company. It is of great importance that the steps
    taken in a matter of such consequence as the resolving to wind up a
    company should be perfectly regular, and in the present case I think
D   that there was no sufficient notice; . . ."

Cairns L.J. said, at p. 195 : " I am of the same opinion, and on the same
grounds." Then a little later he said :

    " In the present case, it appears to me that the provisions of the Act
    have not been complied with; the notice which was given, though
    sufficient for the purpose of passing a resolution requiring confirma-
E   tion, being insufficient for the purpose of passing a resolution
    requiring no confirmation."

    In its context, the reference by Turner L.J. to section 129 (2), as
reported, must, in my opinion, have been intended as a reference to
section 129 (3) of the Act of 1862. I do not think that his judgment
F is of any assistance or relevance in relation to the question whether the
notice given would have been sufficient for the purpose of passing a
special resolution. The only point to be derived from his judgment which
is marginally relevant for present purposes is that by implication it
indicates his view that a notice could be sufficient for the purpose of
passing an extraordinary resolution, within the meaning of section 129
of the Act of 1862, even if it did not specify the precise words of the
G resolution intended to be passed. The difficulty in that case, as the
court thought, was that the members did not have sufficient warning of
the subjects proposed to be considered at the relevant meeting.

    Mr. Instone further relied on the passage in the judgment of
Cairns L.J., in which he expressed the view that the notice was
". . . sufficient for the purpose of passing a resolution requiring confirma-
H tion," in other words, for the purpose of passing a special resolution.
Since, however, this view was expressed by Cairns L.J., obiter, in the
context of an Act which made a subsequent, confirmatory meeting
obligatory, if a special resolution was to be valid and effective, I do not
think that it is of any assistance in the interpretation of section 141 of
the Companies Act 1948, by which the legislature has required no such
confirmatory meeting and therefore might well see fit to require preceding
notices to be in more specific terms.

The next case in order of date relied on by Mr. Instone was *Henderson* **A**
v. *Bank of Australasia* (1890) 45 Ch.D. 330. That case concerned a
bank, which was a deed of settlement company. A proprietor brought
an action to test the validity of certain resolutions altering the deed of
settlement. As appears from pp. 332 to 333 of the report, the advertisement of the proposed meeting had described the proposed resolutions as
" special resolutions " and stated that, if they should be duly passed, they
would be submitted for confirmation to a second extraordinary meeting **B**
of the proprietors, which would be subsequently convened. It also appears,
at p. 333, that the full text of the proposed resolutions had been circulated
before the meeting was held. The plaintiff contended that the resolutions
were invalid, substantially, first, on the ground that no proper notice of the
meeting was given and, secondly, that even supposing the meeting was
duly summoned the resolutions passed at it were invalid, because the **C**
chairman declined to put an amendment which the plaintiff wished to
put. The Court of Appeal, in allowing the plaintiff's appeal from Chitty J.,
was unanimous in the view that the chairman was wrong in refusing to
put the amendment. While Lopes L.J., at p. 349, expressed doubts
whether the notice was sufficient, Cotton L.J., without deciding the point,
expressed the view obiter, at p. 343, that the notice was adequate on the **D**
grounds that it " . . . fairly and reasonably expressed to the shareholders
what matters were going to be discussed at the meeting "; and Fry L.J.
at p. 346 expressed entire agreement with the judgment of Cotton L.J.

Mr. Instone, in effect, relied on this case as authority for two general
propositions: first, that if an amended form of a resolution is proposed
to a meeting and is passed thereat, it may be validly passed, provided
that the amended version does not stray too far from the version contained **E**
in the notice of the meeting; secondly, that this result may ensue,
even though the actual text of the resolution in its unamended form had
been circulated to shareholders before the meeting. I accept that these
particular propositions were, by necessary implication, accepted by the
Court of Appeal on the particular facts of the *Henderson* case. I am,
however, unable to accept that this decision affords any assistance at all **F**
in the construction of section 141 (2) of the Companies Act 1948, if only
for two reasons. First, no statutory provisions were under consideration
by the Court of Appeal in that case, and none were referred to in the
judgments. Everything turned on the provisions of the relevant deed
of settlement, the form of the relevant notices and the course of the
relevant meeting; in other words, it was a decision entirely on its special
facts. Secondly, in my judgment, as I have already indicated, considera- **G**
tions quite different from those applicable to the present case may apply
in considering the sufficiency of a notice convening a meeting at which
there is to be considered a resolution which, if passed, has to be
submitted for confirmation to a second meeting. Correspondingly, in my
judgment, considerations quite different from those applicable to the
Henderson case may apply in considering whether an amendment of a **H**
special resolution, intended to be passed under section 141 of the
Companies Act 1948, may properly be put to a meeting.

Mr. Instone next referred to *In re Teede & Bishop Ltd.* (1901) 84 L.T.
561. In that case notices were sent to the shareholders of a company
stating that an extraordinary general meeting would be held on a stated
date for the purpose of considering and, if thought fit, passing three
resolutions, the text of which was stated in the notices. These resolutions

A   were to the following effect, namely, (1) that a reconstruction of the company was desirable and that the company therefore be wound up voluntarily and that a named person be appointed its liquidator; (2) that the liquidator should be authorised to consent to the registration of a new company; and (3) that the liquidator should be authorised, pursuant to section 161 of the Companies Act 1862, to enter into an agreement with the new company, when incorporated, in the terms of a draft

B   agreement submitted to the meeting. At the subsequent meeting, only one resolution was put to the meeting and purportedly passed as a special resolution under section 51 of the Companies Act 1862. This was a resolution for the voluntary winding up of the company and the appointment of a liquidator. This resolution was subsequently confirmed as a special resolution at another meeting. Certain creditors of the

C   company subsequently claimed that the resolution for the voluntary winding up was invalid, on the ground that the single resolution passed did not accord with the three contemplated resolutions of which notice had been given. Cozens-Hardy J. upheld this claim. Having referred to the three resolutions which had been set out in the notices and the single resolution which was actually put to and passed at the meeting, he said, at p. 562:

D

> " That is altogether different in its results and objects from what was contemplated in the notice, and not such a resolution as an absent shareholder was entitled to suppose would be brought before the meeting, under which he could claim compensation under section 161. It would not bring section 161 into operation, and it would not limit the amount of the expenses; and, in fact, it was not the resolution of
>
> E   which notice had been given. A shareholder receiving the notice might very well say that he would not trouble to attend an ordinary reconstruction meeting, and at the same time might have the strongest objection to an ordinary voluntary winding up, which is something more than a winding up for the limited purpose of reconstructing the company."

F   The decision in *In re Teede & Bishop Ltd.* is of some interest for present purposes, since it does concern a case where a meeting of members of a company purported to pass a special resolution, but the resolution took a different form from the contemplated resolution or resolutions of which the text had previously been circulated to members in the preceding notices. Furthermore, in the event the resolution was held to be invalid.

G   Nevertheless, Mr. Instone sought to derive some assistance from the passage in the judgment of Cozens-Hardy J. which I have already read. If I understood him correctly, he suggested that the corollary of the reasoning of that passage was that if a special resolution was *not altogether different* in its result and object from what was contemplated in the notice, it could be valid, even if it represented an amended version of the text set out in the notices preceding the meeting. He suggested that the

H   decision was, at least by inference, authority for the proposition that, if the text of a special resolution has been circulated, an amendment thereof at the meeting is permissible, if it satisfies the criterion that a shareholder, who had formed a view or intention on the resolution as circulated, could not reasonably adopt a different view on the amended version.

    Possibly this would have been Cozens-Hardy J.'s opinion, but I am unable to draw this inference from the brief report of his judgment. A little later in the same passage, at p. 562, he stated: " in fact, it was not

the resolution of which notice had been given." These words, at least   A
if read in isolation, suggest rather the contrary, namely, that no amendment is permissible.

On any footing, therefore, this case is, in my judgment, of little
assistance to the company in the present case: first, because the amendment of the special resolution was in the event there held impermissible;
secondly, because Cozens-Hardy J. did not clearly specify the circum-   B
stances, if any, in which he would have held an amendment permissible;
and, thirdly, because the decision was based on the construction of the
Act of 1862, section 51 of which differed materially from section 141 (2)
of the Act of 1948.

This third comment also applies in relation to the next decision relied
on by Mr. Instone, namely, *Torbock* v. *Lord Westbury* [1902] 2 Ch. 871.
Subject to this comment, however, this decision provides him with rather   C
more substantial ammunition. In that case the board of a company had
given its members notice that an extraordinary general meeting would be
held for the purpose of considering and, if thought fit, passing a resolution,
the text of which was circulated. This resolution would have provided
for the company's articles of association to be altered by allocating 40 per
cent. of the profits of the company, after payment of certain dividends,   D
by way of remuneration to the directors of the company, in the
proportions 20 per cent. to the managing director and the balance
between the remaining directors in such proportions as they might decide.
The first meeting was held and the proposed resolution was amended by
altering the 40 per cent. to 30 per cent. and reducing the proportions
to be received by the individual directors pro tanto. The amended   E
resolution was passed at the meeting and was confirmed at a subsequent
meeting. The plaintiff claimed that, owing to the amendment, no notice
had been given of the resolution actually passed and that it was therefore
invalid as a special resolution. Mr. Eve K.C., arguing against this claim,
submitted, at p. 873:

> " There is no doubt that an entirely new resolution cannot be proposed
> under the guise of an amendment, but though the point must often   F
> have arisen in similar cases, it has never been contended that an
> amendment in pari materiâ with the resolution specified in the notice
> contravenes the statute and thereby necessitates a fresh notice."

Swinfen Eady J. in effect accepted this submission and rejected the
plaintiff's contention. He said, at pp. 873–874:

> " This contention is not well founded. The resolution confirmed at   G
> the second meeting must no doubt be in the same form as that
> passed at the first meeting. In other words, the second meeting can
> only say Aye or No to the resolution passed at the first meeting.
> But it is not necessary that the resolution passed at the first meeting
> should be in the identical terms of the resolution specified in the
> notice. Section 51 requires a special resolution to be passed ' at any   H
> general meeting of which notice specifying the intention to propose such
> resolution has been duly given.' If, therefore, proper and sufficient
> notice of the intention to propose the resolution is given, nothing
> more is required, and the resolution is not invalidated if, owing to an
> amendment at the first meeting, the resolution passed is not indentical
> with that of the notice. In the present case full notice was given
> to fix the directors' remuneration, and the only difference between

A   the proposed resolution, as set forth in the notice of the first meeting, and the resolution actually passed was the reduction of the proposed remuneration from 40 to 30 per cent., the proportion allocated to the general manager being unaltered. I hold that this alteration did not invalidate the resolution. . . ."

That case is thus, in my judgment, clear authority for the following
B   propositions: (a) If the members of a company passed a special resolution, it could, in appropriate circumstances, be legitimately claimed that " notice specifying the intention to propose such a resolution has been duly given," within the meaning of section 51 of the Act of 1862, even though, owing to an amendment at the first meeting, the resolution passed was not in the identical terms of the resolution referred to in the notice.
C   (b) All that was necessary was that " proper and sufficient notice " of the intention to propose the resolution had been given. (c) The special resolution confirmed at the second meeting had, nevertheless, to be in the identical terms of that passed at the first meeting.

Swinfen Eady J. did not elaborate as to the test which should be applied in deciding whether " proper and sufficient notice " had been given. But it seems plain from his judgment that he regarded it as having
D   been given on the facts of that case, on the grounds that members had been given notice of the intention to fix the directors' remuneration, and the only difference in the resolution passed from that of which notice had been given was a reduction in the amount of the remuneration. I will revert to his judgment hereafter.

Sections 51 and 129 of the Companies Act 1862 were partially repealed
E   by the Companies Act 1907, Schedule 4, but the Companies Act 1907 was itself repealed by the Companies (Consolidation) Act 1908 which introduced entirely new definitions of an " extraordinary resolution " and a " special resolution." Section 69 (1) provided:

" A resolution shall be an extraordinary resolution when it has been passed by a majority of not less than three fourths of such members entitled to vote as are present in person or by proxy (where proxies
F   are allowed) at a general meeting of which notice specifying the intention to propose the resolution as an extraordinary resolution has been duly given."

Section 69 (2) provided:

" A resolution shall be a special resolution when it has been—(a)
G   passed in manner required for the passing of an extraordinary resolution; and (b) confirmed by a majority of such members entitled to vote as are present in person or by proxy (where proxies are allowed) at a subsequent general meeting, of which notice has been duly given, and held after an interval of not less than 14 days, nor more than one month, from the date of the first meeting."

H   The form of section 69 (2) of the Act of 1908 relating to special resolutions thus bears little similarity to section 141 (2) of the Act of 1948. For present purposes, the significance of the Act of 1908 lies rather in the definition of an " extraordinary resolution " in section 69 (1), for two reasons. First, the language of section 141 (1) and (2) of the Act of 1948 clearly derives its descent from this definition. Secondly, this definition itself clearly derives its own descent from the opening limb of section 51 of the Act of 1862—defining a special resolution—which it quite closely resembles but with certain apparently deliberate departures from its A wording. The departure from that wording most significant for present purposes is the substitution of the phrase " notice specifying the intention to propose *the* resolution " for the phrase " notice specifying the intention to propose *such* resolution." (Italics mine).

Mr. Instone submits that this is a distinction without a difference, but I cannot accept this submission. As Miss Arden pointed out, the primary definition of the word " such " to be found in the *Shorter Oxford English* B *Dictionary*, 3rd ed., is " Of the character, degree or extent described, referred to, or implied in what has been said." As the dictionary shows, in appropriate contexts the word can also bear the meaning " the previously described or specified "; but this is not the primary meaning of the word. It must have been, at least, strongly arguable that, in the context of section 51 of the Act of 1862, the word " such " bore its C primary meaning, with the result that it would have sufficed for a notice to specify the intention to propose a special resolution of *the character* which was in fact passed, in other words a resolution in pari materiâ: see, for example, the argument of Mr. Eve K.C. in the *Torbock* case [1902] 2 Ch. 871, 873, already quoted. It seems to me highly probable that in the drafting of section 69 (1) of the Act of 1908 the legislature deliberately abandoned the word " such " and adopted the word " the," D meaning " the aforesaid," so as to make it plain that prior notice of the actual resolution, not merely of the character of the resolution, had to be given if an extraordinary resolution was to be valid. One obvious reason for so providing was that an extraordinary resolution did not require the confirmation by a subsequent meeting, which a special resolution at that time did require. E

This conclusion as to the intention of the legislature in 1908, in my judgment derives a measure of support from a comparison of the wording of section 69 (1) with that of article 49 in Table A in Schedule 1 to that Act. That article so far as material provides:

"Seven days notice at the least . . . specifying the place, the day, and the hour of meeting and, in case of special business, the general F nature of that business shall be given in manner hereinafter mentioned. . . ."

In the case of a special resolution, it was clearly not intended to suffice to specify the " general nature " of the proposed resolution.

The next case referred to by Mr. Instone is a significant one, because it concerned the construction of section 69 (1) of the Act of 1908, the G wording of which closely resembles that of section 141 (2) of the Act of 1948 in all respects material for present purposes. In *MacConnell* v. *E. Prill & Co. Ltd.* [1916] 2 Ch. 57, the articles of the company in question incorporated the last mentioned article 49. The company, which had a nominal share capital of £2,000, sent a notice to shareholders convening an extraordinary general meeting, of which the agenda was stated to be H " to pass resolution to increase capital of the company ": see p. 58. The company subsequently passed an extraordinary resolution that the capital of the company be increased to £3,500 by the creation and issue of 1,500 shares of £1 each. The plaintiff claimed that the notice was insufficient on two grounds, both depending on the language of section 69 of the Act of 1908. Sargant J. summarised the grounds of objection, at p. 61:

A   " In the first place it is said that the notice convening the meeting
did not specify *the* resolution, and in the next place it is said that
the notice did not specify the intention to pass the resolution as
an extraordinary resolution."

Sargant J. held that both objections were well founded. In relation to
the first objection, the material one for present purposes, he said, at p. 61 :

B   " As regards the first objection, it is obvious that the notice signifies
merely an intention to propose some increase or other in the capital
of the company, and not an intention to make the specific increase
embodied in the resolution that was actually passed. It seems to
me of great importance that shareholders should be protected in
matters of this kind by specific notice of what is intended to be
C   done. And there is a marked difference between the very definite
language in this respect of section 69 of the Act of 1908 and the
much looser and general language of article 49 in the Table A of
that Act with regard to notice of any special business that is proposed
to be transacted at a meeting of the company. In the latter case
notice is required only of the general nature of any special business
to be transacted, while in the case of an extraordinary resolution the
D   notice has to specify the resolution."

Mr. Instone, as I understood him, accepted that the decision of Sargant J.
was correct on its particular facts. He submitted, however, that he was
wrong in saying " in the case of an extraordinary resolution the notice has
to specify the resolution." He submitted that this dictum was obiter and
ought to be disregarded as being inconsistent with the *Bridport* (1867) L.R.
E   2 Ch.App. 191; *Henderson* (1890) 45 Ch.D. 330 and *Torbock* [1902] 2 Ch.
871 decisions, the last two of which were not apparently cited to Sargant J.
Mr. Instone submitted that all three decisions show that a resolution can
be validly passed, even if not identical to the notified form. He reminded
me that what had to be notified under the terms of section 69 (1) of the
Act of 1908—as under section 141 (2) of the Act of 1948—was simply the
F   *intention* to propose the relevant resolution. He submitted that there
was no reason why the freedom of the members at the meeting to
translate the intention into action should be fettered by the form of
wording chosen by the conveners.

No authorities subsequent to that of *MacConnell's* case [1916] 2 Ch.
57 directly relevant to the present point were cited to me. After
amendment by the Companies Act 1928, section 29 of the Act of 1908
G   was wholly repealed by the Companies Act 1929, of which section 117
is the forerunner of section 141 of the Act of 1948. In relation to
special resolutions, however, section 117 of the Act of 1929 embodied
at least one important alteration in the law of 1908. Under the Act of
1929—as under the Act of 1948—a second confirmatory meeting was not
made requisite in relation to a special resolution, so that in this respect
H   special resolutions were equated with extraordinary resolutions.

As I have indicated, the source of the wording of section 141 (2) of
the Act of 1948 relating to special resolutions can be traced back to the
wording of section 69 (1) of the Act of 1908, relating to extraordinary
resolutions. In all the circumstances it was, I think, common ground
between counsel that the decision of Sargant J. in *MacConnell's* case in
relation to the construction of section 69 (1) of the Act of 1908 must, so
far as this decision is correct, be applicable to the interpretation of

section 141 (2) of the Act of 1948. This, I conceive is why Mr. Instone A
took such pains to satisfy me that Sargant J. was wrong in stating that,
in the case of an extraordinary resolution, the notice had to " specify the
resolution." In the case of an extraordinary resolution under the Act
of 1908, and in the case of a special resolution under the Act of 1948,
he submitted in effect that all that is necessary is to give notice of the
nature of what the resolution is to do. It is not the law, he submitted,
that the actual wording of the proposed resolution must be notified or B
that, if it is notified, no amendment is permissible. Following the service
of a notice in sufficient form, an amendment of the proposed resolution
at the meeting will be permissible, he submitted, provided only that any
shareholder who had formed a view or intention on the resolution as
circulated could not reasonably have adopted a different view on the
amended version. This latter criterion he conveniently termed the C
" limits of tolerance." In reply, he submitted in the alternative, in
reliance on the *Torbock* case [1902] 2 Ch. 871, that if the effect of an
amendment is merely to " whittle down " the effect of the form of a
special resolution as set out in a notice of a meeting, such an amendment
must prima facie be permissible unless it is so substantial as significantly
to change the nature of the transaction.

Miss Arden drew my attention to an Australian case, *In re Picturesque* D
Atlas and Publishing Co. Ltd. (1892) 13 N.S.W. Eq. 44, on the particular
facts of which the amendment of a special resolution was held not to
affect its validity. While I found this decision interesting, I did not find
it of any real assistance in the present case, since it apparently centred
on the construction of a section of a New South Wales statute, section 83
of the Companies Act 1874 (37 Vic. No. 19), in materially different terms E
from section 141 (2) of the Act of 1948, in particular because it embodied
the phrase " such resolution," not " the resolution." Neither did I derive
much help from the conflicting views of textbook writers.

Having referred to all the authorities cited to me which I consider
directly relevant for present purposes, I shall now attempt to express my
own views on the decision in *MacConnell* v. *E. Prill & Co. Ltd.* [1916] F
2 Ch. 57 and to formulate the principles applicable to the case before me.

If—which I doubt—Sargant J., in stating that " in the case of an
extraordinary resolution the notice has to specify the resolution," intended
to say that the notice must set out the precise text of the proposed
resolution, I would agree with Mr. Instone that he went a little too far.
The relevant condition precedent to the validity of an extraordinary
resolution, as set out in section 69 (1) of the Act of 1908, is that " notice G
specifying the intention to propose the resolution as an extraordinary
resolution has been duly given." Strictly, therefore, it is the relevant
intention of which notice must be given. I do not think it can be possible
to give notice specifying the relevant intention without also specifying
the entire substance of the actual resolution which it is intended to
propose. Nevertheless, as Miss Arden pointed out, it is well established H
that notices are not to be construed with excessive strictness, if they
give reasonable notice of that of which they are supposed to give notice:
see *Buckley on The Companies Acts,* 13th ed. (1957), p. 331, note (*k*),
and the cases there cited. In my judgment, it is perfectly possible to
conceive a form of notice which may properly be said to give notice
specifying the intention to propose a particular resolution, even though
it does not set out in terms the text of the proposed resolution. Provided

A that the notice specifies both *the entire substance* of the intended resolution—that is the entire substance of what is to be decided—and the intention to propose it, it can, in my judgment, be properly claimed that notice has been given " specifying the intention to propose the resolution " within the meaning of section 69 (1) of the Act of 1908 or section 141 (1) or section 141 (2) of the Act of 1948. In such circum-
B stances it can also properly be said that the resolution subsequently passed is " *the* resolution " referred to in the notice.

The fact remains, however, that under the terms of each of these three last-mentioned subsections, if a resolution is to be validly passed, it must be *the* resolution—i.e. the same resolution as that—identified in the preceding notice. This, as I read it, was the crucial point on which the whole of Sargant J.'s reasoning in the *MacConnell* case [1916] 2 Ch.
C 57 was based in the present context and I respectfully agree with it. The difficulty in that case was, as he said at p. 61, that the notice in question signified

"... merely an intention to propose some increase or other in the capital of the company, and not an intention to make the specific increase embodied in the resolution that was actually passed."

D Neither the precise form nor the substance of the intended resolution was communicated to the shareholders, and this necessarily rendered the notice invalid.

With the one possible qualification to which I have referred, I therefore respectfully agree with and adopt the reasoning of Sargant J.'s judgment in the *MacConnell* case. I feel unable to accept Mr. Instone's submission
E that it was inconsistent with the *Bridport*, L.R. 2 Ch.App. 191, *Henderson*, 45 Ch.D. 330 and *Torbock* [1902] 2 Ch. 871 decisions. Sargant J. himself ([1916] 2 Ch. 57, 62) referred to the *Bridport* decision (1867) L.R. 2 Ch.App. 191 as being a case which turned:

... merely on the question whether the notice which had been sent gave shareholders sufficient warning that it was intended to put
F the company into liquidation by a single extraordinary resolution under section 129 (3) of the Act of 1862 rather than by the more normal process of a special resolution."

This entirely accords with my own earlier analysis of this decision. The *Henderson* decision, 45 Ch.D. 330, as I have indicated, was a decision on its own, entirely special, facts. Though it is perhaps regrettable that the
G *Torbock* decision [1902] 2 Ch. 871 was apparently not cited to Sargant J., I cannot think that it would have made any difference to his own decision, bearing in mind that the *Torbock* decision (a) related to section 51 of the Companies Act 1862, which used the phrase " such resolution," as opposed to the words " the resolution," to which Sargant J. in my judgment rightly attached such significance, and (b) concerned a special resolution which, at the time when the *Torbock* case was decided, required
H a second meeting for its confirmation, so that the need for exact precision in the notice calling the first meeting was clearly less acute.

I therefore find nothing in the authorities which precludes me from reaching the conclusion as to the construction of section 141 (2) of the Act of 1948 which I would have reached in the absence of authority and indeed I think this conclusion derives strong support from the *MacConnell* decision [1916] 2 Ch. 57. In the light of this analysis of the authorities and of the wording of section 141 (2), I shall now attempt to summarise what are in my judgment the relevant principles relating to notices of. A and the subsequent amendment of, special resolutions:

(1) If a notice of the intention to propose a special resolution is to be a valid notice for the purposes of section 141 (2), it must identify the intended resolution by specifying either the text or the entire substance of the resolution which it is intended to propose. In the case of a notice of intention to propose a special resolution, nothing is achieved by the addition of such words as "with such amendments and alterations as shall be determined upon at such meeting." B

(2) If a special resolution is to be validly passed in accordance with section 141 (2), the resolution as passed must be the same resolution as that identified in the preceding notice; the phrase "the resolution' in section 141 (2) means 'the aforesaid resolution."

(3) A resolution as passed can properly be regarded as "the resolu- C tion" identified in a preceding notice, even though (a) it departs in some respects from the text of a resolution set out in such notice—for example by correcting those grammatical or clerical errors which can be corrected as a matter of construction, or by reducing the words to more formal language—or (b) it is reduced into the form of a new text, which was not included in the notice, provided only that in either case there is no D departure whatever from the substance.

(4) However, in deciding whether there is complete identity between the substance of a resolution as passed and the substance of an intended resolution as notified, there is no room for the court to apply the de minimis principle or a "limit of tolerance." The substance must be identical. Otherwise the condition precedent to the validity of a special resolution as passed, which is imposed by section 141 (2), namely that E notice has been given "specifying the intention to propose the resolution as a special resolution " is not satisfied.

(5) It necessarily follows from the above propositions that an amendment to the previously circulated text of a special resolution can properly be put to and voted on at a meeting if, but only if, the amendment involves no departure from the substance of the circulated text, in the F sense indicated in propositions (3) and (4) above.

(6) References to notices in the above propositions are intended to include references to circulars accompanying notices. In those cases where notices are so accompanied, the notices and circulars can and should, in my judgment, ordinarily be treated as one document.

(7) All the above propositions may be subject to modification where all the members, or a class of members, of a company unanimously agree G to waive their rights to notice under section 141 (2): see section 143 (4) (d) of the Act of 1948; In re Pearce Duff & Co. Ltd. [1960] 1 W.L.R. 1014 and In re Duomatic Ltd. [1969] 2 Ch. 365.

I would emphasise that these propositions are directed solely to special resolutions. Very different considerations may apply in the case of ordinary resolutions, in relation to which the criteria of permissible H amendments suggested by Mr. Instone could well be very relevant: see, for example, Betts & Co. Ltd. v. Macnaghten [1910] 1 Ch. 430. In relation to special resolutions however, I think that my conclusions of principle accord not only with the wording of the Act of 1948 and with the authorities, but also with the following considerations of public policy. The Act requires a special resolution only in about ten circumstances. Thus, for example, such a resolution is required by section 5

A for the alteration of a company's memorandum, by section 10 for the alteration of its articles, by section 18 (1) for the change of its name, by section 66 for the reduction of its capital, by section 222 (a) for a resolution that the company may be wound up by the court; it is also required for a resolution for voluntary winding up passed under section 278 (1) (b). It may, I think, fairly be said that all the situations in which

B special resolutions are required are special situations, where the resolutions in question are by their nature likely either to affect the company's constitution or to have an important effect on its future. Since the passing of the 1929 legislation, the shareholders of a company, when faced with the intention to propose a special resolution, no longer have the protection of a locus poenitentiae in the shape of a second confirmatory meeting, at which they can accept or reject a special resolution passed at

C the first meeting. It is therefore all the more important that each shareholder should now have clear and precise advance notice of the substance of any special resolution which it is intended to propose, so that he may decide whether he should attend the meeting or is content to absent himself and leave the decision to those who do; the provisions imposed by section 141 (2) of the Act of 1948 must be intended as much

D for the protection of the members who in the event decide to absent themselves as of those who decide to attend: see for example Tiessen v. Henderson [1899] 1 Ch. 861, 866–867 and 870–871 per Kekewich J. If it were open to the members who did attend to propose and vote on a special resolution differing in substance albeit slightly from the resolution of which notice had been given, there would be a risk of unfair prejudice to those members who, after due consideration, had deliberately absented

E themselves. I do not think that their interests would be sufficiently protected by the safeguard suggested by Mr. Instone, namely, that an amendment could properly be put to and voted on by the meeting only if a member, who had formed a view or intention with regard to a resolution as circulated, could not reasonably adopt a different view on the amended version. Nor do I think that the alternative " whittling

F down " criterion suggested by him would offer them adequate protection. In many circumstances, albeit not on the facts of this particular case, either test when applied in practice could involve serious uncertainties and difficult questions of degree. Furthermore, in many cases it would present substantial embarrassment both to the chairman of the meeting who had to apply it and to any persons holding " two-way " proxies on behalf of absent members. The absent members would be correspondingly

G faced with unpredictable risks.

These considerations strengthen my conclusion that the strict interpretation which I have placed on section 141 (2) is likely to represent the true intention of the legislature, as well as the grammatical meaning of the words used. There must be absolute identity, at least in substance, between the intended resolution referred to in the notice and the resolu-

H tion actually passed.

I now turn to apply the seven propositions set out above to the facts of the present case. The qualifications referred to in the last of them are not relevant here, since not all members of the company entitled to vote thereat were present at the meeting of April 26, 1979. While I have no reason to doubt that the amendment to the resolution was put to the meeting in good faith and on legal advice, it was in my judgment improperly put and voted on. Miss Arden accepted, and I

accept, the correctness of the advice given to Mr. Silman, on the facts, A
that no shareholder who had made up his mind how to vote on the
resolution in its original form could reasonably have adopted a different
view in regard to the amended form. For this reason I have a measure
of sympathy with this petition. This point, however, in my judgment
is irrelevant to law. In my judgment, the crucial point is that the
resolution which the meeting of April 26, 1979, approved was not the
same resolution, either in form or in substance, as that of which the text B
had been circulated to shareholders in the notices of April 2, 1979. There
is no room for the application of any de minimis principle; a resolution
to reduce the share premium account of a company to £321 could not
even be deemed to be the same as a resolution to reduce it to £320.

In the circumstances the resolution was not in my judgment validly
passed in accordance with section 141 (2) of the Act of 1948. The court, C
therefore, has no jurisdiction to confirm the reduction of the share
premium account as asked by this petition.

As to the exercise of the court's discretion

The second principal point which has been argued before me relates
to the exercise of the court's discretion and arises in the following D
circumstances. The petition invokes this discretion to approve the
reduction of the share premium account on the grounds that, as alleged
in paragraph 8 of the petition:

" previously to the passing of the said resolution the entire share
premium account of £1,356,900·48 had been lost with the exception
of £321·17 credited thereto in March 1979."   E

The petition is thus founded on loss and echoes the wording of section
66 (1) (*b*) of the Act of 1948.

[His Lordship read the subsection, referred to *In re Hoare & Co.*
[1904] 2 Ch. 208 and *Caldwell* v. *Caldwell & Co.* (*Papermakers*) *Ltd.*
[1916] W.N. 70 and, having stated that any views that he expressed on
the submissions of counsel would be obiter, continued:] I therefore do F
not propose to state how I would have been minded to exercise my
discretion if I had had jurisdiction to approve the proposed reduction.
As things are, I find that, the requirements of section 141 (2) not having
been complied with, I have no jurisdiction to approve it and must
decline to make the order sought.

Petition dismissed.   G

Solicitors: *Nicholson, Graham & Jones; Treasury Solicitor.*

T. C. C. B.

H

A

[FAMILY DIVISION]

*PRACTICE DIRECTION
(PRE-TRIAL REVIEW: FINANCIAL PROVISIONS)

B
*Husband and Wife—Financial provision—Pre-trial review—Pro-
cedure—Property adjustment and lump sum applications—
Consideration of settlement of claim or clarification of issues—
Applicant's affidavit—Matters to be set out—Need for
attendance by counsel or solicitors—Matrimonial Causes Act
1973 (c. 18), ss. 23 (1), 24 (1)*

From April 1, 1980, by way of experiment in the Divorce Registry the
C substantive appointment for directions in all applications for property
adjustment and lump sums will include a pre-trial review at which the
registrar will consider the possibility of settlement of the case, or clarification of the issue. Where the case continues to be contested the registrar
will give directions, particularly as to discovery, designed to elicit all
necessary information but to save costs by excluding over-detailed requests
for it. With a view to achieving these objectives the following procedure
D should be followed in these cases:

1. The applicant's affidavit in support of the application should have
annexed to it a list setting out the capital of the deponent, and any loans
debts and other charges against capital. The list should also set out all
the deponent's sources of income and the income from each source. A
copy of this list with a similar list in respect of the respondent's means,
E set out on the same page, should be annexed to his affidavit. Where
the deponent is employed he should exhibit his last three pay slips, or,
if he is the director of any company, the last three accounts of that
company. Where the deponent is self-employed he should exhibit his
accounts for the past three years or other appropriate information as
to his means.

2. After affidavits have been filed, general mutual discovery should
F take place without order 14 days from the last affidavit, unless some other
period is agreed, with inspection 7 days thereafter.

3. Where a dispute arises as to the value of any property a valuation
should be made by an agreed valuer or, in default of agreement, by an
independent valuer chosen by the President of the Royal Institution of
Chartered Surveyors. The valuation should be produced at the appoint-
G ment for directions and pre-trial review.

4. Any questionnaire should be delivered to the other side at least 21
days before the said appointment. At the pre-trial review directions
will be given by the registrar as to what disputed items on discovery or
in the questionnaire are to be dealt with. Where the registrar considers
that to answer any question would entail considerable expense and that
there is doubt whether the answer would provide any information of
H value, he may make the order for the question to be answered at the
questioner's risk as to costs. The registrar may refuse to order an answer
to a question if he considers that its value would be small in comparison
with the property or income of the party to whom the question is
addressed.

5. If after the pre-trial review there are relevant changes in the income
or capital position of either party, these should be set out in an affidavit
annexing a list of the changes as compared with the earlier list.

6. Where the issue of conduct is raised on the affidavits, the registrar A will inquire whether it is being pursued and, if so, will order particulars to be given of the precise allegations relied on.

7. To ensure the success of this procedure it is essential that pre-trial reviews should be attended either by counsel or by a representative of solicitors who is fully conversant with the facts of the case.

B

R. L. BAYNE-POWELL,
Senior Registrar.

February 12, 1980.

[CHANCERY DIVISION]   C

* *In re* STOTT, DECD.

KLOUDA *v.* LLOYDS BANK LTD. AND OTHERS

[1978 S. No. 957]

1979   May 3; 11   Slade J.   D

*Probate—Pleading—Want of knowledge and approval—Allegations
in support of plea material to unpleaded claim of undue influence—Whether allegations " in support of " plea of undue
influence—Application to strike out—R.S.C., Ord. 76, r. 9 (3)*

The plaintiff, named as residuary beneficiary in what purported to be a will executed by the deceased on February 17,   E
1976, asked that the court should pronounce in favour of the
will. The third defendant named as residuary beneficiary in
what purported to be a will executed by the deceased on May
25, 1972, counterclaimed asking that the court should pronounce
against the will of 1976 and for that of 1972. By paragraph 1
of his defence the third defendant pleaded that at the time of
execution of the will of 1976 the deceased " did not know and
approve of the gift of residue in favour of the plaintiff," and,   F
in support of that plea, particulars were given of the circumstances in which the will of 1976 had been prepared and
executed. Those particulars, while supporting the plea of
want of knowledge and approval, included particulars which
could have been material to a plea of undue influence. By
paragraph 2 the third defendant alleged that the deceased, at
the time when the will purported to have been executed, " was
not of sound mind, memory or understanding." and, by para-   G
graph 3, he put the plaintiff to proof that the deceased knew
and approved of the gift of residue to the plaintiff or that she
was of sound mind, memory or understanding.

On the plaintiff's summons to strike out some of the particulars in paragraph 1 of the defence on the ground that they
had been pleaded in contravention of R.S.C., Ord. 76, r. 9 (3) [1]
since they were "relevant" to an unpleaded claim of undue
influence: —   H

Held, dismissing the summons, that the words, in R.S.C.,
Ord. 76, r. 9 (3), " relevant in support of " a plea of undue
influence were not intended to exclude matters material to a
plea of want of knowledge and approval and, therefore, they
were to be read in a restricted sense as being intended to apply
merely to a case where the pleader was in substance making an
affirmative allegation of undue influence without specifically

[1] R.S.C., Ord. 76, r. 9 (3): see post, p. 250D–F.

A   introducing that plea; that an allegation should not be treated
as "relevant," unless it would establish alone or with other
facts pleaded a claim of undue influence and not merely assist
towards such proof; and that, since the allegations made by the
third defendant, even if they were all established, would not
suffice to prove undue influence, they were not relevant
allegations within the meaning of R.S.C., Ord. 76, r. 9 (3)
(post, pp. 252H—253A, D–G).

B   Dictum of Lord Simonds in *Wintle* v. *Nye* [1959] 1 W.L.R.
284, 294, H.L.(E.) and *In the Estate of Fuld, decd. (No. 3)*
[1968] P. 675 applied.
          In re R., decd. [1951] P. 10 distinguished.

      The following cases are referred to in the judgment:
Barry v. *Butlin* (1838) 2 Moo. P.C.C. 480, P.C.
C   *Fuld, decd. (No. 3), In the Estate of* [1968] P. 675; [1966] 2 W.L.R. 717;
          [1965] 3 All E.R. 776.
      R., decd., In re [1951] P. 10; [1950] 2 All E.R. 117.
      Wintle v. *Nye* [1959] 1 W.L.R. 284; [1959] 1 All E.R. 552, H.L.(E.).

      No additional cases were cited in argument.

D   SUMMONS
      By a writ and statement of claim dated February 27, 1978, the plain-
tiff, Alice Klouda, sought to have established a will dated February 17,
1976, of May, Lady Stott, late of 20, FitzJames Avenue, London W. 14,
in which the plaintiff was named as residuary beneficiary. The testator
died on January 2, 1977. The writ was issued against the first defendant,
E Lloyds Bank Ltd., as the executor named in the will, the second defendant Norman Jones, as the executor of a previous will dated May 25,
1972, and against the third defendant, Herbert Gardner, as a beneficiary
named in the will of 1972, and because he had entered a caveat. By
his defence, the third defendant pleaded by paragraph 1, that the deceased
did not know and approve of the gift of residue in favour of the plaintiff contained in the will of February 17, 1976, and gave particulars
F supporting that plea. By paragraph 2, he pleaded that " further or in
the alternative the deceased at the time when the said alleged will purports to have been executed was not of sound mind, memory or understanding " and, by paragraph 3, he put the plaintiff to proof that the
deceased knew and approved of the gift of residue to the plaintiff, or
alternatively that the deceased was of sound mind, memory and understanding when she purported to execute the will.
G   By a summons dated November 24, 1978, the plaintiff asked that the
particulars given in sub-paragraphs (a), (b), (e), (f), (g) and (h) of paragraph 1 of the third defendant's defence be struck out as contravening
R.S.C., Ord. 76, r. 9 (3), and that the costs of the application be paid
by the third defendant in any event.
      The facts are stated in the judgment.

H
      Peter Rawson for the third defendant.
      J. H. Weeks for the plaintiff.

                                                        Cur. adv. vult.

      May 11. SLADE J. By this summons application is made by the
plaintiff to strike out parts of the defence of the third defendant in an
action. It raises a pleading point which is not easy and is of some general

importance in the context of probate actions. I am surprised that, A
apparently, it has not been decided in any earlier reported case.

The action concerns the estate of the late May, Lady Stott who died
on January 2, 1977. The plaintiff, Mrs. Alice Klouda, is named as the
residuary beneficiary in what purports to be a will executed by Lady
Stott on February 17, 1976, under which she appointed the first defendant,
Lloyds Bank Ltd., executor and trustee. The third defendant, Mr. B
Herbert Gardner, is named as the residuary beneficiary in what purports
to be a will executed by Lady Stott on May 25, 1972, by which she appointed the second defendant, Mr. Norman Jones, executor and trustee.

By her writ, endorsed with a statement of claim in the abbreviated
form commonly used in such cases, the plaintiff propounds the will of
1976. By counterclaim the third defendant, Mr. Gardner asks, inter
alia, that the court should pronounce against the will of 1976, and for C
the will of 1972. The first and second defendants have filed defences
which show that, effectively, they are both adopting a neutral stance in
the proceedings. They have not appeared before me on this application.
The contest is effectively between the plaintiff and the third defendant,
who opposes probate of the will of 1976, first, on the grounds of want of
knowledge and approval of its contents, and secondly, on the ground of
testamentary incapacity. There is no express plea by the third defendant D
of undue influence or fraud.

Paragraph 1 of the third defendant's defence, which contains the
plea of want of knowledge of approval, reads:

"At the time of execution of the alleged will dated February 17,
1976, May Lady Stott (hereinafter called the deceased) did not know
and approve of the gift of residue in favour of the plaintiff contained E
in clause 4 thereof.

"Particulars

"(a) The plaintiff is and has at all material times been the pro-
prietress or manageress of a nursing home at 20, FitzJames Avenue,
London W. 14. (b) The deceased took up residence at the said
nursing home on or about November 14, 1975. (c) At the date of F
taking up residence the deceased was 91 years old and suffering
from senile dementia, so that she was incapable of living by herself.
(d) The deceased gave instructions for the said alleged will by a letter
dated December 5, 1975, to Messrs. Freeborough Slack & Co. At
the date of said letter the deceased was in a confused and disturbed
mental state and was unaware of the extent of her free estate.
(e) The said letter was written with the assistance of one Davey, an G
employee or associate of the plaintiff. (f) By the said letter the
deceased purported to instruct Messrs. Freeborough Slack & Co.,
to prepare a will under which the plaintiff was the sole residuary
beneficiary. There was no good reason why the deceased should
have wished to give her entire residuary estate to the plaintiff. In
three previous wills dated respectively March 2, 1957, October 4, H
1968, and May 25, 1972, the deceased had shown a consistent desire
to benefit the third defendant. (g) The deceased did not at any time
see or speak to any partner or other representative of Messrs. Freeborough Slack & Co., in relation to her said alleged will and received
no independent legal advice from any other source in connection
therewith. The deceased had never previously consulted the said
firm. (h) At the date of the said letter the deceased was under the

The Weekly Law Reports, March 7, 1980

249

1 W.L.R.   **In re Stott, decd. (Ch.D.)**   Slade J.

A   control of the plaintiff and was on the instructions of the plaintiff confined to the said nursing home. The plaintiff kept the doors of the same locked at all times and did not permit the deceased to use the key for the same or to leave the said nursing home unattended. The plaintiff further arranged for the deceased to be accompanied either by herself or by a member of her family or by the said Davey on all occasions when she was visited by friends or relations.

B   (i) The third defendant accordingly puts the plaintiff to proof that the said alleged will was, in respect of the gift of residue contained in clause 4 thereof, the will of a free and capable testatrix who knew and understood the effect thereof."

Paragrah 2 of this defence, containing the plea of testamentary incapa-
C city, begins with the following words:

"Further or in the alternative the deceased at the time when the said alleged will purports to have been executed was not of sound mind, memory or understanding."

There then follow, in paragraph 2, lengthy particulars of the alleged lack of testamentary capacity, such particulars, in certain respects, over-
D lapping with those contained in paragraph 1. Paragraph 3 of this defence reads:

"In the premises the third defendant puts the plaintiff to proof that the deceased knew and approved the contents of clause 4 of the said alleged will or alternatively that the deceased was of sound mind, memory and understanding when she purported to execute
E the same."

The pleading then contains a counterclaim by the third defendant, which I need not read for present purposes.

    By paragraphs 1 and 3 of the defence, the pleader clearly intends to rely on the general principle of law that, where a will is prepared and executed in circumstances which excite the vigilance and suspicion of the
F court, the burden is placed on the person propounding it to remove the suspicion and prove that the testator knew and approved of its contents. In particular this principle is likely to be applied where the court is satisfied on the evidence that a person has, by himself or his agents, been instrumental in preparing a will under which he himself takes a benefit: see for example *Wintle* v. *Nye* [1959] 1 W.L.R. 284.

G   In the light of these principles Mr. Weeks, on behalf of the plaintiff, does not dispute that each and every one of the allegations contained in paragraph 1 of the third defendant's defence is relevant to the plea of want of knowledge and approval. In this important respect, at least, the present case is distinguishable from *In re R., decd.* [1951] P. 10 to which he referred me. In that case the defendants in a probate action alleged, inter alia, that, at the apparent time of execution of the relevant will, the deceased did not know or approve of its contents. Under that
H heading, in their pleadings, they made derogatory allegations concerning the relationship between the beneficiary and the testator. Willmer J. struck out these allegations, primarily on the grounds that they were "scandalous" and might "tend to embarrass or delay the fair trial of the action," within what was then R.S.C., Ord. 19, r. 25 (*a*).

    The grounds of Willmer J.'s decision were that where a question is raised concerning knowledge and approval of the contents of a will:

The Weekly Law Reports, March 7, 1980

250

Slade J.   In re Stott, decd. (Ch.D.)   [1980]

" the circumstances which are held to excite the suspicions of the A
court must be circumstances attending, or at least relevant to, the
preparation and execution of the will itself.": see at p. 17.

He accepted, at p. 20, that the allegations could be relevant to the testamentary capacity of the deceased or to a plea of undue influence. Since
however, the allegations could not be relevant to the issue of want of
knowledge and approval, within the test which he had formulated, he B
struck them out.

In the present case, Mr. Weeks does not dispute that each and every
one of the allegations made in paragraph 1 of the third defendant's
defence is a circumstance attending, or relevant to, the preparation and
execution of the will of 1976 and is thus a material fact in respect of
which the third defendant will, understandably, wish to rely in support
of his plea of want of knowledge and approval, to the extent that such C
fact is provable by evidence and that the rules permit it.

He submits, however, that the allegations pleaded in sub-paragraphs
(a), (b), (e), the second sentence of (f) and sub-paragraphs (g) and (h) of
paragraph 1, though allegations of facts material for purposes of the
said plea, are not allegations which it is permissible for the third defendant to insert in his defence, in its present form, having regard to D
R.S.C., Ord. 76, r. 9 (3). For this reason he seeks to have them struck
out. Order 76, r. 9 (3) provides:

" Without prejudice to Ord. 18, r. 7, any party who pleads that at
the time when a will, the subject of the action, was alleged to have
been executed the testator did not know and approve of its contents
must specify the nature of the case on which he intends to rely, and
no allegation in support of that plea which would be relevant in E
support of any of the following other pleas, that is to say: (a) the
will was not duly executed, (b) that at the time of the execution
of the will the testator was not of sound mind, memory and understanding, and (c) that the execution of the will was obtained by
undue influence or fraud, shall be made by that party unless that
other plea is also pleaded."   F

Mr. Weeks submits that each of the allegations under attack would also
be relevant in support of a plea that the execution of the will of 1976
was obtained by undue influence on the part of the plaintiff. Accordingly,
he submits, Ord. 76, r. 9 (3) (c) must render such allegations impermissible
in a pleading, such as this, where undue influence is not specifically
pleaded. He submits that it would be wrong for the court to allow the G
third defendant to insinuate what is effectively a plea of undue influence
under cover of a plea of want of knowledge and approval. If the third
defendant wants to plead undue influence, Mr. Weeks suggests, he should
do so expressly with all the potential consequences as to costs that such
a pleading may entail. He submits that further support for his general
argument is to be found in a passage from the judgment in In re R.,
decd. [1951] P. 10, 20–21, in which Willmer J. having decided that H
the allegations there sought to be struck out should be struck out under
the then R.S.C., Ord. 19, r. 25 (a), proceeded further to decide that they
should also be struck out as being in direct contravention of the last
sentence of rule 40A of the Contentious Probate Rules 1862.

At the time Willmer J. made this decision, rule 40A was still in
force; he rejected, at p. 20, an argument that it had been entirely superseded by what was then R.S.C., Ord. 19, r. 25 (a). However, the Con-

The Weekly Law Reports, March 7, 1980

251

1 W.L.R.   In re Stott, decd. (Ch.D.)   Slade J.

A tentious Probate Rules 1862 were wholly revoked by the Rules of the
Supreme Court (Revision) Order 1962, which introduced a new, special
order, Order 76, dealing with probate proceedings. This revision was
effected only two or three years after the House of Lords had given its
decision, concerning the plea of want of knowledge and approval, in
Wintle v. *Nye* [1959] 1 W.L.R. 284. It seems to me readily conceivable
B in principle that the revision was intended substantially to alter the rules
of practice and procedure relating to this plea. I therefore think that any
reference to rule 40A of the old Contentious Probate Rules 1862 or to
that part of the judgment of Willmer J. in *In re R., decd.* [1951] P. 10
dealing with that rule, is of little assistance in the present case. The
attack of the plaintiff on the third defendant's pleading must stand or
fall on the wording of the present R.S.C., Ord. 76, r. 9 (3).

C   On a first literal reading of the wording of this rule, I think there is
considerable force in the basic submission of Mr. Weeks, that a party in
a probate action may never plead an allegation in support of a plea of
want of knowledge and approval, if such allegation would in any sense at
all be relevant in support of a plea of undue influence, but a plea of
undue influence is not itself made in the action. This submission however, if correct, would have such surprising results as to make me doubt
D whether this can have been the intention of those responsible for introducing R.S.C., Ord. 76, r. 9 (3).

       For the purpose of testing the correctness of the submission as a
matter of principle, I have to assume that the third defendant would be
in a position to prove at the trial all the allegations of fact which are now
under attack. As I have said, it is not disputed that they are all material
E to a plea of want of knowledge and approval though I would myself raise
a small query, not raised in argument, in relation to the materiality in
this context of the second and third sentences of paragraph 1 (f). With
this one possible exception, it seems to me that all the relevant allegations are matters of fact which, if proved, in conjunction with the other
facts pleaded in paragraph 1 of the third defendant's defence, the trial
judge would be likely to regard as creating a suspicion that fell to be
F removed by the person propounding the will, within the principle of
such cases as *Wintle* v. *Nye* [1959] 1 W.L.R. 284 and the much earlier
decision in *Barry* v. *Butlin* (1838) 2 Moo. P.C.C. 480, 482 *per* Parke B.

       Accordingly, apart from R.S.C., Ord. 76, r. 9 (3), the relevant allega-
tions are eminently suitable matters for a pleader to allege, on instructions,
in support of a plea of want of knowledge and approval; if true, they
G would give rise to reasonable suspicion. Furthermore, R.S.C., Ord. 18,
r. 7, to which Ord. 76, r. 9 (3) is expressly stated to be " without prejudice," expressly provides that every pleading must contain a statement
in summary form of the facts on which the party pleading relies for his
claim, or defence, as the case may be, though " not the evidence by which
those facts are to be proved."

       In contrast, however, an affirmative plea of undue influence ought
H never to be put forward unless the person who pleads it has reasonable
grounds to support it. In the present case the third defendant does not
wish to put forward an affirmative plea of undue influence. It seems a
fair assumption, though I do not actually know, that the reason for this
reluctance is that he and his legal advisers consider that, on the information available to them, there are no sufficient grounds to support such a
plea. The third defendant, after all, presumably has little or no personal
knowledge of the circumstances in which the will of 1976 came to be

The Weekly Law Reports, March 7, 1980

252

Slade J.   **In re Stott, decd. (Ch.D.)**   **[1980]**

made, but must rely on what he has been told by others. Yet, if the A submissions of the plaintiff on the interpretation and effect of R.S.C., Ord. 76, r. 9 (3) are correct, the third defendant, and defendants in a similar position in other probate actions, will find themselves obliged for practical purposes either (a) wholly to abandon a number of material allegations of fact, which are of crucial importance to their plea of want of knowledge and approval or (b) to raise an affirmative plea of undue influence, which they have no reasonable grounds to support. B

The resulting anomalies became even more apparent from references made by Mr. Rawson, on behalf of the third defendant, to cases. First, as appears from the speech of Lord Simonds in *Wintle* v. *Nye* [1959] 1 W.L.R. 284, 294, it is open to a party, alleging want of knowledge and approval, to cross-examine the person propounding the will on matters which may result in establishing fraud on the part of such C person, even though fraud has not been pleaded. The same must, I think, apply to undue influence.

Further, Scarman J., in *In the Estate of Fuld, decd.* (*No.* 3) [1968] P 675, 722c–f, made it clear that he did not regard the failure or deliberate omission of a party, who had raised a plea of want of knowledge and approval in a probate action, also to plead undue influence, as precluding such party from introducing, in support of his plea, matters D of fact which would also, at least in a broad sense, be relevant in support of a plea of undue influence.

These various points guide me towards the conclusion that the basic submission made by Mr. Weeks cannot be right. In my judgment the answer to it is, in the end, a short and simple one.

In my judgment, the second limb of R.S.C., Ord. 76, r. 9 (3), begin- E ning with the words " and no allegation . . .", though not perhaps very happily drafted, must be read in a somewhat restricted sense, as being intended to apply merely to the case where, under cover of a plea of want of knowledge and approval, a pleader is in substance making affirmative allegations of lack of proper execution, or lack of testamentary capacity, or undue influence, or fraud, as the case may be, without specifically introducing the appropriate alternative plea. In other words, F so far as it relates to fraud and undue influence, it is intended to cover the case where the pleader is willing to wound, but afraid to strike.

Willmer J., in *In re R., decd.* [1951] P. 10, 19, himself referred to the principle that the defence of want of knowledge and approval is not to be

> " used as a screen behind which one man is to be at liberty to charge G another with fraud or dishonesty without assuming the responsibility of making that charge in plain terms."

Paragraph (c) of the second limb of R.S.C., Ord. 76, r. 9 (3), in my judgment, reflects this principle. A little later in the same judgment, however Willmer J. observed, at p. 19:

> H
> " It is obvious that in the nature of things a fair measure of latitude must be allowed the pleader in alleging facts in support of a plea of want of knowledge and approval."

By the like token, in construing R.S.C., Ord. 76, r. 9 (3) a reasonably narrow meaning should, I think, be attributed to the phrase " which would be relevant in support of any of the following other pleas." An allegation should not, in my judgment, be treated as being " relevant "

The Weekly Law Reports, March 7, 1980

253

1 W.L.R.   **In re Stott, decd. (Ch.D.)**   Slade J.

A   within this meaning, unless it would, if established either alone or in conjunction with other facts also pleaded, *affirmatively prove* the relevant alternative plea. The mere fact that the allegation, if proved, might constitute evidence that could incidentally assist the proof of the relevant alternative plea, if raised, does not seem to me to bring it within this second limb of R.S.C., Ord. 76, r. 9 (3).

B   If the position were otherwise it is hard to see where the line could be drawn. For in any case there are likely to be numerous facts which, in a broad sense, could be said to be relevant in support of a plea of undue influence, as well as a plea of want of knowledge and approval. Simply for example, on facts similar to those in *Wintle* v. *Nye* [1959] 1 W.L.R. 284, it would not, if the plaintiff's present contentions are correct, even be open to a party, who seeks to assert a plea of want of knowledge and

C   approval without affirmatively alleging fraud or undue influence, to allege that the person who prepared the relevant will, and was the residuary legatee thereunder, was the testator's solicitor. In one sense such an allegation might be said to be " relevant in support of " a plea that the execution of the will was obtained by undue influence or fraud, because the fact alleged would, or might, constitute important evidence of the circumstances and background against which undue influence or

D   fraud was affirmatively alleged. In my judgment, however, it would not be " relevant in support of " such a plea, within the meaning of R.S.C., Ord. 76, r. 9 (3) unless it formed one of a number of allegations which, taken together, would, if established, affirmatively prove undue influence or fraud.

Ord. 76, r. 9 (3) is expressed to operate subject to Ord. 18, r. 7. As

E   Ord. 18, r. 7 itself shows, a crucial distinction is to be drawn between facts on which a party relies to support a plea and the evidence upon which he relies to prove such facts.

In the present case, I can well see that some or all of the allegations made in paragraph 1 of the third defendant's defence would incidentally go some way towards assisting him to make out a case of undue influence, if he were minded to put forward such a plea. However they do not, in

F   my judgment, constitute a screen behind which the third defendant is implicitly charging the plaintiff with undue influence, without expressly alleging it. Even if they were all established, they would not serve affirmatively to prove undue influence, since, even then, they would not necessarily be inconsistent with complete innocence of such a charge on the part of the plaintiff. In these circumstances the relevant allegations

G   are not, in my judgment, allegations which would be " relevant in support of " a plea of undue influence, within the true meaning of Ord. 76, r. 9 (3).

The assertion of a plea of want of knowledge and approval is not by itself treated by the court as an example of an attempt to wound made by someone who is yet afraid to strike. Its very nature is such that it will often be put forward by persons who, through no fault of their own, have very limited information as to the precise circumstances in which the

H   relevant will was made, but who are entitled to submit that the circumstances which *are* known to them should excite the vigilance of the court and place upon the person propounding the will the onus of proving that the testator knew and approved of its contents. The very nature of the plea is also such that the facts upon which the pleader may rely in support of it will often overlap with the evidence which he might wish to adduce in support of an affirmative plea of fraud or undue influence. An analogy is to be found in the case where a person seeks to set aside

a transaction in equity on the alternative grounds of presumed undue   A
influence and of actual undue influence; the facts upon which he will
rely to support the presumption must often overlap with the evidence
with which he will adduce in support of the plea of actual undue influence.

If, however, Ord. 76, r. 9 (3) were to be construed as having the far-
reaching effect contended for by the plaintiff in the present case, this
would, I think, have one or both of two most undesirable results. Either
it would have the effect of emasculating the scope of the plea of want of   B
knowledge and approval, in a manner quite inconsistent with the House
of Lords decision in *Wintle* v. *Nye* [1959] 1 W.L.R. 284 and contrary
to the public interest; alternatively it would encourage parties and their
counsel to put forward specific pleas of fraud or undue influence merely
as a precautionary measure and without sufficient grounds. For the
reasons which I have tried to indicate, I do not think that the construc-   C
tion of the rule suggested on behalf of the plaintiff is either the necessary
or the correct one.

I must, accordingly, dismiss this application.

> *Summons dismissed.*
> *Leave to appeal.*

D

Solicitors: *Farrer & Co.; Speechly, Bircham.*

T. C. C. B.

E

[COURT OF APPEAL]

* STOKE-ON-TRENT CITY COUNCIL *v.* WOOD MITCHELL
& CO. LTD.

1978 July 17, 18; 28   Stephenson, Roskill and Geoffrey Lane L.JJ.   F

Compulsory Purchase—Compensation—" Disturbance " for—Cor-
poration tax—Company reinstating business on acquired land
—Whether corporation tax factor in assessing compensation—
Land Compensation Act 1961 (9 & 10 *Eliz.* 2, *c.* 33), *s.* 5 (6)—
Finance Act 1969 (*c.* 32), *Sch.* 19, *para.* 11

The claimants, who were a company carrying on the busi-   G
ness of printers on land subject to a compulsory purchase
order, were served with a notice to treat. They agreed with
the acquiring authority to sell their land for £6,000 to the
authority and repurchase part of that land for £3,000 for the
purposes of reinstating their business thereon. The agreement
did not include compensation for temporary losses between
1969 and 1971 while their business was being re-established.
The parties agreed that the gross amount of compensation for   H
that disturbance was £12,633·77 of which £405·50 was capital,
leaving a balance of £12,228·27. On a reference to the Lands
Tribunal, the only matter in dispute was whether the gross
sum should be adjusted to take into account corporation tax.
The tribunal held that, in accordance with paragraph 11 of
Schedule 19 to the Finance Act 1969,[1] the balance of £12,228·27
was in the nature of income and to be treated as a trading

¹ Finance Act 1969. Sch. 19 para 11: see post, p. 261F–H.

A   receipt in the hands of the claimants and, therefore, as the
claimants were liable to pay corporation tax on the sum
received, they were entitled to compensation assessed without
deduction of tax.

On appeal by the acquiring authority:—

Held, dismissing the appeal, that under the Finance Acts
1965 and 1969 capital gains tax was payable on compensation
for compulsory acquisition and, since paragraph 11 of Schedule
B   19 to the Finance Act 1969 permitted the breakdown of
compensation into its component parts to enable the capital
element and the income element to be separated by apportionment so that the tax was only payable on the capital element,
compensation was no longer to be treated as a single capital
payment and paragraph 11 had the effect that it freed the
compensation paid to the claimants for loss of temporary
profits from its capital nature and enabled it to be treated as
C   a trading receipt in the hands of the claimant; that, since
corporation tax applied the income tax and capital gains tax
codes to bodies corporate such as the claimants, the claimants
could be liable to both corporation income tax and corporation capital gains tax on the compensation they received and,
therefore, no deduction was to be made in assessing compensation for corporation tax (post, pp. 261F–H, 262D–H, 263c).

D   *West Suffolk County Council* v. *W. Rought Ltd.* [1957]
A.C. 403, H.L.(E.) distinguished.

The following cases are referred to in the judgment of the court:

British Transport Commission v. *Gourley* [1956] A.C. 185; [1956] 2
W.L.R. 41; [1955] 3 All E.R. 796, H.L.(E.).

Horn v. *Sunderland Corporation* [1941] 2 K.B. 26; [1941] 1 All E.R. 480,
E   C.A.

Inland Revenue Commissioners v. *Glasgow and South-Western Railway
Co.* (1887) 12 App.Cas. 315, H.L.(Sc.).

London and Thames Haven Oil Wharves Ltd. v. *Attwooll* [1967] Ch. 772;
[1967] 2 W.L.R. 743; [1967] 2 All E.R. 124, C.A.

West Suffolk County Council v. *W. Rought Ltd.* [1957] A.C. 403; [1956]
3 W.L.R. 589; [1956] 3 All E.R. 216, H.L.(E.).

F
No additional cases were cited in argument.

CASE STATED by the Lands Tribunal.

By virtue of the City of Stoke-on-Trent (Lindop Street, Bucknall New
Road, St. Ann Street and Bucknall Old Road, Hanley) Housing Compulsory Purchase Order 1965, which became operative on March 31,
G   1966, the acquiring authority, Stoke-on-Trent City Council, became entitled to acquire from the claimants, Wood Mitchell & Co. Ltd., office and
warehouse premises at 5, 7 and 9, Lindop Street and a yard and garage
adjoining.   On that land the claimants carried on the business of printers.
Notice to treat was served on them on May 27, 1966, and, by agreement,
the claimants sold the land to the acquiring authority for £6,000 and the
H   claimants purchased back part of the land for £3,000 so that they could
re-establish their office and warehouse thereon.   The parties referred
to the Lands Tribunal the question of compensation to be paid, under
rule (6) of section 5 of the Land Compensation Act 1961, for the loss of
profits and other matters suffered by the claimants as the result of the
disturbance to their business between 1969 and 1971.   The parties agreed
that the compensation was £12,633·77 of which £405·50 was of a capital
nature, leaving a balance of £12,288·27, and the only effective question to

be determined by the tribunal was whether those figures should be adjusted   A
to take into account corporation tax.

The member of the tribunal, Mr. V. G. Wellings Q.C., held that the
effect of paragraph 11 of Schedule 19 to the Finance Act 1969 was that
the sum of £12,228·27 was to be treated as a trading receipt taxable in the
hands of the claimants and, therefore, no deduction should be made to
that figure. He awarded the claimants £12,633·77 together with their
surveyors' fees, if any, and ordered the acquiring authority to pay the   B
claimants' costs of the reference.

The acquiring authority appealed.

The facts are further stated in the judgment.

R. M. Bramwell for the acquiring authority.
D. A. Shirley for the claimants.   C

Cur. adv. vult.

July 28. ROSKILL L.J. read the judgment of the court. This is an
appeal by way of case stated by the Lands Tribunal dated October 3,
1977. The decision was that of Mr. V. G. Wellings Q.C., as a member
of that tribunal which he gave in writing on February 8, 1977, and arose   D
out of a reference to it of a dispute between the claimants, Wood Mitchell
& Co. Ltd. (the respondents in this court), and the acquiring authority, the
Stoke-on-Trent City Council (the appellants in this court), concerning
the quantum of compensation payable by the acquiring authority to the
claimants in respect of the compulsory acquisition by the acquiring authority of certain property belonging to the claimants at Stoke-on-Trent.

The facts which gave rise to the dispute are stated with admirable   E
clarity by the member in his decision, and we gratefully borrow that
statement verbatim:

" By an agreement in writing dated March 13, 1969, the claimants
agreed to sell and the acquiring authority agreed to buy the above
mentioned land and premises at the price of £6,000. In the same
agreement the acquiring authority agreed to sell and the claimants   F
to buy back part of the land and premises acquired by the acquiring
authority and at the price of £3,000. All the land retained by the
acquiring authority after March 13, 1969, was in its possession by
November 1968. The transaction provided for in the agreement
dated March 13, 1969, was completed on July 21, 1970, when conveyances putting the agreement into effect were executed. The   G
purpose of the claimants buying that part of the land and premises
was to enable them to re-establish their offices and warehouse.
Their claim to compensation under rule (6) [of section 5 of the Land
Compensation Act 1961] relates to the temporary losses which they
suffered in the years 1969 to 1971 whilst their offices and warehouse
were being re-established. In the agreement dated March 13, 1969,   H
it was acknowledged by the acquiring authority that the property
acquired by it under the agreement did not take into account any
compensation for disturbance consequent upon the making of the
compulsory purchase order; it was thus agreed that the acquiring
authority should pay to the claimants such sum as might be agreed
in respect of compensation for disturbance, together with any interest
properly payable thereon and in default of agreement such sum as

A   might be fixed in respect thereof by the Lands Tribunal. This reference is therefore to be regarded as a reference by consent. No evidence was called at the hearing because all the facts had been agreed. Indeed the parties were in agreement as to the gross amount of compensation under rule (6) to which the claimants are entitled. It was agreed that that gross amount is £12,633·77. It was further agreed that of that sum items totalling £405·50 are of a capital

B   nature, leaving a balance of £12,228·27. The only question which the tribunal is asked to resolve is whether, and if so, to what extent that balance should be adjusted to take account of corporation tax."

Thus the member had to determine whether the claimants should receive £12,228·27 in addition to the £6,000 and the £405.50 or only some lesser sum arrived at in accordance with the decision of the House of Lords in

C   *West Suffolk County Council* v. *W. Rought Ltd.* [1957] A.C. 403, applying the principles previously laid down by the House in *British Transport Commission* v. *Gourley* [1956] A.C. 185, to payments of compensation under the Acquisition of Land (Assessment of Compensation) Act 1919, the statutory precursor of the Land Compensation Act 1961, under which the claimants' present entitlement to compensation

D   arises. It is not, and indeed could not be, suggested that there was any relevant difference between section 5, rules (2) and (6) of the latter statute and section 2, rules (2) and (6) of the former statute. The argument for the acquiring authority which the member rejected and which was repeated in this court with conspicuous ability by Mr. Bramwell ran:

E   1. Ever since the decisions of the House of Lords in *Inland Revenue Commissioners* v. *Glasgow and South Western Railway Co.* (1887) 12 App.Cas. 315 and of this court in *Horn* v. *Sunderland Corporation* [1941] 2 K.B. 26, it has been the relevant law that compensation for disturbance in connection with the compulsory acquisition of land is to be treated as part of the price payable for the land compulsorily taken: see especially the judgment of Scott L.J. in the latter case, at pp. 43–45.

F   2. Even though that compensation for disturbance might reflect loss of profits which, had they been earned in the ordinary course of business in the absence of that disturbance caused by the compulsory acquisition, would have been chargeable to income tax, nonetheless that compensation being part of the price payable for the compulsory acquisition is not liable to such tax in the hands of the recipient.

G   3. In *West Suffolk County Council* v. *W. Rought Ltd.* [1957] A.C. 403 the Inland Revenue wrote a letter—see p. 407 of the report—stating that they did not regard such compensation as liable to taxation for income tax purposes. Though the Inland Revenue were not parties to that dispute, Lord Morton of Henryton, who delivered the leading speech in the House of Lords, said, at p. 412:

H   "My Lords, the question whether any sum awarded to the respondents under heading 3B is or is not liable to income tax is not before the House, but I see no reason to doubt that the view of the Board of Inland Revenue as expressed in the letter of February 16, 1954, was correct, and I have formed the opinion which I am about to express upon the footing that this is so."

The House accordingly held unanimously that the Lands Tribunal ought to have estimated to the best of their ability the amount of additional

taxation which the claimants in that case would have had to bear if they   A
had actually earned during the period in question the sum awarded to them
as compensation for disturbance and then should have reduced the
award by that amount: see the speech of Lord Morton of Henryton at
p. 413.

4. That principle still applied today to reduce the figure of £12,228·27 by
a sum equal to the amount of corporation income tax calculated at the
rate of 42·5 per cent. which the claimants would have had to pay on   B
that sum had that sum been earned by them as profits during the period
in question. It is convenient to interpose at this point that, for ease of
reference in this judgment, we shall use the phrases " corporation income
tax " and " corporation capital gains tax " in the same sense as did the
member in his decision.

5. This would result in the figure payable for compensation being reduced   C
to £7,031·26.

6. The position established by *West Suffolk County Council* v. *W. Rought
Ltd.* remained unaffected by the introduction in 1965 of capital gains tax
and by the introduction in 1970 of corporation tax. There was still no
liability on the part of the claimants to pay corporation income tax on
this sum, and so far as corporation capital gains tax was concerned paragraph 11 of Schedule 19 to the Finance Act 1969 exempted this sum from   D
liability to corporation capital gains tax in the hands of the claimants.
It was for this reason that the claimants' alternative argument that if
they were liable to suffer any corporation capital gains tax on this sum
at the rate of 30 per cent. then the figure of £7,031·26 should be grossed
up by a multiplier of $^{10}/_7$ to produce a figure of £10,044·65, was erroneous,
since there was no liability for corporation capital gains tax and there-   E
fore no need to introduce such compensatory grossing up.

The claimants contended (perhaps unusually for a taxpayer) that they
were liable for either or both corporation income tax or corporation
capital gains tax on this sum, and that accordingly the principle laid down
in *West Suffolk County Council* v. *W. Rought Ltd.* was no longer
applicable to payments for compensation for disturbance. The position
in relation to liability to tax upon compensation of this kind was now   F
akin to the position established by this court in *London and Thames
Haven Oil Wharves Ltd.* v. *Attwooll* [1967] 1 Ch. 772, where it was held
that so much of the damages received by jetty owners as related to loss
of earnings of, as distinct from compensation for physical damage to, a
jetty was a taxable revenue receipt: see the judgment of Diplock L.J. at
pp. 815 and 816.
                                                                              G
Though in our view in the ultimate analysis our decision turns upon
the true construction of paragraph 11 of Schedule 19 to the Finance Act
1969, it is necessary to examine certain other legislative provisions dealing
with the imposition first of capital gains tax, and then of corporation tax
in order that the somewhat obscurely worded paragraph may be interpreted in its proper setting.

But before we do so, we think it necessary to draw attention to one   H
important distinction between *West Suffolk County Council* v. *W. Rought
Ltd.* [1957] A.C. 403 and the present. In the *West Suffolk County
Council* case, as already pointed out, the Inland Revenue had made plain
that in their view no income tax was chargeable on the compensation in
question, and the House of Lords proceeded upon the assumption that
that view was correct. In the present case the Inland Revenue have
written no such letter nor given any such assurance. On the contrary, an

A exchange of letters between the claimants and one department of the
Inland Revenue suggested that the Inland Revenue would, or at least
might, seek to contend that corporation capital gains tax was payable.
The acquiring authority's counsel read a letter from the solicitor to the
Board of Inland Revenue written to their solicitors after the decision
of the member, declining to take any part in these proceedings, though
B invited to consider doing so. At one point we considered inviting the
Inland Revenue to instruct counsel to appear before us as amicus curiae
in order to give us the benefit of the board's views on the issue we have
to decide, since we were reluctant to give our decision without it. But
having read that letter, we appreciate his reasons for not wishing to take
part in a dispute with which his department is not directly concerned,
and we therefore did not further press the initial suggestion.

C   We regard the position of the Inland Revenue in this case as of
importance. If hereafter an attempt is made by the Inland Revenue to
levy tax in one form or another upon that sum in the hands of the
claimants and that attempt ultimately succeeded, after we in this court
had held, reversing the Lands Tribunal, that some lesser sum were payable by the acquiring authority because of the application of the West
Suffolk County Council case, a grave injustice would have been done
D to the claimants. They would have received a lesser amount from the
acquiring authority on the basis that that which they received would not
be taxable in their hands, and yet they would or might thereafter have to
pay tax at the instance of the Inland Revenue on that lesser amount.
     Since the purpose of decisions such as those in British Transport
Commission v. Gourley [1956] A.C. 185 and West Suffolk County Council
E v. W. Rought Ltd. [1957] A.C. 403 was to secure that a successful
plaintiff or claimant did not get more by way of damages or compensation than would have been received by him in the absence of his injuries
or of the compulsory acquisition in question, as the case might be, it seems
somewhat strange that the principle underlying those decisions should be
able to be invoked by the acquiring authority in order to produce the
result that the claimants, in the absence of any assurance from the
F Inland Revenue that no attempt would be made to levy tax upon this
sum, stood in peril of receiving considerably less than that which they
would have received had their capacity to earn continued unaffected by
compulsory acquisition. In such circumstances the more natural course,
which would avoid any risk of injustice, would be for the claimants to
receive the full sum, leaving the question of liability to tax, if any, to be
G adjusted thereafter between the claimants and the Inland Revenue.
     We take the view that the principles laid down in West Suffolk County
Council v. W. Rought Ltd. can only be applied if after examination of
the relevant statutory provisions it is clear beyond peradventure that the
sum in question would not be taxable in the hands of the claimants. If
that is clear, then it would be wrong to require the acquiring authority
to compensate the claimants beyond the amount of the loss which the
H claimants would in truth suffer. But if it is not, then it seems to us
unjust that in a doubtful situation the acquiring authority can get the
benefit of a reduced payment while leaving the claimants exposed to the
risks we have mentioned. Considerations of abstract justice might be
thought to suggest that the claimants should receive the full sum and
then in due course account to the Inland Revenue for any tax properly
chargeable upon that amount.
     It is against that background that we turn to consider the relevant

statutory provisions. We think it preferable to deal with these in chrono- A
logical rather than perhaps strictly logical order. We start with the
relevant provisions of the Finance Act 1965. We turn first to Part III
which bears the main rubric " Capital gains " and section 19 bears the
title " General." Subsection (1) provides:

> " Tax shall be charged in accordance with this Act in respect of
> capital gains, that is to say chargeable gains computed in accordance B
> with this Act and accruing to a person on the disposal of assets."

Section 22 provides:

> " (1) All forms of property shall be assets for the purposes of this Part
> of this Act, whether situated in the United Kingdom or not, including
> . . . (c) any form of property created by the person disposing of it,
> or otherwise coming to be owned without being acquired. . . . (3) C
> Subject to subsection (6) of this section, and to the exceptions in
> this Part of this Act, there is for the purposes of this Part of this
> Act a disposal of assets by their owner where any capital sum is
> derived from assets notwithstanding that no asset is acquired by the
> person paying the capital sum, and this subsection applies in parti-
> cular to—(a) capital sums received by way of compensation for
> any kind of damage or injury to assets or for the loss, destruction or D
> dissipation of assets, or for any depreciation or risk of depreciation
> of an asset, . . . (9) The amount of the gains accruing on the disposal
> of assets shall be computed in accordance with Part I of Schedule 6
> to this Act, and subject to the further provisions in Schedules 7 and
> 8 to this Act, and in this section ' capital sum ' means any money or
> money's worth which is not excluded from the consideration taken E
> into account in the computation under the said Part I of Schedule
> 6 to this Act."

We turn next to Schedule 6. Paragraph 1 of Part I of this Schedule
provides:

> " The provisions of this Schedule shall have effect for computing
> for the purposes of this Part of this Act the amount of a gain accru- F
> ing on the disposal of an asset."

Paragraph 2 (1) provides:

> " There shall be excluded from the consideration for a disposal
> of assets taken into account in the computation under this Schedule
> of the gain accruing on that disposal any money or money's worth
> charged to income tax as income of . . . the person making the G
> disposal for the purposes of the Income Tax Acts."

Paragraph 21 (4) provides:

> " For the purposes of any computation under this Schedule any
> necessary apportionments shall be made of any consideration or of
> any expenditure and the method of apportionment adopted shall,
> subject to the express provisions of this Schedule, be such method as H
> appears to the inspector or on appeal the commissioners concerned
> to be just and reasonable."

Next the Finance Act 1969: section 42 of that Act provides:

> " Schedule 19 to this Act (which makes further provision for amend-
> ing the enactments relating to long-term and short-term capital
> gains) shall have effect."

A   We turn next to paragraph 11 (1) of Schedule 19 which is the all-important provision for the purposes of the present appeal:

     "Where land or an interest in or a right over land is acquired after April 29, 1969, and the acquisition is, or could have been, made under compulsory powers, then in considering whether, under paragraph 21 (4) of Schedule 6 to the Finance Act 1965, the purchase price or
B   compensation or other consideration for the acquisition should be apportioned and treated in part as a capital sum within section 22 (3) (*a*) of the said Act, whether as compensation for loss of good will or for disturbance or otherwise, or should be apportioned in any other way, the fact that the acquisition is or could have been made compulsorily, and any statutory provision treating the purchase price or other consideration as exclusively paid in respect of the land itself,
C   shall be disregarded."

    Finally, the Income and Corporation Tax Act 1970. We start with section 238 (1) which provides that corporation tax shall be charged upon the profits of companies. Subsection (4) of the same section defines " profits " as " income and chargeable gains." Section 250 provides that subject to certain exceptions the amount of any income of a corporation
D shall for the purpose of corporation tax be computed in accordance with income tax principles. Section 265 which opens Chapter II of Part XI of this statute with the rubric " Companies' capital gains " provides that the amount to be included in respect of chargeable gains in a company's total profits for any accounting period shall be the total amount of chargeable gains accruing to the company in the accounting period after
E deducting allowable losses. Subsection (2) provides, inter alia, that the total amount of such chargeable gains shall for the purposes of corporation tax be computed in accordance with the principles applying to capital gains tax.

    Thus corporation tax is comprised of the two elements, income tax and capital gains tax, the relevant statutory provisions applicable to the calculation of each being applied to the calculation of those two elements
F in corporation tax.

    We think that consideration of the present problem must start from the fact that the decided cases clearly show that compensation payable for compulsory acquisition, whatever its component parts, constitutes a single payment which at least before the Finance Acts 1965 and 1969 was not chargeable to income tax in the hands of the recipient. We
G understood Mr. Bramwell to accept that, but for paragraph 11 of Schedule 19 to the Act of 1969, the whole of that single payment would have been liable to capital gains tax under section 22 of the Finance Act 1965. His argument was that paragraph 11 was directed to permitting a breakdown of this single payment into its component parts and then to exempting that part which related to income from capital gains tax whilst leaving the existing freedom from liability to income tax unaffected. He
H contended that any other view involved that paragraph 11, appearing as it does in legislation dealing only with capital gains tax, would have to be construed as imposing a charge to income tax where such liability had not previously existed, a result which he contended was unsupported at least by the express language of that paragraph. That argument undoubtedly has force, but before it can be accepted, paragraph 11 must be subjected to closer analysis.

    The paragraph is clearly directed to the possibility of and the manner

Stoke-on-Trent City v. Wood Mitchell & Co. (C.A.)   [1980]

of apportionment for the purpose of capital gains tax legislation of " the   A
purchase price or compensation or other consideration for the acquisition " in accordance with paragraph 21 (4) of Schedule 6 to the Finance
Act 1965. The paragraph further clearly contemplates that that apportionment may result in part only of the compensation being treated as a
capital sum within section 22 (3) (a) of that Act (which, as already pointed
out, refers to capital sums received by way of compensation for any kind
of damage or injury to assets) " whether as compensation for loss of   B
goodwill or for disturbance or otherwise." It also provides that that
need not be the only manner of apportionment but contemplates that
apportionment may be made " in any other way." Then if and when
any such apportionment is made the fact of compulsory acquisition and
any statutory provision (a phrase which we think, as the member did, must
extend to cover any judicial interpretation of any statutory provision)   C
shall be disregarded. Paragraph 21 (4) of Schedule 6 to the Finance Act
1965—as already stated—provides that, subject to the provisions of that
Schedule, the method of apportionment shall be such as appears to the
inspector or on appeal to the commissioners concerned to be just and
reasonable.

Construing this paragraph against the background of the judicial
decisions we have mentioned, section 22 and in particular section 22 (3)   D
(a) of the Finance Act 1965, and the reference to the computation of
the amount of a gain accruing on the disposal of an asset in Schedule
6 to that Act, and in particular to paragraphs 1, 2 (1) and 21 (4) of that
Schedule, we think it is impossible to avoid the conclusion that this
legislation is directed, first, to imposing a liability for capital gains tax
on compensation for compulsory acquisition upon the footing that such   E
compensation is a capital sum received upon the disposal of an asset;
secondly, and notwithstanding the antecedent judicial decisions, to permitting a breakdown of that compensation into its component parts so as
to enable what may be called the capital element and the income element
to be separated by apportionment in such manner as the inspector or on
appeal the commissioners may think just and reasonable; thirdly, to
exclude from the computation of the capital gain accruing from such   F
disposal any money charged to income tax as the income of the person
making the disposal; fourthly, to ensure that any such apportionment is
arrived at without regard to the antecedent judicial decisions that such
compensation is to be treated as exclusively, i.e. as a single indivisible
sum, paid in respect of the land itself, so as to abolish the distinction
which certainly since the decision in *London and Thames Haven Oil*   G
Wharves Ltd. v. *Attwooll* [1967] Ch. 772 and perhaps earlier would
seem to have existed—somewhat illogically—between compensation arising from the negligence of a tortfeasor which could be broken down into
its capital and income elements so that income tax was chargeable on the
latter but not on the former, and compensation for compulsory acquisition where seemingly before 1969 such breakdown was not permissible.
Then when corporation tax was introduced in 1970, the existing income   H
tax and capital gains tax codes including provisions of the Finance Acts
1965 and 1969 already discussed were applied in their entirety to bodies
corporate such as the claimants.

Like the member we have arrived at this conclusion as a matter of
the construction of the relevant legislation which in deference to Mr.
Bramwell's argument we have analysed at some length. But we might
have contented ourselves with expressing our complete agreement with

A the succinct single sentence in which the member expressed his conclusion
in the decision:

> " The effect of an apportionment to which paragraph 11 refers,
> though it be made for the purposes of a computation of a capital
> gain, is to free the compensation for loss of temporary profits of
> its capital nature and enable it to be treated for what it in truth is,
B namely, a trading receipt."

We would add that we were referred by counsel to a number of other
decisions. We do not refer to them for we do not think they in any way
help to solve this question of statutory construction. So far then from it
being clear, as it was in *West Suffolk County Council* v. *W. Rought Ltd.*
[1957] A.C. 403, that no part of the sum in question is liable to tax,
C we think the Inland Revenue are entitled to make an apportionment of
the compensation as a consequence of which, subject to any decision
of the commissioners on appeal, some part of the compensation being
compensation for disturbance may become liable in the hands of the
claimants to corporation income tax. The *West Suffolk* case is therefore
clearly distinguishable. We think it clear, therefore, that the acquiring
authority should pay the full sum to the claimants, leaving the claimants
D to account to the Inland Revenue for such sum, if any, as may subsequently be shown to be due from them to the Inland Revenue by way of
corporation income tax or maybe corporation capital gains tax. Our
conclusion makes it unnecessary to consider the alternative argument
about grossing up. The appeal fails and must be dismissed.

E   *Appeal dismissed with costs.*
                                           Leave to appeal refused.

Solicitors: *S. W. Tickener, Solicitor, Stoke-on-Trent City Council;
Breton, Deacon & Co., Longton, Stoke-on-Trent.*

[Reported by EVERARD CORBALLY, ESQ., Barrister-at-Law]

F

[CHANCERY DIVISION]

* *In re* A DEBTOR (No. 13 of 1964),

G   *Ex parte* THE OFFICIAL RECEIVER *v.* THE DEBTOR

1979 May 8, 9; 21   Fox and Browne-Wilkinson JJ.

*Bankruptcy—Discharge—Review of order—Suspended order of dis-
charge with conditions—Conditions continuing after period of
suspension—Whether " discharged "—Whether discharge to be
H deemed absolute from October 1, 1977—Insolvency Act 1976
(c. 60), s. 7 (4) (5)*

Section 7 of the Insolvency Act 1976, which came into
force on October 1, 1977, provides:

> " (4) Where a person has been adjudged bankrupt more
> than five years before the coming into force of this
> section and—(a) has not been discharged in respect of the
> adjudication under section 26 of the [Bankruptcy Act
> 1914] before the relevant date (that is to say, the coming

A
into force of this section or the tenth anniversary of the
date of the adjudication, whichever is the later); . . . the
same results shall ensue as if the court had on the relevant
date granted him an absolute order of discharge. . . .
(5) In subsections . . . (4) (a) above references to discharge
are references to discharge by an absolute order of discharge or by the expiration of the period, or satisfaction
of any requirement, specified by a suspended or conditional
order."

B
An order was made on May 16, 1968, that a debtor, who
had been adjudicated bankrupt in 1964, was to be granted a
discharge suspended for six months and that he be discharged
as from November 16, 1968, subject to conditions that payments totalling £20,000 be made out of after-acquired property.
In 1978, the official receiver applied to the county court for a
review of the order but the judge dismissed the application
on the ground that, by virtue of section 7 (4) of the Insolvency
Act 1976, the debtor had been absolutely discharged on
October 1, 1977.
On appeal by the official receiver:—
Held, allowing the appeal, that " conditional order " in
section 7 (5) of the Act was not to be construed as including
an order of discharge where the attached conditions were
subsequent to the discharge; that, accordingly, " discharge " in
section 7 did not have a restricted meaning and the principle
that a suspended order with attached conditions subsequent
became effective when the period of suspension had elapsed
applied to the section; and that, since the order of bankruptcy
was discharged on November 16, 1968, the debtor was not to
be treated by virtue of section 7 (4) as if he had been granted
an absolute discharge on October 1, 1977, and, therefore, the
case would be remitted to the county court for a review of the
order (post, pp. 266H—267B, 268D–E, 269E–F).
In re A Debtor (No. 946 of 1926) [1939] Ch. 489, C.A.
applied.

C

D

E

The following cases are referred to in the judgment:

Debtor (No. 946 of 1926), In re A [1939] Ch. 489; [1939] 1 All E.R.
735, C.A.
Tabrisky, In re, Ex parte Board of Trade [1947] Ch. 565; [1947] 2
All E.R. 182, C.A.

F

The following additional cases were cited in argument:

Green v. Premier Glynrhonwy Slate Co. [1928] 1 K.B. 561, C.A.
Mills (A Bankrupt), In re, Ex parte The Bankrupt v. The Official Receiver
[1967] 1 W.L.R. 580; [1966] 1 All E.R. 516.
Reed (A Debtor), In re [1979] 3 W.L.R. 345; [1979] 2 All E.R. 22, D.C.

G

APPEAL from Judge Paul Hughes sitting at the Nottingham County
Court in Bankruptcy.

On April 3, 1964, the debtor was adjudicated bankrupt on his own
petition. On May 16, 1968, on the debtor's application, an order was made
granting a discharge subject to six month's suspension and subject to a
condition that the debtor should pay to the official receiver and trustee for
distribution among the creditors the sum of £20,000 by instalments of not
less than £1,000 in each six months' period. The debtor made two payments in accordance with the order and then, with the permission of the
official receiver, made payments of £100 a month from January 1969
until December 1977. Thereafter he made no payments, having been
advised that the condition was no longer operative because of section 7 (4)

H

A of the Insolvency Act 1976. On November 20, 1978, the official receiver applied under section 108 (1) of the Bankruptcy Act 1914 to the Nottingham County Court for a review of the order of May 16, 1968, and on January 16, 1979, the application was dismissed by Judge Paul Hughes. By notice dated February 2, 1979, the official receiver appealed to the High Court, on the ground, inter alia, that the judge had misdirected himself in determining that section 7 (4) of the Insolvency Act 1976 applied to the debtor.

B
The facts are stated in the judgment.

Michael Crystal for the official receiver.
Stephen Lloyd for the debtor.

Cur. adv. vult.

C
May 21. BROWNE-WILKINSON J. read the following judgment. This is an appeal from Judge Paul Hughes, who dismissed an application by the official receiver under section 108 (1) of the Bankruptcy Act 1914 to review an order of discharge of the debtor dated May 16, 1968. The appeal raises a short but difficult point on section 7 (4) of the Insolvency Act 1976.

D
The relevant facts are that the debtor was adjudicated bankrupt on April 3, 1964. In 1968 the debtor applied for his discharge, which was granted by an order dated May 16, 1968. That order recites that certain facts of the kind specified in section 26 (3) of the Bankruptcy Act 1914, as amended, had been proved, and then continues:

"It is ordered that the bankrupt's discharge be granted but suspended
E   for six months and that he be discharged as from November 16, 1968, subject to the following conditions as to his after-acquired property estate and earnings which conditions shall operate concurrently with the aforesaid suspension and shall continue to operate, if necessary, after November 16, 1968, that is to say, the bankrupt shall pay to the official receiver and trustee for distribution among the creditors in the bankruptcy the sum of £20,000 by instalments of
F   not less than £1,000 in each six months period, the first instalment to be paid on or before June 1, 1968."

It is to be noted that the order both suspends the discharge for a specified time and also imposes conditions which are to continue after the date of discharge. After a short while the debtor was unable to continue payments at the rate of £1,000 every six months, but, without dissent by the official
G receiver, made payments of £100 per month. He has paid in all some £12,100. In 1978 the debtor desired to vary the conditions as to payment, saying that his circumstances had changed. He was then advised that by reason of section 7 (4) of the Act of 1976 he had been absolutely discharged and that the condition as to payments contained in the order of May 1968 was no longer operative. The official receiver did not share
H this view, and made an application for review of the 1968 order. The judge decided that the debtor had been absolutely discharged by section 7 (4) and, without going into the circumstances of the case, dismissed the official receiver's application.

Section 7 of the Insolvency Act 1976, which came into force on October 1, 1977, reads:

"(4) Where a person has been adjudged bankrupt more than five years before the coming into force of this section and—(a) has not

been discharged in respect of the adjudication under section 26 of the
said Act of 1914 before the relevant date (that is to say, the coming
into force of this section or the tenth anniversary of the date of the
adjudication, whichever is the later); and (b) the adjudication has not
been annulled before the relevant date under section 21 (2) or 29 of
that Act, the same results shall ensue as if the court had on the
relevant date granted him an absolute order of discharge under the
said section 26.   (5) In subsection (2) (a) and (4) (a) above references
to discharge are references to discharge by an absolute order of discharge or by the expiration of the period, or satisfaction of any
requirement, specified by a suspended or conditional order."

In the present case the debtor was adjudicated more than five years before
October 1, 1977.   Accordingly, if he was not discharged before October
1, 1977, he will be in the same position as if he had obtained an absolute
discharge on October 1, 1977, i.e. from that date onwards the conditions
for payment would cease to apply.   The only question is whether or not,
for the purposes of section 7 of the Act of 1976, the order dated May 16,
1968, is to be treated as having discharged the debtor on November
16, 1968 (i.e. the expiry of the time suspension) or whether he is to be
treated as having remained undischarged on October 1, 1977, the condition as to the payment of £20,000 not having been fully satisfied by
that date.
    I will first consider the position as it would have been apart from
the special definition in section 7 (5) of the Act of 1976.   Section 26 (1)
of the Bankruptcy Act 1914 (as amended) provides for a debtor to apply
for his discharge.   Subsection (2) then provides:

" On the hearing of the application the court shall take into consideration a report of the official receiver as to the bankrupt's conduct
and affairs (including a report as to the bankrupt's conduct during
the proceedings under his bankruptcy), and may either grant or
refuse an absolute order of discharge, or suspend the operation of the
order for a specified time, or grant an order of discharge subject to
any conditions with respect to any earnings or income which may
afterwards become due to the bankrupt, or with respect to his after-
acquired property: Provided that the court shall refuse the discharge
in all cases where the bankrupt has committed any misdemeanour
under this Act, or any enactment repealed by this Act, or
any other misdemeanour connected with his bankruptcy, or where
in any case any of the facts hereinafter mentioned are proved, the
court shall either (i) refuse the discharge; or (ii) suspend the discharge
for such period as the court thinks proper; or (iii) suspend the
discharge until a dividend of not less than ten shillings in the pound
has been paid to the creditors; or (iv) require the bankrupt as a
condition of his discharge to consent to judgment being entered against
him by the official receiver or trustee for any balance or part of any
balance of the debts provable under the bankruptcy which is not
satisfied at the date of the discharge . . ."

There is a second proviso to subsection (2), to which I need not refer.
Then subsection (3) sets out the facts which bring into operation the first
proviso to subsection (2).
    If one were to read subsection (2) without reference to authority, there
would be much to be said for the view that it only authorises the

A imposition of conditions as conditions precedent to the discharge, i.e. if the debtor does a particular act he will thereafter be discharged. But there is a longstanding practice (which the Court of Appeal has considered on at least two occasions) whereby, as in the present case, conditions subsequent are imposed, i.e. the debtor is discharged on condition that thereafter he does certain things. In my judgment it is established that, under the law applicable before 1976, an order such as that of May 16,

B 1968, discharges the debtor as from the date on which the order states that he is to be discharged even though the order imposes conditions to be observed thereafter: *In re A Debtor* [1939] Ch. 489. In that case the Court of Appeal had to consider the validity of a variation of an absolute order for discharge, the variation requiring the debtor to make annual payments. Sir Wilfrid Greene M.R. said, at p. 500:

C   " The bankrupt was discharged: his discharge is effective, and he remains discharged. He is no longer an undischarged bankrupt, and there is nothing in this order which puts him back into that condition. The order is entirely without prejudice to the discharge, and merely does what could admittedly, by a proper form of words, have been provided in the original order for discharge. It continues the

D   personal order against the bankrupt in such a way that it operates after his discharge and imposes upon him liability in respect of after-acquired property which would not vest in his trustee in bankruptcy. Therefore, in my opinion, the suggestion that this in some way interferes with the status of the bankrupt is entirely unjustified."

   See also *In re Tabrisky* [1947] Ch. 565, 567.

E   The question, therefore, is whether the special definition in section 7 (5) of the Insolvency Act 1976 requires the word " discharge " to be given a special meaning. Mr. Lloyd, who argued the case most persuasively for the debtor, urged that we should give effect to the obvious policy of the Act, which he said was to get rid of old bankruptcies and to ensure that the back-log of undischarged bankruptcies would never be repeated. He pointed out that for the future section 7 (1) to (3) provide machinery for

F an automatic discharge after five years if the court decides to invoke the machinery. In cases in which that machinery is not invoked section 8 ensures that there will be a review after five years. Then, he said, in dealing with the past the intention was to wipe the slate clean and give absolute discharges in all cases where no such discharge had been obtained before the section came into force. Against this background, Mr. Lloyd

G submitted that the three types of case referred to in section 7 (5) (i.e. an absolute order, an order suspended for a time, and a conditional order) correspond to the same three types of order referred to in section 26 (2) of the Bankruptcy Act 1914. Therefore, he said, if, as in the present case, there is an order which is conditional, section 7 (5) requires one to say that there has been no discharge until that condition has been satisfied. On this argument the words " conditional order " in section 7 (5) refer to

H orders containing conditions subsequent to discharge as well as conditions precedent. Finally, he says that where a conditional order has been made, for the purposes of section 7 (5) no discharge is to be treated as having occurred until the conditions are fully satisfied, even though the order itself states that the discharge was to take place at some other time.

   Mr. Crystal, who argued equally persuasively for the official receiver, has convinced me that Mr. Lloyd's arguments ought not to be accepted. Mr. Crystal submits, and I accept, that section 7 is designed only to get

rid of the status of bankruptcy as such. There is no good reason why the A
existing rights of creditors under existing conditional orders should be
prejudiced provided that the debtor is no longer labouring under the stigma
and disabilities of being an undischarged bankrupt. In my judgment
there is no general policy behind the Act of 1976 which requires one to
treat someone who had in fact been discharged before 1977 as not having
been discharged.

Section 7 (5) states that " references to discharge are references to dis- B
charge by " one of three methods. The definition by its clear words
requires one to find that one or other of those methods has produced a
discharge. Mr. Lloyd's submission really asks us to overlook this reference
to " a discharge by " certain means, and to read that subsection as
though it said (in relation to cases involving a conditional discharge)
" references to discharge mean the satisfaction of any requirement specified C
by a conditional order." In my judgment that is not legitimate. Subsection (5) requires one to find an effect (discharge) produced by specific
events: it does not say that the occurrence of those events is to be treated
as producing the effect. One has to ask of each order " by what means
was a discharge produced? Was it by an absolute order, or by the expiry
of a time suspension or by the satisfaction of a condition?" In each case
one has to look to see what produced the discharge, not to treat an event D
which did not in fact produce a discharge as though it did. If an order
has imposed only conditions subsequent, there can never be an occasion
when there has been a discharge by satisfaction of the requirements of that
condition: it is not the satisfaction of the condition that produces the
discharge but some other event. Therefore, in my judgment it is only
possible to read the references to conditional orders in subsection (5) as E
references to cases where the condition was imposed as a condition
precedent to the discharge.

Both sides sought to support their arguments by reference to anomalies
which the opposite view would produce. The official receiver pointed
out that, if the debtor's submission is correct, there would be a strange
distinction between those cases where, pursuant to the proviso to section
26 (2) of the Act of 1914, the court had required the debtor to submit F
to judgment before discharging him and cases such as the present. There
is nothing in section 7 of the Act of 1976 to get rid of such a judgment.
On the other side, Mr. Lloyd points out that the official receiver's construction leaves the good bankrupt (who has obtained his discharge subject
to conditions subsequent) under a continuing obligation, whereas the bad
bankrupt (who has not been able to get a discharge on any terms) gets G
away free of any obligations since he gets an absolute discharge on
October 1, 1977. This is true, but to my mind not decisive. The bad
bankrupt has laboured under his disability for 10 years at least: the
good bankrupt has enjoyed the period since his discharge free of any
disability at the price of submitting to the conditions.

Mr. Lloyd also points out that if there were an order which contained H
no time suspension, but gave an immediate discharge subject to conditions
subsequent, on the official receiver's construction the case would not fall
within subsection (5) at all. It would not be a discharge by an absolute
order, nor would there ever be a discharge by any other means mentioned
in subsection (5): therefore, it is said, in such a case the statutory absolute
discharge would operate. I will assume, without deciding, that this is so.
But in my judgment the anomaly would not be sufficient to justify a

A departure from the clear meaning of the words. We were told that, in practice, conditional orders are not normally made except in cases where the mandatory provisions of the first proviso to section 26 (2) apply, i.e. in cases where the discharge has to be suspended (either for a time or until a condition is satisfied) or the bankrupt has to submit to judgment. There-fore, the anomaly, if it exists, will not be one of common occurrence.

B There is one further point which appears to me to support the official receiver's argument, but as it was not argued should be treated with some reserve. The definition in section 7 (5) applies not only to subsection (4) but also to subsection (2). The scheme for automatic discharge in section 7 (1) to (3) is that at the conclusion of the debtor's examination the court can make an order that subsection (2) is to apply. If such an order is made, on the fifth anniversary of his adjudication the debtor is automati-C cally discharged if, but only if, before that date the debtor " is not discharged." It seems to me that if Mr. Lloyd's construction is correct, where the section 7 (2) machinery has been invoked it will be impossible for a court subsequently to grant a discharge subject to effective conditions such as those imposed in this case. Say that an order has been made under subsection (1), but four years after his adjudication a deserving debtor were to apply for his discharge and be prepared to agree to pay D annual sums to the official receiver for the benefit of his creditors. If the court were to impose such conditions, and Mr. Lloyd's construction is right, the debtor would receive an automatic absolute discharge at the expiry of five years after his adjudication free from the conditions imposed by the conditional discharge. In my judgment the legislature should not be taken to have intended such a result, the effect of which would be to E militate against deserving debtors getting an early discharge on terms beneficial both to them and to their creditors.

For these reasons, in my judgment the debtor in this case was dis-charged on the expiry of the suspension to November 16, 1968, provided for in the order of May 16, 1968. Therefore, he was not absolutely dis-charged on October 1, 1977, by virtue of section 7 (4) of the Insolvency Act 1976. Accordingly, the order of May 16, 1978, is still open to review F and the application should be remitted to the county court to consider on its merits.

Fox J. I agree.

Appeal allowed.
Application remitted to Nottingham
G *County Court.*

Solicitors: *Treasury Solicitor; Law & Co., Leicester.*

[Reported by Miss HILARY PEARSON, Barrister-at-Law]

H

A

[COURT OF APPEAL]

* PRACTICE DIRECTION (CRIME: SENTENCE: LOSS OF TIME)

1980 Feb. 14   Lord Widgery C.J., Roskill L.J. and
B
                                                                Caulfield J.

Crime—Sentence—Loss of time—Application on grounds settled by counsel and supported by opinion—Hopeless appeal—Jurisdiction to direct loss of time—Whether to be specially considered —Criminal Appeal Act 1968 (c. 19), ss. 29 (1), 31 (2) (h) [1]

LORD WIDGERY C.J., at the sitting of the court, gave the following   C
practice direction.

In 1970, Lord Parker C.J. found it necessary to issue a reminder of the power, both of the full court and of the single judge, when refusing an application for leave to appeal, to direct that part of the time, during which a person was in custody after lodging his application, should not count towards sentence: see *Practice Direction: Applications for Leave*   D
to Appeal (1970) 54 Cr.App.R 280.

The power was then being exercised only rarely at the single judge stage and the reminder was necessary, due to the serious delays caused to meritorious appeals by the huge number of hopeless appeals which had also to be considered. It led immediately to an improvement in the situation.

A similar reminder is necessary now. Again, meritorious appeals are   E
suffering serious and increasing delays, due to the lodging of huge numbers of hopeless appeals. Again, the power at the single judge stage is being rarely used.

In order to accelerate the hearing of those appeals in which there is some merit, single judges will, from April 15, 1980, give special consideration to the giving of a direction for loss of time, whenever an   F
application for leave to appeal is refused. It may be expected that such a direction will normally be made unless the grounds are not only settled and signed by counsel, but also supported by the written opinion of counsel. Advice on appeal is, of course, often available to prisoners under the legal aid scheme. Counsel should not settle grounds, or support them with written advice, unless he considers that the proposed appeal is properly arguable. It would, therefore, clearly not be appropriate to   G
penalise the appellant in such a case, even if the single judge considered that the appeal was quite hopeless.

It is also necessary to stress that, if an application is refused by the single judge as being wholly devoid of merit, the full court has power, in the event of renewal, both to order loss of time, if the single judge has not done so, and to increase the amount of time ordered to be lost if the   H
single judge has already made a direction, whether or not grounds have

---

[1] Criminal Appeal Act 1968, s. 29 (1): "The time during which an appellant is in custody pending the determination of his appeal shall, subject to any direction which the Court of Appeal may give to the contrary, be reckoned as part of the term of any sentence to which he is for the time being subject."
S. 31: "(1) The powers of the Court of Appeal . . . specified in subsection (2) below may be exercised by a single judge . . . (2) . . . (h) to give directions under section 29 (1) of this Act. . . ."

A been settled and signed by counsel. It may be expected that this power too will, as from April 15, 1980, normally be exercised.

Steps will be taken to see that the terms of this *Practice Direction,* which is made after consultation both with those Lords Justices who habitually preside in this court and with the judges, are brought to the attention of prisoners who contemplate lodging a notice of appeal.

B

L. N. W.

[COURT OF APPEAL]

C * CO-OPERATIVE RETAIL SERVICES LTD. *v.* SECRETARY OF STATE FOR THE ENVIRONMENT AND OTHERS

1979 Oct. 22

Stephenson and Brandon L.JJ.

D *Town Planning—Appeal to Secretary of State—Secretary of State's discretion—Order for public inquiry—Secretary of State's refusal to adjourn date fixed for public inquiry—Whether " decision . . . on an appeal "—Court's jurisdiction to consider application to quash order refusing adjournment—Town and Country Planning Act 1971 (c. 78), ss. 36, 242 (1) (e), (3) (b)*

A company applied to the local planning authority for planning permission to build a supermarket near to the appli-
E cants' existing supermarket. The planning authority did not determine that application within the prescribed period and the company appealed to the Secretary of State, under section 36 of the Town and Country Planning Act 1971, against the deemed refusal of planning permission. A public inquiry was arranged to be held on October 23, 1979. The applicants and the local planning authority applied to the Secretary of State to adjourn the inquiry to enable them to prepare their cases opposing the grant of planning permission. The Secretary of
F State refused their applications to adjourn the inquiry. By notice of motion, the applicants applied, under section 245 of the Act, for an order quashing the Secretary of State's refusals to grant an adjournment of the inquiry. The judge held that he had no jurisdiction to determine the matter by reason of section 242 (1) (e) of the Act [1] because none of the decisions to refuse an adjournment was a " decision of the Secretary of
G State on an appeal under section 36 " within the meaning of section 242 (3) (b) of the Act.

On the applicants' appeal:—

Held, dismissing the appeal, (1) that " any decision . . . on an appeal " in section 242 (3) (b) of the Act had to be a decision made in disposing of the appeal and at least one made in coming to the final decision; that the decision not to postpone the date of the public inquiry, although made in the course of
H the appeal and affecting its procedure, was not one that was made in disposing of the appeal and, accordingly, the judge had correctly held that he had no jurisdiction under section 242 to hear the application brought under section 245 of the Act (post, pp. 275A–C, 276H—277A).

Per Brandon L.J. It is arguable that the phrase " any decision of the Secretary of State on an appeal under section 36 " in section 242 (3) (b) is limited to decisions or orders or

[1] Town and Country Planning Act 1971, s. 242 (1) and (3): see post, p. 274F–H.

final results arrived at under section 36 (3) of the Act (post, A
p. 277c).

Chalgray Ltd. v. Secretary of State for the Environment
(1977) 33 P. & C.R. 10 doubted.

(2) That, alternatively, since the notice given of the date of
the public inquiry was adequate and the inspector holding the
inquiry had a complete discretion to order, if necessary, an
adjournment during the inquiry, the decision of the Secretary
of State did not cause any injustice to the applicants and, there- B
fore, his refusal to adjourn the hearing was not contrary to
natural justice (post, pp. 276A–B, D–F, H—277A).

Dictum of Lord Denning M.R. in Ostreicher v. Secretary of
State for the Environment [1978] 1 W.L.R. 810, 816, C.A.
applied.

Decision of Phillips J. affirmed.

The following cases are referred to in the judgments: C
Button v. Jenkins [1975] 3 All E.R. 585, D.C.
Chalgray Ltd. v. Secretary of State for the Environment (1977) 33 P. &
    C.R. 10.
Ostreicher v. Secretary of State for the Environment [1978] 1 W.L.R.
    810; [1978] 3 All E.R. 82, C.A.

The following additional case was cited in argument: D
Ellinas v. Secretary of State for the Environment [1977] J.P.L. 249.

APPEAL from Phillips J.

The third respondents, William Morrison Supermarkets Ltd., the
owners of supermarkets, applied for planning permission to the local
planning authority, Wakefield City Metropolitan District Council, the
second respondents, to demolish existing brickworks and construct a new E
supermarket and car park on the site of Westgate Brickworks, Dewsbury,
Wakefield. On failing to obtain planning permission, within the prescribed period, the third respondents appealed to the Secretary of State for
the Environment, the first respondent, and a public local inquiry was
arranged for October 23, 1979. By letters dated August 17, September 3,
and October 1 and 2, 1979, the applicants, Retail Services Co-operative
Ltd., who owned a nearby supermarket in Manor Road, Wakefield, 400 F
yards from the proposed site, wrote to the Secretary of State requesting an
adjournment of the inquiry on the basis that a longer period of time was
required to enable them to prepare their opposition to the appeal with
the aid of expert evidence. The applications to adjourn were supported
by the local planning authority. By letters dated August 31, September
7 and October 5, the Secretary of State informed the applicants that the G
inquiry would be held on October 23 as planned.

The applicants applied by motion for an order quashing or suspending
the Secretary of State's refusals to adjourn on the grounds that (1) the
decision was a breach of natural justice since it deprived the applicants of
an opportunity to prepare their case properly and to call expert witnesses
in answer to the third respondents' appeal; (2) the applicants and the
local planning authority would be prejudiced by the inadequate time for H
preparation and by the unavoidable absence of the chief planning officer
on October 23, so that justice would not be done or be seen to be done;
and (3) the Secretary of State misdirected himself in failing to take into
account the applicants' difficulties concerning their ability to present their
case.

The local planning authority supported the applicants' motion. The
Secretary of State applied for the motion to be struck out under R.S.C.,

The Weekly Law Reports, March 7, 1980

273

1 W.L.R.   Co-op. Retail Ltd. v. Environment Sec. (C.A.)

A Ord. 18, r. 19 and under the court's inherent jurisdiction on the ground that no reasonable cause of action had been disclosed and that the application was an abuse of the court's process.

The judge dismissed the applicants' motion on the ground that he had no jurisdiction to hear it since the Secretary of State's refusal was not a decision on an appeal under section 36 of the Town and Country Planning Act 1971, within the meaning of section 242 (3) (b) of the Act.

B The applicants appealed against that decision on the grounds that (1) the judge was wrong in holding that the words " any decision of the Secretary of State on an appeal under section 36 " in section 242 (3) (b) of the Act did not include a decision of the Secretary of State wrongly refusing to grant an adjournment of the inquiry; (2) the judge was wrong in holding that section 242 did not take away or limit the right to challenge

C certain categories of action by the Secretary of State; (3) the judge ought to have held that the words in section 242 (3) (b) did include such a decision; (4) the judge ought to have held that the Secretary of State's decision constituted a breach of natural justice in that its effect was to deprive the applicants and the local planning authority of an opportunity to prepare their case adequately and to call suitably prepared expert evidence in answer to the third respondents' appeal; and (5) the judge

D should have held that the Secretary of State had misdirected himself in failing to have regard to the applicants' difficulties in connection with their ability to present their case at the inquiry.

The facts are stated in the judgment of Stephenson L.J.

Patrick Ground for the applicants.

E *David Latham* for the Secretary of State for the Environment.
Duncan Ouseley for the third respondents.

STEPHENSON L.J. This is an important appeal and I regret that in view of the lateness of the hour and the urgency of the matter I must deal with it shortly and, therefore, run the risk of doing a considerable injustice to the careful submissions made by both counsel, particularly

F those made by Mr. Ground on behalf of the applicants.

What we have before us are orders of Phillips J. made at the end of last week, in effect refusing to interfere with a decision of the Secretary of State for the Environment refusing to grant an adjournment of a public inquiry fixed for tomorrow, October 23, 1979, at the suit of the applicants, the Co-operative Retail Services, and the City of Wakefield Metropolitan

G District Council, the planning authority for the area. The public inquiry is concerned with an appeal by the third respondents, William Morrison (Supermarkets) Ltd. against a decision refusing them planning permission to carry out some demolition work and erect a large supermarket, which is obviously going to have a considerable effect, if it is permitted, on the nearby premises of the applicants, Co-operative Retail Services Ltd., and it could have a considerable effect, one would have thought, on the

H planning of the whole area.

In the correspondence which we have seen, namely, in the months of August and September 1979, the applicants, have been repeatedly attempting to get the Secretary of State to adjourn the hearing and holding of this public inquiry on the ground that they cannot be ready in time. I would not like to be thought insensitive to the difficulties of getting specialist counsel and specialist experts to support opposition to an appeal which, of course, may be unsuccessful even if unopposed, because the

applicants and the planning authority are not appellants, they are resisting   A
this appeal of the third respondents, William Morrison (Supermarkets)
Ltd.

The Secretary of State has, in letters which I shall not read, taken, if
I may say so, a hard line, not always choosing his words particularly well
and being perhaps rash enough to indicate an unbending policy which
might be thought not to take adequate account of the objections that
were being put: but I bear in mind the authority which Mr. Latham for   B
the Secretary of State has cited to us, *Ostreicher* v. *Secretary of State for
the Environment* [1978] 1 W.L.R. 810, and what in particular Lord
Denning M.R. has said, at p. 816:

> ". . . there is a distinction between an administrative inquiry and
> judicial proceedings before a court. An administrative inquiry has
> to be arranged long beforehand. There are many objectors to con-   C
> sider as well as the proponents of the plan. It is a serious matter to
> put all the arrangements aside on the application of one objector
> out of many. The proper way to deal with it, if called upon to do
> so, is to continue with the inquiry and hear all the representatives
> present: and then, if one objector is unavoidably absent, to hear his
> objections on a later day when he can be there. There is ample   D
> power in the rules for the inspector to allow adjournments as and
> when reasonably required."

That, of course, was said in reference to a very different case from this,
but nevertheless it states matters which have to be borne in mind in considering the second ground on which we are asked to allow this appeal by
the applicants.
                                                                          E
Phillips J. dismissed the motion before him on the ground that he
had no jurisdiction to hear it. He was sitting as a single judge of the
High Court to hear an appeal under section 245 of the Town and Country
Planning Act 1971 and by R.S.C., Ord. 94, r. 1 (1), a single judge is the
person to hear a matter of that kind.

What was said by Mr. Ground to the judge, and has been said to us,   F
is that what is being questioned is a decision of the Secretary of State on
an appeal under section 36 of the Town and Country Planning Act 1971
as provided by section 242 (3) (*b*). Section 36 of the Act deals with
appeals against planning decisions and sets out a number of matters.
Section 36 (6) states: " The decision of the Secretary of State on any
appeal under this section shall be final." That, like all the other subsections of the Act has to be read with section 242, which provides by   G
subsection (1):

> " Except as provided by the following provisions of this Part of this
> Act the validity of—. . . (*e*) any such action on the part of the
> Secretary of State as is mentioned in subsection (3) of this section,
> shall not be questioned in any legal proceedings whatsoever."

By section 242 (3) the action referred to in section 242 (1) (*e*) includes: H
" (*b*) any decision of the Secretary of State on an appeal under section
36 of this Act; . . ." The opening words of section 242 (1) let in the provision of section 245 for questioning the validity of, inter alia, such a
decision on an appeal: section 245 (3).

The judge was referred to sections 36, 242 and 245 of the Act and the
first question he had to decide was: " Are these decisions decisions of
the Secretary of State on a appeal under section 36? " The judge said,

The Weekly Law Reports, March 7, 1980

275

1 W.L.R.   Co-op. Retail Ltd. v. Environment Sec. (C.A.)   Stephenson L.J.

A in a note of his judgment which has been agreed but has not been submitted to the judge for approval because it had not been typed:

"It is a short but not necessarily easy question, namely, whether in
section 242 (3) (*b*) they constitute a decision of the Secretary of
State on an appeal. In my judgment, they do not."

B He was referred to *Chalgray Ltd.* v. *Secretary of State for the Environment* (1977) 33 P. & C.R. 10 which is a decision of Slynn J. and to
Button v. *Jenkins* [1975] 3 All E.R. 585 which was applied in that case;
but Phillips J. took the view that what was in contemplation when Parliament referred to a decision on an appeal, both in section 36 (6) and in
section 242 (3) (*b*), was a decision which disposes of an appeal, not a
decision in the course of an appeal but one dealing with its final outcome.
C Then Phillips J. considered that the present decision of the Secretary of
State,—and this cannot be doubted—was not a decision disposing of the
appeal: it was a decision letting the appeal go on but refusing to alter
the date on which the public inquiry was to be started; and so he came to
the conclusion that it was not for him under section 245, which empowered
him to deal with the matter, to grant the relief sought, but it was possible
to apply for judicial review to a Divisional Court.

D It is now conceded that he was right about that possibility and if this
were a decision on an appeal under section 36 there would also be that
possibility because by section 242 (4) it is provided:

"Nothing in this section shall affect the exercise of any jurisdiction
of any court in respect of any refusal or failure on the part of the
Secretary of State to take any such action as is mentioned in sub-
E section (3) of this section."

It seems to me that if the Secretary of State refuses to do his statutory
duty, or fails to do his statutory duty by making a decision which he
ought to make, he is then subject to the supervisory jurisdiction, the
jurisdiction of judicial review, of the Divisional Court.

For my part, after hearing the interesting arguments addressed to us,
F I am in complete agreement with the view of Phillips J. on this point. It
may be in a sense a procedural wrangle. It is a matter, as the judge said,
of some importance, but it seems to me that looking at sections 242 and
245, this decision of the Secretary of State is not a decision on an appeal
under section 36 of the Act. I think some support for the view which the
judge took is to be derived from section 246 of the Act which starts off
G in subsection (1) with these words: "Where the Secretary of State gives
a decision in proceedings on an appeal . . ." *Button* v. *Jenkins* [1975] 3
All E.R. 585 on which Mr. Ground relied, both here and before Phillips
J., was a decision on that section and on those words, and it may well be
that the decision in this case was a decision in proceedings on an appeal,
but it was not, in my view, a decision on appeal.

If there is anything in Slynn J.'s decision in *Chalgray Ltd.* v. *Secretary
H of State for the Environment,* 33 P. & C.R. 10 which indicates a different
view from that taken by Phillips J. or can be taken to define the words
used in a different way to that in which they are defined by Phillips J.,
I would not be disposed to follow it. I see no reason to suppose that the
decision by Slynn J. was wrong and have every reason to suppose that
Phillips J. was right in saying that he was not departing from the decision in the *Chalgray* case in reaching the decision which he did on the
main point. I would, however, like to add, that if I were wrong on this

The Weekly Law Reports, March 7, 1980

276

Stephenson L.J.   Co-op. Retail Ltd. v. Environment Sec. (C.A.)   [1980]

point, and Phillips J. was wrong on this point, we have listened to full A
argument on the question whether the Secretary of State's decision does
result in a breach of the rules of natural justice or, in other words, does
deny justice to the applicants or to the planning authority. In my view, it
does not. It is, of course, true that the inspector will know that the
Secretary of State has repeatedly refused to adjourn the date of this
inquiry, and he will not be able to put that out of his mind. Nevertheless,
he has, as indicated in the passage quoted from Lord Denning M.R.'s B
judgment in *Ostreicher* v. *Secretary of State for the Environment* [1978]
1 W.L.R. 810, 816, a complete discretion of his own under the rules to
adjourn if he thinks it is necessary in the interests of justice to
any objector or any party to do so. We were referred to the terms of
rule 10 (8) of the Town and Country Planning (Inquiries Procedure) Rules
1974 which gives him a wide and unfettered discretion from time to time C
to adjourn. One knows that adjournments are ordered by inspectors
handling public inquiries in order to enable further objections to be
taken or pursued.

I am not indicating in any way whether the inspector should yield to
the arguments addressed to us in the course of this appeal, if and when he
is asked to do what the Secretary of State refuses; but it is very apparent
that the Secretary of State by refusing to delay the start of this inquiry D
has in no way decided that the inquiry is to be continued and to proceed
to a determination by the inspector without adjournments if asked for.

The notice given was adequate. There are, no doubt, great administrative pressures in these cases and I have carefully considered the
possible injustice to the parties who complain that they have not been
given more time. If I thought that they would have no opportunity of E
pressing those objections but would be bound to do the best they could
without any possibility of a further adjournment being granted, I
might feel able to take the view that natural justice was being breached
by the hard line taken by the Secretary of State. But I am not satisfied
on the material we have that it would not be possible for all the parties
to put adequately before the inspector, at any rate before the end of the
inquiry, the objections which they wish to put before him, and I am F
by no means satisfied that if they were to try to persuade the inspector to
grant an adjournment, their attempts would necessarily be defeated.
There seems to be a real possibility that they may be successful in obtaining an adjournment, but that is a matter for the inspector and he has
the duty to consider any applications that may be made to him, and to
decide them independently of what the Secretary of State has already G
decided. There is a difference between a decision to postpone the start
of a widely advertised inquiry which may cause great inconvenience, and
a decision de die in diem to adjourn in order to enable particular points
or material to be put before the inspector as the inquiry goes on. For
those reasons I would dismiss the appeal.

BRANDON L.J. I agree that the appeal should be dismissed on the H
two grounds stated by Stephenson L.J. The first ground is that the
decision of the Secretary of State to refuse a postponement of the inquiry
was not a decision on an appeal under section 36 of the Town and Country
Planning Act 1971, within the meaning of section 242 (3) (b) of that Act.
There was, accordingly, no jurisdiction in the judge to deal with the application. The second ground which is alternative is that, if that is wrong,
then the decision to refuse postponement of the inquiry has not been

The Weekly Law Reports, March 14, 1980

277

1 W.L.R.   Co-op. Retail Ltd. v. Environment Sec. (C.A.)   Brandon L.J.

A shown on the evidence before us to have been contrary to justice. Therefore, the court has no power to interfere with that decision.

I should like to make some observations about *Chalgray Ltd.* v.
Secretary of State for the Environment, 33 P. & C.R. 10, which was
relied on by Mr. Ground for the applicants. In the headnote of that
case, the second part of the decision is stated in this way:

B   " . . . That the words in section 242 (3) (*b*) ' any decision of the Secretary of State on an appeal under section 36 of the Act ' were not
necessarily limited to the decision or orders or final result specified in
section 36 (3); and that the Secretary of State's declining to consider
the appeal was a decision on an appeal under section 36."

Even if that decision made by Slynn J. is correct, it does not assist the
C applicants on the facts of this case because there has not been any refusal
to consider the appeal. I am bound to say, however, that I have doubts
about the correctness of that decision on the law by Slynn J. It seems
to me very arguable that the expression " any decision of the Secretary
of State on an appeal under section 36," as used in section 242 (3) (*b*),
is limited to decisions or orders or final results arrived at under section
36 (3). I further think that, where there is a refusal to consider an appeal,
D the case might well come within section 242 (4) of the Act. It is not,
however, necessary to decide that question in this case. I only wish to
express my doubts about this because the case has been relied on and I
would not like it thought that I regard it as necessarily correct.

Appeal dismissed with costs.
Leave to appeal refused.

E

Solicitors: *Bower, Cotton & Bower for Bury & Walkers, Barnsley;*
Treasury Solicitor; Last Suddards & Co.

[Reported by Miss Henrietta Steinberg, Barrister-at-Law]

F

[HOUSE OF LORDS]

* WOODAR INVESTMENT
        DEVELOPMENT LTD. .   .   .   .   . Respondents
G   AND
WIMPEY CONSTRUCTION U.K. LTD.   .   .   . Appellants

1979 Nov. 19, 20, 21, 22;   Lord Wilberforce, Lord Salmon,
1980 Feb. 14   Lord Russell of Killowen
                                             Lord Keith of Kinkel and
                                                     Lord Scarman
H

Contract — Repudiation — Right to rescind reserved — Purported
   exercise—Held bad in law—Whether contract repudiated
Damages—Contract—Breach—Condition for payment to third party
   —Whether sum recoverable in action by party to contract

On February 21, 1973, the purchasers, W.C. Ltd. entered
into a contract to buy certain land from the vendors, W.I.D.
Ltd. The purchase price was £850,000 of which £150,000 was
to be paid on completion to T.T. Ltd. There was a prospect

of planning permission for development being granted. By a
special condition E (a) (iii) the purchasers reserved the right
to rescind

> " if prior to the date of completion . . . (iii) any authority
> having a statutory power of compulsory purchase shall
> have commenced to negotiate for the acquisition by agree-
> ment or shall have commenced the procedure required by
> law for the compulsory acquisition of the property or
> any part thereof."

On March 20, 1973, the purchasers sent the vendors a notice
purporting to rescind the contract under that provision on
the ground that the Secretary of State for the Environment
had commenced the procedure for compulsory acquisition of
part of the land.

At the date of the contract both parties knew that in 1970
the minister had given the then owner notice of a draft compulsory purchase order. On November 8, 1973, a compulsory
purchase order was made.

The vendors brought an action against the purchasers for
a declaration that the condition gave them no right to rescind.
By their defence the purchasers contended that on the true
construction of the condition the notice of rescision was
valid. In a second action the vendors claimed damages for
breach of contract by the purchasers in serving the notice
and delivering their defence.

Fox J. held that the purchasers were not entitled to invoke
the condition and by doing so had wrongfully repudiated the
contract and that they were accordingly liable for damages
including £150,000 for the use and benefit of T.T. Ltd. The
Court of Appeal affirmed his decision but varied the amount
of the damages.

On appeal by the vendors: —

Held, allowing the appeal (Lord Salmon and Lord Russell
of Killowen dissenting), that a party who took action relying
simply on the terms of the contract in question and not
manifesting by his conduct an ulterior intention to abandon
it was not to be treated as repudiating it; that the whole
circumstances must be looked at and, since it had been
assumed in those proceedings that both sides would abide by
the decision of the court, the evidence of the purchasers'
conduct was insufficient to support a case for repudiation
(post, pp. 280F–G, 282C–D, 283A, D–E, 296E, 297A–C, 298A–C,
299D–F).

Federal Commerce & Navigation Co. Ltd. v. *Molena Alpha
Inc.* [1979] A.C. 757, H.L.(E.) considered.

Per curiam. If vendors made a contract that a sum of
money was to be paid to a third party they could not, without
showing that they had themselves suffered loss or were agents
or trustees for the third party sue for damages for non payment
of that sum (post, pp. 284A–B, 291B–D, 293E, 297D–F, 300D–E).

Jackson v. *Horizon Holidays Ltd.* [1975] 1 W.L.R. 1468,
C.A. disapproved.

Decision of the Court of Appeal reversed.

The following cases are referred to in their Lordships' opinions:

Beswick v. *Beswick* [1968] A.C. 58; [1967] 3 W.L.R. 932; [1967] 2
   All E.R. 1197, H.L.(E.).
Bradley v. *H. Newsom, Sons & Co.* [1919] A.C. 16, H.L.(E.).
Federal Commerce & Navigation Co. Ltd. v. *Molena Alpha Inc.* [1978]
   Q.B. 927; [1978] 3 W.L.R. 309; [1978] 3 All E.R. 1066, C.A.; [1979]
   A.C. 757; [1978] 3 W.L.R. 991; [1979] 1 All E.R. 307, H.L.(E.).
Freeth v. *Burr* (1874) L.R. 9 C.P. 208, D.C.
Frost v. *Knight* (1872) L.R. 7 Ex. 111.
Heyman v. *Darwin's Ltd.* [1942] A.C. 356, H.L.(E.).

A   *Jackson* v. *Horizon Holidays Ltd.* [1975] 1 W.L.R. 1468; [1975] 3 All
          E.R. 92, C.A.
     Johnstone v. *Milling* (1886) 16 Q.B.D. 460, C.A.
     Lloyd's v. *Harper* (1880) 16 Ch.D. 290, C.A.
     Mersey Steel and Iron Co. Ltd. v. *Naylor, Benzon & Co.* (1884) 9
          App.Cas. 434, H.L.(E.).
     New Zealand Shipping Co. Ltd. v. *A. M. Satterthwaite & Co. Ltd.*
B   [1975] A.C. 154; [1974] 2 W.L.R. 865; [1974] 1 All E.R. 1015,
          P.C.
     Radford v. *De Froberville* [1977] 1 W.L.R. 1262; [1978] 1 All E.R. 33.
     Shaffer (James) Ltd. v. *Findlay Durham & Brodie* [1953] 1 W.L.R. 106,
          C.A.
     Smyth (Ross T.) and Co. Ltd. v. *T. D. Bailey, and Son and Co.* (1940)
          164 L.T. 102; [1940] 3 All E.R. 60, H.L.(E.).
     Spettabile Consorzio Veneziano di Armamento e Navigazione v. *North-*
C   *umberland Shipbuilding Co. Ltd.* (1919) 121 L.T. 628, C.A.
     Sweet & Maxwell Ltd. v. *Universal News Services Ltd.* [1964] 2 Q.B.
          699; [1964] 3 W.L.R. 356; [1964] 3 All E.R. 30, C.A.
     Tweddle v. *Atkinson* (1861) 1 B. & S. 393.

     The following additional cases were referred to in argument:

D   *Coulls* v. *Bagot's Executor and Trustee Co. Ltd.* (1967) 40 A.L.J.R. 471.
     General Billposting Co. Ltd. v. *Atkinson* [1909] A.C. 118, H.L.(E.).
     Viles v. *Viles* [1939] S.A.S.R. 164.
     West v. *Houghton* (1879) 4 C.P.D. 197.

     APPEAL from the Court of Appeal.
          This was an appeal by the defendants, Wimpey Construction U.K.
E   Ltd., formerly George Wimpey & Co. Ltd. (the appellants), by leave of
     the Court of Appeal, from an order of the Court of Appeal (Buckley,
     Lawton and Goff L.JJ.) made on October 26, 1978, varying an order
     made by Fox J. on December 21, 1976. By his order Fox J. awarded
     the plaintiffs, Woodar Investment Development Ltd. (the respondents),
     damages for breach of contract in the sum of £462,000 with interest, that
     sum being expressed by the order to include the sum of £150,000 for the
F   use and benefit of Transworld Trade Ltd. By its order the Court of
     Appeal (Buckley L.J. dissenting on the issue of liability) reduced those
     damages to the sum of £272,943 with interest, including therein the
     sum of £135,000 for the use and benefit of Transworld.
          The facts are stated in their Lordships' opinions.

G   *Jonathan Parker Q.C.* and *Stephen Acton* for the appellant company.
          A. Leolin Price Q.C. and *Nicholas Stewart* for the respondent
     company.

          Their Lordships took time for consideration.

H   February 14, 1980. LORD WILBERFORCE. My Lords, the appellants
     (" Wimpey ") are defendants in this action brought by the respondents
     (" Woodar ") upon a contract of sale dated February 21, 1973. This
     contract related to 14·41 acres of land of Cobham, Surrey, near to the site
     later occupied by the Esher by-pass. There was the prospect of planning
     permission being granted for development. The purchase price was
     £850,000 and there was a special condition (condition I) that upon
     completion the purchasers should pay £150,000 to a company called

Lord Wilberforce   **Woodar Ltd. v. Wimpey Ltd. (H.L.(E.))**   **[1980]**

Transworld Trade Ltd. Completion was fixed for the earliest of three A
dates namely (i) two months from the granting of outline planning
permission for the development of the property, (ii) February 21, 1980,
(iii) such date as the purchaser should specify by not less than 14 days'
notice in writing.

The contract contained a special condition E under which there was
reserved to the purchasers power to rescind the contract in either of
three events. The first related to failure to obtain outline planning B
permission, the second to failure to obtain an easement giving access
to the property, the third (E (a) (iii)) was in the following terms:

> ". . . if prior to the date of completion . . . (iii) Any authority
> having a statutory power of compulsory acquisition shall have com-
> menced to negotiate for the acquisition by agreement or shall have
> commenced the procedure required by law for the compulsory C
> acquisition of the property or any part thereof."

On March 20, 1974, the appellants sent to the respondents a notice
in writing purporting to rescind the contract under this provision. The
notice stated that the ground relied on was that the Secretary of State
for the Environment had commenced the procedure required by law
for the compulsory acquisition of 2·3 acres of the property. D

It was in fact known to both parties at the date of the contract that
certain steps had already been taken in relation to these 2·3 acres. In
1970 the Minister had given notice to the then owner of a draft compulsory purchase order, and this fact had been published in the local
press. Notice had been given of the appointment of an inspector to
hold a public inquiry, and this was held. A compulsory purchase order E
was made on November 8, 1973. On these facts, the respondents
contended that special condition E (a) (iii) could not be invoked by the
appellants because the relevant procedure for compulsory purchase had
started before the date of the contract, and so did not come within the
words "shall have commenced." This contention was upheld by Fox J.
at the trial and was not the subject of appeal, so that the appellants'
claim to invoke the condition has failed. F

This gives rise to the first issue in this appeal: whether, by invoking
special condition E (a) (iii), and in the circumstances, the appellants
are to be taken as having repudiated the contract. The respondents so
claim, and assert that they have accepted the repudiation and are entitled
to sue the appellants for damages.

My Lords, I have used the words "in the circumstances" to indicate, G
as I think both sides accept, that in considering whether there has been
a repudiation by one party, it is necessary to look at his conduct as
a whole. Does this indicate an intention to abandon and to refuse
performance of the contract? In the present case, without taking the
appellants' conduct generally into account, the respondents' contention,
that the appellants had repudiated, would be a difficult one. So far
from repudiating the contract, the appellants were relying on it and H
invoking one of its provisions, to which both parties had given their
consent. And unless the invocation of that provision were totally abusive,
or lacking in good faith, (neither of which is contended for), the fact
that it has proved to be wrong in law cannot turn it into a repudiation.
At the lowest, the notice of rescission was a neutral document consistent
either with an intention to preserve or with an intention to abandon
the contract, and I will deal with it on this basis—more favourable to

A the respondents. In order to decide which is correct the appellants' conduct has to be examined.

One point can, in my opinion, be disposed of at once. The respondents, in March 1974 started proceedings against the appellants: this is one of the actions consolidated in the litigation before us. They claimed a declaration that the appellants' notice of rescission was not valid, and
B the appellants, by their defence, asserted the contrary and they counterclaimed for a declaration to that effect. The respondents now contend that if the original notice did not amount to a repudiation, the defence and counterclaim did. I regard this contention as hopeless. The appellants' pleading carried the matter no further: it simply rested the matter on the contract. It showed no intention to abandon the contract whatever the result of the action might be. If the action were to
C succeed (i.e. if the appellants lost) there was no indication that the appellants would not abide by the result and implement the contract.

The facts indicative of the appellants' intention must now be summarised. It is clear in the first place that, subjectively, the appellants, in 1974, wanted to get out of the contract. Land prices had fallen, and they thought that if the contract were dissolved, they could probably
D acquire it at a much lower price. But subjective intention is not decisive: it supplied the motive for serving the notice of rescission: there remains the question whether, objectively regarded, their conduct showed an intention to abandon the contract.

In early 1974, there was a possibility that some planning permission might be granted. If it were, and unless the purchasers could take valid objection to it, completion would (under the conditions) have to follow
E in two months. Therefore, if a notice of rescission were to be given, it had to be served without delay, i.e. before the planning permission arrived. In this situation, the appellants' advisers arranged a meeting with a Mr. Cornwell, who was acting for the vendors, or as an intermediary with power to commit the vendors, to discuss the matter. This took place on March 7, 1974, and is recorded as a disclosed aide mémoire
F dated the next day. This document was prepared by the appellants, and we have not the benefit of Mr. Cornwell's evidence upon it: he had died before the trial. But the rest of the correspondence is fully in line with it and I see no reason to doubt its general accuracy. After recording each side's statement of position, the document contained (inter alia) these passages:

G   " He [Mr. Cornwell] stated that if we attempted to rescind the contract, then he would take us to court and let the judge decide whether the contract could be rescinded on the point we were making."

This " point " was undoubtedly that relating to the compulsory purchase of the 2·5 acres.

H   " I told him that our legal department would be serving the notice to rescind the contract within a short while—this would ensure that the company was fully protected and was prudent. He assured me that he would accept it on that basis and not regard it as a hostile act."

The notice was then served on March 20, 1974. On March 22 the respondents' solicitors wrote that they did not accept its validity. On

May 30, 1974, Mr. Cornwell wrote a long letter to Sir Godfrey Mitchell, A
president of Wimpey.   I refer to one passage:

> ". . . within a few days of the original meeting, a notice of rescission
> was served upon the vendor company by your organisation that the
> contract was to be rescinded.   Simultaneously with that notice or
> rescission, proceedings were instituted and there the matter remains
> so far as the legal situation is concerned and both parties, from the B
> legal point of view, must now await the decision of the court as to
> the validity of the claim made by Messrs. George Wimpey & Co.
> Ltd. that they are entitled to rescind this contract upon the grounds
> which they have so stated."

On June 4, 1974, Mr. Cornwell wrote again:

> ". . . all I need say now is that we will retire to our battle stations C
> and it goes without saying I am sure that you will abide by the
> result as I will."

My Lords, I cannot find anything which carries the matter one inch
beyond, on Wimpey's part, an expressed reliance on the contract (condition E (a) (iii)), on Woodar's side an intention to take the issue of the
validity of the notice (nothing else) to the courts, and an assumption, not D
disputed by Wimpey, that both sides would abide by the decision of the
court.   This is quite insufficient to support the case for repudiation.   There
is only one other matter relied on.   At the date of the contract (February
21, 1973) there were arrangements made for a loan of £165,000 to be
made to the respondents by the National Westminster Bank.   The
appellants guaranteed—subject to three months' notice of termination— E
the respondents' indebtedness to the bank up to £165,000 and agreed
with the bank to meet interest and other charges.   As between the
appellants and the respondents it was agreed that the appellants should
indemnify the respondents against all interest on the loan for seven
years or until the contract should be "fulfilled or discharged."   These
arrangements did not form part of the contract of sale but were collateral
to it. F

When the notice of rescission was served on March 20, 1974, it was
accompanied by a covering letter, of the same date, referring to the
loan arrangements.   It stated:

> "The undertaking was limited to seven years from the date of
> exchange or until the contract was fulfilled or discharged.   As the
> contract is now discharged by the enclosed notice, [Woodar] will G
> now be liable for the charges incurred in respect of this loan."

The appellants also gave three months' notice to the bank terminating
the guarantee.   Again, in my opinion, this carried the matter no further.
It simply drew the attention of Woodar to the consequences which
would follow from rescission of the contract, nothing more.   Woodar,
in fact understood it as such, for they wrote to the bank on April 8, H
1974, stating that proceedings had been instituted against Wimpey for
a declaration "which, if successful, will reinstate the arrangements which
you now give notice you intend to bring to an end."

My Lords, in my opinion, it follows, as a clear conclusion of fact,
that the appellants manifested no intention to abandon, or to refuse
future performance of or to repudiate the contract.   And the issue being
one of fact, citation of other decided cases on the other facts is hardly

A   necessary. I shall simply state that the proposition that a party who takes action relying simply on the terms of the contract, and not manifesting by his conduct an ulterior intention to abandon it, is not to be treated as repudiating it is supported by *James Shaffer Ltd.* v. *Findlay Durham & Brodie* [1953] 1 W.L.R. 106 and *Sweet & Maxwell Ltd.* v. *Universal News Services Ltd.* [1964] 2 Q.B. 699.

B   In contrast to these is the case in this House of *Federal Commerce & Navigation Co. Ltd.* v. *Molena Alpha Inc.* [1979] A.C. 757 which fell on the other side of the line. Of that I said at p. 780:

"The two cases relied on by the appellants (*James Shaffer Ltd.* v. *Findlay Durham & Brodie* [1953] 1 W.L.R. 106 and *Sweet & Maxwell Ltd.* v. *Universal News Services Ltd.* [1964] 2 Q.B. 699) . . . would only be relevant here if the owners' action had been confined to assert-

C   ing their own view—possibly erroneous—as to the effect of the contract. They went, in fact, far beyond this when they threatened a breach of the contract with serious consequences."

The case of *Spettabile Consorzio Veneziano di Armamento e Navigazione* v. *Northumberland Shipbuilding Co. Ltd.* (1919) 121 L.T. 628 though in some factual respects distinguishable from the present, is nevertheless, in

D   my opinion, clear support for the appellants.

In my opinion therefore the appellants are entitled to succeed on the repudiation issue, and I would only add that it would be a regrettable development of the law of contract to hold that a party who bona fide relies upon an express stipulation in a contract in order to rescind or terminate a contract should, by that fact alone, be treated as having

E   repudiated his contractual obligations if he turns out to be mistaken as to his rights. Repudiation is a drastic conclusion which should only be held to arise in clear cases of a refusal, in a matter going to the root of the contract, to perform contractual obligations. To uphold the respondents' contentions in this case would represent an undesirable extension of the doctrine.

The second issue in this appeal is one of damages. Both courts below

F   have allowed Woodar to recover substantial damages in respect of condition I under which £150,000 was payable by Wimpey to Transworld Trade Ltd. on completion. On the view which I take of the repudiation issue, this question does not require decision, but in view of the unsatisfactory state in which the law would be if the Court of Appeal's decision were to stand I must add three observations:

G   1. The majority of the Court of Appeal followed, in the case of Goff L.J. with expressed reluctance, its previous decision in *Jackson* v. *Horizon Holidays Ltd.* [1975] 1 W.L.R. 1468. I am not prepared to dissent from the actual decision in that case. It may be supported either as a broad decision on the measure of damages (per James L.J.) or possibly as an example of a type of contract—examples of which are persons contracting for family holidays, ordering meals in restaurants

H   for a party, hiring a taxi for a group—calling for special treatment. As I suggested in *New Zealand Shipping Co. Ltd.* v. *A. M. Satterthwaite & Co. Ltd.* [1975] A.C. 154, 167, there are many situations of daily life which do not fit neatly into conceptual analysis, but which require some flexibility in the law of contract. *Jackson's* case may well be one.

I cannot however agree with the basis on which Lord Denning M.R. put his decision in that case. The extract on which he relied from the judgment of Lush L.J. in *Lloyd's* v. *Harper* (1880) 16 Ch.D. 290, 321

was part of a passage in which the Lord Justice was stating as an
" established rule of law " that an agent (sc. an insurance broker) may
sue on a contract made by him on behalf of the principal (sc. the assured)
if the contract gives him such a right, and is no authority for the proposition
required in *Jackson's* case, still less for the proposition, required here,
that, if Woodar made a contract for a sum of money to be paid to Transworld, Woodar can, without showing that it has itself suffered loss or that
Woodar was agent or trustee for Transworld, sue for damages for non-
payment of that sum. That would certainly not be an established rule of
law, nor was it quoted as such authority by Lord Pearce in *Beswick* v.
Beswick [1968] A.C. 58.

2. Assuming that *Jackson's* case was correctly decided (as above), it
does not carry the present case, where the factual situation is quite
different. I respectfully think therefore that the Court of Appeal need
not, and should not have followed it.

3. Whether in a situation such as the present—viz. where it is not
shown that Woodar was agent or trustee for Transworld, or that Woodar
itself sustained any loss, Woodar can recover any damages at all, or any
but nominal damages, against Wimpey, and on what principle, is, in my
opinion, a question of great doubt and difficulty—no doubt open in this
House—but one on which I prefer to reserve my opinion.

I would allow the appeal.

LORD SALMON. My Lords, this case raises a point of law of considerable importance in relation to the repudiation of contracts.

Between July 1969 and February 1973 prolonged negotiations took
place between Mr. Ronald Cornwell and the appellants (Wimpey) for the
purchase by Wimpey of 14·41 acres of freehold land known as Mizen's
Nurseries at Cobham. In January 1973 Wimpey learnt from Mr. Cornwell
that the vendors were to be the respondents (Woodar). By February
1973 the purchase price had been agreed at £1m. In that month Mr.
Cornwell proposed that part of the purchase price should be paid to
him as European agent for the Transworld Trade Ltd. (Transworld),
and a few days later it was agreed that that part of the purchase price
should amount to £150,000 and be paid to Transworld direct.

It was also arranged that the contract should provide for a loan of
£165,000, secured by a charge on the land (the subject matter of the
contract) to be made to Woodar by Wimpey through their bank and
that Wimpey should be responsible for servicing the loan. Wimpey
were, however, advised that the loan should be treated separately from
the contract, otherwise the contract might be void as constituting a clog
on the equity of redemption under the charge. Accordingly, on February
21, 1973, Wimpey's bank lent Woodar £165,000 and Woodar executed a
legal charge on the land in respect of the loan. Wimpey gave a written
undertaking to the bank to meet all interest and other charges in respect
of the loan until February 21, 1980, " or until the contract should be
fulfilled or discharged." (The underlining is mine.) The facts which
I have related are all taken out of Wimpey's printed case.

The written contract for the purchase of the land by Wimpey from
Woodar was also executed on February 21, 1973. It specified the
purchase price as £850,000 and laid down at the end of the contract in
special condition I that upon the completion of the purchase of the whole
or any part of this land, Wimpey should pay Transworld £150,000.

A   I will now turn to the material clauses in the contract. Special conditions E (a) so far as relevant reads:

" This contract shall be absolutely binding on both parties . . . for a period of seven years from the date hereof but there shall be reserved to the purchaser only the power to rescind this contract if prior to the date of completion: . . . (iii) any authority having a statutory
B   power of compulsory acquisition shall have commenced to negotiate for the acquisition by agreement or shall have commenced the procedure required by law for the compulsory acquisition of the property or any part thereof."

This clause, quite obviously, refers only to any such negotiation or procedure commenced after the execution of the contract and prior to
C   completion but not to any negotiation or procedure which had commenced and of which both parties were well aware before they executed the contract.

Special condition E (c), so far as relevant, reads:

" The power to rescind reserved to the purchaser by subclause (a) . . . shall be exerciseable by the service of a notice in writing to
D   that effect upon the vendor . . . and the purchaser's liability under . . . this contract shall from the date of service of such notice cease."

Special condition E (g) provides that completion shall take place on the earliest of the three dates it mentions, namely, (i) two months after the date on which outline planning permission for the development of the property is granted; (ii) February 21, 1980, (iii) such date as the purchaser shall
E   specify but not by less than 14 days' written notice.

Returning to special condition E (a) (iii) of the contract, it is common ground that Wimpey and Woodar both knew, well before the contract between them was executed, (1) that in 1970 the Minister of Transport had given notice of a draft compulsory purchase order in respect of 2·3 acres of the 14·41 acres covered by the contract, (2) that this fact had been published in the local press, and (3) that notice had also been
F   given of the appointment of an inspector to hold a public inquiry which he had duly held.

Indeed, there is a provision in the contract under special condition G, which, so far as relevant, reads:

" It is hereby agreed that the vendor shall not require the purchaser to include in the transfer to the purchaser any part . . . of the land
G   hereby agreed to be sold which shall be required by the Surrey County Council . . . or any statutory authority . . . and the purchase price shall be abated at the rate of £70,000 per acre . . . for any part . . . of the land hereby agreed to be sold which shall not be included in the transfer to the purchaser."

H   It is to be observed that if the land is priced in the contract at £70,000 an acre, the 14·41 acres sold under the contract would, in fact, be priced at about £1m.

By March of 1974 there had been a very alarming slump in the value of land. It is quite clear from one of Wimpey's internal memoranda, written at the beginning of that month, that Wimpey had no intention of honouring their contract by paying the agreed price of £70,000 an acre for the land: that they intended to repudiate the contract but would gladly enter into a new contract with Woodar to buy the land at £48,000 A an acre, on otherwise the same terms as those of the existing contract. The relevant part of the memorandum reads as follows:

"Revised broadsheets have been prepared taking account of the reduced selling price of houses and increased building costs and these indicate that currently to show 20% profit we can offer £48,000 per acre, to show 15% profit £53,000 per acre. The indi- B cations are that this piece of land could obtain outline planning permission within the next four months, in which case we as a company would be obliged to perform in accordance with the obligations of our contract to purchase subject to the various conditions. We propose arranging a meeting with Mr. Cornwell to discuss formally with him: (a) Our intention to rescind the contract so that he is obliged to pay the interest on the loan thereafter from that date. C (b) To make him a proposal that we are prepared to proceed with the purchase of the land at the reduced figure of £48,000 per developable acre subject, of course, to the same terms and conditions."

On March 20, 1974, a notice was sent to Woodar by Wimpey in the following terms:

D
"Pursuant to clause E (c) of a contract dated February 21, 1973, and made between Woodar Investment Development Ltd. of the one part and George Wimpey & Co. Ltd. of the other part the said George Wimpey & Co. Ltd. hereby rescinds the said contract on the ground that within the meaning of clause E (a) (iii) of the said contract the Secretary of State for the Environment has commenced the procedure required by law for the compulsory acquisition E of part of the property (a compulsory purchase order relating to the land edged red on the plan annexed hereto having been made)."

I am afraid that I am entirely unable to agree with the proposition that this notice of rescission was a neutral averment consistent either with the intention to preserve or with an intention to abandon the contract. To my mind it was served with the clearly expressed intention F of bringing the contract to an end. This notice was accompanied by a letter of the same date, the last paragraph of which reads as follows:

"When contracts for the sale and purchase of the above land were exchanged, an undertaking was given by the company indemnifying Woodar Investment Development Ltd. against all interest charges payable to the National Westminster Bank Ltd. as a result of a G loan by them to you of a sum of £165,000. The undertaking was limited to seven years from the date of exchange or until the contract was fulfilled or discharged. As the contract is now discharged by the enclosed notice, Woodar Investment Development Ltd. will now be liable for the charges incurred in respect of this loan." (The underlining is mine.)

H
My Lords, it was conceded in this House on behalf of Wimpey that they had no right to rescind, discharge or repudiate the contract. In my respectful opinion, Wimpey had made it crystal clear by their notice and letter of March 20 that they purported to bring their liability under the contract to an end by rescinding and discharging it; and that they had no intention of paying the contract price for the land in question. If this does not go to the root of the contract and evince an unequivocal

A intention no longer to be bound by it, and therefore amounts to a repudiation of the contract, I confess that I cannot imagine what would.

In the court of first instance, Wimpey sought to justify their notice and letter of March 20, 1974, on the ground that prior to the execution of the contract of February 21, 1973, steps had been taken for the compulsory acquisition of 2·3 acres out of the 14·41 acres the subject matter of the contract. I have already described these steps and I

B shall not repeat them. It is common ground that all these steps were well known both to Wimpey and to Woodar at the time they were taken. The point was nevertheless argued on behalf of Wimpey before the trial judge that because of these steps having been taken when they were, Wimpey were entitled under special condition E (a) (iii) of the contract to rescind the contract and refuse to perform it. The learned trial

C judge made short work of that point and decided that it was untenable. The point was so obviously bad that it was wisely decided by counsel on behalf of Wimpey not to be worth taking in the Court of Appeal. It was however accepted by Woodar that on March 20, 1974, Wimpey honestly believed in the point which they later abandoned. I do not understand how Wimpey's honest belief in a bad point of law can in any way avail them. In *Federal Commerce & Navigation Co. Ltd.* v.

D *Molena Alpha Inc.* [1978] Q.B. 927, 979, Lord Denning M.R. said:

" I have yet to learn that a party who breaks a contract can excuse himself by saying that he did it on the advice of his lawyers: or that he was under an honest misapprehension. Nor can he excuse himself on those grounds from the consequences of a repudiation."

E I gratefully adopt that passage which seems to me to be particularly apt in the present case. It certainly was never questioned in your Lordships' House when the appeal from the decision of the Court of Appeal in the *Federal Commerce* case [1979] A.C. 757 was dismissed.

In *Freeth* v. *Burr* (1874) L.R. 9 C.P. 208, 213 Lord Coleridge C.J. said:

F " . . . where the question is whether the one party is set free by the action of the other, the real matter for consideration is whether the acts or conduct of the one do or do not amount to an intimation of an intention to abandon and altogether to refuse performance of the contract."

In *Mersey Steel and Iron Co. Ltd.* v. *Naylor, Benzon & Co.* (1884)

G 9 App.Cas 434 Lord Selborne L.C., after approving of what Lord Coleridge said in *Freeth* v. *Burr* went on to say, at p. 439 :

" . . . you must examine what that conduct is, so as to see whether it amounts to a renunciation, to an absolute refusal to perform the contract, such as would amount to a rescission if he had the power to rescind, and whether the other party may accept it as a reason for not performing his part; "

H In the *Spettabile* case, 121 L.T. 628, 634–635 Atkin L.J. said:

" A repudiation has been defined in different terms—by Lord Selborne as an absolute refusal to perform a contract; by Lord Esher as a total refusal to perform it; by Bowen L.J. in *Johnston* v. *Milling* (1886) 16 Q.B.D. 460 as a declaration of an intention not to carry out a contract when the time arrives, and by Lord Haldane in *Bradley* v. *H. Newsom Sons & Co.* [1919] A.C. 16 as an inten-

tion to treat the obligation as altogether at an end. They all come A
to the same thing, and they all amount at any rate to this, that it
must be shown that the party to the contract made quite plain his
own intention not to perform the contract."

In *Heyman* v. *Darwins Ltd.* [1942] A.C. 356, 378–379, Lord Wright
said:

> "There is, however, a form of repudiation where the party who B
> repudiates does not deny that a contract was intended between the
> parties, but claims that it is not binding because of the failure of
> some condition or the infringement of some duty fundamental to
> the enforceability of the contract, it being expressly provided by
> the contract that the failure of condition or the breach of duty
> should invalidate the contract . . . But perhaps the commonest
> application of the word 'repudiation' is to what is often called C
> the anticipatory breach of a contract where the party by words or
> conduct evinces an intention no longer to be bound and the other
> party accepts the repudiation and rescinds the contract. In such a
> case, if the repudiation is wrongful and the rescission is rightful, the
> contract is ended by the rescission but only as far as concerns
> future performance. It remains alive for the awarding of damages D
> . . . for the breach which constitutes the repudiation."

In my opinion, the repudiation in the present case exactly fits the
repudiation which Lord Wright explains in the passages which I have
just cited.

I do not recall that any of these definitions of a repudiation of a
contract have ever until now, been questioned. The fact that a party E
to a contract mistakenly believes that he has the right to refuse to
perform it cannot avail him. Nor is there any authority for the proposition that if a party to a contract totally refuses to perform it, this refusal
is any the less a repudiation of the contract because he honestly but
mistakenly believes that he is entitled by a condition of the contract
to refuse to perform it.

It would indeed be unfortunate if the law were otherwise. A mistake F
in the construction of a contractual condition, even such a glaringly
obvious mistake as the present can apparently easily be made especially
perhaps when the market price has fallen far below the contract price.
It is acknowledged in this case that the mistake was an honest one. If,
however, a case arose in which a mistake of this kind was alleged to be an
honest mistake, but not acknowledged to be so, it would be extremely G
difficult, if not impossible to prove the contrary.

James Shaffer Ltd. v. *Findlay Durham & Brodie* [1953] 1 W.L.R.
106 and *Sweet & Maxwell Ltd.* v. *Universal News Services Ltd.* [1964]
2 Q.B. 699 were strongly relied upon on behalf of Wimpey. Those two
cases were very different from each other and even more different from
the present case; in my opinion they certainly lend no more support to
Wimpey than they did to the appellants in the *Federal Commerce* case H
[1979] A.C. 757. Indeed, if anything, they are of some help to Woodar.
In the former case, Singleton L.J. said at p. 121: ". . . is it possible
to say that the defendants . . . showed an intention to abandon and
altogether to refuse the performance of the contract? . . . I think not."
Morris L.J. said at p. 124: "I have no doubt that [the defendants]
wanted to go on with the contract." In the latter case [1964] 2 Q.B.
699, 729 Harman L.J. said:

A   " . . . repudiation really is not in the picture here at all, because if the defendants were not wholly justified in the attitude they took up, [on the construction of the agreement] the plaintiffs were not wholly justified in their attitude either, and they could only treat the defendants' refusal to comply with their demands as repudiation if their demands were wholly right. Therefore . . . repudiation does not really arise: but as it was the ground of the judgment of the judge below I think I ought to say something about it . . . there was not that absolute refusal to go on which is necessary . . . to arrive at a conclusion that an agreement . . . has been entirely repudiated."

B

Pearson L.J. said much the same.

C   The present case is, however, quite different from the *James Shaffer* case [1953] 1 W.L.R. 106 and the *Sweet & Maxwell* case [1964] 2 Q.B. 699 because Wimpey made it very plain by their notice and letter of March 20, 1974, that they had no intention to go on with the contract and buy the land at the contract price.

      Spettabile Consorzio Veneziano di Armamento e Navigazione v. *Northumberland Shipbuilding Co. Ltd.,* 121 L.T. 628 was also strongly

D relied upon on behalf of Wimpey. The facts of that case were very strange and clearly distinguishable from the present. Goff L.J. made a long and masterly analysis of that case with which I agree and gratefully adopt. I do not consider that that case is, in reality, of any help to Wimpey.

      I cannot accept that the majority of the Court of Appeal concentrated too much attention on Wimpey's rescission notice of March 20,

E 1974, and not enough upon its surrounding circumstances. In any event, it seems to me that those surrounding circumstances supported Woodar's case rather than Wimpey's. I think that it is obvious from the surrounding circumstances that Wimpey had made up their mind at the beginning of March 1974 (and never changed it) that, in no circumstances would they comply with their contractual obligation to buy the land in question

F at the price of £70,000 per acre. This is made clear by the language of their memorandum which I have already cited and which appears to have been written a day or two before Wimpey's aide mémoire of March 8, 1974, upon which Wimpey rely. I do not understand how that document can be evidence against Woodar, even if Mr. Cornwell were still alive. Nor do I think that even if the document were admissible in evidence it could be accepted as being accurate in every detail.

G Looking at the document as a whole, however, it seems to support Woodar's case rather than Wimpey's. It indicates (1) that Wimpey made plain to Mr. Cornwell what was recorded in the memorandum which I have cited; (2) that Mr. Cornwell was anxious to effect a compromise and suggested that " the money could be paid to him over a period of up to say five years, or that the price could be lowered or

H a combination of both "; (3) that Wimpey replied " the mere extension of five years would not be attractive to us, but that if the land value was vastly reduced we would still like to remain with the deal "; (4) that Mr. Cornwell then said " that he would go away and consider the lowest price that he could afford to sell it to us and that below that price he would fight us through the courts." (The underlining is mine).

      On March 22, 1974, two days after the notice of rescission was served by Wimpey, Woodar's solicitor wrote that they did not accept

its validity.   By a writ of summons endorsed with a statement of claim   A
served on March 29, 1974, Woodar, amongst other things, claimed against
Wimpey a declaration that their notice of March 20, 1974, did not
rescind the contract.   It may well be that Woodar considered that once
they commenced legal proceedings, Wimpey would throw in their hand.
If so, they were mistaken, for Wimpey served a defence and counterclaim on May 18, 1974, alleging that the notice of rescission of March
20, 1974, was valid and counterclaimed a declaration that the contract   B
had been rescinded by that notice.

   Mr. Cornwell, who seems to have done all the negotiations on behalf
of Woodar, was obviously anxious if possible to settle rather than embark
on lengthy and expensive litigation.   He was no doubt disappointed when
Wimpey made it clear by their defence and counterclaim that they
intended to fight.   He probably, I think, wrote his lengthy letter of   C
May 30, 1974, in one last effort to effect a settlement.   Wimpey have
sought to make much of this letter which in my view helps Woodar
rather than Wimpey.   It seems to make it very plain that Mr. Cornwell
had consulted counsel on the notice of rescission and had been advised
that it constituted a wrongful repudiation of the contract.   I cite one
brief passage from it: ". . . unless some compromise is reached and
quickly, then I shall feel obliged to sell immediately in the best possible   D
circumstances with a certain knowledge, so far as counsel's advice is
concerned, that we have a complete redress against" Wimpey.   Of
course there was nothing to stop the parties waiting and doing nothing
until the litigation constituted by the first action was over as Mr. Cornwell
said earlier in his letter.   But there was nothing to prevent Woodar
from selling immediately and bringing another action claiming damages,   E
once they had accepted the repudiation to which I have already referred.

   At the time when Mr. Cornwell's letter of June 4, 1974, was written,
upon which my noble and learned friend, Lord Scarman, places considerable reliance, Woodar had not accepted the repudiation: and a
repudiation, however wrongful is nugatory until accepted by the other
contracting party.

   The result of the first action must have been in Woodar's favour.   F
They could have waited until completion was due under the contract,
which could not have been later than February 21, 1980.   Wimpey might
then perhaps have completed the contract or they might have failed to
complete it, in which event they would have had no defence to an action
for specific performance or damages.   There was, however, nothing to
compel Woodar to confine themselves to the first action.   They had a   G
free choice to do so or to accept the wrongful repudiation which would
enable Woodar to bring the second action claiming damages for an
anticipatory breach of the contract.

   I entirely agree with my noble and learned friend, Lord Wilberforce,
that Wimpey's counterclaim in the first action did not amount to a
repudiation of the contract.   For the reasons I have given, however, their   H
repudiation of the contract had, in my view, been effected by the notice
of rescission dated March 20, 1974, and supported by the letter of the
same date.

   Although I cannot agree with Buckley L.J. that the contract was not
wrongfully repudiated, I do agree with his view that if Wimpey's notice
of the March 20, 1974, did constitute a wrongful repudiation of the
contract of February 21, 1973, the proceedings launched by Woodar

A against Wimpey on March 29, 1974, could not preclude them from accepting that repudiation and bringing another action against Wimpey claiming damages for an anticipatory breach of contract. And this is what Woodar did. On July 10, 1974, through their solicitors, they accepted the wrongful repudiation of March 20, 1974, and then launched their action for damages for an anticipatory breach of contract. The two actions were consolidated and duly tried by Fox J. who found that
B Wimpey had wrongfully repudiated the contract of February 21, 1973, and gave judgment in favour of Woodar for, in all, £462,000 damages.

The Court of Appeal by a majority affirmed Fox J.'s decision on liability but reduced the damages to £272,943.

My Lords, for the reasons I have stated, I would dismiss the appeal on the issue of liability. Since, as I understand, the majority of your
C Lordships are for allowing the appeal on liability, the interesting question in relation to damages in respect of the claim for £150,000 does not now arise. I do, however, agree with what my noble and learned friend, Lord Wilberforce, has said about the finding of the majority of the Court of Appeal (Goff L.J. with reluctance) on this topic. I would add that, in my opinion, the law as it stands at present in relation to damages of this kind is most unsatisfactory; and I can only hope that your Lordships'
D House will soon have an opportunity of reconsidering it unless in the meantime it is altered by statute.

LORD RUSSELL OF KILLOWEN. My Lords, the contention advanced by the purchaser (" Wimpey ") was that it was entitled to rescind the contract by notice of rescission under special condition E (a) (iii) of
E the contract, because the relevant authority had " commenced the procedure " required by law for compulsory acquisition not earlier than the making of the compulsory purchase order on November 8, 1973, subsequent to the contract. Fox J. held that this was incorrect; and that even if it were a correct construction of the contract there should be rectification to make it clear that steps taken by authority in that connection prior to the contract constituted commencement of the
F relevant procedure and were not intended to afford a ground for rescission under the special condition. From that holding there was and is no appeal.

Consequently there was no justification in law for the notice of rescission, and the first question in this appeal is whether the notice of rescission was capable of being accepted by Woodar as a renunciation
G or repudiation of the contract by Wimpey. An affirmative answer to that question was assumed, or not disputed, before Fox J., and was given by the majority in the Court of Appeal (Buckley L.J. dissenting).

The difference of opinion on this point in the Court of Appeal and in your Lordships' House turns upon a question which can be shortly stated. If a party to a contract has a power thereunder totally to rescind
H and renounce all liability to perform any part of its obligations under a contract, and in terms purports absolutely so to rescind and renounce on grounds that in law are not justified, can there ever be circumstances which enable the rescinder to dispute the renunciatory and repudiatory quality of his action?

My Lords, in my opinion the answer to that question is in the negative.

I do not of course dispute that a mistaken concept of the rights of a party under the contract, and action (or inaction) on the basis of

that mistaken concept, need not constitute such a renunciation of the   A
contract as to be capable of being accepted as repudiation of the
contract. Nor do I dispute that repudiation is a serious matter not
lightly to be found. Nor do I dispute that in most cases repudiation or
non-repudiation falls to be decided having regard to all the circumstances
of a case. But I deny that a clear case of the purported exercise of a
power of rescission, a total renunciation of all future obligation to perform
any part of the contract, such as now concerns your Lordships, can by   B
any circumstances be watered down or deprived of its repudiatory quality.
I further assert that it is fallacious to deny that totally renunciatory and
repudiatory quality on the ground that because the action is purportedly
taken under a clause in the contract it is somehow affirming rather
than repudiating the contract. The notice of rescission given in this
case by Wimpey was wholly unequivocal, in effect saying that Wimpey   C
would not in any circumstances fulfil the contract: and that flat statement is not to be regarded as otherwise than renunciatory of the contract
because Wimpey genuinely thought that it was entitled in law to take
that attitude.

It is of course true that in previous discussion with Mr. Cornwell
(for Woodar) it was indicated that Wimpey's right to rescind on the   D
ground suggested would be challenged by Woodar in proceedings. But
I see no ground in that for watering down the absolute nature (or colour)
of the notice of rescission as being somehow conditional upon the
rectitude in law of Wimpey's stance. Indeed I do not accept a view
that the notice of rescission could have been (a) expressed to be conditional upon its justification in law but (b) then operative to terminate
all liability of Wimpey under the contract, as it was manifestly intended   E
to be because it was feared that shortly a planning permission would be
forthcoming (though it did not) which would trap Wimpey irrevocably
into an unprofitable bargain.

I can, my Lords, envisage a situation in which a party in the position
of Woodar might state unequivocally in advance that if Wimpey were to
serve the notice which it did serve, Woodar would not, when it was   F
shown in proceedings that the notice was unjustified, treat it as repudiatory. But that would achieve a position in which Woodar would be
debarred from asserting repudiation, rather than constitute a circumstance
qualifying the fundamental renunciatory character of the purported
exercise by Wimpey of the power. But it cannot be said that such a
position was achieved by anything said by Cornwell in this case.
      G
I am, my Lords, not led to a contrary view by the circumstances of
the *Spettabile* case, 121 L.T. 628 at first instance. There the view was
taken that if originally a communication would have indicated a repudiatory attitude, subsequent approach to the court by the " repudiator "
for a decision upon the rights of the case should be taken as withdrawal
of the original repudiation. That is not this case. The resort to the
court was not by Wimpey, and Wimpey never withdrew its notice of   H
rescission to abide the outcome of the litigation.

It was suggested that the proceedings by Woodar for a declaration
and/or rectification somehow constituted an election not to accept the
rescission as a repudiation, so that Woodar's later purported acceptance
of it as such was ineffective. In common with, I believe, all your
Lordships I cannot accept that. Woodar was obliged to take steps that

A   it did in order to establish that the notice was unjustified in law and
therefore an unjustified repudiation.

Accordingly in my opinion Wimpey wrongfully repudiated the contract
by its notice of rescission, and Woodar accepted that repudiation so as
to entitle it to damages for total breach.

In arriving at my conclusion I do not rely upon the reference to interest
B   payments in the covering letter enclosing the rescission notice: nor upon
the defence or counterclaim of Wimpey. These seem to me to add
nothing to the repudiatory nature of the notice itself.

In conclusion upon this point I cannot agree that, if my opinion were
correct, it would be an unfortunate step in the law. If a party takes such a
bold step he risks disaster. If he plunges in without first testing the
temperature by a construction summons asking whether the rescission
C   remedy is available to him he runs the risk of catching a severe cold.

There is no question on this appeal as to quantum of damage save
under the heading of damages for breach of special condition I, under
which Wimpey agreed on completion of the sale to pay £150,000 to Transworld, a Hong Kong company. Transworld was in some way connected
with Mr. Cornwell, who died before action. No evidence connects Trans-
D   world with Woodar, the party to the contract. No evidence suggests that
Woodar could suffer any damage from a failure by Wimpey to pay
£150,000 to Transworld. It is clear on the authority of Beswick v.
Beswick [1968] A.C. 58, that Woodar on completion could have secured
an order for specific peformance of the agreement to pay £150,000 to
Transworld, which the latter could have enforced. That would not have
been an order for payment to Woodar, nor (contrary to the form of
E   order below) to Woodar for the use and benefit of Transworld. There
was no suggestion of trust or agency of Woodar for Transworld. If it
were necessary to decide the point, which in the light of the views of the
majority of your Lordships on the first point it is not, I would have concluded that no more than nominal damages had been established by Woodar
as a consequence of the refusal by Wimpey to pay Transworld in the
F   light of the law of England as it now stands. I would not have thought
that the reasoning of Oliver J. in Radford v. De Froberville [1977] 1
W.L.R. 1262 supported Woodar's case for substantial damages. Nor do I
think that on this point the Court of Appeal was correct in thinking it
was constrained by Jackson v. Horizon Holidays Ltd. [1975] 1 W.L.R.
1468 to award substantial damages. I do not criticize the outcome of that
case: the plaintiff had bought and paid for a high class family holiday:
G   he did not get it, and therefore he was entitled to substantial damages
for the failure to supply him with one. It is to be observed that the order
of the Court of Appeal as drawn up did not suggest that any part of the
damages awarded to him were " for the use and benefit of " any member
of his family. It was a special case quite different from the instant case
on the Transworld point.
H
I would not, my Lords, wish to leave the Jackson case without adverting
with respectful disapproval to the reliance there placed by Lord Denning
M.R.—not for the first time—on an extract taken from the judgment of
Lush L.J. in Lloyd's v. Harper, 16 Ch.D. 290. That case was plainly
a case in which a trustee or agent was enforcing the rights of a beneficiary
or principal, there being therefore a fiduciary relationship. Lord Denning
in Jackson's case said, at p. 1473:

" The case comes within the principle stated by Lush L.J. in *Lloyd's*   A
v. *Harper* (1880) 16 Ch.D. 290, 321 : ' I consider it to be an established
rule of law that where a contract is made with *A*. for the benefit of
B., *A*. can sue on the contract for the benefit of *B*. and recover all
that *B*. could have recovered if the contract had been made with *B*.
himself '."

Lord Denning continued: "It has been suggested that Lush L.J. was   B
thinking of a contract in which A was trustee for B. But I do not think
so. He was a common lawyer speaking of common law." I have already
indicated that in all the other judgments the matter proceeded upon a
fiduciary relationship between A and B: and Lush L.J. in the same
passage makes it plain that he does also; for he says:

> " It is true that the person [B] who employed him [the broker A]   C
> has a right, if he pleases, to take action himself and sue upon the
> contract made by the broker for him, for he [B] is a principal party
> to the contract."

To ignore that passage is to divorce the passage quoted by Lord Denning
from the fiduciary context in which it was uttered, the context of principal
and agent, a field with which it may be assumed Lush L.J. was familiar.   D
I venture to suggest that the brief quotation should not be used again as
support for a proposition which Lush L.J. cannot have intended to
advance.

In summary therefore, in disagreement with the majority of your
Lordships, I would have dismissed this appeal on repudiation. Had I
been correct I would, as at present advised, have allowed the appeal on
the Transworld point, and awarded only nominal damages on that point to   E
Woodar, and not substantial damages to be paid to Woodar " for the use
and benefit of " Transworld, a form of order which I cannot see was
justified.

LORD KEITH OF KINKEL. My Lords. In deciding the issue of repudiation which arises in this appeal, the guiding principle is that enunciated   F
by Lord Coleridge, C.J. in *Freeth* v. *Burr,* L.R. 9 C.P. 208, 213 :

> " . . . in cases of this sort, where the question is whether the one
> party is set free by the action of the other, the real matter for con-
> sideration is whether the acts or conduct of the one do or do not
> amount to an intimation of an intention to abandon and altogether
> to refuse performance of the contract."
                                                                            G
The matter is to be considered objectively:

> " The claim being for wrongful repudiation of the contract it was
> necessary that the plaintiff's language should amount to a declaration
> of intention not to carry out the contract, or that it should be such that
> the defendant was justified in inferring from it such intention. We
> must construe the language used by the light of the contract and the   H
> circumstances of the case in order to see whether there was in this
> case any such renunciation of the contract." (*Johnstone* v. *Milling*
> (1886) L.R. 16 Q.B.D. 460, 474, *per* Bowen L.J.).

The importance of looking at the whole circumstances of the case was
emphasised by Lord Selborne L.C. in *Mersey Steel and Iron Co. Ltd.* v.
Naylor, Benzon & Co., 9 App.Cas. 434, and by Singleton L.J. in *James
Shaffer Ltd.* v. *Findlay Durham & Brodie* [1953] 1 W.L.R. 106, 116.

A   There is a tract of authority which vouches the proposition that the assertion by one party to the other of a genuinely held but erroneous view as to the validity or effect of a contract does not constitute repudiation. In the *Spettabile* case, 121 L.T. 628, the plaintiffs sent to the defendants a letter claiming that certain contracts were no longer binding upon them and followed it up with a service of a writ seeking declarations to that effect. The Court of Appeal held that the plaintiffs' conduct did
B   not amount to repudiation of the contracts. Warrington L.J. said at p. 633, with reference to the letter:

> " It seems to me that that is not telling the defendants that whatever happens, whatever is the true state of the case, whether the contracts are binding on the plaintiffs or not, they will not perform them : but that they have instructed their solicitors to take proceedings with the
C > object of having it determined that the contracts are not binding upon the plaintiffs and are at an end; . . ."

And with reference to the writ:

> " . . . I think that it is desirable to say this, that in my opinion where one party to a contract conceives that he is no longer bound by the con-
D > tract or has a right to have it rescinded or declared null and void, and issues a writ for the purpose of obtaining that which he believes to be his right, he does not by that mean to repudiate the performance of the contract in any event. It seems to me that he submits to perform it if the court, as the result of the action, comes to the conclusion that he is bound to perform it, and it cannot be taken to be an absolute repudiation."
E
Lord Atkin, at p. 635, after observing that it must be shown that the party to the contract made quite plain his own intention not to be bound by it, said:

> " . . . the substance of [the writ] appears to me to be this : that the plaintiffs in the action are asking the court to declare whether or not they are any longer bound by the contracts. It appears to me that
F > that is an entirely different state of facts altogether from an intimation by the plaintiffs, apart from the courts of law, that they in any event are not going to perform the contracts. It is something quite different from a repudiation. So far from expressing the intention of the parties not to perform the contracts, it appears to me to leave it to the court to say whether or not the contract is to be performed,
G > and if the court says it is, then it impliedly states that it will be performed. I think, therefore, there was no repudiation of the contract.'

In two other cases it was held by the Court of Appeal that the expression by one party to a contract of a genuine but erroneous view as to the obligations which on a proper construction of it were thereby
H   imposed did not infer an intention to repudiate the contract. These cases are *James Shaffer Ltd.* v. *Findlay Durham & Brodie* [1953] 1 W.L.R. 106 and *Sweet & Maxwell Ltd.* v. *Universal News Services Ltd.* [1964] 2 Q.B. 699. Finally, it is worth observing that in *Ross T. Smyth and Co. Ltd.* v. *T. D. Bailey, and Son and Co.* (1940) 164 L.T. 102, 107, Lord Wright said : " . . . a mere honest misapprehension, especially if open to correction, will not justify a charge of repudiation."

So in the present case the question comes to be whether, having A
regard to all the circumstances, the conduct of the appellants in relation to
their invocation of special condition E (a) (iii) of the contract was such
that a reasonable person in the position of the respondents would properly
infer an intention " in any event," to use the expression employed by
Warrington and Atkin L.JJ. in the *Spettabile* case, 121 L.T. 628, to refuse
to perform the contract when the time came for performance.

The terms of special condition E (a) (iii) have been quoted by my noble B
and learned friend Lord Wilberforce. It conferred upon the appellants
the right lawfully to rescind the contract in the event there described. The
appellants had come to find the contract burdensome in view of the
dramatic collapse of the property market. They accordingly desired to be
relieved of it and took legal advice as to whether there existed grounds
upon which they might lawfully do so. The advice received was to the C
effect that special condition E (a) (iii) provided such a ground.

The appellants did not, however, at once give notice of rescission
under the clause. They sought an interview with Mr. Cornwell, as
representing the respondents, which took place on March 7, 1974, and
proceeded on the lines described in the aide mémoire which is in evidence.
The appellants informed Mr. Cornwell of their position as regards the D
application of special condition E (a) (iii) and proposed a renegotiation of
the contract, failing which they stated their intention to serve notice of rescission in terms of the clause. Mr. Cornwell contested the correctness of their
position, and expressed the intention, if the appellants served notice of rescission, of taking the matter to court and obtaining a decision upon their
right to do so. The appellants served their notice of rescission about two
weeks later, clearly in the expectation, which was duly and promptly E
realised, that the respondents would initiate legal proceedings in order to
test its validity. In my opinion there was nothing in the appellants' conduct up to this point, there being no dispute about the genuineness of their
belief that they were entitled to terminate the contract upon the stated
ground, which might reasonably be treated as inferring that it was their
intention to refuse performance in the event of a judicial determination
that that belief was erroneous. The letters written by Mr. Cornwell to F
Sir Godfrey Mitchell on May 30, and June 6, 1974, the material parts of
which have been quoted by my noble and learned friend, clearly indicate
that he himself did not draw any such inference. I am unable to regard
the appellants' conduct as evincing an intention " altogether to refuse performance of the contract " as Lord Coleridge put it in *Freeth* v. *Burr*,
L.R. 9 C.P. 208, 213 or as constituting an absolute " repudiation " in the G
sense in which Atkin L.J. used that expression in the *Spettabile* case,
121 L.T. 628.

I would accept without hesitation the statement of Lord Denning M.R.
in *Federal Commerce & Navigation Co. Ltd.* v. *Molena Alpha Inc.* [1978]
1 Q.B. 927, 979 that a party who breaks a contract cannot excuse himself
by saying that he did it on the advice of his lawyers, or that he was under
an honest misapprehension. If in the present case the time for performance H
had passed while the appellants were still maintaining their position based
on the erroneous interpretation of special condition E (a) (iii), they would
have been in breach of contract and liable in damages accordingly. Lord
Denning goes on to say: " Nor can he excuse himself on those grounds
from the consequences of a repudiation." That may be so, but it is first
necessary to determine whether or not there has been a repudiation.

The doctrine of repudiatory breach is largely founded upon considera-

A tions of convenience and the opportunities which it affords for mitigating
loss, as observed by Cockburn C.J. in *Frost* v. *Knight* (1872) L.R. 7 Ex.
111, 114.   It enables one party to a contract, when faced with a clear
indication by the other that he does not intend to perform his obligations
under it when the time for performance arrives, to treat the contract, if he
so chooses, as there and then at an end and to claim damages as for actual
breach.   Where one party, honestly but erroneously, intimates to the other
B reliance upon a term of the contract which, if properly applicable, would
entitle him lawfully to rescind the contract, in circumstances which do not
and are not reasonably understood to infer that he will refuse to perform
his obligations even if it should be established that he is not so entitled,
legal proceedings to decide that issue being in contemplation, I do not
consider it in accordance with ordinary concepts of justice that the other
C party should be allowed to treat such conduct as a repudiation.   Nor, in
my opinion, are there any considerations of convenience which favour that
course.

I would add that in my view the lodging by the appellants of their
defence and counterclaim in answer to the respondents' first writ did not
constitute further conduct on their part which can itself be regarded as
having a repudiatory character.   They thereby demonstrated nothing
D more than an adherence to their position as they had earlier expressed
it.   Further, the action taken by the appellants in relation to the
guarantee arrangements with the National Westminster Bank appear to
me to have been no more than a natural consequence of the view taken
by the appellants as to their right to terminate the contract.

In the circumstances the issue regarding the respondents' right to
E damages in respect of alleged breach of the appellants' obligation under
the contract to pay £150,000 to Transworld does not arise for decision.
It is desirable, however, that I should express my agreement with my
noble and learned friend, Lord Wilberforce, that the decision in favour
of the respondents upon this issue, arrived at by the majority of the
Court of Appeal, was not capable of being supported by *Jackson* v.
Horizon Holidays Ltd. [1975] 1 W.L.R. 1468.   That case is capable of
F being regarded as rightly decided upon a reasonable view of the measure
of damages due to the plaintiff as the original contracting party, and
not as laying down any rule of law regarding the recovery of damages
for the benefit of third parties.   There may be a certain class of cases
where third parties stand to gain indirectly by virtue of a contract, and
where their deprivation of that gain can properly be regarded as no more
G than a consequence of the loss suffered by one of the contracting
parties.   In that situation there may be no question of the third parties
having any claim to damages in their own right, but yet it may be proper
to take into account in assessing the damages recoverable by the contracting party an element in respect of expense incurred by him in
replacing by other means benefits of which the third parties have been
H deprived or in mitigating the consequences of that deprivation.   The
decision in *Jackson* v. *Horizon Holidays Ltd.* is not, however, in my
opinion, capable of being supported upon the basis of the true ratio
decidendi in *Lloyd's* v. *Harper,* 16 Ch.D. 290, which rested entirely on the
principles of agency.

I would also associate myself with the observations of my noble and
learned friend, Lord Scarman, as to the desirability of this House having

an opportunity of reviewing, in some appropriate future case, the general A
attitude of English law towards the topic of jus quaesitum tertio.

My Lords, I would allow the appeal.

LORD SCARMAN. My Lords. For the reasons given by my noble and
learned friend, Lord Wilberforce, I would allow the defendants' appeal.
In my judgment the defendants did not commit, or threaten to commit,
a repudiatory breach of contract. The principle of the modern law is now   B
" perspicuous," as my noble and learned friend observed in *Federal Commerce & Navigation Co. Ltd.* v. *Molena Alpha Inc.* [1979] A.C. 757, 778.
To be repudiatory, the breach, or threatened breach, must go to the root of
the contract. If an anticipatory breach is relied on, the renunciation
must be " an intimation of an intention to abandon and altogether to
refuse performance of the contract "; or, put in other but equally   C
clear words, " the true question is whether the acts and conduct of the
party evince an intention no longer to be bound by the contract ": Lord
Coleridge C.J. in *Freeth* v. *Burr*, L.R. 9 C.P. 208, 213. The emphasis
upon communication of the party's intention by his acts and conduct
is a recurring theme in the abundant case law. Two well-known cases
illustrative of the emphasis are *Mersey Steel and Iron Co. Ltd.* v. *Naylor,
Benzon & Co.*, 9 App.Cas. 434 and *Bradley* v. *H. Newsom, Sons &*   D
Co. [1919] A.C. 16 (see in particular the speech of Lord Wrenbury).

Difficulty, however, does arise in the application of the principle to
particular facts—as the difference in judicial opinion in the present case
shows. The dividing line between what is repudiatory and what is not
emerges from three very persuasive dicta to be found in the case law.
When the *Federal Commerce* case [1979] A.C. 757 was in the Court of   E
Appeal, Lord Denning M.R. said [1978] Q.B. 927, 979 :

" I have yet to learn that a party who breaks a contract can excuse
himself by saying that he did it on the advice of his lawyers: or
that he was under an honest misapprehension . . . I would go by
the principle . . . that if the party's conduct " " contract " must be a
misprint "—objectively considered in its impact on the other party—   F
is such as to evince an intention no longer to be bound by his
contractual obligations, then it is open to the other party to accept
his repudiation and treat the contract as discharged from that time
onwards."

In the *Spettabile* case, 121 L.T. 628, 634–635, Atkin L.J. said of the
various definitions of repudiations :   G

" They all come to the same thing, and they all amount at any rate
to this, that it must be shown that the party to the contract made
quite plain [emphasis supplied] his own intention not to perform
the contract."

In *James Shaffer Ltd.* v. *Findlay Durham & Brodie* [1953] 1 W.L.R.   H
106 the Court of Appeal had under consideration a breach of a long-term
supply contract where the defendant, who had undertaken to pass on
orders of not less than a specified value each year, failed to do so.
He honestly believed his failure was not a breach of contract: but the
Court of Appeal held that it was, his construction of the contract being
erroneous in law. The court held, however, that the breach did not
evince an intention not to be bound by the contract. Singleton L.J., who

A referred to *Freeth* v. *Burr*, L.R. 9 C.P. 208 and the *Spettabile* case, 121 L.T. 628 made this comment, at p. 120:

"Streatfield J. said that this was a very difficult case and near the line. I think that that is a true description. Sometimes when a case is put in one particular way it has great appeal, and, when it is put in the other way, it has an almost equal appeal. I do not think
B that it is right to look at the interview of May 18 alone; as I understand the law, it is our duty to have regard to the circumstances."

Morris L.J. (bottom of p. 124) and Upjohn J. (p. 127) said the same thing.

My Lords, as I see it, the error of the majority of the Court of Appeal in the instant case was, notwithstanding some dicta to the contrary, to concentrate attention on one act, i.e. the notice of rescission
C with its accompanying letter. They failed to give the consideration which the law requires of all the acts and conduct of the defendants in their dealings with Mr. Cornwell—the " alter ego " of the plaintiff company. The law requires that there be assessed not only the party's conduct but also, " objectively considered," its impact on the other party. The error is neatly exposed in Goff L.J.'s terse conclusion: " In my judgment
D rescission is repudiation, and if it cannot be justified by the terms of the contract it is wrongful and a breach." The learned Lord Justice was, with respect, concentrating too much attention on one act isolated from its surrounding circumstances and failing to pay proper regard to the impact of the party's conduct upon the other party.

In this case the contract provided for the possibility of rescission by the defendants. But the notice of rescission, which the defendants gave,
E was not, in the circumstances which existed when it was given, one which the defendants had any contractual right to give. But they honestly believed the contract did give them the right. When one examines the totality of their conduct and its impact upon Mr. Cornwell it is plain, as shown by my noble and learned friend's analysis of the facts, that the defendants, though claiming mistakenly to exercise a power given them
F by the contract to bring it to an end, were not evincing an intention not to be bound by the contract. On the contrary, they believed they were acting pursuant to the contract. And Mr. Cornwell well understood the situation. As he put it in his final letter to Sir Godfrey Mitchell, the president of the defendants,

"... all I need say now it that we will retire to our battle stations
G   and it goes without saying I am sure that you will abide by the result as I will."

It never occurred to Mr. Cornwell that the defendants, if held not to have been entitled to give notice of rescission, would refuse to perform the contract. In fact, it would seem that he believed exactly the contrary.
H Such was the impact upon him of the defendants' conduct.

It being the view of the majority of the House that there was no repudiation, the appeal must be allowed, with the result that there is no need to consider the other issues raised. But, because of its importance, I propose to say a few words on the question of damages.

The plaintiff company agreed to sell the land to the defendants for £850,000. They also required the defendants to pay £150,000 to a third party. The covenant for this payment was in the following terms:

"I. Upon completion of the purchase of the whole or any part A
of the land the purchaser shall pay to Transworld Trade Ltd. of
25 Jermyn Street, London, S.W.1 a sum of £150,000."

No relationship of trust or agency was proved to exist between the
plaintiff company and Transworld Trade Ltd. No doubt, it suited Mr.
Cornwell to split up the moneys payable under the contract between
the two companies: but it is not known, let alone established by evidence B
(though an intelligent guess is possible) why he did so, or why the
plaintiffs desired this money to be paid to Transworld Trade. It is simply
a case of B agreeing with A to pay a sum of money to C.

B, in breach of his contract with A, has failed to pay C. C, it is said,
has no remedy, because the English law of contract recognises no "jus
quaesitum tertio": *Tweddle* v. *Atkinson* (1861) 1 B. & S. 393. No
doubt, it was for this reason that Transworld Trade is not a party to the C
suit. A, it is acknowledged, could in certain circumstances obtain specific
performance of the promise to pay C: *Beswick* v. *Beswick* [1968] A.C.
58. But, since the contract in the present case is admitted (for reasons
which do not fall to be considered by the House) to be no longer in
existence, specific performance is not available. A's remedy lies only in
an award of damages to himself. It is submitted that, in the absence of D
any evidence that A has suffered loss by reason of B's failure to pay C,
A is only entitled to nominal damages.

I wish to add nothing to what your Lordships have already said about
the authorities which the Court of Appeal cited as leading to the
conclusion that the plaintiff company is entitled to substantial damages
for the defendants' failure to pay Transworld Trade. I agree that they
do not support the conclusion. But I regret that this House has not yet E
found the opportunity to reconsider the two rules which effectually
prevent A or C recovering that which B, for value, has agreed to provide.

First, the "jus quaesitum tertio." I respectfully agree with Lord Reid
that the denial by English law of a "jus quaesitum tertio" calls for
reconsideration. In *Beswick* v. *Beswick* [1968] A.C. 58, 72 Lord Reid,
after referring to the Law Revision Committee's recommendation in F
1937 (Cmnd. 5449) p. 31 that the third party should be able to enforce
a contractual promise taken by another for his benefit, observed:

"And, if one had to contemplate a further long period of Parliamentary procrastination, this House might find it necessary to deal
with this matter."

The committee reported in 1937: *Beswick* v. *Beswick* was decided in G
1967. It is now 1979: but nothing has been done. If the opportunity
arises, I hope the House will reconsider *Tweddle* v. *Atkinson*, 1 B. & S. 393
and the other cases which stand guard over this unjust rule.

Likewise, I believe it open to the House to declare that, in the absence
of evidence to show that he has suffered no loss, A, who has contracted
for a payment to be made to C, may rely on the fact that he required H
the payment to be made as prima facie evidence that the promise for
which he contracted was a benefit to him and that the measure of his
loss in the event of non-payment is the benefit which he intended for C
but which has not been received. Whatever the reason, he must have
desired the payment to be made to C and he must have been relying on B
to make it. If B fails to make the payment, A must find the money from
other funds if he is to confer the benefit which he sought by his contract

A　to confer upon C. Without expressing a final opinion on a question which is clearly difficult, I think the point is one which does require consideration by your Lordships' House.

　　Certainly the crude proposition for which the defendants contend, namely that the state of English law is such that neither C for whom the benefit was intended nor A who contracted for it can recover it, if the contract is terminated by B's refusal to perform, calls for review: and

B　now, not forty years on.

Appeal allowed.

　　Solicitors: *P. J. Ward; Sharpe, Pritchard & Co.*

F .C.

C

[FAMILY DIVISION]

* PRACTICE DIRECTION (CHILD: JOINT CUSTODY ORDER)

D　*Husband and Wife—Divorce—Children—Practice—Joint custody*
order—Procedure to secure uniformity of practice in making
order—Matrimonial Causes Act 1973 (c. 18), s. 41

　　It sometimes happens that the judge who is considering the arrangements for the children under section 41 of the Matrimonial Causes Act 1973 is invited by one or both parties to make a joint custody order. Such orders are being sought more often now than formerly and

E　variations of practice have been noticed in different parts of the country. With a view to securing uniformity of approach it is hereby directed as follows:

　　1. Where a petitioner and a respondent have reached an agreement as to which of them should have care and control of the child, or children, and are further agreed that legal custody should be vested in the two

F　of them jointly and only one of them appears on the appointment, the court ought not on that appointment to make an order which is inconsistent with the agreement. If the court is unwilling to make the agreed order, it should adjourn the matter to give each party the opportunity to be heard.

　　2. Where a petition contains a prayer for custody and the respondent has indicated in writing (in the acknowledgment of service or otherwise)

G　that he (or she) wishes to apply for custody to be vested in the two of them jointly, the court should proceed on the basis that the question of custody is in issue, and should not make an order for custody, or joint custody, except with the agreement of both parties or after giving each of them the opportunity to be heard.

　　This direction is issued with the concurrence of the Lord Chancellor.

H

Sir John Arnold P.

February 18, 1980.

[1980]

[HOUSE OF LORDS]   A

* ENGINEERS' AND MANAGERS'
    ASSOCIATION and Others . . . . Respondents

AND

ADVISORY, CONCILIATION AND
    ARBITRATION SERVICE . . . . Appellants   B

1979   Dec. 5, 6, 10   Lord Wilberforce, Lord Diplock,
1980   March 6   Lord Edmund-Davies, Lord Keith of Kinkel
                                                  and Lord Scarman

Trade Union — Recognition issue — Reference to Acas — Award   C
    earlier made by disputes committee of T.U.C. under Brid-
    lington agreement — Award subject matter of complaint to
    T.U.C. and of High Court action—Acas resolving to defer its
    inquiries—Whether Acas bound to proceed with reference—
    Employment Protection Act 1975 (c. 71), ss. 11, 12

    Rivalry existed in the engineering industry between three
trade unions, E.M.A., T.A.S.S. and U.K.A.P.E. Both E.M.A.
and T.A.S.S. were affiliated to the T.U.C. and when E.M.A.   D
started a recruiting campaign at a factory in order to get
recognition for collective bargaining T.A.S.S. complained to
the T.U.C. On March 16, 1977, the disputes committee of
the T.U.C. found that E.M.A. had infringed T.U.C. disputes
principles, said that its members at the factory should join
T.A.S.S. and ordered that E.M.A. should not proceed with
its recognition claim at the factory. On April 27, 1977, E.M.A.
applied for the reference of a recognition issue to Acas under   E
section 11 of the Employment Protection Act 1975. Acas
had already received a similar recognition application from
U.K.A.P.E. On September 15, 1977, Acas resolved to proceed
with the inquiry and agreed a questionnaire to be completed
by employees at the factory stating their wishes as regards
union representation.
    On October 13, 1977, E.M.A. issued a writ against the
T.U.C. claiming that the award of their disputes committee   F
was invalid. In view of the issue of the writ, on December 14,
1977, Acas resolved " not to proceed, for the time being "
with the recognition references and declined to alter that
decision despite protests from professional employees at the
factory.
    On January 25, 1978, E.M.A. issued a writ against Acas
for declarations that Acas was in breach of its statutory duties
in refusing and/or failing to investigate and/or report on   G
the recognition issue of April 27, 1977. On April 7, 1978,
Oliver J. held that Acas had a discretion to defer consideration
of the recognition issue and that, since in December 1977
there could have been an early disposal of the action between
E.M.A. and the T.U.C., Acas had not exercised that discretion
unreasonably. The Court of Appeal reversed his decision.
    On appeal by Acas: —
    Held, allowing the appeal, (1) that although Acas had a   H
discretion to suspend its inquiries and defer the preparation
of its report if it was of opinion that a period of suspension
would promote the improvement of industrial relations, it could
not under the guise of deferment refuse to complete its
inquiries (post, pp. 308C–E, 311G–H, 318A–C, D–E).
    (2) (Lord Diplock and Lord Keith of Kinkel dissenting)
that the test of whether Acas had abdicated its statutory
functions being whether no reasonable advisory, conciliation
and arbitration service could have continued the deferment,

A   in the confused situation the continued deferment did not amount to an abdication by Acas of its functions (post, pp. 311H, 312A, 318G–H, 320A–B, C–D).

    Per curiam. If justice required it the Court of Appeal and the House of Lords might, in determining an appeal, have regard to events subsequent to the trial (post, pp. 306G–H, 310F–G, 320E).

    Decision of the Court of Appeal [1979] 1 W.L.R. 1113;
B   [1979] I.C.R. 637; [1979] 3 All E.R. 223 reversed.

    The following cases are referred to in their Lordships' opinions:

    Grunwick Processing Laboratories Ltd. v. *Advisory, Conciliation and Arbitration Service* [1978] A.C. 655; [1978] 2 W.L.R. 277; [1978] I.C.R. 231; [1978] 1 All E.R. 338, H.L.(E.).

C   *Lim Poh Choo* v. *Camden and Islington Area Health Authority* [1980] A.C. 174; [1979] 3 W.L.R. 44; [1979] 2 All E.R. 910, H.L.(E.).

    United Kingdom Association of Professional Engineers v. *Advisory, Conciliation and Arbitration Service* [1980] 2 W.L.R. 254; [1980] 1 All E.R. 612, H.L.(E.).

    The following additional cases were cited in argument:

D   *Attorney-General* v. *Birmingham, Tame and Rea District Drainage Board* [1912] A.C. 788, H.L.(E.).

    B. v. *W. (Wardship: Appeal)* [1979] 1 W.L.R. 1041; [1979] 3 All E.R. 83, H.L.(E.).

    Carter v. *Credit Change Ltd.* [1979] I.C.R. 908, C.A.

    Ibeneweka v. *Egbuna* [1964] 1 W.L.R. 219, P.C.

    Jeffrey v. *Jeffrey (No. 2)* [1952] P. 122; [1952] 1 All E.R. 790, C.A.

    Maxwell v. *Keun* [1928] 1 K.B. 645, C.A.

E   *National Employers Life Assurance Co. Ltd.* v. *Advisory, Conciliation and Arbitration Service* [1979] I.C.R. 620.

    New Brunswick Railway Co. v. *British and French Trust Corporation Ltd.* [1939] A.C. 1; [1938] 4 All E.R. 747, H.L.(E.).

    Reg. v. *Adamson* (1875) 1 Q.B.D. 201.

    Rex v. *Central Professional Committee for Opticians, Ex parte Brown* (1949) 65 T.L.R. 599; [1949] 2 All E.R. 519, D.C.

F   *Rex* v. *Commonwealth Court of Conciliation and Arbitration, Ex parte Amalgamated Engineering Union* (1949) 80 C.L.R. 164.

    Rothwell v. *Association of Professional Executive Clerical and Computer Staff* [1976] I.C.R. 211.

    Russian Commercial and Industrial Bank v. *British Bank for Foreign Trade Ltd.* [1921] 2 A.C. 438, H.L.(E.).

    Wilson v. *Dagnall* [1972] 1 Q.B. 509; [1972] 2 W.L.R. 823; [1972] 2 All E.R. 44, C.A.

G   *Yates' Settlement Trusts, In re* [1954] 1 W.L.R. 564; [1954] 1 All E.R. 619, C.A.

    APPEAL from the Court of Appeal.

    This was an appeal by the Advisory, Conciliation and Arbitration Service from an order of the Court of Appeal (Lord Denning M.R.,
H Lawton and Cumming-Bruce L.JJ.) given on May 14, 1979, whereby the court allowed an appeal by the first respondents, the Engineers' and Managers' Association, against the judgment and order of Oliver J. given on April 7, 1978, and declared that the Service was bound in pursuance of its statutory duties under section 12 of the Employment Protection Act 1975 to investigate and/or report upon the issue referred to in the writ of summons (namely a " recognition issue " concerning certain of the employees of a company known as G.E.C. Reactor Equipment Ltd.

employed at its premises at Whetstone near Leicester) and ordered that   A
the Service pay the first respondents their costs of the action and of the
appeal. By that order the Court of Appeal refused the Service leave to
appeal to the House of Lords, but on June 27, 1979, the Appeal Committee of the House of Lords granted the Service leave to appeal. The
second respondents, the United Kingdom Association of Professional
Engineers, were an independent trade union, the second named defendants   B
in the proceedings.

The facts are stated in their Lordships' opinions.

P. D. J. Scott Q.C. and *Henry Brooke* for the appellants.
Simon Goldblatt Q.C. and *Peter Clark* for the first respondents.
Charles Hickling, deputy general secretary of the United Kingdom
Association of Professional Engineers, appeared for U.K.A.P.E.   C

Their Lordships took time for consideration.

March 6. LORD WILBERFORCE. My Lords, I agree that this appeal
must be allowed for the reasons given by my noble and learned friend,
Lord Scarman.   D

LORD DIPLOCK. My Lords, this appeal raises the question whether
the Advisory, Conciliation and Arbitration Service (" Acas ") was in
breach of its statutory duties under sections 12 and 14 of the Employment
Protection Act 1975, when over a period of two years from December
1977 to December 1979 it refused to proceed with its inquiries into a
recognition dispute that had been referred to it by a trade union, the   E
Engineers' and Managers' Association (" E.M.A.") in April 1977.

Largely owing to uncertainty as to what happened at the hearing in
the Court of Appeal, I have found this a difficult case to decide. My
mind has wavered often both during the hearing in this House and
thereafter. Moreover, since the hearing an event has occurred which
makes the outcome of this appeal to your Lordships' House of no   F
practical importance to either party to it. The reason on which Acas
relied as justifying the lengthy suspension of its inquiries into the recognition dispute was the contemporaneous existence throughout that period
of a pending action between E.M.A. and the Trades Union Congress
(" T.U.C."name). That action has now been settled and what Acas regarded
as a continuing obstacle to its proceeding expeditiously with its inquiries   G
has been removed.

In these circumstances it might be thought that a body of whose title
" conciliation " forms a conspicuous part might have withdrawn its
appeal, even after the conclusion of the hearing, when an event occurred
which deprived success or failure in it of any practical consequences
other than in the incidence of costs. Acas, however, has expressed a
wish that this House should proceed to delivery of judgment. The   H
reason why Acas wants this to be done is for its own guidance as to
the limits of its discretion to suspend its inquiries into particular recognition disputes if circumstances should again arise that are analogous to
those which were present in the instant case.

My Lords, the appeal is one on which, as will appear, your Lordships
are narrowly divided and that division of opinion is, in the main, due to
incertitude as to what happened in the course of the hearing in the Court

A of Appeal. I fear that this may diminish any guidance which this House is able to give.

The relevant facts are to be found set out in the speech of my noble and learned friend, Lord Scarman, to which reference may be made. I will not take time in repeating them here.

No one disputes that Acas has a very wide discretion as to how it will conduct a recognition issue that has been referred to it under
B section 11 of the Employment Protection Act 1975; but conduct it, in some way or another, it must. It cannot decline to proceed on a reference, untimely though it may think the reference to be, except in the limited circumstances described in section 12 (2) which have no application to the instant case. Having started on a reference, Acas cannot abdicate its functions under sections 12 and 14 to examine the
C issue and to consult all parties who it considers will be affected by the outcome, to ascertain the opinions of workers to whom the issue relates, to make such other inquiries as it thinks fit and to make a written report conformably with section 12 (4). The crucial question for the Court of Appeal and for this House is whether Acas's refusals since November and December 1977 to proceed further with the conjoined references of the United Kingdom Association of Professional Engineers (" U.K.A.P.E.")
D and E.M.A. (which I will refer to as " the reference ") does amount to an abdication if its statutory functions, or, as the majority of your Lordships think, was a mere adjournment of the proceedings on the reference in the lawful exercise of a statutory discretion to decide how references can best be conducted.

My Lords, the Court of Appeal were greatly influenced by the
E consideration that the persons most vitally affected by Acas's decision to postpone proceeding with the reference were the group of more than 300 professional engineers in the two highest grades employed at Whetstone (" the unrepresented engineers ") who were excluded from a place at the collective bargaining table with their employers but wanted to be represented there by a trade union of their own choice. They were not parties to the reference; they had no means of hastening its progress;
F yet so long as the recognition issue remained pending before Acas and Acas were unwilling to issue a report, their right to be represented at a collective bargaining would remain in limbo. This is because with two rival unions, E.M.A. and U.K.A.P.E. as claimants for recognition by the employers against the opposition of yet a third union, the Technical Administrative and Supervisory Section (" T.A.S.S."), the employers
G could not safely settle the issue by agreement with either of the claimant unions, lest Acas in its report should ultimately recommend recognition of the other, with all the consequences which that would entail under sections 15 and 16 of the Act.

A recognition issue relating to the unrepresented engineers had been referred to Acas by U.K.A.P.E. as long ago as July 1976. The rival claim of E.M.A. to represent the same group was referred to Acas as
H a recognition issue in April 1977. By the time the question of the lawfulness of Acas's inaction since November 1977 came before the Court of Appeal in May 1979, the unrepresented engineers' right of representation at collective bargaining had already been in limbo for close on three years covering successive round of pay bargaining during a period of inflation and erosion of differentials. Unless Acas were to change its mind their representation would remain in limbo until March 1980 at the earliest. By then Acas's failure to proceed with the reference would

have lasted for some two-and-a-half years and the reference itself for
nearly four years without any report being forthcoming.

My Lords, the long title of the Act of 1975 makes it clear that the
purpose of Part I is to establish machinery for the improvement of
industrial relations. Acas provides the most important part of that
machinery and section 1 (2), which defines the functions of Acas, makes
clear the intention of Parliament in 1975 that, so far as practicable,
collective bargaining as to terms and conditions of employment should
be extended. To the great majority of the people of this country their
contracts of employment are the most important contracts in their lives.
The wages for which these contracts provide determine the material
standard of living which they and their dependent families can enjoy.
In providing, by means of the reference of recognition issues to Acas,
machinery for coercing employers to recognise trade unions as representing groups of workers in collective bargaining the dominant intention of
Parliament must have been to benefit the groups of represented rather
than to subordinate this to increasing the power of the trade unions;
though such increased power might be an inevitable and not unwelcome
by-product.

If this be so, Acas in exercising its functions in relation to recognition
issues referred to it under section 12 where there are rival trade unions
seeking to represent the workers to whom the issue relates, cannot,
consistently with the policy of the Act, sit back and passively await the
outcome of a power struggle between rival unions fought out in some
other forum of their choice and in their own good time. Once the issue
has been referred to it Acas is, in my view, required to play a more
active role than this in protecting the interests of those workers whom
Parliament intended to be the primary beneficiaries of the machinery
which the Act provides for dealing with recognition. In particular Acas
should bear in mind that where there are rival unions claiming to be
recognised the practical effect of prolonging the reference by its own
inaction will be to prolong the period during which those workers will,
for the reasons I have indicated, continue to be deprived of the possibility
of acquiring the right to be represented at all in collective bargaining
about the terms of their contracts of employment. Acas is in my view
under a duty to play an active part in ending the impasse.

The continuing deprivation suffered by the unrepresented engineers
of any practical possibility of obtaining representation in collective
bargaining with the employers so long as Acas refrained from issuing a
report, seems to me to be relevant also to the question whether the
Court of Appeal were right in taking into consideration events that had
occurred and in particular the time that had elapsed since the final
judgment of Oliver J. against which the appeal was brought. Additionally
to the reasons given by your Lordships for holding that the Court of
Appeal were entitled to do so, provided that it could be done without
unfairness to Acas, I would add the fact that the unrepresented engineers,
two-thirds of whom had in December 1977 petitioned Acas to proceed
with the reference and report before March 1978, had no means themselves of hurrying up the progress either of the reference itself or of
the action by E.M.A. against the T.U.C. upon which Acas had decided
that any further progress in the reference should depend.

My Lords, I do not underestimate the difficulty of the task that
confronted Acas when called upon to examine and report upon the
recognition issues that had been referred to it by U.K.A.P.E. and E.M.A.

A   The problem of what trade union, if any, should represent the unrepresented engineers in collective bargaining with their employers was bedevilled by the rivalry of the three trade unions who had been engaging in competitive recruiting campaigns among them. Longest on the scene had been T.A.S.S., a union affiliated to the T.U.C., a member of the Confederation of Shipbuilding and Engineering Unions (" C.S.E.U.") and, as such, a party to the industry-wide procedural agreement with

B   Engineering Employers Federation (" E.E.F.") and to the existing collective bargaining agreements at Whetstone as representing inter alios some lower grades of engineers. Its recruiting campaign among the unrepresented engineers however had had but minimal success despite the fact that it had extended over several years. E.M.A. was affiliated to the T.U.C. but it was not a member of the C.S.E.U., as its membership

C   had until recently been confined to comparable grades of employees in the electricity supply industry. It had succeeded in recruiting rather more than one-third of the unrepresented engineers at Whetstone. The third claimant union was U.K.A.P.E.; it is not affiliated to the T.U.C. and is not a member of the C.S.E.U. It had been less successful in recruiting the unrepresented engineers than E.M.A. but, in the short time that it had been on the scene, it had already done better than T.A.S.S. The

D   consequences of this inter-union rivalry was complicated by the intervention of the T.U.C. in application of the Bridlington principles. By the time E.M.A. had become a party to the reference in April 1977 conciliation between E.M.A. and T.A.S.S. by use of T.U.C. machinery had failed and E.M.A. had already been directed by an award of a disputes committee of the T.U.C. to cease recruiting at Whetstone and

E   not to proceed with any claim for recognition. These directions were confirmed on September 28, 1977, by the general council of the T.U.C. under threat of disaffiliation. So there was the possibility that if E.M.A. persisted in continuing as a party to the reference it would do so as an unaffiliated union. The initiation by E.M.A. of its action against the T.U.C. claiming that these directions were invalid and T.U.C.'s undertaking given upon the application for an interlocutory injunction meant

F   that the question whether E.M.A. would continue to be a union affiliated to the T.U.C. would not be answered for an indefinite period dependent upon when E.M.A.'s action against the T.U.C. was settled or came on for trial and judgment was delivered in it. At the time of Acas's decision in December 1977 to put a halt for the time being to the proceedings on the reference, it was justifiably thought by Acas that the period of

G   uncertainty would be short; but by the time the matter came before the Court of Appeal it was plain that it would continue until at least March 1980, and from what had been told them in the course of the hearing the court were under the impression, whether mistakenly or not, that Acas's continuing intention, from which it had never deviated was to await the decision of that action before proceeding any further with the reference.

H   My Lords, the difficulties arising out of doubts as to the future status of E.M.A. as a trade union affiliated to the T.U.C. or as to whether if its then current action against the T.U.C. should fail, E.M.A. would continue to be a party to the reference, may well have needed to be resolved before Acas felt justified in deciding whether to make a recommendation for the recognition of either of the claimants in the reference, E.M.A. or U.K.A.P.E. But the Act requires Acas to come to a decision *whether or not* to make a recommendation for recognition

in the circumstance as they exist when the reference is proceeding, not   A
to wait indefinitely for those circumstances to change. Even if the
circumstances are such that it finds itself unable to make any recommendation it must none the less prepare a written report which must set
out its reasons for not making any recommendation for recognition, the
findings upon which these reasons are based and any advice it thinks
appropriate to give in connection with those findings. Its advice need
not be directed only to the trade unions and employers who are the   B
parties to the reference, but may be proffered also to the persons most
vitally affected by the report—the workers to whom the recognition issue
related. The advice may indicate what change of circumstances would
be likely to lead Acas to recommend the recognition of some particular
trade union for the purpose of collective bargaining on behalf of the
unrepresented engineers, whether that union was claimant in the reference   C
or not. This, as I pointed out, was what in effect Acas did in the case
of *United Kingdom Association of Professional Engineers* v. *Advisory,
Conciliation and Arbitration Service* [1980] 2 W.L.R. 254 which this
House heard immediately before the instant case.

    This is not to say that Acas has no discretion to postpone further
progress with a reference for a reasonable time if it thinks that the
postponement is likely to enable it to make a recommendation or to   D
ascertain with greater certainty the circumstances which are likely to
exist when its decision either to make or not to make a recommendation
will take effect. But the existence of uncertainty as to the status of
one of the claimant unions as an affiliate of the T.U.C. is in itself a
relevant circumstance which may justify making no recommendation for
recognition; and once it is plain that the uncertainty is likely to continue   E
for so long a period that it will cover successive rounds of negotiations
of pay claims, Acas in my view would be abdicating its functions under
section 12 if it did not then proceed with the reference.

    In the instant case it was not plain that E.M.A.'s status as an
affiliated union would remain undecided for more than a very few months
when Acas made its decision in December 1977 not to proceed with the
next step in the reference until the action by E.M.A. against the T.U.C.   F
had been disposed of; nor do I think that it was plain in April 1978
when the trial took place before Oliver J. By May 1979, however,
when the matter came before the Court of Appeal it had become
abundantly clear that E.M.A.'s future status as an affiliated union of the
T.U.C. would not be decided until March 1980 at the earliest and not
even then if the action, as well it might be, were taken to appeal. It   G
may be that the Court of Appeal was mistaken in its belief that Acas
had by that date already reached a final decision that, unless required
by the court to do so, it would take no further step in the reference
until E.M.A.'s affiliated status had been resolved; but another eight
months elapsed before the matter came before this House. It was then
plain that Acas from first to last had never once deviated from that
policy and had no present intention of departing from it. So, in view   H
of the light that its conduct since May 1978 has thrown upon its
intentions then, I would uphold the judgment of the Court of Appeal
declaring that Acas was under a statutory duty to get on with the next
step in the reference, and this involved ascertaining the opinions of the
unrepresented engineers.

    It remains to deal with the two grounds on which Acas has relied to
justify its policy of waiting until the action between E.M.A. and the

A T.U.C. had been disposed of. Both of them as it seems to me confirm Acas's failure to appreciate what the Act of 1975 requires of it. The first is Acas's contention that the blame for the long delay in ascertaining E.M.A.'s future status as an affiliated union rests with E.M.A. itself for "dragging its feet" in its action against the T.U.C. This may be so; it was a matter of disputed fact before the Court of Appeal; but like Cumming-Bruce L.J. I do not think it matters whether it is so or not.

B A reference of a recognition issue to Acas bears no resemblance to a lis between the employers and the trade unions whose claim to recognition by those employers has been refused. It may affect the interests of other unions and of many other persons; it is bound to affect vitally the interests of the workers to whom the issue relates. In granting a wide discretion to Acas as to the way a reference is to be conducted Parliament

C should not be taken to have intended that the workers' interests in the outcome of the reference should be subordinated to those of the trade unions who were seeking to be recognised as representing them or should be allowed to suffer because of tactics adopted in the reference by any of those unions. Part of Acas's functions must surely be to do its best to prevent this happening.

D The second matter is Acas's claim that to proceed to the next stage in the reference, the ascertainment of the opinions of workers to whom the issue relates, would have necessitated the putting of hypothetical questions so long as the action between E.M.A. and the T.U.C. was undecided; and that hypothetical questions would not produce answers that Acas could treat as reliable. The unrepresented engineers are men with professional qualifications and presumably not of the lowest level

E of intelligence. I do not find it credible that they are incapable of understanding and answering the simple questions posed in the questionnaire that Acas had prepared in September 1977 or, if Acas thinks fit, additional questions involving the hypotheses (a) that E.M.A. would be disaffiliated from the T.U.C. or (b) that it would withdraw its claim to recognition. The answers to those questions would represent the current opinions of the workers on them, however ill-informed their opinions

F might appear to be to Acas with its great experience of industrial relations. From the various ways in which it has been put by Acas in argument, it is clear to me that Acas's real objection to proceeding to ascertain the opinions of the unrepresented engineers whether by means of a questionnaire or in some other way, is that it did not think that those opinions, if obtained at a time when E.M.A.'s affiliated status

G was undecided, would provide material on which they would feel able to base any recommendation for recognition. Assuming that this were so, and Acas must be the judge of this, it may be a reason for its reporting that it does not make any recommendation for recognition. It is not in my view a valid reason for refusing to comply with its statutory duty under section 14 to ascertain the opinions of workers to whom the issue relates in the circumstances as they now exist, which included

H uncertainty as to E.M.A.'s status.

So, on the ground that Acas had by May 1979, demonstrated that it had not simply exercised a discretion as to how the reference should be conducted but had abdicated its statutory functions under section 12 to go on with the reference, I would have dismissed this appeal.

LORD EDMUND-DAVIES. My Lords, this appeal is concerned with the duties and responsibilities imposed upon Acas by the Employment

310

Protection Act 1975 and the extent to which their manner of discharging   A
(or neglecting) those duties and responsibilities are open to be controlled
by the courts. The outcome of the appeal turns, in particular, upon
whether Acas is fettered in deferring the disposal of a recognition issue
referred to it under section 11 (1) of the Act.

The relevant dates are startling. For it was as long ago as July 9,
1976, that U.K.A.P.E. referred its recognition issue to Acas, and it was
on April 27, 1977, that the rival claim of E.M.A. was similarly referred.   B
On December 14, 1977, Acas resolved not to proceed " for the time
being " with its inquiries into those recognition issues. By a writ dated
January 25, 1978, E.M.A. claimed declarations that Acas was in breach
of its statutory duties in not prosecuting them. On February 10, 1978,
E.M.A. gave notice of motion for interim relief, and, when the matter
came before Oliver J. on April 7, this was treated by consent as the trial   C
of the action. In the result, the learned judge decided in favour of Acas,
and I am in respectful agreement with your Lordships that, on the facts
as they then stood, that judgment was unimpeachable. Nevertheless, it
may well be that (as my noble and learned friend, Lord Keith, observed
in the course of counsel's submissions) at least some of the later complications would have been avoided had the motion not been so treated
and the action had proceeded to trial in the ordinary and more formal   D
manner. Be that as it may, there is little room for doubt that, later
on, lassitude largely took control over Acas. So much so that, when
the case reached the Court of Appeal in May 1979, Acas had not taken
a single step towards resolving E.M.A.'s reference, and by the time this
appeal came before this House last December, absolutely no progress
had been made.   E

This is a lamentable tale, and, had what exactly happened in the
Court of Appeal been beyond all doubt, I should have been driven to
the conclusion that the unanimous view of that court that Acas had
unwarrantably failed in its statutory duties was right and, indeed,
inevitable. For, although Acas indubitably has an inherent right of
deferment and postponement in proper cases, such extraordinary delay
as occurred here called for a clear and convincing explanation. But the   F
conclusion of the Court of Appeal was that the case presented for Acas
itself demonstrated that, so far from reasonably postponing the disposal
of E.M.A.'s recognition issue, that body had, in effect, abandoned the
task. They rightly held that, although an appellate court, they were in
all the circumstances entitled to have regard to what had happened not
only after the issue of the writ but also to events (and non-events) since   G
the hearing before Oliver J. They concluded therefrom that Acas had
manifestly decided to postpone dealing with the recognition issue until
such time as E.M.A.'s case against the T.U.C. had been finally disposed of.

Now, had that been so, virtual abandonment of their statutory duty
would have been clear and E.M.A.'s entitlement to the relief sought
established. The funereal course of events (both in the past and in
the foreseeable future) leading to that inexorable conclusion was thus   H
described by Cumming-Bruce L.J. [1979] 1 W.L.R. 1113, 1130D:

"... on any view, if the first instance trial [of E.M.A. v. T.U.C.]
takes place in March 1980, even assuming (which is a very big
assumption) that there is no appeal to this court, there then remains
before finality on the question of the affiliation of E.M.A. with the
T.U.C. the many steps to be taken ... So that now it does not look

A   as if there is any prospect of the uncertainty arising from the decision of E.M.A. to claim a declaration against the T.U.C. being resolved certainly for another 18 months, and I would have thought probably for a good deal longer. So the effect of the decision taken by Acas in December 1977 is now seen in this court to involve necessarily . . . a decision to keep the applications for recognition both by E.M.A. and by U.K.A.P.E. on ice for a period not less than about *three* years from the date of the applications before even proceeding to inquire of the opinion of workers."

These depressing factors led the learned Lord Justice to say:

"I cannot accept that such a long postponement can be regarded as a proper exercise of the undoubted discretion vested in Acas to determine its manner of proceeding and how to set about finding out the opinion of workers and its undoubted discretion to give itself reasonable time before attempting to proceed to inquiry."

Now that conclusion, which was arrived at also by Lord Denning M.R. and by Lawton L.J. seems to have been based substantially on the belief that learned counsel for Acas had informed the Court of Appeal that, as Cumming-Bruce L.J. put it, at p. 1130H:

". . . it is *not* the intention of Acas to proceed to inquiry stage until the uncertainties flowing from the litigation and the dispute between E.M.A. and the T.U.C. have been *finally* resolved . . ."

But learned counsel himself has in strenuous terms informed your Lordships that this belief entertained by the members of the Court of Appeal was quite mistaken. He asserted that, so far from indicating or accepting that Acas had ever adopted a *final* stand, he had intimated to that court that, having decided on December 14, 1977, simply ". . . not to proceed with its inquiries on the references for the *time being* until E.M.A.'s claims against the T.U.C. had been determined in the courts or withdrawn," Acas had thereafter reviewed the position periodically and had throughout kept an open mind on how and when they should next proceed.

My Lords, the difference between the clear understanding of the Court of Appeal and the distinction drawn before your Lordships by learned counsel may be thought by some to be narrow. But counsel insisted that it is substantial and important, and that justice would be denied Acas were what he asserts was the mistaken view taken by the Court of Appeal to prevail. As he, in effect, put it: To say "Come what may, we, Acas will *not* proceed with the recognition references until the *E.M.A.* v. *T.U.C.* litigation is finally disposed of," is materially different from keeping the matter open, periodically reviewing it, and reaching a fresh conclusion each time in the light of the developing situation; the former involves abandonment by Acas of its statutory duty, the latter merely a reasonable and permissible postponement.

I have naturally found this conflict between court and counsel considerably embarrassing. But, having reflected long on the matter, I feel I cannot exclude from my mind the possibility that the latter attitude may indeed have been the one adopted by Acas. If it was, can it be condemned out of hand as one which no reasonable body, charged with the statutory duties imposed upon Acas, could properly have arrived at? After considerable hesitation, I do not think it can. But, even so, with

the passing of time—much, *much* time—can it be said that what may   A
well have been reasonable at one stage had later become clearly unreasonable? This has proved a far more difficult question. But, having
heard from learned counsel the sort of considerations which Acas believed
relevant to their assessment of the situation, I am unable to say that,
singly or cumulatively, they ought not to have carried some weight.

On the whole, I have therefore come to the conclusion that this appeal   B
should be allowed. But for me it has been a knife-edge decision and one
which Acas should not regard as recognising any sort of right in them
to make a habit of dilatoriness. If they do, they will surely come to
grief. For they are fettered by the requirements of reason, and, if those
are not met, condemnation must follow.

LORD KEITH OF KINKEL. My Lords, I agree with the speech of my   C
noble and learned friend, Lord Diplock, and would accordingly dismiss
the appeal.

LORD SCARMAN. My Lords, the question for the House in this appeal
is whether Acas was entitled in the circumstances in which it found
itself first to take, and then to continue, its decision to defer its inquiries   D
into a recognition issue referred to it pursuant to section 11 (1) of the
Employment Protection Act 1975 by the respondent trade union, the
Engineers' and Managers' Association. A subsidiary question arises as
to the extent of the power of the Court of Appeal and this House to
have regard to events occurring between trial and the hearing of the
appeal.

The history which lies behind the appeal is complex. The motives   E
and intentions of the actors are not always clear. But the facts necessary
for a decision are few.

First, some words as to the parties and persons directly affected by
the appeal.

The House has under consideration a further chapter in the chequered
and complicated story of the struggle between a number of unions to   F
secure recognition as the collective bargaining agent of the professional
engineers (and others of comparable status) employed in the engineering
industry. The unions in contention are the United Kingdom Association
of Professional Engineers (U.K.A.P.E.), the Engineers and Managers
Association (E.M.A.), and the Technical, Administrative and Supervisory
Section (T.A.S.S.) of the Amalgamated Union of Engineering Workers
(A.U.E.W.). The employees, for whose favour the unions compete, are   G
vitally affected by, but not participants in the struggle. They are " in
consimili casu " with my fair lady at a mediaeval tourney, for whose
favour the jousting champions compete. Apart from voicing their
opinions, hopes and expectations, they stand, like her, upon the sidelines,
watching and waiting for the master of the tournament—for them Acas
—to decide upon which competitor to confer the accolade of recognition,   H
i.e., the right to be treated as their champion.

In the present case, there are some 300 workers to whom the recognition issue relates. They are professional, or equivalently high grade,
engineers employed by the General Electric Co. Ltd. at Whetstone, near
Leicester. Over 100 of them are members of E.M.A.: some 90 of them
belong to no union: the remaining 100 are, it appears, more or less
equally divided between U.K.A.P.E. and T.A.S.S. In other words, at

A least 200 of them wish to be represented by a union, and E.M.A. has a membership which is double that of any other union.

The engineering industry has had for many years a number of "procedural" agreements with staff unions who are members of the Confederation of Shipbuilding and Engineering Unions (C.S.E.U.). T.A.S.S. as a section of the A.U.E.W., is a party to these agreements.

B They establish negotiating arrangements for the purpose of collective bargaining as to the terms and conditions of employment of a great number of workers; but they do not cover senior professional engineers. T.A.S.S., though it includes some qualified engineers amongst its members, has not made headway in its effort to extend its membership amongst the more highly qualified workers at Whetstone. U.K.A.P.E., a union which is not affiliated to the T.U.C. and whose rules limit membership

C of the union to professional engineers and other employees of comparable status, has had some success in attracting members amongst the workers with whom this case is concerned and would do much better if it could secure recognition by the employers. E.M.A., a union which prior to April 22, 1977, was known as the Electrical Power Engineers Association and is the plaintiff in the present case, is, like T.A.S.S.,

D affiliated to the T.U.C. In recent years it has sought to extend to the engineering industry. In its campaign to recruit senior engineers and managers as members, it has caused offence to T.A.S.S.

The struggle between the unions burst into flame in the late seventies. It may be told, so far as this appeal is concerned, by setting out the critical dates and noting against them the relevant facts.

E *July 9, 1976.* U.K.A.P.E. refers to Acas a recognition issue arising from its rejected request to be recognised by the company for the purpose of collective bargaining on behalf of graduate engineering staff employed at Whetstone.

March 16, 1977. Award by T.U.C. disputes committee in favour of T.A.S.S. upon a complaint that E.M.A. by recruiting for members at Whetstone was in breach of "the Bridlington agreement" which since

F 1939 has regulated inter-union disputes between unions affiliated to the T.U.C. The award imposed a ban on E.M.A. recruiting.

April 22, 1977. E.M.A. changes its name from the Electrical Power Engineers Association to E.M.A.

April 27, 1977. In defiance of a requirement of the Bridlington agreement not to invoke the Act without consultation and agreement

G with other affiliated union(s) affected, E.M.A. refers its recognition issue to Acas, who, with the consent of U.K.A.P.E. and E.M.A., decide to conduct the two references together.

July—early October 1977. Acas proceeds with its examination and inquiries. In particular, Acas with the help of those interested in the reference prepares a draft questionnaire designed to ascertain the opinions

H of the workers concerned.

September 28, 1977. T.U.C. inform E.M.A. that the union must either comply with the award or face disciplinary proceedings. In other words, T.U.C. serves notice on E.M.A. that, if it continues to recruit and to proceed with its reference, it faces the possibility of expulsion from the T.U.C. E.M.A. requests Acas to suspend its inquiries while it considers its position. Acas agrees.

October 13, 1977. E.M.A. issues a writ against the T.U.C. (the

T.U.C. action) claiming a declaration that the disputes committee award   A
was invalid.

October 14, 1977. E.M.A. requests Acas to proceed with the reference and to report as soon as possible. E.M.A.'s strategy is clear: to
immobilise the T.U.C. while it seeks a recognition recommendation from
Acas.

November 8, 1977. On E.M.A.'s application for an injunction in   B
the T.U.C. action, the Chancery Court (Browne-Wilkinson J.), upon the
T.U.C. undertaking until judgment or further order not to impose any
penalty upon E.M.A. for non-compliance with the disputes committee
award, and by consent, gives directions intended to make possible an
early trial of the action: the statement of claim is to be delivered within
seven days and, after close of pleadings and exchange of lists of documents, the parties are to attend the master on February 6, 1978, to enable   C
the action to be set down and the parties to apply for an early trial.
E.M.A. in the event took 98 days to deliver a statement of claim: there
were delays associated with discovery; the action has not yet reached
trial, which is now expected in February 1980. The inference is inescapable: that E.M.A. has, to put it kindly, made haste slowly in the
hope that Acas would report with a recommendation in its favour before   D
the court ruled on the validity of the T.U.C. committee's award.

November 9, 1977. Acas decides "to defer its inquiries" for the
present. The anxieties of Acas and the reasons for its decision are best
explained by the words of its press notice of this date:

> " The council of Acas today considered further whether to
> proceed with its inquiries into the references for trade union recog-   E
> nition concerning the United Kingdom Association of Professional
> Engineers (U.K.A.P.E.), the Engineers' and Managers' Association
> (E.M.A.) and G.E.C. Reactor Equipment Ltd., Whetstone.
> " Two references have been made under section 11 of the Employ-
> ment Protection Act 1975. The first by U.K.A.P.E. made on July
> 9, 1976, and the second by E.M.A. on April 27, 1977; both concern
> the same group of engineers employed by G.E.C. R.E.L. at Whet-   F
> stone. It has been agreed with the parties that the two references
> can be conducted together.
> " Apart from the recognition references to Acas, the matter was
> already the subject of a dispute between E.M.A. and T.A.S.S. which
> had been referred to the T.U.C. disputes committee. The award of
> the committee has been challenged and is now the subject of a writ   G
> by the E.M.A. which is still sub judice. However today it is being
> further discussed between the T.U.C. and the E.M.A. with a view
> to seeking a solution. The outcome is not known.
> " In considering whether to proceed with its own inquiries under
> section 12 of the Employment Protection Act the council took
> account of the above position and also of the probability that if it
> decided to go ahead with its inquiries its decision might be the   H
> subject of legal challenge by U.K.A.P.E. whilst if it decided to defer
> inquiries it might be challenged by E.M.A.
> " The council is most anxious to act lawfully and has taken full
> account of the advice of its legal advisers. It is very conscious of
> its duty under section 12 (3) of the Employment Protection Act to
> have regard to the desirability of encouraging a settlement by agree-
> ment and where appropriate by conciliation. It has also taken

A   account of the Code of Practice on Industrial Relations which provides in paragraph 85 that the ' responsibility for avoiding disputes between trades unions about recognition is principally with the unions themselves and, in the case of affiliated unions, with the Trades Union Congress. Unions concerned should make full use of the available procedures.'

B   " The council believes that it would be helpful if the issue between the T.U.C. and the E.M.A. were resolved since the outcome would be one of the factors which the council would need to take into account in its own examination. The council is also anxious not to exacerbate the problem by untimely action of its own, and has decided to defer its inquiries for the present. The council intends in the meantime to seek further legal guidance and will consider

C   the matter at its next meeting."

November 18, 1977. Solicitors for E.M.A. protest against Acas's decision, call for Acas to proceed with the E.M.A. reference and, in particular, for the questionnaire to be sent to the workers concerned. E.M.A.'s consent to its reference being conducted together with that of U.K.A.P.E. is withdrawn.

D   *December 14, 1977.* Acas reaffirms its decision " not to proceed, for the time being," with the two references. A press notice is issued by Acas as follows:

" At its meeting today the council of Acas reconsidered its position with regard to proceeding on the references for trade union recognition concerning the United Kingdom Association of Professional

E   Engineers (U.K.A.P.E.), the Engineers' and Managers' Association (E.M.A.) and G.E.C. Reactor Equipment Ltd. (Whetstone).

" The council decided that it would not proceed, for the time being, with its inquiries on those references. In reaching its decision, it took particular account of the implications of the writ which has been served on the T.U.C. by E.M.A., one of the applicant unions. This writ which is still outstanding seeks to challenge an award by a

F   T.U.C. disputes committee in respect of a recognition and recruitment issue concerning the group of employees who are the subject of the E.M.A. reference."

Almost immediately some 200 of the engineers at Whetstone present a petition of protest to Acas.

G   *January 25, 1978.* E.M.A. issue writ in this action, claiming against Acas declarations that Acas in refusing or failing to proceed upon its reference is in breach of its statutory duties, and that it is bound by section 12 of the Act to examine and report upon E.M.A.'s recognition issue.

February 10, 1978. E.M.A.'s notice of motion for interim relief.

March 8, 1978. The writ is, by leave, amended so as to allow

H   U.K.A.P.E., at its request, to become a defendant. U.K.A.P.E.'s attitude to the case, put lucidly in this House as in the Court of Appeal by one of its officers, is that it is content, indeed it would wish, that Acas proceed with both references, provided it adds to its workers' questionnaire a question designed to discover their second choice of a union for recognition if their first choice fails to secure Acas's recommendation. This represented a change of attitude by U.K.A.P.E: for in a letter dated September 30, 1977, the union had requested Acas to defer the

questionnaire until the issue between the E.M.A. and the T.U.C. had
been resolved.

April 7, 1978. E.M.A.'s motion being treated by consent as the trial
of the action, Oliver J. gives judgment for Acas. The speed in this
action is to be contrasted with the delays in the T.U.C. action.

May 14, 1979. The Court of Appeal allows E.M.A.'s appeal, and
declares that Acas is bound to proceed with the reference and report
upon the recognition issue.

December 1979. Hearing of Acas's appeal in this House.

The chronological table reveals the very serious delay imposed upon
the conduct of the reference by the decision of Acas taken on December
14, 1977, and maintained ever since. For some $3\frac{1}{2}$ to 4 years the workers
affected who wish to be represented by a union have waited: but are still
without any decision upon either reference. The reasons for Acas's
suspension of its inquiries into the two references have been explained
in the press notices and in the evidence of one of its senior officers,
Mr. Norcross. In an affidavit of February 16, 1978, he said:

> " 8. In these circumstances it appeared to the defendants that it
> was inappropriate and untimely to proceed with the next stage of
> their inquiries, which will involve seeking the opinions of workers to
> whom the recognition issues relate, for so long as the plaintiffs'
> challenge to the legal validity of the recruitment bar has not been
> determined by the court or withdrawn by the plaintiffs. The
> defendants considered that it would not have been meaningful to
> put hypothetical questions to workers at a time when it was not
> known whether the recruitment ban was lawfully made and could be
> lawfully enforced, and when it was within the plaintiffs' power to
> break this deadlock by proceeding expeditiously with its action against
> the T.U.C. or by withdrawing their challenge to the legal validity of
> the recruitment bar. Moreover, the U.K.A.P.E. had specifically
> requested the defendants to defer issuing a questionnaire to workers
> until this issue was resolved one way or the other on the grounds that
> the employees could not complete the questionnaire meaningfully in
> such circumstances.
>
> " 9. The defendants were also of the opinion that they could not
> have reached a proper conclusion on the basis of the results of such
> survey. In any case the defendants were of the opinion that they
> were not only entitled but had a duty, on industrial relations grounds,
> to take into account any relevant award of the T.U.C. disputes
> committee before they could reach a conclusion on the plaintiffs'
> reference."

Put shortly, the T.U.C. action was, as Oliver J. observed, the determining
factor. In his second affidavit, sworn March 17, 1978, Mr. Norcross
described the attitude of Acas in these words:

> " Acas would like to proceed with the conduct of the references
> but considers that it would be untimely to do so in the light of the
> legal action between the E.M.A. and the T.U.C., which is still
> pending."

I turn now to consider whether Acas has power to defer or suspend
proceedings on a reference, and, if it has, the extent of the power.
The answer depends upon the interpretation to be put upon sections 11
to 16 of the Act.

A   Section 11 (1) entitles an independent trade union to refer a recognition issue to Acas. A recognition issue arises from a request by a trade union for recognition by an employer for the purpose of collective bargaining: sections 11 (2) and (3). A reference having been made, Acas becomes bound to examine the issue, to consult affected parties, and to make such inquiries as it thinks fit. If the issue is not settled and the reference is not withdrawn, Acas " shall prepare a written report ":

B   sections 12 (1) and (4). Thus the union may settle with the employer at any time, or unilaterally withdraw the reference, in either of which events Acas has nothing further to do: and the workers to whom the issue relates have no right to compel either the union or Acas to proceed. Indeed it is the duty of Acas to seek a settlement of the issue by agreement, using in appropriate cases its statutory powers of conciliation:

C   section 12 (3). If Acas has to prepare a report, it must set out in the report its findings, any advice it chooses to offer in connection with its findings, and any recommendation for recognition it decides to make. Whether it makes, or decides not to make a recommendation, it must give the reasons for its decision in the report: section 12 (4).

         The processing by Acas of a recognition issue is, therefore, not forensic in character though it embodies a judicial element substantial

D   enough to impose upon Acas in the conduct of the reference the obligations of natural justice. Acas can make no order nor, if it recommends recognition, is there available under the law any process which can compel an employer to recognise a trade union. The law provides in sections 15 and 16 of the Act for pressure, which many employers would, no doubt, wish to avert by choosing recognition; but

E   neither Acas nor the central arbitration committee, to whom a trade union may apply if an employer fails to comply with an Acas recommendation, nor the courts of the land can order recognition.

         Accordingly, Acas's power, whatever its extent, to defer its inquiries or the preparation of its report is not to be compared, except in terms of the broadest generality, with a court's discretion to adjourn the hearing of a case. It is a power the nature of which depends upon Acas's

F   statutory functions, duties and responsibilities.

         Acas, it can be said with confidence, has the following duties. It must do what the statute says it shall do. It must exercise its powers in a way in which in the circumstances of each particular case it considers best suited to advance the purpose and policy of the statute. These are the improvement of industrial relations, and the extension of collective

G   bargaining. It must ensure that those whom it consults—and it is under a statutory duty to " consult all parties who it considers will be affected " (section 12 (1)), e.g., other trade unions, the T.U.C., employers' associations, and to " ascertain the opinions of workers to whom the issue relates " (section 14 (1))—have a proper opportunity of making their views known. But subject to the mandatory duties imposed upon it by the statute it may conduct its examination of the issue and its

H   inquiries in whatever way it thinks best.

         The statute, as my noble and learned friend, Lord Diplock, observed in *Grunwick Processing Laboratories Ltd.* v. *Advisory, Conciliation and Arbitration Service* [1978] A.C. 655, 688, imposes no time limit upon the conduct of the reference. Acas is clearly under a duty, arising from the mandatory words of section 12 subsections (1) and (4), to proceed with reasonable expedition: but equally clearly it has a power to defer its inquiries and consultations. If, for example, Acas thinks

there is a chance of the settlement of the issue by agreement, it may   A
defer its inquiries and must defer the preparation of a report until it
knows whether it will be necessary to report upon the issue. Equally
clearly, Acas has a power to defer the preparation of a report until it
has made the inquiries which it thinks appropriate to the reference.

To sum up the effect of the statute, I interpret it as conferring upon
Acas a discretion to suspend inquiry or to defer the preparation of its
report if it is of the opinion that a period of suspension or deferment   B
would promote the improvement of industrial relations (including the
extension of *collective* bargaining: my emphasis). Conversely if Acas
should be of the opinion that industrial relations would be worsened
(or *collective* bargaining put at risk) if it did not for a period suspend
inquiries or defer preparation of its report, it has the power, at its discretion, to defer action. Since ascertainment of the views of the workers   C
to whom the recognition issue relates is a part, albeit a mandatory part,
of its inquiries, this discretionary power extends also to this phase of
the inquiry.

Both the chance of settlement of the issue and (as with E.M.A. in
early October 1977) the possibility of withdrawal of the reference are
instances in which the power may be exercised. But the power is not
limited. It is a general power to be exercised reasonably, and consis-   D
tently with the general duty imposed upon Acas by section 1 (2) of the
Act as construed by this House in the immediately preceding appeal of
United Kingdom Association of Professional Engineers v. *Advisory,*
Conciliation and Arbitration Service [1980] 2 W.L.R. 254.

The statute imposes no cut-off point, no time limit. If, however,
under the guise of deferment Acas in effect terminates its conduct of the   E
reference, refusing to complete its examination or to proceed to a report,
it will be acting ultra vires the statute: for it can terminate proceedings
only if the issue has been settled or the reference has been withdrawn.

In my judgment, therefore, Acas has a discretion to defer inquiries
for a period. For the reasons given in *United Kingdom Association of*
Professional Engineers v. *Advisory, Conciliation and Arbitration Service,*
the exercise of its discretion is not reviewable by the courts unless Acas   F
can be shown either to have misdirected itself in law; or to have failed to
observe the requirements of natural justice, or to have failed to consider
relevant matters; or to have conducted the reference in a way in which
no reasonable advisory conciliation or arbitration service, paying due
regard to the statute, could have conducted it. I, therefore, agree with
the formulation by my noble and learned friend, Lord Diplock, of the   G
crucial question presented by the appeal: has Acas by the deferment in
this case abdicated its statutory function to proceed with the reference?
The courts cannot intervene, unless satisfied that it has.

The test of reasonableness being not what the court, or this House,
thinks would have been the reasonable course to have pursued but
whether it has been shown that no reasonable advisory, conciliation and
arbitration service could properly have made and then continued its   H
deferment decision in the circumstances in which Acas found itself, it
is not possible, in the light of Mr. Norcross's evidence, and applying this
test, to hold that the decision of December 14, 1977, was unreasonable.
I agree on this point with the trial judge. Indeed, I find only one error
in his judgment. He said [1978] I.C.R. 875, 893B that he had to
look to the time when the decision was taken, and not as it was at trial.
For reasons, which I shall mention briefly when dealing with the subsidiary

A question, I think that he should have considered the reasonableness not
only of the initial decision to defer but also of the decision to maintain
the deferment in the circumstances which existed at trial. Nevertheless
the case for deferment was much the same in April 1978 when he gave
judgment as it had been in December 1977. In particular, there was
still, notwithstanding " E.M.A.'s own dilatoriness" (the judge's com-
B ment, with which I agree), a reasonable prospect of an early, or at
least a not too distant trial in the T.U.C. action. The matters to which
Acas had attached importance in the previous November and December
remained relevant and real. Their weight was in April 1978, as at the
earlier time, not for the court but for Acas to decide.

It is submitted, however, that 13 months later, when the case reached
the Court of Appeal, the lapse of time was such that it was now
C unreasonable on the part of Acas to persist any longer in deferring proceedings on the reference. This was the view of all three members of
the Court of Appeal. It is unfortunate that this question was dealt
with not on the basis of evidence directed to the situation then obtaining
but upon statements by counsel. Nevertheless enough is known to enable
a conclusion to be reached. The Court of Appeal understood counsel for
Acas to have said that " his instructions were that Acas was not going
D to proceed with its inquiries until the validity of the award [i.e. the award
of the disputes committee which was the subject of the T.U.C. action]
was determined ": see Lord Denning M.R. [1979] 1 W.L.R. 1113, 1124–
1125 and Cumming-Bruce L.J., at p. 1130. Exactly what counsel said is
a matter of doubt. But he did not intend to convey, nor, as we have
been told and I accept, was it Acas's view that, come what may, it would
E in no circumstances resume its inquiries until the validity or invalidity of
the award was finally determined. Misunderstanding of Acas's view arose
because evidence was not taken, as it should have been if matters subsequent to trial were to be relied on, as to what its view was in May 1979.
But, my Lords, it cannot be doubted that Acas's view in May 1979, and
indeed today, remains the same as it had been on December 14, 1977,
namely, that " it would not proceed, for the time being, with its inquiries "
F and that it was taking " particular account of the implications of " the
T.U.C. action.

The question, therefore, is whether in May 1979 the various factors
referred to by Mr. Norcross in the evidence to which I have referred
and, in particular, the difficulties created by the T.U.C. action were
such that, notwithstanding the lapse of another 18 months without a
G decision in that action, Acas could reasonably refuse to resume the
conduct of the reference. All the factors mentioned by Mr. Norcross
remained relevant: but there now had to be weighed in the balance the
serious frustrations of the workers concerned arising from the delay.
And there was one further relevant consideration: trial in the T.U.C.
action was not expected in February or March 1980.

The passage of time had not lessened the difficulties of eliciting the
H opinions of the workers fairly and accurately. Because of the failure
of E.M.A. to bring the T.U.C. action to trial, Acas was in no better
position in 1979 than it had been in 1977 either to reach a proper
conclusion on the survey of workers' opinion or to report. The difficulty
in the way of making a recommendation for recognition remained as
formidable as it had been in 1977. If Acas proceeded to a report, it
might well find it impossible to make any recommendation—a result
which would do little to relieve the frustrations of the workers. And it still

remained Acas's duty, on industrial relations grounds, to take account A
of the T.U.C. award, if lawful, before determining E.M.A.'s reference:
see paragraph 85 of the Code of Practice to which reference was made
in the press notice of November 9, 1977.

Can it, therefore, be said that Acas in May 1979 was acting as no
reasonable body with its statutory duties could properly act? Was its
decision to continue with the deferment an abdication of its statutory B
function? In my judgment, no. Workers do not have a right to have
the trade union of which they are members recognised for the purpose of
collective bargaining, even if a substantial number of them belong to
the union: for no employer can be compelled to recognise a trade union.
The opinions of the workers are a relevant matter of great importance,
which Acas is bound to ascertain before it recommends, or refuses to
recommend, recognition. But Acas is not bound to recommend in C
accordance with their opinion. Acas has to form its view as to what
is best for the promotion of improved industrial relations and the extension of collective bargaining. The Court of Appeal erred in substituting
its judgment for that of Acas. In the confused situation which E.M.A.
had allowed to persist by not pursuing the T.U.C. action with sufficient
expedition it was not unreasonable of Acas to continue the suspension
of its inquiries: and it may well remain in the true interests of the D
workers to defer a report until the facts exist in which a recognition
recommendation can be made.

The appeal reached this House in December 1979. Trial in the T.U.C.
action was then only a few months away. It must now be reasonable
to await the outcome of the trial, if there be any validity in the reasons
adduced by Mr. Norcross for the decision to defer inquiries. E

For these reasons, my Lords, I would allow the appeal.

My Lords, I have reached my conclusion on the merits of the appeal
as I see them. In so doing I have assumed that the answer to the
subsidiary question is that the Court of Appeal and this House may,
if justice requires it, have regard to events subsequent to trial in determining an appeal. In my view, the assumption is sound in law. I agree
with Lord Denning M.R. that the Court of Appeal was in duty bound, F
if it thought it necessary in order to do justice, " to re-hear the case
as at the time of re-hearing: and ought to give such judgment
as ought to be given if the case came *at that time* before the court
of first instance " [1979] 1 W.L.R. 1113; 1126. By parity of reasoning, it is the duty of a trial judge to take account of the situation
of the parties as it exists at the time of trial. I think, however, the G
proposition is not as general as might appear from the judgment of
the Master of the Rolls. I know of no case of authority in the
books in which an appellate court has reversed a judgment for the
defendant where there was no cause of action, actual, imminent, or
threatened when the writ was issued: and, if there be any such case,
I think it would be wrong in principle. The power to reverse or modify
a judgment at first instance in the light of subsequent events arises most H
frequently in connection with the remedy or relief to be granted. If
it be damages, the appeal court can and, if justice so requires, ought to
take account of developments since trial: see *Lim Poh Choo* v. *Camden
and Islington Area Health Authority* [1980] A.C. 174. If the relief is
equitable, e.g., injunction or specific performance, the duty is well
established. If the relief sought, as here, is declaratory, it is a matter
of discretion. But, if an appellate court is disposed to allow an appeal

A on the basis of events subsequent to trial, it must be astute to ensure that it does so on evidence. Evidence, of course, embraces admissions, including admissions by counsel. However, in the present case, a statement by counsel was an insecure foundation for forming a view as to whether Acas, a statutory body whose duties lay in a complex and specialised field, had since trial abdicated its statutory functions. The Court of Appeal did less than justice to Acas in relying on what it

B understood counsel to be saying. Justice required that the court made plain the view it was likely to form in the absence of further evidence as to events subsequent to trial and invited Acas to file evidence. We now know that, had this been done, Mr. Norcross would have sworn a further affidavit explaining the attitude of Acas in 1979. I have no doubt that he would have had plenty to say. Fortunately, for the reasons

C already given, enough is known of Acas's position to enable a judgment to be formed as to whether in May 1979 it was abdicating its statutory function. In my opinion, it was not.

Appeal allowed.

Solicitors: *Treasury Solicitor; Lawford & Co.*

D

F. C.

E

* PRACTICE DIRECTION (CHILD: APPLICATION TO REGISTRAR) (No. 2)

Minor—Practice—Custody applications—Applications for agreed custody and access orders—Wardship and guardianship proceedings in Principal Registry—Applications to registrar

F

By a practice direction of November 3, 1977, *Practice Direction (Child: Application to Registrar)* [1977] 1 W.L.R. 1226, it was provided that on an application in a matrimonial cause for an agreed custody order or for an order for access to a child where the only question at issue is the extent of such access, the application should in the first instance be made to a registrar, unless there are exceptional

G circumstances making it desirable for the matter to be brought before a judge for decision.

The judges of the Family Division are of the opinion, and it is accordingly hereby directed, that applications of like nature made in wardship and guardianship cases proceeding in the Principal Registry including applications for an agreed care and control order should be

H dealt with in the same manner.

Issued with the approval of the President.

R. L. BAYNE-POWELL,
Senior Registrar.

March 4, 1980.

322

A

[FAMILY DIVISION]

* PRACTICE DIRECTION (FAMILY DIVISION: LIBERTY TO APPLY)

Husband and Wife—Practice—Liberty to apply—Family Division—Procedure where " liberty to apply " granted—Procedure applicable to non-contentious probate—Matrimonial Causes Rules 1977 (S.I. 1977 No. 344 (L. 6)), r. 122

B

Liberty to apply

Judges and registrars of the Family Division have found that there is misunderstanding among practitioners as to the meaning of the above words. In one sense there is always liberty to apply since the court can always be applied to by using the proper procedure, but it is emphasised that, except in a few special cases, the words " Liberty to apply " do not give the right to apply to the court without using the procedures comprised in rule 122 of the Matrimonial Causes Rules 1977 and in the Non-Contentious Probate Rules, passim.

C

Under a summons for directions there is always liberty to apply for further directions without taking out a further summons. The court may give liberty to apply as to terms of compromise or as to the minor terms where property is settled. These examples are not exhaustive, but, in general applications should not be made under liberty to apply without using the procedures laid down by the Rules referred to.

D

R. L. BAYNE-POWELL,
Senior Registrar.

E

March 4, 1980.

[FAMILY DIVISION]

F

* TOMLINSON v. TOMLINSON

1979 Oct. 22   Sir John Arnold P. and Wood J.

Husband and Wife—Justices—Evidence—Witness present in court —No order excluding witnesses from court—Admissibility of evidence—Practice in matrimonial proceedings

G

The parties were divorced in 1978. The wife was granted a periodical payments order of £12 a week which was registered in the magistrates' court. The husband sought variation of that order to a nominal order on the ground that the wife was cohabiting and being maintained by another man. At the hearing the wife, who was unrepresented, wished to call the other man as a witness in order to refute the allegation. The husband's solicitor objected to the witness on the ground that the witness had been present in court from the commencement of the hearing. The justices upheld that objection. The justices found the husband's allegations proved and varied the periodical payments order to 5p a week.

H

On appeal by the wife: —

Held, allowing the appeal, that, in the absence of an order that witnesses should withdraw from the court until they were called to give evidence, there was no justification for excluding

A   the evidence of the wife's witness and, since his evidence was material, the decision of the justices could not stand and the case would be remitted for a rehearing.

    Per curiam. The proper course in domestic proceedings before justices was (1) that witnesses should not be under any obligation to leave the court unless an order was made by the bench excluding them; (2) that if an application was made to exclude a witness the justices should grant the application unless

B   they were satisfied that such an order in the circumstances was inappropriate; (3) where a party was unrepresented and the justices considered it appropriate that a witness should be excluded then the justices should invite the unrepresented party to make the application to exclude the witness; and (4) that where a witness against whom the justices had made an exclusion order remained in court the justices had a discretion to admit the evidence (post, pp. 326H—327c).

C

The following cases are referred to in the judgment of Sir John Arnold P.:

Nightingale, decd., (Practice Note), In re [1975] 1 W.L.R. 80.
Practice Note (1908) 24 T.L.R. 263.
Rex v. *Briggs* (1930) 22 Cr.App.R. 68, C.C.A.
Selfe v. *Isaacson* (1858) 1 F. & F. 194.

D   No additional cases were cited in argument.

APPEAL from Wigan justices.
    Following divorce, the husband was ordered to make weekly periodical payments of £12 to his former wife by the Wigan Divorce County Court. The order was registered in the Wigan Magistrates' Court on August 22,

E   1978. The husband sought variation of the periodical payments order to a nominal order on the ground that the wife was cohabiting with and being maintained by another man.
    At the hearing on March 9, 1979, the wife was unrepresented. She denied the allegation and wished to call the other man as a witness. The husband's solicitor objected on the ground that the witness had been present in court from the commencement of the hearing. The witness did not give

F   evidence. The justices found the husband's allegation proved. The periodical payments order was varied to a nominal order of 5p a week.
    The wife appealed on the grounds (1) that there was no evidence or no sufficient evidence for the justices to find that she was cohabiting or being maintained by another man; (2) that the justices had no evidence of the income of the man with whom the husband alleged that the wife was co-habiting; and (3) that the justices were wrong in law or, alternatively, in

G   the exercise of their discretion to refuse to allow the wife to call her witness in support of the contention that the wife was neither cohabiting with nor being maintained by the witness.
    The facts are stated in the judgment of Sir John Arnold P.

    Martyn Bennett for the wife.
H   *Simeon Thrower* for the husband.

    SIR JOHN ARNOLD P. This is an appeal from the Wigan Magistrates' Court. On March 9, 1979, the justices heard an application by Mr. Tomlinson for a reduction of the maintenance which he had been ordered to pay to his wife. His application was based on the proposition that his wife was cohabiting with and being maintained by another man. The other man in question was one Mr. Holmes. There has been no dispute on

the hearing of the appeal that in order for such a ground to be a valid A
ground for the reduction of the amount of a maintenance order it is necessary to satisfy both of the requirements in proof before the justices; namely,
that the person being maintained is cohabiting with another man and that
she is being maintained by that other man.

The justices made the order sought and reduced the amount of maintenance to a purely nominal sum. From that order the wife appeals. She B
brings forward three grounds for her appeal. She says that there was no
or no sufficient evidence to enable the justices to find that she was cohabiting with and being maintained by Mr. Holmes. Upon refinement of that
proposition in argument it is found to be simply that the second part of
the combined proposition was not supported by the evidence. There was
no doubt that there was sufficient evidence for the justices to find, if they
were so disposed, that the wife was cohabiting with Mr. Holmes.   C

The second ground is that there was no evidence before the justices
of the income of Mr. Holmes. The way that point arises is this: in the
absence of any direct evidence of payments by Mr. Holmes to the wife for
any purpose which could justly be regarded as maintenance, there might
have been—it is thought by the husband—some possibility that the court
might have inferred the fact of such maintenance from a consideration of D
the availability of the wherewithal to maintain.

Thirdly, that the justices were wrong in law or alternatively in the
exercise of their discretion to refuse to permit the wife to call Mr. Holmes
as a witness of fact, in support of her contention that she was neither cohabiting with nor being maintained by him.

It is that last matter which seems to me not only to be the most impor- E
tant of the matters which were raised in the notice of appeal but also to
give rise to wider considerations than those which intimately affect this
particular case.

The facts which were adduced in evidence as regards the proposition
that the wife was being maintained by Mr. Holmes were two, and two
only. One was that Mr. Holmes from time to time bought toys for the
wife's children, and the other was that on occasions Mr. Holmes left his F
van at the wife's premises to enable her to run her mother about, there
being evidence that she was looking after her mother to some extent.

It is for consideration whether, without more, those two matters could
really be enough to enable justices to hold that they were facts from which
the inference of some degree of maintenance could be drawn.

But they are very much bound up with the rest of the matter because G
if Mr. Holmes had been called those two matters could—and could with
propriety—have been more deeply investigated. For my part, I have preferred to place my judgment in this appeal upon the basis not of the first
ground—that is, there being no evidence from which the justices could
legitimately infer the fact of maintenance—but upon the matter of the
evidence of Mr. Holmes. Similarly, in relation to the second ground of H
appeal, the fact that there was no evidence of the income of Mr. Holmes
must be intimately bound up with the fact that Mr. Holmes gave no
evidence at all.

I come then to the third ground. What happened was this: the wife,
after some hesitation, it seems, not having a solicitor present in the court,
decided that she would go through the trial unrepresented. Of course,
the justices knew that perfectly well.

A   At the beginning of the evidence, when the husband was in the witness box, within a matter of minutes of starting his evidence he said—according to the notes of evidence taken down by the clerk: "I want the order reduced because another man has been living with my wife. His name is Derek Holmes. He is in court today." Then the husband gave his evidence. He was cross-examined by his wife and then a Mr. Worthington, an inquiry agent, gave his evidence about the comings and goings of Mr. Holmes from the wife's premises.

B

The wife then gave her evidence. In the words of the justices in their reasons, the wife proposed to call a witness—that was Mr. Holmes—but it was pointed out by the husband's solicitor that the witness had been in court throughout the hearing and the wife did not pursue her intention of calling him as a witness but in fact, as we heard from both sides today, C the reason why the wife did not pursue her intention of calling him as a witness was because she was told by the justices that she would not be allowed to do so. That in my judgment was an absolutely wrong thing for the justices to do. Since it seems to me to be tolerably clear that the evidence of Mr. Holmes, if it had been given, might have altered the view which the justices took, the refusal to permit him to be called appears to D me to be a fatal defect and one which must necessarily involve a further hearing of this complaint.

In the course of the argument on the appeal it has been brought to our attention that there is something of a confusion in the various authoritative pronouncements which have been made concerning the general matter of the presence or otherwise of witnesses in court during the hearing of a matter of controversy in the magistrates' court. As long ago as January 21, E 1908, Sir John Gorrell Barnes P. said that with regard to contested probate and matrimonial cases his view was that the old Admiralty rule should be adopted: namely, that all witnesses should remain out of court until they had given their evidence. He then noticed that it might be unpleasant for counsel to have to apply for a direction that the witnesses should remain out of court and concluded that in future in all contested cases the wit- F nesses should remain out of court, subject of course to a relaxation of that rule where there was no need for it to be enforced: see *Practice Note* (1908) 24 T.L.R. 263.

That was plainly intended to be a ruling as to the practice in the High Court in the Probate, Divorce and Admiralty Division over which Sir John Gorrell Barnes P. presided. But it would be very bad practice that there G should be different rules pertaining in different courts. Therefore, it is plainly desirable that there should be a degree of consistency in the matter.

In *The Supreme Court Practice* vol. 2, p. 444, para. 1666, there is a note to be found on this subject in relation to the Matrimonial Causes Rules 1957, which were the rules then in operation. The note is appended to the rule which provided that evidence should in ordinary circumstances H be given orally and in open court. The direction given by Sir John Gorrell Barnes P. in 1908 is noted and then the comment in *The Supreme Court Practice* (1967) is:

"This practice has fallen into desuetude and the present practice in probate and divorce suits is to allow the exclusion of witnesses to depend on the discretion of the judge, either on the application of counsel or at the judge's own instance."

In *Stone's Justices' Manual* 1979, vol. 1, p. 535, the matter is discussed   A
in relation to proceedings in magistrates' courts generally. The note states:

  " It is a common practice when a case is called on for hearing to order
  the witnesses on both sides to leave the court; but if a person who has
  disobeyed such order by remaining in the room should be offered in
  evidence by either party, his testimony cannot, it seems, be excluded."

But there is no authority given for that statement at all.   B

The note then observes that in accordance with a ruling given by Byles J.
in *Selfe* v. *Isaacson* (1858) 1 F. & F. 194 the plaintiff himself could not be
included in the order to withdraw. There is a further note that, in the
absence of an order, a witness may stay in court until he is called: see
Rex v. *Briggs* (1930) 22 Cr.App.R. 68.

Finally in *The Supreme Court Practice* (1979), vol. 1, p. 589 under the   C
rubric 38/1/4 the note is to this effect:

  " On the application of either party the court may at any time order
  all witnesses on both sides, other than the one under examination, to
  withdraw, but not to leave the court again after giving evidence so as
  to communicate with other witnesses before they give evidence."

The only other matter which I think it is necessary to mention is   D
In re Nightingale, decd. [1975] 1 W.L.R. 80 in which a direction was given
by Goulding J. during the hearing of a probate action in the Chancery
Division. Goulding J. merely says that the practice note by Sir John
Gorrell Barnes P. appears never to have been overruled and it was not
thenceforth to apply to the trial of probate actions in the Chancery Division, where the ordinary practice stated in *The Supreme Court Practice*   E
(1973), vol. 1, note 38/1/4 (which we are told is the same as that which
I have quoted from 1979) should be followed.

In those circumstances, it is apparent that by excluding the evidence of
witnesses who had been in court during the hearing of a case in relation
to which there had never been any order whatever that the witnesses
should withdraw, the justices were going beyond what on any of the   F
various practices which I have indicated could possibly be justified. In my
judgment, that is by itself enough to make it imperative that this case should
be reheard. However, it is desirable to take this opportunity of indicating
what I think should be the practice in matrimonial proceedings in magistrates' courts.

I do not think that it is enough in relation to proceedings in which
parties are frequently unrepresented merely to say that the court should be   G
permitted to exclude witnesses upon an application being made, because
necessarily if the matter is to be limited to that, unrepresented parties would
be very likely to omit to make an application out of sheer ignorance where
an application ought to be made in accordance with the best principles
of the administration of justice.

It seems to me that the right course is this: witnesses should not be   H
under any obligation to leave the court, except where an order is made
excluding them. The proper course for justices to pursue, if an application is made to them, would be to exclude the witnesses, unless they were
satisfied that that would not be an appropriate step to take; but if
they think it is a case in which perhaps the witnesses should be excluded,
then where a party is not represented to suggest that perhaps they might
like to make an application to that effect.

A　　This of course does not apply and never has applied to the parties themselves or their solicitors or their expert witnesses. Those are never excluded from the court.

There is one more matter to be considered: what should happen if a witness remains in court or a person remains in court after an order has been made excluding witnesses and his testimony is then offered to the

B　court? In that case there should it seems to me be—and there is some indication that there already is—a discretion to admit that witness's evidence, notwithstanding that he has remained in court in apparent defiance of a ruling. Of course the justices, if they were satisfied that contumacy or deception was involved, would be likely to exercise their discretion by excluding the testimony. But, on the other hand, if the case were one in which the possibility of that person being called as a witness was not

C　apparent at the time when the exclusion order was made and the person remained, then they might well exercise their discretion the other way. But it being a discretion, it would have to be exercised in every case in accordance with the merits of the occasion.

Section 57 (2) of the Magistrates' Courts Act 1952 provides that no person shall be present during the hearing and determination in the magis-

D　trates' court of any domestic proceedings except, among others, parties to the case, witnesses and other persons directly concerned in the case. Then in subsection (6) it is provided that nothing in the section is to affect the exercise by a magistrates' court of the power to direct that witnesses shall be excluded until they are called for examination. If the discretion which I have suggested should be exercised in fact exists, as I think it does exist, then there is nothing in the section to render it inoperable.

E

WOOD J. I agree.

Appeal allowed.
Remitted to fresh panel of justices for
re-hearing.

F

Solicitors: *G. Isherwood & Co., Wigan; White & Leonard for Taylors, Bridge, Baron & Sykes, Wigan.*

M. B. D.

G

H

[PRIVY COUNCIL]

* PATRICK JOSEPH McENIFF . . . . APPELLANT

AND

GENERAL DENTAL COUNCIL . . . . . RESPONDENT

[ON APPEAL FROM THE DISCIPLINARY COMMITTEE OF THE
GENERAL DENTAL COUNCIL]

1979 Oct. 11;
Nov. 27

Lord Edmund-Davies, Lord Scarman
and Lord Lane

Dentist—Infamous conduct in professional respect—Assessor's advice—Assessor advising disciplinary committee—Whether advice amounting to misdirection invalidating committee's decision—Sentence—Principles applicable—Dentists Act 1957 (5 & 6 Eliz. 2, c. 28), s. 25 (1) (b)

The appellant, a registered dentist, permitted unqualified staff to insert filling materials into the teeth of a patient. He was charged with having been guilty of infamous or disgraceful conduct in a professional respect. At the hearing before the Disciplinary Committee of the General Dental Council, the legal assessor advised the committee that " infamous conduct " meant " serious conduct in a professional respect," and that in deciding whether the conduct had been serious the committee should apply the ordinary standard of the profession, and not a special standard greater than was ordinarily to be expected. The committee found the appellant guilty of the charge and, pursuant to section 25 (1) (b) of the Dentists Act 1957,[1] ordered his name to be erased from the register.

On appeal by the appellant to the Judicial Committee against the finding of guilt, on the ground, inter alia, that the assessor had misdirected the Disciplinary Committee by making no distinction between negligent and infamous or disgraceful conduct, and against the sentence: —

Held, dismissing the appeal, (1) that a dentist could only be found guilty of infamous or disgraceful conduct in a professional respect if the conduct was such as to deserve the strongest reprobation; that it was for the committee to determine whether in law and in fact the appellant had been guilty of such conduct and, since the committee had been reminded of several decisions which accurately stated the law, the advice tendered by the assessor had not had sufficient significance to the result to invalidate the committee's decision and, therefore, it could not be a ground for quashing the finding of guilt (post, pp. 331H—332B, C–F).

Dicta of Lord Jenkins in *Felix* v. *General Dental Council* [1960] A.C. 704, 720, P.C. and Lord Guest in *Sivarajah* v. *General Medical Council* [1964] 1 W.L.R. 112, 117, P.C. applied.

Per curiam. The Judicial Committee regard Lord Jenkins' exposition in *Felix* v. *General Dental Council* [1960] A.C. 704, 720, as so valuable that, without going so far as to say that his words should invariably be cited in every disciplinary case, they think that to do so would be a commendable course (post, p. 332c–d).

(2) That, since the Disciplinary Committee was in the best position to weigh the seriousness of professional misconduct,

[1] Dentists Act 1957, s. 25 (1) (b): see post, p. 330A–B.

A   the Judicial Committee would only interfere with the exercise
by the Disciplinary Committee of its discretion as to sentence
if the sentence was wrong or unjustified; and that, although the
sentence of erasure passed on the appellant was undoubtedly
severe, it could not be said to be wrong or unjustified (post,
pp. 333F—334B).

      Dicta of Lord Upjohn in *McCoan* v. *General Medical
Council* [1964] 1 W.L.R. 1107, 1112, P.C. applied.

B   *Per curiam.* The penalty provisions of the Dentists Act
1957 need to be reconsidered in the light of the fact that
unlike the corresponding statutory provisions applicable to
doctors the Act has not been amended to permit the imposition
of the milder penalty of suspension for a period not longer
than 12 months in cases involving what may properly be
regarded as the less serious breaches of the professional code
(post, pp. 332H—333A).

C

    The following cases are referred to in the judgment of their Lordships:

Allinson v. *General Council of Medical Education and Registration* [1894]
    1 Q.B. 750, C.A.
Dubois v. *General Dental Council* (unreported), March 12, 1979, Privy
    Council Appeal No. 18 of 1978.
Felix v. *General Dental Council* [1960] A.C. 704; [1960] 2 W.L.R. 934;
D   [1960] 2 All E.R. 391, P.C.
Fox v. *General Medical Council* [1960] 1 W.L.R. 1017; [1960] 3 All
    E.R. 225, P.C.
McCoan v. *General Medical Council* [1964] 1 W.L.R. 1107; [1964] 3
    All E.R. 143, P.C.
Sivarajah v. *General Medical Council* [1964] 1 W.L.R. 112; [1964] 1
    All E.R. 504, P.C.

E

    The following additional cases were cited in argument:

Bhattacharya v. *General Medical Council* [1967] 2 A.C. 259; [1967] 3
    W.L.R. 498, P.C.
Rex v. *General Medical Council* [1930] 1 K.B. 562, C.A.

F   APPEAL (No. 14 of 1979) by the appellant, Patrick Joseph McEniff,
from a determination of the Disciplinary Committee of the General
Dental Council (Sir Rodney Swiss presiding) on May 16, 1979, finding
that the appellant had been guilty of infamous or disgraceful conduct
in a professional respect, and ordering that his name be erased from the
register.

    The facts are stated in the judgment of their Lordships.

G   *Roy Beldam Q.C.* and *Bernard Hargrove* for the appellant.
    Anthony Hidden Q.C. and *Timothy Straker* for the General Dental
Council.

                                               Cur. adv. vult.

H   November 27. The judgment of their Lordships was delivered by
LORD EDMUND-DAVIES.

    This is an appeal from a determination of the Disciplinary Committee
of the General Dental Council, made on May 16, 1979, by which the
appellant, Mr. Patrick Joseph McEniff, a registered dentist, was found
to have been guilty of infamous or disgraceful conduct in a professional
respect and his name was ordered to be erased from the register.

    The appeal (which is against both finding and sentence) is said to

involve the construction of section 25 of the Dentists Act 1957, the A
relevant parts of which read as follows:

"(1) A registered dentist who either before or after registration—
. . . (b) has been guilty of any infamous or disgraceful conduct in a
professional respect, shall be liable to have his name erased from
the register. (2) A person's name shall not be erased under this
section—. . . (c) on account of his adopting or refraining from B
adopting any particular theory of dentistry."

The appellant was charged in the following terms:

"That being a registered dentist, between about October 1, 1975,
and January 3, 1976, you knowingly enabled persons employed by
you who were not registered medical or dental practitioners or
enrolled ancillary dental workers to carry out work amounting to C
the practice of dentistry as defined in section 33 of the Dentists Act
1957; and that in relation to the facts alleged you have been guilty
of infamous or disgraceful conduct in a professional respect."

The facts can be shortly stated. The appellant qualified in 1964 and
has practised for many years in Northern Ireland. The charge arose
from a complaint originally made by Miss Teresa Elizabeth McGrath by D
a letter which she sent to the Central Services Agency in Northern
Ireland. The nature of her complaint was that, in treating Miss McGrath
as a patient, on approximately nine or ten occasions the appellant
had drilled her teeth but the fillings were inserted by unqualified staff.
It was said on the appellant's behalf that he had tried unsuccessfully for
two years to recruit qualified staff and had in consequence to manage E
with a Mrs. Blake, who was a qualified dental surgery assistant, and
a Miss Ellis, a receptionist. It was not suggested on his behalf that either
of them was an " ancillary dental worker " within the meaning of section
41 of the Act of 1957. A hearing of Miss McGrath's complaint took
place before the Services Committee of the Central Services Agency on
October 3, 1978, and this led to a report being presented to the Disciplinary Committee by the Department of Health and Social Services. F

It was admitted on behalf of the appellant that on four occasions—
namely, October 24, December 11, December 19, 1975, and January 23,
1976—Miss McGrath attended the appellant's surgery as a patient and
was treated by him, and that on each of these occasions either Miss
Ellis or Mrs. Blake treated her by inserting the filling after drilling had
been completed by the appellant. He claimed that he always inspected G
the work done before Miss McGrath left the surgery, but accepted that
in treating her in this way he was not offering the full services of
professional dentistry, and that by allowing unqualified persons to do the
packing he was increasing the risk of a filling becoming loose, with
resultant pain, discomfort, or waste of the patient's time.

The conviction has been attacked on two grounds: (1) that the legal H
assessor misdirected the Disciplinary Committee as to what constituted
infamous or disgraceful conduct in a professional respect; and (2) that
the appellant's maltreatment of Miss McGrath could not be so stigma-
tized.

As to (1), reference must first be had to the opening of the case
before the Disciplinary Committee by Mr. Hidden. Having outlined the
facts, he continued:

A   " May I pause now only to say one or two words on the law, of which you will be fully familiar, and no doubt you will be advised by your learned legal assessor in any event. You will remember that the test of what is infamous conduct in a professional respect was laid down clearly in the case of *Allinson* v. *General Council of Medical Education and Registration* [1894] 1 Q.B. 750, 763. Lopes

B   L.J. in fact devised the test, with the assistance of the other judges, and the immortal words are these: ' " If it is shown that a medical man, in the pursuit of his profession, has done something with regard to it which would be reasonably regarded as disgraceful or dishonourable by his professional brethren of good repute and competency," then it is open to the General Medical Council to say that he has been guilty of " infamous conduct in a profes-

C   sional respect." ' There is some assistance equally in the case of *Rex* v. *General Medical Council* [1930] 1 K.B. 562. Scrutton L.J. said, at p. 569: ' It is a great pity that the word " infamous " is used to describe the conduct of a medical practitioner who advertises. As in the case of the Bar so in the medical profession advertising is serious misconduct in a professional respect and that is all that is meant by the phrase " infamous conduct; " it

D   means no more than serious misconduct judged according to the rules written or unwritten governing the profession.' Your committee will be aware of the case of *Felix* v. *General Dental Council* [1960] A.C. 704."

At the conclusion of the evidence and speeches of counsel, the legal assessor, exercising his indubitable right under rule 4 of the

E   General Dental Council Disciplinary Committee (Legal Assessor) Rules 1957 (S.I. 1957 No. 1470) to advise the Disciplinary Committee of his own motion where it appears desirable to do so, concluded his short observations by saying:

" As far as what constitutes infamous or disgraceful conduct is concerned, to which both advocates have referred, for me the

F   words of Scrutton L.J. of ' serious misconduct in a professional respect ' mean quite plainly that it is for the committee, applying their own knowledge and experience, to decide what is the appropriate standard each practitioner should adhere to, not a special standard greater than is ordinarily to be expected, but the ordinary standard of the profession. I think I have said very little

G   that is in any way new to any member of the committee, but having regard to the submissions made to you I thought I ought at least to say what I have said."

These observations have been criticised as wrong in law in that they failed to draw a distinction between mere negligent conduct and infamous or disgraceful conduct. The submission is that there was a

H   misdirection, in that, although in his opening remarks counsel for the Disciplinary Committee had made passing reference to *Felix* v. *General Dental Council* [1960] A.C. 704, the legal assessor failed to remind the Disciplinary Committee of an important passage in the speech of Lord Jenkins, who, in delivering the judgment of this Board in that case, said at p. 720:

" Granted that . . . the full derogatory force of the adjectives ' infamous ' and ' disgraceful ' in section 25 of the Act of 1957

must be qualified by the consideration that what is being judged   A
is the conduct of a dentist in a professional respect, which falls to
be judged in relation to the accepted ethical standards of his
profession, it appears to their Lordships that these two adjectives
nevertheless remain as terms denoting *conduct deserving of the
strongest reprobation,* and indeed so heinous as to merit, when
proved, the extreme professional penalty of striking-off."
(Emphasis added.)   B

Although the facts in *Felix* were quite unlike those of the present
case, these observations are of compelling significance. For it has
respectfully to be said that, although prolonged veneration of the oft-
quoted words of Lopes L.J. has clothed them with an authority
approaching that of a statute, they are not particularly illuminating. It is   C
for this reason that their Lordships regard Lord Jenkins' exposition
as so valuable that, without going as far as to say that his words should
invariably be cited in every disciplinary case, they think that to do so
would be a commendable course. But, having said that, it has to be
added that the committee in the instant case were duly reminded of
decisions which have long been approved of by this Board as accurately
stating the relevant law. And their Lordships have in mind in this   D
context the following observations of Lord Guest in *Sivarajah* v.
General Medical Council [1964] 1 W.L.R. 112, 117:

> " The committee are masters both of the law and of the facts.
> Thus what might amount to a misdirection in law by a judge to
> a jury at a criminal trial does not necessarily invalidate the com-
> mittee's decision. The question is whether it can ' fairly be thought   E
> to have been of sufficient significance to the result to invalidate
> the committee's decision ' (*Fox* v. *General Medical Council* [1960]
> 1 W.L.R. 1017, 1023)."

In their Lordships' judgment, it cannot be said that the advice tendered
by the legal assessor in this case contained such a defect, and the first
ground of criticism must therefore be rejected.   F

Little needs to be added regarding the second ground of appeal
against finding. Whether the misconduct of the appellant—freely
admitted by him with complete candour—was such as to justify his
being convicted as charged was essentially for the committee. Their
Lordships' desire to say no more than that had a finding of not guilty
been pronounced it could well have been greeted by surprise. Indeed,
by allowing his unqualified staff to insert fillings, the appellant impli-   G
cated both himself and them in contravention of section 34 of the
Act of 1957 and all three of them could have been subjected to
summary proceedings in a magistrate's court.

Their Lordships turn accordingly to the appeal against sentence, it
being urged that, in all the circumstances of the case, the penalty of
erasure was excessive. It has to be said, and not for the first time, that   H
the penalty provisions of the Dentists Act 1957 need to be reconsidered.
As recently as this year the matter was raised by Lord Diplock in *Dubois*
v. *General Dental Council* (unreported), March 12, 1979, in the following words which their Lordships respectfully regard as well worthy to be
recorded:

> " . . . under section 25 of the Dentists Act 1957 the *only* punish-
> ment for professional misconduct which the Disciplinary Com-

A　　mittee has jurisdiction to impose is to erase the dentist's name from the register. Unlike the corresponding statutory provisions applicable to doctors the Act has not been amended to permit the imposition of the milder penalty of suspension for a period not longer than 12 months in cases involving what may properly be regarded as the less serious breaches of the professional code. In the case of dentists the only way in which the gravity of the offence

B　　can be reflected in the punishment he is compelled to undergo by reason of the erasure of his name from the register, is the length of time that he is made to wait before an application for restoration of his name to the register under section 30 of the Act, is granted; but the minimum period that must elapse before he can make such application is ten months."

C　　Section 25 provides merely that a registered dentist found guilty under subsection (1) (b) " shall be *liable* to have his name erased from the register." The committee is therefore free to do no more than deliver a homily in suitable cases, and it appears that this is by no means uncommon. Or it may resort to the device of postponing sentence to a date sufficiently far distant to enable the committee in due course to

D　　judge whether the wrongdoer has learnt his lesson, and then at the adjourned hearing to do no more than deliver what is again in the nature of an unofficial admonition. But if the committee does not regard either of these courses as appropriate, it has no alternative but to order erasure from the register.

　　In all the mitigating circumstances of the present case, their Lordships would have been in no degree surprised had the Disciplinary

E　　Committee elected to postpone sentence, but that course evidently did not commend itself. The only remaining alternative to erasure would therefore be to take no action at all in respect of the section 25 finding, save, in effect, to grant an absolute discharge and accompany it possibly by a homily if such were deemed desirable. Section 29 of the Act of 1957 provides that appeals in disciplinary cases lie to this Board, and,

F　　in relation to a similar provision contained in section 36 of the Medical Act 1956, it was held in *Fox* v. *General Medical Council* [1960] 1 W.L.R. 1017 that the Board's position in such appeals is analogous to that of the Court of Appeal hearing an appeal from a judge sitting alone. Their Lordships can see no reason for holding that similar appeals, brought under the Dentists Act 1957, should be regarded any differently. The attitude to be adopted by this Board in these circum-

G　　stances is well-established by such decisions as *McCoan* v. *General Medical Council* [1964] 1 W.L.R. 1107, where Lord Upjohn said, at pp. 1112–1113 :

　　　" The powers of the Board to correct the determination of the committee on the hearing of such an appeal are in terms unlimited, but in principle, where a professional body is entrusted with a dis-

H　　　cretion as to the imposition of the sentence of erasure their Lordships should be very slow to interfere with the exercise of that discretion . . . Their Lordships are of opinion that Lord Parker C.J. may have gone too far in *In re a Solicitor* [1960] 2 Q.B. 212 when he said that the appellate court would never differ from sentence in cases of professional misconduct, but their Lordships agree with Lord Goddard C.J. in *In re a Solicitor* [1956] 1 W.L.R. 1312 when he said that it would require a very

A strong case to interfere with sentence in such a case, because the Disciplinary Committee are the best possible people for weighing the seriousness of the professional misconduct. No general test can be laid down, for each case must depend entirely on its own particular circumstances. All that can be said is that if it is to be set aside the sentence of erasure must appear to their Lordships to be wrong and unjustified."

B

Adopting that test and applying it to the proved circumstances of the present case, their Lordships, while adhering to the view earlier expressed regarding the severe sentence of erasure, are unable to say that it was wrong or unjustified.

It follows that, in relation to both finding and sentence, their Lordships must humbly advise Her Majesty that the appeal should be dismissed. There will be no order as to costs.

C

Solicitors: *Hempsons; Waterhouse & Co.*

[Reported by MICHAEL HAWKINGS, ESQ., Barrister-at-Law]

D

[FAMILY DIVISION]

* PRACTICE DIRECTION (CHILD: SUPERVISED ACCESS)

Minor—Custody order—Access—Supervised access—Supervision by person agreed by both parties—Parties' duty to find suitable person

E

Where application is made to the court for access to be supervised, every effort should be made, before the matter comes before the court, to obtain the consent of a person likely to be agreeable to both parties to supervise the access. Mutual friends, unprejudiced relatives and godparents are examples of the classes of person who should be approached.

F

Only when every effort has been made to enlist the help of such persons and has been unsuccessful should welfare officers and similar persons be involved. Application for such persons to supervise access should never be made without obtaining the consent of the person concerned and every effort should be made to avoid asking them to exercise supervision on Saturdays or Sundays.

In the few instances where it is necessary to ask that supervision should be carried out by welfare officers, the supervision should be confined to a very few occasions, the number of which should be specified in the order. Care must be taken to arrange a place of access which does not cause the welfare officer undue travelling difficulties.

G

Issued with the concurrence of the Lord Chancellor.

H

SIR JOHN ARNOLD P.
March 12, 1980.

A

[HOUSE OF LORDS]

*AIR-INDIA . . . . PETITIONERS

AND

WIGGINS . . . . RESPONDENT

B

1980 Feb. 21   Lord Diplock, Lord Salmon and Lord Scarman

Petition by the defendants for leave to appeal to the House of Lords from the decision of the Divisional Court of the Queen's Bench Division [1980] 1 W.L.R. 102.

C   The Appeal Committee allowed the petition.

M. G.

D

[COURTS-MARTIAL APPEAL COURT]

* REGINA v. BISSET

1979 Oct. 12   Lawton L.J., Tudor Evans
                                        and McNeill JJ.

E   *Military Law—Civil offence—Condonation—Adjutant in reliance
    on informal information stating that accused unlikely to be
    charged — Squadron commander relating information to
    accused—Whether offence condoned—Army Act 1955 (3 & 4
    Eliz. 2, c. 18), s. 134*

The accused, a lance-corporal in a tank regiment, was on duty in a squadron club when an altercation took place in which he intervened, and broke a glass in the face of a trooper
F   involved in the altercation. He had, as was later discovered, been drinking while on duty. The incident was made known to the accused's squadron commander and the adjutant. The adjutant, relying on an informal conversation with a member of the military police, informed the squadron commander that the accused was unlikely to be charged with an offence in respect of the wounding. The squadron commander related
G   that information to the accused, adding that he hoped the matter had ended. He dealt summarily with the offence of drinking while on duty, which was an offence against the regiment's standing orders. Subsequently the accused was charged under section 70 of the Army Act 1955 with committing a civil offence, namely, wounding, contrary to section 20 of the Offences against the Person Act 1861. He offered a plea in bar of trial on the ground that the offence had been
H   condoned by his commanding officer within the meaning of section 134 of the Act of 1955.[1] The judge-advocate dis-

[1] Army Act 1955, s. 134: " (1) Where a person subject to military law— . . . . (c) has had an offence condoned by his commanding officer . . . , he shall not be liable in respect of that offence to be tried by court-martial . . . (2) For the purposes of this section— . . . (d) an offence shall be deemed to have been condoned by the commanding officer of a person alleged to have committed the offence if, and only if, that officer or any officer authorised by him to act in relation to the alleged offence has with knowledge of all relevant circumstances informed him that he will not be charged therewith; . . ."

allowed the plea on the ground that it was not supported by A
the evidence and, following that ruling, the accused was
convicted and sentenced.

On the accused's appeal against conviction: —

Held, dismissing the appeal, (1) that for an offence to
be deemed to be condoned under section 134 of the Army
Act 1955, the accused's commanding officer or an officer
authorised by him in relation to the alleged offence had, with
knowledge of all the relevant circumstances, to inform the B
accused that he would not be charged therewith; that since
the accused's commanding officer, who for the purposes of
section 134 was the officer commanding the tank regiment,
had not made any investigation into the relevant circumstances
of the case nor had he authorised the squadron commander
to act in relation to the offence, it followed that the squadron
commander could not be said to be communicating to the
accused a decision by the commanding officer or some other C
authorised officer to condone the offence of wounding.

(2) That the adjutant had no jurisdiction in the absence
of formal authority to deal with a question of misconduct,
but that even if he had been acting with the authority of the
commanding officer, the general circumstances of the case did
not bring the power of condonation into operation, since
information from an informal source could not constitute the
authority for the exercise of that power.   D

Per curiam. The very nature of the power of condonation
indicates that it is one which should only be used in exceptional
circumstances, especially in relation to civil offences. In
normal peace time conditions the circumstances which call for
its exercise must be exceptional. There should be formality
about its use and a record made of what has been done (post,
pp. 339H—340B).

E

No cases are referred to in the judgment.

The following case was cited in argument:

Reg. v. *Durkin* [1953] 2 Q.B. 364; [1953] 3 W.L.R. 479; [1953] 2 All
E.R. 685, Ct.-M.A.C.

APPEAL against conviction.   F

The accused, Lance-Corporal James William Bisset, was convicted
of unlawful wounding by a district court-martial at Munster, West
Germany, on March 29, 1979. He presented a petition against conviction
and sentence to the Army Board of the Defence Council on the ground,
inter alia, that the deputy judge-advocate, Mr. S. B. Spence, should have
allowed his plea in bar of trial submitted under section 134 (2) (*d*) of the G
Army Act 1955, such plea being based on the fact that he had been
informed by the officer commanding " D " Squadron, 4th Royal Tank
Regiment, that he would not be charged with any further offences in
respect of an incident which had occurred in the squadron club and that
any such further offence or offences were thereby condoned.

The facts are stated in the judgment of the court.

H

Leonard Krikler for the accused.
Michael Hucker for the Crown.

LAWTON L.J. On March 29, 1979, at a district court-martial held at
Munster, the accused, a lance-corporal, was convicted of maliciously
wounding a trooper, and was sentenced to six months' imprisonment and
to be dismissed from the service after reduction to the ranks.

A   At his trial there was an unusual development. He was represented by a solicitor, who raised a plea in bar, namely, that the offence charged had been condoned by the accused's commanding officer.

    At all material times the accused had been serving in the 4th Royal Tank Regiment. On November 16, 1978, he had been duty sergeant in a squadron club. It had been his responsibility to ensure that there was orderly behaviour there. An altercation of some kind took place. The

B cause of that altercation was probably a trooper named Galligan. The accused as duty sergeant intervened. There were some words between him and Galligan. The incident ended with the accused breaking a glass in Galligan's face. Galligan was badly cut and had to have 34 stitches to suture the wounds. The military police were called in. They later brought in the special investigation branch.

C   That there had been this altercation in a squadron club and that the military police had been called in became known to the adjutant, a Captain Spellar, and to the accused's squadron commander, a Major Williams. The adjutant was concerned about the incident for two reasons: first, if charges were preferred, it would mean that the accused would be unable to go with his squadron to the tank ranges early in December, and secondly, the accused's posting to another regiment,

D which the accused wanted to join, would be held up, because postings of that kind cannot take place when a court-martial charge is under consideration.

    The adjutant got in touch with someone in the Royal Military Police. The channel of communication is not known. The court infers that it was probably by telephone. As a result of what was said Captain Spellar

E formed the opinion that no charges were likely to be preferred against the accused. On December 1 he told Major Williams what he had learnt. Major Williams then had the accused brought before him. It had been discovered in the meantime that on the night of this incident the accused had broken the regiment's standing orders by drinking whilst on duty. Major Williams informed the accused what he had been told by Captain Spellar and went on to ask him if he would consent to a charge of

F conduct contrary to good order and military discipline being dealt with summarily. The accused said he would and thereupon he was found guilty of such conduct by drinking whilst on duty, and fined £40.

    About a week later a report came from the special investigation branch. We have not seen that report, nor did the court-martial. But the inference to be drawn from what happened afterwards is that it

G recommended that charges under section 20 of the Offences against the Person Act 1861 and section 70 of the Army Act 1955 should be preferred against the accused. They were preferred and thereafter the ordinary military procedure was followed. In due course a court-martial was convened.

    The details of the evidence in support of the plea in bar are important. Major Williams's recollection was as follows: that he informed the

H accused that as far as he knew there would be no charges in respect of the incident with Trooper Galligan. He said that he thought the words he used were: " To the best of my knowledge no charges will be laid on you and I hope that's the end of the matter."

    Captain Spellar gave more details. He said that on December 1, 1978, he telephoned Major Williams to tell him that there were to be no charges against the accused in relation to the incident involving Trooper Galligan. But, he said, he added the proviso that he wanted confirmation

in writing, as he had not yet received a final report of the investigation. A
He said that in telephoning Major Williams he was acting on behalf of
the commanding officer; but he went on to say that he would not have
made a final decision until he had received a report from the military
police and until he had had advice from the Directorate of Army Legal
Services.

Mr. Krikler in this court opened the appeal by submitting that, what- B
ever may have been the authority of Captain Spellar to communicate in
the terms he did with Major Williams, Major Williams in fact investigated
the incident which had happened on November 16. He took account of
what he had been told by Captain Spellar about the attitude of the
military police. In those circumstances, in saying what he did to the
accused, he condoned the offence. He sought to rely on section 134 of
the Army Act, the relevant parts of which are in these terms: C

"(1) Where a person subject to military law— . . . (c) has had an
offence condoned by his commanding officer (whether military, naval
or air-force), he shall not be liable in respect of that offence to be
tried by court-martial or to have the case dealt with summarily by
his commanding officer or the appropriate superior authority.
(2) For the purposes of this section— . . . (d) an offence shall be D
deemed to have been condoned by the commanding officer of a
person alleged to have committed the offence if, and only if, that
officer or any officer authorised by him to act in relation to the
alleged offence has with knowledge of all relevant circumstances
informed him that he will not be charged therewith; . . ."

Mr. Krikler submitted that the adjutant purporting to act in the name E
of the commanding officer, and being authorised so to act, was a person
authorised by the commanding officer of the regiment to act in relation
to the offence and in those circumstances what he was doing was communicating the decision of the commanding officer to Major Williams,
which he put into effect.

The first point which arises is whether Captain Spellar was in law
authorised to do what Mr. Krikler on behalf of the accused said he was F
doing. For this purpose it is necessary to look at the Army Act and
regulations made under it to discover who was the accused's commanding
officer. The relevant provisions are to be found in section 82 of the
Army Act and in regulation 5 of the Army Summary Jurisdiction Regulations 1972. It is clear from the Act and the regulations that the accused's
commanding officer was the officer commanding the 4th Royal Tank
Regiment. It was not Major Williams. It follows therefore that any- G
thing Major Williams did, he could only have done if he was authorised
by the commanding officer to do it. There was no evidence that he was
so authorised, save Captain Spellar's assertion in the witness box that he
was acting in the name of the commanding officer.

Adjutants in the army perform many functions. Most of them are of
an executive kind. When they are performing executive functions they H
are normally acting in the name of the commanding officer and with his
authority, either express or implied. There is nothing in the Army Act
1955, however, which authorises an adjutant to exercise the legal jurisdiction over persons subject to military law which is entrusted by the Act
and the regulations made under it to a commanding officer. If, for
example, a commanding officer goes on leave, he cannot properly say to
his adjutant: "Whilst I am away will you deal with all the cases of

A misconduct which I as commanding officer would normally deal with."
The jurisdiction to deal with misconduct whilst the commanding officer
is on leave has to be dealt with by some other officer of senior rank duly
and formally authorised by the commanding officer to perform that
function. In this case the adjutant had no jurisdiction or authority to
make any decision about condonation; and on the facts of this case there
is no evidence that the commanding officer of the 4th Royal Tank
B Regiment had made any investigation into the relevant circumstances.
The words of the statute are unusually emphatic: the power to condone
civil offences only arises

"... if, and only if, [the commanding] officer or any officer
authorised by him to act in relation to the alleged offence has with
knowledge of all relevant circumstances informed him that he will
C not be charged therewith; ..."

A question has arisen in this case, as to what is meant by the statutory
words " all relevant circumstances." It was submitted at one stage that
those words related solely to knowledge of the incident itself. Both
counsel in the end accepted that the words must have a wider meaning
than that, because a commanding officer who has the duty of investigating
incidents of this kind has not only to inform himself of what happened,
D but of all the relevant circumstances. In relation to civil offences, he
may have to seek the advice of the military police and the Directorate of
Army Legal Services. We say " may," because in many cases the
commanding officer may be able to deal with the situation with knowledge which comes to him from within his own command: as for example
when he is told what has happened by the regimental sergeant major, this
E being the situation most commonly occurring within regiments. What
happened in this case could not possibly have amounted to condonation
in law.

Even if Captain Spellar was acting on behalf of the commanding
officer, which we adjudge he was not, the general circumstances of this
case were not sufficient to bring into operation the concept of con-
F donation. Captain Spellar seems to have got his information as to what
the Royal Military Police were minded to recommend in some informal
way. What he was doing was passing on some informal information to
the accused's squadron commander. This commonly happens in army
life, but experienced officers know, or should know, how unwise it is to
act on informal information. Such information may be of help in
G getting ready to act: it cannot constitute authority to act. Captain
Spellar knew this as his evidence shows. It follows therefore, without
recourse to the legal problem of delegation of powers to which we have
referred, the evidence itself, as the deputy judge-advocate found, did not
support the plea in bar which was raised by the accused.

We wish to stress that the jurisdiction to condone offences given by
section 134 of the Army Act is a most unusual one. In effect it is a
H power to dispense soldiers from the consequences of breaking the law, a
power which was taken away from Ministers of the Crown by the Bill of
Rights 1688 save under the authority of Parliament. The very nature of
the power indicates that it is one which should only be used in
exceptional circumstances, especially in relation to civil offences. When
Parliament gave this power to commanding officers it probably had in
mind that when those subject to military law are on active service, and in
particular when they are on operations, condonation of offences, whether

civil or military, may be necessary in order to secure military efficiency. **A**
But it is a power which in normal peace time conditions should seldom
be used for civil offences and sparingly for military offences. We say " in
normal peace time conditions," because even then exceptional circumstances may arise which call for the exercise of the power; but the
circumstances must be exceptional. When the power is used there should
be some formality about its use. A record should be made of what has
been done.   **B**

The Adjutant-General will no doubt bring to the attention of all
officers the need to have regard to what we have said in this judgment.

The appeal is dismissed.

Appeal dismissed.

Solicitors: *Registrar of Criminal Appeals; Director of Army Legal*   **C**
Services.

B. O. A.

[COURT OF APPEAL]   **D**

* BELL *v.* ALFRED FRANKS & BARTLETT CO. LTD.

AND ANOTHER

1979 Nov. 7, 8   Megaw, Shaw and Waller L.JJ.
                                                                      E

Landlord and Tenant—Business premises (security of tenure)—
Occupation for purposes of tenant's business—Garage let to
company for standing private cars only—Used to store samples
and for garaging cars for conveyance of customers—Landlord's
predecessor in title not objecting to use—Whether " consent "
to prohibited use—Landlord and Tenant Act 1954 (2 & 3 Eliz.
2, c. 56), s. 23 (1) (4)

By an agreement dated September 23, 1964, the plaintiff's   **F**
predecessor in title, the leasehold owner of a flat and garage,
demised the premises to the defendant company for a term of
three and a quarter years from September 29, 1964. Under
the agreement the company covenanted to use the garage for
standing a private car only and the flat as and for a private
dwelling. The covenant was subsequently relaxed to allow the
garage to be used for standing two private cars. After the   **G**
agreement expired the company continued to pay the rent.
They sublet the flat but always retained the use of the garage
in which, for many years, they stored cartons of samples in
connection with their business. They also used it for the
standing of company cars which were used for conveying
customers from place to place and for conveying samples. The
landlord, the plaintiff's predecessor in title, knew of the purposes to which the garage was put and never objected nor did   **H**
he ask for the use to be discontinued. In 1975 the reversion of
the lease was assigned to the plaintiff. On April 29, 1977, the
plaintiff served notice to quit on the company and brought an
action for possession of the premises. The company claimed
that at all material times since the date of the 1964 agreement
they had occupied the garage for the purposes of their business,
so that the tenancy was one to which Part II of the Landlord
and Tenant Act 1954 applied and that the notice to quit was
ineffective since it did not comply with the form required by

A   section 25 of that Act. Judge Leslie found that the garage had
      been used for business purposes by virtue of the storage of
      samples therein, and that the plaintiff's predecessor in title
      had consented to that use. He accordingly held that section
      23 (4) of the Act of 1954 [1] applied, and that the notice to quit
      was invalid. He refused to make an order for possession of
      either the garage or the flat which he held was lawfully sublet
      to the second defendant who was entitled to the protection
B   of the Rent Act 1977.

          On appeal by the plaintiff against the refusal to make an
      order for possession of the garage, and on a cross-appeal by
      the defendant company who sought to uphold the judgment
      on the ground also that the garage had been used for business
      purposes because the cars they garaged there were used for
      business purposes: —

          Held, dismissing the cross-appeal, (1) that in the context
C   of the agreement under which the defendant company held
      the garage the words " private car," read in conjunction with
      the reference to the use of the flat as a private dwelling, meant
      a car not merely constructed for but used for some personal
      or domestic purpose and that a car used to a substantial degree
      for business purposes was not a private car and to house it in
      the garage was an infringement of the covenant (post, pp.
      346D–G, 348C, 349C, H—350A).

D   (2) Allowing the appeal, that in the context of section 23 (4)
      of the Act of 1954 " consent " was put in plain antithesis to
      " acquiescence "; that whereas acquiescence meant a passive
      attitude by a person with knowledge of a breach of a prohibi-
      tion, " consent " involved a positive demonstrative act of an
      affirmative nature, which could be either in writing, oral, or by
      conduct, but there must be something more than a mere stand-
E   ing by and absence of objection; that the proper inference to
      be drawn from the history of the matter was that the plaintiff's
      predecessor in title had acquiesced but had not consented to
      the breach of covenant by the company in the use of the garage
      and since it was conceded that there was no acquiescence on
      the part of the plaintiff the requirements of the Act of 1954
      were not called into play, the notice to quit was effective to
      terminate the tenancy, and the plaintiff was entitled to an order
F   for possession of the garage (post, pp. 347A–D, G, 348B, 349A–C,
      350A–C).

      No cases are referred to in the judgments.

      The following cases were cited in argument:

      Atkins v. *Rose* [1923] 1 Ch. 522.
G   *Blackstone (David) Ltd.* v. *Burnetts (West End) Ltd.* [1973] 1 W.L.R.
          1487; [1973] 3 All E.R. 782.
      Chapman v. *Freeman* [1978] 1 W.L.R. 1298; [1978] 3 All E.R. 878, C.A.
      Cheryl Investments v. *Saldanha* [1978] 1 W.L.R. 1329; [1979] 1 All E.R.
          5, C.A.
      City and Westminster Properties (1934) *Ltd.* v. *Mudd* [1959] Ch. 129;
          [1958] 3 W.L.R. 312; [1958] 2 All E.R. 733.

H
      [1] Landlord and Tenant Act 1954, s. 23: " (1) Subject to the provisions of this
      Act, this Part [Part II] of this Act applies to any tenancy where the property com-
      prised in the tenancy is or includes premises which are occupied by the tenant and
      are so occupied for the purposes of a business carried on by him or for those and
      other purposes. . . . (4) Where the tenant is carrying on a business, in all or any
      part of the property comprised in a tenancy, in breach of a prohibition (however
      expressed) of use for business purposes which subsists under the terms of the tenancy
      and extends to the whole of that property, this Part of this Act shall not apply to
      the tenancy unless the immediate landlord or his predecessor in title has consented
      to the breach or the immediate landlord has acquiesced therein."

Daimar Investments Ltd. v. *Jones* (1962) 112 L.J. 424. A

Doe d. *Sheppard* v. *Allen* (1810) 3 Taunt. 78.

Hillil Properties and Investment Co. Ltd. v. *Naraine Pharmacy Ltd.* (1979) 123 S. J. 437, C.A.

McGill v. *Robson* [1972] 1 W.L.R. 237; [1972] 1 All E.R. 362.

Sayers v. *Collyer* (1884) 28 Ch.D. 103, C.A.

APPEAL from Judge Leslie sitting at Bloomsbury and Marylebone B
County Court.

The plaintiff, John Arnaud Bell, the leasehold owner of premises known as South Garage together with a second floor flat of property situated at and known as 9, Devonshire Close, London, W.1, brought an action in the county court claiming possession of the premises against the defendants, Alfred Franks & Bartlett Co. Ltd. (the defendant company) and C
Mr. David Blank.

By his amended particulars of claim dated November 8, 1978, the plaintiff claimed that by an agreement in writing dated September 23, 1964, made between his predecessor in title, Harold John Allen, as the landlord, and the defendant company, the premises were let to the company for a term of three and a quarter years from September 29, 1964, at a yearly rent of £450 payable quarterly in advance. The reversion expectant upon D
the determination of the term was assigned to him, the plaintiff, on September 29, 1975. The agreement expired by effluxion of time on September 25, 1967, and thereafter the defendant company continued to pay rent and there arose by implication of law a periodic yearly tenancy subject to the same terms and conditions contained in the agreement.

By a notice to quit dated April 28, 1977, and served on the defendant E
company on April 29, the plaintiff determined the tenancy on December 25, 1977, or at the expiration of the year of the tenancy which should expire next after the end of one half year from the service of the notice, yet the defendant company had remained in occupation of the premises as trespassers.

The plaintiff alleged breaches by the defendant company of repairing F
covenants contained in the tenancy agreement by reason whereof he alleged that he had suffered damage and that the value of his reversion had been diminished. He also alleged that there were arrears of rent due and owing from the company from the period September 29, 1977, to December 25, 1977, and such other sum as should be found due.

He claimed that the defendant company, a limited company, was not entitled to the benefit of protection of the security of tenure afforded by G
the Rent Act 1977.

The claim for possession of the flat, which was occupied by the second defendant, Mr. Blank, under an agreement made with the defendant company in 1971, is not relevant to this report because there was no appeal against the judge's decision that the second defendant was a lawful subtenant and that the plaintiff's claim for possession against him should be H
dismissed.

By their amended defence the defendants denied that the plaintiff was entitled to possession of the garage or the flat. The defendant company agreed that by the agreement the garage was to be used for standing a private car only, but they claimed that at all material times since the date of the agreement the company had occupied and now occupied it for the purposes of a business carried on by them.

A   They relied on the following matters: (1) that since the date of the
agreement the company, for the purposes of their business, had kept private
cars from time to time belonging to them in the garage; (2) that they had
also kept samples, papers and other articles connected with their business
in the garage and that the use thereof for those purposes and for storage
was known to and permitted by the plaintiff's predecessor in title, Mr.
Allen, since about February 1951, and acquiesced to by the plaintiff since
B   about September 1975.
        In the premises the defendants contended that the tenancy created by
the agreement was a business tenancy within Part II of the Landlord and
Tenant Act 1954; that upon the expiry of the term of the agreement on
December 29, 1967, the tenancy continued under section 24 of the Act of
1954 and that they had continued to pay the rent.
C   Further, or in the alternative if (which was not admitted) a yearly
tenancy had been created in December 1967 they would contend that such
yearly tenancy was at its inception or became in about September 1975 a
business tenancy within the ambit of Part II of the Act of 1954.
        They denied that the notice to quit was effective to determine their
tenancy of the premises in that it was not given in the form prescribed by
D   section 25 of the Act of 1954. They denied that they were trespassers in
the garage.
        By his reply the plaintiff denied, inter alia, that the defendant company
occupied the garage for the purposes of a business or that the tenancy
created by the agreement was a business tenancy, or that the use of the
premises for storage purposes was known to or permitted by his predecessor in title.
E   The trial of the action took place in April 1979. On April 24 Judge
Leslie found that the defendant company had been using the garage for
the purposes of a business, namely, for the storage of cartons of samples
although contrary to the lease and the head lease and that the plaintiff's
predecessor in title, Mr. Allen, knew of the use and must have waived the
breach. He held that section 23 (4) applied; that since the premises had
F   been used for business purposes notwithstanding the prohibition and that
use had been consented to by the plaintiff's predecessor, the notice to quit
did not operate to determine the tenancy because it did not satisfy the
requirements of the Act of 1954. He gave judgment for the defendants
because the contractual tenancy continued after the original term of the
lease and had never been validly determined.
G   The plaintiff appealed only in relation to the garage on the grounds,
inter alia, that there was no evidence upon which the judge could have
held that the defendant company occupied the garage for the purposes of
a business within the meaning of Part II of the Landlord and Tenant Act
1954; that there was no evidence upon which the judge could have held that
the plaintiff's predecessor in title had consented to the use of the premises
by the defendant company in breach of covenant thereby giving rise to a
H   business tenancy within the meaning of section 23 (4) of the Act of 1954;
that the judge ought to have held that upon the evidence his predecessor
in title had only acquiesced in the use of the premises in breach of the
user covenant contained in the lease and that such acquiescence was not
sufficient to create a business tenancy within the meaning of section 23 (4).
        By a respondent's notice, the defendant company sought to contend that
the judgment of the judge should be affirmed on the additional ground that
the judge should have held that the company occupied the garage for the

purposes of a business because they used the premises to garage their **A**
Rolls-Royce car which they used for business purposes.

The facts are stated in the judgment of Shaw L.J.

Andrew Pugh for the plaintiff.
J. J. Davis for the defendants.

MEGAW L.J. I will ask Shaw L.J. to deliver the first judgment.   **B**

SHAW L.J. This is an appeal from that part of a judgment of Judge
Leslie given on January 11, 1979, at the Bloomsbury and Marylebone
County Court which dismissed the plaintiff's claim for possession of a
garage at 9, Devonshire Close in the West End of London. At the
hearing a flat in proximity to the garage was also the subject-matter of   **C**
the litigation, but this appeal is concerned only with the garage. The
matter in contention was whether that garage had been occupied by
the first defendants for business purposes. That issue arises because the
plaintiff purported to give a notice to quit which was not in the form
required by the Landlord and Tenant Act 1954 in relation to a business
tenancy and, therefore, would have been abortive if the garage had in   **D**
fact been occupied for business purposes.

The history which was dealt with by the judge is a long one and it is
not necessary to recount it in the detail with which it was necessary for
Mr. Pugh to present it to this court. As long ago as the end of 1949 a
gentleman named Ward, who occupied No. 94, Harley Street (which is
adjacent to 9, Devonshire Close), let the garage there to the first
defendants (whom I shall call " the defendant company "). In 1954 Mr.   **E**
Ward assigned, or agreed to assign, the lease to a gentleman named Allen,
who was a dental surgeon practising at No. 94, and in 1964 Mr. Allen, by
a written agreement, let the garage in question together with the flat to
which I have referred to the first defendants. The term was for three-and-
a-quarter years beginning in September 1964 and therefore it expired by
effluxion of time somewhere at the end of December 1967. The agree-   **F**
ment, by clause 2 paragraph (4), setting out the tenant's covenants,
provided that the tenant undertook to " use the said garage for standing a private car only " and then, since the agreement comprised the
flat also, it went on to say " and the flat only as and for a private dwelling
house." It is important to note that the same word " private " is used in
relation to the car and also in relation to the dwelling house, because the
question arises as to whether " *private* car " was merely a description of   **G**
the character of the vehicle or was a reference to the nature of the use
to which it would normally be put.

In September 1975 there was an assignment of Mr. Allen's lease to
the plaintiff. By that time the covenant to which I have just referred had
been relaxed because it was amended so as to provide that two private
motor cars might stand there instead of one. For some long time before   **H**
the assignment to the plaintiff there is no question but that a Mr. Franks
—who was a moving spirit in the defendant company—had used the garage
from time to time to take in and store samples collected for his company's
business. Two cars which were put there—one a Bentley and another a
Rolls-Royce—were used, so the evidence went, in order to assist the objects
of the company by carrying prospective customers to and fro and also for
the purpose of conveying samples. That was the business use which was

A relied upon in order to establish the character of the occupation of the garage as being for business purposes within the provisions of section 23 of the Landlord and Tenant Act 1954.

The plaintiff, having given the notice to quit, discontinued the action which he had started. It was not until December 15, 1977, that the action under which the present appeal arises was begun. In that action the plaintiff claimed possession of the flat (which is not now in issue) and also of the garage. This was on the ground that the agreement under which the defendant company held, made in 1964, had expired at the end of December 1967. The defence, in general terms, was that the notice was ineffective because it was not such a notice as is required in the case of a business tenancy by the Landlord and Tenant Act 1954. In that way the critical issue from the standpoint of this appeal is whether the judge was right in finding, as he did, that the occupancy of the garage was within the Act of 1954.

C Section 23, which is the first section in Part II of the Act, which is headed "Tenancies to which Part II applies," by subsection (1) provides:

D "Subject to the provisions of this Act, this Part of this Act applies to any tenancy where the property comprised in the tenancy is or includes premises which are occupied by the tenant and are so occupied for the purposes of a business carried on by him or for those and other purposes."

If a business is carried on in contravention of a covenant excluding such user, subsection (4) provides:

E "Where the tenant is carrying on a business, in all or any part of the property comprised in a tenancy, in breach of a prohibition (however expressed) of use for business purposes which subsists under the terms of the tenancy and extends to the whole of that property, this Part of this Act shall not apply to the tenancy unless the immediate landlord or his predecessor in title has consented to the breach or the immediate landlord has acquiesced therein."

F Thus if a breach of the prohibition has occurred but it can be said to have been acquiesced in by the immediate landlord the activity constituting the breach will nonetheless give rise to a business tenancy. If the acquiescence of the immediate landlord is not relied upon—and it was not in this case, as is conceded—one has to look back to his predecessor in title (who in the present case was Mr. Allen) and see whether he consented to that use.

G Mere acquiescence by a predecessor in title would not be sufficient to confer upon the tenant the protection of the Act of 1954 afforded to a tenant of business premises.

Mr. Allen—who is unfortunately now deceased—had a long and friendly association with Mr. Franks. Mr. Allen carried on his practice as a dentist at 94, Harley Street and he very often was in the vicinity of the garage; he

H was able to observe what was going on there; he was able to see that from time to time there were parcels containing samples left there; and he also saw from time to time one or other of the vehicles which the company used, namely, the Rolls-Royce or the Bentley, but not a van, or a lorry, or anything of the nature that might be called a commercial vehicle. It is contended that as over this long history Mr. Allen did not require that activities of that kind in the garage should stop as being in contravention of the tenant's covenants in the agreement, that amounted to consent.

That is really the short point which the judge had to decide so far as A
the occupancy of the garage was concerned. Two matters were relied upon
before him by counsel on behalf of the defendants to show that there was
a business user of the premises and that there had been consent to that
use. One was the presence of cartons containing samples for the business,
fortified by conversations—which were part of the evidence—between Mr.
Allen and Mr. Franks and which had reference to the contents of the
cartons, such as sunglasses and things of that kind. The other was the B
fact that the cars themselves were used in order to convey customers of
the defendant company as well as goods belonging to it.

The first question is: did those activities constitute a business use?
There can be no doubt that the bringing in of samples in cartons, and so
forth, might well constitute such a business use even though it was intermittent and not continuous. The evidence suggested that there was nearly C
always something of that kind there—and the judge held that that was
in this respect such a use. He made no finding as to the effect of the presence
of these motor cars from time to time. That prompted Mr. Davis to submit, on the basis of the cross-notice, that he should have found that the
motor cars were there for business purposes, so that upon that foundation
also the premises were occupied for such purposes and, therefore, there D
existed a business tenancy which was protected under the Landlord and
Tenant Act 1954.

It is convenient to deal with that part of his submission first because it
raises the narrow question of interpretation of the meaning of the word
" private " car in the context of the agreement under which the defendant
company held the garage. It seems to me that in conjunction with the
sentence which follows it, which refers to the use of the flat as a " private " E
dwelling house, " private " there must mean used for some personal or
domestic purpose; not merely a car which is constructed for such purpose,
but which is indeed used for such purpose. A dwelling house, of course,
is a house which people normally dwell in. A " private " dwelling house is
one actually used for domestic purposes. So construing that agreement,
one has got to take note of the conjunction of the use of that word in two F
different aspects, one relating to the garage and the other relating to the
flat, No. 9. It would follow that use of the word " private " there means
for private purposes. The fact that it used the phrase " for standing two
private cars " did not mean two private cars used for business purposes
thus introducing the element of business occupancy into the letting of the
garage any more than it did into the letting of the flat at the same time.
So I would hold against Mr. Davis's submission on that matter under his G
cross-notice.

That leaves for decision only the question whether there had been at
some stage in the history a consent to the use of the garage against the
prohibition contained in the agreement. This is a semantic and philosophical question which requires definition of the distinction between
acquiescence and consent. It is quite clear that what section 23 (4) of H
the Act of 1954 intended was to ensure that the immediate landlord
should not be bound by mere—and I use that word deliberately—
acquiescence on the part of the immediate predecessor in title, because
that goes far to giving to the tenant a protection and exposing the immediate landlord to an undue risk to which he ought not to be exposed.
What is meant by acquiescence? It may involve no more than a merely
passive attitude, doing nothing at all. It requires as an essential factor

A that there was knowledge of what was acquiesced in. In this case it is not in controversy that there was such knowledge on the part of the plaintiff's predecessor in title that the garage was used in the way in which it was.

If acquiescence is something passive in the face of knowledge, what does " consent " mean? In the context of the contrast implicit in sub-section (4), the only practical and sensible distinction that can be drawn is that if acquiescence can arise out of passive failure to do anything, consent
B must involve a positive demonstrative act, something of an affirmative kind. It is not to be implied, because the resort to implication betokens an absence of express affirmation. The only sense in which there can be implied consent is where a consent is demonstrated, not by language but by some positive act other than words which amounts to an affirmation of what is being done and goes beyond mere acquiescence in it. It may lead, in this
C context, to a false conclusion to speak of " implied consent," which is what the judge said was the proper inference to be drawn from the long history of acquiescence. I would prefer for myself to say " consent " involves something which is of a positive affirmative kind and that is what is required by section 23 (4) if the immediate landlord is to be deprived of the opportunity of taking advantage of a breach of a prohibition contained
D in the terms of the tenancy.

The judge, in his very careful judgment, having examined the evidence, expressed himself in this way in regard to the garage: " The question is whether the plaintiff's notice to quit was effective to terminate the letting to the first defendants, and that depends on the use of the garage." He then stated the contentions of the parties and went on to say:

E   " It is true that the plaintiff and his witnesses saw no cartons, but having heard the evidence I find that the defendants have been using the premises for the purposes of a business, namely for the storage of cartons containing samples and goods, although contrary to the lease and contrary to the head lease. Mr. Allen "—he was the predecessor in title of the plaintiff—" knew of this and must have waived the breach. It is possible that the plaintiff is entitled to bring proceedings
F   for forfeiture but that is not what the court is concerned with in the present case."

Then having set out section 23 (4) in his judgment he said " and in my view that section applies in this case." That was following what he had previously said, that Mr. Allen knew what was going on " and must have waived the breach." However, the inference from the history of Mr. Allen's
G relationship with Mr. Franks and his knowledge of the activities of the defendant company gives rise, so it seems to me, to no stronger inference than that there was acquiescence on the part of Mr. Allen. An examination of the evidence as a whole reveals nowhere that any such positive consent, positive affirmation or permission was actually given at any time. So far as the immediate landlord is concerned, that appears to be fortified by the
H earlier part of the history when Mr. Franks—who was himself, incidentally, a solicitor although he was engaged in business as well—had asked that the tenancy should be in the name of his company. That was not necessarily because the company wanted it. There might have been convenience, or financial advantage, in having the company as the tenant of the garage instead of Mr. Franks himself.

I have not here dealt with all the elaborate submissions that Mr. Pugh presented before this court. That is not to say that they were without

interest, but it seems to me that the only ones that really go to the heart of A
this case are: first, the issue as to whether or not the judge was right in
coming to the conclusion that there had been a business use; secondly,
whether he was right in saying that the premises were occupied for the
purposes of the business; and, thirdly, whether he was right in finding, as
he did, that there had been a consent within the meaning of section 23 (4).
In my view, what is decisive of the appeal is that there was no acquiescence on the part of the plaintiff and no consent by Mr. Allen. Accord-   B
ingly, the requirements of the Act of 1954 were not called into play. The
notice to quit was effective to terminate the tenancy and the plaintiff was
entitled to an order for possession of the garage premises.

I would allow the appeal.

WALLER L.J. I agree, and I agree with the judgment which Shaw L.J. C
has just delivered. I only add a few words on the question of consent
because we are differing from a very experienced judge on that one finding
which he made.

Shaw L.J. has already read section 23 of the Landlord and Tenant Act
1954 and in particular subsection (4), and I only repeat the last three lines
of that subsection which state: " . . . this Part of this Act shall not apply to D
the tenancy unless the immediate landlord or his predecessor in title has
consented to the breach or the immediate landlord has acquiesced therein."
The judge, in considering that part of the case, made the finding already
quoted by Shaw L.J., namely, having dealt with the storage of cartons
about which evidence was given by Mr. Franks, he said:

" Mr. Allen knew of this and must have waived the breach. It is   E
possible that the plaintiff is entitled to bring proceedings for forfeiture,
but that is not what the court is concerned with in the present case."

So that, in effect, was the view that the judge formed in that paragraph, and
then he went on to consider whether or not the consent had to be formal
and said:

" When a landlord knows about a breach as Allen did, and the breach   F
clearly goes on for a substantial period of time, as this one did, and
the landlord can even accept a sample which should not be there, then
one can only infer that he did consent. The parties were on amicable
terms and Mr. Allen took no steps to cause this wrongful user to cease
and he never even objected. I find, therefore, that the premises were
used for business purposes notwithstanding the prohibition and that it   G
was consented to by Mr. Allen."

When one looks at the evidence on which the judge made that finding,
perhaps the high-water mark is shown in a quotation from the evidence of
Mr. Franks. He said at the end of his evidence-in-chief " He never
objected." Although there are other passages which clearly show acquiescence that answer is the only one upon which the judge could found   H
the finding that there was consent.

Shaw L.J. has already mentioned—and I do not wish to repeat it, but
I would emphasise—the distinction which is drawn in section 23 (4)
between the predecessor of the landlord and the immediate landlord. In
order to avoid being taken out of the Act the tenant has to show that the
immediate predecessor consented to the breach whereas it would be sufficient for him to show acquiescence on the part of the present landlord.

A The contrast between those words is, in my view, significant. Aquiescence clearly can cover a great many matters, and it seems to me the words of the judge where he says " Mr. Allen knew of this and must have waived the breach " was very clear evidence of acquiescence; but acquiescence is something which has to be contrasted with consent and, in my judgment, consent requires some positive action on the part of the landlord or his predecessor, usually no doubt, in words perhaps in writing, possibly by gestures if these

B were absolutely clear but, in my view, careful proof of such an intention would be required. Normally one would look for some express statement, either in writing or oral, by the landlord. The answer which I have quoted clearly shows something far short of that, because there is the answer " He "—that is Allen—" never objected." In my judgment, having regard to the matters that I have mentioned, it is not possible to draw an

C inference from that evidence that the predecessor consented to the use for business purposes. Accordingly, I also would allow the appeal.

MEGAW L.J. I agree with the conclusions reached by Shaw and Waller L.JJ. and with the reasons given by them. We did not consider it necessary to trouble Mr. Davis to make submissions on a number of points

D which had been raised by Mr. Pugh for the plaintiff in support of the appeal. That was because it was apparent, and accepted by counsel, that if Mr. Davis, for the defendants, were wrong on the point which he wished to raise in the cross-notice and were wrong on the issue as to consent, then none of those other issues fell to be decided.

One of those issues on which we did not hear Mr. Davis and on which,

E therefore, I do not find it necessary to express anything in the nature of a concluded view, was the conclusion reached by the judge that here it was shown on the evidence that the premises were occupied for the purposes of the business carried on by the defendants. I will assume, therefore, without expressing any view on it, that the judge was right in deciding that question in favour of the defendant company, the tenants. On that

F assumption, Mr. Davis put forward, by virtue of his cross-notice, as I understood it, the proposition that the case thus inevitably fell within the purview of section 23 (1) and (2) of the Landlord and Tenant Act 1954 and then he went on to submit that for one simple reason section 23 (4) did not apply to take it out again. Subsection (4) depends upon the carrying on of a business having been in breach of a prohibition on use for business purposes; and, said Mr. Davis, here there was no covenant in the

G relevant tenancy agreement which in any way precluded the defendant company from using the garage for business purposes. That was a point which depended upon the construction of subclause (4) of the agreement of September 23, 1964, which imposed an obligation on the tenant " To use the said garage for standing a private car only and the flat only as and for a private dwelling house." Whatever may be the meaning of " private "

H or " private car " in other contexts, I am satisfied that on the true construction of the words of that clause, first the keeping of cartons of goods in the garage was in breach of that covenant to use the garage for standing a private car only; and, secondly, that the using of the garage in order to keep one or more cars there which were used to a substantial degree for the business of the defendant company (being a limited liability company) was an infringement of that covenant. If a car is used to a substantial degree for business purposes it is not a private car for the purposes of this

covenant any more than the use of a house for purposes of business would A
be the using of the house as a private dwelling house.

That point having gone, then unless the judge was right in the view
which he has taken that there was here consent on the part of the plaintiff's predecessor in title, the plaintiff was entitled to succeed. I agree with
Shaw and Waller L.JJ. that in the context of section 23 (4) of the Act of
1954 whatever consent or acquiescence may mean in different contexts,
in that context " consent " is put in plain antithesis to " acquiescence "; and B
that, therefore, if something falls within the description " acquiescence,"
it is not consent. The difference which is pointed out between the two in
this context is that " consent " involves some affirmative acceptance, not
merely a standing by and absence of objection. The affirmative acceptance may be in writing, which is obviously the clearest; it may be oral;
it may conceivably even be by conduct, such as nodding the head in a C
specific way in response to an express request for consent. But it must be
something more than merely standing by and not objecting.

I agree that the appeal falls to be allowed.

> *Appeal allowed with costs of appeal.*
> *Judge's order varied so as to provide* D
> *that no costs of court below shall be*
> *payable by either side to either side*
> *so far as plaintiff and first defend-*
> *ants are concerned.*
> *Order for possession against first*
> *defendants; order to be stayed for* E
> *28 days.*

Solicitors: *Manches & Co.; Franks, Charlesly & Co.*

E. M. W.

F

[PRIVY COUNCIL]

*** BANK OF AMERICA NATIONAL TRUST AND
SAVINGS ASSOCIATION** . . . . . . **APPELLANT**

AND   G

CHAI YEN . . . . **RESPONDENT**

[ON APPEAL FROM THE FEDERAL COURT OF MALAYSIA]

1979 Oct. 29;   Lord Edmund-Davies, Lord Fraser of Tullybelton,
      Dec. 3   Lord Russell of Killowen, Lord Keith of
                                        Kinkel and Lord Lane H

*Malaysia—Federal Court—Appeal to—Decision of judge in cham-
bers—Appeal brought after judge's refusal to hear further
argument—Whether appeal brought within time limit—Federal
Court (Civil Appeals) (Transitional) Rules 1963 (L.N. 242),
r. 13 (a)—Rules of the Supreme Court 1957, Ord. 54, r. 22A*

Rule 13 of the Federal Court (Civil Appeals) (Transitional)
Rules 1963 provides:

A
" No appeal shall, except by special leave of the full court, be brought after the expiration of one month—(a) in the case of an appeal from an order in chambers, from the date when such order was pronounced or when the appellant first had notice thereof. . ."

Ord. 54, r. 22A of the Rules of the Supreme Court 1957 provides:

B
" Any party dissatisfied with any order made by a judge in chambers may apply . . . within four days from the day of the order in writing . . . for the adjournment of the matter into court for further argument; and on such application, the judge may either adjourn the matter into court and hear further argument, or may certify in writing that he requires no further argument. . ."

C
On September 6, 1976, a judge in chambers adjudicated in favour of the appellant in its action against the respondent. On September 8, the respondent's solicitors sent a request to the High Court, under Ord. 54, r. 22A, for the matter to be adjourned into open court for further argument before the judge. On October 14, some five weeks after the original determination, the court informed the respondent's solicitors that the judge declined to hear further argument. On November 1 the respondent filed a notice of appeal to the Federal

D
Court from the decision of September 6. Before the hearing of the substantive appeal, the appellant raised the issue whether the respondent's notice of appeal was out of time under the provisions of rule 13 (a) of the Rules of 1963. The Federal Court ruled that the appeal had not been brought out of time.

On appeal by the appellant to the Judicial Committee:—

Held, dismissing the appeal, that where an order was made

E
in chambers and an application for further argument under Ord. 54, r. 22A was lodged within the time allowed, the time for appealing to the Federal Court under rule 13 (a) of the Rules of 1963 ran from the date on which the judge's decision not to hear further argument was communicated to the applicant, and not from the date of the order; and that, accordingly, the respondent had filed her notice of appeal in time.

Decision of the Federal Court of Malaysia affirmed.

F
No cases are referred to in the judgment of their Lordships.

The following cases were cited in argument:

Bozson v. *Altrincham Urban District Council* [1903] 1 K.B. 547, C.A.
Hong Kim Sui v. *Malayan Banking BHD.* [1971] 1 M.L.J. 289.
Sri Jaya Transport Co. Ltd. v. *Fernandez* [1970] 1 M.L.J. 87.

G
APPEAL (No. 39 of 1978) by Bank of America National Trust and Savings Association from a decision dated August 16, 1978, of the Federal Court of Malaysia (Raja Azlan Shah, Wan Suleiman and Chang Min Tat F.JJ.) dismissing, on a preliminary point, the appellant's contention that the appeal to the Federal Court by Chai Yen (married woman) from a decision of Mohd. Azmi J. given in chambers in the High Court on Sep-

H
tember 6, 1976, had not been brought within the time prescribed by rule 13 (a) of the Federal Court (Civil Appeals) (Transitional) Rules 1963.

The facts are stated in the judgment of their Lordships.

K. Thayalan (of the Malaysian Bar) for the appellant.
G. T. Rajan (of the Malaysian Bar) for the respondent.

Cur. adv. vult.

Bank of America v. Chai Yen (P.C.)   **[1980]**

December 3.   The judgment of their Lordships was delivered by   A
LORD LANE.

This is an appeal from the Federal Court of Malaysia who had upheld
the decision of Mohd. Azmi J. in the High Court. The short point is
whether under the rules the respondent is out of time for, and accordingly
barred from, appealing to the Federal Court.

The history of events is as follows. The appellant in December 1975   B
filed an originating summons to set in motion foreclosure proceedings in
respect of certain lands charged by the respondent to the appellant. Somewhat surprisingly, in view of the allegation of fraud and undue influence
made by the respondent, the matter was decided by the judge on
affidavit evidence. Sitting in chambers on September 6, 1976, he made
the various orders for which the appellant prayed, including an order that
the lands should be sold by public auction on December 13, 1976, for the   C
recovery of the moneys owing. On September 8, 1976, the respondent's
solicitors wrote to the High Court requesting that the judge should hear
further arguments in open court. On October 14, 1976, that is to say some
five weeks after the original determination, the High Court informed the
respondent's solicitors that the judge declined to hear further argument
and sent them a certificate to that effect. On November 1, 1976, that is to   D
say some two weeks after the judge's refusal but about seven weeks after
the original determination, the respondent filed a notice of appeal to the
Federal Court from the decision of Mohd. Azmi J. of September 6. On
May 31, 1978, before the hearing proper of the appeal, the appellant raised
the preliminary objection that the appeal had not been brought within the
time prescribed by rule 13 (a) of the Federal Court (Civil Appeals) (Transitional) Rules 1963. Rule 13 (a) provides: E

" No appeal shall, except by special leave of the full court, be brought
after the expiration of one month—(a) in the case of an appeal from
an order in chambers, from the date when such order was pronounced
or when the appellant first had notice thereof . . ."

It was common ground that the respondent had not sought from any court   F
any leave to appeal. Consequently the appellant's argument was simple.
The appeal was brought more than one month from the date when the
judge pronounced his order and so is caught by the plain words of rule
13 (a) and is out of time.

The matter is however not so simple as that. The application, already
mentioned, by the respondent's solicitors on September 8, 1976, for the
hearing of further argument by the judge was made under the provisions   G
of Ord. 54, r. 22A of the Rules of the Supreme Court of 1957. That runs:

" Any party dissatisfied with any order made by a judge in chambers
may apply, at the time the order is made, orally, or at any time within four days from the day of the order in writing to the registrar, for
the adjournment of the matter into court for further argument; and
on such application, the judge may either adjourn the matter into court   H
and hear further argument, or may certify in writing that he requires
no further argument. If the judge hears further argument he may set
aside the order previously made, and make such other order as he
thinks fit."

It is not difficult to see that there is potentially an inherent conflict
between the terms of that Order and those of rule 13 (a). There is no

A time limit imposed upon the judge under Order 54 within which he must grant or refuse the application for further argument. If he takes more than a month to make up his mind, what is the applicant to do? If she (the applicant being a woman in this case) files notice of appeal in accordance with rule 13 (*a*) that might be taken as an abandonment of her application to the judge. Indeed, Mr. Thayalan for the appellant firmly contended that such would be the result. If on the other hand she awaits the

B judge's decision before filing a notice of appeal she will be met, as here, by the argument that rule 13 (*a*) is clear, and that the other party should not be deprived of its safety under that rule by what is called by Mr. Thayalan "the unilateral act" of the present respondent in applying to the judge under Order 54.

No doubt this problem was not present to the minds of those who were
C responsible for the drafting of the Rules of 1963, but somehow or other the dilemma has to be resolved.

It seems to their Lordships that no litigant should be put in the position of having to elect between two different remedies by something entirely outside the litigant's control, namely, the length of time taken by a judge to reach or pronounce his conclusion. The essence of any rule of procedure

D must be fairness, and to apply stringently the provisions of rule 13 (*a*) would in circumstances such as the present work manifest injustice to the respondent. She might be forced, in short, to abandon a perfectly proper and relatively inexpensive application to the judge to hear further argument for a costly and possibly unnecessary appeal to the Federal Court. Nor are their Lordships impressed by the suggestion that the respondent could have put matters right by applying for special leave under rule 13 (*a*).

E She should not have that burden thrust upon her.

Their Lordships do not consider it necessary to embark upon an examination of the perennially difficult question whether the decision of Mohd. Azmi J. was a final or an interlocutory order. Assuming without deciding that it was final, nevertheless immediately the timeous application of September 8, 1976, was made to the court to hear further argument the

F whole matter entered a state of suspended animation until the judge ruled one way or the other upon the application. True it is that the application did not act as an automatic stay, but if the judge had failed to make his ruling by the time the date fixed for sale had arrived on December 13, 1976, an application to stay the sale could not have been other than successful.

G Their Lordships are of the view, therefore, that the Federal Court came to the right conclusion in this matter, and that the only way in which it is possible with fairness to reconcile the provisions of rule 13 (*a*) on the one hand and of Ord. 54, r. 22A on the other is to hold that in the case of an order made in chambers in which an application under Ord. 54, r. 22A has been lodged within the time allowed, the time for appealing under rule 13 (*a*) runs from the date when the judge's decision not to require

H further argument is communicated to the applicant and not from the date of his original order.

Their Lordships would wish to add this comment. Even if they had not been in agreement with the reasoning and conclusions of the Federal Court (as in fact they are), they would have felt reluctant to differ from that court on a matter which is eminently procedural and eminently a matter in this case to be left to the courts of Malaysia to decide.

A

Their Lordships accordingly advise His Majesty the Yang di-Pertuan Agong that the appeal should be dismissed with costs.

Solicitors: *Stephenson, Harwood; Philip Conway, Thomas & Co.*

[Reported by MICHAEL HAWKINGS, ESQ., Barrister-at-Law]

B

[FAMILY DIVISION]

* PRACTICE DIRECTION (MAINTENANCE: REGISTRATION OF ORDERS)

C

*Husband and Wife—Justices—Maintenance—Registration order—
Leave to register maintenance orders in magistrates' courts—
Order for payment direct to child—Form of order—Magistrates'
Courts Act 1952 (15 & 16 Geo. 6 & 1 Eliz. 2, c. 55), s. 53A (as
amended by Domestic Proceedings and Magistrates' Courts
Act 1978 (c. 22), s. 77)*

(a) *Children's orders*

D

Section 77 of the Domestic Proceedings and Magistrates' Courts Act 1978, which came into operation on November 1, 1979, added a new section 53A to the Magistrates' Courts Act 1952. This makes provision, inter alia, for a magistrates' clerk to transmit payments under a maintenance order registered in his court, which provides for payment directly to a child, either directly to that child or to the person with whom the child has his home. It also provides that that person may proceed in his own name for variation, revival or revocation of the order and may enforce non-payment either in his own name or by requesting the magistrates to do so.

E

It is therefore no longer necessary for the High Court or the divorce county court when granting an application for registration to place on the order the wording required by the practice direction of November 2, 1977, *Practice Direction (Child: Maintenance Payment)* [1977] 1 W.L.R. 1222, and that direction is hereby cancelled.

F

The registration in a magistrates' court of an order made direct to a child entails a considerable amount of work. Accordingly, when the court is considering the form of an order where there are children, care should be taken not to make orders for payment direct where such orders would be of no benefit to the parties or where the parties would derive no immediate tax advantage.

G

(b) *Nominal orders for spouses*

Applications for leave to register orders for nominal amounts in favour of spouses only should not be allowed and, except in special circumstances, leave to register should not be granted in respect of orders for maintenance pending suit and interim orders.

H

Issued with the concurrence of the Lord Chancellor.

R. L. BAYNE-POWELL
Senior Registrar

March 10, 1980.

A

[FAMILY DIVISION]

* KHAN (SAJID) *v.* KHAN (SAJID)

1979   Oct. 16   Sir John Arnold P. and Waterhouse J.

B   *Husband and Wife—Justices—Maintenance—Quantum—Young un-*
    qualified wife without experience of employment—Jurisdiction
    to make order limited in time — Matrimonial Proceedings
    (Magistrates' Courts) Act 1960 (8 & 9 *Eliz.* 2, *c.* 48), *s.* 2 (1) (*b*)

The parties married in May 1977.   At the time the wife
was aged 17 years, she had not completed her studies and had
never worked.   The husband was in his twenties.   They lived
C   with the husband's sister.   In February 1978 the wife returned
to her parental home.   The wife did not work but she was
studying by means of a correspondence course.   The husband
earned £3,844 gross a year.   On March 27, 1979, the stipendiary
magistrate found the wife's complaints of the husband's desertion and of his wilful neglect to maintain her proved and
made an order requiring the husband to pay a weekly sum
of £18.   The husband appealed on the question of quantum
D   on the ground that the order should have been made for a
limited period only.
On the question whether under section 2 (1) (*b*) of the
Matrimonial Proceedings (Magistrates' Courts) Act 1960 [1] the
court had jurisdiction to make an order limited in time: —
Held, allowing the appeal, that the jurisdiction of the court
to order the payment of " such weekly sum " as was reasonable,
under section 2 (1) (*b*) of the Matrimonial Proceedings (Magis-
E   trates' Courts) Act 1960, included not only a power to fix the
amount of payment but also the duration of that payment;
that the wife required a reasonable period in which to train
herself and find employment and, therefore, in the circumstances, the order would be varied by inserting a time limit
of a year into the order for payment of £18 a week and,
thereafter, the husband would only be required to pay £5 a
week.
F

The following cases are referred to in the judgments:

Chesworth v. *Chesworth* (1974) 118 S.J. 183.
Graves v. *Graves* (1973) 117 S.J. 679.

No additional cases were cited in argument.

G

APPEAL from the Birmingham stipendiary magistrate.
On March 27, 1979, following complaints by the wife, Fazeelath Sajid
Khan, that her husband, Mohammed Sajid Kahn, had deserted her on
February 15, 1978, and had wilfully neglected to maintain her from May 2,
1978.   The stipendiary magistrate found the complaints proved and made
H   an order requiring the husband to pay her the weekly sum of £18 for her
maintenance.   The husband appealed on the question of quantum only.
The facts are stated in the judgment of Waterhouse J.

[1] Matrimonial Proceedings (Magistrates' Courts) Act 1960, s. 2: "(1) . . . on hearing a complaint under . . . section 1 by either of the parties to a marriage the court
may make an order (in this Act referred to as a ' matrimonial order ') containing any
one or more of the following provisions, namely— . . . (*b*) a provision that the
husband shall pay to the wife such weekly sum . . . as the court considers reasonable in all the circumstances of the case; . . ."

Eleanor Platt for the husband.   A

John Freeman for the wife.

WATERHOUSE J. This is an appeal from a decision made by the stipendiary magistrate at Birmingham Magistrates' Court on March 27, 1979. He had before him complaints by a wife of desertion by her husband from February 15, 1978, and of wilful neglect to maintain her from May 2, 1978. The magistrate found both the complaints proved. There is no child   B of the marriage and, accordingly, his order was limited to maintenance of the wife, which he assessed at £18 per week. I should interpolate that, since the order, the husband has paid an average of about £6 per week pending the outcome of the present appeal.

The notice of appeal includes grounds of appeal directed to the magistrate's findings on both complaints and an appeal on quantum in   C relation to the maintenance order itself. Miss Platt, on behalf of the husband, has now said that he wishes to proceed only with the appeal on quantum, and it is on that footing that I will deal with the matter.

The marriage was short-lived. Both parties are Muslims and were natives of India, although the wife came to England at a young age. She was only about 17 years old when she married and her husband was in   D his twenties. The marriage took place on May 14, 1977, and the final separation occurred only nine months later on February 15, 1978. After the parting, the wife went to live with her parents and the husband went to live with his sister. It is perhaps material to mention that the magistrate, in setting out the reasons for his decision, gave some account of the married life in which he said that the wife not only had no home of her own during the marriage, because they were living with the husband's   E sister, but had no allowance from him and no money of her own. She told the court that no attempt was made to provide her with a home of her own. The wife's father said that he had agreed to provide £1,000 towards a house, of which he had paid £500. The husband said that they looked at flats and houses but the magistrate was satisfied that no serious attempt had been made to find independent accommodation.   F

The finding of the magistrate in relation to the charge of desertion was that the husband constructively deserted his wife in February 1978. The basic facts were that the wife's father, who was a building contractor in Birmingham, went to Croydon and had a long interview with the husband. The latter said that he would not have his wife back if she attended a marriage ceremony that she wished to attend. The husband said to the father that if the wife went to the wedding she was not to   G come back, and in front of the wife herself said: " I am telling you in front of your father, you are not to come back again." It was in those circumstances that the father took his daughter back to Birmingham where she has lived ever since; and the magistrate went on to find that there was no genuine offer by the husband to return.

At the stage when the matter came before the magistrate, the wife   H had received no maintenance in the intervening period, and the magistrate said that the wife had suffered humiliation in her married life: no house or income had been supplied, and she had been told to go.

In the course of the hearing, the evidence was mainly directed to the circumstances in which the parting had occurred, and the events that followed. The evidence about the means of the parties and the potential income of the wife was brief. The magistrate took the view that it was a

A straightforward case where there should be an order for maintenance. The evidence before him indicated that the husband's income was £2,580 net per annum, and, grossed up, that would produce a figure between £3,300 and £3,500. With the consent of the wife, there has been produced to us in court today the income tax form P.60 for the year to April 1979, which indicates that the husband's gross income was £3,844, subject to a deduction of £250 in respect of national insurance and no doubt some

B further small deductions appropriate to cover the travelling expenses incurred by the husband in earning his income. He is employed, and has at all material times been employed, by the Commonwealth Secretariat.

The wife's position was that she had never worked; in cross-examination she said that she learned housework at school and that she took C.S.E.'s but had no time to take O levels. She had been to a college

C after school until her marriage. She said also that it was her idea to go to college during the marriage, and she did start in September 1977, but she only went to two classes because a quarrel with her husband caused her to discontinue the course. She said that she would have liked to go on and pass O levels, but she told the magistrate that she was taking a correspondence course because she could not get into college. The court

D has been told that she has continued with that correspondence course since the magistrates' court hearing. There was very little evidence, therefore, before the magistrate as to the real potential of the wife and her earning capacity. The husband concentrated in his evidence upon the details of the history of the marriage, and did not supply any additional information about his wife's capacity, or indeed about Muslim practice in relation to employment.

E It has been urged on behalf of the wife throughout that it is not Muslim practice for a married woman to go out to earn an income, and the court has been invited to take judicial notice of this practice on the assumption that it continues to apply to parties who are separated and not continuing to cohabit. For my part, I am quite unable to accept the argument that one should take judicial notice of the Muslim practice

F in this regard. It is plainly a matter about which there should be evidence if it is to be relied on as a relevant factor.

Thus, the position in this case was that the wife had been deserted in February 1978 and by the time the matter came before the magistrate she had been deserted for a period of 15 months. She had had the advantage of living with her parents during that period, and it is clearly a case in which serious consideration had to be given to her earning

G capacity in the future. The general principle applicable to a case of this kind was stated in Graves v. Graves (1973) 117 S.J. 679. In that case, the parting had occurred only about 12 months after the marriage; there was no child; and both parties were in their early twenties. Ormrod J. said:

H "that the appeal emphasised the difference in the approach of justices and that of the judges of the Family Division when considering financial matters in similar circumstances. Where a marriage was of short duration and the parties were young a nominal order was the appropriate order unless there were children or the wife was handicapped in some way which prevented her from working. At the time of the hearing before the justices, the wife was not working but she was a state enrolled nurse and the justices should have taken into account her potential earning capacity. The wife was now employed full time A in a hospital."

The present case is, of course, plainly distinguishable from *Graves* v. *Graves* because there the young wife had a profession, and indeed, by the time of the hearing of the appeal to the Divisional Court, she had been able to resume that profession. The present wife is in receipt of social security benefits totalling £13·90 per week, but she has no additional income, B and there was no evidence before the magistrate that she was, as yet, in a position to earn her living outside her parents' home. One would infer, however, from the fact that she was living with her parents that she must have been providing some services in the home in return for the board and lodging afforded to her by them.

On behalf of the husband, it has been urged by Miss Platt that the C approach of the magistrate should have been that the wife was capable of earning an income in the near future, and that the order should have catered for that finding of fact. Miss Platt suggests that, either the order should have been for a limited period in order to encourage the wife to train herself for employment at an early date, or that it should have been assessed at such a modest level that there would be active encouragement to the wife to find employment at the earliest opportunity. D

The jurisdiction of the court to make an order for a limited term has been stated in *Chesworth* v. *Chesworth* (1974) 118 S.J. 183. The dicta in that case were obiter because the court, comprising Sir George Baker P. and Dunn J., was dealing with an offer of maintenance for a limited period; but Sir George Baker P. said:

"It was accepted by the wife's counsel that only a nominal order was E appropriate. The husband was willing to pay £3·50 a week to the wife for a limited period of nine months while she reorganised her life. Doubts had been expressed whether justices had power to make such an order limited in time. Justices had power to make orders unlimited in time and it was common sense to make limited orders as well."

I agree with what was said by Sir George Baker P. Section 2 (1) of F the Matrimonial Proceedings (Magistrates' Courts) Act 1960 provides that the court may make a matrimonial order containing any one or more of the following provisions, namely, "(b) a provision that the husband shall pay to the wife such weekly sum . . . as the court considers reasonable in all the circumstances of the case." In the absence of any express fetter, it seems abundantly clear that the order may be either G unlimited in time or limited in time; and there is no such fetter in the statute

Looking at the whole of the facts of this case, and the rather limited evidence about the parties' finances that was before the stipendiary magistrate, I consider that it is a case in which it is right for a time limit to be placed upon the order for maintenance. The amount of H £18 per week was assessed at a level rather less than one third of the joint incomes, and provides adequately for the wife in her particular circumstances whilst she is seeking to train herself and obtain satisfactory employment. However, a substantial period has now elapsed since the desertion occurred in February 1978. For my part, I think that, if the order of the magistrate had been limited to a period of 12 months from the date thereof, that would have provided satisfactory maintenance for

A the wife for an adequate period, that is just over two years from the date of the desertion, and that any maintenance thereafter should be at a reduced rate.

I consider, therefore, that this is a case in which the appeal should be allowed, simply to the extent of inserting in the magistrates' court order a time limit of twelve months, so that the maintenance at the rate of £18 a week will terminate at the end of March 1980. The position thereafter

B requires separate consideration. It is right that there should continue to be some small maintenance for the wife but it should be assessed on an entirely different basis. Having regard to the whole of the history and the obligations and means of the parties, I would propose that from March 27, 1980, the rate of maintenance should be £5 per week.

C   SIR JOHN ARNOLD P. I agree. I would like just to add a word in relation to the matter which was considered in *Chesworth* v. *Chesworth* (1974) 118 S.J. 183 to which Waterhouse J. has referred. The provision in the Matrimonial Proceedings (Magistrates' Courts) Act 1960 is a provision that the husband shall pay to the wife " such weekly sum . . . as the court considers reasonable in all the circumstances of the case."

D   In my view, the word " such " is not limited to defining the amount of the weekly sum but carries with it an ability to qualify that sum in every relevant respect; in terms of duration in particular so far as this case is concerned, as well as amount. Nor does there seem to me to be anything inconsistent with that provision in making the weekly payments of a variable nature, in relation to successive periods. The order which we make in the terms suggested by Waterhouse J. is, of course, in line with

E what we regard as reasonable and expectable in the present circumstances. If we are wrong, and there is a really valid reason why, at the end of the twelve-month period, the wife is not able to earn an adequate living, then she can deploy those matters on an application to vary before the magistrate; and equally, if the basis upon which the continuing payment of £5 a week is ordered, namely, that the expectation that the wife will at any rate for some little time to come be earning less than she might otherwise

F have earned if she had been more experienced and therefore some small subsidy would be appropriate, turns out to be a pessimistic point of view, then equally the husband can apply for an appropriate variation.

Accordingly, the appeal will be allowed to the extent indicated.

Appeal allowed.
G   *Legal aid taxation.*

Solicitors: *Stocken & Co.; Evershed & Tomkinson, Birmingham.*

M. B. D.

H

A

[CHANCERY DIVISION]

* *In re* GRANT'S WILL TRUSTS

HARRIS AND OTHERS *v.* ANDERSON AND OTHERS

[1977 G. No. 2060]

B

1978   Dec. 18, 19;   Vinelott J.
1979   March 16

Will—Construction—Gift to non-charitable association—Gift to
" Labour Party property committee " for benefit of constituency
labour party—Rules of association alterable by outside body
—Whether legacy valid

C

The testator had for many years been a member of the
Labour Party and financial secretary of the Chertsey Constituency Labour Party. In 1959 a property was bought to serve as
the constituency party headquarters and held on trust to deal
with the property as directed by the general management committee of the constituency party, and if that party should cease
to exist, on trust for the Labour Party absolutely. In 1970,   D
following the reorganisation of constituency boundaries, the
constituency ceased to exist and the constituency party was
dissolved. A new constituency party, the Chertsey and Walton
Constituency Labour Party, was then formed, and on February
8, 1975, a set of rules was adopted in the form laid down by
the National Executive Committee of the Labour Party (the
N.E.C.). Those rules provided, inter alia, that the constituency
party should be managed by a general committee which should   E
accept and make such changes in the rules as might be agreed
to by the annual party conference or made by the N.E.C., and
the committee's power to make changes in the rules was limited
to changes which did not contravene their spirit and intention.
The general committee was to have power, subject to the
approval of the N.E.C., to buy property and to appoint trustees
to hold it on behalf of the constituency party. The 1959
headquarters continued to be held by the original trustees and   F
was managed by a property committee made up of members
from three local Labour Parties pending the resolution of the
question of ownership of the property. After the testator's
death an arrangement was made whereby the headquarters
passed to the new constituency party.

By his will dated May 12, 1975, the testator appointed
the trustees of the headquarters his executors and devised all   G
his real and personal estate to " the Labour Party property
committee " for the benefit of the Chertsey headquarters of
the new constituency party, provided that such headquarters
remained in what was " the Chertsey Urban District Council
Area (1972)," with a gift over in default of such condition to
the National Labour Party absolutely. At all material times
the headquarters of the new constituency party remained in the
Chertsey Urban District Council Area (1972). It was common   H
ground that by " the Labour Party property committee " the
testator meant the committee which had been managing the
headquarters since the reorganisation.

On the executor's application to the court to determine
the validity of the gift and to ascertain the beneficiaries
thereunder : —

Held, (1) that unless the terms of the gift to the Labour
Party property committee could be construed as a gift to the
existing members of an unincorporated body either as joint

A   tenants or for their benefit subject to their contractual rights
and obligations as members of the association, there must be a
trust created in order for the gift to be valid; that, since the
testator had indicated that the gift was to the property committee and not to the trustees of the 1959 trust and had also
envisaged, by the proviso and the gift over to the National
Labour Party, a situation where the constituency party would
no longer need headquarters, the terms of the will could not be
B   construed as granting a gift to be held under the terms of the
1959 trust deed and, accordingly, no valid trust had been
created (post, pp. 365G, 368E–H, 371C–F).
        (2) That, if the gift was to the existing members of the
constituency association with a direction, not amounting to a
trust, to use the property for " headquarters purposes ", it was
invalid (i) because on the construction of the clause, the gift
could not be to existing members of the association as joint
C   tenants and, therefore, to be valid the gift had to be for the
benefit of the existing members subject to the contractual
rights and obligations as members, and for that purpose it was
essential that the members who received such a gift should be
free to dispose of the fund in any way they thought fit in
furtherance of the testator's intentions or to divide it beneficially
among themselves, and that the rules of the constituency
association made it plain that its members were controlled by
D   an outside body and did not have such powers; and (ii)
because the gift was expressed to be to the Labour Party
property committee and not the members of the association
(post, pp. 374B–D, 375A–C).
        Leahy v. Attorney-General of New South Wales [1959]
A.C. 457, P.C. applied.
        Neville Estates Ltd. v. Madden [1962] Ch. 832; In re
Recher's Will Trusts [1972] Ch. 526 and In re Denley's Trust
E   Deed [1969] 1 Ch. 373 considered.
        In re Lipinski's Will Trusts [1976] Ch. 235 distinguished.
        (3) That the gift could not be construed as a gift to the
members of the National Labour Party with a direction to
permit it to be used by the Chertsey and Walton Constituency
Labour Party because of the gift over to the National Labour
Party and, accordingly, the gift was void and the estate
devolved as on intestacy (post, p. 375A).
F
The following cases are referred to in the judgment:

Denley's Trust Deed, In re [1969] 1 Ch. 373; [1968] 3 W.L.R. 457;
        [1968] 3 All E.R. 65.
Drummond, In re [1914] 2 Ch. 90.
Leahy v. Attorney-General of New South Wales [1959] A.C. 457; [1959]
        2 W.L.R. 722; [1959] 2 All E.R. 300, P.C.
G   Lipinski's Will Trusts, In re [1976] Ch. 235; [1976] 3 W.L.R. 522; [1977]
        1 All E.R. 33.
Neville Estates Ltd. v. Madden [1962] Ch. 832; [1961] 3 W.L.R. 999;
        [1961] 3 All E.R. 769.
Price, In re [1943] Ch. 422; [1943] 2 All E.R. 505.
Recher's Will Trusts, In re [1972] Ch. 526; [1971] 3 W.L.R. 321; [1971]
        3 All E.R. 401.
H   Turkington, In re [1937] 4 All E.R. 501.

The following additional cases were cited in argument:

Astor's Settlement Trusts, In re [1952] Ch. 534; [1952] 1 All E.R. 1067.
Endacott, decd., In re [1960] Ch. 232; [1959] 3 W.L.R. 799; [1959] 3
        All E.R. 562, C.A.
Macaulay's Estate, In re [1943] Ch. 435.
Ogden, In re [1933] Ch. 678.

SUMMONS

A

By an originating summons dated July 12, 1977, the plaintiffs, Bertram Henry Harris, Keith Jeffery Joseph Thompson and Denis Wood, the executors of the will of Wilson Phelps Grant deceased, sought determination of the questions (1) whether the expression " the Labour Party Committee " was void for uncertainty and, if not void, who constituted the committee; (2) whether the gift to the Labour Party property committee for the benefit of the Chertsey headquarters of the Chertsey B and Walton Constituency Labour Party was a valid gift to the committee or to some other body or whether it was void for uncertainty, want of a beneficiary, perpetuity or some other reason; and (3) if the gift was void, whether the gift over took effect or whether the estate was undisposed of and passed as on intestacy.   The first defendant, Anthony Sidney Anderson, was sued on his own behalf and on behalf of all the members C of the Chertsey and Walton Constituency Labour Party, the second defendant, Ronald George Hayward, was sued on his own behalf and on behalf of all the members of the Labour Party, the third defendant, Margery Godden, represented the persons entitled to the testator's estate upon intestacy.

The facts are set out in the judgment.

D

Nicholas Stewart for the plaintiffs.
J. H. G. Sunnucks for the first and second defendants.
Jonathan Simpkiss for the third defendant.

Cur. adv. vult.

E

March 16, 1979. VINELOTT J. read the following judgment.   The testator, Wilson Phelps Grant, died on June 6, 1975.   By his will dated May 12, 1975, he appointed: " The trustees of 36, Guildford Street, Chertsey, to be the executors of this my will."   At the date of the will, and of the testator's death, the property, 36, Guildford Street, Chertsey, was the headquarters of the Chertsey and Walton Constituency Labour Party.   The plaintiffs were registered as proprietors with an absolute F title, and as hereafter appears they held the property as trustees of a trust deed dated June 26, 1959.   The plaintiffs duly proved the will, which was never altered or revoked, on December 8, 1975.

After the appointment of the executors, the will continues as follows:

" I give all my real and personal estate to the Labour Party property committee for the benefit of the Chertsey Headquarters of the G Chertsey and Walton Constituency Labour Party provided that such headquarters remain in what was the Chertsey Urban District Council Area (1972), if not, I declare that the foregoing provision shall not take effect and in lieu thereof I give all my said estate to the National Labour Party absolutely."

The factual background which forms the context in which these H words have to be construed is shortly as follows.   The testator was a member of the Labour Party for upwards of 24 years.   He played an active part in the affairs of his local constituency party which until shortly before his death was the Chertsey Constituency Labour Party (which I shall abbreviate to " the Chertsey C.L.P.").   In the redistribution of Parliamentary constituency boundaries in 1970 Chertsey constituency ceased to exist; part is now in North-West Surrey, part is in the Chertsey

A and Walton constituency. The Chertsey C.L.P. was accordingly dissolved. The general management committee of the Chertsey C.L.P. held its last meeting on January 29, 1971. The testator was present. He was the C.L.P.'s financial secretary. The last sentence of the minutes records ". . . that this meeting dissolves the Chertsey Constituency Labour Party."

B Some time later a new constituency party, the Chertsey and Walton C.L.P., was formed. Its rules, which are in the form of model rules prescribed by the National Labour Party, were adopted by the general committee of the new C.L.P. on February 28, 1975. I shall have to return to examine these rules in detail later in this judgment. I should mention at this stage the testator was also the financial secretary of the Chertsey and Walton C.L.P., an office which he continued to hold until C his death.

The property, 36, Guildford Street, was bought by the old Chertsey C.L.P. in 1959. A trust deed was executed on June 26, 1959, the parties being Arthur Imisson and Charles Frederick Huggins as trustees of the one part, and Roy Goodall, vice-chairman of the general management committee of the Chertsey C.L.P., on behalf of himself and all the D members of the general management committee, who are named in the first schedule and include the testator, of the other part. The trust deed recited that by the instrument of transfer specified in the second schedule, the property, 36, Guildford Street, had been transferred to the trustees who had been registered as proprietors with an absolute title. In fact, as appears from subsequent documents, the transfer was not registered until October 16, 1959, and was in favour of Messrs. Imisson, Huggins and E Goodall. The trust deed recited that the property had been purchased out of moneys provided by the Chertsey C.L.P., and that under its rules it was provided that the management of the affairs of the Chertsey C.L.P. should be vested in its general management committee. Clause 2 contains a declaration that the trustees:

F ". . . shall hold the said property until the same shall be sold or otherwise disposed of upon trust for the party absolutely and shall deal with the same as the committee shall from time to time by resolution direct."

I should mention in passing that " the party " is defined as the Chertsey C.L.P. It continues:

G " The trustees shall have full power with the approval of a resolution of the committee to raise money for any purpose connected with the said property including the provision of the whole or any part of the cost of purchasing the said property, or erecting enlarging or improving any building for the time-being thereon."

Of the remaining provisions of the trust deed only two require to be H mentioned. Clause 9 provides:

" The trustees shall until otherwise directed by the committee hold all trust moneys whether income or capital moneys and howsoever same shall arise in the joint names of the trustees and may invest them or any part of them in any securities authorised by law for the investment of trust funds in the joint names of the trustees, and shall pay the income of such investments and the rent and profits of any hereditaments to the account of the party with the bank."

Clause 15 provides:

A

"If the party shall cease to exist for any reason the said property shall be held by the trustees upon trust for the Labour Party absolutely and the National Executive Committee of the Labour Party shall thereafter exercise all of their powers now vested in the committee hereunder."

The plaintiffs were appointed trustees of the trust deed on April 6, 1975. From April 6, 1975, until the testator's death they remained the trustees thereof. They were clearly the persons designated by the phrase, ". . . the trustees of 36, Guildford Street," in the testator's will and, as I have said, they duly proved the will.

B

The property was purchased with the help of a mortgage from a building society, which was discharged on April 24, 1975, very shortly before the date of the will. The testator as financial secretary of the Chertsey C.L.P. and later of the Chertsey and Walton C.L.P., must have been well aware of this history. As I have said, he was a member of the general management committee at the time of the purchase.

C

There is one other fact which I should mention before I turn to explain what happened to 36, Guildford Street on the reorganisation of the Chertsey C.L.P. 36, Guildford Street was in the language of a proviso to the will ". . . in what was the Chertsey Urban District Council Area (1972)." Since the local authority reorganisation in 1974 it has been within the geographical area of the Runnymead district. It has at all material times been the office, and the only office, of the Chertsey and Walton C.L.P.

D

An affidavit has been sworn by Anthony Sidney Anderson, the first defendant, who is joined to represent the members of the Chertsey and Walton C.L.P., and who is an officer and general election agent designate of the Chertsey and Walton C.L.P., explaining the arrangements made with regard to the ownership of 36, Guildford Street following the redistribution of Parliamentary constituency boundaries in 1970, and the dissolution of the Chertsey C.L.P. on January 29, 1971. It appears that at the time of the redistribution the management of 36, Guildford Street was put into the hands of a property committee consisting of delegates from each of the three local Labour Parties, namely, those of Egham, Bagshot and Chertsey. Although the Chertsey C.L.P. was dissolved the local Labour Parties did not cease to exist, and of course the plaintiffs continued to hold the property as trustees. This arrangement for managing 36, Guildford Street was intended as a temporary arrangement pending resolution of the ownership of the property. That question remained unresolved at the testator's death, though since his death an arrangement has been made under which the ownership of 36, Guildford Street will pass to the Chertsey and Walton C.L.P. subject to the payment of a sum of £4,000 to the North-West Surrey C.L.P. in recognition of the part played by former members of the Chertsey C.L.P. within the North-West Surrey C.L.P. in the acquisition and maintenance of 36, Guildford Street. It is common ground that in these circumstances the testator when he spoke of " the Labour Party property committee " must have intended to refer to the property committee formed to manage 36, Guildford Street, after dissolution of the Chertsey C.L.P. and pending resolution of the question of ownership.

E

F

G

H

The question raised by the summons is whether the gift in the will of the testator's real and personal estate is a valid gift, or is void for

A　uncertainty or for perpetuity or otherwise; and if it is a valid gift, who are the persons entitled to benefit thereunder?

Before turning to this question, it will be convenient to explain what are in my judgment the principles which govern the validity of a gift to an unincorporated association. A convenient starting point is a passage in the decision of Cross J. in *Neville Estates Ltd.* v. *Madden* [1962] Ch. 832, 849 which is often cited. He said:

B

> "The question of the construction and effect of gifts to or in trust for unincorporated associations was recently considered by the Privy Council in *Leahy* v. *Attorney-General for New South Wales* [1959] A.C. 457. The position, as I understand it, is as follows. Such a gift may take effect in one or other of three quite different ways. In the first place, it may, on its true construction, be a gift to the members
>
> C of the association at the relevant date as joint tenants, so that any member can sever his share and claim it whether or not he continues to be a member of the association. Secondly, it may be a gift to the existing members not as joint tenants, but subject to their respective contractual rights and liabilities towards one another as members of the association. In such a case a member cannot sever his share.
>
> D It would accrue to the other members on his death or resignation, even though such members include persons who become members after the gift took effect. If this is the effect of the gift, it will not be open to objection on the score of perpetuity or uncertainty unless there is something in its terms or circumstances or in the rules of the association which precludes the members at any given time from dividing the subject of the gift between them on the footing that they
>
> E are solely entitled to it in equity. Thirdly, the terms or circumstances of the gift or the rules of the association may show that the property in question is not to be at the disposal of the members for the time being, but is to be held in trust for or applied for the purposes of the association as a quasi-corporate entity. In this case the gift will fail unless the association is a charitable body. If the
>
> F gift is of the second class, i.e., one which the members of the association for the time being are entitled to divide among themselves, then, even if the objects of the association are in themselves charitable, the gift would not, I think, be a charitable gift."

This statement, though it may require amplification in the light of subsequent authorities, is still, as I see it, an accurate statement of the law.

G　In a case in the first category, that is a gift which, on its true construction, is a gift to members of an association who take as joint tenants, any member being able to sever his share, the association is used in effect as a convenient label or definition of the class which is intended to take; but, the class being ascertained, each member takes as joint tenant free from any contractual fetter. So, for instance, a testator might give a legacy or share of residue to a dining or social club of which he had
H been a member with the intention of giving to each of the other members an interest as joint tenant, capable of being severed, in the subject-matter of the gift. Cases within this category are relatively uncommon. A gift to an association will be more frequently found to fall within the second category. There the gift is to members of an association, but the property is given as an accretion to the funds of the association so that the property becomes subject to the contract (normally evidenced by the rules of the association) which govern the rights of the members inter se.

Each member is thus in a position to ensure that the subject-matter of the A
gift is applied in accordance with the rules of the association, in the same
way as any other funds of the association. This category is well
illustrated by the decision of Brightman J. in *In re Recher's Will Trusts*
[1972] Ch. 526. There a share of residue was given to " The Anti-
Vivisection Society, 76 Victoria Street, London, S.W.1." The society in
fact ceased to exist, being amalgamated with another society, during the
testatrix's lifetime. Brightman J. first examined whether the gift would B
have been valid if the society had continued to exist. He said, at p. 538:

" A trust for non-charitable purposes, as distinct from a trust for
individuals, is clearly void because there is no beneficiary. It does
not, however, follow that persons cannot band themselves together
as an association or society, pay subscriptions and validly devote
their funds in pursuit of some lawful non-charitable purpose. An C
obvious example is a members' social club. But it is not essential
that the members should only intend to secure direct personal
advantages to themselves. The association may be one in which
personal advantages to members are combined with the pursuit of
some outside purpose. Or the association may be one which offers
no personal benefit at all to the members, the funds of the association D
being applied exclusively to the pursuit of some outside purpose.
Such an association of persons is bound, I would think, to have
some sort of constitution; that is to say, the rights and liabilities
of the members of the association would inevitably depend upon
some form of contract inter se, usually evidenced by a set of rules.
In the present case it appears to be clear that the life members, the
ordinary members and the associate members of the London and E
Provincial society were bound together by a contract inter se. Any
such member was entitled to the rights and subject to the liabilities
defined by the rules. If the committee acted contrary to the rules,
an individual member would be entitled to take proceedings in the
courts to compel observance of the rules or to recover damages for
any loss he had suffered as a result of the breach of contract. As F
and when a member paid his subscription to the association, he
would be subjecting his money to the disposition and expenditure
thereof laid down by the rules. That is to say, a member would be
bound to permit, and entitled to require, the honorary trustees and
other members of the society to deal with that subscription in
accordance with the lawful directions of the committee. Those
directions would include the expenditure of that subscription, as G
part of the general funds of the association, in furthering the
objects of the association. The resultant situation, on analysis, is
that the London and Provincial society represented an organisation
of individuals bound together by a contract under which their
subscriptions became, as it were, mandated towards a certain type of
expenditure as adumbrated in rule 1. Just as the two parties to a H
bi-partite bargain can vary or terminate their contract by mutual
assent, so it must follow that the life members, ordinary members
and associate members of the London and Provincial society could,
at any moment of time, by unanimous agreement (or by majority
vote, if the rules so prescribe), vary or terminate their multi-partite
contract. There would be no limit to the type of variation or
termination to which all might agree. There is no private trust or

trust for charitable purposes or other trust to hinder the process. It follows that if all members agreed, they could decide to wind up the London and Provincial society and divide the net assets among themselves beneficially. No one would have any locus standi to stop them so doing. The contract is the same as any other contract and concerns only those who are parties to it, that is to say, the members of the society.

"The funds of such an association may, of course, be derived not only from subscriptions of the contracting parties but also from donations from non-contracting parties and legacies from persons who have died. In the case of a donation which is not accompanied by any words which purport to impose a trust, it seems to me that the gift takes effect in favour of the existing members of the association as an accretion to the funds which are the subject-matter of the contract which such members have made inter se, and falls to be dealt with in precisely the same way as the funds which the members themselves have subscribed. So, in the case of a legacy. In the absence of words which purport to impose a trust, the legacy is a gift to the members beneficially, not as joint tenants or as tenants in common so as to entitle each member to an immediate distributive share, but as an accretion to the funds which are the subject matter of the contract which the members have made inter se."

Two points should be noted. First, as Brightman J. pointed out, it is immaterial in considering whether a gift falls within this category that the members of an association have not joined together for a social and recreational purpose, or to secure some personal advantage, but in pursuit of some altruistic purpose. The motive which led the testator to make the gift may have been, indeed most frequently will have been, a desire to further that purpose. It may be said that in that sense the gift is made for the furtherance of the purpose. But the testator has chosen as the means of furthering the purpose to make a gift to an association formed for the pursuit of that purpose in the expectation that the subject matter of the gift will be so used, without imposing or attempting to impose any trust or obligation on the members, or the trustees, or the committee of the association. Indeed, there are cases where the gift has been expressed as a gift for the purposes, or one of the purposes, of the association, and nonetheless has been held not to impose any purported trust. Two examples will suffice. In *In re Turkington* [1937] 4 All E.R. 501, the gift was expressed as a gift to the Staffordshire Knot Masonic Lodge No. 726 as a fund to build a suitable temple in Stafford. Luxmoore J. construed the gift as a gift to the members of the lodge and construed the words ". . . to build a suitable temple in Stafford " as—and I cite from his judgment, at p. 504:

". . . simply an indication by the testator of the purposes for which he would like the money to be expended, without imposing any trust on the beneficiary."

In the recent decision of Oliver J. in *In re Lipinski's Will Trusts* [1976] Ch. 235, the gift was:

". . . for the Hull Judeans (Maccabi) Association in memory of my late wife, to be used solely in work of constructing new buildings for the association and/or improvements to the said buildings."

Oliver J. said, at p. 246:

A

" If a valid gift may be made to an unincorporated body as a simple accretion to the funds which are the subject matter of the contract which the members have made inter se—and *Neville Estates Ltd.* v. *Madden* [1962] Ch. 832 and *In re Recher's Will Trusts* [1972] Ch. 526 show that it may—I do not really see why such a gift, which specifies a purpose which is within the powers of the association and of which the members of the association are beneficiaries, should fail. Why are not the beneficiaries able to enforce the trust or, indeed, in the exercise of their contractual rights, to terminate the trust for their own benefit? Where the donee association is itself the beneficiary of the prescribed purpose, there seems to me to be the strongest argument in common sense for saying that the gift should be construed as an absolute one within the second category —the more so where, if the purpose is carried out, the members can by appropriate action vest the resulting property in themselves, for here the trustees and the beneficiaries are the same persons."

B

C

As I read his judgment, Oliver J. construed the gift as one under which the members of the association could have resolved to use the property for some other purpose, or, indeed, have divided it amongst themselves. He said, at p. 249:

D

" There is an additional factor. This is a case in which, under the constitution of the association, the members could, by the appropriate majority, alter their constitution so as to provide, if they wished, for the division of the association's assets among themselves."

E

That leads to the second point. It must, as I see it, be a necessary characteristic of any gift within the second category that the members of the association can by an appropriate majority, if the rules so provide, or acting unanimously if they do not, alter their rules so as to provide that the funds, or part of them, should be applied for some new purpose, or even distributed amongst the members for their own benefit. For the validity of a gift within this category rests essentially upon the fact that the testator has set out to further a purpose by making a gift to the members of an association formed for the furtherance of that purpose in the expectation that although the members at the date when the gift takes effect will be free, by a majority if the rules so provide or acting unanimously if they do not, to dispose of the fund in any way they may think fit, they and any future members of the association will not in fact do so but will employ the property in the furtherance of the purpose of the association and will honour any special condition attached to the gift.

F

G

Turning to the third category, the testator may seek to further the purpose by giving a legacy to an association as a quasi-corporate entity, that is, to present and future members indefinitely, or by purporting to impose a trust. In the former case the gift will fail for perpetuity, unless confined within an appropriate period; though if it is so confined and if the members for the time being within the perpetuity period are free to alter the purposes for which the property is to be used and to distribute the income amongst themselves it will not, as I see it, fail upon any other ground. In the latter case, the gift will fail upon the ground that the court cannot compel the use of the property in furtherance of a stated purpose unless, of course, the purpose is a charitable one. As

H

A   Vicount Simonds said in *Leahy* v. *Attorney-General for New South Wales* [1959] A.C. 457, 478:

> " If the words ' for the general purposes of the association ' were held to import a trust, the question would have to be asked, what is the trust and who are the beneficiaries? A gift can be made to persons (including a corporation) but it cannot be made to a purpose
B   or to an object: so also, a trust may be created for the benefit of persons as cestuis que trust but not for a purpose or object unless the purpose or object be charitable. For a purpose or object cannot sue, but, if it be charitable, the Attorney-General can sue to enforce it. (Upon this point something will be said later). It is therefore by disregarding the words ' for the general purposes of the association ' (which are assumed not to be charitable purposes) and treating the
C   gift as an absolute gift to individuals that it can be sustained."

There are two cases in which, if this analysis is correct, the reasons given for the decision, though possibly not the decision itself, are not well-founded. First, there is a decision of Eve J. in *In re Drummond* [1914] 2 Ch. 90, where the testator gave his residuary estate upon trust for the Old Bradfordians' Club, London, and by a codicil directed that
D   the moneys:

> ". . . should be utilised by the club for such purpose as the committee for the time being might determine, the object and intent of the bequest being to benefit old boys of the Bradford Grammar School residing in London or members of the club, and to enable the committee, if possible, to acquire premises to be used as a clubhouse for
E   the use of members, being old boys of Bradford Grammar School, with power to the committee to make rules and regulations as to residence in or use of the same, and further that it was the object of the bequest that the moneys should be utilised in founding scholarships or otherwise in such manner as the committee for the time being should think best in the interests of the club, or the
F   school."

Eve J. held that he could not say that the gift was a gift to the members of the club, but he said, at p. 97:

> " There was, in his opinion, a trust, but there was abundant authority for holding it was not such a trust as would render the legacy void as tending to a perpetuity: *In re Clarke* [1901] 2 Ch. 110. The legacy
G   was not subject to any trust which would prevent the committee of the club from spending it in any manner they might decide for the benefit of the class intended. In his opinion, therefore, there was a valid gift to the club for such purposes as the committee should determine for the benefit of the old boys or members of the club."

The second is *In re Price* [1943] Ch. 422, where Cohen J. held that a
H   gift of a share of residue to the Anthroposophical Society of Great Britain ". . . to be used at the discretion of the chairman and executive council of the society for carrying on the teachings of the founder, Dr. Rudolf Steiner " was a valid gift. There the only question considered by the judge was whether the gift tended to a perpetuity, and having held that it did not he held the gift was a valid gift, without considering whether it was not void as creating a trust for a non-charitable purpose. It is to be observed that he said, at p. 435: " Had it been necessary for

370

me to deal with this point, I would have inclined to uphold the gift to the   A
Anthroposophical Society as a valid charitable gift."

I have also been referred to the recent decision of Goff J. in *In re
Denley's Trust Deed* [1969] 1 Ch. 373. There by clause 2 of a trust deed
trustees were given powers of sale over land held by them and were
directed to hold the land while unsold during a defined perpetuity period
on trust, that

B

> ". . . (c) The said land shall be maintained and used as and for the
> purpose of a recreation or sports ground primarily for the benefit of
> the employees of the company and secondarily for the benefit of
> such other person or persons (if any) as the trustees may allow to
> use the same with power to the trustees from time to time to make
> any alterations they shall think proper with regard to the laying out
> of the ground or the preparation of parts thereof for special purposes   C
> or otherwise provided always that the trustees shall not at any time be
> bound to execute any works in or upon the said land or in or to any
> buildings erections or works thereon or otherwise to incur any
> expenses in relation to the said land unless funds shall be provided by
> the employees of the company or other users of the said land and there
> shall for the time being be in hand a sum which shall in the opinion   D
> of the trustees be available and sufficient to answer the costs of the
> said works or to meet such expenses. (d) The trustees shall have
> power from time to time to make rules and regulations with regard
> to the times and manner of user of the said land and subject to such
> rules and regulations as shall from time to time be made by the
> trustees the employees of the company shall be entitled to the use
> and enjoyment of the said land."

E

It was also provided:

> " (j) If at any time the number of employees subscribing shall be less
> than 75 per cent. of the total number of employees at any given time
> (subscribing at the rate of twopence per week per man) or if the said
> land shall at any time cease to be required or to be used by the said
> employees as a sports ground or if the company should go into   F
> liquidation then the trustees shall notwithstanding anything that
> shall or may have been done or partly accomplished and subject to
> repayment to the company of the aforesaid sum of £400 with interest
> thereon convey the said land to the General Hospital Cheltenham or
> as it shall direct."

G

Goff J., having held that the words " secondarily for the benefit of such
other person or persons if any as the trustees may allow to use the same,"
conferred on the trustees a power operating in partial defeasance of a trust
in favour of the employees, held that the trust deed created a valid trust
for the benefit of the employees, the benefit being the right to use the
land subject to and in accordance with the rules made by the trustees.
That case on a proper analysis, in my judgment, falls altogether outside   H
the categories of gifts to unincorporated association and purpose trusts.
I can see no distinction in principle between a trust to permit a class
defined by reference to employment to use and enjoy land in accordance
with rules to be made at the discretion of trustees on the one hand, and,
on the other hand, a trust to distribute income at the discretion of
trustees amongst a class, defined by reference to, for example, relationship
to the settlor. In both cases the benefit to be taken by any member of

A the class is at the discretion of the trustees, but any member of the class can apply to the court to compel the trustees to administer the trust in accordance with its terms. As Goff J. pointed out, at p. 388:

"The same kind of problem is equally capable of arising in the case of a trust to permit a number of persons—for example, all the unmarried children of a testator or settlor—to use or occupy a B house or to have the use of certain chattels; nor can I assume that in such cases agreement between the parties concerned would be more likely, even if that be a sufficient distinction, yet no one would suggest, I fancy, that such a trust would be void."

With those principles in mind, I return to the testator's will. Mr. Sunnucks, who appeared both for the first defendant (joined to represent C the members of the Chertsey and Walton C.L.P.) and the second defendant, Ronald George Hayward (joined to represent all members of the National Labour Party), argued, first, that the gift should be construed as a gift upon the trusts of the trust deed so that the residuary estate would be an accretion to and follow in all respects the devolution of 36, Guildford Street or the proceeds of sale thereof. The intention of D the testator in making the gift, said Mr. Sunnucks, may have been to provide a fund which could be used both as to capital and income for the enlargement, improvement and maintenance of 36, Guildford Street. But the terms of the proviso seem to me to place an insuperable obstacle in the way of this construction, for it is clear from the proviso that the testator contemplated that 36, Guildford Street might not continue to be the headquarters of the Chertsey and Walton C.L.P. The residuary E estate was, nonetheless, to be held ". . . by the Labour Party property committee for the benefit of the Chertsey Headquarters of the Chertsey and Walton Constituency Labour Party provided the headquarters remained within the geographical limits of the former Chertsey Urban District Council." There are two other considerations which also weigh heavily against this construction. First, although the trustees of 36, Guildford Street are appointed executors of the will, the gift is for F ". . . the Labour Party property committee." If the testator had intended his residuary estate to be held on the trusts applicable to 36, Guildford Street, or the proceeds of sale thereof, one would have expected the testator to have given it to the trustees of 36, Guildford Street. Secondly, it is clear from the affidavit of Mr. Anderson, to which I have referred, that the question as to the ownership and the use of 36, G Guildford Street, following the reorganisation of constituency boundaries, remained unresolved until after the testator's death.

Mr. Sunnucks' second submission was that the gift should be construed by analogy with In re Lipinski's Will Trusts [1976] Ch. 235 as a gift to the members of the Chertsey and Walton C.L.P., with a superadded direction, not imposing any trust, that it should be used for what may be broadly expressed as headquarters' purposes rather than general H purposes, which might include, for instance, the cost of an election campaign; but subject, nevertheless, to a gift to the National Labour Party in defeasance of the prior gift in the event that at the testator's death the headquarters of the Chertsey and Walton C.L.P. should be outside the geographical limits of the old Chertsey Urban District Council. I observe in passing that construed as a gift over operating at any time, the gift over would have been void under the rule against perpetuities, though the initial gift would then stand free from the proviso.

Before examining this submission, it is first necessary to look at the   A
rules governing the Chertsey and Walton C.L.P. Those rules, as I have
said, were in the form of model rules prescribed by the National Labour
Party. The provisions which appear to be material are as follows.
Clause I defines the Chertsey and Walton C.L.P. as " the party." Clause
II sets out the objects of the party. Sub-clause (1) sets out the familiar
objects of the National Labour Party under the heading " National ";
and under the heading " Constituency " sub-clause (2) reads: B

" (a) To unite the forces of Labour within the constituency and to
    ensure the establishment of, and to keep in active operation, branches
    throughout the constituency, and to co-ordinate their activities; and
    (b) To secure the return of Labour representatives to Parliament and
    local government bodies."
                                                                             C
Clause III deals with membership. It provides: " (1) There shall be two
classes of members namely:—(a) affiliated organisations (b) individual
members. . ." Affiliated organisations are to consist of trade unions and
co-operative societies, branches of socialist societies affiliated to the Labour
Party nationally and :

" (d) branches of other organisations which, in the opinion of the   D
    National Executive Committee, have interests consistent with those
    of other affiliated organisations and which are affiliated to the
    Labour Party nationally. (e) The Trades Council. (f) Any other
    organisation or branch thereof which the National Executive Com-
    mittee deems eligible for affiliation. . . . (3) Individual members shall
    be British subjects or citizens of Eire, or other persons resident in
    Great Britain for more than one year, who are not less than fifteen   E
    years of age and who subscribe to the conditions of membership."

Clause IV prescribes the conditions of membership:

" (1) Each affiliated organisation must: — (a) Accept the programme,
    principles and policy of the Labour Party. (b) Agree to conform
    to the constitution and standing orders of the Labour Party and the
    rules of this party."   F

Each individual member must accept the same obligation and, if
eligible, be a member of a trades union affiliated to the T.U.C.
    Clause IX deals with management. By sub-clause (1) the manage-
ment is put into the hands of a general committee of delegates elected by
affiliated organisations, branches of individual members, women's sections and Young Socialist branches. Sub-clause (2) sets out the basis of   G
representation. Sub-clauses (3) and (4) I must read in full:

" (3) The general committee shall accept and make such changes in
    the rules of this party as may be agreed to by the Annual Party
    Conference or made by the National Executive Committee in
    accordance with the powers conferred upon it under clause VIII (j)
    of the Party Constitution, and shall, further, subject to the approval   H
    in writing of the National Executive Committee, have power itself
    to make alterations, amendments or deletions in these rules, provided
    that such changes do not contravene their spirit or intention as
    accepted by Annual Party Conferences or alter the objects, basis or
    conditions of affiliated and individual membership, or vary the
    procedure for the selection of Parliamentary candidates (otherwise
    than is provided in the rules of this party) or effect a change in the

A   relationship of constituency Labour Parties with the Labour Party.
(4) The general committee shall, subject to the approval in writing
of the National Executive Committee, have power either itself or to
authorise the executive committee of this party on its behalf—(a) to
buy freehold or leasehold land and to erect buildings thereon and/or
freehold or leasehold premises and to borrow money on mortgage or
B   otherwise on the security thereof; (b) to appoint trustees to hold any
land and property so acquired for and on behalf of this party; and (c)
to define the powers of any trustees so appointed and to lay down
the manner in which such power shall be exercised."

Clause VIII (2) of the Party Constitution reads as follows:

C   "(j) To sanction, where local circumstances render it necessary,
modifications in the rules laid down by the Annual Party Conference
for the various classes of party organisations, provided that such
modifications comply with the spirit and intention of the Annual
Party Conference and do not alter the objects, basis or conditions
of affiliated and individual membership, vary the procedure for the
selection of Parliamentary candidates (except as provided in the
D   rules) or effect a change in the relationship of Constituency Labour
Parties with the Labour Party."

Thus, under clause IX (3) of the Chertsey and Walton C.L.P. rules, the
general committee are bound to change the rules to accord with changes
". . . agreed at the Annual Party Conference." The words ". . . as
agreed at the Annual Party Conference," must, I think, refer to the
approval by the Annual Party Conference of proposals made by the
E   Executive Committee of the National Labour Committee under clause
VIII (2) (g) of the Party Constitution, which reads as follows:

"(g) To propose to the Annual Party Conference such amendments
to the constitution, rules and standing orders as may be deemed
desirable and to submit to the Annual Party Conference or to any
special party conference, called in accordance with the standing
F   orders, such resolutions and declarations affecting the programme,
principles and policy of the party as in its view may be necessitated
by political circumstances."

Secondly, the General Committee of the C.L.P. must make any
changes prescribed by the National Executive Committee in accordance
with the powers conferred by clause VIII (2) (j) of the Party Constitution.
G   Lastly, the general committee of the C.L.P. have power to change the
rules of the C.L.P., but only with the approval of the National Executive
Committee, and provided that the changes do not contravene the spirit or
intention of the Annual Party Conference or alter the objects, basis or
conditions of affiliated and individual membership, or vary the procedure
for the selection of Parliamentary candidates (otherwise than is provided
H   in the rules of the party) or effect a change in the relationship of
Constituency Labour Parties with the Labour Party.

Clause XI is headed " Affiliation Fees and Members' Contributions."
Under sub-clause (1):

"The affiliation fees payable by this party to the National Labour
Party shall be at such rate as may be laid down by the Annual Party
Conference from time to time."

Affiliation fees and contributions to the C.L.P. are payable at the rate A
prescribed by sub-clause (2). In the case of individual members fees are
payable to the appropriate officer as determined by the C.L.P. The rules
contain no provision as to what is to happen to any property purchased
under clause IX (4) or to any surplus of affiliation fees and members' fees
in the event of the dissolution of the party. Subject to any amendment
to the rules approved by the Annual Party Conference or made by the B
National Executive Committee, or by the general committee of the
C.L.P. and approved by the National Executive Committee, such
property or moneys would prima facie be held in the resulting trust for
the persons by whom they were contributed.

Reading the gift in the will in the light of the rules governing the
Chertsey and Walton C.L.P., it is, in my judgment, impossible to
construe the gift as a gift made to the members of the Chertsey and C
Walton C.L.P. at the date of the testator's death with the intention that
it should belong to them as a collection of individuals, though in the
expectation that they and any other members subsequently admitted
would ensure that it was in fact used for what in broad terms has been
labelled " headquarters' purposes " of the Chertsey and Walton C.L.P.

I base this conclusion on two grounds. First, the members of the D
Chertsey and Walton C.L.P. do not control the property, given by
subscription or otherwise, to the C.L.P. The rules which govern the
C.L.P. are capable of being altered by an outside body which could direct
an alteration under which the general committee of the C.L.P. would be
bound to transfer any property for the time being held for the benefit of
the C.L.P. to the National Labour Party for national purposes. The
members of the Chertsey and Walton C.L.P. could not alter the rules so E
as to make the property bequeathed by the testator applicable for some
purpose other than that provided by the rules; nor could they direct that
property to be divided amongst themselves beneficially.

Brightman J. observed in *In re Recher's Will Trusts* [1972] Ch. 526,
536:

> " It would astonish a layman to be told there was a difficulty in his F
> giving a legacy to an unincorporated non-charitable society which
> he had, or could have, supported without trouble during his lifetime."

The answer to this apparent paradox is, it seems to me, that subscriptions
by members of the Chertsey and Walton C.L.P. must be taken as made
upon terms that they will be applied by the general committee in
accordance with the rules for the time being including any modifications G
imposed by the Annual Party Conference or the National Executive
Committee. In the event of the dissolution of the Chertsey and Walton
C.L.P. any remaining fund representing subscriptions would (as the rules
now stand) be held on a resulting trust for the original subscribers. Thus,
although the members of the C.L.P. may not be able themselves to alter
the purposes for which a fund representing subscriptions is to be used or
to alter the rules so as to make such a fund divisible amongst themselves, H
the ultimate proprietary right of the original subscribers remains. There
is, therefore, no perpetuity and no non-charitable purpose trust. But if
that analysis of the terms on which subscriptions are held is correct, it is
fatal to the argument that the gift in the testator's will should be construed
as a gift to the members of the Chertsey and Walton C.L.P. at the
testator's death, subject to a direction not amounting to a trust that it
be used for headquarters' purposes. Equally it is in my judgment

A   impossible, in particular having regard to the gift over to the National
Labour Party, to read the gift as a gift to the members of the National
Labour Party at the testator's death, with a direction not amounting to a
trust, for the National Party to permit it to be used by the Chertsey and
Walton C.L.P. for headquarters' purposes.

   That first ground is of itself conclusive, but there is another ground
which reinforces this conclusion.   The gift is not in terms a gift to the
B   Chertsey and Walton C.L.P., but to the Labour Party property committee,
who are to hold the property for the benefit of, that is in trust for, the
Chertsey headquarters of the Chertsey and Walton C.L.P.   The fact that
a gift is a gift to trustees and not in terms to an unincorporated association, militates against construing it as a gift to the members of the
association at the date when the gift takes effect, and against construing
C   the words indicating the purposes for which the property is to be used as
expressing the testator's intention or motive in making the gift and not
as imposing any trust.   This was, indeed, one of the considerations
which led the Privy Council in *Leahy's* case [1959] A.C. 457, to hold
that the gift ". . . upon trust for such Order of Nuns of the Catholic
Church or the Christian Brothers as my executors and trustees should
select " would, apart from the Australian equivalent of the Charitable
D   Trusts Validation Act, have been invalid.

   I am, therefore, compelled to the conclusion that the gift of the
testator's estate fails, and that his estate accordingly devolves as on
intestacy.   I will make the usual order that the costs of the plaintiffs as
trustees, and the defendants on a common fund basis, be taxed and paid
out of the estate in due course of administration.

E
                                                    Order accordingly.

   Solicitors: *Cripps, Harries, Willis & Carter for Clive Fisher & Co.,
Addlestone; Milners Curry and Gaskell; Penman Johnson & Ewins,
Watford.*

F   [Reported by MISS HILARY PEARSON, Barrister-at-Law]

[1980]

[COURT OF APPEAL]   A

* REGINA v. WILSON (JAMES)

1979 Dec. 18   Lawton L.J., Chapman and Woolf JJ.

Crime—Court of Appeal—Sentence, appeal against—Committal to
Crown Court for sentence — Breach of suspended sentence   B
admitted — Sentence for offence and activation of varied
suspended sentence—Total sentence less than six months—
Whether jurisdiction on appeal limited to suspended sentence
—Criminal Appeal Act 1968 (c. 19), s. 10 (3) (a) (c) (as
amended by Courts Act 1971 (c. 23), s. 56 (1), Sch. 8, para.
57, Criminal Justice Act 1972 (c. 71), s. 64 (1), Sch. 5, and
Powers of Criminal Courts Act 1973 (c. 62), s. 56 (1), Sch. 5,
para. 28)   C

The appellant, who was subject to a suspended sentence of
six months' imprisonment, pleaded guilty to committing an
offence during the period of suspension. He was committed
for sentence to the Crown Court, where he was sentenced to
one month's imprisonment for the offence to which he had
pleaded guilty and the suspended sentence was varied to two
months' imprisonment and ordered to be effective consecutively. D
On appeal against sentence in reliance on section 10 (3) of
the Criminal Appeal Act 1968 [1] : —
Held, allowing the appeal, that on the true construction
of section 10 (3) of the Criminal Appeal Act 1968 as amended,
when a suspended sentence was brought into effect by a Crown
Court, an appeal could be brought against not only the suspended sentence but also the sentence for the offence which
brought the suspended sentence into effect, albeit the sentence E
appealed was for imprisonment of less than " six months or
more " within section 10 (3) (a); and that, in the circumstances,
the sentences of imprisonment would be quashed and a fine
substituted.

The following case is referred to in the judgment:
Reg. v. Keelan (1975) 61 Cr.App.R. 202, C.A.
                                                                    F
No additional cases were cited in argument.

APPEAL against sentence.

On April 1, 1977, at Brighton Crown Court the appellant, James
Andrew McNaughten Wilson, was sentenced to six months' imprisonment suspended for two years and was fined £500. On May 31, 1979,
at Reading Magistrates' Court the appellant pleaded guilty to being   G
knowingly concerned in the fraudulent evasion of the prohibition of the
importation of cannabis on January 18, 1979. He was committed for
sentence to the Crown Court. On July 13, 1979, at Reading Crown
Court the appellant was sentenced to one month's imprisonment for the
offence to which he had pleaded guilty; he admitted being in breach of
the suspended sentence imposed on April 1, 1977, and it was varied to H
two months' imprisonment ordered to be put into effect consecutively
to the one month's sentence. He appealed against severity of sentence.
The facts are stated in the judgment.

Philip Cox Q.C. and Basil Hillman for the appellant.
David Jeffreys for the Crown.

[1] Criminal Appeal Act 1968, s. 10 (3): see post, pp. 377G—378A.

A   LAWTON L.J. gave the following judgment of the court. On May 31, 1979, at Reading Magistrates' Court, the appellant, James Andrew McNaughten Wilson, pleaded guilty to being knowingly concerned in the fraudulent evasion of the prohibition of the importation of cannabis. He was committed to the Crown Court for sentence pursuant to section 29 of the Magistrates' Courts Act 1952. The offence for which he was committed was the one for which he was sentenced by the Crown Court.

B   On July 13, 1979, at the Reading Crown Court he admitted to the breach of a six months' suspended sentence of imprisonment which had been passed by Brighton Crown Court on April 1, 1977. The recorder sentenced him to one month's imprisonment. The suspended sentence was varied to one of two months' imprisonment and was ordered to be put into effect consecutively. The result was that the Crown Court sentenced him to a total of three months' imprisonment.

C   He now appeals against that sentence by leave of the single judge. A point has arisen as to whether there is jurisdiction in this court to hear his appeal. The problem arises under section 10 of the Criminal Appeal Act 1968, as amended by the Courts Act 1971, the Criminal Justice Act 1972 and the Powers of Criminal Courts Act 1973. Section 10 (1) of the Act of 1968 as amended reads:

D   " This section has effect in providing rights of appeal against sentence when a person is dealt with by the Crown Court (otherwise than on appeal from the magistrates' court) for an offence of which he was not convicted on indictment."

The offence for which this appellant was convicted was not, of course, on indictment. The relevant part of subsection (2) is as follows:

E   " The proceedings from which an appeal against sentence lies under this section are those where an offender convicted of an offence by a magistrates' court, is committed by the court to be dealt with for his offence before the Crown Court . . ."

It is relevant to point out that the opening words of subsection (2) are: " The proceedings from which an appeal against sentence lies . . .; " and
F   the use of the words " against sentence " contrast with the later words in the subsection, namely, " . . . where an offender is convicted of an offence . . ."

It follows from subsection (2) that, prima facie, anyone who is sentenced by a Crown Court after committal pursuant to section 29 of the Magistrates' Courts Act 1952, has a right of appeal; but Parliament seems to have intended that that right should be restricted.
G   The restrictions are to be found in section 10 (3); the relevant parts read:

       " (3) An offender dealt with for an offence before the Crown Court in a proceeding to which subsection (2) of this section applies, may appeal to the Court of Appeal against sentence in any of the following cases:— (a) where either for that offence alone or for
H   that offence and other offences for which sentence is passed in the same proceeding, he is sentenced to imprisonment for a term of six months or more; or . . . (c) where the court in dealing with him for the offence makes in respect of him—(i) a recommendation for deportation; or (ii) an order disqualifying him for holding or obtaining a licence to drive a motor vehicle under Part III of the Road Traffic Act 1972; or "—and this is the important part— " (iii) an order under section 23 of the Powers of Criminal Courts

Act 1973 (orders as to existing suspended sentence when person A subject to the sentence is again convicted)."

Mr. Cox, on behalf of the appellant, has submitted that the object of paragraph (c) of subsection (3) is to set out cases where, although the sentence is for a term of less than six months, nevertheless, there is a right of appeal. He submits that the right of appeal exists when the person appealing has been made subject to an order under section 23 B of the Powers of Criminal Courts Act. That arises from the wording of the section and in particular from the use of the phrase: "may appeal to the Court of Appeal against sentence," the argument being that, once the appellant is before the court, because he comes under one of the exceptions in subsection (3), then the court has power to deal with the whole of his sentence, even though the totality of the sentence may be less than six months. C

Mr. Jeffreys has appeared before us not to oppose the application, but to help the court with the construction of this section of the Criminal Appeal Act 1968 as amended. He has suggested that there is an alternative construction to be put upon subsection (3), namely, that paragraph (c) (iii) only entitles this court to look at and deal with that part of a sentence which is the suspended sentence and if that be so, it D follows that the court would not have jurisdiction to deal with the substantive offence in respect of which the appellant was committed under section 29 of the Act of 1952.

That would be a very odd situation indeed, because it would mean that this court, when dealing with a suspended part of a sentence, would only be dealing with part of it. The general policy of the Criminal Appeal Act 1968 is that, when anyone appeals against sentence, the E whole sentencing position must be looked at by the court. Under section 11 of the Act of 1968 an appellant cannot appeal against one of a number of sentences. The court is empowered to look at all the sentences passed upon him.

Mr. Jeffreys suggests and submitted that this construction was in line with the policy of the Act, viz., that appeals are restricted to this court when the sentence is less than six months. F

It may well be that what paragraph (a) of subsection (3) was intending to deal with was not suspended sentences at all. Our attention was drawn to the fact that under the Powers of Criminal Courts Act 1973, which was passed some years after the Criminal Appeal Act 1968, section 23 (9) reads:

"For the purposes of any enactment conferring rights of appeal G in criminal cases any order made by a court with respect to a suspended sentence shall be treated as a sentence passed on the offender by that court for the offence for which the suspended sentence was passed."

We have to construe section 10 (3) (a) of the Act of 1968 in the light of that general provision in the Powers of Criminal Courts Act H 1973, which does make the construction of section 10 (3) difficult, because it seems that with one hand Parliament is restricting appeals against sentences under section 10 (3) (a), because a suspended sentence does come under that paragraph, but with the other hand it is giving a power of appeal against a suspended sentence. In our judgment a sensible construction of this statute is that when there is a suspended sentence brought into effect, the appellant can appeal not only against

A the suspended sentence, but against the sentence which has brought the suspended sentence into effect.

It follows, in the circumstances of this case, that there is a right of appeal.

We call attention to the fact that this decision does not in any way, in our judgment, conflict with the decision of this court in *Reg.* v. *Keelan* (1975) 61 Cr.App.R. 202. Sentences of detention, with which

B that case was concerned, do not come within the exceptions set out in section 10 (3) of the Act of 1968.

We turn now to the facts of this case. On January 18, 1979, the appellant sent from South Africa to his elder brother, who was a student at Reading University, a parcel containing 5.3 grammes of cannabis which was enough to make about 20 reefer cigarettes. The sending was

C accomplished by hollowing out the inside of a book. The parcel was intercepted at Reading post office and its contents examined. In due course the appellant's brother was arrested and is, we understand, awaiting to be dealt with by the court for this offence. The appellant himself was questioned on February 15, 1979. He admitted his guilt and made a written statement in the course of which he described how he and his brother were in South Africa for Christmas 1978 and whilst there they

D came into possession of some cannabis. The pair of them discussed sending some of it back to England when the brother returned.

The difficulty in this case is this: in 1977 this appellant was charged and convicted of a serious offence relating to drugs. In respect of that offence he received the suspended sentence of six months' imprisonment. We have been told by Mr. Cox, who appears on his behalf, that in

E addition he was fined £500. It follows that this offence was committed whilst the period of the suspension was still operating.

Unfortunately, at the Crown Court, the recorder and the justices sitting with him, seem to have thought that this offence was committed eight months after the imposition of the suspended sentence. The recorder said to the appellant when sentencing him: ". . . Within a period of eight months you deliberately cut out that book and sent off

F that cannabis, and a suspended sentence is something which should not be interfered with. . ." Mr. Cox, who appeared for the appellant at once got up and pointed out that it was not a period of eight months, it was a period of 20 months. Even Mr. Cox was wrong: it was a period of nearly 22 months; in other words, the period covered by the suspended sentence was almost exhausted. In those circumstances, it

G seems to us that there would be a good ground for saying that the rigour of the law ought to have been mitigated substantially in relation to the suspended sentence.

The recorder and his magisterial colleagues did mitigate the sentence, but perhaps in the unusual circumstances of this case, having regard to the passage of time, it might not have been necessary to bring the suspended sentence into effect at all.

H The problem still arises, however, as to what should have been done to the appellant, who is now 22 years of age, for deliberately importing into this country a small quantity of cannabis. We stress that the quantity was small, 5.3 grammes, enough to make 20 reefer cigarettes. Anyone who brings drugs into this country is asking to be dealt with severely and anyone introducing drugs into a university is asking to be dealt with very severely. Drug addiction amongst the young in universities is a problem and our courts have got to do their best to

eradicate it; but the fact remains that the cannabis was sent by this A
young man to his brother and the quantity was such that it seems to us
unlikely that there was any element of trafficking in drugs. The probability seems to be that any reefer cigarettes made from the cannabis
were intended for his brother. It is possible, we suppose, that they might
have been handed round amongst a small circle, but they could not have
been handed round very much if there was only enough to make the
equivalent of a packet of cigarettes. B

What is the right course to take? The appellant, save for these two
drug offences, has led a blameless life. He is a hard-working young man
who has established himself in the catering trade and at the present time
is doing well in that trade. He has risked his liberty. He has seen the
inside of a prison for a few days. It is to be hoped that the clanging of
prison doors behind him has had a salutary effect upon him. C

With considerable hesitation, we have come to the conclusion, that
in all the circumstances of this case, the sentence for the substantive
offence and the suspended sentence, can be quashed. There will be
substituted for the substantive offence a fine of £500.

Appeal allowed.
Sentence varied. D

Solicitors: *Nightingale & Francis, Reading; Director of Public
Prosecutions.*

L. N. W.

E

[CHANCERY DIVISION]

* BUCKINGHAM (INSPECTOR OF TAXES) *v.* SECURITAS
PROPERTIES LTD. F

1979 Nov. 30
Dec. 3 Slade J.

*Revenue—Corporation tax—Capital allowances—Industrial build-
ing—Security area for wage-packeting and cash storage by
security company — Whether expenditure on construction* G
*expenditure on " industrial building " to qualify for allowance
—Whether coins and notes of currency " goods "—Whether
wage-packeting activity subjection of " goods " to " any
process "—Capital Allowances Act 1968 (c. 3), ss. 1 (1),
7 (1) (e)*

The taxpayer company leased premises near Newcastle-
upon-Tyne to a security company. Part of those premises was H
specially constructed by the taxpayer company as a security
area which was used by the security company for wage packeting, storage of money and a communications centre for the
whole building. The area contained a wage packeting area, a
strong room, a generator room, a store room and a loading
and service bay for the armoured vehicles used in the security
company's trade. About 10,000 wage packets were handled
in the security area each week, the money being drawn by
cheque at the bank and then brought to the security area where

A   packeters would fill each wage packet with the exact amount
and break down of notes specified by the various employers
who used the security company's services. The filled wage
packets were then distributed by the security company in
various ways according to each employer's orders. The taxpayer company appealed against an assessment to corporation
tax of £4,601 for the accounting period ended December 31,
1976, claiming an allowance under sections 1 (1) and 7 (1) (e)
B   of the Capital Allowances Act 1968,[1] in respect of the expenditure incurred by them on the construction of the security area.
The general commissioners, allowing the appeal, held that as
the wage packeting activities of the security company constituted " the subjection of goods or materials to any process,"
the security area was within the definition of an " industrial
building or structure " and thus the expenditure incurred on it
C   qualified for the allowance.
      On appeal by the Crown : —
      Held, allowing the appeal, that in its context in section 7 (1)
(e) " goods " meant " merchandise " or " wares " and did not
include money used in the sense of currency; accordingly,
although the wage packeting activities carried out by the
security company in the security area might constitute the
subjection of coins and notes to a " process," the taxpayer
D   company were not entitled to capital allowance relief under
section 7 (1) (e) because the security company was dealing
with the money as currency, and therefore it did not constitute
" goods " for the purposes of the capital allowances legislation
(post, pp. 388B–D, 389D–F).
      Per curiam. The phrase " subjection of goods or materials
to any process " might well be capable of including coins and
notes when not being dealt with as currency; e.g. a building
E   used for preparing antique coins for sale by a cleansing operation might qualify for the allowance (post, p. 388D–E).

The following cases are referred to in the judgment:

Bourne v. *Norwich Crematorium Ltd.* [1967] 1 W.L.R. 691; [1967] 2
      All E.R. 576; 44 T.C. 164.
F   *Kilmarnock Equitable Co-operative Society Ltd.* v. *Inland Revenue Com-
      missioners* (1966) 42 T.C. 675.
Noordam, The (No. 2) [1920] A.C. 904, P.C.
Reg. v. *Vanek, Ex parte Cross* (1969) 6 D.L.R. (3d) 591.
Reg. v. *Behm* (1969) 12 D.L.R. (3d.) 260.

The following additional case was cited in argument:

G   *Saxone Lilley & Skinner (Holdings) Ltd.* v. *Inland Revenue Commissioners*
      (1966) 44 T.C. 122.

CASE STATED by the Commissioners for the General Purposes of the
Income Tax Acts.
      The taxpayer company, Securitas Properties Ltd., leased a building at
Felling, Newcastle-upon-Tyne, to Group 4 Total Security Ltd. It had
H   incurred capital expenditure on the construction of part of that building as
a security area which Group 4 used to store money and to fill wage packets
for various employers. The taxpayer company appealed against an assessment to corporation tax in the sum of £4,601 for the accounting period
ended December 31, 1976, claiming entitlement to an allowance under
the Capital Allowances Act 1968 in respect of the expenditure by it on

[1] Capital Allowances Act 1968, s. 7 (1): post, pp. 382G—383A.

the security area. The commissioners by a majority allowed the appeal A
holding that having regard to the definition of " industrial building or
structure " in section 7 of the Capital Allowances Act 1968 (i) because (a)
the money which was wage packeted was collected from the bank and
delivered to the security company's premises in bulk, (b) it was movable
property and (c) there was no definition excluding money from the Act,
that money could in the context of the present case be classified as goods;
(ii) that the breaking down of bulk money into individual wage packets and B
the other activities connected with the operation constituted the subjection
of those goods to a process and (iii) because the whole of the claim area
was specifically designed and purpose built as a highly secure complex, that
the building (excluding the service bay) fell within the definition of
industrial building or structure.

The findings of fact in the case stated are set out in the judgment, at C
p. 383E et seq.

Michael Hart for the Crown.
Barry Pinson Q.C. for the taxpayer company.

SLADE J. This is an appeal by the Crown from a decision of the D
commissioners for the general purposes of income tax in favour of a
company known as Securitas Properties Ltd. the taxpayer company. The
appeal concerns part of a building at Felling, near Newcastle-upon-Tyne,
which was leased by the taxpayer company to a company known as
Group 4 Total Security Ltd. (" Group 4 "). Briefly, the issue is whether
the relevant part of the building known as " the security area," was at
the relevant time an " industrial building or structure " within the meaning E
of the Capital Allowances Act 1968 so as to entitle the taxpayer company
to allowances under Chapter I, Part I, of that Act in respect of capital
expenditure incurred by it on the construction of the security area. Under
section 1 (1) of the Act of 1968, the relevant relief is given

"where a person incurs capital expenditure on the construction of
a building or structure which is to be an industrial building or structure F
occupied for the purposes of a trade carried on either by that person
or by such a lessee as is mentioned in subsection (3) of this
section. . . . "

Section 7 of the Act contains a definition of " industrial building or
structure." For present purposes everything turns on the question whether
the security area is an " industrial building or structure " within this G
definition, as the taxpayer company contends and the Crown denies.

It will be convenient to begin by reading the relevant provisions of
section 7:

"(1) Subject to the provisions of this section, in this Chapter
'industrial building or structure' means a building or structure in
use—(a) for the purposes of a trade carried on in a mill, factory or H
other similar premises, or (b) for the purposes of a transport, dock,
inland navigation, water, electricity or hydraulic power undertaking
. . . (e) for the purposes of a trade which consists in the manufacture
of goods or materials or the subjection of goods or materials to any
process, or (f) for the purposes of a trade which consists in the storage
—(i) of goods or materials which are to be used in the manufacture of
other goods or materials, or (ii) of goods or materials which are to be

The Weekly Law Reports, April 18, 1980

383

1 W.L.R.   Buckingham v. Securitas Properties Ltd. (Ch.D.)   Slade J.

A   subjected, in the course of a trade, to any process, or (iii) of goods or
materials which, having been manufactured or produced or subjected,
in the course of a trade, to any process, have not yet been delivered
to any purchaser, or (iv) of goods or materials on their arrival by
sea or air into any part of the United Kingdom. . . .

" (2) The provisions of subsection (1) of this section shall apply in
B   relation to a part of a trade or undertaking as they apply in relation
to a trade or undertaking: Provided that where part only of a trade
or undertaking complies with the conditions set out in the said provisions, a building or structure shall not, by virtue of this subsection,
be an industrial building or structure unless it is in use for the purposes
of that part of that trade or undertaking."

C   Section 7 (3) begins with the following words:

" Notwithstanding anything in subsection (1) or subsection (2) of
this section, but subject to the provisions of subsection (4) of this
section, ' industrial building or structure ' does not include any building
or structure in use as, or as part of, a dwelling-house, retail shop,
showroom, hotel or office or for any purpose ancillary to the purposes
D   of a dwelling-house, retail shop, showroom, hotel or office: . . . ."

There follows a proviso which is not material for present purposes. The
Crown sought to argue before the commissioners, inter alia, that the
security area was in any event excluded from the relevant exemption as
being in use as an office within this subsection (3). The point, however, has
not been pursued before me. Since neither side has placed any reliance
E   on subsection (4) of section 7, I need not read it.

The relevant facts are set out in the case stated. Those most material for
present purposes are as follows. Three main activities took place in the
security area; namely, (i) wage packeting, (ii) storage of money, some of
which was and some of which was not held for wage packeting, and (iii) the
activities of the control room, which was the communications centre for
the whole division, as well as guarding the security area. The security area
F   comprised part of a purpose-built block. Entry into it was through an
external air lock entrance, and was controlled by means of closed circuit
television from a control room. The security area comprised a wage packeting area with ancillary kitchen and toilets, a strong room or vault, a control
room with its own kitchen and toilets, a generator room, a room containing
the main distribution frame for electronics and telephone equipment, a
separate store room for other technical equipment, together with a loading
G   and unloading bay and a service bay for the armoured vehicles used in
the trade. For security reasons the security area had no windows and its
own air supply. The findings of fact made by the commissioners in relation
to the wage packeting activities are to be found set out in paragraphs 5 (b)
to (i) of the case stated, from which I quote verbatim:

H   " (b) As to the wage packeting, this was a service provided for a fee
by Group 4 to employers. The employer supplied Group 4 with a
cheque for the total payroll and individual payslips for each employee.
Group 4 then presented the cheque at the bank and drew the money
in the required breakdown which would have been notified to the
bank by the employer. A bulk check would be carried out and
the case would then be sealed into containers and transported to the
premises at Felling in a bullion vehicle. The contents of each container

were subject to a limit by value, for insurance reasons. (c) On the A
journey to Felling the vehicle would be in two-way radio communication with the control room. On arrival it would be admitted into the
unloading bay (which was guarded by electrically operated shutters)
by staff in the control room. The shutters would be closed and the
cash would then be passed through a rotary hatch between the
unloading bay and the wage packeting area. Usually the money would
then be stored in the vault under the supervision and control of the B
vault officer. (d) When the time came to packet the money it would
be taken from the vault by the vault officer and handed to the wage
packeting supervisor. The supervisor and her wage packeters were
all female; the latter were all part-time workers. The supervisor would
count the money by bundles and then break it down by section for
payroll analysis. Each section (i.e. corresponding to a section of C
employees) would then be put into an individual bag along with the
relevant pay slips, and given to one of the packeters. (e) The packeter
would then do an exact count, and fill each wage packet with the
amount and the breakdown specified by the employer in question.
When all the packets were filled, provided the balance was exactly
right, the packets would be sealed. If the balance was not right, all D
the packets in that section would have to be emptied and refilled until
it was. The packets were designed and sealed in such a way that the
recipient could check the contents without breaking the seal. Care was
taken to ensure that the notes in a wage packet were not all of large
denomination: for example, a £60 wage packet was not made up
of 3 notes of £20 each; there would be a combination of £5 and £1
notes. (f) The packets were then sealed in boxes in the correct sequence E
and returned to the vault pending distribution. Wage packets were
distributed in various ways, according to the employer's orders. Some
were delivered in bulk to the employer; some were posted in greater
or lesser bulk, Group 4 delivering them to the post office; some were
distributed directly by Group 4. (g) This pattern was sometimes varied
to comply with the wishes of a particular customer. For example F
some employers required deductions to be made from the wage
packets for advance wages, union dues and the like; some supplied
their own wage packets; some wanted circulars to their employees to
be inserted into the packets. Sometimes there was a shortfall of cash
delivered, or the case included torn or defaced notes or foreign
coins which were removed and replaced. A float of £50 was kept for
such contingencies. (h) About 10,000 wage packets were handled G
each week, mostly between 8 p.m. on Wednesdays and 2 a.m. on Thurs-
days; and 8 a.m. to 6 p.m. on Thursdays. The packeters were trained
by Group 4 and the skills required were numeracy and accuracy when
counting at speed. A kitchen and toilets were provided because the
staff were not allowed to leave the area until the packets were filled
and the cash had balanced, for security reasons. The only machinery H
employed in this area was a coin-counting machine worth about £3,000–
£4,000. (i) Wage packeting was a task which, if it were not contracted to Group 4, would in all probability be done by the employer's
wages office, but no employer could match Group 4's security."

In paragraphs 5 (j), 5 (k) and 5 (l) of the case stated the commissioners
further recorded a number of specific findings of fact in relation to the

The Weekly Law Reports, April 18, 1980

385

1 W.L.R.   Buckingham v. Securitas Properties Ltd. (Ch.D.)   Slade J.

A vault, the control room, the generator and the service bay. It was common ground before the commissioners, as it has been before me, that the character of the security area should be determined without regard to the remainder of the premises of which it formed part, and that nothing turned on the circumstance that the taxpayer company was not itself in occupation. It was also conceded on behalf of the Crown that the vehicle service

B bay qualified as an "industrial building" under section 7 (1) (b) of the Act of 1968, as being in use for the purpose of a transport undertaking. There is therefore no dispute in regard to the service bay.

At a meeting of the commissioners held on July 3, 1978, the taxpayer company appealed against an assessment to corporation tax in the sum of £4,601·48 for the accounting period ending December 31, 1976. The commissioners, by a majority, held that the security area fell within the

C definition of "industrial building or structure" contained in section 7 (1) (e) of the Act of 1968, and allowed the taxpayer company's appeal. The grounds on which the commissioners reached this decision are to be found set out in paragraph 9 of the case stated. The commissioners accordingly determined the corporation tax assessment at an agreed figure of nil. The Crown required a case to be stated for the opinion of the High Court

D pursuant to section 56 (2) of the Taxes Management Act 1970. The question for the opinion of the High Court is whether, on the facts stated in the case stated, the commissioners were entitled to reach the decision reached by them.

The arguments, which were attractively urged on this court by Mr. Pinson in support of the commissioners' decision and constitute a more developed version of the commissioners' own reasons, may I think be

E fairly summarised as follows: (i) The trade of Group 4 consisted substantially in wage packeting and the security area in which it was carried on was erected for the specific purpose of accommodating this wage packeting operation. (ii) The coins and notes being handled in the wage packeting area were "goods" within the meaning of that word as used in section 7 (1) (e) of the Act of 1968. (iii) The wage packeting area was

F an area in which such goods were being subjected to a process, namely, that of breaking down bulk coins and notes into individual wage packets, which had to be prepared to the specific requirements of respective employers and had to exclude torn or defaced notes or foreign coins. (iv) The wage packeting area was thus a building or structure in use for the purposes of a trade consisting in the subjection of goods (in the shape of coins and notes) to a process (namely, the breaking down of bulk coins and notes

G into individual wage packets). (v) Furthermore, each and every other part of the security area, on the facts, served the purposes of and was thus in use for the purposes of the like trade. (iv) Accordingly the whole of the security area qualifies for relief under section 7 (1) (e). No dispute I think arises in relation to Mr. Pinson's first proposition. I therefore turn to consider his second and third propositions, which are the critically

H important ones in the present context.

The Act of 1968 contains no definition of the words "use" or "process." Mr. Hart, on behalf of the Crown, submitted that, even if the subject matter of the wage packeting operations carried out by Group 4 constituted "goods" within the meaning of section 7 (1) (e), the operations did not constitute "the subjection of goods to any process," within the meaning of the subsection, because nothing was done to the notes and

coins to enhance their value or make them more marketable, or to alter A
their substance.

Mr. Pinson, however, relied, inter alia, on what was said by Lord
Cameron in *Kilmarnock Equitable Co-operative Society Ltd.* v. *Inland
Revenue Commissioners* (1966) 42 T.C. 675, which was a decision of the
Court of Session concerning section 271 (1) (c) of the Income Tax Act 1952,
a forerunner of section 7 (1) (e) of the Act of 1968. Lord Cameron said,
at p. 685:   B

> " The word ' process ' in its ordinary connotation seems to me to mean
> no more than the application of a method of manufacture or adapta-
> tion of goods or materials towards a particular use, purpose or end,
> while ' to subject ' means no more than to treat in some manner or
> other."
>   C

Mr. Pinson also referred me to one of the definitions of the word
" process " which is to be found in the *Shorter Oxford English Dictionary*,
3rd ed. (1944), p. 1677. It reads as follows: " A continuous and regular
action or succession of actions, taking place or carried on in a definite
manner; a continuous (natural or artificial) operation or series of operations." One of the definitions of the word " subject " to be found in the
same dictionary is: " To bring under the operation of an agent, agency, or D
process; to submit to certain treatment; to cause to undergo or experience
something."

I would be inclined to accept Mr. Pinson's submission that, if the
subject matter of Group 4's activities in the wage packeting area constituted " goods," then such activities constituted a subjection of such
goods to a process, within the meaning of the subsection. As he pointed E
out, the coins and notes came into the security area in bulk form and left
it reduced to individual wage packets, after being dealt with through the
activities of a staff, requiring numeracy and accuracy, who had to take care
that each wage packet contained the right amount and selection of notes
and coins, broken down according to the employer's specifications. I am
inclined to think that these activities did involve the subjection of the
coins and notes to a " process, " within the ordinary meaning of words F
and within the meaning of the subsection, even though it could not be
said that their texture, substance or value was altered by such activities.
I derive some support from the *Kilmarnock* case, where Lord President
Clyde specifically said, at p. 679, that in his view alteration of the material
in question, in that case coal, was not essential to involve subjecting it to
a process.   G

Nevertheless, I think that in the present case the meaning of the phrase
" subjection to any process " in the subsection cannot be satisfactorily
considered in isolation from the word " goods "; and, indeed, vice versa.
The phrase " subjection of goods to any process " must be considered as a
whole. I respectfully agree and adopt an observation of Stamp J. in *Bourne*
v. *Norwich Crematorium Ltd.* [1967] 1 W.L.R. 691. This, though a decision H
on section 271 (1) (c) of the Income Tax Act 1952 gives little direct
guidance here, since the facts were very different, concerning as they
did the question whether the consumption by fire in a crematorium of
human remains constituted " the subjection of goods or materials to any
process," within section 271 (1) (c). Stamp J., deciding that it did not,
observed, at p. 696:

> " Sentences are not mere collections of words to be taken out of the

The Weekly Law Reports, April 18, 1980

387

1 W.L.R.   Buckingham v. Securitas Properties Ltd. (Ch.D.)   Slade J.

A sentence, defined separately by reference to the dictionary or decided cases, and then put back again into the sentence with the meaning which one has assigned to them as separate words, so as to give the sentence or phrase a meaning which as a sentence or phrase it cannot bear without distortion of the English language."

B For this reason I approach with some caution the one Privy Council decision, two Canadian decisions and two English statutes to which I have been referred by way of guidance in interpreting the word " goods." From them, however, I think there can be derived a number of helpful guidelines in the present context, which I will attempt to state. First, " . . . the content of the word ' goods ' differs greatly according to the context in which it is found and the instrument in which it occurs ": see *The Noordam* (*No*. 2)
C [1920] A.C. 904, 909 *per* Lord Sumner. Secondly, a distinction has to be made between (i) the case where coins and notes are referred to in their character as currency, by which I mean a medium of exchange, and (ii) the case where they are referred to by reason of the intrinsic nature of the substances from which they are made or the other uses to which they may be put. In the latter case, coins and notes may readily fall within the description of " goods " in ordinary parlance. There is, for example, little difficulty
D in regarding antique coins and notes that are bought and sold in retail shops as " goods " according to legal terminology. Similarly, in any case where coin metal is considered without reference to its coinage but simply as bullion, when its value as bullion may be very different from its value as money, there may be little difficulty in regarding it as " goods." I refer generally in this context to the judgment of Osler J. in a decision of the
E Ontario High Court, *Reg*. v. *Vanek, Ex parte Cross* (1969) 6 D.L.R. (3d) 591, 594—595, and to the judgment of Tremblay C.J.Q. in a decision of the Quebec Court of Appeal, *Reg*. v. *Behm* (1969) 12 D.L.R. (3d) 260, 262– 263. As was said in the latter judgment at p. 263: " Metal and paper are objects which can be bought and sold." This, in my view, is none the less so because the metal happens to take the form of a coin or the paper happens to take the form of a currency note. Thirdly, however, I think
F at least in the context of an English statute which contains no further definition of the word " goods," the word would not ordinarily, and in the absence of a special context, include money in the sense of currency. Section 4 (2) of the Criminal Justice Administration Act 1914 provides one clear example of the legislature's assumption that money in the sense of currency and " goods " are different and distinct things. It provides:

G " Where a warrant of distress is issued by a court of summary jurisdiction it shall authorise the person charged with the execution thereof to take any money as well as any goods of the person against whom the distress is levied, and any money so taken shall be treated as if it were the proceeds of sale of goods taken under the warrant, and the provisions of the Summary Jurisdiction Acts shall apply accordingly."

H The Sale of Goods Act 1893 likewise draws a distinction between the goods which are the subject matter of a sale and the price which is the monetary consideration therefor. Thus, section 1 (1) defines a contract of sale of goods as being " a contract whereby the seller transfers or agrees to transfer the property in goods to the buyer for a money consideration, called the price." Section 62 (1) defines " goods " as including " all chattels personal other than things in action and money, and in Scotland

all corporeal moveables except money." This statutory definition of A
" goods " tallies closely with ordinary English usage, as is apparent from
the definition of the plural word " goods " to be found in the *Shorter
Oxford English Dictionary,* which is referred to in the *Behm* case, 12
D.L.R. (3d) 260, 266. This definition reads : " merchandise; wares; now
chiefly manufactured articles." " Merchandise," in turn, is defined in the
same dictionary as : " the commodities of commerce; moveables which
may be bought and sold." B

Reverting to the wording of section 7 (1) (*e*) of the Act of 1968, this
clearly contemplates that the category of an industrial building may include
a place where goods or materials are subjected to a process which falls
short of the actual manufacturing of a new article: see *Kilmarnock
Equitable Co-operative Society Ltd.* v. *Inland Revenue Commissioners*
(1966) 42 T.C. 675, *per* Lord President Clyde at p. 679. Nevertheless, in C
the subsection it is significant that the phrase " subjection of goods or
materials to any process " appears in close proximity to the phrase
" manufacture of goods or materials." This is, in my judgment, a fairly
persuasive reason for concluding that the word " goods " in this context
is intended to bear its ordinary dictionary meaning of " merchandise " or
" wares." I cannot think that the legislature, in employing the word D
" goods " in either phrase, was intending to include money in the sense of
currency that can be offered in the payment of the price on the sale of the
merchandise or wares.

I accept that the phrase " subjection of goods to any process " could
well be capable of including coins and notes when *not* being dealt with as
money. If, for example, a building was used for the purpose of preparing
antique coins for sale by a cleansing operation, it might well be said that E
it was being used for the subjection of goods to a process. Mr. Pinson
suggested as a hypothetical example a building attached to the Royal Mint
where coins were packaged. Perhaps also in this case it could be said that
the building was being used for the subjection of goods to a process, for
in this instance it could be argued that the coins were being handled as
goods in the same way as any other industrial, physical substance, by shape F
and size, but without regard to their intrinsic value as currency, and that
they would become money only when they were made available for public
use as legal tender. I do not feel much doubt, however, that a dealing with
coins or notes simply as currency cannot constitute the subjection of goods
to a process within the meaning of section 7 (1) (*e*).

If the reasoning thus far is correct, the present issue seems to me to
resolve itself to this short question. Assuming in favour of the taxpayer G
company that the coins and notes which are dealt with by Group 4 in the
security area are being " subjected to a process," are they being dealt with
merely as money in the sense of currency of the realm or are they being
dealt with as goods? Though Mr. Pinson submitted to the contrary, it
seems to me that the former alternative must be the correct answer to this
question. The case stated says that wage packeting was a task which, if it H
were not contracted to Group 4, would in all probability be done by the
employer's wages office. If the work were done in the employer's office,
there could be no doubt that the coins and notes were being dealt with as
money, and this I think would be so even if an independent contractor,
such as Group 4, were hired to perform the task in this office. I cannot see
that it makes any essential difference that the task is performed in Group
4's own building. Nor do two other factors specifically referred to by the

The Weekly Law Reports, April 18, 1980

389

1 W.L.R.   **Buckingham v. Securitas Properties Ltd. (Ch.D.)**   Slade J.

A   commissioners in the reasons for their decision, namely (i) that the whole of the area was " specifically designed and purpose built as a highly secure complex," or (ii) that the money was collected from the bank and delivered to the security area in bulk. Throughout the whole of the operation carried out by Group 4 in the security area, beginning with the time when the money was drawn from the bank and ending with the time when the wage

B   packets were finally delivered to their ultimate recipients, the coins and notes were, I think, being dealt with as money in the sense of currency rather than as goods. The very attention which had to be paid by the staff of Group 4 to the denomination of the notes, the need to replace torn or defaced notes and foreign coins which would or might not constitute acceptable currency, the need to fill each wage packet with the exact amount and according to the breakdown specified by the employer in

C   question, seem to me to highlight the fact that the notes and coins were continuously being dealt with as money or currency. The mere circumstance that the operation of wage packeting was a very large and complex one, involving a number of stages, may afford additional grounds for arguing that a " process " was involved, but no additional ground for submitting that the subject matter of that process was " goods " within

D   the meaning of the subsection.

   In response to Mr. Pinson's second and third propositions, my conclusions must therefore be these. Even if the wage packeting operations of Group 4 constituted a process within the meaning of section 7 (1) (e), they did not involve " the subjection of goods to any process " within such meaning, since the subject matter of the process was not " goods " but money, because the coins and notes involved in these operations were

E   throughout being dealt with by Group 4 as currency, not as goods. This conclusion makes it unnecessary to consider Mr. Pinson's remaining propositions of law. It also makes it unnecessary to consider the alternative argument of the Crown. This was that the security area has to be looked at in parts, and that in any event it could not be said that either the vault or the loading bay, or the room containing the technical equipment frame or

F   the room containing the main distribution frame, were in use for the wage packeting process, if process there was.

   For the reasons I have attempted to explain, I think that, on the facts stated, the commissioners were not entitled in law to reach the decision which the majority of them did reach. I must accordingly allow this appeal.

G
               Appeal allowed with costs.
               Case remitted to the commissioners for
               figures to be determined.

   Solicitors: *Solicitor of Inland Revenue; Cameron, Kemm, Nordon &*
Co.

   [Reported by MRS. HARRIET DUTTON, Barrister-at-Law]

H

A

[COURT OF APPEAL]

*CARTER v. CARTER

1979 Dec. 13, 14   Orr, Ormrod and Goff L.JJ.

B

*Husband and Wife — Financial provision — Dismissal of claim —
Absence of consent—Wife claiming periodical payments for
self and children—Dismissal of claim without consent—
Whether court having jurisdiction to dismiss claim for children
or for wife—Matrimonial Causes Act 1973 (c. 18), s. 23 (1)*

At the conclusion of the hearing of an application for
ancillary relief following a decree of divorce, the judge ordered
that the matrimonial home be held on trust for the wife and the
children of the family, subject to a charge of £5,250 in favour
of the husband, and made " no order for periodical payments " for the wife or children. The form in which the
order was eventually drawn up was unsatisfactory, and the
judge restored the case to his list in order to deal with a
matter that had been omitted from the order. After a long
discussion between counsel for both parties and the judge, the
judge, purporting to act under Ord. 15, r. 12, of the County
Court Rules, the slip rule, varied the order by, inter alia,
dismissing the wife's claim for periodical payments for herself
and the children. The wife had not consented to such
dismissal.

On appeal by the wife against the dismissal of the claim
for periodical payments: —

Held, allowing the appeal, that section 23 (1) of the
Matrimonial Causes Act 1973 conferred a right to apply for
any of the orders therein set out, and that right could not
be taken away by order of the court unless the party concerned
consented to such an order; that, since there was no one who
could consent on behalf of the children to the dismissal of their
claim for periodical payments, and the wife had not consented
in respect of her own rights, the judge had not had jurisdiction
to dismiss the wife's claim for periodical payments for herself
or the children of the family (post, p. 393B–C); and that, in
any event, the second order introduced a major change in the
original order and as such was outside the provisions of
Ord. 15, r. 12, of the County Court Rules (post, p. 393F–G).

Minton v. *Minton* [1979] A.C. 593, H.L.(E.) considered.

Per curiam. The phrase " no order for periodical payments " is ambiguous. It is extremely important that legal
advisers and the court should make it clear whether the
intention is that the wife should be barred from making any
further claim for periodical payments or any other relief or
whether the matter is being left open (post, p. 395C–E).

C

D

E

F

G

The following cases are referred to in the judgment:

Jessel v. *Jessel* [1979] 1 W.L.R. 1148; [1979] 3 All E.R. 645, C.A.
Minton v. *Minton* [1979] A.C. 593; [1979] 2 W.L.R. 31; [1979] 1 All
E.R. 65, H.L.(E.).

H

No additional cases were cited in argument.

APPEAL from Judge Smithies sitting at Bournemouth County Court.

On June 8, 1979, at Bournemouth County Court, on an application
for ancillary relief by the petitioner wife, Judge Smithies ordered, inter
alia, that the matrimonial home be held on trust for the petitioner

A absolutely subject to a charge of £5,250 in favour of the respondent husband, and that there be no order for periodical payments. On October 30, 1979, having restored the case to the list to remedy an omission from the order, the judge, purporting to act under the slip rule, Ord. 15, r. 12 of the County Court Rules, varied the order of June 8, and in particular ordered that the claim for periodical payments for the wife and children of the family be dismissed.

B The wife appealed on the ground, inter alia, that the judge, having found that the order of June 8 was valid and effective, had no jurisdiction to make an order dismissing the claim for periodical payments.

The facts are stated in the judgment of Ormrod L.J.

Bruce Mauleverer for the wife.
C *T. G. Field-Fisher Q.C.* and *Sheila McKinney* for the husband.

ORMROD L.J. This is in form an appeal from an order made on October 30, 1979, by Judge Smithies at Bournemouth County Court in ancillary proceedings following a divorce between the husband and wife.

It is not necessary to go into the history either of this marriage or of the preceding litigation between the parties beyond saying that both the marriage and the litigation seem to have been quite unusually stormy.
D Matters came almost to a head on June 8, 1979, when the judge had before him a claim by the wife for a property adjustment order, a periodical payments order and other ancillary relief. There had previously been an order for periodical payments for the wife and children, the last of those orders being on December 14, 1977, when an order was made for £37 per week to be paid to the wife, the wife assuming responsibility
E for the mortgage repayments on the matrimonial home, and a total of £20 per week in all for the children, of whom there are effectively two. The proceedings in June were mainly about the former matrimonial home. It is a house owned by the parties jointly and it is subject to a mortgage.

The judge, having heard the evidence, which was voluminous so far
F as affidavits went, and also having heard oral evidence, did not give a reasoned judgment. I do not for a moment criticise him for that. What he did do at the end of the argument was to say what his conclusions were. We are very much assisted by a helpful note which was taken by Miss McKinney who was then counsel for the husband. Her note of what the judge said reads:

"I value the equity at £21,000. I order that the petitioner and
G respondent hold the former matrimonial home on trust for the petitioner and children subject to a charge in favour of the respondent in the sum of £5,250. I make no order for periodical payments for the petitioner or children. Liberty to the respondent to apply to enforce the charge when a home is no longer required for the petitioner and children unless the parties otherwise agree, or on death
H or re-marriage or co-habitation with another man, without leave of the court."

Then there is an order as to costs which does not matter. The judge then invited the parties' counsel and solicitors between them to draw up minutes of order. In the events which have now come to light the parties have come, at the 59th minute of the 11th hour, to an arrangement between themselves which makes it unnecessary to go in great detail through the matter.

There are, however, at least one or two important points which have A
arisen in the course of argument in this case and it would be, I think,
right for this court to express a view about them. It is clear that the
judge intended that the legal representatives of the parties should draft
the order. Unfortunately a muddle occurred in the court office. Counsel
went away and proceeded to draw up minutes of the order. Whether
they were finally settled or not we have not been told, nor have we seen
a draft (no doubt rightly), because unknown to counsel and solicitors B
acting for the wife the order was in fact being drawn up in the court
office. The court officer drew up the order, no doubt thinking that it was
an ordinary case, and this order appears in our papers. The parts of it
which matter are these:

> " Upon hearing counsel for both parties . . . It is declared that the
> petitioner and respondent hold the matrimonial home, . . . on trust C
> for the petitioner absolutely subject to a charge in favour of the
> respondent in the sum of £5,250.
> " It is ordered that the said charge be not enforced otherwise on
> death, marriage or co-habitation of the petitioner without leave of
> the court.
> " Liberty to the respondent to apply if the property for the time D
> being subject to the charge is not reasonably required for both the
> petitioner and the children of the family."

Then this is the important part: " And it is ordered that there be no
order for periodical payments."

That order as drawn did not satisfy either party when it appeared.
It does not seem to have met with the judge's approval either because E
he himself, we are told, restored the matter to his list to deal with an
item which had been overlooked, namely, the outstanding arrears of
periodical payments which amounted, we are told, to something like
£2,000. So that led to the case being restored, but meanwhile it seems
clear that neither side was satisfied with the order in the form in which
it appears.

So the matter came back before the judge on October 30, 1979, as F
I have already mentioned. There was a long discussion between counsel
and the judge and he gave a long judgment. The upshot was that he
varied the order of June 8 in some considerable detail purporting to act
under the slip rule. The first part of the order of October 30 is not now
of particular significance. It rewrote the provisions relating to the former
matrimonial home without very materially altering them. The important G
change made in the order related to the periodical payments. The June
order, as I have already said, specifically provided that there be no order
for periodical payments for the wife or the children. The order as varied
on October 30 by the judge deleted the words " there be no order for
periodical payments " and substituted for them: " The petitioner's application for periodical payments for herself and the dependent children of H
the family be dismissed."

In my judgment, for two quite separate reasons, the judge had no
jurisdiction to make the order in that latter form. First, it is conceded
by Mr. Field-Fisher, very properly, that the one thing the judge clearly
had no jurisdiction to do was to dismiss the children's claim for periodical
payments. In my judgment neither had he jurisdiction to dismiss the
wife's claim for periodical payments unless she consented to it, which she

A   did not. My reason for saying that is simply this: section 23 (1) of the Matrimonial Causes Act 1973 provides:

> "On granting a decree of divorce, a decree of nullity of marriage or a decree of judicial separation or at any time thereafter . . . the court may make any one or more of the following orders . . ."

B   Then the various periodical payments orders are set out. Reference is made to a lump sum order and various other matters are dealt with. In my judgment the effect of section 23 (1) is to give the parties concerned a statutory right to apply for one or other of the orders set out in that section. That statutory right, as I see it, cannot be taken away by the court unless the party concerned consents to such an order. There is no one who could possibly consent in such circumstances on behalf C   of the children, and the wife did not consent in respect of her own rights. So, in my view, the judge never had any power to dismiss the wife's claim for periodical payments in the circumstances of this particular case. She had offered to agree to forgo her claim to periodical payments in return for the transfer to her of the husband's half share in the house. She never agreed—and was never asked to agree—to forgo her claim for periodical payments in return for a transfer of the husband's share of the D   house to her subject to a charge, which means in effect that the husband would transfer half his interest (that is one quarter of the whole) to the wife, leaving a quarter of the value of the house in his hands. It is true, of course, that if inflation proceeds at the present rate the wife would have got progressively a greater and greater proportion of the house in the end, because of course the real value of the charge, expressed E   as it is in a sum of money, would progressively decrease.

The second reason is that in my judgment it was miles outside the provisions of this slip rule. The slip rule is Ord. 15, r. 12 in the County Court Rules. It reads:

> "Clerical mistakes in judgments or orders or errors arising therein from any accidental slip or omission may at any time be corrected by the court."

F

Having regard to what the judge said at the conclusion of the submissions to him, as recorded by Miss McKinney, it could not conceivably be referred to as a "clerical mistake" or an "accidental slip." It may be accidental in the sense that the judge did not express what he had in his mind with sufficient clarity, but however that may be the order of G   October 30 introduces a major change in the order as drawn on June 8, so it was, in my judgment, way outside the slip rule.

Reference was made in the course of argument, quite rightly, to a judgment in the House of Lords in *Minton* v. *Minton* [1979] A.C. 593. That case, in my judgment, decides two propositions only. The first proposition—and the important one—is that a party with a claim to financial relief under either section 23 or 24 of the Matrimonial Causes H   Act 1973 may validly agree to forgo any such claim for ever in the future. The issue that was before the House in *Minton* v. *Minton* was whether, there being no order in terms dismissing the wife's claim for periodical payments, the court retained nonetheless, in spite of the agreement between the parties, jurisdiction to entertain a new application for periodical payments. The House of Lords, and it is all set out in Lord Scarman's speech, decided that an adult party could bar his or her claim under those two sections by making an appropriate agreement. There is nothing in *Minton* v. *Minton* to suggest that such a claim can be barred in any A other way.

The other proposition which *Minton* v. *Minton* decides is that it is not necessary for the court specifically to dismiss the claim. Whether or not the claim is barred depends on the construction of the agreement between the parties. In *Minton* v. *Minton* what had happened was that an agreement had been reached between the parties which provided, inter alia, for payment by the husband to the wife of maintenance of the rate of B five pence per annum until the matrimonial home was conveyed to her. Obviously the purpose was to preserve her right to claim periodical payments in the event of anything going wrong with the conveyance. The agreement went on to provide that when the matrimonial home had been conveyed to her such nominal payment should cease. The construction placed on that agreement—and for my part I would say the only possible C construction—was that the wife was agreeing that on the conveyance to her of the former matrimonial home, her application for periodical payments would in effect be dismissed. The House held that that was good enough. In my judgment there is nothing else established by *Minton* v. *Minton*, often quoted as it now is in this and many other courts for all sorts of other propositions. For my part I respectfully agree with the observations on *Minton* v. *Minton* to be found in the judgments of D Lord Denning M.R. and Geoffrey Lane L.J. in *Jessel* v. *Jessel* [1979] 1 W.L.R. 1148. That deals with the relevant parts of the appeal in relation to the order of October 30. The judge had no power, in my view, to make an order dismissing either the wife's claim for periodical payments or the children's claim. So that necessitates the allowing of this appeal from that order. E

Fortunately, with the great assistance of counsel on both sides, these parties, who have been warring for years, have now realised that it is essential to tidy up their affairs and they have reached an agreement. What has been agreed between the parties now is this, that the husband will now agree to the order which the wife originally suggested in her affidavit in May 1978, namely, that he should transfer to her his interest in the former matrimonial home, subject to the mortgage, in respect F of which she will undertake to indemnify him in respect of all sums falling due under that mortgage. She has not consented to an order dismissing her claim for periodical payments in full because there is one outstanding matter which neither counsel can deal with by consent, nor we in this court, and that is this: these two parties have been carrying on a business of a butcher and fish and chip shop in partnership together. G That business has collapsed for one reason or another. There were substantial debts, and we are told by Mr. Field-Fisher that there are some debts, the amount of which is not entirely clear, still outstanding. In respect of those debts, of course, under the law the husband and wife are both responsible.

Mr. Mauleverer, on behalf of the wife, would be prepared to consent to her claim for periodical payments being dismissed if she could get H an indemnity from the husband against any claim made against her in respect of the partnership debts. Mr. Field-Fisher has not the necessary instructions to consent to that, so we are not able at the moment to go as far as dismissing her claim for periodical payments, but it has been agreed by counsel that the best we can do in the circumstances is to make the order I have indicated transferring the husband's interest to the wife and an order for nominal maintenance for the wife of

A　five pence a year, such order to be discharged and her claim dismissed if and when she receives the necessary undertaking from her former husband to indemnify her against any partnership liability which may fall on her. In order to do that, it will be necessary to give leave to the wife to appeal against the order of June 8. For some reason the judge did not seem to think that he had power to give her leave to appeal. He clearly had. He did not have the power to give her leave

B　to appeal out of time, but we can do that, so I would give her leave to appeal and to extend her time for appealing until today (no doubt the notice of appeal can be amended) and vary the order of June 8 in the way I have indicated.

There may be other details of this order to be settled by counsel. There are a number of other minor matters outstanding which we ought

C　to deal with if we can.

There is only one other point I would like to mention and that is that the phrase in the order of June 8 " no order for periodical payments " is ambiguous. Whether the judge intended to discharge the order of December 1977 or not one does not know. One can only presume that he did, but if he did, the order does not say so; it simply says " no order." It is arguable that, having said " no order " the original order

D　stands. It should be emphasised that where agreements are made between husband and wife for disposal of their financial claims, one upon the other, it is extremely important that the legal advisers to both sides and the court, whether it be registrar or judge, should make it perfectly clear whether the intention is that the wife should be barred from making any further claim for periodical payments or any other relief, or whether the

E　matter is being left open. That means that for the sake of clarity these orders should state clearly either that the claim for periodical payments or other relief is to be dismissed, or that it is left open. We will have to go back to the old " nominal order " in order to make it perfectly clear that the claim remains in existence. Parties must make up their minds which of the two alternatives they want, otherwise the court will have great difficulty in construing some of these agreements to decide

F　whether or not there is, or was, the necessary consent to forgo the statutory right of the parties concerned.

In those circumstances I would allow the appeal. I would discharge the order of October 30, 1979, in whole or in part, depending on how much of it Mr. Field-Fisher wishes to retain in respect of the other matters. I would give leave to appeal from the order of June 8, 1979,

G　and set that order aside and substitute for it an order that the husband within 14 days (or whatever is the convenient time) transfers his interest in the former matrimonial home to the wife absolutely, she undertaking to indemnify him in respect of all debts arising under the existing mortgage. I would make a nominal order for periodical payments for the wife and for the children on the basis that she is now free to apply for maintenance whenever she is so advised for the children. There will

H　be a further order that, in the event of the husband giving an undertaking in writing to indemnify the wife against liability for any outstanding partnership debts, the nominal order for periodical payments for the wife shall be dismissed. That I feel is all that we need do.

ORR L.J. I agree.

GOFF L.J. I agree. One of the minor matters to be provided for

in the order is what is to be done about the application for periodical   A
payments for the children. Ormrod L.J. has pointed out that that could
not be dismissed and therefore the paragraph in the order of October 30,
1979, which was a new paragraph purporting to dismiss the petitioner's
application of June 8, 1979, will have to be discharged or varied to enable
her to make application for periodical payments for the children or to
vary the order as to herself in the event of her failing to get the undertaking. Mr. Mauleverer has suggested that the proper way would be to   B
give her liberty to apply to the registrar for directions as to the claim
in respect of the children. That, speaking for myself, would appear to
be the right thing to do so far as she is concerned. Of course there will
be no application if she gets the undertaking unless circumstances change.

> *Appeal allowed with costs of appeal*   C
> *and of hearing below, not to be*
> *enforced without leave of the*
> *county court.*
> *Legal aid taxation.*

Solicitors: *Gregory, Rowcliffe & Co. for Humphries, Kirk & Miller,*
Wareham; Jacobs & Reeves, Poole.   D

[Reported by ROBERT WILLIAMS, ESQ., Barrister-at-Law]

[QUEEN'S BENCH DIVISION]   E

* REGINA *v.* WILKINSON (ROBERT)

1979 Oct. 3, 4, 5, 8, 9;   Robert Goff J., sitting with assessors
     Nov. 21   F

Crime—Costs—Taxation—Legal aid—Law Society booklet propos-
ing system for assessment of solicitors' costs—Solicitors' claim
based on system—Whether solicitor's court attendance to be
remunerated by fee or by hourly charge plus sum for care
and conduct—Whether valid basis for assessment—Legal Aid
in Criminal Proceedings (Fees and Expenses) Regulations 1968
(S.I. 1968 No. 1230), regs. 2, 7 (6), Sch. (as amended by Legal
Aid in Criminal Proceedings (Fees and Expenses) (Amendment)   G
Regulations 1977 (S.I. 1977 No. 875), reg. 2

Solicitors were instructed to act on behalf of a legally aided
defendant in criminal proceedings in the Crown Court. At the
conclusion of the trial, which lasted four days, they submitted
their bill of costs to the clerk of the court for taxation, basing
their calculations on a Law Society booklet entitled *The*
Expense of Time, which proposed a system for calculating   H
the expense to the solicitor of doing his work. The system
depended on assumptions relating to chargeable hours, which
were hours occupied directly on work for clients, and on
notional salaries for profit-sharing partners. It was suggested
that pending the calculation of accurate figures for each firm,
it would be reasonable to work on the basis of 1,000 chargeable
hours a year, and also that notional salaries for profit-sharing
partners should be based on the salary scale of career-grade
lawyers in the Civil Service. The solicitors claimed £8,142·34

A in respect of preparation for trial. For attendance at the trial they claimed £945·98, based on attendance by a partner for the whole trial at a rate of £22·66 an hour, attendance by an assistant solicitor and a secretary for part of the trial at rates of £12·43 and £10 respectively, and a small claim of £11·33 in respect of attendance by the partner at a bail application. The taxing officer allowed only £2,733 for preparation for trial and £207 for court attendance. In accordance with the taxation

B practice for court attendance such attendance was remunerated on the basis of a fee, and no additional sum was allowed in respect of care and conduct. The solicitors asked for a review of the taxation, but apart from a minor item the taxing officer made no change in his assessment. They then applied for review to the taxing master, submitting that calculations based on *The Expense of Time* were capable of providing sufficient evidence of the broad average direct cost

C of work done by a principal solicitor in a particular area at a particular time. The taxing master granted the application only to the extent of allowing £4,283 for preparation for trial as against the £8,142·34 claimed. The amount allowed for court attendance remained unchanged.

On an appeal by the solicitors to the High Court: —

Held, refusing the application, (1) that the evidence did not establish that the proposed figure of 1,000 chargeable

D hours was a sound basis on which to calculate the expense of time pending the calculation of accurate figures for each firm; that in determining the notional salary for profit-sharing partners salaries paid to lawyers in the Civil Service were not comparable and did not reflect the market value for the different types of work undertaken by solicitors in private practice; and that for those and other reasons, *The Expense of Time*, in its present form, did not provide a reliable basis

E for the taxation of costs (post, pp. 401H, 402H—403A, 405H—406A, F–H, 407G–H, 408C).

Per curiam. *The Expense of Time* contains many useful features and constitutes a most valuable step towards the more scientific assessment of solicitors' costs. The Law Society might consider re-examination of the booklet and then invite the Lord Chancellor's Department to consider with them whether it is possible to arrive at more acceptable figures for

F solicitors' hourly expense rates for various types of work in various areas (post, pp. 403G, 409E–F).

(2) That the present practice to allow a solicitor a daily fee for court attendance without mark-up for care and conduct derived from regulation 2 of the Legal Aid in Criminal Proceedings (Fees and Expenses) Regulations 1968; that, although the argument that a solicitor's court attendance should be remunerated by an hourly charge plus a sum for care and

G conduct was persuasive, it would be wrong for the court to introduce so fundamental a change in taxation practice which was contrary to the basis contemplated by the Regulations and confined to legally-aided criminal proceedings (post, pp. 410B–C, 411G–H, 412B–C).

Per curiam. The figures specified in the Schedule to the Regulations of 1968 have remained unaltered since 1960 and so have remained unaltered throughout one of the worst

H periods of inflation in the history of this country. By today's standards the figures can only be regarded as derisory. The time for change must be long overdue (post, pp. 410F, 411G).

The following cases are referred to in the judgment:

Eastwood, In re [1975] Ch. 112; [1974] 3 W.L.R. 454; [1974] 3 All E.R. 603, C.A.

Lazarus (Leopold) Ltd. v. *Secretary of State for Trade and Industry,* The Times, April 9, 1976.

The following additional cases were cited in argument: A

Eastwood, In re [1975] Ch. 112; [1973] 3 W.L.R. 795; [1973] 3 All E.R.
     1079.
Reg. v. *Dunwoodie* [1978] 1 All E.R. 923.

APPEAL from taxing master.

By originating summons dated May 11, 1979, the appellants, Stunt
& Son, solicitors of Chelmsford, applied for an order that the decision   B
of Master Clews contained in his certificate dated January 26, 1979, of
his review of the taxation of the solicitors' bill of costs payable under
a legal aid order made in 1977 in proceedings in the Chelmsford Crown
Court, be amended, and that the solicitors be allowed (*a*) such fees and
expenses as appeared to be fair remuneration for work actually and
reasonably done, and that the taxing officer ought to accept, as suffi-   C
cient evidence of the broad average direct cost of work done in the
Chelmsford area by a principal solicitor in 1977 the expense rates
shown in the tables prepared by a group of solicitors practising in the
Chelmsford Crown Court, on the basis of the method suggested in the
Law Society publication, *The Expense of Time,* 2nd ed. (1976), and (*b*)
for attendance at court at the trial, an amount ascertained by multiplying the time actually and reasonably engaged in any one day by the   D
relevant expense rate of the appropriate fee-earner and adding to it a
further sum for care and conduct calculated as a percentage of the
time charged. Master Clews, by a certificate dated May 1, 1979, had
certified that the questions to be decided involved points of principle of
general importance.

The facts are stated in the judgment.   E

Robert Gatehouse Q.C. and *A. J. C. Sumption* for the solicitors.
Mark Potter for the Attorney-General.

                                           Cur. adv. vult.

November 21. ROBERT GOFF J. read the following judgment. This
is an appeal by a firm of solicitors from a decision on a review by a   F
taxing master, Master Clews, of an assessment by a taxing officer of their
fees incurred in a criminal case, *Reg.* v. *Wilkinson.*

The matter arises as follows. The defendant in the criminal proceedings was charged with attempting to murder his wife on July 18,
1977, by dropping a live electric hair-dryer into her bath while she was
bathing. Legal aid was granted to the defendant, and the solicitors   G
were instructed to act on his behalf, Mr. Kemp being the partner
concerned. The trial took place at Chelmsford Crown Court on
November 24, 25, 28 and 29, 1977; the defendant was represented by
junior counsel and at the conclusion of the trial was acquitted. On
January 13, 1978, the solicitors submitted their bill of costs to the clerk
of the Crown Court at Chelmsford for taxation. In their bill of costs,
they claimed a sum of £4,949·73 in respect of preparation for trial,   H
plus a 50 per cent. mark up for care and conduct, and a further £717·75
for typing and copying—making a total of £8,142·34 in respect of preparation for trial. For attendance at the trial, they claimed a total of £945·98,
based on attendance by the partner concerned (Mr. Kemp) for the whole
trial at a rate of £22·66 per hour, attendance by an assistant solicitor
and secretary for part of the trial at rates of £12·43 and £10 per hour
respectively, and a small claim of £11·33 in respect of attendance by

The Weekly Law Reports, April 18, 1980

399

1 W.L.R.   Reg. v. Wilkinson (Robert) (Q.B.D.)   Robert Goff J.

A Mr. Kemp on the occasion of a bail application before a judge; on these sums, a mark up of one third was claimed for profit, bringing the total claim for attendance at court to £945·98. The taxing officer at the Crown Court however allowed only £2,733 for preparation for trial, and £207 for attendance at court. The principal differences between the sums claimed and the sums allowed were as follows:

B   (1) *Preparation for trial*: The claim was based on an expense rate for partners of £22·66 per hour; the taxing officer allowed only £15 per hour. £1·50 a page was claimed for letters written, but they were allowed at a rate of 75p for short letters and £1·50 for long letters. 35p a page was claimed for letters received, but these were allowed at 35p for short letters and 70p for long letters. Routine untimed telephone calls were claimed and allowed at £1 each. Only part of the time C claimed in respect of attendance by a partner on the defendant and his witnesses, and of his preparation and consideration of the documents for trial, was allowed. The effect of these, and certain other minor, reductions was to reduce the basic expense claimed from £4,949·73 to £1,630. The 50 per cent. mark up was allowed; but the reduction in the expense from £4,949·73 to £1,630 meant that the mark up was only £815 instead of the £2,474·86 claimed. The taxing officer allowed D £100 (instead of £248) for typing; and £187 (instead of £469·75) for copying. Hence the total of £2,733 allowed.

      (2) *Attendance at court*: The taxing officer allowed a daily attendance fee of £50 per day for the partner, and £7 for the bail application; nothing was allowed for the assistant solicitor or secretary, and no mark up was given. Hence the total of £207 was allowed.

E   The solicitors were dissatisfied with this assessment, and on April 28, 1978, Mr. Kemp wrote to the chief clerk of the Crown Court at Chelmsford asking for a review of the taxation. On June 1, 1978, the taxing officer replied; apart from a trivial item, he made no changes in his assessment. He gave his reasons for his decision in a document dated June 21, 1978. The solicitors then exercised their right to F apply for review of the decision to the Chief Taxing Master under regulation 9 of the Legal Aid in Criminal Proceedings (Fees and Expenses) Regulations 1968 (S.I. 1968 No. 1230). The application was heard by Master Clews, and on January 26, 1979, he published his decision in which to some extent he allowed the application. He revised the figure allowed for partner's time in preparation for trial from £15 to £16 per hour; and he restored periods of time (9½ hours G and 50 hours) in respect of partner's time spent on attendance on the defendant and his witnesses and in preparation and consideration of documents. The effect of these revisions was to increase the total sum allowed for preparation for trial by £1,550, so that a total of £4,283 (instead of £2,733) was allowed, as against £8,142·34 claimed. The amount allowed for attendance at court remained unchanged at H £207, as against £945·98 claimed.

      Following the decision of Master Clews, the solicitors by letter dated February 9, 1979, requested a certificate from the master under regulation 10 (1) of the Regulations and in response to that request Master Clews issued a certificate on May 1, 1979, in respect of two specific points of principle of general importance (to which I shall refer later) and at the same time expanded his reasons for his earlier decision. Pursuant to that certificate the solicitors now appeal to the High Court.

Such in bald outline is the background to this appeal. Behind A
it however lies a circumstance which explains the importance which
Master Clews attached to the appeal. In 1972 the Law Society
published a booklet entitled *The Expense of Time*; a second edition
of the booklet was published in 1976. In the preface to the booklet the
author, Mr. Thomas Woodcock, stated that it dealt with "the first
but essential stage in deciding what is fair and reasonable remuneration,
namely, establishing the expense to the solicitor of doing his work." B
Mr. Kemp based his calculation of the expense rate of his own time
(£22·66 per hour), which was used in drawing up his firm's bill of costs
submitted to the taxing officer, on the formula proposed in *The Expense
of Time*; and he subsequently sought to provide justification for that
approach by adducing in evidence expense rates for partners in other
firms of solicitors in Chelmsford calculated on the same basis. This C
approach was however rejected both by the taxing officer and by Master
Clews. The taxing officer, in his letter of June 1, stated that he felt
the booklet had little relevance to taxation of costs in the Crown Court;
and Master Clews gave detailed reasons why he considered that *The
Expense of Time* did not provide a satisfactory basis for taxation of
solicitors' costs. The appeal before me, which enjoyed the support of
the Law Society, was really directed towards persuading the court D
to reject the reasoning of Master Clews, and to give its seal of approval
to the approach in *The Expense of Time*. Indeed, one of the two
questions which Master Clews certified as involving a point of principle
of general importance was the question whether

"... the taxing officer ought to accept, as sufficient evidence of
the broad average direct cost of work done in the Chelmsford area E
by a principal solicitor in the year 1977, the expense rates shown
in the tables prepared by a group of solicitors practising in the
Chelmsford Crown Court, on the basis of the method suggested
in the publication of the Law Society entitled *The Expense of Time*
(2nd ed., 1976)."

There is, however, a second question of principle raised in the case. F
Hitherto, the practice has been for taxing officers and taxing masters to
approach taxation of costs for court attendance on a different basis
from that adopted in taxation of other costs. The general principle
of taxation, following *In re Eastwood* [1975] Ch. 112 and *Leopold
Lazarus Ltd.* v. *Secretary of State for Trade and Industry,* The Times,
April 9, 1976, has been that a solicitor's remuneration should consist G
of two elements—first, a sum computed on the basis of an hourly rate
which represents the "broad average direct cost" of undertaking the
work; and second, a sum, usually expressed as a percentage mark up
of the broad average direct cost, for care and conduct. The first
element is generally known as the "A" factor: the second as the
"B" factor. The total of the A factor and the B factor (if any)
constitutes the solicitor's total remuneration. However, for court H
attendances in all criminal and civil cases the practice has been to allow
a daily fee; furthermore no addition has been made to the daily fee for
care and conduct, though the taxing officer may take this omission into
account, in an appropriate case, in assessing the B factor to be awarded
in respect of the work done in preparing the case for trial. In the
present case the solicitors, again with the support of the Law Society,
sought to challenge this practice; they submitted that solicitors' costs

The Weekly Law Reports, April 18, 1980

401

1 W.L.R.   Reg. v. Wilkinson (Robert) (Q.B.D.)   Robert Goff J.

A for attendance at court should be assessed in the same way as other costs, viz. on the basis of the broad average direct cost expressed as an hourly rate plus a percentage mark up for care and conduct. Accordingly, the second question certified by Master Clews was whether the solicitors should be allowed:

B " . . . for attendance at court on the trial an amount ascertained by multiplying the time actually and reasonably engaged in any one day by the relevant expense rate of the appropriate fee-earner and adding to that a further sum for care and conduct calculated as a percentage of the time charge."

Since both questions are of fundamental importance to the calcula-tion of solicitors' charges, the Attorney-General intervened in the action, and the court has had the assistance of counsel, Mr. Mark Potter, who
C appeared on behalf of the Attorney-General, instructed by the Treasury Solicitor. The court wishes to express its indebtedness to Mr. Potter, and also to Mr. Gatehouse who appeared on behalf of the solicitors, instructed by the Law Society, for their assistance in elucidating the problems in the case, which are of considerable complexity. I also wish to express my gratitude to the two assessors who sat with me—the Chief
D Taxing Master (Master Matthews) and Mr. Thum—for the extremely helpful advice which they have provided to the court.

I propose to deal with the matter as follows. First, I shall consider the Law Society's submission based on *The Expense of Time.* Second, I shall consider the Law Society's submission concerning the daily fee for court attendance. Third, I shall consider whether, in the light of
E my conclusion on the first two points, I should interfere in the taxation of the solicitors' costs in the present case.

1. *The Expense of Time*

I must first summarise the system proposed in *The Expense of Time* for establishing the expense to the solicitor of doing his work. The aim of the system is expressed to be " to produce an *hourly expense rate* for
F each *time recorder.*" Both these expressions are defined. A time recorder is defined as

" a partner, assistant solicitor, legal executive, clerk or articled clerk whose time is occupied directly on work for clients and who records on a time record sheet details of all time spent."

G The hourly expense rate is defined as

" the actual expense of one hour of a time recorder's chargeable time "—chargeable time being itself defined as " time occupied directly on work for clients."

The booklet proposes that the hourly expense rate for any particular firm should be established as follows: (1) First, the relevant figure for
H chargeable time has to be established. The booklet points out that where an office works a 35 hour week (i.e. 5 working days per week of 7 hours each) then 1,820 hours are worked in a year. It continues:

" The number of working hours representing *chargeable time* varies from firm to firm. The correct figure for any particular firm will appear in due course from its own records. In the meantime the number of chargeable hours might reasonably be estimated at 1,000 per annum . . . "

For the purposes of computing the actual chargeable time used in any   A
one firm, it is recommended that *all* chargeable time should be recorded
in the time record sheet, except for short letters and short telephone calls,
which should be allowed for at the rate of six minutes for each such
letter or call. It is not clear from the booklet whether " overtime " (i.e.
time spent directly on work for clients outside usual office hours)
should be included in chargeable time: the definition of " chargeable   B
time " suggests that it should, but the estimate of 1,000 hours appears
to be based on a proportion of the office working hours (apparently
making allowance for such matters as hours not so spent by reason of
other work, holidays, sickness, etc.) which would not include overtime,
and this appears to be the view taken by the Law Society.

   (2) Next, the expenses of the firm have to be established. This is
done by adjusting the expense figure in the latest profit and loss account   C
of the firm in five respects (I quote from p. 8 of the booklet):

> " (i) The addition of a *notional salary* for each partner to reflect
> the fact that partners make a working contribution which justifies a
> basic reward. (ii) A provision for partners' pensions to reflect the
> fact that the recommendation for determining *notional salaries* is
> based on a salary scale which includes a non-contributory pension   D
> funded entirely by the employer. (iii) Updating salaries and other
> items of normal expenditure either by the substitution of known
> current figures or by a percentage increase to the figures for the
> previous year based on the current rate of inflation. (iv) The sub-
> stitution of the *market rent* of the office premises for the figure
> (if any) which appears in the latest profit and loss account. This
> adjustment is appropriate only where no rent is paid, or where the   E
> office premises are rented but the landlord/tenant relationship is
> such (for example where the landlord is a partner or a relative of a
> partner or former partner in the firm) that the rent actually payable
> was not fixed by reference to normal market factors. (v) Interest
> on the *working capital* provided by the partners."

In the glossary to the booklet, notional salary is defined as   F

> " the amount used in the various calculations to represent the salary
> which a partner would receive as an employee for the working
> contribution he makes."

However, in the text it is stressed that, since the object is to calculate
an expense rate and not the amount actually to be charged to the   G
client, it is better to have one uniform hourly expense rate for all the
more experienced partners in a firm, and another for the less experienced
partners: where partners do exceptional work, this can be reflected in
the amount actually to be charged, over and above the expense rate. The
booklet makes the following proposal for fixing notional salaries:

> " The best criterion for fixing *notional salaries* would be the market   H
> value of assistant solicitors in private practice with equivalent age
> and experience. As this market is a limited one these *notional
> salaries* can perhaps best be estimated by reference to scales of
> salaries paid to solicitors employed outside private practice. The
> council suggest the *notional salaries* for profit sharing partners are
> based on the scale of salary of the career grade of lawyers in the
> Civil Service current from time to time with the addition where

The Weekly Law Reports, April 18, 1980

403

1 W.L.R.   Reg. v. Wilkinson (Robert) (Q.B.D.)   Robert Goff J.

A   appropriate of the London weighting allowance. The present career
grade is that of senior legal assistant."

However, the booklet adds the caveat that, although the council's
suggestions are likely to be suitable for most firms, it is for each firm to
select the figures it calculates to be appropriate bearing in mind that in
the end the firm may be called upon to justify the figures by reference
B to market factors.

(3) Next, the hourly expense rate for each time recorder is calculated
as follows (I quote from p. 10 of the booklet):

" Step 1.   Calculate the total of all *time recorders' salaries, actual
              or notional.*
" Step 2.   Calculate the total of *adjusted expenses.*
C   " Step 3.   Calculate the total of the *other overheads* by deducting
              the total of all *time recorders' salaries, actual or
              notional,* from the total of *adjusted expenses.*
" Sept. 4.   *Hourly expense rates* are calculated for each *time
              recorder* by allocating to each *time recorder* his own
              salary, actual or *notional,* a per capita share of one
D   half of the *other overheads* and a proportionate to
              salary share of the other half of the *other overheads*
              and dividing the resultant sum by the *time recorder's*
              number of hours worked on client's matters (his
              chargeable time)."

The booklet then goes on to consider how, taking into account the
E expense to the firm of dealing with it, calculated on the basis of the
time spent and the hourly expense rate, any particular matter should
be charged out to the client. For this, the booklet recommends that all
the relevant circumstances should be taken into account, including for
example complexity, skill, the amount involved, the importance of the
matter to the client, etc.

Such is the system proposed in *The Expense of Time.* Its origin and
F purpose were explained to the court in a helpful affidavit sworn by
Mr. Woodcock himself. There is no doubt that the booklet constitutes
a most praiseworthy effort to promote the calculation of the expense
of time to solicitors on a scientific and uniform basis, primarily for
managerial purposes, but also as a means to assist solicitors in calculating
their charges and justifying them on taxation. Inevitably, during the
G course of the argument, it was subjected to critical examination, both
by counsel for the Attorney-General and by the court; and certain
criticisms will be made of it in this judgment. This does not alter the
fact that the booklet, which must be the fruit of very considerable work,
contains many useful features and constitutes a most valuable step
towards the more scientific assessment of solicitors' costs.

In the course of his argument, however, Mr. Gatehouse, on behalf of
H the Law Society, made certain claims for the booklet which were not
justified. He claimed that it had received the seal of approval from
the Royal Commission on Legal Services, October 1979 (Cmnd. 7648):
I do not consider that, on a fair reading of the report of that body, such a
claim can be justified. He also claimed that the booklet had, after study,
been approved by Messrs. Peat, Marwick, Mitchell & Co., the accountants,
as a method of calculating solicitors' expense rates. I consider that that
also was putting the case for the document too high. There was placed

before the court a helpful report on the document by Messrs. Peat's, in A
which it is stated :

> " the basis set out in *The Expense of Time* is a practical method
> of calculating expense rates although it is acknowledged that in
> theory at least it would be possible to adopt a more sophisticated
> approach."

The report goes on to approve certain features of the system, but also B
proposes certain qualifications regarding overtime, interest on clients'
accounts and articled clerks.   I do not consider that this report can
reasonably be said to constitute approval of the system.   It is true, however, that *The Expense of Time* formed in part the basis of a remuneration
survey carried out by the Law Society in 1976 for the purpose of their
evidence to the Royal Commission. The survey recorded that, of the total of C
6,485 firms which received the Law Society's questionnaire, answers were
received from 4,230 firms (about two-thirds) which formed the basis of the
survey.   Of these firms, 2,185 kept time sheets; but only 1,592 kept time
sheets for all fee earners, and only 527 kept time sheets for all work, and it
was stated that only 446 firms maintained a full time recording system.
The survey also recorded that, of the 4,230 firms which provided answers,
1,174 used *The Expense of Time* basis for calculating hourly expense D
rates.   It is, however, plain from the figures I have already given that
among these 1,174 firms the methods of time keeping must have varied.
Furthermore, the survey recorded that those who used *The Expense of Time*
basis interpreted the expression " chargeable hours " in a number of
different ways, including (a) the number of hours worked in normal
office time directly chargeable to clients; (b) the number of hours whether E
worked in or out of normal office time directly chargeable to clients;
or (c) the number of hours actually spent on the business of the firm
whether in or out of normal office time and whether directly chargeable
to clients or not.   Of these, comments the survey, *The Expense of Time*
requires the calculation to be done on the first basis—a conclusion which,
of course, excludes all " overtime."   It is however apparent that figures
for average hourly expense rates set out in this survey based on these F
samples cannot provide any very precise guide to the expense rates
which would derive from a widespread uniform application of *The
Expense of Time,* first because of the statistically small size of the
relevant sample, and secondly because of the variations in the methods
of time keeping and calculation used by the firms concerned.   Nor does
the survey provide information about the profitability of different G
categories of work.

    I now turn to consider whether *The Expense of Time* can provide
a useful basis for the taxation of solicitors' costs.   It is clear from the
question certified by Master Clews, and indeed from the correspondence
upon which that question was based, that the submission made to him
was that calculations founded upon *The Expense of Time* were capable
of providing " sufficient evidence " of the broad average direct cost of H
work done by a principal solicitor in the relevant area at the relevant
time.   However, in the course of argument, Mr. Gatehouse did not put
his argument in such an extreme form, recognising that to do so would
place an undue fetter upon the taxing officer's discretion: his submission
was rather that *The Expense of Time* should be taken into account by
the taxing officer in exercising his discretion, though it was plain from
his argument that the purpose of the Law Society's submission was to

The Weekly Law Reports, April 18, 1980

405

1 W.L.R.   Reg. v. Wilkinson (Robert) (Q.B.D.)   Robert Goff J.

A persuade the court to hold that *The Expense of Time* did provide a reliable guide for the calculation of the expense rate, to which taxing officers should attach great importance in the taxation of costs. However, after careful consideration of the document and of the submissions of counsel, I have come to the conclusion that there are very serious difficulties in the way of Mr. Gatehouse's submission.

B The first criticism derives from the system itself. The system proposed by *The Expense of Time* is dependent upon assumptions relating to the number of chargeable hours and notional salaries for profit sharing partners. It proposes that (pending the calculation of accurate figures for each firm in the light of experience) it would be reasonable for firms to work on the basis of 1,000 chargeable hours per annum; and it proposes that notional salaries for profit sharing partners should be

C based on the scale of salary of career grade lawyers (senior legal assistants) in the Civil Service. The incorporation in the system of each of these assumption makes it, in my judgment, unreliable as a scientific guide to the assessment of solicitors' hourly expense rates.

I take first the assumption relating to the number of chargeable hours. Mr. Gatehouse sought to defend the recommended estimate of 1,000

D chargeable hours per annum. He relied on three matters—certain paragraphs in the Law Society's remuneration survey, certain evidence from Centre-File Ltd. which provides computer services for (inter alios) solicitors, and the evidence of Mr. Kemp himself. The survey recorded that the average chargeable hours per annum of very large firms, which kept time records by computer, were (for principals) 985 hours for firms with 15–19 principals, and 1,080 hours for firms with more than

E 20 principals. Somewhat higher figures were given for salaried partners, assistant solicitors and legal executives; and lower figures for articled clerks. The Law Society sought justification for these figures by pointing out that, with deductions for weekends, bank holidays, etc., leave and sick leave, there were 223 working days in the year making 1,561 normal working hours per annum, and by stating that it was clear from records

F maintained by Centre-File Ltd. that one-third of normal working time cannot be charged directly to clients. From all this they inferred that 1,040 chargeable hours " cannot be far wrong." It is however fair to point out that this conclusion was based on a statistically small sample of one type of firm and that it ignored overtime altogether. If the Law Society's figures are right, and overtime is taken into account, the figures should be considerably higher than 1,040; but I must confess that

G I doubt if there is a sufficiently firm statistical basis for the Law Society's figures. The evidence of Mr. Gladstone of Centre-File Ltd. was that, on the basis of records kept for 125 firms, the average annual chargeable hours recorded by full time fee-earners (including partners) was 1,005, and for partners alone 970. The figures included overtime. From the recorded figures for partners in 11 firms, with 10, 11 or 12 partners,

H the average figure was 912 hours. It was pointed out that firms using this service had every incentive to record their hours, since otherwise they could not bill their clients; even so there must be doubt whether all had done so, and the statistical basis of this evidence is a very small sample of firms. Indeed it is not easy to reconcile Mr. Gladstone's evidence with the Law Society's remuneration survey. Finally, there were Mr. Kemp's own figures of 967 chargeable hours per annum.

Mr. Gatehouse's submission was that these matters contributed the

only really hard evidence available, and that they provided strong A
support for the estimated average figure of 1,000 hours. I am bound
to say that I am unable to accept this submission. I cannot say that
the figure of 1,000 hours is necessarily wrong: I can only say that
the evidence available is insufficient to establish it as a reliable figure.
It is plain that the taxing masters do not accept it. I was informed
by the assessors that a very wide range of figures is used by various B
firms of solicitors, ranging from 800 to 1,400 hours per annum at the
extremes. Mr. Thum, the solicitor assessor who sat with me, told the
court that he personally worked on a figure (including overtime) of
1,200 hours, though this was calculated on a somewhat optimistic basis.
Master Clews works on 1,100 hours; and the Chief Taxing Master told
the court that, although until recently they worked on 1,200 hours, the
figure of 1,100 hours was now widely used by taxing masters, the figure C
being founded upon their general experience of what they learn from
solicitors in the innumerable taxations which take place. It is right
to observe that overtime can make a considerable difference—an average
of one hour overtime a day on each working day could lead to an extra
200 chargeable hours a year, quite apart from overtime worked at
weekends. In all the circumstances, it is impossible for me to hold
that there is a satisfactory basis for the Law Society's figure of 1,000 D
hours; likewise, it is impossible for me to hold that Master Clews erred
in proceeding on the basis of 1,100 hours.

I turn next to the recommendation made in *The Expense of Time*
that the notional salary for each partner should be based on the scale
of salary of the career grade of lawyers in the Civil Service, i.e. senior
legal assistant; for partners outside London the appropriate notional E
salary so derived would in 1976 have been £8,750 for senior partners,
and £7,914 for junior partners. Now Mr. Gatehouse found this adoption
of Civil Service salaries as the appropriate criterion very difficult to
defend. *The Expense of Time* itself states that the best criterion for
fixing notional salaries would be "the market value of assistant solicitors
in private practice with equivalent age and experience" (see p. 9); and
I am satisfied that the Civil Service salaries provide no useful guide to F
such market value, because they simply are not comparable. Putting
on one side such matters as non-contributory pensions, the Civil Servant's
salary represents his full remuneration for work of a different kind, in
a profession to which entry is gained on a competitive basis, which will
involve promotion in graduated steps, and which provides no opportunity
to make extra profits but does provide a certain security. G

I cannot see how in these circumstances the salary paid to a lawyer
in the Civil Service, of any grade, can provide any useful guide to what
might be the market value of an assistant solicitor in private practice,
or to the notional salary for a partner in a firm of solicitors, particularly
as there has to be added to the solicitor's notional salary the " B " factor
for care and conduct. Even if it were useful to have regard to the
Civil Service rates of salary, I suspect that the grade chosen is too H
high. But the choice appears to me to be an arbitrary one; and
calculations founded upon it cannot, in my judgment, provide a reliable
guide to solicitors' expense rates for the purpose of taxation of costs.

When he found himself driven into a corner on this point,
Mr. Gatehouse had recourse to certain figures published in the Report of
the Royal Commission on Legal Services, October 1979 (Cmnd. 7648)
which, I was told, were not available at the time of the preparation of

The Weekly Law Reports, April 18, 1980

407

1 W.L.R.   Reg. v. Wilkinson (Robert) (Q.B.D.)   Robert Goff J.

A the second edition of *The Expense of Time*. These figures are to be found in Table 16.76 at p. 526 of volume II of the report, and relate to November 1976 salaries of full-time salaried partners and assistant solicitors by year of admission. Mr. Gatehouse concentrated upon the column concerned with solicitors admitted in the 10 years 1961–1970, which showed the following figures for November 1976 salaries:

B
Average	£6,379
Highest decile	£9,871
3rd decile	£7,590
Median	£6,050
7th decile	£5,010
Lowest decile	£3,832

C Mr. Gatehouse submitted that these figures provided the best evidence available for assessing notional salaries for partners of Mr. Kemp's standing by reference to the market value for assistant solicitors in private practice, as recommended by *The Expense of Time*, subject to an increment to allow for inflation between November 1976 and the date when the work was done. He further submitted that the appropriate rate to take was the figure for the highest decile (£9,871). I

D do not however feel able to accept this submission. In the first place the table relates to full-time salaried partners as well as assistant solicitors; the formula in *The Expense of Time* relates only to the latter. Next, the table draws no distinction between the various types of assistant solicitor, or the types of work they do. It is notorious that highly intelligent and well qualified young men in large firms, who have not

E yet achieved a partnership, may be highly paid; so also may assistant solicitors engaged on difficult or highly profitable work, such as commercial work or conveyancing. It does not follow, with all respect to Mr. Kemp, that an assistant solicitor in private practice with equivalent age and experience to his would command a salary in the highest decile. Support for this view is to be found in Table 16.75 on the previous page, which relates the salary figures to the size of the

F firm; it is significant that for firms of three to four partners, the salary figure given for the highest decile is £5,999, whereas for firms with 10 or more partners it is £8,748. The salary figure of £5,999 in Table 16.75 is very close to the median figure of £6,050 in Table 16.76. Accordingly, if it is right to use these tables as a guide, they point to a figure in the region of £6,000 in November 1976, which is significantly lower than the

G Civil Service salaries for senior legal assistants current at that time. But I feel that, without further information, it would be unwise to place too much reliance on these figures as providing, in any particular case, an appropriate guide for the assessment of notional salaries under the system advocated in *The Expense of Time*. Indeed, such evidence as was available to the court of salaries paid to assistant solicitors in firms in Chelmsford indicated a level of salary considerably lower than that for

H which Mr. Gatehouse contended.

For these two reasons alone, I am unable to say that *The Expense of Time* in its present form provides a sufficiently reliable guide to be used as a basis for taxation of solicitors' costs. It is right that I should record that figures were placed before the court by Mr. Potter which showed that, if calculations were made on the basis of 1,100 hours' chargeable time and partners' notional salary of £6,000 (as opposed to 1,000 hours and the recommended Civil Service rates in 1976), this would

effect a very significant reduction (in some cases of almost one-third) A
in the hourly expense rate, primarily due to the difference in notional
salary; I need not go into the details of this calculation in my judgment,
since the figures as such were unchallenged, but I comment that
comparatively small variations in chargeable hours and notional salary
can affect substantially the resultant expense rate, which points to the
need for maximum precision in this exercise. The Chief Taxing Master
also produced calculations of partners' profits based on the charging B
rates adopted by Mr. Kemp in the present case, on the basis of *The
Expense of Time.* These calculations were necessarily hypothetical to
some degree; but they tended to the conclusion that the resulting
profits of partners would, if based on fees so calculated, be surprisingly
high compared with the median profits recorded in the Law Society's
survey as having been actually received by solicitors in 1976. My C
conclusion is however simply based on the demonstrated facts that the
figure of 1,000 hours lacks sufficient evidence to support it, and that the
adoption of Civil Service rates for assessing partners' notional salaries
is likely to be positively misleading; but I wish to point out that any
error arising from the adoption of an inaccurate basis for the calculation
of expense rates will be compounded when the " B " factor is applied to
the figure so calculated. D

I should add that there are certain other criticisms of *The Expense
of Time* which are, in my judgment, well founded. In particular, no
provision is made for the necessarily speculative element of interest on
clients' account, and clarification is needed of the method of treating
articled clerks, who are in any event unlikely to work for 1,000 chargeable hours (as apparently envisaged on p. 16 of the booklet). I have E
already referred to the omission of overtime in dealing with the question
of chargeable hours; and it has not been established how " non-chargeable
time " has been calculated, or whether it has been calculated consistently. It is also doubtful whether any allowance should be made for
the provision for partners' pensions or, if any such allowance should be
made, whether it should be based on the net amounts actually paid in
previous years. However, on the positive side I wish to add that, on the F
evidence before me, I consider it right that an allowance should be made
for interest on working capital, and that rent for offices should be
allowed at the " market rent " in those cases in which no rent is paid or
the rent paid is not fixed by reference to normal market factors.

There are however other more fundamental objections to the submission advanced by Mr. Gatehouse on behalf of the Law Society. If G
a taxing officer is presented by a firm of solicitors with a particular
expense rate calculated on the basis of *The Expense of Time,* it is in
practice impossible for him to check whether it is accurate or not. He
may well possess neither the time nor the training to enable him to
check the relevant accounts on which the calculations are based, or
indeed the calculations themselves. This problem is compounded by
two further factors. First, as is apparent from the Law Society's H
remuneration survey, there is at present no consistency in the method
of operating the system, in particular in the method of assessing the
number of chargeable hours; there is also, on the evidence before the
court, some variation in the practice of attributing overheads to fee
earners. Second, the taxing officer's task will be made all the more
difficult if he is required to consider not only the calculation of the
hourly expense rate of a partner in one firm, but also (as in the present

The Weekly Law Reports, April 18, 1980

409

1 W.L.R.   Reg. v. Wilkinson (Robert) (Q.B.D.)   Robert Goff J.

A case) the calculation of the rates of partners of other firms in the neighbourhood. In this connection, it is to be borne in mind that an ordinary Crown Court taxation does not take place on an opposed hearing, so that there is no adversary to assist the taxing officer in the detection of shortcomings or errors in the figures presented to him.

Another point is that *The Expense of Time* system produces no separate figures for different types of work. All the overheads of each
B firm are attributed to all the fee earners, without regard to the type of work done, whether the work be of a type which in fact attracts small overheads (e.g. legal aid criminal work) or larger overheads (e.g. commercial work, including commercial conveyancing work). Finally, there is a point of a more general nature. If a taxation of costs were to be based up on a system such as *The Expense of Time*, taxed costs would
C tend to float on the actual expenses of the relevant firm, rather in the manner of an index-linked pension. Now it can be said with force that there are market forces which militate against solicitors allowing their expenses to rise uncontrolled; the taxation of costs by an independent body, unfettered by any rigid system of computing expense rates, does however impose an element of discipline which, together with market forces, provides some resistance to uncontrolled increases in
D expense rates.

For all these reasons, I have come to the conclusion that *The Expense of Time*, laudable though it is in many way, does not in its present form provide a reliable basis for the taxation of costs; and I also conclude that it will be difficult in practice for any such system to form such a basis without some prior monitoring by an appropriate
E body. I reach this conclusion with some regret, because I regard with considerable sympathy the aim of the Law Society to place the calculation of solicitors' charges on a more scientific basis, and I have great respect for the work which has been done under their auspices. I very much hope that this judgment, negative though it is, will assist rather than impede the continuation of that work. One solution of the problem which may prove attractive to all concerned would be for the Law
F Society to re-examine *The Expense of Time* in the light of this judgment and then invite the Lord Chancellor's Department to consider with them, no doubt with the aid of accountants, and possibly also with the aid of the Chief Taxing Master, whether it is possible to arrive at more acceptable figures, or ranges of figures, for solicitors' hourly expense rates for various types of work in various areas, for the general guidance of taxing
G officers. Whether such figures are capable of being produced, I do not know, though the implementation of the recommendations of the Royal Commission in paragraph 37 of their Report might assist in their production, and might also assist in such figures being kept up to date. I do not envisage that such figures, even if produced, would deprive the taxing officer of his overall discretion; but they might introduce an element of greater certainty into the present system, and might also serve
H to reduce the feeling among many solicitors, which I have no doubt is sincerely felt, that they are being under-remunerated under the present system for criminal legal aid work.

In the result I answer the first question certified by Master Clews in the negative. I only wish to add this. I am not saying that taxing officers should necessarily disregard altogether calculations of hourly expense rates submitted to them based upon *The Expense of Time*; but I do consider that they should regard such calculations with some reserve,

Robert Goff J.   **Reg. v. Wilkinson (Robert) (Q.B.D.)**   [1980]

having regard to the comments made in this judgment, and that they A should at present treat them as no more than one matter to be taken into account when they come to tax costs.

I do not wish to leave this part of the case without paying a tribute to the very carefully drafted reasons prepared by Master Clews, which formed the basis of much of the discussion before the court. It is unnecessary for me to refer to these reasons in any detail; but in fact much of the criticism advanced by Master Clews in his reasons has B survived the argument and is now reflected in this judgment.

2. *The daily fee for court attendance*

The present practice of taxing masters and taxing officers is to allow a solicitor a daily fee for court attendance, without any mark-up for care and conduct. This practice is challenged in the present case, the C proposal of the Law Society being that court attendance should be remunerated on the same basis as preparation for trial.

The practice derives from regulation 2 of the Legal Aid in Criminal Proceedings (Fee and Expenses) Regulations 1968. Regulation 2 (1) and (3) provide:

> " (1) Where a person is granted legal aid under the provisions of D section 73 of the Criminal Justice Act 1967 . . . his solicitor and counsel shall (subject to the following provisions of these Regulations) be allowed basic fees in accordance with the provisions of the Schedule to these Regulations. . . . (3) Where a hearing has not been concluded on the day on which it started, there shall be allowed to the solicitor, in respect of the second or every subsequent E day or part thereof, a daily fee in accordance with the provisions of the Schedule to these Regulations."

So I turn to the Schedule. Under the heading " Solicitor," fees are specified in two columns, relating respectively to (1) basic fee for hearing and preparation therefor, and (2) daily fee, and related to (a) the Court of Appeal, (b) the Crown Court and (c) magistrates' courts. I was F astonished to learn that the figures specified in this Schedule have remained unaltered since 1960, and so have remained unaltered throughout one of the worst periods of inflation in the history of this country. In the result, by today's standards the figures can only be regarded as derisory. Thus the solicitor's daily fee in the Court of Appeal is specified as not exceeding £15·75; in the Crown Court, not exceeding £21 where no counsel is instructed and in other cases not exceeding £15·75; in the G magistrates' courts, not exceeding £9·45 where no counsel is instructed.

The only concession which has been made by those responsible for this legislation is an amendment made in 1977 to regulation 7 of the Regulations. Regulation 7 (6) of the Regulations originally provided:

> " (6) If it appears to the taxing authority having taken into account all the relevant circumstances referred to in paragraph (1) of this H regulation that nevertheless owing to exceptional circumstances the sums payable by virtue of these Regulations or any of them would not provide fair remuneration for the work actually and reasonably done by the solicitor or counsel, as the case may be (whether in respect of the whole work or a particular item of work, including work done in respect of advice on appeal or giving notice of appeal or application for leave to appeal), he shall certify accordingly; and,

The Weekly Law Reports, April 18, 1980

411

1 W.L.R.   **Reg. v. Wilkinson (Robert) (Q.B.D.)**   Robert Goff J.

A   where he so certifies, any limitation contained in these Regulations on the amount of any fee payable shall not apply."

In 1977, by regulation 2 of the Legal Aid in Criminal Proceedings (Fees and Expenses) (Amendment) Regulations 1977, this was replaced by the following paragraph:

B   " (6) If it appears to the taxing authority having taken into account all the relevant circumstances referred to in paragraph (1) of this regulation that the nature, importance, complexity or difficulty of the work or the time involved, including time spent at the court on any day waiting for the case to be heard if the case was in that day's list, was such that the sums payable by virtue of these Regulations or any of them would not provide fair remuneration C   for the work actually and reasonably done by the solicitor or counsel, as the case may be (whether in respect of the whole work or a particular item of work, including work done in respect of advice on appeal or giving notice of appeal or application for leave to appeal), he shall certify accordingly; and, where he so certifies, any limitation contained in these Regulations on the amount of any fee payable shall not apply."

D

This amendment was no doubt intended to ameliorate the position created by the retention of the long-outdated figures in the Schedule. I was not surprised to learn, however, that this method of amending legislation has placed taxing officers in a position of great difficulty. On its face, the new paragraph appears to contemplate that the taxing authority should give a certificate where the case exhibits features which E   require him to do so; in practice, taxing officers treat it as a means of escape from the straitjacket of the Schedule, all interpreting the new regulation 7 (6) very liberally, and some in consequence now disregarding the Schedule altogether. This attitude is most understandable in the circumstances; but the present situation cannot be described as satisfactory. The court has every sympathy for those government departF   ments whose duty it is to do all they can to keep inflation under control, and Mr. Potter did his valiant best to defend the Schedule; but the result of preserving fixed scales unchanged over the past 19 years has not only been to provoke justified resentment on the part of the legal profession and measured criticism by the Royal Commission, but to drive those responsible for the taxation of costs to shut their eyes to what has become oppressive legislation. The time for change must be G   long overdue; indeed, it is difficult to see how fixed scales of fees can be justified at all in an inflationary age, unless machinery is provided for their regular scrutiny and frequent revision.

At all events, the preservation of the scales in the Schedule added an edge to the Law Society's argument that solicitor's court attendance should be remunerated on the same basis as his preparation for the H   trial. The argument so advanced by them appears to me, in practical terms, most persuasive. First, solicitors generally bill their clients on the basis of an hourly expense rate; it is difficult to see why this should not apply to court work as much as to other work. Second, the principles applicable to the assessment of costs for preparatory work, with the built-in- " B " factor for care and conduct, are as well fitted to the assessment of costs for court appearance. Third, by assessing costs on an hourly expense rate, the taxing officer can make a more scientific assessment based on the length of the solicitor's court **A** attendance, including waiting time and travelling time. Fourth, under the present system, under which the taxing officer allows no mark-up for care and conduct on court attendances, he is driven to reflect the lack of such mark-up in the " B " factor allowed on preparation for trial; such a system is somewhat crude and unscientific, and it would be far better to provide for a separate mark-up on court attendances, especially as there must be many cases where counsel is instructed for **B** the court hearing and the mark-up on a solicitor's preparatory work would be justifiably higher than his mark-up on his attendance in court.

Having regard to the force of these arguments, I feel greatly tempted to accede to the Law Society's submissions on this point. But on reflection, I do not think it would be right for a court to introduce this fundamental change, particularly as any such change as I made in this **C** case would be confined to legally aided criminal proceedings. The assessment of a solicitor's costs in such proceedings is regulated by the Regulations of 1968 and those Regulations contemplate that his attendance in court should be remunerated on the basis of a daily fee. This is so not only in cases where the Schedule applies (as to which see regulation 2 (1) and (3), quoted above), but also in cases where, by **D** virtue of a certificate granted under regulation 7 (6), the scales in the Schedule do not apply, for the paragraph provides that in such event " any limitation contained in these Regulations *on the amount of any fee payable* shall not apply." For years, it has been the practice for the taxing masters and taxing officers so to assess costs; this practice is reflected in paragraph 95 et seq. of the *Taxing Officers' Notes for Guidance in Crown Court Cases* (1979). It would be a fundamental **E** change for taxing officers to adjust their practice to the assessment of all solicitors' costs in legally aided criminal cases in the manner now proposed by the Law Society. How fundamental this change would be is illustrated by the fact that, at present, a daily fee is allowed whether or not the person from the solicitor's office in court is a qualified solicitor, articled clerk or legal executive, or is some other employee from the office; if costs were to be assessed on the basis of **F** an hourly expense rate, it is at least possible that no costs would be allowed where the person attending court was not a fee-earner, because the costs of such a person attending court would form part of the firm's overheads and would therefore be reflected in the hourly expense rates of the solicitors and articled clerks in the firm. I do not consider that it is open to me to make so fundamental a change. I **G** must therefore answer the second question certified by Master Clews in the negative.

But once again I wish to express the hope that this judgment, though negative, may not be unproductive. I wish to draw to the attention of those concerned the comments I have made on the continuance in force of the Schedule to the Regulations of 1968, and invite them to consider **H** whether, in the light of this judgment, it is desirable that the Schedule should in any event be allowed to stand in its present form. It is possible that, if consultations take place between the Lord Chancellor's Department and the Law Society on the lines I have already envisaged in the first part of this judgment, their scope might be widened to embrace the whole question of solicitors' remuneration for court attendances, and in particular the question whether such remuneration should no

The Weekly Law Reports, April 18, 1980

413

1 W.L.R.   Reg. v. Wilkinson (Robert) (Q.B.D.)   Robert Goff J.

A longer be on the basis of a fee but rather on the basis of an hourly expense rate plus a mark-up for care and conduct.

3. *Review of the taxation of the solicitors' costs in the present case.*

The argument before me was directed towards the two questions certified by Master Clews. Having answered both those questions in the negative, I do not consider that it would be right for me to interfere
B with the costs assessed by Master Clews on his review of the taxing officer's taxation.

Appeal dismissed.

Solicitors: *The Law Society*; *Treasury Solicitor.*

C   R. D.

D   [CHANCERY DIVISION]

                * WARNETT (INSPECTOR OF TAXES) *v.* JONES

1979 Nov. 20   Slade J.

Revenue — Income tax — Employment — Payment on termination
E *of employment—Award by industrial tribunal for unfair*
   dismissal—Employee incurring expenditure on seeking new
   employment and on legal representation before tribunal—
   Whether expenditure deductible in computing liability to tax
   —Income and Corporation Taxes Act 1970 (c. 10), s. 187 (1) (2)

In 1976 the taxpayer's employment as a general manager
   was terminated with a payment being made to him of £2,250,
   being three months' salary in lieu of notice. At a subsequent
   hearing before an industrial tribunal the taxpayer was found
F to have been unfairly dismissed and was awarded the statutory
   maximum limit of £5,200 compensation, being in addition to
   the payment he had received in lieu of notice. The tribunal
   found that the taxpayer had spent £500 in seeking other
   employment and it had not been disputed that he had paid
   £1,300 for legal representation at the hearing. The tribunal
   declined to make an order for costs in the taxpayer's favour.
G The taxpayer appealed against an assessment to Schedule E,
   Case I, income tax for 1975–76 in the sum of £12,214. The
   general commissioners reduced the assessment to £9,494, upholding his claim that under section 187 of the Income and
   Corporation Taxes Act 1970 [1] only the net amount of the
   payments received by him on the termination of his employment, namely, the total payment made by his former employer
   less the £500 and £1,300, fell within the charge to tax.
H   On appeal by the Crown:—
      Held, allowing the appeal, that section 187 (1) charged tax
   in respect of " any payment " made to the taxpayer on the
   termination of his employment and did not restrict the tax
   exigible under Schedule E to payments representing " profit "
   accruing to him; that, accordingly, tax was payable on the full
   amount of the compensation payment subject to a deduction
   of £5,000 allowed by section 187 (3) of the Act of 1970, but

[1] Income and Corporation Taxes Act 1970, s. 187 (1) (2): see post, p. 416A–D.

without deduction being made for the expenditure incurred   A
by the taxpayer (post, pp. 418D–E, H—419A).

No cases are referred to in the judgment.

The following cases were cited in argument:

Cape Brandy Syndicate v. *Inland Revenue Commissioners* [1921] 2 K.B.
403; 12 T.C. 358, C.A.   B
Eagles v. *Levy* (1934) 19 T.C. 23.

CASE STATED by the Commissioners for the General Purposes of the
Income Tax Acts.

The taxpayer, Herbert Kenneth Jones, was employed as general
manager by Richards & Wallington (London) Ltd. In January 1976, his
employment was terminated with a payment of £2,250 being made to   C
him by the company. In July 1976, an industrial tribunal held that the
taxpayer had been unfairly dismissed and awarded him compensation of
£5,200. No order was made by the tribunal in respect of costs. He
appealed against an estimated assessment to income tax under Case I
of Schedule E in an amount of £12,214 for 1975–76. The commissioners
upheld his case that the expenses he had incurred in seeking other   D
employment and in obtaining compensation against his former employers
were deductible in computing his emoluments for the purposes of
Schedule E. They reduced the assessment to £9,494. The Crown
appealed.

The facts are stated in the judgment.

C. H. McCall for the Crown.   E
The taxpayer in person.

SLADE J. At a meeting of the commissioners for the general purposes
of income tax held on January 12, 1978, the taxpayer, Mr. Herbert
Kenneth Jones, appealed against an estimated assessment to income tax
under Case I of Schedule E for the year 1975–76. The commissioners   F
allowed the appeal to the extent of reducing the estimated assessment
from £12,214 to £9,494. The Crown now appeals from the decision of
the commissioners by way of case stated.

The relevant facts as appearing from the case stated are as follows.
The taxpayer had been employed as general manager of a company
known as Richards & Wallington (London) Ltd., which I shall call " the
company." On January 31, 1976, his employment was terminated with   G
a payment of three months' salary in lieu of notice of £2,250. At a
hearing before an industrial tribunal on July 21, 1976, the taxpayer was
held to have been unfairly dismissed by the company. The tribunal made
an award comprising seven items totalling £6,059, made up as follows: a
further six months' salary less social security received, £2,766; pension
contributions lost, £198; BUPA contributions lost, £105; use of car lost,   H
£360; expenses in seeking other employment, £500; expected net loss of
salary over two further years, £2,000; and loss of accrued redundancy and
protection, £130. The final award was, however, restricted to £5,200,
which constituted the statutory maximum. This was additional to the
payment in lieu of notice. No order was made as to costs. One of the
findings of the tribunal was that the taxpayer had incurred or would
incur a total of £500 in seeking other employment, and this sum, as I

A have shown, was one of the constituent parts of the award. He further incurred costs of £1,300 for representation by a solicitor and counsel at the tribunal. Though the tribunal accepted that the company had not discharged the burden of proof which lay on it to show that the tax-payer had been fairly dismissed, it declined to make an order for costs in his favour because, in its view, the company had a presentable case and had not acted vexatiously or frivolously in resisting his application

B for a redundancy payment. The taxpayer, who had no legal knowledge or experience of industrial tribunals, had attended a number of hearings before his own case was heard in order to become familiar with the procedure and to prepare his own case, and in every instance the employer had been represented by counsel. He therefore came to the conclusion that, unless he was professionally represented, he would

C stand little chance of success against his former employers, who were represented at his hearing by Queen's Counsel.

As appears from this summary of the facts, the taxpayer thus received a payment of £2,250 from the company in lieu of notice and a further £5,200 as a result of the tribunal's award. The question of law at issue previously before the commissioners and now before this court sub-stantially resolves itself to the question whether tax falls to be charged

D under Schedule E in respect of all or only part, and, if so, what part, of these aggregate payments of £7,450.

The provisions relating to tax under Schedule E are to be found in Part VIII, section 181 and the succeeding sections, of the Income and Corporation Taxes Act 1970. I shall refer to this Act, as amended, as "the Taxes Act 1970." Under section 181, tax under Schedule E falls

E to be charged "in respect of any office or employment on emoluments therefrom which fall under one, or more than one, of the following Cases." Case I, the only relevant Case for present purposes, is defined, omitting immaterial words, as applying "where the person holding the office or employment is resident and ordinarily resident in the United Kingdom . . ." Section 183 (1) of the Taxes Act 1970, defines the scope of the charge to tax under Case I of Schedule 1. It provides that it

F shall:

"except as hereinafter mentioned, be chargeable on the full amount of the emoluments falling under that Case, subject to such deductions only as may be authorised by the Tax Acts."

It further defines the expression "emoluments" as including "all

G salaries, fees, wages, perquisites and profits whatsoever." Wide though this definition is, I think it would not prima facie include payments made to a person on retirement or removal from office or employment. I am inclined to accept the taxpayer's submission that the words "salaries, fees, wages, perquisites" would not be apt to cover the award of £5,200 made to him, and that if all or any part of this sum were capable of

H being brought into charge by section 183 (1), which I doubt, this could only be by virtue of the word "profits." However, I do not have to decide this point as, before me, the Crown has placed no reliance on section 183.

The charging section which it invokes is the quite separate and inde-pendent section 187, which contains provisions specially designed to deal with payments made to a person on retirement or removal from office or employment. Section 187 reads:

" (1) Subject to the provisions of this section and section 188 below, A
tax shall be charged under Schedule E in respect of any payment to
which this section applies which is made to the holder or past holder
of any office or employment, or to his executors or administrators,
whether made by the person under whom he holds or held the office
or employment or by any other person. (2) This section applies
to any payment (not otherwise chargeable to tax) which is made, B
whether in pursuance of any legal obligation or not, either directly
or indirectly in consideration or in consequence of, or otherwise in
connection with, the termination of the holding of the office or
employment or any change in its functions or emoluments, including
any payment in commutation of annual or periodical payments
(whether chargeable to tax or not) which would otherwise have been
made as aforesaid. . . . (4) Any payment which is chargeable to tax C
by virtue of this section shall be treated as income received on the
following date, that is to say—(a) in the case of a payment in commutation of annual or other periodical payments, the date on which
the commutation is effected, and (b) in the case of any other
payment, the date of the termination or change in respect of which
the payment is made, and shall be treated as emoluments of the
holder or past holder of the office or employment assessable to tax D
under Schedule E; and any such payment shall be treated for all
the purposes of the Income Tax Acts as earned income."

Section 188 contains a number of exemptions and reliefs which are
applicable solely in respect of tax that would otherwise be payable under
section 187. Only one of these subsections is relevant and has been
relied on by either party in the present proceedings. That is sub- E
section (3). This subsection, omitting an immaterial proviso, in the
form which it took in relation to the relevant fiscal year, reads:

" Tax shall not be charged by virtue of section 187 above in respect
of a payment of an amount not exceeding £5,000, and in the case
of a payment which exceeds that amount shall be charged only in
respect of the excess . . ."   F

The limit of £5,000 has since been increased to £10,000.

Finally, section 189 (1) of the Taxes Act 1970 confers certain reliefs
where the holder of an office or employment is necessarily obliged to
expend money wholly, exclusively and necessarily in the performance of
the duties thereof. It reads: G

" If the holder of an office or employment is necessarily obliged to
incur and defray out of the emoluments thereof the expenses of
travelling in the performance of the duties of the office or employment, or of keeping and maintaining a horse to enable him to
perform the same, or otherwise to expend money wholly, exclusively
and necessarily in the performance of the said duties, there may
be deducted from the emoluments to be assessed the expenses so H
necessarily incurred and defrayed."

In my judgment, however—and indeed this is common ground—
section 189 (1) has no relevance in respect of the legal expenses of £1,300
and the £500 expenses in seeking other employment incurred or to be
incurred by the taxpayer. The duties referred to in the subsection are,
I think, manifestly duties owed to the employer in question. In my

A judgment, it cannot be said that expenses of prosecuting legal proceedings against the employer after the employment has terminated are incurred wholly and exclusively in the performance of such duties: nor can it be said that expenses in seeking employment with employer " B " are incurred wholly, exclusively and necessarily in the performance of an employee's duties to employer " A." The taxpayer himself has placed no reliance on section 189, and the commissioners likewise took the view

B that no relief was available to him under that particular section on the facts of the present case, so I need refer to it no more.

The commissioners' decision on the point of principle put to them was given in writing on January 12, 1978, and is to be found summarised in paragraph 8 of the case stated, in these terms:

C " We find that the appellant's emoluments from Richards & Wallington (London) Ltd. as defined in sections 183 (1) and 187 (4) of the Taxes Act 1970 comprised his normal salary £7,250 and a ' profit ' which resulted from the hearing—of the dispute with his former employers—by an industrial tribunal. Giving the word ' profit ' its normal meaning we find that the sum to be taken into account under section 187 is £7,450 less expenses £1,800, i.e., £5,650. We

D leave the determination of the appeal in figures to the agreement of the parties."

The commissioners were later informed that the parties had agreed that, in the light of their decision in principle, the assessment should be determined in the sum of £9,494. The manner of arriving at this sum is to be found set out in paragraph 9 of the case stated. They accord-

E ingly reduced the assessment of £12,214 to £9,494. The question of law for the opinion of this court is whether the commissioners' decision on the point of principle was correct.

The essential reasons for this decision are, I think, to be found in the first three sentences of paragraph 7 of the case stated. They say:

" We, the commissioners who heard the appeal, were of the opinion

F that Mr. Jones's action in obtaining professional representation at the industrial tribunal hearing had a direct bearing on the amount of compensation awarded to him and that being so, the amount of ' profit ' (resulting from the award) within the definition of ' emoluments ' contained in section 183 (1) of the Income and Corporation Taxes Act 1970 was the net amount of £3,400 i.e. after deduction of the expenses of £1,800. We were unable to draw any distinction

G between the £500 expenses which the tribunal found Mr. Jones had incurred or would incur in seeking other employment and the £1,300 he paid for legal representation at the hearing. Both reduced the amount he ultimately received as compensation and in our view only the net amount of £3,400 should be carried back to the terminal date as an emolument of the office."

H As I have already stated, part of the award of compensation made by the industrial tribunal—namely £500—was intended to recompense the taxpayer for expenses incurred or to be incurred in finding other employment. Furthermore, the case stated shows that he had to pay £1,300 in respect of legal costs in connection with the tribunal hearing. Furthermore, though the tribunal made no express finding of fact to this effect, I would be prepared to infer in the taxpayer's favour that in all the circumstances the employment of a solicitor and counsel by him was reasonable. I therefore think there is much to be said for the proposition that, in commercial reality, the net benefit to him which resulted from the payment in lieu of notice and the tribunal's subsequent award was not £7,450 but £5,650, that is to say, £2,250 plus £5,200 less £1,300 less £500. This was apparently the proposition urged by him on the commissioners, and in due course accepted by them.

In the circumstances, I would not have been surprised to discover in the Taxes Act 1970, a provision which operated to render the tax payable under Case I of Schedule E, not on the gross sum of £7,450 but on the net sum of £5,650—subject, of course, to the relief afforded by section 188 (3). Such a provision would not have seemed to me unreasonable in principle. The court, however, is not at liberty to disregard the clear words of a taxing statute simply in order to achieve what it may happen to consider a fair or reasonable result: it is bound to construe and then apply the language actually used. In the wording of this statute I can find no provision of such a nature as I have just mentioned. It appears from paragraph 8 of the case stated that the general commissioners regarded the tax exigible under Schedule E as being payable only in respect of a " profit," the relevant " profit " in the present case being treated by them as being £5,650. With respect to them, however, I think this involves a misconception. Section 187 (1), which is the principal charging section, by its terms renders tax chargeable under Schedule E in respect, not of " profits " but of " any payment to which this section applies." Furthermore, under section 187 (2), the section is expressed to apply to " any payment (not otherwise chargeable to tax) which is made . . . either directly or indirectly in consideration or in consequence of, or otherwise in connection with, the termination of the holding of the office or employment." It cannot, I think, be denied that the full sums of £5,200 and £2,250 were " paid " to the taxpayer, and were paid to him " in connection with the termination of his employment." To hold otherwise would be to fly in the face of the facts.

The only possible escape route available to the taxpayer therefore appears to me to lie in the opening words of section 187 (1), which express the liability to tax imposed by that section to be imposed " Subject to the provisions of this section and section 188 below." No subsequent provisions of section 187, however, are of any avail to the taxpayer on the facts of the present case; and the only provision of section 188 which assists him is subsection (3), which exempts from tax the first £5,000 of the £7,450 received by him. It follows that in my judgment the balance of £2,450 must be chargeable to tax by virtue of section 187 (1). By virtue of section 187 (4) (b) it will fall to be treated as earned income received on January 31, 1976, and will be treated under that subsection as an emolument of his employment assessable to tax under Schedule E.

In my judgment, in focussing their attention on the word " profits " in section 183, the commissioners were directing their attention to the wrong section, since section 187, not section 183, is the relevant charging section relied on. The wording of section 183 (1), so far from assisting the taxpayer, as the commissioners apparently thought, in my judgment places a further obstacle in his path, so far as it is relevant at all. For it expressly provides that tax under Case I shall, except as provided by the later provisions of the Act, be chargeable on " the full amount of the emoluments falling under that Case, subject to such deductions only

A as may be authorised by the Tax Acts." As I have already indicated,
I think that, having regard to section 187 (1) and (2), the "full amount
of the emoluments falling under" Case I in the present instance can
only be treated as being £7,450, rather than £5,650. Furthermore, I can
find no relevant deduction authorised by the wording of the Taxes Act
1970 save that embodied in section 188 (3), the application of which
the Crown has at all material times conceded.

B   I must therefore allow this appeal.

> *Appeal allowed.*
> *Assessment increased to £11,294.*
> *No application for costs.*

C   Solicitors: *Solicitor of Inland Revenue.*

[Reported by MRS. HARRIET DUTTON, Barrister-at-Law]

D

[QUEEN'S BENCH DIVISION]

* HAWKINS *v.* BEPEY AND OTHERS

1979   Oct. 23, 24;   Browne L.J. and Watkins J.
E   Nov. 2

*Police—Duties—Law enforcement—Informations laid by officer
made responsible therefor by chief constable—Appeal against
dismissal of informations—Death of officer before appeal heard
—Whether officer sole prosecutor—Whether appeal lapsed*

F   A police chief inspector who, under instructions issued by
his chief constable, was responsible for laying informations
in magistrates' courts on behalf of the police force, gave notice
of appeal against the dismissal by the justices of informations
laid by him. Before the appeal, by way of case stated, could
be heard the chief inspector died.
    On the hearing of the appeal the defendants submitted
that the chief inspector had been the sole prosecutor in the
case and, therefore, the appeal had lapsed on his death.
G   On the question whether the court had jurisdiction to hear
the appeal: —
    Held, that the chief inspector represented the chief constable
when he laid the informations in obedience to the instructions
of the chief constable; that, therefore, the real prosecutor in
the case was either the chief constable or the force under his
direction and control, and accordingly the appeal had not lapsed
since no party to it had died in a real sense, and the court
H   had jurisdiction to deal with it.
    Reg. v. *Truelove* (1880) 5 Q.B.D. 336, D.C. and *Reg.* v.
Burt, Ex parte Presburg [1960] 1 Q.B. 625, D.C. considered.

The following cases are referred to in the judgment:

Reg. v. *Burt, Ex parte Presburg* [1960] 1 Q.B. 625; [1960] 2 W.L.R. 398;
    [1960] 1 All E.R. 424, D.C.
Reg. v. *Commissioner of Police of the Metropolis, Ex parte Blackburn*
    [1968] 2 Q.B. 118; [1968] 2 W.L.R. 893; [1968] 1 All E.R. 763, C.A.

Reg. v. *Jefferies* [1969] 1 Q.B. 120; [1968] 3 W.L.R. 830; [1968] 3 All
    E.R. 238, C.A.
Reg. v. *Truelove* (1880) 5 Q.B.D. 336, D.C.

The following additional cases were cited in argument:

Finchley Urban District Council v. *Blyton* (1913) 77 J.P. 556, D.C.
Garnsworthy v. *Pyne* (1870) 35 J.P. 21, D.C.
Hodgson v. *Lakeman* [1943] 1 K.B. 15, D.C.
Reg. v. *Rowe* [1955] 1 Q.B. 573; [1955] 2 W.L.R. 1056; [1955] 2 All
    E.R. 234, C.C.A.
Rex v. *Kettle, Ex parte Ellis* [1905] 1 K.B. 212, D.C.
Rex v. *Newport (Salop) Justices, Ex parte Wright* [1929] 2 K.B. 416,
    D.C.
Rex v. *Spokes, Ex parte Buckley* (1912) 76 J.P. 354, D.C.
Richards v. *Bloxham (Binks)* (1968) 66 L.G.R. 739, D.C.

CASE STATED by Kent justices sitting at Tunbridge Wells.

On June 24, 1976, informations were laid by the prosecutor, Chief
Inspector Ernest Walter Hawkins, of Kent Police Force, alleging that
the first two defendants, Derek Jeffrey Bepey and Bepey Transport
Services Ltd., on March 26, 1976, at Frant Road, Tunbridge Wells, used
on a road a motor vehicle for the purpose of towing a broken down
vehicle of an excessive weight, being a purpose for which it was so
unsuitable as to cause or be likely to cause danger to persons on a road,
contrary to regulation 90 (3) of the Motor Vehicles (Construction and
Use) Regulations 1973 and sections 40 (5) and 177 of the Road Traffic
Act 1972. An information was laid on the same date alleging that the
third defendant, Wendy Carr, aided, abetted, counselled and procured
the commission of the offence by the first defendant.

By consent the justices heard all the informations together on April
4, 1977. At the end of the evidence called on behalf of the prosecutor
it was argued on behalf of the three defendants that there was no case
to answer. The justices accepted the submission and dismissed the
informations.

The prosecutor appealed.

A case was stated on August 1, 1977, and on October 15, 1978, the
chief inspector died. The appeal came on for hearing in October 1979.
The only question calling for a report is whether the court lacked jurisdiction to hear the appeal on the ground that the prosecutor had died and
the appeal had therefore lapsed.

Stephen Hockman for the prosecutor.
Camden Pratt for the defendants.

Cur. adv. vult.

November 2. BROWNE L.J. I will ask Watkins J. to give the first
judgment.

WATKINS J. read the following judgment. This is an appeal by case
stated from a decision of justices sitting at Tunbridge Wells Magistrates'
Court on April 4, 1977. On that day they heard informations laid against
the defendants, Derek Jeffrey Bepey, Bepey Transport Services Ltd. and
Wendy Carr, alleging that the two first named defendants did, on March
26, 1976, at Frant Road, Tunbridge Wells, use on a road a motor vehicle
for the purpose of towing a broken down vehicle of an excessive weight,

A being a purpose for which it was so unsuitable as to cause or be likely to cause danger to persons on a road, contrary to regulation 90 (3) of the Motor Vehicles (Construction and Use) Regulations 1973 and sections 40 (5) and 177 of the Road Traffic Act 1972. The third defendant was alleged to have aided, abetted, counselled and procured the commission of this offence by the first defendant.

B At the conclusion of the prosecution's evidence the justices, in response to a submission to that effect made to them on behalf of all the defendants, found there was no case to answer and dismissed the informations. The prosecutor appealed against the decision. He asked the justices to state a case. This they have done and invite this court to decide, inter alia, whether they were correct in law in finding there was no case to answer and whether an order for costs made in favour of the defendants was

C legally proper.

Before expressing an opinion upon these matters it is necessary to examine a very different question, namely, whether this court has jurisdiction to hear the appeal since the police officer who laid the informations died on October 15, 1978, which was over a year after the case had been stated. He was Chief Inspector Ernest Walter Hawkins of the Kent Police Force. That this appeal was not heard before his death is due to no lack

D of diligence on his part in prosecuting it. Nor is it attributable to any fault of the defendants.

It is submitted by counsel on their behalf that, however regrettable the effect of this may be, the appeal lapsed upon the death of Chief Inspector Hawkins. Accordingly, if that be right, we have no power to hear it and presumably no power to make any order whatsoever concerning it

E save in respect of costs. He asserts that the chief inspector and none other was the prosecutor. Upon laying the informations he did so of his own volition and determination. He acted neither at the behest nor on behalf of anyone. He entered into a personal recognizance to prosecute this appeal without delay as he was by law called upon to do when requesting the justices to state a case. This was enforceable against him and is now enforceable against his estate. No other person can be made respon-

F sible for it. When a party to an appeal who is a prosecutor in a criminal matter dies, public policy demands that thereupon the appeal should be terminated. It would be unconscionable or otherwise wrong to allow some other person to take the place of the deceased chief inspector on the basis that he is an " aggrieved " person for the purpose of section 87 (1) of the Magistrates' Courts Act 1952 or upon any other basis. The deceased chief inspector's estate has no interest, pecuniary or other, in

G the appeal since no one will make demands upon that, no matter what be the outcome of these proceedings.

Counsel for the defendants and counsel instructed by the prosecuting solicitor for the Chief Constable of the Kent Police Force have referred us to a large number of authorities, most of which raised the question of the effect of the death of a respondent to an appeal upon its con-

H tinued existence. In some cases personal representatives of the deceased respondents have been allowed by this court to continue appeals, upon establishing a pecuniary interest in the subject matter on appeal. This court does not derive its jurisdiction and powers entirely from statute. Widgery L.J. in Reg. v. Jefferies [1969] 1 Q.B. 120, 124 said of the courts which do derive jurisdiction from statute:

" Whatever may be the powers of courts exercising a jurisdiction that does not derive from statute, the powers of this court are derived

from, and confined to, those given by the Criminal Appeal Act of A
1907. We take it to be a general principle that whenever a party to
proceedings dies, the proceedings must abate, unless his personal
representatives both have an interest in the subject matter and can
by virtue of the express terms of a statute (or from rules of court
made by virtue of jurisdiction given by a statute) take the appropriate
steps to have themselves substituted for the deceased as a party to
the proceedings." B

Jefferies died following his conviction of conspiracy to cheat and defraud
and before his application for leave to appeal could be heard. The
court held that it had no jurisdiction to allow his widow and executrix
to continue the application since neither the Criminal Appeal Act 1907
nor rules made thereunder made provision for the continuance of an
appeal after the death of the " person convicted." The right of appeal C
under the Act was strictly personal to the person convicted and there
was no inherent power in the court to permit an appeal to continue
after his death.

Regardless of the matter of inherent power, it is further submitted on
the defendants' behalf that it would be grossly unjust to permit an appeal
to continue following the death of a prosecutor and to deny the like consent D
to the personal representatives of a convicted person.

How this court would have viewed an application on behalf of a
personal representative with an interest to continue an appeal following,
let me suppose, the death of either the first or third defendant had that
person been convicted does not arise for determination. However, as
I understand the status and power of this court, it would have by its
inherent jurisdiction the right in its discretion to grant such an application. E
The fate of the application would, I think, depend upon the nature and
extent of the interest, probably pecuniary only, in the subject matter of the
appeal proved by the personal representative.

Since this is not the issue before us I do not see the necessity to
recite the authorities which appear to support this proposition. Nor do I
deem it necessary to embark upon a review of all those authorities and F
matters of argument and submission which counsel for the chief constable
provided. He maintains that the chief constable and the personal representative of the chief inspector are " aggrieved " persons. Thus either one
is entitled to continue the appeal. Whether this be so or not, this court
as a matter of practice will allow the appeal to proceed wherever it is
just and convenient to do so. Whilst those propositions might prove to
be meritorious if closely examined, since I believe the jurisdiction to hear G
this appeal can be securely founded upon a wholly different basis, I do
no more than make mention of them.

There is no doubt that the Kent Police Force is under the direction
and control of its chief constable: see section 5 (1) of the Police Act
1964. Using those powers the chief constable has by No. 45 of his
instructions to the force ruled: H

"Officers in charge of divisions will as a general rule arrange that
all informations relative to proceedings in magistrates' courts shall be
laid by the chief inspector or inspectors."

No one suggests that that instruction is in any way improper. A similar
instruction exists in other police forces. There is a sound administrative,
if no other, reason for it. By obeying this instruction, does a chief
inspector who lays an information, having had no connection with investi-

A gating the offence involved, become *the* prosecutor, that is to say, the one and only person thereafter to be so regarded for all purposes? I think not. I believe that in carrying out force instruction No. 45 Chief Inspector Hawkins was acting in a representative capacity. He was representing his chief constable, whose orders he had to obey, not as a result of the relationship of master and servant but as a duty arising out of the chief constable's power and obligation to direct and control the force.

B

In *Reg.* v. *Commissioner of Police of the Metropolis, Ex parte Blackburn* [1968] 2 Q.B. 118, 136, Lord Denning M.R. said:

" Although the chief officers of police are answerable to the law, there are many fields in which they have a discretion with which the law will not interfere. For instance, it is for the Commissioner of Police of the Metropolis, or the chief constable, as the case may be, to decide in any particular case whether inquiries should be pursued, or whether an arrest should be made, or a prosecution brought. It must be for him to decide on the disposition of his force and the concentration of his resources on any particular crime or area. No court can or should give him direction on such a matter."

C

D The real prosecutor of these defendants was, in my opinion, the Chief Constable of Kent or the Kent Police Force. So, as counsel for the chief constable has submitted, in a real sense no party to this appeal has died. The recognizance entered into by the chief inspector was tendered by him on behalf of the chief constable, who is answerable for all the consequences of it.

E In coming to this conclusion I have gathered support for it from the following cases which were heard in this court, the facts of which are, as one would expect, different from those in the instant case. So are the legal implications which arise from the very different offences and issues involved in them. But whilst the quotations I use must be viewed in the context of the whole of the judgment from which they are taken. I regard the principle which emerges from them as being of general application in circumstances where a police officer dies after laying an information and before the relevant proceedings before the court.

F

In *Reg.* v. *Truelove* (1880) 5 Q.B.D. 336, 340, Lush J. said:

" The counsel for the defendant mainly relied upon these last words, as shewing that it is essential that there should be a complainant to appeal against. But I cannot see why, if upon the death of the complainant some other person takes up the prosecution, he should not be liable to pay costs if the appeal should be successful. It could readily be ascertained as a matter of fact who was the party virtually prosecuting the appeal. There is nothing to shew that the same person who originally made the complaint must always be party to the appeal."

G

H In *Truelove's* case the complainant died before a summons concerning the sale of obscene books was heard in the magistrates' court.

In *Reg.* v. *Burt, Ex parte Presburg* [1960] 1 Q.B. 625 Lord Parker C.J. said, at p. 635:

" That is really an end of this case, but I would like to say this, and I should have said it earlier. It has been conceded that, although the information was laid by a particular police constable, he must be taken in laying that information to be acting on behalf of the

Metropolitan Police; it would be quite artificial to treat him as a A
private individual and to say that as a private individual he had been
put to no expense or loss or trouble because he himself was being
paid all the time. Not only would that be an artificial approach,
but if one looks at section 17 (1) of the [Costs in Criminal Cases
Act 1952], it is expressly provided: ' " Prosecutor " includes any
person who appears to the court to be a person at whose instance the
prosecution has been instituted, or under whose conduct the prosecu- B
tion is at any time carried on.' Accordingly, [counsel for the
applicant], quite rightly, has conceded that the prosecutor here and
the person entitled to costs, if costs be payable, is the Commissioner
of Metropolitan Police or the Metropolitan Police Force. Accordingly, in my judgment, this application fails."

The subsequent repeal of the Act of 1952 by the Costs in Criminal C
Cases Act 1973 does not, in my opinion, affect in any way the principle
which clearly emerges as a general proposition from what Lord Parker
C.J. said. I hold, therefore, that the actual prosecutor in this case now
before this court is either the chief constable or the Kent Police Force.
I will assume him to be the chief constable for the purpose of dealing,
as I now do, with the substantive issues in the appeal in the belief that D
this court is competent to do so. [His Lordship went on to consider the
substantive appeal.]

BROWNE L.J.   I agree.

Ruling accordingly.
E
Solicitors: *Sharpe, Pritchard & Co. for R. A. Crabb, Maidstone;
Buss, Stone & Co., Tunbridge Wells.*

B. O. A.

A

[CHANCERY DIVISION]

* FROBISHER (SECOND INVESTMENTS) LTD. *v.* KILORAN
TRUST CO. LTD. AND ANOTHER

B

[1979 C. No. 5389]

1979 Nov. 22

Walton J.

*Landlord and Tenant—Maintenance—Tenant's contribution—
Annual contribution payable to landlords for maintaining
building—Tenant making interim payments before amount of
contribution ascertained—Whether interim payments illegal
service charges—Whether tenant liable for interest on moneys
borrowed—Housing Finance Act 1972 (c. 47), s. 91A (as
amended by Housing Act 1974 (c. 44), s. 124 (1))*

C

The plaintiff landlords held the reversion of the lease of a
flat to which the Rent Acts did not apply since the lease was a
long one at a low rent. Under the terms of the lease, the
defendant tenants covenanted to pay a "contribution" defined
as a percentage of the amount which the landlords had
expended during the preceding year on maintenance. The
lease also provided for a payment to be made on account of
the contribution twice yearly. At the end of the year when
the correct amount of the contribution had been ascertained, the
interim sums paid on account would be set against it or, if the
balance was in favour of the tenants, such balance would be
refunded. The contribution was a service charge for the
purposes of section 91A of the Housing Finance Act 1972.[1]

D

E

On the questions (1) whether the interim sums were
service charges to which section 91A of the Housing Finance
Act 1972 applied and therefore only recoverable after the
expenditure had been incurred and (2) whether the landlords
could recover interest payable on money borrowed by the
landlords or their agents, or any fee paid to their agents in
respect of obtaining a loan, pending the recovering of the
expenditure from the tenants: —

F

Held, (1) that, since the contribution was a service charge
for the purposes of section 91A of the Housing Finance Act
1972 and the interim sums were paid on account of the contribution, the interim sums were also service charges for the
purposes of the section and, accordingly, the landlords could
not demand those sums from the tenants in advance of the
actual expenditure on maintaining the property (post,
pp. 428D–E, 429C–D).

G

(2) That, in the absence of an express term in the lease
permitting the landlords to recover interest on borrowing
moneys to meet the cost of maintaining the property, no
term could be implied into the lease for payments arising as
a result of a statute intervening to alter the contractual terms
agreed between the parties to the lease and, therefore, the
tenants were not liable for such interest charges whether
incurred by the landlords themselves or their agents (post,
pp. 431A–D, 432A–C, E—433B).

H

The following cases are referred to in the judgment:

Finchbourne Ltd. v. *Rodrigues* [1976] 3 All E.R. 581, C.A.
Moorcock, The (1889) 14 P.D. 64, C.A.

[1] Housing Finance Act 1972, s. 91A (7): see post, p. 428F.

The following additional case was cited in argument:

Quistclose Investments Ltd. v. *Rolls Razor Ltd.* [1970] A.C. 567; [1968] 3 W.L.R. 1097; [1968] 3 All E.R. 651, H.L.(E.).

SUMMONS

The plaintiffs, Frobisher (Second Investments) Ltd., were the reversioners of a lease of Flat 34, Campden House, 29, Sheffield Terrace, London W.8, and the lease was vested in the defendants, Kiloran Trust Co. Ltd. and Vernon Aidan Ravenscroft. The Rent Acts did not apply to the lease. By a summons issued on August 16, 1979, the plaintiffs sought determination whether the interim payments provided for in the lease were charges to which section 91A of the Housing Finance Act 1972 applied; and whether the plaintiffs were entitled to require such payments to be made in advance and whether they could recover from the defendants the appropriate proportion of the costs of borrowing money for the expenditures incurred by the plaintiffs during the year and to recover the fees paid to their agents in that respect.

The facts are stated in the judgment.

Benjamin Levy for the plaintiff landlords.
Paul de la Piquerie for the defendant tenants.

WALTON J. The matter before me arises out of the impact of section 91A of the Housing Finance Act 1972, which was added by section 124 (1) of the Housing Act 1974, upon a lease in a fairly standard form. The lease was made on November 25, 1965, between Campden House Chambers Ltd., as lessors, and George Maylam and Deborah Smith, as lessees. The reversion is now vested in the plaintiffs, Frobisher (Second Investments) Ltd., and the lease is now vested in the defendants, Kiloran Trust Co. Ltd. and Vernon Aidan Ravenscroft.

The lease was a demise in consideration of the payment of a premium of a flat in a block of property described in the first schedule to the lease as Campden House, no. 29, Sheffield Terrace in the Royal Borough of Kensington. The lease is a long lease at a low rent, so that the provisions of the Rent Acts do not apply to it. By the fourth clause of the lease the lessors covenanted with the lessee:

"from time to time and at all times during the said term to observe and perform each and every of the obligations on the lessors' part set out in the seventh schedule hereto."

That is in substance the services to be provided by the lessors, which I will have a look at a little more closely in a moment. The lessees undertook to pay in respect of that "the contribution," and we will see in a moment how "the contribution" is in fact defined.

The schedule of matters which the landlord undertook to do were the kind of things that one frequently finds in a block of flats; for example, keeping the reserved property in good order, repair and condition, keeping the property insured, paying all premiums necessary for effecting and maintaining insurance, to apply all moneys received under insurance in respect of loss or damage in rebuilding and reinstating the property, to pay the charges incurred in the water rates on the whole of the property, electricity charges in connection with part of the property, the cost of maintaining and renting a public GPO telephone, and a clause, to which I shall have to refer in more detail later, but for present

A   purposes may be taken as the reasonable and proper fees payable by the lessors to its managing agents for the time being for carrying out the general management and administration of the property. Then there was another clause concerning the cleaning and maintaining of part of the reserved property, the dustbins, paying the rent and performing the covenants in the head lease. Then there are two matters with which we are not concerned, employing and maintaining a porter, providing

B   a supply of hot water, and repairing and keeping in running order the lifts.

    Now, one of the covenants on the part of the lessee contained in the sixth schedule is that the lessee will pay the rent and " the contribution " and interim sums on the days and in the manner stipulated in this lease. That takes us on to the eighth schedule, which deals with " the con-

C   tribution," and " the contribution " is a yearly sum equal to a percentage, which would vary from flat to flat, but in the case of the flat with which we are concerned is 0·3 per centum:

> " of the amount which the lessors shall from time to time have
> expended during the year immediately preceding the date next
> hereunder mentioned in (a) meeting the outgoings costs expenses
> and liabilities incurred by them in carrying out their obligations
D   > under the provisions of the seventh schedule hereto (except para-
> graphs 6 and 7 thereof) and (b) in paying from time to time the
> costs and expenses of and incidental to making repairing maintaining
> amending and cleansing all or any ways roads pavements gutters
> sewers channels drains pipes watercourses walls party walls party
> structures fences and other conveniences which shall belong to or
E   > be used for the premises in common with any other part or parts
> of the property or which shall form part of the reserved property
> such contribution to be paid on March 25 in every year The
> amount of such contribution shall be ascertained and certified by
> the lessors' managing agents acting as experts and not as arbitrators
> once each year throughout the term on March 25 in each year
F   > (or if such ascertainment shall not take place on the said March
> 25 then the said amount shall be ascertained as soon thereafter as
> may be possible as though such amount had been ascertained on
> March 25) commencing on March 25, 1964, and such certificate
> shall contain full details and figures relating to all the component
> elements comprised therein and a copy thereof shall be supplied to
G   > the lessee at the request of the lessee and without charge to him
> (but not more frequently than once in every yearly period . . .)."

Then it is provided first of all:

> " That the lessee shall (if required by the lessors) pay such a sum
> on account of the contribution payable by the lessee under this
> schedule as the lessors' managing agents shall certify as being a
H   > reasonable interim sum (in this lease referred to as ' interim sum '
> or in the plural as ' interim sums ') to be paid on account of the
> contribution such interim sums shall be paid (if required as afore-
> said) half yearly in advance on March 25 and September 29 in
> every year commencing on the quarter day next following the date
> of this lease in respect of the period from the date hereof to the
> next following half yearly day."

Then (2):   A

> "That the contribution payable by the lessee hereunder (or such
> balance as shall remain after giving credit for any interim sum)
> shall be paid by the lessee or any proper balance found to be
> repayable to the lessee shall be so repaid to him on June 24 next
> following the year ending on March 25 to which such contributions
> shall relate or as soon thereafter as may be possible. . . ."   B

Then there is a proviso limiting the contribution for a comparatively
short period from the commencement of the lease; and it is finally
provided:

> "That (without prejudice to any other remedy or right) the lessors
> shall not be entitled to re-enter under the provisions in that behalf
> herein contained in respect of non-payment only of any interim   C
> sum."

So the general scheme is quite clear: twice a year, on March 25 and
September 29, the lessees are required to pay interim sums certified by
the managing agents as being reasonable. At the end of the year at
the next March 25 or shortly thereafter there is worked out what the
contribution properly comes to. The sums which have been paid on   D
account are set against that, and then either the lessee has to pay the
balance, if it is a balance against him, or if it is a balance in his favour,
he receives the balance back.

There can, I think, be no doubt whatsoever, and it is not challenged
in any way, that the contribution proper is in fact a service charge.
For present purposes—that is to say, for the purposes of section 91A
of the Housing Finance Act 1972—the expression "service charge"   E
means:

> "any charge for services, repairs, maintenance or insurance, being
> a charge which is payable as part of, or in addition to, the rent,
> and which varies or may vary according to any costs (including
> charges for overheads) incurred from time to time by or on behalf
> of the landlord or any superior landlord."   F

That is a definition to be found in section 90 (12) of the Housing
Finance Act 1972 and it applies to section 91A, because in section
91A (7) there is to be found this definition:

> "In this section 'chargeable items' means any items for which a
> service charge may be payable, and other expressions used in this
> section have the meanings assigned to them by section 90 (12) above."   G

The difficulty which is created by section 91A lies in this, that if one
reads the opening words of section 91A, it is I think abundantly clear
that a service charge strictu sensu can only be recovered in respect of
expenditure which has already been incurred or defrayed by the landlord and cannot be recovered in respect of prospective matters, however
clear it is that those matters, when actually carried out, will be properly   H
chargeable items and costs proper to be brought into account as part of
the service charge. That is because section 91A in its opening words
—and I only intend to read the opening words because there are very
grave difficulties thereafter, with which, fortunately, I am in no wise
concerned in this case—begins as follows:

> "(1) A service charge shall only be recoverable from the tenant
> of a flat—(a) in respect of the provision of chargeable items to a

A   reasonable standard; and (b) to the extent that the liability incurred
     or amount defrayed by the landlord in respect of the provision
     of such items is reasonable; . . ."

     Mr. de la Piquerie, on behalf of the tenants, has argued that the
result is brought about not only by the wording of section 91A (1) (b)
but also by the wording of section 91A (1) (a) that a service charge shall
B   only be recoverable from the tenant of a flat " in respect of the provision
of chargeable items to a reasonable standard."   But, in my judgment, he
is putting too great a burden on that wording, and if that wording stood
alone, there would be no reason to restrict the service charge that may
be recovered to past items.   But however, when one gets to paragraph (b),
" to the extent that the liability incurred or amount defrayed by the
C   landlord in respect of the provision of such items is reasonable; " it
appears to me perfectly clear that the landlord must have defrayed the
cost, or at any rate incurred liability to pay the cost, before it can be
recovered from the tenant.

     Therefore, I am faced in this case with the simple point—simple,
that is, to state, but difficult to solve—as to whether the interim sums are
or are not properly to be designated as a service charge.   In my judgment,
D   they are to be so designated.   It seems to me that the wording of the
lease is too strong to enable me to do anything else, because the first
proviso to the eighth schedule which I have already read, provides that
the interim sums are to be paid on account of the contribution or,
spelling that out, the interim sums are sums paid on account of the
service charge, and it appears to me that sums paid on account of the
E   service charge are part of the service charge.

     Mr. Levy, for the landlords, has sought to argue that the interim
sums are a kind of trust fund or moneys held by the lessors' managing
agents as stakeholders, and that therefore they really have nothing to do
with the service charge, save that when the contribution is ascertained
and becomes payable, then the lessors' managing agents, on behalf of the
tenants, are entitled to put those moneys towards the discharge of the
F   contribution, and that is the first time that those moneys become part of
or are used to discharge the service charge.

     But that seems to me to ignore the realities of the matter.   Clearly
the interim sums are paid so as to enable the managing agents to have
money in hand to discharge the costs of the lessors, which are properly
recoverable by means of the contribution, as and when they arise without
G   waiting for the contribution to be ascertained; and because that is so, it
appears to me that the suggested analogies of the lessors' managing
agents being stakeholders or alternatively trustees of the money just will
not fit the circumstances of the case in any way at all.   They are not
stakeholders of the money, because stakeholders hold the money of
third parties, to be applied in a particular way when a particular event
happens.   But I cannot see that there is anything in the lease to prevent
H   the lessors' managing agents from applying the moneys as they receive
them to whatever appropriate purpose they think fit.   Indeed, we know
that that is precisely what happens, because in fact the managing agents
maintain a separate service charge bank account, and they maintain that
to meet the day to day costs during the year.   Similarly it seems to me
that there is no possibility here of treating the moneys as trust moneys in
any way.   First of all, one does not import the question of trust into a
matter of this nature, which is a purely commercial matter, unless one

has to do so, but, even more importantly, if those moneys were trust **A**
moneys to be applied in the way that has been suggested, only at the end
of the year in meeting the contribution, it seems to me that it would be
the duty of the managing agents to keep all those moneys together all
during the year until the specified event happened, and that that is
not what is intended is perfectly apparent.

So it seems to me that the provision for repayment if by any chance
the interim sums do exceed the contribution payable by the lessee is a **B**
matter which very sensibly rests purely in contract as between the landlord and the tenant, and does not in any way rest in trust or on some
concept of the managing agents being stakeholders.

I realise, of course, that that is a most unfortunate conclusion so far
as the landlords are concerned, but I have reached that conclusion
on the argument which has been placed before me. Having reached that **C**
conclusion, I did not require counsel to address me upon it, but I am by
no means certain that that is the only way of putting the matter against
the landlords. At the very lowest, the interim sums are some form of
security for the fact that the contribution will ultimately be paid; and
the opening words of section 91A are that a service charge shall only
be recoverable from the tenant of a flat to the extent that the liability **D**
incurred, etc; and it seems to me that even if one could, by some attribution of a label, call the interim sums something other than " service
charge," the exemption of the interim sums would still be a matter of
recovering the service charge and thus invalidated by the opening words
of section 91A (1).

This now leads me on to the second point, which is this: Mr. Levy
says: " Well, if now it is impossible to recover the costs in advance in **E**
this way, this is going to create very difficult problems for the landlords,"
and I should not like the landlords to think that I do not fully sympathise
with the fact that that is precisely and exactly what my decision will do.
I can see their very great difficulties which will result. What Mr. Levy
says is that it will mean that the landlords, or the landlords' managing
agents, will have to borrow moneys in order to carry out their obligations
under the lease, and he naturally wishes on behalf of the landlords to **F**
include the costs of the borrowed money—that is to say, the interest
which will be payable upon it—in the matters which can be recovered
from the tenants.

The only clause in the lease, I think it is fair to say, to which he can
really point as providing any ground for such a submission is to be found
in clause 3 (iv) of the seventh schedule. Of course, if it is in clause 3 (iv) **G**
of the seventh schedule, then it will be one of the matters which the
tenant will have to reimburse pursuant to the provisions of the eighth
schedule. But I must now read the clause in detail:

> " The reasonable and proper fees payable by the lessors to its mana-
> ging agents for the time being for carrying out the general manage-
> ment and administration of the property including (but without **H**
> prejudice to the generality of the foregoing) all fees payable to such
> agents in connection with the collection of the rents the contribution
> and the interim sums payable by the respective owners of the flats
> the payment of the rent under the head lease and other outgoings
> payable by the lessors in respect of the property or any part thereof
> and the preparation of all accounts in connection with the calcula-
> tion and assessment of the contribution and interim sums and

A   arrangements for the supervision of any works which may be carried out pursuant to paragraph 1 of this schedule and (if undertaken by such agents) preparation of specifications in connection therewith."

I am afraid that at the end of the day I cannot find in there any real reference of any description to "interest." It seems to me what that clause is dealing with are the fees payable to the managing agents. They B are fees payable for carrying out the general management and administration of the property. Then the clause goes on to specify, without prejudice to the generality of that phrase, various matters: fees payable to the agents in connection with the collection of the rents, fees payable to the agents in connection with the collection of the contribution, fees payable to the agents in connection with the collection of the interim sums, fees payable to the agents in connection with the payment of the C rent under the head lease, fees payable to the agents in connection with the payment of other bills payable by the lessors in respect of the property or any part thereof, fees payable to the agents in respect of the preparation of accounts and in connection with the calculation and assessment of the contribution and interim sums and fees payable to the agents in respect of the arrangements for the supervision of any works D and preparations of specifications. It does not seem to me that one can fairly say that in that wording there is any general phrase which one could fairly read as including interest payments of the general nature with which we are dealing.

    Moreover, it would be very surprising indeed if one could, and for this reason: it may very well be that the present landlord is an impecunious landlord—I know not—but the landlord might, far from being impecu- E nious, have very large sums of money under his control, in which case he would not need to borrow any other money at all; and if that were the situation and interest was going to be charged, one would have expected to find a clause specifically dealing with it and mentioning the interest on sums expended, or words to that effect, somewhere in the lease, and one does not, unfortunately, find any such words.

F   Mr. Levy then says: "Well, be that so, it must be implied as a matter of necessary implication, following the doctrine of *The Moorcock* (1889) 14 P.D. 64, in this lease that if the statute were to render the payment of the service charge in advance unlawful, the tenant would immediately start paying interest upon moneys expended in the manner in which it will now become necessary for the landlord to incur that interest."

G   While the doctrine of *The Moorcock* is a very useful doctrine indeed, and I would be the last person to refuse to apply it if I thought it could be properly applied, Mr. de la Piquerie for the tenant says that so far from the tenant saying "Of course that must be the case," if he was asked at the commencement of the lease "Supposing the statute intervened to make your payments in advance unlawful, I assume that you will H be quite willing to pay interest upon the moneys that the landlord has to borrow?" the tenant might very well reply "Well, I don't know about that. I shall want to know a very great deal more about the whole matter. I am not sure I am going to agree to that."

    Whether that be so or not, I do not think that in fact one can apply the doctrine of *The Moorcock,* because I know of no case—and Mr. Levy has been unable to cite any case to me—in which the doctrine of *The Moorcock* has been applied when there has been a disturbance to

contractual arrangements as the result of a statute. It seems to me that A
if there is a disturbance of contractual relationships because a statute
intervenes, then it must be left to the statute to say what is to happen
consequentially upon its intervention, and that one cannot foist upon
the parties what some outside body thinks would have been what they
would have agreed to in circumstances which neither of them can
possibly have contemplated under any circumstances. Indeed, if I am
right on the construction that I have given to section 91A—and I say B
" if I am right," because, unfortunately, this appears to be the first case
on that section, and it is likely, I imagine, to go to a higher court—the
legislature has set its face against the tenant paying in advance for anything except liabilities actually incurred by the landlord; and in order to
imply a clause taking the fullest possible advantage of that fact, which
could undoubtedly be done in future leases, one would have to reconstruct C
the whole system of liability completely; and it seems to me that it is
not a proper use of *The Moorcock* to imply a term reconstructing the
position as between the landlord and tenant only partially.

Therefore, for those reasons, I feel unable to accept Mr. Levy's
submission on *The Moorcock* on that point of principle. Moreover,
although I do not, having done that, need to decide it, I feel at any
rate a lurking suspicion that if the tenant had been asked " What are the D
parties going to do if statute intervenes to frustrate any part of your
bargain? " he would have said " Well, that must be left to statute.
I am not going to agree to any particular term in advance," because it
must be recalled that implied terms do not, as it were, get written into
the contract as one goes along. One goes back to the inception of the
contract and asks the question then and says " Is that the term to which E
both of you would agree if asked by the officious bystander? " It seems
to me that it must at the very least be dubious whether the tenant would
not have said, " Well, if statute intervenes, I shall have to read the
statute and see what it says. I am not going to agree in advance what is
going to happen."

Mr. Levy pressed me on this aspect of the case very much with the
decision in *Finchbourne Ltd.* v. *Rodrigues* [1976] 3 All E.R. 581, where F
the Court of Appeal had no hesitation in implying a term that various
matters should be carried out fairly and reasonably in a lease and that
maintenance of the property should not be left to the landlords' discretion
to adopt the highest conceivable standard of maintenance for the block
of flats and to charge the tenant with that cost. It seems to me that that
case, as it were, speaks for itself. Obviously, in order to give business G
efficacy to a block of flats leased in the Mile End Road, one assumes a
Mile End Road standard of maintenance, just as if the flats were in
Park Lane on would assume a Park Lane standard of maintenance. It
seems to me that the readiness of the Court of Appeal to adopt, as it
were, the current standard for the block of flats in that particular case
does not in any way assist me in this matter at all.

Therefore, at the end of the day, for those reasons, I have come to H
the conclusion that the interim payments for which provision is made in
the proviso to the eighth schedule to the lease are charges to which
section 91A of the Housing Finance Act 1972 applies, and I have come
to the conclusion that the plaintiff is not entitled to require the said, or
any, interim payments to be made in advance on account of estimated or
proposed expenditure to be incurred for the purposes referred to in the
seventh schedule to the lease, or for any of such purposes, before

A such expenditure has been incurred; and also I have come to the conclusion that the plaintiff is not entitled to recover from the defendants as lessees the appropriate proportion of the cost of borrowing in the financial market the moneys required to make the expenditure referred to in the seventh and eighth schedules until such time as the payments referred to in the eighth schedule are made to the plaintiff, nor would that in the slightest be changed if instead of the plaintiffs as lessors incurring the interest charges, those charges were incurred by the managing agents themselves.

Declarations accordingly.

Solicitors: *Lieberman, Leigh & Co.; Thwaytes.*

C   [Reported by Mrs. F. ALLEN McLEAN, Barrister-at-Law]

[COURT OF APPEAL]

D   * DODD PROPERTIES LTD. AND ANOTHER *v.*
CANTERBURY CITY COUNCIL AND OTHERS

[1973 D. No. 444]

1978   June 19, 20, 21, 22, 23,   Cantley J.
        26, 27, 29, 30;
E   July 28

1979   Dec. 10, 11, 12; 21   Megaw, Browne and
                                                                Donaldson L.JJ.

*Damages—Measure of damages—Building, damage to—Garage
building damaged by neighbours' building operations—Repairs
deferred from 1970 to 1978 while liability disputed—Decision
F   in accordance with comercial good sense—Whether damages
to be assessed on basis of 1970 or 1978 cost of repair—Garage
owners' financial stringency—Relevance*

The first plaintiffs owned a garage, and the second plaintiffs occupied it as their lessees. In 1968, the first defendants erected a multi-storey car park nearby; the second defendants were their main contractors and the third defendants the sub-
G   contractors for the foundations. As a result of the operations, the garage building was damaged, and the plaintiffs brought an action against the defendants for damages for negligence and/or nuisance. The first plaintiffs' claim was based on the cost of the necessary repairs to the building, the second plaintiffs' claim on the prospective interruption of their business while the repairs were carried out. The defendants denied liability, but shortly before the action came on for hearing in
H   1978 the second and third defendants admitted liability, the damages to which the plaintiffs were entitled remaining in issue. The first defendants, who had received an undertaking of indemnity from the second and third defendants, did not formally admit liability, but took no part in the proceedings. They were held liable by Cantley J. At the hearing, the evidence that Cantley J. accepted was that the cost of the necessary repairs to the building, which had not yet been carried out, would in 1978 be £30,327; in 1970 it would have been £11,375. The second plaintiffs' damage would in 1978

be £11,951; in 1970 it would have been £4,108. Cantley J. **A** accepted the evidence of a director of the plaintiff companies that, if there had been no money problem, he would not have spent money on the building before he was sure of recovering the cost from the defendants; it would not have made commercial sense to spend it on a property that would not produce corresponding additional income; so long as there was a dispute as to liability or the amount of compensation he would have done no more than to keep the building weatherproof and " in **B** working order." Cantley J. found that the first plaintiffs could probably have raised the money for repairs but that that would have increased their annual losses and their financial stringency. As a commercial decision, judged exclusively from the point of view of the immediate and short-term welfare of the plaintiff companies, it had been reasonable to postpone the expense of the repairs while no harm was being done to the building and the defendants were denying liability. He held, **C** however, that the general principle that damages must be assessed as at the date when the damage had occurred applied, though in the case of damage to a building repairs could not usually be put in hand at once. He held that the appropriate damages were the cost of repairs at the time when it had been reasonable to begin them, but that whether the time was reasonable must be judged objectively and not taking into account such matters as impecuniosity or financial stringency. **D** On that basis, it had been reasonable for the plaintiffs not to begin the repairs until 1970, and he accordingly awarded the plaintiffs damages on the basis of repair in 1970.

On appeal by the plaintiffs : —

Held, allowing the appeal, (1) that the fundamental principle as to damages was that the measure of damages was that sum of money that would put the injured party in the same position as that in which he would have been if he had not sustained **E** the injury (post, pp. 451c–e, 454e–g, 456g).

Livingstone v. *Rawyards Coal Co.* (1880) 5 App.Cas. 25, H.L.(Sc.) applied.

Per curiam. In any case of doubt, it is desirable that the judge, having decided provisionally as to the amount of damages, should, before finally deciding, consider whether the amount conforms with the requirement of the fundamental principle. If, if it appears not to conform, he should examine **F** the question again to see whether the case falls within one of the exceptions, or whether he is obliged by some binding authority to arrive at a result inconsistent with the fundamental principle (post, p. 451e–f).

(2) That, although as a general rule damages were assessed as at the date of the breach, that rule was subject to many exceptions and qualifications; and that in a case such as the present, where there was a material difference between **G** the cost of repair at the date of the wrongful act and the cost when the repairs could, having regard to all the relevant circumstances, first reasonably have been undertaken, the damages were to be assessed by reference to the cost of repair at the latter time (post, pp. 450h—451c, 454h—455a, 457b–d).

Miliangos v. *George Frank (Textiles) Ltd.* [1976] A.C. 443, H.L.(E.) distinguished.

Dictum of Denning L.J. in *Philips* v. *Ward* [1956] 1 W.L.R. **H** 471, 474, C.A. not followed.

(3) That, if, as Cantley J. had held, the grounds advanced by the plaintiffs for deferment of the repairs until 1978 had been reasonable from their point of view, 1978 had prima facie been the date by reference to which the damages had fallen to be assessed; that, on the facts, it had not been " financial stringency " or " impecuniosity " that had been the cause, or even an effective cause, of the plaintiffs' decision to postpone the repairs, the " financial stringency " that would have been

The Weekly Law Reports, May 2, 1980

435

1 W.L.R.   Dodd Properties v. Canterbury City Council (Q.B.D.)

A   created by carrying out the repairs having been merely one
of a number of factors that had together produced the result
that commercial good sense pointed towards deferment; that,
further, the reasonableness of the deferment was to be equated
with a plaintiff's duty to mitigate his damage and a plaintiff
was not obliged in mitigating his damage to do what he
could not afford to do; and that, accordingly, there was no
reason why the damages should not be assessed on the basis
B   of the 1978 cost of repairs in accordance with fundamental
principle (post, pp. 452A–B, 453A–G, 456A–C, D–E, 459C–F).
             Radford v. *De Froberville* [1977] 1 W.L.R. 1262 applied.
             The Liesbosch [1933] A.C. 449, H.L.(E.) distinguished.
             Per curiam. The ratio of *The Liesbosch* was that, in so
far as the plaintiffs had in fact suffered more than the loss
assessed on a market basis, the excess loss had flowed directly
from their lack of means and not from the tortious act of
C   the defendants, alternatively, it was too remote in law, i.e.
not foreseeable (post, pp. 452H, 456D, 459B–C).
             Decision of Cantley J., post, p. 437B–C et seq. reversed.

The following cases are referred to in the judgments in the Court of
          Appeal:
Clark v. *Woor* [1965] 1 W.L.R. 650; [1965] 2 All E.R. 353.
D   *Clippens Oil Co. Ltd.* v. *Edinburgh and District Water Trustees* [1907]
          A.C. 291, H.L.(Sc.).
Johnson v. *Agnew* [1979] 2 W.L.R. 487; [1979] 1 All E.R. 883, H.L.(E.).
Liesbosch, The [1933] A.C. 449, H.L.(E.).
Livingstone v. *Rawyards Coal Co.* (1880) 5 App.Cas 25, H.L.(Sc.).
Miliangos v. *George Frank (Textiles) Ltd.* [1976] A.C. 443; [1975] 3
          W.L.R. 758; [1975] 3 All E.R. 801, H.L.(E.).
E   *Philips* v. *Ward* [1956] 1 W.L.R. 471; [1956] 1 All E.R. 874, C.A.
Radford v. *De Froberville* [1977] 1 W.L.R. 1262; [1978] 1 All E.R. 33.
West Midland Baptist (Trust) Association (Inc.) v. *Birmingham Corporation*
          [1970] A.C. 874; [1969] 3 W.L.R. 389; [1969] 3 All E.R. 172,
          H.L.(E.).

The following additional cases were cited in argument in the Court of
F   Appeal:
Alberta Caterers Ltd. v. *R. Vollan (Alta.) Ltd.* (1977) 81 D.L.R. (3d) 672.
Applegate v. *Moss* [1971] 1 Q.B. 406; [1971] 2 W.L.R. 541; [1971]
          1 All E.R. 747, C.A.
British Westinghouse Electric and Manufacturing Co. Ltd. v. *Underground
          Electric Railways Co. of London Ltd.* [1912] A.C. 673, H.L.(E.).
Bunclark v. *Hertfordshire County Council* (1977) 243 E.G. 381.
G   *Celia (S.S.) (Owners)* v. *S.S. Volturno (Owners) (The Volturno)* [1920]
          P. 447; 454n., C.A.; [1921] 2 A.C. 544, H.L.(E.).
Di Ferdinando v. *Simon, Smits & Co. Ltd.* [1920] 3 K.B. 409, C.A.
Edison, The [1932] P. 52, C.A.
Jens and Jens v. *Mannix Co. Ltd.* (1978) 5 W.W.R. 486.
Jones v. *Griffith* [1969] 1 W.L.R. 795; [1969] 2 All E.R. 1015, C.A.
H   *Kingsway, The* [1918] P. 344, C.A.
Kitchen v. *Royal Air Force Association* [1958] 1 W.L.R. 563; [1958]
          3 All E.R. 241, C.A.
London, Chatham & Dover Railway Co. v. *South Eastern Railway Co.*
          [1893] A.C. 429, H.L.(E.).
Pickett v. *British Rail Engineering Ltd.* [1980] A.C. 136; [1978] 3 W.L.R.
          955; [1979] 1 All E.R. 774, H.L.(E.).
Taylor (C.R.) (Wholesale) Ltd. v. *Hepworths Ltd.* [1977] 1 W.L.R. 659;
          [1977] 2 All E.R. 784.

Dodd Properties v. Canterbury City Council (Q.B.D.)   **[1980]**

The following cases are referred to in the judgment of Cantley J.:   A

Applegate v. *Moss* [1971] 1 Q.B. 406; [1971] 2 W.L.R. 541; [1971] 1 All E.R. 747, C.A.

Clark v. *Woor* [1965] 1 W.L.R. 650; [1965] 2 All E.R. 353.

Clippens Oil Co. Ltd. v. *Edinburgh and District Water Trustees* [1907] A.C. 291, H.L.(Sc.).

East Ham Corporation v. *Bernard Sunley & Sons Ltd.* [1966] A.C. 406; [1965] 3 W.L.R. 1096; [1965] 3 All E.R. 619, H.L.(E.).   B

Hoare & Co. v. *McAlpine* [1923] 1 Ch. 167.

Liesbosch, The [1933] A.C. 449, H.L.(E.).

Lodge Holes Colliery Co. Ltd. v. *Wednesbury Corporation* [1908] A.C. 323, H.L.(E.).

Philips v. *Ward* [1956] 1 W.L.R. 471; [1956] 1 All E.R. 874, C.A.

Rylands v. *Fletcher* (1868) L.R. 3 H.L. 330, H.L.(E.).   C

The following additional cases were cited in argument before Cantley J.:

Bunclark v. *Hertfordshire County Council* (1977) 243 E.G. 381.

Harbutt's "Plasticine" Ltd. v. *Wayne Tank and Pump Co. Ltd.* [1970] 1 Q.B. 447; [1970] 2 W.L.R. 198; [1970] 1 All E.R. 225, C.A.

Hollebone v. *Midhurst and Fernhurst Builders Ltd.* [1968] 1 Lloyd's Rep. 38.   D

Martindale v. *Duncan* [1973] 1 W.L.R. 574; [1973] 2 All E.R. 355, C.A.

Mesters v. *Home Freeholds Co.* [1921] 2 K.B. 526.

Moore v. *DER Ltd.* [1971] 1 W.L.R. 1476; [1971] 3 All E.R. 517, C.A.

Radford v. *De Froberville* [1977] 1 W.L.R. 1262; [1978] 1 All E.R. 33.

Robbins of Putney Ltd. v. *Meek* [1971] R.T.R. 345.

E

ACTION

By writ dated February 20, 1973, the plaintiffs, Dodd Properties (Kent) Ltd. and Marlowe Garage (Canterbury) Ltd., claimed against the defendants, the Canterbury City Council, Truscon Ltd. and Frankipile Ltd., damage for negligence and/or nuisance by the defendants and each of them in the course of construction of a multi-storey car park on land adjacent to the plaintiffs' premises known as Marlowe Garage,   F
Rose Lane, Canterbury, on or about April 1968.

The defendants denied liability. Shortly before the hearing of the action, however, liability was admitted in nuisance by the second and third defendants. The first defendants did not formally admit liability, but they took no part in the proceedings, having received an undertaking of indemnity from the second and third defendants. The issues at the   G
trial were, accordingly, as to damages. The second and third defendants contended, inter alia, that the plaintiffs were only entitled to recover damages in respect of such damage to their premises as they might prove due to the matters complained of on the basis of the reasonable cost of the reasonably necessary works of repair thereto (and the reasonable cost of any reasonably necessary alternative accommodation and any loss of profit reasonably or necessarily incurred, neither of which the   H
defendants admitted to be the case); in particular, the reasonable time for performing such works had been in 1968; further and/or alternatively, if the plaintiffs' failure thereafter to perform the works of repair had been due to their impecuniosity, such additional loss and damage due to the later performance of the works was in law irrecoverable.

The facts are stated by Cantley J.

A   *Roger Titheridge Q.C.* and *Michael McMullan* for the plaintiffs.
Michael Wright Q.C. and *John Crowley* for the first defendants.
Oliver Popplewell Q.C. and *Stephen Desch* for the second and third
defendants.

Cur. adv. vult.

B   July 28, 1978. CANTLEY J. read the following judgment. The first
plaintiffs, Dodd Properties (Kent) Ltd., are and always have been the
owners of a building in Rose Lane, Canterbury, which was erected in
1958. It is known as " Marlowe Garage." The second plaintiffs, Marlowe Garage (Canterbury) Ltd., are and at all material times have been
the occupiers of that building as lessees of the first plaintiffs under a 20-
year lease. As their title indicates, the second plaintiffs carry on at
C Marlowe Garage the general business of garage proprietors, and the business
includes the selling and buying and repairing of motor cars and selling
petrol, oil and motor car accessories.

There is and always has been close connection between the two
companies. During his lifetime, the late Mr. John Dodd controlled both
companies and he and his family held all the shares in both companies.
D Mr. Dodd died in September 1970 and, after his death, the beneficial
interest in the shares in both companies remained in members of his
family.

About 1966, the first plaintiffs erected another building called
" Watling House " alongside Marlowe Garage. The ground floor of
Watling House is used as a motor car show-room by the second plaintiffs
and the upper floors are let as offices. Watling House and Marlowe
E Garage are structurally joined together.

I have been told, and no one has disputed, that Marlowe Garage and
Watling House were erected in conformity with the by-laws and regulations of the local authority who are the first defendants in this action.
Indeed, the presumption would be that the buildings were erected in
accordance with all relevant by-laws and regulations.

F   Beginning in 1968, the first defendants erected a massive multi-storey
car park along the other side of Marlowe Garage, separated from
Marlowe Garage by no more than a few feet. The relationship between
the buildings, the car park and Watling House with Marlowe Garage
in the middle, is shown in an exhibited photograph.

The method adopted by the defendants in the building of the car park
involved excavation and pile-driving in the close vicinity of the founda-
G tions of Marlowe Garage. The second defendants were the main
contractors to the building operations and the third defendants were
subcontractors to the second defendants for the pile-driving.

From the outset, it was appreciated, and, indeed, must have been
obvious, that the pile-driving operations would involve some risk of
damage to the structure of Marlowe Garage. In a report prepared by
H the third defendants and dated November 16, 1967, the danger from
vibration was described as " . . . a fair risk for driven piles provided we
take precautionary measures to avoid vibration for 28 piles." I do not
know from whose point of view the risk was being assessed as fair; one
would naturally assume that it would be from the point of view of the
third defendants but for the fact that their subsequent correspondence
with the plaintiffs and their pleadings in this action until almost the eve
of trial implied that the whole risk ought to be borne by the plaintiffs.

However, a letter dated May 2, 1968, from the first defendants'   A
structural engineers to the third defendants confirms " . . . the importance
of ensuring that every possible precaution is taken to obviate disturbance
and damage to the premises of Messrs. Marlowe Motors." The minutes
of a site meeting of representatives of all three defendants on May 30,
1968, record as follows:

> " The city architects advised Messrs. Truscon " (that is, the second   B
> defendants) " and Frankipile " (that is, the third defendants) " . . . to
> exercise every care concerning possible damage to Marlowe Motors
> and suggested that it would be in their interests to make arrange-
> ments for a schedule of defects to be drawn up at an early date by
> an independant firm of consultants."

Even at that stage litigation was being provided for.

Pile-driving began in June 1968, and the adventurers' apprehensions   C
as to the possible effects were duly realised in the summer of 1968. I
accept the expert evidence of Mr. Moors and Mr. Wootton and the
evidence of Mr. Cryer from his personal experience in the building at
the time that the pile-driving caused severe vibration in Marlowe Garage.
This resulted in a volumetric change in the strata below the foundations
of Marlowe Garage.   D

The resultant damage to the building is set out in Mr. Moors's report
of May 29, 1970, and in the plaintiffs' further and better particulars of
their statement of claim. Apart from minor damage, there were cracks
in the walls and in the concrete floor. Furthermore, the building had
been constructed round a steel girder frame with vertical steel columns
on concrete blocks. Consequent on the defendants' operations, settlement   E
and movement of the foundations occurred and caused distortion of this
steel frame. The steel columns are now out of plumb, leaning slightly
in the direction of the top. According to Mr. Wootton, the structural
engineer, the worst one is seven-eighths of an inch from the vertical.
The columns are 20 feet high to the underside of the roof and the
distortion is not really perceptible to the naked eye. The steel roof
trusses are now out of horizontal although not seriously so. According   F
to Mr. Marshall, a very highly qualified civil engineer called by the
defendants, the worst one is two inches out of horizontal. As the length
of the trusses is 50 feet, this is equivalent to a slope of 1: 300 and is not
perceptible to the naked eye.

However, one practical effect of the distortion of the steel frame is
that the roof which was formerly nearly a flat roof is now sloping slightly
in the wrong direction, away from the gutter.   G

All the defendants have steadily denied liability for this damage both
in correspondence and in their pleadings. The third defendants in their
defence contended that the damage was not reasonably foreseeable and was
due to unusual susceptibility of the plaintiffs' building by reason of its
having been built on insufficiently consolidated ground with foundations
insufficiently deep.   H

On June 15, 1978, a matter of a few days before the trial of this action
began, they formally admitted liability for most of the damage. They
excepted from their admission certain cracks in the walls of Marlowe
Garage in the vicinity of Watling House. These cracks are the only
items of which the causation was seriously contested before me. I may
as well dispose of that issue at once. I find that they were caused by
the defendants' operations. Mr. Cryer, the second plaintiffs' managing

The Weekly Law Reports, May 2, 1980

439

1 W.L.R.   Dodd Properties v. Canterbury City Council (Q.B.D.)   Cantley J.

A director, who was there at the time, said that they actually happened during the piling operation and that while the piling was going on near the building the whole building vibrated. If confirmation of his evidence were needed, I would find it in the fact that these cracks were not listed in the defects found after careful examination of the building on behalf of the third defendants before the pile-driving began. Those walls may

B have been vulnerable, as Mr. Marshall suggested, but they were not cracked. I find that the third defendants' operations caused all the ascertained physical damage to the building of which the plaintiffs complain.

The first and second defendants, on the plaintiffs' undertaking that they would not seek against those defendants any damages other than the damages sought against the third defendants, have not taken part in

C the trial. However, while not contesting liability, they have not admitted it. Although their attitude has at this stage achieved a very sensible saving of costs, it does not absolve me from making a decision as to their liability. I hold them liable. The third defendants were independent contractors, but they were employed to carry out an extra-hazardous operation, by which I mean one which, by its very nature, involved

D risk of damage to the building in its close vicinity and not an operation which only involved such risk if done negligently. They did it on advice that it was a fair risk, but it is they who must take the risk.

I also hold that the operation which they authorised amounted to a nuisance as is illustrated by Mr. Cryer's evidence in addition to the expert evidence which I have heard as to the volumetric change which the vibrations were likely to cause in the strata below the building. The

E third defendants were employed to carry out an operation from which it was reasonably to be foreseen, and, indeed, from which it was foreseen, that damage to the adjoining building was likely to occur. In *Hoare & Co.* v. *McAlpine* [1923] 1 Ch. 167, Astbury J. held that the principle of *Rylands* v. *Fletcher* (1868) L.R. 3 H.L. 330 applied to the escape of vibrations from pile-driving, but, on the facts of this case, I do not

F find it necessary to decide whether that principle does apply to vibrations.

It remains, therefore, to assess the damages to which the plaintiffs are entitled. That is a question which has occupied nearly the whole of the time of this trial. It has been accepted by the defendants that, so far as damage to the structure of the building is concerned, the appropriate measure of damages is the reasonable cost of repairing it. The first plaintiffs' claim is based on the cost of repairing the building.

G The execution of the repairs will necessarily interfere with the second plaintiffs' business while the repairs are being carried out and the second plaintiffs' claim is for the expense and loss of profit which would be caused to them during the execution of the repairs.

I have two matters to decide: (1) the extent of the repair work for which the defendants are liable, and (2) the time at which the damages

H should be calculated by reference to the cost of doing the work.

The plaintiffs and the defendants are agreed that the defendants are liable for the cost of such repairs as are reasonable. They differ radically as to what repairs are reasonable. The plaintiffs, supported by their respectable and sincere expert witness, Mr. Moors, claim that they are entitled to restore the building so far as is physically possible to the exact state in which it was before the damage was done. The defendants contend that less extensive repairs—those recommended by their experts,

440

Mr. Knight and Mr. Marshall—will reasonably and properly compensate A
the plaintiffs for the damage. Happily for me, the respective calculations
in money on the basis of adopting what I will call Mr. Moors's proposal
and Mr. Knight's proposal became substantially agreed in the course of
the hearing. The main differences between the two proposals are these.

Mr. Moors proposes to take off and subsequently reconstruct the
roof, to straighten the vertical steel columns to a plumb position and to B
refix the roof trusses so that they are on a level line as originally
constructed. He also proposes a more extensive inspection of the foundations than Mr. Knight and Mr. Marshall, the defendants' structural
engineer, consider necessary or reasonable. Mr. Knight and Mr. Marshall
also consider that the distortion of the steel framework is too slight to
justify the correction which Mr. Moors proposes and that it is unnecessary
to remove the roof. So far as the roof is concerned, their proposal C
is not to remove it but to regrade it so as at least to restore it to its
former slope.

Quite extensive work is proposed and it is as follows, from the evidence
of Mr. Marshall. The present felt and insulation board will be left in
place after inspecting it for any defects. On top of the present felt there
will be a sheet of polystyrene of appropriate thickness. Bonded to this D
there will be a single layer of thin-grade felt. On top of this there will
be insulation boards 13 mm. thick. On top of that there will be three
layers of bituminous roofing felt and, finally, chippings.

Mr. Marshall says that the life of this would be much the same as
that of the original roof and the roof as reconstructed in accordance with
his proposals would be as good as before, or, indeed better. I accept
his opinion. I have already mentioned that the distortion of the frame- E
work is of a degree which is discoverable by expert measurement but
not by ordinary observation. Mr. Marshall went so far as to say that
he doubted whether even a surveyor inspecting the building for a
prospective purchaser would notice it. What is more important is
whether the strength of the building has been significantly diminished
by the distortion of the steel framework.
                                                                          F
It seems to me that in the end there was no real dispute about
that matter. The plaintiffs' structural engineer, Mr. Wootton, made a
calculation which is set out in his report of September 19, 1970. He
calculated that there was a loss of some 5 per cent. of the factor of safety,
but, in cross-examination, he conceded that there was no reason to
suppose that the factor of safety had thereby been rendered inadequate.

I accept Mr. Marshall's opinion that, so far as safety is concerned, G
there is no need to do anything to the steel framework and that the
defendants' operations have not significantly diminished the strength of
the building. I also accept Mr. Marshall's opinion that a prospective
purchaser, scrupulously informed of the degree of distortion of the
framework, would not be put off if, as would be likely in a transaction
of that size, he took expert advice as to whether the structure was H
satisfactory.

A point was made on behalf of the plaintiffs that the distortion of
the framework would prevent the building owner from carrying out a
project to put a first floor in the building, a project for which planning
permission, long since expired, was obtained in 1963. I am not satisfied
as a matter of probability that the present plaintiffs will ever proceed
with this project. Mr. Moors told me that in 1966 the cost of carrying

The Weekly Law Reports, May 2, 1980

441

1 W.L.R.   Dodd Properties v. Canterbury City Council (Q.B.D.)   Cantley J.

A   it out would have been £35,000 to £40,000, and Mr. Willis, a chartered quantity surveyor called by the plaintiffs, told me that building prices have increased by about 100 per cent. since 1973. Building prices were increasing, though at a less startling rate, before 1973, and it would seem that the cost now would be in the region of £100,000. The plaintiffs have never been disposed to spend that sort of money even if they could find it without crippling themselves with debt.

B   In any event, I am satisfied, on the evidence of Mr. Knight and Mr. Marshall, that, if the building is dealt with in accordance with their proposals, it is as capable of taking the extra floor satisfactorily as it was before it was damaged. They expressed no opinion as to whether it will take the extra floor satisfactorily, because that is a matter on which no calculations have been made by them. But, so far as the

C existing building is concerned, it is as fit for it as it was before. It is true that, owing to the slight slope of the roof trusses, 1: 300, there would probably have to be a corresponding slight adjustment in the construction of the floor and of the walls of the new first floor, but this would not present any real difficulty for the builder or spoil the appearance or utility of the new first floor when constructed.

D   So far as the proposed investigation of the foundations is concerned, I accept the view of Mr. Knight and Mr. Marshall that no further investigation or work on the foundations is called for. Nothing has gone wrong since 1968.

  There was a great difference between the cost of Mr. Moors's proposals and Mr. Knight's. To carry out the work recommended by Mr. Moors would cost about twice as much as that recommended by

E Mr. Knight, and both are big figures. Today, it would cost about £30,000 to carry out Mr. Knight's scheme and over £70,000 to carry out Mr. Moors's scheme. Moreover, the work in carrying out Mr. Moors's scheme would take three times as long as the work in carrying out Mr. Knight's scheme. There would be correspondingly longer dislocation of the second plaintiffs' business.

F   As Lord Loreburn L.C. said in *Lodge Holes Colliery Co. Ltd.* v. *Wednesbury Corporation* [1908] A.C. 323, 326: " Even those who have been wronged must act reasonably, however wide the latitude of discretion that is allowed to them within the bounds of reason." The plaintiffs are entitled to the reasonable cost of doing reasonable work of restoration and repair. They are, of course, not bound to accept a shoddy job or put up with an inferior building for the sake of saving expense to the

G defendants. But I do not consider that they are entitled to insist on complete and meticulous restoration when a reasonable building owner would be content with less extensive work which produces a result which does not diminish to any, or any significant, extent the appearance, life or utility of the building and when there is also a vast difference in the cost of such work and the cost of meticulous restoration.

H   In my judgment, the cost of the repairs to the building must be assessed on the basis of the work proposed by Mr. Knight and Mr. Marshall.

  I have next to consider at what time this cost has to be ascertained. It is now no less than 10 years since the damage occurred and nothing has yet been done to put it right. There are various reasons. One which has not been emphasised by the plaintiffs is that there has been no further deterioration of the building since 1968 and the second plaintiffs have

been able to carry on business there as usual all the time. Another is A
that, although the plaintiffs understandably do not accept that they ought
to be described as impecunious, they have been very short of ready cash.

Mr. Smith, the director of each of the plaintiff companies, also told
me that if money had been no problem he would not have spent it on
repairing the building before he was sure of recovering the cost from the
defendants. The building is still watertight and it would not, in his view—
and he is a chartered accountant—have made commercial sense to spend B
this amount of money on a property which would not produce any
corresponding additional income. So long as the defendants' liability
was in dispute, or even if the only dispute had been as to the amount of
compensation, he would not have done any repairs except such as might
have been necessary to make the building weatherproof and to keep it in
working order. C

In case it ever becomes necessary hereafter for me to have to make
a finding as to the plaintiffs' financial position, I will do so. On Mr.
Smith's evidence, I find that the only way in which the first plaintiffs
could have found the cash for repairs was by borrowing on second or
third mortgages on their various properties. They had sufficient remaining equities in those properties to secure such mortgages, but it might D
have been difficult to find a lender and interest rates would have been
about 3½ per cent. over the current bank rate.

The first plaintiffs have been running at a substantial annual loss
from 1967 to 1973. The second plaintiffs are not impecunious, but they
have been trading on a bank overdraft for some years; they have made
profits and have improved their cash position as the years have gone by.
They have assets. E

I find that the first plaintiffs could probably have raised the money
for repairs but that this would have increased their annual losses and
their financial stringency. As a commercial decision, judged exclusively
from the point of view of the immediate and short-term welfare of the
companies, it was reasonable to postpone incurring the very considerable
expense of these repairs while no harm was being done to the building by F
the delay in repairing it and while these three rich defendants with
apparent if not genuine belief in the validity of their defences were
firmly denying liability to make even a contribution.

The effect of the delay has however been startling. Inflation has been
continuing ever since 1968, but it accelerated strikingly from 1973
onwards. The cost of doing the work on the basis that I have accepted
was £10,817 in 1968. In 1970, it was over £11,000. In 1978, it is £30,327. G

Mr. Titheridge has boldly argued that the plaintiffs are entitled to
have their damages assessed at the time of hearing as in the case of a
personal injuries action, subject only to its being proved against them
that they failed to act reasonably to mitigate their loss. He relies on
the dictum of Lord Collins in *Clippens Oil Co. Ltd.* v. *Edinburgh and
District Water Trustees* [1907] A.C. 291, 303: H

" It was contended that this implied that the defenders were entitled
to measure the damages on the footing that it was the duty of the
company to do all that was reasonably possible to mitigate the loss,
and that if, through lack of funds, they were unable to incur the
necessary expense of such remedial measures the defenders ought
not to suffer for it. If this were the true construction to put upon
the passage cited, I think there would be force in the observation,

The Weekly Law Reports, May 2, 1980

443

1 W.L.R.   Dodd Properties v. Canterbury City Council (Q.B.D.)   Cantley J.

A   for in my opinion the wrongdoer must take his victim talem qualem, and if the position of the latter is aggravated because he is without the means of mitigating it, so much the worse for the wrongdoer, who has got to be answerable for the consequences flowing from his tortious act."

That dictum was referred to with approval and not, as the headnote B suggests, with disapproval in the well known case of *The Liesbosch* [1933] A.C. 449. Of Lord Collins's dictum, Lord Wright said, at p. 461:

"But, as I think it is clear that Lord Collins is here dealing not with measure of damage, but with the victim's duty to minimize damage, which is quite a different matter, the dictum is not in point."

If it is not impertinent to say that I agree with Lord Wright, then I will C do so.

This principle enunciated by Lord Collins applies when one is considering the duty to mitigate the damage. However, one must first ascertain the measure of damage before considering whether the victim has unreasonably failed to minimise that damage. In the case of destruction of a chattel, the normal measure of the damage is its market value D at the time of the loss. That was the measure of damage applied in *The Liesbosch.* I do not suppose that it would have made any difference in that case if the unfortunate owners of that elderly dredger had done nothing to replace it for 10 years except to go on trying to save up enough money to buy another similar dredger and had then claimed the current cost of one on a risen market. They would, I suppose, have recovered the market value at the time of loss. If they also were given E interest on the money that they ought to have received 10 years before, that might have bought them another similar dredger. As Mr. Titheridge has pointed out, it is when the rate of inflation exceeds the rate of interest that it becomes important to have your damages assessed at the date of hearing.

A similar rule as to the measure of damage applies where chattels are F damaged as opposed to destroyed and it is reasonable to deal with the damage by way of repair.

Philips v. *Ward* [1956] 1 W.L.R. 471 was an action for damages against a surveyor who had made a negligent report about the condition of a house which was bought by the plaintiff on his advice. The measure of damages claimed for the plaintiff in that action was the cost of repairing the house at prices ruling at the date of hearing. In the event, G the plaintiff was not awarded damages on that basis but on the basis of the difference between the value of the house in its actual condition when he had bought it and the price that he had then paid for it. But the court made some observations on the claim for the cost of repairs which I find of assistance. Denning L.J. said, at p. 474:

"Another point arose about the time at which the damages should H be assessed. The cost of repair has risen considerably since the house was bought, and it will cost Mr. Philips a good deal more than £7,000 now to put his house right. The £7,000 is based on 1952 costs, not 1956 costs . . . I think that it is right to assess the damages as at 1952 prices. The general principle of English law is that damages must be assessed as at the date when the damage occurs, which is usually the same day as the cause of action arises, but may be later: see *Cummings* v. *London Bullion Co. Ltd.* [1952]

1 K.B. 327. A fall thereafter in the value of money does not in A
law affect the figure, for the simple reason that sterling is taken
to be constant in value: see *Di Ferdinando* v. *Simon, Smits & Co.
Ltd.* [1920] 3 K.B. 409 . . . *S.S. Celia (Owners)* v. *S.S. Volturno
(Owners) (The Volturno)* [1921] 2 A.C. 544 . . . *Bishop* v. *Cunard
White Star Co. Ltd.* [1950] P. 240 . . . In the case of continuing
damage (as in personal injury cases) the award for permanent disability can and usually does take into account the fall in the value B
of money since the accident; but that is because much of the damage
has accrued and will accrue since that date."

Denning L.J. was there not only stating the general principle but pointing
out the reason why it is not followed as a rule in cases where the plaintiff
is claiming damages for personal injury.

In the same case, Romer L.J. said at the end of his judgment, C
referring to the plaintiff's claim for the cost of repairs, at p. 478:

". . . I would only add that even if I had been able to accept the
principle on which it was based, I can see no warrant for the plaintiff's submission that the sum should be increased so as to reflect the
diminution in the value of the pound since 1952."

Denning L.J.'s dictum in *Philips* v. *Ward* was followed and applied by D
Lawton J. in *Clark* v. *Woor* [1965] 1 W.L.R. 650. This was an action for
damages for breach of a building contract where the measure of damages
applied was the cost of repairs. The cost of repairs had greatly increased
between the time when the plaintiff had first discovered the cause of
action and the date of trial four years later, but the damages were
assessed at the date when the plaintiff first discovered the cause of action. E

No authority has been cited to me, and in my very limited opportunity
lately I have discovered none for myself, where a court has considered
the time at which damages are to be assessed in the cases of buildings
damaged and put in need of repair by a tortious act. If there is no
authority on that precise point, it may be because no one has ever before
thought to contend that the general principle did not apply to it. The F
general principle is that damages must be assessed as at the date when
the damage occurs. In my view, that general principle applies here. It
is not, of course, to be rigidly applied as a rule of thumb, fixing the
time rigidly by the calendar and the clock. The damage may be
concealed by some fault of the wrongdoer or not reasonably discoverable
by the victim until some time after it has first appeared: see, for example,
East Ham Corporation v. *Bernard Sunley & Sons Ltd.* [1966] A.C. 406 G
and *Applegate* v. *Moss* [1971] 1 Q.B. 406.

Moreover, repairs cannot usually be put in hand at once and at prices
ruling at the very date of damage. There may have to be inspections
and specifications and tenders and an available contractor may have to
be found before the work can be started.

Furthermore, the nature and circumstances of the damage may be H
such that it would be imprudent and possibly wasteful to begin the work
before waiting longer to ensure that no further damage is going to develop
from the same cause. This is particularly true when the foundations of a
building have been disturbed by vibrations.

I would put it in this way. The appropriate damages are the cost of
repairs at the time when it was reasonable to begin repairs. Whether
the time is reasonable must be judged objectively and not taking into

The Weekly Law Reports, May 2, 1980

445

1 W.L.R.   Dodd Properties v. Canterbury City Council (Q.B.D.)   Cantley J.

A account such matters as impecuniosity or financial stringency which, in the words of Lord Wright in *The Liesbosch* [1933] A.C. 449, 460, 461, are extrinsic.

This seems to have been the view of Lord Upjohn in *East Ham Corporation* v. *Bernard Sunley & Sons Ltd.* [1966] A.C. 406 where he said, at p. 445:

B   " Where the cost of reinstatement is the proper measure of damages it necessarily follows as a matter of common sense that in the ordinary case the cost must be assessed at the time when the defect is discovered and put right, and it is not suggested here that the building owner unreasonably delayed the work of repair after discovery of the defect. So prima facie the damages ought to be assessed as the actual cost of repair in 1960 . . . "

C

In the present case, the damage was discovered in 1968 but the experts on both sides are agreed that it was reasonable not to begin repairs until 1970. Mr. Marshall, the defendants' civil engineer, said that if he had had reason to think that there had been a horizontal slip he would have advised the plaintiffs to wait a year or two. He went on to say that, in his view, there was reason to guard against that possibility in this case

D and that he thought that it was right to wait until September 1970. That was the reasonable stage at which the work should have been begun.

Accordingly, I adopt as the measure of damage the cost of repairs done in accordance with the recommendations of Mr. Knight and Mr. Marshall and cost it on the prices ruling in 1970. Bearing in mind, as I must do throughout this case, that these costings which go down to the

E nearest pound are in fact only estimates of work that has not even been started, I propose to take the rough and ready course of taking figures supplied by the plaintiffs and the defendants, £11,402 and £11,349 respectively, and dividing them by two and awarding the result, which comes to £11,375.

I next have to consider the claim of the second plaintiffs' loss to be caused by dislocation of their business during the execution of the works.

F The relevant works will be those recommended by Mr. Knight and Mr. Marshall, so that the period of disturbance is nine weeks.

There are two preliminary matters which I have to decide. First, Mr. Popplewell submits that it is fundamental to the second plaintiffs' claim that the work of repairs will be done, and he suggests that it is not at all certain that the works will be done. During part of Mr. Smith's

G evidence, I developed suspicions that perhaps the work would not be done and the first plaintiffs would be content to pocket the cost of repairs as awarded and the second plaintiffs delighted to pocket the estimated loss of profits on the conjectural repairs. After all, they have both got along very well for the last 10 years without doing anything. However, Mr. Smith, who I think was being careful to say no more than the truth and no more than he knew, said that in all probability the

H repairs will be done. I have been troubled about this, for, although the first plaintiffs are entitled to the reasonable costs of repairs to their building and can lawfully please themselves whether they do the repairs or accept the money and the diminution in the value of their unrepaired building, the second plaintiffs will not suffer any of the loss which they have claimed unless the repairs are done. Having regard to what Mr. Smith said, I think that the probability, which is all that is necessary in a civil case, is just about established for the benefit of both plaintiffs

although I would be more confident of the extent of the second plaintiffs'   A
loss if the first plaintiffs were recovering the present day cost of the
repairs so that they could, with a light heart, carry out the full repairs
recommended by Mr. Knight and Mr. Marshall.

Mr. Titheridge, on the other hand, says that, as the second plaintiffs
will suffer no loss until the first plaintiffs begin repairs, their loss must
at least be assessed at present day costs. He might, on the same basis,   B
ask for 1979 or 1980 prices having regard to the tempo up to date. It
is a profoundly unsatisfactory feature of the whole case that no repairs
whatever have been done and all those careful calculations of costs to
the nearest pound are no more than skilled estimates. It cannot be
right that the first plaintiffs, by postponing the repairs till 1979 or 1984,
can increase the second plaintiffs' damages, and I am not going to allow
it. I know, as Mr. Titheridge reminded me, that each of the plaintiffs   C
is a separate independent entity, but it would be unrealistic to ignore
the very close community between them to which I have already referred.
In this action they have joined together to claim separate heads of
damage resulting from the same wrong. The basis of the second plaintiffs' claim is that they are and were the occupiers of the building. They
are the natural and primary plaintiffs in so far as this is an action for
nuisance. Their cause of action arose in 1968, and their present claim   D
is one selected aspect of it. I have not seen the lease, and no party in
this action has relied on any of its terms, but I have learned in the course
of the evidence that the second plaintiffs had a 20-year lease which had
10 years to run at the date when the damage was discovered and that
they had been promised a new lease for 15 years. Up to the present, it
is they who have suffered any inconvenience or loss of amenity due to   E
the damage to the building which they occupy. Under their lease I am
informed that they are obliged to keep the building in tenantable repair.
I have not been informed of any specific exception to that obligation. It
seems to me they could have claimed for the cost of repairing the building in their own right or joined with the first plaintiffs in that claim.

In my view, their present claim must be founded on the assumption   F
that they were entitled to be compensated for dislocation of their business
by repairs done within a reasonable time of the accrual of the cause of
action on which their claim is founded, namely, 1968. For the reasons
already stated, I consider that the reasonable time had arrived in 1970,
and that is the time by reference to which I shall assess their loss. They
cannot attribute to the defendants the loss due to the fall in the value of
money since 1970. [Cantley J. awarded the second plaintiffs damages of   G
£4,108. He further awarded the plaintiffs interest at the short term
investment account rate from the date of service of the writ, in sums
agreed at £5,504·20 and £1,987 respectively, making total awards of
£16,879·20 and £6,095 respectively.]

Order accordingly.

H

Solicitors: *Lewis & Dick; Ponsford & Devenish, Tivendale & Munday;
Hewitt, Woollacott & Chown.*

The plaintiffs appealed, contending that the defendants should be
ordered to pay them damages of £30,327 and £11,951 respectively, alternatively, that they should be ordered to pay them interest on the
respective sums of damages at a commercial rate from the date at which

The Weekly Law Reports, May 2, 1980

447

1 W.L.R.   Dodd Properties v. Canterbury City Council (Q.B.D.)

A the damage was assessed, namely, from 1970, on the grounds that Cantley J. had been wrong in law in that, having found as a fact that the plaintiffs and each of them had acted reasonably in not repairing the premises before the date of the hearing, he had held that the first plaintiffs were entitled to damages reflecting only the cost of repairs in 1970 (the earliest date at which repairs could have been carried out) and not the cost of repairs at the time of the hearing (1978) and that the second plaintiffs were entitled to damages reflecting only the loss of profits that they would have suffered if the repairs had been carried out in 1970 as opposed to the loss of profits calculated at 1978 figures; that he had been wrong in law in holding that the general principle for the assessment of damages was that damages must be assessed at the date when the damage occurred; alternatively, if he had not been wrong in the above

C respects, that he had been wrong in law and/or in the exercise of his discretion in ordering that (a) the defendants pay interest only from the date of service of the writ and not from the date at which the damage was assessed; (b) the rate of interest to be paid by the defendants be that of the short term investment account instead of at a commercial rate which was applicable in a case of this type.

D The defendants cross-appealed, seeking an order that judgment might be entered for the plaintiffs in such lesser sum than that awarded by Cantley J., if any, as the court might hold just and proper, on the ground that Cantley J. had been wrong in law in that, having held that it was only just a probability that the second plaintiffs would lose profits of £4,108 or any profits due to the matters complained of and that they might not lose any profits at all on that account, he had held that they

E were entitled to recover such profits in full instead of holding that they were only entitled to recover a lesser sum, if any, to allow for the contingency of the profits not being lost at all due to the matters complained of if the repairs had not been carried out.

Roger Titheridge Q.C. and *Michael McMullan* for the plaintiffs.
F *Oliver Popplewell Q.C., Stephen Desch* and *Antony Edwards-Stuart* for the second and third defendants.

Cur. adv. vult.

December 21, 1979. The following judgments were read.

MEGAW L.J. This is an appeal from a judgment of Cantley J.
G The first plaintiffs, Dodd Properties (Kent) Ltd., are the owners of a building in Rose Lane, Canterbury, known as Marlowe Garage. The second plaintiffs, Marlowe Garage (Canterbury) Ltd., have been the occupiers of Marlowe Garage as lessees of the first plaintiffs. They carry on their business there as motor car dealers and they sell petrol, oil and accessories.

In 1968 the first defendants, the mayor, aldermen and citizens of the
H city of Canterbury, erected a large multi-storey car park close to Marlowe Garage. The second defendants, Truscon Ltd., were the main contractors; the third defendants, Frankipile Ltd., were their subcontractors for the foundations of the car park. As a result of their operations, damage was caused to the plaintiffs' building. Liability was for long denied, but shortly before the action came on for hearing before Cantley J. in 1978 liability was admitted in nuisance by the second and third defendants, though the extent of the damage was in issue and also the

Megaw L.J.   **Dodd Properties v. Canterbury City Council (C.A.)**   **[1980]**

basis of assessment of the amount of the damages to which the plaintiffs A
were entitled. The first defendants did not formally admit liability, but
they took no part in the proceedings, having received an undertaking
of indemnity from the other defendants.

Cantley J. held that the first defendants also were liable. They are not
parties to the appeal. There is no dispute as to liability. The issues are
as to damages.

No question of fact is now in dispute; Cantley J.'s findings of fact B
are accepted as to the extent of the physical damage and as to other
matters.

On the question of the extent of the damage, Cantley J. to a large
degree accepted the evidence of the defendants' experts. On their
evidence, the necessary repairs would, at the prices prevailing at the time
of the hearing in 1978, cost about £30,000. On the evidence of the C
plaintiffs' expert, the repairs required were much greater and the cost
much higher.

The question which remained, and which is the primary issue before
us, is this: by reference to which of two dates is the cost of the repairs
to be ascertained, for purposes of arriving at the amount of the defendants' liability for their tort? The plaintiffs say that the relevant date D
for this purpose is the date of the hearing, or of the judgment: that
is, that the 1978 prices are relevant and decisive. The defendants say
that the relevant date is 1970 and the relevant prices are the 1970 prices.
As a result of inflation, the difference between the computations at those
respective dates is very large. The 1978 figure, for the repairs which
Cantley J. held to be required, is £30,327. The 1970 figure, for the
same work, is approximately £11,375. E

The second plaintiffs also have a claim. It gives rise to the same
issue as to the proper date of assessment. The second plaintiffs' claim
arises out of prospective interruption of their business during the time
that would be required for the carrying out of the appropriate repairs,
if and when that work is done. The figure, if the repairs were to be
carried out in 1978, would be £11,951. In 1970 the corresponding amount F
would have been £4,108.

Taking the first and second plaintiffs' potential entitlements together,
the sums payable by the defendants as damages (apart from any question
of interest) would be: on the 1970 assessment, £15,483; on the 1978
assessment, £42,278.

Cantley J. held that in law, in the circumstances, judgment had to
be given on the 1970 basis. He also awarded interest, making the total G
payable by the defendants to the first and second plaintiffs £22,974·20.

Against that judgment, the plaintiffs appeal and the defendants cross-
appeal. The plaintiffs say that Cantley J. was wrong in law to make his
assessment of damages on the basis of the cost of the repairs in 1970.
They say that he should have taken the 1978 computation. They say,
in the alternative, that, if they should be wrong on this, which is their H
first and main contention, then he ought to have awarded interest from
an earlier date and at a higher rate. The accept that, if they are right
on their first contention—that is, the acceptance of 1978 as the date by
reference to which the cost of the repairs is to be assessed—then they
could not claim interest.

The defendants' cross-appeal raises an issue affecting the damages
of the second plaintiffs only. The defendants say that, since Cantley J.

The Weekly Law Reports, May 2, 1980

449

1 W.L.R.   Dodd Properties v. Canterbury City Council (C.A.)   Megaw L.J.

A held that it was only " just about established " that it was probable that the repairs would in fact be carried out after his judgment, he ought not to have awarded to the second plaintiffs the full amount of the prospective loss to them arising from the interruption of their business which would be caused by those potential repairs. He, say the defendants, should have awarded the second plaintiffs only, say, 60 per cent. of the total prospective loss by interruption, because the chance that the loss

B would in fact occur was no greater than a chance of that order.

On the first, and main, issue raised by the plaintiffs, it is necessary to see what Cantley J. found were the reasons why the repairs for this damage to Marlowe Garage, caused in 1968, had still not been carried out when the action was heard in 1978. Because I think it is important to see precisely what Cantley J. held in this respect, I shall quote his own

C words, ante, p. 442e–f:

> " I find that the first plaintiffs could probably have raised the money for repairs but this would have increased their annual losses and their financial stringency. As a commercial decision, judged exclusively from the point of view of the immediate and short-term welfare of the companies, it was reasonable to postpone incurring
> D the very considerable expense of these repairs while no harm was being done to the building by the delay in repairing it and while these three rich defendants with apparent if not genuine belief in the validity of their defences were firmly denying liability to make even a contribution."

Cantley J. then referred to the well known, much discussed, case,
E *The Liesbosch* [1933] A.C. 449. He said, ante, p. 443c: " In the case of destruction of a chattel, the normal measure of the damage is the market value at the time of the loss. That was the measure of damage applied in *The Liesbosch.*" He then cited from the judgment of Denning L.J. in *Philips* v. *Ward* [1956] 1 W.L.R. 471, 474:

> " The general principle of English law is that damages must be assessed as at the date when the damage occurs, which is usually the
> F same day as the cause of action arises, . . . A fall thereafter in the value of money does not in law affect the figure, for the simple reason that sterling is taken to be constant in value: . . ."

Although this may not affect the statement of " the general principle," I think that the reasoning as to sterling having to be taken to be constant in value is unfortunately no longer good law, having regard to the facts
G of life and the recent authoritative decisions, including *Miliangos* v. *George Frank (Textiles) Ltd.* [1976] A.C. 443.

Cantley J. then said:

> " No authority has been cited to me, and in my very limited opportunity lately I have discovered none for myself, where a court has considered the time at which damages are to be assessed in
> H the cases of buildings damaged and put in need of repair by a tortious act. If there is no authority on that precise point, it may be because no one has ever before thought to contend that the general principle did not apply to it. The general principle is that damages must be assessed as at the date when the damage occurs. In my view, that general principle applies here. It is not, of course, to be rigidly applied as a rule of thumb, fixing the time rigidly by the calendar and the clock. The damage may be concealed by some

fault of the wrongdoer or not reasonably discoverable by the victim   A
until some time after it has first appeared: see, for example, *East
Ham Corporation* v. *Bernard Sunley & Sons Ltd.* [1966] A.C. 406 and
Applegate v. *Moss* [1971] 1 Q.B. 406. Moreover, repairs cannot
usually be put in hand at once and at prices ruling at the very date of
damage. There may have to be inspections and specifications and
tenders and an available contractor may have to be found before the
work can be started. Furthermore, the nature and circumstances of   B
the damage may be such that it would be imprudent and possibly
wasteful to begin the work before waiting longer to ensure that no
further damage is going to develop from the same cause. This is
particularly true when the foundations of a building have been
disturbed by vibrations. I would put it in this way. The appropriate
damages are the cost of repairs at the time when it was reasonable to   C
begin repairs. Whether the time is reasonable must be judged
objectively and not taking into account such matters as impecuniosity
or financial stringency which, in the words of Lord Wright in *The
Liesbosch* [1933] A.C. 449, 460, 461, are extrinsic."

He then held that it had been reasonable for the plaintiffs not to begin
repairs until 1970 even though the damage had all occurred, and had   D
been known, in 1968. On that basis he adopted " as the measure of
damage the cost of repairs . . . on the prices ruling in 1970 "; that is,
£11,375.

There is no dispute in this case but that the appropriate measure of
damages on this claim of the first plaintiffs is by reference to the cost of
the repairs required.

The defendants do not challenge Cantley J.'s acceptance of the 1970   E
figures. That means that they do not now contend that he should
have taken the lower prices for the repair work prevailing in 1968 when
the tort was committed.

It is important to bear in mind that we are not concerned with any
suggestion that the plaintiffs were under a duty towards the defendants
to repair the premises damaged by the defendants' wrongdoing. The   F
plaintiffs did not lose their right to recover damages from the defendants
because they did not effect the repairs. True, in certain circumstances
with which we are not concerned here, such as the building being
destroyed by fire before the repairs had been carried out, the amount of
the plaintiffs' entitlement to damages might have become nil. But what we
are concerned with here is: by reference to what date is the amount of
the recoverable loss to be calculated, during a period when the cost of   G
the necessary work is rising as time goes on? Since the defendants do
not suggest that Cantley J. was wrong in taking the 1970 prices instead
of the 1968 prices, it is accepted, and I think necessarily and rightly
accepted, by the defendants that there are circumstances in which the
proper amount of damages, where, as here, the damages are to be
computed by reference to the cost of repairs, has to be computed by   H
reference to that cost at a date later than the date of the wrongdoing
which caused the damage.

The general principle, referred to in many authorities, has recently
been recognised by Lord Wilberforce in *Miliangos* v. *George Frank
(Textiles) Ltd.* [1976] A.C. 443, 468, namely, that " . . . as a general
rule in English law damages for tort or for breach of contract are
assessed as at the date of the breach . . . " But in the very passage in

The Weekly Law Reports, May 2, 1980

451

1 W.L.R.   Dodd Properties v. Canterbury City Council (C.A.)   Megaw L.J.

A   which this " general rule " is there stated, it is stressed that it is not a universal rule. That it is subject to many exceptions and qualifications is clear. Cantley J. in the present case rightly recognised that that was so, in the passage from his judgment which I have recently read.

Indeed, where, as in the present case, there is serious structural damage to a building, it would be patently absurd, and contrary to the general principle on which damages fall to be assessed, that a plaintiff,
B   in a time of rising prices, should be limited to recovery on the basis of the prices of repair at the time of the wrongdoing, on the facts here being two years, at least, before the time when, acting with all reasonable speed, he could first have been able to put the repairs in hand. Once that is accepted, as it must be, little of practical reality remains in postulating that, in a tort such as this, the " general rule " is applicable.
C   The damages are not required by English law to be assessed as at the date of breach.

The true rule is that, where there is a material difference between the cost of repair at the date of the wrongful act and the cost of repair when the repairs can, having regard to all relevant circumstances, first reasonably be undertaken, it is the latter time by reference to which the cost of repair is to be taken in assessing damages. That rule conforms
D   with the broad and fundamental principle as to damages, as stated in Lord Blackburn's speech in *Livingstone* v. *Rawyards Coal Co.* (1880) 5 App.Cas. 25, 39, where he said that the measure of damages is

"... that sum of money which will put the party who has been injured, or who has suffered, in the same position as he would have been in if he had not sustained the wrong for which he is now
E   getting his compensation or reparation."

In any case of doubt, it is desirable that the judge, having decided provisionally as to the amount of damages, should, before finally deciding, consider whether the amount conforms with the requirement of Lord Blackburn's fundamental principle. If it appears not to conform, the judge should examine the question again to see whether the particular
F   case falls within one of the exceptions of which Lord Blackburn gave examples, or whether he is obliged by some binding authority to arrive at a result which is inconsistent with the fundamental principle. I propose to carry out that exercise later in this judgment.

Cantley J. has held, in a passage which I have already read, that as a commercial decision, judged exclusively from the plaintiffs' point of
G   view, it was reasonable to postpone incurring expense of the repairs up to—for so I understand what Cantley J. says—the time when the action had been heard and liability decided, resulting in a judgment which, when complied with, would have put the plaintiffs in funds. The reasons why that deferment of repairs was reasonable from the plaintiffs' point of view included the fact, not that they were " impecunious," meaning poverty-stricken or unable to raise the necessary money, but that the
H   provision of the money for repairs would have involved for them a measure of " financial stringency." Other reasons, consistent with commercial good sense, why the repairs should have been deferred include those mentioned in evidence by a director of the plaintiff companies, whose evidence was accepted by Cantley J. as truthful and reliable. If there had been no money problem, he said, he would still not have spent money on the building before he was sure of recovering the cost from the defendants. It would not have made commercial sense to spend this

money on a property which would not produce corresponding additional A income. So long as there was a dispute, either as to liability or as to the amount of compensation, he would have done no more than to keep the building weatherproof and " in working order."

If that was, as Cantley J. held, reasonable from the point of view of the plaintiffs as being grounds for deferring the carrying out of repairs, and if the time at which the cost of the repairs falls to be computed in order to ascertain the amount of damages is the time when B it has become reasonable to do the repairs, why did Cantley J. reject 1978, for which the plaintiffs contended, and accept 1970 for which the defendants contended?

There are, as I see it, two possible answers to that question. The first answer is that what is reasonable has to be looked at from the point of view of both parties and a balance struck. Cantley J.'s finding C of reasonableness of the deferment from the point of view of the plaintiffs does not, therefore, conclude the matter. But I do not think that that was the answer intended to be given by Cantley J. He nowhere refers to the question in any such form and there is no indication of any attempt by him to strike a balance. If a balance had to be struck, surely it would be right, even in a climate of indulgence to contract-breakers or D tortfeasors, that the scales should move heavily in the favour of the innocent party as against the wrongdoer, in any comparison of respective disadvantages or unfairnesses? It has to be borne in mind that these were defendants who were wrongly maintaining a denial of any liability and thereby leaving the plaintiffs faced with all the potentially heavy expenditure of money required for the mere purpose of establishing by litigation what we now know to have been their rights. Moreover, as the E plaintiffs concede, they could not claim interest on the amount of their compensation starting to run before the date when the money was expended on repairs. So the defendants, being liable, as we now know, to recompense the plaintiffs for the tort which the defendants committed in 1968, will have enjoyed the free use for their own account of the money which would have been the appropriate compensation at that date, with the opportunity of earning compound interest thereon, from F 1968 until the date of judgment. If that were the ground on which Cantley J. held in favour of the defendants on this issue, I would respectfully hold that it was a wrong ground. But I do not think that he did so hold.

The second possible answer is that which I believe to have influenced Cantley J. He thought that the decision in *The Liesbosch* [1933] A.C. 449 G precluded him from taking into account, in considering the reasonableness of the deferment of repairs, any part of the deferment which was caused by " financial stringency."

The Liesbosch has been the subject of much debate and much speculation, and a considerable measure of disagreement, as to its ratio decidendi and the scope of its application, particularly in the light of later House of H Lords decisions: see, for example, the discussion of the case by the learned author of the article on " Damages " in *Halsbury's Laws of England*, 4th ed., vol. 12 (1975), para. 1144, footnote 4. I agree with the analysis of *The Liesbosch* and the comments thereon in the judgment which Donaldson L.J. will deliver hereafter. I do not think that, on any fair view of the ratio decidendi of *The Liesbosch,* it applies to the issue with which we are concerned. Amongst other reasons, there are these

The Weekly Law Reports, May 2, 1980

453

1 W.L.R.   Dodd Properties v. Canterbury City Council (C.A.)   Megaw L.J.

A two. First, it was not " financial stringency," let alone " impecuniousness " as in *The Liesbosch*, which on any fair view, on Cantley J.'s findings, was *the* cause, or even, I think, an effective cause, of the decision to postpone repairs. The " financial stringency " which would have been created by carrying out the repairs was merely one factor among a number of factors which together produced the result that commercial good sense pointed towards deferment of the repairs. The second reason

B which I would mention is that, once it is accepted that the plaintiff was not in any breach of any duty owed by him to the defendant in failing to carry out repairs earlier than the time when it was reasonable for the repairs to be put in hand, this becomes, for all practical purposes, if not in theory, equated with a plaintiff's ordinary duty to mitigate his damages Lord Wright in his speech in *The Liesbosch,* at p. 461, accepted Lord

C Collins's dictum in *Clippens Oil Co. Ltd.* v. *Edinburgh and District Water Trustees* [1907] A.C. 291, 303:

> " . . . in my opinion the wrongdoer must take his victim talem qualem, and if the position of the latter is aggravated because he is without the means of mitigating it, so much the worse for the wrongdoer, . . ."

D I agree with the observations of Oliver J. in *Radford* v. *De Froberville* [1977] 1 W.L.R. 1262, 1268 as to the relationship between the duty to mitigate and the measure, or amount, of damages in relation to a question such as the question with which we are here concerned. A plaintiff who is under a duty to mitigate is not obliged, in order to reduce the damages, to do that which he cannot afford to do: particularly where, as here, the

E plaintiffs' " financial stringency," so far as it was relevant at all, arose, as a matter of common sense, if not as a matter of law, solely as a consequence of the defendants' wrongdoing.

My provisional answer to the question raised in the first issue would, thus, be that the damages in this case are to be assessed by reference to the 1978 cost of repairs. I now carry out that exercise which I mentioned earlier. Once it is accepted, as it is accepted by the parties,

F that the damages fall to be computed by reference to the cost of repairs to the building, and once *The Liesbosch* [1933] A.C. 449 and *Philips* v. *Ward* [1956] 1 W.L.R. 471 are out of the reckoning, there is no exception of which I am aware which is relevant here to exclude application of Lord Blackburn's fundamental principle. On the relevant facts as found by Cantley J., the 1978 cost of the repairs gives the answer which accords

G with that principle. The calculation of damages by reference to the 1970 cost of repairs would not so accord.

On that issue, I would allow the appeal.

The result is that the plaintiffs' alternative ground of appeal, as to the appropriate calculation of interest, does not arise. For it is a necessary part of their submission on the first issue that, damages being

H referable to the deferment of repairs, interest is not payable up to the date of the hearing. In the circumstances, I think it better to say nothing on that point, on which the argument on either side was commendably brief.

If I am right on my conclusion on the main issue in the appeal, I think that the cross-appeal, whatever its merits in law might otherwise have been, ceases to have validity. Early in this judgment, I summarised the issue raised by the cross-appeal. I need not repeat it. I find difficulty

in reconciling two passages in the judgment as to the probability of repairs A
being carried out. Cantley J., referring to the evidence of Mr. Smith
a director of the plaintiff companies, said, ante, p. 445G–H: " However,
Mr. Smith, who I think was being careful to say no more than the truth
and no more than he knew, said that in all probability the repairs will be
done." The acceptance of the truthfulness and the reliability of that evidence by the man who was in the best position to give the best evidence on
that question would appear to be conclusive. How then can Cantley J.'s B
acceptance of it be reconciled with what he says a few lines later:
" Having regard to what Mr. Smith said, I think the probability . . . is
just about established . . . "? If Mr. Smith was truthful and reliable in
saying " in all probability," that results in much more than probability
being " just about established."

However, fortunately, it is not necessary to resolve that difficulty, C
since Cantley J. went on to say: " . . . although I would be more confident
of the extent of the second plaintiffs' loss if the first plaintiffs were
recovering the present day costs of the repairs so that they could, with a
light heart, carry out the full repairs. . . ." As in my judgment the
plaintiffs are entitled to recover the 1978 cost of the repairs, this court
should not remit this Methuselah of an action for a further hearing by
Cantley J. on that issue. We should make our own assessment what the D
discount, if any, should be. In my opinion, the discount, if the law
requires any discount—I do not find it necessary to decide this—would be
de minimis. As the law requires us to disregard the trivial, I propose
to disregard it, as I think Cantley J. would have disregarded it, if he had
reached the same conclusion as I have reached on the main issue.

So I would allow the appeal, and direct that judgment be entered E
for the first plaintiffs for £30,327, without interest up to the date of
Cantley J.'s judgment, and for the second plaintiffs for £11,951, also
without interest up to that date. I would dismiss the cross-appeal.

BROWNE L.J. I agree that this appeal should be allowed and the
cross-appeal dismissed, for the reasons given by Megaw L.J. and the
reasons which will be given by Donaldson L.J. in the judgment he will F
deliver very soon. I can summarise my own reasons fairly shortly,
because they are in substance the same as theirs.

The first principle for the assessment of damages is that the injured
person should, so far as money can do it, be put in the same position as
if the wrong—in this case the tort—had not been committed against him:
see Halsbury's Laws of England, 4th ed., vol. 12, title " Damages," para.
1129, and—for example—the authority cited by Megaw L.J., Livingstone G
v. Rawyards Coal Co., 5 App.Cas. 25, per Lord Blackburn, at p. 39. This
the damages of £11,375 awarded to the first plaintiffs, for the cost of
repairs in 1970, glaringly fail to do. By the time of the hearing in 1978
the cost had risen to £30,327. In fact, the repairs had not been done
by that time, and the cost will probably have risen still further by the
time they are done, but the plaintiffs do not make any further claim H
beyond the cost at the date of the hearing.

It is not disputed that in this case the measure of the first plaintiffs'
damages is the cost of repair, as opposed to the other possible measure
in a case of this sort, i.e. the diminution in the value of the building.
The only question is the time as at which that cost shall be taken.

The general rule, both in contract and tort, is that damages should
be assessed as at the date when the cause of action arises, but they may

The Weekly Law Reports, May 2, 1980

455

1 W.L.R.   Dodd Properties v. Canterbury City Council (C.A.)   Browne L.J.

A be assessed as at some later date. In my view, Cantley J. was plainly
right in saying, ante, pp. 444H—445A: " The appropriate damages are the
cost of repairs at the time when it was reasonable to begin repairs." In
Johnson v. *Agnew* [1979] 2 W.L.R. 487 Lord Wilberforce said, at p. 499:

> " The general principle for the assessment of damages is com-
B   pensatory, i.e. that the innocent party is to be placed, so far as
>   money can do so, in the same position as if the contract had been
>   performed. Where the contract is one of sale, this principle normally
>   leads to assessment of damages as at the date of the breach—a
>   principle recognised and embodied in section 51 of the Sale of Goods
>   Act 1893. But this is not an absolute rule: if to follow it would
>   give rise to injustice, the court has power to fix such other date as
>   may be appropriate in the circumstances. In cases where a breach
C   of a contract for sale has occurred, and the innocent party reasonably
>   continues to try to have the contract completed, it would to me
>   appear more logical and just rather than tie him to the date of the
>   original breach, to assess damages at at the date when (otherwise
>   than by his default) the contract is lost. Support for this approach
>   is to be found in the cases. In *Ogle* v. *Earl Vane* (1867)
D   L.R. 2 Q.B. 275; (1868) L.R. 3 Q.B. 272 the date was fixed by
>   reference to the time when the innocent party, acting reasonably,
>   went into the market; in *Hickman* v. *Haynes* (1875) L.R. 10 C.P. 598
>   at a reasonable time after the last request of the defendants (buyers)
>   to withhold delivery. In *Radford* v. *De Froberville* [1977] 1 W.L.R.
>   1262, where the defendant had covenanted to build a wall, damages
>   were held measurable as at the date of the hearing rather than at
E   the date of the defendant's breach, unless the plaintiff ought reason-
>   ably to have mitigated the breach at an earlier date."

Lord Wilberforce, of course, was there speaking of damages for
breach of contract, but I have no doubt that the same principle applies
to this case, where it is common ground that the measure of damages is
the cost of repairs. I think this view is supported by analogy by the
F decision of the House of Lords in *West Midland Baptist (Trust) Association (Inc.)* v. *Birmingham Corporation* [1970] A.C. 874.

In this case, it was common ground, and Cantley J. accepted, that it
had been reasonable to postpone the doing of the repairs from 1968,
when damage had first been discovered, until 1970, and that 1970 was
the earliest date as at which the cost of repairs should be assessed. The
G defendants contended that the assessment should not be any further
postponed; Cantley J. accepted this contention, and assessed the damages
on the cost of repairs in 1970.

In the course of the passage in his judgment which Megaw L.J. has
already read, ante, pp. 442E–F, 449C–D, he held that:

> " As a commercial decision, judged exclusively from the point of
H   view of the immediate and short-term welfare of the companies, it
>   was reasonable to postpone incurring the very considerable expense
>   of these repairs . . . "

Like Megaw L.J., I understand this to mean that it was in this sense
reasonable to postpone doing the repairs until after the hearing. This
was based on the evidence of Mr. Smith, a director of both the plaintiff
companies and a chartered accountant, which is set out in Cantley J.'s
judgment and has been summarised already by Megaw L.J. Cantley J.

gave a number of reasons for the decision. Only one of what he said **A** were the relevant factors was financial, and I think that his finding on this point falls far short of " impecuniosity " or " financial embarrassment " in the *Liesbosch* sense.

Cantley J. said, ante, pp. 444E—445A:

" Whether the time is reasonable must be judged objectively and not taking into account such matters as impecuniosity or financial stringency **B** which, in the words of Lord Wright in *The Liesbosch* [1933] A.C. 449, 460, 461, are extrinsic."

I am afraid I do not clearly understand what Cantley J. meant by " objectively " in that sentence. If he meant that the decision to postpone, although reasonable from the point of view of the plaintiff companies, was not reasonable from the point of view of a hypothetical reasonable commercial man, I cannot agree; it seems to me that any commercial man in the **C** circumstances with which Mr. Smith was faced could reasonably, and probably would, have come to the same decision.

The judge relied on *Philips* v. *Ward* [1956] 1 W.L.R. 471 and *Clark* v. *Woor* [1965] 1 W.L.R. 650, in which Lawton J. simply followed and applied *Philips* v. *Ward.* I agree with Megaw L.J. that the reasoning of Lord Denning M.R. in *Philips* v. *Ward,* at p. 474, can no longer be **D** regarded as good law.

That leaves only *The Liesbosch* [1933] A.C. 449. I do not propose to analyse that difficult case, because I entirely agree with Megaw L.J. and Donaldson L.J. that, for the reasons they give, it did not compel Cantley J. to take the 1970 cost of repairs. I will only say that, like Megaw L.J., I agree with the observations of Oliver J. in *Radford* v. *De Froberville* **E** [1977] 1 W.L.R. 1262, 1272 as to the relationship between the duty to mitigate and the measure of damages in a case such as this.

I would, therefore, allow the first plaintiffs' appeal and vary the judgment by substituting £30,327 for £11,375. I think it necessarily follows that the appeal of the second plaintiffs should also be allowed, and their damages increased from £4,108 to £11,951.

The plaintiffs' alternative ground of appeal as to interest therefore **F** does not arise, and, like Megaw L.J., I think it better to say nothing on that point.

I agree that the cross-appeal should be dismissed, for the reasons given by Megaw L.J.

DONALDSON L.J. The general object underlying the rules for the **G** assessment of damages is, so far as is possible by means of a monetary award, to place the plaintiff in the position which he would have occupied if he had not suffered the wrong complained of, be that wrong a tort or a breach of contract. In the case of a tort causing damage to real property, this object is achieved by the application of one or other of two quite different measures of damage, or, occasionally, a combination of the two. The first is to take the capital value of the property in an **H** undamaged state and to compare it with its value in a damaged state. The second is to take the cost of repair or reinstatement. Which is appropriate will depend upon a number of factors, such as the plaintiff's future intentions as to the use of the property and the reasonableness of those intentions. If he reasonably intends to sell the property in its damaged state, clearly the diminution in capital value is the true measure of damage. If he reasonably intends to continue to occupy it and to

The Weekly Law Reports, May 16, 1980

457

1 W.L.R.   Dodd Properties v. Canterbury City Council (C.A.) Donaldson L.J.

A repair the damage, clearly the cost of repairs is the true measure. And there may be in-between situations.

Happily there is no issue in the present case as to which measure of damage falls to be applied. It is the cost of reinstatement. The primary issue is as to how and, more particularly, on what date those costs are to be assessed. This is a very significant issue in the light of the increase in costs over the period between the occurrence of the damage in
B 1968 and the trial in 1978.

Mr. Popplewell, for the defendants, submits, and I for my part would readily accept, that the general rule is that damages fall to be assessed as at the date when the cause of action arose. The rule is so stated by Lord Wilberforce in *Miliangos* v. *George Frank (Textiles) Ltd.* [1976] A.C. 443, 468. And I am inclined to think that in normal circumstances this would
C be applicable where the relevant measure of damage was diminution in the capital value of the property. But it is only a general or basic rule and is subject to many exceptions. Thus damages for personal injury, excluding consequential loss to which other principles apply, are assessed in the light of the value of money at the date of the hearing. The issue here is whether the assessment of damages based upon the cost of repair or reinstatement is another exception as Mr. Titheridge for the plaintiffs
D contends. I think that it is.

In *West Midland Baptist (Trust) Association (Inc.)* v. *Birmingham Corporation* [1970] A.C. 874, the House of Lords was faced with the problem of whether the reasonable cost of equivalent reinstatement, which was the basis of compensation under the Land Compensation Act 1961, involved taking costs which prevailed at the date of the notice to
E treat or those which prevailed at the earliest date when the claimants might reasonably have begun rebuilding. The decision was in favour of the latter. Lord Reid, at p. 894, cites with approval various statements on the measure of compensation which assume that the assessed cost of reinstatement would be sufficient to enable the owner to undertake the work if he acted reasonably. In an era of rising costs, this could only happen if compensation was assessed on the basis of costs applicable at
F the time at which reinstatement would in fact occur, on the assumption that the owner acted reasonably. Again Lord Morris of Borth-y-Gest said, at p. 903:

"The reasonable cost, depending upon the facts of particular cases, will be the actual reasonable cost which a claimant has incurred or can be expected to incur; it will be such cost at the time when
G equivalent reinstatement reasonably does or should take place."

Whilst this is not a decision on the measure of damages in tort, I think that the reasoning is directly applicable to the present problem. It is also only common sense, for, as Mr. Titheridge pointed out, it would be wholly unfair to the defendant to charge him with the costs applicable to reinstatement in 1968 when the damage occurred, if the actual
H reinstatement took place at a later date when improved technology had reduced the cost. That this happy situation has not in fact arisen does not affect the point of principle.

In the absence of special and extraneous factors, there is no divergence between the interest of a plaintiff and a defendant on the choice of the most propitious moment at which to effect reinstatement. Both wish to achieve the maximum economy, at least so long as the plaintiff is in doubt whether he will be entitled to a full indemnity from the defendant.

Donaldson L.J.   Dodd Properties v. Canterbury City Council (C.A.)   **[1980]**

It follows that, in a case in which a plaintiff has reinstated his property A before the hearing, the costs prevailing at the date of that operation which were reasonably incurred by him are prima facie those which are relevant. Equally in a case in which a plaintiff has *not* effected reinstatement by the time of the hearing, there is a prima facie presumption that the costs then prevailing are those which should be adopted in ascertaining the cost of reinstatement. There may indeed be cases in which the court has to estimate costs at some future time as being the reasonable B time at which to reinstate, but that is not this case.

This is, however, only a prima facie approach. It may appear on the evidence that the plaintiff, acting reasonably, should have undertaken the reinstatement at some date earlier than that in fact adopted or, as the case may be, earlier than the hearing. If so, the relevant costs are those ruling at that earlier date. Whether this is regarded as arising out of the C primary measure of damage, i.e. that the relevant time is when the property should have been reinstated, or whether it is regarded as being a reflection of a plaintiff's duty to mitigate his loss, may not matter.

In the present case Cantley J. accepted that the relevant date was when it was reasonable to begin repairs. However, in deciding what was reasonable, he considered himself bound by the decision of the House of Lords in *The Liesbosch* [1933] A.C. 449 to disregard such factors as D impecuniosity or financial stringency experienced by the plaintiffs. Accordingly, although he considered that the plaintiffs had acted reasonably in deferring reinstatement until after the hearing, he felt constrained to adopt September 1970 costs, the delay until then being justified exclusively on other grounds, namely, the need to make sure that no further damage would occur before repairs were started. Dealing with the E latter delay he said, ante, p. 442E–F.:

" I find that the first plaintiffs could probably have raised the money for repairs but this would have increased their annual losses and their financial stringency. As a commercial decision, judged exclusively from the point of view of the immediate and short-term welfare of the companies, it was reasonable to postpone incurring the very F considerable expense of these repairs while no harm was being done to the building by the delay in repairing it and while these three rich defendants with apparent if not genuine belief in the validity of their defences were firmly denying liability to make even a contribution."

Whatever the difficulties inherent in the *Liesbosch* decision—and it is not at once apparent why a tortfeasor must take his victim as he finds G him in terms of exceptionally high or low profit-earning capacity, but not in terms of pecuniosity or impecuniosity which may be their manifestation—it binds this court as much as it bound Cantley J. unless and until it is reviewed by the House of Lords. However, it is important to see precisely what it did decide.

The *Edison* fouled the *Liesbosch's* moorings, carried her out to sea and sank her. The ordinary measure of damage was the cost of buying H another similar vessel, the cost of getting her to the *Liesbosch's* old moorings and any loss of profit consequent upon the disruption of commercial operations whilst the substitute vessel was being obtained and delivered. However, the plaintiffs contended for a different and special measure of damage. Substitute dredgers were available for purchase but the plaintiffs could not afford to buy them. Instead they hired another dredger, the *Adria,* which was larger than the *Liesbosch*

The Weekly Law Reports, May 16, 1980

459

1 W.L.R.   Dodd Properties v. Canterbury City Council (C.A.)   Donaldson L.J.

A and more expensive to operate and for which they had to pay a very high rate of hire. Eventually the port authority, for whom the plaintiffs were working, bought the *Adria* and resold her to the plaintiffs under a credit sale contract. The plaintiffs claimed the cost of hiring the *Adria* until the port authority bought and resold her to them, the cost of purchasing the *Adria* and the excess cost of working her as compared with the *Liesbosch* together with unrecovered overhead charges and lost profit
B whilst they were without any dredger. The ordinary measure of damage is based upon market rates. The measure of damage claimed by the plaintiffs was quite different, namely, one based upon their actual loss and expenditure.

As I understand Lord Wright's speech, he took the view that, in so far as the plaintiffs had in fact suffered more than the loss assessed on a market
C basis, the excess loss flowed directly from their lack of means and not from the tortious act, or alternatively it was too remote in law. In modern terms, I think that he would have said that it was not foreseeable.

The position of the plaintiffs in the present case seems to me to be quite different. They were not impecunious in the *Liesbosch* sense of one who could not go out into the market. On the contrary, they were financially able to carry out the work of reinstatement in 1970. However,
D on Cantley J.'s findings, they were commercially prudent in not incurring the cash flow deficiency which would have resulted from their undertaking the work in the autumn of 1970 and waiting for reimbursement until after the hearing, particularly when the defendants were denying liability and there was a dispute as to what works could and should be done by way of reinstatement. In my judgment, the decision in *The Liesbosch* has no
E application to such a situation which is distinguishable.

If the decision whether to adopt 1970 or 1978 costs turns upon whether, bearing in mind the likelihood that prices would rise, the plaintiffs should have undertaken the work in 1970 in pursuance of their duty to mitigate their damage, there is another ground for distinguishing *The Liesbosch* [1933] A.C. 449 and for taking full account of the plaintiffs' financial position. This is that Lord Wright's explanation, at
F p. 461, of the decision in *Clippens Oil Co. Ltd.* v. *Edinburgh and District Water Trustees* [1907] A.C. 291, where Lord Collins, at p. 303, said that the tortfeasor must take his victim as he found him, including any lack of means, was that that decision represented the rule in relation to the duty to minimise damage.

I would therefore allow the appeal by the plaintiffs and, for the reasons
G stated by Megaw L.J., would dismiss the defendants' cross-appeal.

> *Appeal allowed. Judgment below*
> *varied by substituting as amount of*
> *damages, for first plaintiffs, £30,327,*
> *and, for second plaintiffs, £11,951.*
> *Cross-appeal dismissed.*
H *Plaintiffs to have full costs below and*
> *costs of appeal and cross-appeal.*
> *Leave to appeal refused.*

Solicitors: *Lewis & Dick; Hewitt, Woollacott & Chown.*

M. G.

A

* STEWART CHARTERING LTD. *v.* C. & O. MANAGEMENTS
S.A. AND ANOTHER

[1979 S. No. 3986]

PRACTICE NOTE

B

1979 Dec. 21   Robert Goff J.

*Practice—Judgment in default of appearance—Mareva injunction
—Claim for liquidated damages and Mareva injunction—
Mareva injunction granted—Application for leave to sign
judgment in default of appearance—Court's jurisdiction to
grant leave and continue Mareva injunction—R.S.C., Ord. 13,
r. 6* [1]

C

APPLICATION for leave to enter judgment in default of appearance.

By a specially indorsed writ dated August 22, 1979, the plaintiffs, Stewart
Chartering Ltd., claimed against the defendants, C. & O. Managements S.A.
of Greece and Palirima Shipping Co. Ltd. of Cyprus, £23,101·33 in respect of   D
services rendered, and an injunction to restrain the defendants from, inter
alia, removing from the jurisdiction any of their assets, save in so far as such
assets exceeded £32,500.

By orders of the same date, Judge Hawser, sitting as a commercial judge,
Queen's Bench Division, granted the injunction and gave leave to serve notice
of the writ on the defendants outside the jurisdiction.

The defendants failed to enter an appearance and on December 13, 1979,   E
the plaintiffs, notwithstanding that a claim for an injunction was not mentioned
in R.S.C., Ord. 13, rr. 1 to 4, applied ex parte in chambers to Robert Goff J.
for leave to enter judgment in default of appearance.

No cases are referred to in the judgment or were cited in argument.

Jonathan Hirst for the plaintiffs.

F

ROBERT GOFF J. read the following judgment in open court.   There is
before the court an ex parte application for leave to sign judgment in default
of appearance in an action for a liquidated sum brought against the defendants outside the jurisdiction who have been properly served with proceedings
pursuant to leave granted under R.S.C., Ord. 11.   In the ordinary course, no
appearance having been entered, judgment could be entered for the sum   G
claimed without leave of the court; but the matter is complicated by the fact
that, in order to obtain a Mareva injunction, the writ is indorsed in addition
with a claim for an injunction.   In such circumstances, having regard to the
provisions of R.S.C., Ord. 13, r. 6, it is not possible for the plaintiffs simply to
enter judgment in default of appearance; and in the present case, the chief
clerk in the judgment room has quite rightly declined to permit the plaintiffs
so to proceed.

I am therefore presented with the paradoxical situation that, because the   H
plaintiffs have obtained an injunction designed to prevent the defendants from
removing assets from the jurisdiction in order to prevent the plaintiffs from
satisfying any judgment, they are inhibited from signing judgment in default of

---

[1] R.S.C., Ord. 13, r. 6: "(1) Where a writ is indorsed with a claim of a description not mentioned in rules 1 to 4, then, if any defendant fails to enter an appearance, the plaintiff may, . . . proceed with the action as if that defendant had entered
an appearance."

The Weekly Law Reports, May 16, 1980

461

1 W.L.R.   Stewart Chartering v. C. & O. Managements (Q.B.D.)   Robert Goff J.

A   appearance which is, in the present situation, the next step which would
ordinarily be taken by them with a view to enforcing their claim.

The solution to this problem lies, in my judgment, in the inherent jurisdiction of the court to control its own process, and in particular to prevent any
possible abuse of that process. If the plaintiffs were unable to obtain a judgment in the present case without abandoning their Mareva injunction, it would
be open to a defendant to defeat the very purpose of the proceedings simply
B   by declining to enter an appearance. Such conduct would be an abuse of the
process of the court; and in my judgment the court has power to take the
necessary steps, by virtue of its inherent jurisdiction, to prevent any such abuse
of its process. The appropriate action to be taken by the court in such circumstances is, in my judgment, to grant leave to the plaintiffs, in an appropriate case, to enter judgment in default of appearance, notwithstanding that
the writ is indorsed with a claim for an injunction. If the court so acts, it
C   can also order that the Mareva injunction continue in force until after the
judgment, in aid of execution. The purpose of a Mareva injunction is to
prevent a defendant from removing his assets from the jurisdiction so as to
prevent the plaintiff from obtaining the fruits of his judgment; from this it
follows that the policy underlying the Mareva jurisdiction can only be given
effect to if the court has power to continue the Mareva injunction after judgment in aid of execution.

D   In my judgment, the present case is an appropriate case for the court so
to proceed. I therefore give leave to the plaintiffs to enter judgment; and I
shall also order that the Mareva injunction continue in force in aid of
execution.

Application granted with costs.
Order that plaintiffs have liberty to enter
judgment for £23,101·33 and costs to
E   *be taxed and that injunction be con-*
tinued with liberty to defendants to
apply.

Solicitors: *Constant & Constant.*

B. O. A.

F

[QUEEN'S BENCH DIVISION]

*ROCHDALE METROPOLITAN BOROUGH COUNCIL *v.*
F.M.C. (MEAT) LTD.

G

1980   Jan. 28;   Lord Widgery C.J. and Woolf J.
       Feb. 1

Food and Drugs — Food — Purchase with warranty — Chicken
purchased and invoiced under brand name of supplier—No
written warranty—Chicken unfit for human consumption
H   *when sold to customer—Whether brand name amounting*
to written warranty—Food and Drugs Act 1955 (4 Eliz. 2,
c. 16), s. 115 (1) (5)

Section 115 of the Food and Drugs Act 1955 provides:
" (1) . . . in any proceedings for an offence under this
Act . . . being an offence consisting of selling . . . any
article . . . , it shall be a defence for the defendant to
prove—(*a*) that he purchased it as being an article . . .
which could lawfully be sold or . . . could lawfully be

so sold or dealt with under the name or description or A
for the purpose under or for which he sold or dealt
with it, and with a written warranty to that effect, and
(b) that he had no reason to believe at the time of the
commission of the alleged offence that it was otherwise,
and (c) that it was then in the same state as when he
purchased it. . . . (5) For the purposes of this . . .
section, a name or description entered in an invoice shall
be deemed to be a written warranty that the article or B
substance to which the entry refers can be sold or
otherwise dealt with under that name or description by
any person without contravening any of the provisions
of this Act. . . ."

A frozen chicken was sold through a succession of
suppliers to a local authority. The immediate supplier had
purchased the chicken from the defendants, who, in turn, had C
purchased it under an invoice in which it was described under
the brand name of the original suppliers. The invoice contained no written warranties. The chicken was found to be
unfit for human consumption, and the local authority laid
an information against the immediate suppliers alleging an
offence under section 8 (1) of the Food and Drugs Act 1955.
The suppliers joined the defendants in accordance with the
provisions of section 113 of the Act.[1] The defendants relied
on the defence provided by section 115 (1) of the Act, on the D
basis that the brand name in the invoice amounted to a
warranty by virtue of section 115 (5). The justices dismissed
the information.

On appeal by the local authority: —

Held, dismissing the appeal, that on the literal interpretation of the words of section 115 (1) of the Act it was a
necessary ingredient of a defence under the section that a
defendant should prove that he had purchased the article as E
being one which could lawfully be sold under the name under
which he sold it and that he had purchased it with a warranty
to that effect; that the defence was available in " any proceedings " for an offence under the Act, which clearly included
an offence under section 8 (1); that the entry of a name or
description in an invoice was deemed by section 115 (5) to be a
written warranty that the article to which the entry referred
could be sold under that name without contravening any F
provisions of the Act, and that the effect of the subsection
was not limited to cases where the offence related to the name
or description of the article only, and, the defendants having,
as the justices found, proved all the necessary facts to establish
a defence under the section, the justices had come to the
correct conclusion.

No cases are referred to in the judgment or were cited in argument.   G

CASE STATED by Greater Manchester justices.

On June 17, 1977, an information was laid by the local authority
against Louis C. Edwards Ltd. that they did on March 11, 1977, sell to
Rochdale Borough Council certain food, namely one chicken, which was
intended for, but was unfit for human consumption, contrary to section H
8 (1) of the Food and Drugs Act 1955. On September 2, 1977, an

---

[1] Food and Drugs Act 1955, s. 113 (1): " A person against whom proceedings
are brought under this Act shall, . . . be entitled to have any person to whose act
or default he alleges that the contravention of the provisions in question was
due brought before the court in the proceedings; and if, after the contravention
has been proved, the original defendant proves that the contravention was due
to the act or default of that other person, that other person may be convicted of
the offence, . . ."

A information was laid by Louis C. Edwards Ltd. against F.M.C. (Meat) Ltd., the defendants, alleging that the contravention of the provisions of section 8 (1) of the Food and Drugs Act 1955 was due to the act or default of the defendants. On October 19, 1977, the defendants served notice on Louis C. Edwards Ltd. and T. N. Green & Sons (Poultry) Ltd. that at the hearing of the summons against the defendants, the defendants would rely on a warranty under section 115 (5) of the Food B and Drugs Act 1955 given by T. N. Green & Sons (Poultry) Ltd., by invoices numbered 54946 and 54947 dated February 24, 1977.

The justices heard the informations on November 10, 1977, and found the following facts. Louis C. Edwards Ltd. on March 11, 1977, sold to the local authority, inter alia, a chicken which was unfit for human consumption. The chicken had been sold and delivered by C the defendants to Louis C. Edwards Ltd. on March 8 or 9, 1977. The chicken had been frozen and packed by G. W. Padley Ltd., Anwick Village, Sleaford, Lincolnshire, the exclusive owners of the brand name " Saxon Chix," a firm that all parties including the local authority, conceded enjoyed the highest of reputations as frozen poultry suppliers. G. W. Padley Ltd. had sold the chickens to T. N. Green & Sons D (Poultry) Ltd. of Manchester abattoir; T. N. Green & Sons (Poultry) Ltd. sold the chickens to the defendants, who also traded from the Manchester abattoir, in what was merely a paper transaction. T. N. Green & Sons (Poultry) Ltd. directed the suppliers, G. W. Padley Ltd., to deliver the chickens direct to the defendants, who then had the chickens stored by Trafford Park Cold Storage Ltd., Manchester, and E thereafter either at Trafford Park cold store, their own Manchester Abattoir cold store, or refrigerated transport until delivered to Louis C. Edwards Ltd. Trafford Park Cold Storage Ltd., an independent cold store company, was recognised by all parties, including the local authority, to be a firm of great experience and expertise in the handling of frozen meat; Trafford Park Cold Storage Ltd. reserved a special bay for goods handled by them on behalf of the defendants. Mr. Frost, the F defendants' manager at the Manchester abattoir, satisfied the justices that the name " Saxon Chix " was one of the major factors that determined his decision to purchase the chickens; that by previous trading with G. W. Padley Ltd. he had on a personal basis established that they were a brand name he could trust regarding the quality of chickens he was purchasing, a fact that was also confirmed by Mr. Edwards of Louis C. Edwards Ltd. in determining his decisions to purchase the chickens.

G It was contended by the local authority that the warranty relied on by the defendants was the warranty, deemed by section 115 (5) of the Food and Drugs Act 1955 in relation to the words " Saxon Chix " in the invoices, and that that was insufficient to amount to a warranty that the chicken in question was fit for human consumption.

It was contended by the defendants (a) that the warranty relied on H was the warranty deemed by section 115 (5) of the Food and Drugs Act 1955 in relation to the words " Saxon Chix " in the invoices. The defendants purchased the chicken from T. N. Green & Sons (Poultry) Ltd. as being an article or substance which could lawfully be sold or otherwise dealt with under the name of " Saxon Chix " without contravening section 8 (1) of the Food and Drugs Act 1955; (b) that evidence had been given to the effect that there was no visible indication that that chicken had been defrosted and refrozen, which evidence indicated

that the fault occurred before the chicken came into the control of the   A
defendants, and that view was confirmed by the evidence of Mr. Edwards
of Louis C. Edwards Ltd. who in his opinion as an expert butcher of
many years standing, suggested that the chicken had been incorrectly
butchered and that the deterioration of the bird had taken place before
freezing, therefore the defendants had no reason to believe at the time
of the commission of the alleged offence that the said chicken was
otherwise than in the same state as when they purchased it.   B

The justices were of the opinion that (a) the words " Saxon Chix "
referred to a distinctive brand of frozen poultry, a brand that all parties
were agreed came from a firm who enjoyed the highest of reputations;
(b) frozen goods by their very nature were difficult to check up on
before they reached the hands of the eventual consumer and that all
firms, the defendants, Trafford Park Cold Storage Ltd., and sub-   C
sequently Louis C. Edwards Ltd. had exercised reasonableness in their
handling of the chicken and that at no time while in any of their
possessions had anything happened that could have reasonably led
them to believe that the state of that chicken had changed; (c) the
defendants' contention was correct and, therefore, the defendants
having proved the other conditions laid down in section 115 (1) of the
Food and Drugs Act 1955 were entitled to rely upon the defence   D
specified in section 115 (1) of the Food and Drugs Act 1955 and the
justices, therefore, acquitted the defendants.

The prosecutor appealed.

The question for the opinion of the High Court was whether on the
facts found the justices were correct in holding that the words " Saxon
Chix " in the invoices were deemed under section 115 (5) of the Food   E
and Drugs Act 1955 to be a written warranty for the purposes of
section 115 (1) of the Act that the article or substance so referred to
could be sold or otherwise dealt with under that name or description
by any person without contravening section 8 (1) of the Act.

S. J. Sauvain for the local authority.   F
J. J. Finney for the defendants.

Cur. adv. vult.

February 1. WOOLF J. read the following judgment of the court.
This is an appeal by way of case stated by Greater Manchester justices.
On November 10, 1977 those justices acquitted the defendants of an
offence under section 8 (1) of the Food and Drugs Act 1955, in   G
respect of the sale of a chicken which was intended for, but was unfit
for, human consumption, on the ground that the defendants were
entitled to rely upon the statutory defence provided by section 115 of
the Food and Drugs Act 1955. There is no dispute that, but for the
provisions of section 115, the chicken which had been frozen and pre-
packed was unfit for human consumption and an offence contrary to   H
section 8 had been committed. The appeal therefore turns on the
construction of section 115 of the Food and Drugs Act 1955 and
raises a point on which there is no previous authority. The relevant
provisions of section 115 are as follows:

" (1) Subject to the provisions of this section, in any proceedings
    for an offence under this Act or any regulations made thereunder,
    being an offence consisting of selling, or offering, exposing or

A   advertising for sale, or having in possession for the purpose of sale, any article or substance, it shall be a defence for the defendant to prove—(a) that he purchased it as being an article or substance which could lawfully be sold or otherwise dealt with as aforesaid, or, as the case may be, could lawfully be so sold or dealt with under the name or description or for the purpose under or for which he sold or dealt with it, and with a written

B   warranty to that effect, and (b) that he had no reason to believe at the time of the commission of the alleged offence that it was otherwise, and (c) that it was then in the same state as when he purchased it. (2) A warranty shall only be a defence in proceedings under this Act if—(a) the defendant—(i) has, not later than three clear days before the date of the hearing, sent to the prosecutor a copy of the warranty with a notice stating that he intends to

C   rely on it and specifying the name and address of the person from whom he received it and (ii) has also sent a like notice of his intention to that person, . . . (5) For the purposes of this and the next following section, a name or description entered in an invoice shall be deemed to be a written warranty that the article or substance to which the entry refers can be sold or otherwise dealt with

D   under that name or description by any person without contravening any of the provisions of this Act or of regulations made thereunder."

The requirement under section 115 (2) that the defendant shall give notice, inter alia, to the prosecutor, is partly explained by the fact that section 116 of the Act creates offences in relation to warranties.

E   The chicken, the sale of which gave rise to the proceedings, had, on paper at any rate, passed through a number of hands before it reached the ultimate purchaser which was the Rochdale Metropolitan Borough Council, the present appellants. It had originally been sold by G. W. Padley Ltd. to T. N. Green & Sons (Poultry) Ltd.; T. N. Green & Sons (Poultry) Ltd. had sold the chicken to the defendants,

F   F.M.C. (Meat) Ltd., and the defendants had sold the chicken to Louis C. Edwards Ltd. who had sold it to the local authority. The local authority accordingly commenced proceedings by laying an information against Louis C. Edwards Ltd. and that company then joined the present defendants under section 113 of the Act.

The sale by T. N. Green & Sons (Poultry) Ltd. to the defendants had been with an invoice which referred to the chicken as " Saxon

G   Chix " which is the brand name used by G. W. Padley Ltd. for their frozen poultry. It is recited in the case that all parties were agreed that this brand came from a firm who enjoyed the highest of reputations.

Apart from the reference in the invoice to " Saxon Chix " there was no written warranty on which the defendants could rely and the issue

H   before this court is whether the reference to " Saxon Chix " in the invoice amounted to a sufficient warranty for the purposes of section 115. Subject to this the justices were of the opinion that the other conditions laid down in section 115 were complied with and the defendants were entitled to rely upon the defence specified in that section. The local authority do not challenge that conclusion and confine their argument as to the effect of the reference to " Saxon Chix " in the invoice.

Rochdale Council v. F.M.C. Ltd. (D.C.) [1980]

Although this may initially seem surprising, on the literal interpre- A
tation of the words used in section 115, we have come to the conclusion
that the justices came to the correct decision. In interpreting section
115 (5) it is necessary to read that section with section 115 (1). The
scope of the defence is set-out in subsection (1). The relevant words
of that subsection are: " In *any* proceedings for an offence under this
Act . . ., being an offence consisting of selling . . . any article or
substance, it shall be a defence. . . ." So subsection (1) clearly applies B
to proceedings in respect of offences under section 8 of the Act.

Under section 115 (1) (*a*) it is up to a defendant to prove two
matters, in addition to the other requirements of the section: first that
he made his purchase of the article or substance as being one where
the article or substance could lawfully be sold or otherwise dealt with
or, as the case may be, could lawfully be sold or dealt with under the C
name or description or for the purpose under or for which he sold or
dealt with it and secondly (in each case) that he purchased it with a
written warranty to that effect.

Pausing for a moment at subsection (1) (*a*), the use of the words
" or, as the case may be " indicates that it is sufficient if either alternative is fulfilled.

So far as the requirement of subsection (1) of " a written warranty D
to that effect " is concerned, subsection (5) deems the entry of a
name or description in an invoice to be a written warranty that the article
or substance to which the entry refers can be sold or otherwise dealt
with under that name or description by any person without contravening any of the provisions of the Act. Again, " any provisions of this
Act " must include section 8, so the deemed warranty in the case of E
named articles in an invoice has to be treated as though there was an
express warranty that the article could be sold under a name or
description specified in an invoice without contravening the provisions of the Act, including section 8. An invoice bearing the name of
the article is therefore deemed to be a written warranty; that so far as
the provisions of the Act are concerned, that article could lawfully
be sold under that name. It is therefore a warranty to one of the effects F
specified in subsection (1) (*a*).

It was contended on behalf of the local authority that this cannot
be the right interpretation as it would give far too wide an effect to
section 115. We do not accept that this is the case. First of all it has
to be remembered that, in addition to section 115, a defendant has to
establish that he complies with section 115 (1) (*b*) and (*c*) and G
magistrates should be careful to ensure those requirements have been
satisfied before acquitting a defendant. In many cases this will not be
possible and the prosecution will succeed because of this. In this case
the magistrates were satisfied but that was because of the high reputation of the brand concerned. It is also to be remembered that proceedings can not only be brought against the person who relied upon
the warranty, proceedings can also be brought against the person H
who gave the warranty. Those proceedings can allege one of the
number of offences created by section 116, which include giving a false
warranty. It is true that the wording of section 116 is not all that
wide. However, in addition to bringing proceedings under section 116,
the prosecuting authority could also proceed against the seller of the
warranty for one of the substantive offences created, inter alia, under
section 8.

A   A further argument advanced on behalf of the local authority rested upon a comparison of the language of section 84 of the Food and Drugs Act 1938, which was the predecessor of section 115 of the Food and Drugs Act 1955, with section 115. It was pointed out that the Act of 1955 was a consolidating Act and it was said that a change of substance would not be made in a consolidating Act. Undoubtedly section 115 is wider than section 84 of the Food and Drugs Act 1938,

B   which only applied to what would now be offences under section 2 of the Food and Drugs Act 1955, namely, offences alleging that food was not of the nature or of the substance or of the quality demanded and the defence under section 84 of the Food and Drugs Act 1938 did not extend to prosecutions under section 9 of that Act which is the corresponding section to section 8 of the Act of 1955. However any sub-

C   stance in this contention is destroyed by section 36 and Schedule 3 to the Food and Drugs Amendment Act 1954, which amended section 84 of the Act of 1938 so that it was, for all practical purposes, in the same terms and had the same scope as the present section 115.

The local authority construes section 115 (5) so that where the name or description of an article is all that appears in an invoice, the application of the warranty defence is limited to those cases where the

D   charge is one which related to the name or description of the article. This restrictive interpretation is contrary to the express language used and would not be justified in the case of a section which provides a defence to criminal offences, many of which are absolute offences not dependent upon any lack of care of the alleged offender. It would also be out of accord with contemporary marketing practice where

E   frequently the trade name of an item of food is the best guarantee of its quality and it is often difficult, if not impossible, for those engaged in distribution to do other than rely on the reputation of the original supplier.

Accordingly we would dismiss this appeal.

Appeal dismissed with costs.
Certificate that point of law of
general public importance
involved, namely: " Whether
the effect of section 115 (5) of
the Food and Drugs Act 1955
is such that any name or des-
cription entered in an invoice
is deemed to be a written
warranty that the article is
fit for human consumption so
as to provide a defence under
section 115 (1) of the Act to
a prosecution under section 8
(1) of the Act "
Leave to appeal refused.

Solicitors: *Sharpe, Pritchard & Co.* for *J. Malcolm Russum, Roch-*
dale Metropolitan Borough Council; *Richards, Butler & Co.*

[Reported by D. L. LAWUMI, ESQ., Barrister-at-Law.]

A

[COURT OF APPEAL]

* VON ERNST & CIE S.A. AND OTHERS v. INLAND REVENUE
COMMISSIONERS

1979 Nov. 22, 23, 26, 27; 30   Buckley, Bridge and Templeman L.JJ.

B

*Revenue—Capital transfer tax—Settled property—Capital distribu-
tions—Exemption for government securities held by non-
resident trustees—Non-resident beneficiaries becoming entitled
to interests in possession—Whether status as " excluded
property " determined immediately before taxable event—
Whether charities beneficially entitled to interest in possession
—Finance Act 1975 (c. 7), Sch. 5, para. 6 (2) (4), Sch. 7, para.
3 (1) (2)* [1]

C

Under the terms of a settlement made in 1967, property
was held by the taxpayers as trustees on discretionary trusts
for the benefit of any children of the settlor. On a failure of
those trusts the property was to be held on constructive
discretionary trusts for two United Kingdom charities, one
being a limited company with exclusively charitable objects and
the other an unincorporated charitable foundation. Neither
the taxpayers nor the two children subsequently born to the
settlor were domiciled or resident in the United Kingdom.
On March 22, 1976, the taxpayers purchased £4,205,875
Treasury stock which were exempt gilt-edged securities. By
a further settlement dated March 24, 1976, the taxpayers as
trustees held the fund in trust for such of the settlor's
children as they might appoint and, subject to that power, on
discretionary trusts for those children for a trust period. On
the same day, exercising their powers of advancement, the
taxpayers directed that the Treasury stock be held on the
trusts of the 1976 settlement. On the following day the taxpayers appointed the trust funds subject to the 1976 settlement on trust to be divided into two equal parts and the
income of each part to be paid to the settlor's two children
with remainders over in favour of the two charities.

In consequence of that appointment the taxpayers received
notices of determination that, under paragraph 6 (2) of
Schedule 5 to the Finance Act 1975, there had been a
capital distribution and they were liable under paragraph 6 (4)
to capital transfer tax of £2,900,993. They appealed under
paragraph 7 (3) of Schedule 4 direct to the High Court seeking a declaration, inter alia, that no capital transfer tax was
payable because the Treasury stock constituted " excluded
property " under paragraph 3 (1) of Schedule 7 as it was
settled property to which persons neither domiciled nor
resident in the United Kingdom were entitled to interests in
possession. Browne-Wilkinson J. dismissed the appeal holding that because at the time immediately before the appointment there was no interest in possession in the Treasury stock it
was not " excluded property " within the meaning of paragraph 3 (1) (*b*) of Schedule 7 and accordingly not exempted
by paragraph 11 (11) of Schedule 5 from the provisions of
paragraph 6 charging capital distributions to the tax.

On appeal by the taxpayers: —

Held, (1) that whether the capital distributions were exempt
from liability to the tax arising by virtue of paragraph 6 of
Schedule 5 depended on whether at the time immediately
before the distribution was made the Treasury stock was

D

E

F

G

H

[1] Finance Act 1975, Sch. 5, para. 6 (1) (2) (4): see post, p. 473A–C.
Sch. 7, para. 3 (1) (2): see post, pp. 472C–D, 474G–H.

A   " excluded property " under paragraph 3 (1) (*b*) of Schedule
7; that since no interest in possession existed in the stock at
that time, it did not fall within that exempting provision
unless, under paragraph 3 (2), the known persons beneficially
entitled to an interest in possession were neither domiciled
nor ordinarily resident in the United Kingdom (post, pp.
473H—474E, 478A–B, C–E).

     (2) Allowing the appeal, that immediately before the 1976
B   appointment paragraph 3 (2) of Schedule 7 applied so as to
make the stock " excluded property " because the known
individuals beneficially entitled were neither domiciled nor
resident in the United Kingdom and the two charities were
not capable of being benefited or of becoming beneficially
entitled to the stock being merely the machinery used to carry
on exclusively charitable activities and, accordingly, the taxpayers were not liable for capital transfer tax (post, pp.
C   475G—476C, 480A–E).

     Decision of Browne-Wilkinson J. [1979] 1 W.L.R. 1325
reversed on point not argued below.

The following cases are referred to in the judgments:

Construction Industry Training Board v. *Attorney-General* [1973] Ch. 173;
     [1972] 3 W.L.R. 187; [1972] 2 All E.R. 1339, C.A.
D   *Finger's Will Trusts, In re* [1972] Ch. 286; [1971] 3 W.L.R. 775; [1971]
     3 All E.R. 1050.
French Protestant Hospital, In re [1951] Ch. 567; [1951] 1 All E.R. 938.
Inland Revenue Commissioners v. *Graham's Trustees* 1971 S.L.T. 46,
     H.L.(Sc.).
Larter v. *Skone James* [1976] 1 W.L.R. 607; [1976] 2 All E.R. 615.
Smith, decd., In re [1951] Ch. 360; [1951] 1 All E.R. 146.
Soldiers', Sailors' and Airmen's Families Association v. *Attorney-General*
E   [1968] 1 W.L.R. 313; [1968] 1 All E.R. 448.

The following additional cases were cited in argument:

Ayerst v. *C. & K. (Construction) Ltd.* [1976] A.C. 167; [1975] 3 W.L.R.
     16; [1975] 2 All E.R. 537, H.L.(E.).
Camille & Henry Dreyfus Foundation Inc. v. *Inland Revenue Commis-
     sioners* [1956] A.C. 39; [1955] 3 W.L.R. 451; [1955] 3 All E.R.
F   97, H.L.(E.).
Gasque v. *Inland Revenue Commissioners* [1940] 2 K.B. 80; 23 T.C. 210.

APPEAL from Browne-Wilkinson J.
     The taxpayers, Von Ernst & Cie S.A., Jean-Paul Aeschimann and
Kenneth Porter, were the trustees of two settlements made by Mrs.
G   Vivien Louise Duffield in 1967 and 1976. As trustees of the 1967 settlement, they executed a deed on March 24, 1976, whereby £4,205,875
nominal 10½ per cent. Treasury stock 1976 were appointed to be held
on the trusts of the 1976 settlement, and the following day, as trustees
of the 1976 settlement, they appointed the funds to be divided into two
equal parts and the income therefrom to be paid to the settlor's two
children with remainders over in favour of two United Kingdom charities,
H   Annacastle Ltd. and the Charles Clore Foundation. On February 2, 1978,
the taxpayers received notices of determination under paragraph 6 of
Schedule 4 to the Finance Act 1975 that in consequence of the deed of
appointment they were liable for capital transfer tax of £2,900,993
together with interest thereon from October 1, 1976.

     The taxpayers issued an originating summons pursuant to paragraph
7 (3) of Schedule 4 to the Finance Act 1975 seeking declarations, inter
alia, that in ascertaining the liability, if any, of the taxpayers to capital

transfer tax under paragraph 6 (2) of Schedule 5 to the Act of 1975 in A consequence of the deed of appointment made by the taxpayers on March 25, 1976, the part of the trust fund which consisted of the Treasury stock did not fall to be taken into account; and that no capital transfer tax was chargeable in consequence of the deed of a appointment.

Browne-Wilkinson J. declined to make the declaration sought by the taxpayers holding that immediately before the 1976 appointment there was no interest in possession in the Treasury stock with the result that B it was not " excluded property " within the meaning of paragraph 3 (1) (b) of Schedule 7 and thus not exempt from the charge imposed by the provisions of paragraph 6 of Schedule 5.

The taxpayers appealed on the grounds (1) that when the taxpayers executed the deed of appointment on March 25, 1976, the holding of 10½ per cent. Treasury stock held by them constituted " excluded property " C within paragraph 3 (1) (b) or alternatively paragraph 3 (2) of Schedule 7 to the Finance Act 1975 and accordingly was not comprised in the settled property chargeable with capital transfer tax in consequence of the deed of appointment; (2) that by reason of section 22 (1) (b) of the Finance (No. 2) Act 1931 the holding of Treasury stock was in any event not liable to capital transfer tax; (3) that the judge had no jurisdiction to make an order confirming the determination of capital D transfer tax.

The facts are set out in the judgment of Browne-Wilkinson J. [1979] 1 W.L.R. 1325, 1326–1327.

C. N. Beattie Q.C. and Robert Walker for the taxpayers.
D. J. Nicholls Q.C. and Peter Gibson for the Crown. E

Cur. adv. vult.

November 30. The following judgments were read.

BUCKLEY L.J. I have asked Bridge L.J. to deliver the first judgment in this case. F

BRIDGE L.J. This is an appeal from a judgment of Browne-Wilkinson J. given on March 26, 1979, refusing the declarations sought by the taxpayers in their originating summons and confirming the determination by the Board of Inland Revenue (subject to an agreed variation of the figures) that a capital distribution had been made by the taxpayers attracting capital transfer tax under paragraph 6 of G Schedule 5 to the Finance Act 1975.

The facts are concisely and accurately summarised in the judgment of Browne-Wilkinson J. [1979] 1 W.L.R. 1325, 1326–1327 and I need not repeat them. The point at issue relates to a transaction affecting a holding of 10½ per cent. Treasury stock 1976. These are securities issued subject to a condition, authorised by section 22 (1) of the Finance H (No. 2) Act 1931, that they shall be exempt from taxation so long as the securities are in the beneficial ownership of persons neither domiciled nor ordinarily resident in the United Kingdom. It will be convenient to refer to them as exempt securities. For the purposes of capital transfer tax, imposed by Part III of the Finance Act 1975, the effect of section 29 and paragraph 3 (1) (b) of Schedule 7 is to provide that exempt securities are excluded property:

A
"if they are settled property and a person neither domiciled nor ordinarily resident in the United Kingdom is beneficially entitled to an interest in possession in them."

Immediately before March 25, 1976, the exempt securities with which we are concerned were held on discretionary trusts and were thus comprised in a settlement in which no interest in possession subsisted.

B By a deed of appointment made on March 25, 1976, two named individuals, neither of them domiciled nor ordinarily resident in the United Kingdom, became entitled to interests in possession in the exempt securities. The question at issue is whether in consequence of this appointment capital transfer tax became chargeable under paragraph 6 (4) of Schedule 5 to the Finance Act 1975 "as on the value transferred by a chargeable transfer." Three distinct points have been canvassed before

C us. First, is the transaction exempt from tax by virtue of paragraph 3 (1) (b) of Schedule 7 to the Act of 1975? Secondly, is the transaction exempt from tax independently of the provisions of the Finance Act 1975 by the operation of section 22 (1) of the Finance (No. 2) Act 1931? Thirdly, is the transaction exempt from tax by virtue of paragraph 3 (2) of Schedule 7 to the Act of 1975? The second and third points were

D raised for the first time in this court.

I have set out the points in the order in which they were argued before us for the taxpayers but I find it convenient to dispose of the second point first since this can be done in a few sentences. It is to my mind clear beyond argument that whether or not any particular transaction affecting exempt securities is exempt from capital transfer tax must

E depend on the true construction of the specific provisions applicable to such a transaction contained in the Finance Act 1975. If those provisions provide exemption, well and good; if those provisions do not provide exemption, the taxing provisions of the Finance Act 1975 come into operation and the provisions of the Finance (No. 2) Act 1931 cannot provide any exemption from them.

F I turn now to the first point which the judge decided in favour of the Crown. This point depends on the true construction of the provisions of paragraph 6 of Schedule 5, but to see the overall scheme of the Act of which the crucial provisions form part it is convenient to set out the main taxing provisions and in particular to see how they operate in relation to exempt securities. I shall read them, omitting immaterial words.

G Section 19 (1) reads as follows: "A tax, to be known as capital transfer tax, shall be charged on the value transferred by a chargeable transfer." Section 20 (2) reads:

"Subject to subsections (3) and (4) below, a transfer of value is any disposition made by a person ('the transferor') as a result of which the value of his estate immediately after the disposition is less than it would be but for the disposition; and the amount by which it is

H less is the value transferred by the transfer."

Section 20 (3) reads:

"For the purposes of subsection (2) above no account shall be taken of the value of excluded property which ceases to form part of a person's estate as a result of a disposition."

Section 22 (1) reads:

"On the death of any person after the passing of this Act tax A shall be charged as if, immediately before his death, he had made a transfer of value and the value transferred by it had been equal to the value of his estate immediately before his death, but subject to the following provisions of this section."

Section 23 (1) reads:

"For the purposes of this Part of this Act, a person's estate is the B aggregate of all the property to which he is beneficially entitled, except that the estate of a person immediately before his death does not include excluded property."

Section 24 contains general provisions relating to "excluded property" but the relevant definition of "excluded property" for present purposes is in paragraph 3 (1) of Schedule 7 to which I have already referred. C It reads:

"Where securities have been issued by the Treasury subject to a condition authorised by section 22 of the Finance (No. 2) Act 1931 (or section 47 of the Finance (No. 2) Act 1915) for exemption from taxation so long as the securities are in the beneficial ownership of persons neither domiciled nor ordinarily resident in the United D Kingdom the securities are excluded property—(a) if they are not settled property and are in the beneficial ownership of such a person; or (b) if they are settled property and such a person is beneficially entitled to an interest in possession in them."

Pausing there, it is in my judgment abundantly clear from the language of the provisions I have read that the question whether a particular E property escapes taxation on a transfer inter vivos or on the death of the owner as "excluded property" depends on whether it correctly answers to that description in the hands of the transferor or the deceased, not on whether it will answer to that description in the hands of the transferee or the beneficiary who inherits on death. I found Mr. Beattie's contention to the contrary, with respect, to be quite unarguable.

Against that background I turn to Schedule 5, which is brought into F effect by section 20 (1). Paragraph 1 (1) provides:

"The following provisions of this paragraph apply for determining what is to be taken for the purposes of capital transfer tax to be a settlement, and what property is, accordingly, referred to as property comprised in a settlement or as settled property; and who is the settlor and a trustee in relation to a settlement." G

It was common ground that the phrases "property comprised in a settlement" and "settled property" are synonymous. Paragraph 3 (1) provides:

"A person beneficially entitled to an interest in possession in settled property shall be treated as beneficially entitled to the property in which the interest subsists." H

This provision, it will be observed, has the effect, together with section 22, of charging capital transfer tax on settled property on the death of the life tenant unless he is entitled to exemption as a non-resident holder of exempt securities under paragraph 3 (1) (b) of Schedule 7 or unless the property is otherwise excluded property. Paragraph 4 contains provisions for imposing tax on the disposal or other termination inter vivos of

A   interests held under a settlement, but again gives exemption in favour
of the non-resident beneficiary on the disposal or termination of his
interest in exempt securities or other excluded property. Paragraph 6
provides:

"(1) Where a distribution payment is made out of property com-
B   prised in a settlement and at the time the payment is made no interest
in possession subsists in the property or in the part of it out of which
the payment is made, the payment is in this Schedule referred to as a
capital distribution. (2) Where a person becomes entitled to an
interest in possession in the whole or any part of the property comprised in a settlement at a time when no such interest subsists in
the property or that part, a capital distribution shall be treated as
being made out of the property or that part of the property; and
C   the amount of the distribution shall be taken to be equal to the
value at that time of the property or, if the interest is in part only of
that property, of that part. . . . (4) Tax shall be charged on any capital
distribution as on the value transferred by a chargeable transfer . . . "

These provisions must be read in conjunction with paragraph 11, which
provides:

D   "(7) 'Distribution payment' means, subject to sub-paragraph (8)
below, any payment which—(a) is not income of any person for any
of the purposes of income tax and would not for any of those
purposes be income of a person not resident in the United Kingdom
if he were so resident; and (b) is not a payment in respect of costs
or expenses; and 'payment' includes the transfer of assets other than
E   money . . . (11) References to settled property shall be construed
as referring only to property which is not excluded property."

The argument of Mr. Beattie for the taxpayers was essentially a
simple one. He submitted that when the appointment of March 25, 1976,
took effect, the beneficiaries thereunder did not "become entitled to an
interest in possession in . . . property comprised in a settlement" under
F   paragraph 6 (2) because at the very moment of their entitlement arising
the property in question ceased to be "settled property" under paragraph 6 by virtue of paragraph 11 (11). Mr. Beattie sought to support his
argument by extracting from certain earlier authorities relating to estate
duty and capital gains tax the general principle that in applying what
has been called a mutation tax, one must always determine the incidence
and amount of the tax by reference to the state of affairs existing after,
G   not before, the occurrence of the event relied on as giving rise to the
charge to tax. He relied on In re Smith, decd. [1951] Ch. 360; Inland
Revenue Commissioners v. Graham's Trustees, 1971 S.L.T. 46 and
Larter v. Skone James [1976] 1 W.L.R. 607. In reference to a taxing
statute which left the matter at large, or threw up an ambiguity on the
point which could not otherwise be resolved, I can appreciate that it
H   would be proper to pray in aid the principle derived from these
decisions. But if the provisions of the particular statute on their true
construction, point to an opposite conclusion these decisions are, in
my judgment, of no relevance.

As Browne-Wilkinson J. [1979] 1 W.L.R. 1325, 1329, pointed out,
paragraph 6 (2) of Schedule 5, read quite literally, contemplates a
logical impossibility, viz. a person becoming entitled to an interest in
possession at a time when no such interest subsists. The sequence con-

templated must clearly be first the existence of settled property in which   A
no interest in possession subsists, secondly the creation of an interest in
possession in that property. When that sequence of events occurs the sub-
paragraph provides that " a capital distribution shall be treated as being
made out of the property." The property out of which the capital
distribution is treated as being made is property in which no interest in
possession subsists. This brings paragraph 6 (2) into line with sub-paragraph (1), which provides in effect a definition of what amounts to a   B
capital distribution. The two elements essential to a capital distribution
are (i) a payment out of property comprised in a settlement and (ii) the
making of the payment at a time when no interest in possession subsists
in the property. Mr. Beattie conceded, I think, that a distribution
payment out of property held on discretionary trusts to a beneficiary for
an absolute interest would be an actual capital distribution under   C
paragraph 6 (1) which, subject to the new point raised under paragraph
3 (2) of Schedule 7, would inevitably attract tax under paragraph 6 (4).
This concession being rightly and, as I think inescapably, made, it follows
in my judgment equally inescapably that the capital distribution which
is to be treated as being made in the event contemplated by paragraph
6 (2) attracts tax in exactly the same way. This construction would, in
my judgment, be the right one to apply to the language of paragraph 6   D
considered in isolation. But it is powerfully reinforced by the consideration that it brings the paragraph wholly into line with the rest of the
Act as looking at the state of affairs before rather than after the event
giving rise to a potential charge to tax in order to determine whether
any relevant exclusion from liability is applicable.

Accordingly, on the only point which was argued before Browne-   E
Wilkinson J., I reach a conclusion entirely in accord with his. I have
attempted to set out my reasons for doing so in my own language but I
would also wish gratefully to adopt the judge's admirably lucid and to my
mind wholly convincing reasoning.

All that has been said so far in this judgment has been based on the
assumption, which was accepted as correct in the court below, that the
taxpayers cannot claim exemption from capital transfer tax in respect   F
of the appointment made on March 25, 1976, in reliance on paragraph
3 (2) of Schedule 7. But now in this court that assumption is challenged
and it is submitted that even if one must, in applying paragraph 6 (2)
and paragraph 11 (11) of Schedule 5, consider whether the exempt
securities were excluded property when still subject to a discretionary
trust, one can reach a conclusion in favour of the exemption claimed by   G
applying paragraph 3 (2) of Schedule 7 to the facts of the case. That
sub-paragraph provides:

> " If the securities are settled property and no interest in possession
> subsists in them the condition of sub-paragraph (1) (b) above shall be
> treated as satisfied if it is shown that all known persons for whose
> benefit the settled property or income from it has been or might be   H
> applied or who might become beneficially entitled to an interest in
> possession in it are persons neither domiciled nor ordinarily resident
> in the United Kingdom."

For the purpose of considering the application of this provision, we
have to look at the facts as they were immediately before the appointment
of March 25, 1976. The exempt securities were then subject to discretionary trusts of which the only individual beneficiaries were neither

domiciled nor ordinarily resident in the United Kingdom. But it was common ground that on failure of the trusts in favour of those beneficiaries the property would have been held on constructive discretionary trusts for two named charities in the United Kingdom, one a company limited by guarantee with exclusively charitable objects, the other an unincorporated charitable foundation. I should add that the limited company was qualified to take under the discretionary trusts only so long as its objects remained exclusively charitable.

A number of questions have been canvassed on the construction of paragraph 3 (2) of Schedule 7, but the only question I find it necessary to decide is whether either or both the charities who might have received payment of the income or capital out of the exempt securities fall within the words " known persons for whose benefit the settled property or income from it . . . might be applied or who might become beneficially entitled to an interest in possession in it."

Mr. Walker, junior counsel for the taxpayers, submitted in summary that the trustees of an unincorporated charity have no " benefit " from, nor " beneficial entitlement " to, trust moneys within the meaning of this provision and that likewise a company with exclusively charitable objects has no " benefit " from, nor " beneficial entitlement " to, the company's assets. The true beneficiaries in each case, Mr. Walker submitted, are the objects of the charity. This submission was developed by reference to a number of authorities concerned with various aspects of the status, functions and duties of charitable corporations. I do not refer to these in detail since, in my view, they certainly do not resolve nor in the end throw much significant light on the question we have to decide which depends on the true construction of the particular statutory provision to be applied.

Mr. Nicholls, for the Crown, understandably concentrated his argument on the charitable company, though he did not concede that the trustees of the unincorporated charity were not " known persons for whose benefit the settled property or income from it . . . might be applied or who might become beneficially entitled to an interest in possession in it." With respect to the company, he submitted that a company formed under the Companies Acts, though its objects may be exclusively charitable, is nevertheless not a trustee of its assets. I assume for the purpose of this judgment that that submission is well founded. It must inevitably follow from that, according to Mr. Nicholls's submission, that all receipts by the company are for its benefit and that the company is beneficially entitled to all its assets.

In the end this question falls to be decided according to the proper meaning to be given to the concepts of " benefit " and " beneficial entitlement " in paragraph 3 (2) of Schedule 7. I find it difficult to see how it could properly be said that the trustees of an unincorporated charity " might become beneficially entitled " to property within the meaning of the provision and consequently I should be inclined equally to exclude them from the scope of the phrase " known persons for whose benefit the settled property . . . might be applied." If this view is right and the inclusion of an unincorporated charity as the possible object of a discretionary trust is not fatal to the exemption given by paragraph 3 (2) of Schedule 7, if it is otherwise applicable, I should be reluctant to find myself driven to the opposite conclusion if the charity which may take under the discretionary trust is a limited company qualified to take only so long as its objects remain exclusively charitable. I can imagine no

possible ground of fiscal policy which could make such a distinction A
sensible or reasonable. But the decisive factor which has confirmed me
in the conclusion that this point should be decided in favour of the
taxpayers is derived from a consideration of another provision in the Act.
Paragraph 10 (2) and (3) of Schedule 6 provides:

> " (2) Notwithstanding anything in paragraph 6 of Schedule 5 to this
> Act, where property is given to a charity by the making of a distribu-   B
> tion payment within the meaning of that paragraph, the distribution
> payment is not a capital distribution for the purposes of that Schedule.
> (3) For the purposes of this paragraph property is given to charities
> if it becomes the property of charities or is held on trust for charitable
> purposes only."

It follows from this that no payment out of a discretionary trust in favour   C
of a charity attracts capital transfer tax at all. That being so, it would
seem to me utterly paradoxical that the mere possibility of such a payment
being made out of a particular discretionary trust should deprive that
trust of the immunity from taxation which it would otherwise enjoy
under paragraph 3 (2) of Schedule 7 on a capital distribution of exempt
securities.

On that short ground I would accordingly allow the appeal and   D
substitute for the judge's order a declaration in the terms claimed in
paragraph 1 of the taxpayers' originating summons.

TEMPLEMAN L.J. I agree with the judgment that has just been
delivered and, having had an opportunity of reading in draft the judgment
which Buckley L.J. is about to deliver, I agree with that also.   E

BUCKLEY L.J. I agree with the judgment which Bridge L.J. has
delivered, but as the case may be one of some general interest, I propose
to state my reasons in my own language.

The question in this case is whether in the circumstances of the case
the 10½ per cent. Treasury stock comprised in the settled fund was
" excluded property " for the purposes of Part III of the Finance Act 1975   F
on March 25, 1976, when the settlor's two children, whom I shall call
Arabella and George, became entitled to interests in possession in the
settled fund under the appointment of that date. It was common ground
that the fund in question was " property comprised in a settlement "
and " settled property " for the purposes of the Act. By virtue of section
21, Schedule 5 to the Act applies to such property.

Immediately before March 25, 1976, the fund was held on discretionary   G
trusts, and it was common ground that in that state of affairs no interest
in possession subsisted in the fund within the meaning of the Act.
Accordingly under paragraph 6 (2) of the Schedule a " capital distribution " must be treated as having been made out of the property comprised
in the settlement on Arabella and George becoming entitled to interests
in possession. The label " a capital distribution " is given by paragraph   H
6 (1) of the Schedule to a " distribution payment " made out of settled
property at a time when no interest in possession subsists in it; and by
virtue of paragraph 11 (4) of the Schedule " distribution payment "
means, putting it shortly, any payment, which may include a transfer of
assets other than money, which is not the income of any person for
income tax purposes and would not be so if he was resident in the
United Kingdom. The combined effect of these provisions is that on

A March 25, 1976, payments of a capital nature are to be treated as having been made out of the trust fund to Arabella and George together equal to the value at that time of the settled property except to the extent that the settled property consisted of " excluded property ": see paragraph 11 (11). Tax became payable under paragraph 6 (4) on the value so ascertained.

B Section 29 of the Act gives statutory effect to certain exemptions and reliefs contained in Schedule 7 to the Act. The relevant paragraph of that Schedule for present purposes is paragraph 3, which specifies in what circumstances securities issued upon such conditions as in fact apply to the $10\frac{1}{2}$ per cent. Treasury stock in the present case constitute " excluded property." Sub-paragraph (1) (b) of that paragraph provides that such securities are excluded property if they are settled property C and a person who is neither domiciled nor ordinarily resident in the United Kingdom (a qualification which both Arabella and George had at all material times) is beneficially entitled to an interest in possession in them. Paragraph 3 (2) contains an alternative ground upon which such securities may qualify as excluded property, to which I must return later.

D Mr. Beattie, relying on In re Smith, decd. [1951] Ch. 360; Inland Revenue Commissioners v. Graham's Trustees, 1971 S.L.T. 46 and Larter v. Skone James [1976] 1 W.L.R. 607, contended that for the purposes of paragraph 3 (1) (b) of Schedule 7 one must consider the beneficial interests which arise on the event which occasions the charge to tax; that is to say that in the present case it is the interests in possession which arose in Araballa and George on the execution of the appointment E that are relevant, and not the discretionary trusts which were in operation immediately before that appointment. His argument can, I hope, be fairly summarised thus. A capital distribution is only to be treated under paragraph 6 (2) of Schedule 5 as being made if and when a person becomes entitled to an interest in possession in settled property. At that moment the settlement is transmuted from being one under which no interest in possession subsists to being one under which a person is F entitled to an interest in possession. Since this transmutation is the cause of the charge to tax arising, the charge to tax must be regarded as arising after—no doubt immediately after, but nevertheless after—the transmutation. Therefore the taxing provisions must be applied in the light of the interests subsisting as the result of the transmutation, not of those which subsisted immediately before the transmutation.

G Mr. Beattie suggested that precisely the same principles must also apply to other cases in which a transfer of value occurs, or is to be treated as having occurred, for the purposes of the tax. Thus in a case of an out and out transfer of property by a transfer inter vivos, to which section 20 is applicable, Mr. Beattie said that whether exempt securities are excluded property must depend not on the domicile and ordinary residence of the transferor, but of the transferee. In the same H way on a transfer on death, to which section 22 is applicable, he said that the answer to the question must depend on the state of affairs following the death and not on that immediately preceding the death. In the case of a change in beneficial ownership occurring on a cesser of a life interest, to which paragraph 3 (1) of Schedule 5 and section 23 and section 22 (1) are applicable, Mr. Beattie said that the answer must depend on the state of affairs following the death of the life tenant and not on that immediately preceding his death. In my judgment none

of these contentions can stand up against the express language of the A
relevant provisions.   Section 20 (3) provides that no account shall be
taken of the value of excluded property " which ceases to form part of
(the transferor's) estate " as a result of a disposition.   Section 23, which
falls to be read with section 22, provides that the estate of the deceased
immediately before his death does not for the purposes of the Act
include excluded property.   The same provision is applicable on the
termination of a life interest.   This language, in my opinion, clearly B
points to the identification of excluded property by reference to the state
of affairs while the property in question forms part of the estate of the
transferor or of the deceased owner or life tenant.   In my judgment,
analysis of paragraph 6 (1) and (2) of Schedule 5 leads to the same
conclusion.   When a person becomes entitled to an interest in possession
in settled property in which no such interest has hitherto subsisted, what C
is to be treated as being made out of that property is a " capital distribution," which by definition (see paragraph 6 (1)) is a payment out of
settled property at a time when no interest in possession in it subsists.
This, in my opinion, focuses attention on the state of affairs which
existed immediately before the transmutation.   At that stage in the
present case no one who was neither domiciled nor ordinarily resident
in the United Kingdom had any interest in possession in the Treasury D
stock.   Indeed at that stage no one at all had any interest in possession
in the stock.   If anyone had had such an interest, paragraph 6 would
not have applied.   I consequently reach the conclusion that the Treasury
stock was not excluded property by virtue of paragraph 3 (1) (*b*) of
Schedule 7 for the purposes of the charge to tax which arose in this
case on the appointment taking effect.   The cases referred to earlier, on E
which Mr. Beattie relied, are decisions on other statutes.   I reach my
conclusion on this part of the present case on the construction of the
language used in the relevant provisions of the Finance Act 1975.   I do
not think the cases are of assistance on that question of construction.

I turn, therefore, to paragraph 3 (2) of Schedule 7, which has already
been read by Bridge L.J.   No point was taken on this before Browne-
Wilkinson J.   The question here is whether in the present case it can F
be said that immediately before the appointment took effect, " all known
persons for whose benefit the settled property or income from it has
been or might be applied or who might become beneficially entitled to
an interest in possession in it " were persons who were neither domiciled
nor ordinarily resident in the United Kingdom.   At that stage the
settled fund was held on a discretionary trust for a class of discretionary G
objects consisting of Arabella and George and their respective issue, of
whom there were and never have been any in existence, subject to a
power of appointment in favour or for the benefit of Arabella and
George or either of them.   If no appointment had been made under
that power, and if Arabella and George had both died before the end
of the last mentioned trust period without issue, or their issue failing
during that trust period, the trusts of the 1976 settlement would have H
become exhausted and one would be thrown back on the trusts of the
1967 settlement then capable of subsisting, under which an incorporated
charity called Annacastle Ltd., which was introduced to the 1967 settlement by the variation of trusts order of December 14, 1972, and an
unincorporated charity called the Charles Clore Foundation, would have
become objects of the trusts.

The appointment of March 25, 1976, was made under the power of

A appointment contained in the 1976 settlement. As, in accordance with my judgment already expressed, the question whether the Treasury stock was " excluded property " for the purposes of the notional capital distribution which must be treated as having been made on that appointment taking effect has to be answered in reference to the state of affairs which existed immediately before the appointment took effect, I need not consider in detail the terms of that appointment. The only known

B persons or bodies who might have to be taken into account for the purposes of paragraph 3 (2) of Schedule 7 in relation to that notional capital distribution are Arabella, George, Annacastle Ltd. and the Charles Clore Foundation. Annacastle Ltd. is a company incorporated under the Companies Act 1948 having objects of a wide character but exclusively charitable. Its memorandum of association forbids in a familiar

C form any payment or transfer of assets directly or indirectly to any member of the company and provides that on liquidation surplus assets shall not be paid to or distributed among the members but shall be applied for charitable purposes. The company has power in law to alter its objects and so could introduce non-charitable objects: but this is, I think, irrelevant because the variation of trusts order makes Annacastle Ltd. an object of the trusts of the 1967 settlement for so long only as

D its objects remain exclusively charitable. In these circumstances the question arises whether Annacastle Ltd. was, at March 25, 1976, a " known person for whose benefit the settled property or income from it had been or might be applied or who might become beneficially entitled to an interest in possession in it."

Mr. Walker, who argued this part of the case on behalf of the tax-

E payers and did so, if I may say so, very well, accepted that Annacastle Ltd. was a known person, but contended that it was not a person capable of being benefited or of becoming beneficially entitled for the purpose of paragraph 3 (2). He said that the only persons or purposes capable of benefiting from money or property received by Annacastle Ltd. are the objects of the charitable purposes of the company, and these are unascertained purposes and unknown persons. Mr. Nicholls, for the

F Crown, submitted that Annacastle Ltd. is not a trustee of its assets; it owns its assets absolutely and can do what it likes with them within its statutory powers like any other company incorporated under the Companies Acts. It can, he said, own property beneficially.

We were referred to certain authorities which give support to the view that a company incorporated for exclusively charitable purposes is

G in the position of a trustee of its funds or at least in an analogous position. The authorities were In re French Protestant Hospital [1951] Ch. 567; Soldiers', Sailors' and Airmen's Families Association v. Attorney-General [1968] 1 W.L.R. 313; Construction Industry Training Board v. Attorney-General [1973] Ch. 173 and In re Finger's Will Trusts [1972] Ch. 286. In the first two of these cases it seems to me that it was assumed, rather than decided, that a corporate charity

H was in the position of a trustee of its funds. In the third, the question was what was meant by the words " in the exercise of the court's jurisdiction with respect to charities " in section 45 (1) of the Charities Act 1960. In the court of my judgment in that case I certainly did express the view that the court would exercise its jurisdiction over corporate charities on the basis that their assets were held on charitable trusts and it appears to me that Plowman J., as I understand his very short judgment, agreed with me in that respect. In re Finger's

Will Trusts turned on a question of whether or not a bequest to a   A
charitable corporation, which ceased to exist in the testatrix's lifetime,
demonstrated a general charitable intention capable of permitting a
cy-près application. I do not think that it is a decision which is of
assistance for present purposes.

On this part of the case, as on the earlier part, I do not think that
authority helps us much. We have to construe paragraph 3 (2). In
my judgment a corporation which is by its constitution debarred from   B
using or acquiring assets for the purpose of making or obtaining any
profit for itself or its corporators, and which serves the purpose only
of machinery for carrying on exclusively charitable activities, is not an
object for whose benefit settled property or income from it can be
applied or which might become beneficially entitled to an interest in
possession in settled property within the meaning of paragraph 3 (2).   C
For the purposes of applying paragraph 3 (2) I think one must look at
the character of such a body to see whether it, rather than the purposes
which it exists to serve, is capable of benefiting within the meaning of
the paragraph and, in my judgment, it is not capable of doing so. It is
a mere conduit pipe, just as in my view the trustees of an unincorporated
charity are.

It is, in my view, significant that by paragraph 10 of Schedule 6   D
property given to charity is not a capital distribution for the purposes
of Schedule 5. If settled property given to charity is exempt, it would
be strange if the inclusion of a charity in a discretionary class could
render exempt securities held on discretionary trusts for that class non-
excluded if those securities would otherwise be excluded property. I
would consequently allow this appeal on this latter ground.   E

On the point which has been argued under the Finance (No. 2) Act
1931, I am in entire agreement with Bridge L.J.

> *Appeal allowed.*
> *Taxpayers to have their costs of*
> *hearing.*
> *Order for costs below not disturbed.*   F
> *Leave to appeal.*

Solicitors: *Titmuss, Sainer & Webb; Solicitor of Inland Revenue.*

[Reported by MRS. HARRIET DUTTON, Barrister-at-Law]   G

A

[COURT OF APPEAL]

* HALL *v.* AVON AREA HEALTH AUTHORITY (TEACHING)

1979 Dec. 3, 4   Stephenson, Waller and Cumming-Bruce L.JJ.

B *Damages—Personal injuries—Medical examination of plaintiff—
Defendants' request for examination—Agreement conditional
on plaintiff's nominated doctor being present—Defendants'
objection—Whether plaintiff entitled to insist on presence of
own doctor*

The plaintiff, a woman aged 52 years, who was employed
by a health authority as a domestic at a hospital, sustained
C   injuries when she slipped and fell while walking along a
driveway at the hospital. She brought an action against the
health authority for breach of duty of care, claiming damages
for pain and shock, and a major rupture of the right shoulder.
The health authority, denying liability, alleged contributory
negligence. The master ordered a mutual exchange of medical
reports. The plaintiff agreed to be examined by an orthopaedic
surgeon named by the health authority on condition that the
examination took place in the presence of a doctor nominated
D   by her solicitors. On the health authority's summons, the
deputy district registrar ordered that the plaintiff's action
should be stayed until she submitted to a medical examination
without a doctor nominated by her being present. On the
plaintiff's appeal, the judge held that the plaintiff's request
that a doctor nominated by her should be present at the
examination by the health authority's doctor was reasonable
E   in the case of a female plaintiff of 52 years of age and that
since she was only asking that her doctor be present to safeguard her interests and not to take part in the examination,
the order would provide that the examination by the health
authority's surgeon should take place in the presence of a
surgeon nominated by the plaintiff.
On the health authority's application for leave to appeal
and, leave having been granted, on appeal: —
F   *Held,* allowing the appeal, that the reasons suggested for
the imposition of the condition were not sufficient to outweigh the disadvantages in increased expenses or delay which
would be caused by requiring one surgeon to be present while
another was carrying out an examination; that while there
might be cases where a plaintiff might require the help and
comfort of a third party, the court ought to be given good
or substantial reasons before imposing such a condition on a
G   reasonable request for a medical examination of a plaintiff by
a doctor named by a defendant; accordingly, the condition in
the judge's order would be set aside and the action stayed
until the plaintiff submitted to the examination unconditionally
(post, pp. 491G–H, 492B, E–H, 494G—495A).
Starr v. *National Coal Board* [1977] 1 W.L.R. 63, C.A.
considered.

H   The following cases are referred to in the judgments:

Edmeades v. *Thames Board Mills Ltd.* [1969] 2 Q.B. 67; [1969] 2 W.L.R.
      668; [1969] 2 All E.R. 127, C.A.
Lane v. *Willis* [1972] 1 W.L.R. 326; [1972] 1 All E.R. 430, C.A.
Pickett v. *Bristol Aeroplane Co. Ltd.,* March 16, 1961; Court of Appeal
      (Civil Division) Transcript No. 114 of 1961, C.A.
Starr v. *National Coal Board* [1977] 1 W.L.R. 63; [1977] 1 All E.R. 243,
      C.A.

Hall v. Avon Health Authority (C.A.) [1980]

The following additional cases were cited in argument:

Clarke v. *Martlew* [1973] Q.B. 58; [1972] 3 W.L.R. 653; [1972] 3 All E.R. 764, C.A.

McGinley v. *Burke* [1973] 1 W.L.R. 990; [1973] 2 All E.R. 1010.

Murphy v. *Ford Motor Co. Ltd.* (1970) 114 S.J. 886, C.A.

Worrall v. *Reich* [1955] 1 Q.B. 296; [1955] 2 W.L.R. 338; [1955] 1 All E.R. 363, C.A.

INTERLOCUTORY APPEAL from Kenneth Jones J.

The plaintiff, Mrs. Betty Hall, was employed by the defendants, the Avon Area Health Authority (Teaching), as a domestic at the Hortham Hospital, Almondsbury, Bristol. On November 8, 1977, the plaintiff, then aged 52 years, was walking along a drive leading to the Avon Ward when she slipped on mud and wet leaves, and fell. By her statement of claim dated September 15, 1978, she contended that her fall was caused by the negligence and/or breach of statutory duty of the health authority, and that she had suffered personal injuries, loss and damage. By the particulars, she alleged, inter alia, that the health authority had failed to take adequate steps to prevent vehicles from using the driveway and strewing mud over the surface; that they had failed to clear up the mud or to collect the leaves which had fallen on the driveway; that they had failed to inspect the state of the driveway and warn her of the hazard of mud and fallen leaves; and had failed to provide her with a safe place of work or were in breach of their duty as occupiers. The particulars of injury alleged shock and severe pain, and major rupture of the rotator cuff of the right shoulder. The statement of claim further indicated that details of the plaintiff's injuries appeared in a medical report of June 26, 1978, by Mr. W. G. J. Hampson to the effect that she would have a permanent marked limitation of movement in the right shoulder. By their defence dated November 8, 1978, the health authority denied liability and alleged that the plaintiff had been guilty of contributory negligence in failing to look where she was walking, or in walking deliberately or carelessly on the alleged patch of mud and wet leaves. At all relevant times the health authority were the occupiers of the premises and the plaintiff, being in the course of her employment, was a visitor.

On January 4, 1979, Master Lubbock ordered the parties mutually to disclose medical reports within 28 days. By a letter dated January 19, 1979, the health authority's solicitors wrote to the plaintiff's solicitors suggesting a medical examination of the plaintiff by an orthopaedic surgeon, Mr. M. P. McCormack. By a letter dated January 25, 1979, the plaintiff's solicitors replied that the plaintiff was willing to be examined on condition, inter alia, that a doctor nominated by them was present. On the health authority's summons, on March 21, 1979, the deputy district registrar, Mr. R. L. Sansbury, ordered, inter alia, that the plaintiff's action should be stayed until such time as she was prepared to be medically examined by the health authority's consultant without the attendance of the plaintiff's medical adviser at the examination. On the plaintiff's appeal, Kenneth Jones J. on July 27, 1979, setting aside the order of the deputy district registrar, ordered (see post, p. 487c–e), inter alia, that all further proceedings in the action should be stayed until such time as the plaintiff should have been medically examined by Mr. M. P. McCormack F.R.C.S., provided that such examination should take place in the presence of Mr. P. J.

A Witherow F.R.C.S., a surgeon nominated by the plaintiff, and that there should be mutual disclosure of the medical reports obtained.

The health authority gave notice of their intention to apply for leave to appeal against that order and, if leave should be granted, of their intention to appeal immediately.

By their notice of appeal of August 17, 1979, the health authority appealed against the judge's decision on the grounds that (1) the judge B was wrong in law in holding that the plaintiff or her solicitors had a legal right to insist on a doctor nominated by the solicitors to be present at the medical examination by the health authority's orthopaedic surgeon; (2) that there was no ground on which the judge could properly have exercised his discretion in favour of the plaintiff by imposing such a condition on the medical examination by the health authority's surgeon; (3) the judge C should have held that, the health authority having made a reasonable request for a medical examination by a surgeon to whom no objection had been raised (a) the plaintiff had no legal right to insist as a condition of consenting to an examination, on her own named practitioner being present; (b) since no reason for such a condition was given by the plaintiff herself, or by her legal advisers, and there was no evidence to suggest that there were any reasonable grounds for imposing it, the plaintiff was not D entitled to have it inserted as a term of the order; and (c) the mere fact that the plaintiff was a female aged 52 years was not a sufficient reason for the court to exercise its discretion by inserting such a condition in the order; and that (4) in the premises, the order made by the deputy district registrar for a stay of the action ought to have been upheld without any condition being imposed. Accordingly, the health authority sought an order E that paragraphs 2 (a) (examination should take place in the presence of Mr. Witherow) and 3 (costs) of the judge's order should be set aside.

C. S. Rawlins for the health authority.
Edward Bailey for the plaintiff.

F STEPHENSON L.J. The plaintiff, Mrs. Hall, in this action has refused to undergo a medical examination by an orthopaedic surgeon nominated by the defendants, the Avon Area Health Authority, unless the examination is conducted in the presence of a doctor nominated by her or her solicitors.

Kenneth Jones J. held on July 27, 1979, that she was entitled to refuse on that condition. He allowed her appeal from an order of the deputy district registrar staying her action, or intending to stay her action, until G she submitted to that examination without her doctor being present, and he subjected the stay to the proviso that (among other things) the examination should take place in the presence of a surgeon nominated by her. Was the judge plainly wrong?

Mr. Rawlins has submitted for the health authority that he was and that we should remove the condition. Mr. Bailey has submitted for the plaintiff H that the judge was right and we should not interfere with his exercise of his discretion.

I am bound to say that my first reaction to this application for leave to appeal was hostile. Why should not the plaintiff have her doctor or surgeon there? Why should she be prevented from pursuing her claim unless she agreed to be examined without him? What injustice could possibly result from her insisting on his presence? And even if I might have reached a different decision, how could it be said that the judge was not

entitled to exercise his discretion as he did? But Mr. Rawlins has per- A
suaded me, in spite of my reluctance to reverse an exercise of discretion
by this judge and of all that Mr. Bailey has forcibly urged in support of
his order, that we ought to give leave to appeal and to allow the appeal.

The plaintiff's case is an uncomplicated one, as appears from paragraphs 1 and 2 of her statement of claim which was served on September 15,
1978:

> " At all material times the plaintiff was employed by the [health auth- B
> ority] as a domestic at their premises Hortham Hospital, Almondsbury,
> Bristol of which premises the [health authority] were at all relevant
> times the occupiers and on which the plaintiff, during the course of
> her said employment, was a visitor. On November 8, 1977, at about
> 8.05 a.m. the plaintiff was walking along the driveway leading towards
> Avon Ward when she was caused to slip and fall to the ground by a C
> patch of mud and wet leaves which were lying on the said driveway."

Then it was alleged that her fall was caused by the negligence and/or
breach of statutory duty of the health authority and it was alleged in paragraph 4 that, by reason of the health authority's negligence and/or breach
of duty as employer or occupier, the plaintiff sustained personal injury and
suffered loss and damage, the only particulars given being " (a) Shock and D
severe pain. (b) Major rupture of the rotator cuff of the right shoulder."
Paragraph 4 goes on:

> " The plaintiff was aged 52 at the time of the accident. Details of
> her injuries and treatment therefore appear in a medical report dated
> June 26, 1978, by Mr. W. G. J. Hampson. The plaintiff will have a
> permanent marked limitation of movement in her right shoulder and E
> this may well prevent her from continuing her employment as a
> domestic and will restrict her ability to obtain other employment."

The report referred to in that paragraph was, by a mistake, not in fact
delivered with the statement of claim to the health authority's solicitors
and, of course, it was a report of an examination made not in the presence
of any representative, medical or otherwise, of the health authority. Mr. F
Hampson, who was the author of that report, unfortunately died before
these proceedings came on for trial. His death was not immediately
known to the plaintiff's solicitors.

The defence delivered on November 8, 1978, is in ordinary form, denying liability and damage and alleging contributory negligence on the part
of the plaintiff. G

On January 4, 1979, Master Lubbock made an order for directions and
by paragraph 1 he ordered:

> " The plaintiff and the [health authority] do mutually disclose medical
> reports within 28 days after setting down. Such reports be agreed if
> possible. Unless such reports are agreed, the parties be at liberty to
> call medical witnesses limited to one witness for each party whose H
> report has been so disclosed."

That order for mutual disclosure was in accordance with the practice
laid down in the R.S.C., Ord. 38, r. 37. That provides:

> " (1) Where in an action for personal injuries an application is made
> under rule 36 (1) in respect of oral expert evidence relating to
> medical matters, then, unless the court considers that there is

The Weekly Law Reports, May 16, 1980

485

1 W.L.R.   Hall v. Avon Health Authority (C.A.)   Stephenson L.J.

A   sufficient reason for not doing so, it shall direct that the substance of the evidence be disclosed in the form of a written report or reports to such other parties and within such period as the court may specify."

Orders made under that rule provide now for the mutual exchange of medical reports contemporaneously on the principle of reciprocity which

B   is recognised also, for instance, in Ord. 38, rr. 36 and 38, and in Ord. 25, r. 6 (1). In the *Supreme Court Practice* (1979), pp. 441 and 622, will be found valuable notes, 25/6/2 and 38/35/5, referring to the authorities which establish this principle and explaining the machinery of simultaneous exchange and its reason.

On January 19, 1979 (well before the end of the period laid down in

C   the order for directions, to which I have referred), the health authority's solicitors wrote to the plaintiff's solicitors:

"As you know, we do not yet have a medical report on your client. We would like to instruct Mr. M. P. McCormack, orthopaedic surgeon, of 18, Richmond Hill, Bristol 8, to examine your client and prepare a report on her for the purpose of defending the action. Would you please ascertain whether your client has any personal objections to

D   Mr. McCormack and, if she has not, please confirm this and we will instruct him."

To that the plaintiff's solicitors replied on January 25:

"We confirm that facilities will be available to you to have our client examined by Mr. McCormack on the usual terms, namely: 1. A

E   doctor nominated by us is present. 2. You agree to meet the fees of the doctor nominated by us. 3. You agree to reimburse our client her reasonable expenses including any loss of wages for attending the medical examination. 4. You agree to let us have a sight of your doctor's report. We note that you are waiting to hear from counsel and we await hearing from you as soon as possible."

F   So there the plaintiff's solicitors are putting forward four (what they call) "usual terms," which are conditions precedent to the plaintiff's being examined by Mr. McCormack, the orthopaedic surgeon nominated by the health authority to whom they, by their silence, have no personal objections. It is admitted, and the judge so found, that the request contained in the health authority's solicitors' letter of January 19 was a reasonable request.

G   Thereafter, the solicitors for the health authority took out a summons and the deputy district registrar made an order, neither of which I need read.

On June 26, the plaintiff appealed against the registrar's order as it was intended to be made, to stay the plaintiff's action unless she submitted to an examination by Mr. McCormack without the presence of a doctor

H   nominated by her. On June 26, apparently, the judge had his first hearing of the plaintiff's appeal. The hearing dealt mainly with the question of reciprocity in making any report by Mr. McCormack available to the plaintiff and any report by a doctor nominated by the plaintiff available to the health authority. But on July 27, when the hearing was resumed, that matter had been resolved and the sole issue was the first condition which the plaintiff's solicitors were seeking to impose on the examination as a "usual term."

We have the advantage of a full note of the judge's judgment, approved   A
by him, and that note begins with these two sentences:

"This matter can be taken shortly. The [health authority] wish to have
the plaintiff examined by their own doctor. The plaintiff started by
agreeing or consenting to such examination only on certain conditions,
these conditions being . . . " and then he sets out the four conditions.

In a note appended to the agreed note of his judgment, on September 5,   B
1979, the judge added:

"According to my recollection the only issue here was whether condition 1 "—i.e. the first ' usual term '—" was reasonable. I decided
that it was. On that basis the [health authority] agreed that
conditions 3 and 4 were reasonable. The plaintiff at the outset
abandoned condition 2."   C

The plaintiff's solicitors had given an undertaking in accordance with all
the cases which were cited to us, ending with Starr v. National Coal Board
[1977] 1 W.L.R. 63. The reasonableness of condition 1 was the only outstanding issue between the parties.
      The judge referred to Starr's case [1977] 1 W.L.R. 63 and quoted
from it what Scarman L.J. had said, at p. 70:   D

"So what is the principle of the matter to be gleaned from those cases?
In my judgment the court can order a stay if, in the words of Lord
Denning M.R. in Edmeades's case [1969] 2 Q.B. 67, 70, the conduct of
the plaintiff in refusing a reasonable request for medical examination
is such as to prevent the just determination of the cause. I think
that those words contain the principle of the matter. We are, of course, E
in the realm of discretion. It is a matter for the discretion of the judge,
exercised judicially upon the facts of the case, whether or not a
stay should be ordered."

Kenneth Jones J. went on to say:

"In this case it is not disputed that the defendants' request for a
medical examination is a reasonable request. . . . Really the question   F
is whether the conduct of the plaintiff in insisting on these two conditions (1 and 4) prevents a just determination of the cause. I have
no doubt that the court has to see whether these conditions are reasonable in all the circumstances of the case."

Further he added:

"It seems to me abundantly obvious that it is reasonable. She is not   G
insisting on a joint examination. She is not insisting that her doctor
should in any way impede or interfere with the examination. She is
only asking that he be present to protect her interests in the widest
sense. It seems to me that that is a very modest request indeed and I
am surprised that any defendant looking at it dispassionately can really
contend otherwise. It seems entirely reasonable that a lady aged 52   H
should be accompanied at a medical examination. It is better that
the person to accompany her should possess some professional skill.
She might have asked for her solicitors to be present but it is obviously
right that the person should be another doctor. He can safeguard her
interests. He can witness the examination as it takes place, witness
what is said by the plaintiff to the defendants' doctor and he can in
due course confirm whether the defendants' doctor's account is an

The Weekly Law Reports, May 16, 1980

487

1 W.L.R.   **Hall v. Avon Health Authority (C.A.)**   Stephenson L.J.

accurate one. It may be that the defendants' doctor has recorded her answers not quite accurately. He may have to report that the defendants' doctor's account is not quite accurate but that is not necessarily impropriety. That is all part of the examination. The matter is so completely obvious that it does not require further elaboration. It is urged on me that I should require evidence of why a doctor nominated by her should be present and that affidavits should be sworn. I see no need for evidence where a female plaintiff of 52 is required to undergo a medical examination. If she was requiring her doctor to take some part in the examination that would be different."

So, with the undertaking given to get rid of condition 4, the order of July 27 was made by the judge. By that order he ordered:

"1. The plaintiff's appeal be allowed and the order made by Mr. Deputy District Registrar Sansbury on March 21, 1979, be set aside. 2. All further proceedings in this action be stayed until such time as the plaintiff shall have been medically examined by Mr. M. P. McCormack F.R.C.S. provided that (a) such examination shall take place in the presence of Mr. P. J. Witherow F.R.C.S., a surgeon nominated by the plaintiff." Mr. Witherow was nominated to take the place of the deceased Mr. Hampson. "(b) The [health authority] do pay the plaintiff's own reasonable expenses of attending such examination. (c) The [health authority] shall disclose to the plaintiff's solicitors a copy of any report which they obtain from Mr. M. P. McCormack in exchange for any report which the plaintiff's solicitors may obtain from Mr. P. J. Witherow and any other reports on which the plaintiff intends to rely. 3. The costs of the plaintiff's appeal and of the [health authority's] application to the deputy district registrar be the plaintiff's in any event. 4. Leave to appeal be refused."

I need not, I think, refer to any of the cases to which Mr. Rawlins for the health authority has directed our attention: most of them are cited in the notes at pp. 441, 622 of the *Supreme Court Practice* (1979), to which I have already referred. None of those cases, including *Starr's* case [1977] 1 W.L.R. 63, deals with a conditional refusal of this kind. The observations which were made by the members of this court in *Starr's* case relate to an unconditional refusal. That is made plain by what Scarman L.J. said, at p. 56:

"The question which the judge had to decide, and which is now before this court, is whether the plaintiff was entitled to refuse to be examined by a particular doctor."

Then Scarman L.J. said, at p. 67:

"There are a number of propositions of law which are not in dispute, and I mention them straight away so that one may approach and consider that which is in issue between the parties. It is accepted that where a plaintiff refuses to undergo a medical examination requested by a defendant, the court has an inherent jurisdiction to grant a stay until such time as he submits to such examination when it is just and reasonable so to do. It is also recognised that a stay, if granted, either shuts out the plaintiff from the seat of justice or compels him against his will to submit to a medical examination; and, of course, that is an invasion of his personal liberty."

Then he said, at p. 70: " So what is the principle of the matter to be gleaned   A
from those cases? In my judgment the court can order a stay if, in the
words of Lord Denning M.R. in *Edmeades's* case [1969] 2 Q.B. 67,"
and then he goes on to cite the rest of the passage which has already
been read in a quotation from the judgment of the judge in this case.
After that passage Scarman L.J. said, at pp. 70–71:

> " For myself, I find talk about onus of proof in such a case inappro-   B
> priate. There is, I think, clearly a general rule that he who seeks a
> stay of an action must satisfy the court that justice requires the imposi-
> tion of a stay.
> " In the exercise of the discretion in this class of case, where a
> plaintiff has refused a medical examination, I think the court does have
> to recognise (and here I think *Pickett* v. *Bristol Aeroplane Co. Ltd.,*
> Court of Appeal (Civil Division) Transcript No. 114 of 1961 is helpful)   C
> that in the balance there are, amongst many other factors, two funda-
> mental rights which are cherished by the common law and to which
> attention has to be directed by the court. First, as mentioned in
> *Pickett's* case by Wilmer and Donovan L.JJ. and by Sachs L.J. in
> *Lane* v. *Willis* [1972] 1 W.L.R. 326, there is the plaintiff's right to
> personal liberty. But on the other side there is an equally funda-   D
> mental right—the defendant's right to defend himself in the litigation
> as he and his advisers think fit; and this is a right which includes the
> freedom to choose the witnesses that he will call. It is particularly
> important that a defendant should be able to choose his own expert
> witnesses, if the case be one in which expert testimony is significant."

Then Scarman L.J. said, at p. 71:   E

> " And so in every case, as I see it, the particular facts of the case up-
> on which the discretion has to be exercised are all-important. The dis-
> cretion cannot be exercised unless each party does expose the reasons
> for his action. I have already indicated that I do not regard this as a
> question of onus of proof. There is, in my judgment, a duty upon
> each party in such a situation to provide the court with the neces-   F
> sary material known to him, so that the court, fully informed, can
> exercise its discretion properly. However, I would add this
> comment: that at the end of the day it must be for him who seeks
> the stay to show that, in the discretion of the court, it should be
> imposed."

He then applies those principles and states the first question to be: G
" was the defendants' request for the examination of the plaintiff by
Dr. X a reasonable request? " He found that it was. He asked himself the second question: " granted the reasonableness of the defendants'
request, was the plaintiff's refusal of it unreasonable? " He answers
that question: " Yes, it was."

The judgments of Geoffrey Lane and Cairns L.JJ. each contain a pas-   H
sage to which I will refer. Geoffrey Lane L.J. said at p. 75:

> " One has to do one's best to extract from the decisions such principles
> as seem best to accord with reason and with practice and with fairness.
> The court clearly has inherent jurisdiction to order a stay when the
> justice of the case demands such a stay. There are not infrequent occa-
> sions when justice demands that the plaintiff should undergo medical
> examination by a doctor appointed on behalf of the defendants. There

The Weekly Law Reports, May 16, 1980

489

1 W.L.R.   Hall v. Avon Health Authority (C.A.)   Stephenson L.J.

A   are circumstances in which refusal by the plaintiff to undergo such examination should in justice be met by the imposition of a stay."

Cairns L.J. said, at p. 78:

"If the defendant has put forward the name of a particular doctor and can show that an examination by a doctor is necessary in his interests and that this particular doctor is apparently well qualified to
B   examine the plaintiff, the plaintiff then has to give reasons for objecting to him. He must at least be able to show that there is some substantial ground on which he or his advisers have formed the opinion that the doctor in question lacks the proper qualifications or is likely to conduct his examination and to make his reports unkindly or unfairly."

C   In their notice of appeal the health authority complained that the judge had held that the plaintiff had a legal right to insist on her nominated doctor being present at her examination by the health authority's nominated surgeon. I can find nothing of the kind in the judge's judgment. He quoted Scarman L.J.'s observations that the matter is a matter of discretion and it seems to me that the judge treated it throughout as a matter of dis-
D   cretion. I therefore would not read ground (1) of the notice of appeal,

"(2) That there were no grounds or material upon which the judge could properly have exercised any discretion vested in him in favour of the plaintiff by making it a condition of any examination by the said Mr. McCormack on behalf of the [health authority] that it should only take place in the presence of the said Mr. Witherow. . . . (3) The
E   learned judge should have held that, the [health authority] having made a reasonable request for a medical examination by an orthopaedic surgeon to whom the plaintiff raised no objection: . . . (b) As no reason for imposing such a condition was given by the plaintiff herself, or by her solicitors or by her counsel and no evidence was tendered to suggest that there were any or reasonable grounds for imposing it, the plaintiff was not entitled to have it inserted as a term of the order.
F   (c) The mere fact that the plaintiff was a female aged 52 was not a sufficient reason for the court to exercise its discretion in her favour by inserting the condition in the order."

Mr. Rawlins relies on those grounds and submits that, by claiming condition 1 to be a " usual term " required by solicitors, wider considerations are raised and, if the judge's judgment is upheld, this court will be decid-
G   ing that the court is absolved from finding reasons for a particular plaintiff insisting on this term or condition; that it is a usually reasonable requirement which the courts should not remove but enforce. So here we are not concerned with this case in isolation but with the effect which our decision may have on other cases and other plaintiffs, and in particular members of the trade union which has acted for this plaintiff and instructed these
H   solicitors of hers will be taking the same point if the judge's order stands.

Mr. Rawlins, accordingly, submits first that the interests of justice and the just determination of personal injuries litigation involve four things: first, that the imposition of this condition should be the exception rather than the rule: second, that if a plaintiff refuses to undergo an examination unless this condition is performed, he or she must disclose his or her reasons for seeking to do so. I think he relies on *Starr's* case [1977] 1 W.L.R. 63 and, in particular, some of the passages I have quoted from the judgments of all three Lords Justices. Those principles, he submits, **A** apply to any condition which involves the court's exercise of its discretion.

The third thing is that the principle of reciprocity must not be infringed. It is a consistent theme running through the disclosure and exchange of medical reports and to depart from it can cause an injustice or an imbalance of justice in the determination of personal injuries litigation. He points out that, in this case as in others, it would be quite impracticable for **B** the health authority to have their medical man present at the first examination or the early examinations of a plaintiff by his or her nominated medical man. Yet this condition requires the presence of the plaintiff's medical man at the health authority's medical man's first examination.

Fourth, if allowed to become a general rule of practice, and not the exception, the imposition of this condition would have the inevitable consequence that there will be a widespread adoption of this practice and that **C** will cause delay in getting medical reports and will cause injustice and extra expense. He added that it will cause the alienation of medical men from assisting the court in litigation of this kind. They may not always easily be persuaded to examine the parties to litigation, knowing that if they do they may or will have to take time off from their practices to give evidence in support of their reports. Their reluctance will be increased if **D** they are called upon to be present with (as it were) a watching brief at medical examinations in which they can take no part. They may find that a burdensome and frustrating duty and be further deterred from giving their assistance in this type of litigation.

Those submissions are, of course, in addition to those which he elaborated in his grounds of appeal, namely, that in this case no good **E** reason has been put forward for this lady requiring this medical man to be present at her examination by this other medical man. He submits, on the authority particularly of *Starr's* case, that such reasons must be put forward and they must be reasons sufficient to outweigh, when it comes to the exercise of the court's discretion, those increases in delay and costs, which may ultimately fall on the health authority, caused by **F** insisting on this condition, and those other consequences—the one-sided presence of the other side's doctor after an earlier examination where only the plaintiff's side has been present, and the possible deterrent effect on doctors generally.

Mr. Bailey for the plaintiff does not shrink from our treating this case as a test case. He submits that the experience of his instructing solicitors is that members of this union with a background like the plaintiff's, a union **G** for whom they have acted in claims against other defendants, have during the last nine months to a year complained of the medical examinations to which they have been submitted by doctors nominated by defendants, in the absence of anybody on their own side. It is in consequence of this general experience of those solicitors that they have evolved this practice of requiring this condition, without consulting each plaintiff for whom they are **H** acting, although each plaintiff is, of course, informed by them of what they are doing or have done to protect the plaintiff's interests in this way. By this condition Mr. Bailey's instructing solicitors hope to protect unskilled and uneducated plaintiffs from being badgered or upset, as he put it, by medical examinations in the absence of anybody representing their own side, and from being led to feel that they are being unjustly treated, even if their feelings are irrational. They also hope, by this condition, to

The Weekly Law Reports, May 16, 1980

491

1 W.L.R.   Hall v. Avon Health Authority (C.A.)   Stephenson L.J.

A increase the chances of agreement between the medical men on each side
and of the consequent settlement of their claims.

He frankly conceded that this condition would be required where a
plaintiff was not a woman of 52 but a man of 25, provided that he came
from the same unskilled, uneducated sort of background as this lady; but
he submitted that it was even more reasonable to require such a condition
for a 52-year-old woman.

B Mr. Bailey did not argue that the court should enforce unreasonable
conditions if justice would, nonetheless, not be thereby prevented from being
done; but he did claim that it was reasonable for a party like the plaintiff
to stand on his or her right to personal liberty by having his or her own
nominated doctor present when it could not prejudice the health authority
or their nominated doctor's examination or cause them any injustice.

C He conceded that the costs of the attendance of a medical man like
Mr. Witherow might be relevant to the exercise of the judge's discretion,
but he submitted that any delay resulting from the adoption of this practice
was minimal and that the question of possibly deterring the medical profession if this practice were to be adopted was not put to the judge or supported by anything but speculation. He pointed out that the taxing master
could disallow the costs of the attendance of such a medical man if he
D thought proper, but on any view these considerations on which Mr. Rawlins
relies could not outweigh the importance of protecting an unskilled working
man or woman, and this plaintiff in particular, not only from injustice but
from any sense of injustice, however unreasonable, which medical examination by the other side's medical man alone might implant in their minds.

Mr. Bailey argued that the judge was entitled to hold, as he undoubtedly
E did, that the plaintiff's age and sex justified the solicitors requiring this
condition without any reason, substantial or otherwise, being put before
him on affidavit or in argument. And he did not throw over what seems
to have been the other ground on which the judge decided in the plaintiff's
favour, namely, that her own surgeon would be able to check any inaccuracy in the health authority's surgeon's report of his examination of
F her. But, as I understand him, he rested his case mainly on the experience
of his solicitors in other cases that other such clients felt aggrieved by such
medical examinations; a submission he was prevented from making to the
judge, because the judge stopped him and called on Mr. Rawlins before he
could make it. From the note of the judgment the judge clearly regarded
this as a plain case and that is confirmed by his having asked Mr. Rawlins
(so he told us) whether the plaintiff was not entitled to have someone to
G protect her interests when she went into the " den of lions ".

In my judgment, the court ought to have good or substantial reasons
put before it on instructions or, in an appropriate case, on affidavit, if it is
to impose conditions of this kind on a reasonable request for a medical
examination of a plaintiff by a doctor nominated by a defendant. This is
just as necessary in a case like the present as in cases, like *Starr's* [1977]
H 1 W.L.R. 63, of out-and-out refusal. The judge rightly treated this conditional acceptance as a refusal of a reasonable request, but I cannot agree
with his opinion that it was a reasonable refusal because the plaintiff was a
woman of 52 or because the surgeon nominated by her solicitors might
have testified to the inaccuracy of the other surgeon's report. Nor would it
have been reasonable because in other cases other previously injured parties
had been injured in their feelings by the way in which they were examined
by other doctors for other defendants. All professions have their black

sheep and good men have " off days." Courts of law, as well as the parties   A
to litigation and their solicitors, must give a Fellow of the Royal College
of Surgeons, of high standing in his profession of orthopaedic surgeon, credit
for being fair and considerate in his treatment of those whom he examines
on behalf of the other side and fair and accurate in his recording of such
examination, and for needing no third party, whether medically qualified
or not, to prevent him from misleading the court by inaccuracies or, I
would add, to restrain him, as was suggested (though not by the judge),   B
from confusing the party examined by unfair interrogation.

None of the reasons advanced to support the practice, which alone can
justify the judge's order, makes this plaintiff's conditional refusal to be
examined reasonable or outweighs the disadvantages in increased expenses
and delay which it may cause, even in such a simple case as this. I do not
put into the scale the lack of reciprocity necessarily resulting, or the possible   C
deterrent effect on the medical profession's willingness to take part in examinations of parties if they are required to hold a watching brief at an
examination in which they take no part, because I think there is nothing in
the first factor and not much in the second; though I may be under-estimat-
ing that consideration.

I accept that the plaintiff's solicitors require this (I think) unreasonable   D
condition in what they conceive to be the best interests of this plaintiff and
other parties for whom they act. And I am not to be taken as saying that
it would be unreasonable in every case or that it could never be imposed by
a judge. I do, however, find it difficult to see what advantage a medical
man has over a solicitor or a friend in the protection of a plaintiff from
being harassed or disturbed or inaccurately reported. I cannot understand
why a partner or legal executive in the firm of solicitors, handling this   E
plaintiff's case as local agents, would not have secured the purpose of her
union's solicitors better than Mr. Witherow, a specialist, who, by the accident of Mr. Hampson's death, was as unfamiliar to her as was Mr.
McCormack, the health authority's specialist.

What I have said about this condition is not intended to deprive the
plaintiff of the help and comfort of any third party's presence at any medical   F
examination by any doctor on behalf of any defendant. If, for example, the
particular plaintiff were in a nervous state or confused by a serious head
injury, or if the defendant's nominated doctor had a reputation for a fierce
examining manner, or if the plaintiff asked for her nominated doctor to be
present, it might be reasonable for her solicitors to insist, for her, on such a
condition, though the need for it might often be met, I would have thought,
by a joint medical examination, which was never suggested by the plaintiff's   G
advisers and which Mr. Bailey submitted was something which the health
authority's advisers ought to have suggested. But there is nothing of that
kind here. On the bare facts of this case, and they are perhaps so bare as to
make it a good test case, I can find no reason for not staying the plaintiff's
action unless she submits to this examination by Mr. McCormack unconditionally.   H

I would, accordingly, grant the health authority leave to appeal, allow
the appeal and set aside paragraph 2 (a) of the judge's order. That
would leave the stay subject to sub-paragraphs (b) and (c) only: see
ante, p. 487c–e.

WALLER L.J. I agree with the judgment of Stephenson L.J. I would
only add this. In my experience, the order which was sought here is an

unusual order and, although the plaintiff's solicitors in their letter describe
the terms as "usual terms," Mr. Bailey, for the plaintiff, frankly said that
it was only for the last nine months that those instructing him had sought
to enforce this condition. It has become clear in the course of the argument that this is not a special case; it is an attempt to change the practice.
In my judgment, the case for change has not been made out. If this change
were to be made it would cost money and the extent of the cost over the
country as a whole would be or might be great.

Mr. Bailey has based his case on the members of the union for whom
those instructing him appear, but that case would apply very widely indeed
to members of other unions throughout the country. If this became a
common order it might well make doctors less ready to involve themselves
in personal injury litigation, because it would involve highly-skilled professional men sitting quietly while one of their fellow consultants was making
an examination. It would also cause delays, because, although Mr. Bailey
rather minimised this, there would be the difficulty of two busy professional
men having to make an appointment which fitted them both rather than
just one, and that would cause delay.

There may be cases where such an order would be justifiable: for
example, a very nervous plaintiff. In such a case it might well be, indeed
it probably would be, preferable to have some other person present rather
than a consultant whom he or she has probably only seen once. Another
case might be the sort of case which arose in *Starr* v. *National Coal Board*
[1977] 1 W.L.R. 63 where it was thought that the consultant whom the
defendants wished to examine the plaintiff was one who tended to be hostile
to plaintiffs. In such circumstances it might (I do not say it would) be a
good ground for saying that the consultant on the other side should be
present.

Starr v. *National Coal Board* is authority for the view that it is not a
ground for refusing but it might be a good ground for having somebody
present. In this case there were no such grounds and, although the judge
has based his decision on the age and sex of the plaintiff, when one asks
where the line has to be drawn, Mr. Bailey promptly concedes that he would
be making a similar application even if the age and sex were both different.
The real grounds put before us are that plaintiffs sometimes come back from
medical examination by the defendant's consultant unhappy and worried;
a worry which may be irrational.

Having heard the argument—because, like Stephenson L.J. initially I
was disposed to uphold the judge's decision—in my view there were in fact
no grounds on which the judge could properly exercise his discretion as he
did. Furthermore, if he had been told the real grounds on which the application was made, it would not have strengthened the case in any way.
Indeed, those real grounds would have demonstrated the flimsy nature of
the case for this change of practice. I would allow the appeal.

CUMMING-BRUCE L.J. I agree. It is clear now that in this court we have
obtained a much more comprehensive picture of the history of the conditions
that the plaintiff's solicitors sought in their letter of January 25, 1979, than
was available to the judge. Mr. Bailey for the plaintiff told this court that
most of the time at the hearing before the judge was taken up with discussion
of the notice of appeal and when Mr. Bailey was himself addressing the

judge it was very quickly apparent that the judge, partly as a matter of first
impression, had formed a strong view in his favour, which emerges from the
judgment. So Mr. Bailey did not have the opportunity of developing his
argument in the way in which it has been developed in this court. But it
emerged from Mr. Bailey's candid submission to this court that the conditions sought to be imposed on January 25, 1979, were not in any sense the
result of any initiative or sense of need on the part of the particular plaintiff, but were founded entirely upon the experience of the plaintiff's solicitors
in the conduct of litigation.

I agree with Stephenson and Waller L.JJ. that such initiative on the part
of the solicitors is entirely within their professional competence and I would
not for a moment criticise them for the initiative that they took in this case.
But, as appears from Mr. Bailey's submission in this court, the strongest
consideration which moved the solicitors to ask for the conditions on which
they tried to insist was a subjective feeling of which they had become aware
on the part of previous clients who had complained about the way in which
they had been received, examined and treated in the course of the examination, although an analysis of the reaction of those clients showed that
frequently their reaction had been irrational. It was in order to give a
reasonable reassurance to clients who had to be subjected to a medical
examination on the part of the defendant's doctors that the conditions put
forward in the letter were prompted.

It may be too dramatic a metaphor, but it seems to me that the remedy
proposed by the solicitors was a sledge-hammer to crack a nut. It seems to
me entirely reasonable that solicitors, as a result of their professional experience in litigation, should advise plaintiffs that it would be sensible to
have someone with them to reassure them when they go to a medical examination, whether the examination be by a doctor nominated on their behalf
by their own solicitors or examination by a doctor nominated by the defendants. The person who could usually give such reassurance, perfectly
adequately, would be a relative or a friend, who in the ordinary way would
not expect any remuneration, or in some (perhaps rare) cases a member of
the staff of the plaintiff's solicitors' firm, preferably someone to whom the
plaintiff had previously been introduced in order to gain confidence.

Such a solution would avoid the objections which Mr. Rawlins for the
health authority has so forcibly brought to our notice about the conditions
required by the plaintiff's solicitors in this case. To require a medical consultant to be present to act as a chaperone, although he has no personal
function to perform in the course of the examination by the health authority's surgeon, seems to me to be a serious addition to the costs of the
litigation and also an inexcusable requirement, on the part of the processes
of litigation and justice, of the precious time of highly qualified consultants,
whose professional business includes the examination of litigants for the
purposes of litigation, but whose primary concern is with diagnosis and
treatment of patients in order to alleviate their sufferings.

In my view, the court should hesitate long before encouraging or permitting any such addition to the time and expense in the conduct of personal
injury cases as is proposed by the solicitors in this case.

For those reasons, in addition to the reasons stated by Stephenson and

The Weekly Law Reports, May 16, 1980

495

1 W.L.R.   Hall v. Avon Health Authority (C.A.)   Cumming Bruce L.J.

A Waller L.JJ. with which I fully agree, I agree that this appeal should be allowed.

Leave to appeal granted.

Appeal allowed with costs in Court of Appeal, of appeal before judge and of application to deputy district registrar.

B

Para. 2 (a) of judge's order regarding proviso as to medical examination and para. 3 concerning costs set aside.

Leave to appeal refused.

C Solicitors: *Bevan, Hancock & Co.*, Bristol; *Gillhams.*

[Reported by MISS HENRIETTA STEINBERG, Barrister-at-Law]

D

[COURT OF APPEAL]

* M. GOLODETZ & CO. INC. *v.* CZARNIKOW-RIONDA CO. INC.

1978 Nov. 2, 3; 20   Donaldson J.
E 1979 Oct. 31;   Megaw, Shaw and Waller L.JJ.
      Nov. 1

Shipping—Bill of lading—Clean bill—Sugar damaged by fire after shipment—Notation added to bill of lading recording damaged state of sugar—Whether bill of lading clean

The sellers, who had agreed to sell sugar c. & f. free out Bandarshapur, Iran, chartered a vessel to carry the sugar from Kandla in India to Iran. Four days after the vessel had arrived in Kandla, and when the sugar was partly loaded, fire broke out, destroying 200 tons of it. Under the terms of the contract for the sale of the sugar, which incorporated the rules of the Refined Sugar Association, the sellers were entitled to be paid the price on tender of a clean " on board " bill of lading. A bill of lading relating to the lost sugar was tendered to the buyers in the standard form, which by printed clauses acknowledged the shipment of the sugar in apparent good order and condition. Added to it was a typewritten notation recording the state of the sugar after shipment and after the fire damage had occurred. The buyers, who had failed to insure the goods, contrary to the association's rules, rejected the bill of lading and, asserting that the loss of the sugar should fall on the sellers, took the matter before the association's board of appeal. The board held that the loss must fall on the sellers. On the arbitrators stating their award in the form of a special case, Donaldson J. held, giving judgment for the sellers, that, as the bill of lading had been merchantable in that, when properly read and understood, it had called for no further inquiry and had not invited litigation and as it had neither cast doubt on the condition of the goods at the time of shipment nor asserted that at the time of shipment the shipowner had had any claim against the goods, it had been a clean bill

of lading and that, having been clean at the time of shipment, *A*
it could not be rendered unclean by the addition to it at a
later stage of a notation recording the fate of the goods after
shipment.

On appeal by the buyers: —

Held, dismissing the appeal, that a clean bill of lading was
one in which there was nothing to qualify the admission that
the goods had been in apparent good order and condition at
the time of shipment; that the bill of lading in the present *B*
case had been a clean bill in that sense and the arbitrators
had erred in law in finding that it had not been; and that,
while there was a further requirement in law that a bill of
lading, to be " clean," must be a document that would ordinarily and properly be accepted in the trade as being a merchantable document, on the true construction of their award
the arbitrators had not found that the form of the bill of
lading in the present case was not clean in the sense of being *C*
unacceptable in the trade (post, pp. 518H, 519B–C, E–G, 520A–B,
H—521B).

Hansson v. *Hamel and Horley Ltd.* [1922] 2 A.C. 36,
H.L.(E.) applied.

Decision of Donaldson J., post, p. 505B *et seq*; [1979]
2 All E.R. 726 affirmed.

The following case is referred to in the judgment of Megaw L.J.: *D*

Hansson v. *Hamel and Horley Ltd.* [1922] 2 A.C. 36, H.L.(E.).

The following additional cases were cited in argument in the Court of
Appeal:

Astrovlanis Compania Naviera S.A. v. *Linard* [1972] 2 Q.B. 611; [1972]
2 W.L.R. 1414; [1972] 2 All E.R. 647; [1972] 1 Lloyd's Rep. 331, *E*
C.A.
Biddell Brothers v. *E. Clemens Horst Co.* [1911] 1 K.B. 214.
British and Foreign Marine Insurance Co. Ltd. v. *Gaunt* [1921] 2 A.C.
41, H.L.(E.).
British Imex Industries Ltd. v. *Midland Bank Ltd.* [1958] 1 Q.B. 542;
[1958] 2 W.L.R. 103; [1958] 1 All E.R. 264.
Canada and Dominion Sugar Co. Ltd. v. *Canadian National (West Indies)* *F*
Steamships Ltd. [1947] A.C. 46, P.C.
Horn v. *Minister of Food* [1948] 2 All E.R. 1036.
Munro, Brice & Co. v. *War Risks Association Ltd.* [1918] 2 K.B. 78.
Panchaud Frères S.A. v. *Etablissements General Grain Co.* [1970] 1
Lloyd's Rep. 53, C.A.
Restitution Steamship Co. v. *Sir John Pirie & Co.* (1889) 61 L.T. 330.
Rugg v. *Minett* (1809) 11 East 210.
Slattery v. *Mance* [1962] 1 Q.B. 676; [1962] 2 W.L.R. 569; [1962] 1 All *G*
E.R. 525; [1962] 1 Lloyd's Rep. 60.
Spillers Ltd. v. *J. W. Mitchell Ltd.* (1929) 33 Ll.L.Rep. 89.
Yeoman's Executrix v. *Ferries,* 1967 S.L.T. 332.

The following cases are referred to in the judgment of Donaldson J.:

Arnhold Karberg & Co. v. *Blythe, Green, Jourdain & Co.* [1916] 1 K.B. *H*
495, C.A.
British and Foreign Marine Insurance Co. Ltd. v. *Gaunt* [1921] 2 A.C. 41,
H.L.(E).
British Imex Industries Ltd. v. *Midland Bank Ltd.* [1958] 1 Q.B. 542;
[1958] 2 W.L.R. 103; [1958] 1 All E.R. 264.
Hansson v. *Hamel and Horley Ltd.* [1922] 2 A.C. 36, H.L.(E.).
Munro, Brice & Co. v. *War Risks Association Ltd.* [1918] 2 K.B. 78.
Restitution Steamship Co. v. *Sir John Pirie & Co.* (1889) 61 L.T. 330.

1 W.L.R.   M. Golodetz & Co. v. Czarnikow-Rionda (Q.B.D.)

Sassoon (E. D.) & Co. Ltd. v. Yorkshire Insurance Co. Ltd. (1923) 14
    Ll.L.Rep. 167; 16 Ll.L.Rep. 129, C.A.
Slattery v. Mance [1962] 1 Q.B. 676; [1962] 2 W.L.R. 569; [1962] 1 All
    E.R. 525.

The following additional cases were cited in argument before Donaldson J.:

Macdonald v. Refuge Assurance Co. Ltd. (1890) 17 R. (Ct. of Sess.) 955.
Theodorou v. Chester [1951] 1 Lloyd's Rep. 204.

SPECIAL PAPER

By a contract in writing dated February 26, 1975, the sellers,
M. Golodetz & Co. Inc., sold sugar to the buyers, Czarnikow-Rionda Co.
Inc. The contract incorporated the rules of the Refined Sugar Association including the rules relating to arbitration and the rules relating to
contracts. Disputes arose between the parties and arbitrators were appointed
by the association's council to act on its behalf in relation to the determination of those disputes. A hearing took place on November 30 and
December 1, 1976. The matters referred to arbitration were (a) a claim by
the sellers for U.S. $180,720 representing the price of 2,008 bags of sugar
or alternatively damages of the same amount in respect of the buyers'
alleged failure to accept the goods or to take up and pay for the shipping
documents; (b) a counterclaim by the buyers for $3,012 as damages in
respect of the sellers' alleged failure to present documents to the buyers in
respect of the 2,008 bags of sugar in conformity with the contract; (c) a
claim by the sellers (in the event that the claim under head (a) did not
succeed) for damages in respect of the buyers' alleged failure to comply
with the provisions of the contract as to insurance. The parties asked the
arbitrators to make an interim award (" the first award ") in respect of the
claim and counterclaim referred to under heads (a) and (b) in the form of
a special case.

The arbitrators in an award dated February 14, 1977, found the following facts. By the contract dated February 26, 1975, the sellers sold to the
buyers minimum 12,000 metric tons maximum 13,200 metric tons in
sellers' option of omnibus white and/or refined sugar packed in new jute
bags for shipment during March/April 1975. The contract price was $900
per metric ton c. & f. free out Bandarshapur, Iran, and payment was by
cash against documents on first presentation in New York. Other terms
and conditions of the contract were in accordance with the rules of the
Refined Sugar Association. By a contract dated February 24, 1975, the
buyers had sold to Foreign Transactions Co., Teheran, 12,000 metric tons
10 per cent. more or less at sellers' option of omnibus white sugar for
shipment during March/April 1975 in sellers' option. The contract price
was U.S. $915 per metric ton c. & f. free out Bandarshapur. The contract
further provided:

" Payment by irrevocable letter of credit to be opened immediately
    and confirmed in London by first class British or U.S. bank (we
    recommend Chase Manhattan Bank, London) for value 12,000 tons
    plus 10 per cent."

Other terms were as per the rules of the Refined Sugar Association. At the
time when the sellers entered into their contract with the buyers, they were
not aware of the existence of the sub-contract that the buyers had made
with Foreign Transactions Co., Teheran, or of its terms. In order to perform their contract with the buyers, on March 7, 1975, the sellers agreed

to buy from the State Trading Corporation of India Ltd. ("STC") 12,600 metric tons plus or minus 5 per cent. at buyers' option of Indian white crystal sugar of 1974/1975 crop for shipment in April/May 1975 at buyers' option. The price was £292 per metric ton f.o.b. stowed one Indian port. The contract provided, inter alia, for 100 per cent. payment by letter of credit to be opened immediately. In order to perform their contracts with the buyers and STC, the sellers chartered the *Galatia* on March 14, 1975, and by a Telex message sent to the buyers on the same day they nominated that vessel to carry Indian sugar of the contract description. The charterparty included the following provisions:

" 16. Mate's receipts to be signed for each parcel of sugar when on board, and master to sign bills of lading in accordance therewith, as requested by charterers or shippers. . . . 44. The master or his authorised representative shall issue ' mate's receipts ' acknowledging the receipt of cargo on board the vessel, at the end of each shift or day as required by the shipper or his agents. In exchange of the 'mate's receipts,' the bill of lading shall be issued promptly on demand of the shipper or his agents by the master or owners' agents, after loading of the sugar is completed on board of the vessel, for the quantity as determined by the shippers' surveyors. If owners elect to hold a draft survey of the vessel, it will be at their own expense and costs but the loaded quantity as determined by such surveyor shall not be mentioned in the bill of lading. Once cargo is accepted on board the vessel, the master or the owners' agent shall issue clean ' mate's receipts ' bill of lading.'

On March 17, 1975, the sellers' bankers issued a letter of credit in accordance with the provisions of the sellers' contract with STC. The vessel arrived at Kandla on March 20, 1975, and a number of bags of sugar of the contract description were placed alongside. On or before March 24, 1975, 2,008 bags (200·8 metric tons) out of the number placed alongside were loaded into no. 1 lower hold of the *Galatia* in apparent good order and condition and clean mate's receipts were issued in respect of them. The 2,008 bags were loaded in part performance of the contract between the sellers and the buyers. On March 24, 1975, subsequent to the loading of the 2,008 bags, a fire occurred on board the vessel. The 2,008 bags were damaged by the fire and by water used to extinguish it. The bags were unloaded on March 29 and 30, 1975. No. 1 hold was then cleaned and dried, but the 2,008 bags were never reloaded or replaced. Consideration was given to reprocessing the damaged sugar or selling it locally, but the costs involved in either of those courses would have exceeded the value of the sugar. Consideration was also given to reloading the damaged sugar, but that was impractical because it was too wet and there was insufficient space on the vessel to stow it separately. A bill of lading (numbered 2 and dated April 6, 1975) was issued in respect of the 2,008 bags. It stated that the goods had been shipped in apparent good order, and condition and contained the following notation:

" Cargo covered by this bill of lading has been discharged Kandla view damaged by fire and/or water used to extinguish fire for which general average declared."

The bill of lading was stamped " freight to pay " so as to accord with the letter of credit provisions under the contract between the sellers and

STC. On balance of probabilities the arbitrators found that the three originals of the bill of lading had also been stamped with the words " freight prepaid " or like wording. The words " freight prepaid " were plainly intended to supersede the words " freight to pay " even though there was no evidence that the latter words had ever been deleted. In consequence of the notation referred to above it was necessary for the sellers to amend the terms of the letter of credit opened pursuant to their contract with STC. On April 21, 1975, the sellers presented to the buyers a complete set of documents relating to the 2,008 bags, for payment in accordance with the contract between them. In a letter to the sellers dated April 22, 1975, the buyers rejected those documents on the ground that the bills of lading bore the notation referred to above. On April 28, 1975, the documents in respect of the 2,008 bags were again presented by the sellers to the buyers. On May 13, 1975, the buyers agreed to take them up and to present them for negotiation under the letter of credit opened by their sub-buyers. They did so on the understanding that their taking up of the documents and indorsement of the bills of lading was without prejudice and was in no way an admission of liability on their part. The documents were then presented by them for payment to their sub-purchasers' confirming bank (the Chase Manhattan Bank N.A.) but that bank refused payment because the bills of lading showed the notation referred to above. Until shortly before the arbitration hearing the buyers contested the sellers' claim solely on the ground that the bills of lading were not " clean " and so conducted themselves as to lead the sellers to believe that they, the buyers, were not contesting the presentation of documents on any other ground. It was common ground that, if the buyers were not entitled to reject the documents, the damages recoverable by the sellers amounted to U.S. $180,720 representing the price of the goods covered thereby. No dispute arose between the parties as to the balance of the contract covering 12,999·20 metric tons of goods of the contract description, shipped on the *Galatia* under a separate bill of lading which was also dated April 6, 1975, documents in respect whereof were taken up and paid for by the buyers. The contract between the sellers and the buyers gave the sellers the option of delivering minimum 12,000 metric tons, maximum 13,200 metric tons, of sugar. The sellers did not exercise their option under that contract to deliver any additional quantity of sugar in excess of the 12,999·20 metric tons. There was no evidence that the market price of the sugar on April 21, 1975, or when the vessel would in the ordinary course have arrived at Bandarshapur had exceeded the price under the contract between the sellers and the buyers.

The questions of law for the decision of the court were on the facts found and on the true construction of the contract (1) whether the sellers were entitled to the price of the 2,008 bags of sugar, alternatively to damages for the buyers' failure to accept the same or to take up and pay for the shipping documents in respect thereof; if the answer to (1) were " no," (2) whether the buyers were entitled to any, and if so what, damages against the sellers for the sellers' failure to make a contractual presentation of documents in respect of the 2,008 bags of sugar. Subject to the decision of the court on the questions of law, the arbitrators found and held as follows. (a) Under the contract between the sellers and the buyers bills of lading presented for payment were required to be clean " on board " bills of lading evidencing freight having been paid. (b) The bills of lading presented by the sellers in respect of the 2,008 bags of sugar were bills of

lading evidencing freight having been paid. (c) The bills of lading were
not clean " on board " bills of lading within the meaning of the contract
by reason of the notation referred to. (d) The buyers had been entitled
to reject the documents in respect of the 2,008 bags on the ground that
the bills of lading were not clean " on board " bills of lading. (e) The
buyers were now estopped or precluded from contending that the documents were capable of rejection on any other ground except that mentioned in (d) above. (f) The sellers were not entitled to the price of the
2,008 bags of sugar or to damages for the buyers' failure to accept the
same or to take up and pay for the shipping documents in respect of them.
(g) The sellers had not been under any obligation to tender documents
in respect of any quantity in excess of the 12,999·20 metric tons, and the
buyers were not entitled to damages in respect of the sellers' failure to
deliver more than that quantity or in respect of their failure to tender a
clean " on board " bill of lading in respect of the 2,008 bags. Accordingly,
the arbitrators awarded and adjudged that the claim by the sellers under
head (a) and the counterclaim by the buyers under head (b) both failed.
If, however, the court should answer the first question of law in the
affirmative, they awarded and adjudged that the buyers should forthwith
pay to the sellers the sum of U.S.$180,720 together with interest at the
rate of 6 per cent. from April 21, 1975, to the date of the award. If the
court should answer the second question of law in a manner different
from that mentioned in paragraph (g) above, they requested that the court
remit the award to them under section 22 of the Arbitration Act 1950,
with the appropriate directions.

On March 30, 1977, a hearing took place in relation to a further claim
by the sellers not dealt with in the arbitrators' first award. The buyers
asked the arbitrators to make their further award in the form of a special
case. The arbitrators, in a further award dated September 9, 1977, in which,
by agreement of the parties, the findings of fact in the first award were
treated as if they were repeated and the documents annexed to that award
were treated as annexed to and forming part of it, found, in so far as they
were questions of fact, and held, in so far as they were questions of law,
subject to the opinion of the court on the questions of law stated, as
follows. Under the terms of the contract dated February 26, 1975, it was
the obligation of the buyers to cover marine and war risk insurance in
accordance with rule 22 (see post, p. 506B–C) of the rules relating
to contracts. The first question that the arbitrators were asked to
decide concerned the nature and extent of the obligation imposed
by rule 22. The buyers contended that their obligation was defined
by the fourth paragraph of that rule and that the arbitrators should
not treat the first paragraph as having any relevance to a contract on
c. & f. terms. The sellers contended that the marine insurance policy
referred to in the fourth paragraph had to comply with the requirements set out in the first paragraph. Alternatively, they contended that
it had to be one that was usual in the trade (referring to Benjamin's Sale
of Goods (1974), para. 1525, p. 786). The arbitrators rejected the buyers'
contention and held that the insurance to be effected by them under the
contract had to comply with the requirements set out in the first paragraph
of rule 22 as well as those set out in the fourth paragraph. The next
question that they were asked to decide was whether the buyers had
effected marine insurance in accordance with such requirements. The
buyers produced an incomplete document issued by the Iran Insurance

A Co. in favour of Foreign Transactions Co. dated March 16, 1975, purporting to cover 12,000 tons of white sugar to be shipped from the U.S.A. to the port of Shahpour. There was an issue as to whether that was a relevant policy of insurance or had been issued pursuant to Foreign Transactions Co.'s obligations to the buyers under their contract dated February 24, 1975, or at all. On balance of probabilities the arbitrators found and/or held that it was a relevant policy of insurance in the sense that it had
B been intended to apply to the parcel of sugar that was the subject of Foreign Transactions Co.'s contract with the buyers and the buyers' contract with the sellers. It was not disputed that the buyers could satisfy their obligations as to insurance either by effecting a policy that complied with the requirements of rule 22 or by procuring their sub-buyers to do so. The sellers contended that the policy effected by Foreign Transactions Co.
C was defective in the following respects. (a) That Iran Insurance Co. was not a first-class insurance company. No evidence was given in support of that contention. (b) That the policy contained no provision whereby it was to be for the sellers' protection. (c) That the policy related to a shipment from the U.S.A. and not from India. (d) That the document covered only 12,000 tons of white sugar and failed to cover 13,200 metric tons being
D the maximum quantity that the sellers had the right to supply. (e) That the policy provided for claims to be investigated in Teheran and to be paid in rials rather than in the currency of the contract and did not provide that claims would be submitted, admitted and settled in London. The arbitrators found and/or held that the policy was defective in all the respects enumerated, other than that in (a). They further found and/or held that the policy was not one that was usual or merchantable in the
E trade. There was no evidence to show that the document had been amended in any way after March 16, 1975, either to cure the defects referred to or at all. Accordingly, the arbitrators found and/or held that the buyers were in breach of their contract with the sellers in failing to comply with its provisions regarding insurance. The next question that they were asked to decide was whether the sellers had suffered any loss by
F reason of the buyers' breach. The sellers contended that the loss that they had suffered was the value of the claim that would have been available to them under a proper policy of insurance. They further contended that the value of such claim was U.S.$180,720 (being the invoice value of the 2,008 bags) plus 2 per cent. and that the onus was on the buyers to show that a first-class insurance company would have sought or would have been able to defeat or to reduce any claim on the insurance. The sellers
G limited their claim to U.S.$180,720 and did not seek to recover the additional 2 per cent. The buyers contended that the sellers had suffered no loss by reason of any defects in the policy of insurance. The first argument relied on by the buyers in support of that contention was to the following effect. The sellers had been entitled to insist that a clean bill of lading be issued in respect of the 2,008 bags of sugar in question. Instead
H of doing so, they had amended the letter of credit in favour of their seller, State Trading Corporation of India Ltd. (" STC ") to permit payment against a claused bill of lading. Had they not amended the letter of credit, no payment would have been made to STC. Alternatively, payment to STC would only have been made against presentation of an unclaused bill of lading, and the sellers would then have been able to obtain payment from the buyers. Accordingly, it was argued, the sellers could have avoided all loss if they had acted as they were entitled to do, and should have done,

and any loss that they had incurred had therefore been a voluntary loss. **A**
The sellers contended that the obligation to insure was independent of the
payment provisions in their contract with the buyers. They also argued
that their failure to obtain an unclaused bill of lading and their action in
amending the letter of credit in favour of STC had been reasonable in
all the circumstances of the case and that they ought not to be deprived
of the benefit of the insurance that they had contracted for merely because **B**
they could have avoided all loss if they had acted differently. They further
contended that, if payment had not been made to STC, they would have
incurred a liability to STC in respect of the same defects in the insurance
policy which formed the basis of their claim against the buyers. The
arbitrators accepted the sellers' contentions and found and/or held that
(a) the buyers' obligation to insure was independent of the other provisions
in the contract (in particular, the payment provisions) and (b) the sellers' **C**
conduct had been reasonable and not such as to make any loss that they
had suffered in respect of defects in the insurance policy a voluntary loss
or a loss that they could and should reasonably have avoided; (c) if payment had not been made to STC as aforesaid STC would, in all probability,
have made a claim against the sellers for £59,806·27 (being the invoice
value of the 2,008 bags under the contract between STC and the sellers
plus 2 per cent.) in respect of the defects in the insurance policy. The **D**
second argument relied on by the buyers in support of their contention that
the sellers had suffered no recoverable loss was that the sellers had failed
to show that, even if rule 22 had been complied with, they would have
received payment from the insurers. The sellers contended, on the other
hand, that the buyers stood in the same position as the underwriters would
have been in if a claim had been made against them under a policy in the **E**
proper form. Accordingly, they argued that, once it was shown that the
goods had been damaged by fire, the onus was on the buyers to show that
the underwriters could have invoked some exception or defence under the
terms of the policy. The arbitrators held that the sellers' contentions with
regard to the onus of proof were correct. As stated in their first award,
they found that the 2,008 bags had been damaged by fire and by water **F**
used to extinguish it. In those circumstances, if the marine insurance had
been effected on the Institute Cargo Clauses (All Risks) there would prima
facie have been a claim against the insurers in respect of such damage.
The buyers contended, however, that the insurers could have rejected such
a claim on the grounds that (a) the parcel had been damaged through
" inherent vice or nature of the subject matter insured " within the meaning of clause 5 of the Institute Cargo Clauses (All Risks); the sellers had **G**
failed to comply with the requirement in clause 9 of those clauses (the
bailee clause) that all rights against " carriers, bailees or other third parties
are properly preserved and exercised." As to the question of "inherent
vice," the sellers contended that the buyers were not entitled to make such
an allegation. They said that, in the course of the hearing preceding the
arbitrators' first award, the buyers had accepted the proposition that, if **H**
the sellers were held to be right on the question of whether the bill of
lading was "clean," then they would be entitled to the full price of the
goods, and that that could only have been on the basis that there was no
contention that the goods were unmerchantable or worth anything less than
the full price. The sellers therefore argued that the buyers were estopped
from asserting that the damage to the goods had arisen from inherent vice.
The buyers denied that what they had said at the previous hearing had that

A   effect, and the arbitrators considered that, because of the confusion as to
the effect of what had been said, it would not be right to hold that the
buyers were estopped from raising the issue of inherent vice in relation to
the insurance question. In any event, the sellers said that they did not wish
to rest their case on a technicality provided that they could adduce the
evidence that had been available at the previous hearing, and arrange-
B   ments were agreed for written evidence on that question to be submitted
by both parties after the oral hearing before the arbitrators. In support of
their allegation that the damage in question had been caused by inherent
vice, the buyers relied on a report dated June 18, 1975, by a firm of surveyors named Ericson & Richards. That report was stated to have been
made " at the request of the P. & I. Services of India," and the arbitrators
found that it had been commissioned on behalf of the owners of the
C   vessel. The report contained the following passage:

   " *Probable cause of fire :* The chief officer of the vessel was closely
   interrogated by us as he was the first among the ship's officers to have
   noticed the fire and the labourers coming out. He informed us that
   flames were observed in different locations all over the hatch at the
   same time. He emphasised that the fire occurred spontaneously and
D   all of a sudden. The master of the vessel also stated that the fire was
   spontaneous. In the course of our investigations, we observed charred
   bags in different locations of the hatch and at different depths. This
   clearly ruled out smoking to be the probable cause of fire. We also
   checked the hatch for possible electrical short circuits and found no
   evidence to suggest fire due to this cause. The fire-affected bags were
E   closely examined and it was found that the burning or charring of the
   bags was largely at the mouths and along ' dog's-ears ' suggesting that
   the stitching twine used for closing the mouths of the bags was
   ' suspect.' In a similar fire recently (in February 1975), in a cargo
   of Indian groundnut h.p.s. kernels, samples of sacking and twine were
   analysed when it was found to contain a steam volatile oil ' flammable
   at temperatures slightly higher than room temperature.' Chemical tests
F   on the samples also gave positive indication of the presence of oxidis-
   ing reagent. It is known that certain types of oils are used in processing jute. Having careful regard to the above findings and our own
   observations of the cargo after the fire, we are of the opinion that the
   fire in this consignment of sugar was spontaneous and probably caused
   by the oil used in processing jute. *Cargo :* The cargo had suffered con-
G   siderable damage on account of the use of seawater for extinguishing the fire. As has been stated elsewhere in this report, there were
   pools of water in the after part of the hatch, on top of the cargo, in
   spite of pumping out the bilges. It was thus evident that considerable
   amounts of water had been poured to extinguish the fire."

There was no other evidence as to the cause of the fire from anyone who
H   had witnessed either the fire itself or its effects. The evidence submitted
to the arbitrators after the oral hearing comprised reports by technical
experts, based on examination of documents, and by cargo surveyors with
long experience of handling shipments of sugar in India. At the oral
hearing, there had also been much discussion about a Lloyd's survey
report that had not been produced. In relation to that, the arbitrators found
that on March 25, 1975, the sellers had undertaken at the buyers' request
to obtain such a survey report on the damaged parcel, but that they had

failed to do so, despite repeated reminders. No explanation of that failure A had been given, except that there appeared to have been a " muddle," that is to say, some misunderstanding within the sellers themselves or between the sellers and persons with whom they had been in communication in India. On the evidence before them, the arbitrators found that it was not possible to determine the true cause of the fire. They had grave doubts as to whether the explanation given by Ericson & Richards was correct, but B the only other evidence submitted to them was too remote from the actual circumstances of the fire to form the basis of any firm conclusion. The policy effected by Foreign Transactions Co. contained a provision that " no request for payment of claim will be valid without an investigation certificate," meaning, in the context, a survey report from a Lloyd's surveyor at the port of loading. It would also have been a normal requirement for making a claim under a policy of the type referred to in rule 22 C that steps be taken to obtain a report from a Lloyd's surveyor. In the arbitrators' judgment, any insurer dealing with a claim in respect of the damage in question would have required evidence as to the circumstances of the fire from a Lloyd's surveyor or at least from a reputable independent source. In view of the allegation in the Ericson & Richards report that the fire was attributable to the characteristics of the packing, the arbitrators D did not consider that the insurer would have paid a claim without that evidence. They found and/or held that the claim would have failed for that reason and that responsibility for the fact that such evidence had not been and was not available must be laid at the sellers' door. As to whether the sellers had complied with the bailee clause, the buyers contended that the sellers had (a) failed to take proceedings against the owners of the vessel on their bill of lading in respect of the parcel within the time limited E by the Hague Rules incorporated therein, so that by article III, rule 6, of those rules the carrier and the ship had been discharged from all liability in respect of loss or damage to the goods, and (b) failed to pursue a claim in general average against the vessel in respect of damage caused to the parcel by water used to extinguish the fire, and (c) failed to act as a prudent uninsured who would have insisted on his right to the issue of a F clean bill of lading to ensure payment by the buyers. The evidence before the arbitrators did not support the suggestion that a claim against the insurers would have been rejected on any of those grounds, and they found and/or held that it would not have been rejected by reason of any failure to comply with the bailee clause. A further point raised by the buyers was that the damaged cargo had or might have had some residual value. That argument had not been raised until after the oral hearing, and the G arbitrators would have rejected it for that reason alone. Further, that matter had already been decided in their first award. However, even if they had been able to take into account the additional evidence on that point submitted after the oral hearing, their finding would still be as set out in their first award. The questions of law for the decision of the court were whether on the facts found and on the true construction of the H contract between the parties: (1) the buyers had fulfilled their obligations to effect insurance cover, and, if not, (2) whether the sellers were entitled to any, and if so what, damages for the buyers' breach of contract. Subject to the decision of the court on the questions of law, the arbitrators found and held (1) that the buyers had failed to comply with their obligations in relation to the insurance of the 2,008 bags; (2) that the sellers had not suffered any loss by reason of such failure because any

A claim against the insurers would, on balance of probabilities, have failed for the reason given. Accordingly, the arbitrators awarded and adjudged that the claim by the sellers that was the subject of the award failed.

   Kenneth Rokison Q.C. and *David Grace* for the sellers.
   David Johnson Q.C. and *Christopher C. Russell* for the buyers.

B
                                                    Cur. adv. vult.

   November 20. DONALDSON J. read the following judgment.

   The dispute
       The parties to this dispute are household names in the world trade in
C sugar. Both are based on New York. The sugar concerned was to be shipped from Kandla in India to Iran. The reason why the matter comes to the English Commercial Court is that the contract incorporated the rules of the Refined Sugar Association and provided for arbitration in London.
       The problem which has arisen must be unusual and is certainly not without legal interest. The sellers agreed to sell 12,000/13,200 metric tons (sellers'
D option) of omnibus white and/or refined sugar in new jute bags, c. & f. free out Bandarshapur, Iran, shipment March/April 1975. Czarnikow-Rionda Co. Inc. were the buyers. The sellers chartered the *Galatia* to carry the sugar and she arrived at Kandla on March 20, 1975. Four days later, when the vessel was partly loaded, fire broke out and 2,008 bags (200·8 tons) of sugar were damaged by the fire itself or by water used in extinguishing it. This sugar was discharged, but was condemned as it was
E not commercially practicable to recondition it. The balance of the cargo, amounting to 12,999·20 metric tons, was safely loaded and carried to its destination.
       The question at issue is, of course, who is to stand the loss in respect of the 200 tons of sugar which was destroyed by or as a consequence of the fire? The board of appeal of the Refined Sugar Association has held
F that the loss must fall upon the sellers. The sellers now appeal.
       Although this is the general issue, I have to consider it under the three heads which constitute the effective questions of law set out in the award. These are (i) whether the sellers are entitled to be paid the price of the sugar or, alternatively, to recover damages for the buyers' failure to accept the sugar and to take up and pay for the shipping documents; (ii) whether the buyers fulfilled their obligations in respect of insuring the sugar; and
G (iii) if not, whether the sellers are entitled to any, and if so what, damages for this failure. There was a fourth question. This is the obverse of the first question, namely, whether, if the sellers were in breach of contract in connection with the presentation of the documents, the buyers are entitled to damages. As the board have found facts which on this hypothesis negative any loss by the buyers, the question no longer arises.

   The contract
       The starting point is the contract. The terms of payment were as follows. The contract itself provided for cash against documents upon first presentation in New York. The rules of the Refined Sugar Association, which were incorporated in the contract, expanded this obligation as follows (in the rules relating to contracts):
       " 23. Payment for the sugar shall be made by cash, ship lost or not

lost, if sold . . . (b) c. & f. against a complete set, or satisfactory A
guarantee for any missing copies, of signed clean ' on board ' bills of
lading evidencing freight having been paid or against ship's clean
delivery order."

Under a c. & f. contract, unlike a c.i.f. contract, it is usually for each party
to decide whether to insure its own interest. However, the rules of the
Refined Sugar Association provide: B

"22. Insurance shall be covered for the invoice value plus 2 per
cent. by a Lloyd's policy or by a policy with a first class insurance
company under which a claim can be submitted, admitted and settled
in London. Marine insurance shall be effected on institute cargo
clauses (all risks) including institute strikes, riot and civil commotions
clauses. . . . In a contract on c. & f. terms the buyer's risk shall C
commence immediately the sugar is alongside the export vessel. The
buyer shall cover marine and war risk insurance and policies shall
be for the seller's protection until payment is made. The buyer shall
furnish evidence of compliance if requested by the seller."

Performance of the contract
D
The sellers duly procured the sugar necessary for the performance of
the contract. They also chartered the *Galatia* to carry it from Kandla to
Bandarshapur. The terms of the charterparty provided:

"16. Mate's receipts to be signed for each parcel of sugar when on
board, and master to sign bills of lading in accordance therewith, as
requested by charterers or shippers. . . . 44. The master or his auth- E
orised representative shall issue ' mate's receipts ' acknowledging the
receipt of cargo on board the vessel, at the end of each shift or day
as required by the shipper or his agents. In exchange of the ' mate's
receipts,' the bill of lading shall be issued promptly on demand of
the shipper or his agents by the master or owners' agents, after loading
of the sugar is completed on board of the vessel, for the quantity as
determined by the shipper's surveyors. If owners elect to hold a draft F
survey of the vessel, it will be at their own expense and costs but the
loaded quantity as determined by such surveyor shall not be mentioned in the bill of lading. Once cargo is accepted on board the
vessel, the master or the owners' agent shall issue clean ' mate's
receipts '/bill of lading."

The *Galatia* arrived at Kandla on March 20, 1975, and in due course began G
loading the sugar. The 200 tons was stowed in no. 1 lower hold in apparent
good order and condition and clean mate's receipts were issued accordingly. The fire occurred on March 24 and this, and the water used to
extinguish it, severely damaged the sugar. It was unloaded on March 29
and 30. Although consideration was given to reprocessing it or to selling it locally, the costs were such that it was condemned as a total loss. H
The remainder of the cargo was loaded without incident and this amounted
to 12,999·20 tons which was more than the minimum quantity called for by
the contract.

Two bills of lading were issued dated April 6, 1975. One related to
the 200 tons and the other to the balance of the cargo. The latter was taken
up and paid for by the buyers and needs no further consideration. That
relating to the 200 tons was rejected by the buyers.

The Weekly Law Reports, May 16, 1980

507

1 W.L.R.   M. Golodetz & Co. v. Czarnikow-Rionda (Q.B.D.)   Donaldson J.

A   The 200-ton bill of lading was on the "Congenbill" form, which by printed clauses acknowledges the shipment of the goods in apparent good order and condition "weight, measure, quantity, condition, contents and value unknown." It bore a typewritten notation:

"Cargo covered by this bill of lading has been discharged Kandla view damaged by fire and/or water used to extinguish fire for which
B   general average declared."

In the light of the provisions of clauses 16 and 44 of the charterparty, it is difficult to see what possible justification there can have been for including this notation. However, it was included and has given rise to the whole of the present litigation.

The documents attached to the award include a non-negotiable copy
C   of this bill of lading with the typewritten notation "freight to pay." However, the board has found that the negotiable copies were also overstamped "freight prepaid" and that "the words 'freight prepaid' were plainly intended to supersede the words 'freight to pay' even though there was no evidence that the latter words were ever deleted."

The buyers were entitled themselves to effect the insurance called for
D   by clause 22 of the contract or to leave it to others to do so on their behalf. In the event, the buyers elected to leave it to the sub-buyers from them. This was an unfortunate decision for, as is now admitted, the insurance effected by the sub-buyers was not in conformity with the contract. The rights of the parties have, therefore, to be considered as if the buyers had failed to insure the cargo.

E   *The cause of the fire*

Fires may be caused accidentally or deliberately or they may arise spontaneously due to the composition of the materials concerned. There is no suggestion that this fire was caused deliberately, but the board heard evidence on the issue of whether the fire was caused accidentally or was the result of spontaneous combustion. If it was a case of spontaneous
F   combustion, it was not the sugar but the stitching twine used for closing the mouths of the bags which was the villain of the piece. The board's conclusion was that: "On the evidence before us, we find that it is not possible to determine the true cause of the fire."

The sellers' claim to the price

G   Under the terms of the contract, the sellers are entitled to be paid the price upon tender of "clean 'on board' bills of lading evidencing freight having been paid." Mr. Rokison, for the sellers, submitted that this bill of lading qualified for this description, notwithstanding the notation recording that the sugar had been discharged fire-damaged and notwithstanding the conflicting references to "freight prepaid" and "freight to pay." In
I   his submission, the sellers, having tendered this bill of lading, were entitled to be paid the price. Alternatively, the sugar was at the risk of the buyers when it was destroyed and, that being so, the sellers were entitled to be paid the price whether or not they tendered this or any other bill of lading.

Mr. Johnson, who appeared for the buyers, challenged these submissions root and branch. In his submission, there were no less than eight reasons why the sellers were not entitled to be paid the price. It is, of course, for the sellers to make out their case, but, in all the circumstances,

it is convenient to consider whether they have done so in the context of
Mr. Johnson's objections.

(a) That the bill of lading was not " clean "

(i) *The practical test.* Mr. Johnson submits that there are two
possible tests to be applied, the practical and the legal. The practical test
is whether a bill of lading in this form is acceptable to banks generally as
being a " clean " bill of lading. Since 1962, virtually all banks have
accepted the international rules set out in a document issued by the
International Chamber of Commerce entitled " Uniform Customs and
Practice for Documentary Credits." Rule 16 provides:

> " A clean shipping document is one which bears no superimposed
> clause or notation which expressly declares a defective condition of
> the goods and/or the packaging. Banks will refuse shipping docu-
> ments bearing such clauses or notations unless the credit expressly
> states clauses or notation which may be accepted."

This definition fails to specify the time with respect to which the notation speaks. The bill of lading and any notations speak *at* the date of issue,
but they may speak *about* a state of affairs which then exists or about an
earlier state of affairs or both. If the rule refers to notations about the
state of affairs at the time of the issue of the bill of lading or, indeed, at
any time after shipment of the 200 tons was completed, the bill of lading
is not " clean " within the meaning of that word in the rule for the notation clearly draws attention to the cargo being damaged. If, however, it
refers to notations about the state of affairs upon completion of shipment,
the bill of lading is equally clearly clean for it shows that the goods were
in apparent good order and condition on shipment and suggests only that
they were damaged after shipment.

Mr. Johnson draws attention to the fact that this bill of lading was
rejected by two different banks. The first rejection was by the sellers' own
bank when the bill of lading was tendered by the shippers under the
f.o.b. supply contract. The second rejection was by the buyers' sub-purchasers when it was tendered to them by the buyers without prejudice to
the rights of the parties as between sellers and buyers. On these facts,
Mr. Johnson invites me to hold that this bill of lading is not a " clean "
bill in commercial or practical terms.

Let me first consider this " practical " test. The information as to what
prompted the banks' action is somewhat sparse. So far as the supply contract is concerned, the award states only that in consequence of the offending clause, the sellers had to amend the letter of credit opened in favour
of their suppliers and appends the letter of credit and the Telexed amendment. The letter of credit calls for " full set 3/3 clean on board charterparty bills of lading plus seven copies issued to order blank indorsed
evidencing shipment from India to Bandarshapur, Iran." The amendment
covers two separate changes, namely, (a) that there should be two complete
sets of bills of lading, the first relating to 12,999·2 tons and the second to
200·8 tons, and (b) that the latter set is to be acceptable with the offending clause. This letter of credit is not in terms subject to the Uniform
Customs and Practice (" U.C.P.").

The award exhibits the letter of credit opened by the sub-buyers in
favour of the buyers. This calls for a " full set of clean on board bill of
lading marked freight prepaid " and is expressly subject to the U.C.P.

The Weekly Law Reports, May 16, 1980

509

1 W.L.R.   M. Golodetz & Co. v. Czarnikow-Rionda (Q.B.D.)   Donaldson J.

A   There is no contemporary note of why the bank refused to accept the documents, but there is a letter dated March 24, 1976, reading:

"Your draft and documents valued $183,732.00, payment for which was not effected because bills of lading showing the following clause 'Cargo covered by this bill of lading has been discharged at Kandla view damaged by fire and/or water used to extinguish fire for

B   which general average declared,' whereas credit calls for clean (unclaused) bills of lading."

It is not uninteresting that it was not the buyers' bank which rejected the documents, but the buyers themselves: see their letter of April 22, 1975, attached to the award. Furthermore, although they gave as a reason the fact that the clause prejudiced their ability to negotiate

C   the documents with their buyers, the letter of March 24, 1976, set out above suggests that the documents were only rejected by the sub-buyers' bank some weeks later on May 13, 1975. However, there may have been more than one rejection.

It is clear that the sub-buyers' bank thought that a letter of credit incorporating the U.C.P. rules and calling for " clean " bills of lading was

D   only satisfied if the bills were wholly unclaused. This goes further than the U.C.P. rules justify since they appear to take exception only to a "superimposed clause or notation which expressly declares a defective condition of the goods and/or the packaging," whatever that may mean.

There is, I think, more than one answer to this " practical test " objection. First, the contract called for cash against documents, which no doubt assumes a documentary credit. But the board has not found that it

E   was a custom of the trade, and the contract does not provide, that the documents shall be such as to satisfy the U.C.P. rules as to " clean " bills of lading, which rules do not have the force of law. Furthermore, if there is ambiguity as to the meaning of those rules, that ambiguity should if possible be resolved in a way which will result in the rules reflecting the position under general maritime and commercial law. So construed they

F   add nothing to the legal test which I consider hereafter.

Second, the evidence does not disclose that banks generally would reject such a bill of lading as that relating to the 200 tons as not being a " clean " bill of lading or that, if they would do so, it would be for any better reason than that they were applying what they thought the U.C.P. rules required.

G   Third, I am not satisfied that it is right to apply a practical test, other than in the context of the merchantability of the documents to which I will return hereafter. What is really being said here is that the very fact that the buyers and two banks rejected these documents proves that they are not " clean." This is a proposition which I decline to accept.

(ii) *The legal test.* I, therefore, proceed to apply the legal test. As

H   Salmon J. remarked in *British Imex Industries Ltd.* v. *Midland Bank Ltd.* [1958] 1 Q.B. 542, 551, a " clean bill of lading " has never been exhaustively defined. I have been referred to a number of textbooks and authorities which support the proposition that a " clean " bill of lading is one in which there is nothing to qualify the admission that the goods were in apparent good order and condition and that the seller has no claim against the goods except in relation to freight. Some clearly regard the relevant time as being that of shipment. Some are silent as to what is the relevant time. None refers expressly to **A** any time subsequent to shipment.

As between the shipowner and the shipper (including those claiming through the shipper as holders of the bill of lading) the crucial time is shipment. The shipowner's prime obligation is to deliver the goods at the contractual destination in the like good order and condition as when shipped. The cleanliness of the bill of lading may give rise to an estoppel **B** and the terms of the bill of lading contract may exempt the shipowner from a breach of this obligation, but everything stems from the state of the goods as shipped. As between seller and c.i.f. or c. & f. buyer, the property and risk normally pass upon the negotiation of the bill of lading, but do so as from shipment. Thus, the fact that the ship and goods have been lost after shipment or that a liability to contribute in general average or salvage has arisen is no reason for refusing to take up and pay for the **C** documents.

In these circumstances, it is not surprising that there appears to be no case in which the courts or the textbook writers have had to consider a bill of lading which records the fate of the goods subsequent to shipment and, indeed, I have never seen or heard of a bill of lading like that in the present case. Nor is it surprising that some of the judgments and textbooks **D** do not in terms say that when reference is made to the condition of the goods what is meant is their condition on shipment.

However, I have no doubt that this is the position. The bill of lading with which I am concerned casts no doubt whatsoever on the condition of the goods at that time and does not assert that at that time the shipowner had any claim whatsoever against the goods. It follows that in my judgment this bill of lading, unusual though it is, passes the legal test of clean- **E** liness.

(b) That the bill of lading was rightly rejected as being unmerchantable

Mr. Johnson submits that documents tendered under a c. & f. contract must be merchantable and that, in the context of a bill of lading, this may be a factor of cleanliness or an independent quality which is required. He **F** seeks to support this proposition by reference to *Hansson* v. *Hamel and Horley Ltd.* [1922] 2 A.C. 36, in which Lord Sumner said, at p. 46:

> "When documents are to be taken up the buyer is entitled to documents which substantially confer protective rights throughout. He is not buying a litigation, as Lord Trevethin (then A. T. Lawrence J.) says in [*In re General Trading Co. Ltd. and van Stolk's Commissi-* **G** *chandel* (1911) 16 Com.Cas. 95, 101]. These documents have to be handled by banks, they have to be taken up or rejected promptly and without any opportunity for prolonged inquiry, they have to be such as can be re-tendered to sub-purchasers, and it is essential that they should so conform to the accustomed shipping documents as to be reasonably and readily fit to pass current in commerce."
>   **H**

I need hardly say that I accept this proposition unreservedly. A tender of documents which, properly read and understood, call for further inquiry or are such as to invite litigation is clearly a bad tender. But the operative words are " properly read and understood." I fully accept that the clause on this bill of lading makes it unusual, but properly read and understood it calls for no inquiry and it casts no doubt at all upon the fact that the goods were shipped in apparent good order and condition

The Weekly Law Reports, May 16, 1980

511

1 W.L.R.   M. Golodetz & Co. v. Czarnikow-Rionda (Q.B.D.)   Donaldson J.

A or upon the protection which anyone is entitled to expect when taking up such a document whether as a purchaser or as a lender on the security of the bill. The bill of lading in *Hansson*'s case was of quite a different character since, for the reasons which Lord Sumner gave, at p. 45, it was very doubtful whether and to what extent the bill protected the holder in respect of perils operating during the 13-day voyage from Norway to Hamburg.

B The only ground for holding that the bill of lading was not " reasonably and readily fit to pass current in commerce " is that the form is unusual and that two banks and the buyers rejected it. If the buyers wanted bills of lading which were not only " clean," but also " in usual form," they should have contracted accordingly. They did not do so and I am not prepared to hold that the bill was unmerchantable.

C
(c) That the bill of lading does not evidence freight having been paid

This is unarguable in the light of the board's findings that the bill of lading as tendered was overstamped " freight pre-paid," whether or not the words " freight to pay " were deleted. It was no different from a receipted account.

D
(d) That the bill of lading did not evidence an effective contract of affreightment

At first sight, it may seem obvious that the bill of lading should evidence an effective contract of carriage. But this is not necessarily true. Thus a bill of lading relating to the carriage of goods which have been lost on the voyage is a good tender. And this is so even if the ship has also been lost.

E In such cases the contract is clearly ineffective. In *Arnhold Karberg & Co.* v. *Blythe, Green, Jourdain & Co.* [1916] 1 K.B. 495, 509, the expression used by Bankes L.J. was a " subsisting " contract of carriage. There the further performance of the contract had become illegal as a result of the war. But I am not sure that even " subsisting " is always the right word, because the loss of the ship and goods might be said to put an end to the

F contract. " Enforceable " might be a better term, because although the further performance of the contract may be at an end, the holder of the bill of lading will have rights against the shipowner. In the *Arnhold Karberg* case, the contract was unenforceable for reasons of public policy.

This bill undoubtedly evidences an enforceable contract, whether or not the shipowners had a complete defence on the facts.

G
(e) That the bill of lading should have been, but was not, a receipt of goods on board the ship

Mr. Johnson, in a picturesque phrase, submitted that the buyers were entitled to a bill of lading instead of a bill of unlading. But this did not cease to be a bill of lading just because the goods had necessarily to be discharged as a result of a casualty which occurred after shipment. It duly

H evidenced the shipment of the goods and the contract under which they were to be carried. Anything else was surplusage, because the clause does not suggest that the shippers had taken delivery of the goods. So far as the bill showed, the goods were still in the custody of the shipowners.

(f) That the offending clause would or might adversely affect the holder's rights against the ship

Mr. Johnson suggested that the presence of the clause might make it

more difficult for the holder of the bill of lading to call for delivery of the   A
goods in the like good order as when shipped. I cannot see why it should.
He could call for delivery, the shipowner would reply that this was impossible because of the casualty and the bill of lading holder's claim would fall
to be decided on the terms of the contract and the facts affecting the
casualty. But this would have been the position with or without the clause.
The estoppel in the bill of lading as to apparent condition on shipment
would remain fully effective.   B

(g) *That the bill of lading was stale, having been issued on April 6 whereas
     loading of the 200 tons was completed on or before March 24.*
     At first I thought that this was a good point, because this is prima facie
a long interval of time and 13 days' delay was held to be fatal in *Hansson*
v. *Hamel and Horley Ltd.* [1922] 2 A.C. 36. However, as Mr. Rokison   C
pointed out, in that case the bill of lading was issued not only after the ship
had sailed, but after it had arrived in another country. There is no obligation to issue bills of lading hold by hold. All that is required is that they
should be issued within a reasonable time of completing loading. Here the
intention was that there should be a single bill of lading covering the whole
parcel. This would have been issued on or about April 6 when loading was   D
completed. In the event, the bill of lading was split and both bills were
issued on this date. The buyers did not object to the other bill of lading
as being stale and I do not think that they can object to this one on this
ground. It was issued as soon as reasonably practicable after the completion of the loading of the whole parcel and at or about the time when
the ship sailed.
                                                                                   E

(h) *That the bill of lading was objectionable because it was claused
     " weight, measure, quantity, condition, contents and value unknown "*
     In *Restitution Steamship Co.* v. *Sir John Pirie & Co.* (1889) 61 L.T.
330, 333, Cave J. cited *Maude and Pollock, A Compendium of the Law
of Merchant Shipping,* 4th ed. (1881) for the proposition that a clean
bill of lading is one which contains nothing in the margin qualifying   F
the words in the bill of lading itself. Now this is a printed form of bill
of lading and the words complained of are not a superadded clause in
the margin but part of the bill of lading itself. This may distinguish
it. But however that may be, what is acknowledged is goods " said to
weigh " 200·8 tons. " Weight unknown " does not qualify this acknowledgment. Nor is any conflict produced by the other words in the
phrase. " Measure " and " quantity " must both, I think, relate to the   G
sugar itself rather than to the number of bags and there is no
acknowledgment as to the measure or quantity of sugar shipped. " Condition unknown " does not qualify an acknowledgment of *apparent* condition
and there is no acknowledgment of value.
     Accordingly, I do not think that this common printed clause contains
any qualification of the acknowledgment contained in the bill of lading   H
rendering it otherwise than " clean." I am not unhappy to reach this
conclusion since " weight unknown " provisions occur in most printed forms
of bill of lading, but are not objected to. Indeed, the buyers themselves
did not demur at these words in the bill of lading for the bulk of the shipment for which they paid or in this bill of lading. Their objections were
limited to the typewritten clause. This objection seems to be something in
the nature of a Temple afterthought.

The Weekly Law Reports, May 16, 1980

513

1 W.L.R.   M. Golodetz & Co. v. Czarnikow-Rionda (Q.B.D.)   Donaldson J.

A *Conclusion*

For the reasons which I have sought to express, I consider that this was a " clean " bill of lading and that the buyers should have accepted it and paid the price. In reaching this conclusion, I have, regretfully, to disagree with the decision of the board of appeal. That decision seems to me to have been based solely on considerations of law. Had it been a conclusion based upon trade practice and included, for example, a finding that a bill of lading in this form was not acceptable in the trade, my decision would, of course, have been different.

The insurance point

My conclusion that the sellers should have been paid the price renders it unnecessary to decide this point. However, in the light of the full argument which was addressed to me it is right that I should express a view.

It being admitted that the buyers failed to insure the goods contrary to rule 22 of the association's rules, they are liable to pay the sellers such sum as would have been recoverable under the terms of the insurance which should have been effected.

The insurance should have been on the terms of the Institute Cargo Clauses (All Risks). Clause 5 is in these terms:

" This insurance is against all risks of loss of or damage to the subject matter insured but shall in no case be deemed to extend to cover loss damage or expense proximately caused by delay or inherent vice or nature of the subject matter insured. Claims recoverable hereunder shall be payable irrespective of percentage."

Mr. Johnson submits that it is for the assured to prove a loss proximately caused by a peril insured against and that for present purposes the sellers are to be treated as being the assured. This is right. He goes on to submit that there is a distinction to be drawn between insurance against a peril subject to exceptions and insurance against a limited peril. In the former case the burden of proof lies on the assured to prove a loss by the peril and upon the underwriter to prove that the facts fall within the exception. In the latter case it is for the assured to show a loss falling within the limited peril: see *Colinvaux, The Law of Insurance,* 3rd ed. (1970), pp. 82–83. Again I agree. Mr. Johnson then submits that clause 5 provides for insurance against a limited range of perils and that the assured would have to negative the possibility that the proximate cause of the loss was inherent vice or nature of the subject matter insured. This, of course, the sellers cannot do.

The classic authority on the cover afforded by a marine policy insuring against " all risks " is *British and Foreign Marine Insurance Co. Ltd.* v. *Gaunt* [1921] 2 A.C. 41. The headnote to the report rightly summarises the decision as being that a plaintiff who sues under an " all risks " policy must prove that the loss was due to an accident or casualty, but is not bound to prove the exact nature of the accident or casualty. However, as Lord Sumner pointed out, at pp. 57–58:

" There are, of course, limits to ' all risks ' . . . the expression does not cover inherent vice or mere wear and tear or British capture. It covers a risk, not a certainty; it is something, which happens to the subject matter from without, not the natural behaviour of that subject matter, being what it is, in the circumstances under which it is carried. Nor is it a loss which the assured brings about by his own act, for then he

514

has not merely exposed the goods to the chance of injury, he has A
injured them himself. Finally the description ' all risks ' does not alter
the general law; only risks are covered which it is lawful to cover, and
the onus of proof remains where it would have been on a policy
against ordinary sea perils.

  " I think, however, that the quasi-universality of the description
does affect the onus of proof in one way. The claimant insured against
and averring a loss by fire must prove loss by fire, which involves B
proving that it is not by something else. When he avers loss by some
risk coming within ' all risks,' as used in this policy, he need only
give evidence reasonably showing that the loss was due to a casualty,
not to a certainty or to inherent vice or to wear and tear. That is
easily done."

This seems to me to establish that if an assured claims under an all C
risks policy on the basis that a loss has occurred due to some accident or
casualty without proof of its exact nature, he will necessarily be relying
upon a change in the condition of the goods rather than upon direct
evidence of what occurred and that in such circumstances he must prove
that this change was not due to the natural behaviour of the subject matter.
If he does not prove this, he will be unable to prove the essentially acci- D
dental nature of the broad cover provided.

  However, a claim under an all risks policy can be pursued in a different
way. As Lord Sumner also pointed out, at p. 57: " ' All risks '
has the same effect as if all insurable risks were separately enumerated."
The assured can, therefore, claim on the basis that he was insured, inter
alia, against loss or damage by fire. E

  The question then becomes that of whether insurance against " fire "
is unlimited but subject to exceptions for inherent vice or is limited to fire
which does not arise from the inherent nature of the goods insured.

  I was referred to Slattery v. Mance [1962] 1 Q.B. 676, 680 as authority for the proposition that " fire " is not confined to accidental fire, but
extends to intentional fires, the exclusion of cover where the author is the F
assured depending not upon the width of the cover, but upon the principle that no man can take advantage of his own wrong. This is clearly
right, but I doubt whether it assists in deciding the width of " fire " in the
context of inherent vice.

  The difference between qualified promises and promises subject to exceptions was considered very fully by Bailhache J. in Munro, Brice & Co.
v. War Risks Association Ltd. [1918] 2 K.B. 78. His conclusions, which G
I respectfully adopt, are set out at pp. 88 and 89. In my judgment, an
insurance against " fire " is an unqualified promise which is subject to the
exceptions set out in section 55 (2) (c) of the Marine Insurance Act 1906,
namely:

  " Unless the policy otherwise provides, the insurer is not liable for
  ordinary wear and tear, ordinary leakage and breakage, inherent vice H
  or nature of the subject matter insured, or for any loss proximately
  caused by rats or vermin, or for any injury to machinery not proximately caused by maritime perils."

It does not seem to me that the proviso in clause 5 of the Institute clauses
does more than make it clear that the insurance against " all risks " is not
intended to override this exception. This conclusion is in line with the

The Weekly Law Reports, May 16, 1980

515

1 W.L.R.   M. Golodetz & Co. v. Czarnikow-Rionda (Q.B.D.)   Donaldson J.

A view expressed in *Phillips on the Law of Insurance*, 4th ed. (1854), that proof of fire suffices to prove a casualty for which the underwriters are liable unless they can show that it occurred as a result of inherent vice: see *Arnould, Marine Insurance (British Shipping Laws,* vol. 10), 15th ed. (1961), para. 858 and *E. D. Sassoon & Co. Ltd.* v. *Yorkshire Insurance Co. Ltd.* (1923) 14 Ll.L.Rep. 167; (1923) 16 Ll.L.Rep. 129.

B   Accordingly, I should, if necessary, have been prepared to hold that the sellers were entitled to recover an amount equal to the price as damages for the buyers' failure to insure the goods.

The claim based upon the goods being at the buyers' risk

This point does not arise for decision unless I am wrong both on the issue of whether this was a " clean " bill of lading and on that concerning
C the scope of " all risks " cover under the Institute clause.

On the facts of this case and the construction which I put on the Institute clause, it would be sufficient to conclude that the provision that " in a contract on c. & f. terms the buyer's risk shall commence immediately the sugar is alongside the export vessel " is included in order to give the sellers an insurable interest before the property in the sugar passes to them.
D Another view is that it constitutes the buyers " all risks " insurers of the sugar while the succeeding sentence of rule 22 requires the buyers to re-insure that risk for the protection of the sellers in the event of the buyers' insolvency.

But if the Institute clause has a narrower construction, there may be a separate claim under this " risk " provision. Mr. Rokison uses it as a basis for claiming payment of the price without tendering a clean bill of
E lading. This argument is certainly open on the questions of law submitted to the court. But I doubt whether technically it is right. The entitlement to the price arises only on and against the tender of contractual documents, the only qualification being that the buyers cannot insist upon such a tender if it is their action which has prevented its being made. That is not this case. The claim under the " risk " provision may well be for an
F amount equal to the price, i.e., the value of the goods to the sellers, but it is not, I think, for the price itself. This in turn raises the question of whether such a claim is open to the sellers on the form of this special case.

If it is open, and if I am wrong about the cleanliness of the bill of lading and the scope of the " all risks " cover, I think that the sellers should succeed under this head. The words are clear. The goods are wholly at the
G risk of the buyers as soon as they are alongside. The cause of the loss or damage is wholly irrelevant, save to the extent that it may found a counterclaim. But the buyers will have to prove that counterclaim. For present purposes, they would have to prove that the loss arose from the goods being unfit for carriage to their destination by sea and this they cannot do.

Accordingly, for the reasons which I have expressed, I answer the questions of law in favour of the sellers.

H
                    *Judgment for sellers with costs of
                          hearing.
                    Leave to appeal.*

Solicitors: *Thomas Cooper & Stibbard; Ince & Co.*

                                                      R. D.

APPEAL from Donaldson J.   A

The buyers appealed, seeking an order that the answer to question
(1) in the arbitrators' award dated February 14, 1977, be " yes " and that
their award in that award be upheld; that the answer to question (2) of the
arbitrators' award dated September 9, 1977, be " no " or " nominal " and
that their award in that award be upheld; and that there be no remission
of the latter award, on the grounds that Donaldson J. had been wrong in   B
holding that the sole test of whether the bill of lading had been " clean "
within the meaning of the sale contract between the parties was whether
there had been an unqualified admission by the shipowners in the bill that
the goods had been in apparent good order and condition when shipped;
that he, having observed that he had " never seen or heard of any bill of
lading " like the bill of lading and having rightly accepted that the clause
on the bill of lading made it unusual and that *Hansson* v. *Hamel & Horley* C
Ltd. [1922] A.C. 36 established that it was " essential that [shipping docu-
ments] should so conform to the accustomed shipping documents as to be
reasonably and readily fit to pass current in commerce," had been wrong in
holding that if the buyers wanted bills of lading that were in " usual form "
they should have contracted accordingly; that he had been wrong in holding that the tender of documents need not have satisfied the Uniform   D
Customs and Practice for Documentary Credits in respect of the rules as
to clean bills of lading, that the evidence did not disclose that banks
would generally reject a bill of lading of the kind tendered, that, on the
evidence, the bill of lading evidenced freight having been paid,
that the bill of lading evidenced an effective contract of affreightment,
that the bill of lading did not show that the goods were other than in   E
the custody of the shipowners and that it was a receipt for goods on
board the ship, that the clause on the bill of lading would not adversely
affect the holder's rights against the ship, that the bill of lading had
been issued as soon as reasonably practicable after loading, that the
buyers could not have objected to its date and that in all the circumstances it had not been stale, that the buyers had not been entitled   F
to reject the documents on the ground that the bill of lading was
claused " weight, measure, quantity, condition, contents and value unknown " and that the bill of lading was a contractual bill and that the
answer to question (1) of the arbitrators' first award was in the affirmative;
that he, having correctly accepted the statement in *British and Foreign
Marine Insurance Co. Ltd.* v. *Gaunt* [1921] 2 A.C. 41, 58 to the effect G
that, when a claimant insured against some risk coming within " all risks,"
he must give evidence that the loss was due to a casualty, not to a certainty
or to inherent vice, had been wrong in law in holding that a claimant
insured under an all risks policy did not have the onus of proving that the
loss had not been due to inherent vice; and that he had been wrong in law
in holding that the sellers were entitled to recover an amount equal to the
price in damages for the buyers' failure to insure the goods, that the   H
answer to question (2) in the arbitrators' award dated September 9, 1977,
was in the affirmative and that the buyers would have been entitled to
payment of an amount equal to the price even in the event of a non-
contractual tender of documents by reason of the provision that the goods
were to be at the buyers' risk " immediately the sugar is alongside the
export vessel."

A   *A. G. S. Pollock Q.C.* and *Christopher C. Russell* for the buyers.
Kenneth Rokison Q.C. and *Martin Moore-Bick* for the sellers.

MEGAW L.J. This is an appeal from the judgment of Donaldson J.
delivered on November 20, 1978, wherein he gave his decisions on two
awards, each in the form of a special case stated by the council of the
Refined Sugar Association to whose arbitration disputes had been referred
B by the parties to a contract. That contract was dated February 26, 1975, and
by its express terms that contract was made subject to the rules of that association. The parties were, respectively, the sellers under the contract in
question, M. Golodetz & Co. Inc., New York, and the buyers under the
contract, Czarnikow-Rionda Co. Inc., New York. The two awards were
dated respectively February 14, 1977, and September 9, 1977. The arbitral
C tribunal, members of the council of the Refined Sugar Association (I shall
call them " the arbitrators "), decided in favour of the buyers in both awards.
Donaldson J., on the cases stated, decided both in favour of the
sellers. As requested by the parties, he heard the arguments on the
two special cases together and gave one single judgment, though
separate formal orders were made. That was a proper and sensible
D procedure. The first of the two awards was expressed to be an interim
award and the second of them a supplementary award.
    It is not necessary for me to go in any detail into the facts. The text
of the two awards (ante, pp. 497E—500D, E–505A), as well as the judgment of Donaldson J. (ante, pp. 505B—515G), will be found reported in
[1979] 2 All E.R. 726. On the view that I take of this appeal, no
important question of principle falls to be decided. The decision is
E one that depends on special and unusual facts.
    A number of the contentions that were raised before Donaldson J.
have not been renewed in argument in this court, I have no doubt for good
and sufficient reason.
    The contract was for the sale of 12,000–13,000 tonnes of sugar on
c. & f. terms to Bandarshapur in Iran. Though the contract did not so
F specify, shipment took place from an Indian port, Kandla. Payment under
the contract was to be made cash against documents upon first presentation in New York. The shipment period was March/April 1975. The
contract provided that its terms and conditions were to be in accordance
with the rules of the Refined Sugar Association. The relevant parts of
the relevant rules, rules 22 and 23 of the rules relating to contracts,
headed respectively " Insurance " and " Payment," are set out in the
G judgment appealed from. Rule 23 included provision that, in respect
of a c. & f. contract, payment was to be " . . . against a complete set
. . . of signed clean ' on board ' bills of lading evidencing freight having
been paid. . . "
    It was arranged by or on behalf of the sellers that the sugar would be
carried in a vessel, the *Galatia.* She arrived at Kandla on March 20,
H 1975. On March 24, by which time part of the sugar had been loaded, a
fire broke out on board and 2,008 bags, that is, 200·8 tonnes of sugar, were
damaged by fire and water. The sugar was discharged. It could not be
made suitable for reloading. The rest of the cargo, which totalled 12,999·2
tonnes, was safely loaded and was carried to Bandarshapur in the
Galatia.
    The intention had been, apparently, that there should be one single set
of three bills of lading, but, following the fire, two separate sets of bills

of lading were prepared and signed on behalf of the shipowners and made   A
available to the sellers. (For simplicity, I shall refer to the set of three
bills of lading as " a " bill of lading). One of the bills of lading was for
12,999·2 tonnes. No question arises about it or about that part of the
contract goods. The other bill of lading was for 200·8 tonnes.

There were in the course of the arbitration various other complaints
about that bill of lading. One by one they have dropped away, but the   B
complaint that was the original complaint, when the bills of lading were
first tendered by the sellers to the buyers and when the 200 tonnes bill of
lading was rejected, still remains. That complaint relates to the fact that,
on the face of the bill of lading, presumably before the signature was put
on the bill, there was put on it a typewritten notation, which was in these
terms: " Cargo covered by this bill of lading has been discharged at Kandla
view damaged by fire and/or water used to extinguish fire for which   C
general average declared." That notation accurately stated the facts. It
was contended on behalf of the buyers, in rejecting that bill of lading, that
it was not a " clean " bill of lading. I do not find it necessary to refer to
the precise terms of the various ways in which that contention was
expressed in the correspondence that passed between the parties at the
time of the rejection.

The issue in the first arbitration was, and the first issue before us is,   D
whether the buyers were entitled to reject that bill of lading. The award
made by the arbitrators reads: ". . . (c) The said bills of lading were not
clean ' on board' bills of lading within the meaning of the said contract
by reason of the notation referred to in paragraph A.8 hereof " (that is, the
notation above set out).

The relevant question of law that was stated for the decision of the   E
court in that award is:

> " on the facts found and on the true construction of the contract
> (1) whether the sellers are entitled to the price of the 2,008 bags of
> sugar alternatively to damages for the buyers' failure to accept the
> same or to take up and pay for the shipping documents in respect
> thereof."   F

A further question was stated, which does not now call for an answer.

Donaldson J. held that the correct answer to the question was in the
affirmative. That was because, in his view, the bill of lading was a clean
bill of lading and the buyers should have accepted it and paid the price.

I think that, without disrespect to the very interesting and careful arguments that have been put before us by counsel on that issue, I can deal   G
with them quite shortly.

Donaldson J. was asked, on behalf of the buyers, to uphold the arbitrators' view of the matter on a large number of grounds. The first ground
was that the bill of lading was not " clean " and that, therefore, it did not
comply with the provisions of the contract for a clean " on board " bill of
lading; and that, indeed, was what the arbitrators appear to have held in   H
their award. Donaldson J., having gone into the authorities, arrived at
the conclusion that a clean bill of lading is one in which there is nothing
to qualify the admission that the goods were in apparent good order
and condition at the time of shipment.

Mr. Pollock, for the buyers, accepted in this court that that meaning of
" clean," in respect of " clean bill of lading," was indeed, as he put it, the
correct meaning of the word " clean." There is also authority to that

The Weekly Law Reports, May 16, 1980

519

1 W.L.R.   M. Golodetz & Co. v. Czarnikow-Rionda (C.A.)   Megaw L.J.

effect. But, said Mr. Pollock, though that is the correct meaning of " clean," it has another, wider, meaning in which it can be used: namely, that a bill of lading is not " clean " if it contains a clause the effect of which is to make the bill of lading unacceptable or unmerchantable, so that it would not be accepted in the ordinary way in the trade as being a proper document. Mr. Pollock says that, on the true construction of the award with which we are concerned, the arbitrators ought to be taken to have been using the words " not clean " in that wider sense. They ought not to be taken to have been using the words in the narrower sense.

I have no doubt but that Donaldson J. was right in saying that, on the correct approach in law, this bill of lading, with the typewritten notation on it, was a " clean " bill of lading in the proper sense of that word; and, therefore, if, indeed, the arbitrators' finding that it was not a " clean " bill of lading was a finding that had got to be treated as using the word " clean " in its proper legal sense, the arbitrators had erred in law. That is the view that Donaldson J. took.

However, Mr. Pollock, as I have said, submits that, on the construction of the award as a whole and by reference to various documents that passed between the parties and, I think he also submits, as a matter of ordinary good sense, the arbitrators ought, by way of necessary inference, to be taken as saying that the bill of lading was not " clean " in the sense that it was not a document that would ordinarily and properly have been accepted in the trade as being an appropriate document. That there is such a requirement in relation to bills of lading is, I think, sufficiently clear. The authority in that regard that is usually quoted, and that was quoted by Donaldson J. in this case, is a passage from the speech of Lord Sumner in *Hansson* v. *Hamel and Horley Ltd.* [1922] 2 A.C. 36, 46. The passage cited by Donaldson J. contains these words:

"These documents have to be handled by banks, they have to be taken up or rejected promptly and without any opportunity for prolonged inquiry, they have to be such as can be re-tendered to sub-purchasers, and it is essential that they should so conform to the accustomed shipping documents as to be reasonably and readily fit to pass current in commerce."

Donaldson J. unreservedly accepted that proposition. He said that, if the arbitrators had found that a bill of lading in this form was not acceptable in the trade, his decision " would, of course, have been different " (ante, p. 513A–B). In that event, he would have upheld their decision on this issue. But he found himself unable to take the view that that was what the arbitrators were to be treated as having said, either by the words that they had used or by any inference that could properly be drawn in respect of them from the award as a whole or any relevant matters referred to therein.

For myself, I find that view supported by the fact that, in the second award dealing with what has been called the " insurance " issue, the self-same arbitrators, in dealing with the question whether a policy of insurance taken out by the buyers was in accordance with the contract, made an express finding, first, that the policy was defective in certain stated respects, and then went on to say: " We further find and/or hold that the policy was not one which was usual or merchantable in the trade."

The arbitrators, therefore, when they were minded to find that a document was not one that was usual or merchantable in the trade, were prepared to express that view specifically. That lends strength, in my view, to

the conclusion reached by Donaldson J. I would agree with him, in any   A
event, that here it cannot be assumed or accepted, even on a balance of
probability (if that were the appropriate test), that the arbitrators were
intending to say: " We, having considered this matter, find here that this
document is one that was unusual and that was not merchantable in the
trade." In my judgment, accepting the conclusion of Donaldson J., the
arbitrators here must be taken, incorrectly as a matter of law, to have held
that the bill of lading in question was not " clean " by reason of the nota-   B
tion referred to. If the arbitrators have not found that this bill of lading,
with its notation, is not reasonably and readily fit to pass current in commerce, there is no reason for the court so to hold.

No other grounds are now put forward in favour of the buyers on this
issue. I am satisfied that the decision of Donaldson J. was correct on this
issue.   C

However, I should say, as we have had interesting submissions on each
side as to whether or not this bill of lading could properly be regarded as
one that should have been, in some way, unacceptable, that I think that there
is great force in the submissions that Mr. Rokison put forward on behalf of
the sellers. In saying that, however, I am not departing in any way from
the view that the judge expressed that if that had been what the arbitrators   D
had said he would have accepted it. So would I, on that hypothesis.

That being so, it is agreed between the parties that, so far as this court
is concerned, the answer on this first issue makes it unnecessary to decide
the other two issues. As to one of them, Donaldson J. (ante, p. 515B)
would have decided it in favour of the sellers if it had arisen, but it did
not arise, if his decision on the first issue was right. As to the third
issue (ante, p. 515F), it may be that he was disposed to the view that   E
it would not, in any event, have been open to the sellers to argue it,
in view of the form of the question of law, but the third issue also does
not arise, if the first issue is decided in favour of the sellers.

I merely mention that the second question was the question as to the
right of the sellers to obtain damages from the buyers, having regard to the
fact, which was strongly contested before the arbitrators, but which is now   F
not challenged on behalf of the buyers, that the insurance policy that they
purported to take out, in compliance with their duty under the contract
(for the contract by incorporating rule 22 of the rules of the association
put the duty of insuring the goods on the buyers), was not a policy that
fulfilled their own contractual obligation under the contract. Though that
is accepted, it is said in this court that the only damages to which the
sellers would be entitled by reason of that breach of contract by the buyers   G
would be the loss of the chance, whatever the chance might have been, that,
if a proper insurance policy had been taken out, the sellers would, if they
were wrong on the first issue, have been entitled to recover their loss from
the insurers under the proper policy of insurance. It was said that, in the
circumstances and having regard to what were said to be facts as found by
the arbitrators, the arbitrators must be taken to have arrived at a conclusion   H
of fact that, if the proper policy had been issued, the sellers would not have
been able to recover one penny of the insurance money from the insurers
in respect of the 200 tonnes that had been destroyed by fire.

Since this hypothetical question does not arise if the sellers are right
on the first issue, I find it unnecessary to consider it. We have had interesting argument on it from Mr. Pollock. We have not heard Mr. Rokison
on it. I therefore express no view about it. By reason of what I regard as

The Weekly Law Reports, May 23, 1980

521

1 W.L.R.   M. Golodetz & Co. v. Czarnikow-Rionda (C.A.)   Megaw L.J.

A being the correct decision of Donaldson J. on the first issue, however, I would dismiss the appeal.

SHAW L.J. For the reasons given by Megaw L.J., I agree that this appeal should be dismissed.

B WALLER L.J. I also agree.

Appeal dismissed with costs.

Solicitors: *Ince & Co.; Thomas Cooper & Stibbard.*

C   M. G.

D   [CHANCERY DIVISION]

                                    * CARGILL v. GOTTS

                                      [1977 C. No. 1189]

E 1979   Oct. 22, 23, 24, 25, 26; 29   H. E. Francis Q.C., sitting as a
                                                    deputy judge of the Chancery Division

*Easement—Right to draw water—Statutory restriction—Use of
    water from mill-pond forming part of river—Occupier of
    dominant tenement having no statutory licence to abstract
    water—Increase of user during prescriptive period—Whether
    bar to prescription—Effect of statute—Water Resources Act*
F *1963 (c. 38), ss. 23 (1), 24 (1)*

        In 1928, the plaintiff became tenant of a 400-acre farm
    which he farmed as tenant until he purchased the freehold in
    1942 and he had been in continuous occupation ever since.
    In 1977 the defendant bought some land, which included a
    mill-pond forming part of a river. Since 1928 the plaintiff or
    his employees had been in the habit of drawing water from
G the pond for use on the farm for watering cattle and for
    spraying. The quantity of water abstracted had increased over
    the years from about 200 gallons a day to as much as 4,000
    gallons in a single day. In the early days a horse-drawn cart
    with a capacity of about 100 gallons was used; at the time
    of the action the plaintiff used a " bowser " with a metal tank
    added, which had a capacity of 1,400 gallons. The plaintiff did
    not have a licence under the Water Resources Act 1963 to
H abstract water, and was thus prohibited by section 23 (1) [1] from
    abstracting water except in a quantity not exceeding 1,000
    gallons under the terms of section 24 (1) of the Act.
        On the plaintiff's claim for a declaration that he had an
    easement to draw water from the pond, an injunction preventing
    the defendant from interfering with that easement and damages
    for interference: —

─────────
[1] Water Resources Act 1963, s. 23 (1): see post, p. 526D–E.
   S. 24 (1): see post, p. 526G.

Cargill v. Gotts (Ch.D.) [1980]

Held, (1) that immediately prior to the Water Resources Act A
1963 the plaintiff had been entitled to an easement at common
law to draw water from the mill-pond for use on his farm for
agricultural purposes; that the Act did not extinguish that right
but merely controlled its exercise by means of restrictions,
imposed for the benefit of the public at large, which precluded
the abstraction of water otherwise than in accordance with a
licence granted by the river authority or within the limits
imposed by section 24 (1) of the Act, but that the servient owner B
as such had no right to enforce the restrictions imposed by the
Act (post, p. 527c–e).

(2) That an increase of user was no bar to prescription unless
it was of a different kind or for a different purpose or unless
it was so great that the practical burden imposed on the servient
tenement was drastically increased, and, in the absence of
evidence that the increase in the quantity of water abstracted
had materially affected the level or flow of water in the pond, C
the plaintiff was entitled to the declaration and injunction
sought and to £50 damages for interference with his right
(post, p. 528b–f).

Hulley v. *Silversprings Bleaching and Dyeing Co. Ltd.* [1922]
2 Ch. 268 distinguished.

British Railways Board v. *Glass* [1965] Ch. 538, C.A. and
Woodhouse & Co. Ltd. v. *Kirkland (Derby) Ltd.* [1970] 1 D
W.L.R. 1185 applied.

Per curiam. A succession of abstractions on quite separate
occasions, each made for the purpose of meeting an additional
need for water on a farm, would not constitute a " series of
operations " within the meaning of section 24 (1) of the Water
Resources Act 1963 (post, p. 527f).

The following cases are referred to in the judgment: E

British Railways Board v. *Glass* [1965] Ch. 538; [1964] 3 W.L.R. 913;
    [1964] 3 All E.R. 418, C.A.
Hulley v. *Silversprings Bleaching and Dyeing Co. Ltd.* [1922] 2 Ch. 268.
Woodhouse & Co. Ltd. v. *Kirkland (Derby) Ltd.* [1970] 1 W.L.R. 1185;
    [1970] 2 All E.R. 587.

F

The following additional cases were cited in argument:

Blackburne v. *Somers* (1879) 5 L.R.Ir. 1.
Cawkwell v. *Russell* (1856) 26 L.J.Ex. 34.
Chasemore v. *Richards* (1859) 7 H.L.Cas. 349, H.L.(E.).
Millington v. *Griffiths* (1874) 30 L.T. 65.
Neaverson v. *Peterborough Rural District Council* [1902] 1 Ch. 557, C.A.
Phillips v. *Britannia Hygienic Laundry Co. Ltd.* [1923] 2 K.B. 832, C.A. G
R.P.C. Holdings Ltd. v. *Rogers* [1953] 1 All E.R. 1029.
Traill v. *M'Allister* (1890) 25 L.R.Ir. 524.

ACTION

By a writ dated December 6, 1977, the plaintiff, David Cargill,
who was the occupier of Grove Farm, Gimingham, Norfolk, sought (1) H
a declaration that he was entitled either at common law or under section
2 of the Prescription Act 1832 to draw water for use appertaining to the
dominant tenement, Grove Farm, from the mill-pond at Gimingham,
which belonged to the defendant, Brown Gordon Gotts; (2) alternatively, a
declaration that he was entitled to the right to draw water by virtue of
the doctrine of lost modern grant; and (3) an injunction restraining the

A defendant from preventing the plaintiff from drawing water from the mill-pond and (4) damages.

The facts are stated in the judgment.

Vivian Chapman for the plaintiff.
Sonia Proudman for the defendant.

B   *Cur. adv. vult.*

October 29. Mr. H. E. FRANCIS Q.C. read the following judgment. The plaintiff, Mr. David Cargill, is the lessee and occupier of a farm nearly 400 acres in extent, known as Grove Farm, which is situated near the village of Gimingham, Norfolk. The plaintiff, who is now 81 years of age, became the tenant of the farm in 1928 and he farmed it as a
C tenant until 1942 when he bought the freehold. In 1959 he granted a lease of the farm to himself and one David Henderson for a term of 35 years from April 6, 1958. This lease was assigned in 1963 to the plaintiff and his son, Alan Milne Cargill, and in 1972 it was assigned to the plaintiff. Since 1965 the freehold of the farm has been vested in Alan Milne Cargill. Nothing turns on these various dealings with the farm, it being
D common ground that since the purchase in 1942 the plaintiff has been in continuous occupation of the farm either as the freeholder or as a lessee.

The defendant, Mr. Brown Gordon Gotts, is the fee simple owner of a piece of land at Gimingham just under seven acres in extent, which includes the mill-pond and dam, serving or formerly serving Gimingham mill. The pond has been referred to in this action as the mill-pond but
E it is, in fact, part of the river Mun, which, at the north-eastern extremity of the pond passes through a grille under the highway which runs along the eastern side of the pond, and through or alongside the mill premises on the other side of the road, where, until the mill closed in about 1977, there was a sluice by means of which the water in the river could be dammed and released for the purpose of working the turbine at the mill.
F Mr. Gotts bought this property in 1977, and it is common ground that he is the owner of the bed of the mill-pond and of the land surrounding it, including the narrow strip of land which lies between the pond and the highway on the eastern side of the pond. It follows that Mr. Gotts has the natural rights of a riparian owner with respect to the water in the pond.

The dispute which has unfortunately arisen between the parties is this.
G The pond is about 500 yards away from the nearest point of Grove Farm and, as I shall presently relate more fully, there is no doubt that the plaintiff has been in the habit for a long time of abstracting water from the pond for agricultural use on Grove Farm, such as watering cattle and spraying crops with insecticides and other chemical liquids. Since he bought the pond, Mr. Gotts has challenged the plaintiff's right
H to abstract water from the pond. The upshot is this action, in which the plaintiff claims, first, a declaration that he has an easement to abstract water from the pond for agricultural use on Grove Farm, either by prescription at common law, or by statutory prescription under section 2 of the Prescription Act 1832, or under the doctrine of lost modern grant; secondly, an injunction restraining the defendant from preventing the plaintiff from drawing water from the pond for that purpose; and, thirdly, damages.

The salient facts are not seriously in dispute. The principal witnesses **A**
as to user were the plaintiff and his employees, Mr. Thurlborne and Mr.
Waite. The plaintiff told me that his employees started to draw water from
the pond from the time when he became tenant at Grove Farm in 1928.
A horse-drawn water-cart with a capacity of about 100 gallons was
taken down to the pond and filled by means of buckets. In dry periods
the water cart would go down to the pond two or three times a day.
In winter they did not use the pond nearly so much because sufficient water **B**
was available from a pond on Grove Farm. The abstracted water was
then used mainly for watering horses and bullocks; in the 1930s the
plaintiff had about 100 bullocks on the farm. This use continued until
after the Second World War when the plaintiff bought a water tanker,
formerly used by the Royal Air Force, with a capacity of some 900
gallons. By this time he had started to use water for spraying chemicals **C**
to destroy weeds, such as docks. The plaintiff said that the user was
quite open, and that the owner of the mill and pond never took any
objection to it. He said that he never asked for permission to take water
from the pond. He also mentioned that smallholders and villagers who
kept horses or pigs took water from the pond.

Mr. Thurlborne has been employed by the plaintiff as a farm worker **D**
at Grove Farm and other farms since 1948, and throughout that period
he has lived at Gimingham. He told me that he started to take water
from the mill pond for use on Grove Farm from the beginning of his
employment. He never asked for permission to draw water from the
pond. At first the water container was a wooden barrel with a capacity
of 50 to 60 gallons, but as the years went by the water tanks became
larger. For a time they used a water cart with a capacity of 250 gallons. **E**
Later, an ex-Royal Air Force water tanker—referred to during the trial
as a " bowser "—with a capacity of 900 gallons was used. Later still, a
square metal tank was added to the bowser increasing the capacity to
some 1,400 gallons. He told me that during the first five years of his
employment the water was used mainly for watering cattle, and that
little spraying was done. From 1953 onwards, however, it became the **F**
practice to spray crops with insecticides and other chemical liquids and
the use of the abstracted water for this purpose was increased very
considerably over the years. It used to be the practice to spray crops
only at springtime but, latterly, spraying was done at intervals throughout the year. In the result the quantity of water abstracted from the pond
for use on Grove Farm has increased substantially since the 1950s. In **G**
cross-examination Mr. Thurlborne admitted that since the middle 1950s
the quantity of water abstracted by him from the pond for spraying had
increased tenfold by 1977. By this time the water was used not only for
Grove Farm, but also for other farms belonging to or managed by the
plaintiff, that is, Knapton Farm, Dunton Park and Alley Farm. Occasionally, Mr. Thurlborne drew three full tanker loads of water, that is about
4,000 gallons, in a single day. **H**

No claim is made in this action in respect of the three other farms
because they are no longer farmed by the plaintiff. I am concerned only
with the claim made in respect of Grove Farm.

Mr. Waite, who was born in Gimingham in 1913 and has lived there
for practically the whole of his life, has been employed on Grove Farm
since 1927, first as an ordinary farmworker and for some years past as a

A   foreman. He told me that water has been drawn from the mill pond for use on Grove Farm since before 1927. His grandfather had been employed at Grove Farm for many years prior to 1927, and he remembers going down to the pond as a small boy with his grandfather in a horse-drawn cart for the purpose of drawing water from the pond for use on Grove Farm. He said that he was allowed to ride on the back of the horse. The water tank was filled by means of a bucket. At one time a wine

B   barrel with a capacity of 120 gallons was used as a water container, the barrel being carried on a horse-drawn cart. Before the war the water cart was taken to the pond about four times a week. The water was used mainly for watering horses and cattle on Grove Farm. Some time after the war the bowser was acquired, but before this a water tank with a capacity of 250 gallons to 300 gallons had been used instead of the wine barrel. The

C   bowser was filled by means of a pipe or hose through which the water was pumped into the bowser by a mechanical pump mounted on the side of the bowser. After the war the water was abstracted for spraying operations on Grove Farm as well as for watering livestock. Formerly, spraying took place only in April and May but, latterly, far more spraying had been done. Mr. Waite said that he never asked for anyone's per-

D   mission to draw the water from the pond and, so far as he knew, no one else did.

Important evidence was also given by Mr. Ottewell, an independent witness now retired, who has lived in Gimingham since 1927. From 1949 to 1969 he was employed at Gimingham mill. He remembered that in the days before the war farmers came to the pond with water carts to draw water, especially at threshing time when steam engines were in

E   use, and for watering cattle. He told me that in those days there was a place for animals on the roadside near the southern end of the pond to drink water from the pond. People did not ask the miller for permission. After 1949 he saw Mr. Thurlborne draw water on numerous occasions by pumping water from the pond into a tanker. Sometimes he saw him draw water twice a day, then he might not see him again for several days.

F   This continued to happen until 1970. He also told me that the manager at the mill, a Mr. Paine, told him that they could not stop farmers drawing water from the pond so far as it was needed for agricultural purposes.

I am satisfied that the four witnesses to whom I have referred were honest witnesses, and I have no hesitation in accepting their evidence as to user. Their evidence so far as summarised above was not really contradicted by the defendant or his witnesses. It was plain to me that

G   the defendant and his witnesses were not in a position to do so.

The evidence called for the defendant was directed mainly to the state of affairs after 1970. There was evidence that the condition of the pond between the late 1960s and the purchase of it by the defendant had deteriorated very considerably through lack of attention. Little if anything had been done for some years to keep it clean, and the result was

H   that a good deal of silt had accumulated on the bed of the pond and it became partly overgrown with rushes and algae. It also seems that some rubbish was thrown into it. The water in dry periods became very shallow. In my judgment, however, little turns on this because I am satisfied that the plaintiff and his employees continued to draw water from the pond for use at Grove Farm, although at times there may have been some difficulty in finding and reaching clear water of sufficient depth for pumping.

Another matter that was canvassed by the defendant and his witnesses   A
was the pollution of the pond by chemicals. It was alleged by the defendant
that on more than one occasion from the summer of 1976 onwards, Mr.
Thurlborne washed out his chemical sprayer, which was a red plastic
tank attached to the rear of his tractor, into the pond thereby causing
the water to be polluted by a chemical solution. Mr. Thurlborne strongly
denied that he ever did this. He conceded that he filled the sprayer with   B
water on one or two occasions when he was drawing water from the pond,
but he asserted that on no occasion did he wash out the chemical residue
in the sprayer into the pond. There is a direct conflict of evidence here
between Mr. Thurlborne and the defendant. Although I have felt some
doubt as to where the truth lies, it has not been proved to my satisfaction
that Mr. Thurlborne was lying when he told me that he never washed
out his sprayer into the pond. I am quite satisfied that he did not make a   C
practice of it and that normally he would wash out the sprayer on some
rough ground at Grove Farm or another farm where he had been spraying.
In any event, I do not consider that the alleged pollution in and after
1976 has any bearing on the issues which arise in this action.

I now turn to the Water Resources Act 1963, upon which much
reliance was placed by Miss Proudman in her admirable argument for   D
the defendant. This Act was passed on July 31, 1963, for the purpose,
inter alia, of securing the protection and proper use of inland waters.
Section 23 (1) provides:

> "Subject to the following provisions of this Part of this Act, as
> from the end of the period of three months beginning with the
> second appointed day (in this Act referred to as ' the initial period ')   E
> no person shall abstract water from any source of supply in a river
> authority area, or cause or permit any other person so to abstract
> any water, except in pursuance of a licence under this Act granted
> by the river authority and in accordance with the provisions of that
> licence."

The mill pond, being part of the river Mun, is plainly a source of supply   F
within the meaning of this subsection. The second appointed day was
April 1, 1965, so that the prohibition took effect as from July 1, 1965.
The plaintiff did not in fact obtain a licence under the Act in respect of
the abstraction of water from the mill pond. The prohibition in section
23 (1) is subject to certain exceptions, of which the only material exception
in this case is that contained in section 24 (1) which provides:

> "The restriction imposed by subsection (1) of the last preceding
> section does not apply to any abstraction of a quantity of water not
> exceeding 1,000 gallons, if it does not form part of a continuous
> operation, or of a series of operations, whereby in the aggregate
> more than 1,000 gallons of water are abstracted."

Section 49 makes it an offence to contravene section 23 (1). Section 118   H
provides:

> "(1) It shall be the duty of a river authority to enforce the
> provisions of this Act in relation to the area of the authority. (2) No
> proceedings for any offence under this Act shall be instituted except
> (a) by a river authority, or (b) by, or with the consent of, the Director
> of Public Prosecutions."

A   Miss Proudman has submitted that all the abstractions of water made by or on behalf of the plaintiff since June 30, 1965, have been illegal, either as being an abstraction of a quantity of water exceeding 1,000 gallons by a continuous operation (as undoubtedly happened on numerous occasions when Mr. Thurlborne took away a full load in the bowser), or as being an aggregate abstraction in excess of 1,000 gallons by successive abstractions forming part of a series of operations. On that footing it

B   is argued that the plaintiff cannot prove user as of right since June 1965 and that his claim based on prescription and his claim under the doctrine of lost modern grant must fail. Moreover, argues Miss Proudman, any grant presumed from the previous user must be limited to the lawful user, and any illegal user would be excessive and beyond the scope of the fictional grant.

C   I do not feel able to accept these submissions. In my judgment immediately before July 1, 1965, the plaintiff was entitled at common law to an easement to draw water from the mill pond for use on Grove Farm for agricultural or farming purposes. The Act of 1963 did not extinguish that right. It did not, as I see it, alter the rights of the dominant and servient owners, inter se. What it did was to control the exercise of

D   the easement by means of restrictions imposed, not for the benefit of the servient owner as such, but for the benefit of the public at large. The Act precludes the dominant owner from abstracting water otherwise than in accordance with the provisions of the Act, namely, either under and according to a licence granted by the river authority or within the limits specified in section 24 (1). If the dominant owner fails to observe the statutory restrictions then the remedy lies with the river authority.

E   The servient owner as such has no right to enforce the restrictions.

   I do not accept Miss Proudman's submission that the abstractions of water made by or on behalf of the plaintiff constituted a series of operations within the meaning of that phrase in section 24 (1). The phrase would no doubt cover the case of a tanker with a capacity exceeding 1,000 gallons being filled by means of a bucket, since each bucketful would

F   constitute an " abstraction " as defined in section 135 (1). In my judgment, a succession of abstractions on quite separate occasions, each made for the purpose of meeting an additional need for water on a farm, would not constitute a series of operations within the meaning of the Act. It follows that it is open to the plaintiff to abstract water from the mill pond consistently with the provisions of the Act of 1963 provided he does not draw out more than 1,000 gallons on any one occasion. It may be that

G   the plaintiff would be well advised to use a water tanker with a capacity not exceeding 1,000 gallons.

   The other major submission made by Miss Proudman was that the user required to support a prescriptive right must be certain and uniform in its extent and nature throughout the relevant prescriptive period. In other words, the burden on the servient tenement must remain substanti-

H   ally the same. In this case the quantity of water abstracted and the corresponding burden on the servient tenant had increased very substantially over the years, especially during the past 10 to 15 years. That there has been a very substantial increase in the quantity of water abstracted as compared with what was abstracted up to the middle 1950s or thereabouts is plain. In support of this submission, Miss Proudman referred me to *Hulley* v. *Silversprings Bleaching and Dyeing Co. Ltd.* [1922] 2 Ch. 268. In that case the defendants claimed a prescriptive

easement to pollute a natural stream by discharging into it the effluent A
from their bleaching and dyeing works.   The claim was rejected by Eve J.
inter alia on the ground stated at p. 281, where he said:

> " The progressive increase in the plant in the defendants' mill and in
> the volume of water polluted is destructive of that certainty and
> uniformity essential for the measurement . . . of the user by which
> the extent of the prescriptive right is to be ascertained."
                                                                         B

Miss Proudman argued that there is no distinction in principle between
an easement to pollute and an easement to abstract water.

On the other hand, Mr. Chapman submitted on behalf of the plaintiff
that an increase in the user is no bar to prescription unless it is user of a
different kind or for a different purpose, or unless the increase is so great
that the practical burden on the servient tenement is drastically increased. C
In the present case, argued Mr. Chapman, water was abstracted throughout for farming purposes at Grove Farm, and the increased burden on
the servient tenement was of no great significance, there being no evidence
to show that the increase in the quantity of water abstracted had materially affected the level or flow of water in the pond. In support of his
submission Mr. Chapman referred me to *British Railways Board* v. *Glass*
[1965] Ch. 538 and *Woodhouse & Co. Ltd.* v. *Kirkland (Derby) Ltd.* D
[1970] 1 W.L.R. 1185, both concerning rights of way, where it was held
that the mere increase in the use of the right of way during the
prescriptive period did not vitiate the prescriptive claim.   Mr. Chapman's
submission appears to me to be correct and I accept it.

In the result, I hold that subject and without prejudice to the provisions
of the Water Resources Act 1963 the plaintiff is entitled at common law E
to an easement to draw water from the mill pond for farming purposes
on Grove Farm, and I will make a declaration accordingly. I also grant
him an injunction to restrain the defendant from preventing the plaintiff
or his servants or agents from drawing water in exercise of that easement
from the mill pond.

As regards the claim for damages, I am not satisfied that the plaintiff
has suffered much loss, but I consider that he is entitled to some general F
damages for the interference with his right. I therefore award him £50
damages. The defendant must pay the costs.

> *Declaration and injunction accord-*
> *ingly.*
> *Judgment for plaintiff for £50 with* G
> *costs.*

Solicitors: *Rooks Rider & Co. for Daynes, Chittock & Back, Norwich;*
Mills & Reeve, Norwich.

T. C. C. B.

                                                                         H

A

[COURT OF APPEAL]

* NABI *v.* BRITISH LEYLAND (U.K.) LTD.

[1976 N. No. 3748]

B 1979 Nov. 12, 13; 30   Megaw, Browne and
Brightman L.JJ.

*Damages—Earnings, loss of—Unemployment benefit—Employee
injured in industrial accident—Receipt of unemployment benefit
—Whether benefit deductible from special damages—Social
Security Act 1975 (c. 14), s. 12 (1) (a)*

C
An employee was injured as the result of an industrial
accident. In an action against his employers for damages for
negligence and/or breach of statutory duty, the trial judge
held that the employers were liable. In assessing damages,
the judge assessed the special damages for loss of earnings to
date at £4,724. He then deducted £1,062 for unemployment
benefit received by the employee under section 12 (1) (a) of
D the Social Security Act 1975 and accordingly awarded £3,662
under that head of damages.

On the employee's appeal against the deduction: —

Held, dismissing the appeal, that although statutory provisions regulated the amount of certain contributory benefits
to be taken into account in the assessment of damages, no
such provision had been made in relation to unemployment
benefit; that while the proceeds of insurance or benevolence
were to be disregarded in assessing damages, unemployment
E benefit, which was received by an employee by virtue of
contributions made by his employer as well as himself, could
not be regarded as comparable to benefits received under a
personal insurance policy, because the employer, having made
a contribution, should be entitled to the benefit of it in as
much as the loss suffered by the employee was diminished by
the resulting benefit and, accordingly, the sum of £1,062
F received as unemployment benefit should be deducted from
the award of £4,724 in respect of loss of earnings (post, pp.
531G–H, 532C–D, 534E–F, H, 535B).

Parsons v. *B.N.M. Laboratories Ltd.* [1964] 1 Q.B. 95,
C.A. followed.

Parry v. *Cleaver* [1970] A.C. 1, H.L.(E.) considered.

Per curiam. The time has come for *Parsons'* case to be
reviewed, as was indeed indicated in *Parry's* case, but such
review cannot properly be conducted by this court. The law
G in relation to unemployment benefit is at present laid down
in *Parsons'* case, and so it must remain until the House of
Lords or the legislature decides otherwise (post, pp. 538H—
539A).

Decision of Smith J. affirmed.

The following cases are referred to in the judgment of the court:

H *Bougeois* v. *Tzrop* (1957) 9 D.L.R. (2d) 214.
Bowker v. *Rose,* February 2, 1978; Court of Appeal (Civil Division)
Transcript No. 164 of 1978, C.A.
Bradburn v. *Great Western Railway Co.* (1874) L.R. 10 Ex. 1.
British Transport Commission v. *Gourley* [1956] A.C. 185; [1956] 2
W.L.R. 41; [1955] 3 All E.R. 796, H.L.(E.).
Daish v. *Wauton* [1972] 2 Q.B. 262; [1972] 2 W.L.R. 29; [1972] 1 All
E.R. 25, C.A.
Eldridge v. *Videtta* (1964) 108 S.J. 137.

Fitzpatrick v. *Moore* [1962] N.I. 152.   A
Foxley v. *Olton* [1965] 2 Q.B. 306; [1964] 3 W.L.R. 1155; [1964] 3 All
    E.R. 248.
Hewson v. *Downs* [1970] 1 Q.B. 73; [1969] 2 W.L.R. 1169; [1969] 3
    All E.R. 193.
Lindstedt v. *Wimbourne Steamship Co. Ltd.* (1949) 83 Ll.L.R. 19.
Parry v. *Cleaver* [1968] 1 Q.B. 195; [1967] 3 W.L.R. 739; [1967] 2 All
    E.R. 1168, C.A.; [1970] A.C. 1; [1969] 2 W.L.R. 821; [1969] 1 All   B
    E.R. 555, H.L.(E.).
Parsons v. *B.N.M. Laboratories Ltd.* [1964] 1 Q.B. 95; [1963] 2 W.L.R.
    1273; [1963] 2 All E.R. 658, C.A.
Payne v. *Railway Executive* [1952] 1 K.B. 26; [1951] 1 All E.R. 1034;
    [1951] 2 All E.R. 910, C.A.
Redpath v. *Belfast and County Down Railway* [1947] N.I. 167.
Shaw v. *Cape Insulation Co. Ltd.* (unreported), July 18, 1977, Hollings J.   C

The following additional cases were cited in argument:
Brooks v. *Gloucestershire County Council* (1967) 66 L.G.R. 386, D.C.
Cheeseman v. *Bowaters United Kingdom Paper Mills Ltd.* [1971] 1
    W.L.R. 1773; [1971] 3 All E.R. 513, C.A.
Cunningham v. *Harrison* [1973] Q.B. 942; [1973] 3 W.L.R. 97; [1973]
    3 All E.R. 463, C.A.   D
Eley v. *Bedford* [1972] 1 Q.B. 155; [1971] 3 W.L.R. 563; [1971] 3 All
    E.R. 285.
Gohery v. *Durham County Council,* April 26, 1978; Court of Appeal
    (Civil Division) Transcript No. 236 of 1978, C.A.
Turner v. *Ministry of Defence* (1969) 113 S.J. 585.

APPEAL from Smith J.   E
By writ dated April 29, 1976, the employee, Guhulam Nabi, claimed
damages against the employers, British Leyland (U.K.) Ltd., for personal
injuries suffered and losses and expenses incurred as a result of an
accident which occurred on or about June 10, 1975, at the defendants'
premises arising out of the negligence and/or breach of the statutory
duty of the employers.
    On July 13, 1978, Smith J. awarded the employee the sum of £4,724   F
under section 2 of the Law Reform (Personal Injuries) Act 1948 for
loss of earnings to the date of the trial. The judge deducted the sum
of £1,062 received by the employee under section 12 (1) (*a*) of the Social
Security Act 1975 and awarded the difference in the sums, namely £3,662.
    By notice of appeal, dated September 4, 1978, the employee appealed
on the grounds that the judge erred in law when he deducted the un-   G
employment benefits received by the plaintiff from the loss of earnings
to the date of trial.
    The facts are stated in the judgment of the court.

    T. P. Russell Q.C. and *Janet Smith* for the employee.
    Christopher Rose Q.C. and *Keith Goddard Q.C.* for the employers.
                                                                                   H
Cur. adv. vult.

    November 30. MEGAW L.J. The judgment which Brightman L.J.
is about to read is the judgment of the court.

    BRIGHTMAN L.J. This appeal raises the question whether sums received
by an injured workman by way of unemployment benefit under section

A 12 (1) (a) of the Social Security Act 1975 ought to be taken into account in assessing as against his negligent employers the damages to be awarded for his consequent loss of earnings. Smith J. held that such sums should be taken into account and the damages reduced accordingly.

The employee was injured by an accident which occurred during the course of his employment on June 10, 1975. The accident was held by the trial judge to be due to the fault of the employers who had left dangerous

B machinery unfenced in breach of their statutory duty. Damages were awarded under three heads (leaving aside interest): general damages for pain and suffering and loss of amenity; special damages in respect of loss of earnings to date; and special damages in respect of loss of future earnings. The first head of special damages was calculated as follows. The judge assessed the loss of earnings at £4,724 without regard to social

C security. He then took into account the fact that the plaintiff had received the sum of £1,062 by way of unemployment benefit, and reduced the sum of £4,724 by that amount, thereby arriving at a figure of £3,662. The question at issue, as already indicated, is whether the judge correctly had regard to that sum of £1,062.

The Social Security Act 1975 came into force in April of that year.

D The scheme of the Act, so far as relevant for present purposes, is as follows. The funds required for paying benefits are provided by means of contributions payable by employers, self-employed persons and others, together with supplements paid by the Treasury. Employers and employees make what are called Class 1 contributions: section 1. A Class 1 contribution is a percentage of the employee's earnings subject to upper and lower limits; the employer's contribution is somewhat larger than the

E employee's contribution: section 4. Section 12 specifies the eight contributory benefits payable. One of these is unemployment benefit. To qualify for unemployment benefit, a claimant must have made a certain minimum number of contributions: section 14. The duration of the benefit is confined to a year (section 18, the 312 days therein mentioned being the equivalent of a year). The claimant is thereafter disqualified

F from unemployment benefit until he has resumed employment for a certain period and thus made further Class 1 contributions. It is evident from this brief outline of the scheme that, in relation to unemployment benefit, it bears some similarity to an insurance scheme, in that payments are made by a person which have the effect of entitling him to a benefit upon the happening of an event which may or may not occur.

As regards some of the contributory benefits described in section 12,

G the sort of issue which arises in the instant case has been resolved by statute. Section 2 of the Law Reform (Personal Injuries) Act 1948 (as amended by the National Insurance Act 1971) provides that in assessing damages for personal injuries, one half of sickness benefit and invalidity benefit shall be taken into account against loss of earnings. Widow's benefit and death grant are to be left wholly out of account under section

H 2 of the Fatal Accidents Act 1959 (as amended by the Social Security Act 1975). Unemployment benefit and retirement pensions are however untouched by statute in this context.

In order to reach a reasoned conclusion as to whether unemployment benefit should or should not be taken into account in assessing the damages payable to a person who is unemployed in consequence of the wrongful act of another, one needs to search for the principle to be applied. Prima facie damages are compensation for net loss. If the victim of a personal

injury or any other wrong is in receipt of a benefit which he would not   A
have received had the wrongful act not been done, that benefit, in a
broad sense, reduces his loss and is usually intended to do so.

As pointed out by Lord Reid in *Parry* v. *Cleaver* [1970] A.C. 1, 13,
there are three questions to be answered in this type of case; first, what
did the plaintiff lose as a result of the accident, i.e. what are the sums
which he would have received but for the accident and which by reason of   B
the accident he can no longer get? The answer in the present case, down
to date of judgment, is £4,724. Secondly, what are the sums which he did
in fact receive as a result of the accident, i.e. sums which he would not
have received but for the accident? It may be convenient to refer to
such sums as post-accident receipts. In the instant case, the answer is
£1,062 so far as relevant for present purposes. Thirdly, should the latter
sum be deducted from the former in assessing the damages? So analysed   C
the problem we have to consider is not resolved by *British Transport
Commission* v. *Gourley* [1956] A.C. 185, which only governs the answer
to question 1.

There are two large and clearly defined areas in which post-accident
receipts are disregarded at common law, that is to say, the proceeds of
insurance and the proceeds of benevolence. The first exception is usually   D
considered to have been established by *Bradburn* v. *Great Western
Railway Co.* (1874) L.R. 10 Ex. 1, although, as Lord Reid pointed out in
Parry's case, it was recognised in Scotland as long ago as 1818. The ratio
of Bramwell B.'s decision, at p. 2, in the *Bradburn* case was that: ". . . the
plaintiff is entitled to retain the benefit which he has paid for. . . ." The
approach of Pigott B., at p. 3, was that:
                                                                          E
"He does not receive that sum of money because of the accident,
but because he has made a contract providing for the contingency;
an accident must occur to entitle him to it, but it is not the accident,
but his contract, which is the cause of his receiving it."

There is probably no substantial distinction between the two reasons.
The victim of an injury can keep for himself a benefit for which he has   F
paid; the wrongdoer cannot appropriate it to himself by way of a reduction in his liability. For the exclusion of the proceeds of benevolence it
is convenient to turn to *Redpath* v. *Belfast and County Down Railway*
[1947] N.I. 167, a decision of Sir James Andrews L.C.J. A railway
company, in an action by a passenger for personal injuries, sought unsuccessfully to administer interrogatories to elicit whether the plaintiff had
been the recipient of benefit out of a distress fund raised locally for the   G
victims of the accident. The decision in favour of the plaintiff was based
on a number of grounds; it was not the accident but an extraneous factor,
namely, the existence of the charity fund, which gave the plaintiff his
advantage, echoing the approach of Pigott B.; the circumstance relied
upon in mitigation of damages arose independently of the cause of action
and was not actually attributable to it; admittedly a sequence but not a   H
consequence, it arose as a result of a novus actus interveniens.

In *Parry* v. *Cleaver* [1970] A.C. 1, Lord Reid expressed the view, at
p. 19, that unemployment benefit could be regarded as a combination of
insurance and national benevolence. There is no sensible reason for
distinguishing between public and private benevolence; so said by this
court in *Daish* v. *Wauton* [1972] 2 Q.B. 262, which established the
non-deductibility from lost future earnings of the benefit of state main-

A   tenance under the National Health Service legislation. If both insurance payments and the fruits of public and private benevolence are to be disregarded, one may ask oneself why it is logical to take into account payments which can properly be regarded as a combination of insurance and benevolence.

B   So far as reported decisions are concerned, the question of deductibility of unemployment benefit against lost earnings arose in Northern Ireland about a year before the same point arose in this country. In *Fitzpatrick* v. *Moore* [1962] N.I. 152, the plaintiff had suffered personal injuries as the result of the admitted negligence of his employers. The defendants sought to deduct from damages for loss of earnings the unemployment benefits received by the plaintiff before he resumed employment. We were told by counsel that the Northern Irish legislation under which this

C   case was decided did not materially differ from the English legislation applicable to the appellant's case. In *Fitzpatrick's* case Lord MacDermott C.J. said, at p. 159:

"While the plaintiff, during the second period of his unemployment"—nothing turns on the word "second"—"was suffering a loss of earnings because of the accident, he was not receiving his

D   unemployment benefits because of the accident. He was receiving them, while he remained in benefit by virtue of his contributions, because he was unemployed, and neither the defendants' negligence nor the accident which resulted therefrom had anything directly to do with his entitlement to those benefits. The fact that his contributions and his benefits were exacted and granted under statute

E   does not, in my opinion, affect the matter. To distinguish on that score between the present case and *Bradburn's* case would be to ignore the principle of remoteness and to raise fine distinctions which the law relating to damages can very well do without."

There is also a Canadian case *Bourgeois* v. *Tzrop* (1957) 9 D.L.R. (2d) 214, in which the Appeal Division of the New Brunswick Supreme Court

F   reached the same conclusion. The plaintiff's claim was for damages for personal injuries suffered while being carried as a passenger in a car owned and driven by the defendant. The question arose whether the unemployment insurance benefits received by the plaintiff should be applied to reduce the damages for which the defendant was liable in respect of the plaintiff's loss of earnings. It was said that this point had not previously

G   been decided by any Canadian court. It was held that the benefits were not deductible. After a review of the authorities, including the English cases, the reasons were expressed as follows in the judgment of the court given by Ritchie J., at p. 224:

"The amount of $159 paid to the plaintiff under the provisions of the Unemployment Insurance Act was derived partly from moneys

H   provided by Parliament, partly from contributions by employed persons, including the plaintiff, and partly from contributions by the employers of those persons. Both Tzrop and his employer, in respect of him made weekly contributions in equal amounts to the Unemployed Insurance Fund. . . . The benefits, which the plaintiff did receive would have been paid if his injuries had been sustained without any negligence on the part of the defendant. The payments

received by the plaintiff were received not because he was injured
but because he was entitled to unemployment insurance benefits by
reason of having been employed in an occupation coming within
the scope of the Unemployment Insurance Act. The accident in
which the plaintiff was injured was not the causa causans of the
receipt by the plaintiff of the unemployment insurance benefits but
the causa sine qua non. The causa causans was his employment having
been within the scope of the Unemployment Insurance Act. There
is no statutory provision requiring the deduction of unemployment
insurance benefits from damages allowed to an injured employee in
respect to the injuries which caused the employment in respect to
which the benefits were paid. . . . I am unable to distinguish between
unemployment insurance benefits and a pension for naval service. . . .
The wrongdoer should not get the benefit of the fortuitous circumstance that the plaintiff's employment entitled him to unemployment
insurance benefits."

" Naval service " was a reference to the decision of this court in *Payne* v.
Railway Executive [1952] 1 K.B. 26.

The problem came before this court in *Parsons* v. *B.N.M. Laboratories
Ltd.* [1964] 1 Q.B. 95, on appeal from a decision of a Queen's Bench
master who had decided that unemployment benefit should be disregarded.
In that case the plaintiff claimed damages for wrongful dismissal. The
master assessed damages at £1,200 representing the plaintiff's loss of
salary and commission. Unemployment benefit of £59 odd had been
received by the plaintiff under the National Insurance Act 1946, which
was broadly similar to the present legislation. During the course of the
argument the Court of Appeal was referred to *Bourgeois* v. *Tzrop,* 9
D.L.R. (2d) 214 but oddly not to *Fitzpatrick* v. *Moore* [1962] N.I. 152.
The court unanimously reversed the master's decision. Sellers L.J. said,
at pp. 120–121:

" With the employer as a contributing party I do not regard the
payment as comparable to benefits received under a purely personal
insurance policy or by way of pension or benefit arising out of a
man's employment. In the one case the employee has paid a premium
and in the other he has a contract of employment and his services
given under it form the reward (equivalent to a premium) which
entitles him to the benefit. I can see no reason why a defaulting party
should obtain the benefit of a payment for which he has not paid
any part of the premium or given the services which command the
benefit. In such matters I would apply the decision of this court in
Payne v. *Railway Executive* [1952] 1 K.B. 26. That case was applied
in Canada in support of a similar question to that which we have
to consider here, but although I was a party to the decision in *Payne*
at first instance, with respect I would not so apply it but would
distinguish it. I would adhere to what was said in *Payne* and by
Donovan L.J. in *Browning* v. *War Office* [1963] 1 Q.B. 750, 761
but I think that where, as here, the employer has made a contribution
to the unemployment insurance he should get the benefit of it, if
he finds it necesary to put one of his employees into unemployment,
even in circumstances where he is liable to compensate him in
damages."

A   Harman L.J. said, at pp. 130–131:

"Unemployment insurance is a sum receivable by contract made by the employed man and his employer, each of whom contributes to the state upon the footing that if and when the servant is unemployed the state will make good part of his earnings to him. I do not think such payment is truly analogous to insurance moneys, as in the

B   leading case of *Bradburn* v. *Great Western Railway Co.* (1874) L.R. 10 Ex. 1, where there was a purely voluntary contract made by the plaintiff. This is a contribution which he is bound to make with the very object of mitigating the damage which inability to work will do him. It is just as if his employer continued to pay part of his wages. The loss he suffers is pro tanto diminished and therefore cannot be charged against the wrongdoer."

C   Pearson L.J. expressed himself in a similar manner, at pp. 143–144:

"The dismissal caused the plaintiff to become unemployed, and therefore entitled, as a matter of general right under the system of state insurance and not by virtue of any private insurance policy of his own, to receive unemployment benefit. The effect of the dismissal

D   was not to deprive him of all income but to reduce his income by substituting unemployment benefit for his salary. It would be unrealistic to disregard the unemployment benefit, because to do so would confer on the plaintiff, to the extent of £59 2s. 6d. a fortuitous windfall in addition to compensation."

This decision was applied by John Stephenson J. two years later in a

E   personal injuries case, *Foxley* v. *Olton* [1965] 2 Q.B. 306.

We were invited by the employee to review these two decisions in the light of the House of Lords' conclusion in *Parry* v. *Cleaver* [1970] A.C. 1. In that case a police constable had been injured in a traffic accident in January 1963 as a result of the defendant's admitted negligence. On June 30, 1964, he was discharged from the police force as the result of

F   his injuries. In October 1964 he obtained other but less well-paid employment. In the action he claimed damages in respect, inter alia, of his net annual loss of earnings pending normal retirement at 48 in 1975. However, as from July 1, 1974, he received a police disablement pension, called "an ill-health award," payable to him during his life. There was no dispute that he was entitled to damages representing the difference

G   between the wages he would have earned in the force and his civilian wages until he would have retired at the age of 48. The problem was whether, during the period when he was under 48 and was still claiming loss of wages, he must give credit for the disablement pension which he received from his employers during what should have been, but for the accident, his working time on full pay in the force.

H   Although there was no actual disablement pension fund in existence, it was agreed between the parties, and the case proceeded upon the basis, that he should be treated as if there had been a fund in existence to which he contributed, the remainder necessary for paying the benefit being provided by the police authority, so that in effect employer and employee were the contributories, and the sole contributories, to the notional fund.

The House decided by a majority against deductibility; the majority

consisted of Lord Reid, Lord Pearce and Lord Wilberforce. Lord Reid, A
in reviewing the authorities which he described as not consistent with
each other, dealt first with the case of " benevolence." *Redpath* v. *Belfast
and County Down Railway* [1947] N.I. 167 was readily supported ([1970]
A.C. 1, 14) on the ground that:

> " It would be revolting to the ordinary man's sense of justice, and
> therefore contrary to public policy, that the sufferer should have B
> his damages reduced so that he would gain nothing from the bene-
> volence of his friends or relations or of the public at large, and
> that the only gainer would be the wrongdoer. We do not have to
> decide in this case whether these considerations also apply to public
> benevolence in the shape of various uncovenanted benefits from
> the welfare state, but it may be thought that Parliament did not C
> intend them to be for the benefit of the wrongdoer."

As regards insurance Lord Reid said, at p. 14:

> " I think that the real and substantial reason for disregarding them
> is that the plaintiff has bought them and that it would be unjust and
> unreasonable to hold that the money which he prudently spent on D
> premiums and the benefit from it should enure to the benefit of the
> tortfeasor. Here again I think that the explanation that this is too
> remote is artificial and unreal. Why should the plaintiff be left worse
> off than if he had never insured? In that case he would have got
> the benefit of the premium money: if he had not spent it he would
> have had it in his possession at the time of the accident grossed up E
> at compound interest."

A contributory pension is in no different position. The benefits
received, so far as attributable to the employer's contribution, are delayed
remuneration for current work. The pension itself is a form of insurance;
the employee does not get back exactly what he paid in, but an amount
which is dependent on how things turn out; it may be less or more than F
the contributions from himself and his employer. Lord Reid referred to
Parsons' case and *Foxley's* case, but said they were not directly relevant,
and added, at p. 19:

> " In *Foxley* v. *Olton* [1965] 2 Q.B. 306, John Stephenson J. followed
> *Parsons's* case [1964] 1 Q.B. 95 in taking unemployment benefit into G
> consideration, but refused to take national assistance grants into
> consideration following a decision of Veale J. in *Eldridge* v. *Videtta*
> (1964) 108 S.J. 137. I find it difficult to draw a distinction between
> unemployment benefit and national assistance. The former could
> be regarded as a combination of insurance and national benevolence
> while the insurance element is absent from the latter. But there H
> are here other considerations besides those with which I have dealt.
> There has been no full argument about them and I do not propose
> to express any concluded opinion on this matter."

Lord Pearce made no mention of *Parsons'* case or *Foxley's* case. Lord
Wilberforce referred to *Parsons'* case but left the matter open. He said,
at p. 39:

A   " As regards some of the social protections which injured plaintiffs
may enjoy, Parliament has intervened with a compromise solution,
providing that half of certain payments over a period are to be
deducted in assessing the loss—see section 2 of the Law Reform
(Personal Injuries) Act 1948, but this type of solution is not open to
the courts. They have to grapple with each type of benefit as it arises,
and they have done so sometimes by setting themselves to ascertain

B   what is ' fair,' sometimes by attempting to squeeze the appropriate
answer from, or to explain the answer arrived at by reference to, such
words (and I do not wish to depreciate their utility) as ' compensatory,' ' loss,' ' collateral ' or ' caused.' On the whole, reasonably
consistent results have been achieved. As regards private insurance
policies taken out by the injured man, the courts have adhered to

C   Bradburn's case, L.R. 10 Ex. 1—it has been approved in this House
and in other common law jurisdictions: as regards receipts from
voluntary funds it has been decided in Northern Ireland that no
deduction should be made (Redpath v. Belfast and County Down
Railway [1947] N.I. 167). The decision was put either on public
policy or on the intention of the subscribers, see per Sir James Andrews
L.C.J. at p. 170. Decisions have been given regarding some forms of

D   social benefit (for example, Parsons v. B.N.M. Laboratories Ltd.
[1964] 1 Q.B. 95): I do not think that we ought to consider these
at this time."

Lord Morris, in his dissenting judgment, did not refer to Parsons' case.
Lord Pearson said that he adhered to his decision in Parsons.

E   In the instant case Smith J. treated deduction of unemployment
benefit as settled practice. He said:

" All I propose to say upon this issue, which is whether or not a sum
paid by way of unemployment benefit to the plaintiff should or should
not be deducted, is that I am going to follow the reasoning in the
case which Hollings J. decided last year. There is also the authority

F   of the decision of Finer J. Both Hollings and Finer JJ. were in
favour of deductibility. Therefore I am going to say the sum of £1,062
paid by way of unemployment benefit should be deducted from the
plaintiff's damages."

Hollings J.'s case was Shaw v. Insulation Co. Ltd. (unreported) decided
on July 18, 1977. It contains some indication of the current practice.

G   Hollings J. said:

" Now I did have occasion to consider the deductibility of unemployment benefit in an earlier case last year, Washington v. Norwest
Holt Ltd., and gave judgment at Liverpool on July 30, 1976. I have
retained my notes of that judgment, and I have reconsidered it in
the light of the submissions of Mr. Playford and, in particular, of

H   Mr. Russell. I should state that in my judgment the proper way to
deal with these benefits is to deduct unemployment benefit but not
to deduct supplementary benefit, and I will try to make as brief
as possible my reasons for this. This question involves consideration
of previous decisions both of the Court of Appeal and of first instance
and also depends on whether the decision of the House of Lords in
Parry v. Cleaver has had any effect, and if so what effect, upon this
question. . . . In two decisions at first instance in this jurisdiction, it

has been held that unemployment benefit is deductible—Cassels J. A
in *Lindstedt* v. *Wimborne Steamship Co.* (1949) 83 Ll.L.Rep. 19,
and John Stevenson J. in *Foxley* v. *Olton* [1965] 2 Q.B. 306; and I
add there a recent decision of Milmo J. reported in The Times,
though no reason was set out there, when he deducted unemployment
benefit and industrial rehabilitation allowance and supplementary
benefit, in *Cackett* v. *Earl,* The Times, October 15, 1976."

B

He then referred to the cases of *Fitzpatrick, Parsons, Foxley* and *Parry.*
He came to the conclusion that he was bound by the *Parsons'* case but
even apart from such authority he would have so held:

"I agree with the submission that for the period that the plaintiff
received unemployment benefit, the plaintiff did not suffer a complete
loss of earnings; unemployment benefit is paid in lieu of wages or C
when wages cannot be earned for any reason. Taking the views that
I do, that unemployment benefit is a recognised substitute for wages,
provided by statute, and that the insurance element is essentially
notional or even illusory, I consider any sum received should be
deducted."

No transcript or other note was available of Finer J.'s judgment.   D

We were pressed by the employee's counsel to allow this appeal on
the basis that *Parsons'* case [1964] 1 Q.B. 95 was wrongly decided, and
that we were at liberty and indeed obliged to depart from it on the ground
that the ratio decidendi could not be supported in the light of the majority
conclusions in *Parry's* case [1968] 1 Q.B. 195. Unemployment benefit, it
was submitted, was the product in part of contributions made by the E
employee over perhaps many years. It was a form of state insurance, not
an alternative to or continuation of the wages which had been received
by the plaintiff during his employment. The effect of the social security
scheme was that both employee, employer and the state were contributing
to the insurance of the employee against the risk of unemployment. The
benefits therefore partake partly of the character of insurance and partly
of the character of benevolence. Furthermore, social benefits have come F
through a series of decisions of the courts not to be deductible from the
damages payable by the wrongdoer, save so far as they are subject to the
statutory compromise imposed by the Act of 1948: see, for example,
Hewson v. *Downs* [1970] 1 Q.B. 73 (state retirement pension), *Daish* v.
Wauton (maintenance under the National Health Service), *Bowker* v. *Rose*
(unreported), Court of Appeal (Civil Division) Transcript No. 164 of 1978, G
decided by this court on February 2, 1978 (mobility allowance and
attendance allowance). So ran the argument of the employee.

It was also urged upon us that *Parsons'* case was not decisive of the
instant case, because the damages were in respect of breach of contract
and not, as here, in respect of personal injuries. That appears to us to be
a distinction without a difference.   H

We appreciate the force of the employee's main argument. In the
end it comes down to the question whether *Parsons'* case was overruled by
Parry's case. We have no doubt that the time has come for *Parsons'*
case to be reviewed, as indeed was indicated in *Parry's* case, but we do
not think that such review can properly be conducted by this court.
There is no such inconsistency between the two decisions as would entitle
us to depart from our previous decision. The law in relation to unemploy-

A ment benefit is at present that laid down in *Parsons'* case, and so it
must remain until the House of Lords or the legislature decides otherwise.
For these reasons the appeal will be dismissed.

> *Judgment for the employers*
> *with costs.*
> *Leave to appeal.*

B

Solicitors: *Brian Thompson and Partners, Manchester; A. W. Mawer
& Co., Manchester.*

L. G. S.

C

[CHANCERY DIVISION]

* *In re* BOURKE'S WILL TRUSTS

D BARCLAYS BANK LTD. *v.* CANADA PERMANENT TRUST CO.
AND OTHERS

[1975 B. No. 7405]

1979 June 28, 29   Slade J.

E *Will—Construction—Substitutionary gift—Gift of capital to three
named persons after termination of life interests " or their heirs
and surviving issue "—Meaning of " surviving issue " and
" heirs " in context—Whether reversionary interests vesting in
heirs of those predeceasing last life tenant—Whether beneficiaries taking as joint tenants or tenants in common—Law of
Property Act 1925* [1] *(15 & 16 Geo. 5, c. 20), s. 132*

F By a holograph will dated June 11, 1938, the testator, who
died in 1943, bequeathed all his real and personal estate to
trustees on trust as to the income of one half to his wife for life
and the remaining half to his brother for life with the survivor
to receive the whole income " provided always that if there
be issue of my marriage ... such issue shall receive the benefit
on [my wife's] death if previous to my brother of her income
and on my brother's death of his income also and aforesaid
issue shall on reaching the age of 21 succeed to the capital."
The brother died in 1953, and the testator's widow on April
G 18, 1971. There were no children of the marriage and in the
event the operative clause of the will provided: " If no issue
or none reach the age of 21 the capital shall be divided
equally between [three named persons] or their heirs and
surviving issue on the death of my wife and brother." The
three persons so named were (i) the testator's half brother R,
who died in 1958 without having had any issue; (ii) a half
H sister, W, who survived the testator's widow, dying in 1976,
and (iii) a half sister, E, who died intestate in 1969, leaving
three children, 13 grandchildren and two great-grandchildren.
No question arose as to the one third share of W, who survived
the testator's widow but died before the hearing.
On the executor's summons to determine (1) whether R's
share was held (a) on trust for his personal representatives as

[1] Law of Property Act 1925, s. 132: see post, p. 548F–G.

A

part of his estate, (b) for W, or (c) on trust for some other person or persons, and if so in what shares; (2) whether E's share was held (a) for her personal representatives as part of her estate, (b) for her three children and if so whether as joint tenants or as tenants in common, (c) for all the children and remoter issue of E living at her death, and if so whether as joint tenants or as tenants in common, or (d) for some other person or persons and if so in what shares:—

B

Held, (1) that the words " or their heirs and surviving issue " constituted a substitutional gift in favour of the respective heirs and surviving issue of the three persons named in the clause, namely, R, W and E; that in the context of the testator's use of the word " issue " earlier in the will the words " surviving issue " meant surviving children rather than surviving issue of all degrees; that " heirs " must be given its strict pre-1926 meaning, and that by virtue of section 132 of the Law of Property Act 1925 it conferred an equitable interest in the property on those who, before 1926, would have been properly described as " heirs "; that " surviving " meant surviving the praepositus and not surviving the date of distribution; that accordingly, on R's death W and E became entitled to a vested interest in the reversion to R's share of residue as joint tenants, expectant only on the death of the testator's widow, and on E's death her three children became absolutely entitled as beneficial joint tenants to E's share of residue, subject to the life interest of the testator's widow (post, pp. 544H—545C, 549E–H, 551H—552C, H—553A).

C

D

In re Noad, decd. [1951] Ch. 553 applied.
In re Kilvert, decd. [1957] Ch. 388 considered.

(2) that, although prima facie W as the survivor of herself and E would have become entitled to R's share on the death of the testator's widow, since it was possible that E might have severed the joint tenancy before she died her personal representatives would be given liberty to apply within six months from the date of judgment for an inquiry whether there had been a severance, but that in default of any such application the plaintiff would be given liberty to distribute that share of the residuary estate on the footing that there had been no such severance (post, p. 552C–H).

E

In re Osoba, decd. [1979] 1 W.L.R. 247, C.A. applied.

F

The following cases are referred to in the judgment:

Gansloser's Will Trusts, In re [1952] Ch. 30; [1951] 2 All E.R. 936, C.A.
Jones's Estate, In re (1878) 47 L.J. Ch. 775.
Keay v. *Boulton* (1883) 25 Ch.D. 212.
Kilvert, decd., In re [1957] Ch. 388; [1957] 2 W.L.R. 854; [1957] 2 All E.R. 196.
Noad, decd., In re [1951] Ch. 553; [1951] 1 All E.R. 467.

G

Osoba, decd., In re [1979] 1 W.L.R. 247; [1979] 2 All E.R. 393, C.A.
Reed v. *Braithwaite* (1870) L.R. 11 Eq. 514.
Smith v. *Butcher* (1878) 10 Ch.D. 113.
Whitehead, In re [1920] 1 Ch. 298.
Wingfield v. *Wingfield* (1878) 9 Ch.D. 658.

H

The following additional cases were cited in argument:

Brown v. *Gould* [1972] Ch. 53; [1971] 3 W.L.R. 334; [1971] 2 All E.R. 1505.
Browne v. *Moody* [1936] A.C. 635; [1936] 2 All E.R. 1695, P.C.
Manly, decd., In re [1969] 1 W.L.R. 1819; [1969] 3 All E.R. 1011.
Powell v. *Boggis* (1866) 35 Beav. 535.
Ralph v. *Carrick* (1879) 11 Ch.D. 873, C.A.
Sibley's Trusts, In re (1877) 5 Ch.D. 494.

A   ORIGINATING SUMMONS

By his will, dated June 11, 1938, the testator, Isidore McWilliam Bourke, who died domiciled in England on February 2, 1943, appointed as his executors Barclays Bank Ltd. (the plaintiff) and Edward Orford Capon, who predeceased the testator leaving the plaintiff as sole surviving executor.   By clause 1 of the will, the testator bequeathed to his wife, Dorothy Gladys Bourke, a legacy of £300 and a legacy of " £500 for
B   each surviving issue of our marriage."   After bequeathing various other legacies the testator bequeathed " all my real and the residue of my personal estate and effects " on trust for sale and conversion with a power to postpone such sale and conversion and directed his trustees after paying debts and funeral and testamentary expenses

C   " to stand possessed of the proceeds of sale of such investments and of all parts of my estate for the time being unsold (residuary estate) upon trust as to the income of one half to my wife Dorothy Gladys for life and remaining half to my . . . brother John Joseph Fitz Adlem Bourke . . . and on death of either survivor to receive income of whole.   Provided always that if there be issue of my marriage with Dorothy Gladys McW.Bourke such issue shall
D   receive the benefit on her death if previous to my brother of her income and on my brother's death of his income also and aforesaid issue shall on reaching the age of 21 succeed to the capital. If no issue or none reach the age of 21 the capital shall be divided equally between . . . R. R. Bourke, Winifred Louis and Eva Venables or their heirs and surviving issue on the death of my wife and brother."

E   The testator's brother John died in 1953 and the testator's wife died on April 18, 1971.   There were no children of the marriage.

The three named persons between whom the capital fell to be divided were (1) the testator's half-brother, Richard Rowland Bourke, who died without issue in 1958, but leaving a will under which his widow, Rosalind Thelma Bourke, was sole beneficiary.   She died on
F   January 27, 1971, and the sole executor of her will, Canada Permanent Trust Co., (the first defendant) represented both estates.   (2) The testator's half-sister, Winifred Louis, (the second defendant) who survived the testator's widow, but died on June 27, 1976, and whose estate was represented by the seventh defendant, Judith Valentine Winfred Jones.   (3) The testator's other half-sister, Eva Venables, who pre-
G   deceased the testator's widow, died intestate on July 31, 1969, leaving three children, Albert John Venables (the third defendant), May Frances Vernon Reaney (the fourth defendant) and John Michael Venables (the fifth defendant), 13 grandchildren and two great grandchildren all of whom survived the testator's widow and were still living at the date of the proceedings.   One of the adult grandchildren, Jocelyn Comyn Reaney, was joined as sixth defendant to represent all other
H   grandchildren and remoter issue of Eva Venables.

By an originating summons, dated July 31, 1975, the plaintiff sought to determine whether upon the true construction of the will and in the events which happened (i) the share of residue bequeathed to Rowland Richard Bourke was held on trust (a) for his personal representatives as part of his estate, (b) for Winifred Louis or (c) for some other person or persons and if so in what shares; (ii) the share of residue bequeathed to Eva Venables was held on trust (a) for her personal representatives

as part of her estate; (b) for her three children, and if so whether as joint A
tenants or tenants in common; (c) for all her children and remoter issue
living at her death, and if so whether as joint tenants or tenants in
common, or (d) for some other person or persons and if so in what shares.

The facts are stated in the judgment.

John Monckton for the plaintiff.
R. G. Fawls for the first defendant. B
J. L. Munby for the second and seventh defendants.
C. R. Semken for the third, fourth and fifth defendants.
R. de Lacy for the sixth defendant.

SLADE J. This originating summons raises certain questions of construction on the will of the late Isidore McWilliam Bourke. The will was C
dated June 11, 1938. The testator died on February 2, 1943, domiciled
in England, and probate of his will was granted to Barclays Bank Ltd., as
the sole surviving executor named in the will, out of the principal probate
registry on October 30, 1943. On October 1, 1970, the plaintiff, Barclays
Bank Trust Co. Ltd., became sole trustee of the will in the place of
Barclays Bank Ltd.

The will was a holograph document made by a testator who des- D
cribed himself therein as having the qualifications " F.R.C.S., M.R.C.S.
and D.Ph." Though it was apparently a home made one, it was made
by a man who seems to have had considerable knowledge of legal phraseology. It is a concisely drawn will, and, with the exception of one short
phrase which has given rise to all the difficulties in the present case, a
well drawn one.

By clauses 1 to 8 of the will the testator, having appointed as his E
executors Barclays Bank Ltd. and Edward Orford Capon, who pre-
deceased him, gave a number of pecuniary and specific legacies. Of these
clauses, I need only read clauses 1 and 5:

" 1. To my wife Dorothy Gladys £300 and £500 for each surviving
issue of our marriage . . . 5. To my aforesaid brother John my A.C.A.
championship silver bowl as an heirloom and thence to my half F
brother R. R. Bourke, V.C., D.S.O."—and an address is given—
" and thence to Reg Louis and Bert Venables in that order nephews
of R. R. Bourke, V.C., D.S.O."

The will then proceeded:

" I bequeath all my real and the residue of my personal estate and G
effects unto my trustees upon trust to sell, call in and convert the
same into money (with power in their discretion to postpone such
sale, calling in and conversion) and after paying all debts, funeral and
testamentary expenses to stand possessed of the proceeds of sale of
such investments and of all parts of my estate for the time being
unsold (residuary estate) upon trust as to the income of one half to
my wife Dorothy Gladys for life and remaining half to my aforesaid H
brother John Joseph Fitz Adlem Bourke of Eagle, Alaska, U.S.A.,
and on death of either survivor to receive income of whole, provided
always that if there be issue of my marriage with Dorothy Gladys
Mc. W. Bourke such issue shall receive the benefit on her death if
previous to my brother of her income and on my brother's death
of his income also and aforesaid issue shall on reaching the age of
21 succeed to the capital. If no issue or none reach the age of

A 21 the capital shall be divided equally between the aforesaid R. R. Bourke, Winifred Louis and Eva Venables or their heirs and surviving issue on the death of my wife and brother."

In conclusion the will contained two brief administrative provisions which I need not read.

B The testator's widow, Dorothy Gladys Bourke, survived him and died on April 18, 1971. His brother, John Joseph Fitz Adlem Bourke, also survived him but died long before the testator's widow, namely, on December 14, 1953. Accordingly, at the date of her death she was, in accordance with the terms of the will, entitled to receive the whole income of the testator's residuary estate. There were no children of the testator's marriage to her. Accordingly, on her death, the residuary estate fell to be disposed of in accordance with the last sentence of the residuary gift contained in the will, which I read again:

C

"If no issue or none reach the age of 21 the capital shall be divided equally between the aforesaid R. R. Bourke, Winifred Louis and Eva Venables or their heirs and surviving issue on the death of my wife and brother."

D It is now necessary to explain who these three named persons were. The testator's father, who had pre-deceased the testator, had been married twice. The testator and his brother, John Joseph Fitz Adlem Bourke, one of the life tenants of residue named in the will, had been the only two children of the first marriage. Of the second marriage of the testator's father there had been three children, namely, the testator's half brother, Rowland Richard Bourke, and the testator's half sisters, Winifred Louis and Eva Venables.

E

Rowland Richard Bourke died on August 29, 1958, without having had any issue. His will dated April 19, 1952, was proved by his widow, Rosalind Thelma Bourke, the sole executrix named in it and the sole beneficiary thereunder. She herself died on January 27, 1971, and her will dated October 7, 1969, was proved by Canada Permanent Trust Co. the sole executor named in it. Canada Permanent Trust Co. is the first defendant in these proceedings and is there to represent the estates of both Rowland Richard Bourke and Rosalind Thelma Bourke.

F

Winifred Louis was still alive when this originating summons was issued on July 31, 1975, and was joined as second defendant to the proceedings. Since she survived the period of distribution, no questions arise concerning the one-third share of residue bequeathed to her. She died, however, on June 27, 1976. Letters of administration with the will annexed of her estate were granted on March 10, 1978, out of the Supreme Court of British Columbia to Judith Valentine Winifred Jones. Winifred Louis has no personal representative constituted within the jurisdiction of this court. Accordingly, by order of March 22, 1979, Master Gowers appointed Judith Valentine Winifred Jones to represent for the purpose of these proceedings the estate of Winifred Louis and ordered that proceedings be carried on with her as an added defendant. The originating summons has been amended to add her as the seventh defendant.

I

Eva Venables died on July 31, 1969, a widow and intestate, having had three children only, all of whom survived her, namely, the third defendant, Albert John Venables, the fourth defendant, Mary Frances Vernon Reaney, and the fifth defendant, John Michael Venables. At her death she had 13 grandchildren and two great grandchildren, all of whom A survived the testator's widow and are still living. No grant of administration to the estate of Eva Venables has been obtained, but the evidence is that her three children are entitled to any such estate in equal shares. One of the adult grandchildren of Eva Venables is Jocelyn Comyn Reaney, who has been joined as the sixth defendant to these proceedings for the purpose of representing all other grandchildren and remoter issue of Eva Venables.

The two questions asked by paragraph 1 of the amended originating summons are as follows:

" Whether upon the true construction of the said will and in the events which have happened (1) the share of his residuary estate bequeathed by the above-named testator to his half brother Rowland Richard Bourke is held upon trust (a) for the personal representatives C of the said Rowland Richard Bourke as part of his estate, or (b) for the testator's half sister the defendant Winifred Louis, or (c) for some other person or persons and if so in what shares and proportions (2) the share of his residuary estate bequeathed by the above-named testator to his half sister Eva Venables is held upon trust (a) for the personal representatives of the said Eva Venables as part of her D estate, or (b) for the three children of the said Eva Venables and if so whether as joint tenants or as tenants in common in equal shares, or (c) for all the children and remoter issue of the said Eva Venables living at her death and if so whether as joint tenants in common in equal shares, or (d) for some other person or persons and if so in what shares and proportions."

Paragraph 2 (1) of the amended originating summons seeks an order that Canada Permanent Trust Co. may be appointed to represent the estates of Rowland Richard Bourke and Rosalind Thelma Bourke. Paragraph 2 (2) seeks an order that Jocelyn Comyn Reaney may be appointed to represent all other grandchildren and remoter issue of Eva Venables. Paragraph 2 (3) seeks an order that Judith Valentine Winifred Jones may be appointed to represent the estate of Winifred Louis. F

The two problems reflected in paragraph 1 of the originating summons centre round the use by the testator of the phrase:

" If no issue or none reach the age of 21 the capital shall be divided equally between the aforesaid R. R. Bourke, Winifred Louis and Eva Venables or their heirs and surviving issue on the death of my wife and brother." G

More particularly the problems centre round the phrase " or their heirs and surviving issue." While this latter phrase gives rise to a number of doubts and uncertainties, four points are in my judgment reasonably clear, and it will be convenient to state them at once, as a starting point.

First, in view of the use of the word of division " equally " in this phrase, it is obvious that if all of R. R. Bourke, Winifred Louis and Eva H Venables had been alive at the date of ultimate distribution, there would have been a division of the residuary estate into equal third shares. Correspondingly, there is in my judgment no doubht that the words " or their heirs and surviving issue " mean " or the respective heirs and surviving issue of each of them ": compare In re Kilvert, decd. [1957] Ch. 388, 391 per Roxburgh J.

Secondly, the words " or their heirs and surviving issue " constitute

A *substitutional* gifts to the respective " heirs and surviving issue "—whatever that may mean—of the one-third shares of the residuary estate given to R. R. Bourke, Winifred Louis and Eva Venables, intended to take effect if he or she is not still alive to take at the relevant time—whatever that may be. That the gift is substitutional in nature is, I think, made clear not only by the use of the introductory word " *or* ", but also by the nature of the succeeding description of the class that is to
B take. The relevant principles are to be found set out in *Jarman on Wills,* 8th ed. (1951), vol. 2, pp. 1304 to 1305.

Thirdly, the words " on the death of my wife and brother " in my judgment relate back to the phrase " shall be divided equally." As a matter of ordinary grammar, I think that they designate the time of such division. I cannot accept a submission that they fall to be read merely
C with the phrase " their heirs and surviving issue " or, alternatively, with the phrase " surviving issue "; such a construction would seem to me to involve an unnatural distortion of language.

Fourthly, the reference to " surviving issue " must in my judgment be construed in its context as a reference to surviving children rather than surviving issue of all degrees. I accept Mr. Semken's submission to this effect on behalf of the third, fourth and fifth defendants. It is true that,
D as Mr. de Lacy has pointed out on behalf of the sixth defendant, in the absence of any further assisting context, the court will generally construe the word " issue," when used in a will, as meaning issue of all degrees. In my judgment, however, there is an overwhelming context here showing that this testator intended the phrase " surviving issue " to be restricted to children. He had used the word " issue " on five previous occasions
E in this will, and on every single occasion he had in my judgment used it in the sense of " children." By clause 1 he had bequeathed " £500 to each surviving issue of our marriage." I respectfully agree with what Roxburgh J. said in *In re Noad, decd.* [1951] Ch. 553, 557:

" ' Issue of our marriage ' ought to mean to the court, as it undoubtedly would mean to any layman, the children of the person using the words and of the other person to whom he was referring,
F i.e. of himself and his wife."

In this case Roxburgh J. himself followed the decision of Malins V.-C. in *Reed* v. *Braithwaite* (1870) L.R. 11 Eq. 514, and held that, in a gift by a testator to his named wife for life " and upon her death to be equally divided between the issue of our marriage," the phrase " issue of our marriage " meant children.
G Following the decision in *In re Noad, decd.* [1951] Ch. 553. I therefore think that the word " issue " in clause 1 of this will means " children " and indeed the contrary has not been contended in relation to clause 1.

The same interpretation must be given to the word " issue " when it appears in the phrase " issue of my marriage," which is contained in the bequest of the testator's residuary estate. The same interpretation too
H must be given to the phrases " such issue," " aforesaid issue " and " if no issue," which appear in this bequest of residue.

I accept that, where the context furnishes a clear guide to a testator's meaning, the word " issue " may bear the narrower meaning of " children " in the earlier part of a will and the wider meaning of " issue of all degrees " in a later part. Although, in the absence of further guidance, the court will tend to put the same construction on the same word when it occurs twice or more in the same will, that canon of con-

struction will always yield to a contrary context: *Jarman on Wills*, 8th A
ed. (1951) vol. 3, p. 1594. Nevertheless in the will now before me I can
see no sufficient contrary context. The very sentence, in which the crucial phrase " their heirs and surviving issue " appears, is introduced by
the phrase " If no issue . . ." As I have indicated, the word " issue " in
the latter phrase plainly means " children." As Mr. de Lacy has pointed
out on behalf of the sixth defendant, the word " issue " in this phrase
clearly refers back to " issue of my marriage," while the word " issue," B
when appearing for the second time in this sentence of the will, does not
so refer. Nevertheless in my judgment it is more or less inconceivable
that this obviously literate testator would have chosen to use the very
same word in the very same sentence in two quite different senses.

Mr. de Lacy also pointed out that the testator might have foreseen
that the ultimate distribution of his residuary estate would not take C
place until a distant date and that this is one reason for concluding that
he might well have intended issue of his half-brother and half-sisters,
more remote than children, to be qualified to participate. I think, however, that this point is more than outweighed by two others. First, the
testator plainly did not intend that his own issue more remote than
children should participate in the ultimate distribution of residue.
Secondly, he did not direct the distribution among heirs and issue to be D
per stirpes. I would regard it as inherently improbable that he would have
contemplated a distribution among heirs and issue of all degrees per
capita in which parents and children would have competed with one
another.

These are the main reasons which have led me to the fourth conclusion, which I have already described as reasonably clear, namely, that E
the reference to " surviving issue " in the phrase " their heirs and surviving issue " must be construed as a reference to " surviving children."

I now approach territory which is a little less easy to traverse. The
next problem, I think, is whether, on the basis of the conclusions already
reached, the substitutional gift to " their heirs and surviving issue " should
be construed as a gift to the members of a class comprising one composite
category or to the members of a class comprising two categories. Putting F
the point another way, should it be construed as a gift both to the heirs
of the relevant person and also to his or her surviving children? Or
should it be construed as a gift to one class only, namely, to that class
of persons who qualify both as heirs and surviving children of such
person?

In *In re Kilvert, decd.* [1957] Ch. 388, Roxburgh J. had to consider G
a will of which the phraseology bore strong superficial resemblances to
the present case. The headnote reads:

" A testator, by his will, dated June 4, 1948, gave his wife the use
of certain chattels for her life, and then provided that they should
be ' returned to my brothers and sister or their heirs and successors
at her death.' He gave his residuary estate ' to be equally divided H
between my brothers E and W, and my sister S or their heirs and
successors . . .' The testator died in 1954. One brother was alive
at the date of the summons, one brother had predeceased the
testator leaving a wife and son and daughter, and the sister had
survived the testator and his widow, but was now dead."

There then followed a summons to determine who was entitled to take

A under the words " heirs and successors " and in what shares or proportions the persons so entitled took. Roxburgh J. held, at p. 389:

> " (1) that no distinction should be drawn between the gifts of the personalty and realty, and that those entitled were the persons entitled to the real and personal estate under the law of intestate succession as it had stood since January 1, 1926; . . . (2) that the words
B 'heirs and successors' did not constitute such a reference to the Statutes of Disribution as to oust the general rule that members of a class took as joint tenants."

The property in question in that case consisted partly of real estate and partly of personal estate and there was nothing to convert the real estate into personal estate for the purpose of distribution. Roxburgh J. sum-
C marised the three lines of argument that had been put before him as follows, at p. 392:

> " One is that the person entitled is the person who would have been the heir on an intestacy before January 1, 1926. Another view is that there is no differentiation to be made since 1925 between real and personal estate, and that the persons entitled are those who are
D entitled to property undisposed of under the existing law of intestate succession. The third view has been that the words ' and successors ' introduce such a degree of uncertainty as to vitiate not only themselves but their co-partner, the word ' heirs,' and thus produce an intestacy, on the ground of uncertainty."

He held, at p. 393:

E > " It seems to me most probable that, at the present time, in the case of a gift to a class of persons or their heirs, both realty and personalty would be distributed in accordance with the present law of intestate succession, making no distinction between realty and personalty. That, I think, is most probable, but I must not put it higher, because that is not the position here. I have the words ' and successors ';
F and, in my view, the words ' and successors ' are words of a much wider and more general application than the word ' heirs.' There is about them no flavour or savour of realty at all. The word ' heirs,' of course, historically and in a legal vocabulary has a very strong flavour of realty, though no doubt lay people often use it and have used it in connection with personalty; but the word ' successors ' has no such savour. It is no more akin to realty than to personalty; and
G the phrase is ' heirs and successors.' In my judgment, that does not mean the same as ' heirs or successors,' which might have suggested a different construction. I think that where one has the presence of the word ' successors ' as well as the word ' heirs '—and that is what I have to decide—the court will construe those words as referring to the persons entitled to the real and personal estate under the law of intestate succession applicable at the date when the
H testator died."

In the *Kilvert* case [1957] Ch. 388, it seems to have been the implicit assumption of the court and all counsel that, if the gift to " their heirs and successors " took effect at all, it took effect in favour of a class comprising one category only, namely, those persons who qualified as " heirs and successors " of the relevant deceased person. The contrary does not appear to have been argued. That, however, was a case where

the phrase in question was such as to be readily capable of interpretation A
as referring to a class comprising one category, namely, the persons
entitled to the real and personal estate of the relevant deceased person
under the law of intestate succession applicable at the date when the
testator died. This was the construction which Roxburgh J. ultimately
attributed to the phrase.

In contrast, in the present case, the relevant phrase "*their heirs and
surviving issue*" is not in my judgment capable of interpretation as B
referring to a class comprising one single category. In my judgment
there is no such single category to which the words are apt to refer.
For this reason, among others, Mr. Fawls, on behalf of the first defendant,
submitted that the whole of the substitutional gift over is void for
uncertainty. Accordingly, he submitted that, in the events which have
happened, the share of residue bequeathed to Rowland Richard Bourke C
is held upon trust for the estate of Rowland, which has a vested interest
in his share that cannot now be divested. The very fact, however, that
a reference to " heirs and surviving issue," as a class comprising one
single category, would have produced potential uncertainty so obvious
to any intelligent testator is in my judgment a good reason for concluding that he regarded the gift to " their heirs and surviving issue " as
a gift to the members of a class comprising two separate categories, D
namely, first, " heirs " and, secondly, " surviving issue." In my judgment
this is a perfectly reasonable meaning to attribute to the words and is the
proper construction of the phrase.

As any informed layman such as this testator would have realised,
the word " heirs " in any legal document would ordinarily fall to be
construed in a very different sense from the word " issue." Thus in E
my judgment this testator must be deemed to have intended, by the
substitutional gift in question, to benefit two separate, albeit perhaps
overlapping categories, namely, " heirs " and " issue."

In the light of my conclusions so far, I now turn to consider the
meaning of the word " heirs " in the context of this will. Section 132 (1)
of the Law of Property Act 1925 provides:

> " A limitation of real or personal property in favour of the heir, F
> either general or special, of a deceased person which, if limited in
> respect of freehold land before the commencement of this Act,
> would have conferred on the heir an estate in the land by purchase,
> shall operate to confer a corresponding equitable interest in the
> property on the person who would, if the general law in force imme-
> diately before such commencement had remained unaffected, have G
> answered the description of the heir, either general or special, of the
> deceased in respect of his freehold land, either at the death of the
> deceased or at the time named in the limitation, as the case may
> require."

In the relevant clause of this will, one finds a limitation of the real and
the personal property of the testator " in favour of the heir of a deceased H
person," namely, R. R. Bourke, Winifred Louis and Eva Venables, as
the case may be. Applying the wording of section 132 therefore, the
question then arises: if such limitation had been limited in respect of
freehold land before January 1, 1926—this being the hypothesis which
the section poses—would it have conferred on the heir an estate in the
land by purchase? The general rule appertaining before 1926 was as
stated in *Jarman on Wills,* 8th ed., vol. 3, p. 1544:

" Like all other legal terms, the word *heir,* when unexplained and uncontrolled by the context, must be interpreted according to its strict and technical import; in which sense it obviously designates the person or persons appointed by law to succeed to the real estate in question in case of intestacy."

It is said a little later on the same page:

" And the circumstance that the expression is *heir* (in the singular) and that the heirship resides in, and is divided among, several individuals as co-heirs or co-heiresses, would create no difficulty in the application of this rule of construction; the word ' heir ' being in such cases used in a collective sense, as comprehending any number of persons who may happen to answer the description; and which persons, if more than one, would, if there were no words to sever the tenancy, be entitled as joint tenants."

Before 1926, in the absence of the contrary context, the word " heir " was taken to be used in its strict sense, even where the entire subject of the bequest was personal property: see *Jarman,* vol. 3, p. 1565. I have, however, been referred to a number of pre-1926 cases where, on the provisions of particular wills, it was held that this strict interpretation of the word " heir " yielded to a contrary context in regard to personal estate: see *Wingfield* v. *Wingfield* (1878) 9 Ch.D. 658; *Keay* v. *Boulton* (1883) 25 Ch.D. 212 and *In re Whitehead* [1920] 1 Ch. 298, though compare *Smith* v. *Butcher* (1878) 10 Ch.D. 113. In my judgment, however, these cases are of little or no assistance in the present context since they related to mixed gifts of realty and personalty, or personalty alone.

For the purpose of testing the applicability of section 132 of the Law of Property Act 1925 to the substitutional gift contained in this testator's will, I have first to assume that it was a gift limited solely in respect of freehold land, taking effect before January 1, 1926. On this hypothetical assumption, I can see no sufficient context that would have entitled the court to give the word " heirs " anything other than its strict and technical import, as referred to in *Jarman,* vol. 3, p. 1544.

The testator having provided for conversion of all his real estate into personalty could so easily have used the phrase " next of kin," but deliberately chose to use the technical word " heirs." Further, the provisions of clause 5 of his will give some indication, albeit slight, that he was well familiar with the concept of heirship, usually connected with realty, being made applicable in the context of personalty.

On the hypothetical assumption mentioned above, the gift in this will would have conferred on the heir an estate in land by purchase. It follows in my judgment that, by virtue of section 132 of the Law of Property Act 1925, the substitutional gift operates to confer a corresponding equitable interest in the property on the person or persons who, if the general law immediately before January 1, 1926, had remained unaffected, would have answered the description of the heir of the deceased in respect of his freehold land " either at the death of the deceased or at the time named in the limitation as the case may require."

I will consider the relevant date in one moment. Beyond attempting to ascertain them from the language which he has used, I do not attempt to guess at the testator's true intentions in this context or in any other passage of his will. I see no sufficient reason, however, why the use by him of the word " heirs " should not have operated as an effectual invocation of section 132 of the Law of Property Act 1925.

For the sake of clarity, however, I should perhaps add this. In *In re Kilvert, decd.* [1957] Ch. 388 Roxburgh J. referred to *In re Whitehead* [1920] 1 Ch. 298, the effect of which decision he summarised, at p. 393:

" Sargant J. held that where, as in that case, the words ' or their heirs ' were referable to a mixed fund, they were words of substitution and not words of limitation, both in regard to realty and in regard to personalty, and accordingly that personalty went to the statutory next-of-kin and (as far as I can make out) that realty went to the heir-at-law, though that is not expressly stated."

Roxburgh J. then proceeded to make the following observations:

" That would, at any rate, be the position as it was in 1920; but what I have to consider is first of all whether that would be true now and, secondly, even if it would be true of a gift to a class or their heirs, it would be equally true of a gift to a class or their heirs and successors. Of course, the important thing that has happened since 1920 is the assimilation of the devolution of real and personal property on an intestacy. No doubt there are certain saving provisions, but I do not think that they have any application to the present case. It seems to me most probable that, at the present time, in the case of a gift to a class of persons or their heirs, both realty and personalty would be distributed in accordance with the present law of intestate succession, making no distinction between realty and personalty. That, I think, is most probable, but I must not put it higher, because that is not the position here."

The important penultimate sentence of this passage, which I have already read, clearly represented an obiter observation. With great respect to Roxburgh J., I think it should be approached with considerable caution, since it appears to me that to attach inadequate weight to the possible relevance of section 132 of the Law of Property Act 1925, to which he did not refer in his judgment, though it was referred to in argument. I do not suggest that the actual decision in the *Kilvert* case was incorrect, since it might well have been supported on the footing that a substitutional gift of property in favour of " the heirs and successors " of a named praepositus, even if limited in respect of freehold land before 1926, would not have conferred on the heir an estate in the land by purchase, and that therefore section 132 had no application. This presumably was in fact Roxburgh J.'s implicit reasoning. I seek, however, to make it plain that I do not regard the present case as being on all fours with the *Kilvert* case.

Having concluded, as I have concluded, that in the relevant phrase the word " heirs " means heirs in the strict pre-1926 sense and that the word " issue " means children, I now have to consider at what time the relevant classes should be ascertained. The general prima facie rule is that:

" . . . inasmuch as the proper time for the operation of the Statutes of Distribution in relation to the estate of any person is the death of that person, therefore, prima facie, the reference to next of kin according to the statutes involves by implication the ascertainment of those persons at the proper time, namely, the death of the person

A whose next of kin according to the statutes are referred to." *In re Gansloser's Will Trusts* [1952] Ch. 30, 44 *per* Jenkins L.J.: see also *per* Evershed M.R., at p. 37.

On the particular facts of that case, the Court of Appeal held that there was something in the terms of the particular will under consideration which, despite the prima facie rule, showed that it was not intended that B the ascertainment of the next of kin of the relevant person according to the statutes should take place at the death of such person. In my judgment, however, the prima facie rule still applies and must, by parity of reasoning, in the absence of a contrary context be applicable to a gift to the " heirs " of a named person: see *Wingfield* v. *Wingfield*, 9 Ch.D. 658, 666 and *In re Whitehead* [1920] 1 Ch. 298, 304.

C In contrast, the general rule, as stated in *Jarman,* 8th ed. (1951), vol. 2, p. 1304, in relation to substitutional gifts to issue, is, as Mr. Munby pointed out on behalf of the second defendant, as follows:

"The question frequently arises where there is a prior life estate, as in the case of a gift to A for life and after his death to B or his issue; if B dies in the testator's lifetime, the class is ascertained at the testator's death, while if he survives the testator and dies in A's D lifetime, the class consists of all issue coming into existence before the death of the tenant for life."

See, for example, *In re Jones's Estate* (1878) 47 L.J.Ch. 775.

I feel no doubt that the category of " heirs " and the category of " surviving issue " in the present case must each fall to be ascertained E at the same date; for this purpose no differentiation can be made between the two categories. The choice is thus between (a) the death of the relevant praepositus and (b) the date of ultimate distribution, being the date of death of the last surviving tenant for life, April 18, 1971.

An attempt was made to bolster up the argument in favour of construction (b) by inviting me to read the words " on the death of my wife and brother " along with the phrase " or their heirs and surviving issue "; F but I have already indicated that I reject this argument. The phrase " on the death of my wife and brother " in my judgment falls to be read with the phrase " shall be divided equally," and accordingly affords no direct assistance to the argument in favour of construction (b).

In deciding which of the two constructions is correct, the most important point, it seems to me, is that construction (b) would or could in-G volve the treatment of a person for the purpose of this will as being the heir of a praepositus, when he was in no sense his true heir. If, for example, one of R. R. Bourke, Winifred Louis or Eva Venables were to die during the lifetime of the survivor of the testator's widow and his brother John, leaving X as his or her heir in the strict sense, X might predecease such survivor, in which case, for the purpose of applying construction (b), the heir of the praepositus would have to be ascertained H on an entirely artificial hypothesis, namely, that the praepositus had died at a date when he or she did not die.

Construction (a) in contrast involves no artificiality of this kind. Furthermore, it gives rise to no difficulties in construing the phrase " surviving issue," if the word " surviving " is construed,—as I think it readily can and should be construed—as meaning " surviving the praepositus." I do not therefore accept the submission that the word " surviving " necessarily means surviving the date of distribution. Accordingly,

I hold that construction (a) above is the correct one and that the date   A
of ascertainment is the death of the relevant praepositus.

It is in my judgment clear that, under the terms of the will, the members of the class of heirs and surviving issue of each praepositus take as joint tenants rather than as tenants in common. The will contains no express words of severance and nothing which indicates that the testator intended severance: compare *In re Osoba, decd.* [1979] 1 W.L.R. 247,   B
261, *per* Goff L.J.

I will now attempt to apply these conclusions as to the interpretation of the wording of the will to the actual facts of this case. As to the share of Rowland Richard Bourke, this half brother of the testator had died on August 29, 1958, before the testator's widow, leaving no issue but leaving his two sisters, Winifred Louis and Eva Venables as his " heirs " in the strict sense. It follows from my earlier conclusions that   C
on Rowland's death, Winifred Louis and Eva Venables became entitled to a vested interest in the reversion of Rowland's share as joint tenants, expectant only on the death of the testator's widow. Prima facie therefore Winifred Louis, as the survivor of herself and Eva Venables, would have become entitled to Rowland's share on the death of the testator's widow. It is, however, possible that Eva Venables may have severed this joint tenancy before she died. The available evidence gives no indication   D
as to the facts on this point, one way or the other. The situation in this respect is thus substantially the same as that which faced the Court of Appeal in *In re Osoba, decd.* [1979] 1 W.L.R. 247. In that case the court ordered an inquiry whether or not there had, since the death of the testator, been any severance of the relevant joint tenancy; this appears from the report, at p. 257A, and a transcript of the colloquy following   E
the judgments, which I have seen.

I have not been invited in the present case to make an immediate order for a similar inquiry, but have been invited to give the persons interested in the estate of Eva Venables liberty to apply for one. I think that some time limit should be imposed on the period within which this application is to be made, if at all, and that, if the application is to be made, it should be made by Eva Venables' personal representatives, if   F
and when duly constituted.

Subject therefore to the submissions of counsel, I propose to declare, in answer to question 1 of the amended originating summons, that on the true construction of the will, on the death of Rowland Richard Bourke and in the events which had happened, Winifred Louis and Eva Venables became absolutely entitled in reversion, as beneficial joint   G
tenants, to the share of his residuary estate bequeathed by the testator to Rowland, subject only to the life interest therein of Dorothy Gladys Bourke. Subject likewise to the submissions of counsel, I propose further to give the personal representatives of Eva Venables, if and when duly constituted, liberty to apply within six months of today's date for an inquiry whether or not there has, since the death of the testator been any severance of the said joint tenancy. I propose so far as necessary to   H
reserve the costs of any such application and any subsequent inquiry.

In default of any such application being made within the said six months period, I propose to give the plaintiff liberty to distribute this share of the residuary estate on the footing that there has been no such severance.

In answer to question 2 of the amended originating summons, I propose to declare that on the true construction of the will and in the

A events which had happened, on the death of Eva Venables the third, fourth and fifth defendants became absolutely entitled in reversion as beneficial joint tenants to the share of the testator's residuary estate bequeathed to Eva Venables, subject only to the life interest therein of Dorothy Gladys Bourke.

B I propose to make the representation orders sought by paragraphs 2 (1), 2 (2) and 2 (3) of the amended originating summons. Subject to the submissions of counsel, I propose also to make a further representation order to the effect that, for the purpose of the proceedings, the third, fourth and fifth defendants be appointed to represent the estate of Eva Venables.

Declarations and orders accordingly.

C Solicitors: *Sharpe, Pritchard & Co.*

T. C. C. B.

D

[FAMILY DIVISION]

* PRACTICE DIRECTION (PROBATE GRANTS: ZIMBABWE)

E *Probate—Resealing—Zimbabwe—Grants of representation issued in Southern Rhodesia before independence*

By virtue of an Ordinance enacted on December 7, 1979, provision was made for the recognition of any act done in Southern Rhodesia in reliance upon any law or purported law in operation in that country from November 11, 1965, onwards until its independence.

F One of the effects of this provision is that grants of representation issued by the courts in Southern Rhodesia, irrespective of the date of issue, may once more be re-sealed in England and Wales under the Colonial Probates Act 1892.

Accordingly, the registrar's direction of April 7, 1970, *Practice Direction (Rhodesian Grants: Resealing)* [1970] 1 W.L.R. 687, is hereby cancelled.

G On April 18, 1980, Southern Rhodesia became an independent country known as Zimbabwe. Provision has been made in the Act granting such independence for the continued application of the Colonial Probates Act 1892 to grants issued by its courts on and after that date.

R. L. BAYNE-POWELL,
Senior Registrar.

H *April* 23, 1980.

A

[1980]

* REGINA v. SPRATT

1980 March 13; 20   Lord Widgery C.J., Ackner L.J. and O'Connor J.

B

Crime—Court of Appeal—Substitution of verdict—Charge of murder—Defence of diminished responsibility supported by medical evidence—Defective medical evidence in rebuttal—Whether court empowered to substitute verdict of manslaughter—Homicide Act 1957 (5 & 6 Eliz. 2, c. 11), s. 2—Criminal Appeal Act 1968 (c. 19), s. 3

The appellant was charged with murder. He raised a defence of diminished responsibility within section 2 of the Homicide Act 1957 [1] and called medical evidence in support. The Crown called rebuttal medical evidence and the appellant was convicted of murder. He appealed against conviction and the Crown did not seek to rely on the rebuttal medical evidence, which was defective, and accepted that at the time of the offence the appellant was suffering from diminished responsibility.

C

On the question whether the court had power under section 3 of the Criminal Appeal Act 1968 [2] to substitute a verdict of manslaughter:—

D

Held, that since the jury found that the appellant killed the victim and that he did so unlawfully, they must have been satisfied of facts which proved him guilty of manslaughter, for they must have been satisfied of facts which proved that the homicide was neither justifiable nor excusable; and that, accordingly, the court had jurisdiction under section 3 of the Criminal Appeal Act 1968 to substitute a conviction of manslaughter, and a verdict of manslaughter would be substituted.

E

Reg. v. *Deacon* [1973] 1 W.L.R. 696, C.A. distinguished.

The following cases are referred to in the judgment:

Reg. v. *Deacon* [1973] 1 W.L.R. 696; [1973] 2 All E.R. 1145, C.A.
Reg. v. *Matheson* [1958] 1 W.L.R. 474; [1958] 2 All E.R. 87, C.C.A.

F

No additional cases were cited in argument.

APPEAL against conviction.

On September 5, 1978, at St. Albans Crown Court (Melford Stevenson J.) the appellant, Arthur Edward Spratt, was arraigned on a charge of murder. He called Dr. John T. Hutchinson, a consultant psychiatrist, to give medical evidence as to his mental condition. Medical evidence for the prosecution was given by Dr. Manorama Mehar Singh Legha. The sole issue for the jury was whether or not the appellant was at the time of the killing guilty of murder or suffering from such an abnormality of mind arising from injury as substantially to impair his mental responsibility for his acts and omissions in the killing, so as to reduce his offence to manslaughter. On September 7, 1978, the jury returned a unanimous verdict of guilty of murder, and the appellant was sentenced to life im-

G

H

---

[1] Homicide Act 1957, s. 2: "(1) Where a person kills ... another, he shall not be convicted of murder if he was suffering from such abnormality of mind ... as substantially impaired his mental responsibility for his acts and omissions in doing ... the killing ... (3) A person who but for this section would be liable ... to be convicted of murder shall be liable instead to be convicted of manslaughter. ..."

[2] Criminal Appeal Act 1968, s. 3: see post, p. 556C–D.

A prisonment. He appealed against conviction, and the Crown indicated that, at the appeal, reliance would not be sought to be placed on the evidence of Dr. Legha and that it would be accepted that, at the time of the offence, the appellant was suffering from diminished responsibility. On March 13, 1980, the court quashed the verdict of murder and ordered the appellant's immediate release. Judgment was reserved on the question whether there was jurisdiction under section 3 of the Criminal Appeal

B Act 1968 to substitute for the verdict of murder a verdict of manslaughter. Only the decision on jurisdiction calls for report.

The facts are stated in the judgment.

Peter Taylor Q.C. and *John Zieger* for the appellant.
William Howard Q.C. and *Colin Nicholls* for the Crown.

C
                                                    Cur. adv. vult.

March 20. ACKNER L.J. read the following judgment of the court. On Thursday last week, March 13, we quashed the conviction of the appellant, Arthur Edward Spratt, of murder and on compassionate grounds ordered his immediate release. He is suffering from an inoper-

D able complaint as a result of which his life expectancy is very limited. We reserved, however, our judgment on the question as to whether we had power under section 3 of the Criminal Appeal Act 1968 to substitute for the verdict found by the jury a verdict of manslaughter.

In allowing the appeal we dealt in detail with the facts. For the purpose of this decision they can be restated very shortly. On the night of March 20–21, 1978, the appellant killed Mrs. Naughton, a woman

E with whom he had been living since 1973. The sole issue which the jury had to decide was whether he was guilty of murder or whether he was guilty of manslaughter on the ground that at the time of the killing he was suffering from such an abnormality of mind arising from injury as substantially impaired his mental responsibility for his acts and omissions in doing the killing. The principal evidence for the defence was given

F by a consultant psychiatrist Dr. Hutchinson who, having considered earlier medical reports, concluded that as a result of a motor accident in 1966 the appellant suffered serious brain damage resulting in epilepsy and a marked personality deterioration. He was performing at a border line sub-normal level, that is to say, at the level of a child of nine or 10 years of age and his emotions were those of an immature child. He accordingly responded to the provocation which he received that evening

G in a grossly exaggerated way, as a brain-damaged immature individual would.

The prosecution called in rebuttal a Dr. Legha, then medical officer at Brixton Prison. She considered the appellant's intellect to be normal, that he was not suffering from severe brain damage and she doubted whether he had ever so suffered. She was firmly of the view that he was

H not suffering from any abnormality of mind and accordingly his mental responsibility at the time of the killing was not diminished. Subsequent events, which we referred to in some detail when quashing the conviction, led the Director of Public Prosecutions to commission an independent medical report which proved strongly critical of Dr. Legha, who is apparently suspended from her duties. The prosecution no longer rely on the evidence of Dr. Legha and accept that at the time of the offence the appellant was suffering from diminished responsibility.

We therefore concluded that the verdict of murder should be set aside   A
on the ground that it was unsafe and unsatisfactory. If Dr. Hutchinson's
evidence as to diminished responsibility had stood unchallenged, as it
should have been, the jury would have undoubtedly returned a verdict of
manslaughter.

The only issue for the jury to decide being, as previously stated,
whether the appellant was guilty of murder or manslaughter, the logical
step was to substitute for the verdict of murder that of manslaughter.   B
Mr. Taylor, however, drew our attention to *Reg.* v. *Deacon* [1973]
1 W.L.R. 696, an authority which at first sight seemed to show that we
had no power to take this course.

Before dealing with the facts of that case it is convenient to set out
the terms of section 3 of the Criminal Appeal Act 1968 which re-enacted
in almost identical terms section 5 of the Criminal Appeal Act 1907. It   C
provides:

" (1) This section applies on an appeal against conviction, where the
appellant has been convicted of an offence and the jury could on the
indictment have found him guilty of some other offence, and on
the finding of the jury it appears to the Court of Appeal that the jury
must have been satisfied of facts which proved him guilty of the other   D
offence.   (2) The court may, instead of allowing or dismissing the
appeal, substitute for the verdict found by the jury a verdict of guilty
of the other offence, and pass such sentence in substitution for the
sentence passed at the trial as may be authorised by the law for the
other offence, not being a sentence of greater severity."

The facts of *Reg.* v. *Deacon* [1973] 1 W.L.R. 696 were quite unusual.   E
The appellant was charged on two counts. The first count charged him
with the murder of his brother-in-law and the second count with the
attempted murder of his wife. Both counts were tried together. Both
the charge of murder of the brother-in-law and the attempted murder of
the wife arose out of one incident. There were matrimonial problems
between the appellant and his wife who left home for a period taking the
children with her. He wanted her to return. The brother-in-law became   F
involved in the discussions and suggested that the sensible thing would
be, in the first instance, for the appellant to move out of the house and
let the wife and children return there to live. The appellant apparently
agreed to this and a date was set for the move, namely, October 13, 1971.
On that day the brother-in-law and Mrs. Deacon drove with the children
to the matrimonial home. Her account was the only eye witness account
of what happened. Arguments developed in the course of which she   G
noticed that her husband had a double barrelled gun, which he was aiming
at the brother-in-law. Angry words were exchanged and in the midst of
the altercation the appellant, according to his wife, raised the gun and
shot his brother-in-law, injuring him fatally. Thereafter there was a
struggle in which the gun was fired a second time, not hitting Mrs.
Deacon. However, the appellant then went out into the passage and   H
reloaded the gun, pointed it at his wife and shot her through the hand
which she was holding in front of her body to protect herself. The jury
convicted the appellant on the first count and for some unknown reason
were discharged from giving a verdict on the second count.

The wife was not a competent witness on count 1 (the alleged murder
of the brother-in-law) but she was on the second count charging him with
her attempted murder. No formal application was made by the defence

A that the wife should be called as a witness, but in fact she gave evidence relating to both counts. No warning was given to the jury to exclude the wife's evidence when considering the first count. The Court of Appeal accordingly quashed the conviction of murder. They considered whether it was a case to which to apply the proviso to section 2 (1) of the Criminal Appeal Act 1968 but decided that it was not an appropriate case. Although there was plenty of other evidence upon which the jury might

B well have convicted the appellant, if the wife had not given evidence, the wife was the sole eye witness to the scene.

Her evidence that the appellant had deliberately shot at her brother was evidence of such weight and importance that the court could not say that the verdict of the jury would have been the same if either the wife had not been called, or if they had been given a direction to exclude her

C evidence when considering the verdict on count 1. At the trial the defence had raised provocation, diminished responsibility and accident. The court, however, had no doubt that without the evidence of the wife, the jury, if properly instructed, would have at least returned a verdict of manslaughter, observing " the appellant's own evidence goes a long way to show that he was handling the gun in a wholly reckless fashion, and that the killing of the brother-in-law could hardly have been justifiable

D or excusable homicide in the circumstances." Thus if there was power under the Criminal Appeal Act 1968 to substitute a verdict of manslaughter on the footing that this was the verdict which the jury must inevitably have reached had the case been tried in accordance with the law, the Court of Appeal would have substituted that verdict. Having considered section 3 they concluded they had no such power.

E In the words of Lord Widgery C.J., giving the reserved judgment of the court, at pp. 699–700:

"What is necessary is that the findings of the jury themselves must establish the appropriate facts to support the alternative offence. In the instant case the jury were satisfied that the appellant had murdered his brother-in-law, but we cannot do other than assume

F that they were influenced in that finding by the wife's evidence. The improper admission of the wife's evidence seems to us to colour the entire findings of the jury, and we are unable to say that the jury found facts appropriate to a verdict of manslaughter, except on the footing that they received support in their finding from the evidence of the wife."

G In this appeal, however, the jury found first that the appellant did kill Mrs. Naughton, and, secondly, that he did so unlawfully. There never was any issue as to those matters. On these findings, the jury must have been satisfied of facts which proved the appellant guilty of manslaughter. The defective evidence of Dr. Legha was not related to those findings, and if one expunges her evidence, the jury's satisfaction with those facts remains unaffected. True it is that the jury made further findings,

H namely, that the appellant had the necessary murderous intent and that he had failed to establish the defence of diminished responsibility, and accordingly did not bring in a verdict of manslaughter. However, since this court has set aside that verdict for the reasons given, we have to consider, not the totality of the jury's finding, but only whether they must have been satisfied of sufficient facts to prove him guilty of the other offence. We are not substituting a verdict of " guilty of manslaughter by reason of diminished responsibility." There is no such verdict. Of

course judges do ask juries, when they bring in a verdict of manslaughter, A
whether such a verdict is based upon diminished responsibility, in cases
where the defence of no intent and/or provocation is run. This request
is only made for the purpose of considering the appropriate sentence:
see *Reg.* v. *Matheson* [1958] 1 W.L.R. 474, 479–480.

Here the jury's findings justify manslaughter on the basis that they
must have been satisfied of facts which proved that the homicide was
neither justifiable nor excusable. The fact that they rejected the defence B
of diminished responsibility because of the defective medical evidence
called by the prosecution is accordingly irrelevant. We therefore conclude that we have power to substitute a conviction of manslaughter and,
although it is of only academic interest in this case, we think it is right
to exercise this power. In the majority of cases, where a verdict of manslaughter is substituted for murder, a sentence of imprisonment or a C
hospital order usually follows.

We accordingly substitute by way of sentence such period as was
appropriate to have enabled his release which we ordered last week.

Appeal allowed.
Sentence varied.

D

Solicitors: *John Hogan, Harlow; Director of Public Prosecutions.*

L. N. W.

E

[CHANCERY DIVISION]

* ORAM (INSPECTOR OF TAXES) v. JOHNSON

1980   Feb. 11   Walton J. F

*Revenue—Capital gains tax—Computation of gain—Allowable
deductions—Repairs and improvements to cottage by taxpayer
—Capital gain on sale of cottage—Whether notional value of
taxpayer's labour deductible from gain as " amount of any
expenditure " incurred on asset—Finance Act 1965 (c. 25),
s. 22 (9), Sch. 6, para. 4 (1)*[1]

In 1968 the taxpayer bought a derelict cottage for £2,250. G
During the following years the taxpayer himself carried out
extensive work on repairing and improving the property and
transformed it into a four-bedroom cottage with all modern
amenities. At no time was it occupied as the taxpayer's
main residence. He sold it in 1975 for £11,500. He appealed
against an assessment to capital gains tax made on him for
1975–76 in respect of the gain accruing on that sale. The H
general commissioners upheld his contention that he should
be entitled to deduct £1,700 from the gain on the sale as
representing the value of his own personal labour at £1 per
hour on improving the cottage and reduced the assessment.

On appeal by the Crown: —

Held, allowing the appeal, that in the context of revenue
legislation " expenditure " connoted money expenditure or ex-

[1] Finance Act 1965, Sch. 6, para. 4 (1) (*a*) (*b*): see post, pp. 560H, 561B–C.

A   penditure in money's worth in the sense of something which diminished the total assets of the person making the expenditure, and as such it could not include the notional value of the work done on the cottage by the taxpayer; and that accordingly the sum of £1,700 was not, for the purposes of paragraph 4 (1) of Schedule 6 to the Finance Act 1965, "the amount of any expenditure wholly and exclusively incurred on the asset" and it was not deductible in the computation of chargeable B   gains accruing on the sale.

No cases are referred to in the judgment.

The following cases were cited in argument:

Chandris v. *Union of India* [1956] 1 W.L.R. 147; [1956] 1 All E.R. 358, C.A.

C   *Secretan* v. *Hart* [1969] 1 W.L.R. 1599; [1969] 3 All E.R. 1196; 45 T.C. 701.

CASE STATED by the Commissioners for the General Purposes of the Income Tax Acts.

In May 1968 the taxpayer, Keith David Johnson, purchased Yew Tree Cottage, Linton, Ross-on-Wye, for £2,250. He carried out extensive improvement and enlargement works to it, doing most of the work himself D   in his spare time. He sold it in November 1975 for £11,500. He was assessed to capital gains tax on the sale in the amount of £9,250 for 1975–76. On an appeal against the assessment the Crown agreed that the assessment was excessive in that expenditure of £1,501 on the cottage was deductible from the total gain. However it disputed the claim by the taxpayer that further sums of £1,700 and £700 representing the estimated E   expenditure of his own labour and expenditure on paid labour unsupported by receipts, respectively, were also deductible. The commissioners upheld the taxpayer's contention and reduced the assessment to £5,349.

The Crown appealed.

The facts are stated in the judgment.

F   *C. H. McCall* for the Crown.

The taxpayer in person.

WALTON J. This case arises on a case stated under section 56 of the Taxes Management Act 1970 by the general commissioners for Abingdon in the county of Oxford. It arises out of the purchase by the taxpayer, G   Mr. Keith David Bebb Johnson, on May 10, 1968, of a freehold dwelling-house known as Yew Tree Cottage, Linton, Ross-on-Wye, Herefordshire. When the taxpayer acquired the property it was in a pretty poor state, and he acquired it for the sum of only £2,250. He sold the property on November 29, 1975, at a price of £11,500. As he pointed out to me, that is an increase by a factor of 5, whereas during the same period the Government's index of house prices rose 2·15, thus clearly indicating that H   something very much more than inflation was at work—and, indeed, so it was. The property was not at any time the only or main residence of the taxpayer, so there was no question at all but that on his disposal of Yew Tree Cottage he became chargeable on whatever was the capital gain he made on it, computed according to the rules of law largely laid down in the Finance Act 1965.

The argument in front of the commissioners turned really on two matters, and I will get the one which is no longer in issue out of the way.

There was certain expenditure, totalling a sum of £700, which the tax- A
payer estimated was the amount of money that he had actually paid out
for labour and work, but in respect of which he had not got receipts. Of
course, that always poses a difficult problem for the revenue, but suffice
it to say that, having heard the taxpayer, the commissioners were quite
satisfied that that money had been paid out by him, and there is therefore
no doubt but that that £700 is deductible from the sale price in order to
arrive at the amount of the chargeable gain. So also, of course, beyond B
all question, is the original purchase price of £2,250, the expenditure on
materials and labour supported by receipts, which amounted to £980 and
the legal costs and survey fees on acquisition and disposal.

Having taken all that off, the taxpayer now wishes to take off—and the
commissioners found that he was entitled to do so—a further sum of
£1,700. That represents the value of work which the taxpayer himself C
carried out on the property; the product of his own skill and labour
wholly and exclusively spent on the enhancement of the value of the
cottage. He has taken the comparatively modest sum of £1 per hour as
the value of his work in that way, and hence 1,700 hours work out, at
the rate he claims, at £1,700. The commissioners held that he was
entitled to make that deduction, but from that finding the inspector of
taxes has appealed and that is the sole point which is at issue in front of D
me.

The statutory provisions are really very simple, although that is not
to say that they are all that easy to interpret. First of all, if I may go
to section 19 (1) of the Finance Act 1965 that provides:

"Tax shall be charged in accordance with this Act in respect of
capital gains, that is to say chargeable gains computed in accordance E
with this Act and accruing to a person on the disposal of assets."

So that section tells one that, somewhere later in the Act, one will find
rules for computing the chargeable gain. Section 22 (9) then indeed
provides: "The amount of the gains accruing on the disposal of assets
shall be computed in accordance with Part I of Schedule 6 to this Act."
There are various qualifications, but I do not think that they affect F
anything I have to decide.

I therefore go straightaway to paragraph 4 of Schedule 6 to the Act
of 1965. Paragraph 4 (1) says:

"Subject to the following provisions of this Schedule, the sums
allowable as a deduction from the consideration in the computation G
under this Schedule of the gain accruing to a person on the disposal
of an asset shall be restricted to. . . ."

Pausing there for one moment before one comes on to the items to which
they are restricted, it says " sums allowable as a deduction." One will
therefore expect to find in the following sub-subparagraphs matters set out
basically in terms of money, because one can deduct from the consideration in the computation of a gain accruing to a person on the disposal
of an asset only money sums; there is no machinery generally provided
for deducting anything else. Then, sub-sub-paragraph (a) provides:

"the amount or value of the consideration, in money or money's
worth, given by him or on his behalf wholly and exclusively for the
acquisition of the asset. . . ."

A So there one has to reduce to pounds and pence " the amount or value of the consideration, in money or money's worth, given by him or on his behalf wholly and exclusively for the acquisition of the asset," and it goes on to deal with incidental costs and matters of that sort, with which I am not concerned. So there undoubtedly one can take into consideration that which is given in money or money's worth wholly and exclusively for the acquisition of the asset, which might very well be in some B cases services and matters of that nature which otherwise would not easily translate into money.

Next comes sub-sub-paragraph (b), which is the crucial one here:

"the amount of any expenditure wholly and exclusively incurred on the asset by him or on his behalf for the purpose of enhancing the value of the asset, being expenditure reflected in the state or nature C of the asset at the time of the disposal, and any expenditure wholly and exclusively incurred by him in establishing, preserving or defending his title to, or to a right over, the asset."

It is that sub-sub-paragraph which is the one in issue, it being conceded that the taxpayer's work was undoubtedly " reflected in the state or nature D of the asset at the time of the disposal."

Mr. McCall called my attention to paragraph 4 (2), which runs:

"For the purposes of this paragraph and for the purposes of all other provisions of this Part of this Act the incidental costs to the person making the disposal of the acquisition of the asset or of its disposal shall consist of expenditure wholly and exclusively incurred by him E for the purposes of the acquisition or, as the case may be, the disposal, being fees, commission or remuneration paid for the professional services of any surveyor or valuer, or auctioneer, or accountant, or agent or legal adviser and costs of transfer or conveyance (including stamp duty) together—(a) in the case of the acquisition of an asset, with costs of advertising to find a seller, and (b) in the case F of a disposal, with costs of advertising to find a buyer and costs reasonably incurred in making any valuation or apportionment required for the purposes of the computation under this Schedule. . . ."

Mr. McCall submitted to me that sub-paragraph (2) tends to show, without providing a statutory definition, that " expenditure " is intended to be something which is paid out by the person incurring the expenditure. G I see the force of that, but I do not myself think that that really governs the matter sufficiently for me to be able to rely on it.

So I return basically to paragraph 4 (1) (b)—" the amount of any expenditure." It seems to me that, although one does in general terms talk about expenditure of time and expenditure of effort, having regard particularly to the opening words of paragraph 4 (1), where the expendi-H ture is to be " a deduction," the primary matter which is thought of by the legislature in sub-sub-paragraph (b) is something which is passing out from the person who is making the expenditure. That will most normally and naturally be money, accordingly presenting no problems in calculation; but that will not necessarily be the case. I instance the case (it may be fanciful, but I think it is a possible one and tests the principle) of the taxpayer employing a bricklayer to do some casual bricklaying about the premises, the remuneration for the bricklayer being three bottles of whisky at the end of the week. It seems to me that that would be expenditure by the taxpayer, because out of his stock he would have to give something away to the person who was laying the bricks, and I do not think that that would present any real problems of valuation or other difficulty.

But when one comes on to his own labour, it does not seem to me that that is really capable of being quantified in this sort of way. It is not something which diminishes his stock of anything by any precisely ascertainable amount; it is something which would have to be estimated. It has been estimated here by taking the very modest sum of £1 an hour, but the fact that the taxpayer has been modest in his demands does not enable one to escape from the crucial crunch, which is how, in a case which was contested and where the amount claimed was something which was larger than was obviously right, one would test it. It seems to me that there would undoubtedly have to be found in the end some machinery for translating into money terms the work put in by the owner of the asset himself, if that was to be allowable. But it seems to me that that does not fall into the ordinary meaning of " the amount of any expenditure wholly and exclusively incurred on the asset by him or on his behalf." The wording, to my mind, just does not fit that sort of situation.

It is perhaps a matter of first impression based on the impression that the word " expenditure " makes on one; but I think that the whole group of words, " expenditure," " expended," " expenses " and so on and so forth, in a revenue context, mean primarily money expenditure and, secondly, expenditure in money's worth—something which diminishes the total assets of the person making the expenditure—and I do not think that one can bring one's own work, however skilful it may be and however much sweat one may expend on it, within the scope of paragraph 4 (1) (b).

This may seem hard, and I am sure the taxpayer will think it hard, but I think there is another side to the coin. Suppose the taxpayer were, as it were, to be able to charge the revenue up in this way with his notional expenditure of £1,700 worth of work. Would it not then be just that the revenue should charge the taxpayer up with his receipt of the £1,700 as moneys earned by him in his subsidiary trade of a bricklayer, or whatever? I think the revenue would be quite happy to allow him the £1,700 here provided they could add to his notional income for the purposes of income tax, including tax at the higher rates, the sum of £1,700. Of course, in the taxpayer's case that may be an absurd matter, but a solicitor who acts for himself and thus saves himself money on conveyancing might present a case where the adding of a notional sum might look a very real proposition. However, it seems to me, as I say, that although it looks very hard on the taxpayer at first blush that this notional expenditure should be disallowed, I think that, if one follows it through, perhaps the taxpayer has not been so hardly done by as would at first appear.

I am very glad to say that in this case, there being such a narrow point at issue and there being no case which really is of much assistance (although I am very much indebted to Mr. McCall for having cited to me a couple of cases which throw a very fitful light on the subject; but, they being the only cases that exist, it was his duty to cite them to me), it being a matter on which there is no authority down to this moment, the Crown has not asked for costs, and therefore, of course, there will be no order for costs.

> *Appeal allowed.*
> *No order as to costs.*
> *Assessment varied to £7,049.*

Solicitor: *Solicitor of Inland Revenue.*

[Reported by MRS. HARRIET DUTTON, Barrister-at-Law]

[CHANCERY DIVISION]

* SLATER (INSPECTOR OF TAXES) *v.* RICHARDSON & BOTTOMS LTD.

1979   June 22   Oliver J.

Revenue—Income tax—Appeal to commissioners—Construction company failing to make proper deductions from payments to sub-contractors—Collector of taxes refusing to exonerate company—Whether commissioners empowered to review exercise of discretion conferred on collector of taxes—Finance Act 1971 (c. 68), ss. 29 (4), 30 (1)—Income Tax (Payments to Sub-Contractors in the Construction Industry) Regulations 1971 (S.I. 1971, No. 1779), reg. 6 (3)—Taxes Management Act 1970 (c. 9), s. 50 (6)

During the fiscal year 1973–74 the taxpayer company, being a company concerned in the construction industry, made payments to two sub-contractors in respect of construction work carried out by them. Section 29 (4) of the Finance Act 1971 [1] required the taxpayer company to deduct a sum equal to 30 per cent. of those payments and to pay it to the Board (the Commissioners of Inland Revenue) as income tax of the sub-contractors. The two sub-contractors produced certificates in their names, issued under the provisions of section 30 of the Act, exempting them from section 29 and which were valid certificates at the beginning of the fiscal year but which expired shortly thereafter. The taxpayer company failed to notice the expiry dates and continued making payments to them in full during the rest of the year. The collector of taxes, after considering whether to exonerate the taxpayer company from liability for the sums it had failed to deduct, declined to make any such direction under the provisions of regulation 6 (3) of the Income Tax (Payments to Sub-Contractors in the Construction Industry) Regulations 1971.[2] The taxpayer company appealed, under the provisions of section 50 (6) of the Taxes Management Act 1970,[3] against an assessment made on it under regulation 11 (1) of the Regulations of 1971 for payments to sub-contractors in the sum of £3,459. The general commissioners, deciding that the taxpayer company had taken reasonable care to comply with the requirements of the legislation and that

---

[1] Finance Act 1971, s. 29 (4): see post, p. 565D–E.
S. 30 (1): see post, p. 565H.
[2] Income Tax (Payments to Sub-Contractors in the Construction Industry) Regulations 1971, reg. 6 (3): see post, p. 566D–F.
[3] Taxes Management Act 1970, s. 50 (6): see post, p. 568D–E.

A
the non-deduction of the sums in respect of income tax had
arisen through an error made in good faith, allowed the appeal
and discharged the assessment.

On appeal by the Crown: —

Held, allowing the appeal, that the discretion to exonerate
a contractor from liability to make the payments required by
section 29 (4) of the Act of 1971 was conferred by regulation
6 of the Regulations of 1971 only on the collector of taxes;
that neither the provisions of the Act of 1971 nor of section
50 (6) of the Taxes Management Act 1970 enabled commissioners on hearing an appeal against an assessment to review
the exercise of that discretion and that, accordingly, the
commissioners had no power to discharge the assessment made
on the taxpayer company.

B

The following case is referred to in the judgment:

Customs and Excise Commissioners v. *J. H. Corbitt (Numismatists) Ltd.*
[1979] 3 W.L.R. 291, Neill J. and C.A.

C

No additional cases were cited in argument.

CASE STATED by the Commissioners for the General Purposes of the
Income Tax Acts.

D

The taxpayer company, Richardson & Bottoms Ltd., was involved
in the construction industry and during the fiscal year 1973–74 made
payments, inter alia, to two individual sub-contractors who worked for
it on a construction site. The sub-contractors produced certificates
exempting them from having sums in respect of income tax deducted
from the payments which expired on April 30, 1973 and November 19,
1973, respectively. The taxpayer company failed to make deduction
from payments made to them after the date of expiry of those certificates.
It was assessed under regulation 11 (1) of the Income Tax (Payments to
Sub-Contractors in the Construction Industry) Regulations 1971 for
payments to sub-contractors for 1973–74 of £3,479. Its appeal against
the assessment was allowed by the commissioners on the grounds that it
had taken reasonable care to comply with the requirements of the new
legislation and that it would be wrong to penalise it for the loss which
had as its origin the deceit of the sub-contractors concerned and but for
which renewed and valid certificates might have been in force. They
discharged the assessment.

E

F

The Crown appealed.

The facts are stated in the judgment.

G

Brian Davenport for the Crown.
The taxpayer company did not appear and was not represented.

OLIVER J. This is an appeal on the case stated from the general
commissioners at Luton. It is the Crown's appeal against the discharge
by the commissioners of an assessment made against the taxpayer company, which is Richardson & Bottoms Ltd., under the provisions of
regulation 11 (1) of the Income Tax (Payments to Sub-Contractors in the
Construction Industry) Regulations 1971.

H

Before I go on to consider any of the relevant facts as they appear
from the case stated, I ought I think to review the statutory provisions
under which this assessment is made. The construction industry is one
which it is public knowledge has for some time given rise to certain

The Weekly Law Reports, June 6, 1980

565

1 W.L.R.   Slater v. Richardson & Bottoms Ltd. (Ch.D.)   Oliver J.

A problems in the matters of the assessment and collection of tax and provisions were enacted to meet some of those problems and in particular the provisions in force at the material time (that is the time at which this particular appeal was concerned) were the provisions of sections 29 and 30 of the Finance Act 1971. Section 29 (1) sets the stage, as it were, for the application of the provisions and applies:

B " Where a contract relating to construction operations is not a contract of employment, but—(a) one party to the contract is a sub-contractor (as defined in subsection (2) below); and (b) another party to the contract (in this section referred to as the contractor) either is a sub-contractor under another such contract relating to all or any of the construction operations or is a person to whom this paragraph applies; . . ."

C Now it was not in dispute that the taxpayer company was the contractor for the purposes of those provisions and that the two other persons with whom the case is concerned—and I shall have to refer to that later—were sub-contractors within the definition there set out. The next relevant subsection for present purposes is section 29 (4), which provides:

D " On making a payment to which this section applies the contractor shall "—and I pause to note that that is mandatory—" deduct from it a sum equal to 30 per cent."—the figure at the material time—" of so much of the payment as is not shown to represent the direct cost to any other person of materials used or to be used in carrying out construction operations to which the contract under which the payment is made relates; and the sum so deducted shall be paid to the Board and shall be treated for the purposes of income tax—(a) as not diminishing the payment; but (b) as being income tax paid in respect of the profits or gains of the trade, profession or vocation of the person for whose work the contractor makes the payment."

E

So there one sees the frame of the legislation; where you have a sub-contract in the construction industry, the main contractor is responsible for paying to the revenue 30 per cent. of so much of the amount due to the sub-contractor as is not shown to consist of the direct cost of materials used in the construction operations. Then subsection (5) empowers the Board to make regulations. It is in these terms:

F

" The Board shall make regulations with respect to the collection and recovery, whether by assessment or otherwise, of sums required to be deducted from any payments under this section and for the giving of receipts by persons receiving the payments to persons making them; and those regulations may include any matters with respect to which regulations may be made under section 204 (pay as you earn) of the Taxes Act."

G

H So far so good.

Now section 30 provides for exemptions or exceptions from section 29 and, as can be seen, they have a great materiality in this particular case. Section 30 (1) provides:

" A person is excepted from section 29 of this Act if a certificate under this section is in force—(a) in respect of him; or (b) in respect of a firm in which he is a partner; "

566

A

I need not read the rest of the section because it is not a case in which
a partnership is concerned. So the material point for examination here
is whether in this case there was, so far as the sub-contractor is concerned,
a certificate under section 30 in force at the material time. I need not,
I think, read the rest of section 30, save perhaps to refer to the fact that
the Board has, under subsection (7), the power to make regulations
prescribing the period for which certificates are issued and providing for
renewal, and so on.

B

Now the Board did, indeed, under the powers to which I have referred,
make regulations, and those regulations are, or were at the material
time at any rate, the Income Tax (Payments to Sub-Contractors in the
Construction Industry) Regulations 1971 (S.I. 1971 No 1779). Regulation 4 requires certain forms to be completed and regulation 6 requires
the payment of the appropriate sums to the collector. I had better read,
I think, regulation 6 (1):

C

> " Within 14 days of the end of every income tax month the con-
> tractor shall pay to the collector all amounts which he was liable
> under the principal section to deduct from payments made by him
> during that income tax month."

D

The principal section has been previously defined in the Regulations as
section 29 of the Finance Act 1971. Then there is a provision for giving
receipts, and regulation 6 (3) is the critical provision for present purposes,
and it provides:

> " If the amount which the contractor is liable to pay to the collector
> under paragraph (1) of this regulation exceeds the amount actually
> deducted by him from payments made during the relevant month
> but he satisfies the collector that he took reasonable care to comply
> with the provisions of the principal section and of these Regulations
> and that either—(a) the under-deduction was due to an error made
> in good faith, or (b) in spite of such reasonable care as aforesaid, he
> had been led to the genuine belief that a payment made by him,
> which was one to which the principal section applies, was not or
> was not wholly such a payment, then the collector may direct that
> the contractor shall not be liable to pay the said excess to the
> collector."

E

F

Finally I think I ought to refer to regulation 11 (1), which is the provision under which the assessment in the instant case was made, and that
provides:

G

> " Where—(a) there is a dispute between a contractor and a sub-
> contractor as to the amount, if any, deductible by the contractor
> under the principal section from a payment to the sub-contractor
> or his nominee; or (b) the inspector has reason to believe, as a
> result of an inspection under regulation 10 or otherwise, that the
> amount which a contractor is liable to pay to the collector under
> these Regulations is greater than the amount, if any, which he has
> so paid, or (c) the inspector for any other reason sees fit to do so,
> the inspector may at his discretion make an assessment on the
> contractor in the amount which, according to the best of his judg-
> ment, the contractor is liable to pay under these Regulations, and
> all the provisions of the Income Tax Acts regarding appeals, collec-
> tion and recovery shall apply as though it were an assessment to

H

The Weekly Law Reports, June 6, 1980

567

1 W.L.R.   Slater v. Richardson & Bottoms Ltd. (Ch.D.)   Oliver J.

A   income tax, except that the amount charged by the assessment shall be due and payable 14 days after the assessment is made."

Now in the instant case the position is this. The taxpayer company is a company concerned in the construction industry and in the year of assessment 1973–74 it made payments to sub-contractors for construction work from which it was required to deduct the 30 per cent. provided in B   section 29. There were two sub-contractors going under the names of Hayes and Dooley. Several payments were made by the taxpayer company. Those sub-contractors were persons who held exemption certificates or produced exemption certificates applying to Mr. Hayes and Mr. Dooley. I think there is some question as to whether they were the rightful holders of those certificates, but in the event that is not really material to the present case. What is material is this, that the C   certificate issued in the name of Mr. Hayes expired on April 30, 1973, and the certificate in the name of Mr. Dooley expired on November 19, 1973. But unfortunately this was not spotted by those responsible for making the payments within the organisation of the taxpayer company and payments continued to be made in full to those sub-contractors in respect of periods after the expiry of their certificates, when under the D   provisions of section 29 deductions should have been made.

It should be said in fairness that the taxpayer company is in a substantial way of business, as the general commissioners found, and it carries on work at nine different sites. The certificates had to be produced to the site managers. Indeed out of all their work only two cases were found in which the taxpayer company had proved to be at fault, although E   their quarterly payments to sub-contractors amounted to very substantial sums, somewhere between £33,000 and £42,000. The case finds that the taxpayer company had been punctilious in its making of quarterly payment returns and that the collector of taxes had considered, in relation to the circumstances of the instant case, whether he ought to make a direction under regulation 6 (3), to which I have referred, which enables him in certain circumstances to exonerate a company from that F   liability. For reasons which were good no doubt to him—and whether good or bad is not a matter for my judgment—he declined to make any such direction, and the inspector accordingly, under regulation 11 (1), made an assessment. The taxpayer company appealed to the general commissioners against that assessment and the commissioners came to this conclusion: they, having heard the appeal, were of the opinion G   that the taxpayer company had taken reasonable care to comply with the requirements of the new legislation the problem of non-deduction of tax had arisen from an error made in good faith. They went on:

"Moreover, we felt that if it had been practical for earlier attention to have been given to the [taxpayer company's] quarterly returns of payments made, it might have been possible to prevent payments continuing to be made in full on the certificates which turned out H   to be falsely used. In these circumstances we considered that it would be wrong to penalise the [taxpayer company] for the loss which had as its origin the deceit of the sub-contractors concerned and but for which renewed and valid certificates might have been in force."

Accordingly they held that the appeal succeeded and they discharged the assessment. It is from that that the Crown now appeals.

The taxpayer company has not taken part in the appeal, has not turned up to resist it, for reasons which I think have been explained in a letter to the registrar. It is, in any event, immaterial why they have not turned up. I have had the benefit of Mr. Davenport's submissions on behalf of the Crown in which he has very fairly put the case and drawn my attention to all the material points which might be made in the taxpayer company's favour. Having heard those submissions, I have no doubt whatever that this is a case in which the appeal of the Crown must succeed, and for this reason: that it seems to me there is no power in the statute, there is nothing in the provisions of the Finance Act 1971, nor indeed of the Taxes Management Act 1970, which enables, in my judgment, the general commissioners to arrogate to themselves the discretion which is clearly conferred by the regulation to which I have referred on the collector of taxes.

The position is, of course, that the right to appeal arises under section 31 of the Taxes Management Act 1970, which provides that an appeal may be brought against any assessment of tax by notice of appeal in writing given 30 days after the notice of assessment, and subsection (4) of that section allows for the appeal to be made to the general commissioners. The commissioners, when they entertain the appeal have their powers and duties prescribed by Part V of the Taxes Management Act, and section 50 (6) there provides:

"If, on an appeal, it appears to the majority of the commissioners present at the hearing, by examination of the appellant on oath or affirmation, or by other lawful evidence, that the appellant is overcharged by any assessment, the assessment shall be reduced accordingly, but otherwise every such assessment shall stand good."

There is nothing in those words, I think, which can possibly enable the commissioners to discharge an assessment on the ground that the circumstances were such that the collector of taxes ought to have exercised a discretion which is placed on him to remit tax which is clearly payable under the provisions of the section.

Mr. Davenport very fairly drew my attention to a case concerning value added tax, which was an appeal from a decision of Neill J. to the Court of Appeal. It is *Customs and Excise Commissioners* v. *J. H. Corbitt (Numismatists) Ltd.* [1979] 3 W.L.R. 291, in which the majority of the Court of Appeal held that on an appeal to the tribunal, the tribunal was empowered to consider matters which, under the statutory provisions, had been confided to the commissioners. But the wording of the sections was very different from the provisions which I have to consider, and in any event, there the position was that the persons exercising the discretion and the persons making the assessment, namely the commissioners, were the same. Here the discretion is clearly vested not in the inspector of taxes but in the collector of taxes, and I can find nothing in the statutory wording which enables the commissioners or gives to them any power to review the collector's decision, nor any power in the inspector himself to review the collector's decision.

In these circumstances it seems to me that although I have the very greatest sympathy with the taxpayer company and the position in which it found itself as a result of having in good faith under-deducted, there is,

The Weekly Law Reports, June 6, 1980

569

1 W.L.R.   Slater v. Richardson & Bottoms Ltd. (Ch.D.)   Oliver J.

A   I think, no answer to the Crown's claim and the appeal must be allowed and the decision of the commissioners reversed.

Appeal allowed.
No application by Crown for costs.
Case remitted to commissioners for
assessment to be adjusted.

B

Solicitor: *Solicitor of Inland Revenue.*

[Reported by Mrs. Harriet Dutton, Barrister-at-Law]

C

[COURT OF APPEAL]

* REGINA *v.* SECRETARY OF STATE FOR THE
HOME DEPARTMENT, *Ex parte* MANGOO KHAN

D   1980   Jan. 15, 16;   Lord Denning M.R.,
            Feb. 13   Lawton and Ackner L.JJ.

Immigration—Illegal entrant—Certificate of entry—Application for
certificate by unmarried fully dependent son under 21—Entry
visas granted to family to join father six years later when son
over 21—Son's marriage in Pakistan after grant of visa—
Immigration officer asking no questions on arrival—Grant of
E   *indefinite leave to enter—Subsequent arrest and detention of*
son after wife openly joining him—Whether son illegal entrant
—Whether deception to be inferred from not volunteering
information—Statement of Immigration Rules for Control on
Entry: EEC and Other Non-Commonwealth Nationals (1973)
(H.C. 81), paras. 10, 39—Immigration Act 1971 (c. 77),
s. 33 (1) [1]

F   In 1972 a wife and four young children, of whom the
applicant was the eldest, applied in Pakistan to the British
authorities for entry visas to join the father who had
been in England since 1962 and had a right of abode here.
In January 1974, when the applicant was 15, he signed by his
thumb mark an application form printed in English with a
note stating that holders of entry certificates would be pre-
G   sumed by the United Kingdom immigration officer to be
qualified for admission " unless he discovers . . . (b) that a
change of circumstances after issue has removed the basis of
the holder's claim to admission," that being the substance of
paragraph 10 of the Immigration Rules for Control on Entry
relating to non-Commonwealth Nationals (HC81). Paragraph
39 of those rules provided: " Generally, children aged 18 or
over must qualify for admission in their own right; but . . . an
unmarried and fully dependent son under 21 . . . may be
H   admitted if the whole family . . . are being admitted for settlement." Entry visas for the family were not granted until
June 1978, when the applicant was just over 21. Two weeks
before the family flew to Heathrow, the son married in Pakistan, leaving his wife there. On arrival at the airport on
August 13, 1978, he handed the entry certificate endorsed
" Settlement—accompanying mother to join father " and his
passport, showing his age, to the immigration officer who

[1] Immigration Act 1971, s. 33 (1): see post, p. 575C–D.

570

A

asked him only if he was coming to join his father, to which he answered " Yes." She then stamped his passport " Indefinite leave to enter "; and he and the family went to live at his father's house.

Eight months later he in England and his wife in Pakistan took the requisite steps for her to join him. When she arrived he met her at Heathrow; questions were asked; and both stated the facts as to the marriage. Three weeks later he was arrested and detained in prison pending removal to Pakistan, the immigration authorities purporting to act under paragraph 16 (2) of Schedule 2 to the Immigration Act 1971. He applied for a writ of habeas corpus on the ground that he was not an illegal entrant, having been given indefinite leave to enter in August 1978. The affidavit sworn on behalf of the Secretary of State for the Home Department justified his detention on the ground that the applicant had obtained entry on a false basis—as the dependent unmarried son of a father settled here when he was already married—and was to be regarded as a person who had obtained entry by deception in that he had employed for that purpose a visa which he knew related to circumstances which no longer existed and the basis for which had disappeared. The Divisional Court dismissed his application.

On appeal by the applicant : —

Held, allowing the appeal and granting the writ of habeas corpus, that there was no evidence of fraud or deception in obtaining the entrance visa, since, in view of the length of time between his application as a boy of 15 and the grant of his entry visa when he was over 21, it was impossible to say that he had continued to represent that he was a fully dependent unmarried son under 21; that in any event paragraph 39 of the Rules of Entry did not apply to the applicant who, being over 21 when his entry visa was granted, must have been treated as qualifying for entry in his own right; that when he entered he did and said nothing to deceive the immigration officer; that the officer, with the applicant and his documents before her, must, by omitting to question him about his age and dependency, be taken to have waived those requirements and accepted the manifest change of circumstances; and that as she did not ask him about his marital status, there was no logical reason for not assuming that she had also waived the original " unmarried " requirement; and that as there was no evidence of fraud or misrepresentation in obtaining the entry visa or on entry, the deception alleged by the Home Office could not be supported to justify his detention as an " illegal entrant."

Reg. v. *Secretary of State for the Home Department, Ex parte Zamir* [1980] 2 W.L.R. 357, C.A. distinguished.

Per Lord Denning M.R. (i) An " illegal entrant " as defined in section 33 (1) of the Act of 1971 is a person unlawfully entering in breach " of the immigration laws "; and " immigration laws " means the Act, not the rules (post, p. 575D). Breach of the rules is not enough to make a person entering with leave an " illegal entrant " (post, p. 576E–F). (ii) When the holder of an entry clearance presents himself, the immigration officer should examine him to see whether there has been a change of circumstances. There is no duty of disclosure on the entrant, and in the absence of deception, if leave to enter is granted, that leave is good (post, p. 577A–B).

Decision of the Divisional Court of the Queen's Bench Division reversed.

B

C

D

E

F

G

H

The following cases are referred to in the judgments:

Reg. v. *Secretary of State for the Home Department, Ex parte Choudhary* [1978] 1 W.L.R. 1177; [1978] 3 All E.R. 790, C.A.

A   *Reg.* v. *Secretary of State for the Home Department, Ex parte Hussain*
        [1978] 1 W.L.R. 700; [1978] 2 All E.R. 423, D.C. and C.A.
        Reg. v. *Secretary of State for the Home Department, Ex parte Ram*
        [1979] 1 W.L.R. 148; [1979] 1 All E.R. 687, D.C.
        Reg. v. *Secretary of State for the Home Department, Ex parte Zamir*
        [1979] Q.B. 688; [1979] 3 W.L.R. 89; [1979] 2 All E.R. 849, D.C.;
        [1980] 2 W.L.R. 357; [1980] 1 All E.R. 1041, C.A.
B   *With* v. *O'Flanagan* [1936] Ch. 575; [1936] 1 All E.R. 727, C.A.

        The following additional cases were cited in argument:
        Reg. v. *Governor of Brixton Prison, Ex parte Ahsan* [1969] 2 Q.B. 222;
        [1969] 2 W.L.R. 618; [1969] 2 All E.R. 347, D.C.
        Reg. v. *Governor of Pentonville Prison, Ex parte Azam* [1974] A.C. 18;
        [1973] 2 W.L.R. 949; [1973] 2 All E.R. 765, H.L.(E.).
C   *Reg.* v. *Immigration Appeal Tribunal, Ex parte Ekrem Mehmet* [1977]
        1 W.L.R. 795; [1977] 2 All E.R. 602, D.C.
        Reg. v. *Immigration Appeal Tribunal, Ex parte Manek* [1978] 1 W.L.R.
        1190; [1978] 3 All E.R. 641, D.C. and C.A.
        Reg. v. *Preston Supplementary Benefits Appeal Tribunal, Ex parte Moore*
        [1975] 1 W.L.R. 624; [1975] 2 All E.R. 807, C.A.
D   *Reg.* v. *Secretary of State for Home Affairs, Ex parte Hosenball* [1977]
        1 W.L.R. 766; [1977] 3 All E.R. 452, D.C. and C.A.
        Reg v. *Secretary of State for the Home Department, Ex parte Khan*
        [1977] 1 W.L.R. 1466; [1977] 3 All E.R. 538, C.A.
        Reg. v. *Secretary of State for the Home Department, Ex parte Mughal*
        [1974] Q.B. 313; [1973] 3 W.L.R. 647; [1973] 3 All E.R. 796, C.A.
        Reg. v. *Secretary of State for the Home Department and Another, Ex
E   parte Suruk Miah* (C.A. January 29, 1976) unreported.
        Robertson v. *Minister of Pensions* [1949] 1 K.B. 227; [1948] 2 All E.R.
        767.

APPEAL from the Divisional Court of the Queen's Bench Division.
        On August 29, 1979, the applicant, Mangoo Khan, foundry worker,
of 217, Jupiter Drive, Hemel Hempstead, Hertfordshire, applied ex parte
F to Neill J. in the vacation court for leave to apply for a writ of habeas
corpus in respect of his detention in H.M. Prison Pentonville on the
orders of an immigration officer; the application was adjourned for
notice to be given to the Secretary of State for the Home Department
and for application to be made inter partes to the Divisional Court.
By his affidavit in support of his application the applicant stated
that he was the son of Farman Ali Khan, of Jupiter Road, Hemel
G Hempstead, who was settled in the United Kingdom; that he himself was
born in Pakistan on May 20, 1957; that he had applied to the British
Embassy in Islamabad, Pakistan, for an entry certificate to join his father
in the United Kingdom, as his dependent son, first, on September 4, 1972,
secondly, on June 25, 1973, and thirdly, on January 16, 1974; that he
was granted a settlement visa on June 26, 1978, and came to the United
H Kingdom on August 13, 1978, when he was admitted by an immigration
officer for an indefinite period; and that all the aforementioned endorse-
ments and dates were entered in his Pakistan passport which was presently
held by the immigration authorities. He deposed further that after the
issue of the settlement visa his family felt that as he was going to the
United Kingdom permanently, he might weaken or sever his links with
his native land and culture and that to protect those links they arranged

Reg. v. Home Secretary, Ex p. Mangoo Khan (C.A.)   **[1980]**

for him to undergo a ceremony which though in form a marriage   A
ceremony was in fact intended to be and was regarded by him and all
others concerned as a betrothal ceremony to one Meniza Begum on
July 28, 1978, in Pakistan; that that ceremony was not followed by
cohabitation and/or consummation, it being agreed between the two
families that after his arrival in the United Kingdom he would send for
Meniza Begum and register their marriage here, after which cohabitation
as husband and wife would start; and that when he was examined by the   B
immigration officer on his arrival at Heathrow on August 13, 1978, he
had not mentioned the ceremony in Pakistan because he believed it to be
only a betrothal ceremony; that Meniza Begum had come to the United
Kingdom on July 2, 1979, but was refused admission. He continued:

> " I was arrested by the police on July 22, 1979, by order of an im-
> migration officer and I am being detained as an illegal entrant under   C
> the provisions of paragraph 16 (2) of Schedule 2 to the Immigration
> Act 1971. I am not an illegal entrant. I was given leave to enter
> the United Kingdom for an indefinite period on August 13, 1978. I
> submit that my detention is unlawful."

He asked for the issue of a writ of habeas corpus and to be brought before
the court so that the court might determine whether his detention was   D
legal. He also asked for bail pending the final disposal of his application.

    The Divisional Court (Waller L.J. and Park J.) refused the application
on November 13, 1979, holding that there were reasonable grounds for
the Secretary of State coming to the conclusion that the applicant, when
he came into this country, in August 1978, did conceal the fact that he
was married and that if the Secretary of State considered that he   E
deliberately did so, there was evidence on which he could properly come
to that conclusion.

    The applicant, pursuant to leave to appeal granted by the Court of
Appeal, appealed on the grounds, so far as relevant, that as the appeal
procedure following his original application was protracted over a period
of six years and he in no way contributed to that delay, the relevant date
to judge the factual situation of his claim to entry clearance which gave   F
him the statutory right of entry into the United Kingdom was the date of
his application; that he was not an " illegal entrant " within section 33 (1)
of the Immigration Act 1971; and that the marriage which was non-
consummated after the issue of the entry clearance did not amount to
a change of material circumstances such as to vitiate his claim to enter
the United Kingdom; that the Divisional Court, having held that the   G
facts of the present case were not on all fours with *Reg.* v. *Secretary of
State for the Home Department, Ex parte Zamir* [1979] Q.B. 688, should
have granted his application for habeas corpus; and that the court, having
held that it was not necessary to decide whether the applicant had
obtained entry by means of deception or fraud, wrongly held that he had
a duty to disclose a marriage which took place after the issue of the
entry clearance without fully considering whether under the immigration   H
rules he was in any way prevented from bringing a wife from abroad
after having obtained admission to the United Kingdom.

    K. S. Nathan for the applicant.
    David Latham for the Secretary of State.

                                                  Cur. adv. vult.

1 W.L.R.   **Reg. v. Home Secretary, Ex p. Mangoo Khan (C.A.)**

A   February 13. The following judgments were read.

LORD DENNING M.R. Farman Ali was born in a village in Pakistan. He came here as long ago as 1962. He has lived and worked at Hemel Hempstead in Hertfordshire. He has a right of abode here. He went back to Pakistan on visits a couple of times.

B   Ten years afterwards in 1972 he asserted that he had a wife and four children in that same village in Pakistan. He wanted them to come over and join him here in England. She was Rashid Begum, and the children were three boys and one daughter. Farman Ali said he wanted to sponsor them and pay for them here. They applied to the British authorities in Islamabad for entry certificates. The British authorities were very sceptical about their claims. They doubted whether Rashid Begum was really his wife, and they more than doubted whether the children were his children. So they turned down their applications. There were inquiries and appeals. All were turned down until 1978. Until on a final appeal on May 23, 1978, the Immigration Appeal Tribunal allowed their appeal. In their ruling they said:

D   "We have considered all the relevant matters with care and, notwithstanding the inexplicable discrepancies, are satisfied on the balance of probabilities that the appellants are related to the sponsor as claimed. The appeal is accordingly allowed and we direct that the appellants be granted entry certificates to join the sponsor."

The Home Office obeyed that ruling. On June 2, 1978, they sent this telex out to the British Embassy in Islamabad: "Rashid Begum, Mangoo E   Khan, Khalid Khan, Zafar Iqbal, Parveen, Appeals allowed by tribunal. Please issue . . . Settlement Joining Husband/Father (Appeal) . . ."

On June 11, 1978, the British Embassy in Islamabad wrote to them:

"Rashid Begum and children—
"Dear Applicants,
    "With reference to your application for entry clearance, please call F   at this office . . . You should bring with you this letter and your passport."

They were overjoyed. Now after six years they were to get their entry certificates. Of course by this time they were all six years older. In particular the eldest boy, Mangoo Khan (who had been 15 when the application was made in 1972) was now 21. At any rate, mother and G   children went to the Embassy in Islamabad and were granted entry certificate visas on June 26, 1978. Mangoo Khan's was endorsed "Settlement—accompanying mother to join father (appeal)."

Armed with the entry certificates, they made arrangements to come to England in two months' time—to settle here. But in the interval Mangoo Khan got married. It was a family arrangement. On July 28, 1978, he was married to Meniza Begum from the same village in H   Pakistan. He was 21. She was 20. He says that it was only a betrothal and was not followed by cohabitation or consummation. But that point was not pressed before us. It is pretty plain that it was a marriage, and he cannot escape the effect of it by calling it a betrothal.

He did not bring her to England with him. He could not do so. She had no entry certificate. So Mangoo Khan went to England with his mother and the other three children. It was on August 13, 1978, that they arrived at Heathrow. They went before an immigration officer,

Lord Denning M.R.   Reg. v. Home Secretary, Ex p. Mangoo Khan (C.A.)   [1980]

Wendy Boden. She looked at his visa. She saw that it was all in order.
She asked him: "You are coming to join your father?" He said:
"Yes." She granted him "Indefinite leave to enter" and stamped his
passport accordingly.

Now, here is the important point. The immigration officer did not
ask him his age. She did not ask him if he was married. She did not
ask him if he was fully dependent on his father. If she had asked him—
and he had told her that he was a married man—she would have refused
him entry. In order to be eligible under the rules—coming as part of a
family unit—he had to be "an unmarried and fully dependent son under
21": see paragraph 39, Statement of Immigration Rules for Control on
Entry, EEC and other Non-Commonwealth Nationals (1973) (H.C. 81).
Those requisites must be satisfied at the time of entry. Now by
looking at his passport, the immigration officer could see that he was
born on May 20, 1957. So she could have seen that he was over 21. He
was three months over 21 on August 13, 1978, when he presented himself.
By admitting him, the immigration officer certainly waived the requirement that he should be "under 21." By not asking him whether he was
married, did she waive the requirement that he should be "unmarried"?
To this I will return later. The point to notice at the moment is that
here he was in the United Kingdom—a person lawfully here who had
been granted perfectly lawfully "Indefinite leave to enter." So long as
that leave stood unrevoked, he had a perfect right to stay here.

Months passed. Then Mangoo Khan wanted to get his wife, Meniza
Begum, over here to join him. He made the requisite declaration here.
She applied in Islamabad. She was given an entry clearance on May 14,
1979, endorsed "Settlement to join husband." She then arranged her
flight to England and arrived at Heathrow on July 2, 1979. Her husband,
Mangoo Khan, was there to meet her. The immigration officer was
Mrs. Sutton. She asked some questions through an interpreter. Meniza
Begum said she had married Mangoo Khan on July 28, 1978. He
admitted that they had got married after he got his entry certificate. He
said:

> "My mother told me that now I had the entry clearance I should
> get married. I had a say in the arrangements for the marriage. I did
> not bring my wife with me when I came to the United Kingdom in
> August 1978. I decided to leave her behind and call her later. I
> was not asked at Heathrow whether I was married. I arrived with
> my mother, two brothers and my sister."

The immigration authorities felt that, on these answers, they ought to
look further into the matter. They gave the wife temporary admission:
and allowed the husband to go free.

Three weeks later the immigration authorities made up their minds.
They regarded Mangoo Khan as a person who had obtained entry by
deception. On July 22, 1979, he was arrested, taken into custody and
detained in Pentonville Prison. The immigration authorities claimed
authority to do so under paragraph 16 (2) of Schedule 2 to the Immigration Act 1971. At the same time his wife was refused leave to
enter. She lodged an appeal under section 13 (2) of the Act.

After being taken to prison, Mangoo Khan applied for habeas corpus.
In an affidavit of August 14, 1979, he said:

A

" I am not an illegal entrant. I was given leave to enter the United
Kingdom for an indefinite period on 13.8.1978. I submit that my
detention is unlawful."

He was given leave to apply for habeas corpus. On November 13, 1979,
it was refused by a Divisional Court of the Queen's Bench consisting of
Waller L.J. and Park J. He appeals by leave to this court.

B

The relevant provisions

On the return to habeas corpus made by the governor of the prison,
the detention is justified as being authorised under " paragraph 16 (2) of
Schedule 2 to the Immigration Act 1971." That refers back to paragraph
9, which says: " Where an illegal entrant is not given leave to enter or
C remain in the United Kingdom, an immigration officer may give directions," and so forth.

In order to justify the detention, therefore, the immigration officer
must show that Mangoo Khan was " an illegal entrant." That carries us
back to section 33 (1) of the Act of 1971, which says:

D

" . . . ' illegal entrant ' means a person unlawfully entering or seeking to enter in breach of a deportation order or of the immigration
laws, and includes also a person who has so entered; . . ."

" Immigration laws " means this Act—not the rules. The only relevant
immigration law is section 24 (1) (*a*), which makes it a criminal offence—
" if contrary to this Act he knowingly enters the United Kingdom in
breach of a deportation order or without leave."

E

It seems to me, therefore, that, in order to justify the detention of
Mangoo Khan, the immigration officer must show that he entered the
United Kingdom *without leave*.

Did he enter without leave?

On the face of it, Mangoo Khan entered *with leave*. He had an entry
F clearance with a visa endorsed " settlement—accompanying mother to
join father (appeal)." On producing it, the immigration officer granted
him " Indefinite leave to enter." Then how can the immigration authorities say that he entered without leave?

Looking at the matter in principle, it seems to me that everything
depends on whether on August 13, 1978, the grant of " indefinite leave
to enter " was *void* or *voidable*, or *valid*. If it was *void*, it would in law
G be a nullity—from the very beginning. It would be automatically null
and void without more ado. There would in law be no grant of leave at
all. But if it was *voidable*, it would have legal effect up to the time at
which it was set aside. It would, therefore operate so as to be a grant of
leave at the time he entered. If it was valid, clearly he had leave.

Now I can understand that if the immigration officer granted leave
H under a fundamental mistake—as, for instance, if the applicant is guilty
of fraud or misrepresentation of such character as to vitiate the consent—
then the grant of leave is void altogether. Such were the cases of *Reg.* v.
Secretary of State for the Home Department, Ex parte Hussain [1978] 1
W.L.R. 700, and *Reg.* v. *Secretary of State for the Home Department, Ex
parte Choudhary* [1978] 1 W.L.R. 1177. But if he has been guilty of no
fraud or misrepresentation at all—and the mistake is that of the immigration officer alone—then the leave is validly granted, as in *Reg.* v. *Secretary*

Lord Denning M.R.   Reg. v. Home Secretary, Ex p. Mangoo Khan (C.A.)   [1980]

of State for the Home Department, Ex parte Ram [1979] 1 W.L.R. 148.   A
In the present case, I cannot see that Mangoo Khan was guilty of any
fraud or misrepresentation at all.   There had, it is true, been a change
of circumstances.   In 1972, at the age of 15, he was " an unmarried and
fully dependent son under 21 years ": but in 1978 he was married and
independent and over 21 years.   That change of circumstances was such
that the immigration officer might, under the immigration rules, have
refused him leave to enter.   But I do not know that he was under any   B
duty to disclose this change of circumstances to the immigration officer—
unless she asked him.   She could see, by his passport, that he was over
21.   Yet she did not refuse him on that account.   By failing to ask any
questions, she seems to have ignored any change of circumstances—or,
indeed, to have waived any objection on that score.   In any case, I do not
see that this change of circumstances would render the grant of leave void.   C
At most it would render it voidable.   The leave would be good at the time
it was given.   He would not be an illegal entrant at that time.   It would
remain good until set aside.

Test it by assuming that in July 1979 he had gone back to Pakistan
and returned to England bringing his wife with him.   He would be fully
entitled to enter by virtue of his original leave: and he could have
brought her with him.   How then can it be said that the original leave was   D
void?

Mohammed Zamir

Reg. v. *Secretary of State for the Home Department, Ex parte Zamir*
[1980] 2 W.L.R. 357 presents us with a problem.   It was decided on
December 21, 1979.   It appears at first sight to be indistinguishable from   E
the present case.   It is under appeal to the House of Lords.

It seems to me, however, that Stephenson and Brandon L.JJ. inferred
that Zamir obtained leave to enter by deceit.   That was the basis of their
decision.   On the facts of the present case, I would not draw that
inference.   In the absence of deceit, I do not think that this leave should
be regarded as void.   It was valid at the time it was granted.   That means
he was not an " illegal entrant."   Under the statute, an " illegal entrant "   F
is one who *has entered* in breach of the immigration laws.   Mangoo Khan
did not so enter. He may have entered in breach of the immigration rules
(because of the change of circumstances).   But that is not enough.   The
definition in section 33 makes him an illegal entrant only if he is in
breach of the laws, not if he is in breach only of the rules.

G

Conclusion

This case has raised an important point of principle.   It is this.   If a
man arrives at Heathrow with a valid entry clearance honestly obtained,
is he to do more than produce it?   Is he to volunteer more about himself?
Or can he wait until he is asked questions by the immigration officer?

The White Paper issued in November 1979 (Proposals for revision of   H
the Immigration Rules) (Cmnd. 7750) * seems to suggest that it is for
the immigration officer to examine him.   Paragraph 14 says:

" An immigration officer may examine the holder of an entry clearance so far as is necessary to determine whether any of the exceptions
mentioned in paragraph 13 applies, and in determining this question

---

* Not yet laid before Parliament at the date of hearing of the appeal.

The Weekly Law Reports, June 6, 1980

577

1 W.L.R.   Reg. v. Home Secretary, Ex p. Mangoo Khan (C.A.)   Lord Denning M.R.

A   may act on reasonable inferences from the results of that examination and any other information available to him. But the examination should not be carried further than is necessary for this purpose . . ."

This suggests to my mind that, in a case such as the present, when the holder of an entry clearance presents himself, the immigration officer

B   should examine him to see whether there has been a change of circumstances. It should not rest on the man to disclose it. I would hold that there is no duty of disclosure: and that, in the absence of deception, if the man is granted leave to enter, that leave is good. I would, therefore, allow this appeal and grant the habeas corpus.

C   LAWTON L.J. On July 22, 1979, Mangoo Khan was arrested and on July 25, 1979, he was lodged in Pentonville Prison. He had not been charged with a criminal offence nor had he been sent to prison under any order of a court. The authority for detaining him purported to be a detention order issued by an immigration officer under paragraph 16 of Schedule 2 to the Immigration Act 1971. The immigration officer had no power to order his detention unless he was an illegal entrant. The

D   question then is whether he was an illegal entrant. He came into the United Kingdom on August 13, 1978, under an entry certificate which had been granted to him on June 26, 1978. It was endorsed " Settlement —accompanying mother to join father." He was then just over 21, as the British Embassy officials in Islamabad, Pakistan, would have appreciated had they looked at his date of birth as set out in his application for an entry certificate. He did come with his mother and he intended to,

E   and did, join his father. He was interviewed by an immigration officer who did not ask him any questions about either his marital status or his dependency on his father. He was given indefinite leave to stay in the United Kingdom. At that date there was no reason why anyone in the United Kingdom should have thought that he was an illegal immigrant. The Secretary of State, however, alleges that he was.

F   The affidavit upon which the Secretary of State relies, that of Mr. K. V. Osborne, gives the reason. He said:

"... it appeared to the Home Office that the applicant had obtained entry to the United Kingdom in August 1978 on a false basis—that is as the dependent unmarried son of a person settled here when in fact he was already married. Indeed he had stated that his marriage had been deliberately delayed until his visa had been granted. Ac-

G   cordingly he was regarded as a person who had obtained entry by deception in that he had employed for that purpose a visa which he knew related to circumstances which no longer existed and the basis for which had disappeared."

If this allegation was well founded, the applicant was an illegal entrant

H   and his arrest and detention were lawful: see *Reg.* v. *Secretary of State for the Home Department, Ex parte Hussain* [1978] 1 W.L.R. 700.

This way of putting the Secretary of State's case was different from that in which it had been put before the Divisional Court. There it was submitted by counsel (not Mr. Latham) that it had been the duty of the applicant to disclose to the immigration officer at Heathrow that there had been a change of circumstances. In this court, Mr. Latham thought it right to rely upon the ground set out in Mr. Osborne's affidavit. I do

not think it necessary or advisable to make any comments about im- A
migrants having a duty to disclose changes in their circumstances save in
so far as failure to disclose has a bearing on deception.

Whether leave to enter the United Kingdom was obtained by deception is a matter of evidence; and the evidence will vary with each case.
If deception there was, it was practised at Heathrow when the applicant
arrived there on August 13, 1978. It could have been by words or con- B
duct. He said nothing which could have misled the immigration officer.
Beyond presenting his Pakistani passport which was endorsed in the
terms set out in Mr. Osborne's affidavit he did nothing. The only possible
basis for alleging deception is, first, that on January 16, 1974, when he
was 16, he had declared by putting his thumb mark on an application
form for a United Kingdom entry certificate, written in English, that the
information given on it was true and correct and, secondly, that he had C
shown, by getting married when he did, knowledge of the immigration
rules and had arranged his journey to the United Kingdom so as to evade
them.

The Secretary of State has failed to satisfy me that there was anything in the application form which was untrue or incorrect. At the top
of this form there are some notes. One, Note D, is in these terms:
D
> " The holders of entry certificates will be presumed by the im-
> migration officer in the United Kingdom to be qualified for admission
> unless he discovers: (a) that the entry certificate was obtained by
> fraudulent representations or by concealment of facts which the
> applicant knew to be material; or (b) that a change of circumstances
> after issue has removed the basis of the holder's claim to admis-
> sion; ..."
E
In my judgment there is no evidence in this case of fraudulent misrepresentation. There is some evidence that he knew his marriage was
a material fact which he concealed. He married after he got his entry
certificate. That marriage had probably been contemplated for some
time before he got the certificate. He did not bring his wife to the
United Kingdom in August 1978 and when the immigration authorities F
found out about his marriage he claimed untruthfully that he had only
gone through a betrothal ceremony, not a valid marriage. This evidence
must be weighed, however, against the other evidence in the case, which
relates to the way the Embassy staff in Pakistan behaved. When the
official in Islamabad gave the applicant an entry certificate endorsed
" Settlement—accompanying mother to join father " he would have had
the applicant's file in front of him. Had he looked through it, he would G
have appreciated that the applicant was over 21 and had he thought about
what he was doing he would have realised that he was issuing an entry
certificate to a young man who was probably no longer dependent upon
his father but was coming here to find work. Because of the long delays
which had occurred between the making of the application for an entry
certificate and its grant, the circumstances upon which it had been made H
had changed before it was granted, and the likelihood of that change
should have been appreciated by the Embassy official—but he still granted
an entry certificate. He was not granting it under paragraph 39 of the
Immigration Rules because the applicant was over 21 and unlikely still
to be fully dependent on his father. What he was doing was waiving the
rules and granting the applicant an entry certificate as if he were an
adult coming here to work. The basis of the original application had

The Weekly Law Reports, June 6, 1980

579

1 W.L.R.   Reg. v. Home Secretary, Ex p. Mangoo Khan (C.A.)   Lawton L.J.

A gone because of the passing of time and the Embassy official should have appreciated that it had. In my judgment, it would be unreasonable for the Secretary of State to deal with the applicant's case as if he had been someone who had entered the United Kingdom under the rules and in breach of them. He had entered the United Kingdom because an Embassy official in Islamabad had said he could, and he had not deceived the immigration officer at Heathrow by anything he had said or done.

B There was no continuing representation that the circumstances set out in the application for an entry certificate made in 1974 were still continuing so as to impose a duty on the applicant to disclose to the immigration officer that they had changed: see *With* v. *O'Flanagan* [1936] Ch. 575, 584. It was obvious that they had. A duty to disclose not arising out of a representation, if there be any, is far removed in my judgment from the alleged deception upon which the Secretary of State relies.

C I have considered the decision of this court in *Reg.* v. *Secretary of State for the Home Department, Ex parte Zamir* [1980] 2 W.L.R. 357. In that case the applicant was 18 both when he was granted an entry certificate and when he entered the United Kingdom. He did not disclose on entry that he had married after being granted the entry certificate. He was adjudged to be an illegal immigrant. The difference between that

D case and this is that paragraph 39 did apply to Zamir but not to this applicant. Zamir had been granted his entry certificate on the basis that he was a fully dependent son under 21. His marriage was strong evidence that he was no longer " a fully dependent son." This applicant was outside paragraph 39. He had to qualify for entry in his own right.

E The probabilities are that the Embassy official in Islamabad who dealt with him did not read the applicant's file as thoroughly as he should have done; but the applicant was not to know that. If there was slackness in Islamabad on the part of an official which led to the grant of an entry certificate the Secretary of State cannot take advantage of it: see *Reg.* v. *Secretary of State for the Home Department, Ex parte Ram* [1979] 1 W.L.R. 148. In my judgment *Zamir's* case has no relevance to this one.

F I would allow the appeal.

ACKNER L.J. Where a person enters the United Kingdom pursuant to leave to do so which he obtained by deceit, he enters in breach of the immigration laws and is therefore an illegal entrant: *Reg.* v. *Secretary of State for the Home Department, Ex parte Hussain* [1978] 1 W.L.R. 700,

G 707 *per* Geoffrey Lane L.J. The Secretary of State for the Home Department contends that he had reasonable grounds for concluding that the leave to enter obtained by the applicant Mangoo Khan on August 13, 1978, was obtained by deceit. Accordingly when this was discovered, a year later, on July 22, 1979, he was detained under paragraph 16 (2) of Schedule 2 to the Immigration Act 1971. It is therefore contended on behalf of the Secretary of State that this detention was and is lawful.

H The applicant was born in Pakistan on May 20, 1957. He is thus now approaching his 23rd year. When he was 15 years of age his father Farman Ali Khan, who had come and settled in this country in 1962, was anxious that his wife, and his children, that is the applicant, his two brothers and his sister, should join him in this country. An application in writing was therefore made by all five, the wife and the four children, to join Farman Ali in England. The application was first made to the

British Embassy in Islamabad, Pakistan, on September 1, 1972. How- A ever, it was not until after numerous further applications and appeals nearly six years later that the final appeal was heard and determined in favour of the wife and the four children, including the applicant. He was accordingly granted on June 26, 1978, a settlement visa issued by the British Embassy in Islamabad and endorsed " Settlement—accompanying mother to join father."

Although the applicant was 15 years old at the time he made his B application for an entry certificate to join his father, he was a month over 21 when it was granted. This passage of time is, in my view, of considerable relevance. Paragraph 38 of the Statement of Immigration Rules for Control on Entry (H.C. 81) provided that if the requirements of paragraphs 34 and 35 are satisfied (which have no special relevance here), *children under* 18 are to be admitted for settlement if, inter alia, one C parent is settled in the United Kingdom and the other is on the same occasion admitted for settlement. Of course the applicant was within this age limit when his application was made, but well beyond it when the application was granted. Paragraph 39 of the rules provides:

"Generally, children aged 18 or over must qualify for admission in their own right; but, subject to the requirements of *paragraphs* D *34 and 35* an unmarried and fully dependent son under 21 . . . may be admitted if the whole family are settled in the United Kingdom or are being admitted for settlement."

But the applicant was *over 21* and therefore the discretion referred to in this paragraph was not the discretion which was exercised. The visa was not nor could have been granted on the basis that the applicant satisfied E the requirements of this paragraph. Mr. Latham for the Secretary of State concedes that this is so and says that a general overriding discretion was exercised.

Such being the case, it is clear that the requirement that the applicant should be under 21 was waived and it seems to me equally to follow that the requirement that he be fully dependent upon his father was also waived. Mr. Latham did not really seem to argue the contrary. Given F the waiver of those two important factors, it is nevertheless contended that there was no waiver of the third requirement, namely, that the applicant should be unmarried. I am bound to say I do not follow the logic of this. The Secretary of State was bound to concede that the requirement so far as age was concerned had been waived because of the length of time that had gone by. I take it that the waiver with regard G to dependency was on the same basis. Although the representation was sufficiently made in the application form that the applicant, then a boy of 15, was fully dependent upon his father, it would be quite unreal to view that as a continuing representation and to assume, without further inquiry, that six years later it was still the fact. The applicant has ceased to be a boy and has become an adult. There was every reason to assume that by 21 his total dependency had ceased. If reality requires that H approach and accordingly it could not reasonably be said that, six years after the applicant made his application, he was still representing that he qualified for entry either on the grounds of age or dependence, could it reasonably be said that he was still continuing to represent that he was unmarried? I do not consider that after so long a delay between the application for and the grant of the visa any such representation could reasonably be said to have continued. If the applicant's matrimonial

The Weekly Law Reports, June 6, 1980

581

1 W.L.R.   **Reg. v. Home Secretary, Ex p. Mangoo Khan (C.A.)**   Ackner L.J.

A status was then thought to be so important, it should have been inquired into before the grant of the visa.

Some six weeks after he had been granted the visa, the applicant entered the United Kingdom. He came on his own account, although he had a fortnight earlier married Meniza Begum. As far as one can gather from the limited material, on arrival in this country he and his mother, B brothers and sister went to his father's address, 217, Jupiter Drive, Hemel Hempstead, Hertfordshire. Again, as far as the material goes, there is no suggestion that he did not continue to live there until he was arrested on July 22, 1979. When he entered the United Kingdom he was not asked whether he was married and he did not volunteer this information, but on the available material he was complying with the endorsement " Settlement—accompanying mother to join father." On December 28, C 1978, he applied in writing for permission for his wife to come to this country. She arrived on July 2, 1979, but was refused admission on July 22, upon which day, as previously stated, the applicant was arrested.

Mr. Latham for the Secretary of State has argued this appeal on a somewhat different basis to the way in which it was argued by Mr. Simon Brown in the Divisional Court. Mr. Latham has sought to support the D contention put forward by Mr. Osborne, Senior Executive Officer in the Immigration and Nationality Department of the Home Office, that the applicant obtained entry to the United Kingdom in August 1978 on a false basis—that is, as the dependent unmarried son of a person settled here, when in fact he was already married. He thus, it is contended, obtained entry by deception and this nullified the permission that had been granted to him on June 26, 1978. However, the whole foundation E of this submission depends upon the validity of the contention that the application made by Mangoo, when he was 15, operated as a continuing representation that he was unmarried. For the reasons which I have already stated, I do not accept this.

So far as the facts of this case are concerned, they are significantly different from *Reg.* v. *Secretary of State for the Home Department, Ex F parte Zamir* [1979] Q.B. 688 (affirmed on appeal [1980] 2 W.L.R. 357). There, although the application was made when the boy was 15, it was granted when he was 18 and thus the visa was granted on the basis that he satisfied the requirements of paragraph 39 of H.C. 81. Moreover, he admitted that he had come to the United Kingdom principally for work for himself and his wife.

In the Divisional Court the submission which was accepted as the G basis of the refusal of the application for habeas corpus was that there were reasonable grounds for the Secretary of State coming to the conclusion that the applicant Mangoo, when he came into this country in August 1978, concealed the fact that he was married and there was evidence upon which the Secretary of State could properly come to the conclusion that he did so deliberately. Mr. Latham made it clear that H he did not wish to support the decision on those grounds, but upon the much more serious grounds referred to above, which I hold have failed.

Were I wrong in the decision I have reached, then, as I understand the position, if the applicant had entered this country in August 1978 unmarried, it is accepted that he could have then returned by the next plane to Pakistan, married the lady who is his wife, and then lawfully brought her back to this country. That he should destroy both his and the lady's entitlement to live in this country by marrying her just before

he arrived in England would seem to me, in the particular circumstances A
of this case, to be an anomaly that would have done the system no credit.

> *Appeal allowed with costs, including*
> *costs of bail application.*
> *Legal aid taxation of applicant's costs.*
> *Leave to appeal refused.*

B

Solicitors: *Duckney & Co., Southall; Treasury Solicitor.*

M. M. H.

_____

[COURT OF APPEAL]   C

* CINNAMOND AND OTHERS *v.* BRITISH
AIRPORTS AUTHORITY

[1978 C. No. 8971]

1980 Feb. 19, 20, 21, 22   Lord Denning M.R.,   D
                                                Shaw and Brandon L.JJ.

Metropolis—Hackney carriage—London Airport byelaws—" Mini-
cab" drivers with convictions for touting and alleged over-
charging—Ban on entry save as bona fide passenger under
byelaw imposed without prior warning—Whether ban and
byelaw valid—Whether breach of natural justice—Airports E
Authority Act 1975 (c. 78), ss. 2 (1) (3), 9 (1)—Heathrow
Airport—London Byelaws 1972, byelaw 5 (59)

The Airports Authority Act 1975, which consolidates the
Airports Authority Act 1965 and other enactments, provides
by section 1 (1) for the management of Heathrow airport and
other named aerodromes by a body corporate, the British
Airports Authority. By section 2 (1) it is that authority's   F
duty " to provide at its aerodromes such services and facilities as are in its opinion necessary or desirable for their operation " and by subsection (3) the authority " shall have power
to do anything which is calculated to facilitate the discharge
of its duties " under the Act. By section 9 (1), which re-enacts
section 9 (1) of the Act of 1965, the authority " may . . . make
byelaws for regulating the use and operation of the aerodrome
and the conduct of all persons while within the aerodrome . . ." G
  The plaintiffs, six car-hire drivers, after initially setting
down passengers at Heathrow airport, made a practice of
frequenting parts of the airport where passengers arrived in
order to persuade the incoming passengers to hire them for
the journey to the passengers' destinations. The authority,
who received many complaints about the exorbitant fares
charged by such drivers, had tried for some years to stop the
practice, which enabled the drivers to get an advantage over   H
licensed taxi drivers, who charged regular fares. All six
plaintiffs had convictions for offences connected with their
practice at the airport, including loitering and offering services
contrary to byelaws 5 (23) and 5 (55) of the Heathrow Airport
—London Byelaws 1972 [1] (" the byelaws "), made by the

_____

[1] Heathrow Airport—London Byelaws 1972. Byelaw 5 (23): see post, p. 586B.
Byelaw 5 (55): see post, p. 586B–C.
Byelaw 5 (59): see post, p. 589D.

A   authority under the Act of 1965. The total of unpaid fines for
sentences for such convictions in respect of each of the six
plaintiffs ranged from £840 to £2,156.

On November 23, 1978, the authority wrote to each of the
plaintiffs telling him that as from the date of the letter and
" until further notice " he was " prohibited from entering "
the airport save " as a bona fide airline passenger " and that if
in future he was found on the airport except as such a pas-
B   senger the authority would take action under byelaw 5 (59).
Without making any representations to the authority the
plaintiffs issued a writ against the authority claiming declarations that the notice of November 23 was invalid; that byelaw
5 (59) was ultra vires and void and that the authority had no
power to ban them from the parts of the airport to which
the public had access. Forbes J. gave judgment for the
authority.

C   On appeal by the plaintiffs : —
Held, dismissing the appeal, (1) that, since banning the
plaintiffs from entering the airport save as bona fide passengers
was " calculated to facilitate the discharge " of the authority's
duties under section 2 (1) and (3) of the Act of 1975, the
authority had power under the Act to prohibit such entry
indefinitely and it could not be said that the authority acted
unreasonably in making the prohibition (post, pp. 588A–C,
D   591E, G, 592E–F, H).

Associated Provincial Picture Houses Ltd. v. Wednesbury
Corporation [1948] 1 K.B. 223, C.A., considered.

Per Lord Denning M.R. The plaintiffs had abused their
right to enter the airport to set down passengers and became
trespassers ab initio (post, p. 588F).

(2) That (Brandon L.J. dubitante) byelaw 5 (59) sanctioned
a lawful prohibition on entry to the airport by the authority
E   under its powers under the Act of 1975 and was valid (post,
pp. 589H, 591H, 593H—594B).

Per Lord Denning M.R. A byelaw which is desirable for
the operation of an airport should be interpreted so as to
render it valid rather than invalid (post, p. 589F–G).

(3) That since the plaintiffs with their long record of
convictions, unpaid fines and flouting of the regulations had no
F   legitimate expectation of being heard before the ban was
imposed, and moreover had made no immediate representations
to the authority, there had been no breach of natural justice
(post, pp. 590H—591B, 592A–B, 593C–D).

Dicta of Lord Denning M.R. in Reg. v. Gaming Board for
Great Britain, Ex parte Benaim and Khaida [1970] 2 Q.B.
417, 430, C.A. and Norwest Holst Ltd. v. Secretary of State
for Trade [1978] Ch. 201, 224, C.A. applied.

G   Per curiam. The ban on the plaintiffs could be lifted if
they gave suitable undertakings to the authority to comply
with its regulations (post, pp. 589B, 592B, 593B).

Per Brandon L.J. The plaintiffs could not complain of not
having an opportunity to make representations because they
were not prejudiced thereby (post, p. 593F).

Decision of Forbes J. (1979) 77 L.G.R. 730; [1979] R.T.R.
331 affirmed.

H

The following cases are referred to in the judgments:

Associated Provincial Picture Houses Ltd. v. Wednesbury Corporation
    [1948] 1 K.B. 223; [1947] 2 All E.R. 680, C.A.
Barker v. Midland Railway Co. (1856) 18 C.B. 46.
British Trawlers Federation Ltd. v. London and North Eastern Railway
    Co. [1933] 2 K.B. 14, C.A.
Kruse v. Johnson [1898] 2 Q.B. 91, D.C.

Malloch v. *Aberdeen Corporation* [1971] 1 W.L.R. 1578; [1971] 2 All A
    E.R. 1278, H.L.(Sc.).
Norwest Holst Ltd. v. *Secretary of State for Trade* [1978] Ch. 201;
    [1978] 3 W.L.R. 73; [1978] 3 All E.R. 280, C.A.
Perth General Station Committee v. *Ross* [1897] A.C. 479, H.L.(Sc.).
Reg. v. *Gaming Board for Great Britain, Ex parte Benaim and Khaida*
    [1970] 2 Q.B. 417; [1970] 2 W.L.R. 1009; [1970] 2 All E.R.
    528, C.A.
Schmidt v. *Secretary of State for Home Affairs* [1969] 2 Ch. 149; [1969] B
    2 W.L.R. 337; [1969] 1 All E.R. 904, C.A.
Scott v. *Pilliner* [1904] 2 K.B. 855, D.C.
Six Carpenters' Case (1610) 8 Co.Rep. 146a; 1 Smith L.C. 134.
Tarr v. *Tarr* [1973] A.C. 254; [1972] 2 W.L.R. 1068; [1972] 2 All E.R.
    295, H.L.(E.).

The following additional cases were cited in argument: C
Durayappah v. *Fernando* [1967] 2 A.C. 337; [1967] 3 W.L.R. 289;
    [1967] 2 All E.R. 152, P.C.
Mixnam's Properties Ltd. v. *Chertsey Urban District Council* [1965]
    A.C. 735; [1964] 2 W.L.R. 1210; [1964] 2 All E.R. 627, H.L.(E.).
Nagle v. *Feilden* [1966] 2 Q.B. 633; [1966] 2 W.L.R. 1027; [1966] 1 All
    E.R. 689, C.A.
Roberts (Charles) & Co. Ltd. v. *British Railways Board* [1965] 1 W.L.R. D
    396; [1964] 3 All E.R. 651.
Wiseman v. *Borneman* [1971] A.C. 297; [1969] 3 W.L.R. 706; [1969]
    3 All E.R. 275, H.L.(E.).

APPEAL from Forbes J.

By writ of December 1, 1978, the plaintiffs, Norman John Cinnamond, E
Peter Molyneux, and Abdul Aziz Nada, claimed against the British Air-
ways Authority (" the authority "), the defendant, that the notice dated
November 23, 1978, was invalid and an order stopping their banning from
Heathrow Airport until the action was heard. By amendment of April 2,
1979, Hugo Rosato, Thomas Anthony Ryan and Michael Banaster were
added as plaintiffs and declarations were claimed that (1) the notices of
November 23, 1978, were invalid; (2) on its true construction byelaw F
5 (59) of the Heathrow Airport—London Byelaws 1972 did not empower
the authority to ban the plaintiffs from the parts of the airport to which
the public had access; (3) the authority had no power to ban the plaintiffs from such parts; and (4) byelaw 5 (59) was void as being ultra vires
the conferring powers and as being unreasonable. An injunction was
claimed forbidding the authority from making any orders under byelaw
5 (59) with an interim injunction requiring the authority to revoke the G
banning orders, and damages were also claimed.

On April 11, 1979, Forbes J. held that the authority had the power to
ban the plaintiffs from the parts of the airport to which the public had
access and entered judgment for the authority.

The plaintiffs appealed on the grounds that the judge (1) upon the facts
found as to the expectation of the plaintiffs that they could continue to H
bring passengers to the airport and convey passengers to London the
judge should have exercised his discretion so as to make the declarations
asked for; (2) in so far as he held that byelaw 5 (59) of the byelaws was
valid was wrong in law; (3) ought to have held that the authority did
not afford a proper opportunity for the plaintiffs to be heard (contrary
to the rules of natural justice) and that in consequence the operation of
the ban given in the letter of November 23, 1978, was of no effect;

A (4) made no or no sufficient finding of fact that the lawful activities of the plaintiffs were a cloak for illegal activities. If such a finding was made, it was made without regard to the evidence before the court; (5) did not pay sufficient heed to the fact that the authority had on numerous occasions caused the plaintiffs to be prosecuted in the magistrates' courts and that in substance its defence was to seek a civil remedy as in its view the penalities, the maximum amounts of

B which were set out in the authority's Acts, were inadequate; (6) should have held that the appropriate procedure for seeking a civil remedy was through an action moved by the Attorney-General; (7) was wrong in law in so far as he held that the power to ban was valid; (8) made no finding that the power to ban was oppressive and could not be exercised in a reasonable way; (9) should not have refused the declarations or reliefs sought.

C   The facts are stated in the judgment of Lord Denning M.R.

   John Macdonald Q.C. and *Mark Batchelor* for the plaintiffs.
   Richard Fernyhough for the defendant.

D   LORD DENNING M.R. Many years ago Lord Coke had a case about six carpenters. Now we have a case about six car-hire drivers. They have their own cars. They often go to the airport at London Heathrow. On average they go twice a day. They are in touch with hotels in central London. When a passenger wants a car to take him to the airport, the hotel telephones one of these car-hire drivers and he takes the passenger to the airport.

E   Now comes the point. These six car-hire drivers, it is said, hang about the airport and seek to get incoming passengers to hire them for the drive back to London. They thus get ahead of the licensed taxi drivers who are in the feeder parks waiting to be hired. What is worse, it is said that these six car-hire drivers are known to charge the passengers far too much. Whereas the taxi drivers charge the regular fare of about £8, these six car-hire drivers are known to charge £20, £40 or even £100

F for the trip to London.

      Naturally enough, the licensed taxi drivers are incensed because their legitimate business is being " creamed off " in this way. It often happens also that these six car-hire drivers have no legitimate reason to go to the airport. A driver may get up to such a trick as this: he may make out a slip of paper, as if he were engaged to meet an incoming passenger.

G Such as " Mr. Smith, arriving on Flight B.A. 791 due at 11.45 a.m." That slip would be a fake. There would be no Mr. Smith arriving by that flight or any flight. The car-hire driver will not have been employed at all. But the slip of paper serves its turn. By means of it he gets into the airport, and hangs about to " tout " incoming passengers for the trip to London.

      An instance is given in our papers. On March 17, 1979, an overseas

H visitor came from Nigeria at the instance of the British Council. He had on the lapel of his coat a label with " British Council " on it—so as to be able to be picked out by the British Council representative. A car-hire driver came up to him and said, " Hello, British Council. Come with me. I will take you to the Victoria Air Terminal where they are expecting you." At the Victoria Air Terminal he was set down at the entrance. The driver said, " That's £40." When the passenger demurred a little, the car-hire driver said, " It's the recognised fee from the airport."

Other instances are given. Some passengers pay up because they do A
not know the value of English currency. Others because they are
frightened. Others pay up because the driver has the luggage in the
boot and will not allow the passenger to have his luggage until the
payment is made.

The airport authority have for years been trying to stop these car-hire
drivers from doing this. They have prosecuted them for offences under
two byelaws. One byelaw of the Heathrow Airport—London Byelaws B
1972 is no. 5 (23): "No person shall loiter, frequent or remain on the
aerodrome or any part thereof without reasonable cause"—that is the
loitering one. The other byelaw is no. 5 (55):

"No person shall, without the permission of the authority, sell or
distribute anything, offer anything for sale or hire or make any offer
of services"   C

that is the "offering of services" offence: in other words, "touting."

The maximum penalty for breach of any of those byelaws is £100.
The airport authority have prosecuted these six car-hire drivers scores and
scores of times. We have the details given to us in the papers: every few
weeks or so they have been prosecuted, convicted and fined. They do
not pay the fine. They appeal to the Crown Court. That takes 18 D
months or so. The appeal is dismissed. Still they do not pay the fine.
The cases are so numerous that the Crown Court has had to set a limit
to the number of cases they can take. The machinery of collecting fines
is so time-consuming and so fruitless that the car-hire drivers can ignore
them with impunity. We have here the amounts of the fines, and the
totals unpaid. The first driver has £1,715 outstanding: the next one, E
£2,155: the next one, £2,020: the next one £2,156: another £840: and
another £1,476. All outstanding. Even if he paid them, the car-hire
driver would regard them as an expense incurred in the course of his
business—to be set off against his profits.

The prohibition

Seeing that the summonses have proved so useless, the airport F
authority have taken a step which has raised the question in this action.
They go to another byelaw, no. 5 (59):

"No person shall enter the aerodrome, except as a bona fide airline
passenger, whilst having been prohibited from entering by an authorised officer of the authority."   G

Having turned up that byelaw, which they had not used before, on
November 23, 1978, they wrote this letter to each of the six car-hire
drivers in this case:

"Dear Sir,

"The British Airports Authority hereby give you notice that as
from the date of this letter, and until further notice, you are pro- H
hibited from entering Heathrow Airport for any purpose other than
as a bona fide airline passenger.

"If, in future, you are found on Heathrow Airport, except as a
bona fide airline passenger, action will be taken by the British Airports Authority under byelaw 5 (59) of the Heathrow Airport—
London Byelaws 1972, and in addition, the authority will consider
taking injunction proceedings.

The Weekly Law Reports, June 6, 1980

587

1 W.L.R.   Cinnamond v. British Airports Authority (C.A.)   Lord Denning M.R.

A   "A copy of the Heathrow Airport—London Byelaws 1972 is enclosed."

The six car-hire drivers took immediate action. Within seven days they issued a writ, on December 1, 1978, against the airport authority claiming that the notice was invalid and of no effect: and that the byelaw does not empower the authority to ban them from the airport.

B   That raised a very important question for all concerned. Mocatta J. made an order for a preliminary issue. But when it came up before Forbes J. on April 11, 1979, all parties agreed that he should deal with the case as if it were the trial of the action.

Three main points were argued before us. The first was the power of the authority to prohibit entry to the airport—apart altogether from the byelaw. The second was the effect of byelaw 5 (59). The third was the requirements of natural justice.

The power of the authority apart from the byelaws

Mr. Fernyhough submitted that the airport authority was in the same position as a private landlord: and, if it wished, it could prohibit anyone from entering the airport. The only restriction upon the airport authority was its own self-interest—to let people in when it suited them because of their trade. For this proposition he relied on two cases about the railway companies in the last century. One was *Barker* v. *Midland Railway Co.* (1856) 18 C.B. 46, where an omnibus proprietor wanted to carry passengers and their luggage for hire to and from a railway station. When the company refused to allow him to drive his omnibus into the station yard, the court held that the company could stop him. He had no right to come in. The other case was *Perth General Station Committee* v. *Ross* [1897] A.C. 479. The railway had its own hotel in Perth next to the station. Some hotel porters from other hotels in Perth wanted to come into the railway station to collect passengers and their luggage. They wanted to wear their own special hotel livery. The railway company said "No," because they had their own hotel there and did not want the others to compete with them. The House of Lords seems to have held that the railway company had power, like a private landowner, to prohibit anyone they wanted to from coming into the station premises. The only restriction on it was their own self-interest.

To my mind those cases have no application whatever to the statutory corporation here—the airport authority. It is of a different character altogether from the railway companies of the last century. The rights of individuals coming to it are to be found by reference to the words of the statute itself: and for this purpose I would rely upon the more recent case of *British Trawlers Federation Ltd.* v. *London and North Eastern Railway Co.* [1933] 2 K.B. 14, particularly to the passages of Scrutton L.J. at pp. 35 and 36 and Lawrence L.J. at pp. 46 and 47.

So I will turn to the statute itself. Section 2 (1) of the Airports Authority Act 1975 provides:

> "It shall be the duty of the authority to provide at its aerodromes such services and facilities as are in its opinion necessary or desirable for their operation."

Those words "in its opinion" no doubt give the authority a discretion as to the extent of the services and facilities it provides. But once they are provided, it seems to me that there is a right in the travelling public to

The Weekly Law Reports, June 6, 1980

take advantage of those services and facilities. If a bona fide airline   A
passenger comes to the airport, they cannot turn him back—at their own
discretion without rhyme or reason—as a private landowner can. Nor
can they turn back the driver of the car. Nor the friends who come to
help him with the luggage. Nor the relatives who come to see him off.
Save for an exception which is implicit in section 2 (3). It says: " The
authority shall have power to do anything which is calculated to facilitate
the discharge of its duties under this Act." On a proper interpretation   B
of that power, I think that the airport authority can turn a passenger
back, and others too, if the circumstances are such as fairly and reasonably to warrant it. By " reasonably " I take the ordinary meaning of
the word and not the extraordinary meaning which some have placed on
it, and which Mr. Fernyhough asked us to adopt following *Associated
Provincial Picture Houses Ltd.* v.*Wednesbury Corporation* [1948] 1 K.B.   C
223. If that is the position, as I believe it to be, then the airport authority have power to forbid entry if the circumstances fairly and reasonably
warrant that step being taken.

     Take one or two instances: Suppose there is acute congestion of
traffic coming into the airport. The authority can say that only licensed
taxi-cabs are to enter: That they are to be parked in a feeder park in the
aerodrome: and queue up to take on passengers. To avoid congestion,   D
the authority can prohibit the car-hire drivers from jumping the queue
and getting ahead of the regular taxi drivers. Again, if there is an alert
because of terrorist activities, the airport authority can intervene. They
can stop a car to see if the driver or passengers are above suspicion or
not. There are many circumstances in which it is fair and reasonable for
the airport authority to restrict or prohibit entry. Any right to come on   E
to the premises must be subject to that restriction. Entry can be restricted
if the circumstances are such as fairly and reasonably to warrant it.

     Applying that principle to this case, it seems to me that when one of
these car-hire drivers picks up a passenger at a London hotel and drives
to the airport, he has a right to enter so as to drop his passenger and
luggage. But the driver has no right whatever to hang about there so as
to " tout " for a return fare. By so doing he is abusing the right which   F
is given to him by the law: and that automatically makes him a trespasser from the beginning. That is why I referred to the *Six Carpenters'
Case* (1610) 8 Co.Rep. 146a; 1 Smith L.C. 134. It has its parallel here. The
six carpenters went into a wine tavern in the City of London called the
Queen's Head. They had a right by law to enter into it, it being a
common tavern. When they got in there, they ordered a quart of wine   G
and a penny-worth of bread, amounting to 8d. They refused to pay, and
would not pay. The inference was that from the beginning they went in
with the intention of having the wine and the bread and not paying for it.
The court held that they were guilty of a trespass from the beginning.
It was resolved, said Lord Coke at p. 135, that " when entry, authority,
or licence is given to anyone by the law, and he abuses it, he shall be a
trespasser ab initio "—from the beginning. So here. These car-hire   H
drivers abused the authority given to them by the law by hanging about
and " touting." So they became trespassers from the beginning, and can
be turned out. Whether they come with a passenger—and then stop to
" tout "—or whether they come with a faked slip— they are abusing
the authority given by the law. They become trespassers from the
beginning and can be turned out.

The Weekly Law Reports, June 6, 1980

589

1 W.L.R.   Cinnamond v. British Airports Authority (C.A.)   Lord Denning M.R.

A   Such is the position on any single occasion. But, if it goes on time after time—week after week—then it seems to me that, apart from any byelaw, the law gives the airport authority the right to say, " You are prohibited from coming on to these premises any more: because, time after time, you have abused the authority given by law." Apart from the byelaw altogether, I would hold that the airport authority were perfectly in order, and within their rights, in writing the letter of November 23, 1978, in which they prohibited these car-hire drivers from entering the airport until further notice. Mark you—only until further notice. If they show an intention to abide by the law in the future—if they are ready to give an undertaking—there is no doubt that the prohibition will be withdrawn. That has not happened. We have been told that, despite Forbes J.'s decision, these six car-hire drivers have been going on in the same way even since that decision in April 1979 until this very day.

C

The byelaws

The power to make byelaws is given by section 9 of the Airports Authority Act 1975: which contains many safeguards in Schedule 2 to see that they are properly made. Byelaw 5 (59) is invoked by the airport authority:

D

" No person shall enter the aerodrome, except as a bona fide airline passenger, whilst having been prohibited from entering by an authorised officer of the authority."

Is that byelaw valid or not? Mr. Macdonald referred us to *Kruse* v. *Johnson* [1898] 2 Q.B. 91 and *Scott* v. *Pilliner* [1904] 2 K.B. 855. Many years ago I had to consider those cases when I drafted the byelaws for the Southern Railway Co. In those days the courts used to interpret railway byelaws with a jealous eye. Almost malevolently. Prepared to strike them down if on their literal interpretation they could be said to be too wide or too uncertain. To my mind, that approach is entirely out of date—at any rate, in regard to byelaws made by this great statutory authority (the airport authority), with its chairman and board specially selected with all the safeguards required by the statute: and the byelaws confirmed, as they have to be, by the Secretary of State. It seems to me that the approach nowadays should be different in regard to modern byelaws. If the byelaw is of such a nature that something of this kind is necessary or desirable for the operation of the airport, then the courts should endeavour to interpret the byelaw so as to render it valid rather than invalid. The Latin maxim is Ut res magis valeat quam pereat—It is better for a thing to have effect than to be made void. If it is drafted in words which on a strict interpretation may be said to be too wide, or too uncertain, or to be unreasonable, then the court—so long as the words permit it—should discard the strict interpretation and interpret them with any reasonable implications or qualifications which may be necessary so as to produce a just and proper result.

H   So with byelaw 5 (59). In the course of the argument Brandon L.J. suggested that in front of the word " prohibited " we should read " lawfully "—a suggestion with which I entirely concur. It is a lawful prohibition if it is one which is fairly and reasonably warranted by the circumstances of the case. If a lawful prohibition is imposed, and is broken, the person who breaks it is guilty of an offence against the byelaw and in a proper case, he may be arrested: see section 9 (5) and (6) of the Act of 1975. In my opinion the byelaw is valid.

Natural justice

A

I now turn to the last point. What does natural justice demand in such a case as this? Mr. Macdonald said, quite rightly, that nowadays the rules of natural justice apply not only to people doing a judicial act: they often apply to people exercising an administrative power. I should like to say that it depends upon the nature of the administrative power which is being exercised. In *Schmidt* v. *Secretary of State for Home Affairs* [1969] 2 Ch. 149, 170, I said:

B

". . . an administrative body may, in a proper case, be bound to give a person who is affected by their decision an opportunity of making representations. It all depends on whether he has some right or interest, or, I would add, some legitimate expectation of which it would not be fair to deprive him without hearing what he has to say."

C

That is the sort of administrative power upon which a person should be entitled to make representations.

Mr. Macdonald urged us to say that this was such a case: that there ought to have been an opportunity given to these six car-hire drivers so that they could be heard. They might give reasons on which the prohibition order might be modified; or they might be given a little time; or they might be ready to give an undertaking which might be acceptable—to behave properly in future. When it was said that a fair hearing would make no difference, Mr. Macdonald cited a passage from Professor Wade's book *Administrative Law*, 4th ed. (1977), p. 455:

D

". . . in the case of a discretionary administrative decision, such as the dismissal of a teacher or the expulsion of a student, hearing his case will often soften the heart of the authority and alter their decision, even though it is clear from the outset that punitive action would be justified."

E

I can see the force of that argument. But it only applies when there is a legitimate expectation of being heard. In cases where there is no legitimate expectation, there is no call for a hearing. We have given some illustrations in earlier cases. I ventured to give two in *Reg.* v. *Gaming Board for Great Britain, Ex parte Benaim and Khaida* [1970] 2 Q.B. 417, 430. I instanced the Board of Trade when they granted industrial development certificates, or the television authorities when they awarded television programme contracts. In administrative decisions of that kind, a hearing does not have to be given to those who may be disappointed. Only recently in *Norwest Holst Ltd.* v. *Secretary of State for Trade* [1978] Ch. 201, 224 I gave the instance of a police officer who is suspended for misconduct. Pending investigations, he is suspended on full pay. He is not given any notice of the charge at that stage, nor any opportunity of being heard. Likewise the Stock Exchange may suspend dealings in a broker's shares. In none of these cases is it necessary to have a hearing.

F

G

Applying those principles: suppose that these car-hire drivers were of good character and had for years been coming into the airport under an implied licence to do so. If in that case there was suddenly a prohibition order preventing them from entering, then it would seem only fair that they should be given a hearing and a chance to put their case. But that is not this case. These men have a long record of convictions. They have large fines outstanding. They are continuing to engage in conduct which they must know is unlawful and contrary to the byelaws. When

H

The Weekly Law Reports, June 6, 1980

591

1 W.L.R.   Cinnamond v. British Airports Authority (C.A.)   Lord Denning M.R.

A they were summonsed for past offences, they put their case, no doubt, to the justices and to the Crown Court. Now when the patience of the authority is exhausted, it seems to me that the authority can properly suspend them until further notice—just like the police officer I mentioned. In the circumstances they had no legitimate expectation of being heard. It is not a necessary preliminary that they should have a hearing or be given a further chance to explain. Remembering always this: that it
B must have been apparent to them why the prohibition was ordered: and equally apparent that, if they had a change of heart and were ready to comply with the rules, no doubt the prohibition would be withdrawn. They could have made representations immediately, if they wished, in answer to the prohibition order. That they did not do.

The simple duty of the airport authority was to act fairly and reason-
C ably. It seems to me that they have acted fairly and reasonably. I find nothing wrong in the course which they have taken. I find myself in substantial agreement with the judge, and I would dismiss the appeal.

SHAW L.J. I agree. Like Lord Denning M.R. I am of the opinion that in order to decide the issue raised on these appeals it is unnecessary, and indeed it would be wrong, to look outside the provisions of the
D Airports Authority Act 1975 which is a comprehensive statute. Section 1 provides: " There shall continue to be a body corporate called the British Airports Authority . . . which shall manage the aerodromes " mentioned in the subsection, including Heathrow. By section 2 (1) the function and duty of the authority are defined; and by subsection (3) of that section the powers which are relative to that function and duty are
E concisely stated: " The authority shall have power to do anything which is calculated to facilitate the discharge of its duties under this Act."

In my view, unless something which is done can be held not to be reasonably within the purview of the power defined in the term " anything which is calculated to facilitate the discharge of its duties," then the authority could not be challenged in doing what for example they have done in the present case.

F Section 9 which confers a power to make byelaws adds sanctions to the powers of management and administration set out in the earlier sections. It is true that subsection (1) of that section provides that the authority may " make byelaws for regulating the use and operation of the aerodrome and the conduct of all persons while within the aerodrome," but it seems to me that managing the use and operation of the aerodrome involves also a power to exclude altogether persons who have proved
G themselves not to be amenable to having their conduct regulated when they are inside the aerodrome. So on the first point of whether there was a power to exclude, I agree with Lord Denning M.R. and with the judge below that that power did exist.

It is submitted also that byelaw 5 (59) is ultra vires because it goes beyond anything that comes within any power conferred by the Act; but,
H properly understood, byelaw 5 (59) is saying that if there has been a prohibition which can be justified and supported as being within section 2 (3) of the Act, that is, something " calculated to facilitate the discharge " of these duties imposed upon the authority, then a sanction may be added in order to enforce what is a valid and lawful prohibition. I do not look at that byelaw as giving rise to a power to prohibit entry but simply as adding a sanction for the exercise of that power which is derived from section 2 and not from section 9.

As to the suggestion of unfairness in that the drivers were not given an   A
opportunity of making representations, it is clear on the history of this
matter that the drivers put themselves so far outside the limits of tolerable
conduct as to disentitle themselves to expect that any further representations on their part could have any influence or relevance. The long
history of contraventions, of flouting the regulations, and of totally disregarding the penalties demonstrate that in this particular case there was
no effective deterrent. The only way of dealing with the situation was   B
by excluding them altogether.

It does not follow that the attitude of the authority may not change
if they can be persuaded by representations on behalf of the drivers that
they are minded in future to comply with the regulations.

Forbes J. came to the right conclusion, and I too would dismiss the
appeal.   C

BRANDON L.J. I would divide the points arising on this appeal into
five. The first question is whether the prohibition against entry into the
airport was valid. It was submitted that the airport authority had power
to issue that prohibition because they were owners of the land comprising the airport, and on that ground alone they were entitled to exclude
anybody except, as I understand it, a would-be passenger. Reliance was   D
placed in that connection on the railway cases to which Lord Denning
M.R. referred in his judgment.

For my part I would prefer to express no opinion on the question as
to whether those railway cases are applicable to the present case or not
because I do not find it necessary to do so.

It was submitted in the alternative that the airport authority had   E
power to prohibit entry under the powers conferred on them by section
2 (1) and (3) of the Act of 1975. It seems to me that that submission is
well-founded. The authority were entitled to exclude any person if that
was calculated to facilitate the discharge of their duties under the Act.
They took the view that to exclude these minicab drivers after their
previous conduct over many years was calculated to facilitate the discharge of their duties under the Act. So it seems to me that, subject to   F
such restraints as are imposed by the requirement not to act arbitrarily,
and so on, the airport authority had power to exclude these minicab
drivers from the aerodrome.

The second question is whether, having that power, they abused it in
any way by exceeding it or by acting on improper material or by not
having regard to proper material in coming to their decision. It was   G
common ground between counsel that the test of whether they abused
their powers or not was governed by the principles laid down in the
Wednesbury Corporation case [1948] 1 K.B. 223. For the minicab
drivers it was argued that the prohibition was an abuse of power in that
it was too wide. It was said that it was too wide because it prohibited
entry for all purposes save travelling as a bona fide air passenger; it was
not necessary to have such an extensive prohibition in order to achieve   H
the aim of the airport authority. Then it was said that it was too wide
because it was indefinite as to time; it should have been for a limited
period.

I do not accept these submissions. It seems to me that it would be
quite impossible to say that the airport authority in the circumstances of
this case was acting in a way that no reasonable airport authority could
act in making the prohibition as extensive as they did. So far as exclud-

The Weekly Law Reports, June 13, 1980

593

1 W.L.R.   Cinnamond v. British Airports Authority (C.A.)   Brandon L.J.

A ing entry for any purpose other than travelling as a bona fide passenger is concerned, it seems to me that the previous conduct of the minicab drivers has shown that, if they are allowed to enter on any pretext whatsoever, they will be likely to abuse their position. Nor was there any evidence that they had ever desired in the past, or would ever desire in the future, to use the airport for any other purposes than those for which they had abused it in the past.

B As regards the question of time, this is not a permanent prohibition. It is an indefinite prohibition. It is always open to the minicab drivers to apply for it to be ended. The position is that they had a licence for many years to come into the airport, and that licence has been revoked. If they desire the licence to be renewed, there is nothing to stop them applying to the airport authority to ask for a renewal subject to suitable C undertakings.

So I cannot see that there was any abuse by the airport authority of its power to exclude persons from the aerodrome.

The third question which was argued before us was that of natural justice. So far as that is concerned, I agree with what has been said by Lord Denning M.R. and Shaw L.J. I do not think that in the circum-D stances of this case there was any need to give these minicab drivers an opportunity to make representations to the authority before they issued the ban. The reason for the ban must have been well known when the letters were received. Any representations which were desired to be made could have been made immediately by letter. None were. The truth is that no representations other than representations which included satisfactory undertakings about future behaviour would have been of the E slightest use.

If I am wrong in thinking that some opportunity should have been given, then it seems to me that no prejudice was suffered by the minicab drivers as a result of not being given that opportunity. It is quite evident that they were not prepared then, and are not even prepared now, to give any satisfactory undertakings about their future conduct. Only if F they were would representations be of any use. I would rely on what was said in *Malloch* v. *Aberdeen Corporation* [1971] 1 W.L.R. 1578, first *per* Lord Reid at p. 1582 and secondly *per* Lord Wilberforce at p. 1595. The effect of what Lord Wilberforce said is that no one can complain of not being given an opportunity to make representations if such an opportunity would have availed him nothing.

G The fourth point argued was the validity of byelaw 5 (59). I must confess that I have felt considerable difficulty about the question whether this byelaw is within the powers conferred by section 9 of the Act of 1975. That section empowers the authority to make byelaws regulating the use and operation of the aerodrome. That is a general power, and the section also gives power in particular to make byelaws prohibiting or restricting access to any part of the aerodrome.

H It has been laid down by the House of Lords that in general the expression " regulating " does not include prohibiting unless the context specially requires it: *Tarr* v. *Tarr* [1973] A.C. 254. I have some difficulty in construing the words " regulating the use of the aerodrome " as including prohibiting its use by someone. Then as to the particular power to make byelaws " prohibiting or restricting access to any part of the aerodrome," it seems to me that that is intended to deal with the prevention of someone who has entered the aerodrome going to a parti-

cular part of it rather than the prevention of someone going into the
aerodrome at all. If the latter meaning were intended, one would expect
the words to be "prohibiting or restricting access to the aerodrome or
any part of it."

On the other hand, it is necessary to consider the broad purposes of
the Act and the great problems which the airport authorities face in
maintaining security and control at an airport. Bearing in mind these
considerations, I am not sufficiently persuaded, on the basis of the points
which I have mentioned, to disagree with Lord Denning M.R. and Shaw
L.J. that this byelaw was within the powers of section 9. I have doubts
about it, but I am not prepared to disagree on the matter.

The fifth and last point which was argued was in regard to the power
of the court, even if it were thought that either the ban or the byelaw
were invalid, nevertheless to refuse relief in its discretion because the
claim came from persons with so little merit. Since I take the view that
there is nothing to declare void or invalid, I do not think it is necessary
to express any opinion on that further question.

For the reasons which I have given, I also would dismiss the appeal.

> *Appeal dismissed with costs.*
> *Leave to appeal refused.*

Solicitors: *Somers & Leyne; Richard Everitt.*

A. H. B.

May 1, 1980. The Appeal Committee of the House of Lords (Lord
Wilberforce, Viscount Dilhorne and Lord Scarman) dismissed a petition
by the plaintiffs for leave to appeal.

[COURT OF APPEAL]

* FEDERATED HOMES LTD. *v.* MILL LODGE PROPERTIES LTD.

[1978 F. No. 1296]

1979 Nov. 23, 26, 27, 28, 29   Megaw, Browne and Brightman L.JJ.

*Restrictive Covenant—Enforceability—Annexation—Conveyances
from common owner—Defendants as original purchasers of
one part subject to restrictive covenant — Plaintiffs as successors in title of original purchasers entitled to benefit of
covenant—Conveyance of part to plaintiffs containing express
assignment of benefit—Other part registered — Transfer of
second part containing no express assignment — Whether
covenant personal to common owner — Whether covenant
annexed to land—Law of Property Act 1925 (15 & 16 Geo.
5, c. 20), s. 78*[1]

In September 1970 M. Ltd. bought four equal-sized areas
of land (" red, green, pink and blue land ") and obtained
outline planning permission on the conditions, inter alia, that
applications for the planning authority's approval, where
necessary, should be made in writing within three years and

[1] Law of Property Act 1925, s. 78: see post, p. 604A–B.

A that the permission was to enure for the benefit of M. Ltd. and their subsidiaries and related to, among others, approximately 1,250 private residential dwellings. M. Ltd. simultaneously entered into a phasing agreement with the planning authority whereby provisions were made for the disclosure of the agreement on a sale, for M. Ltd. to assign the burden and benefit of the agreement and for the rate of development

B so that the development would be completed by 1980. On February 26, 1971, M. Ltd. conveyed the blue land to the defendant expressly making it subject to the phasing agreement. By clause 5 (iv) the defendant covenanted with M. Ltd. that, in carrying out the development of the blue land the defendant would not build at a greater density than 300 dwellings so as not to reduce the number of units which M. Ltd. might eventually erect on the retained land under the existing planning permission. Clause 2 of the defendant's conveyance

C contained a reference to the retained land as " any adjoining or adjacent property retained by " M. Ltd. By a conveyance dated March 25, 1971, the red and green land was conveyed to B. Ltd. who conveyed the green land to the plaintiff. Both conveyances contained express assignments of the benefit of the covenant in the defendant's conveyance. B. Ltd. conveyed the red land to another purchaser assigning the benefit of the covenants. The title to that land was registered at the Land

D Registry. The purchaser transferred it to the plaintiff but the transfer did not contain any express assignment of the benefit of the covenant. The outline planning permission lapsed in 1973. The defendant carried out development of the blue land under new planning permissions granted to them in 1971 and 1972 for a total of 300 dwellings. In 1977 the plaintiff applied for planning permission in respect of the red and green land and discovered that the defendant had obtained planning

E permission for the erection of 32 additional dwellings on the blue land and that adversely affected the development on the plaintiff's land. On September 20, 1978, the plaintiff issued a writ seeking to restrain the defendant from building on the blue land at a greater density than 300 dwellings. The deputy High Court judge granted the injunction.

On appeal by the defendant: —

Held, dismissing the appeal, (1) that since the planning

F permission by its terms was available to a subsidiary of M. Ltd. it was not exclusive to M. Ltd. and its benefit was therefore assignable; that the restrictive covenant contained in clause 5 of the defendant's conveyance was not personal to M. Ltd. but, in accordance with business realities, its benefit was assignable and that it was not spent for the covenant and the original planning permission were not rigidly linked together and it was more natural and businesslike to read the reference

G to the existing planning permission as explanatory and not as controlling so that the benefit of the covenant in relation to the green land reached the plaintiff through an unbroken chain of assignments and that was sufficient to entitle the plaintiff to relief (post, pp. 601G–H, 602A–C, 603A–B, 607G–H).

(2) That on the true construction of section 78 of the Law of Property Act 1925, providing that the condition precedent of a covenant relating to the land of the covenantee in the

H sense of touching and concerning the land was fulfilled, the benefit of that covenant ran with the land and was annexed to it; accordingly, since the condition precedent was satisfied, the plaintiff could enforce the covenant against the defendant in respect of the red land as well as the green land and, there being no adequate ground for refusal of an injunction, the injunction should be upheld (post, pp. 603H, 604F–G, 607C–F, G–H).

Shelfer v. *City of London Electric Lighting Co.* [1895] 1 Ch. 287 applied.

Decision of John Mills Q.C. sitting as a deputy judge of A
the Chancery Division affirmed.

The following cases are referred to in the judgments:

Drake v. *Gray* [1936] Ch. 451; [1936] 1 All E.R. 363, C.A.
Rogers v. *Hosegood* [1900] 2 Ch. 388, C.A.
Russell v. *Archdale* [1964] Ch. 38; [1962] 3 W.L.R. 192; [1962] 2 All
E.R. 305.
B
Sefton v. *Tophams Ltd.* [1967] 1 A.C. 50; [1966] 2 W.L.R. 814; [1966]
1 All E.R. 1039, H.L.(E.).
Shelfer v. *City of London Electric Lighting Co.* [1895] 1 Ch. 287, Keke-
wich J. and C.A.
Smith and Snipes Hall Farm Ltd. v. *River Douglas Catchment Board*
[1949] 2 K.B. 500; *sub nom. Smith* v. *River Douglas Catchment
Board* [1949] 2 All E.R. 179, C.A.
Union of London and Smith's Bank Ltd.'s Conveyance, In re [1933] Ch.
C
611, C.A.
Williams v. *Unit Construction Co. Ltd.* (1951) 19 Conveyancer 262, C.A.

The following additional cases were cited in argument:

Doherty v. *Allman* (1878) 3 App.Cas. 709, H.L.(I.).
Ecclesiastical Commissioners for England's Conveyance, In re [1936] Ch.
D
430.
Goldberg v. *Edwards* [1950] Ch. 247, C.A.
Green v. *Ashco Horticulturist Ltd.* [1966] 1 W.L.R. 889; [1966] 2 All
E.R. 232.
Johnson v. *Agnew* [1979] 2 W.L.R. 487; [1979] 1 All E.R. 883, H.L.(E.).
Kelly v. *Barrett* [1924] 2 Ch. 379, C.A.
Marten v. *Flight Refuelling Ltd.* [1962] Ch. 115; [1961] 2 W.L.R. 1018;
[1961] 2 All E.R. 696.
E
Prenn v. *Simmonds* [1971] 1 W.L.R. 1381; [1971] 3 All E.R. 237,
H.L.(E.).
Reardon Smith Line Ltd. v. *Yngvar Hansen-Tangen* [1976] 1 W.L.R.
989; [1976] 3 All E.R. 570, H.L.(E.).
Shayler v. *Woolf* [1946] Ch. 320; [1946] 2 All E.R. 54, C.A.
Suisse Atlantique Société d'Armement Maritime S.A. v. *N.V. Rotter-
damsche Kolen Centrale* [1967] 1 A.C. 361; [1966] 2 W.L.R. 944;
F
[1966] 2 All E.R. 61, H.L.(E.).

APPEAL from John Mills Q.C. sitting as a deputy judge of the
Chancery Division.

On September 20, 1978, the plaintiff, Federated Homes Ltd., issued a
writ seeking to restrain the defendant, Mill Lodge Properties Ltd. (" Mill
G
Lodge "), from building or attempting to build at a greater density than
a total of 300 dwellings in carrying out the development of the land in the
parish of Newport Pagnell, Buckinghamshire, containing 35.93 acres or
thereabouts which was described as " the blue land " in the conveyance
dated February 26, 1971, and made between Mackenzie Hill Ltd. of the
first part, Wm. Brandt's Sons and Co. Ltd. of the second part and Mill
Lodge of the third part.
H
Mr. John Mills gave judgment on June 29, 1979, holding that the
covenant or proviso contained in clause 5 (iv) of the conveyance related
to land and enured for the benefit of successors in title of the covenantee
and that the plaintiff was entitled in equity to the benefit of such covenant
or proviso and accordingly entitled to enforce the same against Mill
Lodge. His Lordship ordered that Mill Lodge be restrained from building
or attempting to build more than 300 dwellings on the blue land.

A   By a notice of appeal dated July 4, 1979, Mill Lodge appealed on the grounds, inter alia, that the judge was wrong in holding (a) that the benefit of the covenant or proviso was not personal to the covenantee and was assignable; (b) that the covenant related to land; and (c) that the covenant related to land and accordingly enured for the benefit of successors in title of the covenantee. Furthermore, the judge, in construing the covenant, misdirected himself in giving no weight or insufficent weight to the terms
B   and conditions of the outline planning permission of the Buckinghamshire County Council dated September 18, 1970, which was expressly referred to in the covenant. The judge was wrong in holding that the plaintiff was entitled in equity to the benefit of the covenant and that section 62 of the Law of Property Act 1925 incorporated into a transfer dated March 18, 1975, and made between U.D.T. Properties Ltd. of the first part and the
C   plaintiff of the second part the benefit of the covenant to the plaintiff not-withstanding the absence of express words of assignment in the transfer. The judge in granting an injunction exercised his discretion perversely in that having regard to the manifest purpose of the covenant or proviso and to the evidence before him damages were the appropriate remedy.

      The facts are stated by Brightman L.J.

D
      Leolin Price Q.C. and *Martin Mann* for Mill Lodge.
      M. A. F. Lyndon-Stanford Q.C. and *R. G. B. McCombe* for the plaintiff.

      MEGAW L.J. I shall ask Brightman L.J. to deliver the first judgment in this matter.

E   BRIGHTMAN L.J. This is an appeal from a judgment of Mr. Mills Q.C., sitting as a deputy High Court judge of the Chancery Division. The dispute relates to a large development site near Newport Pagnell in Buckinghamshire. This site consists of four areas of land of roughly equal size which can for convenience, be called the red, green, pink and blue land. There were also included in the development site certain
F   additional bits of land which I shall ignore.
      The plaintiff company is now owner of the red and the green land. The defendant company, Mill Lodge Properties Ltd. (which I shall call " Mill Lodge "), is the owner of the blue land. The plaintiff claims to be entitled to the benefit of a restrictive covenant which is said to debar Mill Lodge from building more than 300 houses on the blue land. Mill Lodge is in the process of exceeding that density by building an additional 32
G   houses in conformity with a new planning permission which it has obtained. The judge decided against Mill Lodge and granted an injunction.
      In September 1970 a company called Mackenzie Hill Ltd. (which I shall refer to as " Mackenzie Hill ") was about to become the owner of the site. On September 18 the Buckinghamshire County Council, as planning authority acting through the Newport Pagnell Urban District Council as its
H   agent, granted outline planning permission to Mackenzie Hill to develop the site by the provision of housing and associated amenities.
      There were a number of conditions attached to the permission, of which the important ones were these:

      " 1. The approval of the county council shall be obtained to the number, siting, design and external appearance of the buildings, (except the schools), and the means of access thereto before the development is commenced. . . . 2. This permission shall be null and void if the

approval of the county council to all the matters referred to in the last A
preceding condition has not been applied for in writing within three
years. . . ."—i.e., by September 1973. " 4. This permission shall
enure only for the benefit of the applicants and their subsidiaries.
5. This permission shall relate to the erection of a church/community
centre, a shopping cluster, a petrol filling station, a public house, and
approximately 1,250 private residential dwellings. . . ."
                                                                        B
Condition 8 specified the rate of development, but this topic was covered
in a revised form by the agreement to which I shall next refer.

On the same day as the planning permission Mackenzie Hill entered
into an agreement with the urban district council, which has been called
the phasing agreement. By this agreement the council undertook to
construct roads and sewers through the site and Mackenzie Hill agreed C
to contribute towards the cost. Clause 7, so far as material, reads as
follows (in the clause the expression " developers " means Mackenzie Hill
and " H.1." means the development site):

" (a) If the developers shall desire to sell the whole or any part of
H.1. they shall forthwith inform the council and the terms and
conditions of such sale or sales shall include the disclosure of this
agreement to the purchasers and provisions to safeguard the council's D
position under this agreement which shall be to the satisfaction of
the council . . . provided that this sub-clause shall not apply to the
sale of any single completed dwelling to an individual purchaser.
(b) The developers shall have the right to assign the burden and
benefit of this agreement but shall not be released from their
obligations hereunder on any such assignment unless the proposed E
assignees shall have first furnished the council with a bond . . ."

By clause 9 (a) Mackenzie Hill agreed that the rate of development
should not exceed 50 houses by the end of 1970 and a further 125 houses
in each of the years 1971 and 1972. The rate of development was then
to be reviewed with the possibility of an increase, but not a decrease,
in the rate. On that basis the development would be completed in or F
before 1980 according to whether or not the rate of development
ultimately exceeded a minimum of 125 houses a year. That rate of
development differed slightly from the rate laid down in the planning
permission and that, no doubt, was the reason for clause 9 (e) of
the phasing agreement, whereunder Mackenzie Hill covenanted with the
council that they would enter into an agreement under seal with the G
council on or before December 14, 1970, incorporating the terms of
clause 9 (a).

It seems to me, reading clauses 7 and 9 (e), that the urban district
council contemplated that Mackenzie Hill might not itself develop, but
might part with the development in favour of someone else. Furthermore, as it was the urban district council which had, on the same day H
as the phasing agreement, in its capacity as agent for the Buckinghamshire County Council, granted the planning permission to Mackenzie
Hill, the planning permission ought fairly to be read in conjunction with
the phasing agreement.

On February 26, 1971, Mackenzie Hill and its mortgagee sold and
conveyed the blue land to Mill Lodge. By clause 3 the conveyance was
expressed to be subject to and with the benefit of the phasing agreement.

The Weekly Law Reports, June 13, 1980

599

1 W.L.R.   Federated Homes Ltd. v. Mill Lodge Ltd. (C.A.)   Brightman L.J.

A Clause 5 (iv) set out the covenant which is the subject matter of this action. It reads:

> "The purchaser hereby covenants with the vendor that . . . (iv) in carrying out the development of the 'blue' land the purchaser shall not build at a greater density than a total of 300 dwellings so as not to reduce the number of units which the vendor might eventually
>
> B erect on the retained land under the existing planning consent."

There was a simultaneous conveyance of the pink land to a company called Gough Cooper (Midland) Ltd. (which I shall abbreviate to " Gough Cooper "). Clause 6 of the Mill Lodge conveyance provided that the blue land was sold with the benefit, so far as the same related to the blue land, of the agreements and undertakings on the part of Gough Cooper C contained in the Gough Cooper conveyance. Clause 7 of the Mill Lodge conveyance contained a covenant by Mackenzie Hill with Mill Lodge expressed to be for the benefit of the blue land and every part thereof that Mackenzie Hill would not build houses on the red and green land, with an immaterial exception, before the date on which Mill Lodge had erected or had permission from the planning authority under any revised phasing agreement to erect 300 dwellings on the blue land or January 1, D 1975, whichever should happen first, but not in any event earlier than January 1, 1974.

The Mill Lodge conveyance contains no express definition of the retained land. There is, however, a reference in clause 2 to " any adjoining or adjacent property retained by the vendor." I read " the retained land " in clause 5 (iv) as meaning just that. I do not accept E the submission of the plaintiff's counsel that the retained land included the pink land; clause 6 makes it clear that the pink land was not retained, but was being simultaneously conveyed to Gough Cooper. Counsel invited us to look at the contract of sale to Mill Lodge for the purpose of resolving an ambiguity as to the meaning of the retained land, but I see no ambiguity. I, therefore, conclude that the retained land means the red and the green land and the small additional areas comprised in the F site, other, of course, than the blue and the pink land. To avoid confusion, I think I ought to explain that the expression " the green land " is made use of in the Mill Lodge conveyance, but it means both the red and green land as I use those expressions in this judgment.

The Gough Cooper conveyance is not, in my view, relevant to the construction of the Mill Lodge conveyance, but it is permissible to refer G to it as part of the backcloth against which the Mill Lodge conveyance was made, since the Gough Cooper conveyance is referred to in the Mill Lodge conveyance as a document of simultaneous execution. Clause 4 of this conveyance was obviously intended to cover the same subject matter as clause 5 (iv) of the Mill Lodge conveyance and was in the following terms:

H
> "The purchaser for itself and its successors in title hereby covenants with the vendor and its successors in title that the purchaser shall not build on the land hereby conveyed at a greater density than a total of 300 dwellings so as not to reduce the number of units which the vendor might eventually erect on the land edged green on the said plan under the existing planning consent obtained by the vendor in respect of the whole of the land edged red edged blue and edged green on the said plan."

Clause 6 of the Gough Cooper conveyance is the counterpart of and has   A
much the same wording as clause 7 of the Mill Lodge conveyance, in
effect binding Mackenzie Hill to give precedence to the purchasers'
building programme in the operation of the phasing agreement.

A month later Mackenzie Hill sold and conveyed the red and the
green land to William Brandt's Sons & Co. Ltd. (which I shall call
" Brandt's "). Brandt's was in fact Mackenzie Hill's mortgagee of the
blue and the pink land at the time of the earlier conveyance, but nothing   B
turns on that. The conveyance to Brandt's was dated March 25, and it
contained an express assignment of the benefit of the covenant contained
in the Mill Lodge and the Gough Cooper conveyance.

Just under a year later Brandt's sold and conveyed the green land to
the plaintiff. This conveyance, which was dated February 25, 1972,
likewise contained an express assignment of the benefit of those covenants.   C

Shortly afterwards Brandt's and the plaintiff conveyed the red land
to B.T.A. Trading Co. Ltd. In that conveyance the plaintiff was the
purchaser and B.T.A. was the sub-purchaser. This conveyance, which
is dated March 1, 1972, also contained an express assignment of the
benefit of the covenants. Following that conveyance B.T.A.'s title
became registered at the Land Registry.   D

On March 18, 1975, B.T.A., which by then had changed its name to
U.D.T. Properties Ltd., sold and conveyed the red land to the plaintiff.
This conveyance was in the form of a transfer applicable to registered
land. It did not contain any express assignment of the benefit of the
covenants in the Mill Lodge and the Gough Cooper conveyances.

The original outline planning permission granted in 1970 lapsed in
1973 because approval of the county council to all the matters referred   E
to in condition 1 had not been applied for in respect of the total site
within three years. In fact, Mill Lodge proceeded with the separate
development of the blue land under new planning permissions granted in
1971 and 1972 for a total of 300 dwellings.

Towards the end of 1977 the plaintiff applied for planning permission
in respect of the red and the green land. The balance of density left   F
available for these areas, having regard to the Mill Lodge and Gough
Cooper conveyances, was approximately 650 dwellings if the principle of
the 1970 planning permission still applied. The application was, in fact,
for a much greater density, but after a planning inquiry the 1970 density
of about 1,250 dwellings for the entire site was reaffirmed. It was at
about this time that the plaintiff discovered that, on January 9, 1975,
Mill Lodge had obtained planning permission for the erection of an   G
additional 32 dwellings on the blue land. It is not in dispute that the
existence of such additional dwellings would or might prejudice the
plaintiff in relation to the development that might be permitted on
the red and the green land; and, therefore, if the plaintiff's rights would
be infringed by the building of the further 32 dwellings, the plaintiff
would suffer damage.   H

In September 1978, after much prevarication on the part of Mill
Lodge, the plaintiff issued a writ to restrain Mill Lodge from building on
the blue land at a greater density than a total of 300 dwellings in breach,
it was alleged, of clause 5 (iv) of the Mill Lodge conveyance. The
defences raised by Mill Lodge so far as relied upon in this appeal were
as follows: (1) the covenant in clause 5 (iv) was said to be personal to
Mackenzie Hill so that the benefit thereof was incapable of assignment

The Weekly Law Reports, June 13, 1980

601

1 W.L.R.   Federated Homes Ltd. v. Mill Lodge Ltd. (C.A.)   Brightman L.J.

A to the plaintiff; (2) alternatively, it was said that the covenant became spent when the 1970 planning permission became void at the end of the three-year period; and (3) it was said that, if the covenant was assignable and was not spent, then the benefit had not become vested in the plaintiff by assignment or otherwise.

That, in broad effect, was how the defence was pleaded so far as relevant for present purposes. In a reserved judgment Mr. Mills held
B that the covenant was not personal to Mackenzie Hill and was not spent when the original planning permission lapsed. As regards the transmission of the benefit of the covenant, he held that the benefit was not annexed to the red and the green land, so that it did not automatically pass upon conveyances of the red and the green land. However, he found, as was clearly the fact, that there was an unbroken chain of
C assignments between transferor and transferee of the green land, so that the benefit of the covenant was now vested, by reason of such assignments, in the plaintiff as the present owner of the green land. There was no such unbroken chain of assignments in the case of the red land; but the judge considered that section 62 of the Law of Property Act 1925, which implies general words into a conveyance of land, was apt to carry the benefit of the covenant from U.D.T. Properties Ltd., the previous
D assignee of such benefit, to the plaintiff when the registered transfer in its favour was made. The defence, therefore, failed. The judge rejected a submission that damages would be the proper remedy. He granted an injunction against building in excess of the permitted density and gave liberty to apply for a mandatory injunction.

I deal first with the question of construction, upon which two issues
E arise: whether the covenant was personal to Mackenzie Hill, and whether it is spent.

Mr. Price, for Mill Lodge pointed out that the planning permission was expressed by condition 4 to enure for the benefit of Mackenzie Hill and its subsidiaries. That meant that a purchaser from Mackenzie Hill, not being a subsidiary company, had no legal right as between itself and the Buckinghamshire County Council to rely on the planning permission
F as authority to carry out development which would otherwise be contrary to planning legislation. Possibly the condition was inserted to enable the planning authority to object to development by somebody of whom it did not approve. Mr. Price sought to argue from this that the covenant in the Mill Lodge conveyance was personal to Mackenzie Hill and not assignable. It was designed, he submitted, to protect a non-assignable
G planning permission and therefore should itself be treated as non-assignable.

I do not think that Mill Lodge can gain much comfort from the form of the planning permission. The planning permission was certainly not exclusive to Mackenzie Hill because it was available to a subsidiary of Mackenzie Hill; so the benefit was clearly assignable to that extent.
H Theoretically, and not I think as a matter of reality, there was nothing in the planning permission to prevent the assignment of the benefit. The only restriction was that the proprietor who ultimately relied upon the permission would have to be either Mackenzie Hill or a subsidiary. There could, in theory, be any number of intermediate transfers of the land, with the benefit of the permission, through persons who would not have been themselves qualified to rely upon the permission. I think this is a narrow point and I do not stress it.

Mr. Price also relied upon the fact that clause 5 is penned as a covenant with the vendor (no mention of assigns) and that it is linked with the number of dwellings which the vendor (again no mention of assigns) might erect on the retained land.

But, apart from these considerations, I entirely agree with Mr. Mills when he said that it is neither necessary nor natural nor sensible to read the covenant as personal to Mackenzie Hill. Generally speaking, the benefit of a contract between businessmen is assignable without mention of assignability unless the contract is of a personal nature, which the restrictive covenant was not. Furthermore, clause 3 of the Mill Lodge conveyance stated that the property was sold subject to and with the benefit of the phasing agreement and, as I have already mentioned, clauses 7 and 9 (e) of that agreement in terms contemplated that Mackenzie Hill might sell the development site in whole or part. So it is hardly possible to argue that the parties *must* have contracted on the basis that Mackenzie Hill personally would develop the retained land. I conclude that the restrictive covenant was not personal, but was assignable, which seems to me to correspond with business realities.

If there were still any doubt, section 78 of the Law of Property Act 1925, in my view, sets that doubt at rest. For it provides that a covenant relating to any land of the covenantee shall be deemed to have been made with the covenantee and his successors in title, which presupposes assignability. I shall have occasion in due course to examine this section at greater length.

I turn to the defence that the covenant is now spent as the 1970 planning permission has lapsed. The concluding words of clause 5 (iv) are: " so as not to reduce the number of units which the vendor might eventually erect on the retained land under the existing planning consent." As no dwellings can now be erected in reliance upon the original planning consent, the covenant has, it was argued, lost its purpose. This resolves itself into the question whether the concluding words form an integral part of the restrictive covenant or are merely explanatory of the covenant without controlling it. I think that the answer is largely a matter of impression and is not susceptible of prolonged argument. It does, however, seem to me a little unlikely that the parties intended to tie the restrictive covenant to the original planning permission so that the covenant and the permission should stand and fall together. There would seem no purpose in such rigidity. There must always have been a strong possibility, if not a likelihood, that a developer would have to apply for a new planning permission at some stage (as happened) because the three-year deadline for seeking planning approval for the siting, design and external appearance of the buildings and the means of access thereto does not fit easily into the 10-year phasing of the development.

There is the additional consideration that, if the covenant were linked to the 1970 planning permission, it is difficult to see its value. The 1970 planning permission was to become void if detailed approval were not applied for in relation to the entire site within three years. As Mackenzie Hill was selling off and therefore not developing the blue and the pink land, the 1970 planning permission seems to me to have had a very doubtful future. It could hardly have been anticipated that Mackenzie Hill would be applying for detailed approval for the development of land which was going to be developed by others. There was no covenant by Mill Lodge or Gough Cooper to apply for detailed approval

The Weekly Law Reports, June 13, 1980

603

1 W.L.R.   Federated Homes Ltd. v. Mill Lodge Ltd. (C.A.)   Brightman L.J.

A within the three-year period; so the covenant, if linked to and dependent upon the 1970 planning permission, becomes somewhat of a nonsense as Mr. Price was, I think, constrained to admit. I think that the more natural and businesslike construction of the subclause is to read the reference to the existing planning permission as explanatory and not as controlling.

B Having reached the conclusion that the restrictive covenant was capable of assignment and is not spent, I turn to the question whether the benefit has safely reached the hands of the plaintiff. The green land has no problem, owing to the unbroken chain of assignments. I am disposed to think that that is sufficient to entitle the plaintiff to relief, and that the plaintiff's right to relief would be no greater at the present time if it were held that it also had the benefit of the covenant in its

C capacity as owner of the red land. However, the judge dealt with both areas of land and I propose to do the same.

An express assignment of the benefit of a covenant is not necessary if the benefit of the covenant is annexed to the land. In that event, the benefit will pass automatically on a conveyance of the land, without express mention, because it is annexed to the land and runs with it. So the issue of annexation is logically the next to be considered.

D The judge said in his judgment:

" The next heading with which I must deal is ' annexation,' to which I will now come. It is a somewhat technical thing in the law of restrictive covenants. A good deal of argument was addressed to me on annexation by both sides. Submissions were made about express annexation, implied annexation, that is to say, annexation

E implied from surrounding circumstances, and annexation by assignment. In my judgment, there was in this case no ' annexation ' of the benefit of the covenant to the retained land or any part of it. Section 78, in particular, of the Law of Property Act 1925 does not have the effect of annexing the benefit of the covenant to anything. It is simply a statutory shorthand for the shortening of conveyances,

F which it perhaps has done to some extent in this case. Annexation depends upon appropriate drafting, which is not here in this case, in spite of a recent process which can perhaps be called ' a widening of the law ' in these matters. The attendant circumstances moreover, positively militate against annexation because, as Mr. Price rightly pointed out to me (though he did so in the course of his argument on construction) the restriction in this particular case is of limited

G duration and plainly not applicable to ultimate purchasers of plots of the land intended to be benefited. ' Annexation,' in my judgment, is for the parties to the covenant itself to achieve if they wish to, and (though parties may no doubt provide for annexation at a later stage) I am not satisfied or prepared to hold that there is any such thing as ' delayed annexation by assignment ' to which the convenantor is

H not party or privy."

The reference to " delayed annexation by assignment " is to a proposition that a covenant can, on a later assignment, thereby become annexed to the land by the act of the assignor and the assignee alone.

In my judgment the benefit of this covenant was annexed to the retained land, and I think that this is a consequence of section 78 of the Act of 1925, which reads:

Brightman L.J.   Federated Homes Ltd. v. Mill Lodge Ltd. (C.A.)   [1980]

" (1) A covenant relating to any land of the covenantee shall be A deemed to be made with the covenantee and his successors in title and the persons deriving title under him or them, and shall have effect as if such successors and other persons were expressed. For the purposes of this subsection in connexion with covenants restrictive of the user of land ' successors in title ' shall be deemed to include the owners and occupiers for the time being of the land of the covenantee intended to be benefited. (2) This section applies B to covenants made after the commencement of this Act, but the repeal of section 58 of the Conveyancing Act 1881 does not affect the operation of covenants to which that section applied."

Mr. Price submitted that there were three possible views about section 78. One view, which he described as " the orthodox view " hitherto held, is that it is merely a statutory shorthand for reducing the length of legal C documents. A second view, which was the one that Mr. Price was inclined to place in the forefront of his argument, is that the section only applies, or at any rate only achieves annexation, when the land intended to be benefited is signified in the document by express words or necessary implication as the intended beneficiary of the covenant. A third view is that the section applies if the covenant in fact touches and concerns D the land of the covenantee, whether that be gleaned from the document itself or from evidence outside the document.

For myself, I reject the narrowest interpretation of section 78, the supposed orthodox view, which seems to me to fly in the face of the wording of the section. Before I express my reasons I will say that I do not find it necessary to choose between the second and third views E because, in my opinion, this covenant relates to land of the covenantee on either interpretation of section 78. Clause 5 (iv) shows clearly that the covenant is for the protection of the retained land and that land is described in clause 2 as " any adjoining or adjacent property retained by the vendor." This formulation is sufficient for annexation purposes: see *Rogers* v. *Hosegood* [1900] 2 Ch. 388.

There is in my judgment no doubt that this covenant " related to the F land of the covenantee," or, to use the old-fashioned expression, that it touched and concerned the land, even if Mr. Price is correct in his submission that the document must show an intention to benefit identified land. The result of such application is that one must read clause 5 (iv) as if it were written: " The purchaser hereby covenants with the vendor and its successors in title and the persons deriving title under it or them, including the owners and occupiers for the time being of the retained G land, that in carrying out the development of the blue land the purchaser shall not build at a greater density than a total 300 dwellings so as not to reduce, etc." I leave out of consideration section 79 as unnecessary to be considered in this context, since Mill Lodge is the original covenantor.

The first point to notice about section 78 (1) is that the wording is H significantly different from the wording of its predecessor section 58 (1) of the Conveyancing Act 1881. The distinction is underlined by section 78 (2), which applies section 78 (1) only to covenants made after the commencement of the Act. Section 58 (1) of the Act of 1881 did not include the covenantee's successors in title or persons deriving title under him or them, or the owner or occupiers for the time being of the land of the covenantee intended to be benefited. The section was confined, in

The Weekly Law Reports, June 13, 1980

605

1 W.L.R.   Federated Homes Ltd. v. Mill Lodge Ltd. (C.A.)   Brightman J.

A relation to realty, to the covenantee, his heirs and assigns, words which suggest a more limited scope of operation than is found in section 78.

If, as the language of section 78 implies, a covenant relating to land which is restrictive of the user thereof is enforceable at the suit of (1) a successor in title of the covenantee, (2) a person deriving title under the covenantee or under his successors in title, and (3) the owner or occupier of the land intended to be benefited by the covenant, it must, in my view,
B follow that the covenant runs with the land, because ex hypothesi every successor in title to the land, every derivative proprietor of the land and every other owner and occupier has a right by statute to the covenant. In other words, if the condition precedent of section 78 is satisfied—that is to say, there exists a covenant which touches and concerns the land of the covenantee—that covenant runs with the land for the benefit of
C his successors in title, persons deriving title under him or them and other owners and occupiers.

This approach to section 78 has been advocated by distinguished textbook writers; see Dr. Radcliffe's article " Some Problems of the Law Relating to Restrictive Covenants " (1941) 57 L.Q.R. 203, Professor Wade's article, " Covenants—A Broad and Reasonable View " and the apt cross-heading " What is wrong with section 78? " [1972B] C.L.J. 151,
D 171, and Megarry and Wade, The Law of Real Property, 4th ed. (1975), p. 764. Counsel pointed out to us that the fourth edition of Megarry and Wade indicates a change of mind on this topic since the third edition.

Although the section does not seem to have been extensively used in the course of argument in this type of case, the construction of section 78 which appeals to me appears to be consistent with at least two cases
E decided in this court. The first is Smith and Snipes Hall Farm Ltd. v. River Douglas Catchment Board [1949] 2 K.B. 500. In that case an agreement was made in April 1938 between certain landowners and the catchment board under which the catchment board undertook to make good the banks of a certain brook and to maintain the same, and the landowners undertook to contribute towards the cost. In 1940 the first
F plaintiff took a conveyance from one of the landowners of a part of the land together with an express assignment of the benefit of the agreement. In 1944 the second plaintiff took a tenancy of that land without any express assignment of the benefit of the agreement. In 1946 the brook burst its banks and the land owned by the first plaintiff and tenanted by the second plaintiff was inundated. The two important points are that the agreement was not expressed to be for the benefit of the landowner's
G successors in title; and there was no assignment of the benefit of the agreement in favour of the second plaintiff, the tenant. In reliance, as I understand the case, upon section 78 of the Act of 1925, it was held that the second plaintiff was entitled to sue the catchment board for damages for breach of the agreement. It seems to me that that conclusion can only have been reached on the basis that section 78 had the
H effect of causing the benefit of the agreement to run with the land so as to be capable of being sued upon by the tenant.

The other case, Williams v. Unit Construction Co. Ltd. (unreported in the usual series of law reports but fully set out in 19 Conveyancer 262), was decided by this court in 1951. There a company had acquired a building estate and had underleased four plots to Cubbin for 999 years. The underlessors arranged for the defendant company to build houses on the four plots. The defendant covenanted with Cubbin to keep the

adjacent road in repair until adopted. Cubbin granted a weekly tenancy
of one house to the plaintiff without any express assignment of the
benefit of the covenant. The plaintiff was injured owing to the disrepair
of the road. She was held entitled to recover damages from the defendant
for breach of the covenant.

We were referred to observations in the speeches of Lord Upjohn
and Lord Wilberforce in *Sefton* v. *Tophams Ltd.* [1967] 1 A.C. 50, 73
and 81, to the effect that section 79 of the Act of 1925, relating to the
burden of covenants, achieved no more than the introduction of statutory
shorthand into the drafting of covenants. Section 79, in my view,
involves quite different considerations and I do not think that it provides
a helpful analogy.

It was suggested by Mr. Price that, if this covenant ought to be read
as enuring for the benefit of the retained land, it should be read as enuring
only for the benefit of the retained land as a whole and not for the
benefit of every part of it; with the apparent result that there is no
annexation of the benefit to a part of the retained land when any
severance takes place. He referred us to a passage in *In re Union of
London and Smith's Bank Ltd.'s Conveyance* [1933] Ch. 611, 628, which
I do not think it is necessary for me to read.

The problem is alluded to in *Megarry and Wade, The Law of Real
Property*, 4th ed., p. 763.

" In drafting restrictive covenants it is therefore desirable to annex
them to the covenantee's land ' or any part or parts thereof.' An
additional reason for using this form of words is that, if there is
no indication to the contrary, the benefit may be held to be annexed
only to the whole of the covenantee's land, so that it will not pass
with portions of it disposed of separately. But even without such
words the court may find that the covenant is intended to benefit
any part of the retained land; and small indications may suffice,
since the rule that presumes annexation to the whole only is arbitrary
and inconvenient. In principle it conflicts with the rule for assignments, which allows a benefit annexed to the whole to be assigned
with part, and it also conflicts with the corresponding rule for
easements."

I find the idea of the annexation of a covenant to the whole of the
land but not to a part of it a difficult conception fully to grasp. I can
understand that a covenantee may expressly or by necessary implication
retain the benefit of a covenant wholly under his own control, so that
the benefit will not pass unless the covenantee chooses to assign; but I
would have thought, if the benefit of a covenant is, on a proper construction of a document, annexed to the land, prima facie it is annexed to
every part thereof, unless the contrary clearly appears. It is difficult to
see how this court can have reached its decision in *Williams* v. *Unit
Construction Co. Ltd.*, 19 Conveyancer 262, unless this is right. The
covenant was, by inference, annexed to every part of the land and not
merely to the whole, because it will be recalled that the plaintiff was a
tenant of only one of the four houses which had the benefit of the
covenant.

There is also this observation by Romer L.J. in *Drake* v. *Gray* [1936]
Ch. 451, 465. He was dealing with the enuring of the benefit of a
restrictive covenant and he said:

The Weekly Law Reports, June 13, 1980

607

1 W.L.R.   Federated Homes Ltd. v. Mill Lodge Ltd. (C.A.)   Brightman J.

A

" . . . where one finds not ' the land coloured yellow ' or ' the estate '
or ' the field named so and so ' or anything of that kind, but ' the
lands retained by the vendor,' it appears to me that there is a
sufficient indication that the benefit of the covenant enures to every
one of the lands retained by the vendor, and if a plaintiff in a
subsequent action to enforce a covenant can say: ' I am the owner
of a piece of land that belonged to the vendor at the time of the

B

conveyance,' he is entitled to enforce the covenant."

In the instant case the judge in the course of his judgment appears
to have dismissed the notion that any individual plot-holder would be
entitled, even by assignment, to have the benefit of the covenant that
I have been considering. I express no view about that. I only say this,
that I am not convinced that his conclusion on that point is correct. I

C

say no more about it.

In the end, I come to the conclusion that section 78 of the Law of
Property Act 1925 caused the benefit of the restrictive covenant in
question to run with the red land and therefore to be annexed to it, with
the result that the plaintiff is able to enforce the covenant against Mill
Lodge, not only in its capacity as owner of the green land, but also in

D

its capacity as owner of the red land.

For these reasons I think that the judge reached the correct view on
the right of the plaintiff to enforce the covenant, although in part he
arrived there by a different route.

There remains only the question whether we ought to interfere with
the remedy granted by the judge of an injunction against the building

E

of the 32 extra dwellings. *Shelfer* v. *City of London Electric Lighting
Co.* [1895] 1 Ch. 287 is authority for the proposition that a person
who has the benefit of a restrictive covenant is, as a general rule, entitled
to an injunction on the trial of the action as distinct from an award
of damages unless (1) the injury to the plaintiff's legal rights is small,
(2) it is capable of being estimated in terms of money, (3) it can
adequately be compensated for by a small payment, and (4) it would be

F

oppressive to the defendant to grant an injunction. In my view, the
first, third and fourth of these conditions have not been shown to be
satisfied.

I would therefore, uphold the injunction and I would dismiss this
appeal.

G

BROWNE L.J. I agree that this appeal should be dismissed for the
reasons given by Brightman L.J. I agree so entirely with the judgment
that he has delivered that there is nothing I can usefully add.

MEGAW L.J. I also agree with the conclusion reached by Brightman
L.J. for the reasons given by him. There is only one matter on
which I would desire to add a few words. That is in respect of the

H

passage quoted by Brightman L.J. towards the end of his judgment from
the judgment of Romer L.J. in *Drake* v. *Gray* [1936] Ch. 451, 465. It
is right to observe that the passage which Brightman L.J. read has been
the subject of criticism by Buckley J. in *Russell* v. *Archdale* [1964]
Ch. 38, 47. Buckley J. suggested that the passage in question in
Romer L.J.'s judgment was obiter dictum and that there was difficulty
in accepting the distinction which Romer L.J. there drew between, on
the one hand, land described as the land marked yellow on the plan or

Megaw L.J.   Federated Homes Ltd. v. Mill Lodge Ltd. (C.A.)   [1980]

the estate of the vendor known as such and such a name and, on the   A
other hand, reference to the remaining land or retained land. It is,
however, right to point out that Buckley J. said, at p. 47: "No doubt
every case of this kind, being one of construction, must be determined on
the facts and the actual language used," and he went on to say that,
with the utmost respect to Romer L.J. he could not see that the distinction was a valid one.

For myself, I would regard the observations made in the passage   B
which Brightman L.J. read from *Megarry and Wade, The Law of
Real Property*, 4th ed., p. 763, as being powerful reasons, and I find
great difficulty in understanding how, either as a matter of principle,
or as a matter of practical good sense in relation to a legal relationship
of this sort, it can be said that a covenant, which ex hypothesi has been
annexed to the land as a whole, is somehow or other not annexed to the
individual parts of that land. I agree that the appeal should be dismissed.   C

> *Appeal dismissed with costs.*
> *Leave to appeal refused.*

Solicitors: *Blyth, Dutton, Holloway for Coffin, Mew & Clover, Havant;
Eatons.*
D

A. R.

<hr>

[EMPLOYMENT APPEAL TRIBUNAL]

** GREATER LONDON COUNCIL v. FARRAR   E

1979 Nov. 19   Slynn J., Miss J. Collerson
and Mr. A. C. Blyghton

*Discrimination, Sex—Employment—Statutory authority—Wrestling
licences issued under local authority statute—Prohibition on
women's wrestling—Woman wrestler refused employment by   F
promotions company—Industrial tribunal's finding that local
authority to be treated as committing act of discrimination—
Whether discrimination in compliance with requirements of
instrument made under prior statute lawful—Sex Discrimination Act 1975 (c. 65), ss. 42 (1), 44, 51 (1)*

Pursuant to the local authority's right to impose restrictions
on wrestling licences, in accordance with Schedule 12 to the   G
London Government Act 1963, licences were issued for
premises, subject to a provision prohibiting women's wrestling.
The complainant, a woman wrestler, was refused employment
by a promotions company because of the restriction in the
licence. She applied to an industrial tribunal for a declaration
against the local authority that they had discriminated against
her on the ground of her sex in that by prohibiting women's
wrestling they had knowingly aided the promotions company   H
to do an act made unlawful by the Sex Discrimination Act
1975 and, as a result of section 42 (1) of the Act,[1] they were
to be treated as doing the unlawful act themselves.

<hr>

[1] Sex Discrimination Act 1975, s. 42: "(1) A person who knowingly aids
another person to do an act made unlawful by this Act shall be treated for the
purposes of this Act as himself doing an unlawful act of the like description."
S. 44: see post, p. 613B–C.
S. 51 (1): see post, p. 611A.

A   The tribunal found that since the passing of the Sex Discrimination Act 1975 a condition prohibiting women's wrestling was unlawful and that by imposing the restriction in the licence the local authority had aided the company in the commission of an unlawful act within the meaning of section 42. They further found that section 44 of the Act did not operate so as to exclude women's wrestling from the provisions of the statute since the section did not include sport where

B   women were matched against other women. The tribunal held that the complainant was entitled to a declaration that she had been unlawfully discriminated against.

      On an appeal by the local authority on the grounds that they were entitled to rely on the statutory defence contained in section 51 (1) and that women's wrestling was excluded under section 44: —

C   *Held*, allowing the appeal, that a local authority licence was an instrument made or approved under an Act within the meaning of section 51 (1) (*b*) of the Act of 1975; that the relevant question was not whether the condition in the licence was unlawful but whether it was intra vires the Act under which it was made; and that since the local authority were empowered under the London Government Act 1963 to impose restrictions on wrestling licences, the provisions of

D   section 51 (1) applied and the company was entitled to refuse to employ the complainant in order to comply with the terms of the licence even where the licence was issued after the enactment of the Sex Discrimination Act 1975 (post, pp. 611E–H).

      Per curiam. Section 44 is dealing with a situation in which men and women might both be playing in the same game or taking part in the same event. It is not dealing with the situation where it is desired that a girl should play a game

E   against a girl or where teams of girls are to play teams of girls (post, p. 613G–H).

      Quaere. Whether " aids " in section 42 (1) should be construed as meaning " aiding and abetting " in the technical sense used in criminal statutes or as " assisting or supporting " (post, p. 612H—613A).

      The following cases are referred to in the judgment:

F   *Associated Provincial Picture Houses Ltd.* v. *Wednesbury Corporation* [1948] 1 K.B. 223; [1947] 2 All E.R. 680, C.A.
      Bennett v. *Football Association Ltd.,* July 28, 1978; Court of Appeal (Civil Division) Transcript No. 591 of 1978, C.A.

      No additional cases were cited in argument.

G   APPEAL from an industrial tribunal sitting in London.
      The local authority, the Greater London Council, appealed from a decision of the industrial tribunal on February 26, 1979, granting an application for relief for unlawful discrimination on the ground of sex by the complainant, Marjorie Farrar. They appealed on the grounds that the industrial tribunal had erred in law in their construction of sections

H   42 (1), 44 and 51 (1) of the Sex Discrimination Act 1975.
      The facts are stated in the judgment.

      Gerald Angel for the local authority.
      Frederic Reynold for the complainant.

      SLYNN J. delivered the following judgment of the appeal tribunal. The complainant, Mrs. Farrar, is a professional wrestler. She wrote to a

A company called Verdun Leslie Promotions asking for an engagement in wrestling productions arranged by them. They told her that they had absolutely nothing against her as a wrestler but that the wrestling licence issued by the Greater London Council, the local authority in respect of the particular premises at which the programmes were to take place, forbade the use of women wrestlers.

B The complainant applied to an industrial tribunal for a declaration against the local authority that they had discriminated against her on the ground of her sex. The tribunal which heard the matter came to the conclusion that they had jurisdiction to hear the application, and, having gone, with obvious care, into the matters which were raised by the parties, they concluded that the case had been made out.

C An industrial tribunal has jurisdiction to deal with claims under this legislation where an application is brought under Part II of the Sex Discrimination Act 1975, alleging that there has been discrimination in the field of employment. But, in addition, a complainant may go to a tribunal if by virtue of either section 41 or section 42 of the Act a person is to be treated as having himself done the act. There is, of course, here, no question of the local authority itself employing or refusing employment to the complainant. What was said here was that the local authority had knowingly aided another person to do an act made unlawful by the Act of 1975 and so was to be treated as itself having done that act.

D The case comes about in this way. Under the London Government Act 1963 there are provisions as to the licensing of theatres and other places of public entertainment. Section 52 (3) of the Act takes one to Schedule 12; there we find specific provisions about the licensing of premises for boxing and wrestling. Paragraph 4 (2) of the Schedule provides that wrestling is not to take place otherwise than at premises licensed for the purpose in accordance with the provisions of paragraph 4 of the Schedule and in accordance with the terms of the licence. Paragraph 9 of the Schedule provides that the council may make regulations prescribing the terms, conditions and restrictions subject to which licences are to be granted. The licences which are granted by the local authority for premises where wrestling is to take place contain a provision which prohibits women from wrestling there. That apparently has been the policy of the local authority both before and after the passing of the Act of 1975.

E The first matter that really arose for decision before the industrial tribunal was whether this condition contained in the licence was in itself lawful. The industrial tribunal considered that even though before the Act of 1975 it would have been open to the local authority to include this condition, it could not after the Act include a condition or restriction which was not lawful in the sense that it was a contravention of the Act. So they said that the condition which was imposed was unlawful. The tribunal also went on to decide that by imposing this condition the local authority had aided the company in the commission of an unlawful act, on the basis that it was the local authority which had instigated and caused the company to discriminate against the complainant.

The local authority appeal against that decision. They contend that the industrial tribunal has failed to give proper effect to the provisions of the Act of 1975. They rely upon the terms of section 51 (1) of the Act of 1975:

A " Nothing in Parts II to IV shall render unlawful any act done by a person if it was necessary for him to do it in order to comply with a requirement—(a) of an Act passed before this Act: or (b) of an instrument made or approved (whether before or after the passing of this Act) by or under an Act passed before this Act."

It is conceded here, as obviously it must be, that this policy adopted
B by the local authority does in fact discriminate against woman wrestlers because they are women. But, it is said, that is not the end of the case: the question is first whether what is done is unlawful on the part of the company and, secondly, whether the local authority aided within the meaning of section 42 of the Act. And so it is said that even if, here, men are treated more favourably than women on the ground of their sex, and even if, but for the provisions of section 51, it would have been
C unlawful for the company to refuse the complainant employment because she was a woman, nonetheless section 51 means that their refusal is lawful.

It is accepted on behalf of the complainant—we think rightly accepted —by Mr. Reynold that a licence, which is given by the local authority under the London Government Act 1963, is an instrument made or
D approved under an Act of Parliament. But, Mr. Reynold says, even assuming that that is correct, here the condition imposed since the passing of the Act of 1975 is not one which can validly be included; it is accordingly void; it must therefore be ignored when looking at the act of the company in refusing the complainant employment and, accordingly, no reliance can be placed on section 51 of the Act.

The industrial tribunal, acceded to this submission. They appear to
E have been of the view that, now, conditions cannot be included in licences of this kind if they permit conduct which would be in conflict with the Act of 1975.

We take the view that the question in any case is whether what has been done by the instrument is something which falls within the powers of the Act under which it was made. There is no doubt here that this
F licence was granted, and thereby made or approved, under an Act of Parliament on the face of it clearly giving powers to the local authority to include such terms as they thought right for the granting of the licence. Parliament, by section 51, has excluded from the ambit of Parts II to IV of the Act of 1975 acts necessary to comply with a requirement of a statute passed before the Act of 1975 or an instrument made or approved under it. It does not seem to us that the Act under which
G the instrument is made must itself specifically require that the act of the kind which is complained about shall be done. But for the provisions of the Act of 1975 it is not suggested that the licence was other than intra vires. The question is whether the Act of 1975 requires as a matter of law that this condition shall be removed. It does not seem to us that the Act of 1975 does require the condition to be removed. On the contrary,
H as long as it is valid within the Act of 1963, it seems to us that Parliament has expressly validated or excluded from the area of illegality anything which is done as a result of a requirement in that Act or an instrument made under it.

Mr. Reynold says that in continuing to include this condition the local authority have violated the principle set out in Associated Provincial Picture Houses Ltd. v. Wednesbury Corporation [1948] 1 K.B. 223. That case stresses that where discretion is given to an authority the courts will not interfere except in a limited number of cases. For this A purpose the relevant ones are where the authority has failed to have regard to matters to which it should have had regard or has taken into account wholly irrelevant matters. Now it is clear here that the local authority did consider the effect of the 1975 legislation upon what had been their policy. They considered the matter in committee and before the council, and eventually, after a decision of the council by a majority, it was decided that they should preserve the conditions of the licence B which were accepted to be otherwise intra vires under the London Government Act 1963. So it cannot be said here that they have left the matter out of account altogether. Can it be said that the decision of the local authority in this case is so unreasonable that they must have misdirected themselves in some way? To some people this policy—which apparently is not followed by some authorities, although it is followed by others— C may in the present climate of opinion be surprising; and it may be a policy with which some people do not agree. But the matter has been gone into, as we see it, at length and in depth, as the voting and discussion in council and in committee reveal. Whatever our own views individually as members of this appeal tribunal may be, whatever we may think about it, we do not find it possible to say here that this decision of the local authority is so unreasonable that there must have been some D misdirection or misapplication of the discretion which is vested in them.

Then Mr. Reynold says that, here, the inclusion of this condition is unlawful because it is the instructing by the local authority of another person to do an unlawful act by virtue of Part II and therefore is an instruction to discriminate within the meaning of section 39 of the Act; alternatively, that it is the exercising of pressure to discriminate contrary E to section 40 of the Act. We do not agree with those submissions. It seems to us that the industrial tribunal erred when they said that before a condition can be included it has to be one which is not contrary to the principles or provisions of the Act of 1975. It seems to us that section 51 (1) (b) is expressly keeping alive instruments which can be made intra vires under previously existing legislation whether those instruments were made before or after the Act. It does not seem to us that if an F authority makes an instrument under the provisions of the Act of 1963 which itself would contravene or lead to the contravention of the Act of 1975 but for the instrument, that that amounts to an instruction to discriminate or pressure to discriminate within the meaning of section 39 or 40 of the Act. If Parliament had intended that all instruments made subsequent to the Act of 1975 were to comply with the provisions G of that Act and that other legislation should be treated as amended accordingly, it would have said so. It seems to us that it said precisely the opposite. The question of the policy to be applied in situations like the present is, of course, one for the local authority and we say no more about it.

If that is right and the licence validated the refusal by the company of employment because the complainant could not lawfully appear at H these particular premises in London, then there can be no question of the local authority knowingly aiding another person to do an act made unlawful by the Act of 1975.

There has been some argument before us as to the meaning of the word " aids " in the present case. We would be reluctant to construe the word " aids " as meaning aiding and abetting in the technical sense which has been adopted in many criminal statutes and to introduce it

A into this legislation. For the purposes of this case we would accept the
submission made by Mr. Angel, and accepted as a matter of first impression by Mr. Reynold, that " aiding " here means assisting or supporting.
We do, however, leave this matter open for another occasion because we
see force in Mr. Reynold's submission that if it is construed in this way
there may be gaps in the legislation. That however can wait for another
day.

B   The other matter which is put forward by the local authority, to
exempt them from any liability under this legislation, is the provision
contained in section 44 of the Act of 1975:

    " Nothing in Parts II to IV shall, in relation to any sport, game
    or other activity of a competitive nature where the physical strength,
C   stamina of physique of the average woman puts her at a disadvantage
    to the average man, render unlawful any act related to the partici-
    pation of a person as a competitor in events involving that activity
    which are confined to competitors of one sex."

    The industrial tribunal said that they found the section was not very
easy to construe and we confess that we find ourselves in the same
D position. The Court of Appeal has considered it in *Bennett* v. *Football
Association Ltd.* (unreported), July 28, 1978. That was a case where
a 12-year-old girl wanted to play football either in a mixed team or in
teams which would be playing against boys. The Court of Appeal had
no doubt that her claim failed. Lord Denning M.R. said, Court of
Appeal Civil Division Transcript No. 591 of 1978:

E   " Just reading [section 44], it seems to me that football is a
    game which is excepted from this statute. It is a game which on
    all the evidence here the average woman is at a disadvantage to the
    average man because she has not got the stamina or physique to
    stand up to men in regard to it."

On two further occasions Lord Denning M.R. said that football was a
F game which was completely outside the Sex Discrimination Act 1975.
The other members of the Court of Appeal (as we read it) agreed with
him. We have no doubt, on the basis of that decision, and from our
own reading of the section, that in a case where it is desired to exclude,
for example, a girl from a mixed team, or to exclude girls from playing in
teams against other boys or men, such an exclusion would not be unlawful for the purposes of the Act of 1975.

G   But it seems to us that this section is dealing with a situation in which
men and women might both be playing in the same game or taking part
in the same event. It is in that situation that the disadvantage of the
woman because of physical strength, stamina or physique would become
a relevant matter. It does not seem to us that this section is dealing
with the situation where it is desired that a girl should play a game
H against a girl, or where teams of girls are to play teams of girls.
Accordingly on this point we accept the submissions of Mr. Reynold.
We read the decision of the Court of Appeal as applying to the particular
facts before it. Had we been in the complainant's favour on the
section 51 point, we would also have been in her favour on this point.
But, in the circumstances, it seems to us that the words of section
51 (1) (*b*) do expressly contemplate that provisions may be made under
instruments even after the passing of the Act of 1975 which prevent

A

from being unlawful acts which otherwise would be unlawful under the
provisions of Part II of the Act.

Appeal allowed.
Leave to appeal

Solicitors: *R. A. Lanham; Birdman & Partners.*

B

J. W.

[COURT OF APPEAL]

C

* GAMLEN CHEMICAL CO. (U.K.) LTD. *v.*
ROCHEM LTD. AND OTHERS

[1974 G. No. 3313]

1979 Dec. 3, 4, 5, 6, 7   Goff and Templeman L.JJ.

D

*Solicitor — Costs — Lien — Plaintiffs joining defendants' solicitors'
partner as defendant — Solicitors informing defendants of
difficulties in conducting defence and requesting payment of
fees up to date—Fees disputed—Summons for removal from
record—Whether solicitors discharging themselves—Whether
possessory lien lost—R.S.C., Ord. 67, r. 6 (1)*

Solicitors were retained to act for all the defendants in
a complicated action and it was agreed that the defendants
would make periodical payments to the solicitors on account
of costs. The plaintiffs then joined one of the partners in
the solicitors' firm as a defendant to the action. On counsel's
advice, the solicitors arranged for the partner to be separately
represented and informed the first three defendants that unless
the partner was dismissed from the action it would be
impossible for the solicitors to act for any of the defendants.
The solicitors also called upon the defendants to pay their
professional charges to date. The defendants disputed the
amount of the charges, paid some money but refused to pay
any more. On February 23, 1979, the solicitors wrote stating
that unless their costs were paid by March 2, they would
issue a summons on March 5, later extended to March 14,
applying to be removed from the record. By a letter of
June 25 they again notified the defendants that unless they
were paid they would apply to the court to be removed from
the record and on the same day they issued a summons under
R.S.C., Ord. 67, r. 6 (1), applying for such an order. On
July 9 the defendants instructed other solicitors and they duly
gave notice of change. On a notice of motion by the first
three defendants seeking the delivery of documents to the new
solicitors Oliver J. made the order sought.

On appeal by the solicitors: —

Held, dismissing the appeal, that where a client discharged
a solicitor the court had no power to call upon the solicitor to
hand over documents because the solicitor's lien endured,
but where the solicitor discharged himself in the course of an
action his possessory lien over the documents became subject
to the practice of the court, and the court would order the
documents to be handed over to the new solicitors subject
to the lien unless exceptional circumstances existed when the
court might be justified in imposing terms; accordingly, since
the right inference from the facts was that the solicitors had

E

F

G

H

A discharged themselves and as there were no exceptional circumstances to cause a modification of the usual practice, the solicitors were bound to hand over the documents to the defendants' new solicitors (post, pp. 620D–F, H—621B, 624D–G, 625C–D, 626G—627A).

 Heslop v. *Metcalfe* (1837) 3 My. & C. 183 and *Robins* v. *Goldingham* (1872) L.R. 13 Eq. 440 applied.

B   *Per curiam.* R.S.C., Ord. 67, r. 6 (1) is not dealing with the relationship between the solicitor and his client but with the position between other parties to the litigation and the client (post, p. 623C–D, 626E–F).

 Decision of Oliver J. affirmed.

The following cases are referred to in the judgments:

Bluck v. *Lovering & Co.* (1886) 35 W.R. 232, D.C.
Heslop v. *Metcalfe* (1837) 3 My. & C. 183.
C *Hughes* v. *Hughes* [1958] P. 224; [1958] 3 W.L.R. 500; [1958] 3 All E.R. 179, C.A.
Robins v. *Goldingham* (1872) L.R. 13 Eq. 440; 25 L.T. 900.
Webster v. *Le Hunt* (1861) 9 W.R. 804.

The following additional cases were cited in argument:

D *Boughton, In re* (1883) 23 Ch.D. 169.
Davidson v. *Leslie* (1845) 9 Beav. 104.
Faithful, In re (1868) L.R. 6 Eq. 325.
Steele v. *Scott* (1828) 2 Hog. 141.
Wright v. *King* (1846) 9 Beav. 161.

APPEAL from Oliver J.

E On July 23, 1979, three of the thirteen defendants in the action, Rochem Ltd., Rochem International Ltd. and Rochem (Equipment) Ltd., gave a notice of motion seeking an order against their former solicitors, Amhurst, Brown, Martin & Nicholson (" the appellants "), on the defendants' present solicitors giving an undertaking to hold all the documents delivered to them by the appellants subject to the appellants' lien for costs, that the appellants should deliver, on oath if required, F to the defendants' present solicitors all papers in the action and all other documents in their custody or power relating to the action against the defendants by Gamlen Chemical Co. (U.K.) Ltd. (" the plaintiffs ") and belonging to the defendants or any of them. On July 24, Oliver J. made the order sought.

By a notice of appeal dated August 2 the appellants appealed on the G grounds, inter alia, that the judge's finding was against the weight of the evidence and/or was wrong in law in that the appellants, having declared that they would cease to act unless they were put in funds and having issued a summons seeking an order under R.S.C., Ord. 67, r. 6 (1), that they had ceased to act, had discharged themselves from acting for the defendants; and in that, having regard to the filing of notice of change dated July 10, 1979, by the defendants' present solicitors, the H defendants had not discharged the appellants; and further, that the judge was wrong in law in holding that the appellants, having stated that they would cease to act for the defendants but having continued on record and continued to act after the issue of the summons for an order under Ord. 67, r. 6 (1), declaring that they had ceased to act, were to be regarded as having discharged themselves before the making of any such order and that a solicitor, who ceased or alternatively threatened to cease to act as a result of his not being put in funds,

whether or not such cesser or threatened cesser amounted to his dis-   A
charging himself, thereby lost his right to retain actual physical custody
of his clients' papers and documents although retaining his lien thereon.

The facts are stated by Goff L.J.

Antonio Bueno and *Elizabeth Gumbel* for the appellants.
J. L. Munby for the defendants.
                                                                        B

GOFF L.J. This is an appeal from an order of Oliver J. dated July
24, 1979, which he made upon a motion, whereby he ordered as follows:

> " Upon the undertaking of counsel for the defendants Rochem
> Ltd., Rochem International Ltd. and Rochem (Equipment) Ltd., on
> behalf of the solicitors for the said defendants (1) to hold all papers
> and documents delivered to them by Amhurst, Brown, Martin &   C
> Nicholson under this order subject to the lien of the said Amhurst
> Brown, Martin & Nicholson for costs (2) to afford the said Amhurst,
> Brown, Martin & Nicholson and their costs draftsman reasonable
> access to the said papers and documents for the purpose of preparing
> their bill of costs (3) to defend this action in an active manner and
> (4) to re-deliver the said papers and documents to the said Amhurst,   D
> Brown, Martin & Nicholson after the conclusion of this action.
> Let the said Amhurst, Brown, Martin & Nicholson so soon as may
> be reasonably practicable and in any event forthwith upon the
> receipt by them of written authorities from the defendants "—then
> a number of defendants are named—" deliver (on oath if required)
> to Douglas Goldberg & Co. all papers in this action and all other
> documents in the custody or power of the said Amhurst, Brown,   E
> Martin & Nicholson relating to this action and belonging to the
> said defendants or any of them."

Messrs. Amhurst, Brown, Martin & Nicholson, whom I will call the
appellants, now appeal against that order.

The action is a very complicated one in which the plaintiffs, who are
associated with a large American organisation called Sybron, are suing   F
the three English companies whose names I have just read out, and a
number of individual defendants. I need not go into the details of
the action, but shortly, the plaintiffs allege a conspiracy against all
the defendants, and also various torts and breaches of contract or
abuse of fiduciary duty or confidence against individual defendants.

The appellants acted as solicitors for all the defendants, and it was   G
an express term of the retainer that the defendants would make periodical
payments on account of costs. I do not think it would make much
difference if that were not so, as in my view a solicitor cannot be
required to go on with long and complicated litigation, without being put
in funds, unless, of course, he has expressly agreed so to do.

But here, as I say, there was in fact an express agreement to keep
the appellants in funds.   H

In February 1979, a complication presented itself in that the plaintiffs
joined one of the partners in the appellants, as a defendant, alleging
that he was a party to the conspiracy. I wish to make it clear that
at this stage nothing whatever has been proved against him; but in
the circumstances, leading counsel advised that he should be separately
represented, and further that the appellants might not be able to go
on acting themselves.

The Weekly Law Reports, June 13, 1980

617

1 W.L.R.   Gamlen Chemical Ltd. v. Rochem Ltd. (C.A.)   Goff L.J.

A   I read from their letter of February 2, 1979, reporting the position
to the defendant, Mr. Bove, who appears to control or to be the moving
spirit of the three defendant companies. They said:

"... As you know, Adrian Churchward was served with the
amended writ in this action on January 16 and as a firm, we have
since taken the advice of Mr. Hamilton Q.C., whose opinion is that
B   Adrian should be separately represented both by solicitors and
counsel; Messrs. Reynolds Porter Chamberlain and Co. have
accordingly been instructed to act on his behalf. Mr. Adrian
Hamilton further advised that Adrian Churchward's solicitors
should serve a searching request for further and better particulars
of the amended statement of claim as soon as it has been served
and, depending on the answers thereto, seriously consider mounting
C   an application to strike out the statement of claim on the ground
that it discloses no cause of action. He also advised that in the
course of argument at the hearing of a search application we
should point out that unless Adrian Churchward is dismissed from
the action it will be impossible for Amhurst, Brown, Martin &
Nicholson to continue to act for any of the other defendants,
D   which means that they will all have to go away and find separate
solicitors ..."

About the same time a dispute arose between the appellants and
Mr. Bove who asserted that the appellants' charges were grossly
excessive. Again, we cannot try that issue which can only be resolved
by taxation. He also said he had no intention of paying any costs until
E   he should know if the action against Mr. Adrian Churchward be
dismissed.

I read from his letter of February 21:

"... I have carefully considered your letter dated February 2,
1979, and can only come to the conclusion that Amhurst, Brown
would be happy to desert this case. Your charge of almost £20,000
F   for the period from April 1 to December 31 is almost equal to
your firm's estimated charges for the entire trial put forward in
your letter of June 9, 1973. May I remind you that we have not
yet been through a 60-day trial and that you have not prepared briefs
for counsel, just to point out two of the more significant items
that I assume were included in the £25,000 estimate. My layman's
evaluation of the work involved during the 9 month period would
G   be an amount similar to your charges presented on April 25, 1978,
for the period from September 1974 to March 31, 1978, specifically
£5,000 to £6,000. Consequently, I am left exasperated concerning
your £20,000 bill and do not know how to proceed. This is
especially true when I consider the origins of this entire case and
the manner in which it has developed. In addition to the above,
H   you leave me with a situation pregnant with the possibility that we
will have to seek new solicitors anyway due to Adrian's position.
At that time we will have to go out and pay entrance fees to new
solicitors to learn what we have already paid you to learn. ... To
be fair, I must point out that until I know if the action against
Adrian is dismissed, I have no intention of paying anything more
than the £5,000 already paid on account. ..."

The suggestion that the appellants would be happy to desert the A
case is, of course, refuted and was immediately refuted in the correspondence, and some further payments were made but, in the upshot, first no
steps have been taken to get Mr. Churchward out of the action, and
secondly there is a balance due to the appellants, according to their
bills of costs, of £12,961, which does not include any disbursements
and which the defendants refuse to pay.

On February 23, 1979, the appellants wrote a long letter to Mr. Bove, B
and in the course of that letter they said:

". . . If you wish to come and discuss the matter, I am perfectly
prepared so to do but I would make it clear at this stage that I am not
prepared to entertain any reduction in the amount of my firm's fees
so that if your reason for suggesting such a meeting is with a view
to try to persuade me to agree such a reduction then we will be C
wasting each other's time. Having said that, as you obviously
consider that our bill is excessive, you are entitled to have the same
vetted by a taxing master and I would be perfectly happy for this
to be done. If my firm's costs are not reduced by more than one
fifth, then you would have to pay the costs of the taxation in
addition to the amount allowed on taxation. However, this opera- D
tion would take several months and does not solve the present
problem, namely that unless my firm's bill is paid in the very
near future, then we shall have no alternative but to apply to the
court to be removed from the record. In these circumstances, I
am perfectly willing to agree that you should pay the amount of
my firm's costs and disbursements without prejudice to your right
to call upon us to have the same taxed as aforesaid. As I have E
said, the matter is now rather urgent as we must instruct counsel
to settle an amended defence, but I am not prepared to incur any
further counsel's fees until my firm's costs have been paid. I regret
therefore that I must ask you to accept this letter as formal notice
to the three defendant companies that if the balance of my firm's
costs and disbursements as set out in my firm's bill dated February 2, F
1979, namely the sum of £16,336 "—and I interpose there that that
was the figure at that time—" is not paid to us by Friday, March 2,
1979, we will issue a summons on Monday, March 5, 1979, applying
for this firm to be removed from the record as solicitors for the
three defendant companies. . . ."

As Mr. Bove was then abroad, the appellants extended the deadline G
until March 14, 1979, and on March 8, 1979, they wrote accordingly:

". . . I am prepared to extend the deadline from Monday, March
5, 1979, until Wednesday next March 14, 1979, but if I have heard
nothing by that date then I regret it will be necessary to take the
course outlined in my letter of February 23."

The dispute dragged on after that, and as I have said certain payments H
were made but the net balance increased to the figure I have mentioned,
over £12,000, and on June 25, 1979, the appellants wrote as follows:

". . . These circumstances leave me no alternative but to apply
to the court for my firm to be removed from the record as solicitors
for the three defendant companies and a copy of the summons will
be served upon the companies direct. Furthermore, as my firm's

The Weekly Law Reports, June 13, 1980

619

1 W.L.R.   Gamlen Chemical Ltd. v. Rochem Ltd. (C.A.)   Goff L.J.

A position as regards costs has not been secured, I am writing to all the personal defendants for whom my firm acts informing them that my firm can no longer act for them unless our position as regards costs is secured satisfactorily . . ."

and they did, in fact, issue a summons that very day, under R.S.C., Ord. 67, r. 6, the return day of which was July 26, and they served it the B next day. That summons, as far as material, read:

" . . . for an order declaring that the said Amhurst, Brown, Martin & Nicholson have ceased to be the solicitors acting for the said defendants in the above action and that the costs of this application be taxed and paid by the said defendants."

C They also applied for similar relief against the individual defendants.

The matter came before Master Ball on July 31, 1979, and was adjourned by him to give the individual defendants an opportunity of reconsidering their position, but before then letters were written to each defendant on July 3, in precisely the same form, and I quote from one of them:

D " . . . Although Rochem International Ltd. have paid our costs and disbursements in respect of the period from the commencement of the action down to and including March 31, 1978, we regret to inform you that a substantial part of our costs for the period from April 1, 1978, down to April 30, 1979, remains unpaid. We hope you will readily appreciate that we cannot continue to act either for you or any of the other defendants in regard to this action E unless our position in respect of costs is secured. We have accordingly issued a summons for an order declaring that we have ceased being the solicitors acting for you in this action and we enclose a copy of such summons herewith. . . . If the whole of our outstanding costs have been paid before the said summons comes on for hearing, then we will be happy to continue to act for you in this action and will withdraw the said summons. However, if F such costs are not paid, then we regret that we shall have no alternative but to seek the order mentioned in such summons."

After the matter had come before Master Ball and he had adjourned it, a letter was written to the individual defendants asking four questions:

" . . . (1) Do you wish us to continue to act for you in this action? G (2) If so, have you any proposals to make with regard to the satisfaction of the costs dealing with your individual defence? (3) If you have no such proposals to make, do you intend to appoint other solicitors to act for you in this action in our stead? (4) If you do not intend to instruct other solicitors to act for you in this action in our stead, do you intend to file notice that you will be acting in person in this action in our stead? "

H The matter came again before Master Chamberlain on September 3, when he made the order as asked against the individual defendants. In the meantime, the appellants' summons against the companies was overtaken by events as, on July 9, the first three defendants instructed new solicitors who duly gave notice of change and applied for and obtained the order now under appeal.

At this stage I must read the relevant rule, which is R.S.C., Ord. 67,

r. 6, and so far as material it is in these terms. It is headed " Withdrawal   A
of solicitor who has ceased to act for party."

" 6 (1) Where a solicitor who has acted for a party in a cause or
matter has ceased so to act and the party has not given notice
of change in accordance with rule 1, . . . the solicitor may apply
to the court for an order declaring that the solicitor has ceased
to be the solicitor acting for the party in the cause or matter,   B
and the court or the Court of Appeal, as the case may be, may make
an order accordingly, but unless and until the solicitor—(a) serves
on every party to the cause or matter (not being a party in default
as to entry of appearance) a copy of the order, and (b) procures the
order to be entered in the district registry or other appropriate
office mentioned in rule 1 (2), and (c) leaves at that office a copy of
the order and a certificate signed by him that the order has been   C
duly served as aforesaid, he shall, subject to the foregoing provisions
of this Order, be considered the solicitor of the party till the final
conclusion of the cause or matter, whether in the High Court or
Court of Appeal."

Oliver J. based his judgment on an old case, *Robins* v. *Goldingham*
(1872) L.R. 13 Eq. 440, and he said: D

" The principles, I think, are fairly clear; that is to say, that if a
client discharges a solicitor the solicitor's lien endures and the
court has no right—or no title—to call for the documents to be
handed over. But, if the solicitor has discharged himself in the
course of an action, then the order which is sought on this motion
seems to follow as a course, and there is authority for that in   E
Robins v. *Goldingham* . . . to which I have been referred." Then,
after reviewing that case, he went on: " I am bound to say, I find
the present case really almost wholly indistinguishable from
Robins v. *Goldingham*. Mr. Bueno, on behalf of the solicitors,
has forcefully argued that as a result of the rule to which I have
referred, Messrs. Amhurst Brown remained on the record, but I do
not think that is the point. It seems to me that they have   F
unequivocally intimated, both by taking out the summons on June
25 and then in their further letter of July 3, that they were not
prepared to go on unless some arrangement was made as to their
costs. That seems to me to be a clear case of the solicitor discharging himself."

Mr. Bueno, who has argued this case very forcefully before this court   G
also, and has said all that can possibly be said on behalf of his clients'
case, takes three points on that judgment: first, he says that in so far
as *Robins* v. *Goldingham* was a decision on the facts, it is distinguishable
and he submits that Oliver J. should have drawn the opposite inference
on the facts of this case. Secondly, he says that *Robins* v. *Goldingham*
was wrongly decided and he asks us to overrule it, and thirdly, he   H
repeats the submission referred to in the extract which I have read from
the judgment on the construction of the rule.

I am wholly unable to accept the first of these contentions. He
suggested the following grounds for distinguishing the two cases: first,
here the correspondence shows that the appellants were willing to
continue if their costs were paid, whereas the report of *Robins* v.
Goldingham in 25 L.T. 900 shows that a later letter was written in

The Weekly Law Reports, June 13, 1980

621

1 W.L.R.   Gamlen Chemical Ltd. v. Rochem Ltd. (C.A.)   Goff L.J.

A   which the solicitors in that case positively refused to go on. Secondly, he points to the initial agreement in the present case to pay by instalments as the matter progressed, which he said was not so in *Robins* v. *Goldingham*; and thirdly, he points out that we have in the present case the additional element that Mr. Bove invoked Mr. Churchward's position as a ground for refusing to pay the costs.

B   I agree that each case must depend upon its own facts, but in my judgment Oliver J.'s view of the inference to be drawn from the facts in the present case was clearly right.

Mr. Bueno said that all his clients were doing was to fire " warning shots " across the defendants' " bow," but after earlier warnings they took up a categorical position by their letter of June 25 and by issuing and serving a summons forthwith and that under a rule which applies

C   where a solicitor has ceased to act and, as Oliver J. pointed out, they emphasised that position in their letters of July 3.

For my part, I do not think that they can complain and say "We did not discharge ourselves; you discharged us," because the defendants, not being willing to meet the bill, took the appellants at their word and instructed other solicitors and therefore I see nothing in the first suggested ground of distinction.

D   The second is, in my judgment, really insignificant because an agreement to make interim payment would ordinarily be implied, but in any event there was such an express bargain in *Bluck* v. *Lovering & Co.* (1886) 35 W.R. 232 in which *Robins* v. *Goldingham*, L.R. 13 Eq. 440, was followed, and with all respect to the argument, the third point seems to me to be quite irrelevant as a ground of distinction.

E   The attack upon *Robins* v. *Goldingham* is mounted on several grounds. First, it is said, that the court assumed that the solicitor would keep his lien if he was ordered to deliver up the document without prejudice to it, and upon an undertaking to return them, which may be technically right, but is not so in fact, and therefore (so the argument runs) the premise upon which the case proceeded was bad.

F   Secondly, he relies upon the hardship which will be inflicted upon a solicitor if his lien is whittled away in this way, but that again has to be balanced against the hardship which will be inflicted on the client if, in the middle of the case, he has to change his solicitor and is unable to get hold of the relevant papers.

Thirdly, he said that the position is now quite different because when *Robins* v. *Goldingham* was decided, one was faced with impov-

G   erished litigants, whereas now there is no such problem because of legal aid.

Fourthly, he pointed out, perfectly correctly, that prior to 1932, a solicitor could not get himself removed from the record, but I cannot see how that point affects the matter, save possibly with regard to the third limb of the appellants' case, the construction of the rule.

H   Fifthly, Mr. Bueno said the client can secure the costs pending taxation, but that does not necessarily save him from hardship or even disaster.

So far as legal aid is concerned, I cannot accept that as any ground for saying the law should now be different or that we should overrule *Robins* v. *Goldingham* because it is well known that there are many litigants whose capital or income is sufficiently large to disqualify them for legal aid, but not sufficient to enable them to proceed with compli-

Goff L.J.   **Gamlen Chemical Ltd. v. Rochem Ltd. (C.A.)**   **[1980]**

cated litigation without great difficulty and hardship, and in any case   A
in the present case, we are dealing with companies who are not entitled
to legal aid. The problem may have ceased to apply to a number,
perhaps a large number, of litigants, but the problem is still there and the
decision on principle must, as has been observed, fit all cases.

So it really comes down to the first two points: that the order which
has been made, if allowed to stand, will whittle away the lien contrary
to the assumed basis upon which *Robins* v. *Goldingham* proceeded and,   B
secondly, the question of hardship.

In the course of the argument it turned out, although it did not
appear from the judgment itself, that *Robins* v. *Goldingham* was one
of a number of cases all pointing in the same direction. There is
Bluck v. *Lovering & Co.*, 35 W.R. 232, which I have already mentioned,
and *Webster* v. *Le Hunt* (1861) 9 W.R. 804, to which we were also   C
referred.

We did not call upon Mr. Munby but he told us that he would have
cited many more such cases. Be that as it may, the distinction upon
which *Robins* v. *Goldingham,* L.R. 13 Eq. 440, proceeded between a
solicitor who is discharged by his client and is, therefore, entitled to
retain the papers even in the course of litigation, and the solicitor who   D
discharges himself, was clearly recognised in Mr. Ormrod's argument,
as late as 1958, in *Hughes* v. *Hughes* [1958] P. 224, 226, where he said:
"An important distinction is drawn between (1) a solicitor who discharges himself, (2) a solicitor who is still acting, and (3) a solicitor who
is discharged by his client."

Mr. Ormrod cited three cases in support of that analysis, and we
have been referred to one of them, namely *Heslop* v. *Metcalfe* (1837)   E
3 My. & C. 183 which seems to me to be of the utmost significance
in this case, and to afford conclusive reasons why we should not at this
late stage reverse the decision in *Robins* v. *Goldingham,* because *Heslop*
v. *Metcalfe* shows quite clearly that in those days the court had fully
adverted to the factual effect upon the lien on the making of such an
order, and to the hardship which it would impose upon a solicitor.   F
Lord Cottenham L.C., giving judgment, said at pp. 188–190:

"Undoubtedly, that doctrine may expose a solicitor to very great
inconvenience and hardship, if, after embarking in a cause, he
finds that he cannot get the necessary funds wherewith to carry it
on. But, on the other hand, extreme hardship might arise to the
client, if,—to take the case which is not uncommon in the smaller   G
practice in the country,—a solicitor, who finds a poor man having a
good claim, and having but a small sum of money at his command,
may go on until that fund is exhausted, and then, refusing to proceed
further, may hang up the cause by withholding the papers in his
hands. That would be great grievance and means of oppression to
a poor client who, with the clearest right in the world, might still
be without the means of employing another solicitor. The rule of   H
the court must be adapted to every case that may occur, and be
calculated to protect suitors against such conduct . . . I then take the
law as laid down by Lord Eldon, and, adopting that law, must hold
that Mr. Blunt is not to be permitted to impose upon the plaintiff
the necessity of carrying on his cause in an expensive, inconvenient
and disadvantageous manner. I think the principle should be, that

The Weekly Law Reports, June 13, 1980

623

1 W.L.R.   Gamlen Chemical Ltd. v. Rochem Ltd. (C.A.)   Goff L.J.

A   the solicitor claiming the lien, should have every security not inconsistent with the progress of the cause."

So all the misgivings that one might have in one's mind, which I confess I have had in my mind during certain stages of the argument, were there considered and set at rest. In my judgment, therefore, I would not think it right to overrule *Robins* v. *Goldingham,* L.R. 13

B Eq. 440.

That leaves the third head of the argument which is this: that having regard to the latter part of Ord. 67, r. 6 (1), the appellants necessarily continued as the solicitors for the defendants for all purposes, no order having been obtained on their summons and, therefore, the steps referred to in the earlier part of the order of necessity not having been taken. Mr. Bueno relies on the words

C

"... shall, subject to the foregoing provisions of this Order, be considered the solicitor of the party till the final conclusion of the cause or matter, whether in the High Court or Court of Appeal."

In my judgment, however, that rule is not dealing with the relationship between the solicitor on the record and his client, but the position

D as between other parties to the litigation and the client; they being entitled, until the appropriate steps have been taken to change the record, to regard the solicitor as being still the solicitor, and to serve him with pleadings, notices and so forth.

I think that must be the right conclusion for two reasons: first, the opening words of the order refer to a solicitor who has ceased to act, so that the argument would mean that the latter part of the order was

E inconsistent with the former; and secondly, the qualifications which I have read under the headings (*a*), (*b*) and (*c*) show quite clearly that the order is dealing only with matters of procedure.

These reasons are sufficient to dispose of this appeal, but before I conclude my judgment, I think I should say a few words about two other points which Mr. Bueno took in his persuasive argument. He

F said, as is true, that a solicitor can withdraw for good cause and " good cause " is " non-payment." But we cannot decide the questions which the defendants have raised when they say that the appellants' charges are excessive, and also a further charge which they have made, of some kind of negligence or breach of duty on the part of the appellants. They have not yet formulated that in any definite terms, but one way is suggested in the correspondence in that they allowed their partner, then

G an assistant solicitor, to become so involved that the plaintiffs have seen fit to add him as a defendant. There may be absolutely nothing in this at all, but Mr. Churchward still remains a party, and the allegation that he joined the conspiracy still remains upon the record. As it seems to me, we cannot decide the question of " good cause " either on the point of the allegation that the charges are excessive, or on the second ground.

H The other point is this; Mr. Bueno submits that we should protect the lien until these questions can be decided but that, as it seems to me, merely brings us back again to the question of hardship, with which I have already dealt, the overriding principle being that a solicitor who has discharged himself is not allowed so to exert his lien as to interfere with the course of justice—he has, as it has been put, only a qualified lien. Finally, he argued that the conduct of the defendants was repudiatory in refusing to pay the costs, and he says that the appellants have accepted that repudiation, but that again can only be right if the A defendants are wrong on the points which they have taken, and I do not see how it can affect our judgment at this stage.

For these reasons I agree with the judgment given by Oliver J., and I would dismiss this appeal.

TEMPLEMAN L.J.   I entirely agree. This appeal illustrates the difficulties which arise when a client and his solicitor part company in B the midst of litigation. A solicitor who accepts a retainer to act for a client in the prosecution or defence of an action engages that he will continue to act until the action is ended, subject however to his costs being paid. That principle was re-affirmed in *Bluck* v. *Lovering & Co.*, 35 W.R. 232, 233.

If before the action is ended, the client determines the retainer, the C solicitor may, subject to certain exceptions not here material, exercise a possessory lien over the client's papers until payment of the solicitor's costs and disbursements. Thus, in *Hughes* v. *Hughes* [1958] P. 224, 227–228, Hodson L.J. said:

" There is no doubt that a solicitor who is discharged by his client during an action, otherwise than for misconduct, can retain any papers in the cause in his possession until his costs have been D paid . . . This rule applies, as the authorities show, whether the client's papers are of any intrinsic value or not, . . ."

The solicitor himself may determine his retainer during an action for reasonable cause, such as the failure of the client to keep the solicitor in funds to meet his costs and disbursements; but in that case the E solicitor's possessory lien, i.e. his right to retain the client's papers of any intrinsic value or not, is subject to the practice of the court which, in order to save the client's litigation from catastrophe, orders the solicitor to hand over the client's papers to the client's new solicitors, provided the new solicitors undertake to preserve the original solicitor's lien and to return the papers to the original solicitor, for what they are worth, after the end of the litigation. F

This practice was settled many years ago, and as Goff L.J. has shown, from the citation which he gave of *Heslop* v. *Metcalfe*, 3 My. & C. 183, 188, there are convincing reasons why the practice should be followed, and it has been followed, at least in the cases Goff L.J. has cited, *Webster* v. *Le Hunt* (1861) 9 W.R. 804; *Robins* v. *Goldingham*, L.R. 13 Eq. 440, and is to be found also in the argument of counsel in *Hughes* v. *Hughes* [1958] P. 224. G

Where the solicitor has himself discharged his retainer, the court then will normally make a mandatory order obliging the original solicitor to hand over the client's papers to the new solicitor against an undertaking by the new solicitor to preserve the lien of the original solicitor.

I wish to guard myself against possible exceptions to this general rule. The court in fact is asked to make a mandatory order obliging H the original solicitor to hand over the papers to the new solicitor. An automatic order is inconsistent with the inherent, albeit judicial, discretion of the court to grant or withhold a remedy which is equitable in character. It may be, therefore, that in exceptional cases the court might impose terms where justice so required. For example, if the papers are valueless after the litigation is ended and if the client accepts that he is indebted to the original solicitor for an agreed sum and has

The Weekly Law Reports, June 13, 1980

625

1 W.L.R.　　　　　Gamlen Chemical Ltd. v. Rochem Ltd. (C.A.)　　　Templeman L.J.

A　no counterclaim, or accepts that the solicitor has admittedly paid out reasonable and proper disbursements, which must be repaid, the court might make an order which would only compel the original solicitor to hand over the papers to the new solicitor providing that in the first place the client pays to the original solicitor a sum, fixed by the court, representing the whole or part of the moneys admittedly due from the client to the original solicitor.　Much would depend on the nature of

B　the case, the stage which the litigation had reached, the conduct of the solicitor and the client respectively, and the balance of hardship which might result from the order the court is asked to make.

　　Applying those principles, the following questions arise in the present case: first, did the solicitor discharge the client or did the client discharge the solicitor?　Secondly, if the solicitor discharged the client, was there

C　reasonable cause for the solicitor to do so?　Thirdly, if there was reasonable cause for the solicitor to discharge the client, and the solicitor did so, should the court impose terms on the delivery of the client's papers and documents by the solicitor to the new solicitor, other than the term which requires the new solicitor to undertake to preserve the lien of the original solicitor?

D　　As to the first question, in my judgment the evidence clearly shows that it was the solicitor who discharged the client.　The writ was issued in August 1974; the relevant clients gave and the solicitor accepted, a retainer to represent the defendants in the action.　The clients paid large sums for disbursements and costs necessarily incurred in complicated interlocutory and other matters to April 1, 1978.

　　Goff L.J. has read the letter dated February 2, 1979, in which the

E　appellants warned the defendants that it might be necessary for all the defendants to have separate representation.　At the same time, the appellants did not at that stage take the step of advising the defendants to go elsewhere, and it was in that letter, as Goff L.J. has said, that the appellants put in a bill for £21,523.　The defendants replied, protesting that the charge ought to be £5,000 or £6,000 and not £20,000, and complaining that: " In addition to the above, you leave me with a

F　situation pregnant with the possibility that we will have to seek new solicitors anyway."

　　On February 23, 1979, again in a letter which Goff L.J. has read, the appellants pointed out that the defendants were entitled to taxation and continued: "However, this operation would take several months," and asked the defendants to accept the letter as formal notice that if

G　the balance then due exceeding £16,000 was not paid by Friday, March 2, they would issue a summons on March 5 applying for the appellants' firm to be removed from the record as solicitors for the three defendant companies.　The deadline was extended until March 14, 1979; there was then a certain amount of correspondence and payment on account; a further bill was rendered, and on June 11, 1979, the appellants gave a

H　seven-day ultimatum saying that if it was not complied with, they would have no alternative but to apply to the court to be removed from the record.

　　Finally the appellants on June 25, 1979, said they were going to apply to the court, and they did apply to the court by summons on the same day, returnable in July 1979.

　　In my judgment, not later than the issue and service of this summons, the appellants had discharged themselves from their retainer by the

defendants, subject to the defendants accepting the position or paying
the appellants the amount which they demanded exceeding £12,000 odd.
The defendants elected to accept the situation and did so; they accepted
that the appellants had withdrawn, and not unnaturally in those circumstances consulted fresh solicitors who, on July 10 and 11, 1979, gave a
written notice of change and asked the appellants to confirm that the
summons dated June 25, 1979, would be withdrawn.

As a result, the appellants wrote saying that they did not propose
to proceed with the summons. It follows that the defendants besides
disputing the amount of costs which the appellants claimed, also felt a
grievance, rightly or wrongly, revolving round the complication caused
by the allegations that a partner in the appellants' firm had become
involved personally in the litigation, and the delay which had taken place
clarifying the position with regard to representation and conflict of
interest. At present, there are no means of knowing whether the
appellants will be held to be entitled to recover the whole or part of
the costs which they claim. They have been paid their disbursements.

Mr. Bueno, for the appellants, submitted that all the correspondence
which Goff L.J. has read, and the issue of the summons, did not amount
to the discharge of the client by the solicitors. The solicitors, he said,
were discharged by the client when the client instructed fresh solicitors,
and that new firm gave notice of change. Goff L.J. has already dealt
with that argument, and I agree that on a plain reading of the correspondence, it was the appellants who, as between themselves and the
defendants, discharged the defendants. The defendants then took the
step which they were entitled to do, of accepting the repudiation by the
appellants, and instructed fresh solicitors.

Mr. Bueno submitted that, as a matter of law, the appellants would
only have discharged themselves if they had proceeded with the summons
and obtained an order under Ord. 67, r. 6.

That rule has been read and analysed by Goff L.J. and I agree that
it governs the position as between the litigants and third parties but has
nothing to do with the position as between a client and his own solicitor.
The rule plainly implied that a summons will be taken out and an order
will be made after the solicitors have ceased to act, and the provisos to
the rule make clear its object, which is to safeguard third parties. It is
not a rule which is appropriate to prevent the ending of the relationship
of solicitor and client as between them, before an order is made under
the rule.

I have no doubt that in the present circumstances it was the appellants
who discharged their retainer from the defendants.

The second question is whether the solicitors had reasonable cause to
discharge themselves? They were unable to obtain payment of the costs
which the appellants claimed to be due, or to reach agreement about the
payment of future costs and disbursements. For the purposes of this
motion I assume they were not bound to go on. But if the appellants
had reasonable cause to discharge themselves, and did so, they are,
nevertheless, for the reasons given in *Heslop* v. *Metcalfe*, 3 My. & C.
183, to which I have already referred and which Goff L.J. has read,
bound to hand over the papers of the clients to their new solicitors,
against the undertaking of the new solicitors to preserve the lien, for
what it is worth, unless there are exceptional circumstances which justify
some modification of the usual practice.

The Weekly Law Reports, June 13, 1980

627

1 W.L.R.   Gamlen Chemical Ltd. v. Rochem Ltd. (C.A.)   Templeman L.J.

A   That raises the third question, namely, are there exceptional reasons why the court should impose terms on the defendants modifying the usual practice? In my judgment, there are no grounds for modifying the usual practice. This action was begun in 1974; the appellants acted until June 1979 and the action was set down for March 1980—possibly a little optimistically. Whether the defendants this day can lay their hands on the money to pay the appellants' demands, I know not, but
B   the defendants dispute the appellants' right to be paid in principle and in quantum. It would be disastrous for the defendants if their new solicitors could not, at this stage, obtain the papers held by the appellants.

For these reasons, and the reasons given by Oliver J. and by Goff L.J., I agree that the appeal must be dismissed.

C   *Appeal dismissed with costs.*

Solicitors: *Amhurst, Brown, Martin & Nicholson; Douglas Goldberg & Co.*

A. R.

D
                            [HOUSE OF LORDS]

*LONRHO LTD. AND ANOTHER .   .   .   .   .   APPELLANTS

                              AND

SHELL PETROLEUM CO. LTD. AND ANOTHER .   . RESPONDENTS
E   (FIRST APPEAL)

LONRHO LTD. AND ANOTHER .   .   .   .   .   APPELLANTS

                              AND

SHELL PETROLEUM CO. LTD. AND ANOTHER .   . RESPONDENTS
F   (SECOND APPEAL)

                         [1980 L. No. 202]

1980 April 23, 24, 28, 29;   Lord Diplock, Lord Edmund-Davies,
       May 22   Lord Fraser of Tullybelton,
                                    Lord Russell of Killowen and
G   Lord Keith of Kinkel

Company — Powers — Foreign subsidiaries — Discovery — Multi-
   national company—Subsidiaries' refusal to disclose documents
   in their possession—Whether " power " in company to compel
   disclosure—R.S.C., Ord. 24, rr. 2 (1), 3 (1) [1]
Crown — Privilege — Objection to produce documents — Statutory
H *inquiry—Confidential information volunteered to inquiry—*
   Public interest in persons giving evidence voluntarily to
   inquiry—Whether outweighing public interest that decision
   in proceedings be based on all relevant facts

[1] R.S.C., Ord. 24, r. 2 (1): " . . . each party must . . . make and serve on [the] other party a list of the documents which are or have been in his possession, custody or power relating to any matter in question between them in the action."
R. 3 (1): " . . . the court may order any party . . . to make and serve on any other party a list of the documents which are or have been in his possession, custody or power relating to any matter in question in the cause or matter, . . ."

Lonrho Ltd. v. Shell Petroleum (H.L.(E.))   [1980]

The plaintiffs were the owners of an oil pipeline running   A
from Beira in Mozambique to Umtali in Zimbabwe, then
called Rhodesia. It was completed in January 1965 and was
operated under an agreement between the plaintiffs and a
number of major oil companies including the defendants. On
November 11, 1965, Rhodesia unilaterally declared its independence of the United Kingdom (" U.D.I.") and, as a result
of sanctions imposed on the direction of the United Nations,
the pipeline could not be used for importing oil into Rhodesia   B
so long as U.D.I. continued. The plaintiffs consequently
suffered loss of profits. Oil continued, however, to reach
Rhodesia by other routes. In 1977, pursuant to article 15
of and Schedule 1 to the Southern Rhodesia (United Nations
Sanctions) (No. 2) Order 1968, the Secretary of State for
Foreign and Commonwealth Affairs appointed a private inquiry
to conduct an investigation into the supply of petroleum and
petroleum products to Rhodesia since the coming into force   C
on December 17, 1965, of the Southern Rhodesia (Petroleum)
Order 1965. The defendants agreed to cooperate fully with
the inquiry. On May 31, 1977, the plaintiffs commenced an
action against the defendants and 31 others, the substance of
their claim being that the defendants and others had conspired together to supply oil to Rhodesia in breach of the
Order of 1965, that by doing so they had enabled the rebel
government of Rhodesia to prolong U.D.I. and that they had   D
thereby made it impossible for use of the pipeline to be
resumed.   They claimed damages for unlawful conspiracy,
alternatively for breach of implied covenants in the agreement.
On July 27, 1977, the chairman of the inquiry said in a
letter to the second defendants that the members appreciated
that on commercial grounds and because of the proceedings
commenced by the plaintiffs certain of the answers to their
questions might well involve information that the second   E
defendants would regard as confidential and that if, in answering, they would indicate any areas of particular concern, the
members would do their utmost, consistently with the duty
laid on them by the Secretary of State, to respect that confidentiality. After receiving the inquiry's report in August
1978, the government announced its intention of publishing
it as soon as the necessary consents to disclosure required
under the Order of 1968 had been obtained. On September   F
5, 1978, the Foreign and Commonwealth Office wrote to
the defendants asking for their consent to the disclosure in
the report of information and documents furnished by them
to the inquiry. They consented subject to the qualification
that their consent applied to the disclosure of information
and documents to the extent only that they were contained
in the report and any appendices thereto; they did not consent
to publication of any more extensive information or docu-   G
ments that could then be available for the purposes of other
proceedings.
The plaintiff's action having been stayed as against the
defendants and their claim against them sent to arbitration
the arbitrators made directions for discovery of documents,
but the plaintiffs were dissatisfied with the discovery made by
the defendants and took out the originating summons against
them that was the subject of these appeals. The summons   H
was heard by Robert Goff J. in two parts.
The summons related, first, to documents in the possession
of subsidiary companies in the defendants' groups of companies
in Rhodesia, South Africa and Mozambique. In the case of
Rhodesia and South Africa, the boards of the subsidiaries
refused to disclose the documents of which the plaintiffs sought
discovery to do so on the grounds that it would constitute
a criminal offence to do so without a ministerial licence and

A that, in any event, it would not be in the companies' best interests. In the case of the Mozambique subsidiary, the defendants offered to do their best to facilitate the plaintiffs' inspection of the documents in Mozambique between March 3 and April 3, 1980, but their offer was not accepted by the plaintiffs. The plaintiffs' application for discovery of the documents was dismissed by Robert Goff J., and the Court of Appeal dismissed an appeal by the plaintiffs from his

B decision. They gave the plaintiffs leave to appeal.

The summons secondly related to documents that had come into existence in connection with or for the purposes of the inquiry. The defendants refused disclosure of those documents on the ground of public interest immunity, supported by a certificate of the Lord Privy Seal lodged by the Attorney-General, who was given leave to intervene in the proceedings to assert the immunity of the documents from disclosure on

C behalf of the Crown. The documents included copies of the transcripts of the oral evidence of witnesses including managers and directors of the subsidiaries in Southern Africa, written submissions made by the defendants to the inquiry and correspondence between the defendants and the Foreign Office and the members of the inquiry. The plaintiffs' application for disclosure of those documents was also dismissed by Robert Goff J., and an appeal by the plaintiffs was dismissed by the

D Court of Appeal, who again gave the plaintiffs leave to appeal.

On the first appeal: —

Held, dismissing the appeal, that on the true construction of R.S.C., Ord. 24, a party had a document in his " power " only if he had a presently enforceable legal right to obtain inspection of the document from whoever actually held it without the need to obtain the consent of anyone else; and that, since the documents in the possession of the subsidiaries

E could not be obtained without their consent (failing alteration of their articles of association) and, in the case of the subsidiaries in Rhodesia and South Africa, ministerial consent, they were not in the power of the defendants (post, pp. 635E— 636A, F–H).

Decision of the Court of Appeal [1980] 2 W.L.R. 367 affirmed.

On the second appeal: —

F *Held*, dismissing the appeal, that, since the likelihood of success of an inquiry of the kind in question in discovering the truth as to what had happened was greatly facilitated if those persons who knew what had happened came forward to volunteer information, and since without an assurance of complete confidentiality information was less likely to be volunteered, particularly where the inquiry was directed to

G matters that were the subject matter of a pending civil action to which the possessor of the information was a defendant, the judge's decision that in the particular circumstances of the case the public interest against disclosure of the documents outweighed the general public interest that in the administration of justice the decision should be based on all the relevant facts should be upheld (post, pp. 637G–H, 638G–H).

Decision of the Court of Appeal affirmed.

H *Per curiam.* In neither of these cases was it appropriate to give leave to appeal to the House of Lords against concurrent and unanimous judgments of the judge and of the Court of Appeal. If the size of the damages claimed in the arbitration, of the order of £100,000,000, was thought to justify giving leave to appeal, that is not a valid reason in an appeal on an interlocutory matter, such as discovery, which would not have qualified for leave on any other grounds, particularly where the discovery is sought in an arbitration (post, pp. 631H, 632C–D).

Lonrho Ltd. v. Shell Petroleum (H.L.(E.))   **[1980]**

The following case is referred to in the opinion of Lord Diplock: A

Conway v. *Rimmer* [1968] A.C. 910; [1968] 2 W.L.R. 998; [1968] 1 All E.R. 874, H.L.(E.).

The following additional cases were cited in argument:

B. v. *B.* (*Matrimonial Proceedings: Discovery*) [1978] Fam. 181; [1978] 3 W.L.R. 624; [1979] 1 All E.R. 801.

Bartlett v. *Barclays Bank Trust Co. Ltd.* (*Nos. 1 and 2*) [1980] 2 W.L.R. 430; [1980] 1 All E.R. 139.

B

Burmah Oil Co. Ltd. v. *Governor and Company of the Bank of England* [1979] 3 W.L.R. 722; [1979] 3 All E.R. 700, H.L.(E.).

Clinch v. *Financial Corporation* (1866) L.R. 2 Eq. 271.

D. v. *National Society for the Prevention of Cruelty to Children* [1978] A.C. 171; [1977] 2 W.L.R. 201; [1977] 1 All E.R. 589, H.L.(E.).

Daimler Co. Ltd. v. *Continental Tyre and Rubber Co.* (*Great Britain*) C *Ltd.* [1916] 2 A.C. 307, H.L.(E.).

Mertens v. *Haigh* (1863) 3 De G.J. & Sm. 528.

Mustad (*O.*) & *Son* v. *Dosen* (*Note*) [1964] 1 W.L.R. 109; [1963] 3 All E.R. 416, H.L.(E.).

Revlon Inc. v. *Cripps & Lee Ltd.*, November 22, 1979; Court of Appeal (Civil Division) Transcript No. 601 of 1979, C.A.

Sankey v. *Whitlam* (1978) 21 A.L.R. 505.   D

Science Research Council v. *Nassé* [1979] 3 W.L.R. 762; [1979] I.C.R. 921; [1979] 3 All E.R. 673, H.L.(E.).

Taylor v. *Rundell* (1841) Cr. & Ph. 104.

Woolfson v. *Strathclyde Regional Council* (1978) 38 P. & C.R. 521; 1978 S.L.T. 159, H.L.(Sc.).

APPEALS from the Court of Appeal.   E

By writ of May 31, 1977, the plaintiffs, Lonrho Ltd. and Companhia Do Pipeline Moçambique Rodesia S.A.R.L. (a company incorporated under the laws of Mozambique) claimed against the defendants, Shell Petroleum Co. Ltd. (" Shell ") and British Petroleum Co. Ltd. (" B.P."), 28 other oil companies and three individual defendants (1) an injunction restraining the defendants from (i) conspiring with each other or with any other person in breach of the Southern Rhodesia (Petroleum) Order   F 1965 or otherwise unlawfully to supply or agree to supply petroleum to any person, (ii) committing or participating in any breach of an agreement of October 30, 1962, between the plaintiffs and the first four defendants, (iii) by the supply of petroleum unlawfully causing damage and loss to the plaintiffs; (2) damages for breach of contract, unlawful interference with contract, conspiracy, negligence and the committing of   G unlawful acts causing loss and injury. By order of Brightman J. in January 1978 the action was stayed so far as concerned Shell and B.P. and the proceedings against those two defendants went on by way of arbitration.

By originating summons issued on January 18, 1980, the plaintiffs applied for orders for further discovery by the defendants of, inter alia,   H documents in the possession of subsidiaries in the defendants' groups of companies in Rhodesia, South Africa and Mozambique, and documents including the written submissions of the defendants and any of their subsidiaries to the Bingham inquiry, copies of the transcripts of the oral evidence given by officers and employees of the defendants and the subsidiaries to the inquiry and certain correspondence between the defendants and the Foreign Office and the members of the inquiry. The

A summons was heard by Robert Goff J. in two parts. On January 25, 1980, he refused the plaintiffs' application in so far as it related to documents in the possession of the subsidiaries, giving the plaintiffs leave to appeal. They appealed, on the grounds that he had been wrong in law and on the facts in holding that the documents in question were not within the power of the defendants for the purposes of R.S.C., Ord. 24, r. 3. The Court of Appeal (Lord Denning M.R., Shaw and Brandon
B L.JJ.) on February 12, 1980, dismissed the appeal, giving the plaintiffs leave to appeal. They appealed. On March 4, 1980, Robert Goff J. refused the plaintiffs' application in so far as it related to the Bingham inquiry documents and dismissed the summons, giving the plaintiffs leave to appeal. They appealed, on the grounds that the judge had been wrong in law and fact in holding that the documents in question should
C not be disclosed on the ground of public interest. The Court of Appeal (Lord Denning M.R., Waller and Dunn L.JJ.) on March 12, 1980, dismissed the appeal, giving the plaintiffs leave to appeal. They appealed.

The appeals were heard consecutively. The facts are set out in the opinion of Lord Diplock.

D *Mark Littman* Q.C., *Charles Sparrow* Q.C., *Gavin Lightman* Q.C. and *Alan Boyle* for the plaintiffs.

Peter Curry Q.C., *Brian Davenport* Q.C. and *Gordon Langley* for the first defendants, Shell Petroleum Co. Ltd.

Robert Alexander Q.C., *Roger Buckley* Q.C., *Jonathan Sumption* and *Stephen Ruttle* for the second defendants, British Petroleum Co. Ltd.

Simon D. Brown and *John Laws* for the Attorney-General.

E
Their Lordships took time for consideration.

May 22. LORD DIPLOCK. My Lords, these two appeals, which have occupied four days of your Lordships' time despite the fact that it was not found necessary to call on the respondents save briefly on a minor
F point in one of the appeals, are both about discovery of documents. The discovery sought is for the purposes of an arbitration and so required the issue of an originating summons by the appellants (whom I will refer to collectively as " Lonrho "); but the essential nature of the orders sought was interlocutory. The summons was heard by Robert Goff J. in two parts. In decisions or January 25 and March 5, 1980, he refused the orders sought by Lonrho. In each case Lonrho appealed to the
G Court of Appeal. The first appeal (which I will call " the subsidiaries appeal ") came before a court consisting of Lord Denning M.R. and Shaw and Brandon L.JJ.; the second (which I will call " the Bingham appeal ") came before a court consisting of Lord Denning M.R. and Waller and Dunn L.JJ. In each appeal the judgment of the court dismissing the appeal was unanimous.

H It is very rarely that your Lordships would yourselves give leave to appeal to this House on a question that is essentially interlocutory, in the sense that the answer to it will not dispose finally of the main proceedings either in law or as a matter of practical reality—as may be the case with some other orders granting or refusing interlocutory injunctions. In neither of the instant cases would I myself have thought it appropriate to give leave to appeal to this House against concurrent and unanimous judgments of the judge and of the Court of Appeal. The

circumstances which have given rise to the disputes about discovery are   **A**
quite exceptional; they are unlikely to recur in any other case and, for
that reason, they do not in my view provide a suitable occasion for any
general disquisition by this House upon the principles of law applicable
to the discovery of documents.   This was also the view that was taken
in the courts below.   In the subsidiaries appeal Robert Goff J. delivered
an ex tempore judgment which cited no authorities, and, in the Court
of Appeal, although a few authorities were referred to in the judgments   **B**
of Lord Denning M.R., that court was at pains to make it clear that
their judgment was directed to the particular facts of the case before
them.   In the Bingham appeal, except for a minor cavilling against one
adverb that the judge had used, as savouring of hyperbole, there was no
dispute about the law that was applicable.   All that was in issue was
the application of well-settled law to very special facts.   One is left to   **C**
suppose that the size of the damages claimed in the arbitration, which
are of the order of £100,000,000, may have been thought to justify
giving leave to appeal in a case in which, if the amount at stake had
been smaller, leave would have been refused.   For my part, I do not
accept this as a valid reason for giving leave to appeal to this House,
in *an appeal upon an interlocutory matter,* such as discovery, which
would not have qualified for leave on any other grounds.   This is   **D**
particularly so where the discovery is sought in an arbitration.   In reflects
discredit upon English arbitral procedure that so much delay and so
much costs (which in the instant appeal, in which 13 counsel were
engaged, must have been enormous) should be permitted to be incurred
by reason of the intervention of a court in matters that are merely
preparatory to the hearing of the arbitration by the arbitrators of the   **E**
parties' choice.

The relevant allegations in the claim made by Lonrho against the
two respondents ("Shell" and "B.P.") in the arbitration need be stated
in barest outline only.   Lonrho are the owners of an oil pipeline which
runs from the port of Beira in Mozambique to a refinery at Umtali in
Zimbabwe, then called Rhodesia.   It came on stream a few months   **F**
before the unilateral declaration of independence by Rhodesia ("U.D.I.")
and was operated under an agreement ("the shippers' agreement")
between Lonrho and a number of major oil companies including Shell
and B.P.   As a result of sanctions imposed on the direction of the United
Nations the pipeline could not be used for importing oil into Rhodesia
so long as U.D.I. continued; so Lonrho lost the profits that it would
have made under the shippers' agreement if the pipeline had remained   **G**
in use.   As a matter of public knowledge, however, despite the sanctions,
oil continued throughout the period of U.D.I. to reach Rhodesia by other
routes.

Lonrho started an action in the High Court on May 31, 1977, against
Shell and B.P. and 31 other defendants including all those subsidiary
companies belonging to the Shell and/or B.P. groups disclosure of whose   **H**
documents is sought in the subsidiaries appeal.   The substance of the
claim was that the 33 defendants had conspired together to supply oil
to Rhodesia in breach of the Southern Rhodesia (Petroleum) Order 1965,
that by doing so they enabled the rebel government of Rhodesia to
prolong U.D.I., and thereby made it impossible for use of the pipeline
to be resumed.   The losses incurred by Lonrho through inability to use
the pipeline during the resulting prolongation of U.D.I. were claimed

A in the alternative as damages for unlawful conspiracy or for breach of implied covenants in the shippers' agreement.

The shippers' agreement, to which Shell and B.P. were parties, contained an arbitration clause. As this was not a domestic arbitration agreement within the meaning of the Arbitration Act 1975, Shell and B.P. successfully applied to have the action stayed as against them, and
B this was done in January 1978. The action apparently remains on foot against the other defendants including the subsidiary companies of the Shell and/or B.P. groups; but it has been allowed to go to sleep. In the meantime the arbitration between Lonrho and Shell and B.P. has started before a distinguished team of two arbitrators and an umpire, (the " arbitrators "), by whom the usual directions for pleading and discovery of documents were made in February 1979, and dates have now been
C fixed for the hearing of the reference from June 23 running through to October 1980. If the hearing were to be postponed it would be another two years before the same arbitrators would be available for what is expected to be a very protracted hearing—if it is ever held.

On December 18, 1979, Lonrho expressed dissatisfaction with the discovery made by Shell and B.P. in a number of respects (of which
D your Lordships are concerned only with those that have given rise to the subsidiaries appeal and the Bingham appeal respectively) and applied for a hearing before the arbitrators for directions for further discovery. January 18 and 19, 1980, were fixed by the arbitrators for the hearing of the application; but on January 18 Lonrho issued its originating summons in the High Court.

E *The Bingham report*

As is well known, an investigation into the supply of petroleum and petroleum products to Rhodesia since the Southern Rhodesia (Petroleum) Order 1965 came into force was undertaken by Mr. Bingham Q.C., as he then was, and Mr. Gray, a chartered accountant. They were appointed for this purpose by the Secretary of State for Foreign and Commonwealth
F Affairs pursuant to article 15 of and Schedule 1 to the Southern Rhodesia (United Nations Sanctions) (No. 2) Order 1968. This investigation, in which Shell and B.P. cooperated upon terms to which I shall have to refer later when I come to the Bingham appeal, started in the summer of 1977 and ended with the publication of " the Bingham report " in August 1978. It contains some useful charts of the complicated company structure of the Shell and B.P. groups so far as their operations in
G Southern Africa, including Rhodesia, are concerned. Reference may be had to these if what I have to say later about subsidiary companies of the groups lacks clarity.

The subsidiaries appeal

The relevant rule of the Supreme Court dealing with the discovery
H that is sought in the subsidiaries appeal is Ord. 24, r. 3, which empowers the court to make an order upon any party to a cause or matter to make and serve on any other party a list of the documents " which are or have been in his possession, custody or power relating to any matter in question in the cause or matter, . . ." The documents of which discovery is sought are documents which, although they do relate to matters in question in the arbitration, are not and never have been in the possession or custody of Shell or B.P. They are and always have

been in the sole possession and custody of the subsidiary companies of A
the groups which operated in Southern Africa and, with only one
exception that has been drawn to your Lordships' attention, are resident
in South Africa or Rhodesia and, for the most part, also incorporated
there. Lonrho's contention in the subsidiaries appeal is that because
of the company structure of the groups these documents are in the
" power " of either Shell or B.P. severally or Shell and B.P. jointly.

My Lords, neither Shell nor B.P. is a direct shareholder in any of the B
relevant subsidiary companies. In some Shell is a shareholder at one
remove and B.P. at two removes through a company, the Consolidated
Petroleum Co. Ltd. (" Consolidated "), in which Shell holds 50 per cent. of
the share capital and B.P., through a wholly-owned subsidiary, Britannic
Estates Ltd., holds the remaining 50 per cent. Some of the operating
companies in Southern Africa are wholly-owned subsidiaries of Consoli- C
dated; Shell Moçambique Ltd. is one of these. In others the shares are
held by subsidiaries of Consolidated and in yet others the shares are held
not through Consolidated at all but as to 50 per cent. by another wholly-
owned subsidiary of Shell and as to the remaining 50 per cent. by another
wholly-owned subsidiary of B.P.

It is unnecessary for present purposes to distinguish between sub- D
sidiaries that are incorporated in the United Kingdom and those incorporated in South Africa or Rhodesia. The company law of those two
countries is substantially the same as that to be found in the Companies
Act 1948; and the articles of association of each of the subsidiaries
contain the usual " short cut " provisions appropriate to subsidiaries,
enabling the shareholders by unanimous agreement in writing to exercise
all the powers of a general meeting of the company. E

The articles of association of all the subsidiaries vest the management
of the company in its board of directors. It is the board that has control
of the company's documents on its behalf; the shareholders as such have
no legal right to inspect or to take copies of them. If requested to
allow inspection of the company's documents, whether by a shareholder
or by a third party, it is the duty of the board to consider whether to F
accede to the request would be in the best interests of the company.
These are not exclusively those of its shareholders but may include those
of its creditors. Needless to say, if the local law of the country in
which the company is resident forbids disclosure, the company through
its board must comply with that local law.

Such is the case with the subsidiaries that are resident in South
Africa or Rhodesia. In each of those countries it would have been a G
criminal offence for the board of a subsidiary to disclose the company's
documents to Shell or B.P. unless they could obtain a ministerial licence
permitting them to do so. Shell and B.P. did in fact inquire of the
boards of the subsidiary companies resident in South Africa and Rhodesia
whether they were willing to disclose their companies' documents of
which Lonrho seeks discovery in the subsidiaries appeal. The boards H
refused upon the grounds that it would constitute a criminal offence to
do so and that, in any event, it would not be in the best interests of
the company.

My Lords, in the circumstances it seems to me to be quite unarguable
that the documents of subsidiaries resident in South Africa or Rhodesia
are or have ever been in the " power " of Shell or B.P. within the
meaning of R.S.C., Ord. 24. Nevertheless your Lordships were pressed

A with the contention that there were a series of steps open to Shell and B.P. which, if taken, might have the result of giving them a legal right to inspect and take copies of documents belonging to those subsidiaries. I can restrict myself to those operating companies which are subsidiaries of Consolidated, since the steps suggested in respect of the other operating companies were essentially the same. The suggested steps would be

B for Shell and B.P., as holders between them of all the shares in Consolidated, to procure the board of Consolidated to exercise that company's power to alter the articles of association of each of those companies of which Consolidated is itself the sole shareholder, so as to entitle the shareholders to inspect and take copies of the documents of any of the subsidiaries or sub-subsidiaries of Consolidated. Any copies taken by Consolidated would be the property of that company; so a similar

C alteration at least would be needed in the articles of association of Consolidated itself; nor is it clear how the board of Consolidated could be procured to act as suggested in relation to its subsidiaries if it did not consider that it was in the best interest of Consolidated to do so. Clearly, however, no alteration in the articles of association of the operating subsidiaries could overcome the obstacle of the prohibition upon disclosure of the documents imposed by the local law. So, it is said, Shell

D and B.P. ought to procure Consolidated to procure the operating subsidiaries to apply for a ministerial licence permitting the disclosure. It is Lonrho's contention that until all this has been done and the licence has actually been refused, neither Shell nor B.P. will be in a position to say that the documents in the possession of the operating subsidiaries are not in Shell and B.P.'s own power.

E My Lords, this argument only requires to be stated to be rejected. Your Lordships are not concerned with any other consequences of the relationship between parent and subsidiary companies than those which affect the duty of a parent company of a multi-national group, whose company structure is that of the Shell or B.P. groups, to give discovery of documents under R.S.C., Ord. 24; and this, as I have pointed out,

F depends upon the true construction of the word " power " in the phrase " the documents which are or have been in his possession, custody or power."

The phrase, as the Court of Appeal pointed out, looks to the present and the past, not to the future. As a first stage in discovery, which is the stage with which the subsidiaries appeal is concerned, it requires a party

G to provide a list, identifying documents relating to any matter in question in the cause of matter in which discovery is ordered. Identification of documents requires that they must be or have at one time been available to be looked at by the person upon whom the duty lies to provide the list. Such is the case when they are or have been in the possession or custody of that person; and in the context of the phrase " possession,

H custody or power " the expression " power " must, in my view, mean a presently enforceable legal right to obtain from whoever actually holds the document inspection of it without the need to obtain the consent of anyone else. Provided that the right is presently enforceable, the fact that for physical reasons it may not be possible for the person entitled to it to obtain immediate inspection would not prevent the document from being within his power; but in the absence of a presently enforceable right there is, in my view, nothing in Order 24 to compel a party

to a cause or matter to take steps that will enable him to acquire one   A
in the future.

I turn then to the case of Shell Moçambique Ltd., the only subsidiary
of Consolidated that is not resident in South Africa or Rhodesia but is
incorporated in the United Kingdom and resident in Mozambique—a
country in which the local law does not prohibit the disclosure of that
company's documents.   Shell Moçambique is a defendant to the original
High Court action and before that action went to sleep steps were taken   B
by its solicitors, who are also solicitors to B.P. in the arbitration,
preparatory to Shell Moçambique's giving discovery on its own behalf
in the High Court action.   Some political and physical obstacles were
encountered but in spite of these a list of documents was obtained
together with somewhat illegible copies of some of the documents in
the list.   In an affidavit sworn on behalf of B.P. on January 10, 1980,   C
for the purpose of the hearing of the application to the arbitrators for
further discovery that had been fixed for January 18 and 19, the list
and copies of documents were exhibited, and an offer was made to
Lonrho that if the arbitrators took the view that discovery of these
documents should be made, then " without prejudice to whatever the
legal position may be " B.P. would do their best to facilitate the inspection
by Lonrho of Shell Moçambique's documents in Mozambique where   D
they were situated, provided that the inspection took place between
March 3 and April 3, 1980.   The limitation as to date was to prevent
lateness of discovery providing an excuse for postponing the date of
hearing of the arbitration.

As already mentioned, the hearing before the arbitrators accomplished nothing, as Lonrho had by then decided to proceed by originating   E
summons in the High Court.   For what, in the absence of any plausible
explanation, I can only suppose to have been tactical reasons, the offer
was never accepted before the time stipulated for inspection in Mozambique had expired.   Shell and B.P. are therefore now entitled to stand
upon their legal rights if as a matter of arbitral tactics they think fit to
do so.
                                                                        F
For the reasons already indicated Shell Moçambique's documents are
not in my opinion within the " power " of either of Shell or B.P. within
the meaning of R.S.C., Ord. 24.   They could only be brought within
their power either (1) by their taking steps to alter the articles of association of Consolidated and procuring Consolidated through its own board
of directors to take steps to alter the articles of association of Shell
Moçambique, which Order 24 does not require them to do; or (2) by   G
obtaining the voluntary consent of the board of Shell Moçambique to
let them take copies of the documents.   It may well be that such
consent could be obtained; but Shell and B.P. are not required by Order
24 to seek it, any more than a natural person is obliged to ask a close
relative or anyone else who is a stranger to the suit to provide him
with copies of documents in the ownership and possession of that other   H
person, however likely he might be to comply voluntarily with the
request if it were made.

In dismissing the subsidiaries appeal on its own special facts, I
expressly decline any invitation to roam any further into the general
law of discovery.   In particular, I say nothing about one-man companies
in which a natural person and/or his nominees are the sole share-

A holders and directors. It may be that, depending upon their own particular facts, different considerations may apply to these.

The Bingham appeal

This appeal relates to documents which only came into existence in connection with or for the purposes of the Bingham inquiry. The only

B ground on which disclosure is refused is public interest immunity. This is supported by a certificate of Sir Ian Gilmour, the Lord Privy Seal, which was lodged by the Attorney-General who was given leave to intervene in the proceedings to assert on behalf of the Crown an immunity from disclosure of a kind which used to be called " Crown privilege."

C At the Bingham inquiry, as has already been mentioned, both the Shell group and the B.P. group cooperated fully. They produced to the inquiry many contemporaneous documents. All of these have also been disclosed to Lonrho in the current arbitration. They arranged for many witnesses including managers and directors of subsidiary companies operating in Southern Africa to appear at the inquiry and to give oral evidence. Three new classes of documents came into existence and

D into the possession of Shell and B.P. in the course of the inquiry: (1) copies of the transcripts of the oral evidence of those witnesses, (2) written submissions made by Shell and B.P. to the inquiry and (3) certain correspondence between Shell and B.P. and the Foreign Office and the members of the inquiry. It is of these documents, which I shall call "the Bingham documents," that discovery is sought in the Bingham

E appeal.

Schedule 1 to the Southern Rhodesia (United Nations Sanctions) (No. 2) Order 1968, under which the Bingham inquiry was held, makes it an offence for anyone to refuse to furnish to the persons appointed to conduct an inquiry under the Order any document or information requested by them; but it protects from disclosure to any third party (such as Lonrho) who is not charged with official duties in connection

F with the enforcement of sanctions any document or information furnished to the inquiry without the consent of the person who furnished it, or, when he did so in the capacity of an employee or agent, without the consent of his employer or principal. So the consent of Shell and B.P. was required to the disclosure of the Bingham documents to Lonrho.

Many judges have at some time in their lives had experience of

G conducting official inquiries or investigations in private. Even without the Minister's certificate I should not have needed evidence to satisfy me that the likelihood of success of an inquiry of this kind in discovering the truth as to what happened is greatly facilitated if those persons who know what happened come forward to volunteer information rather than waiting to be identified by the inquiry itself as likely to possess

H relevant information and having it extracted from them by question and answer. Nor would I need any evidence to satisfy me that without an assurance of complete confidentiality information is less likely to be volunteered; particularly where the inquiry is directed to matters that are the subject matter of a pending civil action to which the possessor of the information is a defendant.

Mr. Bingham himself was well aware of this and, in a letter to B.P. of July 27, 1977, expressing his pleasure at learning from the Foreign

Secretary that B.P. had undertaken to cooperate fully in the investigation, he added the following paragraph:

> " We appreciate that on commercial grounds and because of civil proceedings recently commenced by Lonrho and C.P.M.R. certain of the answers to our questions may well involve information which your company would regard as confidential. If, in answering, you will indicate any areas of particular concern, we will do our utmost (consistent with the duty laid upon us by the Secretary of State) to respect this confidentiality."

My Lords, as was fully recognised by the judge and the Court of Appeal, this claim to public interest immunity from discovery was a claim for non-disclosure not because of the contents of the individual documents but because of the class to which they belong. Like all class claims the basis of it is pour encourager les autres. As the Minister put it in his certificate:

> " It is important to the proper working of such an investigation as that chaired by Mr. Bingham and also of many other bodies who have the statutory duty of investigation and of finding facts, that witnesses should not be discouraged from coming forward to give evidence or from giving evidence fully and freely. In my opinion, there is serious risk that such witnesses would be discouraged if, despite express or implied assurances of confidentiality, the information which they provide could be made public, and they themselves laid open to possible attack at the suit of anyone with whom they may have business dealings, including competitors. In my opinion, the disclosure of information and documents furnished and produced to Mr. Bingham and Mr. Gray would impede the work of any body which may be set up in the future to obtain evidence and information or to establish whether or not any offences may have been committed in similar circumstances. In my view, it is necessary for the proper and efficient functioning of such an investigation that the [Bingham documents] should be withheld from production."

Robert Goff J. accepted that, while weight ought to be given to this certificate, it was for him not for the Minister to decide whether the public interest against disclosure relied on by the Minister outweighed the general public interest that in the administration of justice, whether by courts of law or by arbitrators, the decision should be based upon all the facts that are relevant, to the fullest extent that available procedures enable them to be ascertained. The various matters that he ought to take into consideration in balancing the one public interest against the other are summarised in his judgment with clarity and accuracy by reference to the relevant authorities dating from *Conway* v. *Rimmer* [1968] A.C. 910. He came to the confident conclusion that the public interest immunity from disclosure ought to prevail in the particular circumstances of the instant case. The Court of Appeal unanimously agreed with him—and so do I.

I can deal briefly with an alternative submission on behalf of Lornho that, whatever confidentiality may have attached initially to the Bingham documents, Shell and B.P. forfeited their right to it when they consented to the publication of the Bingham report. Although this submission does not appear to have loomed large before the learned judge it was

A put in the forefront of the argument advanced on behalf of Lonrho before this House and argued forcefully.

After receiving the Bingham report in August 1978, the government announced its intention of publishing it as soon as the necessary consents to disclosure required under the Southern Rhodesian (United Nations Sanctions) (No. 2) Order 1968 had been obtained. Those factual parts of the report which dealt with the activities of the Shell and B.P. groups **B** had been shown to Shell and B.P. in draft; and, on September 5, 1978, the Foreign and Commonwealth Office wrote to Shell and to B.P. asking for their consent to the disclosure which would be made in the report when it was published of information and documents furnished by Shell and B.P. to the inquiry. Such consent was given; but it was subject to a qualification expressed by Shell in the following terms in its reply of **C** September 8, 1978:

> " Every consent expressed in this letter is subject to two general qualifications: (a) It applies to the disclosure of information and documents to the extent only that they are contained in the report of the inquiry and any appendices thereto. Our reason for specifying this is that we do not consent to publication of any more extensive **D** information or documents which could then be available for the purposes of other proceedings."

B.P.'s reply was to the same effect. Nothing could be plainer.

My Lords, in the face of this express qualification, it appears to me to be too plain for argument that the consent to disclosure did not extend to the Bingham documents. I would therefore dismiss the Bingham **E** appeal as well.

LORD EDMUND-DAVIES. My Lords, I have had the advantage of reading in draft the speech prepared by my noble and learned friend, Lord Diplock. For the reasons he gives, which I entirely accept, I concur in holding that these two appeals should be dismissed.

F LORD FRASER OF TULLYBELTON. My Lords, I have had the advantage of reading in draft the speech prepared by my noble and learned friend Lord Diplock. I entirely agree with it, and, for the reasons therein stated, I would dismiss these appeals.

LORD RUSSELL OF KILLOWEN. My Lords, I have had the advantage **G** of reading in draft the speech of my noble and learned friend Lord Diplock stating his reasons for the dismissal of these appeals. I agree that these appeals should be dismissed for the reasons given by him.

LORD KEITH OF KINKEL. My Lords, for the reasons given in the speech of my noble and learned friend Lord Diplock, which I have had the opportunity of reading in draft and with which I agree entirely, **H** I too would dismiss these appeals.

Appeals dismissed with costs.

Solicitors: *Cameron Kemm Nordon; Slaughter & May; Linklaters & Paines; Treasury Solicitor.*

M. G.

A

[COURT OF APPEAL]

* MILLICAN AND ANOTHER *v.* TUCKER AND OTHERS

[1975 M. No. 6262]

1979 Oct. 29;   Browne-Wilkinson J.   B
     Nov. 1; 26
1980 Jan. 15, 16; 23   Buckley and Donaldson L.JJ.

*Legal Aid—Costs—Successful unassisted party—Counterclaim by
legally aided defendant—Dispute settled—Counterclaim dismissed — Whether counterclaim separate " proceedings " —
Whether costs recoverable from legal aid fund by unassisted*   C
*party—Whether restricted to costs of counterclaim additional
to costs of claim—Legal Aid Act* 1974 (c. 4), s. 13 (1)

The plaintiffs who were successful entertainers were induced
to enter into management contracts with the two individual
defendants and the defendant company. They issued a writ
seeking declarations that the contracts were obtained by oppression and fraud and were not binding on them, and an account.
The individual defendants were legally aided with nil contribu-   D
tions to defend the action and the legal aid certificate of the
first defendant was extended to cover a counterclaim. By
his counterclaim the first defendant sought a declaration that
the management contracts were binding and, by a subsequent
amendment, he added an alternative seeking remuneration on
a quantum meruit basis. The company made a similar
counterclaim. In March 1979 the hearing began but after   E
some negotiations between the parties the dispute was settled
on terms that the plaintiffs withdrew their allegations of fraud
and the defendants accepted that the contracts were not binding
but, the company being insolvent, the plaintiffs had to accept
a judgment against the individual defendants for £2,000.
Against that they had incurred costs of over £6,000, of which
the major part had been incurred in relation to the claim
alone, and they also faced claims by third parties. The   F
plaintiffs sought an order for costs under section 13 (1) of
the Legal Aid Act 1974 [1] against the legal aid fund. Browne-
Wilkinson J. held, inter alia, that as the counterclaim constituted a separate proceeding for the purposes of section 13, he
could properly order the payment of the costs of the counterclaim and that since the claim and counterclaim raised the
same issues it was legitimate to treat the costs as incurred
partly on the claim and partly on the counterclaim; accord-   G
ingly, in making an order against the legal aid fund he
directed that the costs incurred after the date of the counterclaim on the issues common to both claim and counterclaim
should be divided equally between the costs of the claim
and those of the counterclaim.
On appeal by The Law Society: —
Held, allowing the appeal, that where an assisted party
instituted a counterclaim, the court's power under section   H
13 (1) of the Legal Aid Act 1974 to make an order for
payment out of the legal aid fund to the unassisted party
in respect of costs incurred in " those proceedings " related
to the counterclaim only; that costs incurred in connection
with a claim remained part of the costs of the claim and
however dealt with could not become costs of the counterclaim; accordingly, although the judge's order might have

[1] Legal Aid Act 1974, s. 13: see post, pp. 644H—645D.

A   been a proper order if made inter partes, there was no power to order the legal aid fund to pay part of the costs of the plaintiffs' claim (post, pp. 654C–F, 655F—656B).

       Atlas Metal Co. v. *Miller* [1898] 2 Q.B. 500, C.A. and *Medway Oil and Storage Co. Ltd.* v. *Continental Contractors Ltd.* [1929] A.C. 88, H.L.(E.) applied.

      Saner v. *Bilton* (1879) 11 Ch.D. 416 considered.

      Decision of Browne-Wilkinson J., post, p. 643B et seq.

B   reversed.

     The following cases are referred to in the judgment of Donaldson L.J.:

Atlas Metal Co. v. *Miller* [1898] 2 Q.B. 500, C.A.

Medway Oil and Storage Co. Ltd. v. *Continental Contractors Ltd.* [1929] A.C. 88, H.L. (E.).

Saner v. *Bilton* (1879) 11 Ch.D. 416.

C   *Stentor, The* [1934] P. 133, C.A.

     The following additional cases were cited in argument in the Court of Appeal:

Christie v. *Platt* [1921] 2 K.B. 17, C.A.

Cinema Press Ltd. v. *Pictures & Pleasures Ltd.* [1945] K.B. 356; [1945]
D   1 All E.R. 440, C.A.

     The following cases are referred to in the judgment of Browne-Wilkinson J.:

Cinema Press Ltd. v. *Pictures & Pleasures Ltd.* [1945] K.B. 356; [1945] 1 All E.R. 440, C.A.

Medway Oil and Storage Co. Ltd. v. *Continental Contractors Ltd.* [1929]
E   A.C. 88, H.L.(E.).

Mills & Mills [1963] P. 329; [1963] 2 W.L.R. 831; [1963] 2 All E.R. 237, C.A.

Saner v. *Bilton* (1879) 11 Ch.D. 416.

Stentor, The [1934] P. 133, C.A.

     The following additional cases were cited in argument before Browne-
F   Wilkinson J.:

Atlas Metal Co. v. *Miller* [1898] 2 Q.B. 500, C.A.

Hanning v. *Maitland (No. 2)* [1970] 1 Q.B. 580; [1970] 2 W.L.R. 151; [1970] 1 All E.R. 812, C.A.

Neck v. *Taylor (A Married Woman)* (1893) 9 T.L.R. 547.

New Fenix Compagnie Anonyme D'Assurances De Madrid v. *General Accident, Fire and Life Assurance Corporation Ltd.* [1911] 2 K.B.
G   619, C.A.

S. v. *S. (Unassisted Party's Costs)* [1978] 1 W.L.R. 11; [1978] 1 All E.R. 934, Latey J. and C.A.

Visco v. *Minter* [1969] P. 82; [1969] 3 W.L.R. 70; [1969] 2 All E.R. 714.

APPLICATION

H   By a writ dated October 7, 1965, the plaintiffs, Alan Millican and Thomas Nesbitt sought (1) a declaration that the agreements between each of them and the first defendant, Leonard William Jesse Tucker, dated January 20, 1974, were void as being unconscionable and/or in unreasonable restraint of trade or as having been procured by the undue influence of the first defendant; (2) alternatively a declaration that the plaintiffs had been discharged from their duty to perform their respective obligations under the agreements by reason of the first defendant's breach of his express and/or implied obligations thereunder; **A** (3) a declaration that the argeement between the second defendant, Mardistar Ltd., the first defendant and the plaintiffs dated December 21, 1974, was void as being unconscionable and/or in unreasonable restraint of trade or as having been procured by the fraud or undue influence of the first defendant and/or of the third defendant, James Patrick Houlihan; (4) a declaration that the first and second defendants had no interest or claim to moneys held or owing by Bernard Delfont Ltd., **B** or any other person in respect of performances by the plaintiffs; (5) an order that the first defendant pay to the plaintiffs all moneys received or collected by him or by any other person on his behalf pursuant to the agreements of January 20, 1974, subject to deduction of expenses properly incurred by the first defendant on behalf of the plaintiffs and of reasonable remuneration for time spent by him in or about the **C** affairs of the plaintiffs; (6) an order that the second defendant pay to the plaintiffs all moneys received or collected by it or by any person on its behalf in respect of performances by the plaintiffs, subject to deduction of expenses properly incurred by the second defendant on behalf of the plaintiffs; (7) a declaration that the first and third defendants were accountable as constructive trustees for all moneys received or collected by or on behalf of the second defendant as afore- **D** said and an order for payment by the first and third defendants accordingly; (8) against the first defendant damages for the breach of the agreements of January 20, 1974; (9) against the first and third defendants damages for fraud and/or breach of fiduciary duty in inducing the plaintiffs to enter into the arrangements embodied or recorded in the Mardistar agreement of December 21, 1974, and in **E** the minutes of the board meeting of the second defendant dated September 20, 1974; (10) all necessary accounts and inquiries; (11) interest, costs and further or other relief.

By an amended defence and counterclaim dated June 27, 1977, the first defendant counterclaimed for (i) a declaration that the agreements of January 20, 1974, were valid and subsisting; (ii) an account of all **F** sums received by or due to the plaintiffs as earnings from January 20, 1974; (iii) payment of such sums as were found due pursuant to those agreements upon the taking of such account, or alternatively damages; (iv) costs and further or other relief. The second defendant counter-claimed for (i) a declaration that the Mardistar contract was valid and subsisting (ii) an account of all sums received by or due to the plaintiffs as earnings from December 21, 1974; (iii) payment of such sums as **G** were found due pursuant to the Mardistar contract upon the taking of such account, or alternatively damages; costs and further or other relief.

The case was heard by Browne-Wilkinson J. on March 19, 20, 21, 22, 23, and 26, April 25 and 26, and July 10, 1979. The case was settled on terms which in fact amounted to a complete surrender by the **H** defendants. The defendants acknowledged that the management contracts of January 20, 1974, and the Mardistar contract were not binding. The plaintiffs withdrew any allegations of fraud or mis-representation against the defendants. They did not obtain a full account but the terms included a payment of some £2000 to the plaintiffs. The defendants' counterclaim, which was re-amended during the hearing to claim remuneration on a quantum meruit basis, was dismissed.

A The first and third defendants were legally aided, having nil contributions. No order for costs to be paid personally by them was made.

The plaintiffs applied for an order that certain of their costs should be paid out of the legal aid fund, and the matter was heard on October 29, November 1 and 26, 1979.

The facts are stated in the judgment.

B *William Goodhart Q.C.* for the plaintiffs.
Duncan Matheson for The Law Society.

Cur. adv. vult.

November 26, 1979. BROWNE-WILKINSON J. read the following judg-
C ment. This is an application by the plaintiffs for an order that certain of their costs be paid out of the legal aid fund.

The background facts are these. Until 1973 the plaintiffs were both coal miners who used to sing as entertainers in their spare time. In 1973—when they were in their late forties—they appeared on a television programme, " Opportunity Knocks," with great success on a number of occasions. They were approached by the first defendant, Mr. Tucker,
D who said he could arrange for a recording contract with Pye Records Ltd. Mr. Tucker was in business with Mr. Houlihan, who is also a defendant. Mr. Tucker required the plaintiffs to sign a management contract (which I will refer to as " the first contract ") under which he was appointed their exclusive manager at remuneration which gave him 30 per cent. of their gross receipts. The first contract was for one
E year only. Shortly afterwards the plaintiffs were persuaded to enter into a new management contract (" the second contract ") under which Mr. Tucker received remuneration at the rate of 35 per cent. of gross receipts. The plaintiffs, on the advice of Mr. Tucker, also entered into a recording contract with Pye Records Ltd. under which a sum on account of royalties was paid to the defendants as the plaintiffs' agents. This sum was returnable if the actual royalties earned did not
F equal the amount of the advance.

The plaintiffs were very successful—at least one of their records did very well in the charts, and they also appeared with success as performers in clubs. All the plaintiffs' earnings were paid to the defendants who gave the plaintiffs and their wives some cash weekly. The rest of the plaintiffs' earnings, which amounted to many thousands of
G pounds, have not been accounted for.

Not content with these arrangements Mr. Tucker suggested that a company should be formed to exploit the earning potential of the plaintiffs and possibly others. The defendant company, Mardistar, was incorporated. The plaintiffs between them had 60 per cent. of the issued shares: Mr. Tucker and Mr. Houlihan 40 per cent. In circumstances which have never been explained, in December 1974,
H the plaintiffs signed certain documents which had the effect of altering the shareholdings in Mardistar, so that between them Mr. Tucker and Mr. Houlihan became the majority shareholders in Mardistar.

Simultaneously the plaintiffs signed a further contract (" the Mardistar contract ") under which they bound themselves to provide their services exclusively to Mardistar for five years from June 11, 1974, at a salary of £520 per annum. The result of these transactions, as alleged by the defendants, was that the plaintiffs were bound to provide their services for

five years to a company in which they were minority shareholders in return A
for an assured income of only £520 per annum, the defendants taking 35
per cent. of the plaintiffs' gross receipts under the second management
contract and the balance of the gross receipts going to a company in which,
as I say, the plaintiffs were only minority shareholders. All this had
occurred without the plaintiffs, who were entirely unversed in business
matters, receiving any independent advice at all.

The action was started by writ issued in October 1975. The plaintiffs B
claimed declarations that the second management contract and the
Mardistar contract were not binding on them, declarations that the
transactions which caused them to become minority shareholders were
void, and an account of all moneys received by the defendants. The
defendants obtained legal aid to defend that claim and put in a
defence on April 1, 1976, denying all the allegations. Subsequently C
the legal aid certificate was amended so as to permit the defendants
to counterclaim, and a counterclaim was put in on June 27, 1977, claiming declarations that the second management contract and the
Mardistar contract were valid and subsisting and an account of sums
received by the plaintiffs which ought to have been paid to the
defendants under those contracts. At an early stage during the hearing
before me the counterclaim was further amended to claim remuneration D
on the basis of a quantum meruit.

The case was heard by me on March 19, 20, 21, 22, 23 and 26, 1979.
On March 26 the time had come for Mr. Tucker to go into the witness
box, but he became ill and after some delay a medical certificate was
produced. The hearing was therefore adjourned. The hearing was
resumed on April 25 and Mr. Tucker went into the witness box. On E
April 26 I was told that it was hoped to settle the action and I
adjourned the matter again. The matter was finally mentioned on
July 10, 1979, when I was informed that the action had been settled
on the terms that the plaintiffs' claim was stayed on terms endorsed
on counsel's brief—which I understand included the payment of some
£2,000 by the defendants to the plaintiffs—and the defendants acknowledged that the management contracts and the Mardistar contract were F
not binding. The plaintiffs withdrew any allegation of fraud or misrepresentation against the defendants, and the counterclaim was dismissed. Apart from not submitting to a full account and the
withdrawal of the allegations of fraud these terms in fact amounted to a
complete surrender by the defendants.

On July 10 the plaintiffs indicated that they intended to apply for G
costs of the counterclaim to be paid out of the legal aid fund. Since
the legal aid certificates showed that the defendants had nil contributions I determined on that date to make no order for the costs of the
counterclaim to be paid by the defendants personally. I then stood
over the application as to costs to come on with The Law Society
represented. This judgment is concerned with the matters argued on
that adjourned hearing after hearing argument on behalf of The Law H
Society.

The power to award costs out of the legal aid fund is contained in
section 13 of the Legal Aid Act 1974 which, so far as material, reads:

"(1) Where a party receives legal aid in connection with any
proceedings between him and a party not receiving legal aid (in this
and section 14 below referred to as ' the unassisted party ') and those

A   proceedings are finally decided in favour of the unassisted party, the court by which the proceedings are so decided may, subject to the provisions of this section, make an order for the payment to the unassisted party out of the legal aid fund of the whole or any part of the costs incurred by him in those proceedings. (2) An order may be made under this section in respect of any costs if (and only if) the court is satisfied that it is just and equitable in all the circumstances that provision for those costs should be made out of public funds; and before making such an order the court shall in every case (whether or not application is made in that behalf) consider what orders should be made for costs against the party receiving legal aid and for determining his liability in respect of such costs. (3) Without prejudice to subsection (2) above, no order shall be made under this section in respect of costs incurred in a court of first instance, whether by that court or by any appellate court, unless—(a) the proceedings in the court of first instance were instituted by the party receiving legal aid; and (b) the court is satisfied that the unassisted party will suffer severe financial hardship unless the order is made. (4) An order under this section shall not be made by any court in respect of costs incurred by the unassisted party in any proceedings in which, apart from this section, no order would be made for the payment of his costs. . . . (6) In this section 'costs' means costs as between party and party; but the costs in respect of which an order may be made under this section include the costs of applying for that order."

In order to bring a case within those provisions of section 13 there are six conditions which have to be satisfied, viz: (1) the proceedings in the court of first instance must have been started by the assisted party; (2) the unassisted party must have succeeded; (3) the court must have considered what order for costs should be made against the assisted party; (4) irrespective of the Legal Aid Act 1974 an order would have been made for payment of the unassisted party's costs; (5) the unassisted party will otherwise suffer severe financial hardship; (6) it must be just and equitable for an order to be made.

It is not disputed that, even though I never had to give a judgment in the case because, in effect, the defence collapsed, the proceedings were "finally decided" in favour of the plaintiffs. Nor has it been disputed that apart from legal aid an order for costs of the counterclaim would have been made against the defendants. I have already decided that an order for costs should not in fact be made against the defendants personally. That leaves three matters that are in dispute. First, whether it is possible under section 13 for the court to order that the costs of the counterclaim be paid out of the legal aid fund, i.e., whether for the purposes of section 13 (3) the counterclaim can be treated as separate proceedings instituted by the defendants; secondly, whether the plaintiffs will suffer severe financial hardship; and thirdly, whether it is just and equitable to make the desired order.

First, can a counterclaim constitute separate proceedings for the purposes of section 13 (3) of the Act? Section 14 (1) (a) of the Act provides for the making of regulations. The relevant regulations made under the predecessor of section 14 are the Legal Aid (Costs of Successful Unassisted Parties) Regulations 1964 (S.I. 1964, No. 1276). Regulation 2 of those regulations is as follows:

" Any proceedings in respect of which a separate civil aid certifi-   A
cate could properly be issued under the General Regulations to a
person receiving legal aid shall be treated as separate proceedings
for the purposes of the Act."

Therefore if a separate legal aid certificate *could* have been—not was—
issued covering the counterclaim, the counterclaim is to be treated as a
separate proceeding for the purpose of section 13 of the Act. Regula-   B
tion 6 (1) (*b*) of the Legal Aid (General) Regulations 1971 (S.I. 1971,
No. 62 (L.1.) provides that a certificate may be issued in respect of " the
whole or part of proceedings in a court of first instance." Regulation
6 (2) (*b*) provides that

" Unless a certificate otherwise provides it shall not without the
authority of the appropriate committee given under regulation 15 (1)   C
extend to . . . (*b*) any steps having the same effect as a cross-action
or a reply thereto or to a cross-appeal; . . ."

On these regulations it seems to me clear that, whatever would otherwise have been the proper meaning to attach to the word " proceedings "
in section 13, a counterclaim does constitute a separate proceeding for
the purpose of section 13 (3). Although the normal practice may be   D
to amend the certificate covering the defence so as to extend it to cover
a counterclaim—as was done in this case—it seems to me clear that a
separate certificate could properly be issued to cover the counterclaim
alone, since such counterclaim is certainly part of the whole litigation.
The Law Society suggested that I should give a more restricted meaning
to regulation 6 of the General Regulations since otherwise any small
interlocutory step for which a separate certificate *could* have been   E
issued might fall to be treated as separate proceedings for the purposes
of section 13 which, it was said, would be ridiculous. But I cannot make
any such implied limitation. Say there was a case in which a legally
aided defendant brought a counterclaim raising wholly different issues
from those raised by the claim. Why should not the court order the
costs of such counterclaim to be paid out of the legal aid fund? Yet if   F
I were to limit the words in the way suggested by The Law Society so as
to exclude counterclaims entirely, no order could be made in such
a case.

The plaintiffs also contended, in reliance on *Mills* v. *Mills* [1963]
P. 329, that even without the special definition in regulation 2 of the
regulations of 1964, a counterclaim could properly be described as
" separate proceedings." In view of my decision on the effect of   G
regulation 2 it is unnecessary for me to express any view on this point.

The next question is whether the plaintiffs will suffer severe financial
hardship if the order is not made. Until it is known what order the
court can and should make under section 13, it is impossible to say
whether the refusal of the order will cause severe financial hardship.
There is no exact calculation of the plaintiffs' costs of the claim and the   H
counterclaim, but they are estimated at between £6,000 and £7,000.
If an order under section 13 would relieve the plaintiffs of a liability to
pay, say, £2,000 of their costs, the financial hardship involved would
be much greater in refusing such order than if the order would produce
only, say, £50 towards the total costs.

It is this factor which is the basis of the principal submissions made
by The Law Society, which are as follows: (1) that under section 13 (1)

A the court only has jurisdiction to award the costs incurred by the defendants on the counterclaim; (2) that it is established by the so-called rule in *Saner* v. *Bilton* (1879) 11 Ch.D. 416 that the costs of a counterclaim include only those costs which are additional to the costs of the claim; (3) that in this case the majority of the costs were incurred on the claim; (4) that accordingly the court has jurisdiction only to award the very small costs which were properly called costs of the counterclaim; (5) alternatively, that even if the court has jurisdiction to award more than *Saner* v. *Bilton* costs, it should not in the exercise of its discretion do so; (6) that the failure to receive the small sums which the court could award under section 13 could not amount to severe financial hardship to the plaintiffs, and therefore no order could be made under section 13.

C   I will deal with these submissions in turn. (1) It was not really disputed that the court only has jurisdiction to award the costs of the plaintiffs incurred in the counterclaim. The dispute is as to what those costs can consist of.

       (2) The Law Society submitted that the decision in *Medway Oil and Storage Co. Ltd.* v. *Continental Contractors Ltd.* [1929] A.C. 88 finally established that, in working out an order to tax the costs of a counterclaim, the costs of a counterclaim are only those costs which are additional to the costs of the claim and that it is not legitimate to apportion costs incurred partly in relation to the claim and partly in relation to the counterclaim, treating part of such costs as costs of the counterclaim. Mr. Goodhart for the plaintiffs suggested that this was not the effect of the *Medway Oil* case and pointed to certain passages— for example at pp. 92 and 100 (where Viscount Haldane of Cloan referred to costs incurred in common) for example a brief fee—being divided between the claim and the counterclaim. These passages, submitted Mr. Goodhart, show that there is no such absolute rule that costs incurred on the claim cannot be attributed in part to the counterclaim.

       I accept The Law Society's submissions on this point. Although some of the language used by Viscount Haldane is not altogether clear, there can be no doubt that all their Lordships were approving and applying the rule in *Saner* v. *Bilton,* 11 Ch.D. 416 and the *Medway Oil* decision [1929] A.C. 88, has since been treated as establishing that rule: see *The Stentor* [1934] P. 133; *Cinema Press Ltd.* v. *Pictures & Pleasures Ltd.* [1945] K.B. 356. In my judgment the rule operates as follows. Where the court has not made any special order as to costs but simply allowed or dismissed both the claim and the counterclaim with costs, in taxing those costs the first step is to discover what were the issues which arose on the claim which I will call "the claim issues." All costs incurred on the claim issues are to be taxed exclusively as costs of the claim, notwithstanding that the same issues arose on the counterclaim. No part of the costs incurred on the claim issues can be attributed to the counterclaim. Then the taxing master must discover any additional issues which were raised exclusively by the counterclaim which I will call "the additional counterclaim issues." If money has been expended for the purpose both of the claim issues and the additional counterclaim issues (for example, the brief fee) then and then only can the expenditure be divided so as to attribute to the costs of the counterclaim the part of that expenditure properly attributable to the additional counterclaim issues.

However, it is to be noted that all the cases point out that the rule in   A
Saner v. *Bilton*, 11 Ch.D. 416 only applies to the simple case where both
claim and counterclaim have been dismissed or allowed with costs,
and that the trial judge both can and should make some special order as
to costs if the strict application of the rule would not produce the fair
result.

(3) It is common ground in this case that, until the late amendment
raising the quantum meruit claim, the issues on the claim and the   B
counterclaim were identical. The plaintiffs were claiming declarations
that the second contract, the Mardistar contract, and the share transactions were invalid and relief consequential thereon: the defendants were
counterclaiming that those contracts and transactions were valid and for
relief flowing from their validity. Accordingly if the rule in *Saner* v.
Bilton is applied in its full rigour an order directing the legal aid fund   C
to pay the costs of the counterclaim (being only the costs on the
quantum meruit claim) would produce very little cash for the plaintiffs.

(4) The Law Society submit that, accordingly, I only have jurisdiction to award costs of the counterclaim taxed in accordance with the
rule in *Saner* v. *Bilton.* I do not accept this submission. Section 13 (1)
simply refers to " costs incurred . . . in those proceedings," that is the
counterclaim. It does not define those words and I can see no good   D
reason for limiting the statutory words, which are dealing with the
award of costs, so as to make them bear the meaning that they would
have for the taxing master in working out an award of costs already
made. As I have said, the rule in *Saner* v. *Bilton* only applies if the
judge, in making the order for costs, has not given special directions. I
do not see why the court should not give special directions under   E
section 13 as much as in proceedings which are not legally aided provided
that he goes no further than to award costs which can fairly be regarded
as costs incurred on the counterclaim.

The position I think can be illustrated by a case in which the
plaintiffs' claim raises a point as a minor, but not vital, issue on the
claim, and the same issue is fundamental to the counterclaim. A judge
who dismissed both claim and counterclaim might well take the view that   F
it was not fair to saddle the unsuccessful plaintiff with all the costs of
that issue and direct that the costs of that issue be treated as wholly or
largely costs of the counterclaim to be borne by the defendant. If
that could be done in proceedings where there is no legal aid why
should Parliament have intended that the court should be precluded from
ordering the costs of a legally aided defendant from being treated in   G
the same way? I accordingly hold that under section 13 the court is not
limited to awarding the costs of a counterclaim taxed in accordance with
the rule in *Saner* v. *Bilton.*

(5) How should the court exercise its discretion in this case?
Although I have held that the " costs incurred . . . in those proceedings "
referred to in section 13 (1) of the Act are not as a matter of jurisdiction   H
limited to those costs of a counterclaim which would be allowed under
the rule in *Saner* v. *Bilton,* it does not follow that I have carte blanche
to make such order as I think just in relation to all the costs of the
claim and the counterclaim. I emphasise two points. First, I can only
properly order the payment of costs which on the ordinary meaning
of the words can properly be called costs of the counterclaim. Second,

A   Parliament has made it very clear that the legal aid fund is not to bear any part of the costs of the claim made by an unassisted person.

In my judgment when a claim and counterclaim raise the same issues it is legitimate to treat costs incurred in those issues as incurred partly on the claim and partly on the counterclaim. The extent to which such costs are properly attributable to the counterclaim must depend on the circumstances of each case. In the present case there are two factors
B   which persuade me that it is right to attribute part of the costs of common issues to the counterclaim. First, once the counterclaim was brought, the unassisted plaintiffs lost the option of simply discontinuing the action if they thought that the costs were getting too large. Secondly, the counterclaim made positive claims by Mardistar and by Mr. Tucker to recover moneys from the plaintiffs: it was not merely defensive.
C   For those reasons I think it is quite proper to regard costs incurred after the date of the service of the counterclaim on the issues common to the claim and the counterclaim as being incurred half on the claim and half on the counterclaim, and I so direct.

(6) The estimate of the plaintiffs' total costs is between £,6000 and £7,000. Therefore it is reasonable to assume that, on the basis of equal division of common costs, the plaintiffs will receive something in
D   the region of £2,000 if I make an order under section 13.

The plaintiffs' means are quite moderate. The period of their great financial success is past and although they remain popular entertainers at the clubs, their incomes are not great, being in the region of £5,700 net before tax. Mr. Goodhart suggested that this was less than they would be earning if they had stayed in the pits. They own their own
E   houses which, after deduction of the mortgage debts, have a value of about £12,000. They each own a car and have small personal savings.

From these assets they will in any event have to meet the costs of the claim say £4,000 to £5,000, and accountants' charges of £3,460. In addition there is a sum of £8,142 repayable to Pye Records Ltd. on account of advance royalties overpaid. In fact their commitments exceed their
F   assets unless they sell up their homes. Both of them would now qualify for legal aid under the new financial tests introduced this year. In the circumstances I can feel no doubt that if they were not to be relieved of the liability to pay a further £2,000, that would constitute a severe financial hardship to each of them.

Finally, is it just and equitable to make the order? In the circumstances of this case, I have no doubt that it is. In fact the plaintiffs have
G   been reduced to their present financial straits by the now admittedly wrongful acts of the defendants; they have to repay to Pye Records Ltd. moneys which the defendants received, and they have been unable to recover these moneys from the defendants. It is a hard case.

I therefore propose to order that the plaintiffs be paid their costs of the counterclaim out of the legal aid fund and to direct that in taxing
H   such costs, costs incurred after the date of the counterclaim on issues common to both claim and counterclaim should be divided equally between the costs of the claim and the costs of the counterclaim. Of course the plaintiffs will be left to bear the remainder of their costs and I wish to point out what to my mind is an injustice in the present statutory provisions.

Section 13 (3) of the Act prohibits a judge of first instance from making any order for the payment out of the legal aid fund of the

plaintiffs' costs of his successful claim against a legally aided defendant. A
So far as I am aware the only reason that has been advanced for this
rule is that it is up to a plaintiff to decide whether or not to sue a
man who is not good for the costs and if he chooses to do so he should
not be in a better position than he would have been apart from legal aid.

Whatever the merits of this argument in a normal case, as to which
I have some doubts, it is an argument which only applies in cases
where the plaintiff has a genuine option whether to sue or not, for B
example whether to claim damages for a past wrong. To my mind it
has little validity in such a case as this, that is to say a case where a
plaintiff is forced to sue to rid himself of some contractual or other legal
obligation which extends into the future. In such a case a plaintiff
either has to endure the unlawful fetter for the future or sue. If he sues,
as surely in justice he ought to be able to, those who have ensnared C
him in the alleged illegal obligation are assisted by the state to maintain
what is eventually held to be a wrongful obligation. If no legal aid
had been available the wrongdoer might well have given in at an earlier
stage or not fought the case at all. Yet the plaintiff is left with a bill
for many thousands of pounds which in most cases will constitute a
severe financial hardship as the price he has to pay to free himself from D
the wrongful fetter.

Take this case. I saw the plaintiffs give their evidence in the witness
box and there is no doubt in my mind that they were both men of
the highest integrity—men whom in every way I admire. Equally
obviously they were totally without business acumen. Their success on
" Opportunity Knocks " led them into the dubious fringes of the entertainment industry where, through no fault of their own, they not only E
lost the greater part of the fruits of their success but found themselves
bound, hand and foot, to work for four years for a company controlled
by the defendants. In reality they had no option but to sue to get rid
of those iniquitous transactions. Yet at the end of the day they are left
without the fruits of their success and burdened with a bill of many
thousands of pounds as the price of their freedom. I express the hope F
that Parliament may look again generally at the case for giving an
unassisted plaintiff wider rights to be paid his costs out of the legal aid
fund, and in particular to consider whether the court might not be given
some discretion to order costs out of the legal aid fund where a
successful plaintiff has, in effect, been forced to sue a legally aid
defendant in order to set aside a transaction which imposes a continuing
fetter on the plaintiff. G

I make it clear that I am not in any way criticising the legal aid
committee in this case. They granted legal aid in reliance on the facts
and matters as presented to them by the defendants. If those were not
the true facts the legal aid committee is not in any way to blame.

*Costs of counterclaim to be paid out H
of legal aid fund, and to include
half costs of issues common to both
claim and counterclaim.
Leave to The Law Society to appeal.*

Solicitors: *Bartlett & Gluckstein; The Law Society.*

T. C. C. B.

1 W.L.R.   **Millican v. Tucker (C.A.)**

A   APPEAL from Browne-Wilkinson J.

By a notice of appeal dated December 11, 1979, The Law Society
appealed from the judgment of Browne-Wilkinson J. on the ground that
the judge erred in law and/or misdirected himself in holding that
although by reason of the provisions of section 13 (3) (a) of the Legal
Aid Act 1974 the court had jurisdiction only to order that the plaintiffs'
costs of and connected with the counterclaim be paid out of the legal
B   aid fund, and although the effect of the decisions in *Saner* v. *Bilton*
(1879) 11 Ch.D. 416 and *Medway Oil and Storage Co. Ltd.* v. *Continental
Contractors Ltd.* [1929] A.C. 88 was that the costs of the counterclaim
were limited to the costs of those issues which were exclusively referable
to the counterclaim and that amount by which the costs of other issues
had been increased by reason of there being a counterclaim, both of
C   which points were accepted by the judge, nevertheless the court was
entitled when considering an application for costs to be paid out of the
legal aid fund to make a special order or direction that on taxation of
the costs, the costs of issues common to both claim and counterclaim
should be apportioned equally. The judge had no jurisdiction to make
such a direction and was wrong so to direct.

D   *Duncan Matheson* for The Law Society.
William Goodhart Q.C. for the plaintiffs.
The defendants were not parties to the appeal.

The appeal was heard by Buckley, Goff and Donaldson L.JJ. Goff
L.J. died on January 17, 1980, before the judgments were delivered.

E
                                                    Cur. adv. vult.

January 23. The following judgments were read.

BUCKLEY L.J.   I have asked Donaldson L.J. to deliver the first
F   judgment in this case.

DONALDSON L.J.   In this appeal the legal aid fund challenges an
order for costs made against it by Browne-Wilkinson J. The plaintiffs
were coal miners and part time entertainers. In 1973 they appeared on
more than one occasion as singers on the television programme
"Opportunity Knocks." They were a great success. This success did
G   not pass unnoticed. The individual defendants in the action decided
that they would share in that success. They induced the plaintiffs to
appoint them as managers for a year. Under this contract the
defendants' remuneration was no less than 30 per cent. of the plaintiffs'
gross receipts.

The plaintiffs greatly impressed the judge as men of the highest
H   integrity—men whom the judge said that he admired in every way.
Unfortunately (and this is no criticism of them) they lacked all business
acumen. This led them not only to accept the original management
contract, but also a suggestion from the defendants that this should
be superseded by another contract under which the defendants received
35 per cent. of the plaintiffs' gross receipts for a period of three years.
But even this did not satisfy the defendants. They negotiated a contract
with Pye, under which a large sum was paid to them on behalf of the

Donaldson L.J.   **Millican v. Tucker (C.A.)**   **[1980]**

plaintiffs as advance royalties. They then formed a company, Mardistar A
Ltd., the second defendant, in which the plaintiffs had only a 60 per
cent. interest, later reduced to a minority interest. The remaining
shareholders were, of course, the individual defendants. The plaintiffs
were induced to agree that what remained of their gross earnings after
paying the 35 per cent. management fee would be paid to Mardistar
Ltd. in exchange for a salary of £10 per week, and that this arrangement should continue for five years.   B

The plaintiffs eventually took legal advice. As a result they sued
the defendants for declarations that the second management contract
and the contract with Mardistar had been induced by oppression and
fraud and were not binding on them. They also claimed an account
of all sums received by the defendants on their behalf. Pending the
trial of the action they took such steps as were open to them to   C
ensure that they and not the defendants received fees payable to them
in respect of their activities as entertainers.

The individual defendants obtained legal aid. In April 1976 they
delivered a defence denying all the plaintiffs' allegations. A year later
Mr. Tucker obtained an extension of his legal aid certificate entitling
him to counterclaim against the plaintiffs. The defence was then
amended and a counterclaim delivered. By the counterclaim Mr.   D
Tucker sought a declaration that the second management contract was
binding. The company, for its part, sought a similar declaration that
its contract was binding. Both Mr. Tucker and the company also
claimed an account from the plaintiffs. At the trial Mr. Tucker added
an alternative counterclaim for remuneration on the basis of a quantum
meruit.   E

The hearing began in March 1979, but after two adjournments,
the dispute was settled. The plaintiffs withdrew their allegations of
fraud, but, subject to that, the settlement amounted to a total surrender
by the defendants. But it was a hollow victory. The three-year life
of the second management contract had already expired and the
Mardistar contract was due to expire shortly. The large sums of   F
money received by the defendants had evaporated. Mardistar was
insolvent and the plaintiffs had to accept a judgment against the
individual defendants for no more than £2,000. Against this they had
incurred costs amounting to between £6,000 and £7,000, and, the
defendants being legally aided with nil contributions, no part of these
costs could be recovered from them. In addition, the plaintiffs were
faced with a claim by Pye's for the repayment of £8,000 of advance   G
royalties—money which had gone to the defendants. As the judge
rightly said, it was a very hard case.

In these circumstances, the plaintiffs sought an order for costs
against the legal aid fund under section 13 of the Legal Aid Act 1974.
They were successful. Browne-Wilkinson J. ordered the payment by
the fund of the plaintiffs' costs of the counterclaim and directed that H
in taxing those costs, the costs incurred after the date of the counterclaim on issues common to both claim and counterclaim should be
divided equally between the costs of the claim and those of the counterclaim. The legal aid fund now challenges the jurisdiction of the judge
to make this order.

Let it be said at once, as the judge himself said, that there is no

A criticism of The Law Society for granting legal aid to the defendants.
At the stage at which legal aid had to be granted or refused, those
concerned did not know the true facts. They had to rely upon what
they were told by the defendants.

The making of an order for costs against the legal aid fund at first
instance is exceptional, because no less than six conditions have to be
B satisfied. These are as follows:

(1) The proceeding in the court of first instance must have been
started by the assisted party. It is now accepted that this condition
is met in that the counterclaim, which was instituted by Mr. Tucker,
is to be regarded as a proceeding separate from the claim.

(2) The unassisted party must have succeeded. The counterclaim
was settled by abandonment, but it is accepted that this constituted
C success by the plaintiffs for the purposes of the section.

(3) The court must have considered what order for costs should
be made against the assisted party. Browne-Wilkinson J. did so and
decided that no order for costs should be made, because Mr. Tucker
was an assisted person with a nil contribution.

D (4) Apart from the fetter imposed by the Act of 1974, an order
for costs would have been made against the assisted party for the
payment of the unassisted party's costs. This condition is satisfied.

(5) In the absence of an order against the legal aid fund, the
unassisted party will suffer severe financial hardship. If Browne-
Wilkinson J.'s order is right, the plaintiffs will recover something of the
order of £2,000. Clearly the refusal to make an order having this effect
E would cause the plaintiffs severe financial hardship, for their means are
such that they are now themselves eligible for legal aid. If, however,
the order is wrong, any other order would entitle the plaintiffs to some
quite insignificant sum and no hardship would be caused by refusing to
make it.

(6) It must be just and equitable in all the circumstances that provi-
F sion for the costs incurred by the unassisted party in the proceedings
in which the other party was assisted should be made out of public
funds. In the most unfortunate circumstances of the present case, it
has not been contended that it would be other than just and equitable that the plaintiffs' costs should be met out of public funds.

Where a court orders that claim and counterclaim be dismissed,
G or allowed, with costs, the rule of taxation is that the claim should be
treated as if it stood alone and the counterclaim should bear only the
amount by which the costs of the proceedings have been increased by
it. This is the rule in Saner v. Bilton (1879) 11 Ch.D. 416 which was
approved by the House of Lords in Medway Oil and Storage Co. Ltd.
v. Continental Contractors Ltd. [1929] A.C. 88. In the present case
H almost the whole of the plaintiffs' costs would have been incurred if the
claim had stood alone, because the counterclaim did little more than
claim declarations which were the mirror image of those claimed by
the plaintiffs. This is not to say that the counterclaim was unnecessary.
Only that it scarcely added to the costs. The counterclaim for an
account would, if successful, have added to the costs at the later stage
of an inquiry, but that stage was never reached. Whilst it is true that

the counterclaim for remuneration on the basis of a quantum meruit A did raise a new issue, it is unlikely that it involved the plaintiffs in any significant increase in their costs. A simple order that the legal aid fund pay the plaintiffs' costs of the counterclaim would therefore produce very little benefit.

A trial judge has a wide discretion in deciding what order as to costs should be made inter partes. Browne-Wilkinson J. considered that to make such an order in this case would do less than justice to B the plaintiffs for two reasons. First, whilst the bringing of the counterclaim may not have appreciably increased the plaintiffs' costs, it made it much more difficult for the plaintiffs to discontinue the action if they thought that the costs were becoming too large; and second, the counterclaim was a matter of real substance since it made positive claims to recover moneys from the plaintiffs and was not merely C defensive. In the circumstances, he thought it right to make a special direction that the costs of common issues be divided equally between the costs of the claim and the counterclaim.

If this order had been made inter partes, it would have been well within the judge's discretion. But it was not. It was made between the plaintiffs and the legal aid fund, which was not a party to the D proceedings, and it was made pursuant to a statutory power and not in the exercise of the inherent jurisdiction of the court. The judge recognised this distinction. Section 13 (1) of the Legal Aid Act 1974 authorises the court to " make an order for the payment to the unassisted party out of the legal aid fund of the whole or any part of the costs incurred by him in those proceedings." In a case in which the E assisted party institutes the counterclaim rather than the claim " those proceedings " means the counterclaim. Browne-Wilkinson J. therefore directed himself that he could only properly order the payment of costs which, on the ordinary meaning of the words, can properly be called costs of the counterclaim and that the section made it clear that, in the context of this action, the legal aid fund was not to bear any part of F the costs of the claim by the plaintiffs.

I agree that *Saner* v. *Bilton*, 11 Ch.D. 416, viewed in isolation, might be thought to do no more than define what is meant by the words " costs of the counterclaim " where the counterclaim is allowed or dismissed with costs. However, I do not think that it is possible to take so narrow a view of the later cases. For present purposes the G most important of these is *Atlas Metal Co.* v. *Miller* [1898] 2 Q.B. 500. It is not mentioned in the judgment and may not specifically have been brought to the attention of the judge. It was, however, referred to and approved in *Medway Oil and Storage Co. Ltd.* v. *Continental Contractors Ltd.* [1929] A.C. 88, 97–99, 105, 106.

Sir Nathaniel Lindley M.R. giving the judgment of the Court of H Appeal in *Atlas Metal Co.* v. *Miller*, said, at p. 505–506:

" What are costs of a counterclaim? The answer must be the costs occasioned by it. No costs not incurred by reason of the counterclaim can be costs of the counterclaim. The fact that if there had been no action the costs of the counterclaim would have been larger, because the defendant would then have had to

A   issue a write and take other proceedings, does not make costs
not incurred costs incurred, and in considering what the costs of
a counterclaim really have been in any particular case, the costs
saved by not bringing a cross-action cannot be treated as costs
incurred.   The introduction of counterclaims has given litigants
advantages in this respect.   Counter-claims, although cross-actions
for all purposes of procedure and evidence, cost less than actions, and
B   the party who has to pay the costs of a counterclaim gets the benefit
of the cheaper procedure.   To include in the costs of a counterclaim any costs not occasioned by its being a counterclaim, but
saved by its being what it is, appears to us wrong in principle and
opposed to *Saner* v. *Bilton,* 11 Ch.D. 416, and *In re Brown* (1883)
23 Ch.D. 377."

C   The order under appeal seeks by the special direction to include
in the costs of the counterclaim costs which were not occasioned by it,
but were saved because the issues had already been raised by the claim
and defence.   This is permissible inter partes, because all that the
judge is then doing is to make an order that one party should pay part
D   of the costs both of the claim and of the counterclaim.   Indeed, it may
often be right to do so, because where, as here, both parties are seeking
inconsistent declarations as to their rights, it may be largely a matter
of chance, financial ballast or enthusiasm that determines which party
initiates the claim and which the counterclaim.   It was to such an
order that Scrutton L.J. referred in *The Stentor* [1934] P. 133, 140,
E   when he said:

     " Each judge, under the present system now set up by Ord. 65,
     r. 1, has discretion, and he can make such order as he likes.   If
     he makes an order in common form, it is no doubt important that
     it should be known what the order, in common form means; but
     nothing is to bind this division or any other division to make any
F   particular form of order.   If the judge thinks a better result will
     be obtained, as in *The Bremen* [1931] P. 166, by saying no costs,
     or by making an express order as to apportionment, he is perfectly
     at liberty to do it."

     But it is quite clear from *Atlas Metal Co.* v. *Miller* [1898] 2 Q.B.
G   500 and *Medway Oil and Storage Co. Ltd.* v. *Continental Contractors
Ltd.* [1929] A.C. 88 that costs incurred in connection with the claim
can never be appropriated to the counterclaim, either wholly or by
apportionment, so as to become part of the costs of the counterclaim.
However dealt with by the judge's order, they remain part of the
costs of the claim.   If costs are incurred in connection with the claim
and further costs are incurred in connection with the counterclaim,
H   but the parties have aggregated those costs, for example, fees payable
to counsel or to the solicitor for instructions to counsel, the judge or
the taxing master can divide them on the basis of attributing to the
counterclaim the increase in the costs occasioned by the existence of
that counterclaim.   This is not, however, an exercise of judicial discretion; it is merely doing what the parties ought really to have done
themselves.

In my judgment, Browne-Wilkinson J. has, inadvertently, done A
precisely what he set out to avoid, namely to order the legal aid fund
to pay part of the plaintiffs' costs of the claim. Accordingly, I would
allow the appeal.

BUCKLEY L.J. I entirely agree with the judgment which Donaldson
L.J. has just delivered and, although we are differing from Browne- B
Wilkinson J., I do not think that any useful purpose would be served
by my re-stating in my own words the reasons which Donaldson L.J.
has given. I would however suggest that consideration should be given,
when an appropriate opportunity arises, to amending the Legal Aid Act
1974, section 13, to enable a judge to order payment out of the legal
aid fund of any costs incurred by an unassisted person in proceedings C
against an assisted person which the assisted person would, if he had
not been assisted, have been ordered to pay to the unassisted person by
reason of the assisted person's having commenced proceedings against
the unassisted person, whether such costs are strictly costs of the
proceedings so commenced or not.

D

> *Appeal allowed.*
> *No order as to costs sought.*
> *Judge's order as to costs discharged.*
> *Leave to appeal refused.*

Solicitors: *The Law Society; Bartlett & Gluckstein, Crawley & de Reya.* E

A. R.

May 1, 1980. The Appeal Committee of the House of Lords (Lord
Wilberforce, Viscount and Lord Scarman) dismissed a petition by the
plaintiffs for leave to appeal.

F

[CHANCERY DIVISION]

* PRACTICE NOTE (COMPANIES: ADVERTISEMENT OF PETITION)

1980 April 21   Vinelott J.

Company—Winding up—Petition—Advertisement—Procedure and form of advertisement — Companies (Winding-up) (Amendment) Rules 1979 (S.I. 1979 No. 209), rr. 3, 10, 11

Vinelott J. made the following statement in the Companies Court:

(1) During the period while the " London Gazette " was not being distributed on time Oliver J. and later Dillon J. directed that petitioners might advertise either in a London or in a local newspaper according to the particular circumstances. The difficulties experienced by the " London Gazette " have happily been resolved and from today advertisements must be made in accordance with the Companies (Winding-up) (Amendment) Rules 1979 (S.I. 1979 No. 209) introduced on April 1, 1979.

(2) Experience shows that advertisements are still being made in the old form and not in the shorter form introduced by the new rules. The new rules *must* be observed and petitioners who do not advertise in the correct form may suffer the penalty of being required to re-advertise.

(3) Cases have arisen and are becoming more frequent in which a petition has been advertised less than seven days after it has been served on the company. The breach of these rules can cause serious injustice by unduly restricting the period within which a company may apply to restrain advertisement. I draw attention to this rule in the expectation that this will not occur in the future. If it does a petitioner may be deprived of part of his costs.

T. C. C. B.

[BLACKBURN CONSISTORY COURT]

* *In re* ST. MARY'S, LANCASTER

1979 Oct. 22, 23;
      Dec. 10   Edwards Ch.

Ecclesiastical Law—Faculty—Organ—Pipe organ of historic and artistic importance—Petition for faculty to replace with electrostatic organ—Removal of organ part of larger scheme to extend church facilities—Relevant considerations—Preferability of petition to cover whole scheme—Disclosure of expert evidence prior to hearing

The vicar and churchwardens of a parish church petitioned for a faculty to dismantle the existing Harrison pipe organ and to replace it with a " Westmorland " electrostatic organ. The church, a beautiful and historic building, attracted many visitors, and the parish had plans for major alterations to the vestry, including the provision of a new meeting room. The organ occupied space required for the proposed new accommodation and to resite it would cost considerably more than to install a new electrostatic organ. Though the petition was unopposed, the opinion of witnesses from the Diocesan Advisory Committee and the Council for Places of Worship was that the Harrison organ, which was of historic and artistic importance, should be preserved.

On the petition: —

Held, (1) that the issues raised by the petition had to be determined in the context of the larger scheme contemplated by the petitioners; and that it would have been preferable for the petition to have covered the whole scheme rather than to have related to the organ alone (post, p. 659A–C).

(2) That, in view of the importance to the work of the church in the parish of the proposals embodied in the larger scheme, the price of preserving the Harrison organ was greater than the parish could reasonably be asked to pay in the light of the difference between the Harrison organ and the electrostatic organ, which, on the evidence, was a fine musical instrument in its own right (post, pp. 661A, 662H); and that, accordingly, a faculty as sought would be granted subject to the conditions, inter alia, that a petition for the execution of works of alteration to the vestries and organ chamber of the church be lodged on or before October 1, 1980, and that no work should be executed on the existing organ until an order authorising such works was made (post, pp. 664G—665B).

Per curiam. In future cases before this Consistory Court, directions for the hearing will be given, following, so far as desirable and necessary, the provisions of R.S.C., Ord. 38, rr. 35 to 44 and, in the absence of special circumstances, for a copy of the report of any expert witness whom a party proposes to call to be delivered before the hearing to the Diocesan Advisory Committee and to any witness entitled or required to attend to assist the court under the Faculty Jurisdiction Rules (post, p. 664B–D).

No cases are referred to in the judgment.

PETITION

The vicar and churchwardens of St. Mary's Church, Lancaster, petitioned for a faculty to dismantle the existing Harrison organ and replace it with a Compton-Makin electronic organ designed for the needs of the church. The petition was supported by a unanimous resolution of the parochial church council. No appearance was entered in opposition to the petition.

The facts are stated in the judgment of the chancellor.

J. L. Gillibrand, solicitor, for the petitioners.
J. R. Gower-Jones, solicitor, for the Archdeacon.

Cur. adv. vult.

December 10. EDWARDS Ch. delivered the following judgment. The amended petition of the vicar and churchwardens of St. Mary's Church, Lancaster, widely known as Lancaster Priory, is for a faculty " to dismantle the existing Harrison organ and replace it with a Compton-Makin electronic organ designed for the needs of the church." The petition is supported by a unanimous resolution of the parochial church council. The removal of the existing pipe organ and its replacement by an electronic, or, more properly, electrostatic, organ is only a part of a much larger scheme upon which the petitioners and the parochial church

A council wish to embark. This is the alteration and extension of the vestry on the north side of the church to provide a new meeting room and an office on the ground floor, two enlarged vestries on the first floor as well as sanitary and storage facilities and also the replacement of the existing heating system. During the hearing of this cause it occurred to me that it would have been preferable if the whole scheme, including the proposals relating to the organ, had been included in one petition.

B However, the incumbent, Canon Tomlinson, has explained that the petitioners considered that they must know how they stand with regard to the organ before committing themselves, the parochial church council and the parish to the whole scheme. While I understand the reason for thus petitioning about the organ alone, I remain doubtful whether it was the best course and return to this question at the conclusion of this judg-

C ment. Nevertheless, it follows from what I have said that all the evidence and arguments have had to be weighed and the issues determined in the context of the scheme as a whole.

I should like at the outset to pay tribute to the assistance I have received from all those who have given evidence in this case. Although no appearance in opposition to this petition was made, I directed that in view of the historic and artistic importance of the organ of the church

D there should be a hearing in open court and that the member of the Diocesan Advisory Committee with special responsibility for organs and not more than one other member of the committee, if the committee so wished, should give evidence under rule 6 of the Faculty Jurisdiction Rules 1967 and 1975. I also directed service of the petition and accompanying papers upon the Council for Places of Worship which, under those rules, made applications that three members of its organs advisory

E committee should give evidence. As all five of the witnesses who came to assist the court from the Diocesan Advisory Committee and the Council for Places of Worship expressed the considered opinion that the Harrison organ should be preserved the case has had the nature of a contested cause. However, all witnesses, including those called on behalf of the petitioners, expressed themselves with charity and restraint and I

F have been much helped. While it would be invidious to distinguish between them I am especially indebted to Mr. Charles Myers, the organ adviser to the diocese, and to the three witnesses from the Council for Places of Worship, all of whom have gone to much trouble and given up much time to qualify themselves to give evidence.

The musical instrument at the heart of the controversy in this case is

G the organ now installed in Lancaster Priory. Not all material facts of its history are known but I find that the relevant facts for the purposes of this case are these. The basis of the present organ was an instrument built by William Hill 1873. He certainly re-used a number of pipes from the organ which was then in the church, which was by George Pike England and was built in about 1812. William Hill's organ was rebuilt,

H though without alteration to the case, by Harrison and Harrison, the well-known organ builders of Durham, in 1922. Their specification was not then completed; the work was finished in 1965, largely with the help of a notable donation by the late Alderman Garnett, to which I shall hereafter refer. This organ, which is on the north side of the choir, occupies space which, if the proposals of the petitioners are to take effect, is required for the new accommodation to be provided under the major scheme. Accordingly, the petitioners and the parochial church council

were, in the early days of their planning, resolved to remove the whole A
instrument to the gallery at the west end of the church, where an organ,
possibly the predecessor of this organ in the years before 1873, had been.
When, however, they appreciated what such a removal would cost they
then proposed to store and later to dispose of the existing organ as best
they could and to place a Compton-Makin "Westmorland" electrostatic organ partly in the west gallery and partly within the existing organ
case, which instrument they could so install at a fraction of the estimated B
cost of the reinstallation of the existing organ.

There can be no shirking the fact that if a faculty for these purposes
is granted the present Harrison organ will be lost for ever. All the witnesses from the Diocesan Advisory Committee and the Council for Places
of Worship expressed as their opinions that this loss would be so great
that, notwithstanding the pastoral, financial and musical arguments C
advanced on behalf of the parish by the petitioners the faculty should not
be granted. Those witnesses presented to me the wider interests of
diocese and province, indeed of the Church of England as a whole. They
were concerned that visitors to this famous church might find here the
heritage of past worshippers and benefactors worthily preserved. When
a church has, as this church has, they said, an organ as noble and fine
and well-known as this, then the parish, in its own interest, in the interest D
of future parishioners and in order that the Church's sacred duty to
worship Almighty God as worthily as possible might be fulfilled, should so
order its affairs and care for its buildings that the organ might be saved
for the present generation and for those to come. Those witnesses urged
upon me that, by its very nature, an electrostratic organ would never
adequately take the place of a pipe organ of such quality as this organ. E

The witnesses from the Diocesan Advisory Committee and the
Council for Places of Worship certainly persuaded me of the importance
of pipe organs in the musical life of the Church. During the hearing some
of the witnesses described electrostatic organs as "fake" or "imitation"
organs. Such epithets are, and were intended to be, pejorative and I
do not adopt them, but they serve to illuminate the fact that pipe organs
set the standard against which all organs in places of worship are judged. F
Electrostatic organs, or, at any rate those which are put forward as being
suitable for installation in churches, are held out by their manufacturers
as simulating the sound made by a pipe organ. The simulation may be
so effective that even a trained ear cannot detect that the sound is produced electrically rather than by wind, but it remains simulation. It
follows that, if the Church is to preserve its existing tradition of music as G
an accompaniment and enrichment of worship, there must be pipe organs
played and heard at as many places as possible where the services of the
Church are sung. By "as possible" I mean as is consistent with the
exercise of the informed, collective conscience of the Church in the use
and deployment of its forces and resources, whether spiritual, financial or
material. No doubt, therefore, the Church will continue to look to its H
cathedrals and collegiate churches especially, though not only to them
but to all foundations where there is a living tradition of church music,
to keep, and to build where necessary, pipe organs which will speak to
the glory of God and uplift the hearts of all those who hear and sing with
them.

Lancaster Priory is first and foremost a parish church in a parish of
about 8,000 souls. It has its own people who come from the parish itself

A and beyond. It has, because it is a beautiful and historic building, so grandly set upon a hill above an ancient city, many visitors—their number has been estimated at over 150,000 a year. Canon Tomlinson, the incumbent, supported as he has been by the evidence of the archdeacon, has persuaded me that for the church to do its work as the centre of worship for the parish, his congregation and the visitors, more accommodation is needed. The meeting room proposed would be a most
B valuable room for use in conjunction with the church; first, it could accommodate the Sunday school, now attended by some 35 to 40 children who accompany their parents to the weekly family communion; second, in it refreshments could be served to the many visitors to the church and some of the interesting objects belonging to the church displayed; third, it could serve as a convenient place for meetings of parishioners for
C many different purposes. I have briefly described the other aspects of the larger scheme of the parish. I am anxious not to prejudge the matter lest there should be opposition to the petition, which has still to be presented, for a faculty to execute the necessary works. It suffices to say for present purposes that, in my judgment, the alterations and enlargements are desirable in that they will further the work of the Church in Lancaster. Indeed, it should be said that the Diocesan Advisory Com-
D mittee have considered the scheme as a whole and would wholeheartedly recommend it to the court in principle if the existing organ could be preserved.

If the scheme is to be brought into effect the only way the organ can be preserved is by moving it to the west gallery. Two estimates of the cost of this have been obtained. In the end I am left with approximate
E figures; both estimates have to be treated as the basis for an increased or uplifted figure, because the continuing fall in the value of money has already made them out of date, an estimate of the cost of funding, viz. of interest payments, cost of an appeal, etc., has had to be made, and there are differences of opinion as to the extent and nature of the work which is required. Mr. W. G. Thwaite, the parish's funding consultant, has put the present figures at £112,242, being the uplifted figure on the
F estimate from Harrison and Harrison, and £65,625, being the figure, similarly uplifted, from George Sixsmith. He said further that both figures should be further increased by 12½ per cent. having regard to the inevitable rise in costs and in borrowing charges in 1980. The bracket is therefore in round figures £73,500 to £125,500, the mean figure being £99,500. To this must be added the cost of the steel platform which
G would have to be built to support the organ since the gallery itself is not thought by the church's architects to be strong enough for the purpose. This, with value added tax, is cautiously estimated at £9,315.

As against these figures is to be set the cost of a new Compton-Makin organ. This figure, given a similar uplift, was put by Mr. W. G. Thwaite at £30,268 and I accept his evidence. To it must be added the cost, which
H seems to have been left out of account by the petitioners, of removing and refixing—since that is part of their proposals—the case of the existing organ. This was tentatively estimated during the hearing at £3,000 but may well cost more. The total cost of the electrostatic organ is therefore likely to be, in round figures, £35,000.

The statement of these figures shows that if the parish are to go ahead with the major scheme and if they are, having provided the new and additional accommodation under the scheme, to have an organ thereafter, the extra sum which they will have to find to make sure that such organ will still be their present Harrison organ is £73,815. That sum is arrived at by taking the mean figure I have mentioned, viz. £99,500 and adding to it the cost of the structural work to the gallery, viz. £9,315 and deducting from the sum of those two figures, viz. £108,815, the estimated total cost of installing the electrostatic organ, viz. £35,000. It appears from the evidence that the extra sum required might be considerably more than £73,800 and on any footing will not be less than £47,815. In blunt terms this extra sum, however, much it may be, is the price to the parish of retaining the Harrison organ.

That I have jurisdiction to require the parish to pay this price as part of the cost of embarking upon the major scheme I have no doubt. A consistory court may decline a faculty sought at the behest of the present generation of incumbent, churchwardens, parochial church councillors, parishioners and those upon the electoral roll, however united and eager they may be, in the interests of those who will come after them and of diocese and province at large and indeed on the ground that those seeking the faculty have misunderstood their own obligations and their Christian duty. But before taking the grave step of refusing this unopposed faculty I must take the following into account—first, the mere fact that it *is* an unopposed petition of incumbent and churchwardens supported by the parochial church council; secondly, the disadvantage to Lancaster Priory, its parish and its visitors of the loss of the organ compared with the merits of the larger scheme; thirdly, whether it is reasonable to require the parish to pay the price I have mentioned to save the Harrison organ, having regard to its musical qualities, compared with those of the " Westmorland " organ, and its historic importance; and fourthly, whether the requirement of the price mentioned would place the achievement of the major scheme beyond the capacities of the parish.

With regard to the third matter some criticism has been made of the musical qualities of electrostatic organs. But I have not, so far, mentioned the cogent evidence called on behalf of the petitioners as to the musical merits of the particular organ which the petitioners propose should be installed, namely a " Westmorland " organ, made by J. & J. Makin (Organs) Ltd. The present organist of Lancaster Priory, Mr. J. B. Wishart-Hodgson, was firmly opposed to the introduction of such an organ, or indeed any electrostatic organ, into the church until he actually played one. He then became a warm enthusiast. I also heard evidence from Dr. B. Hesford, a well-known organist, musical journalist and organist of the Priory from 1970–1972, from Mr. Heys, F.R.C.O., organist of St. Mary, Stockport, in which a Compton-Makin organ is installed, and from Mr. D. H. Cox, A.R.C.O., organist of Sedbergh School, who also played on such an organ at Sedbergh. This evidence convinced me of the merit of the " Westmorland " organ; if organists of the experience and standing of these witnesses declare it to be a fine musical instrument, to be played and heard in its own right as a notable organ and barely distinguishable from a pipe organ, then I do not consider that I should be justified in stigmatising it as unworthy of Lancaster Priory. To put the matter bluntly: the evidence has convinced me that the petitioners are justified in pressing on with the major scheme and that the price to the parish of preserving the Harrison organ as part of that scheme is greater than the parish can reasonably be asked to pay in the light of the difference between the one instrument and the other.

A   In reaching this conclusion I have taken into account the four matters I have mentioned. I am conscious that there will be many lovers of the musical tradition of the Church as a whole, and of Lancaster Priory in particular, who will be deeply sorry to see the organ go, but on the other hand many who work for the Priory would be frustrated and disappointed in their worthy plans for the church's advancement if the petition were refused. It must be a matter for judgment between many conflicting
B   principles. I have had to set the importance of the retention of the existing organ against the desirability of executing the major scheme. I say against the larger scheme because the evidence for the petitioners is really to the effect that if they were required to pay for the removal and re-installation of the Harrison organ they would have to abandon the larger scheme. Mr. Thwaites, the petitioners' funding consultant,
C   whose evidence I accept, made the point that the appeal for the sum required for the whole scheme could not be successfully made if it included the cost of moving the Harrison organ. It follows that if I were to refuse this petition the parish would have to abandon the proposals which I have mentioned, whereas they are, in my judgment, of sufficient importance to the work of the church in the parish to justify the loss of the organ, taking all the other considerations which have been urged
D   upon me into account.

Finally, a matter which has troubled me a good deal is the receipt by the parish of donations towards the fund raised to complete the organ in 1965. The witnesses from the Diocesan Advisory Committee drew attention to this fund and in particular to the donation of £6,500 towards it by the late Alderman Garnett. It was rightly put to me that a con-
E   sistory court should not so exercise its jurisdiction that the generosity and expectations of benefactors of the Church are frustrated. Those who give to the Church are entitled to expect that what has been given will be respected and husbanded. I have had some assistance as to the particular circumstances of this gift from Mr. J. Glenn, the verger of the Priory, and it seems to me that, taking all matters into account, I should not refuse to grant a faculty which I believe to be in the interests of the
F   work of Lancaster Priory, because of Alderman Garnett's response to the appeal for the organ 14 years ago. As a general rule I deprecate speculation upon the intentions of deceased donors and the use of such speculation as a basis for decisions upon the disposition of their bene- factions. But here Alderman Garnett was not the sole benefactor; he was completing a work begun in earlier generations by others and, having
G   heard Mr. Glenn, who knew Alderman Garnett well, I feel entitled to hold that the gifts he made were on the footing that the parish would do the best it could in the future to maintain the work of Lancaster Priory and the larger work of the Church in city and county.

In the course of the hearing it appeared to me that the witnesses from the Diocesan Advisory Committee and the Council for Places of Worship
H   were at an unnecessary disadvantage in assisting the court in that they had no prior written notice of the expert evidence called on behalf of the petitioners. While the disadvantage in relation to the expert musicians was very slight it was more noticeable when they had to deal with the evidence of Mr. John Pilling, the managing director of J. & J. Makin (Organs) Ltd., who not only testified as to the nature of the " Westmor- land " organ but also how and where it might be installed. As this was not a contested case and the archdeacon, who was represented, supported

the case for the petitioners, there could not, in any real sense, be cross- A
examination of Mr. John Pilling. Thus, without cross-examination or the
opportunity for the study of figures and plans put forward, albeit orally,
by such a witness as Mr. John Pilling the witnesses who came to advise
the court may have been unable to help the court as fully as they would
have liked, so far as a critical analysis of his evidence was concerned.

Experience in the civil courts has shown the value of the new pro- B
cedure introduced by Part IV of R.S.C., Ord. 38 which comprises rules
35 to 44 of that Order and which were added, by amendment, with effect
from June 1, 1974. These rules make provision for the disclosure of an
expert witness's report before he is called at a hearing. A similar practice
should be adopted in this consistory court and it is my intention in future
cases which require to be heard in open court to give directions for the
hearing which will follow, so far as is desirable or necessary, the pro- C
visions of Part IV of R.S.C., Ord. 38. These directions will, in the
absence of special circumstances, include a direction that a copy of the
report of any expert witness whom a party to the cause proposes to call
shall be delivered in due time before the hearing to the Diocesan Advisory
Committee and to any witness who is entitled or required to attend to
assist the court under the Faculty Jurisdiction Rules.
                                                                            D
Having taken a decision upon this petition in principle some further
matters arise. One of the difficulties of the course which the petitioners
have taken in severing the question of the disposal of the Harrison organ
from the question of the execution of the works I have mentioned is that
precise proposals for the installation of the " Westmorland " organ have
not yet been formulated. There was considerable vagueness in the evidence for the petitioners concerning the disposition of the sound pro- E
ducing apparatus of the organ; in the end all that was clear was that some
of it was to be placed at the back of the gallery in the west end of the
church and some of it behind the case of the existing organ on the north
side of the church. I am satisfied that the petitioners are right in wishing
to retain the case which is a worthy embellishment of the church. However, if it is to be retained it must first be dismantled, set aside in proper F
condition and then re-erected, all at a cost which has not really been
taken into account by the petitioners.

This petition is presented in order to obtain my ruling upon the matter
of principle to which I have referred, viz. that the appeal for funds in aid
of the major scheme may be made, and the petition for a faculty for the
scheme lodged, on the footing that the provision of a new " Westmorland " organ, as a replacement of the existing organ, be an integral part G
of the scheme. I have given judgment on this matter of principle but
decline to anticipate my judgment upon the petition yet to be lodged
either in principle, since there may be objections to it, or in detail, since
no adequate particulars of the works proposed, so far as the organ is
concerned, have been formulated. Accordingly, the order which will be
made on this amended petition is that the petitioners may dismantle the H
existing Harrison organ and replace it with a Compton-Makin " Westmorland " organ, subject to the conditions (1) that a petition for the
execution of works of alteration to the vestries and organ chamber of
the church be lodged on or before October 1, 1980; (2) that the petition
referred to in (1) above shall contain or refer to full particulars of works
necessary to dismantle the existing organ and install the " Westmorland "
organ and of all works to be executed upon the case of the existing

A organ; (3) that no work other than running repairs shall be executed upon the existing organ or its case unless and until an order authorising such works is made upon the instant petition or the petition referred to in (1) above; (4) that the works referred to in (2) above shall be executed within such time as may be allowed in such order, if any, as shall be made upon the petition referred to in (1) above; and (5) that if the works mentioned in (1) above are not begun on or before October 1, 1982, this order shall

B stand revoked. The petitioners are to have liberty to apply to vary the above conditions and are to pay the court costs.

Order accordingly.

C Solicitors: *Oglethorpe, Sturton & Gillibrand, Lancaster; Foysters, Altrincham.*

C. N.

D [CHANCERY DIVISION]

* *In re* A DEBTOR (No. 44 of 1978),
Ex parte THE DEBTOR *v.* CHANTRY MOUNT AND
HAWTHORNS LTD.

E 1979 May 10, 11   Fox and Browne-Wilkinson JJ.

Bankruptcy — Receiving order — Jurisdiction to make — Petition based on non-compliance with bankruptcy notice—Debtor's application to set aside bankruptcy notice determined by registrar after hearing—Appeal against registrar's refusal to set aside notice pending when order made—Whether application " heard " if appeal pending—Discretion to stand over

F *application for receiving order while appeal being pursued——Bankruptcy Rules 1952 (S.I. 1952 No. 2113), r. 179*

Rule 179 of the Bankruptcy Rules 1952 provides:
" Where the act of bankruptcy alleged in the petition is non-compliance with the requirements of a bankruptcy notice, then—(*a*) if the debtor has applied to set aside the notice, no receiving order shall be made against him until the application has been heard. . . ."

G The petitioning creditors obtained summary judgment under Order 14 against the debtor on March 13, 1978, and on September 14 served a bankruptcy notice in respect of the amount of the judgment and costs remaining unpaid. The debtor applied to have the bankruptcy notice set aside, and on October 4 the registrar heard and dismissed the application. The debtor gave notice of appeal against that decision, but

H did not set the appeal down despite being granted several extensions of time in which to do so. On November 1 the creditors presented their petition based on non-compliance with the bankruptcy notice and on December 15 the registrar made a receiving order. At that time the appeal against the refusal to set aside the bankruptcy notice was still pending. The debtor gave notice of appeal against the making of the receiving order on the ground, inter alia, that the registrar had not taken into account when making the receiving order the fact that the appeal against his refusal to set aside the bankruptcy

notice was pending. On March 6, 1979, before the appeal
was heard, the Court of Appeal dismissed the debtor's appeal
against the Order 14 judgment.

On the question whether the receiving order should have
been made in view of rule 179 of the Bankruptcy Rules
1952:—

Held, that once there had been an actual hearing and
decision by the registrar the application to set aside the
bankruptcy notice had been "heard" for the purposes of rule
179, so that a receiving order could properly be made even
though an appeal against the refusal to set aside the bankruptcy
notice was pending (post, pp. 670H, 673c).

In re A Debtor (No. 10 of 1953), Ex parte The Debtor v.
Ampthill Rural District Council [1953] 1 W.L.R. 1050 applied.

Per curiam. Ordinarily a court dealing with an application
to make a receiving order will stand the application over until
the appeal against the refusal to set aside the bankruptcy notice
has been determined, provided that that appeal is bona fide and
pursued with diligence (post, p. 671D).

The following cases are referred to in the judgments:

Debtor (No. 10 of 1953), In re A, Ex parte The Debtor v. Ampthill
    Rural District Council [1953] 1 W.L.R. 1050; [1953] 2 All E.R.
    561, D.C.
Marendez, In re, Re a Debtor (No. 10 of 1978), Ex parte the Debtor v.
    Ready Mixed Concrete (Lincolnshire) Ltd. (unreported), February 2,
    1979, D.C.

No additional cases were cited in argument.

APPEAL from the Bournemouth County Court in Bankruptcy.

By a notice of appeal dated January 5, 1979, the debtor, Reginald
Willam Wolsey-Neech, appealed against a receiving order made against
him on December 15, 1978, on the petition dated November 1, 1978, of
the petitioning creditor, Chantry Mount and Hawthorns Ltd. The
petition was based upon the debtor's non-compliance with a bankruptcy
notice dated September 14, 1978.

The facts are stated in the judgment of Browne-Wilkinson J.

The debtor appeared in person.
Christopher Brougham for the petitioning creditors.

May 11. BROWNE-WILKINSON J. read the following judgment. This
is an appeal by the debtor from a receiving order made by the registrar
of Bournemouth County Court on December 15, 1978, on the petition of
Chantry Mount and Hawthorns Ltd. (which I will call "the company").

I can state the background very shortly. The debtor and his wife
owned and carried on a school which appears to have got into some
financial difficulties. In 1975 they entered into an agreement with,
amongst other people, the company, under which for a limited time the
financial but not the scholastic management of the school was vested in
the company as attorneys. Under that agreement, the debtor and his
wife bound themselves to pay over to the company all the school fees
which were payable, and the company in its turn made various disbursements provided for and entered into certain contracts. The agreement
provided that the debtor and his wife would indemnify the company
against any liability. For reasons which it is not necessary for me to go

The Weekly Law Reports, June 20, 1980

667

1 W.L.R.   In re A Debtor (No. 44 of 1978) (D.C.)   Browne-Wilkinson J.

A into, a disagreement of a serious nature emerged between the debtor and his wife on the one hand and the company on the other. Shortly, it appears that the company had alleged that it was not receiving all fees and in acting under the agreement it had incurred liabilities. The matter culminated in a writ in the Queen's Bench Division, issued on December 15, 1977, under which the company claimed a fixed sum by way of indemnity against liabilities they had incurred. The company proceeded under R.S.C., Ord. 14, to obtain judgment, which was obtained after a hearing before the master in the Queen's Division on March 13, 1978, at which both parties were represented by counsel. The judgment was for the sum of £17,130 odd, but execution on that judgment was stayed. The stay was removed on May 4, 1978. The debtor has told us that during that period he was suffering from severe illness. The judgment remaining unsatisfied, on September 14, 1978, the company served a bankruptcy notice based on that judgment and claiming the sum of £10,360·82, being the amount of the judgment plus costs, less two sums which they had received from third parties in reduction of the judgment debt.

On October 4, 1978, the registrar in the Bournemouth County Court refused an application by the debtor to set aside the bankruptcy notice. It is to be noted that there was an actual hearing of that application. On October 23, the debtor gave notice of appeal to this court against the registrar's refusal to set aside the bankruptcy notice, but took no immediate steps to set down that appeal. On October 30, he obtained an extension of time for 30 days for setting down his appeal to the Divisional Court. On November 1, the company presented the petition on which the receiving order was based, relying on failure to comply with the bankruptcy notice. On November 28, the debtor obtained a further extension to December 21 for setting down his appeal against the order of October 4. On both occasions the explanation was that the debtor was applying for legal aid which he expected to get shortly.

On December 15, 1978, the receiving order was made by the registrar. On December 20 (that is to say, after the date of the receiving order), the debtor gave notice of appeal against the Order 14 judgment, being an appeal to the Queen's Bench judge in chambers, and on the same date he obtained yet another extension of time for setting down his appeal to this court against the refusal to set aside the bankruptcy notice. That final extension of time expired on January 15, 1979.

On January 5, 1979, the debtor gave the notice of appeal against the receiving order which is the appeal before us today. A week later, on January 12, the Queen's Bench judge in chambers dismissed the debtor's appeal against the Order 14 judgment. The debtor then appealed against the order of the Queen's Bench judge in chambers. His appeal was heard on March 6, and the Court of Appeal dismissed his appeal. Accordingly, the Queen's Bench judgment under the Order 14 proceedings is final and unappealable.

H The notice of appeal given by the debtor states the following grounds for the appeal:

"1. That the debtor denies he is indebted for £10,360·82p. 2. That the registrar having been informed by the debtor that he proposed to appeal against the judgment of March 13, 1978, on which the petition debt was based did not adjourn the hearing of the petition in order that that could be done. 3. The registrar failed to take any or any proper account of the copy of legal aid certificate [which he

identifies] to enable the debtor to prosecute properly for damages for A
breach of contract and for negligence against [five persons, including the company] or to counsel's opinion with particular reference
to the nature of the proceedings and identity of the defendants. 4.
The registrar erred in his discretion in failing to give the debtor an
opportunity to file evidence disputing the petition debt. 5. The
registrar failed to take any or any proper account of the debtor's
appeal against the order of Mr. Registrar Wood dated October 4, B
1978, whereby he dismissed the debtor's application to set aside the
bankruptcy notice. . . ."

I will deal first with the fifth ground of appeal, because it raises a
point which was not apparent to the debtor (who presented his case in
person), involving, as it does, a point turning on the construction of the
Bankruptcy Rules 1952 and two earlier decisions of this court.   C

It will be noted that when the receiving order was made in this case
on December 15, 1978, the debtor's appeal against the registrar's refusal
to set aside the bankruptcy notice was still outstanding. Rule 179 of the
Bankruptcy Rules 1952 provides as follows:

"Where the act of bankruptcy alleged in the petition is non-
compliance with the requirements of a bankruptcy notice, then (a) D
if the debtor has applied to set aside the notice, no receiving order
shall be made against him until the application has been heard; and
(b) if the notice is set aside or while proceedings are stayed, no
receiving order shall be made; and the petition shall be adjourned or
dismissed as the court thinks fit."

In an unreported judgment of this court, In re Marendez, Re a E
Debtor (No. 10 of 1978), Ex parte the Debtor v. Ready Mixed Concrete
(Linconshire) Ltd. delivered on February 2, 1979, the reasoning in the
judgment of the court suggests that, for the purposes of rule 179, the
application to set aside the bankruptcy notice may not have been
" heard " within the meaning of that word in the rule so long as an appeal
against the registrar's decision is outstanding. It appeared to us that, if F
the decision in In re Marendez covered this present case, the debtor's
appeal would be bound to succeed.

In a particularly persuasive argument Mr. Brougham (for the petitioning creditors) has persuaded me that the decision in In re Marendez does
not in terms cover the present case and that there is an earlier decision
of this court which is directly in point which was not cited to the
Divisional Court in In re Marendez.   G

In order to understand the argument, I must refer to certain other
bankruptcy rules. Rules 137 and 138 require a bankruptcy notice to be
indorsed with a statement that if the debtor has a counterclaim, set-off
or cross-demand which could not have been raised in the original action
on which the judgment was founded he must file an affidavit within three
days. Rule 139 then reads as follows: H

" (1) The filing of the affidavit referred to in rule 137 shall operate
as an application to set aside the bankruptcy notice, and thereupon
the registrar shall, if he is satisfied that sufficient cause is shown, fix
a time and place for hearing the application, and shall give not less
than three clear days' notice thereof to the debtor, the creditor, and
their respective solicitors if known. (2) If the application cannot be
heard before the time specified in the notice for compliance with its

The Weekly Law Reports, June 20, 1980

669

1 W.L.R.   In re A Debtor (No. 44 of 1978) (D.C.)   Browne-Wilkinson J.

A   requirements, the registrar shall extend the time, and no act of bankruptcy shall be deemed to have been committed under the notice until the application has been heard and determined."

In *In re A Debtor* (*No. 10 of 1953*) *Ex parte The Debtor* v. *Ampthill Rural District Council* [1953] 1 W.L.R. 1050 the Divisional Court had to consider the meaning of what is now rule 139. The headnote reads B as follows:

"On September 10, 1952, the registrar dismissed an application by a debtor to set aside a bankruptcy notice which began to run from that date. On appeal to the Divisional Court the registrar's order was discharged, but on February 10, 1953, the Court of Appeal reversed the decision of the Divisional Court and directed that the registrar's C   order of September 10, 1952, be restored. On March 10, 1953, a petition was presented, founded on the act of bankruptcy which was complete on September 10, 1952:—*Held,* that as the time for the validity of the bankruptcy notice (namely, three months) began to run at the latest on September 11, 1952, and the Court of Appeal had reversed the decision of the Divisional Court and restored the registrar's judgment, that judgment accordingly remained standing D   as from the date when it was given, namely September 10, 1952, and the petition was out of time and must be dismissed."

That headnote is not altogether accurate, but for present purposes the point in question is accurately summarised by Harman J., at p. 1053:

"The second ground taken was that the act of bankruptcy was E   complete on September 10, 1952, when the registrar made his order and therefore was not available as a foundation for a petition filed more than three months thereafter, namely, on March 10, 1953."

He then deals with that point at p. 1054, where he says:

"As to the second point, it is enough to remember the two dates appearing on the face of the receiving order, namely, August 22, F   1952 (the date of service of the notice) and February 10, 1953 (the date of failure to comply), suggest at once the conclusion that the interval is too great. The notice in the ordinary course expired on August 29, and it was admittedly extended by the registrar, under rule 141 of 1915 to September 10. On that date prima facie the act of bankruptcy was complete and the three months then began G   to run. It was, however, argued for the respondents that either the notice of appeal filed by the appellant on October 18 or the order of this court on November 10, discharging the order of September 10 and setting aside the bankruptcy notice in some way suspended the running of time, and that time remained so suspended until the final determination of the matter by the Court of Appeal on February 10, 1953. That order allowed the appeal, rescinded the H   order of this court of November 10 and restored the registrar's order, and it is said the respondents had three months from that date to enter their petition, and complied by filing it on March 10. We are unable to accede to this argument. In our judgment, it follows from the terms of rule 141 of 1915 (replaced now without material alteration in this respect by rule 139 of 1952) that the only person who can extend the time for complying with the bankruptcy notice is the registrar, or, having regard to the definition in rule 3, his

deputy. The rule is directory and compels the registrar to extend A
it " until the application has been heard and determined." These
words can only apply, in our judgment, to the determination before
the registrar of the application to set aside the bankruptcy notice
made by filing the affidavit mentioned in the rule and cannot apply
to its determination either by this court or by the Court of Appeal.
It seems to us, therefore, that the time began to run at the latest on
September 11, 1952. There were in fact, on any view, two months B
during which the registrar's order stood and in which a petition
could have been presented. Of course when this court set aside the
bankruptcy notice it would also have set aside the petition, but
the order of the Court of Appeal would have restored both."

In my judgment, this is a clear decision that for the purposes of
rule 139, where there has been an actual hearing by the registrar of an C
application to set aside a bankruptcy notice, that application is " heard
and determined " at the date of the registrar's decision and that the only
power to extend the time for complying with the bankruptcy notice is
that contained in rule 139, the maximum period of extension being until
the registrar, and not any appellate court, has heard the application.

In In re Marendez (unreported) February 2, 1979, the debtor had D
apparently applied to set aside the bankruptcy notice by an affidavit as
required by rule 139. There was no actual hearing of that application,
because the registrar had refused to fix a day for the hearing, presumably
on the grounds that no sufficient cause was shown. The debtor appealed
to the Divisional Court against the refusal to set aside the bankruptcy
notice, but whilst that appeal was pending a receiving order was made.
The Divisional Court was hearing an appeal against a refusal to rescind E
the receiving order, and held that the appeal should be allowed since the
receiving order was made in contravention of rule 179. There is no
transcript of the judgment of the Divisional Court before us, but we have
a note of the judgment made by the registrar, which includes the following
passage:

"Rule uses ' heard.' Literal construction of ' heard.' ' Heard ' F
when heard by registrar. Too narrow a construction. Seems that
rule prohibits receiving order whilst still pending issue as to validity
of notice. Counsel argues might enable debtor to prolong by appeal.
Quite true. Might be said. Equally one must consider injustice
suffered by the debtor. Severe injustice if receiving order made
because in the event registrar might wrongly have refused to set aside. G
Don't think rule relates to registrars only. Rule comprehends whole
course of proceedings, statutory and non-statutory. No reason
limiting ' hearing ' to initial hearing."

I have in one respect altered the note to make it read comprehensibly.
The decision in In re A Debtor (No. 10 of 1953) [1953] 1 W.L.R. 1050
was not drawn to the court's attention in In re Marendez. Since the H
former decision was concerned with the exact point we have to decide
today, in my judgment it covers the present case, that is, where there has
been an actual hearing by the registrar, the application has been " heard "
for the purposes of the rule once the registrar has given his decision,
notwithstanding that there is an appeal pending against that decision. It
is true that the decision in In re A Debtor (No. 10 of 1953) was concerned
with rule 139 and not rule 179, which is the rule with which we are

The Weekly Law Reports, June 20, 1980

671

1 W.L.R.   In re A Debtor (No. 44 of 1978) (D.C.)   Browne-Wilkinson J.

A concerned, but unless there is a good reason shown to the contrary in my judgment the same words appearing in the same set of rules and dealing with the same subject matter ought to be given the same meaning.

In *In re Marendez* (unreported) February 2, 1979, the court was dealing with a case where there had been no hearing at all of the application to set aside the bankruptcy notice. The part of the judgment in *In re Marendez* which I have read may suggest that, even where there has been actual hearing by the registrar, the matter cannot be treated as having been " heard " for the purposes of rule 179 if an appeal is pending. In my judgment, if so, the reasoning goes too far since it is inconsistent with the decision in *In re a Debtor (No. 10 of 1953)*. In my view, if that decision had been before the Divisional Court in *In re Marendez,* that would not have formed one of the grounds for its decision.

C But for the present purposes it is sufficient to say that *In re Marendez* was dealing with a case different from that before us, since in *In re Marendez* there had not been any hearing of any kind of the application to set aside the bankruptcy notice.

Although, in my judgment, rule 179 does not preclude the making of a receiving order once the hearing by the registrar to set aside the bankruptcy notice has been completed, of course in the ordinary event a court dealing with an application to make a receiving order will stand over that application until the appeal against the refusal to set aside the bankruptcy notice has been finally dealt with. But that will only be the case if there is a bona fide appeal being pursued with due diligence. If there is no bona fide appeal or there is no diligence in pursuing it, then, in my judgment, rule 179 does not preclude a receiving order from being made. Once it is held that rule 179 provided no absolute bar to the making of the receiving order in this case, in my judgment the fact that theoretically there was such an appeal on foot does not provided any ground for overturning the receiving order in this case. The debtor's appeal against the refusal to set aside the bankruptcy notice was being pursued with anything but diligence. Moreover, any possibility of such an appeal now being brought has disappeared since, even with the three extensions of time that he was granted, the time for setting down such an appeal expired on the January 15, 1979.

I turn next to the first and fourth grounds which the debtor has urged for setting aside the receiving order. These were really the grounds that he developed in argument before us. He sought to show, by miscellaneous pieces of evidence, that at the date of the Order 14 judgment the company held funds belonging to himself and his wife more than sufficient to offset the amount owed by him to the company. On the view that I take of the matter, it is not necessary to go into the details of his submissions on the point. I can perhaps illustrate it by reference to one item which he alleges reduced the indebtedness due at that date. He says that at that date the petitioning creditors' solicitors were holding a substantial sum of money, which ought to be credited against the liability of himself and his wife to the company. But the petitioning creditors' solicitors state that they were holding no moneys on behalf of the debtor or his wife: what they were holding were moneys paid to them by the debtor in satisfaction of other orders for costs. This illustrates the unsatisfactory nature of the case the debtor is trying to make; he takes the judgment debt as the only indebtedness and then says that, by showing that there were other funds available at the time, the whole of that indebtedness has been offset. I am not satisfied that in any case the sum was not due. But in my A judgment that is not the point. What the debtor is trying to do is either to show that there was no debt, or to show that he had a set off which extinguished an existing debt.

To the extent that he is seeking to show that there was no debt, it seems to me impossible for this court to entertain such an argument. There is the judgment of the master, the judge in chambers, and the Court of Appeal that the debt is due; there is a judgment for that sum. B He has shown no grounds for going behind that judgment, save that in one respect he says that the material that he has put before us was not available in his hands until recently. There is no evidence of the date at which the material came to him. Indeed, in relation to the majority of the material, it is quite clear that it has been in his hands for a considerable period. C

If the debtor is seeking to set up these matters by way of set off, the set off plainly arises out of the same transaction namely, the agreement between him and the company, and it could and should have been set up in the action in which the judgment was given. This was not done, though the debtor appears to have been given considerable leeway to put up such a set off even after the Order 14 judgment.

Turning to the third ground of appeal, this appears to be a claim D based on a counterclaim. No argument was developed by the debtor before us based on any such counterclaim. No opinion of counsel was produced to us. There is no evidence of any kind to substantiate the existence of such a counterclaim. In any event, for the same reasons that I have given in relation to set off, the matter should have been raised by way of counterclaim in the original action and is not open as E a ground now for attacking the receiving order.

As to the second ground of appeal, namely, that he proposed to appeal against the judgment of March 13, 1978, in my judgment the registrar was fully at liberty, bearing in mind the time-table I have set out, to disregard that matter. In any event, the appeal has now taken place and the appeal has been dismissed.

Finally, the debtor in his reply (but not to my understanding in the F course of his opening) put forward some suggestion that the Order 14 judgment had been obtained either by fraud or by the perjury of deponents to the affidavits which were sworn in support of the Order 14 summons. Nothing that he has said suggests that he has even a prima facie case of fraud. What he is saying is that he was not indebted in the sum. In any event, having pursued his appeal against the Queen's G Bench judgment to the Court of Appeal without previously raising any allegation of fraud, in my judgment he is too late to raise that matter now, unless he shows that there is new material which prevented him from raising the point earlier. As I have said, there is no indication that there is such material.

For these reasons, I would myself dismiss the appeal.

H

Fox J. I add only some observations about In re Marendez, Re a Debtor (No. 10 of 1978), Ex parte the Debtor v. Ready Mixed Concrete (Lincolnshire) Ltd. (unreported) February 2, 1979. In that case, the debtor had filed an affidavit under rule 137 of the Bankruptcy Rules 1952 asserting a counterclaim or a set off. Under rule 139, that operates as an application to set aside the bankruptcy notice, and, under the same rule, the registrar, if satisfied that sufficient cause is shown, is to fix a

A time and place for hearing the application. In *In re Marendez* the registrar refused to fix the time and place for hearing. The debtor appealed against that. The appeal was not heard until after the receiving order. At the time the receiving order was made therefore, the application to set aside the bankruptcy notice had never been heard at all. The refusal to fix a hearing was effected merely by the registrar indorsing the affidavit " No cause shown," or some similar words, and without a
B hearing. Rule 179 prohibits the making of a receiving order until the application to set aside the bankruptcy notice has been heard. As I have said, when the receiving order was made in *In re Marendez*, the application had not been heard, the registrar having refused to fix a date and time for hearing. Thus the issue in *In re Marendez* was whether the application could be said to have been heard prior to the
C determination of the appeal by the Divisional Court. That being said, and although we have only a very brief note of the judgment in *In re Marendez*, I think it is very probable that my observations were on any view too widely expressed, having regard in particular to *In re A Debtor (No. 10 of 1953), Ex parte the Debtor* v. *Ampthill Rural District Council* [1953] 1 W.L.R. 1050 which was not cited to the court in *In re Marendez*. I agree with Browne-Wilkinson J. that the latter case, *In re A Debtor*
D *(No. 10 of 1953)*, is directly in point in the present case and covers the present point.

In the circumstances, I agree that the appeal must be dismissed.

Appeal dismissed with costs.

E Solicitors: *Adlers and Aberstones.*

[Reported by MISS HILARY PEARSON, Barrister-at-Law]

F
[COURT OF APPEAL]

* ASHBY AND ANOTHER *v.* SECRETARY OF STATE
FOR THE ENVIRONMENT AND ANOTHER

G 1979 Oct. 31;   Stephenson, Goff and Eveleigh L.JJ.
   Nov. 1;
   Dec. 11

Highway — Public path — Diversion order — Housing development
obstructing footpath begun before diversion order published—
Whether Secretary of State empowered to confirm order—Town
and Country Planning Act 1971 (c. 78), ss. 209 (1), 210 (1)

H
In 1962 outline planning permission was granted to a developer for a housing development of 40 houses on a plot through which a public footpath ran. When detailed approval was sought, consideration was given to diverting the footpath. Permission was given to the developer and work commenced in 1976. A diversion order was made in respect of the footpath under sections 209 (1) and 210 (1) of the Town and Country Planning Act 1971. That was confirmed by the Secretary of State after a public inquiry in 1977. The applicants applied to

A the Queen's Bench Division for an order quashing the Secretary of State's decision on the ground that some of the houses were nearly complete and it was not within his powers under section 209 (1) to validate development that had begun. After finding that some permitted development remained to be completed, the deputy judge refused to quash the decision, holding that the diversion order was necessary to enable the remaining work to be completed and that the Secretary of State could confirm the diversion of a footpath under section 209 (1) if he were B satisfied that it was necessary to enable the development to be carried out in accordance with planning permission.

On appeal by the applicants: —

Held, dismissing the appeal, that the confirmation of the diversion order was valid as (*per* Eveleigh L.J.) on the true construction of section 209 (1) of the Town and Country Planning Act 1971 the Secretary of State might confirm the order stopping up or diverting the footpath if he were satisfied C that it was necessary in order to enable development which had been carried out on the ground to be legalised (post, pp. 678 D–F, 679H) or (*per* Stephenson and Goff L.JJ.) the development on the footpath not having been completed, what remained to be done showed that it was necessary for the purposes of section 209 (1) to make an order to enable the development to be carried out (post, pp. 681E–G, 683A–B).

Decision of Sir Douglas Frank Q.C. sitting as a deputy D judge of the Queen's Bench Division affirmed.

The following case is referred to in the judgment of Goff L.J.:

Wood v. *Secretary of State for the Environment* (unreported), June 27, 1975.

The following additional cases were cited in argument: E

Jones v. *Bates* [1938] 2 All E.R. 237, C.A.

Lucas (F.) & Sons Ltd. v. *Dorking and Horley Rural District Council* (1964) 62 L.G.R. 491.

Reg. v. *Secretary of State for the Environment, Ex parte Hood* [1975] Q.B. 891; [1975] 3 W.L.R. 172; [1975] 3 All E.R. 243, C.A.

Thomas David (Porthcawl) Ltd. v. *Penybont Rural District Council* [1972] 1 W.L.R. 1526; [1972] 3 All E.R. 1092, C.A. F

APPEAL from Sir Douglas Frank Q.C. sitting as a deputy judge of the Queen's Bench Division.

The applicants, Kenneth Ashby and Andrew Dolby, suing on their own behalf and on behalf of the Ramblers' Association, by a notice of motion dated March 9, 1978, sought an order to quash and set aside the order G of the Secretary of State for the Environment dated November 2, 1977, whereby he confirmed the order of the planning authority, the Kirklees Metropolitan District Council, made under section 210 of the Town and Country Planning Act 1971, known as the Kirklees (Broad Lane Estate, Upperthong) Public Path Diversion Order 1976. The grounds of the application were: (1) that the Secretary of State's decision was not within his powers under the Act of 1971; (2) that, the footpath being obstructed H so as to be impassable, the Secretary of State and the planning authority could not be satisfied that it was necessary to divert the footpath in order to enable development to be carried out in accordance with planning permission under Part III of the Act; (3) that the Secretary of State and the planning authority were wrong in holding that they could be so satisfied if any development remained to be completed; (4) that they should have held that, once development had taken place to an extent that it

A obstructed the footpath, then they could not be so satisfied; (5) that, alternatively, the Secretary of State wrongly held that the permitted development had not been completed by reason of the internal works to some of the houses and the layout of land in curtilages; and (6) that there was no evidence on which the Secretary of State could reasonably conclude that the layout of the land in curtilages formed any part of the permitted development which remained to be completed.

B The deputy judge dismissed the application on July 13, 1978, holding, inter alia, that the Secretary of State could authorise the diversion of a footpath under section 209 (1) of the Act if he was satisfied that it was necessary to enable development to be carried out lawfully in accordance with planning permission and that the order had been properly confirmed by the Secretary of State. The applicants appealed against the deputy

C judge's decision on the grounds that (1) on a proper construction of section 209 (1) of the Act of 1971, the power to authorise the diversion of a public footpath was to facilitate the proposed development and that the powers created under sections 209 and 210 of the Act could not be exercised so as to validate development already carried out; (2) the deputy judge was wrong in holding that he was entitled to consider another part of the development, not directly affected by the footpath, in deciding

D whether the development had been carried out; and (3) the proper procedure should have been an application under section 111 of the Highways Act 1959, in which case objectors would have been entitled to invite the Secretary of State to consider other criteria; whereas the procedure adopted effectively encouraged developers to carry out unlawful development, thereby prejudicing the objectors' rights and the considera-

E tion of the merits of their objections.

The facts are stated in the judgment of Eveleigh L.J.

Barry Payton for the applicants.
Jeremy Sullivan for the Secretary of State.
The planning authority was not represented.

F
Cur. adv. vult.

December 11. The following judgments were read.

STEPHENSON L.J. I will read first the judgment of Eveleigh L.J. who
G is not able to be here this morning.

EVELEIGH L.J. This is an appeal against the refusal of the deputy judge to quash a decision by the Secretary of State concerning a footpath diversion order made by the Kirklees Metropolitan District Council, the planning authority under section 210 of the Town and Country Planning Act 1971.

H In 1962 outline planning permission was granted for housing develop-ment on an area of land through which ran a public footpath. Approval of the details of residential development for 40 houses was given on September 5, 1975, to a Mr. Woodhead, a builder. The proposed development involved obstruction of the footpath at a number of points and so the question of diversion arose. On September 4, 1975, the advisory panel on footpaths of the planning accepted a proposed route for the diversion. In January 1976 the builder laid out an alternative

footpath and started work on a house, No. 25, which obstructed the foot-   A
path before the planning authority had published a diversion order and
of course before any application was made to the Secretary of State. For
that he was fined £80 and ordered to pay £100 costs.

On March 15, 1976, the planning authority made a diversion order in
respect of a new route. After objections had been received and a public
meeting had rejected this diversion, the planning authority devised   B
another route for the footpath which became the subject of the Kirklees
(Broad Lane Estate, Upperthong) Public Path Diversion Order 1976.
After a local inquiry, the Secretary of State confirmed the order. It is
this decision which is the subject of the present appeal.

Section 210 (1) of the Town and Country Planning Act 1971 reads:

"Subject to section 217 of this Act, a competent authority may by
order authorise the stopping up or diversion of any footpath or   C
bridleway if they are satisfied as mentioned in section 209 (1) of this
Act."

Section 217 (1) reads:

"An order made under section 210 . . . of this Act shall not take
effect unless confirmed by the Secretary of State, or unless confirmed,   D
as an unopposed order, by the authority who made it."

As the order made under section 210 was opposed, confirmation by the
Secretary of State was required. Section 217 (2) reads:

"The Secretary of State shall not confirm any such order unless
satisfied as to every matter of which the authority making the order
are required under section 210 . . . to be satisfied."   E

Thus, the planning authority and the Secretary of State have to be satisfied of the matters referred to in section 209. Section 209 (1) reads:

"The Secretary of State may by order authorise the stopping up or
diversion of any highway if he is satisfied that it is necessary to do
so in order to enable development to be carried out in accordance
with planning permission granted under Part III of this Act, or to   F
be carried out by a government department."

It is on the interpretation of this subsection that this appeal depends. For
the applicants, Kenneth Ashby and Andrew Dolby, suing on their own
behalf and on behalf of the Ramblers' Association, emphasis is placed
upon the words "to be carried out." It is said that these words relate
to the future and cannot apply where development has begun or, alter-   G
natively and a fortiori, where development has been completed. It is
argued that there is no power to ratify past activities which would only
encourage developers to "jump the gun." The whole of Part X of the
Act in which the relevant sections are contained and provisions in
Schedule 20 and section 215 of the Act for objectors to be heard and
inquiries to be held indicate that the purpose of those provisions is to   H
prevent premature unlawful development where a highway will be
obstructed. In the present case, therefore, the order and the Secretary
of State's decision were invalid and the developer's only course is to apply
under section 111 of the Highways Act 1959 for an order for the diversion
of the highway.

The Secretary of State (the planning authority does not appear) claims
that section 209 of the Act of 1971 on its proper construction does give

The Weekly Law Reports, June 20, 1980

677

1 W.L.R.   Ashby v. Environment Secretary (C.A.)   Eveleigh L.J.

A power to the Secretary of State to act although development has been completed and although the highway has already been obstructed. Alternatively, it is claimed that all of the permitted development had not been completed, that development in accordance with planning permission remained to be done and that, consequently, there was a situation where the Secretary of State's decision could enable development to be carried out in the future.

B The alternative submission makes it necessary to see what work had actually been done. Work on house, No. 25, was begun in January 1976 and part of the house went over the footpath. Two houses, Nos. 20 and 21, were about 18 feet apart and one was on the east of the footpath and the other on the west. The tarmac drives to the garages of these houses were linked or merged and between them covered the line of the footpath

C over the distance from the pavement to the garages. The footpath crossed the gardens of these houses and also the plots of two further houses, Nos. 34 and 36, which were to the north of Nos. 20 and 21. Although the public could still walk along the footpath line, save that No. 25 encroached over it, the path would be totally isolated from public use when the various plots were fenced.

D The house numbered 25, appeared to have been completed externally but inside it had not been decorated. A floorboard 14 feet long was missing and some cupboards had not been completely installed in the kitchen. The houses numbered 20 and 21 also appear to have been completed from the outside but inside neither had been decorated. Radiators and sanitary fittings had not been installed in house, No. 21, and floorboards had not been nailed down in the larder of house, No. 20.

E In his report to the Secretary of State the inspector remarked that the footpath had not yet been legally diverted and said:

" For this reason Mr. Woodhead [the builder] is unable to sell the three plots and houses and to complete the development so far as he is concerned and so to enable the buildings to be occupied as dwelling-houses. So long as the public has a right to walk through these plots people are not likely to buy the houses. The development permitted

F on plan C, away from the line of the path, is also incomplete and cannot be completed until the alternative route is known along which the path will be diverted."

He went on to say that he considered that it would be unfair to the developer to require him to pull down house, No. 25, (and possibly another house).

G An application to stop up or divert a highway may be made with the Secretary of State's consent to a magistrates' court under sections 110 and 111 of the Highways Act 1959.

Part X of the Town and Country Planning Act 1971 contains provisions for stopping up and diverting highways and provisions for safeguarding the public interest before a final order is made. The

H considerations governing the making of an order are not precisely the same as those under the Highways Act 1959, although in some situations the order might well be obtainable under the procedure of either Act. The effect of Part X of the Town and Country Planning Act 1971 is to provide a comprehensive scheme in that Act for the development of land and the consequential interference with highways under the supervision of the Secretary of State. It is tidy and logical and ensures a consistent approach in deciding the merits of conflicting interests.

I turn now to consider the construction of section 209. The Secretary A
of State is empowered to " authorise the stopping up or diversion of any
highway." Stopping up or diversion may refer to the past or the future.
The words are as applicable to a highway which has already been diverted
as to one which it is intended to divert. I cannot accept the argument
that the word " authorise " is inappropriate to something already done.
The first meaning in the *Shorter Oxford Dictionary* 3rd ed. (1944) vol. 1,
p. 125, for the verb " to authorise " is given as " To set up or acknowledge B
as authoritative. To give legal force to; to sanction, countenance."
Where " authorise " embodies the idea of future conduct, it is defined in
the second meaning in that dictionary. I read section 209 as saying that
the Secretary of State may acknowledge as authoritative or give legal
force to or sanction the stopping up and, consequently, he may deal with
a highway that has been stopped up or one that will be stopped up. C
Indeed, the above meaning of the word is borne out by section 209 (4),
which provides:

"An order may be made under this section authorising the stopping
up or diversion of any highway which is temporarily stopped up or
diverted under any other enactment."

The Secretary of State has to be " satisfied that it is necessary to do D
so." This means that it is necessary to authorise the stopping up or the
diversion. We then come to the words so strongly relied on by the
applicants " in order to enable development to be carried out in
accordance with planning permission granted under Part III of this Act,"
etc. Mr. Payton for the applicants would have us read this as though
" carried out " were equivalent to " begun." I cannot so read it. For
something to be carried out it must of course be begun, but bearing in E
mind the use of the past participle it must also contemplate completion.
Section 209 of the Act is not concerned with the possibility of the works
being carried out from a physical or practical point of view. It is an
enabling section and is concerned to remove what would otherwise be a
legal obstacle (not a physical obstacle) to development. In other words,
the authorisation has to be necessary in order to enable development to be F
carried out lawfully. If it has not yet been carried out lawfully, the
purpose for which the Secretary of State is given power to " authorise "
is still there as the basis for the exercise of that power. Thus far, then,
I see nothing in the words of the section themselves to prevent the
Secretary of State from authorising an already existing obstruction of the
highway caused by development already carried out to completion. Mr.
Payton, however, says that Parliament must be taken to have intended G
to discourage unlawful development and furthermore to deny assistance
in any way to a developer who, as he put it, " has jumped the gun."

The development covered by the section is " development . . . in
accordance with planning permission granted under Part III " of the Act.
It is relevant therefore to see what development may be permitted under
Part III. Section 32 (1) reads: H

"An application for planning permission may relate to buildings or
works constructed or carried out, or a use of land instituted, before
the date of the application, whether—(*a*) the buildings or works
were constructed or carried out, . . . or (*b*) the application is for
permission to retain the buildings or works, or continue the use of
the land, without complying with some condition subject to which
a previous planning permission was granted."

The Weekly Law Reports, June 20, 1980

679

1 W.L.R.   Ashby v. Environment Secretary (C.A.)   Eveleigh L.J.

A Clearly the legislature did envisage the possibility of legalising that which had already been done without permission. There is, however, no reference in section 32 to the obstruction of a highway. As the Act of 1971 envisages authorisation by the Secretary of State for development purposes and provides a comprehensive scheme (as I have already stated), it seems to me illogical that in a particular case where planning permission may be granted, namely under section 32, the Secretary of State should

B have no power to authorise the stopping up. This would presumably be the case if " to be carried out " made authorisation impossible when the work had already obstructed the highway.

If the construction of section 209 is in any way ambiguous, I would resolve the ambiguity in favour of consistency in the operation of the scheme for every kind of permitted development envisaged by the Act.

C Developers who act unlawfully would have to be dealt with by the penal provisions applicable to their conduct.

The matter does not stop there, however. Section 32 (2) reads:

" Any power to grant planning permission to develop land under this Act shall include power to grant planning permission for the retention on land of buildings or works constructed or carried out, or for the continuance of a use of land instituted, as mentioned in

D subsection (1) of this section; and references in this Act to planning permission to develop land or to carry out any development of land, and to applications for such permission, shall be construed accordingly."

The words " and references in this Act to planning permission to develop land or to carry out any development of land," etc., are of importance.

E The references are not limited to the sections contained in Part III of the Act. It is true that " applications for such permission " will be made under Part III, but there are references to " planning permission to develop land " and to " the carrying out of any development of land " elsewhere than in Part III. Section 209 refers to " development to be carried out in accordance with planning permission granted under

F Part III "; that is to say, " planning permission to develop land," the expression used in section 32. Putting it another way, " planning permission granted under Part III of this Act " (the words of section 209) *is* " planning permission to develop land." Consequently, by virtue of section 32 (2), the words in section 209 must be construed to include planning permission for the retention on land of buildings or works constructed or carried out, etc., as mentioned in subsection (1) of section

G 32. This makes it quite clear to my mind that Parliament cannot be said to have intended that there should be no authorisation when a highway had already been obstructed or when the development had already been carried out. In other words, it emphasises that what is being applied for is an order to enable development to be carried out lawfully. This must be so because ex hypothesi in a case to which section 32 refers,

H the development has already been carried out on the ground. It is perfectly permissible, consequently, to read section 209 as saying that the Secretary of State may authorise the stopping up of any highway if he is satisfied that it is necessary to do so in order to enable development which has been carried out on the ground to be legalised.

I appreciate that it can be argued that the power of the Secretary of State to authorise development ex post facto should be limited to a case where planning permission has been applied for by virtue of section 32

itself. However, once one recognises that section 209 can apply to an   A
application under section 32, the future tense as contended for by Mr.
Payton cannot be upheld. An argument seeking to limit retrospective
authorisation to the section 32 case can only be based on the argument
that the developer who " jumps the gun " must be denied the procedure
under section 209 if it is conceivably possible to do so. Such an argument
really rests on an inferred intention to penalise such a person by forcing
upon him the procedure provided by the Highways Act 1959. While the   B
conditions for the exercise of the power to make an order under the
Highways Act 1959 are not the same as those contained in the Town and
Country Planning Act 1971, there are many cases where an order could
be made under either Act.

Mr. Payton has contended for the applicants that in this present case
the application falls to be deal with under section 111 of the Highways   C
Act 1959. I do not see that any worthwhile advantage is to be obtained
in this way. It is surely better for the Secretary of State who may have
to consider the merits of the development permission, to consider at the
same time the highway question. Moreover, it does not always follow
that the developer is blameworthy. Genuine mistakes can occur. A
builder might be prepared to say that he will pull the house down and
start again. Why should not the Secretary of State give his authority   D
in such a case? I regard section 209 as saying that if development is of
the kind which involves obstruction of a highway, then the Secretary of
State can give his authority so that the development can be carried out
legally. Until his authority is given development, although carried out on
the ground, has not been carried out legally. The Secretary of State is
concerned to give legal status to a development of which he approves.   E
He is not concerned to inquire how far, if at all, the work has been done.

I would dismiss this appeal.

GOFF L.J. I much regret that I am unable to accept Eveleigh L.J.'s
conclusion that section 209 of the Town and Country Planning Act 1971
includes power for the Secretary of State to make a completely retrospec-   F
tive order, although on a more restricted construction of the section which
I am prepared to adopt, I agree that this appeal should be dismissed.

I feel the force of his argument and I would like to adopt it, or any
other process of reasoning which would enable me to arrive at the
conclusion that the Secretary of State's powers under section 209 are
fully retrospective, since that would avoid the possible anomaly which
will arise if (ignoring de minimis) an order may be made where the work   G
is nearly finished, although not if it has been completed. It would also
protect an innocent wrondoer, as in *Wood* v. *Secretary of State for the
Environment* (unreported), June 27, 1975, where an order had actually
been obtained before work started, but it was void for a technical
irregularity and it was assumed that a further order could not be made
under section 209 or 210.   H

However, I am driven to the conclusion that this is not possible in
view of the words of futurity " to be carried out " which occur in section
209 (1), and I think this is emphasised by the sharp contrast with the
expression in section 32 (1) " constructed or carried out, or a use of land
instituted, before the date of the application."

Moreover, with all respect, I do not think that any anomaly is
involved, in that if the work be started without planning permission, the

A developer will have to have recourse to section 32, and that contains no provision for authorising work upon the highway. The answer, to my mind, is that if the work has been finished sections 209 and 210 do not apply, whether or not planning permission was obtained before the work was done or started, and if it has not been finished the permission granted would have to be not only under section 32 to retain the work so far done, but also to authorise the rest, and that would bring in sections 209

B and 210. I do not see how the planning authority or the Secretary of State can be satisfied that an order is necessary " in order to enable development to be carried out " without ascertaining the factual situation in order to see whether there is in fact any part of the relevant permitted development left to be carried out or whether it has all been completed.

Moreover, one cannot escape this difficulty by holding that in law

C there has been no development until the work is completed, because development occurs as soon as any work is done, and to say otherwise for the purposes of sections 209 and 210 would be inconsistent with the definition of development in section 22 (1), and with section 23 (1). Any work is a development, even if contrary to planning control: see section 87 (2). It cannot be any the less a development because it is unlawful for

D an entirely extraneous reason, namely, that it is built upon the highway. Nor, I think, can it be said that the planning authority or the Secretary of State has to perform a paper exercise, looking only at the plan and ignoring the facts. This is possibly what the legislature ought to have said, but it has not said it. It would be necessary to do unwarranted violence to the language. One would have to read the section as if it said " to be carried out or remain," or " it is or was necessary."

E So I turn to the more limited alternative. Can it be said that if development on the highway has not been completed, then what remains to be done does show that it is necessary to make an order to enable development to be carried out, none the less so because the order will as from its date validate the unlawful exercise?

In my judgment, the answer to that question should be in the affirma-

F tive, on the simple ground that what remains to be done cannot be carried out so long as what has already been done remains unlawful and liable to be removed, at all events where the new cannot physically stand alone. It would be a very narrow distinction to draw between that kind of case, for example, building an upper storey or putting on a roof, and a case where what remains to be done can stand alone but is only an adjunct, for example, a garage, of what has to be removed, the house.

G If necessary, I would say that any further building on the site of the highway, even although it is physically stopped up by what has been done already, is itself a further obstruction which cannot be carried out without an order.

Much reliance was placed by the applicants on paragraph 1 (2) (c) of Schedule 20 to the Town and Country Planning Act 1971, but I do not

H think that that presents any unsurmountable difficulty. The words " is to be stopped up, diverted or extinguished " clearly refer only to the effect of an order, because the paragraph reads on " by virtue of the order." So it is in no way inconsistent with an order being made to give validity to what remains to be done and indirectly to what has been done in fact but unlawfully. The positioning of the notice is a little more difficult, because the ends or an end of the relevant part of the highway may already have disappeared, but the notice can still be given on the face of whatever obstruction has been constructed. The general sense of the paragraph is A perhaps against my construction, but it is only an administrative provision and certainly does not, in my view, exclude it.

Section 90 (1), which draws a distinction between carrying out and continuing, has caused me some difficulty, but this distinction is not repeated in the final provision in subsection (5) and I do not feel driven by this section from the alternative construction which I have proposed, B which is beneficial and which I would adopt.

When it comes to the exercise of discretion, in my view the planning authority or the Secretary of State should disregard the fact that the highway has already been obstructed, for he ought not on the one hand to make an order he otherwise would not have made because the loss to the developer if no order be made would be out of all proportion to the loss to the public occasioned by the making of the order, for that C loss the developer has brought upon himself, nor on the other hand should the planning authority or the Secretary of State, in order to punish the developer, refuse to make an order which he otherwise would have made. Punishment for the encroachment, which must in any event be invalid for the period down to the making of the order, is for the criminal law.

I should add finally that Mr. Payton for the applicants made much D of the public policy of preserving amenities for ramblers; but in many cases this is not the point, because even if no order be made the developer may well, either before or after development starts, be able to obtain planning consent for revised plans and develop the site, so making the highway no longer a place for a ramble. The relevant considerations will be the desirability (if any) of keeping any substituted way off the estate E roads, and the convenience of the way as a short cut, whether or not to a place where one can ramble, and if a diversion is proposed the relative convenience of the old and the new way, whether any different diversion would be better and whether in suitable cases diversion is necessary or whether the way may simply be stopped up.

For these reasons, I agree that this appeal should be dismissed. F

STEPHENSON L.J. I am attracted by the construction put by Eveleigh L.J. on section 209 of the Town and Country Planning Act 1971, but I agree with Goff L.J. that it does violence to the language of the section and, for the reasons he gives, I cannot accept it.

Sections 209 and 210 require the Secretary of State or the planning G authority to be satisfied that to authorise a diversion order *is* necessary in order to enable development *to be carried out* in accordance with planning permission granted under Part III of the Act. They do not require, or permit, either to be satisfied that it *was* necessary to authorise a diversion order, or that it is necessary to authorise one ex post facto, in order to enable development *to have been carried out.* I cannot give what seem to me reasonably plain words that strained meaning unless H it can be confidently inferred from their context or other provisions in the Act that that meaning would express Parliament's intention. And I do not find in any of the provisions of this Act to which we have been referred, including section 32, or in the provisions of the Highways Act 1959, any clear indication that what appears to be a requirement that the Secretary of State or a planning authority should be satisfied on the facts that something cannot be done in the future without a diversion order is

The Weekly Law Reports, June 20, 1980

683

1 W.L.R.   Ashby v. Environment Secretary (C.A.)   Stephenson L.J.

A intended to be a requirement that the Secretary of State or a planning authority should be satisfied on paper that something done in the past unlawfully needs to be legalised by a diversion order.

I am, however, in agreement with the view that, on the facts of this case, development was still being carried out which necessitated the authorisation of a diversion order at the time when the diversion order was authorised and confirmed. I agree with the deputy judge that on the
B inspector's findings of fact it was then still necessary to enable a by no means minimal part of the permitted development to be carried out.

In my judgment, development which consists of building operations— and it may be development which consists of change of use, as to which I express no concluded opinion—is a process with a beginning and an end; once it is begun, it continues to be carried out until it is completed
C or substantially completed. That fact of life may produce the deplorable result that the earlier the developer " jumps the gun " the better his chance of completing the development before the Secretary of State or the planning authority comes to consider whether it is necessary to authorise a diversion order. But it may not save the developer from unpleasant consequences and it does not enable me to attribute to the legislature an intention which it has not expressed.
D I agree that the appeal fails.

Appeal dismissed.
Secretary of State's costs to be paid
by applicants.

E Solicitors: *Franks, Charlesly & Co. for Pearlman Grazin & Co. Leeds:*
Treasury Solicitor.

[Reported by Miss Henrietta Steinberg, Barrister-at-Law]

F
[CHANCERY DIVISION]

* WESTMINSTER CITY COUNCIL *v.* HAYMARKET
PUBLISHING LTD.

[1979 W. No. 1223]

G
1979 Oct. 17, 18   Dillon J.

Rating—Unoccupied hereditament—Surcharge—Commercial build-
ing unoccupied for more than six months—Legal charge in
favour of mortgagee prior in time to rating authority's charge
—Whether rating authority's charge on all interests in land
H *—Whether binding on purchasers from mortgagee—General*
Rate Act 1967 (c. 9), s. 17A (as amended by Local Govern-
ment Act 1974 (c. 7), s. 16)

On January 3, 1974, a company acquired certain commercial premises, which it charged by way of legal mortgage in favour of a bank, to secure all moneys and indebtedness present and future owing by the company to the bank. The premises remained empty and unused for a period extending beyond October 24, 1975, and a rating surcharge amounting to £16,940·93 became

payable under section 17A (1) of the General Rate Act 1967.[1]   A
On March 19, 1976, the bank served a demand for payment of
the amount due under the bank's legal charge. In April 1976
the rating authority demanded payment of the surcharge and
registered it in the land charges registry as a local charge. In
August 1977 the bank, in exercise of its powers as legal
mortgagee, sold the premises to the defendants. In the contract
of sale the bank agreed to indemnify the defendants against
the rating surcharge, if that charge was binding on them.   B

On the rating authority's summons, seeking, inter alia, a
declaration that the surcharge was charged on the land and a
declaration that it had priority over (a) the defendants' interest
in the land and (b) the entirety of the interests therein: —

Held, granting the declarations, that the rating surcharge
was a charge on all interests in the premises, including the
bank's interest as mortgagee, and it had priority over the
defendants' and all other interests in the land.   C

Birmingham Corporation v. *Baker* (1881) 17 Ch.D. 782 and
Guardians of Tendring Union v. *Dowton* [1891] 3 Ch. 265, C.A.
applied.

The following cases are referred to in the judgment:
Birmingham Corporation v. *Baker* (1881) 17 Ch.D. 782.
Tendring Union (Guardians of) v. *Dowton* [1891] 3 Ch. 265, C.A.   D

The following additional cases were cited in argument:
Banister v. *Islington London Borough Council* (1972) 71 L.G.R. 239, D.C.
Brent London Borough Council v. *Alfa Romeo (Great Britain) Ltd.*
   (1977) 75 L.G.R. 685, D.C.
Bristol Corporation v. *Virgin* [1928] 2 K.B. 622.
Paddington Borough Council v. *Finucane* [1928] Ch. 567.
Tottenham Local Board of Health v. *Rowell* (1880) 15 Ch.D. 378, C.A.   E

ORIGINATING SUMMONS

By an originating summons dated May 14, 1979, the rating
authority, Westminster City Council, claimed against the defendants,
Haymarket Publishing Ltd., the following relief, viz. (1) payment
of £16,940·93, being the amount of a surcharge payable to the rating   F
authority by virtue of sections 17A and 17B of the General Rate
Act 1967; (2) a declaration that under or by virtue of those statutory
provisions and of section 7 of the Local Land Charges Act 1975, the
sum of £16,940·93 was charged on the land, (3) a declaration that the
rating authority's charge, being registered in the local land charges register
on April 22, 1976, had priority over (a) the interest of the defendants in   G
the land and (b) the entirety of the interests therein; (4) possession of the
land; (5) an order that the charge be enforced by sale of the land; (6)
interest at such rate and for such period as the court might think fit;
(7) further or other relief; and (8) costs.

The facts are stated in the judgment.

W. J. Mowbray Q.C. and *Colin Braham* for the rating authority.   H
Peter Millett Q.C. and *G. Hill* for the defendants.

DILLON J. I am concerned in this case with the scope and priority
of the charge in respect of the rating surcharge on unused commercial
property, which is imposed by sections 17A and 17B of the General Rate

---

[1] General Rate Act 1967, s. 17A (1): see post, p. 685A–B.

The Weekly Law Reports, June 20, 1980

685

1 W.L.R.   Westminster Council v. Haymarket Publishing Ltd. (Ch.D.)   Dillon J.

A   Act 1967. These sections were introduced into the Act of 1967 by the
Local Government Act 1974 and have effect from February 8, 1974.
Their relevant provisions are as follows:

> "17A (1).   If for a continuous period exceeding six months a
> commercial building is not used for the purpose for which it was
> constructed or has been adapted, its owner shall pay in respect of
> B   that period (the 'period of non-use') a surcharge additional to the
> rates (if any) payable apart from this section.   (2) Subsection (1)
> of this section shall not apply where—(a) the owner has tried his
> best to let the building, or (b). . . ." another condition which is not
> relevant in the present case.

In subsections (3) and (4) there are alternative conditions. Subsection
C   (3) applies where the owner is in occupation of the building throughout
the period of non-use, and subsection (4) applies where the owner is not
in occupation of the building throughout the period of non-use.
     Section 17B (3) provides:

> "A surcharge imposed under section 17A of this Act in respect of a
> hereditament shall until recovered be a charge on the land comprised
> D   in the hereditament; and for the purposes of the application to such
> a charge of section 15 (registration of local land charges) of the
> Land Charges Act 1925 this Act shall be deemed to be a similar
> statute to the Acts mentioned in subsection (1) of that section."

Section 17B (6) makes Schedule 1 to the General Rate Act 1967 apply for
the purposes of section 17A with minor modifications, and then section
E   17B (7) provides that in sections 17A and 17B " owner " means the person
entitled to possession, and while different persons are entitled to possession of a hereditament during different parts of a period of non-use a
surcharge in respect of that period shall be apportioned between them
according to the length of each part and levied accordingly. In Schedule
1 to the General Rate Act 1967, paragraph 13 provides:

> F   " Any amount due . . . shall, without prejudice to the operation of
> any other enactment under which it is recoverable, be recoverable
> as a simple contract debt in any court of competent jurisdiction."

The premises with which I am concerned in these proceedings are no.
17 Lancaster Gate and nos. 12 and 13 Lancaster Mews, London W.2.
These premises were acquired in fee simple by Shop Investments Ltd.,
G   which I shall call " the company," on January 3, 1974, and on the next
day they were charged by the company by way of legal mortgage with
the payment to National Westminster Bank Ltd., which I shall call
" the bank," of all moneys and indebtedness due from the company
to the bank.   The legal charge to the bank contains nothing to cut down
the ordinary immediate right of a legal mortgagee to possession of the
H   mortgaged property.
     On February 8, 1974, when sections 17A and 17B came into effect,
the premises, which were commercial premises, were empty and unused,
and it is common ground that they remained empty and unused until
October 24, 1975, and that the rating surcharge is payable by the owner
in respect of the premises for the period. The total amount is £16,940·93.
The premises remained empty after October 24, 1975, but it is common
ground that no surcharge is payable in respect of time after that date

because of the efforts then being made to let the premises. On March 19, 1976, the bank served a demand on the company for the payment of the amount due under the legal charge. This amount was at all material times in excess of £6,000,000 because the company had guaranteed its parent company's obligations to the bank. On April 21, 1976, the rating authority served a demand on the company for the payment of the £16,940·93 rating surcharge, and on the following day the rating authority's charge in respect of the surcharge was duly registered in the land charges registry as a local land charge. The amount has not yet been paid.

On July 15, 1977, the bank in exercise of its powers as legal mortgagee contracted to sell the premises to the present defendants, Haymarket Publishing Ltd., for a sum of £220,000. A few weeks later this contract was duly completed and the defendants are now the registered proprietors of the premises at H.M. Land Registry. In the contract of July 1977 the bank agreed to indemnify the defendants against the rating authority's charge for the rating surcharge if that charge is binding on the defendants.

By virtue of section 17B (3) of the General Rate Act 1967 the surcharge while unpaid is declared to be a charge on the land. It is common ground between Mr. Mowbray, for the rating authority, and Mr. Millett, for the defendants, that this wording can only mean either (1) a charge on all interests, legal or equitable, in the premises including the bank's interest as mortgagee, or (2) merely a charge on the interest, such as it was at the relevant time, of the " owner," in the premises.

Mr. Mowbray's first contention is that the charge is a charge on all interests in the premises including the bank's. It is common ground that if this is correct the charge binds the defendants because the charge on this contention had priority to the bank's interests and the defendants claim under the bank. Mr. Mowbray's second contention is that, even if the charge is only a charge on the interest of the owner in the premises, the bank was at all relevant times an owner or the owner of the premises whether or not the company was also an owner. It is common ground that, if this is right, again the charge binds the defendants.

Mr. Millett by contrast contends that the charge is only a charge on the interest of the owner in the premises, that under the scheme of the Act only one interest at any one time can be the interest of " the owner " and that " the owner " at the relevant times was the company whose interest was merely the equity of redemption subject to the bank's charge. Mr. Mowbray concedes that, if that is right, the defendants are freed from the rating authority's charge.

In support of his second contention Mr. Mowbray relies on the well-established rule that by virtue of his legal estate a legal mortgagee is entitled to possession of the mortgaged property even before the ink is dry on the mortgage; certainly before demand and before any default on the part of the mortgagor. I prefer Mr. Millett's view that it is inconsistent with the scheme of the Act for there to be several owners of a property at the same time, not being mere joint owners of the same legal estate like partners or trustees.

Subsections (3) and (4) of section 17A are concerned in the alternative with the situation where the owner is or is not in occupation of the premises, and I do not find these readily workable if there is one owner who is in occupation and another owner in respect of a different interest who is not in occupation. Subsection (2) refers to the situation where

The Weekly Law Reports, June 20, 1980

687

1 W.L.R.   Westminster Council v. Haymarket Publishing Ltd. (Ch.D.)   Dillon J.

A the owner had tried his best to let the building and this hardly fits the situation where there is one owner, the mortgagor, who is trying his best to let and another owner, the mortgagee, who has not been concerned to do anything because the interest under his mortgage had been duly paid. Moreover, I cannot conceive that Parliament intended to impose a personal liability to pay the surcharge recoverable as a simple contract
B debt on a mortgagee, let alone a second or subsequent mortgagee, who was not at the relevant time a mortgagee in possession in the accepted sense of that term. However, it is unnecessary for me to express any final view on this since I have reached a clear conclusion that Mr. Mowbray is right on his first contention.

In support of this contention Mr. Mowbray has referred me to a line of established authorities on earlier Acts, such as Public Health Acts
C and Highways Acts, where charges on land created by statute in favour of local authorities had been held to be charges on all the interests in the land, including the interests of chargees under subsisting mortgages, and not merely charges on the equity of redemption subject to all prior mortgages: see particularly *Birmingham Corporation* v. *Baker* (1881) 17 Ch.D. 782. The terms of the relevant statute are set out as follows, at
D p. 783:

"... the Public Health Act 1875 enacts that 'Where any local authority have incurred expenses for the repayment whereof the owner of the premises for or in respect of which the same are incurred is made liable under this Act or by any agreement with the local authority, such expenses may be recovered, together with
E interest at a rate not exceeding £5 per centum per annum, from the date of service of a demand for the same till payment thereof, from any person who is the owner of such premises when the works are completed for which such expenses have been incurred, and until recovery of such expenses and interest the same shall be a charge on the premises in respect of which they were incurred ...'"

F Sir George Jessel M.R. said, at p. 786:

"Now, the houses per se being inanimate, they cannot bear the burden. If there be a charge on the houses it is a charge on the total ownership—if I may call it so, on the proprietorship; not on any particular section or portion of the proprietorship, but on the whole."

G See also the judgment of Fry L.J. in *Guardians of Tendring Union* v. *Dowton* [1891] 3 Ch. 265 where he said, at p. 269: "All the Act does is to create a charge on the premises—that is, on the land—that is, on all the interests of the owners of the land." He went on to explain that the charge did not override a restrictive covenant in favour of the owners of other property for reasons which are not relevant to this present case.

H   Mr. Millett has sought to distinguish these authorities. He has said, correctly, that they were decisions under other Acts, and under those other Acts the definition of the term " the owner " was somewhat different. He has pointed out that under recent Public Health Acts and Highways Acts the charge is expressly stated in the Act to be on the land and each and every interest in the land: see section 291 (1) of the Public Health Act 1936, and section 264 (1) of the Highways Act 1959. But this does not, in my judgment, invalidate the reasoning of the earlier decisions

under the earlier Acts. Mr. Millett has contended in particular as a ground   A
for distinguishing the earlier decisions, that in all those cases moneys had
been laid out by the local authorities in carrying out works which were
calculated to benefit the owners of all interests in the relevant premises
including mortgagees. It is quite true that in the reported cases the
judges have pointed out that the works concerned would benefit the
owners of all interests in the premises. But I think they have done so not   B
as the ratio of their decisions but as an indication why the decisions they
have reached are intelligible or in accordance with commercial sense:
see Lord Halsbury L.C. in *Guardians of Tendring Union* v. *Dowton*
[1891] 3 Ch. 265, 268. The real ratio is that the words in the relevant
statute " charge on the land " naturally import a charge on all interests
in the land, that is to say, a charge on the proprietorship or total ownership. The emphasis of the judgments is on the interests rather than on the   C
benefits. It would be impossible for the court, in applying such sections
which create statutory charges, to enter on an inquiry whether the matters
which have brought about the creation of the statutory charge were or
were not beneficial to the owners of all or any of the interests in the
land concerned. The true beneficiaries may well be other sections of the
community, users of the public highway or occupiers of neighbouring   D
premises, and any benefit to any owner of an interest in the subject
premises may on any view be incidental. It would be equally impossible
as a matter of construction for the meaning of such words as " a charge
on the land " in a public statute to vary from case to case, depending on
whether or not the matters which had given rise to the imposition of
the charge were or were not in some sense beneficial to the owners of
particular interests in the land.   E

I conclude, therefore, that the rating authority's charge for £16,940·93
under section 17B has priority over and binds the defendants' interest
in the land and all other interests in the land and I will so declare.

Declarations accordingly.

Solicitors: *Solicitor, Westminster City Council; Wilde Sapte.*   F

T. C. C. B.

[CHANCERY DIVISION]

G

* INLAND REVENUE COMMISSIONERS v. REGENT TRUST CO.
LTD.

1979 Nov. 22, 23   Slade J.

Revenue—Income tax—Discretionary trusts, income of—Charge at   H
additional rate—Settled property held on discretionary trust—
Non-resident trustee — Trust income including distributions
from United Kingdom companies—Distributions not charge-
able to basic rate tax in hands of non-resident trustee—
Whether chargeable at additional rate — Finance Act 1973
(c. 51), s. 16 (1)

Section 16 (1) of the Finance Act 1973 provides:
" So far as income arising to trustees is income to which
this section applies it shall, in addition to being charge-

A   able to income tax at the basic rate, be chargeable at
the additional rate."

         Under the terms of a discretionary trust established in 1970
under the law of Jersey, the settlor vested funds solely in a
non-resident trustee company for the benefit of members of his
family who resided in the United Kingdom. The settled fund
included ordinary shareholdings in United Kingdom companies
and the dividends paid in respect of them were received by
B the trustee company. Those dividends were "qualifying
distributions" for the purposes of the Finance Act 1972 but
under sections 86 (5) and 87 (5) of that Act,[1] income tax at
the basic rate was not payable on such distributions in the
hands of non-resident trustees. The trustee company received
three estimated assessments to income tax at the additional
rate imposed by section 16 (1) of the Finance Act 1973 for the
years from 1973 to 1976 in respect of the distributions it had
C received from the United Kingdom companies. The trustee
company appealed. The special commissioners allowed the
appeal holding that section 16 (1) of the Act of 1973 imposed
liability to tax at the additional rate only in respect of income
which was chargeable at the basic rate.

         On appeal by the Crown: —

         Held, allowing the appeal, that the phrase "in addition to
being chargeable to income tax at the basic rate" had been
D incorporated into section 16 (1) of the Finance Act 1973 to
make it clear that the additional rate charge did not supersede
the basic rate charge; that the subsection could not be construed so that the additional rate tax was only chargeable if
basic rate tax was payable and, accordingly, the trustee company
was liable to tax at the additional rate on the distributions
it had received (post, pp. 694A–c, 696E–F).

E No cases are referred to in the judgment.

The following cases were cited in argument:

Cockerline (W. H.) & Co. v. *Inland Revenue Commissioners* (1930) 16
     T.C. 1, C.A.
Hallamshire Industrial Finance Trust Ltd. v. *Inland Revenue Commis-*
F   *sioners* [1979] 1 W.L.R. 620; [1979] 2 All E.R. 433.
Income Tax General Purposes Commissioners for City of London v.
     Gibbs [1942] A.C. 402; [1942] 1 All E.R. 415, H.L.(E.).
Whitney v. *Inland Revenue Commissioners* [1926] A.C. 37; (1925) 10
     T.C. 88, H.L.(E.).

CASE STATED by the Commissioners for the Special Purposes of the
G Income Tax Acts.

         In 1970 an initial sum of £10,000 was settled by Sir Ralph Ellis Brook
on a non-resident trustee company, the Regent Trustee Co. Ltd. The
trustee company had power to pay income of the fund to any of the
United Kingdom beneficiaries of the settlement. Included in the trust
fund were holdings of ordinary shares in United Kingdom companies.
H The trustee company was assessed on an estimated basis under section
16 (1) of the Finance Act 1973 to additional rate income tax in respect
of dividends that it had received from those companies for the years
from 1973 to 1976 each in an amount of £2,000. The commissioners,
allowing the appeal and discharging the assessments, held that the trustee

---

[1] Finance Act 1972, s. 86 (5): see post, p. 691G.
   S. 87 (5): see post, p. 692D.

company was not chargeable under section 16 (1) to additional rate tax on the distributions from United Kingdom companies.

The Crown appealed.

The facts are set out in the judgment.

Peter Gibson for the Crown.

C. H. McCall for the trustee company.

SLADE J. This is an appeal by the Crown from a decision of the Commissioners for the Special Purposes of the Income Tax Acts. At a meeting of the commissioners held on February 1, 1978, the trustee company, Regent Trust Co. Ltd., which was the sole trustee of a settlement made by Sir Ralph Ellis Brook on March 26, 1970, appealed against three assessments to income tax at the additional rate which had been made against it on an estimated basis under section 16 of the Finance Act 1973. These assessments were for the respective years of assessment 1973–74, 1974–75 and 1975–76, and each of them was in the sum of £2,000. The commissioners allowed the appeal and discharged the assessments. The Crown now appeals from their decision by way of case stated.

The relevant facts are common ground. The settlement in question is of a discretionary nature. It was made to provide for the settlor's daughter, Mrs. Butt, her husband, both of whom were, at the date of the settlement, resident and domiciled in London, and their children and remoter issue. The trustee company is a company registered and resident in Jersey, and is the sole trustee of the settlement. Until a far distant vesting day as defined in the settlement, the trustee company has power to transfer, pay or apply the income of the trust fund for the benefit of any of the class of beneficiaries, who comprise Mr. and Mrs. Butt, their children and remoter issue already in being or born before the vesting day, and subject thereto has power to accumulate the income. During the relevant years the trust fund included ordinary shares in United Kingdom companies, dividends from which had been received by the trustee company. In these circumstances, the Inland Revenue raised assessments against the trustee of the nature and amount which I have indicated. The special commissioners found as a fact that the four conditions set out in section 16 (2) of the Finance Act 1973, to which I shall revert later, were satisfied. Shortly stated, the question for decision by this court, as by the commissioners, is whether trustees of a discretionary trust not resident in the United Kingdom are chargeable under section 16 of the Finance Act 1973 to income tax at the additional rate on distributions from companies resident in the United Kingdom.

The Finance Act 1971 introduced what is commonly known as the unified tax system, though it was not to come into force until the year 1973–74. It will be convenient to refer chronologically to some of the relevant statutory provisions. Section 32 (1) (*a*) of that Act provides that income tax shall be charged in respect of any income not falling within paragraph (*b*) " at such rate, to be known as the basic rate, as Parliament may determine." Paragraph (*b*) provides that income tax shall be charged " in respect of so much of an individual's total income as exceeds such amount as Parliament may determine, at such higher rate or rates as Parliament may determine." Finally, section 32 (1) provides:

A
" . . . where an individual's total income includes investment income and that investment income exceeds such amount as Parliament may determine, income tax shall also be charged in respect of the excess at such additional rate or rates as Parliament may determine."

Section 32 thus introduces the concepts of basic rates, higher rates and additional rates of tax. However, this particular section was not expressed
B to apply to trustees.

Section 66 of the Finance Act 1972 then specified the amount of the basic rates, higher rates and additional rates for the year 1973–74. By section 84 of that Act the legislature, as part of its reform of the structure of corporation tax, specified the circumstances in which a company has to make a payment in advance of corporation tax, and the manner in which the payment is to be calculated. Liability to pay an
C amount of what is called therein " advance corporation tax " is imposed by section 84 (1) on a company resident in the United Kingdom which makes what is there called " a qualifying distribution " after April 5, 1973. By section 84 (4) " qualifying distribution " is in effect defined as including distributions other than certain bonus issues of shares and securities. Section 84 (2) imposes the general rule that advance corpora-
D tion tax shall be payable on an amount equal to the amount or value of the distribution at a rate which, for the period April 6, 1973, to March 31, 1974, shall be three-sevenths, and thereafter such fraction as Parliament may determine. Section 85 provides for payment of advance corporation tax to be set against a company's liability to corporation tax on its income.

E
Section 86 (1) provides that where a company resident in the United Kingdom makes a qualifying distribution after April 5, 1973, and the person or company receiving the distribution is resident in the United Kingdom, the recipient shall be entitled to receive what is called a " tax credit." Section 86 (2) provides:

F
" The tax credit in respect of a distribution shall be available for the purposes specified in this section and the subsequent provisions of this Act, and shall be equal to such proportion of the amount or value of the distribution as corresponds to the rate of advance corporation tax in force for the financial year in which the distribution is made."

By virtue of section 86 (4), a person other than a company resident in the United Kingdom who is entitled to a tax credit may in effect set this
G off against his total tax bill for the year of assessment in which the distribution is received. Section 86 (5) provides, inter alia:

" . . . where any such distribution is income of a United Kingdom trust the trustees shall be entitled to a tax credit in respect of it if no other person falls to be treated for the purposes of this section as receiving the distribution."

H
The phrase " United Kingdom trust," however, is defined by section 110 (1) of the same Act in terms such that it would not include the trust in the present case, so that the trustee cannot claim the benefit of a tax credit under that subsection.

Section 87 contains provisions relating to income tax on distributions by a company which are to have effect for the year 1973–74 and subsequent years of assessment. Section 87 (2) substitutes for the Schedule

F as set out in section 232 (1) of the Income and Corporation Taxes Act A 1970 the following provision:

"Schedule F. 1. Income tax under this Schedule shall be chargeable for any year of assessment in respect of all dividends and other distributions in that year of a company resident in the United Kingdom which are not specially excluded from income tax, and for the purposes of income tax all such distributions shall be regarded B as income however they fall to be dealt with in the hands of the recipient. 2. For the purposes of this Schedule and all other purposes of the Tax Acts any such distribution as aforesaid in respect of which a person is entitled to a tax credit shall be treated as representing income equal to the aggregate of the amount or value of that distribution and the amount of that credit, and income tax under this Schedule shall accordingly be charged on that aggregate." C

Section 87 (3) provides:

"No distribution which is chargeable under the said Schedule F shall be chargeable under any other provision of the Income Tax Acts."

Section 87 (5) reads: D

"Where in any year of assessment the income of a person, not being a company resident in the United Kingdom, includes a distribution in respect of which that person is not entitled to a tax credit—(a) no assessment shall be made on that person in respect of income tax at the basic rate on the amount or value of the distribution; . . ." E

This subsection contains two other paragraphs, (b) and (c), which I think I need not read.

There next followed the Finance Act 1973. Section 16 (1) of that Act, which is the subsection in issue in the present case, states:

"So far as income arising to trustees is income to which this section F applies it shall, in addition to being chargeable to income tax at the basic rate, be chargeable at the additional rate."

Subsection (2) states:

"This section applies to income arising to trustees in any year of assessment so far as it—(a) is income which is to be accumulated or which is payable at the discretion of the trustees or any other person G (whether or not the trustees have power to accumulate it); and (b) is neither (before being distributed) the income of any person other than the trustees nor treated for any of the purposes of the Income Tax Acts as the income of a settlor; and (c) is not income arising under a trust established for charitable purposes only or income from investments, deposits or other property held for the purposes H of a fund or scheme established for the sole purpose of providing relevant benefits within the meaning of section 26 of the Finance Act 1970; and (d) exceeds the income applied in defraying the expenses of the trustees in that year which are properly chargeable to income (or would be so chargeable but for any express provisions of the trust)."

A Subsection (3) reads:

"This section also applies to sums apportioned to the trustees under paragraph 1 of Schedule 16 to the Finance Act 1972 and treated, under paragraph 5 (2) of that Schedule as applied by subsection (4) below, as income received by the trustees."

B It will thus be seen that section 16 (2) sets out four conditions which have to be satisfied if section 16 (1) is to be capable of applying so as to render income arising to trustees chargeable to income tax at the additional rate. The commissioners' finding that all these four conditions were satisfied in relation to the relevant income in the present case has not been challenged. In these circumstances, there could I think be no doubt that if the relevant income received by the trustee company was "chargeable to income tax at the basic rate" within the meaning of subsection (1), it will be caught by subsection (1). It is, however, common ground that the trustee company is not assessable to income tax at the basic rate in respect of the relevant dividends, for this short reason: this not being a United Kingdom trust, the trustee is not entitled to a tax credit in respect of the relevant dividends under section 86 (5) of the Finance Act 1972; this being the case, section 87 (5) (a) of that Act prevents any assessment from being made on the trustee in respect of income tax at the basic rate on the amount of the relevant dividends.

Does this fact prevent the amount of such dividends from being chargeable at the additional rate by virtue of section 16 (1) of the Finance Act 1973? Mr. McCall, on behalf of the trustee company, submitted that it does, on two principal grounds, which were substantially the grounds argued before the commissioners, on which the trustee company succeeded. First, he submitted that section 16 (1), on its true construction, can apply only to income which is "chargeable to income tax at the basic rate" within the meaning of that subsection. If income is not so chargeable, he submitted, the subsection cannot apply at all. Secondly, he submitted that the relevant income, on the particular facts of the present case, is not "chargeable to income tax at the basic rate" within the meaning of subsection (1), because no assessment can be made against the trustee in respect of it, and chargeability and assessability in this particular context, he suggested, must be equated. It follows from these two points, in his submission, that section 16 (1) cannot bite on the facts of the present case. It is common ground that this must follow if each of his two propositions is correct. For his part, however, he accepted that he must establish the correctness of each of them if he is to succeed in resisting this appeal.

The first point in the context of section 16 (1) essentially turns on the force to be attributed to the crucial phrase, "in addition to being chargeable to income tax at the basic rate." In the course of argument, two points have I think emerged as common ground. First, the phrase is not itself a charging provision; it does not itself operate to charge anything to income tax at the basic rate or any other rate. Under section 87 (3) of the Finance Act 1972 no distribution such as this, which is chargeable under Schedule F, is chargeable under any other provision of the Income Tax Acts. Secondly, one of the functions of the phrase must necessarily be to make it clear that the charge to tax at the additional rate thereby imposed is to be on top of, and not in substitution for, any charge to income tax at the basic rate. This was a point which obviously had to be covered by the legislation somewhere.

In the present context, the dispute really centres round the question A
whether this crucial phrase has any further function. Mr. McCall, on
behalf of the trustee company, submitted that indeed it has. He submitted
that the phrase has the function of rendering the charge to income tax at
the additional rate imposed by the subsection conditional on the income in
question being chargeable to income tax at the basic rate. He invited me,
as a matter of statutory interpretation, to interpolate the words " if and "
immediately before the words " in addition to being chargeable at the B
basic rate." Mr. Gibson, on behalf of the Crown, submitted, in contrast,
that the crucial phrase is no more than a parenthesis, intended to make
it clear that the charge at the additional rate imposed by the subsection
is not intended to supersede the charge at the basic rate.

Beginning, as I do, by reading section 16 in isolation, I have no
hesitation in preferring the Crown's construction of subsection (1) as a C
matter of ordinary language. The words " in addition to being chargeable to income tax at the basic rate," at least at first sight, would appear
to me quite inappropriate to embody a condition; I think this is implicitly
accepted by Mr. McCall when he invited me to read into the subsection
the words " if and." If the legislature had intended to render the phrase
a condition, there are surely many ways in which it could so easily
have expressed this. Subsection (2) already sets out four conditions which D
have to be present before the section can apply to income arising to
trustees in any year of assessment. A condition that the income must be
chargeable to income tax at the basic rate could have easily been added
as a fifth condition, though no doubt the presence of the phrase in subsection (1) would still have been required, so as to make it plain that the
charge at the additional rate was not intended to supersede the charge at E
the basic rate. Alternatively, if the legislature had intended to impose
such a condition, it could have inserted it in express terms in section 16 (1).
In the event, I can hardly think of less appropriate language than that
of section 16 (1) to introduce a condition, if condition had been intended.
Though the sense of the subsection might have been made clearer still if
the crucial phrase had read " in addition to being chargeable, if at all, to
income tax at the basic rate," I do not regard the Crown's construction F
of the language as depending on the interpolation of the words " if at all,"
or some such words, as a matter of statutory interpretation. It seems
to me that, as a matter of ordinary language, the words of the subsection,
at least if read in isolation, would obviously fall to be read in this sense,
even in the absence of the words " if at all." I am not therefore able to
accept Mr. McCall's submission that the Crown's contention involves G
what he calls " doing violence to the language " of the subsection. In
my judgment, the trustee company's interpretation, which it is accepted
must involve the interpolation of the words " if and " as a matter of
construction, must do much greater violence by altering the entire sense
of the subsection.

This being my view of the construction of section 16 (1) when read
in isolation, I now have to see whether there is any context in the other H
provisions of the Act of 1973 sufficient to displace what seems to me its
clear prima facie meaning. At this point it will be convenient to see how
the commissioners dealt with what is now the first of Mr. McCall's two
principal points on this appeal. In their decision they said:

" . . . we have to choose between two possible constructions of
section 16 (1) of the Finance Act 1973. While the appellant contends

A that it imposes liability to tax at the additional rate only in respect of income which is also chargeable at the basic rate, the revenue contends that the reference to the basic rate charge is a mere parenthesis: it explains only that tax at the additional rate is to be imposed on top of, and not in place of, any charge to tax at the basic rate. We find the wording far from clear but we prefer, on balance, the appellant's construction. This is at any rate consistent

B with the wording of section 17 (3) (a), where it appears to be assumed that income of the trustees which has been charged at the additional rate will also have been taxed at the basic rate."

The commissioners thus attached some importance to section 17 (3) (a), as did Mr. McCall in his argument. Section 17 (1) directs that the following provisions of the section shall apply with respect to certain

C payments under discretionary trusts in lieu of section 52 or section 53 of the Taxes Act 1970. Section 17 (2) provides:

"The payment shall be treated as a net amount corresponding to a gross amount from which tax has been deducted at a rate equal to the sum of the basic rate and the additional rate in force for the year in which the payment is made; and the sum treated as so

D deducted shall be treated—(a) as income tax paid by the person to whom the payment is made; and (b) so far as not set off under the following provisions of this section, as income tax assessable on the trustees."

Subsection (3) specifies, in paragraphs (a), (b), (c) and (d) thereof, the amounts which, so far as not previously allowed, shall be set against the

E amount that would otherwise be assessable on the trustees under subsection (2). Subsection (3) (a) reads:

"(a) the amount of any tax on income arising to the trustees and charged at the additional as well as at the basic rate in pursuance of section 16 of this Act; ..."

F The commissioners, as has appeared, took the view that this subsection (3) (a) assumes that income of the trustees which has been charged at the additional rate under section 16 will also have been taxed at the basic rate. I think it is fair to say that the phrase " as well as at the basic rate," appearing in subsection (3) (a), does seem to assume that income which has been charged at the additional rate will also have been charged at the additional rate will also have been charged

G at the additional rate. I deliberately use the word " charged " rather than " taxed," the word used by the commissioners, because the argument involved in Mr. McCall's second principal point illustrates that there may be a distinction between the two. In my judgment, however, the phrase " as well as at the basic rate " appearing in section 17 (3) (a) merely echoes the phrase " in addition to being chargeable to income tax at the basic rate " appearing in section 16 (1). I would accept that the

H draftsman of the latter subsection similarly appears to assume that income which is chargeable at the additional rate will also be chargeable at the basic rate. The mere fact, however, that the draftsman of sections 16 (1) and 17 (3) (a) may have made both these assumptions does not seem to me to justify the court in inferring a condition in section 16 (1), which he has signally failed to express in words. It was common ground between counsel that section 17 itself gives rise to many difficult problems of interpretation. In my judgment, the language of section 17 (3) (a) provides no sufficient context or justification for the court to read into A section 16 (1) a condition that is not there.

It remains, then, to consider whether there is any general context, apart from section 17, which compels the court to the conclusion that, notwithstanding the language used, a condition of the nature suggested must be read into section 16 (1) as a matter of construction. Mr. Gibson pointed out two results that would ensue if the trustee company's interpretation is correct. First, it would mean that this trustee company and all other B non-United Kingdom trustees in a similar position would escape liability to tax at the additional rate on dividends, albeit arising in this country, merely because they were resident outside the United Kingdom. Furthermore, it would mean that trustees, whether inside or outside the United Kingdom, would escape liability to tax at the additional rate in respect of non-qualifying distributions. For section 87 (5) (a) of the Finance Act C 1972 prevents any assessment from being made on a person in respect of income tax at the basic rate on the value of a distribution in respect of which such a person is not entitled to a tax credit; and section 86 of that Act makes tax credits available only for qualifying distributions.

I agree with Mr. McCall's comment that a comparison of anomalies is a dangerous approach to the construction of any tax statute, and I accept that other anomalies can be detected if the Crown's construction of D section 16 (1) is correct. Nevertheless, I think he has been able to suggest no purpose which the legislature might have wished to achieve by inserting in that subsection a condition of the nature asserted, and which was both sensible and consistent with the other provisions of the Act. It is I think significant that foreign as well as United Kingdom trustees may unquestionably find themselves chargeable to tax at the additional rate E under the complicated provisions of section 16 (3) in respect of *deemed* distributions consisting of the income of a close company apportioned on a short-fall apportionment and treated as income received by them.

For all these reasons I conclude that there is no sufficient context to displace what I regard as the clear meaning of the words of section 16 (1) of the Finance Act 1973. Despite Mr. McCall's persuasive argument, therefore, I must reject his first principal point. I accept the Crown's F submission that the phrase " in addition to being chargeable to income tax at the basic rate " has no further function than to make it clear that the charge to income tax at the additional rate is not to supersede the charge, if any, to tax at the basic rate. It is therefore unnecessary to consider Mr. McCall's second principal point. Though I heard some interesting and instructive argument from both counsel on this point with reference G to a number of statutory provisions and some authority, I hope that they will forgive me if I make no comment on it save one obiter observation, which is this. Mr. McCall's defence to the Crown's present claim in one sense depends, it seems to me, partly on section 87 (5) (a) of the Finance Act 1972, which by its terms absolves the trustee from an assessment in respect of income tax at the basic rate on the amount of the relevant H dividends. However, this very same section as drafted appears to me prima facie to contemplate that, notwithstanding the exemption from assessment, the same distribution will remain " chargeable " within the meaning of the word as used in section 87 (2) and (3). For this reason, among a number of others, I am not sure that, if the point had been relevant, I would have been able to accept Mr. McCall's invitation, in effect, to equate in the particular context of section 16 (1) of the Finance Act

A 1973 the words "chargeable" and "assessable," which he accepts are frequently, if not normally, used in two distinct senses in taxing statutes. Nor am I sure that I would have been able to accept the conclusion of the commissioners, expressed in their decision:

"If the relevant statutory provisions, read as a whole, impose no liability to basic rate tax there is, in our opinion, nothing which can
B sensibly be called a charge to tax at that rate on the income in question."

However, I do not in the event have to decide this point, and I do not do so. As things are, I must allow this appeal.

C
Appeal allowed.
No application for costs.
Case remitted to commissioners to
determine amounts of assessments.

Solicitors: *Solicitor of Inland Revenue; Allen & Overy.*

[Reported by MRS. HARRIET DUTTON, Barrister-at-Law]

D

[COURT OF APPEAL]

E
* PRACTICE DIRECTION (CROWN COURT: COSTS OF
PROSECUTION)

1980   June 3   Lord Lane C.J., Boreham and Gibson JJ.

Crime—Costs—Central funds—Crown Court—Discretion to order
payment of costs of prosecution out of central funds

F
LORD LANE C.J. at the sitting of the court, announced publication of the following practice direction.

1. Paragraph 4 (a) of the *Practice Direction* (*Crown Court*: *Costs*) [1977] 1 W.L.R. 181 of February 7, 1977, requires the court to have regard to the principle that an order will normally be made for prosecution costs in the Crown Court to be paid out of central funds, unless the
G proceedings have been instituted or presented without reasonable cause. It has become the practice to assume that such an order has been made unless the court orders to the contrary.

2. That practice will no longer prevail. An application for costs is to be made by the prosecution in each case. This will serve to remind the court that where proceedings have been instituted or continued when
H they should not have been, the court has a discretion not to order the costs of the prosecution to be borne by central funds.

3. This practice direction is to take effect from Monday, June 30, 1980.

L. N. W.

A

[QUEEN'S BENCH DIVISION]

*SEAMARK v. PROUSE

1980 Jan. 29   Lord Widgery C.J. and Woolf J.

B

Crime—Firearms—Drunk in possession of loaded firearm—Air
rifle—Whether "firearm" includes air rifle—Licensing Act
1872 (35 & 36 Vict c. 94), s. 12

Informations were preferred against two defendants alleging
that each was drunk in possession of a loaded firearm, namely
an air rifle, contrary to section 12 of the Licensing Act 1872.
The justices were of the opinion that an air rifle was not a
firearm for the purposes of the Act of 1872, and dismissed   C
the informations.

On the prosecutor's appeal: —

Held, allowing the appeal, that in the absence of a definition of "firearm" in the Licensing Act 1872 and of any
assistance which might be derived from later legislation, the
ordinary meaning of the word "firearm" must be applied to
the terms of the Licensing Act 1872; that applying that
ordinary meaning, the word "firearm" included an air rifle;   D
accordingly, the justices had erred in their conclusion and
the case should be remitted with a direction to continue the
hearing.

No cases are referred to in the judgment.

The following cases were cited in argument: E

Moore v. Gooderham [1960] 1 W.L.R. 1308; [1960] 3 All E.R. 575.
Ormond Investment Co. Ltd. v. Betts [1928] A.C. 143, H.L.(E.).

CASE STATED by Devon justices sitting at Okehampton.

On June 17, 1977, informations were preferred by the prosecutor,
Christopher Clifford Leslie Seamark against each of the defendants,   F
Clifford Cecil Prouse and Romley John Prowse, that at North Tawton,
Devon, on May 10, 1977, he was drunk in possession of a loaded firearm,
namely, an air rifle, contrary to section 12 of the Licensing Act 1872.
The defendants pleaded not guilty and agreed that the two informations
should be tried together.

The following facts were agreed. At approximately 11.15 p.m. on
Tuesday, May 10, 1977, each of the defendants was in possession of   G
a B.S.A. ·22 air rifle in the vicinity of their home in Arundell Road,
North Tawton, Devon. On their own admission each defendant fired
one lead pellet at a bottle which they had perched on top of a van parked
in Arundell Road. The defendants, however, were in the garden of their
home when they fired the air rifles at the bottle. Several neighbours
were disturbed by the noisy behaviour of the defendants. The prosecutor   H
alleged that the defendants, who had been drinking intoxicating liquor,
were drunk; but that particular fact was not admitted on behalf of the
defendants.

It was contended on behalf of the prosecutor that the expression
"firearm" had the same meaning as contained in section 57 of the
Firearms Act 1968, explained in Moore v. Gooderham [1960] 1 W.L.R.
1308. For the defendants, it was contended that the interpretation of

A   the expression " firearm " was not governed by section 57 of the Fire-
arms Act 1968, by virtue of the opening words of the section, namely,
" In this Act . . ." which confined any definition therein to the Firearms
Act 1968.

The justices retired to consider the issue and came to the conclusion
(a) that section 57 of the Firearms Act 1968, had no effect on the interpretation of the word " firearms " in the Licensing Act 1872, and (b)
B   that the words " loaded firearms " in the Licensing Act 1872 could not
in their ordinary meaning be construed to include a loaded air rifle. The
justices dismissed both of the informations.

The prosecutor appealed. The question for the opinion of the High
Court was whether the justices were right in deciding that a loaded air
rifle was not a loaded firearm for the purposes of the Licensing Act 1872.

C
    Roger Backhouse for the prosecutor.
    The defendants did not appear and were not represented.

    LORD WIDGERY C.J.   This is an appeal by case stated by Devon
justices acting for the petty sessional division of Okehampton and sitting
at Okehampton in September 1977. They there had before them an
D   information preferred by the prosecutor against the defendants that at
North Tawton on May 10, 1977, the defendants were drunk in possession
of a loaded firearm, namely, an air rifle, contrary to section 12 of the
Licensing Act 1872.

The facts of the case are contained in those three or four lines
because the whole issue was whether that which the defendants had in
E   their possession was a loaded firearm. One looks naturally enough to
the definition clause of the statute creating the offence in the hope of
there finding an answer to the problem.

We look, therefore, at the Act in question which is the Licensing
Act 1872, and we find there is no statutory definition of a firearm at
all. One must work in some other way.

F   The next thing to do is to inquire whether there is any later legislation
which assists us in interpreting this phrase and, if so, considering to
what extent we can take advantage of it. But there is, in my judgment,
no legislation, contemporary or otherwise, which fills the gap in the Act
of 1872.

We have been referred to more than one canon of construction
dealing with circumstances in which a later Act within the same subject
G   matter can be used to construe an earlier Act. Putting it bluntly and
briefly, such a comparison is allowed where there is an ambiguity in the
earlier Act and where it is clear that that ambiguity can be resolved by
reference to the later Act.

But that, in my judgment, does not apply here. I do not think
that the ambiguity is apparent enough or that there is sufficient similarity
H   between the two subject matters to make it safe and wise to try to
obtain guidance from that source. If we reject that, as I think we
should, we are left with only one method of approaching the problem,
and that is to ask ourselves " What is the ordinary meaning of the word
' firearm '? " and apply that meaning to the terms of the Act.

It is not altogether easy to decide how this matter should be dealt
with. We have had a reference to the *Shorter Oxford English Dictionary*
in which " firearm " is described as " a weapon from which missiles are

propelled by an explosive, e.g. gunpowder." I venture to think that the A
modern meaning of "firearm" at all events is somewhat wider than
that.

If one compares the air gun, which was the weapon carried by the
defendants in this case, with a modern rifle, one can say with confidence
that the two weapons are substantially identical, save only for the nature
of the propellant, i.e. save only for the fact that the propellant in one
case is compressed air and in the other case is cordite.   B

One puts oneself in the position when an airgun has become part of
the modern armoury of sport, and one tries to envisage the discussions
which would take place when this new-fangled weapon had been taken
into use and Parliament had been accustomed to it.

For my part, I think that the attitude at that time would have been
for people to compare the similarity of the two weapons, to observe, as   C
I have observed, that it is only the nature of the propellant which distinguishes them, and I do not think that the use of the phrase "firearm"
should be regarded as unsuitable for an airgun because of that difference
in the propellant.

In my judgment, the ordinary meaning of the word requires us to
say that the expression "firearm" does include an airgun. The justices
having found in the contrary sense, I think this appeal should be allowed D
and the case must go back with a direction to continue the hearing on
the matters upon which a decision has not yet been reached.

WOOLF J.   I agree.

Appeal allowed with costs out of
central funds.   E
Case remitted to justices with direc-
tion to continue hearing.

Solicitor: *Neville Jennings, Exeter.*

[Reported by MISS EIRA CARYL THOMAS, Barrister-at-Law]   F

[COURT OF APPEAL]

* THAMES WATER AUTHORITY *v.*
BLUE AND WHITE LAUNDERETTES LTD.   G

1979 Nov. 23, 26;   Stephenson, Eveleigh and
      Dec. 20   Brandon L.JJ.

Rating—Sewerage—Right to charge—Launderette—Liquid dis-
charged from washing machines—Whether trade effluent—
Whether exempted from charge as "domestic sewage"—Public   H
Health (Drainage of Trade Premises) Act 1937 (1 *Edw.* 8 & 1
Geo. 6, *c.* 40), *s.* 14 (1)

Section 14 (1) of the Public Health (Drainage of Trade
Premises) Act 1937 provides:
"...'trade effluent' means any liquid, either with or
without particles of matter in suspension therein, which
is wholly or in part produced in the course of any trade

A   or industry carried on at trade premises and, in relation
to any trade premises, means any such liquid as aforesaid
which is so produced in the course of any trade or industry
carried on at those premises, but does not include domestic
sewage; . . ."

A water authority, claiming that effluent discharged from
nine premises owned by the respondents and used as launderettes was trade effluent, brought proceedings in the county
B   court to recover from the respondents charges of £1,355·27 in
respect of trade effluent discharged from those premises. The
judge dismissed the claim on the ground that the liquid discharged from the washing machines was domestic sewage and,
therefore, exempted from the definition of trade effluent in
section 14 (1) of the Act.

On appeal by the water authority: —

Held, allowing the appeal, that the exception of " domestic
C   sewage " in section 14 (1) of the Act related to the household
or domestic activities carried on at trade premises as opposed
to the effect of the business activities; that, although the
liquid discharged from the washing machines in a launderette
was identical to the liquid discharged from domestic washing
machines, the purpose for which the activity was carried on
was relevant, and, accordingly, since all the effluent produced
at the launderettes was directly produced in the course of the
D   trade or business of a launderette, it did not come within the
exception of domestic sewage and was chargeable as trade
effluent (post, pp. 703c–G, 706A, 710c–E).

Metropolitan Water Board v. *Avery* [1914] A.C. 118,
H.L.(E.) considered.

The following cases are referred to in the judgments:

E   *Colley's Patents Ltd.* v. *Metropolitan Water Board* [1911] 2 K.B. 38,
C.A.; [1912] A.C. 24, H.L.(E.).
Iron Trades Mutual Employers Insurance Association Ltd. v. *Sheffield
Corporation* [1974] 1 W.L.R. 107; [1974] 1 All E.R. 182, D.C.
Lyons (J.) & Co. Ltd. v. *London Corporation* [1909] 2 K.B. 588, D.C.
Metropolitan Water Board v. *Avery* [1913] 2 K.B. 257; [1914] A.C. 118,
D.C. and H.L.(E.).
F   *Oddenino* v. *Metropolitan Water Board* [1914] 2 Ch. 734.
Pidgeon v. *Great Yarmouth Waterworks Co.* [1902] 1 K.B. 310, D.C.
South Suburban Gas Co. v. *Metropolitan Water Board* [1914] 2 Ch. 734.

The following additional cases were cited in argument:

Barnard Castle Urban District Council v. *Wilson* [1902] 2 Ch. 746, C.A.
Garfield v. *Yorkshire Laundries* (1905) 3 L.G.R. 1192, D.C.
G   *Metropolitan Water Board* v. *London, Brighton and South Coast Railway
Co.* [1910] 2 K.B. 890, C.A.
South-West Suburban Water Co. v. *St. Marylebone Guardians* [1904]
2 K.B. 174.

APPEAL from Judge Dow sitting at Clerkenwell County Court.

H   The appellants, Thames Water Authority, appealed from the dismissal
on October 16, 1978, by Judge Dow, in the Clerkenwell County Court,
of their claim for £1,355·27, being charges in respect of the discharge of
effluent from nine launderette premises owned by the respondents, Blue
and White Launderettes Ltd.

The grounds of the appeal were, inter alia, that the judge was wrong
in law in holding that the liquid discharged from the respondents' premises
was " domestic sewage " within the meaning of section 14 (1) of the

A

Public Health (Drainage of Trade Premises) Act 1937; and that he was
wrong in law in considering solely the purpose for which the liquid
had been used and not the nature of the premises in which it had been
used.

The facts are stated in the judgment of Eveleigh L.J.

B

David Widdicombe Q.C. and *John Laws* for the appellants.
J. P. Gorman Q.C. and *John Foy* for the respondents.

Cur. adv. vult.

December 20, 1979. The following judgments were read.

C

EVELEIGH L.J. (read by Stephenson L.J.). This is an appeal from
the judgment of Judge Dow sitting at Clerkenwell County Court whereby
he dismissed the plaintiffs' claim for £1,355·27, being charges in respect
of the discharge of effluent from nine different launderette premises.
He did so on the basis that the effluent which came from the washing
machines on the premises was domestic sewage within the meaning of
section 14 of the Public Health (Drainage of Trade Premises) Act 1937
and therefore not chargeable as trade effluent. The relevant part of
section 14 (1) of the Act reads:

D

"'trade effluent' means any liquid, either with or without particles
of matter in suspension therein, which is wholly or in part produced
in the course of any trade or industry carried on at trade premises
and, in relation to any trade premises, means any such liquid as
aforesaid which is so produced in the course of any trade or industry
carried on at those premises, but does not include domestic sewage;
'trade premises' means any premises used or intended to be used
for carrying on any trade or industry."

E

This appeal is solely concerned with the question whether or not the
effluent is in relation to those premises trade effluent or domestic sewage
within the meaning of that section. It is admitted that the premises are
trade premises but for completeness and no doubt mindful of judicial
ignorance a description of a launderette has been placed before the court.
It is as follows:

F

"A shop-like premises, equipped with a number of large automatic
washing machines, which may or may not be coin operated, supplied
with hot water from a central source, and with about one tumbler
dryer for about each three washing machines. There may or may
not be an attendant to undertake 'service washing' (i.e. the customer
leaves the washing with the attendant, who puts it through the
machines, to be collected later). Soap can usually be bought from
a dispenser on the premises. There may or may not be staff facilities,
such as an office, lavatories or rest room."

G

H

Further it was agreed between the parties that for the purposes of the
action and this appeal the discharge from an ordinary householder's
washing machine is similar to that from a washing machine in a launderette
in both its constituents and its strength.

I turn to consider the meaning of trade effluent in the Act without
regard to any authorities there might be on the matter. I read the

The Weekly Law Reports, June 27, 1980

703

1 W.L.R.   Thames Water v. Launderettes Ltd. (C.A.)   Eveleigh L.J.

A definition as giving two meanings to trade effluent. The first is to apply generally and the second is applicable only when the matter has to be considered in relation to trade premises. The words " but does not include domestic sewage " in my opinion, apply only to the second meaning. I say this because the words which follow the phrase " in relation to any trade premises " have exactly the same meaning as those which appear before the phrase, save for the reference to " domestic
B sewage." The relevant part of the definition may therefore be stated as saying that in relation to any trade premises trade effluent does not include domestic sewage. We are therefore concerned to ask whether the effluent from the washing machines is domestic sewage in relation to the premises on which those machines stand.

Counsel for the respondent has submitted that the water discharged
C from a washing machine in a house must be domestic sewage and the liquid in the present case is identical and must therefore be covered by the same description. Such an approach would, in my opinion, lead to the conclusion that almost anything which could be classified as domestic sewage when emanating from a house must of necessity be domestic sewage when coming from a factory in spite of its being used only in the process of manufacture carried on in that factory. Counsel has argued
D that this would not be a necessary conclusion because the process of washing the clothes is one which is done in what is virtually an identical way in a similar machine in the home. In my opinion, however, that comparison does not go far enough. One should ask also the purpose for which the activity is carried on. No doubt clothes may be washed for a reward in a private home. However, when one asks whether washing
E water is domestic sewage or not one decides in favour of that description not by having regard to the possibility of use for business purposes, but on the basis of its use for domestic purposes.

Upon trade premises one would expect there to be a source of effluent that is not related to the trading or industrial process carried on there. The establishment will have its domestic side as well as its truly
F business side. The words " wholly or in part produced in the course of any trade " are almost wide enough to include anything which comes from the premises used by people working there. " In the course of " is a phrase often considered by lawyers and has been shown to have a wide embrace. Washing room activities for personal cleanliness might well be said to give rise to effluent in the course of trade or industry carried
G on at the premises. In my opinion the exclusion of domestic sewage is intended to relate to the household activities on the premises, the domestic activities of those who work there as opposed to the effects of the business activities. I would, therefore, conclude from the words of section 14 itself that the water discharged from the washing machine in a launderette is trade effluent within the meaning of the section, and not domestic
H sewage.

I gain support for this conclusion from sections 1 and 4 of the Act. Section 1 (1) provides:

    ". . . the occupier of any trade premises within the district of a local
    authority may, with the consent of the local authority . . . discharge
    into the public sewers of the local authority any trade effluent pro-
    ceeding from those premises."

Section 4 (4) (now repealed) provides:

> "The consent of a local authority to the discharge, from any premises into a sewer of the local authority, of any liquid produced solely in the course of laundering articles on those premises shall not be necessary for the purposes of this Act."

Certainly in so far as that subsection is concerned it would appear that liquid produced solely in the course of laundering articles on trade premises is regarded as trade effluent.

The distinction between domestic sewage and a liquid produced in a manufacturing process is indicated by the proviso to section 34 (1) of the Public Health Act 1936 which reads:

> "Provided that nothing in this subsection shall entitle any person— (a) to discharge directly or indirectly into any public sewer—(i) any liquid from a factory, other than domestic sewage or surface or storm water, or any liquid from a manufacturing process; . . ."

We have been referred on behalf of the respondents to a number of authorities in which counsel submits the court has treated water as domestic even though it was used for business purposes. Foremost among these is *Metropolitan Water Board* v. *Avery* [1914] A.C. 118. That case and the others to which we were referred dealt with the provisions of section 25 of the Metropolitan Water Board (Charges) Act 1907. Various reasons were given in those cases for treating the water as being supplied for domestic purposes prominent among which was that use for business purposes did not detract from the domestic use for which the water was in any event supplied. In *Metropolitan Water Board* v. *Avery* water was supplied to the licensee of a public house where luncheons were served and the water was used for cooking the food and washing up the plates and dishes. It was held that the water was used for domestic purposes within the meaning of section 25 of the Metropolitan Water Board (Charges) Act 1907. That section, which was not strictly a definition section, stated that the expression "domestic purposes" should be deemed to include certain uses but should not include a supply of water for a specified number of purposes of which "any trade manufacture or business" was one. Lord Dunedin, in a passage much relied upon by counsel for the respondent, said, at p. 124:

> "On the other hand, the test of the quality of the use in itself so tersely put by Buckley L.J. 'The test is not whether water is consumed or used in the course of the trade, but whether the user of the water is in its nature domestic'—is not only easy of application but is automatic in checking abuse. For purposes truly domestic cannot be amplified, and when the consumption on such heads is large it is invariably attended by an increase in the rating value of the premises which brings with it an increased water rate."

I do not regard him as saying that a use which might be found to exist domestically will be properly called domestic wherever found and no matter the extent and purpose of the use from the point of view of the person to be charged. This follows, in my opinion, from a further passage from Lord Dunedin's speech where he considered public baths or public water closets carried on for profit. He said, at p. 125:

> "My Lords, I think such extreme cases—for such establishments, at least of the second class, are not common—may be left to be

The Weekly Law Reports, June 27, 1980

705

1 W.L.R.   Thames Water v. Launderettes Ltd. (C.A.)   Eveleigh L.J.

A dealt with till they arise within the metropolitan area. But when they do I think the solution may be suggested by a phrase in the judgment of Bray J. He says: ' If the water is used for a purpose which is common to all domestic establishments it is none the less used for domestic purposes because it is ancillary to a trade, manufacture, or business.' In the case supposed the use of the water would not be ancillary to the business, it would be the business itself, and I should

B personally be prepared to hold—again, I venture to think, taking a common sense view of the situation—that the trade use of the water was so pre-eminent that it could not be said that in those establishments there was truly a use for a domestic purpose at all."

Lord Atkinson said, at p. 129:

C " And when one has to construe this clumsily drawn and puzzling statute, one may well ask oneself, if the water supplied is at the same moment used, and intended to be used, for both purposes, and it is impossible to separate the one purpose from the other, which consideration is to prevail? Is the domestic purpose to be treated as the real and dominant purpose, and the business purpose to be ignored, or vice versa?"

D He in fact held that the character of the purpose for which the water was supplied was domestic and that the business carried on by the respondent was not a business at all within the meaning of section 25.

In section 14 the emphasis is the other way round to that found in section 25 of the Metropolitan Water Board (Charges) Act 1907. We start with trade effluent as being a liquid produced in the course of trade

E and then proceed to exclude it if it is domestic sewage. Thus the words of Buckley L.J., " The test is not whether the water is consumed or used in the course of the trade, . . ." are not applicable to our case. This only goes to emphasise how misleading it may be to apply a meaning of words in one case as though they came from a universal dictionary applicable to all cases.

F Counsel also referred to J. Lyons & Co. Ltd. v. London Corporation [1909] 2 K.B. 588. In that case the refuse of a restaurant, consisting of ashes, clinkers, coffee grounds, etc., was held to be " house refuse " within the meaning of section 30 of the Public Health (London) Act 1891. Section 141 provided:

G " In this Act, unless the context otherwise requires . . . the expression ' house refuse ' means ashes, cinders, breeze, rubbish, night soil, and filth, but does not include ' trade refuse ': The expression ' trade refuse ' means the refuse of any trade, manufacture or business or of any building materials."

So the court decided that the refuse was not trade refuse as envisaged by the Act and consequently was not excluded from the definition of

H " house refuse." Sutton J. said, at p. 598:

" As regards trade refuse I think the cases show clearly that that means the residue of the manufacture and does not include all matters necessary to carry on the manufacture."

For my part the support claimed by the respondents from that case is purely superficial. The court was not deciding what was house refuse in any general sense of the term but whether the material in question fell

within the words of the particular statute. I do not, therefore, find it   A
possible to draw any analogy between domestic sewage in our present case
and the house refuse in the case quoted.

There is nothing in any of the decided cases to govern the interpretation of the section with which we are concerned. Consequently, for the
reasons I have given I do not think that the washing liquid in this case
was domestic sewage and I would allow the appeal.

                                                                          B

STEPHENSON L.J. The respondents' launderettes are admitted to be
" trade premises " within the Public Health (Drainage of Trade Premises)
Act 1937 because they are " premises used or intended to be used for
carrying on any trade or industry ": see section 14 (1).

The respondents admittedly occupied them within the appellants'
district and accordingly have a right under section 1 of the Act, with   C
the appellants' consent, to discharge into the appellants' public sewers
any trade effluent proceeding from those premises, subject to the restrictions imposed by section 2.

Furthermore, it is admitted on behalf of the respondents that any
liquid which is wholly or in part produced in the course of any trade or
industry carried on at those premises would be " trade effluent," within   D
the meaning given to those two words by section 14 (1), if it were not
" domestic sewage." But, say the respondents, it is all domestic sewage as
the judge has held, whereas the appellants say it is not, or not all, domestic
sewage.

There is in the Act of 1937 no definition of domestic sewage, but I
think that its meaning can be derived from proviso (a) (i) to section 34 (1)   E
of the Public Health Act 1936. In Part II of that Act there are or were
sections dealing with sewage and sewage disposal, of which section 26
(repealed by section 1 (3) of the Act of 1937) requires local authorities to
afford facilities for factories to drain into public sewers, and section 34
(still in force) confers on the owner or occupier of any premises within
the district of a local authority a right to have his private drains made to
communicate with the authority's public sewers, and thereby to discharge   F
foul water and surface water from those premises. But that right is
subject to (among other provisos) a proviso:

  " . . . nothing in this subsection shall entitle any person—(a) to
  discharge directly or indirectly into a public sewer—(i) any liquid
  from a factory, other than domestic sewage or surface or storm
  water, or any liquid from a manufacturing process; . . ."   G

" Domestic sewage " is not defined in the Act of 1936, though many
expressions in the statute, including " factory," are defined in section
343 (1). But in its context I have no doubt that it means the liquid
from water closets and baths, lavatories and sanitary conveniences, used
by work people in a factory.

The distinction between that liquid and liquid from a manufacturing   H
process is roughly the same as the distinction between water supplied
(to a factory) for domestic purposes and water supplied for other than
domestic purposes as those purposes are defined in " the slovenly and
inaccurate language " of the Metropolitan Water Board (Charges) Act
1907 as Lord Loreburn L.C. described it in Colley's Patents Ltd. v. Metropolitan Water Board [1912] A.C. 24, 31: compare South Suburban Gas
Co. v. Metropolitan Water Board [1909] 2 Ch. 666. That distinction will

The Weekly Law Reports, June 27, 1980

707

1 W.L.R.   Thames Water v. Launderettes Ltd. (C.A.)   Stephenson L.J.

A have to be considered in the light of such cases on the same Act of 1907
as *Metropolitan Water Board* v. *Avery* [1914] A.C. 118, to see whether
it puts the effluent from the respondents' launderettes on the domestic or
the trade side of the line. But it clearly gives domestic sewage a meaning
which could cover lavatories and washing facilities for the respondents'
staff at their premises, whether or not it also covers the washing machines
with which the respondents carry on their trade. The former would clearly
B be ordinary house sewage—the words used in section 56 (1) (*a*) of the
Public Health (London) Act 1936 to express the same well-known concept.

There remains the crucial question, to be answered, in my judgment,
in the light of its meaning in section 34 (1) of the Act of 1936: is the
effluent from the launderettes' washing machines or, in the judge's words,
the liquid discharged from washing machines in a launderette, domestic
C sewage, as the judge held, or is it not, as the appellants submit?

The basis of the judge's decision is that the same or similar liquid
discharged into a sewer from the same or a similar washing machine
installed in a dwelling house would be beyond question domestic sewage.
Indeed, it would not be a trade effluent at all. Why should it be transformed into a trade effluent which is not domestic sewage if it is dis-
D charged, with or without the help of staff employed by the occupier, from
the same or similar machines installed in a launderette?

There is some support for answering this question, as the judge did,
in the respondents' favour to be obtained from authorities concerned with
the supply of water for domestic and other purposes and, less directly,
from authorities concerned with the removal of house refuse and trade
refuse. It is accepted by the appellants for the purposes of this action
E that the discharge from an ordinary householder's washing machine is
similar to that from a washing machine in a launderette in both its
constituents and its strength (what in section 2 of the Act of 1937 is
called " the nature or composition of the trade effluent ") though not in
its quality or rate of discharge (where maxima are shown by that section
to be matters of concern to a sewage authority).

F But several of the judgments given in those cases recognise the
difficulty, not resolved but rather perhaps increased by statutory provisions, of regarding water or other liquids used or discharged in the
course of activities which could be carried out by householders at home
as still necessarily domestic when carried out elsewhere for profit.

Section 25 of the Metropolitan Water Board (Charges) Act 1907 itself
G declared that " domestic purposes " should not include a supply of water
for a number of purposes ending with " any trade manufacture or
business " sandwiched in between " public pumps, baths or wash houses "
and " any bath constructed . . . to be capable of containing . . . more
than 80 gallons." There is an echo of that definition in paragraph 1 (1)
of Schedule 3 to the Water Act 1945, which declares:

H   " . . . ' a supply of water for domestic purposes ' means a sufficient
supply for drinking, washing, cooking and sanitary purposes, but
not for any bath having a capacity . . . in excess of fifty gallons; and
includes—(*a*) a supply for the purposes of a profession carried on in
any premises the greater part whereof is used as a house; . . . Provided that it does not include a supply of water for the business of a
laundry or a business of preparing food or beverages for consumption
otherwise than on the premises; . . ."

Section 4 (4) of the Act of 1936 exempted the discharge from any premises, A
into a sewer of a local authority, of any liquid produced solely in the
course of laundering articles on those premises from requiring the local
authority's consent; and the exemption of such premises from the
imposition of any charge or condition in relation to the discharge of a
trade effluent from such premises was preserved by section 65 (7) of the
Public Health Act 1961. The Water Act 1937, however, transferred to
water authorities the duty to provide sewerage and sewage disposal, B
including sewers for domestic purposes (sections 14 and 16), and abolished
the exemption of laundries from the need for consent to discharges
(section 40 and Schedule 8, paragraph 44).

Clearly the premises of a laundry, where articles were bought or
sent by the public, laundered and taken or sent back to the customer,
were regarded by the legislature as trade premises and premises to which C
water was not supplied for domestic purposes.

A launderette is a modern invention and differs from a laundry—to
supply the deficiencies in the evidence from common knowledge—in the
range of its washing activities, the washing and cleaning materials it uses
and the amount of self service which it leaves to the customer. But
the customer's washing is still brought to the premises, done there and D
taken away. Indeed, the respondents' own memorandum of association
describes themselves as proprietors of coin-operated and self-service
laundries and their business as " the business of laundry proprietors . . ."
When they inconsistently gave the appellants a trade effluent notice, they
gave the nature of their business as " launderette," the trade premises
from which trade effluent would result as " use of washing machines by
the public "; and the nature and composition of the trade effluent as E
" drainage from washing machines, i.e. soapy water."

The position of premises where the clothes of members of the public
are washed has been considered, for example, by Darling J., in *Pidgeon* v.
Great Yarmouth Waterworks Co. [1902] 1 K.B. 310, 315, where he stated
his opinion that water supplied to a boarding-house keeper for the purpose
of washing, drinking, cooking and sanitary purposes within the house F
would be supplied and used for domestic purposes but for business purposes if used " for the purpose of washing clothes which were delivered to
people outside." In *Metropolitan Water Board* v. *Avery* [1913] 2 K.B. 257,
268–269, Channell J. treated a supply of water for a bath proprietor as
possibly a trade supply and water supplied for a laundry or a dyer's and
cleaner's business as probably a trade supply, because the water was,
" as it were, the raw material of the trade " directly used for trade G
purposes. And in the same case Lord Atkinson [1914] A.C. 118, 131,
adopted Channell J.'s words about the raw material of the trade and
dealt with counsel's argument (at p. 121) that

" Nothing could be more domestic than washing clothes, but washing clothes for people in general—people outside the house—would
not be a domestic purpose within [section 25 of the Act of 1907] H
because a trade purpose " in this way. " [Counsel] urged that
[public laundries] render services for their customers which are
usually rendered in one's home. I do not think the cases are
analogous," that is the case of public laundries and the case before
him of a public house where water was used for cooking luncheons
and washing up plates and dishes " and it is unnecessary to decide
the point."

The Weekly Law Reports, July 4, 1980

709

1 W.L.R.   Thames Water v. Launderettes Ltd. (C.A.)   Stephenson L.J.

A   Ever since *Avery's* case hotels and restaurants have occupied a favoured position. They are not to this day charged for their effluent, we are told, presumably on the basis that they merely render services usually rendered in the home of the public who patronise them: food and drink, accommodation, sleeping and washing and sanitary facilities. And their refuse has been held to be not "trade refuse" but "house refuse" which the sanitary authority was bound under the Public Health (London) Act B 1891 to remove without payment. But Sargant J., in *Oddenino* v. *Metropolitan Water Board* [1914] 2 Ch. 734 held that the Imperial Restaurant was being used for a trade purpose, namely, carrying on the business of a restaurant for which water was used so that the Metropolitan Water Board was entitled, on his construction of section 20 of the Act of 1907 (which differed from section 25), to refuse a supply of water otherwise C than by meter.

     That case illustrates the importance of the particular statutory provisions on which those earlier authorities were based and the dangers of applying them without caution to different statutory provisions. *Colley's* case [1912] A.C. 24 is, to my mind, the safest guide to the solution of our problem, because, as I have indicated, it is from that decision that the first statutory provision for domestic sewage comes into section 34 (1) D of the Act of 1936. And it is in that case that Lord Loreburn L.C., at p. 31, clearly points to the distinction between water supplied "for use in the trade, manufacture or business" of the factory and water supplied for ordinary domestic use in the factory by the factory's workmen.

     In *Avery's* case [1914] A.C. 118 the Earl of Halsbury L.C. followed E Lord Loreburn's judgment in *Colley's* case, though there appears to have been a divergence of opinion between the other two noble lords on the test which Mr. Widdicombe asked us to extract from the opinions of Lord Loreburn L.C. and Lord Dunedin and to apply to the decision of this appeal.

     In rejecting the argument of Avery's counsel by analogy not from F public laundries (which I have already quoted), but from public baths or water closets (which is not set out in the report but appears to have been the same), Lord Dunedin [1914] A.C. 118, 125 thought that the solution of such extreme cases when they arose might be suggested in a phrase in the judgment of Bray J. which Eveleigh L.J. has quoted [1913] 2 K.B. 257, 265:

G   "If the water is used for a purpose which is common to all ordinary domestic establishments, it is none the less used for domestic purposes because it is ancillary to a trade, manufacture or business."

And Lord Dunedin went on to say:

     ". . . the use of the water would not be ancillary to the business, it would be the business itself, and I should personally be prepared to hold . . . that the trade use of the water was so pre-eminent that it H   could not be said that in those establishments there was truly a use for a domestic purpose at all."

Lord Atkinson, on the other hand (at p. 131 of his speech already quoted) apparently rejected the test, or at least rejected its application to the facts of the case before him: and Lord Dunedin was in agreement that it was inapplicable, as the unanimous decision of their Lordships' House demonstrated.

A   As eminent judges have felt able to distinguish hotels and restaurants from public laundries and baths, I do not feel bound by any authority or the Act of 1907 to hold that all the soapy water discharged from a launderette is necessarily domestic, though I recognise that the operations of a launderette are nearer to those of a householder than are the operations of a laundry. Nor do I feel bound by any authority or the Act of 1891 to hold that the refuse of a launderette could not be " trade refuse "
B   within section 73 of the Act of 1936. Even if the question whether the discharge from a launderette is domestic sewage within section 14 (1) of Act of 1937 could be answered by answering the question whether the refuse from a launderette was house refuse within section 72 of the Act of 1936, Bridge J. in *Iron Trades Mutual Employers Insurance Association Ltd.* v. *Sheffield Corporation* [1974] 1 W.L.R. 107, 112 felt
C   free to approach the distinction between house refuse and trade refuse afresh. Following his lead, I feel free to decide that everything directly produced in the course of the trade or business of a launderette, whether for the trade purpose of washing or laundering clothing or for the trade purpose preferred by Mr. Gorman for the respondents of hiring out washing machines and providing soap and water-softener, is a trade effluent, except the effluent from any lavatories or wash basins or water
D   closets or baths provided as ancillary to the trade use of the launderette. And that exception is domestic sewage.

The exception is made in order to prevent domestic effluent, if separately discharged, being classed and charged as trade effluent because it might be considered to be produced in the course of the trade carried on at trade premises. But it does not follow that because all liquid
E   discharged from particular trade premises is not trade effluent none of it is. And the definition prevents Lord Dunedin's suggestion of all or none applying not only to factories but to trade premises, including launderettes.

For these reasons, I would give a different answer from that given by the judge to the question whether the effluent from the machines at the launderettes is domestic sewage. In my judgment, it is not. I too would allow the appeal.
F
BRANDON L.J. I agree with both judgments.

Appeal allowed.
Judgment for plaintiffs for £1,355·27
with costs of appeal and below on
county court scale 4.
G   *Leave to appeal refused.*

Solicitors: *R. A. R. Gray; Swatton, Hughes & Co., Tring.*

[Reported by ROBERT WILLIAMS, ESQ., Barrister-at-Law.]
H
February 21, 1980. The Appeal Committee of the House of Lords (Lord Diplock, Lord Salmon and Lord Scarman) dismissed a petition by the respondents for leave to appeal.

In re Gray's Inn Construction (C.A.)

A

[COURT OF APPEAL]

In re GRAY'S INN CONSTRUCTION CO. LTD.

[No. 001437 of 1977]

B 1979 Oct. 16, 17, 18;   Buckley and Goff L.JJ.
  Dec. 5   and Sir David Cairns

Company — Winding up — Disposition of property — Company's
 bank account overdrawn—Bank accepting payments into and
 out of account between presentation of petition and winding
 up order—Whether payments void as dispositions of company's
C *property — Discretion of court to validate transactions —*
 Companies Act 1948 (11 & 12 *Geo.* 6, *c.* 38), *s.* 227 [1]

  A company incorporated in 1969 carried on a building
business. The company's current bank account was normally
overdrawn and unsecured by the company but guaranteed by
the managing director whose guarantee was secured. On
August 3, 1972, a creditor presented a petition for the wind-
D ing up of the company. The petition was advertised on
August 10 and on August 17 it came to the notice of the
bank manager, although it came to the notice of the head
office of the bank a day or two earlier. On October 9 the
court made a compulsory winding up order. The bank did
not require the company, after the commencement of the
winding up, to operate a separate account but continued to
accept payments into and out of the company's current
E account from August 3 to October 9. The bank attempted
to ensure that all the cheques were drawn in the ordinary
course of the company's business but did not distinguish
between pre- and post-liquidation debts. It did not apply to
the court for a prospective validating order under section 227
of the Companies Act 1948.
  In October 1976 the liquidator issued a summons for a
declaration that the amounts credited and/or debited to the
F account by the bank during the period in question constituted
dispositions of the company's property which were void pursuant to section 227, and sought an order that the bank pay
those moneys to the liquidator with interest. The liquidator,
at the hearing, limited the claim to the amount which the
company lost by remaining in business after the presentation
of the petition. Templeman J. held that the payments of
moneys to the credit of a company's account, whether or not
G in credit, did not constitute a disposition of the company's
property and that as the decision by the bank to allow facilities
for normal trade was a reasonable decision in the circumstances, was made by a bank manager with sufficient knowledge
of the company's affairs and was supported by proper safeguards on the operation of that account, the loss could not be
recovered from the bank and the dealings on the account for
the period from August 3 to October 9, 1972, would be
H validated.
  On appeal by the liquidator:—
  Held, allowing the appeal, (1) that where a company paid
money into its overdrawn bank account, it discharged its
indebtedness to the bank pro tanto and in those circumstances
there was clearly a disposition by the company to the bank of
the amount paid in and that, unless validated under section 227
of the Companies Act 1948, all payments into and payments

[1] Companies Act 1948, s. 227: see post, p. 715G.

out of the account during the period August 3 to October 9, **A**
1972, were invalid (post, pp. 715H—716A, C–E).

(2) That the court should exercise its discretion under section
227 in validating otherwise invalid dispositions in order to
ensure that the interests of unprotected creditors would not be
prejudiced and, accordingly, the order made by the judge
resulting in the preferential discharge of the existing overdraft
should not have been made; that the correct course, in view of
the failure of the bank to protect its own position, was to con-   **B**
sider what the position would have been had the overdraft been
frozen on August 3 and all subsequent transactions been dealt
with through a new account; and, accordingly, the court would
validate the sums credited to the account before the advertisement of the petition and before the bank became aware of
the presentation of the petition, but, thereafter, credits to the
account should not be validated and, in the circumstances, the
bank was liable to restore to the company the amount lost by   **C**
post-liquidation unprofitable trading (post, pp. 718A–B, 719D–G,
721A–H, 724B–C, F–H).

In re Steane's (Bournemouth) Ltd. [1950] 1 All E.R. 21
considered.

Order of Templeman J. discharged.

The following cases are referred to in the judgment of Buckley L.J.:

D
Civil Service and General Store Ltd., In re (1888) 58 L.T. 220.
Clayton's Case, Devaynes v. Noble (1816) 1 Mer. 572.
Clifton Place Garage Ltd., In re [1970] Ch. 477; [1970] 2 W.L.R. 243;
   [1970] 1 All E.R. 353, C.A.
Leslie (J.) Engineers Co. Ltd., In re [1976] 1 W.L.R. 292; [1976] 2 All
   E.R. 85.
Levy (A. I.) (Holdings) Ltd., In re [1964] Ch. 19; [1963] 2 W.L.R. 1464;
   [1963] 2 All E.R. 556.   **E**
Liverpool Civil Service Association, In re, Ex parte Greenwood (1874)
   L.R. 9 Ch.App. 511.
Neath Harbour Smelting and Rolling Works, In re (1887) 56 L.T. 727.
Park Ward & Co., In re [1926] Ch. 828.
Steane's (Bournemouth) Ltd., In re [1950] 1 All E.R. 21.
Wiltshire Iron Co., In re., Ex parte Pearson (1868) L.R. 3 Ch.App. 443.

F
The following additional cases were cited in argument:

Fryer v. Ewart [1902] A.C. 187; [1901] 1 Ch. 499, H.L.(E.).
Mal Bower's Macquarie Electrical Centre Pty. Ltd., In re [1974] 1
   N.S.W.L.R. 254.
Millar v. National Bank of Scotland Ltd. (1891) 28 S.L.R. 884.
Operator Control Cabs Ltd., In re [1970] 3 All E.R. 657.   **G**
Repertoire Opera Co., In re (1895) 2 Manson 314.
T.W. Construction Ltd., In re [1954] 1 W.L.R. 540; [1954] 1 All E.R. 744.
Yeovil Glove Co. Ltd., In re [1963] Ch. 528; [1962] 3 W.L.R. 900;
   [1962] 3 All E.R. 400; [1965] Ch. 148; [1964] 3 W.L.R. 406; [1964]
   2 All E.R. 849, C.A.

APPEAL from Templeman J.   **H**

The company, Gray's Inn Construction Co. Ltd., traded as builders and
contractors and maintained a current account with the National Westminster Bank Ltd. On August 3, 1972, Field-Davis Ltd., a creditor of the
company, sought an order for the compulsory winding up of the company
on the ground of insolvency. The petition was presented on August 3,
1972, and advertised on August 10, 1972, and the company was wound up
by the court on October 9, 1972.

A   The liquidator, Mr. Richard Eaglesfield Lloyd, appointed by the court
on December 14, 1972, sought (1) a declaration that the sums received by
the bank from the company between August 3 and October 9, 1972,
amounting to £22,183 constituted dispositions of the company's property
and were void pursuant to section 227 of the Companies Act 1948; (2)
an order that the bank should pay the liquidator the sum of £22,183
together with interest at such rate as the court deemed fit; (3) alternatively
B   to (1) and (2), a declaration that debits caused or permitted by the bank to
be made to the company's account between August 3 and October 9, 1972,
totalling £21,693 and/or the payments to which they related constituted
dispositions of property of the company which were void pursuant to section
227 of the Act of 1948; and (4) (further to (3)) an order that the bank
should pay the liquidator the sum of £21,693 with interest at such rate as
C   the court deemed fit.

     On July 18, 1978, Templeman J. made an order validating all trans-
actions on the current banking account of the company made between
August 3 and October 9, 1972.

     The liquidator appealed, inter alia, on the gounds that (1) whenever a
banker credited to the overdrawn account of a customer the proceeds of a
cheque left with the banker by the customer for collection, the property
D   or assets of the customer were thereby reduced to the extent to which the
credit reduced or extinguished the amount by which the account was overdrawn; (2) the judge erred in law in holding that payment of moneys to the
credit of a company's overdrawn account did not constitute a disposition
of the property of the company within the meaning of section 227 of the
Companies Act 1948; (3) upon the true construction of section 227 and
E   upon principle, no disposition of any property of any company which would
otherwise be void by virtue of that section should be validated by the court
unless (i) the person purporting to make the disposition on behalf of the
company and/or the person receiving the benefit of it believed at the time
when the disposition was effected that there was no reasonable prospect
of the general body of creditors of the company being thereby prejudiced
and had reasonable grounds for such belief, or (ii) the interests of the general
F   body of creditors were not thereby prejudiced; (4) as a matter of construction of the section and upon both principle and authority, the onus of
establishing that belief and the reasonable grounds therefor and/or the
absence in fact of any prejudice lay upon the party seeking validation; (5)
the judge erred in law in holding that a banker faced with a request by a
corporate customer, against which a petition for winding up had been
G   presented, to continue to cause or permit the making of entries to the credit
of an overdrawn account of the customer against the proceeds of cheques
payable to the customer and collected by the banker, or to continue to
cause or permit payments by the banker, or to continue to cause or permit
payments by the customer to be debited to an account of the customer
whether overdrawn or not, had only to consider in deciding whether or not
to accede to such request whether harm was likely to be caused to the
H   creditors of the company in so causing or permitting; (6) the judge erred
in law in failing to hold that the onus of proving that belief and the reasonable grounds therefor and/or the absence in fact of any such prejudice,
alternatively that such consideration as the judge held ought to be given
was in fact given, lay upon the bank; (7) the judge erred in law in holding
that in order to succeed upon the application, the liquidator should be
required to identify any payment either to the credit or to the debit of the
account of the company which was unusual, or otherwise than for the

714

purpose of a bona fide trading transaction in the ordinary course of busi- **A**
ness, or to identify any pattern of payments into or out of such account
from August 17, 1972, onwards which ought to have alarmed the bank.

The facts are stated in the judgment of Buckley L.J.

David Oliver for the liquidator.
Philip Heslop for the bank.

B

Cur. adv. vult.

December 5. BUCKLEY L.J. read the following judgment. This is
an appeal from an order of Templeman J. under the Companies Act 1948,
section 227, validating all transactions on the current banking account of
the company, Gray's Inn Construction Co. Ltd., between August 3, 1972,
when a petition for the compulsory winding up of the company was pre- **C**
sented by a creditor, and October 9, 1972, when an order was made on that
petition for the winding up of the company.

The company, which was incorporated in 1969, carried on a building
business. It maintained a current account with the National Westminster
Bank at its Tavistock Square branch in London. It seems that the company did not engage in large building projects or in speculative building on **D**
its own account, but mainly undertook relatively small contracts of which
it seems to have secured a considerable number. The company's current
account appears to have been normally overdrawn. At any rate it was in
debit throughout the period covered by the evidence, and it is apparent
that the company found difficulty in keeping within the overdraft limit
of £5,000 imposed by the bank. The overdraft was unsecured by the
company, but was guaranteed by Mr. Chapman, the managing director, **E**
whose guarantee was secured.

The company was indebted to another company, named Field-Davis
Ltd., of which it had at one time been a subsidiary, in a sum of over £4,000.
The origin of this debt does not appear from the evidence, but it seems
possible that it may have been a loan made by Field-Davis Ltd. to the
company to provide working capital in the company's early days. On **F**
August 3, 1972, Field-Davis Ltd. presented a petition for the winding up
of the company founded upon that debt. The petition was advertised
on August 10, 1972, and came to the notice of the manager of the Tavistock
Square branch of the bank on August 17. It is, however, evident that it
must have come to the notice of the head office of the bank before August
17, though on what date is not clear. On October 9, 1972, the court made
a compulsory winding up order. The bank continued throughout the period **G**
August 3 to October 9, 1972, to accept payments into the account, mainly
if not entirely in the form of third parties' cheques paid in by the company
and collected by the bank; it also continued to honour cheques drawn on
the account, making sure, so far as it was able to do so, that all such
cheques were drawn in the ordinary course of the company's business but
without attempting to distinguish between pre-liquidation debts and post-
liquidation debts. In so doing the branch manager was acting in accor- **H**
dance with an internal directive issued by the bank's head office to all
branches. This dealt as follows with the action to be taken on notice of
presentation of a petition:

" Normally the acount whether overdrawn or in credit may be continued for all bona fide transactions which are in the normal course of
business, *i.e.* wages and current purchases until a winding up order is

A   made. The bank is accepting some risk in adopting this course as the winding up will, if pursued, commence from the date of the petition and the bank is relying on the court to confirm those transactions which are allowed on the account after notice of the petition and before the winding-up order is made. Managers must therefore advise the area manager as soon as notice is received. All entries on the account during this period must be scrutinised very carefully and where

B   there are unusual transactions, further reference should be made to the area manager."

   Immediately before August 3, 1972, the account was overdrawn to the extent of £5,322 (I ignore pence). At October 9, 1972, it was overdrawn to the extent of £4,464. Sums amounting to £25,313 had been paid in during this period: sums amounting to £24,129 had been paid out and the

C   bank had debited the account with sums amounting to £326 for interest and bank charges. The amount of the overdraft during this period fluctuated, the highest figure being in excess of £7,000 and the lowest less than £3,600.

   On October 27, 1976, the liquidator issued a summons for a declaration that the receipt by the bank from the company between August 3 and

D   October 9, 1972 (inclusive), of the amounts credited to the account during that period constituted dispositions of the property of the company which were void pursuant to the Companies Act 1948, section 227, and an order that the bank should pay the amount of those sums to the liquidator with interest; alternatively, a declaration that the amounts debited to the account during the period constituted dispositions of property of the company which were likewise void, and an order that the bank should pay the amount of

E   those sums to the liquidator with interest. At the hearing, however, the liquidator did not press for this relief in full; he limited his claim to the amount which the company lost by remaining in business after the presentation of the petition, which the liquidator calculated to amount to £13,260. The judge said that reconstruction (and I think he was referring to reconstruction of the trading figures during the relevant period) was difficult on

F   the information before the court; that it was not possible to be certain that harm was caused by the company continuing in business after August 3, 1972; that the probability was that creditors were worse off by not less than £4,000 or more than £8,000; and that for the purposes of the summons he assumed and found that the creditors were worse off to the extent of £5,000. That finding is not now sought to be disturbed. It was, I think, a finding that there had been a trading loss of £5,000.

G   The Companies Act 1948, section 227, is in the following terms:

     " In a winding up by the court, any disposition of the property of the company, including things in action, and any transfer of shares, or alteration in the status of the members of the company, made after the commencement of the winding up, shall, unless the court otherwise orders, be void."

H
   The judge proceeded on the basis, which he held to be the position in law, that payment of moneys to the credit of a company's account, whether it is in credit or not, do not constitute, a disposition of the company's property. That is a view with which, with deference to the judge, I feel unable to agree. When a customer's account with his banker is overdrawn he is a debtor to his banker for the amount of the overdraft. When he pays a sum of money into the account, whether in cash or by payment in

of a third party's cheque, he discharges his indebtedness to the bank pro   A
tanto. There is clearly in these circumstances, in my judgment, a disposition by the company to the bank of the amount of the cash or of the
cheque. It may well be the case, as Mr. Heslop has submitted, that in
clearing a third party's cheque and collecting the amount due upon it, the
bank acts as the customer's agent, but as soon as it credits the amount
collected in reduction of the customer's overdraft, as in the ordinary course
of banking business it has authority to do in the absence of any contrary   B
instruction from the customer, it makes a disposition on the customer's
behalf in its own favour discharging pro tanto the customer's liability on
the overdraft. Mr. Heslop was constrained in the course of the argument
to accept that this is so. In the present case the company's account with
the bank was overdrawn, so I need not consider what the position would
have been if any cheque had been paid in when the account was in credit,   C
but I doubt whether even in those circumstances it could be properly said
that the payment in did not constitute a disposition of the amount of the
cheque in favour of the bank.

Mr. Heslop does not dispute that all payments out of the company's
account to third parties, not being payments to agents of the company as
such, are dispositions of the company's property; but he contends (as I
understand his argument) that they are only relevant for the purposes of   D
section 227 to the extent that payments out during the relevant period
exceed payments in. That all such payments out must be dispositions of
the company's property is, I think, indisputable, but I cannot accept Mr.
Heslop's contention. The section must, in my judgment, invalidate every
transaction to which it applies at the instant at which that transaction
purports to have taken place. I cannot see any ground for saying that the   E
invalidation can be negatived by any subsequent transaction.

It follows, in my judgment, that unless validated under the section all
the payments into and all the payments out of the company's account
during the period August 3 to October 9, 1972, were invalid. No one,
however, suggests that the bank should repay to the liquidator £25,313 and
that all the recipients of the £24,129 should repay to the liquidator the
sums so received by them. The problem is how in these circumstances   F
the discretionary power of the court under the section to validate dispositions which would otherwise be invalid should be exercised.

Templeman J. said in the course of his judgment:

> "This present case, however, inevitably involves consideration of the
> dilemma which confronts a bank when a company requests the con-
> tinuation of banking facilities after the presentation of a winding up   G
> petition, but there are no plain indications on the one hand that the
> petition is misconceived or on the other hand that the company ought
> to be immobilised immediately."

He went on to say that a bank faced with such a request should weigh the
likely benefits and dangers of the company continuing in business against
the benefits and losses which may be the consequence of an immediate   H
cessation of business, and that, if the bank comes to the conclusion that
the risks of allowing the company to continue in business are worth taking
in the interests of the company and its creditors, the bank must thereafter
remain satisfied that the company does not make payments which are not
normal and reasonable expenditure in the ordinary course of business, and
that there are no indications that the financial position of the company is
deteriorating and no signs that the confidence of the bank in the directors

A   is misplaced.   He reviewed the facts of the present case and concluded that
the decision to allow banking facilities for normal trade was made after
proper consideration by a prudent and conscientious bank manager who
knew sufficient about the company's affairs to reach a reasonable conclusion, and who prescribed and enforced proper safeguards for the operation
of the company's banking account.   If in the event the creditors were
worse off by £5,000 or more, that loss could not, he said, fairly be recovered
B   from the bank.   On these grounds he validated all the dealings on the
account during the period August 3 to October 9, 1972.

In *In re Steane's (Bournemouth) Ltd.* [1950] 1 All E.R. 21, Vaisey J.
said, at p. 25 :

" The legislature, by omitting to indicate any particular principles
which should govern the exercise of the discretion vested in the court,
C   [by the section] must be deemed to have left it entirely at large, and
controlled only by the general principles which apply to every kind
of judicial discretion."

I do not at all dissent from that statement beyond saying that the discretion
must, in my opinion, be exercised in the context of the liquidation provisions of the Companies Act 1948.

D   It is a basic concept of our law governing the liquidation of insolvent
estates, whether in bankruptcy or under the Companies Acts, that the
free assets of the insolvent at the commencement of the liquidation shall
be distributed rateably amongst the insolvent's unsecured creditors as at
that date.   In bankruptcy this is achieved by the relation of the trustee's
title to the bankrupt's assets back to the commencement of the bankruptcy.
E   In a company's compulsory winding up it is achieved by section 227.
There may be occasions, however, when it would be beneficial, not only
for the company but also for its unsecured creditors, that the company
should be enabled to dispose of some of its property during the period
after the petition has been presented but before a winding up order has
been made.   An obvious example is if the company has an opportunity
by acting speedily to dispose of some piece of property at an exceptionally
F   good price.   Many applications for validation under the section relate to
specific transactions of this kind or analogous kinds.   It may sometimes be
beneficial to the company and its creditors that the company should be
enabled to complete a particular contract or project, or to continue to carry
on its business generally in its ordinary course with a view to a sale of the
business as a going concern.   In any such case the court has power under
section 227 of the Companies Act 1948 to validate the particular trans-
G   action, or the completion of the particular contract or project, or the
continuance of the company's business in its ordinary course, as the case
may be.   In considering whether to make a validating order the court must
always, in my opinion, do its best to ensure that the interests of the
unsecured creditors will not be prejudiced.   Where the application relates
to a specific transaction this may be susceptible of positive proof.   In a case
H   of completion of a contract or project the proof may perhaps be less
positive but nevertheless be cogent enough to satisfy the court that in the
interests of the creditors the company should be enabled to proceed, or at
any rate that proceeding in the manner proposed would not prejudice them
in any respect.   The desirability of the company being enabled to carry on
its business generally is likely to be more speculative and will be likely to
depend on whether a sale of the business as a going concern will probably
be more beneficial than a break-up realisation of the company's assets.   In

each case, I think, the court must necessarily carry out a balancing exercise   A
of the kind envisaged by Templeman J. in his judgment. Each case must
depend upon its own particular facts.

Since the policy of the law is to procure so far as practicable rateable
payments of the unsecured creditors' claims, it is, in my opinion, clear that
the court should not validate any transaction or series of transactions which
might result in one or more pre-liquidation creditors being paid in full at
the expense of other creditors, who will only receive a dividend, in the   B
absence of special circumstances making such a course desirable in the
interests of the unsecured creditors as a body. If, for example, it were in
the interests of the creditors generally that the company's business should
be carried on, and this could only be achieved by paying for goods already
supplied to the company when the petition is presented but not yet paid
for, the court might think fit in the exercise of its discretion to validate   C
payment for those goods.

Where a third party proposes to enter into a transaction with a company
which is liable to be invalidated under section 227 of the Companies Act
1948, the third party can decline to do so until the company has obtained
a validating order, or it might itself seek a validating order, or it can enter
into the transaction in anticipation of the court making a retroactive validating order at a later date. In the present case the bank adopted the last   D
course. A third party who does that takes the risk of the court refusing
to make the order.

It may not always be feasible, or desirable, that a validating order
should be sought before the transaction in question is carried out. The
parties may be unaware at the time when the transaction is entered into
that a petition has been presented; or the need for speedy action may be   E
such as to preclude an anticipatory application; or the beneficial character
of the transaction may be so obvious that there is no real prospect of a
liquidator seeking to set it aside, so that an application to the court would
waste time, money and effort. But in any case in which the transaction is
carried out without an anticipatory validating order the disponee is at
risk of the court declining to validate the transaction. It follows, in my
view, that the parties when entering into the transaction, if they are   F
aware that it is liable to be invalidated by the section, should have in
mind the sort of considerations which would influence the court's decision.

A disposition carried out in good faith in the ordinary course of business
at a time when the parties are unaware that a petition has been presented
may, it seems, normally be validated by the court (see In re Wiltshire Iron
Co. (1868) L.R. 3 Ch.App. 443; In re Neath Harbour Smelting and   G
Rolling Works (1887) 56 L.T. 727, 729; In re Liverpool Civil Service
Association (1874) L.R. 9 Ch.App. 511, 512) unless there is any ground
for thinking that the transaction may involve an attempt to prefer the
disponee, in which case the transaction would probably not be validated.
In a number of cases reference has been made to the relevance of the
policy of ensuring rateable distribution of the assets In re Civil Service   H
and General Store Ltd. (1888) 58 L.T. 220; In re Liverpool Civil Service
Association, L.R. 9 Ch.App. 511 and In re J. Leslie Engineers Co. Ltd.
[1976] 1 W.L.R. 292. In the last-mentioned case Oliver J. said, at
p. 304:

    " I think that in exercising discretion the court must keep in view
    the evident purpose of the section which, as Chitty J. said in In re

A   *Civil Service and General Store Ltd.,* 58 L.T. 220, 221, is to ensure
that the creditors are paid pari passu."

But although that policy might disincline the court to ratify any transaction which involved preferring a pre-liquidation creditor, it has no
relevance to a transaction which is entirely post-liquidation, as for instance
a sale of an asset at its full market value after presentation of a petition.
B   Such a transaction involves no dissipation of the company's assets, for it
does not reduce the value of those assets. It cannot harm the creditors
and there would seem to be no reason why the court should not in the
exercise of its discretion validate it. A fortiori, the court would be inclined
to validate a transaction which would increase or has increased, the value
of the company's assets, or which would preserve, or has preserved, the
value of the company's assets from harm which would result from the
C   company's business being paralysed: *In re Wiltshire Iron Co.* (1868) L.R.
3 Ch.App. 443; *In re Park Ward & Co. Ltd.* [1926] Ch. 828, where the
business of the company was eventually sold as a going concern, presumably to the advantage of the creditors; *In re Clifton Place Garage Ltd.*
[1970] Ch. 477. In *In re A. I. Levy (Holdings) Ltd.* [1964] Ch. 19 the
court validated a sale of a lease which was liable to forfeiture in the event
D   of the tenant company being wound up, and also validated, as part of the
transaction, payment out of the proceeds of sale of arrears of rent which
had accrued before the presentation of the petition for the compulsory
liquidation of the company. If that case was rightly decided, as I trust
that it was, the court can in appropriate circumstances validate payment
in full of an unsecured pre-liquidation debt which constitutes a necessary
part of a transaction which as a whole is beneficial to the general body of
E   unsecured creditors. But we have been referred to no case in which the
court has validated payment in full of an unsecured pre-liquidation debt
where there was no such special circumstance, and in my opinion it would
not normally be right to do so, because such a payment would prefer the
creditor whose debt is paid over the other creditors of equal degree.

So I ask myself what the court would have done if an application had
F   been made at or about August 10, 1972, for an order that all dealings in
the ordinary course of business on the company's current account pending
an order for the winding up of the company should be valid? For this
purpose I will assume that the court would have been satisfied that it would
be in the interests of the general body of creditors that the company should
be permitted to continue trading and to use the services of the bank for that
purpose. In such circumstances the court should not, and would not in my
G   judgment, have made an order which would result in the preferential discharge of the existing overdraft on the company's account. The proper
course in such circumstances, in my opinion, would be to be freeze the
existing overdraft as at August 3, 1972. The practical method of achieving
this in accordance with normal banking practice would, I imagine, be to
discontinue all further dealings on that account as from August 3, 1972, and
H   to require all subsequent dealings to be on a new and separate account.
The effect of such an order would have been that at and after August 3,
1972, the old account would have remained overdrawn to the extent of
£5,322, which would be provable in the winding up. The new account
would initially have been neither in debit nor in credit. Upon this footing
the court might well have been disposed to allow the bank to operate the
new account subject to safeguards directed to ensuring that it would only
do so for so long as the company was trading at a profit or that continued

Buckley L.J.   In re Gray's Inn Construction (C.A.)   [1980]

trading would be likely to benefit the general body of creditors. A bank   A
cannot, of course, spend all or even a great deal of its time in conducting
a day-to-day surveillance of a customer's business, and the court, if asked
to make a prospective order, must do its best to make a realistic assessment
of the risk involved of any system of safeguards falling short of failing
safe; but we are not in this case concerned with a prospective order. It
seems to me that, when the matter came before Templeman J., he was
bound to deal with it in the light of all the facts then known to him, includ-   B
ing the fact, according to his finding, that the company had traded at a loss.
The bank, having taken the risk of going on without the protection of a
validating order, must, it seems to me, take the consequences.

If the old account had been frozen in the way I have supposed, between
August 3 and October 9, 1972, the credits to the new account would have
been £25,313; the debits, including interest and charges, would have   C
amounted to £24,455: so that, if the post-liquidation operations were
segregated from the pre-liquidation current account, the new account would
have been in credit at October 9, 1972, to the extent of £858, to which
amount the liquidator would have been entitled as an asset of the company.

Templeman J. took the view that, as the bank had acted in good faith
in the belief that the petition would be dismissed and that the company
would continue in business, it would be unfair to the bank to make the   D
bank answerable for any of the £5,000 loss. He said that the bank could
not be required to insure the creditors against loss. Having come to the
conclusion that harm would have resulted if the company had ceased to
trade and that it did not appear to the bank manager that harm would be
occasioned if the company were allowed banking facilities after August 17,
1972, for the purpose of continuing normal trade, he made the order   E
appealed from. I ask myself, however, why the creditors should suffer for
the loss, the bank not having protected itself by the precaution of obtaining
an order of the court. In my judgment, the judge should in principle have
ensured that the creditors did not suffer. On the other hand I see no reason
why the bank should be penalised further than may be necessary to restore
to the fund of assets available for distribution among the creditors the
amount of the loss.   F

It may be suggested that this approach is one which must increase the
dilemma referred to by the judge in a passage which I have cited from his
judgment. I do not think that this is really so. If a bank decides to continue to afford facilities to a corporate customer against whom a winding
up petition has been presented, having an account in debit at the date of
the presentation of the petition, the bank can itself freeze that account and   G
insist upon all subsequent dealings being dealt with on a separate account.
It can require personal assurances from the directors of the company that
no payments out of the new account will be made in discharge of pre-
liquidation debts and that all payments out of the new account shall be in
respect of liabilities incurred in the ordinary course of business subsequent
to the presentation of the petition. It can institute such checks upon the
profitability of the company's trading as it thinks fit.   H

Having regard to the way in which the current account was operated
in the present case, under the rule in *Clayton's Case* (1816) 1 Mer. 572,
the earliest credits on and after August 3, 1972, up to an aggregate amount
of £5,322, if valid, would be treated as appropriated to discharge pro tanto
the overdraft existing immediately before August 3, 1972. Sums amounting
to £2,570 were credited to the account between August 3, 1972, and
August 9, 1972 (both included); further sums amounting to £4,666 were

A credited to the account before August 17, 1972. Sums amounting to
£2,928 were debited to the account between August 3 and August 9 (both
included) and further sums amounting to £3,483 were debited before
August 17, 1972.

On the facts of this case it seems to me that it was proper for the judge
in the exercise of his discretion to validate the credits amounting to £2,570
which were credited to the account before advertisement of the petition.

B Of the credits to the account between August 10 and August 17, 1972, £100
was credited on August 11 and £4,566 on August 15. Although the branch
manager was not aware of the presentation of the petition until August 17,
I think that the bank must be treated as having been aware of the presentation of the petition before August 15. In these circumstances I would
not disturb the validation of the £100. The aggregate amount of £2,670

C so validated would have the effect of reducing the pre-liquidation overdraft
of £5,322 to £2,652. In my judgment, the bank was not justified in appropriating any subsequent credits to the discharge of this outstanding pre-
liquidation debt. I would accordingly refuse to validate the next credits
to the account after August 11, 1972, up to a sum of £2,652, and would
order repayment of that sum by the bank to the liquidator but without
prejudice to the right of the bank (if any) to prove in the liquidation in

D respect of that sum as part of the £5,322 due to the bank on the overdraft
at the commencement of the winding up.

It appears from the affidavit of Mr. Cookey-Gam, and particularly
from the exhibit to that affidavit, that during the period August 3 to
October 9, 1972, the company paid out of its current account with the
bank for goods and services supplied before the commencement of the

E winding up an aggregate sum of £4,824. These payments were a consequence of the failure of the bank to take any steps to ensure so far as
it could, as in my judgment it should have done, that no payments were
made out of the current account after the commencement of the winding
up in payment of pre-liquidation debts. In these circumstances, in my
judgment, subject to the qualification I shall mention in a moment, the
bank is vulnerable to a refusal to validate the next £4,824 of credits

F to the account and to an order for repayment of that sum by the bank
to the liquidator.

It seems to me, however, that primarily these sums, amounting in
the aggregate to £4,824, should be recovered from the creditors to whom
they were paid, and that the bank should in any event only be required
to repay them to the extent that the amounts, if any, which prove to be

G irrecoverable from those creditors exceed the dividends which would be
payable in respect of them.

These repayments of £2,670 and £4,824 would restore to the fund of
assets available for distribution amongst the unsecured creditors all the
sums mistakenly applied in payment of pre-liquidation debts, but those
from whom they have been recovered will be entitled to prove in the

H winding up in respect of the amounts recovered.

This, however, would not restore the fund of assets distributable
amongst the unsecured creditors to its state as at August 3, 1972. There
is still the trading loss of £5,000 to be considered. Before expressing my
own view about this, it is right that I should indicate how the judge
approched this problem. He said:

" It follows that before a bank allows a company to continue to
operate its bank account, the bank must know enough about the

company's finances to be able to determine whether there is a
reasonable chance that the company will avoid or mitigate the
effects of compulsory liquidation. The bank must know enough
about the company's activities to be able to determine the probable
effect of an immediate cessation of business and the probable effect
of remaining in business until the winding up petition is heard. The
bank must have grounds for trusting the integrity and competence
of the directors. . . . If in the event the decision taken by the bank
involves the creditors in loss, the court will nevertheless absolve the
bank from liability provided the decision was based on adequate
information and was reasonable at the time."

The judge found that the branch manager lectured the directors from
time to time on the danger of over-trading and the need to press for
prompt payment from debtors in order to keep within the overdraft
limit, but he also found that there were no indications of serious
over-trading, and that there was no evidence of unprofitable trading.
The directors assured the branch manager that proposals for clearing the
petitioner's debt over a period had been submitted to and agreed by
the petitioner. No creditors gave notice of an intention to support
the petition.

The judge made the following findings:

"The directors informed the bank manager that they were optimistic
for the future of the company: current turnover was £15,000 to
£16,000 per month, with monthly outgoings in the region of £10,000.
Order books were full. Work in progress amounted to £168,000.
Debtors stood at £24,000 and new contracts totalling £102,500 had
been signed. The current account was expected to move into
permanent credit in the foreseeable future. The liquidator agrees
that the factual information given by the directors to the bank
manager was broadly accurate."

He found that the branch manager warned the directors that until
the petition was withdrawn the company's account would be under close
scrutiny and that only bona fide trading transactions would be permitted
and that he also stressed that borrowing must in no circumstance exceed
the overdraft limit of £5,000. In fact, from August 3 to 15 the overdraft
was substantially in excess of £5,000 by a margin of around £2,000; on
August 17 and 22 it was more than £500 in excess of £5,000, and on
August 30 and 31 it was again in excess of £5,000, the excess on the latter
date being more than £1,100, notwithstanding that the account was
scrutinised by the bank every day. Templeman J. said:

". . . the bank manager did ask himself whether it would be
beneficial to the company to be allowed to continue to operate its
bank account and to continue in business and he had sufficient
information with which to answer that question. If it was beneficial
to the company to continue, it was beneficial to the creditors. The
bank manager was informed that an agreement had been reached
which would result in the petition being dismissed. The bank
manager was provided with figures from which it appeared that the
company was trading at a profit. The bank manager was not told
how much the company owed but he was told that the bank account
would be in credit in the foreseeable future. The bank manager had

A   no reason to suppose from this information that the company was trading at a loss or was over-trading or was for any reason insolvent. The liquidator admits that the information given to the bank manager was in general accurate. If the bank manager had asked for more detailed information the result would have been the same. At the least there appeared a reasonable chance that the company would avoid liquidation and that the creditors would be paid in full.

B   " The information that work in progress amounted to £168,000 and new contracts for £102,000 had been signed, signified that if the company immediately ceased to trade the results could be disastrous to the company and thus to the creditors. At the least it appeared that the effects of remaining in business, even if the winding up petition succeeded, were likely to be less harmful than the effects

C of an immediate cessation of business. The bank manager had no reason to distrust the integrity or competence of the directors. The danger of over-trading which had manifested itself in the past appeared to have been averted judging by the history of the past months. Provided that the company kept within its existing overdraft of £5,000 and made no unusual payments there was no reason to think that the financial position of the company would

D deteriorate."

and Templeman J. continued:

    " In my judgment the circumstances of this company were such that harm would have resulted if the company had ceased to trade on August 3 or 10 or 17. It did not appear that harm would be

E occasioned if the company were allowed banking facilities after August 17 for the purpose of continuing its normal trade. It is not certain that any greater harm resulted from the decision to continue in business than the harm which would have been suffered if the company had ceased to carry on business."

    The correctness of the judge's conclusion in respect of the trading loss

F depends, I think, upon whether he was right in saying that if in the event the decision taken by the bank involved the creditors in loss, the court would nevertheless absolve the bank from liability provided that the decision was based on adequate information and was reasonable at the time. In my judgment, and with deference to the judge, that is too benevolent a view, particularly in a case in which the bank was unsuccessful in putting into operation precautions which would effectively alert

G the bank to the fact that the company was trading at a loss.

    It is evident that the judge had prominently in mind what was said by Cairns L.J. in In re Wiltshire Iron Co., L.R. 3 Ch.App. 443, 447:

    " But where a company actually trading, which it is the interest of every one to preserve, and ultimately to sell, as a going concern, is made an object of a winding up petition, which may fail or may

H succeed, if it were to be supposed that transactions in the ordinary course of its current trade, bona fide entered into and completed, would be avoided, and would not, in the discretion given to the court, be maintained, the result would be that the presentation of a petition, groundless or well-founded, would, ipso facto, paralyse the trade of the company, and great injury, without any counterbalance of advantage, would be done to those interested in the assets of the company."

It will be observed that Cairns L.J. there supposes a case of a company   A
actually trading which it is in the interests of everyone to preserve and
ultimately to sell as a going concern. It has not been suggested in the
present case that anyone ever addressed his mind to the question whether
it would be in the interests of the unsecured creditors that the company's
business should be continued with a view to a sale as a going concern
nothwithstanding the possibility of trading losses meanwhile.

If the bank had applied for a prospective validating order at or   B
about August 10 or 17, 1972, it is possible that the court would have
been prepared to authorise continued banking facilities subject to certain
precautions. Precisely what those precautions would have been I cannot
say, but they would or should have been devised to ensure, as far as
was practicable, that the company would not be supported in unprofitable
trading unless this would be likely to benefit the general body of creditors.   C
The bank made no such application; as I have already said, it took the
risk of going on without an order. It is accordingly in my judgment
also vulnerable to an order to restore to the company the amount lost
by post-liquidation unprofitable trading, viz. £5,000.

The liquidator has been moderate in his demands on this appeal. In
saying so, I do not intend in any way to criticise him for the course he
has taken in what has been, I think, a difficult case. By his notice of   D
appeal he has claimed repayment by the bank of three alternative sums,
which he asserts to have been the amounts to the extent of which the
creditors have been prejudiced. They are £13,259·92, which was the
liquidator's estimate of the trading loss during the relevant period;
alternatively £5,000, which was the amount of the loss as found by the
judge, and in the further alternative £1,184·91, which was the amount   E
by which credits exceeded debits on the current account during the
period August 3 to October 10, 1972, plus the £326 debited in respect
of bank charges and interest. The liquidator now accepts the judge's
finding that the loss amounted to £5,000. Accordingly he does not claim
repayment of more than that sum.

In these circumstances I would allow this appeal, discharging the order   F
of Templeman J. and substituting an order to the following effect: (1)
validating payments into the company's current account with the bank
on and after August 3, 1972, in order of priority of date up to a sum of
£2,670; (2) declaring invalid the payment into that account of the next
£5,000 paid in after August 3, 1972, and ordering repayment of that sum
by the bank to the liquidator for the account of the company without
prejudice to the right (if any) of the bank to prove in the liquidation in   G
respect of a sum of £2,652 as part of the £5,322 due by the company
to the bank immediately before August 3, 1972; and (3) validating as
between the company and the bank all other transactions on the account
on and after August 3, 1972, but on the footing that no credits to the
account which are so validated shall be treated as discharging any part
of the £2,652.

I have made no reference to any interest on the sum repayable to   H
the liquidator. I would like to hear submissions by counsel upon that
point.

Counsel for the liquidator has submitted that certain of the findings
of the judge were unjustified by the evidence. I do not think that I need
deal with those submissions in any detail. I need only say that I have
not been satisfied upon any of the findings in question that there was

A   not sufficient evidence before the judge upon which he could make such finding. I differ from the judge, not on the basis of fact, but on the principles upon which the discretion under the section should be exercised.

GOFF L.J. Having had the advantage of reading Buckley L.J.'s judgment whilst it was still in draft, and of discussing the case with him on several occasions, I am happy to say, with respect, that I agree in its entirety with the judgment which Buckley L.J. has just delivered.

B

SIR DAVID CAIRNS. I also am in the position of being able to agree.

> *Appeal allowed with costs below and in Court of Appeal.*
C
> *Order of Templeman J. discharged and order substituted in terms set out in judgment of Buckley L.J.*
> *Leave to appeal on undertaking by bank not to disturb order for costs or seek order for costs in House of*
D
> *Lords and to pay costs of liquidator on appeal on common fund basis.*

Solicitors: *Wm. F. Prior & Co.; Wilde, Sapte & Co.*

L. G. S.

E
_____

[EMPLOYMENT APPEAL TRIBUNAL]

* KIRBY *v.* MANPOWER SERVICES COMMISSION

F   1980 Feb. 5   Slynn J., Mr. A. C. Blyghton and
                                                       Mrs. M. E. Sunderland

*Discrimination, Race — Employment — Victimisation — Job centre
clerk reporting employers to local community relations council
—Clerk demoted by employers for breach of confidence—
Whether victimisation " by reference to this Act "—Race*
G   *Relations Act 1976 (c. 74), ss. 2 (1) (c) (d), 4 (2)*

The complainant was employed at a job centre run by the respondent employers, a government agency, as a first tier clerk interviewing applicants for jobs. Information that he received from would be employers and employees was to be treated as confidential. On different occasions he reported to the local Council for Community Relations that prospective employers
H   were discriminating against coloured applicants, in particular, that a bus company had refused to interview a black man, that a nursing home had asked whether an applicant was black and that a club had refused to employ a black girl. The club was subsequently successfully prosecuted under the Race Relations Act 1976. The manager of the job centre, hearing of the applicant's action in reporting the bus company and the nursing home, moved the complaint to a job as filing clerk where he had no contact with the public. He complained to an industrial tribunal that he had been victimised within the meaning of

section 2 of the Act of 1976.[1]   The tribunal found that,   A
although the report of the club's discrimination and the
subsequent prosecution were not known to the employers at
the time of the alleged victimisation, the report was information " in connection with proceedings " within the meaning
of section 2 (1) (b) of the Act, and was done " under or
by reference " to the Act in relation to another person within
the meaning of section 2 (1) (c).   They further found that
the allegation against the club was an allegation of conduct   B
which would amount to a contravention of the Act within
the meaning of section 2 (1) (d).   The tribunal concluded that
by demoting the complainant to less interesting work the
employers had subjected him to a detriment so that any
discrimination would be unlawful under section 4 (2) (c), but
they dismissed the complaint, since the complainant had failed
to show, under section 2 (1), that he had been treated less
favourably than other persons would have been treated if   C
they had disclosed confidential information to an outside body.
   On the complainants' appeal: —
   Held, (1) that the phrase " in any circumstances relevant
for the purposes of any provision of this Act " in section 2 (1)
of the Race Relations Act 1976, referred to discrimination
in any field covered by the statute, including employment,
education and the provision of goods, facilities and premises,
and that the section was not restricted to the particular areas   D
of discrimination contained in section 4 (post, p. 424c).
   (2) That since the employers did not know of the
complainant's report of the club's alleged discrimination when
they demoted him and since the prosecution against the club
took place after the demotion that incident could not have
affected the employers' action and the complainant could not
rely on the report as being an allegation that an act had been
committed which amounted to a contravention of the statute   E
within the meaning of section 2 (1) (d) or as " evidence or
information in connection with proceedings " within the
meaning of section 2 (1) (b) so as to show victimisation; but
that the reports of the incidents concerning the nursing home
and the bus company which the employers knew about before
the alleged victimisation were acts done " by reference " to
the statute in relation to " any other person," namely the
subject of the discrimination, within the meaning of section 2   F
(1) (c) and the complainant was entitled to rely on those acts
as showing victimisation under the section (post, pp. 730c–e,
731c–d, h—732a).
   (3) That having regard to the industrial tribunal's finding
that it was contrary to the employers' interests and prejudicial
to race relations that confidential information should be disclosed to an outside body, they were justified in holding that
the complainant had failed to show, as required by section   G
2 (1), that he had been treated less favourably than someone
else would have been treated in the circumstances and,
accordingly, the industrial tribunal had not erred in law in
dismissing the complaint (post, p. 733b–c).

The following case is referred to in the judgment:

Ministry of Defence v. Jeremiah [1980] Q.B. 87; [1979] 3 W.L.R. 857;   H
   [1980] I.C.R. 13, C.A.

No additional cases were cited in argument.

[1] Race Relations Act 1976, s. 2: see post, p. 728c–f.
S. 4: " (2) It is unlawful for a person, in the case of a person employed by him
at an establishment in Great Britain, to discriminate against that employee . .
(c) by dismissing him, or subjecting him to any other detriment."

A APPEAL from an industrial tribunal sitting at Bristol.

The complainant, Steven John Kirby, appealed from a decision of
the industrial tribunal on August 20, 1979, dismissing his complaint of
unlawful racial discrimination against his employers, Manpower Services
Commission, on the ground that the industrial tribunal had erred in
law in their interpretation of section 2 of the Race Relations Act 1976.

B The facts are stated in the judgment.

Kuttan Menon, legal officer, Commission for Racial Equality, for
the complainant.

William Crowther for the employers.

C SLYNN J. delivered the following judgment of the appeal tribunal. In
September 1978, Mr. Kirby, the complainant, who had been a civil
servant for some three years and who apparently had signed a declaration
under the Official Secrets Act, was appointed to work at a job centre.
Job centres are run by the Manpower Services Commission which is a
government agency and is to be treated as a statutory body.

The complainant was given the job of acting as a "first tier clerk."
D That involves interviewing people who come to the job centre who are
looking for work and employers who are looking for employees. If
someone comes in who wants a job, the first tier clerk will get in touch
with an employer who may have vacancies and will give details of the
prospective employee. If necessary, he will arrange an appointment.
It is apparently the policy of those responsible for running the job centres
that first tier clerks, who are in touch with both employers and employees,
E should adopt as neutral an attitude as possible. It is their task to collect
information and put people in touch with each other, but they are discouraged from becoming too involved either with the affairs of the
employer or the employee. There is a code laid down which gives
guidance to civil servants about the implementation of the Race Relations
Act 1976, but this case has proceeded on the basis that the complainant
F may well not have seen a copy of that. It is, however, accepted that
when he began to do this work he was told that if he wanted further
information or was unsure about any matter, he should ask the person
in the rank immediately above him, namely, a second tier officer.

The complainant, who was at the relevant time 23 years of age,
felt very strongly about racial discrimination and in the course of his
job he apparently came across three incidents which troubled him very
G much.

He was on one occasion in September 1978 working at his desk
when he was overheard by another first tier clerk telephoning to the
Council for Community Relations in Bristol. This caused some concern
to the other clerk. Then there was another incident when apparently
another employee at the job centre got to know that he had been in
H touch with the Bristol Council for Community Relations and, as a
result, the matter was brought to the attention of Mr. Frost, who was
the senior manager at the job centre. As a result of the interview which
they had, Mr. Frost decided that the complainant should no longer
work as a first tier clerk. He caused him to be moved to another job
in the department. This was a job which someone of his rank would
be doing but it was said was of a very much less interesting nature—in
effect, he was made to do the work of a filing clerk.

As a result of this, the complainant brought proceedings before an A
industrial tribunal alleging that he had been victimised contrary to
section 2 of the Race Relations Act 1976. The case was heard by an
industrial tribunal who, in the end, dismissed his claim. He now appeals
to this appeal tribunal.

The case turns on the proper construction of sections 2 and 4 of
the Act of 1976. Section 4 is dealing with discrimination by employers
in the employment field and it provides, amongst other things, that it B
is unlawful for a person to discriminate against an employee by dismissing
him or subjecting him to any other detriment. "Discrimination" is
defined in section 1 of the Act as including the treating on racial grounds
of another person less favourably than the employer treats or would
treat other people. Section 2 reads:

> "(1) A person . . . discriminates against another person . . . C
> in any circumstances relevant for the purposes of any provision of
> this Act if he treats the person victimised less favourably than in
> those circumstances he treats or would treat other persons, and
> does so by reason that the person victimised has—(a) brought
> proceedings . . . or . . . (b) given evidence or information in
> connection with proceedings brought by any person against the D
> discriminator or any other person under this Act; or (c) otherwise
> done anything under or by reference to this Act in relation to the
> discriminator or any other person; or (d) alleged that the dis-
> criminator or any other person has committed an act which (whether
> or not the allegation so states) would amount to a contravention
> of this Act . . ."
>   E

In addition, the subsection provides that if the discriminator knows that
the person victimised intends to do any of those things and he treats
him less favourably, that too is brought within the ambit of the Act.
Subsection (2) provides:

> "Subsection (1) does not apply to treatment of a person by
> reason of any allegation made by him if the allegation was false F
> and not made in good faith."

Now what is said here is that the complainant gave information
"in connection with proceedings" brought by some person against
another person under the statute. Alternatively, he had otherwise done
something "under or by reference to the Act in relation to some other
person. And, thirdly, that he had "alleged that the discriminator" or G
some other person "has committed an act which (whether or not the
allegation so states) would amount to a contravention of the Act."

It all turned on three cases which were referred to the Bristol Council
for Community Relations. One of them involved the Bristol Omnibus
Co. and there the complainant reported to the Council for Community
Relations that a representative of the bus company had asked if the
applicant for the job was black; when told that he was black and that H
the applicant had been living in Jamaica for the last year, the representative of the bus company refused to give an interview. The second
case involved a nursing home where the person looking for a part-time
nurse asked whether the applicant for the job was black; asked why, she
said, "Just like to know what to expect;" but, as the applicant for the
job was white, the interview was arranged. The third case involved a
coloured girl who wanted a part-time job as a barmaid at a club. Once

A the coloured girl came for interview, although the manager was prepared to take her, he told the complainant that the chairman of the club had told him that they must not take on a black girl because it might upset a few of the members.

The complainant's case, accordingly, was that he had given part of the information "in connection with proceedings" because in the third case the girl concerned had brought proceedings before an industrial

B tribunal alleging a breach of the Race Relations Act 1976 and she had succeeded. He said that he had done things "by reference to the Act" in relation to other persons because he had given the information to the Council for Community Relations in order that they might consider taking proceedings under the Race Relations Act. He also said that he had alleged that the bus company, the nursing home and the club

C had committed acts which would amount to a contravention of the Act. He was discriminated against in that he was moved for doing these things.

The section, it seems to us, has to be construed as a whole. On the argument we have heard, the first matter to consider is what is meant by the words in section 2 (1) "in any circumstances relevant for the purposes of any provision of this Act." Mr. Crowther, who has appeared on behalf of the employers, was disposed at first to argue that the

D relevant circumstances in the present case are those which are set out in section 4 of the Act and that the relevant one here is subjecting the complainant to a detriment; that one has to ask whether here the employers have treated the complainant less favourably than they would have treated other persons. We do not consider, as we think in the end Mr. Crowther himself accepts, that that is the right approach. It seems to us that the

E words "any circumstances relevant for the purposes of any provision of this Act" which appear not only in section 2 but also section 1 are referring to the areas with which this Act is concerned. "Any circumstances relevant for the purposes of any provision of this Act" include the field of employment, they include education, they include the provision of goods, facilities, service and premises, and a number of other matters which are specified in the Act. It is only if it is so con-

F strued that it is possible to read the phrases "in any circumstances" and "in those circumstances" in a way which seems to us to make sense. So for the present case we have to ask whether there has been discrimination in relation to employment by a person in an establishment in Great Britain of another person. And one then has to ask the question whether the discriminator has treated the person victimised in

G the circumstance of employment at the establishment in Great Britain less favourably than other persons by reason of one of the matters alleged. So really two questions have to be looked at. The first question is whether a person (the person victimised) has been treated in the employment field less favourably than the employer would treat other persons in that field. The second question which has to be looked at

H is whether the employer (the discriminator) has done so by reason of one of the specified matters.

The industrial tribunal were quite satisfied that although the complainant had given evidence in the case brought by Miss Pasley against the club in March 1969, that was long after his removal to the filing clerk job on October 31, 1978. So they said whether he had been treated less favourably or not did not matter because he had given evidence too late for it to be relied upon.

Then, however, they said that he had given evidence or information A
" in connection with proceedings " brought by persons against the various
bodies to which we have referred. The industrial tribunal there thought
it right to read these words " in connection with proceedings " in a wide
way. They said it was enough that information should be given which
led to proceedings. We are sympathetic to that approach, because one
should not strive to cut down the language which Parliament has used
in this field. But the question remains whether the person alleged to B
have victimised did so by reason that the person victimised had given
information " in connection with proceedings " brought by any person
" against any other person under the Act." No proceedings ever were
brought against the bus company or against the nursing home, so they,
it seems to us, cannot be said to qualify for this purpose. The industrial
tribunal, however, took the view that because on October 30 (that is C
before Mr. Frost moved the complainant to the filing clerk job) the
complainant had given information to the Council for Community Relations about the club, that was enough. We entirely accept that the
giving of information prior to the commencement of proceedings may
fall within the section, but it seems to us that before an allegation of
victimisation can be made it must be shown that the victimisation has
occurred at a time when proceedings have actually been brought. The D
relevant question is, had the proceedings been brought? If they had,
it does not matter whether the information was given before or after
the commencement of proceedings so long as it is something which is
relied upon by the discriminator as a reason for the victimisation. Here
the proceedings (which were heard in March) did not, however, begin
until January 3, 1979; that was after the complainant was moved. E
So, accordingly, we consider that in finding that the employers had
moved the complainant to the new job because he had given information
in connection with proceedings brought, the industrial tribunal erred.

They went on to say that the making of a report of alleged discrimination by the club against Miss Pasley was an act done " by
reference to " the Act in relation to another person; alternatively it
appears that they are saying that if it was not done by reference to, it F
was done " under " the Act. We are quite satisfied here that the making
of a report to the Council for Community Relations cannot be said to
be something which is done under the Act. For it to be done under the
Act one must find a specific statutory provision under which the report
was made, and there is none. The words " by reference to " are much
more difficult. If it is enough simply to refer to the statute for some G
act to be done " by reference to " it, clearly it is possible that a very
wide range of activities might be included. If that were so and section
2 (1) (c) were intended to be a sweep-up clause, one would have expected
it to have followed sub-paragraph (d); and the argument is that because
the substance of (d) comes after paragraph (c), one should really construe
" by reference to " in very much the same way as one construes the word
" under." The argument is that one should look for a specific section H
of the Act and, even though it does not provide for a power to do
something, one should ask whether there has been conduct which is only
referable to, or explicable by reference to, that particular section.

We have been referred to section 72 as an example. It is said that
if reliance is placed upon a term of the contract as being void pursuant
to that section, that is an act which is done by reference to the statute

A   in relation to any other person. We do not find it an easy matter to assess the precise limits of this provision " by reference to the Act in relation to . . . any other person," but we are prepared to assume, as the industrial tribunal did—and we consider rightly did—that if a report is made to the Commission for Racial Equality—that facts are available which ought to be investigated and which indicate a possible breach of the provisions of the Race Relations Act 1976, then the making of that

B   report is an act done by reference to the statute in relation to the person against whom it is said discrimination might have occurred. We realise that that is to some extent an overlap with the provisions of paragraph (d), but in our judgment the phrase an act done " by reference to " the statute is wide enough to include such a report.

  So the question is whether there was here a report by reference to

C   the statute in relation to any other person. It is clear that there was a report about these three incidents. One of them—the third one, the one which led to the proceedings—however, as the industrial tribunal found, was not known to Mr. Frost when he moved the complainant to the filing clerk's job. Accordingly, it does not seem to us that it can be said that he moved him by reason that he had reported that third incident to the Council for Community Relations. On the other hand, the com-

D   plainant did tell Mr. Frost of the first two cases—those involving the bus company and the nursing home—and it seems to us that the report of those matters was an act done by reference to the statute in relation to the persons there involved. So we would on that ground, but not on the ground that something was done under the statute, uphold the decision of the industrial tribunal on that matter.

E   But the industrial tribunal went further. They found that there had been here an allegation that the discriminator had committed an act which would amount to a contravention of the statute. They were in some doubt about the first two incidents. No doubt they were not sure whether the refusal of the bus company to hold the interview was due to the fact that the applicant was black or whether it was due to the fact that he had been absent in Jamaica for a period of a year. No

F   doubt they had also some anxiety as to whether merely asking for information whether or not somebody was black was itself a contravention of the Act. So they merely said that those two incidents may have amounted to a contravention of the Act. We think they were right not to be satisfied that those two incidents would have amounted, had they been assuming them to be true, to a contravention of the Act. It seems

G   to us that what has to be done in these cases is to consider whether the allegation which is made, which must be assumed for present purposes to be true, does amount to an act which would amount to a contravention of the Act. It seems to us that here the tribunal was rightly not satisfied that those two first incidents would amount to such a contravention.

  The third one, the tribunal were quite satisfied, would amount to a

H   contravention and there really can be no doubt about that. But, as in the case of paragraph (c), it appears that when Mr. Frost took his decision he did not know about the third incident. He was only told about it some weeks later when the complainant prepared his report. So, it seems to us, on our approach to the construction of this section, that Mr. Frost cannot be said to have acted as he did by reason that the complainant had alleged that there had been a contravention of the Act in respect of Miss Pasley. So, accordingly, we think that under paragraph

A

(*d*), as under paragraph (*c*), the industrial tribunal came to a conclusion on their own findings of fact which cannot stand with what we see to be the correct interpretation of the opening words of the section.

But, the complainant succeeds in holding the finding under paragraph (*c*), that what was done had been done by reason of the fact that he had done an act, i.e., had made a report in relation to the people to whom we have referred. So the next question, taking the sequence adopted by the industrial tribunal, is to go on and ask whether the Manpower Services Commission treated the complainant less favourably than they treated, or would treat, other persons by reason of the report which he had made. The proper approach to this part of the section has led to considerable argument before us, as it undoubtedly did before the industrial tribunal. It seems to us that one thing is plain: that it is not right simply to ask whether the complainant was treated in the same way as other people who did one of these acts which are set out in paragraphs (*a*), (*b*), (*c*) and (*d*). If that were law, then the employer could only escape if he could show that he had victimised all the relevant people; he would fail if it were shown that he had only victimised some of them. Nor, on the view which we have taken, is it enough simply to consider whether the detriment which is imposed is the same in all these cases. It seems to us that what has to be looked at is the reason given by the employer for the dismissal or removal and to ask whether other persons who committed an act of a similar kind would be treated in the same way or less favourably.

Now the tribunal rejected any suggestion here that the complainant's move had nothing to do with the telephone calls to the Council for Community Relations. They were quite satisfied that he would not have been moved but for his communicating with the Council for Community Relations. But the reason why he was moved was accepted to be that he had given away information which had come to him in confidence as an employee of the job centre. It was felt by those in charge, and indeed by the industrial tribunal, that it was quite wrong for this information which came in confidence to be disclosed to other people. Indeed, the tribunal appear to have been of the view that however well-intentioned the complainant was, he really might have done quite serious harm to race relations in this particular area by reporting the matter and, more important, it is said he might have discouraged employees, who ought to be encouraged to come to job centres, from so coming. If information about employees and their personal backgrounds (nothing to do with race) is given away, then employees might be deterred from coming. Equally, if employers cannot go to a job centre without information they have given in confidence being used and given for other purposes, then it is said that they will be deterred from coming and in the end harm will be done to the work of the Manpower Services Commission.

The question, it seems to us, which arises in this case for decision is whether it has been shown that these employers treated the complainant less favourably than they would have treated someone in their employment who gave away confidential information whatever its kind. The industrial tribunal looked into this matter. They were quite satisfied that Mr. Frost had caused the complainant to be taken away from the job at the desk of a first tier clerk and to be made a filing clerk because he did not consider that he was suitable for this particular work since he had breached the confidence entrusted in him and shown, in the view of his

B

C

D

E

F

G

H

A superiors, an error of judgment. Now the question is, would other persons giving confidential information away have been treated any more favourably? This industrial tribunal found that Mr. Frost, the manager, would have the same view if confidential information had been given to any outside person or body by the complainant or any other civil servant who had not been authorised to give that information. Although they talk only about Mr. Frost, we read their decision as meaning here

B Mr. Frost, the manager of the job centre, on behalf of the Manpower Services Commission. Once that evidence is accepted, it seems to us to follow that the tribunal here were not satisfied that the complainant had been treated less favourably than anybody else who gave confidential information away. On the contrary, they were satisfied that he was treated in the same way as they would have been. In those circumstances,

C even if the complainant was moved because he had made his report to the Bristol Council for Community Relations, he was not " victimised " within the meaning of this section. It seems to us that the tribunal was entitled on the material before it clearly to come to that conclusion.

We have heard many references to the position of the Official Secrets Act. It has been said that if the motive of the employer, the Crown,

D is to deal with someone who has committed breaches of the Official Secrets Act, or has violated the special confidence which must obtain in an agency of this kind, that is enough to defeat a claim under this Act. We do not think that it is enough. It may be that even if someone has committed an act which is a breach of the Official Secrets Act, the employer still may do something which falls foul of the Race Relations Act 1976. It seems to us that that is not the right question. The right

E question in our view is that which we have posed, namely, whether people who give away information of this kind or information which is received in confidence would be treated on broadly the same basis.

It is necessary to add just two short points. We have heard argument as to whether there was here any detriment in any event in so far as that is relevant to the decision in the case. It is suggested that the

F moving of the complainant from the job as a front clerk to a filing clerk was de minimis and cannot amount to a detriment. Mr. Crowther, in our view rightly, has abandoned the argument which was advanced before the tribunal that detriment has to be construed ejusdem generis with dismissal. It seems to us that we should follow what was said in the Court of Appeal in *Ministry of Defence* v. *Jeremiah* [1980] Q.B. 87. There, Brandon L.J. at p. 99 interpreted " detriment " as meaning putting

G under a disadvantage. Lord Denning M.R. at p. 97 clearly took the view that to require someone to work in less attractive conditions was itself capable of being a detriment. There is here a finding that this work of filing was less interesting, less responsible and less varied than was the work of a first tier clerk, and we have no doubt here that the tribunal was quite right in its conclusion that there was here a subjecting to a

H detriment within the meaning of section 4 (2) (c).

Then, finally, the industrial tribunal make references to the reasons which led the complainant to reveal information to the Bristol Council for Community Relations. Despite those remarks, they have found that the allegations which were made were made by him in good faith. Mr. Crowther has accepted that the complaints which were made, the allegations which were made, were made honestly even if, in the view of the employers, mistakenly and so, accordingly, this claim would not have

been barred had it otherwise been entitled to succeed by virtue of the A
provisions of section 2 (2) of the Act. In the result, however, despite
Mr. Menon's admirable arguments on behalf of the complainant, this
appeal fails.

Appeal dismissed.

Solicitors: *Osborne, Clarke, Bristol.*

J. W.

B

[COURT OF APPEAL]

* O'BRIEN AND OTHERS *v.* SIM-CHEM LTD.

1979 Dec. 5, 6, 7, 10, 11, 12; 21   Stephenson, Waller and
Cumming-Bruce L.JJ.

C

Discrimination, Sex—Equal pay—Evaluation study—Scheme to
remunerate employees in accordance with evaluation study
and merit assessment schemes—Evaluation study completed
but not implemented—Merit assessment scheme incomplete—
Whether women's remuneration determined by " rating of the   D
work "—Whether women entitled to equal pay as men in
same grade—Equal Pay Act 1970 (c. 41), s. 1 (2) (b) (as
amended by Sex Discrimination Act 1975 (c. 65), s. 8)
Discrimination, Sex—Equal pay—European Economic Community
—Effect of Community law on municipal law—Directive on
equal pay for equivalent work—E.E.C. Treaty (Cmnd.
5179—II), art. 119—E.E.C. Council Directive 75/117/E.E.C.,   E
art. 1

A job evaluation committee representing management and
union was established by the employers to devise a job
evaluation scheme. By March 1976 the grading of the jobs
was completed and the relevant employees, including the
three applicants, were informed of their new job grade and
salary range for the grade. They were informed of their
right of appeal in respect of the job grading. In the absence F
of an appeal the grade would be confirmed with effect from
April 26, 1976, and their contracts of employment would be
amended accordingly. The employers also intended that,
before the job evaluation scheme was applied and employees
were paid in accordance with their grading, a merit assessment scheme should be introduced. Owing to difficulties
arising from the implementation of the government's pay
policy, the employees were never remunerated in accordance G
with the new job evaluated salary structure nor was the
position of any individual employee determined on the basis
of a merit assessment scheme.
    The applicants claimed that they were entitled to equal pay
on the basis that a job evaluation study had been completed
and that their jobs were rated as equivalent with that of men
in the same employment, who in each case, were paid more
than they were. An industrial tribunal dismissed their appli- H
cations on the ground that the job evaluation study as a
whole had not been completed and that it had not been
adopted or accepted.
    The applicants appealed claiming that they were entitled
to equal pay under the provisions of section 1 (2) (b) of the
Equal Pay Act 1970,[1] as amended, even though the job

[1] Equal Pay Act 1970, as amended, s. 1: see post, p. 740D–H.

evaluation scheme had not been implemented, and that their claim was supported by article 119 of the E.E.C. Treaty and Directive 75/117/E.E.C. adopted by the Council on February 10, 1975. Allowing the applicants' appeal, the appeal tribunal ordered that, since there was a valid job evaluation scheme in all respects other than regarding merit rating, the applicants should have a declaration that they were entitled to a salary appropriate to the grade for their job, the level of the job to be negotiated by the parties and, basing its decision on section 1 (2) (b) of the Act without considering E.E.C. legislation, held that the job evaluation scheme was relevant to the contracts, and that each applicant's contract of employment as to remuneration should be treated as modified so as to be no less favourable than a similar term in the contract of a man whose job had been given an equal grading.

On the employers' appeal: —

Held, allowing the appeal, (1) that " a term . . . determined by the rating of the work " in section 1 (2) (b) (ii) of the Act was to be given its normal meaning and the past participle " determined " carried a causal implication; that, accordingly, there had to be a job evaluation scheme accepted and implemented before the terms of a contract could be determined by the rating for the job and, since none of the employees' contracts had been modified as a result of the job evaluation scheme, an equality clause based on equivalent work could not be introduced into the applicants' contracts under the provisions of section 1 (2) (b) (ii) of the Act (post, pp. 743E–F, 744C–D, 745E–F, 748H—749C, G–H).

(2) That, although article 1 of Directive 75/117/E.E.C. provided for member states to legislate on equal pay for work of equal value, in the absence of such national legislation the Directive was not directly applicable in the English courts and, therefore, the applicants could not rely on its provisions as a means of interpreting section 1 (2) (b) (ii) of the Act (post, pp. 747F–G, 748A, 750A–B, E).

Defrenne v. *Sabena* [1976] I.C.R. 547, E.C.J. applied.

Decision of the Employment Appeal Tribunal [1979] I.C.R. 13 reversed.

The following cases are referred to in the judgments:

Defrenne v. *Sabena* [1976] I.C.R. 547, E.C.J.

Macarthys Ltd. v. *Smith* [1978] 1 W.L.R. 849; [1978] I.C.R. 500; [1978] 2 All E.R. 746, E.A.T.; [1979] 1 W.L.R. 1189; [1979] I.C.R. 785; [1979] 3 All E.R. 325, C.A.

Shields v. *E. Coomes (Holdings) Ltd.* [1978] 1 W.L.R. 1408; [1978] I.C.R. 1159; [1979] 1 All E.R. 456, C.A.

Van Duyn v. *Home Office* [1975] Ch. 358; [1975] 2 W.L.R. 760; [1975] 3 All E.R. 190, E.C.J.

The following additional cases were cited in argument:

Capper Pass Ltd. v. *Lawton* [1977] Q.B. 852; [1977] 2 W.L.R. 26; [1977] I.C.R. 83; [1977] 2 All E.R. 11, E.A.T.

Clay Cross (Quarry Services) Ltd. v. *Fletcher* [1978] 1 W.L.R. 1429; [1978] I.C.R. 1; [1978] 1 All E.R. 474, C.A.

Eaton Ltd. v. *Nuttall* [1977] 1 W.L.R. 549; [1977] I.C.R. 272; [1977] 3 All E.R. 1131, E.A.T.

Greene v. *Broxtowe District Council* [1977] I.C.R. 241; [1977] 1 All E.R. 694, E.A.T.

Hebbes v. *Rank Precision Industries Ltd.* [1978] I.C.R. 489, E.A.T.

Snoxell v. *Vauxhall Motors Ltd.* [1978] Q.B. 11; [1977] 3 W.L.R. 189; [1977] I.C.R. 700; [1977] 3 All E.R. 770, E.A.T.

O'Brien v. Sim-Chem Ltd. (C.A.)   **[1980]**

Waddington v. *Leicester Council for Voluntary Service* [1977] 1 W.L.R.   A
544; [1977] I.C.R. 266; [1977] 2 All E.R. 633, E.A.T.
Worringham v. *Lloyds Bank Ltd.* [1979] I.C.R. 174, E.A.T.

APPEAL from the Employment Appeal Tribunal.

The applicants, Patricia O'Brien, a travel agent, Doris Lloyd Coleman,
a telephonist, and Isobel Mary Clarkson, a comptometer operator, appealed
from a decision of the industrial tribunal sitting at Manchester on October   B
11, 1977, that since a job evaluation scheme had not been completed and
implemented, the applicants were not entitled to equality of pay with
men employed on work rated as equivalent to them and also employed
by the employers, Sim-Chem Ltd.

The applicant's grounds of appeal were, inter alia, that the industrial
tribunal erred in law in finding that because the results of a job evaluation   C
scheme had not been implemented by the employers, the applicants were
thereby not entitled to equal pay under the provisions of section 1 (2) (*b*)
of the Equal Pay Act 1970; and that the tribunal erred in law in its
application of section 1 (2) (*b*) of the Act to the facts of the case.

On July 28, 1978, the Employment Appeal Tribunal (Phillips J.,
Mr. S. C. Marley and Mrs. A. L. T. Taylor) allowed the applicants'   D
appeal, [1979] I.C.R. 13, and by an amended order of August 23, 1978,
ordered that the term of each applicant's contract of employment relating to remuneration should be treated as so modified as to be not less
favourable than the similar term in the contract of employment of any
man whose job had been given an equal value to her job in the job
evaluation scheme dated April 26,1976, in so far as grading was concerned
and that the position within the grading was to be determined by agree-   E
ment. The appeal tribunal further stated that its order should not be
enforced until October 31, 1978, without prejudice to any agreement
being reached as to its being enforced at an earlier date, or as relating
back to an earlier date; and granted liberty to apply as to the form of the
order.

The employers, with the leave of the Employment Appeal Tribunal,   F
appealed from its decision asking for the order of the industrial tribunal
to be restored on the grounds (1) that on the facts as found by the
industrial tribunal, namely, that the job evaluation scheme did not
govern the pay received by any male employee, but that all male
employees were paid in accordance with existing pay scales, the appeal
tribunal was wrong in holding that section 1 (2) (*b*) of the Equal Pay
Act 1970 entitled the applicants to an order that their contracts of   G
employment be treated as modified in that there was no relevant term in
the contract under which a man was employed which was determined by
the rating of the work; (2) on the facts as found by the industrial tribunal,
namely, that the employers had intended to carry out a job evaluation
scheme which not only graded each employee's job but also assessed
personal performance in each grade, and that such assessment was neces-   H
sary before each employee could be placed in a grade so that the
appropriate salary could be identified, and on the further finding that the
employers had not completed the scheme in that they had not carried out
such assessment, the appeal tribunal was wrong in holding that a job
evaluation scheme had been accepted or adopted or was a scheme in force
so as to bring into effect section 1 (2) (*b*) of the Act of 1970; and (3) that
the appeal tribunal was wrong in holding that, if a new employee were

A recruited, he would receive remuneration at the rate currently in force appropriate to his grade, since there was no evidence to that effect.

The facts are stated in the judgment of Cumming-Bruce L.J.

Martin Collins Q.C. and *G. W. Wingate-Saul* for the employers.
Eldred Tabachnik for the applicants.

B   *Cur. adv. vult.*

December 21. The following judgments were read.

CUMMING-BRUCE L.J. Parts of this judgment I am afraid are still drafted in a kind of legal jargon which may later have to be translated **C** into English, and I hope it is intelligible. On May 20, 1977, the applicants, three women employed by Sim-Chem Ltd., applied to an industrial tribunal for a decision that their employers had refused since October 1975 to pay them for their work remuneration equal to the remuneration paid to men whose work had been rated as equivalent to theirs by virtue of a job evaluation study which the employers had **D** accepted as an accurate assessment of equivalent work The industrial tribunal dismissed their applications stating that it did so with regret. The applicants appealed to the Employment Appeal Tribunal. On August 23, 1978, the appeal tribunal allowed their appeal and made the following order:

E " In the case of each [applicant] the term of her contract of employment relating to remuneration should be treated as so modified as to be not less favourable than the similar terms in the contract of employment of any man whose job has been given an equal value to her job in the job evaluation scheme dated April 26, 1976, in so far as grading is concerned and that the position within the grade is to be determined by agreement."

F And the appeal tribunal further ordered that their order should not be enforced until October 31, 1978, without prejudice to any agreement being reached to its being enforced at any earlier date, or as relating back to an earlier date. The tribunal gave liberty to apply as to the form of the order and gave leave to appeal to this court. The employers appeal.

G *The facts*

At all material times the employers, Sim-Chem Ltd., employed 125 clerical employees upon 70 different jobs at their head office in Stockport. The Equal Pay Act 1970 as amended by the Sex Discrimination Act 1975 came into force on December 29, 1975. Before that date the employers had identified those members of their clerical staff at the headquarters **H** office who were employed upon like work to an employee of the opposite sex, and had introduced modifications to their pay structure which complied with the equal pay provisions of the legislation relating to persons employed on like work within the meaning of section 1 (4) of the Equal Pay Act 1970, as amended. But many female clerical employees were not doing work of the same or similar nature to any male employee. With a view to the introduction of a pay structure which would provide that men and women who were doing equivalent work were paid equally without discrimination based on sex, the employers set up a committee charged with the duty of evaluating the jobs done by clerical employees in terms of the demands made upon them by their jobs. This committee produced its report on October 8, 1975.

They had included in their proposed job evaluation scheme all relevant employees save those in the shipping department from whom further information was required, but the proposed scheme included the jobs of the three applicants to the industrial tribunal. The committee proposed that all the clerical jobs should be graded into one of six grades. The grades were related only to the demands of the job, and no grades were related to sex. They recommended that within the scheme provision should be made for determination of individual salaries on the basis of how well the job was being performed by the individual as opposed to what job was being performed. The employers accepted the grading of jobs proposed by the committee, and negotiated with the clerical staff trade union a range of salaries to be applied to each grade. The intention of the employers and the union was that the precise place of each individual employee within the salary range appropriate to his or her grade would be negotiated after a procedure to decide the merit rating of the individual concerned. Salary ranges were such that a salary might be increased by as much as one-third in the case of an employee who attained the highest merit rating.

On receipt of the job evaluation scheme the employers encountered a problem. At the material time Her Majesty's Government were trying to operate a policy of voluntary restraint of increases of pay and salaries. The employers thought that if they introduced the new graded pay structure, with the application of the range of salary agreed with the union for each grade, the Department of Employment would take the view that some at least of the resulting salaries infringed the guide lines of the pay policy. This could imperil the business of the employers because Her Majesty's Government had stated that such a breach of their policy might be followed by sanctions in various forms, including withdrawal of government contracts and loss of discretionary grants or loans from which the employers might derive benefit.

Against this background the employers wrote to the applicants and to 40 other clerical employees to be affected by the new pay structure the letters dated March 24, 1976. In the letter, the employee was told the new grade of the job, and the salary range that had been negotiated for that grade with the union. Paragraphs 2, 4, 6, 7 and 8 are quoted below:

"2. As a result of this evaluation your job description form (attached) No. 4/A/   has received the following grading:
    Grade: . . .
    Salary Range: . . .
    Provisional/Permanent: . . .

"4. Although the procedure (see Appendix ' C,' paragraph 2 (e)) indicates that an appeal should be lodged within ten days, it is possible that minor queries will be raised by Heads of Departments and staff initially. *For the introduction of the scheme only,* therefore, appeals should be lodged not later than April 23, 1976. In the absence of an appeal this grade is confirmed and with effect from April 26, 1976, your contract of employment will be amended accordingly.

"6. The proposed salary range has been negotiated with

A.C.T.S.S. the clerical staff trade union, and certain undertakings have been given in order to effect a smooth introduction to the scheme. (a) Staff whose salaries are below the stated minimum level for their grade, will receive the new basic rate as soon as the government restriction on earnings is removed. (Please note that no salary adjustments can be made at present). (b) Staff who are paid a salary above the maximum for their grade will retain any excess on a personal basis; such staff will be entitled to receive any future general salary award applicable to their grade.

" 7. The aims and purpose of the job evaluation scheme are as follows: (a) Job evaluation is a method of comparing jobs, one with another, (rather than assessing a single job in isolation) and producing a job grading structure. *The complete job is assessed and not the individual who undertakes the work.* It is immaterial whether the job is carried out by a man or woman. Job evaluation is not a technique for determining rates of pay. Salary negotiations start when the job evaluation exercise is finished. (b) The purpose of the exercise has been to rank jobs in their true value and importance throughout the company. *Job evaluation does not seek to establish a salary rate which recognises the performance of any employee— this is merit rating.*

" 8. The job evaluation scheme including the formal procedure is introduced at Cheadle with effect from April 26, 1976, although no adjustments can be made to salary for the time being."

Individual employees continued to be paid in accordance with their existing contracts, with such uplifts as were regarded by the employers as consistent with the government's pay policy. No one was paid by reference to the grading of jobs described in the letter of March 24, 1976. There followed a period of negotiation between the union and the management. The union argued that equal pay rises that would have followed introduction of the job grading structure and the salary ranges agreed for each grade should be implemented at once. The employers disagreed, taking its stand on the danger of infringing the government pay policy. On March 30, 1977, the employers consulted the Department of Employment. On April 14, 1977, the Department replied and that letter stated: " In our view, therefore, it would be unacceptable for increases to be awarded under the new structure over and above the new pay policy limits."

Meanwhile the union had been in touch with the Department of Employment, pressing the case of those women who would not receive the equal pay for work graded as equivalent under the job grading scheme and the related salary ranges. On July 22, 1977, two months after the application had been made to an industrial tribunal, the Department gave its blessing to any award of an increase in pay made by an industrial tribunal on an application under the Equal Pay Act 1970. So the matter rested at the date of the dismissal by the industrial tribunal of the three applications, and at the date of the order of the Employment Appeal Tribunal. Today the pay policy is no more. The practical effect of the appeal is now limited to the arrears of pay to which the applicants and others in a similar position are entitled if the order of the appeal tribunal is upheld. The issue of principle may however be of more general interest.

The questions

A

The questions that arise or might arise for decision are these. (a) Is the meaning of the English legislation clear? If so, what is it? (b) If that meaning is uncertain, is the problem of construction helped (i) by reference to article 119 of the E.E.C. Treaty; (ii) by reference also to the Council Directive dated February 10, 1975? If the answer is " Yes," with what result? (c) Is the English legislation inconsistent with article B 119? If so, does the European article override the municipal law? (d) Is the English legislation inconsistent with the Directive? If so, what is the result?

The industrial tribunal decided to dismiss the applications without consideration of European law. The appeal tribunal decided that the meaning of the Equal Pay Act 1970 was clear and in favour of the applicants. Though it was argued before them that article 119 points C to a construction of the English statute that supported the applicants, the appeal tribunal appears to have founded its decision on the construction of the English statute without seeking aid from Community law.

The English statute

The relevant provisions of section 1 of the Equal Pay Act 1970 (as D amended) are as follows:

" (1) If the terms of a contract under which a woman is employed at an establishment in Great Britain do not include (directly or by reference to a collective agreement or otherwise) an equality clause they shall be deemed to include one. (2) An equality clause is a provision which relates to terms (whether concerned with pay or E not) of a contract under which a woman is employed (the ' woman's contract '), and has the effect that . . . (b) where the woman is employed on work rated as equivalent with that of a man in the same employment—(i) if (apart from the equality clause) any term of the woman's contract determined by the rating of the work is or becomes less favourable to the woman than a term of a similar kind in the contract under which that man is employed, that term F of the woman's contract shall be treated as so modified as not to be less favourable, and (ii) if (apart from the equality clause) at any time the woman's contract does not include a term corresponding to a term benefiting that man included in the contract under which he is employed and determined by the rating of the work, the woman's contract shall be treated as including such a term. (3) An G equality clause shall not operate in relation to a variation between the woman's contract and the man's contract if the employer proves that the variation is genuinely due to a material difference (other than the difference of sex) between her case and his. . . . (5) A woman is to be regarded as employed on work rated as equivalent with that of any men if, but only if, her job and their job have H been given an equal value, in terms of the demand made on a worker under various headings (for instance effort, skill, decision), on a study undertaken with a view to evaluating in those terms the jobs to be done by all or any of the employees in an undertaking or group of undertakings, or would have been given an equal value but for the evaluation being made on a system setting different values for men and women on the same demand under any heading."

A *The case for the employers*

By the English legislation the equality clause is mandatory whenever a man and a woman are employed on like work as defined in section 1 (4). If on the facts an industrial tribunal determines that their work is like work, the equality clause in section 1 (2) (*a*) automatically applies. But in the case of equivalent work the structure of the Act is different.

B First the tribunal has to decide pursuant to section 1 (5) whether the woman's job and the man's job

> " have been given an equal value, in terms of the demand made on a worker under various headings . . . on a study undertaken with a view to evaluating in those terms the jobs to be done . . ."

On the facts of this case, this condition was satisfied when the employers

C on March 24, 1976, told the applicants of the grading given to their jobs by the job evaluation scheme, and informed them that in the absence of an appeal their grades were confirmed and with effect from April 26, 1976, their contracts of employment would be amended accordingly. These applicants did not appeal, and accepted the proposed variation of their contracts of employment. Secondly, the industrial

D tribunal has to be satisfied that section 1 (2) (*b*) applied to the facts of the applicants' cases. Parliament has not made the equality clause mandatory whenever section 1 (5) applies, but only if the facts bring the case within the provisions of section 1 (2) (*b*). The question to be answered, in the language of the subsection, is: Is any term of the woman's contract determined by the rating of the work less favourable to the woman than a term of a similar kind in the contract under which

E that man is employed? Or, alternatively, has it become less favourable?

The rating of the work as equivalent work does not in a literal sense fix anyone's remuneration. Two processes have to be completed before the remuneration of an individual employee is fixed. First a range of salary has to be negotiated for each grade of equivalent jobs. Second, the position of each individual worker has commonly to be decided by

F means of an assessment of " the merit " of the individual. This assessment, commonly called " the merit rating " has regard to those material differences between individual cases which are not related to sex, but to ability, experience, seniority and so on. By means of the merit rating fine differences between individuals doing equivalent work can be given effect by placing them appropriately towards the top or bottom figure in the range of salaries fixed by the employers for each grade of equivalent

G work. Mr. Collins, for the employers, did not argue that the absence of a merit assessment would of itself prevent the rating of the work determining any term of their male or female employees' contracts. His submission was that the fact that the employers never proceeded to the stage of assessing the merit ratings was explained by the fact that the employers never introduced the new system of salary ranges proper to

H the six new grades of equivalent work which the employers had made a term of the contracts of relevant male and female employees. He conceded that " determined " in section 1 (2) did not mean " solely determined "; the subsection contemplated that the rating of the work had a significant causal effect on the processes involved in fixing the terms of the contracts relating to remuneration of the men and the women. On the facts the rating placed on the work by the job evaluation scheme had never had any influence on the terms of any employee's

A
contract. Their remuneration was founded on factors which as a matter
of history had nothing to do with the rating of the work. So the comparison between the term of the woman's contract determined by the
rating of the work and the term in the man's contract determined by
the rating of the work was an impossible exercise; neither derived any
benefit by reason of the rating of the work. For practical purposes it
would have no effect on anything until the employers introduced a
method of fixing remuneration totally different from that which had
hitherto prevailed. And that had not happened at the date of the
applications.

B

The applicants' case

Mr Tabachnik for the applicants submitted that the phrase " term . . .
determined by the rating of the work " did not in the context carry the
narrow causative implication proposed by the employers. It was common
ground that " determined by " did not have the literal meaning " solely
determined by " or " fixed by." The contract pointed to the meaning
preferred by the appeal tribunal. All that any job evaluation study
can do is to rate work as equivalent. When work has been rated as
equivalent, as it was in the cases of these male and female employees
on March 24, 1976, section 1 (2) (b) directs the tribunal to identify the
term in the woman's contract which refers to the work rated as equivalent,
then to identify the term in the man's contract which refers to the work
rated as equivalent, and to compare the two. If it then appears that
the woman is paid less than the man after making full allowance for
genuine material differences (other than sex) between her case and his,
the inference is that she is paid less for doing work equivalent to the
man's work. In that situation the pay term in her contract which has
been identified as referable to the work rated as equivalent to his work
is a term less favourable to her than the term of a similar kind in his
contract, i.e., the pay term in his contract. He submitted that the
structure of section 1 is really quite simple once it is appreciated that its
object is to prevent discrimination as regards terms and conditions of
employment between men and women as stated in the short title, and
he explained the statutory scheme as follows. (a) As regards like work,
the equality clause comes into play as soon as the tribunal finds that a man
and a woman are doing like work as defined in subsection (4). (b) As
regards equivalent work, as Mr. Collins agreed, the first task for the
tribunal is to see if the woman's work has been rated as equivalent with
that of a man, by means of a job evaluation study which has complied
with the terms of subsection (5). (c) Where, as here, everyone has
accepted the validity of the six grades of equivalent work worked out
by the job evaluation study, the next stage is to discover the terms in
her contract which are manifestly related to the job rated as equivalent,
and the similar terms in the man's contract. (d) Having identified those
terms, material differences (other than sex) between her case and his
are to be discounted. This eliminates the kind of factors which are
relevant to merit rating. They are personal to the individual employee
and have nothing to do with the job itself. (e) Then if there are any
differences between the terms of their contracts which reward each of
them respectively for doing work, now rated as equivalent, and those
differences have the effect that she is less favourably treated than he is,

C

D

E

F

G

H

A the statutory discrimination between the sexes is proven. (f) The equality clause comes into play.

As a matter of drafting the phrase " rating of the work " in section 1 (2) (b) (i) and (ii) is used to mean " the work rated as equivalent by the job evaluation study." So section 1 (2) (b) (ii) applies whenever there is a term in his contract benefiting him and that term when judged in the light of the equivalence of their work is part of the consideration moving
B from the employers to the man for doing the work, and there is no such term in her contract for doing the equivalent work.

Community law

Mr. Tabachnik made two submissions upon Community law. First, he relied upon article 119 of the E.E.C. Treaty as expanded in
C Directive 75/117/E.E.C. of February 10, 1975, in aid of the proper construction of section 1 (2) (b), if this court holds that the words of the subsection are ambiguous. Secondly, he submits that the construction relied on by the employers is repugnant to Community law as collected from article 119 and the Directive, and that Community law should prevail. If there is doubt about the interpretation of Community law a question should be referred by this court to the European
D Court of Justice in Luxembourg. I examine these submissions after expressing my opinion on the meaning of section 1 (2) (b) without the aid of Community law in construing the English statute.

My conclusions
The meaning of section 1 (2) (b)
E
In the context of section 1 (2) (b) (i) the phrase " if any term of the woman's contract determined by the rating of the work," and in the context of section 1 (2) (b) (ii) " a term . . . determined by the rating of the work," the past participle " determined " has a usual meaning, and that meaning carries a causal implication. If the phrase is converted into the active voice it would read " the rating of the work determines
F the term." In the context of a job classification study, the phrase should be expanded to read: " The rating of the work into equivalent grades determines a term in the woman's contract " in section 1 (2) (b) (i); and to read " The rating of the work into equivalent grades determines a term benefiting that man included in the contract under which he is employed " in section 1 (2) (b) (ii). If Parliament was contemplating
G the elimination of sex discrimination in a case in which a job evaluation study had been completed and had been put into operation so as to regulate the remuneration and other contractual terms of persons employed, the meaning is clear. The remedy (the equality clause) eliminates discrimination built into the new structure for wages or other benefits. Merit rating will probably be involved, and section 1 (3) looks after that. The meaning for which the applicants contend, and which
H commended itself to the appeal tribunal is, with respect, a meaning which subjects both the participle " determined " and the noun " rating " to a greater strain than either can bear.

The applicants justify the strain put on the meaning of both these words by reference to the mischief and the object of the Act. They contend that the meaning which is, in my view, ordinary and natural, is so restrictive that it defeats or quite unduly narrows the remedy afforded by the Act in cases in which a job evaluation study has

744

established, as it did on these facts, grades of equivalent work. But I   A
am not at all convinced that Parliament was contemplating the situation
which developed in this case, or any similar situation. It must, I believe,
be quite extraordinary for an employer to co-operate with his employees
in promoting a job evaluation study, to negotiate and agree salary ranges
for those grades, to proceed to incorporate the equivalent grades of jobs
into the contracts of the employees, and then to postpone indefinitely
the occasion of introduction of the resulting wage structure. The   B
applicants contend that though the pressure of the government pay
policy may have been an unusual intervening event, there may be many
employers who may take this course for reasons of their own, including
opposition from the men on their shop floor. There is no evidence of
such an industrial phenomenon, and no indication of it in the reasons
of the industrial tribunal or in the judgment of the appeal tribunal. I   C
can readily appreciate the possibility of masculine opposition to a job
evaluation system which is likely to achieve equality for women's wages
and other terms of employment. But I would expect it to be made
manifest at a stage long before the achievement of an agreed job
evaluation study. The intention of Parliament to be collected from the
words of section 1 (2) (b) is to legislate for the situation in which an
employer has agreed and implemented revised terms of employment   D
based upon and related to a job evaluation study. Until a system of
equivalent jobs has been brought into force so that wages and other
terms of employment are based upon it, it remains a thing writ in water.
The anomalies so ably collected by Mr. Tabachnik are, in my view,
based on assumptions about industrial relations and behaviour which, by
reason perhaps of my very limited experience, I find unreal. But I   E
have found no hint in the judgments below of a different experience or
expectation.

    In my judgment the difference in the constructions of section 1
between the applicants and the employers is not due to any ambiguity
in the language of the Act, but to a difference of approach to the object
of subsection (2) and to the mischief which Parliament by the subsection   F
seeks to prevent or remove. As I think the meaning of those words is
reasonably plain, there is, on ordinary principles of construction, no
occasion to look to the Community legislation as an aid to interpretation.

    I also find some difficulty in appreciating the effect of the order
made by the appeal tribunal. As the salary ranges which had been agreed
for each grade for equivalent work had not been made contractual terms,
the situation prevailing in the head office was that 125 members of the   G
clerical staff were employed on their 70 different jobs. Whatever their
pay and other terms were related to, they had no causal connection with
the salary ranges for the six grades agreed in the job evaluation scheme.
As I understand the order of the appeal tribunal the applicant, Mrs.
O'Brien, who is a comptometer operator, is to point to the men whose
jobs have been rated by the clerical grading scheme as grade 5 jobs and   H
then her pay is to be raised until it is not less than the pay of one of
those men on October 31, 1978.

    The words " the position within the grade is to be determined by
agreement " (which I quote from the order of the appeal tribunal)
presumably contemplate that a merit rating will be carried out of the
applicants on the one side and of the men whose jobs have been graded
as equivalent on the other side. Then Mrs. O'Brien (for example) can

A point to a man whose job is in the same grade, and whose merit rating is the same as hers, and claim to be paid as much as the man. If the merit ratings vary, an appropriate variation can be permitted as a differential in her salary. One practical difficulty is that when Mrs. O'Brien has had her pay thus raised, any man with a job in the same grade will then be able to insist on his pay being raised to the same level as hers, subject to merit rating. As I understand that the employers are

B in fact introducing, or attempting to negotiate the introduction of their original job evaluation scheme, these problems may in practice be ironed out in negotiation. But the exercise of back dating such novel revision of the pay structure, so that the arrears are paid from May 20, 1977, will be of curious difficulty.

C If the employers fail or refuse to try to carry out a May 1977 merit rating of all the men whose jobs were then rated as equivalent, it will be impracticable to find the individual salary to which Mrs. O'Brien's salary should have corresponded in May 1977 and for the next two and a half years. These practical problems are an inevitable consequence of an attempt to apply section 1 (2) (b) to a job classification exercise that was never implemented so as to introduce the new kind of pay structure that it contemplated.

D This leads me to a further consideration which illustrates the practical consequences which flow from the meaning that Mr. Tabachnik proposes. If " determined " is to be understood as meaning " identified by reference to," the effect of section 1 is the same for equivalent work as for like work. A woman could apply to an industrial tribunal for a ruling that her work is rated as equivalent to that of a man in the same under-

E taking and, upon a finding of the tribunal that her work is equivalent to his, the equality clause would operate to eliminate differences in pay which the employer could not bring within section 1 (3). The effect could be to dislocate the whole wage structure of the undertaking.

I would, therefore, affirm the order of the industrial tribunal, unless the Equal Pay Act 1970, thus construed, is in conflict with Community law binding upon us. To that question I now turn.

F

Conflict with Community law

I take it to be established law that, where an article of the E.E.C. Treaty applies directly to the facts of the case, the law enacted in the article is binding on the English court and the subject has the right to apply to the English court for the European remedy: see *Defrenne* v.

G *Sabena* [1976] I.C.R. 547, 568, and *Shields* v. *E. Coomes (Holdings) Ltd.* [1978] 1 W.L.R. 1408.

Do the provisions of article 119 of themselves entitle those three applicants to the industrial tribunal to be paid a remuneration not less favourable than that of a man whose job has been rated in the job evaluation scheme as equivalent to theirs? By its terms article 119 lays

H down a principle that each member state shall during the first stage ensure and subsequently maintain the application of the principle that men and women should receive equal pay for equal work. The definition of equal pay without discrimination based on sex relates only to pay for the same work or for the same job.

The judgment in *Defrenne* v. *Sabena* [1976] I.C.R. 547 clearly distinguishes between the direct and the indirect effects of article 119. It is the direct effects which may be invoked in the national courts independently of national legislation. This direct discrimination is A identified in paragraph 18 of the judgment, at p. 566, as that which can be identified solely with the aid of the criteria based on equal work and equal pay in article 119. The discrimination which is thus identified is that relating to pay for the same work, i.e. " like work " in English statutory language. So in *Macarthys Ltd.* v. *Smith* 1 W.L.R. 1189, in connection with a " like work " claim, this court referred to the B European Court of Justice in Luxembourg questions relating to interpretation and direct applicability of article 119. A question was also put as to the direct applicability of Directive 75/117/E.E.C. as it could by the reference to the same work in article 1 of that Directive affect the " like work " problem under consideration in that case: see *Macarthys Ltd.* v. *Smith* [1978] 1 W.L.R. 849, and the questions put in that case reported in [1979] 1 W.L.R. 1189. C

In *Defrenne* v. *Sabena* [1976] I.C.R. 547, 566, in the same paragraph 18 " indirect and disguised discrimination " is identified as that kind of discrimination which can only be identified by reference to more explicit implementing provisions of a Community or national character. By paragraph 18, in answer to the first question set out in paragraph 4:

> " For the purposes of the implementation of these provisions a D distinction must be drawn within the whole area of application of article 119 between, first, direct and overt discrimination which may be identified solely with the aid of the criteria based on equal work and equal pay referred to by the article in question and, secondly, indirect and disguised discrimination which can only be identified by reference to more explicit implementing provisions of a Community or national character." E

By paragraph 19:

> " It is impossible not to recognise that the complete implementation of the aim pursued by article 119, by means of the elimination of all discrimination, direct or indirect, between men and women workers, not only as regards individual undertakings but also entire F branches of industry and even of the economic system as a whole, may in certain cases involve the elaboration of criteria whose implementation necessitates the taking of appropriate measures at Community and national level."

The second question put to the European Court of Justice in the *Defrenne* case was, at pp. 550–551: G

> " Has article 119 become applicable to the internal law of the member states by virtue of measures adopted by the authorities of the E.E.C. (if so, which, and as from what date?) or must the national legislature be regarded as alone competent in this matter? "

In its answer to this question, at pp. 568–571, the European Court of Justice gave a concise history of the important differences between the H various states in the implementation of the principle of equal pay, and of the measures taken to promote uniform implementation in each of the member states. These measures culminated in the adoption by the Council on February 10, 1975, of Directive 75/117/E.E.C. " on the approximation of the laws of the member states relating to the application of the principle of equal pay for men and women." The last recital of the preamble to this Directive reads:

A
" Whereas differences continue to exist in the various member states despite the efforts made to apply the resolution of the conference of the member states of December 30, 1961, on equal pay for men and women and whereas, therefore, the national provisions should be approximated as regards application of the principle of equal pay."

Article 1 of the Directive establishes a new criterion, not found in
B article 119, and I quote, leaving out irrelevant words:

". . . for work to which equal value is attributed, the elimination of all discrimination on grounds of sex with regard to all aspects and conditions of remuneration. In particular, where a job classification system is used for determining pay, it must be based on the same criteria for both men and women and so drawn up as to exclude any
C   discrimination on grounds of sex."

The following articles of the Directive give directions to the member states as to the specific action that they are to take on a stated time-table to enact the national legislation required to put the Directive into effect. Article 6 recognises that the measures will vary according to the national circumstances and legal systems of the member states.
D The Directive was issued on February 10, 1975. The English legislation (Schedule 1 to the Sex Discrimination Act 1975) came into force on December 29, 1975. We were shown a background report issued by the Commission on April 20, 1979, in which there is a statement that the Commission has written to Her Majesty's Government outlining why it considers that the Equal Pay Act 1970 (as amended) did not conform
E with the Directive. The complaint is based on the restricted effect of section 1 (2) (b), " because a worker may only request equal pay for equivalent work if a job evaluation scheme is practised in the firm in which he is employed." The word " not " which appears in print is evidently a misprint and should be deleted. The report recites that Her Majesty's Government has maintained that our legislation fully conforms with Community legislation.
F The only relevance of this debate between the Commission and Her Majesty's Government is that it appears to be the kind of follow-up to article 1 of Directive 75/117/E.E.C. which is contemplated by articles 8 and 9 of that Directive.

I am satisfied that the Directive is what it professes to be, i.e. a directive to governments to take national measures to approximate their
G laws in order to give effect to the new criteria expressed in article 1 of the Directive. The discrimination identified by the application of the criterion in that article is not directly applicable in national courts until it is implemented in national legislation. Paragraph 68 of the judgment in the Defrenne case [1976] I.C.R. 547, 571, makes it necessary to make one qualification of that conclusion:

H   " Even in the areas in which article 119 has no direct effect, that provision cannot be interpreted as reserving to the national legislature exclusive power to implement the principle of equal pay since, to the extent to which such implementation is necessary, it may be relieved by a combination of Community and national measures."

In my view this paragraph contemplates the combination of Community and national measures and affirms the jurisdiction to decide

Cumming-Bruce L.J.   O'Brien v. Sim-Chem Ltd. (C.A.)   **[1980]**

whether national measures comply with the Treaty and with relevant
Directives, even if such Directives are not directly applicable.

So I would hold that article 1 of Directive 75/117/E.E.C. is not
directly applicable in relation to equivalent work in an English court, and
the applicants cannot rely on it. It is, therefore, unnecessary for me to
express an opinion upon the difference revealed in the background report
between Her Majesty's Government and the Commission on the interpretation and effect of Directive 75/117.

The applicants relied on the judgment of the European court in *Van
Duyn* v. *Home Office* [1975] Ch. 358. That case was concerned with
Directive 64/221/E.E.C., made by the Commission for the purpose of
implementing article 48 of the Treaty. It is clear that the ruling of the
court that that Directive was directly applicable in the courts of the
member states has no relevance to the question whether Directive 75/117
made under article 119 is directly applicable.

For these reasons I would allow the appeals, quash the order of the
appeal tribunal, and restore the orders of the industrial tribunal.

I would like to take the opportunity of saying that I was greatly
indebted to the assistance that I derived from the arguments of both
Mr. Collins and Mr. Tabachnik.

WALLER L.J. I agree with the judgment which has just been delivered.
I only add a few words of my own because we are differing from the
appeal tribunal.

The important words to be considered are those contained in section
1 (2) (*b*) (i), namely " if . . . any term of the woman's contract determined
by the rating of the work . . ." The employers contend that the words
should be interpreted more or less literally. In other words that there
cannot be a term determined by the rating of the work until the contract
has been modified as a result of the job evaluation scheme. The word
" determined " should be given a causative meaning. The applicants'
construction, on the other hand, is that the word " determined " simply
means measured by reference to or ascertained by reference to or judged
in the light of the job evaluation scheme. In the circumstances of the
present case where the valuation of the job has been carried out but has
not been implemented the employers' construction would have no effect
on the employees' rate of pay. The applicants' construction however
would, in the same circumstances, result in the employee being able to
make a claim based on job evaluation.

The necessity to make a decision in this case is only caused by the
accident of the pay freeze in 1975. Were it not for that the whole
scheme would have been carried into effect and the rates of pay of all
the employees would have been modified in accordance with the job
evaluation scheme. It is argued by Mr. Tabachnik for the applicants,
however, that the decision of this case would not only apply to employees
of the appellant employers but would have more far reaching implications.
He submits that there may be cases where a job evaluation scheme having
been carried to the point of evaluation the employer might then flinch
from putting it into effect because of the cost of so doing. I am bound
to say that I regard this as a very remote possibility.

In my opinion the employers' construction requires (i) a causative
element to be imported into the word " determined " and (ii) a term
in the contract which has brought equivalence into it, i.e. a term which

A prescribes that pay will be based on the grade of the particular employee. On the other hand the applicants' construction requires (i) no causative element in the word " determined," and (ii) no actual modified term, i.e. a term would not be interpreted as meaning the words of the term but simply the nature of the term, e.g., pay or pension. These terms, and there might well be others, would be in contradistinction to terms which are not affected by the rating. There can be no doubt that the word

B " determined " can properly be interpreted with a causal meaning. The *Shorter Oxford English Dictionary* gives one meaning of " determine " as " To fix or decide causally." Therefore the construction urged by the employers is one which involves no great strain because the term imputing equal value would be determined at least in part by the value of the work. The employers further say that there is no reason for giving a strained

C meaning to this clause because an employer is not under an obligation to have a job evaluation scheme and may decide not to do so.

The applicants' case, however, is that the object of the Equal Pay Act 1970 was to provide equality between men and women and, it having been ascertained that each applicant in this case is in a particular grade, she should at once be entitled to be paid in accordance with that grade. It is further submitted that it would be wrong that an employer should

D be able to avoid the consequences of a job evaluation scheme by stopping at the stage which has been reached in this particular case, albeit by reason of the accident of government intervention. The argument on behalf of the applicants was conducted on the basis that each applicant would be put into the category in which her job evaluation places her and the consequences would be that her pay, for example, would be based

E on that category. The words of section 1 (2) (*b*) (i) however say, " where the woman is employed on work rated as equivalent with that of a man in the same employment," and then go on to say that any term in her contract shall be treated as to be modified so as to be not less favourable than a similar term in a man's contract. This does not involve, at the stage where contracts have not been modified, comparison with a category but involves direct comparison with a man. A woman

F wishing to argue that her contract was less favourable than that of a man in the same category might well choose a man with the highest possible pay in that category. This could have unforeseen results increasing the woman's pay beyond that which would be proper if it were merely categorised. The consequences of doing that would then react on other men in the group who would be able to claim similar

G equality with her new rate of pay.

I have come to the conclusion that this consequence cannot have been contemplated by Parliament in enacting section 1. Furthermore, this being voluntary to the employers, I am satisfied that there is no good reason for departing from the literal meaning of the words. This is the more so when departure involves not only giving a strained

H meaning to " determined " but also giving a strained meaning to " term," because the word " term " would normally mean the wording of the term, whereas the applicants' construction requires " term " to be interpreted as the nature of the term or the title of the term. An example of this construction could be " wages " or perhaps " pension provision."

Accordingly, I am of opinion that there cannot be a term determined by the rating of the work until the contract has been modified to give effect to a job evaluation scheme. There will then be a term of the

amended contract which will be determined, at least in part, by the rating A
of the work.

Although the question of Community law was not before the appeal
tribunal I should add that I entirely agree with the judgment of
Cumming-Bruce L.J. on this. In *Defrenne* v. *Sabena* [1976] I.C.R. 547,
571, in paragraph 68, already quoted by Cumming-Bruce L.J., the
European Court of Justice makes it clear that there is an area where
article 119 has a direct effect and also an area where it has no direct B
effect. In my opinion, equivalent work as opposed to like work is an
area where article 119 has no direct effect, and Directive 75/117 is
addressed to the national legislatures for them to implement the equal
pay provisions where the work is equivalent work and not like work.
The Equal Pay Act, with which we are concerned, is the national measure
designed to implement this part of the policy.　　　　　　　　　　C

Equivalent work is not readily ascertainable. It requires considerable
argument and no doubt requires give and take between the parties. If
equivalence were to be left to a tribunal to decide, the difficulties would
be enormous and the Equal Pay Act scheme set out in section 1 (2) (*b*)
and section 1 (5) is a way of achieving the desired result without those
difficulties. But this scheme clearly involves adjustments and provides D
justice between various groups. To call it rough justice would be unfair,
but absolute justice between different groups is probably unattainable.
In my opinion, therefore, the whole scheme must be put into effect in
order to implement the Directive. To try to impose the categories
without the whole scheme being put into effect would, in my view,
produce interminable arguments, which would be avoided if the whole
scheme is put into effect.　　　　　　　　　　　　　　　　　E

I only add these observations to indicate that the analysis of
Community law made by Cumming-Bruce L.J. is wholly consistent with,
and indeed supports, the construction of section 1 (2) (*b*) given by him.

I agree with the order proposed by Cumming-Bruce L.J.

STEPHENSON L.J. I agree with both judgments and I have nothing to F
add to them.

> *Appeal allowed.*
> *Order of appeal tribunal quashed.*
> *Orders of industrial tribunal restored.*
> *Leave to appeal refused.*

Solicitors: *C. H. G. MacKenzie, Stockport*; *Pattinson & Brewer.* G

[Reported by MISS HENRIETTA STEINBERG, Barrister-at-Law]

March 27, 1980. The Appeal Committee of the House of Lords
(Lord Wilberforce, Lord Keith of Kinkel and Lord Lane) allowed a H
petition by the applicants for leave to appeal.

A

[CHANCERY DIVISION]

* PRACTICE DIRECTION (CHANCERY DIVISION:
MOTIONS PROCEDURE)

B

[No. 2 of 1980]

*Practice—Chancery Division—Motion—Revised procedure for
listing and hearing motions*

The judges of the Chancery Division have decided that as from
October 1, 1980, the procedure for bringing motions in the Chancery
C Division should be revised. The new procedure is set out below. It
is substantially on the lines of the proposals which were circulated in
the profession for comment last year. The new procedure will apply
until further notice, though it will be kept under review, and will, if
necessary, be revised in the light of experience.

1. *Motion days*

D Instead of the normal motion days being Tuesdays and Fridays, every
week-day (except the last day of each sittings) will be a motion day.

2. *Motion judges*

(a) For each sittings, two judges will, as at present, be assigned to
hear motions. One of these judges (" the motions judge ") will sit to
hear all motions, whether in Group A or Group B, on each court day
for a period of two weeks. If the volume of motions requires it, the
E other judge (" the stand-by judge ") or any other judge then available
to assist with motions will hear such motions as the motions judge directs.

(b) Subject to this, the stand-by judge will hear such of the ordinary
work of the Division (usually the short non-witness work hitherto heard
by the motions judges on Mondays, Wednesdays and Thursdays) as may
be required.

F (c) At the end of the first two weeks, the motions judge and the
stand-by judge will exchange functions for the ensuing two weeks, and
so on until the end of the sittings. As at present, the Easter and Trinity
Sittings will for this purpose be treated as a single sittings.

(d) Minor variations in these periods may be made from time to
time, e.g., to equalise the burdens on the judges. Notices in the Term
G List or Daily Cause List will show the periods for which each judge will
be motions judge and stand-by judge.

3. *Notices of motion*

Notices of motion will continue to be given for the same period as
at present, though they may be given for any court day, whether or
not a Tuesday or Friday, except the last day of each sittings.

H 4. *Listing motions*

(a) *Motions book.* As far as possible, all motions will be listed. For
this purpose, the clerk to the motions judge for the time being will
maintain a motions book.

(b) *Entry in motions book.* A motion will be entered in the motions
book only if (i) two copies of the writ, (ii) two copies of the notice of
motion, and (iii) the best estimate of duration that counsel can given,
signed by counsel for the applicant, are lodged with the clerk to the

motions judge not later than 12 noon on the day before the date for   A
which notice of motion has been given, or on the preceding Friday if
the notice has been given for a Monday. If there is any difficulty in
reaching the clerk to the motions judge, the documents may instead be
lodged with the Clerk of the Lists (Room 165), who will record the time
of lodging and transmit the documents to the clerk to the motions judge.

(c) *Revised estimate of duration.* Counsel for the applicant must   B
ensure that the clerk to the motions judge is at once informed of any
material revision to an estimate of duration entered in the motions book.
This applies equally to shortening, as where the parties come to terms
or agree an adjournment, and lengthening, as where substantial last-
minute affidavits are to be adduced. If a revised estimate is given
orally, it should be confirmed in writing as soon as possible.

(d) *" Short " motions.* As soon as it becomes apparent that a motion   C
will take less than 5 minutes to dispose of, as where terms have been
agreed or the motion is to be stood over, the clerk to the motions judge
should be informed and requested to mark the motion " short " in the
motions book. This will not alter the sequence of motions in the book,
but it will usually ensure that the motion will be taken before the more
lengthy motions: see paragraph 6 below.

(e) *Daily Cause List.* Each motion duly entered in the motions book   D
will be listed in the Daily Cause List for the day on which it is to be
heard. Where possible, the motions judge will direct the later motions
in the list to be marked " Not before " a stated time, though in view of
the unpredictability of motions, this will be done only where counsel for
all parties have given the clerk to the motions judge telephone numbers
which will make it possible for counsel to be in court on ten minutes   E
notice. There will be no warned list of motions, but information about
motions listed for future days can be obtained from the clerk to the
motions judge.

5. *Standing over and saving motions*

(a) *In court.* When a motion is stood over in court, or it is saved
in court, the clerk to the motions judge will forthwith enter it in the   F
motions book for the day for which it has been stood over or saved;
and in due course the motion will be listed for that day.

(b) *Out of court.* If a motion is saved by agreement, or if by consent
it is stood over before a registrar (see *Practice Direction (Chancery
Division: Motions)* [1976] 1 W.L.R. 441 and *Practice Direction
(Chancery Division: Motions) (No. 2)* [1977] 1 W.L.R. 228), it will
be entered in the motions book for the day for which it has been stood   G
over or saved only when the clerk to the motions judge has been notified
of this by the parties, and the documents mentioned in paragraph 4 (b)
above have been lodged with him, if that has not already been done.
Before arranging the future date, it will normally be advisable for the
parties to consult the clerk to the motions judge in order to ascertain
what other motions there will be on that date.   H

6. *Order of hearing*

The judge hearing motions will continue to exercise his discretion as
to the order in which he hears them, so that he may, for instance, give
priority to any application that he considers to be sufficiently urgent, as
may be the case with some ex parte applications. Subject to this—
(a) motions affecting the liberty of the subject will continue to take
priority over all other motions. (b) Motions marked " Short " in the

A motions book will usually be taken next. If it becomes apparent that a motion is not in fact " short," the judge will normally cease to hear it and let it resume its normal priority. (c) All other listed motions will be heard in the order of listing, irrespective of the seniority (or juniority) of counsel. (d) All unlisted motions will then be heard, according to the seniority (or juniority) of counsel as at present. But if the clerk to the motions judge or the registrar in court is informed

B that an unlisted motion is or has become " short " (see paragraph 4 (d) above), he will mention this to the judge, and the judge may take it after motions listed as " short " and before other listed motions. (e) Motions likely to last more than three hours will still normally be made motions by order unless the state of work permits the judge to deal with them as they arise. (f) When another judge is available to assist with

C motions, the motions judge may transfer to him such motions as he considers appropriate, irrespective of priority. (g) Any motion which at the end of a day is part-heard will normally head the listed motions for the next court day, followed by any listed motions that have not been reached. (h) The judge will usually give effect to any variation in this order of priority which is agreed by all who are affected.

D 7. *Ex parte motions*

The procedure under this practice direction will apply to ex parte motions. If it is desired to have an ex parte motion listed, two copies of the order sought should be lodged under paragraph 4 (b) (ii) above in place of a notice of motion. If the application is to be made otherwise than in open court, it can be listed under the applicant's name alone, without that of the defendant. Where it may be unjust to the defendant

E or some other party if the application is heard in public, the judge may exercise his discretion to sit otherwise than in open court. Where an application is very urgent and the motions judge is unable to hear it promptly, it may be heard, as at present, by any judge who is available, though the request for this must be made to the clerk to the motions judge, or, in default, to the Clerk of the Lists.

F 8. *Excepted motions*

This new procedure is intended to apply only to what may be called ordinary interlocutory motions made during the usual sittings. It does not apply to motions made during the vacations, nor to motions for judgment, or motions in the Patents Court, in the Companies Court, in bankruptcy, or in the revenue paper. In all these matters, the present

G procedure will remain unchanged. The same applies to originating motions, save that applications for directions as to the hearing of such motions which at present come before the judge hearing motions may be made under the procedure of this direction, with the originating notice of motion taking the place of the writ and notice of motion under paragraph 4 (b) above; and agreed directions may be given out of court under paragraph 9 below.

H 9. *Trade marks: agreed directions on originating motions*

(a) Certain proceedings by originating motion at present come before the judge hearing motions for directions as to the conduct of the proceedings. Where the parties are agreed as to the directions that should be given, then instead of being obliged to obtain those directions from a judge in court, they may obtain them from a registrar of the Division out of court, subject to the registrar's discretion to require the application

to be made in court. This is an extension of the procedure for agreed A
adjournments of motions by a registrar: see the practice directions
cited in paragraph 5 above.

(b) Any application under this head must be made to the registrar
in chambers either by counsel or solicitors for all parties, or else by
counsel or solicitors for any party producing a consent or consents signed
by counsel or solicitors representing all parties. The applicant must
produce a document setting out the agreed directions; and these, where B
appropriate, may include liberty to apply to the master if any further
directions are required. On this being done, the registrar will give the
necessary direction to the Clerk of the Lists for setting the matter down
in the appropriate list for hearing. In simple cases it will not be necessary
for any order to be drawn up.

(c) This procedure applies to the following proceedings—(i) any C
appeal from the Registrar of Trade Marks under Order 100 from the
refusal of an application to register a trade mark, or from his decision
in opposition or rectification proceedings; (ii) any application for rectification of the register of trade marks under the Trade Marks Act 1938,
sections 26, 27 or 32; and (iii) any case referred to the court by the
Registrar of Trade Marks or the Board of Trade under sections 12 (2),
53 or 54 of that Act. D

By the direction of the Vice-Chancellor.

EDMUND HEWARD,
Chief Master.

June 23, 1980.

E

[CHANCERY DIVISION]

* PRACTICE DIRECTION (CHANCERY: BESPEAKING ORDERS)

F

[No. 1 of 1980]

1980 June 12   Sir Robert Megarry V.-C.

*Practice—Chancery Division—Bespeaking order—Duty to bespeak
judgment or order within seven days—Undue delay—Applications for leave to draw up order where excessive delay—* G
Costs of application—R.S.C., Ord. 42, r. 7 (2) (3)

SIR ROBERT MEGARRY V.-C. gave the following direction in open
court. The attention of practitioners is drawn to the importance of
bespeaking judgments and orders in the Chancery Division promptly in
accordance with R.S.C., Ord. 42, r. 7. Rule 7 (2) provides that within
seven days of the judgment being given or the order being made, it H
should be bespoken and the necessary documents lodged. If this is not
done, rule 7 (3) authorises the registrar to decline to draw up the
judgment or order without the leave of the court.

It is recognised that it is not always practicable for there to be strict
compliance with the seven days rule, especially where the court has
directed that there should be minutes of order; and in such cases the
registrars have always exercised their discretion under the rule. However,

A in too many cases delays of many weeks or months in bespeaking judgments or orders have been occurring without any apparent justification, sometimes to the prejudice of the litigants concerned.

I have therefore directed the Chancery registrars that if in future there appears to have been undue delay in bespeaking a judgment or order, then unless the registrar is satisfied that there is an adequate justification for the delay he should forthwith refer the matter to the
B Chief Registrar. Subject to any action that the Chief Registrar may take, he will then arrange for the case to be listed, normally before me on a Wednesday morning at 9.45 a.m., as an application in open court for leave to draw up the judgment or order notwithstanding the delay. On such an application, a full explanation of the delay must be before the court; and the court may direct affidavits to be filed. One of the matters
C that the court will consider is how the costs of the application should be borne, and whether steps should be taken under Ord. 62, r. 8, with a view to an order being made against the solicitors personally.

At present this direction does not apply to judgments or orders which are to be drawn up in district registries.

A. R.

D

_____

[CHANCERY DIVISION]

E * ROBINSON (INSPECTOR OF TAXES) *v.* SCOTT BADER CO. LTD.

1980   Feb. 13; 21   Walton J.

Revenue—Corporation tax—Expenses of trade—Parent company seconding employee to work for overseas subsidiary—Expenditure incurred by parent company in its own interest—Subsidiary
F *benefiting from expenditure—Whether expenditure wholly and exclusively for purposes of parent company's trade—Income and Corporation Taxes Act 1970 (c. 10), s. 130 (a)*

Section 130 of the Income and Corporation Taxes Act 1970 provides:
"... in computing the amount of the profits or gains to be charged under Case I or Case II of Schedule D, no sum shall be deducted in respect of—(*a*) any disbursements or expenses, not being money wholly and exclusively
G laid out or expended for the purposes of the trade, profession or vocation, ..."

The taxpayer company manufactured chemicals and synthetic resins for the glass fibre industry. It had three subsidiary companies in Europe including a French company in which it had a 50 per cent. interest and which was making losses and showing marked lack of success. At a board meeting
H of the taxpayer company in November 1974 it was resolved to give strong support and financial backing to the French subsidiary for the purpose of furthering its own business in France and in Europe. Towards that end it decided to send one of its employees to act as manager in France to provide the subsidiary with the necessary technical and marketing expertise. Following that meeting the taxpayer company acquired the remaining 50 per cent. interest in the French subsidiary. During its accounting period ending in July 1976

Robinson v. Scott Bader Ltd. (Ch.D.)   **[1980]**

A

the taxpayer company expended a total of £16,354 on the salary, expenses and social costs of its employee whilst he was working abroad. It appealed against an assessment to corporation tax made on it for that period seeking to deduct that sum from its taxable profits. The general commissioners allowed the appeal on the ground that section 130 (a) of the Income and Corporation Taxes Act 1970 did not preclude the deduction of £16,354 from the taxpayer company's profits.

On appeal by the Crown : —

B

Held, dismissing the appeal, that, since the exclusive object of the taxpayer company in making the expenditure was to further its own overseas business and not to benefit the subsidiary company, the incidental benefit received by the subsidiary in consequence of the parent company's action did not alter the fact that the expenditure had been shown to have been made solely for the purposes of the taxpayer company's trade and, therefore, the provisions of section 130 (a) of the Act did not apply and the expense was deductible (post, pp. 758e–f, 761b, d–f).

C

Bentleys, Stokes & Lowless v. *Beeson* [1952] 2 All E.R. 82, C.A. applied.

The following cases are referred to in the judgment:

Bentleys, Stokes & Lowless v. *Beeson* [1952] 2 All E.R. 82; 33 T.C. 491, C.A.

D

Marshall Richards Machine Co. Ltd. v. *Jewitt* (1956) 36 T.C. 511.

Odhams Press Ltd. v. *Cook* [1940] 3 All E.R. 15; 23 T.C. 233, H.L.(E.).

The following additional cases were cited in argument:

Inland Revenue Commissioners v. *Huntley & Palmers Ltd.* (1928) 12 T.C. 1209.

E

Milnes v. *J. Beam Group Ltd.* (1975) 50 T.C. 675.

CASE STATED by the Commissioners for the General Purposes of the Income Tax Acts for the Division of Wellingborough.

During its accounting period ended July 2, 1976, the taxpayer company, Scott Bader Co. Ltd., whose registered office was Wollaston Hall, Wollaston, Northamptonshire, expended £16,354 on seconding one of its employees to work as manager of its French subsidiary company, Scott Bader S.A., during the first period of its 100 per cent. ownership of that company. The taxpayer company appealed against an assessment to corporation tax of £486,000 for that accounting period claiming to deduct the £16,354 from its taxable profits. The commissioners found that, notwithstanding the provisions of section 130 (a) of the Income and Corporation Taxes Act 1970, the expenditure was an allowable deduction having been made " wholly and exclusively for the purpose of the taxpayer company's trade ". They accordingly determined the taxpayer company's taxable profits in the sum of £485,910.

F

G

The Crown appealed.

The facts are set out in the judgment.

H

Michael Hart for the Crown.

J. M. Tallon for the taxpayer company.

Cur. adv. vult.

February 21. WALTON J. read the following judgment. This case is concerned with the correct ascertainment of the profits of the taxpayer

A company for its accounting period ended July 2, 1976, for the purposes of corporation tax. The principal activity of the taxpayer company at the relevant time, and indeed subsequently, was the manufacture and marketing of chemical intermediates and synthetic resins, principally, perhaps exclusively, for glass fibre making. It provides its synthetics as raw materials for its subsidiary company, associated companies, licensees and other customers for their manufacturing trades. It has one wholly

B owned subsidiary company incorporated in England, two partly owned associated companies in Sweden and Germany, and a wholly owned subsidiary incorporated in France, now known as Scott Bader Societé Anonyme. It is in connection with this French subsidiary company that the problem arises. Originally, the taxpayer company held only a 50 per cent. interest in this French company, and at this stage, on November

C 25, 1974, a special board meeting of the taxpayer company was held to examine the position of the French company and to decide on action as necessary. The minutes of that meeting, so far as relevant, read:

"Papers were before the meeting from Mr. Truman setting out the position and from Mr. Broome itemising the points for and against the continuing operations in France. Mr. Truman and Mr. Fearon

D attended the meeting and opened the discussion by presenting SBS from the point of view of resources in France (site—capacities—people) and the present operation position in France (economy—market—prices—costs—labour relations). Mr. Fearon also had available at this meeting a budget for 1975 and Mr. Leyland briefly drew attention to certain points that this budget highlighted, the main ones being that whereas the operation appeared to be carried

E out in France in a very lean manner as far as staff were concerned, and output was high, the margin on sales was low and, if these margins could not be increased, added throughput would be needed to get above break-even level. The various matters raised were thoroughly ventilated. (Mr. Truman and Mr. Fearson left the meeting at the lunch break). After further discussion, particularly on the

F desirability for our continuing operation in Europe, it was unanimously agreed to go ahead with Scott Bader Sturge S.A. with strong support and backing from Wollaston."

"Backing from Wollaston" was a reference to backing from the taxpayer company, Wollaston Hall being its registered office. Following on that special meeting, on March 31, 1975, the taxpayer company

G acquired the other 50 per cent. interest in the French company, and, following the departure of the former managing director, Mr. S. Fearon, an employee of the taxpayer company, was seconded to the French company to act as its manager, this providing that company with the necessary technical and marketing expertise. The basis of this secondment was that the taxpayer company would pay his salary, expenses and

H social costs while he was in France. These, in the accounting year in question, amounted to the sum of £16,354, and it is this sum which is in dispute. The taxpayer company seeks to deduct this sum from its profits for the purposes of corporation tax. The Crown is unwilling to allow this deduction.

I shall first mention, in order to put them on one side before I come to the crucial question in this case, one or two submissions made on behalf of the Crown in relation to this sum which I consider to be wholly

untenable. By a notice dated December 19, 1979, the Crown gave notice **A**
that it would be contended on its behalf that the expenditure was not a
permissible deduction by reason of section 130 (*e*) and/or (*f*) of the
Income and Corporation Taxes Act 1970, and/or was a capital sum.
Paragraph (*e*) prevents the deduction of any loss not connected with or
arising out of the trade, profession or vocation. It appears to me that
there is here no possibility of classing Mr. Fearon's wages as a "loss."
Paragraph (*f*) prevents the deduction of sums intended to be employed **B**
as capital, or withdrawn from capital, in the trade, profession or vocation. Once again, this does not come within miles of describing Mr.
Fearon's wages. As regards the possibility of his wages being regarded
as a capital sum which was simply given by the taxpayer company to the
French company, if the liability to pay Mr. Fearon's wages had been
the responsibility of the French company I could have understood the **C**
argument; but such was not in any event the case. The taxpayer
company neither paid the French company anything, nor did they relieve
that company from any liability which would otherwise have fallen
on it. What it did do was to make a present of Mr. Fearon's services to
the French company, and in order to do just that it had to pay Mr.
Fearon's wages. I cannot imagine anything less like a capital sum viewed **D**
from the point of view of the taxpayer company, Mr. Fearon and, I
doubt not, the French revenue authorities.

I therefore think that at the end of the day the whole question turns
on the provisions of section 130 (*a*) of the Income and Corporation Taxes
Act 1970, which prohibits the deduction of any disbursements "not
being money wholly and exclusively laid out or expended for the purposes
of the trade, profession or vocation." On this crucial point I have had **E**
excellent arguments addressed to me by Mr. Hart for the Crown, and Mr.
Tallon for the taxpayer company, and I am much indebted to both of
them.

It appears to me to be recognised in all the authorities that where
a parent company affords financial or other assistance, of whatever
nature, to a subsidiary company, there are three possible situations: (i) **F**
the parent company is providing such assistance solely in the interests
of the subsidiary company: (ii) the parent company is providing such
assistance partly in the interests of the subsidiary company and partly
in its own interests: and (iii) the parent company is providing such
assistance solely in its own interests. On this point I would refer to the
speech of Lord Maugham in *Odhams Press Ltd.* v. *Cook* [1940] 3
All E.R. 15, and to the judgment of Upjohn J. in *Marshall Richards* **G**
Machine Co. Ltd. v. *Jewitt* (1956) 36 T.C. 511, 525. The clear taxation implication is that in cases (i) and (ii) the parent company cannot
deduct the expenditure in question from its profits, whereas in case (iii)
it can. However, one must be very clear about this: even if the
expenditure is incurred by the parent company solely in its own interests,
it will of necessity still to some extent benefit the subsidiary company. **H**
That is virtually inevitable. How, then, is the distinction between cases
(ii) and (iii) to be made, since the wholly objective situation, unless for
some wholly exceptional reason in either case the projected benefit to
the subsidiary company is not realised, is basically the same; that is to say,
benefit to each? The answer in my judgment is to be found in the
well known judgment of Romer L.J. in *Bentleys, Stokes & Lowless* v.
Beeson [1952] 2 All E.R. 82, 84–86:

A   " The relevant words of rule 3 (a) of the Rules Applicable to Cases
I and II—' wholly and exclusively laid out or expended for the
purposes of the . . . profession '—appear straightforward enough. It
is conceded that the first adverb—' wholly '—is in reference to the
quantum of the money expended and has no relevance to the present
case. The sole question is whether the expenditure in question was
' exclusively ' laid out for business purposes, that is: What was the

B   motive or object in the mind of the two individuals responsible for
the activities in question? It is well established that the question is
one of fact: and again, therefore, the problem seems simple enough.
The difficulty however arises, as we think, from the nature of the
activity in question. Entertaining involves inevitably the characteristic of hospitality: giving to charity or subscribing to a staff

C   pension fund involves inevitably the object of benefaction: an
undertaking to guarantee to a limited amount a national exhibition
involves inevitably supporting that exhibition and the purposes for
which it has been organised. But the question in all such cases is:
Was the entertaining, the charitable subscription, the guarantee,
undertaken *solely* for the purposes of business, that is, solely with
the object of promoting the business or its profit-earning capacity?

D   It is, as we have said, a question of fact. And it is quite clear that
the purpose must be the sole purpose. The paragraph says so in
clear terms. If the activity be undertaken with the object both of
promoting business and also with some other purpose, for example,
with the object of indulging an independent wish of entertaining a
friend or stranger or of supporting a charitable or benevolent object,

E   then the paragraph is not satisfied though in the mind of the actor
the business motive may predominate. For the statute so prescribes.
Per contra, if, in truth, the sole object is business promotion, the
expenditure is not disqualified because the nature of the activity
necessarily involves some other result, or the attainment or furtherance of some other objective, since the latter result or objective

F   is necessarily inherent in the act.

    " The matter may be illustrated by simple cases which were
given in argument. A London solicitor may hear that an old friend
and client whom he has not for a long time seen has arrived in
London. He says to himself: ' I would like to see my friend again,
and I know he may wish to talk business with me. I will ask him
to have lunch with me and then we can discuss any business he has

G   at the same time. I can kill two birds with one stone.' A London
solicitor may hear from the representative of a foreign firm, old
clients of his own, that the representative is in London and urgently
desires to see him on some matter of business, but that his time is
very short—and he cannot come to the solicitor's office, and is only
free at lunch time. The solicitor, to enable the client to get the

H   advice, asks him to lunch at his club or a restaurant. In the first case
it appears to us clear that the expenditure could not be justified
under the paragraph even though it turned out that the friend
spent the whole of the lunch time seeking the solicitor's advice on
his private affairs. On the other hand, it would appear to us
reasonably clear that in the second case the expenditure (so far,
at any rate, as reasonable) must be allowable. The difficulty, of

course, arises in the large area between the two examples when it is A
a question of fact in each case to determine what was the real
motive or purpose of the entertaining. But in both examples we have
given there is present inevitably the motive or purpose of hospitality
—that is, the solicitor in inviting the friend or the foreign representative to lunch does so with the purpose of giving him lunch.
That motive is unavoidably involved in the activity itself. A man, B
to oblige a friend who is a Roman Catholic priest, may agree to
participate in a church bazaar organised for the purpose of
promoting the interests of the Catholic Church, though he has
himself no desire whatever to support that Church, to which he may
be religiously opposed. In such a case the subsidiary purpose is no
part of the conscious or deliberate motive of the actor.

" So much, indeed, counsel for the Crown concedes, for other- C
wise it would follow that all entertaining expenses, all charitable
donations, would be necessarily excluded. Counsel admits, as we
understand him, that in such a case as the present there must be a
deliberate and independent wish or motive, that is, independent of
the business purposes to be served, to entertain the guest, and for
simplicity counsel has described this independent motive as ' private D
hospitality '. Thus, we return to the question: In the case before us,
was this element of private hospitality in some degree present?
Many cases were properly cited to us, but on such a matter we
cannot think that, by and large, they are of much assistance. It is
not relevant to the present matter that the business purpose must be
related to its profit-earning capacity: *Strong & Co. Ltd.* v. *Woodifield*
[1906] A.C. 448. Nor are we assisted by cases in which there is E
involved not so much duality of purpose, as duality of capacity—
cases, for example, where the question has been, whether the activity
is at least in part attributable to the doer's character, not as
proprietor of, or partner in, a business but to his character as an
ordinary citizen—cases relating to the costs of litigation, like *Smith's
Potato Estates Ltd.* v. *Bolland* [1948] A.C. 508 . . . *Spofforth & Prince* F
v. *Golder* [1945] 1 All E.R. 363, and cases of particular charitable
donations such as *Bourne & Hollingsworth Ltd.* v. *Ogden* (1929)
14 T.C. 349. If we have correctly analysed the problem, then the
present question remains one of fact to be determined in the light of
its own circumstances, and we agree with the Crown's contention
that it is for the taxpayer to satisfy the tribunal of fact on his claim.
More important, it is a firm rule in tax cases that, if the tribunal G
of fact has found the fact, the court will not disturb its conclusion
unless it is clear either that the tribunal has misapplied the law to
the facts found or that there was no evidence whatever to support
the finding. The first essential question, then, in the present case is:
What have the Special Commissioners found? "

H

So that judgment, which was the judgment of the court, establishes
that the mere fact that the subsidiary company receives a benefit is
nihil ad rem for this purpose if the object of the expenditure is the
exclusive benefiting of the parent company. It will be observed that
Romer L.J. uses three purpose words in the passage I have read:
" object," " motive," " purpose." I am not at all sure that these words
are always used in the cases in the sense in which he there uses them,

A but he poses the central question as, "What is the object of the expenditure?", and uses the words "motive or purpose" to describe the factual result—in the case before him, "hospitality." I think that Upjohn J. in *Marshall Richards Machine Co. Ltd.* v. *Jewitt* (1956) 36 T.C. 511, 526, uses the word "motive" in the same sense as it is used by Romer L.J., but uses the word "purpose" where Romer L.J. uses

B "object." Otherwise, I can make no sense of his pronouncement, but, read in that light, it is all of a piece with the judgment of the Court of Appeal. It follows from all this that (i) the test is a subjective, not an objective one—i.e., the relevant question is, "What was the object of the person making the disbursement in making it?," not, "What was the effect of the disbursement when made?"—and (ii) that this is, in all cases, a pure question of fact.

C In the present case the taxpayer company appealed to the general commissioners for the Division of Wellingborough against the disallowance by the inspector of the disbursements here in question, and the commissioners allowed its appeal. Among the commissioners' primary findings of fact is this one:

D "The position of the French company vis-à-vis the respondent was unique, the rescue operation being undertaken to further the respondent's business in France and in Europe."

Now this being a primary finding of fact, I am by no means certain that in any event I am at liberty to go behind it. In plain terms the commissioners have found that the object of the expenditure on Mr. Fearon's wages and other benefits was to further the taxpayer company's, not the

E subsidiary company's business in France and in Europe, and that should be conclusive. Presumably, that finding of primary fact was based on the evidence of a Mr. Leyland, a director, and formerly company secretary, of the taxpayer company. It has not been suggested to me that this primary conclusion of fact was in any manner inconsistent with, or not justified by, the evidence he gave to the commissioners. Assuming

F for one moment, however, that I am in the position where I have to ascertain, based on other primary facts, whether the conclusion so reached is one which reasonable commissioners properly instructed in the law could have reached, it appears to me that the answer must unhesitatingly be in the affirmative.

It appears from the other primary facts found by the commissioners

G that one of the taxpayer company's most important customers in France was a concern known as Wauquier Societé Anonyme. To this concern the taxpayer company sold its specialist products, I think directly; but whether such sales were made directly or indirectly through the French company, this was a customer which the taxpayer company did not wish to lose. In addition to the specialist products, in order to produce whatever was the finished product that Wauquier Societé Anonyme produced

H that concern required what are described as "prerequisite basic products." There was no question of the taxpayer company supplying these to Wauquier S.A.; this was ruled out because of transportation costs. Hence, it was essential if the taxpayer company was to maintain its business in France, that Wauquier S.A. should have a source of supply of the basic products, and that source was, in practical terms, the French company. Hence, if the taxpayer company allowed the French

company to continue as it was, not reaching a break-even level, it was   A
obvious that in the long run the whole of the taxpayer company's
business in France, at any rate, was in jeopardy. In these circumstances,
it is as plain as a pikestaff that a rescue operation for the French company was capable of being mounted with the object of furthering the
taxpayer company's business in France, and therefore a finding to this
effect is one which it is quite impossible for this court to overturn, even
if it be regarded as a secondary finding, which in my judgment it is in   B
any event not.

I think that Mr. Hart had several very pertinent criticisms of the way
in which the taxpayer company originally put its case through the mouths
of its advisers, its accountants, who appear to have placed their case on
the basis that what the taxpayer company was doing was to protect its
investment in the French company, which is, of course, the very reverse   C
of seeking to protect its own trade. However, this is a point which must
have been present to the minds of the commissioners, since they set out
the relevant letters in the case stated, and at the end of the day they paid
no attention to this, and, indeed, prior, inept formulations of the taxpayer
company's case. In this I think they were clearly correct, because long
before any question arose, namely—in the minutes of the board meeting   D
of the taxpayer company held on November 25, 1974—it is recorded
that what the board were considering in connection with the French
company was " our continuing operation in Europe."

Mr. Hart also criticised the actual form in which the commissioners
set out their decisions. This reads:

" We decided on the evidence . . . that: (a) the [taxpayer company]   E
and the French company contribute to and are dependent upon an
international unitary business. (b) The nature of that business
includes marketing and extension of markets. (c) The deduction of
£16,354 from the [taxpayer company's] profits should be allowed."

I do not fully understand (a). Strictly there could be an " international
unitary business " only if all the activities of the French company had   F
been undertaken solely as agents for the taxpayer company, and this is
plainly not the case. If, however, all it means, and I suspect this to be
the case, is that, having regard to the needs of customers, it was essential
for the taxpayer company's business that there should be a supplier
of basic products, and that supplier was the French company, whose
survival was therefore essential to the continued business of the taxpayer
company in France and possibly elsewhere, then of course it is fully   G
in line with the primary findings of fact made by the commissioners.
As regards (b), this seems to me to be a statement of the obvious, so far
as any manufacturing company is concerned; but, once again, I think
that what the commissioners are really saying is no more than that what
the taxpayer company was protecting in making the services of Mr.
Fearon available to the French company was its continued ability to sell   H
its products, and doubtless expand its sales, in France and elsewhere in
Europe—again, fully in line with the primary facts found by them.
And (c), of course, is no more than an inevitable consequence of their
primary finding of fact that the rescue operation was undertaken to
further the taxpayer company's own business in France and in Europe.

Accordingly, for these reasons, it appears to me that the commissioners came to a conclusion on this matter from which I am not at

A liberty to depart but from which, even if I were at such liberty, I could not properly depart. It follows that this appeal by the Crown from their decision must be dismissed.

Appeal dismissed with costs.

Solicitors: *Solicitor of Inland Revenue; Jaques & Co.*

B   [Reported by MRS. HARRIET DUTTON, Barrister-at-Law]

C   [COURT OF APPEAL]

* REGINA *v.* MACHIN

1980 March 18; 28   Lord Widgery C.J., Eveleigh L.J. and O'Connor J.

D *Crime—Common law offence—Attempt to pervert course of justice —Statement made to police—Plan for evidence to be given at trial that statement induced by physical violence—Plan not pursued—Whether substantive offence committed*

The appellant was charged with attempting to pervert the course of public justice in having fabricated evidence of a false allegation of assault by police officers on him and inciting others to give false evidence in relation to certain charges preferred against him. Although he had started to act on E the plan to fabricate evidence, he did not pursue it and, at his trial, he submitted that the acts alleged did not amount to an attempt since they were insufficiently proximate to the offence of perverting the course of public justice. The submission was rejected and the jury were directed to consider the tendency of the appellant's conduct and his intention. He was convicted and appealed.

F   On the question whether attempting to pervert the course of justice was a substantive offence: —

Held, dismissing the appeal, (1) that the gist of the offence was conduct which might lead to a miscarriage of justice, whether or not a miscarriage actually occurred; and that use of the word " attempt " in such a context did no more than describe a substantive offence consisting of conduct which had a tendency to, and was intended to, pervert the course of G justice.

(2) That a jury was not to be directed to assess the conduct of a defendant in terms of proximity to an ultimate offence but should be left to consider the tendency of the conduct and the intention of the defendant; and that, accordingly, the jury had been properly directed and their verdict was supported by the evidence.

Reg. v. *Vreones* [1891] 1 Q.B. 360; *Reg.* v. *Andrews* [1973]
H Q.B. 422, C.A. and *Reg.* v. *Rowell* [1978] 1 W.L.R. 132, C.A. considered.

Per curiam. The word " attempt " is convenient for use in the case where it cannot be proved that the course of justice was actually perverted (post, p. 767B).

The following cases are referred to in the judgment:

Reg. v. *Andrews* [1973] Q.B. 422; [1973] 2 W.L.R. 116; [1973] 1 All E.R. 857, C.A.

Reg. v. *Rowell* [1978] 1 W.L.R. 132; [1978] 1 All E.R. 665, C.A.   **A**
Reg. v. *Vreones* [1891] 1 Q.B. 360.

The following additional cases were cited in argument:
Reg. v. *Britton* [1973] R.T.R. 502, C.A.
Reg. v. *Grimes (Note)* [1968] 3 All E.R. 179.
Reg. v. *Kellett* [1976] Q.B. 372; [1975] 3 W.L.R. 713; [1975] 3 All E.R.
   468, C.A.   **B**
Reg. v. *Panayiotou* [1973] 1 W.L.R. 1032; [1973] 3 All E.R. 112, C.A.
Reg. v. *Thomas (Derek)* [1979] Q.B. 326; [1979] 2 W.L.R. 144; [1979]
   1 All E.R. 577, C.A.

APPEAL against conviction.

On October 5, 1979, at Doncaster Crown Court (Judge Michael
Walker) the appellant, Lawrence Machin, was convicted of attempting to **C**
pervert the course of public justice:

"... by fabricating evidence of a false allegation that he had been
assaulted on September 10, 1978, by Stevan Lavin and Timothy John
Miskell [two police officers], and by inciting Brian Allen to give false
evidence in proceedings against the appellant for offences of permitting a vehicle to be used on a road without insurance, that the **D**
appellant had sustained an injury to his face in Frederick Street
Police Station, Rotherham, on September 10, 1978."

He was sentenced to nine months' imprisonment. He appealed against
conviction on the grounds that (1) the judge was wrong to reject a submission at the close of the prosecution's case that there was no case to
answer, alternatively that the case should be withdrawn from the jury **E**
because (i) an attempt to pervert the course of justice was to be treated
in the same manner as other attempts and, therefore, governed by the same
rules as to proximity; (ii) the facts proved were insufficiently proximate
to a perversion of the course of justice to amount to the offence charged
of attempting to pervert it; (iii) if, contrary to the appellant's submission,
an attempt to pervert the course of justice was a substantive offence in
its own right and if the judicial definition of it as an act having a tendency **F**
and which was intended to pervert it (*Reg.* v. *Rowell* [1978] 1 W.L.R.
132) was correct, even so "tendency" and "intended" were to be
defined by essentially the same proximity tests as attempts generally; (iv)
alternatively and in any event the facts proved neither met the proximity
test nor any other reasonable definition of "having a tendency," nor did
they prove, or sufficiently prove, an intention to pervert the course of **G**
justice; and (2) further or alternatively, the direction to the jury was
wrong that the offence was made out by acts which had a tendency and
were intended to pervert the course of justice.

The facts are stated in the judgment.

Lionel Scott (assigned by the Registrar of Criminal Appeals) for the **H**
appellant.
R. M. Harrison for the Crown.

Cur. adv. vult.

March 28. EVELEIGH L.J. read the following judgment of the court.
On October 5, 1979, in the Doncaster Crown Court the appellant was
convicted of attempting to pervert the course of public justice and was

A sentenced to nine months' imprisonment. He now appeals against
conviction.

On August 10, 1978, police officers on two separate occasions stopped
a motor vehicle belonging to the appellant. On each occasion it was driven
by a different man and neither of them held a valid driving licence. On
August 19 the appellant made written statements to the police claiming
that neither man had permission to use the vehicle. On September 10 he
B went to the police station in connection with another matter. Two friends,
Brian Allen and Keith Shaw, waited outside. In the station the appellant
dictated two statements to the effect that he had given the two men permission to drive the vehicle and that he was aware that they did not hold
licences and were not covered by insurance.

Thereafter the prosecution's case was as follows. When the appellant
C left the police station he asked Allen to punch him in the eye. This Allen
did causing the eye to swell. The appellant told Shaw and Mrs. Shaw that
the police officers had hit him. He said the same thing to his own wife
and told her to telephone the Doncaster police and lodge a complaint.
This she did. He made similar allegations to a hospital doctor and to his
solicitor. He went to a photographer who photographed the eye. He asked
D Allen to give evidence that the police had caused his injury and Allen
agreed. Later however Allen changed his mind. The appellant did not in
fact collect the photograph.

The appellant made a written statement admitting these facts, but in
evidence he said that the statement had been composed by the police and
that he had signed it because the police had threatened to have his children
put into care if he did not sign. He denied the facts alleged by the
E prosecution.

At the close of the prosecution case counsel submitted to the judge that
the facts alleged did not go far enough to amount to an attempt. Before
this court he has argued that to charge the offence of attempting to pervert
the course of public justice is to charge an inchoate offence and that the
jury should be given directions as to how they may decide whether or not
F an act is sufficiently proximate to amount to an attempt.

The judge addressed the jury as follows:

" Now, what is attempting to pervert the course of public justice?
It is this. It is the doing of an act or series of acts which have a
tendency and are intended to pervert the course of justice. Now, as
to the course of justice, members of the jury, nobody disputes in
G this particular case that the course of justice in relation to the
alleged offence of permitting this motor car to be used without
insurance, nobody disputes that the course of justice had begun . . .
What is perverting the course of public justice? Members of the
jury it is the doing of something—or attempting to pervert the course
of justice is doing something which is designed to lead to a false
conclusion if the matter goes the whole way, and doing an act or a
H series of acts which have a tendency to, and are intended to, pervert
the course of public justice is this offence of attempting to pervert the
course of public justice. . . ."

Counsel has also submitted that if his primary submission is wrong the
acts alleged in any event did not have a tendency to pervert the course
of justice.

In directing the jury as he did the judge was following the words of

Pollock B. in *Reg.* v. *Vreones* [1891] 1 Q.B. 360. There the defendant A
had tampered with wheat samples taken for submission to arbitrators to
be appointed to determine any dispute that might arise as to the quality
of the consignment. He was convicted of a common law misdemeanour
of attempting by the manufacture of false evidence to mislead a judicial
tribunal. Pollock B. said, at p. 369: " The real offence here is the doing
of some act which has a tendency and is intended to pervert the administration of public justice."   B

In *Reg.* v. *Andrews* [1973] Q.B. 422 the accused sought to persuade a
Mr. Reeves, the defendant in a motor accident prosecution, to pay him to
give false evidence at the trial. Lord Widgery C.J., referring to *Reg.* v.
Vreones, said, at p. 425:

" So that the question arose whether it was possible to have an
attempt to pervert the course of justice. Lord Coleridge C.J. said, C
at pp. 366, 367: ' The first count of the indictment in substance
charges the defendant with the misdemeanour of attempting, by the
manufacture of false evidence, to mislead a judicial tribunal which
might come into existence. If the act itself of the defendant was
completed, I cannot doubt that to manufacture false evidence for
the purpose of misleading a judicial tribunal is a misdemeanour . . . D
I think that an attempt to pervert the course of justice is in itself a
punishable misdemeanour; and though I should myself have thought
so on the grounds of sense and reason, there is also plenty of authority
to show that it is a misdemeanour in point of law.' Accordingly, to
produce false evidence with a view to misleading the court and perverting the course of justice is a substantive offence; an attempt so
to act can be charged as such, and in our judgment an incitement E
so to act is also a charge known to the law and properly to be
preferred in appropriate circumstances."

In *Reg.* v. *Rowell* [1978] 1 W.L.R. 132 Ormrod L.J. said, at p. 138:
" The remaining grounds of appeal, namely duplicity in the indictment and the lack of sufficiently proximate acts to constitute an F
attempt, are both based, in our opinion, on the same false premise,
which arises from the description of the offence as ' attempting to
pervert the course of public justice.' The use of the word ' attempt '
in this context is misleading. The defendant was not charged with an
attempt to commit a substantive offence but with the substantive
offence itself, which is more accurately, if less compendiously,
described in Pollock B.'s words which we have already quoted, G
namely the doing of an act (or we would add a series of acts) which
has a tendency and is intended to pervert the course of justice. Lord
Coleridge C.J. in *Reg.* v. *Vreones* [1891] 1 Q.B. 360, 367, said:
' I think that an attempt to pervert the course of justice is in itself
a punishable misdemeanour . . .'."

The law is concerned to forbid unlawful conduct which may result in a H
miscarriage of justice. There are specific common law offences such as
embracery and personating a juryman. There are statutory offences, for
example, the concealing of information for reward about an arrestable
offence contrary to section 5 (1) of the Criminal Law Act 1967. On the
other hand, as is pointed out in the Law Commission Report on offences
relating to interference with the course of justice (Law Com. No. 96),
the common law recognises a wide general offence variously referred

A to as perverting or obstructing the course of justice, obstructing or interfering with the administration of justice, and defeating the due course,
or the ends of justice. The particular acts or conduct in question may
take many different forms including conduct that amounts in itself to
some other criminal offence or attempt thereat in the strict sense of an
inchoate offence. The gist of the offence is conduct which may lead and
is intended to lead to a miscarriage of justice whether or not a miscarriage
B actually occurs. We therefore respectfully agree that the use of the word
"attempt" in the present context is misleading as was said in Reg. v.
Rowell [1978] 1 W.L.R. 132, 138. The word is convenient for use in the
case where it cannot be proved that the course of justice was actually perverted but it does no more than describe a substantive offence which
consists of conduct which has tendency and is intended to pervert the
C course of justice. To do an act with the intention of perverting the
course of justice is not of itself enough. The act must also have that
tendency.
    We are, therefore, of the opinion that the jury should not be directed
to assess the defendant's conduct in terms of proximity to an ultimate
offence but should be left to consider its tendency and the intention of
the defendant, as was done in this case. In our opinion, the acts alleged
D did have a tendency to pervert the course of justice even though the
appellant's plan was not pursued to a final successful conclusion and the
verdict of the jury was clearly supported by the evidence.
    Consequently this appeal is dismissed.

Appeal dismissed.

E Solicitor: *M. J. Rose, Sheffield.*

L. N. W.

F [PRIVY COUNCIL]

* MUKTA BEN AND ANOTHER . . . . . . APPELLANTS

AND

SUVA CITY COUNCIL . . . . RESPONDENT

G [ON APPEAL FROM THE COURT OF APPEAL OF FIJI]

1979 Oct. 15, 16, 17, 18, 22, 23;   Lord Wilberforce, Lord Edmund-Davies,
       Dec. 12   Lord Russell of Killowen, Lord Keith
                                        of Kinkel and Lord Lane

*Fiji—Land—Compulsory acquisition—Council's right to purchase
    compulsorily if unable to acquire by "agreement . . . on
H   reasonable terms"—Notice of acquisition to be served describ-
    ing subject land—Whether sketch plan in notice sufficient
    description—Failure to publish notice in Gazette and news-
    paper—Validity of acquisition—Towns Ordinance (Laws of
    Fiji, 1967 rev., c. 106), s. 136 (1)—Crown Acquisition of Lands
    Ordinance (Laws of Fiji, 1967 rev., c. 119), s. 7 (4), Sch.*

    In 1964 the appellants contracted to buy a plot of land
outside the Suva City boundaries. In 1966 negotiations were
begun for the sale by the appellants of part of the land to the

Suva City Council ("the council"), which wished to build a power station thereon. The appellants asked what they regarded as a reasonable market price for the land, but the council took the view that it was too high. Since agreement could not be reached, the council applied to the Governor in Council for authority to acquire the land compulsorily under section 136 (1) of the Towns Ordinance [1] on the ground that it was "unable to purchase by agreement and on reasonable terms." Although the appellants were aware that the council was likely to seek powers of compulsory acquisition, they were not informed that the application was being made or invited to make representations. The Governor gave his authority, and pursuant to section 5 of the Crown Acquisition of Lands Ordinance [2] the council served notices of acquisition on the appellants and on the vendor to the appellants, who was still the registered proprietor, but it did not publish the notice in the Gazette and in a newspaper, as required by section 7 (4) of that Ordinance. The notices described the subject land as 20 acres at the eastern end of the plot "as delineated on the sketch plan hereinafter appearing." The sketch plan, which was not to scale and not the result of a survey, indicated an area stated to be 20 acres. There was evidence that if the plan was treated as a scale plan, the area depicted by it was in fact more than 20 acres. The council subsequently completed the acquisition and built the power station.

The appellants brought an action against the council for, inter alia, a declaration that the acquisition was unlawful and ultra vires and for damages for trespass. The Supreme Court of Fiji gave judgment for the council, and the appellants' appeal was dismissed by the Court of Appeal of Fiji.

On appeal by the appellants to the Judicial Committee: —

Held, dismissing the appeal, (1) that the requirement in the Schedule to the Crown Acquisition of Lands Ordinance that the form of notice of compulsory acquisition should describe the subject land " giving measurements and showing boundaries whenever practicable," was satisfied in an appropriate case if the land was denoted by a sketch plan, as long as its position and extent could be ascertained therefrom; and that the description in the council's notice was sufficiently precise, and it was irrelevant that the area on the plan, if measured to scale, did not correspond exactly with the stated area (post, p. 777E–F).

(2) That, although section 136 (1) of the Towns Ordinance did not expressly empower the council to acquire land outside the boundaries of the city, the land that the council could acquire compulsorily under the subsection was land that it could have acquired by agreement under the previous provisions of the Ordinance; that, since those earlier provisions permitted a council to acquire land outside its boundaries, section 136 (1) permitted the council, in default of agreement, to compulsorily acquire the appellants' land (post, pp. 777H—778B).

(3) That section 7 (4) of the Crown Acquisition of Lands Ordinance was not imperative in the sense that the council's failure to publish the acquisition notice in the Gazette or a newspaper vitiated the acquisition and since sufficient notice

---

[1] Towns Ordinance, s. 136 (1): see post, pp. 770G—771B.

[2] Crown Acquisition of Lands Ordinance, s. 5: " Whenever the Governor resolves that any lands are required for a public purpose the [town clerk] shall give notice to the registered proprietors of the said lands and to the mortgagees, encumbrancees and lessees thereof or to such of them as shall after reasonable inquiry be known to him, which notice may be in the form in the Schedule hereto or to the like effect."

S. 7 (4): see post, p. 771D.

Sch.: see post, p. 771G–H.

A   had been given to the only persons interested in the land,
non-compliance with section 7 (4) should not invalidate the
acquisition of the land (post, p. 778c).

(4) That the condition precedent to the activation of the
compulsory acquisition procedure, that the council should have
been unable to purchase " by agreement and on reasonable
terms," imported that there should have been an irreconcilable
difference of opinion between the parties as to what were

B   reasonable terms and that, accordingly, the contention that the
appellants' asking price was, in the circumstances, reasonable
had no bearing on the validity of the compulsory acquisition
(post, pp. 778f—779c).

(5) That the acquisition could not be impugned on any
ground of natural justice, since the legislation imposed no
obligation to inform the appellants that an application for
compulsory acquisition was contemplated or to invite them

C   to make representations to the Governor, and the Governor had
in no way acted unfairly in regard to the appellants (post,
pp. 779g—780b); and since none of the appellants' other
grounds of objection was sustainable, the land had been validly
acquired.

Decision of the Court of Appeal of Fiji affirmed.

No case is referred to in the judgment of their Lordships.

D

The following cases were cited in argument:

Amstad v. *Brisbane City Council (No.* 2) [1968] Qd.R. 343.
Attorney-General v. *Mersey Railway Co.* [1907] 1 Ch. 81, C.A.
Ayres v. *Chacos* (1972) 19 F.L.R. 468.
Banks v. *Transport Regulation Board (Victoria)* (1968) 119 C.L.R. 222.
Bristol Corpn. v. *Sinnott* [1917] 2 Ch. 340.

E   *Coles* v. *County of Matamata* (unreported) appeal No. 69/74 of 1976,
      Court of Appeal of New Zealand.
Company of Horners v. *Barlow* (1688) 3 Mod.Rep. 159.
Cullimore v. *Lyme Regis Corporation* [1962] 1 Q.B. 718; [1961] 3 W.L.R.
      1340; [1961] 3 All E.R. 1008.
Delta Properties Pty. Ltd. v. *Brisbane City Council* (1955) 95 C.L.R. 11.
De Verteuil v. *Knaggs* [1918] A.C. 557, P.C.

F   *Durayappah* v. *Fernando* [1967] 2 A.C. 337; [1967] 3 W.L.R. 289; [1967]
      2 All E.R. 152, P.C.
Foster v. *Saskatchewan Telecommunications* (unreported), July 26, 1978,
      Court of Queen's Bench, Regina, Saskatchewan.
Furnell v. *Whangarei High Schools Board* [1973] A.C. 660; [1973] 2
      W.L.R. 92; [1973] 1 All E.R. 400, P.C.
Gaiman v. *National Association for Mental Health* [1971] Ch. 317.

G   *Garbin* v. *Wild* [1965] W.A.R. 72.
Garland v. *Minister of Housing and Local Government* (1968) 67 L.G.R.
      77; 20 P. & C.R. 93, C.A.
Gresham Life Assurance Society v. *Crowther* [1914] 2 Ch. 219.
Hawtin v. *Shire of Doncaster and Templestowe* [1959] V.R. 494.
Hughes v. *Sutherland* (1881) 7 Q.B.D. 160, D.C.
Jones v. *Commonwealth of Australia* (1963) 109 C.L.R. 475.

H   *Li Hong Mi* v. *Attorney-General for Hong Kong* [1920] A.C. 735, P.C.
London and Westcliff Properties Ltd. v. *Minister of Housing and Local
      Government* [1961] 1 W.L.R. 519; [1961] 1 All E.R. 610.
Lower Hutt City Council v. *Bank* [1974] 1 N.Z.L.R. 545.
Lynch v. *Commissioners of Sewers of the City of London* (1886) 32 Ch.D.
      72, C.A.
Manukau City v. *Attorney-General ex rel. Burns* [1973] 1 N.Z.L.R. 25.
McCurrie v. *Nazia* (1900) 2 W.A.R. 15.
North Shore Railway Co. v. *Pion* (1889) 14 App.Cas. 612, P.C.

Ocean Estates Ltd. v. *Pinder* [1969] 2 A.C. 19; [1969] 2 W.L.R. 1359, A
P.C.
Parkdale Corporation v. *West* (1887) 12 App.Cas. 602, P.C.
Patel v. *Premabhai* [1954] A.C. 35; [1953] 3 W.L.R. 836, P.C.
Plimmer v. *Wellington Corporation* (1884) 9 App.Cas. 699, P.C.
Prentice v. *Brisbane City Council* [1966] Qd.R. 394.
Ridge v. *Baldwin* [1964] A.C. 40; [1963] 2 W.L.R. 935; [1963] 2 All
E.R. 66, H.L.(E.).
B
Roberts v. *Board of Land and Works* [1965] V.R. 265.
Robinson v. *Montgomeryshire Brewery Co. Ltd.* [1896] 2 Ch. 841.
Sandringham Corporation v. *Rayment* (1928) 40 C.L.R. 510.
Saunby v. *London (Ontario) Water Commissioners* [1906] A.C. 110, P.C.
Treasury Gate Pty. Ltd. v. *Rice* [1972] V.R. 148.
Webb v. *Minister of Housing and Local Government* [1965] 1 W.L.R.
755; [1965] 2 All E.R. 193, C.A.
C
West Midland Baptist (Trust) Association (Inc.) v. *Birmingham Corpor-*
ation [1970] A.C. 874; [1969] 3 W.L.R. 389; [1969] 3 All E.R. 172,
H.L.(E.).

APPEAL (No. 19 of 1977) by the appellants, Mukta Ben (daughter
of Bhovan) and Shanta Ben (daughter of Bhimji), from a judgment of the
Court of Appeal of Fiji (Gould V.P., Marsack J.A. and O'Regan J.) D
given on February 18, 1977, dismissing an appeal by the appellants from
a judgment dated August 26, 1975, of the Supreme Court of Fiji (Stuart J.)
dismissing the appellants' claim for, inter alia, a declaration that a purported compulsory acquisition by the respondent, the Suva City Council,
of part of the appellants' land was unlawful and ultra vires, and for
damages for trespass.

The facts are stated in the judgment of their Lordships.
E

Kenneth H. Gifford Q.C. and *Dr. R. Sundberg* (both of the Victoria
Bar) for the appellants.
T. F. F. Hughes Q.C. and *Catharine Weigall* (both of the New South
Wales Bar) for the council.

Cur. adv. vult. F

December 12. The judgment of their Lordships was delivered by
LORD RUSSELL OF KILLOWEN.

This appeal from the Court of Appeal of Fiji involves an attempt by
the appellant landowners to challenge under a number of heads the
validity of a compulsory acquisition of 20 acres of their land for the
purpose of the erection of an auxiliary power station by the respondent, G
the Suva City Council (" the council "). The purported compulsory
acquisition was under the provisions of section 136 of the Towns Ordinance
(c. 106) which is in the following terms:

" (1) If a town council are unable to purchase by agreement and on
reasonable terms suitable land for any purpose for which they are
authorised to acquire land the council may represent the case to the H
Governor in Council and if the Governor in Council is satisfied, after
such inquiry, if any, as he may deem expedient, that suitable land
for the said purpose cannot be purchased on reasonable terms by
agreement and that the circumstances are such as to justify the
compulsory acquisition of the land for the said purpose and that
the said purpose is a public purpose within the meaning of the Crown
Acquisition of Lands Ordinance he may authorise the council to

A acquire the land compulsorily. (2) The provisions of the Crown Acquisition of Lands Ordinance shall apply to the compulsory acquisition of land by a town council under the provisions of this section, and in the application of the provisions of that Ordinance to such acquisition reference to 'the Crown,' 'the Governor' or 'Government' shall be deemed to be reference to a town council authorised to acquire land under the provisions of this section and

B reference to 'the Director of Lands' shall be deemed to be reference to the Town Clerk."

Section 5 of the Crown Acquisition of Lands Ordinance, as applied by section 136 (2) above, requires the town clerk of the council, authorisation for the compulsory acquisition having been given under section 136 (1), to give noitce:

C ". . . to the registered proprietors of the said lands and to the mortgagees, encumbrances (sic) and lessees thereof . . . which notice may be in the form in the Schedule hereto or to the like effect."

Section 7 of the Crown Acquisition of Lands Ordinance contains provisions for service of the notice, and section 7 (4) additionally provides:

D "All notices served under the provisions of this Ordinance shall be inserted once at least in the Gazette and in a newspaper circulating in Fiji."

In the instant case that last provision was not complied with.

Section 6 of that last Ordinance enables the town clerk to direct the yielding up of possession of the land within a period to be stated in the notice. Section 12 provides for the determination of the amount

E of compensation to be awarded for the land compulsorily acquired, matters to be taken into consideration including (expectedly) market value at date of notice of intention to take, damage due to severance at the taking of possession, and injurious affection. The present appeal is not concerned, directly, with quantum of compensation; it concerns only the contention of the appellants that the purported compulsory acquisition is

F and always was invalid and that therefore the council has trespassed on their land and still so trespasses and should be ordered to vacate it and the power station and other buildings which the council has erected upon it. Before leaving the Crown Acquisition of Lands Ordinance it is to be noted that section 17 imposes penalties for wilful hindrance or obstruction of the taking or retaining of possession of the lands pursuant to the

G Ordinance. Further, the Schedule to the Ordinance, giving the form of notice, is as follows:

"Notice is hereby given that the following lands (*describe lands, giving measurements and showing boundaries whenever practicable*) are required by [the council] for public purposes. . . . Any person claiming to have any right or interest in the said land is required

H within three months from the date of this notice to send to [the town clerk] a statement of his right and interest and of the evidence thereof, and of any claim made by him in respect of such right or interest. . . ."

The form continues (see section 6) with a notice of intention "to enter into possession of the said lands at the expiration of [*blank*] weeks . . . ," and adds a warning in terms of section 17. One point taken by the appellants is that the notice insufficiently defined the land.

Mukta Ben v. Suva Council (P.C.)   [1980]

The facts of this matter are in outline these. Land C.T.8316 is of A somewhat irregular shape with its east boundary at high water mark of the sea and its west boundary at a riverside, comprising some 94 acres. It was owned by one Sukhichand and in July 1964 was contracted by the appellants to be bought from him, save a small portion near his house, possession to be given much later. From 1963 onwards the council was looking for a suitable site for an auxiliary power station to serve the city and possibly in due course to serve an area outside the B then city limits. In October 1964 the council was in search of an area of some 50 to 70 acres for this purpose, partly depending on future expansion and partly on the nature of the terrain. The appellants offered to make a gift of five acres out of C.T.8316, and said they were prepared to negotiate for a sale of 30 acres. In April 1966 the council wanted the whole (or substantially the whole) of C.T.8316, and offered to buy it, no C price being named. The appellants offered on April 22, 1966, to sell 50 acres of the eastern portion at a price of £200 per acre, saying that they were unwilling to sell the whole since they contemplated subdividing the western end of C.T.8316 for industrial use subject to planning approval. The whole of C.T.8316 was then in use by Sukhichand for dairy farming. The appellants also offered access to the eastern end through the retained western end on terms that the council would build and maintain the road, D which would of course serve also as access to any subdivision of the retained land.

There were then further conversations in which it appeared that the council then preferred land at the western end of C.T. 8316 and on May 13, 1966, the appellants' solicitor (Warren) wrote to the council's solicitor (McFarlane) noting that the council now preferred the western end, offer- E ing 40 to 50 acres at that end at £300 per acre, the price having increased because they had intended to subdivide the western area. The letter stipulated that the council would provide without cost to the appellants a formed public road from the King's Road to the western end of the appellants' retained eastern land. In August 1966 the council wrote to say that £300 was very high and that the council considered that £110 was a fair and reasonable price, and offering that rate for 40 acres, the F area to be subject to survey. The same letter said that the council would form the public road access to the appellants' retained land. The letter finished:

> " If your client cannot accept the above price, then we are instructed
> to serve the appropriate notice of acquisition and proceed compulsorily
> to acquire and use the procedure set out in the Ordinance."   G

The appellants' solicitor (who also acted for Sukhichand) replied that £110 was quite unacceptable and unrealistic, and concluded: " As there seems to be no prospect of *further* negotiation on price, the [council] will presumably now proceed with a compulsory acquisition." (Emphasis supplied.) A point sought to be made for the appellants in connection with section 136 of the Towns Ordinance was that there had been no H negotiation for the acquisition of land by agreement. Their Lordships do not accept that contention. Negotiations may be protracted but they may also be brief, and their Lordships are content to accept the view of the appellants' solicitor which finds expression in his use of the word " further." The other matter that emerges from that letter is that the appellants had no objection to compulsory acquisition of up to 40 acres of their land, and were concerned only with price (if to be agreed) and

A compensation (if not). At this stage the matter of acquisition had as noted switched from the eastern end (by the sea) to the western end (by the river).

On September 8, 1966, the council's solicitor applied by letter under section 136 of the Towns Ordinance for authority of the Governor in Council to acquire compulsorily approximately 40 acres for its new power station. Their Lordships observe at this juncture that there is no pro-
B vision in the legislation for notification of such application to those interested in the land in question and no provision for the hearing of any objections. The only legislative requirements are in connection with the giving of notices after the compulsory acquisition has been authorised, and those requirements are directed solely to the later assessment of compensa-
tion. This is not of course to say that if there is ground for holding the
C authorisation to be invalid, the owner or owners cannot resort to the court for the purpose of asserting that invalidity, but prima facie a lack of notification, or of opportunity to object in advance to the authorisation, is not, since none is required by the legislation, ground for asserting such invalidity. And the only reference in section 136 of the Towns Ordinance to inquiry by the Governor is to " such inquiry, if any, as he may deem expedient."

D   The application letter of September 8, 1966, pointed out the need for a new power station. It referred to negotiations with the appellants, who had in 1964 bought approximately 88 acres, including the 40 acres the acquisition of which was now sought, at approximately £90 an acre. It said that the appellants had asked for £300 an acre, which was considered highly excessive in view of that last-mentioned fact and of a
E 1964 valuation by a Mr. Tetzner of adjoining property. It said that after consideration the council had offered £110 per acre, which had been refused, " and as the [appellants'] solicitors say there seems no prospect of any further negotiations." It said that there was little likelihood of the appellants agreeing to reduce their price much below £300, and that the writers had advised the council having regard to knowledge of the land and of valuations in that area that £110 was then a reasonable market
F price. It added that the land was then used as a dairy farm. It stressed that the matter was of some urgency. It said : " the site would be used exclusively for erection of buildings in connection with the power house and all purposes incidental thereto." On September 19, 1966, this application letter was followed by questions from the Director of Lands, to whom the Governor in Council would turn for advice in such matters. He suggested that it would be appropriate for the application to be made
G under section 15 of the Suva Electricity Ordinance, whose provisions need not be investigated since that suggestion was not taken up. With a view however to an application under the last-mentioned section the Director of Lands asked for a plan showing clearly the 88 acres acquired by the appellants in 1964 and the 40 acres required by the council, and also details of access to the 40 acres and of the access which would be
H available to the balance of the 88 acres—these matters not having been shown clearly on the sketch plan sent on September 8. The Director of Lands also asked the following questions :

" (b) what other sites, if any, council has investigated for the new power station; (c) full details of the reasons why city council consider it necessary to acquire as much as 40 acres for a power station; (d) if the 40 acres will not be wholly utilised to accommodate a new power station what other uses the council propose to put the land;

(e) whether or not the relevant rural local authority and/or the town planning board has been consulted on council's proposal to use this particular land for a power station, and if so, what were their observations; (f) whether or not the council has obtained an assessment of the value of the 40 acres from a professional valuer in terms of 1966 land prices, and if so, what this amounts to; (g) whether or not any attempt has been made to reach an agreement on a compromised price somewhere between council's offer of £110 an acre and [the appellants'] demand of £300 an acre; (h) whether or not the [appellants] have raised any objection to council's proposal to use the 40 acres as a power station site. In other words, whether or not it is reasonable to conclude that the only point of disagreement between the parties is the matter of price to be paid for the land."

The council's solicitor having referred these matters to the town clerk and, through him, to the city electrical engineer, received a letter from the former on October 4, a copy of which was later sent to the Director of Lands. It described other sites investigated and found unsuitable for various reasons. Paragraphs 2 and 3 of the town clerk's letter of October 4 were as follows:

"2. An area of 40 acres was considered to be the minimum which should be obtained, to allow for future expansion, the provision of suitable storage areas for stores and fuel, suitable working areas for maintenance, and for running ancillaries such as water cooling towers etc., and adequate isolation of the station from existing and future development in the immediate vicinity of the area. Owing to the undulating nature of the topography of the particular area, the most suitable position for the station building is near the southern boundary of the portion of C.T.8316. The purchase of this site together with the portion of C.T.8315 required will permit the siting of the station virtually in the centre of the whole block thus acquired. The section of C.T.8315 adjacent to the Samabula River would enable the installation of fuel oil handling and storage facilities, and permit fuel oil deliveries to be made by barge from Suva. This would be very much cheaper than using road transport It is possible that some living quarters may be provided on the perimeter of the area for the housing of breakdown and shift staff. 3. It was hoped that some industry could be established immediately adjacent to the station which could use waste heat in the form of steam. This could materially reduce the cost of the electricity supply."

There was then an interview between the Director of Lands, the chief electrical engineer of the city, and the council's solicitor. On October 26, the council's solicitor wrote to the Director in answer to his letter of September 19. He enclosed plans (which showed also a further 40 acres desired out of adjoining land C.T.8315) with proposed roads A and B. He said:

"It was agreed with the owner of Title 8316 that if the [council] acquired the area out of the title a road would be provided to give access to the balance area."

The balance area at this stage was the eastern part of C.T.8316. In answer to queries (b), (c) and (d) in the letter of September 19 a copy of the town clerk's letter of October 4 was enclosed. On value, the letter referred to a 1964 valuation by Tetzner of adjacent land, also dairy

A land, at £75 per acre, and said that the latter had told the writer that the figure of £300 asked was ridiculous. The council's offer of £110 was considered by the council to be the ultimate price it could offer:

" The dairy farm land in that area is worth no more than £100 an acre today, having regard to the use to which it is now put. . . . It was pointed out to the [appellants] that the balance areas in the title
B [C.T.8316] would be considerably increased in value due to the [council] erecting a power station there and giving good road access, thus enabling the [appellants] to subdivide. . . . There is no objection to the [council's] proposal to acquire by either [appellant], but each wants as much as possible, so that the only point of disagreement is one of price. . . . As we pointed out to you the electrical engineer considers this is the most suitable site, and the [council] must have
C room for expansion and requires the land proposed as a buffer area. . . . The proposed site . . . will be really in another decade more or less in the centre of Suva and its environs."

On March 1, 1967, the Governor in Council authorised the compulsory acquisition of 20 acres for a power station under section 136 of the Towns Ordinance (or rather under its then equivalent), having considered that
D 20 acres was sufficient for the purpose, and the council was so notified on March 16, 1967, by the office of the Secretary for Fijian Affairs and Local Government. This was of course in relation to the west end of C.T.8316.

No further step was taken by the council on the basis of that authorisation. The council then decided that it would prefer 20 acres at the eastern end by the sea. On June 7, 1967, the solicitor wrote on behalf of the
E council saying this and asking for authority to acquire such area, enclosing a sketch plan indicating a required access road to the area from the north through native and crown land to King's Road. The letter stated that the appellants had already asked much more than the council was prepared to pay for what the land was worth: this presumably was a reference to £200 an acre which was the figure required for land at the eastern end.
F On July 18, 1967, the council was notified that the Governor in Council had on July 5, 1967, signified his approval under the relevant section to compulsory acquisition as requested, and also to compulsory acquisition of such land as is necessary " following either of the two routes proposed " to give access to the new power station site from King's Road. The record does not make it plain what were the two routes, nor when they were proposed, but the letter indicates that there were discussions
G between the town clerk and advisers of the Governor in which the council indicated that it would follow " the access route from King's Road through the Kinoya Subdivision." There is no mention of the access road serving also the balance land to the west.

On July 25, 1967, the council accordingly served notices of acquisition on the appellants and Sukhichand under the Crown Acquisition of Lands
H Ordinance (as applied), requiring possession within eight weeks. The land required was referred to in the notice as land containing 20 acres at the eastern end of C.T.8316 " as delineated on the sketch plan hereinafter appearing." That sketch plan indicated an area, stated to be the 20 acres, to be acquired bounded on the east by what is obviously intended to be high water mark, on the north and south by those limits of C.T.8316 and on the west by a straight line apparently at right angles to those north and south boundaries. Of course it did not purport to be more than a

Mukta Ben v. Suva Council (P.C.) [1980]

sketch plan. It was not the result of a detailed survey, and the high   A
water mark line was apparently taken for its purpose from the deposited
plan of C.T.8316, since when it would have varied by accretions to the
land. But a detailed survey of the then high water mark could suffice
to place the west boundary with exactitude so as to contain 20 acres of
C.T.8316 as added to by accretion.

It would appear that Sukhichand, then the registered proprietor of   B
C.T.8316, in late September 1967 in connection with survey activities conducted on behalf of the council on the subject land, erected a fence on what
he took to be the west boundary of the subject land and withdrew his
cattle to the west thereof. On October 16, 1967, the appellants were
registered as proprietors of that part (the greater part) of C.T.8316 that
they had agreed in 1964 to buy from Sukhichand, including of course the
subject land. Meanwhile surveyors on behalf of the council were making a   C
survey of the subject land. On October 25, 1967, Warren formally claimed
compensation on behalf of the appellants. On October 24, 1967, a
plan, the result of the above survey, was submitted to Warren for signature
by Naranji (attorney under power of the appellants), specifying both the
subject land and the balance of C.T.8316. This was with a view to subdivision and registration. Neither the sketch plan with the notice of
acquisition nor this survey plan indicated any access road either to the   D
subject land or to the balance land on the west. This was queried on
behalf of the appellants, and the solicitor for the council produced a
locality map which indicated in colour a proposed access road from King's
Road (to the north) to the subject land and also adjoining the balance
land so as to afford access thereto. On that understanding Naranji signed
the subdivision plan, which itself contained no indication of the access   E
road. It would not of course do so, since the intended road would be
outside C.T.8316 on crown and native land. In fact that plan has not
been used by the council. On October 26, 1967, Warren returned the
plan signed and also the locality map, enclosed with a letter saying that it
was signed:

> " on the understanding that it is the [council's] intention to establish
> access from King's Road to the 20 acre area by means of a public   F
> road as shown in red on the map returned herewith, portion of which
> will run along and touch the northern boundary of our clients' land
> for a distance of about 18 chains."

That letter was not answered. The bona fides of the council is not in
issue, so that it is to be assumed that at that time the council did intend
to procure that public road access to the balance land. But not long   G
afterwards the council changed its mind, for what reason does not appear,
a fact which has led to this extensive litigation in an attempt to challenge
the validity of the compulsory acquisition under a number of heads. In
February 1968 a surveyor (Knuckey) who pegged out the centre line of
the road from the north to the subject land was expressly instructed that
it was nowhere to abut on the balance land, and as later constructed it   H
does not. When formerly there were negotiations for the acquisition
by the council of land at the eastern end the suggestion had been that
road access to the eastern end should be from a bridge over Naivula
Creek through the western land, such road to be constructed and maintained by the council. That was quite different from the proposal in
October 1967.

According to Warren's evidence, Naranji was told by Carter Rees &

A   Associates (who were conducting all the survey work for the council) in May 1968 that the road to the subject land would not abut anywhere on the balance land and would not give access thereto. The idea then (internal to Naranji and Warren) was that in that case the compensation claim should be increased from £400 to £600 per acre. Warren agreed in evidence that probably he told McFarlane (solicitor to the council) in September 1968 that if no road access to the balance land were provided
B   the compensation claim would be increased.

Their Lordships do not pause to add to the strictures made below on the council's behaviour in relation to its unexplained failure to provide public road access to the balance land in accordance with the locality map, or some other such access. A feeling of some unease is perhaps reflected in the fact that the council has since undertaken to pay to the
C   appellants in that connection a sum of $11,000, albeit subject to deduction of such costs of this litigation as are ordered to be paid by the appellants to the council.

Their Lordships turn now to the various and varied grounds upon which the appellants seek to set aside as invalid the compulsory acquisition, with the result (if they succeed) that the council has from the outset trespassed upon the appellants' land and erected and operated upon it the
D   power station and auxiliary building, which no doubt would much enhance any claim for compensation if the council sought to start again.

(1) *The notice of acquisition lacked sufficient definition of the subject land*

Their Lordships do not accept that contention. It is no doubt true
E   that there was power in the council to conduct a full survey of the 20-acre area to be acquired before operating the acquisition machinery, based upon the then situation of the high water mark boundary of C.T.8316; but their Lordships do not consider that the words in parenthesis in the Schedule to the Crown Acquisition of Lands Ordinance forbid in the case of an area such as this a notice of acquisition based upon a sketched plan. The notice made it clear that the subject land was to be 20 acres
F   of C.T.8316 inward from high water mark, and that was capable of ascertainment. Evidence that the sketch plan, if treated not as a sketch plan but as a scaled plan, resulting from survey, contained more than 20 acres as the land to be acquired appears to their Lordships to be irrelevant. Nor are they persuaded that exactitude is required by the fact that a penalty may be incurred if there be resistance to or hindrance of the taking of possession of land of which notice of acquisition and taking has
G   been given: such an offence must be wilful.

(2) *There was no power in the council to acquire compulsorily land outside the town boundaries*

This contention depended upon the language of the Towns Ordinance. In this opinion reference is made to sections of the Towns Ordinance,
H   though at the relevant time, before a revision, identical provisions of an earlier Ordinance applied; hence reference in the documents to section 137 of the Local Government (Towns) Ordinance (c. 78) instead of to section 136 of the Towns Ordinance (c. 106). The argument was that section 132 in authorising a town council to construct and maintain public works necessary or beneficial to the town expressly says " whether within or without the boundaries of the town." Further, section 133 (1) authorises a town council to acquire by agreement, whether by way of purchase,

lease or exchange, any land for the purpose of any of their functions, "whether situate within or without the boundaries of the town." But, it was said, when you come to compulsory acquisition under section 136 there is no such reference to topography.

In their Lordships' opinion this contention is unsound. Section 136 has already been quoted, and in their Lordships' opinion it reads on to embrace all land which under the earlier provisions the council is authorised to acquire, but is unable to do so by agreement.

(3) The council failed to publish the notice of acquisition either in the Gazette or in a newspaper, pursuant to section 7 (4) of the Crown Acquisition of Lands Ordinance

The appellants contended that, notwithstanding that the notice was duly served upon them (and upon Sukhichand), this was a necessary requirement for the validity of the acquisition. In their Lordships' opinion this requirement of the legislation was not imperative in the sense that non-compliance stultified the process of compulsory acquisition; and having regard to the fact that notice of acquisition was duly given to the only persons interested in the land total non-compliance with the direction should not have that effect. In this respect their Lordships find themselves in accord with the views expressed in greater detail by O'Regan J.

(4) The council had in addition to the actual power station built on the subject land housing for employees engaged in it

It was suggested for the appellants that this was in excess of the authority for compulsory acquisition, and consequently either a circumstance vitiating that acquisition, or pro tanto a trespass. Their Lordships reject those contentions. In their Lordships' opinion the use of part of the subject land for such a purpose is obviously sensibly and reasonably incidental to the operation of a power station in that area.

(5) Purchase by agreement on reasonable terms

It was contended by the appellants that the authorisation for the compulsory acquisition was invalidated because in terms of section 136 of the Towns Ordinance it was not correct to say that the condition precedent—that the council was unable to purchase the subject land on reasonable terms—to such authorisation had been fulfilled. Evidence was called to support the view that the value per acre was greatly in excess of the sum per acre which the appellants were asking; therefore, it was said, it was established that the council could have purchased the subject land by agreement on reasonable terms, and section 136 could have no operation. This argument is based upon the submission that that requirement of the section is simply objective.

Their Lordships do not accept that submission. Here is a case in which there was a genuine difference of opinion in negotiation for purchase by agreement on the question of reasonable terms. The purely objective test would make the section virtually unworkable. In rejecting this submission their Lordships are content to accept the views of Gould V.P., which were never satisfactorily dealt with for the appellants. He said:

"Mr. Hughes's argument on behalf of the council was that the intention of the section was to make available the compulsory acquisition procedure in any case where the two parties—landowner and council—

A   were unable to agree on what was a reasonable price. Such dis-
agreements were of daily occurrence between would-be vendors and
purchasers. The objective construction urged by the appellants would
mean that if in the event of compulsory acquisition proceedings it were
decided that the compensation payable should be as much as or more
than the owner had asked for the land, the owner could have the whole
proceedings set aside. This would entail that a council would have to
B   predict whether the land owner's asking price would be held to be
reasonable. If the council considered it would, of course the price
could be accepted and section 136 becomes irrelevant. If the council
considered the asking price too high and was later shown to be
wrong the proceedings could be rendered nugatory: such an interpretation would stultify the legislation. The alternative construction,
that is, that the section applies if the parties are unable to agree upon
C   what are reasonable terms, would render it workable."

(6) *It was contended in that last connection that the Governor in Council
was misled by the council*

Their Lordships do not accept that contention. The council acted
D   bona fide in its views as to a reasonable price per acre for the subject
land. In the wisdom of hindsight it may have undervalued, as may
according to the evidence also the appellants. The Governor in Council
formed an opinion under section 136 on the point, and having formed an
opinion decided upon authorisation. Their Lordships see no ground for
treating the authority and the acquisition as a nullity under this head.

E   (7) *The failure to afford access to the balance land to the west*

In their Lordships' opinion this cannot be a ground for holding that the
authorisation of the Governor in Council, and consequently the compulsory
acquisition, was a nullity or is to be treated as such. The council at all
stages in the negotiations intended to provide such access, and so informed
the Governor's advisers. Assuming that that information was to be
F   regarded as extending also to access to the balance land after the switch
of the subject land from west to east in the application to the Governor there
is no ground (granted the bona fides of the council) for thinking that the
council did not then intend to provide access to the balance (western)
land or misled the Governor on that point. Whether the failure to
provide such access would affect the quantum of compensation, their
Lordships do not pause to consider; but they are clearly of opinion that
G   it cannot serve to deny the validity of the compulsory acquisition.

(8) *The appellants contended that in all the circumstances the requirements
of natural justice were not observed*

This, to be a valid point, must be such as to undermine the decision by
the Governor in Council to authorise the acquisition. But in what respect
H   can it be said that the Governor acted unfairly to the appellants? There
is no obligation under the legislation to give to them notice of the application for authority to acquire, or of the representations made by the council
in support of that application. Their Lordships fail to see how it could
have occurred to the Governor that he was acting unfairly. It was
argued that if the appellants had been informed of the representations that
were being made they might have made criticisms or counter-representa-
tions on questions such as reasonable terms and the extent of the land

required for the particular purpose. But nobody for the appellants gave A evidence that they would (or even might) have then taken such steps. Moreover they had been prepared for a much larger area than 20 acres to go; and finally it was plain that at that time they were content with (or resigned to) compulsory acquisition, the only matter with which they were concerned being the amount of compensation, a matter not to be dealt with by the Governor. Their Lordships reject this appeal to the principles of natural justice.   B

(9) *Twenty acres an excessive area for the purpose*

The next attack for the appellants on the validity of the compulsory acquisition was based upon the contention that 20 acres was greatly in excess of the area required for the establishment and operation of the power station. It was pointed out that even with inclusion of the employees' C housing and other ancillary buildings the area at present actually occupied is much less than the 20 acres to which the Governor on advice reduced the application for authority for 40 acres. Their Lordships recall once more that the council must be regarded as having formed a bona fide view of the acreage desirable, and it is obvious that for such a project a view may be formed of the need for future expansion, the nature of the terrain, D and matters such as the desirability of a surrounding buffer area in which other development might otherwise lead to complaints of nuisance. Their Lordships do not accept that this complaint can serve to invalidate the compulsory acquisition. It was held by Marsack J. that the approval of the Governor in Council should be set aside not in toto but to the extent that it covers a greater area than that required by the council for the specific purposes for which that approval was granted. He thought that this might E be to the extent of 15 acres, leaving the council with 5 acres. This might appear to be a reasonable solution but their Lordships do not consider it to lie within the powers of the court. An alteration in the area to be taken could only be made by the Governor in Council.

(10) *The final challenge by the appellants is based upon the provisions of* F *the Subdivision of Land Ordinance*

Their Lordships say at once that if and in so far as there may have been a failure to comply with the provisions of that legislation that cannot suffice to invalidate the compulsory acquisition of the subject land. It may be that the Ordinance does not apply to a case of compulsory acquisition. It may be that the council has done nothing that comes within the G definition of subdivision, or that the council is not the " applicant " within that Ordinance. It may be that someone, including the council, has incurred penalties under section 18 of that Ordinance. It may be that the council has to take further steps before it can be registered as proprietor of the subject land. Their Lordships do not consider it necessary, or desirable, in this case to decide such matters, nor therefore to rehearse the facts which raise the points, for they are of opinion that if all the H points hereunder were to be decided in favour of the contentions of the appellants it would still leave the appellants unable to assert, as they seek to do, the invalidity of the compulsory acquisition.

For the council, it was contended that, if the appellants were right on all (or any) of the points taken for them, they would be estopped by their actions (or inactions) from contending for the invalidity of the compulsory acquisition. The arguments on this point were interesting and perhaps

A   nicely balanced. Their Lordships have not found it necessary to rehearse all the facts relevant to that submission, and do not find it necessary to rule upon it.

Their Lordships will accordingly humbly advise Her Majesty that this appeal be dismissed with costs.

B   Solicitors: *Wray, Smith & Co.; A. L. Philips & Co.*

[Reported by MICHAEL HAWKINGS, ESQ., Barrister-at-Law]

C   [COURT OF APPEAL]

* LIFF v. PEASLEY AND ANOTHER

[1975 L. No. 3066]

1979   Oct. 19, 22, 23, 24;   Stephenson and Brandon L.JJ.
D   Nov. 14

Practice—Parties—Joinder—Joinder of defendant to action after claim against him statute-barred—Unconditional appearance to amended writ — Whether waiver of irregularity — Whether properly joined as party to action—R.S.C., Ord. 15, r. 6 (2) (a)
Limitation of Action — Personal injuries — Time limit, power to override — Passenger injured when two cars in collision —
E   *Passenger's action against one driver — Insurers repudiating liability — Second driver made party to action after claim against him statute-barred—Court's discretion to extend period — Whether insurance position to be taken into account — Limitation Act 1939 (2 & 3 Geo. 6, c. 21) (as amended by Limitation Act 1975 (c. 54), s. 1), ss. 2A, 2D*

On October 25, 1973, the plaintiff sustained injuries when a
F   motor car, in which he was a passenger and which was being driven by the second defendant, collided with a motor car being driven by the first defendant. Two independent witnesses made statements placing responsibility for the collision on the first defendant, who was subsequently convicted of careless driving. In August 1975, the plaintiff issued a writ against the first defendant for damages for personal injuries and loss arising out of the accident. The first defendant's insurers repudiated liability and informed the Motor Insurers Bureau
G   that they had done so. The bureau nominated another insurance company to act on its behalf in the matter and that company sought to bring the second defendant into the action so that, if a finding of negligence was made against him, the plaintiff could recover damages through the insurers indemnifying the second defendant. After the three year period of limitation under section 2A of the Limitation Act 1939 [1] had

H   _____

[1] Limitation Act 1939, as amended, s. 2A: "(1) This section applies to any action for damage for negligence, . . . where the damages claimed by the plaintiff for the negligence, . . . consist of or include damages in respect of personal injuries to the plaintiff. . . . (3) Subject to section 2D below, an action to which this section applies shall not be brought after the expiration of the period specified in subsections (4) and (5) below. (4) Except where subsection (5) applies, the said period is three years from—(a) the date on which, the cause of action accrued, . . ."
S. 2D: "(1) If it appears to the court that it would be equitable to allow an action to proceed having regard to the degree to which—(a) the provisions of section 2A or 2B of this Act prejudice the plaintiff or any person whom he represents, and

A
expired in 1976, the first defendant delivered his defence claiming that the collision was caused wholly or partly by the
negligence of the second defendant.

On the plaintiff's ex parte application made five years after
the accident, the master ordered that the second defendant
should be joined as a party to the action and he gave leave for
the plaintiff to amend the statement of claim and the first
defendant to serve an amended defence. Later, an order was
made giving the plaintiff leave to amend the writ to include the   B
second defendant. The second defendant's solicitors then
entered on his behalf an unconditional appearance to the writ
and served a defence which contained a plea that the action
was statute-barred. The second defendant then applied to have
the claim against him struck out as being statute-barred and
that he should be struck out as a defendant to the action on the
ground that he had been improperly joined within the meaning
of R.S.C., Ord. 15, r. 6 (2) (a) ² or on the ground of want of   C
prosecution. The judge made no order on the application to
have the claim struck out and dismissed the other applications.

On appeal by the second defendant : —

Held, allowing the appeal, that it was an established rule of
practice that the court would not permit a person to be added
as a defendant to an action at a time when he could rely on a
period of limitation as barring the plaintiff from bringing a
fresh action against him; that, although the entry of an un-   D
conditional appearance to the writ on behalf of the second
defendant would act as a waiver of a mere irregularity, it could
not waive an established rule of practice and, in any event, he
was a person who had been improperly made a party within
the meaning of R.S.C., Ord. 15, r. 6 (2) (a) or, if he had been
properly made a party because on the ex parte application
it was not known whether he would plead the Statute of
Limitations, he had ceased to be a proper party for the purposes   E
of that rule as soon as he had made clear his intention to rely
on that defence; and that, accordingly, he was entitled to an
order under rule 6 (2) (a) that he should cease to be a party
to the action (post, pp. 797c–e, 798a–f, 799b, 800f—801b).

Byron v. *Cooper* (1844) 11 Cl. & Fin. 556, H.L.(E.); *Mabro*
v. *Eagle Star and British Dominions Insurance Co. Ltd.* [1932]
1 K.B. 485, C.A.; *Davies* v. *Elsby Brothers Ltd.* [1961] 1
W.L.R. 170, C.A. and *Seabridge* v. *H. Cox & Sons (Plant*   F
Hire) Ltd. [1968] 2 Q.B. 46, C.A. applied.

Lucy v. *W. T. Henleys Telegraph Works Co. Ltd.* [1970]
1 Q.B. 393, C.A. and *Gawthrop* v. *Boulton* [1979] 1 W.L.R.
268 considered.

Per Stephenson L.J. The second defendant was properly
joined as a party because when the order was made it was not
known whether he would plead section 2 of the Limitation Act
1939 (post, p. 789h).

Held, further, that, although it was equitable to consider   G
the insurance position when determining whether the plaintiff
would be prejudiced if the time limit was not extended under
section 2D of the Limitation Act 1939, it had not been proved
on the affidavit evidence before the court that the plaintiff
would be prejudiced if he was not able to pursue his claim
against the second defendant and, therefore, the court had no
discretion under the section to disapply the three year period   H
of limitation fixed by section 2A of the Act (post, pp. 788h—
789c, e–g, 799a).

(b) any decision of the court under this subsection would prejudice the defendant
or any person whom he represents, the court may direct that those provisions shall
not apply to the action, or shall not apply to any specified cause of action to which
the action relates. . . . (3) In acting under this section the court shall have regard to
all the circumstances of the case . . ."

² R.S.C., Ord. 15, r. 6: see post, p. 790f–h.

A *Per curiam.* The reason for the rule of practice of not permitting a person to be added as a defendant to an action after the claim against him was statute-barred was either that the action against the added defendant related back to the date of the original writ so that he was barred from relying on the statute or because the action began against him at the date when he was added as a party and so he could rely on the statute as barring the plaintiff's claim. The latter reason for
B the rule was to be preferred (post, pp. 791C–D, 795H—796A, 799C–E, 804D).

Decision of T. P. Russell Q.C. sitting as a deputy judge of the Queen's Bench Division reversed.

The following cases are referred to in the judgments:

Ashley v. *Taylor* (1878) 10 Ch.D. 768.
C *Braniff* v. *Holland & Hannen and Cubitts (Southern) Ltd.* [1969] 1 W.L.R. 1533; [1969] 3 All E.R. 959, C.A.
Byron v. *Cooper* (1844) 11 Cl. & Fin. 556, H.L.(E.).
Challinor v. *Roder* (1885) 1 T.L.R. 527.
Davies v. *Elsby Brothers Ltd.* [1961] 1 W.L.R. 170; [1961] 1 All E.R. 672, C.A.
Firman v. *Ellis* [1978] Q.B. 886; [1978] 3 W.L.R. 1; [1978] 2 All E.R. 851, C.A.
D *Gawthrop* v. *Boulton* [1979] 1 W.L.R. 268; [1978] 2 All E.R. 615.
Hattam v. *National Coal Board*, The Times, October 28, 1978.
Lucy v. *W. T. Henleys Telegraph Works Co. Ltd.* [1970] 1 Q.B. 393; [1969] 3 W.L.R. 588; [1969] 3 All E.R. 456, C.A.
Mabro v. *Eagle Star and British Dominions Insurance Co. Ltd.* [1932] 1 K.B. 485, C.A.
Marubeni Corporation v. *Pearlstone Shipping Corporation (The Puerto*
E *Acevedo)* [1978] 1 Lloyd's Rep. 38, C.A.
Mitchell v. *Harris Engineering Co. Ltd.* [1967] 2 Q.B. 703; [1967] 3 W.L.R. 447; [1967] 2 All E.R. 682, C.A.
Plowden v. *Thorpe* (1840) 7 Cl. & Fin. 137, H.L.(E.)
Riches v. *Director of Public Prosecutions* [1973] 1 W.L.R. 1019; [1973] 2 All E.R. 935, C.A.
Seabridge v. *H. Cox & Sons (Plant Hire) Ltd.* [1968] 2 Q.B. 46; [1968]
F 2 W.L.R. 629; [1968] 1 All E.R. 570, C.A.
Sneade v. *Wotherton Barytes and Lead Mining Co.* [1904] 1 K.B. 295, C.A.
Sterman v. *E. W. & W. J. Moore* [1970] 1 Q.B. 596; [1970] 2 W.L.R. 386; [1970] 1 All E.R. 581, C.A.
Walkley v. *Precision Forgings Ltd.* [1979] 1 W.L.R. 606; [1979] 2 All E.R. 548, H.L.(E.).
G *Weldon* v. *Neal* (1887) 19 Q.B.D. 394, C.A.

The following additional cases were cited in argument:

Bower v. *Cooper* (1843) 2 Hare 408.
Browes v. *Jones & Middleton* (1979) 123 Sol.J. 489.
Steward v. *North Metropolitan Tramways Co.* (1886) 16 Q.B.D. 556, C.A.
Vallance v. *Birmingham and Midland Land and Investment Corporation*
H (1876) 2 Ch.D. 369.

INTERLOCUTORY APPEAL from T. P. Russell Q.C., sitting as a deputy judge of the Queen's Bench Division.

The plaintiff, Raymond Jack Liff, was injured on October 25, 1973, when the Ford Cortina motor car in which he was a passenger and which was being driven by the second defendant, Timothy John Spinks, was in collision with a Triumph 2000 being driven by the first defendant, Ian

Liff v. Peasley (C.A.) [1980]

Stanley Peasley. The accident occurred at the junction of Hampton Road
and Sixth Cross Road, Twickenham, Middlesex. By a writ dated August
14, 1975, the plaintiff brought an action against the first defendant only for
damages for personal injuries and consequential loss caused by his negligent
driving. By his statement of claim delivered on June 27, 1977, the plaintiff
alleged, inter alia, that the accident had been caused by the first defendant's
negligence; that the first defendant had been convicted of careless driving
on May 24, 1974, on a summons arising out of the accident; and that the
plaintiff had suffered injury, loss and damage. By his defence of September
22, 1977, the defendant denied negligence and contended that the collision
was caused wholly or partly by the negligence of the second defendant.

On October 5, 1978, Master Warren ordered that the second defendant
be joined in the action and gave the plaintiff leave to amend the statement
of claim and the first defendant leave to serve an amended defence. By the
amended statement of claim served on October 17, 1978, the plaintiff
claimed that the collision was caused by the negligence of the first defendant
or, alternatively, by the negligence of the second defendant. On January
22, 1979, Master Creightmore gave leave for the writ to be amended and
a copy was sent to the second defendant's solicitors, who then entered an
unconditional appearance on his behalf. By his defence of March 2, 1979,
the second defendant denied negligence, alleged that the collision was
caused by the first defendant's negligence and, relying on section 2 of the
Limitation Act 1939, as amended, contended that the plaintiff's cause of
action was statute-barred.

By his amended summons of July 29, 1979, the second defendant sought
an order that (1) the plaintiff's claim against the second defendant be struck
out as being statute-barred, notwithstanding section 2 of the Act of 1939,
as amended; (2) alternatively, that the second defendant should be struck
out of the action, having been improperly joined; or (3) alternatively, that
the action should be struck out for want of prosecution. The deputy judge
made no order under item (1) of the amended summons, dismissed items
(2) and (3) and granted leave to appeal.

By his notice of appeal, the second defendant appealed against the
judge's decision, seeking an order that (1) the provisions of section 2A of
the Limitation Act 1939, as amended, were applicable to the plaintiff's
action against the second defendant and that the claim was statute-barred;
(2) that, under R.S.C., Ord. 15, r. 6, the second defendant had improperly
been made a party to the proceedings in that he was joined after the expiry
of the limitation period and that he should cease to be a party; and (3)
that the action against the second defendant should be dismissed for want
of prosecution.

The facts are stated in the judgment of Stephenson L.J.

John Cherry for the second defendant.
Mark Tennant for the plaintiff.
Jonathan Woods for the first defendant.

Cur. adv. vult.

November 14, 1979. The following judgments were read.

STEPHENSON L.J. This is an appeal by leave of Mr. T. P. Russell Q.C.,
sitting as a deputy judge of the High Court in the Queen's Bench Division
from his refusal on July 26, 1979, to grant three applications by Mr.
Timothy John Spinks, the appellant.

A   Mr. Spinks has been joined as a defendant to an action brought against the first defendant, Mr. Peasley, by the plaintiff, Mr. Liff, by writ issued on August 14, 1975. The plaintiff was injured in a cross-roads collision between a Ford Cortina motor car driven by Mr. Spinks, in which he was a passenger, and a Triumph motor car driven by the first defendant on October 25, 1973. By summons dated March 12, 1979, Mr. Spinks asked the judge in chambers to order: " 1. That notwithstanding section 2 of the Limitation Act 1939 as amended, the plaintiff's claim against the second defendant be struck out as being statute-barred." By amendment at the hearing of the summons on July 26, 1979, he asked the deputy judge to order two other things:

"2. That further or in the alternative that the second defendant be struck out of the action having been improperly joined. 3. Further or in the alternative the action against the second defendant be dismissed for want of prosecution."

The deputy judge made no order on the application under item 1, and dismissed the applications under items 2 and 3.

By his notice of appeal Mr. Spinks asks this court for the same three things, two in slightly different form:

"1. For an order that the provisions of section 2A of the Limitation Act 1939 as amended shall apply to the plaintiff's cause of action against the second defendant and that the plaintiff's claim against the second defendant is statute-barred. 2. Further or in the alternative for an order under R.S.C., Ord. 15, r. 6 that the second defendant was improperly made a party to the proceedings in that he was joined after the expiry of the limitation period and that the second defendant cease to be a party to the proceedings. 3. Further or in the alternative for an order that the action against the second defendant be dismissed for want of prosecution."

In this court Mr. Cherry has submitted that Mr. Spinks was improperly joined as a party, because he was joined too late according to the Rules of the Supreme Court and to the practice established by binding authority. His submissions and those of counsel for the plaintiff and the first defendant require consideration of the peculiar history of the plaintiff's action, of the rules of court and of a number of decided cases.

First the history. The accident which injured the plaintiff took place on October 25, 1973. The Cortina Mr. Spinks was driving was apparently owned by his brother and insured with the Norwich Union (" the Norwich "). They acted promptly and on November 18, 1973, obtained a statement from an independent eye-witness named Kennard blaming the first defendant only. Traffic lights were not working at the time of the accident, but Mr. Spinks stopped and tried to cross carefully while the first defendant tried to cross much too fast without stopping. On December 8, 1973, the police obtained a statement from another independent eye-witness named Stevens which was equally favourable to Mr. Spinks.

On May 28, 1974, the first defendant was convicted of careless driving. On September 3, 1974, his insurers, Zurich Insurance (" the Zurich ") notified the Norwich of the plaintiff's claim against their insured. On August 1, 1975, the plaintiff issued his writ against the first defendant alone, and on September 1, 1975, the Norwich heard again from the Zurich. After a further year's silence the Norwich wrote again to the Zurich on October 2, 1976, and heard from the Zurich on December 9, 1976, that

Stephenson L.J.   **Liff v. Peasley (C.A.)**   [1980]

the Zurich was not involved.   By that time the three years' primary period   A
of limitation had expired on October 2, 1976.   The Zurich had in fact
repudiated liability and brought the matter to the attention of the Motor
Insurers Bureau (" the M.I.B."), who nominated the Sun Alliance (" the
Sun ") as insurer concerned for the first defendant.

This action appears to have been taken at the end of 1975 and the
beginning of 1976, but the Zurich did not advise the first defendant's
solicitors until June 1977 and the Sun did not approach the Norwich until   B
January 1978.   Meanwhile on June 27, 1977, the plaintiff delivered his
statement of claim against the first defendant, and on September 22, 1977,
the first defendant delivered his defence claiming that the collision was
caused wholly or partly by the negligence of Mr. Spinks.

On January 23, 1978, 4½ years after the accident, the Sun wrote to the
Norwich as follows: C

" Your insured T. J. Spinks.   R. J. Liff v. I. S. Peasley.   Motor
accident October 25, 1973.   It would appear from our papers that
this is the first time we have approached you in the above connection.
You will be familiar with the circumstances of the accident and will
therefore have knowledge of how the various parties are involved.
Our interest arises on behalf of the Motor Insurers Bureau who are   D
undertaking Mr. Peasley's defence following the decision of his insurers
not to indemnify.   An action has been started by Mr. R. J. Liff who
was a passenger in your insured's Ford Cortina MVK 201E against
Mr. Peasley for the injuries he received and we have had a defence
entered.   You will be aware, we trust, that the M.I.B. agreement
relieves them of any responsibility to satisfy any judgment if there is
any other known party upon whom a minimum of 1 per cent. con-   E
tributory negligence can be proven.   It will be the duty of that person's
insurers to satisfy any judgment.   Your insured is not yet named in
the proceedings but our solicitors consider this step should be taken
and notwithstanding the possibility that the limitation defence will be
raised on his behalf it is felt that the court would, in its discretion,
allow the action to proceed against him.   In this event we are satisfied   F
the required degree of negligence could be held to attach.   We are
therefore providing you with the opportunity to consider your position
and to ask whether or not you wish to take over the handling of the
claim that has been brought by Mr. Liff.   May we have your decision
as quickly as possible as our solicitors have asked for our further
instructions."
                                                                             G
It is clear from this letter that it was at the instance of the M.I.B. that
the plaintiff brought Mr. Spinks into his action.   At the same time the Sun
suggested to the plaintiff's solicitors that they should join Mr. Spinks as a
defendant.

On October 5, 1978, Master Warren made the order: it is headed:

" Liff—plaintiff, Peasley—first defendant and Spinks—second defen-   H
dant.   Upon hearing the solicitors for the parties it is ordered that
Timothy John Spinks be joined as second defendant in this action and
that the plaintiff has leave to amend the statement of claim as shown
in the documents initialled by the master and to re-serve the amended
statement within 14 days with leave to the defendant to serve an
amended defence (if so advised) in 14 days thereafter and the costs
incurred and thrown away by the amendments be costs in the cause."

A   That order calls for the following comments: (1) The " solicitors for the parties " were the solicitors for the plaintiff and first defendant, although Mr. Spinks was wrongly entitled a party as second defendant. For as far as he was concerned, the application was ex parte and he was not represented at its hearing. (2) The order gives the plaintiff leave to amend the statement of claim, but not the writ, and gives the defendant (presumably the first defendant) leave to serve an amended defence, but gives no B directions as to service on the newly joined second defendant.

  On October 13, 1978, the plaintiff's solicitors informed Mr. Spinks' brother that Mr. Spinks had been joined as a second defendant and asked him to pass their letter to his insurers. So the Norwich were informed and instructed solicitors, who wrote to the plaintiff's solicitors on December 11, 1978:

C   " With reference to our telephone call on the 8th instant, we confirm that on the instructions of his motor insurers, the Norwich Union, we act for the second defendant. Before we enter an appearance we should be grateful if you would let us have a copy of the amended writ which presumably you served but which must have gone astray. We have a copy of the amended statement of claim and of the first defendant's defence; should there be any other pleadings, we should D   welcome copies of them as well. No doubt you will extend our time for appearing pending receipt of the above documents."

  A reminder on December 19, 1978, apparently stirred the plaintiff's solicitors into appreciating that, perhaps in consequence of the form of Master Warren's order, the writ had not been amended as required by R.S.C., Ord. 15, r. 8 (1). So on January 22, 1979, they got Master Creightmore E to give leave to amend the writ and sent Mr. Spinks' solicitors a copy on January 25. On January 30, Mr. Spinks' solicitors wrote to the plaintiff's solicitors:

      " We acknowledge receipt of your letter of the 25th instant. We enclose our memorandum of appearance on behalf of the second defendant on your assurance that the writ has been served. Unfor- F   tunately we have been unable so far to trace the whereabouts of Mr. Spinks and any information which your client or you can give us in that respect would be appreciated."

  Then there is a postscript which says:

      " The endorsement as to service on your writ specifies that service was on November 30 but the amendment is said to have been made on G   January 22. Which is wrong please? We do not have a copy of the amending order. May we have one? "

  The appearance they entered was unhappily unconditional. The reply of February 1 from the plaintiff's solicitors explained how the writ had not been amended but not how the endorsement of service antedated the H leave to amend, and asked Mr. Spinks' solicitors to accept service of the statement of claim. On February 2, Mr. Spinks' solicitors wrote to the plaintiff's solicitors:

      " Thank you for your letter of February 1. A copy of the amending order was not, however, enclosed. In the particular circumstances of this case, whilst we will continue our preparations, we shall need an order amending the writ, before we can accept service of the statement of claim. Thereafter, we would like a fixed date. We suggest

that you should have the date vacated, and at the same time apply to A
the clerk of the lists for a new fixture. The sooner this is done the
earlier the fixture is likely to be. Please keep us closely informed
about this."

It was not until February 6, 1979, that they wrote:

" We have now seen counsel on this matter. Counsel advises that as
and when our client is properly joined in the action, we should make B
an early application to strike out your client's claim against our client,
by reason of delay. This will be a summons for the judge in chambers,
supported by affidavit. We shall therefore be proceeding accordingly."

On March 2, in response to a further letter they wrote:

" We accept service of the amended statement of claim, and enclose
defence, service of which please accept by post and acknowledge. We
have served the defence, as counsel settled the same a little while ago,
whilst we were waiting to hear from you, so that the pleadings can be
in proper order. We are however forthwith applying to the judge in
chambers to strike out the plaintiff's claim, as we told you we would
in our letter of February 6. The summons and supporting affidavit D
will be served in the course of the next few posts."

On March 5, they served Mr. Spinks' defence, which ended with a plea
that the plaintiff's cause of action was statute-barred by section 2 of the
Limitation Act 1939.

I take first the last point which we have been asked to consider, not
because it comes first in logic or in argument but because I find it the E
easiest to decide. This is the point under section 2D of the Limitation
Act 1939 introduced into that Act by section 1 of the Limitation Act 1975:
would it be equitable to allow the plaintiff's action to proceed against
Mr. Spinks having regard to the provisions of section 2D and to prevent
Mr. Spinks from relying on the expiry of the primary limitation period of
three years provided by section 2A if it is otherwise available to him as a F
defence to this action? See the speech of Lord Diplock in *Walkley* v.
Precision Forgings Ltd. [1979] 1 W.L.R. 606, 616. We have heard argument on a subsidiary point whether this question should be decided on a
summons to strike out the claim against the added defendant, or at the
trial, or after a separate action has been directed to be brought, and we
have been referred to the views expressed in *Firman* v. *Ellis* [1978] Q.B.
886, 909E, 913D, 916G: in *Walkley's* case [1979] 1 W.L.R. 606, especially G
per Lord Wilberforce at p. 610A and in *Hattam* v. *National Coal Board,*
The Times, October 28, 1978.

In the course of what turned out to be a long hearing we were supplied
with fresh evidence to enable us to decide whether it was equitable to
override the three years' time limit and " disapply " the provisions of
section 2A. I have come to the conclusion that, if Mr. Spinks can rely H
on the primary limitation period, the plaintiff ought not to be allowed to
override it. If in refusing to make any order on paragraph 1 of the
summons the judge exercised his discretion to grant to the plaintiff a discretionary limitation period on the material and submissions before him,
on the material before us I would refuse to grant the plaintiff that relief.

I can state my reasons shortly. I am first not satisfied that the provisions of section 2A have prejudiced the plaintiff to any degree, so the

A   condition required by section 2D (1) (*a*) for exercising the discretion is not fulfilled: compare *Walkley* v. *Precision Forging Ltd.* [1979] 1 W.L.R. 606. The plaintiff has a cast-iron case against the first defendant. His claim may turn out to be beyond the first defendant's means to satisfy. We have affidavit evidence that he has only limited resources in capital and income, but we have no evidence to suggest that the M.I.B. will not satisfy any judgment against the first defendant. We have evidence in a statement made

B to the police by Mr. Spinks himself and in statements from other witnesses of matters which might prove some contributory negligence on Mr. Spinks' part. Hence the M.I.B.'s request to the plaintiff to join him in his action. But we have seen the M.I.B. agreement of November 22, 1972, which does not " relieve them of any responsibility to satisfy any judgment if there is any other known party upon whom a minimum of 1 per cent. contributory

C negligence can be proved," as stated in the Sun's letter dated January 23, 1978, which I have read. This appears to be a misleading reference to clause 5 " Conditions Precedent to Liability " and the provision:

> " (1) M.I.B. shall not incur any liability under clause 2 of this agreement unless . . . (c) *if so required by M.I.B.* and subject to full indemnity from M.I.B. as to costs the person bringing the proceedings
D has taken all reasonable steps to obtain judgment against all the persons liable in respect of the injury or death of the third party, and, in the event of such a person being a servant or agent, against his principal."

What the plaintiff or his legal advisers did or did not do *before* they were first required by the M.I.B. to do anything is not a ground for relying on

E this condition; and Mr. Woods, for the first defendant, and instructed on behalf of the Sun and the M.I.B., did not suggest any failure to take all reasonable steps to obtain judgment against Mr. Spinks *after* being so required.

    Mr. Woods submitted that in " having regard to all the circumstances of the case," as required by section 2D (3), we should disregard the insurance position, or if we had regard to it we should disregard the

F presence of the M.I.B. I would consider it unrealistic and inequitable to disregard the insurance position or the important part of it occupied by the M.I.B. Ormrod and Geoffrey Lane L.JJ. both considered the insurance position in *Firman* v. *Ellis* [1978] Q.B. 886, 912F, 916B. I would do the same, not least in an appeal which would never have come before the court but for the M.I.B. I make no criticism of their action in initiating

G the joinder of Mr. Spinks, but I regard it as an important circumstance which tells against granting the plaintiff a discretionary limitation period.

    On the view I take of the outcome of the plaintiff's claim against the first defendant and the M.I.B.'s liability to satisfy it, I need not consider any prejudice to Mr. Spinks under section 2D (1) (*b*) or any other matters under section 2D (3).

    I can go back to consider the question whether Mr. Spinks was

H properly or improperly joined. I have no doubt that he was properly joined by Master Warren's order of March 2, 1978. Whatever the defects in the form of that order, it was properly made, because when made it was not known whether Mr. Spinks would plead section 2 of the Act of 1939, and it was properly made ex parte: see for example *Marubeni Corporation* v. *Pearlstone Shipping Corporation (The Puerto Acevedo)* [1978] 1 Lloyd's Rep. 38 and *Ashley* v. *Taylor* (1878) 10 Ch.D. 768.

    But when Mr. Spinks' solicitors were notified through his brother

and his insurers of the joinder they did not enter a conditional appearance A
—or no appearance—and apply under R.S.C., Ord. 12, r. 8 to set aside
or discharge Master Warren's order.   That rule provides:

"(1) A defendant to an action may at any time before entering an
appearance therein, or, if he has entered a conditional appearance,
within 14 days after entering the appearance, apply to the court for
an order setting aside the writ or service of the writ, or notice of B
the writ on him, or declaring that the writ or notice has not been
duly served on him or discharging any order giving leave to serve
the writ or notice on him out of the jurisdiction.   (2) An application
under this rule must be made (*a*) in an Admiralty action in rem, by
motion; (*b*) in any other action in the Queen's Bench Division, by
summons; (*c*) in any other action, by summons or motion."
                                                                          C
Instead, they entered an unconditional appearance and proceeded to serve
a defence before intimating their intention to take out a summons to
strike out the claim against them.   The effect of entering an unconditional
appearance is stated in the notes to the R.S.C., Ord. 12, r. 1 in *The
Supreme Court Practice* (1979).   Note 12/1/3 reads:

"Where a defendant enters an ordinary appearance, without any
condition or protest reserving his right to object to the irregularity D
of the writ or service, or the jurisdiction of the court, he is debarred
from raising an objection afterwards.   The effect therefore, of
ordinary or unconditional appearance is a waiver of irregularity, if
any, as well as submission to the jurisdiction of the court."

Then note 12/1/4 reads:
                                                                          E
"On the other hand, the effect of an unconditional appearance is
not a waiver of the defendant's right to dispute the plaintiff's claim,
though it is sometimes a waiver of the right to raise a defence
against the validity of the action."

It is submitted by Mr. Woods on behalf of the first defendant and by
Mr. Tennant on behalf of the plaintiff that by their action Mr. Spinks'
solicitors have waived his objection to his joinder, have lost his right F
to challenge it and cannot now apply under Ord. 15, r. 6 to have the
plaintiff's claim against him struck out.   The judge was therefore right
to dismiss the second application.   Ord. 15, r. 6 provides:

"(1) No cause or matter shall be defeated by reason of the misjoinder
or nonjoinder of any party; and the court may in any cause or
matter determine the issues or questions in dispute so far as they G
affect the rights and interests of the persons who are parties to the
cause or matter.   (2) At any stage of the proceedings in any cause
or matter the court may on such terms as it thinks just and either
of its own motion or on application—(*a*) order any person who
has been improperly or unnecessarily made a party or who has for
any reason ceased to be a proper or necessary party, to cease to be a
party; . . . (3) An application by any person for an order under H
paragraph (2) adding him as a party must, except with the leave
of the court, be supported by an affidavit showing his interest in the
matters in dispute in the cause or matter, or, as the case may be,
the question or issue to be determined as between him and any party
to the cause or matter."

On the wording of this rule we are asked on the one hand to say

A   by a restrictive interpretation and application of it that Mr. Spinks is not improperly or unnecessarily made a party to the plaintiff's action. On the other hand Mr. Cherry for Mr. Spinks asks us to hold that Mr. Spinks is improperly or unnecessarily made a party or, on the suggestion of Brandon L.J., has ceased to be a party properly or necessarily joined. Mr. Cherry concedes that there is no other rule under which he can now get Mr. Spinks out of the plaintiff's action but asks us to give the

B   rule a sensible or even generous construction. So we have to decide whether Mr. Spinks can now be said to be improperly before the court as defendant, and to decide that question we have to examine the practice relating to defendants in Mr. Spinks' situation and the reasons for the practice.

There is no doubt about the practice long established before the

C   Limitation Act 1975. It is not to permit a person to be made a defendant in an existing action at a time when he could have relied on a statute of limitation as barring the plaintiff from bringing a fresh action against him. The reason for this practice—or rather the way in which this practice is justified or the legal basis on which it is rested—is, curiously, more doubtful. There appear to be two alternative bases. (1) The action against the added defendant relates back to the date of the original writ,

D   the plaintiff is deemed to have begun his action against the defendant when he began it against the original defendant, and so the defendant is deprived of his right to rely on the statute of limitation. (2) The action against the added defendant is begun at the date of the amendment joining him in the action, and so he can rely on the statute as barring the plaintiff from suing him. In most cases it will not matter which

E   of the two possible dates is regarded as the date of the commencement of the action brought against the added defendant. If he applies to set aside the order joining him as co-defendant, he will succeed, either because he would be deprived of his right to rely on the statute if the earlier date were preferred or because he would able to rely on the statute and defeat the plaintiff's claim if the later date were preferred. But in this case the added defendant has elected to plead the statute in

F   answer to the plaintiff's claim before challenging the plaintiff's right to make him a defendant. Can be at that later stage allege that his joinder, though properly made in the first instance, is improper if, and only if, he can successfully rely on the statute because he was not sued until the later date, so that it would be pointless and unnecessary that he should be, or remain, a defendant? But if he cannot rely on the statute

G   because he is deemed to have been sued from the earlier date, how can he then deny that he is, and remains, a proper and necessary party to the action?

There is a formidable line of authority which appears to rest the practice on relating the introduction of a new defendant, or a new plaintiff, or a new cause of action, into an existing action back to the date when that action first began. And that amendments relate back

H   to the date of the claim they amend is a principle not confined to statutes of limitation: *Sneade* v. *Wotherton Barytes and Lead Mining Co.* [1904] 1 K.B. 295, 297 *per* Lord Collins M.R.

There are, however, at least three decisions, one at first instance, one in this court and one in the House of Lords, which decide or seem to decide that an action is not brought against a new defendant (whatever may be the date for a new plaintiff or a new cause of action) until he

is brought into the action by amendment; and the later date derives A
support from the wording of some rules and from some judgments in
this court.

It was by 1887 the settled rule of practice that amendments were not
admissible when they prejudiced the rights of the opposite party as
existing on the date of such amendments. So said Lord Esher M.R.
in *Weldon* v. *Neal* (1887) 19 Q.B.D. 394, where this court, consisting of B
Lord Esher M.R. and Lindley and Lopes L.JJ., affirmed a decision of the
Divisional Court striking out paragraphs adding to a statement of claim
fresh causes of action because the amendments would deprive the defendant of the benefit of the Statute of Limitations.

In *Mabro* v. *Eagle Star and British Dominions Insurance Co. Ltd.*
[1932] 1 K.B. 485, this court upheld a refusal to join a plaintiff on the
same ground. Scrutton L.J. restated that practice and that basis of it C
at p. 487:

> " In my experience the court has always refused to allow a party
> or a cause of action to be added where, if it were allowed, the
> defence of the Statute of Limitations would be defeated. The court
> has never treated it as just to deprive a defendant of a legal defence."

And Greer L.J., at p. 489, made it clear that D

> " the objection to joining [the new plaintiff] was that if he were
> joined and treated as a plaintiff from the time the writ was issued the
> defendants would be deprived of the benefit of the Statute of
> Limitations."

The decision concerned a new plaintiff, but not only did Scrutton L.J. E
state the rule as covering any new party or cause of action but he
expressly disapproved the decision in *Challinor* v. *Roder* (1885) 1 T.L.R.
527 that a new defendant could be joined after the statute had run and
approved the opinion of Grove J. that he could not be so joined and
deprived of the benefit of the statute.

In *Davies* v. *Elsby Brothers Ltd.* [1961] 1 W.L.R. 170, this court F
followed the principle of *Mabro's* case [1932] 1 K.B. 485 and applied it to
the substitution of a defendant, Pearce L.J. in a rather obscure passage, at
p. 173, considering the purpose of the addition or substitution of a new
defendant to be to deprive him of the benefit of the statute.

This " long line of authority " was referred to by Lord Denning M.R.
and by Russell L.J. in *Mitchell* v. *Harris Engineering Co. Ltd.* [1967]
2 Q.B. 703, 717, 721, with comments which suggest it must be considered G
in the light of the rules of court, to which I shall return.

Finally, *Mabro's* case [1932] 1 K.B. 485, the reasoning which appears
to underlie it and the principle enunciated in it were approved and
applied to dismiss applications to join new defendants by Mackenna J.
and a majority of this court after a consideration of all the relevant
rules in *Lucy* v. *W. T. Henleys Telegraph Works Co. Ltd.* [1970] 1 Q.B. H
393, 399, 405, 411–412. Megaw L.J., with whose judgment Edmund
Davies L.J. agreed, said, at p. 411:

> " I am unaware of any case in which leave to amend a writ has
> been given in such circumstances; namely where the joinder of a
> new defendant would be calculated to defeat a right as to limitation
> which he would have had if an action were to be brought by the
> plaintiff against him alone. As I understand it, *Mabro's* case [1932]

A   1 K.B. 485 is authority for the proposition that it cannot be done.
     That case was concerned with an application to amend the writ
     so as to join a plaintiff. It was held that leave would not be granted
     where the effect would be to prevent the defendant from relying
     on the Statute of Limitations. The same principle applies in relation
     to the joinder of a defendant. Where, as here, a direct action
     against a proposed defendant can be defeated by a plea of limitation,
B   the plaintiff cannot escape that consequence by seeking to join the
     proposed defendant as a party in pre-existing proceedings."

And then, at p. 412: " . . . an amendment to add a completely new and
different defendant is not permissible where a relevant period of limitation
affecting the proposed defendant has expired."

C   In *Marubeni Corporation* v. *Pearlstone Shipping Corporation* (*The
     Puerto Acevedo*) [1978] 1 Lloyd's Rep. 38, Lord Denning M.R.
     reiterated his dissenting view in *Lucy's* case [1970] 1 Q.B. 393, 404—and
     in other cases: see for example *Sterman* v. *E. W. & W. J. Moore* [1970]
     1 Q.B. 596, 604—that the practice had changed since *Mabro's* case
     [1932] 1 K.B. 485 was decided, and all three members of this court gave
     leave to a plaintiff to join a defendant ex parte, Bridge L.J. expressly
D   preserving the new defendant's right to apply to set the joinder aside.

     In *Gawthrop* v. *Boulton* [1979] 1 W.L.R. 268, Walton J. felt able
to hold—and I read from the headnote, at p. 269:

     " (2) That when leave to join an additional defendant to an existing
     action was given, the joinder took effect as from the date when
     the order for joinder was stamped in the Central Office and had no
E   retrospective effect back to the date of issue of the writ; and that
     the joinder of K as a defendant would not therefore prejudice any
     defence which K might have under the Limitation Act 1939; . . . "

He, accordingly, added K as a defendant. In an interesting judgment he
based his decision on principle and a decision of this court in *Seabridge*
v. *H. Cox & Sons* (*Plant Hire*) *Ltd.* [1968] 2 Q.B. 46. He considered
F   that a later decision of this court, in *Braniff* v. *Holland & Hannen and
     Cubitts* (*Southern*) *Ltd.* [1969] 1 W.L.R. 1533, left open the question
     whether the Statute of Limitations ceased to run against an additional
     defendant from the date of the issue of the writ or from the date when
     he is added as a party, and he distinguished *Mabro* v. *Eagle Star and
     British Dominions Insurance Co. Ltd.* [1932] 1 K.B. 485 and *Lucy* v.
G   *W. T. Henleys Telegraph Works Co. Ltd.* [1970] 1 Q.B. 393.

     In *Seabridge's* case [1968] 2 Q.B. 46 this court held:

     " allowing the appeal, that, on the construction of the new rule 8 (4)
     of Ord. 15, a writ amended in the prescribed manner by being taken
     to the central office, filed and stamped, took effect against the added
     defendant at the moment when it was stamped at the central office;
H   that under Ord. 15, r. 8 (2) once the writ was amended the rules
     as to service applied as against the added defendant as they did to
     an original defendant on the issue of a writ, so that a plaintiff had
     12 months from the date when the amendment was made within
     which to serve the added defendant; and that, accordingly, since
     the amendment had been made within three years of the accident,
     the service was regular and the writs were not statute-barred."

By R.S.C., Ord. 15, r. 8:

> " (1) Where an order is made under rule 6 the writ by which the action in question was begun must be amended accordingly and must be endorsed with (a) a reference to the order in pursuance of which the amendment is made, and (b) the date on which the amendment is made; and the amendment must be made within such period as may be specified in the order or, if no period is so specified, within 14 days after the making of the order. (2) Where by an order under rule 6 a person is to be made a defendant, the rules as to service of a writ of summons shall apply accordingly to service of the amended writ on him, but before serving the writ on him the person on whose application the order was made must procure the order to be noted in the cause book. . . . (4) Where by an order under rule 6 or 7 a person is to be added as a party or is to be made a party in substitution for some other party, that party shall not become a party until—(a) where the order is made under rule 6 the writ has been amended in relation to him under this rule and, (if he is a defendant) has been served on him . . .—and where by virtue of the foregoing provision a person becomes a party in substitution for some other party, all things done in the course of the proceedings before the making of the order shall have effect in relation to the new party as they had in relation to the old, except that entry of appearance by the old party shall not dispense with entry of appearance by the new."

In *Seabridge's* case the amended writ was stamped in the Central Office on the very day when the three year limitation period expired, but it was not served on the added defendant until a few days later. The court was referred to the old rule, R.S.C., Ord. 16, r. 11, which had provided that the proceedings against a party added should " be deemed to have begun only on the service of such writ," and to Ord. 15, r. 2 of the County Court Rules 1936 which was in the same terms; compare *Mitchell* v. *Harris Engineering Co. Ltd.* [1967] 2 Q.B. 703, 711 and 720, *per* Russell L.J. *Mabro's* case [1932] 1 K.B. 485, *Mitchell's* case [1967] 2 Q.B. 703 and *Davies'* case [1961] 1 W.L.R. 170 were all cited. But this court held that the action against the added defendant was begun in time because the writ had been amended in time, though not served in time. The whole argument was addressed to the question whether the writ dated from when the defendant was added or from when he was served. It was not argued that it dated from the issue of the original writ and that possibility was not referred to in the judgment of Lord Denning M.R. with which Diplock and Salmon L.JJ. agreed. The decision rested simply on the wording of the rule and the fact that the limitation period had not expired at the date of the amendment. As a result of the decision, County Court Rules, Ord. 15, r. 2 was amended to read:

> " (2) Where any person is added or substituted as defendant, except under rule 11 of this Order, the amended originating process shall be served on the added or substituted defendant according to the rules applicable to the service of the originating process, and the proceedings as against him shall be deemed to have begun on the date of the amendment."

A Rule 11 is not without interest, for it reads:

" Where a person other than the defendant appears on the return day and admits that he is the person whom the plaintiff intended to sue, or ought to have sued, he may, if the plaintiff consents, be substituted for the defendant, and the proceedings shall continue as if he had originally been made defendant."

B In *Braniff's* case [1969] 1 W.L.R. 1533 this court affirmed a judge's order setting aside a writ and service, where the master had granted an extension of time for amending the writ to add a defendant so as to keep alive or create a cause of action otherwise barred by the Limitation Act 1939. In the leading judgment, with which Davies L.J. agreed, Widgery L.J. stated that the provisions of R.S.C., Ord. 20, r. 5, including C specific exemptions enabling the court to allow amendments " after any relevant period of limitation current at the date of issue of the writ has expired," did not mean that in general there was any relaxation of the principle in *Weldon* v. *Neal,* 19 Q.B.D. 394. But he went on to follow *Seabridge's* case [1968] 2 Q.B. 46 in holding that the amended writ takes effect against the added defendant only when the amendment is completed in accordance with Ord. 15, r. 8. From that he concluded that there was D no writ available against the added defendant, but he left open what he appears to have regarded as a separate question, whether there was no action brought against the added defendant until the final amendment of the writ.

Cross L.J., with whom also Davies L.J. agreed, reserved the question whether the amendment of the writ by adding the second defendant E could relate back to the date of the issue of the writ against the first defendant, but on the assumption that it did relate back thought the master wrong and the judge right.

In *Lucy's* case [1970] 1 Q.B. 393 this court held, by a majority, that writs in actions requiring leave within section 1 (1) of the Limitation Act 1963, which had not been " brought before the end of the period of 12 months from the date on which the deceased died " as required F by section 3 (4) of the Act, could not be amended by adding another defendant as the joinder would deprive the added defendant of the defence afforded by section 3 (4). *Mabro's* case [1932] 1 K.B. 485, *Davies'* case [1961] 1 W.L.R. 170, and *Seabridge's* case [1968] 2 Q.B. 46 were cited, and, as I have said earlier, *Mabro's* case was approved and followed, unaffected by the provisions of Ord. 15, r. 6 and Ord. 20, r. 5 and G (though the judgments do not refer to it) by the decision in *Seabridge's* case [1968] 2 Q.B. 46.

I regret that I am unable to reconcile *Seabridge's* case [1968] 2 Q.B. 46 and *Lucy's* case [1970] 1 Q.B. 393 in the way suggested by Walton J. The decision in *Seabridge's* case [1968] 2 Q.B. 46 is not inconsistent with the decision in *Lucy's* case [1970] 1 Q.B. 393 but their ratios are.

Again I find it difficult to see any distinction in principle between H adding a plaintiff or a defendant—or a cause of action—when deciding the question when an action is brought or begun. But were it not for the authorities to which I have referred I would have no difficulty in holding that the wording of Ord. 15, r. 8 determines that question as it was decided in *Seabridge's* case [1968] 2 Q.B. 46 and *Gawthrop's* case [1979] 1 W.L.R. 268 and regulates the practice concerning the joinder of defendants in a manner which may distinguish the practice concerning the joinder of plaintiffs or causes of action.

The settled practice is, in my judgment, the important matter, not   A
the legal basis of it, which in most cases is of no relevance. But if that
basis is of importance, there is, I think, high, if not overriding, authority
for the opinion that for the purpose of considering whether an action
is statute-barred it is brought or begun against an additional defendant
at the date of his being brought into it. In the middle of the last
century, the House of Lords (Lord Cottenham L.C. and Lord Brougham)   B
had twice to consider whether persons who had been added by an order
of the court as defendants to a bill for tithes filed within one year
after the date fixed by section 3 of the Tithes Act 1832 were defendants
in a suit or action commenced within that time.

On the first occasion Lord Cottenham L.C. expressed strong doubts
about the question whether they could not claim the benefit of section
3, without deciding it: *Plowden* v. *Thorpe* (1840) 7 Cl. & Fin. 137, 164.   C
On the second they decided that the suit, as against such defendants,
must be taken to have commenced at the date at which they were actually
introduced into the bill; that they could not, by relation backwards be
treated as defendants to the original bill, and that they were consequently
entitled to the protection of the provisions of the statute: *Byron* v.
Cooper (1844) 11 Cl. & Fin. 556. Lord Brougham said, at p. 579:
                                                                          D

" The first miscarriage in the court below, however, was to consider
    the whole defendants to the suit, the whole nine appellants, as
    excluded from the operation of the Act. The ground of this opinion
    was that the bill being originally filed before August 16, 1833, and
    the four last named appellants being, under an order of the Court
    of Exchequer, made defendants to that same bill, were as much
    excluded by the third section of the Act as if they had been made   E
    originally defendants to the bill filed on August 5, 1833. This is as
    great and as manifest an error as could well be committed. It is
    contrary to the whole nature and constitution of a tithe suit, and
    to the very species of rights which come in question in such a suit.
    There is no privity whatever between the different defendants. There
    could be no objection taken for the omission of one or more by the   F
    others being made parties to the bill. The defences may be quite
    separate, and are necessarily quite independent one of the other.
    One defence may be of a totally different kind from the others.
    One defendant or class of defendants may set up a former
    modus; one defendant or class of defendants may set up a com-
    position real, which covers his land and none other in the parish.
    One may set up a defence de non decimando, and no modus at all,   G
    as showing that his lands were abbey lands. In short, it is quite
    clear that each party may stand in a different relation towards the
    plaintiff and towards the suit, from all his co-defendants. No more
    need be said to prove how erroneous is the view taken of the case
    below, whereby this is considered as one suit and one defence. The
    parson is permitted to add new defendants to his amended bill, in   H
    order to save delay and expense; but each defendant so added is to
    be considered as sued by the proceeding which makes him a
    defendant, and the date of his being added is the date of the suit's
    commencement quoad him; consequently the four last named and
    last added defendants in this case were only sued in November
    1834, and quoad them the bill and the suit bear the date of November
    1834. They do not fall, therefore, within the description of the third

A   section of the statute. They are not defendants, to use the words of that statute, ' in a suit or action commenced within one year ' after August 16, 1832, being the last day of the session in which the Act passed."

Lord Brougham then continued: " As against them, therefore, the bill should have been at once dismissed, and with costs."

B   I approach and apply that case with caution, but Mr. Woods has not succeeded in persuading me that there was anything in the peculiarities of a tithe suit or in the rules of procedure and practice of the 1840's which weakens the authority of that decision for the proposition which it appears to support that when a defendant has a separate defence he should not be added after the relevant period of limitation has expired C because the date of his being added to a suit commenced in time is the date of the suit's commencement quoad him. That proposition seems to me to accord with what is restated in R.S.C., Ord. 15, r. 8 (4).

How then can effect be given in this case to the practice that a person in Mr. Spinks' position should not be added by the court to defend himself against a claim brought against another in good time but not against him until the time for suing him has long run out?

D   In none of the cases in which the practice of protecting a defendant has operated has it been necessary for the court to decide when the action is brought or commenced or when or how the defendant must claim the protection of the practice. Plaintiffs have been allowed to correct their mistakes, defendants have been allowed to set aside service of writs under Ord. 12, rr. 7 and 8, but never has a defendant been E deprived of the protection. That he may be deprived by exceptional circumstances other than those provided for by Ord. 20, r. 5 is, I think, still a minority view—a minority view which has distinguished support (see the references given in *The Supreme Court Practice* (1979), p. 346, note 20/5-8/7) and which is itself based on the need to relax the doctrine of relation back. I would apply to the present case the two sentences from Rees J.'s judgment in *Pheasant* v. *S. T. H. Smith (Tyres) Ltd.* cited F by Lord Denning M.R. on the hearing of the appeal: see *Firman* v. *Ellis* [1978] Q.B. 886, 907:

" ' . . . On the present state of the authorities, I am not satisfied that power exists to add a defendant after a limitation period was expired . . . even if the power did exist, I am not satisfied that it should be exercised otherwise than in exceptional circumstances, and G I can find no such circumstances in the present case.' "

If free to do so I would hold that Mr. Spinks can plead the Limitation Act 1939 successfully because the plaintiff's action had not been brought against him until he was joined.

.   It would then be a waste of time to let the action against him go to trial provided he made clear his intention to plead the statute. Unless there H were some special reason, I would not think it right to do what Walton J. did in *Gawthrop's* case [1979] 1 W.L.R. 268 and join him as a defendant but would dismiss the action against him at the earliest opportunity: compare *Riches* v. *Director of Public Prosecutions* [1973] 1 W.L.R. 1019, where one of the grounds on which an action was struck out as vexatious and an abuse of the process of the court was that it was bound to be defeated by a plea of the Limitation Act.

If, however, it was rightly conceded that Mr. Spinks must bring himself   A
within Ord. 15, r. 6, I would hold that Mr. Spinks has been improperly
and/or unnecessarily made a party, or has by reason of his pleaded
defence of section 2 of the Limitation Act 1939 ceased to be a proper
or necessary party, and order him to cease to be a party under Ord. 15,
r. 6 (2) (a).

But that is the order which I would make if I am compelled by   B
the weight of authority to hold that the action was brought against Mr.
Spinks when brought against the first defendant.

I am not satisfied that the joinder of Mr. Spinks was an irregularity
within Ord. 2, r. 1 to which objection can only be taken under Ord. 2,
r. 2, or a failure to comply with the rules, or made without jurisdiction;
I am satisfied that by submitting to the jurisdiction there has been no
waiver of the benefit accrued to him by lapse of the primary limitation   C
period, notwithstanding the steps which his legal advisers took and their
failure to apply to set the joinder aside.   It is true that that was the
procedure adopted in most if not all of the cases where a defendant has
succeeded in defeating such a joinder.   But if he was sued by a separate
writ he could choose whether to apply to set it aside or to enter an
appearance and serve a defence pleading the statute.   An unconditional   D
appearance would not then waive his right to plead the statute and be
dismissed from the action.   There would be nothing like the assent
provided for by the County Court Rules, Ord. 15, r. 11.   It would be
unjust, in my judgment, if he should be in a worse position when he
has lost his right to defend the claim if allowed to go on against him
simply because his legal advisers may have made a procedural slip or
have chosen to pursue his right to the benefit of the statute by a less   E
summary or inexpensive method than is open to them under the rules.
In this case of all cases, where the plaintiff has made no mistake in not
suing a second defendant initially, and has only sought to add him at
the instance of a stranger to the action, it would be ridiculous to depart
from the established practice of protecting a person in Mr. Spinks' position
by permitting the plaintiff to take advantage of a procedural error which   F
was made many years later and has prejudiced no one.

I am also satisfied that it is open to Mr. Spinks' advisers to apply
now under Ord. 15, r. 6 on a properly liberal construction of its wording
to make an order under rule 6 (2) (a), whatever the orthodox legal basis
for protecting a person joined as Mr. Spinks was.

Having had the privilege of reading the draft of the judgment which
Brandon L.J. is about to deliver, I am convinced, more especially by his   G
comments on the assumption underlying Ord. 20, r. 5, that we should
allow the appeal on this ground alone without expressing any final opinion
on the true foundation for the practice of protecting persons in Mr.
Spinks's position.   I would allow the appeal and order that Mr. Spinks
ceases to be a party.

I should add that I would not dismiss the action against him for want   H
of prosecution.   That ground of application, as Mr. Cherry submitted,
highlights the absurdity of relating the action against Mr. Spinks back
to the beginning of the action against the first defendant.   For if deemed
to have started his action against Mr. Spinks in 1975 the plaintiff has
indeed been dilatory in prosecuting it by taking no step at all until 1978,
yet he would be in a stronger position to resist its dismissal than a plaintiff
who had in fact sued both in 1975.

A   BRANDON L.J. I agree with Stephenson L.J. that this is not a case
in which the court should exercise its discretionary power under section
2D of the Limitation Act 1939 as amended to extend the primary period
of limitation of three years prescribed by section 2A (4) (a). It follows
that the case must be approached on the footing that the time allowed
to the plaintiff for beginning an action against Mr. Spinks in respect of
the collision expired in October 1976, long before the writ was amended
B   so as to add Mr. Spinks as defendant.

It is an established rule of practice that the court will not allow a
person to be added as defendant to an existing action if the claim sought
to be made against him is already statute-barred and he desires to rely
on that circumstance as a defence to the claim. Alternatively, if the
court has allowed such addition to be made ex parte in the first place, it
C   will not, on objection then being taken by the person added, allow the
addition to stand. I shall refer to that established rule of practice as
" the rule of practice."

There are two alternative bases on which the rule of practice can be
justified. The first basis is that, if the addition were allowed, it would
relate back, so that the action would be deemed to have been begun as
against the person added, not on the date of amendment, but on the
D   date of the original writ; that the effect of such relation back would be to
deprive the person added of an accrued defence to the claim on the
ground that it was statute-barred; and that this would be unjust to that
person. I shall refer to this first basis of the rule of practice as the
" relation back " theory.

The second and alternative basis for the rule is that, where a person
E   is added as defendant in an existing action, the action is only deemed
to have been begun as against him on the date of amendment of the
writ; that the defence that the claim is statute-barred therefore remains
available to him; and that, since such defence affords a complete answer
to the claim, it would serve no useful purpose to allow the addition to
be made. I shall refer to this second and alternative basis of the rule
of practice as the " no useful purpose " theory.

F   An application by a plaintiff for leave to add a person as defendant
in an existing action is, or should ordinarily be made ex parte under
R.S.C., Ord. 15, r. 6 (2) (b). If the application is allowed, the writ must
then be amended under rule 8 (1), and served on the person added under
rule 8 (2), of the same Order. If the person added as defendant, having
had the amended writ served on him, objects to being added on the
G   ground that the claim against him was already statute-barred before the
writ was amended, the ordinary practice is for him to enter a conditional
appearance under Ord. 12, r. 7, and then to apply to set aside the
amended writ and the service of it on him under Ord. 12, r. 8. Then,
if he establishes that the claim against him was statute-barred before the
writ was amended, he is entitled as of right, in accordance with the rule
of practice, to the relief for which he has asked, unless the case is of the
H   special kind covered by Ord. 20, r. 5 (3).

Provided that the person added as defendant follows the ordinary
practice described above, he gets the benefit of the rule of practice, and
it is not material to consider which of the two alternative bases for that
rule, that is to say, the " relation back " theory on the one hand or the
" no useful purpose " theory on the other, is the true one. In the present
case, however, the solicitors acting for Mr. Spinks did not follow the
ordinary practice. Instead, after they had accepted service on him of the

amended writ, they entered an unconditional appearance in the action on A his behalf, and later, after accepting service of the amended statement of claim, they served a defence containing a plea that the claim against him was statute-barred.

It was contended for the plaintiff and the original defendant, Mr. Peasley, that, because the solicitors for Mr. Spinks dealt with the matter in this way, he had now lost his right either (a) to have the addition of him as defendant set aside or otherwise got rid of or (b) to rely on the B defence that the claim against him was statute-barred.

This contention was based on two propositions. The first proposition was that, because the solicitors for Mr. Spinks had entered an unconditional appearance on his behalf, instead of entering a conditional appearance and then applying to set aside the amended writ and service of it, it was now too late for him to contend that he should not have been C added as defendant in the first place. The second proposition was that, since the true basis of the rule of practice was the " relation back " theory, the action must now be deemed to have been begun as against Mr. Spinks on the date of the original writ; it must be deemed therefore to have been begun in time, so that the plea that the action was statute-barred was no longer available to him. D

I should regard it as very unjust if these consequences should flow from what, if the argument is correct, was no more than a procedural error on the part of the solicitors for Mr. Spinks. The solution in that case might be to allow Mr. Spinks to amend his appearance so as to make it conditional instead of unconditional and to apply belatedly to set aside. Leaving aside that possible solution, however, the question to be considered is whether the argument relied on for the plaintiff and the E original defendant is correct or not.

I consider, first, whether, because the solicitors for Mr. Spinks entered an unconditional appearance on his behalf, he is now precluded from contending that he should not have been added as a defendant in the first place. The argument that he was so precluded was put in two ways. It was said, first, that the entry of an unconditional appearance operated F as a waiver of any right to have the addition set aside. It was said, secondly, that, apart from Ord. 12, rr. 7 and 8, there was no rule of court under which an application to set aside, or otherwise get rid of, the addition could now be made by Mr. Spinks or allowed by the court.

I do not accept either of these arguments. With regard to the first argument, the entry of an unconditional appearance operates, no doubt, as a waiver of any irregularity in the process of which the person entering G it was, or should have been, aware. In my view, however, the addition of a person as defendant contrary to the rule of practice is not, and should not be treated as being, a mere irregularity. Such addition involves rather, if the " relation back " theory is correct, the taking away of an accrued right of defence, and the right to complain of it cannot therefore be waived in such a manner. With regard to the second argu- H ment, I think that there is another rule of court, besides Ord. 12, rr. 7 and 8, under which an application to get rid of the addition can be made by Mr. Spinks and allowed by the court. That rule is Ord. 15, r. 6 (2) (a), which provides:

" At any stage of the proceedings in any cause or matter the court may on such terms as it thinks just and either of its own motion or on application—(a) order any person who has been improperly or

A   unnecessarily made a party or who has for any reason ceased to be a proper or necessary party, to cease to be a party."

In my view, since the claim against Mr. Spinks was already statute-barred before he was added as defendant, and he desired to rely on that circumstance as a defence to the claim, he is a person who has been improperly made a party within the meaning of Ord. 15, r. 6 (2) (*a*);

B alternatively, if he was properly made a party on the ex parte application, because it was not then known for certain whether he wished to rely on the claim being statute-barred, then, as soon as it became apparent that he did wish to rely on that defence, he ceased to be a proper party within the meaning of that rule. Either way an order that he cease to be a party should be made.

C   If the view about Ord. 15, r. 6 (2) (*a*), which I have just expressed is correct, it is sufficient to dispose of this case, and it becomes unnecessary to go on to consider the correctness of the second limb of the argument for the plaintiff and the original defendant based on the " relation back " theory. Since the matter was argued at some length before us, however, I think that I should express some provisional views on it.

The crucial question here is this. When the original writ in an action

D is amended by adding a person as defendant, on what date is the action deemed to have been begun, for the purposes of any relevant statute of limitation, as against the person added? Is it the date of the original writ or is it the date of the amendment?

This problem arises not only in relation to amendments involving the addition of a person as defendant. It also arises in relation to amendments

E involving the addition of a person as plaintiff or the addition of a new cause of action. It does not, however, follow necessarily from this that the problem falls to be resolved in the same way in all three cases, although one might well expect this to be so.

Disregarding for the moment the case law on the subject, I should have thought that, if a relevant rule of court prescribed at what time an action is to be deemed to have been begun as against a person added

F as defendant, that is the time which should be taken for the purpose of answering the question posed above.

In fact the relevant rules of court, both in the High Court and the county court do, as I understand them, prescribe in terms the time at which an action is to be deemed to have been begun as against a person added as defendant. In the High Court, R.S.C., Ord. 15, r. 8 (4) provides:

G   " Where by an order under rule 6 or rule 7, a person is to be added as a party or is to be made a party in substitution for some other party, that person shall not become a party until—(*a*) where the order is made under rule 6, the writ has been amended in relation to him under this rule and (if he is a defendant) has been served on him . . ."

In the county court, Ord. 15, r. 2, of the County Court Rules 1936, as

H amended, provides:

    ' Where any person is added or substituted as defendant, except under rule 11 of this Order, the amended originating process shall be served on the added or substituted defendant . . . and the proceedings as against him shall be deemed to have been begun on the date of amendment."

The exception under Ord. 15, r. 11, referred to in this rule, is not directly

relevant for present purposes, although it is, as Stephenson L.J. has said, A
not without interest.

Both these rules, in their present form, are of comparatively recent
origin. The earlier High Court rule, then Ord. 16, r. 11, provided that
proceedings should be deemed to have been begun as against a person
added as defendant on the date of service of the amended writ. The
earlier county court rule contained a similar provision.

It was held by this court in *Seabridge* v. *H. Cox & Sons (Plant Hire)* B
Ltd. [1968] 2 Q.B. 46 that the effect of the present High Court rule,
Ord. 15, r. 8 (4) (*a*) set out above, is that, where a person is added as
defendant, the action is deemed to have been begun as against him on the
date of amendment of the writ, and not, as under the earlier High Court
rule, then Ord. 16, r. 11, on the date of service of the amended writ on
him. The present county court rule, Ord. 15, r. 2, is a revised version of C
the earlier rule, designed to bring the position in the county court into
line with the position in the High Court as it was declared to be in
Seabridge v. *H. Cox & Sons (Plant Hire) Ltd.* There are, perhaps,
difficulties about the interpretation put on the present High Court rule in
that case. Since we are bound by it, however, no purpose would be
served by referring to them.

It seems to me that the " relation back " theory, which involves that the D
date on which an action is deemed to have been begun as against a person
added as a defendant is the date of the original writ, is inconsistent with
the rules of court, both in the High Court and the county court, to which
I have just referred. By contrast it seems to me that the " no useful
purpose " theory, which involves that the date on which an action is
deemed to have been begun as against a person added as a defendant is E
the date of amendment of the writ, is consistent with those rules. If it
were permissible, therefore, to choose between the two theories by reference
to the relevant rules of court alone, without regard to the case law on
the subject, I should have no hesitation in concluding that the " no useful
purpose " theory was the correct one.

Much of the case law, however, though by no means all, supports the
opposite conclusion. The " relation back " theory was treated as the true F
basis of the rule of practice by this court in *Mabro* v. *Eagle Star and
British Dominions Insurance Co. Ltd.* [1932] 1 K.B. 485, (a case of adding
a plaintiff) and again in *Lucy* v. *W. T. Henleys Telegraph Works Co. Ltd.*
[1970] 1 Q.B. 393 (a case, like the present one, of adding a defendant).
The " relation back " theory is also supported, in relation to adding a new
cause of action, by *Weldon* v. *Neal,* 19 Q.B.D. 394, another decision of G
this court.

There are other cases in this court, however, the judgments in which
support, or tend to support, the " no useful purpose " theory rather than
the " relation back " theory. These are *Mitchell* v. *Harris Engineering Co.
Ltd.* [1967] 2 Q.B. 703, 720, *per* Russell L.J. and *Seabridge* v. *H. Cox
& Sons (Plant Hire) Ltd.* [1968] 2 Q.B. 46. The latter case was applied
at first instance in *Gawthrop* v. *Boulton* [1979] 1 W.L.R. 268. H

Other relevant cases in this court are *Davies* v. *Elsby Brothers Ltd.*
[1961] 1 W.L.R. 170, in which the judgment of Pearce L.J. at p. 173 seems
to lend some support to either theory in turn, and *Braniff* v. *Holland &
Hannen and Cubitts (Southern) Ltd.* [1969] 1 W.L.R. 1533, in which the
question whether the " relation back " theory was correct was expressly
left open.

Finally I would refer to *Byron* v. *Cooper,* 11 Cl. & Fin. 556, a decision

A   of the House of Lords which, though it relates to a special statute and an earlier mode of procedure, appears to me to be inconsistent, in principle, with the " relation back " theory.

There is one other matter to be mentioned. The rule committee, in framing the new provisions of the present R.S.C., Ord. 20, r. 5, appears to have assumed that the " relation back " theory was the true basis of

B   the rule of practice. I say that because paragraphs (2), (3), (4) and (5) are designed to allow amendments in certain circumstances which would or might otherwise infringe the rule of practice, and these paragraphs would not serve their intended purpose of defeating a defence of time-bar if the amendments allowed under them did not relate back to the date of the original writ but only took effect from the date of amendment. The fact that the rule committee made that assumption is clearly a matter

C   of some weight to be taken into account. It cannot, however, of itself be decisive of the question under discussion.

There is, in my view, a high degree of artificiality and unreality about the " relation back " theory. There is no reason to quarrel with the general proposition that an amendment of a writ or a pleading relates back to the original date of the document amended, as stated by Lord

D   Collins M.R. in *Sneade* v. *Wotherton Barytes & Lead Mining Co.* [1904] 1 K.B. 295, 297. This seems to me to be an entirely sensible proposition so long as the amendment concerned does not involve the addition of a new party, either as plaintiff or defendant, or the raising of a new cause of action, but involves only the modification, by addition, deletion or substitution, of pleas or averments made between existing parties in respect of a cause or causes of action already raised. Where, however,

E   the amendment concerned involves the addition of a new party or the raising of a new cause of action, it appears to me to be unrealistic and contrary to the common sense of the matter to treat it as relating back in the same way.

The artificiality and unreality of the " relation back " theory to which I have just referred cannot be more forcibly illustrated than by the nature

F   of the relief asked for in the alternative by Mr. Spinks in his amended summons in this case. In paragraph 3 he asks for an order that the action against him be dismissed for want of prosecution. He asks for that order on the footing that, if the action against him is to be treated as having been begun on the date of the original writ, that is to say, August 1, 1975, then the plaintiff has been guilty of inexcusable delay over about 3½ years in prosecuting such action. To such absurdities do artificiality and unreality inevitably lead.

G   The " relation back " theory also creates problems in cases where there is an arguable question whether the claim against the person added or sought to be added as defendant is statute-barred or not. Such a question may arise where there is doubt about the date on which the relevant cause of action arose, or an issue as to whether the plaintiff can rely on suspension or interruption of the relevant period of limitation on one ground or another. In such cases it will not usually be possible to

H   resolve the question whether the claim is statute-barred or not on the hearing of the ex parte application by the plaintiff to add the new defendant, or, if leave is then given, on the hearing of the subsequent inter parties application by the new defendant to set aside the order by which he was added. It will instead be necessary to have pleadings and discovery on the question and a proper trial of it. If the " relation back "

theory applies, and no special order is made, the addition of the new   A
defendant will of itself take away his right to rely on the time bar, and
so make the question whether he would, before such addition, have been
entitled to rely on it or not a purely academic question. In order to
get over this difficulty the order giving leave to add the new defendant
will have to be made on special terms, namely, that the addition shall
not relate back but shall take effect from the date of amendment of the   B
writ only. These considerations again point to the inappropriateness of
treating amendments which involve the addition of a new party or the
raising of a new cause of action as relating back.

This court is undoubtedly bound by the authorities to which I have
referred to hold that the rule of practice exists and to continue to apply
it. I do not consider, however, that this court is also bound to hold that
the " relation back " theory is the true basis of that rule, and that for   C
two reasons. The first reason is that it was never necessary for the
decision in any of the reported cases from 1877 onwards to decide whether
the one theory or the other was the true one. It was sufficient simply to
formulate and apply the rule. The second reason is that the authorities
do not, as I have indicated, speak with one voice on the subject, but on
the contrary provide support both for and against both theories.   D

Feeling free, therefore, to form my own opinion on the matter, I have
reached the provisional conclusion—it is not necessary to reach a final
conclusion—that the " no useful purpose " theory, rather than the " relation back " theory, should be regarded as the true basis of the rule of
practice.

I appreciate that this view, if correct, creates problems with regard
to the effectiveness of paragraph (3), and possibly but not necessarily also   E
paragraphs (4) and (5), of Ord. 20, r. 5, as at present framed. These
difficulties could, however, be overcome by adding an express provision
that, where amendments of the kinds covered by those three paragraphs
are made, they shall relate back to the date of the original writ. This
is, after all, the result which those new provisions of the rule are, in
substance, intended to achieve.   F

The argument against Mr. Spinks was, as I indicated earlier, based on
two propositions. The first proposition was that, because his solicitors
had entered an unconditional appearance on his behalf, he was now
precluded from complaining about his being added as defendant. The
second proposition was that, since the addition of Mr. Spinks as defendant
related back to the date of the original writ, the defence that the claim
was statute-barred was no longer available to him.   G

For the reasons given earlier I have reached the conclusion that the
first proposition is erroneous. I hold that Mr. Spinks is not precluded
from complaining of his being added as defendant, but is on the contrary
entitled to an order under Ord. 15, r. 6 (2) (a), that he cease to be a party.
I am further content to decide the appeal on that ground alone, without
expressing any final view with regard to the second proposition.

If I had reached the conclusion, however, that the first proposition was
correct, I should have been prepared to decide the appeal on the alternative ground that the second proposition was erroneous. I should in
that event not merely have expressed the provisional view, but held as a
matter of decision, that the addition of Mr. Spinks as defendant did not
relate back to the date of the original writ but took effect only from the
date of amendment, so that the defence that the claim was statute-barred

A   remained available to him. On that basis I should again have allowed the appeal and made an order summarily dismissing the action as against Mr. Spinks on the ground that the claim raised against him in it was statute-barred and was therefore bound to fail: see *Riches* v. *Director of Public Prosecutions* [1973] 1 W.L.R. 1019.

B
                              Appeal allowed.
                              Half appellant's costs in Court of
                                 Appeal and below to be paid by
                                 first defendant.
                              No order as to respondent plaintiff's
                                 costs.
                              Leave to appeal.

C   Solicitors: *Greenwood & Co.; Outred & Co.; Stevensons.*

    [Reported by MISS HENRIETTA STEINBERG, Barrister-at-Law]

D   [CHANCERY DIVISION]

                   * *In re* R-R REALISATIONS LTD.
                      (FORMERLY ROLLS-ROYCE LTD.)

E   1979 Nov. 21, 22; 26   Sir Robert Megarry V.-C.

Company—Winding up—Distribution of assets—Voluntary wind-
   ing up—Liquidators given leave to distribute without regard
   to late claims—Late claim resulting from accident on behalf
   of victims and relatives—Whether just to permit distribution—
   Companies Act 1948 (11 & 12 *Geo.* 6, *c.* 38), *s.* 307 [1]

F   The three joint liquidators of a company in voluntary liquidation since October 1971 were able, after selling its assets, to pay all the company's known debts and to pay substantial sums to the stockholders. On January 20, 1975, they were given leave to distribute the assets without regard to any claims made after February 15, 1975. A deed of indemnity dated December 22, 1975, and a policy of insurance covered the company against various liabilities arising from any accident. On October 8, 1979, it was announced that a final distribution

G   of some £5.5 million would be made to ordinary stockholders on December 6, 1979.
         Meanwhile, following the publication on September 22, 1978, of the results of an inquiry into an accident at Bombay airport in 1976 involving an aircraft powered by the company's engines, writs against the company were issued but not served on behalf of victims or their families. In September and

H   October 1979, letters by solicitors acting on their behalf referred to possible proceedings against the company to which on November 6, 1979, solicitors for the company and the liquidators replied. A summons by the joint liquidators dated November 2, 1979, asked the Companies Court for leave to distribute the company's assets remaining in their hands among creditors and stockholders without providing for the payment from those assets of any "debt claim or liability" which

---

[1] Companies Act 1948, s. 307: see post, p. 811E–G.

In re R-R Realisations Ltd. (Ch.D.)   [1980]

might be owing by the company arising from the Bombay A
accident. The registrar dismissed the summons.

On appeal by the liquidators, asking that the registrar's
order should be discharged: —

Held, (1) that in deciding under section 307 of the Companies Act 1948 whether to authorise a distribution of the
assets without regard to late claims made by those who
asserted that they were creditors, the test was whether in all
the circumstances it would be just to make the order; there B
was no requirement that the claimants should first establish
that they were innocent of any wilful default or lack of due
diligence, although those would usually be important factors
in determining what was just (post, pp. 813H—814B).

David v. *Frowd* (1833) 1 Myl. & K. 200 and *In re House
Property and Investment Co. Ltd.* [1954] Ch. 576 considered.

(2) That where the claimants were asking the court to
refuse or suspend such an order, any contention that that C
should be done only on terms that the claimants should bear
the expenses thrown away by their tardiness in asserting their
claims should itself be subject to the test of what was just
(post, p. 814B–C).

(3) That the inconvenience of halting the distribution in
mid-course had to be weighed against the injustice of shutting
out claimants who had not been guilty of any unreasonable
delay from making any effective claim, there being no certainty D
that the claims would be met under the policy of insurance;
that the court would be slower to make an order authorising
a distribution to members where the late claim was made by
creditors rather than by other members; and that it would
therefore not be just to make the order, so that the appeal
would be dismissed (post, pp. 814C–E, G–H).

E

The following cases are referred to in the judgment:

Angell v. *Haddon* (1816) 1 Madd. 529.
Butler v. *Broadhead* [1975] Ch. 97; [1974] 3 W.L.R. 27; [1974] 2 All
E.R. 401.
Cattell v. *Simons* (1845) 8 Beav. 243.
David v. *Frowd* (1833) 1 Myl. & K. 200.
House Property and Investment Co. Ltd., In re [1954] Ch. 576; [1953] F
3 W.L.R. 1037; [1953] 2 All E.R. 1525.
Hull v. *Falconer* (1865) 11 L.T. 761; sub nom. *Hull* v. *Falkoner* (1865)
5 N.R. 266.
McMurdo, In re [1902] 2 Ch. 684, C.A.
Ministry of Health v. *Simpson* [1951] A.C. 251; [1951] 2 All E.R. 1137,
H.L.(E.).
Sale Continuation Ltd., In re (unreported), November 24, 1977, G
Brightman J.

The following additional case was cited in argument:

Rolls Razor Ltd., In re (No. 2) [1970] Ch. 576; [1970] 2 W.L.R. 100;
[1969] 3 All E.R. 1386.

SUMMONS   H

By summons dated November 2, 1979, Edward Rupert Nicholson,
Sir William Kenneth MacLeod Slimmings, and Keith David Wickenden,
the three joint liquidators of R-R Realisations Ltd. (formerly Rolls-Royce
Ltd.) sought, inter alia, an order in the Companies Court that they should
be at liberty to distribute assets remaining in their hands among creditors
and stockholders of the company without providing for the payment

A from those assets of any debt claim or liability which might be owing
by the company arising from an aircraft accident at Bombay airport
in October 1976 including in particular any claim for damages in actions
commenced in the Queen's Bench Division against the company and
others by, amongst others, the respondents to the summons, Nicholas
Brian Baker and David Christopher Willis.

B   On November 16, 1979, Mr. Registrar Hunt dismissed the summons.
The joint liquidators appealed by motion, asking that the registrar's
order should be discharged except for that part of the order (as prayed
in paragraph 2 of the summons) which appointed the respondents to
represent, for the purposes of the application, all the plaintiffs in the
proceedings in the Queen's Bench Division.

    The facts are stated in the judgment.

C
    William Stubbs Q.C. and David Richards for the joint liquidators.
    Alan Heyman Q.C. and M. K. Kennedy for the respondents to the
summons.

                                            Cur. adv. vult.

D   November 26. SIR ROBERT MEGARRY V.-C. read the following
judgment. This is an appeal from a decision of Mr. Registrar Hunt
dated November 16, 1979, whereby he dismissed the summons issued
on November 2, 1979, by the three joint liquidators of R-R Realisations
Ltd., a company formerly entitled Rolls-Royce Ltd. I shall call it " the
company." The company ran into financial difficulties towards the end
of 1970, and after it had been in receivership early in 1971, it went into
E a creditors' voluntary liquidation on October 4, 1971. The receivers sold
the company's aero-engine division to a company originally called Rolls-
Royce (1971) Ltd. and subsequently called Rolls-Royce Ltd. I shall call
this " the new company." The receivers also sold the motor division to
Rolls-Royce Motor Holdings Ltd., a company to which I need not refer
again. Largely as a result of these sales, the liquidators were able to pay
F all the company's debts of which they knew, and pay substantial sums
to the stockholders. The holders of workers' stock were satisfied in full,
and the holders of the ordinary stock have received 55p in the £. On
January 20, 1975, an order was made giving the liquidators leave to
distribute the assets without regard to any claims made after February
15, 1975; but there were still some difficulties in what was plainly a very
substantial and complex liquidation, and further orders dealing with
G specific problems were made in 1978 and 1979. Finally the liquidators
began to make detailed provisions for the final distribution to the
ordinary stockholders, said to be some 80,000 in number. On October 8,
1979, there was a press announcement that a final distribution of 8·41p
in the £ would be made to ordinary stockholders; and it is proposed to
pay this on December 6, 1979. Some £5·5m is to be distributed in this
H way.

    It is against this background that the summons has to be considered.
It arises out of an aircraft accident at Bombay airport in India on
October 12, 1976, in which a Caravelle aircraft powered by Rolls-Royce
engines was destroyed, with the loss of the lives of the 95 persons on
board. The starboard engine, which the company had manufactured
some 10 or 12 years earlier, failed shortly after take-off, due to a crack
in the engine's 10th stage compressor disc; and the consequent fire was

aggravated by the failure of the aircrew to cut off the fuel supply to the A
engine. I make no findings on these facts, but state the essentials of the
findings of Bhasme J. of the High Court of Bombay. He conducted an
inquiry into the causes of the accident, and his report was published
on September 22, 1978. Nothing that could be regarded as a claim against
the company or its liquidators was made on behalf of any of the victims
of the accident or their families until a short solicitors' letter dated
September 26, 1979, was delivered by hand, addressed to a firm of B
accountants and marked for the attention of " R. Nicholson Esq.," who
was one of the joint liquidators. This letter enclosed a copy of a letter
to the new company, asking various questions about the provenance of
the starboard engine of the Caravelle, and concluding with a statement
that if the information was not provided, it might be necessary " to bring
proceedings against all existing Rolls Royce companies as might remotely C
be thought to be involved." No reply to this letter was sent on behalf
of the liquidators, and so on October 15, 1979, the solicitors sent a long
letter to Mr. Nicholson, with copies to the other liquidators and to a
partner in the firm of accountants. There was no reply to this letter
either, and so on October 31, 1979, the solicitors sent to the partner in
the firm of accountants what might be called a telex before action. D
Finally, on November 6, 1979, solicitors for the liquidators and the
company replied to the solicitors' communications. This delay in dealing
with what was plainly a possible claim is most regrettable, and although
it was not explained in evidence, I was told on instructions that Mr.
Nicholson had been on holiday until the end of October; and although the
first letter was opened, it was apparently put on one side and not given
to anyone to reply to or otherwise deal with. However, I do not think E
that this makes much difference, save that if the letter had been treated
more responsibly, the liquidators might well have postponed taking some
of the steps that they took, and in particular the making of the press
announcement on October 8, 1979.

The present state of the claims arising out of the accident is as
follows. 55 writs have been issued, although four of these appear not to F
have been issued until the limitation period expired on October 12, 1979.
However, in these four cases (and in others) the plaintiffs may be able
to obtain leave to sue out of time. The writs have not been served, but
a copy of one writ is in evidence. In this, Mr. N. B. Baker and Mr. D. C.
Willis, who are both partners in a well-known firm of London solicitors,
sue as administrators of one of the victims of the accident. There are
five other plaintiffs, consisting of the deceased's widow, and four infants, G
each suing by Mr. Baker as his or her next friend. These plaintiffs are,
I understand, children of the deceased. There are eight defendants, the
company and the new company being the first two, and the others being
airlines or aviation authorities. The writ is generally indorsed with claims
under the Fatal Accidents Act 1976 for damages for the death of the
deceased and under the Law Reform (Miscellaneous Provisions) Act H
1934 for damages for the loss of expectation of life, earning capacity and
consequential loss. All save the administrators claim damages for personal
injuries, shock, distress and consequential loss and damage. The claims
are based on negligence and breach of statutory duty in, inter alia, the
design, manufacture, assembly and maintenance of the aircraft and its
starboard engine, and in failing to advise as to the correct maintenance

The Weekly Law Reports, July 18, 1980

809

1 W.L.R.   In re R-R Realisations Ltd. (Ch.D.)   Sir Robert
                                                              Megarry V.-C.

A and servicing procedures to be carried out in respect of it. I state the claim as it particularly relates to the company, and with the omission of the ten "and/ors" with which the two sentences of the indorsement are bespattered. During the hearing it was generally accepted that the other writs were in a closely similar form; and there was no contention that the actions could not properly be brought in England. I should add that all writs were issued under emergency legal aid certificates.

B One other matter that I should mention is that of insurance. The combined effect of various transactions, and in particular a deed of indemnity dated December 22, 1975, and a policy of insurance numbered TP(S) 14,211,602, is that the company is entitled, through the new company, to the benefit of an insurance policy for US $115m in respect of any liability arising out of any accident caused by any defect in

C products sold, supplied, repaired or worked upon, or any neglect, error or omission in connection with any advice given or any report supplied: I state it shortly.

In those circumstances, Mr. Stubbs, on behalf of the liquidators, contends that the liquidators ought to be granted the relief that they seek by their summons, and that Mr. Registrar Hunt was wrong in

D dismissing the summons. The relief sought is that the liquidators should be given liberty to distribute the remaining assets of the company without regard to any claims arising out of the aircraft disaster on October 12, 1976: I summarise it. In essence, the substance of Mr. Stubbs' case is that the claims of the plaintiffs against the company were at present very general and unparticularised, but so far as they could be judged, they were unlikely to succeed; that in any event the insurance cover of

E US $115m (which comes to nearly £53m) was virtually certain to cover any successful claims, since it was inconceivable that more than an average of £1m would be recovered in each action; that much time and money had been expended in preparing for the final distribution next month, and that this would be wasted if the distribution was postponed. The direct costs already incurred for printing and data processing are

F said to be about £14,700, and all of this would be wasted if there had to be a postponement. There is also the cost of maintaining a registrar's department, estimated at a little over £250 a day. A document not in evidence gives £86,500 as the estimated cost of a six month delay, though there is an obvious difficulty in substantiating all of this as being wholly wasted expenditure which would be caused by the postponement of the distribution.

G During his opening, Mr. Stubbs helpfully provided a typewritten summary of his submissions on the law. I will not set them out in full, but I shall summarise their main thrust. They fall under two heads. The primary submission was that the liquidators should in any event be granted the liberty to distribute that they sought. The reason was that they were under an implied statutory duty to complete the liquidation

H and to effect a final distribution of the assets within a reasonable time. This imposed a correlative duty on creditors to make their claims with all reasonable diligence, and if a claim was made at a late stage in the liquidation, the burden lay on the creditor to show that he had acted with such diligence. The plaintiffs in the actions had not done this, and so the liquidators should be granted the leave to distribute that they sought.

The secondary submission, made in the alternative, was that the order

giving the liquidators the liberty to distribute that they sought should, A
in effect, instead of being an order absolute, be an order nisi. If a late
claim is made, the court may impose terms on the claimant in order to
prevent injustice to others being caused by postponing the distribution.
Here, substantial sums of money would be wasted if the distribution
was halted, both in barren expenditure already incurred and in the
additional costs of a prolonged liquidation; and even if the plaintiffs'
claims all failed, no order for costs in the actions could include these B
sums. Accordingly, the liquidators should be given the leave to distribute
that they sought unless the plaintiffs made proper provision for the
payment of the additional expenses that would be entailed by a postponement of the proposed distribution. I may add that Mr. Stubbs very
properly accepted that the order dated January 20, 1975, giving the
liquidators leave to distribute the assets without regard to subsequent C
claims could not properly be relied on in respect of claims such as those
made by the plaintiffs, which had not come into existence until after
the date of the order.

It was common ground between Mr. Stubbs and Mr. Heyman, who
appeared for the respondents, Mr. Baker and Mr. Willis, that there was no
authority at all closely in point. But Mr. Stubbs cited a number of cases D
on the administration of estates as providing helpful analogies. Thus
Mr. Stubbs relied on *David* v. *Frowd* (1833) 1 Myl. & K. 200, especially at
pp. 209, 210, as supporting the view that a creditor with a late claim must
establish that he has been guilty of no wilful default and has shown no
want of reasonable diligence. He also relied on *Angell* v. *Haddon* (1816)
1 Madd. 529 and *Cattell* v. *Simons* (1845) 8 Beav. 243 as supporting his
alternative contention that if a creditor is permitted to come in late, he E
will have to bear the costs of revising the distribution.

I think that one has to exercise considerable caution in applying
cases on the administration of the estate of a deceased person to a
voluntary liquidation. One reason is that the effect of a distribution in a
voluntary liquidation is quite different from that of a distribution in the
administration of estates. The *Diplock* principle of tracing assets into the F
hands of the beneficiaries under a will (see *Ministry of Health* v. *Simpson*
[1951] A.C. 251 *) has no application to the recipients, whether creditors
or members, under a distribution of the assets of a company in voluntary
liquidation: see *Butler* v. *Broadhead* [1975] Ch. 97. Once the liquidators
have duly advertised for creditors, any creditor who could have proved his
debt in the liquidation has no claim against any of the assets in the hands of
the creditors or the members of the company to whom that distribution G
has been made. What has gone has gone. There is no question of
reopening the distribution so as to let in the late claimant, in the way
that was done, for example, in *David* v. *Frowd,* 1 Myl. & K. 200. If the
order that Mr. Stubbs seeks is made, and the distribution is duly made
under it, that will be the end of any claim made by the plaintiffs against
the company. Mr. Stubbs also cited *Hull* v. *Falkoner* (1865) 5 N.R. 266, H
an ill-reported case; but even when the better report sub nom. *Hull* v.
Falconer (1865) 11 L.T. 761 is examined, I do not think that it helps
Mr. Stubbs. The case was a plain case of laches by a creditor who had
herself instituted a second suit for administration and yet refrained from

* Affirming the decision of the Court of Appeal sub nom. *In re Diplock, Diplock*
v. *Wintle* [1948] Ch. 465.

The Weekly Law Reports, July 18, 1980

811

1 W.L.R.   In re R-R Realisations Ltd. (Ch.D.)   Sir Robert
                                                              Megarry V.-C.

A proving her debt in the first suit even after she had failed to proceed on her own suit. *In re McMurdo* [1902] 2 Ch. 684 if anything assists Mr. Heyman, in that a creditor in the administration of an insolvent estate was held to be entitled to come in and prove at any time if there were assets still undistributed and no injustice would be caused. I do not think that Mr. Stubbs could get much more out of that case than that in such cases the court can impose terms on a creditor who seeks to come in and prove late.

B

There is another point which I think must be carefully borne in mind in considering the cases on administration of estates, and that is the standing of the claimant in relation to those to whom the distribution is to be made. If the claimant is a creditor, it may well be right to be slower to shut him out if the distribution is to be made to beneficiaries

C than it is if the distribution is to be made to other creditors. Correspondingly, in the voluntary liquidation of a company, it may well be right to give the claimant greater latitude if the distribution is to be to members rather than to other creditors. Just as a man should seek to be just before he affects to be generous, so I think that an especial care is needed to ensure that all creditors are paid before distributions are

D made to the members. It is only subject to the satisfaction of the company's liabilities that the company's property is distributable among the members: see section 302 of the Companies Act 1948. I do not, of course, say that a creditor has an absolute right to come in at any time, however gross his delay, whatever his conduct, and however unjust this would be to others. But I do say that the court should be slower to shut out a creditor as against members than as against other creditors.

E In considering what is the appropriate approach in a voluntary winding up, some assistance can, I think, be obtained from the section of the Companies Act 1948 which confers jurisdiction, section 307. The first two subsections run as follows:

F "(1) The liquidator or any contributory or creditor may apply to the court to determine any question arising in the winding up of a company, or to exercise, as respects the enforcing of calls or any other matter, all or any of the powers which the court might exercise if the company were being wound up by the court. (2) The court, if satisfied that the determination of the question or the required exercise of power will be just and beneficial, may accede wholly or partially to the application on such terms and conditions as it thinks fit or may make such other order on the application as it

G thinks just."

It will be observed that subsection (2) is phrased in terms of what is "just and beneficial," with a power to impose such terms and conditions as the court "thinks fit," and to make such other order as the court "thinks just." The section is, indeed, in very wide terms, and is capable

H of application to a great variety of cases; but nevertheless the language chosen is expressed in terms of what is just. That, I think, is plainly something different from mere convenience.

With that in mind, I turn to the only two cases cited to me which deal with voluntary liquidations. *In re House Property and Investment Co. Ltd.* [1954] Ch. 576 was very different. In it, Roxburgh J. rejected a claim by a lessor to have enough of the assets of the company (which was an original lessee) set aside to meet all future liabilities for the

In re R-R Realisations Ltd. (Ch.D.)

payment of rent and the due performance of the covenants in the lease. A
Instead, it was held that the lessor should prove in the liquidation for
the difference in value of the lease with the benefit of the original lessee's
covenants and its value without that benefit. That, of course, is very
far away from the present case; but in his judgment Roxburgh J., at
p. 612, referred ot the implied obligation imposed by the Companies Act
1948 on liquidators to complete the liquidation and effect a final distribution of the assets within a reasonable time. I fully accept this; but I do B
not think that there flows from this duty any corresponding duty on
creditors to make their claims with all reasonable diligence. Obviously
both prudence and convenience require them to do so: but that is not
the same as saying that there is a legal obligation to do so. I think that
the courts must be cautious in laying down any rules which would in
effect shorten the periods available to a claimant under the Statutes of C
Limitation. In the case of a company in voluntary liquidation where a
final distribution is in contemplation, the practical effect would be to
substitute an undefined period of diligence for whatever was the appropriate statutory period of years. A doctrine of laches may be appropriate
enough in claims made in equity in the administration of estates, but I do
not think that it should be admitted without compelling reasons in D
claims at law made in the statutory process of voluntary liquidation;
and I can see no compelling reasons.

The other case on voluntary liquidation is *In re Sale Continuation
Ltd.* (unreported) November 24, 1977, Brightman J. This is much more
in point. I am indebted to Mr. Stubbs for a transcript of the judgment.
There, the assets of the company had sufficed to pay 33·5p in the £ in a
creditors' voluntary liquidation. The liquidator wished to pay a final E
dividend, to convene final meetings, and to make his final returns; but
there was a claimant whose " excessively stale claims " had " long ago
been rejected by the liquidator," who sought to have the distribution
postponed until he had litigated his claims. The claimant had neither
lodged a formal proof nor commenced proceedings in support of his
claims; and the periods of delay, which varied with different claims, were F
of the order of five or seven or nine years or more, with intermittent
activity in some cases, and some periods of complete dormancy for five
or seven years. In those circumstances, Brightman J., who described
the delay as " grotesque," granted an application by the liquidator
under section 307 of the Act of 1948 for an order authorising him to
distribute the assets without providing for any claims of the claimant
which had not been established. The judge rejected any idea that a G
claimant could keep a voluntary liquidator on tenterhooks for an
indefinite period by deciding neither to sue nor to prove nor to proceed
under section 307 nor to abandon his claim.

That case differs from the present case in at least two important
respects. First, the delay there was " grotesque," and that cannot be
said of any delay in the present case. Second, the case was one of an H
alleged creditor against other creditors, and not as against members.
The judge mentioned as being " instructive " the words in *David* v.
Frowd, 1 Myl. & K. 200 which require from a tardy creditor in the
administration of the estate of a deceased person proof of no wilful
default and no want of reasonable diligence; but I am not at all sure that
in making his decision the judge relied on these words as providing
anything of a test for voluntary liquidation. To say that this burden rests

The Weekly Law Reports, July 18, 1980

813

1 W.L.R.   **In re R-R Realisations Ltd. (Ch.D.)**   Sir Robert
Megarry V.-C.

A on a person who seeks to recover assets which have already been distributed in the administration of the estate of a deceased person by no means leads to the conclusion that the same burden lies on a person who seeks to be included in a distribution of a company's assets which has yet to be made.

I return to the case before me. The accident occurred on October 12, 1976. Mr. Registrar Hunt regarded it as being not merely excusable but
B eminently reasonable that the plaintiffs should have awaited the publication of the report of the inquiry held by Bhasme J. in India; and this did not occur until September 22, 1978. In this, I entirely agree with the registrar. Even if the plaintiffs knew that the company was in liquidation, I can see no reason why, in such a technical matter as the cause of an aircraft accident, the plaintiffs should not take advantage of the pending
C inquiry as a means of discovering the persons and companies against which the claims should be made. True, every conceivable defendant (including the company) could have been notified on a provisional basis; but I do not think that it would have been reasonable to expect this to be done. The first letter to one of the liquidators, delivered on September 26, 1979, contained an enclosure which in its last sentence might well be
D thought to give warning of a possible claim; and in any case the letter of October 15, 1979, is explicit enough. It was no fault of the plaintiffs that neither of these letters provoked any activity on the part of the liquidators until the following month, or that the liquidators should in the meantime have been proceeding with their arrangements for the final distribution. Of course it would have been better if an earlier notification of possible claims had been sent to the liquidators; but with the complications that
E arise from the subject matter being an aircraft accident in India and the multiplicity of plaintiffs I find it impossible to regard the 12 or 13 months in question as being a period of time that ought to bar the plaintiffs' claim. If the claim had been made before the process of arranging the final distribution had begun in June 1979, it would be unthinkable to shut out the plaintiffs. It seems highly probable that the
F real complaint of the liquidators is founded on the time and money expended during the next three or four months, and in particular on the press announcement having been made on October 8, 1979.

I turn to the subject of insurance. On the facts as I know them at present, it seems highly improbable that an insurance cover of over £50m would not suffice to meet any claims that succeed. But I know
G very little of the facts, and I most certainly cannot say that I am sure that the cover will be enough. More important, I do not know whether the insurance company will accept responsibility under the policy if the liability of the company is established. It indeed looks probable that the combined effect of the deed of indemnity and the policy itself will make the insurance company responsible. But questions may arise as to the precise effect of the language of the deed and the language of the
H policy in relation to the as yet unascertained facts in each individual case. In those circumstances, ought the court to make an order which will in effect destroy any chances of success for the plaintiffs if their claims against the company are well founded but the insurance company escapes liability? To me, the question almost answers itself.

In the result, I would summarise my conclusions as follows. (1) In deciding whether to make an order under section 307 authorising

liquidators of a company in a voluntary liquidation to distribute the
assets of a company among the company's members, notwithstanding
a last-minute claim by persons who contend that they are creditors, the
test to be applied is whether in all the circumstances of the case it is
just to make such an order. There is no rule that the claimants must
establish that they have been guilty of no wilful default and no want of
due diligence, although the presence or absence of any such default or
lack of diligence will of course be a factor, and normally an important
factor, in determining what is just. (2) On making such an order the
court may impose such terms and conditions as in all the circumstances
of the case it considers fitting, or may make such other order as it
thinks just. Where the court is asked to refuse or suspend such an order,
any contention that this should be done only on terms that the claimants
should bear the expenses thrown away by their tardiness in asserting their
claims should itself be subject to the test of what is fitting and just. (3)
Where the order is sought in order to facilitate a distribution among
members, the court will be more reluctant to grant it than if the distribution
is to be made to creditors.

If I apply those conclusions to the present case, it becomes plain that
the application must be refused. I do not think that it would be just to
make the order and so shut out the plaintiffs from making any effective
claim against the company, particularly as the proposed distribution is
to members and not creditors. I can well appreciate that it is highly
inconvenient to have the proposed distribution halted in mid-course, and
postponed for an indefinite period, with the attendant wasted and
additional cost. I do not say that inconvenience and expense may not be
of such a degree as to amount to an injustice: but when this is weighed
against the proposed virtual extinction of the plaintiffs' claims against the
company's assets, I have no doubt where the balance of justice lies. As
between injustice and inconvenience of anything like equal degree, it is
injustice that must be rejected. As matters stand, I cannot regard the
rights of insurance as providing any sufficient substitute. When the claims
of the plaintiffs have been sufficiently particularised (and I do not forget
that it is not the fault of the liquidators that they lack anything more
than the broad indications given by the writ that I have mentioned),
it may be possible to get the insurance company to accept the claims
subject to liability being established; and the failure of the present
application would be no bar to the making of a renewed application when
the facts are better known. I would add that if, contrary to my views,
the plaintiffs are required to establish that they were guilty of no wilful
default and no want of due diligence, I would hold that I can see
nothing to establish wilful default, and, with a little hesitation, I would
hold that due diligence had been established. " Due diligence " is a
concept which has to be considered in relation to all the facts of the
case: and the complications of the air accident, differences of countries
and the multiplicity of claims seem to me to regulate the " diligence "
that is " due."

As for requiring the plaintiffs to reimburse the wasted expenditure
as the price of having the order refused, or some other order made,
I need only say that I think that it would be neither just nor fitting to
impose any such terms. I know nothing of the financial status of the
plaintiffs, and I would not draw any extensive inferences from the fact
that the writs were issued under emergency legal aid certificates. Those

The Weekly Law Reports, July 18, 1980

815

1 W.L.R.   In re R-R Realisations Ltd. (Ch.D.)   Sir Robert
                                                                      Megarry V.-C.

A with no assets in England may be wealthy in India. But any such term might exclude the poor in favour of the wealthy, or require the wealthy to bear more than their fair share. In any case, I do not think that such delay as there has been suffices for any requirement to bear any costs. Furthermore, the expenses thrown away are relatively modest in relation to the £5·5m to be distributed. The liquidators' estimate of the direct costs already incurred which would have to be incurred again if

B distribution is postponed is £14,700, but Mr. Heyman may be right when he says that not all of this has been thrown away by the delay. At all events, I do not think that it would be right to accede to Mr. Stubbs' application that unless the plaintiffs within so many days pay a specified sum to the liquidators the order that he sought should be made. At one stage Mr. Stubbs put this sum at £32,300, and at another stage £80,100,

C though in the end I think he had to accept that he could not sustain the larger sum.

In the result, I think that Mr. Registrar Hunt was right in the conclusion that he reached, and I dismiss the appeal. I understand that he made a representation order as prayed in paragraph 2 of the summons, and that order stands. Subject to that, I dismiss the summons.

D
                                                      Order accordingly.
                                                      Liberty to apply.

Solicitors: *Linklaters & Paines; Frere Cholmeley.*

E   K. N. B.

                              [HOUSE OF LORDS]

F
* AIR-INDIA . . . . APPELLANTS

                                   AND

WIGGINS . . . . RESPONDENT

1980 June 9;   Lord Diplock, Lord Edmund-Davies,
      July 3   Lord Keith of Kinkel, Lord Scarman
G   and Lord Roskill

*Animal — Transit of animal — Carrier's duty — Birds carried by
   Indian airline from India to England — Failure to ventilate
   aircraft causing unnecessary suffering—Failure occurring outside English airspace—Whether English courts having jurisdiction — Diseases of Animals Act* 1950 (14 *Geo.* 6, *c.* 36),
H s. 23 (*as amended by Agriculture (Miscellaneous Provisions)
   Act* 1954 (2 & 3 *Eliz.* 2, *c.* 39), *s.* 11, *Sch.* 2, *para.* 1 (1))—
   Transit of Animals (General) Order 1973 (*S.I.* 1973 *No.* 1377),
   arts. 3 (3), 5 (2)

    Section 23 of the Diseases of Animals Act 1950, as amended
by section 11 of and Schedule 2, paragraph 1 (1) to the Agriculture (Miscellaneous Provisions) Act 1954, provides, and the
Act makes contravention an offence:
    " The minister may make such orders as he thinks fit . . .

(b) for ensuring for animals carried by sea or by air a A
proper supply of food and water and proper ventilation
during the passage and on landing; (c) for protecting
them from unnecessary suffering during the passage and
on landing."

Article 3 (3) of he Transit of Animals (General) Order
1973 provides:

"In relation to carriage by sea or air, the provisions
of this order shall apply to animals carried on any vessel B
or aircraft to or from a port or airport in Great Britain,
whether or not such animals are loaded or unloaded at
such port or airport."

Article 5 (2) provides:

"No person shall carry any animal by sea, air, road or
rail, or cause or permit any animal to be so carried, in
a way which is likely to cause injury or unnecessary C
suffering to the said animal."

The defendant airline carried a cargo of live birds consigned for transport from India to Heathrow Airport. Owing
to lack of ventilation during a delay at Kuwait, the greater
part of them probably died there of asphyxiation, being
already dead when the aircraft entered British airspace. The
defendants were charged with contravening article 5 (2) of
the Transit of Animals (General) Order 1973 made by virtue D
of powers contained in section 23 (b) of the Diseases of
Animals Act 1950 by carrying the birds in such a way as
was likely to cause them injury or unnecessary suffering.

The justices convicted the defendants, holding that by
virtue of article 3 (3) proceedings could be brought against
foreign nationals for offences committed abroad. The Crown
Court upheld the conviction. The Divisional Court of the
Queen's Bench Division dismissed the defendants' appeal. The E
appeal was concerned only with the birds which had died.

On appeal by the defendants: —

Held, allowing the appeal, (per Lord Diplock, Lord
Edmund-Davies, Lord Keith of Kinkel and Lord Roskill)
that section 23 of the Act, on its true construction and
having regard to the presumption that an offence-creating
statute was not intended to cover conduct outside the Crown's
territorial jurisdiction, did not confer on the minister the F
power to create extra-territorial offences and, since the birds
were dead when they entered British airspace, no offence
involving causing them suffering within the Act had been
committed (post, pp. 819A, F, 820 A–C, D–E, 822H—823A).

Cox v. Army Council [1963] A.C. 48, H.L.(E.) and Reg.
v. Jameson [1896] 2 Q.B. 425, D.C. applied.

Per Lord Scarman. The language of section 23 can be
construed as covering extra-territorial conduct, provided the G
animals in question were on passage from, or landed at, a
British port or airport. The act which founds the jurisdiction would be the landing, but the birds were dead on arrival,
only their carcases were landed, and article 5 (2) did not cover
the landing of carcases (post, p. 822E–G).

Decision of the Divisional Court of the Queen's Bench
Division [1980] 1 W.L.R. 102; [1980] 1 All E.R. 192, D.C.
reversed. H

The following cases are referred to in their Lordships' opinions:

Cox v. Army Council [1963] A.C. 48; [1962] 2 W.L.R. 950; [1962] 1
All E.R. 880, H.L.(E.).

Practice Statement (Judicial Precedent) [1966] 1 W.L.R. 1234; [1966]
3 All E.R. 77, H.L.(E.).

Reg. v. Jameson [1896] 2 Q.B. 425, D.C.

A   The following additional case was cited in argument:

Reg. v. *Treacy* [1971] A.C. 537; [1971] 2 W.L.R. 112; [1971] 1 All
E.R. 110, H.L.(E.).

Appeal from the Divisional Court of the Queen's Bench Division.

This was an appeal from the Divisional Court of the Queen's Bench
Division (Lord Widgery C.J., Eveleigh L.J. and Kilner Brown J.) dated
B   October 15, 1979, dismissing an appeal from a decision of the Middlesex
Crown Court on October 28, 1976. The order of the Crown Court was
made on the hearing of appeals by the appellants, Air-India, against
conviction by the justices of the peace for the petty sessional division
of Uxbridge sitting at Uxbridge Magistrates' Court on June 17, 1976, on
the hearing of summonses preferred by the respondent, Geoffrey Stuart
C   Wiggins, as prosecutor under the Transit of Animals (General Order)
1973 and the Diseases of Animals Act 1950.

The facts are stated in the opinion of Lord Diplock.

Keith Evans, Frank Panford and *J. Downing* for the appellants.
E. A. Machin Q.C. and *Roger Cox* for the respondent.

D   Their Lordships took time for consideration.

July 3. LORD DIPLOCK. My Lords, in September 1975 Air-India,
the national air line of India and a subject of that sovereign state,
carried a cargo of some 2,000 live parakeets upon a flight from India
to London, Heathrow, which involved a scheduled stop at Kuwait.
E   While the aircraft was at Kuwait a fault was discovered in an engine.
In consequence of this the aircraft was delayed for 31 hours on the
tarmac at Kuwait. The 12 crates in which the parakeets were being
transported remained in the hold untended throughout this period. As
a result only 89 were found to be alive when the aircraft eventually
arrived at Heathrow. The remainder, nearly 2,000 of them, were
found to have died from asphyxiation. It was subsequently found by the
F   Crown Court that it was highly probable that these deaths occurred as
a result of the heat and lack of ventilation to which the birds were
subjected in Kuwait and that they were already dead before the aircraft
entered British airspace.

Air-India were charged before the Uxbridge Magistrates' Court with
36 offences under the Transit of Animals (General) Order 1973. For
G   the purposes of this Order " animals " include all species of birds. Your
Lordships are concerned only with the 12 charges of contraventions of
article 5 (2) of that Order, which provides:

" No person shall carry any animal by sea, air, road or rail, or
cause or permit any animal to be so carried, in a way which is
likely to cause injury or unnecessary suffering to the said animal."

H   Each of these charges related to birds packed in a single crate. All the
crates contained dead birds on arrival at Heathrow, but there was no
evidence to identify which of them contained any of the 89 birds that
survived.

Air-India were convicted on each of these 12 charges by the magistrates' court as well as on the other 24 charges. They appealed to the
Middlesex Guildhall Crown Court. That court allowed the appeal on
the other 24 charges but upheld the 12 convictions under article 5 (2)

Lord Diplock   **Air-India v. Wiggins (H.L.(E.))**   **[1980]**

of the Order. It stated for the opinion of the High Court the following   A
question of law:

> " Were we correct in holding that the provisions of the Transit of
> Animals (General) Order 1973 apply to acts done by foreign nationals
> in foreign territory provided that the vessel or aircraft in which such
> acts are done lands or docks in Great Britain during or at the
> conclusion of the same voyage? "
B

The Divisional Court in a short extempore judgment answered that
question: " Yes,"; and dismissed Air-India's appeal but certified as a
point of law of general public importance a redrafted version of the
question stated by the Crown Court, viz.:

> " Is there an offence punishable in England under the Diseases of
> Animals Act 1950 and regulations made thereunder if an airline   C
> carries animals from India to London Airport in conditions which
> constitute a breach of such regulations but the animals are dead
> before the aircraft enters English airspace? "

The matter comes before your Lordships by leave granted by this House.
    My Lords, article 5 (2) of the Transit of Animals (General) Order
1973 was made by the Minister of Agriculture, Fisheries and Food, in   D
the exercise of powers conferred upon him by section 23 (*b*) and (*c*)
of the Diseases of Animals Act 1950, as amended and applied to air
transport by section 11 of and Schedule 2, paragraph 1 (1) to the Agriculture
(Miscellaneous Provisions) Act 1954. The relevant empowering provisions in the Act of 1950 as so amended read as follows:

> " 23. The minister may make such orders as he thinks fit . . . (*b*) for   E
> ensuring for animals carried by sea or by air a proper supply of
> food and water and proper ventilation during the passage and on
> landing; (*c*) for protecting them from unnecessary suffering during
> the passage and on landing."

The Act provides by section 78 (1) (v) that any person shall be guilty
of an offence against the Act " if he does or omits anything, the doing   F
or omission whereof is declared . . . by an order of the minister to be
an offence by him against this Act; . . ." So section 23 empowers the
minister to make orders creating criminal offences.
    Article 5 (2) of the Transit of Animals (General) Order 1973, the
terms of which I have already cited, was made in exercise of the powers
conferred upon the minister by section 23. Non-compliance with its   G
provisions is declared to be an offence against the Act by article 11 of
the Order. So what the minister is purporting to do by article 5 (2) is
to make the conduct therein described a criminal offence; but there is
nothing in that article itself to suggest that it was intended to have
extra-territorial effect.
    Article 3 (3) which deals with the interpretation of the Order, con-   H
tains the provision relied on by the Divisional Court as making things
done or omitted to be done by foreign nationals in foreign countries
offences under the Act. It is in the following terms:

> " In relation to carriage by sea or air, the provisions of this order
> shall apply to animals carried on any vessel or aircraft to or from
> a port or airport in Great Britain, whether or not such animals
> are loaded or unloaded at such port or airport."

A   My Lords, in construing Acts of Parliament there is a well-established presumption that, in the absence of clear and specific words to the contrary, an " offence-creating section " of an Act of Parliament (to borrow an expression used by this House in *Cox* v. *Army Council* [1963] A.C. 48, 67) was not intended to make conduct taking place outside the territorial jurisdiction of the Crown an offence triable in an English criminal court. As Viscount Simonds put it, at p. 67:

B
"... apart from those exceptional cases in which specific provision is made in regard to acts committed abroad, the whole body of the criminal law of England deals with acts committed in England."

Cox v. *Army Council* was concerned with a statute which in the plainest possible words made acts committed abroad by serving members of the British Army offences triable by court-martial. The presumption against
C   a parliamentary intention to make acts *done by foreigners abroad* offences triable by English criminal courts is even stronger. As Lord Russell of Killowen C.J. said in *Reg.* v. *Jameson* [1896] 2 Q.B. 425, 430:

"One other general canon of construction is this—that if any construction otherwise be possible, an Act will not be construed as applying to foreigners in respect to acts done by them outside the
D   dominions of the sovereign power enacting."

Two consequences follow from these principles of statutory construction: the first is that if the minister had power to make an Order under the statute, making acts done by foreigners abroad offences triable in English criminal courts, such power must have been conferred upon him by words in the statute so clear and specific as to be incapable of any
E   other meaning; the second is that the words of the Order must themselves be explicable only as a clear and unambiguous exercise of that power. If either the empowering words of section 23 (*b*) of the Act or the enacting words of article 3 (3) of the Order would have a sensible content if restricted to acts done within the territorial jurisdiction of the Crown, they must be so construed.

F   So far as section 23 (*b*) is concerned it clearly has a sensible content if the passage of the vessel or aircraft there referred to is over the territorial airspace or waters of the United Kingdom and not beyond and the landing is at a port or airport in the United Kingdom. So no power to create extra-territorial offences is conferred on the minister by the Act. If he had purported to do so by article 5 (2) of the Order read in conjunction with article 3 (3) he would have acted ultra vires: but
G   upon its true construction read in the light of the presumptions to which I have referred the effect of article 3 (3) is not to extend but, on the contrary, to limit the ambit of article 5 (2). Article 5 (2) if it were not subject to qualification, would apply to animals carried by aircraft overflying United Kingdom airspace without landing here at all, although there would be practical difficulties in detecting and punishing
H   contraventions of the article in cases of carriage of this kind. What article 3 (3) does is to confine the application of article 5 to carriage of animals in aircraft which actually land at an airport in Great Britain whether for the purpose of loading or unloading the animals or merely in transit from one foreign airport to another.

My Lords, it is conceded by the prosecution that the offence created by article 5 (2) is a " conduct crime " not a " result crime." It was no

doubt a continuing offence so long as the parakeets were being carried A
on the aircraft in such a way as to cause or to be likely to cause suffering
to them; but the commission of the offence ceased at the moment when
their suffering and all likelihood of their further suffering ended with
their death. It is conceded by the prosecution that, except in the case
of the 89 survivors, this must have occurred at Kuwait and before the
aircraft entered United Kingdom airspace. So no offence was committed B
by Air-India in respect of the birds which were dead on arrival at
Heathrow. It is not disputed by Air India that offences were committed
in respect of the 89 birds that were still alive; but it is not possible to
identify the individual crates which contained any live birds and consequently it is not possible to identify which counts charged offences in
which any live birds were involved. In these circumstances it is common
ground that if the appeal is allowed and the question of law stated by C
the Crown Court is answered " No," all 12 convictions must be quashed.

I would allow the appeal, answer in the negative both the question
certified by the Divisional Court and stated by the Middlesex Guildhall
Crown Court, and accordingly would quash the convictions.

LORD EDMUND DAVIES. My Lords, for the reasons indicated in the D
speech of my noble and learned friend, Lord Diplock, which I have had
the advantage of reading in draft and with which I am in complete
agreement, I would quash the convictions and allow this appeal.

LORD KEITH OF KINKEL. My Lords, I agree with the speech of my
noble and learned friend, Lord Diplock, which I have had the opportunity
of considering in draft, and would accordingly allow the appeal and E
quash the convictions.

LORD SCARMAN. My Lords, the facts I need not repeat: they are
set out in the speech of my noble and learned friend, Lord Diplock. It
is with regret, and a sense of frustration, that I agree that the House
must allow the appeal. Unfortunately it is not a case in which the F
House can invoke the *Practice Statement (Judicial Precedent)* [1966] 1
W.L.R. 1234. If a rule is to be formulated which will solve the problem
raised by the case, it can only be done by creating an exception to a
generally sound principle of the common law: and that is legislative,
not judicial, work. My Lords, I would think it wrong to be led by the
shock of the present case to undermine in any way the general principle
that the criminal law of England " deals only with acts committed in G
England ": Viscount Simonds, *Cox* v. *Army Council* [1963] A.C. 48, 67.
The difficulty of the case is that the neglect which caused unnecessary
suffering and injury to the 2,000 parakeets and mynah birds on passage
with Air-India occurred in Kuwait, and led to their death long before
they entered British air space. Indeed the overwhelming probability is
that they died on the ground (but in the hold) at Kuwait. H

There are, as my noble and learned friend, Lord Diplock, has said,
two canons of construction to be observed when interpreting a statute
alleged to have extra-territorial effect. The first is a presumption that
an offence-creating section was not intended by Parliament to cover
conduct outside the territorial jurisdiction of the Crown: *Cox* v. *Army
Council* [1963] A.C. 48. The second is a presumption that a statute
will not be construed as applying to foreigners in respect of acts done

A   by them abroad: *Reg.* v. *Jameson* [1896] 2 Q.B. 425. Each presumption, is, however, rebuttable: and the strength of each will largely depend upon the subject matter of the statute under consideration. Certainly, Viscount Simonds, in *Cox's* case at p. 67, used words to suggest that specific provision in regard to acts committed abroad is necessary to rebut the presumption against extra-territoriality. But I do not think this will always be so: and, specifically, I do not think it is the correct

B   approach when the courts are faced, as in this case, with a statute which imposes, or authorises a minister to impose by order, criminal liability in respect of movements to, from, or through British ports by sea or air. In order to determine whether such a statute imposes, or authorises the imposition by order, of criminal liability in respect of conduct outside territorial limits, it is necessary to put a fair and reason-

C   able construction upon the language used in the statute, bearing in mind not only the two presumptions, which are to be treated as a general guide to Parliament's purpose, but also the nature of the specific purpose served by the statute.

This is, in my judgment, the correct approach to the interpretation of section 23 of the Diseases of Animals Act 1950. The section as amended in 1954, has been set out by my noble and learned friend,

D   Lord Diplock: and section 78 of the Act of 1950 empowers the minister to create, by order, criminal offences for infringements of the Act—which the minister has done in the Transit of Animals (General) Order 1973. The ambit of any offences created by the minister must depend upon the extent of the power conferred upon him by the Act. The offences, of which Air-India, a foreign corporation, was convicted, were

E   created by article 5 (2) of the Order. Upon a broad construction of the article, read together with article 3 (3), an offence would be committed even if the suffering or injury was caused abroad, provided always that the animals were carried to or from a British port or airport. Upon a narrow construction, the offence would be limited to suffering or injury inflicted within British air space or territorial waters or on land-

F   ing. Which is correct depends upon the construction to be put upon section 23 of the Act.

If the power conferred by the section is limited to acts occurring within territorial limits, so also is the Order. If the power is to be construed as allowing the inclusion of extra-territorial conduct, the words of the Order are wide enough to include such conduct.

G   Section 20 of the Act, as amended, covers the transit of animals by land, sea, or air, within the territorial limits of the United Kingdom. Unless section 23 has some extra-territorial effect, it serves, therefore only a very limited purpose, if any at all. International carriage by sea of live animals has been a well-known traffic for a very long time: and it is to be presumed that Parliament was well aware of its existence, when it first enacted the provision, which now appears as section 23 of

H   the Act of 1950. When Parliament added carriage by air to the section in 1954, it did so, one must infer, because it intended that the minister should be enabled to impose the same duties upon air carriers engaged in the same sort of traffic. And I would think it inconceivable that Parliament did not have in mind the need to impose a measure of control upon international sea and air carriage which included a stop in the United Kingdom.

Lord Scarman Air-India v. Wiggins (H.L.(E.)) [1980]

A more general look at the legislation, of which section 23 is part, **A** certainly does not negative, and might be thought to support, this approach to the construction of the section. The Diseases of Animals Act 1950 is a consolidating Act. The provisions now to be found in paragraphs (b) and (c) of section 23 found a place in the Contagious Diseases (Animals) Act 1878. Part II of that Act dealt with England (Parts III and IV with Scotland and Ireland). It contained elaborate **B** provisions prohibiting the landing of diseased foreign animals and requir- ing the slaughter or quarantine of any that were landed, all of which provisions, with some amendment, are to be found in the Act of 1950. It included a section empowering the Privy Council to make orders for a number of purposes, including (b) and (c) of section 23 of the Act of 1950: see section 32 (xxiii) and (xxiv). There was a consolidating Act in 1894, in which these provisions and others were re-enacted: see **C** Diseases of Animals Act 1894, section 22 (xxiii), (xxiv) and (xxv), which included paragraph (a) as well as (b) and (c) of section 23. It is impossible to read this legislation without appreciating the importance Parliament must have attached to ensuring that animals, on arrival in the United Kingdom, not only were free of disease, but also had not suffered un- necessarily by neglect during their passage and landing. Jurisdiction **D** would not—indeed could not—arise until the animals were landed: but, once landed, the inference may fairly and reasonably be drawn that Parliament intended that events or conduct, wherever occurring, could properly be included in an offence created by ministerial order, provided always that it was conduct occurring during passage to or from Britain. There is, therefore, good reason for doubting whether the presump- tions against extra-territoriality are to have full force and effect when **E** construing section 23. And the section can be construed as covering extra-territorial conduct, provided always the animals were on passage from, or landed at, a British port or airport. So to construe the section gives it a fair and reasonable meaning and, while permitting an exception, maintains the general rule that criminal jurisdiction is territorial in character. The act which founds the jurisdiction in a case such as the present would be the landing of the animals in England. **F**

But the animals in this case never were landed here: only their carcases arrived, a tragic memorial that they had once lived. All, there- fore, that can be established is that in consequence of their treatment at an airport far distant from England the birds died—almost certainly while at the airport.

Had the birds in this case, therefore, arrived at London Airport, I **G** would have held that offences were proved under article 5 (2) of the Order. But they did not. They died before they entered British air space. Their carcases arrived: but I find it impossible to construe either article 5 (2) or the section as covering the landing of carcases. Both are concerned with the living: and to extend either to cover the dead **H** would be to destroy the territorial link which enables the presumption against extra-territoriality to be modified in construing the section and the Order.

For these reasons I would allow the appeal.

LORD ROSKILL. My Lords, I have had the advantage of reading in draft the speech of my noble and learned friend, Lord Diplock. For

A the reasons therein contained, I agree that this appeal should be allowed
and the relevant convictions quashed.

Appeal allowed.

Solicitors: *Bulcraig & Davis; Comptroller and City Solicitor.*

B   F. C.

C   [QUEEN'S BENCH DIVISION : MANCHESTER]

* ROBERTS AND OTHERS *v.* RAMSBOTTOM

1979   Jan. 31;   Neill J.
       Feb. 7

D *Road Traffic—Negligence—Automatism as defence—Collision—*
   Motorist unknowingly suffering from stroke unaware of un-
   fitness to drive—Consciousness impaired or clouded but some
   awareness of surroundings and traffic conditions—Whether
   automatism—Whether negligence

The defendant, who suffered a cerebral haemorrhage unknown to himself, entered and drove his car on a road in a
town; he was unaware throughout that he was unfit to drive
E but his consciousness was impaired or clouded, he had some
awareness of his surroundings and the traffic conditions and
made a series of deliberate and voluntary though inefficient
movements with his hands and legs to manipulate the car controls. He suddenly experienced feelings of queerness and
collided with a stationary van. Still unaware that he was unfit
to drive, he drove away and then into collision with a vehicle
F which was parked at the roadside on his near side; as a result
the parked vehicle was damaged and its driver and a passenger
were injured. The plaintiffs, the vehicle owner, the driver and
the passenger, claimed damages from the defendant for loss
and personal injuries caused by his negligent driving. The
defendant denied negligence and pleaded that he was acting
in a state of automatism and was not responsible for his
actions.

G   On the question of liability: —
       Held, giving judgment for the plaintiffs, that in an action
for negligence against a car driver the standard of care by
which his actions were to be judged was an objective standard;
and that, albeit he would be able to escape liability if his
actions at the relevant time were wholly beyond his control so
as to amount to automatism in law, he could not avoid
liability on the basis that, owing to some brain malfunction,
H his consciousness was impaired; that, therefore, the defendant
was liable, for in law a state of automatism involved complete
loss of consciousness, and in any event, he was guilty of
negligence since he continued to drive with awareness of his
disabling symptoms and of his collision with the stationary
van even though he was unable to appreciate their proper
significance (post, pp. 829G, 832E–H, 833A–B).
       Hill v. *Baxter* [1958] 1 Q.B. 277, D.C.; *Watmore* v.
Jenkins [1962] 2 Q.B. 572, D.C. and *Nettleship* v. *Weston*
[1971] 2 Q.B. 691, C.A. applied.

Roberts v. Ramsbottom (Q.B.D.) [1980]

The following cases are referred to in the judgment:

Glasgow Corporation v. *Muir* [1943] A.C. 448; [1943] 2 All E.R. 44, H.L.(Sc.).

Gordon v. *Wallace* (1973) 42 D.L.R. (3d) 342.

Hill v. *Baxter* [1958] 1 Q.B. 277; [1958] 2 W.L.R. 76; [1958] 1 All E.R. 193, D.C.

Jones v. *Dennison* [1971] R.T.R. 174, C.A.

Nettleship v. *Weston* [1971] 2 Q.B. 691; [1971] 3 W.L.R. 370; [1971] 3 All E.R. 581, C.A.

Reg. v. *Gosney* [1971] 2 Q.B. 674; [1971] 3 W.L.R. 343; [1971] 3 All E.R. 220, C.A.

Reg. v. *Isitt* [1978] R.T.R. 211, C.A.

Reg. v. *Spurge* [1961] 2 Q.B. 205; [1961] 3 W.L.R. 23; [1961] 2 All E.R. 688, C.C.A.

Watmore v. *Jenkins* [1962] 2 Q.B. 572; [1962] 2 W.L.R. 463; [1962] 2 All E.R. 868, D.C.

Waugh v. *James K. Allan Ltd.* [1964] 2 Lloyd's Rep. 1, H.L.(Sc.).

No additional cases were cited in argument.

ACTION

By writ issued on June 30, 1976, the first plaintiff, Jack Roberts, the second plaintiff, Jean Roberts, wife of the first plaintiff, and the third plaintiff, Karen Jane Roberts, daughter of the first and second plaintiffs, suing by her father and next friend, brought against the defendant, Arthur Ramsbottom, an action for damages for personal injuries and loss caused by the defendant's negligent driving of a Volvo motor car on June 4, 1976, in Bolton Road, Bury, Lancashire, when it collided with a stationary Triumph motor car owned by the first plaintiff and caused injuries to the second and third plaintiffs. The defendant denied negligence.

The facts are stated in the judgment.

John Stannard for the plaintiffs.

H. K. Goddard and *R. D. Machell* for the defendant.

Cur. adv. vult.

February 7, 1979. NEILL J. read the following judgment. Mr. and Mrs. Roberts live at 171, Ainsworth Road, Bury. On June 4, 1976, Mrs. Roberts drove in her husband's Triumph car to a launderette in Bolton Road, Bury. Her daughter, Karen, who was born on February 1, 1964, was with her sitting in the front passenger seat. The launderette was called Laundercentre. It was on the south side of Bolton Road between Buxton Street and Fountain Street. Mrs. Roberts approached the shop from the south-west, that is, from the direction of Bolton. She waited for a gap in the traffic and then drove across to the off side of the road and parked outside Laundercentre facing towards Bury. Mrs. Roberts opened the door and prepared to get out on to the pavement. She turned to pick up her handbag. A moment later she was thrown out on to the pavement. A Volvo car driven by the defendant had come up the road from the direction of Bury and had collided head-on with the Triumph car driven by Mrs. Roberts. Karen had seen the car approaching and had ducked beneath the dashboard but the windscreen of the Triumph car was shattered and Karen was seriously injured by broken glass. Mrs.

A Roberts also was injured but less seriously. The Triumph car was damaged beyond repair. The collision took place at about 10.20 a.m.

No criticism whatever is made of Mrs. Roberts's driving. It is accepted on behalf of the defendant that the facts which I have outlined and which are not in dispute would, if unexplained, entitle the plaintiffs to damages caused by negligent driving by the defendant. The first plaintiff, Mr. Jack Roberts, sues in respect of the damage to his car and in respect

B of certain other loss resulting from the collision. His claim is agreed subject to liability at £968·87. The second plaintiff is Mrs. Jean Roberts. She was the driver. She sues in respect of the injuries she suffered. The third plaintiff is Miss Karen Roberts, the daughter. She also sues for damages for personal injuries.

The defendant is Mr. Arthur Ramsbottom. He lives at 396, Brandles-

C holme Road, Bury. He was born on December 2, 1902. He was there-fore 73 at the date of the collision. His defence is that approximately 20 minutes before the collision he suffered a stroke, that is, a cerebral haemorrhage, which so clouded his consciousness that from that moment he was, through no fault of his own, unable properly to control his car or to appreciate that he was no longer fit to drive. Accordingly, argued Mr. Goddard on behalf of the defendant, the defendant was not negligent.

D It is therefore necessary for me to consider the evidence as to the defendant's driving before the collision and the medical evidence as to the effect of his stroke. It is also necessary for me to consider the relevant principles of law.

The defendant's journey to Bolton Road

E By profession the defendant was an accountant. When he was 65 he retired from full-time work but he continued to go to work for part of the day. He used to drive every day from his home at 396, Brandlesholme Road to his office in East Street in Bury. It was a journey of about two miles or a little more. Sometimes his wife went with him in order to go shopping. On June 4, 1976, he got ready to leave about 10 o'clock. It was

F a day his wife was going to go with him. Mrs. Ramsbottom went up-stairs to get her coat. She came down. She found that her husband had gone without her. She was astonished because he had never gone off like this before, leaving her behind when he had arranged to take her. It was so unusual an event that after a time she telephoned the police.

Meanwhile, the defendant had set off towards the centre of Bury in his

G blue Volvo car. There was no evidence before me relating to the earlier part of his journey. The defendant himself cannot now remember any part of his journey or any of the events of that morning and no other witness threw light on the defendant's movement before he reached Irwell Street. I am entitled to infer, however, and I do infer, that the defendant drove down Brandlesholme Road from his home at number 396 and then along Crostons Road into Bolton Street and round the roundabout into

H the continuation of Bolton Street on the east side of the roundabout. If he had followed his usual route the defendant would have then continued eastwards to the Market Place, turned right into Market Street and then driven into Angouleme Way and Spring Street to his office in East Street. On that morning, however, instead of following his usual route, the defendant turned south just beyond the roundabout in Bolton Street and went down Irwell Street.

About half-way along Irwell Street on the east side there is a police

station. About 10.15 a.m. on June 4, 1976, there was a van parked out- A
side the police station. Sitting in the van were Mr. Kay and Mr. Banks.
They were waiting for a colleague. Both Mr. Kay and Mr. Banks gave
evidence and there was some conflict of recollection between them about
what they saw. I prefer the evidence of Mr. Banks and I accept his
account of what happened. This is what he said. He was sitting in the
van when he felt a bang at the rear of the van. He got out and saw that
the off side corner at the back of the van had been hit by a blue Volvo. B
It was the defendant's car. The Volvo was at an angle as though it had
been trying to overtake too late. The defendant tried to reverse. He had
difficulty in getting into gear and when he reversed he moved the car in a
jerky manner. Mr. Banks walked back to where the car was. By then
the defendant had got out and was walking across the road to the path
on the other side. As he crossed the road the defendant was narrowly C
missed by a gas board van. Mr. Banks asked him if he was all right. He
said, " Yes, yes, yes." Mr. Banks asked him if he was sure. " Yes, yes,"
he said. The defendant gave Mr. Banks the impression that he was slightly
dazed and his speech seemed slightly slurred. Mr. Banks noticed when
the defendant crossed the road that he had an uneven gait. The defendant got back in his car and moved forward. He pulled up just behind
the van, only a foot away. Once more he had to reverse. Mr. Banks D
again asked him if he was all right and he said he was. " Are you sure
now? " said Mr. Banks. " Yes," said the defendant. After he had
reversed the second time the defendant drove forward. On this occasion
he avoided the van by a good margin and drove off down Irwell Street.
As the defendant went down the road, however, Mr. Banks saw that he
narrowly missed two men working in the road who waved and shouted. E
The defendant passed from view. A few minutes later Mr. Banks was
joined by the third man in the van and he drove off. By chance his route
took him to Bolton Road. There he saw the blue Volvo again. It was
outside the Laundercentre. It had collided with the Triumph. The
defendant was walking about in the road in a dazed condition.

It is clear that from Irwell Street the defendant had driven across into F
Tenterden Street and had then turned right into Millett Street. At the
end of Millett Street he turned left into Bolton Street and then along
Bolton Road. In Bolton Road, about 100 yards or so before he collided
with the Triumph, the defendant's car brushed past a boy on a bicycle.
The boy, young Mr. Hardman, was just by the Manchester Motor Mart
in Bolton Road. He was riding a few inches from the kerb. He was
knocked off his bicycle and fell on the pavement. There was plenty of G
room in the road for the defendant to have passed him normally. A few
moments later Mr. Hardman saw the defendant's car crash into the
Triumph.

The distance travelled by the defendant from his home to where he
collided with the Triumph car was about two-and-a-half miles and involved travelling round a busy part of Bury and going round a number of H
corners.

The events following the collision

After the collision Mrs. Roberts, Karen and the defendant were taken
together by ambulance to hospital. At the hospital it was not appreciated
at once that the defendant had had a stroke.

A   At 11.30 a.m. he was seen at the hospital by Police Constable Flanagan.
No criticism whatever can be made of the constable for interviewing the
defendant. He had asked a nurse if he could see the defendant and had
been told that he could. He described the defendant as appearing to be
dazed. Constable Flanagan told the defendant that he was making inquiries
about the collision. He cautioned the defendant. This is what the
defendant told him: " I suddenly felt queer and I ran into the van. I felt
B all right after that and I carried on. I felt queer again later and I hit the
car." A little later he said: " I felt a bit queer before I ran into the van.
I went away and felt all right. After that I felt a bit queer again and
I hit the other car." The defendant that morning was also questioned by
the medical staff at the hospital. I have not seen the hospital notes but
it is common ground that the relevant parts of the hospital notes were
C reproduced by Dr. Riley in a letter which he wrote to the defendant's
insurers dated August 24, 1976. The second paragraph of that letter
contains these sentences:

> "He was then driving his car at about 10 a.m. when he felt rather
> dizzy for about 15 minutes and then nauseated. He kept on driving
> and then he remembers crashing his car before losing consciousness
D > and he was apparently unconscious for about two minutes. He was
> admitted to Bury General Hospital."

I am satisfied that the information in that paragraph and in the hospital notes must have come originally from the defendant. I consider,
however, that there is force in Mr. Goddard's argument, which was supported by the medical evidence, that the information may well have been
E based on questions and answers and the defendant may have done no
more than say yes to various questions which were put to him. I do not
therefore attach great importance to what the defendant appears to have
told the doctors. But I do attach considerable significance to the defendant's interview with Constable Flanagan. There is no suggestion that
the police officer put any words into the defendant's mouth.

F
The medical evidence

      On the day after the collision the defendant was seen by Dr. M. E.
Benaim, a consultant physician at Bury General Hospital, where the
defendant had been detained. By this stage the defendant was unable to
remember anything about his journey to Bolton Road. I understand it is
typical for a stroke to be followed by progressive amnesia. He told Dr.
G Benaim he had blacked out and could not remember any more. The
defendant was under Dr. Benaim's care at the hospital. He was very
confused for several days and was discharged after about a fortnight.
Dr. Benaim was satisfied that the defendant had had a stroke and also
thought at one time that he might have had an epileptic attack as well.
He agreed with Dr. Evans (to whose evidence I shall have to refer later)
H that the stroke probably started just before the defendant left home. He
expressed the following opinions. First, that once the stroke had started
the defendant would not have been completely normal and he would not
have been able to judge the quality of his own driving. Secondly, that the
defendant's mental condition following the onset of the stroke could be
correctly termed a clouding of consciousness. Thirdly, in order to drive
in traffic it is necessary for a driver to exercise his will and his capacity
to think, and that when stopping and giving way to approaching traffic a

deliberate decision has to be made. Fourthly, on the subject of what the   A
defendant said to the police officer and may have told the medical staff
on June 4, 1976, Dr. Benaim said that he was not certain that the defendant would in fact have felt dizzy and that when he saw the defendant the
next day, he himself would not have placed any reliance on what the
defendant said. In cross-examination, however, he agreed that the case
notes might be an accurate account of what the defendant actually experienced and, further, that he had no reason to doubt that what the   B
defendant said to the police officer was accurate.

The main medical evidence called on behalf of the defendant was the
evidence of Dr. John Evans, who is a consultant neurologist of the Salford
Group of Hospitals and a lecturer in medicine at the University of Manchester. In addition to giving oral evidence he produced a medical report
dated July 11, 1977. In the witness box Dr. Evans told me that he   C
remained of the opinion expressed in that report. I shall therefore refer
to that part of his report under the heading " Conclusion: "

> " At my examination today "—that is July 11, 1977—" Mr. Rams-
> bottom shows evidence of a moderately severe left hemiparesis with
> sensory loss down the left side of the body and sensory inattention
> to visual stimuli in the left half of his visual field. In addition he   D
> shows an impairment of intellect characterised by a marked impair-
> ment of short term memory. These neurological signs have been
> present since the episode on June 4, 1976. I am of the opinion that
> while his wife was upstairs changing preparatory to going out, Mr.
> Ramsbottom sustained a stroke causing severe disorientation of
> thought and impairment of memory, weakness of the left side of the   E
> body and inattention of his left visual field. It was in this disorien-
> tated condition that he went off in his car, forgetting to take his wife
> with him, and it was in the same disorientated state that he collided
> with the bicycle and the van and the car. It is clear that Mr. Rams-
> bottom was ill at the time of this incident, he did not fully appreciate
> what he was doing and he had no full control over his movements.
> He was, in effect, acting in a state of automatism and he was not   F
> responsible for his actions. At the same time Mr. Ramsbottom was
> not aware of the severity of his incapacity and he was not in a posi-
> tion to judge whether or not he was fit enough to take the wheel of
> his car. He has made a partial recovery from his stroke but still
> remains severely incapacitated. He is not fit to drive a car. He will
> continue to need help and care and attention from his wife."   G

Then Dr. Evans dealt with the suggestion that the defendant might have
suffered an epileptic fit and expressed the view that in his opinion he had
not.

In his evidence-in-chief Dr. Evans repeated what he had said in his
report about automatism. He said that in his view there was no evidence
in favour of an epileptic fit having occurred and that he was certain when   H
the defendant had been driving along he was not capable of forming any
rational opinion as to whether he was able to drive. And later he said
that the clouding of consciousness resulted in the defendant being unable to
appreciate fully what had happened or to appreciate that he was incapable
of driving the car properly. He described, as I have said, the defendant's
condition as a clouding of consciousness. He also expressed the opinion
that a person in the defendant's condition on June 4 following his stroke

A would have given a most misleading account to a police officer or anyone else as to what had happened. In cross-examination, however, Dr. Evans accepted that a person in the defendant's condition might have felt queer and rather dizzy and might have experienced a feeling of nausea. He also agreed that the defendant could have experienced what he described to the police officer.

B He was also questioned about the extent of the defendant's consciousness. He agreed that the defendant was not unconscious but that his consciousness was impaired or clouded from the time he set out. He accepted that the defendant's movements in driving were deliberate movements and that to drive along the route which the defendant followed involved purposeful acts. He described the defendant's state at the time of collision with the Triumph as a state of impaired consciousness. Nevertheless, Dr. Evans remained unshaken in his evidence that the defendant

C did not know that he was driving badly or that he was unfit to drive. He told me that after the initial onset of the stroke further damage to the brain would have occurred all the time during the next hour or so. During that period the defendant's capacity to drive might have fluctuated somewhat but his physical condition must have got worse.

D I have summarised the main points of the evidence and I must now state my findings of fact in relation to the defendant's driving and his condition when driving. It is not in dispute that the circumstances of the collision establish a prima facie case of negligence. I can set out my findings shortly as follows.

First, I find that the defendant suffered a stroke on June 4, 1976, and that the onset of the stroke began shortly before he left home at about

E 10 a.m. Second, before he suffered that stroke the defendant had had no previous symptoms or warning signs. Third, that following the onset of the stroke the defendant's consciousness was impaired. Fourth, that this state of impaired or clouded consciousness continued throughout the defendant's journey from his home to the point of impact in Bolton Road. Fifth, that the defendant did experience the feelings of queerness which he described to the police officer and did know at the time it hap-

F pened that he had hit the van. Sixth, that throughout the journey to Bolton Road and up to the moment of impact with the Triumph car the defendant was sufficiently in possession of his faculties (a) to have some though an impaired awareness of his surroundings and the traffic conditions; and (b) to make a series of deliberate and voluntary though inefficient movements of his hands and legs to manipulate the controls

G of his car. Seventh, that the defendant was at no time aware of the fact that he was unfit to drive; accordingly no moral blame can be attached to him for continuing to do so.

I must turn therefore to consider the law applicable to these facts. The standard of care by which a driver's actions are to be judged in an action based on negligence is an objective standard. Every driver, includ-

H ing a learner driver:

" must drive in as good a manner as a driver of skill, experience and care, who is sound in wind and limb, who makes no errors of judgment, has good eyesight and hearing and is free from any infirmity: . . . "
see Lord Denning M.R. in *Nettleship* v. *Weston* [1971] 2 Q.B. 691, 699.

It is the same standard as that which is applied in the criminal law in relation to offences of dangerous driving and driving without due care

and attention. The standard "eliminates the personal equation and is   A
independent of the idiosyncrasies of the particular person whose conduct
is in question": see the speech of Lord Macmillan in *Glasgow Corporation* v. *Muir* [1943] A.C. 448, 457.

As Salmon L.J. said in *Nettleship* v. *Weston* [1971] 2 Q.B. 691, 703:
"On grounds of public policy, neither the criminal nor civil responsibility
is affected by the fact that the driver in question may be a learner, infirm
or drunk." The liability of a driver in tort is not, however, a strict liability   B
Nor is the offence of dangerous driving an absolute offence. In *Reg.* v.
Gosney [1971] 2 Q.B. 674 Megaw L.J., in relation to a charge of dangerous driving, said, at p. 680:

"It is not an absolute offence. In order to justify a conviction there
must be, not only a situation which, viewed objectively, was dangerous, but there must also have been some fault on the part of the   C
driver, causing that situation. 'Fault' certainly does not necessarily
involve deliberate misconduct or recklessness or intention to drive in
a manner inconsistent with proper standards of driving. Nor does
fault necessarily involve moral blame. Thus there is fault if an inexperienced or a naturally poor driver, while straining every nerve to
do the right thing, falls below the standard of a competent and care-   D
ful driver. Fault indicates a failure, a falling below the care or skill
of a competent and experienced driver, in relation to the manner of
the driving and to the relevant circumstances of the case. A fault in
that sense, even though it be slight, even though it be a momentary
lapse, even though normally no danger would have arisen from it,
is sufficient."
                                                                           E
As Megaw L.J. said a little later in his judgment in *Reg* v. *Gosney* [1971]
2 Q.B. 674, 680: "Such a fault will often be sufficiently proved as an
inference from the very facts of the situation." But there may be cases
where the driver will be able to raise some matter sufficient to avoid the
inference of fault.

In the criminal cases concerned with dangerous driving guidance is   F
given as to the circumstances in which some sudden event will provide
a defence. In *Reg.* v. *Spurge* [1961] 2 Q.B. 205 Salmon J., in delivering
the judgment of the Court of Criminal Appeal, said, at p. 210:

"If, however, a motor-car endangers the public solely by reason of
some sudden overwhelming misfortune suffered by the man at the
wheel for which he is in no way to blame—if, for example, he suddenly has an epileptic fit or passes into a coma, or is attacked by a   G
swarm of bees or stunned by a blow on the head from a stone, then
he is not guilty of driving in a manner dangerous to the public . . . It
would be otherwise if he had felt an illness coming on but still continued to drive, for that would have been a manifestly dangerous
thing to do."
                                                                           H
A little later, in relation to a defect in the vehicle, he went on, at
pp. 210–211:

"There does not seem to this court to be any real distinction between
a man being suddenly deprived of all control of a motor-car by some
sudden affliction of his person and being so deprived by some defect
suddenly manifesting itself in the motor-car. In both cases the motor-
car is suddenly out of control of its driver through no fault of his."

A   In the course of his judgment, at p. 210, Salmon J. also explained that the defendant in what may be called the " sudden affliction " cases may be able to escape liability on the additional ground that he was not driving at all. It was this ground which was considered by the Divisional Court in *Hill* v. *Baxter* [1958] 1 Q.B. 277. Lord Goddard C.J. said, at p. 283 : ". . . there may be cases where the circumstances are such that the accused could not really be said to be driving at all." And Pearson J. put the

B matter in these terms, at p. 286 :

> " In any ordinary case, when once it has been proved that the accused was in the driving seat of a moving car, there is, prima facie, an obvious and irresistible inference that he was driving it. No dispute or doubt will arise on that point unless and until there is evidence tending to show that by some extraordinariy mischance he was ren-
>
C > dered unconscious or otherwise incapacitated from controlling the car."

    In civil cases too a defendant may be able to rebut a prima facie case of negligence by showing that a sudden affliction has rendered him unconscious or otherwise wholly incapable of controlling the vehicle. In *Waugh*

D *v. James K. Allan Ltd.* [1964] 2 Lloyd's Rep. 1 it was contended in the Inner House of the Court of Session that the driver had been driving negligently. But Lord Clyde L.P., in his judgment in the Inner House of the Court of Session, said, at p. 2 :

> " In the first place it was contended that Gemmell was driving his lorry in a negligent and dangerous manner and was therefore guilty of negligence. But it seems to me clear on the evidence that the
>
E > driver was at the time of the accident to the pursuer so completely disabled by the sudden onset of the coronary thrombosis as to have ceased to be responsible for the alarming manoeuvres of his lorry, and the Lord Ordinary had ample evidence upon which he was entitled to negative this ground of fault."

F This ground of negligence was not pursued in the House of Lords, where the only question which was debated was whether the driver should have realised that he was unfit to drive.

    Jones v. *Dennison* [1971] R.T.R. 174 is a similar case. The driver, who was an epileptic, had a sudden blackout but the argument in the Court of Appeal was concerned wholly with the question whether he was or ought reasonably to have been aware of a tendency on his part to

G suffer a blackout : see also the Canadian case of *Gordon* v. *Wallace* (1973) 42 D.L.R. (3d) 342, and the cases there referred to.

    In the present case, however, I am not concerned with a total loss of consciousness but with a clouding or impairment of consciousness. I must turn again for assistance to the criminal cases where specific consideration has been given to what is called the defence of automatism.

H   In *Watmore* v. *Jenkins* [1962] 2 Q.B. 572 the defendant was charged with three offences including dangerous driving and driving without due care and attention. The defendant was a diabetic who had had an attack of infective hepatitis. In the course of driving home from his office he suffered a hypoglycaemic episode and in a gradually worsening state of concussion he drove from Mitcham to a point about five miles away in Coulsdon where he crashed into the back of a car. The defendant had no recollection of this part of his journey and had had no warning of the

onset of the episode. The justices acquitted the defendant on the grounds A
that at all material times he was in a state of automatism. The Divisional
Court, consisting of five judges presided over by Lord Parker C.J., remitted
the case to the justices with a direction to convict. Winn J. who delivered
the judgment of the court, said, at p. 586:

" It is . . . a question of law what constitutes a state of automatism
. . . this expression is no more than a modern catch-phrase which the B
courts have not accepted as connoting any wider or looser concept
than involuntary movement of the body or limbs of a person."

And later, at p. 587, he referred to " such a complete destruction of voluntary control as could constitute in law automatism."

To the same effect was the judgment of the Court of Appeal in *Reg.* v.
Isitt [1978] R.T.R. 211. Lawton L.J. referred to acts done during an C
epileptic attack and continued, at p. 216: " What the accused does in
those circumstances is involuntary. Acts performed involuntarily have
come to be known as automatism." But he added, at p. 216:

" It is a matter of human experience that the mind does not always
operate in top gear. There may be some difficulty in functioning. If
the difficulty does not amount in law to either insanity or automatism, D
is the accused to be entitled to say ' I am not guilty because my mind
was not working in top gear '? In our judgment he is not."

In *Reg.* v. *Isitt* [1978] R.T.R. 211 there was medical evidence that at the
material time the defendant was suffering from some malfunction of the
mind. But the facts showed that he had driven in that state for a considerable distance and his driving was described by Lawton L.J., at p. 216, E
as " purposeful driving."

Finally, the decision of the Divisional Court in *Hill* v. *Baxter* [1958]
1 Q.B. 277 to which I have already referred, provides additional support
for the proposition that in law a state of automatism involves a complete
loss of consciousness.

I am satisfied that in a civil action a similar approach should be F
adopted. The driver will be able to escape liability if his actions at the
relevant time were wholly beyond his control. The most obvious case is
sudden unconsciousness. But if he retained some control, albeit imperfect control, and his driving, judged objectively, was below the required
standard, he remains liable. His position is the same as a driver who is
old or infirm. In my judgment unless the facts establish what the law
recognises as automatism the driver cannot avoid liability on the basis that G
owing to some malfunction of the brain his consciousness was impaired.
Mr. Stannard put the matter accurately, as I see it, when he said: " One
cannot accept as exculpation anything less than total loss of consciousness."

It is true that in the present case Dr. Evans described the defendant's
condition as one of automatism. I am satisfied, however, that his con- H
dition did not amount to automatism as that word has been used in the
decided cases.

I therefore consider that the defendant is liable in law for his driving
when he collided with the Triumph car in Bolton Road.

I also consider that the plaintiffs would be entitled to succeed, if necessary, on the alternative ground put forward, that is, that the defendant
continued to drive when he was unfit to do so and when he should have

A been aware of his unfitness. He was aware that he had been feeling queer and had hit the van. Owing to his mental state he was unable to appreciate that he should have stopped. As I have said, and I repeat, the defendant was in no way morally to blame, but that is irrelevant to the question of legal liability in this case. An impairment of judgment does not provide a defence. I consider that the defendant was in law guilty of negligence in continuing to drive because he was aware of his disabling

B symptoms and of his first collision even though he was not able to appreciate their proper significance.

I turn therefore to the question of damages. [His Lordship considered the evidence relating to damages, and continued:] In those circumstances the damages will be as I have already stated: that is, for the first plaintiff £968·87; for the second plaintiff £700; and for the third plaintiff

C £2,500.

> Judgment for plaintiffs accordingly
> together with interest to be agreed
> and costs.
> Liberty to apply.
> Legal aid taxation of plaintiffs' costs.
> Stay for 28 days.

D

Solicitors: Frederick Howarth Son & Maitland, Bury; A. W. Mawer & Co., Manchester.

L. N. W.

E

[COURT OF APPEAL]

* CASTANHO v. BROWN AND ROOT (U.K.) LTD.
AND ANOTHER

F [1977 C. No. 8927]

1979 Oct. 29, 30; Nov. 19   Parker J.

1980 Feb. 13, 14, 15, 18, 19;   Lord Denning M.R., Shaw
          April 22   and Brandon L.JJ.

G Practice—Discontinuance of action—Interim payments, effect of—
          Portuguese plaintiff injured on American ship in English port—
          English personal injuries action—Defendants making interim
          payments—Notice of discontinuance without leave—Injunc-
          tion to restrain proceedings for higher damages in United
          States—Whether notice of discontinuance and injunction valid
          —R.S.C., Ord. 21, r. 2 (1) (2); Ord. 29, r. 9
    Practice — Stay of proceedings — Jurisdiction — Personal injuries—
          Portuguese plaintiff injured on American ship in English port—
H   Action begun in England—Proceedings in United States for
          higher damages on contingency fee basis—Whether injunction
          to stay proceedings in foreign forum valid

    The plaintiff, a Portuguese subject, was rendered a quadri-
plegic by an accident in February 1977 while he was employed
by the second defendants, a Panamanian company, on an
American ship lying in an English port which was serviced
by the first defendants, an English company. Both defendants
were associates of a large Texas based group of companies.

Castanho v. Brown & Root Ltd. (C.A.)   **[1980]**

While the plaintiff was in hospital in England a writ was
issued in September 1977 by English solicitors claiming damages
for his severe injuries. In November 1977 the plaintiff was
taken back to Portugal. On March 22, 1978, at the invitation
of the defendant's solicitors a consent order was made under
R.S.C., Ord. 29, r. 9,[1] for an interim payment of £7,250 to
the plaintiff and a further order for an interim payment of
£20,000 was made on December 8, 1978.

During 1978 a firm of Texan attorneys contacted the
plaintiff in order to persuade him to bring proceedings in
Texas where higher damages could be obtained. On February
8, 1979, the plaintiff executed a power of attorney giving the
Texan firm exclusive powers to prosecute his claim in the
United States and providing for them to be paid one-third of
the sum recovered in an out of court settlement and 40 per
cent. if a petition were filed; and further providing that the
English action was not to be concluded prior to the decision
in the United States. On April 30, 1979, after proceedings
on the plaintiff's behalf had been commenced in a Texas
state court, the defendants delivered a defence in the English
action in which liability was admitted by the second defendants.

On May 14, 1979, the plaintiff's English solicitors served
notice of discontinuance on the defendants under R.S.C.,
Ord. 21, r. 2(1).[2] In July 1979 a fresh action claiming
compensatory and punitive damages was started on the plaintiff's behalf in a United States federal court in Texas and
the proceedings in the state court were ended by filing a
non-suit.

Parker J. struck out the notice of discontinuance as being
an abuse of process of the court and granted an injunction
restraining the plaintiff from commencing or continuing proceedings in the United States in respect of a claim for damages
for the personal injuries he had sustained in the accident.

On appeal by the plaintiff, who had issued a fresh writ in
England to protect his position in case the court in Texas
declined jurisdiction: —

Held, allowing the appeal (Lord Denning M.R. dissenting),
that (*per* Shaw L.J.), since the plaintiff had complied with
the explicit requirements of R.S.C., Ord. 21, r. 2 (1) and there
had been no abuse of the process of the court, the notice of
May 14, 1979, was a valid notice of discontinuance, the English
proceedings were validly terminated and the judge's orders
should be discharged (post, pp. 864D–E, H—865B, 866G); (*per*
Brandon L.J.) that, on the assumption that after the notice of
discontinuance the court had jurisdiction to grant the injunction, the great advantage to the plaintiff in suing in Texas
where much higher damages were obtainable outweighed the
disadvantages to the defendants of his being allowed to do so
and that, provided the interim payments were repaid and the
protective English action stayed, justice required that he should
be left free to sue in Texas and, accordingly, subject to those
two conditions, the judge's orders should be set aside (post pp.
868B–D, 872H—873C).

Per Lord Denning M.R. Once interim payments have
been sought, received and spent, a plaintiff cannot discontinue
without the leave of the court; alternatively, it is an abuse

[1] R.S.C., Ord. 29, r. 9: ". . . 'interim payment,' in relation to a defendant,
means a payment on account of any damages in respect of personal injuries to the
plaintiff. . . ."

R. 10: "In an action for personal injuries the plaintiff may, at any time after
the writ has been served on a defendant . . . apply to the court for an order
requiring that defendant to make an interim payment."

[2] R.S.C., Ord. 21, r. 2: "(1) The plaintiff in an action begun by writ may,
without the leave of the court, discontinue the action . . . at any time not later than
14 days after service of the defence on him. . . ."

A   of the process of the court to discontinue without such leave
which, since the financial arrangements with the Texan lawyers
were champertous, and the plaintiff had elected to litigate in
England, should not be given (post, pp. 854H—856A, F–G, H—
856A, C).
      A declaration that the notice of discontinuance was invalid
should be substituted for the injunction (post, pp. 856H—857A).
      A summons for committal for contempt cannot be served out
B   of the jurisdiction in any circumstances (post, p. 856H).
      Per curiam. (i) There is a lacuna in the Rules of the
Supreme Court which make no provision for the position where
interim payments are made under R.S.C., Ord. 29, rr. 9–17,
by a defendant who subsequently gives notice of discontinuance
under R.S.C., Ord. 21, r. 2 (1) (post, pp. 854D–F, H, 863C–D,
871A–C).
      (ii) The jurisdiction to grant an injunction restraining a
C   person from suing in a foreign forum is one which should be
exercised with great caution (post, pp. 856F, 865G–H, 869B).
      Decision of Parker J., post, p. 837A reversed.

      The following cases are referred to in the judgments in the Court of
      Appeal:
      Atlantic Star, The [1974] A.C. 436; [1973] 2 W.L.R. 795; [1973] 2 All
D   E.R. 175, H.L.(E.).
      Busfield, In re (1886) 32 Ch.D. 123, C.A.
      Carron Iron Co. Proprietors v. *Maclaren* (1855) 5 H.L.Cas. 416, H.L.(E.).
      Chaparral, The [1972] 2 Lloyds Rep. 315.
      Christiansborg, The (1885) 10 P.D. 141, C.A.
      Cohen v. *Rothfield* [1919] 1 K.B. 410, C.A.
      Fox v. *Star Newspaper Co. Ltd.* [1898] 1 Q.B. 636, C.A.; [1900] A.C.
E   19, H.L.(E.).
      Goldsmith v. *Sperrings Ltd.* [1977] 1 W.L.R. 478; [1977] 2 All E.R. 566,
          C.A.
      Hess v. *Labouchere* (1898) 14 T.L.R. 350, C.A.
      Mackender v. *Feldia A.G.* [1967] 2 Q.B. 590; [1967] 2 W.L.R. 119;
          [1966] 3 All E.R. 847, C.A.
      Mackey v. *James Henry Monks (Preston) Ltd.* [1918] A.C. 59, H.L.(I.)
      MacShannon v. *Rockware Glass Ltd.* [1978] A.C. 795; [1978] 2 W.L.R.
F   362; [1978] 1 All E.R. 625, H.L.(E.).
      Settlement Corporation v. *Hochschild* [1966] Ch. 10; [1965] 3 W.L.R.
          1150; [1965] 3 All E.R. 486.
      Tropaioforos, The (No. 2) [1962] 1 Lloyd's Rep. 410.
      United Australia Ltd. v. *Barclays Bank Ltd.* [1941] A.C. 1; [1940] 4
          All E.R. 20, H.L.(E.).

G   The following additional cases were cited in argument in the Court of
      Appeal:
      Acrow (Automation) Ltd. v. *Rex Chainbelt Inc.* [1971] 1 W.L.R. 1676;
          [1971] 3 All E.R. 1175, C.A.
      Conybeare v. *Lewis* (1880) 13 Ch.D. 469, C.A.
      Hartlepool, The (1950) 84 Ll.L.R. 145.
      Hospital for Sick Children (Board of Governors) v. *Walt Disney Produc-*
H   *tions Inc.* [1968] Ch. 52; [1967] 2 W.L.R. 1250; [1967] 1 All E.R.
          1005, C.A.
      Ionian Bank Ltd. v. *Couvreur* [1969] 1 W.L.R. 781; [1969] 2 All E.R.
          651, C.A.
      Kinnaird (Lord) v. *Field,* [1905] 2 Ch. 306, C.A.
      Liddell's Settlement Trusts, In re [1936] Ch. 365, C.A.
      M'Elroy v. *M'Allister,* 1949 S.C. 110.
      McHenry v. *Lewis* (1882) 22 Ch.D. 397, C.A.
      Metropolitan Bank Ltd. v. *Pooley* (1885) 10 App.Cas 210, H.L.(E.).

Mundy v. *Butterley Co. Ltd.* [1932] 2 Ch. 227.   A
Newcomen v. *Coulson* (1878) 7 Ch.D. 764.
Peruvian Guano Co. v. *Bockwoldt* (1883) 23 Ch.D. 225, C.A.
Raymond v. *Tapson* (1882) 22 Ch.D. 430, C.A.
Sayers v. *International Drilling Co. N.V.* [1971] 1 W.L.R. 1176; [1971]
    3 All E.R. 163, C.A.
Senior v. *Holdsworth, Ex parte Independent Television News Ltd.* [1976]
    Q.B. 23; [1975] 2 W.L.R. 987; [1975] 2 All E.R. 1009, C.A.   B
Siskina (Owners of cargo lately laden on board) v. *Distos Compania
    Naviera S.A.* [1979] A.C. 210; [1977] 3 W.L.R. 818; [1977] 3 All
    E.R. 803, H.L.(E.).
Soya Margareta, The [1961] 1 W.L.R. 709; [1960] 2 All E.R. 756.

The following cases are referred to in the judgment of Parker J.:

Atlantic Star, The [1974] A.C. 436; [1973] 2 W.L.R. 795; [1973] 2 All   C
    E.R. 175, H.L.(E.).
Christiansborg, The (1885) 10 P.D. 141, C.A.
Conybeare v. *Lewis* (1880) 13 Ch.D. 469, C.A.
MacShannon v. *Rockware Glass Ltd.* [1978] A.C. 795; [1978] 2 W.L.R.
    362; [1978] 1 All E.R. 625, H.L.(E.).
Newcomen v. *Coulson* (1878) 7 Ch.D. 764.
Tropaioforos, The (*No.* 2) [1962] 1 Lloyd's Rep. 410.   D

APPLICATIONS

By writ of September 29, 1977, the plaintiff, Inocencio Fernando
Castanho, claimed against the defendants, Brown and Root (U.K.) Ltd.
and (by amendment of the writ) Jackson Marine S.A., damages for
personal injuries suffered and losses and expenses incurred as a result of
an accident which occurred on or about February 11, 1977, on the   E
American Moon at Great Yarmouth, Norfolk, arising out of the negligence and/or breach of statutory duty of the defendants, their servants
or agents.

The defendants applied by summons for orders to strike out the
plaintiff's notice of discontinuance of May 14, 1979, and for an injunction
restraining the plaintiff his servants or agents (1) from continuing or   F
prosecuting or causing to be continued or prosecuted certain proceedings
commenced by him or on his behalf in the District Court of Harris
County, Texas, United States of America, entitled *Castanho* v. *Jackson
Marine Inc., Jackson Marine S.A., Jackson Marine Services N.V., Jackson
Marine Nederland B.V., Brown & Root Inc. and Brown and Root (U.K.)
Ltd.* (79—5719) and (2) from commencing or causing to be commenced   G
any further or other proceedings in the United States of America or elsewhere against the defendants to that action (79—5719) or any of them
directed to his obtaining damages for personal injuries in respect of his
accident on February 11, 1977, on the *American Moon* save for enforcing
any judgment of the court in the action 1977 C. No. 8927.

The applications were heard in chambers and judgment was given in
open court.   H

The facts are stated in the judgments of Parker J. and in the Court of
Appeal.

Timothy Walker for the defendants.
J. *Melville Williams Q.C.* and *John Hendy* for the plaintiff.

                                                        Cur. adv. vult.

A   November 19, 1979. PARKER J. read the following judgment. These are two chambers applications in an action commenced by writ dated September 29, 1977. In the action the plaintiff claims damages for very severe personal injuries suffered in an accident which occurred on February 11, 1977. He is now a quadriplegic. Both applications raise points of considerable general importance. For that reason, and with the agreement of the parties, this judgment is given in open court.

B   The plaintiff is of Portuguese nationality and resides in Portugal. The first defendants are a United Kingdom company and the second defendants are a Panamanian company. The accident took place aboard the *American Moon* at Great Yarmouth. It is admitted in the action that this vessel was owned by the second defendants and that they employed the plaintiff thereon as an oiler. After the accident the plaintiff was in C hospital in England until, in about October 1977, he returned to Portugal on the advice of his doctors. He has remained there ever since.

Until February 1979 the action proceeded without unusual incident, the principal events being as follows. (1) On March 22, 1978, there was an order by consent that the second defendants should pay £7,250 by way of interim payment under R.S.C., Ord. 29, rr. 10–12, and this sum was duly paid. (2) On March 28, 1978, the statement of claim was D delivered. (3) On June 9, 1978, the second defendants admitted liability by letter. (4) On December 8, 1978, there was an order, not by consent, that the second defendants should make a further interim payment of £20,000. This like the earlier sum, was paid, the date of payment being December 18, 1978.

Two months later, on February 7, 1979, process, allegedly on the E authority of the plaintiff, was issued in the District Court of Harris County, Texas, claiming damages in respect of the same accident. Such process was issued by an American firm of attorneys, Benton Musslewhite Inc. The defendants named were the defendants in the action here and also three other Jackson Marine companies and Brown and Root Inc.

The evidence does not reveal how this firm came to get in touch F with the plaintiff in the first instance, but it is plain, and not disputed by Mr. Williams for the plaintiff, that they approached him on their own initiative, that is to say they were " touting " for work on an international scale. However they may have learnt that contact with the plaintiff might be profitable, by June 1978 contact had been made and the evidence reveals that in June and July 1978 the plaintiff was being pressed to hand over his case to them and to sign a power of attorney G giving them full authority to enforce his claim in America on a contingency fee basis. Such fee was to be one third of all recovery if the claim were settled before filing suit and 40 per cent. if suit were filed before any settlement were achieved. Nothing was to be paid in the event of failure of the claim.

Quite apart from the question of the desirability or otherwise of H contingency fees as such, this arrangement would appear to be a direct incentive to lawyers not to settle before filing suit, however favourable might be the terms obtainable, and thus one which a properly advised plaintiff would be unwilling to accept.

Despite the efforts of the American lawyers, the plaintiff did not, at that time, yield to their persuasion and expressed himself to the second defendants' loss adjuster's Portuguese agents as wishing his claims to

remain with those then handling them, that is to say B.M. Birnberg & A
Co. (" Birnbergs "), his solicitors in the action here.

When Birnbergs first heard of the activities of the American lawyers
is not clear, but it was before November 27, 1978, when they issued a
summons for the second interim payment, and was in fact not later than
about September 5, 1978, when the defendants' solicitors wrote to them
drawing attention to the fact that the plaintiff was being approached.

In December 1978, Birnbergs were visited by the American firm and B
had inconclusive discussions with them. In January 1979 there were
further discussions between the two sets of lawyers, this time in the
presence, or partly in the presence, of the plaintiff and his wife, in
Portugal. As a result of those discussions and subsequent events which
I shall mention shortly, the plaintiff, on February 8, 1979, the day after
process had been issued in the Texan state court, signed a power of C
attorney in favour of Benton Musslewhite and also an agreement with
Birnbergs. Before committing themselves to any association with the
American lawyers or any special agreement with the plaintiff, Birnbergs
took advice both from Mr. Williams and the Law Society. The exchange
of letters with the Law Society dated December 12 and 14, 1978, was
exhibited. The advice which they received was, in effect, that they would
be acting properly so long as they charged properly for all work done D
and so long as it was provided that their charges would be paid either by
the American lawyers or by the plaintiff, whatever the result of the
claims. I have not quoted from their letter to the Law Society but
it is right that I should state that it makes it clear that the object of
the exercise so far as they were concerned was simply to try to obtain
the highest possible damages for the plaintiff. E

As the conduct of Birnbergs has been the subject of very serious
criticism on behalf of the defendants and as they were concerned not
merely in the making of their own agreement with the plaintiff but also
with the content of the power of attorney in favour of the American
lawyers, it would in any event be necessary to consider those documents
closely. Quite apart from the conduct of Birnbergs, however, the documents have an important bearing on other matters. I consider the two F
documents in turn.

The power of attorney followed, but was more extensive than, the
document previously submitted to the plaintiff for signature. It gave
to the American lawyers exclusive powers to represent him in the
prosecution of his claim in America in respect of his accident and, like
its predecessor, provided for them to be paid one third of all amounts G
received or recovered by out of court settlement or other means if the
claims were settled prior to the filing of judicial petition, and 40 per
cent. if a petition were filed; for them to advance all moneys necessary
for preparation for trial or settlement and for nothing to be payable by
the plaintiff in respect thereof in the event of failure of his claim.

It went, however, further than its predecessor in a number of respects. H
It provided (1) for Birnbergs to be used by the American lawyers in
connection with the American action and for their fees in this connection
to be liquidated by the American lawyers out of their contingency fees.
(2) For the American lawyers to communicate with the plaintiff exclusively through Birnbergs. (3) For Birnbergs to have exclusive authority
to engage any specialist necessary for the construction for the plaintiff
of any special accommodation or facilities in Portugal. (4) For the

A American lawyers to pay the plaintiff's wages pending final settlement in the event that his employers ceased to do so. (5) For sums expended in the case other than general legal costs, to be limited to U.S. $10,000 (except with the express consent of Birnbergs), and to be deducted from any recovery. (6) For the action here not to be concluded prior to a decision in the United States and that, in the event that the action here should be re-activated by the defendants, the course to be followed should

B be decided by agreement between the American lawyers and Birnbergs or, in default of agreement, by Birnbergs.

This power of attorney, as ultimately granted on February 8, contained certain amendments which had not been agreed by the American lawyers when they were in Portugal, but they were agreed by telephone between Mrs. Bowden of Birnbergs and the American lawyers on February 5, and

C Mrs. Bowden then instructed the American lawyers to proceed with the action in Texas and asked a Mr. Valente, the architect employed in connection with the plaintiff's accommodation, to have it sworn by the plaintiff as soon as possible.

It was, as I have said, on February 7, that the American action was launched and not until February 8 that the power of attorney was

D granted. Hence the American action was commenced on Mrs. Bowden's instructions by telephone. Whether this was sufficient authority in Texas it is unnecessary to investigate or decide, because the action then in being has since come to an end by a non-suit being filed. It is, however, to be noted (1) that Mrs. Bowden's instructions were given without any attempt at settlement having been made and that as a result she was committing her client to a 40 per cent. fee notwithstanding

E that a satisfactory settlement attracting the lesser one third fee was never attempted. (2) That the power of attorney provides not only for the American lawyers to finance the action but also, if necessary, to finance the plaintiff personally. (3) That it expressly provides for the action here to be kept alive. (4) That it appears to contemplate that Birnbergs' remuneration will come wholly out of the American lawyers

F contingency fees.

Item (2) above, the provision for personal finance, is provided for in a clause which was covered over when the power of attorney was produced in connection with the Texas proceedings and also as originally produced in the proceedings before me. However, the full text was finally put in evidence and there was also produced Birnbergs' agreement with the plaintiff which provided that in the event of their fees not being paid

G by the American lawyers they would be paid by the plaintiff. This disposes of the defendants' charge that Birnberg were themselves acting on a contingency fee basis, a charge which, in view of the terms of the power of attorney and Birnbergs' failure to disclose their own arrangements, was entirely understandable.

Why the clause providing for personal finance was covered up I do

H not know. It may well have been because it was felt that, if disclosed, it would encourage the second defendants to cease paying the plaintiff's wages, or it may be because, although contingency fees are permissible in America, the same is not or was feared not, to be true of agreements to provide personal financial support. There was some suggestion that the latter was the true reason but on the evidence I can draw no such conclusion. For the purpose of these applications I regard both the existence of the clause itself and its non-disclosure as neutral matters.

One further clause only of Birnbergs' agreement with the plaintiff A
calls for mention, namely, clause 1 which specifically provided that the
action here should be continued but not determined pending the determination of the American action.

With this account of how the action in the Texas court came to be
launched I can now continue the chronological history of events. On
April 6, 1979, the defendants in the American action (other than the
two who were American corporations), that is to say including the B
defendants in the action here, entered a special appearance objecting to
the jurisdiction of the Texas court.

On April 30 (effectively May 1), the defendants delivered their defence
in the action here in which the second defendants formally admitted
liability and on May 1, they (1) issued a summons for directions in the
action here, and (2) issued a summons in the action here seeking an C
injunction to restrain the plaintiff from continuing the American action
and from commencing further proceedings in the United States or
elsewhere in respect of his accident.

At that time it is not disputed that this court had jurisdiction to grant
such an injunction and that it continued to do so until, on May 14,
Birnbergs gave notice of discontinuance which, it is now accepted, was D
within the time limit by R.S.C., Ord. 21, r. 2. Prima facie the effect
of this notice was to terminate the action here, but under the terms of
Ord. 21, r. 4, the plaintiff would subsequently be able, if he wished, to
commence a fresh action. The plaintiff's prime contention is that the
effect of the discontinuance is to deprive this court of jurisdiction to
grant the injunction sought.

In face of the terms of both the power of attorney and the plaintiff's E
agreement with Birnbergs it would appear that Birnbergs had no authority
to discontinue the action here. Towards the end of the hearing, however,
a further affidavit on behalf of the plaintiff was put in and also, on an
undertaking to have it sworn, a draft affidavit to be sworn by the plaintiff.
It was in due course duly sworn and filed. In that affidavit the plaintiff
states that he wishes to proceed in America rather than in England and F
that the action of Birnbergs in discontinuing the English action so as to
proceed in America as quickly as possible was done with his full consent
and authority. This appeared somewhat doubtful in the light of the
contents of an affidavit of Mr. P. J. Farthing sworn on behalf of the
defendants, but was sought to be supported by a last minute affidavit of
Mrs. Monjardino of the Portuguese consulate who, due to language
difficulties, acted as the channel of communication between Mrs. Bowden G
of Birnbergs and the plaintiff, an earlier affidavit by the deponent not
being satisfactory on the point.

In her second affidavit Mrs. Monjardino states that some days before
attending a meeting with Mrs. Bowden and the American lawyers on
May 16, she had spoken to the plaintiff by telephone about the possibility
of the action in England having to be stopped in order that the American H
action might proceed, and that he had expressed himself as agreeable
if Mrs. Bowden so advised. Mrs. Monjardino does not mention having
passed this information to Mrs. Bowden before the meeting on May 16,
and unless she did so it is plain that in discontinuing on May 14, Mrs.
Bowden was acting contrary to the specific terms of clause 1 of the
agreement between the plaintiff and Birnbergs without any justification.
To have taken such action without authority would, however, be a serious

A matter and it may be that Mrs. Monjardino, in the flurry of filing additional evidence in the closing stages of the hearing, merely omitted some communication which she had with Mrs. Bowden. Had the matter of such authority in the event turned out to be of crucial importance I should have felt it necessary to investigate the matter further. In view, however, of the fact that I have not found it of crucial importance it was

B unnecessary to pursue it or to make any finding on the question of authority. For the purposes of these applications I treat the notice as having been given with authority.

The defendants' summons for directions came on for hearing on June 6, when it was directed to be treated as an application to strike out the plaintiff's notice of discontinuance and adjourned for a date to be fixed.

C On June 18, both the second defendants' solicitor and Mr. Williams gave evidence in Texas on the effect of a notice of discontinuance of the action here. This was in connection with the defendants' attempt to stay the Texas proceedings, but there was no attempt then to obtain any decision. The plaintiff's memorandum of authorities to the Texas court, however, shows that, in order to persuade the Texas court not to stay

D the action there, it was important for the plaintiff to establish that the action here had been terminated and it was not disputed that the notice of discontinuance here was expressly for the purpose of improving the plaintiff's position in resisting the defendants' efforts to stay the Texas proceedings.

On June 26, the defendants in Texas filed a notice under rule 12 of the Civil Procedure Rules in Texas calling upon the plaintiff's attorney

E to show his authority to bring the American action and there then occurred a most remarkable manoeuvre. On July 18, while the original action was still pending, the American lawyers launched an action in the Beaumont Division of the Federal District Court for the Eastern District of Texas in respect of the same accident. There were fewer defendants, the first defendants in the action here being amongst those not included,

F but the second defendants here were still included. In these proceedings the plaintiff claimed $5 million compensatory damages and $10 million punitive damages and requested trial by jury. On the following day the original American action was brought to an end by the filing of a non-suit. Service of the second American action was effected on August 22, and on September 11, the defendants filed motion to dismiss and to show authority for bringing the action.

G The last procedural events are that on October 2, Master Elton referred the application to strike out the notice of discontinuance to be heard by the judge in chambers at the same time as the summons for an injunction and that I gave leave to amend that summons so as to cover the second American action.

Before coming to the issues between the parties I must mention certain

H further matters. The reasons for proceedings in America were said to be the prospect of greater damages there than are likely to be obtained here and increased ease and certainty of enforcing any judgment obtained. The reasons for stopping in the Texas state court and starting afresh in the federal court was stated to be that such courts were more liberal in accepting jurisdiction over foreigners and that an earlier hearing date was likely, it being stated that the motion to stay was likely to be heard in November and tried before the end of January.

That awards of damages in America are higher than in this country   A
I accept, but the evidence before me, which on this point I do not
rehearse, does not convince me that there will be any difficulty in obtaining satisfaction of a judgment obtained in the courts of this country.   As
to hearing date, the evidence shows that the estimates of hearing dates
are unlikely to be fulfilled.   So far as liberality in relation to extended
jurisdiction is concerned I had no satisfactory evidence as to the likelihood
of the federal court accepting jurisdiction on the facts of this case.   What   B
appears to me to matter is the attitude which would be adopted by the
court when acquainted fully with the facts, including in particular (1)
that the plaintiff apparently required considerable persuasion before allowing the American lawyers to embark on an action at all; (2) that by the
time he was so persuaded he had already obtained orders for and been
paid £27,250 in an English action; (3) that the original action had been   C
commenced whilst the English action was pending; (4) that having given
notice of discontinuance in the English action the federal action was
commenced while the original American action was still pending; (5) that
in addition to financing the original action, which is apparently perfectly
proper in America, the American lawyers had undertaken to finance
the plaintiff personally during its pendency; (6) that in proceedings before   D
me it was stated (a) that the plaintiff was prepared to submit to orders
(i) setting aside the notice of discontinuance unless the £27,250 were
repaid within 28 days, and (ii) restraining the federal action until it was
repaid; and (b) that the American lawyers proposed to make this repayment, the plaintiff's authority both for submitting to such orders and
making such payments being considered to derive solely from the power
of attorney of February 8, 1978; and finally (c) that if the federal court   E
declined jurisdiction the plaintiff would consider himself free to and would
seek to start over again in England.

As to the likely attitude of the federal court in such circumstances,
I had no evidence but it appears to me that they are matters which,
however liberal the federal court might be in general, might cause them
to have some doubt in the present instance.   Furthermore, the federal
court will, on the motion, have to consider the authority to bring the   F
action and also possibly to discontinue the original action.

I have set out the history at considerable length for I am being asked
to strike out a notice of discontinuance which, under the rules, the
plaintiff was entitled to serve without leave, and to restrain proceedings
in a foreign court when, if the notice of discontinuance is not struck out,
the defendant applicants will, it is said, not be engaged in an action   G
pending here.

I shall consider first the question of striking out the notice of discontinuance, the giving of which without leave was only possible due to
the fact that, as the events and correspondence reveal, the defendants
were hoping to settle and had not delivered their defence either within
the time limited, or within extensions granted.   H

That a notice of discontinuance terminates an action in the ordinary
way is beyond doubt, but it does not determine altogether the jurisdictions
of the courts in the action, for in every case the defendant is, under
R.S.C., Ord. 62, r. 10, entitled to tax his costs and, if the taxed costs are
not paid within four days, the defendant may sign judgment for them.
Also, if such costs are not paid, the court may stay any fresh action for
the same or substantially the same cause of action until such costs are

A   paid. Furthermore, the court may, after discontinuance, make such order as may be necessary to give effect to rights acquired by the defendant during the course of the proceedings, such as rights under an undertaking in damages: see *Newcomen* v. *Coulson* (1878) 7 Ch.D. 764. In general, however, a notice of discontinuance terminates the action and thus will, for example, automatically terminate an appeal: *Conybeare* v. *Lewis* (1880) 13 Ch.D. 469.

B   Where interim payments have been made under R.S.C., Ord. 29, the rules contain no provision to cover the case of discontinuance. Ord. 29, r. 16 only provides for the court to make orders with respect to interim payments on giving or making a final judgment or order determining the defendants' liability to the plaintiff and for giving effect to that determination. This rule cannot apply to a discontinuance, for the essence of such

C   procedure is that the claim is not determined at all and that the plaintiff is free to bring a fresh action unless leave is required and it is made a term of leave that no such action shall be brought. There can be no doubt that if, in any case where interim payments had been made, leave to discontinue were required, the court could, under R.S.C., Ord. r. 21, 3 (1), make it a term of giving leave that the payments should be repaid. There can also be no doubt that a court has power under the same rule

D   to make it a term of the grant of leave that the plaintiff shall bring no fresh action for the same or substantially the same cause of action.

    If, therefore, the notice of discontinuance had been one day later or delivery of the defence one day earlier, so that the plaintiff required leave to discontinue, there would have been power to adopt either or both of these courses. Furthermore, where leave is required the court would

E   also, in my judgment, as an alternative to making it a term that no fresh action should be brought, make it a term that no foreign proceedings should be instituted or continued. This must follow from the existence of the power in the courts to put a plaintiff to his election whether to proceed in this country or in a foreign court: see *The Christiansborg* (1885) 10 P.D. 141, 153.

F   Although, however, the above powers would exist in such circumstances, it does not follow that all or any of them would be exercised. A plaintiff is in the ordinary way entitled to discontinue on payment of taxed costs and still be free to commence a fresh action later. If he has received interim payments he would in the absence of special circumstances no doubt also be ordered to repay them as a term of the grant of leave unless the defendant were content, provided that the

G   plaintiff were prohibited from bringing a fresh action, to let him retain them. Assuming, however, that the plaintiff were prepared to repay, possibly with interest, the question arises as to the circumstances in which, under the general power in R.S.C., Ord 21, r. 3, to impose such terms as it thinks just, a court would make it a term either that no fresh proceedings be brought here or that no foreign proceedings should be

H   instituted or continued.

    That a plaintiff may in certain circumstances conduct proceedings both in this country and in a foreign court is clear on the authorities. Where he seeks to do so the question whether one and if so which set of proceedings should be stayed depends upon what, in the particular circumstances of each case, justice demands: see *MacShannon* v. *Rockware Glass Ltd.* [1978] A.C. 795.

    In the circumstances of this particular case justice would in my

judgment have demanded at least that discontinuance be allowed only on A
terms that no fresh action should be brought in England. It would in
such circumstances be an injustice to the defendants, even on repayment
of the interim payments with interest, to allow a discontinuance desired
for the purpose of strengthening the plaintiff's case for persuading the
foreign court to accept jurisdiction, yet leave him open to be pursued
again in these courts if the American courts, despite the fact that there
was no pending action in England, declined jurisdiction. To impose B
such a term would not work injustice to the plaintiff. He could accept
the term and discontinue or he could continue the action here and seek
to continue or institute American proceedings. Unless he were certain
of being able to continue the proceedings in America he would clearly
not accept the term and discontinue for by so doing he would be
committing himself to a possible chance of recovering a greater sum at C
the price of repaying money received and, with liability admitted, the
certainty of a large award here in a comparatively short time. Hence,
had an application for leave been necessary, I conclude that it would only
have been granted on terms that the plaintiff would not have accepted
and consequently that leave would have been refused.

I have considered the powers available on an application for leave
and the probable result of such an application, for they have an important D
bearing on the application to strike out. On such an application the
power to order repayment of the interim payments must, if it exists,
depend on the inherent jurisdiction of the courts to prevent an abuse of
their own process. Such jurisdiction has been used in many connections
but never in circumstances such as are here present. I have, however,
no doubt that it covers such a case for nothing could be more clearly an E
abuse of process than for a plaintiff, having received interim payments,
to discontinue without repaying them. Indeed this is not disputed, for
Mr. Williams, by offering to submit to an order to strike out unless the
repayments are made, accepts the jurisdiction to make such an order.
If the jurisdiction is there at all it must be wide enough to allow the
making of an unconditional order to strike out if that is necessary to
prevent an abuse of process. In my judgment it is an abuse of process F
to use the machinery of discontinuance without leave to improve the
plaintiff's position in American proceedings if he is then left free, on
failure of those proceedings, to commence afresh here. This would be
the case on discontinuance without leave. I have already held that it
would be unjust on an application for leave to allow such a result, and
for the same reason I consider it to be an abuse of process. I accordingly G
order that the notice of discontinuance be struck out with the result that
the action here remains in being.

The next question is whether an injunction restraining the continuance
of the American proceedings or the institution of other proceedings
should be granted. If my conclusion on the application to strike out is
correct it is not disputed that jurisdiction exists, but, since this case may H
go further, I express my views shortly on the question whether there is
jurisdiction here, even assuming that the action here has terminated save
for taxation of costs and any order for the repayment of the interim
payments. In such event the situation would be that of a foreign national
resident outside the jurisdiction, with no assets here and with no action
proceeding here, seeking an injunction to restrain proceedings in a foreign
court. This situation arose in *The Tropaioforos (No.* 2) [1962] 1 Lloyd's

A Rep. 410. In that case Megaw J. held that there was jurisdiction on two grounds, one of which does not arise here, but the other of which was that the connection of the applicant with this country was sufficient to ground jurisdiction notwithstanding that an action which he had brought in England had finally terminated in a decision adverse to him. Adopting this test I hold that the plaintiff has, even if the action has terminated, sufficient connection with this country to ground jurisdiction.

B His claim is in respect of a tort committed within the jurisdiction, the natural forum for trying which is in England. He has and retains payments made in the English proceedings. He has solicitors here and is subject to the jurisdiction of the courts here in respect of costs and orders for repayment. His arrangements with the American lawyers and Birnbergs are such that the American proceedings can only be

C advanced with the assistance of Birnbergs, and in any event much of the evidence, documentary and oral, must be obtained from England. This, in my judgment, is sufficient connection to ground jurisdiction even if the action has been terminated. Should an injunction then be granted? Mr. Williams submits that it should not on the basis (1) that a plaintiff is prima facie entitled to proceed both here and elsewhere concurrently; (2) that proceeding in America gives him the legitimate advantage of

D the prospect of very much higher compensatory damages (even after deduction of the American lawyers' 40 per cent.) and the separate additional remedy of very large punitive damages; and (3) that it will work no injustice to the defendants if the action there is allowed to proceed.

Mr. Walker, on the other hand, submits (1) that it would be an

E injustice to the defendants if the action is allowed to proceed, because they have admitted liability here which they might not have done in America; (2) they have paid moneys here that would not have been obtainable in America; (3) the American proceedings would be more expensive and are being pursued for the benefit of the American lawyers and not the plaintiff; and (4) the American proceedings are brought without authority.

F I find it unnecessary to decide whether the federal action was brought without authority for an injunction on this ground would be valueless. With regard to the allegation that the proceedings are being pursued for the benefit of the American lawyers and not the plaintiff, it is plain that they will if they continue, probably be of great benefit to the American lawyers. The total claims in the federal action are for $15 million ($5

G million compensatory damages and $10 million punitive damages) and the evidence is that recent awards for quadriplegia have been between $2 million and $4 million, with the exception of one award of $638,000. It is therefore plain that the American lawyers stand to make a very large sum out of American proceedings. If, for example, the jury were to award $4 million compensatory damages to the plaintiff the American

H lawyers would retain $1.6 million, and even if the award were as low as the exceptional $638,000, they would retain $255,200, leaving the plaintiff in this event with $382,000, or approximately £190,000. Bearing in mind recent very large awards in the courts here it is therefore at least possible that an award in America will leave the plaintiff with less than he might obtain here. Furthermore, it must be borne in mind that, had there been no American proceedings, the action here might well have already determined with a large award already paid and the plaintiff

might by now have the action with all its worries behind him. When A
there is added to this the fact that the American lawyers are prepared,
without reference to the plaintiff and for the purpose of assisting them
in persuading the American court to accept jurisdiction, to pay £27,250
in order to achieve discontinuance of an action which could result in a
large award in favour of the plaintiff in a very short time, there is clearly
much force in Mr. Walker's argument. I am, however, not prepared
on the evidence to hold that the American action is being pursued in B
disregard of the plaintiff's interests. Although is is plainly of great benefit
to the American lawyers that it should be pursued and their advice to
the plaintiff may, as a result, be less than objective, I am prepared to
accept that they do consider it to be in his interests as well as their own
that the action should proceed. I am satisfied that Birnbergs so consider.

    This leaves for consideration the questions whether, assuming authority C
and that the American action is being pursued for the plaintiff's benefit,
that action and any other proceedings should be restricted by injunction.

    The authorities for the most part concern the question of staying an
action in these courts, but they nevertheless afford valuable guidance.
In *The Atlantic Star* [1974] A.C. 436, the question was whether, where
an action had been commenced in the Belgian courts, an action here in
respect of the same matters should be stayed. The House of Lords D
decided that it should be, on the basis that taking into account advantages
to the plaintiff on the one hand and disadvantages to the defendants on
the other the defendants ought not to be required to face proceedings
here as well.

    In *MacShannon* v. *Rockware Glass Ltd.* [1978] A.C. 795, Scotsmen
living and working in Scotland and having suffered personal injuries in E
Scotland sought to proceed in England but were not permitted to do so
and were left to pursue their claims in Scotland. Lord Diplock stated the
rule, at p. 812:

    "' In order to justify a stay two conditions must be satisfied, one
    positive and the other negative: (*a*) the defendant must satisfy the
    court that there is another forum to whose jurisdiction he is amen- F
    able in which justice can be done between the parties at substantially
    less inconvenience or expense, and (*b*) the stay must not deprive
    the plaintiff of a legitimate personal or juridical advantage which
    would be available to him if he invoked the jurisdiction of the English
    court '."

So stated the rule does not take into account prejudice or injustice to G
the defendant, but it is plain from the speeches in the case that this
factor comes equally into consideration. If, with necessary amendments,
this is applied to the present case it appears to me that the defendants
clearly satisfy head (*a*) of the rule. The questions therefore to be determined are in my judgment (1) will an injunction deprive the plaintiff
of a legitimate personal or juridical advantage he would have in the
American proceedings? (2) Will the refusal of an injunction cause H
prejudice or injustice to the defendant? (3) Weighing up the above two
matters, does justice between the parties require an injunction?

    The legitimate advantages which the plaintiff claims and of which he
will be deprived if an injunction is granted are the increased damages
which he is likely to get in an American court. That increased damages
can be a legitimate advantage I have already said I accept. It was indeed
recognised in *MacShannon* v. *Rockware Glass Ltd.* The importance of

A such a matter will, however, inevitably vary not only with the amount or size of the expected increase and the certainty or otherwise of obtaining it, but with other matters as well, such as whether, in a particular case, early termination of the case is more important medically than higher damages which may be obtained if termination in delayed. Even, however, in cases where the expected increase is very considerable and relatively certain it may be of little weight. The object of the court is to

B see that justice is done between the parties. If, for example, two English plaintiffs residing in England suffer identical industrial injuries in respect of which both can and do sue in England, but one, by the accident that the defendant in his case has an office and assets in Texas, can sue in Texas also, the fact that he could recover more compensation in Texas and perhaps punitive damages also cannot in my judgment, even if it is

C a legitimate advantage, be regarded as of much weight. The object of damages is to provide just compensation and what is required for this purpose must vary between country and country according to their respective costs and standards of living. In the case supposed both plaintiffs will obtain here an award considered just by the courts of this country in the circumstances prevailing here. I can see no injustice in preventing one of the two plaintiffs from seeking to obtain an award, which although

D it might be just, reasonable and necessary in the light of costs and standards prevailing in Texas, would be grossly excessive here. If this is not right there is a direct encouragement to " forum shopping " which has been frequently criticised by the courts and which Lord Reid in *The Atlantic Star* [1974] A.C. 436, 454 regarded as undesirable. The question of real importance appears to me to be, not whether the plaintiff will

E obtain a higher award in another jurisdiction but whether the award he is likely to obtain here is likely to be lower than awards in the country where he lives, in this case Portugal. If this were so, and it is not suggested here, the fact that, by going to Texas, he could obtain an award more in line with awards in his own country would no doubt be a legitimate and considerable advantage. As there was nothing here by way of suggestion or evidence to lead me to the conclusion that an

F English award would be regarded as unjustly low in Portugal, where the plaintiff resides and intends to reside, and as an award here is likely to be obtained more quickly and less expensively than a probably higher award in Texas, I regard any advantage to the plaintiff in this respect as being, even if legitimate, of little weight.

What then of the defendants? They have admitted liability here

G and accorded the plaintiff here the advantage of interim payments which he could not have obtained in America. The plaintiff deliberately sued them here and if the proceedings continue in America they will undoubtedly be put to extra expense. It would, I consider, be unjust to expose them to an action in America and I so consider whether or not I am right in deciding that the action here is still in being. If it is not the plaintiff can start again here, pursue his claim in its natural forum

H and obtain economically an award which is not shown to be any less than justice requires.

I should mention also two further matters. Where a foreign plaintiff seeks to sue in his own country as well as here the case is different from that in which a foreign plaintiff seeks to sue in another country, not his own. The latter is a pure case of forum shopping and is the present case. Furthermore, the case is different again where the plaintiff has already

Parker J.   **Castanho v. Brown & Root Ltd. (C.A.)**   **[1980]**

put the defendants to expense in resisting one attempted action in the A
other country, has then abandoned that action and is seeking to proceed
with another, and thereby put the defendants to yet further expense.
That is also the situation here. These matters added to those already
mentioned satisfy me that justice demands in the present case that an
injunction should be granted and I accordingly grant an injunction in
the terms of the summons as amended.

B

> *Notice of discontinuance struck out*
> *with costs including costs reserved*
> *by Master Elton.*
> *Injunction granted with costs.*
> *Leave to appeal.*
> *Application to suspend operation of* C
> *injunction refused.*

Solicitors: *Clyde & Co.; B. M. Birnberg & Co.*

[Reported by MISS ISOBEL COLLINS, Barrister-at-Law]

APPEAL from Parker J.   D

The plaintiff appealed from the order of Parker J. that the notice of
discontinuance be struck out and that the plaintiff by himself his servants
or agents be restrained from commencing or causing to be commenced or
continuing or prosecuting any further proceedings in the United States of
America or elsewhere against the six defendants named in the summons
(ante, p. 836F) or any of them directed to his obtaining damages for E
personal injuries suffered as a result of the accident on February 11, 1977,
save for enforcing any judgment in the action 1977 C. No. 8927.

The grounds of appeal were that the judge (1) had no jurisdiction to
set aside the notice of discontinuance; (2) had no jurisdiction to set aside
the notice of discontinuance on the ground that it was an abuse by the
process of the court; (3) misdirected himself or erred in law in holding
that the notice of discontinuance was an abuse of the process of the F
court; (4) had no jurisdiction to grant the injunction after the notice of
discontinuance had been served; (5) misdirected himself or erred in law
in holding that the plaintiff had sufficient connection with this country
to ground jurisdiction for the making of the injunction; (6) misdirected
himself or erred in law in holding: (a) that the legitimate advantage of
the plaintiff in proceeding in America was of little weight; (b) that the
American proceedings would prejudice or cause injustice to the defendants G
substantially or at all; (c) that justice demanded the injunction and in
making the injunction in all the circumstances; (7) erred in law in
taking into consideration and attaching weight to the matters: (a) that
an award of damages in England was not likely to be lower than an
award in Portugal where the plaintiff lived; (b) that the plaintiff was
foreign both to this country and to the United States of America; (c) H
that the plaintiff discontinued his first action in America; (8) erred in
law in not holding that communications and arrangements between the
plaintiff and his solicitors in England, B.M. Birnberg & Co. (" Birnbergs ")
and between the plaintiff and his American lawyers, Benton Musslewhite
Inc. and Friedman and Chaffin were privileged and irrelevant; (9) misdirected himself and was wrong in finding (a) that Benton Musslewhite
Inc. touted for work on an international scale, or at all, or in the instant

A   case; (b) that a properly advised plaintiff would be unwilling to accept the agreement reached between the plaintiff and the American lawyers; (c) that Mrs. Bowden of Birnbergs instructed the American lawyers to proceed with an action in Texas without direct authority from the plaintiff and/or without an attempt at settlement (d) that the hearing dates in America were unlikely to be fulfilled.

B   By a respondents notice under R.S.C., Ord. 29, r. 6 (2) the defendants contended that the orders should be affirmed on the additional grounds that (1) the American proceedings were being pursued for the benefit of the plaintiff's American lawyers and not the plaintiff; (2) that the plaintiff's American lawyers were financing the plaintiff personally, an arrangement contrary to the Rules of the American Bar Association and the Bar Rules of Texas.

C
    J. Melville Williams Q.C., George Newman and *John Hendy* for the plaintiff.
    Christopher Bathurst Q.C. and *Michael Lerego* for the defendants.

                                                              Cur. adv. vult.

D
    April 22.   The following judgments were read.

    LORD DENNING M.R.   " A Texas-style claim is big business."   That is how the newspaper put it.   The managers of the business are two attorneys of Houston, Texas.   They keep a look-out for men injured on the North Sea oil rigs.   The worse a man is injured, the better for
E   business.   Especially when he has been rendered a quadriplegic and his employers have no answer to his claim.   Their look-out man tells the Texan attorneys.   They come across to England.   They see the injured man and say to him: " Do not bring your action in England or Scotland. You will only get £150,000 there.   Let us bring it in Texas.   We can get you £2,500,000 in Texas."   If he agrees, they get him to sign a power
F   of attorney which provides for their reward.   Under it the attorneys are to get 40 per cent. of any damages recovered.   That is £1,200,000 for themselves.   Big business indeed!

    In our present case, however, the Texan attorneys struck a snag. Their look-out man was too late.   The injured man had already gone to solicitors in England before the Texan attorneys got to know of it.   His English solicitors had already started an action for him against his
G   employers.   They had succeeded so well that they had already obtained from the English court orders for interim payments amounting to £27,250. He had spent that sum on buying land and putting a house on it.   How were the Texan lawyers to overcome that snag?   Could they legitimately start an action in Texas when the English proceedings had got so far?

    They devised a plan.   They said to the English solicitors: " Let us
H   arrange things together.   You drop the action in England and let us help one another in an action in Texas.   We will ourselves pay back the £27,250 out of our own pocket.   We will pay him his salary and everything.   We will pay you all your proper costs for the actual work you do.   We will recoup it out of the £2,500,000 we get in Texas." So they would get their 40 per cent.   The English solicitors would get their proper costs.   A clever plan indeed.   But will it work?   That is the question in this case.

Lord Denning M.R.   **Castanho v. Brown & Root Ltd. (C.A.)**   **[1980]**

In detail   A

A motor vessel called the *American Moon* was engaged in carrying supplies to oil rigs in the North Sea. On February 11, 1977, she was lying at Great Yarmouth in Norfolk. One of her crew was the plaintiff, Inocencio Castanho, a Portuguese. He was transferring oil from a drum to a tank—by a pipe with compressed air. A valve flew off and went into his neck. It penetrated his spinal cord. He was completely paralysed B in his arms and legs—a quadriplegic. He is completely dependent on others for everything. Both by day and night.

He was in Stoke Mandeville hospital for nine months from February 1977 to November 1977. He was well looked after there. The employers treated him very well. They continued to pay him his full salary of $690 a month. They arranged for members of his family to visit him from Portugal. They paid all their expenses. Their representative visited C him regularly once a month to see to his welfare. After nine months, the doctors thought it would be better for him to be with his wife and family in Portugal. So his employers arranged for a specially fitted plane to take him back to Portugal. They also provided special equipment at his home in Portugal—so as to enable him to get about. Their representative in Lisbon visited him at his home—so as to do all they D could for him and and his family. His wife has been very good. She is doing everything for him. The only thing outstanding is the amount of compensation to be paid to him.

The legal history in England up to June 1978

Soon after the accident, his wife and brother came to see him at Stoke E Mandeville. They asked the Portuguese consulate to find a solicitor for him to claim compensation. The Portuguese consulate suggested B. M. Birnberg & Co. ("Birnbergs"), solicitors, of London. They were instructed on May 4, 1977. They got into touch with the employers' solicitors, Clyde & Co. ("Clydes") of London. No doubt Clydes were aware of the Texas-style claims made by some injured men. So they F were glad the proceedings were started in England rather than America. They did everything they could to keep them in England. They said they would willingly make an interim payment on account. This was arranged and everything done properly. A writ was issued in September 1977. An order by consent was made on March 22, 1978, for £7,250 to be paid as an interim payment. A statement of claim was delivered on March 28, 1978. But no defence was delivered at that time. It was G deferred by consent till later.

The Texans come on the scene

The Texans came on the scene in June 1978. Someone told them of the accident to the plaintiff. They did not know his address in Portugal. So they wrote to Stoke Mandeville and got them to forward it to him. H Then things moved rapidly. No expense was spared. The Texan lawyers were ready to pay out large sums themselves out of their own pocket—without security—because of the 40 per cent. contingency fee opening up before them. They were ready to cast their bread upon the waters in the expectancy of the £1,200,000 fee which would be theirs.

One of their top men, Bob Chaffin (he had been named in the newspapers), went to Portugal to see the plaintiff. Bob Chaffin was closely

The Weekly Law Reports, July 18, 1980

851

1 W.L.R.   Castanho v. Brown & Root Ltd. (C.A.)   Lord Denning M.R.

A associated with the firm of Benton Musslewhite Inc. of Houston, Texas. Bob Chaffin pressed the plaintiff to let their firm take over the claim. He succeeded so far that on July 3, 1978, their firm, Benton Musslewhite, sent the plaintiff a power of attorney to sign authorising them to institute proceedings in Texas. They told him to sign it where marked " X " and to return it to them.

B The plaintiff seems to have been a little uncertain. He did not sign the power of attorney at that time. Instead, in August 1978, he got in touch with the employers' representative in Lisbon. He told him " he would like the case to rest with the people (in London) who are handling it."

This made the Texan lawyers very concerned. They had not got the power of attorney back signed by the plaintiff. So they took quick C action. Early in September 1978 Mr. Benton Musslewhite himself went over to Portugal. He saw the plaintiff and told him the advantage of proceeding in the United States. He then went from Portugal over to London and saw Mrs. Margaret Bowden, the managing clerk from Birnbergs. He told her how American law operated. He told her that, if they were permitted to sue in the United States, they would make advance payments to the plaintiff so as to cover all his needs: and that D they were confident of success: and that they would expect the damages to come up to $5,000,000. Mrs. Bowden was impressed and asked him to send her his credentials. He did so. He went back and sent her a batch of papers showing the successes which Benton Musslewhite and Bob Chaffin had achieved in the cases they had handled: and in addition a draft claim which they proposed to file on behalf of the plaintiff in the E American court.

This was followed up by another visit to England by Mr. Benton Musslewhite in December 1978. He had meetings again with Mrs. Margaret Bowden: and also with counsel, Mr. Melville Williams. It was then decided that the American lawyers should be instructed to pursue a claim in the United States of America where the potential F damages were very much greater. Counsel advised that " the English action should proceed, though not to judgment, as this would be a bar to the American action," that Birnbergs should co-operate with the American lawyers in the interests of the plaintiff, but should only get their proper costs. Benton Musslewhite were to pay the English lawyers their proper costs for work done, charged in the ordinary way, win or lose.

G That decision was duly implemented. So much so that on January 31, 1979, Mrs. Bowden herself visited the plaintiff at his home in Portugal, taking with her various papers including a power of attorney in Portuguese for him to sign in favour of Benton Musslewhite—prepared by Benton Musslewhite.

H *The power of attorney*

The power of attorney in Portuguese was executed in the plaintiff's hamlet of Varzim. By it the plaintiff conferred on Benton Musslewhite exclusive powers to represent him judicially in the United States: and promised to pay them, if settled out of court, one third part of the moneys received: and 40 per cent. if the petition were filed in the court. Any expenses that were incurred on behalf of the plaintiff were to come out of the sums he received. If he got nothing, he had to pay nothing. There

was an express clause that: " It is understood that the process initiated   A
in England will not be concluded prior to the decision in the United
States." The object of that provision was, no doubt, to keep the English
proceedings alive in case the American proceedings were unsuccessful.

The power of attorney also contained a provision by which Benton
Musslewhite agreed to pay the plaintiff his salary—if the employers
stopped paying it: and also agreed to repay any amounts received by
the plaintiff by way of interim payments in the English proceedings: also   B
any extra cost necessary to complete the house, etc. in Portugal. All
these payments were no doubt being made by Benton Musslewhite out
of their own pocket—in view of the large contingency fee which they
hoped to receive in due course.

To English eyes that power of attorney was champertous in the
extreme. The Texan lawyers were maintaining the proceedings in the   C
United States—laying out large sums in support of it—and stipulating
in return for 40 per cent. of the damages received: if they lost, they were
to get nothing. And the English lawyers were helping them—going out
to Portugal to get the power of attorney signed—and so forth. If such
an agreement was made in regard to English proceedings, it would be
invalid as contrary to public policy. But I would assume that it was not
invalid by the law of the United States.   D

The English proceedings still continue

Whilst the American lawyers were pressing the plaintiff to proceed
in the United States, the English proceedings were still going on. As I
have said, the solicitors had already received an interim payment of
£7,250. In October 1978—knowing full well of the American approach—   E
they decided to apply in the English proceedings for a further interim
payment of £20,000. On October 10, 1978, they wrote to Clydes:

" The cost of building a pre-fabricated bungalow will be £7,000 but
the plot of land will cost £19,000. It is imperative that our client
is re-housed immediately . . . We are instructed to ask for a further
interim payment of £20,000 to cover these immediate costs."   F

Birnbergs took out a summons. On December 8, 1978, Master Elton
made an order for interim payment of £20,000. That sum was paid. The
plot of land was bought. Arrangements were made for the erection of
the bungalow.

The two proceedings going on together   G

For a time proceedings went on in Texas and England together. On
February 7, 1979, the plaintiff issued a suit in the Texas state court. He
claimed damages for his injuries on the ground that the employers were
guilty of gross negligence. The claim was for $5,000,000.

On April 30, 1979, the defendants delivered a defence in the English
action. They admitted that the plaintiff was employed by the second   H
defendants, Jackson Marine S.A., and that the accident was caused by
the negligence of the chief engineer who was their servant. Thus leaving
only the question of damages.

On May 1, 1979, the defendants took out two summonses in the
English action. One was a summons for an injunction to restrain the
plaintiff from continuing with the proceedings in Texas or any other
proceedings there. The other was a summons asking for directions as

A to the trial of the English action. Before these summonses were heard,
however, the plaintiff's lawyers took a step which is of crucial importance
in the case. They gave notice of discontinuance of the English action.

The notice of discontinuance

Now you will remember that in the Portuguese power of attorney
B it was stipulated that the English action was not to be concluded prior
to the decision of the United States' courts. The lawyers advising the
plaintiff seem to have had second thoughts about this. It might give rise
to difficulties in the American courts. So long as the English action was
alive, the American courts might not let the Texan action go ahead. So
they decided to bring the English proceedings to an end. They looked
up the *Supreme Court Practice* and found that under R.S.C., Ord. 21,
C r. 2 (1), the plaintiff could discontinue the proceedings without leave at
any time within 14 days after service of the defence. But after 14 days,
leave would be necessary—and the English court might not give leave—so
the English action would remain alive.

Now the defence had been served on April 30, 1979. On the very
last day, May 14, 1979, the English lawyers served this document:

D   " Notice of Discontinuance pursuant to Order 21, rule 2
      Take notice that the plaintiff hereby discontinues this action
      against the first and second defendants pursuant to Order 21, rule 2.
      14 days have not elapsed since date of service of defence.
      Dated May 14, 1979.
                                      B. M. Birnberg & Co."

E
Was it authorised?

At once the query arises: did the solicitors have authority to give
this notice of discontinuance—having regard to the terms of the power
of attorney? There is nothing in writing to show that the plaintiff
authorised the notice of discontinuance, but it is said that he authorised
F it over the telephone. Parker J. doubted the validity of this. I too
doubt it. The agency created by the power of attorney was governed
presumably by the law of Portugal: see *Dicey & Morris, Conflict of
Laws,* 9th ed. (1973), rule 167, p. 869. If it is the same as English law,
I doubt whether parol evidence would be admissible to contradict the
express terms of the power of attorney. So the notice of discontinuance
may be invalid on the simple ground that it was not authorised.

G
The Texan actions

Soon afterwards the employers applied to stay the first Texan action.
There was a hearing in Houston on June 18, 1979. English lawyers went
over to give evidence about the position in the English action. No doubt
Benton Musslewhite paid the costs of their English lawyers. But the
H application seems to have left some misgivings on the Texan side. At any
rate, on July 19, 1979, the Texan lawyers filed a notice of non-suit in their
action and started a fresh action. This was in the federal court, the United
States District Court for Texas. They claimed $5 million compensatory
damages and $10 million punitive damages and requested trial by jury.
Since that time there have been voluminous proceedings in the federal
court—motions for judgment—motions to stay—and motions of all sorts.
It is not necessary to describe them here. Save to say that there is a vista

of prolonged and expensive litigation in the United States before a   A
conclusion is reached.

The English proceedings

Returing now to the English proceedings, the summonses came on for
hearing before Master Elton. He thought the notice of discontinuance
was open to question. He treated the summons for directions as a sum-   B
mons to set it aside. He referred both summonses to the judge. On
November 19, 1979, Parker J. struck out the notice of discontinuance
with the result that the English action remained in being. He also granted
an injunction restraining the plaintiff from continuing the proceedings in
America. He gave a reasoned judgment which will repay perusal. Now
there is an appeal to this court.

C

Was the notice of discontinuance valid?

The judge held that, in giving the notice of discontinuance, the plaintiff's advisers were guilty of an abuse of process of the court. This was
because the plaintiff had received interim payments of £27,250 in the
English action. He himself had expended them and could not repay
them. But the American lawyers had offered to repay them—out of their   D
own pocket. In the judge's view this offer of repayment did not cure the
abuse of process.

In giving the notice of discontinuance, the plaintiff's advisers relied on
R.S.C., Ord. 21, r. 2 (1), which says that the plaintiff may, *without* the
leave of the court, discontinue the action at any time not later than 14 days
after service of the defence. That rule goes back several years—long   E
before interim payments were thought of. Interim payments were introduced in 1970 as a result of the Administration of Justice Act 1969, section
20, and R.S.C., Ord. 29, rr. 12–17. Those provisions enable the court,
in personal injury cases—where the plaintiff was likely to succeed—to
order a defendant to make interim payments on account of any damages
for which the defendant may be liable " if a final judgment . . . is given "
for the plaintiff. There is no provision for repayment except that " on   F
giving or making a final judgment " the court may order the repayment of
any sum by which the interim payment exceeds the amount which the
defendant is liable to pay to the plaintiff. There is no provision for
repayment in the case of discontinuance.

The legislative purpose is clear. It was to enable the plaintiff to
receive interim payments—and spend them on his own immediate needs   G
and expenses—rather than have to wait for years until trial. The legislature did not contemplate that he should ever be called upon to repay
them—on discontinuance, or at any other time—except in the unlikely
event that he got less at the trial.

How does that legislative purpose fit in with R.S.C., Ord. 21, r. 2 (1)
which enables a plaintiff to discontinue, without the leave of the court,
within 14 days after defence? I fear that the draftsmen of interim pay-   H
ments forgot all about notices of discontinuance. Interim payments are
quite inconsistent with a right to discontinue without leave. It is inconceivable that a plaintiff can be allowed to give notice of discontinuance—
and walk off with the interim payments—which he has already spent—
and then start a fresh action for damages—without so much as by your
leave. The only way of reconciling the provisions is to hold that, once

The Weekly Law Reports, July 18, 1980

855

1 W.L.R.   Castanho v. Brown & Root Ltd. (C.A.)   Lord Denning M.R.

A interim payments have been sought and received and spent, the plaintiff
can no longer discontinue without the leave of the court.

Another way of reaching the same result is to hold, as Parker J. did
(ante, p. 844D–E), that, once interim payments have been sought and
received and spent, it is an abuse of the process of the court to discontinue the proceedings without the leave of the court. I summarised
the cases on " abuse of process " in *Goldsmith* v. *Sperrings Ltd.* [1977]
B 1 W.L.R. 478, 489–490. I said: " On the face of it, in any particular
case, the legal process may appear to be entirely proper and correct." So
here the notice of discontinuance, on the face of it, is in time and
correctly done without leave. " What makes it wrongful," I added, " is
the purpose for which it is used." If it is used for the purpose of the party
obtaining some collateral advantage for himself, and not for the purpose for
C which such proceedings are properly designed and exist, he will be held
guilty of abuse of the process of the court. So here the notice of discontinuance was done without leave—so as to aid the American lawyers
in obtaining 40 per cent. for themselves out of the American litigation.
That was an abuse of the process of the English court.

If I am right in thinking that leave is necessary, then the court can
do what is right and just. It can insist on repayment—at once in cash
D —as a condition of giving leave to discontinue; or alternatively it can
allow the plaintiff to retain the interim payments (and not repay them)
on condition that no other action shall be brought for the same cause
(see *Hess* v. *Labouchere* (1898) 14 T.L.R. 350, *per* A. L. Smith L.J.); or
it can refuse leave and insist on the case going to judgment (see *Fox*
v. *Star Newspapers Co. Ltd.* [1898] 1 Q.B. 636; [1900] A.C. 19). There
E are some words of Chitty L.J. [1898] 1 Q.B. 636, 639, which fit this
case:

  " The principle of the rule is plain. It is that after the proceedings
  have reached a certain stage the plaintiff, who has brought his
  adversary into court, shall not be able to escape by a side door and
  avoid the contest. He is then to be no longer dominus litis, and
F it is for the judge to say whether the action shall be discontinued
  or not and upon what terms."

The " certain stage " in this case is when interim payments have been
sought and received and spent.

Mr. Melville Williams sought to overcome this argument by offering
to repay the interim payments. That does not impress me in the least.
G It is not the plaintiff who is offering to repay them. It is the American
lawyers out of their own pocket—looking forward eventually to their 40
per cent. of the damages. That very offer of repayment—made in an
English action—is champertous. It is invalid at any rate in the eyes
of an English court. It is the English courts which have jurisdiction over
the English action. The cause of action here is situate in England: see
Dicey & Morris, Conflict of Laws, 9th ed., rule 78, p. 506. In *Mackender*
H v. *Feldia A.G.* [1967] 2 Q.B. 590, 601 Diplock L.J. said: " English courts
will not enforce an agreement, whatever be its proper law, if it is contrary
to English law, whether statute law or common law; . . ." So they will not
countenance this champertous offer—which is contrary to English law.

There is yet another way of reaching the same result. It is by the
doctrine of election. The plaintiff here had only one cause of action.
He had a choice before him—either to litigate it here in England—or to
pursue it in the United States. At the beginning he did not know of

the choice: but in September 1978 he and his advisers knew that it was A
open to him. Yet in October 1978 they made an application in the
English action for interim payment of another £20,000. They got it—
and he spent it. That was an unequivocal act—deciding to pursue his
right of action in England—in lieu of his right of action in America.
It comes within the words of Lord Atkin in *United Australia Ltd.* v.
Barclays Bank Ltd. [1941] A.C. 1, 30:
                                                                                        B
"... if a man is entitled to one of two inconsistent rights it is fitting
that when with full knowledge he has done an unequivocal act
showing that he has chosen the one he cannot afterwards pursue the
other, which after the first choice is by reason of the inconsistency
no longer his to choose."

On all these grounds, therefore, I would support the decision of the C
judge that the notice of discontinuance was invalid. The defendants
were entitled—and are entitled—to insist on the English action going on
to judgment. If this be so, then clearly the Texan action should no
longer be proceeded with.

Injunction
                                                                                        D
The judge granted an injunction to stop the plaintiff from proceeding
further with his action in the United States. At first sight this seemed
to me to be an extraordinary thing to do. It looked like an interference
with the courts of the United States. But on examination I find that
these courts can and do grant injunctions of this kind: on the ground
that they operate only against the party and not against the court. The
authorities are *Carron Iron Co. Proprietors* v. *Maclaren* (1855) 5 H.L.Cas. E
416, 436, *per* Lord Cranworth L.C.; *The Christianborg* (1885) 10 P.D. 141,
152–153, *per* Bagallay L.J. and *The Tropaioforos* (*No. 2*) [1962] 1 Lloyd's
Rep. 410 where Megaw J. gave a valuable review of all the cases. And
I am interested to see that the Supreme Court of the United States
has affirmed an injunction to restrain proceedings in an English court:
see *The Chaparral* [1972] 2 Lloyd's Rep. 315. This jurisdiction, however, should only be granted with great caution so as to avoid even F
the appearance of undue interference with another court: see *Cohen* v.
Rothfield [1919] 1 K.B. 410 and *Settlement Corporation* v. *Hochschild*
[1966] Ch. 10. I feel this so strongly that I would not myself do as the
judge did. I would not grant an injunction. But, even if it were right to
grant an injunction, I think that there would be great difficulty in enforcing
it. In our present case the defendants' solicitors applied to a judge in G
chamber, for leave to serve a summons for contempt on Mr. Benton
Musslewhite and on Mr. Chaffin, in Houston, Texas. The judge granted
leave and in pursuance of it we are told that summonses for contempt of
the English court were served in the streets of Houston, Texas, on Mr.
Benton Musslewhite and Mr. Robert Chaffin. They asked for them to be
committed to Pentonville Prison here in London, England. That cannot
be right. The common law does not permit any service of process out of H
the jurisdiction on a person out of the jurisdiction even in the case of the
service of a writ claiming damages: see *In re Busfield* (1886) 32 Ch.D. 123.
A fortiori it does not permit a summons to commit to be served out of
the jurisdiction. The only cases in which service can be made out of the
jurisdiction are those set out in R.S.C., Ord. 11, and they do not apply here.
There is, however, an alternative open. I see no reason why, in lieu

The Weekly Law Reports, July 18, 1980

857

1 W.L.R.   Castanho v. Brown & Root Ltd. (C.A.)   Lord Denning M.R.

A   of an injunction, the court should not grant a declaration that the notice of discontinuance was invalid: and that the English action was and still is a pending action: that it is open to the plaintiff to proceed to trial and get judgment for the amount of damages assessed by the English court: or, if the plaintiff does not choose to proceed, for the defendants to ask for judgment to be entered for them.

B   If such a declaration were granted by the English court, I should expect that the courts of the United States would themselves not allow the Texan action to continue. The cause of action arose in England. It was properly cognisable and enforceable in the English courts. The plaintiff sued in the English courts on that cause of action. A final judgment in the English courts on that cause of action would, I should think, be recognised by the courts of the United States: just as we C   would recognise a final judgment by a court in the United States: see *Dicey & Morris, The Conflict of Law,* 9th ed., rule 184, p. 1018.

Conclusion

I find myself in substantial agreement with Parker J. save that I would grant a declaration instead of an injunction.

D   Seeing that Shaw and Brandon L.JJ. take a different view, I would like to state how I see the justice of this case. Here is a Portuguese citizen who has a cause of action against his employers. The cause of action undoubtedly arose in England. At Great Yarmouth in Norfolk. He was treated for months in an English hospital. The Portuguese consulate advised him to sue in England. His chose in action is situate E   in England, because England is the country where it is properly recoverable and can be enforced: see *Dicey & Morris, The Conflict of Laws,* 9th ed., rule 78, p. 506. He brought his action in England and got interim payments of £27,250 in England on account of the damages recoverable here. By so doing he reduced his chose of action into possession in England. If his action had proceeded to trial in England—or be settled—he would soon have recovered compensation F   amounting to £150,000 or £200,000—a sum which most people in Portugal or England would have considered reasonable, and even generous. Yet that course was interrupted by the lawyers from Texas. They persuaded him to suspend his English action and to bring proceedings in Texas—in the hope that he would get an award of £2,500,000— out of which the Texan lawyers would get £1,200,000. They would finance it at their own cost entirely. They would charge him nothing G   if they failed in the United States. He could then revert to his action in England. To our English eyes that arrangement with him savoured of champerty. The Texan lawyers were conducting the litigation in the United States—and directing the litigation in England—on the footing that they would get 40 per cent. of the spoils if they won and nothing if they lost. In so far as these arrangements affected the chose in H   action, they are governed by the lex situs: see *Dicey & Morris, The Conflict of Laws,* 9th ed., rules 78 and 83, pp. 506 and 547. The lex situs was English law: and by English law they were contrary to public policy and should not be enforced. This very case is a good example of the evils to which champerty can give rise. There has been voluminous and expensive litigation in the United States already: and there is a vista of much more to come before the plaintiff can get anything there: if he ever does. He would have been better advised to take the bird in

Lord Denning M.R.   Castanho v. Brown & Root Ltd. (C.A.)   [1980]

the hand in England rather than the dozen in the bush in the United A
States—where the bush is a thicket full of sharp thorns. Simple justice
to him would be for the employers to pay him £200,000 to settle the
English action: and for the proceedings in the United States to be
dropped. That is what the judge felt. It is what I feel too. I would
therefore dismiss the appeal and let the plaintiff be compensated here
and now by a payment of £200,000. But as Shaw and Brandon L.JJ.
think otherwise, he will have to wait till the proceedings end in the B
United States: and that may be a very long time. He may be dead by
then.

SHAW L.J. This case has a complicated history. I need not recount
the detail of it for that has been done already. It has also developed
some extraordinary features. It is in regard to them that I add my C
own observations to what has been said in the judgment of Lord
Denning M.R. as I find myself differing from his conclusions and from
those of Parker J.

The plaintiff is a Portuguese subject. This fact is not without significance since it makes him a foreigner equally in England and in the
United States of America. In the course of his employment he D
suffered a tragic accident which has reduced him to utter helplessness
and made him wholly dependent on others. Apart from being paralysed
in his upper and lower limbs, almost every bodily function has been
impaired. He was little more than 30 years old when this catastrophe
befell him, and he has the responsibility of a wife and children to
maintain. There can be no true measure of compensation in such a
case. The minimum requirement is to provide for his care for what life E
he has still to live; and there must be made good also the loss of
earnings resulting from his incapacity. These elements are capable more
or less of calculation or estimation; but what of amends for pain and
suffering and the loss of enjoyment of life? No process of computation
will serve to provide a real answer or an effective one. The response
of the courts to the challenge presented by this problem is inevitably F
imbued with a conventional quality; and in different societies and environ-
ments different conventions prevail. It cannot be said that any are
necessarily more right than others. If someone who has been reduced
to a human wreck can seek amends in a more generous environment,
his misfortune is the more offset by that fortuitous circumstance. At
least the victim will have the satisfaction of knowing that the destruction of his own capacity to derive enjoyment from physical life has had G
the consequence of augmenting his family's prospects of living securely
on a good standard. It must not be thought that this is to compensate
the dependants of the victim. The satisfaction is *his*, and is an important
aspect of the amends he is entitled to receive. The pursuit of that
satisfaction is in my opinion to be commended as justifiable and not
condemned as avaricious; and the provision of a munificent measure of H
compensation is to be applauded and should not be denigrated as extra-
vagant or exorbitant. It would in my view be less than humane to
deny to such a victim the opportunity to pursue his claim for compensation wherever it will evoke the most generous response. Yet this
is exactly what has been and is being attempted in the course of this
litigation in which the unattractive aspects are by no means all on one
side.

A   With these preliminary observations, I turn to the salient features in the history. The disaster happened on February 11, 1977. The plaintiff was paralysed from the neck downwards. He was given such treatment as medical science can provide at Stoke Mandeville Hospital. The Portuguese consul took up his case. As the locus of the accident was a vessel in English waters, a firm of solicitors in London was consulted. They ascertained who were the ostensible employers and who might be responsible
B   for any negligence which might be the cause of the plaintiff's appalling injuries. So far as they could ascertain, at any rate superficially, an English company called Brown and Root (U.K.) Ltd. which provided shore services for the *American Moon* bore the liability. The solicitors retained for the plaintiff can hardly be blamed for not then discovering that Brown and Root (U.K.) Ltd. was part of a vast complex based in Texas
C   and that it, together with a number of other corporate bodies, operated under the aegis of a Texan corporation called Jackson Marine Inc. So on May 9, 1977, they addressed a letter to Brown and Root (U.K.) Ltd. saying that they held that company liable to compensate the plaintiff for his injuries. It has emerged in these proceedings that all the corporations comprised in the Jackson empire are insured with the same insurers. In England Clyde & Co. ("Clydes") act for those insurers. It is notorious
D   that in the United States the scale of damages for injuries of the magnitude sustained by the plaintiff is something in the region of ten times what is regarded as appropriate by the conventional standards of the courts of this country. One can almost hear the sigh of mingled astonishment and relief breathed by those concerned for the insurers for Jacksons (as I shall call the combination of corporate bodies) when proceedings
E   were proposed in England. No better policy could be pursued from the insurers' point of view than to encourage the issue of those proceedings in this country and to confine them there. In pursuing this policy Clydes were acting in the best interests of their insurer clients, no doubt absolutely correctly in accordance with their professional duty.

On June 1, 1977, they wrote in response to the letter which had been sent to Brown and Root (U.K.) Ltd. by B. M. Birnberg & Co. ("Birnbergs"), the plaintiff's solicitors. That letter read:
F

"Dear Sirs, *Mr. I. F. da Costa Castanho.* Your letter of May 9, addressed to Brown and Root (U.K.) Ltd. has been passed to us for our attention. We are investigating the matter, and in due course shall write to you again. In the meantime, liability is not admitted."

G   They followed that letter up by another dated June 28. I read the full text:

"We refer to our letter of June 1, and write to say that we have now had the opportunity of investigating this matter. We are not, of course, in a position to admit liability, but it would appear that some degree of liability may rest on Jackson Marine Corporation, for whom we act. That being the case, as we expect you are aware, Jackson
H   Marine continue to pay Mr. Castanho's salary, and have paid the expenses incurred by members of his family who have travelled from Portugal to visit him. However, our clients recognise that in the very difficult circumstances now facing Mr. Castanho, further expense of a more general nature is likely to be incurred, and we therefore invite you to suggest a figure by way of interim payment to assist Mr. Castanho and his family, which we shall put to our clients for their consideration. We are, of course, authorised to accept service of pro-

860

ceedings, which in any event must be issued for the purpose of the　A
interim payment. We recognise that it will be a considerable time
before you will be in a position accurately to formulate your client's
claim, but we are sure that you will keep us informed of all material
developments.

"We expect you know, but we feel that we ought to place on
record, that about once a month Mr. Castro, a representative of the
Highlands Insurance Co., and of the Brown and Root Group, visits　B
Mr. Castanho in hospital. These visits are purely to inquire after his
progress, and to ensure that the welfare of himself and his family is
properly looked after. Legal matters are not discussed. We hope
that you will have no objection to the continuation of these visits, but
if you do, perhaps you will let us know. In the meantime, we await
to hear from you on the subject of the interim payment."　　　　　　C

An interesting feature of this early communication from Clydes is the
reiterated reference to the prospect of an interim payment and the
indication that the institution of proceedings was necessary to make such
a payment possible. Birnbergs' reply dated July 13 was not entirely satisfactory for it suggested an interim payment before writ. On the very next
day Clydes wrote in answer. Again their letter deserves to be read in full.　D
After acknowledging Birnbergs' letter of the day before, they continued in
these terms:

"We will accept service on behalf of Jackson Marine Corporation.
We do not think that any liability rests upon Brown and Root (U.K.)
Ltd., and we do not at present have instructions to accept service on
their behalf. However, if you will kindly send us the writ, we expect　E
to have instructions to accept service on behalf of both defendants.

"As we said in our letter of June 28, we shall certainly take instructions on the question of an interim payment, and note that you
consider that £7,000 would be a suitable figure. We shall write to
you again as soon as we have instructions on this point. We certainly
agree with you that there is no bar to our settling an interim payment
at this stage, but we should like to have a formal order from the court　F
in respect of it. We cannot exclude the possibility that at some later
stage we may fail to agree on quantum, and in that connection we
should like to draw your attention to the notes to R.S.C., Ord. 29. . . .
There, the editors suggest that a defendant who makes an interim
payment voluntarily, and without an order of the court, is not entitled
to take that interim payment into account when making a payment　G
into court. We would wish to avoid this problem, and therefore ask
that at the appropriate stage you issue a summons. Naturally, there
will be no opposition to your summons in respect of the agreed amount.

"We shall now take our clients' instructions, and look forward
to hearing from you with your writ. We shall also deal with the
question of your client's salary, and write to you in more detail."　　H

The once more repeated reference to the prospect of an interim payment
was again related to a persistent and insistent suggestion as to the issue
of a writ. In the light of the ensuing history this assumes a special
significance.

The carrot of an interim payment and of the other solicitudes
proffered could hardly be resisted when dangled so assiduously. It was
seized with avidity. The plaintiff's plight was a desperate one. He had

A   been an ordinary seaman and had few resources to cope with his predicament. On October 13, 1977, Birnbergs sent the original writ to Clydes together with a copy. There were now proceedings started in England, and there, if the then and any other prospective defendant had their way, the proceedings would also finish. On October 26 Clydes were writing:

B   " We refer to our conversation with Mrs. Bowden on October 24, and write to confirm what we then told you. According to the information with which our clients have provided us, your client was employed by a company called Jackson Marine S.A. . . . We therefore consider that this company are the proper defendants to this action, and although we cannot prevent you from suing Brown and Root (U.K.) Ltd., we think that you ought to sue Jackson
C   Marine S.A. As arranged, we are returning the writ to you so that Jackson Marine S.A. may be added as defendants, and so that this amendment can be effected before service, and so with the least expense and trouble. If you will kindly return the amended writ to us, we will accept service on behalf of both defendants and will let you have an appearance as soon as possible. You will thereafter be able to issue the summons for an interim payment."
D
Then it goes on to deal with the visits to the plaintiff in hospital.

The company suggested as the proper defendants were not a part of Jacksons incorporated in Texas; their registration and their domicile were in Panama. The writ which had been issued on September 29 was amended in accordance with Clydes' suggestion and the added defendants
E   admitted liability. On March 22, 1978, on the application of the plaintiff and at the invitation if not instigation of Clydes, an order was made by consent against Jackson Marine S.A. under R.S.C., Ord. 29, r. 9, for an interim payment by them of £7,250, those defendants having admitted liability.

The action could now be regarded as firmly and irremovably established in the English jurisdiction. It may be that it was this consideration
F   which caused the defendants to oppose a second application made in November 1978 for a further £20,000 which the plaintiff urgently needed to buy a suitable house in Portugal. As even by English standards the damages were likely to be many times that sum, it is at least peculiar that the application should have been resisted by a corporate member of a wealthy complex such as Jacksons, the more so as liability had been
G   admitted. It permits at least the surmise that the earlier show of solicitude had not been disinterested and was tactical rather than humanitarian. Now that the action was tied (or apparently so) to the courts of this country, there was no point in providing any more carrots. However the plaintiff did continue to receive his salary via the second defendants, and his medical expenses were paid by them.

At that time or soon afterwards (that is, about the end of 1978 and
H   the beginning of 1979) a dramatic change deformed the scene. The plaintiff had been approached by the American lawyers. They advised that he could and should pursue his claim not in England but in the state of Texas, U.S.A. They promised greatly magnified damages. They offered also pending the recovery of those damages financial support for the plaintiff on a comprehensive and liberal scale. True, they required as payment for their services 40 per cent. of any damages he would be awarded and the return of their money advances; but only if he won,

as they were confident he would. Even so he would be left very substan- A
tially better off than he could hope to be at the highest with a judgment
in this country. The practice of exacting payment on a contingency
basis for legal services is not only foreign to English concepts but is
viewed here with positive disapproval. None the less it does not behove
English legal institutions, whether solicitors or the Bar or the judiciary,
to adopt a lofty, let alone a pious, attitude in regard to the contingency
system. It is accepted by the legal institutions of the United States and B
they are entitled not only to hold to their views on the matter but to apply
them in practice, as they regularly do. It is no business of ours, and
we must allow that they know theirs.

Faced with the prospect of vastly adding to the measure of satisfaction
he might expect by pursuing his claim in Texas instead of in England,
it seems that the plaintiff may have hesitated at first. Perhaps that C
prospect seemed too good to be true. However he did not hesitate long.
Self-interest prevailed and the American lawyers were instructed on his
behalf to institute proceedings in Texas and to pursue them there. In
February 1979 the plaintiff executed a power of attorney in favour of
the American lawyers. Their first act on his behalf was to issue
proceedings in the state court of Texas which they did during February.
In addition to the defendants in the original action, others of the Jackson D
corporations were sued as well.

Meanwhile in England the defendants in the action brought here
served their defence on April 30, 1979. Brown and Root (U.K.) Ltd.
denied liability but it was admitted by Jackson Marine S.A. By this
time the action was no longer of interest to the plaintiff. His English
solicitors served a notice of discontinuance on May 14, 1979, just within E
14 days of the service of the defence. In view of the suggested doubt
as to their authority to serve that notice, it is pertinent to recall that
they were then (and still are) on the record as the plaintiff's solicitors
in whatever proceedings inure in England. However wide the terms
of the power of attorney given to the American lawyers, they could not
be invested with authority to take any part in those proceedings on
behalf of the then plaintiff; and conversely that power of attorney could F
not per se divest Birnbergs of their general authority to do in the
English action on behalf of their client what appeared to them at the
time to be in his best interests. I see no real basis for misgiving as to
whether the notice of discontinuance was within Birnbergs' authority
at the time it was served. What then was its effect?

R.S.C., Ord. 21, r. 2 (1), provides: G

"The plaintiff in an action begun by writ may, without the leave
of the court, discontinue the action . . . as against any or all of the
defendants at any time not later than 14 days after service of the
defence on him. . . ."

I have omitted the immaterial parts of the rule. There could ordinarily H
be no question but that this notice brought the action to a summary
end. All that was left of it is to be found in R.S.C., Ord. 62, which
deals with costs and nothing else. R.S.C., Ord. 62, r. 10 (1) provides:

"Where a plaintiff by notice in writing and without leave . . . discontinues his action against any defendant . . . the defendant may
tax his costs of the action . . . and, if the taxed costs are not paid
within 4 days after taxation, he may sign judgment for them."

A   In this way it is contemplated that the position between the parties will be restored to what it was before the action was started; and there is a sanction against the erstwhile plaintiff starting another action based on substantially the same cause of action. R.S.C., Ord. 21, r. 5 provides that if he does start another action before he has paid the defendant's costs in the discontinued action, the court may order the proceedings in the second action to be stayed until those costs are paid. This is

B the only sanction to be found in the rules. It seems to me to be clear that this compact code is designed to bring about what can properly be regarded as a restitutio in integrum restoring the respective parties to the positions they occupied before the first action was brought. No other adjustment or redress is contemplated or called for. The first note to the rules in Order 21 in *The Supreme Court Practice 1979,*

C vol. 1, p. 362 says that " these rules constitute a complete code on the subject of withdrawal and discontinuance of . . . an action . . ."

  In the present case a complication has been introduced in the form of the interim payments under R.S.C., Ord. 29, rr. 9–17. That Order says nothing about what is to happen to such payments if the action is discontinued without leave within the time limited by R.S.C., Ord. 21. Is the right to discontinue without leave in any way affected? The question

D was raised in a very odd way.

  By the time the defendants came to serve their defence, their advisers had become aware of the institution of proceedings in the state court of Texas. I daresay they were outraged. All had appeared set for a trial in England with a comparatively moderate assessment of damages. Now all was threatened. It was quite intolerable to the insurers that their expec-

E tations should be thus thwarted. On May 12, 1979, that is, the day after serving their defence—the defendants served a summons for directions and asked for an injunction to restrain the proceedings in Texas. The application for directions came before the master on June 6. The plaintiff had by that date served his notice of discontinuance so he did not attend. The master having been told something of the history of the matter decided that the summons for directions should be treated as an appli-

F cation to strike out the notice of discontinuance as being an abuse of process. It is questionable whether the defendants were at that stage entitled to take out a summons for directions at all, but in the light of the master's order this has no importance other than showing the state of consternation into which the defendants or their insurers were thrown by the proceedings in Texas. In the state court there strenuous efforts were made

G to stay the plaintiff's action. His advisers thought it expedient to abandon the action in the state court and to institute fresh proceedings in the Texas federal court. This they did in July 1979. They considered the federal court would be more ready to accept jurisdiction. The proceedings in that court also provoked an application for a stay; but when it was dealt with some months later it was unsuccessful. There is an appeal pending

H against the refusal of a stay, but by the rules of procedure in Texas the appeal on the issue of jurisdiction will be heard only after the substantive issues in the action have been resolved. I mention this merely as part of the narrative. In my view, for reasons I shall seek to explain later, what is happening or may happen in the courts of Texas has nothing to do with us. The material consideration is that since the end of 1979 and up to the present time the federal court of the state of Texas in the United States of. America has accepted jurisdiction to try an action at the suit of the plaintiff claiming damages compensatory and punitive against Jacksons for the injuries he sustained on the *American Moon.*

In England the long vacation had interrupted the progress of events. It was not until October 2, that the adjourned summons to strike out the notice of discontinuance came again before the master. The application for an injunction to restrain the plaintiff from pursuing his proceedings in Texas was then pending before the judge in chambers. The master therefore adjourned the summons to strike out to the judge so that he might deal with all the matters involved at one and the same time. The matter came before Parker J. on October 29. Both sides were represented by counsel and their argument and submissions occupied some two days. Judgment was reserved and was given in open court on November 19. In the result it was ordered that the notice of discontinuance be struck out under the inherent jurisdiction of the court as being an abuse of process. The judge also granted an injunction whereby the plaintiff and anyone acting on his behalf, including his American lawyers, were enjoined not to pursue the proceedings in the federal court of Texas or to take any part in them on the plaintiff's behalf.

I have read Parker J.'s careful and elaborate judgment with respectful admiration; but I find it impossible to agree with his conclusions or to accept the reasons on which they are founded.

I deal first, as did the judge, with the notice of discontinuance. To begin with, it seems an inversion of logic to speak of an act which purports to terminate a process as being an abuse of that process. It may be that to seek to retain or to take advantage of some benefit which accrued while the process was in being would constitute an abuse, but I find it difficult to see how giving a process its quietus can be an abuse of it. The right accorded by R.S.C., Ord. 21, r. 2 (1) is explicit and unqualified. The note to rule 2 in *The Supreme Court Practice 1979*, vol. 1, p. 363 sets out the three conditions which must be fulfilled if the notice of discontinuance is to be effective. There is no hint that there may be circumstances in which although the specified conditions are satisfied the discontinuance will be ineffectual or may be declared by the court to be so.

It is of value to recall the corresponding rule before the revision of the Rules of the Supreme Court in 1962. It was then in the following form (R.S.C., Ord. 26, r. 1):

> " The plaintiff may, at any time before receipt of the defendant's defence, or after the receipt thereof before taking any other proceeding in the action (save any interlocutory application), by notice in writing, wholly discontinue his action . . ."

In those days there was no provision elsewhere in the rules for interim payments. I doubt whether, if there had been, an application for such payments would have been regarded as other than interlocutory so that the absolute right to discontinue would have prevailed notwithstanding such payments. The rule in the old form had the disadvantage of giving rise to much contention as to what might in a particular case constitute " taking any other proceedings in the action." Accordingly the rule was modified by substituting a simple time limit.

It is said in the present case that although the plaintiff complied with the rules he has abused the process of the court. How and why I fail to see. It is true that he obtained two interim payments amounting to a substantial sum. They were paid on the basis that a judgment in favour of the plaintiff was probable and that it would be for a

A substantially larger amount. The defendant who made the payment could, as I see it, seek to recover the sums so paid as moneys paid to his use for a consideration which has failed. In any case I see no real incipient financial prejudice, for if the plaintiff successfully pursues his claim in Texas, the federal court there will be apprised of and impose the necessary terms of adjustment for the £27,250 already received by the plaintiff, if indeed he has not by then paid it back. We are told by

B counsel for the plaintiff that he, with the assistance no doubt of his American lawyers, will pay that sum back forthwith. I see no reason to make that repayment a condition of preserving the operation of a regular and valid notice of discontinuance. I do not think the court has any power to impose such a condition where discontinuance is possible without leave under the rules.

C   Then it is said that the plaintiff has procured the advantage of an admission of liability by Jackson Marine S.A. If the admission was honest, it can have done nobody any harm. If it was part of a tactical plan, so much the worse for those who employed such tactics. Any judicial tribunal that functions in a civilised community will not in its independent jurisdiction do other than form its own judgment on what is admitted or proved before that tribunal and not elsewhere in a foreign

D jurisdiction.

    There remains the injunction. It was in these terms:

    " It is . . . ordered and directed that the plaintiff . . . by himself his servants or agents or otherwise howsoever be perpetually restrained and an injunction is hereby granted perpetually restraining him from commencing or causing to be commenced or continuing

E   or prosecuting any further or other proceedings in the United States of America or elsewhere against . . . "

and there follow the names of the various Jackson companies made defendants in the proceedings in Texas.

    A crop of question marks and not a few exclamation marks spring to the mind on reading the terms of this order. In the first place, it

F could have no just foundation unless the plaintiff is held by the scruff of his neck to an action in England that he wished to abandon and which he had in my opinion effectively discontinued.

    Even, however, if the English action remained alive and a concurrent action in relation to the same subject matter is brought in another jurisdiction, what should the attitude of the English courts be if they are asked to regularise that situation? There is much law as to

G the principles which should be applied in seeking to preserve the balance of justice. I do not canvass the authorities but seek to apply the result of examining them. There is little doubt that the question for an English court is whether or not to stay the proceedings in this country. It is over *those* proceedings that they have the authority and the power to exercise control. *They* are within its jurisdiction. To attempt in

H effect to stay proceedings in a foreign jurisdiction is to usurp the function of the courts of that jurisdiction. Whatever moral or ethical considerations may inspire (or cloud) the judgment of an English court, it must not seek to meddle officiously with the jurisdiction of foreign tribunals in regard to matters which they consider to be within the province of that jurisdiction. The only apparent (but not real) exception is where the parties to litigation have contracted to sue only in the courts of this country. In such a case the courts might grant an injunction if proceedings were to be instituted abroad, but this would **A** be no more than the enforcement of an English contract not to sue abroad.

The exclamation marks which I have envisaged come to the mind on many grounds. The plaintiff in the federal court of Texas is a Portuguese subject; he is unlikely, especially having regard to his physical state, ever to be in England. His American lawyers are in **B** duty bound to act in his best interests in pursuing the action in Texas. They must regard an order of an English court which forbids them to do their professional duty in America as an unwarranted and ridiculous charade. They too are outside the jurisdiction. We were told that two of the American attorneys acting for the plaintiff have been served in Texas with a notice of motion for their committal to prison for " contempt in aiding and abetting [the plaintiff] in prosecuting pro- **C** ceedings in the United States District Court for the Eastern District of Texas."

I do not permit myself the luxury of conjecturing what they said and are saying about that absurd episode. It was probably derisive. Even if they came to England, I wonder who would dare to pursue such a motion; and I shrink from the contemplation of the proceedings **D** in court, and their inevitable outcome.

In the course of the appeal it was urged upon this court that the striking out of the notice of discontinuance and the granting of the injunction were justified as a means of countering improprieties and breaches of professional codes of conduct by the American attorneys. Even if the allegations of misconduct were well-founded, and I am in no position to express any opinion upon this topic and would not **E** even if I were, what business is it of an English court in relation to matters which have taken place outside England? The courts and the professional bodies of the United States must deal with that if and when it arises. Maintenance and champerty have ugly connotations in English law, but the emotive use of such expressions does not confer upon an English court a universal moral supervision of legal institutions **F** in other countries. The allegations of impropriety were yet another desperate and disingenuous effort to keep the plaintiff's claim within the relatively moderate limits now current in the courts of England. Fortunately American corporations, like their insurers, are aware of the scale of damages in the United States and they arrange their policies and the premiums accordingly.

This is a case about money, not morality. I see no warrant for the **G** injunction and I would discharge it. In my judgment the appeal should be allowed in its entirety.

BRANDON L.J., whose judgment was read by Shaw L.J. The detailed history of this case is fully set out in the judgment of Parker J. (ante p. 837A) and it is not necessary therefore that I should do more than **H** give a brief outline of it.

In February 1977 the plaintiff, who is Portuguese, was employed as an oiler on board the oil rig service ship *American Moon*. On February 11, when the ship was lying alongside in the Port of Great Yarmouth, the plaintiff sustained a very serious accident which has left him a quadriplegic.

The *American Moon* was owned and operated by Jackson Marine

A Corporation (" J.M.C."), a company incorporated in the state of Texas. J.M.C. carries on its activities, which are world-wide, either directly or indirectly through the medium of various subsidiary companies which are wholly owned and controlled by it. Some of these subsidiary companies are also incorporated in Texas. Others are incorporated in various countries outside the United States, including Panama, the Netherlands Antilles, Holland and England.

B The plaintiff, acting through English solicitors, began by suing his employers in England, naming as defendants two companies in the J.M.C. group, one Panamanian and the other English. That was in November 1977. Later, in February 1979, after proceeding with his action here for over a year, and obtaining two interim payments from the second defendants in the course of doing so, he sued his employers

C afresh in Texas. He first sued them in a state court, naming as defendants J.M.C. and five other companies in the J.M.C. group, including the two already sued in England. Then in July 1979 he withdrew his action in the state court and began another action in a federal court in the same state, naming as defendants J.M.C. and two only of the five subsidiaries previously sued in the state court.

D The reason why the plaintiff sued his employers afresh in Texas was that, after his action in England had already got under way, he had been informed by U.S. attorneys (who subsequently acted for him) that he would, if successful, recover far higher damages in Texas than in England. The reason why his action in Texas was switched from the state court to the federal court was that his U.S. attorneys thought that the latter court was more likely to accept jurisdiction than the

E former.

When the plaintiff had first sued his employers afresh in Texas in February 1979, he had left his action in England alive, though in abeyance. Later, however after the defendants in the English action had on May 1, 1979, applied for an injunction restraining him from proceeding in Texas, and for directions for trial, the plaintiff on May 14, 1979, discontinued his action here. This was something which, by

F reason of what I think can fairly be described as a procedural quirk, he was entitled to do without leave under the relevant rule of court. The defendants' response to the discontinuance was to convert their application for directions for trial into an application to strike out the notice of discontinuance as an abuse of the process of the court.

In the result the judge had before him in November 1979 two

G applications by the defendants. The first was for an injunction restraining the plaintiff from proceeding further against his employers in Texas or elsewhere outside England. The second was for an order striking out the notice of discontinuance as an abuse of the process of the court. The judge granted both applications and the plaintiff now appeals against his decision.

H So far as the jurisdiction of the court generally in matters of this kind is concerned, it has long been established that there may be circumstances in which an English court will (i) compel a plaintiff, who desires to sue in England, to sue in another forum elsewhere instead, or (ii) compel a plaintiff, who desires to sue in another forum elsewhere, to sue in England instead. In case (i) the court achieves its purpose by staying any proceedings which the plaintiff has brought here, so leaving him with the only practical alternative of beginning or continuing

proceedings in the other forum. In case (ii) the court achieves its A
purpose by granting an injunction restraining the plaintiff from beginning or continuing proceedings in the other forum, leaving him with
the only practical alternative of beginning or continuing proceedings
here.

It follows that, when on May 1, 1979, the defendants in the action
here applied for an injunction restraining the plaintiff from proceeding
against his employers in Texas or elsewhere outside England, the court B
certainly had jurisdiction to intervene in the manner sought. Difficult
questions arise, however, as to the effect on that jurisdiction of the
discontinuance of the action by the plaintiff on May 14, 1979. Did
the discontinuance, by bringing the action to an end, also bring to an
end the court's jurisdiction to intervene? If so, does the court have
power to restore that jurisdiction, as it were, by striking out the notice C
of discontinuance as an abuse of its process? If so, ought the court
to exercise that power in the circumstances of the case?

These questions do not need to be answered unless the court
considers that, if it had jurisdiction to intervene by granting the injunction sought, it ought to do so. I propose therefore to leave them
on one side for the time being, to assume that the necessary jurisdiction D
exists, and to consider whether, on that assumption, it ought to be
exercised.

The circumstances in which an English court will compel a plaintiff,
who desires to sue in England, to sue in another forum elsewhere instead
were examined in two recent cases in the House of Lords: *The Atlantic
Star* [1974] A.C. 436 and *MacShannon* v. *Rockware Glass Ltd.* [1978]
A.C. 795. In the second of these two cases Lord Diplock stated the criteria E
applicable in this way, at p. 812:

"'In order to justify a stay two conditions must be satisfied, one
positive and the other negative: (*a*) the defendant must satisfy the
court that there is another forum to whose jurisdiction he is amenable in which justice can be done between the parties at substantially
less inconvenience or expense, and (*b*) the stay must not deprive the F
plaintiff of a legitimate personal or juridical advantage which would
be available to him if he invoked the jurisdiction of the English
court' . . ."

It is clear from *The Atlantic Star* [1974] A.C. 436 that, if the positive
condition at (*a*) above is satisfied, but the negative condition (*b*) above is
not, the court has to carry out a balancing operation. It has to weigh in G
the one scale the advantage to the plaintiff of suing in England, and in the
other scale the disadvantage to the defendant of being sued there, and then
decide which of the two should, as a matter of justice, prevail. In carrying
out that balancing operation the court must have regard to all the relevant
circumstances of the particular case.

It was submitted for the defendants on this appeal that there is no H
difference, in principle, between compelling a plaintiff, who desires to sue
in England, to sue in another forum elsewhere (as was done in the two
House of Lords cases referred to above), and compelling a plaintiff, who
desires to sue in another forum elsewhere, to sue or go on suing in England
(as it sought to compel the plaintiff to do in the present case); and that
the same criteria should therefore apply, mutatis mutandis, to the exercise
of the court's power of compulsion in either case.

A   I would accept this submission as a broad proposition. In my opinion, however, some qualification of it is necessary for this reason. Where a stay is granted of an action here, the English court is doing no more than exercise control over its own proceedings. By contrast, where an injunction is granted restraining a person from suing in another forum elsewhere, the English court is interfering, albeit indirectly, with proceedings in another jurisdiction.

B   This distinction led Scrutton L.J. to say, in *Cohen* v. *Rothfield* [1919] 1 K.B. 410, 413, that the power to grant injunctions in such cases " should be exercised with great caution to avoid even the appearance of undue interference with another court." I agree with that observation and consider that, while the power to compel a plaintiff to sue in another forum elsewhere by staying proceedings here should itself (as the authorities show) C be exercised with caution, the power to compel a plaintiff to sue here by restraining him from proceeding in another forum elsewhere should be exercised with even greater caution.

    Bearing this qualification in mind, I propose to consider, first, whether the criteria laid down by Lord Diplock in *MacShannon* v. *Rockware Glass Ltd.* [1978] A.C. 795, 812, are satisfied, mutatis mutandis, in the present case.

D   So far as criterion (*a*) is concerned, the question is whether the English court is a forum to whose jurisdiction the employers are amenable in which justice can be done between the parties at substantially less inconvenience and expense than in Texas. The answer to this question must clearly be in the affirmative. The action in England is well advanced, with liability of one of the two defendants admitted and the amount of damages E only in issue. It should be possible to bring it to trial and to obtain a final judgment in it within a comparatively short time and without any further great expense. The action in Texas, on the other hand, is only in its early stages. Issues are raised in it with regard to punitive as well as compensatory damages and a full-dress trial before a jury is contemplated. Witnesses will have to be brought from abroad, or depositions obtained F from them. From these and other matters, it is clear that the determination of the claim in Texas is bound to involve much greater inconvenience and expense than its determination in England.

    So far as criterion (*b*) is concerned, the question is whether an injunction restraining the plaintiff from proceeding in Texas would deprive him of a legitimate personal or juridical advantage which would be available to him if he continued his action there. The answer to this question G must also clearly be in the affirmative: he stands to recover, even after allowing for the contingency fees of his U.S. attorneys, at least five times more by way of damages in Texas than in England, and, if he can get that very great advantage by suing his employers in their own state, it seems to me entirely legitimate for him to seek to do so.

H   We have a situation, therefore, where criterion (*a*) is satisfied but criterion (*b*) is not, so that the balancing operation to which I referred earlier has to be carried out, and carried out with due regard to all the relevant circumstances of the case.

    If it were merely a question of weighing in the one scale the advantage to the plaintiff of being able to recover at least five times as large an amount of damages in Texas as in England, and in the other scale the much increased inconvenience and expense to the J.M.C. group of having to contest the claim in Texas, I should have no doubt whatever that the **A** advantage to the plaintiff should prevail.

I say that for the following reasons. It would always have been open to the plaintiff, if he had been so advised early enough to sue the J.M.C. group in Texas first, and never to have brought any action against them in England at all. If he had done so, the J.M.C. group could not, so far as I can see, have compelled him to sue in England, and would have had **B** to incur the inconvenience and expense of contesting the claim in Texas in any event. The only additional expenses which the J.M.C. group will have incurred, if the plaintiff is now allowed to go on in Texas after beginning an action in England and later discontinuing it, are the costs incurred by the defendants in the English action. These costs, however, are recoverable by the defendants from the plaintiff under R.S.C., Ord. 62, r. 10, so that they can be disregarded.   **C**

It follows that, if the scales are to be tilted in favour of granting an injunction against the plaintiff, it must be by reason of other factors in the case which would make it just that this should happen. A number of such other factors were indeed relied on by the defendants and it is necessary that I should now state what they are and consider what weight, if any, should be given to them.   **D**

One matter relied on by the defendants was that England is the natural and proper forum for the determination of the claim. As to this, I would accept that England is a natural and proper forum for two reasons: first, the accident took place in an English port; and, secondly, much of the medical evidence is to be found, immediately at any rate, in this country. The plaintiff, however, is not English but Portuguese, and the J.M.C. group by which he was employed is based, **E** directly or indirectly, in Texas. In these circumstances I consider that Texas is also a natural and proper forum for the determination of the claim: no more so, perhaps, than England, but no less so either.

A second matter relied on by the defendants was that the second defendants had made an admission of liability in the English action which would prejudice the J.M.C. group in the action in Texas. If **F** this was a case in which the employers had any reasonable prospect of success on the issue of liability for compensatory damages at least, there might be something in the point. On the evidence about the accident, however, it is clear beyond doubt that it was caused by negligence of the ship's chief engineer for which the employers must be vicariously liable, whether the claim is determined in England or Texas. In these circumstances I do not consider that the likelihood of **G** any prejudice to the J.M.C. group arising from the admission has been made out.

A third matter relied on by the defendants, and relied on as being of great weight, was the receipt by the plaintiff of two interim payments in the action in England. With regard to these there is a curious situation. Two interim payments were made under R.S.C., Ord. 29, **H** rr. 9-12. The first payment was for £7,250, made pursuant to an order dated March 22, 1978. This was a consent order asked for by the plaintiff's solicitors largely at the prompting of the defendants' solicitors. The second payment was for £20,000 made pursuant to an order (not by consent) dated December 8, 1978. The purpose of the second payment was to enable the plaintiff to buy a plot of land and build a suitable pre-fabricated bungalow on it.

A   The question arises whether, following the discontinuance of the action on May 14, 1979, these interim payments became repayable. Examination of the relevant rules reveals a strange lacuna in them. R.S.C., Ord. 29, r. 9, defines an interim payment as meaning a payment on account of any damages in respect of personal injuries which a defendant may be held liable to pay to a plaintiff. Rule 12 provides that one situation in which interim payments may be ordered

B is where a defendant has admitted liability for a plaintiff's claim. Rule 16 provides for adjustment of the amount payable on final judgment or order by taking into account any interim payments previously made. There is, however, no rule covering the situation where interim payments are made by a defendant to a plaintiff, and the plaintiff, being entitled to do so, then discontinues the action without leave, so that the

C stage of final judgment or order is never reached.

     It seems to me that, even though there is no express rule in R.S.C., Ord. 29 authorising the court to order repayment in such circumstances, the court must have inherent jurisdiction, in the interests of justice, to do so. The payments are ordered and made on account of a sum to be awarded on final judgment or order. If, by the choice of the plaintiff who has received them, there will never be a final judgment

D or order, justice requires that he should repay them.

     While it follows from what I have just said that I consider that the court has power in the present case to order the plaintiff to repay the interim payments, the question whether it has such power or not does not really matter. This is because counsel for the plaintiff has indicated that his client is willing to repay the interim payments, and will either

E submit to an order to repay them if the court has power to make it, or else give an undertaking to repay them if the court has no such power.

     It is clear that any repayment of the interim payments would in practice be financed not by the plaintiff himself, but by his U.S. attorneys by way of advance against his ultimate recovery in Texas.

F Thus was objected to as improper by the defendants, but I do not see that, if the interim payments are repaid, it matters from what source the repayment, so long as it is authorised by the plaintiff, is made. The point is one which relates, and relates only, to the propriety of the professional conduct of the plaintiff's U.S. attorneys, a matter which, for reasons which I shall develop later, is in my view outside the purview of this court.

G   The defendants' case with regard to these interim payments was really this. The plaintiff had, it was said, come to the English court and there gained an important advantage which he could not have gained if he had sued his employers only in Texas. Then, having gained that important advantage, he had abandoned the English court and gone off to the Texas court in order to recover there much higher final

H damages than he could have got by continuing in the English court. By so acting he was getting, or trying to get, the best of both worlds, and it was unjust to the employers that he should be allowed to do so.

     I see the force of this argument. The answer to it, however, seems to me to be that, if the interim payments are repaid, the employers will be no worse off in this respect than if the English action had never been begun. No injustice to the employers in relation to the interim payments will, therefore, enure.

A fourth matter relied on for the defendants was that, following A the discontinuance of the plaintiff's action in England, he would be entitled, if the Texas court declined jurisdiction, to begin a further action here, and that it was unjust that he should be able to keep his options open in this way.

The practical position with regard to this matter is as follows. The plaintiff has issued a fresh writ here to protect his position in the event of the Texas court declining jurisdiction. This possibility is, however, B extremely remote. The Texas court has, since the hearing before Parker J. in November 1979, dismissed applications by the defendants there to stay the action on jurisdictional grounds. We have been told that this decision may be open to review on a final appeal after trial, but there was no evidence to show that, if such a review took place, a reversal of the decision was at all likely. In these circumstances it C seems extremely unlikely that the plaintiff would ever wish to prosecute the further action begun by the protective writ referred to earlier.

In so far, however, as the existence of this further action poses a threat, even if a remote one, to the defendants, it can, I think, be taken care of by ordering a stay of the action concerned. I understood counsel for the plaintiff to be willing to submit to such an order being made forthwith. D

The defendants directed a good deal of criticism at the conduct of the plaintiff's U.S. attorneys. They were, of course, retained by the plaintiff on a contingency fee basis. This is normal practice in the United States, and no objection could properly be taken to it. The U.S. attorneys are, however, helping to finance the plaintiff in other ways, first, by agreeing to pay his salary if his employers cease doing E so, and secondly—a point to which I have already referred earlier— by offering to repay the interim payments if that should become necessary.

Evidence was adduced to show that, in acting in these last two ways, the attorneys might be in breach of one or more of the codes of professional conduct (those of the American Bar Association and the Texas Bar Association) by which their behaviour should be governed. F

In my opinion, this court is not concerned with, and ought not to inquire into, questions of that kind. The plaintiff has done what he has done, in suing his employers in Texas and in discontinuing his action here, on the combined advice of his English solicitors and counsel on the one hand and his U.S. attorneys on the other. If the latter have in some way offended against the professional codes which apply to them in G their own country, it must be left to the courts of that country or the associations concerned to take such action, if any, as they think fit.

In this connection it is to be observed that maintenance has never been a ground for staying an action in England: see *Mackey* v. *James Henry Monks (Preston) Ltd.* [1918] A.C. 59, 91, *per* Lord Parker of Waddington. Even less can it be a ground for restraining proceedings H in another forum elsewhere.

Accordingly I do not consider that the conduct of the plaintiff's attorneys, so far as it is criticised by the defendants, is a relevant matter to be weighed in the scales against him.

Having weighed in one scale the very great advantage to the plaintiff of suing his employers in Texas rather than in England, and in the other scale all the various matters relied on by the defendants as being

A   disadvantages to them of his being allowed to do so, or as otherwise making it unjust that he should be allowed to do so, I have reached the conclusion that the balance comes down clearly in the plaintiff's favour.

    I am not persuaded that, provided the interim payments are repaid, and the protective action recently begun by the plaintiff here is stayed,
B there is anything unjust about the plaintiff being allowed to continue his proceedings in Texas. On the contrary I think that justice requires that, subject to these two matters, he should be left free to do so.

    Since I should not think it right, assuming the court had jurisdiction to do so, to grant the injunction sought by the defendants, it is unnecessary for me to decide the difficult questions which I posed earlier as to the effect of the discontinuance of the action on that jurisdiction.
C I shall, therefore, express no opinion one way or the other on those questions.

    For the reasons which I have given, and subject to the two conditions which I have mentioned, I would allow the appeal and set aside the orders of the judge made on November 19, 1979.

D

> *Appeal allowed with costs in Court of Appeal and below.*
> *Order of Parker J. striking out notice of discontinuance set aside and injunction discharged.*
> *Second protective writ stayed meanwhile.*

E

> *Taxation of defendants' costs up to notice of discontinuance and of plaintiff's costs thereafter—set off.*
> *Order not to be drawn up for 14 days to enable interim payments*
F *to be offered or tendered by plaintiff.*
> *Leave to appeal.*

    Solicitors: *B. M. Birnberg & Co; Clyde & Co.*

A. H. B.
G

H

A

[COURT OF APPEAL]

* REGINA *v.* CHATWOOD AND OTHERS

1979 Oct. 19   Bridge L.J., Forbes and Sheldon JJ.

B

Crime—Evidence—Confession—Admissions by experienced drug-taker of possession of controlled drug—Whether evidence of nature of substance possessed—Misuse of Drugs Act 1971 (c. 38), s. 5 (1) [1]

Appellants, who were experienced in unlawful use of drugs, were questioned by police and each appellant made oral and written admissions that he had injected himself with drugs including heroin. Each appellant pleaded not guilty to contravening section 5 (1) of the Misuse of Drugs Act 1971 by unlawful possession of the drugs which he had admitted having used for injecting himself. The prosecution adduced no analysis evidence. A submission by the appellants at the close of the prosecution's evidence, that there was no case to answer in the absence of scientific evidence as to the nature of the substance injected was rejected. Only one appellant gave evidence, in which he stated that the substance with which he had injected himself was flour. The appellants were convicted.

C

D

On appeal against conviction: —

Held, dismissing the appeals, that, since the appellants were experienced drug-takers, their statements to the police were sufficient to provide prima facie evidence of the nature of the substance which had been in their possession; so that they had a case to answer; and that, in view of the jury's verdict, they disbelieved the evidence by the appellant that he had used flour and they believed his admissions to the police.

E

The following cases are referred to in the judgment:

Bird v. *Adams* [1972] Crim.L.R. 174, D.C.
Mieras v. *Rees* [1975] Crim.L.R. 224, D.C.
Reg. v. *Smith (Roger)* [1975] A.C. 476; [1974] 2 W.L.R. 1; [1973] 3 All E.R. 1109, H.L.(E.).
Reg. v. *Wells* [1976] Crim.L.R. 518, D.C.

F

No additional cases were cited in argument.

APPEALS against conviction.
APPLICATION for leave to appeal against sentence.

G

On March 28, 1979, at Preston Crown Court (Judge Openshaw) the appellants, Roy Chatwood, Christopher Michael Patrick Egan, Paul Thomas Flaherty and Harry Proctor, were convicted of contravening section 5 (1) of the Misuse of Drugs Act 1971. They appealed against conviction on the ground that, in the absence of analysis evidence of the substance possessed, they had no case to answer. The applicant, Anthony William Kenneth Walker, who pleaded guilty to supplying a Class A controlled drug, was sentenced on March 26, 1979, to three years' imprisonment. He applied for leave to appeal against severity of sentence.

H

The facts are stated in the judgment.

[1] Misuse of Drugs Act 1971, s. 5: " (1) Subject to any regulations ... in force, it shall not be lawful for a person to have a controlled drug in his possession."

A   *R. C. W. Bennett* (assigned by the Registrar of Criminal Appeals) for the appellants Chatwood, Egan and Flaherty.

Edmund Perez (assigned by the Registrar of Criminal Appeals) for the appellant Proctor.

A. R. D. Stuttard for the Crown.

The applicant Walker did not appear and was not represented.

B
FORBES J. gave the following judgment of the court. On March 26, 1979, at the Crown Court at Preston, the four appellants pleaded not guilty to a number of related offences concerned with the possession of controlled drugs. In addition, the appellant Egan was charged with theft.

The case arose out of the finding of the body of a drug addict named Fisher by the side of a motorway in Lancashire in the middle of June C 1978. Subsequently the police made extensive inquiries among those involved in the abuse of drugs in the area, including the four appellants— Chatwood, Egan, Flaherty and Proctor. Each of them denied having anything to do with Fisher's death, but each admitted, orally and in writing, to police officers, that they had been in possession of the various drugs specified in the indictment. The appellant Egan too admitted that D he had stolen £3 from the wallet of the dead youth, apparently to pay for the transport of the body to the motorway.

The case was complicated by the fact that both the forensic scientist called for the Crown and one of the experienced police officers from the drug squad were asked questions about the nature of the drug heroin itself. The forensic scientist (cautious as scientists usually are) said that he could not tell whether a substance was heroin without analysing it. E The police officer (with nine years' experience with the drug squad) said effectively that while he might have a pretty good suspicion about a substance being heroin, he could not be certain.

On the basis of that evidence, submissions were made to the trial judge that there was insufficient evidence to go to the jury in the case of the appellants, because the only evidence against them was their own F belief that the drug that they had administered to themselves was heroin or pethidine (whichever it may have been in the individual cases) and that that belief was not good enough.

Those submissions were supported by reference to a number of cases, one or two of which I shall have to turn to in a moment.

The three appellants Chatwood, Egan and Flaherty did not give evidence but the appellant Proctor did. He, in his evidence, maintained G that the substance with which he had injected himself was flour. The cogency of that evidence was somewhat eroded, because evidence had been given by the detective sergeant in the prosecution case that during the course of questioning the appellant Proctor, having admitted possessing heroin, had gone on to say:

H   "How can you prove it was heroin? I could say it was flour: in fact I probably will say it was flour when it comes to court. It was poor stuff, it made me sick after cranking it."

"Cranking it" is the cant term for injecting it, as I understand it. The evidence of the interview goes on:

(Q) "How long have you been abusing drugs?" (A) "Since I was about 13 years old. I'm not as fit now as when I first started I'll tell you that. They do say it's habit forming. I was a registered addict

at one time." (Q) " If you have been taking drugs for this length of A
time, you of all people should know the difference between heroin
and flour." (A) " I know the difference all right; that was heroin I
got off that lad. Poor stuff, I know, but you "—i.e., the police—
" have got to be one step ahead. You have to prove it was heroin."

In face of that statement, that he knew perfectly well that it was heroin,
the jury convicted him, quite clearly disbelieving his evidence that he B
thought it was flour and accepting the evidence of that statement that it
was heroin.

There is that distinction between the case of the appellant Proctor
and the others, that he did give evidence—unlike the others—and that
the jury were able to test that evidence against what he had said in his
statement.

The case got off—if one may put it this way—on the wrong foot by C
the fact that in their submissions counsel for the appellants relied on
Reg. v. *Smith* (*Roger*) [1975] A.C. 476. *Reg.* v. *Smith* was a case
concerned with the question whether a person could be guilty of an
attempt to commit a crime (in that case handling stolen goods) when his
belief that he was committing it turned out to be erroneous. I need not
go into the details of their Lordships' opinions in the House. It is suffi- D
cient to say that really the proposition which that case established was
that merely to have an intention to commit a crime, without more, could
not be a crime. If I may turn round the usual aphorism, mens non facit
reum nisi actus sit reus. The case was not concerned in any way with any
question of proof that the goods were stolen, or of whether an admission
by a defendant that the goods were stolen goods amounted to evidence
of that fact, or anything of that kind at all. It was a case concerned E
solely with this issue about attempt. In fact of course in that case, and
I need not go into the facts, the prosecution had established by their
evidence that the goods were not stolen at the time they were handled.

Mieras v. *Rees* [1975] Crim.L.R. 224, on which much reliance was
placed in the Crown Court, was a case to the like effect. The account of
that case in that publication is inaccurate. The defendant was not F
charged, as is said there, with unlawfully supplying a substance, believing
it to be a controlled drug: he was, in fact, charged with attempting (under
section 19 of the Misuse of Drugs Act 1971) to commit an offence under
section 4 (3) by unlawfully supplying a substance believing it to be a controlled drug, in that case one called STP. The only evidence against him
was his own statement that he supplied the substance believing it to be
STP, but had subsequently been told that it was not in fact STP, but G
something similar. Once again that case was clearly concerned with
attempt and not with whether there was prima facie evidence that the
substance supplied was a controlled drug. Had there been such evidence,
the proper charge would have been one of supplying it under section 4
(3), as was pointed out by Michael Davies J. in the judgment of that
case. Having dealt with the defendant's statement to which I have just H
referred, he goes on:

" It is perfectly plain that the difficulty which the prosecution were
in was apparent to them before the informations were laid, the difficulty being that the prosecution was quite unable to prove that the
substance which had been supplied by the appellant was STP. If
they had been able so to prove, the appropriate charge which no
doubt would have been brought would have been one of actually

A   supplying that substance. So it was thought with ingenuity, but in my judgment without any justification as a matter of law and fact, that the prosecution's difficulty could be overcome by preferring informations alleging an attempt to commit an offence even though, as I have said, the court would be bound to conclude that the appellant had not indeed supplied STP."

B   Then Michael Davies J. goes on to refer to the opinion of Lord Reid in *Reg.* v. *Smith* [1975] A.C. 476, 497 and of Lord Morris, at p. 500, and to point out that the decision in *Reg.* v. *Smith* effectively disposed of the argument, in the circumstances set out in *Mieras* v. *Rees* [1975] Crim.L.R. 224, that this could properly be an attempt to commit a crime at all. *Mieras* v. *Rees* has nothing whatever to do with any question of evidence. It was not a question of whether there was prima facie
C evidence led by the prosecution. In *Mieras* v. *Rees*, in fact, the only evidence of the nature of the substance was the statement by the defendant that he had been told that it was not in fact STP. The decision is based on acceptance of that statement as evidence of the nature of the substance. The Divisional Court was apparently content to do this without hesitation and untroubled by any nice question about whether or not the
D statement was admissible as being based on hearsay.

    The case which is in fact concerned with the question of whether an admission of possession of a controlled drug in prima facie evidence that the substance was in fact such a drug is *Bird* v. *Adams* [1972] Crim.L.R. 174. In that case the appellant had been charged with unlawful possession of a controlled drug. The only evidence as to the substance, in possession of which he was found, was his own admission that it was LSD. I take
E up the tale from the transcript of the judgment of Lord Widgery C.J. in that case:

    " Now when the case was heard before the justices, at the conclusion of the prosecution case, which really consisted of nothing more than the evidence of the police officer to which I have referred, there was a submission of no case to answer, and the basis of the submission was
F   this, that although the appellant had admitted possession of what he thought to be LSD, there was no independent proof that the drug was in fact LSD, and that it might have been some innocuous substance sold to the appellant under a fraudulent description, and so it was submitted that there was no case to answer because the vital element of the prosecution case, namely, that the drug was a prohibited drug, had not been established by an admission of the appel-
G   lant who himself could not know whether that which he carried was or was not the genuine drug. Now the justices rejected that suggestion, at least they were not influenced by it. They held there was a case to answer and on the case proceeding the appellant gave no evidence and he was duly convicted. Mr. Reney-Davies before us today returns to the original submission in the case and says that the
H   justices should have upheld the submission of no case because the admission of the appellant in the circumstances of this case was of no evidential value at all. Now it is clear from the authorities which have been put before us that there are many instances where an admission made by an accused person on a matter of law in respect of which he is not an expert is really no admission at all. There are bigamy cases where a man has admitted a ceremony of marriage in circumstances in which he could not possibly have known whether

in truth he had been married or not because he was no expert on the A
marriage ceremonial appropriate in the particular place. It is quite
clear that there are cases of that kind where the person making the
admission lacks the necessary background knowledge to be able to
make the admission at all. Again we have been referred to the
Comptroller of Customs v. *Western Lectric Co. Ltd.* [1966] A.C.
367, where a man made an admission in regard to the country of B
origin of certain goods when he had no idea at all where the goods
had come from. Again it was held that this admission was worthless
because it was an admission of a fact as to which he had no knowledge
at all, and in respect of which no valid admission can be made.
Mr. Reney-Davies submitted that the present case is a like case with
that, but in my judgment this is not so. If a man admits possession
of a substance which he says is a dangerous drug, if he admits it in C
circumstances like the present where he also admits that he has been
peddling the drug, it is of course possible that the item in question
was not a specific drug at all but the admission in those circumstances is not an admission of some fact about which the admitter
knows nothing. This is the kind of case in which the appellant had
certainly sufficient knowledge of the circumstances of his conduct to
make his admission at least prima facie evidence of its truth and D
that was all that was required at the stage of the proceedings at which
the submission to the justices was made."

In view of some remarks about subsequent cases involving handling
stolen goods, which Mr. Bennett submitted on behalf of the first three
appellants, I think perhaps I should read a short passage from the judgment of Lawson J. which followed. He said: E

" I would just add this, that the situation in my judgment seems very
similar to the situation which can and frequently does arise when
people are charged with handling stolen goods under section 22 of
the Theft Act 1968. In many cases it is not possible for those responsible for prosecutions to prove that goods are in fact stolen goods. It
may not be known from what source they emanate, but if the person F
charged has made some statement relating to the circumstances in
which he acquired possession of these goods, it is quite legitimate and
proper for inferences to be drawn from evidence of that statement
that the goods are in fact stolen. This is in fact a common situation
and a situation which seems to me to be very close to the present
case."
G
It should be said that in *Archbold Pleading Evidence and Practice in
Criminal Cases*, 40th ed. (1979), paragraph 1398 there is a note of the
decision in *Bird* v. *Adams* [1972] Crim.L.R. 174 followed by this statement: " In *Mieras* v. *Rees*, on very similar facts, the defendant's appeal
was allowed." From what has been said above, it will be apparent that
neither the facts nor the principles of law in *Mieras* v. *Rees* were at all H
similar to those in *Bird* v. *Adams*.

The last case to which I shall refer is *Reg.* v. *Wells* [1976] Crim.L.R.
518. When examined, that case proceeds entirely on the same reasoning
as *Bird* v. *Adams* [1972] Crim.L.R. 174. Ormrod L.J., giving the
judgment of the court, said:

" The point in this case is, in our view, this. At no time has it been
suggested by Miss Wells that her belief that she had smoked canna-

A   bis with Mr. Cooke and that she had taken 'speed' with him was
erroneous.   There is even now no suggestion by her that she might
have been mistaken about that admission.   All that is said is it is on
the prosecution to prove positively that she had been, at the relevant
time or times, in possession of either cannabis or amphetamine as
the case may be.   But the best evidence that she has been in possession of these articles at some time might well be her admission, parti-
B   cularly when her admission is still not retracted."

It is true that at one point he said that, unlike the case he was dealing
with, *Mieras* v. *Rees* [1975] Crim.L.R. 224 was a plea of not guilty.
But in its context this remark was necessary only to draw the distinction
between that situation and the situation where there was a plea of guilty,
because Ormrod L.J. had just been outlining the principles on which the
C   courts allow a plea of guilty to be withdrawn; principles which the court
in *Mieras* v. *Rees* [1975] Crim.L.R. 224 had not had to consider.   He
went on to point out that *Mieras* v. *Rees* was a case concerned with
attempt, which was the true distinction between that case and the one
before him.   He continued by saying:

D   " What is said is that the prosecution in a drug case must identify
the drugs in question positively by scientific evidence before a court
can accept a plea of guilty to possession.   One has only got to state
the proposition in those terms to see how absurd it must be.   If one
needs to take it to its logical conclusion, it is necessary to point out
it is no answer to say this young woman was convicted on her own
expression of opinion.   In the last analysis all the evidence as to the
E   nature of the substance is an expression of opinion.   Scientists perhaps express more reliable opinions than people who have not got
the advantages of scientific techniques of identifying substances.   But
in the last analysis, everybody is expressing an opinion."

So here these drug abusers were expressing an opinion, and an informed
opinion, that, having used the substance which they did use, it was indeed
F   heroin, because they were experienced in the effects of heroin.

The difficulty is that the commentary in the Criminal Law Review
on *Reg.* v. *Wells* [1976] Crim.L.R. 518 misunderstands both the ratio of
that case and, indeed, the facts of *Mieras* v. *Rees* [1975] Crim.L.R. 224.
This commentary appears to have misled also the editor of *Phipson on
Evidence*, 12th ed. (1976), 2nd Supplement, for the second supplement
reiterates the inaccurate summary given in the Criminal Law Review.
G   This court considers that the law is stated, if we may say so respectfully, with complete accuracy by Lord Widgery C.J. in *Bird* v. *Adams*
[1972] Crim.L.R. 174 in the passage to which I have referred.   Applying
that law to this case, it is apparent that the statements of the appellants in
this case, either orally to the police officer, or when reduced to writing,
were sufficient to provide prima facie evidence of the nature of the sub-
H   stance which had been in their possession.   One of them, Proctor, as I
have indicated, gave evidence, but what I have said about his statement
to the police and the fact that he was found guilty by the jury indicates
quite clearly that the jury disbelieved his explanation that it was flour and
believed his earlier statement to the police that he knew it was heroin.

This court is of the view that the statements of the appellants provide,
having regard to the circumstances of this case, prima facie evidence of
the identity of the substance.   As that is the only point on the appeals

against conviction, the appeals against conviction are accordingly **A**
dismissed.

The court also has before it an application by one other person who
was concerned in this matter, the applicant Walker. He in fact pleaded
guilty to possessing controlled drugs and also to supplying a Class A controlled drug. He was sentenced to three years' imprisonment on the
supply charge and six months' imprisonment concurrent on each of the **B**
possession counts, but consecutive to the three years. There is an application for leave to appeal against that sentence on the ground that it was
excessive. A sentence of three years for supplying heroin cannot, in
the view of this court, be regarded as excessive or as wrong in principle.
The application is accordingly refused.

Appeals dismissed.
Application refused.   **C**

Solicitors: *L. & R. Blackburn.*

L. N. W.

[PRIVY COUNCIL]   **D**

* TREVOR STONE . . . . APPELLANT

AND

THE QUEEN . . . . RESPONDENT

[APPEAL FROM THE COURT OF APPEAL OF JAMAICA]   **E**

1980 Jan. 14;   Lord Diplock, Lord Salmon,
     March 4   Lord Elwyn-Jones, Lord Russell of Killowen
                                       and Lord Keith of Kinkel

Jamaica — Constitution — Gun Court — Firearms offences — Trial   **F**
before judge sitting without jury—Whether right to trial by jury
entrenched in Constitution—Jamaica (Constitution) Order in
Council 1962 (S.I. 1962 No. 1550), s. 13 (1), Sch. 2, s. 97 (1)—
Gun Court Act (No. 8 of 1974), ss. 4 (b), 5 (2), 9 (b)—Gun
Court (Amendment) Act 1976 (No. 1 of 1976), ss. 2, 3, 5

Section 13 of the Jamaica (Constitution) Order in Council
1962 provides:
    " (1) The Supreme Court in existence immediately before **G**
    the commencement of this Order shall be the Supreme
    Court for the purposes of the Constitution . . ."
Section 97 of the Constitution of Jamaica provides:
    " (1) There shall be a Supreme Court for Jamaica which
    shall have such jurisdiction and powers as may be con-
    ferred upon it by this Constitution or any other law."
    The Constitution also provides, by section 49, for a **H**
special procedure for the passage through Parliament of Bills
which alter any entrenched provisions of the Constitution.
    The defendant was charged on indictment in the High
Court Division of the Gun Court with three firearms offences
which at the time when the Constitution of Jamaica came into
force would have been triable by a Supreme Court judge
sitting with a jury. The trial took place on May 11, 1976,
before a Supreme Court judge sitting without a jury, as provided by sections 4 (b), 5 (2) and 9 (b) of the Gun Court Act

A   (as amended by the Gun Court (Amendment) Act 1976).
None of those provisions had been enacted in accordance with
the special procedure provided by section 49 of the Constitution. The defendant was convicted of illegal possession of a
firearm and robbery with aggravation. He applied to the
Court of Appeal for leave to appeal against his conviction.
The Court of Appeal refused leave to appeal but gave the
defendant leave to appeal to the Judicial Committee against
B   that refusal.
     On the question whether section 13 (1) of the Jamaica
(Constitution) Order in Council 1962, read together with
section 97 (1) of the Constitution, had the effect of entrenching
the right to trial by jury in the Constitution so as to render
the trial of a firearms offence by a judge sitting without a jury
inconsistent with the Constitution and void: —
     Held, that a right to trial by jury was not entrenched in the
C   Constitution by any necessary implication from the terms of
section 13 (1) of the Order in Council read with section 97 (1)
of the Constitution, and it was not therefore necessary for the
validity of sections 4 (*b*), 5 (2) and 9 (*b*) of the Gun Court Act
that they should have been enacted by Parliament using the
special procedure appropriate for altering entrenched rights;
and that, accordingly, the defendant's trial had not been
unconstitutional and the Court of Appeal had rightly refused
D   the defendant leave to appeal.
     Decision of the Court of Appeal of Jamaica affirmed.

     The following case is referred to in the judgment of their Lordships:
     Hinds v. *The Queen* [1977] A.C. 195; [1976] 2 W.L.R. 366; [1976] 1 All
          E.R. 353, P.C.

E   The following additional case was cited in argument:
     Ward v. *James* [1966] 1 Q.B. 273; [1965] 2 W.L.R. 455; [1965] 1 All E.R.
          568, C.A.

     APPEAL (No. 11 of 1978) by the defendant, Trevor Stone, from a
judgment (July 29, 1977) of the Court of Appeal of Jamaica (Zacca
and Henry JJ.A. and Rowe J.A. (Ag.)) refusing the defendant's applica-
F   tion for leave to appeal against his conviction on May 11, 1976, of illegal
possession of a firearm and robbery with aggravation by Melville J.
sitting without a jury in the High Court Division of the Gun Court. On
March 15, 1978, the Court of Appeal gave leave to the defendant to
appeal to Her Majesty in Council against that refusal.
     The facts are stated in the judgment of their Lordships.

G   *Ian Ramsay* (of the Jamaica Bar) and *William Glossop* for the
defendant.
     Henderson Downer (of the Jamaica Bar) for the Crown.

                                        Cur. adv. vult.

H   March 4. The judgment of their Lordships was delivered by LORD
DIPLOCK.
     The defendant, Trevor Stone, was tried on May 11, 1976, before
Melville J., sitting without a jury, as a High Court Division of the Gun
Court, upon an indictment which charged him (1) with illegal possession
of a firearm contrary to section 20 (1) (*b*) of the Firearms Act; (2) with
robbery with aggravation contrary to section 37 (1) (*a*) of the Larceny
Act; and (3) with shooting with intent to cause grievous bodily harm. All

three counts related to offences which fall within the jurisdiction conferred   A
upon a High Court Division of the Gun Court under section 5 (2) of
the Gun Court Act as amended by the Gun Court (Amendment) Act 1976
(" the amended Act "). The judge convicted the defendant on the first
two counts and acquitted him on the third. On the first count the judge
imposed a sentence of imprisonment for life, which is mandatory under
section 8 (2) of the amended Act; on the second count he imposed a
sentence of 20 years' imprisonment and six strokes. Against these con-   B
victions the defendant applied to the Court of Appeal for leave to appeal
on a number of grounds, one of which raised a question of interpretation
of the Constitution of Jamaica. His application was refused by the
Court of Appeal on July 29, 1977, and leave to appeal to Her Majesty
in Council against such refusal was granted by the Court of Appeal on
March 15, 1978. The only ground of appeal that has been relied on   C
before this Board is that which raises a question as to the interpretation
of the Constitution—the constitutional point.

Put in summary form the submission made on behalf of the
defendant is that the right of an accused to trial by jury in the case
of grave crimes is entrenched in the Constitution of Jamaica; it can
only be withdrawn or restricted by an Act of Parliament passed in
accordance with the special procedure prescribed by section 49 of the   D
Constitution; neither the Gun Court Act nor the Gun Court (Amendment) Act 1976 was passed in accordance with those procedures, therefore, in so far as sections 4 (*b*), 5 (2) and 9 (*b*) of the amended Act
purport to provide for the trial of grave crimes (i.e. firearm offences) by
a Supreme Court judge *sitting without a jury* they are inconsistent with
the Constitution and void: see section 2 of the Constitution. In the   E
reasons for judgment of the Court of Appeal delivered by Rowe J.A.
(Ag.) the grounds on which this submission must be rejected are set out
compendiously. Their Lordships, since they are in full agreement with
the reasoning of the Court of Appeal, feel able to deal with the matter
briefly.

The entrenched constitutional rights of a person charged with a
criminal offence are to be found in section 20 of the Constitution.   F
They entitle him to be tried " by an independent and impartial court
established by law." The section contains no mention of trial by
jury; though this is where one would expect to find such a right if it were
intended to be entrenched. The defendant is accordingly driven to rely
upon section 97 (1) of the Constitution:

> " There shall be a Supreme Court for Jamaica which shall have   G
> such jurisdiction and powers as may be conferred upon it by this
> Constitution or any other law."

His submission is that because at the date of coming into force of the
Constitution grave crimes were tried in circuit courts by a judge of the
Supreme Court sitting with a jury, the reference in this section to a
Supreme Court coupled with the provision in section 13 (1) of the   H
Jamaica (Constitution) Order in Council 1962 that " The Supreme Court
in existence immediately before the commencement of this Order shall
be the Supreme Court for the purposes of the Constitution . . ." by
necessary implication entrenched in the Constitution the then existing
right to be tried by jury in the Supreme Court in all cases of grave
crimes.

Their Lordships see no ground for any such implication. As was

A pointed out by the Judicial Committee in *Hinds* v. *The Queen* [1977]
A.C. 195, 213, the expression " Supreme Court " in the Constitution
is used as a collective description of all those individual judges who,
whether sitting alone or with other judges, or with a jury, are entitled to
exercise the jurisdiction which was exercised by the Supreme Court of
Judicature of Jamaica before the Constitution came into force.   The
B power of Parliament under section 48 (1) of the Constitution to make
laws for the peace, order and good government of Jamaica, embraces a
power to establish new courts, to confer jurisdiction upon them and
to regulate their practice and procedure and those of courts already in
existence at the time the Constitution came into force.   This Parliament
may do by ordinary law unless either (1) it would be inconsistent with
sections 20 or 25 of the Constitution (in which case it must be passed
C in the manner prescribed by section 50); or (2) it would conflict with
what this Board in *Hinds* v. *The Queen* held to be a necessary implication from Chapter VII of the Constitution: that jurisdiction to try
crimes of great gravity (as reflected by the sentences which they attract)
may not be conferred upon a court, by whatever label it is described,
unless the individual judges of the court are judges of the Supreme Court
or have been appointed in the same manner and upon the same terms
D of tenure as those to which judges of the Supreme Court are entitled
under Chapter VII.   A High Court Division of the Gun Court does
consist of a Supreme Court judge.   So there is no conflict with the
Constitution under that head.

That when exercising the criminal jurisdiction conferred upon him
by section 5 (2) of the amended Act, the Supreme Court judge sits
E without a jury is, in their Lordships' view, more aptly described as a
matter of practice and procedure rather than " jurisdiction " or
" powers " as those expressions are used in section 97 of the Constitution.   The only fetters upon Parliament's power to regulate the practice
and procedure to be followed by courts of law in exercising their jurisdiction are those contained in sections 20 and 25 of the Constitution;
and it is rightly conceded that these provisions do not confer any
F entrenched right to trial by jury for criminal offences.

Moreover, even if the mode of trial, in the instant case by a Supreme
Court judge sitting without a jury, were, on a liberal interpretation,
capable of falling within the expressions " jurisdiction " or " powers,"
section 97 would, in their Lordships' view, be of no avail to the defendant;
since, if while sitting under the description of a " High Court Division " of
G the Gun Court a Supreme Court judge is in substance exercising the
jurisdiction of the Supreme Court, as their Lordships consider he is,
section 97 (1) by its reference to " any other law " authorises Parliament
to extend the jurisdiction or powers of the Supreme Court, as it existed
at the commencement of the Constitution, to try grave crimes by a judge
of that court when sitting with a jury, by adding to it jurisdiction or
power to try such crimes when sitting without a jury.
H In their Lordships' view the constitutional point is without substance.
They are in full agreement with the reasons given by the Court of Appeal
for refusing the defendant leave to appeal to that court.   They will
humbly advise Her Majesty that this appeal should be dismissed.

Solicitors: *Philip Conway Thomas & Co.; Charles Russell & Co.*

T. J. M.

A

[QUEEN'S BENCH DIVISION]

* BARKER *v.* WILSON

1980 Feb. 1   Bridge L.J. and Caulfield J.

Evidence—Documentary—" Bankers' books "—Bank's records on   B
microfilm—Whether photographic record " bankers' book "—
Bankers' Books Evidence Act 1879 (42 & 43 *Vict. c.* 11), *s.* 9

A police officer, who was investigating an alleged theft by
the defendant over a period of time of moneys from his
employer, had seen the statements in the possession of the
defendant relating to his account with a bank. Those statements did not include the names of persons to whom cheques   C
had been paid by the defendant and the bank's records giving
the names of the payees were on microfilm. The police officer
applied to the justices for an order to inspect and take copies
of entries in the bankers' books relating to the defendant's
account. The justices decided that microfilm was included in
the definition of " bankers' books " in section 9 of the Bankers'
Books Evidence Act 1879 [1] and made an order, under the
Act, permitting the police officer to inspect and take copies   D
of entries in the bankers' books including books containing
records, whether photographic or otherwise, of the names of
all payees of cheques drawn upon the defendant's account.
On appeal by the defendant:—
Held, dismissing the appeal, that the definition of " bankers'
books " in section 9 of the Act and the phrase " an entry in
a banker's book " in section 4 were wide enough to include any
form of permanent record kept by the bank of transactions   E
relating to the bank's business; that where microfilm was used
by a bank to record the payment of cheques by photographing
the names of the payee and other matters, the microfilm was
itself an entry in a banker's book and, accordingly, the justices
had jurisdiction to order inspection of the bank's records
including photographic records.

No cases are referred to in the judgments or were cited in argument.   F

CASE STATED by North Yorkshire justices sitting at York.
On April 20, 1979, a notice was issued on behalf of the respondent,
Detective Constable Michael Wilson, against the defendant, Alan William
Barker, that the police officer be at liberty to inspect and take copies of
certain entries in the bankers' books at the Parliament Street (York) branch   G
of Barclays Bank Ltd., relating to the account with the bank of the
defendant.
The justices heard the application on April 25, 1979, and found that
the police officer was a detective officer of the North Yorkshire Police
and had the duty of investigating the alleged theft of £38,947·09 from
the York Wholesale Fruit Co. Ltd., over a period of 12 to 13 years,   H
terminating on February 27, 1978. The defendant's solicitors agreed to
the time and date of the appointment for the defendant to be charged for
the convenience of the defendant and the police officer. A notice had
been issued to the defendant and the bank, dated April 20, 1979, informing

[1] Bankers' Books Evidence Act 1879, s. 4: see post p. 886G–H.
S. 9: ". . . 'bankers' books ' include ledgers, day books, cash books, account
books and all other books used in the ordinary business of the bank."

A them of the application. On the evidence of the police officer and the witness for the defendant, the defendant had had money to which, prima facie, he was not entitled; indeed he had paid some money back to the company, but a very large amount was still outstanding. Bank statements had been handed by the defendant to the police officer and they were produced to the justices and the justices saw there was a close and regular relationship between payments into and out of his bank; and that

B was consistent with the police officer's evidence. It was impossible for the police officer to specify the payees of the cheques from the defendant's bank account without seeing that bank account or the cheques. The order would enable the police officer to make more clear the evidence in his possession. The defendant had made admissions to other persons that he was responsible for the deficit. The justices heard the uncontra-

C dicted evidence of one of those persons and indeed the defendant accepted that there was other evidence to support the charge.

It was contended by the defendant that the application was a " fishing " expedition, although it was accepted that there was other evidence in support of the charge preferred; that the period of time to be covered by any order, if one were to be granted, could not go back much beyond the date

D of the alleged offence, i.e. February 27, 1978; that the definition of " bankers' books " in section 9 of the Bankers' Books Evidence Act 1879 did not include modern day microfilm and cheques; and that sections 4 and 5 of the Act, read in conjunction with section 9, did not include cheques.

It was contended by the police officer that in accordance with *Williams v. Summerfield* [1972] 2 Q.B. 512, the proceedings had properly been

E commenced and the application did not constitute a fishing expedition; that there was other evidence to support the charge preferred; that it was accepted practice in the High Court to charge a continuing offence as having been committed on the date when the money had to be accounted for, rather than between specified dates; and that the definition of " bankers' books " in section 9 of the Act of 1879 was capable of covering com-

F mercial book-keeping and office practices that might exist a century later.

The justices were of the opinion that the police officer was a party to the proceedings; that the proceedings had properly been begun; that it was impossible to specify the payees of cheques from the defendant's bank account without an order; that there was other evidence to support the charge preferred and the application was not a " fishing " expedition; that the word " includes " in section 9 of the Act of 1879 was not exhaustive,

G there was no reason to exclude from the definition of " bankers' books," modern day microfilm and cheques, indeed, microfilm and cheques were acceptable in all modern day accountancy and auditing techniques. The justices, therefore, applied some robust common sense to the definition. The application was a matter which they could properly deal with and they firmly declined to refer it to the High Court. Accordingly, they granted

H the application that the police officer be at liberty to inspect and take copies of entries in the bankers' books of Barclays Bank Ltd., relating to the account at the bank of the defendant, between January 1, 1966, and February 28, 1978, such books to include books containing records, whether photographic or otherwise, of the names of all payees of cheques drawn upon the account. They also ordered, in accordance with section 8 of the Act of 1879, that the defendant pay £50 costs.

Barker v. Wilson (D.C.)   **[1980]**

The defendant appealed. The question for the High Court was whether   A
the justices came to a correct determination in law.

J. W. Bullimore for the defendant.
Peter Collier for the respondent police officer.

BRIDGE L.J. I will ask Caulfield J. to give the first judgment.   B

CAULFIELD J. On April 20, 1979, a notice was issued on behalf of the
respondent, who is a police officer, against the defendant, because the
police officer wanted liberty to inspect and take copies of certain entries
in the bankers' books at the Parliament Street (York) branch of Barclays
Bank Ltd., relating to the defendant's account with the bank.

The defendant was charged on April 23, three days later, with certain   C
offences, which he is alleged to have committed, of taking a substantial
amount of money from his employers. It was being alleged, and will be
alleged in the proceedings, that he had taken this money over a period of
years.

The police included in their investigations an examination of bank
statements, which were provided by the defendant himself to the police,   D
showing the records of cheques paid into his account and cheques met.
But, of course, the records which the defendant disclosed to the police
did not identify the names of the payees of those cheques. Indeed only a
very few banks now do include, in their records to customers, the details
of the payees of the cheques. So the police were in a quandary. They
needed to know, in order to link up the evidence, the identity of the
payees of the cheques which had been drawn by the defendant over a   E
period of years. The deficit, which is the subject of the charge, is believed
to have accumulated over a period from about 1966 onwards.

The point was taken before the justices that microfilm and cheques,
if kept by the bank, were not included in the definition of " bankers'
books " which is contained in section 9 of the Bankers' Books Evidence
Act 1879. The justices came to the conclusion, and they put their con-   F
clusion in the terms that they adopted some robust common sense, that
section 9 did include microfilm, which is a modern process of producing
bankers' records. It is probable that no modern bank in this country now
maintains the old-fashioned books which were maintained at the time of
the passing of the Act of 1879, and possibly maintained for many years
after 1879.
                                                                         G
The other relevant section to this appeal is section 4 of the Bankers'
Books Evidence Act 1879. It reads:

" A copy of an entry in a banker's book shall not be received in
evidence under this Act unless it be first proved that the book was at
the time of the making of the entry one of the ordinary books of the
bank, and that the entry was made in the usual and ordinary course
of business, and that the book is in the custody or control of the bank.   H
Such proof may be given by . . . [an] officer of the bank, and may
be given orally or by an affidavit sworn before any commissioner or
person authorised to take affidavits."

That section enables evidence to be admissible in a court by the production of copies of entries, as distinct from the original books which would
be maintained by the bank. That section is obviously necessary, other-

A   wise—certainly in 1879—the business of the bank would probably be held up for days while the books were at court, which would be an absurd situation. One can see the reason for section 4. Section 4 operates today, as it always has done, enabling banks to produce copies of their entries, as long as those copies are certified by an officer of the bank, within the meaning of that term as used in the Bankers' Books Evidence Act 1879.

B   The justices in this case made the order in these terms: that the police officer could inspect such books at the bank, to include books containing records, whether photographic or otherwise, of the names of all payees of cheques drawn upon the account of the defendant. That was the order made. There is no reference in that order to cheques. Of course until very recently cheques were not retained by a bank, but were returned to the customers. It may well be that the cheques in this particular case

C   have been returned to the customer, who is the defendant, but that is beside the point. Cheques are not included in the order which has been made by the justices. For myself, I would not like, without further argument, to include in this judgment any view as to whether cheques come within the meaning of the word " book " as used in section 9, the definition section of the Bankers' Books Evidence Act 1879. But I have no doubt whatso-

D   ever that the definition section does include microfilm, if microfilm is used by a bank to record the payment of cheques by photographing the name of the payee and other matters. As far as I can see (and indeed it is a matter of common sense) the microfilm is itself an entry which is maintained by the bank in respect of a customer's account.

Therefore if in this particular case the books which are held by the bank in respect of the defendant's account are really a microfilm process

E   of the transactions which the customer (that is the defendant) has carried out at his bank, then that microfilm itself is within the definition contained in section 9 of the Bankers' Books Evidence Act 1879, although it would not be called in ordinary language a book. A banker's book in ordinary language would not be called a book. A book is a word which is used in many contexts. But I have no doubt at all that actual microfilming of

F   actual transactions and actual cheques do come within the definition of " bankers' books " in section 9.

Therefore I think that this order which was made by the justices was wholly justified. I would dismiss this appeal.

BRIDGE L.J. I agree. The Bankers' Books Evidence Act 1879 was enacted with the practice of bankers in 1879 in mind. It must be con-

G   strued in 1980 in relation to the practice of bankers as we now understand it. So construing the definition of " bankers' books " and the phrase " an entry in a banker's books," it seems to me that clearly both phrases are apt to include any form of permanent record kept by the bank of transactions relating to the bank's business, made by any of the methods which modern technology makes available, including, in particular, microfilm.

H   I agree that this appeal should be dismissed.

Appeal dismissed with costs.

Solicitors: *Harrowells, York; Ashworth, Tetlow & Co., York.*

B. O. A.

A

* ALLOWAY v. PHILLIPS (INSPECTOR OF TAXES)

1980 March 13, 14, 17   Lord Denning M.R., Waller and Dunn L.JJ.

B

*Revenue—Income tax—Schedule D, Case VI—Agreement made in
United Kingdom—Non-resident wife of criminal selling life
story to newspaper—Whether money received by her capital
or income—Whether profits or gains arising or accruing from
property in United Kingdom—Income and Corporation Taxes
Act 1970 (c. 10), s. 108* [1]

A man was convicted and imprisoned for robbery. He   C
escaped from prison and fled to Canada where, sometime
before April 1967, he was joined by his wife. In January
1968 he was re-arrested and returned to prison in England.
The wife remained in Canada until after the end of the fiscal
year 1967–68. In February 1968 an agreement enforceable
in England and purported to be made between an English
newspaper and the wife and her husband, both said to be
acting through an agent in London, was executed whereby   D
the wife was to supply information about her life and experi-
ences with her husband for publication in return for payment
in England of £39,000. A reporter from the newspaper then
visited the wife at her home in Canada and was given the
information from which a series of articles was prepared and
published in the newspaper. The £39,000 was paid by the
newspaper to a firm of London solicitors and was in 1973
paid over to the wife who had by then returned to live in   E
England. She was assessed to income tax for the year 1967–68
under Case VI of Schedule D in respect of that payment.
Her appeal against that assessment was dismissed by the
special commissioners. Brightman J. upheld their decision on
the ground that the payment of £39,000 was an income receipt
in the hands of the wife and that the rights contained in
the agreement were property situated in the United Kingdom
and the payment of £39,000 was profit arising from that   F
property within the meaning of section 108 of the Income
and Corporation Taxes Act 1970 and accordingly liable to
Schedule D income tax.

On appeal by the wife: —

Held, dismissing the appeal, (1) that the wife, having
ratified the agreement by adopting the acts of her London
agent, acquired property in the United Kingdom in the form
of a chose in action whereby she became entitled to receive   G
£39,000 from the newspaper; and that the payment of that
sum was not derived from services rendered by her in Canada
but was a profit or gain arising from that United Kingdom
property and, accordingly, liable to income tax under Case VI
of Schedule D for the year 1967–68 (post, pp. 891B–D, 892H—
893A, 894D, F, 895F–G, 897F).

Stainer's Executors v. *Purchase* [1952] A.C. 280, H.L.(E.);
Carson v. *Cheyney's Executor* [1959] A.C. 412, H.L.(E.) and   H
Hume v. *Asquith* [1969] 2 Ch. 58, distinguished.

(2) That the findings of fact by the commissioners that the
payment was received as income and not capital was amply
supported by the evidence and should not be disturbed (post,
pp. 895H, 896E).

Decision of Brightman J. [1979] 1 W.L.R. 564 affirmed.

[1] Income and Corporation Taxes Act 1970, s. 108: see post, p. 891F.

A   The following cases are referred to in the judgments:

  Carson v. *Cheyney's Executor* [1959] A.C. 412; [1958] 3 W.L.R. 740;
    [1958] 3 All E.R. 573, H.L.(E.).
  Edwards v. *Bairstow* [1956] A.C. 14; [1955] 3 W.L.R. 410; [1955] 3 All
    E.R. 48; 36 T.C. 207, H.L.(E.).
  English Scottish and Australian Bank Ltd. v. *Inland Revenue Commis-
    sioners* [1932] A.C. 238, H.L.(E.).

B *Firestone Tyre and Rubber Co. Ltd.* v. *Lewellin* [1957] 1 W.L.R. 464;
    [1957] 1 All E.R. 561; 37 T.C. 111, H.L.(E.).
  Housden v. *Marshall* [1959] 1 W.L.R. 1; [1958] 3 All E.R. 639; 38 T.C.
    233.
  Hume v. *Asquith* [1969] 2 Ch. 58; [1969] 2 W.L.R. 225; [1969] 1 All E.R.
    868; 45 T.C. 251.
  Marsh v. *Joseph* [1897] 1 Ch. 213; C.A.
C *New York Life Insurance Co.* v. *Public Trustee* [1924] 2 Ch. 101, C.A.
  Stainer's Executors v. *Purchase* (1950) 32 T.C. 367, C.A.; [1952] A.C.
    280; [1951] 2 All E.R. 1071, H.L.(E.).

    The following additional cases were cited in argument:

  Craven-Ellis v. *Canons Ltd.* [1936] 2 K.B. 403; [1936] 2 All E.R. 1066,
    C.A.
D *Fitzgerald* v. *Inland Revenue Commissioners* [1919] 2 K.B. 154; 7 T.C.
    284.
  Haig's (Earl) Trustees v. *Inland Revenue Commissioners,* 1939 S.C. 676;
    22 T.C. 725.
  Inland Revenue Commissioners v. *Gardner, Mountain and D'Ambumenil
    Ltd.* [1947] 1 All E.R. 650; 29 T.C. 69, H.L.(E.).
  Luxor (Eastbourne) Ltd. v. *Cooper* [1941] A.C. 108; [1941] 1 All E.R. 33,
    H.L.(E.).
E *Phipps* v. *Boardman* [1965] Ch. 992; [1965] 2 W.L.R. 839; [1965] 1 All
    E.R. 849, C.A.

    APPEAL from Brightman J.
    The taxpayer, Patricia Alloway, was the wife of Charles Wilson, who
was convicted and imprisoned for taking part in a robbery from a train.
F He escaped and went to Canada where he was joined by the taxpayer.
Following his arrest in 1968, the taxpayer, who remained living in Canada,
agreed with the News of the World Ltd. to provide information for a
series of articles in return for payment of £39,000. She was assessed to
income tax for the year 1967–68 under Case VI of Schedule D in the
sum of £39,100. Her appeal against that assessment was dismissed by
the special commissioners who held that the payment was, within the
G meaning of section 108 of the Income and Corporation Taxes Act 1970,
annual profits or gains arising to the taxpayer, a non-resident, from
property in the United Kingdom. They upheld the assessment in principle
but reduced the amount to £39,000. An appeal from that decision was
dismissed by Brightman J.
    The taxpayer appealed on the grounds that the commissioners and
H Brightman J. had misdirected themselves in law in holding that the
relevant receipts were on revenue account and/or in failing to hold that
the receipts were on capital account. Alternatively, it was said that the
commissioners and Brightman J. misdirected themselves in law in holding
that the receipts accrued to the taxpayer and/or arose from property in
the United Kingdom in the context of Case VI of Schedule D and/or
in failing to hold that the receipts accrued to and/or arose for the taxpayer from services, as opposed to property, such services being performed

outside the jurisdiction and/or that the contractual arrangements, if any, A
to which the taxpayer was party had no independent vitality susceptible
of generating taxable receipts and/or that such contractual obligations,
if any, regulated the service which in turn generated the alleged revenue.

The facts are set out in the judgment of Lord Denning M.R.

Marcus Jones for the taxpayer.   B
Brian Davenport for the Crown.

LORD DENNING M.R.   On August 8, 1963, there was the Great Train
Robbery.   Over 2½ million pounds were stolen.   The robbers were caught.
They were tried in 1964 at the Aylesbury Assizes.   One of the gang
was Charles Frank Wilson.   He was convicted and sentenced to 30 years'
imprisonment.   But he escaped from prison and went to Canada.   His   C
wife joined him there.   They hid there living under the names of Mr. and
Mrs. Alloway.   In January 1968 the police discovered them.   Charles
Wilson was arrested, brought back to England, and put back in prison
again.   (We are told that he has since been released on parole.)

Now his wife remained for a few months in Canada. She was very
nervous and taking sleeping pills. But in February 1968, soon after her   D
husband had been taken back to England, someone telephoned her from
England—and told her that a reporter from the *News of the World* was
coming to see her—that she should speak to him—and that she would be
paid for doing so. A little later the reporter arrived. He brought a typewriter with him. He stayed in her house for about a week. He talked
with her and her friends. He saw the papers and photographs that she
had with her. He wrote up a story in journalese about Charles Wilson's   E
part in the robbery, of his life " on the run," and so forth. The first
instalment appeared in the *News of the World* on Sunday, February 25,
1968, and the remaining instalments on the five following Sundays finishing on Sunday, March 31, 1968.

The newspaper paid well for her help. They paid solicitors named
Sampson & Co. in the City of London two cheques. One for £19,000   F
and the other for £20,000. The solicitors cashed the cheques and put them,
I expect, into their client's account. Charles Wilson made a claim to the
money, but they did not pay it to him. His wife came back to England
some time in 1968 after April 5—when the tax year ended. She tried to get
the money, but found it very difficult. She asked a friend of her husband
to deal with it. Eventually after four or five years in 1973 she was paid a
lump sum of £28,000 and, in addition, a house at East Horsley in Surrey   G
was purchased in her name.

Now the *News of the World* had, I expect, in their tax returns
included the payment of £39,000 as part of their expenditure for the
year 1967–68. I also expect that the revenue authorities discovered in 1973
that the wife had received payment of that sum or its equivalent. At
any rate, in 1974 the revenue authorities assessed her for income tax on   H
£39,000: just within the six years after it had been paid by the *News of
the World* to her solicitors. Then there came to light a written agreement.
It was dated February 10, 1968, and purported to have been made between
the *News of the World* and Charles Wilson and his wife. Her address
was given as Rigaud, Quebec, Canada. His was given as " care of
11, St. Bride Street " in the City of London. That was the address of
Sampson & Co. the solicitors. They were presumably, at that time, his

A solicitors as well as hers. But they were not described as agents. A man
called Emanuel Fryde, a South African attorney, was described as the
agent of the husband and wife. Under this agreement the wife agreed to
co-operate in the writing of articles for the newspaper: and the newspaper
agreed to pay her £19,000 on delivery of typescript with her approval
endorsed thereon: and on publication of the first instalment another
£20,000. It also provided that the agreement was to be construed in
B accordance with English law, and the High Court of Justice in England
should be the court having jurisdiction over the matter.

The first question is whether that agreement was binding or not. The
special commissioners found that the wife did not expressly authorise
it: but they found that she ratified it—by all that she did in implementing
it—namely by receiving the telephone call from London; and acting on it
C by receiving the newspaper reporter into her home; and seeking payment
of the sums provided for in the contract. I wondered at first whether
she had sufficient knowledge of the contents of the document to warrant
a finding of ratification: but I think the circumstances were such as
to warrant the clear inference that she was adopting the supposed agent's
acts whatever they were: see Marsh v. Joseph [1897] 1 Ch. 213, 247
per Lord Russell of Killowen C.J. And on ratification the agreement
D became just as binding on the parties as if she had previously authorised it.

Next arises the question: was she liable to pay tax on it for the year
1967–68 when it was paid over to Sampson & Co.? Or for the year 1973–74
when they paid it over to her? The answer is, I think, that, if she is liable
at all, it is for the year 1967–68. It is a general principle that receipts are
to be taken as accruing in the period in which the money is earned,
E even though it is not paid or received till a later period. These sums were
certainly earned in the year 1967–68.

Now here is the point in the case: at that time, in February or March
1968, the wife was not resident in the United Kingdom. She was
resident in Canada. In order that she should be made liable for tax on
the £39,000, it must be brought within the Schedule D charge in section
F 108, paragraph 1 (a) (iii) of the Income and Corporation Taxes Act 1970,
as being:

"the annual profits or gains arising or accruing— . . . to any person,
whether a British subject or not, although not resident in the United
Kingdom, from any property whatever in the United Kingdom . . ."

and under Case VI as being "tax in respect of any annual profits or
G gains not falling under any other Case of Schedule D . . ." The crucial
question is whether this £39,000 was an annual profit or gain accruing
to her on any property whatever in the United Kingdom.

Mr. Marcus Jones submitted two interesting propositions to us. First,
he submitted that the wife here had no property in the United Kingdom.
She derived her profits from the services that she had rendered in Canada.
Second, he submitted that her rights under the contract were not property
H in the United Kingdom. The contract was only machinery for collecting
the reward for her services. It had no independent vitality.

For his first proposition Mr. Marcus Jones referred us to Housden v.
Marshall [1959] 1 W.L.R. 1. That was a case where a jockey sold his
reminiscences to a reporter of the Sunday Chronicle and was paid £750
for an article. Harman J. held that he had to pay tax on it as an "annual
profit or gain." I will read—because it is interesting and typical of

Harman J.—what he had to say about services of this kind. He said, at   **A**
pp. 5–6.

" This kind of case arises either as a result of something emanating
from the famous, as, for instance, Lord Haig, the soldier, and Steve
Donoghue, the jockey; or from the infamous, William Cooper Hobbs
(blackmail, forgery and arson). Either category can produce money,
particularly, I think, from the Sunday newspapers, because the public   **B**
likes to read at its ease before the fireside sensational reminiscences of
either of these two categories of persons. They are not usually, in fact,
strictly speaking, reminiscences of these persons at all; they are
written by what are called ' ghost ' writers. The celebrated or notorious
character communicates this or that to the ' ghost ' and may, as here,
allow his signature to be used to give an air of reality to an other-   **C**
wise bald and unconvincing narrative.
     " The question here is agreed to be capable of a simple statement :
was the transaction on the one side the sale by the taxpayer of some
property of his, or was he really agreeing to perform services for the
newspaper for a reward? "

As a result, Harman J. said, he was paid a sum of money for services   **D**
rendered : that is a taxable subject matter : and the jockey was held
liable to pay tax on the sum. That was the case which Mr. Marcus Jones
submitted for his first proposition that the wife had derived her profits
from the services that she had rendered.
     For his second proposition Mr. Marcus Jones submitted that rights
under the contract were not property. The contract did not matter because
it was mere machinery : it had no independant vitality. For that proposition   **E**
he referred us to a case concerning Mr. Leslie Howard, the actor : see
Stainer's Executors v. *Purchase* [1952] A.C. 280. Mr. Leslie Howard was
a film actor, acting for money. He was paid lump sums, and a share of
the profits, under a contract. Lord Asquith of Bishopstone said, at p. 291 :

" The contracts in the present case enjoy, in my view, no such
independent vitality. The consideration for what Mr. Howard was   **F**
to do—to act or manage—was not the grant of a contract or contracts but the payment of money under the terms of those contracts.
Mr. Howard acted for money; he did not act for contracts. The contracts were mere incidental machinery regulating the measure of
the services to be rendered by him on the one hand and, on the
other, that of the payments to be made by his employers; they were   **G**
not the source, but the instrument of payment . . ."

Those two propositions seem to carry Mr. Marcus Jones quite a
long way. He cited other cases on his second proposition: See *Carson*
v. *Cheyney's Executor* [1959] A.C. 412, 424; and the decision of
Pennycuick J. in *Hume* v. *Asquith* [1969] 2 Ch. 58.
     It seems to me that those cases are entirely distinguishable from the   **H**
present case. They were cases where people were resident in the United
Kingdom—rendering services here in return for payment here. The
question was whether the royalties were classified under Cases II or III
of Schedule D. It seems to me that they have no application at all to the
present case where the wife was resident in Canada—rendering services
there in return for payment here. This case comes under Case VI of
Schedule D. It seems to me clear that the wife had property in the United

A Kingdom. She had a chose in action here. She had a right to receive from the *News of the World* the sum of £39,000. That was situate in England. *Dicey & Morris, The Conflict of Laws,* 9th ed. (1973), rule 78, p. 506 says: " Choses in action generally are situate in the country where they are properly recoverable or can be enforced." It seems to me that she had her chose of action in this country worth an actual gain of £39,000. I would have thought the same would apply if there were an implied B contract by which, in return for services in Canada, she was to be paid a quantum meruit payable in England. The truth is that she had a chose in action in England. It was property in England: but she had no property at all in Canada. She had no copyright there. She only had the information in her head which she told to the newspaper reporter. That is not a species of property known to the law of England—nor, I expect, to the C law of Canada. If the revenue law of Canada is the same as that of England, she would not be liable to pay tax there on the sum of £39,000. She was not carrying on any profession or vocation there. She would only be liable if she had property there—and she had none.

In conclusion I may say that many people regret the practice of such newspapers in paying money to criminals or their wives—so as to get a sensational story to publish. There is nothing illegal in it, so far as I know. D But on one point I am clear: if the criminals or their wives get money by relating their stories to newspapers, they ought to pay tax on their profits and gains. That is this very case. The wife is now in England. She is outside the jurisdiction of the Canadian courts. She received the money here and ought to pay tax here on the sums she received here.

I think that the commissioners and the judge were quite right, and I E would dismiss the appeal.

WALLER L.J. I agree. The question which arises in this case is whether or not this sum of £39,000 is taxable in the United Kingdom. Mr. Marcus Jones has submitted that it is not because he said the source of the profit arose wholly in Canada during the visit of the *News of the* F *World* representative with his typewriter in early 1968. He submitted that it is wrong to hold that the contract was property in the United Kingdom. There was also an argument before us as to the nature of the contract and whether it could be said to have been ratified. Finally Mr. Marcus Jones said that if he was wrong on all these points he would submit that the £39,000 was capital and not income and therefore was G not taxable.

So the first question is, was this contract properly ratified? The commissioners found that it was. They were in doubt as to whether further evidence should have been called from the taxpayer's husband, and they decided to deal with the case without him. They said that they accepted the taxpayer's evidence subject to qualifications. The qualifications were:

H " In our view Mrs. Alloway was made acquainted at some stage between the re-arrest of her husband and the arrival of the newspaper's reporter (either by letters from her husband or a telephone call from one of his associates) that arrangements were being made on her behalf for the sale of her story and of their general tenor— although she may not have known in detail the terms of the purported agreement or of Mr. Fryde's participation in it."

Then later in the same passage the commissioners say: A

"We find therefore that Mr. Fryde did not enter into the purported agreement with Mrs. Alloway's prior authority expressly given. Whether Mr. Fryde had her implied authority is a more difficult question which we are unable to determine on the facts before us, since we have heard insufficient evidence of the circumstances which led up to the conclusion of the purported agreement. However that B may be, we have no doubt that Mrs. Alloway adopted the arrangements to which Mr. Fryde had put his signature when she acquiesced is these arrangements following the telephone call from London and performed her part of the agreement by receiving the newspaper's representative into her home and providing the services described in the contract. The agency was therefore validated by ratification and Mrs. Alloway was in our view entitled to seek, as she subsequently C did, payment of the sums provided for in the contract in England."

There was also a term in the contract which said that the sum of £19,000 was to be paid on the delivery to the company of the final typescript with the approval in writing of the contributor, the agent and the company endorsed thereon. So she had had to sign her approval on the typescript, no doubt before the representative left Canada. In my opinion there was D ample evidence to support the finding of the commissioners that she adopted that contract.

The next question was whether or not the contract was made in the United Kingdom. Lord Denning M.R. has already quoted the passage from *Dicey & Morris*: "Choses in action generally are situate in the country where they are properly recoverable or can be enforced," a proposition E that was approved by this court in *New York Life Insurance Co.* v. *Public Trustee* [1924] 2 Ch. 101, 109. There can be no question but that the debtor was in the United Kingdom. The contract provided that payment be made to Sampson & Co.'s office in London. The rights under the contract are therefore property situate in the United Kingdom.

Mr. Marcus Jones submitted that under the authority of the three cases, two of which Lord Denning M.R. has already mentioned—*Stainer's* F *Executors* v. *Purchase* [1952] A.C. 280, *Carson* v. *Cheyney's Executor* [1959] A.C. 412 and *Hume* v. *Asquith* [1969] 2 Ch. 58—that the rights made under such a contract did not represent property for taxation purposes; but consideration of those cases does not support his argument. In the last of those cases, *Hume* v. *Asquith*, Pennycuick J. was considering a similar problem. He said, at p. 78, on a matter which had given him G some perplexity:

"That is the position which arises where a professional man, having entered into a royalty contract, and while still carrying on his profession, proceeds to assign the benefit of that royalty contract. In such a case it seems clear, at first sight, to say no more, that the royalties could not be treated as part of the professional income of the person who has made the disposition, because they are no longer his income. On H the other hand, it appears that, representing as they do uncollected income owing to the person carrying on the profession, they could equally not be taxed in the hands of the assignee."

Then later on the same page Pennycuick J. quoted from the judgment of Jenkins L.J. in *Stainer's* case (1950) 32 T.C. 367, where he said, at p. 401:

A
"It is I think reasonably plain that periodical payments in respect of a contractual right to a share in the receipts or profits of the distribution of a film acquired otherwise than in the course of a trade, profession or vocation falling within Cases I or II of Schedule D would be taxable under Case III, Rule 1 (*a*), as falling within the words 'Any . . . annual payment . . .'."

B Pennycuick J. went on to say [1969] 2 Ch. 58, 78:

"Counsel for the Crown was at first disposed to say that in that paragraph Jenkins L.J. was deciding the present case, but I think that when one looks at that paragraph one sees that what the judge is addressing himself to is a contractual right which is acquired upon its creation otherwise than in the course of a profession; i.e., at the date
C of the contract the contracting party is not carrying on a profession."

So the distinction which Pennycuick J. was making was that between where there is income from a profession or a trade and where there is no profession or trade. It is the difference between assessments made under Case I or Case II and, in this case, Case VI. These cases make it clear that as the law stood at that time a man in a profession was assessed
D under Case I and the mode of assessment did not change at his death. Accordingly at that time earnings after his death were not taxable and it was not possible to argue that the case should change. They were still professional earnings even though paid after death.

This case is not concerned with professional earnings or with trading profits because the taxpayer was not carrying on a trade or profession.
E Section 108, paragraph 1 of the Income and Corporation Taxes Act 1970 says:

"Tax under this Schedule [Schedule D] shall be charged in respect of—(*a*) the annual profits or gains arising or accruing—. . . (iii) to any person, whether a British subject or not, although not resident in the United Kingdom, from any property whatever in the United
F Kingdom . . ."

The property in that case is not associated with a trade or profession.

This contract gave to the taxpayer a number of rights on which she could have sued in the United Kingdom if necessary. She had no property in Canada capable of producing profits. The information about her husband was not property. It required this contract to convert it into
G property. This sum of £39,000 was in my opinion a profit or gain arising from property in the United Kingdom. It is entirely within section 108, paragraph 1 (*a*) (iii). It does not fall within any other class of Schedule D, and therefore is correctly charged under Case VI.

Finally there was Mr. Marcus Jones' submission that this was capital and not income. The commissioners found that this was income
H and not capital. I do not accept the argument of Mr. Marcus Jones that once the sum was paid the rights under the contract ceased to exist. The commissioners made a finding of fact that this was income, and there was ample evidence on which they could so find; and, in my view, it is impossible to interfere with their finding.

I agree with the judgment of Brightman J., and I would dismiss this appeal.

DUNN L.J. I also agree. The special commissioners made two important findings of fact: first, the taxpayer ratified the agreement purported to have been made on her behalf on February 10, 1968; and, secondly, that the sums payable under that agreement constituted income and not capital. The circumstances in which the court will interfere with findings of fact made by commissioners was stated by Lord Radcliffe in *Edwards* v. *Bairstow* [1956] A.C. 14, 36 in the following terms:

" If the case contains anything ex facie which is bad law and which bears upon the determination, it is, obviously, erroneous in point of law. But, without any such misconception appearing ex facie, it may be that the facts found are such that no person acting judicially and properly instructed as to the relevant law could have come to the determination under appeal. In those circumstances, too, the court must intervene. It has no option but to assume that there has been some misconception of the law and that this has been responsible for the determination. So there, too, there has been error in point of law. I do not think that it much matters whether this state of affairs is described as one in which there is no evidence to support the determination or as one in which the evidence is inconsistent with and contradictory of the determination, or as one in which the true and only reasonable conclusion contradicts the determination. Rightly understood, each phrase propounds the same test. For my part, I prefer the last of the three, since I think that it is rather misleading to speak of there being no evidence to support a conclusion when in cases such as these many of the facts are likely to be neutral in themselves, and only to take their colour from the combination of circumstances in which they are found to occur."

Applying that test, I agree with the judge that there was no ground for interfering with the findings of fact of the commissioners.

But it was said that even accepting that the agreement was ratified by the taxpayer and that the moneys payable thereunder were income, yet no tax was chargeable because the source of income was not the agreement but the services provided by the taxpayer in making her knowledge and information available to the *News of the World*, and those services were provided outside the jurisdiction at a time when she resided in Canada. It was said that the agreement was no more than incidental machinery regulating the method of paying the income and had no independent vitality of its own.

Reliance for this proposition was placed on three House of Lords cases, *Firestone Tyre and Rubber Co. Ltd.* v. *Lewellin* [1957] 1 W.L.R. 464, *Stainer's Executors* v. *Purchase* [1952] A.C. 280 and *Carson* v. *Cheyney's Executor* [1959] A.C. 412. Special reliance was placed on the speech of Lord Asquith of Bishopstone in *Stainer's Executors* v. *Purchase* at p. 291, the passage cited by Lord Denning M.R. In those cases, however, tax was charged under Cases I and II of Schedule D set out in section 109 (2) of the Income and Corporation Taxes Act 1970, being tax in respect of any trade, profession or vocation carried on in the United Kingdom. The limitation of the cases was explained by Pennycuick J. in the passage cited by Waller L.J. in *Hume* v. *Asquith* [1969] 2 Ch. 58, 78. In my judgment, the principle contended for on behalf of the taxpayer applies only to cases where tax is charged under Cases I and II in respect of profits of any trade, business or profession. In the instant case tax was

A charged under Case VI, which has been described as a sweeping up case. The particular provision relied on by the Crown is section 108, paragraph 1 (*a*) (iii), and I will read the material words:

> " . . . the annual profits or gains arising or accruing— . . . (iii) to any person, whether a British subject or not, although not resident in the United Kingdom . . ."

B   Mr. Davenport in his able argument on behalf of the Crown pointed out that the bundle of rights, as he called it, and in particular the right to receive payment arising from the agreement, constituted a chose in action. Section 205 of the Law of Property Act 1925 includes choses in action in the definition of property. Now a chose in action has a location as much as any other species of property. *Dicey & Morris, The Conflict* C *of Laws* (9th ed.), state the rule in this way at p. 506: " Choses in action generally are situate in the country where they are properly recoverable or can be enforced," see *English Scottish and Australian Bank Ltd.* v. *Inland Revenue Commissioners* [1932] A.C. 238. Lord Buckmaster stated the proposition in this way, at p. 246:

> " If, however, once it be assumed that a debt must have a local situa-
> D tion, as I think it must, it can only be where the debtor or the creditor resides, and the fact that it has for other and similar purposes been assumed to be determined by the residence of the debtor and not the creditor is a sufficient reason for holding that that is its situation for the purpose of the statute."

And Lord Warrington of Clyffe said, at p. 248:

E
> " So far back as the reign of Elizabeth in *Byron* v. *Byron* (1596) 1 Cro.Eliz. 472 Anderson J. is reported as saying: ' The debt ' (namely, that in question in that case) ' is where the bond is, being upon a speciality; but debt upon a contract follows the person of the debtor; and this difference hath been oftentimes agreed '."

In the instant case the debtor was the *News of the World*, and the *News* F *of the World* is resident in England. Moreover the agreement expressly provided that it was to be construed in accordance with English law and the High Court in England should be the court of jurisdiction. In these circumstances, the taxpayer's right to recover the payment under the agreement constituted property in the United Kingdom, and she was properly charged to tax upon those payments.

    For those reasons, and for the reasons given by Lord Denning M.R. G and Waller L.J., I too would dismiss the appeal.

Appeal dismissed with costs.

Solicitors: *David Lewis & Co.; Solicitor of Inland Revenue.*

H   [Reported by Mrs. HARRIET DUTTON, Barrister-at-Law]

A

[HOUSE OF LORDS]

* NOTTINGHAM JUSTICES . . . . . . RESPONDENTS

AND

DAVIES . . . . PETITIONER

B

1980 July 3   Lord Diplock, Viscount Dilhorne
                     and Lord Russell of Killowen

PETITION by the applicant for leave to appeal to the House of Lords
from the decision of the Divisional Court of the Queen's Bench Division
in *Reg.* v. *Nottingham Justices, Ex parte Davies* [1980] 3 W.L.R. 15.
The Appeal Committee dismissed the petition.

C

J. A. G.

_____

[HOUSE OF LORDS]

D

* HUNTER . . . . PETITIONER

AND

CHIEF CONSTABLE OF THE WEST
        MIDLANDS AND OTHERS . . . . . RESPONDENTS

E

1980 July 3   Lord Diplock, Viscount Dilhorne
                     and Lord Russell of Killowen

PETITION by the plaintiff for leave to appeal from the decision of
the Court of Appeal in *McIlkenny* v. *Chief Constable of the West
Midlands* [1980] 2 W.L.R. 689.
The Appeal Committee allowed the petition.

F

J. A. G.

_____

[COURT OF APPEAL]

G

* ELSDEN AND ANOTHER *v.* PICK

[1977 E. No. 2286]

1980 March 3, 4, 5, 6, 7; 28   Buckley, Shaw and
                                      Brightman L.JJ.

H

*Agricultural Holding—Notice to quit—Validity—Tenant's notice to
    determine tenancy—Length of notice less than 12 months—
    Landlord agreeing to treat notice as valid—Whether notice
    effective to terminate tenancy—Agricultural Holdings Act 1948
    (11 & 12 Geo. 6, c. 63), s. 23 (1)*

The defendant was the tenant of a farm under an agreement which was determinable on one year's notice in writing
expiring on April 6 in any year. On April 4, 1977, the tenant

A   discussed with the landlords' agent the possibility of his having
to give up the farm, and on April 7 he delivered to the agent
a notice of his intention to quit the farm in April 1978
together with a letter requesting the agent to accept the notice.
The agent agreed to treat the notice as valid notwithstanding
that the length of the notice was short. When, later, the
tenant contended that the notice was ineffective to determine
his tenancy, the landlords brought an action for a declaration
B   that they were entitled to possession of the farm in April 1978.
The judge held that the tenant's notice was invalid as it contravened section 23 (1) of the Agricultural Holdings Act 1948,[1]
and he dismissed the landlords' action.

    On appeal by the landlords: —

    Held, allowing the appeal, that, when a notice to quit had
been given for a period shorter than 12 months, the landlord
and tenant were not precluded by section 23 (1) of the Agricul-
C   tural Holdings Act 1948 from agreeing that it should nevertheless take effect as a valid notice determining the tenancy
(post, pp. 906D–E, 908A–B, H); and that, as on the evidence
the parties had so agreed, the tenant's notice was effective to
determine the tenancy.

    Per Shaw L.J. I do not read *Steadman* v. *Steadman* [1976]
A.C. 536 as enlarging the fundamental concept of acts of part
performance. Such acts must still be in furtherance of the
D   contract and not merely a recognition of its existence or its
contemplation (post, p. 905B–C).

    Decision of Robert Wright Q.C. sitting as a deputy High
Court judge in the Queen's Bench Division reversed.

    The following cases are referred to in the judgments:

Johnstone v. *Hudlestone* (1825) 4 B. & C. 922.

E   *Steadman* v. *Steadman* [1976] A.C. 536; [1974] 3 W.L.R. 56; [1974] 2 All
    E.R. 977, H.L.(E.).

    The following additional cases were cited in argument:

Alan (W. J.) & Co. Ltd. v. *El Nasr Export and Import Co.* [1972] 2
    Q.B. 189; [1972] 2 W.L.R. 800; [1972] 2 All E.R. 127, C.A.

F   *Beesly* v. *Hallwood Estates Ltd.* [1960] 1 W.L.R. 549; [1960] 2 All E.R.
    314.

Bremer Handelsgesellschaft m.b.H. v. *Vanden Avenne-Izegem P.V.B.A.*
    [1977] 1 Lloyd's Rep. 133; [1978] 2 Lloyd's Rep. 109, H.L.(E.).

Clerk v. *Wright* (1737) 1 Atk. 12.

Crabb v. *Arun District Council* [1976] Ch. 179; [1975] 3 W.L.R. 847;
    [1975] 3 All E.R. 865, C.A.

G   *Doe d. Murrell* v. *Milward* (1838) 3 M. & W. 328.

Flather v. *Hood* (1928) 44 T.L.R. 698.

Hankly v. *Clavering* [1942] 2 K.B. 326; [1942] 2 All E.R. 311, C.A.

Hughes v. *Metropolitan Railway Co.* (1877) 2 App.Cas. 439, H.L.(E.).

Johnson v. *Moreton* [1980] A.C. 37; [1978] 3 W.L.R. 538; [1978] 3 All
    E.R. 37, H.L.(E.).

H   *Kammins Ballrooms Co. Ltd.* v. *Zenith Investments (Torquay) Ltd.*
    [1971] A.C. 850; [1970] 3 W.L.R. 287; [1970] 2 All E.R. 871,
    H.L.(E.).

Levey & Co. v. *Goldberg* [1922] 1 K.B. 688.

    [1] Agricultural Holdings Act 1948, s. 23: " (1) A notice to quit an agricultural
holding or part of an agricultural holding shall (notwithstanding any provision to
the contrary in the contract of tenancy of the holding) be invalid if it purports to
terminate the tenancy before the expiration of 12 months from the end of the
then current year of tenancy: . . ."

Ogle v. *Earl Vane* (1868) L.R. 3 Q.B. 272.
O'Reilly v. *Thompson* (1791) 2 Cox Eq.Cas. 271.
Phillips v. *Edwards* (1864) 33 Beav. 440.

A

APPEAL from Robert Wright Q.C. sitting as a deputy High Court judge in the Queen's Bench Division.

By writ dated December 1, 1977, the plaintiff landlords, Richard William Hilary Elsden and Charles Michael Watson-Smith, sought a declaration that they would be entitled to possession of Woodside Farm, Newton, Lincs, on April 6, 1978, in reliance on an agreement between the landlords and the defendant tenant, John Shelbourn Pick, that the tenancy of the farm would expire on April 5, 1978. On February 26, 1979, the judge dismissed the action.

B

By notice of appeal dated June 28, 1979, the landlords appealed on the grounds that (1) the offer made by the landlords through their agent on April 4, 1977, to allow the tenant to terminate his tenancy by giving on or before April 9, 1977, a notice in writing terminating it as at April 5, 1978, and the tenant's acceptance of that offer by giving such notice on April 7, 1977, effected a valid termination of the tenancy as at April 5, 1978; (2) (i) that offer and acceptance constituted an agreement to surrender the tenancy on April 5, 1978, (ii) the judge was wrong in law in holding (or, alternatively, held contrary to the evidence) that the notice given by the tenant was (or was intended by the parties to be) a notice terminating the tenancy pursuant to the provisions of the tenant's contract of tenancy, (iii) the judge was wrong in law in holding that the notice given by the tenant in acceptance of the landlords' offer was a notice to quit for the purpose of section 23 (1) of the Agricultural Holdings Act 1948; (3) alternatively, if the agreement between the parties was that they would treat the notice as valid and effective the judge was wrong in law in holding that such agreement was invalid by reason of section 23 (1); and (4) (i) in the further alternative, the landlords' acceptance of the tenant's notice terminating his tenancy was a waiver of their right to 12 months' notice ending on April 5, 1978, under section 23 (1) and under the contract of tenancy of the farm, (ii) the judge was wrong in holding (or alternatively held contrary to the evidence) that the landlords' acceptance did not constitute such a waiver, (iii) the judge was wrong in law holding that the landlords were prohibited by section 23 (1) from waiving their right.

C

D

E

F

By a respondent's notice dated July 20, 1979, the tenant gave notice of his desire to contend that the judgment should be affirmed on the additional ground that if (contrary to the contentions of the tenant and the findings of the judge) the tenant and the landlords agreed respectively to effect and to accept a surrender of the tenant's tenancy, such agreement was nevertheless unenforceable for want of consideration moving from the landlords and for want of any sufficient memorandum or act of part performance within the meaning and for the purposes of section 40 of the Law of Property Act 1925.

G

H

The facts are stated in the judgment of Shaw L.J.

Maurice Price Q.C. and *Henry Harrod* for the appellant landlords.
Jonathan Parker Q.C. for the respondent tenant.

Cur. adv. vult.

A   March 28. The following judgments were read.

SHAW L.J. delivering the first judgment. This is an appeal by the
plaintiff landlords from a judgment of Mr. Robert Wright Q.C., sitting
as a deputy High Court judge, given on February 26, 1979, whereby he
refused their claim for a declaration that they were entitled to possession
of Woodside Farm, Newton, Lincolnshire, as on April 6, 1978.
B
     The plaintiffs were at all material times the trustees of a settlement
which included the Welby Estate. The principal beneficiary under the
settlement is Sir Bruno Welby. He was concerned with the management
of the estate, of which a Mr. Cawthra was the land agent.
     Included in the estate were a number of farms some of which were
let to tenant farmers. Two, which were known respectively as Woodside
C Farm and Welby Warren Farm, were so let to the defendant tenant,
Mr. Pick, who by 1977 had occupied them for many years. For reasons
which are not relevant to the present appeal, the Welby Estate had at
some time towards the end of the 1960's adopted the policy of not
reletting farms on the estate when they fell vacant. Sir Bruno had formed
a family company called D. & S. Farms Ltd.; it took over the tenancies
D of such farms and farmed them in partnership with a Mr. Giles Halfhead
under the partnership title Sapperton Farming Co.
     At the beginning of 1977 the tenant, who had until then farmed Welby
Warren Farm and Woodside Farm with reasonable success, found himself
surrounded by misfortune both matrimonial and financial. His wife was
in process of divorcing him. He was confronted by burdensome obligations and liabilities. He was in a state of great mental stress and consulted
E his solicitor about his various troubles. On April 1, 1977, the solicitor
wrote advising him that from what he had been told there was a real
possibility that the tenant might have to cease business. The tenant
himself foresaw that he might find himself so destitute of resources that
he would not be able to pay the rent of his farm, or at any rate the rents
of both of them. In that situation he did what an honourable man would
F do. On April 4, which was a Monday, he went to see Mr. Cawthra,
who acted as agent for the landlord trustees and told him what his
position was. Their respective versions of what took place as recounted
in their evidence before the judge did not altogether tally. The judge's
assessment of them as witnesses was that each was honestly seeking to
recall what was arranged between them at that meeting but that the
agent's recollection was the more reliable. This assessment is not
G challenged. According to the agent he was shown the letter from the
tenant's solicitor. A half year's rent in respect of each of the two farms
held by the tenant was to fall due on April 14. He was concerned as to
whether he should give notice to terminate one or both tenancies. The
requisite notice was one year's notice in writing, expiring on April 6
in any year. If, therefore, the tenant wished to bring either tenancy to
an end by notice he would have to give that notice before April 6, 1977,
H so as to expire on April 6, 1978.
     The agent was not then anxious to recover possession of the farms
held by the tenant, who had been over many years a good tenant as well
as a good farmer. He suggested that the tenant might bide his time at
least for a few days before coming to a final decision as to relinquishing
either or both of his tenancies. In pursuance of this suggestion he
proposed that the tenant should make out notices in respect of each farm,

dated April 4, 1977, to expire on April 5, 1978. This latter date was A
erroneous as it should have been April 6, but this slip appears to have
passed unnoticed even at the trial and has not been the foundation of
any of the many submissions addressed to this court. The agent's
suggestion was that if by the end of the week (that is by Saturday, April
9, 1977) the tenant had resolved to give notice to determine one or both
of his tenancies he might then give the notice antedated as proposed and
it would be accepted. The agent, when cross-examined at the trial, said B
he was not absolutely certain whether or not late service would invalidate
the notice. He said, " I thought if we agreed delayed service it would
be valid." According to the judge's findings, the tenant accepted the
agent's proposals and went away to consider them in relation to his own
financial circumstances and prospects.

It seems also that the agent promised that if later on the tenant's C
position improved and he wished after all to continue as before, then he
would recommend to the landlords that the tenant be allowed to retract
his notice.

On Thursday, April 7, the tenant returned to the agent's office. He
took with him two letters. Each bore the date stamp " April 4, 1977."
The first letter read:
D
> " Dear Mr. Cawthra, Following our conversation this morning, after
> giving more thought to it, and talking to father about it, I enclose
> a form of words which I hope you will accept as notice on the
> Newton Farm [Woodside Farm]. The Welby Farm, I think, I
> should not give up unless I have to. I need a little more time to
> work out the implications on that one. Many thanks for your
> sympathy and understanding. Yours sincerely, John Pick." E

The second document was a notice in respect of Woodside Farm; it was
in these terms:

> " To the Trustees of the Newton Settlement, the Estate Office,
> Denton. I, John Shelbourn Pick, tenant of the farm known as
> Woodside Farm, situate at Newton, near Sleaford in the County of F
> Lincolnshire hereby give you notice of my intention to terminate my
> tenancy of the above holding on April 5, 1978. Dated April 4, 1977.
> Signed J. S. Pick, Woodside Farm, Newton, Sleaford."

The agent inquired whether that notice represented the tenant's final
decision. The tenant said it did. He asked for some grace in regard to
the payment of rent due for Woodside Farm on April 12, and was G
accorded it. In the event the rent for each of the farms was duly paid
by the tenant. According to his version of the arrangement between
him and the agent the notice to quit should then have been torn up.
However this assertion was rejected by the judge and it is unnecessary
to consider it further. However, when early in the following August
he got a letter from the agent the contents of which indicated that his
tenancy was regarded as coming to an end, he wrote a reproachful H
reply. It was dated August 12, 1977, and read:

> " Dear Mr. Cawthra, I am very distressed by your letter received
> this morning. I cannot believe that you would do this, after 40
> years here as loyal tenants, because of a hasty, unnecessary act
> done without any advice. I was very close to a nervous breakdown
> at the time, a time of extreme stress the reasons for which I dis-

A cussed with you, and I must appeal to you not to try to hold me to the consequences of such an irrational action. Perhaps we could discuss the matter. Incidentally, I trust that this will now be treated reasonably confidentially . . . "—and he goes on to say why.

It is evident from the tone and tenor of that missive that the tenant believed that he had given a notice which would be effective to deter-
B mine his tenancy of Woodside Farm if it was to be taken at its face value. The agent's response was that matters had progressed too far to allow the notice to quit to be retracted.

Thereafter the tenant, having procured a copy of that notice, consulted his solicitors. He has since maintained that the purported notice was ineffective and did not determine his tenancy. Accordingly he has asserted a right to remain in possession. Hence the claim for a
C declaration. The tenant's basic contention has been that the purported notice to quit Woodside Farm was not an effective notice because it was not in conformity with the requirements of the tenancy agreement and contravened section 23 (1) of the Agricultural Holdings Act 1948, which I now read:

D " A notice to quit an agricultural holding or part of an agricultural holding shall (notwithstanding any provision to the contrary in the contract of tenancy of the holding) be invalid if it purports to terminate the tenancy before the expiration of 12 months from the end of the then current year of tenancy: . . ."

This is the root of the controversy which was ventilated in the court below. The judge came to the conclusion that the effect of that
E statutory provision was to vitiate a notice which did not conform to the requirement of being a year's notice expiring on April 5 (sic). The judge regarded the provision as mandatory and as permitting of no contractual relaxation in any circumstances. He dismissed the landlords' contention that the arrangement or agreement made between their agent and the tenant served to validate the notice as and when
F served in these terms:

" Finally, as matter of legal analysis, whereas in this case the tenancy agreement provides for 12 months' notice, I find difficulty in seeing how an arrangement to accept short notice can be treated otherwise than as a variation of the tenancy. If so, it falls within the prohibition in section 23 against contracting out."

G As I have said, this was the primary issue; but the landlords were not without other resources. Apart from any question of due statutory notice, Mr. Price contended on their behalf that a tenant could at any time surrender his interest and if that surrender was accepted the interest would thereupon cease. This contention was rejected on the ground that the parties had not got a surrender in contemplation. The judge
H said:

" I am afraid I cannot accept it because as a matter of fact the tenant and the agent did not intend to enter into a conditional contract of surrender. The agent thought he was accepting late service of a notice under the tenancy agreement. This is made clear by the passage from his evidence which I have set out above: ' I thought if we agreed delayed service it would be valid.' His requirement that the notice should be dated before April 5 points

in that direction. So also does his evidence generally. He told me A
that he considered that this was going to be a termination of the
tenancy in the ordinary way. This is also confirmed by the agent's
attitude when he had written to the tenant the letter dated August
10, 1977, and it had become apparent that the tenant did not wish
to leave. The agent wrote in a letter dated August 15, 1977: '. . .
it would appear that you are now asking for the notice to quit
Woodside Farm next Lady Day to be withdrawn.' In a letter of B
September 7, 1977, he wrote that the tenant on a certain occasion
had not even suggested that he might 'be regretting giving his
notice.' The form of the notice to quit which I have already read
indicates a notice to quit under the tenancy agreement. That was
also the tenant's understanding of the position. I find this to be
so on the evidence of what took place on this point at the meeting C
of April 4. There is really no dispute about this part of what took
place. On this basis the notice falls fairly and squarely within the
prohibition in section 23."

The judge goes on to say:

"I realise, however, that what the parties may have said is not
conclusive. They are not lawyers. It is the duty of the court to D
ascertain the legal consequences of what has been done. The name
parties give to a transaction may not determine its legal nature.
Nevertheless, a contract is a matter of the intention of the parties.
In this case I am satisfied that the intention was to give a notice
under the tenancy agreement but to accept service of it late. I do
not think the court can hold the arrangement to be a contract of E
surrender. That would be to distort what I find to be the agreement which the parties reached.

"Moreover, I do not think the court ought to be astute to
analyse a transaction so as to bring it outside a statutory provision
when the consequence would be (a) to distort the true intention of
the parties and (b) to drive a coach and four through the statutory
provision. Having reached that conclusion it is unnecessary for me F
to deal with the questions of law which arose on the basis that the
contract was one of surrender."

In this connection there had arisen also problems as to consideration
and whether or not there was a sufficient memorandum in writing to
satisfy section 40 of the Law of Property Act 1925, since a surrender G
involved, if only incidentally, the transfer of an interest in land. As to
consideration, Mr. Price submitted that mutual promises to forego
existing contractual rights constituted consideration passing from each
of the parties related as landlord and tenant. The judge accepted this,
but was of the view it did not resolve the problem. Mr. Price conceded
that there was no sufficient memorandum in writing. This appeared to
me, as to the other members of this court, a somewhat surprising con- H
cession since the notice dated April 4, and the letter which accompanied
it, contained all the essential elements of a memorandum for the
purposes of section 40. Mr. Price asked leave to retract his concession
and as it was made in relation to the construction of documents, which
is a matter of law, that leave was granted. If, therefore, surrender may
provide a solution there is no inhibiting evidential factor. This being
so, it is unnecessary to pursue the somewhat desperate proposition, as

A it seeems to me, that there was part performance on the part of the
landlords which was sufficient to support their claim to specific performance of the agreement betweeen them and the tenant, that he
would surrender his tenancy on April 5, 1978. The part performance
relied upon consisted of acts done by the landlords in relation to
collateral matters such as employing the services of a valuer to arrive at
figures for the tenant's interest so as to determine compensation and so
B on. It was contended that these acts done, not in pursuance of the
contract of surrender itself, but in reliance on its having been made and
fulfilled, came within the concept of acts of part performance as
delineated in *Steadman* v. *Steadman* [1976] A.C. 536. I do not myself
read their Lordships' opinions in that case as enlarging the fundamental
concept of acts of part performance. Such acts must still be in further-
C ance of the contract and not merely a recognition of its existence or its
contemplation. However it is unnecessary, in the light of the view I
have reached as to the primary issue, to dwell further on this aspect. I
content myself by saying that I do not regard the speeches in *Steadman*
v. *Steadman* as introducing a radical change in the basic concept of
what may be regarded as an act of part performance. It must still
necessarily be an act in furtherance of the contract alleged to have been
D made, although it may not go so far as to amount to the discharge of
any primary obligation imposed by it.

Another argument for the landlords was founded on estoppel. In
this court it was enlarged so as to take in the subtle ramifications of
promissory estoppel. Mr. Parker, who appeared for the tenant before
the judge as well as on this appeal, met this with the retort that estoppel
E cannot aid a party to overcome what was a statutory prohibition. This
was indeed the essential theme of the tenant's case in refutation of
every contrary argument. It was the simple statement that section
23 (1) of the Agricultural Holdings Act 1948 precluded the efficacy of
any notice to quit which was of less than 12 months' duration and that
was the end of any argument.

I therefore turn back to the section itself in order to examine its
F language and to deduce its true tenor. It is clear that it is designed
principally to protect the tenant farmer from peremptory or unduly
prejudicial ejectment on the part of the landlord. Nonetheless it serves
also to protect a landlord from the abandonment of a tenancy in
circumstances which may cause a discontinuity in cultivation or a lapse
from proper standards of husbandry. Thus the time for the ending of a
G tenancy is a matter of common interest both to a landlord and to his
tenant. It may suit them both to determine a tenancy without waiting
for what may be as long as nearly two years to bring it to an end. No
statute could have so absurd an intention as to constrain a landlord and
a tenant of an agricultural holding to remain bound in that relationship
at a time when neither desires that it should endure. If they are in
accord, can it matter whether they demonstrate that accord by an
H agreement to surrender or an agreement to accept short notice?

I have read section 23 (1); the first matter to observe is that the
subsection uses the word "invalid" and not "unlawful." Thus there
is no penal prohibition; it is simply that provision in the tenancy agreement for a shorter notice than 12 months is nugatory. So also any
variation of a tenancy agreement in relation to an agricultural holding
which purports to make a shorter period of notice than 12 months

effective will fail of its purpose. This produces the situation that there **A** can be no operative provision whereby notice can in prospect be made effective if it is less than 12 months; but a notice is of course a unilateral act available to one party or the other without the ad hoc consent of the party to whom the notice is given. There seems to me to be no impediment created by section 23 (1) to the party in receipt of a notice to quit to waive his strict right that the notice should expire on a particular day or that it should be of particular duration. A contractual **B** provision which enures for the benefit of a party can be waived by that party albeit that his right to that benefit is reinforced by statute. There may be circumstances which might qualify this situation, as where an element of public interest is involved, but in such a case one would expect the statutory provision to speak in terms of illegality (thus: " it shall be unlawful ") rather than of mere invalidity.   **C**

I would wish to pay respectful tribute to the careful analysis by the judge; but, in my judgment, he erred in concluding that as between the landlord and the tenant of an agricultural holding there could not be a waiver of the requisite term of notice. The statutory provisions do not extend to a situation such as that which developed between the agent, acting on behalf of the landlords, and the tenant. The outcome of their discussions on April 4 and the acceptance by the agent of the **D** notice and the accompanying letter handed to him on April 7 was that the landlords effectively waived, as I am of the view that they were entitled to do, the requirements of the tenancy agreement as to the term and the expiry of the notice. The landlords were not precluded from such waiver by section 23 (1) of the Agricultural Holdings Act 1948 or in any other way. It follows that, in my judgment, the tenant's **E** tenancy was duly determined as at April 5, 1978, and that the landlords were entitled to the declaration claimed in their writ.

I would allow the appeal and make that declaration in their favour.

BRIGHTMAN L.J. On April 7, 1977, in the circumstances outlined by Shaw L.J., the tenant of Woodside Farm, Newton, handed to the landlords' agent his notice of intention to quit, dated April 4. Accord- **F** ingly, the length of the notice fell short of one year by a matter of three days. The notice was accompanied by a letter from the tenant to the agent:

" . . . I enclose a form of words which I hope you will accept as notice on the Newton Farm. The Welby Farm, I think, I should not give up unless I have to."   **G**

Both the landlords' agent and the tenant fully understood that less than one year's notice was being given. The agent agreed with the tenant that he would accept the notice to quit as a valid notice nowithstanding that the length of the notice was short. The landlords' agent also accepted the notice despite another defect, namely, that the notice did not strictly accord with the tenancy agreement in that the **H** date of termination was expressed to be April 5 and not April 6 (a point which was probably not appreciated by either side, and upon which nothing turns). It was the intention of the landlords' agent, and also the intention of the tenant, that the tenancy should end on April 5, 1978, by virtue of the defective notice so given.

The tenant now seeks to resile from the mutually intended con- sequence of the defective notice to quit. To do so the tenant relies on

A section 23 of the Agricultural Holdings Act 1948. The question is whether he can lawfully do so. The trial judge held that he could.

Section 23 (1) provides that a notice to quit an agricultural holding shall be invalid if it purports to terminate the tenancy before the expiration of 12 months from the end of the then current year of the tenancy. If, for example, an agricultural holding is held on a yearly tenancy which is silent as to the length of notice to quit required to
B terminate the tenancy, the notice will be invalid if it purports to be less than a 12 months' notice, calculated in the specified manner, although only a six months' notice is required at common law. Even if the tenancy agreement specifies that a shorter length of notice may be given, a notice of less than 12 months would still be invalid, because the subsection has effect "notwithstanding any provision to the
C contrary in the contract of tenancy of the holding."

In the instant case the tenant's counsel argued that a notice which is defective because it is short, is defective in all circumstances and for all purposes, and is incapable of valid acceptance by the recipient. If a notice served by the tenant is short by a day, but the landlord is content to accept it and so agrees with the tenant, nevertheless the notice is waste paper and the agreement of the parties is valueless. It is no good
D the tenant saying, "Please accept this notice as a valid notice to quit although it is short by a day" and the landlord saying, "I am willing to accept it." They have to go off to their solicitors and ask for a written agreement to be drawn up to end the tenancy. Such an agreement, says counsel, will be perfectly valid. But not an agreement by the recipient of the notice to accept the notice though defective in length.

E Take this extreme case. The landlord serves on his tenant notice to quit. The notice is one day short of the statutory 12 months. The tenant spots the defect and informs the landlord of it, but states that he will accept the notice despite the defect. The tenant intends to emigrate and makes all his plans to leave the country. I will assume that the landlord does not know about the tenant's plans, so as to avoid any complications about estoppel. A day before the notice expires the
F landlord tells the tenant that the notice to quit was indeed invalid, but that the invalidity was not cured by the landlord's express acceptance of the notice and that the tenant is legally liable for another year's rent and performance of the covenants, or more likely two years having regard to the timing which I have assumed in this extreme example. On the argument put forward by the tenant's counsel, the landlord will
G have a cast-iron case against his tenant.

I ask myself whether this can possibly be the law. I do not think it can be. What section 23 means is that a short notice to quit is invalid as against the recipient. A tenant is not bound to accept less than the statutory 12 months' notice to quit served by his landlord (nor vice versa) even if the tenancy agreement so provides. If the tenant
H chooses to do so, he can simply ignore a short notice served on him and resist any attempt by the landlord to recover possession on the strength of it. But if the tenant wishes to do so, he can bind himself to accept it. The parties are entitled to agree that the notice shall be treated in all respects as if it were a notice of the statutory length. If the parties so agree, the tenancy will come to an end on the agreed date by virtue of the defective notice to quit which it is agreed shall be treated as valid. Such an agreement could not effectively be made before a notice to

quit it served, because the parties cannot agree that the tenancy shall A
be capable of being terminated by a short notice. Neither the landlord
nor the tenant can bind himself in advance to accept a short notice
from the other of them. That would be a " provision to the contrary "
in, or supplemental to, the contract of tenancy and would not be
effective. But once an invalid notice has been served, which the
recipient is entitled to ignore, I see nothing in section 23 to prohibit an
agreement between landlord and tenant that the notice shall be followed B
by the same consequences as if it were valid.

There is an alternative approach, which in my view is equally
tenable. Although in the instant case the notice to quit is invalid qua
notice to quit, it contains all the ingredients which are needed to
constitute a valid written acceptance on April 7 of the oral offer made
on April 4 by the landlords' agent, or (if this is the correct interpreta- C
tion of the events) a valid written offer on April 7 which the landlords'
agent accepted orally on the same day. The difference between the
two interpretations is of no moment because the legal consequences are
the same. On the assumption that the latter interpretation is correct,
the defective notice was an expression of the intention, and therefore
of the willingness, of the tenant that the tenancy agreement should
terminate on April 5, 1978, which intention the tenant communicated D
to the landlords' agent in the hope or expectation that the agent would
accede thereto. The agent did accede thereto, as a result of which
there was consensus ad idem between tenant and agent that the tenancy
should end on April 5, 1978. Such a course of dealing seems to me on
analysis to be indistinguishable in any relevant respect from an offer
by the tenant to terminate the tenancy on April 5, 1978, which offer is E
accepted by the landlords. Such an agreement is clearly outside section
23.

I find support for this approach in the judgment of Bayley J. in
Johnstone v. *Hudlestone* (1825) 4 B. & C. 922, 935, decided in the
Court of King's Bench, to which Buckley L.J. invited counsel's attention
during the course of the argument.

For myself, I do not mind which way the case is put and I doubt F
whether there is any substantial difference between the two interpretations of the events.

I would allow the appeal for the reasons which I have endeavoured
to express.

BUCKLEY L.J. The Agricultural Holdings Act 1948, section 23, is G
clearly designed to protect an agricultural tenant against eviction from
his holding against his will by shorter notice than the section prescribes.
It may also confer advantages upon the landlord by ensuring that he
will receive at least 12 months' notice from the tenant of termination
of the tenancy. It does not, like sections 3 and 24 of the Landlord
and Tenant Act 1954, provide that a tenancy shall not come to an H
end except by being terminated in accordance with the provisions of
the Act. It does not, in my judgment, preclude determination of an
agricultural tenancy on shorter notice than the Act requires if both
parties agree to this. Mr. Parker concedes, rightly in my view, that
the parties to an agricultural tenancy can bring the tenancy to an end
by an agreement that the tenant shall surrender the tenancy to the
landlord forthwith or by an agreement that the tenancy shall come to

A an end at some future date which is less remote than the earliest
date at which it could be brought to an end by a notice to quit in
accordance with the section.

In a case which is unregulated by any statutory provision, if a tenant
gives notice to quit in circumstances which make the notice ineffective
—perhaps because it is too short or because it is given for the wrong
day—the landlord can, if he chooses, agree to accept the notice as valid
B notwithstanding the defect in it: he can waive his right to rely on the
defect. If he does so in a manner which is legally binding, the notice
will take effect as if it were not defective. There is, in my opinion,
nothing in section 23 of the Act of 1948 to prevent the parties to an
agricultural tenancy from waiving any defect in a notice to quit,
including a failure to comply with the requirements of the section itself.

C It is, in my opinion, clear upon the evidence that both the landlords'
agent and the tenant thought that the notice to quit handed by the
tenant to the agent on April 7, 1977, was an effective notice, notwithstanding that it was a day late, because the agent on the landlords'
behalf agreed to accept it as effective. The agent in evidence said that
he had had some doubts about this, but the judge found that the agent
believed that the notice would terminate the tenancy. What then
D occurred cannot, in my judgment, have constituted a surrender of the
tenancy, for it is well settled that a tenancy cannot be surrendered in
futuro. I agree with the judge that in the circumstances of this case
one could not find that there was an agreement for a future surrender
of the tenancy. An agreement to surrender a term or to terminate
the relation of landlord and tenant on a particular date and an effective
E notice to terminate the tenancy on that date may have the same legal
effect, but they are different transactions; one operates bilaterally by
way of contract, the other unilaterally by setting a term to a contract
(viz. the tenancy) in exercise of a power under that contract.

A contract to render an existing defective notice to quit effective by
waiving the defect is not, in my view, a contract to vary the tenancy
F agreement. An agricultural tenancy could not, consistently with section
23, be modified by agreement between the parties in such a way that
either party to it could terminate it by a notice to quit which did not
accord with the terms of the section. Such an agreement would conflict
with the words of the section which are within brackets. But it does
not follow from this that, when a notice to quit has been given which
fails to satisfy the requirements of the section, the parties cannot
G effectually agree that, notwithstanding the defect in the notice, it shall
take effect as though it were a valid notice. Such an agreement would
not, in my opinion, conflict with any part of the section. It would not
alter any of the terms of the tenancy agreement. Its effect is that
the parties agree to the tenancy coming to an end on the date specified
in the notice, subject to which the tenancy remains in full force and
H effect. So viewed—and, in my opinion, rightly so viewed—the agreement comes within Mr. Parker's concession.

I therefore agree with the judge that in the present case the intention of the parties was that the tenant should give notice under the
tenancy agreement and that consequently the acceptance by the agent
of late service of the notice did not give rise to a contract for the
surrender of the tenancy. With deference, however, I do not agree
with him that the agreement to accept short notice involved a variation

of the tenancy falling within the prohibition in section 23 against   A
contracting out of the section. In my judgment, the agent's agreement
on the landlords' behalf on April 7, 1977, to accept the notice to quit
as a valid notice effectually determining the tenancy on April 5, 1978,
had the effect of a binding waiver of any defect in the notice and of a
binding agreement that the tenancy should accordingly come to an
end on April 5, 1978. Such waiver and such agreement did not, in my
judgment, conflict with section 23. It is not contended that, if that   B
transaction can legally take effect, it was not contractually binding and
supported by mutual consideration. It is consequently, in my judgment,
binding on the defendant.

For these reasons and for those contained in the judgments already
delivered, with which I agree, I would consequently allow this appeal.

C
Appeal allowed.
Costs below and three-quarters
costs of appeal plaintiffs' costs.
Leave to appeal refused.

Solicitors: *Dawson & Co.; Roythorne & Co., Spalding.*
D
C. N.

E

[HOUSE OF LORDS]

* YUILL . . . . APPELLANT AND
CROSS-RESPONDENT

AND

WILSON (INSPECTOR OF TAXES) . . . RESPONDENT AND   F
CROSS-APPELLANT

1980 May 12, 13, 14;   Viscount Dilhorne, Lord Salmon, Lord
       July 10   Edmund-Davies, Lord Russell of Killowen
                                    and Lord Keith of Kinkel

G
Revenue—Income tax—Tax avoidance—Artificial transactions in
land—Scheme designed and carried out whereby gains arising
on sale of land in United Kingdom realised by non-resident
companies—Taxpayer director of United Kingdom companies
through which scheme implemented—Whether "opportunity
of realising a gain, provided directly or indirectly" by tax-
payer—Whether taxpayer liable to tax on part of gains still
unrealised—Income and Corporation Taxes Act 1970 (c. 10),   H
ss. 488 (2) (3) (6) (8), 489 (13) [1]

The taxpayer was the founder and managing director of
Y. Ltd., a large and prosperous building business in the North-
East of England. A substantial number of the shares in that

_____
[1] Income and Corporation Taxes Act 1970, s. 488 (2) (3) (6) (8): see post,
pp. 913c–914A.
S. 489 (13): see post, p. 914B–c.

A   company were held either by the taxpayer or by trustees for the benefit of the taxpayer's family. Together the shareholdings constituted a controlling interest. In 1958 Y. Ltd. purchased fen land which in 1961 it conveyed to P. Ltd., one of its subsidiary companies, for £4,050. Subsequently farm land was purchased by Y. Ltd. in 1968, a part of which was sold on in 1972 to a development company, D. Ltd., for £48,600. The taxpayer and the trustees together had the controlling share-

B   holding in both P. Ltd. and D. Ltd. In 1972, the taxpayer formed, for the benefit of members of his family, a settlement with trustees who were resident in Guernsey. Thereafter those trustees formed two companies in Guernsey, M. Ltd. and C. Ltd., for the purpose of buying land. The shares in those two companies were held by the Guernsey trustees as trust property. The purpose of those companies was to limit the personal liability of the trustees should anything go wrong financially

C   with the transactions involved in the scheme. In 1972 part of the fen land was conveyed by P. Ltd. to C. Ltd. for £40,000 and shortly afterwards M. Ltd. bought part of the farm land owned by D. Ltd. for £81,000 and paid £100 to Y. Ltd. for the benefit of a contract that it had to purchase the remaining area of farm land. Those transactions were carried out with the sole or main object of realising gains from the disposal of that land once planning permission in respect of it had been

D   acquired. In 1973 the trustees of the various English settlements that the taxpayer had formed for the benefit of his family retired and were replaced by the Guernsey trustees. In 1974 those trustees sold all the shares in C. Ltd. and M. Ltd. to V. Ltd., another Guernsey company in which they held interests, for £65,000 and £200 respectively. Soon after planning permission was granted in respect of the fen land and C. Ltd. contracted to sell it back to Y. Ltd. for £700,000.

E   On the same day M. Ltd. contracted to sell all its interest in the farm land to Y. Ltd. for £648,000. Both those contracts provided for a part-repayment of the purchase price in the event of land nationalisation or compulsory purchase within a period of five years. Substantial parts of the purchase prices were not paid to C. Ltd. and M. Ltd. but left outstanding as loans repayable by instalments.

    The taxpayer was assessed to income tax for 1973–74

F   under Case VI of Schedule D in the sum of £1,129,800 on the basis that the capital gains that had accrued to C. Ltd. and M. Ltd. on the sale of the land fell to be taxed as his income by virtue of section 488 (3) and (8) of the Income and Corporation Taxes Act 1970. The general commissioners dismissed his appeal holding that all the transactions had been carried out as part of a pre-arranged scheme whereby the taxpayer had provided C. Ltd. with the opportunity of realising

G   gains and by virtue of the provisions of section 488 (8) it was he who fell to be substituted for the non-resident companies as the person to be taxed in respect of those gains.

    An appeal by the taxpayer was dismissed by Templeman J. who held that there was ample and cogent evidence on which the commissioners had been entitled to conclude that the taxpayer, acting in the interests of his family, had provided C.

H   Ltd. and M. Ltd. with the opportunity of making the capital gains. Further, he held that as section 488 (3) required the whole of the gain to be treated as income arising when the gain was realised, that the contingent liability of C. Ltd. and M. Ltd. to repay in subsequent years part of the purchase money should certain events occur, was not a factor altering the amount of the gain realised and to be treated as the taxpayer's income for the year 1973–74. The Court of Appeal remitted the case to the commissioners to make further findings.

    On appeal and cross-appeal: —

Held, (1) allowing, in part, the revenue's cross-appeal, that A
a " gain is realised " within section 488 (3) (*b*) of the Income
and Corporation Taxes Act 1970 only when it could be
effectively enjoyed and disposed of and, since, under the terms
of the agreement for the sale of the land, the only gain so
realised in 1973–74 by one of the two vendor companies was
£1,417 the assessment on the taxpayer should be reduced to
that amount, there being a sufficient finding of fact by the
commissioners in the case stated that he had provided the B
opportunity to realise that gain within section 488 (8) (post,
pp. 916F–G, 918B–E, 919H—920A, 927B–D, 928H, 930D–E, 931B–C,
D–E).

(2) Allowing the taxpayer's appeal, that since the revenue
had not at the hearing before the commissioners put forward
the alternative contention that to the amounts at the disposal
of the companies should be added the value of the rights they
had in future years to receive the sums deposited, the case C
should not be remitted to the commissioners for further findings of fact on that point (post, pp. 918G—919B, 921H, 929A–B,
D–E, 931G–H).

Decision of the Court of Appeal [1979] 1 W.L.R. 987;
[1979] 2 All E.R. 1205 varied.

The following cases are referred to in their Lordships' opinions:

Bird (*R.A.*) & *Co.* v. *Inland Revenue Commissioners,* 1925 S.C. 186; 12 D
  T.C. 785.
Bradshaw v. *Blunden* (*No.* 2) (1960) 39 T.C. 73.
Foulsham v. *Pickles* [1925] A.C. 458, H.L.(E.).
Leeming v. *Jones* [1930] 1 K.B. 279.
Moriarty v. *Evans Medical Supplies Ltd.* [1958] 1 W.L.R. 66; [1957] 3
  All E.R. 718, H.L.(E.)
Sungei Rinching Rubber Co. v. *Inland Revenue Commissioners* (1925) 94 E
  L.J.K.B. 865, C.A.
Vestey v. *Inland Revenue Commissioners* [1979] 3 W.L.R. 915; [1979]
  3 All E.R. 976, H.L.(E.).
Vestey's (*Lord*) *Executors* v. *Inland Revenue Commissioners* [1949] 1
  All E.R. 1108; 31 T.C. 1, H.L.(E.).

The following additional cases were cited in argument: F

Edwards v. *Bairstow* [1956] A.C. 14; [1955] 3 W.L.R. 410; [1955] 3 All
  E.R. 48, H.L.(E.).
Harrison v. *John Cronk & Sons Ltd.* [1937] A.C. 185; [1936] 3 All E.R.
  747, H.L.(E.).
Oppenheimer v. *Cattermole* [1976] A.C. 249; [1975] 2 W.L.R. 347;
  [1975] 1 All E.R. 538, H.L.(E.).
Willingale v. *International Commercial Bank Ltd.* [1978] A.C. 834; [1978] G
  2 W.L.R. 452; [1978] 1 All E.R. 754, H.L.(E.).

APPEAL and CROSS-APPEAL from the Court of Appeal.

This was an appeal by leave of the Court of Appeal (Buckley, Goff and
Eveleigh L.JJ.) from an order of that court [1979] 1 W.L.R. 987 made on
December 21, 1978, after hearings on November 29, 30, and December 1, H
1978, allowing the appeal of Cecil Mortley Yuill, the appellant, from an
order of the High Court (Templeman J.) [1979] 1 W.L.R. 987 dated
July 29, 1977, whereby the appeal of the appellant from a determination
of the Commissioners for the General Purposes of the Income Tax Acts
for the Division of Hartlepool was dismissed and the decision of those
commissioners upheld. There was also a cross-appeal by the respondent
Thomas Wilson, inspector of taxes.

A   The facts are stated in the opinions of Viscount Dilhorne and Lord Russell of Killowen.

A. Leolin Price Q.C. and *C. W. Koenigsberger* for the appellant.
D. C. Potter Q.C. and *Christopher McCall* for the Crown.

B   Their Lordships took time for consideration.

July 10. VISCOUNT DILHORNE. My Lords, the appellant, Mr. Cecil Mortley Yuill, was assessed to income tax under Case VI of Schedule D in the sum of £1,129,800 for 1973–74. He appealed to the general commissioners at Hartlepool and during the hearing of his appeal, the revenue contended that that figure should be adjusted to £1,095,853.

C   The assessment was made under section 488 of the Income and Corporation Taxes Act 1970, the relevant provisions of which read as follows:

> " (1) This section is enacted to prevent the avoidance of tax by persons concerned with land or the development of land. (2) This section applies wherever—(a) land, or any property deriving its value from land,
D   is acquired with the sole or main object of realising a gain from disposing of the land, or (b) land is held as trading stock, or (c) land is developed with the sole or main object of realising a gain from disposing of the land when developed, and any gain of a capital nature is obtained from the disposal of the land—(i) by the person acquiring, holding or developing the land, or by any connected person, or (ii)
E   where any arrangement or scheme is effected as respects the land which enables a gain to be realised by any indirect method, or by any series of transactions, by any person who is a party to, or concerned in, the arrangement or scheme; and this subsection applies whether any such person obtains the gain for himself or for any other person. (3) Where this section applies, the whole of any such gain shall for all the purposes of the Tax Acts be treated—(a) as being income
F   which arises when the gain is realised, and which constitutes profits or gains chargeable to tax under Case VI of Schedule D for the chargeable period in which the gain is realised, and (b) subject to the following provisions of this section, as being income of the person by whom the gain is realised. (4) For the purposes of this section . . . (5) . . . (a) where, whether by a premature sale or otherwise, a person directly or indirectly transmits the opportunity of making a gain to
G   another person, that other person's gain is obtained for him by the first-mentioned person, and (b) any number of transactions may be regarded as constituting a single arrangement or scheme if a common purpose can be discerned in them, or if there is other sufficient evidence of a common purpose. (6) For the purposes of this section such method of computing a gain shall be adopted as is just and reasonable in the
H   circumstances, taking into account the value of what is obtained for disposing of the land, and allowing only such expenses as are attributable to the land disposed of, . . . (8) If all or any part of the gain accruing to any person is derived from value, or an opportunity of realising a gain, provided directly or indirectly by some other person, whether or not put at the disposal of the first-mentioned person, subsection (3) (b) of this section shall apply to the gain, or that part of it, with the substitution of that other person for the person by whom the

gain was realised. . . (13) This section shall apply to all persons, A
whether resident in the United Kingdom or not, if all or any part of
the land in question is situated in the United Kingdom."

This section, which has the marginal note " Artificial transactions in
land " is in Part XVII of the Act which is headed " Tax avoidance."

Section 489 supplements section 487 (which dealt with the sale by an
individual of income derived from his personal activities) and section 488. B
Subsection (13) of that section reads as follows:

" For the purposes of the principal sections and this section—' capital
amount ' means any amount, in money or money's worth . . . ' company ' includes any body corporate, ' share ' includes stock, and for the
said purposes any amount in money or money's worth shall not be
regarded as having become receivable by some person until that person C
can effectively enjoy or dispose of it."

Some 50 years ago Mr. Yuill founded what is now a large and prosperous building business in Hartlepool. For many years the business was
carried on by a company called Cecil M. Yuill Ltd. (hereby referred to as
" Yuill ") and until about 1965 he was its managing director. He was
succeeded in that office by a younger man but he continued to take an D
active interest in the affairs of the company and to play a part in it, and did
so at the time of the transactions which led to the assessment being made
on him. He is a substantial shareholder in the company and a substantial
number of shares in it are held by family trusts for the benefit of his
family. The combined shareholding constitute a controlling interest.

Owton Fens Development Co. Ltd. (hereafter called " the development
company ") was formed in 1972 to hold and acquire land for Yuill. The E
appellant's four children were shareholders and the appellant and Mr.
Grieveson, who was also a director of Yuill, were directors.

In 1966 Yuill had agreed to buy 108 acres of land known as Quarry
Farm for £194,400. The purchase of a quarter of that land for £48,600
was to be completed by March 31, 1972, and the purchase of the remaining
three-quarters was to be completed on later dates. F

On May, 10, 1972, on the direction of Yuill the first quarter was conveyed to the development company for £48,600.

Owten Fens Properties Ltd. (hereafter called the ' property company ')
was another company associated with Yuill. The appellant, his wife and
the trustees of a family settlement set up by the appellant were its shareholders and the appellant and his wife were directors with Mr. Grieveson
its secretary. It was formed to take over from Yuill 67 acres of land G
at Owton Fens Farm and did so in March 1961 for the sum of £4,050.
This case is concerned with 48 acres of this land.

Between 1955 and 1962 the appellant created four settlements for
the benefits of members of his family, reserving to himself power to
appoint new trustees. In 1973 he exercised that power in relation to three
of the settlements, appointing as trustees thereof Mr. de Putron, Mr. H
M. J. Wilson and Channel Executor and Trustee Co. Ltd. (later known
as Hillcrest Executor and Trustee Co. Ltd.). These new trustees have
at all times resided in Guernsey. Each trust held a large number of shares
in Yuill.

On September 20, 1972, the appellant made a fifth settlement for
the benefit of members of his family. Its trustees were Mr. de Putron
and a Mr. Bagley, also a resident in Guernsey. These trustees formed

A two companies in Guernsey named Mayville Ltd. and Ceville Ltd. All the shares in those companies were trust property and Mr. and Mrs. Bagley were directors of the companies of which the trustees had complete control. The commissioners said that the companies " were merely a legal vehicle to be used by and on behalf of the trustees so as to limit the liability of the trustees should anything go wrong . . . "

B   On December 28, 1972, the property company sold its 48 acres to Ceville Ltd. for £40,000 and on March 25, 1974, Ceville sold them to Yuill for £700,000.

       On January 30, 1973, the development sold to Mayville Ltd. the quarter of the land at Quarry Farm which had been conveyed to it for £81,000 and Mayville bought from Yuill its rights in relation to the remaining three-quarters. On March 30, 1973, and on March 25, 1974,

C Mayville bought two more quarters, each for £48,600. On March 23, 1974, Mayville sold three-quarters of that land to Yuill for £648,000 and on March 25, the three-quarters were conveyed to Yuill.

       So of the Quarry Farm land which Yuill had agreed to buy for £194,000, the three-quarters of which had been sold to Mayville for £178,200 again became the property of Yuill at a cost of £648,000 and

D the 48 acres which Yuill had held, again became its property for £700,000.

       The revenue contended that by virtue of section 488 the gains made by Ceville and Mayville on the sale of these lands were to be treated as income of the appellant. It was not disputed that the appellant and the Yuill companies were concerned either directly or indirectly with land and its development and the commissioners found that Ceville and Mayville acquired the lands with the sole or main object of realising a

E gain from the disposal of them, so subsection (2) of the section applies if any gain was " obtained " from the disposal either (i) by the person acquiring the land or by any connected person or (ii) where any arrangement or scheme enabled a gain to be realised, by any person who was a party to or concerned in the arrangement or scheme; and the subsection applies whether that person " obtains " the gain for himself or for any

F other person.

       The commissioners found that there was a scheme or arrangement or a series of transactions which enabled capital gains to be made by Mayville and Ceville upon the sale of the lands to Yuill and that the appellant " either directly or through his companies, and with the help of his Guernsey trustees obtained for those companies the said gains . . . " They thus held that the case came within (ii) of subsection (2) and they

G upheld the assessment.

       The appellant's appeal was heard by Templeman J., as he then was [1979] 1 W.L.R. 987. There it was argued for the appellant, as it was in the Court of Appeal [1979] 1 W.L.R. 987, on each occasion without success, and it was contended in this House that the sales to Ceville and Mayville were at market value and that this prevented the section from

H applying. If this submission was well founded, a sale at market value in the chain of transactions leading to a gain being realised would provide an easy method of evading the operation of this section. I am satisfied that it does not do so for the reasons given by Templeman J. and by Buckley L.J. and Goff L.J. in the Court of Appeal.

       Subsection (2) while defining the scope of the section, does not state upon whom liability to pay the tax is to fall. That is done by subsection (3) (b) which provides that subject to the following provisions of the

section, the gain is to be treated as the income of the person by whom   A
the gain was realised. Those persons were Ceville and Mayville, neither
of whom were liable to pay United Kingdom income tax.

So the liability of the appellant depends on whether he is caught by
subsection (8) as having provided Ceville and Mayville directly or
indirectly with an opportunity of realising a gain.

The appellant contends that the assessment should be set aside as,   B
though the commissioners found that he obtained gains for those
companies, they did not find that he had provided them with the
opportunity of realising those gains.

This contention was rejected by Templeman J. but found more favour
in the Court of Appeal, Buckley L.J. stressing the importance of explicit
findings of fact. He thought [1979] 1 W.L.R. 987, 1008 that if the
question of the taxpayer's liability under subsection (8) was to be pursued,   C
the case should be sent back to the commissioners

" . . . with liberty for both the taxpayer and the inspector to adduce
further evidence, with the object of allowing the commissioners to
make such further findings of fact as in the light of the judgments
in this court and of the evidence as a whole may seem to them to be
appropriate."   D

He deliberately forebore from suggesting on what particular matters they
should make findings. Goff L.J. agreed that the case should be sent back
to the commissioners for them to make such further findings of fact as
they might consider appropriate in the light of the judgments and that
each side should have liberty to call further evidence. Eveleigh L.J.
agreed with both judgments. So the Court of Appeal allowed the appeal   E
and set aside the commissioners' determination and sent the case back to
the commissioners.

The case stated shows that it was contended for the revenue that the
appellant had " put Ceville and Mayville into a position where they could
acquire the land and thereafter make a gain from selling it, so that he
provided them with the opportunity of realising the gain." I, for my
part, think it inconceivable that the commissioners failed to appreciate   F
that the appellant's liability depended on whether he had provided that
opportunity. They found as a fact that he had obtained the gains for
these companies. He can hardly have done that without providing them
with the opportunity of realising the gains. I cannot conclude that they
directed their attention solely to subsection (2) and ignored subsection (8).
In my view it necessarily follows from their finding that he obtained the   G
gains for them, that they found that he provided them with that
opportunity and I see no need to remit the case to the commissioners for
them to make a further finding on this point.

Subsection (3) provides that the whole of the gain is to be treated
as income which arises when the gain is realised and that it is chargeable
to tax under Case V of Schedule D for the chargeable period in which the   H
gain is realised. So the question now to be considered is, was any gain
realised by Ceville and Mayville in 1973–74?

Under the similar and curious agreements for sale entered into by Ceville
and Mayville, the sales were conditional upon each of those companies
arranging loans at 10 per cent. interest to Yuill, the loans being secured
by mortgages on the lands. Ceville undertook to arrange a loan to Yuill
of £655,000 and Mayville to arrange one of £445,000. Each loan was to

A be available on the date fixed for completion and if there was failure to arrange a loan at that time, the agreement for sale was to be null and void.

It was also agreed that in partial re-imbursement of the interest to be paid by Yuill on the loans, each company would make payments on specified dates to Yuill. Ceville was to pay Yuill £15,000 on July 14, 1974, £30,000 on January 14, 1975, and £15,000 on July 14, 1975, a total of £60,000. Mayville was to pay Yuill £10,000 on July 14, 1974, £20,000
B on January 14, 1975, July 14, 1975, January 14, 1976, July 14, 1976, and January 14, 1977, and £10,000 on July 14, 1977, a total of £120,000.

Why these companies should have undertaken to pay Yuill part of the interest payable by Yuill on the loans was not explained and fortunately is not necessary to understand for the purposes of this case.

The fact that the price to be paid by Yuill was found by borrowing
C money in no way affects the question whether any, and if so what, gain was realised by these two companies in 1973–74.

Under each agreement the vendors of the lands, Ceville and Mayville undertook that in the event of nationalisation or compulsory acquisition of the land sold, they would make repayments to Yuill of the purchase price. If nationalisation or compulsory acquisition took place within three years of
D the agreement, Ceville was to repay £660,000 of the total purchase price of £700,000 and Mayville £460,000 of the total purchase price of £468,000. If that took place after the expiry of the third year and before the expiry of the fourth, Ceville was to repay £440,000 and Mayville £345,000, if it took place between the fourth and fifth years Ceville was to repay £220,000 and Mayville £230,000 and if that occurred between the fifth and sixth years Mayville was to repay £115,000.

E Ceville undertook to deposit as security for its obligations to repay £655,000 and Mayville to deposit as security for its obligations £445,000. Each sum was to be deposited with a person to be agreed on by the parties or in default of agreement by the auditors of the companies. Any interest on the sums deposited was to be the property of Ceville and Mayville. The sums were, it was stated, deposited with Channel Finance Ltd., a Guernsey
F company which made the loans to Yuill.

If nationalisation or compulsory acquisition did not take place in three years Ceville was to be repaid £215,000 of the sum deposited and Mayville £100,000; if it did not occur in four years Ceville was to be repaid £220,000 and Mayville £115,000; if it did not happen in five years, Ceville was to be repaid the balance of the £655,000 deposited and Mayville £115,000 and if the land sold by Mayville was not nationalised or so acquired within six
G years, Mayville was to be repaid the balance of the sum deposited.

If the lands were nationalised or compulsorily acquired within three years, the total sums deposited were to be paid to Yuill. If that happened between the third and fourth years £435,000 of the sum deposited by Ceville and £330,000 of that deposited by Mayville was to be paid to Yuill. If it happened between the fourth and fifth years, £215,000 of the sum
H deposited by Ceville and £215,000 of that deposited by Mayville were to be paid to Yuill and if between the fifth and sixth years, £100,000 of the sum deposited by Mayville was to be paid to Yuill.

If the lands were nationalised or compulsorily acquired within these periods, Yuill would presumably receive compensation for them and it is not easy to understand why in that event Ceville and Mayville should have agreed that these repayments should be made to Yuill.

Whatever the reason may be, it is apparent that under these agreements

only a very small part of the total purchase prices was at the disposal of   A
Ceville and Mayville on the completion of the sales and that if there was
no nationalisation or compulsory acquisition, they would get the balance
of the purchase price instalments over a period of years. On the other
hand if there was nationalisation or compulsory acquisition within the
periods specified, the whole or part of the sums deposited would never
come under their control but would be paid to Yuill.

In these circumstances it is, I think, wholly unreal to say that in 1973–74   B
Ceville and Mayville realised a gain of the total purchase price less the
cost of acquisition of the land and the expenses of its sale. They only
realised a gain in that year if the sums at their disposal in that year were
in excess of the cost of acquisition and those expenses.

The amount of the purchase price which was at the disposal of Ceville
in 1973–74 appears to have been £45,000. The price paid by that company   C
for the land and the expenses of its sale appears to have been £50,564
so there does not appear to have been any gain by that company in that
year. The amount of the purchase price which was then at the disposal of
Mayville appears to have been £203,000. The cost of the land and the
expenses of sale appear to have amounted to £201,583 so in that year
Mayville appear to have made a gain of £1,417.

It was contended for the revenue that, as the two companies would   D
only have realised the total purchase price over a period of years, the cost
of acquisition of the land and the expenses of its sale should be spread over
the same period. I can see no justification for this and I reject this contention. Gains will have been made by these companies as and when the
instalments became repayable to them on demand and the appellant will be
chargeable to income tax under Case VI in the years in which those sums   E
became payable.

The revenue also contended that to the amounts at the disposal of
Ceville and Mayville in 1973–74, there should be added the value of the
rights they had in future years to receive the sums deposited. Whether
those rights were capable of valuation is open to doubt, bearing in mind that
the whole or part of the sums deposited might be returnable to Yuill.
Mr. de Putron testified that they could not be valued by actuarial or other   F
methods. No finding was made by the commissioners on this and it does
not appear that any evidence on it was given before them on behalf of the
revenue. Buckley L.J. in the course of his judgment said that the Crown
must be entitled to a finding on this question of fact if it is so desired,
and it would seem that it was thought that this might be one of the matters
with which the commissioners might deal if the case was remitted to them.   G

My Lords, it would not in my opinion be right to remit the case to the
commissioners for them to make a finding of fact on this issue when the
revenue could at the hearing before them, if they had thought fit to do
so, have put forward the contention as an alternative to their main
contention, that if the two companies had not realised a gain on the
completion of the sales of the full purchase price, they had realised the
moneys which they were able to enjoy and of which they were free to   H
dispose and the value of the contingent rights to the balance of the purchase price, and have called evidence with regard thereto.

I cannot think it right that the revenue should now be given the
opportunity of supplementing the case they presented against Mr. Yuill and
of calling fresh evidence with regard thereto.

In my opinion the case should not be remitted to the commissioners
on this or any other point. The power to remit given by the Taxes

A Management Act 1970, section 56 (6) and (7) is wide but I have not known it exercised so as to enable the revenue to obtain a re-hearing and to call fresh evidence in order to obtain a finding on a question which could have been raised at the first hearing; nor have I known prior to this case of any instance of a court remitting a case to allow commissioners to make such further findings of fact and to hear further evidence as they might deem appropriate in the light of the judgment of the court. I do not think that the Court of Appeal was right to remit the case to the commissioners for that purpose.

B

I have based my conclusions on the meaning which I think should be given to the expression " the gain is realised." Section 489 of the Act is, as I have said, intended to supplement sections 487 and 488. Subsection (13) of section 489 is a definition subsection and, inter alia, states that for the purposes of section 487 and 488 " any amount in money or money's worth shall not be regarded as having become receivable by some person until that person can effectively enjoy or dispose of it." The operation of section 488 does not depend on whether money or money's worth is receivable. One does not find in it any reference to money or money's worth being receivable. It depends on whether a gain is obtained or realised. So the operation of this definition is, to say the least, obscure in relation to section 488.

C

D

It, however, accords with the meaning which I think should be given to the word " realised," that is to say, that a gain is not realised until it can be effectively enjoyed or disposed of.

There is one other matter to which I must refer. On January 22, 1974 the shares in Mayville and Ceville were sold by the trustees for £65,000 and £200 respectively to a Guernsey company called Valnord Investments Ltd., all of whose shares were owned by a trust of which Hillcrest Executor and Trustee Co. Ltd. was a trustee. This sale was rightly described by Templeman J. [1979] 1 W.L.R. 987, 999 as " mysterious and unexplained." It does not in my opinion relieve the appellant of liability to be assessed to income tax in respect of gains realised by Ceville and Mayville in respect of the sale of the lands to Yuill.

E

F

The Court of Appeal while remitting the case to the commissioners, discharged their determination that the appellant should be assessed to income tax in the sum of £1,095,853. In my opinion that determination should be restored and varied by being reduced to £1,417 being the gain realised in 1973–74 on the sale by Mayville to Yuill of the Quarry Farm land.

G

As the appellant has substantially succeeded in this appeal, I think that the proper order as to costs should be that the respondent should pay his costs on the appeal and cross-appeal here and also below.

LORD SALMON. My Lords, I have had the opportunity of reading in draft the speech prepared by my noble and learned friend Viscount Dilhorne, with which I entirely agree. The appeal should be allowed and the cross-appeal allowed to the extent indicated in the speech of my noble and learned friend, Viscount Dilhorne.

H

LORD EDMUND-DAVIES. My Lords, I am in respectful agreement with my noble and learned friends, Viscount Dilhorne and Lord Russell of Killowen, that the general commissioners sufficiently indicated in paragraph 11 (2) of the stated case their clear conclusion that any gains

Lord Edmund-Davies   **Yuill v. Wilson (H.L.(E.))**   **[1980]**

accruing to Mayville and Ceville by selling the Owton Fens and Quarry   A
Farm land to Cecil M. Yuill Ltd. in 1974 were derived from the
opportunity indirectly provided by the taxpayer. I am furthermore
satisfied that this was the right conclusion on the evidence. But the
Court of Appeal [1979] 1 W.L.R. 987 held that the finding was insufficiently definite to justify the taxpayer being mulcted. They accordingly
allowed the appeal from the judgment of Templeman J. which had upheld
the commissioners' determination, and they set aside that determination.   B

But unfortunately they did not stop there. Instead, and (as we were
informed) to the surprise of counsel for both parties, they ordered that
the matter be remitted to the commissioners, " for them to act upon in
the light of the judgment of this court . . . with liberty to either party
to adduce further evidence." The appellant's primary submission to this
House is that, the Court of Appeal having set aside the commissioners'   C
determination, there was no point, purpose or propriety in nevertheless
remitting the matter back to them. I propose to restrict my remarks
solely to a consideration of that submission, prefacing it by saying that I
am in respectful agreement with my noble and learned friends, Viscount
Dilhorne and Lord Russell of Killowen, in the reason they give for
allowing the appeal.

The relevant statutory provisions are in these days to be found in   D
section 56 of the Taxes Management Act 1970, and in particular the
following subsections:

> " (6) The High Court shall hear and determine any question or
> questions of law arising on the case, and shall reverse, affirm or
> amend the determination in respect of which the case has been
> stated, or shall remit the matter to the commissioners with the   E
> opinion of the court thereon, or may make such other order in
> relation to the matter as to the court may seem fit. (7) The High
> Court may cause the case to be sent back for amendment, and
> thereupon the case shall be amended accordingly, and judgment shall
> be delivered after it has been amended."

No question of amendment being involved, we can concentrate on the   F
ambit of subsection (6). Its terminal words are wide, but, even so, the
court ordering remitter is not the final arbiter of the propriety of making
such an order. For, as Lord Buckmaster said in *Foulsham* v. *Pickles*
[1925] A.C. 458, 469:

> " Remission is not a matter of right but of discretion—a discretion
> to be carefully exercised in each case and dependent upon the special   G
> circumstances in which it stands."

So in *Sungei Rinching Rubber Co.* v. *Inland Revenue Commissioners*
(1925) 94 L.J.K.B. 865, 872, Pollock M.R. said:

> " It appears . . . to me impossible to accede to the suggestion of
> the appellants now made that the case ought to go back before the   H
> commissioners to deal with a new contention of the appellants. . . ."

While the court may remit a case to the commissioners for further
findings if these be necessary to determine a point of law raised in the
case (see *Leeming* v. *Jones* [1930] 1 K.B. 279, 284), Lord Denning said
in this House in *Moriarty* v. *Evans Medical Supplies Ltd.* [1958] 1
W.L.R. 66, 88:

A
" The general rule of every appellate court is not to allow a new point to be raised except on a question of law which no evidence could alter: and this applies equally to a case stated under a statute worded like section 64 (6) of the Income Tax Act 1952. . . ."

So it was that in *Lord Vestey's Executors* v. *Inland Revenue Commissioners* [1949] 1 All E.R. 1108, 1117 Lord Simonds observed:

B
" If it is a condition of the taxpayer's liability that certain facts should be proved, nothing is more necessary, nor anything more easy, than that there should be a clear and explicit finding . . . It may be that they are not found because the special commissioners did not feel justified in finding them. Ought the case then to be remitted for further findings? I think not. It was open to the parties, when C the case was settled, to obtain a more explicit statement, if indeed the special commissioners thought that the circumstances warranted it. After this lapse of time . . . I do not think that your Lordships would be justified in remitting the case."

By way of final reference to the authorities, it is well to recall that Pennycuick J. said in *Bradshaw* v. *Blunden* (*No. 2*) (1960) 39 T.C. 73, D 80:

" It is a well-established and salutary rule that the parties to an appeal to the court should not, in the absence of special circumstances, be enabled to go back to the commissioners and call fresh evidence on issues which were raised in the original proceedings and as to which they had full opportunity of calling such evidence E as they might be advised (see *per* Tucker L.J. in the case of *Murphy* v. *Australian Machinery & Investment Co. Ltd.* (1948) 30 T.C. 244, 260)."

I would however, let the Lord President (Clyde) have the last word on the matter of remitter. In *R. A. Bird & Co.* v. *Inland Revenue Commissioners* 1925 S.C. 186, 191 he said:

F
" It is quite plain from the case, and from what parties say, that the appellant did not put before the commissioners any material, other than what is reproduced in the case, bearing on the alleged inadequacy. It seems to me that, if we were to send this case back for further information about this, we might be exposed, in almost any case, to an exactly similar application—whenever, in short, the appellant has not presented his case to the commissioners in a way G which brings out the point he ultimately desires to make before the Court of Appeal. That would never do. No doubt, if there had been a misunderstanding, we should strain a point to put that right; and, if the commissioners had failed to include, or to allude sufficiently to, some topic that was brought before them by way of evidence, we should remit the case in order to have that put right. But . . . it is H impossible to grant the appellant the indulgence which he asks for in the circumstances of this case."

My Lords, in the light of these and similar authorities, it is clear that exercise of the power of remitter provided for in section 56 (6) of the Act of 1970 calls for a cautious approach. I have already indicated that, in my judgment no remitter was here justifiable. But, even had any been called for, I have respectfully to say that it could not properly have given rise to the unrestricted order made by the Court of Appeal

in this case. This left unspecified the point or points upon which it A
desired the commissioners to deliberate; these, it seems, were left to be
somehow divined "in the light of the judgment of [the Court of
Appeal]." And the parties were granted wholly unrestricted liberty to
adduce further evidence, so that they would not have breached the order
even had they called new evidence on new points, and in the result the
commissioners could with strict propriety have embarked upon a virtual
rehearing of the whole case. Learned counsel for the respondent, while B
seeking to uphold the remitter, expressly disclaimed any desire to
implement that part of it which authorised the calling of further evidence.
But that concession need not have been made, for the order, as it stands,
permits not only the raising of entirely new contentions but also the
adducing of evidence in relation to it.

It is not, I think, relevant to hazard that what the Court of Appeal C
principally had in mind was the calling of evidence for the Crown before
the commissioners with a view to establishing that the contingent rights
of Mayville and Ceville in the deposited sums had a realisable value to
them in the year 1973—74. But if this was indeed so, my noble and
learned friend, Lord Russell of Killowen, has rightly pointed out that
the Crown had argued only for an assessment on the basis of 100 per
cent. of the purchase price. Furthermore, they had adopted those tactics D
in the face of evidence called for the taxpayer to the effect that no lesser
value could be placed on those contingent interests in March 1974. The
appellant is therefore entitled to castigate as "improper and unjust"
any liberty extended to the Crown to support the assessment by
substituting new figures.

I would therefore hold that the direction to remit cannot stand. The E
determination of the commissioners should be restored, but the amount
thereof should, for the reasons indicated in the speech of my noble and
learned friend, Viscount Dilhorne, be reduced from £1,095,853 to £1,417,
the latter being the amount of the gain realised in the year of
assessment 1973–74 by Mayville on the sale of the Quarry Farm land.
I would thus allow the appeal and allow the cross-appeal to the extent
already indicated in my speech and that of the noble and learned Lord F
on the Woolsack, and I would award the appellant costs here and in the
two lower courts.

LORD RUSSELL OF KILLOWEN. My Lords, this appeal concerns an
assessment to income tax on Mr. Cecil Mortley Yuill (" the taxpayer ")
on sums said by the Crown to fall to be treated as his income for the
year 1973–74 by virtue of section 488 of the Income and Corporation G
Taxes Act 1970 (" the Act "). Subsection (1) of that section states: " This
section is enacted to prevent the avoidance of tax by persons concerned
with land or the development of land." Stated very briefly it was asserted
by the Crown that on sales of lands in March 1974 to Cecil M. Yuill Ltd.
(" Y Ltd. ") by two Guernsey companies Ceville Ltd. (" C ") and Mayville
Ltd. (" M ") those companies made a capital profit of over £1m., and H
that the taxpayer was liable to income tax on that amount as having—
to use a general phrase—put them in the way of making that profit
having particular regard to subsection (8) of section 488.

On appeal to the general commissioners by the taxpayer the latter
determined the assessment at a slightly downward adjusted figure still of
over £1m. On a case stated Templeman J. upheld the determination of
the commissioners. On appeal the Court of Appeal set aside the decision

A of Templeman J. and the determination of the commissioners (but not the assessment) but remitted the matter to the commissioners for further consideration on two aspects of the matter with leave to call further evidence: [1979] 1 W.L.R. 987.

It is desirable to set out something of the factual background leading to the acquisition by C and M of the lands in England that they sold in March 1974 to Y Ltd.

B The taxpayer was the founder of Y Ltd. which carried on a prosperous business of building land development in north east England. He and the trustees in England of family settlements created by him controlled Y Ltd. of which he was director and chairman, and also an associated company Owton Fens Properties Ltd. (" Properties "). There was another company, Owton Fens Development Ltd. (" Development ") the shares in which were C owned by children of the taxpayer.

The settlements made by the taxpayer were the following: (1) January 1955: 999 £1 ordinary shares in Y Ltd.: English trustees: ordinary trusts for three then infant children: statutory power to appoint new trustees in taxpayer. (2) October 1959: 333 of such shares on a recently born daughter: otherwise as above. (3) March 1962: £100 initially: beneficiaries descendants of taxpayer: trusts more sophisticated: similar power D to appoint new trustees. (4) September 1972: £5,000: beneficiaries descendants of taxpayer: fairly sophisticated trusts: power in trustees by deed to exclude any class of beneficiaries, a power which was exercised on January 21, 1974, by excluding the taxpayer's four children. The trustees were two Guernsey residents, Mr. de Putron and Mr. Bagley. This was the first step taken by the taxpayer in the direction of Guernsey.

E On March 29, 1973, the English trustees of the 1955 settlement retired and the taxpayer appointed in their place Mr. de Putron, a Mr. M. J. Wilson also a Guernsey resident (both chartered accountants) and a Guernsey company Channel Executor and Trustee Co. Ltd. At that time the trust funds were 1499 £1 ordinary shares and 56,943 " A " £1 ordinary shares in Y Ltd. On the same day the same Guernsey trustees F were appointed of the 1959 settlement, of which the trust funds were then 499 £1 ordinary shares and 18,901 " A " £1 ordinary shares in Y Ltd. On the same day the same three Guernsey trustees were appointed in place of the English trustees of the 1962 settlement, of which the trust funds were then 65,493 " A " £1 ordinary shares in Y Ltd. and 100 £1 ordinary shares in Development. Thus by then all the relevant family settlements were in the hands of Guernsey trustees.

G I return to the history of the lands ultimately sold by C and M to Y Ltd. in March 1974, being respectively Owton Fen lands and Quarry Farm land.

Owton Fen lands, in total some 210 acres, had been bought by Y Ltd. in 1958 and 1959 for a total of £40,000. In 1961 Properties was formed with an issued capital of 300 shares: 60 allotted to the taxpayer: 60 to H his wife: and 180 to the trustees of a 1961 family settlement not relevant to this appeal. Y Ltd. in 1961 sold 67 acres of the Owton Fen lands to Properties for £4,050. Properties (having sold elsewhere 19 acres thereof) on December 28, 1972, sold the remaining 48 acres of the Owton Fen lands to C for £40,000: it was these 48 acres that C sold in March 1974 to Y Ltd. for a price of £700,000. C had been formed in Guernsey by the Guernsey trustees of the 1972 (£5,000) family settlement, de Putron and Bagley.

Quarry Farm lands, 108 acres, were agreed to be bought by Y Ltd. in   A
1968 for the price of £1,800 per acre, total £194,400. Completion was
to be in four quarters by March 31, 1972, 1973, 1974 and 1975, in each
case for a payment of £48,600. £5,000 deposit was paid on contract.
Development having been formed, the first quarter was in 1972 on the
direction of Y Ltd. conveyed to Development. M, a Guernsey company,
was then formed by the Guernsey trustees of the 1972 (£5,000) family   B
settlement. On January 30, 1973, Development sold the first quarter
of Quarry Farm lands to M for £81,000. At the same time M bought
from Y Ltd. for £100 the right to buy the other three quarters when
completion (at £48,600 a quarter) became due. At the same time M
orally agreed, subject to conditions, that Y Ltd. (which was after all a
development builder) should have the development contract for the
Quarry land. In the event M on the direction of Y Ltd. acquired the   C
second and third quarters of the Quarry land (from the original vendor to
Y Ltd.) at £48,600 a time in March 1973 and March 1974. It was these
three quarters of the Quarry land that in March 1974 M sold to Y Ltd.
at a price of £648,000, having paid £178,200 in acquiring them.

I move now, my Lords, to the two transactions in March 1974 of sale
to Y Ltd. by C of 48 acres of Owton Fen for £700,000, and by M of   D
three quarters of the Quarry land for £648,000, the capital profits on
which sales, though not taxable in the hands of the Guernsey companies
C and M, are claimed by the Crown to be, under section 488 of the Act,
assessable as income of the taxpayer in 1973–74 on the ground (in broad
terms) that he indirectly procured those capital profits.

By a contract dated March 23, 1974, Y Ltd. agreed to buy and C
agreed to sell 48 acres of land at Owton Fens. The purchase price was   E
stated to be the sum of £700,000 " but subject to reductions provided by
clause 7 hereof and also subject to the deposit by the vendor of part of
the purchase price as provided by clause 8 hereof." The sale was also
expressed to be conditional upon C arranging a loan to Y Ltd. of
£655,000 on a first mortgage of the land such loan to be available on the
date fixed for completion at interest of 10 per cent. per annum. On failure   F
by C to comply with the condition the contract was to be null and void.
Clause 6 provided that: " The sale and purchase shall be completed on
March 25, 1974, when the whole of the purchase money shall be paid.
Time shall be of the essence of the contract." Clause 7 contained undertakings by C to remain in effect notwithstanding completion. One such
undertaking was that C should pay to Y Ltd. £15,000 on July 14, 1974,
£30,000 on January 14, 1975, and £15,000 on July 14, 1975, in partial   G
reimbursement of the interest to be paid by Y Ltd. upon the said loan
during its first year outstanding. The further undertakings by C were
that in the event of nationalisation or compulsory acquisition of the
land within three years C should repay to Y Ltd. £660,000 of the purchase
price of £700,000: that in the event of nationalisation or compulsory
acquisition of the land between three and four years C should repay to   H
Y Ltd. £440,000: that in the event of nationalisation or compulsory
acquisition of the land between four and five years C should repay to
Y Ltd. £220,000. By clause 8, C undertook that as security for its
obligations under clause 7 C would deposit £655,000 (part of the purchase
price of £700,000) with a mutually agreed depository (or one nominated
by C's auditors) accompanied by an irrevocable letter forbidding the
release to C of any part of the sum deposited without the written

A authority of Y Ltd. It was further provided that Y Ltd. would authorise release to C as follows: if no nationalisation etc. by the end of three years—£215,000: if none by the end of four years—a further £220,000: if none by the end of five years—the balance remaining of the deposited £655,000, viz. £230,000. C on the other hand undertook to authorise the depository to release to Y Ltd. sums as follows: if nationalisation etc. within three years—the whole £655,000; if between three and four
B years—£435,000; if between four and five years—£215,000. The other point to be noted is that any interest earned on the deposit was to belong to C.

It appears from an answer on September 8, 1975, to a request for information by the Inland Revenue that the lender to Y Ltd. of £655,000 was Channel Finance Ltd. of Guernsey which was also the depository
C of the £655,000. It is I think to be assumed in the circumstances that at completion the loan and the deposit were simultaneous with payment of the purchase price.

In the result therefore in March 1974 on completion C received in its pocket £45,000, but was unable to get its hands on the £655,000 deposit except in the future and contingently upon the events of nationalisation, etc. If such an event took place in three years the deposit of £655,000
D would never reach C's pocket, and C would additionally have to pay £5,000 to Y Ltd. If the three years passed without such an event C would have £215,000 in its pocket, but the remaining deposit of £440,000 could only be claimed by C contingently and in the future at the expiration of the fourth and fifth years. C however was entitled to the interest earned from time to time by the deposit, though obliged to contribute
E to Y Ltd. a total of some £45,000 over a period to the latter's loan interest obligations. (I do not quite understand what was intended as to the £5,000 balance of the deposit that would have remained had there been nationalisation etc. in the fourth year, or in the fifth year: but I do not think it matters).

Simultaneously with the sale by C to Y Ltd. of the Owton Fen land,
F M sold three quarters of Quarry Farm land to Y Ltd. (completion was on the same day, March 25, 1974, as completion by M of the purchase of the third quarter from the original vendor of Quarry Farm land). The agreement follows the same plan. The price was £648,000. The loan to be arranged for Y Ltd. by M was £445,000. The reimbursements of loan interest were to total £120,000. The deposit was to be £445,000. It is not necessary to spell out the figures for releases to M or Y Ltd. of
G the deposit moneys. The lender and depository was also Channel Finance Ltd. My comments on the outcome of that completion are the same as in the case of the C transaction.

A particular point is to be noticed in this connection. In January 1974 the entire shareholdings in both C and M had been sold by the trustees of the 1972 settlement to another Guernsey company, Valnord
H Ltd., for £200 and £65,000 respectively. Mr. de Putron in evidence said that Valnord was trustee of an overseas trust with overseas beneficiaries who did not include any member of the taxpayer's family. In the light of the fact that within two months the purchases at £700,000 and £648,000 from those two companies took place, the transaction appears strange, and an unfortunate circumstance for the beneficiaries under the 1972 settlement. (It will be recalled that on January 21, 1974, the settlement trustees exercised their power to exclude the taxpayer's children from

all beneficial entitlement under that settlement, and it appears that there   A
were as yet no remote issue in existence). However in my clear opinion
it would be irrelevant for the purposes of the liability of the taxpayer
under section 488 of the Act that profits made by C and M on the
sales in March 1974 would not enure to the benefit of the taxpayer or
any member of his family, and accordingly such mystery as may attend
the sale of the shares in C and M by the 1972 settlement trustees need   B
not be further probed.

    I turn now to the statutory provisions. I have already referred to
subsection (1) of section 488: there can be no doubt that the events
already outlined come within the mischief aimed at, since the profits
of C and M on the March 1974 sales to Y Ltd. are not amenable
to U.K. taxation, they being Guernsey companies. By subsection (2) it is
provided that the section applies: C

    ". . . wherever—(a) land . . . is acquired with the sole or main object
    of realising a gain from disposing of the land . . . and any gain of
    a capital nature is obtained from the disposal of the land—(i) by
    the person acquiring . . . the land . . ."

It is clear that both C and M fall within the description of such a person
so acquiring the lands which they subsequently in March 1974 sold to   D
Y Ltd. It is also clear that over the years which have passed without
nationalisation etc. since then each will have obtained substantial gains
of a capital nature by the disposals, though whether this is so in respect
of the year of the relevant assessment 1973–74 is for later consideration.

    Subsection (3) provides that the whole of such gain (of a capital
nature) shall for all the purposes of the Tax Acts be treated   E

    ". . . (a) as being income which arises when the gain is realised, and
    which constitutes profits or gains chargeable to tax under Case VI
    of Schedule D for the chargeable period in which the gain is realised,
    and (b) subject to the following provisions of this section, as being
    income of the person by whom the gain is realised."

    Thus far it is to be observed that the provisions cannot be operated   F
against C and M since they are Guernsey companies, and that the taxpayer is not yet touched. However subsection (8) is in the following
terms:

    "If . . the gain accruing to any person is derived from . . . an
    opportunity of realising a gain, provided directly or indirectly by
    some other person . . . subsection (3) (b) of this section shall apply   G
    to the gain . . . with the substitution of that other person for the
    person by whom the gain was realised."

    The general commissioners clearly in my opinion concluded, in their
determination upholding (subject to an agreed downward adjustment) the
assessment, that any gains accruing to C and M from their disposal of
the lands to Y Ltd. in 1974 were derived from an opportunity of realising   H
it provided indirectly by the taxpayer. It is true that in paragraph 11 (2)
of the case stated they did not rehearse in its identical terms the language
of subsection (8): they there said:

    "We are satisfied that there was a scheme or arrangement or a
    series of transactions here which enabled 'capital' gains to be made
    by Mayville and Ceville upon the sale of the Owton Fens land and
    Quarry Farm land to Cecil M. Yuill Ltd. and that the appellant

A   [taxpayer], either directly or through his companies, and with the
       help of his Guernsey trustees obtained for those companies the said
       gains which fall within the provisions of section 488 . . . ."

       The Court of Appeal [1979] 1 W.L.R. 987 took the view that this
finding was, in view of the penal nature of subsection (8), not sufficiently
reliable or definite as a finding against the taxpayer thereunder. I do not,
B with respect, agree. It may be that there was some elision in the expressions of the commissioners with subsection (2) (ii) which I have not quoted:
but I cannot think that it is other than a fair and obvious reading of paragraph 11 (2) of the case stated that the commissioners found that subsection
(8) was satisfied in relation to the taxpayer: indeed that was the crux of
the case. On this point the Court of Appeal, being not satisfied that the
finding was sufficiently precise, remitted the matter to the commissioners
C with liberty to call further evidence. I cannot think, in any event, that
this was right: if at all they should have remitted the matter with the
request that the commissioners should state whether on the evidence
already adduced before them they found or did not find that any gain
accruing to C or M on the sales in March 1974 to Y Ltd. derived from
an opportunity of realising the gain provided directly or indirectly by
D the taxpayer. Accordingly I would consider the remittal on this point
unnecessary and erroneous.
       At this stage it is necessary to refer to three points taken on behalf
of the taxpayer in disputing liability.
       First: it was contended that since according to the evidence the
acquisitions of land by C and M were at market value, the section does
not bite. Sale, it was said, at market value is not provision or trans-
E mission of a relevant opportunity. This contention failed, in my opinion
rightly, in both courts below.
       Second: it was contended that the relevant avoidance of tax must
be at the time tax is avoided: here, by March 1974, there was no question
of tax since C and M were Guernsey companies not subject to U.K.
taxation This point is, I think, connected with the point earlier men-
F tioned that no benefit could enure to any member of the taxpayer's
family having regard to the sales to Valnord Ltd. I reject these contentions.
       Third: that if a relevant opportunity was provided to C and M it was
directly provided by Y Ltd. when it enabled M to acquire the Quarry
land (and indeed when it agreed to buy that land in 1974 from M) and
was directly provided by Properties when Properties sold the Owton Fens
G land to C, and indeed by Y Ltd. when Y Ltd. agreed to buy from C.
It was contended that if there was a case of a direct provision of an
opportunity the Crown could not be entitled to pick and choose between
a direct provider and an indirect provider as an administrative choice,
and indeed should be required to plump for the direct provider. Hereunder some reliance was placed on the recent case in this House of
H *Vestey* v. *Inland Revenue Commissioners* [1979] 3 W.L.R. 915. I cannot,
my Lords, accept these contentions, nor the relevance of the very different
case of *Vestey.*
       There remains the crucial question whether in respect of the fiscal
year 1973–74 the assessment was justified, the assessment being based
upon the supposition that *on the completion on March* 25, 1974, C and
M realised gains measured by the difference between what the lands sold
by them to Y Ltd. had cost them (plus expenses in relation to such

Yuill v. Wilson (H.L.(E.)) [1980]

land) and the stated purchase prices of £700,000 and £648,000. This A
depends upon the language of section 488 coupled in my opinion with
the provisions of section 489 (13).

I have already analysed the substance of the outcome of the contracts
for sale (and their completion) in March 1974 by C and M to Y Ltd.
Section 488 (2) speaks of an occasion when a "*gain* of a capital nature
is *obtained* from the disposal of the land . . ." Section 488 (3) requires that B
the *gain* so *obtained* shall be treated as income which arises "*when the
gain is realised*" and for the chargeable period "*in which the gain is
realised*," and as being income of the person "by whom *the gain is
realised.*" Subsection (8) refers in substituting a person such as the
taxpayer also to a person by whom a "*gain was realised.*"

My Lords, I would incline to the view that on the language so far C
used it would in the circumstances be an exaggeration to say that C and
M either obtained or realised on March 25, 1974, a gain calculated by
reference to that part of the purchase price which they were obliged to
deposit, and in respect of which their ability to demand payment—their
entitlement to receive it—was future and contingent. The fact that
while the moneys remain on deposit they were entitled to interest earned
—subject to a contra obligation to reimburse Y Ltd. certain sums for
which Y Ltd. became liable for interest on the loan—does not in my D
opinion alter that fact.

There is in my opinion a further provision in section 489 (13) which
supports the view that the whole difference between cost (and expenses)
and total purchase prices is not attributable to the year 1973–74. That
section is in the following terms:

"For the purposes of the principal sections and this section— E
'capital amount' means any amount, in money or money's worth,
which, apart from the principal sections, does not fall to be included
in any computation of income for purposes of the Tax Acts, and
other expressions including the word 'capital' shall be construed
accordingly, 'company' includes any body corporate, 'share' includes stock, and for the said purposes any amount in money or F
money's worth shall not be regarded as having become receivable
by some person until that person can effectively enjoy or dispose
of it."

It was contended for the Crown that though the principal sections
included section 488, the last part of that subsection had no applicability
to section 488. I do not accept that: it is as if that last part expressly G
said "for the purposes of sections 487, 488, and 489." Applying in
March 1974 the language of that last part to the sums compulsorily
deposited, I do not think C and M could then effectively enjoy or
dispose of them, and that they are not to be regarded as having then
become receivable by them. If that be so, I find it even more difficult
to hold that they then realised a gain in the calculation of which the
deposited sums should figure. H

If that be so, then on the figures of cost and expenses of the lands,
compared with such parts of the total purchase price as was not required
to be deposited, no capital gain by C and little by M emerges in the
year 1973–74.

The Court of Appeal, however, remitted the case to the commissioners,
with power to call further evidence, with a view to enabling the Crown
to establish if it could that the future and contingent rights of C and M

A in the deposited sums had a realisable value to C and M in March 1974. Before the commissioners the Crown had argued only for 100 per cent. of the purchase price. The Crown made no attempt to adduce evidence in support of some intermediate figure: and evidence was led for the taxpayer to suggest that no such intermediate value could be placed on those future and contingent interests in March 1974. In those circum-
B stances it was in my opinion wrong to remit the case on this point to the commissioners and oppressive of the taxpayer to enable the Crown to reopen an alternative approach on new evidence after deliberately declining to put forward that approach.

I must mention two final points suggested by the Crown. The first was that cost and expenses of the lands should be apportioned to the various "instalments" and not brought wholly into the calculation of
C the gains (if any) resulting from what was paid and not deposited: I cannot accept that as a correct method of assessment for 1973–74: in that year non constat that any part of the deposits would ever reach C and M: in that event the taxpayer would have been liable in respect of 1973–74 though no capital gain might be made by C and M, without there being any provision for reclaim by him. The other point made was
D that by the time the case reached this House the full period of five years had run without nationalisation, etc., and valuation or prophesy was no longer needed. But in my opinion that cannot affect the situation on the taxpayer's liability which fell to be assessed in the year of assessment.

On the figures submitted for the appellant the C transaction showed a loss for 1973–74 of £5,564 and the M transaction showed a gain for 1973–74 of £1,417. It was suggested for the taxpayer that by amalgama-
E tion of these the assessment on the taxpayer should be nil. In my opinion the language of section 488 subsections (3) and (8) does not permit such amalgamation, and the figure of £1,417 is the correct basis of assessment on the taxpayer in respect of the year 1973–74. I imagine that in the long run it will make little difference.

Accordingly, in my opinion the appeal should be allowed and the cross-
F appeal dealt with on that basis. In some respects I have expressed disagreement with points put forward for the taxpayer, but that should not deprive him of his costs here and in the Court of Appeal and before Templeman J.

LORD KEITH OF KINKEL. My Lords, the facts of this case and the
G circumstances under which it comes before your Lordships' House have been fully stated by my noble and learned friend, Viscount Dilhorne, and I need not rehearse them.

The first main point in the appeal is concerned with the significance of the finding which, in paragraph 11 (2) of the case stated, the commissioners made in these terms:

H   "We are satisfied that there was a scheme or arrangement or a series of transactions here which enabled 'capital' gains to be made by Mayville and Ceville upon the sale of the Owton Fens land and Quarry Farm land to Cecil M. Yuill Ltd. and that the appellant, either directly or through his companies, and with the help of his Guernsey trustees obtained for those companies the said gains which fall within the provisions of section 488 of the Income and Corporation Taxes Act 1970."

The question is whether this finding is relevant and sufficiently specific A
for the purpose of attracting the application to the appellant of section
488 (8) of the Act of 1970, which provides:

"If . . . the gain accruing to any person is derived from value, or
an opportunity of realising a gain, provided directly or indirectly by
some other person, . . . subsection (3) (b) of this section shall apply
to the gain . . . with the substitution of that other person for the B
person by whom the gain was realised."

It is true that there can be discerned in the commissioners' finding an
echo of the language of subsection (2) (ii), which refers to the situation
where an arrangement or scheme is effected as respects land which enables
a gain to be realised by any series of transactions by any person who is
a party to the arrangement or scheme, and of the concluding words of the C
same subsection, to the effect that it is to apply whether any such person
obtains the gain for himself or for any other person. These provisions
would not, having regard to the terms of subsection (3), suffice in
themselves to fix the appellant with liability to tax. The application of
subsection (8) is essential for that purpose. But the contentions for the
revenue, as set out in the case stated, make it clear that reliance was
placed on subsection (8). There can be no question of the commissioners D
having overlooked subsection (8), and in all the circumstances I am of
opinion that the passage which I have quoted from paragraph 11 (2) of
the case stated, read along with their findings of primary fact, necessarily
implies a finding that the appellant provided Mayville and Ceville with
the opportunity of realising the gains in question, such as to attract
application of subsection (8). E
The Court of Appeal [1979] 1 W.L.R. 987, taking the view that the
finding was not sufficiently specific, remitted the case to the commissioners
for the purpose, inter alia of their supplementing the finding, with leave to
hear further evidence. In my opinion the remittal for this purpose was
unnecessary, and it was in any event inappropriate that the commissioners
should be authorised to hear further evidence.
The second main point in the appeal in concerned with the extent, if F
any, to which Mayville and Ceville realised gains upon the completion, on
March 25, 1974, of the transactions whereby they disposed of the lands
to Cecil M. Yuill Ltd. The answer to this point turns upon the proper
construction of section 488 (3), which in my opinion is to be arrived at in
the light of section 489 (13).
Section 488 (3), which is the charging provision is in these terms: G

"Where this section applies, the whole of any such gain shall for
all the purposes of the Tax Acts be treated—(a) as being income
which arises when the gain is realised, and which constitutes profits
or gains chargeable to tax under Case VI of Schedule D for the
chargeable period in which the gain is realised, and (b) subject to
the following provisions of this section, as being income of the H
person by whom the gain is realised."

Section 489 (13), so far as relevant, provides:

"For the purposes of the principal sections [sc. sections 487 and 488]
and this section . . . any amount in money or money's worth shall
not be regarded as having become receivable by some person until
that person can effectively enjoy or dispose of it."

A   I think there can be no doubt that some content for that provision of section 489 (13) must be capable of being found in section 488, and that its application is not, as was contended for the Revenue, confined to section 487. In my opinion such content is to be found in the references, in subsection (3) of section 488 and also elsewhere therein, to a gain being realised. No gain can realised until some consideration in money or money's worth has at least become receivable. Further, it is to be observed
B   that section 489 (8) gives a right of relief, where a person is assessed to tax under either section 487 or section 488 in respect of " consideration receivable " by another person, against that other person. So far as section 488 is concerned, the relevant liability must be that imposed by subsection (8). So it is clearly contemplated that a gain realised by another person, under such circumstances as to attract the application
C   of subsection (8), involves a consideration having " become receivable " by that other person in the sense of section 489 (13).

          When the contracts for the sale of the lands were completed in March 1974, Ceville received immediately the sum of £45,000 and Mayville that of £203,000. In each case the balance of the purchase price was tied up under the provisions of the contracts which have been fully set out by my
D   noble and learned friend, Viscount Dilhorne, and there was no question of either Mayville or Ceville becoming entitled to receive any further sums in the tax year 1973–74, with which alone this appeal is concerned. In the circumstances I am of opinion that neither Mayville nor Ceville was able during that year effectively to enjoy or dispose of the balance of the purchase price of the lands respectively sold by them. It follows that in
E   neither case is such balance to be taken into computation for the purpose of ascertaining the amount of any gain realised in that year on disposal of the lands. I have not overlooked that Mayville and Ceville were entitled to interest on the sums deposited by them until such time as they might be released. In my opinion that circumstance did not give them effective enjoyment of the deposits, and they certainly could not
F   dispose of them.

          It was argued for the revenue that Mayville's and Ceville's contingent future rights to receive the deposits should be valued and the resultant figures added to the sums which they actually received in 1973–74. No such contention was advanced before the commissioners, and the revenue led no evidence of such value. There was some evidence from the
G   appellant's side that no such valuation could be satisfactorily made. The Court of Appeal took the view that the revenue were entitled to a finding of fact upon this matter, and it appears that one of the purposes of the remittal ordered to be made was to enable such a finding to be arrived at, in the light, if need be, of further evidence.

          In my opinion the remittal for that purpose was misconceived, and it
H   was not at all proper that the revenue should be given the opportunity of opening up a fresh hearing before the commissioners, and leading new evidence upon, a point which they had not taken at the original hearing. There is ample authority, to which my noble and learned friend, Lord Edmund-Davies, has drawn attention, against the propriety of such a course

          Upon all the other points argued in the appeal I am in full agreement with the views expressed by my noble and learned friend, Viscount

The Weekly Law Reports, August 8, 1980

932

Lord Keith
of Kinkel

Yuill v. Wilson (H.L.(E.))

[1980]

Dilhorne. I would accordingly concur in the allowance of the appeal and A
in the making of an order on the cross-appeal in the terms which he has
proposed.

Appeal allowed.
Determination varied.

Solicitors: *Sinclair, Roche & Temperley for Tilly, Bailey & Irvine,*
Hartlepool; Solicitor of Inland Revenue. B

F. C.

C

[COURT OF APPEAL]

* EALING LONDON BOROUGH COUNCIL v.
EL ISAAC AND ANOTHER

1980 March 18, 19   Megaw and Templeman L.JJ. and
Sir Patrick Browne D

Interest—County court judgment—Jurisdiction to award interest—
Claim by council for repayment of improvement grant—Judg-
ment for sum claimed plus interest up to date of judgment
—Amount to be paid by instalments—Statute providing for
interest to be paid up to date of repayment—Whether doctrine
of merger applicable—Housing Act 1969 (c. 33), s. 6 (4) [1]
Law Reform — Whether necessary — County court — Interest on E
judgments

A borough council which had paid the defendants two
instalments of a housing improvement grant under Part I of
the Housing Act 1969 demanded repayment of the money
because the work was not completed within the specified time.
The defendants failed to pay whereupon the council brought
proceedings in the county court. The registrar struck out the F
defence, which alleged that the defendants had paid money to
a builder who had failed to carry out the work, and gave
judgment for the council for the sum claimed plus interest
up to the date of judgment (at the rate prescribed by section
171 of the Local Government Act 1972) and costs, amounting
in all to £1,158·54. He directed that the defendants should
execute a legal charge on their house in favour of the council
but ordered that the charge should not be enforced while the
defendants paid £20 a month. He rejected a submission made G
on behalf of the council that under section 6 (4) of the Act
of 1969 [1] interest should continue up to the actual date of
repayment of the sum outstanding. The council appealed but
Judge Bernard Lewis drew attention to the long-established
rule that interest was not payable on county court judgments,
held that the interest to which the council were entitled
merged in the judgment, and dismissed the appeal. H

[1] Housing Act 1969, s. 6: " (4) If an instalment of an improvement grant is
paid before the completion of the works and the works are not completed within
the time specified in subsection (5) of this section [12 months from the date on which
the instalment is paid or such further time as the local authority may allow] that
instalment and any further sums paid by the local authority as part of the grant
shall, on being demanded by the local authority, forthwith become repayable to them
by the person to whom the instalment was paid and shall carry interest at such rate
as may be prescribed from the date on which it was paid by the local authority until
repayment."

A   On appeal by the council:—

Held, allowing the appeal, that the doctrine of merger only applied to contracts and covenants and could not be allowed to contradict a statute; that the council were entitled to interest up to the actual date of repayment by virtue of the express provisions of section 6 (4) of the Housing Act 1969 and it was the duty of the Court of Appeal and of the county court to order the defendants to pay that which the statute
B   required them to pay; accordingly the case would be remitted to the county court for determination of the effect of the court's order on the order of the registrar (post, pp. 937H—938B, 939A–B).

In re Sneyd, Ex parte Fewings (1883) 25 Ch.D. 338, C.A. 3 distinguished.

Economic Life Assurance Society v. Usborne [1902] A.C. 147, H.L.(E.) considered.

C   Per curiam. The question whether and in what circumstances interest should be payable on county court judgments requires urgent consideration by Parliament or the Law Commission or both (post, pp. 938C–E, 939A–B, E–F).

Reg. v. Essex County Court Judge (1887) 18 Q.B.D. 704, C.A. considered.

D   The following cases are referred to in the judgments:

Economic Life Assurance Society v. Usborne [1902] A.C. 147, H.L.(E.).
K. v. K. (Divorce Costs: Interest) [1977] Fam. 39; [1977] 2 W.L.R. 55; [1977] 1 All E.R. 576, C.A.
Reg. v. Essex County Court Judge (1887) 18 Q.B.D. 704, C.A.
Sewing Machine Rentals Ltd. v. Wilson [1976] 1 W.L.R. 37; [1975] 3 All E.R. 553, C.A.
E   Sneyd, In re, Ex parte Fewings (1883) 25 Ch.D. 338, C.A.

The following additional case was cited in argument:
Berkeley v. Elderkin (1853) 1 E. & B. 805.

APPEAL from Judge Bernard Lewis sitting at Brentford County Court.

In July 1978 the Ealing London Borough Council issued a summons
F   in the Brentford County Court claiming from the defendants, Taha De Al Muhammed El Isaac and his wife, Amina Josephine El Isaac, the sum of £675, being two instalments of a £1,000 improvement grant paid to them pursuant to the Housing Act 1969, the Act in force at the relevant time, and interest up to the date of judgment, calculated in accordance with section 171 of the Local Government Act 1972, and costs.

G   By their particulars of claim the council stated that they had approved an application dated June 11, 1973, for an improvement grant for works to property situate at 74 Carr Road, Northolt in the London Borough of Ealing subject to the condition, inter alia, that the grant would be paid subject to the specified works being completed to the satisfaction of the council within 12 months or such further time as the council might allow. Two interim payments were made, £315 on July 10, 1974, and
H   £360 on January 7, 1975. The work was not completed within the specified time, which had been extended by three months to March 16, 1975, and the council claimed that they were entitled to recover the interim payments of the grant together with interest thereon pursuant to section 6 (4) of the Housing Act 1969 and paragraph 7 (1) of Schedule 14 to the Housing Act 1974.

The defendants delivered a defence in which they alleged that they had given money to builders who had refused to carry out the work or

to refund the money and they counterclaimed for the balance of the   A
£1,000.

On January 21, 1979, Mr. Registrar Rees ordered that the defence and
counterclaim be struck out. He entered judgment for the council on the
claim and counterclaim and adjourned the assessment of interest until
March 1. On that date he ordered that there be judgment for the council for £675 plus £412·54 interest and £71 costs making a total of £1,158·54.
He further ordered that the defendants should execute a legal charge in   B
favour of the council on the property to secure the payment, the charge
to contain a covenant that the council would not enforce the charge while
the defendants paid the £1,158·54 by instalments of £20 a month beginning
on April 1, 1979, or such higher order as the court might substitute on
application by either party. He rejected a submission put forward on
behalf of the council that under section 6 (4) of the Housing Act 1969   C
interest should be awarded up to the date of repayment of the sum outstanding. He had assessed the interest up to the date of judgment.

The council appealed to the judge on the grounds that the registrar
was wrong in law in deciding that the interest payable by virtue of the
statute terminated on the entry of judgment. On February 12, 1980,
Judge Bernard Lewis dismissed the council's appeal.

The council appealed on the grounds (1) that the judge had misdirected   D
himself in holding that upon the proper construction of section 6 (4) of
the Act of 1969 the interest expressed therein should cease upon judgment
of the court on the debt and that the true construction was that interest
should continue until such time as repayment was made whensoever that
might be; (2) that the judge was wrong to apply the exclusion of section
17 of the Judgments Act 1838 as found in *Reg.* v. *Essex County Court*   E
Judge (1887) 18 Q.B.D. 704 to the council's claim to interest.

In a note for the Court of Appeal Judge Bernard Lewis said that the
solicitor for the council had invited him to give effect to what he submitted was the only interpretation capable of being applied to the relevant section of the Act. His attention had not been drawn to the decision
referred to in the notice of appeal or any other decision. He had drawn
the solicitor's attention to the long-established rule that, subject only to   F
certain specific exceptions, county court judgments could not provide
for interest after the date of the judgment (*Sewing Machine Rentals
Ltd.* v. *Wilson* [1976] 1 W.L.R. 37). He had taken the view that the
undoubted rights of the council as to repayment of the grant and the
accumulated interest to the date of the judgment merged in the judgment,
but did not prevent the council from recovering further interest in the   G
case of non-payment of the judgment debt by a further claim for subsequent interest. The question appeared to him to be, not the council's
ability to recover interest until the date of repayment, but the limits of
the county court's jurisdiction.

Further facts are stated in the judgment of Templeman L.J.

Patrick Clarkson for the council.   H
Robin Campbell for the defendants.

MEGAW L.J. I shall ask Templeman L.J. to deliver the first judgment.

TEMPLEMAN L.J. This is an appeal from a decision of Judge Bernard
Lewis given in the Brentford County Court on April 25, 1979. The
question is whether the judge had power to order payment by the defen-

A dants to the council of interest after the date of the judgment on an improvement grant which had become repayable by the defendants to the council.

On December 17, 1973, the council sanctioned a grant of £1,000, under Part I of the Housing Act 1969, for works to be carried out at 74, Carr Road, Northolt, subject to the works being carried out to the satisfaction of the council within 12 months or such further time as the council might B allow. On July 10, 1974, the council made an interim payment of £315 to the defendants, that sum being part of the £1,000 grant; and on January 7, 1975, they made a further interim payment of £360, so that the defendants received £675 in all. The period for completion of the works was extended to March 16, 1975, but the defendants failed to complete the works to the satisfaction of the council. So the balance C outstanding of the £1,000 grant was not paid.

By section 6 (4) of the Housing Act 1969, which applied to this grant:

" If an instalment of an improvement grant is paid before the completion of the works and the works are not completed within the time specified . . . , that instalment and any further sums paid by the local authority as part of the grant shall, on being demanded by the local D authority, forthwith become repayable to them by the person to whom the instalment was paid and shall carry interest at such rate as may be prescribed from the date on which it was paid by the local authority until repayment."

The council demanded repayment under that subsection and, failing to get it, issued particulars of claim in the Brentford County Court dated July 14, 1978. By those particulars the council claimed the sum of £675 and E interest up to July 14, 1978, and thereafter to judgment. It is common ground that, by virtue of section 171 of the Local Government Act 1972 and determinations of the Treasury applicable thereunder, the rate of interest payable in respect of the first interim payment of £315 is 14¾ per cent. per annum running from July 10, 1974; and in respect of the second interim payment of £360 the rate of interest is 14½ per cent. per annum F running from January 15, 1975.

The defendants served a defence and counterclaim pleading that they had been let down by builders, who had taken the money but not completed the work. Whether this be so or not, and councils and householders usually require some substantial progress before making interim payments, there was no effective defence to the council's claim.

G Accordingly, on January 25, 1979, the registrar of the court struck out the defence and counterclaim and gave judgment for the council for principal and interest to be assessed. On March 1, 1979, the registrar calculated and awarded interest to the council down to the date of judgment. He gave judgment for the principal sum of £675, for interest which he calculated at £412·54, and for costs which he had assessed on scale four at £71: so that the total judgment was for £1,158·54. At the H same time the registrar ordered the defendants to execute a legal charge in favour of the council on the property to secure the payment, and he directed that the charge was to contain a covenant that the council would not enforce the charge while the defendants paid the sum of £1,158·54 by instalments of £20 per month, commencing on April 1, 1979, or such higher order as the court might substitute on application of either party. At the hearing before the registrar the solicitor who appeared for the council argued that the order should provide for interest to continue to

run and to be payable for the period between the date of the judgment   A
and the date of the actual payment on so much of the two sums amounting to £675 as should, from time to time, be outstanding.   The defendants
appeared in person and we do not know what part they played in the
argument, but at any rate the matter was argued.   The registrar rejected
the council's submissions and the council appealed to the judge.

On April 25, 1979, the solicitor appeared for the council; the defen-   B
dants were not represented and did not appear.   There was full argument
on the council's submission that interest was still running and ought to
be made payable from the date of the judgment on the principal sum.
The judge rejected that submission and dismissed the council's appeal.
From his decision the appeal to this court is brought.

The first point taken by Mr. Campbell on behalf of the defendants in
this court is that the particulars of claim did not seek interest beyond the   C
date of the judgment.   It appears, however, that the dispute before the
registrar on March 1, 1979, and before the judge on April 25, 1979,
involved the question whether or not interest was payable after judgment
and that, before this appeal, no one had raised an objection based on the
state of the pleadings, that an amendment (if sought) must have been
granted and that the defendants have not been prejudiced.   That being   D
so, we proceeded to consider the appeal on its merits and as though the
particulars had claimed interest on the principal sum between judgment
and actual repayment.

The claim by the council is within the financial jurisdiction of the
county court, because, as is conceded, in considering whether the financial
limits of that court are exceeded, the amount of interest must be
disregarded.   E

Mr. Campbell then submitted, as the judge had held: first, that the
right of the council to repayment of principal and interest merged in the
judgment, so that no interest is payable after the judgment; and secondly,
that no interest is payable on a county court judgment.

In view of the fact that the registrar, in effect, debarred the council
from recovering save by instalments of £20 per month if such instalments   F
are paid, the defendants will, if Mr. Campbell is correct, have the benefit
of paying the principal sum, accrued interest and costs over a period of
roughly five years, interest-free.   So far as the principal sum is concerned,
this is a surprising result, in view of the terms of section 6 (4) of the
Housing Act 1969, and puts the defendants in a much better position
than if they had in fact raised the money from a building society on
mortgage.   G

The argument as to merger is derived from the decision of this court
in *In re Sneyd, Ex parte Fewings* (1883) 25 Ch.D. 338.   In that case
there was a covenant in a mortgage deed to pay interest on the principal
sum, or so much thereof as should, for the time being, remain unpaid, at
5 per cent.   The mortgagee recovered judgment on the covenant for the
principal sum and interest in arrear and it was held that, the covenant   H
being merged in the judgment, the mortgagee was, as from the date of
the judgment, entitled only to interest on the judgment debt at the rate
of 4 per cent. and was not entitled on the covenant to interest at the rate
of 5 per cent. on the principal sum, which the mortgagor had covenanted
to pay in the mortgage deed.

The Court of Appeal were unanimous as to the result and I cite the
passage from Lindley L.J., where he said, at p. 353:

A   " That is a question of some importance, and it turns on the construction of the covenant. The use of the word ' unpaid ' in the covenant is relied upon. The covenant is to pay 5 per cent. so long as the principal or any part thereof shall remain unpaid. The question is what does ' unpaid ' mean? It cannot mean exclusively payment in cash. Nobody would pretend that, if the debt was satisfied in any other way than by payment in cash, the interest at 5 per cent.

B would still run on. I take it that the true construction is that, so long as the debt is due under the covenant, interest at 5 per cent. shall run. Now it may be technical, but it is well settled, that, if there is a debt secured by a covenant, and judgment is recovered on the covenant, the debt on the covenant merges in the judgment debt. In point of law the £2,200 "—that is the principal sum—" is no longer

C payable under the covenant, it is payable under the judgment; the covenant to pay interest is gone, and the judgment debt bears interest only at 4 per cent. It is said that the effect of this will be to vary the contract between the parties. I think it may vary the contract, but it must be borne in mind that the creditor who obtains a judgment for principal and interest gets compound interest; his judgment carries interest at 4 per cent. upon the arrears of interest, as well as

D upon the principal."

I do not for myself understand how a debt payable with interest until actual repayment can be merged in a judgment without interest or with a different rate of interest payable thereafter. The merger doctrine, which was upheld by this court in *In re Sneyd*, may be due to the fact that, in former ages, high rates of interest marked the progress of the individual

E on the path to perdition; whereas, in this day and age, high interest rates mark the road towards national prosperity.

Merger does not apply where there is an independent covenant, nor does it apply to a security as distinct from a contract. That appears from *Economic Life Assurance Society* v. *Usborne* [1902] A.C. 147. There again there was a mortgage with a covenant to pay interest half-yearly

F on so much of the principal as should remain unpaid. The mortgagors defaulted and the mortgagees recovered judgment against them for principal and interest. It was held:

"that though the personal remedy on a covenant to pay a debt merges in a judgment and a judgment carries only 4 per cent. interest yet upon the true construction of this mortgage deed the mortgagees

G were entitled to retain their security until they were paid the principal sum and interest at 5 per cent."

Lord Davey, referring to preceding authorities, says at p. 152 that the question to be considered is " whether the covenant for the payment of the interest was an independent covenant or a covenant which was merely ancillary to the payment of the principal money;" and the conclusion is

H that it is " an independent covenant which is not merged in or extinguished by the judgment obtained upon the principal covenant."

It appears, therefore, that merger has a very restricted operation. It does not, as appears from the 1902 case which I have just cited, apply to a security. It does not apply to what is said to be an independent covenant and in most mortgages and deeds of borrowing these days care is taken to make the covenant an independent covenant. So that, in practice, the number of times on which interest ceases to run from a date of judgment is very small. But on principle and on the authorities, it seems to A me, the merger doctrine only applies to contracts and covenants.

In my judgment, that doctrine of merger cannot be allowed to contradict statute. Section 6 (4) of the Housing Act 1969 provides plainly for the payment of interest on any instalments or other sums constituting the whole or part of an improvement grant, if it becomes repayable, such interest to be paid until repayment. In these circumstances, it seems to me that it is the duty of this court, and of the county court, to order the B defendants to pay that which the statute plainly requires the defendants to pay in the particular instance.

In these circumstances, it is unnecessary to decide the alternative submission made on behalf of the council, that interest is payable on county court judgments notwithstanding the decision of this court (now some 93 years ago) in *Reg.* v. *Essex County Court Judge* (1887) 18 Q.B.D. C 704, which decided that a county court judgment debt does not carry interest under section 17 of the Judgments Act 1838 (1 & 2 Vict. c. 110). I support, however, the suggestion made by Stephenson L.J. in *K.* v. *K.* (*Divorce Costs: Interest*) [1977] Fam. 39, 57. Stephenson L.J. expressed the hope that Parliament might find time to consider replacing sections 17 and 18 of the Judgments Act 1838 by legislation which would make interest D on judgment debts and costs, beyond doubt, a matter to be regulated by Rules of the Supreme Court and providing for interest on judgment debts and costs in the county court. This suggestion, or a similar suggestion, has also been made by Megaw L.J. There are, of course, many cases, which would require consideration either by the Law Commission or Parliament, or both, in which it is unfair to a plaintiff to deprive him of interest on a county court judgment, and there are other cases, particu- E larly small cases, in which the costs and burden of awarding, assessing and collecting interest would be too great to warrant the infliction of an order which carries interest.

In the present case, I am satisfied that the council are entitled to the interest by virtue of the express provisions of the Housing Act 1969. I would allow the appeal and refer the case back to the county court to F determine the amounts payable. There is no difficulty in calculating the amount of interest which is accruing every day since the judgment until repayment, so that the defendants and the bailiff may know how much is owing on any particular day. The High Court, and the county court for that matter, make similar orders in mortgage actions as a matter of course, for every standard mortgage contains a covenant in a form which negatives merger. There is also no difficulty, if the county court thinks G fit, in providing for payment by equal periodical instalments of capital and interest over a specified period of years, whether five years or any other period of years. Every repayment building society mortgage contains provisions and a specified amount for the repayment of capital and interest over a particular period. If that is desired, the order in the present case can be calculated and completed accordingly: indeed, with more H certainty than the ordinary building society mortgage, because in this case the appropriate rates of interest have been fixed by the statute and the Treasury once and for all and cannot be altered.

Accordingly, I would allow the appeal and remit the case to the county court for determination of the exact effect of this order on the terms of the order made by the registrar.

A   SIR PATRICK BROWNE. I agree that this appeal should be allowed, for
the reasons given by Templeman L.J. and that the court should make
the order which he has proposed. I agree so entirely with his reasons
that I do not find anything I can usefully add.

MEGAW L.J. I also agree with the order proposed by Templeman L.J.,
for the reasons given by him, with which I wholly agree.

B   There are two matters on which I wish to add short observations.
First, the court took the point, in the course of submissions to us on
behalf of the council, whether the particulars of claim in this case,
remaining unamended, were so framed as to warrant the consideration
by the court of the question of the payment of interest subsequent to the
date of judgment. It may well be that the submission made on behalf

C   of the council was right, that there was no need for the particulars of
claims to include specifically in the prayer a specific claim for such interest.
I observe also that in the body of the particulars of claim there is a reference, in paragraph 13, to the provisions of section 6 (4) of the Housing
Act 1969 in relation to interest. However that may be, I also agree entirely with Templeman L.J.'s view that it would not be of the slightest
practical benefit to the defendants in this case if the court had felt obliged

D   to hold that, technically, the pleadings of the plaintiffs were defective,
because in the end the result would, inevitably, have been the same, with
additional costs incurred.

The other matter on which I wish to add my observations is in relation to the submission that was presented to us that the decision of this
court in Reg. v. Essex County Court Judge, 18 Q.B.D. 704 is no longer

E   good law. As at present advised, I do not think that is so, but that is
not a concluded view. However that may be, I am convinced that, if it
be desirable in the circumstances that exist today that interest should be
payable on county court judgments, that is a matter which would require
to be dealt with by Parliament, in order to make sure that the provisions
in relation to the payment of such interest, if it were thought right that
that should be introduced, should be properly adjusted to the particular

F   circumstances which exist in relation to county court judgments. I
repeat what I said in this regard in Sewing Machines Rentals Ltd. v.
Wilson [1976] 1 W.L.R. 37, 43H. This question requires urgent consideration by those who are responsible for such matters.

                              Appeal allowed with costs.
G   Order for costs not to be enforced
                                 without leave of court.
                              Case remitted to county court for
                                 determination of effect of Court of
                                 Appeal's order on order made by
                                 registrar.
                              Liberty to apply to Court of Appeal.
H   Leave to appeal refused.
                              Legal aid taxation of defendants' costs.

    Solicitors: N. L. Green, Chief Solicitor, Ealing London Borough
Council; Camerons, South Harrow.

                                                        E. M. W.

A

[CHANCERY DIVISION]

* ANG v. PARRISH (INSPECTOR OF TAXES)

1980 Feb. 20;
March 7   Walton J.

B

Revenue—Income tax—Settlement—Annual payments to parents
under deeds of covenant—Payments made out of covenantor's
earned income—Whether investment income chargeable to tax
at additional rates—Income and Corporation Taxes Act 1970
(c. 10), ss. 454 (1) (3), 457 (as amended by Finance Act 1971
(c. 68), Sch. 6, para. 67)

During the fiscal year ending April 5, 1975, the taxpayer and   C
his wife's earned income amounted to £6,504. He had also
received investment income from a building society of £46
(net £31). In that year he and his wife executed two deeds
whereby they covenanted to make annual payments totalling
£2,200 in favour of their parents who lived in Singapore. He
was assessed to income tax for the year 1974–75 in respect of
settlement income and building society interest in the sum of
£2,215. On appeal against the assessment the general com-   D
missioners rejected the taxpayer's argument that as the sums
of £2,200 were paid out of his earned income, section 457 of
the Income and Corporation Taxes Act 1970 [1] should not be
construed in such a way as to make those payments bear tax
on the basis of their being the investment income of the
taxpayer.
On appeal by the taxpayer:—   E
Held, dismissing the appeal, that by virtue of section 454
(3) of the Act the payments made under the deeds of
covenant were " income arising under a settlement " falling
within the definition of " investment income "; that section 457
required that the taxpayer's earned income be reduced by the
amount of the payments and then those payments to be added
back so as to ascertain the amount of the total income for
the purposes of computing the taxpayer's liability to tax at   F
the rate appertaining to settlement income (post, pp. 943A–C,
946C–E).
Inland Revenue Commissioners v. Coathew Investments
Ltd. [1966] 1 W.L.R. 716, H.L.(E.) considered.

The following cases are referred to in the judgment:

Allchin v. South Shields Corporation [1943] 2 K.B. 228, C.A.; [1943]   G
A.C. 607; [1943] 2 All E.R. 352; 25 T.C. 445, H.L.(E.).
Inland Revenue Commissioners v. Coathew Investments Ltd. [1966]
1 W.L.R. 716; [1966] 1 All E.R. 1032; 43 T.C. 301, H.L.(E.).
Inland Revenue Commissioners v. Frere [1965] A.C. 402; [1964] 3 W.L.R.
1193; [1964] 3 All E.R. 796; 42 T.C. 125, H.L.(E.).

The following additional cases were cited in argument: H

Bingham v. Inland Revenue Commissioners [1956] Ch. 95; [1955] 3 W.L.R.
663; [1955] 3 All E.R. 321; 36 T.C. 254.
Cape Brandy Syndicate v. Inland Revenue Commissioners [1921] 2 K.B.
403; 12 T.C. 358, C.A.

[1] Income and Corporation Taxes Act 1970, s. 454: see post, p. 942A.
S. 457: see post, p. 942B–C.

A   CASE STATED by the Commissioners for the General Purposes of the
Income Tax for the Division of Uxbridge.

During the fiscal year 1974–75 the taxpayer, Victor Ang, and his wife
had earned income of £4,536 and £1,968 respectively. They also had net
investment income of £31. Under two deeds of covenant made during
that year they paid to their parents in Singapore the sums of £1,000 and
£1,200 repectively. The taxpayer appealed against an assessment to
B   income tax in respect of settlement income and building society interest
for 1974–75 in the sum of £2,215 on the ground that the covenanted
sums should not be regarded as " investment income " for the purposes
of section 32 of the Finance Act 1971 chargeable to tax at the additional
rates. The commissioners dismissed the appeal, holding that the payments
" were investment income and were liable at additional rates of income
C   tax under section 32 (1) of the Finance Act 1971."

The taxpayer appealed.

The facts are set out in the judgment.

Andrew Thornhill for the taxpayer.
Peter Gibson for the Crown.

D   *Cur. adv. vult.*

March 7. WALTON J. read the following judgment. This case raises
a very curious point, well set out in the second paragraph of the case
stated by the general commissioners for the division of Uxbridge. It
reads:

E   " The issue before the commissioners was whether the sums of £2,200
paid in the said year under two deeds of covenant dated October 1,
1974, and December 1, 1974, made by the appellant and his wife in
favour respectively of the parents of the wife of the appellant, who
were resident in Singapore, and in favour of the appellant's parents,
also resident in Singapore (to which the provisions of section 457
of the Income and Corporation Taxes Act 1970 applied), was ' invest-
F   ment income ' for the purposes of section 32 of the Finance Act 1971
and thus chargeable to tax at additional rates on the appellant under
that section."

The case arises because of the distinction, for the purposes of income
tax, between " investment income " and other kinds of income. " Investment income " is defined as " any income other than earned income ":
G   section 32 (3) of the Finance Act 1971. Income arising under a " settlement " is not earned income: section 530 (1) of the Income and Corporation Taxes Act 1970. Investment income is subject to a surcharge over
the ordinary rates of tax if it is in excess of a certain figure, and it was
agreed between the parties in the present case that if the £2,200 in question
is properly to be described as " investment income " then the assessment
H   was a valid one. The whole question is whether what started out as part
of the taxpayer's earned income was, for tax purposes, transmuted into
investment income by the provisions of section 457 of the Income and
Corporation Taxes Act 1970. Section 457 is to be found in Chapter IV
of Part XVI of the Income and Corporation Taxes Act 1970 and it is
provided by section 459 (1), which forms part of the same Chapter, that
therein " income arising under a settlement," " settlement " and " settlor "
have the meanings assigned to them for the purposes of Chapter III by

A

section 454. Subsection (3) of that section defines " settlement " as including any disposition, trust or covenant; and " settlor " as the person by whom the settlement was made. " Income arising under a settlement " is defined by section 454 (1) (a):

B

" any income chargeable to income tax by deduction or otherwise, and any income which would have been so chargeable if it had been received in the United Kingdom by a person domiciled, resident and ordinarily resident in the United Kingdom."

Section 457 (as amended) then provides:

" (1) Where, during the life of the settlor, income arising under a settlement made on or after April 7, 1965, is, under the settlement and in the events that occur, payable to or applicable for the benefit of any person other than the settlor, then, unless, under the settlement and in the said events, the income either "—and then various alternatives, none of which applies, are set out—" the income shall, for the purposes of excess liability, be treated as the income of the settlor and not as the income of any other person. In this subsection ' excess liability ' means the excess of liability to income tax over what it would be if all income tax were charged at the basic rate to the exclusion of any other rate."

C

D

The first thing it is necessary to know is in what manner and why the income payable under the two covenants is deductible from the tax-payer's income in the first place, because, quite clearly, if it were not there would, in the case of a simple covenant of the present nature, be a double charge to taxation. The answer is given in the speech of Lord Radcliffe in *Inland Revenue Commissioners* v. *Frere* [1965] A.C. 402, 421:

E

" The first statutory use of our current phrase ' total income from all sources ' seems to have been in section 8 of the Customs and Inland Revenue Act 1876 and this, significantly, occurs in an exemption section. When super-tax was introduced in 1910, its basis of charge was, as we know, the total income of an individual from all sources ' estimated in the same manner as the total income from all sources is estimated for the purposes of exemptions or abatements under the Income Tax Acts ' (see Finance (1909–10) Act 1910, s. 66 (2)). It is not in dispute, therefore, that, though we are now dealing with a claim to make deductions from or reductions of total income for the purposes of surtax, the test of what is to be brought into that computation is derived from the test of what formed aggregate or total income for the purposes of exemption, relief or abatement under the original income tax system. This assumption is the basis of the decision of the Court of Appeal in *Earl Howe* v. *Inland Revenue Commissioners* [1919] 2 K.B. 336, and there is no need to enlarge upon it further. It was also the basis of the court's decision in that case that, in arriving at the figure of total income, only those annual payments could be allowed as deductions which were themselves payable under deduction and retention of tax as between payer and payee. The decision itself is very well known, and I must say that until this case I had never heard it questioned that the principle the court had proceeded upon was the correct one."

F

G

H

There is clearly no change under the Income and Corporation Taxes Act 1970 for section 528 (1) provides:

A   " In the Income Tax Acts ' total income,' in relation to any person, means the total income of that person from all sources estimated . . . in accordance with the provisions of the Income Tax Acts."

Lord Radcliffe's test throws one back to what is now section 52 of the Income and Corporation Taxes Act 1970. I need not read this section, but, quite clearly, the payments which the taxpayer made under the two

B deeds of covenant would be reduced by the amount of tax at the basic rate pursuant to that section, and hence be deductible from his total income for the purposes of tax in excess of the basic rate: see section 32 (1) (b) of the Finance Act 1971.

So I think one commences with the taxpayer's income being reduced, when one comes to consider what is his " total income," by the amount of the payments under the deeds of covenant. But then, pursuant to

C section 457, in order to ascertain the amount of his total income it is necessary to add back the payments made under the two deeds. It is at this precise point, however, said Mr. Thornhill for the taxpayer, that one must examine carefully the philosophy behind section 457, for what it does, in his submission, is no more and no less than to cut at the root of the principle of deduction as hitherto explained, and to say, in substance,

D that there shall simply be no deduction. That produces the result that, for the purposes of excess rates of taxation, the taxpayer's income remains of precisely the same nature as it always was; and as the sums paid under the deeds of covenant are most suitably paid (subject to another of Mr. Thornhill's submissions, made on the supposition that he is wrong about this one, which I must consider later) out of his earned income, the

E moneys payable under the deeds of covenant remain earned income.

Mr. Thornhill helpfully explored other, somewhat similar, provisions of the Income and Corporation Taxes Act 1970 dealing with a settlor's liability to income tax on income arising under settlements of various types, notably the provisions of Chapter I (relating to dispositions of income for short periods), Chapter II (settlements on children) and Chapter III (revocable settlements), and submitted that under those chapters it

F could be argued that there was a principle of simple non-deduction, and that principle should be implied in Chapter IV. The difficulty, of course, in discerning any consistent pattern in the various chapters of Part XVI of the Act of 1970 is that they all spring from totally different origins, and thus do not in any sense represent what would obviously be highly desirable—namely, a " code "—in any shape or form. Further, Mr.

G Gibson pointed out that for a very considerable period of time now the pattern of the income tax legislation has been to deprive any income paid under a deed of covenant of its character of earned income: see, for example, section 221 of the Income Tax Act 1952 and section 25 of the Income and Corporation Taxes Act 1970. He accordingly submitted that it would be somewhat extraordinary if section 457 on its true construction did swim against the tide on this matter. However, quite

H clearly there is no express provision in the Act of 1970 or elsewhere which, by itself, enables the question at issue to be determined beyond all possible doubt.

I must now turn to consider the one decided case which may be said to have a possible direct bearing on the present one; namely, the decision of the House of Lords in *Inland Revenue Commissioners* v. *Coathew Investments Ltd.* [1966] 1 W.L.R. 716. The question in that case was whether a deduction could be made in respect of a payment by a controlled

investment company to a charity when computing its income for the pur-　A
pose of that income being apportioned between its members for the purposes of surtax. The section under consideration was what is now section
457, and the real question at issue was as I have already stated, it being
provided by what was then section 262 (a) of the Income Tax Act 1970
that no deduction should be allowed in computing the actual income from
all sources of the company which would not have been allowed in computing the total income of an individual. I think there is no burking the　B
fact that their Lordships approached their conclusion that no such deduction was allowable by rather different routes. Viscount Dilhorne said, at
p. 723:

". . . despite the ingenious argument advanced by Mr. Heyworth
Talbot, I have come to the conclusion that although the language of
sections 407 and 415 (1) is different, its effect is the same, namely,　C
to prevent certain deductions being allowable. Willmer L.J. in the
course of his judgment said [1965] 1 W.L.R. 583, 594: ' In the case
of an individual making payments under a covenant such as that in
the present case, section 415 says that such payments are to be treated
for surtax purposes as his income. That means that he is not allowed
to say for surtax purposes that his income is diminished by the amount　D
of those payments. In other words, the plain meaning is that he is not
allowed for surtax purposes to deduct the payments from what would
otherwise be his total income for surtax purposes.' Pearson L.J., as
he then was, put the matter even more succinctly when he said, at
p. 596: ' If that income is to be treated as the income of the settlor,
it must follow that it is not an allowable deduction.' I agree with
them. Not being an allowable deduction in the case of an individual,　E
the proviso to section 262 prevents it being deducted in computing the
actual income of the appellant company."

Lord Cohen at p. 724 agreed with Viscount Dilhorne and Lord Upjohn.
Lord Hodson put the matter thus, at pp. 724–725:

"Since there is no mention of deductions in the section which applies　F
to individuals it is argued that the section can have no application to
the deductions referred to in the proviso to section 262 (2). No
other section comes into play and the argument is reinforced by the
application of the principle that there can be no taxation without
clear words and that the statute has many examples of items being
treated as income in contradistinction to items being allowed as
deductions: (see ss. 405, 407, 408). By way of explanation it should　G
be stated that section 415 had to be drafted in a somewhat roundabout way so as to cover settlements in the ordinary conveyancing
sense of the word by which the settlor disposes of a capital sum and
settles it upon successive interests. No question of deduction in
such a case arises but a covenant is by definition a settlement "
—and he quotes the definition section—" and is thus caught by the　H
language of section 415. The effect, of course, is that the covenantor
cannot deduct the income paid away under the covenant when he is
computing his total income for surtax purposes, although the route by
which that position is arrived at is a devious one. Theoretically he
deducts the covenanted payment as an annual payment under
Schedule 24 and then gets it disallowed by virtue of the covenanted
payment being treated for the purposes of surtax as his income.

A   Arithmetically the result is the same whether one uses the word
' deduction ' or not, and I find myself unable to accept the argument
that because the word ' deduction ' is not employed in section 415
(contrast section 78 of the Finance Act 1965), the section is inapplicable and the taxpaying company is accordingly free from any
restriction as to deduction in the case of this charitable covenant."

B   Lord Guest had this to say, at p. 726:

    " The Crown contends that section 415 prohibits the deduction from
    an individual's total income for surtax purposes of income under cer-
    tain settlements of which it is admitted the present is one. But when one
    refers to section 415 one finds that deductions are not mentioned.
    The section provides as follows: ' (1) Where, during the life of the
C   settlor, income arising under a settlement made on or after April
    10, 1946, is, under the settlement and in the events that occur,
    payable to or applicable for the benefit of any person other than
    the settlor, then . . . the income shall be treated for the purposes
    of surtax as the income of the settlor and not as the income of any
    other person.' The section is directed to an entirely different end.
    Before the predecessor to section 415 appeared on the Statute Book
D   an individual's total income would have been diminished by the
    settlement income. His ' total income ' would have been arrived at
    under the predecessor to section 524 and ascertained by applying
    the rules and directions in force. But the result of section 415 was
    in the case of an individual to nullify the effect of the diminution of
    the individual's income by including in his total income the settlement
E   income. The mechanics of the calculation would then be that in the
    individual's income in the first place would be included the settle-
    ment income in virtue of section 415 and the settlement income
    would then be deducted as an annual payment under Schedule 24.
    The arithmetical result would be in effect to disallow any allowance
    of the settlement income by adding it back for the purpose of ascer-
    taining the total income. But the steps which would according to the
F   Act have to be taken would be as I have stated."

In fact he differed in the end result and would have allowed the appeal,
because section 415 had no effect on section 262 (a). Finally, Lord Upjohn
put the matter in this way, at pp. 728–729:

    " The argument is that the section is not dealing with deductions at
G   all. It is argued that in accordance with general income tax principles
    the taxpayer can deduct from his total income payments of covenanted
    annual sums because his income is thereby diminished. But the
    effect of section 415 is that to this diminished income there must be
    added the sum he has already deducted, for it is to be treated as his
    income and not that of any other person. Hence the permitted
H   deduction and the compulsory addition balance out and the individual
    taxpayer cannot diminish his total income for the purposes of surtax
    by the covenanted annual payment. That, as I have said, is not in
    dispute, but the argument runs that as there is nothing in section
    415 which prohibits deductions and all it has done is to nullify the
    permitted deduction by making an addition, so the proviso to section
    262 (2) does not operate, for it is only dealing with deductions not
    allowable in the case of individuals and there are none. I cannot

accept this argument. The main purpose of section 415 is no doubt A
to deal with settlements as they are ordinarily understood, i.e. settlements where the settlor transfers out-and-out capital sums to trustees
upon various trusts so that the income ceases to be his. Therefore
section 415 was framed to reach the desired tax result by providing
that nevertheless such income was to be treated as his. But when a
settlement is made by definition to include a covenant, a somewhat
artificial though now very familiar concept, the sum has to be worked B
out purely as a matter of mental process in the way in which it has
been argued on behalf of the appellant company, but this leads to
the result which, in my opinion, may be accurately stated in legal
language by saying that the individual taxpayer cannot for surtax
purposes deduct from his total income annual payments made by
him under covenant for charitable purposes. Proviso (a) makes it C
plain that the investment company cannot do so either. That seems
to me to have been the clear intention of Parliament."

Both counsel disclaimed any intention of suggesting that that case
decided the present, but it does seem to me that the balance of the
opinions—that is to say, Lords Hodson, Guest and Upjohn, as against
Viscount Dilhorne, with Lord Cohen keeping a foot in either pan of the D
scales—is in favour of the view that, strictly speaking, the exercise is to
deduct and add back, not simply not to deduct. I have come to the
conclusion that this is, indeed, the correct approach. I think the fallacy
which underlies Mr. Thornhill's valiant attempts to argue for the contrary
approach lies in the fact that the two economically equivalent sums—
the sums paid by the taxpayer pursuant to the deeds of covenant and the E
income arising under the settlement—are not of the same nature. One
can test this very simply by imagining that some Finance Act imposed a
tax on income arising under a settlement, without otherwise altering the
law. It would then be quite clear that what would be added to the taxpayer's income at the end of the day would be the settlement income
less the amount of the special tax. There would be no way in which
it could successfully be argued that there was simply no deduction at all F
to be made from his income. Perhaps the matter can be put even more
simply by saying that, on a fair construction of section 457, the income
arising under the notional settlement is a part of the taxpayer's income,
and unless he is entitled to a deduction in respect of the payments made
under the deeds of covenant he would be liable twice over; and, given
that deduction, the settlement income, which is unearned, remains as his. G

On this basis the appeal from the general commissioners would fall to
be dismissed, but Mr. Thornhill had an entirely different shot in his
locker. It relates to the attribution of a particular outgoing to a particular tranche of income. This is, of course, an accountant's, and not
a lawyer's, conception. As a matter of pure fact, for example, some
instalments of an annuity, or even the whole, may be paid out of the proceeds of sale of a capital item in the hands of the person due to make the H
payments. But that does not prevent him, at the end of the day, attributing those payments to a source of income brought into charge to income
tax, assuming that, when his accounts for the relevant period come to be
made up, he has a sufficient source of such income. That this was perfectly proper so far as the tax position between the taxpayer and the
revenue was concerned has been well recognised for a long time : see,

A for example, *Allchin* v. *South Shields Corporation* [1943] A.C. 607. This
was a decision of the House of Lords, but it was in the Court of Appeal
[1942] 2 K.B. 228 that Lord Greene M.R. gave the well known graphic
illustration of the principle, at p. 236:

> " A trader may spend the whole of his profits for the year in buying
B > himself a house, with the result that he has to borrow money in order
> to pay his mortgage interest. This does not disentitle him from say-
> ing that, as between himself and the revenue, he is entitled to debit
> the interest paid to the fund representing the amount in which his
> profits for the year are assessed."

So, in the present case, Mr. Thornhill submitted that in the taxpayer's
accounts with the revenue he is entitled to show on the credit side " income
C arising under the settlement " and on the debit side " payments under
the two deeds of covenant paid out of the income arising under the settlement per contra," thus leaving the earned income position wholly
unchanged by the manoeuvres forced upon him by section 457.

This is a very attractive argument indeed, and it is with considerable
regret that I find myself unable to give effect to it. The crucial difficulty
which I feel is that there is no income arising under the settlement until
D the sums due under the covenants have in fact been paid. In other words,
there is a situation in which payment A must of necessity be made before
receipt B arises. This is, of course, not the case in any manner with the
kind of case in which the *Allchin* principle applies. It is not, of course,
the timing as such which is important (I have no doubt that in an *Allchin*
case the profits might all have been earned subsequent to the payments
E being made), but the logicality; the necessity that payment A be made
before receipt B arises as a matter of absolute and incontrovertible necessity. As an alternative, the matter might perhaps be put in this way;
namely, that the section says that the income arising from the settlement is
to be part of the settlor's income. If it is to be part of his income, it
cannot also at the same time be appropriated to something which is going
F to be deducted from his income. Or, if it is, the deduction will be
nugatory, as that income itself will still, according to the wording of the
section, remain his income. So that the only effect of appropriating the
income of the settlement to meet the sums due on the covenant would be
to increase the taxpayer's total liability for income tax by the basic rate on
the settlement income. Accordingly, I find myself unable to accept this
alternative argument and, in the result, in my judgment, this appeal falls
G to be dismissed.

Appeal dismissed.
No application for costs.

Solicitors: *Pothecary & Barratt*; *Solicitor of Inland Revenue.*

H [Reported by MRS. HARRIET DUTTON, Barrister-at-Law]

A

[CHANCERY DIVISION]

* LONDON & COUNTY SECURITIES LTD. AND OTHERS
v. NICHOLSON AND OTHERS

1980   Jan. 22, 23, 24, 25, 28   Browne-Wilkinson J.

B

*Company—Investigation of affairs—Evidence—Evidence given to
inspectors appointed by Board of Trade — Subsequent civil
proceedings brought by company against witnesses—Whether
evidence to be admitted in evidence — Companies Act 1948
(11 & 12 Geo. 6, c. 38), s. 167—Companies Act 1967 (c. 81),
s. 50*

C

The first and second plaintiff companies went into liquidation, and the third and fourth plaintiffs, respectively, were
appointed as their liquidators. The defendants were members
of a firm of accountants which had acted as auditors to the
two companies, and had produced audited accounts for the
year ended March 31, 1973. In 1974, the Board of Trade,
acting under section 165 of the Companies Act 1948, appointed
inspectors to investigate the affairs of the first plaintiff. The   D
inspectors took evidence on oath from four of the defendants,
and also from an employee of the defendant firm. That
evidence was amplified in correspondence passing between the
inspectors and the solicitors acting for the defendants. The
inspectors' report was signed on March 7, 1976, and was published by H.M. Stationery Office a year later. No express
assurances were given to the witnesses that their evidence
would be treated as confidential. The plaintiffs sought damages   E
for alleged negligence by the defendants in conducting the
companies' audits for the year ending March 31, 1973. The
material gathered by the inspectors was lodged with the
Department of Trade and Industry. Pursuant to an order made
on October 29, 1975, by the Registrar of the Companies Court
the department handed over certain documents to the liquidator
of the first plaintiff, who gave an undertaking that the
contents would be treated as confidential and would not be   F
disclosed to any person other than his legal advisers and
accountants " except to the extent that such disclosure
shall be necessary for the performance of his duties in conducting litigation as liquidator. . . ." The defendants' solicitors
had previously been notified of the department's intention to
hand over the documents to the liquidator, but no objection
had been taken by them. On the hearing of the action, the
question arose whether the transcripts of the oral evidence   G
given to the inspectors and the correspondence passing between
the inspectors and the defendants' solicitors should be admitted
in evidence: —
    Held, (1) that in general, apart from any question of confi-
dentiality, evidence given to inspectors appointed under section
165 of the Companies Act 1948, whether sworn or unsworn,
was admissible against the witness in subsequent criminal proceedings, both under the general law and by virtue of section   H
50 of the Companies Act 1967, and such evidence must therefore, a fortiori, be admissible against him in subsequent civil
proceedings (post, p. 953E–F).
    In re Rolls Razor Ltd. [1968] 3 All E.R. 698; *Reg.* v.
Harris (Richard) [1970] 1 W.L.R. 1252 and *Reg.* v. *Scott*
(1856) Dears. & B. 47 applied.
    Karak Rubber Co. Ltd. v. *Burden* [1971] 1 W.L.R. 1748
distinguished.
    (2) That in considering whether evidence given to inspectors

A   appointed under section 165 of the Companies Act 1948 was
admissible in subsequent proceedings by a company or its
liquidator it was the court's duty to balance two public
interests against each other, namely, the public interest in
having all available evidence before the court and the public
interest in preserving the confidentiality of the evidence or
information given in order that such evidence or information
would be given freely to inspectors without the witnesses
B   fearing to expose themselves to subsequent proceedings; that
it was not to be presumed that Parliament intended to ensure
as much confidentiality as possible and, accordingly, unless
the public interest in excluding evidence clearly outweighed
the public interest in admitting it, the latter ought to prevail
and, since in the present case there was no sufficient public
interest to exclude the relevant evidence contained in the
transcripts and the subsequent correspondence, that evidence
C   was admissible (post, pp. 956B–F, 957G).
          D. v. *National Society for the Prevention of Cruelty to
Children* [1978] A.C. 171, H.L.(E.) and *Reg.* v. *Lewes
Justices, Ex parte Secretary of State for the Home Department* [1973] A.C. 388, H.L.(E.) applied.
          In re *Pergamon Press Ltd.* [1971] Ch. 388, C.A. and
Reg. v. *Cheltenham Justices, Ex parte Secretary of State
for Trade* [1977] 1 W.L.R. 95, D.C. distinguished.

D
          The following cases are referred to in the judgment:

D. v. *National Society for the Prevention of Cruelty to Children* [1978]
          A.C. 171; [1977] 2 W.L.R. 201; [1977] 1 All E.R. 589, H.L.(E.).
Karak Rubber Co. Ltd. v. *Burden* [1971] 1 W.L.R. 1748; [1971] 3 All
          E.R. 1118.
Pergamon Press Ltd, In re [1971] Ch. 388; [1970] 3 W.L.R. 792;
E   [1970] 3 All E.R. 535, C.A.
Reg. v. *Cheltenham Justices, Ex parte Secretary of State for Trade*
          [1977] 1 W.L.R. 95; [1977] 1 All E.R. 460, D.C.
Reg. v. *Harris* (*Richard*) [1970] 1 W.L.R. 1252; [1970] 3 All E.R. 746.
Reg. v. *Lewes Justices, Ex parte Secretary of State for the Home
          Department* [1973] A.C. 388; [1972] 3 W.L.R. 279; [1972] 2 All
          E.R. 1057, H.L.(E.).
F   *Reg.* v. *Scott* (1856) Dears. & B. 47.
Rolls Razor Ltd., In re [1968] 3 All E.R. 698.

          The following additional cases were cited in argument:

Ashburton (*Lord*) v. *Pape* [1913] 2 Ch. 469, C.A.
Butler v. *Board of Trade* [1971] Ch. 680; [1970] 3 W.L.R. 822; [1970]
          3 All E.R. 593.
G   *Calcraft* v. *Guest* [1898] 1 Q.B. 759, C.A.
Grosvenor and West-End Railway Terminus Hotel Co. Ltd., In re (1897)
          76 L.T. 337, C.A.
Medway v. *Doublelock Ltd.* [1978] 1 W.L.R. 710; [1978] 1 All E.R.
          1261.
S.B.A. Properties Ltd., In re [1967] 1 W.L.R. 799; [1967] 2 All E.R.
          615.
H   *Selangor United Rubber Estates Ltd.* v. *Cradock* (*No.* 2) [1968] 1
          W.L.R. 319; [1968] 1 All E.R. 567.

APPLICATION.
          By a writ dated May 4, 1977, and an amended statement of claim,
the second plaintiff, London and County Securities Group Ltd. and ten
of its subsidiary companies including the first plaintiff, London and County
Securities Ltd., claimed, against Hugh Thayer Nicholson and 28 other

former partners in the firm of Harmood Banner, accountants, damages for   A
alleged negligence in conducting the audits for the first and second companies for the year ended March 31, 1973.

In 1974, the Board of Trade, acting under section 165 of the Companies
Act 1948, had appointed inspectors to investigate the affairs of the first
plaintiff, and in the course of the investigation took oral evidence from
four of the defendants and from one of their employees, and transcripts
were taken of such evidence. That was supplemented by correspondence   B
passing between the inspectors and the defendants' solicitors. The
inspectors' report was published in 1976.

At the hearing of the action, the plaintiffs sought to introduce in evidence, the transcripts, the correspondence and the inspectors' report, but
the defendants objected that none of those documents was admissible.
The parties agreed that the report itself was not admissible, but that   C
passages in the report could be put to witnesses in cross-examination, and
that if a witness agreed with those passages they became part of that
witness's evidence. As to transcripts and the correspondence Browne-
Wilkinson J. delivered a judgment on admissibility, which is the subject of
this report.

The facts are stated in the judgment.
                                                                          D

Donald Nicholls Q.C., Andrew Morritt Q.C. and *David Oliver* for the
plaintiffs.
Adrian Hamilton Q.C. and *Patrick Phillips* for the defendants.

                                                    Cur. adv. vult.
                                                                          E

BROWNE-WILKINSON J. read the following judgment. In this action the
plaintiff companies are suing the defendants, who are partners in Messrs.
Harmood Banner, accountants, for alleged negligence in conducting the
audits for the first and second plaintiff companies for the year ending
March 31, 1973. Both those companies are in liquidation: Mr. Langdon
is the liquidator of the first; the official receiver is the liquidator of the   F
second. I have now to decide difficult questions on admissibility of
documents which have been elaborately and exceptionally well argued.

In January 1974, the Board of Trade, acting under section 165 of
the Companies Act 1948, appointed inspectors to investigate the affairs
of the first plaintiff. In the course of the investigation the inspectors
took oral evidence on oath from four of the defendants, partners in
Messrs. Harmood Banner, and from an employee of that firm. There   G
are transcripts of that evidence, and that oral evidence was later amplified
in correspondence passing between the inspectors on the one hand and
solicitors, Messrs. Linklaters & Paines, acting for the defendants on
the other hand. No express assurance was given to the witnesses that
their evidence would be treated as confidential. The inspectors signed
their report on March 7, 1976, and it was published by H.M. Stationery   H
Office one year later.

The plaintiffs in opening the case, asked me to look at three separate
categories of docments arising from the investigation. Those have been
prepared in three bundles: bundle 4A which contains the inspectors'
report; bundle 4B which contains transcripts of the oral evidence given
on oath to the inspectors by the four defendants and the employee of
the defendants; and bundle 4C which contains the correspondence to

The Weekly Law Reports, August 8, 1980

951

1 W.L.R.   London Securities Ltd. v. Nicholson (Ch.D.)   Browne-Wilkinson J.

A which I have referred. The defendants object that none of these documents is admissible, and I have not yet looked at any of them.

In the course of the argument, it emerged that there was in fact no immediate point for me to decide on the inspectors' report. It is agreed that the report as such is not admissible evidence on the issues I have to decide. References to the report in the experts' proofs of evidence are to be deleted. It is agreed that passages in the report can be put B to witnesses in cross-examination and that if a witness agrees with those passages they become part of that witness's evidence. The parties are not agreed as to the position which will arise if the witness does not agree with the passage put to him. I shall have to decide that point when and if it arises in the light of the actual circumstances.

As to the transcripts of evidence and written replies, section 167 (2) C of the Companies Act 1948 confers on inspectors power to examine on oath officers and agents of the company; " agents " includes the auditors. The Act of 1948 did not in terms provide that such evidence could be used in subsequent legal proceedings, although section 167 (4) provided that evidence given by persons other than officers or agents could be so used. However, section 50 of the Companies Act 1967 provides, so D far as material:

" An answer given by a person to a question put to him in exercise of powers conferred by—(a) section 167 of the principal Act (as originally enacted or as applied by section 172 of that Act or section 32 of this Act); or (b) general rules made under section 365 (1) of the principal Act for carrying into effect the objects of that Act so far as relates to the winding up of companies; may be E used in evidence against him, and a statement required by section 235 of the principal Act (statement of company's affairs to be made to official receiver) may be used in evidence against any person making or concurring in making it."

The plaintiffs say that these documents are admissible both under the general law and by reason of the express statutory enactment in section F 50. The defendants contend, however, that they are not admissible notwithstanding section 50. Shortly, the steps in the defendants' argument are as follows. First, that evidence given to the inspectors appointed under the Companies Act 1948 is given in confidence; secondly, that the plaintiffs have obtained the evidence in breach of that confidence; and thirdly, that the court should therefore not admit such evidence since G confidential information of this type is not admissible on the principles recently expounded by the House of Lords in D. v. National Society for the Prevention of Cruelty to Children [1978] A.C. 171. The defendants do not seek to distinguish between the evidence of the four defendants themselves and the evidence given by their employee.

Before considering these arguments I must state further facts. It H appears that after the conclusion of the investigation the material gathered by the inspectors was lodged with the Department of Trade and Industry. In October 1975, the liquidator obtained an order of the Companies Court for the private examination of a Mr. Osborne, an officer of the Department of Trade and Industry. On October 29, 1975, on an application to which the defendants were not parties, the Registrar of the Companies Court ordered:

"(1) the Department of Trade is directed by the court that before
there is handed over to the said liquidator (a) any transcript of
the hearing before the inspectors appointed by the Department of
Trade, and (b) any statements made by witnesses, letters written by
them or documents produced by them to the said inspectors otherwise
than with the agreement of the witness who gave evidence at that
hearing or the witnesses who made such statements or wrote such
letters or produced such documents to notify such witness by writing
to him at his last known address or to the solicitors who represented
him at that hearing that it is proposed to hand over a copy of such
transcript, letters, statements or documents in accordance with the
undertaking hereinafter given, unless within 14 days the witness
applies to the court to discharge such undertaking.   (2) the said
Michael Charles Anthony Osborne "undertakes to the court that
subject to the advice of counsel he will hand over to the liquidator
copies of the transcripts of hearings before the said inspectors and
such further or other documents requested by the said liquidator
as the Department of Trade releases to him, and (3) the liquidator
[who is named] by his counsel undertakes to the court to treat the
contents of all documents which the said Michael Charles Anthony
Osborne may disclosure to him pursuant to the undertaking given
by him to the court in the course of the said examination as confidential and not to disclose their contents to any person other than
the legal advisers and accountants to [the liquidator] as such
liquidator except to the extent that such disclosure shall be necessary
for the performance of his duties in conducting litigation as liquidator
of the above-named company and upon the footing that any such
disclosure (other than in the course of litigation) is confidential."

That order was plainly made in reliance on the decision of Buckley J.
in *In re Rolls Razor Ltd.* [1968] 3 All E.R. 698.   Pursuant to that
order on November 4, 1975, the Treasury Solicitor wrote to Messrs.
Linklaters & Paines giving them notice that the department was
considering handing over the documents and inviting them to make
representations to the department within ten days.   The letter stated
that the department would consider any representations so made but if,
notwithstanding those representations, they decided to release the documents it would defer such release for 14 days to enable the defendants
to apply to the court.   A reminder was sent to Messrs. Linklaters &
Paines on November 24, and on November 25 there was a telephone
call between Mr. Pickthorn of Linklaters & Paines and Mr. Dean of
the Treasury Solicitor's office.   Mr. Dean made a note of that telephone
call which reads, so far as material, as follows:

"Pickthorn of Linklaters & Paines 'phoned.   1. Would we keep
a note of what handed over?   Would do so but might have difficulty
in identifying the documents from Harmood Banner.   But would
keep a note.   2. Why does liquidator want documents?   Says don't
know.   Section 268 application ex parte but investigate company.
Could be claim against auditors.   3. Would documents be kept
confidential?   Yes.   Gave him particulars of the undertaking to the
court given by the liquidator.   Pickthorn will write confirming above
and that no objection to production."

The Weekly Law Reports, August 8, 1980

953

1 W.L.R.   London Securities Ltd. v. Nicholson (Ch.D.)   Browne-Wilkinson J.

A   As that attendance note forecasts, on the same day Mr. Pickthorn wrote a letter in these terms:

"Thank you for your letters of November 4 and 24. As discussed on the telephone our clients have no objection to the release to Mr. Osborne for production to the liquidator of the documents to which you refer on the understanding that the liquidator gave an under-
B   taking to the court that he would treat the contents confidentially and that a record will be kept (which will be made available to us if requested) of what documents have been handed over."

The evidence of Mr. Pickthorn and the defendants is that they did not by that letter intend to waive any right they had to object to the use of such evidence in subsequent proceedings against them. In due course
C   the documents were handed over to the liquidator.

It is convenient, before turning to the submissions on the public interest point, first to consider whether the sworn and unsworn evidence given to the inspectors is otherwise admissible in evidence in subsequent proceedings. There are two decisions directly in point, and one, *In re Rolls Razor Ltd.* [1968] 3 All E.R. 698, in which the admissibility of such evidence is a tacit assumption underlying the actual decision. In *Reg.*
D   v. *Harris (Richard)* [1970] 1 W.L.R. 1252 MacKenna J. held that, quite apart from section 50 of the Act of 1967, sworn evidence given by a witness to inspectors appointed under the Companies Act 1948 was admissible against that witness in subsequent criminal proceedings. He relied largely on the decision of the Court of Criminal Appeal in *Reg.* v. *Scott* (1856) Dears. & B. 47, which held that unsworn evidence given
E   by a bankrupt on his examination was admissible against him on a subsequent criminal charge. In my judgment these cases establish that, even without section 50 both sworn and unsworn evidence given to inspectors is admissible against the witnesses in subsequent criminal proceedings.

Mr. Hamilton, for the defendants, urged that the decisions were only dealing with evidence in criminal cases. But in my judgment if such
F   evidence is admissible against a man to incriminate himself in criminal proceedings it must, a fortiori, be admissible against him in civil proceed-ings. Unfortunately *Reg.* v. *Harris (Richard)* [1970] 1 W.L.R. 1252 and *Reg.* v. *Scott,* Dears. & B. 47 were not cited to Brightman J. in *Karak Rubber Co. Ltd.* v. *Burden* [1971] 1 W.L.R. 1748. In that case Brightman J. decided in similar litigation brought by the Board of Trade
G   in the name of the company under its statutory powers, that only sworn evidence given to inspectors was admissible and he excluded unsworn evidence. It is clear that the only argument addressed to Brightman J. was on the construction of section 50 of the Act of 1967 and section 167 of the Act of 1948. As the point decided in *Reg.* v. *Harris* [1970] 1 W.L.R. 1252 and *Reg.* v. *Scott,* Dears. & B. 47 was not before him I cannot regard Brightman J.'s decision as impairing those earlier decisions
H   in any way. I therefore approach the question of confidentiality on the basis that both the sworn and unsworn evidence given to the inspectors would otherwise be admissible.

In none of the cases I have so far referred to was any point taken that the evidence was inadmissible on the grounds that it was given to the inspectors in confidence. Mr. Hamilton's submission is that the evidence was given by the witnesses to the inspectors in confidence and that it is therefore not admissible. He accepts that for relevant evidence

to be excluded on these grounds communication in confidence by itself   A
is not enough; it has also to be shown that the confidence is of a kind
which the public interest requires to be protected: see *D. v. National
Society for the Prevention of Cruelty to Children* [1978] A.C. 171, 218.
There is considerable authority supporting the broad proposition that
evidence given to inspectors appointed under the Companies Act 1948 is
given in confidence, and that the public interest requires that confidence to
be protected: see *Reg. v. Cheltenham Justices, Ex parte Secretary of State*   B
for Trade [1977] 1 W.L.R. 95 and *In re Pergamon Press Ltd.* [1971]
Ch. 388. As those cases show, the public interest is to ensure that so far
as possible people will give information and evidence frankly to inspectors
without fear that by so doing they will expose themselves to subsequent
actions by other persons who are or may be adversely affected by their
evidence.   C

    However, it is of fundamental importance that, unlike any other
instance cited to me in which evidence was excluded on this ground,
it is clear that in the case of evidence given to inspectors the confidentiality
of the evidence is not complete. The potential witness will, on any
footing, know that his evidence and identity may be disclosed in any of
the following ways: (1) By his evidence being put by the inspectors to
other witnesses. (2) By being incorporated in the inspectors' report,   D
which under section 168 is or may be distributed to the company, to
members and creditors of the company, and to persons who applied for
the investigation; it may be published by H.M. Stationery Office. (3) In
criminal or civil proceedings against him.

    Therefore the public interest in this case is not the same as that
which protects the confidentiality of police and other informers. In   E
the case of informers, the public interest is to provide the informant
with *total* confidentiality, which apparently cannot be waived, so as to
ensure that informers as a class will know that they cannot be identified.
In the present case, express statutory provisions show that in the view of
Parliament there are other interests which outweigh the public interest
in giving potential witnesses the assurance of complete confidentiality.   F

    Mr. Hamilton's argument runs as follows. He says first, that the
authorities show that there is a public interest in preserving the confidentiality of evidence given to inspectors, and that accordingly Parliament
must be taken not to have intended to breach such confidentiality, save
to the extent that statutory provisions expressly authorise such breach.
Then he says that although section 50 of the Companies Act 1967 plainly
envisages disclosure in some legal proceedings, properly construed the   G
only proceedings referred to in section 50 are proceedings brought in
the public interest, i.e. criminal proceedings, winding up proceedings
brought by the department under section 35 of the Act of 1967, and
proceedings brought by the department under section 37 in the name of
the company. On this construction Parliament has not shown any
intention that such evidence can be used in proceedings such as these   H
brought by a company or by a liquidator of a company.

    I will for the moment assume Mr. Hamilton is correct in his primary
submission that Parliament is to be presumed to prefer the public interest
in preserving confidentiality to the public interest in all relevant evidence
being available to the court. Even on that assumption I cannot accept
Mr. Hamilton's submission for the following reasons.

    First, under the general law, evidence given to inspectors would be

The Weekly Law Reports, August 8, 1980

955

1 W.L.R.   London Securities Ltd. v. Nicholson (Ch.D.)   Browne-Wilkinson J.

A   admissible. If Parliament intended a different result I would have expected it expressly so to have provided. See, for example, the express restrictions on disclosure of information legislated for in a similar field by section 111 of the Act of 1967, but which do not preclude the use of such information in litigation: section 109 (5) of the Act of 1967.

   Secondly, the words of section 50 are entirely general. Any restriction as to the type of proceedings in which the evidence is to be admitted B has to be by way of implied restriction on the generality of those words. On ordinary principles such an implication is not to be made unless the circumstances make such restriction a necessity.

   Thirdly, the assurance of confidentiality is admittedly breached by the fact that the evidence can be admitted in proceedings brought by the department under section 37 of the Ac of 1967 in the name of the C company. How will the public interest in preserving confidentiality be preserved by drawing a distinction between such proceedings and proceedings brought by the company itself or by the liquidator? In terms of a potential witness's confidence that his evidence will not be disclosed or used against him, it does not matter who brings the proceedings. Once a potential witness knows that his evidence may be used against him in any proceedings brought by anyone his assurance is gone.
D
   Mr. Hamilton says correctly that, by the express terms of sections 35 and 37, the department can only bring proceedings " in the public interest," and from this deduces that Parliament only intended company investigations, and the evidence gathered under compulsion during its conduct, to be used when a public body considers it in the public interest to take proceedings. But at least part of the purpose of company E investigations is to protect the individual rights of members and creditors of the company. Under section 165 of the Act of 1948 the department is bound to appoint inspectors if the company so resolves by special resolution, and may do so if one-tenth of the members request it to. In the latter case such members may be required to bear at least part of the cost. Again, the department has power to appoint inspectors of its F own motion if it considers that there are circumstances suggesting that the company is being conducted in fraud of its creditors or there is misfeasance. All this suggests that Parliament was having regard not solely to the public interest in discovering criminal conduct but also to enabling members and creditors of the company to protect their individual rights. I can see no reason why Parliament should not have intended the fruits of such investigation to be available for use by the company G in redressing the wrongs which such investigation has disclosed.

   Fourthly, section 50 makes admissible not only evidence given to inspectors but also the statement of affairs required under section 235 of the Companies Act 1948 and the observations of the official receiver on it, provided for by rule 126 of the Companies (Winding-up) Rules 1949. The official receiver's observations can, and frequently do, refer to H information given to him in personal interviews conducted under rule 52 of the Companies (Winding up) Rules 1949 which the officers of the company are under a statutory duty to give. As I understand it, Mr. Hamilton accepts that section 50 applies to these other types of information so as to make them admissible in any proceedings, whether or not brought by a public authority, since there is no element of confidentiality in such information. But he contends that section 50 must be construed so as to make the words " used in evidence against him " have a different

effect according to the type of information it is dealing with. I think A
this is too subtle and prefer the view that Parliament in enacting section
50 considered that all information of the various kinds referred to in
the section was to be treated on the same footing.

So far I have accepted Mr. Hamilton's fundamental submission that
Parliament is to be taken to have intended to prefer the confidentiality
of evidence given to inspectors to the public interest in having all available B
evidence before the court. But I do not think such submission is correct.
The decision of the House of Lords in *D.* v. *National Society for
the Prevention of Cruelty to Children* [1978] A.C. 171 establishes that
there is a presumption that the public interest in all relevant evidence
being available to the court ought to prevail: see for example, per
Lord Hailsham of St. Marylebone at p. 223D and 225D and *per* Lord
Edmund-Davies at p. 242B; see also *Reg.* v. *Lewes Justices, Ex parte* C
Secretary of State for the Home Department [1973] A.C. 388, 400E.
If such evidence is to be excluded it must be shown that there is
another counter-availing public interest which necessitates the exclusion
of the evidence and that such counter-availing public interest outweighs
the public interest in admitting it. For this reason I do not accept that
the court should first assume that Parliament intended to assure as much
confidentiality as possible and that such confidentiality should only be D
impaired to the extent that Parliament has expressly so provided.

In my judgment, *D.* v. *National Society for the Prevention of Cruelty
to Children* [1978] A.C. 171, requires me to balance the two public interests
against each other; but unless the public interest in excluding the evidence
clearly outweighs the public interest in admitting it, the latter is to prevail.
On this basis, even if—contrary to my view—Mr. Hamilton is correct that E
on its true construction section 50 of the Companies Act 1967 only expressly
applies to proceedings brought by a public authority, I am left with the
question how to balance the two public interests. For this purpose I must
identify what those interests are. In my judgment they are (1) the public
interest in having all relevant evidence before the court, and (2) the loss of
confidence which potential witnesses will feel if they know that their F
evidence can be used in proceedings brought against them by the company
or its liquidator, and not only in proceedings brought by the department
under the powers of section 37 of the Act of 1967.

If I have rightly identified the public interests to be balanced I have
little doubt that the impairment of the public interest involved in disclosing the evidence to the liquidator and allowing it to be used by him
in proceedings does not outweigh the other public interest. There is no G
evidence from any minister or public servant that the public interest
would be harmed; indeed the fact that the department released the
evidence to the liquidator without protest on terms which permitted its
use by the liquidator in legal proceedings indicates that no injury to the
public interest was then foreseen.

In the absence of such evidence I must use my own judgment on the H
point guided by such authority as there is. For myself I cannot see that
any potential witness who knows that his evidence may be used against
him in proceedings brought in the name of the company under section
37 is going to be appreciably further deterred from giving full and frank
evidence to the inspectors by knowing that such proceedings might be
brought by the company itself without the assistance of the department.
As I have said, it is not the identity of the bringer of the subsequent

The Weekly Law Reports, August 8, 1980

957

1 W.L.R.   London Securities Ltd. v. Nicholson (Ch.D.)   Browne-Wilkinson J.

A proceedings but the fact that his evidence may be used against him in any proceedings which will deter the potential witness.

There are two decisions which deal directly with the public interest in maintaining the confidentially of evidence given to inspectors. In *In re Pergamon Press Ltd.* [1971] Ch. 388 the Court of Appeal undoubtedly relied on there being a public interest in maintaining such confidentiality.

B But the court was there dealing with a case in which, unlike the present, the inspectors had given to the witnesses an express assurance that their evidence would be treated as confidential. Different considerations may aply to such a case. More importantly, the Court of Appeal was not dealing with the admissibility of such evidence in subsequent proceedings; indeed Sachs L.J. in terms referred to the public interest being to preserve confidentiality " unless and until court proceedings eventuate ": see at

C p. 404G. In my judgment that decision establishes that there is a public interest in preserving confidentiality but provides no support for the proposition that such public interest is to outweigh the public interest that all relevant evidence should be before the court.

In *Reg.* v. *Cheltenham Justices, Ex parte Secretary of State for Trade* [1977] 1 W.L.R. 95 there had been an investigation under section 167 (2) of the Act of 1948. Subsequently criminal proceedings were brought

D against one of the witnesses. He obtained a witness summons requiring one of the inspectors to produce transcripts of the other witnesses' evidence to the inspectors and certain other documents. The Department of Trade and Industry applied to quash the summons on two grounds: first, that the evidence given by the other witnesses would not be admissible at the trial, and secondly, that the production of such evidence would

E be contrary to the public interest. The second contention was supported by a certificate from the Secretary of State. The Divisional Court quashed the witness summons on the first ground but indicated that it would also have upheld the department's contention on the second ground. In that case there was evidence of the public interest since the department was itself asserting it with support of a certificate from the

F Minister. Moreover the court was having to weigh the public interest in maintaining confidentiality against depriving a litigant not of relevant admissible evidence but of material for cross-examination. I can well understand that the balance in such a case might produce a different result from the one I have reached in this case.

For these reasons I hold that there is no sufficient public interest to exclude the the relevant evidence contained in bundles B and C. It is

G therefore unnecessary for me to consider the plaintiff's alternative submission that, if in the ordinary case such evidence would have been excluded, the fact that the defendants did not object to the evidence being released by the department to the liquidator alters the position.

I would add two points. First, I have only considered the admissibility of this evidence in relation to proceedings brought by a company or its

H liquidator to right wrongs allegedly done to the company; I am not deciding whether such evidence is admissible in proceedings, such as defamation proceedings, brought by a private individual to right a wrong done to him individually. It may well be that different considerations would apply to such a case. Secondly, although I have decided that the evidence is admissible, the weight to be attached to it will depend on what the evidence is, bearing in mind that it was given under compulsion,

Browne-Wilkinson J.   London Securities Ltd. v. Nicholson (Ch.D.)   [1980]

or threat of compulsion, at a time when no claim had been formulated against the defendants.

Order accordingly.

Solicitors: *Herbert Smith & Co.; Barlow, Lyde & Gilbert.*

T. C. C. B.

[COURT OF APPEAL]

* CHAPPELL *v.* COOPER

PLAYER *v.* BRUGUIERE

[1978 C. No. 639] [1978 P. No. 0668] [1974 P. No. 3647]

1979   July 6   Roskill and Ormrod L.JJ. and Sir David Cairns

Limitation of Action—Personal injuries—Time limit, power to override—Writ issued but not served within limitation period —Second writ issued after expiry of limitation period—Trial of preliminary issue as to right to proceed on second writ— Judge's direction that action proceed—Whether plaintiff prejudiced by statutory time limits—Whether discretion in judge to permit action to proceed—Limitation Act 1939 (2 & 3 Geo. 6, c. 21) (as amended by Limitation Act 1975 (c. 54), s. 1), ss. 2A, 2D

Practice—Writ—Extension of time—Writ issued but not served within limitation period—Failure to apply for extension of time within 12 months of expiry of writ—Whether statutory provisions giving court discretion to extend limitation period affecting court's power to grant extension—R.S.C., Ord. 6, r. 8 (2)

The plaintiffs in two actions, who had both been injured in road accidents in 1971, issued writs against the respective defendants claiming damages for negligence, but neither writ was served within the three-year statutory time limit imposed by section 2A of the Limitation Act 1939, as amended by the Limitation Act 1975. A second writ was issued in each case, outside the time limit. In the first action the second writ was served on May 24, 1978, nearly seven years after the accident. The defendant pleaded the Limitation Act 1939. At the trial of the preliminary issue, whether it would be equitable to allow the action to continue under the Act of 1939, as amended, Bush J., in the exercise of the discretion granted by section 2D of the Act of 1939, as amended,[1] directed that the plaintiff should have leave to proceed.

---

[1] Limitation Act 1939 (as amended), s. 2D: " (1) If it appears to the court that it would be equitable to allow an action to proceed having regard to the degree to which—(*a*) the provisions of section 2A [new time limits] or 2B [time limit for actions under the Fatal Accidents Act 1846] of this Act prejudice the plaintiff or any person whom he represents, and (*b*) any decision of the court under this subsection would prejudice the defendant or any person whom he represents, the court may direct that those provisions shall not apply to the action, or shall not apply to any specified cause of action to which the action relates.... (3) In acting under this section the court shall have regard to all the circumstances of the case and in particular to—(*a*) the length of, and the reasons for, the delay on the part of the plaintiff; (*b*) the extent to which, having regard to the delay, the evidence adduced or likely to be adduced by the plaintiff or the defendant is or is likely to be less cogent than if the action had been brought within the time allowed by section 2A [three years from the date on which the cause of action accrued, or the date (if

A   In the second action, the second writ, issued on April 4, 1978, was struck out by the district registrar on the ground that it was out of time. The plaintiff appealed to Park J., who allowed the appeal. Knowing that the defendant intended appealing against that decision to the Court of Appeal, the plaintiff applied ex parte to the district registrar to extend the validity of the first writ under R.S.C., Ord. 6, r. 8,[2] four and a half years after its issue, and outside the maximum period

B   for which a timeous extension might be allowed. Her application was refused, and her appeal to Kenneth Jones J. against that decision was dismissed.

On appeal by the defendants in both actions against the decisions to allow the proceedings begun by the second writs to continue, and on a cross-appeal by the plaintiff in the second action against the decision not to extend the validity of the first writ : —

C   Held, (1) allowing the appeals, that if a plaintiff started an action, but for any reason failed to proceed with it, it was not thereafter open to him to seek to take advantage of the provisions of section 2D of the Limitation Act 1939, as amended, because the cause of his prejudice was not the existence of the primary limitation period under section 2A, but was his own or his solicitors' act or omission in acting or failing to act as he or they should have done in relation to that action;

D   accordingly, the directions given in the courts below that the provisions of section 2A be disapplied must be set aside (post, p. 964c–d).

Walkley v. Precision Forgings Ltd. [1979] 1 W.L.R. 606, H.L.(E.) applied.

Per curiam. Firman v. Ellis (1978) Q.B. 886, C.A. no longer good law.

E   Per curiam. Firman v. Ellis can no longer be treated as guiding or binding authority on this branch of the law (post, p. 965c–d).

Per Ormrod L.J. The whole of the judgment in Firman v. Ellis has gone except perhaps for one remaining point, that in the exercise of the discretion under section 2D, in the form as now limited by the House of Lords, the discretion is one which is to be exercised generally and not in the restricted fashion

F   which the appellants in Firman v. Ellis were arguing for (post, p. 967g–h).

(2) Dismissing the cross-appeal, that the general rule that the court would not exercise its discretion in favour of the renewal of a writ after the period allowed for service had expired if the effect of doing so would be to deprive the defendant of the benefit of a limitation which accrued, remained unaffected by the introduction of the Limitation Act 1975, and

G   that the court had no power to grant the extension sought; and that, accordingly, where a plaintiff who had failed timeously to issue and serve his writ wished to obtain an extension under R.S.C., Ord. 6, r. 8, he had to comply with the principles and the practice under which the court granted such extensions. If he could not do so he could not avail himself of the benefits

H   later) of the plaintiff's knowledge] . . .; (c) the conduct of the defendant after the cause of action arose, including the extent if any to which he responded to requests reasonably made by the plaintiff for information or inspection for the purpose of ascertaining facts which were or might be relevant to the plaintiff's cause of action against the defendant; (d) the duration of any disability of the plaintiff arising after the date of the accrual of the cause of action; (e) the extent to which the plaintiff acted promptly and reasonably once he knew whether or not the act or omission of the defendant, to which the injury was attributable, might be capable at that time of giving rise to an action for damages; (f) the steps, if any, taken by the plaintiff to obtain medical, legal or other expert advice and the nature of any such advice he may have received."

[2] R.S.C., Ord. 6, r. 8: see post, p. 966a–b.

and privileges extended by the Act of 1975 (*post*, pp. 965E,   **A**
967c–D).
> *Heaven* v. *Road and Rail Wagons Ltd.* [1965] 2 Q.B. 355
> approved.
> Decisions of Bush J. and Park J. reversed.
> Decision of Kenneth Jones J. affirmed.

The following cases are referred to in the judgments:

Firman v. *Ellis* [1978] Q.B. 886; [1978] 3 W.L.R. 1; [1978] 2 All E.R. 851,   **B**
    C.A.

Heaven v. *Road and Rail Wagons Ltd.* [1965] 2 Q.B. 355; [1965] 2 W.L.R.
    1249; [1965] 2 All E.R. 409.

Walkley v. *Precision Forgings Ltd.* [1978] 1 W.L.R. 1228; [1979] 1 All
    E.R. 102, C.A.; [1979] 1 W.L.R. 606; [1979] 2 All E.R. 548, H.L.(E.).

  C

No additional cases were cited in argument.

CHAPPELL *v.* COOPER

INTERLOCUTORY APPEAL from Bush J.

The plaintiff, Ronald Chappell, was injured in a road accident on   **D**
August 11, 1971, and claimed damages for personal injuries against the
defendant, June Cooper, by a writ dated June 25, 1974. The writ was
not served within the time limit imposed by the Limitation Act 1939, as
amended by the Limitation Act 1975, and the action became statute-
barred. By order of the court on December 6, 1976, the writ was extended for 12 months, and was served on the defendant on January 10,   **E**
1977. On April 26, 1977, the defendant successfully applied to the court
for the service of the writ to be set aside and for the action to be dismissed. The plaintiff instructed new solicitors to make a claim for negligence against his original solicitors, and to issue a new writ against the
defendants. A second writ, 1978 C. No. 639, was issued and served by
the new solicitors against the defendants on May 24, 1978. A preliminary issue with regard to the limitation period was tried before Bush J.,   **F**
who directed that the plaintiff should have leave to proceed.

The defendant appealed on the ground, inter alia, that no prejudice
such as was referred to in section 2D of the Limitation Act 1939, as
amended, had been caused to the plaintiff by reason of the requirement
of section 2A of the Act that he should commence any action within
three years of the accrual of his cause of action, and that any prejudice   **G**
suffered by the plaintiff was consequent upon the failure of the plaintiff's
first solicitors to renew the writ issued in accordance with the Rules of
the Supreme Court.

PLAYER *v.* BRUGUIERE

  H

INTERLOCUTORY APPEALS from Park J. and Kenneth Jones J.

The plaintiff, Marjorie Ellen Player, was injured in a road accident
on December 9, 1971. She began an action for damages against the defendant, Michel Bruguiere, and a writ was issued on December 6, 1974.
That writ was never served. On April 4, 1978, the plaintiff issued a
second writ, and on February 5, 1979, that writ was struck out by the
order of the district registrar on the ground that it was out of time. The

A plaintiff appealed to Park J. on May 9, 1979. He allowed the appeal and
the defendant appealed against his decision to the Court of Appeal on the
ground, inter alia, that the judge was wrong in holding that where the
plaintiff had commenced an action within the primary limitation period,
section 2D of the Limitation Act 1939, as amended by the Limitation Act
1975, applied to a second action brought by the plaintiff in respect of the
same cause of action. Since, if the Court of Appeal were to reverse Park
B J.'s decision the action based on the second writ would come to an end,
the plaintiff applied ex parte to the district registrar on June 13, 1979,
to extend the validity of the first writ. The application was refused, and
the plaintiff appealed ex parte to Kenneth Jones J. on June 20, 1979, but
the appeal was dismissed. The plaintiff appealed against Kenneth Jones
J.'s decision on the ground, inter alia, that the provisions of section 2A
C to 2D of the Limitation Act 1939, as amended, had undermined the
former principles applicable to renewal of writs so that the court now
had an unfettered discretion to renew a writ in any action to which
section 2A applied. The Court of Appeal heard the plaintiff's appeal
against Kenneth Jones J.'s decision at the same time as it heard the
defendant's appeal against Park J.'s decision.

D
Piers Ashworth Q.C. and *Stephen Grime* for the defendant Cooper.
P. J. M. Kennedy Q.C. and *Roydon Thomas* for the plaintiff Chappell.
Michael Turner Q.C. and *Christopher Rawlins* for the plaintiff Player.
William Crowther for the defendant Bruguiere.

ROSKILL L.J. We have before us one appeal, that is in *Chappell* v.
E *Cooper*, which we gave leave to bring out of time last Monday. We have
also before us an application for leave to appeal in *Player* v. *Bruguiere*.
That application, as we have already indicated, will be granted. Therefore we have in addition the appeal in *Player* v. *Bruguiere*. Finally we
have what is in form an ex parte application on behalf of Mrs. Player,
the plaintiff in *Player* v. *Bruguiere*, for leave to extend the validity of the
writ which was issued in the action as long ago as December 6, 1974, but
F which was not only not served within 12 months of that date but has
never been served up to and including today, July 6, 1979. So that this
application is being made some four and a half years after the date of
the issue of the writ. We propose to give one judgment covering all the
matters that have been argued, but in relation to that last application I
should say that it has been argued inter partes.

G The appeal in *Chappell* v. *Cooper* is against a decision of Bush J.
given at Sheffield on May 10, 1979. The appeal in *Player* v. *Bruguiere*
is an appeal against a decision of Park J. given at Bristol on May 9, 1979.
The application for leave to extend the validity of the writ came before
Kenneth Jones J. also at Bristol on June 20 of this year, when he, for
reasons which he has set out in a very careful judgment, refused the
H application, but gave leave to appeal to this court.

The problems with which we are concerned arise out of the recent
decision of the House of Lords in *Walkley* v. *Precision Forgings Ltd.*
[1979] 1 W.L.R. 606. That decision was given on May 17, 1979. Therefore it was given a few days after the decisions of Park J. and Bush J.,
with which we are concerned, and both those judges did not have the
advantage of the speeches of their Lordships. But, of course Kenneth
Jones J.'s decision was after the date of their Lordships' decision.

Roskill L.J. Chappell v. Cooper (C.A.) **[1980]**

The problems arise because of the views expressed by their Lordships, by which of course we are bound in this court, as to the effect of section 2A, B and D of the Limitation Act 1939 as amended by the Limitation Act 1975. One of the problems is that seemingly their Lordships did not consider an earlier decision of this court (Lord Denning M.R., Ormrod and Geoffrey Lane L.JJ.) in *Firman* v. *Ellis* [1978] Q.B. 886, a decision given on February 6, 1978. We are told by counsel who argued the case for the appellant in *Walkley* v. *Precision Holdings Ltd.* in the House of Lords, Mr. Piers Ashworth, that *Firman* v. *Ellis* was mentioned in the appellant's printed case but that it was not referred to in any detail or indeed at all in argument before their Lordships for this reason; that the point upon which the appellant succeeded in *Walkley* v. *Precision Forgings Ltd.* [1979] 1 W.L.R. 606 was, it was said, a point taken for the first time in the House of Lords, and that when their Lordships were told that the point had never been taken in *Firman* v. *Ellis* they expressed no further interest in nor required further reference to *Firman* v. *Ellis*. Accordingly one point which we have to consider is the extent to which (if at all) *Firman* v. *Ellis* must still in certain respects be treated as good law.

It is easiest if I start with *Walkley* v. *Precision Forgings Ltd.* [1979] 1 W.L.R. 606. In that case the House reversed a majority decision of this court. The case was one where a writ had been issued by a plaintiff, who alleged that he had contracted an industrial disease between 1966 and 1971, on October 7, 1971. That writ was served, but on December 6, 1976, a fresh writ was issued beginning a second action asserting the same cause of action as that asserted by the 1971 writ. The second writ and statement of claim were then served on the defendants, who entered a conditional appearance. They applied to the master to strike out the second writ and to dismiss the action which that second writ instituted. The master made the order sought, but the judge in chambers allowed the plaintiff's appeal and restored the second action on the plaintiff's undertaking to discontinue the first action. The majority of this court dismissed the defendant's appeal on the ground that although the court would have been entitled to dismiss the first action for want of prosecution the criteria which were relevant to the court's decision were not the same as those under section 2D of the Act of 1939 as amended by the Act of 1975, and that accordingly the plaintiff was entitled to have the question whether the second action should be allowed to proceed tested by reference to the criteria in that Act. The House reversed that decision, and it is, in view of some of the arguments of which we have had the advantage in this court, necessary to see precisely upon what grounds their Lordships decided *Walkley*, for it has been strenuously argued by Mr. Kennedy for the plaintiff in the first appeal and by Mr. Michael Turner for the plaintiff in the second appeal, that *Walkley* is only a decision upon the particular facts of that case, and is not of general application. It is said that the present case can be distinguished because there was no question of striking out the first action, no question of discontinuing the first action; here the first action was never pursued because the writ in question was never served.

In *Walkley's* case Lord Wilberforce dealt with the main issue at p. 609 and after setting out the relevant part of section 2D said:

"The provisions of section 2A are those which require an action for personal injuries to be brought within three years. So subsection (1) (*a*) must be contemplating a case in which, because the three years

A have expired without an action being brought, section 2A applies to the prejudice of the plaintiff. But if the plaintiff has brought his action within the three years, how has he been prejudiced by section 2A? This I fail to understand. If this argument is sound, the respondent's case fails in limine. He brought his first action within the normal limitation period, and if he has suffered any prejudice, it is by his own inaction and not by the operation of the Act."

B

Lord Wilberforce then went on to deal with the other issue, namely, whether the judge's decision below was a correct exercise of his discretion.

Viscount Dilhorne dealt with the same issue at pp. 613 and 614. His Lordship, after setting out the whole of section 2D, said, at p. 613:

C "The effect, as I see it, of this section is that the ban imposed by section 2A remains unless and until the court in the exercise of its powers under this section directs that the provisions of section 2A shall not apply and so removes the ban. The court can only so direct when it appears to the court equitable to do so, and in deciding that, the court must have regard to the degree to which the provisions of section 2A prejudice the plaintiff. If they do not do so, the court can hardly regard it as equitable to allow the action to go on for it D must be prejudicial to a defendant to allow an action to proceed if it is started after the three year period has elapsed."

Viscount Dilhorne said, at p. 614:

"In my opinion this appeal should be allowed for it cannot be said that it was the provisions of section 2A (that is to say, the imposition of the three year period after which an action such as this cannot E be proceeded with without the directions of the court) which prejudiced the respondent when within that period he brought an action for damages for the same personal injuries and in respect of the same cause of action as in his second action. He was prejudiced by his delay in proceeding with the first action and by his discontinuance of that action, not by the provisions of section 2A."

F

Lord Diplock dealt with this issue at pp. 617–619. He said, at p. 618: "So the real question in the instant appeal is as to the application of section 2D to the action started by the second writ."
At p. 619:

"My Lords, in my opinion, once a plaintiff has started an action (the first action) within the primary limitation period it is only in G the most exceptional circumstances that he would be able to bring himself within section 2D in respect of a second action brought to enforce the same cause of action. If the first action is still in existence, as it was in the instant case when the matter was before the master and the judge, cadit quaestio; he has not been prevented from starting his action by section 2A or section 2B at all, so the H provisions of those sections cannot have caused him any prejudice. Does it make any difference that the first action is no longer in existence at the time of the application under section 2D either because it has been struck out for want of prosecution or because it has been discontinued by the plaintiff of his own volition? In my view, it does not. These are self-inflicted wounds. The provisions of section 2A caused him no prejudice at all; he was able to start his action. The only cause of the prejudice to him in the case

of dismissal for want of prosecution is dilatoriness which took place   A
after the action was started whether on his own part or on the part
of his legal advisers. In the case of discontinuance the only cause
of the prejudice is his own act. The only exception I have been able
to think of where it might be proper to give a direction under section
2D, despite the fact that the plaintiff had previously started an action
within the primary limitation period but had subsequently discontinued it, would be a case in which the plaintiff had been induced to   B
discontinue by a misrepresentation or other improper conduct by
the defendant; but there is no suggestion of this in the instant case."

Lord Edmund-Davies and Lord Keith of Kinkel said that they agreed
with both Lord Wilberforce and Lord Diplock's speeches.

With great respect to Mr. Kennedy and to Mr. Turner I cannot accept
the submission that this is a decision only upon the facts of that case.   C
It seems to me plainly a decision on principle that if a plaintiff starts but
then does not for any reason proceed with an action, whether it is because
the plaintiff chooses not to serve or his solicitors fail to serve the writ
timeously or because the action is subsequently struck out for want of
prosecution, or because for good reason or bad the plaintiff or his solicitors give notice of discontinuance, it is not open to a plaintiff thereafter   D
to seek to take advantage of the provisions of section 2D of the Limitation Act 1939, as amended, because, as their Lordships have laid down
(and we are of course bound by their decision) the cause of his prejudice
is not the provisions of section 2A, that is to say, the existence of the
primary limitation period, but is the act or ommission of himself or his
solicitors in acting or failing to act as he or they have done in relation
to that action.   E

It is said that that point was argued for the first time in the House of
Lords. When one looks at the report of *Walkley* v. *Precision Forgings*
Ltd. [1978] 1 W.L.R. 1228 in this court, in the majority judgment given
by Megaw L.J., this very point appears to have been adumbrated by him,
at p. 1235:

"If on the true interpretation of the Act of 1975 it could be said   F
that section 2D can have no application to a second action, where a
first action, started in time by the issue of a writ within the primary
period of limitation, has been discontinued or dismissed, then the
answer to the question raised by the present appeal would be simple.
Section 2D would have no application. There would be nothing in
the *Birkett* v. *James* [1978] A.C. 297 principle which would apply.   G
But that simple answer cannot, as I see it, be given in this case. It
was not submitted by Mr. Walker for the defendants that section 2D
can be construed as having no application to a case where a first writ
has been issued within the primary period and that first action has
been discontinued or dismissed."

So though it seems that the point upon which the House of Lords decided   H
Walkley must have been present in the mind of Megaw L.J. nobody took
the point in this court. It was ultimately taken by Mr. Ashworth for the
first time in their Lordships' House and succeeded, notwithstanding that
seemingly it had never previously been taken in any of the numerous
cases that have come either before judges in chambers or this court under
the Limitation Act 1975.

It is against that background that I turn to *Firman* v. *Ellis* [1978]

A Q.B. 886, to which I have already referred. If one looks at the argument of counsel for the appellant in *Firman* v. *Ellis* (there were four cases before this court of which *Firman* v. *Ellis* was the first) at p. 893 one sees the concession he made:

"It is conceded that on the facts and the history of the action the only prejudice to the defendant is being deprived of the benefit of
B the statutory defence under the limitation statutes. It is also conceded that the Act of 1975 has by section 2D given the court an overriding discretion to allow an action to proceed by having regard to the matters set out in subsection (3) (*a*) to (*f*)."

Thus in this court *Firman* v. *Ellis* was argued upon the basis that the court had a wholly unfettered discretion, within of course the limits of
C the relevant considerations laid down by the statute, to decide whether or not the primary limitation period might, to use the word which the draftsman of this statute has seen fit to use, be "disapplied." But that is not the view which their Lordships took in *Walkley*, and therefore with profound respect to the members of this court in *Firman* v. *Ellis,* in my view *Firman* v. *Ellis* can be no longer treated as guiding or binding authority in this branch of the law. What binds us is their Lordships'
D decision in *Walkley.*

In view of this it is clear that the two appeals, the one in *Chappell* v. *Cooper* and the other in *Player* v. *Bruguiere,* must be allowed and the directions given in the court below, that the provisions of section 2A be "disapplied," set aside.

That leaves the appeal from Kenneth Jones J. This has led to an
E interesting argument from Mr. Michael Turner. It has long been the law, and the law was authoritatively stated by Megaw J. in *Heaven* v. *Road and Rail Wagons Ltd.* [1965] 2 Q.B. 355, that in general in the absence of good or sufficient reason the court will not exercise its discretion in favour of the renewal of a writ after the period allowed for service has expired if the effect of doing so will be to deprive the defendant of the benefit of a limitation period which has accrued. I take that summary
F of the effect of the decision in *Heaven* from note 6/8/3 to R.S.C., Ord. 6, r. 8, in the Supreme Court Practice 1979 p. 57. Megaw J.'s decision has been accepted as correct many times in this court. But it has been strenuously argued that as a result of the introduction of the Limitation Act 1975 *Heaven* is no longer binding, and that it is open to this court, and indeed necessary for this court, wholly to reconsider its practice—for
G this is basically a matter of practice rather than substantive law—regarding granting leave to extend the time for service of the writ which has ceased to be valid because it has not been timeously served. It is said that it is now open to us to reconsider the position and to grant the requisite extension of time in any case where it seems equitable for us to do so, notwithstanding that so to do would be to deprive a defendant
H of the accrued benefit of a period of limitation prescribed by the Limitation Act 1939 as subsequently amended. The argument is designed to put a plaintiff who has failed timeously to serve his writ and who ex hypothesi is unable to obtain the benefit of section 2D in the same position as if he had obtained that benefit, because although he cannot successfully pursue a second action, as he cannot have the relevant limitation provisions "disapplied," he nonetheless, so the argument runs, can be allowed to go on with his first action and serve that writ many, many

months, or indeed years, after that writ ought to have been, but was not, **A**
served.

There is one short answer to this submission. That was given by Mr.
Crowther at the outset of his submissions on behalf of the respondent.
That answer turns on the true construction of R.S.C., Ord. 6, r. 8 (2):

"Where a writ has not been served on a defendant, the court may **B**
by order extend the validity of the writ from time to time for such
period, not exceeding 12 months at any one time, beginning with
the day next following that on which it would otherwise expire, as
may be specified in the order, if an application for extension is made
to the court before that day or such later day (if any) as the court
may allow."

Let me give the dates. The writ in the action of *Player* v. *Bruguiere* was **C**
issued on December 6, 1974. The 12 months therefore expired on
December 5, 1975, and the second period of 12 months, which would
be the maximum for which a timeous extension might be allowed, would
have run out on December 5, 1976. But the affidavit in support of this
application was not sworn until June 13, 1979, some three and a half years
after that last date. In view of those dates it seems to me clear, with all
respect to Mr. Turner, beyond doubt that we have no power under the **D**
rules to grant the extension sought.

That is enough to dispose of this appeal, but having regard to the importance of the issue I think it right not only to rest my judgment on
that conclusion. It was strenuously argued that the foundation of Megaw
J.'s decision was that in 1965 there was an absolute entitlement (save only
for the provisions of the Act of 1963 which are not presently relevant), **E**
on the part of a defendant to a three-year limitation period, and that save
in very exceptional circumstances the court would not at that date grant
an extension the effect of which would be to deprive him of that accrued
right. That, it is said, was the foundation of the judge's decision. It is
argued that since 1975 and because of the provisions of section 2D there
is now no absolute entitlement on the part of a defendant to the period
of limitation. The court has, subject to the decision in *Walkley* v. *Pre-* **F**
cision Forgings Ltd. [1979] 1 W.L.R. 606, a discretion to "disapply" the
relevant limitation period. Therefore it is argued that the foundation
for *Heaven* having gone we are free to reconsider—and should reconsider—the practice of the court.

Our attention has been drawn to one passage in the judgment of
Ormrod L.J. at pp. 912–913 and to another in the judgment of Geoffrey **G**
Lane L.J. at p. 916 in *Firman* v. *Ellis* [1978] Q.B. 886. Geoffrey Lane L.J.
in the latter passage, after referring to the decision in *Heaven,* said:

"The decision in *Heaven's* case would no longer constrain him "—
that is the master—" to dismiss the application, because the basis
of that decision, entirely correct when it was made, has been undermined and destroyed by the provisions of the Act of 1975. No longer **H**
is it true to say, as Megaw J. said [1965] 2 Q.B. 355, 358: ' It follows
that, if the validity of the writ were not to be extended, and if the
plaintiff were left to issue a fresh writ, the defendants would have an
unanswerable defence by virtue of the three-year period of limitation
prescribed by the Law Reform (Limitation of Actions, etc.) Act
1954 '."

A That was the relevant limitation statute in force at that time. With great respect to the views then expressed by both Ormrod L.J. and Geoffrey Lane L.J. it is difficult to take the same view today in the light of what the House of Lords has decided in *Walkley* v. *Precision Forgings Ltd.* [1979] 1 W.L.R. 606. I think, as Mr. Crowther submitted, that Megaw J.'s decision is perfectly consistent with and can stand alongside the decision of their Lordships' House. Had *Firman* v. *Ellis* [1978] Q.B. 886

B remained good law the position might have been otherwise, but for the reasons I have already given I do not think that *Firman* v. *Ellis* can still be said to be good law; and accordingly their Lordships having accepted that restrictive interpretation of the relevant provisions of the Act of 1975, it is not and would not be right for this court to by-pass their Lordships' decision by altering the practice that has long existed both before

C and since *Heaven* v. *Road and Rail Wagons Ltd.* [1965] 2 Q.B. 355 by granting long extensions of time to serve a writ which has not been timeously served, even if that were permissible under R.S.C., Ord. 6, r. 8 (2). The principles upon which extensions of time for the service of a writ beyond the initial 12 months can be granted have long been laid down. Those principles seem to me to remain unaffected. Accordingly if a plaintiff who has failed timeously to issue and serve his writ wishes

D to obtain an extension under Ord. 6, r. 8, he must comply with the principles and the practice under which the court grants such extensions. If he cannot do so, and also cannot avail himself of the benefits and privileges extended by the Act of 1975 that is his misfortune and he must look for redress elsewhere than to the proposed defendant, if indeed such other redress is open to him.

E   For those reasons the appeal from Kenneth Jones J.'s order must fail and be dismissed. In the result therefore the appeal in *Chappell* v. *Cooper* will be allowed; the first appeal in *Player* v. *Bruguiere* will be allowed but the second will be dismissed.

F   ORMROD L.J. I agree. I was foolish enough in the course of giving judgment in *Firman* v. *Ellis* [1978] Q.B. 886 to think that at a third attempt Parliament had succeeded in reforming this branch of the law. Now it is apparent that a fourth attempt will be necessary, if the law on this topic is to be rationalised. I see no alternative to Roskill L.J.'s view as to the effect of *Walkley* v. *Precision Forgings Ltd.* [1979] 1 W.L.R. 606 on the judgment in *Firman* v. *Ellis*. *Firman* v. *Ellis* proceeded on the basis, conceded expressly in one case and implicitly in the others, that

G the court had full discretion on the facts of all those four cases, all of which involved second actions. The point taken in *Walkley's* case was not adverted to in any way at all, and consequently the whole of the judgment in *Firman* v. *Ellis* as far as I can see has gone except perhaps for one remaining point, which is that in the exercise of the discretion under the Act of 1975 in the form as now limited by the House of Lords, the discretion is one which is to be exercised generally and not in the

H restricted fashion which the appellants in *Firman* v. *Ellis* were arguing for. That is all I think that can be said to survive from *Firman* v. *Ellis*. The result is that the game will continue to be played between defendants' insurance companies and solicitors' insurance companies. That is not a situation which I personally find at all satisfactory, but it is not for this court to try and resolve the problem. The House of Lords having adopted a restrictive construction of section 2D there is no alternative but to

Ormrod L.J.   Chappell v. Cooper (C.A.)   [1980]

accept the consequences which are as I have said; the old game will A
continue.

I see no alternative to the order proposed by Roskill L.J.

SIR DAVID CAIRNS. I agree that the defendants' appeal in *Chappell* v.
Cooper and *Player* v. *Bruguiere* should be allowed, and the plaintiff's
appeal in *Player* v. *Bruguiere* should be dismissed for the reasons which
have already been given and to which I have nothing of my own to add. B

> *Appeals allowed with costs.*
> *Cross-appeal dismissed with*
> *costs.*

Solicitors: *W. R. Kirk, Manchester; Keeble, Hawson, Steele Carr & Co.,* C
Sheffield; Bevan Hancock & Co., Bristol; Stanley, Wasbrough & Co.,
Bristol.

R. D.

[COURT OF APPEAL]   D

* SIMPSON v. NORWEST HOLST SOUTHERN LTD.

1980 Feb. 21, 22;   Lawton, Ormrod and
       March 14   Brightman L.JJ.

Limitation of Action—Personal injuries—Time limit, power to   E
   override—Employee injured at work—Identity of employer not
   known until end of primary period of limitation—Writ issued
   14 days out of time—Application to strike out and dismiss
   action as abuse of process—Court's discretion to override
   normal three-year period of limitation—Whether restricted
   to exceptional cases—Whether equitable to allow action to
   proceed—Limitation Act 1939 (2 & 3 Geo. 6, c. 21) (as
   amended by Limitation Act 1975 (c. 54), s. 1), s. 2A (4) (6)   F
   (c) (8) [1]

The plaintiff, who started work as a carpenter on a building
site in July 1976, received the statutory notice setting out his
terms of employment which gave the name of his employers as
a " group " which was in fact formed from four limited com-

[1] Limitation Act 1939 (as amended), s. 2A:— " (1) This section applies to any G
action for damage for negligence, . . . or breach of duty . . . where the damages
claimed by the plaintiff for the negligence . . . or breach of duty consist of or include
damages in respect of personal injuries to the plaintiff . . . (3) Subject to section 2D
below, an action to which this section applies shall not be brought after the expiration of the period specified in subsections (4) and (5) below. (4) Except where subsection (5) applies [if the person injured dies], the said period is three years from—
(a) the date on which the cause of action accrued, or (b) the date (if later) of the
plaintiff's knowledge . . . (6) In this section . . . references to a person's date of
knowledge are references to the date on which he first had knowledge of . . . (c) the   H
identity of the defendant . . . (8) . . . a person's knowledge includes knowledge which
he might reasonably have been expected to acquire—(a) from facts observable or
ascertainable by him, or (b) from facts ascertainable by him with the help of medical
or other appropriate expert advice which it is reasonable for him to seek. . . ."
     S. 2D: " (1) If it appears to the court that it would be equitable to allow an
action to proceed having regard to the degree to which—(a) the provisions of section
2A [new time limits] or 2B [time limit for actions under the Fatal Accidents Act
1846] . . . prejudice the plaintiff . . . and (b) any decision of the court under this subsection would prejudice the defendant . . . the court may direct that those provisions
shall not apply to the action . . . (3) In acting under this section the court shall have

A panies. On August 4, 1976, the plaintiff injured his leg while at work. He consulted solicitors who, on September 16, wrote to one of the companies in the group who they believed to be the plaintiff's employers, making a claim for damages on his behalf. They received a reply from insurers under the name of another of the companies in the group. Correspondence took place between the plaintiff's solicitors and the insurers but it was not until July 4, 1979, that the solicitors were able

B to discover the correct name of the plaintiff's employers. The solicitors, who had overlooked the fact that the three years' limitation period following the plaintiff's accident had expired at midnight on August 3, 1979, issued a summons in the county court on August 17 claiming damages for personal injuries against the defendants. The defendants applied to strike out the particulars of claim and have the action dismissed under Ord. 13, r. 6 of the County Court Rules 1936, on the grounds

C that the claim disclosed no reasonable cause of action, was an abuse of the process of the court and that the facts and matters relied on had occurred more than three years before the issue of the summons and that the action was barred by the Limitation Act 1939. The registrar dismissed the application. The defendants appealed to Judge Vowden who took the view that the delay in issuing the summons was not due to the negligence of the plaintiff's solicitors but that the case fell within section

D 2A of the Act of 1939, as amended, and that accordingly he had a discretion under section 2D to decide whether to allow the action to continue. He held that it would be equitable to allow the action to proceed and dismissed the defendants' application.

 On appeal by the defendants on the ground, inter alia, that the judge was wrong in law in holding that the plaintiff was prejudiced by section 2A and that therefore he had no dis-

E cretion under section 2D, and on a respondent's notice by the plaintiff, with the leave of the Court of Appeal, seeking to uphold the judgment on the additional ground that he had not known the identity of his employers until after August 17, 1976: —

 Held, dismissing the appeal, (1) that when the plaintiff injured himself on August 4, 1976, he did not know the identity of his employers and could not, before August 17, 1976,

F reasonably have been expected to have acquired that knowledge, and accordingly, having regard to section 2A (4), (6) (c) and (8) of the Limitation Act 1939, as amended, his action was not barred by effluxion of time (post, p. 974B–D, G).

 (2) That, even if the plaintiff's action were barred, the court had jurisdiction under section 2D to override the time limits, since the subsection contained no restrictive words and none could be implied, and it therefore gave the court a wide dis-

G cretion: the subsection could not and should not be read in any restrictive sense so as to apply only to exceptional cases (post, p. 976F–G).

regard to all the circumstances of the case and in particular to—(*a*) the length of, and the reasons for, the delay on the part of the plaintiff; (*b*) the extent to which, having regard to the delay, the evidence adduced or likely to be adduced by the plaintiff or the defendant is or is likely to be less cogent than if the action had been

H brought within the time allowed by section 2A or as the case may be 2B; (*c*) the conduct of the defendant after the cause of action arose, including the extent if any to which he responded to requests reasonably made by the plaintiff for information or inspection for the purpose of ascertaining facts which were or might be relevant to the plaintiff's cause of action against the defendant; (*d*) the duration of any disability of the plaintiff arising after the date of the accrual of the cause of action; (*e*) the extent to which the plaintiff acted promptly and reasonably once he knew whether or not the act or omission of the defendant, to which the injury was attributable, might be capable at that time of giving rise to an action for damages; (*f*) the steps, if any, taken by the plaintiff to obtain ... expert advice and the nature of any such advice he may have received."

Firman v. *Ellis* [1978] Q.B. 886, C.A. and *Chappell* v. A
Cooper [1980] 1 W.L.R. 000, C.A. considered.

(3) That the plaintiff had been prejudiced by section 2A
since by August 4, 1979, his claim was likely to be barred by
a limitation plea and though the defendants had also been
prejudiced because they would have to defend a claim which
they thought was barred by effluxion of time there was ample
evidence on which the judge could come to the conclusion that
it would be equitable to allow the action to proceed, he had B
exercised his discretion in a proper manner, and the court
could not interfere (post, p. 977A–C).

The following cases are referred to in the judgment:

Chappell v. *Cooper* [1980] 1 W.L.R. 958; [1980] 2 All E.R. 463, C.A.
Firman v. *Ellis* [1978] Q.B. 886; [1978] 3 W.L.R. 1; [1978] 2 All E.R. 851,
  C.A.   C
Walkley v. *Precision Forgings Ltd.* [1978] 1 W.L.R. 1228; [1979] 1 All E.R.
  102, C.A.; [1979] 1 W.L.R. 606; [1979] 2 All E.R. 548, H.L.(E.).

The following additional cases were cited in argument:

Cartledge v. *E. Jopling & Sons Ltd.* [1963] A.C. 758; [1963] 2 W.L.R. 210;
  [1963] 1 All E.R. 341, H.L.(E.).
Clark v. *Forbes Stuart (Thames Steel) Ltd., In re* [1964] 1 W.L.R. 836; D
  [1964] 2 All E.R. 282, C.A.
Davies v. *Elsby Brothers Ltd.* [1961] 1 W.L.R. 170; [1961] 1 All E.R. 672,
  C.A.
Rodriguez v. *R. J. Parker (Male)* [1967] 1 Q.B. 116; [1966] 3 W.L.R. 546;
  [1966] 2 All E.R. 349.
Smith v. *Central Asbestos Co. Ltd.* [1973] A.C. 518; [1972] 3 W.L.R. 333;
  [1972] 2 All E.R. 1135, H.L.(E.).   E
Tolley v. *Morris* [1979] 1 W.L.R. 592; [1979] 2 All E.R. 561, H.L.(E.).
Whittam v. *W. J. Daniel & Co. Ltd.* [1962] 1 Q.B. 271; [1961] 3 W.L.R.
  1123; [1961] 3 All E.R. 796, C.A.

APPEAL from Judge Vowden sitting at Swindon County Court.

By a summons dated August 17, 1979, the plaintiff, Clive Joseph Simpson, claimed damages from the defendants, Norwest Holst Southern Ltd., F
his employers, for personal injuries. By his particulars of claim he
alleged that he had sustained an injury to his leg on August 4, 1976, while
working on a scaffold on the defendants' building site in Swindon to
which the Construction (Working Places) Regulations 1966 applied, and
that his injury was due to the breach by the defendants of certain of the
regulations. He also alleged negligence on their part.

The defendants applied to the registrar of the county court under G
Ord. 13, r. 6 of the County Court Rules 1936 for the particulars of claim
to be struck out and for the action to be dismissed on the grounds that
(1) it disclosed no reasonable cause of action; (2) it was vexatious and
an abuse of the process of the court; and (3) that the facts and matters
relied on had occurred more than three years before the issue of the
summons and the claim (which was denied) was barred by the Limitation H
Act 1939.

At the hearing of the application before Mr. Registrar Trayburn it
was contended for the plaintiff that it was a suitable case for the exercise
of the court's discretion under section 2D of the Act of 1939 as amended
by the Act of 1975.

In a reserved judgment delivered on November 8, 1979, the registrar
exercised his discretion under section 2D in favour of the plaintiff, direc-

A ted that the provisions of section 2A of the Act of 1939, as amended, should not apply to the action and dismissed the defendants' application.

The defendants appealed to Judge Vowden who, on January 3, 1980, distinguished the present case from *Walkley* v. *Precision Forgings Ltd.* [1979] 1 W.L.R. 606, and held that section 2A applied and that therefore section 2D applied. He took the view that the prejudice to the defen-
B dants by the issue of the summons 14 days outside the three-year period was minimal and that the prejudice to the plaintiff if the action were not allowed to continue far outweighed it. Taking into account all the circumstances of the case as required by section 2D he held that it would be equitable to allow the action to proceed. He accordingly dismissed the defendants' appeal but gave them leave to appeal.

The defendants appealed on the grounds, inter alia, that the judge
C was wrong in law in holding that although the plaintiff and his solicitors had the requisite knowledge of the facts for the purpose of section 2A (6) of the Act of 1939, as amended, before the expiry of the primary period of limitation the plaintiff was prejudiced by section 2A (4); that the judge was wrong in law in failing to hold that the purposive construction given to the Act by the House of Lords in *Walkley's* case did not apply to the circumstances of the present case, namely, that any prejudice suffered by
D the plaintiff arose simply by virtue of his solicitors' failure to issue the summons and/or not out of any of the matters referred to in section 2D of the Act; and that the judge was wrong in holding that the failure to issue the summons within the primary period of limitation had prejudiced the plaintiff more than it had caused prejudice to them, the defendants.

At the hearing of the appeal, the court granted counsel for the plain-
E tiff leave to serve a respondent's notice asking that the decision of Judge Vowden should be affirmed on the additional grounds (1) that the plaintiff first had knowledge of the identity of his employers within the meaning of section 2A (6) (c) of the Act of 1939, as amended, on a date later than August 17, 1976; (2) that, in the premises, the time limit pursuant to section 2A (4) of the Act, within which the plaintiff had the right to commence the proceedings, had not expired at the time of the commence-
F ment of them; and (3) that in the premises, at all material times the plaintiff had an indefeasible right to commence the proceedings.

Further facts are stated in the judgment of the court.

Michael Turner Q.C. and *David Paton* for the defendants.
Adrian Palmer for the plaintiff.

G
                                            Cur. adv. vult.

March 14. The following judgment was read.

LAWTON L.J. The judgment I am about to deliver is the judgment of the court.

H On July 19, 1976, the plaintiff started work as a carpenter on the Brunel Plaza building site at Swindon. His employers gave him a statement purporting to be under the Contracts of Employment Act 1963, as amended (it should have been under the Contracts of Employment Act 1972) which set out his terms of employment. This notice stated that "the employing company" was "Norwest Holst Group." The statutory obligation on the employers under section 4 (1) of the Act of 1972 was to give him a written statement "identifying the parties." This the notice

did not do as the words " Norwest Holst Group " do not identify any legal   A
entity.   There seem to have been at least four companies forming that
Group, namely, Norwest Holst Ltd., Norwest Construction Co. Ltd.,
Norwest Holst Southern Ltd. and Norwest Holst Group Administration
Ltd.

On August 4, 1976, the plaintiff hurt his left leg whilst at work.   He
alleges that it was due to his employers' breaches of statutory duty under   B
the Construction (Working Places) Regulations 1966 and to their negligence.   Shortly afterwards he consulted solicitors.   On September 16,
1976, they wrote to " Norwest Holst Ltd." making a claim for damages
on behalf of the plaintiff.   This identified the plaintiff and the date, time
and place of the accident.   It described the plaintiff as being employed
" as a carpenter at your site at the Brunel Plaza, Swindon " and " working
under your foreman " at that site.   C

The recipients of this letter did not reply to it but passed it on to their
insurers who answered by a letter dated October 1, 1976.   This letter
gave the plaintiff's claim a reference number and was headed " Norest "—
that was clearly a spelling mistake as it turns out—" Construction Co.
Ltd."   It referred to the solicitors' letter as having been addressed to
" Norwest Holst."   Thereafter letters passed between the solicitors and
the insurers at a leisurely pace which were headed either " Norest   D
Construction Co. Ltd." or " Norwest Construction Co. Ltd."

There was a gap in the correspondence between November 11, 1976,
and August 9, 1978.   On the latter date the solicitors wrote to the insurers
telling them that the plaintiff had obtained legal aid for proceedings against
" Norwest Construction Co. Ltd." and asking how such proceedings
should be served.   The insurers did not reply to this letter.   E

About this date the solicitors had doubts as to whether the employers
were Norwest Holst Ltd. or Norwest Construction Co. Ltd.   They made
a company search to discover the whereabouts of the registered offices of
these two companies.   On October 31, 1978, the solicitors had a meeting
with a representative of the insurers.   He was asked who the defendants
to any proceedings ought to be.   On the same day the solicitors asked   F
the plaintiff to let them have his pay slips.   He produced some.   They
showed his employers as " Norwest Holst."

By this time the solicitors were puzzled as to who were the plaintiff's
employers.   They expressed this puzzlement in a letter to the plaintiff
dated November 10, 1978, and told him that they thought it would be
safer to see what information the insurance company could give.   The
insurers gave none until much later.   G

Some time about May 1979 there was some discussion between the
solicitors and the insurers.   We infer that it was about a medical report
and the whereabouts of the employers' registered office.   By letter dated
May 24, 1979, the insurers referred to this discussion. The last sentence
of this letter was as follows: " . . . we can advise you that our insured's
registered office is 35, Chesham Place, London."   That letter gave the   H
same claims reference number as before but had after it the words " Norwest Holst."   By letter dated June 11, 1979, the solicitors sent the insurers
copies of two medical reports.   The letter ended in these terms:

" We are obliged to you for the address of your insured's registered
office but we shall be most grateful if you will confirm to us that the
correct title of your insured in this case is indeed Norwest Holst Ltd.
We have discovered some confusion during the course of our investi-

A   gations, as apparently there are several interlinked companies operating together."

The insurers did not reply to this letter until July 4, 1979. They have
not explained why they took so long to do so. In their answer they said
that the "correct title of our insured in this case is Norwest Holst
Southern Ltd."

B   This was the first time that the name of this company had been mentioned. It was not on the plaintiff's statutory written statement of the
plaintiff's terms of employment, as it should have been, nor on his payslips. On July 9, 1979, the solicitors wrote to the Law Society asking for
the name of the proposed defendant on the legal aid certificate to be
altered from Norwest Construction Co. Ltd. to Norwest Holst Southern

C Ltd.
     On August 17, 1979, the solicitors issued a summons in the Swindon
County Court claiming damages for personal injuries on behalf of the
plaintiff against Norwest Holst Southern Ltd. The three years' period of
limitation under the Limitation Act 1939, as amended, had expired at
midnight on August 3, 1979. The solicitors informed the insurers by
letter dated August 21, 1979, that proceedings had been started.

D   The defendants were quick enough now in taking action. On October 8, 1979, they applied to the registrar of the Swindon County Court
to strike out the particulars of claim and dismiss the action pursuant to
Ord. 13, r. 6 of the County Court Rules 1936. The plaintiff asked for
the exercise of the court's discretion in his favour under section 2D of
the Limitation Act 1939, as amended by the Limitation Act 1975. On
November 8, 1979, the registrar dismissed the defendants' application and
E directed that the provisions of section 2A of the Limitation Act 1939, as
amended by the Act of 1975, should not apply to the action.
     The defendants appealed to the judge in the county court, Judge
Vowden. He heard the appeal on January 3, 1980, and dismissed it. He
gave leave to appeal to this court and the defendants have appealed.
     Both before the registrar and the judge, and at first before this court,
F the plaintiff asked for the exercise of the powers given to courts by section 2D to override time limits. The defendants came to this court intending to argue that section 2D had no application to this case. Whilst Mr.
Turner on behalf of the defendants was making his submissions before
us, Brightman L.J. called his attention to the possible application of section 2A (4) and (6) to the facts of this case. Both he and Mr. Palmer on
behalf of the plaintiff were given an opportunity of considering this point
G during an overnight adjournment. The next day Mr. Palmer applied for
leave to serve a respondent's notice asking that the order of Judge
Vowden should be affirmed on grounds additional to those relied on in
the court below, namely, that the plaintiff first had knowledge of the
identity of the defendants within the meaning of section 2A (6) (c) of the
Limitation Act 1939, as amended, on a date later than August 17, 1976.
H Mr. Turner did not oppose the application. We granted it.
     In these circumstances, the following issues have required considera-
tion. First, when did the plaintiff first have knowledge of the identity
of the defendants? Secondly, if he first had actual knowledge when his
solicitors received the defendants' insurers' letter dated July 4, 1979,
might he reasonably have been expected to acquire knowledge of the
identity of his employers before August 17, 1976, from facts observable
or ascertainable by him? Thirdly, have the provisions of section 2A

prejudiced the plaintiff? Fourthly, would the decision of the court under A
section 2D (1) prejudice the defendants? Fifthly, would it be equitable
to allow the action to proceed having regard to the degrees of prejudice
to both parties? If the answers to questions 1 and 2 are in favour of the
plaintiff, there would be no need to answer the other questions as time
would not have begun to run against the plaintiff until he first had knowledge of the identity of the defendants. We have decided, however, to
answer all five questions.   B

Section 2A applies to any action for negligence or breach of duty. It
follows that it applies to this action. Subject to section 2D an action to
which section 2A applies should not be brought after the expiration of
the periods specified in subsections (4) and (5): see subsection (3). Subsection (4) provides that the relevant period in this case is three years
from (a) the date on which the cause of the action accrued, or (b) the   C
date (if later) of the plaintiff's knowledge. By subsection (6), references
to a person's date of knowledge are references to the date on which he
first had knowledge of certain facts, including under paragraph (c) the
identity of the defendant. By subsection (8) a person's knowledge

" includes knowledge which he might reasonably have been expected
to acquire—(a) from facts observable or ascertainable by him, or   D
(b) from facts ascertainable by him with the help of medical or other
appropriate expert advice which it is reasonable for him to seek . . ."

In the circumstances of this case all the plaintiff has to show is that he
first had knowledge of the identity of the defendants after August 17,
1976, bearing in mind what knowledge he might reasonably have been
expected to acquire.   E

When a man takes a job, he might reasonably be expected to find out
who is employing him; and the employers have a statutory duty to identify themselves to the employee in the written statement which they must
give him pursuant to section 4 (1) of the Contracts of Employment Act
1972. The defendants hid their identity from the plaintiff under the
words " Norwest Holst Group." The plaintiff could not reasonably have
been expected to ask for further and better particulars of the identity of   F
his employers. We do not know what, if any, notices there were on the
building site indicating who the contractors were. There was probably
one, may be more than one, which bore the name Norwest Holst. That
was the name on the plaintiff's pay slips and it seems to have been the
name which he gave the solicitors when he consulted them in September
1976. Either he or they, probably they, inferred in September 1976 that   G
Norwest Holst was a limited company. In our judgment, when the plaintiff hurt himself at work, on August 4, 1976, he did not know the identity
of his employers and could not before August 17, 1976, reasonably have
been expected to acquire the knowledge. The only sources from which
he could ascertain the knowledge, namely, the statutory written statement
of the terms of his employment and his pay slips did not give him any
information usable in legal proceedings. Since the plaintiff had no know-   H
ledge of the identity of his employers on August 17, 1976, it is unnecessary
to decide when thereafter through his solicitors he might reasonably have
been expected to acquire it. It suffices to say that for some time after
October 1, 1976, the plaintiff's solicitors acted reasonably in assuming
that his employers were Norest Construction Co. Ltd. It follows that on
August 17, 1979, the plaintiff's action was not barred by the effluxion of
time.

A   If it was, had Judge Vowden any jurisdiction to overrule the time limits? This was the point the insurers behind the defendants wanted decided. Mr. Turner told us that the insurance issue is this: when solicitors fail to start proceedings coming within section 2A (1) should claims be paid under professional indemnity policies or under accident indemnity policies? If courts have jurisdiction in cases such as this to overrule time limits, then claims will fall upon insurers under accident indemnity poli-

B   cies and insurers under professional indemnity policies will avoid liability for the very risks in respect of which they have been paid premiums. We appreciate the commercial importance of such an issue. Whether this appeal will provide an answer is not for us to say. We have to decide the appeal on the facts before us.

Judge Vowden's jurisdiction, if any, was derived from section 2D.

C   We have to construe that section and in doing so we have to consider the words used. This is a commonplace observation to make but a necessary one in this case. Section 2D has a history, the details of which are set out in the judgment of Lord Denning M.R. in *Firman* v. *Ellis* [1978] Q.B. 886, 903–905. We do not consider it necessary to go over that history again. It suffices to say that the last committee which re-

D   ported on the problems arising out of the limitation of actions, that presided over by Orr L.J., recommended in May 1974 [Law Reform Committee 20th Report (Interim Report on Limitation of Actions: In Personal Injury Claims)] (Cmnd. 5630) that the court should have a discretion in some " exceptional cases " to extend the time within which actions could be brought. The Limitation Act 1975 followed. It contained section 2D. Ever since attempts have been made to persuade courts that section 2D

E   should be construed so as to apply only to exceptional cases, the assumption being that Parliament intended to enact the Orr committee's proposals.

The first of these attempts seems to have been in *Firman* v. *Ellis.* No less than four appeals raising substantially the same kind of points were heard together. In each of the cases the court had to consider the effect of issuing new writs after the expiration of the limitation period.

F   In three of the cases writs had been issued within the limitation period but had not been served within a year as provided under the Rules of the Supreme Court. In the fourth an application to join a third party had been made one day out of time. None of the counsel appearing seem to have argued that the prejudice suffered by the four plaintiffs arose from the failure of their solicitors to get on with the actions started

G   within time and not from the provisions of section 2A. The court did, however, decide that section 2D gave the court a wide discretion to override time limits and that the relevant words of the section were so clear that they cannot be construed restrictively as applying only to exceptional cases. The orders made by this court in *Firman* v. *Ellis* cannot, however, now be regarded as correctly made because of the decision of the House

H   of Lords in *Walkley* v. *Precision Forgings Ltd.* [1979] 1 W.L.R. 606.

In that case the plaintiff's solicitors issued a writ on October 7, 1971, claiming damages for personal injuries caused by the alleged negligence and/or breach of duty of the defendants. No statement of claim was ever delivered. The action went to sleep. On December 6, 1976, a new firm of solicitors issued another writ for the same cause of action. The defendants applied to have the second writ struck out and the action dismissed. The master made the order. The judge in chambers allowed an

appeal by the plaintiff on his undertaking to discontinue the first action. A
An appeal by the defendants to this court was dismissed, Waller L.J. dissenting: see [1978] 1 W.L.R. 1228. The submission before this court
seems to have been based upon the assumption that the plaintiff had been
prejudiced by the application of section 2A. In the House of Lords it
was adjudged that since the plaintiff had previously started an action for
the same cause of action within the primary limitation period prescribed
by section 2A, he could not bring himself within section 2D at all. Any B
prejudice arising to the plaintiff by the discontinuance of the first action was
his own act: see the speech of Lord Wilberforce at p. 609D–E; that of
Viscount Dilhorne at p. 614B; and that of Lord Diplock at p. 619B–D.
The House was not concerned with the construction of section 2D; but
Lord Diplock did make some general observations at p. 618H. Both
Lord Wilberforce and Lord Diplock expressed approval of Waller L.J.'s C
dissenting judgment; but it seems clear that the approval was directed to
his assessment of the evidence as demonstrating that it would have been
inequitable to allow the second action to proceed and that no further
evidence could exist which was capable of leading to a contrary conclusion: see the speech of Lord Diplock at p. 616D. Save for Lord Diplock's
general observation about section 2D, to which we have already referred,
Walkley's case provides us with no guidance on the construction of that D
section.

The point upon which Walkley's case turned led this court in Chappell
v. Cooper [1980] 1 W.L.R. 958, to adjudge that Firman v. Ellis
[1978] Q.B. 886 could no longer be treated as a guiding or binding
authority. This was clearly right as to the orders made in that case.
Had this court's attention been invited to the point upon which Walkley's E
case [1979] 1 W.L.R. 606 was decided, those orders would not have been
made. Nevertheless, as Ormrod L.J. pointed out in Chappell v. Cooper,
the construction which this court in Firman v. Ellis gave to section 2D
may perhaps survive. As we have no wish for the purposes of this judgment to become involved in the niceties of the principle of stare decisis,
we will treat Firman v. Ellis as a persuasive authority on the construction
of section 2D. We refer particularly to the judgment of Geoffrey Lane F
L.J.

The opening words of section 2D are " If it appears to the court that
it would be equitable to allow an action to proceed . . ." having regard
to two specified factors, " the court may direct that those provisions (i.e.
section 2A or 2B) shall not apply to the action. . . ." No restrictive words
are to be found here; and in our judgment none can be implied because G
subsection (3) provides that even when acting under this section " the
court shall have regard to all the circumstances of the case " and in
particular to six specific matters. In our judgment section 2D cannot,
and should not, be read in any restrictive sense so as to apply only to
exceptional cases.

Mr. Turner also submitted that whether section 2D was construed H
restrictively or generally, the plaintiff has not shown that the provisions
of section 2A have prejudiced him whereas the overriding of time limits
by the court would prejudice the defendants. They would have to defend
a claim which on August 4, 1979, they thought had been barred by
effluxion of time. Mr. Turner contended that what had prejudiced the
plaintiff for the purposes of section 2D was his solicitors' delay in issuing
a summons, not the provisions of section 2A. This cannot be right.

A Until midnight on August 3, 1979, the plaintiff had a claim against the
defendants which could not be defeated by a plea based on the Limitation
Act 1939, as amended. His chances of success may have been reduced
by his solicitors' delays but the viability of his claim was not affected
thereby. By August 4, 1979, his claim was likely to be barred by a limitation plea. This was due to the provisions of section 2A, not to his
solicitors' delays. There being prejudice to both the plaintiff and the
B defendants, Judge Vowden had to decide whether it would be equitable
to allow the action to proceed. He had, under subsection (3), to have
regard to all the circumstances of the case and in particular to the matters
set out in paragraphs (a) to (f). In our judgment, there was ample evidence
upon which he could properly come to the decision he did. He did not
misdirect himself. In our judgment, there is no reason why this court
C should interfere with his decision. Anyway, he exercised his discretion
as we would have done. The claim was only 14 days out of time. One
reason for the delay was the difficulty, due to the act of the insurers,
which the plaintiff's solicitors had had in identifying the defendants. The
defendants had had an early opportunity of investigating the claim after
the alleged accident and of getting their evidence together. They were
in no worse position to defend the claim when the summons was issued
D on August 17 than they would have been had proceedings started on
August 3, 1979.

The appeal is dismissed.

Appeal dismissed with costs.
Leave to appeal refused.
Legal aid taxation of plaintiff's costs.

E

Solicitors: *Wansbroughs, Bristol; Clarke Dale & Collis, Swindon.*

E. M. W.

F

[QUEEN'S BENCH DIVISION]

* ELLIOTT AND ANOTHER *v.* DIRECTOR GENERAL
OF FAIR TRADING

G 1980 May 16   Lord Lane C.J. and Woolf J.

*Sale of Goods — Consumer credit — Credit-token — Advertising
material sent to members of public—Card purporting to be
credit card for immediate use—Additional steps required to
obtain credit — Whether " credit-token " — Consumer Credit
Act 1974 (c. 39), ss. 14 (1), 51 (1)*

Section 14 (1) of the Consumer Credit Act 1974 provides:
H " A credit-token is a card, check, voucher, coupon, stamp,
form, booklet or other document or thing given to an
individual by a person carrying on a consumer credit
business, who undertakes—(a) that on the production of
it (whether or not some other action is also required) he
will supply cash, goods and services (or any of them) on
credit . . ."
The first defendant was a director of the defendant
company of footwear retailers. The company instituted a

A

promotional scheme whereby certain members of the public
were sent unsolicited an envelope containing a number of
items. The material one was a plasticised card which stated
on its face "The Elliott Account," the company's name,
dates during which the card was valid and a series of figures
similar to those printed by a computer, although they were
not embossed. On the reverse the card displayed a box for
the recipient's signature, then stated that it was a credit
card valid for immediate use, the sole requirement being a
signature and means of identification and that credit was

B

immediately available if the recipient had a bank account.
In fact before a holder of the card could obtain credit from the
defendant company, he would have to obtain the company's
account card, sign a direct debiting mandate and enter into a
credit sale agreement. The Director General of Fair Trading
preferred four informations against the first defendant and
four against the company alleging that they had given credit-
tokens to persons who had not asked for them contrary to

C

section 51 (1) of the Consumer Credit Act 1974. The justices
held that the cards were credit-tokens within section 14 (1)
of the Act and convicted the defendants.

On appeal by the defendants: —

Held, dismissing the appeal, that the test to be applied
was whether on the face or back of the card the company
undertook that on production of the card cash, goods and

D

services (or any of them) would be supplied on credit; that
since the card stated that it was a credit card valid for
immediate use, the sole requirement being a signature and
that credit was immediately available if the recipient had a
bank account, the defendants had undertaken to give credit
and the card was a credit-token within the meaning of section
14 (1); that the fact that those statements were untrue did
not alter the nature of the card and, in any event, the words

E

"whether or not some other action is also required" in
section 14 (1) brought the card within the subsection since
it covered the additional steps which the recipient needed to
take, including the signing of a direct debiting mandate to
his bank, in order to obtain credit from the company; and
accordingly the defendants had been properly convicted under
section 51 (1).

F

No cases are referred to in the judgment.

The following case was cited in argument:

Scammell (G.) & Nephew Ltd. v. *H.C. and T.G. Ouston* [1941] A.C.
251; [1941] 1 All E.R. 14, H.L.(E.).

G

CASE STATED by Surrey justices sitting at Kingston-upon-Thames.

The first defendant, Adrian Thomas Marchant Elliott, was a director
of the defendant company, T. Elliott & Sons Ltd., who were retailers of,
inter alia, ladies shoes with a registered office at Ernest Elliott House,
112 Westbourne Grove, London W.2. The prosecutor, Director General
of Fair Trading, was an official appointed under section 1 of the Fair

H

Trading Act 1973, who had various functions and duties to perform
under the Consumer Credit Act 1974 including, where necessary or
expedient, himself to take steps to enforce the Act.

On January 27, 1978, the prosecutor preferred four informations
against the first defendant and four informations against the defendant
company. The informations each alleged that the defendants had given
an individual named therein (" the consumer ") a credit token for which

A she had not asked contrary to the provisions of section 51 (1) of that
Act.

The justices heard the informations on March 22, 1978, when both
defendants and the prosecutor were represented by counsel, and found
the following facts. At various dates in 1977, set out in the informations,
the defendant company sent to each of the consumers an envelope with
writing upon the interior thereof, and with enclosures consisting of a
B card (" the card ") together with a covering letter (" the promotional
package "). None of the consumers had asked that the promotional
package or any part thereof should be sent to them, whether in writing
or otherwise. In answer to questions from a trading standards officer,
the first defendant asserted that upon the production of such card the
defendant company, would not automatically supply goods on credit to
C the producer thereof. The company would require such a person to
(i) apply for and acquire an " Elliott account card " (ii) sign a " direct
debiting mandate " (iii) enter into a credit sale agreement, all by completion of the form (" the form ") before supplying such a person goods
on credit. The prosecutor did not seek to challenge that. The first
defendant was at all material times a director of the defendant company
and arranged for the sending of the promotional packages.
D
The defendants contended that the defendant company did not in
the promotional package make any offer to the consumers that was
intended to be and/or was capable of being accepted thereby so as to
impose upon the defendant company the legally binding obligation to
supply goods thereto on credit on production of a card; and that, in
the premises, they did not " undertake " to do so within the meaning
E of section 14 (1) of the Act and upon its true and proper construction.
Further the requirements that such a person should carry out the steps
referred to above was not " some other action also required " within
the meaning of section 14 (1) of the Act and upon its true and proper
construction since the " other action " contemplated thereby was the
completion of some procedure ancillary to the production of the card
(which should itself provide entitlement to the credit), and not an entry
F into an agreement, without which no entitlement to credit would arise.

The prosecutor contended that the defendant company did by the
promotional package " undertake " to supply goods on credit upon
production of the card within the meaning of section 14 (1) of the Act
and upon its true and proper construction, and that it was irrelevant
whether they made an offer to the consumer thereby that was intended
G to be and/or was capable of being accepted thereby so as to impose
upon the defendant company the legally binding obligation to do so.
The requirement that the consumers carry out the steps referred to
above was " some other action . . . also required " within the meaning
of section 14 (1) of the Act.

The justices accepted the prosecutor's arguments as to the proper
H construction of section 14 (1) of the Act. Accordingly the justices held
on the basis of the facts found by them (i) that the card was a credit
token within the meaning of section 14 (1) of the Act (ii) that accordingly the defendants were guilty of the offences under section 51 (1) of
the Act with which they were charged.

The defendants appealed. The question for the opinion of the
Divisional Court was whether the justices came to a correct determination and decision in point of law and, if not, the court was respectfully

requested to reverse or amend the same or to remit the matter to the   A
justices with the opinion of the court thereof.

Michael Beloff for the defendants.
David Tudor Price for the prosecutor.

LORD LANE C.J.   This is an appeal by way of case stated from Surrey   B
justices sitting at Kingston and arises under the provisions of the Consumer Credit Act 1974.   The facts are scarcely in dispute and they are
these.   The defendant company deals in footwear and the first defendant,
Mr. Elliott, is a director of the company.   There is no dispute that the
guilt or innocence of the director depends upon the guilt or innocence
of the company.   C

The company devised an idea to increase its sales of footwear to the
public.   The method adopted which has come under the scrutiny of the
Director General of Fair Trading was as follows.   There was sent to
selected members of the public an envelope containing certain materials.
The envelope itself was, so to speak, an advertising ploy because it
contained, when opened out and cut away, first of all an illustrated
advertisement for the Elliott Caterpillar shoe and then the only other   D
material part was an insert in the centre of the piece of paper which
represented the envelope saying:

> " Your Elliott credit account card valid for immediate use.   With
> your card in your hand, walk into any Elliott shop: give us your
> signature, show us simple identification, such as a cheque card and
> walk out of the shop with your purchase *and all the credit you need.*   E
> Please remember to sign your card as soon as you receive it.   It is
> perfectly secure; it cannot be used by anyone until we have their
> signature in the shop."

At the head of that page where it is cut away, it says, with two arrows,
" Cut away front of envelope to see offer inside."   Inside there were a
number of other documents.   First of all, there was a document stating: F

> " Elliott will pay your fare one way from any part of the British
> Isles to the value of half a cheap day return rail ticket against the
> purchase of a pair of Elliott boots, or the equivalent in shoes, bags
> or leather clothes.   This is an unconditional offer.   Valid during
> 1977 only."

On the other side it repeats the information: G

> " If you have bought a cheap day return ticket, show it to your
> assistant when you purchase, and half the purchase price of the
> ticket will be deducted from your bill " and so on.

The other item which was contained in the envelope is the centre
feature of the case.   It is a piece of paper measuring about two inches   H
by three or thereabouts, the size and shape of the ordinary credit card.
It may not be plastic, but it is plasticised and gives the appearance at
any rate of being a plastic card, again like the ordinary bank credit card.
On the face of it it contains this lettering: " The Elliott Account T. Elliott
& Sons Ltd. London valid September 1, 1977—August 30, 1978,"
and below that are a series of what I may describe as computer figures
or figures which are intended to look like computer figures again as, for

The Weekly Law Reports, August 15, 1980

981

1 W.L.R.   Elliott v. Director Gen. of Fair Trading (D.C.)   Lord Lane C.J.

A example, on an American Express card, but nothing, be it noted, embossed.

On the reverse side appears this: first of all, the word " signature " and then a box again such as you get on a credit card designed obviously for the signature to be placed in it, and then these words:

B "1. This credit card is valid for immediate use. 2. The sole requirement is your signature and means of identification. 3. Credit is
immediately available if you have a bank account. Sign the card
as soon as you receive it; it is perfectly secure because it can only
be used when a signature has been accepted at an Elliott shop.
T. ELLIOTT & SONS."

C In those circumstances the Director General of Fair Trading preferred four informations against the first defendant and four informations against the company, each based upon an allegation that those documents, including that card, had been sent to specified individuals in contravention of section 51 (1) of the Consumer Credit Act 1974, which reads: "It is an offence to give a person a credit-token if he has not asked for it."

D There is no dispute that these documents were sent to the persons alleged. There is no doubt that the persons alleged had not asked for them. The only question is: was this a credit-token within the meaning of the Act. In order to discover the definition of " credit-token," one turns to section 14 (1) of the same statute and that reads:

"A credit-token is a card, check, voucher, coupon, stamp, form,
booklet or other document or thing given to an individual by a
E person carrying on a consumer credit business, who undertakes—
(a) that on the production of it (whether or not some other action
is also required) he will supply cash, goods and services (or any of
them) on credit . . ."

To narrow the problem down still further, the real contest in this case is whether the word " undertakes " in that definition has been fulfilled
F by the defendants to these summonses.

The defendants' case, argued as always by Mr. Beloff with great skill and persuasion and charm, is this. Mr. Beloff submits that the word " undertakes " means " makes an offer which is capable of being accepted by the customer so as to impose upon the trader a legally binding obligation to supply to the customer goods on credit." He goes on to
G submit that, since the production of the card here did not entitle the customer to the supply of goods on credit but only enabled him to apply for a credit card which would be given when he had signed a certain form of mandate to which I will come in a minute and also other documents, on that basis what the justices found to be a credit card, namely, this little bit of board which I have described before, was not in fact a credit card at all. In fact, despite the wording on this card which I have
H already read, the credit card was not valid for immediate use. The sole requirement was not the customer's signature and means of identification. Credit was not immediately available if the customer had a bank account. Thus, one reaches the interesting, if somewhat unattractive, proposition that, because those statements on the back of the card are not true, therefore this document, which prima facie appears to be a credit-token, is not in fact one at all. The fact of the matter was that when the customer arrived at the shop, before any credit was in fact

extended to the customer, he or she would have to fill in a direct debiting **A**
mandate to the bank, and would have to sign other documents.

The submission made by Mr. Beloff is that, since all those other
matters had to be carried out before credit could be extended, therefore
this card cannot constitute a credit-token agreement within the Act.

In my judgment, that argument fails at the outset. The word is
" undertakes," and there is no necessity for any contractual agreement
or possibility of contractual agreement to exist. One looks at the card **B**
and one asks oneself whether, on the face or on the back of that card,
the defendant company is undertaking that on the production of the
card cash, goods and services (or any of them) will be supplied on
credit. The answer is yes. The card says " This credit card is valid
for immediate use. The sole requirement is your signature. . . . Credit
is immediately available if you have a bank account." The fact that **C**
none of those statements is true does not absolve the card from being
what it purports to be, namely, a credit-token card.

The argument of Mr. Beloff that it is so obvious to anybody who
stops to think for a moment that this card cannot do what it says without
further agreements being entered into strikes me as being irrelevant.
The card on the face of it and the back of it is a credit-token card, and
that is all that is required. On that basis alone I would dismiss this **D**
appeal.

But there is a further basis on which I would found my judgment.
Assume for the purposes of argument that the first half of Mr. Beloff's
argument is correct and that this cannot amount to the necessary undertaking. One then turns to inquire what about the rest of the agreements
and so on which have to be signed before credit in truth can be obtained **E**
by the customer.

I repeat the words of section 14 (1):

" A credit-token is a card, check, voucher, coupon, stamp, form,
booklet or other document or thing given to an individual by a
person carrying on a consumer credit business, who undertakes—
(a) that on the production of it (whether or not some other action **F**
is also required) he will supply cash, goods and services . . . on
credit . . ."

The other matters which had to be filled in, in my judgment, plainly fall
within the words " (whether or not some other action is also required)."
Even if the card cannot be looked at on its own, as I believe it can,
nevertheless the further matters which have to be completed before **G**
credit is extended fall clearly within the words and parenthesis which
I have read. On that basis too the justices were right in coming to the
conclusion that they did. For those reasons I would dismiss this appeal.

WOOLF J.   I agree.

Appeal dismissed with costs.
H

Solicitors: *Royds, Barfield; Treasury Solicitor.*

[Reported by SUSAN DENNY, Barrister-at-Law]

A

[HOUSE OF LORDS]

* MARREN (INSPECTOR OF TAXES) . . . RESPONDENT

AND

B INGLES . . . . APPELLANT

1980   June 18, 19, 23;   Lord Wilberforce,
         July 24   Viscount Dillhorne, Lord Salmon,
                  Lord Fraser of Tullybelton and Lord Russell of Killowen

Revenue—Capital gains tax—Disposal of assets—Sale of shares for
C   *fixed price immediately payable plus deferred consideration in*
    undetermined amount—Gain accruing on receipt of deferred
    consideration—Whether initial value of right to deferred con-
    sideration chargeable to tax at time of sale—Whether taxable
    as deemed disposal of assets on entitlement to deferred con-
    sideration matured—Whether right to deferred consideration
    within exemption from chargeable gains for " debts "—Finance
    Act 1965 (c. 25), s. 22 (1) (3), Sch. 7, para. 11 (1) (as amended
D   *by Finance Act 1968 (c. 44), Sch. 12, para. 8 (1)) [1]*

By an agreement in writing dated September 15, 1970, the
appellant and two other taxpayers undertook to sell to F
Ltd., inter alia, certain ordinary shares in a private company
in consideration of an immediate payment of £750 per share
and a right to a future cash payment (the deferred considera-
E   tion) that was to be calculated by reference to the sale price
quoted for those shares on the first day of dealing on the
Stock Exchange following the flotation of that company. The
flotation of the company took place on November 29, 1972, and
after December 5, the first day of dealing in the shares, the
taxpayers became entitled under the terms of the agreement
to receive in respect of each of the shares a deferred consideration of £2,825.   The taxpayers appealed against assessments to
capital gains tax for 1970–71 and 1972–73 that had been made
F   on them in respect of chargeable gains accruing on the sale
of the shares. It was conceded that a gain was realised by the
taxpayers when they sold the shares in 1970, but the taxpayers
contended that the receipt of the deferred consideration could
not itself give rise to a charge to the tax in 1972–73 although
the value of the right to that deferred consideration in September 1970 fell to be included in the assessment for 1970–71.
Alternatively, they argued that the right to the deferred con-
G   sideration was a debt to which paragraph 11 of Schedule 7 to
the Finance Act 1965 applied and was thus exempt from
liability to the charge to the tax.   The special commissioners
upheld the appeals in principle on the first of the taxpayers'
contentions.
An appeal by the Crown was dismissed by Slade J. On
appeal, the Court of Appeal allowed the appeal.
On appeal by the appellant: —
H   *Held,* dismissing the appeal, (1) that the right to the deferred
consideration was incorporeal property within the definition
of " assets " in section 22 (1) (*a*) of the Act which the taxpayers could have sold at any time after September 15, 1970,
and that when, in 1972, that right matured and the taxpayers
became entitled to receive the deferred consideration, an asset,

[1] Finance Act 1965, s. 22 (1): see post, p. 988F.
S. 22 (3): see post, p. 985F.
Sch. 7, para. 11 (1) (as amended): see post, p. 985G.

namely the incorporeal property, was deemed to have been A
disposed of by the taxpayers to F Ltd. and a chargeable gain
arose by virtue of the provisions of section 22 (3) which for the
purposes of that subsection established and extended a " disposal " to cases to which the subsection would not otherwise
apply and in which a " disposal " would not naturally be
thought to exist (post, pp. 986A–B, F–G, 987E–F, 989C–D, G–H,
991A).

Dicta of Walton J. in *Inland Revenue Commissioners* v. B
Montgomery [1975] Ch. 266, 271–272 disapproved.

(2) That in the circumstances the taxpayers' right to the deferred consideration did not amount to a " debt " within the
meaning of paragraph 11 (1) of Schedule 7 to the Act and was
accordingly not exempt from the charge to tax (post, pp. 986H
—987C, E–F, 990D–E, 991A).

Decision of the Court of Appeal [1979] 1 W.L.R. 1131
affirmed.   C

The following cases are referred to in their Lordships' opinions.

Inland Revenue Commissioners v. *Montgomery* [1975] Ch. 266; [1975]
    2 W.L.R. 326; [1975] 1 All E.R. 664; 49 T.C. 679.
Mortimore v. *Inland Revenue Commissioners* (1864) 2 H. & C. 838.
O'Brien v. *Benson's Hosiery (Holdings) Ltd.* [1979] Ch. 152; [1978] 3
    W.L.R. 609; [1978] 3 All E.R. 1057, C.A.; [1979] 3 W.L.R. 572; D
    [1979] 3 All E.R. 652, H.L.(E.).
O'Driscoll v. *Manchester Insurance Committee* [1915] 3 K.B. 499, C.A.

The following additional cases were cited in argument:

Aberdeen Construction Group Ltd. v. *Inland Revenue Commissioners*
    [1978] A.C. 885; [1978] 2 W.L.R. 648; [1978] 1 All E.R. 962, H.L.(Sc.).
Aldora, The [1975] Q.B. 748; [1975] 2 W.L.R. 791; [1975] 2 All E.R. 69. E
Inland Revenue Commissioners v. *Bagnall Ltd.* [1944] 1 All E.R. 204.
Ogdens Ltd. v. *Weinberg* (1906) 95 L.T. 567, H.L.(E.).
Seabrook Estate Co. Ltd. v. *Ford* [1949] 2 All E.R. 94.

APPEAL from the Court of Appeal.

This was an appeal by the appellant, James Leslie Ingles, from an order F
dated May 14, 1979, of the Court of Appeal (Ormrod and Templeman L.JJ.
and Sir David Cairns) allowing an appeal from an order dated July 10, 1978,
of Slade J. [1979] 1 W.L.R. 1131 dismissing an appeal by the respondent,
Bertram Kenneth John Marren (H.M. Inspector of Taxes), by way of case
stated under section 56 of the Taxes Management Act 1970 from a decision
of the Commissioners for the Special Purposes of the Income Tax Acts
who had decided in favour of the appellant.   G

The facts are set out in the opinions of Lord Wilberforce and Lord
Fraser of Tullybelton.

Leolin Price Q.C. and *David Ritchie* for the appellant.
Michael Nolan Q.C. and *Christopher McCall* for the respondent.

H

Their Lordships took time for consideration.

July 24. LORD WILBERFORCE. My Lords, in this appeal Mr. J. L.
Ingles is contesting an assessment to capital gains tax which arises out of a
contract made in September 1970. He succeeded before the special commissioners and in the High Court (Slade J.) but lost in the Court of Appeal
[1979] 1 W.L.R. 1131. The transaction giving rise to the claim for tax is

A comparatively simple, not so the relevant provisions of the Finance Act 1965.

By a contract of September 15, 1970, Mr. Ingles, as one of several vendors, agreed to sell to the Industrial and Commercial Finance Corporation Ltd. (" I.C.F.C.") 69 shares in J. L. Ingles (Holdings) Ltd. For 41 of these shares I.C.F.C. agreed to pay a cash price of £1,500 per share. For

B the remaining 28 shares I.C.F.C. agreed to pay an immediate cash price of £750 per share plus a sum to be paid at a future date defined as " half of the profit." This was to be one half of the amount by which the sale price should exceed £750. The sale price was, broadly, to represent the middle market price on the first day of dealings after a flotation of the company, if a flotation should occur. Thus, for the 28 shares in question, there was a consideration consisting of (i) an immediate ascertained cash

C sum (ii) a conditional and unquantified amount payable at an unascertained future date.

In fact there was a flotation in November 1972 and dealings commenced on December 5, 1972. On that date (allowing for a subdivision which had occurred of the shares) the " half of the profit " amounted to £2,825 per (original) share. The question is whether, on that date, or

D when the money was paid, a charge to capital gains tax arose by reference to the sum receivable by the taxpayer. The exact amount of the tax (if any) remains to be fixed.

The contentions are as follows. The taxpayer focuses attention on September 15, 1970, the date of the agreement. He accepts that there was on that date a " disposal " of all 69 shares, and agrees that a charge to capital gains tax then arose. As regards the 28 shares, this tax, he con-

E tends (and I do not understand the revenue to differ) should be based upon the cash sum of £750, plus the value, to be assessed as on that date, of his contingent right to receive the deferred price, less, of course, the cost of the shares, apparently £1 per share. This, he says, represents the totality of his liability in respect of the 28 shares. The revenue, on the other hand, while claiming tax for the year 1970–71 on the basis already

F described, makes an additional claim for 1972–73 based on the deferred consideration received in that year. They base this claim upon section 22 (3) of the Finance Act 1965, the relevant part of which reads:

"there is for the purposes of this Part of this Act a disposal of assets by their owner where any capital sum is derived from assets notwithstanding that no asset is acquired by the person paying the capital sum . . ."

G

The taxpayer contends that this subsection does not apply, briefly because an asset was acquired by I.C.F.C.—namely the shares. In the alternative, if the subsection is capable of applying, he says that he is taken out of it by paragraph 11 (1) of Schedule 7:

"Where a person incurs a debt to another . . . no chargeable gain

H   shall accrue to that (that is the original) creditor . . . on a disposal of the debt, except in the case of the [sic] debt on a security. . ."

The first question, that concerning section 22 (3), involves consideration of the words " notwithstanding that no asset is acquired . . . ," for the rest of the paragraph gives rise to no difficulty. There was an asset in the form of the obligation (a chose in action) to pay the deferred consideration. The deferred consideration when it was paid, in 1972, was, it is difficult to deny, a capital sum derived from that asset. Section 22 (1)

(a) of the Act expressly provides that incorporeal property, of which a chose in action is an undoubted example, is an asset for the purposes of the tax. I do not think that there is any doubt or problem up to this point. But the question remains whether the taxpayer can succeed in the contention that the words " notwithstanding that no asset is acquired " introduce a condition of a limiting character, with the result if an asset *is acquired* the subsection does not apply. For the purposes of this argument I shall assume that an asset was aquired by the payer of the capital sum (viz. I.C.F.C.), though there is much to be said for the contrary view and indeed the Court of Appeal accepted it. Support for the taxpayer's contention is given by a passage from the judgment of Walton J. in *Inland Revenue Commissioners* v. *Montgomery* [1975] Ch. 266, 271–272, which was followed and applied by Slade J. and which led him to accept the taxpayer's contention. But I regret that I am unable to agree. Section 22 (3), after the provision which I have quoted, goes on to provide some examples, to which in particular the subsection is stated to apply. These are:

> " (a) capital sums received by way of compensation for any kind of damage or injury to assets or for the loss, destruction or dissipation of assets or for any depreciation or risk of depreciation of an asset, (b) capital sums received under a policy of insurance of the risk of any kind of damage or injury to, or the loss or depreciation of, assets, (c) capital sums received in return for forfeiture or surrender of rights, or for refraining from exercising rights, and, (d) capital sums received as consideration for use or exploitation of assets."

Now it is obvious that in some, if not most of these examples there is the possibility that an asset *may* be acquired by the person paying the capital sum. The clearest of these is (d), if the sum is paid for the grant of a licence or a profit: but also under (b), if the payer of the sum acquires rights by subrogation, or under (a) if after payment of damages the property in respect of which they were paid vests in the payer. The observations of Walton J. in *Inland Revenue Commissioners* v. *Montgomery* [1975] Ch. 266 do not take account of these possibilities (to which others could be added) and to that extent must be too wide. But apart from this, I cannot read the words in question (" notwithstanding . . ." etc.) as pointing in the direction desired by the taxpayer. In my understanding they are evidently words not of limitation, but of extension, the purpose of which is to apply the subsection (so as to establish a " disposal "), to cases to which it would not otherwise apply and in which a " disposal " would not naturally be thought to exist. In other words they mean, in my opinion, " Whether or not an asset is acquired." With this meaning the examples given under (a) to (d) easily fit.

I, therefore, consider that, in the absence of a contrary or exempting provision, section 22 (3) applies to the case.

Then is the taxpayer exempted by paragraph 11 (1) of Schedule 7? This is a provision of notable obscurity, the purpose and philosophy of which it is difficult to detect. It has to be examined at two points in time.

First, was there a debt in September 1970? In my opinion there was not. No case was cited, and I should be surprised if one could be found, in which a contingent right (which might never be realised) to receive an unascertainable amount of money at an unknown date has been considered to be a debt—and no meaning however untechnical of that word could, to my satisfaction, include such a right. The legislation does, of

A course, make provision for debts not immediately payable; it does so by the draconian method of charging them, when a charge arises, without any allowance for deferral (Schedule 6, paragraph 14 (5)): and I would, for the purpose of argument, be prepared to agree that a contingent debt might come within the paragraph. In *Mortimore* v. *Inland Revenue Commissioners* (1864) 2 H. & C. 838—a case concerned with stamp duty —Martin B. so held. But from this it would be a large step to hold to be

B included an unascertainable sum payable, if a contingency happens, at an unascertainable date, a step which I am unable to take. I adopt in this part of the case—as did the Court of Appeal—the reasoning of the learned judge.

Then, secondly, was there a debt on December 5, 1972, when the contingency arrived, the date became fixed, and the amount became ascer-

C tained? I think there was, though I am not so sure that a debt was then " incurred." But it remains the fact that the amount of the debt was derived from the asset (the chose in action) created in 1972, and is sought to be charged on that basis—under section 22 (3). I cannot accept that the exemption in paragraph 11 (1) applies in such a case. If it were otherwise, and if the taxpayer's contention were correct, no charge under section 22 could arise in any case where the person making the disposal

D did not receive immediate payment. That would largely nullify the section. Whatever paragraph 11 (1) does mean, it cannot have been intended to have so wide an effect. I think that the revenue is correct in analysing this transaction into an acquisition of an asset (viz. a chose in action) in 1970 from which a capital sum arose in 1972 and that there is no question of a debt being disposed of at any time.

E I would dismiss the appeal.

VISCOUNT DILHORNE. My Lords, as I agree with all that my noble and learned friend, Lord Wilberforce, has said in his speech which I have seen in draft, there is no point in my writing a speech to the same effect.

For the reasons he gives this appeal should be dismissed.

F LORD SALMON. My Lords, I have had the advantage of reading in draft the speech of my noble and learned friend Lord Wilberforce with which I entirely agree. I would therefore dismiss the appeal.

LORD FRASER OF TULLYBELTON. My Lords, this appeal raises questions of construction of the capital gains tax provisions in Part III of the

G Finance Act 1965. They arise out of an agreement made on September 15, 1970, between the appellant taxpayer and two other persons (" the vendors ") on one side and the I.C.F.C. (" the purchaser ") on the other. All three vendors were parties to the proceedings in the courts below, but in order to save costs it has been agreed that this appeal will govern all three cases. Nevertheless, I find it convenient to refer to the vendors collectively and to the total number of their shares.

H By the agreement the vendors agreed to sell and the purchaser agreed to purchase 167 " A " Ordinary Shares of £1 each in a private company, J. L. Ingles (Holdings) Ltd. Completion took place on September 15, 1970. As to 107 of the shares the price was £1,500 per share. It was duly paid and no question arises about it. As to the remaining 60 shares, of which 28 belonged to the appellant, the price was agreed at £750 plus " half of the profit." The £750 was paid in cash on completion. The expression " half of the profit " was defined as meaning one half of the

Lord Fraser
of Tullybelton

Marren v. Ingles (H.L.(E.))

[1980]

amount by which " the sale price " exceeded £750. " The sale price " A
was elaborately defined according to various possible future events, one of
which was flotation of the company by the grant of permission to deal in
its shares on a recognised stock exchange in the United Kingdom before
December 31, 1975. Flotation did take place on November 29, 1972, and
the definition of the sale price which came into effect in consequence of
that event, was the middle-market price of the shares on the first day of
dealings after flotation, namely, December 5, 1972. By that date the B
original shares had been subdivided and a scrip issue had been made, with
the result that the original " A " Ordinary Shares had come to be represented by 480,000 shares of 5p each in the company. The middle-market
price on December 5, 1972, was equivalent to a price of £6,400 for each
of the original shares. " Half of the profit " therefore was £2,825, being
one half of the amount by which £6,400 exceeds £750. The figures are C
not in dispute.

The agreement gave rise to immediate disposals of all 167 shares,
within the meaning of the capital gains tax provisions of the Finance Act
1965. The cost of acquisition by the vendors had been £1 per share.
Accordingly, the vendors were assessed to CGT on the 107 shares sold at
£1,500 each on a chargeable gain of £1,499 per share. As to that there is
no dispute. The dispute arises in connection with the other 60 shares D
(referred to in the agreement and hereinafter as " the shareholdings ").
It is agreed that, in respect of the shareholdings, the vendors ought to
have been assessed on the footing that in the fiscal year 1970–71 they had
made a chargeable gain of the difference between the cost price of £1 and
the consideration received for each share, made up of £750 in cash plus
the value on September 15, 1970, of their contingent right to half of the E
profit. The value of that right on September 15, 1970, has not yet been
assessed; indeed, there is a suggestion that it may be impossible to assess,
and nothing that I say is intended to indicate any opinion on the valuation of the right as at September 15, 1970.

Capital gains tax was imposed by section 19 (1) of the Finance Act
1965 on chargeable gains accruing to a person " on the disposal of assets."
Section 22 (1) of the Act provides, inter alia, as follows: F

" All forms of property shall be assets for the purposes of this Part
of this Act . . . including—(a) options, debts and incorporeal property
generally . . ."

Subsection (3) of section 22 is the provision on which the Crown's claim
is directly based. The relevant part of it has been quoted by my noble G
and learned friend Lord Wilberforce.

The Crown has made assessments for the fiscal year 1972–73 in respect
of the receipt by the vendors of the capital sum equivalent to £2,825 per
original share. The assessment was made on the basis that on December
5, 1972, the vendors made a disposal of a separate asset consisting of the
right to receive that sum. The claim by the Crown was negatived by the
special commissioners and, on appeal by stated case, by Slade J. but the H
Court of Appeal (Templeman and Ormrod L.JJ. and Sir David Cairns)
reversed that decision [1979] 1 W.L.R. 1131 and upheld the claim.

The first question is whether the right to half of the profit is properly
to be regarded as a separate asset, or simply as a deferred part of the
price of the shareholdings. In my opinion, the former view is correct.
" Asset " is defined in section 22 (1) in the widest terms, to mean all
forms of property and it has been construed accordingly—see *O'Brien* v.

A *Benson's Hosiery (Holdings) Ltd.* [1979] 3 W.L.R. 572, 575—by my noble and learned friend Lord Russell of Killowen. It is therefore apt to include the incorporeal right to money's worth which was part of the consideration given for the shareholdings in 1970. The vendors could have disposed of the right at any time after September 15, 1970, by selling it or giving it away and assigning it. If they had done so, there would have been an actual disposal of an asset and the vendors would have
B been liable for capital gains tax on the amount, if any, by which the price or value of the asset at the date of disposal exceeded its value on September 15, 1970. Of course, if the price or value had been less than the value on September 15, 1970, they would have made a chargeable loss which they could have set off against gains in the same or future fiscal years. So there is nothing unfair in treating it as an asset. In fact, they did not dispose of the right but they held it until it matured on December 5, 1972.
C If the right was an " asset," then the sum which the vendors received on that date was " derived from " the asset. There was therefore, by virtue of section 22 (3), a disposal of the asset, notwithstanding that no asset was acquired by the " person paying the capital sum," the purchaser. The sum was paid to satisfy or extinguish the right and not as any part of the consideration for the shareholdings; full consideration for them
D had already been given on September 15, 1970. The capital sum is therefore not in any relevant sense derived from the shareholdings, and the appellant's complaint that he was being assessed to capital gains tax twice over on the price is misconceived. The position is no different in principle from what it would have been if the vendors had received new shares in another company as part of the consideration for the shareholdings and had later disposed of the new shares.
E In my opinion, Slade J. was mistaken in treating the receipt of the shareholdings by the purchasers as relevant for the purposes of section 22 (3). The reference there to no asset being " acquired by " the person paying the capital sum must be to an asset acquired in exchange for the capital sum, and the shareholdings were not acquired by the purchaser in exchange for the capital sum paid in December 1972. The material
F question is not whether acquisition of the asset and payment of the capital sum were contemporaneous or not, but whether one was consideration for the other. Moreover Slade J., following a decision of Walton J. in *Inland Revenue Commissioners* v. *Montgomery* [1975] Ch. 266, 271, held that the words " notwithstanding that no asset is acquired by the person paying the capital sum " in section 22 (3) meant that the application of the subsection was confined to cases where no asset was
G acquired. I am unable to agree. The ordinary meaning of the word " notwithstanding " according to the *Shorter Oxford English Dictionary* is " despite, in spite of." One might perhaps suggest also " whether or not." It is a word of extension not of limitation, and I see no reason to read it here in a limiting sense. The comprehensive provisions of subsections (1) and (2) of section 22 may render it not strictly necessary
H for subsection (3) to apply to cases where an asset is acquired by the person paying the capital sum, but even if there is some overlapping, that is not uncommon in fiscal legislation, in order to avoid leaving a loophole. In my opinion subsection (3) applies whether or not an asset is acquired by the person paying the capital sum. That construction is, if anything, fortified by reference to the examples given in paragraphs (a) to (d) of subsection (3), some of which are of cases where payment of the capital sum might well attract corresponding assets. Thus, looking at paragraph

(*b*), where a capital sum is paid under a policy of insurance the insurers will often acquire by subrogation an asset consisting of the assured's right of action against a wrongdoer. Accordingly, I consider that the decision in *Montgomery* on this point was erroneous.

There remains the second question in the case: was the vendor's right to " half of the profit " a debt in the sense of paragraph 11 of Schedule 7 to the Finance Act 1965 (as amended), which provides as follows:

" (1) Where a person incurs a debt to another, whether in sterling or in some other currency, no chargeable gain shall accrue to that (that is the original) creditor or his personal representative or legatee on a disposal of the debt, except in the case of the debt on a security . . . (2) Subject to the provisions of paragraphs 5 and 6 of this Schedule (and subject to the foregoing sub-paragraph) the satisfaction of a debt or part of it . . . shall be treated as a disposal of the debt or of that part by the creditor made at the time when the debt or that part is satisfied."

If this asset was a " debt " the vendors were the original creditors and subparagraph (1) would therefore apply, so that no chargeable gain would accrue to them. The meaning of the word debt depends very much on its context. It is capable of including a contingent debt which may never become payable: *Mortimore* v. *Inland Revenue Commissioners,* 2 H. & C. 838. It is also capable of including a sum of which the amount is not ascertained: *O'Driscoll* v. *Manchester Insurance Committee* [1915] 3 K.B. 499. But I agree with Slade J. and with Templeman L.J., both of whom held that that the word " debt " in paragraph 11 does not apply to the obligation of the purchaser under this agreement, which was described by Templeman L.J. [1979] 1 W.L.R. 1131, 1147 as " a *possible* liability to pay an *unidentifiable* sum at an *unascertainable* date." The words to which I have added emphasis bring out the three factors of this obligation which cumulatively prevents its being a debt in the sense of paragraph 11. Further, the reference to a person who " incurs " a debt " whether in sterling or in some other currency " points, in my opinion, towards the debt being definite, or at least ascertainable, in amount. Similarly, paragraph 14 of Schedule 6 to the Act of 1965, dealing with consideration payable by instalments which, by paragraph 14 (5), is to be brought into account initially without regard to inter alia " a risk of any part of the consideration being irrecoverable," seems clearly to be referring to consideration of an ascertained amount. It is appropriate for dealing with a debt which cannot increase in value, but may decrease if it proves to be partly irrecoverable. Both paragraph 11 of Schedule 7 and paragraph 14 of Schedule 6 are to be contrasted with section 22 (3) which applies to an asset which might either rise or fall in value.

Finally, it was suggested that even if the right to receive half of the profits was not a debt at first, it became one when it was quantified and became immediately payable on December 5, 1972. I agree with Slade J. and Templeman L.J. that that cannot be right because it would lead to absurd results. Every obligation that is ultimately discharged by a money payment must be quantified before payment, and on this argument, capital gains tax would always be excluded when a definite price became payable. In my opinion, paragraph 11 of Schedule 7 only applies to an obligation which has been a debt from the time it came into existence, or at least from the time when it was acquired by the taxpayer.

I would refuse the appeal.

A   LORD RUSSELL OF KILLOWEN. My Lords, I have had the advantage
of reading in draft the speech delivered by my noble and learned friend
Lord Fraser of Tullybelton. I agree with it and with his conclusion that
this appeal should be dismissed.

Appeal dismissed.

B   Solicitors: *Hancock & Willis for Wragge & Co., Birmingham; Solicitor
of Inland Revenue.*

J. A. G.

_____

C   [COURT OF APPEAL]

* REGINA v. WATSON (CAMPBELL)

1980 Jan. 24;   Cumming-Bruce L.J., Thompson and Smith JJ.
      Feb. 12

D *Crime—Evidence—Confession—Admissibility—Judge ruling that
statement admissible—Subsequent evidence concerning voluntary
nature of statement—Whether power to reconsider ruling as
to admissibility of statement*

The defendant was charged on indictment with offences of
burglary and theft. During the trial his counsel challenged the
voluntary character of written statements made by the
E   defendant. There was a trial within a trial and the judge ruled
that the statements were voluntary and admissible. The trial
continued in the presence of the jury and during cross-
examination of a police officer by counsel for a co-defendant
further evidence emerged which counsel for the defendant
regarded as inconsistent with that given at the trial within a
trial. He applied to the judge to reconsider his earlier ruling
but the judge refused, holding that he had no power to do so.
F   The defendant was convicted.

On appeal by the defendant against conviction: —
Held, dismissing the appeal, that it was the duty of a judge
to exclude from the jury's consideration evidence that was
inadmissible and, therefore, he retained throughout the trial
the power to reconsider the admissibility of evidence upon
which he had already ruled; and that, accordingly, the judge
should have considered the submission that the further
G   evidence of the police officer indicated that the defendant's
statements were not voluntary, but the submission failed on
the merits.

Reg. v. Murphy [1965] N.I. 138, Ct.-M.A.C. applied.
Per curiam. The occasions on which a judge should allow
counsel to invite him to reconsider a ruling already made
are likely to be extremely rare. Judges should continue to
discourage counsel from making submissions of law founded
on a tenuous evidential base (post, p. 995c–d).

The following cases are referred to in the judgment:

Reg. v. Gregory; *Reg. v. Mills (Practice Note)* [1969] 1 W.L.R. 455;
[1969] 2 All E.R. 174, C.A.
Reg. v. Murphy [1965] N.I. 138, Ct.-M.A.C.

No additional cases were cited in argument.

Reg. v. Watson (Campbell) (C.A.) [1980]

APPEAL against conviction and sentence.

On July 27, 1979, in the Kingston-upon-Thames Crown Court, the defendant, Campbell Louis Watson, was convicted of three counts of burglary and one count of theft on the first of two indictments. On the same day he pleaded guilty on the second indictment to three counts of burglary, one of theft and one of taking a conveyance without authority. On the first indictment he was sentenced to three years' imprisonment for the burglary offence and six months, to run consecutively, for the theft. On the second indictment, he was sentenced to concurrent terms of imprisonment for burglary and theft and six months to run consecutively for taking a conveyance, an overall total of four years' imprisonment. Twenty-six other offences were taken into consideration.

The defendant appealed against conviction on the ground, inter alia, that the judge was wrong in law in holding that he had no power to rule on the admissibility of written statements at the end of the prosecution case because he had already ruled on it at the conclusion of the trial within a trial. The defendant also applied for leave to appeal against sentence on the grounds that four years' imprisonment was too severe and that the judge was wrong in making a sentence of six months' imprisonment on the second indictment run consecutively to the total of 3½ years' imprisonment imposed on the first indictment.

The facts are stated in the judgment.

Peter Digney for the defendant.
Richard Germain for the Crown.

Cur. adv. vult.

February 12. CUMMING-BRUCE L.J. read the judgment of the court. On July 27, 1979, at Kingston Crown Court, Judge Figgis presiding, the defendant was convicted of four counts on the first of two indictments after a trial lasting 16 days. On the same day he pleaded guilty to five counts on the second indictment.

He was sentenced as follows: first indictment (No. 790636): counts 1 to 3, burglary, three years' imprisonment (concurrent); count 5, theft, six months' imprisonment (consecutive). Second indictment (No. 790891): counts 1, 3 and 5, burglary, three years' imprisonment (concurrent); count 2, theft, six months' imprisonment (concurrent); count 4, taking a conveyance without the owner's consent, six months' imprisonment (consecutive) and licence endorsed. He had 26 other offences taken into consideration (eight burglaries, three thefts, seven taking a conveyance without the owner's consent, two attempted burglaries and six attempted thefts).

He appeals against conviction by leave of the single judge who also referred to the full court his application for leave to appeal against sentence. The first ground of appeal against conviction is:

"The judge was wrong in law in holding that he had no power to rule on the admissibility of evidence at the end of the prosecution case because he had ruled on it in the trial within a trial, even though there were relevant matters that came to light in the trial that had not done so in the trial within a trial."

The evidence against the defendant upon the counts upon which he was convicted was evidence that goods stolen in the three burglaries

A and by the theft alleged in count 5 had been found partly in his house and partly in the house or garden shed of two co-defendants in which he was alleged to have been living for part of the material time; parol admissions made by him to police officers investigating the offences; and two written statements signed by him.

B He gave evidence giving an explanation of the presence of the stolen goods at the two addresses where they were found. In his evidence he said that the alleged oral admissions had been concocted by the police officers who gave evidence about them, and his case, supported by his evidence, was that he had been induced against his will to sign the alleged written statements by promises of favour. These promises included promises that he would be given bail, that there would be no charge arising from the fact that a shotgun had been found in one of the two C relevant addresses, and that no proceedings, save a charge of handling 14 belts, would be taken against one Janet Laver with whom the defendant was cohabiting, in spite of the fact that the investigating police officers had at the time evidence implicating her in other offences of dishonesty with which she was in fact charged many months later.

When Detective Constable Packington was in the witness box, counsel D for the defendant having challenged the voluntary character of the two written statements, there was a trial within a trial. Detective Constable Packington and Detective Sergeant Massey gave evidence and were cross-examined. The defendant gave evidence describing the inducements alleged. The judge ruled that the statements were voluntary.

The trial proceeded in the presence of the jury. When Detective Constable Packington was in the witness box counsel for co-defendant E Janet Laver cross-examined him, and in his answers to those questions gave certain evidence. Counsel for the defendant regarded that evidence as inconsistent with the evidence that the constable had given at the trial within a trial, and as strengthening the case on which he had earlier founded his submission that the written statements were not voluntary. The evidence related to the issue whether the police officers had promised F to turn a blind eye to the evidence implicating Janet Laver in offences other and more serious than the offence of dishonestly handling 14 belts.

Counsel for the defendant then submitted to the judge that he should reconsider the ruling that he gave at the end of the trial within a trial, in the light of the evidence of Packington in the presence of the jury, which appeared to contradict the evidence given by the witness four days earlier. G Counsel asked the judge now to rule that the disputed written statements were inadmissible. The judge refused to reconsider his ruling, intimating that the question whether the statements were voluntary had been finally determined in the trial within a trial.

In this court Mr. Digney's first submission is that the judge wrongly ruled that he had no power to consider the question whether the written statements were not voluntary and therefore inadmissible in the light of H the evidence given in the presence of the jury in answer to questions put by counsel appearing for Janet Laver, who had not been concerned in the trial within a trial. He relied upon the simple propositions that admissibility is a matter for the judge, a trial within a trial is a practical expedient to enable the court to prevent evidence then ruled to be inadmissible from coming to the notice of the jury, and if at any stage thereafter evidence is given which satisfies, or should satisfy, the judge

that the evidence upon which he has already ruled is inadmissible, the **A**
judge must take the appropriate steps to prevent the jury acting upon it.

In our view the judge was wrong to rule as he evidently did that he
had no power to consider the relevance of evidence, given after the
trial within a trial, upon the issue whether the written statements were not
voluntary and therefore inadmissible. He should have allowed counsel to
develop his submission and should have ruled upon its merits.

B

It is the duty of the judge to exclude from the jury's consideration
evidence which is inadmissible. In the case of a written statement, made
or signed by the accused, the judge must be satisfied that the prosecution
have proved that the contested statement was voluntary, before allowing
the jury to decide whether to act upon it. Experience has shown that
where the question of the voluntary character of a statement has been
investigated and decided at a trial within a trial, it is only in very rare **C**
and unusual cases that further evidence later emerges which may cause
the judge to reconsider the question whether he is still satisfied that the
statement was voluntary and admissible. But where there is such further
evidence, the judge has power to consider the relevance of the admissibility of evidence upon which he has already ruled.

We are not aware of any English decision directly upon the point, **D**
but we accept the reasoning expressed in a passage in a judgment of the
Northern Ireland Courts-Martial Appeal Court in *Reg.* v. *Murphy*
[1965] N.I. 138, 143, delivered by Lord MacDermott L.C.J., which,
though immediately concerned with a question of discretionary exclusion,
is equally relevant to exclusion on the ground of legal inadmissibility:

" Is the discretion spent once it has been exercised against the **E**
accused and the evidence has been admitted? We are not aware of
any authority on this question, but on general principles we are of
opinion that the court's discretionary powers are not necessarily
at an end when the relevant evidence has been admitted. Sometimes
the true bearing of evidence said to operate unfairly against an
accused person may only appear clearly to do so when seen in the
light of evidence adduced at a later stage of the trial and after the **F**
material objected to has become part of the record. To say that it is
then too late to reconsider the objection would, we think, be to run
the risk of letting the technicalities of the situation prevail over the
requirements of justice. The admission of a confession as voluntary,
on evidence heard in the absence of the jury, may be shown by
subsequent evidence to have been clearly involuntary and therefore **G**
inadmissible. In such circumstances we consider it would undoubtedly
be within the province of the court either to instruct the jury to
disregard the evidence as no longer admissible or, in the absence of
other evidence capable of sustaining the charge, to direct an
acquittal. If this is right, we can see no reason for making a
distinction between what becomes inadmissible after being thought **H**
admissible and what is seen to be unfair after an earlier view to the
contrary. We are, therefore, of opinion that the discretion under
discussion may, in certain circumstances, properly be the subject of
reconsideration. "

The matter is discussed in *Cross on Evidence*, 5th ed. (1979), p. 72
in which reference is made to *Reg.* v. *Murphy*:

A   " The judge retains his control over the evidence ultimately to be submitted to the jury throughout the trial. Accordingly, if, having admitted a confession as voluntary on evidence given in the absence of the jury, the judge concludes, in the light of subsequent evidence, that the confession was not voluntary, he may either direct the jury to disregard it, or, where there is no other sufficient evidence against the accused, direct an acquittal, or, presumably, direct a new trial. "

B   We accept the accuracy of this statement of the law.

[His Lordship stated that the court, having considered the transcript of the evidence of Detective Constable Packington given at the trial within a trial, and the extract from the evidence which he gave before the jury when he was being cross-examined by counsel for the co-defendant Laver, were satisfied that the evidence of Packington given in answer to counsel

C for the co-defendant Laver was not such as to render the evidence inadmissible, and upheld the conviction. His Lordship continued :] We would emphasise that though as a matter of law the judge has throughout a trial the responsibility of doing what is practicable to prevent a jury acting upon evidence which the judge holds, or should hold, to be inadmissible, the occasions on which a judge should allow counsel to invite him to

D reconsider a ruling already made are likely to be extremely rare. Judges should continue to discourage counsel from making submissions of law founded on a tenuous evidential base. We do not criticise Mr. Digney for seeking to make a further submission in this case, though after hearing his argument we have rejected it.

     The court does not accept that the verdicts of the jury by which they held the defendant and his co-defendant not guilty of other counts in the

E indictment are to be regarded as necessarily inconsistent with the verdicts on which the defendant was found guilty. We are not satisfied that the third pleaded ground of appeal against conviction has been made out.

     Upon the application for leave to appeal against sentence, the court grants leave to appeal. There is no ground to vary any of the sentences save the order that the sentence of six months' imprisonment imposed on

F count 4 of the second indictment should be consecutive to the sentences imposed on the other counts of that indictment. This consecutive sentence should be made concurrent for the reasons given by this court in *Reg.* v. *Gregory; Reg.* v. *Mills* [1969] 1 W.L.R. 455. The total sentence to be served will be 3½ years' imprisonment.

G
Appeal against conviction dismissed.
Appeal against sentence allowed in part; concurrent sentence substituted for consecutive sentence.

     Solicitors: *Registrar of Criminal Appeals; Solicitor, Metropolitan Police.*

H
[Reported by Mrs. Clare Barsby, Barrister-at-Law]

[COURT OF APPEAL]

A

* SIOUX INC. *v.* CHINA SALVAGE CO., KWANGCHOW BRANCH

AND ANOTHER

[1979 S. No. 785]

B

1979 Dec. 10, 11, 12   Lord Denning M.R., Bridge L.J. and
                                     Sir David Cairns

*Arbitration—Time bar—Extension of time—Lloyd's standard
salvage agreement—Practice oversight—Whether " claims " confined to causes of action—Whether bar " undue hardship "—
Security and payment on account of salvage award—Whether
such as " justice of the case may require "—Arbitration Act
1950 (14 & 15 Geo. 6, c. 27), s. 27*
Ships' names—American Sioux

C

The defendant salvors entered into a Lloyd's standard
form salvage agreement on a " no cure—no pay " basis with
the plaintiff owners of the *American Sioux,* which had stranded
in the South China Sea, to use their best endeavours to salve
her and her cargo. By clause 6 of the agreement, where security
was given " any claim for arbitration must be made . . . and
must be received by the Committee of Lloyd's within 42 days
from the date of completion of such security ": if such a claim
were not made the committee were required after the expiry
of the 42 days to see that the amount of the security after
realisation was paid to the salvors. The salvors required the
owners to give security in the sum of U.S. \$2,400,000, and
such security was provided on July 27, 1979. The salvage
services ended after the salvors had effected a cure in August
1979. Owing to an oversight Lloyd's failed to observe their
usual practice and did not notify the owners that the 42 day
period from the date of completion of the security would
expire on September 6, 1979, and, therefore, the owners made
no claim to arbitration within that period. Three weeks later
the salvors requested that the amount of the security be paid
to them. On October 1, 1979, the owners gave late notice of
application for arbitration and applied to the court for an
extension of time under section 27 of the Arbitration Act 1950.[1]
Sheen J. dismissed the application holding that the word
" claims " in section 27 of the Act of 1950 referred to causes
of actions and, therefore, the section did not apply to the
arbitration clause in the Lloyd's form. He said that if the
court had had jurisdiction, the justice of the case would have
required that the owners, who had already paid \$200,000 on
account, be granted an extension of time on terms that they
should pay a further sum of \$200,000 as it was " inconceiv-
able " that the salvors' award would be less than \$400,000.

On appeal by the owners: —

Held, allowing the appeal, (1) that the word " claims "
in section 27 of the Arbitration Act 1950, which should be
given a liberal interpretation, applied to the owners' claim to
arbitration to fix the amount of the salvage award and so to
recover part of the security which they had provided ; and that
in the circumstances " undue hardship " within the meaning
of the section would be caused to the owners if they were not
granted an extension of time (post, pp. 1000g, h—1001c, g–h,
1002f–h).

D

E

F

G

H

[1] Arbitration Act 1950, s. 27: see post, p. 1000b–d.

A   *Consolidated Investment & Contracting Co.* v. *Saponaria
         Shipping Co. Ltd.* [1978] 1 W.L.R. 986, C.A. applied.
             (2) That " the justice of the case " within the meaning of
         section 27 did not require that the owners should be required
         to pay a further $200,000 or to provide further security: it
         would be sufficient if they paid (as they had agreed to do) a
         further $115,000 on account of the salvage award (post, pp.
         1001D–F, 1002C, 1003B–C).
B   *Per* Sir David Cairns. A judge should not estimate what
         he thinks will be the lowest sum likely to be awarded and
         make it a condition of extending the time under section 27
         that the owners should make such a payment on account,
         which would not be recoverable if his estimate were wrong
         (post, p. 1003A–B).
             Judgment of Sheen J. reversed.

C   The following cases are referred to in the judgments:

         Consolidated Investment & Contracting Co. v. *Saponaria Shipping Co.
             Ltd. (The Virgo)* [1978] 1 W.L.R. 986; [1978] 3 All E.R. 988, C.A.
         Liberian Shipping Corporation " Pegasus " v. *A. King & Sons Ltd.* [1967]
             2 Q.B. 86; [1967] 2 W.L.R. 856; [1967] 1 All E.R. 934; [1967] 1
             Lloyd's Rep. 302, C.A.
         Nea Agrex S.A. v. *Baltic Shipping Co. Ltd.* [1976] Q.B. 933; [1976] 2
D   W.L.R. 925; [1976] 2 All E.R. 842, C.A.
         Rolimpex (Ch.E.) Ltd. v. *Avra Shipping Co. Ltd. (The Angeliki)* [1973]
             2 Lloyd's Rep. 226.
         S.I. Pension Trustees Ltd. v. *William Hudson Ltd.* (1977) 35 P. & C.R. 54.

         The following additional cases were cited in argument:

E   *Bunge S.A.* v. *Kruse* [1979] 1 Lloyd's Rep. 279.
         Nestlé Co. Ltd. v. *E. Biggins & Co. Ltd.* [1958] 1 Lloyd's Rep. 398, D.C.
         Shordiche-Churchward v. *Cordle* [1959] 1 W.L.R. 351; [1959] 1 All E.R.
             599, C.A.

         APPEAL from Sheen J.
             By originating summons the plaintiff owners, Sioux Inc., applied for
F   an order that the time for claiming arbitration under a Lloyd's standard
         form of salvage agreement entered into between the owners and the
         defendant salvors, China Salvage Co., Kwangchow Branch, and Transpac
         Marine S.A., and dated September 25, 1978, be extended pursuant to
         section 27 of the Arbitration Act 1950.
             On November 20, 1979, Sheen J. accepted the salvors' submissions
G   that section 27 of the Act did not apply and that accordingly the court
         had no jurisdiction to extend the period of 42 days referred to in
         clause 6 of the agreement, said that it seemed " clear beyond doubt that
         the claims referred to in section 27 must be claims made by a person
         seeking some payment, such as the claim made by a salvor who has
         successfully rendered salvage services " and dismissed the application.
         In case he should be held to be wrong, Sheen J. went on to consider the
H   question of undue hardship and, having concluded that " the hardship
         which the plaintiffs would suffer if the time was not extended was out of
         proportion to the fault which has prevented them from making a claim
         for arbitration," said that the justice of the case required that an exten-
         sion of time should only be granted on terms that the owners should be
         required to make a further payment on account of $200,000, it being
         " inconceivable that the salvors' award will be fixed at less than $400,000 "
         and should be required to give security in the further sum of $500,000.

The owners appealed on the grounds that the judge (1) was wrong in A
holding that he had no jurisdiction under section 27 of the Arbitration
Act 1950 to extend the time for claiming arbitration; (2) ought to have
held that he had such jurisdiction and extended the time for claiming
arbitration unconditionally until October 1, 1979.

The facts are stated in the judgment of Lord Denning M.R.

Gordon Pollock Q.C. and *Nigel Teare* for the owners.   B
Michael Thomas Q.C. and *David Steel* for the salvors.
Charles Macdonald for the Corporation of Lloyd's.

Lord Denning M.R. The *American Sioux* was newly built in 1978.
She was on her first voyage. She was carrying containers. She stranded
on a reef near the Paracel Islands in the South China Sea. That was on C
September 24, 1978. The news soon reached Hong Kong—300 miles
away. Two salvage companies sent out tugs to the rescue at once. Each
signed a Lloyd's standard form of salvage agreement upon the principle
of " no cure—no pay."

It turned out to be a big job. The containers had to be taken off to
lighten her. After some months, she was got off the reef and towed in D
her damaged state to Hong Kong. She was re-delivered to the owners on
August 20, 1979. It took about 11 months. She has not yet been
repaired. The salvors claim a reward which they say would be over
$2 million for their work in saving the hull apart from the cargo. The
shipowners say that the ship in its damaged state in Hong Kong was only
worth $500,000: and that it is a recognised principle of salvage law that
the reward cannot exceed the salvage value, and that at least 10 per cent. E
or 20 per cent. should be left for the owners. So the owners say that the
award should be even less than $500,000.

Now for the dispute. In June 1979, before the salvage operation was
completed, the salvors notified the Committee of Lloyd's that they required
the owners to put up security in the sum of $2,400,000. This was to
cover, according to Lloyd's form, costs, expenses and interest. The ship- F
owners protested that that was excessive. But, nevertheless, they arranged
to provide it through the Bank of America in London. At the same time
they negotiated with a view to paying $200,000 cash down to the salvors in
part payment in anticipation of the arbitration award.

Now comes the point. On July 27, 1979, the security was completed.
The shipowners provided at that date security in the sum of $2,400,000.
Thenceforward, under the Lloyd's standard form of salvage agreement, G
the time started running for claiming arbitration. The owners had 42
days in which to claim arbitration. If they did not do so there was a
provision in the form that Lloyd's were to pay over the amount to the
salvors. It is clause 6 of the standard form. As everything depends on
it in this case, I will read it fully:

" Where security is given to the Committee of Lloyd's any claim for H
    arbitration must be made in writing or by telegram or by telex and
    must be received by the Committee of Lloyd's within 42 days from
    the date of completion of such security. If such a claim is not made
    by any of the parties entitled or authorised to make a claim for
    arbitration in respect of the salved property on behalf of which
    security has been given, the Committee of Lloyd's shall after the
    expiry of the said 42 days call upon the party or parties concerned

The Weekly Law Reports, August 15, 1980

999

1 W.L.R.   Sioux Inc. v. China Salvage (C.A.)   Lord Denning M.R.

A   to pay the amount thereof and in the event of nonpayment shall
realize or enforce the security and pay over the amount thereof to the
contractor.   The receipt of the contractor shall be a good discharge
to the Committee of Lloyd's for any moneys so paid and it shall incur
no responsibility to any of the parties concerned for making such
payment.   No claim for arbitration shall be entertained or acted
upon unless received by the Committee of Lloyd's within 42 days
B   from the date of completion of the security."

The 42 days expired on September 6, 1979. The shipowners did not
make their claim within the 42 days. They were 25 days late. Now they
seek an extension under section 27 of the Arbitration Act 1950. The
salvors say that that section does not apply to a Lloyd's salvage agree-
C   ment: and that the six weeks are imperative and unalterable: and the
shipowners cannot now get any extension of time. Having failed to
claim arbitration within the 42 days, they can do nothing more, and the
salvors can claim the whole security of $2,400,000.

Before dealing with the law, I must explain why the shipowners were
25 days late. It was not their fault. It was all due to an oversight at
Lloyd's.   In these cases it is the practice of Lloyd's, as soon as the
D   security is completed, to notify the parties concerned and tell them
when the 42-day period would expire. In this case the salvors demanded
security of the cargo interest. It was provided. Lloyd's carried out
their usual practice with regard to cargo interests, and told them when
the 42-day period would expire. So the cargo interest knew all about
it. But, by some oversight, Lloyd's did not send the 42-day letter to
E   the shipowners. The clerk at Lloyd's, in an affidavit, explains it in
this way:

"I did not write any letter to Norton Rose "—the solicitors for the
shipowners—" at this time or send them a copy of the letter I wrote
to Constants "—they were for the cargo interest. "This was an
oversight on my part. If I had followed the usual practice adopted
in the department I would have written a 42-day letter to Norton
F   Rose with reference to the ship security."

We are told that it is also the practice of Lloyd's to telephone the
parties about a week or two before the 42 days have expired in order
to warn them of that fact. That too was not done in this case—again
apparently by an oversight.

G   The owners were dismayed, of course, when the salvors applied in the
circumstances for the security to be released to them. As soon as the
shipowners got to know of this, they applied, on October 1, 1979, for an
extension of time. This is the telex which they sent:

"On Friday September 28 the undersigned spoke to Mr. Dollimore "
—of Lloyd's—" to inquire when satisfactory security had in fact
H   been lodged and when 42-day period expired and was told July 29 last
and September 6 respectively. We accordingly hereby give late notice
of application for arbitration on behalf of shipowners. We also
request to be advised name of arbitrator appointed in accordance
with the application already made by one of the parties."

So they applied to the court—25 days late—for an extension of time
under section 27.

1000

Sheen J. held that section 27 did not apply to this arbitration clause. A
He did so because he thought the word "claim" in clause 6 was to be
interpreted as meaning a cause of action: and that it did not apply in
favour of the shipowners here because they had no cause of action at all.
From that decision, the shipowners have appealed to this court.

It raises a question under section 27. That section was first introduced in 1934 following the Report of the Committee on the Law of
Arbitration presided over by Mackinnon J. in 1927 (Cmd. 2817). Section B
27 says:

> "Where the terms of an agreement to refer future disputes to
> arbitration provide that any claims to which the agreement applies
> shall be barred unless notice to appoint an arbitrator is given . . .
> within a time fixed . . . and a dispute arises to which the agreement
> applies, the High Court,"—and these are the important words—" if C
> it is of opinion that in the circumstances of the case undue hardship
> would otherwise be caused, and notwithstanding that the time so fixed
> has expired, may, on such terms, if any, as the justice of the case may
> require, but without prejudice to the provisions of any enactment
> limiting the time for the commencement of arbitration proceedings,
> extend the time for such period as it thinks proper."
D

So the High Court has power to extend the time. In the early days
that section was restrictively interpreted. But, ever since *Liberian Shipping Corporation " Pegasus "* v. *A. King & Sons Ltd.* [1967] 2 Q.B. 86, it
has been construed more liberally. We were taken by Mr. Pollock
through a number of cases since 1967 in which attempts have been made
to restrict its application: but all these attempts have failed. Thus in E
Ch. E. Rolimpex Ltd. v. *Avra Shipping Co. Ltd. (The Angeliki)* [1973]
2 Lloyd's Rep. 226 Kerr J. held that section 27 did not apply to the time
limit under the Hague Rules: but we have since held that it does; see
Nea Agrex S.A. v. *Baltic Shipping Co. Ltd.* [1976] Q.B. 933. In *Consolidated Investment & Contracting Co.* v. *Saponaria Shipping Co. Ltd.
(The Virgo)* [1978] 1 W.L.R. 986 it was submitted that section 27 did not
apply to cases where the right was barred: but we held in this court that F
it did not matter whether the right or the remedy was barred. In any case
the section applied. Then there was *S. I. Pension Trustees Ltd.* v.
William Hudson Ltd. (1977) 35 P. & C.R. 54 before Forbes J. where he
held that section 27 applied.

I need not go further through the cases because this case is not
governed by any of them. It is to be dealt with on the construction of G
clause 6 itself. It seems to me that the word "claim" there is not confined to causes of action, as the judge said. It applies to a claim for
arbitration so as to fix the amount of the salvage award. Suppose, for
instance, in this case that within the 42 days the salvors claimed an
award in excess of the amount of the security—in excess of the $2,400,000
—clearly they would be entitled to have an arbitration on that matter.
Seeing that the salvors could claim arbitration within the 42 days on H
the ground that the sum should be more, surely the shipowners could
claim arbitration within the 42 days on the ground that it should be
less. What is sauce for the goose is sauce for the gander! What is
sauce for the salvors is sauce for the shipowners too! The word "claim,"
in my opinion, here means simply a claim for the salvage award to be
assessed by arbitration. The claim which the shipowners make here
(that it should be less than the $2,400,000) is a claim for arbitration. It

A is a claim which, under clause 6 of the agreement, would be barred if not made within six weeks. Then section 27 comes in: and, as I have often said, it is virtually to be regarded as written into all these arbitration agreements. It says that if the court is of opinion that undue hardship would be caused, it can extend the time.

B The judge found that undue hardship would be caused to the shipowners. His finding on that point is not challenged in this court. That is clearly right. It is no fault of the shipowners that the 25 days elapsed. Those days elapsed because of the oversight of a clerk at Lloyd's. The salvors have suffered no prejudice in any way because of that lapse of 25 days. They are just as well able to contest the case. They know everything about it, as they would have done if the claim had been made within the 42 days. So, on the matter of jurisdiction, I hold that there C is jurisdiction to grant the extension of time.

Now I come to the next point—" on such terms as the justice of the case may require." The judge did not have to give a decision on it—but he considered the terms. He said that, if he had had jurisdiction, he would only have granted it on the terms that the shipowners should pay a further sum of $200,000 within 28 days—they have already paid the D first $200,000—and also give security in a further sum of $500,000.

He said as to the additional $200,000: " It is inconceivable that the salvor's award will be fixed at less than $400,000." I am not sure that that is correct. On the evidence before us, it is arguable that it would be less than $400,000. It must be remembered that a payment would be the equivalent of an unconditional judgment for the amount. It could not be recovered back. So it should not be made a term unless it was un-E arguably due. For present purposes it is sufficient to accept the offer made on behalf of the owners that they are ready to pay another $115,000 on account of the salvage award. That seems to me to meet the case entirely on that point.

As to the sum of $500,000 as further security, it seems to me that that was incorrect. The salvors put their initial figure at $2,400,000—no doubt F on the generous side. They have taken into account the delay in assessing it, the loss of interest, and so forth. It is not appropriate to add a further sum by way of security.

The costs of this application should, of course, be borne by the shipowners because they are applying for an extension of time. They must pay all the costs at all events in the court below. They must also pay the $115,000 which I have mentioned. Those are terms which seem to me G would be justified. The extension of time should be allowed.

BRIDGE L.J. The point raised on the construction of section 27 of the Arbitration Act 1950 is a short one. Having regard to the mischief which that section is intended to remedy, I think it is right to give the word " claims " in the section a wide and liberal interpretation. In my judg-H ment, any claim to have determined by arbitration a matter in issue between the parties upon which the rights of the party making the claim depend is a claim within the meaning of the section. So here the determination by arbitration of the proper amount of the salvors' remuneration directly governs the right of the plaintiff shipowners to recover part of the security they were required to provide for the release of their ship. The shipowners' claim to such a determination is, in my view, clearly one to which the section applies. That being so, I think it is now conceded

that the mere fact of the plaintiffs bringing these proceedings for an   A
extension of time to commence the arbitration is sufficient to satisfy the
requirement of the section that a dispute arises to which the agreement
applies. I therefore respectfully disagree with Sheen J.'s conclusion that
we have no jurisdiction to extend the plaintiffs' time.

On the question of terms, there are in my view far too many im-
ponderables which may affect the eventual outcome of the arbitration to
make it appropriate to order the shipowners to make to the salvors a   B
payment on account (which, once made, would be irrecoverable) of any
greater sum than they have offered so far.

With regard to security, its amount was fixed by the salvors in June.
There can have been no significant change in the circumstances affecting
the appropriateness of the figure then fixed between June and October.
Moreover the delay of 25 days on the part of the shipowners in claiming   C
arbitration was neither occasioned by any significant fault on their part,
nor the cause of any significant prejudice to the salvors. Accordingly,
it would in my judgment be inappropriate to order any increase in the
amount of the security.

For these reasons, I too would allow the appeal and order that the
plaintiffs' time be extended unconditionally.

  D

SIR DAVID CAIRNS. In my opinion, when the shipowners gave notice
of their claim to arbitration, they were in effect making a claim that their
liability to salvage was something less than $2,400,000, the total of the
security they had given and the sum they had paid on account.

Mr. Thomas, on behalf of the salvors, conceded that if the salvors
had wished to obtain *more* than $2,400,000 from the shipowners and had   E
given notice claiming arbitration after the expiration of the 42 days, they
would have been making a claim and could have applied to the court
under section 27 of the Arbitration Act 1950 for an extension of time.
He could give no ground in common fairness why one party should be
able to apply for extra time in order to get *more* money whereas the other
party should not be able to apply in order to have to pay less. He simply   F
relied on the language of section 27 which he contended could have no
other meaning than that upon which he relied.

I, like Lord Denning M.R. and Bridge L.J., take a different view of the
construction of the section. I consider that the word " claim " is fully
capable of bearing the meaning to which I referred at the beginning of
this judgment. I accept that the narrower meaning as found by Sheen J.
is a possible one, but it would be so unjust that I cannot believe it was the   G
meaning intended by Parliament.

If there was a claim by the shipowners, it was obviously not a claim
which the salvors were willing to accede to, and accordingly there was a
dispute between them. I therefore conclude that the judge was wrong in
holding that he had no jurisdiction to extend the time. It is conceded
that he was right in his opinion that the case was one of hardship and   H
that there should be an extension of time if the court had jurisdiction
to grant it.

There remains the question of terms. Here, with very great respect
to Sheen J., I am satisfied that he erred in principle in respect to both the
conditions which he imposed. As to payment on account, it has to be
borne in mind that no *order* for payment on account could be made
either by an arbitrator or by a judge. If it were admitted that the right

A figure for a salvage award would be at least £X, it would be reasonable to
make the payment of £X on account a *condition* of extending the time
under section 27. If an estimate advanced on behalf of the shipowners
were plainly bogus, then again such a condition would be appropriate.
Otherwise I cannot think that it is right for a judge to form an estimate
of what he considers the lowest sum likely to be awarded and to make
the condition that the shipowners shall make a payment on account ac-
B cordingly, a payment which would not be recoverable if the judge's estimate turned out to be too high. I would therefore limit the additional
sum to be paid on account to $115,000, to which the owners agreed.

As to the condition of giving a further $500,000 security, this was
something which was not asked for by the salvors and there was no
material before the judge to indicate that any change had occurred since
C they themselves fixed the figure for security at $2,400,000. I would there-
fore omit that condition altogether.

For those reasons I too would allow the appeal and make the order
proposed by Lord Denning M.R. and Bridge L.J.

Appeal allowed with costs in Court of
Appeal.
D   *Owners to pay costs below.*
Leave to appeal refused.

Solicitors: *Norton, Rose, Botterell & Roche; Constant & Constant;*
William A. Crump & Son; Waltons & Morse.

A. H. B.
E

[COURT OF APPEAL]

* CUSTOMS AND EXCISE COMMISSIONERS *v.*
F   GEORGE WIMPEY & CO. LTD.

[1978 C. No. 7007]

1980 March 12, 13   Lord Denning M.R.,
Waller and Dunn L.JJ.

G *Revenue—Customs and excise—Duty chargeable—Rebate on heavy*
oil duty for certain uses—Specific penalties for misuse and pro-
vision entitling commissioners to recover amount equal to
rebate—Pecuniary penalties recoverable in magistrates' court—
Whether jurisdiction in civil courts to entertain commissioners'
action to recover unpaid amount of rebate—Hydrocarbon Oil
(Customs & Excise) Act 1971 (c. 12), s. 11 (1)

H   The Hydrocarbon Oil (Customs & Excise) Act 1971, a
consolidating Act, provides by section 9 for a rebate of customs
or excise duty " at the time of delivery " on heavy oil delivered
" for home use "; but by section 10 (1) and (2), if it is intended
to use " rebated " oil for vehicles constructed or adapted for
use on roads (except vehicles specified in Schedule 1 to the
Act) a declaration to that effect has to be made; and by subsection (3) [1] no rebated heavy oil shall be used as fuel for

vehicles to which section 10 applies unless an amount equal
to the rebate on like oil has been paid to the Customs and
Excise Commissioners. Section 11 provides:

"(1) A person who (a) uses heavy oil in contravention of
section 10 (3) . . . shall be liable to a penalty of three
times the value of the oil or £100, whichever is the greater ;
and the commissioners may recover from him an amount
equal to the rebate on like oil at the rate in force at the
time of the contravention."

The commissioners began an action in the High Court
against the defendant, a civil engineering company, claiming
that it had since 1971 operated tractors adapted for use on
roads fueled by heavy oil on which a rebate of duty had been
allowed ; some instances were given of such use of tractors
observed by customs officers and further discovery was sought
in order to calculate the amount of rebate alleged to be due
and unpaid. The statement of claim added that the company
wrongly contended that it was entitled to use the rebated oil
for tractors engaged in brushing public roads. It asked for a
declaration that if the company used rebated fuel as alleged
the amount of the rebate had to be paid to the commissioners ; it also sought an account of the amount due in
respect of contraventions of section 10 (3), an order for payment of the amount found due, and other consequential relief.

The company applied to have the action struck out on the
ground that the High Court had no jurisdiction to entertain it,
since on the proper construction of section 11 (1), in the
context of all the relevant Customs and Excise legislation,
the two parts of subsection (1) must be read together so that
the "amount equal to the rebate . . ." which the commissioners
sought to recover in the High Court action was a pecuniary
penalty for a customs offence, additional to the penalties of
"three times the value of the oil or £100 " and recoverable
only in the magistrates' court within three years. The master
and May J. on appeal refused to strike out the action, the
judge holding that the penalties were specified before the
semicolon in section 11 (1) ; that the following words entitled
the commissioners to recover unpaid rebate in any way the
law permitted ; and that the High Court had jurisdiction to
decide the matter.

On appeal by the company: —

Held, dismissing the appeal, that the second part of section
11 (1) was not to be construed as an additional penalty hinged
on to those in the first part but as providing a separate method
by which the commissioners could recover from a person who
contravened the provisions of section 10 an amount equal to
the rebate on like oils at the rate in force at the time of the
contravention ; that such proceedings could be brought in any
court, including the High Court ; that the commissioners were
therefore entitled to seek the declaration they asked for, and
if the tractors were vehicles used on roads in contravention
of section 10 (3), to obtain from the company discovery as to
the number of such tractors they had been using for brushing public roads and for how long ; and by that procedure
could recover the precise amount of any duty which ought
to have been paid on the rebated heavy oil used in them.

Barraclough v. Brown [1897] A.C. 615, H.L.(E.) distinguished.

Decision of May J. affirmed.

The following cases are referred to in the judgments:

Barraclough v. Brown [1897] A.C. 615, H.L.(E.).
Pyx Granite Co. Ltd. v. Minister of Housing and Local Government [1960]
A.C. 260; [1959] 3 W.L.R. 346; [1959] 3 All E.R. 1, H.L.(E.).

A   The following additional cases were cited in argument:

Brown v. *Allweather Mechanical Grouting Co. Ltd.* [1954] 2 Q.B. 443 ;
[1953] 2 W.L.R. 402 ; [1953] 1 All E.R. 474, D.C.

Customs and Excise Commissioners v. *Sokolow's Trustee* [1954] 2 Q.B.
336; [1954] 2 W.L.R. 575; [1954] 2 All E.R. 5.

Director of Public Prosecutions v. *Schildkamp* [1971] A.C. 1 ; [1970] 2
W.L.R. 279 ; [1969] 3 All E.R. 1640, H.L.(E.).

B   *Farrell* v. *Alexander* [1977] A.C. 59 ; [1976] 3 W.L.R. 145 ; [1976] 2 All
E.R. 721, H.L.(E.).

Qualter, Hall & Co. Ltd. v. *Board of Trade* [1962] Ch. 273 ; [1961] 3
W.L.R. 825; [1961] 3 All E.R. 389, C.A.

INTERLOCUTORY APPEAL from May J.

C   The Customs and Excise Commissioners, by a writ issued on September 18, 1978, and statement of claim endorsed thereon, claimed that at all
material times the defendant, George Wimpey & Co. Ltd., very large civil
engineers, carried on its business at various sites throughout the United
Kingdom; that in connection with that business, the company operated a
number of tractors which used as fuel heavy oil in respect of which a
rebate of duty had been allowed at the rate of 1p per gallon less than the
D   rate at which the duty was for the time being chargeable thereon pursuant
to section 9 of the Hydrocarbon Oil (Customs & Excise) Act 1971; that
section 10 (3) of the Act provided that no heavy oil on the delivery of
which rebate had been allowed should be used as fuel for a vehicle to
which section 10 applied, or be taken into such a vehicle as uel, unless an
amount equal to the amount for the time being allowable in respect of
E   rebate on like oil had been paid to the commissioners in accordance with
regulations made for the purposes of that section; that section 10 applied to
any vehicle constructed or adapted for use on roads except any vehicle
specified in Schedule 1 to the Act of 1971; and that by section 11 (1) of
the Act, the commissioners were entitled to recover from a person who
used heavy oil in contravention of section 10 (3) or was liable for heavy
oil being taken into a vehicle in contravention of that subsection, an amount
F   equal to the rebate on like oil at the rate in force at the time of the
contravention.

The commissioners alleged that on occasions which they were unable
to identify, save as were set out in attached particulars, the company had
from time to time since 1971 operated on roads tractors, constructed or
adapted for use on the roads, when the tractors had taken in and used as
G   fuel heavy oil on the delivery of which a rebate on the oil had been
allowed.

The particulars specified three occasions in 1976, at Newcastle-upon-
Tyne, Darlington, and Leven, in Scotland, when identified tractors had
been observed in use and claimed that from information made available
by the company the amount due to the commissioners as rebate of duty
in respect of tractors operated in the Newcastle-upon-Tyne area from
H   1971 was £1,128·75, calculated in accordance with a schedule annexed to
the statement of claim. They alleged that the company wrongfully contended that it was entitled to use the fuel without paying the amount of
the rebate in the case of tractors engaged on brushing public roads.

The commissioners claimed (1) a declaration that if the company
used fuel in respect of which a rebate had been allowed as aforesaid, in
tractors engaged on brushing public roads, the amount of the rebate had
to be paid to them; (2) the sum of £1,128; (3) an account of the amount

due to them from the company, other than the £1,128, in respect of the **A**
company's contraventions of section 10 (3); (4) an order for the payment
of the amount found due on taking such account; and other ancillary
relief.

In response to requests for further and better particulars, the commissioners, while supplying further details of the occasions already specified, stated that they could not comply with the requests until after **B**
discovery in the action.

The company applied to Master Bickford-Smith in chambers by a
summons dated March 1, 1979, asking that the action by the commissioners be struck out on the ground that the court had no jurisdiction to
entertain the claim; alternatively that on the commissioners' admission
that they could not substantiate their alleged claim without discovery and
inspection of documents, the company were unable to plead to the claim **C**
before particulars were given; that it was not incumbent on the company
to provide discovery and inspection of documents to enable the commissioners to substantiate their alleged claim; and that such discovery
might not be required of them until the commissioners had delivered full
particulars of their claim, The master on March 19, 1979, ordered that
unless the company served a defence within 21 days, the commissioners
should have leave to enter judgment for a sum to be assessed. The **D**
company appealed to May J., who on November 8, 1979, dismissed
the appeal and refused to strike out the action, holding on the principal
submission for the company that on the true construction of section 11 (1)
the penalties for misuse of rebated heavy oil were provided before the
semi-colon, and that the words after it went on to provide that the commissioners might recover that which ex hypothesi ought previously to **E**
have been paid to them. He continued:

"Taking that view, I do not think that the only place in which that
debt can be recovered is the magistrates' court. Indeed, as presently
advised, I do not think that the statute entitles the commissioners to
go to the magistrates' court to recover the amount of the rebate.
They may recover in the way or form which the law permits and, **F**
if it permits, in the High Court. I do not accept this contention nor
think that the statement of claim can be faulted on these grounds,
or on the grounds that this court has no jurisdiction to decide the
matter."

The judge granted the company leave to appeal provided that a defence
was served within 21 days, notice of appeal given within 14 days and the **G**
appeal prosecuted with reasonable despatch.

The company having delivered a defence dated November 20, 1979,
filed a notice of appeal from the judge's order, on the grounds (1) that the
judge was wrong in law in failing to hold that on a true construction of
the provisions of the Hydrocarbon Oil (Customs & Excise) Act 1971, the
Customs and Excise Act 1952, the Finance Act 1953, the Magistrates' **H**
Courts Act 1952, and the Justices of the Peace Act 1949, the commissioners' claim to recover "the amount equal to the rebate on like
oil at the rate in force at the time of contravention" could only be
brought in a magistrates' court and therefore the High Court had no
jurisdiction to entertain the claim; and (2) that the judge misdirected
himself in failing to hold that any sums recoverable by the commissioners
pursuant to section 11 (1) of the Act of 1971 could only be recovered in

A proceedings for an offence pursuant to section 283 of the Customs and Excise Act 1952.

Patrick Medd Q.C. and *Graham Garner* for the defendant company.
Simon D. Brown for the commissioners.

LORD DENNING M.R. George Wimpey & Co. are big contractors up
B and down the country. In the course of their work, they often leave
mud and dirt about the roads. It has to be cleared up. For that purpose,
they use tractors to brush the roads. Those tractors use what is called
" heavy oil." Wimpeys have been paying tax at a lower rate on that
" heavy oil " on the basis that the tax is only a penny a gallon: whereas
on other vehicles used on the road with heavy oil, the tax is 22½p a gallon.

C   The Customs and Excise Commissioners say that Wimpeys are not
entitled to pay tax at a lower rate: and they claim the amount of the
rebate which has been allowed to them. It was not until February 1976
that the commissioners discovered what Wimpeys were doing. Then, on
February 19, 1976, one of their officers went to Brunton Lane in Newcastle-upon-Tyne. He found there a tractor, registration no. ELR 299J,
brushing the road. He thought that the proper rate of tax had not been
D paid on the heavy oil used in that tractor. So he got into touch with
Wimpeys in order to find out how often they had been using this tractor
over the years and other tractors like it. The commissioners then estimated that the rebate of duty in respect of tractors operated in the
Newcastle area from 1971 came to £1,128·75. The commissioners discovered that tractors were being used in the same way in other areas.
E They discovered one in Darlington, and another in Scotland.
     Being of opinion that the proper duty had not been paid on the heavy
oil, on September 18, 1978, the Customs and Excise Commissioners
brought an action claiming a declaration that Wimpeys had not been
paying the proper amount for the fuel. That issue having been joined
in the High Court, Wimpeys took the point that no such declaration
could be obtained from the High Court. That point was argued before
F the judge, and it has been argued before us here today. Wimpeys say
that the only remedy is for the Customs and Excise Commissioners to
prosecute them in the magistrates' court: on the ground that that is the
only place where the commissioners are entitled to go to recover these
sums. If this contention is correct, it is to the advantage of Wimpeys.
In the magistrates' court, they are not compelled to give discovery.
G Whereas in the High Court, they may have to give discovery: and a
declaration can be made against them.
     Mr. Medd has put forward an interesting argument before us, with his
usual care and skill. I will not go through all the numerous statutes to
which we have been referred: but the Hydrocarbon Oil (Customs &
Excise) Act 1971 provides for differences in tax on oil according to the
vehicle in which it is used. A high rate has to be paid on heavy oil used
H in vehicles which are used on the roads such as motor cars. A low rate
of tax is payable on vehicles which are used in fields and on land such as
farm tractors and digging machines. In this case the eventual issue is:
into what category do these tractors fall? Wimpeys say that they are
digging machines, and therefore they are only obliged to pay the lower
rate of tax. Whereas the commissioners say they are used on the roads
and ought to pay the higher rate. The issue depends on the use to which
the vehicle is put.

The machinery for recovering the tax depends on sections 10 and 11 **A**
of the Hydrocarbon Oil (Customs & Excise) Act 1971. Section 10 is very
complicated but the effect of it is that if a person does use a tractor for
brushing roads without paying the proper duty on the heavy oil, he is
guilty of an offence. The question for us today is whether, in addition
to that person being guilty of an offence, proceedings can be brought for
the recovery of the amount which should have been paid. Section 11 (1)
provides: **B**

> " A person who—(a) uses heavy oil in contravention of section 10 (3)
> of this Act . . . shall be liable to a penalty of three times the value of
> the oil or £100, whichever is the greater; and the commissioners may
> recover from him an amount equal to the rebate on like oil at the
> rate in force at the time of the contravention."

C

Mr. Medd has argued before us that the second part of that subsection—" may recover from him an amount equal to the rebate on like
oil "—is hinged on to the first part. He maintains that the second part is
really an additional pecuniary penalty. That section is one of the many
provisions in the Customs and Excise Act 1952 and the Finance Acts
dealing with offences against the customs and excise. Section 283 (1) of **D**
the Act of 1952 provides:

> " . . . any proceedings for an offence under the said Acts may be
> commenced at any time within, and shall not be commenced later
> than, three years from the date of the commission of the offence."

And those proceedings are to be commenced before the magistrates.
Section 273 (1) provides: **E**

> " Without prejudice to any other provision of this Act, any amount
> due by way of customs or excise duty may be recovered as a debt
> due to the Crown."

It was urged—and I thought at first that there was something in it—
that under the Customs and Excise Acts proceedings can either be taken
under section 273 for a debt due to the Crown, or under section 283 as **F**
proceedings before the magistrates. And that those are the only two
proceedings available. As a result of the discussion before us, I was satisfied that, although those two sections provide two methods by which
money can be dealt with or recovered, nevertheless there is a third method.
It is contained in the second part of section 11 (1) of the Hydrocarbon
Oil (Customs & Excise) Act 1971 that " the commissioners may recover **G**
from him an amount equal to the rebate on like oil at the rate in force
at the time of the contravention." That is a method of recovery which
can be taken by the commissioners in any of the ordinary courts of the
land. Indeed, I doubt very much whether they could recover the amount
before the magistrates.

Although we have been through all the sections from 1935 onwards, **H**
this afternoon Mr. Brown drew our attention to a most interesting section.
It is section 9 (6) of the Finance Act 1960, which provides:

> " Where a person contravenes the said subsection (2) in respect of
> any oils, then without prejudice to any penalty or forfeiture the
> commissioners may recover from him an amount equal to the rebate
> on like oils at the rate in force at the time of the contravention."

The Weekly Law Reports, August 15, 1980

1009

1 W.L.R.   Customs & Excise v. Geo. Wimpey & Co. (C.A.)   Lord Denning M.R.

A   That is the predecessor of section 11 (2) of the present consolidation Act
of 1971. The words " without prejudice to any penalty or forfeiture "
show that this particular provision is not a penalty or forfeiture at all.
It is open to the commissioners to recover the amount in any of the courts
in the land.

In this context, Mr. Brown referred us to *Pyx Granite Co. Ltd.* v.
Ministry of Housing and Local Government [1960] A.C. 260, and par-
B   ticularly to the observations of Viscount Simonds, at p. 286. He distinguished *Barraclough* v. *Brown* [1897] A.C. 615 on the ground that there
the remedy and the right were inextricably bound together. You only got
the right by going to the magistrates' court. Whereas here they are not so
bound together.

It is quite plain that the commissioners can recover these amounts in
C   proceedings in the High Court. They can obtain a declaration such as
they seek. They can, if need be, obtain discovery from Wimpeys as to
the number of tractors they have been using and for how long. In that
way they can recover the amount of duty which ought to be paid with
regard to the heavy oil used in them. I see no objection to the jurisdiction of the High Court. I would dismiss the appeal accordingly.

D   WALLER L.J. I agree with the judgment of Lord Denning M.R. The
provisions relating to hydrocarbon oil appear to be very complicated. It
seems that hydrocarbon oil is divided by statute between heavy and light;
and the heavy oil, if it is for home use, does not have to pay the full duty.
The full duty, as Lord Denning M.R. has said, is 22½p; but, if it is required
and used for home use, there is a rebate which reduces that 22½p to one
E   penny; and the provisions that we are concerned to consider here are the
provisions of sections 10 and 11 of the Hydrocarbon Oil (Customs &
Excise) Act 1971, and in particular section 11. Lord Denning M.R. has
already read subsection (1) of that section, the important part of it being
the distinction between the words

     " shall be liable to a penalty of three times the value of the oil or
     £100, whichever is the greater; and the commissioners may recover
F   from him an amount equal to the rebate on like oil at the rate in
     force at the time of the contravention."

Mr. Medd made two other points, apart from his submissions about
section 273 of the Customs and Excise Act 1952, which Lord Denning
M.R. has already read. He submitted that this was a penalty because it
was contained in a section with the side note " Penalties for misuse of
G   rebated heavy oil." Secondly he submitted that it was a penalty because
it was not exact compensation for the duty which was lost. He relied on
the words " an amount equal to the rebate on like oil at the rate in force
at the time of the contravention." In my judgment, looking at the
section without considering the history (the history, incidentally, strenth-
ens this conclusion), the subsection deals with the penalties and then, as a
H   completely separate sentence, sets out this provision for recovery. Therefor it seems to me that it is probably not a penalty.

But when you go to the second part of Mr. Medd's submission that
the provision is not being made for exact compensation, in my judgment
the conclusion is the exact opposite, because, when one looks at section
10 (3), which is the section creating the offence the penalties for which are
set out in section 11 (1), section 10 (3) says: " No heavy oil on the delivery
of which for home use rebate has been allowed "—if I may just interpose

there, that means that oil has arrived in this country, it has gone to a   A
refinery, and it has come out of the refinery as a delivery of heavy oil for
home use; and, therefore, instead of the 22½p which was due, there was
a rebate of 21½p, leaving only one penny to be paid. So that section 10
(3) reads:

> " No heavy oil on the delivery of which home use rebate has been
> allowed shall—(a) be used as fuel for a vehicle to which this section   B
> applies . . . unless an amount equal to the amount for the time being
> allowable in respect of rebate on like oil has been paid to the com-
> missioners in accordance with regulations made for the purposes of
> this section."

And we have been told that the regulations made for the purposes of the
section require that the commissioners shall have authorised in writing   C
such a payment to be made.

One can see the common sense of the arrangement because, if the
rate of duty varies from year to year, it may be very difficult to ascertain
precisely what duty has been paid; and, as Mr. Brown pointed out, if
there is a large tank, there may be some oil in it which has borne one rate
of duty and part of which has borne a different rate. So the subsection
provides that a payment should be made before the vehicle is used, being   D
" an amount equal to the amount for the time being allowable in respect
of rebate on like oil "—in other words, a current rebate. That is not only
the sensible way of dealing with it; but, when the vehicle is being used
without that payment being made, that is what the commissioners have
actually lost. So the provision in the second part of section 11 (1) exactly
defines the loss which the commissioners have made. That strengthens   E
the case for saying that this is not a penalty but is a provision for ensuring
as far as possible that the commissioners may recover that rebate which
would have been made at that particular time.

I am quite satisfied that this provision is not a provision for a penalty.
Furthermore, when the argument is made that this is a sum which should
be recovered as part of the proceedings in a court of summary jurisdiction, there is no provision restricting this to a court of summary jurisdic-   F
tion. I would reserve my opinion as to whether or not it is possible to
recover in such proceedings. It seems improbable that it is, and, in my
view, the claim which is made in this case in the High Court is one which
is properly made, and I would dismiss this appeal.

DUNN L.J.   I agree with both judgments delivered by my Lords.   G

Appeal dismissed with costs.
Leave to appeal refused.

Solicitors: *P. J. Ward; Solicitor, Customs and Excise.*

M. M. H.   H

A

[HOUSE OF LORDS]

* O'BRIEN AND OTHERS . . . . APPELLANTS

AND

SIM-CHEM LTD. . . . . RESPONDENTS

B
1980 July 7, 8; 30
Lord Diplock, Viscount Dilhorne,
Lord Salmon, Lord Russell of Killowen
and Lord Keith of Kinkel

*Discrimination, Sex—Equal pay—Evaluation study—Scheme to
remunerate employees in accordance with evaluation study and
merit assessment schemes—Evaluation study completed but not
implemented—Merit assessment scheme incomplete—Whether
women's remuneration determined by " rating of the work "—
Whether women entitled to equal pay as men in same grade—
Equal Pay Act 1970 (c. 41), s. 1 (2) (b) (as amended by Sex
Discrimination Act 1975 (c. 65), s. 8)*

A job evaluation committee representing management and
union was established by the employers to devise a job evaluation scheme. By March 1976 the grading of the jobs was
completed and the relevant employees, including the three
applicants, were informed of their new job grade and salary
range for the grade. They were informed of their right of
appeal in respect of the job grading. In the absence of an
appeal the grade would be confirmed with effect from April 26,
1976, and their contracts of employment would be amended
accordingly. The employers also intended that, before the job
evaluation scheme was applied and employees were paid in
accordance with their grading, a merit assessment scheme should
be introduced. Owing to difficulties arising from the implementation of the government's pay policy, the employees were never
remunerated in accordance with the new job evaluated salary
structure nor was the position of any individual employee
determined on the basis of a merit assessment scheme.

The applicants claimed that they were entitled to equal pay
on the basis that a job evaluation study had been completed
and that their jobs were rated as equivalent with that of men
in the same employment, who in each case, were paid more
than they were. An industrial tribunal dismissed their applications on the ground that the job evaluation study as a whole
had not been completed and that it had not been adopted or
accepted.

The applicants appealed claiming that they were entitled to
equal pay under the provisions of section 1 (2) (b) of the Equal
Pay Act 1970,[1] as amended, even though the job evaluation
scheme had not been implemented. Allowing the applicants'
appeal, the Employment Appeal Tribunal ordered that, since
there was a valid job evaluation scheme in all respects other
than regarding merit rating, the applicants should have a
declaration that they were entitled to a salary appropriate to
the grade for their job, the level of the job to be negotiated
by the parties and, basing its decision on section 1 (2) (b) of
the Act, held that the job evaluation scheme was relevant to
the contracts, and that each applicant's contract of employment as to remuneration should be treated as modified so as
to be no less favourable than a similar term in the contract
of a man whose job had been given an equal grading. The
Court of Appeal allowed the employers' appeal.

O'Brien v. Sim-Chem Ltd. (H.L.(E.))   **[1980]**

On appeal by the applicants: —   A

Held, allowing the appeal and restoring the order of the
appeal tribunal, that once a job evaluation study had been
undertaken and had resulted in a conclusion that the job of
the woman had been evaluated under section 1 (5) of the Act
as of equal value with the job of the man, then the comparison of the respective terms of their contracts of employment was made feasible and a decision could be made (subject
to section 1 (3) whether modification under section 1 (2) (*b*) (i)   B
or treatment under section 1 (2) (*b*) (ii) was called for by
the equality clause deemed to be included in the woman's
contract pursuant to section 1 (1), for it was at that stage when
comparison first became feasible, and discrimination could first
be detected that the provisions of paragraph (*b*) of section
1 (2) was intended to bite, and bite at once, and that it mattered
not that the job evaluation study had been undertaken voluntarily by the employer (post, pp. 1014G, 1016G–H, 1017E).   C

Decision of the Court of Appeal [1980] 1 W.L.R. 734;
[1980] I.C.R. 429; [1980] 2 All E.R. 307 reversed.

The following case is referred to in the opinion of Lord Russell of
Killowen:

Bank of England v. *Vagliano Brothers* [1891] A.C. 107, H.L.(E.).

                                                                        D
The following cases were cited in argument:

Eaton Ltd. v. *Nuttall* [1977] 1 W.L.R. 549; [1977] I.C.R. 272; [1977]
3 All E.R. 1131, E.A.T.
England v. *Bromley London Borough Council* [1978] I.C.R. 1, E.A.T.
Graviner v. *Hughes* (unreported), June 9, 1978, E.A.T.
Greene v. *Broxtowe District Council* [1977] I.C.R. 241; [1977] 1 All E.R.
694, E.A.T.   E
Hebbes v. *Rank Precision Industries Ltd.* [1978] I.C.R. 489, E.A.T.

APPEAL from the Court of Appeal.

This was an appeal by the appellants, Patricia O'Brien, Doris Lloyd
Coleman and Isobel Mary Clarkson, by leave of the House of Lords from
a judgment and order of the Court of Appeal (Stephenson, Waller and
Cumming-Bruce L.JJ.) [1980] 1 W.L.R. 734 dated December 21, 1979,   F
reversing the decision of the Employment Appeal Tribunal (Phillips J.
(President), Mr. S. C. Marley and Mrs. A. L. T. Taylor) [1979] I.C.R. 13
given on July 28, 1978. In that decision the Employment Appeal Tribunal
had itself reversed the decision of an industrial tribunal sitting at Manchester
which held on November 4, 1977, that the appellants' claims under section
1 (2) (*b*) of the Equal Pay Act 1970, as amended by the Sex Discrimination   G
Act 1975 were not well founded.

The following facts were common ground between the parties. At
all material times the respondents, Sim-Chem Ltd., employed 125 clerical
employees upon 79 different jobs at their head office in Stockport. The
three appellants were three female employees of the respondents at the time
of their originating applications to the industrial tribunal.

Before the coming into force on December 29, 1975, of the Equal Pay H
Act 1970, as amended by the Sex Discrimination Act 1975, the respondent
employers had introduced equal pay for all female employees who were
employed on " like work," within the meaning of section 1 (4) of the Equal
Pay Act 1970, with male employees. A number of female employees were
not employed on like work with male employees and accordingly a committee was set up by the respondents with the agreement of the employees'
trade union to evaluate the jobs done by clerical employees in terms of

A the demands made by those jobs. The purpose of that exercise was to produce a pay structure which would ensure that men and women engaged in work rated as equivalent under a job evaluation study would receive equal pay without discrimination based on sex.

The committee, which comprised representatives both of management and of the employees, produced its report on October 8, 1975. The report recommended that all clerical jobs should be graded into one of six grades,
B each grade being related only to the demands of the job and not being related to sex. The report further recommended that individual salaries within each grade should be determined on the basis of how well the job was being performed by each individual on the basis of an individual merit-rating.

The grading of jobs proposed by the committee was accepted by the
C respondents and the employees' trade union. A range of salaries appropriate to each grade was then negotiated, it being intended that the precise place of each employee within the salary range would be decided by a merit rating of the individual concerned.

On March 24, 1976, the respondents wrote to the appellants and a number of other employees informing them of the new grade of the job, and the salary range negotiated for that grade.
D At the time of the job evaluation scheme Her Majesty's Government were operating a policy of voluntary pay and salary restraint. The respondents were apprehensive that the introduction of the new graded pay structure might infringe the government's pay policy and that in consequence it could be subjected to sanctions in various forms.

The respondents did not implement the results of the job evaluation study
E and individual employees (including the appellants) continued to be paid in accordance with their existing contracts and without reference either to the job evaluation study or to the grading of jobs described in the letter of March 24, 1976.

The industrial tribunal dismissed the appellants' applications. The Employment Appeal Tribunal in allowing their appeals [1979] I.C.R. 13 made the following order:
F
"... the tribunal orders that the appeals be allowed.

"The tribunal further orders that in the case of each appellant the term of her contract of employment relating to remuneration should be treated as so modified as to be not less favourable than the similar term in the contract of employment of any man whose job has been given an equal value to her job in the job evaluation scheme dated
G April 26, 1976, in so far as grading is concerned and that the position within the grade is to be determined by agreement.

"And the tribunal further orders that the aforesaid order be not enforced until October 31, 1978, without prejudice to any agreement being reached to its being enforced at an earlier date, or as relating back to an earlier date
H "Liberty to apply as to the form of the aforesaid order. ..."

On appeal by the respondents, the Court of Appeal in allowing the appeal [1980] 1 W.L.R. 734 discharged the above order.

The appellants appealed.

The appeal raised two main issues. The first issue was the proper construction of section 1 (2) (b) (i) of the Equal Pay Act 1970, as amended. That in turn raised two particular questions: first, the proper construction of the word " determined " in section 1 (2) (b) of the Act; second, whether

1014

O'Brien v. Sim-Chem Ltd. (H.L.(E.))   [1980]

a woman employed in work rated as equivalent with that of a man in the A
same employment was entitled to the same contractual rate of pay, even
though the results of the rating of the work had not been incorporated into
the terms of her contract or his. The second issue was whether the construction of section 1 (2) (b) contained in the judgments of the Court of
Appeal was contrary to the principle of equal pay contained in article 119
of the E.E.C. Treaty and article 1 of the Council Directive 75/117/E.E.C.
of February 10, 1975. In the event, the second issue was not considered by B
their Lordships.

Anthony Lester Q.C. and Eldred Tabachnik for the appellants.
Martin Collins Q.C. and G. W. Wingate-Saul for the respondents.

Their Lordships took time for consideration.   C

July 30, 1980. LORD DIPLOCK. My Lords, I have had the advantage
of reading in draft the speech prepared by my noble and learned friend
Lord Russell of Killowen with which I agree, and I too would allow
the appeals.

D

VISCOUNT DILHORNE. My Lords, I agree with the speech of my
noble and learned friend Lord Russell of Killowen which I have seen
in draft.
I would allow the appeals and restore the order of the Employment
Appeal Tribunal with the variations he proposes.

LORD SALMON. My Lords, I have had the advantage of reading in E
draft the speech prepared by my noble and learned friend Lord Russell
of Killowen with which I agree. I too would allow the appeal.

LORD RUSSELL OF KILLOWEN. My Lords, the Equal Pay Act 1970
came into force on December 29, 1975, simultaneously with the Sex
Discrimination Act 1975, as amended by that latter Act. The Equal F
Pay Act 1970 (" the Act ") in its amended form is conveniently set out
in Part II of Schedule 1 to that latter Act. The Act is entitled " An
Act to prevent discrimination, as regards terms and conditions of employment, between men and women." It deals so far as concerns these
appeals with two situations. The first is where a woman is employed
on " like work " with a man in the same employment: the second
(with which these appeals are directly concerned) is where a woman is G
employed on work " rated as equivalent " with that of a man in the
same employment.
By section 1 (1) of the Act each woman's contract now in question
became deemed to include " an equality clause." Whether such an
equality clause has any and if so what effect depends upon the particular
circumstances.   H
It is convenient to consider first the provisions affecting a " like
work " case. A " like work " case is described in section 1 (4) as
follows:

" A woman is to be regarded as employed on like work with men if,
but only if, her work and theirs is of the same or a broadly similar
nature, and the differences (if any) between the things she does and
the things they do are not of practical importance in relation to

A   terms and conditions of employment; and accordingly in comparing her work with theirs regard shall be had to the frequency or otherwise with which any such differences occur in practice as well as to the nature and extent of the differences."

Section 1 (2) provides:

B   "An equality clause is a provision which relates to terms (whether concerned with pay or not) of a contract under which a woman is employed (the 'woman's contract'), and has the effect that—(a) where the woman is employed on like work with a man in the same employment—(i) if (apart from the equality clause) any term of the woman's contract is or becomes less favourable to the woman than a term of a similar kind in the contract under which that man is employed,

C   that term of the woman's contract shall be treated as so modified as not to be less favourable, and (ii) if (apart from the equality clause) at any time the woman's contract does not include a term corresponding to a term benefiting that man included in the contract under which he is employed, the woman's contract shall be treated as including such a term; . . ."

D   It is to be observed that the question whether there is a case of " like work " is an objective fact which in the case of a woman's contract at the coming into force of the Act either exists or does not exist. It is for the relevant tribunal to decide that question (if there be dispute), and also to decide whether modification or addition is required under paragraph (a) (i) and (ii) as a result of the deemed equality provision. In short, the exercise requires a comparison of the terms and conditions

E   of employment of the woman and of the man in a case of " like work." There is, be it noted, a further possible consideration in a " like work " case under section 1 (3), which provides:

"An equality clause shall not operate in relation to a variation between the woman's contract and the man's contract if the employer proves that the variation is genuinely due to a material difference

F   (other than the difference of sex) between her case and his."

The function of that subsection is to enable the employer to show on what may be called a merit basis that the man in the " like work " is as one *individual* entitled to preferential treatment: an example might be long service.

I turn now to subsections (2) (b) (i) and (ii) and (5) of section 1 which

G   deal with cases where the woman and the man are employed on jobs which, though not " like work," have been " rated as equivalent " as a result of a job evaluation study. Subsection (5) provides:

"A woman is to be regarded as employed on work rated as equivalent with that of any men if, but only if, her job and their job have been given an equal value, in terms of the demand made on a worker

H   under various headings (for instance effort, skill, decision), on a study undertaken with a view to evaluating in those terms the jobs to be done by all or any of the employees in an undertaking or group of undertakings, or would have been given an equal value but for the evaluation being made on a system setting different values for men and women on the same demand under any heading."

Job evaluation studies with a view to pinpointing equivalents and differences are not confined to the Act: they are in more general use in industry in an attempt to achieve a broadly sound pay structure. Reference may be made to a document placed before us " Acas Guide No. 1 —Job Evaluation."

It is of importance to note that a job evaluation study cannot be carried out without the agreement of the relevant parties—including of course the employer—that there shall be one. Maybe it was recognised that such a study could not sensibly be made compulsory.

I note at this stage that section 1 (3) already quoted, which might be described as providing for permissible merit variation, applies also to a case of equivalent job rating.

I turn finally to the provisions of section 1 (2) (b) which deals with a case where there is not " like work " but where work of a woman has by the application of section 1 (5) been rated as equivalent with that of a man. Section 1 (2) provides as follows:

" An equality clause is a provision which relates to terms (whether concerned with pay or not) of a contract under which a woman is employed (the ' woman's contract '), and has the effect that—. . . (b) where the woman is employed on work rated as equivalent with that of a man in the same employment—(i) if (apart from the equality clause) any term of the woman's contract determined by the rating of the work is or becomes less favourable to the woman than a term of a similar kind in the contract under which that man is employed, that term of the woman's contract shall be treated as so modified as not to be less favourable, and (ii) if (apart from the equality clause) at any time the woman's contract does not include a term corresponding to a term benefiting that man included in the contract under which he is employed and determined by the rating of the work, the woman's contract shall be treated as including such a term."

It is to be observed that paragraph (b) follows exactly the pattern of paragraph (a), but contains additionally in sub-paragraph (i) the words " determined by the rating of the work " and in sub-paragraph (ii) the words " and determined by the rating of the work." It is over the meaning (if any) to be given to those words that argument has ranged.

Taking a general approach to the legislation, I find that the " like work " provisions operate on a situation in which comparison of terms and conditions, under respectively the woman's and the man's contract, is necessarily feasible, and as soon as that comparison is made it can be decided whether there is a relevant discrimination between the woman and the man, subject of course to the provisions of section 1 (3). Once a job evaluation study has been undertaken and has resulted in a conclusion that the job of the woman has been evaluated under section 1 (5) as of equal value with the job of the man, then the comparison of the respective terms of their contracts of employment is made feasible and a decision can be made (subject of course to section 1 (3)) whether " modification " under (b) (i) or " treatment " under (b) (ii) is called for by the equality clause. I would expect that at that stage when comparison becomes first feasible, and discrimination can first be detected, that the provisions of paragraph (b) would be intended to bite, and bite at once. Comparison of terms and conditions of employment must be at the heart of the legislation: and I cannot imagine any reason why Parliament should postpone to a later stage the operation of paragraph (b).

A　　In the present case the pay structure of the employers was not adjusted as a result of the conclusions of the equivalent jobs value study. (The reason for this is not relevant to the decision of these appeals.) It was in fact anxiety lest a conflict with government pay policy would be involved, with consequences adverse to the commercial interests of the employers. The employers contend that unless and until there is such a resulting adjustment you do not reach the stage of deciding whether paragraph (b) B is operative, and for this they rely upon the presence of the phrases " term . . . determined by the rating of the work. . . ." They say that some effect must be given to them: that unless the employers' contention is correct no effect is given to them, since without their presence paragraph (b) would have exactly the same effect as is contended for by the appellant employees. That last submission is, I think, correct. The employers C argue that " the rating of the work " in sub-paragraphs (i) and (ii) refers to something different from " work rated as equivalent " in the first line of paragraph (b) (and in section 1 (5)): this I am wholly unable to accept, despite the suggested element of tautology.

　　The fact is that the exercise of equivalent work rating pursuant to a study undertaken under section 1 (5) does not determine in any sense any term of the woman's contract, nor determine in any sense any term of the D man's contract beneficial to him but absent from that of the woman. That is not a function of the exercise.

　　The employers based an argument on the fact that they were under no statutory obligation to participate in a job evaluation exercise, which is true, and which I have already suggested may be due to an impossibility of enforcing it. Therefore, it is contended, that the employers should not be E assumed to be under compulsion just because they have co-operated in a voluntary exercise. I do not agree. It seems to me eminently sensible that Parliament should impose the requirements of paragraph (b) at the moment when the evaluation study and exercise has made available a comparison which can show discrimination.

　　In summary, therefore, I am of opinion that the words in dispute cannot F have the result contended for by the employers. We were offered a number of dictionary substitutes for " determined " none of which appealed to me. The best that I can do is to take the phrase as indicating that the very outcome of the equivalent job rating is to show the term to be less favourable. The next best that I can do is to echo the words of Lord Bramwell in Bank of England v. Vagliano Brothers [1891] A.C. 107, 138: " This beats me," and jettison the words in dispute as making no contribu-G tion to the manifest intention of Parliament.

　　I would therefore allow the appeals and restore the order of the Employment Appeal Tribunal (ante, p. 1013F–G) with the following variations:

　　(1) Add after " modified " the words " with effect from April 26, 1976."

　　(2) Add before " to be determined by agreement " the words " if H possible."

　　(3) Delete " October 31, 1978 " and substitute " the expiration of three months after the decision of the appeal in the House of Lords."

　　(4) Delete words after " Liberty to apply " in the same sentence.

　　LORD KEITH OF KINKEL. My Lords, I have had the advantage of reading in draft the speech of my noble and learned friend Lord Russell of Killowen. I agree entirely with his reasoning and his conclusion that the

1018

appeal should be allowed and an order made in the terms which he has
proposed.

Appeal allowed.

Solicitors: *Pattinson & Brewer; C. G. H. Mackenzie.*

J. A. G.

[COURT OF APPEAL]

* SIDDIQUI AND ANOTHER *v.* RASHID

1980 May 22   Stephenson and Dunn L.JJ.
                      and Sir David Cairns

*Landlord and Tenant—Rent restriction—Alternative accommoda-
tion—Tenant living in London and having cultural, religious
and social ties there—Place of work in Luton—Whether flat
in Luton " suitable alternative accommodation "—Rent Act
1977 (c. 42), s. 98 (1), Sch. 15, para. 5 (1) (b)*

> The defendant, a Muslim, was a protected tenant in a flat
> owned by a charitable trust of which the plaintiffs were trustees.
> The flat was in London, where the defendant had friends and
> attended a mosque and cultural centre, but the defendant's
> place of work was in Luton. The plaintiffs wished to sell
> the property containing the flat in order to further their
> charitable work, and in order to sell it with vacant possession
> they offered the defendant alternative accommodation and
> sought a possession order in accordance with the provisions of
> section 98 (1) of the Rent Act 1977.[1] The alternative
> accommodation was in Luton, near to the defendant's work,
> and the question arose whether the alternative accommodation
> was " reasonably suitable . . . to the needs of the tenant . . . as
> regards . . . character; . . ." as required by paragraph 5 (1) (b)
> of Schedule 15 to the Act of 1977. The judge held that
> " character " of a property referred to the property itself, and
> did not include consideration of the tenant's leisure activities or
> proximity to friends, and he made an order for possession.
>   On appeal by the defendant: —
>   *Held,* dismissing the appeal, that " character " in paragraph
> 5 (1) (b) of Schedule 15 to the Rent Act 1977 was confined
> to the character of the property, and although that might be
> affected by environmental matters, such as noise and smell,
> which would directly affect the tenant in the enjoyment of
> the property, it did not extend to the society of friends or
> cultural interests of the tenant, and it was impossible to say that
> the accommodation offered in Luton was not such that the
> defendant could not live there in reasonably comfortable
> conditions suitable to the style of life he had been leading
> in London, and, in the circumstances, it was reasonable to
> grant a possession order.
>   *Redspring Ltd.* v. *Francis* [1973] 1 W.L.R. 134, C.A.
> applied.

The following case is referred to in the judgment of Stephenson L.J.:

Redspring Ltd. v. *Francis* [1973] 1 W.L.R. 134; [1973] 1 All E.R. 640,
    C.A.

---

[1] Rent Act 1977, s. 98 (1): see post, p. 1020A–B.
Sch. 15, para. 5 (1) (b): see post, p. 1020H.

A   No additional cases were cited in argument.

APPEAL from Judge Dow sitting at Clerkenwell County Court.

The defendant, Ghulam Rashid, appealed from a decision of Judge Dow in the Clerkenwell County Court given on January 9, 1980, whereby he granted a possession order relating to premises known as First Floor Rear Room, 148, Liverpool Road, London N.1 to the plaintiffs, Rashid Ahmad
B   Siddiqui and Habib-Ur Rehman, trustees of the United Kingdom Islamic Mission.

The grounds of the appeal were, inter alia, (1) that the judge misdirected himself in holding that he could not take into account the fact that the alternative accommodation offered by the plaintiffs was so situated that if the defendant resided there he would be living a long way from his social,
C   cultural and religious life and in an area where he had no friends when considering whether the accommodation was suitable alternative accommodation within the meaning of section 98 (1) of the Rent Act 1977; (2) that the judge misdirected himself in construing paragraph 5 (1) of Schedule 15 to the Act as being an exclusive definition of suitable alternative accommodation; and (3) that the judge erred in law in holding that for the purposes of that paragraph the fact that the alternative accommodation
D   was so situated as to be wholly inappropriate for the defendant's cultural, social and religious life and so far as the location of his friends was concerned was not a factor which could be taken into account.

The facts are stated in the judgment of Stephenson L.J.

Paul Morgan for the defendant.
E   *Julian Fulbrook* for the plaintiffs.

STEPHENSON L.J.   This is an appeal from an order for possession of a flat in London, a first floor rear room at 148, Liverpool Road, London N.1, which the judge made against the defendant, Mr. Rashid, at the suit of Mr. Siddiqui and Mr. Rehman, who are the trustees of the United Kingdom Islamic Mission.   They wanted to sell the property in which this
F   room is, in order to buy a larger property for their charitable work and they were able to offer to the defendant alternative accommodation in another room in a house not in London but in Luton, at 128, Oak Road. As the judge said in the agreed note of his judgment which we have, but which, by a misunderstanding of the practice, has not been referred to him for approval:

G   " On the face of it this sounds odd—it is a long way from where he
         lives—quite a long way at any rate, but the whole point is that he
         works in Luton and so far as I know will continue to do so."

That may be an over-simplification of the point of the case and of the point of this appeal, but that is the position, that a tenant, who, according to the evidence, had been living in London since 1964 and had been
H   working in Luton since 1967, is objecting to being compelled by the order of the judge to leave his room in London, far from his work, and take up residence in a room in Luton much nearer to his work.

As is well known, the relevant statutory provisions require a judge, before he makes an order evicting a protected tenant, as the defendant admittedly was, to be satisfied that it is reasonable to make the order and that suitable alternative accommodation has been offered and is available to the tenant.   Those provisions are now contained in the consolidating

Rent Act 1977. Part VII of that Act, which deals with security of tenure, A
opens with section 98, which provides:

" (1) Subject to this Part of this Act, a court shall not make an order
for possession of a dwellinghouse which is for the time being let on a
protected tenancy . . . unless the court considers it reasonable to make
such an order and either—(a) the court is satisfied that suitable alternative accommodation is available for the tenant or will be available B
for him when the order in question takes effect, or (b) the circumstances are as specified in any of the Cases in Part I of Schedule 15
to this Act."

It is paragraph (a) of the subsection which is relevant in this case. Subsection (4) provides:

" Part IV of Schedule 15 shall have effect for determining whether, C
for the purposes of subsection (1) (a) above, suitable alternative
accommodation is or will be available for a tenant."

Part IV of Schedule 15 begins with paragraph 3:

" 3. For the purposes of section 98 (1) (a) of this Act, a certificate
of the housing authority for the district in which the dwellinghouse
in question is situated, certifying that the authority will provide D
suitable alternative accommodation for the tenant by a date specified
in the certificate, shall be conclusive evidence that suitable alternative
accommodation will be available for him by that date. 4. Where no
such certificate as is mentioned in paragraph 3 above is produced to
the court, accommodation shall be deemed to be suitable for the
purposes of section 98 (1) (a) of this Act if it consists of either—(a) E
premises which are to be let as a separate dwelling such that they will
then be let on a protected tenancy, or (b) premises to be let as a
separate dwelling on terms which will, in the opinion of the court,
afford to the tenant security of tenure reasonably equivalent to the
security afforded by Part VII of this Act in the case of a protected
tenancy, and, in the opinion of the court, the accommodation fulfils F
the relevant conditions as defined in paragraph 5 below."

No question arises under paragraph 3; it is a paragraph 4 situation, and
sub-paragraphs (a) and (b) of that paragraph are also immaterial because
satisfied. But the question is whether the accommodation which the plaintiffs offered fulfilled the relevant conditions as defined in paragraph 5:

" (1) For the purposes of paragraph 4 above, the relevant conditions G
are that the accommodation is reasonably suitable " (that adverb
has been introduced) " to the needs of the tenant and his family as
regards proximity to place of work, and either—(a) similar as regards
rental and extent to the accommodation afforded by dwellinghouses
provided in the neighbourhood by any housing authority for persons
whose needs as regards extent are, in the opinion of the court, similar
to those of the tenant and of his family; or (b) reasonably suitable to H
the means of the tenant and to the needs of the tenant and his family
as regards extent and character; . . ."

No question arises as to this room in Luton being reasonably suitable
to the needs of the defendant as regards proximity to place of work.
Equally no dispute arises as to the suitability of this room as regards rental
and extent; and no question arises as to its reasonable suitability to the

A defendant's means. But what is in dispute is whether this room would be reasonably suitable to the needs of the defendant and his family as regards character. The judge, as I said, made an order for possession and was satisfied that it was reasonably suitable accommodation as regards character to the needs of the defendant, and he has found that it was reasonable for him to make the order.

B Mr. Morgan, in his interesting argument before us, has submitted that the judge was wrong on the first point, but I think he would agree that he is not able any longer to maintain that if he was right on the first point, he was wrong on the second point, or so plainly wrong, at any rate, that this court could interfere and substitute its view of what was reasonable for the judge's view. The judge considered suitability in this way:

C " The defendant did not suggest that the alternative premises were not suitable as regards extent, but has endeavoured to persuade me that ' character ' must be given a wide interpretation and that if you move a person from the place where he carries out his leisure activities and where his friends are, that can be brought under the heading of character. I totally disagree. In *Redspring Ltd.* v. *Francis* [1973] 1 W.L.R. 134 character was clearly defined in the headnote by reference D to the premises being ' somewhere where [the tenant] could live in reasonably comfortable conditions suitable to the style of life which he led; . . .' This is reflected in the judgment of Buckley L.J. at p. 138D, where he went on to say that ' environmental matters must inevitably affect the suitability of offered accommodation to provide him with the sort of conditions in which it is reasonable that he should live.' Having viewed 128, Oak Road, I am perfectly satisfied that the defen- E dant could lead a perfectly good life in accordance with his present style. I am totally unable to accept the submission that the upsetting effect that the move would have, and that although he would be near his work, he would be further from the mosque he so often attends and where his friends are, can be included in ' character.' I cannot be moved. I must follow the words of the statute. The character of the F property refers to the property itself. I have had the advantage of seeing both properties and have made notes." (Those notes are before us). " In my view, the alternative premises at Oak Road are pre- ferable; furthermore, another room which has not been let would be available for the defendant if he wished it. Furthermore, he will have exclusive use of the kitchen, the sink, and a very nice modern bath- room." (He had had to share in the London premises).

G He then went on to consider " reasonableness," and said:

" That is more arguable, but one must consider the plaintiffs' side. They are trying to help the members of the Muslim community; they are trying to sell 148, Liverpool Road to pay back a loan to buy a larger property in the Euston area. It is obvious that they will get H more for the property with vacant possession than with a tenant. I cannot accept the argument that anyone would be prepared to offer as much if the defendant were there. It is perfectly reasonable for the plaintiffs to seek an order for possession so that they can sell the pro- perty at the best price available. The plaintiffs have amply proved their case and I make an order for possession in 28 days."

We are bound by authority not to give a very narrow construction to the word " character " in paragraph 5 (1) (*b*) of Schedule 15 to the Act of

1977. The wording of the relevant statutory provisions which this court had to consider in *Redspring Ltd.* v. *Francis* [1973] 1 W.L.R. 134 was the same, and in that case this court rejected the argument that the character to which the court must have regard did not include what the county court judge in that case called " environmental aspects or peripheral amenities." That was a case which in some respects resembled this. Buckley L.J. in the leading judgment, said, at p. 137:

> " So we have to consider whether in the present case the accommodation offered at 108, Fleet Road is reasonably suitable to the needs of Mrs. Francis as regards extent and character. No point arises in this case in relation to proximity to the place of work or the means of the tenant. We are concerned only with the question whether the accommodation is reasonably suitable to her needs as regards extent and character. Extent, as I have already stated, is conceded. So the question is whether the accommodation is reasonably suited to her needs in respects of its character."

That was exactly the same position as in this case. There the judge had made an order for possession, because he took the view that equally good accommodation next to a smelly fish and chip shop and a good deal of motor traffic and noise was suitable alternative accommodation to similar premises in a quiet street not far off which Mrs. Francis had been occupying for 30 years. He was able to take that view because of the narrow view which he took of the meaning of the word " character." In his judgment, quoted by Buckley L.J. at p. 137, he had said:

> " ' The " needs " contemplated by paragraph 3 (1) (*b*) of Part IV of Schedule 3 to the Rent Act 1968, cited in argument, are not the same as tastes and inclinations: they are needs of an urgent, compelling nature—space, transport, a bathroom, etc. Peripheral amenities are of a different category; by this I am not saying that Mrs. Francis's objections are fanciful, but I find that her needs are met, apart from the environmental aspect. One must look at the whole of the picture, and I have not forgotten the hospital, the fish and chip shop, the public house and the cinema.' "

This court held that in spite of that last sentence the judge really had forgotten, or, at any rate, put out of the picture, the hospital, the fish and chip shop, the public house and the cinema, and the smells and the noises that all that the proximity of a busy road provide; and was wrong in excluding from his consideration the question whether the accommodation offered was reasonably suited to Mrs. Francis's needs in respect of its character. Buckley L.J. lists " environmental matters " at p. 139:

> " . . . environmental matters such as the smell from the fish and chip shop, the noise from the public house, noise perhaps from vehicles going to and from the hospital and matters of that kind. In so doing, with respect to the judge, I think he misdirected himself. Those, I think, are all matters properly to be taken into consideration in connection with the making of such an order as was sought in this case."

Orr L.J. agreed and Sachs L.J. also agreed, and added some observations to the effect that for there to be a difference in character that must of course normally relate to a difference in kind rather than a difference of lesser degree; and in that case he held that there was a difference in kind between the character of the two premises.

A   As was pointed out in the course of the argument, the statutory provisions say nothing of difference in character, but Mr. Morgan has submitted that it was only if there could be shown to be some difference in character between the two premises that this question of suitability of alternative accommodation to the needs of the tenant as regards character could arise. What he submits—and he did not appear in the county

B   court, but it was submitted in the county court—is that the court must look at environmental aspects, and that means the respective locations of the two premises, and see whether the tenant's needs are satisfied as regards the new location. Those needs are not merely physical needs, it was submitted, but such needs as were given in evidence here; need for a devout Muslim to keep in touch with his local mosque and cultural centre (in this case the mosque and cultural centre in Regent's Park) and need to enjoy

C   the company of friends whom he had made in the course of his many years' residence in London. The judge was not wholly satisfied, according to a note which he made in the course of his notes of the evidence, with the defendant's evidence as to his attendances and need to attend at the Regent's Park mosque, but he ruled that the need of the defendant to visit that mosque and the cultural centre there, and to keep in touch with his London friends, did not relate to the character of the property, as environ-

D   mental aspects had to relate if they were to be a relevant consideration to the question of the suitability of the alternative accommodation.

      The Act does not say that the alternative accommodation must be reasonably suitable to the needs of the tenant as regards location or, of course as regards environment, and for my part I would regard the judge as right in this case in confining " character " to the " character of the

E   property." I find nothing in the judgment of this court in *Redspring Ltd. v. Francis* [1973] 1 W.L.R. 134 to indicate that that is wrong, or to extend the meaning of " character " beyond character of the property. The character of the property was directly affected by the environmental matters which were the subject of Mrs. Francis's objection to her move. I have read them from Buckley L.J.'s judgment; noise and smell were matters which would directly affect the tenant in the enjoyment of her property, so

F   they could well be said to relate to the character of the property. I cannot think that Parliament intended to include such matters as the society of friends, or cultural interest, in using the language that it did in the particular word " character." Nor can I accept that Buckley L.J. had any such considerations in mind when he referred, in the passages which the judge quoted from his judgment [1973] 1 W.L.R. 134, 138, to the

G   needs of the tenant to have " somewhere where [the tenant] can live in reasonably comfortable conditions suitable to the style of life which he leads . . ." and referred to the accommodation providing him with the sort of conditions in which it is reasonable that he should live. To extend the character of the property to cover the two matters on which the defendant relies, namely, his friends in London and his mosque and cultural centre would, in my judgment, be unwarranted. The defendant said he did not

H   want to leave London or to live in Luton, although he worked there, but it is clear that this preference for London and objection to Luton was based on those two considerations.

      In my judgment it would be impossible to say that the room in Luton was not one in which he could live in reasonably comfortable conditions suitable to the style of life which he was leading in London, or that it did not provide him with the sort of conditions in which it was reasonable that he should live.

He implied that his workmates in Luton were not as much friends of   A
his as his friends in London, but he agreed that his workmates were friends.
However that may be, I do not think that the court is required to go into
such questions in considering suitability. I would therefore hold that the
judge was right in the conclusion which he reached as to the reasonable
suitability of the alternative accommodation in Luton which the plaintiffs
offered to the defendant.

That would not conclude the matter if Mr. Morgan had felt able to   B
challenge the judge's view of what was reasonable. The language of the
judge, which I have read, when he went on to consider " reasonableness "
may not be the language in which he would have put his consideration of
the matter in a reserved judgment; but I am not satisfied that he was
indicating that the leisure activities and the spiritual needs of this defendant,
or any defendant, would be irrelevant to the question of overall reasonable-   C
ness. What he was clearly deciding was that it was perfectly reasonable
for the plaintiffs to seek an order for possession and it was reasonable for
him to grant it. I need not detail the evidence that was given as to the
work of the mission, of the trustees who were seeking possession; but the
judge was quite satisfied that they needed to sell these premises to carry
on their charitable work, that they had had to borrow money to acquire
the larger property which they needed to carry on that work, and that   D
they could repay the loan if they could sell the property in which the
defendant was living with vacant possession.

For these reasons, in my judgment, the judge came to the right conclusion and I would dismiss the appeal.

DUNN L.J. I agree.   E

SIR DAVID CAIRNS. I also agree.

Appeal dismissed with costs.

Solicitors: *J. P. Malnick & Co.; Munir & Co.*

[Reported by ROBERT WILLIAMS, Esq., Barrister-at Law]   F

[COURT OF APPEAL]

* REGINA *v.* LANCASHIRE COUNTY COUNCIL, *Ex parte* GUYER   G

1980 Feb. 6, 7   Stephenson and Ackner L.JJ. and
                                                    Sir David Cairns

Highway—Right of way—Protection of—Member of public claim-
ing right of way over footpath—Highway authority not satis-
fied that public using path as of right—Whether highway   H
authority under duty to assert right of public over path—High-
ways Act 1959 (7 & 8 Eliz. 2, c. 25), s. 116 (1) (as amended by
Highways Act 1971 (c. 41), s. 70 and by Local Government
Act 1972 (c. 70), ss. 188 (2), 272 (1), Sch. 21, para. 34, Sch. 30)

A footpath, which had been used by members of the public
but was not shown as a public right of way on the plan prepared pursuant to the National Parks and Access to the
Countryside Act 1949, was blocked by one of the owners of the

The Weekly Law Reports, August 15, 1980

1025

1 W.L.R.   Reg. v. Lancs. C.C., Ex p. Guyer (C.A.)

A   land over which the path ran. The applicant, who maintained that the footpath was presumed to be dedicated as a highway after uninterrupted public use as of right for 20 years under section 34 (1) of the Highways Act 1959, requested the county council, as the highway authority, to exercise their duty under section 116 (1) of the Act [1] to " assert and protect " the rights of the public to the use and enjoyment of the highway. He supported his claim with statements from local residents that

B they had used the path over many years. The county council, not being satisfied that the path had been used by the public as of right, refused to act in the matter. The applicant by notice of motion sought an order of mandamus directed to the county council requiring them to exercise their duty pursuant to section 116 (1) of the Act. Prior to the hearing of the motion, the county council directed one of their officers to hold an inquiry. The evidence heard at the inquiry was con-

C flicting as to whether the path was public or not and included evidence that a gate across the path was locked once a year. The officer recommended that the appropriate committee of the council should accept that the path was not a public footpath. The committee resolved that the legal status of the path should be determined by the court with the council responding to any High Court proceedings. In October 1977, the Divisional Court of the Queen's Bench Division refused the application

D for an order of mandamus.
    On appeal by the applicant: —
    Held, dismissing the appeal, that subsection (1) of section 116 of the Act imposed a duty on a highway authority to assert and protect the rights of the public in the case of a highway which was clearly in existence and for which they were responsible; that the phrase [to] " assert and protect " did not have the effect of requiring an authority to assert claims made by

E members of the public in which they had no faith and, therefore, since there was a serious dispute concerning the nature of the footpath with conflicting evidence as to whether it was public or private, the council had been under no duty to assert the applicant's claim (post, pp. 1031D, 1033C–G, 1035A–B, 1036B–C).
    Decision of the Divisional Court of the Queen's Bench Division (1977) 76 L.G.R. 290 affirmed.

F
    The following cases are referred to in the judgments:
Holloway v. *Egham Urban District Council* (1908) 72 J.P. 433.
Reg. v. *Surrey County Council, Ex parte Send Parish Council* (unreported), May 17, 1979, D.C.

G
    The following additional case was cited in argument:
Reynolds v. *Presteign Urban District Council* [1896] 1 Q.B. 604.

    APPEAL from the Divisional Court of the Queen's Bench Division.
    By a motion dated October 5, 1976, the applicant, Jack Guyer, of 12, Sydney Avenue, Whalley, Lancashire, sought an order of mandamus directed to the Lancashire County Council requiring them to exercise their

H duty under section 116 (1) of the Highways Act 1959, as amended, to assert and protect a particular public right of way within its district, namely, a public footpath running from King Street, Whalley, and following the northern bank of the River Calder upstream. On October 31, 1977, the Divisional Court of the Queen's Bench Decision (Lord Widgery C.J., Talbot and Boreham JJ.) refused the application.

---

[1] Highways Act 1959, s. 116: see post, pp. 1029H—1030D.

1026

The Weekly Law Reports, August 15, 1980

Reg. v. Lancs. C.C., Ex p. Guyer (C.A.)   [1980]

The applicant appealed against that refusal on the grounds that (1) the   A
Divisional Court had wrongly held that the county council's duty to assert
and protect public rights to the use and enjoyment of highways in their
district as laid down by section 116 (1) of the Highways Act 1959 did not
involve a primary duty to decide the status of a footpath where the existence of a public right of way was in dispute; (2) the Divisional Court had
wrongly held that section 116 (5) of the Act imposed a discretion on the
county council which overrode their general duty under section 116 (1)   B
of the Act; (3) the Divisional Court should have held that any discretion
imposed on the council by section 116 (5) to institute or defend legal
proceedings was subject to their general duty under section 116 (1) to
assert and protect public rights over highways in their district; (4) the
Divisional Court should have held that the expression " assert and protect "
in section 116 (1) involved a duty, whenever there was a substantial case   C
for the existence of a public right of way, to assert the public status of a
footpath, notwithstanding that that status was in dispute; and (5) that the
effect of the Divisional Court's decision would inevitably be that, whenever the existence of a footpath was in dispute, there would be no means,
or no effective means, whereby the status of a footpath and any rights
which the public might have to its use and enjoyment, might be deter-   D
mined.

The facts are stated in the judgment of Stephenson L.J.

Charles Bloom for the applicant.
Michael Tillett for the county council.

STEPHENSON L.J.   On October 31, 1977, the Divisional Court of the   E
Queen's Bench Division refused the applicant, Mr. Guyer, judicial review
in the shape of an order of mandamus directed to the Lancashire County
Council requiring the council to exercise the duty imposed on them by
section 116 (1) of the Highways Act 1959 to assert and protect a particular
public right of way within its district, namely, a public footpath running
from King Street, Whalley, in the County of Lancaster at the north-easterly   F
side of Whalley Bridge and proceeding in a generally easterly direction
following the northern bank of the River Calder upstream.

The applicant is a public-spirited resident of Whalley, a small town of
some 4,000 inhabitants, in Lancashire.   He has lived there since 1961 and
in that neighbourhood for all the 70-odd years of his life.

If you cross the River Calder over Whalley bridge in a north-easterly
direction into King Street, a footpath runs eastwards to your right along   G
the northern bank of the River Calder for a distance of between 100 and
200 yards until it joins an admittedly public footpath which carries on
eastwards to a weir.   Many people have used this first stretch of footpath
over the years of this century.   The applicant's case is that this footpath
is presumed to be dedicated as a highway after uninterrupted public use
as of right for 20 years under section 34 (1) of the Highways Act 1959.   He   H
says that the council have a statutory duty to assert that right for him
under section 116 (1) of the Act of 1959, as amended by the Local
Government Act 1972.

He entered into correspondence with the council in March 1975 in an
effort to get them to take up his case and assert that right to use this footpath.   The council informed him that the footpath had not been marked
as a public footpath under the National Parks and Access to the Country-

The Weekly Law Reports, August 15, 1980

1027

1 W.L.R.   Reg. v. Lancs. C.C., Ex p. Guyer (C.A.)   Stephenson L.J.

A side Act 1949 and that there would not be any further review of the matter of footpaths under the Act for quite a few years.

On June 12, 1975, the chief executive of the council wrote to him saying :

> " There appears to be little doubt that this footpath has been used on numerous occasions by members of the public but be that as it may, I am not altogether convinced that this use has been ' as of right.' "

B

He referred to the fact that over a period of years a gate had been locked at least once a year, a gate giving access to the footpath, and concluded :

> " Whilst it is a duty of the council to assert the rights of the public under the amended section 116 of the Highways Act 1959, this assertion presupposes that there is a public right of way in existence in the first place and where there is doubt, as in the present case, the onus of proving the existence of a public right of way rests on the person alleging the same, namely yourself."

C

In a later letter, it was pointed out that many people in Whalley considered the footpath to be private and at the end of that letter the same officer of the council described the operative word in section 116 as being a " highway " and stated :

D

> " . . . before the council can assert any rights, they must be satisfied that the road or path in question is a ' highway ' within the meaning of the Act. If the council is not satisfied that the footpath in question is a highway then obviously they will take no action under section 116 as amended because, in their opinion, there will be no rights to assert."

E

In a letter of August 29, 1975, the chief executive wrote:

> " I am sure you will appreciate that as highway authority the county council must listen to all sides of the argument and it is for this very reason and the fact that there are just too many people who consider the footpath to be private that the council cannot simply purport to assert the rights of the public and dismiss without question the assertion of, above all, the landowners."

F

The applicant supported his case in correspondence with 56 statements of local residents, mainly elderly, as to the use they had made of this footpath over many years, and some of them said that there had never been any gate or notice indicating that the path was private until 1968. I think all are agreed that a barrier had been put up at the King Street, or western, end of the footpath, with notices marking the path as private—" no footpath, no fishing "—in 1974.

G

In June 1976 the Whalley Parish Council did not take the applicant's part. They decided that the disputed stretch of his footpath was in fact private property. The applicant's solicitors took the matter up with the chief executive of the council in a letter of June 3, 1976. They referred to the fact that they had taken counsel's opinion and said:

H

> " We have no doubt that these numerous statements establish at least an extremely strong case for the existence of a public right of way."

They asked for the names of persons, other than the landowners, who were disputing the existence of a public right of way, and were told that there were three landowners who were making that claim. Their letter continued :

"It is our view, supported by counsel, that your duty to assert and A protect the rights of the public to the use and enjoyment of any highway, for which you are the highway authority, must include the taking of such steps as are necessary so as to determine the existence of such a right of way where that is in dispute, provided at least that there is a strong prima facie case for the existence of such a right of way. Any other view would defeat the object of section 116 of the Highways Act 1959." B

They suggested it was a proper case for the council to take proceedings in the High Court under R.S.C., Ord. 15, r. 16 for a declaration that the footpath was a public right of way, and concluded:

"Unless you indicate within the next 14 days that you are prepared to take this course or at least some other appropriate course in exer- C cise of your duty under section 116 (1) of the Act, our instructions are to proceed by way of mandamus."

Hence the applicant took the matter to the Divisional Court by a notice of motion of October 6, 1976.

Pending the hearing in the Divisional Court, the applicant's persistence was rewarded—though I do not think he looked upon it in that light— D by the council instituting a public local inquiry. That was conducted on February 28, 1977, by the council's chief legal officer. At that inquiry 17 people gave evidence, excluding the landowners. Five people gave evidence as to why they thought the path was public.

"Mr. Guyer and his solicitors had been invited to attend but had previously indicated that despite the fact that the landowners' solicitors E intended to represent their clients formally at the hearing, they would rely on the evidence already submitted to the county council in written form."

That is a quotation, its accuracy not disputed, from the report that was made by the officer who presided over that inquiry. He referred as of vital importance to the evidence given by the two daughters of a previous F owner, Mr. Forman, ". . . that a gate at the King Street end of the path was locked at least once a year on November 26, the then landowner's birthday." That seems to have been the procedure which, according to the evidence of those two ladies, was carried out annually from the time when their father bought the property in 1919 until one of them ceased to live there in 1970.

The officer who presided over that inquiry suggested that the highways G and transportation committee of the council should make a recommendation as follows:

"(a) That, having regard to all the evidence available, the committee accept that the path is not public, and therefore not a highway in respect of which action should be taken under section 116 of the Highways Act 1959; and (b) that the chief executive clerk be authorised H to continue to resist the proceedings commenced against the county council."

That recommendation was not adopted by the highways and transportation committee but in March 1977 they resolved:

"That, having regard to the conflicting evidence presented to the committee, the committee feel that the legal status of the path should

The Weekly Law Reports, August 15, 1980

1029

1 W.L.R.   Reg. v. Lancs. C.C., Ex p. Guyer (C.A.)   Stephenson L.J.

A   be determined by the courts and that accordingly the chief executive-clerk be authorised to continue to respond to the High Court proceedings on the basis that the path is not one in respect of which the council has a duty to act under section 116 of the Highways Act 1959."

B   There has been a dispute as to the meaning of that resolution and some criticism of the way in which it was interpreted by Lord Widgery C.J. in the judgment of the Divisional Court refusing the order for mandamus: see 76 L.G.R. 290, 291. I find it unnecessary to go into that resolution, or Lord Widgery C.J.'s interpretation of it, except to say that his interpretation seems to me to accord with the language of the resolution, and that neither side can get out of the resolution any assistance in decid-

C ing the question that we have to decide, which is whether or not the council have failed to do their duty under section 116 of the Act.

    That resolution having been passed, the applicant had to proceed with his application to the Divisional Court, which was, as I have said, dismissed in October 1977. Hoping to save further expense, which he could ill afford, the applicant waited, before deciding whether to appeal from the decision of the Divisional Court, for them to decide *Reg.* v. *Surrey*

D *County Council, Ex parte Send Parish Council* (unreported), May 17, 1979, in the hope that that decision would be favourable to his case. That case was decided by the Divisional Court on May 17, 1979, but it did not help him or alter the council's decision; hence this unfortunately but understandably tardy appeal, by leave given by this court to extend the time.

    The duty under section 116 (1), as amended, is the only duty which in

E his notice of motion the applicant has asked the court to require the council to perform. In the judgment of Lord Widgery C.J. in the Divisional Court, his application is treated—in most cases at any rate—solely as an application to order them to perform their duty by taking proceedings, which would appear to be legal proceedings; but Mr. Bloom, on the applicant's behalf, tells us that he argued (or at any rate intended to argue) in the Divisional Court that the council should, as an alternative to taking

F legal proceedings for instance for a declaration, take other proceedings or action which he need not specify, but which might be for the removal after notice of the barrier and/or gates set up at the ends of the footpath under section 124 of the Act of 1959. And he wished to argue, and has been allowed to argue without objection from Mr. Tillett on behalf of the council, in this court that the council should be required also to perform

G the statutory duty imposed on them by section 116 (3) of the Act.

    I read section 116 (as amended by section 70 (1) of the Highways Act 1971, as well as by the Local Government Act 1972, section 188 (2) and Schedule 21, paragraph 34, and section 272 (1) and Schedule 30) omitting only subsection (2) which is irrelevant and subsections (7) and (8) which have been repealed. Section 116 deals with " Protection of public rights ":

H   " (1) It shall be the duty of the highway authority to assert and protect the rights of the public to the use and enjoyment of any highway for which they are the highway authority, including any roadside waste which forms part of it. . . . (3) Without prejudice to subsections (1) and (2) of this section, it shall be the duty of a council which is a highway authority to prevent, as far as possible, the stopping up or obstruction of highways for which they are the highway authority, and the duty imposed by this subsection on a council which is a highway authority

The Weekly Law Reports, August 15, 1980

1030

Stephenson L.J.   Reg. v. Lancs. C.C., Ex p. Guyer (C.A.)   [1980]

shall extend to a highway for which they are not the highway auth-   A
ority if, in the opinion of the council, the stopping up or obstruction
of that highway would be prejudicial to the interests of their area.
(4) Without prejudice to the foregoing provisions of this section, it
shall be the duty of a local highway authority to prevent any unlawful
encroachment on any roadside waste comprised in a highway for
which they are the highway authority. (5) Without prejudice to their   B
powers under section 276 of the Local Government Act 1933 a council
may, in the performance of their functions under the foregoing provisions of this section, institute legal proceedings in their own name
defend any legal proceedings and generally take such steps as they
deem expedient. (6) If the council of a parish, or community or, in
the case of a parish or community which does not have a separate
parish or community council, the parish meeting or a community   C
meeting, represent to a local highway authority—(a) that a highway,
being one as to which the local highway authority have the duty
imposed by subsection (3) of this section, has been unlawfully stopped
up or obstructed, or (b) that an unlawful encroachment has taken
place on a roadside waste comprised in a highway for which the
authority are the highway authority, it shall be the duty of the council
of that distinct unless satisfied that the allegations are incorrect,   D
to take proper proceedings accordingly and they may do so in their
own name. . . . (9) Any proceedings or steps taken by a council in
relation to an alleged right of way shall not be treated as unauthorised
by reason only that the alleged right is found not to exist."

There are two questions for this court. First, have the council failed
to do their duty under subsection (1) or subsection (3) of section 116?   E
Secondly, if the answer is " yes " in either case, ought the court to exercise
its discretion to grant an order of mandamus requiring them to do their
duty?

The rival contentions appear from the correspondence, parts of which
I have read, and from the judgments of Lord Widgery C.J. and Talbot J.
below with which Boreham J. agreed; and they have been extended and   F
clarified in the longer hearing in this court. They rest ultimately on the
base of rival constructions of section 116 (1) of the Act. The construction
put forward by Mr. Bloom, on behalf of the applicant, is that if anyone
makes out a solid case, as he puts it, or a strong prima facie case as it
is put in the solicitors' letter, which I have already read, that a
way is a public highway, subsection (1) imposes a duty on the highway   G
authority, which the council admit they are under, to assert and protect
public rights to use it. No evidence rests on the applicant to satisfy the
council that it is a highway. It is the overriding policy of the Act laid
down first in the Local Government Act 1894, section 26 (1), and now in
section 116 (1) of the Act of 1959, that a highway authority should do
what a citizen cannot afford to do—put forward, and push forward by
legal proceedings, or lesser action of its own choosing, each and every   H
seriously arguable claim to public rights of way. " Highway " in subsection (1) and other sections means a disputed highway, or an alleged highway, and it matters not whether or not the highway authority are satisfied
that it is a highway. To require the highway authority to be so satisfied
is to read words into the section, words which introduce complications as
to the standard of proof required, and when the satisfaction of a highway
authority is required, it is expressed as in subsection (6). The council,

The Weekly Law Reports, August 15, 1980

1031

1 W.L.R.   Reg. v. Lancs. C.C., Ex p. Guyer (C.A.)   Stephenson L.J.

A submits Mr. Bloom, cannot sit on the fence and refuse to decide whether there is a prima facie case, or a solid case, but must take the applicant's side on the material provided and if, having taken up his case they are found by a decision of the court to have been mistaken and lose the case, they are protected by subsection (9).

B He submits that the addition of the words "assert and" before the word "protect" in section 116 must add something to the duty which that subsection imposes. The words were not in the Act of 1894, and Parliament, by adding those words, must have intended to add a duty upon the highway authority to vindicate claims, he says, relying upon the dictionary definition of the word "assert," whether those claims are justified, substantial, or believed in by the authority or not.

C He relies on some observations of Geoffrey Lane L.J. in *Reg.* v. *Surrey County Council, Ex parte Send Parish Council* (unreported), to which I will come, for the overriding duty which is the main object of this legislation which is contained in section 116 (1), and he relies also on some words in the judgment of Neville J. in *Holloway* v. *Egham Urban District Council* (1908) 72 J.P. 433, 434, to which I will also refer.

D The council, on the other hand, take their stand on the interpretation of section 116 (1) and maintain that the subsection only imposes a duty if there is a highway, giving rise to rights to be asserted and protected under subsection (1), and subsidiary rights under subsections (3), (4) and (5).

That is the view of the duty succinctly expressed in the judgment of Talbot J. in the Divisional Court in which he said, 76 L.G.R. 290, 294:

E "It was a part of Mr. Bloom's submission that, looking at section 116 (1) the county council had a primary duty to decide the status of the footpath. I will not read that section because Lord Widgery C.J. has already done so. I only say this, that there is nothing in the wording of that section, as I read it, to require the county council to come to any such decision. They merely have a duty to assert and protect where there is a highway."

F Mr. Tillett, for the council, concedes that a duty may be imposed on an authority where there is a dispute as to the existence of a public right of way but the dispute is such an unreal dispute that no reasonable authority could take the view that there was no highway, that the way was private and that they were consequently under no duty to assert a public right to use and enjoy it. Where, however, there is a real dispute, there is no such duty.

G Support for that view is given by what was said by Geoffrey Lane L.J., in *Reg.* v. *Surrey County Council, Ex parte Send Parish Council* (unreported). In giving the leading judgment, he said:

"We do not have to decide in this court whether this is a public footpath or not. The basis upon which we can apporach the problem is that the evidence that it is a public footpath is very strong indeed, . . ."

H Later, Geoffrey Lane L.J. is dealing with the limits of the authority's discretion: and it must be remembered that he is dealing with the limits of the authority's discretion to take proper proceedings under section 116 (6), and it is in that connection that he asks the question:

". . . what are the limits of that discretion? Those limits must be culled from the words of the Act themselves. The local authority must at all times act with the object of protecting the highway and of

The Weekly Law Reports, August 15, 1980

1032

Stephenson L.J.　　　Reg. v. Lancs. C.C., Ex p. Guyer (C.A.)　　　[1980]

preventing or removing any obstruction, and more broadly speaking, A
of promoting the interests of those who enjoy the highway or should
be enjoying the right of way; and the county council must likewise
operate against the interests of those who seek to interrupt such
enjoyment of the highway. It is trite law now, and needs hardly to
be expressed, that this court must not, and will not, interfere merely
because it thinks, if it had been a local authority, it would have acted
in a different way. Before we can properly interfere by way of B
mandamus, or indeed by any other method, we must be satisfied that
the local authority have acted under a misapprehension as to their
duties or else in a way in which no reasonable local authority could
have acted had they had their duties as set out in the Act of 1959
properly in mind."

That was a very different case from this. What the county council C
were proposing to do was to extinguish a footpath which there was a very
strong case for saying was a public footpath, and it was not disputed that
the council were not satisfied that the allegations made by the Send Parish
Council's representation were incorrect. Section 116 (6) imposed a duty
on the highway authority, in that case the Surrey County Council, to take
proper proceedings if there was a representation by the parish council, D
unless they, the county council, were satisfied that the allegations made in
the representation—in that case that there was an unlawful stopping up or
obstruction of a highway—were incorrect : though it cannot, with all
respect, have been a very difficult decision to arrive at, that the county
council, in proposing to extinguish a highway when they were not satisfied that allegations that it had been stopped up unlawfully were incorrect, E
were failing to carry out their duty; and that is plain from the judgment
of Ackner J. But the only help that Mr. Bloom for the applicant can
derive from that case is Geoffrey Lane L.J.'s statement, made, it is true,
in connection with the discretion of the council as to what proceedings
were proper under subsection (6) as to the overriding duty imposed on a
highway authority by subsection (1) of section 116.

The council in this case rely on the well-known principle stated by F
Geoffrey Lane L.J. as to the courts' powers and duties to interfere with a
decision of a local authority in a matter of this kind. Both sides rely on
some general observations of Neville J. in the very different case of
Holloway v. Egham Urban District Council, 72 J.P. 433, to which I have
already referred. At the start of his judgment in that case, Neville J. said,
at p. 434 :　　　　　　　　　　　　　　　　　　　　　　　　　　G

" In my opinion the provisions in the Local Government Acts which
give to local authorities the right and impose upon them the duty of
maintaining public rights of road and way are of the greatest possible
importance to the public, and were much needed at the time when
the Acts were passed, because undoubtedly in parts of the country
where the population was increasing and the value of land was grow- H
ing, there was a very great danger of public rights being invaded by
individual proprietors, who acted in furtherance of their own interests,
whereas it was rare to find a member of the public sufficiently wealthy
and sufficiently public-spirited to take proceedings and to fight for the
very infinitesimal interest that it usually was for him, though it was
of much larger interest to the individual landowner."

The Weekly Law Reports, August 15, 1980

1033

1 W.L.R.   Reg. v. Lancs. C.C., Ex p. Guyer (C.A.)   Stephenson L.J.

A Then comes the passage cited in the judgment of Lord Widgery C.J. in this case, 76 L.G.R. 290, 294, and relied on by the council:

" At the same time, of course, the power given to the local authorities is one which ought to be treated in the nature of a trust, and local authorities I have no doubt are, and they certainly should be, exceed-
B ingly careful of the kind of case they take up before they employ the ratepayers' money for the purpose of establishing rights of way."

Mr. Tillett resists Mr. Bloom's construction of the subsection which would make a highway authority a body to decide what should be decided by the courts in a relator action or an action brought by a member of the public suffering special damage from interference with his use or enjoyment of an alleged public right of way. He says that subsection (9) does
C not assist Mr. Bloom on his construction because it is necessary to have a provision of that kind, going back to the Local Government Act 1894, to protect an authority from the consequences of making a mistake and bringing, for instance, proceedings which end in failure.

I accept the council's construction of the section and their inter-
pretation of the statutory duty it imposes. Section 116 must be read as a whole. I agree that subsection (1) imposes an overriding obligation,
D whatever those words precisely mean. Without recourse to subsection (5), I find it difficult to read the subsection as protecting rights in anything but highways which are beyond serious dispute highways. There is a serious dispute about this footpath and conflicting evidence pointing to its being public and pointing to its being private, whether or not the evidence pointing to uninterrupted user as of right is stronger or weaker than the
E evidence pointing in the opposite direction. I do not think it is a question of adding words to the section. It may be said that both sides are seeking to add words to the section, but to my mind it is a question simply of interpreting the words which are actually used in the subsection as it stands. It is not easy to see why Parliament added " assertion " to " protection." We are told there is no decision of the court which can
F explain the addition, but in my judgment Parliament cannot have meant the addition of those words to require an authority to assert claims in which they have no faith. It may be that the words stress the importance of authorities regarding their duty as not merely passive or defensive to action taken by others, but as requiring them at times to initiate action; something which might be held not to be clearly expressed or implicit in
G a duty merely to protect rights of the public for the use and enjoyment of a highway.

Subsection (6), by contrast, clearly imposes a duty on an authority to take proper proceedings in certain circumstances; namely, when a parish council or other named body make a representation, and if the authority are not satisfied that what is alleged by the representation is incorrect. If a
H council are in doubt whether a highway is a highway or not, in those cir-
cumstances subsection (6) requires them to take proper proceedings. There is no such requirement in subsection (1) that if a council are in doubt whether a highway is a highway or not, they must assert by proceedings, or by some other form of action, the rights which a member of the public alleges to exist.

There is, therefore, no call for an order of mandamus here because there has been no breach of statutory duty. If there were a breach and it

was necessary to decide whether mandamus should go, Mr. Bloom's sub-   A
mission that the court's direction should be almost as imprecise as Nelson's
Trafalgar signal and direct the council to do their statutory duty would, in
my opinion, be likely to prove fatal to the exercise of the court's discretion
in favour of the applicant.

I would dismiss the appeal.

ACKNER L.J. In the statement filed by the applicant, pursuant to R.S.C.,   B
Ord. 53 to support the application for mandamus, the following is asserted,
if I may borrow a word on which Mr. Bloom so strongly relies from
section 116 (1):

> "(ii) Within the district of the Lancashire County Council is a par-
> ticular footpath which proceeds from the north-easterly side of Whalley
> Bridge, Whalley, in a generally easterly direction following the northern   C
> bank of the River Calder upstream for approximately one-quarter of
> a mile and then leaves the river bank and proceeds in a northerly
> direction to Accrington Road. (iii) Throughout living human memory
> that footpath has been used and enjoyed by members of the public
> as of right openly and without interruption. (iv) From and since
> about the month of October 1974 G. Wilson the owner of the land   D
> adjacent to Whalley Bridge, over which part of the said footpath
> lies, has prevented access to the said footpaths over a distance
> of approximately 150 yards by the erection of a fixed wooden
> barrier and has denied and continues to deny the existence of a
> public right of way over that part of the footpath. . . . (v) Despite
> numerous requests made in writing to Lancashire County Council by   E
> the applicant and his solicitors that the said council exercise their duty
> under section 116 (1) of the Highways Act 1959 to assert and protect
> the said public right of way, the said council have failed and/or
> refused so to do."

If the facts were as simple as are there set out, there would be no problem
in the way of the applicant obtaining mandamus. Unfortunately from his   F
point of view that is not the true situation.

As Stephenson L.J. has already mentioned, there was an informal
inquiry held on February 28, 1977, and some of the evidence given clearly
indicates that there was a serious dispute as to whether or not the footpath
had been used and enjoyed by members of the public as of right, openly
and without interruption. In that situation Mr. Bloom contends that the   G
section upon which he principally relies, section 116 (1) of the Highways
Act 1959, as amended, should be read essentially in this way. Where there
is a strong prima facie case, or as he prefers, a solid case, that there is a
highway for which the highway authority are responsible, then it is the duty
of the highway authority to assert and protect the alleged rights of the
public to its use and enjoyment. He really relies in his strenuous and   H
skilful argument on the word "assert" as giving him the real foundation
for that submission.

I take the word "assert" in the context of subsection (1) to mean in
essence to claim that there exists. It may well involve action which falls
short of the normally accepted use of the word "protect." Let me give a
simple example. If I find what I consider to be a public footpath, ob-

The Weekly Law Reports, August 15, 1980

1035

1 W.L.R.   Reg. v. Lancs. C.C., Ex p. Guyer (C.A.)   Ackner L.J.

A structed, and go to the council and provide them with information which seems to suggest that it is a public footpath, they may well be prepared to write a letter to the person obstructing it, saying: " From the inquiries we have made to-date, we think that this is a public footpath." That seems to me to be a mere assertion and may fall short of an obligation, if an obligation exists, to protect.

B I do not consider that we can read into the section the words that Mr. Bloom suggests. To my mind the section is quite clear. It refers in terms to that which it is the obligation of the highway authority " to assert or protect." The subject matter is a highway for which the highway authority are responsible. I do not, by that, intend to suggest that a council can merely say : " We have had a suggestion made that this is not a highway and, therefore, we do not propose to take any action." If the basis

C of the dispute has no substance at all—in other words that there is no reasonably disputable evidence—then in my judgment that would be a perverse behaviour by the council and it would be no answer to a demand that they carry out their statutory duty.

Mr. Bloom submitted that there was support to be found for his contentions in Reg. v. Surrey County Council, Ex parte Send Parish Council (unreported) in the Divisional Court, decided on May 17, 1979.

D That was a case which concerned itself with section 116 (6), to the terms of which Stephenson L.J. has already referred. In that case a representation was made by the Send Parish Council to the county council that a footpath from Highcotts Lane to Dedswell Drive in West Clandon, Surrey, was a highway, being one as to which the local authority, that is, the county council, had a duty imposed by section 116 (3), and that it had been

E unlawfully stopped up or obstructed. On receipt of that representation the council had a duty to take proper proceedings unless, and only unless, they were satisfied that the allegations were incorrect. So far from being so satisfied, the evidence pointed in that case almost conclusively to the situation that the council were satisfied that the representations were correct. In those circumstances the council were obliged to take the

F proper proceedings. And that is why, as I understand the judgment of Geoffrey Lane L.J., the statement occurs in his judgment, " We " (that is the Divisional Court) " do not have to decide whether this is a public footpath or not."

Section 116 (6) so far from lending support to the applicant's case seems to me to do precisely the reverse. The parish council, or such other body referred to in that subsection, are put in a privileged position, presumably

G because it is assumed that they can be relied upon to act responsibly. Their representation must be acted upon unless a highway authority are satisfied that it is incorrect. There is no such subsection which applies to the individual, but as I understand Mr. Bloom's submission the individual is in as good a position as a parish council, save only this, that the obligation, following a representation from the parish council, is on the highway

H authority to take proper proceedings, which Mr. Bloom interprets and I do not, as meaning legal proceedings. Significantly in this case the Whalley Parish Council decided that the disputed stretch was, in fact, private property and, therefore, no representation was made by them.

Mr. Bloom finally relies on section 116 (9) of the Act. To my mind that subsection was put in merely to cover the situation that a council, a highway authority, firmly convinced that a way was a highway, pursuant

The Weekly Law Reports, August 15, 1980

1036

Ackner L.J.   Reg. v. Lancs. C.C., Ex p. Guyer (C.A.)   [1980]

to their obligation might take proceedings in order to protect that way, and   A
yet could find ultimately in those proceedings that they were wrong: a situation which in this type of litigation could easily arise where evidence that
might well not have been available when the council made their decision,
comes to light in the course of the proceedings.

I agree accordingly that no valid complaint can be made against the
county council that they have failed to carry out their statutory obligations
and I therefore agree that this appeal should be dismissed.   B

SIR DAVID CAIRNS. I agree that this appeal should be dismissed for
the reasons which have been given in the two judgments which have already
been delivered. I will add a few words of my own out of respect for the
argument which was addressed to this court by Mr. Bloom.

The county council's duty under section 116 (1) of the Highways Act   C
1959 as amended, can, in my view, only come into play if the highway
authority are satisfied that there is a public right of way which is threatened.
In this respect subsection (1) is to be contrasted with subsection (6) of the
same section.

I am prepared to assume that if it is alleged by a member of the public
to the highway authority that a certain road or path is a highway, and that   D
the public's enjoyment of it is being interfered with, there may be a duty
on the part of the authority to consider whether the allegation is true unless
it is obviously insupportable. If there is such a duty it was amply fulfilled in this case. I do not consider that, if it is strongly contended on
the one hand that the path is a public way and strongly contended on the
other hand that the path is a private way, the authority, if left in doubt, are
bound to assert the existence of a public right of way of which they are not   E
convinced, or to protect what from their point of view is not an established
right but merely a claimed right. Nor do I consider that the authority,
when they are not satisfied that a highway exists, have any duty to take any
of the steps provided for in subsections (3) and (5) of section 116, or in
section 124 of the Highways Act.

For those reasons, in addition to those given by Stephenson and   F
Ackner L.JJ., I would dismiss this appeal.

Appeal dismissed with costs.
Leave to appeal refused.

Solicitors: *Eric H. Smith, Burnley; Chief Executive/Clerk, Lancashire*   G
County Council.

[Reported by MISS HENRIETTA STEINBERG, Barrister-at-Law]

H

A

[COURT OF APPEAL]

* REGINA *v.* IMMIGRATION APPEAL TRIBUNAL,

Ex parte KASSAM

B   1980 Feb. 18;   Stephenson and Ackner L.JJ.
         March 14   and Sir David Cairns

Commonwealth Immigrant — Admission — Refusal of — Student's
wife to be granted leave to enter during student's authorised
stay — Application by husband for admission during wife's
authorised stay as student refused—Whether refusal amount-
C   *ing to sex discrimination—Statement of Immigration Rules*
for Control on Entry: Commonwealth Citizens (1973) (*H.C.*
79), para. 22
Discrimination, Sex—Act of 1975 *— Application—Immigration—*
Whether statute applicable to make discrimination against
student's husband unlawful — Whether Secretary of State's
powers relating to immigration concerned with provision of
" facilities . . . to the public "—Sex Discrimination Act 1975
D   (*c.* 65), *s.* 29 (1)

The applicant was a Commonwealth citizen who was originally given leave to enter the United Kingdom for six months
as a visitor in 1972. Applications to remain were refused after
a long delay in 1975, and again in 1976. On January 22,
1977, he married a Pakistani citizen who had been given leave
to enter as a student for a limited period expiring in May
1977. In April 1977 the Secretary of State decided to deport
E   the applicant, and his appeal against that decision was finally
rejected by the Immigration Appeal Tribunal on September 12,
1978. He applied to the Divisional Court of the Queen's Bench
Division for judicial review in the form of orders of certiorari
and mandamus on the ground that under the Immigration
Rules a wife was permitted to enter for the period of her
husband's authorised stay as a student, and that the rule
offended against the Sex Discrimination Act 1975 [1] unless it
F   also applied to allow a husband to enter for the period of his
wife's authorised stay. The application was refused.
On appeal by the applicant: —
Held, dismissing the appeal, (1) that discrimination as
defined in Part I of the Sex Discrimination Act 1975 did not
make discrimination unlawful but described the discrimination
to which the Act applied; that Parts II to IV of the Act were
G   exhaustive of the circumstances in which sex discrimination
was unlawful, and, accordingly, since the Act made no reference to the performance of the duties of the Secretary of State
under the Immigration Act 1971, it had no application in the
present case (post, pp. 1040c, 1041E–H, 1043F–G, 1044c–E).
(2) That when giving leave to enter or remain in the United
Kingdom in the exercise of his powers under the Immigration
Act 1971 or the rules made thereunder, the Secretary of State
H   was not " any person concerned with the provision . . . of . . .
facilities . . . to the public " within the meaning of section
29 (1) of the Act, since the kind of facilities with which the
section was concerned were facilities akin to goods or services,
and not the grant or refusal of leave under the Act of 1971
or the Immigration Rules; accordingly, the Secretary of State
could not be said to have discriminated unlawfully against
the applicant (post, pp. 1042H—1043c, H—1044B, c–E).

[1] Sex Discrimination Act 1975, s. 29 (1): see post, p. 1042B–D.

Reg. v. Immigration Appeal Tribunal, Ex p. Kassam   [1980]

Decision of the Divisional Court of the Queen's Bench   A
Division affirmed.

The following case is referred to in the judgments:
Reg. v. *Immigration Appeal Tribunal, Ex parte Ahluwalia* (unreported),
February 22, 1979, D.C.

No additional cases were cited in argument.   B

APPEAL from the Divisional Court of the Queen's Bench Division.

The applicant, Azim Ebrahim Kassam, applied for a judicial review in
the form of orders of certiorari and mandamus to quash the determination
of the Immigration Appeal Tribunal dated September 12, 1978, dismissing
his appeal against the decision of the Secretary of State for the Home   C
Department to deport him, and to direct that tribunal to hear and determine the appeal according to the Immigration Rules. The grounds of the
application were, inter alia, that the tribunal had erred in law in concluding
that the Immigration Rules, which provided for a wife to be admitted
during her husband's stay as a student but did not expressly authorise a
husband to be admitted during his wife's stay as a student, did not con-   D
travene the Sex Discrimination Act 1975.

The Divisional Court (Lord Widgery C.J., Eveleigh L.J. and Stephen
Brown J.) on February 22, 1979, refused the orders on the ground that the
Sex Discrimination Act 1975 had no application to the Secretary of State
in performing his functions under the Immigration Act 1971. The applicant appealed on the ground that the Divisional Court had erred in law in
coming to that conclusion.   E

The facts are stated in the judgment of Stephenson L.J.

Charles Fletcher-Cooke Q.C. and *K. S. Nathan* for the applicant.
David Latham for the Immigration Appeal Tribunal.

Cur. adv. vult.   F

March 14. The following judgments were read.

STEPHENSON L.J. The applicant is a Commonwealth citizen, being a
citizen of Tanzania. He was given leave to enter the United Kingdom in
August 1972 for six months as a visitor. His application to remain here   G
was after a long delay refused in 1975, and after an unsuccessful appeal
from such refusal was repeated and again refused in 1976. On April 17,
1977, the Secretary of State for the Home Department, satisfied that the
applicant had remained here without authority beyond the time limited by
his leave, decided to deport him under section 3 (5) (c) of the Immigration
Act 1971. Again he appealed unsuccessfully in 1978, his appeals being   H
rejected by an adjudicator on March 6 and by the Immigration Appeal
Tribunal on September 12.

Those appeals rested on a number of grounds. The only one which
concerned the Divisional Court or concerns this court arises out of his
marriage on January 22, 1977, to a Pakistani who had been given leave
to enter as a student for a limited period expiring in May 1977. The
relevant Immigration Rule is paragraph 22 of the Statement of Immi-

The Weekly Law Reports, August 15, 1980

1039

1 W.L.R.   Reg. v. Immigration Appeal Tribunal, Ex p. Kassam   Stephenson L.J.

A gration Rules for Control on Entry: Commonwealth Citizens (1973) (H.C. 79) which provides:

" The wife and children under 18 (as defined in paragraphs 41–43) of a person admitted as a student should be given leave to enter for the period of his authorised stay. . . ."

B The applicant's counsel submitted to the adjudicator and to the Immigration Appeal Tribunal that that rule offended against the Sex Discrimination Act 1975 unless it applied to allow a husband to stay here for the period of his wife's authorised stay as a student. On his motion to the Divisional Court of August 20, 1978, to review the Immigration Appeal Tribunal's decision he again raised that ground among others. But his C application for judicial review in the shape of an order for mandamus and certiorari came on for hearing on February 22, 1979, immediately after the Divisional Court had decided in *Reg.* v. *Immigration Appeal Tribunal, Ex parte Ahluwalia* (unreported), February 22, 1979, that the Act of 1975 had " no application whatsoever to this kind of case." Mr. Fletcher-Cooke accordingly, having apparently no faith in the applicant's other D grounds, submitted to judgment and appeals to this court on this one ground:

" The Divisional Court erred in law in coming to the conclusion as they did that the Sex Discrimination Act 1975 has no application to a case under the provisions of the Immigration Act 1971 or rules made thereunder."

E Our decision will not affect *Ahluwalia*'s case because her application for certiorari was granted on other grounds. But the point is of general importance and we have taken time to consider it.

Mr. Fletcher-Cooke attacks the conclusion that the Sex Discrimination Act 1975 has no application to the Immigration Act 1971 and the Immigra-F tion Rules with two submissions: (1) the general principles of sex discrimination set out in Part I, sections 1 and 2, of the Sex Discrimination Act 1975 apply universally except where specific exceptions are enacted by the Act itself, and the provisions of Parts II, III and IV of the Act are not exhaustive; (2) if that is wrong, section 29 (1) in Part III of the Act expressly applies to what the Secretary of State has done in this case.

G I agree with the Divisional Court in *Ahluwalia*'s case that the first submission should be rejected. It is true that particular exceptions are to be found in the Act: in Part II to " Discrimination in the Employment Field " by employers in section 6 (3) to (7) and section 10, and in the " Special Cases " specified in sections 17 and following; and in Part III to " Discrimination in Other Fields " such as education, in sections 26 to H 28, and accommodation in different kinds of premises and/or the provision of all kinds of goods, facilities and services in sections 32 and following. There are also " General Exceptions from Parts II to IV " to be found in Part V in sections 43 and following.

Furthermore, acts done by a Minister of the Crown or government department are not excepted from the Act. On the contrary, section 85 (1) provides:

" This Act applies—(a) to an act done by or for purposes of a A
Minister of the Crown or government department, or (b) to an act
done on behalf of the Crown by a statutory body, or a person holding a statutory office, . . ."

And subsection (4) expressly excepts from the application of the Act
service in the armed forces of the Crown.

Nowhere in the Act of 1975 are the Secretary of State and his exercise
of his statutory powers, or the acts of his immigration officers, under the
Immigration Act 1971 excepted from the application of the Act, and the
right to enforce the Act by an order of certiorari, mandamus or prohibition is expressly preserved by section 62 (2).

All this, however, ignores the primary purpose of the Act, as expressed C
in its language and in the way in which it is set out no less than in its
preamble, namely " to render unlawful certain kinds of sex discrimination
and discrimination on the ground of marriage . . . ." This it effects by first
setting out in Part I what is discrimination to which the Act applies. Discrimination on the ground of marriage is not in question here, and I need
only read the provisions of Part I which relate to sex discrimination against D
women and men. It is of course sex discrimination against a man which
is alleged here. They are sections 1 (1), 2 (1) and, for completeness,
section 5. Section 1 (1) provides:

" A person discriminates against a woman in any circumstances relevant for the purposes of any provision of this Act if—(a) on the
ground of her sex he treats her less favourably than he treats or E
would treat a man, or (b) he applies to her a requirement or condition
which he applies or would apply equally to a man but—(i) which is
such that the proportion of women who can comply with it is considerably smaller than the proportion of men who can comply with
it, and (ii) which he cannot show to be justifiable irrespective of the
sex of the person to whom it is applied, and (iii) which is to her detri- F
ment because she cannot comply with it."

Section 2 (1) provides:

" Section 1, and the provisions of Parts II and III relating to sex discrimination against women, are to be read as applying equally to the
treatment of men, and for that purpose shall have effect with such G
modifications as are requisite."

Section 5 provides:

" (1) In this Act—(a) references to discrimination refer to any discrimination falling within sections 1 to 4; and (b) references to sex
discrimination refer to any discrimination falling within section 1 or H
2, and related expressions shall be construed accordingly. (2) In
this Act—' woman ' includes a female of any age, and ' man '
includes a male of any age. (3) A comparison of the cases of persons
of different sex or marital status under section 1 (1) or 3 (1) must be
such that the relevant circumstances in the one case are the same, or
not materially different, in the other."

The Weekly Law Reports, August 15, 1980

1041

1 W.L.R.   Reg. v. Immigration Appeal Tribunal, Ex p. Kassam   Stephenson L.J.

A Lest there should be any doubt about it section 82 (1) provides that:

> " In this Act, unless the context otherwise requires— . . . ' discrimi-
> nation and related terms shall be construed in accordance with
> section 5 (1); . . ."

And the subsection goes on to repeat the definitions of " man " and
" woman " in section 5 (2).

B   Nothing in Part I of the Act makes any discrimination unlawful, as
Mr. Latham, for the respondent, pointed out. Unlawful discrimination
comes in Parts II, III and IV, which is headed " Other Unlawful Acts "
but which by section 37 makes unlawful " discriminatory practices," and
a " discriminatory practice " is there defined as:

> " . . . the application of a requirement or condition which results in
C   an act of discrimination which is unlawful by virtue of any provision
> of Part II or III taken with section 1 (1) (b). . . ."

The Act only applies to discrimination if the discrimination is " in any
circumstances relevant for the purposes of any provision " of the Act: see
sections 1 (1), 3 (1), 4 (1). This phrase would seem to be an attempted
D improvement on the language of section 1 (1) of the Race Relations Act
1968 and is also to be found in sections 1 (1) and 2 (1) of the Race
Relations Act 1976, which repealed the Act of 1968. The language of the
opening sections of the Sex Discrimination Act 1975 and the Race Relations Act 1976 would appear to express the same intention, namely to confine the discrimination with which the legislature was concerned to those
E practices—including not only acts but deliberate omissions: see section
82 (1)—to which the provisions of Part I applied and which the provisions
of Parts II to IV made unlawful. The introductory references to the " circumstances relevant for the purposes of any provision of this Act " require
the court to take the provisions of Parts II to IV with the provisions of
Part I and make plain that Parts II to IV exhaust the circumstances in
F which sex discrimination (or discrimination on the ground of marriage) as
explained in Part I is unlawful.

On that interpretation of the Act and in particular its opening words
the Act has no application to this case—unless it comes within a provision
in Parts II to IV. That was the view of the Divisional Court in Ahluwalia's
case (unreported), February 22, 1979, where Eveleigh L.J., giving the
G leading judgment, said, after reading sections 1 (1) and 3 (1):

> " It is important to emphasise that both of those sections contain the
> words ' in any circumstances relevant for the purposes ' of the Act.
> They are referring to the sections of the Act which themselves make
> discrimination unlawful. Sections 1 and 2 do not make discrimina-
> tion as such unlawful. It only becomes unlawful in the circum-
H stances set out in what one might call the operative sections for
> that purpose contained in Part II and in other parts of the Act. No-
> where in the Act is there to be found a reference to the performance
> by the Secretary of State of his duties with which we are concerned,
> that is to say under the Immigration Act 1971. For that short reason
> I would hold that the Sex Discrimination Act 1975 has no application
> whatsoever to this kind of case."

That leaves Mr. Fletcher-Cooke's second submission that there has A
been discrimination under section 29 (1). Eveleigh L.J. noted the submission and read the subsection, but neither he nor any other member of
the court referred further to that submission so that we have not got the
benefit of their reasons for rejecting it, as their conclusion implies that
they did.   Section 29 provides:

" (1) It is unlawful for any person concerned with the provision (for B
payment or not) of goods, facilities or services to the public or a section
of the public to discriminate against a woman who seeks to obtain or
use those goods, facilities or services—(a) by refusing or deliberately
omitting to provide her with any of them, or (b) by refusing or
deliberately omitting to provide her with goods, facilities or services of
the like quality, in the like manner and on the like terms as are C
normal in his case in relation to male members of the public or (where
she belongs to a section of the public) to male members of that
section. (2) The following are examples of the facilities and services
mentioned in subsection (1)—(a) access to and use of any place which
members of the public or a section of the public are permitted to
enter; (b) accommodation in a hotel, boarding house or other similar D
establishment; (c) facilities by way of banking or insurance or for
grants, loans, credit or finance; (d) facilities for education; (e) facilities
for entertainment, recreation or refreshment; (f) facilities for transport
or travel; (g) the services of any profession or trade, or any local or
other public authority."

I have found the point so plausible that I have been tempted to accede E
to it. In giving leave to immigrants to enter or remain here is not the Secretary of State a person concerned with the provision of facilities to a section
of the public and discriminating against a man who seeks to obtain or use
those facilities—the facilities which resemble facilities for travel, which the
statute gives as an example? The Immigration Act 1971 itself speaks of a F
person obtaining leave: for instance in section 3 (3) (b) and section 3 (4),
and the language of the Immigration Rules points also to an affirmative
answer. Is not " a passenger seeking entry as a visitor " or " to study in
the United Kingdom " (paragraphs 15 and 18 of H.C. 79) a man or
woman " who seeks to obtain " a facility from such a person?

Mr. Latham concedes that immigrants applying for leave are a section G
of the public, but he submits that the Secretary of State does not provide
facilities and the immigrant does not obtain or use them when he or she
obtains leave from him or his immigration officers. Section 29 is concerned
with what he called " market-place activities." The Secretary of State is
exercising statutory powers to control immigration and any facilities he
may be said in the course of their exercise to provide or to be concerned H
in providing are not within the aim or purview of the section.

I am of the opinion that the Secretary of State is not a person concerned with the provisions of facilities to a section of the public. Section
29 (1) and (2) repeat, mutatis mutandis, section 2 (1) and (2) of the Race
Relations Act 1968 (now repealed and re-enacted in section 20 (1) and (2)
of the Act of 1976) and so are not free from judicial interpretation. But

A read in their natural and ordinary meaning they are not aimed at, and do
not hit, the Secretary of State concerned with giving leave to enter or
remain in the exercise of his powers under the Immigration Act 1971. The
kind of facilities with which the sections of the Acts of 1975 and 1976 are
concerned is of the same order as goods and services, and though it may
not always be easy to say whether a particular person (or body of persons)
B is a person concerned with the provision of any of those three things to the
public or a section of the public and although a Minister of the Crown
or a government department might be such a person (for instance, in
former days the Postmaster General, as Sir David Cairns suggested in
argument), I am clearly of the opinion that the Secretary of State in acting
under the Immigration Act and Rules is not such a person, and he cannot
C be held to have unlawfully discriminated against the applicant by refusing
to give him leave to remain here while his wife was a student, or by refusing to interpret or alter the immigration rule, paragraph 22 of H.C. 79,
which is relevant to this appeal. He is operating in a field outside the fields
in which Parliament has forbidden sex discrimination.

    I therefore find it unnecessary to consider Mr. Latham's submission
D that if the Secretary of State comes within section 29, any discrimination
on his part is saved from being unlawful by section 51 (1) of the Act of
1975.

    For the reasons I have given I would dismiss the appeal.

E   ACKNER L.J. I agree. Paragraph 22 of the Statement of Immigration
Rules (H.C. 79) provides: " the wife and children under 18 . . . of a person
admitted as a student should be given leave to enter for the period of his
authorised stay." There is no similar provision for the husband of a wife
who has been admitted as a student. It is accordingly contended by Mr.
Fletcher-Cooke that the Secretary of State in applying these rules made
F under section 3 (2) of the Immigration Act 1971 is acting in breach of the
Sex Discrimination Act 1975 and is therefore acting unlawfully.

    I respectfully agree with the leading judgment of the Divisional Court
given by Eveleigh L.J. in Reg. v. Immigration Tribunal, Ex parte
Ahluwalia (unreported), February 22, 1979. Sections 1 and 2 of the Act do
not make discrimination as such unlawful. Discrimination is only unlawful
G in the circumstances set out in what one might call the operative sections
for that purpose contained in Parts II, III and IV of the Act. Nowhere in
the Act is there to be found a reference to the performance by the Secretary of State of his duties under the Immigration Act 1971.

    Mr. Fletcher-Cooke, however, relies upon section 29 (1) of the Act
and maintains that the Secretary of State is " concerned with the pro-
H vision of " facilities to the public or a section of the public, such facilities
being permission to enter and stay in the United Kingdom and he has
therefore unlawfully discriminated against the appellant who is seeking
to obtain such facilities.

    In my judgment, when the Secretary of State is exercising his dis-
cretion in relation to powers granted to him by the Immigration Act 1971,
he is not providing a facility within the meaning of section 29 of the Act.
The word " facilities " in that section is flanked on one side by the word

" goods " and on the other by the word " services." This suggests to my
mind that the word " facilities " is not to be given a wholly unrestricted
meaning but must be limited or confined to facilities that are akin to
goods or services. Section 29 (2) provides examples of the facilities and
services mentioned in section 29 (1). These examples support the view
which I have expressed above.

In my judgment when the Secretary of State allows an immigrant to
enter and stay in this country, he is granting a permission, he is not providing a facility. It could, of course, be said that he is conferring a benefit.
Significantly, the word benefit is used in section 34 as additional to
facilities or services: see section 34 (2) (b), " the provision of benefits,
facilities or services . . ." and section 34 (4) " conferring benefits. . . ."

SIR DAVID CAIRNS. I agree with both judgments which have been
given and there is nothing I can usefully add.

Appeal dismissed with costs.
Leave to appeal refused.

Solicitors: *Nazerali & Co.; Treasury Solicitor.*

[Reported by ROBERT WILLIAMS, ESQ. Barrister-at-Law]

May 6. The Appeal Committee of the House of Lords (Lord
Wilberforce, Lord Salmon and Lord Roskill) allowed a petition by the
applicant for leave to appeal.

A

[QUEEN'S BENCH DIVISION]

* REGINA v. BERWYN JUSTICES, Ex parte EDWARDS

1979 Dec. 14;   Lord Widgery C.J., Shaw L.J.,
1980 Jan. 21   Park, Kilner Brown and Woolf JJ.

B

*Licensing — Licensed premises — Special order of exemption —
" Special occasion " — Saturday before bank holiday Monday
— Local knowledge of justices — Whether Saturday before
bank holiday special occasion because of numbers of visitors
attracted to area—Licensing Act* 1964 *(c. 26), s.* 74 (4)

C
The justices made an order, in respect of certain public
houses in their area, granting, under section 74 (4) of the
Licensing Act 1964,[1] applications for extensions of the permitted hours on the two Saturdays respectively preceding the
1979 spring and summer bank holiday Mondays. As the area
contained tourist attractions and was visited by a large number
of people during bank holiday weekends, the justices regarded
the Saturdays forming part of the weekends as special occasions for the purposes of the section. They heard no evidence
on that issue, however, and relied on their own knowledge of
the locality.
D
On an application for an order of certiorari to quash the
justices' order: —
Held, (1) that when considering whether to grant an application for a special order of exemption under section 74 (4)
of the Licensing Act 1964 the justices had first to satisfy themselves that the occasion which was the subject matter of the
application was capable of being a special occasion; if it was,
they had then to consider whether it was in fact a special
occasion in the locality of the licensed premises; if they were
so satisfied, they had finally to ask themselves whether as a
matter of discretion the application should be granted.
E
Martin v. *Spalding* [1979] 1 W.L.R. 1164, D.C. and dictum
of Lord Coleridge C.J. in *Devine* v. *Keeling* (1886) 50 J.P.
551, 552, D.C. applied.
F
(2) Refusing the application, that, for the purposes of
section 74 (4), Saturdays forming part of bank holiday weekends were capable of being special occasions and the justices
were entitled to regard the Saturdays as special occasions in
their area on the basis of their local knowledge and without
hearing evidence on that issue.
Per curiam. The words " special occasion " are ordinary
words in the English language which may be given their ordinary meaning, and if this is done, in the majority of cases it
G
will not be necessary to look at previous authorities in order
to determine whether the particular occasion is capable of
being a special occasion (post, p. 1048c).

The following cases are referred to in the judgment of Woolf J.:

H
Devine v. *Keeling* (1886) 50 J.P. 551, D.C.
Knole Park Golf Club v. *Chief Superintendent, Kent County Constabu-
lary* [1979] 3 All E.R. 829, D.C.
Lemon v. *Sargent (Note)* [1972] 1 W.L.R. 72; [1971] 3 All E.R. 936, D.C.
Martin v. *Spalding* [1979] 1 W.L.R. 1164; [1979] 2 All E.R. 1193, D.C.
Reg. v. *Dewsland and Haverfordwest Licensing Justices*, The Times,
January 28, 1961, D.C.

---

[1] Licensing Act 1964, s. 74 (4): see post, p. 1046H.

Reg. v. *Wenlock Justices, Ex parte Furber*, The Times, July 26, 1978,   **A**
D.C.
Reg. v. *Woodstock Justices, Ex parte Holdsworth* (unreported), May 30,
1977, D.C.

The following additional cases were cited in argument:

Reg. v. *Llanidloes (Lower) Justices, Ex parte Thorogood* [1972] 1 W.L.R.
68; [1971] 3 All E.R. 932, D.C.   **B**
Rex v. *Butt, Ex parte Brooke* (1922) 38 T.L.R. 537, D.C.
Rex v. *Lancashire Justices, Ex parte Customs and Excise Commissioners*
151 L.T. 376, D.C.
Rex v. *Sussex Justices, Ex parte Bubb* [1933] 2 K.B. 707, D.C.

APPLICATION for order of certiorari.   **C**
The applicant, Percy Manning Edwards, a chief superintendent of the
North Wales Police Force, sought an order of certiorari to quash an order
made at Corwen by Berwyn licensing justices, granting applications by
Berwyn Licensed Victuallers Association for the extension, from 11 p.m.
to 11.45 p.m., of the permitted hours in a number of public houses on,
inter alia, the Saturdays, May 26 and August 25, 1979.

The grounds of the application were that the order was wrong in law;   **D**
and that the Saturday before a bank holiday Monday had no particular
character which gave it the quality of a special occasion for the purposes
of section 74 (4) of the Licensing Act 1964 and that in the premises the
justices erred in law in granting the extensions for Saturday, May 26,
and Saturday, August 25, 1979.

The facts are stated in the judgment of Woolf J.   **E**

Martin Thomas Q.C. and *Michael Farmer* for the applicant.
R. J. Harvey Q.C. and *Richard Beckett* for the respondent, the
National Union of Licensed Victuallers.

Cur. adv. vult.   **F**

January 21, 1980. LORD WIDGERY C.J. Woolf J. will give the first
judgment.

WOOLF J. read the following judgment. In this matter Mr. Thomas
moves on behalf of Percy Manning Edwards, a chief superintendent of
the North Wales Police, for an order of certiorari to quash an order made   **G**
by the licensing justices sitting in and for the petty sessional division of
Berwyn on February 9, 1979, granting extensions of permitted hours for
Saturday, May 26, 1979, and Saturday, August 25, 1979, from 11 p.m. to
11.45 p.m., in respect of 48 public houses situated within the division.

The justices in granting the applications purported to act pursuant to
section 74 (4) of the Licensing Act 1964, which provides: **H**

" Justices of the peace may—(*a*) on an application by the holder of
a justices' on-licence for any premises, or (*b*) on an application by
the secretary of a club registered in respect of any premises, make an
order (in this Act referred to as a special order of exemption) adding
such hours as may be specified in the order to the permitted hours
in those premises on such special occasion or occasions as may be so
specified."

The Weekly Law Reports, August 22, 1980

1047

1 W.L.R.   Reg. v. Berwyn Justices, Ex p. Edwards (D.C.)   Woolf J.

A   This case raises again the question of what is the proper approach
which justices should adopt in the case of such applications and the extent
to which this court can interfere with the decisions which they reach. This
is the same question as was considered as recently as May 21, 1979, by
this court in *Martin* v. *Spalding* [1979] 1 W.L.R. 1164. Having heard
numerous authorities cited to the court in that case, Lord Widgery C.J.
and Geoffrey Lane L.J. sought to give general guidance as to the principles
B   to be applied, in the hope that their judgments would assist " materially
to dispose of this recurring problem " : see p. 1168 *per* Lord Widgery C.J.
Lord Widgery C.J. had a reservation as to whether this object would be
achieved, and the present case is not the only justification for that reservation. There has already been at least one other case before this court on
this very provision since *Martin* v. *Spalding.*
C   In the present case counsel have again taken the court through the
relevant authorities starting with *Devine* v. *Keeling* (1886) 50 J.P. 551.
Having considered those authorities, the court considers that the principles set out in the judgments in *Martin* v. *Spalding* [1979] 1 W.L.R.
1164 were correct. In order to try to achieve the same object as was
sought to be achieved in *Martin* v. *Spalding* and with the same reser-
D   vations as to the likelihood of success, we would point out that when
justices are considering applications for a special order of exemption,
there are three questions which they should consider in deciding whether
to grant an application which is made to them in the proper form.
        (1) Is the occasion which is the subject matter of the application
capable of being a " special occasion "? As Lord Widgery C.J. said in
Martin v. *Spalding* [1979] 1 W.L.R. 1164, 1167:
E
        " In other words, the justices must look at this matter like a judge
        looking at a matter of law and ask themselves whether it is open
        to anybody to contend that this is a special occasion."

        (2) If the occasion is capable of being a special occasion, whether, on the
material available to the justices, it is in fact a special occasion in the
F   locality in which the licensed premises in respect of which the application
is made are situated? (3) If it is a special occasion in their locality,
whether as a matter of discretion the application should be granted?
        As will be apparent from the questions, if the justices answer any
question in the negative, it is not necessary for them to go on to consider
the remaining questions. An application can only be granted if all three
questions are answered in the affirmative.
G   The first question is a question of law and if any relief is to be
obtained from a higher court in respect of a decision of the justices, it
will normally be because they have answered the first question in a
manner which is wrong in law. The second question is purely a question
of fact and the court will normally only be able to intervene in the unlikely
event of it being shown that there was no material upon which the justices
could have come to the decision which they did. It is to this question
H   that the passage from the judgment of Lord Coleridge C.J. in *Devine* v.
Keeling, 50 J.P. 551, which is often cited, applies. Lord Coleridge C.J.
stated at p. 552:

        " I think in this case we cannot interfere with the decision of the
        justices, for the question what is a special occasion must necessarily
        be a question of fact in each locality. Each locality may very well
        have its own meaning to those words, and it is for the justices in each

1048

district to say whether a certain time and place come within the description."

Those words should not be taken as applying to the first question. So far as the justices' answer to the third question is concerned, it will be rare indeed that it will be possible to show that the justices have exercised their discretion in a manner which is capable of being challenged in the courts.

It is primarily in relation to the first question, because it involves a question of law, that the previous decisions of the courts can be of assistance. However, even in relation to the first question, the earlier authorities must be approached with some caution. Many of the decisions do not lay down any principle but merely provide examples of what is the appropriate conclusion on their particular facts. They should not be applied rigidly to later situations because the facts are unlikely to be precisely the same. Furthermore, none of the earlier decisions purports to lay down an exhaustive definition as to what is capable of being a special occasion. The words " special occasion " are ordinary words in the English language which may be given their ordinary meaning, and if this is done, in the majority of cases it will not be necessary to look at previous authorities in order to answer the first question. In border-line cases, however, the earlier authorities may be of assistance in giving guidance as to the proper approach to the problem or by laying down markers as to what is, or is not, capable of being a special occasion.

The main guidance which is to be obtained from these authorities can be summarised. (1) The occasion can be special from the national or local point of view. A local occasion can include what might be more aptly described as a personal occasion such as a wedding, but the more local or the more personal the occasion, the more carefully it must be scrutinised: see per Geoffrey Lane L.J. in Martin v. Spalding [1979] 1 W.L.R. 1164, 1168. (2) The more frequent the occasion occurs the less likely it is that it will be a special occasion: see Lemon v. Sargent (Note) [1972] 1 W.L.R. 72. (3) If the occasion is one created by the licensee solely for the purposes of his licensed business, it is unlikely to be capable of being a special occasion. Such a situation must be distinguished from the position of a registered club which creates, for example, sporting occasions which are celebrated at the club and are capable of being special occasions because they are not created solely for the purpose of the licensed business of the club: see Knole Park Golf Club v. Chief Superintendent, Kent County Constabulary [1979] 3 All E.R. 829.

Turning to the facts of the present case, the complaint is in respect of the grant of extensions for permitted hours for Saturday, May 26, 1979, being the Saturday before the spring bank holiday Monday, and Saturday, August 25, 1979, being the Saturday before the summer bank holiday Monday. It is accepted that extensions were properly granted in respect of the bank holiday Mondays themselves, which are agreed to be special occasions. The justices have filed an affidavit in support of their decision. In that affidavit they say in effect that they consider that in their division the whole bank holiday weekend is a continuing special occasion. They point out that the area attracts a large number of visitors during the summer months, and during bank holiday weekends a large number of visitors arrive on Friday evenings and stay over the weekend departing for their homes on bank holiday Monday. Because of the

The Weekly Law Reports, August 22, 1980

1049

1 W.L.R.   Reg. v. Berwyn Justices, Ex p. Edwards (D.C.)   Woolf J.

A tourist attractions of the area the Saturdays prior to the spring and summer bank holidays have a particular character giving them the quality of special occasions. They point out that they came to this conclusion after the case of *Reg.* v. *Wenlock Justices, Ex parte Furber*, The Times, July 26, 1978, to which I will refer later, had been brought to their attention and carefully considered.

B   There is nothing in the evidence which is before the court to suggest that the justices misdirected themselves in any way and if their decision was objectionable it could only be on the basis that the Saturdays in question were not capable of being special occasions. As to this, the court is clearly of the view that it is impossible to say that these particular Saturdays were incapable of being special occasions as they form part of the bank holiday weekends.

C   However, a different view was taken in the *Wenlock Justices* case and this court quashed the justices' decision. The respondent did not appear and was not represented in that case and in *Martin* v. *Spalding* [1979] 1 W.L.R. 1164 Geoffrey Lane L.J. preferred the decision of *Reg.* v. *Woodstock Justices, Ex parte Holdsworth* (unreported), May 30, 1977, which was a decision of this court involving a Saturday before a bank
D holiday weekend in which the court took a different view. Both those cases should be regarded as being decisions on their own facts. What they illustrate is that a Saturday before a bank holiday is close to the border-line of a situation which is not capable of being regarded as a special occasion. An illustration of a case which is beyond the border-line is provided by *Reg.* v. *Dewsland and Haverfordwest Licensing Justices*, The Times, January 28, 1961. In that case the court said that " it was
E impossible to say that because people attended a seaside resort on Thurs-days and Saturdays in the summer months that in law amounted to special occasions."

In support of the application to this court reliance was placed upon an affidavit by Superintendent Pritchard containing in particular more detailed evidence as to the extent to which the area in question is properly
F to be regarded as a holiday area. Quite apart from the fact that the justices had no opportunity of dealing with this affidavit, the court will not go into evidential disputes of this sort in order to review the justices' conclusion on the second question.

Some complaint was made by the applicant that the justices should not have come to the conclusion which they did without hearing evidence
G on the issue. That complaint is not justified. The letter in support of the application which was placed before the justices had attached to it a list which made it clear that the applications for the extension were made because the Saturdays formed part of the holiday weekend and in decid-ing whether or not such a holiday weekend is a special occasion, the licens-ing justices are perfectly entitled to act upon their local knowledge with-
H out having evidence called before them.

The conclusion of the court as to the decision of the justices in this case is that it was one to which they were entitled to come and which they appear to have reached after giving proper consideration to the issues and the material available to them. It follows that the application for an order of certiorari is dismissed.

SHAW L.J. I agree.

LORD WIDGERY C.J. I have the authority of Park J. and Kilner   **A**
Brown J. to say they agree and I also agree.

Application refused.
No order as to costs.

Solicitors: *Sharpe, Pritchard & Co. for William Jones & Talog Davies*   **B**
& Aneurin O. Evans & Co., Ruthin; Lickfolds, Wiley & Powles.

B. O. A.

C

[COURT OF APPEAL]

*REGINA v. ORPIN

1979 Dec. 17, 18;
1980 Feb. 15   Eveleigh L.J., Wien and Drake JJ.

Crime—Arson—Specific intent—Arson endangering life—Offence   **D**
committed while intoxicated—Whether charge of arson with
intent to endanger or reckless as to endangering life crime of
specific intent — Whether drunkenness defence — Criminal
Damage Act 1971 (c. 48), s. 1 [1]

The defendant started two separate fires at about 11 p.m.
one evening in the entrance corridor of a block of holiday
flats. Twelve people who were in the flats were evacuated and   **E**
the fires were put out by the fire brigade. The defendant
admitted starting one fire, knowing that people were in the
flats. Relying upon evidence of drunkenness he pleaded not
guilty to count 1 of an indictment which charged him with
arson with intent to endanger life or being reckless as to
whether life would be endangered, contrary to section 1 (2) and
(3) of the Criminal Damage Act 1971. He pleaded guilty to
count 2 of the indictment, which charged him with simple   **F**
arson, contrary to section 1 (1) and (3) of the Act of 1971. At
the close of the prosecution case, after argument, the trial
judge ruled that the section 1 (2) offence was a crime of basic
intent and, at least in so far as the consideration of recklessness
was concerned, drunkenness was no defence. The defendant
thereupon changed his plea to guilty.

On appeal against conviction: —
Held, allowing the appeal, that although the offence defined   **G**
in subsection (1) of section 1 of the Criminal Damage Act
1971 was a crime of basic intent and while the definition of
the actus reus in the first part of subsection (2) was the same
as in subsection (1), nevertheless the mental element of intention or recklessness in the second part of section 1 (2) was
an aggravating circumstance which added to the gravity of the
actus reus and was to be treated as a specific intent which
had to be established as an ingredient of the offence (post,   **H**
p. 1054B–C); accordingly, the section 1 (2) offence was a crime
of specific intent and evidence of intoxication was a relevant
consideration in determining whether the necessary mental
element existed.
Reg. v. *Majewski* [1977] A.C. 443, H.L.(E.) applied.
Reg. v. *Stephenson* [1979] Q.B. 695, C.A. considered.

[1] Criminal Damage Act 1971, s. 1: see post, p. 1053D–E.

A   The following cases are referred to in the judgment:

Reg. v. *Majewski* [1977] A.C. 443; [1976] 2 W.L.R. 623; [1976] 2 All E.R. 142, H.L.(E.).

Reg. v. *Morgan* [1976] A.C. 182; [1975] 2 W.L.R. 913; [1975] 1 All E.R. 8; [1975] 2 All E.R. 347, C.A. and H.L.(E.).

Reg. v. *O'Driscoll* (1977) 65 Cr.App.R. 50, C.A.

Reg. v. *Stephenson* [1979] Q.B. 695; [1979] 3 W.L.R. 193; [1979] 2 All
B   E.R. 1198, C.A.

The following additional cases were cited in argument:

Leary v. *The Queen* (1977) 74 D.L.R. (3d) 103.

Reg. v. *Hyam* [1975] A.C. 55; [1974] 2 W.L.R. 607; [1974] 2 All E.R. 41, H.L.(E.).

Rex v. *Alexander* (1912) 7 Cr.App.R. 110, C.C.A.
C

APPEAL against conviction.

On July 23, 1979, the defendant, Michael John Orpin, was charged at York Crown Court (Judge Beaumont) with two offences of arson: count 1, contrary to section 1 (2) and (3) of the Criminal Damage Act 1971 (arson with intent to endanger life or being reckless as to whether
D   life would be endangered); and count 2, contrary to section 1 (1) and (3) (simple arson). He pleaded guilty to count 2 but not guilty to count 1, his defence being that he was drunk when he committed the offence. At the close of the prosecution case the judge ruled that the section 1 (2) offence was a crime of basic intent and that drunkenness was no defence, at least in so far as the consideration of recklessness was concerned. The defendant thereupon changed his plea to guilty.

E   He appealed on the grounds (1) that the judge was wrong when he directed that the offence under section 1 (2) of the Criminal Damage Act 1971 was an offence of basic intent within the meaning of *Reg.* v. *Majewski* [1977] A.C. 443; the offence should be classified as one which required a specific intent within the meaning of the *Majewski* case; (2) the effect of the judge's ruling was to exclude all consideration of
F   drunkenness by the jury from the defendant's case, when this would have been his defence; he was therefore advised that he had no defence and changed his plea to guilty of count 1 of the indictment, without having had the opportunity of putting his defence to the jury.

David Bradshaw for the defendant.
P. F. Worsley for the Crown.
G
Cur. adv. vult.

February 15, 1980. EVELEIGH L.J. read the following judgment of the court. We gave leave to appeal in this matter. On July 23, 1979, at York Crown Court the defendant pleaded not guilty to count 1 of the indictment, alleging arson with intent to endanger life, contrary to
H   section 1 (2) and (3) of the Criminal Damage Act 1971. He pleaded guilty to count 2, alleging arson contrary to section 1 (1) and (3). On July 24, at the end of the case for the prosecution, and after legal argument and a ruling by the judge, the defendant changed his plea on count 1 to one of guilty. He was sentenced to eight years' imprisonment on count 1 and to six years' imprisonment concurrent on count 2.

Both charges arose out of an incident at a block of holiday flatlets in Scarborough during the night of April 19–20, 1979. At about 11.20 a

guest noticed smoke coming from the ground floor of the block and A
telephoned the fire brigade. Twelve people were evacuated safely, some
by way of a ladder, others through the main entrance. It was found
that two distinct fires had been burning in the hall and passageway on
the ground floor. Damage estimated at a cost of £4,000 was done. The
defendant admitted starting a fire, but said that he could not remember
starting two. He admitted knowing at the time that there were people B
in residence. He spoke of drinking five or more pints of beer that
evening.

Before the prosecution opened the case counsel for the defence
indicated that on count 1 he would rely upon evidence of drunkenness,
and he invited the judge to rule at that stage whether section 1 (2) was a
crime of specific intent and whether, putting it compendiously, drunkenness could be a defence. The judge declined to give a ruling at that C
stage. At the close of the prosecution case the point was argued and a
ruling was given to the effect that, at least in so far as the consideration
of recklessness was concerned, drunkenness was no defence to the charge
under section 1 (2). Thereupon the defendant changed his plea.

The judge considered himself bound so to hold by the judgment in
Reg. v. *Stephenson* [1979] Q.B. 695, and he said that a passage in the D
judgment of the court in *Reg.* v. *O'Driscoll* (1977) 65 Cr.App.R. 50,
indicating that the offence was one of specific intent, was obiter. The
particular passage in *Reg.* v. *Stephenson* upon which the judge relied
reads, at p. 704:

> " Evidence of self-induced intoxication such as to negative mens rea
> is a defence to a charge which requires proof of a 'specific intent,' E
> but not to a charge of any other crime. The Criminal Damage Act
> 1971, section 1 (1) involves no specific intent: see *Reg.* v. *O'Driscoll*
> (1977) 65 Cr.App.R. 50, 55. Accordingly it is no defence under the
> Act of 1977 for a person to say that he was deprived by self-induced
> intoxication of the ability to foresee or appreciate an obvious risk."

Referring to this passage in his ruling the judge said: " ' Under the Act ' F
—not just under section 1 (1) of the Act."

In *Reg.* v. *O'Driscoll* Waller L.J., delivering the judgment of the
court, said that section 1 (1) created a crime of basic intent, but he went
on to say, at p. 55:

> " It would have been different in our view if the intent had involved
> the question of danger to the life of others, as in subsection (2) of G
> section 1 of the Criminal Damage Act 1971, because that would not
> be inherent in the actus reus if there was an intention to endanger
> the life of another or recklessness as to whether the life of another
> would be endangered or not."

We would say at once that we do not regard the words referred to in H
Reg. v. *Stephenson* [1979] Q.B. 695 as referring to any provision in the
Act other than section 1 (1). The court was only concerned with that
particular offence, and to meet what might be seen to be a logical
difficulty in view of the references in *Reg.* v. *Majewski* [1977] A.C. 443,
to recklessness in the context of drunkenness. The emphasis placed upon
the subjective element of recklessness in the decision in *Reg.* v. *Stephen-*
son might be thought by some to admit drunkenness as a relevant

A consideration in the offence with which the court was concerned. It was therefore pointed out that intoxication was irrelevant to a crime of basic intent, which an offence under section 1 (1) was.

For the Crown it has been argued that, as recklessness must bear the same meaning in section 1 (2) as it does in section 1 (1), then if section 1 (1) is a crime of basic intent so too is section 1 (2). When the court gives a meaning to a particular word it does not by that act of definition

B alone decide another question, that is, whether or not an offence is one of basic or specific intent. Consequently, whatever view the court formed as to the nature of an offence under section 1 (1), that would not decide the question as to the nature of an offence under section 1 (2).

It was right to say that the words of Waller L.J. in *Reg. v. O'Driscoll,* 65 Cr.App.R. 50 also were obiter. There is therefore no binding authority

C on the question before the court.

In *Reg. v. Majewski* [1977] A.C. 443 the House of Lords clearly recognised that drunkenness was a relevant consideration in relation to crimes of specific intent. It is submitted on behalf of the defendant that section 1 (2) is a crime of specific intent, and that is in fact the only issue in this case. Section 1 reads:

D   " (1) A person who without lawful excuse destroys or damages any property belonging to another intending to destroy or damage any such property or being reckless as to whether any such property would be destroyed or damaged shall be guilty of an offence. (2) A person who without lawful excuse destroys or damages any property, whether belonging to himself or another—(a) intending to destroy

E   or damage any property or being reckless as to whether any property would be destroyed or damaged; and (b) intending by the destruction or damage to endanger the life of another or being reckless as to whether the life of another would be thereby endangered; shall be guilty of an offence. (3) An offence committed under this section by destroying or damaging property by fire shall be charged as arson."

F   The first part of subsection (2) reproduces, with differences irrelevant for our purpose, the definition contained in subsection (1). That subsection was held to be a crime of basic intent: see *Reg. v. O'Driscoll.* Indeed the definition's use of the words " intention " and " reckless " coincide almost exactly with the mental element required to be established in the case of assault, as stated by Lord Edmund-Davies in *Reg. v.*

G *Majewski* [1977] A.C. 443, 487, when he adopted the words of Lord Simon of Glaisdale in *Reg. v. Morgan* [1976] A.C. 182, 216–217:

      " I take assault as an example of a crime of basic intent where the consequence is very closely connected with the act. The actus reus of assault is an act which causes another person to apprehend immediate and unlawful violence. The mens rea corresponds exactly.

H   The prosecution must prove that the accused foresaw that his act would probably cause another person to have apprehension of immediate and unlawful violence, or would possibly have that consequence, such being the purpose of the act, or that he was reckless as to whether or not his act caused such apprehension."

It is quite clear that recklessness can be an ingredient in a crime of basic intent.

However, the second part of subsection (2), while introducing the element of intention or recklessness as an ingredient, does not postulate as an essential ingredient a corresponding act. Indeed there is no act referred to in the second part of the definition; unless, of course, the forming of an intent, or a decision to go ahead in spite of a risk, constitutes the act. It may be in a particular case that life has been endangered, but proof of this is not necessary to establish the offence.

The mental element, intention or recklessness, in the second part of subsection (2) is an aggravating circumstance which adds to the gravity of the actus reus which is defined in the first part of that subsection. Although the proof of that additional element will often involve evidence as to possible or actual danger to life, the additional aggravating factor lies in the mind. It is the mental attitude to the consequences of an actus reus. It goes beyond the actus reus itself, and is therefore to be treated as a specific intent which has to be established as an ingredient of the offence. That being so, evidence of intoxication is relevant as one of those matters to be taken into consideration in determining whether or not the necessary mental element existed.

There is nothing inconsistent in treating an offence under subsection (1) as a crime of basic intent and an offence under subsection (2) as one of specific intent. It is only the second part of subsection (2) which introduces a specific intent. The same words are used to denote the attitude of mind, but in the one case there is an act stipulated corresponding to the mental state and manifesting its existence, whilst in the other there is no such act. It seems to this court that there is nothing inconsistent in treating intoxication as irrelevant when considering the liability of a person who has willed himself to do that which the law forbids (for example, to do something which wounds another), and yet to make it relevant when a further mental state is postulated as an aggravating circumstance making the offence even more serious.

This appeal must, therefore, be allowed, and the conviction on the first count will be quashed.

Appeal allowed.

Solicitors: *Medley, Drawbridge & Co., Scarborough; Bedwells, Scarborough.*

[Reported by MISS EIRA CARYL-THOMAS, Barrister-at-Law]

A

[COURT OF APPEAL]

* REGINA v. HOLMES

REGINA v. MERRICK

REGINA v. THORNTON

B

REGINA v. WOOD

1980   March 17;   Ormrod L.J., Jupp and
       April 1   Comyn JJ.

*Crime—Conspiracy—Acquittal or conviction of co-conspirators—
Four defendants charged with conspiring together that two
should steal—Direction that two should both be convicted or
both acquitted—Judge's discretion to give such direction—
Criminal Law Act 1977 (c. 45), s. 5 (8) (9)*

C

Section 5 (8) and (9) of the Criminal Law Act 1977 provides:
" (8) The fact that the person or persons who, so far as
appears from the indictment on which any person has
been convicted of conspiracy, were the only other parties
to the agreement on which his conviction was based have
been acquitted of conspiracy by reference to that agreement (whether after being tried with the person convicted
or separately) shall not be a ground for quashing his
conviction unless under all the circumstances of the case
his conviction is inconsistent with the acquittal of the
other person or persons in question.   (9) Any rule of
law or practice inconsistent with the provisions of subsection (8) above is hereby abolished."

D

E

H., M., T. and W. were charged with conspiracy at common
law by conspiring together that M. and W. should steal goods
from delivery vans.   At their trial, the prosecution adduced
evidence against the defendants, and alleged that W. had made
admissions which, if believed, were damaging to his defence.
W. denied the admissions.   At the end of the evidence, after
submissions made in the absence of the jury, the trial judge
ruled that section 5 (8) and (9) of the Criminal Law Act 1977
did not apply to proceedings which had begun before the subsections came into effect.   He directed the jury that they
should either convict both M. and W. or acquit them both.
All of the defendants were convicted.

F

On M.'s appeal against conviction : —

Held, dismissing the appeal, that the trial judge had wrongly
ruled that section 5 (8) and (9) of the Criminal Law Act 1977
did not apply to the proceedings; but that, although the effect
of section 5 (8) and (9) was that it was no longer necessary
when two persons were accused of conspiring together for a
judge to direct the jury that they must convict both or acquit
both, the trial judge retained a discretion to give such a
direction where there was a serious risk of inconsistent verdicts
and, in all the circumstances, he had been right in the present
case to do so.

G

Director of Public Prosecutions v. *Shannon* [1975] A.C.
717, H.L.(E.) considered.

H

The following cases are referred to in the judgment:

Director of Public Prosecutions v. *Shannon* [1975] A.C. 717; [1974] 3
    W.L.R. 155; [1974] 2 All E.R. 1009, C.A. and H.L.(E.).
Reg. v. *Coughlan (Joseph)* (1976) 64 Cr.App.R. 11, C.A.

No additional cases were cited in argument.

APPEAL against conviction.   A

APPLICATIONS for leave to appeal against convictions.

On February 12, 1979, at Leeds Crown Court before Judge Nevin
and a jury, Brian William Holmes, Francis Paul Merrick, Pauline
Thornton and Maurice Wood were charged with conspiracy to steal.
The particulars of the offence were that the defendants " on divers days
between November 1, 1976, and November 17, 1977, conspired together   B
that Francis Paul Merrick and Maurice Wood should steal cigarettes,
tobacco and other goods from unattended delivery vehicles in the counties of West and South Yorkshire." At the end of the evidence and
after submissions made in the absence of the jury by counsel for Merrick,
the trial judge ruled that section 5 (8) and (9) of the Criminal Law Act
1977 did not apply to Merrick's trial, and he directed the jury that they
could only convict Wood if they also convicted Merrick. On February   C
27, 1979, all the defendants were convicted. Merrick appealed against
his conviction on the ground, inter alia, that the judge misdirected the
jury and erred in law in directing the jury that (a) if they were to bring
in a verdict of guilty of conspiracy, that verdict must be against at least
two out of four accused and (b) they could not convict Wood unless they
convicted Merrick as well, that these two stood or fell together; whereas
he should have directed the jury that in the light of section 5 (8) and (9) D
of the Criminal Law Act 1977 it would be open to them to convict one
of the accused only of conspiracy. Holmes, Thornton and Wood applied
for leave to appeal against their convictions.

The facts are stated in the judgment.

J. S. H. Stewart (assigned by the Registrar of Criminal Appeals) for   E
the defendant Merrick.

R. M. Harrison (assigned by the Registrar of Criminal Appeals) for
the defendants Holmes and Thornton.

Sydney Levine (assigned by the Registrar of Criminal Appeals) for
the defendant Wood.

M. T. Cracknell for the Crown.
                                                                         F
                                                  Cur. adv. vult.

April 1. ORMROD L.J. delivered the following judgment of the court.
In this case four persons, Brian William Holmes, Francis Paul Merrick,
Pauline Thornton and Maurice Wood were convicted on February 27,
1979, at Leeds Crown Court, before Judge Nevin and a jury, on an   G
indictment containing one count, in the following terms: Francis Paul
Merrick, Maurice Wood, Brian William Holmes and Pauline Thornton
on divers days between November 1, 1976, and November 17, 1977,
conspired together that Francis Paul Merrick and Maurice Wood should
steal cigarettes, tobacco and other goods from unattended delivery
vehicles in the counties of West and South Yorkshire.

It should be said that this was a common law conspiracy because the   H
offence was committed before the relevant sections of the Criminal Law
Act 1977 came into force. By the time of the trial, however, they were
in force.

In the case of Merrick, the trial judge certified that the case was fit
for appeal. The other three persons concerned now apply for leave to
appeal against their respective convictions. The judge's certificate states
the grounds as follows:

A   " Was I right to direct the jury that they could only convict Wood if
they also convicted Merrick, and in ruling that section 5 (8) and (9)
of the Criminal Law Act 1977 did not apply to the trial of Merrick? "

The case for the prosecution, briefly summarised, was that Wood and
Merrick had evolved a scheme for stealing from delivery vans which, in
outline, consisted of selecting a delivery van, following or " stalking " it
B   in a car until it stopped to deliver some of its load at a place convenient
for their purpose, waiting until the driver had opened the back of the van
and entered a shop to deliver a parcel or parcels, leaving the back of the
van open or unlocked, and then quickly snatching a package or packages
from the van and driving off. For this purpose they used various cars,
some of which had false number plates to prevent identification, and a
C   garage, rented by Wood in the false name of Walsh, to store the goods
pending their disposal. Holmes was alleged to be the receiver who disposed of the stolen goods. Mrs. Thornton, who was living with Wood,
helped in minor ways, such as driving Wood to meeting places with
Merrick and paying the rent for the garage to the owner.

The case for the prosecution was supported by a great deal of police
evidence from officers who had carried out an elaborate and prolonged
D   surveillance of the movements of Merrick, Wood and Mrs. Thornton,
during which Wood and Merrick were seen to be following vans and
behaving suspiciously in other ways. No actual theft was observed, but
on one such occasion Merrick was seen to jump out of the car, run to
the back of the van, and try to open it while the driver was in the shop;
he was unsuccessful because it was locked. There was evidence that
E   Wood had rented the garage in a false name, that the police found a key
to the garage in possession of Wood, and another in Merrick's possession
and that in the garage were found false number plates and a small quantity of wine and snuff which had been stolen from a van or vans during
deliveries. The evidence against Holmes was mainly the finding of his
finger prints on the stolen wine and snuff in the garage. In addition
there was evidence from police officers of interviews with all four accused.
F   Merrick refused to answer any questions and maintained his refusal
throughout all the interviews; Wood refused to answer any questions at
the first two or three interviews, but eventually gave way, and made a
number of admissions which, if believed by the jury (they were vigorously
denied by Wood), were very damaging to his defence; Holmes gave a
series of facetious answers which did nothing to help his case; and Mrs.
G   Thornton made no significant admissions. All the accused except Mrs.
Thornton gave evidence at the trial and were cross-examined.

At the end of the evidence and before speeches, Mr. Stewart, for
Merrick, asked for and was given an opportunity to make a submission
in the absence of the jury, as to the form of the summing up. At this
stage of the trial, Mr. Stewart's appreciation of the situation was that
the prosecution's case against Wood, due largely to his (disputed) admis-
H   sions to the police officers at the later interviews, was much stronger than
the case against his client Merrick. He foresaw the possibility that if the
judge directed the jury on the lines that they must either convict both
Merrick and Wood, or acquit them both, and that they could not convict
one and acquit the other, Merrick might be pulled down by the weight
of the stronger case against Wood, in spite of warnings that Wood's admissions to the police were not evidence against Merrick. So Mr. Stewart
argued that such a direction should not be given and that the jury should

be told that they could, if they thought fit, acquit Merrick and still A
convict Woods of conspiring with Merrick to steal from delivery vans.
He based his submission on the effect of section 5 (8) and (9) of the
Criminal Law Act 1977, and relied strongly on a passage in the latest
edition of *Smith and Hogan, Criminal Law,* 4th ed. (1978), p. 243. Mr.
Cracknell, for the prosecution, supported his submission which was also
supported by counsel for Holmes, but Mr. Levine, for Wood, argued that
these subsections did not apply in this case which had started before the B
section came into effect. The judge accepted Mr. Levine's submission
and said that in any event he would direct the jury that they should
either convict both Merrick and Wood or acquit them both.

In this court Mr. Stewart put forward the same submission with force
and clarity, Mr. Cracknell adopted a neutral position, but invited the
court, if it was in Mr. Stewart's favour, to consider applying the proviso. C
Mr. Harrison, on behalf of Holmes, and Mr. Levine maintained their
previous submissions. Mr. Stewart contended that the effect of section
5 (8) and (9), particularly subsection (9), was to abolish the practice
hitherto adopted in conspiracy cases of directing the jury either to convict both the persons charged or to acquit both, and that the jury should
be directed to consider the evidence against each defendant separately,
and that it was open to them to convict Wood and acquit Merrick. This D
submission amounts to the proposition that subsection (9) precludes a
judge from directing a jury in a conspiracy case that they must not convict one defendant unless they convict a co-defendant.

The judge gave the following directions to the jury:

"The essential elements of the offence of conspiracy are these—
first, there must be an agreement and that is the real crux of the E
case that you are trying. There must be an agreement. Secondly,
with at least one other person and I stress, members of the jury,
that if you bring in a verdict of guilty it must be against at least
two of the accused. Do not bring in a verdict of guilty against
only one because that cannot be a conspiracy since conspiracy is
an agreement with at least one other person," F

and later he said:

"Well, in so far as it is possible, members of the jury, I must ask
you to consider the evidence against each accused person separately
and before you can convict, as I have said, you must be sure that
two or more of the accused of their own free will agreed to and knew
and intended this illegal scheme of following British Road Service G
lorries and waiting until the lorries were unlocked and the driver had
gone to deliver and then quickly stealing cartons and driving away.
The whole of the charge should be considered and as I have said,
you have it before you in detail and you cannot convict Wood unless
you convict Merrick as well and again, members of the jury, these
two stand or fall together and if you do acquit Wood and Merrick H
well then, members of the jury, you will acquit Holmes and Mrs.
Thornton. If you are in doubt of the guilt of one, well then you will
acquit the other. I hope I have made those matters clear to you."

He went on to warn the jury again and again that statements made to the
police by Wood were not evidence against Merrick.

Section 5 (8) and (9) reads:

A   " (8) The fact that the person or persons who, so far as appears from
      the indictment on which any person has been convicted of con-
      spiracy, were the only other parties to the agreement on which his
      conviction was based have been acquitted of conspiracy by reference
      to that agreement (whether after being tried with the person con-
      victed or separately) shall not be a ground for quashing his convic-
      tion unless under all the circumstances of the case his conviction is
B   inconsistent with the acquittal of the other person or persons in
      question.   (9) Any rule of law or practice inconsistent with the
      provisions of subsection (8) above is hereby abolished."

        In our judgment the effect of these subsections is to complete the
      process begun by the House of Lords in *Director of Public Prosecutions
C   v. Shannon* [1975] A.C. 717, and carried most of the way, of abandoning
      the well-established doctrine of the common law that if two persons are
      accused of conspiring together and one is acquitted and the other con-
      victed, the conviction must be quashed.   It follows that it is no longer
      necessary for trial judges to direct juries that they must convict both or
      acquit both.   But it does not mean that such a direction may not be given
      in proper cases.

D   In the course of their speeches in *Shannon*, their Lordships discussed
      at some length the implications of their decision for trial judges and
      expressed, obiter, conflicting views as to the way in which juries should
      be directed.   All their Lordships, with the exception of Viscount Dilhorne,
      clearly indicated that it was a matter for the discretion of the trial judge,
      depending upon the state of the evidence, whether to direct the jury to
E   find separate verdicts against each conspirator or to find both guilty or
      both not guilty.   Viscount Dilhorne did not specifically refer to cases
      where the evidence against each man was broadly similar.

        The editors of *Smith and Hogan's Criminal Law*, however, have ex-
      pressed the view at p. 243 that the effect of section 5 (8) and (9) of the
      Act of 1977 is that the decision of this court in *Reg. v. Coughlan (Joseph)*
      (1976) 64 Cr.App.R. 11, " is overruled and the opinion of Viscount
F   Dilhorne and Lord Simon of Glaisdale in effect enacted by section 5 (8)
      and (9) of the Act. . . .' "

        With respect, we disagree.   The effect of subsections (8) and (9) in
      our judgment, is to give express statutory effect to what was implicit in
      the decision of the House of Lords in *Director of Public Prosecutions* v.
      Shannon [1975] A.C. 717, namely, that the former practice of automati-
G   cally quashing the conviction of one conspirator where the only other
      alleged conspirator had been acquitted, no longer applies.

        We do not think that these subsections are directed to, or affect the
      situation at trial, except in so far as the abolition of the former practice
      of this court leaves the trial judge with a discretion which he did not
      have under the old law.   The concluding words of subsection (8) preserve
      the power of this court to quash a conviction if, " under all the circum-
H   stances of the case [it] is inconsistent with the acquittal of the other
      person."   It must follow that, if there is a serious risk of inconsistent
      verdicts, the trial judge has a discretion to direct the jury, if he thinks fit,
      to convict both or acquit both.

        The result is that the judge's ruling that subsections (8) and (9) of
      section 5 did not apply to this case because they were not in force when
      the proceedings began was wrong, but the question remains whether his
      decision to direct the jury that they must either convict both Merrick

and Wood, or acquit them both, was correct " under all the circumstances of the case."

The indictment in this case did not charge a conspiracy between Merrick and Wood to steal simpliciter. Instead it charged four persons with conspiring that Merrick and Wood should steal from delivery vans. It was not, therefore, a two-man conspiracy of the *Shannon* type, so that under the old law the judge would not have been obliged to direct the jury to convict both or acquit both, but the unusual wording of the charge made it extremely difficult for the jury to find one guilty and the other not guilty. So the judge was faced with a situation in which there was a real danger that the jury would be seriously confused, and a real risk that they might return inconsistent verdicts. No doubt it was with these dangers in mind that he decided to direct the jury in the terms set out earlier in this judgment. In exercising his discretion, he had, of course, to bear in mind the importance of ensuring that each man was convicted only upon evidence admissible against him.

On the facts of the case there was a considerable amount of evidence, which was equally admissible and cogent as against each of these two men, Merrick and Wood. The additional evidence, which was admissible only as against Wood, were his oral admissions to the interrogating police officers. But these were vigorously denied by Wood and might, for all the judge could tell, have been rejected by the jury. We think that, in any event, the evidence admissible against Merrick, if accepted by the jury, was enough to justify his conviction on the count charged. Moreover, had the jury acquitted Merrick and convicted Wood, Wood might well have appealed to this court on the ground that the verdicts were inconsistent, arguing that the jury must have rejected the evidence of the officers carrying out the surveillance, leaving only the evidence of his admissions at the interviews.

Accordingly, the judge was entitled to take the course that he did. Throughout the summing up he repeatedly emphasised that various statements to the police by Wood were not evidence against Merrick or the others, and he specifically directed the jury, if they were in doubt about the case against either man, to acquit them both. This was enough to ensure that Merrick was not " pulled down " by the evidence of Wood's admissions. Accordingly Merrick's appeal against conviction is dismissed.

So far as the applications by Wood, Holmes, and Mrs. Thornton for leave to appeal against their convictions are concerned, they are all based upon criticisms of details in the summing up. We have carefully considered the grounds of appeal in each case and the submissions of counsel to us in this court but our conclusion is that there is no substance in these criticisms and nothing to lead us to think that these convictions are unsafe. In Mrs. Thornton's case, as we read the summing up, particularly a passage towards the end, the judge was implicitly inviting the jury to acquit her but they did not respond to the invitation. The application in each case, therefore, is refused. The applications for leave to appeal against sentence have not been pursued so they are also refused.

Appeal dismissed.
Applications refused.

Solicitor: *M. D. Shaffner, Wakefield.*

[Reported by MISS EIRA CARYL-THOMAS, Barrister-at-Law]

A

[COURT OF APPEAL]

*DODDS v. WALKER

1980 Feb. 29   Stephenson, Bridge and Templeman L.JJ.

B   *Landlord and Tenant—Business premises (security of tenure)—
    Application for new tenancy—Notice to quit served on
    September 30—Tenant's application for new tenancy made on
    January 31—Whether application made within statutory four
    month period—Landlord and Tenant Act 1954 (2 & 3 Eliz. 2,
    c. 56), s. 29 (3)*

On September 30, 1978, the landlord, under Part II of the
C   Landlord and Tenant Act 1954, gave notice to the tenant to
    determine his tenancy of business premises. Under section 29
    (3) of the Act,[1] the tenant had " four months after the giving
    of the landlord's notice " to apply to the county court for a
    new tenancy. The tenant applied on January 31, 1979. The
    registrar dismissed the application on the basis that it was out
    of time and, on appeal, the judge held that, in computing the
    four months' period under section 29 (3), the day the landlord
D   gave notice was to be excluded but, notwithstanding that
    September was a 30 day month, the period elapsed on the
    corresponding day in the fourth month, namely, January 30,
    and therefore the tenant's application made on the last day
    of January was made one day too late.
        On appeal by the tenant: —
        Held, dismissing the appeal (Bridge L.J. dissenting), that
    under section 29 (3) of the Landlord and Tenant Act 1954, the
E   tenant had four calendar months in which to apply for the
    grant of a new tenancy; that, since in calculating the four
    months' period the day the landlord gave notice was to be
    excluded, the tenant had from midnight on September 30 to
    midnight on the corresponding date in the fourth month in
    which to make his application and, therefore, the tenant had
    made his application one day too late and the county court
    had no jurisdiction to determine whether he should be granted
F   a new tenancy (post, pp. 1066F–G, 1067A, G–H, 1068C–D).
        Migotti v. *Colvill* (1879) 4 C.P.D. 233, C.A. considered.
        Per Bridge L.J. For the purposes of section 29 (3) of the
    Act, the day the landlord served notice to terminate the
    tenancy is to be disregarded and the calculation of the four
    month period begins from the day after the giving of the notice,
    namely, October 1. A period of four calendar months from
    October 1 must expire on January 31 for the reason that the
G   four calendar months which come into computation are the
    actual and entire months of October, November, December
    and January (post, pp. 1064F, H—1065A).

The following cases are referred to in the judgments:

Freeman v. *Read* (1863) 4 B. & S. 174.
Lester v. *Garland* (1808) 15 Ves. 248.
H   *Migotti* v. *Colvill* (1879) 4 C.P.D. 233, Denman J. and C.A.
Webb v. *Fairmaner* (1838) 3 M. & W. 473.

The following additional cases were cited in argument:

Beardmore Motors Ltd. v. *Birch Bros. (Proprietors) Ltd.* [1959] Ch. 298;
    [1958] 2 W.L.R. 975; [1958] 2 All E.R. 311.

[1] Landlord and Tenant Act 1954, s. 29 (3): see post, p. 1063B.

Hodgson v. *Armstrong* [1967] 2 Q.B. 299; [1967] 2 W.L.R. 311; [1967] A
  1 All E.R. 307, C.A.
Marren v. *Dawson Bentley & Co. Ltd.* [1961] 2 Q.B. 135; [1961] 2
  W.L.R. 679; [1961] 1 All E.R. 270.
Radcliffe v. *Bartholomew* [1892] 1 Q.B. 161, D.C.
Rex v. *West Riding of Yorkshire Justices* (1833) 4 B. & Ad. 685.
Young v. *Higgon* (1840) 6 M. & W. 49.

B

APPEAL from Judge Whitehead sitting at Grantham County Court.

By a notice dated September 29, 1978, and served on September 30,
Kenneth Edward Walker, the landlord of business premises at George
Street, Grantham, Lincolnshire, gave notice under section 25 of the
Landlord and Tenant Act 1954 to the tenant, Robert William Dodds
(trading as Cee Bee Autos), to terminate the tenancy on March 31, 1979.
On November 29, 1978, the tenant gave counter-notice under section 29 (2) C
that he was unwilling to give up possession on the expiry date. On January
31, 1979, the tenant applied to the county court for the grant of a new
tenancy pursuant to the provisions of Part II of the Act of 1954. On
February 21, 1979, the landlord gave notice of his intention to apply to the
registrar for an order that the tenant's application should be dismissed on
the ground that he had failed to comply with section 29 (3) of the Act. D
At the hearing on March 23, 1979, the registrar, Mr. A. J. D. Wain, dismissed the tenant's application for the grant of a new lease. On April
27, 1979, the judge dismissed the tenant's appeal against the registrar's
decision on the ground that the tenant's application of January 31, 1979,
had been made out of time for the purposes of section 29 (3) of the Act.

The tenant appealed, asking that his application for renewal of the
tenancy should be heard, on the grounds that the judge was wrong (1) in E
holding that the tenant had failed to comply with the requirements of
section 29 (3) of the Landlord and Tenant Act 1954; and (2) in holding that
the period of four calendar months allowed by the Act following service
of the landlord's notice on September 30, 1978, had expired on January
30, 1979.

F

Mathew Thorpe for the tenant.
James Guthrie for the landlord.

STEPHENSON L.J. I will ask Bridge L.J. to give the first judgment.

BRIDGE L.J. The applicant is the tenant of premises known as 34 G
George Street, Grantham, Lincolnshire. I shall refer to him in this judgment as the tenant. He holds a business tenancy of those premises to
which Part II of the Landlord and Tenant Act 1954 applies.

In September 1978 the respondent, to whom I shall refer as the
landlord, gave notice under section 25 of the Act to determine the tenancy
on March 31, 1979. That notice was dated September 29, but was served
on September 30, 1978. On November 29, 1978, the tenant duly gave H
counter-notice pursuant to section 29 (2) of the Act, intimating that he
would not be willing to give up possession of the premises on the expiry
date mentioned in the landlord's notice. On January 31, 1979, the tenant
made his application pursuant to section 24 of the Act to the Grantham
County Court for the grant of a new tenancy.

On February 21, 1979, the landlord applied to dismiss the tenant's application for a new tenancy on the ground that it had been made out of time

A   under section 29 (3) of the Act. That application was heard by the
registrar on March 23, 1979. He acceded to it and dismissed the tenant's
application as one which the court had no jurisdiction to entertain. The
tenant appealed from the registrar's order to the judge. On April 27,
Judge Whitehead heard that appeal and dismissed it. The tenant now
appeals from the judge's order to this court.

B   I turn at once to the relevant statutory provision, section 29 (3) of the
Landlord and Tenant Act 1954, which provides as far as relevant:

> " No application under subsection (1) of section 24 of this Act shall
> be entertained unless it is made not less than two nor more than four
> months after the giving of the landlord's notice under section 25 of
> this Act . . ."

C   Reading that section, as we must, in the light of the Interpretation Act 1889
the period of four months referred to is a period of four calendar months.
Accordingly the question for decision is this: when a landlord's notice to
determine a tenancy under section 25 of the Act is served on September
30 in any year, when does the four month period after the giving of that
notice within which the tenant is allowed to apply for a new tenancy, expire?
The landlord contends and the registrar and judge have found, that it
D   expires on January 30. The tenant contends that it expires on January
31, the day when he made his application. It is perhaps not inappropriate,
as Stephenson L.J. observed in the course of the argument, that we should
be called on to decide such a point on February 29 in a leap year.

    There is no direct authority on the point, so it falls to be decided, it
seems to me, as one of principle on the proper application to the facts
E   of this case of the provisions of section 29 (3) as correctly construed.

    In calculating the period of four months, to which the subsection refers,
no difficulty whatever arises whenever the landlord's notice in any month
is given on any day in the month from the 1st to the 27th. It is quite
clear on authority that in any such case the four month period will then
expire on the corresponding date in the fourth succeeding month to
the date on which the landlord's notice was served. A calculation made on
F   that basis I will refer to for convenience as a calculation applying the
corresponding date principle. A moment's reflection is sufficient to demonstrate that the corresponding date principle cannot be of universal application. That is most clearly demonstrated by the illustration of a landlord's
notice under section 25 which is served in a non-leap year on either
October 29, 30 or 31. In each of those cases the period of four months
G   after the giving of the notice necessarily expires on February 28 because
the month of February in a non-leap year has no 29, 30 or 31 and to
extend the period beyond the last day of February would be to extend it
beyond the fourth and into the fifth month after the giving of the landlord's notice. So far what I have said it supported by authority and I
need only refer to Migotti v. Colvill (1879) 4 C.P.D. 233. That was a
case where the question in issue was on what date a term of one month's
H   imprisonment expired when sentence had been passed on October 31. It
was common ground in that case that the first day of the sentence of
one calendar month was to be reckoned as the day on which sentence
was passed and the prisoner was taken in custody from the court to the
prison. The court held, contrary to the contention on behalf of the
prisoner, that the period of one calendar month expired on November 30.
I need only read a short passage from the judgment of Cotton L.J., at
p. 238:

"Prisoners cannot always be imprisoned during one particular calendar **A**
month, in the sense of a month the name of which is to be found in the
calendar. What then is the meaning of the term when the sentence
begins otherwise than at the first day of a calendar month?"

(i.e. for the purpose of that case, on October 31). Returning to the
quotation, Cotton L.J. continues, at pp. 238–239:

"Although there are difficulties, I am of the opinion that the right **B**
rule is that which has been laid down by Denman J."—who, I interpose, was the judge at first instance—"and the other members of
this court. The imprisonment ends at 12 o'clock on the day immediately preceding the day in the following month corresponding to
the day on which the imprisonment began."

Again, interposing my own observation, there is what I have called the **C**
"corresponding date principle" being applied; but Cotton L.J. continues:

"If there are not enough days in the second month to satisfy this rule
the calculation is made in favour of the prisoner, and he will be
liberated on the last day of the month."

So if a prisoner had been imprisoned on January 29, 30 and 31, for one
calendar month, he would be released on February 28. The corresponding **D**
date principle could not apply.

The question we have to consider is the converse of that case. The
question we have to consider is what happens when notice is given on the
last day of a short month, here September 30, and the period of four
months after the giving of that notice has to be calculated. Does it take
one to the 30th day of the fourth succeeding month, or does it take one to **E**
the 31st? Exactly the same question would, of course, arise in relation to
a notice served on February 28. Would the period of four months expire
on June 28 or on June 30?

The key to the solution of this problem, to my mind, lies in the principle
for which there is abundant authority, that in calculating the period of
four months after the giving of a notice under section 25 of the Act of 1954,
for the purposes of section 29 (3), one must disregard in the computation **F**
the day of service of the notice and commence to calculate the running
of the four month period from the day after the giving of the notice;
in this case, therefore, October 1. That principle, and its application
to section 29 (3) of the Act of 1954, is not in issue, but, if authority
were required for it, it is sufficient to cite *Halsbury's Laws of England*,
3rd ed., vol. 37 (1962) para. 168, which is headed "Exclusion of first **G**
day," and reads:

"The general rule in cases in which a period is fixed within which a
person must act or take the consequences is that the day of the act or
event from which the period runs should not be counted against him."

We have been taken through a number of cases cited in the footnote to
that proposition which clearly demonstrate that it is well founded. **H**

Accordingly the question we have to decide, restated, in my judgment,
becomes this: when does a period of four calendar months beginning on
the first day of October expire? In my judgment the answer to that
question must be on January 31, for the simple reason that the four
calendar months, and the only four calendar months, which come into the
computation, are the actual and entire months of October, November,
December and January, and I can see no reason whatsoever why the period

A of four months should expire before the expiry of the fourth of those months, namely, on January 31.

We have been referred to a number of authorities. None of them, as I have said, is directly in point, but possibly one throws some light on the matter. That is *Webb* v. *Fairmaner* (1838) 3 M. & W. 473. In that case, goods had been sold on October 5 to be paid for in two months, but the seller issued his writ claiming the price from the buyer on December 5.
B It was held that his action was premature because it could not properly be commenced until the expiration of December 5, in other words, disregarding the day on which the goods were sold as a day not to be computed in the period of two months allowed to the buyer for payment. In its decision *Webb's* case is no more than yet another illustration of the application of the corresponding date principle to a case where a calendar
C month has to be measured as between two broken months, but in my judgment it is not without significance to find Parke B. observing, at p. 476:

"Whatever doubt there might have been upon the point before the decision in *Lester* v. *Garland* (1808) 15 Ves. 248, since that case the rule appears to be that the time is to be calculated exclusively of the day on which the contract was made: the party is to have two
D entire calendar months in which to make payment, exclusively of the day of sale."

Applying that statement of principle to the circumstances of a case arising under section 29 (3) of the Act of 1954, I would say that a party is to have four entire calendar months in which to make application for the grant of a new tenancy, exclusive of the day on which the landlord's notice under
E section 25 was served on him.

An authority, which is said to be an authority the other way, is relied on by Mr. Guthrie for the landlord. It is *Freeman* v. *Read* (1863) 4 B. & S. 174 where an action of a particular kind was one for which one month's notice had to be given. Notice of the action was, in fact, given to the proposed defendant on April 28, 1862, and the action was commenced on May 29, following, and it was there held that notice of action
F was given in due time; again an illustration of the application of the corresponding date principle. But the passage relied on in argument by Mr. Guthrie is a passage from the judgment of Cockburn C.J. where he said, at p. 184:

"In a case like the present where the months are broken," (and I pause to emphasise that phrase, "where the months are broken":
G it seems to govern all that follows) "the day on which the notice was given being excluded, the calendar month or other period of time required is complete when, starting from a given day in the first month, you come to the corresponding day in the succeeding month whatever be the length of either. This is in accordance with common usage, especially with regard to bills of exchange, and with the sense of
H mankind. As Mr. Kingdon argued with great force, you cannot, in reckoning a calendar month, include two days of the same number."

That last sentence was particularly emphasised by Stephenson L.J. but applied to this case that sentence has to be translated; in reckoning four calendar months for the purposes of section 29 (3) you cannot include five days of the same number. In his reply to Mr. Guthrie, Mr. Thorpe asked rhetorically, and to my mind with great force, where, in the computation for which the tenant here contends, concluding the four month period on

January 31, is any day of the same number found appearing for a fifth   **A**
time? The only possible candidate for that role must be September 30;
but ex hypothesi that date is to be disregarded. I appreciate it may be
said that this conclusion leads to anomalies but, whichever way the matter
is decided, there are bound to be anomalies. There could be no greater
anomaly than that to which I have already drawn attention in the circumstances that when, in a non-leap year, a landlord's notice is served on
October 29, 30 or 31, it does not make any difference to the date when   **B**
the tenant's four-month period for making his application expires; in each
case it expires on February 28. The short answer to any argument based
on anomalies is that one must expect anomalies so long as Parliament
chooses to specify periods for taking some action under statute in terms
of calendar months which are in their nature of unequal length.

    Accordingly, I have reached the conclusion that the judge and the   **C**
registrar were wrong, and that the appeal ought to be allowed so that the
tenant's application can proceed and be heard on its merits; but I express
that conclusion with diffidence, not only because I know that it is at variance
with the views of the judge and the registrar, but still more so because I
know also that it is at variance with the views which are about to be
expressed by Stephenson and Templeman L.JJ. Despite the diffidence,
however, I am bound to say that I have no doubt or hesitation in reaching   **D**
my conclusion. It seems to me that the point is abundantly clear and had
it been up to me, I would have allowed the appeal.

    TEMPLEMAN L.J. On September 30, 1978, the landlord served notice
under Part II of the Landlord and Tenant Act 1954 determining the
tenancy of the applicant. By section 29 (3) of the Act, if the tenant   **E**
wished to apply for a new tenancy, he was obliged to apply " not less
than two nor more than four months after the giving of the landlord's
notice . . ."

    The tenant applied to the county court on January 31, 1979, and
Judge Whitehead, sitting in the Grantham County Court on April 27, 1979,
decided that the tenant's application was too late. The tenant appeals to   **F**
this court.

    When time is limited by reference to calendar months no account
can be taken of the fact that some months are longer or shorter than
others. February equals March. In my judgment if an act is authorised to be performed on any arbitrary day in any month of the year,
then one month elapses on the corresponding day of the next month, provided that the day of the act itself is excluded from the computation.   **G**
That is what Bridge L.J. has felicitously referred to, and I understand to
be the corresponding day principle, evolved by the authorities to which
Mr. Guthrie for the landlord referred. I see no reason for engrafting on
that principle an exception which depends on the mere accident of the
particular date of service of a notice and on the particular month which
follows the date of service. It is clear that if a month's notice is served on   **H**
December 31, an application on February 1 would be more than one month
after the giving of the notice. If a month's notice is served on February
15, an application on March 16 would be more than one month after the
giving of the notice in any year, including a leap year. If a month's notice
is served on January 29, 30 or 31, an application on March 1 would be
more than one month after the giving of the notice, whether February has
28 or 29 days.

A   In the present case notice was given on September 30: the relevant corresponding date was January 30. Time began to run when the clock struck midnight on September 30 and expired four months later to the stroke, when the clock struck midnight on the corresponding January 30. In the result, the tenant's application on January 31 was made more than four months after the giving of the landlord's notice on September 30. It does not seem to me that a landlord who happens to choose the last day

B   of February, April, June, September or November, to serve his notice should be in any different position from a landlord who serves his notice on any of the other 360 days. All that the tenant has to do is to look at the day when the notice was served and if he makes his application on a later day than that, when the necessary number of months have expired, then he knows that his application is doomed to failure.

C   In my judgment, the passage which Bridge L.J. read from *Webb* v. *Fairmane*r, 3 M. & W. 473 does not assist the matter one way or the other. It says that time is to be calculated exclusively of the day on which the contract was made. But the question which has to be answered here is whether the application was made more than four months after the giving of the landlord's notice. It also says that the party was to have two entire calendar months in which to make payment exclusively of the day of sale;

D   and in my judgment, once the corresponding day principle is accepted, the tenant in the present case has four entire months in which to make his application. If the landlord had served his notice on September 29, the last available date for application by the tenant would admittedly have been the corresponding January 29. The landlord served his notice on September 30 and therefore the last available date for application by the tenant was

E   the corresponding January 30. By claiming that his last day for application was one day later, namely, January 31, the tenant is breaking the corresponding day principle and is attempting to compensate himself for the non-existence of September 31 by ignoring the existence of January 30. He is not entitled to do this. In conformity with authority and consistency, one or more calendar months' notice may be served on any arbitrary date; all months are assumed to be equal; every non-existing day is ignored; no

F   one is entitled to ignore an existing day or to compensation for any non-existing day; and any relevant corresponding day marks the end of the period of notice.

    Like the judge I have some sympathy with the tenant but he had four months, the statute does not allow more and there are obvious reasons for finality. The moving finger writes and, having writ, moves on and the

G   court, unlike Proust, is unable to transform time lost into time regained. I would dismiss the appeal.

    STEPHENSON L.J. The tenant is required by section 29 (3) of the Act of 1954 to apply for a new tenancy not more than four months after September 30, 1978. He made his application on January 31, 1979. Like Templeman L.J. I agree with the registrar and the judge in the county court that he made it more than four months after September 30 because

H   those four months expired at midnight on January 30, 1979. I know that by the Interpretation Act 1889 those four months are calendar months and that September 30 is excluded by the rule in *Lester* v. *Garland* (1808) 15 Ves. 248, now too well established to be doubted, from counting against the tenant. I accept the statement of the rule which Bridge L.J. had read from *Halsbury's Laws of England*, 3rd ed., vol. 37, para. 168.

I also accept the statement at paragraph 143 of the same volume A
which provides:

"When the period prescribed is a calendar month running from any
arbitrary date the period expires with the day in the succeeding month
immediately preceding the day corresponding to the date upon which
the period starts; save that, if the period starts at the end of a calendar
month which contains more days than the next succeeding month, the
period expires at the end of the latter month."   B

The last sentence is, in my judgment, supported by *Migotti* v. *Colvill*,
4 C.P.D. 233 to which Bridge L.J. referred as a decision on the
corresponding date principle. If the relevant calendar month in which
the period expires is too short to provide a corresponding date, the
period expires on the last day of that month, but if that period expires C
in a calendar month which is long enough to provide a corresponding
date, that date appears to me to be the date on which the period expires.
If the day when the period begins to run is excluded from counting
against the tenant making the application and happens to be the last
day of a shorter month like September, it means that the four months
must be reckoned from midnight on September 30, but does not, in my
opinion, mean that, because the reckoning starts as midnight ushers in D
the first day of a new month, the four months' period runs over that
corresponding date in the longer month into the last day of that month.
     I find much of interest but, like Bridge and Templeman L.JJ., nothing
of direct assistance in the authorities which have been cited to us, though
some touched on other difficulties caused by the awkward fact that the
months of the calendar are uneven in length. I do not find the answer to E
the short question raised by this appeal as easy as Bridge and Templeman
L.JJ., for which I may perhaps be excused, by the difference of opinion
between them on what the right answer is. I am however of the opinion
that there is no sufficient reason for not applying the corresponding date
principle, which I find simple, natural and easy for the tenant to understand, and which, were it not for the different opinion of Bridge L.J., I
would accept as more in accord with what Cockburn C.J. called "the F
sense of mankind," in *Freeman* v. *Read*, 4 B. & S. 174, 184, whether or
not the months to be considered are broken in that they do not run from
the last day of a month. I too, would dismiss the appeal.

*Appeal dismissed with costs, to include
costs reserved by court below.* G
Leave to appeal.

Solicitors: *Norton & Hamilton, Grantham; Roythorne & Co., Spalding.*

[Reported by MISS HENRIETTA STEINBERG, Barrister-at-Law]
                                                                          H

A

[COURT OF APPEAL]

* C.S.I. INTERNATIONAL CO. LTD. *v.* ARCHWAY PERSONNEL
(MIDDLE EAST) LTD.

B

[1978 C. No. 7073]

1980 Feb. 29   Roskill and Eveleigh L.JJ. and Walton J.

*Practice—Pleadings—Counterclaim—Writ issued in respect of dis-
honoured cheque—No defence—Summary judgment for
plaintiffs—Judgment debt satisfied—Defendants purporting to
serve counterclaim—Whether service valid—R.S.C., Ord. 15,
r. 2 (1)*

C

The plaintiff company, incorporated in Thailand, agreed
with the defendants, an English limited company, to recruit
staff for work in the Middle East. The agreement was made
in Thailand. A dispute arose between the parties, in settlement of which the defendants agreed to pay to the plaintiffs
£44,816 by three postdated cheques. The first cheque for
£15,000, payable on July 6, 1978, was dishonoured on presentation. The plaintiffs issued a writ in respect of the
dishonoured cheque, to which there was no defence. The
plaintiffs applied for summary judgment under R.S.C., Ord. 14.
The defendants filed an affidavit seeking a stay of execution
of the judgment the plaintiffs were expected to obtain, and
adverted to a prospective counterclaim. The matter came
before Master Lubbock on November 28, 1978. He gave
judgment with interest for the plaintiffs and refused a stay
of execution. The defendants made no request for directions
with respect to the counterclaim. On April 10, 1979, the
defendants' solicitors sent to the plaintiffs' solicitors a bankers'
draft for the full judgment debt with interest and costs. On
May 1, the defendants' solicitors sent a document entitled
" Defence and Counterclaim " to the plaintiffs' solicitors who
refused to accept service of it. The defendants signed
judgment in default on the counterclaim. Master Lubbock
set aside that judgment on the ground of irregularity. The
defendants appealed to Sir Douglas Frank Q.C., sitting as a
deputy High Court judge, who allowed the appeal and gave
the defendants leave to counterclaim.

On the plaintiffs' appeal: —

Held, allowing the appeal, that where a counterclaim had
been raised but had not been formally pleaded or made the
subject of a summons for directions, once judgment for a
party had been obtained and fully satisfied thereafter there
was no action in existence in which the counterclaim could
be made; and that, accordingly, the defendants were unable
to serve a counterclaim on the plaintiffs.

Decision of Sir Douglas Frank Q.C. sitting as a deputy
High Court judge in the Queen's Bench Division reversed.

D

E

F

G

H

No cases are referred to in the judgment.

The following cases were cited in argument:

General Railway Syndicate, In re (Whiteley's Case) [1900] Ch. 365, C.A.
Gniezno, The [1968] P. 418; [1967] 3 W.L.R. 705; [1967] 2 All E.R.
738.
Hobson v. *Monks* [1884] W.N. 8.

C.S.I. International v. Archway Personnel (C.A.)   **[1980]**

APPEAL from Sir Douglas Frank Q.C. sitting as a deputy High Court   A
judge.

By writ dated September 19, 1978, the plaintiffs claimed against the
defendants as drawers of a cheque for £15,000 dated August 6, 1978,
payable to the plaintiffs, which cheque was dishonoured on presentation.
The plaintiffs applied for summary judgment under R.S.C., Ord. 14.
The defendants filed an affidavit which disclosed no defence but
requested a stay of execution of the expected judgment for the plaintiffs   B
since the defendants intended to enter a counterclaim.   On November
29, 1978, the case came before Master Lubbock who gave judgment
for the plaintiffs with interest and refused a stay of execution.   The
judgment was not satisfied until April 10, 1979, when the defendants'
solicitors sent to the plaintiffs' solicitors a bankers' draft for the entire
sum due, namely the debt, interest and costs, and enclosed a document   C
headed " Counterclaim."   The plaintiffs' solicitors refused to accept
service of the document.   On May 1, 1979, the defendants' solicitors
purported to serve a fresh document entitled " Defence and Counterclaim " of which the plaintiffs' solicitors also refused to accept service.
On May 25, the defendants' solicitors entered judgment in default on
the counterclaim.   The plaintiffs applied to Master Lubbock, who on
July 18, 1979, set aside for irregularity the judgment in default.   The   D
defendant appealed to Sir Douglas Frank Q.C. sitting as a deputy High
Court judge, who allowed the appeal, and gave the defendants leave
to counterclaim.   The plaintiffs appealed.

The facts are stated in the judgment of Roskill L.J.

L. J. Libbert for the plaintiffs.   E
I. E. Jacob for the defendants.

ROSKILL L.J.   This is an appeal from an order of Sir Douglas Frank,
sitting as a deputy High Court judge in chambers on January 18, 1980.
The deputy judge gave judgment in open court at the request of the
parties because he said that the question raised was important, namely,
whether a counterclaim could be served after a final judgment had been   F
obtained by a plaintiff and indeed satisfied.

The facts are a little unusual and raise a curious point under the
Rules of the Supreme Court.   The plaintiffs are a company incorporated
in Thailand; they are C.S.I. International Company Ltd.   The defendants
are an English limited company, Archway Personnel (Middle East) Ltd.
which seems to be the alter ego of a gentleman called Mr. Paschali.   G
Those two companies apparently worked together to provide manpower
for contracting work in the Middle East and, in particular, Saudi Arabia,
and the defendants made arrangements with another company called
Avco Dallah Ltd., which we are told was a consortium of a United
States company and a Saudi Arabian company under which the defendants
supplied such manpower for Avco.

An agreement was made between the plaintiffs and the defendants   H
under which the plaintiffs would recruit persons in Thailand for working
in the Middle East, and it is common ground that that agreement between
the plaintiffs and the defendants was made in Thailand.

Various disputes, with the details of which we are not concerned,
thereafter arose.   On June 6, 1978, a settlement of those disputes was
made.   The terms do not matter save this; paragraph 6 provided that
the defendants would pay the plaintiffs sums totalling £44,816 by three

A postdated cheques endorsed personally by three persons named in the clause. The first cheque was for £15,000 payable on July 6; the second was for a like sum payable on August 6, and the third, the balance of the sum I have already mentioned, namely £13,816, was payable on September 6, 1978.

The first postdated cheque was presented on due date and was dishonoured on presentation. The plaintiffs thereupon issued a writ; at
B the same time there was another writ concerning a dispute between the defendants and Avco, with which we are not concerned.

On the modern authorities, to an action brought in these circumstances on a dishonoured cheque there was no defence. However the defendants put in an affidavit by Mr. Paschali. That affidavit, with all respect to the draftsman—no doubt he did his best—obviously disclosed no defence.
C But it did say that there was an action pending by the defendants against Avco and for that reason the defendants sought a stay of execution upon any Ord. 14 judgment which the plaintiffs were likely to get. Paragraph 11 reads:

"... it is true that the cheque in the sum of £15,000 has not been paid and that the plaintiffs are entitled to judgment for this. However
D   I would ask that the court make an order that this judgment not be enforced until after the hearing of a counterclaim to be brought by [the defendants] against the plaintiffs. The nature of the counterclaim is that the plaintiffs were agents for [the defendants]. From January 1978 whilst the agency agreement was still in existence they dealt with Avco Dallah directly and in breach of their duty of good faith. They claim commission on workers who were in
E   fact recruited by them as our agents and ' stole ' our contract with Avco Dallah. It is the [defendant] company's intention to bring a counterclaim claiming damages for this breach of duty of good faith. However it will take some time for all counsel's requirements as to this to be satisfied and the company cannot make its counterclaim until certain further research has taken place . . .".

F   That affidavit, if I may be forgiven the colloquialism, did not cut much ice with Master Lubbock. He entered judgment for the plaintiffs for £15,000 and interest, making a total of £15,476·71. He refused a stay of execution. There was, on the occasion of that summons for judgment, no request whatever made for directions in connection with a counterclaim which had been—I avoid the use of the word " raised "—but I will say " adumbrated " in that paragraph in that affidavit.
G   That judgment was obtained on November 28, 1978. The plaintiffs were not immediately paid. They took various steps to try to enforce that judgment. On April 10, 1979, the defendants' solicitors wrote a letter to the plaintiffs' solicitors saying that they were glad to tell the plaintiffs' solicitors that their clients had put them in funds to discharge the sums due, totalling £16,016·44 which was the amount of the judgment
H and interest and costs. They sent, under cover of that letter of April 10, a banker's draft for that sum, and they added—and one must note that this was some four months after the date of the judgment—that they enclosed a counterclaim by way of service. The letter goes on:

" Our client is very concerned that your clients are a Thai company and if our client is successful and we believe they will be there will be no assets in this country against which the counterclaim and costs could be enforced."

That counterclaim which has at least the merit of brevity, was settled   A
by Mr. Jacob. It is headed " Counterclaim." That document was not
welcomed by the plaintiffs' solicitors. They wrote back on April 12
saying:

> " The action against [the defendants] is closed, and your clients
> have no right to serve a counterclaim within the context of those
> proceedings. We accordingly return it herewith . . . ".   B

They suggested that fresh proceedings be brought against the plaintiffs
in Thailand. The defendants' solicitors replied on April 18:

> " Prior to serving the counterclaim upon you we discussed the matter
> with counsel who stated we were quite entitled to serve the counter-
> claim in this action despite the fact of the judgment. The counter-
> claim is therefore returned and we should be obliged to know whether   C
> you intend to serve a defence to counterclaim otherwise we will
> proceed with the summons for directions."

The counterclaim was again sent back, on April 24, by the plaintiffs'
solicitors. On April 26, the defendants' solicitors, in a succinct letter
said: " Order 15, rule 3, sub-paragraph 3. Counterclaim returned.
Yours faithfully."   D
On April 27 the plaintiffs' solicitors acknowledged that letter. Once
again they sent the unhappy counterclaim back and drew attention to
one of the rules. Then on May 1 the defendants came back yet again,
agreeing that they had served a counterclaim but not a document which
was also a defence to which the counterclaim was attached. So the
defendants, at that point, had a second bite at the cherry and wrote: E

> " . . . and we therefore serve a defence and counterclaim and agree
> that the counterclaim we have previously served was of no effect
> whatsoever."

Enclosed with that letter was Mr. Jacob's second attempt at a pleading;
it was in exactly the same language as before save that it was headed:
" Defence and Counterclaim." The " defence " says: F

> " The defendant admits the claim and will set off so much of the
> counterclaim as will totally or partially extinguish the plaintiffs'
> claim."

One admires Mr. Jacob's ingenuity, if he will allow me to say so,
since, at that point, judgment had already been signed against his clients   G
and satisfied so there was no liability left to admit. But it was said that
the counterclaim was bad unless it was attached to a defence and so the
battle concerning the counterclaim continued.
Ultimately, the defendants signed judgment in default against the
plaintiffs on that counterclaim. The matter then went back to Master
Lubbock, and he set aside that default judgment on the ground of
irregularity.   H
There was an appeal to Sir Douglas Frank, sitting as a deputy High
Court judge in chambers, and Sir Douglas Frank allowed the appeal to
a limited extent. He purported to say he was setting aside the judgment
" on the merits." We are told that that phrase was used by agreement
between counsel, and not by the court. With respect, it is not a very
happy phrase. But what I think it was intended to convey was that this
counterclaim had been properly served and therefore the plaintiffs should

A be required to serve a defence to counterclaim, for which the deputy judge gave leave.

Sir Douglas, as I have said, delivered his judgment in open court. The plaintiffs appeal saying that Sir Douglas Frank's order was wrong and that the master's order was right. The plaintiffs say that they should not have been required to serve a defence to that counterclaim.

B It will have been observed from the chronology which I have outlined that the so-called defence and counterclaim was not served until after the judgment, which the plaintiffs had obtained against the defendants, had been fully satisfied as to principal, interest and costs. Nonetheless it is said that the defendants were at that time entitled to serve that defence and counterclaim.

In order to consider the merits of the rival submissions, it is neces-C sary to start with the provisions of the Supreme Court of Judicature (Consolidation) Act 1925. The relevant sections start at section 39. The most relevant section, for present purposes, on which the relevant Rules of the Supreme Court are based, is section 39 (1). This provides:

D "The court or judge shall have power to grant to any defendant in respect of any equitable estate or right or other matter or equity, and also in respect of any legal estate, right or title claimed or asserted by him—(a) all such relief against any plaintiff or petitioner as the defendant has properly claimed by his pleading, and as the court or judge might have granted in any suit instituted for that purpose by that defendant against the same plaintiff or petitioner; and (b) all such relief relating to or connected with the original subject of the cause or matter, claimed in like manner against any E other person. . . ."

It is necessary against the background of that statutory provision, which is the foundation for the relevant rules, to look for a moment at certain Rules of the Supreme Court. I need not read Ord. 14, rr. 1 and 2, but r. 3 reads:

F "(1) Unless on the hearing of an application under rule 1 either the court dismisses the application or the defendant satisfies the court with respect to the claim, or the part of a claim, to which the application relates that there is an issue or question in dispute which ought to be tried or that there ought for some other reason to be a trial of that claim or part, the court may give such judgment for the plaintiff against that defendant on that claim or part as may be G just having regard to the nature of the remedy or relief claimed. (2) The court may by order and subject to such conditions, if any, as may be just, stay execution of any judgment given against a defendant under this rule until after the trial of any counterclaim made or raised by the defendant in the action."

H I draw attention to that phrase "made or raised" in contrast to the language of Order 15, to which I now turn. Ord. 15, r. 2, deals with causes of actions and counterclaims against a plaintiff, and provides:

"(1) Subject to rule 5 (2) a defendant in any action who alleges that he has any claim or is entitled to any relief or remedy against a plaintiff in the action in respect of any matter (whenever and however arising) may, instead of bringing a separate action, make a" —notice the word is "make" and not "make or raise"—" counterclaim in respect of that matter; and where he does so he must add A the counterclaim to his defence."

I turn to Ord. 18, r. 3:

"(1) A plaintiff on whom a defendant serves a defence must serve a reply on that defendant if it is needed for compliance with rule 8, and if no reply is served, rule 14 (1) will apply. (2) A plaintiff on whom a defendant serves a counterclaim must, if he intends to B defend it, serve on that defendant a defence to counterclaim."

Various points were argued before the judge and have been repeated by Mr. Libbert in this court. Mr. Libbert put in the forefront of his argument, as he did before the judge, that it was not possible to have a counterclaim in any circumstances unless there was a defence to which that counterclaim could be attached. The judge, after setting out the C rules and orders to which I have referred, said:

"In my judgment these absurdities and anomalies are not necessary if one gives to the rule the meaning that the counterclaim must be added to the defence where a defence has been delivered and to reject the meaning that a counterclaim must be pursued by a separate action where no defence has been delivered. It seems to D me, although it is not necessary to my decision, that the reason for the requirement is to minimise the number of pleadings and that is linked with Ord. 18, r. 3 (3) where a plaintiff is required to serve a defence and reply to a counterclaim in the same document."

On that point I find myself, with respect, in complete agreement with E the judge and I have nothing more to say on that point.

Then Mr. Libbert said there was no power to deliver a counterclaim once there was a judgment given under Order 14 and there was no stay of execution upon that judgment. Of course, in many cases before the master and the judge in chambers, this would not be a live point, as Mr. Libbert accepted, for the reason that no useful purpose would be served by a plaintiff seeking to take this point against a defendant. But here, F plainly, the defendants are in difficulties under Order 11, in serving the plaintiffs in a separate action, and therefore this point (although it would not arise in the ordinary way) is of particular importance. I am bound to say that, for the reasons Sir Douglas gave, I do not think there is anything to stop a defendant serving a counterclaim—and I use the word "serve" as a neutral word but perhaps I should have said G "making" a counterclaim, where there is a judgment against him which has not been stayed, provided that counterclaim falls within the general purview of section 39 of the Act of 1925 and other relevant rules to which I have referred.

But what happened here was that nothing was done about the counterclaim on the Order 14 summons before the master, even if one assumes that paragraph 11 which I have already read from the affidavit, H can be said to "raise" a counterclaim for the purposes of the relevant part of Ord. 14, r. 3 (2). Thereafter month after month elapsed and the judgment in favour of the plaintiffs was wholly satisfied before any attempt was made to advance or serve or, to use the wording of the rule, to make a counterclaim.

Walton J. asked Mr. Jacob what his submission was regarding any possible time limit upon "making" a counterclaim. Mr. Jacob grasped

A the nettle. He said there was no relevant time limit because there was a lacuna in the rules in the case where a judgment had not been stayed. He claimed that a defendant was at liberty at any time thereafter to deliver a counterclaim. Now in a case such as the present that would have most curious results. A counterclaim may be barred by the Limitation Act 1939 but as the notes to Ord. 15, r. 2 in *The Supreme Court Practice* (1979), at p. 166 point out, section 28 of that Act provides

B that

> " a claim by way of set-off or counterclaim is deemed to be a separate action and to have been commenced on the same date as the action in which it is pleaded."

If Mr. Jacob's argument is taken to its logical conclusion, then not-

C withstanding that the plaintiffs had obtained full satisfaction of the judgment, the defendant can, years later, as it were, out of the blue, serve a counterclaim. I do not think that is right. It may be that certain amendments are required and could, with advantage, be made to the rules in order to make clear what the position is. But I rest my decision on this simple point: where a counterclaim, even if it has previously been raised, has not been the subject of a summons for

D directions or when required of a formal pleading before the time when the plaintiff had received full satisfaction of the judgment which he has obtained against the defendants, I do not think there is still extant any action by the plaintiffs in which the defendants could properly counterclaim against them. The action had, for all practical purposes, come to an end when satisfaction of the judgment had been obtained.

E I have considerable sympathy for the defendants; it may be that if other steps had been taken at other times other results might have followed. I do not know, and I express no opinion. Suffice it to say that the master was right and, with great respect to Sir Douglas, I do not think his order was right. I should perhaps say that many of the points taken in this court were not argued fully or perhaps at all before the deputy judge. It may well be that had they been so argued he

F would have reached the same conclusion as we have done.

I would allow the appeal to this extent: I would set aside the default judgment which the defendants obtained against the plaintiffs, and Sir Douglas's order that a defence to the counterclaim should be filed. It seems to me that the counterclaim was not properly served; there was a material irregularity in its service since the defendants had no right

G to serve it; therefore in the result the master's order should stand.

EVELEIGH L.J. Section 36 of the Supreme Court of Judicature (Consolidation) Act 1925 reads:

> " Subject to the express provisions of any other Act, in every civil cause or matter commenced in the High Court, law and equity shall

H be administered by the High Court and the Court of Appeal, as the case may be, according to the provisions of the seven sections of this Act next following."

One such section of course is section 39 which relates to the jurisdiction of the court in relation to a counterclaim. It seems to me that R.S.C., Ord. 15 can only operate under section 39, which itself operates under section 36; in other words, there has to be a cause or matter in which a counterclaim has been or can be properly pleaded in accordance with

the words of section 39, and in the present case it has not been pleaded
even though it may perhaps have been " raised." No directions have
been given relating to a counterclaim before the judgment was satisfied
and consequently in my opinion there was no cause or matter extant
that could cover any proceedings in relation to a counterclaim that
was not yet properly pleaded.

I agree with the order proposed by Roskill L.J.

WALTON J. I agree with both the judgments which have fallen from
Roskill and Eveleigh L.JJ. and I also agree with the order which should
be made.

> *Appeal allowed.*
> *Order of Sir Douglas Frank Q.C. set*
> *aside. Order of Master Lubbock of*
> *November 29, 1978, restored.*
> *No order as to costs.*

Solicitors: *Baker & McKenzie; Eric Cheek & Co*

[Reported by SUSAN DENNY, Barrister-at-Law]

[QUEEN'S BENCH DIVISION]

*** N.V. SLAVENBURG'S BANK v. INTERCONTINENTAL NATURAL
RESOURCES LTD. AND OTHERS**

[1976 N. No. 68]

1979   Feb. 5, 6, 7, 8, 9, 12, 13; 22   Lloyd J.

> *Company—Charge—Registration—Foreign company trading in*
> *England—Company not registered in England—Company*
> *charging property as security for credit facilities from bank—*
> *Bank not registering charge—Company in liquidation—Whether*
> *charges void against liquidators—Whether charges void as un-*
> *registered bills of sale—Companies Act 1948 (11 & 12 Geo. 6,*
> *c. 38), ss. 95, 106—Bills of Sale of Act (1878) Amendment*
> *Act 1882 (45 & 46 Vict., c. 43), s. 17*

The defendant oil company, which was incorporated in
Bermuda in February 1974 and not registered in the United
Kingdom, dealt in crude oil and refined petroleum products.
On June 1, 1974, the defendant oil company entered into a
service agreement with a company incorporated in the United
Kingdom. On June 13, 1974, the oil company entered into
three agreements governed by Dutch law with the plaintiff
bank, which was incorporated in the Netherlands. By a general
credit agreement the bank was to provide credit facilities for
the oil company by means of a current account in return for
collateral securities. By a general agreement of assignment the
oil company assigned all present and future debts to the bank.
By an assignment of stocks as security the oil company assigned

The Weekly Law Reports, August 22, 1980

1077

1 W.L.R.   Slavenburg's Bank v. Intercontinental Ltd. (Q.B.D.)

A   to the bank by way of security its entire business, including present and future trading stocks. The Registrar of Companies was not notified of those charges, since it was not his practice to accept particulars of charges for registration from an overseas company with a place of business in England which was not registered in England under Part X of the Companies Act 1948. The oil company stored petroleum products at the premises of a storage company with bulk

B   storage facilities, which sent the bank storage reports with respect to the quantity of the oil company's products in store. On December 4, 1975, the bank decided to withdraw all credit facilities from the oil company. On December 19 the bank directed the storage company not to deliver any of the oil company's products without the bank's consent. The storage company refused to comply with that direction. On December 29 the oil company ceased trading. On January 9, 1976,

C   the bank's solicitors demanded immediate delivery of all the oil company's products stored by the storage company. On January 12 the bank obtained an ex parte order for the detention and preservation of the goods under R.S.C., Ord. 29, r. 3 and a Mareva injunction restraining the oil company from disposing of the proceeds of any goods sold before January 12. As a result of negotiations the parties opened a joint bank account in the names of the parties' solicitors to preserve the

D   proceeds of sales of the oil. On March 15, 1976, a creditor in Bermuda presented a petition for the compulsory winding up of the oil company. On April 19 a winding up order was made and joint liquidators were appointed on May 27. Interpleader proceedings were commenced in England between the bank, the oil company and the storage company to which the joint liquidators applied to be made parties in May 1977. The application was granted on July 11, 1978.

E   On the question whether the charges created in favour of the bank were void against the liquidators by virtue of sections 95 and 106 of the Companies Act 1948 [1] and whether the charges were void as unregistered bills of sale: —

     Held, (1) that, since on the plain wording of section 106 of the Companies Act 1948 the provisions of section 95 of the Act applied to charges on property in England created by a foreign company with a place of business in England, regis-

F   tration of a charge under section 95 (1) was not dependent on registration of a foreign company under Part X of the Act (post, pp. 1085A–C, 1086D–E); that, although it was the practice of the registrar not to register a charge where a foreign company had failed to comply with the requirements of Part X to register itself, the validity of a charge under section 95 did not depend on whether it had been registered but on whether particulars of the charge and the relevant documentary

G   evidence had been delivered to the registrar within 21 days of its creation and, therefore, the bank to avoid the charges being held null and void should have delivered the necessary particulars within the time limit (post, p. 1086B–D).

     National Provincial and Union Bank of England v. *Charnley* [1924] 1 K.B. 431, C.A. applied.

     (2) That for the purpose of section 106 of the Act of 1948

H   when applied to a foreign company " liquidator " meant either an English liquidator or the foreign equivalent, and accordingly, the joint liquidators appointed in Bermuda came within the meaning of " liquidator " (post, pp. 1086H—1087A).

     (3) That where a charge came within section 106 then by virtue of section 95 it was to be treated as if it were a charge created by an English company, even where the company ceased to have a place of business in England after the charge

[1] Companies Act 1948, s. 106: see post, p. 1084B–C.

had been created and, similarly, by virtue of section 95 float- A
ing charges and charges on future property came within the
provisions of section 106 (post, p. 1089B–H); and that, since the
parties had agreed to hold the proceeds of the sale of the
subject matter of the charges in a joint account, there could
be no question of the charges being spent and, accordingly,
they were void against the liquidators for failure to deliver
particulars to the registrar within 21 days (post, pp. 1092A–B,
1093C–D, F–G).   B

    Held, further, that the Bills of Sale Acts 1878 and 1882
applied only to individuals and not to corporations, and accordingly the charges were not void as unregistered bills of sale
(post, pp. 1098G–H, 1099E, 1101c).

    Read v. *Joannon* (1890) 25 Q.B.D. 300, D.C.; *In re Standard
Manufacturing Co.* [1891] 1 Ch. 627, C.A. and *Clark* v. *Balm,
Hill & Co.* [1908] 1 K.B. 667 applied.

    Great Northern Railway Co. v. *Coal Co-operative Society* C
[1896] 1 Ch. 187 considered.

The following cases are referred to in the judgment:

Asphaltic Wood Pavement Co. Ltd., In re (1883) 49 L.T. 159.
Brocklehurst v. *Railway Printing and Publishing Co.* [1884] W.N. 70.
Clark v. *Balm, Hill & Co.* [1908] 1 K.B. 667.
Cunningham & Co. Ltd., In re (1885) 28 Ch.D. 682.   D
Deffell v. *White* (1866) L.R. 2 C.P. 144.
Edmonds v. *Blaina Furnaces Co.* (1887) 36 Ch.D. 215.
Eichholz, decd., In re [1959] Ch. 708; [1959] 2 W.L.R. 200; [1959] 1
    All E.R. 166.
Farrell v. *Alexander* [1977] A.C. 59; [1976] 3 W.L.R. 145; [1976] 2
    All E.R. 721, H.L.(E.).
Great Northern Railway Co. v. *Coal Co-operative Society* [1896] 1 Ch. E
    187.
Jenkinson v. *Brandley Mining Co.* (1887) 19 Q.B.D. 568.
Levy v. *Abercorris Slate and Slab Co.* (1887) 37 Ch.D. 260.
Lloyds Bank Ltd. v. *Bank of America National Trust and Savings Asso-
    ciation* [1938] 2 K.B. 147, C.A.
Mercantile Bank of India Ltd. v. *Chartered Bank of India, Australia and
    China* [1937] 1 All E.R. 231.   F
National Provincial and Union Bank of England v. *Charnley* [1924] 1 K.B.
    431, C.A.
Nye (C. L.) Ltd., In re [1971] Ch. 442; [1970] 3 W.L.R. 158; [1970] 3
    All E.R. 1061, C.A.
Read v. *Joannon* (1890) 25 Q.B.D. 300, D.C.
Row Dal Constructions Pty. Ltd., In re [1966] V.R. 249.
Royal Marine Hotel Co., Kingstown Ltd., In re [1895] 1 I.R. 368.   G
Shears v. *Jacob* (1866) L.R. 1 C.P. 513.
Standard Manufacturing Co., In re [1891] 1 Ch. 627, C.A.
Welsted (John) and Co. Ltd. v. *Swansea Bank Ltd.* (1889) 5 T.L.R. 332.

The following additional cases were cited in argument:

Cella, The (1888) L.R. 13 P.D. 82, C.A.
Charlesworth v. *Mills* [1892] A.C. 231, H.L.(E.).   H
Contracting (J. & D.) Pty. Ltd., In re [1970] Q.W.N. 101.
Cookson v. *Swire* (1884) 9 App.Cas. 653, H.L.(E.).
Distillers' Co. Ltd. v. *Inland Revenue*, 1899, 36 S.L.R. 538.
Dublin City Distillery Ltd. v. *Doherty* [1914] A.C. 823, H.L.(I.).
Ehrmann Brothers Ltd., In re [1906] 2 Ch. 697, C.A.
Gordon, In re; Ex parte Navalchand [1897] 2 Q.B. 516.
Hall, In re; Ex parte Close (1884) 14 Q.B.D. 386.

The Weekly Law Reports, August 22, 1980

1079

1 W.L.R.   Slavenburg's Bank v. Intercontinental Ltd. (Q.B.D.)

A *Hamilton Young & Co., In re; Ex parte Carter* [1905] 2 K.B. 772, C.A.
Hilleary and Taylor, In re (1887) 36 Ch.D. 262, C.A.
Hubbard, Ex parte; In re Hardwick (1886) 17 Q.B.D. 690, C.A.
Independent Automatic Sales Ltd. v. *Knowles & Foster* [1962] 1 W.L.R. 974; [1962] 3 All E.R. 27.
Inland Revenue Commissioners v. *Hinchy* [1960] A.C. 748; [1960] 2 W.L.R. 448; [1960] 1 All E.R. 505, H.L.(E.).

B *Irrigation Co. of France, In re; Ex parte Fox* (1871) L.R. 6 Ch.App. 176.
Johnson v. *Diprose* [1893] 1 Q.B. 512, C.A.
Knightsbridge Estates Trust Ltd. v. *Byrne* [1940] A.C. 613, H.L.(E.).
Lemon v. *Austin Friars Investment Trust Ltd.* [1926] Ch. 1, Lawrence J. and C.A.
Luke v. *Inland Revenue Commissioners* [1963] A.C. 557; [1963] 2 W.L.R. 559; [1963] 1 All E.R. 655, H.L.(Sc.).

C *Manchester, Sheffield, and Lincolnshire Railway Co.* v. *North Central Wagon Co.* (1888) 13 App.Cas. 554, H.L.(E.).
North Wales Produce and Supply Society Ltd., In re [1922] 2 Ch. 340.
Official Assignee of Madras v. *Mercantile Bank of India Ltd.* [1935] A.C. 53, P.C.
Reg. v. *Federal Steam Navigation Co. Ltd.* [1974] 1 W.L.R. 505; [1974] 2 All E.R. 97, H.L.(E.).

D *Richards* v. *Overseers of Kidderminster* [1896] 2 Ch. 212.
Saunderson and Co. v. *Clark* (1913) 29 T.L.R. 579.
Senanayake v. *Cheng* [1966] A.C. 63; [1965] 3 W.L.R. 715; [1965] 3 All E.R. 296, P.C.
Société Générale de Paris v. *Dreyfus Brothers* (1887) 37 Ch.D. 215, C.A.
Tailby v. *Official Receiver* (1888) 13 App.Cas. 523, H.L.(E.).

E *Tooth, In re* [1934] Ch. 616.
Topham v. *Greenside Glazed Fire-Brick Co.* (1887) 37 Ch.D. 281.
Vita Food Products Inc. v. *Unus Shipping Co. Ltd.* [1939] A.C. 277, P.C.
Westminster Bank Ltd. v. *Zang* [1966] A.C. 182; [1966] 2 W.L.R. 110; [1966] 1 All E.R. 114, H.L.(E.).

F PRELIMINARY ISSUES

The plaintiff bank, N.V. Slavenburg's Bank, a company incorporated according to the laws of the Netherlands, brought an action against the defendants claiming the delivery up of mineral oil, the property of the plaintiffs and stored by the second defendants, Paktank Storage Co. Ltd., in the name of the first defendants, Intercontinental Natural Resources Ltd., and damages for its detention and an injunction against the first
G defendants restraining them by themselves, their servants or agents from disposing of their assets or removing them out of the jurisdiction. An order for the winding up of the first defendants, a company incorporated according to the laws of Bermuda, was made in Bermuda in April 1976 and joint liquidators, Richard William Kempe and Andrew Mark Homan, were appointed in May 1976. The joint liquidators applied to be made
H parties to the action. Kerr J. granted the application and by order of July 26, 1977, Mr. Kempe was added as third defendant and Mr. Homan as fourth defendant to the action. On July 11, 1977, Donaldson J. ordered a trial of the issues on the preliminary questions (1) whether the assignment of stocks as security and/or the storage reports, referred to in the points of claim in the issues were void against the second and third defendants by reason of the provisions of sections 95 and 106 of the Companies Act 1948; and (2) whether the assignment of stocks as security and/or the

storage reports were registrable in England as bills of sale and were un-   A
enforceable for want of registration as such.

The facts are set out in the judgment of Lloyd J.

  W. F. Stubbs Q.C. and David Grace for the bank.
  E. C. Evans-Lombe Q.C. and Laurence Libbert for the oil company
and joint liquidators.
                                                         B
                                                     Cur. adv. vult.

  February 22. LLOYD J. read the following judgment. In this case I
am concerned with preliminary points of law in an interpleader issue
between the plaintiffs, N.V. Slavenburg's Bank, a company incorporated
in the Netherlands, and the defendants, Intercontinental Natural Resources
Ltd., a company incorporated in Bermuda. The order directing the inter-   C
pleader issue was made by Mocatta J. on March 27, 1976. Subsequently
on April 19, 1976, the Supreme Court of Bermuda made an order for the
compulsory winding up of the company. Joint liquidators were appointed
on May 27, 1976. In May 1977 the joint liquidators applied to be made
parties to the English proceedings. The bank resisted the application but
on July 26, 1977, Kerr J. directed that the liquidators be joined as second D
and third defendants in the issues. There then followed pleadings in
which various defences were raised by the joint liquidators. On June 19,
1978, the defendants applied to the court for the trial of certain preliminary
questions of law raised by the pleadings. Again, the application was
resisted by the bank but on July 11, 1978, Donaldson J. granted the application. I need not set out verbatim the preliminary questions of law
which he ordered to be tried, more particularly as they have been varied   E
by subsequent agreement between the parties. But in essence the questions with which I have been concerned are, first, whether certain charges
created in favour of the bank are void against the liquidators by virtue of
section 95 of the Companies Act 1948, and, secondly, whether, if not, the
document, or documents, in question are void as unregistered bills of sale.
Before coming to the questions of law I must first give a short account   F
of the facts.

  The defendant company was incorporated in Bermuda on February 6,
1974. Until it went into liquidation it carried on business in the purchase
and sale of crude oil and refined petroleum products. On June 1, 1974,
it entered into a so-called service agreement with Dycon Petroleum Trading
Ltd., a company incorporated in the United Kingdom. According to an
affidavit filed on behalf of the bank it is the sort of agreement which is not   G
uncommon between an English company and a company incorporated in
a tax haven such as Bermuda.

  On June 13, 1974, the defendant company entered into three agreements
with the bank, all in the Dutch language and all governed by Dutch law.
The first is called " general credit agreement." By that agreement the
bank was to provide the company with credit facilities by way of current   H
account. By clause 9 the company agreed to provide certain collateral
securities, as there set out. The second agreement is called " general
agreement of assignment." By clause 1 the company agreed to assign all
present and future debts to the bank and to execute such assignments in
a form prescribed by the bank. The prescribed form is called " list of
assignment of accounts receivable." The third agreement is called
" assignment of stocks as security." By clauses 1 to 3 the company

The Weekly Law Reports, August 22, 1980

1081

1 W.L.R.   Slavenburg's Bank v. Intercontinental Ltd. (Q.B.D.)   Lloyd J.

A assigned its entire business by way of security to the bank, including present and future trading stocks. By clause 4 (b) the company assigned, or agreed to assign, all claims arising on the sale of its trading stocks. There was also a provision that all cash payments were to be collected by the company as agents for the bank. Those are the three principal agreements on which the bank relies in these proceedings.

B   It was the practice of the company to store petroleum products with a company called Paktank Storage Co. Ltd., which had bulk storage facilities at Grays, Essex, and at East Ham. Paktank are the second defendants in the action and it was as a result of their interpleader summons that Mocatta J. made the order to which I have referred. In the course of 1975 Paktank sent a number of telexes to the bank showing the quantity of the company's products in store at the end of the preceding month.

C On December 3, 1975, Paktank sent a telex in the following terms:

"We hold the following oil products to the account of Intercontinental Natural Resources Ltd., Hamilton, Bermuda, and at your disposal. It being understood that Intercontinental Natural Resources Ltd. has free and complete authority to dispose of all or any part of these products and that we are entirely free to accept their disposal instruc-
D   tions, subject only to contrary instructions from you."

The language of that telex had originally been suggested by the bank, and the bank's request had been passed on by the company to Paktank. Paktank sent a similar telex on December 18, 1975, giving the figures at close of business on the preceding day, showing a total quantity of 12,974 long tons in store. These telexes were referred to as " storage reports."

E   Meanwhile, on December 4, 1975, the bank had decided to withdraw all further facilities from the company. On December 19 the bank sent a telex to Paktank, referring to Paktank's storage report of December 18 and asking Paktank to issue them with a warehouse receipt. The bank went on to direct Paktank not to deliver any products without the bank's consent. On December 19 Paktank declined to accept the bank's direc-
F tions. On December 29 the company ceased trading. On January 9 Linklaters & Paines, on behalf of the bank, demanded immediate delivery of all the company's products stored by Paktank at Grays and East Ham, and on January 12 they obtained an ex parte order from Mocatta J. for the detention and preservation of the goods under R.S.C., Ord. 29, r. 3. They also obtained a Mareva injunction restraining the defendants from parting with the proceeds of any goods sold prior to January 12, 1976. The
G parties then entered into negotiations which resulted in the opening of a joint account at Lloyds Bank in the names of the parties' solicitors. On January 20, 1976, Linklaters & Paines wrote to the solicitors then acting for the company:

"We refer to our various discussions during the past few days, and confirm that our clients, N.V. Slavenburg's Bank, are agreeable to the
H   uplifting on an interim basis by Dycon Petroleum Trading Co. Ltd. of the oil presently stored by Paktank Storage Co. Ltd. in the name of Intercontinental notwithstanding the existence of the order of court of January 12, 1976, pending the signing, it is hoped, of an appropriate written agreement setting out more permanent arrangements for the uplifting of and payment for the oil and the destination of its proceeds pending the conclusion of the present litigation between Slavenburg's, Intercontinental and Paktank. . . . We have opened an

account styled ' Linklaters & Paines/Freshfields ' at the City branch   A
of Lloyds Bank Ltd. . . . Withdrawals from the account can only be
made on seven days' notice and they must be supported by the signatures of one designated partner in Linklaters & Paines and one
designated partner in Freshfields or else by an order of court. . . .
The purpose of these arrangements, it is hardly necessary to add, is
to preserve the proceeds of the oil just as the oil itself is, by means
of the present court order, preserved."   B

The first payment into the joint account was made on January 21 and
payments continued to be made through the rest of January, and in February and March. By April 15 the joint account stood at £905,098·21.
In October 1976 it was converted into a dollar account and now stands,
with interest, at $1,747,327·02. The joint account contains three main   C
elements: first, there is a relatively small sum of £63,068, which was the
company's share of the profit arising out of a joint venture for the sale
of fuel oil to the C.E.G.B. The other party to the joint venture was a
company called Shaw's Fuels Ltd. The defendant company's share of the
profit was specifically assigned to the bank by a " list of assignment "
dated December 16, 1975, and was paid into the joint account on January 29, 1976. The second element in the joint account is £256,607·98   D
being the proceeds of sale of products sold between January 1, 1976, and
the date of Mocatta J.'s order of January 12, 1976. This sum was paid
into the joint account on April 15, 1976. The third element in the joint
account represents proceeds of products sold since January 12, 1976.

The remaining events can be mentioned very briefly. On March 15,
1976, a creditor in Bermuda presented a petition for the compulsory   E
winding up of the company on the basis of a judgment debt of $5,195,832.
On April 19—as already mentioned—a winding up order was made and the
joint liquidators were appointed on May 27, 1976. Meanwhile on April 13,
1976, the company and the bank reached agreement by telex, subsequently
confirmed by letter, as to the terms on which the joint account had been
set up. The joint liquidators were not, of course, parties in their own
names to that agreement, since they had not yet been appointed. Since   F
the agreement is important for an understanding of the bank's submissions,
I will set out the letter of April 15 in full:

" Dear Sirs, this letter confirms our telex of today as follows: Following
legal action taken by you in the High Court in London on January 12,
1976, on behalf of N.V. Slavenburg's Bank arresting all mineral oils
owned by us and stored with Paktank in the U.K. a joint bank account   G
was set up at Lloyds Bank in the names of Linklaters & Paines and
Freshfields into which it was agreed the proceeds of the sale of such
mineral oils should be paid on terms that the right, interest and equities
of each ourselves and N.V. Slavenburg's Bank in such proceeds of sale
should be identical to those in the mineral oils from which the proceeds derived.   H
   " Since January 21, 1976, sales of mineral oils have taken place
with the consent of Slavenburg's and the proceeds of the sale duly
paid to the joint bank account on the terms set out above. In addition on or about January 29, 1976, Shaw's Fuels Ltd. paid into the
joint account £63,068·48. This sum did not represent proceeds of sale
of mineral oils subject to your arrest but was our share of profit on
approximately 40,000 tons of fuel oil delivered to C.E.G.B. in Dec-

The Weekly Law Reports, August 22, 1980

1083

1 W.L.R.   Slavenburg's Bank v. Intercontinental Ltd. (Q.B.D.)   Lloyd J.

A ember 1975 the account receivable in respect of which was purported
to be assigned by us to Slavenburg's. A further 40,000 tons were
delivered to C.E.G.B. in March under the same contract and the
proceeds which will be considerably less than £63,000 are expected to
be paid shortly.

"During the first two weeks of January prior to your court proceedings we sold mineral oils from U.K. storage for a total net sale price
B of £256,607·98 the accounts receivable in respect of these sales were
purported to be assigned by us to Slavenburg's. The sales were made
to Dycon Petroleum Trading Ltd. and that company has deposited
the said sum of £256,607·98 on client account with Messrs. Freshfields
to be released only as follows: 1. In accordance with instructions from
an authorised signatory of Dycon to pay either us or Slavenburg's.
C 2. In accordance with joint instructions from us and Slavenburg's to
pay either of us. 3. In accordance with an order of the High Court
arising from any proceedings between us and Slavenburg's relating
to the moneys in question.

"Against your clients' agreement 1. That the joint account is to
be divided into three parts, the first representing proceeds of sale of
mineral oils subject to their arrest, the second representing payments
D made under the C.E.G.B. contract and the third representing the proceeds of sale of mineral oils to Dycon Petroleum Trading Ltd. prior
to the arrest, and 2. That the rights, titles and interest and equities of
Intercontinental Natural Resources Ltd. and N.V. Slavenburg's Bank
in each part of the account shall be identical to the rights, titles,
interest and equities that each of them held in the mineral oils and
E accounts receivable from which each part derived and against your
clients agreeing to amend their pleadings before the High Court to
reflect this agreement and to enable the court to decide the issues pertaining to each of the three parts we will join with your clients in
instructing Freshfields to pay £256,607·98 into the joint account and
will instruct Shaw's Fuels to pay the balance of the C.E.G.B. moneys
F into the joint account."

A number of facts have been agreed between the parties, and I have
been asked to make a number of assumptions for the purpose of dealing
with the questions of law which are now before the court. It may well be
that the short-cut which the court had in mind when ordering the preliminary questions of law will in the end, in this case as in others, prove to
G have been the longest way round. But, be that as it may, I am satisfied
that the points which are now before the court are in no way academic,
and in those circumstances my proper course is to attempt to deal with
all the points that have been argued.

I now turn to the questions of law. As already mentioned, they fall
into two main groups, the first relating to section 95 of the Companies Act
1948, and the second to the Bills of Sale Acts 1878 and 1882. For the
H purposes of dealing with the first group of questions I am asked to
assume (1) that they are to be determined in accordance with English
law and not Dutch law; (2) that the company had at all material times
an established place of business in England within the meaning of
section 106 of the Companies Act 1948; (3) that the documents relied
on by the bank, that is to say the general credit agreement, the general
agreement of assignment, the assignment of stocks as security, the list
of assignments and storage reports, all create charges within the meaning

of section 95 (2) of the Companies Act 1948; (4) that no particulars of these charges were ever delivered to the registrar for registration pursuant to section 95 (1).

On those assumptions Mr. Evans-Lombe, who appears for the company and the joint liquidators, argues that the charges are all void as against the liquidators by virtue of the combined effect of sections 95 and 106. I need not set out the provisions of sections 95, but section 106 provides:

"Application of Part III to charges created, and property subject to charge acquired, by company incorporated outside England.

"106. The provisions of this Part of this Act shall extend to charges on property in England which are created, and to charges on property in England which is acquired, by a company (whether a company within the meaning of this Act or not) incorporated outside England which has an established place of business in England."

Mr. Stubbs, who appears for the bank, takes five points: first, logically (though not in the order in which he took them) is that section 106 does not apply because on its true construction it only applies to companies incorporated in Scotland and Northern Ireland. Mr. Stubbs supports that argument in a number of ways. First he says that all other provisions relating to overseas companies generally are to be found in Part X of the Act; therefore if section 106 relates to overseas companies generally you would expect to find it in Part X and not at the end of Part III. Secondly, he says that section 103 and section 104 presuppose the existence of a registered office; and other provisions in Part III create offences. It would be absurd—he says—that Parliament should have intended such provisions to apply to all overseas companies. Thirdly, he appeals to the legislative history. He says that the words in brackets " whether a company within the meaning of this Act or not," which, on their face, are fatal to his argument, were first enacted when the legislature was preoccupied with the problem of applying the Companies Acts to Northern Ireland, and that they were introduced for that limited purpose only.

I cannot accept Mr. Stubbs's argument. The language of section 106 is crystal clear. If by " companies incorporated outside England " the legislature had meant companies incorporated in Scotland and Northern Ireland, and nowhere else, it would have been simple enough to say so. Moreover, it is impossible to reconcile Mr. Stubbs's contention with section 461 of the Companies Act 1948 which provides:

"Application to Northern Ireland.

" 461 (1) Nothing in this Act, except the provisions thereof which relate expressly to companies registered or incorporated in Northern Ireland or outside Great Britain, shall apply to or in relation to companies registered or incorporated in Northern Ireland. (2) Nothing in this Act, except where it is expressly provided to the contrary, shall affect the law in force in Northern Ireland at the commencement of this Act."

Nor is it correct to say that all provisions relating to overseas companies are contained in Part X: see Part IX which relates to the winding up of unregistered companies, and, in particular, section 400. None of the standard textbooks on company law suggest that section 106 is confined to Scotland and Northern Ireland, and Buckley on the Companies Acts,

The Weekly Law Reports, August 22, 1980

1085

1 W.L.R.   Slavenburg's Bank v. Intercontinental Ltd. (Q.B.D.)   Lloyd J.

A 13th ed. (1957); *Palmer's Company Law*, 22nd ed. (1976); *Gower, Modern Company Law*, 3rd ed. (1969) and *Pennington, Company Law*, 3rd ed. (1973), all clearly assume the contrary. The editors of *Buckley on the Companies Acts*, 13th ed., in particular, draw attention at p. 247 to the potential difficulty of applying sections 103 and 104, according to their literal terms, to all overseas companies. But they do not draw the con-
B clusion that section 106 is on that account to be treated as inapplicable to all companies incorporated outside England except those incorporated in Scotland and Northern Ireland.

As for the legislative history, I am guided, and indeed bound, by what was said by the House of Lords on the construction of consolidation Acts in *Farrell* v. *Alexander* [1977] A.C. 59, 73, 82 and 97. There is no difficulty or ambiguity in the meaning of section 106. The words in
C brackets make it clear that the section applies to any company whether or not a company as defined in section 455. In those circumstances I do not regard it as desirable to speculate—and it could be no more than speculation—why the words were introduced into the Act of 1929. For those reasons I reject Mr. Stubbs's first argument.

Mr. Stubbs's second argument is that assuming, contrary to his first
D argument, section 106 applies to overseas companies generally, it only applies where they have been registered under Part X. As appears from paragraphs 9 to 12 of Mr. Hathaway's affidavit, sworn on July 21, 1977, this seems to have been the principal argument relied on by the bank in resisting the liquidators' application to be joined as parties to the proceedings. The point is taken in paragraph 3 of the points of reply to the liquidators' points of defence:

E   ". . . if, which is denied, Incon [the first defendant] had an established place of business in England no registration of the said company or place of business pursuant to the provisions of Part X of the Companies Act 1948 was ever effected by or on behalf of the said company. In the premises it was not possible, it was not practicable and it was not necessary to register the plaintiffs' securities pursuant
F   to section 106 of the Companies Act 1948."

Mr. Stubbs, however, did not put the point in the forefront of his argument. He described it as *a* point, not *the* point. He supported it by reference to the practice of the Registrar of Companies as described in a letter dated October 24, 1977. From that letter it appears that, since overseas companies with a place of business in England are obliged to register
G under Part X, the registrar requires the company to comply with Part X before he will accept particulars of charges for registration under Part III. The letter continues:

    "There is no method by which an overseas company can register charges unless it has an established place of business in England and therefore should first register under section 407, unless it informs the
H   registrar that it is in the process of submitting the necessary documents required under that section, in which case the charges would be held for a short period pending registration. If registration was not completed within a short period the charges would be returned."

In contrast, a Scottish company is not, of course, required to register under Part X. In the case of Scottish companies, therefore, wishing to register a charge under section 95, the registrar opens a special file.

Against the background of that practice (which I am to assume has

continued uniformly since 1928) Mr. Stubbs submits, first, that the object
of delivering particulars of charges under section 95 (1) is so that they may
be registered. He stresses the words " for registration," and if the fact is
that charges will not be registered unless the company has first registered
under Part X, then section 95 cannot have been intended to apply to such
charges. Secondly, he submits that a chargee is entitled to know where
he is, and it is unsatisfactory that the validity of his charge in the absence
of registration should depend on something which may be so uncertain as
whether the company has an established place of business in England or
not.

The fallacy in the argument lies in regarding registration of the charge
under Part III as a condition precedent to its validity. It is clear both
from the language of section 95 and from what was said in *National
Provincial and Union Bank of England* v. *Charnley* [1924] 1 K.B. 431
that it is delivery of particulars of the charge, together with the instrument
(if any) by which it is created or evidenced that saves the charge, and not
its registration. In the *National Provincial Bank* case Scrutton L.J. said
at p. 447, after referring to the language of the section: " That makes the
avoidance depend on the neglect to send in the particulars. The neglect
to register the charge will not make it void." Mr. Stubbs reserved the
right to challenge the correctness of that dictum in a higher court. So far
as I am concerned, it seems to follow that the bank could have preserved
the validity of its charges by delivering particulars within 21 days, despite
the unwillingness of the registrar to register the charge without prior
registration by the company under Part X. In those circumstances there
is really nothing left in Mr. Stubbs's argument under this head. There is
certainly nothing in section 106 to suggest that the operation of that section is dependent in any way on the company having registered under
Part X, and I am unwilling to imply any such limitation.

Before leaving the point, I should say that Mr. Evans-Lombe expressly
disclaimed any criticism of the registrar's current practice. Nor would I,
myself, wish to criticise it in any way. His reasons for insisting on the
company first registering under Part X are clear enough. But they cannot
affect the outcome of this case. I reject Mr. Stubbs's second argument.

Mr. Stubbs's third argument is that, assuming section 95 and section 106
apply to the charges in the present case, nevertheless the joint liquidators
cannot take advantage of section 95 because " the liquidator " in section
95 means " the liquidator in an English liquidation," whereas the joint
liquidators were, as I have already mentioned, appointed by the Supreme
Court of Bermuda. Mr. Stubbs's argument is that wherever the word
" liquidator " appears in the Companies Act 1948 it means liquidator in
an English winding up, whether voluntary or compulsory; that section 95
is no exception, and that it cannot be extended to include the person
appointed in a foreign liquidation, even though he may happen to be
called a " liquidator."

I would accept the premise of Mr. Stubbs's argument, but I would not
accept the conclusion. The primary meaning of " liquidator " in section
95 is, no doubt, the liquidator in an English winding up, just as the
primary meaning of "company" in section 95 is an English company.
But when applied to a foreign company by section 106 the word " company " in section 95 must necessarily be given an extended meaning. That
being so, I can see no difficulty in doing the same for the word " liquidator." For the purpose of section 106 (but only of course for the

The Weekly Law Reports, August 22, 1980

1087

1 W.L.R.   Slavenburg's Bank v. Intercontinental Ltd. (Q.B.D.)   Lloyd J.

A purpose of section 106) it means either an English liquidator or the foreign equivalent (whether in place of incorporation or elsewhere) as the case may be. Otherwise section 106 would lose much of its impact. It cannot have been intended that wherever there is a foreign winding up there should always have to be a winding up in England under Part IX before section 95 can be operated for the benefit of unsecured creditors. Certainly there is nothing express to that effect and, again, I cannot see why any such limitation should be implied.

B

There could perhaps be a difficulty where it is uncertain whether a foreign proceeding is in the nature of a winding up. But no such difficulty arises here. I was referred to the Companies Act 1923 of Bermuda. From section 37 it appears that so far as practicable companies in Bermuda are wound up in the manner in which English companies are wound up " under the law and practice in England regulating the winding up of companies . . ." I note that the winding up order in Bermuda was made under the United Kingdom Companies Act 1948 as well as under the Act of 1923, and that one of the two joint liquidators is in fact resident in England. Mr. Stubbs submits that, though I am entitled to read the Bermuda Companies Act 1923, I am not entitled to draw any conclusion as to its meaning. I need not deal with that submission, although it is hardly a submission which commends itself to me. For I only refer to the Companies Act 1923 in the present connection for the limited purpose of satisfying myself (which I should in any event have thought obvious) that a winding up in Bermuda is a proceeding which the English court will recognise or characterise as a winding up for the purposes of section 95. I hold that the joint liquidators come within the meaning of " liquidator " in section 95 as applied to the present case by section 106.

C

D

E

In case I should be against him on that point Mr. Evans-Lombe applied to join Sedgwick Forbes & Co., the well-known insurance brokers, as fourth defendants in the interpleader issue. Even if the joint liquidators cannot, themselves, take the points under section 95 because they are not liquidators appointed in an English liquidation, there can, he said, be no objection to Sedgwick Forbes taking the same points as representative creditors. Mr. Stubbs strenuously resisted the application on the ground that it would be unfair to the bank. The application comes, he says, too late. But the underlying principle is, as stated in R.S.C., Ord. 15, r. 6 (1):

F

G
" No cause or matter shall be defeated by reason of the misjoinder or nonjoinder of any party; and the court may in any cause or matter determine the issues or questions in dispute so far as they affect the rights and interests of the persons who are parties to the cause or matter."

In the present case the proceedings are still only at the stage of preliminary questions of law. It would require a very strong case indeed before I would refuse leave to join a new party at this stage. In fact so far from the defendants being in mercy it is rather the other way round. Paragraph 22 of Mr. Hathaway's affidavit of July 21, 1977, to which I have already referred, shows that one of the points taken by the bank in resisting the application to join the liquidators was that the liquidators would not in any event, as foreign liquidators, be entitled to take " an independent point in the litigation." In the context this must mean a point under section 95. I will read the relevant paragraph:

H

" Further Incon [the first defendant] is a foreign corporation and the **A**
liquidators are acting under a foreign winding up order. No winding
up order has been made in England relating to Incon's assets here,
nor have liquidators been appointed in England. In these circumstances in my respectful submission the liquidators, while they can act
on behalf of Incon and in its name, cannot act separately from it,
take an independent point in litigation, or raise matters which the
company itself could not raise."   **B**

Subsequently Cameron Kemm Nordon, the solicitors acting for the
defendants, wrote as follows on August 22, 1977:

" As you will be aware, one of the points taken by your clients at the
hearing was the question of whether or not the liquidators, being
liquidators appointed by the Supreme Court of Bermuda, had any **C**
locus standi in their own right in the English court. The judge was
not disposed to determine this question on an interlocutory application. It was agreed that it would be open to your clients to take it
by way of defence in the action if they so wished.

" However, having regard to the fact that it is open to our clients
at any time to apply for Incon to be wound up in England (for which
purpose the existence of assets in England would be sufficient) and **D**
that on the making of such a winding up order there would be
liquidators in England who would undoubtedly have locus standi it
seems to us to be pointless to take this step for that purpose alone.
Whatever the result of the litigation between our respective clients,
your clients will in any event at the end of the day still be unsecured
creditors for quite a considerable sum of money and it is not therefore **E**
in their interest that the assets which will in any event be available for
unsecured creditors should be further dissipated by the costs of an
English winding up proceeding.

" We should be glad therefore if you would kindly confirm within
the next 14 days that your clients will not seek to take the locus standi
point by way of defence or by way of appeal from the order of
Kerr J."   **F**

There was no reply to that letter, nor was the point ever pleaded. Mr.
Stubbs says that the point which he is taking upon the construction
of the word " liquidator " in section 95 is entirely separate and distinct
from the so-called locus standi point. For myself, I cannot see the
difference. Certainly there is no difference in substance. Whichever way **G**
the point is put it could have been met by a successful application to the
court for the company to be wound up in England and it was to avoid the
pointless expense of doing that that Cameron Kemm Nordon wrote their
letter of August 22, 1977. So that even if the points are entirely separate,
as Mr. Stubbs maintains, the defendants were justified in thinking that no
technical point of the kind covered by that letter was going to be taken,
which is why the defendants were so surprised (as clearly they were) when **H**
the present point was taken. In those circumstances, I can see no unfairness whatever in allowing the amendment to meet the point by joining
Sedgwick Forbes as representative creditors. Accordingly that application
is allowed. If authority is needed for the course which I have taken it is
to be found in the decision of Harman J. in *In re Eichholz, decd.* [1959]
Ch. 708

Mr. Stubbs's last point under this head is that there is in any event no

The Weekly Law Reports, August 22, 1980

1089

1 W.L.R.   Slavenburg's Bank v. Intercontinental Ltd. (Q.B.D.)   Lloyd J.

A point in joining the creditors because they cannot be in a better position than the English liquidators. I find it difficult to follow that argument. I could understand—though I would not accept—an argument that the creditors have no locus standi in the absence of an English winding up. But Mr. Stubbs expressly disclaims that argument. His argument is that, on the true construction of section 95, they are not creditors at all within
B the meaning of the section. It seems to me that a creditor is either a creditor or he is not. It cannot depend on whether the company is being wound up, and, if so, where.

I now turn to the fourth argument. Mr. Stubbs submits that section 106 only applies to charges on property which is in England at the time the charge is created or the property acquired. I cannot accept that argument either. It would means that all floating charges so far as they relate
C to future property would be outside the scope of the section. Yet section 95 (2) (f) expressly covers floating charges. In applying section 95 to overseas companies Parliament must have intended it to apply to floating charges as well as fixed charges and must therefore have intended it to apply in the case of future property in England as well as existing property in England. I reject Mr. Stubbs's main argument under his fourth head.

D There is, however, a subsidiary argument, that, even if a charge were initially within section 95, by virtue of section 106, it would cease to be within section 95 if at any time the company ceased to have an established place of business in England under section 106. For this purpose I have to qualify the assumption made above, that the company had an established place of business in England at all material times, and assume instead that, having had such a place of business, it ceased to have a place
E of business before the commencement of the winding up in Bermuda on March 15, 1976. The point can be illustrated in the following way: Suppose on day 1 a foreign company with an established place of business in England creates a charge on its assets in England. If it fails to deliver particulars of the charge within 21 days, the charge is potentially void against the liquidator and general creditors. Suppose on day 30 a
F liquidator is appointed. What is the position if on, say, day 25 the company had ceased to have an established place of business in England? Mr. Evans-Lombe submits that the liquidator's rights are unaffected. He would, I think, submit the same even if the company had ceased to have a place of business in England on day 15. Mr. Stubbs, on the other hand, submits that the conditions of section 106 have to be satisfied not only at the date of the creation of the charge but also at the commencement of
G the winding up. For until then there is nobody who is in a position to take advantage of the provisions of section 95. The point is not altogether easy. But on the whole I prefer Mr. Evans-Lombe's submission. Section 106 is, as he says, a triggering section. If its conditions are satisfied it triggers section 95 in relation to charges at the moment of their creation. Thereafter the charge is to be treated as if it were for all purposes a
H charge created by an English company. If that is right, it does not matter that the conditions of section 106 ceased to be satisfied the day after the creation of the charge. Mr. Evans-Lombe referred me to In re C. L. Nye Ltd. [1971] Ch. 442. But I do not find the case particularly helpful in this connection. I prefer to rest my decision on what seems to me the most natural meaning of section 106.

I now turn to the last of the points under section 95. Mr. Stubbs submits that there is nothing here for section 95 to bite on, because the

property charged had all been sold and the proceeds paid into the joint   A
account in the names of the parties' solicitors before the liquidators were
ever appointed. It is settled law, says Mr. Stubbs, that a liquidator cannot avoid a charge that has ceased to exist or become spent, and the
charges here were all spent prior to the appointment of the liquidators,
when the products were sold pursuant to the agreement of January 20,
1976. He further submits that the liquidators cannot, themselves, take
advantage of that agreement since they were not parties to it, and, in   B
those circumstances, the joint liquidators can lay no claim to the fund for
the benefit of the creditors.

    The point was first foreshadowed in the letter from Linklaters &
Paines dated January 16, 1979. As the argument progressed it became an
increasingly important part in the bank's case. It was accepted by both
sides that, for the sake of simplicity, the relevant date should be regarded   C
as the date of the appointment of the liquidators rather than the commencement of the winding up or the date of the winding up order.

    Now, I agree with Mr. Stubbs that once a charge is spent there is
nothing for section 95 to bite on. That appears sufficiently from the
language of the section itself and also from at least two authorities that
were cited. In *Mercantile Bank of India Ltd.* v. *Chartered Bank of*   D
India, Australia and China [1937] 1 All E.R. 231, two banks had lent
money to a company on the security of certain documents variously
called letters of hypothecation and letters of lien. The company subsequently went into liquidation. The banks each alleged against the
other that the other's securities were void for non-registration. Prior to
the liquidation the defendant bank had seized the company's assets
under the terms of its security. One of the questions was whether   E
the defendant's security should be regarded as a floating charge or not.
Porter J. said, at p. 235:

    " I do not propose finally to decide that question, because I think
    it is admitted, . . . that, the goods having been seized, the Chartered
    Bank [that is the defendant bank] has put itself in a different
    position; and has brought down, as it were, on the floating charge a   F
    perfecting of the charge upon those goods, whatever they may be . . ."

Later on in the same judgment, after referring to a number of authorities,
he said, at p. 241:

    " On the authority of those cases, it appears that once seizure has
    taken place, at a time before liquidation, at any rate, of the company,
    the security, even if it were originally a floating security, has ceased   G
    to be so describable. It has become a definite charge which has been
    perfected by the seizure of the goods. Therefore, in so far as the
    Chartered Bank has seized the goods rightfully, it is entitled, in my
    view, to the benefit of its security."

Porter J.'s decision is authority for the view that once a charge has been
perfected by seizure of the goods charged it is too late for the liquidator   H
to intervene.

    Mr. Stubbs had some doubt whether the decision of Porter J. goes all
the way for him. But the point was not really contested by Mr. Evans-
Lombe, so that I need not consider whether his doubts are justified.
Certainly it is too late for the liquidators to intervene if the chargee has
already been paid prior to the liquidation. That appears from the other
decision to which I was referred, namely, *In re Row Dal Constructions*

The Weekly Law Reports, August 22, 1980

1091

1 W.L.R.   Slavenburg's Bank v. Intercontinental Ltd. (Q.B.D.)   Lloyd J.

A *Pty. Ltd.* [1966] V.R. 249, a decision of the Supreme Court of Victoria. In that case a bank had lent money to a company on the security of certain book debts which were assigned to the bank. The company subsequently went into liquidation. But before it went into liquidation the bank had been paid the amount of its loan under the assignment. The liquidator sought to recover from the bank the amount paid under the assignment on the ground that the assignment was void as against him
B for non-registration. It was held that he could not succeed as the bank had already been paid before he came on the scene. The non-registration was therefore irrelevant. Herring C.J. said, at p. 258:

"Had liquidation in this case intervened before the payment of the £6,000 actually paid . . . on May 31, no doubt in that event there would have been a contest as to the destination of this sum, the
C liquidator claiming it as property of the company and relying upon non-registration of the assignment to defeat the bank's claim and the bank for its part claiming it as its property by reason of the absolute assignment. But as things are the liquidator can derive no assistance from the failure to register under section 72 [of the Companies Act 1958 of Victoria]. When he was appointed on
D July 6, 1962, there was no property of the company upon which the bank claimed any security, and there was consequently no basis upon which he could call in aid section 72 to defeat the bank's assignment. These considerations are, in my opinion, sufficient to dispose of this point."

Mr. Stubbs laid particular stress on the penultimate sentence of that
E passage which I have just read. He says that the position is precisely the same here because the only property of the company upon which the bank claimed security had been sold and the proceeds paid into the joint account before the liquidators were appointed.

The real dispute, as it seems to me, on this part of the case is not as to what is the effect in law of the charge being spent, because it is largely common ground that if a charge is spent before liquidation
F section 95 has nothing to bite on. The real dispute is whether the charges were indeed spent, or whether the bank can be heard to say that they were spent, on the facts of this case; for, if Mr. Stubbs is wrong about that, then the rest of his argument falls to the ground.

There are, I think, considerable difficulties in the way of his sub-mission. In the first place it is to be noted that the facts of the present
G case are very different from those in the two cases to which I have just referred. The bank has not seized or taken possession of the property in any way, as in the former case, nor has it been paid, as in the latter. The money is still in the joint account. It is no more within the control of the bank than it is within the control of the company. In the absence of agreement between the parties to this action, the destination of the
H fund in the joint account is subject to the decision of this court. Secondly, when one looks at the bank's pleading, it is clear, as Mr. Evans-Lombe points out, that the basis of the bank's claim to be entitled to the amount in the joint account are the very charges which the liquidators seek to impugn. It hardly lies in the bank's mouth to say that the charges are spent, when, at the same time, it asserts their existence and validity as the basis of its claim against the company.

But I am prepared to assume that the bank could get over both those

difficulties. The real objection to Mr. Stubbs's argument, as it seems to A
me, lies in the agreement of January 20, 1976, by virtue of which these
products came to be sold. It is accepted by both parties that one must
construe that agreement as amplified by the letter of April 15, 1976, to
which I have already referred. What does that agreement provide? It
provides quite simply that the rights of each party to the proceeds of sale
shall be the same as its rights in the oil. One therefore asks oneself the
question: What rights would the bank have had to the oil if it had still B
existed? The answer must be that the bank's rights would have been
liable to have been defeated by the very arguments which the liquidators
are now advancing.

Mr. Stubbs puts forward a number of counter-arguments against that
simple view. First, he submits that you must look at the rights of the bank
immediately *prior* to the sale of the products, at which time the liquida- C
tors had not been appointed. He draws attention to the language of the
relevant passage in the letter of April 15:

" That the rights, titles and interests and equities of Intercontinental
Natural Resources Ltd. and N.V. Slavenburg's Bank, in each part
of the account, shall be identical to the rights, titles, interest and
equities that each of them held in the mineral oils and accounts D
receivable from which each part derived . . ."

He says that the word " held " shows that you are not to look at future
events. It seems to me that that is reading far too much into a single
word; and it is to be noted that that word does not appear when the
effect of the agreement is set out in the first paragraph of the letter. I
can see no justification for treating the parties' rights as having been E
frozen when the agreement was made, still less for treating them as
having been frozen in relation to any particular quantity of petroleum
products immediately prior to the sale of that quantity.

Mr. Stubbs's second argument was that " the bank's rights " means its
rights as against the only other party to the agreement at the time it was
made, namely, the company. The bank's rights cannot, he said, be F
affected by any " rights " which the liquidators may acquire under section
95, since the liquidators were not, themselves, parties to the agreement.
But that is to draw an entirely artificial distinction between the rights
which the liquidators assert in the name of the company for the general
benefit of its creditors, which rights are indisputably preserved by the
agreement, and the additional rights which they, and they alone, can
assert for the benefit of creditors under section 95. G

Thirdly, Mr. Stubbs argues that I cannot assume that a liquidation
was inevitable on January 20, 1976, or even likely. But, as Mr. Evans-
Lombe pointed out, the company can have had no motive for entering
into the agreement of January 20, 1976, other than to benefit the general
creditors. There was never any doubt about the existence of the company's debt to the bank or its amount. From the start the only dispute H
has been whether, and if so to what extent, the bank's debt is secured.
This must have been as obvious to the bank as it was to the company.
It may well be, as Mr. Stubbs asserts, that a liquidation was not inevitable. But it does not follow, in my judgment, that the liquidators are to
be regarded as strangers to the agreement.

Mr. Stubbs's fourth, and final, argument was that, whatever the parties
may have agreed, the petroleum products did in fact cease to be the

The Weekly Law Reports, August 22, 1980

1093

1 W.L.R.   Slavenburg's Bank v. Intercontinental Ltd. (Q.B.D.)   Lloyd J.

A property of the company when they were sold, and that thereafter there was nothing to which the charge could apply. The money in the joint account is not " the company's property " within the meaning of section 95. The parties cannot by their private agreement make section 95 apply to something to which, on its true construction, it does not apply. It seems to me that there is a short answer to that argument. Of course the parties cannot by their private agreement contract themselves out of a public

B statute. But that is not what these parties have sought to do. They are, in effect, agreeing to be bound by a statute as if it applied, which is a very different thing. I can see no reason why they should not make such an agreement. Indeed such agreements are matters of everyday experience in the commercial world as, for instance, where parties agree to apply the Carriage of Goods by Sea Act 1971 to a bill of lading to

C which it would not otherwise apply; or to a charterparty, which the Act specifically excludes from its operation. For the above reasons, I cannot accept any of Mr. Stubbs's submissions as to the construction and effect of the agreement of January 20, 1976. To my mind the meaning is, as I have already said, clear enough, namely, that you look at the rights of the parties (and that means all the parties to this litigation, including the

D liquidators) as if the petroleum products were still in existence. If that is right, then it follows that Mr. Stubbs's argument that section 95 has nothing to bite on must be rejected.

There was some further discussion in the course of the hearing as to the nature of the bank's claim to the sums standing in the joint account. I have already mentioned that in their pleading they claim as assignees or chargees. The alternative is to regard them as beneficiaries under a

E trust. I do not find it necessary to consider that question further, because I take it to have been conceded that if the bank should fail on all the points that have been argued, then, on the assumptions I have been asked to make, the sum in the joint account would fall to be paid out to the defendants. If that is not conceded, I would so decide.

That concludes the various points which have been argued in relation to section 95, all of which I have decided against the bank. On the

F assumptions which I have been asked to make, I hold that the charges created by the documents on which the bank relies are all void, so far as any security was conferred thereby, against the second and third defendants, as joint liquidators, and against the fourth defendants, as representative creditors of the company. It follows on the same assumptions that the defendants are entitled to have paid out to them the sum

G standing in the joint account.

I now come to the second group of questions, namely, whether the documents on which the bank relies are void as unregistered bills of sale. If I am right so far, that is to say, if its charges are all void against the liquidators or representative creditors under section 95, then the point does not arise. But as I am dealing with preliminary questions of law

H on a number of assumed facts, some or all of which may not be established at the trial. Mr. Evans-Lombe naturally wishes to be able to support his attack on alternative grounds. In any event, having heard full argument (more than 50 authorities were cited) it is obviously right to express my conclusion, if only quite shortly.

The first main issue in relation to the Bills of Sale Acts 1978 and 1882 is whether they apply to companies at all. Mr. Stubbs says they do not. Mr. Evans-Lombe says they do but not if the charge falls to be registered

under section 95. If for any of the reasons which Mr. Stubbs has advanced A
the present charges are not void under section 95, then, says Mr. Evans-
Lombe, the defendants can fall back on the Bills of Sale Acts 1878 and
1882.

The general pattern of the Bills of Sale legislation is very well set out
in *Halsbury's Laws of England*, 4th ed., vol. 4 (1973), paras. 605–606.
Very briefly, the Act of 1878 is the sole Act in force in relation to absolute
bills. It is also in force in relation to bills given by way of security, to B
the rather limited extent that it has not been amended by the Bills of Sale
(1878) Amendment Act 1882. It is agreed by all parties that the documents on which the bank rely, if they are bills of sale at all, are bills of
sale given by way of security and not absolute bills. Accordingly, I am
concerned primarily with the Act of 1882. I need only refer to one
section of it. Section 17 provides: C

" Debentures to which Act not to apply.

" 17. Nothing in this Act shall apply to any debentures issued by
any mortgage, loan, or other incorporated company, and secured upon
the capital stock or goods, chattels, and effects of such company."

While I am primarily concerned with the Act of 1882, I am also concerned
indirectly with the Act of 1878 to the extent that it throws light on the D
question whether the Bills of Sale Acts as a whole (since they are to be
read as one) apply to companies as well as individuals, and also to the
limited extent to which, as I have already said, it still applies in relation
to security bills.

Before dealing with the submissions on either side, I must refer, in
order to make the submissions intelligible, to the five principal cases in this E
field. I can start with *Read* v. *Joannon* (1890) 25 Q.B.D. 300. Prior to
Read v. *Joannon* there were cases in which it had been said, or more often
assumed, that the Bills of Sale Acts applied to companies as well as
individuals: see *Shears* v. *Jacob* (1866) L.R. 1 C.P. 513; *Deffell* v. *White*
(1866) L.R. 2 C.P. 144; *In re Cunningham & Co. Ltd.* (1885) 28 Ch.D.
682; *Edmonds* v. *Blaina Furnaces Co.* (1887) 36 Ch.D. 215; *Levy* v. F
Abercorris Slate and Slab Co. (1887) 37 Ch.D. 260; *Jenkinson* v. *Brandley
Mining Co.* (1887) 19 Q.B.D. 568 and *Brocklehurst* v. *Railway Printing
and Publishing Co.* [1884] W.N. 70. There were also cases the other
way: see *In re Asphaltic Wood Pavement Co. Ltd.* (1883) 49 L.T. 159
and *John Welsted and Co. Ltd.* v. *Swansea Bank Ltd.* (1889) 5 T.L.R.
332.

In *Read* v. *Joannon*, 25 Q.B.D. 300 the question arose in relation G
to an ordinary company debenture. It had been held in the City of
London court that the debenture was void as against an execution creditor,
under the Act of 1878, notwithstanding section 17 of the Act of 1882. The
matter then came on appeal before the Divisional Court in July 1890. In
an unreserved judgment Lord Coleridge C.J. said, at p. 303:

" The question is, whether a debenture of an incorporated company H
requires registration as a bill of sale. I am of opinion—and I think
it right to say that my opinion does not stand alone, but is supported
by that of a judge of much greater authority than myself, whom I
have had the opportunity of consulting—that such debentures are not
bills of sale, and are not struck at by either of these Acts of Parliament—that they were never within the Act of 1878, and are expressly
exempted from the operation of the Act of 1882."

The Weekly Law Reports, August 22, 1980

1095

1 W.L.R.   Slavenburg's Bank v. Intercontinental Ltd. (Q.B.D.)   Lloyd J.

A Wills J. said, at pp. 304–305:

"I am of the same opinion; and I agree with my Lord, upon consideration, that debentures of an incorporated company are not, and
were never intended to be, within the operation of the Act of 1878."

Both judgments went on to hold that even if the debenture had fallen
within the Act of 1878 considered on its own it was taken out of the Act
B of 1878 by section 17 of the Act of 1882.

In the course of the next term precisely the same question came before
the Court of Appeal, consisting of Lord Halsbury L.C., Bowen and Fry
L.JJ., in In re Standard Manufacturing Co. [1891] 1 Ch. 627. There was
a very full argument lasting four days. In the course of the argument for
the execution creditors it was submitted that debentures were registrable
C as bills of sale and that that had been the general understanding prior to
Read v. Joannon, 25 Q.B.D. 300. It was submitted for the debenture
holders that limited liability companies never were within the operation
or policy of the Bills of Sale Acts, quite apart from section 17 of the Act
of 1882. The point was thus directly before the Court of Appeal. The
judgment of the court was given the following February by Bowen L.J.
The court held that the debentures were expressly excepted by section 17
D from the Act of 1882. But the court went on to consider the position
under the Act of 1878. The court held that company debentures are not
within the Act of 1878. There are three strands to be found in the
reasoning. In the first place company debentures are not within the
mischief of the Act. The Act was designed to prevent frauds on
creditors by secret bills of sale. Company debentures could hardly be
E described as "secret documents" since there already existed provision
for their registration under the Companies Clauses Consolidation Act
1845 and the Companies Act 1862. Secondly, the language of the Act
seemed much more appropriate to individuals than companies; thus in
section 12 there is provision that the index of bills of sale to be kept by
the registrar is to be arranged according to the "surnames" of their
grantors; thirdly, the court referred to previous authority. The judgment
F concludes with the following paragraph at pp. 647–648:

"The view that debentures like the present are not within the Bills
of Sale Act of 1878 was that adopted by Pollock B. in the case of
John Welsted and Co. Ltd. v. Swansea Bank Ltd., 5 T.L.R. 332, and
by Lord Coleridge C.J. and Wills J. in the case of Read v. Joannon,
25 Q.B.D. 300: see also Edmonds v. Blaina Furnaces Co., 36 Ch.D.
G 215 and Levy v. Abercorris Slate and Slab Co., 37 Ch.D. 260. We
agree with this view, and we think that this appeal should, therefore,
be allowed with costs both here and below, on the ground that the
mortgages or charges of any incorporated company for the registration of which other provisions have been made by the Companies
Clauses Act 1845 or the Companies Act 1862 are not within the
H Bills of Sale Act of 1878."

In re Standard Manufacturing Co. [1891] 1 Ch. 627 was followed a
year later in an Irish case, In re Royal Marine Hotel Co., Kingstown Ltd.
[1895] 1 I.R. 368. Porter M.R. stated the ground of the decision in
In re Standard Manufacturing Co. [1891] 1 Ch. 627 as follows, at p. 375:

"It was there decided by the Court of Appeal that a debenture charging the chattels of a limited company was not void as against execution creditors because it was not registered under the Bills of Sale Acts,

on the ground that under the Companies Act of 1862 a company is A
bound to keep a register of its mortgages and charges, and that the
debenture should have been placed upon such register, and that the
legislature having enacted this particular provision for registering
charges given by a company on its property, impliedly relieved a
company from registering such charges under the Bills of Sale Acts.
I agree with Mr. Fleming that this may be a far-reaching decision,
but I am bound by it."   B

Then in 1896 *In re Standard Manufacturing Co.* [1891] 1 Ch. 627 was
distinguished by Vaughan Williams J. in *Great Northern Railway Co.* v.
Coal Co-operative Society [1896] 1 Ch. 187. The case concerned debentures issued by a society registered under the Industrial and Provident
Societies Act 1876. By virtue of its registration the society became a body C
corporate with perpetual succession, a common seal and limited liability.
But it was not a limited company within the Companies Act 1862, so that
it was not obliged to keep a register of mortgages or charges under
section 43 of that Act or under any other Act. Vaughan Williams J.
held that the debentures were void against the liquidator for non-registration. The primary ground of his decision was that the society, although
a corporation, was not an incorporated company within the meaning of D
section 17 of the Bills of Sale (1878) Amendment Act 1882. He said, at
p. 194:

"The word 'company' has come to have a very well recognised meaning. There are various legal companies, but this industrial society does
not come within the connotation of that word in any of its accepted
legal meanings. And I think that that alone would be sufficient ground E
for saying that the section was designed by the legislature in favour
of companies, and that if the legislature had intended to exclude from
the operation of the Bills of Sale Act all sorts of corporations, nothing
would have been easier for the legislature to do than to say so in plain
terms."

But Vaughan Williams J. went on to consider the broader question whether F
corporations, be they limited companies within the Companies Act 1862
or not, are within the Bills of Sale Acts at all. He treated the decision in
In re Standard Manufacturing Co. [1891] 1 Ch. 627 as being confined
to companies for which other provisions for registration had been made
in the Companies Clauses Consolidation Act 1845 or the Act of 1862.
The question whether the Bills of Sale Act could ever apply to corporations had been "deliberately and studiously [left] . . . open." He said, G
at p. 197:

"I think I have now been through the authorities on this point. There
is the judgment of the Court of Appeal delivered by Bowen L.J. in
In re Standard Manufacturing Co. [1891] 1 Ch. 627, which decides
that companies for the registration of the mortgages of which provision is made are not within the Act of 1878, and I am asked to H
go a step further and say that no corporations are within the Bills
of Sale Acts. I do not feel disposed to go that step."

He then concluded, at p. 198:

"Under those circumstances I am disposed to hold that there is
nothing in the Bills of Sale Acts generally or in section 17 of the Act
of 1882 which excludes from the operation of the Bills of Sale Acts

The Weekly Law Reports, August 22, 1980

1097

1 W.L.R.   Slavenburg's Bank v. Intercontinental Ltd. (Q.B.D.)   Lloyd J.

A   debentures issued by an industrial society like the present, and I therefore decide in favour of the liquidator."

The last case to which I must refer is *Clark* v. *Balm, Hill & Co.* [1908]
1 K.B. 667, a decision of Phillimore J. The case concerned a series of
debentures issued by a company incorporated in Guernsey but charged on
property in England. The question was whether the debentures were void
B for want of registration. The company was not obliged by the law of
Guernsey to keep a register of charges. Phillimore J. held, nevertheless,
in favour of the debenture holders. His conclusion as to the Act of 1878
is expressed in the very start of his judgment, namely, that all debentures
of all incorporated bodies are outside the Act of 1878 and there is " a little
error " in the judgment of Vaughan Williams J. in *Great Northern Railway*
C *Co.* v. *Coal Co-operative Society* [1896] 1 Ch. 187. As for section 17 of
the Act of 1882, he accepted that the Court of Appeal in *In re Standard
Manufacturing Co.* [1891] 1 Ch. 627 had not gone the full length and had
rightly guarded itself against deciding more than it need by limiting its
decision to companies which keep a register of mortgages or charges.
Nevertheless he regarded that distinction as being unsatisfactory. He therefore decided the point left open by the Court of Appeal in accordance
D with the earlier decision of the Divisional Court in *Read* v. *Joannon*,
25 Q.B.D. 300. He said, at p. 671:

> " I myself think that, though the Court of Appeal rightly guarded
> itself against deciding more than it need do in *In re Standard Manu-
> facturing Co.* [1891] 1 Ch. 627, I ought to follow and am bound by
> *Read* v. *Joannon*, 25 Q.B.D. 300, which is wider in its terms; and
E   > I must say that the reasoning of Wills J. in that case commends
> itself to my mind."

He also considered, and rejected, the argument that " incorporated company " in section 17 means " company incorporated in the United
Kingdom."

In the light of those cases, all decided within a relatively short space
F of time, Mr. Evans-Lombe submits, first, that the overriding authority is
that of the Court of Appeal in *In re Standard Manufacturing Co.* [1891]
1 Ch. 627. *Read* v. *Joannon*, 25 Q.B.D. 300 was approved but only on
the limited ground that the company in that case was one for which the
Act of 1862 had provided an alternative system of registration. In the
absence of an alternative system of registration the Bills of Sale Act
G applies to individuals and corporations alike. They are all within the
mischief of the Act. It follows that, if, for any reason the charges in
the present case are not registrable under section 95 of the Companies
Act 1948 they are caught by the Bills of Sale Acts just as charges given
by companies registered under the Industrial and Provident Societies Act
1876 were held to be within the Acts by Vaughan Williams J. In
particular it would, he said, be absurd that an overseas company with
H an established place of business in England which failed to register under
Part X should, as a result of its own failure, escape registration of its
charges altogether, i.e. under the Bills of Sale Acts as well as under
the Companies Act. As for section 17 of the Act of 1882, he says that
it shows conclusively, or is at least a very strong indication, that, but
for section 17, companies are within the Bills of Sale Act. Otherwise
it serves no useful purpose.

These are forceful arguments but I do not think they ought to prevail.

The real difficulty in Mr. Evans-Lombe's path is the decision of Philli- A
more J. in *Clark* v. *Balm, Hill & Co.* [1908] 1 K.B. 667. That decision is
for all practical purposes the latest decision in the field. It has stood now
for 70 years. Even if I thought it wrong (which I do not) I would be most
reluctant not to follow it. So far as I know, it has never been criticised
in any of the standard textbooks. It is treated as good law in the most
recent textbook on the topic, *Gough, Company Charges* (1978), pp. 381–
382, nn. 4–6, a book to which I am much indebted. The only support B
which Mr. Evans-Lombe could find for the opposite view was a single
reference in *Halsbury's Laws of England*, 4th ed., vol. 4, para. 800. If
Clark v. *Balm, Hill & Co.* [1908] 1 K.B. 667 is rightly decided, as I
believe it to be, then it is clear that the present case cannot be distinguished.
Both concerned foreign companies. Both concerned companies for which,
on the assumption that I am making, there was no alternative system of C
registration. Mr. Evans-Lombe tried to persuade me that *Clark* v. *Balm,
Hill & Co.* [1908] 1 K.B. 667 was wrongly decided. If he could have
shown that the decision was inconsistent with what had been held by the
Court of Appeal in *In re Standard Manufacturing Co.* [1891] 1 Ch. 627,
he would, so far as I am concerned, have succeeded. But there is no such
inconsistency. The Court of Appeal decided that certain corporations were
outside the Bills of Sale Act. It did not decide that all other corporations D
are within the Act. It left the point open; and it was the point which was
left open by the Court of Appeal which Phillimore J. decided in the negative.

It is true, of course, that the reasoning in *Clark* v. *Balm, Hill & Co.*
[1908] 1 K.B. 667 is difficult, even impossible, to reconcile with the decision of Vaughan Williams J. in *Great Northern Railway Co.* v. *Coal* E
Co-operative Society [1896] 1 Ch. 187. It is also true that Vaughan
Williams J. was an acknowledged expert in this field. But as between the
two, and with the humility which any judge must feel in the circumstances,
I would prefer the decision of Phillimore J. In the first place, as I have
already mentioned, it is the latest in point of time. Secondly, like Phillimore J. I find it difficult to see that the publicity afforded by the Act of F
1862 registration system was ever a very sound basis for distinguishing
between debentures of corporations which fall within the Act of 1862 and
those that do not. Thirdly, I would attach rather more importance than
did Vaughan Williams J. to the infelicity of the language of the Bills of
Sale Act when applied to corporations. It seems to me clear that, as
Bowen L.J. says, the draftsman cannot have had corporations in mind.
As for section 17 of the Act of 1882, the obvious explanation is that given G
by Phillimore J., namely, that it was inserted per majorem cautelam.

It may perhaps be possible to reconcile the two cases on the narrow
ground that, while a foreign company is an incorporated company within
the meaning of section 17, a society registered under the Industrial and
Provident Societies Act 1876, though incorporated, is not an incorporated
company. But I would prefer to put my decision on the broad ground H
indicated by Phillimore J., namely, that Bills of Sale Acts apply to individuals only and not to corporations at all.

There is a further point which weighs with me, and which I must
mention, even though it did not find much favour with Mr. Stubbs.
Even if *Great Northern Railway Co.* v. *Coal Co-operative Society* [1896]
1 Ch. 187 was correctly decided, and even if the Court of Appeal in *In re
Standard Manufacturing Co.* [1891] 1 Ch. 627 is to be taken as having

The Weekly Law Reports, August 22, 1980

1099

1 W.L.R.   Slavenburg's Bank v. Intercontinental Ltd. (Q.B.D.)   Lloyd J.

A held that the only corporations outside the Act are those for which Parliament has provided an alternative system of registration, then it seems to me that Parliament *has* provided just such a system in the present case by virtue of Part III of the Companies Act 1948. Mr. Evans-Lombe's argument in effect came to this, that the Bills of Sale Acts are a catchall, which apply to all bills of sale as defined unless a charge created by a particular bill of sale happens to be registrable under the Companies Act

B 1948; so that if, for instance, Parliament had provided for a system of registration of charges, but a particular charge, while coming broadly within the system, fell through an unforeseen gap, for example, by non-registration of an overseas company under Part X of the Companies Act 1948, then it would be caught by the Bills of Sale Act.

I think this is to attribute far too meticulous an intention to the legis-

C lature. Assuming Parliament did not intend to exclude all corporations when they enacted the Bills of Sale Acts, as I have held that they did, the intention must have been to exclude certain broad categories of corporation, namely, those for whom a separate system of registration was provided by the Companies Acts in force from time to time. You then look at the current Companies Act and ask yourself: is the company in question within the registration provisions? If it is, then the Bills of Sale Acts

D on their true construction do not apply, and it is irrelevant that the particular charge may not be registrable. In other words, you look at the company and not at the charge.

If that is right, then it seems to me that on all except one of Mr. Stubbs's arguments the present company falls outside the Bills of Sale Acts even if the charges were not registrable under the Companies Act.

E The one exception is Mr. Stubbs's argument that section 106 only applies to companies incorporated in Scotland and Ireland. On all the other arguments the company is within the registration provisions of the Companies Act 1948 even if the particular charge is not registrable, and, accordingly, the Bills of Sale Acts do not apply.

I now turn to the second main issue under the Bills of Sale Acts.

F Assuming the Bills of Sale Acts are capable of applying to companies, are the documents in the present case debentures issued by an incorporated company within the meaning of section 17 of the Act of 1882? The point does not arise as a separate point if I am right on the first issue, so I can deal with it quite briefly. Mr. Evans-Lombe argues, first, that " incorporated company " does not include a company incorporated abroad. In *Clark* v. *Balm, Hill & Co.* [1908] 1 K.B. 667 Phillimore J. held that

G " incorporated company " at least included a company which, if not a company incorporated according to the law of the United Kingdom, was nevertheless incorporated according to the laws in force in one portion of the British Empire under the sanction of the common Sovereign. Although the British Empire no longer exists, I see no reason for not applying what Phillimore J. said to a company incorporated in Bermuda.

H Secondly, Mr. Evans-Lombe argued that the documents are not debentures within the meaning of section 17. A debenture, he said, is a document which creates or acknowledges an indebtedness. It is of the essence of a debenture that it identifies the particular sum which is due. Accordingly, a document which relates to future indebtedness, that is to say to a debt which is unquantified at the date of the creation of the document and may never arise, cannot be a debenture. Thus it was said that the ordinary form of bank debenture which is taken by a bank as security for sums to

be advanced on current account—sometimes called an "all-moneys" A
debenture, as opposed to a "fixed sum" debenture—is not a debenture
at all.

I was referred to a number of cases. I note that in many of them
judges of great eminence have declined to attempt a definition of what is
meant by a debenture. I certainly do not propose to rush in where they
have feared to tread. No doubt it is true that in general a debenture is a
document of which it can usually be said that it creates or acknowledges   B
an indebtedness. But there is no hard and fast definition. Certainly none
of the cases to which I was referred decide that a document cannot be a
debenture unless the debt to which it relates is quantified at the date of its
creation. I am unwilling to be the first so to decide. Had it been necessary for my decision I would have held that all the documents on which
the bank relies in the present case, with the exception of the storage   C
reports, are debentures of an incorporated company within the meaning
of section 17 of the Act of 1882.

I now come to the last question of all. Assuming the documents on
which the bank relies are otherwise within the Bills of Sale Acts 1878 and
1882, are they exempt by virtue of the Bills of Sale Act 1890? Section 1
of the Act, as amended by section 1 of the Bills of Sale Act 1891, provides: D

"Exemption of letters of hypothecation of imported goods. . . .

"1 An instrument charging or creating any security on or
declaring trusts of imported goods given or executed at any time
prior to their deposit in a warehouse, factory, or store, or to their
being reshipped for export, or delivered to a purchaser not being
the person giving or executing such instrument, shall not be deemed
a bill of sale within the meaning of the Bills of Sale Acts 1878   E
and 1882."

For the purpose of dealing with questions under the Act of 1890, I am to
assume (1) that the relevant petroleum products are imported goods, and
(2) that the assignment of stocks as security was executed prior to their
deposit with Paktank. In those circumstances, Mr. Stubbs argues that the
assignment of stocks as security is to be deemed not to be a bill of sale.   F
Mr. Evans-Lombe, on the other hand, submits that the Act of 1890 is
not dealing with future goods at all, that is to say with instruments which
charge or create any security on goods generally, but only with particular
goods which can be identified at the time of the creation of the charge,
for example a consignment of goods arriving by a particular ship. In
Halsbury's Laws of England, 4th ed., vol. 4, para. 636, there is a footnote   G
which reads:

". . . It would seem that the statutory provisions contemplate an
instrument referring to a specific consignment of goods, rather than
a general letter of pledge covering all goods that may from time to
time be imported by the pledgor."

Counsel were unable to refer to any other authority. The point is a very   H
short one. On the whole I agree with Mr. Evans-Lombe's contention on
this point. It seems to me that what the section contemplates is the sort
of document sometimes called a letter of hypothecation, but more usually
called a trust receipt, which a bank takes when releasing bills of lading
held under a documentary credit in order to enable the merchant to take
delivery of the goods from the ship's side. In Lloyds Bank Ltd. v. Bank
of America National Trust and Savings Association [1938] 2 K.B. 147, the

The Weekly Law Reports, August 22, 1980

1101

1 W.L.R.   Slavenburg's Bank v. Intercontinental Ltd. (Q.B.D.)   Lloyd J.

A practice in relation to such documents was described as well-established and of very long standing. I do not say that the section is necessarily confined to such documents. But I do decide that it was not meant to cover a document which creates, or purports to create, a general charge on all future goods, whether imported or not. I would therefore agree with what is said in the footnote in *Halsbury's Laws of England*, 4th ed.,

B vol. 4, to which I have already referred, with a proviso that the word "specific" might prove misleading. For the goods do not have to be specific goods in the strict Sale of Goods Act 1893 sense, provided the consignment is sufficiently identified. With regard to the storage reports, Mr. Stubbs agreed that they could not come within the section because they were only issued after the petroleum products had been deposited with Paktank.

C On this last issue, therefore, I decide in favour of the defendants. But on the other issues in relation to the Bills of Sale Acts 1878 and 1882, I decide in favour of the bank.

The overall result is that, on the assumptions I have been asked to make, the defendants win outright on the first group of issues, that is to say in relation to section 95 of the Companies Act 1948. But on their

D alternative case under the Bills of Sale Acts 1878 and 1882 they fail.

Judgment for defendants.

Solicitors: *Linklaters & Paines; Cameron Kemm Nordon.*

[Reported by SUSAN DENNY, Barrister-at-Law]

E

F

[FAMILY DIVISION]

* W. *v.* SUNDERLAND METROPOLITAN BOROUGH COUNCIL

1980 Jan. 28   Sir John Arnold P. and Butler-Sloss J.

G *Children and Young Persons—Care of—Child received into care by local authority—Endeavour to establish bond between mother and child with view to reunion—Decision by social workers to abandon endeavour—Whether resolution vesting parental rights and duties in local authority not to lapse—Matters to be established — Whether mother "consistently" failing in parental obligations—Whether proper for justices to see social worker privately before hearing—Children Act 1948 (11 & 12 Geo. 6, c. 43), s. 2 (1) (as substituted by Children Act 1975 (c. 72), s. 57)*

H   Section 2 of the Children Act 1948 (as substituted by section 57 of the Children Act 1975) provides:
"(1) Subject to the provisions of this Part of this Act, if it appears to a local authority in relation to any child who is in their care under the foregoing section— ... (b) that a parent of his— ... (v) has so consistently failed without reasonable cause to discharge the obligations of a parent as to be unfit to have the care of the child; ... the local authority may resolve that there shall vest in

them the parental rights and duties with respect to that   A
child . . .

" (5) Where a counter-notice has been served on a
local authority . . . the authority may . . . complain to a
juvenile court . . . and the court may on the hearing of
the complaint order that the resolution shall not lapse by
reason of the service of the counter-notice: Provided that
the court shall not so order unless satisfied—(a) that the
grounds mentioned in subsection (1) of this section on   B
which the local authority purported to pass the resolution
were made out, and (b) that at the time of the hearing
there continued to be grounds on which a resolution under
subsection (1) of this section could be founded, and (c)
that it is in the interests of the child to do so . . ."

Shortly after her birth in October, an illegitimate girl was
placed in the care of the local authority at the request of the
mother. At that time the mother felt unable to accept the   C
responsibility for the child and after a few weeks the child
went to foster parents.   On September 12, 1978, the local
authority passed a resolution under section 2 of the Children
Act 1948 (as substituted by the Children Act 1975) vesting
parental rights and duties in themselves. The mother objected
and the local authority applied to the juvenile court under
section 2 (5) for an order that the resolution should not lapse.
The hearing of the complaint was fixed for October 26, 1978.   D
On that day the justices were told that the local authority
hoped that in time mother and child could be reunited and
with that prospect in view the mother would be encouraged
to see the child frequently. The hearing was adjourned sine die.
The mother was offered the tenancy of a house which was
outside her own area but she was advised that appropriate
accommodation was essential if she was to develop a situation
in which she could have the child back.   She accepted the   E
tenancy in February 1979. The house was in need of repair
and redecoration which should have taken about three weeks
but took considerably longer.   During the winter the mother
visited the child fairly regularly but failed to visit the child
for approximately six weeks between mid-March 1979 and
the end of April 1979.

On May 1, 1979, following a case review the social services
officers decided that the mother had failed to bring about a   F
situation which was likely to lead to a reunion with the child
and that it was in the best interests of the child to abandon
the endeavour. It was envisaged that the child would be
offered eventually for adoption. The juvenile court hearing was
reinstated.   On October 4, 1979, before the hearing of the
complaint, the justices saw the child together with the social
worker immediately in charge of the case in their private room.
The justices confirmed the local authority's resolution.   G

On the mother's appeal: —

Held, allowing the appeal (1) that where an issue arose of
a potentially disputatious character regarding the facts it was
improper for the justices to see in their private room before
the hearing of a complaint a witness who would be giving
evidence (post, p. 1105c).

(2) That the justices had to be satisfied under section   H
2 (1) (b) and (5) of the Children Act 1948 not only that at
the time of the passing of the resolution there were grounds
on which to found a resolution assuming parental rights and
duties but also that at the time of the hearing there continued
to be such grounds and that it was in the interests of the
child that the resolution should not lapse; that the consistent
failure to discharge parental obligations under section 2 (1) (b)
had to be demonstrated by reference only to such period of
time as was appropriate to the facts of the particular case

A   and while there was material such as to enable the justices to find that there had been a parental failure within section 2 (1) (b) (v) before the date of the resolution, in the period following the resolution there was not, in all the circumstances, material from which the justices could reasonably conclude that the mother had consistently failed without reasonable cause to discharge the obligations of a parent so as to be unfit to have care of the child, and, accordingly, the resolution

B   must be allowed to lapse (post, pp. 1105H—1106A, 1107A–B, 1109C–D, H—1110B).

    In re D. (Minors) (Adoption by Parent) [1973] Fam. 209, D.C. considered.

    The following cases are referred to in the judgment of Sir John Arnold P.:

    D. (Minors) (Adoption by Parent), In re [1973] Fam. 209; [1973] 3 W.L.R.

C   595; [1973] 3 All E.R. 1001, D.C.

    T. (An Infant), In re (1974) 118 S.J. 78, D.C.

    The following additional case was cited in argument:

    M. v. Wigan Metropolitan Borough Council [1980] Fam. 36; [1979] 3 W.L.R. 244; [1979] 2 All E.R. 958, D.C.

D   APPEAL from Sunderland Juvenile Court.

    On September 12, 1978, the Sunderland Metropolitan Borough Council by resolution of the social services committee assumed parental rights and duties in respect of an illegitimate girl born on October 13, 1977, on the ground that the mother had so consistently failed without reasonable cause to discharge the obligation of a parent as to be unfit

E   to have the care of the child. The mother objected to the resolution and served a counter-notice on the local authority under section 2 (4) of the Children Act 1948. The local authority sought an order from the juvenile court that the resolution should not lapse. The complaint came before the justices on October 26, 1978, when the hearing was adjourned sine die. On that day the justices were told that it was hoped to establish

F   a bond between mother and child so that eventually the child could be returned to the mother. The mother was encouraged to visit the child regularly at the home of the foster parents. On May 1, 1979, at a case conference the social services officers decided that it was in the child's best interests to remain with the foster parents and eventually to be adopted by them. The mother's visits were restricted to once every three weeks. The adjourned hearing of the complaint was reinstated on

G   October 4, 1979, when the justices upheld the resolution and made the order sought by the local authority.

    The mother appealed against the justices' decision on the grounds, inter alia, (1) that they had failed to take any or sufficient notice of the evidence of a woman social worker who had stated that the mother was a fit person to have the care of the child and that it was in the best

H   interests of the child not to sever the blood tie; (2) that there were no continuing grounds to justify the resolution; and (3) that the mother had resumed teaching in a school and been considered a fit and proper person to have the care and control of children.

    The facts are stated in the judgment of Sir John Arnold P.

    Robert Lamb for the mother.
    A. J. N. Brunner for the local authority.

W. v. Sunderland Council (D.C.) [1980]

SIR JOHN ARNOLD P. On October 13, 1977, the mother, the appellant, had a baby girl. On September 12, 1978, the Sunderland Metropolitan Borough Council passed a resolution under section 2 of the Children Act 1948 vesting the parental rights and duties in respect of the child in themselves. A counter-notice was given under that section by the mother, whereupon the matter was referred to the juvenile court. The matter was listed for hearing later that year, on October 26, 1978. The local authority and the mother came to an arrangement which was designed to see whether a state of affairs could be brought about under which the local authority could feel able not to continue with the resolution but to facilitate the reunion of the mother and child. There would in the meantime be an intensive regime of access between mother and child to see whether that situation could be brought about. It was very sensibly decided to adjourn the court hearing indefinitely.

That was how the matter rested between September 1978 and May 1, 1979. On May 1, 1979, there was a case conference among the officers of the local authority, as a result of which it was determined at that level that the experiment had failed and that it was no longer realistic to expect to bring into being a state of affairs in which the child could be, or should be, returned to the mother. It was decided that the resolution should be implemented by means of long term fostering, in fact with the same foster parents who had had the child in the meantime but under the guise of would-be adopters. The new style of regime should be accompanied no longer by an intensive programme of access, but by the more restrictive programme of three-weekly visits by the mother to the child.

When this decision was indicated to the mother, she determined to reinstate the juvenile court hearing on the question whether the resolution should stand. The issue came before the court on October 4, 1979. On that occasion the justices decided that the resolution should stand. It is from that decision that the mother appeals to us today. That is the history of the litigation, and it now falls upon us to consider whether or not that decision of the justices should stand.

The mother arrived at the juvenile court with her solicitor and a couple of women friends shortly before 10 o'clock on the morning of the hearing. At about the same time there were present in the court building the officer of the social services department of the local authority who had been in immediate charge of the case, a Mr. J. and a superior officer of Mr. J.'s together with Mr. and Mrs. B. who were the foster parents, and the little girl, who was then almost exactly two years old. The mother was told by, I think, Mr. J. and his superior that the justices had expressed a desire to see the child and that she (the mother) could see the child thereafter. That piece of information was passed by the mother to her solicitor, and nothing more transpired except that some little time later—between that event which took place about 10 o'clock and 10.30 when the hearing started—an opportunity was given to the mother to see the child for a very short time. The case was then heard.

In fact, what had happened was that the justices had seen the child in company with the foster parents, who though interested parties were not in fact witnesses, and Mr. J., who was the only important witness for the local authority. There is no material before us to suggest for a moment that anything was said by the foster parents or by Mr. J. which could have had any effect on the minds of the justices. There is no reason

A   to think that there was; certainly there is no material from which we could so judge. Nor is there any reason to suppose that it was necessary for the child to be accompanied either by Mr. J. or by the foster father. It is arguable, and for my part I would be happy to accept, that it was desirable that there should be somebody with the child in case she became distressed or nervous, but no reason at all, that I can see, to think that it should have been anybody other than, or in addition to,

B   the foster mother.

    At no time, until long after the decision of the justices had been made and announced, was it ever brought to the attention of the mother or her solicitors, or anybody else concerned with the case, that the justices had, in fact, had with them before the hearing anybody other than the child. Certainly there was no reason whatever for anybody to

C   suppose that they had had Mr. J. with them. But such was the fact.

    To me it seems plain that in those circumstances justice cannot have been seen to have been done. It cannot be right, in any imaginable circumstances, that where an issue arises of a potentially disputatious character as regard the facts—and if ever there was one it was this one— that the justices should be closeted, for whatever reason, with the very person who is going to give the disputable evidence about the matter.

D   It is, in fact, the case, as has been said in this court, in *In re T. (An Infant)* (1974) 118 S.J. 78, that there is no rule of law which empowers justices to see children in their private room. But it does not necessarily follow that, in any case in which they did do so, that circumstance alone would be sufficient to upset their decision. However that may be, that is not this case.

E   This case is one in which, quite plainly, in view of what happened and what I have described this decision cannot stand.

    We were told by Mr. Brunner, on instructions—and the local authority must be much concerned with appearances in that court—that it was the practice in the juvenile court of the Sunderland Bench always to see the social worker and the child in similar circumstances. I can only say

F   that I regard that as a most unfortunate practice, at least in cases in which the social worker is liable to be called upon to give potentially controversial evidence. If there be any very unusual circumstances in which it is imperative that such a course should be followed, what the justices ought to do is to indicate that this unfortunate incident had occurred so that, at least, everybody in the court knows the fact. It would be very much better if it never happened again.

G   A conclusion that the decision cannot stand as it is does not, of course, mean that the opposite conclusion should necessarily be reached. It would be possible, if this court were not to be convinced that the material led to a conclusion that the resolution should lapse, merely to set aside the decision which had so far been made and to remit the case for another hearing before the justices.

H   It is, therefore, necessary to go on to consider the submissions which are made by the mother as to the merits of the decision. When one looks at section 2 of the Children Act 1948 (as substituted by section 57 of the Children Act 1975) it is to be seen that there are in this case three matters which have to be decided. First of all, in order that the court should direct that the resolution should not lapse, it has to be satisfied in the circumstances of this case that the mother had so consistently failed without reasonable cause to discharge the obligations of a parent

as to be unfit to have the care of the child, on grounds which were already A
made out at the date of the passing of the resolution on September 12,
1978. Secondly, that there continued to be grounds on which that
conclusion ought to be reached at the time of the hearing before the
justices on October 4, 1979. Finally, that it was in the interests of the
child to direct that the resolution should not lapse.

If the local authority failed to make out any one of those three
matters, and the onus was squarely upon them, then the only proper B
conclusion of the justices could have been that the resolution should
lapse.

The history of the matter was this. The mother had had, prior to
the birth, some psychiatric problems about which it is sufficient to say
that on the medical evidence she was cured. Because of that history, the
baby was placed initially, while the mother and baby were still in C
hospital, in the special baby care unit. On October 21, 1977, the mother
was ready for her discharge. She could, on any medical grounds, have
taken the child with her, but she did not. According to the evidence,
she told the nurse in charge that she felt unable to cope with the baby at
home at that stage. Exactly why this was is not very clear; at that early
stage it may very well be attributable to post-natal depression or perhaps D
to the lack of self-confidence which would, not surprisingly, be felt by
a young woman who had had psychiatric troubles in the fairly recent
past.

The mother, quite soon, acquiesced in a fostering of her child, and,
indeed, by the end of a month or so after the birth, the child had been
placed with the foster parents. The mother was, at that time, minded
to wish that the child should be adopted. The result of that was that after E
a reception into care on November 4, 1977, by the local authority,
although it was made quite clear to the mother that she could see the
child she did not, in fact, do so until four months later when, on
March 3, 1978, the mother made an arrangement, quite independently,
on her own account to see the child and did so. That was a surprise to
the social worker who was in communication with the Hexham and F
Newcastle Diocesan Rescue Society and expected any visit to be arranged
through that agency; but it was not.

Then the local authority, through its appropriate officer, was minded
to arrange for further visits. But only one visit after that—or perhaps
two—took place. So matters stood until August 1978 when the mother
gave the sort of intimation which amounts to a request under section
1 (3) of the Children Act 1948 for the return of the child to her. It was G
in those circumstances that the local authority passed its resolution on
September 12, 1978.

The first question then is, "Was there, on the part of the mother,
such a failure to discharge the obligations of a parent as to be unfit to
have the care of the child without showing any reasonable cause
therefor?" There is very little evidence as to exactly what it was which H
caused the contact between mother and child to be so minimal after
March 3, 1978, and up to the date in August 1978 when she asked for
the child back. In the course of her evidence the mother suggested that
access was refused; but there is no indication that it was refused by the
local authority; quite the reverse, they offered to arrange it. And it
seems to me, at any rate, that the justices were, on the material before
them, fully entitled to take the view that the separation of mother and

A   child for that long period of about six months was not explained in any way which should have led them to conclude that there was a reasonable cause for it.

    An unexplained absence of any significant visit to the child over that period seems, at least to me, to be a matter which entitled the justices, if they were so minded, to conclude that there was the sort of failure B which is indicated in section 2 (1) (b) (v) of the Act of 1948. For my part I do not find it possible to say that the justices were wrong in thinking that the first matter had been made out.

    The second matter relates to the period between the resolution of September 12, 1978, and the hearing a little over a year later on October 4, 1979. What had happened was that very soon after the resolution in September some correspondence took place between the C local authority and solicitors who were acting for the mother. The exact details of that have not been referred to, but the upshot, at no very great distance of time—not more than three weeks after the passing of the resolution—was that regular weekly visiting started. The first occasion was, apparently, October 3, 1978.

    The arrangements which had been made betokened twice weekly D visits. The visits which took place from October 3 through to Christmas were, so far as appears from the evidence, absolutely regular once-weekly visits. It seems to me to be quite impossible to say that the difference between once-weekly and twice-weekly visits is a difference involving the sort of failure which is mentioned in paragraph (v) of section 2 (1) (b) of the Children Act 1948.

    So matters fell until Christmas. On December 22, 1978, there was a E telephone call between Mr. J. and the mother. Mr. J. was told by the mother that she had agreed with the foster mother to the child going to her parents' home the next week. This was vetoed by Mr. J. on the ground that he had not visited the parents' home to see whether it was suitable for the child. There was also, as Mr. J. pointed out, a difficulty in that there was a bad personal relationship between him and the F mother's father—a matter about which we know nothing—and that that was an obstacle in the way of his inspecting the house. His language on oath is this: " I said her father had been unwilling to let me visit home." (I suppose " the home.")

    Mr. J. then, for the first time, told the mother that his department might have to make alternative plans if she did not respond to the child G as she should; that the review upon this matter was fixed for May, and that the alternative which he had in mind was long term fostering. That warning, whatever it was based on, cannot have been based on any lack of regular visiting. Visiting had been regular and consistent from October 3, 1978.

    He also told her—which I suppose she knew—that the adjournment of the juvenile court proceedings had been agreed to by his department H to let the reunion process start. Well, there is nothing controversial about that. He arranged for her to visit on January 2, 1979, and on January 5, 1979, she did visit (the visit on January 2 having been cancelled, according to Mr. J., because of blocked roads). She visited on January 5, 16 and 19, so there were three visits within the first 14 days. There was then a small gap, and on February 2 and 6, 1979, she visited. Again, after a gap of three weeks, she visited on February 27, 1979. She visited again on March 6, 9 and 13, 1979.

1108

She had been seen by Mr. J. on February 28, 1979, and he found her very worried and drawn but she refused to elaborate on her anxieties.

In the meantime, on February 19, 1979, she had signed a tenancy agreement for a house. It was a house which was not situated in the part of Sunderland which she particularly favoured—where her church was situated, and where she was deriving, it seems, a good deal of support both from the clergy and the congregation. But on February 2, 1979, the solicitor to the local authority, in a letter which had obviously been written with the close collaboration of Mr. J.—who is freely quoted in it—had pointed out that there was a review coming up in May. That review was liable to lead to a solution which would be unsatisfactory to the mother if at that stage no progress had been made towards the development of a situation in which she could have the child back. Appropriate accommodation was essential, and she would be very wise, therefore, to accept accommodation where she had been offered it, instead of insisting on accommodation in the favoured part of town. That was a sensible suggestion, and she was persuaded, no doubt, by that.

On February 19, 1979, as I have indicated, she obtained accommodation. It was a house which had been occupied by somebody else and was in need of both repair and replacement, that is to say, decorative repair and more substantial matters of which only two are known to the court, one related to a single-drawer sink unit which had to be fitted and the other to some electrical work about which we know nothing.

The matter of the sink unit was slightly complicated in that although it was not technically necessary to delay fitting it until a top was available, according to the general foreman in the public works department, a lay person such as the mother might very well think that it was. Whether for that reason or for any other I do not know, but the fact of the matter is that it took very much longer than the period which the foreman considered appropriate, namely, a period of not more than three weeks, to put the house to rights. At the hearing on October 4, 1979, the mother said it was almost redecorated by then. Mr. J. saw it on May 22, 1979, and it was curtained and wallpapered, and there were three chairs in the sitting room. He does not appear to have gone to any other room; there is no reason why he should. But it was a slow business, and this period after the acquisition to some extent coincided with the falling off in the visits between the mother and her child.

They did continue, as I have already indicated, up to March 13, 1979. Then there was a gap of five or six weeks from March 13, 1979, to April 24, 1979. On April 24, 1979, the mother visited the child again, but on the previous day she had had a meeting with Mr. J. at which they had discussed, in his office, the state of things in the new house. She told Mr. J., according to his evidence, that everything was going well. She told him that she could not visit—or presumably had not been able to visit—as she had been busy. He reminded her of her duty to maintain contact with the child, and he said that the visits had fallen off rather than increased as the department had hoped. These comments seem to have been sufficiently cogent to persuade her to visit on the following day.

In the meantime, as indeed the mother knew, there had been arranged for May 1, 1979—a week away—the case review. She knew about it

A because, according to the evidence, on the occasion of the meeting on April 23, 1979, she had mentioned bringing a friend with her to attend the review. On May 1, 1979, it was decided that she had failed in her endeavour to bring about a situation which would lead, or be likely to lead, to a reunion with her child. From that moment on that was abandoned. The three-weekly visit was substituted in conjunction with the long term fostering project. So final was that departure that the

B justices did not consider it necessary to consider any question of whether there had been any failure in the duty indicated in section 2 (1) of the Children Act 1948 at any time after May 1, 1979. Not unreasonably, perhaps, but certainly they regarded that as the watershed. They regarded the die as cast upon that date.

The question that we have to consider under this head is whether

C the justices were entitled to regard the local authority as having discharged the onus, in respect of the period theoretically between September 12, 1978, and October 4, 1979, practically, having regard to the way they set about their task between September 12, 1978, and May 1, 1979, of demonstrating the failure concerned.

It has to be not only a consistent failure, but such a failure as to

D render the parent unfit to have the care of the child. Both those postulates have to be satisfied. The phrase is not the same as the phrase which is used in the Adoption Act 1958. It is pointed out in the case to which our attention has been directed that there is a distinction between the use of the word " persistent " in the adoption section and the word " consistent " used in section 2 (1) of the Children Act 1948. The difference which is relevant, so far as this case is concerned, is that the

E period for a persistent failure has to be a substantially longer period, whereas in the section we are considering the consistency has to be demonstrated only by reference to such period of time as is appropriate to the matters which arise in the particular case.

Two aspects of failure are put forward by the local authority on this appeal. One is—though faintly comprehending the period between the

F beginning of October and Christmas, more pertinently related to the period between Christmas and the end of April—that there had been such gaps in the mother's visiting programme, such inadequacies of excuse, that the failure was made out in respect of that period on the basis, purely, of the failure to keep contact. The other is the failure between February 19, 1979, and May 1, 1979, to carry out expeditiously the maximum of three weeks' work, according to the foreman, which

G was required to render the house habitable so as to provide a place to which the mother could, if properly minded to discharge her duties to her child, have been able to take that child if and when she had earned her right to do so by an effective reunion by visiting the child.

In re D. (Minors) (Adoption by Parent) [1973] Fam. 209, was a case which required a consideration of whether the father had " persistently

H failed without reasonable cause to discharge the obligations of a parent " in terms of section 5 (2) of the Adoption Act 1958. I do not think that on the question of whether the failure was persistent or not I can derive any assistance in the present case, precisely because of the difference which is pointed out—as I have already mentioned—between a persistent failure and a consistent failure in the relevant context. What *In re D.* does show, in my view, is that this appellate court is entitled to review the justices' decision in such a matter, in order to see whether there was

1110

material upon which the justices could reasonably have concluded that the A
failure had been demonstrated. Having given the best consideration that
I can to the present case, my conclusion is that there was not, between
September 12, 1978, and May 1, 1979—or more relevantly between
Christmas 1978 and May 1, 1979—material upon which the justices could
reasonably conclude that the failure had been made out in terms of
section 2 (1) (a) (v) of the Children Act 1948. In my judgment, therefore, B
this court ought to reverse the justices' decision and direct that the
resolution should lapse.

BUTLER-SLOSS J.   I agree.

Appeal allowed.
Resolution to lapse.

C

Solicitors: *Collyer-Bristow for Goodswens, Middlesbrough; J. M.*
Trebble, Sunderland.

M. B. D.

D

[QUEEN'S BENCH DIVISION]

* REGINA v. GOVERNOR OF PENTONVILLE PRISON,
Ex parte BUDLONG
* REGINA v. GOVERNOR OF HOLLOWAY PRISON,
Ex parte KEMBER

E

1979 Nov. 12, 13, 14, 15, 16, 19; 30   Lord Widgery C.J. and
Griffiths J.

Extradition—Treaty—Construction—Burglary of confidential docu-
ments from United States government department—No formal
document with particulars constituting offence according to
English law—Whether substantial similarity of offences suffi- F
cient to constitute double criminality—Whether offence of
political character—Whether attempted enforcement of public
law—Extradition Act 1870 (33 & 34 Vict. c. 52), ss. 3 (1), 26 [1]
—United States of America (Extradition) Order 1976 (S.I.
1976 No. 2144), Sch. 1, art. III [2] *European Court of Justice—*
Reference to—Whether necessary—Extradition from United
Kingdom of own national—Whether requiring justification on
public policy grounds—Whether question requiring ruling by G
European Court—E.E.C. Treaty (Cmnd. 5179—II), art. 48 (3)

Members of the Church of Scientology entered various
government offices in the District of Columbia, United States
of America, and there stole confidential material relating to
the church and its adherents; they revealed that they acted
on the instructions of the applicants, B (an American) and K
(a United Kingdom national), who were senior members of H
the church residing in England. The applicants were charged
with burglary, in respect of which the United States Government made a requisition for their surrender, and the Home
Secretary authorised a metropolitan stipendiary magistrate to
issue warrants for their arrest. The documents placed before

[1] Extradition Act 1870, s. 3 (1): see post, p. 1125G–H.
S. 26: see post, p. 1122C.
[2] United States of America (Extradition) Order 1976, Sch. 1, art. III: see post,
pp. 1121H–1122A.

The Weekly Law Reports, October 3, 1980

1111

1 W.L.R.   Reg. v. Pentonville Prison Governor, Ex p. Budlong (D.C.)

A   the magistrate did not allege entry by the burglars as trespassers, but the magistrate concluded that there was a prima facie case of burglary under the relevant laws, both American and English, and, since burglary was an extraditable offence under the Extradition Treaty between the United Kingdom and the United States as set out in Schedule 1 to the United States of America (Extradition) Order 1976, he issued warrants committing the applicants to prison to await extradition.

B   The applicants applied for writs of habeas corpus on the ground that the extradition warrants were unlawful. They both contended that the magistrate erred in considering the evidence without there being a formal document containing sufficient particulars to constitute burglary according to English law; that the American and English definitions of the crime ought to have been identical since, in accordance with the principle of double criminality, the offence had to be

C   established under both American and English law; that the offence as committed was of a political character; and that the real purpose of the requisition was to enforce a public law protecting government information. K also sought a reference to the European Court of Justice for a preliminary ruling on the question whether her extradition had to be justified on public policy grounds under article 48 (3) of the E.E.C. Treaty.[3]

D   On the applications: —

Held, refusing the applications, (1) that the only formal documents required to be put before the magistrate in extradition proceedings were the Secretary of State's order, giving, inter alia, the name of the crime and the foreign warrant authorising the arrest; neither of those documents was required to set out all the particulars of offence and no other documents were necessary because it was for the magistrate to

E   see whether there were sufficient facts established to constitute an offence contrary to English law (post, p. 1115F–G).

Reg. v. *Jacobi and Hiller* (1881) 46 L.T. 595, D.C. applied.

Reg. v. *Governor of Brixton Prison, Ex parte Gardner* [1968] 2 Q.B. 399, D.C. distinguished.

(2) That on the true construction of article III of the Extradition Treaty and section 26 of the Extradition Act 1870 double criminality in the English law of extradition was

F   satisfied if the offence for which extradition was demanded and the offence for which it was granted would be recognised as substantially similar in the foreign country and England, even though the definitions of the offences in the laws of the two countries were not identical; accordingly, the applicants could be extradited notwithstanding that entry as a trespasser was not an ingredient of burglary in American law (post, pp. 1118G, 1122A, C–E, H, 1123A).

G   *In re Bellencontre* [1891] 2 Q.B. 122, D.C. and *In re Arton (No. 2)* [1896] 1 Q.B. 509, D.C. applied.

(3) That, since the purpose of the burglaries was not to challenge the political control or government of a country, they were not offences of a political character and, accordingly, section 3 (1) of the Act and the rule whereby a foreign public law would not be enforced did not apply (post, pp. 1123G–H, 1124H—1125A, D–E, 1125H—1126A).

H   *Reg.* v. *Governor of Brixton Prison, Ex parte Schtraks* [1964] A.C. 556, H.L.(E.).

(4) That, extradition being closely analogous to the implementation of domestic criminal law, common sense dictated that article 48 should be interpreted as not intended to apply to the exercise by the United Kingdom of the power to extradite

---

[3] E.E.C. Treaty, art. 48: "1. Freedom of Movement for Workers . . . 3. It shall entail the right, subject to limitations justified on grounds of public policy, . . . (b) to move freely within the territory of member states for this purpose; . . ."

Reg. v. Pentonville Prison Governor, Ex p. Budlong (D.C.)   [1980]

an accused person; and that, as the point was reasonably clear   A
and free from doubt, no reference would be made to the
European Court (post, pp. 1127E, 1128C–D).

  H. P. Bulmer Ltd. v. *Bollinger S.A.* [1974] Ch. 401, C.A.
applied.

The following cases are referred to in the judgment:

Arton, In re [1896] 1 Q.B. 108, D.C.   B
Arton (No. 2), In re [1896] 1 Q.B. 509, D.C.
Bellencontre, In re [1891] 2 Q.B. 122, D.C.
Bulmer (H. P.) Ltd. v. *J. Bollinger S.A.* [1974] Ch. 401; [1974] 3 W.L.R.
    202; [1974] 2 All E.R. 1226, C.A.
Castioni, In re [1891] 1 Q.B. 149, D.C.
Factor v. *Laubenheimer* (1933) 290 U.S. 276.
Knoors v. *Secretary of State for Economic Affairs* [1979] 2 C.M.L.R. 357,   C
    E.C.J.
Reg. v. *Bouchereau* [1978] Q.B. 732; [1978] 2 W.L.R. 250, E.C.J.
Reg. v. *Governor of Brixton Prison, Ex parte Gardner* [1968] 2 Q.B.
    399; [1968] 2 W.L.R. 512; [1968] 1 All E.R. 636, D.C.
Reg. v. *Governor of Brixton Prison, Ex parte Kolczynski* [1955] 1 Q.B.
    540; [1955] 2 W.L.R. 116; [1955] 1 All E.R. 31, D.C.
Reg. v. *Governor of Brixton Prison, Ex parte Schtraks* [1963] 1 Q.B. 55;
    [1962] 2 W.L.R. 976; [1962] 2 All E.R. 176, D.C.; [1964] A.C. 556;   D
    [1962] 3 W.L.R. 1013; [1962] 3 All E.R. 529, H.L.(E.).
Reg. v. *Governor of Pentonville Prison, Ex parte Cheng* [1973] A.C.
    931; [1973] 2 W.L.R. 746; [1973] 1 All E.R. 935; [1973] 2 All E.R.
    204, D.C. and H.L.(E.).
Reg. v. *Governor of Pentonville Prison, Ex parte Ecke* [1974] Crim.L.R.
    102, D.C.
Reg. v. *Governor of Pentonville Prison, Ex parte Myers* (unreported),   E
    December 6, 1972, D.C.
Reg. v. *Jacobi and Hiller* (1881) 46 L.T. 595, D.C.
Reg. v. *Saunders* [1979] 3 W.L.R. 359; [1979] 2 All E.R. 267, E.C.J.
Rex v. *Dix* (1902) 18 T.L.R. 231, D.C.
Shapiro v. *Ferrandina* (1973) 478 F. 2d 894.
Windsor, In re (1865) 6 B. & S. 522.
Wright v. *Henkel* (1902) 190 U.S. 40.   F

The following additional cases were cited in argument:

Government of India, Ministry of Finance (Revenue Division) v. *Taylor*
    [1955] A.C. 491; [1955] 2 W.L.R. 303; [1955] 1 All E.R. 292, H.L.(E.).
Huntington v. *Attrill* [1893] A.C. 150, P.C.
Kakis v. *Government of the Republic of Cyprus* [1978] 1 W.L.R. 779;
    [1978] 2 All E.R. 634, H.L.(E.).   G
Malone v. *Metropolitan Police Commissioner* [1979] Ch. 344; [1979]
    2 W.L.R. 700; [1979] 2 All E.R. 620.
Reg. v. *Chief Immigration Officer, Heathrow Airport, Ex parte Salamat
    Bibi* [1976] 1 W.L.R. 979; [1976] 3 All E.R. 843, C.A.
Reg. v. *Governor of Brixton Prison, Ex parte Soblen* [1963] 2 Q.B.
    243; [1962] 3 W.L.R. 1154; [1962] 3 All E.R. 641, Stephenson J. and
    C.A.   H
Reg. v. *Governor of Winson Green Prison, Birmingham, Ex parte
    Littlejohn* [1975] 1 W.L.R. 893; [1975] 3 All E.R. 208, D.C.
Reg. v. *Thompson* (1979) 69 Cr.App.R. 22, E.C.J.
Schemmer v. *Property Resources Ltd.* [1975] Ch. 273; [1974] 3 W.L.R.
    406; [1974] 3All E.R. 451.
Van Duyn v. *Home Office* [1975] Ch. 358; [1975] 2 W.L.R. 760; [1975]
    3 All E.R. 190, E.C.J.
Wyatt v. *McLoughlin* [1974] I.R. 378.

The Weekly Law Reports, October 3, 1980

1113

1 W.L.R.   Reg. v. Pentonville Prison Governor, Ex p. Budlong (D.C.)

A   APPLICATIONS for writs of habeas corpus.

The applicants, Morrison Budlong and Jane Kember, who had been committed to Pentonville Prison and Holloway Prison, respectively, pending their extradition to the United States of America, under an order made at Wells Street Magistrates' Court by a metropolitan stipendiary magistrate (W. E. C. Robins), each moved for a writ of habeas corpus directed to the prison governor concerned with that applicant.

B   The facts are stated in the judgment of Griffiths J.

Louis Blom-Cooper Q.C., *Alan Newman* and *Hannah Burton* for the applicant Kember.

William Denny Q.C. and *Anthony Hooper* for the applicant Budlong.

C   *David Tudor Price* and *Colin Nicholls* for the United States Government.

Nicholas Bratza as amicus curiae.

Cur. adv. vult.

D   November 30. LORD WIDGERY C.J.   I will ask Griffiths J. to read the judgment of the court.

GRIFFTHS J.   In these proceedings the applicants move for writs of habeas corpus on the ground that the extradition warrants issued by the metropolitan magistrate, Mr. Robins, dated May 25, 1979, and upon which they are held pending extradition to the United States of America E   are unlawful.

The Government of the United States seeks the extradition of the applicants to face 10 charges of burglary committed between January and May 1976 and for which they were indicted by a grand jury on August 15, 1978.   The evidence placed before the magistrate revealed the following facts.   Between January and May 1976 members of the F   Church of Scientology unlawfully as trespassers entered various offices of the United States Internal Revenue Service and the United States Department of Justice in the District of Columbia and therein, making use of government property, took photocopies of the contents of confidential government files relating to the affairs of the Church of Scientology and its adherents.   They replaced the original documents in the files but stole the photocopies.   Eventually the actual burglars were G   caught red-handed and they then revealed that they were acting on the written instructions of the applicants who are senior members in the hierarchy of the Church of Scientology residing in this country.

The magistrate, being satisfied that the facts revealed a prima facie case of burglary against the applicants, both according to the relevant law of the United States, namely, sections 1801 (*b*) and 105 of Title 22, H   District of Columbia Code, and according to English law, and that burglary was an extraditable crime within the Extradition Treaty made between the Government of the United Kingdom and the Government of the United States of America, he issued warrants committing the applicants to prison to await extradition.   They have in fact both since been allowed bail pending the outcome of these proceedings.

In this court the magistrate's warrants have been attacked on a variety of grounds, but there has been no suggestion that the evidence

before the magistrate did not establish a prima facie case of burglary   A
against the applicants both according to American and English law.

The pleading point

The first ground of attack was conveniently described by counsel for
the applicants as the pleading point. His complaint is that there was no
formal document before the magistrate that contained sufficient parti-   B
culars of the applicants' offence to show that it constituted the crime of
burglary according to English law. It is submitted that before the magistrate can begin to consider the evidence in support of the application
for an extradition warrant he must have all the necessary ingredients to
establish the English offence formally set out in some document; and, as
there was no formal document in this case that alleged the burglars
entered " as trespassers," the magistrate should have refused to consider C
the matter further because trespass is an essential element of the English
crime of burglary: see Theft Act 1968.

In order to examine this submission it is necessary to consider the
steps by which extradition is obtained to see what formal documents are
required to be placed before the magistrate. The first step is the request
for extradition. This is made through the diplomatic channel and the   D
material that must accompany the request is set out in article VII of the
Extradition Treaty between the two governments: see Schedule 1 to the
United States of America (Extradition) Order 1976. This is the material
upon which the legal advisers in the Home Office will consider whether
they should advise the Secretary of State to take the next step in the
extradition procedure which is to refer the request to a metropolitan
magistrate pursuant to section 7 of the Extradition Act 1870 which   E
provides:

" A requisition for the surrender of a fugitive criminal of any foreign
state, who is in or suspected of being in the United Kingdom, shall
be made to a Secretary of State by some person recognised by the
Secretary of State as a diplomatic representative of that foreign state.   F
A Secretary of State may, by order under his hand and seal, signify
to a police magistrate that such a requisition has been made, and
require him to issue his warrant for the apprehension of the fugitive
criminal.

" If the Secretary of State is of opinion that the offence is one
of a political character, he may, if he think fit, refuse to send any   G
such order, and may also at any time order a fugitive criminal
accused or convicted of such offence to be discharged from custody."

When the magistrate receives the order from the Secretary of State
it is his duty to inquire into the evidence and, if sufficient, to issue his
warrant, as plainly appears from the terms of sections 8 and 10. Section
8 provides: H

" A warrant for the apprehension of a fugitive criminal, whether
accused or convicted of crime, who is in or suspected of being in the
United Kingdom, may be issued—1. by a police magistrate on the
receipt of the said order of the Secretary of State, and on such evidence as would in his opinion justify the issue of the warrant if the
crime had been committed or the criminal convicted in England; . . ."

The Weekly Law Reports, October 3, 1980

1115

1 W.L.R.   Reg. v. Pentonville Prison Governor, Ex p. Budlong (D.C.)

A   Section 10 provides:

"In the case of a fugitive criminal accused of an extradition crime, if the foreign warrant authorising the arrest of such criminal is duly authenticated, and such evidence is produced as (subject to the provisions of this Act) would, according to the law of England, justify the committal for trial of the prisoner if the the crime of which he is
B   accused had been committed in England, the police magistrate shall commit him to prison, but otherwise shall order him to be discharged."

The form of the Secretary of State's order is prescribed by section 20, which provides:

C   "The forms set forth in Schedule 2 to this Act, or forms as near thereto as circumstances admit, may be used in all matters to which such forms refer, and in the case of a British possession may be so used, mutatis mutandis, and when used shall be deemed to be valid and sufficient in law."

The "form of order of Secretary of State to the police magistrate" contained in Schedule 2 requires the Secretary of State to do no more than
D   insert the name of the crime for which extradition is asked. The order in the present case is in the form prescribed by Schedule 2 and names the crime as burglary. As such it is deemed to be valid and sufficient in law by section 20.

The only other document of a formal nature that is required to be before the magistrate is the foreign warrant authorising the arrest of the
E   criminal. It cannot have been intended that this foreign warrant should set out all the ingredients of the English offence for, as Stephen J. said in Reg. v. Jacobi and Hiller (1881) 46 L.T. 595:

"If it were necessary for the warrant to set forth precisely the crime . . . every foreign magistrate who issued a warrant . . . would have to be acquainted with the law of England."

F   Such an oppressive requirement would, of course, make extradition unworkable. There is nothing in the Treaty that requires any other formal document to be before the magistrate and no authority has been cited to show that extradition has ever been refused on this ground. I am quite satisfied that in extradition proceedings there is no requirement for any formal documents to be before the magistrate other than the order of the
G   Secretary of State and the warrant of arrest, neither of which, for the reasons I have given, are required to set out all the particulars of the English offence. It is to the evidence that the magistrate is directed to look to see whether there are sufficient facts established to constitute an offence contrary to English law and not to any formal document. I am glad to find that this is so, for it would be deplorable if the technicalities of English procedure were introduced to thwart an otherwise
H   proper request for extradition.

In support of his submission, Mr. Denny relied upon the decision of this court in Reg. v. Governor of Brixton Prison, Ex parte Gardner [1968] 2 Q.B. 399, followed in this court in Reg. v. Governor of Pentonville Prison, Ex parte Myers (unreported), December 6, 1972. Gardner's case is a decision under the Fugitive Offenders Act 1967, as was Myers's case, which Act provides for the return from the United Kingdom of persons who have committed crimes in the Commonwealth.

The facts of *Gardner's* case were that warrants had been issued in   A
New Zealand alleging against Gardner the offence of obtaining by false
pretences. Because the warrants only disclosed a pretence as to future
conduct they did not at that date disclose any offence according to
English law. The Fugitive Offenders Act 1967 makes provision for the
arrest and return of persons accused in a Commonwealth country of a
" relevant offence." A relevant offence is defined in the terms in section
3 (1) of the Act: B

> " For the purposes of this Act an offence of which a person is
> accused or has been convicted in a designated Commonwealth country
> or United Kingdom dependency is a relevant offence if—(*a*) in the
> case of an offence against the law of a designated Commonwealth
> country, it is an offence which, however described in that law, falls
> within any of the descriptions set out in Schedule 1 to this Act, and C
> is punishable under that law with imprisonment for a term of 12
> months or any greater punishment; (*b*) in the case of an offence
> against the law of a United Kingdom dependency, it is punishable
> under that law, on conviction by or before a superior court, with
> imprisonment for a term of 12 months or any greater punishment;
> and (*c*) in any case, the act or omission constituting the offence, or D
> the equivalent act or omission, would constitute an offence against
> the law of the United Kingdom if it took place within the United
> Kingdom or, in the case of an extra-territorial offence, in corres-
> ponding circumstances outside the United Kingdom."

Section 5 requires the requesting country to furnish the Secretary of
State with the following information: E

> " (2) . . . (*a*) in the case of a person accused of an offence, a warrant
> for his arrest issued in that country; . . . together . . . with parti-
> culars of the person whose return is requested and of the facts upon
> which and the law under which he is accused or was convicted, and
> evidence sufficient to justify the issue of a warrant for his arrest
> under section 6 of this Act. (3) On receipt of such a request the
> Secretary of State may issue an authority to proceed unless it appears F
> to him that an order for the return of the person concerned could
> not lawfully be made, or would not in fact be made, in accordance
> with the provisions of this Act."

Section 6 then provides that a magistrate on receipt of the authority
to proceed may issue a warrant of arrest and section 7 provides for the
committal if, after hearing evidence, the court is satisfied that the   G
offence in respect of which the authority to proceed has been issued is a
relevant offence and that the evidence discloses a prima facie case.

Nowhere in the Act is there any requirement as to the form in which
the authority to proceed should be drawn. This is, as I have already
illustrated, in contrast to the Extradition Act 1870 which does prescribe
the form in which the order of the Secretary of State should be drawn.   H

Lord Parker C.J., having considered the general framework of the
Act, concluded that the authority to proceed had to be drawn with
sufficient particularity to disclose all the ingredients of a relevant offence.
He said, at p. 415:

> " It seems to me that what is clearly contemplated here is that a
> request coming forward to the Secretary of State must set out in
> some form, and no doubt the most usual form is the warrant or

The Weekly Law Reports, October 3, 1980

1117

1 W.L.R.   Reg. v. Pentonville Prison Governor, Ex p. Budlong (D.C.)

A   warrants for arrest, the offence or offences of which the fugitive is accused in this case in New Zealand. Not only must it supply a general description which will fulfil the provisions of section 3 (1) (a) but it must condescend to sufficient detail to enable the matter to be considered under section 3 (1) (c). Similarly, as it seems to me, it is contemplated that the Secretary of State in giving his authority to proceed under section 5 (1) should again set out the offences to
B   which his authority is to relate in sufficient detail for the matter to be considered again not only under paragraph (a) but also under paragraph (c) of section 3 (1)."

The authority to proceed in Gardner's case stated (see p. 413):

C   " Request having been made to the Secretary of State by or on behalf of the Government of New Zealand for the return to that country of [the applicant] who is accused of the offences of obtaining money by false pretences; attempting to obtain money by false pretences . . . the Secretary of State hereby orders that a metropolitan stipendiary magistrate proceed with the case in accordance with the provisions of the Fugitive Offenders Act 1967."

D   Lord Parker C.J. continued, at p. 415:

" So far as this case is concerned, as I have said the authority to proceed was in perfectly general terms, and this court naturally has not seen and could not look at the request from the Commonwealth power. But it seems to me perfectly plain that this authority to proceed, albeit in general terms, must be taken as relating to the
E   offences of which this applicant was accused in New Zealand, and upon which the request was made for his return."

As those offences did not disclose an offence known to English law, which is an essential element of a " relevant offence," it was held that the authority to proceed was not in respect of a relevant offence and the application succeeded.

F   I can see no reason why these decisions should be applied to proceedings under the Extradition Act 1870. They turn upon the construction of the Fugitive Offenders Act 1967, the shape and provisions of which are not in any way on all fours with the Extradition Act 1870. However, the applicants submit that because article III of the Treaty requires similar information to be submitted to the Secretary of State by the country requesting extradition to that required to be submitted
G   by a Commonwealth country under section 3 of the Fugitive Offenders Act 1967, it follows that the Secretary of State's order under the Extradition Act 1870 shall contain the same particulars as, pursuant to Gardner's case, are required to be set out in the authority to proceed under the Fugitive Offenders Act 1967. I cannot see why that result should necessarily follow, but the conclusive answer to the submission is
H   to be found in the terms of section 20 of the Extradition Act 1870 which expressly provides that the order shall be valid if it follows the form prescribed in Schedule 2, which form does not require the order to do other than state the general description of the crime for which extradition is asked.

The point is also covered by authority. In In re Bellencontre [1891] 2 Q.B. 122, Cave J. said, at p. 136:

A

" The duty of the Secretary of State is to call the attention of the police magistrate to what he is required to do under the Extradition Treaty, and it is enough if he draws attention to the particular crime under article 3 of the Extradition Treaty, and that is fraud by a bailee, which expresses in general terms what is expressed rather more specifically in the French warrant."

B

Because, in my view, *Gardner's* case and *Myers's* case do not support the applicants' argument, it is not necessary to consider if they were correctly decided. But I would not wish anything I have said to be taken as expressing my own endorsement of the decisions. It seems to me that they lead to the surprising conclusion that the success or failure of a Commonwealth country to extradite a criminal who has offended against their laws may depend on the drafting of particulars in a document, namely, the authority to proceed, for which they are not responsible.

C

For the reasons I have given the pleading point fails.

Double criminality

The second submission is founded upon the fact that under the relevant American law, section 1801 (*b*) of Title 22 District of Columbia Code, entry as a trespasser is not an essential element of the crime of burglary whereas under English law trespass is an essential element of the crime: see section 9 of the Theft Act 1968.

D

It is admitted that the facts of this case show that the burglars obtained entry to the various government offices as trespassers, but it is argued that because the applicants, when they are tried in America could be convicted without proof that the entry involved a trespass, they are thereby placed in peril of being convicted of a crime in America for which they could not be convicted in this country. The applicants submit that this offends against the principle of double criminality under which a criminal is only to be extradited for the commission of a crime punishable by the laws of both countries.

E

The prosecution submit that the true rule is that a criminal is to be extradited if his crime falls within the general description of a crime specified in the Extradition Treaty and the facts of the offence—that is, the conduct complained of—show it to be a criminal offence punishable by the laws of both countries. As the facts of these offences show a prima facie case of burglary against both the laws of the District of Columbia and this country, the prosecution submit that extradition should be ordered.

F

The law of extradition depends not upon any common law principles, but upon statute. Ultimately the question before this court has to be solved by deciding whether upon their true construction the Treaty and the Extradition Act 1870, which by the United States of America (Extradition) Order 1976 is applied to the Treaty, permit extradition in this case. None of the authorities that have been cited bear directly upon the question we have to decide, but I believe they provide valuable guidance to the correct approach to the construction of the statutory provisions.

G

In *In re Windsor* (1865) 6 B. & S. 522 extradition to the United States was demanded under a treaty making forgery an extraditable offence. The facts alleged against a bank teller revealed that he had made a false entry in a bank book for fraudulent purposes which would amount to forgery under the definition in the New York statute; they did not, how-

H

The Weekly Law Reports, October 3, 1980

1119

1 W.L.R.   Reg. v. Pentonville Prison Governor, Ex p. Budlong (D.C.)

A   ever, constitute the offence of forgery in English law. The principal
ground given for refusing extradition was that the local statute of
New York did not make the offence forgery by the general law of the
United States and, hence, the crime of forgery had not been committed
in either country. This ground has been disapproved by the Supreme
Court of the United States, see *Wright* v. *Henkel* (1902) 190 U.S. 40, and
is not relied upon in this case. There are, however, two short passages
B   dealing with the concept of double criminality. Cockburn C.J. said,
at p. 528:

"The true construction of this statute is, that its terms, specifying
the offences for which persons may be given up, must be understood
to apply to offences which have some common element in the legislation of both countries."

C
Blackburn J. said, at p. 530: "Forgery is one of the crimes specified, and
that must be understood to mean any crimes recognised throughout the
United States and in *England* as being in the nature of forgery." From
the two expressions "some common element" and "in the nature of"
it is apparent that the court was not looking for the crime to be defined
in identical terms in both countries.

D
In *In re Bellencontre* [1891] 2 Q.B. 122 the French authorities demanded extradition of a French subject accused in France of 19 separate
charges of embezzling or misappropriating money delivered to him as a
notary. The court found that as to 15 of the charges the evidence disclosed no crime punishable by English law, but that in the case of the
four remaining charges the evidence did show an offence contrary to the
E   French Penal Code and English law within the Extradition Treaty and that
extradition ought to be granted in respect of those four charges. In the
course of his judgment Wills J. said, at pp. 140–141:

"The substance of the Extradition Act 33 & 34 Vict. c. 52, seems
to me to require that the person whose extradition is sought
should have been accused in a foreign country of something which is
a crime by English law, and that there should be a prima facie case
F   made out that he is guilty of a crime under the foreign law, and also
of a crime under English law. If those conditions are satisfied,
the extradition ought to be granted. We cannot expect that the
definitions or descriptions of the crime when translated into the
language of the two countries respectively, should exactly correspond. The definitions may have grown up under widely different
G   circumstances in the two countries; and if an exact correspondence
were required in mere matter of definition, probably there would be
great difficulty in laying down what crimes could be made the
subjects of extradition. Now this difficulty has been met, as it
seems to me, by the first Schedule to the Extradition Act 1870 (33
& 34 Vict. c. 52), which describes what are the various extradition
H   crimes. In this case, the man has been accused of a number of
things which clearly fall within article 408 of the French Code, and
therefore are crimes in France, and crimes which clearly fall under
number 18 in the French part of the Treaty of Extradition. One
looks, then, to see whether in the corresponding English section,
No. 18 of article 3, there is a crime described by English law which
crime has been made out by the evidence. It seems to me that
there is no difficulty in saying which of the definitions it falls under."

This passage clearly indicates that in considering extradition it is the A actual facts of the offence which are all important rather than the definition of the crime in the foreign law.

In *In re Arton (No. 2)* [1896] 1 Q.B. 509 extradition was demanded for " faux," which is the French equivalent of forgery. The facts did not disclose the offence of forgery according to English law, but did disclose the offence of falsification of accounts, which is an extradition crime and within the French and English treaties. Lord Russell said, B at p. 517:

> " Is extradition to be refused in respect of acts covered by the treaty, and gravely criminal according to the law of both countries, because in the particular case the falsification of accounts is not forgery according to English law, but falls under that head according to French law? I think not. To decide so would be to hinder the C working and narrow the operation of most salutary international arrangements."

Here again the emphasis is placed not in the definition of the crime but on the acts that constitute the criminal conduct. In a later passage he continued, at p. 517:

> " We are here dealing with a crime alleged to have been committed D against the law of France; and if we find, as I hold that we do, that such a crime is a crime against the law of both countries, and is, in substance, to be found in each version of the treaty, although under different heads, we are bound to give effect to the claim for extradition."

Here, too, it is the substance of the two offences that must correspond, E not their precise definitions.

Rex v. *Dix* (1902) 18 T.L.R. 231 is another case in which the description of the crime was different in the two countries, but the facts revealed criminal acts punishable under the laws of both countries and within the Extradition Treaty. The accused was charged with larceny by embezzlement according to American law. It was held that as the evidence showed fraud by a bailee banker under the Larceny Act—an offence F within the treaty—the accused could be extradited. Darling J. said, at p. 232: " . . . the essential thing was to see whether what the evidence showed prima facie that the prisoner had done was a crime in both countries and within the treaty." Once more the court is looking to the actual criminal conduct to decide if extradition should be granted.

The case most comparable to the present facts is the decision of this G court in *Reg.* v. *Governor of Pentonville Prison, Ex parte Ecke* [1974] Crim.L.R. 102. The German Government asked that the accused should be extradited upon a number of charges of fraudulent trading, the dishonesty alleged being a false representation as to a future intention and not as to an existing fact. The date of the Treaty was 1960 at which date a false representation as to a future intention was not a criminal offence in England. Article 2 of the Treaty provided: H

> " Extradition shall be reciprocally granted for the following crimes, provided that the crime charged constitutes an extradiction crime according to the laws of the territory from which and to which extradition is desired."

The list of crimes included in the English version under paragraph 17 are:

The Weekly Law Reports, October 3, 1980

1121

1 W.L.R.   Reg. v. Pentonville Prison Governor, Ex p. Budlong (D.C.)

A   " fraud by a bailee, banker, agent, factor or trustee, or by a doctor, member or public officer of any company; fraudulent conversion; or obtaining money, valuables, security, or goods by false pretences."

In the German version paragraph 17 consisted of two words meaning, in English, " fraud."

It was submitted that an offence could not be an extraditable offence
B within the meaning of the Treaty unless it was an offence with all its English constituents, and that as a false pretence as to a future event was not an English offence in 1960, when the Treaty was made, it was not an extradition crime under the Treaty. The fact that, since the Theft Act 1968, a misrepresentation as to a future event will found a criminal charge was said to be beside the point for to accept it as now coming
C within the Treaty would be to amend the Treaty unilaterally. This argument was rejected: the court held that the words descriptive of the offence in the Treaty were to be given their general meaning, general to the lawyer and layman alike, their ordinary international meaning, and not a particular meaning they may have attracted in England. Giving the words a liberal meaning, treating them not as words of art but words of general description, the accused's activities came within both the
D English and German versions of article 17. The court pointed out that the requirement that the facts alleged must amount to an offence in English law would have protected him from extradition if his offences had been committed before 1968.

It was helpful to have citation of three American authorities, two decisions of the Supreme Court, *Wright* v. *Henkel* (1902) 190 U.S. 40 and
E *Factor* v. *Laubenheimer* (1933) 290 U.S. 276, and one decision of the Court of Appeal of the second circuit, *Shapiro* v. *Ferrandina* (1973) 478 F. 2d 894. None of them bear directly on the problem in this case, but they show no difference in their general approach to extradition to that adopted by the courts in this country. I will do no more than cite briefly from the opinion of the court in *Wright* v. *Henkel,* at pp. 57–58:

F   " Treaties must receive a fair interpretation, according to the intention of the contracting parties, and so as to carry out their manifest purpose. The ordinary technicalities of criminal proceedings are applicable to proceedings in extradition only to a limited extent . . . The general principle of international law is that in all cases of extradition the act done on account of which extradition is demanded must be considered a crime by both parties."

G Finally, in reference to the definition of the crime under the American and British statutes, at p. 58: " Absolute identity is not required. The essential character of the transaction is the same, and made criminal by both statutes."

With the guidance of these authorities I turn back to the statutory provisions. Article III of the Treaty provides:

H   " (1) Extradition shall be granted for an act or omission the facts of which disclose an offence within any of the descriptions listed in the Schedule annexed to this Treaty, which is an integral part of the Treaty, or any other offence, if: (*a*) the offence is punishable under the laws of both parties by imprisonment or other form of detention for more than one year or by the death penalty; (*b*) the offence is extraditable under the relevant law, being the law of the United Kingdom or other territory to which this Treaty applies by

virtue of sub-paragraph (1) (*a*) *of* article II; and (*c*) the offence   A
constitutes a felony under the law of the United States of America."

The first requirement is satisfied—burglary is in the Schedule. The
facts do disclose acts that would be recognised by layman and lawyer
alike as falling within the concept of burglary, and it matters not that
the two crimes are not identically defined.

Sub-paragraphs (*a*) and (*c*) are satisfied. Burglary in both countries is   B
punishable by imprisonment for more than one year and it is a felony
under American law.

I turn to sub-paragraph (*b*). For the offence to be extraditable under
the law of the United Kingdom it must be an extradition crime as
defined by section 26 of the Extradition Act 1870, for it is only in respect
of an extradition crime that the magistrate has power to commit an   C
accused person under section 8. The definition in section 26 reads:

"The term 'extradition crime' means a crime which, if committed
in England or within English jurisdiction, would be one of the crimes
described in the first Schedule to this Act: . . ."

Now I come to what I consider to be the nub of the case. Is this
definition to be construed as meaning that the crime as defined in the   D
foreign law must contain all the essential ingredients of one of the English
crimes described in the Schedule, in which case the applicants' submission succeeds because the American definition of burglary does not
require trespass as an essential element?

Alternatively, does the definition mean that an " extradition crime "
has been committed if that which the accused has done would have
amounted to the commission of one of the crimes in the Schedule if it had   E
been done in England? If this is the true meaning of the definition, the
applicants fail for the evidence shows that they committed the crime of
burglary according to English law.

In my judgment, the second construction is to be preferred. The
first construction would give rise to all the difficulties inherent in attempting to apply extradition upon the unlikely foundation that foreign defini-   F
tions of crimes often in different languages and operating in very different
legal systems will accord with English definitions. The authorities show
that the courts do not expect or look for such identity of definition.

On the other hand, an English court should have no difficulty in
deciding whether a given set of facts does or does not constitute a crime
according to English law. The authorities that have been cited stress   G
the importance that the facts of the case should disclose an offence against
the law of both countries and appear to me to lean heavily towards this
interpretation of the definition. I appreciate that this construction may
in theory result in the possibility of conviction in a foreign country which
would not occur here. Although a theoretical possibility, it is I think
a very unlikely result and, certainly so far as I can see, there is not a
remote chance of it in the present case. This construction still leaves   H
the accused with the protection that he is only to be extradited for a
crime that is substantially similar in concept in both countries and I do
not believe that this will result in any injustice.

I therefore summarise by saying that double criminality in our law of
extradition is satisfied if it is shown: (1) that the crime for which extradition is demanded would be recognised as substantially similar in both
countries; (2) that there is a prima facie case that the conduct of the

A   accused amounted to the commission of the crime according to English law.

I therefore conclude that double criminality does not have the meaning contended for by the applicants and their objection fails.

Are the offences of a political character?

B   Extradition will not be granted if the offence with which the accused is charged is of a political character. An offence of a political character is an elusive concept and probably defies any completely satisfactory definition. It is probably not desirable to attempt one because, as Lord Radcliffe said in *Reg.* v. *Governor of Brixton Prison, Ex parte Schtraks* [1964] A.C. 556, it is virtually impossible to find one that does not cover too wide a range. It is submitted that the offences were of a political C   character because the applicants were engaged in an attempt to change the policy of the United States Government towards the Church of Scientology and that the burglaries were committed to further this end. The applicants rely upon passages in the opinions in *Schtraks's* case and *Reg.* v. *Governor of Pentonville Prison, Ex parte Cheng* [1973] A.C. 931 which refer to an offence of a political character being one aimed at D   changing the policy of the foreign government: see Lord Reid in *Schtraks's* case at p. 583 and Lord Diplock in *Cheng's* case at p. 945. But these words of their Lordships must be read in the full context of their speeches which make it clear that they were considering offences committed in the course of a struggle against a foreign government from which the accused had sought asylum in this country. As society becomes more sophisticated, and populations increase, so the scope of government E   increases with the inevitable result that the policies of government affect the everyday life of the individual over an ever widening range of his daily activities.

In respect of any government policy there will probably be a substantial number of people who disagree with it and would wish to change it, but it should not be thought that if they commit a crime to achieve F   their ends it necessarily becomes an offence of a political character. In only two of the reported cases have our courts held that the offence was of a political character: in *In re Castioni* [1891] 1 Q.B. 149 in which the accused had killed a member of the government in the course of an armed uprising that overthrew the government, and in *Reg.* v. *Governor of Brixton Prison, Ex parte Kolczynski* [1955] 1 Q.B. 540 in which a number of Polish seamen mutinied and sailed their vessel to England where they G   sought asylum, for they feared prosecution for their political opinions if they should be returned to Poland. The idea underlying an offence of a political character is expressed by Lord Radcliffe in *Reg.* v. *Governor of Brixton Prison, Ex parte Schtraks* [1964] A.C. 556 in the following language, at p. 591:

H   " In my opinion the idea that lies behind the phrase ' offence of a political character ' is that the fugitive is at odds with the state that applies for his extradition on some issue connected with the political control or government of the country. The analogy of ' political ' in this context is with ' political ' in such phrases as ' political refugee,' ' political asylum ' or ' political prisoner.' "

Mr. Blom-Cooper has taken the court through a great deal of evidence in the course of his submission upon this aspect of the case. The evidence reveals that the Church of Scientology has been engaged in a pro-

tracted struggle with the Internal Revenue Services Department of the A
United States (IRS) to secure exemption from taxes on the ground that it
is a religious foundation, and that it has also fought another long battle
through the courts against the Food and Drugs Administration to establish
that they were entitled to use a device known as an E-Meter as a part of
their religious practice. It is also apparent from the documents that the
IRS and the Food and Drugs Administration entertained grave doubts B
about the bona fides of the Scientologists and that they had received a
number of reports suggesting various forms of criminal activity and
chicanery on the part of the church and its members. The material
before us also shows that these departments of the United States Government were not alone in their distrust of Scientology and its practices.
The State of Victoria passed legislation against it and this country has
refused to permit entry to those wishing to enter the employment of the C
Church of Scientology. It should, however, be stated that the Church of
Scientology has achieved a substantial degree of success in the American
litigation; the IRS in June and July 1975 finally conceded exempt status
for tax purposes to all but one of its churches in the United States, and
subject to certain safeguards the courts have permitted the use of the
E-Meter.

Mr. Blom-Cooper submitted that the burglaries were planned in order D
to gain access to the information that had been collected by the IRS and
the Department of Justice so that the Church of Scientology could inform
themselves as to the false reports circulating about it between government departments, and identify and deal with the particular persons within
the departments who were hostile to the church.

I am prepared to accept that this was one motive for the burglaries. E
Guardian order 1361 dated October 21, 1974, which seems to be the
seminal document that initiated the break-ins, does refer to employees
of the government departments concerned as " suppressive psychotics
utilising the IRS as a substitute for standard justice procedures on
scientology; "—and later it refers to the—" suppressive psychotics being
identified and handled." We were not told just how it was proposed to
handle them. But this was only one of the guardian orders put in F
evidence, and it is manifest from the terms of other orders that a
very important purpose of the burglaries was to obtain information
that would help in the litigation. By way of examples only, I quote
from guardian order dated December 5, 1975: " Place an agent in the
US Attorneys Office DC as a first action as this office should cover all
federal agencies that we are in litigation with or may be in the litigation G
with," and guardian order dated March 27, 1976; " An excellent BI
success over the last year was the obtaining of non-FOI data that
resulted in aiding our overall strategy to get the CofS tax exemptions."

I am unable to accept that organising burglaries either for the purpose
of identifying persons in government offices hostile to the Scientologists,
or for the purpose of gaining an advantage in litigation, or even for the
wider purpose of refuting false allegations thus enabling a better image H
of the Church of Scientology to be projected to the public, comes anywhere near being an offence of a political character within the meaning
of the Extradition Act.

The applicants did not order these burglaries to take place in order
to challenge the political control or government of the United States;
they did so to further the interests of the Church of Scientology and its
members, and in particular the interest of Ron L. Hubbard, the founder

The Weekly Law Reports, October 3, 1980

1125

1 W.L.R.   Reg. v. Pentonville Prison Governor, Ex p. Budlong (D.C.)

A   of Scientology.   In my view, it would be ridiculous to regard the applicants as political refugees seeking asylum in this country, and I reject the submission that these were offences of a political character.

The public law argument

It is a well established rule that our courts will not enforce a foreign
B   revenue, penal or public law.   This means that our courts will not try and either punish or give a remedy for the breach of such a law committed in a foreign country.   Mr. Blom-Cooper submits that the United States Government is attempting by indirect means to enforce a public law of the United States, namely, the Freedom of Information Act.   He says the real purpose behind the request for extradition is to punish the applicants not for burglary but for stealing confidential government
C   information protected by the Freedom of Information Act.   This could not be achieved by extradition proceedings because a breach of that Act is not an extradition crime, and so, it is said, resort is had to the offence of burglary.   Although in the course of his argument Mr. Blom-Cooper said he was not suggesting any bad faith on the part of the Government of the United States, it seems to me that bad faith is
D   necessarily implicit in this submission.   Under the Treaty the United States give their undertaking that the accused will not be tried for any offence other than that for which they are extradited; if in the face of this undertaking they were ostensibly tried for burglary but in fact punished for the commission of a different offence, I should regard that as flagrant bad faith.   When the offence has not been shown to be of a political character our courts will not entertain allegations of bad faith on the
E   part of the requesting country: see In re Arton [1896] 1 Q.B. 108 and Reg. v. Governor of Brixton Prison, Ex parte Kolczynski [1955] 1 Q.B. 540.

This is sufficient to dispose of the submission, but there is in fact a further ground for rejecting it.   In the course of the proceedings in the United States Judge Richey has given the following ruling:

F   " The government will not be permitted to rely on any alleged
        conversion of government information for a violation of section 641
        in this case.   However the government may proceed on the theory
        that copies made from government resources are owned by the
        government."

This makes it doubly unthinkable that their punishment will not be for
G   burglary but for stealing confidential information.   This objection therefore fails.

The construction of section 3 (1) of the Extradition Act 1870

Section 3 provides:

        " (1) A fugitive criminal shall not be surrendered if the offence in
H   respect of which his surrender is demanded is one of a political
        character, or if he prove to the satisfaction of the police magistrate
        or the court before whom he is brought on habeas corpus, or to
        the Secretary of State, that the requisition for his surrender has in
        fact been made with a view to try or punish him for an offence of a
        political character: . . ."

Mr. Blom-Cooper addressed an argument to the court on the construction of section 3 (1).   He submitted that stealing confidential information was

a political act and that the requisition for surrender was made with a A
view to punishing the applicants for this offence, and that they were thus
protected by the second limb of section 3 (1). For the reasons I have
already given this submission would fail on the facts, but it is also bound
to fail on the construction of the section. It is submitted that, even if the
crime for which extradition is asked is not an offence of a political
character within the first limb of the section, the second limb allows the
fugitive criminal to show that the requesting country intends to try or B
punish him for some other political offence. This was the construction
of the section adopted by Lord Russell C.J. in *In re Arton* [1896] 1 Q.B.
108. But since that date the section has been construed in two modern
authorities: by Lord Goddard C.J. in *Reg.* v. *Governor of Brixton
Prison, Ex parte Kolczynski* [1955] 1 Q.B. 540, by Lord Parker C.J. in
Reg. v. *Governor of Brixton Prison, Ex parte Schtraks* [1963] 1 Q.B. C
55 in the Divisional Court and by Lord Radcliffe, Lord Reid and Lord
Evershed in *Schtraks's* case [1964] A.C. 556 in the House of Lords.
They have all rejected Lord Russell's construction and held that the
second limb of the section does no more than permit the accused to show
by evidence that the offence for which extradition is asked is in truth of a
political character, although it might not appear to be so from the evidence produced by the country requesting extradition. In my judgment, D
this court is bound by that weight of authority to apply this construction.

The law of the European Economic Community

The final submission is made on behalf of Mrs. Kember only and by
virtue of her status as a national of the United Kingdom. It is submitted that the order of committal to await extradition is a restriction E
on her right to move freely between countries within the Community
guaranteed by article 48 of the Treaty of Rome and can only be justified on grounds of public policy under article 48 (3), and in accordance
with the provisions of Council Directive 64/221/EEC of February 25,
1964.

The basis of this submission is that extradition is closely analogous to F
deportation. In *Reg.* v. *Bouchereau* [1978] Q.B. 732 the European Court
of Justice on a reference from the Marlborough Street Magistrates'
Court held that a recommendation for deportation made by a criminal
court in this country was a " measure " within the meaning of article
3 (1) and (2) of E.E.C. Directive 64/221 and could only be made on
grounds of public policy. The case concerned a French national convicted of the unlawful possession of drugs and it was accepted that a G
deportation order would constitute a restriction upon his freedom of
movement within article 48. Directive 64/221 applies only to foreign
nationals and therefore has no direct application to the facts of the
present case; it is concerned with the behaviour of member states towards
foreign nationals in relation to entry to or expulsion from their territory.
However, it has been argued that a member state is under a duty to H
treat its own nationals no less favourably than foreign nationals, for which
the authority of *Knoors* v. *Secretary of State for Economic Affairs* [1979]
2 C.M.L.R. 357 was cited, and that as extradition is equivalent to
deportation, a member state can only extradite one of its own nationals,
if it applies the same criteria as it is required to apply by Directive 64/221
in the case of foreign nationals.

The Weekly Law Reports, October 3, 1980

1127

1 W.L.R.   Reg. v. Pentonville Prison Governor, Ex p. Budlong (D.C.)

A   If this submission is right, it will impose a formidable fetter upon extradition. It will mean that extradition can only be ordered on grounds of public policy based exclusively on the personal conduct of the individual concerned; see article 3 of the Directive. In *Reg.* v. *Bouchereau* [1978] Q.B. 732 the European Court said in the course of their judgment, at p. 759:

B   " The existence of a previous criminal conviction can, therefore, only be taken into account in so far as the circumstances which gave rise to that conviction are evidence of personal conduct constituting a present threat to the requirements of public policy . . . Although, in general, a finding that such a threat exists implies the existence in the individual concerned of a propensity to act in the same way in the future, it is possible that past conduct alone may constitute C   such a threat to the requirements of public policy."

This concept is easily understood in the case of deportation. A man should not be banished for a crime for which he has been punished unless he remains a present threat to society. But how do you apply it to extradition? The whole basis of extradition is that the accused has offended against society in another country; in all probability he is no D   threat to our society. Does that then mean he is not to be extradited to face justice where he has committed the crime? I cannot believe that it can have been the intention of those who drew the Treaty of Rome that it should have the effect of so emasculating the process of extradition.

It is submitted by Mr. Bratza, who appeared as amicus curiae, that the restrictions on the freedom of an individual imposed by extradition E   are unaffected by article 48. In *Reg.* v. *Saunders* [1979] 3 W.L.R. 359 the European Court of Justice held that article 48 did not aim to restrict the power of member states to lay down restrictions, within their own territory, on the freedom of movement of all persons subject to their jurisdiction in the implementation of domestic criminal law. I regard extradition as far more closely analogous to the implementation of domestic criminal law than to deportation. It is in no true sense a banishment F   from our shores as is deportation; indeed section 3 (2) of the Extradition Act specifically provides that there will be no extradition unless the foreign state undertakes to allow the accused to return to this country after he has been dealt with for the extradition crime. Extradition is no more than a step that assists in the implementation of the domestic criminal law of the foreign state.

G   This country has extradition treaties with other member states entered into before the Treaty of Rome. Article 234 of the Treaty provides:

" The rights and obligations arising from agreements concluded before the entry into force of this Treaty between one or more member states on the one hand, and one or more third countries on the other, shall not be affected by the provisions of this Treaty."

H   It would be a curious result if extradition could be granted upon generally accepted principles between member states who had entered into extradition treaties before the Treaty of Rome but upon very different principles, introducing the concept of public policy already discussed, between member states who made or, I suppose, amended, extradition treaties after the Treaty of Rome. Again I cannot think that this result can have been intended.

Mr. Blom-Cooper wishes us to refer to the European Court of Justice   A
the following question:

" Whether a member state, in considering an application for the
extradition (whether to another member state or to a third party)
of a worker who is a national of that first member state, must have
regard to the provisions of article 48 (3) of the Treaty establishing
the E.E.C."

B

Article 48 (3) requires the justification to be on grounds of public
policy. If we did refer this question we should undoubtedly have to refer
a number of supplementary questions to elucidate how the concept of
public policy was to be applied to extradition. Lord Denning
M.R. in *H. P. Bulmer Ltd.* v. *Bollinger* S.A. [1974] Ch. 401 laid down
guidelines to assist the courts in deciding whether to refer a question to   C
the European Court of Justice. The court should refer the point unless
it considers it to be reasonably clear and free from doubt.

I have come to the clear conclusion that, borrowing the words of the
Advocate General Jean-Pierre Warner from his opinion in *Reg.* v.
Saunders [1979] 3 W.L.R. 359, 366 " it is common sense that dictates
that article 48 should be interpreted as manifestly not intended to " apply
to the exercise of the power of this country to extradite an accused person   D
to the United States of America. Accordingly I would not make any
reference to the European Court of Justice.

For the reasons I have given I would refuse the writ of habeas corpus
to these applicants.

Applications refused.   E
Leave to appeal refused.
Bail granted on existing terms.
Costs out of central funds.

Solicitors: *Stephen M. Bird, East Grinstead; Director of Public
Prosecutions; Treasury Solicitor.*

F

B. O. A.

February 7, 1980. The Appeal Committee of the House of Lords
(Lord Edmund-Davies, Lord Fraser of Tullybelton and Lord Russell of
Killowen) dismissed a petition by the applicants for leave to appeal.

G

H

[HOUSE OF LORDS]

* HYUNDAI HEAVY INDUSTRIES CO. LTD. . . RESPONDENTS
(FORMERLY HYUNDAI SHIPBUILDING AND HEAVY
INDUSTRIES CO. LTD.)

AND

PAPADOPOULOS AND OTHERS . . . . . APPELLANTS

1980 Feb. 13, 14, 18, 19;   Viscount Dilhorne, Lord Edmund-Davies,
April 1   Lord Fraser of Tullybelton,
                       Lord Russell of Killowen
                    and Lord Keith of Kinkel

*Guarantee—Debt—Contract for payment by instalments—Ship-
building contract—Buyers' default in payment—Shipbuilders
rescinding contract—Issue of writ after date of rescission—
Liability of guarantors for unpaid instalments due before date
of rescission*
*Shipping — Shipbuilding — Contract — Payment by instalments —
Buyers defaulting in payment—Shipbuilders rescinding contract—Issue of writ after date of rescission—Whether accrued
right to unpaid instalments due before date of rescission*

    The respondents contracted with a Liberian company to
build and sell them a ship. The appellants gave a letter of
guarantee which provided, inter alia,
    " . . . we hereby jointly and severally irrevocably guarantee
    the payment in accordance with the terms of the contract
    of all sums due or to become due by the buyer under the
    contract and in case the buyer is in default of any such
    payment we will forthwith make the payment in default
    on behalf of the buyer."
    Article 11 of the contract gave the respondents a right to
rescind the contract and further provided that the rights
given by the article were " . . . in addition to such other
rights powers and remedies as the builder may have elsewhere
in this contract and/or at law, at equity or otherwise." The
purchase price of the vessel was payable by instalments. On
default by the buyers of payment of the second instalment the
respondents rescinded the contract and sued the appellants
under the letter of guarantee. The appellants contested
liability on the grounds, inter alia, that cancellation of
the contract by the respondents was founded on the contractual right to rescind under article 11, and that accordingly
the contract having been rescinded before the date of the
issue of the writ, there was on that date no accrued right to
unpaid instalments which had become due before the date of
the rescission. Lloyd J. held that the appellants had no
arguable defence. On appeal, the Court of Appeal dismissed
the appeal.
    On appeal by the appellants: —
    Held, dismissing the appeal, (1) (Lord Russell of Killowen
and Lord Keith of Kinkel dubitante) that save in the cases
of sales of land and goods where there had been a total
failure of consideration, the cancellation or rescission of a
contract in consequence of repudiation did not affect accrued
rights to the payment of instalments of the contract price,
unless the contract so provided; that the present contract
on its true construction was akin to a building contract or
a contract for hire, and that accordingly, the buyers remained
liable for the second instalment despite the cancellation under

Hyundai Industries v. Papadopoulos (H.L.(E.))   **[1980]**

article 11 and the appellants remained liable for that instalment under the guarantee (post, pp. 1134G, 1136A–B, 1137F, 1141G—1142A, E–F, 1148H—1149A, 1150A, 1152H—1153A, D–C).

(2) That even if the cancellation deprived the respondents of their accrued rights to payment by the buyers of the second instalment that did not deprive them of the right to have recourse to the appellants for the amount of that instalment in view of the terms of the letter of guarantee (post, pp. 1137F–H, 1142H—1143A, 1144G, 1152B–C, 1153A–B, C).

Hyundai Shipbuilding & Heavy Industries Co. Ltd. v. *Pournaras* [1978] 2 Lloyd's Rep. 502, C.A. applied.

Dies v. *British and International Mining and Finance Corporation Ltd.* [1939] 1 K.B. 724 distinguished.

Lep Air Services Ltd. v. *Rolloswin Investments Ltd.* [1973] A.C. 331, H.L.(E.) considered.

Decision of the Court of Appeal [1979] 1 Lloyd's Rep. 130 affirmed.

The following cases are referred to in their Lordships' opinions:

Bradley v. *H. Newsom, Sons & Co.* [1919] A.C. 16, H.L.(E.).
Brooks v. *Beirnstein* [1909] 1 K.B. 98, D.C.
Chatterton v. *Maclean* [1951] 1 All E.R. 761.
Dies v. *British and International Mining and Finance Corporation Ltd.* [1939] 1 K.B. 724.
Hyundai Shipbuilding & Heavy Industries Co. Ltd. v. *Pournaras* (unreported), November 29, 1977, Donaldson J.; [1978] 2 Lloyd's Rep. 502, C.A.
Johnson v. *Agnew* [1980] A.C. 367; [1979] 2 W.L.R. 487; [1979] 1 All E.R. 883, H.L.(E.).
Lep Air Services Ltd. v. *Rolloswin Investments Ltd.* [1971] 1 W.L.R. 934; [1971] 3 All E.R. 45, C.A.; [1973] A.C. 331; [1972] 2 W.L.R. 1175; [1972] 2 All E.R. 393, H.L.(E.).
Leslie Shipping Co. v. *Welstead* [1921] 3 K.B. 420.
McDonald v. *Dennys Lascelles Ltd.* (1933) 48 C.L.R. 457.
Newfoundland Government v. *Newfoundland Railway Co.* (1888) 13 App.Cas. 199, P.C.
Palmer v. *Temple* (1839) 9 A. & E. 508.
Prenn v. *Simmonds* [1971] 1 W.L.R. 1381; [1971] 3 All E.R. 237, H.L.(E.).

The following additional cases were cited in argument:

Bechervaise v. *Lewis* (1872) L.R. 7 C.P. 372.
Heyman v. *Darwins Ltd.* [1942] A.C. 356; [1942] 1 All E.R. 337, H.L.(E.).
Mardorf Peach & Co. Ltd. v. *Attica Sea Carriers Corporation of Liberia* [1977] A.C. 850; [1977] 2 W.L.R. 286; [1977] 1 All E.R. 315, H.L.(E.).
Photo Production Ltd. v. *Securicor Transport Ltd.* [1980] 2 W.L.R. 283; [1980] 1 All E.R. 556, H.L.(E.).
Scottish Midland Guarantee Trust v. *Woolley* (1964) 114 L.J. 272.
Wehner v. *Dene Steam Shipping Co.* [1905] 2 K.B. 92.

APPEAL from the Court of Appeal.

This was an appeal by the appellants, Petros Papadopoulos, Charalambos Paraskevopoulos and George Papanastassopoulos from an order dated October 6, 1978, of the Court of Appeal (Roskill, Geoffrey Lane and Bridge L.JJ.) dismissing an appeal by the appellants from a decision of Lloyd J. dated July 14, 1978, giving summary judgment for the

A respondents, Hyundai Heavy Industries Co. Ltd. for the sum of U.S. $357,000 plus interest against the appellants under the terms of a letter of guarantee given by the appellants in respect of the payments due under a shipbuilding contract entered into between the respondents and Pitria Pride Navigation Co. Inc., a Liberian company.

The facts are set out in their Lordships' opinions.

B
Peter Curry Q.C. and *N. J. M. Teare* for the appellants.
Adrian Hamilton Q.C. and *T. P. D. Saloman* for the respondents.

Their Lordships took time for consideration.

April 1. VISCOUNT DILHORNE. My Lords, on August 30, 1975, a
C contract was made between Pitria Pride Navigation Co. Inc., a Liberian company, (hereafter referred to as " the buyer ") and the respondent, (hereafter referred to as " the builder ") whereby it was agreed that the builder should " build, launch, equip and complete " a 24,000 ton deadweight multi-purpose cargo ship and " deliver and sell " her to the buyer for U.S. $14,300,000. It was a term of the contract that con-
D struction of the vessel should proceed continuously from keel laying to delivery.

Article 10 of the contract provided that the price should be paid in five instalments, the first of 2·5 per cent. of the contract price i.e. $357,500; the second of the same amount to be paid on July 15, 1976; the third of 10 per cent. of the contract price; the fourth, of 17·5 per cent. of the contract price and the fifth and final instalment of 67·5
E per cent. plus or minus any increase or decrease due to modifications to be paid at least three days prior to the scheduled delivery date of the vessel.

The date stipulated for payment of each instalment was referred to as " the due date " and this litigation arises from the non-payment of the second instalment on the due date.

F It was also agreed in article 10 that:

" all payment under the provisions of this article shall not be delayed or withheld by the buyer due to any dispute of whatever nature arising between the builder and the buyer hereto, unless the buyer shall have claimed to cancel the contract under the terms thereof or in the case of the last payment, have rejected the vessel."

G This provision is indicative of the importance attached to payment of the instalments on the due dates; and the increasing amount of the instalments shows that they were intended to reflect the increasing costs incurred in the building of the vessel.

Article 10 also provided that the payments made by the buyer prior to delivery of the vessel should constitute advances to the builder, and
H that if the contract was cancelled or rescinded otherwise than in accordance with the provisions of article 11 " the full amount of total sums paid by the buyer to the builder in advance of delivery " should be refunded to the buyer.

Article 11 stated at its commencement that:

" The buyer shall be deemed to be in default under this contract . . . in the case of . . . the second . . . instalment, if such instalment is not received within the period of 30 days following the due date . . .

or if the buyer fails to be in punctual, due and full compliance A with any of its obligations under this contract."

It is not necessary in this case to decide whether the buyer was in default when payment was not made on the due date, July 15, or only became in default 30 days thereafter.

The article then went on to say:

"In case the buyer is in default of any of its obligations under this B contract, the builder is entitled to and shall have the following right, power and remedies in addition to such other rights, powers and remedies as the builder may have elsewhere in this contract and/or at law, at equity or otherwise."

It was thus provided that the rights, powers and remedies given to the builder by this article were to be in addition to and not exclusive of C any other rights, powers and remedies he might have in consequence of default on the part of the buyer.

This article then went on to provide that if an instalment remained unpaid for more than three days after the due date, the builder should notify the buyer of that, and that if the default continued for seven days after the builder's notification, the builder might "rescind" the contract D by giving notice of rescission. In the case of the second instalment it was provided that:

"the said seven days notice to cancel this contract may be given at any time after the 23rd day following the due date . . . and shall be effective upon the expiry of the said seven day period if the buyer is at the expiry of seven day period in default."

E

The second instalment not having been paid on the due date or thereafter, the contract was cancelled on September 6, 1976, by notice given by the builder in accordance with this article.

This article stated that on cancellation the builder should be:

"entitled to retain the instalments already paid by the buyer to the builder which shall be applied to recovery of the builder's loss and damage including, but not being limited to, reasonable estimated F profit due to the buyer's default and the cancellation of this contract."

The contract did not state what was to happen with regard to rights which had accrued prior to cancellation. I do not think that this express provision relating to instalments already paid, which was perhaps thought G necessary in view of the obligation under article 10 to refund all such instalments if the contract was terminated otherwise than under article 11, throws any light on the consequences of cancellation with regard to instalments which had become due and had not been paid.

That article also gave the builder if he cancelled the contract in accordance with its provisions, the right either to complete or not to complete the vessel and to sell her in either a complete or incomplete H state. It contained detailed provisions as to the application of the proceeds of sale if the builder decided to sell her and provided that if, after compensating the builder, there was any balance left, that should be paid to the buyer.

Contemporaneously with this contract the appellants (hereafter referred to as "the guarantors") gave the builder the following guarantee:

A
" In consideration of your entering into the shipbuilding contract
... with Pitria Pride Navigation Co. Inc., Liberia, (' the buyer '), we
hereby jointly and severally irrevocably guarantee the payment in
accordance with the terms of the contract of all sums due or to
become due by the buyer to you under the contract, and in case
the buyer is in default of any such payment we will forthwith
make the payment in default on behalf of the buyer. Our liability
B
under this guarantee shall cease upon delivery of the vessel or upon
the previous assignment (with your consent) by the buyer to a third
party of this contract upon terms that the assignee shall adopt to
the exclusion of the buyer all rights and obligations of the buyer
towards you under the contract."

C
Payment of the second instalment not having been received, the
builder on March 14, 1978, issued a writ against the guarantors claiming
the sum of U.S. $420,879·95, the amount of that instalment and interest
thereon as provided by the contract. Lloyd J. gave judgment for the
builder under R.S.C., Ord. 14. The buyer's appeal to the Court of
Appeal was dismissed on October 6, 1978. On May 17, 1978, *Hyundai
Shipbuilding & Heavy Industries Co. Ltd.* v. *Pournaras* [1978] 2 Lloyd's
D
Rep. 502 had come before a differently constituted Court of Appeal.
In that case the contracts were similar in all material respects to that
in this case; guarantees were given in the same terms and there had
been default in the payment of instalments in consequence of which the
builder had treated the contracts as repudiated and had accepted the
repudiation.

E
Roskill L.J., with whose judgment Stephenson L.J. agreed, said that
in his view the true meaning of the guarantees was that if the buyer
did not pay on time, the guarantors would pay. To hold otherwise was
in his opinion to fly in the face of the obvious commercial purpose of
the guarantees. He rejected the argument that once the contracts had
come to an end, liability to pay instalments which had become due and
had not been paid ceased and was replaced by a claim not in debt but
F
in damages. In his opinion the ending of the contracts did not free the
buyer from the obligation to pay the instalments liability for the payment
of which had already accrued, and did not free the guarantors from
liability under the guarantees.

The two main differences between that case and this are, first, that
in that case the builder did not invoke article 11 but treated the non-
payment of instalments by the buyer as entitling it to treat the contracts
G
as terminated and in the present case the builder had cancelled under
article 11; and, secondly that in that case the writ was issued against
the guarantors before the repudiation was accepted whereas in this case
it was issued after the cancellation.

Mr. Curry for the appellants contended that that case could on these
grounds be distinguished from the present case, and if that were not so,
H
that the decision in that case was wrong. He conceded that prior to the
cancellation on September 6, neither the buyer nor the guarantors had
any answer to a claim for payment of the second instalment due on
July 15, but he contended that the effect of cancellation by the builder
was to relieve the buyer of the obligation to pay that instalment. Cancellation meant that that instalment was no longer due and not being
due from the buyer, the guarantors were not under any liability to pay
it. Cancellation meant that the builder was deprived of his accrued

right to payment of the second instalment either from the buyer or A under the guarantee.

If this argument is well founded, one curious consequence would appear to be that the very ground for cancellation was destroyed by the act of cancellation.

The first question for consideration appears to me to be, does cancellation of the contract under article 11 or the acceptance of a repudiation destroy accrued rights?

In this connection Mr. Curry placed great reliance on *Dies* v. *British and International Mining and Finance Corporation Ltd.* [1939] 1 K.B. 724, a decision of Stable J. In that case the defendants entered into a contract to sell rifles and ammunition for £270,000 and on the date the agreement was made, the purchaser paid £100,000 to the defendants in prepayment of part of the purchase price. The purchaser failed to accept delivery of the goods and the defendants elected to treat the contract as at an end. The purchaser and his assignee then claimed repayment of the £100,000 less a sum for liquidated damages for the breach of contract by the purchaser and it was held that their claim succeeded. Stable J. at p. 743 referred to *Benjamin on Sale,* 7th ed. (1931), p. 989 where it was stated: " In ordinary circumstances, unless the contract otherwise provides, the seller on rescission following the buyer's default, becomes liable to repay the part of the price paid " and said:

> " If this passage accurately states the law, as in my judgment, it does where the language used in a contract is neutral, the general rule is that the law confers on the purchaser the right to recover his money, and that to enable the seller to keep it he must be able to point to some language in the contract from which the inference to be drawn is that the parties intended and agreed that he should."

Stable J. did not think that the foundation of the right of the purchaser to recover the money he had paid was that there had been a total failure of consideration. He held that there had not been.

Mr. Curry contended that in the light of this decision the buyer was entitled to be repaid the instalment paid on cancellation and would have been entitled to be repaid the amount of the second instalment if that had been paid; and that being so, after cancellation the second instalment ceased to be due from the buyer and the guarantors.

I do not find it necessary in the present case to consider whether the *Dies* case [1939] 1 K.B. 724, was rightly decided for in this case the contract was not just for the sale of a ship. As I have said, it was a contract to " build, launch, equip and complete " a vessel and " to deliver and sell " her. The contract price included " all costs and expenses for designing and supplying all necessary drawings for the vessel..." It was a contract which was not simply one of sale but which so far as the construction of the vessel was concerned, resembled a building contract.

Hudson's Building and Engineering Contracts, 10th ed. (1970), p. 255 under the heading " Express terms for payment by instalments " states:

> " Where the contractor has become entitled to an instalment payment, he will not normally forfeit his right to such payment by a subsequent abandonment or repudiation of the contract, but will be entitled to sue for any unpaid instalment, if he has satisfied the

conditions for it to become due, subject, of course, to the employer's right to counterclaim for damages for breach of contract. In *Taylor* v. *Laird* (1856) 25 L.J.Ex. 329 the plaintiff undertook to serve as a commander of a vessel at pay of £50 per month but wrongfully abandoned the contract after eight months having been paid for seven only. The court held that the plaintiff was entitled to recover £50 for the eighth month, Pollock C.B. saying ' There (i.e. in the contract) " per month " means each month or monthly and gives a cause of action as each month accrues which once vested is not subsequently lost or divested by the plaintiff's desertion or abandonement of his contract.' "

Hudson then cites the following passage from Salmond and *Winfield, The Law of Contract* (1927), p. 286:

" Every obligation which has accrued due between the parties before the rescission of the contract, and which so creates a then existing cause of action, remains unaffected by the rescission and can still be enforced. It makes no difference in this respect whether such accrued obligation and existing cause of action is one in favour of the party rescinding the contract or is one in favour of the other party."

and states that this passage was quoted with approval in two Australian cases *Ettridge* v. *Vermin Board of the District of Murat Bay* [1928] S.A.S.R. 124 and *McLachlan* v. *Nourse* [1928] S.A.S.R. 230.

Hudson then states that there are two qualifications to this general principle, one being that there may be a determination clause in the contract which if exercised by the employer will expressly deprive the contractor of an accrued right to an instalment, and it may well be that article 10 of the contract in this case would deprive the builder of the right to an accrued instalment in the event of cancellation or rescission otherwise than under article 11.

In *Brooks* v. *Beirnstein* [1909] 1 K.B. 98 a hirer of furniture at a monthly rent was in arrear with the rent and the owners of the furniture retook possession of it as they were entitled to do under the contract. They then sued for the arrears of rent. Bigham J. said that the agreement for hire in conferring the right to retake possession on a breach by the hirer, did not take away any other rights which the law gave to the owners, among which rights was that of suing for the monthly rent which had already accrued. He went on to say, at p. 102:

" If it could be said that by taking away the goods the owners had deprived the hirer of all consideration for the rent, then I could understand that the accrued cause of action would be gone."

Chatterton v. *Maclean* [1951] 1 All E.R. 761 was a decision to the like effect. In that case the guarantor of a hire purchase agreement relating to a motor car disclaimed liability on the ground that by accepting the hirer's breach of contract as repudiation of the agreement, the company had released all its rights under that agreement. It was held by Parker J. that the hirer remained under any liability which had already accrued at the date of the repudiation and said, at p. 764:

" If he remained liable for the accrued liability—and, of course, it was only right that he should remain liable, because he had had the benefit of the car for the period relating to it—prima facie, he being liable and the sum not having been paid, the guarantor is liable under his guarantee."

In the light of these decisions and of what was said in *Hudson,* I conclude that save in the case of sales of land and goods and where there has been a total failure of consideration, it was the law prior to the decision in *Lep Air Services Ltd.* v. *Rolloswin Investments Ltd.* [1973] A.C. 331 that cancellation or rescission of a contract in consequence of repudiation did not affect accrued rights to the payment of instalments of the contract price unless the contract provided that it was to do so. It follows that the differences between the *Pournaras* case [1978] 2 Lloyd's Rep. 502 and the present case are immaterial.

In the *Lep Air Services* case [1973] A.C. 331 in consideration for relinquishing a lien the debtor agreed to pay £40,000 he then owed by weekly instalments of £6,000. The contract included a guarantee by Mr. Moschi. The debtor defaulted in his obligations from the outset. The creditors treated his breaches of contracts as repudiation and accepted it. They then sued the debtor for damages and the guarantor for the full amount of the weekly instalments less what had been paid. At the time the action was commenced, a number of instalments had accrued due. They claimed against the guarantor the amounts which had become due and those which would have become due if the debtor's repudiation had not been accepted, that is to say, the total amount.

In the Court of Appeal [1971] 1 W.L.R. 934 Megaw L.J. delivering the judgment of the court, said at p. 941:

"It is we think, plain beyond any real argument that an accrued liability for breaches of contract does not change its character so as to release the guarantor from his already existing liability in respect thereof, merely because the creditor has elected to exercise the right which is given to him as an incident of the general law of contract: the right, namely, to accept the wrongful repudiation constituted by those breaches, and thus to be enabled to treat the principal debtor's future obligations under the contract as having been irrevocably broken as from that moment. The mere fact that the creditor is thereupon entitled to additional damages in respect of the resulting immediate breach by the principal debtor of future obligations under the contract cannot have the effect of releasing the guarantor from his already existing liability referable to that already existing accrued liability of the principal debtor. The essential nature of that accrued liability is in no way changed."

In this House [1973] A.C. 331, this part of his judgment was not subjected to any criticism or comment. The guarantor's appeal on the ground that his obligation was discharged by the respondent's acceptance of the repudiation was dismissed. Lord Reid said that the guarantor's next argument was more formidable. He summarised it as follows, at p. 344:

"He" (the guarantor) "says, look at clause (XIII). It merely guarantees that each instalment of £6,000 shall be duly paid. But by reason of the accepted repudiation the contract was brought to an end before the later instalments became payable. So they never did become payable. All that remained after the contract was

A   terminated was a claim for damages. But I never guaranteed to pay damages. If the creditor chooses to act so that future instalments are not payable by the debtor, he cannot recover them from me."

This passage shows that the issue was as to liability for future instalments and not in relation to instalments the right to payment of
B   which had already accrued.

My noble and learned friend Lord Diplock began his speech by holding that four instalments had become due when the creditor elected to treat the contract as rescinded. He went on to say, at p. 346:

"... as there has been no previous case upon the effect that the rescission of a contract has upon the liability of a guarantor in
C   respect of the obligations of the principal debtor of which performance had not fallen due at the date of the rescission, I propose to make some observations about the general principles of the law of guarantee which, in my view, govern this situation."

My noble and learned friend Lord Simon of Glaisdale at p. 354 referred to the appellant's contention that the acceptance of repudiation
D   discharged the guarantor from liability in respect of accrued instalments. That he said, at p. 355:

"would make nonsense of the whole commercial purpose of suretyship: you would lose your guarantor at the very moment you most need him—namely, at the moment of fundamental breach by the principal promisor."

E   My Lords, none of their Lordships referred to the passage I have cited from Megaw L.J.'s judgment. They surely would have done so if they had disagreed with it. The decision was concerned with future instalments and I find nothing in the speeches to lead me to the conclusion that the law with regard to accrued instalments was altered by that decision.

F   If, as I hold, in the present case the buyer remained liable for the second instalment which had accrued despite the cancellation under article 11, there is in my opinion no doubt that the guarantors remained liable under the guarantee for that instalment.

If, contrary to my view, cancellation deprived the builder of his accrued right to payment by the buyer of the second instalment, would
G   that also deprive the builder of the right to have recourse to the guarantors for the amount of that instalment? In my opinion the answer is in the negative. If the terms of the guarantee are such, as they clearly are in this case, as to guarantee payment of that instalment on the due date, the builder had an accrued right to payment by the guarantors. It was conceded that the builder had had an accrued right to payment of that sum by the buyer and by the guarantors. In my view the fact,
H   if it was the fact, that the builder lost his right as against the buyer on cancellation, would not deprive the builder of his accrued right against the guarantors.

It was also contended on behalf of the guarantors as it was in the *Pournaras* case [1978] 2 Lloyd's Rep. 502 that they were entitled to set off against a claim by the builder for loss and damage the second instalment if due at the date of the issue of the writ, and also that they should be given some equitable relief against having to pay the second instalment. For the reasons given by Roskill L.J. in the *Pournaras* case, I think as he did, that these contentions should be rejected.

In my opinion for the reasons I have stated, this appeal should be dismissed.

LORD EDMUND-DAVIES. My Lords, this appeal is from a decision of the Court of Appeal dismissing an appeal by the present appellants (who were guarantors of sums due or to become due under a shipbuilding contract) from the summary judgment of Lloyd J. who had awarded the respondent shipbuilders U.S. $357,500 with interest under the terms of a letter of guarantee. In so deciding Lloyd J. and the Court of Appeal held that the facts in the instant case were substantially indistinguishable from those of *Hyundai Shipbuilding & Heavy Industries Co. Ltd.* v. *Pournaras* [1978] 2 Lloyd's Rep. 502 in which the Court of Appeal upheld an order for summary judgment against guarantors given by Donaldson J. (unreported), November 29, 1977, on a similarly worded guarantee.

These are the salient facts: by a shipbuilding contract (" the ship contract ") dated August 30, 1975, the respondents (" the builders ") agreed to build a 24,000 ton deadweight dry cargo ship for Pitria Pride Navigation Co. Inc., a Liberian company (" the buyers "). This was one of a series of four contracts of the same date, whereby the builders agreed to build identical ships for associated companies of the buyers. The contracts were expressly governed by English law.

By letters of guarantee (which were also expressly subject to English law) annexed to each of the shipbuilding contracts the appellants (" the guarantors ") provided the builders with a guarantee in the following terms:

" From: Petros Papadopoulos
          Charalambos Paraskevopoulos
          George Papathanassopoulos
" To: Hyundai Shipbuilding and Heavy Industries Co. Ltd.
" Date: (August 30, 1975)
                    " LETTER OF GUARANTEE
" Dear Sirs,
" In consideration of your entering into the shipbuilding contract, its present and future form, relating to your Hull No. 2338 ('the contract ') with Pitria Pride Navigation Co. Inc., Liberia, ('the buyer '), we hereby jointly and severally irrevocably guarantee the payment in accordance with the terms of the contract of all sums due or to become due by the buyer to you under the contract, and in case the buyer is in default of any such payment we will forthwith make the payment in default on behalf of the buyer.

" Our liability under this guarantee shall cease upon delivery of the vessel or upon the previous assignment (with your consent) by the buyer to a third party of this contract upon terms that the assignee shall adopt to the exclusion of the buyer all rights and obligations of the buyer towards you under the contract.

"This guarantee shall be governed by and construed in all respects in accordance with the law of England.

"Yours faithfully,

(1) *Petros Papadopoulos*
(2) *Charalambos Paraskevopoulos*
(3) *George Papathanassopoulos*"

The payment scheme under the ship contract is of particular importance and must therefore be described in a little detail. The contract price of the vessel was U.S. $14,300,000, subject to such adjustment or modification as was indicated in the contract. The terms of payment were these: the first instalment of $357,000 (being 2·5 per cent. of the price) was payable within 7 days of receipt of export licence; the second instalment of the same amount was payable on July 15, 1976; the third instalment for $1,430,000 (10 per cent.) was payable on August 31, 1976; the fourth for $2,502,000 (17·5 per cent.) was payable on the launching of the vessel or on January 31, 1977, whichever was the later; and the fifth and final instalment of $9,652,500 (67·5 per cent.), plus or minus any increase or decrease due to modifications or adjustment, was payable "at least three days prior to the scheduled delivery date of the vessel," which was fixed for June 30, 1977.

Although the builders warranted that construction would proceed on a continuous basis from keel-laying to delivery, it followed from the foregoing that the builders would have to wait for 67·5 per cent. of the contract price until three days before delivery. Punctual payment of earlier instalments was therefore of importance, and this was emphasised in article 10 (b), which provided that:

"It is understood and agreed upon by the builder and the buyer that all payments under the provisions of this article shall not be delayed or withheld by the buyer due to any dispute of whatever nature arising between the builder and the buyer hereto, unless the buyer shall have claimed to cancel the contract under the terms thereof or in case of the last payment, have [sic] rejected the vessel."

The first instalment was punctually paid, but the second instalment (due on July 15, 1976) was never met. Article 11 (a) of the shipbuilding contract provided that:

"In case the buyer is in default of any of its obligations under this contract, the builder is entitled to and shall have the following right, power and remedies in addition to such other rights, powers and remedies as the builder may have elsewhere in this contract and/or at law, at equity or otherwise."

Article 11 (b) (iii), which was restricted to cases of the buyers' default in *payment,* provided that if any instalment was unpaid for more than three days after the due date, the builders must give notice of that fact to the buyers. There followed elaborate provisions which need not now be entered into; their effect being that, if the default in payment continued the builders became entitled to give the buyers what was variously described as "notice of rescission" and "notice to cancel" the contract. Article 11 (b) (iv) provided that:

"In the event of such cancellation by the builder of this contract due to default in payment of the ... second ... instalment ... the

builder shall be entitled to retain the instalments already paid by
the buyer to the builder which shall be applied to recovery of the
builder's loss and damage ... and at the same time the builder
shall have the full right and power either to complete or not to
complete the vessel which is the sole property of the builder as he
deems fit, and to sell the vessel at public auction ... The sale of
the vessel at auction ... shall be without prejudice to any right of
the builder to recover damages from the buyer for its default ..."

It was later provided in the ship contract that the proceeds received by
the builders from the sale were to be applied (in addition to the retained
instalments) in the following manner: (1) for paying expenses incurred
in holding the sale; (2) in recouping the builders for the unpaid balance
of the contract price if the vessel had been completed before sale, or
for the cost of work done if the vessel was sold in an uncompleted
state; (3) any remaining balance would go to the buyers, who would
remain liable to the builders in the event of the sums retained by them
under (1) and (2) being insufficient to meet their entitlement under the
contract.

The buyers having defaulted in respect of the second instalment due
on July 15, 1976, the builders exercised on September 6, their right to
rescind, and by a specially endorsed writ issued on March 14, 1978,
they sued the guarantors under the letter of guarantee for the amount of
that instalment plus interest. Lloyd J. in the Commercial Court and
the Court of Appeal held that, in the light of the decision in *Hyundai
Shipbuilding & Heavy Industries Co. Ltd.* v. *Pournaras* [1978] 2 Lloyd's
Rep. 502 there was no arguable defence and that the builders were
entitled to judgment. It is against that holding that the guarantors now
appeal, urging (a) that the *Pournaras* case is distinguishable from the
present case, and (b) in any event, the decision in that case was wrong.

Mr. Curry at the outset of submissions so formidable as to call
for close examination, conceded that from default up until the builders'
cancellation of the contract on September 6, 1976, both buyers and
guarantors were liable under their respective contracts for payment of
the second instalment. But, so the argument proceeded, upon such
cancellation the buyers' only rights and obligations were those under
article 11 (b) (iv), which could be summarised in this way. (1) The
builders were entitled to retain the first instalment which the buyers
had duly paid, but only in order to meet (in whole or in part) their
" loss or damage." (2) The builders' right under article 11 (b) (iii) to
cancel the ship contract for instalments due and unpaid, when contrasted with their express right to retain instalments due and unpaid,
manifested that they had no right to sue for the former after
cancellation. (3) In respect of instalments already due, the right to
retain those already paid before cancellation of the contract, or to
recover by any means those still unpaid depended on the builders proving
" loss or damage." This they had not attempted to do, and they were
accordingly not entitled either to retain instalments paid or to sue for
those unpaid. (4) As to the guarantors, the only sums they had
guaranteed were those " due or to become due " from the buyers under
the ship contract. But it followed from the foregoing that, when the
writ against them was issued on March 14, 1978, the builders' exercise
several months earlier (i.e. on September 6, 1976) of their right to
cancel the ship contract had terminated their right to demand payment

A   of the second instalment, which had therefore ceased to be "due." Substituted therefore was the builders' right to recover damages against the buyers—if they could prove them. But, even if they could, the guarantee extended only to "sums due or to become due by the buyer . . . under the contract, and in case the buyer is in default of any such payment." It had no operation in relation to any right to damages. (5) In the result, at the date of the writ no instalments were

B   due from the buyers under the ship contract, and it followed that there was no liability of the appellants under their guarantee.

My Lords, despite the persuasive manner of their presentation, I find these submissions unacceptable. It has to be said, at the outset, that the assertion that the builders' exercise of their undoubted right to cancel the ship contract terminated it for *all* purposes and, in particular,

C   rendered the second instalment no longer exigible, is an irrational assumption unsupported by any direct authority. It is true that upon cancellation the builders acquired a right to recover damages for such injury flowing from the buyers' default as, in due course and upon proper accounts being taken and a balance struck, the builders could establish. But there is no warrant for saying that such right was acquired in *substitution* for their accrued right to recover the due but

D   unpaid second instalment. On the contrary, having regard to what Lord Wilberforce once called "the matrix of facts" (*Prenn* v. *Simmonds* [1971] 1 W.L.R. 1381, 1384A), there are sound commercial reasons for holding that a vested and indubitable right to prompt payment on a specified date of a specified sum, expressly provided for in the contract, should *not* be supplanted by or merged in or substituted by a right to

E   recover at some future date such indefinite sum by way of damages as, on balance and on proof, might be awarded to the builders, following upon a scrutiny of the parties' respective rights and obligations under the contract as a whole.

In my judgment there is ample authority and judicial support for the proposition stated in *Treitel, The Law of Contract,* 5th ed. (1979), p. 641 that:

F   "Rescission . . . releases the party in breach for the future from his primary obligations to perform. But he is not released from primary obligations already due at the time of rescission, and he also comes under a secondary liability to pay damages. His liability may thus relate both to breaches committed before rescission and to losses suffered by the victim as a result of the defaulting party's

G   repudiation of future obligations."

In *McDonald* v. *Dennys Lascelles Ltd.* (1933) 48 C.L.R. 457, 476, Dixon J. said, in a judgment unanimously approved of by this House in *Johnson* v. *Agnew* [1980] A.C. 367, 396:

        "When a party to a simple contract, upon a breach by the other contracting party of a condition of the contract, elects to treat the

H   contract as no longer binding upon him, the contract is not rescinded as from the beginning. Both parties are discharged from the further performance of the contract, but rights are not divested or discharged which have already been unconditionally acquired. Rights and obligations which arise from the partial execution of the contract and causes of action which have accrued from its breach alike continue unaffected."

Despite an attempt by Mr. Curry to show that hire-purchase agree- A ments are to be distinguished from the ship contract with which this House is presently concerned, they clearly fall within the general pro- position propounded by Dixon J. It is true that in such cases the hirer has received consideration in the shape of use for a limited period of the subject matter of the contract, but that is taken care of by the limited nature of his payment towards the ultimate purchase-price. It has become well established that in such contracts the finance company B is entitled not only to retain instalments paid at the time of cancellation but also to recover instalments accrued due before that date: see *Guest, The Law of Hire Purchase* (1966), paras. 431 and 473. So in *Brooks* v. *Beirnstein* [1909] 1 K.B. 98, 102, Bigham J. held that, when the owners of furniture, hired out with an option to purchase, retook possession under the terms of the contract where the hirer had defaulted C in payment of the agreed monthly rent:

"The agreement, in so conferring the right to retake possession on a breach by the hirer, does not take away any other rights which the law gives to the owners, among which rights is that of suing for the monthly rent which had already accrued."

And in *Chatterton* v. *Maclean* [1951] 1 All E.R. 761, where the D hirer of a car defaulted under a hire-purchase agreement and the owners exercised their right to repossess, Parker J. said, at p. 764:

"The hirer remains under any liability that has already accrued at the date of the acceptance of the repudiation. That is put beyond all doubt by *Brooks* v. *Beirnstein*."

That the legal position is similar in relation to a time charterparty E was common ground between counsel and manifestly approved of by Greer J. in *Leslie Shipping Co.* v. *Welstead* [1921] 3 K.B. 420.

In the light of the foregoing I have been led to the conclusion that, notwithstanding the notice of cancellation of the ship contract given by the builders on September 6, 1976, when they issued their writ against the guarantors on March 6, 1978, under that contract the second instal- F ment of $357,500 was still due from the buyers to the builders.

But, my Lords, what if I am wrong so far—that is to say, what if, although the second instalment was undoubtedly due from the buyers until September 6, 1976, the builders' notice of cancellation of the ship contract on that date destroyed the builders' right to recover the sum and replaced it by a right to sue the buyers for damages? In those G circumstances, would the guarantors nevertheless be liable under their letter of guarantee? Upon that hypothesis, can it still be said, that, after September 6, 1976, the guarantors were still under an obligation to pay "forthwith" $357,500 to the builders? It is to those questions that I now turn.

The appellants sought to place reliance on the decision of Stable J. in *Dies* v. *British and International Mining and Finance Corporation* H *Ltd.* [1939] 1 K.B. 724, a decision which has been described as "not easy to reconcile with earlier authority": see *Goff and Jones, The Law of Restitution*, 2nd ed. (1978), p. 381. But in my judgment, the exiguous nature of the known facts in the present case renders it wholly unrealistic to think that a single payment of a mere 2·5 per cent. of the contract price of the vessel could bring about the sort of case dealt with in the *Dies* case, and I am in respectful agreement with Roskill

A L.J. in *Hyundai Shipbuilding & Heavy Industries Co. Ltd.* v. *Pournaras*
[1978] 2 Lloyd's Rep. 502, 508, that the avowed object of the letter of
guarantee was:

"to enable the yard to recover from the guarantors the amount
due irrespective of the position between yard and buyers, so that the
yard gets its money from the guarantors without difficulty if the
B   yard cannot get it from the buyers."

Having said that, I can conveniently return to *Chatterton* v. *Maclean*
[1951] 1 All E.R. 761. I have already spoken of it, but without
referring to the fact that the defendant there was not the hirer of the
motor-car but his guarantor. Of the latter's position Parker J. had
this to say, at pp. 764–765:

C   "Counsel for the defendant urges... that the very acceptance, the
very treating of the hirer's conduct as a repudiation of the contract,
amounts to a new contract. That leads to the rather startling
conclusion that a guarantor of the performance of a contract is
always released when the creditor does what he is lawfully entitled
to do, namely, to treat the principal debtor's breach as a repu-
D   diation. It would mean that whenever a creditor exercised his
ordinary rights a guarantor was released, not merely in respect of
future liabilities, but in respect of accrued liabilities."

The learned judge then quoted some words of Lord Wrenbury in
Bradley v. *H. Newson, Sons & Co.* [1919] A.C. 16, a case to which
neither side has referred in this appeal, and continued:

E   "... I find it very difficult to think that those words can be used
to support the proposition that by that consensual act a new
contract is made which impinges on the rights of the guarantor. It
seems to me that it is merely bringing the contract to an end—
something which the creditor is lawfully entitled to do—and that
the guarantor cannot complain of it."

F   *Lep Air Services Ltd.* v. *Rolloswin Investments Ltd.* [1973] A.C. 331,
related to liabilities not yet accrued, but the report contains observations highly apposite to such accrued liabilities as are the subject matter
of this appeal. I begin with Lord Diplock, who said, at p. 351:

"The guarantor's obligation under his contract of guarantee does
not... depend upon the debtor's primary obligation continuing to
exist after the contract had been rescinded. Nor is it affected by
G   whether the debtor's secondary obligation which was substituted
for it by operation of law is classified as an obligation to pay
damages or as an obligation to pay the debt. It was the debtor's
failure to perform his primary obligation to pay the instalments
in circumstances which put an end to it that constituted a failure
by the guarantor to perform his own primary obligation to the
H   creditor to see that the instalments were paid by the debtor, and
substituted for it a secondary obligation of the guarantor to pay
to the creditor a sum of money for the loss he thereby sustained.
It is the guarantor's own secondary obligation, not that of the
debtor, that the creditor is enforcing in his claim for damages for
breach of his contract of guarantee."

Lord Simon of Glaisdale said, at p. 355B:

Lord Edmund Davies Hyundai Industries v. Papadopoulos (H.L.(E.))   **[1980]**

" The acceptance of the repudiation of an agreement does not   A
alter its terms in any way—it merely transmutes the primary obligation of the promisor to perform the terms contractually into a
secondary obligation, imposed by law, to pay damages for their
breach. Moreover, the suggested rule would make nonsense of the
whole commercial purpose of suretyship: you would lose your
guarantor at the very moment you most need him—namely, at the
moment of fundamental breach by the principal promisor."   B

The noble and learned Lord went on to describe as " absurd " the notion
that the guarantor of a bank overdraft was discharged from his liability
upon the bank customer repudiating his obligation to pay off his overdraft by instalments and the bank then closing the account and so
terminating the contractual relationship of banker and customer.
    It needs to be added simply that Lord Kilbrandon, also citing   C
Chatterton v. *Maclean* [1951] 1 All E.R. 761 with approval, was of a
like mind, and that Lord Reid had at the outset dealt summarily with
the guarantor's contention (viz., that he was under no liability to pay
anything because his obligations were discharged by the action of the
creditors in accepting the debtor's repudiation and so bringing the contract to an end), by saying, at p. 344:   D

" He supports this startling contention by relying on the principle
that if a creditor agrees to a variation of the debtor's contract he
thereby discharges a guarantor from liability. He argues that
acceptance of a repudiation should be regarded as equivalent to a
variation of the contract. I agree with your Lordships that there
is no substance in this argument and I reject it."   E

    My Lords, with respect, so do I. It is well established that notice of
a principal debtor's default need not be given to his guarantor, who is
liable without being requested to pay (see the cases cited in *Halsbury's
Laws of England*, 4th ed., vol. 20 (1978), title " Guarantee and Indemnity," paragraph 159). That liability is emphasised in the present case
by the guarantors' express undertaking to pay " forthwith " upon the
buyers being in default in payment, a factor to which Donaldson J.   F
rightly attached importance in his unreported judgment in the *Pournaras*
case. Even were the result of the builders' cancellation of the ship
contract to submerge their entitlement to be paid the second instalment
by the buyers into a claim for damages (contrary to the view I have
earlier expressed), it would not impinge on the guarantors' liability in
any way. I respectfully adopt Roskill L.J.'s summary of the matter   G
[1979] 2 Lloyd's Rep. 502, 506, namely that:

" the commercial purport and obvious intent and true construction
of this document is such that the contrary, as in effect the judge
said, is not really arguable. The true meaning is that if the buyer
does not pay in time . . . the guarantor will pay."

    For these reasons I would dismiss this appeal.   H

    LORD FRASER OF TULLYBELTON. My Lords, this appeal raises a
question as to the effect of cancellation of a contract by one of the
parties to it, in the exercise of a right provided in the contract, because
of a default by the other party in paying an instalment of the contract
price, upon the liability of guarantors under a letter of guarantee for
payment of the instalment in default.

A   The respondents ("the builder") are shipbuilders in South Korea. They are the plaintiffs in the action. On August 30, 1975, they contracted with a Liberian company called Pitria Pride Navigation Co. ("the buyer") to build and sell to them a ship designated by the builder as hull no. 2338. About the same date the appellants, who are individuals apparently having some connection with the buyer, granted a letter of guarantee, the terms of which will require careful attention, guaranteeing payment in accordance with the terms of the contract of all sums due or to become due by the buyer under the contract. The buyer defaulted on the second instalment, which was due on July 15, 1976, and the builder cancelled the contract with effect from September 6, 1976, as they were entitled to do under the contract. The builder now claims immediate payment of the second instalment from the guarantors. Both the shipbuilding contract and the letter of guarantee contain express declarations that they are to be governed in all respects by the law of England.

The case for the guarantors has two stages which are in outline as follows. First they say that when the contract was cancelled, all the primary obligations of the buyer, including the obligation to pay the second instalment, came to an end. They were replaced by secondary obligations under the contract which may be summarised with sufficient accuracy for the present as obligations to pay any deficiency brought out on a final accounting. This stage of the argument depends mainly on construction of the shipbuilding contract. The second stage of the argument is that, immediately the liability of the buyer to pay the second instalment came to an end, the liability of the guarantors to pay it on their behalf also came to an end. This stage depends mainly upon construction of the letter of guarantee.

The builder traverses both stages of the argument for the guarantors. It also maintains that, even if the liability of the buyer for the second instalment did come to an end upon cancellation of the contract, the liability of the guarantors continues unaffected.

F   The instant case follows an earlier case—*Hyundai Shipbuilding & Heavy Industries Co. Ltd.* v. *Pournaras* (to which I shall refer as "*Pournaras*") in which the plaintiffs were the same company as the plaintiffs in the present action, and in which the issues were similar to but not identical with the issues in the present action. In *Pournaras* Donaldson J. (unreported), November 29, 1977, decided against the guarantors and his decision was upheld by the Court of Appeal (Stephenson and Roskill L.JJ.) [1978] 2 Lloyd's Rep. 502. In the present case Lloyd J. held that *Pournaras* could not be distinguished and the Court of Appeal (Roskill, Geoffrey Lane and Bridge L.JJ.) upheld his decision. They therefore decided in favour of the builder and against the guarantors. The opinions of Lloyd J. and of the Lords Justices in the present case are limited to explaining the reasons why it cannot be distinguished from *Pournaras* and it is therefore necessary to look at the *Pournaras* case for their reasoning on the main issues raised in this appeal.

Liability of the buyer for the second instalment

I shall consider first the effect of cancellation of the contract upon the liability of the buyer for the second instalment. Article 10 of the shipbuilding contract is headed "Payment" and it provides that the

contract price (U.S. $14,300,000) was to be payable in five instalments. **A**
The first instalment of U.S. $357,500 (2·5 per cent. of the contract
price) was duly paid and no question arises on it. The later instalments
were payable as follows: second instalment 2·5 per cent. of contract
price payable on July 15, 1976: third instalment 10 per cent. of contract
price payable on August 31, 1976: fourth instalment 17·5 per cent.
of contract price payable on notification by the builders that launching
would be completed within 30 days or on January 31, 1977, whichever **B**
was later, and fifth instalment 67·5 per cent. of contract price payable
three days before the scheduled delivery date (June 30, 1977). The date
stipulated for each payment was referred to in the contract as "the
due date." The second instalment was not paid on the due date. The
builder immediately set in motion the elaborate machinery provided by
article 11 of the contract for that event, machinery which could, and **C**
in this case did, end up in the contract being cancelled. Article 11(a)
provides that:

> "The buyer shall be deemed to be in default under this contract . . .
> in the case of either the second, the third, or the fourth instalment,
> if such instalment is not received within the period of 30 days
> following the due date." **D**

It further provides that in case the buyer is in default of any of its
obligations under the contract:

> ". . . the builder is entitled to and shall have the following right,
> power and remedies in addition to such other rights, powers and
> remedies as the builder may have elsewhere in this contract and/or
> at law, at equity or otherwise." **E**

Article 11(b) provides that if the buyer shall be in default as provided
in paragraph (a) in payment of any of the instalments, then in the case
of inter alia the second instalment, seven days' notice to cancel the
contract may be given:

> ". . . at any other time after the 23rd day following the due date
> of that instalment and shall be effective upon the expiry of the **F**
> said seven day period if the buyer is at the expiry of seven day
> period in default."

It is common ground that seven day's notice was given and that it
expired on September 6, 1976. Sub-paragraph (iv) of article 11 (b) provides as follows:

> "(iv) In the event of such cancellation by the builder of this **G**
> contract due to default in payment of the . . . second . . . instalment
> as provided for in paragraph (a) above, the builder shall be
> entitled to retain the instalments *already paid* by the buyer to the
> builder which shall be applied to recovery of the builder's loss and
> damage including, but not being limited to, reasonable estimated
> profit due to the buyer's default and the cancellation of this con-
> tract and at the same time the builder shall have the full right and **H**
> power either to complete or not to complete the vessel which is the
> sole property of the builder as he deems fit, and to sell the vessel
> at public auction either in a complete or in an incomplete state . . ."
> (My italics).

There is further provision that the proceeds received by the builder
from the sale shall be applied, in addition to the retained instalments

A (*first*) in payment of all reasonable expenses of the sale (*second*) (if the
vessel has been completed) in or towards satisfaction of the unpaid
balance of the contract price and the cost of any extra work or (if the
vessel has not been completed) in or towards satisfaction of the cost
incurred by the builder and reasonable estimated profit and (*third*),
finally, that the balance of the proceeds, if any, shall belong to the
buyer, but that if the proceeds of the sale together with retained instal-
B ments are insufficient to pay the builder what is due to him, the buyer
shall be liable for the deficiency and shall pay the same to the builder
on demand. This is the provision to which I have referred as a final
accounting.

The provision in article 11 (b) (iv) that instalments " already paid "
are to be retained and applied by the builders is not matched by any
C provision as to other instalments. Other instalments are not mentioned
at all, but nobody has suggested that future instalments (that is, instalments which have not fallen due for payment by the date of cancellation
of the contract) are payable. It is, I think, clear that they cease to be
payable as instalments, and are replaced by the buyer's obligation to pay
any deficiency brought out in the final accounting. But the position is
less clear in the case of instalments which had accrued and become due
D for payment before the date of cancellation of the contract. Counsel
for the guarantors drew our attention to article 10 (e) of the shipbuilding
contract which is headed " Refund " and which includes a provision
that " The payments made by the buyer to the builder prior to delivery
of the vessel shall constitute *advances* to the builder " (my italics). That
shows that such payments, which would of course have included the
E second instalment if it had been paid, are not earnests of ability to pay
but advances of part of the price. But, said counsel, once the contract
has been cancelled the price must cease to be payable; the purchaser
can no longer be liable to pay the price for a vessel which the builder
is no longer obliged to sell to him, and which he has said he has no
intention of selling to him. The argument was supported by reference
to a statement by Lord Denman C.J. in *Palmer* v. *Temple* (1839) 9
F A. & E. 508, 520–521, where he said:

"But the very idea of payment falls to the ground when both
[parties] have treated the bargain as at an end; and from that
moment the vendor holds the money advanced to the use of the
purchaser."

G *Palmer* v. *Temple* was a case where the plaintiff had contracted to
purchase landed property and had paid a sum " by way of deposit, and
in part of £5,500," which was the purchase price, and had then failed
to pay the balance of the price or to complete the contract. He was
held to be entitled to recover his deposit, but the actual decision turned
on the terms of the particular contract. In *Dies* v. *British and International Mining and Finance Corporation Ltd.* [1939] 1 K.B. 724, where
H a passage from Lord Denman's judgment in *Palmer* v. *Temple* including
the statement that I have quoted was relied on by Stable J. at pp. 740
to 742, the contract was again purely one of sale—in that case of rifles
and ammunition. The vendor was a merchant or middle-man who
had intended to buy the goods from the manufacturer and to resell
them to the purchaser at a profit. Stable J. held that the purchaser
who had paid a large sum as an advance of the purchase price, and who
had then failed to complete payment or to take delivery of the goods,

was entitled to recover his advance payment under deduction of an A
agreed sum of liquidated damages. Counsel for the guarantors in the
instant case argued that if the buyer in the *Dies* case was entitled to
recover an advance which had already been paid, then a fortiori the
buyer in the instant case could not be liable to make an advance that
was due but unpaid; if he did make it, said counsel, he would be entitled
to immediate repayment of it.

I do not accept that argument. In my opinion the *Dies* case [1939] B
1 K.B. 724 and *Palmer* v. *Temple,* 9 A. & E. 508 are both distinguishable
from the present case because in both these cases the contracts were
simply contracts of sale which did not require the vendor to perform any
work or incur any expense on the subjects of sale. But the contract in
the instant case is not of that comparatievly simple character. The obligations of the buyer were not confined to selling the vessel but they C
included designing and building it and there were special provisions
(article 2) that the contract price " shall include payment for services
in the inspection, tests, survey and classification of the vessel " and also
" all costs and expenses for designing and supplying all necessary
drawings for the vessel in accordance with the specifications." Accordingly the builder was obliged to carry out work and to incur expense,
starting from the moment that the contract had been signed, including D
the wages of designers and workmen, fees for inspection and for cost
of purchasing materials. It seems very likely that the increasing proportions of the contract price represented by the five instalments bore
some relation to the anticipated rate of expenditure, but we have no
information on which to make any nice comparison between the amount
of expenses that the builder would have to bear from time to time, and E
the amounts of the instalments payable by the buyer. I do not think
that such comparisons are necessary. It is enough that the builder was
bound to incur considerable expense in carrying out his part of the
contract long before the actual sale could take place. That no doubt
is the explanation for the provision in article 10 (b) of the shipbuilding
contract that:

> " . . . all payments under the provisions of this article shall not be F
> delayed or withheld by the buyer due to any dispute of whatever
> nature arising between the builder and the buyer hereto, unless
> the buyer shall have claimed to cancel the contract under the terms
> thereof. . . ."

The importance evidently attached by the parties to maintaining the G
cash flow seems to support my view of the contract.

There was no evidence either way as to whether the builders had
in fact carried out their obligations to start designing and building the
vessel, but in my opinion we must assume, in the absence of evidence
or even averment to the contrary, that they had carried out their part
of the bargain up till the date of cancellation.

Much of the plausibility of the argument on behalf of the guaran- H
tors seemed to me to be derived from the assumption that the *contract*
price was simply a *purchase* price. That is not so, and once that
misconception has been removed I think it is clear that the shipbuilding
contract has little similarity with a contract of sale and much more
similarity, so far as the present issues are concerned, with contracts in
which the party entitled to be paid had either performed work or pro

A   vided services for which payment is due by the date of cancellation. In contracts of the latter class, which of course includes building and construction contracts, accrued rights to payment are not (in the absence of express provisions) destroyed by cancellation of the contract. Thus in *Newfoundland Government* v. *Newfoundland Railway Co.* (1888) 13 App.Cas.199 the company had contracted to build a railway line within five years, and thereafter to maintain and operate it. The

B government contracted to pay the company a certain subsidy and to pay a proportionate part of the total as each five-mile section of the railway was completed and operated. The company completed a portion of the line and received some payments but it then broke its contract and the government refused further payments. The company claimed sums due for a completed portion of the line. The question then arose

C "whether by the non-completion of the whole railway within the time stipulated, the company forfeit their right to the payment of the subsidy in respect of so much of the line as is completed and operated?" The Judicial Committee answered that question in the negative holding at p. 207: "that each claim to a grant must be treated as complete from the time when the section which has earned it was completed."

D   The same principle applies to hire-purchase contracts. The principle was stated by Parker J. in *Chatterton* v. *Maclean* [1951] 1 All E.R. 761. In that case the hirer of a motor car had failed to pay an instalment of hire timeously and the finance company had resumed possession of the car. Parker J. said, at p. 764:

E   "I think the true effect of what happened was that they chose to treat the hirer's conduct as a repudiation of the hire-purchase agreement. . . . What is the effect of that? The hirer remains under any liability that has already accrued at the date of the acceptance of the repudiation. That is put beyond all doubt by *Brooks* v. *Beirnstein* [1909] 1 K.B. 98. The hirer would also remain liable for any damages for breach of contract. If he remained liable for the accrued liability—and, of course, it was

F   only right that he should remain liable, because he had had the benefit of the car for the period relating to it—prima facie, he being liable and the sum not having been paid, the guarantor is liable under his guarantee."

    The reason given by Parker J. in that case, namely that the hirer had had the benefit of the car, was also the reason given in *Brooks* v.

G *Beirnstein* [1909] 1 K.B. 98 (another hire-purchase case) where Bigham J. said, at p. 102:

    "The agreement, in so conferring the right to retake possession on a breach by the hirer, does not take away any other rights which the law gives to the owners, among which rights is that of suing for the monthly rent which had already accrued."

H A little further down the page he said:

    "If it could be said that by taking away the goods the owners had deprived the hirer of all consideration for the rent, then I could understand that the accrued cause of action would be gone. But in truth the hirer has enjoyed the use of the furniture which was the consideration for the rent, and I can see no reason why he should not be liable to pay the arrears claimed."

In the instant case the buyer has not actually enjoyed any benefit A
from the work which the builder has performed, but it has been performed, (or at least we must so assume, in the absence of evidence to
the contrary) on the faith of the buyer's promise to pay the instalments
on the due dates. The builder had acquired a vested right to the debt
which was owed by the buyer at the date of cancellation and I see
no reason for holding it to be cancelled.

Lep Air Services Ltd. v. Rolloswin Investments Ltd. [1973] A.C. B
331 was concerned with the position of a guarantor and I shall have
to return to it in that connection, but I note here that Lord Simon of
Glaisdale and Lord Kilbrandon both referred to Chatterton v. Maclean
[1951] 1 All E.R. 761, so far as it dealt with the guarantor's liability
with approval. If they had thought that the observation by Parker J.
which I have quoted above was wrong I think they would certainly C
have said so.

For these reasons I am of opinion that the cancellation of the
contract did not release the buyer from his liability for the second
instalment, the due date for payment of which had passed before cancellation. That remained, and still remains, a debt due by the buyer
to the builder. If that is right then the appellants must fail. But even
if it was wrong, I think that they still fail because of the terms of the D
letter of guarantee to which I now turn.

Liability of the guarantors for the second instalment

I proceed now on the assumption, contrary to my opinion, that the
buyer was released from his liability for the second instalment by the
cancellation of the contract and I consider whether that would lead E
to the guarantors also being released. In the Lep Air Services case
[1973] A.C. 331, 344–345, Lord Reid said:

" I would not proceed by saying this is a contract of guarantee
and there is a general rule applicable to all guarantees. Parties are
free to make any agreement they like and we must I think determine just what this agreement means. With regard to making F
good to the creditor payments of instalments by the principal
debtor there are at least two possible forms of agreement. A
person might undertake no more than that if the principal debtor
fails to pay any instalment he will pay it. That would be a conditional agreement. There would be no prestable obligation unless
and until the debtor failed to pay. There would then on the
debtor's failure arise an obligation to pay. If for any reason the G
debtor ceased to have any obligation to pay the instalment on the
due date then he could not fail to pay it on that date. The
condition attached to the undertaking would never be purified and
the subsidiary obligation would never arise. On the other hand,
the guarantor's obligation might be of a different kind. He might
undertake that the principal debtor will carry out his contract. H
Then if at any time and for any reason the principal debtor acts
or fails to act as required by his contract, he not only breaks his
own contract but he also puts the guarantor in breach of his contract of guarantee. Then the creditor can sue the guarantor, not
for the unpaid instalment but for damages. His contract being
that the principal debtor would carry out the principal contract,
the damages payable by the guarantor must then be the loss

A
suffered by the creditor due to the principal debtor having failed
to do what the guarantor undertook that he would do."

There is, so far as I can see, no reason why both types of guarantee
should not be included in one document and I think that in the letter
of guarantee in the instant case both forms are included. The first
limb of the agreement was stated thus:

B
"... we hereby jointly and severally irrevocably guarantee the payment in accordance with the terms of the contract of all sums
due or to become due by the buyer to you under the contract."

That falls into the second of Lord Reid's classes and it would entitle
the builder to sue the guarantors for damages if the buyer defaulted
C
The second limb of the agreement was stated thus: "... and in case
the buyer is in default of any such payment we will forthwith make
the payment in default on behalf of the buyer." That is a conditional
agreement to make any "payment in default" and falls into Lord
Reid's first class.

It is admitted that the buyer was in default in respect of the second
instalment when it was not received within the period of 30 days following
D
the due date: see article 11 (a) of the shipbuilding contract. That
situation arose on either August 14 or 15, 1976 (the choice between
those dates being immaterial for present purposes). Counsel for the
guarantors accepted that the guarantors became liable on August 14
or 15 to make the payment and that their liability continued so long
as the shipbuilding contract had not been cancelled, but counsel argued
that when the contract was cancelled the liability of the guarantors,
E
like that of the buyer, was destroyed. It was said that once the contract had been cancelled there was no longer any sum due by the buyer
"under the contract," except possibly such sum as might be brought
out in the final accounting. So the guarantor's liability for the instalment under the first limb of the guarantee was said to have been
destroyed. With regard to liability under the second limb it was said
F
that as the buyer was, ex hypothesi of this argument, no longer liable
for the second instalment there was no longer any payment in default
for which the guarantors were liable " on behalf of the buyer."

There may be some doubt whether the word "default" in the letter
of guarantee bears the same meaning as it does in the definition in
article 10 (a) of the shipbuilding contract. In the letter of guarantee
default may refer simply to a payment not being made on the due date;
G
if that is correct then the buyer was in default on July 15. I do not
think it is necessary to come to any conclusion on this question
because whether the default began on July 15 or on August 14 or 15,
the argument for the guarantors would be the same, viz., that it terminated when the contract was cancelled.

My Lords, I cannot accept that argument. It seems to offend
H
against both common sense and authority. As regards common sense,
I find it difficult to believe that commercial men can have intended that
the guarantors were to be released from their liability for payments
already due and in default just because the builder used his remedy
of cancelling the shipbuilding contract for the future. The argument
for the guarantors on this part of the case seems to me, with all respect
to those who think otherwise, to be based on reading the letter of
guarantee in a way that is altogether too subtle to be appropriate for

such a document. The default by the buyer was the very event that
gave rise to the guarantor's liability under their letter of guarantee and
it also gave rise to the builder's right to cancel the shipbuilding contract
under article 11. If it had been intended that the builder's use of the
latter remedy was to put an end to the guarantor's liability that would
surely have been stated in the letter of guarantee, especially having
regard to the provision in the second paragraph of the letter that
liability was to cease upon the occurrence of other events there
specified. The guarantors' promise that they would "forthwith" make
the payment in default shows that the obligation became prestable
immediately upon default by the buyer, and was not merely an obligation to pay any deficiency brought out in the final accounting. I
agree with the view expressed by Roskill L.J. in *Hyundai Shipbuilding
& Heavy Industries Ltd.* v. *Pournaras* [1978] 2 Lloyd's Rep. 502, 508
that the purpose of the guarantee was that the yard "gets its money
from the guarantors without difficulty if the yard cannot get it from
the buyers," and that any other construction of the letter of guarantee
would mean that its commercial utility would be at least largely nullified.

As regards authority, I gratefully adopt the words of my noble and
learned friend Lord Simon of Glaisdale in *Lep Air Services Ltd.* v.
Rolloswin Investments Ltd. [1973] A.C. 331 where, after rejecting an
argument that acceptance of repudiation of a contract was equivalent
to its variation so as to release a guarantor from his obligations, he
went on to say at p. 355:

"Moreover, the suggested rule would make nonsense of the whole
commercial purpose of suretyship: you would lose your guarantor
at the very moment you most need him—namely, at the moment
of fundamental breach by the principal promisor. Take a usual
case giving rise to suretyship—that of a trader with a bank overdraft. The bank forbears to close the account (so as to put the
trader into bankruptcy or liquidation) in consideration of the
trader finding a guarantor of the overdraft and agreeing to pay
it off by instalments. The trader thereafter repudiates his obligation to pay off the overdraft by instalments; whereupon the
bank closes the account, so terminating the contractual relationship of banker and customer. It would be absurd to suppose that
the guarantor of the overdraft was thereby discharged from his
liability as surety. Finally, if authority were needed *Chatterton* v.
Maclean [1951] 1 All E.R. 761 is against the appellant's proposition. . ."

Lord Simon then referred to the passage from Parker J.'s judgment
which I have cited above. The considerations referred to by Lord
Simon in that case seem to me to be equally applicable to the cancellation of the shipbuilding contract under article 11 in the instant
case. I am therefore of opinion that cancellation of the contract did
not put an end to the guarantor's liability under the letter of
guarantee.

For these reasons I would dismiss the appeal.

LORD RUSSELL OF KILLOWEN. My Lords, I have had the advantage
of studying the speeches in this appeal of my noble and learned
friends Lord Edmund-Davies and Lord Fraser of Tullybelton.
As at present advised, I am not persuaded of the correctness of

A their conclusions on the construction of the shipbuilding contract, whether after giving notice of cancellation the builders are technically entitled to sue the purchasers for the overdue second instalment.

I need not, however, elaborate upon that point. Both for the reasons given by them, conclude that in any event there is no answer to the claim against the guarantors: and I am persuaded by those reasons that this is a correct conclusion. Accordingly I also would dismiss this appeal.

B

LORD KEITH OF KINKEL. My Lords, I share the doubts expressed by my noble and learned friend Lord Russell of Killowen as to the correctness of the conclusion by the majority of your Lordships that the cancellation by the builders of the shipbuilding contract did not have the effect of terminating the buyers' obligation to pay the second instalment.

C

But however that may be, I agree that, having regard to the particular terms of the guarantee, the cancellation did not put an end to the guarantors' own crystallised obligation to pay the instalment in question.

I would accordingly concur in dismissing the appeal.

D

Appeal dismissed.

Solicitors: *Constant & Constant; Norton, Rose, Botterell & Roche.*

J. A. G.

E

F

[COURT OF APPEAL]

* PERROT *v.* SUPPLEMENTARY BENEFITS COMMISSION

1980 May 1; 23   Stephenson and Brightman L.JJ. and
Dame Elizabeth Lane

G

*Social Security—Supplementary benefit—Entitlement—Claimant
engaged in own business—Expenses of business exceeding
receipts—Whether claimant engaged in " remunerative full-
time work "—Supplementary Benefits Act 1976 (c. 71), s. 6 (1)*

The claimant left her previous employment owing to ill-health, and, having exhausted her right to unemployment benefit, began, in October 1975, to claim supplementary benefit. Subsequently she set up in business on her own account, but continued to claim supplementary benefit since the expenses of the business exceeded the fees received in respect of the services provided during the relevant period. On June 5, 1978, the Supplementary Benefits Commission decided that the claimant was disqualified from receiving supplementary benefit by section 6 (1) of the Supplementary Benefits Act 1976 [1]

H

[1] Supplementary Benefits Act 1976, s. 6 (1): see post, p. 1155F–H.

since she was engaged in " remunerative full-time work "   A
within the meaning of the section. The South London Appeals
Tribunal upheld the commission's decision by a majority, and
on the claimant's appeal to the High Court, Judge Stabb
affirmed the decision of the appeal tribunal, the only issue being
whether the claimant's work was " remunerative."

On the claimant's appeal: —

Held, dismissing the appeal, that on the true construction of section 6 of the Supplementary Benefits Act 1976   B
" remunerative," in the phrase " remunerative full-time work "
qualified the work itself, not the commercial result of it,
and notwithstanding that in ordinary speech " remunerative "
meant " profitable " in a broad and general sense, that meaning was vague and imprecise, and, in the context of the section,
remunerative work meant work which brought remuneration,
i.e., work which was paid for, and the claimant's work was
remunerative within the meaning of the subsection (post, pp.   C
1157B–D, 1159A–C, F–G, 1160D, 1161D–F, 1162A).

Decision of Judge Stabb sitting as a judge of the Queen's
Bench Division affirmed.

The following cases are referred to in the judgments:

Cozens v. *Brutus* [1973] A.C. 854; [1972] 3 W.L.R. 521; [1972] 2 All
E.R. 1297, H.L.(E.).   D

Reg. v. *Postmaster General, Ex parte Saunders* (1876) 1 Q.B.D. 658, D.C.

Vandyk v. *Minister of Pensions and National Insurance* [1955] 1 Q.B. 29;
[1954] 3 W.L.R. 342; [1954] 2 All E.R. 723.

The following additional case was cited in argument:

Aspen v. *Seddon* (1875) 10 Ch.App. 394.

E

APPEAL from Judge Stabb sitting as a judge of the Queen's Bench
Division.

The claimant, Mireille Berthe-Louise Perrot, appealed from a decision
of Judge Stabb, given on May 17, 1979, whereby he dismissed her appeal
against a decision of the South London Appeals Tribunal dated October
19, 1978, affirming a determination of the Supplementary Benefits Commis-   F
sion that she was not entitled to supplementary benefit on the ground that
she was engaged in remunerative full-time employment and was therefore
disentitled to benefit by section 6 (1) of the Supplementary Benefits Act
1976.

The grounds of the appeal were (1) that the tribunal having found that
the work on which the claimant was engaged yielded no remuneration either
in the short or long term, as a matter of law the claimant was not engaged   G
in " remunerative full-time work " within the meaning of section 6 (1) of
the Supplementary Benefits Act 1976; (2) that in the premises the claimant
had a right to benefit under section 1 of the Act corresponding to the
amount by which her needs exceeded her resources; (3) that the judge was
wrong in holding that because the claimant's work was paid for it was
remunerative notwithstanding that no remuneration of any kind reached   H
or could have reached her; and (4) that remunerative work in section 6 (1)
meant work from which a person derived remuneration.

The facts are stated in the judgment of Brightman L.J.

Stephen Sedley for the claimant.
David Latham for the commission.

Cur. adv. vult.

A   May 23. The following judgments were read.

BRIGHTMAN L.J. This is an appeal from a decision of Judge Stabb
sitting as a judge of the High Court, given on May 17, 1979. It
concerns the construction of section 6 of the Supplementary Benefits Act
1976. The question is whether the claimant, who was in business on her
own account as the proprietor of a translation agency, was engaged in
B "remunerative work" notwithstanding that her expenses in conducting
the business of the agency exceeded the remuneration received in respect
of the services provided by the agency.

The claimant was formerly in the employ of a publishing company.
She left owing to ill-health. In October 1975, having exhausted her right
to payments by way of unemployment benefit, she began to receive supple-
C mentary benefit under the Act of 1976. She was the owner of the house
in which she lived, and she decided to set up business there on her own
account as a translation agency. She traded under the name of
"Unimessage," which she changed to "Unimessage International" when
she opened a branch in Paris. In 1976 her gross receipts were £1,048, and
expenses £2,171, leading to a net loss for the year of £1,123. In 1977 the
D comparable figures were gross receipts £1,387, expenses £1,696 and net
loss £309.

On June 5, 1978, the Supplementary Benefits Commission decided that
the claimant was not entitled to benefit as from June 2, 1978, because she
was engaged in remunerative full-time work. The claimant appealed from
that decision to the South London Appeals Tribunal and thence to the
High Court, but before I deal with those appeals I will turn to some of
E the provisions of the Act of 1976 and the regulations made thereunder.

Section 1 of the Act provides that, subject to the provisions of the Act,
every person in Great Britain of or over the age of 16 years whose resources
are insufficient to meet his requirements shall be entitled to a supplementary
pension if of pensionable age, or to a supplementary allowance if under
pensionable age. Under section 2 the Supplementary Benefits Commission
F determines the right to, and the amount of, the supplementary benefits.
Section 6 excludes certain persons from entitlement to supplementary
benefit. The section reads:

"(1) Except as provided in the following provisions of this section
and in section 9 (1) of this Act (supplementary benefit paid after a
return to full-time employment following a trade dispute), for any
period during which a person is engaged in remunerative full-time
G work he shall not be entitled to supplementary benefit. (2) The
Secretary of State may, by regulations made under this subsection,
make provision for postponing the exclusion of persons becoming
engaged in remunerative full-time work from a right to supplementary
benefit under subsection (1) above for such period from the beginning
of their engagement as may be specified in the regulations. (3) There
H is no exclusion from a right to supplementary benefit under subsection
(1) above where the earning power of a self-employed person is, by
reason of a disability, substantially reduced in comparison with that
of other persons similarly occupied. In this subsection 'self-employed
person' means a person engaged in any work otherwise than under
a contract of service."

A measure of flexibility is introduced by section 4, which provides
that section 6 shall not prevent the payment of supplementary benefit in

an urgent case. Under paragraph 1 of Schedule 1, the amount of any   A
supplementary benefit to which a person is entitled shall be the
amount by which his resources fall short of his requirements. Requirements are to be calculated on a weekly basis, and the supplementary
benefit is a weekly amount. Paragraphs 5 to 16 deal with the method of
calculating a person's " requirements " and paragraphs 17 to 30 deal with
the mode of calculating a person's " resources."   Paragraph 21 reads:
                                                                      B
"For the purposes of this Schedule a person's net weekly earnings
shall be calculated or estimated in such manner as the Secretary of
State may, by regulations made under this paragraph, prescribe."

The Secretary of State has issued the Supplementary Benefits (General)
Regulations 1977 (S.I. 1977 No. 1141). Regulation 5 reads as follows:

"(1) For the purposes of Schedule 1 to the Act a person's net weekly   C
earnings shall be the net remuneration or profit, calculated on a
weekly basis, derived by him from any occupation or occupations and,
in particular, in so far as the earnings consist of salary or wages, there
shall be deducted—(a) any sum the deduction of which from salary or
wages is authorised by statute; and (b) any expenses reasonably
incurred by him in connection with his employment. (2) Where the   D
actual earnings of a person for a week are not immediately ascertainable for the purposes of calculating his net weekly earnings under
paragraph (1), his net weekly earnings shall be estimated on the basis
of such information as he is able to supply and such other relevant
information as is available."

The question at issue is whether the claimant is disqualified by section   E
6 of the Act. For the disqualification to apply it must be established that
the applicant is, for the period in question, engaged in work which is
(a) remunerative and (b) full-time.

The appeal was dismissed by the South London Appeals Tribunal by
a majority decision. The three members of the tribunal accepted that the
claimant was engaged in remunerative work. But one member considered
that she was not engaged in full-time work since the work carried out by   F
her would have taken less than 30 hours a week.

The claimant appealed to the High Court. The only point taken before
Judge Stabb was that the tribunal was wrong in law in concluding that
"remunerative work" meant work for which a person was remunerated
notwithstanding that it was not "profitable." The judge decided against
the claimant and expressed his conclusion as follows: G

"Mr. Carnwath, on behalf of the claimant, contended that the word
'remunerative' connotes, or must be shown to connote, some profit
element, and that section 6 only takes effect when it is shown that the
money received overtops the necessary expenses. Quite apart from the
practical difficulty or indeed impossibility of administering the provisions of this Act on a weekly basis in a case such as this, if such a   H
contention were right, I am of the opinion that 'remunerative employment' means, and can only mean, employment which is gainful in
the sense that it is employment where money is paid for the service
which is rendered. . . . I think that the appeal tribunal quite correctly
interpreted section 6 and as the claimant's work was undoubtedly paid
for, although the business unhappily did not show a net profit at the
end of the year, the employment was accordingly remunerative, and

The Weekly Law Reports, October 10, 1980

1157

1 W.L.R.   Perrot v. Supplementary Benefits Com. (C.A.)   Brightman L.J.

A   section 6 must accordingly apply. In those circumstances I confirm the decision of the appeal tribunal."

The *Oxford English Dictionary* gives one obsolete meaning to the word " remunerative," which I shall ignore, and two current meanings: " 2. That remunerates or rewards." The literary illustrations which follow are however unhelpful for, and, I think, inappropriate to, present purposes.
B   " 3. That brings remuneration; profitable." The meaning " brings remuneration " indicates to me that " remunerative work " can be interpreted, without abuse of language, as work which brings remuneration, i.e., is paid for.

However, I have no doubt that the sense in which ordinary persons use the word " remunerative " in ordinary conversation is " profitable "
C   in a broad and general sense, not just a net profit of £1 a year after deducting expenses, but an appreciable profit appropriate to the context in which the word is used. If the accounts of a business concern show that its receipts exceed its expenditure by the sum of £1, the concern would theoretically be in profit, though infinitessimal. It would not usually be described as a remunerative concern. The word "remunerative," meaning
D   profitable, so used by ordinary people in ordinary conversation, is vague and ambiguous. In the same context it can mean quite different things to different people. The meaning verges on the subjective.

Mr. Latham, for the commission, described the " profitable " meaning of the word " remunerative " as the " colloquial " meaning that is to say, belonging to familiar speech as distinct from its meaning in formal or
E   elevated language (as the *Concise Oxford Dictionary* defines non-colloquial use). But so elevated did that non-colloquial use of the word " remunerative " prove to be that Mr. Latham was quite unable to conjure up a single example of its use in ordinary speech to indicate payment as distinct from profitability.

In urging upon us the meaning " profitable," Mr. Sedley for the claimant argued that the object of the Act of 1976 is to meet cases of actual
F   need and that the Act focuses on the adequacy or inadequacy of a person's resources. As the word " remunerative " can bear the meaning " profitable," it should be given that meaning in the statute because one would expect the Act only to be concerned with " work " which produces " resources." " Work " which does not add to the worker's " resources," because expenditure overtakes receipts, leaves a person as much in need as
G   if he were not engaged in any work. One would not therefore expect a person unprofitably engaged in work to be disqualified from benefit. The word " remunerative " more naturally means " profitable " than " paid." It is the antithesis of " unremunerative " which means unprofitable and, so far as I am aware, is not confined to " unpaid." So ran the argument.

Mr. Latham's argument for the commision was that " remunerative work " was work which brings " remuneration." Section 6 defines the type
H   of work which disqualifies, i.e., paid work, and is not looking to the commercial result of the work which may vary between profit and loss week by week. It is the character of the work which is being defined, not the economic result of the work. If " remunerative " means " profitable," then inevitably the question arises, how profitable? It would be unreal and arbitrary to treat work as remunerative in the sense of " profitable " if receipts exceed expenses by £1, but not remunerative if expenses exceed receipts by £1. In ordinary parlance the word " remunerative " would

1158

never be attributed to a business which made a profit of £1 in the course   A
of a year. So ran the commission's argument.

It is appropriate to refer, if only to show that it has not been overlooked, to *Vandyk* v. *Minister of Pensions and National Insurance* [1955]
1 Q.B. 29. That was concerned with the definition of " insured persons,"
who were divided for the purposes of section 1 (2) of the National
Insurance Act 1946 into three classes as follows: B

". . . (a) employed persons, that is to say persons gainfully occupied in
employment in Great Britain, being employed under a contract of
service; (b) self-employed persons, that is to say persons gainfully
occupied in employment in Great Britain who are not employed
persons; (c) non-employed persons, that is to say persons who are not
employed or self-employed persons."
                                                                               C

The appellant, who was physically incapacitated, was employed at a salary
with allowances of £375 a year, but incurred necessary expenses in relation
to that employment which exceeded £375. It was decided by Slade J. that
he was nevertheless gainfully employed. In the course of his judgment he
said, at p. 36:

" It seems to me that there are many difficulties in accepting the con-   D
struction contended for by [the appellant's counsel], and I will deal with
those before I put my own construction. First, it is obvious that if
' gainfully occupied in employment ' means striking a balance between
the receipts and the expenditure to see which of the two exceeds the
other, the position (as Mr. Ashworth put it in argument) might fluctuate
de die in dem, that is to say, an insured person would be an ' em-   E
ployed person ' whenever the receipts exceeded the expenditure by
the smallest amount, and he would automatically cease to be an
' employed person ' whenever by like amount the expenditure exceeded
the receipts. Secondly, it would postulate some means of ascertaining
by what standard or criterion the expenditure which was incurred was
to be assessed. In this case I am, of course, assuming that it was all
reasonably incurred, but is the test to be reasonableness or must it be   F
not only reasonably, but exclusively, incurred or necessarily incurred,
or what is the standard by which the expenditure is to be assessed to
see whether or not it ever over-tops the receipts? "

The second difficulty adverted to by the judge does not arise in the
instant case, because regulation 5, to which I have referred, defines deductible expenses as " expenses reasonably incurred by him in connection with   G
his employment." The judge came to the conclusion that the question was
not whether the employed person was " getting something out of it " but
whether he was " getting something for it," and the words " gainfully
occupied " were really in contradistinction to a contract of employment
in an honorary and unpaid capacity. The reasoning of the case is equally
applicable to self-employment.   H

That decision is useful as illustrative of the problems which can face
the court if a statute uses ambiguous words such as " gainful," but it is
not conclusive of the meaning of a different word in a different statute. It
also serves to remind us that we are not at liberty to interpret a statute by
reference to regulations made under it: see [1955] 1 Q.B. 29, 37. Counsel
for the claimant concedes that he cannot argue, from the reference in
regulation 5 of the Regulations of 1977 to " net remuneration or profit "

The Weekly Law Reports, October 10, 1980

1159

1 W.L.R.   Perrot v. Supplementary Benefits Com. (C.A.)   Brightman L.J.

A struck after deduction of "any expenses reasonably incurred," that section 6 must be looking at profitability rather than payment.

I think that the arguments are finely balanced, but I have come to the conclusion that the argument of the commission is correct. What has weighed most with me, is that the claimant's submission inevitably means that £1 net profit is enough to make work "remunerative" in the sense of "profitable." That concession (and it was expressly conceded) is to my B mind fatal because it involves the use of the word "remunerative" in a highly artificial sense in which the word would in fact never be used by anyone. The failure to make the concession would be equally fatal. If "remunerative" is used in the ordinary sense of "profitable," meaning broadly profitable, it is totally devoid of precision. I therefore find myself constrained to adopt the permissible, though unusual, if not pedagogic, C meaning of "work which brings remuneration" or, as I would prefer to put it, "work which is paid for."

I would dismiss the appeal.

STEPHENSON L.J. The question raised by this appeal is whether it is an error of law to hold that the claimant was "engaged in remunera- D tive full-time work" when she was denied supplementary benefit by the commission. If she was then engaged in remunerative full-time work, she was not entitled to it because section 6 (1) of the Supplementary Benefits Act 1976 says so and the appeal must be dismissed. If she was not so engaged, she was entitled, and her appeal should be allowed.

It is admitted that she was engaged in full-time work. Was she so E engaged in remunerative work on the facts and on the meaning of those words in the subsection? She was in fact remunerated for the work by being paid fees for it. But during the relevant period the expenses she incurred in her work exceeded those fees, which were used to repay her overdraft with her bank. If work is remunerative when it brings remuneration, she was engaged in remunerative work: if work is not remunerative unless it is profitable, she was not.

F The dictionary to which we were referred (*Oxford English Dictionary*) shows that "remunerative" can mean "that brings remuneration" or "profitable." In my opinion Mr. Latham for the commission was right to accept that in ordinary speech (he preferred to call it "colloquially" but got no support from the dictionary for that adverb) "remunerative" means "profitable." Remunerative work or a remunerative enterprise is G one which pays, and pays not simply in the sense that payment is received for it or in the course of it but pays in the sense that it pays enough to make it worth doing or undertaking. "It pays to advertise" would not be true if advertising cost so much that the advertiser was out of pocket at the end of a reasonable time, but it could be true, I suppose, if the resources of the advertiser enabled him to continue advertising until its rewards exceeded its expenses and to wait for the day when it showed a profit. So it is H commonly, and I would agree colloquially, said in these days of the welfare state, high taxation and inflation-indexed pensions of an unemployed person or a person who has earned a retirement pension that it pays him *not* to work, because though he is in each case paid for the work he would be "better off" if he drew unemployment benefit or his retirement pension. It is in that sense of "paying" that work is commonly said to be remunerative (or perhaps lucrative); and it is in that sense, for instance, that the word was used by the Duke of Plaza-Toro when he sang:

"To help unhappy commoners, and add to their enjoyment,   A
Affords a man of noble rank congenial employment;
Of our attempts we offer you examples illustrative:
The work is light, and, I may add, it's most remunerative."

And the "examples illustrative" in the following duet indicate how 'very
paying" the work was: see The Gondoliers, Act II.

Supplementary benefit is for those whose resources are insufficient to B
meet their requirements: see section 1 (1) of the Act of 1976. So Mr.
Sedley submits for the claimant that a person unprofitably self-employed
like the claimant should be entitled to supplementary benefit and the statute
should be construed accordingly to meet her need. He referred us to other
provisions in the Act and the Supplementary Benefits (General) Regulations
1977, including those in which the same expression is used: section 4 (3)
and Schedule 1, Part I, paragraph 22 (3): compare also section 1 (1) (g)   C
of the Family Income Supplements Act 1970. But I do not get any help
from them in construing the expression. Is anything more needed to
support the claimant's interpretation of it than the admission that it is its
ordinary meaning and Lord Reid's observations in *Cozens* v. *Brutus* [1973]
A.C. 854, 861 that the usual question is "whether . . . the words of the
statute do or do not as a matter of ordinary usage of the English language D
cover or apply to the facts which have been proved "?

In my judgment, the word "remunerative" still retains its natural
meaning of "remunerating; bringing remuneration" and it is in that sense
that it is used in the expression "remunerative full-time work" in the Acts
of 1976 and 1970. Work or employment (the marginal note to section 6
indicates that there is no difference between the two words) may be for a   E
consideration or for nothing, paid or unpaid, for gain or for love or duty.
That is a simple dichotomy illustrated by the illuminating judgment of
Slade J. in *Vandyk* v. *Minister of Pensions and National Insurance* [1955]
1 Q.B. 29 in construing different words, "gainfully occupied in employment," in a different statute, the National Insurance Act 1946. But I find
that some of the considerations which militate against Parliament limiting
gainful occupation to an occupation which shows a net gain or profit before F
insurance contributions are payable are also apt to defeat the possibility of
its intending to limit remunerative full-time work to work which shows a
net gain or profit. Parliament has not excluded persons engaged or
occupied in *gainful* full-time work from entitlement to supplementary benefit
or family income supplement. But in considering the object of the exclusion from entitlement to supplementary benefit Parliament would surely   G
have recognised that persons do not engage in unpaid full-time work unless
they have private means, or in paid full-time work unless it fulfils the
hope that induced them to do it and really pays them in the sense
that they not merely take something for it but make something out
of it. *Part-time* work, paid or unpaid, remunerated or unremunerated, may
well be more likely to leave resources insufficient to meet requirements.
But full-time paid or remunerative work is unlikely to create such a   H
condition of need even for the limited class of self-employed persons clearly
contemplated by section 6 (3). The Act of 1976 does not use the expression "*paid* full-time work," perhaps because remuneration may take other
forms than payment of money: see *Reg.* v. *Postmaster General, Ex parte
Saunders* (1876) 1 Q.B.D. 658, 663.

I do not think any material distinction could be drawn between
remunerative, remunerating and remunerated work. The first two seem to

The Weekly Law Reports, October 10, 1980

1161

1 W.L.R.   Perrot v. Supplementary Benefits Com. (C.A.)   Stephenson L.J.

A mean the same and the third could be used if you regarded the work as remunerated (or paid) rather than the person who does it as remunerated (or paid) for it. But what I find an impracticable distinction is between a job which makes a net profit of £1 and a job which makes a net loss of £1 at any particular time. To call the first remunerative and the second not is difficult enough; to suppose that the legislature meant to exclude the first from entitlement to supplementary benefit but the second not is to my mind

B impossible. Both are, in my opinion, remunerative, regardless of the question whether the weekly, monthly or yearly balance sheet shows a credit or a debit balance, just as the paid worker is engaged in remunerative work regardless of what he would get if he went out of work or into retirement. What the remunerated worker, whether self-employed or employed by others, does with his or her remuneration, whether by choice or under

C compulsion or by choice determined by the compulsion of economic necessity, is irrelevant to the remunerative character of the work and the commission's statutory duty under section 6 (1).

What, it may be asked, of the person whose earnings are all attached by an order of the court, or all paid into his or her bank in reduction of an overdraft, before ever they reach his or her pocket? And what of the

D person, employed not by himself but by another, whose wages or salary are not paid until after he has spent them (or more or less than them) on outgoings to a greater or lesser extent required for his work? I answer that all those cases are distinguishable from the claimant's on the facts and may or may not be distinguishable in the application of the statutory exclusion to them. They do not enable me to regard the claimant's full-time work as unremunerative. It was, in my judgment, remunerative, as

E the commission, the tribunal and the judge all thought. I agree with them. I agree with Brightman L.J. that the claimant's construction of the word "remunerative" impales her on the horns of the dilemma expounded at the end of his judgment which are fatal to her case. I agree that the appeal should accordingly be dismissed.

F DAME ELIZABETH LANE (read by Stephenson L.J.). I have had the advantage of reading the judgments being given by Stephenson and Brightman L.JJ., with which I agree.

It seems that the word "remunerative" in section 6 (1) of the Supplementary Benefits Act 1976 may be interpreted as descriptive either of the financial results of full-time work or alternatively of the work itself. If the former be the correct interpretation, it is difficult to understand why

G Parliament did not make this clear by the use of some such words as "remunerative full-time work resulting in a profit."

I refer to the concession made on behalf of the claimant that, on the existing wording of the subsection, a profit of £1 net would bring into operation the exclusion from supplementary benefit whereas a loss of £1 net would not do so. Surely this would give such an anomalous, not to say

H absurd, effect to the subsection that Parliament cannot have intended it.

Further, as supplementary benefit is calculated on a weekly basis, it is difficult to see how payment or withholding, of benefit could be correctly achieved without weekly accounting in cases where the work done involved incurring expenses. Yet a person might be engaged in full-time work for weeks or months on end without receiving any payment at all, although thereafter entitled to be paid what would amount to a handsome net profit for the period concerned. In the case of a person in the position of

the claimant, the receipt of supplementary benefits would, no doubt, pro-   A
vide a convenient, interest-free source of money to assist in building up
a business, but this would hardly be consonant with the intention of the Act.

I have come to the conclusion that the word " remunerative " as used
in section 6 (1) is descriptive of the work itself and not of its financial
results.

I would also dismiss this appeal.
                                                                              B

> *Appeal dismissed.*
> *No order as to costs save legal aid taxation.*
> *Leave to appeal refused.*

Solicitors: *Evill & Coleman; Solicitor, Department of Health and*   C
Social Security.

[Reported by ROBERT WILLIMS, ESQ., Barrister-at-Law]

                                                                              D

[CHANCERY DIVISION]

* STANTON (INSPECTOR OF TAXES) *v.*
DRAYTON COMMERCIAL INVESTMENT CO. LTD.

1980 Feb. 25, 26;   Vinelott J.   E
       March 24

> *Revenue—Corporation tax—Chargeable gains—Allowable deduc-*
> *tions—Investment company acquiring securities in exchange*
> *for issue of its own shares—Conditional agreement stipulating*
> *price of securities and number of shares to be issued in*
> *exchange—Market value of shares falling before completion of*   F
> *agreement—Value of consideration given for securities—*
> *Finance Act 1965 (c. 25), Sch. 6, para. 4 (1) (a).*

In 1972 the taxpayer company entered into a conditional
agreement with E Ltd. to purchase from it securities at an
agreed price of £3,937,962. That purchase price was to be
satisfied by the allotment by the taxpayer company to E Ltd. of
2,461,226 of its ordinary shares of 25p each, " the issue price of
each such share for the purpose of satisfying the consideration   G
being 160p." That price had been agreed by reference to
the middle market quotations for those securities on the Stock
Exchange as at August 31, 1972. The agreement was conditional on the members of the taxpayer company passing a
resolution to create the consideration shares and on the Stock
Exchange granting permission to deal in and quotation for
the consideration shares before October 31, 1972. By October   H
11, 1972, those two conditions were satisfied and the securities
specified in the agreement were exchanged for the shares in
the taxpayer company. On the following day the Stock
Exchange quoted price for the taxpayer company's shares
had fallen to 125p. During the taxpayer company's accounting periods ending December 1972 and December 1973 some
of the securities that they had acquired under the agreement
were sold at a profit. In consequence of the sales they were
assessed to corporation tax in respect of chargeable gains for

A   the relevant years on the basis that the amount of the gains
accruing on the disposals of the securities were to be ascertained by reference to the market price of their shares at the
date when the agreement became unconditional, namely, 125p
and not at the price stated in the agreement of 160p. An
appeal against the assessments was allowed by the special
commissioners who upheld the taxpayer company's case that
the value of the consideration for the purpose of paragraph

B   4 (1) (a) of Schedule 6 to the Finance Act 1965 [1] was £3,937,692
being the consideration expressed in the agreement and based
on Stock Exchange quotations on August 31, 1972, of 160p
per share.

On appeal by the Crown: —

Held, allowing the appeal, that paragraph 4 (1) (a) of
Schedule 6 to the Act restricted the sums allowable as deductions in computing the amount of a gain accruing on the

C   disposal of assets to the amount or market value of the consideration given for the acquisition of the asset; that although
the cost entered into the taxpayer company's accounts as the
price of acquiring the assets was the agreed sum of £3,937,692
based on a share value of 160p, the market value of the consideration given by the taxpayer company for the assets was
the value of their shares at the time they were received by the
vendor on the date that the agreement became unconditional;

D   that, accordingly, the market value of the consideration that
was to be deducted in computing the gains was the Stock
Exchange middle market quotation on the day after the agreement became unconditional of 125p per share subject to the
argument that the true value of the shares was greater than
the market value (post, pp. 1170H—1171A, C–D, 1174H—1175A).

E   The following cases are referred to in the judgment:

Aberdeen Construction Group Ltd. v. *Inland Revenue Commissioners*
[1978] A.C. 885; [1978] 2 W.L.R. 648; [1978] 1 All E.R. 962,
H.L.(Sc.).
Brooklands Selangor Holdings Ltd. v. *Inland Revenue Commissioners*
[1970] 1 W.L.R. 429 ; [1970] 2 All E.R. 76.
Craddock v. *Zevo Finance Co. Ltd.* [1944] 1 All E.R. 566; 27 T.C. 267,

F   C.A.; [1946] 1 All E.R. 523n; 27 T.C. 267, H.L.(E.).
Crane Fruehauf Ltd. v. *Inland Revenue Commissioners* [1974] 1 All E.R.
811 ; [1975] 1 All E.R. 429 ; C.A.
Osborne v. *Steel Barrel Co. Ltd.* [1942] 1 All E.R. 634; 24 T.C. 293,
C.A.
Varty v. *British South Africa Co.* [1966] A.C. 381 ; [1965] 3 W.L.R. 47 ;
[1965] 2 All E.R. 395 ; 42 T.C. 406, H.L.(E.).

G   The following additional cases were cited in argument:

Astley v. *Inland Revenue Commissioners* [1975] 3 All E.R. 696, C.A.
Lap Shun Textiles Industrial Co. Ltd. v. *Collector of Stamp Revenue*
[1976] A.C. 530 ; [1976] 2 W.L.R. 817; [1976] 1 All E.R. 833, P.C.
Smirk v. *Lyndale Developments Ltd.* [1975] Ch. 317 ; [1975] 2 W.L.R. 495 ;
[1975] 1 All E.R. 690, C.A.

H   *Wilkins* v. *Rogerson* [1961] Ch. 133, [1961] 2 W.L.R. 102 ; [1961] 1 All
E.R. 358; 39 T.C. 244, C.A.
Wragg Ltd., In re [1897] 1 Ch. 796, C.A.

CASE STATED by the Commissioners for the Special Purposes of the
Income Tax Acts.

[1] Finance Act 1965, Sch. 6, para. 4 (1) (a): see post, p. 1166A.

On September 21, 1972, the taxpayer company, Drayton Commercial   A
Investment Co. Ltd. (then called Union Commercial Investment Co. Ltd.),
negotiated a conditional agreement with Eagle Star Insurance Co. Ltd. to
purchase a portfolio of securities for £3,937,962 to be satisfied by the
allotment by the taxpayer company of 2,461,226 of its ordinary shares of
25p. The agreement stated that " the issue price of each such share for
the purpose of satisfying the consideration being 160p." By October 11,
1972, the conditions were satisfied and the agreement completed. On   B
October 12, 1972, the Stock Exchange middle market quotation of those
shares was 125p. During the accounting periods ended December 31,
1972, and December 31, 1973, the taxpayer company disposed of some of
the securities comprised in the portfolio. It appealed against assessments
to corporation tax for those two periods in sums of £178,011 and £440,000
respectively.   C
    The commissioners upheld the contention that in ascertaining the
chargeable gains accruing to the taxpayer company on the disposal of the
securities that it had acquired for a price satisfied by the allotment of
ordinary shares, the value of the shares so allotted was, for the purpose
of paragraph 4 (1) (a) of Schedule 6 to the Finance Act 1965, 160p
(being their par value plus the premium at which they were allotted) and
not their market value of 125p at the time they were first quoted on the   D
Stock Exchange following the allotment. They reduced the assessment
for the period ending December 31, 1972, to nil and that for the period to
December 31, 1973, to £349,429.
    The Crown appealed.
    The facts are set out in the judgment.
                                                                     E
    Peter Gibson for the Crown.
    Michael Nolan Q.C. and *Robert Venables* for the taxpayer company.

                                                  Cur. adv. vult.

    March 24. VINELOTT J. read the following judgment. By clause 1
of an agreement for sale date September 21, 1972, and made between   F
Eagle Star Insurance Co. Ltd. (which I shall call " Eagle Star ") of
the one part, and the taxpayer company, Drayton Commercial Investment Co. Ltd. (which was then known as Union Commercial Investment
Co. Ltd.) of the other part, Eagle Star agreed to sell and the taxpayer
company to purchase a portfolio of investments specified in an agreed
schedule at the price of £3,937,962 :   G

    " to be satisfied by the allotment by the purchaser to the vendor of
    2,461,226 ordinary shares of 25 pence each in the purchaser the
    issue price of each such share for the purpose of satisfying the
    consideration being 160 pence."

The ordinary shares were to be issued credited as fully paid up, and were
to rank pari passu with the then existing ordinary shares of the taxpayer   H
company save that they were not to participate in any final dividend paid
on the ordinary shares in respect of the year ending December 31, 1972.
The vendor was to be entitled, in lieu of such dividend, to a gross dividend
equal to the aggregate of the gross dividends paid to the taxpayer company, or which would have been paid but for any disposal, in respect of
the investments comprised in the portfolio during the period from
September 1, 1972, to December 31, 1972, after deducting gross dividends

The Weekly Law Reports, October 10, 1980

1165

1 W.L.R.   Stanton v. Drayton Investment Co. (Ch.D.)   Vinelott J.

A received by the taxpayer company but claimed by Eagle Star on investments quoted ex-dividend on August 31, 1972.

It was provided by clause 2 that the agreement was conditional on:

" (i) the members of the purchaser passing the necessary resolution of the company in general meeting creating the new shares in the purchaser required to satisfy the consideration above mentioned; (ii)
B the Stock Exchange (London) granting permission to deal in and quotation for such new shares subject to allotment before October 31, 1972."

Clause 3 provided that the agreement should be completed within seven days after these conditions were both satisfied. In the event, the necessary resolution was passed at an extraordinary general meeting of the
C taxpayer company on October 9, 1972, and permission to deal in and a quotation for the shares to be issued by the taxpayer company was given by the Stock Exchange on October 11, 1972. The agreement was completed on October 11, 1972, when the shares which the taxpayer company had agreed to issue were allotted to Eagle Star. The shares so allotted were first quoted on the Stock Exchange on October 12, 1972. Clause 4 provided that, as the portfolio had been valued at mid-market quotations
D on August 31, 1972, Eagle Star was to be entitled to all the dividends and interest on investments quoted ex-dividend on that day, and the taxpayer company to dividends and interest declared and paid after that day.

Between October 11, 1972, and October 31, 1972, and during 1973, the taxpayer company disposed of certain of the investments comprised in the portfolio. Assessments to corporation tax were made on the footing that, in ascertaining the chargeable gains accruing to the taxpayer
E company on the disposal of these investments, the value of the portfolio should be taken as equal to the market value of the shares issued by the taxpayer company ascertained in accordance with Stock Exchange quoted prices on the day on which the shares were first quoted in the Stock Exchange Official List after the allotment. The taxpayer company successfully appealed against those assessments on the ground that the value
F of the shares allotted was the price at which they were issued; that is, the par value plus the premium entered into the taxpayer company's books. As I have said, the issue price was ascertained by reference to mid-market prices of the investments comprised in the portfolio quoted on the Stock Exchange on August 31, 1972. On that day the mid-market price of the taxpayer company's ordinary shares was 142p. If that price is applied to
G the shares which the taxpayer company agreed to issue as consideration for the acquisition of the portfolio, the portfolio was effectively purchased for £3,494,941, representing a discount of 11·25 per cent. on its value. On September 21, 1972, the mid-market quoted price of shares of the taxpayer company was 134p and, on October 12, 125p.

Corporation tax is chargeable in respect of chargeable gains of companies computed in accordance with the principles applicable to capital
H gains tax: see sections 238 and 265 of the Income and Corporation Taxes Act 1970. Schedule 6 to the Finance Act 1965 contains provisions governing the computation of the amount of a gain accruing on the disposal of an asset. Paragraph 4 (1) restricts the sums allowable as a deduction from the consideration for the disposal to sums falling under three heads, one of which, embodied in sub-paragraph (a), allows the deduction of the consideration given for the acquisition. It allows the deduction by the taxpayer, in terms of sub-paragraph (a), of

" the amount or value of the consideration, in money or money's   A
worth, given by him or on his behalf wholly and exclusively for the
acquisition of the asset . . . "

The main issue in this appeal is simply whether the amount or value of
the consideration given by the taxpayer company for the portfolio of
investments was the price—namely, £3,937,962—which under the terms
of clause 1 was to be satisfied by the allotment of 2,461,226 shares of the   B
taxpayer company or the value of those shares. Although the paragraph
does not specifically so provide, " value " must, I think, mean market
value. There is a subsidiary question whether, if the answer to this question is that " the amount or value of the consideration " was the market
value of the shares of the taxpayer company issued in satisfaction of the
sum of £3,937,950, the market value should be ascertained at September
21 or at October 11, 1972; and, in the latter event, whether it should be   C
ascertained by reference to prices quoted on the Stock Exchange on
October 12, 1972.

The Crown's contention is that under the agreement the consideration
for the portfolio given by the taxpayer company consisted of the shares
of the taxpayer company which they were contractually bound to issue.
As the agreement was conditional, the disposal of the portfolio by Eagle   D
Star and its acquisition by the taxpayer company must both be taken to
have been made when the conditions in clause 2 were first satisfied (see
paragraph 10 (2) of Schedule 10 to the Finance Act 1971); that is, October
11. The market value on October 11 must be ascertained by reference
to the price at which the shares were first quoted on the Stock Exchange
on October 12, either by analogy to section 44 (3) of the Act of 1965 or
because quoted prices must be taken as the prima facie measure of value   E
—although, of course, as section 44 (3) recognises, there may be special
circumstances which make it inappropriate as a measure of market value.

The argument for the taxpayer company, which, as I have said, persuaded the commissioners, was shortly as follows. It was said that where
a company acquires property in return for the issue of its shares then,
unless the contract for the acquisition of the property is merely colourable   F
or is illusory or fraudulent, the amount or value of the consideration given
by the company is the amount of the credit which it gives to the vendor
of the property for the value of the property acquired. That amount or
value falls to be determined by reference to the terms of the contract.
This proposition was said to be established by the decisions of the Court
of Appeal in *Osborne* v. *Steel Barrel Co. Ltd.* [1942] 1 All E.R. 634 and
Craddock v. *Zevo Finance Co. Ltd.* [1944] 1 All E.R. 566, and to these   G
cases I now turn.

In *Osborne* v. *Steel Barrel Co. Ltd.*, a Mr. Hood Barrs, a well-known
figure to those familiar with the tax cases, entered into a contract with
the receiver of a company in liquidation (which I shall call " the old
company ") for the purchase of its business premises, goodwill, stock in
trade and effects at the price of £10,500. Subsequently, he entered into   H
an agreement with the respondent company under which the respondent
company in effect took the benefit of the contract with the receiver, Mr.
Hood Barrs constituting himself a trustee thereof; and, in consideration
therefor and for other services performed by Mr. Hood Barrs on its behalf,
and of his agreement to serve the respondent company as managing
director in the future, the respondent company allotted him 29,997 shares
credited as fully paid. On completion of the agreement with the receiver,

A the business and assets of the old company were entered into the books of the respondent company at £10,500, the price paid to the receiver, which, of course, the respondent company became liable to pay under the original agreement. Of that sum, £2,493 was apportioned to stock. Subsequently, the stock was revalued, and the opening figure of the stock was entered at £21,375 19s. 8d. The special commissioners found that the value of the stock when the respondent company acquired it was £10,000,
B and that the profits of the respondent company for the year ended April 5, 1933, and subsequent years should be determined on that footing. An appeal by the Crown was allowed by Macnaghten J. on the ground (to quote the summary in the judgment of Lord Greene M.R. in the report on the subsequent appeal [1942] 1 All E.R. 634, 637):

C "the issue of the shares did not cost the appellant company anything, that accordingly the shares issued in respect of the stock added nothing to the price, and the only thing that the company paid for the stock was a proportionate part of the cash"

that is, of the £10,500 paid under the original agreement. In relation to this argument Lord Greene M.R., in a passage which has often been cited and which I hope I shall be forgiven for citing again, said, at
D pp. 637–638:

"It was strenuously argued on behalf of the Crown that, if a company acquires stock in consideration of the issue of fully-paid shares to the vendor, that stock must, for the purpose of ascertaining the company's profits, be treated as having been acquired for nothing, with the result that, when it comes to be sold, the revenue is entitled
E to treat the whole of the purchase price obtained on the sale as profit. This is a remarkable contention, and it would require conclusive authority before we could accept it. The cases relied on in its support were *Inland Revenue Commissioners* v. *Blott* [1921] 2 A.C. 171 and *Lowry* v. *Consolidated African Selection Trust Ltd.* [1940] A.C. 648, neither of which, in our view, has any bearing on the
F point. The argument really rests on a misconception as to what happens when a company issues shares credited as fully paid for a consideration other than cash. The primary liability of an allottee of shares is to pay for them in cash; but, when shares are allotted credited as fully paid, this primary liability is satisfied by a consideration other than cash passing from the allottee. A company, therefore, when, in pursuance of such a transaction, it agrees to credit
G the shares as fully paid, is giving up what it would otherwise have had—namely, the right to call on the allottee for payment of the par value in cash. A company cannot issue £1,000 nominal worth of shares for stock of the market value of £500, since shares cannot be issued at a discount. Accordingly, when fully-paid shares are properly issued for a consideration other than cash, the consideration moving from the company must be at the least equal in value to the
H par value of the shares and must be based on an honest estimate by the directors of the value of the assets acquired."

In retrospect, and with the benefit of Lord Greene M.R.'s analysis, it can be seen that the argument advanced by the Crown was an absurd one. It amounted to saying that whenever a company acquires property (the relevant "property" being in that case the benefit of the contract with the receiver) and issues its own shares in exchange for

it then because it pays nothing in cash it gives nothing for the pro- A
perty. The same fallacy, in a more subtle form, underlay the argument
of the Crown in *Craddock* v. *Zevo Finance Co. Ltd.* [1944] 1 All E.R.
566. In that case, the respondent company, a finance dealing company,
was formed to take over a portfolio of investments belonging to another
investment dealing company. The investments in the portfolio were purchased by the respondent company at the prices at which they stood in
the books of the vendor company, though that was a figure far in excess B
of the value of the portfolio ascertained in accordance with mid-market
prices quoted on the Stock Exchange. Under the agreement for the purchase of the portfolio, the agreed price was satisfied in part by the assumption by the respondent company of certain liabilities of the vendor
company, and in part by the allotment of shares of the respondent company which were credited as fully paid. It was argued by the Crown that C
in computing the profits of the respondent company the amount to be
debited as the cost of the investments, being stock in trade of the respondent company, was their market value and not, as the respondent
company contended, the price which the respondent company paid;
namely, the aggregate of the liabilities which the respondent company
took over and the amount credited as paid up on the shares of the company which were issued at par. That, as Lord Greene M.R. pointed out, D
necessarily led to the conclusion that the shares issued by the respondent
company were issued at a discount, and he said, at pp. 569–570:

> "The fallacy, if I may respectfully so call it, which underlies the
> argument, is to be found in the assertion that where a company issues
> its own shares as consideration for the acquisition of property, those
> shares are to be treated as money's worth as though they were shares E
> in another company altogether, transferred by way of consideration
> for the acquisition. This proposition amounts to saying that con-
> sideration in the form of fully-paid shares allotted by a company must
> be treated as being of the value of the shares, no more and no less.
> Such a contention will not bear a moment's examination where the
> transaction is a straightforward one and not a mere device for issu- F
> ing shares at a discount. In the everyday case of reconstruction, the
> shares in the new company allotted to the shareholders of the old
> company as fully-paid will often, if not in most cases, fetch sub-
> stantially less than their nominal value if sold in the market. But
> this does not mean that they are to be treated as having been issued
> at a discount; or that the price paid by the new company for the
> assets which it acquires from the old company ought to be treated G
> as something less than the nominal value of the fully-paid shares.
> The Crown in this case is in fact attempting to depart from the rule
> (the correctness of which it itself admits) that the figure at which
> stock in trade is to be brought in is its cost to the trader and to
> substitute the alleged market value of the stock for its cost. Of
> course, in a case where stock which a company proposes to acquire H
> for shares is deliberately over-valued for the purpose of issuing an
> inflated amount of share capital, very different considerations apply.
> But nothing of the kind is present in this case which, as I have
> already pointed out, is a perfectly proper and normal reconstruction.
> The propriety of the course adopted is manifest when the uncertainty
> as to the value of the investments, which is pointed out by the
> commissioners, is borne in mind. It is, I think, true as a general

The Weekly Law Reports, October 10, 1980

1169

1 W.L.R.   Stanton v. Drayton Investment Co. (Ch.D.)   Vinelott J.

A proposition that, where a company acquires property for fully-paid shares of its own, the price paid by the company is, prima facie, the nominal value of the shares. It is for those who assert the contrary to establish it, as could be done, for example, in the suggested case of a deliberately inflated valuation. In the present case the Crown has failed to establish the contrary on the facts as found; and there is no justification for the proposition that, on these facts, the com-
B missioners were bound in law to decide the appeal in favour of the Crown."

The decision of the Court of Appeal was affirmed in the House of Lords (1946) 27 T.C. 267. I do not propose to cite extensively from the speeches there. Viscount Simon said, at p. 287:

C "The crucial transaction, albeit in a reconstruction, is a transaction of sale and purchase, and the proper figure to be debited in respect of the purchased investments is the cost thereof to the respondent. That cost is set out in the agreement between the Zevo Syndicate and its liquidator of the one part and the respondent of the other part dated June 15, 1932, and the shares allotted as part of the purchase price are allotted ' credited as fully paid up.' " Then, after
D citing from the judgment of Lord Greene M.R. at p. 277 he continued: "The contrary proposition amounts to saying that consideration in the form of its fully paid shares allotted by a company must be treated as being the value of the shares, no more and no less. I agree with Lord Greene M.R. that such a contention will not bear a moment's examination when the transaction is a straightforward one and not a
E mere device for issuing shares at a discount. To put the matter in its simplest form, the profit or loss to a trader in dealing with his stock-in-trade is arrived at for income tax purposes by comparing what his stock in fact cost him with what he in fact realised on resale. It is unsound to substitute alleged market values for what it in fact cost him."

F Lord Wright said, at p. 289:

"It is well established that the issue of shares at a discount is illegal. It has also been held that, if the consideration for the issue of shares is a sum of money which is less than the nominal value of the shares, the shares will be treated as issued at a discount. If, on the other hand, the shares are issued for something other than a money con-
G sideration, the position is different because the court does not inquire into the adequacy of the consideration so long as the transaction is a genuine and honest agreement deliberately entered into between two persons or companies."

I have set out the facts in Steel Barrel and Craddock, and extracts from the judgments and speeches, at some length because examinations
H of them shows that, far from supporting the proposition for which the taxpayer company relies on them, they are in fact inconsistent with it. The cost of the portfolio to the taxpayer company was unquestionably the sum of £3,937,962. It could be nothing else. That was the cost that had to be entered into their books to balance the sums which were in part applied in paying up shares at par and in part credited to share premium account. If the taxpayer company had been a share dealing company and if the portfolio had been acquired as stock in trade, that is the sum

that would have been debited against sums realised on subsequent dis- A
posals in order to ascertain its trading profit. But in ascertaining the
amount of the gain to be computed in accordance with Part III of the
Finance Act 1965, the amount to be deducted in respect of the consideration for the acquisition is the amount or value of that consideration.
To equate the cost to the taxpayer company of issuing the shares in
satisfaction of the agreed price with the " amount or value " of that
consideration is in my judgment to repeat the fallacy which Lord Greene B
M.R. found to underlie the arguments of the Crown in the *Steel Barrel*
and *Craddock* cases. To repeat what Lord Greene M.R. said in *Craddock*
v. *Zevo Finance Co. Ltd.* [1944] 1 All E.R. 566, 569:

> " In the everyday case of reconstruction, the shares in the new com-
> pany allotted to the shareholders of the old company as fully-paid
> will often, if not in most cases, fetch substantially less than their C
> nominal value if sold in the market."

Mr. Nolan sought support for his submission in the observation of
Lord Wilberforce in *Aberdeen Construction Group Ltd.* v. *Inland
Revenue Commissioners* [1978] A.C. 885, 892–893:

> " The capital gains tax is of comparatively recent origin. The legis- D
> lation imposing it, mainly the Finance Act 1965, is necessarily com-
> plicated, and the detailed provisions, as they affect this or any other
> case, must of course be looked at with care. But a guiding principle
> must underlie any interpretation of the Act, namely, that its purpose
> is to tax capital gains and to make allowance for capital losses, each
> of which ought to be arrived at upon normal business principles. No
> doubt anomalies may occur, but in straightforward situations, such E
> as this, the courts should hesitate before accepting results which are
> paradoxical and contrary to business sense. To paraphrase a famous
> cliché, the capital gains tax is a tax upon gains: it is not a tax upon
> arithmetical differences."

As the price of £3,937,962 was entered, and admittedly properly
entered, into the books of the taxpayer company as the cost of the shares, F
that figure should, Mr. Nolan said, be taken on proper accounting principles as the base from which the gain to the taxpayer company should be
calculated. But in the *Aberdeen Construction Group Ltd.* case the total
investment of the appellant company in another company consisted in
part of share capital and in part of a loan. It sold the shares at a price
in excess of the price it had paid for them, by way of subscription, but on
terms that it would " waive the loan." The aggregate of the price it had G
paid for the shares and the loan which was to be waived exceeded the
cash price at which it sold the shares. In the House of Lords the opinion
of the majority of their Lordships who heard the appeal was that the
" business reality " was that the appellant company had made a loss on
the disposal of its total investment. Here, it seems to me, the " business
reality " is that, while the cost entered into the books of the taxpayer H
company as the price of the acquisition of the portfolio was and could
only have been the agreed sum of £3,937,692, the value of the consideration which it gave for the portfolio was the value of the shares which
it was entitled and bound to issue in satisfaction of that price. That was
the value received by Eagle Star, which would of course go into its books
as arising on the disposal of the portfolio. As I see it, for capital gains
tax purposes it is the value of the consideration given by the taxpayer

The Weekly Law Reports, October 10, 1980

1171

1 W.L.R.   Stanton v. Drayton Investment Co. (Ch.D.)   Vinelott J.

A company and not the cost of the consideration to them which is deductible under paragraph 4 (1) (a) of Schedule 6.

Mr. Nolan submitted in the alternative that the amount or value of the consideration should be determined for commercial as well as for tax purposes at the date of the agreement. For this proposition, he relied on the decision of the House of Lords in *Varty* v. *British South Africa Co.* [1966] A.C. 381. That, again, was a Schedule D case. The question
B was whether, when the respondent company, which acquired an option to subscribe for shares of another company, exercised the option, it realised a profit, the profit being the difference between the price at which it was entitled to subscribe for the shares and their market value at the time of the exercise of the option. It paid nothing for the option, which was granted as part of a wider transaction. It was held in the House of
C Lords that it did not. I can see nothing in that decision which in any way supports Mr. Nolan's submission. Paragraph 10 of Schedule 10 to the Finance Act 1971 requires that in the case of a conditional contract the contract is to be treated as coming into existence when it became unconditional. Paragraph 4 (1) (a) requires that the amount to be deducted in respect of consideration be limited to the amount or value of the consideration, and that must be the amount or value of the consideration at
D the date of the contract, that latter date being, in accordance with paragraph 10, the date when it becomes unconditional.

In my judgment, therefore, the Crown's contentions are well founded. I reach that conclusion simply upon the language of paragraph 4 (1) (a) of Schedule 6 to the Finance Act 1965 and paragraph 10 of Schedule 10 to the Finance Act 1971. But Mr. Gibson, for the Crown, referred me
E to two cases in the field of stamp duty which lend some support to this conclusion. In *Brooklands Selangor Holdings Ltd.* v. *Inland Revenue Commissioners* [1970] 1 W.L.R. 429, the question was whether a very elaborate scheme was " a scheme for the reconstruction of any company or companies or the amalgamation of any companies " within section 55 of the Finance Act 1927; and, if so, whether it satisfied the conditions
F for exemption from stamp duty contained in that section. It was held by the commissioners that it was not a scheme of reconstruction or amalgamation within section 55, and that decision was upheld by Pennycuick J. The commissioners also decided in favour of the Crown on another ground; namely, that one of the conditions in section 55 was not satisfied. That condition (section 55 (1) (c) (ii)), so far as material, required that the consideration for the acquisition of not less than 90 per cent. of the share
G capital of an existing company must consist

" as to not less than 90 per cent. thereof . . . in the issue of shares in the transferee company to the holders of shares in the existing company in exchange for the shares held by them in the existing company; . . ."

In *Brooklands,* the consideration that was relevant for the purposes of the
H condition consisted of 3,003,991 stock units of £1 each plus £115,593 in cash. The commissioners held that the condition was not satisfied on the ground that the market value of the stock units was £722,835, so that the cash element was more than 10 per cent. of the aggregate. In his judgment, Pennycuick J. said, at p. 447 :

" I am wholly unpersuaded that the contention advanced on behalf of the commissioners on this point is well founded. In the first place I am not persuaded that the word ' consideration ' in paragraph (c)

of section 55 (1) means anything other than the expressed consider-   A
ation. I do not find it necessary to equate, and I do not think I
would be justified in equating, that word ' consideration ' there with
the expression ' amount or value of the consideration ' in the charge
for transfer duty."

He then referred to the passage in the speech of Lord Greene M.R. in the
Zevo Finance case which I have cited and commented at p. 448 that " that   B
passage goes some way towards meeting the contention of the commissioners in this case."

In the case now before me, the commissioners seem to have taken the
view that these observations by Pennycuick J. supported the case advanced
by the taxpayer company. But it seems to me that in that passage Pennycuick J. is drawing precisely the distinction between the " consideration "   C
entered into the books of a company which acquires property in exchange
for its own shares and the " amount or value " of the shares so given
which is fundamental to the Crown's case.

The other case is the decision of Templeman J. in Crane Fruehauf
Ltd. v. Inland Revenue Commissioners [1974] 1 All E.R. 811; [1975] 1
All E.R. 429 and of the Court of Appeal affirming his decision. That was
another case which turned on section 55 of the Finance Act 1927. The   D
directors of Crane Fruehauf (which I shall call " Crane ") negotiated the
acquisition of the entire shareholding of Boden Trailers Ltd. (which I
shall call " Boden "), the consideration being the issue of 1·8 million
shares of Crane and £100,000 cash. But one of the shareholders of Crane
was a company called Fruehauf International Ltd. (which I shall call
" F.I.L."), which held one-third of the shares of Crane and did not want   E
to see its proportionate shareholding watered down by the issue of shares
to the Boden shareholders. That was something it was in a position to
prevent because it had a shareholding sufficient to stop the necessary
increase in the capital of Crane. To satisfy F.I.L., an arrangement was
entered into under which the shareholders of Boden agreed to sell their
shares to Crane in exchange for the issue of 1·8 million ordinary shares of
£1 each and £100,000 cash, and under which F.I.L. was given an option   F
to acquire from each of the Boden shareholders one-third of the newly
issued Crane shares (600,000 in all) at £1 per share. The option was
exercised before the shares were issued. The purchase of the Boden
shares by Crane and the purchase of one-third of the new Crane shares
by F.I.L. were completed on the same day, the new Crane shares being
issued to the Boden shareholders, who then executed transfers of 600,000   G
of them and delivered the transfers and share certificates to F.I.L. The
question was whether Crane were entitled to relief under section 55, and
that question turned on whether it could be said that the consideration
for the acquisition of the Boden shares consisted as to not less than 90
per cent. in the issue of shares of Crane. It was held by Templeman J.
and by the Court of Appeal that it did not so consist because, in the words
of Russell L.J. [1975] 1 All E.R. 429, 433, the consideration was   H

" . . . 1,200,000 shares plus £100,000, plus 600,000 shares subject to an
immediate obligation (which the very mechanics of the transaction
made inescapable) and right to receive £600,000; and this situation
was procured by Crane in the bargain offered by Crane to the Boden
shareholders."

But there was a subsidiary question. On the footing that section 55

The Weekly Law Reports, October 10, 1980

1173

1 W.L.R.   Stanton v. Drayton Investment Co. (Ch.D.)   Vinelott J.

A did not apply, the transfers of the Boden shares attracted ad valorem stamp duty, and under section 55 of the Stamp Act 1891 the value on which ad valorem duty was payable included the value of the 1·8 million shares of Crane, which were part of the consideration for the Boden shares. It was conceded by the Crown that the 600,000 shares which were subject to F.I.L.'s option fell to be valued at the option price of £600,000. As to the balance of 1·2 million shares, it was argued that those shares

B ought to be valued at the price at which they were issued, that being the cost brought into the accounts of Crane. That argument precisely reflects the argument advanced on behalf of the taxpayer company in the present case. The *Brooklands* and *Craddock* cases were cited to Templeman J., although he does not refer to them in his judgment [1974] 1 All E.R. 811. At pp. 822–823 he rejected the argument on the ground that Crane's

C accounts

"are not decisive of the real value of the Crane shares required to be assessed by section 55 of the Stamp Act 1891. By section 6 of that Act the value must be assessed as on ' the date of the instrument.' The date of the instrument is either the date when each transfer was signed between September 1 and 22, as counsel for

D Crane contends, on October 12, when the transfers were delivered to Crane. In my judgment the value is the Stock Exchange value on the correct date, which is October 12. Before that date each instrument was in escrow, conditional on Crane issuing 1,800,000 Crane shares and paying £100,000. On that date each share could have been sold for the Stock Exchange price."

E   That decision was affirmed in the Court of Appeal. Russell L.J. said, [1975] 1 All E.R. 429, 434:

"On the basis that Crane was not entitled to relief under section 55 of the Act of 1927 it was submitted on behalf of Crane, as well in this court as before Templeman J., that the appropriate dates for valuing the 1,200,000 Crane shares, being part of the consideration

F for the transfer of the Boden shares within section 55 of the Act of 1891, were the respective dates on which the transfers of the Boden shares were signed by the holders. Section 6 of the Stamp Act 1891 provides that where an instrument is chargeable with ad valorem duty in respect of any stock (which includes shares)—' the duty shall be calculated on the value, on the day of the date of the instrument . . .

G of the stock or security according to the average price thereof.' At the respective dates when the Boden shareholders signed the transfers of their shares the Crane shares had not been issued and accordingly, so the argument ran, section 6 had no application and the value of the Crane shares ought to be taken to be the issue price attributed to those shares in the books of Crane. Templeman J. rejected these submissions, taking the view that until the issue of the Crane shares

H on October 12, 1967, each of the transfers of the Boden shares was in escrow conditional on the issue of the Crane shares. The date of the several transfers was accordingly October 12, 1967, on which date each share could have been sold for the stock exchange price. In my judgment, Templeman J. came to a correct conclusion for the reason which he gave. I would, however, add this. Where section 6 of the Act of 1891 does not apply, the commissioners must do the best they can and, if it were correct that the transfers were executed prior to

the issue of the Crane shares, the market value of the latter at the   A
moment of their issue plus the cash payable to the vendors would in
my view be a good indication of the amount or value of the consideration for the transfers."

The special commissioners distinguished *Crane Fruehauf* on the ground
that
  B

" *Crane Fruehauf* is not, it seems to us, of assistance because that
case was concerned with the valuation, for the purpose of ad valorem
' conveyance or transfer on sale ' stamp duty, of ' the consideration
for the sale,' in other words the valuation of the consideration
received by the vendor (Finance Act 1963, section 55, as amended,
and Stamp Act 1891, section 6), whereas in the present case we are   C
concerned with the valuation of the consideration moving from the
purchaser."

I cannot see that that can be a valid ground of distinction. Under the
joint effect of section 55 of the Finance Act 1963, and of section 55 (1)
of the Stamp Act 1891, the ad valorem duty payable on the transfer of
the Boden shares fell to be computed by reference to the value of the   D
Crane shares, and that in turn fell to be ascertained " on the value, on
the day of the date of the instrument " of the Crane shares " according
to the average price thereof." The argument before Templeman J. and
before the Court of Appeal was that the value of the Crane shares ought
to be taken as the issue price brought into its books. It may be that in
the Court of Appeal, at least, that argument was put forward, not as a   E
general proposition but as an exception founded on the special circumstance that when the Boden shareholders signed their transfer the Crane
shares had not been issued, so that (as I envisage the argument) the issue
price was the only available measure of value. But however the argument
was put in the *Crane Fruehauf* case, the decision of Templeman J. and
of the Court of Appeal, as I see it, is inconsistent with the general pro-   F
position that when shares of a company are issued at par or at a premium
in consideration for the acquisition of property, the value of the consideration is the cost to the company of the acquisition of the property,
that is, the par value of the issued shares plus any premium.

Mr. Gibson also relied on the contrast between the provisions of the
now defunct short-term capital gains tax, under which the base for   G
ascertaining capital gains was ascertained in accordance with Schedule D
principles—that is, the cost to the company—and the very different
approach in the Act of 1965. As I have reached the clear conclusion
from the language of paragraph 4 (1) (*a*) alone that this appeal succeeds, I
do not propose to enter into any comparison of the contrast between these
two very different fiscal structures.
  H

It was common ground that the taxpayer company is entitled to
adduce evidence and argument in favour of its contention that the market
value of its shares when issued to Eagle Star was in excess of the value
arrived at by mere multiplication of Stock Exchange prices. In these
circumstances, I propose to refer the assessments back to the commissioners for the determination of their value; and, unless I hear any

The Weekly Law Reports, October 10, 1980

1175

1 W.L.R.   Stanton v. Drayton Investment Co. (Ch.D.)   Vinelott J.

A argument to the contrary, I shall make the usual order that the taxpayer company pay the Crown their costs of the appeal.

> *Appeal allowed with costs.*
> *Assessments referred to commis-*
> *sioners for determination.*

B Solicitors: *Solicitor of Inland Revenue; Ashurst, Morris, Crisp & Co.*

[Reported by MRS. HARRIET DUTTON, Barrister-at-Law]

C [COURT OF APPEAL]

* WORSFOLD v. HOWE

1979 Dec. 13   Megaw, Browne and Donaldson L.JJ.

D *Road Traffic—Negligence—Collision—Accident in town traffic—*
Car driver edging out blind across stationary tankers to turn
right into main street—Motor cyclist approaching along main
street past stationary tankers—Car and motor cycle colliding—
Whether car driver to blame

The plaintiff motor cyclist was riding along the main street
E of a town one evening while it was still daylight. The roads
were dry, visibility was good but traffic was heavy. After
stopping at a pedestrian crossing controlled by traffic lights,
the motor cyclist positioned himself towards the middle of
the road in order later to turn to the right. He overtook
two stationary tankers waiting at a second set of traffic lights,
where he intended to turn right. The defendant car driver
was emerging from a station yard on the near side of the
stationary tankers, and was attempting to turn right across
F the main street. The stationary tankers obscured his view
so he was unable to see whether the road was clear. The
car driver understood from a wave of the tanker driver's hand
that the tanker driver would leave a gap through which the
car driver could cross the road when it was safe to do so.
The car driver moved slowly forward and edged past the
leading tanker into the motor cyclist's path. In the ensuing
collision the motor cyclist sustained injuries. He brought an
G action for negligence claiming damages against the car driver.
At the trial the judge formed the view on the evidence that
each party was 50 per cent. to blame for the collision. He
was then referred to *Clarke* v. *Winchurch* [1969] 1 W.L.R.
69 and regarded it as a binding precedent requiring him to
absolve the car driver from liability and give judgment for
him.

On appeal by the motor cyclist: —
H *Held*, allowing the appeal, that, *Clarke* v. *Winchurch* but
was a decision laid down no principle of law on its own facts
so that the judge erred in law in considering himself to be
bound by it; that accordingly liability should be apportioned
on the basis of the view that the judge originally formed on
hearing the evidence, namely, that each party was 50 per cent.
to blame.

Garston Warehousing Co. Ltd. v. *O. F. Smart (Liverpool)*
Ltd. [1973] R.T.R. 377, C.A. applied.

Clarke v. *Winchurch* [1969] 1 W.L.R. 69, C.A. considered.

Worsfold v. Howe (C.A.) [1980]

The following cases are referred to in the judgment:

Clarke v. *Winchurch* [1969] 1 W.L.R. 69; [1969] 1 All E.R. 275, C.A.
Garston Warehousing Co. Ltd. v. *O. F. Smart (Liverpool) Ltd.* [1973] R.T.R. 377, C.A.

The following additional case was cited in argument:

Leeson v. *Bevis & Tolchard Ltd.* [1972] R.T.R. 373, C.A.

APPEAL from Judge Jones sitting at Lincoln County Court.

By a plaint dated September 9, 1977, the plaintiff motor cyclist, Mark Worsfold, brought against the defendant car driver, Henry Cecil Howe, an action claiming damages for personal injuries and damage caused by the defendant's negligent driving in the High Street, Lincoln on September 1, 1975. The action was founded on a collision between a Suzuki motor cycle owned and driven by the plaintiff and a Hillman Hunter motor car owned and driven by the defendant, who denied negligence. He alleged that the collision was caused or contributed to by the plaintiff's negligent driving.

The action came on for hearing on November 9, 1978, at Lincoln County Court before Judge Jones who, after hearing the evidence, considered each party to be 50 per cent. to blame for the collision. *Clarke* v. *Winchurch* [1969] 1 W.L.R. 69 was then cited and the judge took the view that that case was a binding precedent obliging him to hold that the defendant had done all he reasonably could in the circumstances to avoid a collision. He gave judgment for the defendant.

The plaintiff appealed on the grounds, inter alia, (1) that the judge, having found as a fact that the plaintiff was exposed to danger and having directed himself to consider whether the defendant took reasonable care for the plaintiff's safety, failed properly or at all to consider whether in law the defendant had a duty to avoid or reduce that danger; and (2) that the judge was wrong to hold that he was bound by *Clarke* v. *Winchurch* to find that the defendant had done all he reasonably could to avoid colliding with the plaintiff.

The facts are stated in the judgment of Browne L.J.

Richard Burns for the plaintiff motor cyclist.
Bernard Livesey for the defendant car driver.

MEGAW L.J. I shall ask Browne L.J. to deliver the first judgment.

BROWNE L.J. This is an appeal from the decision of Judge Jones in the Lincoln County Court, given on November 9, 1978. He gave judgment for the defendant on a claim arising from a collision between the plaintiff's motor bicycle and the defendant's car, and the plaintiff appeals. We are concerned only with liability, the damages having been agreed at £1,200, subject of course to the question of liability. The plaintiff, in his notice of appeal, asks that judgment should be entered for him for £1,200, or alternatively that there should be a new trial.

The accident took place on September 1, 1975, at about 8 p.m. It was daylight, though getting dusk, and the road was dry and visibility was good. The accident took place in the High Street of Lincoln. We have two photographs showing the scene of the accident, looking in opposite directions. At that point High Street, Lincoln, runs roughly north and

A south. The plaintiff on his motor bicycle was travelling from south to
north on the road.

Looking at the position as the plaintiff was going, first of all, there was
a pedestrian crossing controlled by a traffic light. Having passed that
traffic light going towards the city centre one comes to a level crossing.
Then on the left as the plaintiff was going north, there is the entrance to
B a station yard. There is a junction further up between the High Street
and a street going off to the right, also controlled by traffic lights. There
are two lanes of traffic as one approaches that traffic light and there are
arrows on the road showing, in the right-hand lane, an arrow indicating
a right turn and, in the left-hand lane, an arrow indicating straight on or
turn left.

What happened at the time of the accident was that the plaintiff was
C going north. He was then aged 17½. He stopped at the first lot of traffic
lights, that is, the pedestrian crossing. When the lights changed he moved
over towards the off side of his half of the road because he was going
to turn right when he got to the second lot of traffic lights.

There was traffic in his near side lane and, in particular, there were
two petrol tankers, each about 40 feet long, stopped on their near side of
D the road pointing north because traffic had backed up from the second
lot of traffic lights. The first of those two tankers had stopped on the
south side of the entrance to the station yard, no doubt to let traffic get
into or out of the station yard.

The defendant, in his car, was intending to come out from the station
entrance and turn to his right in order to go south. There was a good
deal of traffic about at the time, though it was not the rush hour.
E What happened was that the driver of the leading tanker, that is, the
one that was stopped just south of the station yard entrance, made some
sort of sign to the defendant, but the defendant said that he did not regard
that as being a signal that it was safe for him to go across the road and
turn right. It was merely a signal that, so far as the tanker driver was
concerned, he was going to wait for the defendant. The defendant did
F move out and when the nose of his car was a foot or two feet beyond the
tanker, the plaintiff on his motor cycle ran into the off side front of the car.
The defendant's evidence was that he had stopped his car at the time
of the accident. The plaintiff in his evidence said that the car was
moving when he ran into it.

The judge eventually found for the defendant. Having described the
circumstances of the accident he said:
G

"I am quite satisfied that the speed of the motor cycle was neither
10 miles per hour nor 30 miles per hour, but that it was something
in between."

—I should pause there and say that there was some conflicting evidence
about the speed of the motor bicycle. The judge went on—

H   "I cannot say precisely how fast it was travelling. It is not necessary for me to come to any conclusion as to the precise speed. It is
sufficient to say that the plaintiff was in my judgment travelling too
fast to enable him to stop when he saw something emerging from the
gap. I do not think that the defendant's car was stationary. I think
that it was moving forward all the time. The defendant is not a liar
but I think he is mistaken. I think his recollection is clouded, perhaps by the shock of the collision, perhaps by the passage of time.

He did what he said he did. I think he decided to move out through A
the gap. He could not see and so he inched forward. I find that he
was at an angle of greater than 5 degrees."

Pausing there, the defendant had said that his car was only at an angle
of five degrees. The judge went on:

"He allowed his car to move forward very, very slowly indeed. I
think 'inching' forward is the best way to describe what he did. At B
the time of impact I find the vehicle was projecting more than one
foot and probably beyond two feet from the tanker. I cannot think
that the plaintiff would be riding within one foot of the tanker or
indeed within two feet of the tanker."

Then having described the state of the traffic and saying that the
plaintiff had stopped at the far pedestrian crossing and he then moved C
over towards the middle of his side of the road, the judge went on:

"As [the plaintiff] moved alongside the leading tanker he could see
the gap [into the station yard] ahead. He assumed that this gap was
for vehicles turning right from the station yard. I accept that he
contemplated the possibility that vehicles might turn out of the yard
and that he did not see any vehicle turning out of the yard and D
thought the way ahead was clear. At this stage I am quite sure that
he was travelling at a speed which was too fast to enable him to stop
or otherwise avoid a collision if any vehicle did emerge from the gap
and he did not reduce his speed to such a speed. At the same time
as the plaintiff is thus travelling along the length of the two tankers
the defendant's car is moving through the gap in the traffic and the
plaintiff does not see it. Suddenly the plaintiff sees it and then it is E
too late. He tries to avoid it but he is too close and travelling too
fast. All he can do is to raise his leg in an attempt to mitigate injury
to it. Maybe he lost control. I make no finding about this. The
important finding is that he was travelling too fast and this was the
cause of this accident. In my judgment—and I am quite clear what
was the cause of the accident—the plaintiff suddenly saw the defend- F
ant inching out and was going too fast to do anything about it. He
drove at this speed even though he contemplated that cars might
emerge from the gap.

"What is the effect in law? I have been referred to Clarke v.
Winchurch [1969] 1 W.L.R. 69. I need not repeat the facts of that
case. This case is distinguishable from Clarke's case because this
plaintiff was not queue-jumping. But any vehicle travelling along G
a line of stationary traffic has a very heavy duty of care. He must
contemplate the possibility of vehicles giving warning of their presence
by inching out and must so organise his driving as to guard against
this possibility. This plaintiff did not do that, so he fell short of the
heavy duty on him and he was to blame for the accident. But the
real issue is whether the defendant carries any blame. Now I must H
say that when I first heard counsel for the plaintiff opening this case
I took the view that a person who emerges from a minor into a
major road ought not to proceed beyond the line of his vision and
that if he does so, he does so at his own risk and could not rely on
other vehicles seeing him. That would have continued to be my view
of the matter had I not been referred to Clarke v. Winchurch. Had
it not been for Clarke v. Winchurch, I would have found the parties

A   50-50 to blame, on the basis that the plaintiff had been going too fast
and the defendant had gone beyond the line of his vision. I confess
to having my confidence shattered by the Court of Appeal's decision
in *Clarke.* It is clear that their Lordships' extensive experience
extended numerically more largely in areas other than running down
actions, although the basis of the decision was common sense rather
than anything else. The facts in *Clarke* were almost on all fours with
B   this particular case. The only material distinction was that the facts
in *Clarke's* case occurred at the rush hour but that is not the case
here although the road was busy. All their Lordships discussed, in
Clarke's case, the duty of a driver who wanted to drive across a line
of stationary traffic facing in the direction in which he did not want
to go. Their Lordships even described what a counsel of perfection
C   was."

Then the judge quoted a passage from the judgment of Phillimore L.J.
in that case, and went on:

"I cannot feel that I can make any distinction between *Clarke's* case
and this case. In my judgment the defendant moved out very, very
slowly so that what he did was almost perfect. The only question
D   which exercised me was whether the defendant should have waited
for the tanker to pass. But in my judgment the defendant was only
doing what the defendant in *Clarke's* case did and there is no obligation on him to wait for the tanker to clear before moving out. I do
not think there was any obligation on him to wait. I therefore think
that I am forced to come to the conclusion that he was exercising all
E   the care he should have done and there was nothing more the defendant could have done to avoid this collision. In fact he acted almost
to perfection. Therefore I am driven to the conclusion that he was
not in any way to blame for the accident, because when the plaintiff
saw the defendant inching out he was going too fast to be able to
stop. I therefore am obliged to find against the plaintiff. It may be
no comfort to the plaintiff that I am not at all sure that he was
F   travelling at as great a speed as 30 miles per hour. I find against him
with regret because he is a young man and an honest young man."

Mr. Burns, who appeared for the appellant in this court and the
plaintiff below, submitted that the judge felt that he had been forced by
the doctrine of precedent to do an injustice, and submitted that *Clarke* v.
Winchurch [1969] 1 W.L.R. 69 was not intended to lay down any prin-
G   ciple of law that a driver who inches forward very slowly is entitled to
emerge blind from a minor road on to a major road.

It is quite true that in *Clarke's* case the facts were very like the facts
in the present case. There were certain differences which I do not think
I need go into. That was a case where the first defendant's car was
parked in a parking space on the off side of the road facing oncoming
H   traffic. A bus coming towards him had stopped and flashed its lights.
The first defendant, the driver of the car, started to pull out and a motor
bicycle ridden by the plaintiff came along and ran into him. The plaintiff
in that case had sued the car driver and the bus driver who flashed his
headlights and the bus driver's employer. The trial judge had held that
the bus driver, and through him his employers, were to some extent to
blame for the accident, and that they were one-third to blame, and he
held that the defendant, the car driver, was not to blame at all. But when

the matter got to this court there was an appeal and a cross-appeal, and A
this court held that the bus driver and his employer were not to blame at
all and allowed their appeal, and they dismissed the plaintiff's cross-appeal
holding that the driver of the car was to no extent to blame.

It seems to me that the actual decision in that case was simply that this
court saw no sufficient reason for disagreeing with the finding of the trial
judge that the car driver was not to any extent to blame.

It is quite true that in a passage which is quoted by the judge in the B
present case Phillimore L.J. did say, at p. 74:

"Speaking for myself, that finding seems to me to be a finding that
the first defendant came out extremely slowly and extremely carefully. In effect he inched his way out beyond the line of the bus.
If it be said (and it is the most formidable point that has been made)
that he ought to have just poked his nose out and then stopped, I C
venture to think that the answer is that that is a counsel of perfection; and the difference between doing that, going out for only a
foot or a little more, and travelling very, very slowly for a yard is so
small that it is wrong to say that in the one case it would amount to
negligence, and in the other it would not. I regard the suggestion
of just going out and then stopping as a counsel of perfection. It D
appears to me that for this court to interfere with the judge's finding
that this first defendant did all that he could be expected to do
involves revising other findings of fact which this court is in no
position to do."

Then, having referred to other possibilities, he said, at p. 74:

"But [the trial judge] saw and heard the witnesses, and we have E
not; and in my opinion we are in no position to substitute our findings of fact for those reached by the judge."

Willmer L.J. said, at p. 76:

"On the whole, therefore, accepting (as I think we should) the
findings of fact arrived at by the judge, who saw the witnesses, I do
not think that it would be right for us in this court to impute blame F
to the first defendant."

Russell L.J. dissented and thought that the first defendant should, in
fact, have stopped as soon as the tip of his bonnet was showing.

It seems to me clear that the judge would have come to a different
conclusion but for that decision, and that he did regard that decision as
laying down some principle of law which bound him to find, contrary to G
his own inclination, that the defendant was under no liability at all.

There is, of course, ample high authority about the danger of elevating
decisions on the facts in particular cases into principles of law. For the
purpose of the present case I think it is enough to refer to what was said
in this court in *Garston Warehousing Co. Ltd.* v. *O. F. Smart (Liverpool)
Ltd.* [1973] R.T.R. 377. That again was a case of a car emerging from H
a side road into a main road, and in that case both the plaintiff and the
defendant were held to blame in certain proportions, the emerging car
one-third and the other car two-thirds. Cairns L.J. said, at p. 382:

"It does not appear to me that in this case any question of law arises
at all. Reference has been made to *Clarke* v. *Winchurch* [1969]
1 W.L.R. 69, the circumstances of which bear some resemblance to
those in the present case in that the driver had come out from a side

A   road and, it was said, was negligent in not stopping in very much the
same way as the judge found that the plaintiffs in this case should
have stopped. There it was said that the requirement on the driver
to stop in those circumstances was a counsel of perfection, and the
majority of the Court of Appeal found there was no negligence on his
part at all. Russell L.J., who dissented, would have assessed his
blame for the accident at no more than 20 per cent., and while it is
B   of some assistance to see the way in which this court dealt with the
case which had, as I have said, that feature in common with this
case, I certainly do not think that it was laying down any principle of
law as to whether or not that constitutes negligence."

MacKenna J. did not say anything specifically about this point, but
Buckley L.J. said that he agreed with the judgments that had been
C   delivered and, therefore, was agreeing with what Cairns L.J. had said in
the passage which I have read.

In my judgment, therefore, the judge was not bound by *Clarke* v.
Winchurch [1969] 1 W.L.R. 69, which in my opinion laid down no
principle of law, to reach the conclusion he did.

Mr. Livesey, who appears for the respondent in this court, the
D   defendant, takes another point. I have already read what the judge said,
but I think I should read part of it again. He said:

"Now I must say that when I first heard counsel for the plaintiff
opening this case I took the view that a person who emerges from a
minor into a major road ought not to proceed beyond the line of his
vision and that if he does so, he does so at his own risk and could not
E   rely on other vehicles seeing him. That would have continued to be
my view of the matter had I not been referred to the case of *Clarke*
v. *Winchurch*. Had it not been for *Clarke* v. *Winchurch* I would
have found the parties 50-50 to blame, on the basis that the plaintiff
had been going too fast and the defendant had gone beyond the line
of his vision."

F   Mr. Livesey submits that in that passage the judge is really saying that
the defendant was under an absolute or a strict liability in the circumstances of this case when he was coming out from a side turning in front
of a stationary vehicle. It seems to me that if one reads that sentence
as a whole, and in its context, it is not right to say that the judge was
taking the view that there was a strict or absolute liability. It seems to
me that he was saying no more than that in those circumstances there is
G   a very high duty on a defendant of taking care.

The position therefore, it seems to me, is this: the judge would have
held the parties 50-50 to blame but for the fact that he thought that
Clarke's case either laid down a principle of law or was so close to the
present case on the facts that he had no choice but to come to the same
conclusion as in *Clarke's* case, i.e., that the defendant was under no
H   liability at all. In my judgment, the judge misled himself in that respect.

It seems to me to follow that the right thing for this court to do is to
allow the appeal and make the finding which the judge would have made
if he had not, wrongly in my view, thought he was bound by *Clarke's*
case to come to a different conclusion. I am not saying for a moment
that if I myself had been trying this case I should have apportioned the
responsibility 50-50, but it is not possible for this court to go into the
question of apportionment or alter the judge's view about that. Accord-

1182

ingly, I would allow this appeal and order judgment to be entered for the   A
plaintiff for half the agreed figure of £1,200 damages, that is £600.

DONALDSON L.J.   I agree.

MEGAW L.J.   I also agree. This appeal, if it does nothing else, will I
hope confirm what the court has already said in the passage in the judgment of Cairns L.J., which Browne L.J. has read from *Garston Ware-*   B
housing Co. Ltd. v. *O. F. Smart (Liverpool) Ltd.* [1973] R.T.R. 377, 382,
to the effect that the decision of this court in *Clarke* v. *Winchurch* [1969]
1 W.L.R. 69 was not laying down any principle of law. I also take the
view that it would be quite wrong to treat the words used by the judge
in the county court in such a literal sense as to suggest that what the
judge had had in mind before he saw *Clarke* v. *Winchurch* was that   C
somebody who was carrying out a manoeuvre in a car, as the defendant
was doing in this case, was necessarily and absolutely liable if any
accident happened. That is not what the judge was saying.

I agree with the order proposed and with the reasons for it given
by Browne L.J.

> *Appeal allowed with costs.*   D
> *Judgment for plaintiff for £600 (half*
> *the agreed total damages), interest*
> *agreed at £83 and costs on county*
> *court scale.*
> *Legal aid taxation of plaintiff's costs.*   E

Solicitors: *Royds, Barfield for Anthony T. Clark & Co., Lincoln;
Burton & Co., Lincoln.*

[Reported by SUSAN DENNY, Barrister-at-Law]

F

[CHANCERY DIVISION]

* ATTORNEY-GENERAL *v.* SCHONFELD AND OTHERS

[1979 J. No. 3729]

G

1980 Feb. 26; 28   Sir Robert Megarry V.-C.

Charity—Education—Receiver's powers—Governors of school to
appoint headmaster—Uncertainty as to present governors—
Need to appoint new headmaster—Powers of receiver and
manager appointed to manage charity

The instrument of government made under section 17 (2)   H
of the Education Act 1944 for a voluntary aided secondary
school for boys provided that the governing body should
consist of eight foundation governors to be appointed by the
governors (i.e. the trustees, for the time being of the Jewish
Secondary Schools Movement, a charity) and four representative governors to be appointed by the local education authority. Articles of government made under section 17 (3) of
the Act contained detailed provisions as to the functions of
the governors in relation to, inter alia, the conduct of the

A   school, finance, equipment, condition of the school premises (which were vested in the trustees) and the appointment and dismissal of the headmaster.

A new headmaster was needed for the boys' school but it was not certain who were the present governors. There had been disputes as to the affairs of the charity and by an order of the court made on July 13, 1979, a receiver and manager was appointed to collect all the assets of the charity and to

B   manage its affairs for the time being.

On the receiver's summons asking the court for an order that he be at liberty to advertise, and to invite applications for, the position of head teacher and, in consultation with the local education authority, to appoint such person as he thought fit : —

Held, that the power to appoint a new headmaster being in the hands of the governors, the receiver was in no position

C   to make such an appointment himself, but his power to manage the affairs of the charity must include making proper provision for what had to be done by others and thus ensuring that there were effective foundation governors able to join with the representative governors in appointing a new headmaster; that therefore the receiver had the power to remove the existing foundation governors and appoint new ones in their stead in the interests of the charity and the

D   school; and that the court accordingly would declare that the receiver had the power so stated, and could properly exercise it after taking advice (post, pp. (1186B, H—1187B, D).

The following cases are referred to in the judgment:

Jewish Secondary Schools Movement's Trusts, In re (unreported), October 24, 1979, Sir Robert Megarry V.-C.

E   *Johnson (B.) & Co. (Builders) Ltd., In re* [1955] Ch. 634; [1955] 3 W.L.R. 269; [1955] 2 All E.R. 775, C.A.

No additional cases were cited in argument.

SUMMONS

On July 13, 1979, Walton J. made an order appointing Bernard

F   Garbacz as receiver and manager of the charity known as the Jewish Secondary Schools Movement and empowering him to " collect get in and receive all the assets property and effects " belonging to the charity and also " to manage the affairs of the said charity " until after the substantive hearing of the summons in the proceedings or further order in the meantime.

By summons dated December 4, 1979, (as amended) the receiver

G   applied for an order that he was entitled to be at liberty with the consent of the directorate of educational services of the London Borough of Barnet to advertise the vacancy of head teacher at the Hasmonean School for Boys, to invite applications for the position and to make an appointment of a fit person in consultation with not less than two Rabbis of the Principal Rabbinical Authority of the Union of

H   Orthodox Hebrew Congregations.

The facts are stated in the judgment.

John Mummery for the Attorney-General.
Gavin A. Lightman for the receiver.
The seven defendants in the action named in the summons neither appeared nor were represented.

Cur. adv. vult.

February 28. SIR ROBERT MEGARRY V.-C. read the following judg-   A
ment. This summons raises a question on the powers of a receiver and
manager appointed by the court. I have not found it altogether easy,
particularly as there appears to be no authority anywhere near the
point. There is a charity called the " Jewish Secondary Schools Movement." Its affairs are in a state of disarray and controversy. In 1978
an originating summons was issued, seeking the determination of a
variety of questions relating to the terms of the trusts governing the   B
charity, to who the trustees are, and so on. There seem to be some
nine separate instruments executed between 1935 and 1978, each of
which may or may not regulate the affairs of the charity. In 1979
another originating summons was issued, seeking, inter alia, a scheme.
Both summonses are due to be heard later in this term, with the 1978
summons (the construction summons, as it is called) due to be heard   C
before the 1979 summons. Even if nobody appeals from the decision
on these summonses (an assumption that cannot safely be made), it may
plainly be some while yet before all is settled, especially if a scheme
is directed.

The charity has five schools in the Greater London area, two of
them secondary schools and three of them preparatory schools. What   D
is before me is a summons in the 1979 proceedings relating to one of
the secondary schools, the Hasmonean Grammar School for Boys. By
an order of Walton J. made in these proceedings on July 13, 1979,
Mr. Bernard Garbacz was appointed receiver and manager of the
charity. I have not previously encountered the appointment of a
receiver of a charity, but I do not doubt the power of the court to   E
make such an order in a suitable case such as this. By the order, the
receiver was to " collect get in and receive all the assets property and
effects " belonging to the charity, and also " to manage the affairs of the
said charity " until after the substantive hearing of the originating
summons or further order in the meantime. The summons before me
seeks an order that the receiver should be at liberty (in consultation
with the Directorate of Educational Services of the London Borough   F
of Barnet) to advertise the vacancy of head teacher at the Hasmonean
Grammar School for Boys, to invite applications for this position, and
in consultation with certain specified persons to make an appointment
of such person as the receiver considers fit as such head teacher. I
may say that in this judgment I use the term " receiver " as meaning
someone who, like Mr. Garbacz, has been appointed by the court to   G
be both receiver and manager.

The status of the school under the Education Act 1944 is that it is
a voluntary aided secondary school: see sections 9, 15, and 19. By
virtue of section 17 of the Act, there is an instrument of government
and articles of government for the school, made by the Minister of
Education; these bear the numbers 927 and 882 respectively. The
instrument is almost entirely concerned with the governors of the school   H
and their meetings. There are to be eight " foundation governors "
who are to be appointed and be removable by the " governors for
the time being " of the charity, and four " representative governors "
who are to be appointed and be removable by the local education
authority. The reference to the " governors " of the charity must,
I think, be read as referring to the trustees of the charity. The
articles of government set out detailed provisions for the conduct of

The Weekly Law Reports, October 10, 1980

1185

1 W.L.R.   Attorney-General v. Schonfeld (Ch.D.)   Sir Robert
                                                                 Megarry V.-C.

A the school. The governors have important functions throughout in relation to finance, equipment, the school premises, the appointment and dismissal of the headmaster, the assistant masters and the non-teaching staff, the organisation and curriculum, school holidays, the admission of pupils and so on. The headmaster, of course, has important functions also, but it is abundantly clear that, subject to various obligations as to consultation and so on, the general government of the school rests with the governors.

B Now the present state of affairs is that the headmaster of the school is unwell and is due to retire at the end of next month. It is highly desirable that a new headmaster should be appointed as soon as is reasonably possible. This may take a little while, since if an applicant from some other school is appointed, he will have to give suitable notice to his present school. If the articles of government which are in evidence provide any guide, the notice will have to be of the order of anything from two to four months in length, expiring at the end of a term, the length depending on the position held and the term in question. If it were known with any certainty who are the governors of the school, they, of course, would be the proper persons to make the appointment. But this is not known: it is far from certain who the present governors are. Hence the present application. In it, Mr. Lightman appears on behalf of the receiver and Mr. Mummery on behalf of the Attorney-General, who is one of the defendants in the 1978 originating summons and the plaintiff in the 1979 originating summons. None of the other defendants to the summons now before me has appeared or was represented, though the first defendant, Dr. Solomon Schonfeld, has from time to time taken part in the proceedings under the originating summons, being sometimes represented and sometimes not. He is or was chairman and principal of the trustees of the charity, and also chairman of the governors of the school. It is plain that he is strongly opposed to any attempt to lessen his control of either the charity or the school, and in particular to any appointment of a headmaster save by his agreement. Though represented before the master, he has chosen not to appear before me either by counsel or in person.

The relief sought by the summons was supported rather tentatively by Mr. Lightman, and at first rather more enthusiastically by Mr. Mummery. By the end, however, Mr. Mummery had lost much of his zest for this contention, and it became plain on all hands that, as framed, the application must fail. What was sought was an order that the receiver should make a direct appointment of a headmaster of the school. The receiver, it was said, could do anything that can be done by the trustees of the charity, and so he could appoint a headmaster. When it was objected that the trustees had no power to appoint a headmaster but only power to appoint foundation governors of the school, it was said that the trustees could do directly what they could do indirectly, and so as they, through the appointment of governors, could indirectly appoint a headmaster, so the receiver himself could make the appointment directly.

As I have indicated, this contention was impossible to sustain. I cannot see how power to appoint persons to an office which requires those persons to exercise their skill and judgment in discharging their functions can properly be said to confer on the appointor a power to

do indirectly what the appointees can do directly. True, if an appointee A
displeases the appointor, the appointor may be able to remove him
and appoint someone else: but what the appointee has previously done
has been done, even if it was entirely opposed to the wishes of the
appointor. The argument involves the unreality of treating the direct
acts of the appointee, however unwelcome, as the indirect acts of the
appointor, merely because the appointor has the power of appointment
and removal. I have no hesitation in rejecting this argument. In my B
judgment, the receiver has no power to appoint the headmaster of a
school which is subject to the control of governors under a system of
government such as there is in the present case. If there were no
governors and no such system, but instead the power of appointment
were in the trustees, then the position would be entirely different.
That, indeed, was the position in relation to the girls' school run by the C
charity which came before me in October 1979; and in the circumstances of that case I held that the receiver had the power to advertise
a vacancy in the post of head teacher of that school and, on taking
proper advice, to appoint a suitable person to that post: see *In re
Jewish Secondary Schools Movement's Trusts* (unreported), October 24,
1979. This appointment, I was told, has now been made. But as I
have said, that was an entirely different case. The receiver was doing D
what the trustees could do, and not what they could not do.

That, however, is not the end of the matter. Mr. Lightman,
supported in due course by Mr. Mummery, contended by way of alternative that the receiver could and should exercise the power of the
trustees to remove the existing foundation governors of the school,
whoever they might be, and appoint new foundation governors in their E
stead. These new governors could then join with the existing representative governors, and not only take the appropriate steps to appoint a
new headmaster but also exercise all or any of the other functions
of the governors which at present are clouded by the uncertainty about
who the governors are. This, of course, avoids any reliance on any
argument about doing directly what can be done indirectly. There F
would be no indirection at all: the receiver would be doing directly
what the trustees of the charity clearly have power to do directly. The
question is whether the receiver has power to do this.

In this case, as in many others, it is important to see exactly what
the receiver has been appointed to do. A person appointed to be a
receiver and manager of a company's property is not thereby appointed
to be a manager of the company: see *In re B. Johnson & Co. (Builders)* G
Ltd. [1955] Ch. 634, 646, 661, 662, an authority which Mr. Lightman
helpfully cited. Here, in addition to being appointed to collect, get in
and receive all the assets, property and effects of the charity, the receiver
was appointed "to manage the affairs" of the charity. Those
"affairs" mainly consist of the operation of the charity's schools. The
girls' school is run directly by the trustees. The boys' school with H
which I am now concerned is run by the governors; but the trustees
(in whom, I may say, the school premises are vested) also have
important functions, which include the appointment and removal of the
foundation governors. The boys' school is one of the major assets of
the charity, performing important functions for the charity. Suppose,
for instance, that there were no foundation governors, or that the
foundation governors were in a state of continual deadlock: I should be

The Weekly Law Reports, October 10, 1980

1187

1 W.L.R.   Attorney-General v. Schonfeld (Ch.D.)   Sir Robert
                                                                Megarry V.-C.

A reluctant to say that the power "to manage the affairs" of the charity
did not include power to secure the due management of one of the
charity's schools by doing what was necessary to ensure that there
were effective foundation governors. The power "to manage the
affairs" of the charity must mean the power to manage those affairs
effectively, and that must mean the power of conducting and controlling
those affairs according to their nature. It means conducting and
B controlling directly what can be done directly, and making proper provision for others to conduct and control what has to be done by others.

I have felt considerable hesitation in this case. The appointment and
removal of school governors is not an activity which one is accustomed
to associate with receivers. That hesitation was increased because I
lacked the assistance of hearing any argument against the contentions
C of Mr. Lightman and Mr. Mummery. My hesitation has been entirely
about the powers of the receiver and manager. I feel no hesitation
about the need to bring about the proper operation of this charity and
its schools in accordance with the provisions which govern it: that
seems to me to be quite plain. My doubts have been about the power
of a receiver and manager of the affairs of a charity to exercise
D a power to remove and appoint foundation governors which the
instrument of government, made under statutory authority, confers on
the trustees of the charity. In the end, however, I have reached the
conclusion that I ought to hesitate no more, and hold that the receiver
has the power to remove the existing foundation governors, whoever
they may be, and appoint new foundation governors in their place. I
may say that I see no reason why someone who is or who claims to be
E an existing foundation governor should not be removed in this way
and then be included in those who are then appointed to be foundation
governors, thereby removing any doubt as to his or her title to be
a foundation governor.

In holding that the receiver has this power, I bear in mind that the
power to appoint a receiver is purely equitable in its origin; indeed, it
F was one of the oldest remedies of the Court of Chancery. The remedy
is one to be moulded to the needs of the situation; within proper limits,
a receiver may be given such powers as the court considers to be
appropriate to the particular case. If I am wrong in my conclusion
that the order of Walton J., on its true construction, authorises the
receiver to appoint and remove foundation governors of the school,
then I consider that I can and ought myself now to give that authority:
G and this I do. If that means that I am extending the ambit of a
receiver's functions beyond their existing bounds, then I would say that
this is only part of the process of moulding the functions of a receiver
to the needs of the case which has been going on in equity for centuries.

I must add some caveats. First, I am not deciding that as a matter
of routine the receiver of an educational charity's affairs or assets has
H the power of appointing and removing school governors. Much depends
on the terms of the appointment, the terms of the trusts and other
provisions governing the charity and its assets, and the circumstances
of the case. Certainly in all ordinary circumstances a receiver would
be well advised, if no more, to seek the directions of the court in
such a matter. What I do decide is that this receiver in the circumstances of this case has the power in question. Second, as I suggested
to Mr. Lightman in the course of argument, where a receiver is autho-

1188

rised to exercise such a power, I think that he should do so only after   A
obtaining and duly considering proper advice about the persons who
are to be appointed as governors.   That is particularly important in a
case such as this where there is a considerable degree of controversy
as to the operation of the school.   Mr. Lightman undertook to put
before me proposals to this end, and I shall consider them in due course.
Let me make it clear that the receiver is not bound to accept all the
advice that he is given: indeed, some of it may well be contradictory.   B
What he must do is to obtain the advice, give serious consideration to
it all, and then act as he thinks right and proper in the interests of
the charity and the school.   Third, in exercising his power to remove
the existing foundation governors, the receiver must make it plain
to them that the power of removal is being exercised solely in order
that the school may be properly carried on according to the instrument   C
and articles of government, and that the removal is in no way intended
to be any criticism whatever of any of the governors who are being
removed.   A clean sweep of all who are or claim to be foundation
governors is being made so as to remove uncertainties and to put into
office eight foundation governors whose title is derived from an order
of the court.   Subject to that, I hold that the receiver has the power
that I have stated.   D

> *Order and declaration that the receiver
> and manager of the charity has, and
> may properly exercise, the power vested
> in the governors of the charity to appoint
> and remove foundation governors of the*   E
> *Hasmonean Grammar School for Boys.*

Solicitors: *Treasury Solicitor; Paisner & Co.*

                                                            K. N. B.

A

[COURT OF APPEAL]

* LEUNG *v.* GARBETT

1980 March 17

Megaw and Templeman L.JJ. and
Sir Patrick Browne

B

*County Court—Arbitration—Jurisdiction—Action for damages after
road accident—Award by registrar sitting as arbitrator—Application by defendant to judge to set aside award—Whether judge
entitled to appoint himself arbitrator to hear reference without
consent of parties—County Courts Act 1959 (7 & 8 Eliz. 2,
c. 22) (as amended by Administration of Justice Act 1977
(c. 38), s. 17 (1), s. 92 (3) [1]—County Court Rules 1936 (S.R.
& O. 1936 No. 626/L. 17) (as amended), Ord. 19, r. 1 [2]*

C

After a traffic accident involving vehicles belonging to the
plaintiff and the defendant, the plaintiff brought an action in
the county court claiming damages representing the cost of
repairs to his car which he alleged had been damaged as a result
of the defendant's negligence. The defendant denied liability.
The plaintiff's solicitors asked that the matter should be dealt
with by arbitration and the registrar, treating that request as
being a reference to arbitration and purporting to act under
Ord. 19, r. 1 of the County Court Rules 1936 (as amended)
caused the matter to be referred to himself as arbitrator. After
hearing the evidence of both parties he made an award in favour
of the plaintiff for the full sum claimed. The defendant
applied to Judge Clapham to set aside the award on the ground,
inter alia, that he had not been given an opportunity to address
the court after the evidence had been given. The judge held
that that should be treated as misconduct and set aside the
award. He then appointed himself arbitrator under section
92 of the County Courts Act 1959 and Ord. 19, r. 1 of the
Rules of 1936, came to the conclusion that the plaintiff had
established his case, and made the same award as the registrar
had done.

On appeal by the defendant, on the ground that the judge
had no jurisdiction to appoint himself arbitrator without the
consent of the parties: —

Held, dismissing the appeal, that the words " with the consent of the parties " in the proviso to section 92 (3) of the Act
of 1959 applied only to the judge's power to revoke the reference and not to his power, if he thought fit, having set aside
an award, to order another reference to be made and in that
other reference to appoint himself as arbitrator; accordingly
there was no flaw in the judge's jurisdiction and he was entitled
to hear the reference as arbitrator.

D

E

F

G

No cases are referred to in the judgments.

H

[1] County Courts Act 1959 (as amended), s. 92: " (1) County court rules—(*a*)
may prescribe cases in which proceedings are (without any order of the court)
to be referred to arbitration, . . . (2) County court rules—(*a*) may prescribe cases
in which proceedings may be referred to arbitration by order of the court . . . (3)
On a reference under subsection (1) or (2) above the award of the arbitrator . . .
shall be entered as the judgment in the proceedings and shall be as binding and
effectual to all intents as if given by the judge: Provided that the judge may, if he
thinks fit, on application made to him within such time as may be prescribed, set
aside the award, or may, with the consent of the parties, revoke the reference or
order another reference to be made . . ."

[2] Ord. 19, r. 1 of the County Court Rules 1936 implements the provisions of
s. 92 of the County Courts Act 1959 as amended by s. 17 of the Administration of
Justice Act 1977 concerning the reference to arbitration of cases with and without
order of the court.

The following cases were cited in argument:

Meyer v. *Leanse* [1958] 2 Q.B. 371; [1958] 3 W.L.R. 518; [1958] 3 All E.R. 213, C.A.

Pearce v. *Winkworth* (1873) 28 L.T. 710.

APPEAL from Judge Clapham sitting at Lambeth County Court.

On February 8, 1978 the plaintiff, David Sing Hay Leung, brought an action in the Lambeth County Court against the defendant, Gordon Garbett, claiming damages of £175·80, representing the cost of repairs to his motor vehicle following a collision between his and the defendant's vehicles on June 2, 1977. The defendant denied liability.

The plaintiff asked that the matter should be dealt with by way of arbitration and the registrar, purporting to act under Ord. 19, r. 1 of the County Court Rules 1936 (as amended) caused the matter to be referred to himself as arbitrator. On January 25, 1979, he made an award in favour of the plaintiff for the sum claimed. The defendant applied to Judge Clapham to set aside the award on the ground, inter alia, that he had been given no opportunity to address the court after the evidence had been given. On May 17, 1979, the judge set aside the award and, appointing himself arbitrator under section 92 of the County Courts Act 1959, reheard the matter. He found that the accident had been caused by the negligence of the defendant and he awarded the plaintiff the same sum as the registrar had awarded, namely, £175·80.

The defendant appealed on the ground, inter alia, that the judge, without seeking the consent of the parties, had adopted the role of arbitrator and judge. The defendant contended that the judge had no power to exercise his jurisdiction so as to disable himself from sitting in an appellate capacity to hear and determine the appeal against the registrar's award.

The facts are more fully stated in the judgment of Megaw L.J.

The defendant in person.
Andrew Young for the plaintiff.

MEGAW L.J. This is an appeal brought by Mr. Gordon Garbett who was the defendant in an action brought against him in the county court. The plaintiff was Mr. David Sing Hay Leung. The action apparently arose out of a traffic accident; Mr. Leung complained in the county court alleging in his particulars of claim that the accident had been caused by the negligence of the defendant and the plaintiff claimed damages in the sum of £175·80. The claim was thus for less than £200.

The defendant, denied liability; he said that he was not guilty of any negligence at all, and in his document put in by way of defence he set out what he said were the real facts of the case on the basis of which he was not liable.

The action was in the Lambeth County Court; the registrar, acting or purporting to act under the provisions of Ord. 19, r. 1 of the County Court Rules 1936, caused the matter to be referred to himself as arbitrator. That action he took on the basis of an initiative taken by the plaintiff in the action who, through his solicitors, had written asking that the matter should be dealt with by county court arbitration.

The registrar, in accepting that application, treated it as being a reference to arbitration and appointed himself as arbitrator. In the course of time, the arbitration was heard before the registrar, the defendant representing himself, as, of course, he was entitled to do, and as he has done throughout the proceedings, including the appeal to this court. The registrar heard evidence on one side and the other, and decided in favour of the plaintiff, and made an award to the plaintiff of £175·80 as damages.

It would appear that the registrar, as arbitrator, did not, at any rate formally, invite the defendant or counsel who appeared in the arbitration on behalf of the plaintiff to address him at the conclusion of the evidence. It may be that that was because the defendant—as we are told by counsel for the plaintiff—had in the course of his evidence in the witness box (and this is not a criticism of him) argued the law as well as giving his evidence on the facts, and had made his submissions, and the registrar thus treated the matter as having been argued without formally inviting speeches at the end.

However that may be, the defendant being dissatisfied with the registrar's award, took steps to apply to the judge in the county court to set aside the award. The defendant regards that as being an appeal, and he seems to have some difficulty in understanding the difference between an application to set aside an award and an appeal in an action.

The provisions in relation to applications to set aside appear in the proviso to section 92 (3) of the County Courts Act 1959, that section having been amended by section 7 (1) of the Administration of Justice Act 1973, and section 17 (1) of the Administration of Justice Act 1977. The proviso to subsection (3) reads:

" Provided that the judge may, if he thinks fit, on application made to him within such time as prescribed, set aside the award, or may, with the consent of the parties, revoke the reference or order another reference to be made in the manner aforesaid."

The application to set aside is provided for by Ord. 37, r. 7 of the County Court Rules 1936, which is a rule specifically made under section 92 of the Act of 1959 and which thus refers to proceedings in the county court. It provides:

" (1) An application by a party to set aside the award of an arbitrator to whom proceedings have been referred under section 92 of the Act shall be made on notice stating the grounds of the application, and the notice shall be served within six days from the receipt by the applicant of the copy of the judgment."

The defendant applied to the judge to set aside and in his notice of application, which is to be treated as having been made under Ord. 37, r. 7, he set out his complaint about the award, consisting principally of assertions in relation to the facts and the evidence, and suggesting that the registrar, as arbitrator, had come to the wrong conclusion on the facts. However, he finished his notice by these words:

" However, when the hearing had commenced, the defendant was taken by surprise in that the plaintiff was represented by counsel which in the context of an informal hearing not presided over by a judge was prejudicial to a defendant acting in person."

There is nothing in that point. Then he goes on: " And who otherwise had no opportunity to address the court after the evidence had been given."

It would appear that when the application to set aside came before
Judge Clapham in the Lambeth County Court, the judge took the view
that the defendant, in his application to set aside, had a valid point by
reason of those last few words of his application to set aside, and that
it might be treated as being misconduct. Let me say that I certainly,
myself, would not regard as being misconduct in anything other than a
very technical sense of the word, if it were indeed erroneous at all,
the fact that the defendant had not been given the opportunity to make
a final speech, in the circumstances which I have mentioned.

At any rate, having come to that conclusion, the judge accepted the
defendant's application to the extent in which it was made. He decided
that the registrar's award ought to be set aside.

Now the defendant complains in this court and this to a large extent
is the substance of his complaint, that the judge did not give him the
opportunity to proceed to expound his application to set aside as being
an appeal on the merits. But it is clear that where there is a properly
constituted arbitration in a county court, and an award is made, there is
no appeal in the sense of a re-hearing of the facts, because, as in all other
arbitrations, the arbitrator's conclusions on fact are, subject to very
limited exceptions, to be taken as final and not capable of review by any
court.

The provision in the County Court Rules 1936 in an application to
set aside an award made in a county court arbitration is only if it can be
shown either that there was something which could properly be called
" misconduct " on the part of the arbitrator, which can be said to have
materially prejudiced the party applying for it to be set aside; or that
the award contained a material error of law on its face. The judge,
if he had not had the ground which he seems to have accepted as being
technical misconduct on the part of the registrar, would not have been
entitled to hear the defendant doing what he wanted to do : namely, to
treat the proceeding before him as though it were an appeal from the
registrar's decision in an action, and to re-hear the merits and to apply
his own mind to the evidence. All that the judge could have done at
that stage, apart from what he did do, would have been to set aside the
award and to leave the matter to start again.

But what the judge in fact did was, having held that the registrar's
award should be set aside, thereafter to appoint himself as arbitrator
under section 92 of the County Court Act 1959 and Ord. 19, r. 1 of the
County Court Rules and himself, thereafter, to hear the arbitration as
arbitrator. He heard the evidence tendered on behalf of the plaintiff and
on behalf of the defendant, and having heard that evidence, he himself
gave an award in which he arrived at the conclusion that the plaintiff
had established his case, that he had shown negligence on the part of the
defendant, and that the appropriate amount was the same amount as the
registrar had awarded in the award which the judge had set aside.

The defendant's complaint here, when it is analysed, cannot be a
complaint that the judge did what the defendant asked him to do, namely,
to set aside the registrar's award; his complaint is that the judge thereafter
proceeded without obtaining or requiring the consent of the defendant
himself to make himself an arbitrator and to hear the matter afresh in a
fresh arbitration under the original reference.

For a time it appeared to me that there was substance in the
defendant's complaint by reference to the terms of the proviso to section
92 (3) of the County Courts Act 1959 which I have already read. It

A did appear to me, on the first reading of that statutory provision, that the judge would only have been authorised to turn himself into an arbitrator at that stage with the consent of the parties; but having heard Mr. Young's submissions on this matter, I am quite satisfied that that is wrong, and that the judge did indeed have jurisdiction to do that which he did—namely, having set aside the registrar's award, he was entitled, under Ord. 19, r. 1 to appoint himself as arbitrator to deal with

B the reference and to deal with it and to make an award in place of the award which had been set aside. From that, there would be no appeal on the merits on the assessment of the evidence, any more than there was from the registrar's original award. There would be an appeal to this court from the judge's award only if it could be shown that the judge had no jurisdiction or that there was some error of law on the face of the

C award, or there was some misconduct by the judge.

Looking at the provisions of Ord. 19, r. 1, I see no basis now for suggesting that under the provisions of that rule the judge did not have jurisdiction to make himself arbitrator, having set aside the registrar's award. I am satisfied that in the proviso to section 92 (3) of the Act the words " with the consent of the parties " are applicable only to the provision therein of the judge's power to revoke the reference, and do

D not apply to the judge's power given to him, if he thinks fit, having set aside the award, to order another reference to be made, and in that other reference he was entitled to appoint himself as the arbitrator.

There was here, therefore, no flaw in the jurisdiction of the judge. I think he was entitled to do what he did. There is no substance in the appeal, and I would dismiss it.

E TEMPLEMAN L.J. I agree.

SIR PATRICK BROWNE. I also agree.

Appeal dismissed with costs.

F Solicitors: *R. I. Lewis & Co.*

E. M. W.

[COURT OF APPEAL]

* REGINA v. BIBI

1980 July 21   Lord Lane C.J., Lawton and Shaw L.JJ.

Crime — Sentence — Imprisonment — Sentencing policy — Shortest possible sentence consistent with protecting public interest and punishing and deterring criminal—Uniformity of approach

The appellant, a Kenyan Indian widow aged 49 with an unblemished record and subservient to her brother-in-law at whose home she lived, was on the fringe of an enterprise by him for the illegal import of herbal cannabis. She was convicted of being concerned in the fraudulent evasion of the prohibition on importation of a controlled drug and was sentenced to three years' imprisonment.

On appeal against sentence: —

Meglaw L.J.

Reg. v. Bibi (C.A.) [1980]

A

Held, allowing the appeal, that, since sentencing courts had to be particularly careful to examine each case to ensure that, if an immediate prison sentence was necessary, it was as short as possible consistent only with protecting public interests and punishing and deterring the criminal; that since the appellant was a first offender only on the fringes of the enterprise and any prison sentence would be traumatic for her, the case was typically one where a shorter term would have been appropriate both to offender and offence, and that, accordingly, the sentence would be quashed and a sentence of six month's imprisonment substituted.

B

No cases are referred to in the judgment or were cited in argument.

APPEAL against sentence.

On November 23, 1979, at Croydon Crown Court before the recorder (C. F. Dehn Q.C.) the appellant, Bashir Begum Bibi, was convicted on two counts of being concerned in the fraudulent evasion of the prohibition on importation of a controlled drug. She was sentenced to three years' imprisonment on each count concurrent. She appealed against severity of sentence on the grounds, inter alia, that it did not reflect her lesser involvement in the importation nor her subordinate role.

C

The facts are stated in the judgment.

D

Edward Irving (assigned by the Registrar of Criminal Appeals) for the appellant.

LORD LANE C.J. gave the following judgment of the court. On November 23, 1979, at Croydon Crown Court the appellant, Bashir Begum Bibi, was convicted on two counts of being concerned in the fraudulent evasion of the prohibition on the importation of a controlled drug, which in this case was herbal cannabis. She was sentenced to three years' imprisonment on each of those counts, the terms to run concurrently, three years in all. She now appeals against that sentence by leave of the single judge.

E

There was a person accused with her by name Abdul Ali, who was her brother-in-law. He pleaded guilty to five similar offences and he was sentenced to a total of three and a half years' imprisonment.

F

The facts of the case were these. The appellant at the time of the offence was 48 years of age. She is 49 now. She is a Kenyan Indian. She is a widow and she lived with her brother-in-law, Abdul Ali, and a small grandchild (whom she had in effect adopted at its birth) in a house in Thornton Heath. Both Ali and the appellant had been for a holiday in Kenya, and it is clear that whilst they were there Ali had arranged for a quantity of herbal cannabis to be sent by post from Kenya to the address at Thornton Heath as to a part of it and to another address where a friend lived as to the other part. The cannabis was posted to England. The parcels were intercepted by the customs, and the drugs in some of the parcels were taken out and innocuous material resembling cannabis was substituted. The Post Office delivered the parcels to the Thornton Heath address. This appellant was there and she unpacked the contents That was the extent of her complicity in this crime.

G

H

The social background against which this matter was played out will have to be examined in a moment, but this case opens up wider horizons because it is no secret that our prisons at the moment are dangerously

A overcrowded. So much so that sentencing courts must be particularly careful to examine each case to ensure, if an immediate custodial sentence is necessary, that the sentence is as short as possible, consistent only with the duty to protect the interests of the public and to punish and deter the criminal.

B Many offenders can be dealt with equally justly and effectively by a sentence of six or nine months' imprisonment as by one of 18 months or three years. We have in mind not only the obvious case of the first offender for whom any prison sentence however short may be an adequate punishment and deterrent, but other types of case as well.

The less serious types of factory or shopbreaking; the minor cases of sexual indecency; the more petty frauds where small amounts of money are involved; the fringe participant in more serious crime: all

C these are examples of cases where the shorter sentence would be appropriate.

There are, on the other hand, some offences for which, generally speaking, only the medium or longer sentences will be appropriate. For example, most robberies; most offences involving serious violence; use of a weapon to wound; burglary of private dwelling houses; planned crime

D for wholesale profit; active large scale trafficking in dangerous drugs. These are only examples. It would be impossible to set out a catalogue of those offences which do and those which do not merit more severe treatment. So much will, obviously, depend upon the circumstances of each individual offender and each individual offence.

What the court can and should do is to ask itself whether there is any compelling reason why a short sentence should not be passed. We

E are not aiming at uniformity of sentence; that would be impossible. We are aiming at uniformity of approach.

The present case is an example. Importation of prohibited drugs is a serious offence and the $3\frac{1}{2}$-year sentence passed on Abdul Ali was certainly not too long.

The appellant's role, however, was not that of organiser or carrier.

F There was no question of her being used by Ali because she was a woman and therefore more likely to receive lenient treatment if caught, as one sometimes finds in such cases. Ali was the organiser. She was the person at home when the parcels arrived. She unpacked them and took out what she thought, on the verdict of the jury, to be the cannabis. She was party to the importation. That was a criminal offence and unquestionably deserved an immediate sentence of imprisonment.

G But it is impossible on the facts of this case to overlook the exceptional situation of the appellant, and one turns to the social inquiry report where that is conveniently and accurately set out as follows:

" She is also caring for the 14 month old son of one of her daughters. The arrangement is a permanent one and is not uncommon among Muslim families. Her brother-in-law is totally responsible for her

H welfare and she depends completely upon him for support. As she does not speak any English it is impossible to make a realistic assessment of the Begum Bibi, and it is apparent that she is well socialised into the Muslim traditions and as such has a role subservient to any male figures around her. Contact with society around her is not encouraged and it is her role to remain within the house. Should the Begum Bibi be found guilty of these alleged offences she must undoubtedly find herself in a most serious position. Because she has assumed the traditional role of her culture any involvement in these offences is likely to be the result of being told what to do and the learned need to comply. Traditionally her role revolves completely around her home and as such is probably unaware of a great deal of what is happening in society around her. In view of this I feel she would be totally unable to cope with a period of imprisonment. . . ."

In the light of that history, it would not be safe to credit her with the same independence of mind and action as most women today enjoy. The effect of any term of imprisonment upon her, however short, would inevitably be traumatic, though she seems, it must be said, to have met the difficulties which she has in prison with a remarkable degree of stoicism or fatalism.

On any view of the facts, this woman was on the fringes of the whole enterprise, with very little if any say in the way things were to go. We think that this is a typical case where a shorter term would have been appropriate, both to offender and to offence.

What we accordingly propose to do is to quash the sentence of three years' imprisonment and substitute therefor a term of six months' imprisonment concurrent on each count, making six months altogether, and that will in effect result in her release very shortly, if not immediately. To that extent this appeal is allowed.

Appeal allowed.
Sentence varied accordingly.

L. N. W.

[HOUSE OF LORDS]

* SIMMONS (AS LIQUIDATOR OF
LIONEL SIMMONS PROPERTIES LTD.) . . . . APPELLANT

AND

INLAND REVENUE COMMISSIONERS . . . RESPONDENTS

1980 April 29, 30;   Lord Wilberforce, Viscount Dilhorne,
June 19   Lord Salmon, Lord Scarman
                                      and Lord Roskill

Revenue — Corporation tax — Profits of trade — Acquisition and development of properties—Portfolio of investments—Object to float public company—Adverse business prospects—Sale of properties—Whether proceeds trading profits—Finance Act 1965 (c. 25), ss. 53, 77

A group of companies was formed for the purpose of acquiring properties for development and investment by S. and other individuals associated with him over a period of seven years, the ultimate purpose being to float a public company. In 1966 S. as chairman of the group, having been advised that adverse factors and an unfavourable economic climate made it desirable to sell the properties, decided to liquidate the group. As liquidator he sold various properties

A between 1967 and 1969, producing a surplus of £912,000. The
question arose whether that was assessable to corporation tax
as trading profits. The special commissioners held that three
of the sales produced surplus on capital account and were not
assessable. In respect of four other sales they held that the
proceeds were trading profits. In a case stated for the opinion
of the High Court they said (inter alia) that the acquisitions
of the properties were initially made " primarily for the
B purpose of creating and retaining investments, and not
primarily for the purpose of immediate sales after development " and that the eventual purpose of S. was the flotation
of a public company. They also said that the decision to
liquidate was not " inconsistent with the original aim to create
investments for retention where possible, or where not possible
for turning to account by way of trade." Goulding J. held
that the sums in question were not trading profits. The
C Court of Appeal reversed his decision.
     On appeal by the liquidator: —
     Held, allowing the appeal (Lord Scarman dissenting), that
the commissioners' finding of fact being that the initial intention was " primarily for the purpose of creating and
retaining investments," the subsequent reference to turning
the properties to account by way of trade was not a finding
of fact that there was an original intention to trade, and
D such a finding would have been inconsistent with the previous
finding and with the whole history of the transaction (post,
pp. 1201C–D, G–H, 1202G—1203A, F–H, 1205A).
     Decision of the Court of Appeal [1979] S.T.C. 471
reversed.

The following cases are referred to in their Lordships' opinions:

E Cunliffe v. Goodman [1950] 2 K.B. 237; [1950] 1 All E.R. 720, C.A.
Edwards v. Bairstow [1956] A.C. 14; [1955] 3 W.L.R. 410; [1955] 3
     All E.R. 48, H.L.(E.).
Sharkey v. Wernher [1956] A.C. 58; [1955] 3 W.L.R. 671; [1955] 3 All
     E.R. 493, H.L.(E.).

The following additional cases were cited in argument:

F Chancery Lane Safe Deposit and Offices Co. Ltd. v. Inland Revenue
     Commissioners [1966] A.C. 85; [1966] 2 W.L.R. 251; [1966] 1 All
     E.R. 1, H.L.(E.).
Bowie v. Reg. Dunn (Builders) Ltd. (1974) 49 T.C. 469.
Eames v. Stepnell Properties Ltd. [1967] 1 W.L.R. 593; [1967] 1 All
     E.R. 785, C.A.
Iswera v. Inland Revenue Commissioner [1965] 1 W.L.R. 663, P.C.
G Shadford v. H. Fairweather & Co. Ltd. (1966) 43 T.C. 291.
Smithwick v. National Coal Board [1950] 2 K.B. 335, C.A.

APPEAL from the Court of Appeal.
     This was an appeal from a decision of the Court of Appeal (Orr,
Bridge and Cumming-Bruce L.JJ.) allowing an appeal from a decision
H of Goulding J. on a case stated by the Commissioners for the Special
Purposes of the Income Tax Acts. The appellant was Lionel Simmons
as liquidator of Lionel Simmons Properties Ltd. The company was one
of seven companies which were formed at different times between May
15, 1957, and May 20, 1964, which together ultimately constituted the
Lionel Simmons group of companies of which Lionel Simmons Properties
Ltd. was the parent company.
     The facts are stated in the opinion of Lord Wilberforce.

Michael Nolan Q.C. and *David Shirley* for the appellant.

Patrick Medd Q.C. and *Brian Davenport Q.C.* for the respondents.

Their Lordships took time for consideration.

June 19. LORD WILBERFORCE. My Lords, Lionel Simmons Properties Ltd. (" L.S.P."), whose liquidator, Mr. Lionel Simmons, is the appellant, is one of seven companies formed between 1957–64 which constituted the Lionel Simmons group of companies. Assessments having been made of profits and gains to corporation tax (under Case 1 of Schedule D) and " shortfall " in distribution, five appeals were brought to the special commissioners on behalf of Lionel Simmons Properties Ltd. and other companies in the group namely Polewin Properties Investments Ltd. (" Polewin "), Richhouse Properties Investments Ltd. (" Richhouse "), Centre Town Development (Twickenham) Ltd. (" Twickenham ") and Centre Town Developments (Barnet) Ltd. (" Barnet "). In 1967–69 these companies and two others sold nine blocks of offices and flats. As to two, no question arises, but as to the other seven the question was whether the transactions should be treated as sales of trading stock, or as the sales of permanent investments giving rise to a surplus on capital account. Before the special commissioners the arguments seem to have been on the basis that all these transactions should be treated in the same way so that the surpluses should all be regarded as trading receipts or all as capital receipts. The special commissioners however decided that three (by Polewin and Richhouse) should be treated as sales of investments, and four (namely two involving Lionel Simmons Properties Ltd. and one each of Twickenham and Barnet) as sales of trading stock. The liquidator appealed to the High Court by way of case stated in respect of the latter and his appeals were allowed by Goulding J. But the judge's decision was reversed by the Court of Appeal The liquidator further appeals to this House and the present is his appeal as liquidator of Lionel Simmons Properties Ltd. Appeals in respect of Twickenham and Barnet have been held over.

The facts as regards the whole of the Lionel Simmons group are set out in full detail in the case stated. There is no question here of overruling, or disregarding, the special commissioners' findings of the primary facts. These, which involve the formation and history of each of the companies, the purchase, development and sale of the properties, are accurately and clearly stated. Nor is this, in my opinion, a case in which it is possible to say that the commissioners have reached a decision which no reasonable body of commissioners could have reached, and so have erred in law: see *Edwards* v. *Bairstow* [1956] A.C. 14—a case itself concerned with " trading." Nor I think is this a case which calls for discussion whether the conclusions which the commissioners have reached are themselves findings of secondary facts, or inferences from primary facts: many cases involving the question whether or not there is a trade do so and often there are difficult lines to be drawn.

What I think has to be considered here is, rather, precisely what the commissioners have found as to the companies' intentions, and whether their findings are consistent or intelligible. I do this with, I hope, a proper appreciation of the commissioners' presentation; and a disposition to uphold any decision of theirs on factual matters if I can properly do so.

A   One must ask, first, what the commissioners were required or entitled
to find. Trading requires an intention to trade: normally the question
to be asked is whether this intention existed at the time of the acquisition
of the asset. Was it acquired with the intention of disposing of it at a
profit, or was it acquired as a permanent investment? Often it is
necessary to ask further questions: a permanent investment may be
sold in order to acquire another investment thought to be more satis-
B   factory; that does not involve an operation of trade, whether the first
investment is sold at a profit or at a loss. Intentions may be changed.
What was first an investment may be put into the trading stock—and,
I suppose, vice versa. If findings of this kind are to be made precision
is required, since a shift of an asset from one category to another will
involve changes in the company's accounts, and, possibly, a liability to
C   tax: see *Sharkey* v. *Wernher* [1956] A.C. 58. What I think is not
possible is for an asset to be both trading stock and permanent investment at the same time, nor to possess an indeterminate status—neither
trading stock nor permanent asset. It must be one or other, even though,
and this seems to me legitimate and intelligible, the company, in whatever character it acquires the asset, may reserve an intention to change
its character. To do so would, in fact, amount to little more than making
D   explicit what is necessarily implicit in all commercial operations, namely
that situations are open to review.
     I now approach the critical findings of the commissioners. It must
be borne in mind that these were preceded by a very complete description
of the history of the group which, summarily, amounted to this. Mr.
Simmons, a quantity surveyor, started his property operations in a very
E   small way in the 1950s. About 1955 he came into contact with four
brothers, Chung, wealthy Malayans, who were in London. With their
participation he formed the seven companies in 1957–1964 and through
them set about acquiring properties for development. All the companies,
except one which was a trading company, were formed as property
investment companies. In 1962 an association was formed with a publicly
quoted company, Bishopsgate Property and General Investments Ltd.
F   ("Bishopsgate"), a company associated with Hambros Bank which
specialised in bringing investment (but not trading) companies to the
market, and by 1964 the association with the brothers Chung had virtually
terminated. In 1965 adverse factors developed with the passing of the
Rent Act 1965 and the Finance Act 1965 (introducing the capital gains
tax), and the economic climate became unfavourable. On October 27,
G   1966, the decision in principle was taken to liquidate the group and to
dispose of the properties. At this point, Lionel Simmons Properties
Ltd., which had been incorporated in 1963 as a vehicle for going public
with Bishopsgate's backing, had two properties. 153–155 East Barnet
Road, Barnet, had been acquired in February 1964 and by April 1966
had been let as a whole for 21 years. 27 Greville Street had been
acquired in May 1964 and building was completed in June 1965 but
H   lettings had not been arranged. As regards the other two companies
(their position is relevant for an understanding of the decision) Barnet
had one property (Kingmaker House) which it was formed to and did
acquire in October 1963 and completed, but not let, in March 1965,
and Twickenham had one property (2, Holly Road, Twickenham) which
it was formed to and did acquire in April 1963, completed in April
1964 and let by June 24, 1966. None of these companies had at any

time acquired or sold any property other than those mentioned. All
of these properties were acquired after the association with Bishopsgate
had been arranged, and Bishopsgate, directly, or through Lionel Simmons
Properties Ltd. had an interest in each company. By an agreement
dated October 4, 1963 (inter alia) Mr. Simmons agreed with Bishopsgate not to alter the memorandum or articles of association of Lionel
Simmons Properties Ltd., Twickenham, or Barnet, nor to alter their
business from that of property holding.

In the light of this situation, the commissioners came to their decision.
I must reproduce the relevant passages:

"We accept the evidence of Mr. Simmons, Mr. Phillips and Mr.
Spink, to the effect that the acquisitions with which they were
respectively concerned were initially entered into primarily for the
purposes of creating and retaining investments, and not primarily for
the purposes of immediate sales after development. We also accept
that the overall and eventual ambition or purpose of Mr. Simmons
personally was the flotation of a public company when sufficient
and suitable investments had been gathered together. However, we
do not think acceptance of that evidence is an end of the matter
and automatically puts the eventual disposals into the category of
non-trading.

" The pattern of Mr. Simmons and his associates was to acquire
and develop sites with a view to creating permanent investments,
relying on short and long term loans for the various stages. From
the early transactions of Polewin and Richhouse, and also from
the latter transaction of Hampstead, it is evident that Mr. Simmons
was or had to be prepared to realise one development or part
thereof before it became a completed investment, in order to find
or conserve funds for another development which he thought had
better prospects. It was not until at a late stage in the process, or
until after completion of lettings, that he could be in a position to
decide finally whether to retain or not. We find that the composite
intention to be attributed to the group was to aim at building up a
suitable portfolio of investments but to allow the final decision
whether to retain to await on events.

" It was of the essence of the appellant's case that the minutes of
LSP dated October 27, 1966, incorporating the decision to liquidate
gave effect to change of intention, due to reversal of expectations
which until then had been favourable. By that date the difficulties
and problems facing the group were such that it had for some time
appeared unlikely that the group could become suitable for public
flotation, and the more advantageous course was to sell the group's
properties. The decision to liquidate was in our view not inconsistent with the original aim—to create investments for retention
where possible, or where not possible for turning to account by
way of trade.

" On the above view of the facts it seems to us that the decision
to liquidate only saves surpluses on properties which were retained,
or likely to be retained, as investment before the liquidation was
contemplated: It follows in our view that so far as the uncompleted
investments are concerned the appeals of Barnet and LSP (in respect
of 27 Greville Street) must fail, and we hold that the respective
surpluses of £516,994 and £32,576 were trading profits.

A   " With regard to the appeals of Twickenham and LSP (in respect
of East Barnet Road) the final lettings of the properties were completed approximately only one month and seven months before the
formal decision to liquidate. The decision had been under consideration for some time previously, making the retention of the
properties, which had not begun to produce any surpluses on income
B   accounts, unlikely. In all the circumstances we regard the respective
surpluses of £180,047 and £183,047 as trading profits, and we so
hold."

The revenue, naturally, rely strongly upon the final sentence of the
third paragraph. This they say is a finding of fact which ought not to
be disturbed. If that is right, the appeal can be simply disposed of.
C   But is it right? I must say that I cannot so read it. It does not profess,
in itself, to be a finding as to the " original aim." Rather it assumes,
as was the case, that the original aim has been established already, and
is concerned merely to state that the decision to liquidate was not inconsistent with it. Had they, then, already found that the original aim
was, as stated, to invest for retention where possible, or, where not, to
trade? I cannot find this. The initial intention is stated as " primarily
D   for the purposes of creating and retaining investments " and " not
primarily for the purposes of immediate sales after development." This
is a clear finding of an investment purpose—confirmed by the opening
of the next paragraph. Mr. Simmons, the commissioners proceed, " was
or had to be prepared to realise one development " (meaning I think
any one development) " to find . . . funds for another development "—
E   still quite clearly in the area of investment. In the latter part of the
same paragraph it is said that, with the aim of building up an investment
portfolio, the final decision might have to wait on events—very true—
but far from a finding of an intention to trade. And again, as to the
decision to liquidate; there is no finding that this involved a decision
to trade: that would be a very odd finding indeed, and I find it neither
expressed nor implied. So, when one reads this whole passage, and
F   couples it with the record of each company formed as an investment
company, in two cases to acquire a single property, associated with
Bishopsgate Investment Trust Co., Ltd., a company only interested
in property investment and having an agreement that the investment
status of each company would not be altered, acquiring one property
only, in two cases, and in LSP's two properties, under what is called
G   a primary intention to create and build up a portfolio, I can only ask
where is the finding, or evidence of a trading intention? If there was
such an intention, when was it formed? On the decision to liquidate?
But this did nothing more than put an end to Mr. Simmons' investment
plans. So I cannot avoid the conclusion that the reference to " turning
to account by way of trade " is inconsistent with the whole history and
with the previous finding, and involves an assumption—per saltum—as
H   to what had been found, not supported by the latter, and in any case
not itself a finding of fact.

That this reference is illogical and illfounded appears very clearly
from what follows. This draws a line (not contended for by either side)
between properties retained, or likely to be retained, as investments
before the liquidation was contemplated—which are investments—and
those which had not reached that stage—which are trading stock. But
on what principle, or rationale, can this be based? It seems to pre-

Lord Wilberforce   Simmons v. I.R.C. (H.L.(E.))   **[1980]**

suppose that the properties remained, as it were, in the air, or in limbo, A
until development and letting was completed, and that if the portcullis
of liquidation came down while they were in this state they became
trading stock.   This I find, with respect, incomprehensible.   Before
liquidation they must either have been investments or trading stock: if
the latter, cadit quaestio, but that is not what is found.   If the former,
how was their status changed?   Frustration of a plan for investment, B
which compels realisation, even if foreseen as a possibility, surely cannot
give rise to an intention to trade.   Finally, the distinction, as drawn,
does not even fit the facts.   For in the case of Twickenham and LSP
(East Barnet Road) development and letting *had* been completed before
the liquidation (see above).   But they are found to have been trading,
because retention was " unlikely "—a further gloss upon a strange
rationale. C

My Lords, I regret to have to subject the reasoning of the special
commissioners, over which they evidently took much trouble, to what
may appear to be excessive analysis.   I am less reluctant to differ from
them because their solution was not contended for, nor it seems, tested
by argument.   If it had been, some of the anomaly in it might well
have appeared and suffered reduction.   For myself, having read the D
whole of the case stated, and having, as they did, followed the history
of the group, I find the position, though complicated, reasonably plain.
Mr. Simmons wanted to build up an investment portfolio; he formed
investment companies; allied himself with an investment trust; caused
each (relevant) company to acquire one property, or at most two
properties, to develop and let it, and was forced into a realisation of
these completed investments.   This was simply a realisation of capital. E

Finally as to the decision of the Court of Appeal, the judgment,
delivered by Orr L.J., contains a clear account of the facts, and, in my
respectful opinion, a generally correct statement of the law.   In particular,
it is rightly recognised that a sale of an investment does not render its
disposal a sale in the course of trade unless there has been a change
of intention.   They based their decision largely upon a passage from F
the judgment of Asquith L.J. in *Cunliffe* v. *Goodman* [1950] 2 K.B.
237, which was concerned with the making by a landlord of a provisional
—as contrasted with a conditional—decision.   This they sought to apply
to a very different situation, for there is no basis, either in fact or in
finding, for holding Mr. Simmons' intention to be provisional in the
sense of that word in the judgment.   This led to his critical conclusion: G
" The legal position was that until a decision was taken to treat a
property as an investment, it necessarily followed that the surplus realised
on its sale was assessable as a trading profit."   This must mean that it
was trading stock.   But this is contrary to the whole history of the
matter and goes even further than the commissioners' findings.   I regret
that I cannot agree with it. H

I would allow the appeal.

VISCOUNT DILHORNE.   My Lords, giving the commissioners' conclusion
that the sale of the properties in question was a sale of trading stock
the most favourable consideration that I can, I am unable to find in
the case stated and in their findings any justification for that conclusion.
I have had the advantage of reading in draft the speech of my noble

A and learned friend, Lord Wilberforce. I agree with it and in my opinion
for the reasons he gives, this appeal should be allowed.

LORD SALMON. My Lords, I gratefully adopt and will not repeat my
noble and learned friend, Lord Wilberforce's lucid summary of all the
facts found by the commissioners. Since I concur generally in the
conclusions reached by my noble and learned friend, I shall only add a
B few observations of my own.

I do not believe that this appeal raises any question of law, nor any
question as to whether the commissioners' primary findings of fact can
be overruled. Clearly they cannot. I do not, however, consider that all
the inferences which the commissioners drew from those findings can be
accepted, especially the inference which led them to the conclusion that
C the sale of the relevant properties constituted a sale of trading stock.
This conclusion was plainly wrong and should accordingly be rejected:
see *Edwards* v. *Bairstow* [1956] A.C. 14, 35, 36 *per* Lord Radcliffe.

The Simmons group of companies, bar one, were formed as property
investment companies. The commissioners accepted that the acquisitions
of the properties with which those companies were concerned

D   " were initially entered into primarily for the purposes of creating
       and retaining investments, and not primarily for the purposes of
       immediate sales after development . . . [and that] the overall and
       eventual ambition or purpose of Mr. Simmons personally was the
       flotation of a public company when sufficient and suitable invest-
       ments had been gathered together."

E   In 1962 the Simmons property investment group of companies formed
an association with Bishopsgate Property and General Investment Ltd.
(" Bishopsgate "), an associate of Hambros Bank which specialised in
bringing investment companies to the market. On October 4, 1963, the
Simmons group of companies entered into an agreement with Bishopsgate not to alter their business from that of property holding. Bishopsgate
F had an interest of 25 per cent. in each of the properties acquired by the
Simmons group after its association with Bishopsgate. It is plain that each
of these properties were acquired as an investment. There is certainly
no evidence that they were acquired as trading stock. The decision made
in October 1966 to liquidate the Simmons group of investment companies
was because the prospects of these investments had seriously deteriorated.
In such circumstances, the realisation of capital and withdrawal of the
G investments certainly cannot constitute the sale of trading stock. There
was no evidence and indeed no finding that any of the acquired properties
were acquired or even treated as trading stock. They were acquired
solely as investments which eventually turned out to be unsatisfactory.

The final sentence of the third paragraph of the findings of the
commissioners was strongly relied on by the respondents. It reads:

H   " The decision to liquidate was in our view not inconsistent with
       the original aim—to create investments for retention where possible,
       or where not possible for turning to account by way of trade."

A strange concept indeed. An investment does not turn into trading
stock because it is sold. I entirely agree with my noble and learned
friend, Lord Wilberforce, that no such concept can be accepted.

My Lords, I would accordingly allow the appeal.

LORD SCARMAN. My Lords, I have the misfortune to differ from A
the majority of your Lordships in this appeal. I would dismiss it. But,
since my difference of opinion arises not from any controversy of
principle but only because I have formed a view of the facts found by
the special commissioners and of the inferences to be drawn from them
which differs from that of the majority, I shall be brief. There is no
advantage to the parties and no good done to the law in developing a
minority view of the facts at this stage of the case.   B

There is no error of law in the actual statement of the case by the
commissioners. If they did err in law, the error must be inferred in
this sense: that their determination of the case is explicable only on
the basis of some misconception of the law. To use the formula
preferred by Lord Radcliffe in *Edwards* v. *Bairstow* [1956] A.C. 14, 36,
an appellate court must be satisfied that "the true and only reasonable C
conclusion [upon the facts found] contradicts the determination."

The issue is whether certain property transactions of sale carried
out by a number of separate companies under the control of Mr. Lionel
Simmons and his associates were trading transactions. Or were they
sales negotiated reluctantly and under the pressure of financial difficulties
by a property-investment business which was not engaging in trade or D
any adventure in the nature of trade? The appeal is that of one
company only and relates to two transactions, both of which the commissioners found to be trading transactions. But four other appeals by
four other "Simmons companies" stand or fall by the decision in this
case: and, rightly, the commissioners examined (with a thoroughness
which deserves the highest commendation), ten transactions entered into
by seven companies, all of which were controlled by Mr. Simmons and E
his associates.

The essence of their findings is set out in three paragraphs. [His
Lordship read the findings of the commissioners set out by Lord
Wilberforce, *ante*, p. 1200B–H].

Mr. Simmons lacked capital. He entered the property business, as a
poor man. He had to borrow: and on occasions he had to sell. He F
knew his own weakness and the commissioners have found that he was
prepared to sell in order to find or conserve funds for another development. They summed up the effect of their findings in words of recall
at the end of the passage I have quoted. His aim was "to create investments for retention where possible, or where not possible for turning
to account by way of trade." In other words, Mr. Simmons and his
companies, which were the creatures and the instruments of his will, G
traded when he thought it necessary in the interest of his long-term
objective, which was "to create investments for retention." I find
nothing very extraordinary in such attitude, purpose, and conduct.
Almost every trader looks to his profits to build up a capital position:
the existence of Mr. Simmons' long-term objective is not therefore inconsistent with an intention to trade as part of his business when he H
should judge it necessary.

Whether or not I would have reached the same conclusion as that
of the commissioners is not, of course, the question. The House must
be satisfied that the true and only reasonable conclusion upon the facts
is that the challenged transactions were not trading transactions, and is,
therefore, contradictory of their determination. Notwithstanding the
skilled and detailed analysis of the transactions which have been presented

A to your Lordships by counsel at the bar of the House, I am not so satisfied.
I would, therefore, dismiss the appeal.

LORD ROSKILL. My Lords, I have had the advantage of reading in
draft the speech of my noble and learned friend, Lord Wilberforce. For
the reasons therein contained, I would allow this appeal.

B
Appeal allowed.

Solicitors: *Amhurst, Brown, Martin & Nicholson; Solicitor of Inland
Revenue.*

F. C.

C

                              ───────────

                          [COURT OF APPEAL]

                    * DYSON v. KERRIER DISTRICT COUNCIL

D 1980   June 10, 11; 27   Megaw and Brightman L.JJ. and
                                                     Sir Patrick Browne

*Local Government—Housing—Homeless persons—Applicant with
   priority need living in accommodation on short-term unprotected tenancy—Previous tenancy of council flat in another
   housing area voluntarily surrendered—Housing authority's
   decision that threatened homelessness self-induced—Whether
E becoming " homeless intentionally " referable to past events
   —Whether authority entitled to take into account deliberate
   act in giving up prior accommodation — Housing (Homeless
   Persons) Act 1977 (c. 48), s. 17 (1) (2)* [1]

       In September 1978 the plaintiff, who was expecting a baby,
   went to live with her sister in a council flat in Huntingdon
   where the child was born. Shortly afterwards her sister moved
F to Helston but the plaintiff remained in occupation of the flat
   and on October 2, 1978, the council transferred the tenancy
   into her name. On November 10 the plaintiff signed a tenancy
   agreement for a " winter let " of a flat in Helston which
   expired on March 31, 1979. The tenancy was not protected
   by the Rent Act 1977. She then surrendered the tenancy of the
   flat in Huntingdon. Early in 1979 she applied to the defendant
   council, as housing authority, for accommodation representing
G to them that she was homeless because her sister had left the
   Huntingdon flat. The council having ascertained the true position in relation to that flat informed her through their housing
   officer by a letter dated March 19, after a further application
   by her for accommodation, that her homelessness was going
   to be treated as " self-induced." The plaintiff failed to leave
   the flat at the end of the tenancy and the landlord obtained
   an order for possession on May 18 to take effect on May 25.
H Four days before the order took effect the council informed
   the plaintiff that since this was a case of self-induced homelessness they would provide her with accommodation for one
   month from May 25. In fact they allowed her to remain in
   hotel accommodation until July 6. On July 3 they advised
   her formally of the decision of the housing committee on
   July 2 that she was homeless with a priority need but that she
   had become homeless intentionally.

[1] Housing (Homeless Persons) Act 1977, s. 17 (1) (2): see post, p. 1210D–F.

A The plaintiff brought proceedings against the council in the county court seeking declarations that she had not become homeless intentionally, that the council were in breach of their duty under section 4 (4) of the Housing (Homeless Persons) Act 1977 in failing to ensure that accommodation was available for her from July 6, 1979, an order that the council secure that such accommodation was available, and damages.
B Alternatively, she sought a declaration that the council were in breach of their duty under section 4 (3) of the Act in failing to ensure that accommodation was available to her for such period as would give her a reasonable opportunity of herself securing accommodation. Judge Chope dismissed her claims.

On appeal by the plaintiff: —

Held, dismissing the appeal, (1) that although subsections (1) and (2) of section 17 were drafted in the present and future tenses they were in fact referring to past events; that,
C on the true construction of subsection (1), a person became homeless intentionally if he had deliberately done or failed to do anything in consequence of which he had ceased to occupy accommodation which would have been available for his occupation and which it would have been reasonable for him to continue to occupy; that that formula applied to the Huntingdon flat which the plaintiff had surrendered and accordingly the council were entitled to find that she had
D become homeless intentionally on May 25 in consequence of her deliberate act in surrendering the tenancy of that flat; and therefore their only duty on May 25 was to provide her with short-term accommodation under section 4 (3) (post, pp. 1214F—1215c).

(2) That subsection (2) of section 17 must be similarly construed with the result that the plaintiff, on March 19, as the result of her deliberate act, had become threatened with
E homelessness intentionally within the meaning of the subsection; and in the circumstances the council's only duty on March 19 was to furnish her with advice and assistance under section 4 (2) (post, p. 1215c–F).

(3) That the plaintiff had been given sufficient time to find accommodation since it had been made absolutely clear to her four days before she became homeless that she was being considered as a person who was homeless intentionally with
F a priority need for accommodation and that she was being given a month to find such accommodation, and there was no reason to treat the statutory period under section 4 (3) as beginning on July 3 when the formal letter was sent to her, that letter being merely a confirmation of a decision previously made and communicated to her (post, p. 1216B–D).

G The following cases are referred to in the judgment of the court:

De Falco v. *Crawley Borough Council* [1980] Q.B. 460; [1980] 2 W.L.R. 664; [1980] 1 All E.R. 913, C.A.

Youngs v. *Thanet District Council,* The Times, February 21, 1980.

The following additional case was cited in argument:

Reg. v. *Bristol City Council, Ex parte Browne* [1979] 1 W.L.R. 1437; H [1979] 3 All E.R. 344, D.C.

APPEAL from Judge Chope sitting at Camborne and Redruth County Court.

In August 1979 the plaintiff, Miss Fiona Jane Dyson, brought proceedings in the county court against the Kerrier District Council seeking declarations and damages following alleged breaches by the council of their

A statutory duty under the Housing (Homeless Persons) Act 1977. By her amended particulars of claim dated September 18, 1979, she claimed that from November 10, 1978, to May 25, 1979, she had been resident at no. 10, Church Street, Helston, in the County of Cornwall which was within the area for which the council were the housing authority. By order of the Penzance County Court dated May 18, 1979, she had been ordered to

B vacate the premises and had been rendered homeless on May 25, 1979. On March 31, 1979, and again on May 21, 1979, she had applied to the council for accommodation. In the premises on March 31 and/or May 31, 1979, the council had come under a statutory duty pursuant to section 3 of the Act of 1977 to make appropriate inquiries. She alleged that the council had completed the inquiries on July 2, 1979. She stated that she had a dependent child residing with her, that by reason of the matters aforesaid

C she was homeless, that she had a priority need for accommodation within the meaning of section 2 of the Act and had not become homeless intentionally. She alleged that the council were under a statutory duty under section 4 (4) of the Act to secure that accommodation should become available for her occupation; and that in breach of their statutory duty the council, by letter dated July 3, 1979, had informed her that they would not ensure

D that accommodation should be available for her from and after July 6, 1979, and since that date they had failed to secure that accommodation was available to her.

In the alternative the plaintiff claimed that the council, by the letter of July 3, had informed her that they had decided that she was homeless and had a priority need but that in their opinion she had become homeless intentionally; and in the premises they were under a duty pursuant to

E section 4 (5) of the Act of 1977 to secure that accommodation was made available for her occupation for such period as they considered would give her a reasonable opportunity of herself securing accommodation and that in breach of that duty the council had failed to do so. She alleged that she had suffered loss and damage and claimed (1) a declaration that she did not become homeless intentionally; (2) a declaration that the council were in breach of their duty under section 4 (5) of the Act to secure that

F accommodation should become available for her occupation as from July 6, 1979; (3) an order that the council secure that such accommodation was available; (4) damages in addition to or in lieu of the order; (5) in the alternative, a declaration that the council were in breach of their duty under section 4 (3) of the Act in failing to secure that accommodation was available to her for such period as would give her a reasonable opportunity

G of herself securing accommodation; (6) an order that the council secure that such accommodation was available; and (7) damages in addition to or in lieu of the order.

By their defence the council stated that the plaintiff had applied for accommodation on January 15, 1979. She had been interviewed in connection with the application on February 22 and on March 18, 1979, and

H the council had been informed on May 21, 1979, that the Penzance County Court had made a possession order against the plaintiff and that possession was to be given on May 25, 1979. The council admitted that they were under a statutory duty under section 3 of the Act to make appropriate inquiries as from the date of the plaintiff's application for accommodation. They claimed that they had made those inquiries and completed them by March 1979. They denied that they were in breach of their statutory duty under section 4 (4) of the Act and claimed that they were satisfied

that the plaintiff had become threatened with homelessness intentionally A
and in the premises they were under no duty to secure that accommodation should become available for her occupation under section 4 (4). The
council admitted that they sent the plaintiff the letter dated July 3, 1979,
but denied the alleged breach of statutory duty. They admitted that from
on or about March 19, 1979, they were under a duty to secure that
accommodation was made available for the plaintiff's occupation for such B
period as they considered would give her a reasonable opportunity of
herself securing accommodation and claimed that on May 21 they, the
council, had secured accommodation for the plaintiff under section 4 (3)
for a period of 25 days from May 25, 1979, subsequently extended to
July 6, 1979. They denied the alleged breach of statutory duty. They
denied that the plaintiff had suffered any loss or damages or that she was
entitled to the relief sought or any relief. C

By her amended reply the plaintiff claimed that if, which was denied,
the council purported to be satisfied that she was threatened with
homelessness intentionally the decision took into account matters which
should not properly have been taken into account and was made in
error of law in that the council had wrongly taken into account the
reasons for which she had left her previous accommodation in
Huntingdon on November 10, 1978, and that in the premises the decision D
was one which no reasonable council could have reached.

The matter came before Judge Chope in Camborne and Redruth
County Court in October 1979. On October 24, giving judgment, he was
satisfied that the council had made their decision in relation to the
plaintiff's position on March 19, 1979. He considered section 17 of the
Act of 1977 (which defines " intentional homelessness ") and the Code E
of Guidance issued by the Secretary of State pursuant to section 12 of
the Act and took the view that section 17 (1) included an act or
omission deliberately contrived in respect of other accommodation than
the last occupied by the plaintiff. He was satisfied that the plaintiff
took the accommodation in Helston before she gave up her accommodation in Huntingdon knowing that she would have to leave the
accommodation in Helston on March 31, 1979. She therefore did some- F
thing, namely, give up accommodation in Huntingdon and take on
accommodation in Helston the likely result of which would be that she
would be forced to leave the accommodation in Helston. He found that
whether the council took their decision on March 19, 1979, or July 3,
1979, they had not taken into account any matters excluded under
section 17. He gave judgment for the council. G

The plaintiff appealed on four grounds two of which were not pursued.
The substantive grounds were that the judge was wrong in his interpretation of section 17 of the Act of 1977; and that the judge erred in
law in holding that six weeks from the date that the council decided that
the plaintiff had become homeless or threatened with homelessness intentionally was such period as would give her a reasonable opportunity of
herself securing accommodation for her occupation within the provisions H
of section 4 (3) of the Act.

The facts are stated in the judgment of the court.

J. W. Black Q.C. and *David Fletcher* for the plaintiff.
Konrad Schiemann Q.C. and *John Haines* for the council.

Cur. adv. vult.

A   June 27. BRIGHTMAN L.J. read the following judgment of the court. This is an appeal from a decision of Judge Chope given on October 15, 1979, in the Camborne/Redruth County Court. It raises questions under the Housing (Homeless Persons) Act 1977, and in particular section 17. A dispute arose between the local authority, the Kerrier District Council, and a homeless person, the plaintiff, Miss Fiona Dyson, as a result of which the plaintiff brought an action against the district council for a declaration that they were bound to secure that accommodation was available for her, and also for damages. The judge dismissed the action. Miss Dyson appeals.

We turn first to the Act of 1977. The long title states, as its first purpose, that of making further provision as to the functions of local authorities with respect to persons who are homeless or threatened with homelessness. The material sections are 1 to 4, 8 and 17. It is not necessary to read them at length, except section 17, but we will indicate the general scheme of the Act.

Section 1 (1) defines a person as " homeless " if he has no accommodation if (among other things) there is no accommodation which he is entitled to occupy by virtue of an interest in it or of an order of the court, or which he has an express or implied licence to occupy. Under subsection (3) a person is " threatened with homelessness " if it is likely that he will become homeless within 28 days. Each of such persons is defined by section 2 as having " a priority need for accommodation " if (among other things) he has a dependent child residing with him.

Section 3 imposes certain preliminary duties on housing authorities in cases of possible homelessness. A housing authority is defined as a local authority for the purposes of the Housing Act 1957. In the present case the Kerrier District Council are the housing authority. Under section 3, if a person applies to a housing authority for accommodation, the authority are required to make inquiries in order to satisfy themselves first, whether the applicant is homeless or threatened with homelessness, and, if so, whether he has a priority need and whether he became homeless or threatened with homelessness " intentionally."

Upon completion of their inquiries the housing authority have to make certain decisions. If they are satisfied that the applicant is either homeless or threatened with homelessness, duties are imposed upon them under the somewhat complex provisions of section 4. The nature of these duties varies according to whether the authority are satisfied that the applicant is homeless or is threatened with homelessness, whether they are satisfied that he has a priority need, and whether they are satisfied that he did not become homeless or threatened with homelessness " intentionally." The section, in fact, deals with four categories of applicants who are homeless or threatened with homelessness, although the section is not drafted by reference to categories. Category 1, the applicant who has no priority need; category 2, the applicant who has a priority need but becomes threatened with homelessness " intentionally "; in both these cases the duty of the authority is confined to furnishing him with advice and appropriate assistance (as defined); category 3, the applicant who has a priority need and is homeless " intentionally "; the duty of the authority is not only to furnish advice and appropriate assistance but also " to secure that

accommodation is made available for his occupation for such period as
they consider will give him a reasonable opportunity of himself securing
accommodation for his occupation "; category 4, the applicant who is
threatened with homelessness or is homeless " unintentionally "; the
duty of the authority (put shortly) is to secure that accommodation is
available for his occupation indefinitely.

The applicant for accommodation will need to know where he
stands. So section 8 provides that, on completing their inquiries under
section 3, the housing authority are to notify the applicant of their
decision whether he is homeless or threatened with homelessness, and,
if so, whether he has a priority need, whether he became homeless or
threatened with homelessness " intentionally " and whether they are
notifying any other housing authority. In certain circumstances, not
arising in this case, the housing authority to whom application has been
made may transfer their responsibilities to another housing authority.

Section 17 defines " intentionally " for the purposes of the Act. The
section reads as follows, but only subsections (1) and (2) are material
for present purposes:

" (1) Subject to subsection (3) below, for the purposes of this Act
a person becomes homeless intentionally if he deliberately does or
fails to do anything in consequence of which he ceases to occupy
accommodation which is available for his occupation and which
it would have been reasonable for him to continue to occupy.
(2) Subject to subsection (3) below, for the purposes of this Act a
person becomes threatened with homelessness intentionally if he
deliberately does or fails to do anything the likely result of which
is that he will be forced to leave accommodation which is available for his occupation and which it would have been reasonable
for him to continue to occupy. (3) An act or omission in good
faith on the part of a person who was unaware of any relevant fact
is not to be treated as deliberate for the purposes of subsection (1)
or (2) above. (4) Regard may be had, in determining for the purposes of subsections (1) and (2) above whether it would have been
reasonable for a person to continue to occupy accommodation, to
the general circumstances prevailing in relation to housing in the
area of the housing authority to whom he applied for accommodation or for assistance in obtaining accommodation."

We turn now to the facts. At the beginning of 1978 the plaintiff
was expecting a child. At that time she was living with a friend in a
rented flat, the details of which are not relevant to this appeal. In
July she gave up her flat, and stayed for three weeks in Porthleven with
her mother and her sister Janet. She then went to stay with her sister
Linda, who had a council flat at 61, Essex Road, Huntingdon. The
plaintiff's child Natasha was born in September, when the plaintiff was
living with her sister at the Huntingdon address. At the end of
September the plaintiff's sister Linda left the Huntingdon flat and moved
to other accommodation, no. 10a, Church Street, Helston, Cornwall.
The plaintiff remained for the time being in sole occupation of the
Huntingdon flat. On October 2 or thereabouts the tenancy of the
Huntingdon flat was transferred by the local authority into the plaintiff's
name. The plaintiff soon made up her mind to leave the Huntingdon

A flat and go to Cornwall. On November 10 she signed a tenancy agreement of no. 10, Church Street, Helston, next door to her sister Linda. The tenancy was only for 3½ months, from November 10, 1978, to March 31, 1979. She would have to leave on March 31, 1979, because her tenancy was not protected. It was what is known as a winter letting. It contained a clause under which the tenant acknowledged that she had received notice that the landlord would require possession of
B the property for holiday letting at the expiry of the term thereby created in accordance with Schedule 3, Part II, to the Rent Act 1968, now Part II of Schedule 15 to the Rent Act 1977. The plaintiff was therefore well aware of her position under that agreement. After she had signed the tenancy agreement, she surrendered the Huntingdon flat to the local authority.

C Two months after going to Cornwall, on January 19, 1979, the plaintiff applied to the local housing authority for accommodation. She filled up a printed form and sent it to the Kerrier District Council. She was not quite truthful about the position in her accompanying letter. She represented to the district council that she was homeless because her sister had left the Huntingdon flat. This was not the case.
D On February 22 the plaintiff called on the welfare officer, Mr. Edkins, at Helston. By then the district council had ascertained the true position in relation to the Huntingdon flat and knew that it had been transferred into her name. Mr. Edkins informed the plaintiff that the district council were going to treat her pending homelessness as "self-induced." A letter to this effect was sent to her on the same
E day signed by the housing officer of the district council, but the judge in the county court was not, we think, satisfied that she in fact received it. She called again on March 19, 1979. A letter to the like effect was sent to her on that day. There is no doubt that she received that letter.

The situation on January 19, when the plaintiff first applied to the
F district council, was that the council had no duty towards her under the Act of 1977. She was not at that time homeless. Nor was she threatened with homelessness, because more than 28 days would elapse before she was likely to become homeless. Her tenancy of no. 10 was not due to expire until March 31, 1979. She became "threatened with homelessness" on or immediately after March 3. The duties of the district council under the Act of 1977 accordingly then arose, if
G her previous application for accommodation ought properly to be regarded as brought forward to that date, or at any rate arose when the plaintiff called at the Helston office on March 19 and repeated her application. The judge found as a fact that a decision was taken with relation to the plaintiff on March 19 and that such decision was taken by the housing officer, who signed the letter of March 19, as
H the duly authorised agent of the district council. It is implicit in that letter that the district council had decided that she was threatened with homelessness, and that this was "intentional" within the meaning of the Act of 1977, and it is not in dispute that they recognised that she had a priority need for accommodation within the meaning of the Act.

The plaintiff failed to give up possession of no. 10, Church Street on March 31, 1979. Thereupon she became homeless within the meaning of the Act of 1977, because she was not entitled to occupy the **A** premises by virtue of an interest in it or a licence, or an order of the court. She was a mere trespasser. The landlord was compelled to take proceedings. A possession order was made on May 18, but possession was not ordered to be given up until May 25. Technically, we think that she may have ceased to be homeless between May 18 and 25, because she was then in occupation, in a sense, by virtue of a court order. We will treat May 25, 1979, as the date on which she **B** finally became homeless.

When the plaintiff became homeless, on the assumption that the district council were satisfied, and were properly satisfied, that this was " intentional," they came under a duty under section 4 (3) of the Act of 1977 to secure that accommodation was available for her occupation for such period as they considered would give her **C** a reasonable opportunity of herself securing accommodation for her occupation. Alternatively, if the district council could not properly have decided that she was threatened with homelessness " intentionally," they came under a duty to secure that accommodation was made available for her occupation indefinitely.

On May 21 the district council wrote to inform her that they **D** would assist with accommodation for a period of one month at a hotel in Helston as from May 25, subject to her paying a small weekly amount to the hotel. In fact, the district council allowed the plaintiff to stay on at the hotel until July 6. On July 3, only three days before she was due to leave, the secretary to the district council addressed to her a formal letter, telling her that, at a meeting of the housing committee held on July 2, the following decisions had been reached: **E** (a) that she was homeless, (b) that she had a priority need, (c) that in their opinion she became homeless intentionally, and (d) that they did not propose to notify any other housing authority that her application had been made. The letter also set out the housing committee's reasons for the decision made in paragraph (c).

Two issues arise. First, did the district council correctly construe **F** and apply section 17 in deciding that she became threatened with homelessness, and became homeless, " intentionally "? If so, did they secure that accommodation was made available for her occupation for a period which could properly be considered as giving her a reasonable opportunity of herself securing accommodation for her occupation? The first question is the important one. If the plaintiff's homelessness could not properly be treated as " intentional," then **G** there is no doubt that the district council became and are liable to secure accommodation for her occupation indefinitely. The second question arises under section 4 (3). It depends on whether the district council had completed their statutory inquiries under section 3 and made their decision at the time when they wrote their letter of May 21, and whether such letter was a sufficient notification to the plaintiff **H** of their decision, or whether such decision was not made until July 2, and notified on July 3. In the latter case the period of two or three days allowed to her for making her own arrangements to secure accommodation was admittedly inadequate.

The argument on behalf of the plaintiff before the judge in the county court was that the district council were not entitled under section 17 to look at what had happened at Huntingdon. The council

A were only entitled to look at what the plaintiff had done or omitted to do in relation to the accommodation she was occupying immediately before she became homeless or threatened with homelessness. By taking into account what happened at Huntingdon, the district council considered matters which they were not entitled to consider on a proper interpretation of section 17. The judge came to the conclusion
B that section 17 (1) included an act or omission deliberately contrived in respect of accommodation other than that last occupied by the applicant. Section 17 (2) was to be construed in parallel manner. The district council were therefore entitled to find on March 19, 1979, that she had become threatened with homelessness intentionally; and that, when she became actually homeless, that also was " intentional." He also held that, as she was notified on March 19, 1979, that she was
C being treated as a case of intentional homelessness, she was allowed sufficient time pursuant to section 4 (3) for securing her own accommodation.

There are four grounds of appeal specified in the notice of appeal. First, that there was no sufficient evidence enabling the judge to hold that the district council reached a decision on March 19, 1979. That
D ground was not pursued. Secondly, that the judge was wrong in law in his interpretation of section 17 in holding that the district council were entitled to take the Huntingdon situation into account. Thirdly, that the judge was wrong in holding that the district council were not obliged to follow a statement in the Code of Guidance (1977) issued by the Secretary of State for the Environment under the provisions of section 12 of the Act of 1977, which expresses the view
E that the most immediate cause of homelessness has greater relevance than past events. That ground was not pursued, having regard to the decision of this court in *De Falco* v. *Crawley Borough Council* [1980] Q.B. 460. Fourthly, that the judge erred in law in holding that six weeks from the date that the district council decided that the plaintiff had become homeless or threatened with homelessness intentionally, was such period as would give her a reasonable opportunity
F of securing accommodation for her occupation under section 4 (3) of the Act of 1977. This ground also was not pursued. The point was, however, taken that the statutory period was not capable of starting before July 3, 1979, so that the period allowed was only two or three days.

Certain matters are common ground between the parties, which
G it will be convenient to state. (1) The plaintiff was entitled to occupy the Huntingdon flat and, while she did so, she was not homeless. (2) The plaintiff voluntarily left the Huntingdon flat. (3) The plaintiff knew when she took the Helston flat that her tenancy of it would expire on March 31, 1979. (4) If the plaintiff had not left the Huntington flat in October 1978 she would not have found herself threatened with homelessness in March 1979. (5) She applied to the
H Kerrier District Council for permanent accommodation. (6) This application was refused on the ground that her homelessness was self-induced because she had no need to leave the Huntingdon flat. (7) The court should only interfere if satisfied that the council, when dealing with her application for permanent accommodation in Kerrier, was not entitled to take into account the fact that, if she had not left her Huntingdon flat in October 1978, she would not have found

herself homeless in March 1979. (8) Subsections (1) and (2) of section A 17 of the Act of 1977 should not be construed in such a way that different results are reached before and after homelessness. There are no policy reasons for drawing any distinction between subsection (1) and subsection (2).

As we have already indicated, counsel for the plaintiff submits that, as both subsections (1) and (2) are couched in the present tense, they relate only to the existing home, if one exists, or to the last home B if none exists. That is to say, subsection (1) is directed to the case of a homeless person who loses his *last* home because he has done or failed to do something in consequence of which he ceases to occupy that accommodation which is available for his occupation. Subsection (2) is directed to the case of a person who is threatened with the loss of his *existing* home because he does or fails to do something the likely C result of which is that he will be forced to leave that accommodation which is available for his occupation.

Neither subsection, it was submitted, can apply to this case. The argument is formidable. On March 19, 1979, when the district council made their decision, the plaintiff was threatened with homelessness. Therefore, the relevant subsection is subsection (2). Subsection (2) D says that a person becomes threatened with homelessness " intentionally " if he deliberately does or fails to do anything " the likely result of which is that he *will be* forced to leave accommodation which *is available* for his occupation." The Huntingdon flat cannot be treated as that accommodation, because it was not accommodation which, on March 19, the plaintiff " will be forced to leave." She had already left it. Nor could it be said on March 19 that it was accom- E modation " which is available " for the plaintiff's occupation, because it was not so available. Nor can the Helston flat be treated as accommodation within the subsection. It was not available for her after March 31, 1979. In the result, it was submitted, neither the Huntingdon flat nor the Helston flat was accommodation within subsection (2). Nor does subsection (1) apply. She did not become F finally homeless until May 25, 1979. The accommodation which she then ceased to occupy was not accommodation " which is available " for her occupation.

Although subsections (1) and (2) of section 17 are drafted in the present and future tenses, they are in fact also referring to past events. Subsection (1) reads:

> ". . . a person becomes homeless intentionally if he deliberately G does or fails to do anything in consequence of which he ceases to occupy accommodation which is available for his occupation and which it would have been reasonable for him to continue to occupy."

This subsection is dealing with cause and effect. The subsection states H the effect first. The specified effect is the state of being homeless. The subsection specifies that effect and then describes a particular cause which, if it exists, requires the effect to be treated as intentional. The subsection therefore means

> " a person becomes homeless intentionally if he deliberately *has* done or failed to do anything in consequence of which he *has* ceased to occupy accommodation which *was* available for his

A   occupation and which it would have been reasonable for him to
     continue to occupy."

Does that formulation apply to the Huntingdon flat? In our judgment it does. The district council were entitled to reach the conclusion that the plaintiff became homeless on May 25, 1979, intentionally
because she deliberately had done something (surrendered the Hun-
B tingdon tenancy) in consequence of which she ceased to occupy accommodation (the Huntingdon flat) which was available for her occupation and which it would have been reasonable for her to continue to
occupy; and that, therefore, if she had not done that deliberate act
she would not have become homeless on May 25.

     In the result, when the plaintiff became homeless on May 25, the
district council had no duty under section 4 (5) to house her perma-
C nently.

     We must now consider whether a similar result flows from sub-
section (2). By parity of reasoning this subsection means that a person
becomes threatened with homelessness intentionally if he deliberately
has done or failed to do anything the likely result of which is that
he will be forced to leave accommodation which is available for his
D occupation and which it would have been reasonable for him to continue to occupy. On March 19, 1979, it could properly be said of the
plaintiff that she *had* previously done something (surrendered the
Huntingdon tenancy) the likely and indeed the inevitable result of
which was that she would be forced to leave accommodation (the
Huntingdon flat) which was available for her occupation and which
     it would have been reasonable for her to continue to occupy; as a
E result of which she was, on March 19, 1979, threatened with homelessness on March 31, intentionally. Therefore, the district council
could properly take the view, which they did take, on March 19 that
subsection (2) was satisfied.

     In the result the only duty of the district council on March 19,
1979, when the plaintiff was threatened with homelessness, was to
F furnish advice and appropriate assistance under section 4 (2), and their
only duty on May 25, 1979, when she became homeless, was to secure
short-term accommodation for her under section 4 (3).

     We must refer briefly once more to the *De Falco* case [1980]
Q.B. 460 where it seems possible that a similar point arose, although
it was not taken. The facts were these. Mr. and Mrs. De Falco
G lived in Italy. They decided to come to England to work. They gave
up their home in Italy and arrived in this country in February 1979.
They first took a room rent free with Mrs. De Falco's brother at
Horsham. They left in June because the brother needed the room.
They then went to stay with another relative in Crawley. In
September this relative gave them what is called in the report " a
notice to quit," as the relative needed the room for others. The De
H Falcos then applied to the local authority for accommodation under
the Act of 1977. The authority decided that they were intentionally
homeless within the meaning of section 17. The case came before this
court on appeal from the refusal of a motion for interlocutory relief.
The appeal proceeded on the basis that the accommodation voluntarily given up was the home in Italy. It was not argued that the
only relevant accommodation for the purposes of section 17 was the
last accommodation occupied, namely, the Crawley house, and that

the De Falcos did not give up that accommodation voluntarily. As
the point arising in this case was not argued, and in any event it is
difficult to tell from the report what (if any) interest in, or licence
to occupy, the Horsham and Crawley houses was enjoyed by the De
Falcos, the decision is of no assistance to us on this appeal. We also
had read to us a report of *Youngs* v. *Thanet District Council*, The
Times, February 21, 1980. That also was a case of successive places
of accommodation, but we do not think that there is any similarity
with the case which we have to consider.

The only other point is the sufficiency of the period of accommodation which the district council secured for the plaintiff to enable her
to find her own accommodation. The question, put shortly, is
whether that period ought to be reckoned from July 3, 1979, when the
formal letter was written by the district council to the plaintiff, or
from an earlier date. The temporary accommodation was provided
from May 25, 1979, for a period of one month, subsequently extended.
The letter of May 21, written therefore four days before the plaintiff
became homeless, made it absolutely clear to the plaintiff that she
was being considered as a person " intentionally " homeless who had
a priority need for accommodation. She was, therefore, being given
at least a month in order to find her own accommodation. We can
see no reason for treating the statutory period under section 4 (3) as
commencing on July 3, 1979, when the formal letter was written to
her. That letter was merely confirmation of a decision previously made
and communicated to her, and is of no particular relevance.

For these reasons indicated we dismiss the appeal.

> *Appeal dismissed with costs not to*
> *be enforced without leave of court.*
> *Leave to appeal refused.*

Solicitors: *Randle, Thomas & Thomas, Helston, Cornwall; P. J. A.*
Andrews, Solicitor, Kerrier District Council, Camborne.

E. M. W.

A

[CHANCERY DIVISION]

***In re* BELL'S INDENTURE**

BELL AND ANOTHER *v.* HICKLEY AND OTHERS

[1970 B No. 907]

B

1979   Jan. 16, 17, 18; 26   Vinelott J.

*Trusts—Trustee—Breach of trust—Trustees dissipating trust funds
—Solicitor assisting trustees in contravening terms of trust—
Liability of solicitor's partner for breaches of trust—Trustees
liability to replace assets dissipated—Whether estate duty saving
to be deducted in assessing compensation—Partnership Act*
C   *1890 (53 & 54 Vict., c. 39), ss. 10, 11*

By a marriage settlement, the settlor settled property on
himself for life subject to certain charges and, by his will, he
devised that property to his son, A, for life with various
remainders over. In 1940 A and his mother, the settlor's
widow, became the only trustees of the trusts created by the
marriage settlement and the will and between then and 1947
D   they dissipated the whole trust fund. They did so with the
knowledge and in some instances the active assistance of H,
who was a partner in the firm of solicitors acting for the
trustees. Although H's partner had no knowledge of the
breaches of trust, moneys received and paid in breach of trust
passed through the firm's client account held in the name of
the trustees. One breach of trust was the sale of a farm in
1947 to the trustees, who included H, of a voluntary settlement
made by A. Those trustees sold the farm in 1949 at its market
E   value.

A died in 1959 and the life interest passed to his mother
and, after her death, to a nephew and subsequently to a niece.
The plaintiffs, who had contingent interests under the will
trusts, made inquiries and in 1967 they discovered that A and
his mother had dissipated the trust funds. They brought
proceedings against H, the executors of his partner's estate and
F   the executrix of A's estate claiming the replacement of various
sums and assets dissipated in breach of trust. H died before
the hearing of the action and his executors were joined as
defendants. It was conceded that A was liable as a trustee
for breaches of trust, that H was liable as a constructive trustee
in so far as he assisted in the breaches of trust and that, if the
farm had not been sold in 1947, it would have been properly
sold by the trustees of the marriage settlement and will in 1949
G   for the sum obtained by the trustees of the voluntary settlement.
The Estate Duty Office gave assurances that if any moneys
were recovered, they would not seek to recover duty payable
on the deaths of the life tenants.

On the question whether H's partner was liable either as
constructive trustee or under sections 10 and 11 of the Partnership Act 1890 [1]; the date at which the farm should be valued

H   [1] Partnership Act 1890, s. 10: " Where, by any wrongful act or omission of
any partner acting in the ordinary course of business of the firm, or with the
authority of his co-partners, loss or injury is caused to any person not being a
partner in the firm, or any penalty incurred, the firm is liable therefor to the
same extent as the partner so acting or omitting to act."
S. 11: " In the following cases; namely—(*a*) Where one partner acting within
the scope of his apparent authority receives the money or property of a third
person and misapplies it; and (*b*) Where a firm in the course of its business receives
money or property of a third person, and the money or property so received is
misapplied by one or more of the partners while it is in the custody of the firm;
the firm is liable to make good the loss."

In re Bell's Indenture (Ch.D.)   **[1980]**

and whether the fact that estate duty had been waived should   **A**
be taken into account when assessing liability: —

Held, (1) that a solicitor in the ordinary course of his
practice had the implied authority of his partners to accept
trust moneys as agent of the trustees but he had no implied
authority to accept office as a trustee and so make his
co-partners liable for any misapplication of trust property;
that, therefore, although H was liable in so far as he assisted
with knowledge in the misappropriation of the trust property   **B**
as a constructive trustee, the moneys had not been received
by the partnership as trustees and H's partner was neither
liable as a constructive trustee nor under sections 10 and 11
of the Partnership Act 1890 and that being so, it was immaterial that the moneys had been paid into the firm's client
account (post, pp. 1225H—1226A, 1230c–D, G—1231A).

    Blyth v. *Fladgate* [1891] 1 Ch. 337 distinguished.

    Mara v. *Browne* [1896] 1 Ch. 199, C.A. applied.   **C**

(2) That where a trust asset was sold in breach of trust but
would have been properly sold at a later date, the trustees
were only liable to replace the asset at its value at that date
rather than at the date of judgment (post, p. 1232E–F, H).

    In re Massingberd's Settlement (1890) 63 L.T. 296, C.A.
applied.

Per curiam. The decision in *In re Massingberd's Settlement*
that the date for valuing assets sold in breach of trust was   **D**
the date of issue of the writ was reached per incuriam and the
correct date should be the date of judgment (post, p. 1233F–G).

(3) That a trustee who deliberately misappropriated trust
assets for his own benefit or for the benefit of a third party,
whether an express or a constructive trustee, was liable to
restore the assets without deducting any tax that might have
been paid upon the trust fund if the assets had not been
misappropriated (post, pp. 1235H—1236A, 1237B–c).   **E**

    British Transport Commission v. *Gourley* [1965] A.C. 185,
H.L.(E.) distinguished.

The following cases are referred to in the judgment:

Blyth v. *Fladgate* [1891] 1 Ch. 337.
Brinsden v. *Williams* [1894] 3 Ch. 185.
British Transport Commission v. *Gourley* [1956] A.C. 185; [1956] 2   **F**
    W.L.R. 41: [1955] 3 All E.R. 796, H.L.(E.).
Dornford v. *Dornford* (1806) 12 Ves. 127.
Fryer, In re (1857) 3 K. & J. 317.
Mara v. *Browne* [1896] 1 Ch. 199, C.A.
Massingberd's Settlement, In re (1890) 63 L.T. 296, C.A.
Phillipson v. *Gatty* (1848) 7 Hare 516.
Vyse v. *Foster* (1872) L.R. 8 Ch. App. 309.   **G**

The following additional cases were cited in argument:

Atkinson v. *Mackreth* (1866) L.R. 2 Eq. 570.
Barker, decd., In re (1898) 77 L.T. 712.
Belmont Finance Corporation Ltd. v. *Williams Furniture Ltd.* [1979]
    Ch. 250; [1978] 3 W.L.R. 712; [1979] 1 All E.R. 118, C.A.
Dimes v. *Scott* (1828) 4 Russ. 195.   **H**
Docker v. *Somes* (1834) 2 My. & K. 655.
Kellaway v. *Johnson* (1842) 5 Beav. 319.
Lewis, Ex parte; In re Leonard (1819) 1 Gl. & J. 69.
Pauling's Settlement Trusts, In re [1964] Ch. 303; [1963] 3 W.L.R. 742;
    [1963] 3 All E.R. 1, C.A.
Phipps v. *Boardman* [1967] 2 A.C. 46; [1966] 3 W.L.R. 1009; [1966]
    3 All E.R. 721, H.L.(E.).

A   *Plumer* v. *Gregory* (1874) L.R. 18 Eq. 621.
     Somerset, In re [1894] 1 Ch. 231, C.A.
     Wiles v. *Gresham* (1854) 2 Drew. 258.
     Windsor Steam Coal Co. (1901) *Ltd., In re* [1929] 1 Ch. 151, C.A.

ACTION

B   By a marriage settlement of July 9, 1907, and by his will dated January
22, 1912, the settlor, Matthew Gerald Edward Bell, settled property
known as the Bourne and Milton Estates on his son, Matthew Alexander
Henry Bell (Alexander), for life, with remainders to his sons in tail male,
with remainders over. Alexander died on April 6, 1959, leaving no issue,
and his mother, Mary Bell, took a life interest. On her death on October
7, 1962, the settlor's nephew Lord Sackville, took a life interest, and on
C   his death on July 4, 1965, his sister, Diana Sackville West, later Lady Hall,
took a life interest. On her death without issue on June 23, 1975, after
proceedings had been commenced, the first plaintiff, Cecil George Beresford
Bell, took a life interest with remainders to his issue in tail male. In the
event of the failure of those remainders the second plaintiff, Shurland
Robin Dumergue Bell, would take a life interest with similar remainders
over.

D   On February 6, 1970, the plaintiffs issued a writ claiming against the
first defendant, Anthony North Hickley, the second defendant, Alfred
John Langton Heaver, who had been Mr. Hickley's partner, the third
defendant, Beauchamp Stuart Pell, the surviving executors of Alfred
Heaver and the fourth defendant, Marion Babette Bell, the executrix of Matthew Alexander Henry Bell, replacement of the sum of
E   £25,819 14s. 3d., against Mr. Hickley and Miss Bell the replacement of
the sum of £418 1s. 2d., against Mr. Hickley an account of the profit
made upon the purchase and resale by himself and Mrs. Bell of Churchill
Farm, against Mr. Hickley and Mr. Heaver's executors the replacement
of the sum of £52 18s. 8d., commission on an annuity bought for Mrs.
Bell out of trust funds, against Miss Bell replacement of the sums of
£969 6s. 8d. and £5,000, all those sums representing trust assets dissipated
F   in breach of trust, against Mr. Hickley and Mr. Heaver's executors
damages for negligence and against Mr. Hickley and Miss Bell damages
for conspiracy. The writ also claimed against Miss Bell, the fifth
defendant, Lady Hall, the sixth and seventh and eighth defendants, the
children of the second plaintiff, and the ninth and tenth defendants, the
plaintiffs' sisters, an order for the appointment of trustees of the trusts
G   of the marriage settlement and the will. Mr. Hickley died on September
5, 1972, and by an order of April 5, 1973, the proceedings were carried
on against his executors the eleventh and twelfth defendants. On July
1, 1975, the plaintiffs were by order of the court appointed trustees of
the marriage settlement and the will.

The facts are stated in the judgment.

H   *D. Gidley Scott* for the plaintiffs.
Martin Nourse Q.C. and *Nigel Hague* for the second, third, eleventh
and twelfth defendants.
Roger Horne for the fourth defendant.
The remaining defendants did not appear and were not represented.

Cur. adv. vult.

January 26, 1979. VINELOTT J. read the following judgment. This A
action gives rise to a number of issues of importance which relate to
certain admitted breaches of trust by the Hon. Mary Bell and her son,
Matthew Alexander Henry Bell (whom I will call " Mrs. Bell " and
" Alexander " respectively) in their capacity as the trustees of first a
marriage settlement dated July 9, 1907, and, secondly, the trusts of the
will of Matthew Gerald Edward Bell, who was the settlor of the property
comprised in the marriage settlement and to whom I shall refer as B
" the settlor."

The facts are not in dispute and may be shortly stated as follows. The
marriage settlement was an ante-nuptial settlement and was made between
the settlor of the first part, Mrs. Bell (then a spinster) of the second part,
Kathleen Matilda Bell of the third part and Charles John Sackville West
and the Hon. Alfred Ernest Yorke (as trustees thereof) of the fourth part. C
By the settlement, the settlor conveyed certain freehold lands known as
the Bourne and Milton Estates to the use of the parties thereto of the
fourth part (therein referred to as " the settlement trustees ") for a term
of 500 years commencing from the date of the marriage between the
settlor and Mrs. Bell (which took place on July 11, 1905) upon the trusts
thereinafter declared and subject thereto to the use that from the date of
the said marriage during the remainder of the life of Fanny Cecilia Bell D
(the settlor's grandmother) the settlor so long as he should live and after
his death Mrs. Bell so long as she should live should receive a yearly
rent charge of £500 to be charged upon and issuing out of the said
settled property and subject and charged as aforesaid to the use of
the settlor and his assigns during his life with remainder to the use
that if Mrs. Bell should survive the settlor she should thenceforth during E
the remainder of her life receive a yearly rent charge of £800 to be
charged upon and issuing out of all the said property and subject and
charged as aforesaid to the use of the settlor in fee simple. By clause
3 of the marriage settlement it was provided that the said settled
property was limited to the settlement trustees for the said term
of 500 years upon trust that they should by all or any of the means
therein set forth or by any other reasonable means raise the said F
yearly rent charge of £500. By clause 6 the settlement trustees were
appointed trustees of the marriage settlement and of every compound
settlement consisting of the marriage settlement and of any subsequent
instrument for the purposes of the Settled Land Acts. By clause 7 the
settlor and Mrs. Bell during their joint lives and the survivor of them
during his or her life was given power to appoint a new trustee or new G
trustees of the marriage settlement.

The settlor died on May 8, 1926, leaving Mrs. Bell surviving him.
There was one child only of the marriage, namely, Alexander. By his will
dated January 22, 1912, the settlor appointed Mrs. Bell and Percy Leigh
Pemberton to be his executors and trustees. He devised a dwelling house
known as Oswalds, and the premises occupied therewith to the use of Mrs.
Bell for life and after her death to the uses declared thereafter of and H
concerning the Bourne and Milton Estates. By clause 4 he bequeathed all
his chattels in or about Oswalds in trust to permit Mrs. Bell to have the
use and enjoyment thereof during her life and after her death to hold the
same upon the like trusts as were thereinafter declared of and concerning
the settlor's leasehold, copyhold and customary estates and his plate and
diamonds and furniture in or about his mansion house at Bourne Park.
By clause 5, after reciting the marriage settlement and the death of his

A grandmother, he confirmed the marriage settlement and declared that the provisions intended to be made by the will for Mrs. Bell were in addition to the provision made for her by the marriage settlement, and by clause 6 he devised the Bourne and Milton Estates and his other freehold lands and hereditaments to the use of Alexander for life, with usual remainders to his sons in tail male with divers remainders over which I shall set out in more detail later in this judgment. By clause 7 he declared that if any

B person to whom an estate in tail male by purchase in the Bourne and Milton Estates was thereinbefore limited should be born in his lifetime, such limitation should not take effect and in lieu thereof such person was given a life interest with usual remainders to his sons in tail male and then daughters in tail male successively in order of seniority. Clause 14 and clause 15 contain gifts of leasehold, copyhold and customary estates and

C certain specified chattels and of the residue of his personal estate upon the trusts that would have been applicable thereto if they had been capital moneys arising on the sale of his real estate under the Settled Land Acts.

In the events which happened, the effective limitations of the Bourne and Milton Estates under the joint effect of clauses 6 and 7 of the settlor's will were as follows: first, as I have mentioned, Alexander took a life interest. He died on April 6, 1959. On his death, Mrs. Bell took a life

D interest. She died on October 7, 1962. On her death the settlor's nephew, Edward Charles Sackville West, who later became the fifth Baron Sackville (and to whom I shall refer as Lord Sackville) took a life interest. He died on July 4, 1965. On his death, the settlor's niece, who at the date of the will was Diana Sackville West and who later became Lady Hall, took a life interest. She died on June 23, 1975, after the commencement of these proceedings. On her death, the first plaintiff, Cecil George Beresford

E Bell, son of the settlor's cousin, Shurland Bell, took a life interest with remainder to his sons and then daughters successively according to seniority in tail male. He has not had any issue. On the death of the first plaintiff, and in the event of failure of the limitations to his sons and daughters in tail, the first plaintiff's brother, Shurland Robin Dumergue Bell, if he survives, will take a life interest with remainder to his sons and

F then daughters successively according to seniority in tail male. He has two sons, namely, the sixth and seventh defendants, Matthew Forbes Shurland Bell and Richard John Beresford Bell (a minor), and one daughter, namely, the eighth defendant, Fiona Bell. On the death of the second plaintiff and in the event of the failure of those limitations in tail, the plaintiff's elder sister, Daphne Edith Bridge—the ninth defendant—if she survives will similarly take a life interest with remainders to her sons

G and then daughters successively according to seniority in tail male with remainder to the plaintiff's younger sister, Heather Pauline Nutting, the tenth defendant, with remainders to her sons and then daughters successively according to seniority in tail male. Neither of the plaintiffs' two sisters has had any children. There is an ultimate remainder to the settlor's own right heir who was in the event Alexander.

H The devolution of the trusteeship of the marriage settlement and will is as follows. Probate of the will except settled land was granted on August 7, 1926, to Mrs. Bell and Percy Leigh Pemberton, the executors and trustees appointed by the will. Probate of the will limited to land settled by the marriage settlement was granted to the trustees of the marriage settlement on September 11, 1926. By a deed of appointment dated September 5, 1927, Mrs. Bell appointed herself and Percy Leigh Pemberton to be the trustees of the marriage settlement in place of the trustees originally appointed. On June 24, 1935, Mrs. Bell appointed A Charles Leigh Pemberton to be a trustee of the marriage settlement and of the will in place of Percy Leigh Pemberton who died on March 25, 1934. On April 17, 1940, Mrs. Bell appointed Alexander to be a trustee of the marriage settlement and of the will in place of Charles Leigh Pemberton who thereby retired. Thus from April 17, 1940, Mrs. Bell and Alexander were the trustees of the marriage settlement and the will. No trustees were appointed thereafter until July 1, 1975, when by order of the B court in these proceedings the plaintiffs were appointed trustees of the marriage settlement and the will. As will appear hereafter, by the time of Alexander's death the entirety of the properties subject to the trusts of the marriage settlement and the will had been distributed in breach of trust by Alexander and Mrs. Bell.

There is one other settlement that I should mention. On October 23, C 1930, Alexander made a voluntary settlement, the trust fund comprised therein being settled on protective trusts for himself for life with remainder in favour of his issue. On failure of issue, Alexander was given a general testamentary power of appointment. The first trustees were Mrs. Bell, Percy Leigh Pemberton and Charles Leigh Pemberton. On February 1, 1937, one Anthony North Hickley—to whom I shall refer as Mr. Hickley —was appointed a trustee in place of Charles Leigh Pemberton who, as D I have said, died in 1934. By a deed of appointment dated January 25, 1951, one Edythe Frediswide Gallagher a cousin of Alexander, was appointed a trustee of the voluntary settlement in place of Mr. Hickley.

Mr. Hickley was at all material times a partner in the firm of Clowes Hickley and Heaver. Between 1937 and 1940 the partners in that firm consisted of Mr. Hickley, Sir William Henry Lewthwaite and Alfred E Heaver (to whom I shall refer as Mr. Heaver). From 1940 until Mr. Heaver's death on October 5, 1947, Mr. Hickley and Mr. Heaver were the only partners. From Mr. Heaver's death until April 5, 1951, Mr. Hickley carried on the partnership practice as sole principal. Thereafter the practice was amalgamated with a large London firm.

During a period commencing on or before April 15, 1937, and ending F on or after December 16, 1947, the firm of Clowes Hickley and Heaver acted as solicitors for the trustees of the marriage settlement and of the will and as solicitors for Alexander personally.

As I have said, the entirety of the property, subject to the trusts of the marriage settlement and the will has now disappeared and so far as can now be ascertained had been distributed in breach of trust during Alexander's lifetime. Though it is not directly relevant in these proceed- G ings, it seems probable that the funds comprised in the voluntary settlement were also misappropriated and distributed in breach of trust during Alexander's lifetime. Probate of his will was granted to the fourth defendant, Marion Babette Bell, who was the sole beneficiary under his will and the sole executrix thereby appointed, on February 1, 1960. The nett value of his estate is given in the grant of probate as H £2,756 18s. 2d., and there is no reference to any settled property. No grant has ever been taken out to the estate of Mrs. Bell. Her estate was of negligible value if indeed it was not insolvent.

No steps were taken by Lord Sackville or Lady Hall to ascertain what had happened to the property comprised in the marriage settlement and the will during their respective lifetimes and indeed they may have been unaware of the life interests given to them by the will. Shortly before

A 1967, the plaintiffs, who knew by family repute that there had been a settlement of the Bourne and Milton Estates, obtained copies of the marriage settlement and the will and instituted inquiries to ascertain what had happened to the trust property. The only sources of information they were able to discover were first the books and records, in particular the client's account, of the firm of Clowes Hickley and Heaver which had passed on amalgamation to their successor firm; and, secondly,
B evidence filed in proceedings relating to settled chattels which were heard by Farwell J. in 1935. The records of Clowes Hickley and Heaver show that between August 2, 1940, and February 28, 1947, sums amounting in the aggregate to £38,260 3s. 11d. were paid into the firm's client account to the credit of Mrs. Bell and Alexander as trustees of the marriage settlement and will. Those sums were derived from the sale or realization
C of trust investments, including a farm known as Churchill Farm and of an item of jewellery.

These records also show that out of those sums payments amounting in the aggregate to £26,237 15s. 5d. were made to Alexander, to Mrs. Bell and to the trustees of the voluntary settlement. By far the larger part was paid to Alexander Bell. Payments amounting to £5,361 6s. 6d. were made to Mrs. Bell and payments amounting to £3,043, 17s. were made to
D the trustees of the voluntary settlement. The largest payment to Mrs. Bell was of the sum of £5,293 10s. 10d., and it is clear from other documentary evidence that this sum was applied by her in the purchase of two annuities, the purchase having been arranged by Mr. Hickley, who received a commission of £52 18s. 8d. from the insurance company. In addition, the plaintiffs have discovered two payments to Alexander purport-
E edly by way of loan amounting in aggregate to £969 6s. 8d., which were never repaid. Those payments were made in 1945. It is not alleged that the payments by way of loan passed through the firm's client account or that Mr. Hickley or Mr. Heaver knew anything about them.

As regards the settled chattels, I understand that the evidence before Farwell J. disclosed that there were settled chattels then in the possession of the trustees. The proceeds of sale of one item of jewellery were
F included in the proceeds of sale which passed through the firm's account. Again, it is not contended by the plaintiffs that the proceeds of sale of the remaining chattels passed through the firm's account or that Mr. Hickley or Mr. Heaver knew of any misappropriation of this jewellery. It has been agreed between the plaintiffs and the fourth defendant, representing Alexander's estate, that the value of the jewellery mis-
G appropriated is £2,530 13s. 4d.—that is, of course, in addition to the proceeds of sale which passed through the firm's client account.

I understand that correspondence and other documents disclosed on discovery show that Mr. Hickley knew of the payments out of the client's account to Mrs. Bell, Alexander and the trustees of the voluntary settlement (of whom he was one) amounting to £26,237 15s. 5d. and
H knew—and indeed could not have failed to have known—that those payments were misappropriations by Mrs. Bell and Alexander as trustees of the marriage settlement and will. Indeed, on December 16, 1947, Mr. Hickley was given an indemnity by Alexander and Mrs. Bell by which they authorised and requested him—and I cite:

"... to make available for the use of the said Matthew Alexander Henry Bell all moneys representing capital and income in this settlement which you have had, now have, or in the future will have

in your hands and hereby absolutely indemnify you in respect   A
thereof."

This memorandum is contemporaneous with the last of the misappropriations out of client account that has been discovered, but the memo
concludes with the words:

"This request and authority confirms the verbal or written instructions
to the above effect given by both of us prior to or since March 25,   B
1947."

Further, it is clear from a letter dated February 7, 1947, from Mr.
Hickley to Mrs. Bell that the sale of Churchill Farm, to which I have
referred, was a sale to the trustees of the voluntary settlement and
was made in order to put cash into the hands of Mrs. Bell and Alexander   C
with a view to the distribution of those moneys (amounting to £8,200)
between Mrs. Bell and Alexander. In the words of Mr. Hickley,
Alexander's liabilities were in this way to be " contained in the will trust
leaving the voluntary settlement on a sound basis." It is doubtful whether
even the voluntary settlement remained on a sound basis for much longer.

Mr. Hickley died in 1972 after these proceedings had been commenced
and on April 5, 1973, it was ordered that the proceedings be carried on   D
against his executors, the eleventh and twelfth defendants, Michael
Anthony Petit and Elizabeth North Powell.

It is admitted by Mr. Nourse, on behalf of Mr. Hickley's executors,
that in as much as he assisted with knowledge in the misappropriation of
trust moneys held in the trustees' client account with the firm, he is liable
as a constructive trustee to replace at least the amount of those sums   E
(totalling £26,237 15s. 5d.) paid to Alexander and Mrs. Bell and the
trustees of the voluntary settlement out of moneys in the client account
subject only to a deduction, which it is claimed ought to be made, for
the estate duty which would have been payable on the death of Alexander
and on subsequent deaths, except that of Mrs. Bell, if the trust fund had
remained intact.

The fourth defendant was originally not served with the writ. Her   F
whereabouts at the time were not known and as it was thought at the
time that the assets in Alexander's estate were very small, no serious
efforts were made to trace her. Following Lady Hall's death, substantial
sums fell into Alexander's estate from a settlement in which Lady Hall
had a life interest. Further and successful efforts were made to trace the
fourth defendant who was ultimately found, I understand, in California   G
and a concurrent writ was served on her. She appears by Mr. Roger
Horne, who admits on her behalf that Alexander's estate is liable to
make good at least the sums distributed by him and Mrs. Bell in breach
of trust. Those sums total £29,737, 15s. 5d., being the sum of
£26,237 15s. 5d. paid out of the client account, the loans amounting to
£969 6s. 8d. and the agreed value of chattels misappropriated of £2,530
13s. 4d. But he also claims that a deduction should be made for the   H
estate duty that would have been payable on successive deaths, except
Mrs. Bell's, if the trust fund had remained intact.

On these facts and admissions three issues fall to be determined.
First, it is said by the plaintiffs that Mr. Heaver also became liable, either
as a constructive trustee or as a partner of Mr. Hickley, to make good
the sums wrongly distributed out of his firm's client account. He died
on October 5, 1947. His will was proved on December 4, 1947, by his

A widow, Myra Amelia Heaver, who died before these proceedings were commenced, by the second defendant, Alfred John Langton Heaver, who died on January 21, 1973, and the third defendant, Beauchamp Stewart Pell, who is thus his surviving executor and represents his estate.

Secondly, it is said by the plaintiffs that the liability extends to the present value of Churchill Farm which was sold by the trustees of the marriage settlement and will to the trustees of the voluntary settlement for
B £8,200 on February 24, 1947, or alternatively to the difference between £8,200 and £12,400 which is the price at which Churchill Farm was sold by the trustees of the voluntary settlement in the open market on March 31, 1949.

Thirdly, as I have already indicated, the fourth defendant and Mr. Hickley's executors and, so far as liable, Mr. Heaver's executors, claim
C that in ascertaining the moneys which they are jointly and severally liable to make good to the beneficiaries under the marriage settlement and the will a deduction should be made in respect of the estate duty which would have been paid on the deaths of successive life tenants except that of Mrs. Bell, if no defalcations had taken place. Originally, there was a dispute whether Mr. Hickley or his executors were liable to account for the commission of £52 18s. 8d. received on the purchase of the
D annuities by Mrs. Bell. At first sight if Mr. Hickley is liable to account for this commission, the beneficiaries under the marriage settlement and will will recover the same moneys twice over since the commission was paid by the insurance company from whom the annuities were purchased by Mrs. Bell and Mr. Hickley's estate is admittedly liable to replace the whole of the moneys paid to Mrs. Bell and in large measure used to
E purchase the annuities. However, the amount at stake is very small and Mr. Nourse on behalf of Mr. Hickley's estate does not dispute this liability. I turn therefore to the three main issues.

The first issue

It is admitted on behalf of Mr. Heaver's executors that the moneys for
F the misapplication of which it is sought to make him and his estate liable passed through his firm's client account, and that he had in his possession or had access to documents including copies of the marriage settlement and will and ledger accounts and correspondence between Mrs. Bell, Alexander and Mr. Hickley, inspection of which might have led Mr. Heaver to suspect that breaches of trust were being committed. It is admitted by the plaintiffs that there is nothing to show that Mr. Heaver actually knew of
G these misappropriations and it is not contended that Mr. Heaver failed to exercise a proper degree of supervision over the affairs of the firm or failed to make inquiries which a reasonable solicitor in his position ought to have made and which if made might have led to the discovery of these misapplications. Shortly stated, it is agreed that Mr. Heaver acted throughout honestly and reasonably.

It is argued by Mr. Gidley Scott on behalf of the plaintiffs that Mr.
H Heaver is nonetheless jointly and severally liable to make good the moneys misapplied because, it is said, whenever trust moneys are received by a firm of solicitors and are paid out for a purpose which one of the partners knows to be a breach of trust, all the partners are liable to make good the breach of trust, either as constructive trustees or alternatively under the general principle, embodied in sections 10 and 11 of the Partnership Act 1890, that a firm is liable for the wrongful act of a partner acting in the

ordinary course of business and is liable when a partner, acting within the scope of his authority, receives the property of a third person and misapplies it.

For this, at first sight somewhat surprising, proposition, Mr. Gidley Scott relies primarily on the decision of Stirling J. in *Blyth* v. *Fladgate* [1891] 1 Ch. 337. It is true that there are passages in the judgment of Stirling J. which taken in isolation appear to lend some support to Mr. Gidley Scott's argument. But the passages relied on by Mr. Gidley Scott—to which I shall refer later in this judgment—must be read in the light of the very special facts of that case which were as follows. An antenuptial marriage settlement dated August 20, 1855, was made in consideration of the marriage that shortly afterwards took place between Mr. and Mrs. Blyth. Of the original trustees, one—Archer Thomas Upton—died on January 5, 1875. Another Philip Patten Blyth died on January 30, 1881, and the third, Harry George Gordon, who after the death of Philip Patten Blyth was the sole trustee, died on June 7, 1883. Part of the trust fund was invested in a mortgage which was paid off while Harry George Gordon was the sole trustee, and it was at his direction paid to a firm of solicitors, Messrs. Fladgate, Smith & Fladgate (which I shall call " Fladgates "). By the trustee's direction, Fladgates invested the moneys in Exchequer bills which were deposited with their bankers in their name. Harry George Gordon died and, shortly after his death, the husband, Philip Thomas Blyth interested himself in looking for a suitable mortgage for the investment of the moneys. On October 8, 1883, he asked one Horace William Smith, a partner in Fladgates, to look into a possible mortgage security. Mr. Smith did so and first reported unfavourably. Later, some of the difficulties that had troubled him were surmounted and, prior to February 24, 1884, the Exchequer bills were sold and the proceeds paid to the credit of Fladgates with their bankers. Mr. Smith drew the attention of the husband to the fact that there were no trustees of the marriage settlement. There was delay in getting the consent of one of the trustees proposed by the husband and it was not until April 1884 that new trustees (including Mr. Smith) were appointed. In the meantime, the moneys held by the firm were advanced on mortgage. A mortgage deed was executed in favour of the proposed trustees on March 13, 1884. The advance was imprudent and the security proved insufficient. An action was brought against the trustees in which they were held to be liable to replace the moneys which had been lost. Subsequently, three other actions were brought and heard together, in the first of which a declaration was sought that Mr. Smith's partners in the firm of Fladgates were liable to replace these moneys.

In his judgment, Stirling J. said, at pp. 351–352:

" The defence of the Messrs. Fladgate contained no denial of any part of the allegations made by the statement of claim as to the investment, and regard being had to the admissions in the defence, it must be taken to be admitted by them—first, that the Exchequer bills were in the custody of the firm; secondly, that all the partners knew, or were affected with knowledge that those bills formed part of the funds subject to the trusts of the settlement; and thirdly, that the bills were sold by order of the firm, and that the proceeds were placed to the account of the firm at their bankers. The funds, therefore, came into the custody and under the control of the firm with notice of the trusts upon which they were held; and as against the plaintiffs in *Blyth* v. *Fladgate*, it lay with the firm to discharge themselves by

A showing that the funds were duly applied in accordance with the trusts. That the Messrs. Fladgate attempted to do by saying that the funds were paid over to Mr. Searle by direction of the trustees of the settlement, on the security of mortgages of real estate, a mode of investment which was within the powers of the trustees, and of the impropriety of which they had no notice. It is to be observed that at the date of the payment to Mr. Searle, Messrs. Smith, Philip William

B Blyth, and Morgan had not been appointed trustees, and neither the investment of the funds in their names nor the application of them by their direction could, in the first instance, be a discharge to the firm. Messrs. Smith, Philip William Blyth, and Morgan were however shortly afterwards appointed trustees, and never repudiated the transaction, or disclaimed any interest under the mortgage deed; and under

C these circumstances it was contended, and I think rightly, that they must be treated as having sanctioned the application of the funds.

"That sanction, however, would not avail the partners in the firm of Messrs. Fladgate, Smith & Fladgate if they had knowledge or notice that the investment was one which could not properly be made by duly-constituted trustees. It was admitted that neither Mr. William Mark Fladgate nor Mr. William Francis Fladgate had any actual

D knowledge of the nature of the security taken for the advance made to Mr. Searle; but it was contended that each of them was affected with notice through their partner Mr. Smith, to whom the whole of the facts were known. This point requires careful consideration. As I have already said, the matter was brought before Mr. Smith by Mr. Philip Thomas Blyth, who by his letter of October 8, 1883, asked Mr. Smith

E to " look into this, and see whether this money can be safely lent on it." That letter was addressed to Mr. Smith as a member of the firm of Messrs. Fladgate, Smith & Fladgate, and it is clear from the contemporaneous letter of Mr. Pocock that the advance was to be made by trustees, and consequently that what Mr. Smith was asked to do was to advise whether the security was a safe one for trustees—a matter which falls within the scope of a solicitor's ordinary duties.

F Mr. Smith, as a member of the firm, proceeded to investigate the nature of the security, and ultimately placed himself in communication with Mr. Searle's solicitor, received and perused the abstracts of title, made requisitions thereon, and prepared the securities (which were made to himself, Mr. Philip William Blyth, and Mr. Morgan, the intended new trustees of the settlement), and saw to the due execution of them by the mortgagor. In all that he was acting within the scope

G of his authority as a partner in the firm of Messrs. Fladgate, Smith & Fladgate, and for the work done by Mr. Smith, as such partner, the firm received payment by deducting, in pursuance of an agreement made with Mr. Searle, the mortgagor, the sum of £115 14s. 7d. from the money advanced to Mr. Searle, which passed through their hands. Mr. Smith, therefore, while acting as a member of the firm, became

H acquainted with the nature of the security on which the money under the control of the firm and known by the firm to be a trust fund, was advanced; and the knowledge so acquired by Mr. Smith must, as it seems to me, be imputed to the other partners, whose agent he was, for the purpose of dealing with this trust fund under their control. I think, therefore, that the other partners must be taken to have had notice that the security was not of a character suitable for the

investment of trust funds, and was one which the trustees of the A
settlement could not properly sanction as an investment of the funds
in the custody of the firm. The partners were consequently
implicated in the breach of trust which was committed."

Mr. Gidley Scott relied upon the statement that " In all that [he did]
he [Mr. Smith] was acting within the scope of his authority as a partner
in the firm . . .," and upon the last two sentences of the passages that I B
have cited as a sufficient foundation for the proposition on which he relies.
But, read in the light of the judgment as a whole, and in the light of the
very special facts of that case, these passages are capable of a different
interpretation. When the Exchequer bills were sold and the proceeds
credited to the account of Fladgates with their bankers, the firm (that is,
each and every partner) became a constructive trustee of those moneys. It
was not open to Fladgates to say that they received the moneys as agents C
of the trustees. There were no trustees for whom they could be agents.
It was therefore the duty of the firm to see that the moneys were properly
applied in accordance with the powers in the marriage settlement. As Mr.
Smith, a partner in the firm, negotiated the mortgage and advised as to the
adequacy of the security of the advance, which was in fact an imprudent
one, they could not discharge that duty. The fact that the new trustees, D
when appointed, did not repudiate the transaction and disclaim any interest
under the mortgage deed founded the inference that they had sanctioned
the application of the trust fund. But that could not affect the pre-existing
liability of all the partners in the firm for the breach of trust. That is
the explanation of *Blyth* v. *Fladgate* that was advanced in argument by
Mr. Cozens-Hardy in *Brinsden* v. *Williams* [1894] 3 Ch. 185, 187, when
he said: E

" The case of *Blyth* v. *Fladgate* has been misunderstood. In that case
one member of a firm, acting as a solicitor in such a way that he had
power to bind his partners, took upon himself the management of the
trust; he paid money which was entrusted to the firm at a time when
there were no actual trustees of the fund on an insufficient security,
the sufficiency of which he took upon himself to advise upon. The F
court held that he had constituted himself a trustee, and it was the
duty of the firm of solicitors to see that the money in their hands
was not improperly applied."

That that is the correct explanation is, I think, also clear from the
subsequent decision of the Court of Appeal in *Mara* v. *Browne* [1896] G
1 Ch. 199. In that case, the defendants, Hugh Browne and Arthur Browne,
practised as solicitors in partnership. One of the plaintiffs, Mrs. Mara,
was life tenant under a settlement of August 30, 1875, made on her
first marriage to a Mr. Harold Reeves. Hugh Browne, having been
instructed by Mr. and Mrs. Reeves to investigate the affairs of the trust
fund, found that there had been gross irregularities on the part of one
Bernard Edwin James, a solicitor, and one of the original trustees, his H
co-trustee being one James Walker. On January 7 or 8, 1884, Arthur
Reeves was appointed a trustee in place of Walker but although the deed,
which was undated, was executed by Mr. and Mrs. Harold Reeves, who
had the power of appointing new trustees, it was not executed by Walker
or Arthur Reeves. James remained a trustee on the understanding that
he would be replaced when he had made good certain deficiencies in the
trust assets and would be replaced by Miss Marian Reeves. The deficiencies

A were made good and she was appointed a trustee by a deed executed on May 9, 1884, to act jointly with Arthur Reeves, who was her brother. Between January 1884 and May 9, 1884, moneys were paid by James into a joint account in the name of himself and Arthur Reeves and for the convenience of investment they were paid to Hugh Browne and by him into his private account. He invested the moneys on various mortgages of building land. The investments were made in every case with the approval

B of Mr. and Mrs. Harold Reeves and Arthur Reeves. James knew that the investments were being made out of moneys in the joint account and was content that this should be done, though he was not consulted about the actual investments made. Some of the mortgages were imprudent and made in breach of trust, and it was sought to make Hugh and Arthur Browne liable as constructive trustees. The argument for the

C plaintiffs, which was also put by Mr. Cozens-Hardy and was accepted by North J., was clearly founded on *Blyth* v. *Fladgate*, which was cited. It was said that Arthur Reeves was not a trustee at the time when the moneys were invested by Hugh Browne in the way that I have described, and that Hugh Browne, when he received the moneys, received them as a constructive trustee. As regards that argument, Lord Herschell said,

D at pp. 206–207:

"The moneys sent by Arthur Reeves and James were in every case applied to obtaining the investments for the purpose of which they were sent. James, indeed, probably was not made aware, as Arthur Reeves was, of the particulars of the proposed investments, and perhaps did not trouble himself about them, but he undoubtedly knew that the money was being sent for investment on mortgage securities which

E had been offered, since that very circumstance was employed as a means of putting pressure upon him to complete as speedily as possible payment into the bank of the full value of the trust estate. It was conceded by Mr. Cozens-Hardy, in his argument for the respondents, that, if the transactions now impeached had taken place after the date of the deed of appointment of May 1884, he could not

F have maintained that the defendant Hugh Browne was to be regarded as a constructive trustee. North J. appears to have taken the same view, for he refused relief in respect of advances made when the trusteeship was, as he said, full. In my opinion the distinction made is not a sound one. I do not think that it is correct to say that prior to that date there were no trustees. It appears to me that from the date, at all events, when the account was opened in the names of

G Arthur Reeves and James, down to the appointment by deed in the May following, those two gentlemen were the trustees of the settlement. It may be quite true that, when the circumstances of suspicion in relation to James's conduct became known to Arthur Reeves after January 11, he was unwilling to be joined with James as trustee, and that, if he had not intermeddled with the trust in any way, the deed

H of appointment executed by Mr. and Mrs. Reeves would have been ineffectual. But, in the circumstances which actually occurred, I cannot treat that instrument as a mere nullity Arthur Reeves actually became a joint recipient with James of the whole of the trust funds, and jointly with him disposed of them at a time when James, though he had expressed his willingness to retire, was still a trustee. It is admitted that Arthur Reeves by so doing subjected himself to the responsibilities of a trustee in respect of the trust fund. He became,

it is said, a trustee de son tort. But does it not seem strange thus to A
designate him when he had, immediately before this, been appointed a
trustee with his assent by those who were competent to make the
appointment? It is surely more reasonable to refer his acts as trustee
to this appointment than to treat them as tortious. In my opinion,
therefore, the trusteeship was full during the period covered by the
transactions in question as truly as it was after the subsequent May 9,
and the learned counsel for the respondents made, in my opinion, no B
greater concession than he was compelled to make when he conceded
that, if the money had come into Hugh Browne's hands from duly
appointed trustees for application upon specific investments, his
responsibility would have been that of a solicitor, and not of a trustee."

Any liability of Hugh Browne (or his brother) as a solicitor would of
course have been founded on negligence, and it was accepted that it was C
too late to found an action on that ground. This passage is wholly
inconsistent with the proposition also advanced by Mr. Gidley Scott that
whenever a trustee receives trust moneys, knowing them to be trust moneys,
he, and if the moneys are paid into the firm's client account, his partners,
become liable as constructive trustees and can only escape liability by
showing that the moneys were applied in accordance with the terms of the D
trust.
    Mr. Gidley Scott sought to distinguish *Mara* v. *Browne* on the ground
that the moneys were paid into Hugh Browne's private account. But I do
not think that is a valid ground of distinction. If Mr. Gidley Scott's
proposition were well founded, Hugh Browne, at least, would have been a
constructive trustee. But the decision is of importance for another reason.
At the end of his judgment Lord Herschell said, at p. 208: E

    " What I have already said is sufficient to dispose of the action. But
    I desire to add that, even if in the circumstances of this case Hugh
    Browne had been held liable as a trustee, I should still have come to
    the conclusion that the defendant Arthur Browne was not so liable.
    The only case against him is that, during the period covered by these
    transactions, he was in partnership as a solicitor with the other F
    defendant. He took no part in them, and was ignorant of their nature.
    In my opinion, it is not within the scope of the implied authority of a
    partner in such a business that he should so act as to make himself a
    constructive trustee, and thereby subject his partner to the same
    liability."

A. L. Smith L.J. and Rigby L.J. made observations on the same effect at G
pp. 208 and 214, respectively. Although elliptically expressed, as I understand the judgment, what Lord Herschell is saying is that a solicitor has
the implied authority of his partners to receive trust moneys as agent of the
trustees but does not have any implied authority to constitute himself a
constructive trustee. Nor, I would add, does a solicitor in the ordinary
course of his practice have the implied authority of his co-partners to
accept office as a trustee and so make his co-partners liable for a misapplica- H
tion of the trust property; as to this last point, see *In re Fryer* (1857)
3 K. & J. 317, where it was held that the partners of a solicitor who
received money as a trustees which was lost were not liable for his
default, the moneys having been received by him as trustee and not as
a solicitor.
    If that is the correct principle, it can make no difference to the liability
of the partners of a solicitor who does constitute himself a constructive

A   trustee whether the moneys are paid into his private account or into his firms's client account. In *Blyth* v. *Fladgate* the firm became trustees because there were no trustees at the time when trust moneys were received by them and they could not therefore be considered agents of the trustees.

In my judgment therefore the claim against Mr. Heaver's executors is misconceived.

B   *The second issue*

Churchill Farm was an asset of the compound settlement constituted by the marriage settlement and the will. It was sold on February 24, 1947, to the trustees of the voluntary settlement for the sum of £8,200. It is clear from the letter of February 7, 1947, from Mr. Hickley to Mrs. Bell to which I have referred, that it was sold in order facilitate the distri-
C   bution of the proceeds in breach of trust between Mrs. Bell and Alexander. Churchill Farm was sold by the trustees of the voluntary settlement on March 31, 1949, for the sum of £12,400.

Mr. Gidley Scott contends on behalf of the plaintiffs that the liability of Mrs. Bell, Alexander and Mr. Hickley or their respective estates is to replace the present value of Churchill Farm or alternatively the value of
D   Churchill Farm when it was resold by the trustees of the voluntary settlement. As originally formulated, this claim was founded primarily upon the fact that Mr. Hickley was a trustee of the marriage settlement and the will on the one hand and of the voluntary settlement on the other hand. It was said, I think rightly, that the sale was voidable without proof of undervalue by any beneficiary interested under the marriage settlement and will because a trustee cannot sell to himself or to one of a
E   number which includes himself. As against Mr. Hickley's estate, Mr. Gidley Scott also relied on the fact that Mr. Hickley was solicitor to the trustees of the marriage settlement and will and one of the purchasing trustees. However, in opening his case, Mr. Gidley Scott sought leave to amend to put his case upon the alternative and simpler ground, that as the sale by the trustees of the marriage settlement and the will was made
F   to facilitate a breach of trust, the sale was itself a breach of trust and that the liability of the trustees of Mr. Hickley as constructive trustee is to restore the assets disposed of in breach of trust.

Mr. Nourse on behalf of Mr. Hickley's and Mr. Heaver's executors, and Mr. Horne, on behalf of Alexander's executrix, agreed not to oppose this application on terms that the plaintiffs admitted as a fact that if Churchill Farm had not been sold in breach of trust it would have been
G   sold in the ordinary course of administration of the trusts of the marriage settlement and will at the date and at the price at which it was in fact sold by the trustees of the voluntary settlement. In the absence of an admission, evidence would, I understand, have been called to establish these facts. However, Mr. Gidley Scott, on behalf of the plaintiffs, was prepared to make this admission.

H   Mr. Gidley Scott relied on the well-known decision of the Court of Appeal in *In re Massingberd's Settlement* (1890) 63 L.T. 296. In that case, trustees of a settlement sold a sum of Consols in 1875 in order that the proceeds might be invested in a mortgage. The mortgage was a contributory mortgage on family estates and the investment on a contributory mortgage was not permitted by the powers of investment in the settlement. In 1879 under a re-arrangement of the mortgages on the family estates, a mortgage in the names of the trustees was substituted

1232

for the contributory mortgage but the consent of the tenant for life (which A was required under the settlement to any change of investment) was not obtained. The mortgage was paid off in full in 1887. The question was whether the trustees were liable to replace the Consols sold in 1875. It was also argued that the tenant for life had by his conduct acquiesced in the re-arrangement in 1879, that the mortgage was therefore there-after a proper investment and that the trustee's liability could not extend beyond the sum which would have been necessary to replace B the Consols sold in 1875 at the price of Consols ruling in 1879. It was held by a very strong Court of Appeal (Cotton, Fry and Bowen L.JJ.) that the tenant for life had not consented to the substituted mortgage in 1879 and (following the earlier decision in *Phillipson* v. *Gatty* (1848) 7 Hare 516) that the trustees were liable to replace the Consols sold in 1875 at the higher prices ruling at the date when the proceedings were C commenced.

Mr. Nourse, while reserving the right to challenge the correctness of this decision in a higher court, accepted that it is an authority binding on me for the proposition that if a trust investment is sold with a view to the application of the proceeds in breach of trust, prima facie the liability of the trustees is to replace the investment sold and not merely to make good the proceeds misapplied. He also submitted that it is implicit in the D judgment of the Court of Appeal that if the consent of the tenant for life had been obtained in 1879 to the substituted mortgage, the liability of the trustees would have been limited to the cost of replacing the Consols sold in 1875 at the prices ruling in 1879 on the footing that the Consols would in any event have been sold in 1879 in order to make an investment which, ex hypothesi, would have been a proper one. I accept that submission. E The question whether the substituted investment was made in breach of trust is dealt with at length in the judgment and this question was only relevant on the basis submitted by Mr. Nourse.

Mr. Nourse contends that similarly the liability of Mrs. Bell, Alexander and Mr. Hickley is limited to the value of Churchill Farm at the date when, but for the improper sale, it would admittedly have been sold and properly sold—that is, in 1947—and at the price at which it was sold, F which again is admitted to have been a proper price. Mr. Gidley Scott points out, rightly, that if the farm had been retained and sold with a view to re-investment in 1947, the proceeds might have been invested in another farm, the value of which, like Churchill Farm, probably would have kept pace with the rise in value of agricultural land generally, though he accepts that apart from land, other investments permitted by the marriage settle- G ment and the will would, at least until 1961, have been more likely to have depreciated than to have appreciated in value. He says with considerable force that an order compelling the trustees and Mr. Hickley to make good the present value of Churchill Farm does a kind of rough justice or at least a less rough justice than restoring mere monetary value in 1947.

This is one of the many problems to which inflation gives rise. No H wholly fair solution can, it seems to me, be devised. But I have come to the conclusion, after some hesitation, that Mr. Nourse's submission must be accepted. It is difficult to see how the court could enter into an inquiry into what might have happened to the proceeds of sale of the farm if it had been retained and properly sold with a view to the re-investment of the proceeds. I can see that the court might well be slow to accept evidence that an investment sold with a view to the

A   application of the proceeds of sale in breach of trust would have been sold at a later date if it had not been sold in breach of trust, but in view of the admission made by Mr. Gidley Scott, this difficulty does not arise in the present case.

As regards Mr. Gidley Scott's alternative claims, first that the sale by the trustees of the marriage settlement and will to the trustees of the voluntary settlement was voidable by the beneficiaries under the

B   marriage settlement and will without proof of undervalue, and secondly that Mr. Hickley's estate is liable on the further ground that he was solicitor to the trustees of the marriage settlement and will and one of the trustees of the voluntary settlement, it was accepted by Mr. Gidley Scott, in my judgment rightly, that the measure of compensation could be no greater than that appropriate to the claim founded on *In re*

C   *Massingberd's Settlement*, 63 L.T. 296. I do not propose to say more about these claims except that, without in any way deciding the point, I have some difficulty in seeing how either claim, if otherwise well founded, could extend beyond an account of the actual profit made by the trustees of the voluntary settlement.

There is, however, one other point which I should deal with. In

D   *In re Massingberd's Settlement* the trustees were ordered to make good the difference between the proceeds of the Consols sold in 1875 and the cost of replacing the Consols at the date of the writ. Mr. Gidley Scott argued that the correct date should have been the date of the judgment of Kay J. In *In re Massingberd's Settlement* the real issue was whether, if the trustees were liable at all, they were liable for more than the difference between the proceeds of sale of the Consols sold in 1875 and

E   the cost of replacing the Consols at the date of the substituted mortgage in 1879. No argument was directed to the question whether the appropriate date was the date of the writ or the date of the judgment. It seems likely that, having regard to the stability of the price of Consols over short periods in the 19th century, the difference in price between the date of the writ and the date of the judgment of Kay J. was insignificant.

F   In the case of an action in common law founded in detinue damages for non-return of the chattel are assessed according to the value at the date of the judgment. I have been unable to find any other comparable type of claim where damages are assessed according to value at the issue of a writ. Accordingly, if I had been able to accept Mr. Gidley Scott's main submission, it would, in my judgment, have been open to

G   me to treat the decision of Kay J. and of the Court of Appeal in *In re Massingberd's Settlement,* so far as specifying the date of the writ as the date for ascertaining the value of the property sold in breach of trust to be made good, as an observation made per incuriam and to have substituted the date of judgment.

The third issue

H   I turn to the third and last issue. If the fund subject to the trusts of the marriage settlement and will had not been distributed in breach of trust, estate duty for which the trustees would have been accountable would have been payable on the successive deaths of Alexander (but not Mrs. Bell having regard to the surviving spouse exemption), Lord Sackville and Lady Hall. The estate duty on the death of Alexander would have been small, having regard to his modest estate; but estate

duty would have been payable on the death of Lord Sackville at a rate A
I understand of some 50 or 60 per cent., and on the death of Lady Hall
at a lower but still not inconsiderable rate.

Since these proceedings were commenced, there has been considerable correspondence between on the one hand the several firms of
solicitors acting for the plaintiffs, for the estates of Mr. Hickley and
Mr. Heaver, and for the estate of Alexander, and, on the other hand,
the Estate Duty Office. It is only necessary to refer to two of these B
letters.

In a letter dated May 10, 1974, the Estate Duty Office, in reply to a
letter from the solicitors acting for Mr. Hickley's solicitors, confirmed
that no claim for estate duty would be made " in respect of properties
settled " by the settlor's will on the death of any of the persons who
were given life interests by the will, and:
C

" without retracting the generality of this assurance . . . it proceeds
on the view, which I am content to accept, that it is presently and
practically impossible to recover or reconstitute to any extent the
properties so settled (which was, it is gathered, dissipated in breach
of trust during the lifetime of the first life tenant, Matthew A. H.
Bell)."
D

This assurance was in effect repeated in a letter to the plaintiffs'
solicitors dated September 10, 1974, which is in response to a question
whether estate duty would be payable in respect of moneys recovered
from the estate of Mr. Hickley. The Estate Duty Office said:

" I confirm that this office would not seek to raise claims for estate
duty against the estate of the above named deceased in connection E
with the deaths of Matthew A. H. Bell . . . and the Fifth Baron
Sackville . . . a. if Mr. Hickley's estate is ordered by the court to
replace the missing trust funds; b. if the action is settled by way
of damages payable to or apportioned between, the persons contingently entitled to the remainder; or c. if the action is settled on any
other terms under which the executors of Mr. A. N. Hickley and/or
Mr. A. Heaver should agree to make any payment or payments. F

" I may say that claims would in fact have been raised only if
it had been possible to recover or reconstitute to any extent the
property which was dissipated if such recovery or reconstitution
could have taken place by way of the process known as ' tracing.'
" From the information supplied to this Office, it does not seem
that there is any possibility of the funds or any part of them being G
' traced '."

It is accepted by all the parties that it is not possible—and I quote:
" to recover or reconstitute to any extent the property which was dissipated by any process of ' tracing '."

In these circumstances, it is argued by Mr. Nourse that at least as
regards the claim against Mr. Hickley's estate, the compensation recover- H
able for the breach of trust for which he is liable (that is, in effect, the
payments made out of the client's account to Alexander and Mrs. Bell
and the trustees of the voluntary settlement) should be limited to the
sums wrongly distributed (in the case of Churchill Farm its value in
1947) less the estate duty that would have been payable on the successive
deaths if those moneys or Churchill Farm had been retained (and in
the case of Churchill Farm sold at a proper price in 1947). The principle,

A says Mr. Nourse, is compensation and not punishment. In the case of a trustee, actual or constructive, who has not himself taken the trust property his liability is to make good the fund of which the beneficiaries have been deprived as nearly as possible in the state in which it would have been if no breach of trust had been committed. He found some support, though he did not pretend to find very strong support, in the statement of general principle in *Lewin Trusts,* 16th ed. (1964), p. 664

B where the liability for breach of trust is put in this way:

"If a trustee commits a breach of trust, the beneficiary is entitled to commence civil proceedings against the trustee to recover compensation from him personally for the loss which the trust estate has sustained; and if he has a vested interest and has reason to apprehend that the trustee is going abroad, he may obtain a writ

C of ne exeat regno."

He relied also on the decision of Sir William Grant M.R. in *Dornford* v. *Dornford* (1806) 12 Ves. 127, a case where an executor holding a legacy in trust for an infant with a direction to accumulate became bankrupt and a claim was made against the estate for interest at the rate of 5 per cent. with rests. Sir William Grant M.R. said, at p. 129:

D

" . . . the question is, what is the obligation, which this court attaches upon the breach of such a duty. That obligation is equivalent to the contract of the party. This court says, ' if you neglect your duty, and keep the money yourself, your obligation is to put the infant in the same situation, as if you had not done so.' The court does not inquire into the particular benefit, that has been made; but

E fastens upon the party an obligation to make good the situation of the cestuis que trust."

The obligation, says Mr. Nourse, adopting these words, is not simply to restore the fund without regard to intermediate fiscal charges but to make good the situation of the cestuis que trust by restoring something equivalent to the fund in which, apart from a breach of trust, they would

F have enjoyed their interest.

Mr. Horne, on behalf of Alexander, started by submitting that the same principle should apply to all those breaches of trust to which Alexander was a party including those where he put the trust moneys into his own pocket. He pointed to the fact that if the Estate Duty Office had claimed duty on Lady Hall's death on moneys recovered by

G the plaintiffs from Alexander's estate, they would, in effect, be claiming duty twice on the same death in respect of the same property in as much as Alexander's estate is substantially derived from a reversionary interest under a settlement in which Lady Hall had a life interest. That may be so, but I do not myself see how it advances Mr. Horne's argument. In the course of his argument, Mr. Horne was at least disposed to accept that Alexander's estate was liable to replace all moneys paid to

H Alexander directly or indirectly through the voluntary settlement without any deduction for the estate duty which would have been payable but for his defalcations, though he adopted Mr. Nourse's arguments as regards moneys paid to Mrs. Bell and the difference between the actual proceeds of Churchill Farm received by the trustees of the marriage settlement and will and the proceeds received by the trustees of the voluntary settlement on its subsequent sale.

I find myself unable to accept these submissions. There can to my mind be no doubt that a trustee who has himself defrauded his beneficiaries by taking trust moneys for his own purposes is liable to restore the moneys he has taken without regard to any fiscal liabilities that might have fallen on the trust fund if he had not misappropriated the funds. If, as a result of the decision of the Estate Duty Office not to charge estate duty on the restored fund there is a windfall, the windfall cannot be allowed to benefit the defaulting trustee. Equally, if a trustee has sold an investment in order to misappropriate the proceeds, he must restore the investment or if it is shown or admitted that the investment would have been sold at a later date (as in the case of Churchill Farm) restore its value at that later date.

In my judgment no valid distinction can be drawn between the position of a trustee who has misappropriated for his own benefit and a trustee who has deliberately misappropriated trust moneys for the benefit of someone else. It would to my mind be absurd to impose a lesser liability on a trustee who has deliberately misappropriated trust moneys by paying them to, for instance, his wife or children. And in my judgment a third party who has made himself liable as a constructive trustee by assisting with knowledge of the trust in a misappropriation of trust moneys by the trustee, whether for his own benefit or for the benefit of someone else, can be in no better position than an express trustee. The suggested distinction between a solicitor who is also a trustee and who joins in a misappropriation by his co-trustee on the one hand, and a solicitor acting for trustees who assists with knowledge in a misappropriation by the trustees on the other hand, is to my mind an arbitrary and irrational one.

Mr. Gidley Scott suggested that a distinction can be drawn between a deliberate misappropriation of trust moneys by a trustee, whether for his own benefit or for the benefit of a stranger to the trust, and a breach of trust consciously committed but committed for the benefit of the trust estate, as for instance in *Vyse* v. *Foster* (1872) L.R. 8 Ch.App. 309 and that in this latter case the court might limit the liability of the trustee to such amount as was necessary to reconstitute the fund in the state in which it would have been if no breach of trust had been committed. I can see force in this suggested distinction but it does not arise for decision in this case and I express no opinion on it.

I was, not surprisingly, referred by Mr. Nourse to the decision of the House of Lords in *British Transport Commission* v. *Gourley* [1956] A.C. 185. He urged that the principle established in that case should logically apply to an action by a beneficiary to recover the loss suffered by him personally, for instance, an action by a life tenant or the estate of a deceased life tenant to recover income of which he was deprived by reason of the misappropriation of trust moneys by a trustee. But such an action in my judgment has nothing in common with an action against a defendant who has misappropriated money or property to compel him to restore that which he has wrongfully taken or its value. If an analogy to an action to reconstitute a trust fund is to be found a closer analogy would seem to me to be an action to recover the moneys of a firm which had been misappropriated by an employee if, for example, at a time when the employee was thought to be untraceable or the moneys otherwise irrecoverable the employer had reached an agreement with the revenue under which the moneys were written off thus reducing the employer's taxable profits for that year. The decision in *Gourley's* case does not as I see it entail the conclusion that the

A employer could only recover a net sum equal to the moneys misappropriated less the tax which the employer would have had to pay but for
this misappropriation and the subsequent agreement with the revenue
leaving the fraudulent employee free to enjoy the balance.

Summary

B   In my judgment, therefore, the action so far as brought against
Mr. Heaver's executors is not well founded. The joint and several
liability of Mr. Hickley's executors and Alexander's executrix as regards
Churchill Farm is limited to the replacement of the value of that farm
at the time when it was sold by the voluntary settlement trustees. But
the joint and several liabilities of Mr. Hickley's executors and Alexander's
C executrix to replace trust moneys misappropriated by Alexander and
Mrs. Bell is not affected by the decision of the Estate Duty Office that
the moneys replaced will not attract estate duty on the death of
Alexander, Lord Sackville and Lady Hall.

Orders accordingly.

D   Solicitors: *Macdonald Stacey & Co.; Radcliffes & Co.; Rooks, Rider
& Co.*

[Reported by MISS HILARY PEARSON, Barrister-at-Law]

E   [COURT OF APPEAL]

* MEGARITY *v.* D. J. RYAN & SONS LTD.

[1979 M. No. 80]

F 1980   March 13   Roskill and Ormrod L.JJ.

*Damages—Personal injuries—Medical examination of plaintiff—
Defendants' request for—Plaintiff's agreement conditional on
disclosure of resulting medical report—Defendants' refusal to
accept condition—Whether plaintiff entitled to impose condition — Whether proceedings to be stayed until medical
examination of plaintiff—R.S.C., Ord. 38, r. 37*

G   The plaintiff, who was claiming damages for personal
injuries against the defendants, required, as a condition for
submitting to a medical examination sought by the defendants,
that he should be given a copy of any medical report resulting
from the examination. The defendants rejected the condition
and applied to stay the proceedings until the plaintiff submitted
to the examination. Hollings J., allowing the defendants'
H   appeal from the district registrar's order refusing the application, held that the plaintiff was not entitled to impose the
condition by reason of R.S.C., Ord. 38, r. 37.[1]

[1] R.S.C., Ord. 38, r. 37: " (1) Where in an action for personal injuries an application is made . . . in respect of oral expert evidence relating to medical matters,
then, unless the court considers that there is sufficient reason for not doing so, it
shall direct that the substance of the evidence be disclosed in the form of a written
report or reports to such other parties . . . as the court may specify. (2) The court
may . . . treat any of the following circumstances as a sufficient reason for not
giving a direction under paragraph (1):—(a) that the pleadings contain an allegation

Megarity v. D. J. Ryan & Sons (C.A.)   [1980]

On appeal by the plaintiff: —

Held, dismissing the appeal, that in view of the provisions of R.S.C., Ord. 38, r. 37, a plaintiff in an action for personal injuries was no longer entitled, as a condition of agreeing to submit to a medical examination at the instance of a defendant, to insist upon the disclosure to him of any resulting medical report (post, pp. 1242B–D, 1243D).

Clarke v. *Martlew* [1973] Q.B. 58, C.A. distinguished.

Cluer v. *Chiltern Works (Engineering) Ltd.* (1975) 119 S.J. 85 approved.

The following cases are referred to in the judgment:

Clarke v. *Martlew* [1973] Q.B. 58; [1972] 3 W.L.R. 653; [1972] 3 All E.R. 764, C.A.

Cluer v. *Chiltern Works (Engineering) Ltd.* (1975) 119 S.J. 85.

The following additional cases were cited in argument:

Hall v. *Avon Area Health Authority (Teaching)* [1980] 1 W.L.R. 481; [1980] 1 All E.R. 516, C.A.

Starr v. *National Coal Board* [1977] 1 W.L.R. 63; [1977] 1 All E.R. 243, C.A.

INTERLOCUTORY APPEAL from Hollings J.

The plaintiff, Brian Megarity, by writ dated April 5, 1979, claimed damages for personal injuries against the defendants, D. J. Ryan & Sons Ltd. By an order of February 4, 1980, Hollings J. stayed all further proceedings in the action until such time as the plaintiff had submitted himself for examination by the defendants' appointed medical adviser, such examination not being conditional upon the disclosure of the report(s) of the medical adviser to the plaintiff.

The plaintiff appealed against the decision of Hollings J. on the grounds that (1) the judge misdirected himself in holding that the effect of the decision in *Clarke* v. *Martlew* [1973] Q.B. 58 had been nullified by R.S.C., Ord. 38, Part IV; (2) the judge erred in failing to exercise discretion upon whether it was reasonable for a plaintiff who had suffered personal injury to require to see any medical reports made upon him as a condition of undergoing medical examination at the instance of the defendants; (3) the judge misdirected himself in holding that in matters of law and procedure, and in litigation, the court could not take into consideration the reasonableness of an injured plaintiff's anxiety about his own condition and about a possible need for further treatment which anxiety would be aroused by his knowledge of the existence of a medical report upon him which was not available to him or to his own doctor; and (4) the judge misdirected himself in holding that the plaintiff's undertaking to supply copies of medical reports on which he would rely lacked reciprocity.

The facts are stated in the judgments.

Michael Kershaw for the plaintiff.
Giles Wingate-Saul for the defendants.

ROSKILL L.J. Mr. Kershaw has strenuously urged that we should allow this appeal and reverse the decision which Hollings J. gave when sitting in

of a negligent act or omission in the course of medical treatment; or (*b*) that the expert evidence may contain an expression of opinion—(i) as to the manner in which the personal injuries were sustained; or (ii) as to the genuineness of the symptoms of which complaint is made."

chambers at Manchester on February 4, 1980, but with all respect to the argument, I am clearly of the view that the judgment was correct, for the reasons the judge gave.

The matter arises in this way. The plaintiff brings an action for damages for personal injuries against the defendants. He says in his writ that he was injured in the course of his employment by the defendants at certain premises of Imperial Chemical Industries, as long ago as July 23, 1976. The writ was not in fact issued until April 5, 1979. The statement of claim was duly delivered in the summer of 1979: it was amended in the autumn, and then the defence was served on October 11, 1979. The defendants sought a medical examination of the plaintiff. The plaintiff sought to impose a condition upon his willingness to submit to a medical examination, namely that he and his advisers should be given a copy of any resulting medical report.

The district registrar refused the application which was made on behalf of the defendants on the basis that he was not prepared to make such an order for a medical examination unless there was a disclosure of the report. The defendants appealed, and Hollings J., who gave a long and careful judgment of which we have a transcript, reversed the order of the district registrar. He gave the plaintiff leave to appeal to this court.

The plaintiff in this court has relied strongly upon a well-known decision of this court, *Clarke* v. *Martlew* [1973] Q.B. 58. Of course there are passages in that decision which strongly support the plaintiff's case. There the court had to consider on what terms, if at all, a medical examination should be required of the plaintiff, and the decision of this court (Lord Denning M.R. and Cairns L.J.) is correctly summarised in the headnote which reads:

" *Held,* allowing the appeal, that fairness required that if a defendant sought to have a plaintiff medically examined any report obtained should be disclosed and accordingly the court would only order the action to be stayed for the medical examination of the plaintiff on the condition that the plaintiff was supplied with a copy of the report."

It must be pointed out that at that date, June 23, 1972, there were no relevant Rules of the Supreme Court governing a situation such as this. This is made plain by Lord Denning M.R. in various passages at pp. 62, 63. He points out that it is the defendant who is seeking a privilege by seeking to have a medical examination of the plaintiff, and in his view, the plaintiff should not have to be required to give the defendant that privilege unless the defendant is prepared " to act fairly by it."

Relying upon that, Mr. Kershaw has argued, as he argued before Hollings J., that the plaintiff ought not to be required to submit to a medical examination unless he could receive a copy of the resulting medical report. That was the argument which succeeded before the district registrar but failed before the judge, and in my view it should fail in this court.

Since the judgment in *Clarke* v. *Martlew* [1973] Q.B. 58, the Rules of the Supreme Court have been drastically altered in certain relevant respects. Ord. 38, r. 36 imposes restrictions on adducing expert evidence. Rule 36 (1) reads:

" Except with the leave of the court or where all parties agree, no expert evidence may be adduced at the trial or hearing of any cause or matter unless the party seeking to adduce the evidence has applied

to the court to determine whether a direction should be given under
rule 3, 38 or 41 (whichever is appropriate) and has complied with any
direction given on the application."

Rule 37 bears the rubric "Medical evidence in actions for personal
injuries" and reads:

"(1) Where in an action for personal injuries an application is made
under rule 36 (1) in respect of oral expert evidence relating to medical
matters, then, unless the court considers that there is sufficient reason
for not doing so, it shall direct that the substance of the evidence be
disclosed in the form of a written report or reports to such other
parties and within such period as the court may specify. (2) The
court may, if it thinks fit, treat any of the following circumstances
as a sufficient reason for not giving a direction under paragraph (1):—
(a) that the pleadings contain an allegation of a negligent act or
omission in the course of medical treatment; or (b) that the expert
evidence may contain an expression of opinion—(i) as to the manner
in which the personal injuries were sustained; or (ii) as to the
genuineness of the symptoms of which complaint is made."

Rule 38 goes on:

"(1) Where an application is made under rule 36 (1) in respect of
oral expert evidence to which rule 37 does not apply, the court may,
if satisfied that it is desirable to do so, direct that the substance of
any expert evidence which is to be adduced by any party be disclosed in the form of a written report or reports to such other
parties and within such period as the court may specify."

Thus, the position at the present day and ever since these rules came
in, which was in 1974, is that there has been, as it were, a complete code
dealing with the three conditions which attach to the adducing of expert
evidence at the trial. The whole purpose is to oblige an exchange of
expert reports, medical or otherwise, in order to save time in elaborate
examination-in-chief, and also, of course, to avoid surprise. That applies
just as much to medical expert evidence as to other expert evidence, so
that if the evidence which is obtained by the defendants as a result of a
medical examination to which they required the plaintiff to submit is
going to be used by the defendants at the trial, then, at the summons for
directions stage, the defendants will be obliged to make available a copy
of the report, subject only to the qualification, which I have mentioned, in
rule 37 (2), namely, that they would not have to disclose any part of that
report which contained an expression of opinion, for example, as to the
genuineness of the symptoms of which complaint is made.

Thus the fairness which Lord Denning M.R. rightly, if I may say so,
emphasised in Clarke v. Martlew [1973] Q.B. 58 is now secured, not by
the manner in which it was necessary to secure it in Clarke v. Martlew,
but by the operation of the new rules introduced since. So that looking
at this matter by reference to the rules alone and without troubling about
authority, it seems to me that the judge was clearly right.

But the matter is not free from authority. We have been referred to
a judgment of Cusack J., sitting in chambers, in Cluer v. Chiltern Works
(Engineering) Ltd. (1975) 119 S.J. 85, which was given on October 30,
1974. The report is very abridged. Thanks to the defendants' solicitors,
to whom we are obliged, a transcript of the judgment has been obtained.
The argument advanced on behalf of the plaintiff in that case was

A   almost identical, so far as one can see, with the argument that Mr.
Kershaw has advanced here.   The plaintiff there was claiming damages
for personal injuries.   The defendants sought an order for a medical
examination and Master Ritchie who, if I may say so, is a most experienced master, ordered that the action be stayed until such date as
the plaintiff submitted to a joint medical examination in the presence of
a doctor nominated by the defendants.   No condition was made that the
B   contents of the report should be disclosed to the plaintiff or her advisers.
The judge said:

"The grounds of the appeal are that such disclosure should have
been made a condition.   The matter has hitherto been governed
by the decision of the Court of Appeal in *Clarke* v. *Martlew* [1973]
C   1 Q.B. 58 and the master evidently took the view that *Clarke* v.
Martlew must now be considered in the light of R.S.C., Ord. 38, r. 37
which was added to the Rules of the Supreme Court since that
decision."

He then went on to summarise the effect of *Clarke* v. *Martlew* as I have
done, then set out the new rule, and said:

D   "The plaintiff's counsel submits to me that although the effect of
r. 37 has been to place in the hands of the court a matter which has
hitherto been for the consideration of the parties by requiring the
court to consider whether there should be a mutual waiver of
privilege, r. 37 does not and should not affect the decision in *Clarke*
v. *Martlew* because the problem I am considering arises at quite
a different time from the matters to be dealt with under r. 37 on
E   summons for direction.   On the other hand it is submitted by
[counsel for the defendants] that the stay the master imposed is
correct and should remain . . .   The problem is not an easy one but
[counsel] has urged upon me that the situation is such that it would
lead to unfairness and make nonsense of r. 37 if the former practice
under *Clarke* v. *Martlew* were to be observed still.   I have come
to the conclusion in a case which is by no means easy that in con-
F   sidering the case of *Clarke* v. *Martlew* and the application of r. 37
that Master Ritchie was correct in saying the stay should be imposed.
I bear in mind that if one is dealing simply with the matter under
r. 37 there can be no report to consider unless there has previously
been an examination.   This is of very considerable importance.
Also the plaintiff has always had the privilege to refuse to reveal
G   reports made on the plaintiff's behalf.   I think therefore the master
was right and accordingly dismiss the appeal."

He therefore dismissed the appeal with costs.   The fact that an order
for costs was asked for and obtained; and that leave to appeal was given
suggests, I hope not unfairly, that it was a union case.   The union would
have been unlikely not to have brought that case to the Court of Appeal
H   if they had had serious doubts about the correctness of the decision.
That case therefore is against Mr. Kershaw's submissions.

Hollings J., as I say, in a long and careful judgment, reviewed the
authorities both before and after *Clarke* v. *Martlew* [1973] Q.B. 58 and
went on to consider the rule.   He said:

"But since [the decision in *Clarke* v. *Martlew*], these rules have been
promulgated and lay down a code by which that result can be
achieved with fairness to each party; and so, says Mr. Wingate-Saul

—although he does not use these words—it is not surprising that   A
when the matter came before Cusack J. on this very same point
after the appeal rules had come into force, Cusack J. said, in *Cluer*
v. *Chiltern Works (Engineering) Ltd.* (1975) 119 S.J. 85, that the
condition ought not to be imposed. He said that *Clarke* v. *Martlew*
[1973] Q.B. 58 had hitherto governed the matter, but that the master
confidently took the view that that decision had now to be considered
in the light of R.S.C., Ord. 38, r. 37, which came into operation on   B
June 1, 1974."

Hollings J. went on to summarise Cusack J.'s decision and followed
it. He ended his judgment:

"In the circumstances, the rules providing for exchange of medical
reports under adequate safeguards, as they are thought to be, are the   C
rules which should govern the matter, and those rules, in my judgment, are not consistent with the plaintiff being entitled, as it were,
to impose a condition on allowing himself to be examined by a
doctor on behalf of the defendants, and I think that the district
registrar was wrong in those circumstances in not imposing a stay
until such a medical examination was carried out."
                                                                        D
Quite plainly, what weighed with Cusack J. and Hollings J. was the
position under Ord. 38, r. 37 (2) which entitled the defendant, in a case
to which Ord. 38, r. 37 (2) applies, to withhold part of the contents of
the relevant report on the grounds that it may or does refer to the
genuineness of the symptoms of which complaint is made. Now if Mr.
Kershaw's argument be right, a plaintiff would be entitled to obtain the
entirety of the report at an early stage as a condition of submitting to   E
a medical examination although, at the summons for directions stage, he
would not be entitled to such wide discovery. It seems to me that that
cannot have been the intention of these rules. The plaintiff is, as I see
it, under no obligation, even at the present day, to disclose a report in
his possession unfavourable to himself; and yet, if Mr. Kershaw's argument be right, he could, as a condition of submitting to a medical exami-   F
nation, impose on a defendant an obligation to disclose the resulting
medical report in the hope that the defendants' report, otherwise plainly
a privileged document, would reveal in these circumstances something
more favourable to him than his own medical report would reveal. That
seems to me to be entirely wrong.

I might have contented myself in this case by saying that I wholeheartedly agree with both Cusack J.'s judgment and that of Hollings J.   G
But in deference to Mr. Kershaw's argument, I have dealt with it at a
little more length. I would dismiss the appeal.

I hope nothing in this judgment will be thought as entitling people
to adopt other than sensible attitudes over the exchanging of medical
reports at as early a stage as possible.
                                                                        H
ORMROD L.J. I agree and would add a few words of my own. It is
perfectly easy to understand the plaintiff's feelings and of his wish to
know what the defendants' doctor has said about him; and in terms of
ordinary human response that is perfectly comprehensible and quite
natural. But the question here is whether in litigation it is fair and just
not only to the plaintiff but to both sides. It means quite clearly that
the plaintiff, if he is right, can insist on seeing a copy of the defendants'

The Weekly Law Reports, October 17, 1980

1243

1 W.L.R.   **Megarity v. D. J. Ryan & Sons (C.A.)**   Ormrod L.J.

A doctor's medical report as a condition of submitting to the examination, and if that report is more favourable to his case than his own doctor's, he can call, or be in a position to call that doctor, if so advised. That may be sound enough in terms of fairness, but the corollary is that he, the plaintiff, should disclose all medical reports which he has obtained even if they are unfavourable to his case. I should imagine that most plaintiffs and their advisers would think that that was a major encroach-

B ment on the privileges of a litigant in these courts.

R.S.C., Ord. 38, r. 37, as Roskill L.J. pointed out, clearly contemplates that there are some matters in the medical reports which the parties are not obliged to disclose to the other side. Two items are: views as to the manner in which the personal injuries were sustained, and the genuineness of the symptoms of which complaint is made—both of which

C really are issues going to liability rather than to quantum of damage, although the second one is also part of quantum as well. That rule cannot be made sense of if Mr. Kershaw's argument is right for the reasons which Roskill L.J. has given. It means that a plaintiff could insist, by refusing to submit to an examination, on having material which he could not get under Ord. 38, r. 37, and for that reason and that reason alone it seems to me that *Clarke* v. *Martlew* must be modified.

D Lord Denning M.R., in that case, was not contemplating a situation like this; he was not contemplating the matter on the broad front by which the Rules Committee clearly viewed it, and for my part I do not think, along with Hollings J. and Cusack J., that *Clark* v. *Martlew* can stand since the amendment of the rules.

One suggestion which is put forward in the notice of appeal and

E mentioned by Mr. Kershaw in his argument in this court is that the plaintiff ought to be notified if the defendants' doctor has discovered some more serious condition than the plaintiff's doctor has observed. I have no doubt that is good medicine, but I do not think for a moment that it is good law. The answer to it is that any responsible doctor who found such a condition on a medical examination would certainly him-self wish to communicate his findings to whoever is looking after the

F plaintiff medically, and no doubt it would be proper for him to do it through his ordinary medical channels, if it was a serious matter which was likely to affect the future health of the plaintiff. That is clearly a medical issue, and has nothing whatever to do with the disclosure of reports in a litigation context.

For those reasons, and the reasons given by Roskill L.J., I agree

G that this appeal should be dismissed.

Appeal dismissed with costs.

Solicitors: *Whitehouse, Gibson & Alton for Farley, Parker & Pickles, Blackburn; James Chapman & Co., Manchester.*

H   B. O. A.

[COURT OF APPEAL]

* RAHMAN v. KIRKLEES AREA HEALTH AUTHORITY

PRACTICE NOTE

1979 Nov. 22   Ormrod and Cumming-Bruce L.JJ.

*Damages—Personal injuries—Medical reports—Medical negligence
action—Exchange of medical reports—Whether to be ordered
—R.S.C., Ord. 38, r. 37 (2)*

INTERLOCUTORY APPEAL from Mais J.

The plaintiff in a medical negligence action, Mrs. Joan Rahman, appealed
from a decision of Mais J. given on June 27, 1979, allowing an appeal by the
defendants, Kirklees Area Health Authority, from an order of the district
registrar. Mais J. ordered that there should be deleted from the summons
for directions in the action a direction that medical reports be exchanged
and that if not agreed medical evidence should be limited to one witness for
each party.

No cases are referred to in the judgments or were cited in argument.

John M. Collins for the plaintiff.
Ian A. Kennedy Q.C. and *R. C. Taylor* for the defendants.

CUMMING-BRUCE L.J. gave the first judgment. This is an action for
medical negligence. The negligence alleged is that, by reason of the failure
of the defendants, by their doctors, surgeons or other servants, to exercise
proper skill and care, the plaintiff was subjected to delivery by caesarian
section which, if it could not have been avoided altogether by proper diagnostic
skill, was at any rate not carried out at the right time or at all before the
death of the baby. There is an allegation that, during the period immediately
preceding the birth, there was a want of proper supervision of the patient by
the appropriate specialist eyes or hands; and there is a further allegation that
the defendants re-established a cyntocinon drip without proper consultation
and without proper consideration of harmful effects.

The defence admitted some facts that could not be controverted and
accepted that the plaintiff had had a stillbirth and was found to have suffered
a uterine rupture, which led to drastic surgical interference. The defendants
content themselves with a denial of negligence, putting the plaintiff to proof
of matters of fact alleged.

The summons for directions came before the registrar and, after ordering
discovery of documents, he made the following order: " Medical reports be
exchanged and that if not agreed medical evidence be limited to one witness
for each party whose reports have been exchanged . . . Trial place: Leeds.
Mode: judge alone." There was an appeal of that order and, on the appeal,
the judge allowed the appeal and ordered that " direction no. 23 be deleted
from the summons for directions herein and no limit be imposed on the
number of medical expert witnesses to be called on either side." Item 23
on the summons for directions is the item dealing with the agreement of
medical reports and the restriction of medical witnesses. The plaintiff appeals.

Mr. Collins for the plaintiff appeals two parts of the judge's order. He
seeks an order that: " The plaintiff and defendants do mutually disclose
medical reports within 42 days; such reports be agreed if possible; unless
such reports are agreed the parties be at liberty to call experts on medical
matters limited to those witnesses whose reports have been disclosed and
limited to three witnesses for each party."

The Weekly Law Reports, October 24, 1980

1245

1 W.L.R.   Rahman v. Kirklees Health Authority (C.A.)   Cumming-Bruce L.J.

A   I come first to the appeal in relation to the judge's decision that there should be no mutual disclosure of medical reports. The relevant rule is R.S.C., Ord. 38, r. 37 which appeared in the Rules of the Supreme Court in relation to actions for personal injuries and bears that heading. The rule reads:

"(1) Where in an action for personal injuries an application is made under rule 36 (1) in respect of oral expert evidence relating to medical B   matters, then, unless the court considers that there is sufficient reason for not doing so, it shall direct that the substance of the evidence be disclosed in the form of a written report or reports to such other parties and within such period as the court may specify. (2) The court may, if it thinks fit, treat any of the following circumstances as a sufficient reason for not giving a direction under paragraph (1): —(a) that the pleadings contain an allegation of a negligent act or omission in the C   course of medical treatment; or (b) that the expert evidence may contain an expression of opinion—(i) as to the manner in which the personal injuries were sustained; . . ."

Mr. Collins submitted that, on a scrutiny of paragraph (1), it is clear that the starting point is that the court shall direct disclosure of the reports of expert witnesses subject only to the proviso that such a direction shall not be given " unless the court considers that there is sufficient reason for not D   doing so." He also submitted that paragraph (2) does no more than give some illustrations of certain kinds of case which are not intended to be exhaustive and are selected by the rules committee only as illustrations of certain kinds of situation in which the court may find there is a sufficient reason for refusing disclosure. So construing or explaining Ord. 38, r. 37, Mr. Collins submits that, on the issues in this case—although it is, of course, a medical negligence case because that is what the pleadings allege—when E   the issues raised by the pleadings are considered, there is nothing so special about them as to make it right in the exercise of the judge's duty to find that a sufficient reason for refusing disclosure has been shown.

For myself, I do not accept the explanation and effect of rule 37 propounded by Mr. Collins. Paragraph (2) of that rule goes further than merely indicating as illustrations the kinds of situation which might appropriately be regarded as sufficient reasons for refusing to direct exchange of reports. In F   my view, the rules committee has clearly thought it appropriate expressly to distinguish the situation where expert evidence is being called in other kinds of actions for damages for personal injuries, from the forensic situation that obtains where an allegation of medical negligence is made as a cause of action. For myself, I can see at once the commonsense of that distinction because one of the features of an expert report for the defendants in a medical negligence case is that, in order to found an opinion, it is commonly necessary G   for the expert to be given all or most of the proofs of fact of all those persons whose acts and omissions are under scrutiny in the proceedings. It would be strange indeed if, by means of a direction under Ord. 38, r. 37, the court, on a side wind, made an order in which it was implicit that the defendants' proofs of evidence would be shown to the other side in summary form. The plaintiff has the right, by reference to orders for discovery of documents and interrogatories, to obtain from the defendants such evidence of fact as lies in their possession, subject to the practice of the courts in relation H   to discovery of documents and interrogatories.

Although, as Mr. Collins has rightly stated, the history of procedure in civil actions has been developing over the last generation in that parties are encouraged to hold their cards less closely to their chests, that development has certainly not reached the stage of imposing upon a defendant a duty to disclose his proof of evidence, save insofar as discovery is obtainable through discovery of documents and interrogatories. For the purposes of construing or appreciating the intent of Ord. 38, r. 37 it is helpful, in my view, also to

look at the next rule, rule 38, which has the heading " Other expert evidence." A
It is, I think, helpful to observe that, in Ord. 38, r. 38, paragraph (2) reads:

> " In deciding whether to give a direction under paragraph (1) the court
> shall have regard to all the circumstances and may, to such extent as it
> thinks fit, treat any of the following circumstances as affording a sufficient
> reason for not giving such a direction [for exchange of reports]: —(a)
> that the expert evidence is or will be based to any material extent upon
> a version of the facts in dispute between the parties; or (b) that the B
> expert evidence is or will be based to any material extent upon facts
> which are neither—(i) ascertainable by the expert by the exercise of
> his own powers of observation, nor (ii) within his general professional
> knowledge and experience."

I focus upon Ord. 38, r. 38 (2) (a) and observe that the rules committee,
in relation to other expert evidence—i.e., other than medical evidence in
actions for personal injuries—contemplated that it would not be appropriate C
to exchange reports if the expert evidence will be based to any material extent
upon a version of the facts in dispute between the parties.   Mr. Collins has
submitted that the facts are not really in dispute, because there cannot be a
dispute about the sad history of the plaintiff over the period in June and July
1976 which culminated in the death of the baby and an ensuing hysterectomy.
That is, in my view, a gross over-simplification of the realities.   Matters
in dispute, having regard to the allegations in the statement of claim, are D
likely to be the detail of the history of supervision, diagnosis and treatment
from day to day and, at certain stages, from hour to hour; and there may
very well be the most substantial dispute about what the facts were in relation
to such supervision, diagnosis and treatment.   The experts, whom the defendants would seek to call, are likely to be persons with appropriate professional
qualifications who will state what the proper standards of skill and care are
in relation to the different kinds of problem posed by the patient during the E
relevant period; and, in order to form such an opinion, it will be necessary
for such experts to be given by the defendants' solicitors what may well
amount to a summary of the proofs of all the professional persons who were
responsible for the supervision, diagnosis, medical, surgical and nursing care
of the plaintiff over the relevant period of a month or six weeks.   It is by
reflecting upon such considerations that the decision of the rules committee
to draft Ord. 38, r. 38 (2) (a) in the form in which it was is to be explained. F
For my part I do not accept Mr. Collins' interpretation of Ord. 38, r. 37 (2)
and I can find no reason in the material before the judge which would justify
this court in varying the order that the judge made in deciding not to give
a direction for the disclosure of expert medical reports in this case.   I would
go farther and say that, if I were to consider the subject matter afresh, I
would think that the judge's order was plainly right.
The second matter that arises is on the limitation of medical witnesses. G
In the summons for directions issued by the plaintiff the application was, I
understand, for a limitation of expert evidence to two witnesses to each party.
For some reason which remains obscure to me the registrar made a rather
startling order that the medical reports be " exchanged and that if not agreed
medical evidence be limited to one witness for each party whose reports have
been exchanged."   A mere superficial scrutiny of the issues raised by the
particulars of negligence in the statement of claim is sufficient to show that H
that figure is quite certainly wrong.   It may well be, first, that a number of
different kinds of medical speciality may be involved and, secondly, that both
plaintiff and defendants may reasonably wish to call more than one witness
dealing with any relevant specialist experience connected with the issues in
the case.
The judge decided not to limit the number of witnesses.   Mr. Collins
for the plaintiff submits that that is onerous and subjects the plaintiff, a
mere patient, to the prospect of litigation in which a whole string of men of

The Weekly Law Reports, October 24, 1980

1247

1 W.L.R.   Rahman v. Kirklees Health Authority (C.A.)   Cumming-Bruce L.J.

A medical learning may be marshalled to follow each other into the witness
box to obscure the truth out of a misguided sense of loyalty to a member
or members of their profession charged with negligence. The history of
medical negligence actions, I think, can be said to show that Mr. Collins'
apprehensions are not wholly fanciful but, as against that, this court should
not approach a case on the basis that the defendants, a public authority, will
consciously try to abuse their position. Secondly, having looked at the
B allegations in the statement of claim, it does appear to me—innocent though
I am of professional medical knowledge—to be the kind of case in which the
defendants ought to be at liberty to decide what kinds of medical specialists
to call, and ought also not to be restricted in deciding whether it is necessary
and sensible to call more than one medical witness on any particular kind
of speciality.

   For those reasons I would uphold the judge's order and dismiss the appeal.

C
      ORMROD L.J. I agree and I have only a few words to add of my own.
If Mr. Collins is right in his contention in this case, it produces the most
extraordinary result. Under Ord. 38, r. 37 the court is obliged to order the
exchange of medical reports unless it considers there is sufficient reason for
not doing so. Under Ord. 38, r. 38, on the other hand, the court is simply
left with a general discretion whether to order or not to order the disclosure
of other expert reports. If Mr. Collins' construction of r. 37 is right, it
D would mean that medical negligence cases are singled out from all other
kinds of negligence by experts for quite separate and different treatment.
The court would be prima facie under a duty in medical negligence cases to
order an exchange of reports, whereas in other kinds of professional negligence
cases—such as solicitors or engineers or architects—there would be no such
onus on the court or onus on the persons objecting to the disclosure to make
it good.

E   I am bound to say I do not think that Ord. 38, r. 37 is particularly well
drafted. It appears to me, from the use of the phrase " action for personal
injuries " in the first line of the rule, that the draftsman contemplated what
everybody calls an action for personal injuries, which is a running-down case
or a factory accident or something similar. I do not think I have ever heard
of a medical negligence case spoken about as an action for personal injuries,
although of course in a sense it is. There is no doubt that the burden of
F r. 37 is directed to the case with which we are all so familiar, where the
question is the extent of the injuries suffered by the person as a result of
somebody else's negligence and the prognosis of those injuries—a standard
form of medical report in a personal injury action. Expert evidence in an
action for medical negligence or for professional negligence takes on an
entirely different character, because the evidence is directed not to what the
patient's condition is now or was as a result of the accident or what it is
G going to be in the course of time in order that damages can be assessed. The
expert evidence in this case is directed to the crucial question: was the
treatment correct or reasonable in the circumstances? That is an enormous
difference. No doubt that is why in Ord. 38, r. 37 (2) the draftsman specifically mentioned negligent acts in the course of medical treatment, intending
apparently not to take actions for medical negligence out of the rule altogether,
but to give the court the broadest of hints that the court should not order
H disclosure of reports in such cases unless there is some unusual feature. I
cannot help feeling that it would have been better, if the draftsman intended
there to be an exception, to have made it a clear exception.

   The same comment, with less force, to my mind applies to the provision
in Ord. 38, r. 37 (2) (b) (i), which indicates that the court may if it thinks
fit treat as a sufficient reason for not giving a direction the fact that the expert
evidence may contain an expression of opinion as to the manner in which
the personal injuries were sustained. That is another example of the medical
expert evidence going to liability and not to quantum of damages. The same

applies to Ord. 38, r. 37 (2) (b) (ii) " as to the genuineness of the symptoms   A
of which complaint is made "—that goes to liability. It looks as though the
draftsman of the rule shrank from putting on the court the duty to order
disclosure of the reports when those reports were directed to the issue of
liability as opposed to damages.

In my judgment, the rule is not at all happily phrased and, when one
looks at rule 38—which is permissive in contrast to rule 37—one sees then, as
Cumming-Bruce L.J. has already pointed out, a series of circumstances which   B
will take the expert evidence out of the rule of disclosure.

For all those reasons it seems to me plain that the judge was right in his
view that this was not a case for making any direction at all under rule 37,
and I agree with what Cumming-Bruce L.J. has said as to the number of
witnesses. In a case like this I do not, for my part, see any useful purpose
whatever in limiting the number of witnesses. If the defendants or plaintiff
choose to try to abuse the position by calling an innumerable number of
witnesses they may well end up by damaging their own case in nine out of   C
ten cases, and the trial judge can deal with it himself.

I would dismiss this appeal.

Appeal dismissed.
Defendants' costs in cause.

Solicitors: *Kingsley, Napley & Co. for Stapleton Gardner & Co., Dewsbury;*   D
Hempsons for R. H. D. Chapman, Yorkshire Regional Health Authority.

R. C. W.

[COURT OF APPEAL]   E

* CASTREE *v.* E. R. SQUIBB & SONS LTD. AND ANOTHER

[1978 C. No. 21]

1980 April 24   Buckley, Ackner and Oliver L.JJ.
                                                                              F

> *Tort—Cause of action—Whether arising within jurisdiction—*
> *Personal injuries caused in England by defective machine manu-*
> *factured in Germany—Sale of machine in England—Whether*
> *tort committed by manufacturers within jurisdiction—R.S.C.,*
> *Ord. 11, r. 1 (1) (h)*

> The plaintiff claimed damages against the defendants, her
> employers, for personal injuries she sustained in the course of   G
> her employment when a machine she was using disintegrated.
> The machine had been manufactured in Germany but pur-
> chased by the defendants in England from a firm which was
> said to be the sole agents of the manufacturers. The defend-
> ants sought leave, under R.S.C., Ord. 11, r. 1 (1) (h),[1] to issue
> and serve out of the jurisdiction on the manufacturers a third
> party notice, claiming contribution from them on the basis that,
> on the facts, the plaintiff could have successfully sued them for
> a tort committed by them within the jurisdiction. Leave to   H
> serve the third party notice was granted but later set aside by
> the district registrar. On the defendants' appeal Phillips J.
> reversed the decision of the district registrar.
>   On the manufacturers' appeal: —

---

[1] R.S.C., Ord. 11, r. 1: " (1) . . . service of a writ, . . . out of the jurisdiction is
permissible with the leave of the court . . . (h) if the action begun by the writ is
founded on a tort committed within the jurisdiction; . . . "

A   *Held*, dismissing the appeal, that the plaintiff's cause of
action arose, in substance, not from the defective manufacture
of the machine, but from putting that machine on the English
market with no warning as to its defects and, accordingly,
the action begun by the plaintiff was founded on a tort committed by the manufacturers within the jurisdiction.
          Distillers Co. (Biochemicals) Ltd. v. *Thompson* [1971] A.C.
458, P.C. applied.

B   *George Monro Ltd.* v. *American Cyanamid and Chemical
Corporation* [1944] 1 K.B. 432, C.A. distinguished.
          Decision of Phillips J. affirmed.

The following cases are referred to in the judgment of Ackner L.J.:

Cordova Land Co. Ltd. v. *Victor Brothers Inc.; Cordova Land Co. Ltd.*
     v. *Black Diamond Steamship Corporation* [1966] 1 W.L.R. 793.
C   *Distillers Co. (Biochemicals) Ltd.* v. *Thompson* [1971] A.C. 458; [1971]
     2 W.L.R. 441; [1971] 1 All E.R. 694, P.C.
Donoghue v. *Stevenson* [1932] A.C. 562, H.L.(Sc.).
Monro (George) Ltd. v. *American Cyanamid and Chemical Corporation*
     [1944] 1 K.B. 432; [1944] 1 All E.R. 386, C.A.

The following additional case was cited in argument:

D   *Diamond* v. *Bank of London and Montreal Ltd.* [1979] Q.B. 333; [1979]
     2 W.L.R. 228; [1979] 1 All E.R. 561, C.A.

APPEAL from Phillips J.
     By a writ dated January 20, 1978, the plaintiff, Jayne Susan Castree,
claimed damages for negligence against the defendants, E. R. Squibb &
Sons Ltd., who were granted leave on June 11, 1979, by the district
E   registrar to issue a third party notice against Heraeus-Christe G.m.b.H.,
of West Germany, a company, and to serve the same out of the jurisdiction. The order granting leave was set aside by Mr. District Registrar
Yates on November 7 but restored by Phillips J. on December 20, 1979, on
the defendants' appeal.
     By notice of appeal dated January 22, 1980, the third party appealed
F   on the grounds that the judge was wrong in law in finding that the
defendants had complied with the requirements of R.S.C., Ord. 11,
r. 1 (1) (h); and that the judge was wrong in law in finding that the fact
that the machine was sold in the United Kingdom was a material factor
which he was entitled to take into account.
     The facts are stated in the judgment of Ackner L.J.

G   *Ronald Livesey* for the third party.
William Waldron for the defendants.

ACKNER L.J., delivering the first judgment. This is an appeal by a third
party against a judgment of Phillips J. given on December 20, 1979, when
he reversed a decision of the district registrar of November 7, 1979.
H   The appeal arises in these circumstances. The plaintiff, Miss Jayne
Susan Castree, is suing for damages for personal injuries which she
sustained in August 1976 when she was using a machine, called a centrifuge, for the purpose of separating liquids from solids. She was using
that machine in the course of her employment with the defendants, who
are the respondents to this appeal, and in the course of using that machine
it disintegrated, causing her serious injuries.
     The machine was manufactured in Germany by the appellants, who

are a private German company, and the machine was purchased in this A
country by the defendants. The defendants sought leave to issue and
serve out of the jurisdiction, under R.S.C., Ord. 11, a third party notice
upon the appellants. The basis upon which they sought that leave has
changed, but ultimately—I can put it as shortly as this—the position was
that the defendants contended that the appellants were joint tortfeasors
from whom they were entitled to claim contribution. They did not assert
that they had any remedy against the appellants in contract, but they B
asserted that had the plaintiff sued the appellants in negligence by way
of a *Donoghue* v. *Stevenson* ([1932] A.C. 562) claim she would have
succeeded, and accordingly the basis of the application is that contained
in R.S.C., Ord. 11, r. 1 (1) (*h*), namely, that the action is founded on a tort
committed in the jurisdiction.

The contention of Mr. Livesey, who has argued this case with charac- C
teristic skill, is quite simply that the tortious conduct, if there is any, of
the appellants was all committed out of this country, namely, the defective
design and manufacture of the machinery, and that all that happened in
this country was that the plaintiff sustained damage.

It is important at this stage to make this point in relation to the sale
of the machinery in this country. The judge recites this in his judgment; D
it is alleged, and for the present purpose is to be taken as a fact, that
the defendants purchased the equipment in this country from a firm
acting as sole agents for the appellants. The judge said: " It does seem
important to me that the [appellants have] a distribution system as a
result of which their goods are distributed in this country, . . ." That
assertion is essentially derived from the third party notice as originally
served, in which it was alleged that " the said centrifuge . . . was manu- E
factured . . . and was purchased by the defendants in or about the month
of November 1973 from [the appellants'] United Kingdom agents ";
and from the affidavit in support of the application to serve out of the jurisdiction: " the . . . centrifuge . . . was manufactured by [the appellants]
and was purchased by the defendants from the manufacturers' United
Kingdom agents in or about the month of November 1973." That F
allegation was not controverted in the affidavit which was filed on behalf
of the appellants in support of their application to set aside the order
for service out of the jurisdiction.

In my judgment the judge rightly held that the relevant tort was
committed partly within and partly without the jurisdiction, in that the
product was distributed within, but manufactured outside, the jurisdiction.
He then went on to consider an important authority, namely, *Distillers* G
Co. (*Biochemicals*) *Ltd.* v. *Thompson* [1971] A.C. 458. That was a
case in which an English company, the manufacturers of a drug marketed
under the name of Distaval, which contained the drug thalidomide, had
sold the drug in Australia, as a result of which it was alleged that a woman
who was pregnant suffered, as did the child to whom she subsequently H
gave birth. She sought to sue Distillers in Australia upon the basis that
they committed negligence by virtue of their failure, when they sold the drug,
to give a warning of its dangerous characteristic. The judge cited various
portions of the opinion of the Privy Council as given by Lord Pearson.
He accepted that which Mr. Livesey says is the appropriate approach to
this case (*Distillers Co.* (*Biochemicals*) *Ltd.* v. *Thompson* [1971] A.C.
458, 468):

A   " The right approach is, when the tort is complete, to look back over the series of events constituting it and ask the question, where in substance did this cause of action arise? "

The judge also relied upon a number of other parts of the judgment of Lord Pearson in the *Distillers* case. He said, quoting from p. 468: " It is manifestly just and reasonable that a defendant should have to

B   answer for his wrongdoing in the country where he did the wrong." And in dealing with a suggested test, namely, the test where the last act of negligence occurred, he quoted from p. 467:

" The last event might happen in a particular case to be the determining factor on its own merits, by reason of its inherent importance, but not because it is the last event . . . But when the question is

C   which country's courts should have jurisdiction to try the action, the approach should be different: the search is for the most appropriate court to try the action, and the degree of connection between the cause of action and the country concerned should be the determining factor."

Mr. Livesey relied heavily upon a case in this court, *George Monro*

D   *Ltd.* v. *American Cyanamid and Chemical Corporation* [1944] 1 K.B. 432, and maintained that that was authority for the proposition that where everything else had happened outside the jurisdiction, with the exception of the actual suffering of the damage, then it was not a proper case for proceedings to be brought in this country. That was a case in which I think it can be properly said that the decision of the

E   court was sufficiently founded upon their view that the affidavit had not established that there had been any tort committed within the jurisdiction. That was the view of Winn J. when he considered that case in *Cordova Land Co. Ltd.* v. *Victor Brothers Inc.* and *Cordova Land Co. Ltd.* v. *Black Diamond Steamship Corporation* [1966] 1 W.L.R. 793.

The fundamental point in *George Monro Ltd.* v. *American Cyanamid and Chemical Corporation* [1944] 1 K.B. 432, as it seems to me, is that

F   not only had the negligent manufacture of the product taken place in America, but the goods which were the subject matter of the case were actually sold in America, so that the property passed in America. Thus everything which the company had done, against which complaint could be made, had occurred in America.

There is however some assistance to be obtained from the judgment

G   of du Parcq L.J. in *George Monro Ltd.* v. *American Cyanamid and Chemical Corporation* [1944] 1 K.B. 432, 440–441, where he said:

" . . . I am willing to infer that the negligence alleged is that the corporation put on the market a dangerous substance with written instructions to use it in a dangerous way. That act of commission was done in America and it is highly artificial to say that the tort

H   was committed within the jurisdiction of the English courts. The principle of the rule is plain. Looking at the substance of the matter without regard to any technical consideration, the question is: Where was the wrongful act, from which the damage flows, in fact done? "

Returning to this case and bearing in mind that the application to sue the appellants in this country is based upon the allegation that the plaintiff could successfully sue the appellants, one then asks oneself the question which was posed by du Parcq L.J., and the answer to that

Castree v. Squibb Ltd. (C.A.) [1980]

question seems to me to be clearly this: that which gave, or gives, the A
plaintiff her cause of complaint is not the mere manufacture of the
defective machinery, which of course took place in Germany; the mere
manufacture of the defective machinery is not in my judgment even the
beginning of tort. That manufacture might have been manufacture for
experimental purposes, or it might have been for the development of
some part of the machinery. The substantial wrongdoing in this case B
alleged to have been committed by the appellants is putting on the
English market a defective machine with no warning as to its defects.
That being, in my judgment, the position, and applying the test which is
accepted on all sides to be the appropriate test, namely, to look back
over the series of events constituting the tort and to ask the question
where in substance this cause of action arose, I would conclude that it
arose in this country. C

Accordingly I would dismiss this appeal.

OLIVER L.J. I agree.

BUCKLEY L.J. I also agree and I do not think I can usefully add
anything to what Ackner L.J. has said.
D

Appeal dismissed with costs.

Solicitors: *Hextall Erskine & Co.* for *Laces & Co., Liverpool;*
Weightmans, Liverpool.

B. O. A.
E

[COURT OF APPEAL]

* ALLEN AND OTHERS *v.* JAMBO HOLDINGS LTD. AND OTHERS
F

[1979 A. No. 757]

1979 July 20   Lord Denning M.R., Shaw
and Templeman L.JJ.

Injunction—Interlocutory—Mareva injunction—Claim in negligence
for personal injury—Defendants outside court's jurisdiction— G
Defendants' aircraft sole asset within jurisdiction—Application
to restrain its removal — Plaintiffs' means limited — Whether
relief to be granted

> Following the death of the first plaintiff's husband in an
> accident involving an aircraft, piloted by the second defendant
> and owned by the first defendants, a Nigerian company with
> no other assets within the jurisdiction, the first plaintiff H
> obtained a *Mareva* injunction to restrain the defendants from
> removing the aircraft from the jurisdiction. A writ, claiming
> damages for the dependants and estate of the deceased in
> negligence and under the Fatal Accidents Act 1976, was
> subsequently served on the defendants. Some months later
> the defendants successfully applied to discharge the order,
> contending, inter alia, that, as the first plaintiff was legally
> aided and the deceased's estate of limited value, any cross
> undertaking in damages was of little value to them.

A   On appeal by the first plaintiff: —
        Held, allowing the appeal, that there was no reason in
    principle why a *Mareva* injunction should not be granted in
    a personal injury action as it had been in commercial actions
    (post, pp. 1255E–F, 1258E); that it would be wrong to deny
    the plaintiff a *Mareva* injunction to which she would otherwise
    be entitled on the ground that her cross undertaking in
    damages was of limited value (post, pp. 1256H—1257A, E,
B   1258F–G); and that as it was open to the defendants to secure the
    release of their aircraft by providing alternative security for any
    damages that might be awarded to the plaintiffs, the balance of
    justice and convenience lay in favour of continuing the injunc-
    tion (post, pp. 1257B–C, H—1258A).
        Decision of Bristow J. reversed.

    The following cases are referred to in the judgments:
C
    Rasu Maritima S.A. v. *Perusahaan Pertambangan Minyak Dan Gas Bumi
        Negara (Government of the Republic of Indonesia intervening)
        (Pertamina)* [1978] Q.B. 644; [1977] 3 W.L.R. 518; [1977] 3 All E.R.
        324, C.A.
    Third Chandris Shipping Corporation v. *Unimarine S.A.* [1979] Q.B.
        645; [1979] 3 W.L.R. 122; [1979] 2 All E.R. 972, C.A.

D
    The following additional cases were cited in argument:
    American Cyanamid Co. v. *Ethicon Ltd.* [1975] A.C. 396; [1975] 2
        W.L.R. 316; [1975] 1 All E.R. 504, H.L.(E.).
    Birkett v. *James* [1978] A.C. 297; [1977] 3 W.L.R. 38; [1977] 2 All
        E.R. 801, H.L.(E.).

E   INTERLOCUTORY APPEAL from Bristow J.
        On March 2, 1979, Drake J. granted ex parte to the first plaintiff,
    Ruth Allen, suing for herself and as executrix of the estate of Harry
    Allen deceased and as next friend of the second and third plaintiffs, the
    infants Caroline Commander and Simon Commander, an injunction
    restraining the first and second defendants, Jambo Holdings Ltd. and
    John Eismark, from removing from the jurisdiction or from Leavesden
F   Aerodrome the twin engined Rockwell Commander 685 until March 8,
    1979, or further order. On March 6, 1979, the first, second and third
    plaintiffs, together with the fourth plaintiffs, Arnold Israel and Stephen
    Allen (suing as executors of the estate of Harry Allen deceased), issued
    a writ against the first defendants, the second defendant and the third
    defendants, Rolls Royce Ltd., the owners of Leavesden Aerodrome,
    claiming damages under the Fatal Accidents Act 1976 for the death of
G   the deceased and, on behalf of the deceased's estate, for loss of expectation
    of life and damage to the deceased caused by negligence and/or breach
    of statutory duty of the defendants, their servants or agents at Leavesden
    Aerodrome on January 27, 1979. On March 9, 1979, and March 23, 1979,
    the injunction was continued by consent. On June 19, 1979, the first and
    second defendants issued a summons giving notice of their application to
H   have the injunction discontinued. Bristow J. heard the application and
    discharged the injunction on June 27, 1979.
        The first plaintiff appealed on the grounds that (1) the judge erred
    in failing to conclude that the grant of an injunction would be likely
    to secure an offer by the first defendants of security and/or failed
    adequately or at all to take into account as a resolution of the balance
    of convenience the offering of security by way of bond or otherwise by
    the first defendants; (2) the judge paid regard to a submission that there

might be exchange control difficulties in the provision of security when A
there was no evidence upon which such submission or any inference
could be based; (3) the judge failed to take into account adequately or
at all that the defendants had taken no steps for three and a half months
to discharge the injunction; (4) the judge failed to take into account
adequately or at all that the defendants were only now seeking to discharge the injunction such that they were now likely as a result of the B
injunction to be prepared to give security; and (5) the judge erred in
concluding that there was in law or at all a distinction between the grant
of a *Mareva* injunction in a personal injury or fatal accident action and
in a commercial dispute.

The facts are stated in the judgment of Lord Denning M.R.

Michael Burton for the first plaintiff.   C
Dermod O'Brien for the first and second defendants.
Robert Webb for the third defendants.

LORD DENNING M.R. A man's head got caught in a propeller. He
was decapitated and killed. It was at the Leavesden aerodrome, near
Watford. There was a small twin-engined aircraft there. It belonged to D
a Nigerian company called Jambo Holdings Ltd. It had come into this
country for servicing and to qualify for a certificate of airworthiness.
All was in order for its return to Nigeria. It was due to leave on the
evening of Saturday, January 27, 1979. The first leg to Gatwick, then
on to Nigeria.

The pilot, John Eismark, had agreed to take two passengers with
him on the first leg from Leavesden to Gatwick. Two friends were to E
go to see them off. They were Mr. Harry Allen and his wife Ruth
Allen. Earlier in the evening Mr. Allen himself had gone with the
pilot to the aerodrome to help load some of the heavier luggage into
the aircraft. Afterwards they both returned to fetch the others and
the hand luggage. The pilot went ahead to test the engines. It was a
cold, icy night, and he wanted to see that there was no ice on the wings F
and the propellers, and to see that everything was in order. He was
in the cockpit making those checks when Mr. Allen, his wife and the
two passengers (who were going aboard the aircraft that evening) arrived
by car. As the car approached the aircraft, the pilot switched on the
lights of the aircraft. The car driver had his lights on as he drew near.
The pilot waved him on. The motor car backed to a distance of about
ten yards from the aircraft. Then the passengers and Mr. Allen and G
his wife got out to go to the aircraft. Mr. Allen was carrying a bag on
his shoulder. He went first and the others followed after. It was then
the accident happened. Mr. Allen's head became caught in the propeller.
He was killed. It was a tragedy.

There was an inquest. It was held on March 1, 1979. The coroner
found a verdict of accidental death. As soon as the inquest ended, the H
pilot told the solicitor for the widow that he intended to fly the aircraft
back to Nigeria immediately. The solicitor was afraid that any claim
by the widow for damages would be fruitless if the aircraft was flown
back to Nigeria. It would be very difficult to enforce any judgment in
Nigeria. The solicitors tried to discover whether the aircraft was insured
with an English insurance company, but they failed. So on the next day
they took steps immediately. They instructed counsel. Counsel tele-

A phoned Drake J. and explained the circumstances to him. The judge granted a *Mareva* injunction to restrain the Nigerian company and the pilot from removing the aircraft from the jurisdiction until after the hearing of a summons. The aircraft has remained at Leavesden aerodrome ever since. The injunction was continued by agreement. No request was made for it to be discharged. The reason was because more work had to be done on the aircraft, and further tests were to be made.

B From March until June nothing was done by the Nigerian company or anyone on their behalf to try and discharge the injunction.

Then on June 19, 1979 (that is, last month) a summons was taken out by a well-known firm of solicitors who act for insurance companies in the City of London. They applied for the injunction to be discharged. Affidavits were sworn on both sides. It was heard by Bristow J. He

C realised that it was a new and important case. After careful consideration he decided to discharge the injunction. But he intimated that it was a suitable case for appeal to this court. So he gave leave to appeal.

It is a new case altogether. In the past *Mareva* injunctions have been confined to the commercial court. The judges of that court have granted injunctions to restrain foreign companies from removing moneys

D so as to defeat their creditors. The leading case is *Rasu Maritima S.A. v. Perusahaan Pertambangan Minyak Dan Gas Bumi Negara (Government of the Republic of Indonesia intervening)* [1978] Q.B. 644, coupled with a very recent case, *Third Chandris Shipping Corporation v. Unimarine S.A.* [1979] Q.B. 645. Those were commercial cases. But this is new. Not because it concerns an aircraft. There was one case where a bill was run up for fuel for an aircraft. The bill was not paid. An order

E was made restraining the movement of the aircraft until the bill was paid. But this is the first case we have had of a personal injury (this is a fatal accident case) where a *Mareva* injunction has been sought. The nearest parallel is a ship in an English port where there is an accident causing personal injuries or death. It has been settled for centuries that the claimant can bring an action in rem and arrest the ship. She is not

F allowed to leave the port until security is provided so as to ensure that any proper claim will be duly met.

The question in this case is whether a similar jurisdiction can be exercised in regard to an aircraft. In principle I see no reason why it should not, except that it is to be done by a *Mareva* injunction instead of an action in rem. The real difficulty is that we do not know the rights or wrongs of this accident. The widow alleges that the pilot

G knew that people were coming aboard with the luggage; he knew that they were approaching the doorway close to the propeller; he ought to have warned them, or he ought to have stopped his engines and stopped the propellers going round. On the other hand, it is alleged against Mr. Allen that he ought to have known better; he could hear that the engines were running; and that any person taking reasonable care of

H himself would not have gone close to the propellers as he did.

There are the two sides. It cannot be decided today. It has to be decided in the action. As the judge says, it may be that the owners of the aircraft are wholly liable, or it may be that Mr. Allen was wholly liable; or it may be half and half. All that can be said is that the widow and her children have a good, arguable case for claiming damages on the ground that it was at least in part the fault of the pilot. That is sufficient. We said so in the *Rasu Maritima S.A.* case [1978] Q.B. 644,

663 and, as we also said there, the *Mareva* principle applies not only to A
money but also to goods. So it applies to this aircraft.

On the evening of March 2, 1979, all the plaintiffs knew was that
the aircraft was about to fly off to Nigeria. It was Nigerian owned. For
aught that anyone knew, if the aircraft went off, it might never return.
The widow would have great difficulty in getting any damages if they
were awarded to her. That was quite sufficient to warrant the judge in
granting the *Mareva* injunction.   B

The Nigerian company now come here and ask that that injunction
should be discharged. They do it on these grounds. First, they say in
their affidavit:

"... the first defendant"—that is, the Nigerian company—" is
insured against claims of this nature under Policy No. MA/AHL/
78/HL/0004 issued by the National Corporation of Nigeria of 118,   C
Broad Street, P.O. Box 1100, Lagos, Nigeria, upon whose instructions
the first and second defendants' solicitors herein are acting."

That is all we are told. Nothing is said about whether the insurance
corporation have accepted responsibility. Nothing is said as to their
stability or their backing or as to reinsurance or anything of that kind.
Until more is known about it, it seems to me that the mere assertion of   D
insurance is not sufficient ground for discharging the injunction. If
there had been an undertaking by an English insurance company of
standing, it would be different. But no such undertaking has been offered.

The affidavit goes on to say that this is a new aircraft which was
made in the United States from where it was exported in February 1978.
It was intended to register it in Nigeria. It was worth £½m which is   E
far more than what might be awarded on any claim. No doubt that is
true. But then it goes on to say that, if this injunction remains, the
Nigerian company would suffer great loss. They are a big industrial
group, and if they were deprived of the use of this aircraft they would
have to employ a further 20 senior managers at £50,000 a year each; and
that would raise the group's overheads by £1m a year. That is difficult
to swallow.   F

So the affidavit does not impress me in the least. I can see no reason
in this case, as is done in shipping cases all over the world, why security
should not be given in the way of a bond or an undertaking by a
reputable company or concern in England so as to ensure that any award
of damages to the plaintiffs would be met. If the Nigerian company
are of such high standing, as we are now told they are, if they are ready   G
to accept any liability, as we are told they will, it seems to me that a
bank or an insurance company of standing in this country would back
the Nigerian company by way of security without any difficulty whatsoever. No such security is forthcoming or is mentioned in the affidavit.

We were told, " Ships are different. They have their protection and
indemnity clubs, whereas aircraft have not." I would expect that
insurance policies nowadays would cover the provision of security. But,   H
even if they do not, the sooner they do the better. As with ships, so
with aircraft. The situation is so parallel, the one with the other, that
even though this is a new case, it seems to me that it would be right to
continue the *Mareva* injunction in the expectation that the aircraft will
be released at any moment as soon as security is provided.

There is one other point that I must mention. It is said that whenever a *Mareva* injunction is granted the plaintiff has to give the cross-

A undertaking in damages. Suppose the widow should lose this case altogether. She is legally aided. Her undertaking is worth nothing. I would not assent to that argument. As Shaw L.J. said in the course of the argument, a legally aided plaintiff is by our statutes not to be in any worse position by reason of being legally aided than any other plaintiff would be. I do not see why a poor plaintiff should be denied a *Mareva* injunction just because he is poor, whereas a rich plaintiff would get it.

B One has to look at these matters broadly. As a matter of convenience, balancing one side against the other, it seems to me that an injunction should go to restrain the removal of this aircraft.

The owners of the aerodrome, Rolls-Royce Ltd., are here. They wish for guidance as to what should be done at the aerodrome. This injunction does not prevent any steps being taken so as to see that the

C aircraft is in good order and is kept in good condition and is serviceable. But the injunction does make it clear that the aircraft must not be removed from the jurisdiction or from the aerodrome permanently until further order. It is to be hoped that all difficulties will be resolved in an hour or two by security being provided.

I would allow the appeal accordingly.

D
SHAW L.J. I agree. Mr. O'Brien, who has argued this appeal on behalf of the first and second defendants, has not suggested that there is any real difference in principle between an action for personal injury such as this one and an action in respect of some mercantile transaction. What he has said is that one ought to look more cautiously at the situation because in commercial disputes it is usually the case that a plaintiff will

E be in a position to meet any potential liability under his undertaking in damages if he asks for a *Mareva* injunction and then loses the action. But, as Lord Denning M.R. has pointed out, questions of financial stability ought not to affect the position in regard to what is the essential justice of the case as between the parties.

In the present case the defendants have deposed to their being solvent

F and to the fact that the company has assets which are sufficient to satisfy a judgment. That perfunctory dismissal of the suggestion that the *Mareva* injunction ought not to go in respect of their aircraft makes no reference at all to where those other assets are to be found or what they consist of; nor is account taken of what the magnitude of the judgment may be if the action should go against them. Altogether I found their

G evidence very unimpressive; if one began with any misgivings as to whether the plaintiff if she succeeds in this action will be paid any damages she may be awarded, the defendants' affidavits did not serve to allay those misgivings. They had rather the opposite effect.

One comes back to what is the central principle which should determine whether a *Mareva* injunction should go. It is urged that it would

H be a novel departure from precedent to apply it to an action such as this; but as recently as 1975 it was something of an innovation in regard to mercantile transactions. If one applies the principle that the proper order is one which would result in a due balance of justice and convenience, it would follow that in the circumstances of this case the course to be taken is that which would involve the least risk of ultimate injustice having regard to the actual and potential rights and liabilities of the parties on both sides. This, in my view, will be best achieved by the order proposed by Lord Denning M.R. and I would allow the appeal accordingly.

TEMPLEMAN L.J. I agree. The pilot assumed that the two passengers and the hand baggage would not be brought up to the aircraft. The pilot knew but obviously Mr. Allen did not realise that the clearance between the propeller and the entrance to the aircraft was such as to make it dangerous to attempt to enter while the engines were running. The pilot did not switch off the engines, and Mr. Allen was fatally injured.

The pilot's employers are a foreign corporation with no assets in this country except the aircraft. They resist liability for the death of Mr. Allen; and through counsel they complain that their one asset in this country, the aircraft, has been frozen. They produce evidence, although months have gone by, merely making the bland statement that the pilot's employers are solvent and have assets sufficient to satisfy a judgment. They produce the bland statement that they are insured against claims of this nature. They do not explain why they have not taken what would be the normal precautions to reassure the widow and executors in the circumstances, namely, of producing an undertaking by insurers who are resident in this country or by producing a bond or some form of security. Instead of that they have put forward the proposition that if an injunction is granted and they have to do without the aircraft for a long period they will require 20 senior managers at £50,000 a year, raising their overheads by £1m a year. I am not impressed either by what they have not said, or by what they have said.

So far as the question of jurisdiction is concerned, I can see no difference between a *Mareva* injunction in a commercial action and a *Mareva* injunction for personal injury or any other cause of action save this, that in the kind of actions in which *Mareva* injunctions have been granted, where the contest is between two big commercial concerns, there is usually very little argument about the value of the cross-undertaking in damages, and there are freely available methods of security.

In this case one factor which Mr. O'Brien very properly urged on us—but it is only a factor which we must bear in mind—is the cross-undertaking in damages which must inevitably be limited to the assets of the executors which I understand are no more than the present inflated value of a house. Nevertheless, it seems to me that to deny an injunction in these circumstances would be to deny a measure of assurance to the widow which she is entitled to have. Accordingly, I agree that the injunction should go, and I would suggest that the defendants instead of spending the amount which they have spent on air fares and the amount which they or their insurers have spent on this litigation will now employ their resources in obtaining what it seems to me are perfectly available, feasible and not difficult methods of securing the release of their aircraft by providing the necessary security.

Appeal allowed with costs.
Costs below reserved.
Leave to appeal refused.

Solicitors: *J. Israel, Arnold & Strange; Barlow, Lyde & Gilbert; Beaumont & Son.*

C. N.

A

[CHANCERY DIVISION]

* BARCLAY-JOHNSON *v.* YUILL

[1979 B. No. 3389]

B 1980 April 18, 21   Sir Robert Megarry V.-C.

Injunction — Interlocutory — Mareva injunction — English debtor
absent abroad—Application to restrain removal of debtor's
assets from within jurisdiction pending proceedings for
recovery of debt—Jurisdiction to grant injunction against
non-foreigner not based abroad—Supreme Court of Judicature
C *(Consolidation) Act 1925 (15 & 16 Geo. 5, c. 49), s. 45 (1)* [1]

The plaintiff, associated with the defendant in the business
of acquiring and renovating dilapidated premises, claimed that
he owed her £2,000 following the transfer to him of a penthouse flat on which he had carried out building works to her
order. The sum was agreed but not paid over, and in negotiating the state of the accounts between them the plaintiff
D learnt that the defendant had sold the flat before going abroad,
and was believed to be cruising in the Mediterranean in a
yacht of which he was part owner. The plaintiff knew that
when he was previously in financial difficulties he had gone
to live for some time in the United States of America. She
had begun proceedings for recovery of inter alia the £2,000
but now, fearing that removal of his assets from the jurisdiction would render those proceedings nugatory, she obtained,
in an ex parte application during the vacation, an injunction
E restraining the defendant, who was not a foreigner, from
removing or taking steps to remove out of the jurisdiction, or
dealing with, the proceeds of sale of the flat (represented in part
by a bank balance of some £3,300) otherwise than by paying
them into a bank deposit account within the jurisdiction.
On the plaintiff's application for a continuation of that
injunction : —
F *Held*, (1) that the general principle was still that the court
would not grant an injunction to restrain a defendant from
disposing of his assets merely in order to improve the prospects
of the plaintiff, if successful, in recovering on his judgment
(post, p. 1262H).
Lister & Co. v. *Stubbs* (1890) 45 Ch.D. 1, C.A. considered.
(2) That the *Mareva* injunction formed a limited exception
to that principle, applying where there was a real risk of the
G defendant removing his assets from the jurisdiction, since in
such cases it was " just or convenient " within section 45 of
the Supreme Court of Judicature (Consolidation) Act 1925, to
grant the injunction; and that that applied even if the defendant
was not a foreigner or foreign-based, since the essence of the
injunction was the risk of removal (post, pp. 1263c, 1266c–d).
Mareva Compania Naviera S.A. v. *International Bulk-*
H *carriers S.A.* [1975] 2 Lloyd's Rep. 509, C.A.; *Third Chandris*
Shipping Corporation v. *Unimarine S.A.* [1979] Q.B. 645, C.A.
and *Chartered Bank* v. *Daklouche* [1980] 1 W.L.R. 107, C.A.
considered.
(3) That as the plaintiff had a clearly formulated claim to
£2,000 and had shown that there was a sufficient risk of the

[1] Supreme Court of Judicature (Consolidation) Act 1925, s. 45: " (1) The High
Court may grant . . . an injunction . . . by an interlocutory order in all cases in
which it appears to the court to be just or convenient so to do."

defendant removing his bank balance of £3,300 from the juris- A
diction, the injunction should be continued, though only in
respect of so much of the bank balance as would be required
to satisfy the claim to £2,000, together with a reasonable
additional sum for costs (post, pp. 1266C–D, 1267A–B).

The following cases are referred to in the judgment:

Allen v. *Jambo Holdings Ltd.* [1980] 1 W.L.R. 1252; [1980] 2 All E.R. B
    502, C.A.
Chartered Bank v. *Daklouche* [1980] 1 W.L.R. 107; [1980] 1 All E.R.
    205, C.A.
Etablissement Esefka International Anstalt v. *Central Bank of Nigeria*
    [1979] 1 Lloyd's Rep. 445, C.A.
Gebr Van Weelde Scheepvaart Kantoor B.V. v. *Homeric Marine Services
    Ltd.* (*The Agrabele*) [1979] 2 Lloyd's Rep. 117.   C
Iraqi Ministry of Defence v. *Arcepey Shipping Co. S.A.* [1980] 2 W.L.R.
    488; [1980] 1 All E.R. 480.
Lister & Co. v. *Stubbs* (1890) 45 Ch.D. 1, C.A.
Mareva Compania Naviera S.A. v. *International Bulkcarriers S.A.* [1975]
    2 Lloyd's Rep. 509; [1980] 1 All E.R. 213, C.A.
Montecchi v. *Shimco (U.K.) Ltd.* [1979] 1 W.L.R. 1180, C.A.
Nippon Yusen Kaisha v. *Karageorgis* [1975] 1 W.L.R. 1093; [1975] 3 All D
    E.R. 282; [1975] 2 Lloyd's Rep. 137, C.A.
Rasu Maritima S.A. v. *Perusahaan Pertambangan Minyak Dan Gas Bumi
    Negara* (*Government of the Republic of Indonesia intervening*) (*Per-
    tamina*) [1978] Q.B. 644; [1977] 3 W.L.R. 518; [1977] 3 All E.R.
    324; [1977] 2 Lloyd's Rep. 397, C.A.
Siskina (*Owners of cargo lately laden on board*) v. *Distos Compania
    Naviera S.A.* [1979] A.C. 210; [1977] 3 W.L.R. 818; [1977] 3 All E
    E.R. 803; [1978] 1 Lloyd's Rep. 1, H.L.(E.).
Third Chandris Shipping Corporation v. *Unimarine S.A.* [1979] Q.B.
    645; [1979] 3 W.L.R. 122; [1979] 2 All E.R. 972; [1979] 2 Lloyd's
    Rep. 184, Mustill J. and C.A.

No additional cases were cited in argument.

                                                                          F
MOTION

The plaintiff, Mary Patricia Barclay-Johnson, applied ex parte for
the continuation of an injunction restraining the defendant, Cecil
Mortley Yuill, until trial or further order from removing or taking
steps to remove out of the jurisdiction of the court or disposing of or
transferring charging with any debt or liability or otherwise dealing with
the net proceeds of sale of a leasehold property, The Penthouse Flat, G
12, St. Quintins Avenue, London W.10 otherwise than by paying the
same into and retaining the same separate and apart from all and any
other moneys in a bank deposit account within the jurisdiction. The
plaintiff's application was opposed by the defendant.

The writ dated April 14, 1980, claimed inter alia a declaration that
a sum of £2,000 remained due and owing to the plaintiff in respect of H
the transfer to the defendant of the leasehold flat in August 1978 and
the court was asked for an order that the £2,000 be paid to her together
with such other sums as might be found due to her.

The facts are stated in the judgment.

Christopher Semken for the plaintiff.
D. C. Unwin for the defendant.

A   SIR ROBERT MEGARRY V.-C. This opposed ex parte motion raises the question whether a *Mareva* injunction can and should be granted against a defendant who is in no sense a foreigner. The plaintiff and the defendant have been associated for some while in the business of acquiring dilapidated premises, renovating them, and then selling them. The plaintiff says that she employed the defendant as her agent and building contractor, whereas the defendant alleges that there was a
B   partnership between them. At the centre of the present dispute there is a penthouse flat which the plaintiff says she transferred to the defendant on October 20, 1977, on the terms that the defendant would carry out building works in the flat to the plaintiff's order to the value of £28,000, and then pay the plaintiff a sum which came to be agreed at £2,000. This sum, she says, was never paid, and on or about August
C   30, 1978, her then solicitors registered a caution against dealings in respect of the flat. There was litigation between the parties in which attempts were made to agree the state of accounts between them, but progress was slow: the plaintiff says that she paid some £146,000 to the defendant, and that she believes that the defendant's figure of £73,000 expended by him on the plaintiff's behalf is inflated, so that her claim against him will exceed £73,000.
D   While the negotiations were proceeding, the plaintiff's present solicitors were notified by the defendant's solicitors that their client had either gone abroad or was about to do so: this was on April 2 or 3, 1980. The plaintiff promptly made a telephone call to the penthouse flat in order to speak to the defendant, and the call was answered by a lady who said that she had purchased the flat and knew
E   nothing about any caution. The plaintiff says that neither she nor her former or present solicitors ever applied for the cancellation of the caution or received any notice from the Land Registry about its removal. Inquiries of the Land Registry have elicited the information that no caution is now registered in respect of the flat. The way in which the caution vanished is at present mysterious, though it seems
F   to have been removed on September 18, 1978, in connection in some way with a charge to a bank.
     I pause there to say that both Mr. Semken who appeared for the plaintiff and Mr. Unwin who appeared for the defendant were in a position of some difficulty, though for different reasons. A substantial part of Mr. Semken's papers in this case had gone astray, whereas Mr. Unwin, though instructed generally by the defendant's solicitors, was
G   unable to obtain any specific instructions from the defendant himself. This was because the defendant was abroad, believed to be cruising in the Mediterranean, and could not be reached by his solicitors, who had accepted service on his behalf. The plaintiff says that the defendant is part owner of a 54 foot twin engined diesel yacht. Nevertheless, both counsel did their best to be helpful, and of course I have to deal with
H   the case on the information that is before me. This consists of the writ, issued on April 15, 1980, a notice of motion, and an affidavit sworn by the plaintiff on April 18, the day on which Mr. Semken moved before me. The plaintiff had previously during the vacation obtained an ex parte injunction from Booth J. over April 18 in terms of the notice of motion now before me. Put shortly, this seeks an injunction restraining the defendant from removing or taking steps to remove out of the jurisdiction or dealing with the net proceeds of sale of the penthouse

1262

flat otherwise than by paying them into a bank deposit account within A
the jurisdiction and keeping them separate from any other moneys.
What the plaintiff seeks and the defendant opposes is a continuation
of the ex parte injunction. Mr. Unwin accepts that some £3,300
standing to the credit of the defendant in a bank account in his name
represents the balance of the proceeds of sale of the penthouse flat.

The plaintiff's evidence is that she fears that the defendant will
remove all his assets from the jurisdiction and so render nugatory the B
relief that she seeks in her action. This relief includes a claim to the
£2,000, the taking of accounts, and the payment to the plaintiff of
what is found due to her on taking the accounts. The plaintiff says
that when the defendant was previously in financial difficulties, he
went to live in the United States for a considerable period; this was in
or about 1976. Last summer he told her that he would go abroad C
again, and she fears that he will sell his interests in the United Kingdom
and live on the yacht overseas. He is, of course, out of the jurisdiction
on the yacht at present, so far as is known.

Now in those circumstances, Mr. Unwin, in addition to commenting
adversely on the plaintiff's evidence, took what in effect is a preliminary
point of law. This is simply that no *Mareva* injunction can be granted D
against a defendant who is not a foreigner, and that as the defendant
cannot in any way be described as a foreigner, the injunction ought
not to be continued. During his submissions he conceded that in some
circumstances a person about to depart from the realm, even though
not a foreigner, might be the subject of a *Mareva* injunction. But
basically his submission was that apart from these circumstances,
Mareva injunctions were for foreigners alone. As the argument had E
not concluded at the normal time for adjournment on April 18, I
continued the injunction over today, and the question is whether it
should be further continued or discharged. If Mr. Unwin's point of
law is right, then of course the injunction must be discharged. In
order to decide this I must, I think, examine the basis of the *Mareva*
jurisdiction.
                                                                        F
The *Mareva* jurisdiction takes its name from *Mareva Compania
Naviera S.A.* v. *International Bulkcarriers S.A.* [1975] 2 Lloyd's Rep.
509, a case which concerned the vessel *Mareva*: I shall call it "the
Mareva case." Its immediate precursor was *Nippon Yusen Kaisha* v.
Karageorgis [1975] 1 W.L.R. 1093. Both are decisions of the Court
of Appeal on ex parte applications, and in both cases injunctions of the
type now sought before me were granted against foreign defendants who G
had assets within the jurisdiction. I think that it is the *Mareva* case
which has given its name to the injunction because in the earlier case
the court had not been referred to *Lister & Co.* v. *Stubbs* (1890) 45
Ch.D. 1 or any of the other cases in that line which pointed in the
opposite direction, and it was in the *Mareva* case that the Court of
Appeal held that notwithstanding those authorities, the injunction H
should be granted.

There are thus two lines of authority. First, there is the *Lister* v.
Stubbs line. In broad terms, this establishes the general proposition
that the court will not grant an injunction to restrain a defendant from
parting with his assets so that they may be preserved in case the plaintiff's
claim succeeds. The plaintiff, like other creditors of the defendant,
must obtain his judgment and then enforce it. He cannot prevent

The Weekly Law Reports, October 24, 1980

1263

1 W.L.R.   Barclay-Johnson v. Yuill (Ch.D.)   Sir Robert
                                                                               Megarry V.-C.

A the defendant from disposing of his assets pendente lite merely because
   he fears that by the time he obtains judgment in his favour the
   defendant will have no assets against which the judgment can be
   enforced. Were the law otherwise, the way would lie open to any
   claimant to paralyse the activities of any person or firm against whom
   he makes his claim by obtaining an injunction freezing their assets.
B Of course, the due exercise of the court's discretion would exclude
   flagrant abuses: but the disruptive peril to commercial activities might
   be grave. This refusal to grant injunctions was well settled law before
   1975: see *Siskina* v. *Distos Compania Naviera S.A.* [1979] A.C. 210,
   260, *per* Lord Hailsham of St. Marylebone; and see *Pertamina*
   [1978] Q.B. 644, 659, *per* Lord Denning M.R. (The correct name of
   this case, even omitting the name of the party intervening, is *Rasu*
C *Maritima S.A.* v. *Perusahaan Pertambangan Minyak Dan Gas Bumi
   Negara;* but in mercy to all I impose a short title by reference to the
   name of the company concerned). Furthermore, this doctrine was
   established when the statutory jurisdiction to grant an injunction was,
   as it is now, a power to do so in all cases in which it appeared to
   the court to be " just or convenient " to do so: see the Supreme Court
   of Judicature Act 1873, section 25 (8); Supreme Court of Judicature
D (Consolidation) Act 1925, section 45 (1).
       The other line of authority is, of course, the *Mareva* line. This
   was based on the statutory language that I have just mentioned, and it
   shows that in certain circumstances it is " just or convenient " to grant
   such an injunction. The question is what those circumstances are.
   In the *Siskina* case [1979] A.C. 210, 261 Lord Hailsham referred to
E " foreign based defendants with assets in this country." In *Pertamina*
   [1978] Q.B. 644, 659, Lord Denning M.R. referred to a defendant
   who is " out of the jurisdiction but has assets in this country." The
   contrast is with those who " are within the jurisdiction of the court
   and have assets here ": *Pertamina* at p. 659, *per* Lord Denning M.R.,
   a phrase which in *Chartered Bank* v. *Daklouche* [1980] 1 W.L.R.
F 107, 112, Lord Denning M.R. explained as meaning cases where the
   defendants " were permanently settled here and had their assets here."
   He added: " If a defendant is likely to leave England at short notice, a
   Mareva injunction may well be granted."
       The relevant facts in the *Chartered Bank* case were that the
   defendants were a Lebanese married couple engaged in business in
   the Persian Gulf. The wife bought a house in England and their
G daughters went to school here. The husband then encountered financial
   difficulties and disappeared, but some of his money was transmitted to
   a bank account in the wife's name in England. A bank to which the
   husband owed money then sought and obtained a *Mareva* injunction
   in respect of the money in the wife's bank account here. Eveleigh L.J.
   held that the wife was not an " English based defendant " within Lord
H Hailsham's phrase (see at p. 114), and Lord Denning M.R., as I have
   indicated, did not regard her as being " permanently settled here." The
   case shows that a *Mareva* injunction may be granted against a
   defendant who is within the jurisdiction, even if he or she owns a
   house here, and that the jurisdiction is not confined to those who are
   outside the realm. I know that in *Gebr Van Weelde Scheepvaart Kantoor
   B.V.* v. *Homeric Marine Services Ltd.* (*The Agrabele*) [1979] 2 Lloyd's
   Rep. 117 Lloyd J. held that there was a settled practice against granting

1264

Mareva injunctions against defendants resident within the jurisdiction; A
but in reaching this conclusion the judge had been loyally applying what
Lord Denning M.R. had said in *Pertamina* [1978] Q.B. 644 before,
of course, it had been explained in the *Chartered Bank* case [1980] 1
W.L.R. 107. In any case, for reasons which will appear, I would, with
all respect, hesitate long before accepting that the place of residence
provided any *Mareva* touchstone.

It seems to me that the heart and core of the *Mareva* injunction is B
the risk of the defendant removing his assets from the jurisdiction and
so stultifying any judgment given by the courts in the action. If there
is no real risk of this, such an injunction should be refused; if there is
a real risk, then if the other requirements are satisfied, the injunction
ought to be granted. If the assets are likely to remain in the jurisdiction, then the plaintiff, like all others with claims against the defendant, C
must run the risk, common to all, that the defendant may dissipate his
assets, or consume them in discharging other liabilities, and so leave
nothing with which to satisfy any judgment. On the other hand, if
there is a real risk of the assets being removed from the jurisdiction,
a *Mareva* injunction will prevent their removal. It is not enough for
such an injunction merely to forbid the defendant to remove them
from the jurisdiction, for otherwise he might transfer them to some D
collaborator who would then remove them; accordingly, the injunction
will restrain the defendant from disposing of them even within the
jurisdiction. But that does not mean that the assets will remain sterilised
for the benefit of the plaintiff, for the court will permit the defendant
to use them for paying debts as they fall due: see *Iraqi Ministry of
Defence* v. *Arcepey Shipping Co. S.A.* [1980] 2 W.L.R. 488, especially E
at p. 494, *per* Robert Goff J.

If, then, the essence of the jurisdiction is the risk of the assets being
removed from the jurisdiction, I cannot see why it should be confined to
" foreigners," in any sense of that term. True, expressions such as
" foreign defendant " (see, for example, *Montecchi* v. *Shimco (U.K.)
Ltd.* [1979] 1 W.L.R. 1180, 1183 and the *Siskina* case [1979] A.C.
210, 253), and " foreign based defendants " (see the *Siskina* case at F
p. 261) appear in the cases, and for the most part the cases have concerned those who may fairly be called foreigners. Indeed, in the *Siskina*
case at p. 253, Lord Diplock puts the jurisdiction in terms of a foreign
defendant who does not reside or have a place of business within the
jurisdiction, though I would read this as being descriptive of the past
rather than restrictive of the future. Naturally the risk of removal of G
assets from the jurisdiction will usually be greater or more obvious in
the case of foreign-based defendants, and so the jurisdiction has grown
up in relation to them. But I cannot see why this should make some
requirement of foreignness a pre-requisite of the jurisdiction. If, for
example, an Englishman who has lived and worked all his life in
England is engaged in making arrangements to emigrate and remove all
his assets with him, is the court to say " He is not a foreigner, nor is H
he yet foreign-based, and so no *Mareva* injunction can be granted "?
Why should it make all the difference if instead he had been a foreign
national with a foreign domicile who, after living and working here for
a while, was preparing to leave with his assets? Is it really to be said
that in relation to *Mareva* injunctions, there is one law for the foreigner
and another for the English, and that this flows from a statutory power
to grant an injunction if it appears to the court to be " just or con-

The Weekly Law Reports, October 24, 1980

1265

1 W.L.R.   Barclay-Johnson v. Yuill (Ch.D.)   Sir Robert
                                                           Megarry V.-C.

A venient " to do so? I cannot see any sensible ground for holding that
in this respect there is some privilege or immunity for the English and
Welsh.

In saying this, I do not intend to suggest that matters of nationality,
domicile, residence and so on are irrelevant in *Mareva* applications.
Any or all of them may be of considerable importance in so far as they
bear upon the risk of removal. If the defendant has not even come to
B this country, the risk of his assets here being removed abroad will
normally be high. If a foreign national is here, his nationality will
often make it easier for him at short notice to go abroad with his
assets, and remain there, easier than for a citizen of the United
Kingdom; and his foreign domicile would render it more probable
that he would do this. At the same time, it must be remembered that
C since the first *Mareva* injunction was granted, there has been a significant
change, in that within the last year the abolition of exchange control
has made it easier for everybody to transfer assets abroad.

In the result, I would hold (1) that it is no bar to the grant of a
Mareva injunction that the defendant is not a foreigner, or is not
foreign-based, in any sense of those terms; (2) that it is essential that
there should be a real risk of the defendant's assets being removed
D from the jurisdiction in such a way as to stultify any judgment that
the plaintiff may obtain; and (3) that in determining whether there is
such a risk, questions of the defendant's nationality, domicile, place of
residence and many other matters may be material to a greater or a
lesser degree.

In addition to establishing the existence of a sufficient risk of
E removal of the defendant's assets, the plaintiff must satisfy certain other
requirements. I shall not attempt any comprehensive survey, particularly
in view of the guidelines laid down by Lord Denning M.R. in *Third
Chandris Shipping Corporation* v. *Unimarine S.A.* [1979] Q.B. 645,
668. But I may refer to three of them. One is that it must appear that
there is a danger of default if the assets are removed from the jurisdiction. Even if the risk of removal is great, no *Mareva* injunction
F should be granted unless there is also a danger of default. A reputable
foreign company, accustomed to paying its debts, ought not to be
prevented from removing its assets from the jurisdiction, especially if
it has substantial assets in countries in which English judgments can be
enforced. In commercial cases, it suffices if there are facts

G "from which the Commercial Court, like a prudent, sensible
commercial man, can properly infer a danger of default if assets
are removed from the jurisdiction ": see the *Third Chandris* case
at p. 671, *per* Lawton L.J.

If nothing can be found out about the defendant, that by itself may
suffice: ibid., at p. 672; see also *Etablissement Esefka International
Anstalt* v. *Central Bank of Nigeria* [1979] 1 Lloyd's Rep. 445.

H Second, the plaintiff must establish his claim with sufficient particularity, and show a good arguable case, though he need not demonstrate
that his case is strong enough to entitle him to judgment under R.S.C.,
Ord. 14: see *Pertamina* [1978] Q.B. 644. Third, the case must be
one in which, on weighing the considerations for and against the grant
of an injunction, the balance of convenience is in favour of granting it.
In considering this in *Mareva* cases, I think that some weight must be
given to the principle of *Lister & Co.* v. *Stubbs,* 45 Ch.D. 1: I have

already mentioned this. The *Mareva* prohibition against making any A
disposition of the assets within the country is a normal ancillary of
the prohibition against removing the assets from the country, and if
this is likely to affect the defendant seriously, I think that he is entitled to
have this put into the scales against the grant of the injunction. Much
may depend on the assets in question. If, as in many of the reported
cases, there is merely an isolated asset here, the harm to the defendant
may be small. On the other hand, if he is trading here and the injunc- B
tion would " freeze " his bank account, the injury may be grave. I
think that he should be able to rely on the *Lister* principle except so
far as it cannot be fairly reconciled with the needs of the *Mareva*
doctrine. I would regard the *Lister* principle as remaining the rule,
and the *Mareva* doctrine as constituting a limited exception to it.

I return to the facts of this case. I have already given my reasons C
for rejecting Mr. Unwin's preliminary objection on the law, and for
holding that the defendant's lack of foreignness, if I may so call it,
provides no bar to the granting of the injunction sought. The question
is thus whether on those facts it ought to be granted. Mr. Unwin
realistically accepted that the plaintiff had put forward a clearly formulated claim to the £2,000, but he pointed to an almost complete absence
of particularity in the remainder of the plaintiff's claim. In this, I D
agree with him. I think that the plaintiff's claim attains the requisite
standard of particularity as regards the £2,000, but not as regards anything else.

As for the risk of removal, it seems clear that the £3,300 in the
bank account, like the £70,000 in the *Chartered Bank* case [1980] 1
W.L.R. 107, can, as Lord Denning M.R. put it at p. 113, " be removed E
at the stroke of a pen from England outside the reach of the creditors."
The evidence before me is far from being as cogent as might have
been wished, and mainly consists of simple assertions by the plaintiff
of what she fears the defendant will do. However, the defendant's
previous departure to America, and his present absence on an ocean-
going yacht after selling the flat in which he lived seems to me to
justify an inference that there is a sufficient risk of so easily removable F
an asset as the bank balance being removed from the jurisdiction; and,
in contrast with the Central Bank of Nigeria in the *Etablissement
Esefka* case [1979] 1 Lloyd's Rep. 445, there does not seem to be any
ground on which it could be inferred that the £2,000 would be paid
even if the £3,300 is released. There is nothing to indicate that the
defendant has other assets of any substance except the part-share in G
the yacht which is already outside the jurisdiction; and if he does not
return, there is nothing to indicate where he will go, or whether it will
be to a jurisdiction in which an English judgment will be enforceable.
On the whole, I think that the plaintiff has, by no great margin, made
out a sufficient case under this head. The court, like other human
institutions, must at times take some risks; and in doing so, I think
that it should initially err on the side of conservation rather than dis- H
persion.

On the question of discretion, Mr. Unwin forcefully contended that
the defendant, being in ignorance of the existing injunction, might in
good faith be issuing cheques drawn on the £3,300 in his bank account,
and that his credit would be likely to be gravely impaired if the injunction restrains the bank from honouring those cheques. As *Mareva*
injunctions are normally granted ex parte and without warning to the

The Weekly Law Reports, October 24, 1980

1267

1 W.L.R.   Barclay-Johnson v. Yuill (Ch.D.)   Sir Robert
                                                            Megarry V.-C.

A   defendant so as to ensure that the defendant does not remove the assets
as soon as he learns of the danger, this must be a risk which flows
from many, if not most, of these injunctions, for a greater or a lesser
time. I do not think that such a risk will normally inhibit the grant
of such an injunction. However, in the present case there is a further
point. I cannot see that it would be right to continue the injunction
against the whole of the £3,300 when the claim on which it can properly
B   be based is only £2,000. Allow a reasonable sum for costs, and there
still should be a balance which ought not to be subject to restraint; and
this might well suffice for any incidental cheques that have been drawn
on the account. I shall hear counsel on the matter of quantum.

Accordingly, I propose to continue the injunction. It is not known
when the defendant will return to the jurisdiction, if at all. It was
C   suggested that he might well return in a week's time. In view of the
uncertainty, the proper course may be to continue the present ex parte
injunction until further order, with liberty to the defendant to apply
to vary or discharge it on short notice to the plaintiff. On this, too, I
shall hear counsel; and arrangements must also be made as to the inter
partes motion.

There is one point that I should add. The *Mareva* doctrine grew
D   up in commercial surroundings, particularly in relation to ships. Much
that was said in the judgments reflected that commercial background.
On the other hand, I do not think that there is any authority for confining it to commercial matters, even if it were possible to define them
at all accurately. The case now before me is in some respects commercial in nature, though it is far from being the sort of case that finds
E   its way into the Commercial Court, the true home of the *Mareva*
injunction. However, if, as I think, the foundation of the doctrine is
the need to prevent judgments of the court from being rendered
ineffective by the removal of the defendant's assets from the jurisdiction, then on principle I can see no reason for confining it to commercial
cases. It seems to me to be a doctrine of general application. I have
now found an unreported decision of the Court of Appeal * which
F   plainly seems to me to support this proposition: *Allen* v. *Jambo
Holdings Ltd.,* July 20, 1979; Court of Appeal (Civil Division) Transcript
No. 539 of 1979. I need therefore say no more about that point. All I
shall say is that it seems to me that in the short five years of its life, the
Mareva doctrine has shed all the possible limitations of its origin. It
is now a quite general doctrine, free from any possible requirements of
G   foreignness, commerce or anything else; and in a proper case it depends
only upon the existence of a sufficient risk of the defendant's assets
being removed from the jurisdiction with a consequent danger of the
plaintiff being deprived of the fruits of the judgment that he is seeking.

> *Order that ex parte injunction be
> continued until further order.*
H   > *Liberty to defendant to apply to
> vary or discharge it on short notice
> to plaintiff.*

Solicitors: *Biddle & Co. for Hepworth & Chadwick, Leeds; Jay
Benning & Co.*

K. N. B.

* Now reported [1980] 1 W.L.R. 1252.

A

[COURT OF APPEAL]

* RAHMAN (PRINCE ABDUL) BIN TURKI AL SUDAIRY
v. ABU-TAHA AND ANOTHER

[1980 B. No. 822]

B

1980 June 12   Lord Denning M.R.,
                                                Waller and Dunn L.JJ.

*Injunction—Interlocutory—*Mareva *injunction—Dishonoured cheque
—Order* 14 *proceedings—No disclosure of place of residence—
Foreigners resident within jurisdiction—Risk of disposal of
assets—Jurisdiction to grant injunction to restrain disposal of
assets*

C

By specially indorsed writ the plaintiff claimed £34,000
against the two defendants who stated that they were permanently resident within the jurisdiction. They had originally come from Kuwait and had given the plaintiff a cheque
for £34,000, which had not been honoured on presentation,
in respect of a transaction concerning the sale of a car.
On the plaintiff's summons under R.S.C., Ord. 14, the
defendants' affidavits disclosed substantial assets in England
and gave a business address in Park Lane, London, which
was alleged on the plaintiff's behalf to be empty and deserted.
The affidavits did not state the " place of residence " of the
defendants as required by R.S.C., Ord. 41, r. 1 (4).[1] After
a *Mareva* injunction had been granted and discharged, the
plaintiff's application for an injunction restraining the defendants from removing from the jurisdiction or otherwise disposing of any of their assets was refused.

D

E

On appeal by the plaintiff: —
Held, allowing the appeal, that, since the defendants were
not British subjects, had not disclosed their respective " place
of residence," in accordance with R.S.C., Ord. 41, r. 1 (4),
or the location of their assets and had given a cheque for
£34,000 which had not been met on presentation, there was
a real risk that they would remove their assets from the
jurisdiction or otherwise dispose of them if an injunction
was not granted; and that accordingly an injunction would
be granted in the form sought pending the hearing of the
summons under R.S.C., Ord. 14, notwithstanding that the
defendants were resident within the jurisdiction.

F

Barclay-Johnson v. *Yuill* [1980] 1 W.L.R. 1259, approved.
Gebr Van Weelde Scheepvaart Kantoor B.V. v. *Homeric
Marine Services Ltd.* (*The Agrabele*) [1979] 2 Lloyd's Rep.
117 not followed.

G

Per Lord Denning M.R. A *Mareva* injunction can be
granted against a man even though he is based in this
country if there is a danger of his absconding or a danger of
his assets being removed out of the jurisdiction or disposed
of within the jurisdiction, or otherwise dealt with so that
there is a danger that the plaintiff, if he gets judgment,
will not be able to get it satisfied (post, p. 1273A).

H

Judgment of Patrick Bennett Q.C., sitting as a deputy
High Court judge in the Queen's Bench Division, reversed.

The following cases are referred to in the judgments:
Barclay-Johnson v. *Yuill* [1980] 1 W.L.R. 1259.

[1] R.S.C., Ord. 41, r. 1 (4): " Every affidavit must . . . state the place of residence
of the deponent . . . "

A   *Chartered Bank* v. *Daklouche* [1980] 1 W.L.R. 107; [1980] 1 All E.R.
205, C.A.
Gebr Van Weelde Scheepvaart Kantoor B.V. v. *Homeric Marine Services
Ltd.* (*The Agrabele*) [1979] 2 Lloyd's Rep. 117.
Siskina (Owners of cargo lately laden on board) v. *Distos Compania
Naviera S.A.* [1979] A.C. 210; [1977] 3 W.L.R. 818; [1977] 3
All E.R. 803, H.L.(E.).

B   *Third Chandris Shipping Corporation* v. *Unimarine S.A.* [1979] Q.B.
645; [1979] 3 W.L.R. 122; [1979] 2 All E.R. 972, C.A.

No additional cases were cited in argument.

INTERLOCUTORY APPEAL from Patrick Bennett Q.C. sitting as a deputy
High Court judge in the Queen's Bench Division.

C   By specially indorsed writ of February 6, 1980, the plaintiff, H.R.H.
Prince Abdul Rahman bin Turki al Sudairy, claimed against the defen-
dants, Abu-Taha (male) and Abu-Ghosh (male), £34,000 and interest.
The statement of claim alleged, inter alia, that by a cheque dated
November 25, 1979, drawn on the defendant's bank account of Barclays
Bank Ltd., Park Lane branch, London, in favour of the plaintiff in the
D   sum of £34,000, the defendants purported to repay to the plaintiff
sums owed to him and that the said cheque when presented was
dishonoured and marked " refer to drawer."

On June 6, 1980, the plaintiff applied for an injunction restraining
the defendant and each of them from removing from the jurisdiction
or otherwise disposing of any of their assets including and in particular:
(i) any moneys forming an account in the name of the defendants
E   standing at the branch of Barclays Bank Ltd., at 46, Park Lane,
London, W.1;   (ii) any moneys held to the account of the defendants
by Aston Martin (Sales) Ltd., and/or Aston Martin Lagonda International Ltd., and/or Aston Martin Lagonda (1975) Ltd., and   (iii)
any moneys held to the account of the defendants by Bradshaw Webb
(Sales) Ltd., save in so far as the defendants' assets exceed £34,000
F   until further order and save in so far that the defendants or any of the
named persons by Barclays Bank Ltd., are at liberty to pay to the
plaintiff's solicitors herein, Peter T. James & Co., the sum of £34,000
or any part thereof, or until such time as the defendants or either of
them paid into court the sum of £34,000 or until the hearing of the
plaintiff's application for summary judgment on June 24, 1980.

On June 9, 1980, Patrick Bennett Q.C., sitting, as a deputy judge of
G   the Queen's Bench Division, while accepting that the fact that the
defendants were resident within the jurisdiction did not disentitle the
plaintiff to an injunction, held that he was not satisfied that there was
a real risk of removal of assets sufficient to warrant the grant of an
injunction and refused the application.

The plaintiff appealed on the grounds that (1) the judge erred in
H   failing to attach any or sufficient weight to the plaintiff's contention that
there was a real risk of both defendants removing or transferring their
assets from within the jurisdiction;   (2) in assessing the risk the judge
failed to attach any or sufficient weight to the contents of the affidavits
of Alan Lowe dated June 6, 1980, and June 9, 1980;   (3) the judge
failed to attach any or sufficient weight to the plaintiff's contention that
the risk was increased by reason of the sham and bogus defence set out
in the defendants' affidavits;   (4) the judge in assessing the risk failed

to attach any or sufficient weight to the type of business carried on by   A
the defendants, together with their nationality and domicile;   (5) further
the judge failed to attach any or sufficient weight to the plaintiff's
contention that both defendants were not known as reputable traders
thereby increasing the risk;   (6) the judge failed to attach any or sufficient weight to the plaintiff's contentions that if both defendants removed
their assets from the jurisdiction and the plaintiff subsequently obtained
judgment the plaintiff would find it almost impossible to enforce the   B
same in the Middle East;   (7) the judge in considering the balance of
convenience erred in failing to exercise the same in favour of the
plaintiff.

The facts are stated in the judgments of Lord Denning M.R. and
Waller L.J.

                                                                          C

John Kelly for the plaintiff.
George Laurence for the defendants.

LORD DENNING M.R.   This is an unusual case.   The plaintiff, Prince
Abdul Rahman bin Turki al Sudairy lives in Saudi Arabia.   He is a man
of great wealth.   He entered into negotiations to buy an expensive   D
motor car in England—an Aston Martin Lagonda—for the sum of
£34,000.   He negotiated with two men, the defendants Abu-Taha and
Abu-Ghosh.   They were two young men.   They came originally from
Kuwait.   According to their own accounts they have been in England
for many years and are permanently resident here.   They met when
they both went to the Bath Technical College and took their " A "
levels there.   Abu-Taha went on to Bristol University.   Abu Ghosh   E
went to London University.   They afterwards set up business together
in office premises on the 6th floor, 49 Park Lane, W.1.   That is a block
of offices which houses several Middle East firms.   They carried on
business under the name of Sarco Enterprises.   We know nothing about
that firm except that it is said to be registered in Liechtenstein.

In the course of the negotiations for the Aston Martin Lagonda (for   F
£34,000) Prince Abdul Rahman al Sudairy drew two cheques, one in
favour of Mr. Abu-Ghosh for £12,000 on March 13, 1978; and the other
on February 7, 1979, for £22,000 in favour of Sarco Enterprises.   Both
those cheques were paid into Barclays Bank (Park Lane Branch).

The deal did not go through.   The car was not delivered.   On
November 25, 1979, Abu-Taha purported to return the money.   He
drew a cheque for £34,000 in favour of Prince Abdul Rahman al Sudairy.   G
It was drawn on an account at Barclays Bank (Park Lane Branch) under
the name of Abu-Taha External Account.

The cheque was not honoured.   It was returned marked " Refer to
drawer."   Prince Abdul Rahman al Sudairy sued for his money.   He
issued a writ on February 6, 1980, against the two young men.   He took
out a summons under R.S.C., Ord. 14.   The young men put in affidavits   H
of defence.   They denied that they ever agreed to sell the plaintiff an
Aston Martin Lagonda motor car.   Abu-Taha said that his cheque for
£34,000 was not a repayment.   It was a loan by him to the plaintiff.

The plaintiff, in support of his claim, seeks a *Mareva* injunction
against these two gentlemen.   The summons under Ord. 14 is coming
on in about a fortnight: and he is fearful that any money they have
will have disappeared by the time he gets judgment.   It may be trans-

The Weekly Law Reports, October 24, 1980

1271

1 W.L.R.   Rahman (Prince Abdul) v. Abu-Taha (C.A.) Lord Denning M.R.

A ferred to Kuwait, or somewhere else, and it may be difficult to get hold of it. So he asks for a *Mareva* injunction.

The matter has come before several judges. On February 6, 1980, Smith J. granted a *Mareva* injunction. On February 25, 1980, Robert Goff J. discharged it because the defendants swore that they were resident in England. On June 6, 1980, Peter Pain J. gave leave to
B serve short notice of the plaintiff's further application for a *Mareva* injunction. On June 9, 1980, Mr. Patrick Bennett Q.C., sitting as a deputy judge, refused to grant the injunction sought. The plaintiff appeals to this court asking that a *Mareva* injunction should be granted.

On the hearing before us further affidavits were filed and the case argued inter partes. This further evidence goes far to show that the plaintiff has a strong case for the return of the £34,000. It also shows
C that, although the defendants are permanently resident within the jurisdiction, they are most secretive about their home addresses. In their affidavits both give their addresses as "6th floor, 49 Park Lane, London": but that is a business office. We are told that it is now empty and deserted. Neither of them gives his home address. Abu-Taha says:

D   "I rent a house in North West London, where I live with my wife
       and child. I have no other residence in the U.K. or elsewhere and
       my previous sole residence . . . was in England. I own two motor
       cars. Together with the second defendant I own furniture and
       fittings valued in excess of £25,000."

Abu-Ghosh says:

E   "I own a house in London, where I live with my wife. I bought it
       four years ago. I estimate the value to be between £80,000 and
       £90,000. I have . . . no other residence whether in the U.K. or
       abroad. I own two motor cars valued at approximately £28,000."

So these two young men, on their own statements, have accumulated great wealth during their short time in business. But neither of them
F gives his "place of residence"—as under R.S.C., Ord. 41, r. 1 (4), each ought to have done. Why not? It leads me to think that they are not at all trustworthy. Their houses may be in the names of nominees so as to prevent creditors getting their hands on them. At any rate, the circumstances suggest to my mind that there is a risk that, if the plaintiff should get judgment, he may find that before he can issue execution, the
G defendants may have disposed of their assets. They may have taken them out of the jurisdiction or transferred them to somewhere here.

So the case raises distinctly the question: Can a *Mareva* injunction be granted against a defendant who is resident in this country? In *Gebr Van Weelde Scheepvaart Kantoor B.V.* v. *Homeric Marine Services Ltd.* (*The Agrabele*) [1979] 2 Lloyd's Rep. 117, Lloyd J. held it could not. I can understand his hesitation at first instance in extending the
H principle of *Mareva.* But things are moving rapidly. We consider the position in *Chartered Bank* v. *Daklouche* [1980] 1 W.L.R. 107 and *Third Chandris Shipping Corporation* v. *Unimarine S.A.* [1979] Q.B. 645, 667. I intimated there that a *Mareva* injunction would lie against a person within the jurisdiction. The Report of the Committee on the Enforcement of Judgment Debts (1969) (Cmnd. 3909) presided over by Payne J. considered the problem in paragraphs 1248 to 1255. This illustration was given, at p. 324, para. 1252:

" . . . Under modern conditions of travel, particularly as the cost of   A
air travel is now within the means of many a debtor, the risk of
goods and chattels, or substantial sums of money being taken out
of the country is greatly increased.   It is possible to imagine countless circumstances in which a power to restrain a debtor could be
justified but one will suffice.   A debtor may buy valuable jewellery
on credit, ignore demands for payment and ignore a writ or   B
summons.   The jeweller may not know where the jewellery is.   If
he happens to discover that the debtor has booked an air passage
and proposes to leave England a few days later and before any progress can be made with the action which has been commenced is
there anyone who would argue in these days that the court should
not have power to order that the debtor should not remove the
jewellery from the jurisdiction or otherwise dispose of it? "   C

Very recently Sir Robert Megarry V.-C. has dealt with it fully in
Barclay-Johnson v. *Yuill* [1980] 1 W.L.R. 1259.   As a result, I think
the time has come for us to grasp the nettle.   Lord Hailsham of St.
Marylebone foresaw it when he said in *Siskina* (*Owners of cargo lately
laden on board*) v. *Distos Compania Naviera S.A.* [1979] A.C. 210, 261 :
                                                                      D
"I believe the truth to be that sooner or later the courts or the
legislature will have to choose between two alternatives.   Either
the position of a plaintiff making claim against an English based
defendant will have to be altered or the principle of the *Mareva*
cases will have to be modified."

The courts are now faced with the two alternatives.   We have to   E
make the choice.   I have no doubt what our choice should be.   We must
not modify " the principle of the *Mareva* cases."   It has proved of such
great value to the Commercial Court that it must be retained intact.   So
we must " alter the position of a plaintiff making a claim against an
English-based defendant."   We must do it by putting all defendants
on the same footing, no matter whether they be foreign-based or English-
based.   The same principle applies to both.   It was well stated by Sir   F
Robert Megarry V.-C. in *Barclay-Johnson* v. *Yuill* [1980] 1 W.L.R.
1264A—1265C.

" . . . the heart and core of the *Mareva* injunction is the risk of the
defendant removing his assets from the jurisdiction and so stultifying
any judgment given by the courts in the action . . . the injunction
will restrain the defendant from disposing of [the assets] even within   G
the jurisdiction. . . . If, then, the essence of the jurisdiction is the
risk of assets being removed from the jurisdiction, I cannot see
why it should be confined to 'foreigners,' in any sense of that
term . . . Naturally the risk of removal of assets from the jurisdiction will usually be greater or more obvious in the case of foreign-
based defendants, and so the jurisdiction has grown up in relation   H
to them . . .   Is it really to be said that in relation to *Mareva*
injunctions, there is one law for the foreigner and another for the
English . . . ? . . . I do not intend to suggest that matters of nationality,
domicile, residence and so on are irrelevant. . .   Any or all of them
may be of considerable importance in so far as they bear upon the
risk of removal. . . . within the last year the abolition of exchange
control has made it easier for everybody to transfer assets abroad."

The Weekly Law Reports, October 24, 1980

1273

1 W.L.R.   Rahman (Prince Abdul) v. Abu-Taha (C.A.) Lord Denning M.R.

A   So I would hold that a *Mareva* injunction can be granted against a man even though he is based in this country if the circumstances are such that there is a danger of his absconding, or a danger of the assets being removed out of the jurisdiction or disposed of within the jurisdiction, or otherwise dealt with so that there is a danger that the plaintiff, if he gets judgment, will not be able to get it satisfied.

B   That brings me to the particular circumstances of this case. On their own story, these two young men have done extremely well since they left the technical college. They have much money and many assets available to them. But the strange thing is that they have not said a word as to where they live. They have not given us their addresses at all. They had this Liechtenstein concern: but that has wound up. Then, when it C comes to their assets, one does not know where they are. They are not British nationals. In the circumstances of this case it seems to me that the court may be apprehensive—and the plaintiff may be apprehensive—that, unless something is done to stop them, they may remove their assets from the jurisdiction or otherwise dispose of them. At all events, pending the time when the summons under R.S.C., Ord. 14, has been heard, it D seems to me that the plaintiff should be protected: and there should be an injunction in the usual *Mareva* form restraining the defendants from removing out of the jurisdiction—or otherwise disposing of them within the jurisdiction—any of their assets save in so far as they exceed £34,000.

Of course, £34,000 is the only sum in question here. If they have any E more money here, they can remove it. There is nothing to stop them doing that. All this injunction will restrain them from doing is removing the first £34,000. There will be an injunction in the terms asked, that is, to restrain the defendants from disposing of any moneys or assets held to the account of the defendants by Barclays Bank or by the other named firms. I expect the way in which it will be operated will be for the F plaintiff to notify Barclays Bank and the named firms of the injunction. On the terms of the injunction being notified to the persons concerned, they will of course recognise the injunction: because, if they were to go against it, they themselves would be guilty of a contempt of court.

I would like to add this: when there is a *Mareva* injunction of this kind, if the people who are notified of it are put to any expense in regard G to it, that expense must be paid by the plaintiff.

This is a proper case for the granting of a *Mareva* injunction. I would allow the appeal, accordingly.

WALLER L.J. I agree. I would only add this, that the deputy judge in deciding this case refused to grant a *Mareva* injunction because he was H not satisfied that there was a real risk that assets would be removed if an injunction was not granted. But the facts are these: that the two defendants are both foreigners; they are said to be residing here, but in swearing their affidavits they each say " of 6th floor, 49, Park Lane, London," which are the premises from which they were trading together which are now said to be closed. In addition to that, a cheque for £34,000—the amount at stake—was not met quite recently. In my judgment, that

Waller L.J. **Rahman (Prince Abdul) v. Abu-Taha (C.A.)** **[1980]**

raises a strong inference that assets may be removed from the juris-   A
diction; and I agree that this appeal should be allowed.

DUNN L.J. I also agree.

> *Appeal allowed.*
> *Injunction granted until further order.*   B
> *Costs in action.*
> *Leave to appeal refused.*

Solicitors: *Peter T. James & Co; Joynson-Hicks & Co.*

A. H. B.   C

[COURT OF APPEAL]

* BANKERS TRUST CO. *v.* SHAPIRA AND OTHERS

[1980 B. No. 3116]   D

1980   June 4   Lord Denning M.R., Waller
                                                and Dunn L.JJ.

Practice—Discovery—Motion for Bank's customers obtaining   E
moneys by forgery—Injured party's action seeking reimburse-
ment—Interlocutory claim for bank to disclose confidential
information concerning customers—Customers neither within
jurisdiction nor served with notice of motion—Whether
obligation on bank to assist in tracing action

On September 20, 1979, two men presented to the plaintiff
bank in New York two cheques, each for half a million dollars
purportedly drawn on a bank in Saudi Arabia and made pay-   F
able to one of the men. The bank paid over the million
dollars and on instructions from the two men credited $600,000
and later $108,203 to accounts of the two men at the London
branch of the D bank, the third defendants. In April 1980,
the bank in Saudi Arabia informed the plaintiff bank that
the cheques were obvious forgeries. The plaintiff bank
reimbursed the bank in Saudi Arabia in the sum of one
million dollars, and on May 20, 1980, issued a writ in London   G
with statement of claim in an action to trace and recover
the moneys, and on the same date, by a notice of motion
against the two men (who were by then outside the jurisdiction) and against the D Bank in the Commercial Court, asked,
inter alia, for injunctions to prevent any dealings with the
funds in the D bank. They obtained a Mareva injunction
from Robert Goff J. on May 21; and before Mustill J. sought,
inter alia, an interlocutory order that the D bank should   H
disclose and permit the plaintiff bank to inspect and take
copies of (i) all correspondence between the two men and the
D bank relating to any account in either of the two men's
names, (ii) all cheques drawn on such accounts, and (iii) all
debit vouchers, transfer applications and orders and internal
memoranda relating to any account standing in the names of
either of the two men at the D bank, all as from September
20, 1979, onwards. Mustill J. refused the relief by way of
disclosure of confidential banker/customer information at the

A   early interlocutory stage, a fortiori because the two men had
not been served with notice of the motion.
      On appeal by the plaintiff bank: —
      Held, allowing the appeal and granting the order sought
against the D bank, that though the court would not lightly
use its powers to order disclosure of full information touching
the confidential relationship of banker and customer, such an
order was justified even at the early interlocutory stages of an
B   action where plaintiffs sought to trace funds which in equity
belonged to them and of which there was strong evidence
that they had been fraudulently deprived and delay might
result in the dissipation of the funds before the action came
to trial; and that in the new and developing jurisdiction where
neutral and innocent persons were under a duty to assist
plaintiffs who were the victims of wrongdoing, the court would
not hesitate to make strong orders to ascertain the where-
C   abouts and prevent the disposal of such property; but that the
plaintiffs should be correspondingly bound to undertake that
such information would be used only for the purposes of the
action to trace the funds and not for any other purpose.
      Norwich Pharmacal Co. v. *Customs and Excise Commis-
sioners* [1974] A.C. 133, H.L.(E.) applied.
      Decision of Mustill J. reversed.

D   The following cases are referred to in the judgments:

A v. *C* (unreported), March 18, 1980, Robert Goff J.
Anton Piller K.G. v. *Manufacturing Processes Ltd.* [1976] Ch. 55; [1976]
      2 W.L.R. 162; [1976] 1 All E.R. 779, C.A.
Banque Belge pour L'Etranger v. *Hambrouck* [1921] 1 K.B. 321, C.A.
Initial Services Ltd. v. *Putterill* [1968] 1 Q.B. 396; [1967] 3 W.L.R.
      1032; [1967] 3 All E.R. 145, C.A.
E   *London and Counties Securities Ltd.* (*In Liquidation*) v. *Caplan* (un-
      reported), May 26, 1978, Templeman J.
Mediterranea Raffineria Siciliana Petroli S.p.a. v. *Mabanaft G.m.b.H.*
      December 1, 1978, Court of Appeal (Civil Division) Transcript No. 816
      of 1978, C.A.
Norwich Pharmacal Co. v. *Customs and Excise Commissioners* [1974]
      A.C. 133; [1973] 3 W.L.R. 164; [1973] 2 All E.R. 943, H.L.(E.).
F   *Upmann* v. *Elkan* (1871) L.R. 12 Eq. 140; 7 Ch.App. 130.

The following additional cases were cited in argument:

Chase Manhattan Bank N.A. v. *Israel-British Bank (London) Ltd.* [1980]
      2 W.L.R. 202; [1979] 3 All E.R. 1025.
E.M.I. Ltd. v. *Pandit* [1975] 1 W.L.R. 302; [1975] 1 All E.R. 418.
G   *Third Chandris Shipping Corporation* v. *Unimarine S.A.* [1979] Q.B.
      645; [1979] 3 W.L.R. 122; [1979] 2 All E.R. 972, Mustill J. and
      C.A.
Tournier v. *National Provincial & Union Bank of England* [1924] 1
      K.B. 461, C.A.

INTERLOCUTORY APPEAL from Mustill J.

H   The plaintiffs, the Bankers Trust Co. of New York, a company
incorporated under the laws of the United States and having a place
of business at 9, Queen Victoria Street, London E.C.4, issued a writ
on May 20, 1980, against one Walter Shapira and one Max Frei, as
first and second defendants, and against the Discount Bank (Overseas)
Ltd. (" Discount Bank "), a Swiss bank having a London branch at 63,
Hatton Garden, London E.C.1, as third defendants. They claimed relief
against all three defendants in their statement of claim in an action to trace

Bankers Trust Co. v. Shapira [1980]

funds of $1,000,000 as money had and received by Shapira and Frei to the A
use of the plaintiffs, or alternatively paid to them under a mistake of fact,
and damages for deceit and/or conspiracy as against Shapira and Frei
to defraud the plaintiffs. By a motion of the same date they applied
ex parte in the Commercial Court for relief (A) as against Shapira and
Frei for (1) an injunction restraining them from removing from the
jurisdiction or otherwise disposing of or dealing with any of their assets
within the jurisdiction including and in particular any credit balance or B
balances in any account in either of their names at Discount Bank
save and in so far as such assets did not exceed in value the sum of
U.S. $1,000,000; and (B) as against all three defendants (2) an order that
each of the defendants disclose to the plaintiffs forthwith the sums or
balances at present standing in any account in either of the names of
Shapira and Frei at Discount Bank; (C) as against Discount Bank, the C
third defendants (3) an order that they disclose to the plaintiffs forthwith and permit the plaintiffs to take copies of the following documents
(i) all correspondence passing between Discount Bank and Shapira and
Frei relating to any account at Discount Bank in the names of either
Shapira and/or Frei from July 15, 1979, onwards, (ii) all cheques drawn
on any account at Discount Bank in the names of either Shapira and/or
Frei from July 15, 1979, onwards, (iii) all debit vouchers, transfer appli- D
cations and orders and internal memoranda relating to any account at
Discount Bank in the names of either Shapira and/or Frei from July 15,
1979, onwards; (4) an injunction restraining Discount Bank from making
any payment or transfer out of any account in the name or names of
Shapira and/or Frei at Discount Bank's branch at 63, Hatton Garden,
London E.C.1, or otherwise dealing with such accounts save for payment E
to the plaintiffs of any sum found due to them or otherwise pursuant to
order of the court.

The motion was supported by an affidavit of the legal adviser to the
London branch of Bankers Trust Co. setting out the allegations as to
the matters set out in the judgment of Lord Denning M.R. and adding
that it appears (i) that Shapira was now in jail in Switzerland as a
result of a fraud investigation by the Swiss police; and (ii) Frei was F
presently believed to be in Liechtenstein.

On May 21, 1980, Robert Goff J. in chambers granted *Mareva* injunctions to the plaintiffs ex parte (subject to an undertaking to amend
the writ to include a claim for the injunctions being granted by Robert
Goff J. and to abide by any order the court or a judge might make as
to damages in case it should be held that the defendants or any of them G
should have sustained any damages by reason of the orders) as follows:
(i) that the first and second defendants be restrained from removing
from the jurisdiction or otherwise disposing of or dealing with any of
the assets within the jurisdiction, including any credit balance or balances
in any account in either of their names at Discount Bank (Overseas) Ltd.
save and in so far as such assets did not exceed in value the sum of H
U.S. $1,000,000 until after trial of the action or further order, with
liberty to apply; and (ii) as against Discount Bank (Overseas) Ltd. as
third defendants an injunction restraining the bank from making any payment or transfer out of any account in the name or names of Shapira or
Frei at their Hatton Garden branch or otherwise dealing with such accounts
until after the hearing of a summons returnable on May 22, 1980.

Mustill J. on May 23, 1980, on the hearing of the summons declined

A to make any order under paragraphs (2) and (3) of the statement of claim. His reasons, as noted by counsel for the parties before him, were:

" First, it is a very extreme form of relief and should only be ordered where it is necessary to prevent injustice. This is plain from the judgment of Robert Goff J. in *A* v. *C* (unreported).
B March 18, 1980. Secondly, although a banker can properly be a respondent to such an application care should be taken not unnecessarily to put at risk that confidentiality which is an essential part of banking. The question is where, as here, the true defendants have not been served is it necessary to grant relief against the bank at the present stage? There is no risk of the bank destroying documents. There is no need to make an order for disclosure
C to forestall the disposition of money onwards since the events in question happened eight months ago. The money would have vanished long since. Nor is there any need to grant pre-emptive discovery to support the plaintiff's action against the true defendants or the bank. The actions can proceed in a normal manner, no doubt marked by default on the part of the first two defendants. It
D may be difficult to serve the first two defendants, but substituted service can be granted if necessary. There is no reason why discovery against them should not take place at the normal time. Similarly, in regard to the bank, since the action against it is not necessarily at all a foregone conclusion. It may take the plaintiffs some time to get their money—Discount Bank have disclosed there is some money—but the suggested order would not accelerate the
E process, and even if it would, a court should be very careful not to order a banker to disclose the state of a customer's account unless it is urgently necessary to prevent injustice (which is not the case here), or if the customer is present before the court to make representations. Unlike *A* v. *C* the true defendants are not yet before the court. This is a very important distinction. Accordingly, I
F propose to make no order on the present application at this stage; the plaintiffs can renew their application when the first and second defendants can be present and bound by any decision of the court.
" Leave to appeal to raise questions of principle involved in decision in *A* v. *C*. Costs reserved. Liberty to apply."

The plaintiff bank appealed from so much of the order of Mustill J.
G whereby he made no order on the application of the plaintiffs (a) for an order against all three defendants that each of them disclose to the plaintiffs forthwith the sums or balances at present standing in any account in either of the names of the first or second defendants at the third defendants; (b) for an order against the third defendants that they disclose to the plaintiffs forthwith and permit the plaintiffs to take copies of the documents specified in the order sought in paragraph (2) of the
H notice of appeal, as follows: (1) against the first, second and third defendants that each of them disclose to the plaintiffs forthwith the sums or balances at present standing in any account in either of the names of the first or second defendants at the third defendants; (2) against the third defendants that they disclose to the plaintiffs forthwith and permit the plaintiffs to take copies of the following documents: (i) all correspondence passing between the third defendants and the first and second defendants relating to any account at the third defendants in the names

of either the first and/or second defendants from September 20, 1979, **A**
onwards; (ii) all cheques drawn on any account at the third defendants
in the names of either the first and/or second defendants from September
20, 1979, onwards; (iii) all debit vouchers, transfer applications and orders
and internal memoranda relating to any account at the third defendants
in the names of either the first and/or second defendants from September
20, 1979, onwards.

The grounds of the appeal were that the judge, in making no order **B**
on the plaintiffs' application (a) exercised his discretion wrongly in disregard of principle and/or (b) misdirected himself in law and/or (c)
thereby produced a result leading to injustice to the plaintiffs in support
whereof the plaintiffs would rely, inter alia, upon the following matters—
(i) the plaintiffs' claim, inter alia, to trace, follow and recover such
proportion of the U.S. $1,000,000 paid to the first and/or second defend- **C**
ants on September 20, 1979, and remitted by the first and/or second
defendants to the third defendants within the jurisdiction of the court
and/or thereafter disposed of by the first and/or second defendants elsewhere; (ii) the books, papers and records of the third defendants would
disclose what happened to such proportion of the U.S. $1,000,000 remitted
as aforesaid and thereafter disposed of by the first and/or second **D**
defendants elsewhere; (iii) the judge in requiring the first and/or second
defendants to be served with the proceedings as a pre-requisite to the
making of the order sought by the plaintiffs was thereby giving the first
and/or second defendants even more time to ensure that any dispositions
by them or either of them from any account with the third defendants
could not be capable of being traced, followed and recovered by the
plaintiffs; (iv) as a matter of principle the court should be astute to **E**
provide all such assistance as it properly could to persons in the position
of the plaintiffs to enable them to obtain such information as was
reasonable and proper at the earliest practicable opportunity to enable
them to discover the whereabouts of and/or to follow and recover a
trust fund or any remaining part thereof; (v) the approach of the judge
in determining that the principle of the decision of Robert Goff J. in
A v. *C* (unreported), March 18, 1980, only applied where persons such as **F**
the first and/or second defendants had been served with a notice of an
application such as that made to the judge by the plaintiffs on May 23,
1980, was unnecessarily restrictive of such decision and/or was wrong in
law.

Michael Crystal for the plaintiffs.   **G**
Nicholas Elliott for the third defendants.

LORD DENNING M.R. This is a new case. It illustrates something
that happens from time to time—frauds made upon banks. It appears
that last September—on September 20, 1979—two men (Walter Shapira
and Max Frei) went into a bank in New York, the Bankers Trust Co. **H**
They went into the Middle East section. They presented two apparent
cheques—each for a half a million dollars—for payment. The cheques
purported to be drawn on the Mecca branch of the National Commercial
Bank in Saudi Arabia to the Bankers Trust Co. of 16, Wall Street, New
York. One of them was for $500,000 to be paid to Mr. Shapira. The
other was also for $500,000 to be paid to Mr. Shapira.

The Bankers Trust Co. of New York honoured the cheques. They

A let these men have $1,000,000. They acted on the instructions of the two men. I will not go into detail: but I will mention two particular matters: $600,000 was credited to Mr. Shapira's account at the London branch of a Swiss bank in Hatton Garden—the Discount Bank (Overseas) Ltd. They asked that another sum of $108,203 should be credited to Mr. Frei's account at a bank in the Cayman Islands. But as he had no B such account there, that sum was also transferred to the Discount Bank (Overseas) Ltd. in Hatton Garden. So, on the face of it, $708,203 was sent over to the Discount Bank in Hatton Garden. That was in September 1979.

In some way those cheques got over to the Mecca branch of the Saudi Arabian bank. They apparently honoured them at the time. But six months later, on April 10, 1980, the head office of the National C Commercial Bank in Saudi Arabia found that those two cheques were forgeries. They immediately took the matter up with the Bankers Trust Co. of New York. I will read part of the letter they wrote:

" On looking into these drafts you will find that signatures do not conform in any way to the signatures number 140 and 141 of our officers in our Mecca Branch, that the validating numbers in red do D not compare in any way to our validity machine which has the name of our bank on it, that the draft forms are on poor quality paper while our drafts are printed on safety paper with our logo water mark. We therefore consider these drafts are clearly forged and you should have exercised care in encashing them."

When the Bankers Trust Co. of New York received that letter, they E felt that they were not free from blame themselves. It appears that they did re-credit the Saudi Arabian Bank with the money. So the Bankers Trust Co. of New York have lost $1,000,000.

They then looked round to see if they could find these rogues. (I call them " rogues " although it has not been proved yet: but the prima facie evidence against them is strong). On May 20, 1980, the Bankers Trust Co. of New York brought an action. The first defendant was F Mr. Walter Shapira: the second defendant was Mr. Max Frei: and the third defendant was the Discount Bank (Overseas) Ltd., with which the moneys were deposited. They did not serve the documents on either Mr. Shapira or Mr. Frei. We are told, on the evidence, that they investigated the matter. Mr. Shapira is now in jail in Switzerland as a result of a fraud investigation by the Swiss police. Mr. Frei is presently G believed to be in Liechtenstein. So they have not served those two. But they have served the Discount Bank (Overseas) Ltd. The action they have brought is quite clearly to trace and follow these funds which the Bankers Trust Co. have been fraudulently deprived of. It operates in common law and in equity as a right to follow and trace the moneys. So they brought this action on May 20, 1980.

The Bankers Trust Co. obtained a *Mareva* injunction in the usual H form to stop the bank from disposing of any of the moneys which they had at that time—which Shapira and Frei had paid into the bank. That is common form nowadays in the Commercial Court when it is desired to prevent money being abstracted from the true creditor.

But this case brings out a new point which we have not had before: because the Bankers Trust Co. of New York want more information from the Discount Bank (Overseas) Ltd. They want information as to these accounts. They want to know how much money is now in the

accounts. Money has been taken out in the last six months. They want
to know what has happened to the money in the accounts. It may have
been paid over to third persons: and they may want to follow the money
into the hands of those third persons. So they have asked for discovery
of the documents relating to the moneys which the bank had, and what
has happened to them.

As the question of the form of order has come into question in some
of the cases, I would like to read the actual form of order which is
sought in this regard by the Bankers Trust Co. of New York:

"For an order (1) Against the first, second and third defendants
that each of them do disclose to the plaintiffs forthwith the sums
or balances at present standing in any account in either of the
names of the first or second defendants at the third defendants.
(2) Against the third defendants "—that is, the bank—" that they
do disclose to the plaintiffs forthwith and permit the plaintiffs to
take copies of the following documents: —(i) all correspondence passing between the third defendants and the first and second defendants
relating to any account at the third defendants in the names of either
the first and/or second defendants from September 20, 1979, onwards: (ii) all cheques drawn on any account at the third defendants
in the names of either the first and/or second defendants from
September 20, 1979, onwards: (iii) all debit vouchers, transfer applications and orders and internal memoranda relating to any account
at the third defendants in the names of either the first and/or
second defendants from September 20, 1979, onwards."

That is what they applied for in addition to the ordinary *Mareva* injunction.

The matter came before Mustill J. He refused to make any such
order, his reason being that he thought it should not be made while the
first and second defendants (Mr. Shapira and Mr. Frei) had not been
served.

Mr. Crystal has come here today on behalf of the Bankers Trust Co.
of New York, and asks us to reverse that decision. He has brought to
our attention—very usefully—three recent cases (none of them reported)
in which a similar point has arisen. The first one was on May 26, 1978,
before Templeman J.: *London and Counties Securities (In Liquidation)
v. Caplan.* The plaintiff company had been defrauded by a Mr. Caplan
in the sum of £5,000,000. Mr. Caplan was said to have embezzled it. It
was desired to obtain information as to the whereabouts of the moneys
and what had been done with them. The plaintiffs wanted to trace the
moneys to see where they had gone. Templeman J., having considered
the matter very carefully, made an order under which the bank was to
disclose all the documents and accounts showing where the money had
gone.

Then there was a case before this court on December 1, 1978—
Mediterranea Raffineria Siciliana Petroli S.p.a. v. *Mabanaft G.m.b.H.*
Court of Appeal (Civil Division) Transcript No. 816 of 1978. It was not
a fraud on a bank. Nor a fraud at all. Owing to a mistake in a commercial transaction, moneys payable to the plaintiffs were paid to other
people. It was desired to trace them. A *Mareva* injunction was granted
and also an order for discovery of documents to discover where the
money had gone. Templeman L.J. said:

A   " As Lord Denning M.R. said, it is a strong order, but the plaintiffs'
case is that there is a trust fund of $3,500,000. This has disappeared,
and the gentlemen against whom orders are sought may be able to
give information as to where it is and who is in charge of it. A
court of equity has never hesitated to use the strongest powers to
protect and preserve a trust fund in interlocutory proceedings on
the basis that, if the trust fund disappears by the time the action

B   comes to trial, equity will have been invoked in vain."

The last of the three cases was on March 18, 1980, before Robert
Goff J., entitled *A* v. *C.* That was a case again of a fraud on a bank.
A very large sum of money was involved. It seems to be a case very
similar to the present, but in which the fraudulent rogues—as they may
well turn out to be—had been served. It is on that ground distinguishable

C   from the present case. The rogues were served together with the bank.
Robert Goff J. after considering the two cases which I have mentioned,
said :

" There is no doubt that this jurisdiction is in a process of development; and that it is still in the course of throwing up problems
which have yet to be solved."

D
He granted a *Mareva* injunction: but in addition he made an order
for discovery of documents. He did so in order to enable the plaintiffs
to trace what had happened to the moneys.

Mustill J. had *A* v. *C.* case before him. He thought it was distinguishable on the ground that in that case the " rogues " had been served.
He refused to order discovery in this case: but he gave leave to appeal

E   in order that the questions of principle could be discussed.

We have had the matter fully argued before us. I would like to
express our gratitude to Mr. Crystal for all the submissions he has made
in support of the order. Equally to Mr. Elliott, for the bank, who has
taken a very proper attitude. He said that the bank are neutral in this
matter: but they felt it right to put forward to the court various con-

F   siderations, such as the confidential relationship between the bank and
their customers.

Having heard all that has been said, it seems to me that Mustill J.
was too hesitant in this matter. In order to enable justice to be done—
in order to enable these funds to be traced—it is a very important part
of the court's armoury to be able to order discovery. The powers in this
regard, and the extent to which they have gone, were exemplified in

G   *Norwich Pharmacal Co.* v. *Customs and Excise Commissioners* [1974]
A.C. 133. The Customs authorities were perfectly innocent: but they
had to disclose the names of infringers of patents whose goods had passed
through their hands. Lord Reid said, at p. 175:

" They seem to me to point to a very reasonable principle that if
through no fault of his own a person gets mixed up in the tortious

H   acts of others so as to facilitate their wrong-doing he may incur
no personal liability but he comes under a duty to assist the person
who has been wronged by giving him full information and disclosing
the identity of the wrongdoers "

referring to the views expressed by Lord Romilly M.R. and Lord
Hatherley L.C. in *Upmann* v. *Elkan* (1871) L.R. 12 Eq. 140; 7 Ch.App.
130.

So here the Discount Bank incur no personal liability: but they got mixed up, through no fault of their own, in the tortious or wrongful acts of these two men: and they come under a duty to assist the Bankers Trust Co. of New York by giving them and the court full information and disclosing the identity of the wrongdoers. In this case the particular point is " full information."

This new jurisdiction must, of course, be carefully exercised. It is a strong thing to order a bank to disclose the state of its customer's account and the documents and correspondence relating to it. It should only be done when there is a good ground for thinking the money in the bank is the plaintiff's money—as, for instance, when the customer has got the money by fraud—or other wrongdoing—and paid it into his account at the bank. The plaintiff who has been defrauded has a right in equity to follow the money. He is entitled, in Lord Atkin's words, to lift the latch of the banker's door: see *Banque Belge pour l'Etranger* v. *Hambrouck* [1921] 1 K.B. 321, 355. The customer, who has prima facie been guilty of fraud, cannot bolt the door against him. Owing to his fraud, he is disentitled from relying on the confidential relationship between him and the bank: see *Initial Services Ltd.* v. *Putterill* [1968] 1 Q.B. 396, 405. If the plaintiff's equity is to be of any avail, he must be given access to the bank's books and documents—for that is the only way of tracing the money or of knowing what has happened to it: see *Mediterranea Raffineria Siciliana Petroli S.p.a.* v. *Mabanaft G.m.b.H.* (unreported). So the court, in order to give effect to equity, will be prepared in a proper case to make an order on the bank for their discovery. The plaintiff must of course give an undertaking in damages to the bank and must pay all and any expenses to which the bank is put in making the discovery: and the documents, once seen, must be used solely for the purpose of following and tracing the money: and not for any other purpose. With these safeguards, I think the new jurisdiction—already exercised in the three unreported cases—should be affirmed by this court.

Applying this principle, I think the court should go to the aid of the Bankers Trust Co. It should help them follow the money which is clearly theirs: to follow it to the hands in which it is: and to find out what has become of it since it was put into the Discount Bank (Overseas) Ltd.

If the courts were to wait until these two men were served, goodness knows how many weeks might elapse. Meanwhile, if some of it has got into the hands of third persons, they may dispose of it elsewhere. It seems to me that the fact that these two men have not been served does not deprive the court of its power to make such an order. These two men have gone out of the jurisdiction in circumstances in which it is clear that the court should do all it can to help the innocent people to find out where their money has gone.

In those circumstances—while expressing our indebtedness to both counsel—I would allow the appeal and make the order as asked in the notice of appeal.

WALLER L.J. I agree. I only add a word or two about three points which were made by Mr. Elliott, appearing on behalf of the bank and taking, so far as he could, a neutral attitude in this matter. He first of all emphasised that where the other two parties had not been served, it

A was very strong action on the part of the court to order the bank to break their duty of confidentiality. It was going further, he said, than an *Anton Piller* order [*Anton Piller K.G.* v. *Manufacturing Processes Ltd.* [1976] Ch. 55], because when an *Anton Piller* order is made, there remains the opportunity of disobeying it or appealing against it.

B Clearly it is undesirable that an order such as this should be lightly made. But the answer to this part of Mr. Elliott's submission, in my judgment, is that here there is very strong evidence indeed of fraud on the part of the other two defendants—the first and second defendants. They presented two forged cheques, each for half a million dollars, and as a result a total of $1,000,000 was transferred to accounts in their names or from which they would benefit.

C Secondly, Mr. Elliott submitted that, having regard to the amount of time which had gone by, there was no case for making this order now; it could wait until the normal time for discovery; and indeed Mustill J. in his decision adverted to that. But again, in my opinion, where you have a fraud of this nature, although it may be late and although much or perhaps all of the money may be now gone, the sooner that steps are taken to try and trace where it is the better. If steps are going to be taken, it is important that they should be taken at the earliest

D possible moment.

Thirdly, Mr. Elliott expressed concern at the wideness of the order which it was sought to make—one which required the bank to permit the plaintiffs to take copies of all correspondence, for example, all debit vouchers, transfer applications and orders, and internal memoranda. He submitted that the breadth of that order went far beyond the disclosure

E which would have to be made under the Bankers' Books Evidence Act 1879. Again, in my opinion, an order of that breadth is completely justified in a case of this sort because, unless there is the fullest possible information, the difficulties of tracing the funds will be well-nigh impossible.

On the other side of the coin in relation to that, there must be an implied undertaking on the part of the plaintiffs that the information

F which they obtain will only be used for the purposes of this action and of course will not be disclosed otherwise.

DUNN L.J. I agree for the reasons given by Lord Denning M.R. and Waller L.J. that this appeal should be allowed.

G
                                        Appeal allowed.
                                        No order for costs as between plain-
                                        tiffs and third defendants.
                                        Costs in action reserved.

Solicitors: *Linklaters & Paines; Dawson & Co.*

H
                                                                M. M. H.

[COURT OF APPEAL]   A

* REGINA *v.* HUCKLEBRIDGE

ATTORNEY-GENERAL'S REFERENCE (No. 3 of 1980)

1980 June 10   Lord Lane C.J., Boreham and
                                                        Gibson JJ.   B

*Firearms—Certificate—Ambit—Possession of rifles with rifling
removed—Whether adapted weapon " shot gun "—Whether
firearm certificate required for gun—Firearms Act 1968 (c.
27), ss. 1, 57*

Section 1 of the Firearms Act 1968 provides:

" (1) Subject to any exemption under this Act, it is an   C
offence for a person—(*a*) to have in his possession ... a
firearm to which this section applies without holding a
firearm certificate ... (3) This section applies to every firearm except—(*a*) a shot gun (that is to say a smooth-bore
gun with a barrel not less than 24 inches in length . . ."

Section 57 provides:

" (1) ... the expression ' firearm ' means a lethal barrelled   D
weapon of any description from which any shot, bullet or
other missile can be discharged . . . (4) In this Act— . . .
' shot gun ' has the meaning assigned to it by section
1 (3) (*a*) of this Act . . ."

The appellant had in his possession two Lee-Enfield rifles
which had had their rifling removed and one of the guns had
been rechambered to take shot gun cartridges. He was
charged on an indictment containing two counts of possession   E
of a rifle without a firearm certificate, contrary to section 1 of
the Firearms Act 1968. The judge ruled that the gun adapted
to take cartridges, the subject of count 1, was a shot gun for
which a firearm certificate was not required and he directed
the jury to acquit on that count. The appellant then pleaded
guilty to count 2.

On appeal by the appellant against conviction on count 2
and on a reference to the court by the Attorney-General on   F
the question whether it was possible to adapt a rifle which had
admittedly been a firearm within the definition of section 57
(1) of the Act so as to exclude it from the necessity for a
firearm certificate by reason of section 1 (3) (*a*) of the Act:—

Held, that sections 1 and 57 of the Firearms Act 1968 made
it plain that any " smooth-bore gun with a barrel not less than
24 inches in length " was a shot gun; that provided a gun
came within that definition, it was immaterial that after being   G
adapted it still resembled a rifle and, therefore, the answer to
the question referred to the court was in the affirmative and,
since the adapted guns in the appellant's possession came
within the definition of a shot gun, his appeal would be
allowed and his conviction quashed.

Creaser v. *Tunnicliffe* [1977] 1 W.L.R. 1493, D.C. disapproved.
                                                                          H

The following case is referred to in the judgment:

Creaser v. *Tunnicliffe* [1977] 1 W.L.R. 1493; [1978] 1 All E.R. 569, D.C.

The following additional cases were cited in argument:

Cafferata v. *Wilson* [1936] 3 All E.R. 149; 100 J.P. 489, D.C.
Reg. v. *Freeman* [1970] 1 W.L.R. 788; [1970] 2 All E.R. 413, C.A.
Watson v. *Herman* [1952] 2 All E.R. 70, D.C.

A   APPEAL against conviction.
     REFERENCE by the Attorney-General.
        On July 10, 1979, the appellant, David William Hucklebridge, was
     tried on an indictment at Portsmouth Crown Court with two counts of
     possessing a rifle without a firearm certificate contrary to section 1 of
     the Firearms Act 1968. Both guns had been reproofed as smooth-bore
B   guns and were still capable of firing rifle ammunition albeit at a reduced
     range and accuracy. The gun which was the subject of count 1 had also
     been rechambered. In respect of that gun Judge Galpin, applying
     Creaser v. *Tunnicliffe* [1977] 1 W.L.R. 1493, ruled that a plea of not
     guilty be entered. The appellant changed his plea to guilty on count 2.
     He appealed against conviction on count 2 on the grounds that the judge
     erred in law in holding that a Lee-Enfield rifle still remained a firearm
C   and so subject to the provisions of section 1 (1) of the Firearms Act 1968
     notwithstanding that the rifling had been professionally removed and the
     gun reproofed as a smooth bore gun with a barrel length not less than 24
     inches in length; and that the dissenting judgment of Lord Widgery C.J.
     in *Creaser* v. *Tunnicliffe* [1977] 1 W.L.R. 1493, 1499 was the correct
     interpretation of the law in that once the definition of a shot gun in
     section 1 (3) was satisfied, that was all that had to be proved.
D   As a result of the appellant's acquittal on count 1, the Attorney-
     General, under section 36 of the Criminal Justice Act 1972, referred
     for the opinion of the court the question:

        "Whether it is possible to adapt a Lee-Enfield rifle, which has
        admittedly been a firearm within the definition of section 57 (1) of
        the Firearms Act so as to exclude the said firearm from the necessity
E   for such a certificate by reason of section 1 (3) (*a*) of the same Act."

     The facts are stated in the judgment of the court.

     Stephen Parish for the appellant.
     Brian Leary Q.C. and *James Tabor* for the Crown and the Attorney-
     General.
F

        LORD LANE C.J. gave the following judgment of the court. On July
     10, 1979, at Portsmouth Crown Court, the appellant, David William
     Hucklebridge (who has indicated his lack of objection to his name being
     published, because this is in half as an Attorney-General's reference), was
     convicted on count 2 in the indictment with which we are concerned,
G   charging him with possessing a rifle No. P39869 without a firearm
     certificate, contrary to section 1 of the Firearms Act 1968. He was,
     on the judge's direction, found not guilty of count 1 in the indictment,
     of possessing a rifle No. FB20954 without a firearm certificate contrary
     to the same section. He was sentenced to a fine of £20 or one month's
     imprisonment in default in respect of the count of which he was found
     guilty, namely, count 2. He had originally pleaded not guilty to that
H   count, but in the light of a direction by the judge he, on advice, changed
     his plea.
        Consequently there is one conviction and one acquittal, with both of
     which, rather unusually, this court is now concerned. We are concerned
     with the conviction because on a point of law the appellant appeals
     against that conviction. We are concerned with the acquittal because
     there has been a reference by the Attorney-General to this court in
     respect of the acquittal, both of course arising out of the same trial.

It is necessary to decribe the two guns with which we are concerned. A
Exhibit 1 was the gun in count 1. This had been a Lee-Enfield rifle,
which had been converted to smooth bore by the rifling being reamed out
and had been rechambered to take ·410 shot gun cartridges. But it is
correct to say that it was still capable of firing ·303 cartridges, though,
owing to the obvious increase in bore, it would no longer be so accurate
as it originally was, nor would the range of the rifle be the same, it B
would be very much reduced. The evidence was that it would be lethal
up to about 100 yards. It had been reproofed at the Birmingham Proof
House.

The gun in count 2 had also been a Lee-Enfield ·303 rifle. It had
been converted to smooth bore by the same process as that in respect of
the first count, but this gun had not been rechambered to take shot gun
cartridges. It was still capable of firing ·303 cartridges with the same C
loss of velocity and accuracy as the other gun. It had been reproofed as
a smooth bore gun, but could not, as I say, fire shot gun cartridges.

The facts were not really in dispute and the judge was called upon, as
a matter of submission at the close of the expert evidence as to the guns,
to decide whether or not the rechambered gun had become a shot gun
within the exception of section 1 (3) (a) of the Firearms Act 1968 so that
a firearm certificate was not required in respect of it. So far as that gun D
was concerned, the judge ruled in favour of the appellant.

The appellant appeals against his conviction on count 2. He has a
certificate of the judge in respect of that appeal, although such a certificate was not necessary, this appeal being on a point of law. The
Attorney-General refers this matter in respect of count 1 to this court,
asking the court to rule on the following: E

"Whether it is possible to adapt a Lee-Enfield rifle, which has
admittedly been a firearm within the definition of section 57 (1) of
the Firearms Act so as to exclude the said firearm from the necessity for such a certificate by reason of section 1 (3) (a) of the same
Act."

F
It is necessary therefore to consider the various statutory provisions
which are designed to cover this situation. I turn accordingly to the
Firearms Act 1968. Section 1 has the sidenote " Requirement of firearm
certificate " and reads:

"(1) Subject to any exemption under this Act, it is an offence for a
person—(a) to have in his possession, or to purchase or acquire, a
firearm to which this section applies without holding a firearm G
certificate in force at the time, or otherwise than as authorised by
such a certificate; . . . (3) This section applies to every firearm
except—(a) a shot gun (that is to say a smooth-bore gun with a
barrel not less than 24 inches in length, not being an air gun); . . ."

The question in this case, or put more accurately the two questions in H
this case, depend entirely upon the interpretation to be put on those
words in section 1 (3) (a).

In section 57 (4) of the Act of 1968 shot gun is interpreted as
follows:

"'shot gun' has the meaning assigned to it by section 1 (3) (a) of
this Act and, in sections 3 (1) and 45 (2) of this Act and in the
definition of 'firearms dealer,' includes any component part of a

A   shot gun and any accessory to a shot gun designed or adapted to diminish the noise or flash caused by firing the gun; . . ."

Consequently that interpretation section in a word refers a person desirous of having a definition of shot gun back to section 1 (3) (a), namely " a shot gun (that is to say a smooth-bore gun with a barrel not less than 24 inches in length, not being an air gun)."

B   The contention of Mr. Parish, on behalf of the appellant, is simple. He submits that those two sections taken together, namely, section 57 and section 1, make it perfectly plain that the words in parenthesis in section 1 (3) (a) are, for the purposes of this Act, a definition of what the Act means by shot gun. He goes on to submit that these two guns, each of them, although originally Lee-Enfield rifles properly so called, have ceased to be Lee-Enfield rifles properly so called and have become
C   smooth-bore guns with barrels not less than 24 inches in length. That being the case, says Mr. Parish, they are plainly within section 1 (3) (a) and consequently do not require a firearm certificate. Accordingly, in his submission, the appellant should not only have been acquitted on count 1 but he should have been acquitted on count 2 as well.

        This matter has been considered by the Divisional Court in *Creaser*
D   v. *Tunnicliffe* [1977] 1 W.L.R. 1493. The circumstances in that case were as follows, at p. 1494:

        " Both the defendants collected firearms and both held a number of firearm certificates for specified guns and a shot gun certificate (which covered all shot guns in the certificate holder's possession). They had in their possession certain rifles without firearm certificates
E   from which they had removed the rifling but the gun could still discharge the same ammunition as before the alteration. In respect of those guns, informations were preferred against the defendants that they were in possession of a firearm otherwise than as authorised by a firearm certificate, contrary to section 1 (1) of the Firearms Act 1968. The justices rejected the defendants' contention that the removal of the rifling had the effect of altering the weapon
F   to a smooth-bore gun within the definition of a shot gun in section 1 (3) of the Act. They held that, except in the case of certain antique guns, the defendants required firearm certificates and had committed offences under section 1 (1) of the Act."

The defendants appealed against that conviction. The Divisional Court dismissed the appeal, but Lord Widgery C.J. dissented and held that in
G   his view the appeal should succeed. It was held by the majority:

        " that a rifle from which the rifling had been removed could still be used as a rifle, albeit with a lesser degree of accuracy, and it remained a rifle and, therefore, a firearm as defined by section 57 and subject to the provisions of section 1 (1) of the Act."

H   It seems to this court that what impression the weapon makes upon the court, namely, does it impress the court as being a rifle or does it impress the court as being a shot gun, is an immaterial consideration. What the court has to consider, and I do not apologise for repeating it, is the definition in section 1 (3) (a).

        This court, with respect to the majority in *Creaser* v. *Tunnicliffe*, finds the reasoning of Lord Widgery C.J. compelling. If I may cite a passage from his judgment, at p. 1500:

"When one goes back to examine the circumstances in which a A firearm may be possessed without a firearms certificate, which means going back to section 1 of the Act, one is immediately struck by the fact that the broad distinction drawn between one firearm and another firearm is that the smooth-bore weapon (popularly called a shot gun) goes into one class, and all the rest go into another. Thus all the rifles are in a class described by section 1 of the Act. The reason must be clear enough. It is because the element of risk, B danger and lethal quality which a rifle has when compared to a shot gun is very different. Parliament no doubt had in mind that people may have a legitimate excuse for holding shot guns, but not have any excuse for saying they required a rifle.

"One looks again at the matter which has been mentioned several times by Watkins J., section 1 (3), which contains the vital C definition in these terms: 'This section applies to every firearm except—(a) a shot gun (that is to say a smooth-bore gun with a barrel not less than 24 inches in length . . .); . . .'

"In my imagination I pick up one of these weapons and look at it. I say: has it got a smooth bore? Yes, because the rifling has gone. Is the barrel more than 24 inches in length? Yes, it is. D Therefore it is a shot gun for the purposes of this Act. How is that approach to be faulted? It is said by some that this cannot be a shot gun. This Lee-Enfield with the rifling bored out does not look like a shot gun; one cannot shoot rabbits with it. That may be so. It still seems to me to satisfy the definition of a shot gun in the Act."

With that passage this court respectfully agrees. As I say, it is not for E us to express our view what the particular weapon might look like. That is not the problem. The question is, does it come within the exception as Parliament has set that exception.

Mr. Leary, on behalf of the Attorney-General, draws our attention to section 57 (1), which reads:

"In this Act, the expression 'firearm' means a lethal barrelled weapon of any description from which any shot, bullet or other F missile can be discharged and includes—(a) any prohibited weapon, whether it is such a lethal weapon as aforesaid or not; and (b) any component part of such a lethal or prohibited weapon; and (c) any accessory to any such weapon designed or adapted to diminish the noise or flash caused by firing the weapon; . . ."

He asks us to pay regard to the fact that the component parts of the G Lee-Enfield or most of them are still there. It has only got an adapted barrel and chamber. The rest of the gun remains the same. All the component parts of the gun are the original component parts. Ergo, he says, it is covered by subsection (1) (c).

But that overlooks the words which follow in that subsection, which read: H

"and so much of section 1 of this Act as excludes any description of firearm from the category of firearms to which that section applies shall be construed as also excluding component parts of, and accessories to, firearms of that description."

So that once you have got to the situation—which this court thinks you have—that this is within the definition of shot gun, then all the com-

A ponent parts are likewise protected by the exception. That argument is circular and does not avail the Attorney-General.

Finally Mr. Leary, in his concluding argument, was trying to impress us with the dangerous situation which may result if the Attorney-General's reference does not succeed and if the appeal against conviction on the other count does succeed. He was suggesting to us that that might open the floodgate to undesirable possessors of weapons which could

B take ·303 cartridges and might be detrimental to law-abiding citizens. Some of course think that a shot gun is just as lethal a weapon as a rifle. In certain circumstances it would be. In any event if the holder or possessor of one of these modified weapons desires to discharge from the weapon, albeit inefficiently, a round of ·303 ammunition, he will, we understand, have to possess a firearm certificate before he can obtain

C such ammunition. In any event even if that is not the case, it is not for this court to fly in the face of what we consider to be the plain words of an Act of Parliament. If it is required to close up a possible loophole, that is for Parliament to do and not this court.

Finally there is one other matter to which it is desirable to draw attention, and that is the precise wording of the exception. This is a matter to which the court in *Creaser* v. *Tunnicliffe* [1977] 1 W.L.R. 1493 did

D not advert. The last words, " not being an air gun " seem to this court to have been unnecessary if the Crown's submission is correct, because an air gun would already have been excluded by virtue of the Act; that was a weapon not capable of firing ordinary shot gun ammunition. That particular point is not necessary, strictly speaking, for the decision of this court, but it is by way of comment.

E For these reasons the appeal against conviction on count 2 succeeds and the conviction is quashed. The answer to the Attorney-General's reference, namely " Whether it is possible to adapt a Lee-Enfield rifle, which has admittedly been a firearm within the definition of section 57 (1) of the Firearms Act so as to exclude the said firearm from the necessity for such a certificate by reason of section 1 (3) (*a*) of the same Act " is yes.

F

Appeal allowed.
Question referred to court answered
in affirmative.

G Solicitors: *Gray, Purdue & Co., Waterlooville; Director of Public Prosecutions.*

[Reported by MISS LESLEY HEWLETT, Barrister-at-Law]

H

A

[COURT OF APPEAL]

* WETHERALL v. SMITH AND OTHERS

1980 Feb. 7, 8

Stephenson and Ackner L.JJ.
and Sir David Cairns

B

Agricultural Holding — Tenancy within Act — Abandonment of
agricultural user—Agricultural land used for schooling and
grazing horses—Service of notice to quit—Landlords seeking
possession of land—Proceedings in county court—Jurisdiction
of court to determine whether tenancy ceasing to be agricultural holding—Agricultural Holdings Act 1948 (11 & 12
Geo. 6, c. 63), ss. 1 (1), 94 (1)

C

The tenant, a farmer, was granted a yearly tenancy of a
field in 1956 and it was an agricultural holding within the
meaning of section 1 (1) of the Agricultural Holdings Act
1948.[1] At that time, he was using the field mainly for grazing,
which was an "agriculture" user as defined by section 94 (1)
of the Act, but by 1974 he was also using it for grazing
ponies and horses and as a jumping paddock. In 1976, the
landlords, claiming that the field was only being used as a
jumping paddock and, therefore, had ceased to be an agricultural holding protected by the Act, served a notice to quit
and, after the notice had expired, one of the landlords took
possession of the field.

D

The tenant brought an action claiming that the landlords
were in breach of the implied covenant of quiet enjoyment
and sought damages and an injunction restraining them from
interfering with his occupation of the land. The landlords
counterclaimed for damages for trespass and a declaration
that the tenancy had been terminated by the notice to quit.
The judge found that after 1974 the tenant had continued to
use the field for agricultural purposes, albeit to a small degree,
but the main use had been for grazing and schooling horses.
He held that the tenancy at its inception was protected by
the Act of 1948 and, since any question of its present use
was a matter for the agricultural land tribunal and not for
the court, the tenant was entitled to damages and he made
no order on the landlords' counterclaim.

E

F

On appeal by the landlords: —

Held, allowing the appeal, that where the agricultural user
was substantially or wholly abandoned, the tenancy ceased to
be an agricultural holding protected by the Act of 1948 but,
since a temporary change of user could not take a tenancy
outside the protection of the Act, strong evidence was required
to show that the agricultural user had been abandoned; that,
accordingly, the judge erred in law in not determining whether
the tenancy had ceased to be a protected tenancy under the
Act and, since there was no specific finding that the agricultural user had been abandoned, the case would be remitted
for a rehearing (post, pp. 1299F–G, 1300D–F).

G

Per curiam. Having regard to the nature of the dispute
in this case, it may be necessary for the judge to consider
first, to what extent during about the last two years, up to
the service of the notice to quit, was the field used for the
grazing of cattle, horses, and any other agricultural purposes;
secondly, to what extent was it used for riding lessons and

H

[1] Agricultural Holdings Act 1948, s. 1: see post, p. 1293A–B.
S. 94 (1): see post, p. 1293C.

A   jumping; thirdly, were the horses, while grazed there, used only or mainly for recreation; and fourthly, was any of the land and, if so, what part, used for the purpose of trade or business? (post, p. 1300B–D).

The following cases are referred to in the judgment of Sir David Cairns:

Blackmore v. *Butler* [1954] 2 Q.B. 171; [1954] 3 W.L.R. 62; [1954] 2 All E.R. 403, C.A.

B

Deith v. *Brown* (1956) 167 E.G. 513.

Dunn v. *Fidoe* [1950] 2 All E.R. 685, C.A.

Godfrey v. *Waite* (1951) 157 E.G. 582, C.A.

Hickson & Welch Ltd. v. *Cann*, February 8, 1977; Court of Appeal (Civil Division) Transcript No. 61 of 1977, C.A.

Howkins v. *Jardine* [1951] 1 K.B. 614; [1951] 1 All E.R. 320, C.A.

McClinton v. *McFall* (1974) 232 E.G. 707, C.A.

C

Monson v. *Bound* [1954] 1 W.L.R. 1321; [1954] 3 All E.R. 228.

Normanton (Earl of) v. *Giles* [1980] 1 W.L.R. 28; [1980] 1 All E.R. 106, H.L.(E.).

Price v. *Vaughan* (1958) 172 E.G. 161.

Russell and Harding's Arbitration, In re (1922) 39 T.L.R. 92, C.A.

Wolfe v. *Hogan* [1949] 2 K.B. 194; [1949] 1 All E.R. 570, C.A.

D   No additional cases were cited in argument.

APPEAL from Judge Willcock sitting in the Yeovil County Court.

On March 19, 1956, the plaintiff, Roy Edward Wetherall, was granted the tenancy of a field at Yeovilton, Somersetshire, on a yearly tenancy at a rent of £3 a year, the tenancy amounting to an agricultural holding for
E   the purposes of the Agricultural Holdings Act 1948. On September 8, 1970, the defendants, Peter Charles Smith, Rita Smith, Edward William Evans and Millicent Grace Evans, became the joint owners of the property. In September 1976, they served on the tenant a notice to quit by September 29, 1977. By a counter-notice dated October 5, 1976, the tenant contended that the tenancy continued as an agricultural tenancy protected under the Act of 1948.

F   On March 16, 1977, the tenant brought an action against the defendant landlords, contending that the field was let on a yearly tenancy under the Agricultural Holdings Act 1948 in accordance with the terms of an agreement with the landlords of October 8, 1974, and that the second defendant, Mrs. Smith, had taken possession of the field in breach of the agreement. He claimed damages of £200 (later increased to £500) and an injunction
G   restraining the landlords from interfering with his occupation and enjoyment of the field. By their defence dated January 3, 1978, the landlords, denying that the agreement of October 8, 1974, was a memorandum of a tenancy agreement under the Act of 1948, contended that since that agreement, the tenant had not used the field for agriculture, but only for grazing or riding horses or ponies and that the tenant had changed the nature of the tenancy. They claimed, inter alia, damages for trespass and
H   breach of covenant, an injunction restraining the tenant from entering the landlords' premises and from molesting them, and a declaration that the tenancy had been terminated. By his reply and defence to the counterclaim, the tenant denied allegations of trespass and damage, and asserted that he had used the field as agricultural land throughout the tenancy.

On February 21, 1979, Judge Willcock, holding that the tenancy continued as an agricultural one, gave judgment for the tenant and awarded

him £100 damages for trespass, without making any order on the counter-　A
claim.

The landlords appealed on the grounds that (1) the judge was wrong in
declining to consider the use to which the relevant land was put in the two
years before and at the time when the notice to quit was served on the
tenant on September 28, 1976, and, in particular, when he said that he
had no right to consider the day-to-day conduct of the parties to examine
the use to which the tenant had put the land and that that issue should　B
more properly decided by the agricultural land tribunal; (2) the judge
was wrong in adopting that approach and/or in finding that there was no
reason why an agricultural tenant should not use his land for recreational
purposes; and (3) the judge wrongly held that there was no evidence of any
variation of the terms of the tenancy nor any such variation in fact.

The facts are stated in the judgment of Sir David Cairns.　　　　　　C

R. A. Henderson for the landlords.
Bruce Mauleverer for the tenant.

STEPHENSON L.J. I will ask Sir David Cairns to deliver the first
judgment.

D

SIR DAVID CAIRNS. This is an appeal from a decision of Judge Willcock given on February 21, 1979, at the Yeovil County Court. It relates
to a field or paddock about an acre and a quarter in area which lies near
to a rectory and was part of the glebe land. By a written agreement made
on March 19, 1956, this paddock was let by the rector to the plaintiff in
these proceedings. It was let on a yearly tenancy from Michaelmas 1955　E
at the rent of £3 a year.

By clause 3 of the tenancy agreement it was provided that: " The
tenant shall manage the said land in a good husband-like manner . . ." and
that and other indications in the agreement make it clear that it was at
the start an agricultural tenancy.

In the course of time the reversion passed to the defendants, who are
four in number: a Mr. and Mrs. Smith and a Mr. and Mrs. Evans. Mr.　F
and Mrs. Evans were the parents of Mrs. Smith. There has since been a
divorce between Mr. and Mrs. Smith, but Mrs. Smith and her parents
continue to live at the old rectory.

The question at issue in these proceedings is whether this tenancy,
having begun as an agricultural tenancy protected by the Agricultural
Holdings Act 1948, continues to enjoy that protection. The tenant's claim
was for an injunction to restrain the landlords from interfering with his　G
quiet possession of the paddock. The landlords, by their defence, claimed
that the tenant's tenancy had come to an end and they asked, by a
counterclaim, for, among other relief, a declaration to that effect.

At the trial the judge held that the tenancy continued to be an agricultural one and, accordingly, he found in favour of the tenant and awarded
him £100 damages; and it followed that the landlords' claim was dismissed.　H
The landlords appeal, contending that the holding had ceased to be an
agricultural holding. By their notice of appeal as originally presented—
as it remained up to yesterday—they claimed only a new trial, on the
basis that the judge's findings were not sufficiently clear to justify a firm
decision one way or the other. Leave was granted yesterday for the
notice of appeal to be amended so as to claim in the alternative to a
new trial that judgment should be entered for the landlords.

A   It is convenient to refer straight away to section 1 of the Agricultural Holdings Act 1948 which contains the definition of " agricultural holding " :

"(1) In this Act the expression 'agricultural holding' means the aggregate of the agricultural land comprised in a contract of tenancy, not being a contract under which the said land is let to the tenant during his continuance in any office . . . ."

B   No question arises on the later words of that subsection. Section 1 continues :

"(2) For the purposes of this and the next following section, the expression 'agricultural land' means land used for agriculture which is so used for the purposes of a trade or business . . . ."

C   The remaining words of that subsection are irrelevant. There is a definition in section 94 (1) of " agriculture " in these terms :

". . . 'agriculture' includes horticulture, fruit growing, seed growing, dairy farming and livestock breeding and keeping, the use of land as grazing land, meadow land . . . ."

D   and various other uses but, for the purpose of this appeal, the main words of that definition which are relevant are the words " the use of land as grazing land."

The tenancy agreement having been entered into, it was in 1970 that the reversion passed to the four defendants. Mrs. Smith, the second named defendant, runs a riding school. The plaintiff is a farmer and his farm adjoins the paddock. Relations between the defendants and the tenant, after the defendants had become his landlords, do not seem at any time to

E   have been happy. Acrimonious correspondence began in September 1971. The first defendant Mr. Smith was then asserting, quite wrongly, that the tenancy would end at Michaelmas 1971. The immediate reply on behalf of the tenant was that it was an agricultural tenancy which, at that stage, was accepted on the part of the defendants and, accordingly, in 1973 Mr. Smith gave notice under the Act of 1948 claiming reference to arbitration

F   of the question of increase of rent. Apparently, without the necessity of going to arbitration, it was agreed that the rent should be increased from £3 a year to £4 a year.

Another year passed and in September 1974, Mr. Smith then gave notice claiming arbitration for a further increase of rent. Again, it was unnecessary to go to arbitration because there was an agreement for an increase in the rent to £20 a year, and that agreement was put in writing on

G   October 8, 1974. So, up to that stage, quite clearly the landlords were recognising this as being an agricultural tenancy.

But certain events happened between that time and September 1976 which led the landlords to take the view that the tenancy was no longer an agricultural one and notice to quit was served on the tenant in September 1976, expiring at Michaelmas 1977. It is common ground that that would

H   have been an effective notice except for the provisions of the Act of 1948. The tenant, contending that the holding continued to be an agricultural holding, through his solicitors gave a counter-notice in accordance with the Act of 1948 on October 5, 1976. Thereafter there was correspondence between the solicitors for the two parties as to whether the holding did indeed continue to be an agricultural holding within the meaning of the Act.

In the course of that correspondence the landlords' solicitors wrote on October 26, 1977, contending that the land had been used for a con-

siderable time simply as a jumping paddock. The reply from the tenant's   A
solicitors was that it was continuing its character of an agricultural
holding and was still being used for agricultural purposes.

It can be said at once that, if the use and the only use was as a jumping
paddock with no involvement in any business activity—or, indeed, if it did
involve a business activity—it would not amount to use for agriculture,
because such jumping could be regarded as a recreational purpose and,
within the recent decision of the House of Lords in *Earl of Normanton* v.   B
Giles [1980] 1 W.L.R. 28, would not be use for agriculture.

The tenant started his action in November 1977 and by his particulars
of claim, which were very slightly amended only to increase the amount of
his claim, he set out the circumstances about the yearly tenancy, alleging
that it was a tenancy under the Agricultural Holdings Act 1948, and by
paragraph 2 said: C

> "The defendants are in breach of the covenant for the plaintiff's
> quiet enjoyment implied by law by virtue of the said tenancy. The
> second defendant has taken possession of the above described field
> and by her action has prevented and is preventing the plaintiff from
> using the said field."

It was, in fact, a correct allegation that the second defendant, Mrs. Smith,   D
had indeed taken possession of the field; a letter had been written to the
tenant's solicitors saying that she had done so. The tenant claimed damages, which by then were £500, and an injunction to restrain the landlords
from further interference.

By their defence the landlords alleged that, since the tenancy agreement,
the tenant had not continued to use the land for agriculture, and the pleading   E
went on to say:

> "(6) For a number of years the plaintiff had used the land only for
> grazing horses or ponies and riding the said horses and ponies. (7)
> By his conduct the plaintiff has changed the nature of the tenancy.
> (8) Since the said change of use the defendants accepted rent from the
> plaintiff."   F

The pleading went on to set out a counterclaim, repeating the facts set out
in the defence and saying: "Since the termination of the tenancy the plaintiff has trespassed on the said land. . . ." Damages were claimed in respect
of certain acts the tenant was said to have done on the land, and then there
was a claim for a declaration that the tenancy had been terminated by a
notice to quit. The reply to that pleading denied the allegations of the
defence as to the change of user and said: G

> "The plaintiff has used the land throughout the period of his occupa-
> tion as agricultural land. The said land has been used throughout
> for the grazing of cattle and horses. The plaintiff is entitled to graze
> horses on the said land and relies on the contents of the aforementioned
> agreement. . . ."

By further and better particulars of that reply the tenant said: H

> "Horses have been grazed on the land rented by the plaintiff from
> the defendants as part of his agricultural business, these horses being
> limited to a maximum of two at any one time and the land has also
> been used for grazing of cows, usually for cows in calf, at times in
> conjunction with the plaintiff's adjoining river field with the dividing
> gate being left open. The rented field has also been manured and

A mowed for silage at least on one occasion. The plaintiff has at times erected jumps in the rented field when horses have been ridden and jumped in that field by the defendant's wife and by children."

The matter came before Judge Willcock for hearing on December 11, 1978, and evidence was then given. I do not find it necessary to refer to that except parts of the evidence of the tenant and Mrs. Smith, who was B the principal witness on the defendants' side. The tenant in the course of his evidence said:

"I used it to graze horses and cattle and we may have used a bit also for cows with young calves as a holding paddock. Field is very close to my farm houses. From time to time horses only. From time to time cattle only. We leave gate open to my own home field often. C From time to time jumps for my children. Portable jumps. Two of my children had ponies. We moved jumps about in that field and into other fields. Basically we used the field for grazing."

He was asked when the last cow was in the field and he said:

"October 1977 when I was barred out. We had 30–40 cattle roaming through the three fields, Home Field, this field plus another of mine."

D He also said: "No one rents land from me for horses—what I do is keep someone else's horse from time to time."

Then Mrs. Smith in her evidence made one answer which was originally recorded as "Always discuss jumper," but it has been altered to "Always drums and jumps." She went on:

E "Occasions seen a cow and calf there. Since proper show jumps of Mullins always used just for jumping. They were there when we started riding school 1974. . . . I cannot remember cows and calves being in there regularly. Since 1974 field used as a practice area for Mrs. Wetherall to give lessons, and we used it with permission. . . . Grazed—on occasions, limited, by a cow and calf in our first couple of years"—that would be 1970 to 1972—"Since then only grazing F was by horses, since Mullins' jumps in. Sometimes gates left open and animals would drift in, out of curiosity I would say."

Later on she said:

"After Mullins' jumps put in, it was solely used as a jumping paddock. I would say 1973–77. . . . I have seen ponies and horses put in with G the jumps to graze."

In cross-examination she said: "I don't accept field was used in conjunction with next field. No, jumps not moved in winter. I agree about nine jumps."

The judge did not give judgment on that day, but he did make this note:

H "Facts found: plaintiff continued to use the paddock for agricultural purposes after 1974 to a small degree and that his major use of it was for schooling and grazing horses."

That finding is relied on by both sides here. Mr. Henderson on behalf of the landlords says that, if the use for agricultural purposes is only to a small degree and the major use is for other purposes, then it is no longer an agricultural holding; and Mr. Mauleverer for the tenant says that, if it is

used for agricultural purposes—unless it is really to a de minimis degree, A
which the judge was not finding—it continues to be an agricultural holding.

When the judge came to give judgment on February 21, 1979, it was
not a written judgment. I understand it was given immediately at the
conclusion of argument, and notes were made by a solicitor and submitted
to the judge. The judge said: "First, I accept the submissions of Mr.
George for the plaintiff that this was an agricultural holding from its B
inception." Now, it is not perfectly clear what that means, whether it
means it was an agricultural holding at its inception or it was an agricultural holding at and ever after its inception. The judge continued:

> "Secondly, I accept Mr. George's submission that the correct way to
> put an end to the agricultural tenancy is by the machinery set out in
> the Agricultural Holdings Act."
                                                                          C
That, of course, is only so if it were indeed at the relevant time, whatever
the relevant time may be, an agricultural holding. The judge refers to
clause 3 of the tenancy agreement, setting out the management duties and
so forth and goes on:

> "It is for the defendants to complain to the agricultural tribunal
> if they state that the tenant is in breach. To interpolate, the plain- D
> tiff had continued to use the paddock for agricultural purposes, albeit
> to a small degree, the major use being for grazing and schooling of
> horses and ponies."

That was a repetition of what we had already found previously on
December 11, 1978:

> "If the defendants contend that the mixed use for small agricultural E
> use and major sporting use is in breach of the agreement then it is up
> to them to promote that argument before the agricultural tribunal."

That, with great respect, is really a misunderstanding of the argument on
behalf of the landlords, which was not that it was in breach of the agreement but that, because of the use that had been made of it, it had ceased
to be an agricultural holding and, therefore, had ceased to be something F
which was within the jurisdiction of the agricultural land tribunal at all.
Later on the judge said:

> "It is argued by the defendant that it is open to the court to put aside
> an agricultural tenancy and to examine the question de novo as to
> whether at the date of the notice the user falls within an agricultural
> user."
                                                                          G
That would, I think, be an accurate summary of the argument of the
defendants if the expression "put aside an agricultural tenancy" were
taken to mean to contend that what had orginally been an agricultural
tenancy had ceased to be one; not to say that its origin could be disregarded, but to say that the user, after that time, had had the effect of
changing the character of the tenancy. The judge continues: H

> "[The defendants say] that if you look at the user you see that it is
> ordinary user not agricultural user at that date and the significance
> of that is that the tenant has thrown away the protection afforded to
> him by the Act of 1948 and because he carries on no agricultural
> activity it must be open to the court to say whether or not the tenancy
> is an agricultural tenancy.
> "In the light of what I have said that view cannot prevail. It cannot

A   be right that this court should have the freedom to examine the day by day conduct of the parties to examine the use the tenant has put the land to in order to discover what the tenancy is. It is more properly a question to be decided by the agricultural tribunal whether the use is a proper one under the tenancy.

"As to whether for example some part of the tenancy is agricultural use and some part is not or whether some part is in recreational use and that part is more substantial than the agricultural use are arguments of degree which this court could never resolve."

Now, that seems to me, again with great respect to the judge, to be disclaiming responsibility for making the decision which it really was for him and nobody else at that stage to make, and not one for the agricultural land tribunal to consider.

As I have said, it is common ground that the tenancy was at the outset an agricultural tenancy. If the judge is to be taken as holding, as he seemed to be saying in one part of his judgment, that that was conclusive so far as the court was concerned, then, in my judgment, that was not in accordance with the law as it has been developed; and certainly the suggestion that the matter should go to the agricultural land tribunal for the decision on such a question was inappropriate. The landlords' case here was not that, by departing from agricultural use, the tenant was in breach of the tenancy agreement. Indeed, one of the landlords' contentions was that the change of user had been impliedly assented to; but, whether assented to or not, the landlords' claim that, by the change of user, the tenancy had ceased to be an agricultural tenancy. That is an issue which it was for the court to resolve and not for the agricultural land tribunal.

Mr. Mauleverer, on behalf of the tenants, has not contended that the use which is stated or is to be implied at the beginning of the tenancy is conclusive for the whole period of the tenancy. He concedes, as I think he is bound to do on the authorities, that, notwithstanding what appears in the tenancy agreement, the character of the tenancy can change. That was authoritatively decided, so far as this court is concerned, by *Hickson & Welch Ltd.* v. *Cann* (unreported), February 8, 1977. We have been able to examine the judgment from the transcript obtained from the Supreme Court Library: Court of Appeal (Civil Division) Transcript No. 61 of 1977. But, accepting that there can be such a change, Mr. Mauleverer contends that there is a strong presumption that, if at the start the tenancy is an agricultural one, it continues to have that characteristic, that it takes clear evidence to justify a finding that there has been a change, that the matter has to be decided by considering the whole history of the tenancy, and that the question is one of degree, depending on the extent to which agricultural use has been abandoned and to which any other use has been adopted.

That is, I am afraid, an inadequate summary of the very careful and forceful argument which was developed by Mr. Mauleverer on behalf of the tenant in this case, but I hope it will suffice for the purpose of indicating why I have come to the decision to which I have come. First of all, in my view the period to which attention must be mainly directed in considering whether the tenancy has ceased to be an agricultural one is the time leading up to the service of a notice to quit where a notice to quit has been served. I would not suggest that the change can, in the absence of some very exceptional circumstances, be brought about in a matter of days or weeks; but in *Hickson & Welch Ltd.* v. *Cann* (unreported) all members of this court took the view that the cesser of agricultural activities for the

last two years before the service of the notice to quit was, irrespective of   A
what had gone before, sufficient to deprive the tenant of the right to claim
the protection of the Agricultural Holdings Act 1948. There was no
suggestion in the evidence in that case, so far as appears from the judgments, that there had been any assent to the change of use on the part
of the landlord.

The cases earlier than *Hickson & Welch Ltd.* v. *Cann* are, I think, all   B
consistent with the decision arrived at in that case, though it may be—and
I think it probably is so—that it went further than any of the earlier cases.
Most of the earlier cases that we have been referred to are on the question
whether a tenancy could become an agricultural tenancy by user rather
than the converse.

In the first case that was mentioned, *Dunn* v. *Fidoe* [1950] 2 All E.R.
685, a decision of this court, an inn had been let with an adjoining orchard.   C
It was held to be an agricultural tenancy and Tucker L.J. in the judgment,
which was agreed to by the other members of the court, based his decision
on the fact that the premises were used for the growing of fruit for sale in
addition to the use of the inn for the ordinary purposes of an inn.

In *Howkins* v. *Jardine* [1951] 1 K.B. 614, another decision of this
court, it was held that, where there was a lease which was in substance
that of an agricultural holding, there could be no severance so as to treat   D
part as agricultural holding and part not. The question there was whether
a cottage, which was sublet to persons not engaged in agriculture, was
protected by the Act of 1948. It was held that it was, because the holding
could not cease to be agricultural according to whether a particular part—
in that case the cottage—was occupied for agricultural purposes or not.
In his judgment Jenkins L.J. said, at p. 628:   E

"On this basis one must look at the substance of the matter and see
whether, as a matter of substance, the land comprised in the tenancy,
taken as a whole, is an agricultural holding."

I draw attention to the use of the words "as a matter of substance."
Another word which was relied upon by Mr. Henderson in support of his
argument was the word "is," suggesting that Jenkins L.J. thought that the   F
question should be directed to the present time or something near the
present time rather than to the past when the tenancy began.

A third decision in this court was *Godfrey* v. *Waite* (1951) 157 E.G.
582, and we have seen a transcript of the judgment. That was a case of a
house which was let as a dwelling with a parcel of land adjoining it, but
later the tenant claimed that it had become an agricultural tenancy. Sir
Raymond Evershed M.R. said that, in considering whether the holding   G
was an agricultural one or not, the original purpose of the tenancy was
significant, but if the land had been used for agriculture with the assent of
the landlord, then it might come to be an agricultural holding. Denning L.J.
gave judgment to similar effect, saying that the original purpose might be
decisive but if, after the letting, it was used for agricultural purposes with
the assent of the landlord, it could be brought within the Act. Hodson L.J.   H
agreed and he did not expressly refer in his judgment to any necessity for
the assent of the landlord.

It seems to me that it may well be that, when the question is whether
land which was not an agricultural holding at the beginning had become
an agricultural holding, it can only do so if there were assent of the landlord to the change of use. It by no means necessarily follows that, if
agricultural user is abandoned, the assent of the landlord to such aban-

A donment is necessary in order to reach a conclusion that it had ceased to be an agricultural holding and, indeed, Mr. Mauleverer did not so contend. He was content to say that, if there had clearly been complete abandonment by the tenant of the agricultural use then, apart from any question of assent, the holding would cease to be an agricultural one.

The last of this batch of Court of Appeal cases that I will mention is *Blackmore* v. *Butler* [1954] 2 Q.B. 171. The issue there was as to whether

B two adjoining pieces of land let separately could constitute one agricultural holding. The only assistance that the report gives to this court in the present case is, I think, to be found in the judgment of Somervell L.J. where, after citing at length from *Godfrey* v. *Waite*, 157 E.G. 582, he said, at p. 177:

C " The importance is that the question was held to be one of fact and degree. If it had been let as a farm house for use in connection with the farm, the county court judge could and should have decided that it was an agricultural holding. It was also recognised that the purpose might alter during the currency of the contract."

Another case decided in that year, but this time by McNair J. was *Monson* v. *Bound* [1954] 1 W.L.R. 1321. It was about the letting of a shop and glass conservatory with adjoining garden. The trade that was

D carried on was the sale of flowers and shrubs, of which only about a sixth were grown in the garden adjoining the shop. McNair J. held that there was not an agricultural holding and that, as is clear from the report, was on the basis that only one-sixth of the sales, which amounted to only about one-tenth of the turnover, was within the agricultural business. Therefore, it was not an agricultural holding.

We have been helpfully referred this morning to a number of other

E cases by Mr. Mauleverer. I think they do not do more than give further illustration of the principles laid down in the earlier cases, so I will merely give their references without referring to any details: *In re Russell and Harding's Arbitration* (1922) 39 T.L.R. 92; *Deith* v. *Brown* (1956) 167 E.G. 513, a decision of Pearce J.; *Price* v. *Vaughan* (1958) 172 E.G. 161, a decision in the county court by Sir Donald Hurst and *McClinton* v. *McFall*

F (1974) 232 E.G. 707.

Having referred to those authorities I would respectfully add that, on principle, it is in my judgment right that the protection of the statute should be lost if agricultural activity is wholly or substantially abandoned during the course of the tenancy even if without consent of the landlord. The object of the legislature is surely to maintain continuity in the conduct of farming and horticultural operations rather than to put people, who have

G at some time in the past acquired a particular type of tenancy, in a privileged position. At the same time, the cases show that the tenancy is not to be regarded as alternating between being within and outside the Act of 1948 as minor changes of user take place, and that, when the tenancy is clearly an agricultural one to start with, strong evidence is needed to show that agricultural user has been abandoned.

H I can deal quickly with the amended notice of appeal. I find it impossible to say that there were such findings by the judge as would entitle this court to say that judgment should be entered for the landlords. So far as concerns the matter added to the grounds of appeal, which is in these terms:

" The judge was wrong in fact in holding that there was no evidence of a variation in the terms of the plaintiff's tenancy and wrong in law in holding that there was no such variation."

1300

The only evidence that was relied on to support the proposition that there A had been a variation of the tenancy was that the landlords, with knowledge of the use to which the land was being put by the tenant, accepted rent. It is quite clear that that is not sufficient to bring about the variation in the term of the tenancy. *Wolfe* v. *Hogan* [1949] 2 K.B. 194 is authority to that effect.

However, it remains to be considered whether this is a case in which, B however regrettable it may be, it is necessary for this court to direct that there should be a new trial. As I have indicated, I am of the opinion that the judge here made a wrong approach to the issue that he had to decide and made an error in law in holding that it was not for him to examine what he called the day by day conduct of the parties in order to decide what was the use the tenant was putting the land to. I, of course, accept that minute examination of day to day activities is not required but, C having regard to the nature of the dispute in this case, I consider that it was necessary for the judge to pay attention—it may be among other things—to these points and to reach a conclusion upon them: first, to what extent during about the last two years, up to the service of the notice to quit in September 1976, was the paddock used for the grazing of (a) cattle, (b) horses, (c) for any other agricultural purposes; secondly, to what extent was it used for riding lessons and jumping and other D similar purposes; thirdly, were the horses, while grazed there, used only or mainly for recreation; and, fourthly, was any of the land and, if so, what part, used for the purpose of trade or business?

I suggest those questions, not as intended to bind the judge in any way as to issues of fact to which he should direct his attention, but as being matters that seem to me to be relevant for him to take into account. Because E there are no clear findings by the judge on these various matters and the notes of the evidence would not enable this court to make such findings, in my judgment, the matter must go back for a fresh hearing and, on the basis of the findings that the judge ultimately makes, he should go on to consider whether, during the two years or so leading up to the notice to quit, the land was or was not substantially used for agriculture for the purpose of trade or business, or whether that user had been wholly or F substantially abandoned by the tenant.

It will be convenient and will probably save expense if the matter goes back to the same judge for rehearing and if he is asked to take into account the evidence which he heard before. I consider that the parties should be at liberty to adduce additional evidence, both because it may be that full attention was not paid to the points to which witnesses should address G themselves at the first hearing and because it cannot be expected that at this stage the judge will have a clear recollection of the evidence.

To that extent I would allow the appeal and direct that there should be a fresh hearing.

ACKNER L.J. I agree. Despite the very able argument of Mr. Maul- H everer, I think this case should go back for rehearing by the judge. It is not disputed that the protection of the Agricultural Holdings Act 1948, although enjoyed for many years, can be, as Sir David Cairns has fully demonstrated, lost if the tenant abandons his use of the land for agriculture. The judge erred in his approach to this issue. There was conflicting evidence as to whether any, and if so what, agricultural use was made by the tenant and whether, if so used, the use was for the purpose of trade or

A   business. There were no adequate findings as to whose evidence the judge preferred or generally as to the actual use over the appropriate period. I agree with the order proposed.

STEPHENSON L.J. I agree with both judgments which have been delivered and have nothing to add except my appreciation of the help received by the court from both counsel in reaching an unfortunate but, in my judgment, necessary conclusion.

B

> *Appeal allowed with costs, save for defendants' costs of amendment to notice of appeal.*
>
> *Case remitted for hearing by Judge Willcock.*
>
> *Defendants to amend defence to plead any variations relied on.*
>
> *Plaintiff to give full particulars of business use of land from 1974 to 1976, and produce relevant farm books.*
>
> *Costs below reserved to judge.*

C

D

Solicitors: *Jeremy Wood, Yeovil; Porter, Mangnall & Co., Yeovil.*

[Reported by MISS HENRIETTA STEINBERG, Barrister-at-Law]

E

[COURT OF APPEAL]

F

* UNIVERSITY OF ESSEX v. DJEMAL AND OTHERS

[1980 E. No. 552]

1980 March 14   Buckley, Shaw and
                                                   Brightman L.JJ.

G   *Practice—Possession of land—Order for possession—Students occupying part of university premises—Summary proceedings for possession of land—Whether order for possession to be limited to area occupied by students—R.S.C., Ord. 113, rr. 1, 2*

Students at the plaintiff university occupied part of the university premises and, on February 27, 1980, the university obtained an order for possession which was executed on March 5. Students then went into occupation of another part of the premises and, by an originating summons issued in accordance with the provisions of R.S.C., Ord. 113, the university sought an order for possession of the whole of their premises against the defendants, seven named students and persons unknown. The students vacated the area before the hearing of the summons but threatened further similar action. Walton J. made an order for possession limited to that part of the premises which the students had occupied. The university appealed.

H

A

On the question whether the jurisdiction of the court to make a possession order was limited under the provisions of R.S.C., Ord. 113 to the area that was occupied in adverse possession to the owner's rights:—

Held, allowing the appeal, that R.S.C., Ord. 113 was a procedural order which did not affect the extent or nature of the court's jurisdiction to grant orders for the possession of land; that the jurisdiction of the court extended to the right of a legal owner to the possession of the whole of his property uninterfered with by unauthorised persons in adverse possession, but the extent of any order for possession granted depended on the circumstances and, in the present case, since the defendants threatened further adverse possession, an order would be granted, extending to the whole of the university premises, enforceable against the defendants or any person who might be in adverse possession.

B

C

Order of Walton J. varied.

No cases are referred to in the judgments.

The following case was cited in argument:
Evans v. *Roe* (1820) 4 Moo. C.P. 469.

D

APPEAL from Walton J.

By summons of March 3, 1980, the University of Essex sought an order for possession for the whole of the premises against seven defendants, Amber Djemal, Sheila Margaret Jones, James M. Knights, Michael Mullan, Efstathios Nicolaides, Paul Gareth Rickard, Raymond Horne and persons unknown, who were in adverse possession of part of the premises.

E

On March 11, 1980, Walton J. granted an order for possession of that part of the premises which had been occupied by a body of students, but refused to make an order in the wide terms sought by the university on the grounds that he had jurisdiction under R.S.C., Ord. 113 to make an order extending only to the parts of the premises identified as being in the possession of the defendants.

F

By notice of appeal of March 14, 1980, the university appealed on the ground that the judge erred in law in holding that he had no jurisdiction under R.S.C., Ord. 113 to make an order for possession of premises more extensive than those identified as currently in the occupation of the defendants.

The facts are stated in the judgment of Buckley L.J.

Hugh Laddie and *Martin Howe* for the University.
The defendants in person, through Sheila Margaret Jones.

G

BUCKLEY L.J. This is an appeal from an order made by Walton J. on March 11, 1980; it was an order for possession of part of the premises of the University of Essex, which had been adversely occupied by a body of students by way of protest about certain matters as to which they considered they had grievances; the judge declined to make the order in as wide terms as the university sought.

H

The order which was asked for was an order for possession of "the premises at the University of Essex;" that is to say, an order extending to the whole of the university premises. The judge was only prepared to make the order in respect of that part of those premises which was

A actually in the occupation of the protesting students. This appeal is brought
to this court upon the ground that the judge was in error in holding that
he had no jurisdiction under R.S.C., Ord. 113 to make an order for
possession of premises more extensive than those identified as currently
in the occupation of the students.

The defendants to the proceedings are seven named undergraduates
B of the university and persons unknown, because the university authorities
were only able to identify seven of the protesting students, whose number,
I gather, was considerably larger than seven; in fact it was perhaps a
fluctuating body of students.

The students first went into occupation of part of the administrative
offices of the university on February 27, 1980; on February 29, 1980, a
possession order was obtained in respect of that part of the university
C premises, which was executed on March 5. So the university then
recovered possession of that part of their property.

On that same day, March 5, the students occupied another area of
what is called Level 6 of part of the university buildings. They were
served with a written notice requesting them to leave that area and notifying them that if they failed to do so by 9 o'clock on March 6, the
D university would take legal proceedings. They did not vacate that area
by the time laid down in that notice, and the originating summons which
instituted these proceedings was issued by the university on March 7
against the seven named defendants and other persons unknown.

The matter came before Walton J. first on March 10. At 3 o'clock
on that morning, or at about that time, the students had vacated the
area of the university buildings which they had occupied on the second
E occasion, March 5, so that when the matter came before the court they
had already given up adverse possession of that part of the university
buildings. But they left behind them a document which is headed " occupation statement," in which they said that the Student Union had been in
indefinite occupation for the last ten days and so far the university had
made no concessions at all. They then made reference to the matters
F about which they thought they had grievances, and at the end of the
document they say:

"If the finance committee fails to agree to these demands then we
shall recommend further direct action . . . on Wednesday. Since we
have restored possession of the occupied area to the university there
will be no need for them to proceed with the action in High Court
G this morning."

Not surprisingly, faced with that threat of further action, the university
went on with the legal proceedings.

The judge did not hear the case on March 10; he heard it on the
following day and he then made an order for possession which was
restricted to that part of the university premises which had been occupied
H by the students on March 5. It is from that order that the present appeal
is brought.

From what we have been told—we have not seen any note of his
reasons—the judge seems to have reached his conclusion upon the ground
that by implication the jurisdiction under R.S.C., Ord. 113 is restricted
to making a possession order limited to the particular area which can
be said in the circumstances of the case to be occupied by a person or
persons without the licence or consent of the owner. Mr. Laddie, appear-

ing for the university, has contended that Order 113 is an Order which A
relates to procedural matters only; that it was an Order which was
designed to meet the difficulty which arose out of the need for owners of
property from time to time to seek to obtain possession against defendants
whose identity they could not discover, or the identity of some of whom
they could not discover. The Order permits proceedings to be commenced by originating summons and enables the proceedings to be entertained by the court notwithstanding that the identity of the persons in
adverse possession cannot be ascertained.

I think that that submission by Mr. Laddie is a justified one. Note
113/1—8/1, *The Supreme Court Practice* (1979), says:

> " This Order does not provide a new remedy but rather a new pro-
> cedure for the recovery of possession of land which is in wrongful
> occupation by trespassers. Its machinery is designed to overcome the   C
> apparent shortcomings of the present procedural law in two respects,
> namely, (*a*) by providing the procedure for claiming possession of
> land where not every wrongful occupier can reasonably be identi-
> fied, the Order overcomes the question whether an order for posses-
> sion of land can be made and enforced in ex parte proceedings in
> which no person is named as a defendant . . . or only in proceedings   D
> in which at least one person is named as the defendant."

I think the Order is in fact an Order which deals with procedural matters;
in my judgment it does not affect in any way the extent or nature of the
jurisdiction of the court where the remedy that is sought is a remedy
by way of an order for possession. The jurisdiction in question is a
jurisdiction directed to protecting the right of the owner of property to   E
the possession of the whole of his property, uninterfered with by unauthorised adverse possession. In my judgment the jurisdiction to make a
possession order extends to the whole of the owner's property in respect
of which his right of occupation has been interfered with, but the extent
of the field of operation of any order for possession which the court may
think fit to make will no doubt depend upon the circumstances of the   F
particular case.

In the present case there was, when the matter was before the judge,
a threat to take what is described as " further direct action," which presumably meant similar action to the action which had already been taken,
action which might be taken in respect of any part of the university
property. In those circumstances it would, in my judgment, have been   G
open to the judge to have made an order extending to the whole of the
university property, or he might have made an order extending to particular parts, such as the administrative offices, of the university property.
In my judgment he was in error in thinking that he was bound, by the
terms of R.S.C., Ord. 113, to restrict his order to that particular part of
the university property of which the students were then in actual adverse   H
possession. For these reasons, in my judgment, this appeal is one which
succeeds.

We have, however, been told by Miss Jones, one of the defendants,
who has attended in this court this morning and has spoken as the spokes-
man of the protesting student body, that the students have decided not to
continue this course of so-called direct action because they realise, I think
very sensibly, that it is not a policy which will advance their cause in

A relation to the matters about which they want to negotiate with the university. If that is the position, the order which I would make, and which I think it was open to the judge to have made when the matter was before him, namely, a possession order extending to the whole property of the university and enforceable against the defendants or any other person who might be in unauthorised adverse possession of any part of B the university property, will not in fact incommode the students in any way because, through Miss Jones, they disavow any intention to pursue that policy in the future.

I would allow this appeal and make an order in the wide terms that I have indicated.

C SHAW L.J. I agree. It seems to me also that on its true construction R.S.C., Ord. 113 relates to procedure only and not to the form of redress which the court has jurisdiction to afford in appropriate cases.

The title to the site and building of the University of Essex is vested in the university, which has been incorporated for some years by Royal Charter. Its right of possession seems to me to be indivisible. If it is violated by adverse occupation of any part of the premises, that violation D affects the right of possession of the whole of the premises. It follows that those circumstances would in general justify an order in the terms prayed in the originating summons, namely, ". . . that they do recover possession of the premises at the University of Essex, Wivenhoe Park, Colchester in the County of Essex," without any geographic limitation.

I agree, however, that there may be cases where there is no danger of E actual violation of many, or a succession of, parts of the premises. The order might then be limited in appropriate terms. I do not think that this is such a case.

I would therefore allow the appeal and make an order in the terms proposed by Buckley L.J.

F BRIGHTMAN L.J. For the reasons that have been given by Buckley L.J., I agree that the appeal should be allowed.

Appeal allowed.
Defendants to pay £50 costs.
Order of Walton J. varied.

G Solicitors: *Douglas-Mann & Co.*

L. G. S.

H

A

* GREASLEY AND OTHERS v. COOKE

1980   June 17, 18   Lord Denning M.R., Waller and Dunn L.JJ.

B

Estoppel—Conduct, by—Equitable—Proprietary estoppel—Claim
for possession of house—Occupant originally paid servant—
Remaining in occupation and rendering unpaid services to
family—Assurances by family—Counterclaim for declaration
of right to remain—No evidence by owners—Equitable estoppel
raised by assurances and conduct—Burden of proof of conduct
to her detriment

The owners by inheritance of a dwelling house, H and his   C
two nieces, after serving notices to quit on the defendant,
the sole occupant since 1975, brought a claim for possession
against her in the county court. By her defence the occupant
stated that in 1938 she had entered the house as a living-in
maid to the then owner, a widower with three sons and a
daughter, at a weekly wage of 10s.; that from 1946 she had
cohabited in the house with the son K until his death in 1975;
that after the widower died in 1948, leaving the house in   D
equal shares to K and another son O, she had continued to look
after the house and family, and in particular cared for the
daughter who from 1947 until her death in 1975 was mentally
ill. Having stated that two of the sons, H and O, had left the
house when they married, that O had daughters (the second
and third plaintiffs) who had succeeded to his half share
interest, and that when K died in 1975 he had left his half-
share to his surviving brother H (the first plaintiff), she claimed   E
that she had received no payment from any person for her
services after the death of the widower in 1948 and had not
asked for payment because she reasonably believed and had
been encouraged by members of the family (particularised in
her evidence as K and H) to believe that she could regard the
property as her home for the rest of her life, and that in the
premises the plaintiffs were estopped from evicting her. She   F
counterclaimed for a declaration that she was entitled to
occupy the house rent-free for the rest of her life.
When the case came on for hearing in 1978, the solicitor
for the plaintiffs stated that he was instructed to withdraw
the claim for possession at that stage; and he took no part
by way of defence to the counterclaim. The defendant gave
evidence, and counsel on her behalf based her claim for the
declaration on proprietary estoppel. The judge found that   G
K and H had led the defendant to believe that she would be
able to remain in the house; but he held that the burden of
proving that she had acted to her detriment as a result of
her belief rested on her, and that as there was no evidence
which satisfied him that she had so acted she was not entitled
in equity to the declaration sought.
On appeal by the defendant, on which the plaintiffs were
represented:—   H
Held, allowing the appeal, that once it was shown that the
defendant had relied on the assurances given to her, the burden
of proving that she acted to her detriment in staying on to
look after the house and family without payment did not rest
on her; and in the absence of proof by the plaintiffs to the
contrary, the court would infer that her conduct was induced
by the assurances given to her and declare that in equity she
should be allowed to remain in the house for so long as she
wished.

A
     Reynell v. *Sprye* (1852) 1 De G. M. & G. 660 and *Smith* v. *Chadwick* (1882) 20 Ch.D. 27, C.A. applied.
     Per Lord Denning M.R. Expenditure of money on a property is not a necessary element to establish proprietary estoppel. It is sufficient to raise the equity if the party to whom the assurance is given acts on the faith of it; and it is for the courts of equity to decide in what way the equity should be satisfied (post, pp. 1311F—1312A).

B
The following cases are referred to in the judgments:

Brikom Investments Ltd. v. *Carr* [1979] Q.B. 467; [1979] 2 W.L.R. 737; [1979] 2 All E.R. 753, C.A.

Crabb v. *Arun District Council* [1976] Ch. 179; [1975] 3 W.L.R. 847; [1975] 3 All E.R. 865, C.A.

Moorgate Mercantile Co. Ltd. v. *Twitchings* [1976] Q.B. 225; [1975] 3 W.L.R. 286; [1975] 3 All E.R. 314, C.A.

C
Pascoe v. *Turner* [1979] 1 W.L.R. 431; [1979] 2 All E.R. 945, C.A.

Reynell v. *Sprye* (1852) 1 De G. M. & G. 660.

Smith v. *Chadwick* (1882) 20 Ch.D. 27, C.A.

The following additional cases were cited in argument:

D
Bull v. *Bull* [1955] 1 Q.B. 234; [1955] 2 W.L.R. 78; [1955] 1 All E.R. 253, C.A.

Inwards v. *Baker* [1965] 2 Q.B. 29; [1965] 2 W.L.R. 212; [1965] 1 All E.R. 446, C.A.

Sharpe, (A Bankrupt), In re, Ex parte Trustee of the Bankrupt's Property v. *The Bankrupt* [1980] 1 W.L.R. 219; [1980] 1 All E.R. 198.

E
    APPEAL from Judge Brooke Willis sitting at Alfreton County Court.
    The plaintiffs, Hedley Marsden Greasley, Margaret Mary Greasley and Audrey Jessie Baker, the freehold owners of a dwelling house known as 32, George Street, Riddings, Derbyshire, claimed possession of the house against the defendant, Doris Cooke, who occupied a room rent free in the house by virtue of an agreement made between the original owner, Arthur Greasley, deceased, and the defendant when she entered his

F
employment as a maid aged 16 at 10s. a week.
    By their particulars of claim the plaintiffs stated that the defendant had continued in her employment as a housekeeper under the successive owners of the house after the death of Arthur Greasley but had continued to occupy the house since she ceased her employment, without payment of rent; that she was not protected by the provisions of the Rent Acts

G
because she was not a tenant; that the room was not let as a separate dwelling; and that no rent was paid by her. The claim further stated that by a letter dated June 21, 1977, the defendant had been given one month's notice to vacate the premises but had continued in occupation as a trespasser, and that she had remained there as a trespasser after a further formal notice served on November 17, 1977, and expiring on

H
December 31, 1977.
    By her defence the defendant claimed that (1) the property referred to was owned by Arthur Greasley until his death in 1948; that (2) he was a widower and had four children, namely, the plaintiff Hedley, the late Kenneth, the late Clarice and the late Howard, the father of the second and third plaintiffs; that (3) on July 6, 1938, the defendant had entered into service with Arthur Greasley, had lived at the property ever since July 1938; and that until his death in 1948 he paid her wages for her

services as housekeeper; that (4) the defendant cohabited with Kenneth   A
from 1946 until his death in June 1975; that (5) by his will dated April
21, 1945, Arthur Greasley left the property to Howard and Kenneth in
equal shares and expressed the wish that Clarice, Kenneth and Hedley
should not be disturbed in their occupation of the property; that (6) after
their father's death Clarice and Kenneth continued to live in the property
until they died in 1975, and Hedley lived there until he married in or
around 1950; that (7) from 1948 the defendant kept house for and looked   B
after those members of the family who were living at the property: in
particular she fed, clothed and cared for Clarice who was mentally ill from
1947 until her death in 1975; that (8) the defendant received no payment
from any person for her services after the death of Arthur Greasley in
1948: she reasonably believed and was encouraged by members of the
family to believe that she could regard the property as her home for the   C
rest of her life and accordingly did not ask for any payment; that (9) in
1966 Howard died intestate and the plaintiffs Margaret Mary Greasley
and Audrey Jessie Baker and his widow became beneficially entitled to
his estate including the half share in the property bequeathed to him by
his father's will; that (10) in June 1975 Kenneth died and by his will
left his half share in the property to his brother Hedley; and that (11)   D
in the premises the plaintiffs were estopped from evicting the defendant;
(12) alternatively she claimed that she was entitled to an irrevocable
licence to occupy the property as her home for the rest of her life.

By way of counterclaim the defendant repeated paragraphs 1 to 11 of
the defence, and claimed a declaration that she was entitled to occupy
32, George Street, Riddings, rent free for the remainder of her life, or
alternatively, reasonable remuneration in respect of services rendered.   E

On the date fixed for the hearing of the plaintiffs' claim and the
defendant's counterclaim, the plaintiffs did not appear and their solicitors
on their behalf told Judge Brooke Willis that his clients wished to withdraw the claim, but that he had no instructions to give the defendant
any security of possession. The case proceeded on the counterclaim for
a declaration in terms of the pleadings. The defendant gave evidence   F
but there was no cross-examination, since the plaintiffs' solicitors took no
part in the proceedings. The judge reserved judgment until July 12,
1979, when he ordered that the counterclaim be dismissed.

The defendant appealed on the grounds (1) that the judge misdirected himself in holding that to establish an estoppel the defendant
had to prove that the belief induced by the plaintiffs' predecessors that she   G
could remain in the house was *the* reason for her conduct; and (2) that
he ought to have inferred from the evidence that the belief was *a* reason
for her conduct; and that the judge's order was wrong and ought to be
reversed.

John Weeks for the defendant.
J. H. Leckie (who took no part in the proceedings in the county court)   H
for the plaintiffs.

LORD DENNING M.R. This is a family case. The lady most concerned is Miss Doris Cooke. In 1938, when she was 16, she went as a
maid servant to help in the house of a widower, Mr. Arthur Greasley.
He was a butcher. He had his house and shop at 32, George Street,

A   Riddings in Derbyshire. He had three sons and a daughter. They were
teenagers. Doris Cooke, at the age of 16, went into that house as a maid
servant. She was paid 10 shillings a week.

Ten years later in 1948 the widower died. Doris Cooke stayed on.
She looked after the family for nearly 30 years until 1975. During that
time some members of the family had left: others had died: and she
B   was left alone in the house. The house has become vested in some
surviving members of the family. They wish to turn Doris Cooke out.
She is 59 years old now. This is her home. The judge has ordered her
out. She appeals.

I must tell more of the story. When Doris Cooke was in her twenties,
living in the house, one of the sons (Kenneth) formed an attachment for
C   her. She and Kenneth lived as husband and wife from 1946 onwards.
Kenneth ran the butcher's shop and Doris Cooke—living as his wife—ran
the household. Two other sons left. Hedley left and got married. He
had no children. Howard (another son) left and got married. He had
three children. The daughter Clarice remained. She was very ill mentally. The position was that, for many years, Kenneth was living there
with Doris Cooke as his wife. Clarice, the invalid daughter, was looked
D   after by them both, but particularly by Doris Cooke. Doris Cooke was
entirely one of the family.

The title of the house descended in this way: old Arthur Greasley
(before any of the sons were married or had left) made a will by which he
left the house to two of his sons (Howard and Kenneth) in equal shares.
Howard died. He did not make a will. His half share, on his intestacy,
E   went to his children. Kenneth and Clarice died in 1975. Kenneth left
his half share to Hedley. So the title was in Hedley and the children of
Howard. After Kenneth's death in 1975 they gave Doris Cooke notice
to quit. They brought proceedings to turn her out of the house. They
said that she had no title: she was not a tenant: she paid no rent: and
had no status in the house at all.

F   The matter was taken to the county court. Pleadings passed between
the parties. I will read a paragraph from the defence:

"The defendant received no payment from any person for her
services after the death of Arthur Greasley in 1948. The defendant
reasonably believed and was encouraged by members of the family
to believe that she could regard the property as her home for the rest
G   of her life and accordingly did not ask for any payment."

On that ground, she asked to be allowed to stay in the house for the
rest of her days: and she counterclaimed for a declaration that she was
entitled to occupy it rent free for the rest of her life. Then the case
came on before the judge. It took a most unusual course. The plaintiffs—Hedley and Howard's daughters—had instructed a solicitor. Their
H   solicitor simply got up and said that he withdrew the claim for possession
against Doris Cooke. Mr. Weeks, counsel for Doris Cooke, rose and
said: "But there is my counterclaim to be dealt with." The judge said:
"Yes; you must prove your counterclaim. You must prove that she is
entitled to be there for the rest of her life." So Mr. Weeks called Miss
Doris Cooke and asked her a few questions. Doris Cooke said, according
to the judge's note:

A

" Lived there 42 years. I went there in service to Mr. Arthur
Greasley. I was 16 years "—she went through the story as I have
told it—" Kenneth died: he had no children. Clarice died 20/8/75
mental trouble from 1947. Paid 10s. week by Arthur Greasley. Not
paid wages after that. I looked after house. Kenneth and I looked
after Clarice . . . Kenneth said he would do the right thing by me.
Hedley said no need to worry I'd be looked after."

B

The plaintiffs' solicitor did not cross-examine. He asked no questions.
He said nothing. Mr. Weeks submitted that the counterclaim succeeded
and he should have the declaration sought. The judge was troubled.
He pointed out that Doris Cooke had spent no money on the house.
Mr. Weeks referred to *Pascoe* v. *Turner* [1979] 1 W.L.R. 431: and to
Snell's Principles of Equity, 27th ed. (1973), p. 565. The judge reserved
his decision.

C

On giving judgment the judge rejected Miss Cooke's counterclaim.
She appeals—and for a very good reason. If her counterclaim fails, it
means that she has no right to stay in the house at all. The plaintiffs can
bring an action tomorrow and evict her. Their counsel told us that was
indeed their intention. She will have no answer because the issue will be
res judicata.

D

The judge made this important finding:

" On the facts that I have found I am prepared to accept, although
the evidence is not very strong, that the defendant believed, because
of what was said to her by Kenneth and Hedley, that she would be
allowed to live at and remain in the house as long as she wished
though if Kenneth ' intended to do the right thing by her ' one
might have expected him to do so by his will."

E

Having made that finding, the judge propounded this proposition of law:

" If the defendant is to succeed she has to prove that she acted to
her detriment *as a result of her belief* and that the owners of the
house encouraged her in her actions or stood by knowing that her
actions were because of her belief. In both *Inwards* v. *Baker* [1965]
2 Q.B. 29 and *Pascoe* v. *Turner* [1979] 1 W.L.R. 431 it was the
expenditure of money on the property which raised the equity which
provided the estoppel. There is no question of any expenditure of
money in this case. . . . I have not the slightest doubt that the
defendant did that "—looked after Kenneth and the mentally ill
Clarice—" and that looking after the mentally ill Clarice was an
unpleasant and hard task; but the vital question is: has she proved
that she did that work without payment because of her belief that
she would be entitled to live in the house as long as she wished. Her
belief was induced by what Kenneth and Hedley said to her. . . .
I have accepted that they led her to believe she would be able to
remain in the house. . . . That means that long before any question
as to the defendant's future arose she was doing all those acts
which she has to prove were done relying on her belief that she
would be able to remain in the house as long as she wished. . . .
There is no evidence which satisfies me that the defendant acted in
any way to her detriment as a result of the belief induced in her
mind by the words or conduct of Kenneth or Hedley. That means

F

F

G

H

A   then she is not entitled to call on equity to protect her from what would otherwise be inequitable."

The judge decided the case on that point. Before us Mr. Leckie sought to raise many other points on behalf of the plaintiffs. But we cannot go into them. We must insist that the only points which can be raised on appeal are those which were considered by the judge in the county court.

B   The first point is on the burden of proof. Mr. Weeks referred us to many cases, such as *Reynell* v. *Sprye* (1852) 1 De G. M. & G. 660, 708; *Smith* v. *Chadwick* (1882) 20 Ch.D. 27, 44 and *Brikom Investments Ltd.* v. *Carr* [1979] Q.B. 467, 482–483 where I said that when a person makes a representation intending that another should act on it:

C   " It is no answer for the maker to say: ' You would have gone on with the transaction anyway.' That must be mere speculation. No one can be sure what he would, or would not, have done in a hypothetical state of affairs which never took place. . . . Once it is shown that a representation was calculated to influence the judgment of a reasonable man, the presumption is that he was so influenced."

D   So here. These statements to Miss Cooke were calculated to influence her—so as to put her mind at rest—so that she should not worry about being turned out. No one can say what she would have done if Kenneth and Hedley had not made those statements. It is quite possible that she would have said to herself:

E   " I am not married to Kenneth. I am on my own. What will happen to me if anything happens to him? I had better look out for another job now: rather than stay here where I have no security."

So, instead of looking for another job, she stayed on in the house looking after Kenneth and Clarice. There is a presumption that she did so, relying on the assurances given to her by Kenneth and Hedley. The burden is not on her, but on them, to prove that she did not rely on their F   assurances. They did not prove it, nor did their representatives. So she is presumed to have relied on them. So on the burden of proof it seems to me that the judge was in error.

The second point is about the need for some expenditure of money—some detriment—before a person can acquire any interest in a house or any right to stay in it as long as he wishes. It so happens that in many G   of these cases of proprietary estoppel there has been expenditure of money. But that is not a necessary element. I see that in *Snell's Principles of Equity*, 27th ed. (1973), p. 565, it is said: " A must have incurred expenditure or otherwise have prejudiced himself." But I do not think that that is necessary. It is sufficient if the party, to whom the assurance is given, acts on the faith of it—in such circumstances that it would be unjust and inequitable for the party making the assurance to H   go back on it: see *Moorgate Mercantile Co. Ltd.* v. *Twitchings* [1976] Q.B. 225 and *Crabb* v. *Arun District Council* [1976] Ch. 179, 188. Applying those principles here it can be seen that the assurances given by Kenneth and Hedley to Doris Cooke—leading her to believe that she would be allowed to stay in the house as long as she wished—raised an equity in her favour. There was no need for her to prove that she acted on the faith of those assurances. It is to be presumed that she did so. There is no need for her to prove that she acted to her detriment

or to her prejudice. Suffice it that she stayed on the house—looking   A
after Kenneth and Clarice—when otherwise she might have left and got
a job elsewhere. The equity having thus been raised in her favour, it is
for the courts of equity to decide in what way that equity should be
satisfied. In this case it should be by allowing her to stay on in the
house as long as she wishes.

I would therefore allow the appeal and grant a declaration on the
counterclaim that Miss Cooke is entitled to occupy 32, George Street,   B
Riddings, rent-free so long as she wishes to stay there.

WALLER L.J. I agree. I agree that it was unfortunate that the plaintiffs took no part in the hearing before the judge, but the judge heard
the defendant give evidence on her counterclaim. He was addressed by
Mr. Weeks on her behalf, and he reserved judgment. He clearly found   C
that it was not an easy question to decide, although it appears that at
the time when he reserved judgment he was rather more concerned with
the possibility of detriment and the absence of any specific financial
detriment which the defendant could show. But when he considered
the matter, he delivered his judgment and he made certain clear findings.
He found: " At some time and probably more than once after the death   D
of Arthur Greasley, Kenneth told the defendant he would do the right
thing by her "—Kenneth was the member of the family with whom the
defendant was living. Then another finding: " At some time Hedley
told the defendant that she had no need to worry, she would be looked
after."

The judge did, in considering his reserved judgment, put the onus
fairly and squarely on the defendant. He said: " If the defendant is to   E
succeed she has to prove that she acted to her detriment *as a result of her
belief.*" Then, further on, he said: ". . . has she proved that she did that
work without payment because of her belief that she would be entitled
to live in the house as long as she wished." Then he said again: ". . .
long before any question as to the defendant's future arose she was
doing all those acts which she has to prove were done relying on her   F
belief. . . ." Then he made the findings which Mr. Leckie has submitted
to this court were findings of fact which this court should not interfere
with, namely: " I am satisfied that the defendant looked after Kenneth
and the house in which they lived with Clarice because she was living
with Kenneth as his wife." Then: " There is no evidence which satisfies
me that the defendant acted in any way to her detriment as a result of
the belief induced in her mind by the words or conduct of Kenneth or   G
Hedley."

It was a difficult question—not a simple question—which the judge
had to consider; and one cannot help being sympathetic in that he had
to consider it in the absence of argument from the plaintiffs, and, as an
explanation for his getting the onus of proof wrong in this particular
case, that is probably the main reason. However, I am satisfied that he   H
did, unfortunately, and that he was in error in the way in which he put
the onus of proof. I would just quote the words of Lord Cranworth L.J.
in the case mentioned by Lord Denning M.R.—*Reynell* v. *Sprye,* 1 De G.
M. & G. 660—where, having set out some statements made by one of
the parties, he said, at pp. 707–708:

" Every one of those considerations would be material ingredients
towards enabling Sir T. Reynell to form his judgment as to whether

A   he should or should not accede to the proposal of Capt. Sprye. If he had not received what was equivalent to an assurance that Mr. Yonge considered the proposed division of the property as the usual course of conducting business on such occasions, and if he had not been led to suppose that his interest was contingent, depending on the chance of his surviving Mrs. Williams Reynell, and then only to be recovered by expensive and doubtful litigation, it may well be

B   that he would not have acted as he did;—perhaps he might, perhaps he might not. But this is a matter on which I do not feel called upon or indeed at liberty to speculate."

A similar statement was made by Sir George Jessel, also in a case cited by Lord Denning M.R., *Smith* v. *Chadwick*, 20 Ch.D. 27, 44–45, where he said:

C

"Again, on the question of the materiality of the statement, if the court sees on the face of it that it is of such a nature as would induce a person to enter into the contract, or would tend to induce him to do so, or that it would be a part of the inducement, to enter into the contract, the inference is, if he entered into the contract, that he acted on the inducement so held out, and you want no

D   evidence that he did so act. . . . But unless it is shewn in one way or the other that he did not rely on the statement the inference follows."

In my judgment, if the judge had been referred to those cases, he would have started from a quite different position in considering the facts. He would have had before him the finding of fact which I have just quoted, namely, that Hedley said that she had no need to worry; she

E   would be looked after—which indicates that there was in that conversation the possibility of worry in the defendant's mind. Whether it was said after she said: "I am worried about what is going to happen to me," or whether it was just volunteered, it is certainly something which would tend to induce a course of conduct on her part.

Counsel admitted in the course of argument that a finding the other

F   way could not have been attacked. If the judge had had in mind those cases, he would have come, in my judgment, to a different conclusion, namely, because of the fact that the defendant continued over all those years not only to live with Kenneth but to look after Clarice who was mentally ill, and, as Lord Denning M.R. has said, was a difficult person to look after, he would have come to the conclusion that the evidence showed that there was something which tended to induce a course of

G   conduct, and it would be wrong to speculate what the defendant would have done if those inducements had not existed.

Accordingly I agree with Lord Denning M.R. that this appeal should be allowed and that the declaration should be made in the form asked.

Dunn L.J. I also agree, and would only add this. The circumstances

H   of this case were very exceptional. The plaintiffs withdrew their claim for possession in the county court and, although they were represented by a solicitor, took no part in defending the counterclaim and indeed did not resist it.

The judge considered his judgment and found for the defendant on every point except one, and that is the only point that we can consider on this appeal. It is a narrow point. There is no doubt that for pro-prietary estoppel to arise the person claiming must have incurred expendi-

ture or otherwise have prejudiced himself or acted to his detriment. The A
only question before us is as to the burden of proof of the detriment.
The judge thought that the onus lay on the claimant to prove it. I agree
that in that he fell into error for the reasons given by Lord Denning M.R.,
and I also would allow this appeal.

> *Appeal allowed with costs in Court of* B
> *Appeal and below.*
> *Declaration made as asked in counter-*
> *claim.*
> *Legal aid taxation of defendant's costs.*

Solicitors: *Waterhouse & Co. for Robinsons, Heanor, Derbyshire;*
Dale Parkinson & Co. for Rickards and Cleaver, Alfreton, Derbyshire. C

M. M. H.

D

[QUEEN'S BENCH DIVISION]

* SCHROEDER *v.* ACCOUNTANT GENERAL

1980 March 7   Woolf J. E

Practice—Payment into court—Payment out—Interest—Leave to
defend on condition sum paid into court—Defendant serving
notice of appropriation—Plaintiff not accepting moneys appro-
priated in settlement of claim—Order for money to be paid out
to defendant—Whether payment out to include interest accrued
on sum—Supreme Court Funds Rules 1975 (S.I. 1975 No. 1803
(L. 24)), r. 27 (1) (3) F

In proceedings for summary judgment under R.S.C., Ord.
14, the applicant was given leave to defend the action brought
against her by W on condition that she paid a sum of money
into court. She paid that sum into court and the money was
placed on deposit earning interest. The applicant then served a
notice of appropriation on W in respect of the moneys paid
into court, under rule 27 (1) of the Supreme Court Funds Rules
1975,[1] so that it could be treated as a voluntary payment into G
court which W could accept in satisfaction of his claim. W did
not accept the sum appropriated and, at the trial of the action,
the applicant was successful and the judge ordered that the
sum of £6,000 in court with accrued interest be paid to the
applicant's solicitors. The Accountant General took the view
that, under rule 27 (3) of the Rules of 1975, the accrued interest
had to be paid into the cash account of H.M. Paymaster H
General in accordance with rule 51 (3).
On the applicant's motion for a declaration that she was
entitled to the interest which had accrued on the money paid
into court: —
Held, granting the declaration, that rule 27 (3) was to be
interpreted so that it only applied where the plaintiff in an
action had accepted the money appropriated in satisfaction of

[1] Supreme Court Funds Rules 1975, r. 27: see post, pp. 1316E–G.

A   his claim; that, accordingly, since W had not accepted the money, rule 27 (3) did not apply and the applicant was entitled to the accrued interest in accordance with the order made by the judge (post, p. 1317E–H).

No cases are referred to in the judgment or were cited in argument.

B   APPLICATION
By a notice of motion dated November 26, 1979, the applicant, Wendy Diane Schroeder, applied, under R.S.C., Ord. 20, r. 11, that that part of the judgment, in the action brought by the plaintiff, Robert Cane Winsor, against her, whereby " it was further adjudged that the sum of £6,000 with accrued interest, now in court standing to the credit of this action be paid out to the defendant's solicitors," be amended so as to make it clear and
C   certain that the interest therein referred to included the sum of £741·93 interest which had accrued on June 11, 1979, upon the capital sum of £5,265, which was part of the sum of £6,000 paid into court.
At the hearing of the motion, it was agreed between the parties and the court that the appropriate manner of proceeding was by an application for a declaration that the interest which had accrued on the sum paid into
D   court in accordance with R.S.C., Ord. 14 as a condition of liberty to defend was payable by the Accountant General to the applicant notwithstanding the provisions of rule 27 of the Supreme Court Funds Rules 1975.
The facts are stated in the judgment.

Rudolf Russell for the applicant.
Simon D. Brown for the Accountant General and the Supreme Court
E   Funds Office.

WOOLF J. In this matter Mr. Russell moves on behalf of the applicant, who was the defendant in an action called *Winsor* v. *Schroeder,* for a declaration that interest which has accrued due on a sum which was paid into court in accordance with R.S.C., Ord. 14 as a condition of liberty to
F   defend is payable by the Accountant General to the applicant, notwithstanding the provisions of rule 27 of the Supreme Court Funds Rules 1975. Originally, the applicant was proposing to argue this matter under the provisions of the slip rule but, the difficulties involved in that course having become apparent, with the assistance of Mr. Brown who appears on behalf of the Accountant General it was agreed that the matter should be dealt
G   with in the same way as if there was an application seeking a declaration in the terms which I have just indicated, so that the matter of substance which is before me could be fully explored.
The problem arises in this way. Where money is paid into court as a condition of liberty to defend an action, the money is placed on deposit and while on deposit earns interest which, if nothing further happens in the course of the proceedings, results in the court when it gives judgment in
H   the action being able to deal with the interest which has accrued up to the trial. Where, however, a notice of appropriation is given by a defendant who has paid money into court pursuant to an order of the type to which I have referred, so as to enable the money paid into court pursuant to the order to be treated in the same way as money paid into court voluntarily, the money is taken from deposit, it no longer earns interest, and the Accountant General considers that the interest which had previously accrued has to be transferred and dealt with in accordance with the

requirements of rule 51 (3) of the Supreme Court Funds Rules 1975, so that A
the money, including accrued interest, is transferred to the cash account of
Her Majesty's Paymaster General for the credit of the Administration of
Justice Vote.

If this view of the situation is right it would mean that the giving of a
notice of appropriation could have a very serious consequence to a party
who had been ordered to pay money into court and had complied with
that order. To take this very case: at the date the notice of appropriation B
was given by the applicant the sum which she had paid into court had
earned interest amounting to a total of £741. If the Accountant General
is right in the way he has construed the rule up to this time, the applicant
will lose that money in consequence of her giving the plaintiff an opportunity to take that money out of court as a result of her giving a notice
of appropriation, and also lose that interest where a plaintiff decides not to C
take the money out of court, and the defendant goes on to contest the
action and does so successfully, as was the case with this particular
applicant. That result is one which, in some circumstances, would in my
view quite properly be regarded as unjust. It is right that I should say that
Mr. Brown, who is appearing on behalf of the Accountant General, was at
pains to point out that he was before the court today not to resist the D
argument of the applicant but to assist the court as to the proper interpretation of the Supreme Court Funds Rules 1975, which I have now to
consider, and he has in fact performed that task and assisted me in reaching
the conclusion to which I have come.

The matter turns primarily on the interpretation of rule 27 (1) of the
Supreme Court Funds Rules 1975. I should read that rule which is in these
terms: E

" Where a defendant has lodged money in court in accordance with
Order 14 as a condition of liberty to defend and desires to appropriate
the whole or any part of such money in satisfaction of the whole or
any part of the plaintiff's claim pursuant to Ord. 22, r. 8, he shall
lodge with the Accountant General a notice of appropriation in
Form 5 together with the original receipt for the amount lodged."   F

Then sub-rule (2):

" On receipt of a notice of appropriation the Accountant General shall
note the relevant ledger credit accordingly and shall withdraw the
sum mentioned in the notice from deposit or, where the court has
directed that the money lodged be invested in a short-term investment
account, from that account."   G

Then sub-rule (3):

" For the purposes of payment out of court, the Accountant General
shall deal with the sum appropriated in accordance with rule 43 (1)
and shall transfer any interest accrued in respect of the amount
withdrawn from deposit or a short-term investment account to the
cash account of Her Majesty's Paymaster General in accordance with H
rule 51 (3)."

The difficulty is in rule 27 (3) which, read literally, seems to indicate
that for the purposes of payment out of court the Accountant General has
to deal with the sum appropriated in accordance with rule 43 (1) and has
to transfer any interest accrued in respect of the amount withdrawn from
deposit or a short-term investment account to the cash account of Her

A   Majesty's Paymaster General in accordance with rule 51 (3). That rule can be readily interpreted as dealing with the interest accrued at the time of appropriation by requiring it to be transferred to Her Majesty's Paymaster General. But as a result of the assistance which I have received from counsel I have come to the conclusion that the rule does not have that automatic effect.

B   It is necessary to mention shortly the history of this particular rule. The origin of the rule is rule 43 of the Supreme Court Funds Rules 1927. That rule in its unamended form made no provision with regard to interest, because at that time money which was paid into court pursuant to an order of the court under R.S.C., Ord. 14 was not placed on deposit and did not earn interest. The position was changed by the amendment made to the Rules of 1927, by the Supreme Court Funds (Amendment) Rules 1965.

C That rule quite specifically required the interest which had accrued to be transferred to Her Majesty's Paymaster General. The wording has been altered in the Supreme Court Funds Rules 1975 and the rule re-cast, and it is my view that the literal meaning cannot be given to rule 27 (3) because where money is in court under R.S.C., Ord. 14, and a notice of appropriation has been given by the person who deposited the money but the money is not taken out of court by the plaintiff, the

D Accountant General is incapable of dealing with the money in accordance with rule 43 (1) as rule 27 (3) appears to require.

  That being so, I have come to the conclusion that (although the language does not readily lead to this result) the intent of rule 27 (3) is that which would be achieved if the rule read as follows:

E   " For the purpose of payment out of court, the Accountant General, *in a case where the money appropriated has been accepted by the plaintiff in accordance with Ord. 22, r. 3 (1) of the Rules of the Supreme Court,* shall deal with the sum appropriated in accordance with rule 43 (1) and shall transfer any interest accrued in respect of the amount withdrawn from deposit or a short-term investment account to the cash account of Her Majesty's Paymaster General. . ."

F   Thus the effect of rule 27 (3) is limited to those cases where, on a notice of appropriation being given, the plaintiff accepts the money paid into court in satisfaction of the claim.

  It is pointed out that if the rule is limited in that way no real injustice will be caused because in such circumstances a plaintiff does not normally obtain interest on the money which he accepts; the matter is dealt with

G purely by administrative action and there is no order of the court. In cases where the money is not accepted, then there is an order of the court dealing with payment-out either to the plaintiff or the defendant, and if rule 27 (3) does not apply in such circumstances it will be open to the court, when dealing with the question of payment-out of the money lodged in court, to deal with the interest which has accrued.

H   Accordingly, in the present case where, on the trial, I ordered that the interest which had accrued should be paid out to the defendant, it was an order which applied to the interest which had been earned on the money paid into court while it was deposited in accordance with the order of the master made under R.S.C., Ord. 14.

  It follows that I have come to the conclusion that the applicant is entitled to the declaration which she seeks. I am grateful to both counsel for the considerable assistance they have given me in enabling me to reach

that conclusion, about which I am bound to confess initially I had   A
considerable hesitation.

> *Declaration granted with costs.*
> *Legal aid taxation of applicant's costs.*

B

Solicitors: *Teacher, Stern, Hunter & Selby*; *Treasury Solicitor.*

[Reported by ISOBEL COLLINS, Barrister-at-Law]

C

[COURT OF APPEAL]

* MEGARITY *v.* D. J. RYAN & SONS LTD. (No. 2)

1980   June 27   Lord Roskill and Ormrod L.J.

D

Legal Aid—Costs—Successful unassisted party—Interlocutory appeal
determined against assisted plaintiff—Court of Appeal ordering
defendants' costs to be paid out of legal aid fund—Whether
" proceedings . . . finally decided "—Legal Aid Act 1974 (c. 4),
s. 13 (1)

The plaintiff, who was employed by the defendants, began
proceedings against them for damages for personal injuries   E
allegedly sustained in the course of his employment as a result
of the defendants' negligence and/or breach of statutory duty.
The defendants requested the plaintiff to undergo a medical
examination by their appointed medical adviser. The plaintiff
refused unless the defendants first agreed to furnish him with
a copy of the resulting medical report. The defendants
applied for a stay of the proceedings until the plaintiff submitted unconditionally to the examination. The district   F
registrar dismissed the application and the defendants appealed
to a judge in chambers, who allowed the appeal. The plaintiff
appealed to the Court of Appeal who dismissed the appeal
and ordered that since the plaintiff, who was legally aided,
had no present liability to pay costs, the unassisted defendants'
costs should be borne by the legal aid fund, subject to the
right of the Law Society to object to the order.
On the Law Society's application to the court for a review   G
of the order on the ground that, under section 13 (1) of the
Legal Aid Act 1974,[1] the proceedings had not been finally
decided in favour of the unassisted defendants: —
Held, confirming the order for costs, that on the true
construction of section 13 (1) of the Legal Aid Act 1974, and
having regard to the meaning which the corresponding and
identical provisions of the Legal Aid Act 1964 had previously
been held to bear, the word " proceedings " in that section in-   H
cluded an interlocutory appeal, and that, since the interlocutory appeal had been finally decided in favour of the
unassisted defendants, the court had power to order that their
costs should be paid out of the legal aid fund (post, pp. 1324H,
1325A–B, F–G, 1326 F–H).
General Accident Life and Fire Assurance Corporation Ltd.
v. *Foster* [1973] Q.B. 50, C.A. considered.

---

[1] Legal Aid Act 1974, s. 13 (1): see post, p. 1321C–D.

A   The following cases are referred to in the judgments:

General Accident Life and Fire Assurance Corporation Ltd. v. *Foster*
    [1973] Q.B. 50; [1972] 3 W.L.R. 657; [1972] 3 All E.R. 877, C.A.
Mills v. *Mills* [1963] P. 329; [1963] 2 W.L.R. 831; [1963] 2 All E.R. 237,
    C.A.
Reg. v. *Legal Aid Committee No.* 1 *(London) Legal Aid Area, Ex parte
    Rondel* [1967] 2 Q.B. 482; [1967] 2 W.L.R. 1358; [1967] 2 All E.R.
B   419, D.C.
Wozniak v. *Wozniak* [1953] P. 179; [1953] 2 W.L.R. 1705; [1953]
    1 All E.R. 1192, C.A.

The following additional cases were cited in argument:

Maynard v. *Osmond (No.* 2) [1979] 1 W.L.R. 31; [1979] 1 All E.R. 483,
    C.A.
C   *Shiloh Spinners Ltd.* v. *Harding (No.* 2) [1973] 1 W.L.R. 518; [1973]
    1 All E.R. 966, H.L.(E.).

APPLICATION

By a writ dated April 5, 1979, the legally aided plaintiff, Brian
Megarity, brought an action against his employers, D. J. Ryan & Sons
Ltd., the unassisted defendants, for damages for personal injuries received
D   on two separate occasions in the course of his employment, as a result
of the negligence and/or breach of statutory duty of the defendants,
their servants or agents.   On August 14, 1979, Mr. District Registrar
White of the Blackburn District Registry, dismissed the defendants'
application, dated June 25, 1979, for an order that all further proceedings
be stayed until such time as the plaintiff had submitted himself for
E   examination by the defendants' appointed medical adviser, such examination not being conditional upon the disclosure of the report of the
defendants' medical adviser to the plaintiff.   On February 4, 1980,
Hollings J. sitting in chambers, allowed the defendants' appeal against
the district registrar's decision, but gave leave to the plaintiff to appeal.
The plaintiff appealed and, on March 13, 1980, Lord Roskill and
Ormrod L.J. dismissed the appeal: see [1980] 1 W.L.R. 1237.   They
F   assessed the plaintiff's legal aid contribution as nil, and ordered that
notice should be given to the area secretary of the Law Society of the
court's intention to make an order for the payment to the unassisted
defendants from the legal aid fund of the costs incurred by them in
the proceedings before the Court of Appeal, and that unless the area
secretary of the Law Society objected and sought to be heard within
G   10 weeks, the order would be effective.

By a letter dated May 20, 1980, the area secretary of the Law
Society applied to the Court of Appeal for the consideration by the
court of the Law Society's objections to the order.   The principal objection was that, under section 13 (1) of the Legal Aid Act 1974, the proceedings had not been " finally decided in favour of the unassisted
party."
H

Duncan Matheson for The Law Society.
Giles Wingate-Saul for the defendants.
The plaintiff did not appear and was not represented.

LORD ROSKILL.   On March 13, 1980, there came before this court,
consisting of Ormrod L.J. and myself, an interlocutory appeal from an
order made by Hollings J. sitting in Manchester on February 4, 1980.

The judge had given leave for that appeal. It was an appeal by the **A** plaintiff in a personal injuries case, who objected to submitting to a medical examination at the instance of the defendants unless the defendants first agreed that he (the plaintiff) or his advisers should be given a copy of any resulting medical report. The district registrar upheld the plaintiff's objection, but the judge reversed the district registrar and we in this court, in a judgment which I gave and with which Ormrod L.J. **B** agreed, agreed with Hollings J.; in that respect we followed an earlier judgment of Cussack J.

The plaintiff was legally aided; the defendant was not. We dismissed the appeal without calling upon Mr. Wingate-Saul, who was appearing for the defendants in this court. Mr. Wingate-Saul has reminded us that either in the judgment which I gave or in the course of the argument afterwards I described the appeal as without merit, as indeed from my **C** present recollection of the case I thought it was. As a result, Mr. Wingate-Saul applied for an order that the defendants' costs of this appeal, an interlocutory appeal brought by leave of the judge in chambers, should be paid by the legal aid fund. After some discussion, which is not (quite rightly) recorded in the transcript, we made that order, subject, of course, to the Law Society's usual right to object.

In many of these cases the Law Society do not object; they accept **D** the burden: then the unassisted person's costs in the Court of Appeal come out of the legal aid fund and thus are borne by the taxpayer. But in the instant case the Law Society have objected. We have had the advantage of a very full and careful argument, for which we are greatly indebted, by Mr. Matheson for the Law Society and by Mr. Wingate-Saul for the defendants whether or not the order which Ormrod L.J. and **E** I tentatively made was an order within the powers of the Court of Appeal. Mr. Matheson has grasped the nettle and has said, and it is, so far as I am aware, the first time that this argument has been advanced in this court, but that certainly does not mean that it is wrong, that the Court of Appeal when it dismisses an interlocutory appeal in favour of an unassisted person and against an assisted person who has brought the appeal, has no power at that juncture to make an order, under **F** section 13 (1) of the Legal Aid Act 1974, in favour of the unassisted person and against the legal aid fund. I ought, perhaps, also to say that, to the best of my recollection, the order which this court made in the instant case is one which has been made on interlocutory appeals on a number of previous occasions. We have, therefore, looked at the matter very carefully indeed.

We have been referred to a number of authorities, which I will **G** mention in more detail in a moment, but I want to make this point at this juncture: many were decided under statutes that were on the statute book before the Legal Aid Act 1974 was passed. Before that Act (which was a consolidating Act) the powers of the court in relation to these matters came from at least three different statutes, and most of the cases **H** which came before the court arose either under the Legal Aid and Advice Act 1949, such as *Mills* v. *Mills* [1963] P. 329, or under the Legal Aid Act 1964, such as *General Accident Life and Fire Assurance Corporation Ltd.* v. *Foster* [1973] Q.B. 50. When one looks at the judgments in those cases one sees that the Court of Appeal, on both occasions, referred to, and only to, the language of the statute concerned, which did not cover as wide a field as the Legal Aid Act 1974. They therefore construed what

A   are the crucial words here, namely "any proceedings" and "those proceedings" in section 13 (1) of the Act of 1974 in the context in which the corresponding words appeared in the earlier statutes, the Legal Aid Act 1964 and the Legal Aid and Advice Act 1949. Now, of course, when you have a consolidating Act covering a wider field, it is natural to look at all the places in that statute where those words or the word "proceedings" appear; but it is difficult to think that when Parliament

B   consolidated this legislation it intended the word "proceeding" or "proceedings" in the Act of 1974 to bear any different meaning from that which it had previously been held to bear under the earlier legislation.

With that introduction, let me turn to the relevant statutory provisions. I do not propose to read all that have been referred to. Section 13 of the Legal Aid Act 1974 reads:

C

"(1) Where a party receives legal aid in connection with any proceedings between him and a party not receiving legal aid (in this and section 14 below referred to as 'the unassisted party') and those proceedings are finally decided in favour of the unassisted party, the court by which the proceedings are so decided may, subject to the provisions of this section, make an order for the payment to the

D   unassisted party out of the legal aid fund of the whole or any part of the costs incurred by him in those proceedings. (2) An order may be made under this section in respect of any costs if (and only if) the court is satisfied that it is just and equitable in all the circumstances that provision for those costs should be made out of public funds; and before making such an order the court shall in

E   every case (whether or not application is made in that behalf) consider what orders should be made for costs against the party receiving legal aid and for determining his liability in respect of such costs."

Pausing there, with reference to subsection (2) I would interpose this: first, neither Ormrod L.J. nor I had any doubt but that it was just and

F   equitable in all the circumstances that the respondents' costs should come out of the legal aid fund; secondly, we performed our duty of considering what order should be made against the plaintiff as "the party receiving legal aid"; and our answer was that, in the light of the information we then had, he should not make any contribution. I go on:

"(3) Without prejudice to subsection (2) above, no order shall be

G   made under this section in respect of costs incurred in a court of first instance, whether by that court or by any appellate court, unless . . ."—and I leave out (a) because that deals with courts of first instance—"(b) the court is satisfied that the unassisted party will suffer severe financial hardship unless the order is made. (4) An order under this section shall not be made by any court in respect

H   of costs incurred by the unassisted party in any proceedings in which, apart from this section, no order would be made for the payment of his costs."

Section 14 of the Act of 1974 was relied on. I will read section 14 (1):

"Regulations may make provision—(a) for determining the proceedings which are or are not to be treated as separate proceedings for the purposes of section 13 above . . ."

and I need not read the rest of that. I go to subsection (3) and sub- A
section (4), to which Ormrod L.J. referred during argument. I will not
read (3), but (4) reads:

> " Where a court decides any proceedings in favour of the un-
> assisted party and an appeal lies (with or without leave) against that
> decision, the court may, if it thinks fit, make or refuse to make an
> order under section 13 above forthwith, but any order so made
> shall not take effect—(a) where leave to appeal is required, unless
> the time limited for applications for leave to appeal expires without
> leave being granted; (b) where leave to appeal is granted or is not
> required, unless the time limited for appeal expires without an appeal
> being brought."

I will not read subsection (5), though Mr. Matheson referred us to it, C
or Schedule 1.

I can go to the Legal Aid (General) Regulations 1971 (S.I. 1971
No. 62), which were made under the earlier legislation. Regulation 6
provides:

> " (1) A certificate may be issued in respect of—(a) one or more
> steps to assert or dispute a claim; or (b) the whole or part of—(i) D
> proceedings in a court of first instance, or (ii) proceedings in an
> appellate court; but no certificate shall relate to proceedings (other
> than interlocutory appeals) both in a court of first instance and in
> an appellate court or to proceedings in more than one appellate
> court. (2) Unless a certificate otherwise provides it shall not with-
> out the authority of the appropriate committee given under regu-
> lation 15 (1) extend to . . . (c) lodging an interlocutory appeal, . . ." E

We were referred to regulation 20 but I need not read it. I will go
to the Legal Aid (Costs of Successful Unassisted Parties) Regulations
1964 (S.I. 1964 No. 1276). I need only refer to regulation 2 of those
Regulations:

> " Any proceedings in respect of which a separate civil aid certificate F
> could "—and I emphasise the word " could "—" properly be issued
> under the General Regulations to a person receiving legal aid shall
> be treated as separate proceedings for the purposes of the Act."

In the present case the plaintiff was the beneficiary of a legal aid
certificate for the entirety of his proceedings. He was not issued with
a separate certificate for the instant interlocutory appeal, but authority G
was given for that interlocutory appeal to be brought. But I cannot
think that the answer to the problem we have to resolve can depend upon
the administrative consideration whether or not he was issued with a
single legal aid certificate but one which requires special authority to
bring an interlocutory appeal or with two or more different legal aid
certificates. The essential point, when one looks at section 13 (1) of the
Act of 1974, is whether or not he has received legal aid in connection H
with " any proceedings " and those proceedings are " finally " decided
in favour of the unassisted party.

Mr. Matheson's argument was to this effect: that the plaintiff did
receive legal aid in connection with the action; it is the action which is
" any proceedings " and those proceedings have not been, and will not
be, finally decided in favour of the unassisted party unless and until (if

A ever) there is judgment for the defendant in the action. I should say that liability in this action is still in issue.

Mr. Wingate-Saul's argument is that the plaintiff has received legal aid in connection with this interlocutory appeal; the "any proceedings" are the interlocutory appeal, and "those proceedings" (being the inter-locutory appeal) have been finally decided in favour of the unassisted
B party, namely, the defendant respondents in this appeal.

Both sides have referred us to a number of cases. For my own part, without any disrespect, I doubt if one gets much help from the cases in resolving what is basically a question of construction, but as we have been referred to them I mention some of them if only to dispose of some of the arguments.

In chronological order, the first was *Wozniak* v. *Wozniak* [1953]
C P. 179. The relevant provision in that case was wholly different from the current statutory provisions. Further, what Denning L.J. said had reference only to an order wrongly made by a trial judge; he had not in mind the position of the Court of Appeal.

Next chronologically is *Mills* v. *Mills* [1963] P. 329, again a decision of this court. In proceedings in what was then the Probate, Divorce and
D Admiralty Division, the husband got a limited legal aid certificate enabl-ing him to defend the wife's claim for alimony and maintenance. He was not given legal aid to defend her claim for dissolution of marriage. In due course the judge granted her a decree nisi and ordered the husband to pay the costs of the petition. The husband appealed to this court on the ground that he ought to have had the benefit of his legal aid certificate in respect of all the costs, including the costs of the petition, and not
E merely the costs of contesting the claim for alimony and maintenance. Judge Herbert, sitting as a special commissioner, rejected that argument and this court had no difficulty in affirming the judge without calling upon counsel for the wife. The judgment of the court was given by Diplock L.J. I need only read one passage. After reading the relevant regulations, Diplock L.J. said, at p. 337:

F   "I have a good deal of sympathy with that argument where it applies to petitions for dissolution of marriage in which a petitioner, even in an undefended petition, has to prove his or her case and costs are incurred, and if I could find some way of treating 'pro-ceedings' in paragraph (e) in a different sense from the word 'proceedings' in other parts of the same subsection, I would gladly do so. But, as a matter of construction, that seems to me to be
G   quite impossible. Consequently, the result of the construction con-tended for by Mr. Coningsby would be this: not merely that where an assisted person has a limited certificate limited to disputing part, and part only, of the claim, would he be entitled not to have an order for costs made against him except under the conditions laid down in paragraph (e), but he would also be entitled under para-graph (b) and paragraph (d) to have paid out of the legal aid fund
H   the costs of the very matter in respect of which he was not given a certificate. The result of that construction would mean, so far as I can see, that there would be no power on the part of the legal aid committee to give a certificate limited to part of the proceedings in a court, for such attempted limitation would be a brutum fulmen."

That passage, of course, was not directed to the point currently at issue,

but its underlying philosophy seems to me to be a pointer in the direc-   A
tion of what I regard as the true construction of section 13 (1).

In *Reg.* v. *Legal Aid Committee No.* 1 (*London*) *Legal Aid Area,
Ex parte Rondel* [1967] 2 Q.B. 482, a decision of the Divisional Court,
Lord Parker C.J. said, at p. 491:

> " Mr. Littman in his able argument before this court begins by
> submitting, and for my part I think he is undoubtedly right, that   B
> where ' proceedings ' are referred to in the Act and in the regu-
> lations, those proceedings are not confined to actions but involve all
> proceedings of an interlocutory nature.   I find it unnecessary to
> refer to all the matters to support that view; . . ."

Lord Parker C.J. went on to refer to *Mills* v. *Mills* [1963] P. 329.   Plainly
he had no difficulty in taking the view that " proceedings " in the relevant   C
legislation included interlocutory proceedings.

In *General Accident Fire and Life Assurance Corporation Ltd.* v.
Foster [1973] Q.B. 50, there is this passage in the judgment of Lord
Denning M.R., at p. 55: " The matter is governed by section 1 (1) and
(2) of the Legal Aid Act 1964."   Pausing there, those are the corres-
ponding subsections to section 13 (1) and (2) of the present Act.   Lord
Denning M.R. continued: D

> " The first point is: what are the ' proceedings '?   Are they the
> proceedings from beginning to end—from the very first time when
> legal aid was granted?   I think not.   The only ' proceedings ' with
> which we are concerned is the interlocutory appeal to this court,
> which we heard on January 19, 1971: and for which, no doubt, a
> separate legal aid certificate was granted."   E

Whether Lord Denning M.R. was right in making that last observation
is, if I may say so with respect, doubtful, but it does not matter.

> " The second point is whether ' those proceedings,' i.e., the inter-
> locutory appeal, were ' finally decided in favour of the unassisted
> party ' ?   When are proceedings ' finally decided in favour ' of a party,   F
> especially in a case like this where the result was not wholly in his
> favour? "

It has been pointed out by Mr. Matheson that it was conceded by Mr.
Hames for the Law Society in that case, that " proceedings " included
interlocutory proceedings.   That that concession was made clearly
emerges from the opening sentence of Sachs L.J.'s judgment, where he   G
said, at p. 56:

> " On three preliminary points there was no dispute in this court.
> The first was that the interlocutory appeal to this court was clearly
> a separate proceeding for the purpose of considering the effect of
> section 1 of the Legal Aid Act 1964."

The fact that that concession was made on that occasion does not   H
mean that it was rightly made, and we have looked at the whole matter
de novo.   But it seems to me that if one looks at the relevant words in
section 1 (1) and (2) of the Act of 1964 it was inevitable that Mr. Hames
should have made that concession, and when I look at the corresponding
and identical words in section 13 (1) and (2) of the Act of 1974, I am
unable to give them a different meaning from that which they bore when
that provision appeared in isolation in the Legal Aid Act 1964.   It is

A true that if one goes through, as Mr. Matheson has carefully taken us through, other sections not in the Act of 1964 but in other Acts, now consolidated in the Act of 1974, one can find, as one often does find in statutes, the word " proceedings " used in different senses in different places, but I think the concession was rightly made. I would have no hesitation in construing the words " any proceedings " as including an interlocutory appeal to this court in an ordinary Queen's Bench action.

B If one asks while the interlocutory appeal is going on, " In what proceedings are the plaintiff and the defendant engaging?," I think the man in the street would say " An interlocutory appeal in the Court of Appeal." They would not at that stage say they are engaging in a personal injury action in the High Court. On that point I therefore reject Mr. Matheson's argument.

C It is, perhaps, worth considering what the practical consequences would be if that argument were allowed to succeed. Ormrod L.J. drew attention to those consequences. What is the Court of Appeal to do in a case in which it dismisses an appeal by an assisted person in favour of an unassisted person? It is suggested that the matter would then have to await a decision until after the trial judge finally decides the case. That would involve the trial judge usurping, if I may be forgiven the word, the

D powers of the Court of Appeal over costs in matters before this court. It would involve endless delay. The trial judge would not know what the Court of Appeal would have done if it had had power to do that which ex hypothesi it had not got. It was further said that this court could not finally determine the amount of the assisted person's contribution unless and until the result of the action was known, because his

E means would vary according to the result. It is true his means may so vary, but the Court of Appeal has to take its decision on the best information available to it at the time the appeal is dismissed. After all, if the matter were left to the trial judge it may be that on the day of judgment the plaintiff, if successful, might be worth a certain amount, but the next day he might be worth a great deal more if he had won a football pool or had a successful day at the races. It seems to me that it is

F within the powers of the Court of Appeal to determine this matter once and for all (subject, of course, to due compliance with the other provisions of section 13) at the end of the interlocutory appeal. I have no hesitation in holding that this court does have power, at the conclusion of an interlocutory appeal, to decide this matter, because interlocutory appeals are " any proceedings " between the assisted person and a party not receiving legal aid, and those " proceedings " will have been " finally

G decided," as they were in the present case, in favour of the unassisted party.

Though grateful for Mr. Matheson's excellent argument, I would, therefore, decide this issue in favour of the defendants.

ORMROD L.J. I agree and would only add very few words of my own.

H If Mr. Matheson's argument is right, section 13 (1) of the Legal Aid Act 1974, has to be read: " Where a party receives legal aid in connection with any proceedings "—that is in the sense of an action or claim or some similar proceeding—" between him and a party not receiving legal aid . . . and those proceedings "—that means the whole action—" are finally decided in favour of the unassisted party, the court by which the proceedings "—that is the whole action—" are so decided may, subject to the provisions of this section, make an order for the payment to the

unassisted party out of the legal aid fund of the whole or any part of the A
costs incurred by him in *those* proceedings ", that is the whole action. It
therefore follows, if Mr. Matheson is right, that at the end of the case
the trial judge will be asked to make an order for costs in favour of the
unassisted party, as against the fund in a case such as this, in respect of
part of those costs, namely, the costs of an unsuccessful appeal to this
court. Then the judge would have to deal with the awkward problem
of subsection (3), because the " proceedings " will be proceedings in the B
court of first instance, in which case the court has to be satisfied on the
severe financial hardship point.

The truth is, I think, with respect to Mr. Matheson, that sections 13
and 14 of the Legal Aid Act 1974, as Lord Roskill has said, come from
an entirely separate piece of legislation, the Legal Aid Act 1964, which
was passed expressly to deal with the problem, which had been omitted C
from the Legal Aid and Advice Act 1949, of the unassisted party's costs,
about which there had been a certain amount of feeling and which
eventually was dealt with by the Legal Aid Act 1964 to protect unassisted
parties who were successful. It seems to me that logically we should
construe sections 13 and 14 of the Act of 1974 in exactly the same way as
the court would have construed them when they were in a separate
statute. That was done in *General Accident Life and Fire Assurance* D
Corporation Ltd. v. *Foster* [1973] Q.B. 50, and I, for my part, attach
some significance to the fact that Mr. Hames, who was appearing for the
Law Society in that case, conceded that the interlocutory appeal was a
separate proceeding for the purposes of the Act of 1964. He is a man
who has enormous experience of handling legal aid points and he would
be the last person, I venture to think with respect, to make a concession E
unless it was well-founded. I also obtain a little assistance and a little
comfort from what Sachs L.J. said. He, too, had a long association with
the legal aid scheme, long before 1949, and we find him saying, at p.
56:

" On three preliminary points there was no dispute in this court.
The first was that the interlocutory appeal to this court was clearly F
a separate proceeding for the purpose of considering the effect of
section 1 of the Legal Aid Act 1964."

That, I must confess, impressed me a good deal. It would be very odd if
that concession by Mr. Hames and that view expressed by Sachs L.J.
proved to be wrong. For my part, I would require a lot of convincing
before I came to a different view on the construction of these two sub- G
sections. When one adds to that Mr. Matheson's admission in this court
that the effect of his construction would, if accepted, effectively make it
impossible for this court to make an order for costs in favour of an
assisted party against the legal aid fund in an interlocutory appeal, then
I can only say that before being forced to that conclusion I should
require to see very, very clear statutory provisions leading to that H
conclusion.

I take the same view as Lord Roskill—and, indeed, the view of this
court in the *General Accident* case—that if we look at these two sections
in isolation the answer is obvious. Looked at in the body of the legal
aid legislation as a whole it is easy to get tied in many ways, and Mr.
Matheson is an admirable spinner of webs in that connection. I agree
that the existing order should stand.

A   LORD ROSKILL. May I just add this to my judgment? Mr. Matheson mentioned that the Law Society had not been informed of our tentative order until a considerable number of weeks had elapsed after our judgment on March 13, 1980. I confess that I thought—and I understand Ormrod L.J. shares my view—when this court made such an order, that the court would have informed the Law Society of the order that had been made, but we have been told by the associate that B that is not now the practice. We are told that it was the assisted person's solicitors who notified the Law Society. That cannot be the right way for the Law Society to be notified. But I do not think it is a matter on which we ought to express any final view. Perhaps the Law Society, if they wish to raise it, would be good enough to take it up direct with Lord Denning M.R. It is a matter upon which there should be some C uniform practice.

> *Defendants to recover costs of inter-*
> *locutory appeal against legal aid*
> *fund, such costs to include Law*
> *Society's application.*
> *Leave to appeal refused.*

D
     Solicitors: *The Law Society; Mackrell, & Co. for James Chapman & Co., Manchester.*

[Reported by MISS ISOBEL COLLINS, Barrister-at-Law]

E   ——————

     October 16. The Appeal Committee of the House of Lords (Lord Diplock, Lord Keith of Kinkel and Lord Scarman) allowed a petition by the Law Society for leave to appeal.

F   ——————

[COURT OF APPEAL]

* In re EVERS' TRUST
PAPPS *v.* EVERS

G
1980   May 8; 23   Ormrod, Eveleigh and
                                                   Templeman L.JJ.

Trust for Sale — Power to postpone — Family home — House
purchased by man and woman living together—Parties ceasing
to live together—Woman continuing to occupy house with
H   *children—Man's application for order directing sale—Court's*
discretion—Law of Property Act 1925 (15 & 16 Geo. 5, c. 20),
s. 30

     The parties (" the father " and " the mother "), who had both been previously married and divorced, began to live together in August 1974, in the former matrimonial home of the father. In 1976 a child was born, shortly after which the mother's two children by her previous marriage came to live with them. In April 1978, they bought a cottage for £13,950,

of which £10,000 was obtained on mortgage, £2,400 was pro- A
vided by the mother and £1,050 plus expenses by the father.
The cottage was conveyed into their joint names on a trust
for sale for the benefit of themselves as joint tenants, with
power to postpone sale. In August 1979, they separated. The
mother took out wardship proceedings and was awarded
custody of the child. The father applied under section 30
of the Law of Property Act 1925 [1] for an order for sale of
the cottage. The judge ordered that the property be sold, B
but that sale should be postponed until the child attained the
age of 16 or until further order.

On appeal by the father: —

Held, dismissing the appeal, that in exercising its discretion
on an application under section 30 of the Law of Property
Act 1925 the court had to have regard to the underlying
purpose of the trust for sale and decide whether at the
particular time and in the particular circumstances when the C
application was made, it would be right, having regard to that
underlying purpose, to order a sale; that in considering the
circumstances of the purchase of the cottage, the inference
was irresistible that the parties had purchased it as a family
home for themselves and the three children for the indefinite
future, and, since there was no evidence that the father had
any need to realise his investment whereas the sale of the
property would put the mother in a very difficult position, it D
would be wrong to order a sale at the present time and in
the existing circumstances, and since unpredictable changes
in circumstances might make an order for sale when the
child attained the age of 16 inappropriate, the order should
be varied by dismissing the father's application on the mother's
undertaking to discharge the liability under the mortgage, pay
the outgoings and indemnify the father so long as she occupied
the property, leaving it to either party to make another appli- E
cation if there was a change in circumstances (post, pp.
1330G–H, 1333E–F, 1334B–G).

In re Buchanan-Wollaston's Conveyance [1939] Ch. 738,
C.A.; *Jones* v. *Challenger* [1961] 1 Q.B. 176, C.A.; dicta of
Salmon L.J. in *Rawlings* v. *Rawlings* [1964] P. 398, 419, C.A.
and Lord Denning M.R. in *Williams (J. W.)* v. *Williams
(M. A.)* [1976] Ch. 278, 285, C.A. applied. F

Burke v. *Burke* [1974] 1 W.L.R. 1063, C.A. considered.

Order of Judge Lipfriend, sitting as a deputy judge of the
Family Division, varied.

The following cases are referred to in the judgment of the court:

Browne (formerly Pritchard) v. *Pritchard* [1975] 1 W.L.R. 1366; [1975]
3 All E.R. 721, C.A.
Buchanan-Wollaston's Conveyance, In re [1939] Ch. 217, 738; [1939] 2 G
All E.R. 302, Farwell J. and C.A.
Burke v. *Burke* [1974] 1 W.L.R. 1063; [1974] 2 All E.R. 944, C.A.
Jones v. *Challenger* [1961] 1 Q.B. 176; [1960] 2 W.L.R. 695; [1960]
1 All E.R. 785, C.A.
Martin (B. H.) v. *Martin (D.)* [1978] Fam. 12; [1977] 3 W.L.R. 101;
[1977] 3 All E.R. 762, C.A. H
Mesher v. *Mesher and Hall,* The Times, February 13, 1973; [1980] 1 All
E.R. 126 (Note), C.A.
Rawlings v. *Rawlings* [1964] P. 398; [1964] 3 W.L.R. 294; [1964] 2
All E.R. 804, C.A.
Williams (J. W.) v. *Williams (M. A.)* [1976] Ch. 278; [1976] 3 W.L.R.
494; [1977] 1 All E.R. 28, C.A.

[1] Law of Property Act 1925, s. 30: see post, p. 1330D–E.

A   The following additional cases were cited in argument:

Bull v. *Bull* [1955] 1 Q.B. 234; [1955] 2 W.L.R. 78; [1955] 1 All E.R. 253, C.A.

Cooke v. *Head* [1972] 1 W.L.R. 518; [1972] 2 All E.R. 38, C.A.

Davis v. *Johnson* [1979] A.C. 264; [1978] 2 W.L.R. 553; [1978] 1 All E.R. 1132, H.L.(E.).

B   *Eves* v. *Eves* [1975] 1 W.L.R. 1338; [1975] 3 All E.R. 768, C.A.

Griffith v. *Evans* (1882) 46 L.T. 417, D.C.

Hyde's Conveyance, In re (1952) 102 L.J. 58.

Mayo, In re [1943] Ch. 302; [1943] 2 All E.R. 440.

Spindlow v. *Spindlow* [1979] Fam. 52; [1978] 3 W.L.R. 777; [1979] 1 All E.R. 169, C.A.

Stevens v. *Hutchinson* [1953] Ch. 299; [1953] 2 W.L.R. 545; [1953] 1 All E.R. 699.

C   *Tanner* v. *Tanner* [1975] 1 W.L.R. 1346; [1975] 3 All E.R. 776, C.A.

APPEAL from Judge Lipfriend, sitting as a deputy judge of the Family Division.

The applicant father sought an order under section 30 of the Law of Property Act 1925 directing the sale of a property which was held on trust for sale for the benefit of himself and the mother, the respondent to the application. On December 10, 1979, Judge Lipfriend ordered that
D   the property be sold, but directed that such sale should be postponed until the child of the parties attained the age of 16, or until further order.

The father appealed on the grounds that (1) the judge's decision was wrong in that it did not consider the welfare of the child as the paramount consideration; (2) the judge was wrong in exercising his discretion in
E   favour of the mother; (3) the decision was against the weight of the evidence; (4) the judge erred in law in holding that there was jurisdiction or, if there was jurisdiction, wrongly exercised his discretion in permitting the mother to remain in the property for the next 13 years; and (5) the father's sole obligation was to maintain the child and the purposes of the trusts on which the property had been held had determined.

F   The facts are stated in the judgment of the court.

Quentin Edwards Q.C. and *June Rodgers* for the father.
Roger Gray Q.C. and *David Bodey* for the mother.

Cur. adv. vult.

G   May 23. ORMROD L.J. read the following judgment of the court. This is an appeal by the father from part of the judgment of Judge Lipfriend, sitting as a deputy judge of the Family Division, given on December 10, 1979. The judge had two matters before him, an originating summons in wardship proceedings by the mother, and an application by the father under section 30 of the Law of Property Act 1925 for an order for sale
H   of a cottage near Basingstoke. The judge made an order in the wardship proceedings giving care and control of the child in question to the mother, and in the section 30 proceedings directed that the property be sold, but that such sale be postponed until the child attained the age of 16 years or until further order. The father originally appealed against both orders but at the outset, Mr. Quentin Edwards, for the father, abandoned the appeal in relation to the wardship. The appeal in relation to the section 30 application raises questions of general importance, because it appears

to be the first time that this court has had to consider the application of
section 30 in relation to a property purchased as a home and held in joint
names, by two persons who are not married to one another. This is a
situation which is occurring much more frequently now than in the past,
and is a social development of considerable importance with which the
courts are now likely to have to deal from time to time.

The form of the judge's order bears a close resemblance to, and was
obviously derived from, orders made by this court under section 24 of
the Matrimonial Causes Act 1973, in cases such as *Mesher* v. *Mesher
and Hall*, The Times, February 13, 1973; [1980] 1 All E.R. 126 (Note);
Browne (formerly Pritchard) v. *Pritchard* [1975] 1 W.L.R. 1366 and
Martin (B. H.) v. *Martin (D.)* [1978] Fam. 12, and in fact, the judge
relied expressly on the latter two cases.

At the outset, it must be said that in this respect the judge was in
error. The powers of the court under section 30 of the Law of Property
Act 1925 are different from the powers which it has under section 24
of the Matrimonial Causes Act 1973; the ambit of the discretion is,
consequently, different. Under section 24 the court is empowered to
make orders between former husband and wives, "adjusting" their
respective property rights; under section 30 the court is concerned with
the effect to be given to existing property rights, a much more restricted
function. Cases arising under section 24, therefore, are not relevant to
cases arising under section 30, although some of the considerations to be
taken into account are common to both classes.

Section 30 of the Law of Property Act 1925 is in these terms:

"If the trustees for sale refuse to sell or to exercise any of the
powers conferred by either of the last two sections, or any requisite
consent cannot be obtained, any person interested may apply to the
court for a vesting or other order for giving effect to the proposed
transaction or for an order directing the trustees for sale to give
effect thereto, and the court may make such order as it thinks fit."

The section gives the court a discretion to intervene to deal, inter alia,
with the situation which arises when the trustees under a trust for sale
are unable or unwilling to agree that the property should be sold. In such
circumstances, the court can order a sale of the property, and, if
appropriate, impose terms, or it can decline to make an order, leaving
the property unsold, unless and until the trustees reach agreement, or the
court makes an order at some future date.

The usual practice in these cases has been to order a sale and a
division of the proceeds of sale, thus giving effect to the express purpose
of the trust. But the trust for sale has become a very convenient and
much used conveyancing technique. Combined with the statutory power
in the trustees to postpone the sale, it can be used to meet a variety of
situations, in some of which an actual sale is far from the intentions of
the parties at the time when the trust for sale comes into existence. So,
when asked to exercise its discretionary powers under section 30 to
execute the trust, the court must have regard to its underlying purpose:
see *In re Buchanan-Wollaston's Conveyance* [1939] Ch. 217, and in this
court at p. 738. In that case four adjoining landowners purchased a
plot of land to prevent it being built on and held it on trust for sale. They
also convenanted with one another that the land would not be dealt with
except with the unanimous agreement of the trustees. Subsequently one
of them wished to sell, but some of the other trustees objected so the

A plaintiff applied to the court under section 30 for an order for sale. At first instance, Farwell J. refused the order, saying, at p. 223:

"The question is this: will the court assist the plaintiff to do an act which would be directly contrary to his contract with the other parties, since it was plainly the intention of the parties to the contract that the land should not be sold save with the consent of them all?"

B His decision was upheld in this court, but on a broader basis. Sir Wilfrid Greene M.R. said, at p. 747:

". . . it seems to me that the court of equity, when asked to enforce the trust for sale, whether one created by a settlement or a will or one created by the statute, must look into all the circumstances of the case and consider whether or not, at the particular moment and C in the particular circumstances when the application is made to it, it is right and proper that such an order shall be made. In considering a question of that kind, in circumstances such as these, the court is bound to look at the contract into which the parties have entered and to ask itself the question whether or not the person applying for execution of the trust for sale is a person whose voice should be D allowed to prevail."

Some 20 years later, in *Jones* v. *Challenger* [1961] 1 Q.B. 176, Devlin L.J. reviewed the authorities and affirmed this principle. He said, at p. 181:

"But this simple principle" i.e., that in a trust for sale there is a duty to sell "cannot prevail where the trust itself or the circumstances E in which it was made show that there was a secondary or collateral object besides that of sale. Simonds J., in his judgment in *In re Mayo* [1943] Ch. 302, said that if there were mala fides, the position would be different. If it be not mala fides, it is at any rate wrong and inequitable for one of the parties to the trust to invoke the letter of the trust in order to defeat one of its purposes, whether that F purpose be written or unwritten, and the court will not permit it."

In that case a house had been purchased by a husband and wife jointly as a home. Subsequently, the marriage broke down, the wife left and committed adultery and applied to the court for an order for sale of the property, a leasehold with only a few years to run. The husband continued to live in the house on his own; there were no children. G In these circumstances the court decided that the house should be sold. Devlin L.J., said, at p. 183:

"In the case we have to consider, the house was acquired as the matrimonial home. That was the purpose of the joint tenancy and, for so long as that purpose was still alive, I think, that the right test to be applied would be that in *In re Buchanan-Wollaston's Con-* H *veyance* [1939] Ch. 738. But with the end of the marriage, that purpose was dissolved and the primacy of the duty to sell was restored."

Had there been children whose home was still in the property, the conclusion in that case might have been different. Later Devlin L.J. said, at p. 184: "The true question is whether it is inequitable for the wife, once the matrimonial home has gone, to want to realise her investment."

In *Burke* v. *Burke* [1974] 1 W.L.R. 1063, however, children were
involved. On the husband's application under section 17 of the Married
Women's Property Act 1882 the registrar ordered a sale, but postponed
it for a year or so to give the wife, who had custody of the children, an
opportunity to find an alternative home for them. This court upheld the
registrar's order. The application was actually made under section 17
of the Married Women's Property Act 1882. That section is purely
procedural and the principles are the same as under section 30 of the
Law of Property Act 1925. In giving the leading judgment Buckley L.J.
took the view that the trust for sale was an immediate binding trust subject
to the discretionary power in the court to postpone the execution of the
trust for sale, and that the court must have regard to all the relevant
circumstances of the case and to the situation of both the beneficial
owners. The interests of the children in that case, he thought, were

" . . . interests which are only incidentally to be taken into consideration in that sort of way. They are proper to be taken into
consideration so far as they affect the equities in the matter as
between the two persons entitled to the beneficial interests in the
property. But it is not, I think, right to treat this case as though
the husband was obliged to make provision for his children by
agreeing to retain the property unsold. To do so is, as I think, and
as was urged upon us by Mr. Matheson, to confuse with a problem
relating to property considerations which are relevant to maintenance." (See [1974] 1 W.L.R. 1063, 1067.)

He expressed disagreement with an obiter dictum of Salmon L.J. in
the earlier case of *Rawlings* v. *Rawlings* [1964] P. 398, 419, where he
said:

" If there were young children the position would be different. One
of the purposes of the trust would no doubt have been to provide a
home for them, and whilst that purpose still existed a sale would
not generally be ordered."

Buckley L.J. was plainly anxious to make it clear that the children
themselves in such circumstances were not objects of the trust and,
therefore, had no beneficial interests in the property, and so were in
that sense, only " incidental " to the problem, but we do not think that
Salmon L.J. thought otherwise. The court in *Burke* v. *Burke* [1974]
1 W.L.R. 1063 was not referred to *In re Buchanan-Wollaston's
Conveyance* [1939] Ch. 738, so Buckley L.J. does not seem to have
considered, in so many words, whether or not the primary purpose of
the trust, i.e., for sale, (" the letter of the trust," in Devlin L.J.'s words)
had been affected by the underlying purpose (quoting Devlin L.J. again,
" written or unwritten ") of providing a home, not only for the parents,
but also for the children. Salmon L.J.'s dictum appears, therefore, to be
more, in line with the judgments of this court in *In re Buchanan-
Wollaston's Conveyance* [1939] Ch. 738, and in *Jones* v. *Challenger*
[1961] 1 Q.B. 176. Moreover, it is now supported by a dictum of Lord
Denning M.R. in *Williams (J. W.)* v. *Williams (M. A.)* [1976] Ch. 278,
285: " The court, in executing the trust should regard the primary object
as being to provide a home and not a sale."

This approach to the exercise of the discretion given by section 30
has considerable advantages in these " family " cases. It enables the court
to deal with substance, that is reality, rather than form, that is, con-

A venience of conveyancing; it brings the exercise of the discretion under this section, so far as possible, into line with exercise of the discretion given by section 24 of the Matrimonial Causes Act 1973; and it goes some way to eliminating differences between legitimate and illegitimate children in accordance with present legislative policy: see, for example Part II of the Family Law Reform Act 1969.

B The relevant facts in the present case must now be examined. There is little or no dispute between the parties about them. Both the mother and the father have been married and divorced. The mother had two children of her marriage, both boys, now aged ten and eight. She met the father in May 1974. In August 1974, they began to live together at the father's former matrimonial home; the two boys remained in the care of their father, the mother visiting them regularly. Early in 1976

C the mother became pregnant by the father and gave birth to the child, who is the subject of the wardship proceedings, on December 22, 1976. At about that time, the two older boys joined their mother and from then until the separation in August 1979 all five lived together, at first at the father's former matrimonial home, until in April 1978, the parties jointly acquired the cottage which is the subject of these

D proceedings. This property was purchased for £13,950, of which £10,000 was raised jointly on mortgage. The balance was provided as to £2,400 by the mother and as to £1,050 plus expenses by the father. The mother's contribution was derived from her share of her former matrimonial home. On April 28, 1978, the property was conveyed into their joint names as trustees upon a bare trust for sale with power to postpone the sale in trust for themselves as joint tenants.

E The irresistible inference from these facts is that, as the judge found, they purchased this property as a family home for themselves and the three children. It is difficult to imagine that the mother, then wholly responsible for two children, and partly for the third, would have invested nearly all her capital in the purchase of this property if it was not to be available to her as a home for the children for the indefinite future. It

F is inconceivable that the father, when he agreed to this joint adventure, could have thought otherwise, or contemplated the possibility of an early sale without the consent of the mother. The underlying purpose of the trust was, therefore, to provide a home for all five of them for the indefinite future. Unfortunately, the relationship between the father and the mother broke down very soon, and the parties separated at the

G beginning of August 1979 in circumstances of great bitterness. This is clearly shown by two dates. On July 20, 1979, the mother issued her originating summons in the wardship proceedings; on August 2, 1979, the father issued his application under section 30 for an order for sale of the property.

Mr. Quentin Edwards, for the father, argued that the judge had not

H taken into account that his client's legal liability was limited to providing maintenance for his illegitimate child, and did not extend to providing for the mother. That proposition is correct as the law now stands, though it will not be so when section 50 of the Domestic Proceedings and Magistrates' Courts Act 1978 comes into force. That section amends section 4 of the Affiliation Proceedings Act 1957, by empowering magistrates' courts to take account of the need of the mother. In any event, in the present proceedings the court is not so much concerned

with obligations imposed by law on the father, as with obligations which A
he had assumed or must be taken to have assumed.

It was further argued that the father ought to be allowed to " take
his money out " or " to realise his investment." In point of fact, his
investment amounted to less than one-fifth of the purchase price of the
property, and was smaller than the mother's investment. The major part
of the purchase price was provided by the mortgagees, and the mother is
prepared to accept full responsibility for paying the interest on the B
mortgage, and keeping up the capital re-payments. The father has a
secure home with his mother. There is no evidence that he has any need
to realise his investment. It is an excellent one, combining complete
security with considerable capital appreciation in money terms. His share
is now said to be worth about £5,000, i.e., it has more than doubled in
value in two years. On the other hand, a sale of the property now C
would put the mother into a very difficult position because she cannot
raise the finance to rehouse herself or meet the cost of borrowing money
at present rates. So there is no justification for ordering a sale at the
present time.

For these reasons the judge was right not to order an immediate sale
but the form of his actual order is not satisfactory. Under section 30,
the primary question is whether the court should come to the aid of the D
applicant at the " particular moment and in the particular circumstances
when the application is made to it . . .": see In re Buchanan-Wollaston's
Conveyance [1939] 1 Ch. 738, 747. In the present case, at the present
moment and in the existing circumstances, it would be wrong to order a
sale. But circumstances may change unpredictably. It may not be
appropriate to order a sale when the child reaches 16 years—a purely E
arbitrary date—or it may be become appropriate to do so much sooner,
for example on the mother's remarriage, or on it becoming financially
possible for her to buy the father out. In such circumstances it will
probably be wiser simply to dismiss the application while indicating the
sort of circumstances which would, prima facie, justify a further application. The ensuing uncertainty is unfortunate but, under this section, the
court has no power to adjust property rights or to re-draft the terms of F
the trust. Ideally, the parties should now negotiate a settlement on the
basis that neither of them is in a position to dictate terms. We would
therefore, dismiss the father's appeal, but would vary the order to dismiss
the application on the mother's undertaking to discharge the liability
under the mortgage, to pay the outgoings and maintain the property, and
to indemnify the father so long as she is occupying the property. G

Appeal dismissed.
Leave to appeal refused.

Solicitors: *Lamb, Brooks & Bullock, Basingstoke; Snow & Bispham,
Basingstoke.*

H

July 24, 1980. The Appeal Committee of the House of Lords (Lord
Wilberforce, Lord Salmon and Lord Russell of Killowen) dismissed a
petition by the father for leave to appeal.

R. C. W.

A

[QUEEN'S BENCH DIVISION]

*PRACTICE DIRECTION (LAND REGISTRATION: JUDGMENT CREDITOR) (NO. 2)

B
Land Registration—Register—Judgment creditor—Order for production of register—Ex parte application

The requirement that an application under the Land Registration Rules 1967 (S.I. 1967 No. 761) should be made by summons is hereby revoked and such application may be made ex parte on affidavit.

Accordingly, *Practice Direction (Land Registration: Judgment Creditor)*
C [1970] 1 W.L.R. 1158 should be amended by deleting the words " should be made by summons pursuant to R.S.C., Ord. 32, r. 1 " and substituting therefor the words " may be made by an ex parte application."

This direction is made with the concurrence of the Chief Chancery Master.

SIR JACK I. H. JACOB
Senior Master of the Supreme Court
D *October* 10, 1980.

—

[CHANCERY DIVISION]

E

*SWAIN AND ANOTHER *v.* THE LAW SOCIETY

[1979 S. No. 5105]

1980 Feb. 18, 19, 20, 21;   Slade J.
March 17
F

Solicitor—Compulsory indemnity insurance—Law Society's indemnity insurance scheme—Solicitor's Indemnity Rules 1975–1979 —Whether intra vires Law Society—Entitlement of Law Society to commission—Solicitors Act 1974 (c. 47), s. 37 (2)

Under section 37 of the Solicitors Act 1974 [1] the Council of the Law Society was empowered, with the concurrence of
G the Master of the Rolls, to make rules concerning a compulsory professional indemnity insurance scheme for solicitors. By virtue of section 10 of the Act the Law Society could withhold a practising certificate from any person who did not satisfy it that he, or she, was complying with any indemnity rule or was exempt from the rules. In December 1975, acting on the authority of section 37, and with the concurrence of the Master of the Rolls, the Council of the Law Society made the
H Solicitors' Indemnity Rules 1975 and introduced an Indemnity Insurance Scheme. Under this scheme the Law Society was authorised to take out a master policy and to arrange for a certificate of insurance to be issued to those solicitors to whom the rules applied and who would be required to pay the appropriate premiums. In May 1976 a contract was effected between the Law Society and the Law Society Services Ltd., a company wholly owned by the Law Society, of the first

—

[1] Solicitors Act 1974, s. 37: see post, pp. 1338G—1340A.

part, and London Insurance Brokers Ltd. of the second part A
for the implementation of the insurance scheme and for Law
Society Services Ltd. to retain a commission in respect of
premiums received by the brokers. After September 1, 1976,
the scheme was regarded as compulsory and every solicitor
to whom the rules applied had to produce a certificate of
insurance before receiving an annual practising certificate.
Subsequent rules of a similar nature to those of 1975 were
made in 1978 and 1979. B

On the question whether, upon the true construction of
section 37 of the Solicitors Act 1974 and of the rules of 1975,
1978 and 1979, the rules were ultra vires, and whether
the Law Society was entitled to retain the commission received
by London Insurance Brokers Ltd. in respect of premiums
paid by individual solicitors: —

Held, (1) that on its true construction section 37 (2) (*b*)
of the Solicitors Act 1974 empowered the Council to make C
rules enabling the Law Society to take out and maintain
insurance cover for solicitors with authorised insurers as
trustee of the benefit of the contract and therefore the rules
could not be said to be ultra vires; but since the action was
non-representative there should be no positive declaration as
to the validity of the rules in order to leave the way formally
open for possible further argument on other points in the
future (post, pp. 1348D, 1350E–F). D

(2) That the Law Society " took out " a master policy
within the meaning of the rules as soon as it acquired contractual rights against the insurers and " maintained " such
policies by requiring solicitors to pay premiums on individual
policies and, consequently, had acted in accordance with the
rules (post, pp. 1351H, 1358G–H).

(3) That the Law Society negotiated the master policy
pursuant to its normal function as the solicitors' governing E
body, the negotiating of the contract placing it in a position
to demand the right to participate in the commission received,
but it did not enter into a fiduciary capacity in relation to
the solicitors until after the negotiations had been concluded,
and consequently was not bound to account to the plaintiffs
for any part of the commission received (post, pp. 1360G—
1361A, F–G, 1362F–H—1363A).

F

The following cases are referred to in the judgment:

Blackburn v. *Flavelle* (1881) 6 App.Cas. 628, P.C.
Bray v. *Ford* [1896] A.C. 44, H.L.(E.).
Canadian National Railways v. *Canada Steamship Lines Ltd.* [1945]
 A.C. 204, P.C.
Drinkwater v. *Arthur* (1871) 10 S.C.R. (N.S.W.) 193.
Hooper v. *Exeter Corporation* (1887) 56 L.J.Q.B. 457. G
Morgan v. *Palmer* (1824) 2 B. & C. 729.
Phipps v. *Boardman* [1967] 2 A.C. 46; [1966] 3 W.L.R. 1009; [1966]
 3 All E.R. 721, H.L.(E.).
Regal (Hastings) Ltd. v. *Gulliver* [1942] 1 All E.R. 378; [1967] 2 A.C.
 134N, H.L.(E.).
Shaw v. *Applegate* [1977] 1 W.L.R. 970; [1978] 1 All E.R. 123, C.A.
Thompson v. *Adams* (1889) 23 Q.B.D. 361. H

The following additional cases were cited in argument:

Barclay v. *Cousins* (1802) 2 East. 544.
Dickson v. *Pharmaceutical Society of Great Britain* [1970] A.C. 403;
 [1968] 3 W.L.R. 286; [1978] 2 All E.R. 686, H.L.(E.).
Canning v. *Farquhar* (1885) 16 Q.B.D. 727, C.A.
Fair v. *M'Iver* (1812) 16 East 130.

A   *Jaglom* v. *Excess Insurance Co. Ltd.* [1972] 2 Q.B. 250; [1971] 3 W.L.R.
       594; [1972] 1 All E.R. 267.

SUMMONS

By originating summons dated October 25, 1979, as subsequently
amended, the plaintiffs, James Midwood Swain and Alan Stephen
McLaren, practising solicitors, sought against the defendant, the Law
B   Society, (1) a declaration that upon the true construction of section 37
of the Solicitors Act 1974 and of the Solicitors' Indemnity Rules of 1975,
1978 and 1979 the Council of the Law Society had no power to make
any of the rules and that they were consequently null and void; and
(2) determination of the question whether, upon the true construction
of the Act and rules, the Law Society was entitled to retain for its own
C   purposes the commission received by it from London Insurance Brokers
Ltd. in respect of premiums paid by individual solicitors pursuant to the
Solicitors' Indemnity Insurance Scheme or whether it was accountable
for the commission to such individual solicitors or otherwise. By a
further summons dated January 30, 1980, the plaintiffs sought an order
for inspection of the documents constituting the master policy which the
D   Law Society was empowered by the rules to take out and maintain.

   Leonard Lewis Q.C. and *Martin Roth* for the plaintiffs.
   Robert Alexander Q.C. and *Patrick Phillips* for the Law Society.

                                            Cur. adv. vult.

E   March 17. SLADE J. read the following judgment. In this originating
summons the plaintiffs, Mr. James Swain and Mr. Alan McLaren, are two
practising solicitors and the defendants are the Law Society. The summons
raises two questions relating to the Law Society's Solicitors' Indemnity
Insurance Scheme. These must be of importance to all practising solicitors.
The first challenges the validity of the rules made by the Council of the
F   Law Society, pursuant to which the scheme has been introduced. It is
suggested that the Council had no power to make these rules, from which
it would follow that the scheme itself is not binding on solicitors. The
second question asks the court to decide whether, in the events which have
happened, the Law Society is entitled to retain for its own purposes the
commission received by it in respect of premiums paid by individual
solicitors pursuant to the scheme or whether it is accountable to them for
G   this commission.

The Rules

Until 1975 there existed no general scheme for insurance for solicitors
who wished to obtain indemnity insurance against claims in respect of civil
liability for professional negligence or breach of duty. Solicitors who
H   wished to obtain such insurance sought it on the insurance market, either
with or without the intervention of insurance agents or brokers. They
were free to negotiate terms suiting their individual requirements with such
insurance companies as were prepared to engage in this class of business.
Lloyd's of London and various insurance companies of repute offered
competitive terms.

For some years, however, many persons had been of the opinion that
some form of scheme making professional indemnity insurance for solicitors

compulsory was desirable, having regard to the increasing incidence of   A
claims against solicitors.   In 1972 a special committee of the Law Society
wrote a report for its Council recommending (inter alia) that the introduction of a single compulsory professional indemnity insurance scheme for
all solicitor–principals in private practice should be approved in principle,
subject to satisfactory terms being negotiated and administrative arrangements being made.   It further recommended that any statutory powers   B
required to implement this recommendation should be sought as soon
as possible, after certain consultation.

Statutory provision for the introduction of such a scheme was first
made by section 10 of the Solicitors (Amendment) Act 1974.   That Act,
however, was almost immediately superseded by a consolidating enactment,
the Solicitors Act 1974, which received the Royal Assent on July 31, 1974,
and came into force on May 1, 1975.   I will refer to this as " the Act."   C

The method adopted by the legislature in the Act, so as to enable the
introduction of a compulsory professional indemnity insurance scheme,
essentially embodied two features.   The first was to empower the Council
with the concurrence of the Master of the Rolls to make rules concerning
such indemnity, in such manner as to apply to solicitors or any class of
solicitors.   These rules are referred to in the Act as " indemnity rules."
The second was to empower the Law Society to withhold a practising   D
certificate from any person who does not satisfy it that he is complying
with any indemnity rules or is exempt from them.

Section 1 of the Act disqualifies from acting as a solicitor any person
who does not have a current practising certificate.   Section 10 (1) sets out
the conditions as to which a person must satisfy the Law Society, if he is
to be entitled to a practising certificate.   One of these conditions (set out   E
in sub-paragraph (e)) is that " he is complying with any indemnity rules
or is exempt from them."

There can thus be no doubt that the legislature contemplated that
compliance with any relevant indemnity rules, which the Council of the Law
Society might see fit to make in the proper exercise of its statutory
powers, with the concurrence of the Master of the Rolls, should be an   F
inescapable condition precedent to practice as a solicitor.   However, I
accept the general submission made on behalf of the plaintiffs that the
drastic nature of the sanction which the legislature introduced for non-
compliance affords grounds for concluding that the wording of the
power to make indemnity rules, conferred on the Council by section
37 of the Act, should be construed more narrowly than broadly.

Section 37 (1) reads: G

" The Council, with the concurrence of the Master of the Rolls, may
make rules (in this Act referred to as ' indemnity rules ') concerning
indemnity against loss arising from claims in respect of any description
of civil liability incurred—(a) by a solicitor or former solicitor in
connection with his practice or with any trust of which he is or
formerly was a trustee; (b) by an employee or former employee of a   H
solicitor or former solicitor in connection with that solicitor's practice
or with any trust of which that solicitor or the employee is or
formerly was a trustee."

" The Council " is defined by section 87 of the Act as meaning the Council
of the Law Society.   I pause to observe that the expression " loss arising
from claims," in the context of section 37 (1), plainly refers to loss suffered

A   by *solicitors* as a result of claims made against them, in respect of liability incurred by them. It is not apt to refer to any loss which may be suffered either by their clients or by the Law Society itself.

Section 37 (2) of the Act then proceeds to list three methods which indemnity rules may specify for the purpose of providing for the indemnity. It reads:

B   "For the purpose of providing such indemnity, indemnity rules— (*a*) may authorise or require the Society to establish and maintain a fund or funds; (*b*) may authorise or require the Society to take out and maintain insurance with authorised insurers; (*c*) may require solicitors or any specified class of solicitors to take out and maintain insurance with authorised insurers."

C   With reference to section 37 (2) (*b*) and (*c*), the expression " authorised insurers " is defined by section 87 of the Act as meaning " a person [sic] permitted under the Insurance Companies Act 1974 to carry on liability insurance business or pecuniary loss insurance business; . . ." Thus the Council has no control over the list of " authorised insurers " falling within this definition.

D   Section 37 (3) of the Act contains certain ancillary provisions designed further to define or to extend the rule-making powers of the Council. It provides:

"Without prejudice to the generality of subsections (1) and (2), indemnity rules—(*a*) may specify the terms and conditions on which indemnity is to be available, and any circumstances in which the right to it is to be excluded or modified; (*b*) may provide for the manage-

E   ment, administration and protection of any fund maintained by virtue of subsection (2) (*a*) and require solicitors or any class of solicitors to make payments to any such fund; (*c*) may require solicitors or any class of solicitors to make payments by way of premium on any insurance policy maintained by the Society by virtue of subsection (2) (*b*); (*d*) may prescribe the conditions which an insurance policy

F   must satisfy for the purposes of subsection (2) (*c*); (*e*) may authorise the Society to determine the amount of any payments required by the rules, subject to such limits, or in accordance with such provisions, as may be prescribed by the rules; (*f*) may specify circumstances in which, where a solicitor for whom indemnity is provided has failed to comply with the rules, the Society or insurers may take proceedings

G   against him in respect of sums paid by way of indemnity in connection with a matter in relation to which he has failed to comply; (*g*) may specify circumstances in which solicitors are exempt from the rules; (*h*) may empower the Council to take such steps as they consider necessary or expedient to ascertain whether or not the rules are being complied with; and (*i*) may contain incidental, procedural or supple-

H   mentary provisions."

Section 37 (4) of the Act provides:

"If any solicitor fails to comply with indemnity rules, any person may make a complaint in respect of that failure to the tribunal."

"The tribunal" is defined by section 87 of the Act as meaning the Solicitors Disciplinary Tribunal. Section 37 (5) reads:

" The Society shall have power, without prejudice to any of its other　A
powers, to carry into effect any arrangements which it considers
necessary or expedient for the purpose of indemnity under this section."

It is common ground that section 37 (5) of the Act does not itself give
the Council power to make rules, but that its rule-making powers are to be
found in subsections (1), (2) and (3).　A subsidiary argument has been
advanced in the alternative by Mr. Alexander, on behalf of the Law　B
Society, to the effect that the three permissible methods of providing the
indemnity specified by section 37 (2) do not constitute an exhaustive list
of the methods which may be adopted for this purpose when rules come
to be made.　It is submitted that section 37 (2) takes effect without prejudice to the generality of the rule-making power conferred by section
37 (1).　I think it may be convenient to deal at once with this argument,
which I feel unable to accept.　In my judgment this is a case where the　C
maxim " expressio unius est exclusio alterius " applies.

In *Blackburn* v. *Flavelle* (1881) 6 App.Cas. 628, 634 the Privy Council
approved the following exposition of the principle contained in the judgment of Hargrave J. in *Drinkwater* v. *Arthur* (1871) 10 S.C.R. (N.S.W.)
193:

" ' If there be any one rule of law clearer than another as to the　D
construction of all statutes and all written instruments (as, for example,
sales under powers in deeds and wills) it is this: that where the
legislature or the parties to any instrument have expressly authorised
one or more particular modes of sale or other dealing with property,
such expressions always exclude any other mode, except as specifically
authorised."

　　　　　　　　　　　　　　　　　　　　　　　　　　　　　　　E

As is illustrated by the decision of the Privy Council in *Canadian
National Railways* v. *Canada Steamship Lines Ltd.* [1945] A.C. 204, 211,
the maxim is not one to be applied invariably and regardless of the context.
Nevertheless in the particular context of section 37 (2) of the Act, I think
it reasonably clear that it should be applied, particularly for the following
reasons.　First, as I have already said, the general approach of the court　F
should in my judgment be to construe the rule-making power conferred on
the Council restrictively rather than otherwise.　It seems inherently
improbable that the legislature should have intended to give the Council
carte blanche in selecting methods of providing for the indemnity, subject
only to obtaining the approval of the Master of the Rolls.　Secondly, the
wording of section 37 (2) of the Act, following the same pattern as section
37 (3), could easily have provided that subsection (2) should operate " with-　G
out prejudice to the generality of subsection (1)."　Significantly, subsection
(2) is prefaced with no such provision.　I can see no sufficient ground for
concluding that the list contained in subsection (2) is anything but exhaustive in relation to the permitted methods of providing the indemnity.

There are, however, certain points of construction which are, I think,
common ground in relation to subsection (2) of section 37 of the Act.　H

First, under subsection (2) (*a*), rules could be made authorising the
Law Society to establish and maintain its own indemnity insurance fund.
Furthermore, by virtue of subsection (3) (*b*), rules could require solicitors
or any class of solicitors to make payments to any such fund.

Secondly, under subsection (2) (*c*), rules could be made requiring
solicitors or any specified class of solicitors to take out and maintain their
own insurance with " authorised insurers," as defined by the Act.

A Furthermore, by virtue of subsection (3) (*d*), rules could prescribe the conditions which an insurance policy must satisfy for this purpose.

Thirdly, however, as counsel on its behalf expressly conceded, it would not be open to the Law Society, in reliance on subsections (2) (*c*) and (3) (*d*), to make rules requiring solicitors to take out and maintain insurance with *specified* insurers nominated in the rules. In other words, if rules

B follow the route envisaged by subsections (2) (*c*) and (3) (*d*), the solicitors affected are to be left at liberty to effect insurance with insurers of their own choice, provided only that they are " authorised insurers " as defined by the Act and any conditions prescribed by the rules, as being conditions which a policy must satisfy, are fully complied with.

The present dispute as to the construction of the Act substantially concerns the meaning and effect of subsections (2) (*b*) and (3) (*c*) of section

C 37. What has happened is that the Law Society has made or purported to make rules providing for an indemnity scheme, but these rules, as is common ground, do not on any footing fall within the authority conferred on it by subsection (2) (*a*) or (*c*). It has been submitted as a subsidiary argument on behalf of the Law Society that, quite apart from subsection (2), the general rule-making power conferred by subsection (1) was wide

D enough to authorise the making of these rules. I reject this argument, however, because, for reasons already stated, I think that the alternative methods of providing for the indemnity, which are specified in subsection (2), are exhaustive. It follows that if the rules are to be valid, they must be shown to fall within the authority conferred by subsection (2) (*b*), read in conjunction with subsection (3) (*c*). After this introduction I now turn to the rules themselves.

E On December 12, 1975, the Council of the Law Society, in purported exercise of the authority conferred on it by section 37 of the Act and with the previous concurrence of the Master of the Rolls, made what were named, by rule 1, " the Solicitors' Indemnity Rules 1975." Rule 1 provided that the rules should come into operation immediately, except rule 3, which should come into operation on September 1, 1976. Rules

F 2 and 3 provided:

> " 2. The Society is hereby authorised to take out and maintain with authorised insurers a master policy in the form set out in the Schedule hereto and to arrange for the issue to solicitors to whom these rules apply of certificates of insurance in the form there set out. The provisions of the said master policy and certificate of insurance shall be deemed to form part of these rules. 3. Every

G solicitor to whom these rules apply shall pay the premiums payable by him under the said master policy and certificate of insurance as soon as they fall due and shall comply with such of the provisions of the said master policy and certificate of insurance as apply to him."

H Rule 4 (1) provided that the rules applied to every solicitor " who is, or is held out to the public as, a principal in private practice in England and Wales; . . ." Rule 5 conferred on the Council " power in any case or class of case to waive in writing any of the provisions of these rules and to revoke any such waiver." I need not read the other provisions of the rules themselves.

They were, however, accompanied by explanatory notes. Two of these explanatory notes, though not forming part of the rules, are worth reading

as helping to explain the mechanics of the scheme as envisaged by the   A
Council. The note to rules 1 and 2 explained:

"1. & 2. The master policy referred to in rule 2 is to be taken out
immediately to enable solicitors to whom the rules apply to become
insured under it on a voluntary basis as soon as their current insurance
expires. It will not, however, be compulsory for them to be insured
under the master policy until September 1, 1976, and accordingly   B
rule 3 does not come into operation until that date. Thereafter every
solicitor to whom the rules apply will be required to produce evidence
of compliance with them on applying for a practising certificate."

The note to rule 3 explained:

"3. The amount of indemnity provided under the master policy is the
minimum which must be held by every solicitor to whom the rules   C
apply. That amount will not necessarily reflect what each individual
solicitor and firm as a matter of prudence should consider to be the
amount of indemnity appropriate to their case, in the light of their
commitment."

In the event, since September 1, 1976, the Law Society has regarded
the scheme as having become compulsory and has required every solicitor   D
to whom the rules apply to produce a certificate of insurance on applying
annually for a practising certificate.

On a very first reading, the authority given by rule 2 to the Law Society
to take out and maintain with authorised insurers a master policy would
appear to fall fairly and squarely within the wording of section 37 (2) (b)
of the Act. The provision in rule 3 requiring solicitors to make payments
by way of premium under the master policy would similarly, at first sight,   E
appear to fall fairly and squarely within the wording of section 37 (3) (c).
The position, however, is not as simple as that, if only because the provisions of the proposed master policy and certificate of insurance set out in
the Schedule to the rules are, as is expressly stated, deemed to form part
of them.

I therefore turn to examine first the terms of the proposed master policy   F
scheduled to the rules of 1975. Clause 1 provided:

"The insurers agree with the Law Society on behalf of all solicitors
from time to time required to be insured by indemnity rules made
under section 37 of the Solicitors Act 1974, and on behalf of former
solicitors, to provide such insurance in accordance with the terms of
the certificate attached hereto. Subject as hereinafter appears in respect   G
of former solicitors, such certificate will be issued annually on request
on receipt of the premium payable in accordance with clauses 2 and
3 hereof."

Clause 2 provided:

"This policy commences on December 12, 1975, and shall be extended on September 1, 1976, and September 1, 1977, for a further   H
12 months' period in each case. At each extension date the rates of
premium payable in respect of the year next following shall be the
annual rates of premium applicable in respect of the immediately
preceding period as increased by 12½ per cent., or by 75 per cent. of
the percentage increase in the official retail price index during the
previous year to May 31, whichever percentage shall be the greater.
This policy can be extended subsequently for successive periods of one

A   year on each September 1 subject to the rates of premium for each renewal being agreed by the insurers and the Law Society at least 12 months before such renewal. In the event of any failure so to agree such rates of renewal premium all cover under this policy shall cease on the expiry of the period for which the policy was last extended."

Clause 3 (a) provided:

B   "In respect of the period of insurance prior to September 1, 1976, the premium payable hereunder shall be pro rata to the annual premium of £387·50 per sole practitioner and £310 per partner. For the period of insurance commencing on September 1, 1976, and subsequent periods of insurance the premiums for solicitors who are first required to be insured hereunder during the period of insurance shall

C   be calculated pro rata to the premiums which applied at the beginning of the relevant period of insurance."

(By way of parenthesis, I mention that the equivalent rates of premium agreed between the insurers and the Law Society since the scheme became compulsory on September 1, 1976, were for the year ending August 31, 1977, £435 and £348; and for the year ending August 31, 1978, £490 and

D   £392.)

Clause 3 (b) set out a scale in accordance with which the premiums for part-time sole practitioners would be calculated.

Clause 4 provided that all claims and notices required to be given to the assured under the terms of the attached certificate should be notified to London Insurance Brokers Ltd. on behalf of the insurers. The last-mentioned company was defined by clause 4 as "the brokers." For

E   brevity I shall from time to time refer to it as "L.I.B." Clause 4 also contained a number of provisions in accordance with which L.I.B. was to handle claims. I need only read clause 4 (e):

"In handling claims and potential claims against the assured, the brokers shall act as agents for the assured and, subject to such disclosure as may be necessary to the insurers or as required by them in

F   accordance with the terms of this policy and the attached certificate, shall be under a duty of confidence to the assured; and in particular neither the brokers nor the insurers shall disclose information about any individual or firm to the Law Society without his or their consent."

L.I.B. were thus to act as sole brokers under the scheme, a point which will have some significance in the context of commission.

G   Of the remaining four clauses of the proposed master policy scheduled to the rules of 1975, I need only read clauses 6 and 7:

"6. Authority is hereby given by the insurers to the brokers to issue on behalf of the insurers to solicitors seeking insurance in accordance with clause 1 hereof certificates in the form attached hereto. 7. Expressions used in this policy have the meanings given to them by the

H   certificate attached hereto."

I pause to make a few observations in relation to this form of proposed master policy, and in particular clause 1 thereof, which is of crucial importance in the present case. The phrase:

"... on behalf of all solicitors from time to time required to be insured by indemnity rules made under section 37 of the Solicitors Act 1974, and on behalf of former solicitors ..."

1344

appearing in that clause makes it clear that the Law Society would not be A entering into the agreement on its own behalf and for its own benefit. There have been suggestions on both sides in the present case that the Law Society would be entering into it as *agent* on behalf of the persons from time to time falling into the two categories. A large number of such persons, however, would not be ascertained or capable of ascertainment at the date when the master policy would be effected. As I understand the law, if a contract is to be concluded effectively by a principal as agent B for another party, that party must be both in existence and ascertainable (even if not actually ascertained) at the date of the contract. If he is not in existence and ascertainable at that date the supposed principal cannot even subsequently ratify it: see *Halsbury's Laws of England*, 4th ed., vol. 1 (1973), pp. 454–456, paras. 760 and 761.

A similar restriction, however, does not apply where a person enters C into a contract with another on the footing that he is to hold the benefit of the contract as *trustee* for third parties. The third parties are then beneficiaries under the trust created by the contract and may be entitled to enforce this trust, even though they were unascertained at the date of the contract (see *Halsbury's Laws of England*, 4th ed., vol. 16 (1976), pp. 901, 902, para. 1341, and the cases there cited). In my judgment it is reasonably clear that the effect of the phrase which I have quoted D from clause 1 of the draft master policy is this: on its true construction it indicates the intention of the makers of the rules that the Law Society should enter into the agreement of insurance as *trustees* for the persons, ascertained and unascertained, referred to in that clause, the purpose of the provision being to entitle such persons, as beneficiaries under the trust, to require the insurers to provide them with insurance in accord- E ance with the terms of the proposed certificate, on paying the specified premium.

The form of proposed certificate of insurance scheduled to the rules of 1975 began with the following words:

> " This is to certify that in accordance with the authorisation granted to the undersigned under the master policy referred to in the schedule F by the insurers subscribing such master policy (hereinafter called ' the insurers ') insurance is granted by the insurers in accordance with the terms and conditions following, and in consideration of the payment of the premium stated in the schedule."

There then followed a series of definitions. They included definitions of " the solicitor " as meaning the person named as such in the schedule, G and " the period of insurance " as the period specified in the schedule. " The assured " was defined as meaning:

> " the solicitor, any person employed in connection with the practice (including any articled clerk, and any solicitor who is a consultant or associate in the firm), and the estate and/or the legal representatives of any of the foregoing, to the intent that each of the foregoing shall H be severally insured hereunder."

The expressions " the practice," " the firm " and " partner " were also defined.

Clause 2 (*a*) of the proposed certificate provided that, on the terms and conditions therein contained, the insurers should indemnify the assured against all loss to the assured wheresoever occurring arising from any claim or claims first made against the assured or the firm during the

A period of insurance, in respect of any description of civil liability whatsoever incurred in connection with the practice. This general provision
was followed by a restriction on liability set out in clause 2 (b), which
provided that the liability of the insurers under the certificate and any
other certificate issued under the master policy should not exceed in
respect of each such claim and claimant's costs the sum insured specified
in the schedule, and in addition certain costs and expenses.

B   Clause 3 contained a number of special conditions. Sub-clause (c)
provided (inter alia) that if on the " relevant date " the solicitor was
practising in partnership with one or more solicitors, the schedule should
be deemed to specify as the sum insured in respect of that claim an
amount of £30,000 multiplied by the number in partnership on the
relevant date or on September 1, preceding that date, whichever number

C was greatest. For this purpose the number by which the amount of
£30,000 fell to be multiplied was called " the multiplier." " The relevant
date " was defined substantially as meaning the date when the claim was
first made against the assured or the date, if earlier, when circumstances,
which might give rise thereto, first came to the notice of the solicitor
or of any partners of his.

D   Clause 4 of the proposed certificate contained a number of general
conditions. Sub-clause (d) provided that notices to the insurers to be
given thereunder should be deemed to be properly made if given to L.I.B.
      Clause 5 of the certificate contained a number of general exclusions,
of which sub-clause (a) read as follows:

      " This insurance shall not indemnify the assured in respect of
      the first £250 of any one claim or (in the case of any claim to
E   which special condition (c) applies) the first £250 multiplied by the
      multiplier."

Finally, the form of certificate contained a schedule in the following
form, with a number of blanks left to be completed:

" SCHEDULE

F Certificate No.:   Master Policy No.:
   1. The solicitor:
   2. Address(es) at which the Solicitor practises:
   3. Period of Insurance:
   4. Sum Insured: £50,000 each claim (Sole practitioner)
                     £30,000 each claim (Partner)—see Special
G   Condition 3 (c)
   5. Premium:

      The schedule thus contemplated that, with the exception of item 4,
each item would be completed as appropriate in the individual case.
      Thus the pattern of the form of master policy and certificate of
insurance scheduled to the rules of 1975 was, in my judgment, this.
H The Law Society was to enter into a contract with the insurers on the
terms of the master policy, on the footing that it would hold the benefit
of the contract as trustee for the persons referred to in clause 1 of the
master policy, and that the contract would entitle such persons, as
beneficiaries under the trust, on paying the designated premium, to
require the insurers to issue them a policy on the terms specified in
the certificate of insurance. By virtue of clause 6 of the master policy,
L.I.B. would possess authority from the insurers to issue, on their behalf,

The Weekly Law Reports, November 14, 1980

Slade J.   Swain v. Law Society (Ch.D.)   [1980]

such a certificate to any solicitor seeking insurance in accordance with A
clause 1 of the master policy. Whenever an individual solicitor should
pay to the insurers through L.I.B. the appropriate premium and receive
his certificate of insurance, a further contract would come into being
between him and the insurers, quite separate from that between them and
the Law Society.

In due course, in or about early 1978, the terms of the master policy
and certificate of insurance were renegotiated, in respect of the ensuing B
year beginning on September 1, 1978.

On July 7, 1978, the Council of the Law Society, with the concurrence
of the Master of the Rolls, made the Solicitors' Indemnity Rules 1978,
which were expressed, by rule 1, to come into operation on September 1,
1978, and were designed to incorporate these renegotiated terms. Rules
2 and 3 provided: C

"2. The Solicitors' Indemnity Rules 1975 shall remain in full force
and effect save that the forms of master policy and certificate of
insurance set out in the schedule hereto shall be substituted for
those set out in the schedule to those rules and shall be deemed to
be the forms of master policy and certificate of insurance referred
to in rule 2 of those rules. 3. In all other respects the Solicitors'
Indemnity Rules 1975 are confirmed."   D

The form of master policy scheduled to the rules of 1978 was similar,
though not identical, to the form scheduled to the rules of 1975. I
need only refer to two differences. The policy was expressed to commence
on September 1, 1978. The premiums payable under it were substantially increased, to £658 per solicitor per annum, but for any solicitor
practising within the Inner London area the annual premium was to be   E
£888. The form of certificate scheduled to the rules of 1978 was similar,
though not identical, to the form scheduled to the rules of 1975. One
variation included the substitution of the figure of £400 for the figure
£250 in condition 5 (a).

On July 27, 1979, the Council of the Law Society, with the concurrence of the Master of the Rolls, made the Solicitors' Indemnity F
Rules 1979, which were expressed by rule 1 to come into operation on
September 1, 1979. Their purpose was simply to incorporate the renegotiated terms of the master policy and certificate of insurance, coming
into effect on September 1, 1979. They followed mutatis mutandis the
form of the rules of 1978. The annual premiums were increased to
£926 for those practising in Inner London and to £712 for other solicitors. G

It is common ground that there are no differences between the
respective provisions of the rules of 1975, the rules of 1978 and the rules
of 1979, or the forms respectively scheduled thereto, which are material
for the purpose of the question of construction, which the court has to
decide in relation to the Act and those rules. Accordingly any references
hereafter to "the rules," "the master policy" or "the certificate" are,
save where the context otherwise requires, equally applicable to any one H
of the three sets of rules, master policy and certificate.

A large volume of evidence has been filed on both sides, dealing with
alleged merits or demerits of the present indemnity scheme. These are
clearly matters on which opinions inside the solicitors' branch of the
legal profession can and do greatly vary. This is indicated by the fact
that a poll conducted by the Law Society in November 1975 among
solicitors holding current practising certificates resulted in 10,531 votes

A being cast in favour of the scheme and 7,455 against it. It is understandable that the plaintiffs should have wished to point out what they consider to be a number of disadvantages or anomalies involved in it. I have no doubt that they genuinely consider that, given freedom of choice, they could obtain for themselves better cover from insurance companies of good reputation at a smaller premium than is being charged by the insurers with whom the Law Society has made its arrangements. It

B is equally understandable that the Law Society should have wished to answer such evidence by pointing out anticipated benefits from a group scheme of this kind.

However, I think it neither necessary nor appropriate to enter into the debate or to attempt any evaluation of the merits of the scheme in this judgment, which relates to bare questions of law. The court, in

C construing the Act and the rules, must have regard to any admissible evidence as to surrounding circumstances. In carrying out the process of construction, it is, I think, also entitled to have regard to any self-evident consequences of any particular interpretation. In my judgment, however, for present purposes, it is wholly irrelevant that another kind of scheme might have been either better or worse than that provided for by the rules and the schedules which form part of them.

D Though a number of supporting submissions have been put forward on behalf of the plaintiffs, their challenge to the validity of the rules, as advanced by Mr. Lewis, rests, I think, principally on the following propositions, though I do not reproduce them verbatim from his argument.

(1) Section 37 (2) of the Act contains an exhaustive list of the methods by which indemnity rules may provide for the indemnity required

E to support an indemnity scheme. I have already indicated that I accept this proposition.

(2) Section 37 (2) (*a*) is irrelevant for present purposes. So is section 37 (2) (*c*), because, while this subsection, read in conjunction with section 37 (3) (*d*), empowers the Law Society to make rules requiring solicitors or any class of solicitors to take out and maintain insurance with any " authorised insurers," as defined by section 87 of the Act, on conditions

F prescribed in the rules, section 37 (2) (*c*) does not authorise the making of rules which require insurance to be effected with a *specified* insurer. As I have already indicated, this proposition, unlike the first, is common ground and I accept it.

(3) The Law Society can therefore support the rules as having been made intra vires if, but only if, it can show that they fall within the

G authority given to the Council by section 37 (2) (*b*) and (3) (*c*) of the Act. I accept this proposition.

(4) However, it is submitted, the only authority conferred on the Council of the Law Society by section 37 (2) (*b*) is an authority to make rules authorising or requiring the Law Society to take out and maintain insurance *for itself and on its own behalf*. The subsection does not empower the Council to make rules enabling the Law Society to

H take out and maintain insurance *as agent or trustee for other persons*. If the existing rules and Schedules or any part thereof purport to provide for the " taking out and maintenance " of insurance by the Law Society at all, within the meaning of section 37 (2) (*b*) (which is not admitted), such insurance is not to be effected by the Law Society on its own behalf, but as purported agent or trustee for the individual solicitors concerned. On this ground alone, it is submitted, the rules are ultra vires.

(5) Further or alternatively, it is submitted, the rules are ultra vires,

because they cannot on any footing be said to authorise or require the A
Law Society to "take out and maintain" insurance. The so-called
master policy referred to in the rules, so it is said, would not in truth be
a policy of insurance at all. It would at most represent an undertaking
by the insurers to provide insurance on certain terms, to those solicitors
who paid the premiums. Since the Law Society would have given no
consideration for this undertaking, so it is submitted, it would not be in
a position to enforce it. B

(6) The general effect of the rules, it is submitted, is to do the very
thing which section 37 (2) (c) contemplates shall not be done, namely, to
require solicitors to take out and maintain insurance on prescribed terms
with *specified* insurers of the Law Society's choice, as opposed to any
authorised insurers of their own choice.

I hope and believe that these six propositions fairly embody the C
substance (though not the form) of Mr. Lewis's principal arguments on
question 1 raised by this summons.

Having already dealt with the first three propositions, I shall now
proceed to consider the fourth. It is common ground that the rules and
schedules do not provide for the taking out and maintenance by the Law
Society of insurance *on its own behalf.* The argument on this proposition has therefore centred round the question: is the wording of section D
37 (2) (b) wide enough to permit the making by the Council of rules
which authorise the Law Society to make contractual arrangements for
insurance indemnity against loss of the nature referred to in the section,
not on its own behalf, but on behalf of those solicitors from time to time
required to be insured by rules under the Act and on behalf of former
solicitors? E

Mr. Lewis submitted that the answer to this question must be " No."
As he pointed out, section 37 (2) (b) does not in specific terms provide
that indemnity rules may empower the Law Society to effect and maintain insurance on behalf of other persons. Such a power of insurance,
he observed, would enable it to create a monopoly of insurance in restraint of trade in regard to the solicitors affected. In these circumstances,
he submitted, only the plainest words or inevitable implication would F
justify the interpretation of the subsection as authorising the conferring
of such power. No such inevitable implication, he suggested, arises
here. On the contrary, it was said, section 37 (2) (c) gives a strong indication that the legislature never contemplated that, through the introduction of rules, solicitors should ever find themselves bound to a
particular insurer or insurers selected by the Law Society.

If it be right that section 37 (2) (b) only contemplates the effecting G
and maintenance of insurance by the Law Society on its own behalf, it
is relevant to consider what are the circumstances that the legislature
may be deemed to have had in mind, in which the Law Society might
wish to take out insurance on its own behalf for the purpose of implementing an indemnity insurance scheme. Mr. Lewis suggested two
such circumstances. First, the Law Society might establish its own fund H
for the purpose of meeting claims, as envisaged by section 37 (2) (a).
In this event, it would or might wish to effect insurance on its own
behalf, to protect the fund against the risk of exhaustion by large or
numerous claims and to make sure that it could at all times meet its
commitments. Secondly, the Law Society, without establishing a fund,
might decide that the appropriate course was to give an undertaking to
solicitors to indemnify them against loss. In this event, again it would or

A might wish to take out insurance to protect itself against its own potential liability. These, the plaintiffs submitted, were the two contingencies which the legislature must be deemed to have contemplated in enacting section 37 (2) (b) of the Act; I do not think that any other contingencies were suggested.

A subsidiary argument advanced by Mr. Alexander, on behalf of the Law Society, in opposition to these contentions, was to the effect that,
B even in the two contingencies mentioned, the Law Society would have no insurable interest, within the meaning of the Life Assurance Act 1774, entitling it to take out insurance on its own behalf. I do not, however, need to consider this argument or the submissions advanced by Mr. Lewis in opposition to it, because I am satisfied that there are other more powerful reasons which compel a much broader construction of section 37
C (2) (b) than the plaintiffs attribute to this subsection.

First, the rules which section 37 authorises the Council to make are described by section 37 (1) as rules " concerning indemnity against loss arising from claims " of the nature referred to in the section. As I have already said, the " loss " referred to in this context is loss suffered by solicitors. Prima facie, therefore, I would expect that the insurance envisaged by section 37 (2) (b) would be insurance against loss of the
D nature referred to in the preceding subsection, that is to say, insurance against loss suffered *by solicitors,* not loss suffered by the Law Society.

Secondly, the plaintiffs' argument on the construction of section 37 (2) (b) appears to me to attach inadequate weight to the wording of section 37 (3) (c), which provides that rules may require solicitors to make payments by way of premium on any insurance policy maintained
E by the Society by virtue of subsection (2) (b). I accept that, as Mr. Lewis pointed out, it is a perfectly possible arrangement for X to make payments by way of premium on an insurance policy which is being maintained by Y on Y's own behalf. Nevertheless it seems to me quite unrealistic to suppose that the legislature, in including section 37 (3) (c), was directing its mind to a policy maintained by the Law Society on its
F own behalf. Let it be supposed that the Law Society had either established its own fund or had agreed to indemnify solicitors in the manner suggested by Mr. Lewis. Let it further be supposed that it then wished to insure itself against the commitments which it had thus assumed. It is to my mind inconceivable that it would think it convenient or appropriate to leave the premiums required to maintain a policy of this nature, taken out for its own protection, to be actually paid not by itself, but pro
G rata by the thousands or tens of thousands of individual solicitors concerned. The situation, however, would be quite different, if the insurance were to be arranged by the Law Society simply on behalf of such individual solicitors. In this case there would be nothing in the least inconvenient or inappropriate in leaving each solicitor to pay the premiums applicable to himself. Thus in my judgment the wording of section
H 37 (3) (c) strongly suggests that the type of policy at least primarily (if not solely) envisaged by that subsection is a policy taken out on behalf of solicitors, not on behalf of the Law Society. Correspondingly this wording lends support to the conclusion that a similar type of policy is at least primarily (if not solely) envisaged by section 37 (2) (b).

Thirdly, the argument based on the alleged presumption that the legislature would not have intended to confer on the Law Society the power to create a monopoly of professional indemnity insurance is in my

judgment fallacious. According to the plaintiffs' own submissions, rules   A
could be made empowering the Law Society first to establish its own
indemnity fund, secondly to insure that fund for its own benefit with one
set of insurers of its own choice, and thirdly to require solicitors to pay
the premiums on such insurance. In this event individual solicitors, when
being called on to pay such premiums, would have had no opportunity
whatever to choose their own insurers, so that in this sense a monopoly
of insurance would once again have been arranged by the Law Society.   B
Accordingly the monopoly argument affords no good reason for construing section 37 (2) (*b*) as not referring to the taking out and maintenance by the Law Society of insurance on behalf of solicitors.

Fourthly, I think that common sense suggests that this is the method of
providing the indemnity which the legislature must have had primarily in
mind in enacting section 37 (2) (*b*). It seems to me that three obvious   C
possible alternative routes would have been likely to spring to the mind
of anyone considering methods of providing for a compulsory insurance
scheme for solicitors. The first route would have involved the establishment and maintenance by the Law Society of its own fund, to be financed
by contributions to the fund from solicitors. This route was duly provided for by section 37 (2) (*a*) and (3) (*b*) of the Act. The second route
would have involved a direction to solicitors to take out and maintain   D
insurance on prescribed conditions with authorised insurers. This route
was duly provided for by section 37 (2) (*c*) and (3) (*d*) of the Act. The
third route would have involved the Law Society first itself making group
arrangements with insurers under which the insurers bound themselves
to grant insurance on agreed terms and in an agreed form to individual
solicitors who paid a specified premium and subsequently requiring   E
solicitors to take up the insurance rights thus arranged for them. If
the legislature had omitted to provide for the third route, it would
indeed have been a strange omission. I do not think it did. The route
was in my judgment provided for by section 37 (2) (*b*) and (3) (*c*).

For all these reasons, I conclude that section 37 (2) (*b*) on its true
construction does empower the Council to make rules authorising or
requiring the Law Society to take out and maintain insurance with   F
authorised insurers on behalf of solicitors, on the footing that it is to be
a trustee of the benefit of the contract for the solicitors affected. I
do not think it necessary to decide the further question whether the
subsection would also permit the making of rules enabling the Law
Society to effect insurance on its own behalf. I am inclined to think that
the subsection is not directed to this kind of insurance at all. The Law   G
Society in any event, I understand, has power under its own charter to
insure itself. Furthermore, if it contemplated establishing its own fund
and wished to be given specific power to insure itself in relation to that
fund, such power could no doubt be conferred under section 37 (3) (*i*)
of the Act, under which indemnity rules may contain " incidental, procedural or supplementary provisions." Further or alternatively it would   H
appear to me that section 37 (5) would be wide enough, even in the
absence of any specific rule to this effect, to empower the Law Society
to insure itself in relation to any such fund. However, I leave open this
further point arising on section 37 (2) (*b*), which requires no decision.

I now turn to what I have described as the fifth of the principal propositions put forward on behalf of the plaintiffs. It is clear that, if a
rule is to be justified as falling within the authority given to the Council

A   by section 37 (2) (*b*), it must at very least authorise or require the Law Society to " take out and maintain insurance . . ." The points taken against the Law Society in this context substantially resolve themselves to these. Though the rules in terms authorise the Law Society to take out and maintain with authorised insurers a master policy, the proposed master policy, even if issued by the insurers in the form contemplated, would not, it is suggested, in truth involve the " taking out " of any insurance by

B   the Law Society within the meaning of section 37 (2) (*b*). The taking out of insurance, it is said, necessarily presupposes the existence of enforceable contractual arrangements between the grantor and grantee of the policy in question. Here, it is suggested, the documentation scheduled to the rules envisages no enforceable contractual arrangements between the insurers and the Law Society. The form of master policy

C   even if issued, it is submitted, would constitute at most an undertaking given by the insurers to the Law Society to provide insurance on specified terms to solicitors who paid the appropriate premium. It is submitted that such undertaking could not be enforced by the Law Society, because it would have given no consideration for it.

It is a fact that the form of master policy, like most other insurance policies, in terms imposes obligations solely on the insurers; in terms it

D   imposes none on the Law Society. Nevertheless it seems to me an inevitable inference from the forms of the documents scheduled to the rules that the insurers will have agreed to provide the specified insurance, and will have quoted the rates of premiums payable, on the basis that, during the currency of the master policy, the Law Society will for its part require all solicitors from time to time required to be insured by rules made

E   under section 37 of the Act to effect their insurance with those insurers. The following features to be found in the documentation lead me to this conclusion:

(i) By clause 1 of the master policy, the agreement on the part of the insurers is expressed to be made with the Law Society " on behalf of all solicitors from time to time required to be insured by indemnity rules made under section 37 of the Solicitors Act 1974, and on behalf of

F   former solicitors . . ."

(ii) The master policy makes express reference to the rules and the rules themselves provide that they apply to every solicitor who is or is held out to the public as a principal in private practice in England and Wales. True it is that the rules empower the Council in any case or class of case to waive in writing any of the provisions of the rules; but if the

G   rules are waived in such manner as to exempt a particular solicitor from the requirement to be insured, which is imposed by the rules, such solicitor no longer falls within the ambit of clause 1 of the master policy, so that the insurers have no legitimate ground of complaint. In this respect, as in other respects, the rules themselves and the form of master policy tally with one another.

H   (iii) The rules themselves further provide that every solicitor to whom the rules apply shall pay the premiums payable by him under the master policy and certificate of insurance, as soon as they fall due.

(iv) The rules, as the insurers must be well aware, are made in exercise of an authority conferred by the Act, section 10 of which obliges the Law Society to grant to a solicitor a practising certificate only if it is satisfied that he is complying with the rules or is exempt from them.

Against this background, it seems to me that, from the form of docu-

mentation annexed to the rules, when read with the rules, the inevitable
inference is that the Law Society for its part is implicitly undertaking
with the insurers to enforce the rules during the currency of the master
policy, so as to procure that all solicitors, who are from time to time
required by the rules to be insured, will be insured with those insurers.
It follows that in my judgment the rules and the documentation scheduled
to them envisage that the Law Society will have given consideration for
the agreement on the part of the insurers set out in clause 1 of the master
policy and that the proposed master policy will thus involve mutually
enforceable contractual arrangements.

In my judgment the Law Society can properly be said to " take out
and maintain insurance with authorised insurers," within the meaning
of section 37 (2) (*b*) of the Act, if it enters into contractual arrangements
under which " authorised insurers " agree to provide insurance cover for
solicitors, on specified terms and on the payment by the solicitors of
specified premiums, and if the Law Society subsequently procures that
such premiums are paid. It follows that I must reject what I have
described as the fifth proposition put forward on behalf of the plaintiffs.

Finally in this context, I must deal shortly with their sixth proposition.
I have already accepted that section 37 (2) (*c*) does not contemplate
insurance on prescribed terms to be taken out with specified insurers.
However, to conclude from this that section 37 (2) (*b*) likewise does not
so contemplate seems to me to involve a non sequitur. For practical
purposes, quite different considerations will apply to a group insurance
scheme from those which apply to a system such as is envisaged by
section 37 (2) (*c*). In the case of a system of the latter nature, requiring
solicitors to effect their own insurance on prescribed conditions, but without the protection of any group scheme arranged and maintained by
the Law Society, it would perhaps seem only reasonable that solicitors
should be left free to select their own insurers, provided only that such
insurers fall within the definition of " authorised insurers " and are
prepared to offer insurance on the prescribed conditions. If, however,
a group scheme has been arranged by the Law Society, the commercial
need to preserve such individual freedom of choice is far less compelling
and indeed is likely to be incompatible with the very existence of a
group scheme. The kind of indemnity scheme envisaged by section
37 (2) (*a*) manifestly would not confer the freedom of choice to which
the plaintiffs attach such importance. Likewise, even if the construction
which the plaintiffs themselves place on section 37 (2) (*b*) be the correct
one, a scheme constituted thereunder would not be likely to confer such
freedom. In these circumstances I think there is no substance in the
plaintiffs' sixth proposition.

For all these reasons I conclude that this challenge to the validity of
the rules must fail. Paragraph 1 of the amended originating summons
seeks a declaration:

> " upon the true construction of section 37 of the above-mentioned
> Act and of the rules hereinafter mentioned the Council of the Law
> Society had no power to make all or any of the Solicitors' Indemnity
> Rules 1975, the Solicitors' Indemnity Rules 1978 and the Solicitors'
> Indemnity Rules 1979 and the said rules are accordingly null and
> void."

I must decline to make any such declaration. Since the plaintiffs do not
purport to bring these proceedings in any representative capacity, I do

A not propose to make a declaration in the contrary sense, though I will in due course hear counsel on this point.

Commission

Paragraph 2 of the originating summons asks the question:

B " whether upon the true construction of the said Act and rules and in the events which have happened the Law Society is entitled to retain for its own purposes the commission received by it from London Insurance Brokers Limited in respect of premiums paid by individual solicitors pursuant to the said scheme or whether it is accountable for the same to such individual solicitors or otherwise."

C For the purpose of dealing with this question, unlike the first question, it is necessary to consider the manner in which the rules were actually implemented and the arrangements which were made in regard to the commission. Though the originating summons refers to the commission in question as having been received by the Law Society, the evidence shows that it has in fact been received by the Law Society's wholly-owned company, The Law Society Services Ltd., which I will call " L.S.S.". This company was established several years ago. Through D it the Law Society conducts its various trading activities, the receipt of commissions being one such activity.

By an agreement dated February 6, 1975, the Law Society and L.S.S. had appointed L.I.B. as insurance brokers to L.S.S. and to operate the Law Society's then existing insurance advisory service, on terms (inter alia) that, in the event of the introduction of a compulsory professional E indemnity insurance scheme for solicitors, the provisions of this agreement could be renegotiated at the request of any party.

After the Council of the Law Society had decided to adopt proposals for the introduction of a compulsory scheme by way of a single master policy, taken out by the Society, debate in the profession was encouraged. Two circulars were issued by the Council in May 1975. One of them (part of exhibit " DAM 3 ") summarised in question-and-F answer form the main features of the proposed scheme. It included the question: " what arrangements are proposed under the scheme for commission on premiums? " The answer given was as follows:

" The brokers to the scheme (L.I.B.) will be remunerated on the usual commission basis from which they will meet the major cost of operating the scheme and handling claims. Hitherto the Society, G through the insurance advisory service, has received a share of the brokers' commission and as regards solicitors' professional indemnity business this amounted to approximately £46,000 gross in 1974 (the equivalent of nearly £2 on a practising certificate fee). The existing arrangements with L.I.B. require the Society to provide premises and defray certain quite substantial costs in relation to staff. Under the scheme it is likely that if the existing arrangements are con-H tinued the commission income to the Society will be of the order of £250,000 per annum gross. The benefit of the net excess receipts will inure for the profession as a whole, but, subject to taxation and other important considerations, the Council will consider whether the surplus can be appropriately earmarked for possible future improvements in the scheme. The surplus, however it is generally applied, will correspondingly reduce future calls upon the practising members of the profession."

In October 1975, the President of the Law Society sent to all solicitors A
with practising certificates a letter (part of exhibit " DAM 3 ") setting
out the Council's arguments in favour of the master policy scheme as
recommended by it and enclosing a voting card asking for a " Yes " or
" No " answer to the question whether the recipient was in favour of the
scheme. This letter contained the following paragraph:

> " Although individual solicitors will no longer receive the benefit
> of commission, it will be payable by the insurers, and the Law Society B
> will receive a share after operating expenses have been deducted.
> This will enure for the benefit of the profession, thus mitigating
> future increases in the practising certificate fee."

The result of the vote was published in " The Law Society's Gazette "
in November 1975 and, as I have said, showed a majority in favour of
the scheme. The Law Society, according to the affidavit evidence of C
Mr. D. A. Marshall, its present Vice-President designate, treated this
vote as an endorsement of the proposal that the Law Society should take
the benefit of payments by way of commission as an incident of the
master policy scheme. This proposal had certainly been clearly announced to the profession in the preceding documentation to which I
have referred. D

Normally, as Mr. Marshall states in his first affidavit, professional
indemnity insurance is effected by professional firms, whether solicitors
or otherwise, through an insurance broker, who receives payment by
receipt of brokerage from the insurer with whom the policy is effected.
It made obvious commercial sense that the Law Society, as the price
of permitting L.I.B. to act as sole brokers under the scheme, should E
demand a share of the commission which would otherwise be received
and wholly retained by L.I.B., in respect of premiums paid on policies
effected by solicitors pursuant to the master policy scheme.

On May 11, 1976, a written agreement was entered into between the
Law Society and L.S.S. of the first part, L.I.B. of the second part and
others of the third and fourth parts (" the 1976 agreement "). The
1976 agreement recited (inter alia) the wish of the Law Society and L.S.S. F
to terminate the appointment of L.I.B. as insurance broker to L.S.S.
under the agreement of February 6, 1975, and to enter into a new agreement on the terms thereinafter appearing. The Law Society and L.S.S.
thereby appointed L.I.B. with effect " on and from October 1, 1975 "
as (inter alia) insurance broker to the Law Society for the purposes of the
master policy and insurance broker to L.S.S. in respect of all " solicitors
business," as defined in the agreement, and as managing insurance G
broker of the " service," as therein defined. The 1976 agreement further
provided that L.S.S. should be entitled to a commission in respect of
each year equal to 40 per cent. of the " net brokerage earned by the
service " (as defined therein) up to and including £700,000 and 30 per
cent. of the " net brokerage earned by the service " in excess of £700,000.
This was the broad pattern of the 1976 agreement. I do not think that H
its detailed provisions are material for present purposes.

Mr. Marshall states in an affidavit that, from the outset, it was appreciated by the Law Society that, as all solicitors would be required to pay
premiums for the master policy, benefits received under the agreement with
L.I.B. should demonstrably be applied for the benefit of the profession
as a whole, and not merely of those solicitors who were members of the
Law Society.

A   The consolidated accounts of the Law Society and L.S.S. for the year ended December 31, 1976, show a sum of £412,864 as having been received by L.S.S. under the heading " Insurance Advisory Service—commission receivable." The equivalent figure similarly shown in such accounts for the year ended December 31, 1977, is £365,000. The equivalent figure shown in such accounts for the year ended December 31, 1978, is £670,185, such large increase presumably being principally due to increased rates of premium. The greater part of these sums represented commission in respect of the master policy scheme. The accounts for this most recent year show a sum of £150,000 as set aside for a specific reserve under the heading " professional indemnity insurance." Mr. Marshall explains that this sum has been set aside to be available towards the initial capital of an insurance company, if the profession should wish to adopt an element of self-

C   insurance. His unchallenged evidence is that no part of the commission income received by L.S.S. and attributable to the scheme has been allocated for the sole benefit of members of the Law Society, but that the whole of such income has been allocated for the benefit of the profession as a whole.

Mr. Marshall in his evidence, at least implicitly, suggests that for these reasons, if for no others, the plaintiffs can have no legitimate grounds of complaint in regard to the receipt of these sums by way of commission by

D   the Law Society or by L.S.S. He points out that, but for them, the Law Society would either have been unable to discharge its functions properly or would in fact have raised the income by other means, probably by increasing the cost of a practising certificate. Similar considerations (among others) were urged by the Law Society's counsel.

I see the practical force of submissions along these lines and think

E   they would have been highly relevant if any attack was being made on the integrity of those persons who have been responsible for introducing or administering the Law Society's insurance scheme. No such attack, however, has been made by the plaintiffs. They have not sought in any way to impugn the good faith of these persons or to suggest that full disclosure has not been made to the profession, either of the Law Society's intentions

F   with regard to commission or of its actual receipts and dealings with commission. Their attack on the rights of the Law Society or L.S.S. to retain the share of commission received by it is based not at all on the manner in which the moneys have been dealt with when received, but on quite different grounds, to which I now turn.

The plaintiffs' submissions under this head have been presented on three alternative footings, namely, (1) that the rules are valid and that the Law

G   Society has operated in accordance with them; (2) that the rules are valid, but the Law Society has *not* operated in accordance with them; and (3) that the rules are invalid.

Since I have already decided that the rules have been validly made, the arguments presented on the last of these three footings do not need to be further considered. I think it will be convenient to dispose of the argu-

H   ment presented on the second footing, before reverting to the first, which is in my view by far the more significant.

During the course of Mr. Lewis's opening speech on behalf of the plaintiffs, it became clear (if it had not been made clear before) that one of the reasons why the plaintiffs would be submitting that the Law Society had not operated in accordance with the rules was this. The evidence adduced by the Law Society, it was suggested, did not establish that the insurers had either actually issued to the Law Society any document constituting a master policy or had even contractually bound themselves to A provide insurance on the terms of such a policy.

The submission that no contract existed on the particular facts was in this context based not so much on alleged lack of consideration moving from the Law Society (I have already dealt with this point) as on the alleged absence of any finally agreed arrangements between the parties. The force of this submission, if a good one, would have been that it could hardly be said that the Law Society had " taken out " a master policy in accordance B with the rules, if it had neither received a document issued by the insurers, which could be said to constitute the master policy, nor had the contractual right to require the insurers to provide insurance on the terms of such a policy.

To meet these points, during the course of the hearing, the Law Society put in two further affidavits, both sworn on February 20, 1980, one by C Mr. Marshall and the other by Mr. M. J. Herniman, the managing director of L.I.B. Mr. Marshall and Mr. Herniman were both cross-examined on these affidavits on behalf of the plaintiffs. As a result, there has in the end been a large volume of detailed evidence before the court, describing not only the general practice of Lloyd's with regard to the issue of policies, but also the manner in which the particular arrangements relating to the master policies in the present case were negotiated and implemented. On the basis D of this further evidence, I am satisfied that the suggestion that these arrangements never got beyond the stage of mere negotiation is insupportable in regard to any of the three periods covered by the respective sets of rules. Indeed, as I understood him, Mr. Lewis in his final speech did not seek to persist with this suggestion, his attack then being on a somewhat narrower front. E

In these circumstances, I do not think it necessary to particularise in any detail the evidence as to the manner in which the three sets of contractual arrangements were concluded between the Law Society and the insurers. It will, I think, suffice merely to summarise my conclusions as to these arrangements and to explain the points still taken by the plaintiffs in this context.

I shall begin with the rules of 1975. The cover required for the period F 1975 to August 31, 1978, was provided as to 62·5 per cent. by certain underwriting members of Lloyd's, as to 22·5 per cent. by Guardian Royal Exchange Assurance Ltd. (" Guardian "), as to 7·5 per cent. by Royal Insurance Group, as to 3½ per cent. by Legal & General Assurance Society Ltd. and as to 4 per cent. by General Accident Fire & Life Assurance Corporation Ltd. (" General Accident "). The list of syndicates of Lloyd's G underwriters thus participating, together with the percentages of the risk respectively assumed by them, are to be found set out in a file, containing a binding authority given by the underwriters to L.I.B., a form of master policy and a form of certificate of insurance, which was submitted to the Lloyd's policy signing office (" the L.P.S.O."), stamped and sealed by it and dated March 23, 1976. A copy of this file is exhibit " M.H.2 " in these proceedings. A policy (numbered 892/76/NSPI/P) was in fact issued to H the Law Society by the L.P.S.O. on March 23, 1976, at the same time as it stamped, sealed and dated the file. A copy of this policy is exhibit " M.H.3." A companies' collective policy (numbered 76/NSPI/P) was subsequently issued by the four insurance companies on October 5, 1976. A copy of this policy is exhibit " M.H.4." Each of these two policies had attached to it a copy of the form of master policy scheduled to the rules of 1975. However, the schedule to each policy expressed insurance to be

A afforded thereunder merely in respect of " former partners in accordance
with the attached master policy." The schedules stated that insurance in
respect of solicitors required to be insured under section 37 of the Act
was afforded by individual certificates of insurance. In other words, as I
read them, neither policy purported itself to afford insurance in respect of
such solicitors. In these circumstances, while the purpose of the issue of
these two policies in this particular form is not entirely clear to me, I cannot
B accept the submission of the Law Society that the policies themselves constituted master policies of the nature contemplated by the rules of 1975. They
may have been master policies in ordinary parlance, but were not master
policies of this particular nature. Nor so far as the evidence shows was
any other document issued by the insurers of that nature. I am, however,
satisfied on the evidence that on November 18, 1975, a final draft of the
C rules of 1975 was in existence and on that date a contract was concluded
between the Law Society and the insurers concerned covering the period
from that date until August 31, 1978, and conditional on the rules of 1975
being actually made, which gave the Law Society the same contractual
rights against the insurers as it would have had if a policy in the form of the
master policy scheduled to the rules of 1975 had actually been issued to it.

D   The cover required for the period September 1, 1978, to August 31,
1979, was provided as to 73·5 per cent. by certain underwriting members
of Lloyd's, as to 22·5 per cent. by Guardian and as to 4 per cent. by
General Accident. The list of syndicates of Lloyd's underwriters thus
participating, together with the percentages of the risk respectively assumed
by them, are to be found set out in a copy file, containing a binding
authority given by the underwriters to L.I.B., a form of master policy and
E a form of certificate of insurance, which was submitted to the L.P.S.O.,
stamped and sealed by it and dated January 17, 1979. A copy of this
copy file is exhibit " M.H.6 " in the proceedings. In respect of this
period, no actual Lloyd's policy was issued and no actual companies' collective policy was issued. I am, however, satisfied on the evidence that,
before September 1, 1978, a contract had been concluded between the Law
Society and the insurers concerned, covering the year in question, which
F gave the Law Society the same contractual rights against the insurers as it
would have had if a policy in the form of the master policy scheduled to
the rules of 1978 had been actually issued to it.

     The cover required for the period September 1, 1979, to August 31,
1980, was provided as to 63·5 per cent. by certain underwriting members of
Lloyd's, as to 32·5 per cent. by Guardian and as to 4 per cent. by General
G Accident. The list of syndicates of Lloyd's underwriters thus participating,
together with the percentages of the risk respectively assumed by them, are
to be found set out in a file, containing a binding authority given by the
underwriters to L.I.B., a form of master policy and a form of certificate of
insurance, which was submitted to the L.P.S.O., stamped and sealed by it
and dated January 28, 1980. A copy of this file is exhibit " M.H.7 " in
H these proceedings. In respect of this period, no actual Lloyd's policy has
been issued by the L.P.S.O. and no actual companies' collective policy has
been issued. I am, however, satisfied on the evidence that, before
September 1, 1979, a contract had been concluded between the Law Society
and the insurers concerned, covering the period in question, which gives the
Law Society the same contractual rights against the insurers as it would
have had if a policy in the form of the master policy scheduled to the
rules of 1979 had been actually issued to it.

1358

As I have indicated, Mr. Lewis, as I understood him, having heard   A
all the evidence implicitly accepted that (subject to his point as to lack
of consideration, which I have rejected) the Law Society had acquired
contractual rights against the insurers of the nature which I have indicated, before each set of rules came into force.   In the end, his submissions that the Law Society has been in breach of the rules rested on
much narrower grounds.

First, he submitted in effect that, on the true construction of each   B
set of rules, the authority thereby conferred on the Law Society to implement the scheme was conditional on its actually obtaining a document
issued by the insurers, which could be identified as itself constituting the
proposed master policy referred to in the rules.   It would not suffice, he
submitted, for the Law Society to have entered into a contract with the
insurers, under which the insurers undertook to offer insurance to   C
solicitors on the terms of the master policy; the Society would not have
complied with the rules unless it could point to a specific document
which itself constituted the master policy.   This was no mere technicality,
Mr. Lewis suggested; the Law Society should be in a position on demand
to produce to any careful solicitor, who was called upon to pay a
premium on any policy pursuant to the rules, formal documentation
evidencing the rights which the Law Society had purported to secure on   D
his behalf.

The validity of this line of argument depends on the meaning to be
attributed to the phrase " take out and maintain " in each set of rules.
Special considerations may apply to marine insurance because of the
provisions of the Marine Insurance Act 1906 with which this case is not
concerned.   A contract of non-marine insurance, however, may be con-   E
cluded, and the insurers correspondingly put on risk, as soon as the
parties have reached final agreement to this effect.   A complete and
binding contract may for example be concluded simply by the initialling
by underwriters of a slip containing particulars of the proposed insurance
and showing the risks covered: see for example *Thompson* v. *Adams*
(1889) 23 Q.B.D. 361.   Mr. Herniman's evidence confirms what I think
is a point of common knowledge, namely, that in practice formal policies   F
are frequently not issued for some weeks after payment of the premium
and inception of the risk, and that in many cases formal master policies
are never issued.

In these circumstances, a person may, in my judgment properly be
said to " take out " a policy of insurance in a specified form within
ordinary legal parlance, as soon as he obtains contractual rights against   G
the insurers of the same nature as those which he would have if such
formal policy had actually been issued.   I can see no special context in
the three sets of rules such as to justify attributing to the phrase " take
out " a more restricted meaning than this.   It follows that in my judgment the Law Society " took out " a master policy in the forms set out
in the schedule to each of the respective sets of rules, within the meaning
of such rules, as soon as it acquired contractual rights against the insurers   H
of the same nature as it would have had if a master policy in the relevant
form had been actually issued.   Likewise in my judgment it thereafter
" maintained " such master policies within such meaning, by requiring
solicitors to pay premiums on individual policies in accordance with its
provisions.   Despite their counsel's reference to " careful solicitors,"
there is no evidence that the plaintiffs themselves ever made any
inquiry of the Law Society as to the taking out of the three master

A policies before these proceedings were issued. If, however, they had done so, the nature of the evidence which the Law Society would have been entitled to adduce in answer to this inquiry would not in my judgment have been restricted to formal master policies actually issued by the insurers. It could, for example, have included reference to the originals of exhibits " M.H.2," " M.H.6 " and " M.H.7."

B The second alternative ground upon which Mr. Lewis finally submitted that the Law Society was in breach of the rules was a short one, relating solely to the rules of 1975. Mr. Herniman's evidence shows that, in relation to the Law Society, the insurers finally accepted the risk on November 18, 1975, while the rules of 1975 were not made until December 12, 1975. It was submitted that the authority conferred on the Law Society by those rules only covered the taking out of a policy

C *after* the rules had been made. To use a colloquialism, it was suggested that the Law Society " jumped the gun." I think there is no substance in this point. It was necessary implicit in all the contractual arrangements between the Law Society and the insurers that the operation of these arrangements was to be conditional on the rules of 1975 being finally made in the form envisaged. These arrangements thus became finally operative on December 12, 1975, and not before. This,

D in my judgment, was the date when the Law Society " took out " insurance within the meaning of the rules of 1975.

For these reasons the plaintiffs have not satisfied me that the Law Society has been acting in breach of the rules. I must therefore reject such of their arguments relating to commission as are based on the footing that the Law Society has been in such breach, just as I reject

E their arguments based on the footing that the rules are invalid. This makes it unnecessary to deal with two authorities cited by Mr. Lewis relating to the position where money is improperly obtained under colour of an office, namely *Hooper* v. *Exeter Corporation* (1887) 56 L.J.Q.B. 457 and *Morgan* v. *Palmer* (1824) 2 B. & C. 729.

I now turn to consider the plaintiffs' submissions based on the footing that the rules are valid and that the Law Society has acted in accordance

F with them in taking out and maintaining master policies. The springboard of their arguments in this context is the general principle of equity that a person (such as an agent or trustee) who, by the use of a fiduciary position, derives a profit from a third party, must account to his principal or beneficiary for the profit so obtained. Even where a fiduciary relationship is established, a defendant required to account for

G the profit may successfully resist the claim on the ground that it was received with the knowledge and assent of the principal or beneficiary concerned: see, for example, *Phipps* v. *Boardman* [1967] 2 A.C. 46, 105 *per* Lord Hodson. Furthermore, the right may be lost by a sufficient degree of acquiescence even without express consent. With these exceptions, however, the principle, if applicable at all, is a strict one. As Lord Russell of Killowen said in *Regal (Hastings) Ltd.* v. *Gulliver* [1942]

H 1 All E.R. 378, 386:

" The rule of equity which insists on those, who by use of a fiduciary position make a profit, being liable to account for that profit, in no way depends on fraud, or absence of bona fides; or upon such questions or considerations as whether the profit would or should otherwise have gone to the plaintiff, or whether the profiteer was under a duty to obtain the source of the profit for the plaintiff, or whether he took a risk or acted as he did for the benefit of the plaintiff, or whether the plaintiff has in fact been damaged or benefited by his action. The liability arises from the mere fact of a profit having, in the stated circumstances, been made. The profiteer, however honest and well-intentioned, cannot escape the risk of being called upon to account."

The principle that a person in a fiduciary capacity must not make a profit out of his trust is " part of the wider rule that a trustee must not place himself in a position where his duty and his interest may conflict ": see *Phipps* v. *Boardman* [1967] 2 A.C. 46, 123 *per* Lord Upjohn. Lord Herschell in *Bray* v. *Ford* [1896] A.C. 44, 51 explained the reason for the rule:

" It does not appear to me that this rule is, as has been said, founded upon principles of morality. I regard it rather as based on the consideration that, human nature being what it is, there is danger, in such circumstances, of the person holding a fiduciary position being swayed by interest rather than by duty, and thus prejudicing those whom he was bound to protect."

Mr. Lewis pointed out that, according to the terms of the master policy set out in the schedule to each set of rules, the Law Society was contracting " on behalf of all solicitors from time to time required to be insured by indemnity rules made under section 37 of the Solicitors Act 1974, and on behalf of former solicitors . . ." These very words showed, he submitted, that the Law Society was not contracting with the insurers on its own behalf, but simply as agent or trustee for the solicitors concerned. From this it was suggested that, in contracting, the Law Society must inevitably have been acting in a fiduciary capacity in relation to such solicitors.

Furthermore, it was suggested, there was an inevitable conflict between the interests of such solicitors, who would be concerned to see the premiums on all insurance arranged under the master policy kept as low as possible, and the interests of the Law Society, which would take increased benefits from higher premiums in the form of an increased share of the commission. In these circumstances, while it was not suggested that the Law Society had in fact been influenced by such unworthy motives in making the various arrangements with the insurers, it was submitted that the inflexible rule of equity already mentioned must be applicable in all its rigour, save to the extent that defences, such as acquiescence or waiver, may be available to the Law Society.

If I am right in my conclusion that the Law Society entered into the contract with the insurers on the footing that it was to hold it as trustee for the solicitors concerned, then it does seem to me inevitably to follow that *as soon as the contract had been concluded,* there existed a fiduciary relationship between the Law Society and such solicitors. Thereafter, I think, any such solicitor would have been entitled to call for the Law Society's co-operation, so far as necessary, in enforcing his rights (as beneficiary under the trust created by the contract) to obtain insurance cover from the insurers.

However, proof of a post-contract fiduciary relationship would not itself suffice to entitle the plaintiffs to invoke the equitable principles exemplified in *Phipps* v. *Boardman* [1967] 2 A.C. 46, unless it were shown that the profit in question had been received by the Law Society as a result of the use of this post-contract fiduciary position. I do not

A think that this has been shown. True it is that the 1976 agreement was in point of time actually entered into long after the contract between the Law Society and the insurers had been concluded in 1975. The Law Society, however, found itself in a position in 1976 to conclude the advantageous arrangement relating to commission, not by virtue of its then subsisting fiduciary relationship to the solicitors affected by the scheme, but because of the negotiation of the original contract with the insurers. Under this contract L.I.B. had derived the certain prospect of
B receiving large sums of commission on insurance effected by individual solicitors during the currency of that contract and the hope of receiving further similar large sums if the contract was renewed. It was the negotiation of this contract which placed the Law Society in a position to demand rights to participate in the commission; its subsequent fiduciary position had nothing to do with the matter.
C
In the circumstances, the relevant question seems to me to be whether the Law Society must be treated as having acted in a fiduciary relationship to the solicitors affected, *in negotiating the original contract with the insurers*? If, but only if, the answer to this question be " Yes," the claim of the plaintiffs based on the principle of *Phipps* v. *Boardman* begins to have substantial force in law.

D It might at first sight be assumed that, in any case where A enters into a contract with B on the footing that A is to be trustee for C of any rights acquired under the contract, then A must necessarily be in a fiduciary relationship to C in negotiating the contract. In my judgment, however, any such general assumption would be fallacious. Merely because A is to hold the benefit of the contract, when concluded, as
E trustee for C, it by no means necessarily follows that A was acting in a fiduciary capacity during the stage of negotiation. Everything must depend on the particular circumstances. To take one example, albeit far removed from the present facts: if a grandfather, out of natural love and affection for his grandchild were to enter into a contract with insurers, whereunder he was to hold certain benefits as trustee for his infant grandchild, it could not, I conceive, be suggested that he was
F acting in a fiduciary relationship to the grandchild in negotiating the contract. Correspondingly, even if, as a consequence of negotiating such contract, the grandfather were to obtain commission, or a share of the commission, paid by the insurers in respect of the issue of the relevant policy, it could not be suggested that he was accountable to the grandchild for such commission.

G Thus the mere fact that the Law Society was to hold the benefit of each of the master policy contracts when concluded as trustee for the individual solicitors concerned does not show that it was acting in a fiduciary capacity in relation to such solicitors in negotiating those arrangements. Are there then any other factors which establish the existence of such a fiduciary relationship during the pre-contract stage?

Mr. Lewis emphasised that, as a result of the introduction of the
H master policy scheme, the Law Society has become the possessor of a very substantial new source of income. It would be remarkable, he suggested, if the legislature, in passing the Act and thereby enabling the Law Society to introduce a compulsory scheme, contemplated that the Law Society would thereby be enabled to increase its spendable income by several hundred thousand pounds. This, he suggested, is one reason in itself for concluding that the suggested fiduciary relationship exists.

I do not think there is any substance in this point based on the

supposed intentions of the legislature. First, the express power conferred   A
on the Law Society by section 37 (5) of the Act, which empowered it
to carry into effect any arrangements which it considered expedient for
the purpose of indemnity under the section, was indubitably wide enough
to enable it to enter into a prudent commercial arrangement such as the
1976 agreement. Secondly, the legislature is hardly likely to have
assumed, as does the plaintiffs' argument, that there is an inherent conflict of interest between the Law Society and the members of the solicitors'   B
profession, which the Law Society exists to serve. The suggestion of
conflict of interest on these present facts seems to me an unrealistic one.
The position might be quite different, if the person receiving the commission were an individual and not the professional body which is itself
responsible for the affairs of the solicitors' profession. Thirdly, if the
legislature had directed its mind to the question of commission, it would   C
no doubt have appreciated that the Law Society already has a large
number of powers and duties, which are usually exercised through its
Council and are designed to enable it to advance or protect the interests,
usefulness and efficiency of the profession. Nevertheless, it could not,
I conceive, be argued (and has not been argued in the present case) that
the Law Society or the Council, in the ordinary exercise of its general
powers, acts in a fiduciary capacity in relation to individual solicitors,   D
even in those frequent instances where such exercise is likely to affect
their pockets. If solicitors are dissastisfied with the manner in which the
Council is exercising its powers and discretions, their normal remedy is
by way of exercise of their rights under the Law Society's byelaws, not
by reliance on the principles of equity.

For all these reasons, I see no a priori reason for presuming that the   E
legislature, in conferring on the Council the power to make rules
authorising the Law Society to take out and maintain insurance with
authorised insurers for the purpose of providing indemnity, contemplated
that the Society would be negotiating such insurance in a fiduciary capacity. A similar observation applies to the rules themselves which actually
authorised the taking out of such insurance; at least if read without
reference to the scheduled form of master policy, they do not suggest   F
that the Society will be negotiating any policy otherwise than pursuant
to its normal functions as the governing body of the solicitors' branch of
the legal profession.

In the end, in my judgment, the argument that the Law Society,
in discharging the particular function of negotiating contracts of insurance with the insurers in 1975, 1978, 1979 was acting in a fiduciary   G
capacity in relation to the solicitors concerned, must depend wholly and
exclusively on the phrase " on behalf of all solicitors [etc.] " to be
found in clause 1 of each form of master policy. But for these words,
the argument, I conceive, would not get off the ground. In my judgment,
however, for reasons already appearing, such dependence is ill-founded.
This phrase by itself by no means necessarily imports that the Law
Society was acting in a fiduciary capacity vis-à-vis the individual solicitors   H
concerned, in negotiating contracts; in this respect its import is quite
neutral.

I can see no other sufficient grounds for holding that the performance
of this particular function imposed on the Law Society equitable obligations to individual solicitors of a nature which it would not ordinarily
assume in negotiating commercial contracts, which it considered to be in
the interests of the solicitors' profession. Accordingly in my judgment,

A the existence of the relevant fiduciary relationship at the relevant time, which the plaintiffs must establish if they are to succeed under this head, has not been established.

In these circumstances it is unnecessary to make any decision on the alternative submissions made by the Law Society, to the effect that, on any footing, acquiescence now debars these two particular plaintiffs from seeking to enforce any equitable rights, which they might otherwise
B possess, to compel the Law Society to account for commission. It is common ground that a legal or equitable right may be lost if the situation is such that: "it would be dishonest or unconscionable for the plaintiff, or the person having the right sought to be enforced, to continue to seek to enforce it": see *Shaw* v. *Applegate* [1977] 1 W.L.R. 970, 978 *per* Buckley L.J. Furthermore it appears from the judgment of Goff L.J.
C in that case at p. 132 that it is easier to establish a case of acquiescence where, as in the present case, the right is equitable only.

No attack has been made on the honesty of these two plaintiffs. It has, however, been forcefully submitted on behalf of the Law Society that, as matters stand, it would be unconscionable for the plaintiffs to seek to enforce the rights to participate in commission which they now claim. As I have illustrated, in May and October 1975 the Society made
D full disclosure to solicitors that, if and when the master policy scheme was introduced, it would be receiving a share of the brokers' commission on the relevant policies and that it intended to apply this for the benefit of the profession as a whole (thereby implicitly informing solicitors that it did not intend to account to them individually for it). It is not suggested that the plaintiffs were unaware of these announcements. Subsequently
E every set of annual accounts of the Law Society has disclosed the existence of the commission and its receipt by L.S.S. The evidence shows that all sums thus received have been applied or allocated for the benefit of the whole profession. The plaintiffs have not suggested that they were not, at all material times, aware of the contents of the Law Society's successive sets of accounts and of the manner in which these sums were actually dealt with. And yet until the actual issue of the present origi-
F nating summons, so far as the evidence shows, they did not by any communication to the Law Society dispute or question in any way its right to participate in the commission and to apply it in the manner indicated. It would appear that, so far as the Law Society was concerned, their complaints were directed simply against the existence of a compulsory insurance scheme, which deprived them of the freedom to select their own insurers.
G
In these circumstances, the defence based on acquiescence would in my judgment at least have considerable force in relation to these plaintiffs' claims, if it were necessary to consider it. As things are, however, I express no conclusion on this point.

Subject to the submissions of counsel as to the precise form of relief to be granted, I propose to declare in answer to paragraph 2 of the
H originating summons that, upon the true construction of the Act and the rules, and in the events which have happened, the Law Society is not bound to account to either of the plaintiffs for any part of any commission received by it or by L.S.S. from L.I.B. in respect of premiums paid by individual solicitors pursuant to the solicitors' indemnity insurance scheme. This not being a representative action, I propose not to make any wider declaration than this, but again I will hear counsel on this point.

[There followed further argument.]   A

I think there was a considerable degree of mutual misunderstanding in the correspondence which passed between the plaintiffs' solicitors and the Law Society's solicitors before the issue of the plaintiffs' summons of January 30, 1980.

Looking at the matter very broadly, however, the position as I see it is this. In his affidavit sworn on December 11, 1979, Mr. Marshall had referred to a master policy in terms which could reasonably be read as suggesting that there existed a document constituting a master policy. The plaintiffs' solicitors were therefore entitled under the Rules of the Supreme Court to ask, as they did ask, to inspect such document as constituting a document referred to in an affidavit.

There then followed correspondence between the plaintiffs' solicitors and the Law Society's solicitors, which I read as containing a number   C
of at least implicit suggestions by the Law Society's solicitors that a formal master policy did exist.   Certainly they never said anything to the contrary.

Then on December 28 the Law Society's solicitors wrote a letter to the plaintiffs' solicitors, in which there appeared, in the middle of a paragraph, the sentence: D

"We have in fact supplied your agents with certified copies of the original terms of the master policy and are instructed that, as is usual in cases of this type, a formal printed policy is not issued."

Though this letter did not suggest that it was intended to correct any-thing that had been said before, I suppose that if the matter had stopped there it could be said that the position had been made sufficiently clear   E
by the Law Society's solicitors to the plaintiffs' solicitors.   But the matter did not stop there.   There was further correspondence between the plaintiffs' solicitors and the Law Society's solicitors.   In the course of this correspondence the Law Society's solicitors, in what I am quite sure was a desire to be helpful and to clarify matters, in fact, to my way of thinking, really rather obscured them.   An example of the way   F
in which they were obscured, I think, was this.   The plaintiffs' solicitors wrote to the Law Society's solicitors on January 16 saying:

"You insist upon referring to certified copies of the *terms* of the master policy, whereas you are perfectly well aware that what we have repeatedly requested of you is a certified copy of the original master policy in respect of each of the dates referred to in the first paragraph of your letter under reply.   The first sentence of your   G
letter of December 14, 1979, to our London agents implied that these documents did exist and that for some reason you were reluctant to reveal them to us.   If the original master policies do not exist, would you please say so in plain terms? "

At any rate I would have thought that that paragraph was clear enough. But the Law Society's solicitors wrote back on January 18, saying in   H
answer to it:

"We have no idea whether the original master policies exist or not as we do not know to what you are referring.   What we do know is that the documents recording the contractual relationship between the underwriters and L.I.B. are contained in the documents forwarded under cover of our letter of January 14."

A   I am bound to say that I do not think that this letter of January 18 was particularly helpful or illuminating. By the time that the plaintiffs' summons was issued on January 30, i.e. for the production of the original of the master policy, the position in regard to the existence or otherwise of a formal document constituting the master policy in my view still had not been made fully clear to the plaintiffs.

B   I think that the plaintiffs were entitled to know whether such a document did or did not exist. Likewise, I think they were entitled to know how the relevant contract had been concluded between the Law Society and the insurers, if there was no formal policy document.

The obscurity of the position, even in the minds of the Law Society's advisers, as well as the plaintiffs' advisers, seems to me to be well illustrated by the fact that, having entered court on the first day of the
C   hearing in the belief that there were no documents formally constituting the master policies, the Law Society's representatives then, in the course of the hearing, actually discovered two documents—the originals of exhibits " M.H.3 " and " M.H.4,"—which Mr. Alexander on their behalf then submitted to me were master policies, within the meaning of the rules. The fact that I rejected this submission is neither here nor there
D   for the purposes of the present argument as to costs.

For these purposes it is equally irrelevant, I think, that I have rejected the plaintiffs' submission based on the absence of any document constituting a master policy of the nature referred to in the rules.

The relevant points seem to me these. First, the plaintiffs had originally been led to suppose that a formal policy or policies existed; secondly, they were within their rights in demanding to see any such
E   document which did exist; thirdly, before the issue of the summons, they were neither shown any such documents nor unambiguously informed that they did not exist; fourthly, they were not sufficiently informed of the precise manner in which the relevant contractual arrangements had been concluded until a long way through the hearing of the main summons.

In these circumstances it seems to me that the plaintiffs' summons of
F   January 30 was amply justified, though I entirely accept that the Law Society's solicitors were acting throughout with the very best of intentions, and no-one has attempted to suggest otherwise. I further think that in all the circumstances, because of the way that the matter was conducted on the Law Society's side in relation to the adduction of the evidence to which I have been referring, there has been a certain amount of unnecessary expenditure of time in the hearing itself. I think that both
G   sides are to some extent to blame for the misunderstandings that have occurred, but on the whole I think the fault must be laid more at the Law Society's door in this context.

In these circumstances, therefore, I propose to direct that the Law Society should pay the costs of the summons of January 30, and to direct, in effect, that they make a modest contribution to the plaintiffs'
H   costs of the main summons. Taking all factors into consideration, I think that the proper order will be that the plaintiffs, who have been unsuccessful on the main summons, should be directed to pay four-fifths only of the Law Society's costs of this summons, instead of the whole lot, which I would otherwise have directed them to pay.

In relation to the relief to be granted on the main summons, I think both parties are content that I should make a declaration in answer to paragraph 2 in the form that I have already indicated.

Slade J.   **Swain v. Law Society (Ch.D.)**   **[1980]**

I have considered Mr. Phillips's invitation on behalf of the Law   A
Society that I should make an affirmative declaration in answer to
paragraph 1, but on the whole, in this non-representative action, I remain
of the view that I should not do that, though, by declining to make a
positive declaration that I regard the rules as valid, I do not wish to be
taken in any way as suggesting that I think there is any doubt on the
matter. As will have appeared from my judgment, my own view is that   B
these rules are valid and intra vires; but I think it is right to leave it
formally open to other persons to take such other points on them as
they may see fit to take in the future.

> *Plaintiffs to pay four-fifths of Law*
> *Society's costs of originating sum-*
> *mons of October 25, 1979, with a*   C
> *set off, against those costs, of the*
> *cost of January 30, 1980, summons*
> *the whole of which to be borne*
> *by Law Society.*
>
> *Leave to Law Society to appeal*
> *against order for costs on origi-*
> *nating summons.*   D

Solicitors: *Lovell, Son & Pitfield for Pethybridges, Bodmin; Slaughter*
& May.

[Reported by MRS. F. ALLEN McLEAN, Barrister-at-Law.]

E

[COURT OF APPEAL]

* REGINA *v.* NAZARI

REGINA *v.* DISSANAYAKE   F

REGINA *v.* ANYANWU

REGINA *v.* FERNANDEZ AND ANOTHER

1980 March 14   Lawton L.J., Boreham and Comyn JJ. G

Crime—Sentence—Deportation, recommendations for—Principles
to be applied when considering whether to make recom-
mendation—Immigration Act 1971 *(c. 77), s.* 6 [1]

The defendants, N, D and F, were immigrants who had
been convicted of, or pleaded guilty to, one or more offences,
and, in addition to sentences of imprisonment imposed upon   H
them, were recommended to be deported. The defendant N,
an Iranian, applied for leave to appeal against the recommendation made in respect of him on the ground that the
judge had failed to take fully into account the fact that he
was likely to be executed if he was returned to Iran.
The defendant D, a Sri Lankan national, who pleaded guilty
to manslaughter by reason of diminished responsibility, appealed

[1] Immigration Act 1971, s. 6: see post, p. 1372G–H.

A   against the recommendation that he be deported on the ground that his compulsory return to his country of origin would adversely affect him and his family, and that he would return of his own volition when he had served his term of imprisonment.

     The defendant F, a Spaniard, applied for leave to appeal against his recommendation for deportation on the ground that his removal from the country would cause hardship to his wife,

B   who had resided in England since 1962, and to his children, who had been born in England, attended English schools and were English-speaking.

     On the question whether the recommendations for deportation should be upheld: —

     Held, that before making a recommendation for deportation the court should consider whether the accused's continued presence in the United Kingdom was to its detriment;

C   that the nature of political systems operating in other countries was a matter for the Home Secreary to consider, and not a matter for the court, when determining whether it would be unduly harsh to an accused to make a deportation order compulsorily returning him to his country of origin; that courts should have regard to the effect a recommendation would have upon innocent parties not before the court since courts had no wish to break up families or impose hardship on

D   innocent people (post, pp. 1373c, E, G, 1374A–B); that where there was evidence of mental instability connected with, or resulting in the commission of a serious criminal offence, that was a good reason why a recommendation should be made (post, pp. 1374G); that bearing those considerations in mind the application of the defendant N and the appeal of the defendant D would be dismissed, and the application of the defendant F would be granted and his appeal allowed as his deportation

E   would inevitably cause hardship to his wife and children (post, pp. 1374c, 1375B).

     Reg. v. *Caird* (1970) 54 Cr.App.R. 499, C.A. applied.

     Per curiam. Where an accused was proved to be an illegal immigrant under the Immigration Act 1971, a recommendation for a deportation should normally be made (post, p. 1375A).

F   The following case is referred to in the judgment:

     Reg. v. *Caird* (1970) 54 Cr.App.R. 499, C.A.

     The following additional case was cited in argument:

     Reg. v. *Thoseby* (unreported), July 30, 1979, C.A.

     APPEALS and APPLICATIONS for leave to appeal against sentence.

G   On September 7, 1979, the defendant, Fazlollah Nazari, a citizen of Iran, pleaded guilty at Reading Crown Court before the recorder (J. D. Alliott Q.C.) to being knowingly concerned in the fraudulent evasion of the prohibition on the importation of a controlled drug, contrary to section 3 (1) of the Misuse of Drugs Act 1971. He was sentenced by the recorder to four years' imprisonment and recommended for deport-

H   ation. He applied for leave to appeal against the recommendation on the ground, inter alia, that the recorder had erred in failing to take fully into account the fact that if he was returned to Iran he would probably be executed.

     On March 12, 1979, at the Central Criminal Court, the defendant, Rohan Shivantha Dissanayake, a Sri Lankan national, pleaded guilty to manslaughter by reason of diminished responsibility, having been indicted for murder. He was sentenced by Melford Stevenson J. to five years'

imprisonment and, on March 23, 1979, he was recommended for deport- A
ation. He appealed against his sentence of imprisonment and the
recommendation for deportation. The grounds of appeal in relation to
the recommendation were that his deportation would have an adverse
effect upon himself and his family, and that he would return to Sri Lanka
voluntarily on his release from prison.

On October 2, 1979, at the Kingston-upon-Thames Crown Court, the
defendant, Ebenezer Chukwuma Anyanwu, was convicted of remaining in B
the United Kingdom beyond the time limited by his leave to enter, contrary
to section 24 (1) (b) of the Immigration Act 1971. He was fined £50 or two
months' imprisonment in default by Judge Figgis, and he was recommended
for deportation. He submitted an application for leave to appeal against
sentence one day out of time on November 20, 1979. On January 16, 1980,
he signed a notice of abandonment of appeal. He applied to the Court of C
Appeal for an extension of time in which to apply for leave to appeal against
sentence, asking that the purported abandonment be treated as a nullity.
The grounds of appeal against the recommendation were that deportation
would cause undue hardship to the defendant who wished to remain in the
United Kingdom to conclude his studies.

On September 25, 1979, the defendant, Joseph Fernandez, a citizen of D
Spain, and his co-defendant, Michael Joseph Adamson, were convicted at
the Central Criminal Court of conspiracy to rob and aggravated burglary.
On October 8, 1979, they were sentenced by Judge Argyle to a total of 18
months' and 15 months' imprisonment, respectively, and Fernandez was also
made the subject of a recommendation for deportation. He applied for leave
to appeal against the recommendation on the ground that no recommenda- E
tion should have been made as he had worked well in the United Kingdom
for 14 years; his children were born and schooled here and spoke no
Spanish; he had not been a burden on the state, and the offence was out
of character and unlikely to be repeated. The co-defendant Adamson
applied for an adjournment of his application for leave to appeal against
conviction. F

The facts are stated in the judgment of Lawton L.J.

Richard Harvey for the defendant Nazari.
Simeon Hopkins for the defendant Dissanayake.
C. A. I. Ginikanwa for the defendant Anyanwu.

G

The defendants Fernandez and Adamson were neither present nor
represented.

LAWTON L.J. gave the judgment of the court. These three applicants
and one appellant either appeal or apply for leave to appeal against
sentence, which in each case included a recommendation for deportation. H

During the last decade this court has from time to time indicated the
principles upon which orders recommending deportation should be made.
It has been suggested that some of the decisions are conflicting. As a result,
it was decided that four cases raising different matters for consideration
should be heard one after the other so that the court would have an
opportunity of reviewing the principles which are applicable. It is first
necessary to set out the facts of each case so far as they are relevant.

A   *Reg.* v. *Nazari*

On September 7, 1979, at Reading Crown Court, Fazlollah Nazari pleaded guilty to being knowingly concerned in the fraudulent evasion of the prohibition on the importation of a controlled drug. He was sentenced to four years' imprisonment and recommended for deportation.

He is a young man of Iranian citizenship. In the summer of 1979, he
B   was studying at a polytechnic in London. He arrived at Heathrow Airport on June 19, 1979, carrying a black suitcase. Customs officers were suspicious about the suitcase. He was allowed to pass through the Customs but was kept under observation in case he met somebody and handed over the suitcase. He did not meet anybody. Before he left the airport he was detained. The suitcase was opened and found to contain 1·95 kg of opium in the form of sticks. It was accepted by the prosecution that opium in that
C   form could not be converted into heroin.

There is no application for leave to appeal against the sentence of four years' imprisonment, which was in line with the kind of sentences which are passed upon those who try to smuggle dangerous drugs into the United Kingdom.

Complaint is made about the recommendation for deportation. Mr.
D   Harvey, on this applicant's behalf, has called attention to what might be called the general compassionate grounds relating to this young man. It is said that if he is deported he will not be able to continue his studies in England; that he will probably be separated from the English girl whom he hopes to marry, and that he is not likely to commit this kind of offence again. But the major part of Mr. Harvey's submission was directed to the proposition that if the applicant is deported he will be sent back to Iran,
E   where the present government is likely to take a very serious view of his activities and he may face a court which will have jurisdiction to pass, and may pass, a sentence of death upon him.

The evidence relating to what is likely to happen to the applicant if and when he returns to Iran is unsatisfactory. So far as the trial judge was concerned, a statement to the effect stated above was set out in the social
F   inquiry report. The probation officer who made it said that at some date which he did not specify he had spoken on the telephone to somebody at the Iranian Embassy who had confirmed that very serious consequences would befall this applicant if he returns to Iran. Before this court today Mr. Harvey informed us that he personally had spoken to Professor Coulson, of the School of Oriental Studies of London University, who had told him that the type of consequences which have been indicated
G   might befall the applicant. In addition, Mr. Harvey put in an affidavit sworn by an Iranian holding a degree in law who is at present an articled clerk with a firm of solicitors. He deposed that under Iranian law serious consequences, including the death penalty, could fall upon anyone who imported dangerous drugs. What he meant by importing dangerous drugs was not clear. We do not know whether the deponent was talking about
H   importation into Iran or into the United Kingdom. It seems odd that any Iranian court would have jurisdiction over somebody who was arrested for importing dangerous drugs into the United Kingdom.

In this class of case, when it is suggested that unpleasant consequences are likely to follow for anyone recommended for deportation if the Home Secretary makes an order for deportation, it is essential that proper evidence should be before the court; the court cannot act on the kind of evidence which has been put before it in this case.

Reg. v. *Dissanayake*   A

We turn to the next case, that of Rohan Shivantha Dissanayake. Leave to appeal against sentence has been granted to him by the single judge. Mr. Hopkins, who has appeared on behalf of the appellant, has urged upon us that the sentence of imprisonment, as well as the order recommending deportation, was wrong.

On March 12, 1979, at the Central Criminal Court, before Melford B Stevenson J., the appellant, who had been indicted for murder, pleaded guilty to manslaughter, the basis of his plea being diminished responsibility. There was, in addition, a suggestion, but no more than a suggestion, that he had been provoked into doing that which he did. He was sentenced to five years' imprisonment and recommended for deportation.

[His Lordship stated that the appellant had killed his wife by striking her several times on the head with a heavy wooden ornament, referred to C the circumstances and continued:] In our judgment, men who batter their wives to death should consider themselves fortunate to receive a sentence as light as five years. It could have been much longer without in any way being excessive.

In our judgment there is nothing in that part of the appeal which relates to the sentence of imprisonment. We will consider the recommendation for deportation in the light of the observations that we propose D making after we have recounted the facts of the two other cases.

Reg. v. *Anyanwu*

The case of Ebenezer Chukwuma Anyanwu is very straightforward. On October 22, 1979, at Kingston-upon-Thames Crown Court he was convicted after a four-day trial of remaining in the United Kingdom beyond E the time-limit, contrary to section 24 (1) of the Immigration Act 1971. He was fined £50, with two months' imprisonment in default, and ordered to pay the costs of the prosecution up to a maximum of £150. We find it difficult to understand how a simple case like this could have lasted four whole days but it did. In addition to the fine the applicant was recommended for deportation and detained under the provisions of paragraph (2) F of Schedule 3 to the Immigration Act 1971. He was clearly an illegal immigrant on the finding of the jury.

[His Lordship then considered the facts relating to the defendant's abandonment of his appeal and continued:] We are satisfied that the applicant did abandon his application for leave to appeal against sentence, and accordingly there is nothing for this court to consider.

G

Reg. v. *Fernandez*

We come now to the case of Fernandez and Adamson. Adamson defended himself at the trial. That was by his own choice. He has had legal aid for the purpose of advising him about the procedure to be adopted for appealing against sentence. He now asks for an adjournment so that he can have more advice as to his grounds of appeal. We H feel impelled, albeit with some reluctance, to agree to his application for leave to appeal against conviction being adjourned. It will be adjourned. He will be granted legal aid for the purpose of getting advice about his grounds of appeal. But he should clearly understand that he must get the advice as quickly as he can, and once he has got it the case will be restored to the list as soon as possible thereafter. There will be no further adjournments.

A   Turning now to the case of Fernandez; on September 25, 1979, at the Central Criminal Court, he and Adamson were convicted of conspiracy to rob and aggravated burglary. On October 9, 1979, Fernandez was sentenced to 18 months' imprisonment on each count of the indictment on which he was convicted, and in addition, sentences of three months' and three months' consecutive, suspended for two years on June 10, 1977, were ordered to take effect, varied to a total of three months' imprisonment

B   concurrent. He was also recommended for deportation.

Fernandez applied for leave to appeal against his sentence. The single judge referred his application to the full court, and we grant him leave to appeal against sentence. He himself is not present today, but we have had the benefit (and it has been a great benefit to the court, and indeed to him) to have his wife here to speak for him. He has a statutory right to appear

C   himself but, having regard to what we propose to say about the recommendation for deportation, he will probably not want to come back to this court, though he is at liberty to do so if he wishes.

Fernandez comes from Galicia, in north-west Spain, and has been in this country many years. During most of the time he has been here he has been a waiter. In June 1977, when he was working in a night club, he and

D   others decided to rob his employer of the club takings while he was on his way home with them. He and his co-conspirators (there were four of them altogether) met at a public house and made plans. They reconnoitred the employer's house and agreed to break into it and to overpower anyone who might be there. They were to lie in wait for the employer to come home. They anticipated that he would be carrying takings amounting to about £600. On the night of July 15—16, 1977, Fernandez and one

E   of his co-conspirators purchased some sticky tape. Fernandez made a hood from a pillow case, with holes cut for the eyes, so that the employer would not recognise him. Later that night the conspirators met at the house of the employer, Mr. Leigh, and succeeded in opening a window. They carried with them knives, rope and the tape. A cassette player, radio and silver lighter were removed from the window sill to facilitate entry, and those items were later found in the house of one of the con-

F   spirators. They were, however, disturbed by neighbours, who saw lights on, and they left, intending to return later. Fortunately for justice, a police patrol car saw Fernandez walking around, and as a result of their stopping and questioning him the plot came to light.

Fernandez has not got a clean record in this country, but all his offences to date have kept him out of prison, although in 1977, as we have already

G   recounted, he received a suspended sentence for driving whilst disqualified. His appearance before the courts started in 1972 with two offences, one of attempted deception and the other of theft. Later that year he was convicted of assault occasioning actual bodily harm. Three years later he was again convicted of assault occasioning actual bodily harm. Then he had a few comparatively minor motoring offences. His record is not good. On the other hand, it cannot be said that he has shown by his record

H   that he is a member of the criminal class in this country. He seems generally to be a hard-working man. His family situation is as follows: he has a Spanish wife, who came to this country about 10 years ago. She is a devoted wife. They have two children, the elder of whom is now nine, both born in this country. They are buying their own house, which is in their joint names. Spanish is the language of the home, but, although the children can understand Spanish and can say a few sentences in that

language, they are more English-speaking than Spanish-speaking, and, of   A
course, they go to English schools.

We are satisfied, having heard Mrs. Fernandez, that if the recommendation for deportation is accepted and if her husband is sent back to Spain,
she is going to face a grave dilemma. She feels as a wife that she ought to
go back with her husband, but as a mother she feels that she ought to stay
in England with her children because she is convinced that there is a better
future for them here than there could be in Spain. Clearly she and the   B
children will suffer hardship. On the other hand, if the only matter which
the court should take into consideration is the crime and the circumstances of the crime which Fernandez himself committed, then there are
indications that there should be a recommendation for deportation.

It is against that background of facts that we come to consider the
principles which should be applied in this class of case. The leading   C
authority is *Reg.* v. *Caird* (1970) 54 Cr.App.R. 499. The facts are irrelevant for the purposes of this judgment; we refer to it because a recommendation for deportation had been made in that case, and the court,
which was presided over by Sachs L.J., set out the principles which should
apply. The relevant passage is at p. 510:

" So far as Bodea, however, is concerned, there was also a recom-   D
mendation for deportation. In a case such as is under consideration
the question for the court is whether the potential detriment to this
country of Bodea remaining here has been shown to be such as to
justify the recommendation. This court is of the clear opinion that
upon that basis the recommendation based on this particular isolated
offence cannot be supported and should be cancelled."
                                                                          E
As we are referring to this case I go on to read a paragraph which is
relevant to a matter which arises in the case of the appellant Nazari:

" It desires to emphasise that the courts when considering a recommendation for deportation are normally concerned simply with the
crime committed and the individual's past record and the question as
to what is their effect on the question of potential detriment just men-   F
tioned. It does not embark, and indeed is in no position to embark,
upon the issue as to what is likely to be his life if he goes back to the
country of his origin. That is a matter for the Home Secretary."

It is relevant to point out that the power of a court to make a recommendation for deportation is derived from section 6 of the Immigration Act
1971. Subsections (1) and (2) read: G

" Where under section 3 (6) above a person convicted of an offence
is liable to deportation on the recommendation of a court, he may be
recommended for deportation by any court having power to sentence
him for the offence unless the court commits him to be sentenced or
further dealt with for the offence by another court . . . (2) A court
shall not recommend a person for deportation unless he has been
given not less than seven days' notice in writing stating that a person   H
is not liable to deportation if he is patrial, describing the persons
who are patrial and stating (so far as material) the effect of section
3 (8) above and section 7 below . . ."

Then there are other matters relating to adjournment and the like.

In our judgment it is clear that Parliament in 1971 intended that there
should be full inquiry into a case before any order recommendng deporta-

A tion is made. A person who is likely to be the subject of an order must be given seven clear days' notice of what may happen to him. The object of that is to enable him to prepare his answer to a suggestion that he should be recommended for deportation. It follows that no court should make an order recommending deportation without full inquiry into all the circumstances. It should not be done, as sometimes happened in the past, by adding a sentence as if by an afterthought, at the end of observations

B about any sentence of imprisonment. It would be advisable for judges to invite counsel to address them specifically on the possibility of a recommendation for deportation being made.

We now indicate some guidelines which courts should keep in mind when considering whether to make an order recommending deportation. But we stress that these are guidelines, not rigid rules. There may well

C be considerations which take a particular case out of the guidelines; that is a matter which will depend on the evidence.

First, the court must consider, as was said by Sachs L.J. in *Reg.* v. *Caird,* 54 Cr.App.R. 499, whether the accused's continued presence in the United Kingdom is to its detriment. This country has no use for criminals of other nationalities, particularly if they have committed serious crimes or have long criminal records. That is self-evident. The more serious the

D crime and the longer the record the more obvious it is that there should be an order recommending deportation. On the other hand, a minor offence would not merit an order recommending deportation. In the Greater London area, for example, shoplifting is an offence which is frequently committed by visitors to this country. Normally, an arrest for shoplifting followed by conviction, even if there were more than one

E offence being dealt with, would not merit a recommendation for deportation. But a series of shoplifting offences on different occasions may justify a recommendation for deportation. Even a first offence of shoplifting might merit a recommendation if the offender were a member of a gang carrying out a planned raid on a departmental store.

Secondly, the courts are not concerned with the political systems which

F operate in other countries. They may be harsh; they may be soft; they may be oppressive; they may be the quintessence of democracy. The court has no knowledge of those matters over and above that which is common knowledge; and that may be wrong. In our judgment it would be undesirable for this court or any other court to express views about regimes which exist outside the United Kingdom of Great Britain and Northern Ireland. It is for the Home Secretary to decide in each case

G whether an offender's return to his country of origin would have consequences which would make his compulsory return unduly harsh. The Home Secretary has opportunities of informing himself about what is happening in other countries which the courts do not have. The sort of argument which was put up in this case is one which we did not find attractive. It may well be that the regime in Iran at the present time is

H likely to be unfavourable from the point of view of the applicant. Whether, and how long, it will continue to be so we do not know. Whether it will be so by the end of this man's sentence of imprisonment must be a matter of speculation. When the time comes for him to be released from prison, the Home Secretary, we are sure, will bear in mind the very matters which we have been urged to consider, namely, whether it would be unduly harsh to send him back to his country of origin.

The next matter to which we invite attention by way of guidelines is

the effect that an order recommending deportation will have upon others   A
who are not before the court and who are innocent persons.   This court
and all other courts would have no wish to break up families or impose
hardship on innocent people.   The case of Fernandez illustrates this very
clearly indeed.   Mrs. Fernandez is an admirable person, a good wife and
mother, a credit to herself and someone whom most of us would want
to have in this country.   As we have already indicated, if her husband
is deported she will have a heartrending choice to make; whether she   B
should go with her husband or leave him and look after the interests of
the children.   That is the kind of situation which should be considered
very carefully before a recommendation for deportation is made.

We have considered the case of Fernandez in the light of those considerations and have come to the conclusion that the recommendation for
deportation should be quashed.   We can see no reason for interfering with   C
the sentences of imprisonment.   We had to grant him leave to appeal in
order to quash the recommendation for deportation.   He may, if he so
wishes, exercise his statutory right to be present, but we hold out no hope
that it will do him any good; and we should be grateful if his wife would
make that clear to him.

That concludes all the cases except to say a word in relation to   D
deportation in the case of Dissanayake.   He wants to go back to Sri Lanka,
but says that he does not want to go back under an order of deportation.
It is possible in his case (we make no finding about it) that even if we were
to quash the recommendation the Secretary of State, under the powers
which he has under the Immigration Act 1971, could deport him in any
case, because apparently his stay here is subject to the limitations which
were imposed upon him when he first came to this country.   His wife,   E
whom it is said he married for reasons of convenience, is now dead,
but that is not a matter into which we intend to go.   It is often said in
this class of case that there is no need to recommend deportation, because
the accused is willing to go back of his own free will when he has served
his sentence of imprisonment.   We are not impressed with that argument.
Assertions of intention made in this court are often forgotten on leaving
the court and even more frequently forgotten once the prison gates have   F
opened and the appellant is at large once again.

In our judgment there were very good grounds in the case of
Dissanayake for making a recommendation.   He had committed a serious
offence, and he committed it, according to the case put forward on his
behalf, when he was in a state of diminished responsibility by reason of
what, in his case, must be inherent causes.   Where there is evidence of   G
mental instability connected with, or resulting in the commission of a serious
criminal offence it seems to us, again as a matter of guidelines, that that
in itself is a good reason why a recommendation for deportation should be
made.   Whether it is carried out is entirely a matter for the Home Secretary.

We wish to state clearly and firmly that all a court does when it makes
a recommendation for deportation is to indicate to the Secretary of State   H
that in the opinion of the court it is to the detriment of this country that
the accused should remain here.   The final decision is for the Secretary
of State.   No doubt he will take into account the personal circumstances
of each person whose case he is considering, and that will include the
political situation in the country to which he will have to go if an order of
deportation is made.   These are matters solely for the Secretary of State,
and not for the courts.

A   It follows from what we have said that in the case of Nazari the application will be dismissed. The appeal will be dismissed in all its aspects in
the case of Dissanayake. In the case of Anyanwu there is now no appeal
before the court; but if there had been one we should have upheld the
recommendation because he was proved to have been an illegal immigrant.
In such cases a recommendation should normally be made. In the case
of Fernandez, as has already been indicated, the order recommending
B deportation will be quashed.

Orders accordingly.

Solicitors: *Offenbach & Co.; Philip Kossof & Co.; Stuart A. West
& Co.*

C   [Reported by MISS ISOBEL COLLINS, Barrister-at-Law]

[CHANCERY DIVISION]

*HOWARD E. PERRY & CO. LTD. v.
D   BRITISH RAILWAYS BOARD

[1980 H. No. 1746]

1980 March 14, 17   Sir Robert Megarry V.-C.

E *Conversion Act of Detention of owners' goods—Temporary withholding of goods during period of industrial action—Whether
conversion of goods — Whether fears of further industrial
action justifying withholding of goods — Interlocutory order
for delivery up of goods — Torts (Interference with Goods)
Act 1977 (c. 32), ss. 1, 3 (2) (a); 4 (2)—R.S.C., Ord. 29, r. 2A*

Members of the National Union of Railwaymen, who were
employed by the defendant board, had been instructed by
F   their union to support a strike of steelworkers by refusing to
transport steel. In two of the board's depots were consign-
ments of steel awaiting delivery to the plaintiffs, who were steel
stockholders and to whom the steel belonged. The steel was of
a type which could not be kept for a long period without risk
of becoming unworkable because it would harden and become
unmalleable. As the plaintiffs knew that the board's road
carriers would not cross picket lines, they sought permission
G   from the board to collect the steel themselves but the board,
fearing further industrial action, refused that request. The
plaintiffs claimed, under section 3 of the Torts (Interference
with Goods) Act 1977,[1] an order for the delivery up of the
goods and damages.
On the plaintiffs' motion for an order that the board
deliver up the steel to the plaintiffs:—
Held, (1) that the board, by refusing to release the plain-
H   tiffs' goods during the steelworkers' strike because of a genuine

[1] Torts (Interference with Goods) Act 1977, s. 3: " (1) In proceedings for
wrongful interference against a person who is in possession . . . of the goods relief
may be given in accordance with this section . . . (2) The relief is—(a) an order
for delivery of the goods . . ."
S. 4: " (2) On an application of any person in accordance with rules of court,
the High Court shall, in such circumstances as may be specified in the rules, have
power to make an order providing for the delivery up of any goods which are or
may become the subject matter of subsequent proceedings in the court . . ."

or reasonable fear of further industrial action on the part of A
their employees, were denying the plaintiffs most of the rights
of ownership, including the right to possession, for an
indefinite period; that the fear of industrial action was not a
justification for a temporary withholding of the steel and, by
so doing, the board had committed the tort of conversion and
therefore, there had been a wrongful interference with goods
within the meaning of section 1 of the Torts (Interference with
Goods) Act 1977 (post, pp. 1380B–E, 1381A–C).   B

Hiort v. Bott (1874) L.R. 9 Ex. 86 and Caxton Publishing
Co. Ltd. v. Sutherland Publishing Co. [1939] A.C. 178, H.L.(E.)
considered.

(2) That under section 4 of the Act and R.S.C., Ord. 29, r.
2A, the court had jurisdiction to order the board to deliver up
the steel and that jurisdiction was not limited to cases where
there was a danger that the goods would be disposed of, lost
or destroyed (post, pp. 1382D–F).   C

(3) That since steel was not readily available on the open
market, damages would not compensate the plaintiffs for the
difficulty in continuing to carry on their business; that the
balance between the plaintiffs' need for the steel and the board's
fears of increased industrial action was that the plaintiffs had
made out a strong claim to be permitted to collect their steel
while the board's case was weak and, accordingly, the court
would exercise its discretion to order the board to deliver up D
the steel (post, pp. 1382H—1383B, 1385A–B).

Dicta of Swinfen Eady M.R. in Whiteley Ltd. v. Hilt
[1918] 2 K.B. 808, 819, C.A. and Diplock L.J. in General and
Finance Facilities Ltd. v. Cooks Cars (Romford) Ltd. [1963]
1 W.L.R. 644, 649–650, C.A. applied.

The following cases are referred to in the judgment: E

Beaman v. A.R.T.S. Ltd. [1948] 2 All E.R. 89; [1949] 1 K.B. 550; [1949]
1 All E.R. 465, C.A.

Beatty v. Gillbanks (1882) 9 Q.B.D. 308.

Burroughes v. Bayne (1860) 5 H. & N. 296.

Caxton Publishing Co. Ltd. v. Sutherland Publishing Co. [1939] A.C. 178;
[1938] 4 All E.R. 389, H.L.(E.).

Clayton v. Le Roy [1911] 2 K.B. 1031, C.A.   F

General and Finance Facilities Ltd. v. Cooks Cars (Romford) Ltd.
[1963] 1 W.L.R. 644; [1963] 2 All E.R. 314, C.A.

Hiort v. Bott (1874) L.R. 9 Ex. 86.

Lancashire and Yorkshire Railway Co. v. MacNicoll (1918) 88 L.J.K.B.
601.

Lawrence's Will Trusts, In re [1972] Ch. 418; [1971] 3 W.L.R. 188;
[1971] 3 All E.R. 433.   G

Oakley v. Lyster [1931] 1 K.B. 148, C.A.

Whiteley Ltd. v. Hilt [1918] 2 K.B. 808, C.A.

No additional cases were cited in argument.

MOTION   H

By their notice of motion dated March 11, 1980, the plaintiffs,
Howard E. Perry & Co. Ltd., steel stockholders, sought an order
that the defendants, the British Railways Board, should deliver up 180
tons of the plaintiffs' steel in their Wolverhampton Depot and 300 tons
of the plaintiffs' steel in their Brierley Hill Depot to the plaintiffs forthwith, and that the costs of the application be provided for.

The plaintiffs' claim under the writ was for an order for the delivery

A   of the steel and damages in accordance with section 3 (2) (a) of the Torts (Interference with Goods) Act 1977.

The facts are stated in the judgment.

Alexander Irvine Q.C. and *A. J. G. Dalziel* for the plaintiffs.
D. Gidley Scott for the defendants.

B
SIR ROBERT MEGARRY V.-C. In this motion the plaintiffs, Howard E. Perry & Co. Ltd., seek an order that the defendants, the British Railways Board, should forthwith deliver up certain quantities of steel which lie at the defendants' Wolverhampton and Brierley Hill depots and belong to the plaintiffs. Some 500 tons of steel, worth some £10,000, is there, and some at least is imported. There is no dispute about most
C   of the facts. The steel is admittedly the plaintiffs' property, and they are admittedly entitled to possession of it. The plaintiffs have admittedly demanded the steel from the defendants, and the defendants have admittedly refused to comply with the demands. The reasons for the refusals arise out of the strike of steel-workers which began on January 1, 1980, coupled with the attitude of the National Union of Railwaymen
D   ("N.U.R."), a union to which many of the defendants' employees belong. The argument on this motion lasted after the usual hour for adjournment on Friday, and for that reason, and also to enable me to look into the authorities, I postponed giving judgment until today, Monday.

The plaintiffs carry on business as steel stockholders; and by reason of the strike there is a strong demand for steel by the plaintiffs' customers and many others. The steel in question, say the plaintiffs, cannot
E   be kept for any long period without the risk of it becoming impossible to work through becoming too hard and unmalleable. At first, the plaintiffs were able to continue to receive the steel carried for them by the defendants; but then the drivers employed by the defendants' road carriers refused to cross picket lines. Even then, as late as January 21 or 22, the plaintiffs were able to collect over 100 tons of steel from the
F   defendants by sending the plaintiffs' own men and equipment for it; and members of the N.U.R. assisted in the loading. But then the General Secretary of the N.U.R., Mr. Weighell, sent a letter dated January 23 to all branches of the N.U.R., and to other bodies and officials of the union, stating that in consequence of a further request for assistance from the Iron & Steel Trades Confederation (" I.S.T.C. "), the union engaged in the steel strike, " N.U.R. members are now
G   instructed to refuse to transport all steel, regardless of its origin." This further request was made in view of the decision of I.S.T.C. to extend the strike from the British Steel Corporation to " the private sector " as from January 27.

On behalf of the plaintiffs, Mr. Irvine emphasised that the plaintiffs do not seek to compel the defendants to take any active steps to deliver
H   the steel to the plaintiffs in the sense of loading it, or transporting it to their premises. Notwithstanding the terms of the notice of motion, all that the plaintiffs ask is that the defendants should permit the plaintiffs, with their own vehicles, equipment and employees, to enter the defendants' depots and remove the steel themselves. On behalf of the defendants, Mr. Gidley Scott has not suggested that there would be any objection or difficulty in this, apart from what may compendiously be called trade union difficulties. Mr. Irvine's case was simplicity itself. The

steel is the plaintiffs', and they are entitled to possession of it. It lies   A
on the defendants' property, and yet despite demands for it by the
plaintiffs the defendants have refused and are refusing either to deliver
it in accordance with the terms of the contract between the plaintiffs
and the defendants or to allow the plaintiffs to fetch it for themselves.
The defendants have accordingly committed what used to be called the
tort of conversion and now, by virtue of section 1 of the Torts (Inter-   B
ference with Goods) Act 1977, is called " wrongful interference with
goods." The plaintiffs' claim under the writ is for an order for the
delivery of the steel, and damages, and this accords with section 3 (2) (a)
of the Act. By section 4 (2) and R.S.C., Ord. 29, r. 2A, the court has
power to make an interlocutory order for delivery up of the goods,
and on the facts of the case it is plainly right that such an order
should be made. That was the contention.   C

On behalf of the defendants, Mr. Gidley Scott advanced three main
contentions to the contrary. The first and most fundamental was that
on the admitted facts the defendants had committed no tort, and were
committing none. The second was that under the Rules of the Supreme
Court, no interlocutory order for delivery up would be made when
the goods were merely being detained and there was no risk of their
being disposed of, lost or destroyed, or becoming otherwise unaccounted   D
for. The third contention was that a proper exercise of the court's discretion required the application to be refused, since damages would be
an adequate remedy, and the defendants feared industrial action if the
order was made and they complied with it.

On the first contention, Mr. Gidley Scott accepted that before the Act
of 1977 the defendants would have been guilty of committing the tort   E
of detinue; but he said that this tort had been abolished by the
Act (as indeed it has), and that the new statutory tort of wrongful
interference with goods does not include a mere refusal to deliver goods
to the owner such as had occurred in this case. If this is right, then the
Act of 1977 may, at any rate on one view, be said to have blundered
by removing from the sphere of tort some acts which previously were   F
clearly tortious, without any apparent reason for doing so.

Mr. Gidley Scott's process of reasoning was as follows. Section 1
of the Act defines " wrongful interference with goods " as meaning
" conversion of goods (also called trover)," " trespass to goods " and
negligence or (subject to section 2) any other tort, so far as it results
in damage to goods or to an interest in goods. Detinue is not mentioned. Section 2 (1), which must be one of the shortest subsections on   G
the statute book, simply states " Detinue is abolished," without even a
" hereby." By section 2 (2):

> " An action lies in conversion for loss or destruction of goods which
> a bailee has allowed to happen in breach of his duty to his bailor
> (that is to say it lies in a case which is not otherwise conversion,
> but would have been detinue before detinue was abolished)."   H

In other words, the only form of detinue which the Act converts into
conversion, and so into wrongful interference with goods, is the loss
or destruction of goods which a bailee has allowed to happen in breach
of his duty to the bailor. If there is anything else which used to be
detinue but not conversion or any other tort mentioned in section 1,
the Act has removed it from the field of tort. Mr. Gidley Scott's endea-

The Weekly Law Reports, November 14, 1980

1379

1 W.L.R.   Howard Perry & Co. v. British Railways (Ch.D.)   Sir Robert
                                                                          Megarry V.-C.

A vours were thus directed towards demonstrating that what the defendants had done in the present case, though detinue under the old law,
was not conversion under that law, and so was not wrongful interference
with goods under the present law. As there plainly has been no " loss
or destruction of goods," the case obviously is not one which falls
within section 2 (2).

B   In support of his contention, Mr. Gidley Scott cited a number of
authorities. He set the general background by reading from *Clerk &
Lindsell on Torts,* 14th ed. (1975), pp. 677–680, and he then cited a line
of cases running from *Hiort* v. *Bott* (1874) L.R. 9 Ex. 86, 89, to *Caxton
Publishing Co. Ltd.* v. *Sutherland Publishing Co.* [1939] A.C. 178, 201,
202 and *Beaman* v. *A.R.T.S. Ltd.* [1948] 2 All E.R. 89, 92. This last
decision was reversed on other grounds at [1949] 1 K.B. 550, although
C at p. 570 Somervell L.J. said that some of the statements made on the
point in the court below might be found to need qualification. In the
cases there are a number of definitions or descriptions of the tort of
conversion. Mr. Gidley Scott relied on the approval by Farwell L.J., in
Clayton v. *Le Roy* [1911] 2 K.B. 1031, 1052, of the words of Bramwell
B. in *Burroughes* v. *Bayne* (1860) 5 H. & N. 296, 309, to the effect that
D there must be a withholding of property " in such a way as that it may be
said to be a conversion to a man's own use." This quotation must, I
think, be read in the light of what Bramwell B. said three sentences
further on: " He has claimed a dominion over it inconsistent with
mine."

       Mr. Gidley Scott also relied on the approval by Scrutton L.J. in
E *Oakley* v. *Lyster* [1931] 1 K.B. 148, 153 of a statement by Atkin J. in
Lancashire & Yorkshire Railway Co. v. *MacNicoll* (1918) 88 L.J.K.B.
601, 605, to the effect that there must be a dealing with goods in a
manner inconsistent with the right of the true owner, provided that in
so doing the defendant intends to deny the owner's right or assert a
right inconsistent with it. In the *Caxton* case [1939] A.C. 178, 202, Lord
Porter pointed out that Atkin J. went on to say that where the act done
F was necessarily a denial of the owner's right or an assertion of a right
inconsistent therewith, intention does not matter. Lord Porter added:

> " Another way of reaching the same conclusion would be to say
> that conversion consists in an act intentionally done inconsistent
> with the owner's right, though the doer may not know of or intend
> to challenge the property or possession of the true owner."

G   The main thrust of Mr. Gidley Scott's contentions was that as a mere
refusal in response to a demand was not itself a conversion, though it
could be evidence of a conversion (see *Clerk & Lindsell on Torts,* p. 678),
and the defendants had at no stage denied the plaintiffs' title to the
steel, or attempted to deal with it in any way inconsistent with the
plaintiffs' rights, there had been no conversion within the true meaning
H of that term. There was no conversion, he said, if the reason for the
refusal to release the goods was a genuine or reasonable fear, unless
this meant that the owner could never have his goods. He accepted that
there could be a conversion if the threat induced a withholding of the
goods for a long period, measured in months or years, but not if it was
merely a matter of days or weeks; and he said that the present case
fell into this latter category, though he could not be persuaded to
prophesy when the strike of steel workers would end. This contention

was based to some extent, I think, on words of Bramwell B. in *Hiort* A
v. *Bott* (1874) L.R. 9 Ex. 86, 89. The judge there said that a good
description of what constituted a conversion was " where a man does an
unauthorized act which deprives another of his property permanently or
for an indefinite time "; and I think that Mr. Gidley Scott interpreted
" indefinite time " as meaning a period which was not only uncertain in
length but also of substantial duration.

There seems to me to be considerable force in the observation in B
Clerk & Lindsell on Torts, p. 682 that " It is perhaps impossible to
frame a definition which will cover every conceivable case." What I
have to consider here is a case in which the defendants are in effect
saying to the plaintiffs: " We admit that the steel is yours and that you
are entitled to possession of it. Yet because we fear that industrial
action may be taken against us if we permit you to remove it, we have C
refused to allow you to collect it for some weeks now, despite your
demands, and we will continue to refuse to allow you to collect it until
our fears have been removed." Looking at the matter as one of
principle, I would conclude that this is a clear case of conversion. The
defendants are denying the plaintiffs most of the rights of ownership,
including the right to possession, for a period which clearly is indefinite. D
It may be short, or it may be long; but it is plainly uncertain. I do not
think that a period which will not end until the defendants reach the
conclusion that their fears no longer justify the withholding of the steel
can very well be called " definite." There is a detention of the steel
which is consciously adverse to the plaintiffs' rights, and this seems to
me to be of the essence of at least one form of conversion. A denial
of possession to the plaintiffs does not cease to be a denial by being E
accompanied by a statement that the plaintiffs are entitled to the
possession that is being denied to them.

It seems to me that this view is consistent with the authorities put
before me, and also with some others. The cause of action in conversion
was stated in the Common Law Procedure Act 1852, as follows: " That
the defendant converted to his own use, or wrongfully deprived the plain- F
tiff of the use and possession of the plaintiff's goods." I do not see how
it could be said that the defendants are not at the moment wrongfully
depriving the plaintiffs of the use and possession of the plaintiffs' goods,
unless the defendants' fears of industrial action could be said to prevent
their refusal to release the steel from being wrongful. (The quotation
from the Act, I may say, is from Schedule (B), paragraph 28, to which
section 91 gave force and effect: *Clerk & Lindsell* at p. 671 supports the G
quotation by a reference to section 49, but that seems to have nothing
to do with it. See also *Bullen & Leake's Pleadings,* 3rd ed. (1868), p. 290.)

I have also looked at the *Eighteenth Report of the Law Reform
Committee,* 1971 (Cmnd. 4774), not in order to construe the Act of 1977,
but for the statement of the pre-existing law there set out. In paragraph
8, the report states: H

> " The present position appears to be that conversion will lie in every
> case in which detinue would lie, save only that detinue lies, but
> conversion does not lie, against a bailee of goods who in breach of
> his duty has allowed them to be lost or destroyed."

The report is not, of course, an authority in the sense that a judgment
is: but it was signed by four eminent judges (Lord Pearson, Lord Diplock,

The Weekly Law Reports, November 14, 1980

1381

1 W.L.R.   Howard Perry & Co. v. British Railways (Ch.D.)   Sir Robert
                                                                          Megarry V.-C.

A Buckley L.J., and Orr L.J.), and it certainly represented my views when
I too signed it. If the report is right on this point, that is the end of the
defendants' contention. The report also provides an explanation of the
form taken by section 2 of the Act of 1977.

My conclusion is accordingly that this contention of the defendants
fails. For the defendants to withhold the steel from the plaintiffs is a
B wrongful interference with goods within the Act of 1977 unless the
reason for the withholding provides a justification. I cannot see that
it does. This is no brief withholding made merely in order that the
defendants may verify the plaintiffs' title to the steel, or for some other
purpose to confirm that the delivery of the steel would be proper. This
is a withholding despite the plain right of the plaintiffs to the ownership
and possession of the steel, on the ground that the defendants fear
C unpleasant consequences if they do not deny the plaintiffs what they
are entitled to.

I turn to the second point. Section 4 (2) of the Act of 1977 provides
that on the application of any person in accordance with rules of court,
the High Court is to have power, " in such circumstances as may be
specified in the rules," to make an order providing for the delivery up
D of any goods " which are or may become the subject matter of subsequent proceedings in the court, or as to which any question may
arise in proceedings." By section 4 (3) delivery is to be to the claimant or
to a person appointed by the court for the purpose, as the order may
provide, and is to be on such terms and conditions as may be specified
in the order. By section 4 (4), the rule-making power is to include power
to make rules as to the manner in which an application for such an
E order can be made, and as to the circumstances in which it can be made,
with such incidental, supplementary and consequential provisions as the
rule-making authority may consider necessary or expedient.

This power was exercised by the Rules of the Supreme Court (Amendment No. 3) 1978 (S.I. 1978 No. 579). This Order replaced the existing
R.S.C., Ord. 13, r. 3, and R.S.C., Ord. 19, r. 4, by new rules, and inserted
F a new Ord. 15, r. 10A, Ord. 29, r. 2A, and Ord. 42, r. 1A. Only Ord. 29,
r. 2A, was referred to in argument, though I may mention that Ord. 13,
r. 3, and Ord. 19, r. 4, with their references to a claim " relating to the
detention of goods only " do not easily fit in with Mr. Gidley Scott's
main contention that detention simpliciter is not tortious. R.S.C., Ord.
29, r. 2A, runs as follows:

G   " (1) Without prejudice to rule 2, the court may, on the application
         of any party to a cause or matter, make an order under section 4
         of the Torts (Interference with Goods) Act 1977 for the delivery
         up of any goods which are the subject-matter of the cause or matter
         or as to which any question may arise therein. (2) Paragraphs (2)
         and (3) of rule 1 shall have effect in relation to an application for
         such an order as they have effect in relation to an application for
H   the grant of an injunction."

In order to make this rule intelligible, I should explain the references.
The reference to rule 2 is to the rule which authorises an order to be
made for the detention, custody or preservation of property which is
the subject matter of proceedings, or for its inspection. The reference
to paragraphs (2) and (3) of rule 1 is to the provision for making ex
parte applications for injunctions in urgent cases, and for the grant of

injunctions in cases of urgency even before the issue of the writ or   A
originating summons. What Mr. Gidley Scott relied on was a note to
R.S.C., Ord. 29, r. 2A, in the *Third Cumulative Supplement to The
Supreme Court Practice (1979).* This note states that an order for the
interim delivery up of goods will only be made where the matter is
urgent

> " and there is a real and imminent danger or risk that the goods will   B
>   be disposed of or lost or destroyed or will otherwise be unaccounted
>   for."

In this case, there is no danger that the steel will be disposed of or lost
or destroyed, or will otherwise be unaccounted for, and so, it was said,
no order for the delivery up of the goods should be made. That was the
contention.   C
   Now no authority is cited for the proposition in the note to rule 2A nor
is any reasoning advanced to support it; and Mr. Gidley Scott was not able
to put forward any cogent reason for sustaining it. Suppose, for instance,
the goods in question are gradually deteriorating. It may be a long
while before the deterioration would reach a point where it can be said
that the goods have been " destroyed "; yet if the note is right, the
court will not order the goods to be delivered up. Or suppose that the   D
goods in question are in no peril but are urgently needed by the owner
to avoid other losses. Thus the goods might be the only keys to a strong-
room, or they might be scientific or medical papers relating to some new
process or remedy, or a dozen other things. Why should the court refuse
to make an order for delivery up in such a case? The rule contains
nothing whatever to suggest any limitation or restriction; it simply   E
states that the court " may . . . make an order " under section 4 " for
the delivery up " of the goods in dispute. Of course the court must
exercise a proper judicial discretion in deciding whether or not to
exercise the power; but I can see nothing whatever to put the court in
the strait-jacket which the note proclaims. Accordingly, I reject this
contention of the defendants, and hold that the exercise of the powers   F
under the Act and under R.S.C., Ord. 29, r. 2A, are not fettered in the
way in which the defendants contend. I think that the note is in this
respect wrong.
   Third, there is the court's discretion. The defendants put forward
two contentions in support of the proposition that the court ought not
in its discretion to make any order for delivery up. They were, first,
that damages were an adequate remedy for the plaintiffs, and second,   G
the defendants' fears of industrial action. I will take these in turn.
   I think that it is plain that the making of an order for the delivery
up of goods is in the discretion of the court. Section 3 (2) (*a*) of the Act
of 1977 allows a plaintiff to claim delivery of the goods with consequential
damages, and that is what the plaintiffs have done in this case. Such a
claim does not give the defendant an option to pay damages in lieu of   H
delivering the goods; but section 3 (3) (*b*) provides that relief under section
3 (2) (*a*) " is at the discretion of the court," and I think that any interlocutory order must also be within the discretion of the court, both for
this reason and upon general principles. A principle on which the court
has long acted is not to order delivery of goods which are ordinary
articles of commerce with no special value or interest, whether to the
plaintiff or others, when damages will fully compensate: see *Whiteley*

The Weekly Law Reports, November 14, 1980

1383

1 W.L.R.   **Howard Perry & Co. v. British Railways (Ch.D.)**   Sir Robert
Megarry V.-C.

A *Ltd.* v. *Hilt* [1918] 2 K.B. 808, 819, *per* Sir Charles Swinfen Eady M.R.;
and see also *General and Finance Facilities Ltd.* v. *Cooks Cars (Romford)
Ltd.* [1963] 1 W.L.R. 644, 649, 650, *per* Diplock L.J. If a plaintiff can
easily replace the goods detained by purchasing their equivalent on the
market, then the payment of damages out of which the price of the
equivalent may be paid is adequate compensation to the wronged plaintiff, and there is little or no point in making an order for the delivery of
B the goods. Far better to let the plaintiff fend for himself with the defendant's money.

In normal times, the steel here in dispute might indeed be in this
category; but these times are not normal, and at present steel is obtainable on the market only with great difficulty, if at all. If the equivalent
of what is detained is unobtainable, how can it be said that damages
C are an adequate remedy? They plainly are not. Mr. Irvine observed
that at present " steel is gold," and one can see what he meant. Yet
even that may not do justice to his cause, since as far as I know gold is
still available on the open market to those who pay the price. In one
sense, I suppose, it can be said that as those who trade do so for profit,
damages of a sufficient amount may compensate for any wrong. All that
D the plaintiffs are losing, said Mr. Gidley Scott, is the sale of some steel,
and damages will adequately compensate them for that. I do not think
that this is by any means the whole picture. Damages would be a poor
consolation if the failure of supplies forces a trader to lay off staff and
disappoint his customers (whose affections may be transferred to others)
and ultimately impels him towards insolvency. On the facts of the
present case the perils of the plaintiffs may well not be so great as that
E at present, but such elements cannot be ignored. In any case, I think
that what matters is the adequacy of damages in place of the thing that
ought to have been delivered. Under this head I think that my discretion ought to be exercised in favour of making the order that the
plaintiffs seek.

The other main issue on discretion was that of the defendants' fears
F of industrial action. On behalf of the defendants, there was the evidence
of Mr. Scott. Until February 22, 1980, he had been the area manager
for the defendants of the area which includes the defendants' freight
terminals at Wolverhampton and Brierley Hill, and then he became
divisional operating superintendent for the defendants' division which
includes those terminals. He puts the defendants' reasons succinctly
in his affidavit:
G
> " The board's reasons for not agreeing to the collection of the
> steel by the plaintiffs are:—(i) the fear that it would bring about
> intensified industrial action by the N.U.R. and the board's work-
> people, affecting the conduct of the board's business and thus affect-
> ing other customers of the board; (ii) the fear that in the future
> action might be taken by the I.S.T.C. against the board, with
H > similar results; and (iii) the fear of disorder at and outside the
> board's terminals at Brierley Hill and Wolverhampton."

He also states that on several occasions between January 23 and March
12, 1980, the defendants have asked representatives of their workers at
the two terminals whether they would handle steel for delivery to the
plaintiffs, and whether they would load it on to the plaintiffs' vehicles,
to which in each case the answer has been " No," and also whether

they would object to the plaintiffs loading the steel on to their own   A
vehicles, to which the answer was " Yes."

Now in the motion before me, the first two questions and answers do
not arise, as the plaintiffs do not seek any order requiring the defendants to handle or load the steel. There is thus no more than the statement by representatives of the workers that they would " object " to
the plaintiffs loading the steel themselves. As Mr. Irvine emphasised,   B
there has been no threat of a strike, or a so-called " work to rule," or
any other form of industrial action or inaction in relation to the plaintiffs' proposal to move their own steel. At the same time, one cannot
live very long in England in these days without being aware that anything which an employer does or fails to do may, if it is disliked by a
number of his employees, be proclaimed to be " aggro," and may lead
to the inception and escalation of various forms of industrial disruption.   C
I agree that a mere objection is not the same as a threat; but in this field
the circumstances may make it reasonable to regard it as an indirect
threat, especially where, as here, there is subsisting industrial action by
the defendants' employees in relation to transporting steel generally. I
certainly would not consider it to be unreasonable for the defendants to
regard it as an indirect threat.
                                                                             D
Let me assume, then, that the defendants' fear of intensified industrial action is a real fear in respect of an indirect threat of intensified
industrial action by the N.U.R., that their fear of future action by the
I.S.T.C. against them is a real fear of a possibility, and so is their fear
of disorder at and outside their terminals where the steel lies. Do these
fears of the defendants, either individually or collectively, provide a
sufficient ground for the court, in its discretion, to refuse to make the   E
order for delivery which otherwise ought to be made in favour of the
plaintiffs? Ought the court to be dissuaded from making an order
against a litigant if that litigant has been threatened with unpleasant
consequences if he does what the order requires him to do?

I think that the courts should be very reluctant to answer such
questions with an unqualified " Yes." There may indeed be some cases   F
in which " Yes " would be an appropriate answer. Thus where the
parents of a young child are disputing the custody of that child, the
court, in giving effect to the paramount interests of the child, may
sometimes have to bow to what in effect are threats of lawful action on
one side or the other. At times the courts have to accept matters as
they are, rather than as they ought to be. Again, there may be cases in
which in other respects the scales are only barely tipped in favour of   G
making the order, and the damaging effect of the threats is so great
that the court may then refrain from making the order. But apart from
cases such as these, I think that the court ought not to allow threats to
a litigant, and the litigant's fears of those threats, to dominate the
decision. Possible examples abound. Mr. Irvine suggested the case of a
motorist who had had his car repaired by a garage, and had paid the   H
bill, being then told by the garage proprietor that his staff had just
discovered who the motorist was, and had threatened to strike if he was
allowed to take his car away. I need not pursue the effect on the practice
in granting injunctions if the fear of industrial consequences, or, indeed,
other unpleasant results, were to be allowed to play the part for which
the defendants contend. Nor, I think, need I stress the importance of not
allowing people's rights to be curtailed by fears of disorder, which

The Weekly Law Reports, November 21, 1980

1385

1 W.L.R.   Howard Perry & Co. v. British Railways (Ch.D.)   Sir Robert
                                                                          Megarry V.-C.

A plainly include fears of unlawful assemblies and breaches of the peace. As in *Beatty* v. *Gillbanks* (1882) 9 Q.B.D. 308, I think that it is the unlawful that must yield to the lawful, and not vice versa.

In my judgment, the exercise of the court's discretion calls for a balancing of the considerations on each side. In this case I think that the plaintiffs have a strong case for their claim to be permitted to collect their own steel, and I think that the defendants' case for the court not

B to make the order is weak. I cannot, of course, say whether any industrial action, and if so what, will in fact be taken if in obedience of the order of the court the defendants allow the plaintiffs to collect their steel. The unions and their members will no doubt bear in mind that the defendants will be doing no more than obeying the ordinary law of the land, and not least a direct order of the High Court. All con-

C cerned may take a practical view of the matter, and decide that as only some 500 tons of steel is concerned, and there appears to be small prospect of it being replaced for the time being, there would be little point in mounting industrial action over what may be regarded as a " one-off job." It is not as if a continuing source of supply were in issue.

The unions and their members may also give some weight to a

D petition signed by nearly 100 workers at Brasway Ltd., of Brierley Hill, whose tube division manufactures electrically welded steel tubes, and obtains most of its steel from the plaintiffs. The evidence is that the division can obtain no steel elsewhere, and if it receives no further supplies it will have to lay off 120 employees almost at once. The two main manufacturers that the division supplies have stated that if the division fails to supply them, they will cease to place orders with the company, in which

E case the division would probably have to close, and 120 jobs would be lost. The petitioners not surprisingly state that they cannot see why their jobs should be put at risk because the plaintiffs are unable to obtain their own material. Yet whatever attitude the unions and their members may adopt, it seems quite plain to me that on the evidence and the law I ought to make the order sought by the plaintiffs.

F I shall therefore make the order which the plaintiffs claim. The wording of it is for consideration. The power to order the " delivery " (or, as the rule puts it, the " delivery up ") of goods must be wide enough to cover an order requiring a defendant to allow the plaintiff to collect for himself goods which the defendant is unable or unwilling to deliver to him in the sense of collecting and transporting them, at all events, where, as here, no objection to this course has been suggested.

G " Delivery " must, I think, include the process of merely transferring authority over something in situ, as with the delivery up of possession of land, or livery of seisin. I will only say that I think that there should be a form of wording which will admit of compliance by the defendants without their taking any physical steps to move the steel. On that footing the motion succeeds.

H There are two things that I should add. First, certain terms on which the defendants carry goods and warehouse them were put in evidence; but it soon became common ground that although these might be of some importance in relation to damages, they did not affect anything that I have to decide, and so I say no more about them. Second, although I have cited certain authorities which were not mentioned in argument, I have observed the principle that I stated in *In re Lawrence's Will Trusts* [1972] Ch. 418, 436, 437. If any of these authorities had altered the con-

clusion that I had reached without their aid, then I would have restored A
the case for further argument, so that counsel would have been able to
meet them: a litigant ought not to be defeated by authorities which he
has had no opportunity of controverting or explaining. As in fact those
authorities merely fortified the views that I had formed without them,
there was no need for further argument, and so I called for none.

B

> *Order that defendants permit plaintiffs*
> *to take their steel not before 10 a.m.*
> *on March 18, 1980.*
> *Liberty to apply.*

Solicitors: *Elfords for Cove & Co., Birmingham; Evan Harding.*

C

K. N. B.

[CHANCERY DIVISION]

* PRACTICE DIRECTION (COSTS: ASSESSMENT IN CHAMBERS) D
(No. 2)

[No. 3 of 1980]

Practice—Chancery Division—Costs—Assessment in chambers—
Monetary limit of costs assessed or settled in chambers

E

1. Since 1975 the limit of costs which may be assessed or settled
in chambers by a master has been £500, with defined exceptions.
This limit is now raised to £1,500.

2. *Practice Direction (Costs: Assessment in Chambers)* [1975] 1
W.L.R. 1202 is amended accordingly.

By direction of the Vice-Chancellor.

F

EDMUND HEWARD,
Chief Master.

October 22, 1980.

G

[CHANCERY DIVISION]

* HEYWOOD *v.* BOARD OF VISITORS OF HULL PRISON
AND ANOTHER

[1980 H. No. 1446]

H

1980 April 16   Goulding J.

High Court — Divisions — Jurisdiction — Assignment of business
between divisions—Judicial declarations in Chancery Division
—Alternative proceedings for judicial review in Queen's Bench
Division—When appropriate—R.S.C., Ord. 53

A prisoner at Hull Prison was charged among others with
breaches of discipline during disturbances there. The board

A   of visitors found the charges proved and he suffered a loss of remission of sentence of 250 days. He sought relief from the board's decision, not by way of application for certiorari in the Queen's Bench Division, but by issuing a writ in the Chancery Division for a declaration that the adjudication of the board of visitors in his case was null and void. A motion by the board and the Home Office asked that all further proceedings in the action be stayed or that the action should be B   dismissed as being an abuse of the process of the court and that before the commencement of any proceedings against the board the leave of the Divisional Court of the Queen's Bench Division should have been and should be sought under R.S.C., Ord. 53 [1]: —

Held, that although the court in an appropriate case was not debarred by the existing rules from granting relief by way of judicial declaration in proceedings commenced by writ C   or originating summons, the present type of case where the decision of such a tribunal as the board of prison visitors was being called in question was one more appropriate for judicial review in accordance with the provisions of R.S.C., Ord. 53, and in those circumstances it was the duty of the court to put a stop at an early stage to an action which would by-pass the need for leave of the Divisional Court to bring proceedings in the Queen's Bench Division; accordingly, the D   motion of the board and the Home Office succeeded and further proceedings in the action against them would be stayed (post, pp. 1393C–E, 1395C–E, G–H).

Uppal v. *Home Office,* C.A. (post, pp. 1394A et seq.); Court of Appeal (Civil Division) Transcript No. 719 of 1978 applied.

De Falco v. *Crawley Borough Council* [1980] Q.B. 460, C.A. and *Pyx Granite Co. Ltd.* v. *Ministry of Housing and* E   *Local Government* [1960] A.C. 260, H.L.(E.) considered.

The following cases are referred to in the judgment:

Barnard v. *National Dock Labour Board* [1953] 2 Q.B. 18; [1953] 2 W.L.R. 995; [1953] 1 All E.R. 1113, C.A.

De Falco v. *Crawley Borough Council* [1980] Q.B. 460; [1980] 2 W.L.R. 664; [1980] 1 All E.R. 913, C.A.

F   *Pyx Granite Co. Ltd.* v. *Ministry of Housing and Local Government* [1960] A.C. 260; [1959] 3 W.L.R. 346; [1959] 3 All E.R. 1, H.L.(E.).

Reg. v. *Board of Visitors of Hull Prison, Ex parte St. Germain* [1979] Q.B. 425; [1979] 2 W.L.R. 42; [1979] 1 All E.R. 701, C.A.

Taylor v. *National Assistance Board* [1958] A.C. 532; [1958] 2 W.L.R. 11; [1957] 3 All E.R. 703 H.L.(E.).

G   *Uppal* v. *Home Office,* The Times, October 21, 1978, Sir Robert Megarry V.-C.; The Times, November 11, 1978; Court of Appeal (Civil Division) Transcript No. 719 of 1978, C.A.

The following additional case was cited in argument:

Sirros v. *Moore* [1975] Q.B. 118; [1974] 3 W.L.R. 459; [1974] 3 All E.R. 776, C.A.

H   MOTION

By writ dated February 28, 1980, and statement of claim in the Chancery Division, the plaintiff, Joseph Bernard Paul Michael Heywood of H.M. Prison, Long Lartin, South Littleton, Evesham, claimed a declaration against two defendants, the Board of Visitors of Hull Prison

---

[1] R.S.C., Ord. 53, r. 1: see post, pp. 1389H—1390C.

and the Home Office, that the adjudication of the board made on   A
October 12, 1976, respecting breaches of discipline was in his case null
and void.

By notice of motion dated March 31, 1980, the defendants sought
inter alia an order under the inherent jurisdiction of the court or under
R.S.C., Ord. 18, r. 19 that all further proceedings in the action against
them be stayed or that the endorsement of the writ and statement of
claim should be struck out and the action dismissed as being an abuse   B
of the process of the court, and that before the commencement of proceedings against them the leave of the Divisional Court of the Queen's
Bench Division should have been and should be sought under R.S.C.,
Ord. 53.

Further facts are stated in the judgment.

C
Lord Gifford for the plaintiff.
P. L. Gibson for both defendants.

GOULDING J.   I have before me a motion on the part of two
defendants in an action brought by Joseph Bernard Paul Michael
Heywood as plaintiff against them, namely, the Board of Visitors of
Hull Prison and the Home Office. The plaintiff, Mr. Heywood, was a   D
prisoner at Hull in the summer of 1976 at the time of the well-known
disturbances that then took place there. In consequence of those disturbances, a large number of prisoners were charged with various breaches
of discipline before the board of visitors of Hull Prison, the present
first-named defendants. The plaintiff was charged with two specific
offences alleged to have taken place on August 31, 1976, the charges   E
being laid, as I understand, on October 12, 1976. On the next day,
October 13, the board of visitors found the charges proved and sentenced
the plaintiff to various penalties, including a loss of remission of sentence
amounting to 250 days.

Some of the prisoners who were the subject of disciplinary proceedings after the Hull disturbances sought relief from the decisions of
the board of visitors by way of application for certiorari. The Divisional   F
Court of the Queen's Bench Division took the view that that remedy
was not available in such a case. However, some of those concerned
appealed to the Court of Appeal—that is, to the Civil Division of the
Court of Appeal—and there the decision of the Divisional Court was
reversed and it was held that the determinations of the board of visitors
could be called in question by way of certiorari: *Reg.* v. *Board of*   G
Visitors of Hull Prison, Ex parte St. Germain [1979] Q.B. 425.

After the decision of the Court of Appeal, the plaintiff quickly came
to know of it and took steps to seek legal aid and to endeavour to bring
proceedings for his own benefit. There were, it is conceded, delays on
the plaintiff's side and it is said (though I have no evidence on the
point, but it is said by counsel on his behalf) that he personally was
not to blame in the matter. I will so assume for the purposes of my   H
judgment. However, in the event, the plaintiff did not seek relief by
certiorari proceedings in the Queen's Bench Division, which would
now have to be brought under R.S.C., Ord. 53 by way of an application
for judicial review. Instead, he issued a writ in the Chancery Division
on February 28, 1980. It is endorsed generally for one item of relief
only, namely, "a declaration that the adjudication of the board of
visitors on October 12, 1976, is null and void."

The Weekly Law Reports, November 21, 1980

1389

1 W.L.R.   Heywood v. Hull Prison Visitors (Ch.D.)   Goulding J.

A   On March 26, 1980, the plaintiff gave notice of a motion seeking
an order for a speedy trial of the action. That is plainly a necessary
move on his part, because he is now, so I am informed, only detained
in prison in consequence of the loss of remission of 250 days by the
sentence of the board of visitors. Accordingly, unless he can obtain
relief reasonably quickly, it will be of no benefit to him in that regard.

B   The notice of motion given on behalf of the plaintiff has been overtaken by a cross-notice of motion on the part of both defendants,
the board of visitors and the Home Office, which seeks:

"An order under the inherent jurisdiction of the court or under
R.S.C., Ord. 18, r. 19, that all further proceedings in this action be
stayed or that the endorsement of the writ and the statement of
claim herein be struck out and this action dismissed on the ground
C   that this action is an abuse of the process of the court and that
before the commencement of any proceedings against the defendants in respect of the matters of complaint alleged in the said
writ and statement of claim the leave of the Divisional Court of the
Queen's Bench Division should have been and should be sought
under R.S.C., Ord. 53."

D   Very properly and logically, it has been agreed that I should hear the
defendants' motion first.

Several matters are, in my judgment, quite clear when one comes to
consider the contentions put forward on behalf of the defendants.
First of all, all relief by way of judicial declaration, whether or not
accompanied by relief of a more practical character, is equitable or
E   statutory in origin. The common law of England itself knew of no
such remedy. Secondly, there is ample and indisputable authority that all
declaratory relief is in the discretion of the court, and there is authority of long standing that where the declaration sought is (as it were)
independent—I mean where it is not introductory or ancillary to some
other specific relief—the discretion is to be exercised with caution.
Thirdly, under the Rules of the Supreme Court, which have the force
F   of statute, in the form in which they stand at present and in the circumstances of the present case, there are at least two methods indicated of
seeking a declaration from the court. One is R.S.C., Ord. 15, r. 16,
which says:

"No action or other proceeding shall be open to objection on the
ground that a merely declaratory judgment or order is sought there-
G   by, and the court may make binding declarations of right whether
or not any consequential relief is or could be claimed."

While that applies to all proceedings in the High Court, it looks primarily
at actions—that is, actions in the ordinary sense, begun by writ or
originating summons—and it makes it clear that a writ or originating
summons cannot be objected to merely because it asks for nothing but
H   a declaration. So there is one way indicated of seeking such relief
from the court. But in the present case there is an alternative and
more special mode of approach indicated by R.S.C., Ord. 53, which has
been extensively revised, quite recently, in 1977. I will read R.S.C.,
Ord. 53, r. 1. It is divided into two paragraphs:

"(1) An application for—(a) an order of mandamus, prohibition
or certiorari, or (b) an injunction under section 9 of the Administration of Justice (Miscellaneous Provisions) Act 1938 restraining a

person from acting in any office in which he is not entitled to act, shall be made by way of an application for judicial review in accordance with the provisions of this Order. (2) An application for a declaration or an injunction (not being an injunction mentioned in paragraph (1) (*b*)) may be made by way of an application for judicial review, and on such an application the court may grant the declaration or injunction claimed if it considers that, having regard to—(*a*) the nature of the matters in respect of which relief may be granted by way of an order of mandamus, prohibition or certiorari, (*b*) the nature of the persons and bodies against whom relief may be granted by way of such an order, and (*c*) all the circumstances of the case, it would be just and convenient for the declaration or injunction to be granted on an application for judicial review."

The order goes on to provide for a preliminary ex parte application for leave to bring proceedings by way of judicial review and then for the substantive application to be made by originating notice of motion. Clearly, that procedure is appropriate to the present case. Reference to the facts and the judgment of the Court of Appeal in *St. Germain's* case [1979] Q.B. 425, shows plainly that relief sought against a decision of a board of prison visitors would fall within the scope of rule 1 of R.S.C., Ord. 53 and a declaration might suitably be claimed by an application for judicial review. Fourthly (and I am still dealing with matters that I consider clear), although the present case in its subject matter is clearly and properly within the scope of R.S.C., Ord. 53, the court has jurisdiction to give a declaration in an action commenced by writ or originating summons. The existence of that concurrent jurisdiction seems to me to be sufficiently established by reported cases, of which it will be enough to refer to *Barnard* v. *National Dock Labour Board* [1953] 2 Q.B. 18; *Taylor* v. *National Assistance Board* [1956] A.C. 532 and *De Falco* v. *Crawley Borough Council* [1980] Q.B. 460. The fifth and last of the points which in my judgment are clear is that, looking at the matter from the point of view of a court seeking to apply the existing Rules of the Supreme Court in the interests of justice, it is obviously undesirable that the plaintiff should seek relief by action rather than by application for judicial review.

There are a number of considerations which to my mind justify that opinion. First of all, the Rules of the Supreme Court as they stand must be construed as a whole. Where, in a code of procedural rules, carefully designed machinery is provided for determining a special class of issues or questions, it is in general inconvenient to use some broader form of process designed to cover not only that, but much larger categories of question. Secondly, R.S.C., Ord. 53, r. 5 (1) requires a would-be applicant for judicial review to obtain preliminary leave ex parte from a Divisional Court of the Queen's Bench Division or in vacation from a judge at chambers. There are very good reasons (among them an economy of public time and the avoidance of injustice to persons whom it is desired to make respondents) for that requirement of preliminary leave. If an action commenced by writ or originating summons is used instead of the machinery of R.S.C., Ord. 53, that requirement of leave is circumvented. Thirdly, under rule 4 certain requirements of expedition are laid down to be observed by an applicant for judicial review, though they are not inflexible and

The Weekly Law Reports, November 21, 1980

1391

1 W.L.R.   Heywood v. Hull Prison Visitors (Ch.D.)   Goulding J.

A within limits the court has a discretion as to their application. Once again, there are very good reasons for such a requirement. Once again, the provisions of the rule are obviated if the relief is sought by action instead of by application for judicial review. In the present case the plaintiff or his advisers (for whom he is responsible) have, it may be, been guilty of some delay. It is no recommendation of the plaintiff's application that that has happened, though of course he may
B on investigation be able to excuse himself. Fourthly, rule 9 (4) provides that where an order of certiorari is sought and obtained, the court may, in addition to quashing the decision to which the application relates, remit the matter to the court, tribunal or authority concerned, with a direction to reconsider it and reach a decision in accordance with the findings of the court. No such convenient machinery for remission
C of the cause is available in an action for a declaration. Fifthly, in proceedings seeking a review of a judicial or quasi-judicial determination, the machinery of an action as to discovery and giving of evidence may result in placing members of the tribunal concerned in a position not really compatible with the free and proper discharge of their public functions, or at least in attempts to put them in that position. In the present case counsel for the plaintiff has contemplated the possibi-
D lity (though he by no means says it will be a necessity) of cross-examining members of the board of visitors. In principle, that seems to me an undesirable way of dealing with such questions. Sixthly, proceedings under R.S.C., Ord. 53 have to be brought in the Queen's Bench Division, and that division has had and daily obtains a larger experience in these questions about administrative or quasi-judicial proceedings
E by bodies that are not courts in the full sense, than the Chancery Division has. That last point is of little weight, because it could be met, if necessary, by an order for transfer to the Queen's Bench Division.

Those matters seem to me, as I have said, tolerably plain. But now I leave what is clear for the question that I have to decide. I think I have to ask myself in the end this question: is the impropriety of using the procedure of an action in the present case so gross that the
F court, in exercising its undoubted power to regulate its own business and avoid abuse of its process, can stop an action that is within the court's jurisdiction to determine and that might conceivably succeed, stop it at the earliest stage, when the issues have not yet been defined by pleadings, nor elucidated by particulars or discovery, simply in order to force the plaintiff to use the proper machinery in the light of the
G Rules of the Supreme Court considered as a whole?

Now, this question is not free from previous observations by judges and learned writers. On behalf of the plaintiff, I have been directed, among other things, to the Report of the Law Commission on Remedies in Administrative Law (Law. Com. No. 73) (Cmnd. 6407), which I am told led to the revision of R.S.C., Ord. 53. The report, at para. 34, says:
H
"In the light of our consultation we are clearly of the opinion that the new procedure we envisage in respect of applications to the Divisional Court should not be exclusive in the sense that it would become the only way by which issues relating to the acts or omissions of public authorities could come before the courts."

Consistently with that recommendation R.S.C., Ord. 53, as appears from the passages that I have read, while providing that in a suitable case

an application for a declaration or an injunction may be made by way of A
judicial review, leaves it open, so far as any express words are concerned, to the applicant to proceed by action. There is, in other words,
no rule of exclusion contained in R.S.C., Ord. 53.

Then I was referred also to what Professor de Smith says in his
book, *Judicial Review of Administrative Action*, 3rd ed. (1973), p. 459.
Discussing the remedy of a declaratory judgment in cases of administrative law, the author asks: B

"Is jurisdiction to award a declaration excluded if another non-
statutory remedy is available in the High Court and is equally
or more appropriate?" He answers his question with a citation
from an earlier writer: "There is great force in the view that
'it ought not to make any difference to judges through which door
the petitioner enters the judicial forum, provided he is lawfully C
there and the court is in a position to grant him relief'."

Somewhat similar language was employed by Lord Denning M.R.
in a case relating to the duties of a housing authority under the
Housing (Homeless Persons) Act 1977, namely, *De Falco* v. *Crawley
Borough Council* [1980] Q.B. 460. Lord Denning M.R. said, at p. 476:

D

"During the hearing, a point was raised about the procedure
adopted by the applicants. They issued writs in the High Court
claiming declarations and an injunction. It was suggested that
they should have applied for judicial review: because that was the
more appropriate machinery. Now the interesting thing is that
this new Act, the Housing (Homeless Persons) Act 1977, contains
nothing about remedies. It does not say what is to be done if the E
local authority fails to perform any of the duties imposed by the
statute upon it. It has been held by this court that, if the council
fails to provide accommodation as required by section 3 (4), the
applicant can claim damages in the county court: see *Thornton* v.
Kirklees Metropolitan Borough Council [1979] Q.B. 626. I am
very ready to follow that decision and indeed to carry it further:
because this is a statute which is passed for the protection of private F
persons—in their capacity as private persons. It is not passed for
the benefit of the public at large. In such a case it is well settled
that, if a public authority fails to perform its statutory duty, the
person or persons concerned can bring a civil action for damages
or an injunction: see *Meade* v. *Haringey London Borough Council*
[1979] 1 W.L.R. 637, 646; *Wade, Administrative Law*, 4th ed. (1977), G
pp. 633–634, and the Report of the Law Commission, Law Com.
No. 73, Report on Remedies in Administrative Law 22.12.1975
(Cmnd. 6407), p. 22. No doubt such a person could, at his option,
bring proceedings for judicial review under the new R.S.C., Ord. 53.
In those proceedings he could get a declaration and an injunction
equally well. He could get interim relief also. So the applicant
has an option. He can either go by action in the High Court or H
county court: or by an application for judicial review."

That conclusion, that the plaintiffs in the *De Falco* case had rightly
proceeded by way of action for declarations and an injunction, was
shared by the other two members of the Court of Appeal who decided
the case, Bridge L.J. and Sir David Cairns. It is only, I think, of
limited assistance to the plaintiff in the present case, because Lord

A Denning founded his observations on the hypothesis that the proceedings with which he was concerned were for the enforcement of a statute passed for the protection of private persons, and not passed for the benefit of the public at large. Also, I think the Court of Appeal, in considering that the applicant had an option, were not concerned how far in the preliminary stages of the proceedings the court can interfere with initial freedom of choice. So far as they go, the observations
B in the *De Falco* case reinforce the suggestion in Professor de Smith's book that it ought not to make any difference to judges through which door the petitioner enters the forum.

However, there has been much said that points in the other direction. As long ago as 1960, in *Pyx Granite Co. Ltd.* v. *Ministry of Housing and Local Government* [1960] A.C. 260, 290, Lord Goddard
C said:

"It was also argued that if there was a remedy obtainable in the High Court it must be by way of certiorari. I know of no authority for saying that if an order or decision can be attacked by certiorari the court is debarred from granting a declaration in an appropriate case. The remedies are not mutually exclusive, though
D no doubt there are some orders, notably convictions before justices, where the only appropriate remedy is certiorari."

Thus Lord Goddard recognised the existence of a class of case in which a High Court declaration would not be an appropriate way of attacking a tribunal's decision, and there is at least a sufficient resemblance between the functions of justices of the peace and those of a board
E of prison visitors, operating in either case in the exercise of their judicial functions, for one to be on one's guard after reading what he said.

Now I come to what has been mainly relied on by the defendants in the present case; that is, a pronouncement by the Court of Appeal in an immigration case: *Uppal* v. *Home Office,* The Times, October 21, 1978
F and November 11, 1978. The case is not in the Law Reports but I have been furnished with a transcript of the proceedings (No. 719 of 1978).*
The case was one in which an application for a declaration in a matter of the immigration laws had been made to Sir Robert Megarry V.-C. in the Chancery Division. It failed. One of the grounds argued on behalf of the Home Office against the plaintiffs was that they ought to have proceeded in the Queen's Bench Division. That argument was rejected.
G Sir Robert Megarry V.-C., as will be seen in a moment, thought the proceedings in the Chancery Division were properly brought and should be decided on the merits. When the plaintiffs brought on their appeal in the Court of Appeal they decided, at what appears to have been an early stage, to abandon it and were content to submit to an order dismissing the appeal. The Lords Justices were much concerned at
H certain observations of the judge below and, after some brief discussion with counsel, proceeded to express their views for the guidance, as it would appear, of the profession and the courts. The observations in question were made by Roskill L.J., but can be taken to be those of the court, as Geoffrey Lane L.J. and Sir David Cairns expressed their agreement without qualification. I will read from a transcript of the

* The major part of the transcript is set out in the judgment of Goulding J.

proceedings the greater part of what Roskill L.J. said. After mention-　A
ing the abandonment of the appeal, Roskill L.J. continued:

"There is, however, one difficulty which this court feels it should
refer to, and that relates to the procedure which was adopted in
this case. The relief sought against the Secretary of State was in
form indistinguishable from an application for judicial review under
R.S.C., Ord. 53. But the proceedings were not taken before the　B
Divisional Court: nor was leave sought from the Divisional Court
under R.S.C., Ord. 53. On the contrary, an originating summons
was issued in the Chancery Division, the applicants being the
plaintiffs to that summons and the Secretary of State the
defendant."

Then, a few lines down, Roskill L.J. cites part of Sir Robert Megarry　C
V.-C.'s judgment below, in these terms:

"First, Mr. Gibson said that these were the wrong proceedings
in the wrong division: the plaintiffs ought to have sought some
prerogative order by way of judicial review in the Queen's Bench,
and so no declaration should be granted. I do not accept this; nor
do I accept Mr. Gibson's watered-down version, seeking that I
should make some obiter pronouncement that such cases ought to　D
be brought in the Queen's Bench. Where two or more different
types of proceedings are possible in the same court (and of course
the Chancery Division and the Queen's Bench Division are both
parts of the High Court) then I do not see why the plaintiffs should
not be free to bring whatever type of proceeding they choose. I
readily accept that the Queen's Bench Division has had a far greater　E
experience of immigration cases than the Chancery Division has
had: but that cannot require a plaintiff to proceed for judicial
review in the Queen's Bench if he wishes to proceed for a declaration in the Chancery Division. I do not think the Chancery Division can be regarded as being avid for this jurisdiction: but it would
be wrong to turn away or discourage a plaintiff who elects to
bring one form of proceedings instead of the other."　　F

After reading that from Sir Robert Megarry V.-C.'s judgment, Roskill
L.J. continued:

"With the greatest respect to Sir Robert Megarry V.-C., I find
myself unable to agree with the latter part of that passage. There
is no doubt—and Mr. Gibson before us has not sought to say other-　G
wise—that in theory the Chancery Division has jurisdiction to
entertain an application of this kind. But as I said a moment
ago this application is in principle indistinguishable from an application for judicial review; and, where an application for judicial
review is sought, then as R.S.C., Ord. 53, r. 3 (1), provides, that
application must be made to the Divisional Court. I feel bound
to say that I find it not a little surprising that this form of proce-　H
dure has been chosen rather than an application to the Divisional
Court for judicial review. It is the Divisional Court which is
equipped by reason of its experience, expertise and long practice
to deal with these matters and to deal with them expeditiously;
and I express the hope that in future it is the Divisional Court to
which this type of problem will be submitted and that the temptation to deal with immigration problems by way of an originating

The Weekly Law Reports, November 21, 1980

1395

1 W.L.R.   Heywood v. Hull Prison Visitors (Ch.D.)   Goulding J.

A   summons in proceedings for a declaration in the Chancery Division will be avoided."

Then Roskill L.J. summarised the first rule of Ord. 53, and he concluded:

B   "There is, as I said a moment ago, and Mr. Gibson has not argued otherwise, jurisdiction in the Chancery Division to hear an application of this kind, but it would be wrong that this procedure should be adopted in order to by-pass the need for getting leave from the Divisional Court to move for the relevant order where what in truth is sought is judicial review. As this is a matter of some general importance, I venture to make that criticism of what Sir Robert Megarry V.-C. said with the greatest respect to him."

C   Now it is not possible, in my judgment, to confine the force of the observations in *Uppal* v. *Home Office* to immigration cases. The reasons given by Roskill L.J. in the passage that I have read apply equally to the present case. The observance by applicants of the requirements of R.S.C., Ord. 53 with regard to preliminary leave and as to prompt timing are equally necessary or desirable in attempts to question the decisions of prison visitors as in attempts to question decisions of the immigration authorities. The superior experience and practice of the Queen's Bench Division are equally obvious in the present class of case. The judges of that division, who are accustomed to sit in the Criminal Division of the Court of Appeal and in the Crown Court and in the Queen's Bench Divisional Court itself, have in general quite plainly more acquaintance than the judges of the Chancery Division with this sort of subject matter.

E   Secondly, it was suggested on behalf of the plaintiff that there is no persuasive authority in the pronouncement in *Uppal* v. *Home Office,* because it is inconsistent with the actual decision of the Court of Appeal in *De Falco* v. *Crawley Borough Council* [1980] Q.B. 460. I think that is not so. As I have just shown in referring to the remarks of Lord Denning M.R. in that case, the legislation there under consideration was of a special character directed to the protection of individual homeless persons. Whether or not the language used in the Court of Appeal fits comfortably together in the two cases, there is nothing in the decision in the *De Falco* case that is inconsistent with what was said in *Uppal.* The status of what was said in *Uppal* is, of course, unusual. The appeal was dismissed by consent, but the court felt constrained to express its view that part of the judgment below was erroneous. That being so, whether or not the views of the court are technically binding on me, they are clearly deserving of the greatest respect, because they were made for the guidance of both the profession and the lower courts. It seems to me that if the formulation of the matter in *Uppal* v. *Home Office* is correct, if indeed it is wrong that the procedure of an action should be adopted in order to by-pass the need for getting leave from the Divisional Court, then in the present case it is my duty to put a stop at an early stage to the action. Although I have some sympathy for the opinion expressed by Professor de Smith in his book and by Sir Robert Megarry V.-C. in *Uppal* v. *Home Office* that if the rules appear to leave the plaintiff with a choice of procedure he should be allowed to have it, judicial discipline requires me to follow the view of the whole Court of Appeal in that case, whether technically binding or not. The observance of

Goulding J.   **Heywood v. Hull Prison Visitors (Ch.D.)**   **[1980]**

judicial discipline in the hierarchy of courts in this country seems to   A
me much more important than any particular considerations affecting
the plaintiff in this individual case.

For those reasons, the defendants' motion succeeds and, subject to
any observations of counsel, the proper order will be that I stay all
further proceedings in the action.

Order accordingly.   B

Solicitors: *Sidney Torrance & Co. for Barrington, Black, Austin &
Co., Leeds; Treasury Solicitor.*

K. N. B.

                                                                          C

[COURT OF APPEAL]

* REGINA *v.* CHIEF IMMIGRATION OFFICER, GATWICK
AIRPORT, *Ex parte* KHARRAZI   D

1980   June 30;   Lord Denning M.R., Waller
       July 1; 9   and Dunn L.JJ.

> *Immigration—Refusal of entry—Student—Iranian boy accepted for
> " O " level course at English school — Intention to continue
> education in England thereafter — Immigration officer not   E
> satisfied of student's intention to leave on completion of
> course of study — Whether " full-time course of study "
> restricted to course of study for which student accepted —
> Statement of Changes in Immigration Rules (1980) (H.C. 394),
> paras.* 21, 22

> The applicant, a 13-year-old Iranian boy, arrived in England
> to attend an independent boarding school where he had been
> accepted for a three-year " O " level course. When interviewed   F
> by the immigration officer the applicant said that he expected to
> remain in the United Kingdom for up to 10 years so as to
> complete his education by taking " O " and " A " levels and
> going on to university. The immigration officer refused leave
> to enter on the ground, according to his subsequent affidavit,
> that, having considered paragraphs 21 to 24 of the Statement
> of Changes in Immigration Rules (1980) (H.C. 394) [1] and
> taking into account, inter alia, that the applicant's intentions   G
> were not limited to the three-year course, he " could not be
> satisfied that the applicant intended to leave the United
> Kingdom on completion of his course of study." An application

---

[1] Statement of Changes in Immigration Rules (1980) (H.C. 394), para. 21: " A
passenger seeking entry to study in the United Kingdom should be admitted (subject
to paragraph 13) if he presents a current entry clearance granted for that purpose.
An entry clearance will be granted if the applicant produces evidence which satisfies   H
the entry clearance officer that he has been accepted for a course of study at a
university, a college of education or further education, an independent school or
any bona fide private educational institution; that the course will occupy the whole
or a substantial part of his time; and that he can, without working and without
recourse to public funds, meet the cost of the course and of his own maintenance
and accommodation and that of any dependants during the course."
   Para 22: " An applicant is to be refused an entry clearance as a student if the
entry clearance officer is not satisfied that the applicant is able, and intends, to
follow a full-time course of study and to leave the country on completion of it...."

A   for leave to apply for a judicial review to quash the decision
of the immigration officer was refused by the Divisional Court.
    On appeal by the applicant: —
    Held, allowing the appeal (Waller L.J. dissenting), that
" full-time course of study " in paragraph 22 of the Statement
of Changes in Immigration Rules (1980) (H.C. 394), on completion of which the immigration officer had to be satisfied that
a student seeking entry intended to leave the country, was not
B   restricted to " a course of study," referred to in paragraph 21,
for which the student had been accepted but could include a
coherent and definite educational proposal which the student
could reasonably be expected to complete (post, pp. 1402c–d,
1408e–g); that, accordingly, it was not necessary for the
applicant to satisfy the immigration officer of his intention to
leave the country on completion of his " O " level course; and
that, as, on the evidence, the immigration officer had required
C   to be so satisfied, his decision should be quashed and the matter
remitted to the Chief Immigration Officer at Gatwick Airport
for further consideration (post, pp. 1404b, f, 1409c–e).
    Per Waller L.J. The phrase " full-time course of study " in
paragraph 22 of the Statement of Changes in Immigration
Rules (1980) (H.C. 394) could include more than one course
provided that they were specific parts of a coherent whole
(post, pp. 1406d–e, 1407b).   But, on the facts, the immigration
D   officer had not confined himself to the strict construction of
the words of paragraph 22 but gave them a more liberal
construction.   Accordingly, the applicant failed to show any
error of law in the decision (post, pp. 1406d–e, 1407b).
    Decision of the Divisional Court reversed.

    The following cases are referred to in the judgments:

E   *Anisminic Ltd.* v. *Foreign Compensation Commission* [1969] 2 A.C. 147;
          [1969] 2 W.L.R. 163; [1969] 1 All E.R. 208, H.L.(E.).
      Company, In re A [1980] Ch. 138; [1980] 2 W.L.R. 241; [1980] 1 All
          E.R. 284, C.A.; [1980] 3 W.L.R. 181; [1980] 2 All E.R. 634,
          H.L.(E.): see also *In re Racal Communications Ltd.*
      Pearlman v. *Keepers and Governors of Harrow School* [1979] Q.B. 56;
          [1978] 3 W.L.R. 736; [1979] 1 All E.R. 365, C.A.
F   *Racal Communications Ltd., In re,* The Times, July 4, 1980, H.L.(E.).
      Reg. v. *Governor of Pentonville Prison, Ex parte Azam* [1974] A.C. 18;
          [1973] 2 W.L.R. 1058; [1973] 2 All E.R. 765, H.L.(E.).
      Reg. v. *Hillingdon London Borough Council, Ex parte Royco Homes Ltd.*
          [1974] Q.B. 720; [1974] 2 W.L.R. 805; [1974] 2 All E.R. 643, D.C.
      Reg. v. *Medical Appeal Tribunal, Ex parte Gilmore* [1957] 1 Q.B. 574;
          [1957] 2 W.L.R. 498; [1957] 1 All E.R. 796, C.A.
G   *Reg.* v. *Secretary of State for Home Affairs, Ex parte Hosenball* [1977]
          1 W.L.R. 766; [1977] 3 All E.R. 452, D.C.

    The following additional cases were cited in argument:

      Reg. v. *Chief Immigration Officer Lympne Airport, Ex parte Amrik Singh*
          [1969] Q.B. 333; [1968] 3 W.L.R. 945; [1968] 3 All E.R. 163, D.C.
      Reg. v. *Immigration Appeals Adjudicator, Ex parte Khan* [1972] 1 W.L.R.
H   1058; [1972] 3 All E.R. 297, D.C.

    APPEAL from the Divisional Court of the Queen's Bench Division.
    The applicant, Khashayar Kharrazi, applied by his brother and next
friend, Dariush Kharrazi, on May 20, 1980, for leave to apply for judicial
review for an order of certiorari and mandamus in respect of the refusal
of leave to enter given to him by an immigration officer at Gatwick Airport
on May 16, 1980. On June 6, 1980, the Divisional Court refused the

application without giving reasons. The applicant appealed by leave of A
the Court of Appeal granted on June 13, 1980.

The facts are stated in the judgment of Lord Denning M.R.

Charles Fletcher-Cooke Q.C. and *K. S. Nathan* for the applicant.
Simon D. Brown for the Chief Immigration Officer, Gatwick Airport.

B

Cur. adv. vult.

July 9. The following judgments were read.

LORD DENNING M.R.

Entry for education   C

To be educated in England is an advantage. It is much sought after.
For many years parents in countries overseas have sent their children here
to be educated. If they can afford it. They have sent their sons and
daughters to our public schools and on to our universities. On finishing
here, they have returned to their own countries—often to exercise much
influence there—for good, the most distinguished being Jawaharlal Nehru D
of Harrow and Trinity College, Cambridge. Many have been called to the
English Bar and gone back to be prime ministers and judges. Even
revolutionaries, such as Mahatma Gandhi. Some have come to Sandhurst
and gone back to become generals and heads of military governments, like
Ayub Khan. Successive Home Secretaries have recognised the value of this
beneficent service to the world. Under the immigration rules, we freely
admit boys—and girls—of school age whose parents wish them to be E
educated here and can afford the expense—on the understanding that, when
their education is completed, they will return to their home countries. This
freedom of education is ensured by the special provisions relating to the
entry of students. They are contained in the Statement of Changes in
Immigration Rules (1980) (H.C. 394). We have today to consider their
interpretation.   F

"21. A passenger seeking entry to study in the United Kingdom should
be admitted (subject to paragraph 13) if he presents a current entry
clearance granted for that purpose. An entry clearance will be granted
if the applicant produces evidence which satisfies the entry clearance
officer that he has been accepted for a course of study at a university,
a college of education or further education, an independent school or G
any bona fide private educational institution; that the course will
occupy the whole or a substantial part of his time; and that he can,
without working and without recourse to public funds, meet the cost
of the course and of his own maintenance and accommodation and
that of any dependants during the course.

" 22. An applicant is to be refused an entry clearance as a student
if the entry clearance officer is not satisfied that the applicant is able, H
and intends, to follow a full-time course of study and to leave the
country on completion of it. In assessing the case the officer should
consider such points as whether the applicant's qualifications are
adequate for the course he proposes to follow, and whether there is
any evidence of sponsorship by his home government or any other
official body. As a general rule an entry clearance is not to be granted

The Weekly Law Reports, November 21, 1980

1399

1 W.L.R.   Reg. v. Immigration Officer, Ex p. Kharrazi (C.A.)   Lord Denning M.R.

A   unless the applicant proposes to spend not less than 15 hours a week
in organised daytime study of a single subject or of related subjects,
and is not to be granted for the taking of a correspondence course."

The young Iranian boy

Iran is much in the news. So are Iranian nationals. Here is a young boy
B who seems to have been caught up in the inter-changes of nations. He
is Khashayar Kharrazi. He was born in Iran on April 3, 1967. So he is just
13. His father and mother are in Iran where his father is the executive
manager of a big agricultural concern. They are very well off. They have
three other sons. They have sent all their sons to the United States or
England for their education. One of them went to the United States and
qualified in computer engineering. He has returned to Iran to work. Another
C is studying in the United States, doing a course in aerospace programming.
Yet another is studying in England and is doing a course for the Higher
National Diploma. The fourth and youngest is our present applicant,
Khashayar.

When Khashayar was just 12, in June 1979, his mother took him to the
United States and enrolled him at a junior high school in Tucson, Arizona.
D His teacher there gives him a first-class report showing that he has done
exceedingly well. His mother had originally entered him as a " visitor " to
the United States, but, after the overthrow of the Shah, the American
authorities gave a general permission to Iranian nationals to stay. Later on,
when the hostages were imprisoned in Tehran, the American policy changed
towards Iranian nationals. Things were so uncomfortable there for this
E young boy that the family decided to bring him over to England for his
education if suitable arrangements could be made. His mother and father
had already gone back to Iran. So his brothers did everything. They made
inquiries of the British Consul in Los Angeles and of the Home Office in
London. They were told that, as long as he had a course and sufficient
funds available for his maintenance, he would be granted leave to enter
F as a student. (That seems to be a convenient summary of paragraphs 21
and 22 of H.C. 394.) The family arranged for him to be enrolled as a
student at one of our smaller public schools, Pierrepont School, Frensham,
Farnham, Surrey. The headmaster gave a certificate:

"... Khashayar Kharrazi has enrolled and has been accepted to start
a three year 'O' level course at Pierrepont School as a boarding
G   student with effect from September 1, 1980."

Everything being then in order for England, the family arranged for
him to be granted voluntary departure from the United States. It was done.
His belongings were packed up. His flight booked. All papers got in order
so as to show his good faith. His brother Dariush was to meet him at
Gatwick, and get him settled in.
H

Gatwick—May 16, 1980

On May 16, 1980, the boy arrived at Gatwick Airport. An immigration
officer, Mr. Ladd, interviewed him. The boy was only just 13 but he
answered well and produced all his papers. They showed excellent
credentials. This is the account given by the immigration officer of the
interview:

"The applicant was interviewed throughout in English which he   A
spoke well and there were no language difficulties. I asked the applicant
how long he wished to stay in the United Kingdom. He replied that
he wanted leave to enter for one year as a student and said that he
expected to remain in the United Kingdom for up to 10 years so as to
complete his education, taking ' O ' levels, ' A ' levels and going on to
university."
                                                                        B
The immigration officer then examined the applicant's papers. They showed
he had ample means of support. He had a banker's draft for £1,071·21.
He had a letter from Williams & Glyn's Bank showing that his brother
here had a credit of £12,000. He had the certificate of enrolment at
Pierrepont School for three years. He had a warm letter of support from
a well-placed English resident at Camberley saying: ". . . my wife and I   C
will also be taking more than a passing interest in his well-being, both
socially and as regards education." After questioning the young boy, the
immigration officer then saw his brother Dariush who had come to meet him.
He was accompanied by his English young lady whom he expected to marry.
The immigration officer asked the brother how long he expected the young
boy to remain in England. The brother answered: "Up to 10 years or as
long as it takes to complete his education."   D
    The immigration officer consulted his senior. They then told him that
the boy was refused entry. They served a notice on the boy on May 16,
1980, in these words:

    "Mr. Khashaya Kharrazi
        "You have asked for leave to enter the United Kingdom as a
    student but I am not satisfied that you intend to leave the United   E
    Kingdom when your studies are completed.
        "I therefore refuse you leave to enter the United Kingdom. I have
    given/propose to give directions for your removal to Tehran."

Note the word "studies" in that letter. The brother took that as meaning
the completion of the applicant's studies at school and university. The
brother told the immigration officer that he was prepared to give a bond   F
so as to guarantee that the boy would leave after completion of his studies.
But the immigration officer told him that our law in the United Kingdom
does not authorise him to accept such bonds.
    Having thus refused the boy entry, the immigration officer went off to
make arrangements for the boy to be sent on the first available flight to
Tehran. And he would have gone—but for the intervention of the law.
The brother at once went to solicitors. They telephoned to the immigration   G
officer saying that they were applying to the court. On that intimation the
immigration officer allowed the boy to be temporarily admitted without
prejudice to the position: see Immigration Act 1971, Schedule 2, paragraph 21.
    It so happened that three days later the authorities here put a brake
on the entry of Iranian nationals into this country. They could not enter   H
except with a visa. But that did not apply to this boy. Under the immigration rules, as I read them, he ought to have been admitted.

The application for judicial review

    According to the statute, the boy had a right of appeal to an adjudicator,
but *not* "so long as he is in the United Kingdom." In order to appeal,
the boy would have to go (as ordered) to Iran and to appeal from there:

The Weekly Law Reports, November 21, 1980

1401

1 W.L.R.   Reg. v. Immigration Officer, Ex p. Kharrazi (C.A.)   Lord Denning M.R.

A see section 13 (1) and (3) of the Immigration Act 1971. This would have
been disastrous for the boy's future for several reasons. One is that it would
take a long time for the boy's appeal to be heard by an adjudicator.
Another is that the appeal would have to be decided on paper. The boy
would not be present to speak for himself. His appeal might not be heard
for months. So that his schooling would be gravely interrupted. And on
B the latest information, the Iranian law now forbids a student to leave Iran
under the age of 18 years. So once back in Iran any hope for his education
in England was gone.

In this parlous situation, on May 20, 1980, application was made to
the Divisional Court for judicial review. The application was made by the
applicant's brother as his guardian ad litem. It was made on the grounds
that the refusal of the immigration officer was unreasonable and contrary
C to the immigration rules. The Divisional Court refused the application
without giving any reasons. It was renewed before us. We asked for the
attendance of the immigration authorities. Then for the first time the
immigration officer made an affidavit. This disclosed a new state of affairs.
You will remember that the notice refusing entry said: " I am not
satisfied that you intend to leave the United Kingdom when *your studies*
D *are completed.*" The boy, his brother and we ourselves had all assumed
that this meant when he had finished his full-time education—at school and
university. But the affidavit of the immigration officer shows that he interpreted the rule as meaning that he had to intend to leave for good as soon
as the course at Pierrepont School was completed: and that, as he intended
to go on from school to the university, if he could get in, he was to be
refused entry.

E

The reasoning of the immigration officer

The reasoning of the immigration officer is so important that I will set
it out in full:

" I then considered the matter in the light of the immigration rules
       then applicable, paragraphs 21–24 of the Statement of Changes in
F   Immigration Rules (H.C. 394). It appeared that the applicant had been
       accepted for a course of study for ' O ' levels and had the financial
       means to follow the course. *However both the applicant and his
       brother had indicated that the applicant's intentions were not limited
       to the three year course and it was evident that he expected to stay in
       the United Kingdom for up to 10 years or more.* He had been required
G   to leave the United States of America and had stated that this was
       because of failure to comply with United States immigration rules.
       He was not without family in the United Kingdom and this situation
       was likely to continue since it appeared that his brother would be
       seeking to remain indefinitely. *Taking all these things together I could
       not be satisfied that the applicant intended to leave the United Kingdom
       on completion of his course of study.* I discussed this matter with
H   Chief Immigration Officer S. Woods and with his authority I refused
       the applicant leave to enter."

To my mind that reasoning is only capable of one interpretation: the
immigration officer regards the applicant's course of study as being the
three-year course. In order to gain entry, the boy must intend to leave this
country for good at the end of his three-year course at Pierrepont School:
and that, as he did not intend to do so, but to go on to the university if he

could, he had to be refused entry. If this interpretation of the rules be   A
correct, it means that every boy or girl coming to England—to go to a
public school—hoping to go on to a university—will have to be refused
entry. He can only be admitted if he intends to leave this country for
good—not for a holiday—at the end of his public school course—without
going to a university. Such a rule would exclude all the most promising
students who seek to come to England. All of them want to go on to the
university if they can.   B

The interpretation of the rules

I can understand the way the immigration officer looked at the rules.
He thought that the words " a full-time course of study " in paragraph 22
referred back to " a course of study " in paragraph 21. That is a possible
interpretation but it is a narrow interpretation. So narrow indeed—and so   C
unjust and unfair—that I think it should be rejected. The words " a full-
time course of study " in paragraph 22 should be interpreted as meaning
" a full-time course of study " such as a boy of his age can reasonably
expect to follow through to its completion—that is, to the attainment of a
degree—even though he has not yet been guaranteed or accepted for a
place at a university. If he is able and intends to follow such a course—   D
and to leave for good at the end of it—he comes within paragraph 22.
He may be admitted for an appropriate period depending on the length
of the course of study and on his means. That fits in well with paragraph 97.
The appropriate period might only be for one year. He should then apply
for extensions from time to time under paragraph 98 and they will be
granted to him so long as he is going on with his studies and intends to   E
leave at the end of them.

There is a sentence in paragraph 24 which enables an immigration
officer to admit " for a short period " but that is directed to cases where
a student comes without sufficient means to carry him through—or without
having been actually enrolled for a course of study at a college or school.
He can be admitted for a short period so as to enable him to overcome
those difficulties. But that does not apply to this case.   F

The misdirection by the immigration officer

In my opinion, therefore, the immigration officer misdirected himself
in point of law. He did not interpret paragraph 22 correctly. He gave it too
narrow an interpretation and for that reason refused this boy entry. What
then is to be done? Can the immigration officer's refusal be quashed by   G
the court? Or is the court powerless? Must the boy be sent to Iran and
appeal from there to an adjudicator?

The procedure for judicial review is now governed by R.S.C., Ord. 53.
The first question is this: is an immigration officer " a person or body
against whom relief may be granted by way of an order of mandamus or
certiorari? " To my mind he is. He acts under a power conferred on him   H
by Parliament to give or refuse leave to enter: see section 4 (1) of the
Immigration Act 1971. He is bound to apply the rules made by the Secretary of State under the authority of the statute: see sections 1 (4) and 3 (2)
of the Act. Being a public officer bound to apply statutory rules, he is
amenable to the prerogative writs or, in modern terms, to judicial review.

The next question is whether this is a case where mandamus or
certiorari will lie. If the immigration officer had been entrusted with a

The Weekly Law Reports, November 21, 1980

1403

1 W.L.R.   Reg. v. Immigration Officer, Ex p. Kharrazi (C.A.)   Lord Denning M.R.

A   discretion—and the complaint was only of the manner of its exercise—then it would not lie: see *Reg.* v. *Secretary of State for Home Affairs, Ex parte Hosenball* [1977] 1 W.L.R. 766. But, if the immigration officer interprets the rules wrongly—and on that account asks himself the wrong question—and thus gives the wrong answer to those dependent on it—he does something which he is not empowered to do. He acts ultra vires.

B   That is made clear by the important observations of Lord Diplock in *In re Racal Communications Ltd.,** The Times, July 4, 1980. These do away with long-standing distinctions between errors within the jurisdiction and errors without it. They do it by the simple device which was adumbrated in *Pearlman* v. *Keepers and Governors of Harrow School* [1979] Q.B. 56. No administrative tribunal or administrative authority has jurisdiction to make an error of law on which the decision of the case depends.

C   The House of Lords said in *Racal* that we were wrong to apply that concept to the High Court: but left it intact with regard to administrative tribunals and other administrative authorities. Meaning thereby, as I understand it, all statutory tribunals and authorities other than the regular courts of law. Even if the statute makes the decision " final and conclusive " (*Reg.* v. *Medical Appeal Tribunal, Ex parte Gilmore* [1957] 1 Q.B. 574) or " not to be called in question in any court " (*Anisminic Ltd.* v. *Foreign*

D   *Compensation Commission* [1969] 2 A.C. 147) or, what is the same thing, " not appealable," nevertheless, so far as administrative tribunals and authorities are concerned, that exemption is only given on condition that they interpret their rules—and thus their power—rightly. If it should appear that they make an error of law on which their decision depends, they do that which they have no jurisdiction to do. " No jurisdiction " means " no power."

E   They act ultra vires. This approach renders it unnecessary to inquire whether there is, or is not, error on the face of the record: nor to inquire what is the record and what is not. Such bodies have no record as the courts of law have. Suffice it that it is shown, to the satisfaction of the court, that they have misinterpreted the statute or the rules under which they are empowered to act. By that very misinterpretation they go outside their power. Their decision must be quashed.

F   Incidentally I would make this comment. Although we were wrong—according to the House of Lords—in *Pearlman* v. *Harrow School* [1979] Q.B. 56 and *In re A Company* [1980] Ch. 138, nevertheless we did clear up the legal position. We did give guidance to the judges below as to the way in which the statute in question should be interpreted. Whereas the House of Lords gave no guidance. They left every judge to do as he liked. Each

G   one could interpret the statute as he wished—according to the length of his foot—and no one could correct him. So no one in the profession could advise his client how to act. What a state of affairs!

All that I have just said is, however, subject to this qualification. If there is a convenient remedy by way of appeal to an adjudicator, then certiorari may be refused: and the applicant left to his remedy by way of

H   appeal. But it has been held on countless occasions that the availability of appeal does not debar the court from quashing an order by prerogative writs, either of habeas corpus (see *Reg.* v. *Governor of Pentonville Prison, Ex parte Azam* [1974] A.C. 18, 31) or certiorari: see *Reg.* v. *Hillingdon London Borough Council, Ex parte Royco Homes Ltd.* [1974] 1 Q.B. 720. It depends on the circumstances of each case. In the present case the

* Sub nom. *In re A Company* [1980] 3 W.L.R. 181.

remedy by way of appeal is useless. This boy's education—indeed, his   A
whole future—will be ruined if he is sent off by 'plane to Tehran. Rather
than his future be ruined, it is better to quash the refusal—and let the
Home Secretary reconsider the case.

Applied to this case

The immigration officer misdirected himself on the interpretation of   B
the rule. He asked himself the wrong question. As he interpreted the rule,
he asked himself: " Does this boy intend to leave the country for good
at the end of his three-year course at Pierrepont School?" The answer
was plainly: " No. He intends to stay on in this country, and go on to
university if he can." Owing to asking himself that wrong question, the
immigration officer refused him leave to enter. But, if the immigration
officer had asked himself the right question, he would have asked himself: C
" Does this boy intend to leave this country for good as soon as he has
completed his expected course of study—at school and university? " If the
immigration officer had asked himself that question, he would, I should
have thought, on the evidence before him, have answered it in this way:
" The boy says himself that, after he gets his degree, he intends to go back
to Iran. His brother (who is here) confirmed it. The brother offers a bond   D
to show their good faith. One of his brothers has gone back there already.
We should give them credit for good intentions." On that evidence, the
immigration officer should have been satisfied of the present intention of
the boy and should allow him to come in.

There is, moreover, another way in which the immigration officer went
wrong. As Mr. Fletcher-Cooke submitted to us, the rules require the
immigration officer to look at the *present* intention of the applicant—   E
subjectively—not to his *future* intention—*objectively*. Here the immigration
officer seems to have asked himself: " Am I satisfied that this boy *will*
leave—or is *likely* to leave—at the end of his course of study? " That is
shown by the phrase he used, " this situation was likely to continue." That,
too, was the wrong question, and resulted in the wrong answer. If he had
asked himself the right question: " What is the boy's present intention? "   F
he might well have been satisfied and allowed him to enter.

Seeing that the immigration officer has asked himself the wrong
question, I think his refusal should be quashed. The Home Secretary should
consider the case afresh and decide whether he should be given leave to
enter or not. I hope he will give him leave for one year anyway: and then
extend it if proper. Who knows? If this young boy is admitted here—he
may do brilliantly—he may go back to Iran and become a leader in that   G
troubled country. I would give him that chance. I would allow this appeal.

WALLER L.J. Khashayar Kharrazi, the applicant, is an Iranian citizen
and he is aged 13. He went to the United States with his parents in June
1979, and went to school there in Arizona. As a result first of the fall of
the Shah and secondly of the taking of the American hostages, United   H
States policy towards Iranians in the United States changed. I do not at
this stage go into the details of that save to say that the applicant agreed
voluntarily to leave the country before June 28, 1980. His brother who was
in the United Kingdom made arrangements for him to go to his school
at Farnham to do an " O " level course of three years commencing in
September 1980. Inquiries had been made from the Home Office and his
brother understood that provided sufficient funds were available the

The Weekly Law Reports, November 21, 1980

1405

1 W.L.R.   Reg. v. Immigration Officer, Ex p. Kharrazi (C.A.)   Waller L.J.

A applicant would be granted leave to enter as a student. On May 16, 1980, the applicant arrived at Gatwick Airport, applied for leave to enter as a student and after being interviewed by an immigration officer was refused leave. The refusal stated:

" You have asked for leave to enter the United Kingdom as a student but I am not satisfied that you intend to leave the United Kingdom
B   when your studies are completed."

The applicant now applies for judicial review of that decision with the leave of this court.

     The applicant had a letter showing that his brother had considerable funds in this country and the immigration officer then saw his brother. The brother was a final year student doing a National Diploma course at
C Farnborough Technical College and who had been in the country six years and was accompanied by a United Kingdom citizen, Miss Price, his fiancée. The brother was intending to reside in the United Kingdom after marriage. The brother told the immigration officer that the applicant would be likely to remain in the United Kingdom for 10 years or as long as it took to complete his education. The immigration officer in his affidavit sets out
D fully an account of his interview with the applicant and in particular dealing with the applicant's explanation of the reasons for leaving the United States. The applicant asserted that the only reason was to continue his education in the United Kingdom, but when asked why he had been ordered to leave the United States he said it was because of immigration regulations. The immigration officer, after considering the matter in the light of the Statement of Changes in Immigration Rules (H.C. 394), para-
E graphs 21 to 24, refused the applicant leave to enter in the terms which I have already set out. I will come to the details of his reasoning hereafter.

     The paragraphs of the Statement of Changes in Immigration Rules which apply to this case are paragraphs 21 to 24. Paragraph 21 sets out the conditions under which an entry clearance should be granted. They are: (1) evidence of acceptance for a course of study, (2) that it is whole time,
F (3) that he has funds for his maintenance and accommodation. Paragraph 22 requires the immigration officer to refuse an entry clearance as a student if he is not satisfied of either of two things, namely: (1) that the applicant is able and intends to follow a full-time course of study, and (2) that the applicant intends to leave the country on completion of it. Paragraph 23 has no application to this case. Paragraph 24, in the first part, states that a passenger may be admitted who satisfies the requirements I have already
G set out, and, in the second part, gives a discretion to the immigration officer to admit somebody who he is satisfied has genuine and realistic intentions of studying for a short period to enable further consideration of the case. In my opinion paragraph 24 does not arise if the applicant has been refused an entry clearance because of either of the bars set out in paragraph 22. In other words, if the immigration officer is not satisfied
H that the applicant intends to follow a full-time course and is able to do so or is not satisfied that the applicant is able and intends to leave the country on completion of the course, he must refuse an entry clearance.

     In order to succeed in this case the applicant must show that the immigration officer's conclusion was one to which no reasonable immigration officer could come on the evidence or that in some other respect the decision was wrong in point of law. It has not been argued that no reasonable officer could come to this conclusion. The point of law depends

in part on the construction of paragraphs 21 and 22. In paragraph 21 an　**A**
entry clearance has to be granted if the applicant produces evidence " that
he has been accepted for a course of study at a university, a college of
education, etc.," and in paragraph 22 an applicant is to be refused if the
officer is not satisfied that the applicant " is able and intends to follow
a full-time course of study and to leave the country on completion of
it." Do the words " a full-time course of study " refer to the course of
study at a university, etc., mentioned in paragraph 21, or do they have　**B**
a wider, and if so what, other meaning? Were it not for the consequences
of the strict interpretation, I would have come to the conclusion that the
words " course of study " in paragraph 22 mean the same as " course of
study " in paragraph 21. However, such a construction would lead to rather
surprising results. A boy coming to the United Kingdom planning to go to
school and then to university here, even if those plans were fairly clearly　**C**
fixed, would not be allowed entry because his course at school would
terminate and he would have to have an intention to return to his native
country. If he intended to go on to university, that would be contrary to
the intention and therefore he would have to be refused admission. On the
other hand a more liberal construction might involve the admission of
applicants as students who had rather vague plans for courses, one　**D**
following another, and the intention of the rules would be frustrated. Is the
true construction somewhere between these two extremes? Paragraph 98,
which deals with variation of leave to enter or remain, states: " An
extension should be refused if there is reason to believe that the student
does not intend to leave at the end of his studies." That is a wider phrase
than is used in paragraphs 21 or 22. In my judgment, the phrase " full-
time course of study " in paragraph 22 is not restricted to precisely the　**E**
course of study in paragraph 21. On the other hand it does not mean that
an intention to do more than one course is necessarily covered by the
phrase " full-time course of study." Full time course of study, in my
opinion, could include more than one course provided that they were
specific parts of a coherent whole. In other words, arrangements to go to
a preparatory school followed by a public school might well be a full-time　**F**
course of study. They would require separate arrangements but they would
be part of a coherent whole. Furthermore, perhaps school followed by
university might be a coherent course, but that would depend on the facts,
on the ability of the individual and so on. I have come to this conclusion
with some hesitation but, on the facts as I now consider them, whether that
view is right or whether a restrictive interpretation should be given does
not matter in this case.　**G**

The immigration officer in his affidavit said:

" It appeared that the applicant had been accepted for a course of
study for ' O ' levels and had financial means to follow the course.
However, both the applicant and his brother had indicated that the
applicant's intentions were not limited to the three-year course and
it was evident that he expected to stay in the United Kingdom for　**H**
up to 10 years or more."

The immigration officer clearly, if it were the strict construction that had
to be adopted, was coming to the conclusion that the requirements were
not met. But he did not stop there; he went on to consider the reasons
for leaving the United States; he went on to consider the fact that there
was family in the United Kingdom; he had already set out in detail the

The Weekly Law Reports, November 21, 1980

1407

1 W.L.R.   Reg. v. Immigration Officer, Ex p. Kharrazi (C.A.)   Waller L.J.

A circumstances of his brother in the United Kingdom, and then he said, at the end of the paragraph:

" Taking all these things together I could not be satisfied that the applicant intended to leave the United Kingdom on completion of his course of study."

B There the immigration officer is following the precise words of paragraph 22. If the immigration officer had been confining himself to the strict construction, he would have not gone further than his first statement, but the fact that he went on and took these other matters into consideration shows, in my view, that he was giving a more liberal construction to the words. Accordingly, in my judgment, the applicant fails to show that there was any error of law in the decision of the immigration officer.

C If I had come to the conclusion that the immigration officer had wrongly construed the immigration rules, I would have been in favour of granting the application and of setting the immigration officer's decision aside. Since I am dissenting from Lord Denning M.R. and Dunn L.J. (whose judgment I have seen in advance), I ought to state my view of the effect of granting the application for judicial review. This is not a case of a patrial D or of some other person with a qualified right to enter. The applicant is an Iranian citizen and by section 3 (1) (a) of the Immigration Act 1971: " he shall not enter the United Kingdom unless given leave to do so in accordance with this Act." To say that the refusal was made because of an error of law does not give the applicant a right to enter and this court has no power to grant leave to enter. In my opinion the applicant would be in the situation of an alien asking for leave to enter as a student. He has not been E granted leave to enter and he would not have been refused if the refusal was wrong in law. It would be for the Secretary of State to ensure that the applicant's case is reconsidered applying the right principles.

On the view I take these questions do not arise. I have come to the conclusion that this application fails and should be refused. I should add, however, that on this view there are, I think, certain matters which would F merit the consideration of the Secretary of State in this particular case. They are these. (1) The applicant came here as a result of information given to his brother by the Home Office on the one hand and as a result of information given by the British Consul in Los Angeles on the other. That information was that he would be admitted as a student to do the studies which had been arranged. (2) Because of that information the applicant arrived here although he had not then obtained entry clearance. G (3) In the ordinary way a refusal would mean that an applicant would have to return to his native country and appeal to an adjudicator. In this case however there is information before this court that if the applicant returns to Iran he will not be allowed to leave until he is aged 18. In effect, therefore, the applicant is deprived of a right of appeal. This was something which the immigration officer perhaps did not know. (4) It is also H possible that there was some misunderstanding in the mind of the immigration officer about the position of the applicant vis-à-vis the American immigration authorities. It may have appeared to the immigration officer that the applicant was not being entirely frank with the American authorities whereas there is before this court an affidavit setting out more fully the situation under American law which could possibly lead to a different conclusion. I emphasise that it is possible; I do not suggest that it necessarily was an important part. These matters are only matters which

might be considered by the Secretary of State and do not affect my view   A
that there was no error in law in the immigration officer's decision.

DUNN L.J. If paragraphs 21 and 22 of the Statement of Changes in
Immigration Rules stood alone in a statute I would feel bound to hold that
the words " full-time course of study " in the first sentence of paragraph
22 referred to the course of study for which the applicant had produced   B
evidence that he had been accepted under paragraph 21, whatever the
consequences of that might be. But these rules do not fall to be construed
as a statute. They have to be construed by busy immigration officers at all
the ports of entry. They have to be construed in the light of their intention
which clearly is to afford entry to bona fide students who come here for
the purpose of their education and studies, and who can support themselves so long as they are here. They also have to be read as a whole.   C
Paragraphs 97 to 99 relate to applications by students to extend their
leave for the purpose of continuing their studies, and show that when
considering such applications the immigration officer may look beyond the
particular course of studies for which the applicant was granted leave to
stay, and only refuse leave if he has reason to believe that the student
does not intend to leave at the end of his extended course of studies.   D

If a narrow construction is put upon the words " full-time course of
study " in the first sentence of paragraph 22, it would mean that a student
who came here having been accepted for an initial course of study, but who
honestly told the immigration officer that it was his intention to remain
if possible for a further course of study, could never obtain entry. Whereas
if he falsely told the immigration officer he intended to leave on completion
of his first course of study, or if he changed his mind, he could be granted   E
leave and then apply for an extension. This seems to me to put a premium
on dishonesty and I cannot believe that it was the intention of the rules.

Indeed Mr. Brown does not seriously suggest that it was. He
suggests that the words " full-time course of study " in the first sentence
of paragraph 22 should not be confined to the course of study for which
the applicant has been accepted but should be given a somewhat wider   F
meaning so as to include not only that course but also a coherent definite
educational proposal reasonably capable in the view of the immigration
officer of being carried out by the applicant. The longer the initial course
the more difficult it would be for the applicant to satisfy the immigration
officer that he has a sufficiently definite educational proposal extending
beyond it, so that the immigration officer can be satisfied that the applicant   G
intends to leave the country on completion of his total course of studies.

I accept the submission of Mr. Brown as to the meaning of the
words " full-time course of study " in paragraph 22. The question remains
whether in refusing entry the immigration officer in this case adopted that
meaning or the narrower meaning to which I have referred above. If he
adopted the latter, then he erred in law and his decision cannot stand.
His reasoning is set out in his affidavit of June 27, 1980. It is true that he   H
refers to the fact that the applicant failed to comply with the immigration
rules of the United States of America, and to his family circumstances in
this country, as indications that he did not intend to leave the country on
completion of his course of studies. But he says:

" However both the applicant and his brother had indicated that the
applicant's intentions were not limited to the three-year course and

The Weekly Law Reports, November 21, 1980

1409

1 W.L.R.   Reg. v. Immigration Officer, Ex p. Kharrazi (C.A.)   Dunn L.J.

A   it was evident that he expected to stay in the United Kingdom for up
to 10 years or more."

The reference to staying in the United Kingdom for up to 10 years or more
is referable to an earlier passage in the affidavit when the immigration officer
said:

B   " I asked the applicant how long he wished to stay in the United
Kingdom. He replied he wanted leave to enter for one year as a
student and said that he expected to remain in the United Kingdom
for up to 10 years so as to complete his education, taking ' O ' levels,
' A ' levels, and going on to university."

And later in the affidavit the immigration officer said:

C   " When I asked [the applicant's brother] how long he expected the
applicant to remain in the United Kingdom he said that the period
would be up to 10 years or as long as it took to complete his education."

Although an affidavit of this kind is not to be construed too strictly,
those passages indicate to me that the question to which the immigration
D officer was applying his mind was whether the applicant intended to leave
this country on completion of the three-year course of study for which he
had been accepted, and as the applicant frankly said he expected to remain
here for up to 10 years to complete his education the immigration officer
refused him entry. He did not apply his mind to the question whether the
applicant intended to remain after completion of his full course of
education. In that approach I think the immigration officer erred in law.

E   In reaching that conclusion I attach no blame whatever to the immigration officer. Mr. Brown told us that he was instructed to put forward
the strict or narrow construction of paragraph 22 as being the correct
construction, and it is not unreasonable to assume that it is that narrow
construction that has hitherto been generally accepted by the Home Office
and immigration officers as being correct. Indeed as I have already said it
F was at first my own reaction until I realised the full implications of such
construction and saw paragraphs 97 to 99. And I can well understand why
the immigration officer approached the matter in the way in which he did.
However, for the reasons I have given, his decision cannot stand. I too
would allow the appeal, but I agree with Waller L.J. that this does not
mean that the applicant is now entitled as of right to enter as a student,
and I would welcome the submissions of counsel as to the appropriate
G form of order so that his application can be reconsidered in the light of
the principles enunciated by this court.

Appeal allowed with costs.
Decision of immigration officer
quashed.
H   *Remitted to Chief Immigration Officer,*
Gatwick Airport.

Solicitors: *Donald Nelson & Co.; Treasury Solicitor.*

C. N.

A

[COURT OF APPEAL]

* EDGAR v. EDGAR

[No. 13269 of 1978]

1980   July 2, 3; 23   Ormrod and Oliver L.JJ.   B

*Husband and Wife—Financial provision—Agreement—Jurisdiction
of court — Deed of separation negotiated by parties' legal
advisers — Wife agreeing against legal advice and without
duress not to seek capital payment other than provided by
deed—Whether wife entitled to lump sum award on divorce
—Matrimonial Causes Act 1973 (c. 18), ss. 23, 25 (1)*

C

A deed of separation dated April 1, 1976, embodying
arrangements agreed by negotiations between the parties'
solicitors provided, inter alia, that the husband, a multi-
millionaire, would purchase in the wife's name a specified
house, or some commensurate alternative, make certain other
provisions and pay the wife and four children severally certain
annual sums.   Despite an initial reservation in relation to
capital provision and the advice of her legal advisers that   D
she might get a substantial lump sum payment in divorce
proceedings, by clause 8 the wife acknowledged that she did
not intend to seek any further capital or property provision
from the husband and agreed not to proceed with her claims
for lump sum and property adjustment orders in the event
of divorce.

On the wife's petition the marriage was dissolved.   The
wife applied under section 23 of the Matrimonial Causes Act   E
1973 for a lump sum payment, claiming that she agreed to
clause 8 of the deed because she felt over-powered by the
husband's enormous wealth and position and she desperately
wanted to get away.   There was no evidence, however, to
show that the husband exerted any pressure to accept his terms
during the negotiations prior to the drawing up of the deed.
Eastham J. ordered the husband to pay a substantial lump sum
and discharged the deed.   F

On appeal by the husband: —

Held, (1) that the court had jurisdiction to entertain the
wife's application for a lump sum payment and to make an
order on it notwithstanding her covenant in clause 8 of the
deed of separation not to proceed with such a claim and
that, where such a covenant subsisted, before making an order
the court had to determine the effect of the covenant on the
exercise of its discretion under section 23 of the Matrimonial   G
Causes Act 1973 (post, pp. 1415A–C, 1420E).

Hyman v. *Hyman* [1929] A.C. 601, H.L.(E.) applied.

(2) Allowing the appeal, that section 25 (1) of the Act
required the court to have regard to all the circumstances of
the parties and the existence of a prior agreement was an
important aspect which should be looked at having regard to
the conduct of the two parties, both leading up to the agreement and subsequent thereto, and the court should bear in   H
mind that formal agreements, properly and fairly arrived at
with competent legal advice, should be given effect to unless
good and substantial grounds were shown for concluding
that injustice would be done by holding the parties to the
terms of the agreement; that, although the husband had a
superior bargaining power, he had not been shown to have
exploited it unfairly so as to induce the wife to act to her
disadvantage; and that, accordingly, since there was no
evidence reflecting adversely on the husband's conduct in the

A   negotiations and no adequate explanation of the wife's con-
       duct either in entering into the covenant or in asking the
       court to disregard it, the wife had failed to show sufficient
       grounds to justify the court in going behind the deed of
       separation (post, pp. 1417A–F, 1418E–F, 1419E, 1420A–C, F—
       1421D, 1423F–G, 1424C–D, G).
           Wright v. Wright [1970] 1 W.L.R. 1219, C.A. applied.
           Decision of Eastham J. reversed.

B
       The following cases are referred to in the judgment of Ormrod L.J.:

       Brockwell v. Brockwell, November 5, 1975; Court of Appeal (Civil
           Division) Transcript No. 468 of 1975; The Times, November 11,
           1975, C.A.
       Dipper v. Dipper [1980] 3 W.L.R. 626; [1980] 2 All E.R. 722, C.A.
       Hyman v. Hyman [1929] A.C. 601, H.L.(E.).
C   O'D. v. O'D. [1976] Fam. 83; [1975] 3 W.L.R. 308; [1975] 2 All E.R.
           993, C.A.
       Wright v. Wright [1970] 1 W.L.R. 1219; [1970] 3 All E.R. 209, C.A.

       The following additional cases were cited in argument:

       Backhouse v. Backhouse [1978] 1 W.L.R. 243; [1978] 1 All E.R. 1158.
       Dean v. Dean [1978] Fam. 161; [1978] 3 W.L.R. 288; [1978] 3 All E.R.
D   758.
       Ladbrook v. Ladbrook (1977) 121 S.J. 710.
       Smallman v. Smallman [1972] Fam. 25; [1971] 3 W.L.R. 588; [1971] 3
           All E.R. 717, C.A.
       Wachtel v. Wachtel [1973] Fam. 72; [1973] 2 W.L.R. 366; [1973] 1 All
           E.R. 829, C.A.

E   APPEAL from Eastham J.
       On an application by the petitioner wife, Roberta Hilary Ann Edgar,
Eastham J. ordered on March 27, 1980, that the respondent husband,
Anthony Samuel Edgar, should pay the wife a lump sum of £670,000
on or before July 27, 1980, and that on payment of that sum an earlier
order for periodical payments to the wife and four children of the
family should be discharged, all other financial claims of the wife should
F be dismissed and a deed of separation dated April 1, 1976, and made
between the parties embodying agreed separation arrangements, including financial arrangements, should be discharged. His Lordship gave
leave to appeal to both parties.
       By a notice of appeal dated April 9, 1980, the husband appealed on
the grounds, inter alia, (i) that the judge was wrong in principle in
G declining to give effect to the deed of separation which was an agreement
made by the parties after negotiations by their respective legal advisers
over a period of six months and which was not contrary to public policy
and the husband had met all his obligations under it, that the judge had
a duty to uphold the deed and that he was wrong in not doing so; (ii)
that the judge was wrong in his finding that the deed was not freely
entered into by the wife and, in particular, that there was inequality of
H bargaining power between the husband and the wife since (a) the bulk
of the proposals contained in the deed originated from the wife and
represented what she wanted, (b) she was throughout the antecedent
negotiations leading up to the execution of the deed represented by
competent solicitors, counsel and accountants, (c) she fully understood
all matters canvassed and took an active part in negotiations; (iii)
further, and in the alternative, the judge wrongly exercised his discretion to award the wife a capital payment and, in particular, (a) he

was wrong to hold, bearing in mind that the husband was enormously **A**
wealthy and the wife's lack of contribution towards his wealth, that
the payment by the husband to the wife of a substantial capital sum
placed the parties in the financial position in which they would have
been if the marriage had not irretrieveably broken down and that each
had properly discharged his or her financial responsibilities and obligations towards the other, (b) he was wrong to hold that the wife's standard
of living today fell far short of the standard enjoyed by the parties during **B**
the marriage and, alternatively, he was wrong to redress any imbalance
in the respective standards of living of the parties by a capital payment,
(c) he failed to take into account the fact that the wife did not need
a capital sum, and (d) he was wrong not to deduct from the award the
current value of the wife's property and its contents amounting to
£150,000. **C**

The facts are stated in the judgment of Ormrod L.J.

Joseph Jackson Q.C. and *N. P. R. Wall* for the husband.
Robert Johnson Q.C. and *Nicholas Wilson* for the wife.

Cur. adv. vult. **D**

July 23. The following judgments were read.

ORMROD L.J. This is an appeal by a husband from an order made
on March 27, 1980, by Eastham J. in proceedings for financial provision following a divorce. It is a wholly exceptional case on the facts,
and this judgment must be read in the light of the strange and, in some **E**
ways, unsatisfactory state of the evidence.

The judge was dealing with applications under sections 22 and 23 of
the Matrimonial Causes Act 1973, by the wife of an extremely rich
husband for a lump sum and periodical payments for herself and four
children, of whom she has the custody. The husband is a multi-
millionaire, who is in a position to make a very large payment without
liquidity problems. The main issue at the hearing was the husband's **F**
contention that the court should give effect to an undertaking by the
wife, contained in a deed of separation, not to apply, after divorce, for
additional capital provision, beyond that provided by the deed, which
had been fully complied with by the husband.

After hearing the evidence and argument at length, Eastham J.
decided that he could properly ignore the wife's undertaking, and so **G**
proceeded to assess the lump sum under the provisions of section 25 of
the Act. He ordered the husband to pay the sum of £670,000 by July
27, 1980, and upon payment of this sum (a) the existing order for
periodical payments to the wife and the children be discharged; (b) all
other financial claims of the wife be dismissed; (c) the deed of separation, dated April 1, 1976, be discharged.

The order was made in this form with a view to producing a " clean **H**
break " between the parties, notwithstanding that they have four
children, in whose lives both are playing, and intend to play, as full a
part as they can in the circumstances. The consent of the wife to the
dismissal of her claim to periodical payments was not obtained. *Dipper*
v. *Dipper* [1980] 3 W.L.R. 626, decided by this court on March 5, 1980
was not brought to the attention of Eastham J. Nor, apparently, had she
consented to the discharge of the order for periodical payments to the

A   children, a very unusual, if not unprecedented, order in such circumstances.

    The marriage took place on August 23, 1967, and the four children are aged 12, 9, 8 and 6. The marriage had run into serious difficulties by the summer of 1975, and by October 1975, the wife had made up her mind to leave her husband as soon as arrangements could be made for her to do so. She was extremely anxious to retain the care and control

B   of the children, but had no alternative accommodation and, without her husband's co-operation, had no means of providing an alternative home for herself and the children. The husband wished to keep the marriage going and the family together, and had made it clear to her that he would not agree to her leaving with the children unless she had a proper and suitable home for them.

C   The wife consulted solicitors and, on October 6, 1975, they spoke on the telephone to the husband's solicitors saying she wanted to leave and wanted a divorce. On October 15, 1975, she had a conference with counsel, and on October 16 her solicitors wrote to the husband's solicitors confirming her decision, and setting out her requirements in detail. I will return to this and other letters at a later stage in this judgment. This letter, however, expressly stated that the wife was not

D   asking for a full capital settlement at that stage. However, by November 25, 1975, at the latest, the wife seems to have agreed that she would not ask for any further capital provision in the event of a divorce, and confirmed this in an interview with her husband's solicitor and her own solicitor on that date. On December 5 the husband's solicitors wrote a letter setting out in full proposed heads of agreement,

E   including the following:

> "5. Your client agrees that she will not ask for, now, or in the future, any capital or lump sum payment or provision pending, during or following any divorce proceedings nor during the subsistence of the deed of separation."

    The wife's solicitors sent a long, detailed letter on December 15 dealing

F   with many points in the proposed terms, and in particular in reply to the paragraph quoted above, they wrote:

> "5. As you know our client has been advised not to agree this, but she has instructed us that she is prepared subject to what we write in the final paragraph in this letter not to claim now or in the future any capital or lump sum provision with the exception that should

G   legislation change the tax position regarding husbands paying wives maintenance as referred to by you in your point 9 our client must reserve the right to claim a capital or lump sum provision to compensate her and this must be clearly accepted by your client."

    The final paragraph referred to, read thus:

> "Finally, and this is not intended in any way to be a threat, our

H   client is not prepared to go on bargaining about the position. She has made her situation quite clear. As you will appreciate, if the matters do proceed in accordance with our client's wishes, she is giving up a very sizeable capital payment which she would otherwise, in both counsel's and on our view, receive. She has instructed us that if your client is not prepared to agree the points we have raised in this letter then we are to . . . proceed . . . with the divorce as a matter of urgency."

By the time this stage in the marriage had been reached the wife was A
emotionally involved with another man, possibly with two other men,
with one of whom she had admittedly committed adultery; the husband
had committed adultery on many occasions with a number of women.
Both of them were, therefore, in a position to file a petition immediately.

Negotiations, mainly involving details, continued between solicitors
until the deed of separation was agreed and executed, by both parties, on
April 1, 1976. They were still living together, and continued to do so B
until November 1976, when the wife moved into her own house. Under
the deed, the husband agreed to purchase in the name of the wife a
named house, or some commensurate alternative, to pay for alterations,
to provide accommodation for the wife's mother, to buy the wife a
motor car, and to pay £16,000 per annum less tax to the wife, and
£5,000 per annum less tax to each of the four children. These were, C
substantially, the provisions for which the wife had originally asked in
her solicitors' letter of October 16, 1975. We were told by counsel that
the present value of the capital provisions made for the wife is approximately £100,000. In addition, the deed contained a clause in these
terms:

"8. The wife acknowledges that on transfer to her of the said pro- D
perty referred to in paragraph 2 hereof and on payment of the sums
referred to therein and in paragraph 4 hereof and always provided
that no reconciliation between the wife and husband is effected
she does not intend to seek any further capital or property provision from the husband whether by way of ancillary relief in divorce
proceedings or otherwise and in the event of a decree of divorce
being granted she hereby agrees not to proceed with her claims for E
lump sum and property adjustment orders subject only to her
right to make application to the court for lump sum or property
provision in accordance with paragraph 7 hereof if in the circumstances referred to therein the parties cannot reach agreement
regarding alternative financial provision."

This clause, of course, represented the arrangements made between the F
solicitors in the relevant extracts from their letters, which have already
been quoted.

It was subsequently discovered that the provision in the deed for payment direct to the children of £5,000 per annum each was not effective
for tax purposes. Accordingly, arrangements were made (to use neutral
language) to replace this provision in the deed by consent orders under G
section 27 of the Act of 1973 (the wilful neglect to maintain section),
which were effective for tax purposes.

On November 3, 1978, the wife presented a petition for divorce,
relying on two years' separation and consent. The prayer was in the
usual form, asking for all forms of ancillary relief. Decree nisi was
pronounced on January 24, 1979. Notice of intention to proceed with
the application for all forms of ancillary relief was given on March 7, H
1979, and it was supported by an affidavit of the wife which made it
quite clear that she was claiming a "substantial capital sum." The
affidavit referred to the contents of clause 8 of the deed, and gave some
explanation, but in very general terms, of the wife's change of mind in
relation to claiming further capital provision. I will refer later to this
part of the affidavit in greater detail.

Turning now to the law, it is common ground that the principle laid

A down by the House of Lords in *Hyman* v. *Hyman* [1929] A.C. 601 still
applies. Lord Hailsham L.C. said, at p. 614:

"However this may be, it is sufficient for the decision of the present
case to hold, as I do, that the power of the court to make provision
for a wife on the dissolution of her marriage is a necessary incident
of the power to decree such a dissolution, conferred not merely
B in the interests of the wife, but of the public, and that the wife
cannot by her own covenant preclude herself from invoking the
jurisdiction of the court or preclude the court from the exercise
of that jurisdiction."

Eastham J., therefore, had jurisdiction to entertain the wife's application for a lump sum, and to make the order which he did, notwith-
C standing the provision of clause 8 of the deed, under which the wife
covenanted not to proceed with a claim for a lump sum. The real
question, and it is a difficult one, is to determine the effect, if any, to
be given to such a covenant, when exercising the statutory discretion
under section 23 of the Act of 1973, to order the husband to pay a
lump sum to the wife.

In *Hyman* v. *Hyman* Lord Hailsham L.C., having held that the
D existence of the covenant did not preclude the wife from making an
application to the court, went on to say, at p. 609:

". . . this by no means implies that, when this application is made,
the existence of the deed or its terms are not the most relevant
factors for consideration by the court in reaching a decision."

E This problem was considered in this court in *Wright* v. *Wright*
[1970] 1 W.L.R. 1219. In giving the leading judgment, Sir Gordon
Willmer accepted that the principle of *Hyman* v. *Hyman* applied, notwithstanding that the agreement between the parties had been approved
by the court, under what was then section 5 of the Matrimonial Causes
Act 1963. He said, at pp. 1223–1224:

"There is no doubt that no agreement made inter partes can ever
F deprive the court of its right to review the question of maintenance
for a wife, as was decided by the House of Lords in *Hyman* v.
Hyman [1929] A.C. 601. I do not think that anything contained
in the new provisions of the Act of 1965, giving the court the power
to approve reasonable arrangements between the parties, is such as
to cast any doubt at all upon the continuance in force of the
G doctrine enunciated by the House of Lords in *Hyman* v. *Hyman*.
There is, therefore, scope for two diametrically opposite views. On
the one hand, it may be said that the court has an absolute right to go
behind any agreement between the parties so far as the question of
maintenance for a wife is concerned. On the other hand, there is
the judge's approach to the problem, that is, that where there is
an agreement between the parties approved by the court, effect
H must be given to it. Under the one view, the right to award maintenance would be completely uninhibited, whereas under the other it
would be strictly curtailed by the arrangement made between the
parties and approved by the court at the time of the trial. Mr.
Dean, as I understood his argument, contended for an intermediate
position between those two extremes. As I followed him, he said
that the fact of this arrangement having been made and having
been approved by the court is merely one factor amongst the

numerous factors that have to be taken into consideration when A
the court is called upon to award maintenance to a wife following
a divorce case. I suppose the result of this argument would be to
limit or inhibit to some extent the generosity of the registrar or
judge in making an award of maintenance; that is to say, supposing
he would, without any such arrangement having been made, have
been disposed to award X a week, he must now in deference to the
arrangement made between the parties, to which some effect must B
be given, award only X minus Y. The difference between that and
the judge's view is that the judge held that it would not be right, in
the absence of proof of any unforeseen circumstances of the kind
envisaged by the arrangement, to make any award of maintenance
at all. On behalf of the husband, the judge's conclusion was
vigorously defended by Mr. Anns who said, and said very forcibly, C
that this was a perfectly valid agreement between two parties, both
sui juris, arrived at with the assistance they had from their legal
advisers and approved by the court. It was, therefore, something to
which effect ought to be given unless compelling reasons to the
contrary were shown. He added (I think with a good deal of force)
that the fact that the court had given its approval to the proposed
arrangement had put the stamp of reasonableness on the arrangement D
which was then being made, viz. that there should be no maintenance. . . . " I think, approaching the matter de novo and in the
absence of authority, that the proper view is to say that this was an
agreement entered into with full knowledge of all the circumstances
and on the advice of both parties' legal advisers. It is, therefore,
something to which considerable attention must be paid. I accept that E
it would not be right to say that it has to be construed like a
statute, or that it absolutely forbids any possible award of maintenance, except upon the strictest proof of the existence of the
circumstances mentioned. If and in so far as the judge so decided,
I would not agree wholly with his conclusion. But I do not think
that he went so far as that. I think he was thinking along the
same lines as I myself think, namely, that the existence of this F
agreement, having regard to the circumstances in which it was
arrived at, at least makes it necessary for the wife, if she wants to
justify an award of maintenance, to offer prima facie proof that
there have been unforeseen circumstances, in the true sense, which
make it impossible for her to work or otherwise maintain herself.
If that be right, I think that it is quite plain that the wife here did G
not ever give such prima facie proof."

In *Brockwell* v. *Brockwell* (unreported) November 5, 1975, Court of
Appeal (Civil Division) Transcript No. 468 of 1975, Stamp L.J., having
cited these passages from Sir Gordon Willmer's judgment in *Wright* v.
Wright said:

" Nevertheless, the wife ought in my judgment to have the oppor- H
tunity of showing that in all the circumstances and notwithstanding
the agreement the court should exercise in her favour this discretion to award her some lump sum payment."

That case, of course, arose under the current Matrimonial Causes Act
1973 and, in an attempt to integrate the *Hyman* v. *Hyman* principle
with the new provisions relating to the exercise of the discretion in

A   financial matters, set out in section 25, I suggested in my judgment in that case, that an agreement not to claim a lump sum should be taken into account under the heading of conduct, and added, ". . . when people make an agreement like this it is a very important factor in considering what is the just outcome of the proceedings." I see no reason to resile from that statement.

B   Under section 25 (1) it is the duty of the court to have regard to all the circumstances of the case, and, in particular, to the matters detailed in paragraphs (a) to (g), and to exercise its powers so as to place all parties, so far as practicable, and having regard to their conduct, just to do so, in the financial position they would have been in had the marriage not broken down. The ideal, of course, is rarely if ever, attainable; so, inevitably, in most cases, the phrase " so far as . . . practicable " dominates

C   the issue, modified, where relevant, by conduct.

To decide what weight should be given, in order to reach a just result, to a prior agreement not to claim a lump sum, regard must be had to the conduct of both parties, leading up to the prior agreement, and to their subsequent conduct, in consequence of it. It is not necessary in this connection to think in formal legal terms, such as mis-representation or estoppel; *all* the circumstances as they affect each of

D   two human beings must be considered in the complex relationship of marriage. So, the circumstances surrounding the making of the agreement are relevant. Under pressure by one side, exploitation of a dominant position to secure an unreasonable advantage, inadequate knowledge, possibly bad legal advice, an important change of circumstances, unforeseen or overlooked at the time of making the agreement,

E   are all relevant to the question of justice between the parties. Important too is the general proposition that formal agreements, properly and fairly arrived at with competent legal advice, should not be displaced unless there are good and substantial grounds for concluding that an injustice will be done by holding the parties to the terms of their agreement. There may well be other considerations which affect the justice of this case; the above list is not intended to be an exclusive

F   catalogue.

I agree with Sir Gordon Willmer in *Wright* v. *Wright* [1970] 1 W.L.R. 1219, 1224, that the existence of an agreement,

> ". . . at least makes it necessary for the wife, if she is to justify an award of maintenance, to offer prima facie proof that there have been unforeseen circumstances, in the true sense, which make it

G   impossible for her to work or otherwise maintain herself."

Adapting that statement to the present case, it means that the wife here must offer prima facie evidence of material facts which show that justice requires that she should be relieved from the effects of her covenant in clause 8 of the deed of separation, and awarded further capital provision.

H   Eastham J. in the present case, approached the problem on these lines. He summarised the law in five propositions:

> "(1) . . . (and this is not contested) notwithstanding the deed of April 1, the wife is entitled to pursue a claim under section 23 of the Act. (2) If she does pursue such a claim, the court not only has jurisdiction to entertain it but is bound to take into account all the considerations listed in section 25 of the Act. (3) The existence of an agreement is a very relevant circumstance under section 25

and in the case of an arm's length agreement, based on legal advice　A
between parties of equal bargaining power, is a most important
piece of conduct to be considered under section 25.　(4) Providing
that there is equality above, the mere fact that the wife would
have done better by going to the court, would not generally be a
ground, for giving her more as, in addition to its duty under section
25, the court had a duty also to uphold agreements which do not
offend public policy.　(5) If the court, on the evidence, takes the　B
view that having regard to the disparity of bargaining power, it
would be unjust not to exercise its powers under section 23 (having
regard to the considerations under section 25), it should exercise
such powers even if no fraud, misrepresentation or duress is
established which, at common law, would entitle a wife to avoid
the deed."　　　　　　　　　　　　　　　　　　　　　　　　　　　　　C

　　I agree with these propositions, subject to two reservations.　First,
as to proposition (4), I am not sure that it is helpful to speak of the
court having " a duty " to uphold agreements, although I understand
the sense in which the word was used.　Secondly, the reference to
" disparity of bargaining power " in proposition (5) is incomplete.　It
is derived from a phrase taken from *Brockwell* v. *Brockwell,* and for　D
which I must accept ultimate responsibility.　I used it as a shorthand
way of describing a situation with which all experienced practitioners
are familiar, where one spouse takes an unfair advantage of the other
in the throes of marital breakdown, a time when emotional pressures
are high, and judgment apt to be clouded.　It is unfortunate, because
Eastham J. has based his decision solely on this notion of disparity of
bargaining power as such, and not on the use, if any, made of it by　E
the husband.　The wife, herself, in her affidavit in support of her application, gave as her reasons for disregarding the advice of her counsel
and solicitors, and entering into the covenant not to claim a lump sum,
the fact that she felt overpowered by her husband's enormous wealth
and position, coupled with her fears of losing the children.　There can
be no doubt that in this case, as in so many, there is a disparity of　F
bargaining power.　The crucial question, however, for present purposes,
is not whether the husband had a superior bargaining power, but
whether he exploited it in a way which was unfair to the wife, so as to
induce her to act to her disadvantage.

　　It is at this point that this case becomes so puzzling.　At no time
has the wife alleged that the husband put pressure on her to accept his
terms during the negotiations which led up to the deed, and the judge　G
expressly found as a fact that the husband, " . . . did not make threats
with the intention of forcing his wife to take far less than a court would
award her after a decree."

　　The course of the negotiations for the deed of separation were not
gone into in any detail at the hearing, although both parties gave oral
evidence.　Much time was taken up in investigating the wife's emotional　H
involvements in the summer and autumn of 1975, to show that she might
have been disposed to agree to almost any terms to get away from
her husband, but there was no evidence that the husband was stipulating
for an abandonment by her of her claim to a lump sum as a condition
precedent to arrangements which would enable her to leave.　All we
know is that the wife put forward at the outset, in the letter of October
16, 1975, her detailed demands for a house, a home for her mother, an

A allowance totalling £36,000 a year for herself and the children, and expressly reserved her right to claim a lump sum after divorce. There is a forthrightness and a sense of urgency about this letter, which does not suggest that she was conscious of much disparity in bargaining power. Three weeks later there is a letter from the husband's solicitors, dated November 7, saying that an agreement has apparently been reached by the parties themselves on the basis of the letter of October

B 16 with "appropriate amendments." Then comes the meeting on November 25, 1975, at the wife's solicitors' office between the husband's solicitor, and the wife's solicitor, at which the wife insisted on being present. She again stated her terms. The husband's solicitor, according to his note of the meeting

C "asked it to be made clear that [the wife] would not ask for any further capital or lump sum payments to be made by her husband once the financial arrangements which were now being discussed had been set out in a deed of separation, and in fact implemented. [The wife] said she agreed to this but she was not prepared to wait indefinitely whilst her husband made up his mind before taking any further steps."

D In a revised version of the note he put it more neutrally. "I . . . asked if it was quite clear that . . . she would not ask for any further capital. . . ." These notes were agreed as a fair record of the interview. There is nothing to suggest any pressure on, or exploitation of, the wife by the husband or his solicitor. So the mystery remains unsolved as to why the wife so determinedly rejected the wise advice of her counsel and solicitors not to enter into an agreement to forgo her further claim

E for a lump sum.

In my judgment, therefore, there is no evidence which reflects adversely on the husband's conduct in the negotiations, and no, or no adequate, explanation of the wife's conduct, and no grounds are shown for holding that justice requires the court to relieve her from the effects of the covenant.

F Mr. Johnson, for the wife, in this court has accepted that he cannot point to any evidence of pressure from the husband on the wife to act as she did, and he has not submitted that the disparity in bargaining power is enough by itself to justify this court in ignoring the deed. Instead he has relied on a line of argument foreshadowed by Sir Gordon Willmer in *Wright* v. *Wright* [1970] 1 W.L.R. 1219, 1223E–G, that the court in carrying out its duty under section 25 should look at the facts and

G decide, disregarding the deed at this stage, what provision is required to put the wife into a position she would have been in had the marriage continued, and then take into account the financial provisions of the deed. If this is done, he submits that the shortfall is obvious; the provision in the deed is plainly inadequate; and, therefore, the inference must be that it would be unjust to hold the wife to her agreement not to

H claim a lump sum.

This argument gives no weight at all to the wife's covenant, and tacitly assumes that a wife, in the position of this wife, would be likely to receive a much larger capital provision than that already provided for under the deed, but with no periodical payments, instead of a large order for periodical payments and a relatively small capital sum. This court has not yet had occasion to consider the application of the principles of section 25 to cases involving very rich people although a

little assistance may perhaps be had from *O'D.* v. *O'D.* [1976] Fam. 83, **A**
a case involving a rich, but not extremely rich, husband. The point
does not arise directly for decision in the present case, so I shall not
say any more about it on this occasion.

In the result, I have come to the conclusion that the wife has failed
to show sufficient grounds to justify the court in going behind the
arrangements made in April 1976 and embodied in the deed. No **B**
reasons have been given for the complete change in attitude between
the letter of October 16, 1975, reserving her position in regard to capital
provision, and her acceptance at the meeting on November 25, 1975, in
spite of the advice of her lawyers, that she would make no further claim;
there is no evidence of undue pressure by the husband or of any other
circumstances that led her to act in a way apparently so contrary to
her interests. Similarly, there is no evidence to explain or justify her **C**
later decision in March 1979 to go back on her undertaking and claim a
further lump sum, or any suggestion that her circumstances had changed
in some significant way between April 1976 and March 1979.

At one stage during the argument I thought that it might be appropriate to send the case back to give the wife an opportunity to adduce
further evidence on these lines, but, on reflection, I do not think that
any useful purpose will be served and further costs would be involved. **D**

I can see, therefore, no alternative but to allow the appeal and
dismiss the wife's applications under sections 23 and 24 of the Act of 1973.
We shall have to send the case back for determination, in default of
agreement, of the amounts to be paid to the wife and the children by way
of periodical payments.

E
OLIVER L.J. I agree fully with the judgment of Ormrod L.J. and
I add some observations of my own only in the light of the fact that
we are differing from Eastham J. and in deference to the sustained
arguments which have been advanced by Mr. Johnson in seeking to
uphold his decision in this court.

The principles to be applied are not seriously in dispute. After a
review of the relevant authorities the judge stated them in the five pro- **F**
positions which have already been referred to in the judgment of
Ormrod L.J. and I accept them subject to the same reservations as those
which he has stated and in particular as regards the reference which the
judge made to " equal bargaining power " and " disparity of bargaining
power." If, by these references, Eastham J. meant no more than that
one must look in every case at all the circumstances to see whether
there was some unfair or unconscionable advantage taken of some **G**
factor or of some relationship between the parties which enables the
court to say that an agreement was not truly entered into by one party
or the other as a free agent, then I have no quarrel with them. If,
however, he meant that the court must engage in an exercise of
dissecting the contract and weighing the relative advantages and bargaining position on each side in order to ascertain whether there is some **H**
precise or approximate equilibrium, then I respectfully disagree. Men
and women of full age, education and understanding, acting with competent advice available to them, must be assumed to know and appreciate what they are doing and their actual respective bargaining
strengths will in fact depend in every case upon a subjective evaluation
of their motives for doing it. One may, of course, find that some
unfair advantage has been taken of a judgment impaired by emotion,

A   or that one party is motivated by fear induced by some conduct of the
other or by some misapprehension of a factual or legal position, but
in the absence of some such consideration as that—and these are
examples only—the mere strength of one party's desire for a particular
result or the mere fact that one party has greater wealth than the other
cannot, I think, affect the weight to be attributed to a freely negotiated
bargain.

B
Having said that, I do not, of course, quarrel for one moment with
the proposition that the court in every case must— indeed is enjoined
by statute to—look at all the circumstances in exercising its powers
under section 25 (1) of the Act of 1973 to produce the result directed by
that section.   That is not in issue here, but the extent to which the
court is directed and is able to produce the result of placing all the
C   parties in the financial position in which they would have been if the
marriage had not broken down is controlled first by practicability and
secondly by the consideration of what is just having regard to their
conduct.   In that consideration the existence of a freely negotiated
bargain entered into at the instance of one of the parties and affording
to him or her everything for which he or she has stipulated must be a
most important element of conduct which cannot be lightly ignored.
D   Essentially therefore what is in issue in the instant case is whether, in
exercising the jurisdiction which the statute required him to exercise,
Eastham J. was right to decline to hold the wife to a particular term
of the agreement into which she had entered four years earlier.   I say
" a particular term " because there is really no dispute between the
parties that, if the wife makes out a proper case for additional income
E   payments beyond those specified in the deed of separation, the husband
is willing to provide them.   There may be a lively dispute both about
the necessity and the quantum, but there is, if I understand Mr. Jackson
right, no dispute in principle.   What is in dispute is whether, having
regard to clause 8 of the deed, to which Ormrod L.J. has already
referred, the judge was right to award to the wife the very large capital
sum which he did award.

F
Substantially, the only evidence about how that clause came to be
in the deed is provided by the agreed note of the meeting between the
solicitors for the husband and the wife on November 25, 1975, at which
the wife (who is evidently a lady of some strength of character) insisted
upon being present and in which she took an active part. I will not repeat
the relevant parts of this note which have already been quoted by
G   Ormrod L.J.

Now it seems clear that this was the first occasion upon which this
particular matter was mentioned, and whether it was put forward as this
note suggests as a simple inquiry by Mr. Tamlin, the husband's solicitor,
or (as seems to be suggested by the earlier version of the note) as a
positive stipulation, seems to me to be largely immaterial.   Up to this
H   point the negotiations between the solicitors had, as the correspondence
shows, been on the basis that, upon the marriage being dissolved, the
wife would retain her liberty to claim that provision should be made for
her by way of a lump sum payment.   A letter of November 7, 1975,
seems to indicate that the question of the provision to be made for
the wife had been discussed between her husband and herself personally
and that they had reached broad agreement on the basis of the earlier
correspondence in which this term appeared, and nowhere in her

evidence does the wife suggest that her forgoing this right was, up to this point, something which was insisted upon by her husband or which she was under any pressure to accept. The note of the meeting shows that when it was mentioned she immediately agreed to it and indeed that it was she who was pressing for an agreement to be concluded and threatening proceedings if it was not. Now she could not have been under any misapprehension at all about what she was agreeing to. She had, on October 15, 1975, been taken by her solicitors to a conference with leading counsel and had been clearly advised that in any divorce proceedings she could expect to receive sums very substantially in excess of those which she was then contemplating as acceptable to her and that the provision made by the court would be likely to include an extremely large capital provision having regard to her husband's financial position. Whether the underlying assumption that the court would necessarily be inclined to award a capital sum of the magnitude which she was advised that she might achieve was correct is not something upon which we are called to express an opinion and I do not do so. I observe only that, whilst the statute casts upon the court the burden of forming a view about what the financial position of each of the parties would have been if the marriage had not broken down, I do not find in it anything which necessarily compels a hypothesis of such continued affection, contentment or open-handed generosity as to lead either party to make a gift to the other of a substantial part of his or her fortune.

Now there was never any secret of the fact that she entered into the agreement in deliberate defiance of the advice of her solicitors and counsel and with a full appreciation that she had the possibility of achieving a very much more substantial settlement from her husband if she was prepared to bargain for it.

Nor was it simply a snap decision made in a moment of rashness. The negotiation of the terms of the agreement continued for a full four months after this meeting and indeed there was specific negotiation about the terms of clause 8 having regard to the possibility, then fore-seen by the parties' advisers, that changes in fiscal legislation might require the arrangements to be reviewed. So it is really difficult to imagine a clearer case of knowledge, understanding and assent. Further-more, although as Mr. Johnson has not been slow to point out, the agreement represented for a husband as wealthy as this husband was (and is) a very cheap bargain if one assumes the inevitability of a divorce, the fact is (and the evidence is really indisputable), that he was in fact a very reluctant party to it because what he really wanted was to try to preserve the marriage. This was not a case of a disillusioned husband seeking to rid himself cheaply of a tiresome wife. It was, throughout, she who was keeping up the pressure for an agreement which would enable her to clear out with her children and live her own life independently of him. I say that in no spirit of criticism. No doubt she did find that living with him was intolerable to her, and it is profit-less to inquire whether her reasons for so feeling were objectively justified. But it does mean that one must examine with great care the reasons which she now advances for having entered into the bargain of which she has since repented and which she asks the court to ignore.

In her affidavit of February 28, 1979, she said that she was adamant that she did not feel able to claim the large capital sum which she was advised that she would achieve and wanted simply a house and

A income which, she says, she knew the husband was only prepared to offer. And the reason for disregarding the advice which she was given was, she said, that she felt overpowered by his enormous wealth and position. She said that her husband had told her that unless there was agreement he would contest the custody of the children, and although she was assured about the likely result of custody proceedings she was frightened that she might lose. She also said that she was concerned
B to avoid a bitter matrimonial struggle.

In the light of the correspondence which passed between the parties' advisers, to some of which Ormrod L.J. has already referred, this account of her motives is, to say the least, lacking in conviction although her insistence on the agreement, as it appears from the correspondence, certainly bears out her frank admission that she was desperate to leave.
C She was cross-examined at length and really substantially nothing emerged from her evidence which gave any clue to her ready acceptance of clause 8 in defiance of the advice which she had received. Her own account of the matter was that there were three motivating factors which, in descending order of priority, she stated as being (i) her fears about the custody of the children, (ii) her desire to get away, and (iii) her desire to avoid a messy divorce.
D As to the first, Eastham J. found as a fact that the husband did not make any threats with the intention of forcing his wife to accept less than the court would order. He made it plain that he would fight for the children if agreement was not reached, but there was no finding by the judge—and indeed no evidence to justify any finding—that he ever stipulated what ultimately became enshrined in clause 8 as a sine qua
E non of the agreement. As regards the fear of a scandalous divorce, it is quite evident from the correspondence that that had very little influence upon her—indeed she was herself, through her solicitors, using it as a weapon to force agreement. I need only refer to her solicitors' letter of October 31, 1975, in which they say, ". . . whilst our client does not court publicity, please be under no illusion that she fears it and it may however be that the contrary is the case."
F Having read and re-read the evidence I am driven irresistibly to the conclusion that what motivated the wife was her urgent desire to disencumber herself of the company of a husband with whom, for reasons good or bad, she found it uncomfortable to live. No doubt her love for her children and her sense of responsibility for them tempered her impatience to get away, but in the ultimate analysis what shines through her evidence—and she was devastatingly frank about it—is that her
G driving force was her urgent impulse to leave her husband upon terms which would give her the independence which she sought.

Eastham J. clearly appreciated this. He said:

"The husband's stance relating to the children was, in fact, I find, prompted by his concern for them but it did have the effect of facing the lady with the choice of leaving them behind—which she was not
H prepared to do—or accepting terms which were dictated in the husband's interests by Mr. Tamlin at the meeting which took place in Mr. Tooth's office, the attendance note of which I have read in full."

That the suggestion of what finally emerged as clause 8 emanated from Mr. Tamlin appears from the note itself, but if by "dictated in the husband's interests" the judge intended to draw the inference that

Mr. Tamlin was placing the wife under any pressure to accept, then that A
inference appears to me not only to be unsupported by the evidence
but indeed to have been contradicted by the lady herself. She was
asked, in terms, whether any undue pressure was put upon her at this
meeting and her answer was that certainly none was put upon her by
Mr. Tamlin. The undue pressure, she asserted, came from living in a
house with a man she did not want to live with and the threat of
having her children taken away, with the threat of a messy divorce. B
Indeed Mr. Johnson was, I think, constrained to admit that he really
could not point to any unfair advantage taken by the husband or even
to any insistence on his part upon clause 8 as a term of the deed. The
nearest one came to it was an admission by the husband in cross-
examination that the provision was " of the very greatest importance."

  In the last analysis the attack upon the agreement centres, as C
Eastham J. recognised, not upon any unfair pressure or leverage, but
simply upon the disparity in bargaining power between the parties, that
is to say the inequality in the weapons which were available to them
if they chose to use them and not in the use of them or even threats of
use of them which they actually made. That does not, in my judgment,
constitute any ground for going behind this agreement in the circumstances of this case, where it was, throughout, the wife who, for her D
own convenience, was pressing for it and threatening proceedings if it
was not concluded and implemented. By its terms she achieved the
independence she desired, she obtained the home of her own choosing,
and she obtained a not insubstantial income for the support of herself
and her children. It was a result which commended itself to her at the
time and it does not become an unjust result merely because she could E
have done better if she had taken the professional advice which she was
given. Clearly it did not give her the standard of life which she had
enjoyed in the company of a husband with whom she was no longer
prepared to live, but in a consideration of what is just to be done in the
exercise of the court's powers under the Act of 1973 in the light of the
conduct of the parties, the court must, I think, start from the position
that a solemn and freely negotiated bargain by which a party defines F
her own requirements ought to be adhered to unless some clear and
compelling reason, such as, for instance, a drastic change of circumstances,
is shown to the contrary. No such compelling reason has been demonstrated in the evidence placed before this court. The wife's reasons for
seeking to resile from the agreement, as they emerge from her affidavit,
appear to be that she feels unable to offer her children amenities G
comparable to those which her husband is able to offer and that she would
like to buy a farm and to have a house in London. I find myself wholly
unpersuaded that such considerations furnish any ground for relieving
her of the bargain into which she freely entered and I would hold her
to that bargain. I agree therefore that the appeal should be allowed
and I concur in the course proposed by Ormrod L.J.

                    H

            Appeal allowed.
            No order as to costs.

  Solicitors: *Sharpe, Pritchard & Co. for North, Kirk & Co., Liverpool;*
Raymond Tooth & Co.

                    A. R.

A

[COURT OF APPEAL]

* REGINA v. HILLINGDON LONDON BOROUGH COUNCIL,
Ex parte STREETING

B

1980 Feb. 26, 27   Lord Widgery C.J. and
                                                                Griffiths J.

1980 July 1, 2; 10   Lord Denning M.R., Waller
                                                          and Dunn L.JJ.

C

*Local Government — Housing — Homeless persons — Ethiopian
    refugee in England having no local connection with any area
    in Great Britain—Application to housing authority as home-
    less person—Whether housing authority under duty to provide
    accommodation—Housing (Homeless Persons) Act 1977 (c. 48),
    s. 1 (1)*

D

    Following a short visit to England the applicant, an
Ethiopian, and her young son were refused permission to
return to Greece where they had been living. Unable to live
in Ethiopia for political reasons, the applicant applied to the
respondent council for accommodation as a homeless person
pursuant to section 1 (1) of the Housing (Homeless Persons)
Act 1977.[1] The council, though satisfied that the applicant
was unintentionally homeless and that she had a priority need,
decided that they owed her no duty under the Act as she
had no local connection with the area of any housing authority
within Great Britain. The applicant and her son were subsequently accepted as refugees in the United Kingdom. On a
motion by the applicant for a judicial review of the council's
decision, the Divisional Court quashed the decision, holding
that the council were under a duty to secure that accommodation was available for the occupation of the applicant and
her son.

F

    On appeal by the council:—
    Held, dismissing the appeal, that the duties imposed on a
housing authority by the Housing (Homeless Persons) Act
1977 were owed to any person applying to them pursuant to
the Act who was lawfully in the country, irrespective of
whether such person had a local connection with any housing
area within Great Britain (post, pp. 1433B–C, F–G, 1434C, 1436F,
1439F); and that, accordingly, the respondent council were
under a duty to secure that accommodation was available for
the applicant (post, p. 1434F).

G

    Decision of the Divisional Court of the Queen's Bench
Division (post, p. 1426H et seq.) affirmed.

H

[1] Housing (Homeless Persons) Act 1977, s. 1: " (1) A person is homeless for
the purposes of this Act if he has no accommodation, and a person is to be treated
as having no accommodation for those purposes if there is no accommodation—
(*a*) which he, together with any other person who normally resides with him as a
member of his family or in circumstances in which the housing authority consider
it reasonable for that person to reside with him—(i) is entitled to occupy by virtue
of an interest in it or of an order of a court, or (ii) has, in England or Wales, an
express or implied licence to occupy, or (iii) has, in Scotland, a right or permission,
or an implied right or permission to occupy, or (*b*) which he (together with any such
person) is occupying as a residence by virtue of any enactment or rule of law giving
him the right to remain in occupation or restricting the right of any other person
to recover possession of it."

Reg. v. Hillingdon Council, Ex p. Streeting (D.C.) **[1980]**

The following cases are referred to in the judgments of the Court of A
Appeal:

De Falco v. *Crawley Borough Council* [1980] 2 W.L.R. 664; [1980] 1 All
E.R. 913, C.A.

Dyson v. *Kerrier District Council* [1980] 1 W.L.R. 1205; [1980] 3 All
E.R. 313, C.A.

Jefferys v. *Boosey* (1854) 4 H.L.Cas. 815, H.L.(E.).

Reg. v. *Bristol City Council, Ex parte Browne* [1979] 1 W.L.R. 1437; B
[1979] 3 All E.R. 344, D.C.

Rex v. *Inhabitants of Eastbourne* (1803) 4 East 103.

Stock v. *Frank Jones (Tipton) Ltd.* [1978] 1 W.L.R. 231; [1978] I.C.R.
347; [1978] 1 All E.R. 948, H.L.(E.).

The following additional cases were cited in argument in the Court of
Appeal: C

Draper (C. E. B.) & Son Ltd. v. *Edward Turner & Son Ltd.* [1965] 1 Q.B.
424; [1964] 3 W.L.R. 783; [1963] 3 All E.R. 148, C.A.

Ealing London Borough Council v. *Race Relations Board* [1972] A.C. 342;
[1972] 2 W.L.R. 71; [1972] 1 All E.R. 105, H.L.(E.).

Luke v. *Inland Revenue Commissioners* [1963] A.C. 557; [1963] 2 W.L.R.
559; [1963] 1 All E.R. 655, H.L.(Sc.).

Reg. v. *Bristol Corporation, Ex parte Hendy* [1974] 1 W.L.R. 498; [1974] 1 D
All E.R. 1047, C.A.

The following cases are referred to in the judgment of Griffiths J. in the
Divisional Court:

De Falco v. *Crawley Borough Council* [1980] 2 W.L.R. 664; [1980] 1 All
E.R. 913, C.A.

Reg. v. *Bristol City Council, Ex parte Browne* [1979] 1 W.L.R. 1437; E
[1979] 3 All E.R. 344, D.C.

No additional cases were cited in argument in the Divisional Court.

APPLICATION for judicial review.

By notice of motion dated December 27, 1979, the applicant, Sophia F
Streeting, applied for a judicial review of the refusal of the respondents,
Hillingdon London Borough Council, to provide accommodation for the
applicant and her child, seeking an order of certiorari to quash the
council's decision that no duty under the Housing (Homeless Persons)
Act 1977 was owed to an applicant who had no local connection with
the area of any housing authority within Great Britain and an order of
mandamus to compel the council to secure that accommodation remained G
available for the occupation of the applicant and her child.

The facts are stated in the judgments of Griffiths J. and Lord Denning
M.R.

Andrew Arden for the applicant.
David Fletcher for the respondent council. H

GRIFFITHS J., giving the first judgment. The applicant, Sophia
Streeting, asks for an order of certiorari to quash the decision of the
Hillingdon London Borough Council that they owed no duty under the
Housing (Homeless Persons) Act 1977 to provide accommodation for
her and her child. She also asks for an order of mandamus directing
the authority to provide accommodation for them.

The Weekly Law Reports, November 28, 1980

1427

1 W.L.R.   Reg. v. Hillingdon Council, Ex p. Streeting (D.C.)   Griffiths J.

A   The Housing (Homeless Persons) Act 1977 imposes a duty on local authorities to provide accommodation for homeless persons. The short point that has be decided in these proceedings is whether that duty is owed to all homeless persons lawfully in this country or whether it is limited to homeless persons who have or had a local connection with the area of a housing authority in Great Britain. In other words, is any duty owed to a stranger or is it limited to those who live or have lived in this country?

B

The applicant was born in Ethiopia and lived there until May 1975 when she went through a form of marriage to Alan Streeting, an Englishman. Thereafter she lived with Alan Streeting as his wife and he cared for her child. In fact she later discovered that Alan Streeting was still married at the time that he went through the marriage ceremony with her. The couple lived together abroad, visiting this country for periods of leave. During the last two years of his life he provided a flat in Athens for the applicant and her child whilst he was working in Libya.

C

On April 27, 1979, Alan Streeting died of a heart attack in Libya; his body was flown back to England and the applicant and her son flew over to attend his funeral in Yorkshire. On her arrival in this country the applicant was at first given a limited permission to stay until November 25, 1979, and she was for the first few weeks accommodated in a hotel at the expense of Alan Streeting's employers.

D

She was refused permission to live in Greece, and as a result of the political situation she decided that it was impossible for her to return to Ethiopia. She, therefore, applied to the Home Office to be accepted in this country as a refugee. On November 28 the Home Office gave their decision accepting the applicant and her young son as refugees in the United Kingdom.

E

In the meantime, on June 1, Streeting's employers had refused to continue to provide hotel accommodation, and the applicant applied to the Hillingdon London Borough Council for assistance under the Housing (Homeless Persons) Act 1977. The authority provided temporary accommodation for the applicant and her child and proceeded to make inquiries as to her situation pursuant to section 3 (1) of the Act.

F

As a result of these inquiries the authority concluded that she was homeless, that because of her dependent child she had a priority need, and that she had not become homeless intentionally. These findings would normally oblige the authority to provide accommodation for the applicant and her child: see section 4 (5). But the authority refused to provide such permanent accommodation, giving as their reason that no duty under the Act was " owed to an applicant who has or had no local connection with the area of any housing authority in Great Britain." As a result of interlocutory proceedings between the parties, the applicant is still housed by the authority pending the outcome of this hearing.

G

The phrase " local connection " appears in various sections of the Act and is defined in section 18 (1) in the following terms:

H

" Any reference in this Act to a person having a local connection with an area is a reference to his having a connection with that area —(a) because he is or in the past was normally resident in it and his residence in it is or was of his own choice; or (b) because he is employed in it, or (c) because of family associations, or (d) because of any special circumstances."

It is admitted that the applicant has no local connection with the   A
area of any housing authority within the meaning of this definition, but
it is contended on her behalf that this is of no significance because the
duty to provide accommodation under sections 3 and 4 of the Act is
expressed to be a duty owed to all homeless persons and is in no way
qualified by a requirement that they should have or have had a local
connection with any area. The only purpose of introducing the concept of   B
a local connection into the framework of the Act is, it is said, to enable
the burden of providing accommodation to be fairly shared between local
authorities.

To this end, section 5 provides an elaborate code under which the
authority can pass on the burden of housing a person who has no local
connection with their area to an authority with which they do have a
local connection. The housing authority wishing to pass on this burden,   C
referred to in section 5 as the notifying authority, can only initiate this
procedure if they are of opinion that an applicant has no local connection
with their area. The authority to which they wish to pass the responsibility,
referred to in the section as the notified authority, do not have to accept
the responsibility unless the applicant does have a local connection with
their area.   D

If the applicant does not have a local connection with either area, it
is submitted that the situation is covered specifically by section 5 (5),
which provides:

"In any other case it shall be the duty of the notifying authority
to secure that accommodation becomes available for occupation by
the person to whom the notification relates."   E

In support of this submission reliance is placed upon the Code of Guidance
introduced by section 12 of the Act and issued by the Department of the
Environment, which provides:

"(1) In relation to homeless persons and persons threatened with
homelessness a relevant authority shall have regard in the exercise of
their functions to such guidance as may from time to time be given   F
by the Secretary of State. (2) The Secretary of State may give guidance
either generally or to specified descriptions of authorities."

In the Code of Guidance, paragraph 5.5 the commentary upon section 5 (5)
reads:

"If a person has no local connection with the area of any housing   G
authority in Great Britain, the duty to secure accommodation for him
rests with the authority to whom he applies."

The applicant also relies upon a passage in the annex to the Code of
Guidance, which at paragraph A2.2 reads:

"Applications for help under the Act from people admitted to the   H
country on a temporary or conditional basis may give rise to special
considerations; in dealing with such cases authorities will need to
bear in mind that discrimination on grounds of nationality or citizenship is unlawful. There are, however, a variety of circumstances in
which people are so admitted; for example, some come to take up
approved employment, but for others different requirements are
imposed as a condition of entry. In determining how most appro-

The Weekly Law Reports, November 28, 1980

1429

1 W.L.R.   Reg. v. Hillingdon Council, Ex p. Streeting (D.C.)   Griffiths J.

A   priately to fulfil their obligations under the Act, authorities will need to take account of the particular circumstances of individual cases."

It is clear from these passages that it never occurred to those responsible for drafting the code that the duty would be limited to those having a local connection. The views expressed in the code are not of course conclusive of the construction of the statute, but in this case they accord B with my own view that section 5 (5) contemplates and provides for the situation in which neither authority will accept that the homeless person has a local connection with their area, from which it must follow that this duty is owed to such a person, for the subsection provides that accommodation is to be provided in such cases by the notifying authority.

The authority concede that there are no express words to be found C in the Act limiting the duty to persons having a local connection. But they submit that it cannot have been the intention of Parliament to impose a duty on local authorities to provide accommodation for all and sundry who choose to pour into this country from abroad and then present themselves as homeless. This, they say, would place an intolerable burden upon local authorities, and in particular those like Hillingdon London Borough Council whose area is adjacent to a large airport like Heathrow. They D therefore submit that the Act of 1977 must be read as limited to our own homeless and to exclude those coming from abroad in the situation of this applicant, for to read it in any other way would, they say, produce an absurd and unworkable result.

In support of this submission they rely upon the definition of homelessness in section 1 (1), which, inter alia, refers to a licence to occupy E premises in England and Wales and a right or permission to occupy in Scotland and the lack of reference to any corresponding concept in premises abroad, which they argue indicates that the Act is not concerned with the problem arising from homelessness abroad. They point to the lack of any machinery under section 5 that would enable an authority to pass this responsibility to an authority in the country from which the F applicant had come. They point to the lack of any provisions under which an authority near ports or airports can share the financial burden with other authorities, and finally to the difficulty with which an authority may be faced in trying to determine whether someone coming from abroad has disentitled himself to relief because he has become homeless intentionally.

These submissions might carry more weight if anyone could enter this G country and settle here without let or hindrance; but that is not the case. Immigration is strictly controlled, and it is unrealistic to suppose that large numbers of persons would be allowed to enter this country either on a temporary or permanent basis who have nowhere to stay whilst they are here. Of course occasionally it will happen, as in the case of this applicant whom we have accepted as a refugee, and in such cases H no doubt the burden will tend to fall upon the authorities near airports or seaports, and I have sympathy for them, for it seems hard that the burden should be borne unaided by their ratepayers. But these circumstances were known to Parliament in 1977, and I am wholly unpersuaded by the council's argument that words must be read into this Act to limit the duty to persons with a "local connection." Local authorities will be protected from an influx of homeless from abroad by the operation of the immigration rules, and they have the further pro-

tection that a person abroad cannot give up his accommodation and   A
then expect to be housed by the local authority under this Act because
by intentionally making himself homeless abroad he will have disentitled
himself to relief under the Act: see *De Falco* v. *Crawley Borough Council*
[1980] 2 W.L.R. 664. Nor is there anything to prevent an authority from
discharging their duty by in fact arranging for accommodation to be
provided in the country from which the applicant has come: see *Reg.* v.
Bristol City Council, Ex parte Browne [1979] 1 W.L.R. 1437.   B

In my view, a homeless person in this Act includes a person who has
no local connections with the area of any authority. The council therefore owe a duty to provide this applicant and her child with accommodation. I reach this conclusion with satisfaction, for if ever anyone
needed the succour of this Act it is this young woman and her child,
homeless refugees in a strange country.   C

I would therefore grant an order of certiorari to quash the decision of
the council dated November 13, 1979, to the effect that they owed no
duty under the Housing (Homeless Persons) Act 1977. In the circumstances I doubt if there is any need for mandamus to go, but I would
give liberty to apply if it turned out to be necessary.

D

LORD WIDGERY C.J. I entirely agree and certiorari will go to quash the
decision.

[*Counsel agreed that mandamus was unnecessary.*]

> *Application granted with costs.*
> *Order of certiorari.*   E
> *Liberty to apply for order of man-*
> *damus in case of practical difficulty.*
> *Legal aid taxation.*

Solicitors: *Charles Coleman & Co., Slough*; *J. A. Kosky, Uxbridge.*

B. O. A.   F

APPEAL from Divisional Court of the Queen's Bench Division

The council appealed, by notice of appeal dated March 18, 1980, on
the grounds that (1) the Divisional Court erred in law in finding that the
council owed a duty to house the applicant under the Housing (Homeless G
Persons) Act 1977, having regard to the fact that the applicant had no local
connection with the area of any housing authority in Great Britain, but
did have a local connection with an area outside Great Britain; and (2)
the Divisional Court ought to have held as a matter of law that the Act
had to be read as subject to a limitation excluding from the duties owed
under section 4 of the Act all persons having, at the time of their applica- H
tion for housing, no local connection with the area of any housing authority
in Great Britain and having a local connection with an area outside Great
Britain.

Lionel Read Q.C. and *David Fletcher* for the council.
Andrew Arden for the applicant.

Cur. adv. vult.

A   July 10.   The following judgments were read.

LORD DENNING M.R.   She was born in Ethiopia. Her name was Sophia
Abrahim. In 1975 she was 19 years of age. She had a baby son, David,
aged 2. An Englishman then came to Addis Ababa. He was Alan Streeting.
He was aged 45. He asked Sophia to marry him. He told her he was
B   divorced. They were united in marriage in Addis Ababa on May 17, 1975.
She kept her marriage certificate. He brought her and the baby over to
England where they stayed for some weeks. He was employed by an Ameri-
can company and worked in Libya. He took a flat in Athens in Greece.
Sophia and her child lived there and he went to and fro to them. He
also brought them again to England for a holiday. Then tragedy struck.
In Libya he had a heart attack and died. It was on April 27, 1979. His
C   company flew his body back to England for burial. They arranged for
Sophia and her little boy to come here for the funeral. It was at
Brighouse in Yorkshire. It then transpired that he had not been
divorced at all. His wife was still alive in England. So his marriage to
Sophia was a bigamous marriage. It was a nullity. But his company took
pity on her. They arranged for her to go back to Greece to sort out her
D   affairs there. They paid her fare. But when she arrived at Athens airport, she was not allowed to enter: on the ground that she had not a
valid residency permit. So she returned to England. That was on May
25, 1979. The company then put her and the baby up at an hotel here.
But they could not keep her indefinitely. So they went with her to the
housing department at Hillingdon. That was on June 4, 1979. They
presented her and her child as homeless. The housing department made
E   all sorts of inquiries—from Greece—from Ethiopia—to see if she could
be found a home there. But these were all fruitless. The Hillingdon
housing department arranged for temporary accommodation for her at a
guest house—for bed and breakfast—at £7·75 a night. She also got
supplementary benefit—national assistance—from which she could pay
for her other meals and clothes, etc. But eventually the Hillingdon
F   council decided that they could pay no longer for her accommodation.
On November 13, 1979, the director of housing at Hillingdon wrote this
letter to her:

"*Housing (Homeless Persons) Act 1977*

"I have decided that you are not entitled to assistance of this
G   council pursuant to the Housing (Homeless Persons) Act 1977.
"The duty under the Act is not owed to an applicant who has
or had no local connection with the area of any housing authority
within Great Britain. You have admitted that you have no local
connection and have never had any local connection with the area
of any such housing authority. Further or in the alternative the
duty under the Act is not owed to an applicant who is not entitled
H   to remain permanently in Great Britain. You are entitled to remain
in Great Britain only until November 25, 1979.
"Without prejudice to the above contentions, if the statutory
duty is owed, then for the purposes of section 8 of the Act I confirm
that I have completed my inquiries under the Act and my findings
together with the reasons, where required by law, are as follows:

1. I consider that you are homeless.

2. I am satisfied that you have a priority need.   A

3. I am not satisfied that you became homeless intentionally.

4. I do not propose to notify any other housing authority that your application for assistance in obtaining accommodation has been made."

Although Mrs. Streeting's leave at first extended only until November 25, 1979, she has since been granted "refugee status." That means that   B she is at liberty to remain here indefinitely. But the question is whether the respondent council are bound to house her and her child.

On receiving that letter Mrs. Streeting's advisers applied for judicial review. On an interlocutory application, Kenneth Jones J. ordered the council to ensure that accommodation remained available to her. On the final hearing on February 27, 1980, the Divisional Court made an order   C requiring the council to provide accommodation for Mrs. Streeting and her child. The council appeals to this court.

The case is regarded by local authorities as if it were a test case. Mrs. Sophia Streeting is undoubtedly homeless in this country. She is also homeless elsewhere. But she has no local connection with England at all. Are the respondent council bound to provide accommodation   D for her indefinitely? At their own expense? So that she takes priority over all the other people on their waiting list. The council say that for the seven months from June 5, 1979, to January 14, 1980, they had paid out £1,728·25 for her accommodation: of which she had paid £187·33.

The case raises directly the question: when a man or woman with children come from a foreign country and are homeless here—and are also homeless in their own country—is the housing authority here bound   E under our statute to secure accommodation for them here—and their children?

Mr. Read put his argument attractively in this way. The statute was intended to deal with homelessness in England. It was not intended to deal with homelessness in countries overseas. No person who is homeless overseas should be entitled to come into this country and say: "I am   F homeless in my own country. So you must house me here—at your expense."

He supported this argument by saying that the statute is to be given territorial effect—and not to be construed extra-territorially. I agree with this sentiment. But I think the statute can be given territorial effect by reading section 1 (1) in this way: A person is homeless " in this country " for the purposes of this Act if he has no accommodation " in this   G country "; and a person is to be treated as having no accommodation " in this country " for those purposes if there is no accommodation " in this country " which he is at liberty to occupy and can secure entry peacefully. So read, the exceptions in section 1 (1) (a) (i) and (ii) and (b) and section 2 (1) (a), (b) and (c) are entirely appropriate. They are dealing with a person who is in this country and not elsewhere: and with accom-   H modation in this country and not elsewhere.

Once you confine the statute in this way to homelessness in this country, you are giving it territorial effect. It does not operate extra-territorially. Once this is understood, then I will try to explain—as I sought to do in *De Falco* v. *Crawley Borough Council* [1980] 2 W.L.R. 664—in simple words the position when a person coming from overseas is found to be homeless here. The housing authority comes under an

The Weekly Law Reports, November 28, 1980

1433

1 W.L.R.   Reg. v. Hillingdon Council, Ex p. Streeting (C.A.)   Lord Denning M.R.

A   obligation to make inquiries to see whether he has dependent children with him (and thus has a priority need), and whether his homelessness here is intentional or unintentional. If he has a priority need and his homelessness overseas was *unintentional*, the housing authority comes under a duty to secure that accommodation becomes available for him in this country: see section 4 (5), no matter that he comes here from a country overseas. But, if his homelessness was *intentional*, the housing authority
B   are only bound to house him for a short time: see section 4 (2) (*b*). If he has a home outside this country which he can occupy if he wishes, he can be treated as *intentionally* homeless here. If he has *had* a home outside this country—which he could *have* continued to occupy if he wished—but he has given it up so as to come here— then again he can be treated as *intentionally* homeless here. That was settled by the *De Falco*
C   case [1980] 2 W.L.R. 664. But, if he has not a home elsewhere—and it is not in the least his fault—then he qualifies as being unintentionally homeless: and the housing authority are under a duty to secure that accommodation is available for him indefinitely. But they can perform that duty by finding accommodation for him in the country whence he came and by sending him and the children back there: see *Reg.* v.
D   *Bristol City Council, Ex parte Browne* [1979] 1 W.L.R. 1437.

Mr. Read put forward two extreme cases, each of which he said would be so absurd that the statute cannot have been intended to apply to them. The first was when a foreigner has a home overseas which he is at liberty to occupy—but yet he comes over here and is homeless here. Is the housing authority bound to secure accommodation for him indefinitely? The second was when a foreigner—who had no home in his
E   own country—and yet comes over here and is homeless here. Is the housing authority bound to provide accommodation for every foreigner who comes here—pleading that he is homeless in his own country?

The only sensible solution of those absurdities, said Mr. Read, was to introduce into section 1 an implication to the effect that a person coming from overseas must have some local connection with this country—
F   before he can claim to have the benefit of the statute. He would read into section 1 (1) after " person," " being a person having a local connection with this country." The words " local connection with this country " are so vague that we pressed Mr. Read to define them more closely. He then said they were to be found in section 18 of the Act. The person must have *a local connection with an area* in this country. I cannot accept
G   that suggestion for this simple reason. Many a soldier or sailor in our armed forces has no local connection with any particular area in this country. His parents may be dead. On returning to civilian life he is homeless. He should certainly qualify for the benefits of the statute. And how does he qualify? This is done by the comprehensive words of sections 5 (5):

H   " In any other case it shall be the duty of the notifying authority to secure that accommodation becomes available for occupation by the person to whom the notification relates."

Another point on Mr. Read's argument was this: he acknowledged that, if his submission in this case was correct, it meant that *De Falco's* case [1980] 2 W.L.R. 664 was wrongly decided. The De Falcos came from Italy to stay with a brother here in England. They had therefore a local connection with England within section 18. When the

brother turned them out, they became homeless in England. Under the   A
guidelines that was the homelessness which had to be considered; and,
as it was unintentional, it was the duty of the local authority to house them.
I cannot accept any argument which involves that the *De Falco* case was
wrongly decided.

Rejecting Mr. Read's implication, I think the safeguard against his
suggested absurdities lies in the control exercised by the immigration
authorities. People from foreign countries are not allowed in except   B
under carefully prescribed conditions. For instance, they might have
to have a work permit: and that would not be given without arrangements having been made for their accommodation. Or they might be
admitted as students: and that would not be given unless proper
arrangements had been made. And so forth. It must be comparatively
rarely that a foreigner is allowed to enter when he is homeless overseas,   C
and will be homeless here—with no means to support himself or herself.

Of course if he is an illegal entrant—if he enters unlawfully without
leave—or if he overstays his leave and remains here unlawfully—the
housing authority are under no duty whatever to him. Even though he is
homeless here—even though he has no home elsewhere—nevertheless he
cannot take any advantage of the Acts. As soon as any such illegality   D
appears, the housing authority can turn him down—and report his case
to the immigration authorities. This will exclude many foreigners.

Conclusion

If this Ethiopian lady had been truly married to Alan Streeting—as
she believed she was—she would have been entitled to enter England as
of right. She ought not to suffer by reason of the unknown invalidity   E
of her marriage. She ought to be treated by this country just as if
she had been truly married. If she and her child are homeless, then
the statute should apply to them. All the more so seeing that she has no
home in any other country. Her homelessness is not due to any fault of
hers. It is completely unintentional. In those circumstances, as I read
the statute, the respondent council are under a duty to secure that   F
accommodation is available for her. This duty no doubt puts much
expense on them. They may have other cases too of homeless people
coming into Heathrow Airport for whom they may have to provide accommodation. But it must be remembered that the airport pays rates and
brings money into the area. So the council should shoulder the burden.
True this is a meritorious case. There may be others not so meritorious.
But, meritorious or not, I hold that, if a foreigner, coming here with   G
a child, is homeless in this country—and is homeless in his own country
without his fault—then under the statute the housing authority is under
a duty to provide accommodation for him. I agree with the Divisional
Court and would dismiss the appeal.

WALLER L.J. Sophia Streeting is a refugee from Ethiopa, with a son   H
aged 8, who has been granted refugee status in this country. She claims
against the Hillingdon London Borough Council for accommodation as a
homeless person under the Housing (Homeless Persons) Act 1977. The
council did not accept that they were under a duty to provide accommodation for her and she applied to the Divisional Court for an order
of mandamus directing the council to provide accommodation for her and
her son. On February 27, 1980, the Divisional Court granted an order

A of certiorari to quash the decision of the council, holding that the council were under a duty to Sophia Streeting to provide her with accommodation. The council now appeals to this court on the ground that the duty is not owed to all homeless persons lawfully in this country but only to those who have, or had, a local connection with the area of a housing authority in Great Britain.

B   The decision in this case depends upon a consideration of the Housing (Homeless Persons) Act 1977. Mr. Read submits that a careful reading of the statute leads to the conclusion that duties are only owed to homeless persons who have, or have had, a local connection in this country. He relies, first, on the long title to the Act and, secondly, on the consideration of sections of the Act and in particular section 5 and section 18 (1), the former of which enables a housing authority to transfer the duty to

C house to another authority if that other authority is one with which the applicant has a local connection. And section 18 (1) defines " local connection " by present or past residence or employment in it or because of a family association or special circumstances. Mr. Read submits that there is a presumption that Parliament in passing an Act of Parliament is only dealing with this country and in this particular case was only

D dealing with England and Wales and Scotland which are specified in the Act. It was inherent in his submission that any other interpretation of the Act created anomalies and was unfair to those housing authorities which contained within them either ports or airports of arrival from foreign countries.

        The Divisional Court had dismissed those considerations and found that the Immigration Acts and rules made thereunder were a safeguard

E against the entry of persons from abroad who might claim to be considered as homeless. Careful consideration of the Statement of Changes in Immigration Rules (1980) (H.C. 394) shows that it is not easy for someone to enter this country who is not able to support himself. Futhermore, I do not accept that the anomalies in this case are all on one side nor is there a substantial injustice. An argument was addressed to the court

F that it was unfair that one housing authority should be responsible for an immigrant who had no connection with this country at all and that if anybody was to be responsible it should be a national responsibility. I am satisfied that this argument does not succeed.

        As long ago as 1803 in *Rex* v. *Inhabitants of Eastbourne* (1803) 4 East 103, 107, Lord Ellenborough C.J. in a settlement case said:

G   " As to there being no obligation for maintaining poor foreigners before the statutes ascertaining the different methods of acquiring settlements, the law of humanity, which is anterior to all positive laws, obliges us to afford them relief, to save them from starving; . . ."

Those words, with suitable amendment, would cover precisely the relevant argument in the present case. They also show that a statute would not

H be interpreted so as to exclude benefit to foreigners in this country. The doctrine of extra-territoriality would not apply in such a case.

        There is nothing in the plain meaning of the words of the Housing (Homeless Persons) Act 1977 which imposes the limitation proposed on behalf of the council and I would follow Viscount Dilhorne in *Stock* v. *Frank Jones (Tipton) Ltd.* [1978] 1 W.L.R. 231, 234–235, in quoting Lord Mersey and Lord Loreburn L.C.:

        " ' It is a strong thing to read into an Act of Parliament words

which are not there, and in the absence of clear necessity it is a   A
wrong thing to do ' said Lord Mersey in *Thompson* v. *Goold & Co.*
[1910] A.C. 409, 420. '. . . we are not entitled to read words into an
Act of Parliament unless clear reason for it is to be found within the
four corners of the Act itself' said Lord Loreburn L.C. in *Vickers,
Sons & Maxim Ltd.* v. *Evans* [1910] A.C. 444, 445."

If there were any reason to try to read words into the statute there   B
are two sections which, in my view, show clearly that this statute should
not have the limitation proposed. The first section is section 5 (5).
Section 5 deals with the responsibility as between housing authorities and
by subsection (1) enables an authority with an applicant who has no local
connection with it to notify another where the applicant has an apparent
local connection, and subsections (2), (3) and (4) deal with problems   C
arising under that notification, but subsection (5) then reads:

" In any other case it shall be the duty of the notifying authority
to secure that accommodation becomes available for occupation by
the person to whom the notification relates."

Those words indicate to me that any person without any local connection
will be owed the duty by the housing authority which is the notifying   D
authority.

The second section which supports the same view is section 18 and in
particular section 18 (2). Section 18 (1) defines " local connection " and,
as I have already mentioned, one of the connections may be residence.
But section 18 (2) provides that residence in an area is not of a person's
own choice for the purposes of subsection (1) if he became resident in it
because he was serving in the regular armed forces of the Crown or was   E
detained under the authority of an Act of Parliament. It would follow
that if local connection was essential there might well be ex-soldiers who
have no local connection in the country at all, even though they are
United Kingdom citizens, even though they were born here, because they
will have been in the armed services all their working lives. Accordingly,
I have no doubt that the limitation proposed by the council does not   F
apply and the duty is not limited to those with local connections.

This construction of the Act does not result in a large number of
persons from overseas becoming a burden on local authorities. *Reg.* v.
Bristol City Council, Ex parte Browne [1979] 1 W.L.R. 1437 and *De Falco*
v. *Crawley Borough Council* [1980] 2 W.L.R. 664 indicate that a local
authority may fulfil their duty by giving advice to an applicant to return
to his or her native land where housing will be available or by considering   G
the circumstances in which the applicant came to this country as perhaps
revealing that the applicant was intentionally homeless. These two cases
illustrate that local authorities may make full investigation to solve the
problem in a way which does not involve the local authority with the
obligation of providing housing.

I would dismiss the appeal.   H

DUNN L.J. The definition of "homeless person " in section 1 (1) of
the Housing (Homeless Persons) Act 1977 on the face of it relates to any
person who has no accommodation in Great Britain. It is said by counsel
on behalf of the local authority that this construction produces an absurd
anomaly because it would mean that a person with accommodation abroad
would fall within the definition so that a housing authority would be under a

The Weekly Law Reports, November 28, 1980

1437

1 W.L.R.   Reg. v. Hillingdon Council, Ex p. Streeting (C.A.)   Dunn L.J.

A   duty to house him. It is said that that cannot have been the intention of Parliament, so that it is necessary to construe section 1 (1) so as to enable the housing authority to look at a person's entitlement to accommodation world wide; and in order to do that the subsection should be construed so as to limit the definition of " homeless person " to persons having a " local connection " with some area of Great Britain, the words " local connection " being defined as in section 18 of the Act. This, it is said, would be in accordance with the object and purpose of Parliament as set out in the long title and also in accordance with the principle that statutes should be construed so as to apply territorially and not extra-territorially.

    In order to test this submission it is necessary to construe the section in the light of the other provisions of the Act, and to see the nature and extent of the various duties placed on housing authorities at different stages. I start by taking the words of section 1 (1) according to their natural and ordinary meaning which leads me to the conclusion that a " homeless person " as defined by the subsection is any person who has no accommodation in Great Britain. The only limitation to the word " person " is that he should be a person who is lawfully here, that is to say, a person who does not require leave to enter, either because he is a citizen of the United Kingdom and Colonies not subject to immigration control, or because he has come from some other part of the Common Travel Area comprising in addition to the United Kingdom the Channel Islands, Isle of Man and the Irish Republic. Persons lawfully here also include persons who have been granted leave to enter by the immigration control either for a limited period or for settlement. Such persons, including prospective workers from E.E.C. countries, will generally have had to satisfy immigration control that they can maintain and accommodate themselves and their dependents without recourse to public funds.

    So illegal immigrants are not persons within the meaning of section 1 (1). But if a person lawfully here has no accommodation in Great Britain he may apply to a housing authority and if the authority have reason to believe that in fact he has no accommodation in Great Britain they are at that stage only under a duty to make inquiries to satisfy themselves: (1) whether he has a priority need, and (2) whether he became homeless intentionally. This duty also exists if the person has accommodation but cannot secure entry to it or if occupation of it will probably lead to domestic violence, or if he is likely to become homeless within 28 days. But I will throughout deal with the situation where a person claims to be homeless.

    At that initial stage the housing authority may also make inquiries as to whether the applicant has a local connection with the area of another housing authority, and there are provisions in the Act whereby that other authority may be under a duty to house the applicant. These provisions are not relevant to the circumstances of the present case which assumes that the applicant has no local connection with any other area.

    Even if the person is homeless, if the housing authority is not satisfied that he has a priority need as defined by section 2 (1) they are only under a duty to give the person advice or assistance. If they are so satisfied, they are under a duty to secure that accommodation is made available for him pending their inquiries as to whether he became homeless intentionally.

    Section 17 provides:

"(1) Subject to subsection (3) below, for the purposes of this Act   A
a person becomes homeless intentionally if he deliberately does or
fails to do anything in consequence of which he ceases to occupy
accommodation which is available for his occupation and which it
would have been reasonable for him to continue to occupy. . . . (3)
An act or omission in good faith on the part of a person who was
unaware of any relevant fact is not to be treated as deliberate for the
purposes of subsection (1) or (2) above."   B

It is at this stage for the first time that any foreign element becomes
relevant.   Up to this stage the housing authority will only have been
concerned to ascertain whether the person has accommodation in Great
Britain and whether he has a priority need.   But in considering whether
the person has become homeless intentionally, the housing authority is   C
entitled to make inquiries relating to the country whence he came.   So in
De Falco v. *Crawley Borough Council* [1980] 2 W.L.R. 664 Italian families
with priority needs who had no accommodation in Great Britain were
held to have become homeless intentionally because they voluntarily gave
up accommodation in Italy in order to come to England.   Whether or not
a person becomes homeless intentionally is, like all questions of causation,   D
a matter of fact and degree.   It is for the housing authority to
decide having regard to all the circumstances of the particular case.
Although the most immediate cause of the homelessness may not
have been intentional, the housing authority are entitled to look at past
events including the circumstances in which foreign applicants left accommodation in their own country: see *De Falco* v. *Crawley Borough Council*
and *Dyson* v. *Kerrier District Council* [1980] 1 W.L.R. 1205, where it   E
was held that although the most immediate cause of the homelessness was
that the applicant had been evicted, she was intentionally homeless because
she had surrendered a tenancy of a council flat in order to move into the
accommodation from which she was evicted.

If the housing authority are satisfied that the person became homeless intentionally, then their only duty is to give him advice and assistance.   F
But even if they are not satisfied that he became homeless intentionally,
they can perform their ultimate duty to secure that accommodation
becomes available to him in a number of ways.   They can make available
accommodation held by them under the Housing Act 1957 in which case
he acquires a priority in selection as a tenant by reason of an amendment
to section 113 (2) of the Housing Act 1957; or they can secure that he
obtains accommodation from some other person and give him such advice   G
and assistance as will secure that he obtains accommodation from some
other person: see section 6.   So if he has come from a foreign country
and if as a result of their inquiries the housing authority are satisfied
that some person in the foreign country will provide him with accommodation there, then they can advise him to return to the foreign country and
if necessary assist him by paying his fare.   This was done in *Reg.* v.   H
Bristol City Council, Ex parte Browne [1979] 1 W.L.R. 1437 where Mrs.
Browne arrived in Bristol from Ireland with her children and applied to
the local housing authority for accommodation.   She was homeless in
Great Britain and she had a priority need.   As a result of their inquiries
the housing authority ascertained that the housing authorities in Tralee
would provide her with accommodation.   So they advised her to return to
Tralee and offered to pay her fare.   This was held by the Divisional Court

The Weekly Law Reports, November 28, 1980

1439

1 W.L.R.   Reg. v. Hillingdon Council, Ex p. Streeting (C.A.)   Dunn L.J.

A   to be a perfectly proper fulfilment by them of their duty under section 6 (1) (c) of the Act. If the contention made on behalf of the council in this case is correct, Bristol City Council would have been under no duty to Mrs. Browne at all because she had no local connection with any area of Great Britain, although it is right to say that the Divisional Court decided the case on the narrow ground that the housing authority had fulfilled any duty which they had.

B   The submission that the definition of a homeless person in section 1 (1) should be limited to persons with local connection with an area of Great Britain is also inconsistent with the express provisions of the Act. Section 5 deals with responsibilities as between housing authorities. Subsections (1) to (4) provide that a housing authority to whom application is made by a homeless person, if they are of opinion that the applicant

C   has a local connection with another housing authority's area, may notify that other authority accordingly, and it then becomes the duty of the notified authority to secure accommodation for the applicant. Section 5 (5) provides:

D   "In any other case it shall be the duty of the notifying authority to secure that accommodation becomes available for occupation by the person to whom the notification relates."

Those words mean what they say. They expressly negative the limitation of the word " person " to mean only a person who has a local connection with some area of Great Britain.

But there is another objection to such limitation. Section 18 defines the meaning of " local connection." Subsection (2) excludes from that

E   meaning any regular member of the armed forces of the Crown or any person who has been in prison or detained in a mental hospital from having a local connection with an area because of residence or employment in that area. The limitation sought to be placed by the council on the definition of " homeless person " would therefore exclude from the protection afforded by this Act many members of the regular forces of the

F   Crown and ex-patients from mental hospitals. I regard this anomaly as more absurd than any suggested by the council in this case.

On the construction that I have so far placed on section 1 (1), housing authorities are under the various duties provided by the Act to any person lawfully here, including those who came here from abroad and who have no connection with this country. In a welfare statute of this kind there is nothing wrong in principle with that. In the old settlement cases it was

G   held that a foreigner lawfully here who otherwise qualified was entitled to a settlement under the poor laws: see Rex v. Inhabitants of Eastbourne, 4 East 103. And foreigners lawfully here have been held to be entitled to the protection of English laws of copyright: Jefferys v. Boosey (1854) 4 H.L. Cas. 815, 955.

I do not share the fears expressed on behalf of the council that this

H   construction would place an intolerable burden upon them. Of course it places an additional burden upon them, but I see no reason to suppose that it is not a burden intended by Parliament. The Act must be read in conjunction with the Immigration Act 1971 and the immigration rules made thereunder. It contains the various safeguards for housing authorities to which I have referred and which have been clarified by De Falco v. Crawley Borough Council [1980] 2 W.L.R. 664 and Reg. v. Bristol City Council, Ex parte Browne [1979] 1 W.L.R. 1437. I see no reason

1440

to limit the words of section 1 (1) in the way suggested, and I too would   A
dismiss this appeal.

Appeal dismissed with costs.

Solicitors: *J. A. Kosky; Charles Coleman & Co., Slough.*

C. N.   B

[HOUSE OF LORDS]   C

* BUTTES GAS AND OIL CO. AND ANOTHER . . RESPONDENTS
AND
HAMMER AND ANOTHER . . . . . . PETITIONERS

(No. 3)

1980 Nov. 11   Lord Wilberforce, Lord Keith of Kinkel   D
and Lord Bridge

Petition by the defendants for leave to appeal to the House of Lords
from the decision of the Court of Appeal in *Buttes Gas and Oil Co.* v.
Hammer (*No. 3*) [1980] 3 W.L.R. 668.
The Appeal Committee allowed the petition.   E

M. G.

[HOUSE OF LORDS]   F

* BUTTES GAS AND OIL CO. AND ANOTHER . . PETITIONERS
AND
HAMMER AND ANOTHER . . . . . . RESPONDENTS   G

1980 Nov. 11   Lord Wilberforce, Lord Keith of Kinkel
and Lord Bridge

Petition by the plaintiffs for leave to appeal to the House of Lords
from the decision of the Court of Appeal [1975] Q.B. 557 notwithstanding
that leave previously refused [1975] Q.B. 557, 582.
The Appeal Committee allowed the petition.   H

M. G.

A

[HOUSE OF LORDS]

* DODDS . . . . PETITIONER

AND

WALKER . . . . RESPONDENT

B

1980   Nov. 6   Lord Diplock, Lord Keith of Kinkel
and Lord Scarman

Petition by the tenant for leave to appeal to the House of Lords from
the decision of the Court of Appeal [1980] 1 W.L.R. 1061 notwithstanding
that time limited by Standing Order I had expired.

C

The Appeal Committee allowed the petition.

M. G.

D

[HOUSE OF LORDS]

* DYSON . . . . PETITIONER

AND

KERRIER DISTRICT COUNCIL . . . . . RESPONDENTS

E

1980   Nov. 6   Lord Diplock, Lord Keith of Kinkel
and Lord Scarman

Petition by the plaintiff for leave to appeal to the House of Lords
from the decision of the Court of Appeal [1980] 1 W.L.R. 1205.

The Appeal Committee dismissed the petition.

F

M. G.

G

[FAMILY DIVISION]

* PRACTICE DIRECTION (MINOR: SCHOOL FEES)

*Husband and Wife—Financial provision—Divorce proceedings—
Provision for children—School fees—Order for fees to be
paid direct to school—Tax relief—Form of order*

H

Where a maintenance order to a child includes an element in respect
of school fees, which is paid direct to the school (because, for example,
it is feared that the other spouse might dissipate it), the Inland Revenue
has agreed, subject to the condition hereafter set out, that tax relief will
will be given on that element. The wording of the order should be

" that that part of the order which reflects the school fees shall be
paid to the (headmaster) (bursar) (school secretary) as agent for the
said child and the receipt of that payee shall be sufficient discharge."

The school fees should be paid *in full* and should be paid out of the   A
net amount under the maintenance order after deduction of tax.   Certificates for the full tax deduction should continue to be provided to the
other spouse (or other person referred to in rule 69 of the Matrimonial
Causes Rules 1977) in the normal way.

It is a condition of such an order being acceptable for tax purposes
that the contract for the child's education (which should preferably be
in writing) should be between the child (whose income is being used) and   B
the school and that the fees are received by the officer of the school as
the appointed agent for the child.

A form of contract which is acceptable to the Inland Revenue is as
follows:

" THIS AGREEMENT is made between THE GOVERNORS OF
.... by their duly authorised officer   C
.... (hereinafter called " the
School ") of the first part; ....
and the (headmaster) (bursar) (school secretary) of the second part,
and .... (hereinafter
called " the Child ") of the third part.

WHEREAS/it is proposed to ask the .... D
Court to make an order/
the .... Court has made an order/ in Cause No. ....
that the Father do make periodical payments to the Child at the
rate of £ .... per annum less tax until the Child completes full
time education (or as the case may be) and that that part of the order
which reflects the school fees shall be paid to the (headmaster)
(bursar) (school secretary) as agent for the said Child and the receipt   E
of that agent shall be a sufficient discharge.

1. The Child hereby constitutes the (headmaster) (bursar) (school
secretary) to be his agent for the purpose of receiving the said fees
and the Child agrees to pay the said fees to the said School in
consideration of being educated there.

2. In consideration of the said covenant the (headmaster) (bursar)   F
(school secretary) agrees to accept the said payments by the father as
payments on behalf of the Child and the School agrees to educate
the Child during such time as the said school fees are paid."

Issued with the concurrence of the Lord Chancellor.

R. L. BAYNE-POWELL   G
Senior Registrar

November 10, 1980.

                                                                          H
_____

A   [COURT OF APPEAL]

* BOOTH *v.* ELLARD (INSPECTOR OF TAXES)

1980 May 19, 20   Buckley, Ackner and Oliver L.JJ.

Revenue—Capital gains tax—Disposal of assets—Agreement estab-
B   *lishing trust to hold shares in family company—Power of*
shareholders to dispose of shares to outsiders restricted by
transfer to trustees—Whether shareholder transferring shares
under agreement absolutely entitled as against trustees—
Whether disposal of assets giving rise to chargeable gain—
Finance Act 1965 (c. 25), s. 22 (5)

Following an agreement in 1972, the taxpayer and 11 other
C   members of his family transferred their shareholdings in B Ltd.
to trustees to be held by them for a period of 15 years. The
shareholders each had an interest in the same number of shares
before and after the creation of the trust. Under the terms of
the agreement the shareholders consented, inter alia, to have
their rights to dispose of the shares or to deal with their
beneficial interests in them restricted. The purpose of the
agreement was to ensure that the taxpayer and members of his
D   family retained effective control of B Ltd. at a time when it
was expected that B Ltd. would apply to become a public
quoted company. The taxpayer, who transferred 55,000 shares
under the terms of the agreement, appealed against an assessment to capital gains tax in the sum of £70,000 for the year
1972–73 on the ground that under the terms of the agreement
he was absolutely entitled to the shares as against the
trustees within the meaning of section 22 (5) of the Finance
E   Act 1965.[1] The special commissioners dismissed his appeal
holding that the transfer was a disposal of assets giving rise to
a chargeable gain. Goulding J., who allowed the taxpayer's
appeal, held that he was " absolutely entitled as against the
trustees " to the shares and thus was not within the charge to
tax on the transfer of the shares to the trustees.
On appeal by the revenue: —
Held, dismissing the appeal, that since the shareholders who
F   contributed shares to the trust retained interests in the same
proportions of shares as before the creation of the trust, their
beneficial interests in aggregate amounted to the entire property
subject to the trust and those interests were all concurrent;
together they could put an end to the trust summarily and
hence were jointly entitled absolutely to the whole trust fund
as against the trustees within section 22 (5); and, accordingly,
the taxpayer was not liable to capital gains tax on the transfer
G   of his shares to trustees.
Decision of Goulding J. [1978] 1 W.L.R. 927; [1978] 3
All E.R. 298 affirmed.

The following cases are referred to in the judgment:

Kidson v. *Macdonald* [1974] Ch. 339; [1974] 2 W.L.R. 566; [1974]
1 All E.R. 849; 49 T.C. 503.
H   *Stephenson* v. *Barclays Bank Trust Co. Ltd.* [1975] 1 W.L.R. 882; [1975]
1 All E.R. 625; 50 T.C. 374.

The following additional cases were cited in argument:

Aberdeen Construction Group Ltd. v. *Inland Revenue Commissioners*
[1978] A.C. 885; [1978] 2 W.L.R. 648; [1978] 1 All E.R. 962;
T.C. Leaflet No. 2675, H.L.(Sc.).

[1] Finance Act 1965, s. 22 (5): see post, p. 1445G–H.

Booth v. Ellard (C.A.)   **[1980]**

Hoare Trustees v. *Gardner* [1979] Ch. 10; [1978] 2 W.L.R. 839; [1978] A
   1 All E.R. 791; T.C. Leaflet No. 2663.
Kipping, In re [1914] 1 Ch. 62, C.A.
Weiner, In re [1956] 1 W.L.R. 579; [1956] 2 All E.R. 482.

APPEAL from Goulding J.

By an agreement dated August 29, 1972, the taxpayer, John Sebastian
MacCaulay Booth, transferred 55,000 shares in Booth International Hold- B
ings Ltd., to trustees to be held by them for a period of 15 years on the
terms of the agreement. Other members of the taxpayer's family also
transferred shares in the same company to the trustees under the agreement.
The taxpayer appealed against an assessment to capital gains tax in the
sum of £70,000 for the year 1972–73 made in respect of the transfer on the
ground, inter alia, that he was not liable to pay the tax because he was
" absolutely entitled as against the trustees " to the shares within the C
meaning of section 22 (5) of the Finance Act 1965. The special commissioners dismissed the appeal. Goulding J. allowed the appeal, holding that
section 22 (5) extended to cases where beneficial interests were inter-
dependent by virtue of contractual provisions or trusts where all the
beneficiaries' interests were concurrent and similar in quality, and accordingly the taxpayer was " absolutely entitled as against the trustees " to the D
shares within section 22 (5) and thus was not within the charge to tax on
the transfer of the shares to the trustees.

The revenue appealed.

The facts are stated in the judgment of Buckley L.J.

Andrew Morritt Q.C. and *C. H. McCall* for the revenue.
D. J. Nicholls Q.C., J. E. Holroyd Pearce Q.C. and *Alastair Wilson* E
for the taxpayer.

BUCKLEY L.J. This is an appeal from a judgment of Goulding J.
delivered on February 28, 1978, on an appeal by a taxpayer, Mr. John
Sebastian Macaulay Booth, from a decision of the special commissioners,
who upheld in principle an assessment of the taxpayer to capital gains tax F
for the year 1972–73. The judge allowed the taxpayer's appeal. The
inspector of taxes now appeals to this court from that decision.

The detailed facts are set out in paragraph 4 of the case stated. They
arise out of the circumstances that in August 1972 the taxpayer and
members of his family held, either beneficially or as trustees, 432,299 of
the 600,000 issued shares of a company called Booth International Holdings
Ltd., and that it was then in contemplation that in the near future appli- G
cation would be made for permission to deal in, and for a quotation for,
the company's shares on the London Stock Exchange. This would
necessitate sales on the market of a substantial part of the family's
holdings. The family was anxious to retain effective control of the
company as far as possible. With that object 270,091 shares of the
company held by members of the family (approximately 45 per cent. of H
the issued share capital) were transferred to trustees to be held on the
terms of an agreement set out in full in the case. They included 55,000
shares transferred by the taxpayer. Some of these he owned beneficially
and some he held as trustee, but that is, I think, irrelevant to what we
have to decide.

Stating it as shortly as I can the substance of the agreement is as
follows: the trust is to continue until December 31, 1987, unless deter-

A   mined earlier under clause 3 by a majority, in terms of settled shares, of
the persons entitled under the trust. The income (subject to administrative
expenses) is distributable amongst the participants in the arrangement in
proportion to the number of shares to which they are respectively entitled.
Subject to receiving a prescribed notice, the trustees are to exercise voting
rights on the shares as the several participants direct in respect of the
shares to which they are respectively entitled, subject to which the
B   trustees may vote as they think fit. In the event of any offer being made
to acquire all or any part of the shares, if a specified majority of the
participants wish to dispose of their shares, the trustees are to take
such action as in their opinion is likely to result in all the trust shares
being disposed of to the best advantage. In the event of any duty
becoming payable in respect of any of the trust shares by reason of a
C   death, the trustees are, if so requested, to sell sufficient shares to pay
the duty, and the person entitled to those shares may charge the shares
to raise any such duty. A participant is entitled to dispose of his beneficial
interest in any shares to which he is beneficially entitled under the trust,
subject to restrictions of a kind which are familiar in the regulations of
private companies, involving the giving of a disposal notice and a right of
pre-emption for other participants at a fair value, and provision is made
D   for the personal representatives of a deceased participant to be deemed
to have given a disposal notice in certain circumstances which might
result in the deceased's shares going outside the family circle. Possible
rights issues and bonus issues are also dealt with. Upon the determination
of the trust the shares then held by the trustees are to be transferred to
the participants then respectively entitled to them.

E   The question for decision is whether, by reason of his transferring
55,000 shares of the company to the trustees, the taxpayer became liable
to capital gains tax. That tax was brought into existence by the Finance
Act 1965, Part III. The relevant sections for present purposes are sections
19 (1) and (3), 20 (1), 22 (1), (4) and (5) and 45 (1). Reference should
also be made to paragraph 9 of Schedule 19 to the Finance Act 1969,
which explains the meaning in this context of the expression " absolutely
F   entitled as against the trustee." Section 45 (1) defines " settled property "
as meaning (subject to an irrelevant qualification) " any property held in
trust other than property to which section 22 (5) of this Act applies."
The question in the present case is whether the case falls within section
22 (5) or not. If it does so, the taxpayer is not liable for tax on his
disposal of the 55,000 shares: if it does not, he is.

G   Section 22 (5) is in the following terms:

" In relation to assets held by a person as nominee for another person,
or as trustee for another person absolutely entitled as against the
trustee, or for any person who would be so entitled but for being
an infant or other person under disability (or for two or more persons
who are or would be jointly so entitled), this Part of this Act shall
H   apply as if the property were vested in, and the acts of the nominee
or trustee in relation to the assets were the acts of, the person or
persons for whom he is the nominee or trustee (acquisitions from
or disposals to him by that person or persons being disregarded
accordingly)."

Breaking this down, selecting only the words appropriate to a case such
as the present and reading it first as applicable to a single person absolutely
entitled, the subsection reads:

"In relation to assets held by a person . . . as trustee for another A
person absolutely entitled as against the trustee . . . this Part of
this Act shall apply as if the property were vested in, and the acts
of the . . . trustee in relation to the assets were the acts of, the
person . . . for whom he is . . . trustee."

Let me now read it as it must be read in relation to two or more persons
absolutely entitled; that would read as follows: B

"In relation to assets held by a person as . . . trustee for . . . two
or more persons . . . jointly absolutely entitled as against the
trustee, this Part of this Act shall apply as if the property were
vested in, and acts of the . . . trustee in relation to the assets were
the acts of, the . . . persons for whom he is . . . trustee."

The words in brackets which close the subsection enunciate a consequence C
of what precedes them. They are "(acquisitions from or disposals to
him by that person or persons being disregarded accordingly)." Here
"him" refers to the trustee and "that person or persons" refers to the
person or persons beneficially entitled.

So if A transfers shares into the name of B as his nominee or as
trustee of a trust under which B holds the shares for A absolutely, the   D
shares are to be treated for capital gains tax purposes as though they
remained vested in A, and the disposal by A to B is to be disregarded,
as also is any re-acquisition of the shares by A from B.

The present case is not so simple as that, because there were 12 distinct
settlors, treating joint settlors as single entities. They brought various
numbers of shares into the trust. They did not retain any beneficial   E
interest in the specific shares which they brought in. Each settlor became
entitled, subject to the provisions of the trust, to the number of shares
which he brought in, but the shares to which each settlor was entitled
were unspecified shares in the pool.

The meaning of the word "jointly" in section 22 (5) has been
considered in two cases, the correctness of the decisions in which has not
been questioned before us. In *Kidson* v. *Macdonald* [1974] Ch. 339,   F
Foster J. was concerned with a case in which two gentlemen had bought
land in 1960 and 1961 in their joint names as joint tenants on trust for
sale and to hold the net proceeds of sale in trust for themselves as tenants
in common. In 1966 one of them died and his legal personal representatives sold his share in the land at a profit. The question was whether
the vendors were liable to capital gains tax. That they were so was clear, G
unless they were exempt under paragraph 13 of Schedule 7 to the Act
which, so far as relevant, reads:

"(1) No chargeable gain shall accrue on the disposal of an interest
created by or arising under a settlement . . . by the person for whose
benefit the interest was created by the terms of the settlement . . ."

So, if the interest disposed of by the vendors was one created by or   H
arising under a settlement for the purposes of Part III of the Act, the
vendors were exempt from tax. Having regard to the definition of
"settled property" in section 45 (1), the judge held that the deceased's
interest arose under a settlement unless section 22 (5) was applicable. So
it was in the taxpayer's interest in that case to contend that section 22 (5)
did not apply. Foster J. held that in section 22 (5) "jointly" was not
used in a technical sense, but meant concurrently or in common. So

A   the tenants in common were jointly entitled within the meaning of the subsection and as against the trustee they were together absolutely entitled. On that basis Foster J. held that the taxpayers were not exempt from tax.

In *Stephenson* v. *Barclays Bank Trust Co. Ltd.* [1975] 1 W.L.R. 882 Walton J. was concerned with a fund in which two beneficiaries under a will became absolutely entitled in possession to a fund as tenants in common upon the execution in 1969 of a deed of family arrangement. In the course of his judgment Walton J. drew a distinction between successive beneficial interests and the interests of persons " jointly entitled " within the meaning of section 22 (5). He said, at p. 890:

C   " The definition says ' jointly '; it does not say ' together.' I think this is because it is intended to comprise persons who are, as it were, in the same interest. This is a point which was alluded to by Foster J. in *Kidson* v. *Macdonald* [1974] Ch. 339. If property is settled upon A for life with remainder to B, A and B are ' together ' entitled absolutely as against the trustees, but they are not so entitled ' jointly,' ' concurrently,' or ' as tenants in common.' "

D   In the present case Mr. Morritt, for the revenue, has submitted that section 22 (5) is not applicable because the taxpayer did not transfer his shares to the trustees on trust for himself alone but to be held as part of a pool in which all the participants had interests. Alternatively, he says that if the taxpayer's shares were held specifically in trust for him, he was not entitled to direct the trustees how to deal with them. On the first point Mr. Morritt says that the relevant consideration is whether the trustees held the shares transferred by the taxpayer in trust for him and him alone as a person absolutely entitled as against the trustees.

Mr. Nicholls, for the taxpayer, submits that one should not look at the taxpayer in isolation. Upon the creation of the trust the several settlors who contributed shares to the pool were, Mr. Nicholls says, concurrently and absolutely entitled to the settled property as against F   the trustees; they could, by a unanimous act, have put an end to the settlement at any time and without recourse to any provision for termination contained in the agreement. No beneficial interest passed from anyone to anyone in consequence of the trust. What had previously been owned by several owners in several ownerships coalesced in a trust fund which was held in trust for the same persons and in proportions G   corresponding to the proportions of their previous several ownerships. In such a state of affairs Mr. Nicholls submits that section 22 (5) applies. He does not suggest that this would necessarily be so in any case except one in which (a) the beneficial interests of the several persons beneficially interested under the trust amounted in the aggregate to the whole beneficial interest in the property subject to the trust; and (b) those interests were all concurrent. In the light of the two cases which I have cited, I H   understand " concurrent " in this context to mean co-existent and of the same quality. Taking (a) with (b), it seems to me that this must mean that the interest of every person having a beneficial interest must be an absolute interest in some part of, or share in, the property. Given that such interests amount in the aggregate to the entire beneficial interest in the fund, then, assuming that the persons beneficially interested are all sui juris—and there is no suggestion to the contrary here—it must follow that they have it in their power to put an end to the trust summarily at any moment, notwithstanding any powers or discretions conferred on the trustees by the terms of the trust or by operation of law.

In the circumstances of the present case, Mr. Nicholls submits, all the 12 settlors who contributed shares to the pool comprised in the trust were together collectively and concurrently entitled absolutely to the whole trust fund as against the trustees, within the meaning of section 22 (5). Collectively they could put a summary end to the trust and so destroy or override any discretion or power vested in the trustees. They were consequently jointly entitled to the trust property absolutely as against the trustees within the meaning of section 22 (5). So one must treat the shares as vested in the settlors and treat the acts of the trustees as the acts of the settlors, with the consequence, as Mr. Nicholls contends, that the position must be viewed as though none of the settlors had disposed of his or her or their shares.

The logic of this argument seems to me to be unassailable unless it can be said that by participating in the pooling arrangement the several settlors lost their existing beneficial interest in their own particular shares and became entitled merely to an undivided or unappropriated share in the pool formed by their several contributions and that, because the latter interest was different from the former, there were dispositions not merely of the shares themselves but of the anterior beneficial ownerships of specified shares.

Mr. Nicholls concedes that if A transferred shares to B in trust as to nine-tenths for himself absolutely and as to one-tenth for C absolutely, there would, for the purposes of the Act, be a chargeable disposal of one-tenth of the shares though not of the nine-tenths. This, he submits, is because although A and C would be jointly absolutely entitled to the trust shares as against B, section 22 (5) would require the one-tenth to be treated as vested not in A (which would negative any disposal by A to B) but in C (which could only be the case if A had made a disposal of the shares comprised in the one-tenth). To the extent of that one-tenth, A would have parted with the shares.

Can it, then, be argued successfully that in the present case all the several settlors did in fact make a chargeable disposal of their shares because under section 22 (5) all the shares which are subject to the trust are to be treated as vested in the settlors collectively, whereas before the inception of the trust they were vested in them severally? I think not. The effect of the trust was to subject all the trust shares to powers and discretions conferred upon the trustees for what was conceived to be the collective benefit of the settlors but, subject to those powers and discretions which the settlors collectively could override, the measure of the beneficial interests of the settlors remained unaffected by the trust. There was no transfer of any beneficial interest from any one of them to any other. This is, in my judgment, the answer to Mr. Morritt's first contention to the effect that the taxpayer did not transfer his shares to the trustees in trust for himself alone.

On the true view of the facts the taxpayer, in my view, never lost his interest in 55,000 shares of the company. He subjected that interest to certain restraints, as did the other settlors in respect of their shares, but it was at all times within their collective power to abolish those restraints, whereupon each settlor would become absolutely entitled to the same number of shares as he had brought into the trust.

Mr. Morritt's second submission does not, in my opinion, require

A   consideration. It depends upon the premise that the taxpayer's original 55,000 shares were specifically held on trust for him. This was not, in my opinion, the effect of the agreement.

    Goulding J. [1978] 1 W.L.R. 927, expressed his conclusions and his reasons for them, at p. 935:

B   " Looking at the judgments by which I have to be guided, of Foster J. and Walton J., I find that they appear to lay down at most two requirements for the application of section 22 (5) where there is a plurality of beneficial owners. The first requirement is that the interests of the beneficial owners must be concurrent and not successive, like the interests of a life tenant on the one hand, and a remainderman or reversioner on the other. That is distinctly stated

C   in *Kidson* v. *Macdonald* [1974] Ch. 339, 349 where Foster J. said: ' If, however, one has a trust for A for life with remainder to B absolutely, A and B together are able to direct the trustees how to deal with the settled property, but such a limitation is clearly settled property and is not excluded by section 22 (5).' It was also stated in *Stephenson* v. *Barclays Bank Trust Co. Ltd.* [1975] 1 W.L.R. 882,

D   890 in the passage I have already read. The second requirement for the application of section 22 (5) which may be found in the reported cases is that the interests of the co-owners should be, as Walton J. put it, the same. Again the passage is that to which I have already referred, where the judge said: ' The definition says ' jointly '; it does not say ' together.' I think this is because it is

E   intended to comprise persons who are, as it were, in the same interest.' The reference, I think, is certainly to a similarity of interests in quality, not equality in quantity, because I do not think there is any hint in the decisions that tenants in common in unequal shares should be treated differently from tenants in common in equal shares.

F   " Those two tests appear to me to be satisfied in the present case. The interests of the different shareholders within the agreement are concurrent—that is to say, they all coexist in time during the same period of the agreement—and they are the same in Walton J.'s sense; that is, each shareholder has, pro rata with regard to the size of his original holding, the same sort of rights as every other. Each is subject to a right of pre-emption for the benefit of the others, but

G   each has the benefit of the right of pre-emption against all the others. I can find no warrant in the two reported cases for adding a third requirement, which, as appears from the summary of the argument that I have given, is elusive to conceive and hard to define in words."

  That is, I think, a reference to an argument presented to Goulding J. by Mr. McCall, which is referred to at pp. 934H—935B. Goulding J. went

H on, at pp. 935–936: " Does the language of the statute itself clearly require this third attribute of nominee property? " I pause here to interject that " nominee property " was a term that the judge adopted to describe property falling within section 22 (5). He goes on:

      " I think not. We know that the word ' jointly ' must be taken in a popular sense, not in the technical sense of joint tenancy in English law; and then we have to see what is the relevant character of property falling under section 22 (5)."

He went on to give his reasons for rejecting Mr. McCall's argument, and A
said, at p. 936:

> " Accordingly, while accepting that the word ' jointly ' is not to be
> technically construed and embraces all concurrent interests, and
> while accepting also that the concurrent interests must have a
> qualitative similarity one to another (though it will be for future
> cases, no doubt, to define how far that requirement goes), I see no B
> reason to introduce any further refinement in the test. It follows
> that in my judgment, on the true construction of the agreement and
> the facts found in the present case, the shares comprised in the
> agreement are nominee property and not settled property for the
> purposes of capital gains tax."

With those observations of the judge I fully agree.   C

For these reasons, in my judgment this appeal fails and should be
dismissed.

ACKNER L.J. I agree; there is nothing that I can usefully add.

OLIVER L.J. I also agree. Where several separate owners of property D
pool their property through the medium of a trust in such a way that
their respective beneficial proprietary interests under the trust reflect
precisely the individual property interests which they separately had before
the creation of the trust, nobody would say, I think, using language in its
ordinary sense, that they had disposed of their property except in the
purely technical sense that the legal ownership has been transferred to
the trustees. To tax such a technical disposition as one producing a E
capital gain would be capricious and it seems to me that Mr. Nicholls is
right in saying that section 22 (5) was introduced precisely to avoid so
unreasonable a result. When, of course, a trust is created as a result
of which the beneficial owner disposes of the whole or part of his
beneficial interest, there is pro tanto a disposition attracting capital gains
tax on the interest disposed of. Thus, if A declares himself a trustee of F
a one-tenth share of particular property for B, he has clearly disposed
of the one-tenth and the tax becomes payable on any gain notionally found
to be made on the disposition. If A does the same thing in a different
way, namely by transferring the property to C and D as trustees on trust
for himself and B in the proportions of nine-tenths and one-tenth, it
would be entirely unreasonable to treat the disposition to the trustees
as a disposition attracting tax on a notional gain made on the whole G
interest. Hence section 22 (5), which in effect directs that where assets
are held by trustees either for a single person absolutely entitled as against
the trustee, or for two or more persons who are jointly absolutely entitled
as against the trustees, the position is to be looked at as if the assets
were vested in the beneficiaries, disposals *by those beneficiaries* to the
trustees being disregarded.   H

In other words, you are to look through the trustees to the beneficiaries in this situation to determine whether there has been any
disposition attracting capital gains tax.

This does not, of course, mean that the creation of a trust for the
same persons who previously owned the trust property, but in proportions
different from those in which they previously owned it, will escape tax.
The disposal to the trustees may have to be disregarded under section

A   22 (5), but there will still have been pro tanto a disposal of the beneficial interest.

The revenue does not seek to challenge the construction put by the courts on the words " absolutely entitled as against the trustee " and " jointly so entitled " in section 22 (5), in *Kidson* v. *Macdonald* [1974] Ch. 339 and *Stephenson* v. *Barclays Bank Trust Co. Ltd.* [1975] 1 W.L.R. 882. It seems to me inevitably to follow in the instant case that the trust
B here under consideration was one where the beneficiaries are, and were at all material times, jointly and absolutely entitled as against the trustees to the assets vested in the trustees, since their interests are both concurrent and qualitatively identical, and they can collectively, at any time, terminate the trust and direct the actions of the trustees. The transfers to the trustees, therefore, fall to be ignored, and the question of whether there
C was a taxable disposition has to be determined as between the beneficiaries themselves. On this analysis there was, for the reasons given by Buckley L.J., no such disposal. Their interests in the mass precisely reflect the individual interests which they had before the deed was entered into.

In my judgment, therefore, the judge reached the correct conclusion, and I would dismiss the appeal. I do so with the more satisfaction since
D the result seems to me to be in accordance with the common sense and commercial reality of the matter. This was no more than a shareholders' voting agreement carried out through the medium of a trust, and it would seem capricious and unreasonable to tax these shareholders on a wholly illusory gain simply because of the technical machinery which they chose to adopt to effect an end which involved no quantitative alteration in their separate and individual beneficial entitlements.

E

Appeal dismissed with costs.

Solicitors: *Solicitor of Inland Revenue; Herbert Smith & Co.*

[Reported by SUSAN DENNY, Barrister-at-Law]

F

[CHANCERY DIVISION]

G

* CANE *v.* JONES AND OTHERS

[1977 C. No. 1785]

1979 Nov. 27, 28, 29, 30;   Michael Wheeler Q.C., sitting as a
     Dec. 19   deputy judge of the Chancery Division

H   *Company—Articles of association—Amendment—Corporators all*
     agreeing to amendment—No meeting held or special resolution
     passed—Whether agreement effective to deprive chairman of
     casting vote—Companies Act 1948 (11 & 12 *Geo.* 6, c. 38),
     ss. 10 (1), 141

       Section 10 (1) of the Companies Act 1948 provides:
         " Subject to the provisions of this Act and to the con-
         ditions contained in its memorandum, a company may by
         special resolution alter or add to its articles."

Section 141 provides:

" (1) A resolution shall be an extraordinary resolution when it has been passed by a majority of not less than three fourths of such members as, being entitled so to do, vote in person or, where proxies are allowed, by proxy, at a general meeting of which notice specifying the intention to propose the resolution as an extraordinary resolution has been duly given. (2) A resolution shall be a special resolution when it has been passed by such a majority as is required for the passing of an extraordinary resolution and at a general meeting of which not less than 21 days' notice, specifying the intention to propose the resolution as a special resolution, has been duly given: . . ."

A family company, incorporated in 1946, had an issued capital of £30,000 divided into shares of £1 each, of which 15,000 were vested in the first and second defendants jointly, representing one branch of the family, and the remaining 15,000 in two trustees of a family trust in trust for the plaintiff as sole beneficiary, representing the other branch of the family. The company's articles of association provided for up to six directors; that the brothers, P and H, should be life directors; that the chairman should be elected by the directors, and should have a casting vote at board meetings; and that he should preside over and have a casting vote at general meetings of the company. P was the third defendant and father of the first and second defendants. H was the plaintiff's father. In March 1967 the first and second defendants agreed with the two trustees that the chairman should not have any casting vote.

On the determination of the trust, the trustees transferred 15,000 shares in the company to the plaintiff. Subsequently, a state of deadlock was reached in the management of the company's affairs. The first and third defendants, maintaining that the agreement of March 1967 was unenforceable by the plaintiff who had not been privy to it, sought to enforce the chairman's right to exercise a casting vote. The plaintiff denied that any such right existed as a result of the agreement reached by all the shareholders in March 1967.

On the question whether the agreement of March 1967 was effective to alter the company's articles of association: —

Held, that despite the wording of sections 10 and 141 of the Companies Act 1948 and the fact that there had been neither a meeting nor a resolution in writing, the agreement of March 1967, being an expression of the unanimous will of all the corporators acting together and being intra vires the company, was effective to amend the company's articles of association so as to deprive the chairman of his casting vote (post, pp. 1459G—1460B, H—1461A, 1465A).

In re Duomatic Ltd. [1969] 2 Ch. 365 and *In re Oxted Motor Co. Ltd.* [1921] 3 K.B. 32, D.C. applied.

In re Pearce Duff & Co. Ltd. [1960] 1 W.L.R. 1014 and *In re Moorgate Mercantile Holdings Ltd.* [1980] 1 W.L.R. 227 considered.

The following cases are referred to in the judgment:

Consolidated Nickel Mines Ltd., In re [1914] 1 Ch. 883.
Duomatic Ltd., In re [1969] 2 Ch. 365; [1969] 2 W.L.R. 114; [1969] 1 All E.R. 161.
Express Engineering Works Ltd., In re [1920] 1 Ch. 466, C.A.
MacDougall v. *Gardiner* (1875) 1 Ch.D. 13, C.A.
Moorgate Mercantile Holdings Ltd., In re [1980] 1 W.L.R. 227; [1980] 1 All E.R. 40.
Newman (George) & Co., In re [1895] 1 Ch. 674, C.A.
Oxted Motor Co. Ltd., In re [1921] 3 K.B. 32, D.C.

A   *Parker and Cooper Ltd.* v. *Reading* [1926] Ch. 975.
     Pearce Duff & Co. Ltd., In re [1960] 1 W.L.R. 1014; [1960] 3 All E.R.
        222.
     Wenlock (Baroness) v. *River Dee Co.* (1887) 36 Ch.D. 674.

The following additional cases were cited in argument:

     Bentley-Stevens v. *Jones* [1974] 1 W.L.R. 638; [1974] 2 All E.R. 653.

B   *Beswick* v. *Beswick* [1968] A.C. 58; [1967] 3 W.L.R. 932; [1967] 2 All
        E.R. 1197, H.L.(E.).
     Browne v. *La Trinidad* (1887) 37 Ch.D. 1, C.A.
     Cotter v. *National Union of Seamen* [1929] 2 Ch. 58, C.A.
     Dunlop Pneumatic Tyre Co. Ltd. v. *Selfridge and Co. Ltd.* [1915] A.C.
        847, H.L.(E.).
     Foster v. *Foster* [1916] 1 Ch. 532.

C

ACTION

Kingsway Petrol Station Ltd., the fourth defendant, was incorporated
on June 21, 1946, and in its articles of association the third defendant,
Percival Charles Jones (" Percy ") and his brother, Harold Courtney
Jones (" Harold ") were named as life directors.

At all material times 15,000 of the 30,000 issued shares of £1 each

D were registered in the joint names of the first and second defendants,
Ronald Vivien Courtney Jones (" Ronald ") and Mrs. Maureen Heather
Fooks (" Heather "), a son and a daughter, respectively, of Percy. Since
August 1967 the remaining 15,000 shares had been registered in the name
of the plaintiff, Mrs. Gillian Mary Cane (" Gillian "), who was the
daughter of Harold, the shares having been transferred from Mr. Williams
and Mr. Fooks, the trustees of a family trust of which Gillian was the

E sole beneficiary, and to which she had become absolutely entitled.

Half the shares of the company were thus held by Percy's side of the
family and half by Harold's side. A dispute arose between the two
branches of the family. The chairman of the board of directors, under
the articles of association, had a casting vote at board meetings and
presided over and had a casting vote at general meetings.

F   By a writ dated February 22, 1977, the plaintiff, Gillian, claimed
against the defendants (1) a declaration that Percy and Harold were
and had been since December 31, 1975, the only directors of the
company; (2) a declaration that certain heads of agreement of 1975
between Percy, Ronald, Harold and Mr. Williams were void and of
no effect in so far as they purported to (i) reconstitute the board of

G directors, (ii) alter the company's articles of association, or (iii) amend
the provisions of an agreement made in or about March 1967, to which
Ronald, Heather, Mr. Fooks and Mr. Williams were alleged to be parties,
they being the then registered holders of all the issued shares in the
company, whereby it was allegedly agreed that the chairmen should not
exercise any casting vote at general meetings of the company; (3) a
declaration that the proceedings of a meeting allegedly held on September

H 27, 1976, were a nullity in so far as they purported to constitute a meeting
of the directors, and that the resolutions purportedly passed thereat were
void and of no effect; (4) a declaration that the proceedings at an annual
and an extraordinary general meeting of the company on December 31,
1976, were a nullity in so far as they purported to constitute such annual
general or extraordinary general meeting of the company and that each
of the resolutions passed thereat was void and of no effect; (5) a declaration that at any agreed meeting of the company in the case of an equality

of votes, whether on a show of hands or at which a poll was demanded A
the chairman was not entitled to a second or casting vote; (6) a declaration that the proceedings at each of the meetings of shareholders or
directors on January 26, 1977, were a nullity in so far as they respectively
purported to constitute (i) a meeting or directors, or (ii) an extraordinary
general meeting of the company, and that each of the resolutions passed
thereat was void and of no effect. (7) An injunction restraining Ronald
from acting or holding himself out as a director of the company. (8) An B
injunction restraining the company, whether by its directors, servants,
agents or otherwise, from acting on any of the resolutions declared to be
void and of no effect. (9) Costs. And (10) further or other relief.

The facts are stated in the judgment.

Oliver Weaver for the plaintiff.
Robin Potts for the first and third defendants. C
The second defendant was not represented.
The defendant company took no part in the proceedings.

Cur. adv. vult.

December 19. MICHAEL WHEELER Q.C. read the following judgment. D
This action concerns a dispute in a family company, called Kingsway
Petrol Station Ltd. ("the company"). The family is the Jones family
and I will briefly refer to the family tree. In doing so I shall adopt for
convenience the method adopted by counsel of referring to them (if they
will forgive me) by their Christian names. There are two brothers,
Percy and Harold Jones—Harold is sometimes called "Nick." Percy E
has a son Ronald and a daughter Maureen Heather, more usually referred
to as "Heather," who is now Mrs. Fooks. Harold has a daughter
Gillian, who is Mrs. Cane. Gillian is the plaintiff in this action, and Mr.
Oliver Weaver appears for her. Ronald and Percy are the first and third
defendants, and they appear by Mr. Robin Potts. Heather is the second
defendant, who has entered an appearance but has not been represented
at the hearing, and the company is the fourth defendant, which has taken F
no part at all, for reasons which will become apparent in the course of
this judgment.

The company was incorporated on June 21, 1946, under the Companies
Act 1929, and its articles mainly adopt the 1929 Table A. It was formed
by Percy and Harold and they are named in the articles as life directors.
It has a present issued capital of £30,000 in 30,000 fully paid £1 shares, and G
at all material times 15,000 of these shares have been registered in the
joint names of Ronald and Heather. It is now common ground, although
initially it was in dispute, that since August 1967 the remaining 15,000
shares have been registered in the name of the plaintiff, Gillian, on a
transfer from Mr. T. J. Williams and Mr. J. A. Fooks. They were the
trustees of a family trust of which Gillian was sole beneficiary and to
which she had become absolutely entitled. Mr. T. J. Williams is a H
solicitor and a family friend of Harold's. Mr. Fooks is the company's
secretary and Heather's husband. The position, therefore, is that half
the share capital is held by what I might call Percy's side, in the shape of
Ronald and Heather as joint holders, and the other half is held by
Harold's side, initially by Messrs. Williams and Fooks and more recently
by Gillian.

I will refer briefly to one or two other provisions in the articles:

A   article 13 provides that there be up to six directors. Article 14 provides
for the two life directors, namely, Percy and Harold, who do not retire
by rotation. All other directors do, and regulations 73 to 77 of the 1929
Table A apply to the company. The regulations relating to the chairman
are of importance: the company's articles incorporate four regulations of
the 1929 Table A, namely regulation 84, under which the chairman of
directors is elected by the directors—I shall have to refer to that again
B   later: regulation 81, where the chairman of directors has a casting vote
at board meetings: regulation 47, where the chairman of the board pre-
sides at general meetings: and regulation 50, where the chairman has a
casting vote at general meetings. It will be seen at once that if these
articles are still in force in a company where the shares are held 50/50,
the position of the chairman of directors could be crucial. That is really
C   what this action is all about. The two sides of the family have fallen out.
     The plaintiff (Harold's side) claims that by virtue of an agreement
entered into between all the shareholders in March 1967, (i.e. Ronald and
Heather as joint holders on the one hand and Mr. Williams and Mr.
Fooks as joint holders on the other, the chairman has ceased to be
entitled to exercise a casting vote: alternatively, that there is currently
no chairman, so that on either view there is complete deadlock.
D
     The first and third defendants (Percy's side) claim that the original
articles are still in force, unaltered; that in any event Gillian, not being
a party to the March 1967 agreement, cannot enforce it; and that, on the
facts, Percy is currently the chairman, so that Percy's side have control.
     Mr. Weaver accepts that if Percy is chairman with a casting vote,
Gillian must fail because in that event all the acts complained of are
E   capable of ratification and that, on the principles laid down in *Mac-
Dougall* v. *Gardiner* (1875) 1 Ch.D. 13, the court will not interfere.
I agree with him.
     It is common ground that there were from time to time other directors
who were liable to retire by rotation. It is also common ground that
owing to successive failures to hold annual general meetings the directors
F   who should have retired by rotation in due course automatically ceased
to be directors on the principle recognised in *In re Consolidated Nickel
Mines Ltd.* [1914] 1 Ch. 883. In particular, it is common ground that
although Ronald was for a time a director, he too ceased to hold office
at the latest by December 31, 1978, on the same principle.
     The position now is, therefore, that both sides agree that Percy and
Harold are the only two directors. Percy's side claim that *he* is the
G   chairman with the casting vote, but Harold's side claim that there is no
chairman's casting vote, or alternatively that there is no chairman. I
should add that the issues have been simplified because in the course of
the hearing before me both sides—very properly—abandoned contentions
which clearly were not supported by the evidence.
     With this introduction, I can now go straight to the shareholders'
H   agreement of March 1967 to which I have already briefly referred—
" the 1967 agreement." It is common ground that it was made in March
1967 although the copy in the agreed bundle is not in fact dated. It reads:

     " This agreement is made the " blank " day of " blank " 1967
     between [Ronald and Heather] of the first part [Mr. Fooks and
     Mr. Williams] (as trustees for the deed of settlement in favour of
     Gillian Jones) of the second part and [Mr. Fooks and Mr. Simons]
     of the third part, Whereas this agreement is supplemental to an

agreement (hereinafter called ' the said agreement ') bearing even   A
date herewith and made between " the various people there named
" And whereas at the time of entering into the said agreement it
was agreed by and between the parties thereto to enter into this
agreement also, Now this agreement made in pursuance of the said
agreement and in consideration of the premises witnesseth as follows:
(1) The chairman of Kingsway Petrol Station Ltd. shall not exercise
any casting vote as chairman and in the event of an equality of   B
votes occurring it is agreed by and between the parties hereto that
an independent chairman shall be appointed by them and in default
of agreement upon such appointment the same shall be made by the
President of the Institute of Chartered Accountants (2) [Harold
and Percy] shall continue as directors of Kingsway Petrol Station
Ltd. and shall be paid directors' fees of £500 per annum each and   C
in addition shall be paid a salary of £2,000 each or such lesser sum
as they the said [Harold and Percy] shall both mutually agree upon
provided that either the said [Harold] or the said [Percy] may
renounce their respective salaries or a part or parts thereof in favour
of a member or members of their respective families but so that in
the aggregate the fees and salaries paid to one family shall in no way
exceed those paid to the other family. (3) Upon the death of either   D
the said [Harold] and/or [Percy] the parties hereto shall cause
Kingsway Petrol Station Ltd. to enter into an agreement to pay their
wives Dulcie Jones and Joan Jones a pension of £1,000 per annum
each for and during their respective lives or until their remarriage.
(4) [Ronald and Mr. Fooks] shall be paid by Kingsway Petrol
Station Ltd. " and another company which I need not bother with   E
" a salary based upon and according to the time and services rendered
to those companies by them due regard being paid to the fact that
they will be following full time employment by the new company
(5) The parties hereto shall cause Kingsway Petrol Station Ltd. and
[the other company] to pay out 60 per cent. of their respective net
incomes and profits by way of dividends unless the shareholders
shall otherwise agree. (6) It is hereby declared that the parties hereto   F
shall where the context so admits include their respective successors
in title to all or any of the shares in Kingsway Petrol Station Ltd. and
[the other company] and all references to those companies shall
include any successors or assignees thereof howsoever and whatsoever. (7) The parties hereto hereby jointly and severally agree to do
any act matter or thing necessary to carry into effect the terms of   G
this agreement and also to execute any documents necessary or
required to carry out the terms hereof and also to cause the said
companies to do any such act matter or thing to carry out the terms
hereof "

The other agreement referred to in the 1967 agreement provided for the
re-organisation of a company called S.W.B. Ltd. It is unnecessary for
me to go through the terms of that agreement. It is sufficient to say that   H
clause 1 of the 1967 agreement was the quid pro quo for Harold's side
agreeing to the re-organisation of S.W.B. Ltd.

Now as to the arguments about the effect of the 1967 agreement. Mr.
Weaver contends that it operated as an alteration of the articles on what
was conveniently called in argument " the *Duomatic* principle " based on
In re Duomatic Ltd. [1969] 2 Ch. 365, and the principle is, I think, con-

A veniently summarised in a short passage in the judgment in that case of Buckley J. where he says, at p. 373:

> ". . . I proceed upon the basis that where it can be shown that all shareholders who have a right to attend and vote at a general meeting of the company assent to some matter which a general meeting of the company could carry into effect, that assent is as binding as a resolution in general meeting would be."

B

Applying that principle to the present case, Mr. Weaver says that the agreement of all the shareholders embodied in the 1967 agreement had the effect, so far as requisite, of overriding the articles. In other words, it operated to deprive the chairman for the time being of the right to use his casting vote, except, perhaps, in so far as an independent chairman contemplated by clause (1) might need to do. I should add here that it

C is quite clear that Percy, who was actually chairman of the company at the time, was well aware of the terms of the 1967 agreement.

For the first and third defendants, Mr. Potts has two answers to Mr. Weaver's argument. First, that on its true interpretation in relation to a special or extraordinary resolution the *Duomatic* principle only applies if there has been (i) a resolution, and (ii) a meeting; and that here he says,

D with some truth, there was neither a resolution nor a meeting of the four shareholders. Secondly, he stresses that the agreement does not in terms purport to alter the articles at all: it rests, he says, solely in contract and Gillian, not being a party, cannot take either the benefit or the burden of the agreement.

On the first of these two arguments, Mr. Potts helpfully reminded me

E of the line of cases in which the effect of the unanimous consent of the corporators has been considered, starting with *Baroness Wenlock* v. *River Dee Co.* (1887) 36 Ch.D. 674. I do not propose to refer to all these cases in detail but, for the record, I will list them. The other cases are *In re George Newman & Co.* [1895] 1 Ch. 674; *In re Express Engineering Works Ltd.* [1920] 1 Ch. 466; *In re Oxted Motor Co. Ltd.* [1921] 3 K.B. 32; *Parker and Cooper Ltd.* v. *Reading* [1926] Ch. 975; *In re*

F *Pearce Duff & Co. Ltd.* [1960] 1 W.L.R. 1014; *In re Duomatic Ltd.* [1969] 2 Ch. 365 to which I have already referred, and finally a decision of Slade J. in *In re Moorgate Mercantile Holdings Ltd.* [1980] 1 W.L.R. 227.

Mr. Potts pointed out—correctly—that of these cases only three were concerned with special or extraordinary resolutions, namely, *In re Pearce Duff & Co. Ltd.* [1960] 1 W.L.R. 1014; *In re Moorgate Mercantile*

G *Holdings Ltd.* [1980] 1 W.L.R. 227 (both of which were concerned with special resolutions) and *In re Oxted Motor Co. Ltd.* [1921] 3 K.B. 32, which was concerned with an extraordinary resolution. All the rest were concerned with matters which, if capable of ratification at all, could have been validated by ordinary resolutions.

Mr. Potts's starting point is section 10 of the Companies Act 1948,

H which provides for the alteration of articles by special resolution; and from that he goes on to section 141, mentioning subsections (1) and (2) and including the particular proviso, laying down how special and extra-ordinary resolutions are to be passed. First of all section 10:

> " (1) Subject to the provisions of this Act and to the conditions contained in its memorandum, a company may by special resolution alter or add to its articles. (2) Any alteration or addition so made in the articles shall, subject to the provisions of this Act, be as valid

as if originally contained therein, and be subject in like manner to   A
alteration by special resolution."

Then section 141:

" (1) A resolution shall be an extraordinary resolution when it has
been passed by a majority of not less than three fourths of such
members as, being entitled so to do, vote in person or, where proxies
are allowed, by proxy, at a general meeting of which notice specifying   B
the intention to propose the resolution as an extraordinary resolution
has been duly given.   (2) A resolution shall be a special resolution
when it has been passed by such a majority as is required for the
passing of an extraordinary resolution and at a general meeting of
which not less than 21 days' notice, specifying the intention to propose the resolution as a special resolution, has been duly given: C
Provided that, if it is so agreed by a majority in number of the
members having the right to attend and vote at any such meeting,
being a majority together holding not less than 95 per cent. in nominal
value of the shares giving that right, or, in the case of a company not
having a share capital, together representing not less than 95 per
cent. of the total voting rights at that meeting of all the members, a
resolution may be proposed and passed as a special resolution at a   D
meeting of which less than 21 days' notice has been given . . ."

Thus, says Mr. Potts, you can only alter the articles by special resolution. That is his first argument.   Secondly, that a special resolution must
be passed at a meeting; thirdly, that here there was neither a resolution nor
a meeting.   *In re Pearce Duff & Co. Ltd.* [1960] 1 W.L.R. 1014 he says,   E
does not help Mr. Weaver because in that case there had been a resolution and a meeting: and all that was later cured by the unanimous,
but separate, consents of the shareholders was a defect in the consent
to short notice under the proviso to section 141 (2).   *In re Moorgate
Mercantile Holdings Ltd.* [1980] 1 W.L.R. 227 was concerned with the
extent to which, if at all, a resolution which is to be proposed as a special
resolution could be amended at the meeting, and its relevance for present   F
purposes lies solely in the fact that Slade J. referred to *In re Pearce Duff
& Co. Ltd.* [1960] 1 W.L.R. 1014 and *to In re Duomatic Ltd.* [1969] 2
Ch. 365, and also to section 143 (4) of the Act to which I too shall refer
in a moment, and stated that the proposition which he had laid down
earlier in his judgment for the amendment of special resolutions might
be subject to modification where the members unanimously agreed to   G
waive the requirements of notice.

In re Oxted Motor Co. Ltd. [1921] 3 K.B. 32 was a case of an extraordinary resolution for voluntary winding up.   There were only two
shareholders, who were also the two directors.   They met and passed a
resolution that the company be wound up and they signed a minute to
that effect; but no notice to propose the resolution as an extraordinary   H
resolution had ever given.   The Divisional Court of the Queen's Bench
Division upheld the resolution on the ground that it was competent for the
shareholders of the company acting together to waive the formalities
required by what is now section 141 (1) of the Act of 1948.   In *In re
Pearce Duff & Co. Ltd.* [1960] 1 W.L.R. 1014, which was a petition to
confirm a reduction of capital, Buckley J., after referring to *In re Oxted
Motor Co. Ltd.* [1921] 3 K.B. 32 and also to *Parker and Cooper Ltd.* v.

A *Reading* [1926] Ch. 975 as showing that in certain circumstances all the corporators, if they agree, can bind the company, continued, at p. 1017:

"Those cases, I think, relate to a rather different subject matter from that which I have to consider, because, as I see it, I have to consider not whether these resolutions bound the company as special resolutions but whether any shareholder could now say that the
B resolutions were not properly passed as valid special resolutions. Having regard to the 100 per cent. consent which has been obtained to the resolutions being treated as valid and to the fact that the petition has been presented upon that footing, I do not think that this court ought to hear any of the shareholders to say that those resolutions were not validly passed. In those circumstances, I think, the case being a rather exceptional one, that I am entitled to regard
C this special resolution as sufficient basis for the reduction which the court is asked to confirm; and accordingly, subject to being satisfied on the evidence as to excess of wants, I will confirm the reduction."

It is with very great diffidence that I venture to criticise the reasoning of so distinguished a judge in a short extempore judgment delivered, I notice, on the last Monday of the 1960 Trinity term. But with great
D respect to Buckley J. the problem he was faced with surely was not whether any shareholder could *object* that the resolutions had not been passed as valid special resolutions, but whether as a matter of law they *had* been validly so passed: because unless he had before him a validly passed special resolution he had no jurisdiction to confirm the desired reduction of capital: see section 66 (2) and section 67 (1) of the Act of 1948. I
E do not think, therefore, that I can regard the decision in *In re Pearce Duff & Co. Ltd.* [1960] 1 W.L.R. 1014 as concluding the point which I have to consider.

The first of Mr. Potts's two arguments—namely that there must be a "resolution" and a "meeting"—does not appear to have been raised in any of the three reported cases which were concerned with special or extraordinary resolutions. But it is not an argument to which I would
F readily accede because in my judgment it would create a wholly artificial and unnecessary distinction between those powers which can, and those which cannot, be validly exercised by all the corporators acting together.

For my part I venture to differ from Mr. Potts on the first limb of his argument, namely that articles can *only* be altered by special resolution. In my judgment, section 10 of the Act is merely laying down a procedure
G whereby *some only* of the shareholders can validly alter the articles: and if, as I believe to be the case, it is a basic principle of company law that all the corporators, acting together, can do anything which is intra vires the company, then I see nothing in section 10 to undermine this principle. I accept that the principle requires all the corporators to "act together": but with regard to this I respectfully adopt what Astbury J. said in
H *Parker and Cooper Ltd.* v. *Reading* [1926] Ch. 975, 984:

"Now the view I take of both these decisions"—those were *In re Express Engineering Works Ltd.* [1920] Ch. 466 and *In re George Newman & Co.* [1895] 1 Ch. 674—"is that where the transaction is intra vires and honest, and especially if it is for the benefit of the company, it cannot be upset if the assent of all the corporators is given to it. I do not think it matters in the least whether that assent is given at different times or simultaneously."

See also Younger L.J. in *In re Express Engineering Works Ltd.* [1920] A
Ch. 466, 471, and the passage from the judgment of Buckley J. in *In re
Duomatic Ltd.* [1969] 2 Ch. 365 which I have read earlier in this judgment. I should add that the evidence in the case before me is that the
1967 agreement was signed by " the two sides," if I may call them that,
separately, and that they did not meet together, however informally, for
the purpose of signing the document. But it is clear beyond doubt that
the agreement did represent a meeting of minds which is, after all, the B
essence of a meeting and the passing of a resolution.

Some light is also, I think, thrown on the problem by section 143 (4)
of the Act of 1948. Section 143 deals with the forwarding to the Registrar
of Companies of copies of every resolution or agreement to which the
section applies: and subsection (4) reads:

> " This section shall apply to—(*a*) special resolutions; (*b*) extraordinary C
> resolutions; (*c*) resolutions which have been agreed to by all the
> members of a company, but which, if not so agreed to, would not
> have been effective for their purpose unless, as the case may be,
> they had been passed as special resolutions or as extraordinary
> resolutions; (*d*) resolutions or agreements which have been agreed to
> by all the members of some class of shareholders but which, if not D
> so agreed to, would not have been effective for their purpose unless
> they had been passed by some particular majority or otherwise in
> some particular manner, and all resolutions or agreements which
> effectively bind all the members of any class of shareholders though
> not agreed to by all those members; . . ."

Paragraph (*c*) thus appears to recognise that you can have a resolution, E
at least, which has been agreed to by all the members and is as effective
as a special or extraordinary resolution would have been: but, as Mr.
Potts was quick to point out, paragraph (*c*) says nothing about " agreements " in contrast to paragraph (*d*) which refers to resolutions or
agreements which have been agreed to by all the members of some class
of shareholders. I should say in passing that I think the reference in
paragraph (*d*) to " resolutions or agreements " stems directly from regu- F
lation 4 of Part I of the 1948 Table A, which, dealing with class meetings,
provides briefly:

> " If at any time the share capital is divided into different classes
> of shares, the rights attached to any class (unless otherwise provided
> by the terms of issue of the shares of that class) may, whether or not
> the company is being wound up, be varied with the consent in writing G
> of the holders of three-fourths of the issued shares of that class, or
> with the sanction of an extraordinary resolution passed at a separate
> general meeting of the holders of the shares of the class . . ."

so that you have either a consent which might be termed an agreement
or a resolution.

I cannot regard this difference in drafting between paragraphs (*c*) and H
(*d*) of section 143 (4) as fatal to the basic argument. It may be, as Mr.
Weaver suggested, that a document which is framed as an agreement can
be treated as a " resolution " for the purposes of paragraph (*c*). I
should add in passing that a copy of the 1967 agreement was never, as
far as I am aware, sent to the Registrar of Companies for registration.
It may be that there is a gap in the registration requirements of section
143. But be that as it may, the fact that the 1967 agreement was drafted

A   as an agreement and not as a resolution, and that the four signatories did not sign in each other's presence does not in my view prevent that agreement overriding pro tanto—and so far as necessary—the articles of the company; in my judgment Mr. Potts's first argument fails and unless he can show that the 1967 agreement has been superseded, the chairman of the company has no casting vote at board or general meetings.

B   In view of my conclusion on Mr. Potts's first argument, it is not strictly necessary to consider his second argument that the 1967 agreement does not purport to alter the articles and that its force and effect rest solely in contract so as to preclude Gillian from relying upon it since she did not sign it.

I shall take this argument quite shortly. In the first place it is in my view significant that although in 1967 Percy and Harold were clearly still C   the dominant figures in the company, it was the four *shareholders* who signed the agreement, thus underlining the nature and purpose of the agreement. Nor do I think that clause (7)—under which the parties agreed to do whatever was necessary to carry the agreement into effect— is inconsistent with this view, having regard, for example, to the terms of clause (3), under which, on the death of Harold or Percy, the parties were to procure the company concerned to enter into agreements to pay their D   widows a pension each.

Moreover, I am by no means certain that even if the agreement were regarded as a contract Gillian would be out of court on the privity of contract argument. Messrs. Williams and Fooks were—and were recorded as—acting as her trustees. Clause 6 declares that the parties to the agreement are to include their successors in title to all or any of the E   shares in the company: and I see a good deal of force in Mr. Weaver's argument that the combination of these factors was sufficient to enable Gillian to take the benefit of the agreement when, on the termination of her trust, the 15,000 shares were transferred to her by Mr. Williams and Mr. Fooks: and that she would therefore require Mr. Fooks and Mr. Williams—although Mr. Williams, of course, is now dead—to enforce the F   agreement on her behalf. However, in the circumstances, it is unnecessary to express a concluded opinion on this point and I do not do so.

I can now move forward in time to September 27, 1975. On that day Harold, Percy, Ronald and Mr. Williams signed a document entitled " Heads of agreement, providing for arrangements within S.W.B. Ltd. and Kingsway Petrol Station Ltd. and ancillary matters." It is to be observed that Gillian did not sign this document, although she was, of G   course, by that time the registered holder of her 15,000 shares.

I refer to these Heads of agreement (" the 1975 Heads ") because they purport to affect the composition of the board of the company and also the chairman's casting vote. I do not propose to read the whole of the 1975 Heads since only three clauses are, I think, strictly relevant, namely:

H   " (3) The board of Kingsway Petrol Station Ltd. will be changed forthwith so that the following persons only will be directors: " Ronald, Percy, Harold. (4) Ronald " will be appointed chairman of each of the above companies "—that was the company and S.W.B. Ltd.—" with a second vote in the event of a tie on voting in any situation. (5) The articles of association of each of the above companies will be changed in so far as is necessary to achieve the above."

1462

It must be remembered that at the date of " the 1975 Heads " neither   A
Harold nor Percy were shareholders in the company at all. Ronald
was, of course, joint holder of the 15,000 shares held by Percy's side, and
clause (6) (c) of " the 1975 Heads " provided that Ronald would enter
into an agreement with Gillian to acquire her shares in the company,
such agreement to be a mutual option exercisable within a four to six
year period.

Mr. Potts relied upon " the 1975 Heads " in the following way.   B
Accepting—as he does—that Ronald is now no longer a director of the
company, because of the *Consolidated Nickel Mines Ltd.* [1914] 1 Ch.
883 principle, he nevertheless argues, as I understand it, (i) that " the
1975 Heads " are binding on the signatories; (ii) that those signatories
include the two existing directors of the company, Harold and Percy;
(iii) that as such directors they have power under regulation 15 of the   C
articles to appoint an additional director; (iv) that " the 1975 Heads " are
specifically enforceable; and (v) that I ought to regard Ronald as entitled
to require Percy and Harold to appoint Ronald as additional director.
Mr. Potts does not, of course, worry about a casting vote in these circumstances because, if he can get Ronald on the board, Ronald and Percy
would side together and thus out-vote Harold.

I should add that a good deal of time was taken up in evidence in   D
trying to establish the allegation that Harold, in signing " the 1975
Heads," bound Gillian, either because he had some general or specific   ⁄
prior authority to do so or because she subsequently ratified it. I do not
propose to review the evidence on this aspect in any detail. Gillian's
evidence in particular was very confused. Suffice it to say that I am
entirely satisfied that as a matter of law Gillian was *not* bound by " the
1975 Heads." It may well be that Harold and Mr. Williams thought that   E
" the 1975 Heads " were in Gillian's interest: it may also be that Harold
felt certain that Gillian would do whatever he wanted. And Mr. Fulwell,
solicitor to Percy and Ronald, who actually drafted " the 1975 Heads,"
told me that he considered the agreement to be binding on Gillian. But
in my view he was wrong. The parties took a risk in not getting " the
1975 Heads " signed by Gillian: she never did sign them; nor in my   F
judgment did she either authorise or ratify them: and they are not
binding upon her.

As to Mr. Potts's specific performance argument, I would merely point
out (i) that his case as pleaded does not contain any claim for specific
performance; (ii) that " the 1975 Heads " are already more than four
years old; (iii) that if specific performance were required it would have to
be of the whole of " the 1975 Heads " and not part only—and I do not   G
know whether this is even practicable; and (iv) that specific performance
is in any event an equitable remedy. In short, the argument is not open
on the pleadings, has not been seriously argued before me and is in my
view at best highly suspect.

There remains Mr. Potts's last point, namely that of the two present
directors, i.e. Percy and Harold, Percy is in fact the chairman. This of   H
course will only help him if, contrary to the view which I have expressed
as to the effect of the 1967 agreement, the chairman *has* a casting vote.
It is necessary at this point to refer again to the manner in which under
the 1929 Table A, regulation 84, a chairman is appointed:

"84. The directors may elect a chairman of their meetings and
     determine the period for which he is to hold office; but if no such
     chairman is elected, or if at any meeting the chairman is not present

A   within five minutes after the time appointed for holding the same, the directors present may choose one of their number to be chairman of the meeting."

It is common ground that for a number of years—possibly up to the 1967 agreement—Percy was chairman. By September 27, 1976, at a board meeting, a resolution was purportedly passed instructing the secretary

B   to implement clause (3) of " the 1975 Heads "—that the board was to consist only of Ronald, Percy and Harold. But that meeting was in law a nullity because it was attended only by Percy and Ronald, and Ronald was not—and this is common ground—a director at that time. Nothing was said in the minutes about implementing clause (4)—that Ronald was to be chairman with a casting vote.

C   At the annual general meeting held on December 31, 1976, the minutes record that Mr. Williams and Mrs. Jones, Harold's wife, questioned whether or not Percy had resigned as chairman of the company and that neither of them accepted Ronald as chairman. This annual general meeting was ineffective because only one shareholder, Ronald, was personally present so that there was no quorum. At a board meeting held immediately after this annual general meeting, at which Ronald is

D   shown as chairman, Mr. Williams and Mrs. Jones again objected to Ronald acting as chairman and questioned whether Percy " had ever handed over the chairmanship to Ronald."

At a board meeting on January 26, 1977, at which Percy, Harold and Ronald were all present, Ronald was again shown as chairman and a letter from Gillian's solicitors was produced in which they advised that as a result of the 1967 agreement the only directors were

E   Harold and Percy, and that the chairman would not have a casting vote.

At a board meeting on February 25, 1977—i.e. three days after the issue of the writ in these proceedings—Ronald is again shown as chairman, Percy and Harold also being present, and Harold asked for his objections to the position of Ronald as chairman and director to be recorded. On August 8, 1977, there was another board meeting—the first minutes

F   prepared by Mr. Watson, the new secretary. All three gentlemen were present; none was named as chairman: and the minutes were in fact signed by Percy. On August 16, 1977, at a board meeting, all three were present and the minutes record: " It was unanimously agreed that Mr. P. C. Jones be chairman *for this meeting.*" That was why Percy signed the minutes of the previous board meeting. Mr. Weaver accepts that at this meeting a resolution was validly passed which had the effect

G   of appointing Ronald an additional director. It was also resolved to hold the annual general meeting on September 14, 1977, and—by a majority of two to one against Harold—that Ronald " should be chairman of that meeting."

On August 31, 1977, there was an extraordinary general meeting to increase the company's capital. Ronald was shown as chairman. Ronald

H   was for the resolution and Gillian voted against. Ronald as chairman purported to use his casting vote. Gillian objected and says she does not accept that Ronald was in fact chairman of the meeting. Ronald also took the chair at a board meeting held on the same day. On September 14, 1977, there was a board meeting at which all three were present and Percy was shown as chairman. Minute 3 reads as follows:

" R. V. C. Jones proposed that P. C. Jones be elected chairman of the directors. This was accepted by H. C. Jones on condition that

A no casting vote be used. This was not accepted, but notwithstanding the proposal was carried unanimously."

I find that slightly difficult to understand. At an extraordinary general meeting held on the same day Percy was shown as chairman and purported to use his casting vote, and Harold asked that his objection to this be minuted. Again on the same day there was an *annual general meeting* and Percy was in the chair. The resolution to re-elect Ronald a director B was purportedly carried by the use of Percy's casting vote.

At a *board meeting* on September 27, 1977, when all three were present, Percy was shown as chairman, and Harold asked for the minutes of the last board meeting " to be amended to show Percy as acting temporary chairman ": but this was not done. At a *board meeting* on March 29, 1978—*Harold was not present*—Percy proposed that " in C accordance with the agreement he had signed in September 1975 "—the 1975 Heads—" he should invite Ronald to take the chair. Ronald agreed and the meeting continued under his chairmanship." This meeting was not properly called—and there is no doubt about this—because notice of it had not been given to Harold.

The only other board or general meeting held in 1978 was a board meeting on December 6, 1978. Percy and Ronald were the only two D there: there is no record of either of them acting as chairman. It is common ground—as I have already mentioned—that Ronald ceased to be a director on December 31, 1978.

I have referred to the meetings recorded in the company's minute book in some detail because Mr. Potts claims that, properly analysed, Percy has never lawfully ceased to be chairman and that the purported E appointment of Ronald at the board meeting on March 29, 1978, was a nullity because the meeting had been improperly called. It is slightly ironic that Mr. Potts should be relying on the failure of his clients to give proper notice of the board meeting to Harold. Therefore, says Mr. Potts, if Ronald was not validly appointed, Percy did not effectively resign. F

I find it difficult to accept this argument. True that under the 1929 Table A regulation 84 " the directors " may " elect a chairman of their meetings and determine the period for which he is to hold office ": but the first point I would make is that there is no evidence whatsoever before me of anyone ever having been appointed chairman of the board for any specific period. Moreover, there is nothing in regulation 84 G which requires any specific formality for a chairman of the board to resign that office. In view of this, I have, as it seems to me, to look at the factual history and decide, in the light of that, what those concerned must be taken as having decided. I would also add that one of the most striking features of this case has been the almost total failure of all concerned to observe the simplest requirements of company law.

In the light of these considerations, and of the confused and confusing H attitudes which the various dramatis personae adopted from time to time, I do not feel justified in concluding that there is, or has been for some considerable time, any effective agreement between Percy and Harold that the former should be chairman: or that the original situation, when Percy was admittedly chairman, should be perpetuated or restored. It follows, therefore, in my judgment that even if I am wrong in holding that the 1967 agreement has effectively put the chairman's casting vote

A in baulk, there is, on the facts of this case, at present no chairman who could effectively exercise that casting vote.

I have accordingly reached the conclusion (a) that the 1967 agreement was and is effective to restrict the use of the chairman's casting voting vote, and (b) that if I am wrong in that conclusion and if the chairman has a casting vote, nevertheless there is currently no chairman. These conclusions give me no satisfaction nor, may I add, would it have afforded
B me any satisfaction to have reached a contrary conclusion that Percy's side were in control by virtue only of the casting vote. It seems to me that, unless the parties can pull themselves together and arrive at some practical solution of their family squabble, the company is doomed to one thing and one thing only, namely liquidation and it may be compulsory liquidation and further waste of money.

C As I have said, the conclusions I have reached, even if only one of those main conclusions is correct, means that this is a deadlocked company, and I do not, as at present advised, see any prospect—unless the parties can manage to live together—of the company being able to continue effectively in business. I can quite appreciate there may be monetary difficulties in one side buying the other out, but if that is so it seems to me that both sides have only one sensible course open to them and that
D is to combine together to put the company into voluntary liquidation and realise this undertaking for the best possible price in the interests of both sides of the family.

Declaration accordingly.

E Solicitors: *Rye Naylor & Leman for Meade-King & Co., Bristol; Fulwell & Partners, Bristol.*

T. C. C. B.

F

* REGINA v. CROYDON JUSTICES, *Ex parte*
LEFORE HOLDINGS LTD.

1980 March 19   Lawton and Waller L.JJ.

G *Justices — Case stated — Practice — Application to state case — Question in issue not specifically stated—Justices' refusal to state case — Whether substantial compliance with statutory requirements—Whether case to be stated—Magistrates' Courts Rules 1968 (S.I. 1968 No. 1920 (L. 20)), r. 65 (as amended by Magistrates' Courts (Amendment) (No. 2) Rules 1975 (S.I. 1975 No. 518 (L. 8)), r. 2)*

H   A rating authority applied for a distress warrant for non-payment of rates against the applicants. All the facts were agreed except whether the applicants were in rateable occupation and their evidence to show that they had not been in rateable occupation was uncontested. The justices issued the warrant. The applicants applied to the justices to state a case " setting forth the facts and grounds of . . . determination including evidence upon which the justices made their findings of fact." The justices refused to state a case on the ground that the application failed to comply with rule 65 of the Magi-

strates' Courts Rules 1968,[1] as amended, in that there had not   A
been a proper identification of the question upon which the
case was to be stated. The applicants sought leave to apply
for a judicial review of the decision. The Divisional Court
refused leave. The Court of Appeal on an ex parte application granted leave.

On the application to the Court of Appeal for judicial
review: —

Held, granting the application, (1) that the provisions of   B
rules 65 to 68 of the Magistrates' Courts Rules 1968, as
amended, were to be applied strictly so that their object, the
speeding up of the administration of justice, was enforced;
that the strict enforcement of the rules should not be at the
expense of justice being done and, therefore, the court when
considering a case where a provision of the rules had been
disregarded, had to take into account the importance of that
provision in relation to the object of the rules and whether   C
there had been a substantial compliance with the relevant
rule before deciding whether to enforce the rule strictly (post,
pp. 1470E—1471A).

Dicta of Lord Penzance in *Howard* v. *Bodington* (1877)
2 P.D. 203, 211 and Templeman J. in *Coney* v. *Choyce* [1975]
1 W.L.R. 422, 434 applied.

(2) That, since the application to state a case referred
specifically to the evidence upon which the justices made their   D
findings of fact and there was only one question of fact before
the justices, the justices could have been in no doubt as to the
issue and they could have stated a case on the information
in the application and, accordingly, there had been a substantial
compliance with rule 65 and an order of mandamus would
be granted ordering the justices to state a case (post,
p. 1471C–H).

Decision of the Divisional Court of the Queen's Bench   E
Division reversed.

The following cases are referred to in the judgments:
Coney v. *Choyce* [1975] 1 W.L.R. 422; [1975] 1 All E.R. 979.
Howard v. *Bodington* (1877) 2 P.D. 203.
Reg. v. *Industrial Injuries Commissioner, Ex parte Amalgamated Engineer-*
    ing Union [1966] 2 Q.B. 21; [1966] 2 W.L.R. 91; [1966] 1 All E.R.   F
    97, C.A.

The following additional case was cited in argument:
Michael v. *Gowland* [1977] 1 W.L.R. 296; [1977] 2 All E.R. 328, D.C.

APPLICATION for judicial review.
    On October 2, 1979, the applicants, Lefore Holdings Ltd., applied   G
ex parte to the Divisional Court of the Queen's Bench Division (Lord
Widgery C.J., Eveleigh L.J. and Swanwick J.) for leave to apply for judicial
review for the purpose of obtaining an order of mandamus directed to the
Croydon justices requiring them to state a case for the opinion of the
High Court.
    The grounds on which the applicants sought relief were that the   H
justices had wrongly refused to state a case upon their application dated
December 8, 1978; the justices wrongly decided that the application was
not an application within section 87 of the Magistrates' Courts Act 1952;
they wrongly decided that the application did not comply with the requirements of rule 65 of the Magistrates' Courts Rules 1968 in all the circumstances; they wrongly decided that the application was not capable of

---

[1] Magistrates' Courts Rules 1968, r. 65, as amended: see post, pp. 1469H—1470B.

A   amendment to comply with rule 65; they wrongly held the Magistrates' Courts Rules 1968 to be mandatory as opposed to directory; and they wrongly refused to state their reasons for their decision as required by section 87 (5) of the Act of 1952. The application was refused and, on the same day, the applicants made a similar application to the Court of Appeal.

B   Pursuant to the leave of the Court of Appeal the applicants, by notice of motion dated October 10, 1979, applied to the Court of Appeal for the order of mandamus.

The facts are stated in the judgments.

Graham Clark for the applicants.
Simon D. Brown as amicus curiae.

C

LAWTON L.J.   On October 2, 1979, the applicants, Lefore Holdings Ltd., applied to the Divisional Court of the Queen's Bench Division for leave to apply for a judicial review with the object of obtaining a mandamus against the Croydon justices. That application was refused; the same day, they appealed against the refusal to this court. This court heard that application ex parte and granted leave to apply. We have been informed by D   Mr. Clark on behalf of the applicants, that on the occasion of the refusal, the court directed that the motion, in respect of which leave was required, should be heard by this court. This court clearly has jurisdiction to hear a motion in those circumstances, having regard to its own decision in *Reg.* v. *Industrial Injuries Commissioner, Ex parte Amalgamated Engineering Union* [1966] 2 Q.B. 21.

E   The matter arises out of an application for a distress warrant against the applicants in respect of their rateable occupation of some waste ground at the rear of premises in Croydon. The allegation was that they had been in rateable occupation of that waste ground for approximately a year, namely, from September 1977 to September 1978. The applicants claimed that they had not been in rateable occupation. When the summonses came F   on for hearing in the Croydon Magistrates' Court on October 18, 1978, the applicants appeared by counsel and called evidence to show that they had not been in rateable occupation. We have been informed, and accept for the purposes of this motion, that that evidence was not contested.

There was a subsidiary point in the case, namely, if they had been in rateable occupation, when such occupation had come to an end. We have been informed, and it seems to be a fact, that the rating authority accepted G   that the occupation—if there were any—had come to an end on May 8, 1978, when the National Westminster Bank Ltd. took over the piece of waste ground as tenants of Croydon London Borough Council.

At the end of the hearing on October 18, 1978, the chairman of the bench said that it would be necessary to consult their senior clerk, who had not been in court when the case was being heard, and as a result H   the case would be adjourned. The adjournment was until November 22, 1978. On that day, the chairman of the bench announced the finding of the justices that the applicants had, or could have had, beneficial use of the land in question, and that taking into account the concession made by the rating authority, the justices had decided to issue a distress warrant in the sum of £240·26 together with costs at £3·11.

The applicants were aggrieved by that finding and as a result, by a notice dated December 8, 1978, they applied to the justices to state a case.

Their contention, so we have been told, was that they had not at any A
material time been in possession of land which was of some use, value
or benefit to them, and that there was no evidence before the justices on
which they could so find. Accordingly, so the submission went, there had
been no rateable occupation.

We have been told, and again we accept for the purposes of this
motion, that at the hearing on October 18, 1978, the only contested issue
was whether the evidence called by the applicants, and not disputed by B
the rating authority, had shown any rateable occupation. It is against that
background that we have to consider the application for a case stated.

The relevant parts of the application are:

"Now Lefore Holdings Ltd., being dissatisfied and aggrieved with
your determination upon the hearing of the said information, as being
wrong in law, hereby, pursuant to the provisions of the Magistrates' C
Courts Act 1952, s. 87, apply to you to state and sign a case setting
forth the facts and grounds of such your determination including
evidence upon which the justices made their findings of fact for the
opinion thereon of the Queen's Bench Division of the High Court of
Justice."

We have been told by Mr. Clark, on behalf of the applicants, that whoever D
drafted that notice did so using a precedent in *Oke's Magisterial Formulist,*
19th ed. (1979), pp. 131–132, and numbered 41. That precedent is not
as helpful as the one which is set out in *Stone's Justices' Manual,* 112th ed.
(1980), vol. 3, p. 6174, and numbered 6. If the applicants' advisers had
followed the precendent no. 6, it is doubtful whether this application
would now be before the court.   E

The time in which the application had to be made, under section 87
of the Magistrates' Courts Act 1952, as amended by the Criminal Law
Act 1977, was 21 days. That period expired on December 13, 1978. On
that day, the justices' clerk wrote to the applicants' solicitors in these
terms:

"Dear Sirs, Further to your letter of December 8 enclosing an appli- F
cation to state case, please identify the question or questions of law
or jurisdiction on which the opinion of the High Court is sought in
accordance with rule 65 of the Magistrates' Courts Rules 1968."

That letter seems to have been posted during the Christmas period, and
as a result there was some delay in delivery. It was answered on January
10, 1979, in these terms: G

"It is our understanding that there was only one major finding of
fact, namely, that Lefore Holdings Ltd. had beneficial use or could
have had beneficial use of the ground in question as a car park and
it is that finding of fact which it is claimed cannot be supported by
the evidence before the court."

The clerk to the justices seems to have consulted the justices and to H
have given them advice and as a result, the justices decided that there
had not been any proper identification of the issue in the application to
state a case, as required by rule 65 of the Magistrates' Courts Rules 1968.
It was because of that refusal that the applicants applied to the Divisional
Court for a judicial review.

The problems which have arisen in this case are, first, was the application, dated December 8, 1978, one which complied with section 87 of the

A Magistrates' Courts Act 1952 as amended? Secondly, did it comply
with rule 65 of the Magistrates' Courts Rules? Thirdly, if it did not,
were those rules mandatory or directory? If they were mandatory, any
defects in the application dated December 8, 1978, could not be rectified.
If they were directory and not mandatory, they might, subject to the
discretion of the court, be rectified by subsequent addition or amendment.

B   It is necessary now to look at the terms of the relevant statutes and
rules. Section 87 of the Magistrates' Courts Act 1952, as amended, reads:

> " (1) Any person who was a party to any proceeding before a magi-
> strates' court or is aggrieved by the conviction, order, determination
> or other proceeding of the court may question the proceeding on the
> ground that it is wrong in law or is in excess of jurisdiction by
> applying to the justices composing the court to state a case for the
C > opinion of the High Court on the question of law or jurisdiction
> involved: . . . (2) An application under the preceding subsection shall
> be made within 21 days after the day on which the decision of the
> magistrates' court was given."

It is clear, in our judgment, that the provisions of subsection (2) are
mandatory. There is no power in the Magistrates' Courts Act 1952 to
D extend the time in which an application can be made. It follows, therefore, that if what purports to be an application in law does not amount
to an application, no new application can be made after 21 days.

The first problem, therefore, in this case is whether the application
made on December 8, 1978, was an application for the purposes of section
87 of the Magistrates' Courts Act 1952, as amended. If it were such an
application, the next problem is whether it complied with rule 65 of the
E Magistrates' Courts Rules 1968 as amended by the Magistrates' Courts
(Amendment) (No. 2) Rules 1975. The Magistrates' Courts Rules 1968
dealt with cases stated; rule 65 under those rules was in these terms:

> " An application under section 87 (1) of the Act shall be made
> in writing and shall be delivered to the clerk of the magistrates' court
> whose decision is questioned, or sent to him by post."

F
There were difficulties about the application of that rule. Those difficulties arose in this way. Applicants for a case stated were not bound to
and in general did not state the point upon which they wanted the justices
to state a case. This could lead to the justices wasting a good deal of
effort in reviewing the whole of a case when only one aspect of it was
in issue. Secondly, time was wasted by the practice which had existed for
G many years, up to 1975, whereby normally the applicant for a case drafted
it, submitted it to the respondent, who then either agreed or disagreed with
the draft. There was a good deal of coming and going of the draft between
the applicant and the respondent, and it was only after the pair of them
had agreed the draft that it was sent to the justices' clerk for the justices'
approval. All this took time, and as there were considerable delays in the
H hearing of applications before the Divisional Court, it was thought that
the procedure ought to be made tighter so that these delays could be
obviated.

It is against that background that we come to consider the changes
which were made by the Magistrates' Courts (Amendment) (No. 2) Rules
1975. Rule 2 of the Rules of 1975 provides:

> " For rules 65 to 68 of the Magistrates' Courts Rules 1968, as
> amended, there shall be substituted the following rules:—65—(1) An

application under section 87 (1) of the Act shall be made in writing A
and signed by or on behalf of the applicant and shall identify the
question or questions of law or jurisdiction on which the opinion
of the High Court is sought. (2) Where one of the questions on which
the opinion of the High Court is sought is whether there was evidence
on which the magistrates' court could come to its decision, the particular finding of fact made by the magistrates' court which it is
claimed cannot be supported by the evidence before the magistrates' B
court shall be specified in such application. (3) Any such application
shall be sent to the clerk of the magistrates' court whose decision is
questioned."

Then comes rule 65A, and the substance of that rule, which I need not
set out in detail, is that for the future, justices' clerks are to prepare the
first draft, and the old practice of letting the applicant prepare the first C
draft is to come to an end.

One of the problems which arises in this case is whether the provisions
of rule 65, as amended, are mandatory or directory. Mr. Clark, on behalf
of the applicants, has submitted that they are directory. They are essentially procedural; their object is to ensure that justice is done but done
quickly and that there is no reason to think that Parliament intended, D
when approving those rules, that people should be shut out from the seat
of justice merely because of some failure to observe one of the technical
provisions of the rules.

Mr. Brown, on the other hand, who has appeared as amicus in this
case, has called our attention to the fact that in 1975 Parliament approved
a change in the existing practice and put in its place a more stringent
set of rules, the object of which was to speed up the administration of E
justice. He submitted, in my view rightly, that the intention of Parliament
must not be overriden by any elasticity which this court, on merely
equitable grounds, might seek to apply in circumstances such as arise
in this case.

For my part I accept that this court should be chary about relaxing
what appear to be the strict provisions of the Rules of 1975. Nevertheless, F
as was pointed out by Lord Penzance many years ago in *Howard* v.
Bodington (1877) 2 P.D. 203, 211, the whole scope and purpose of the
enactment must be considered and one must assess " the importance of
the provision that has been disregarded, and the relation of that provision
to the general object intended to be secured by the Act . . ."

Now, the " general object intended to be secured " by the change in
the law was the speeding up of justice. It was not to curtail the oppor- G
tunities for doing justice. I have to bear in mind that all sorts and manner
of persons come before the magistrates' courts; some may be worldly wise,
some may have the benefit of expert legal advice, some may not be
worldly wise; others may have the advice of inexperienced lawyers. It
would be a sad state of affairs if, in matters which are mostly penal and
often include cases which involve the liberty of the subject, a mere failure H
to comply with a procedural rule should in all circumstances keep an
applicant away from the seat of justice.

It seems to me, therefore, that in considering the scope of these
amended rules, to use the words of *Bodington's* case, " the importance of
the provision that has been disregarded, and the relation of that provision
to the general object intended " by the change of the rules should be kept
in mind. Justice has to be done to applicants who may not be familiar

The Weekly Law Reports, December 5, 1980

1471

1 W.L.R.   Reg. v. Croydon JJ., Ex p. Lefore Ltd. (C.A.)   Lawton L.J.

A with the technicalities of the law. Each case, of course, has to be looked at on its merits, and in my judgment the court cannot begin to waive the strict provisions of the law unless there has been, to use Templeman J.'s phrase in *Coney* v. *Choyce* [1975] 1 W.L.R. 422, 434, a " substantial compliance with the regulations."

B The problem, therefore, for this court, as I see it, is to ask whether the application dated December 8, 1978, complied substantially with rule 65 as amended. The rule allows an applicant to raise a question as to whether there was evidence on which the magistrates' court could come to its decision, and then it goes on:

C " the particular finding of fact made by the magistrates' court which it is claimed cannot be supported by the evidence before the magistrates' court shall be specified in such application."

The problem arises whether the application of December 8 identified the kind of point upon which the justices' case was to be founded? It referred specifically to the evidence upon which the justices made their findings of fact, and that, in my judgment, to a clerk to the justices, would have indicated at that date that what the applicants wanted to D argue in the High Court was that, on the only evidence before the justices, the rating authority had not shown that they were in rateable occupation of this waste land. There could not have been any other question upon which the justices were being asked to state a case, because that was the only question at the hearing. In those circumstances, the justices were alerted to what was in issue, and they could, without further information, have stated a case on that application.

E There were unnecessary words in the application, but once again, the clerk to the justices would have appreciated—and I am sure that he did— that those unnecessary words did not take the application any further and would be unlikely to confuse the justices because there was no issue in the case other than that relating to the evidence about rateable occupation. So there was a substantial compliance, in my judgment, with the rule, and F the subsequent events and correspondence clarified the matter for the justices.

Accordingly, I would hold that the justices should be ordered to state a case.

WALLER L.J. I entirely agree. I would only add this, that we are told G that at the hearing before the justices every fact was agreed except the ingredients of rateable occupation, and the only witness called was a witness called on behalf of the applicants. When the distress warrant was ordered to be issued, they were aggrieved and they served the notice that Lawton L.J. has already quoted.

The fact that there was only one witness and only one point before the justices must have indicated clearly when that notice was received, H what the particular point was; and indeed, when one looks at the affidavit of the justices, there appears this paragraph:

" We appreciated that rateable occupation contained four ingredients, namely, (i) actual occupation or possession; (ii) this must be exclusive to the applicants; (iii) this must also be of value or benefit to the applicant; (iv) the period must not be too transient. Item No. (iv) did not cause difficulty, but we wished to give items (i) to (iii) more

detailed consideration than was possible during the time remaining A
to us on October 18 and we therefore adjourned the hearing."

We are told by counsel that items (i) and (ii) were conceded, so there only
was the one point, namely, item (iii): were they satisfied that it was of
value. Indeed, the phrase in *Stone's Justices' Manual*, 112th ed. (1980),
vol. 2, p. 3547, is, " of some use, value or benefit to the [applicant] ", and
that underlines the point that there could only be one possible interpretation B
of the notice which Lawton L.J. has quoted.

Application granted.

Solicitors: *W. G. R. Saunders & Son; Treasury Solicitor.*

B. O. A.   C

[QUEEN'S BENCH DIVISION]

* PARSONS *v.* F. W. WOOLWORTH & CO. LTD.   D

1980 April 24   Donaldson L.J. and Bristow J.

> *Justices—Case stated—Time bar—Application to state case—Draft*
> *case sent to parties more than 21 days after receipt of applica-*
> *tion—Applicant responsible for delay—Whether jurisdiction*
> *in Divisional Court to hear appeal—Magistrates' Courts Rules* E
> *1968 (S.I. 1968 No. 1920), r. 65A (as amended by Magistrates'*
> *Courts (Amendment) (No. 2) Rules 1975 (S.I. 1975 No. 518*
> *(L. 8)), r. 2)*
>
> On September 12, 1977, the Kidderminster justices dismissed
> seven informations alleging that a company had committed
> offences under the Trade Descriptions Act 1968, brought by
> the prosecutor, a trading standards officer. On September 21, F
> the prosecutor applied, pursuant to section 87 (1) of the
> Magistrates' Court Act 1952, for the justices to state and sign
> a case. By October 11, a draft case had been prepared, but at
> the request of the prosecutor, who at that time had not
> received the local authority's permission to pursue the appeal,
> the draft case was not issued to the parties within 21 days of
> the receipt of the application as provided by rule 65A (1) of
> the Magistrates' Courts Rules 1968.[1] G
> On an application by the company that the court should
> not proceed to hear and determine the question raised on the
> case stated because of the failure to comply with the time limit
> in rule 65A : —
> *Held,* that, since the draft of the case stated had been
> prepared and could have been issued to the parties within the
> time limit required by rule 65A, there had been a plain breach
> of that rule; that although a breach of that provision, being H
> directory and not mandatory, did not go to the jurisdiction
> of the Divisional Court to hear and determine the question

---

[1] Magistrates' Courts Rules 1968, r. 65A: " (1) Within 21 days after receipt of
an application made in accordance with rule 65 of these Rules, the clerk of the
magistrates' court whose decision is questioned shall, unless the justices refuse to
state a case . . ., send a draft case in which are stated the matters required under
rule 68 to the applicant or his solicitor and shall send a copy thereof to the respondent
or his solicitor."

A   raised on the case stated, the court would nevertheless decline
to hear and determine the matter where an appellant had
caused or been responsible for the delay and, accordingly, that
principle would be applied in the present case and the court
would dismiss the appeal without considering the merits (post,
pp. 1475D–G, 1476A).

    Moore v. *Hewitt* [1947] K.B. 831, D.C. and *Whittingham* v.
Nattrass (Practice Note) [1958] 1 W.L.R. 1016, D.C. applied.

B

The following cases are referred to in the judgment:

Moore v. *Hewitt* [1947] K.B. 831; [1947] 2 All E.R. 270, D.C.
Rippington v. *Hicks & Son (Oxford) Ltd.* [1949] 1 All E.R. 239, D.C.
Whittingham v. *Nattrass (Practice Note)* [1958] 1 W.L.R. 1016; [1958]
    3 All E.R. 145, D.C.

C
No additional cases were cited in argument.

APPLICATION
    On September 12, 1977, the Hereford justices sitting at Kidderminster
dismissed seven informations brought by the appellant prosecutor, P. G.
Parsons, a trading standards officer, against the respondent company,
D   F. W. Woolworth & Co. Ltd. The informations alleged that the company had offered to supply goods by means of an advertisement which
gave an indication likely to be taken as an indication that the goods were
being offered at a price less than that at which they were in fact being
offered, contrary to section 11 (2) of the Trade Descriptions Act 1968.
    The prosecutor, being dissatisfied with the justices' decision as being
E   wrong in law, applied to the justices pursuant to section 87 (1) of the
Magistrates' Courts Act 1952, to state a case. The justices' clerk prepared
a draft case which was ready to be sent to the parties by October 11,
within the time limit prescribed by rule 65A (1) of the Magistrates' Courts
Rules 1968. At the request of the prosecutor, the draft case was not issued
to the parties within the time prescribed by the Rules. On behalf of the
F   company, an application was made to the Divisional Court that, because
of the non-compliance with the time limit, the court should not hear and
determine the matter.

    Anthony Scrivener Q.C. and *Stephen Martin* for the appellant
prosecutor.
    Susan Jackson for the company.
G

    DONALDSON L.J. This matter comes before the court in the form of a
preliminary application that the court do not proceed to hear a case stated
by the Kidderminster justices at the request of the prosecutor, they having
dismissed seven informations which had been preferred against F. W.
H   Woolworth & Co. Ltd., alleging offences under the Trade Descriptions
Act 1968.
    Unless it be thought from that rather bald description of the matter
that some fearful crime was being alleged against the company, I ought
in fairness to say that the complaint in essence was that the company
had said that certain goods would be offered for sale at a reduced price.
They advertised this information in " Woman's Own " magazine which
comes out weekly, and this particular issue was dated November 27, 1976.

1474

The essence of the matter was whether the company had in fact placed   A
the goods on sale at the reduced price on the date when they should have
done in accordance with the Act. But we are not concerned with that
aspect of the matter.

We are concerned at this stage with the preliminary point that the
timetable required under the Magistrates' Courts Rules 1968 was not
complied with and what was the effect of that non-compliance. The   B
timetable is provided by rules 65, 65A and 66. Each of those rules has
as an adjunct, a separate paragraph in rule 67 dealing with extensions
of time. It is a three-stage operation. Rule 65 is concerned with the
application to the justices by the aggrieved party to state a case. Rule 65A
is concerned with the issue of a draft case and its study by the parties
making representations as to what amendments should be made. Rule 66
consists of the final settlement of the case and its submission to the   C
parties.

Let me go back to rule 65. That requires that an application for the
case stated under section 87 (1) of the Magistrates' Courts Act 1952 shall
be made in writing and signed by or on behalf of the applicant and shall
identify the question or questions of law or jurisdiction on which the
opinion of the High Court is sought. The Act of 1952 itself provides that   D
the application should be made within 14 days after the day of the
magistrates' court decision.

This decision was reached on September 12, 1977. The latest date for
making the application to the justices to state a case was September 26.
The application was made in due time by the appellant prosecutor, Mr.
Parsons, on September 21. Under rule 65A, within 21 days after receipt   E
of an application made in accordance with rule 65, the clerk to the
justices whose decision is questioned shall, unless the justices refuse to
state a case (which was not the position here), send a draft case in which
are stated the matters required under rule 68 to the applicant or his
solicitor and send a copy thereof to the respondent or his solicitor. Then
the parties have 21 days in which to make representations. The justices'
clerk was obliged within 21 days after receipt of the application on   F
September 21, 1977, to issue a draft case to the parties. That step should
have been taken by October 12, 1977.

In fact the draft case was prepared by the justices' clerk and was
ready for issue to the parties on October 11 within due time, so no
criticism can be made of the justices' clerk. However, he was asked by
the prosecutor, who was of course an officer of the local authority, to   G
delay the issue of this draft because authority to pursue these proceedings
was required from a committee of the council and the chairman was not
apparently prepared to take responsibility in the usual way for dealing
with it as a matter of urgency subject to subsequent ratification.

It was not a case of a single delay. There were several delays. There
was a great deal of correspondence. As I say, the prosecutor could not
get backing from his local authority and the justices' clerk sat on the   H
draft case meanwhile.

It would, I think, have been a matter of some criticism of the justices'
clerk if he had been prepared not to issue a draft case merely because an
applicant, and in particular a local authority applicant, chose to ask him
not to do so. It is of the highest importance that justices' clerks realise
that, closely though they may in many cases have to work with the local

A authorities concerned, they are an independent judicial authority, and local authorities are not entitled to any greater consideration than any other litigant or party to a criminal proceeding. But that is not this case because the justices' clerk was entitled to require, and did require, the prosecutor to enter into a recognisance before the draft case was sent forward to the parties. The prosecutor, who could not get backing from his local authority, was naturally not prepared to enter into the

B recognisance, so there was a perfectly good constitutional reason for this draft case not being forwarded to the parties. It was ready to be sent on October 11, but was in fact sent on November 28, well out of time.

Rule 67 (1) deals with the position where there is a failure to comply with the time limits in rule 65A, and it does so in these terms:

C " If the clerk of a magistrates' court is unable to send to the applicant a draft case under paragraph (1) of rule 65A of these rules within the time required by that paragraph, he shall do so as soon as practicable thereafter and the provisions of that rule shall apply accordingly; but in that event the clerk shall attach to the draft case, and to the final case when it is sent to the applicant or his solicitor under rule 66 (3), a statement of the delay and the reasons therefor."

D As I read rule 67 (1) and rule 65A, between them they provide a " 21 days plus " time limit, that is to say 21 days if the justices' clerk can send the draft case out within that time, and " 21 days plus " whatever may be necessary in order to enable him to send it out if he cannot. But of course on the facts of this case he could have sent the draft case out on October 11, so there is no room for any extension of time under rule

E 67 (1). It is not, I may say, an extension of time that he grants or the court grants. It is an automatic extension of time arising by operation of the rule as applied to the facts. There is a plain breach of the rule.

What is the consequence of that? As I understand the authorities under the old Rules (and I refer to *Moore* v. *Hewitt* [1947] K.B. 831; to *Rippington* v. *Hicks & Son (Oxford) Ltd.* [1949] 1 All E.R. 239 and to

F *Whittingham* v. *Nattrass (Practice Note)* [1958] 1 W.L.R. 1016), these Rules or their predecessors, and the same applies to these Rules, do not go to the jurisdiction in this court to hear and adjudicate upon a case stated; they are directory, as Lord Goddard C.J. put it in those cases, and not mandatory. Those cases do show an approach under the old Rules, and I see no reason why the court should adopt a different approach under

G these Rules, that they will decline to hear a case where the party seeking to have the case heard and determined by the Divisional Court has himself been the author of the delay or responsible for the delay in some way. That seems to me to be this case.

I agree with the remarks of Lord Goddard C.J. about the necessity for a prompt trial of criminal matters. Of course it is unfortunately true

H that the delay here is negligible as compared with the delay which has arisen in the Divisional Court list itself. No individual judge can accept responsibility for that, but collectively we must of course appear, as Bristow J. was putting it to Mr. Scrivener, in white gown, if not in sackcloth and ashes. But the fact remains that the principle that there shall be no delay by the parties in bringing these matters forward and complying with the rules is one of vast importance.

Donaldson L.J   Parsons v. Woolworth Ltd. (D.C.)   **[1980]**

For my part, for that reason I would decline to adjudicate upon the   A
case stated. We can discuss the exact form of the order and whether we
dismiss it or not, but I would decline to proceed further with the matter.

BRISTOW J. I agree.

Application allowed with costs.
Appeal dismissed.

B

Solicitors: *Sharpe, Pritchard & Co. for J. W. Renney, Worcester;*
Lovell, White & King.

[Reported by MISS ISOBEL COLLINS, Barrister-at-Law]

C

[QUEEN'S BENCH DIVISION]

* ROBINSON *v.* WHITTLE

1980 May 2   Donaldson L.J. and Bristow J.   D

Justices—Case stated—Time bar—Application to state case within
time limit—Failure to identify question of law—Question of
law identified more than 21 days after justices' decision—
Whether application nullity—Whether jurisdiction in Divisional
Court to hear appeal—Magistrates' Courts Act 1952 (15 & 16
Geo. 6 & 1 Eliz. 2, c. 55), s. 87 (2) (as amended by Criminal
Law Act 1977 (c. 45), s. 65, Sch. 12, para. 7)—Magistrates'   E
Courts Rules 1968 (S.I. 1968 No. 1920), r. 65 (1) (as substi-
tuted by Magistrates' Courts (Amendment) (No. 2) Rules 1975
(S.I. 1975 No. 518 (L. 8)), r. 2)
Animal — Bird — Protection — Offence of laying poison — Farmer
laying poison to protect crops—Whether protection of crops
defence to charge—Protection of Birds Act 1954 (2 & 3 Eliz.
2, c. 30), ss. 5 (1) (b), 4 (2) (a) (as amended by Protection of
Birds Act 1967 (c. 46), ss. 4 (5), 6)   F

The defendant, a farmer, laid poison on his land with the
intention of killing rooks and other wild birds that were
damaging his crops and eating food that he had supplied to
his pigs. The prosecutor laid an information that he had used
a poisonous substance for the purpose of killing wild birds,
contrary to section 5 (1) (*b*) of the Protection of Birds Act
1954.[1] The defendant relied on the defence under section 4   G
(2) (*a*) of the Act that it was necessary to kill the birds to
prevent serious damage to his crops and property. The justices
accepted that defence and dismissed the information.

The prosecutor applied to the justices to state a case within
21 days of their decision in accordance with the provisions of
section 87 (2) of the Magistrates' Courts Act 1952.[2] The application did not specify the question of law for the opinion of
the High Court, as required by rule 65 (1) of the Magistrates'   H
Courts Rules 1968,[3] but a further notice was filed outside the
21-day period which identified the question of law as being
whether the exception in section 4 (2) (*a*) of the Act of 1954
applied to an offence under section 5.

[1] Protection of Birds Act 1954, as amended, s. 5 (1) (*b*): see post, p. 1481G.
S. 4 (2): see post, p. 1481C–D.
[2] Magistrates' Courts Act 1952, s. 87, as amended: see post, p. 1479A–C.
[3] Magistrates' Courts Rules 1968, r. 65 (1), as amended: see post, p. 1479F.

A   On the question whether the court had jurisdiction to hear
the appeal, and on the appeal:—

Held, (1) that the provisions of rule 65 (1) of the Magistrates' Courts Rules 1968 were directory and not mandatory
and, therefore, provided an applicant complied with the mandatory provisions of section 87 of the Magistrates' Courts Act
1952, his application to the justices to state a case was not
a nullity because of a failure to comply with the provisions
B   of the sub-rule; that non-compliance with the sub-rule could
be cured at anytime before the case came before the Divisional
Court and, accordingly, since the prosecutor had corrected his
error before the hearing, the court had jurisdiction to hear
the case on its merits (post, p. 1480D–F).
Moore v. *Hewitt* [1947] K.B. 831, D.C. applied.
(2) Allowing the appeal, that section 4 (2) (*a*) of the Pro-
C   tection of Birds Act 1954 only created a defence to a criminal
offence which consisted of killing birds; that, since the ingredient of the offence created by section 5 (1) (*b*) of the Act
was the laying of poison or using an article for the purpose
of killing birds, whether or not a bird was killed by that means,
the defendant had contravened those provisions and section
4 (2) afforded him no defence to his action (post, pp. 1481F, H).

D   The following cases are referred to in the judgment:

Lockhart v. *St. Albans Corporation* (1888) 21 Q.B.D. 188, C.A.
Michael v. *Gowland* [1977] 1 W.L.R. 296; [1977] 2 All E.R. 328, D.C.
Moore v. *Hewitt* [1947] K.B. 831; [1947] 2 All E.R. 270, D.C.

The following additional case was cited in argument:

Goldman v. *Eade* [1945] K.B. 57; [1945] 1 All E.R. 154, D.C.
E

CASE STATED by Oxfordshire justices sitting at Oxford.
On December 16, 1977, an information was preferred by the prosecutor,
Peter John Robinson, against the defendant, Richard A. B. Whittle, that
he between June 22 and 26, 1977, at Northfield Farm, Burcot in Oxford-
shire, did use a poisonous substance for the purpose of killing wild birds,
F   contrary to section 5 (1) (*b*) of the Protection of Birds Act 1954, as
amended by the Protection of Birds Act 1967 and the Protection of Birds
(Amendment) Act 1976.
The justices heard the information on January 26, 1978, and found
the following facts. The defendant was a farmer between Burcot-on-
Thames and Dorchester in Oxfordshire. His farm was bounded on the
east and north sides by the River Thames. The produce of his farm was
G   partly arable and partly livestock. The arable crops were winter barley,
spring barley, maize and potatoes; in addition he had a breeding herd of
about 280 sows housed in small ark huts on an outdoor system. There
were in trees which stood on the opposite side of the river considerable
rookeries. The rooks and other birds descended from those trees in large
numbers, at times estimated to be 2,000. Those birds caused damage to
H   the defendant's crops and ate his pigs' food, causing the defendant an
estimated loss of £2,000 to £3,000 per annum. Because the trees in which
the rookeries stood were amongst houses on land which was not the
defendant's, it was not possible for him to shoot out those rookeries and,
because of the proximity of the houses, it was not reasonable for him to
use the type of scarer which caused regular explosions. He had experimented with a rotating scarer which was ineffective. There was no other
method available other than poisoning which would effectively prevent

serious damage to the defendant's crops and property. On June 24, 1977, he used for the purpose of killing wild birds, namely rooks, jackdaws and hooded crows, a poisonous substance, namely, Alpha-Chlorelose.

It was contended by the prosecutor that the acts committed by the defendant contravened the terms of the Protection of Birds Act 1954, as amended. The prosecutor's concern was not that the defendant had killed the birds but that he had used poison which was a method of killing prohibited by section 5 of the Act. He further contended that the defendant could not claim to be excepted from its provisions by virtue of section 4 (2) of the Act. Section 10 of the Act as extended by section 8 of the Protection of Birds Act 1967 created a system of licensing enabling the controlled use of poisons for the killing of birds " to prevent serious damage to crops . . . or property " and that to grant the defendant the general exception of section 4 (2) would render the system of licensing the use of poison for the killing or taking of birds included in Schedule 2 without purpose; it would thus become permissible under one section of the Act to do that which, under another section, could only be done with the sanction of a licence.

The defendant contended that his acts were excepted from the prohibition of section 5 (1) by virtue of section 4 (2) of the Act.

The justices were of opinion that the wording of section 4 (2) of the Protection of Birds Act 1954, where relevant, was clear and unambiguous. They found as fact that the only course of action open to the defendant to prevent further damage to his crops and property was to kill the offending birds by the use of a chemical poison. Despite the apparent contradiction of objectives between the general exception of section 4 (2) and the licensing system of section 10, which the justices observed had only been extended to cover serious damage to crops or other property by the Protection of Birds Act 1967, the justices could not be moved from the opinion that the general exception of section 4 (2) appeared to be clear and apparently exactly worded to exclude the defendant's liability under the criminal sanctions of the Act and, accordingly, they dismissed the information.

The prosecutor appealed. The question for the opinion of the High Court was whether the exceptions set out in section 4 (2) (*a*) of the Protection of Birds Act 1954 applied to an offence alleged under section 5 (1) (*b*) of the Act.

When making the application to the justices to state a case, the prosecutor complied with the provisions of section 87 of the Magistrates' Courts Act 1952 but failed to specify the question of law on which the opinion of the High Court was sought, as required by rule 65 (1) of the Magistrates' Courts Rules 1968, as amended. He supplied that information after the 21-day period in which to make the application had expired. The defendant took the preliminary point that, because of the prosecutor's failure to comply with the rule, the court had no jurisdiction to hear the appeal.

Robert Turner for the prosecutor.
Stewart E. Jones for the defendant.

DONALDSON L.J. In this case we are concerned with a preliminary objection going to our jurisdiction to hear an appeal by way of case stated by Oxfordshire justices sitting in Oxford. The basis of the objection is this:

A   section 87 of the Magistrates' Courts Act 1952, as amended by paragraph 7 of Schedule 12 to the Criminal Law Act 1977, provides:

> " (1) Any person who was a party to any proceeding before a magistrates' court or is aggrieved by the conviction, order, determination or other proceeding of the court may question the proceeding on the ground that it is wrong in law or is in excess of jurisdiction by applying to the justices composing the court to state a case for the opinion of the High Court on the question of law or jurisdiction involved: Provided that a person shall not make an application under this section in respect of a decision against which he has a right of appeal to the High Court or which by virtue of any enactment passed after December 31, 1879, is final. (2) An application under the preceding subsection shall be made within 21 days after the day on which the decision of the magistrates' court was given."

Within that period the prosecutor in this case, Mr. Robinson, made an application to the justices in these terms:

> ". . . being dissatisfied and aggrieved with your determination upon the hearing of the said information alleging that the said Richard A. B. Whittle did use a poisonous substance for the purpose of killing wild birds contrary to section 5 (1) (b) of the Protection of Birds Act 1954, as amended by the Protection of Birds Act 1967 and the Protection of Birds (Amendment) Act 1976, as being wrong in law, hereby, pursuant to the provisions of section 87 of the Magistrates' Courts Act 1952, applies to you to state and sign a case setting forth the facts and grounds of your such determination for the opinion thereof of the Queen's Bench Division of the High Court of Justice."

I have quoted the application fully because it complies precisely with the requirements of section 87 (1) of the Magistrates' Courts Act 1952, and it was served on the justices within the time limit provided by subsection (2). But it is said for the defendant that it was a bad notice because it failed to comply with the Magistrates' Courts Rules 1968, and in particular rule 65 (1) which reads:

> " An application under section 87 (1) of the Act shall be made in writing and signed by or on behalf of the applicant and shall identify the question or questions of law or jurisdiction on which the opinion of the High Court is sought."

G   That point was taken by the justices' clerk or somebody below, and in consequence a supplementary notice was filed outside the 21-day period, specifying precisely the point of law. Accordingly, there was compliance with the Magistrates' Courts Rules 1968, but outside the 21-day period provided by the statute. There was compliance with the statute within the 21-day period.

H   It has been held by the Divisional Court of the Family Division, in *Michael* v. *Gowland* [1977] 1 W.L.R. 296, that there is no power in the Divisional Court to extend the time for giving notice under the statute. Thus it is not open to us to regularise the situation by any extension of time. It follows that we are faced with having to decide whether the original notice was a nullity, in which case the second notice would be out of time and we would have no jurisdiction, or whether it was only irregular and, if so, whether the irregularity could be corrected by amending the original notice outside the 21-day period, provided always that the irregu- A larity was corrected before the matter came before this court.

We have been referred to a number of cases under the Summary Juris- diction Act 1879, beginning with *Lockhart* v. *St. Albans Corporation* (1888) 21 Q.B.D. 188. These cases are all distinguishable, because in section 33 of the Summary Jurisdiction Act 1879, which is the equivalent of section 87 of the Magistrates' Courts Act 1952, there was a subsection which provided: B

> " (2) The application "—that is the application referred to in sub- section (1)—" shall be made and the case stated within such time and in such manner as may be from time to time directed by rules under this Act . . ."

There is no such provision in the Magistrates' Courts Act 1952.   C

It follows that we have to consider whether the rule making body which made the Magistrates' Courts Rules 1968 had power to deprive an appli- cant of a plain right conferred upon him by the statute, or whether, when it purported to do this, it was acting ultra vires. The alternative view is that the Rules are directory, and while directions must be complied with, they do not go to jurisdiction.

There is authority, apart from principle, which suggests that the Rules D are directory. It is to be found in *Moore* v. *Hewitt* [1947] K.B. 831. In that case Lord Goddard C.J. was dealing with a different rule which required the justices to state a case within the period of three months, but he said in terms that the court had power in its discretion to allow the case to be heard and that the rule was directory and not mandatory.

In my judgment rule 65 (1) is to be treated as directory and not man- E datory. An application must be made within three weeks to comply with the terms of section 87 of the Act of 1952. If it complies with that section, but does not comply with the Rules, that irregularity can be corrected, even if it is corrected outside the 21-day period specified by the statute provided always that it is corrected before the case comes before this court. In other words the original application in this case was not a nullity. As F it was not a nullity, it can be, and has been, corrected.

BRISTOW J. I agree.

[The court went on to hear submissions on the case]

DONALDSON L.J. We now come to the substance of the case stated by G the Oxfordshire justices sitting in Oxford, against which the prosecutor has appealed.

An information was preferred by the prosecutor charging the defendant with using a poisonous substance for the purpose of killing wild birds con- trary to section 5 (1) (*b*) of the Protection of Birds Act 1954, as amended by the Protection of Birds Act 1967 and the Protection of Birds (Amend- H ment) Act 1976.

The facts found by the justices were these. The defendant was a farmer farming between Burcot-on-Thames and Dorchester. His farm was bounded on the east and north by the River Thames. The produce of his farm was partly arable and partly livestock. The arable crops were winter barley, spring barley, maize and potatoes. In addition he had a breeding herd of about 280 sows housed in small ark huts on an outdoor

A system. There were considerable rookeries in the trees which stood on the opposite side of the river. These rooks and birds from these trees descended in large numbers—by large numbers it appears we are talking of the order of 2,000.

Not surprisingly they caused considerable damage to the defendant's crops and ate his pigs' food, causing an estimated loss of £2,000 to £3,000
B a year. He had a problem because the trees in which the rookeries stood were amongst houses on land which was not his, and it was not possible for him to shoot out these rookeries. Furthermore, because of the nearness of the houses, it was not reasonable for him to use any of the scarers which produce large explosions. Apparently he had experimented with a rotating scarer. That was quite ineffective. So, as the justices found, he either had to put up with his loss and the rooks or he had to get rid of
C them by poisoning and on June 24, 1977, he did just that. He put down a poisonous substance, Alpha-Chlorelose, with a view to killing the rooks.

He was prosecuted and he raised a defence under section 4 (2) of the Act of 1954. Section 4 (2) provides:

> " Notwithstanding any of the provisions of section 1 or of any order
>   made under section 3 of this Act, a person shall not be found guilty
D >   of an offence against this Act—(a) by reason of the killing or injuring
>   of, or an attempt to kill, a wild bird other than a bird included in
>   Schedule 1 to this Act if he satisfies the court before whom he is
>   charged that his action was necessary for the purpose of preventing
>   serious damage to crops, vegetables, fruit, growing timber or any other
>   form of property or to fisheries; . . ."

E The justices found as a fact that the defendant's action was necessary for this purpose. They found that he had killed the rooks. Accordingly they held that this section applied and that the defendant had a complete defence.

I have some sympathy with the justices in reaching that conclusion. At first blush the Act might be thought to say that. But it does not in
F fact say anything of the sort. It is not as clearly drafted as it might be. In fact the general exceptions in section 4 probably apply only to section 1, rules made under section 3 and section 3 itself. But whether that is right or not, they produce a defence only to the offence of killing. The offence with which the defendant was charged was not killing. He is equally guilty under section 5 if not one single rook had taken the poison or if they had only been made ill by it, because the provisions of section 5 are:
G

> " (1) If, save as may be authorised by a licence granted under section
>   10 of this Act, any person . . . (b) uses for the purpose of killing or
>   taking any wild bird any such article as aforesaid "—including poison
>   —" whether or not of such a nature and so placed as aforesaid, or
>   any net, baited board, bird-lime or substance of a like nature to bird-
>   lime . . . he shall be guilty of an offence . . ."
H

It is the placing of the poison which is the offence, not the killing. It follows that section 4 provides no defence.

The defendant should have applied for a licence. We have been told that licences are rarely granted. That may very well be the case for obvious reasons. But this may equally have been a case where the situation is very unusual and the Secretary of State might perhaps have considered it appropriate to allow the defendant to use an appropriate poison. I say

nothing about that. My decision would only be that the justices were   A
wrong.

For reasons which are no fault of either party to the proceedings, this
is a very stale case. The decision was reached in January 1978. In those
circumstances I think, and the prosecutor does not dissent, that it would
be inappropriate to send it back to the justices with a direction to convict.
In fact the prosecutor's only interest is to secure an authoritative construc-   B
tion of the Act. That he has done. Therefore I would make no order
save to answer the question of law in terms of the judgment which I have
given.

BRISTOW J. I agree.

                    Appeal allowed.   C
         Prosecutor's costs to be paid out of
                    central funds.

Solicitors: *Baileys, Shaw & Gillett; A. H. Franklin & Sons, Oxford.*

[Reported by MISS ISOBEL COLLINS, Barrister-at-Law]   D

[COURT OF APPEAL]

* KHAN *v.* GOLECHHA INTERNATIONAL LTD.

1980 Feb. 7, 8   Bridge, Cumming-Bruce and   E
                                        Brightman L.JJ.

*Estoppel—Per rem judicatam—Issue estoppel—Decision that money
for house purchase moneylending transaction—On appeal concession by counsel that transaction not loan—Appeal dismissed
by consent—Whether issue arguable in subsequent proceedings*   F

In December 1972 the plaintiff agreed to purchase a house
from the defendant company, who were licensed moneylenders.
Pursuant to a clause in the agreement, the company on completion advanced the purchase price to the plaintiff on the
terms of a draft legal charge, by a cheque drawn in the
plaintiff's favour. A memorandum of contract was drawn
up and signed, stating that the money was advanced as a
loan and was repayable over a certain period, and a legal   G
charge was executed which provided, inter alia, that the company would not enforce the security as long as the plaintiff
repaid the principal sum by weekly instalments. The plaintiff
indorsed the cheque to the company's solicitors who in turn
indorsed it to the company. The plaintiff defaulted on his
repayments and in 1974 he brought an action seeking to set
aside the contract of loan and the legal charge. On the
issues arising, Thompson J. held that the sum advanced was   H
" money lent " within the meaning of section 6 of the
Moneylenders Act 1927,[1] and that the memorandum of contract satisfied the requirements of that section. On the
plaintiff's appeal the company served a respondents' notice
contending, inter alia, that the judge ought to have ruled that
the transaction was not one of moneylending and was outside

[1] Moneylenders Act 1927, s. 6: see post, p. 1485D.
  S. 13 (1): see post, p. 1484H.

A the scope of the Moneylenders Acts. At the hearing in the Court of Appeal, counsel for the plaintiff conceded the points raised in the respondents' notice and the appeal was dismissed by consent.

In 1977 the plaintiff brought another action against the company, claiming that the debt was statute barred by section 13 (1) of the Act of 1927. Vinelott J. held that the transaction was a loan within the meaning of the Act of
B 1927, that the plaintiff was not estopped by the concessions made on his behalf in the previous proceedings from asserting that it was a loan, and that the limitation period had expired, and he gave judgment for the plaintiff.

On appeal by the company: —

Held, allowing the appeal, that the transaction was a loan (post, pp. 1487G, 1492B, 1493D); but that the principle that issues already adjudicated upon could not be relitigated between
C the parties extended to concessions and admissions made in the Court of Appeal which led to the dismissal of an appeal by consent for they were just as efficacious for the purposes of issue estoppel as a judgment delivered after full argument; and, accordingly, since in the appeal in the previous action the question whether or not the transaction was a loan had been raised by the respondents' notice and the consent order had been made on the basis of counsel's concession that
D there was no loan, the plaintiff was estopped from asserting the contrary in the present proceedings (post, pp. 1490F–G, 1492B, 1493A–C).

Ord v. *Ord* [1923] 2 K.B. 432 and *Hoystead* v. *Commissioner of Taxation* [1926] A.C. 155, P.C. applied.

Jenkins v. *Robertson* (1867) L.R. 1 Sc. & Div. 117, H.L. (Sc.) distinguished.

Decision of Vinelott J. reversed.

E
The following cases are referred to in the judgment of Brightman L.J.:

Carl Zeiss Stiftung v. *Rayner & Keeler Ltd. (No. 2)* [1967] 1 A.C. 853; [1966] 3 W.L.R. 125; [1966] 2 All E.R. 536, H.L.(E.).

Hoystead v. *Commissioner of Taxation* [1926] A.C. 155, P.C.

Jenkins v. *Robertson* (1867) L.R. 1 Sc. & Div. 117, H.L.(Sc.).

Ord v. *Ord* [1923] 2 K.B. 432.
F *Ramsden* v. *Inland Revenue Commissioners* (1957) 37 T.C. 619.

The following additional cases were cited in argument:

Fidelitas Shipping Co. Ltd. v. *V/O Exportchleb* [1966] 1 Q.B. 630; [1965] 2 W.L.R. 1059; [1965] 2 All E.R. 4, C.A.

Greenhalgh v. *Mallard* [1947] 2 All E.R. 255, C.A.

G
APPEAL from Vinelott J.

By an agreement dated December 18, 1972, between the defendants, Golechha International Ltd. (" the company "), as vendor and the plaintiff, Mohammed Goffer Khan, as purchaser, the company agreed to sell a freehold property to the plaintiff for £8,000. Clause 9 of the agreement provided: " The vendor shall at completion advance the sum
H of £8,000 upon the terms of the attached charge." On January 22, 1973, a memorandum of contract was signed by the plaintiff and the conveyance and a legal charge were executed. Both the memorandum and the charge contained terms of repayment. The company advanced the £8,000 to the plaintiff, who paid it to the company.

By a writ dated March 22, 1974, the plaintiff began an action in the Queen's Bench Division (1974 K. No. 395) claiming that the memorandum of contract did not comply with section 6 of the Moneylenders

A

Act 1927, and that it was therefore void and unenforceable, and seeking repayment of £3,950, being moneys paid to the company under the memorandum of contract, and an order that the legal charge was null and void. On July 23, 1975, Thompson J. held that the company had made a loan to the plaintiff in the course of their business as registered moneylenders, and that the memorandum of contract complied with section 6 of the Act of 1927. The plaintiff appealed by notice dated September 1, 1975, on the ground, inter alia, that the judge had erred in holding that the memorandum complied with section 6. The company entered a respondents' notice proposing that the judgment should be affirmed on the grounds (1) that the judge ought to have ruled that the transaction was not a moneylending transaction or in any event was not a transaction arising out of the company's business of moneylending, and was consequently outside the scope of the Moneylenders Acts 1900 to 1927, and (2) that the company had a lien on the property mortgaged to or charged in their favour as unpaid vendors. At the Court of Appeal hearing on May 25, 1977, counsel for the plaintiff told the court (Cairns and Roskill L.JJ. and Sir John Pennycuick) that " . . . the point I would have to argue in front of your Lordships on the respondents' notice is not sustainable." The appeal was dismissed by consent.

B

C

D

By a writ dated July 14, 1977, the plaintiff began the present action in the Chancery Division (1977 K. No. 820) seeking a declaration that the loan and the charge were statute-barred under section 13 of the Act of 1927, and unenforceable. On March 7, 1979, Vinelott J. held that the transaction was a loan, that the plaintiff was not estopped from relying on the transaction being a loan, that the loan was made in the course of the company's business as moneylenders, and that the loan and charge were statute-barred. By a notice dated May 24, 1979, the company appealed. The grounds were, inter alia, that the judge should have held that on the facts there was no loan by the company to the plaintiff, and that the judge should have held that the plaintiff was estopped from contending that the transaction was one of loan.

E

The facts are stated in the judgment of Brightman L.J.

F

Ellis Meyer for the company.
Terence Cullen Q.C. and *Robert Powell-Jones* for the plaintiff.

BRIGHTMAN L.J. delivering the first judgment. This is an appeal from a judgment of Vinelott J. given on March 7, 1979. He decided that a loan made by the defendants, Golechha International Ltd., licensed moneylenders (" the company "), to the plaintiff, Mr. Mohammed Goffer Khan, was statute-barred under section 13 (1) of the Moneylenders Act 1927, which provides:

G

" No proceedings shall lie for the recovery by a moneylender of any money lent by him after the commencement of this Act or of any interest in respect thereof, or for the enforcement of any agreement made or security taken after the commencement of this Act in respect of any loan made by him, unless the proceedings are commenced before the expiration of 12 months from the date on which the cause of action accrued : . . ."

H

The important words are " money lent." It is common ground that there was a debt outstanding which was owed by the plaintiff to the

A company. The principal points at issue are whether that debt comes within the words " money lent "; alternatively, whether it is now open to the plaintiff (the respondent to the appeal) to assert that it was " money lent."

The facts are admirably set out in the judgment of Vinelott J. and for present purposes I can restate them quite shortly. On December 18, 1972, a sale agreement was made between the company as vendors and the plaintiff as purchaser. The agreement related to the sale of a house at Greenwich. The purchase price was £8,000. Completion was to take place in January. The property was sold subject to the National Conditions of Sale. Clause 9 provided: " The vendor shall at completion advance the sum of £8,000 upon the terms of the attached charge." I shall refer to that later. Completion took place on January 22.

C The form of the sale agreement was such that in the normal course of events completion would take place by the following steps, either simultaneously or in sequence. The first thing that had to be done was the signing of a memorandum of contract to comply with section 6 of the Moneylenders Act 1927 on the assumption, which the parties then made, that this was a moneylending transaction. So far as I need read it, D section 6 (1) provides:

" No contract for the repayment by a borrower of money lent to him or to any agent on his behalf by a moneylender after the commencement of this Act or for the payment by him of interest on money so lent and no security given by the borrower or by any such agent as aforesaid in respect of any such contract shall be E enforceable, unless a note or memorandum in writing of the contract be made . . ."

The next step logically was for the sum of £8,000 to be paid by the vendor to the purchaser pursuant to clause 9. The third step would be payment of the £8,000 purchase price to the vendor pursuant to the National Conditions of Sale. The fourth step would be the execution of F a conveyance of the property in the form of a registered transfer, as this was registered land. Lastly, the purchaser, being at this stage the owner, would execute a legal charge in favour of the vendor pursuant to clause 9.

Those steps were taken. The sum of £8,000 was advanced by the company to the plaintiff by a cheque drawn in his favour. The £8,000 purchase money was paid by the plaintiff by his specially indorsing that cheque in favour of the company's solicitors, who clearly had authority G from the company to accept the money. In due course, presumably after their costs had been paid, the solicitors specially indorsed that same cheque to the company. We know it was not in fact passed through the company's banking account, because that was unnecessary.

I will say a brief word about the memorandum of contract of loan. This stated that the £8,000 was advanced to the plaintiff as a loan and H that it should be repaid by instalments over a period of, I think, about four years. It was also provided that the principal should be repaid on demand if default should be made in the payment of any instalment. The accompanying legal charge provided that if the borrower should repay the principal sum by weekly instalments and so long as he should perform his other obligations, the company would accept such weekly payments of principal without payment of any interest and would not enforce the security thereby constituted.

The plaintiff defaulted before the year was out. So far as we know, the company did not seek to enforce the security before the plaintiff began proceedings in the Queen's Bench Division in 1974. He sued the company to set aside the contract of loan and the legal charge. His claim was that the memorandum of contract of loan did not satisfy the requirements of section 6 of the Act of 1927. The company defended the action. They argued that section 6 was satisfied. They also alleged that the transaction was outside section 6 because the sum secured by the contract and by the legal charge was not " money lent." So there were two issues which logically fell to be decided in this order. First, did the company make a loan of £8,000? If so, with the result that the Act of 1927 applied, did the memorandum of contract of loan satisfy section 6?

The matter came to trial before Thompson J. He decided the first issue—loan or no plan—against the company, but the second issue in their favour. The plaintiff was not satisfied. He appealed. We have not got the notice of appeal before us but I think that does not matter. What we have got is the respondents' notice which was served by the company. Although the company had won on what was the principal issue before Thompson J., they appreciated that the Act of 1927 is a somewhat dangerous jungle and that it would be wise to go to the Court of Appeal with more than one string to their bow. I will read the respondents' notice where two further issues were raised:

" (a) That the judge ought to have accepted the submission of the [company] and ruled that the transaction in respect of which this action was brought was not a moneylending transaction or in any event was not a transaction arising out of the [company's] business of moneylending and was consequently outside the scope of the Moneylenders Acts 1900 to 1927. (b) That the [company] had a lien on the property mortgaged to or charged in their favour as unpaid vendors."

In the event the appeal was not heard. It was dismissed by consent. The plaintiff on advice threw in his hand. His advisers took the view that, even if he succeeded on the section 6 issue, nevertheless he would lose on both the issues raised in the respondents' notice, each of which, if decided against him, would be fatal—one issue to a greater extent than the other. So the appeal was dismissed by consent. There is a transcript of what occurred before this court when the court was invited to make that order. Counsel told the court that the best he could expect would be a Pyrrhic victory, and on being asked for elucidation, he said:

" I might have been able to persuade your Lordships that the document did not comply with the Act, but I would not have been able to argue that he [sic] was not entitled in any event to a lien on the property for the amount outstanding. The thing that really clinches it from my point of view is that my friend yesterday referred me to a revenue case in which the analogy for these purposes was total, and it makes it clear that the point I would have to argue in front of your Lordship on the respondents' notice is not sustainable."

In case it might be thought that counsel for the company had been pulling wool over the eyes of counsel for the plaintiff (who was not counsel appearing before us), we were told (and I accept) that all that had happened was that the company's counsel had, in the course of normal

The Weekly Law Reports, December 5, 1980

1487

1 W.L.R.   Khan v. Golechha International (C.A.)   Brightman L.J.

A pre-trial courtesies, handed to the plaintiff's counsel a list of the authorities which he intended to have by him in court. There is no dispute that the revenue case referred to was *Ramsden* v. *Inland Revenue Commissioners* (1957) 37 T.C. 619. It deals with the complicated provisions of section 412 of the Income Tax Act 1952 and concerned a running account between a company and a director. It was a case in which the court held that purchase money allowed to remain outstanding by the vendor is not per se properly described as " on loan " to the purchaser.

B

There the matter rested until the summer of 1977 when the plaintiff again took up cudgels to escape from his obligations. This time he launched a new attack. He claimed that the debt was statute-barred by section 13 of the Act of 1927 which, as I have pointed out, contains a 12 month time limit. The claim involved two main issues; whether the relevant indebtedness arose from a moneylending transaction and, if so, whether the 12 month period had elapsed.

C

There is one paragraph of the defence to which I should refer:

D

"The [company] state that at the hearing of an appeal from the judgment of Thompson J. in proceedings between the same parties ... the plaintiff through counsel conceded that the transaction in question was neither a loan nor moneylending and counsel further conceded that he could not contest the ground in the respondents' notice under R.S.C., Ord. 59, r. 6 (2) (the respondents being the [company]) that there was in fact no loan and that the point he would have to argue in front of the Court of Appeal on that notice was not sustainable. On those concessions being made the [company] did not press their notice to a hearing and the plaintiff's appeal was dismissed, the plaintiff agreeing with the [company] to pay the costs of the appeal including the costs of the respondents' notice. The [company] state and submit that the plaintiff is in any event stopped from contending that there was any loan by the [company] to the plaintiff or that the transaction was a moneylending transaction."

E

F The action was heard by Vinelott J., as I have said, in March 1979. He dealt first with the question whether there was a loan. He decided that question affirmatively. He dealt secondly with the question whether the plaintiff was estopped from relying on the transaction being a loan. He decided the question of estoppel against the company for reasons which I shall come to. Thirdly, he found that the loan was made in the course of the company's business as moneylender. Lastly, he decided that the limitation period had expired. We are not troubled in this court with any argument on that point.

G

So the plaintiff won that round. The company appealed. We have heard argument from Mr. Meyer on behalf of the company principally directed to two points: loan or no loan, and estoppel. I will deal first with loan or no loan. In my view there is no room for doubt. The indebtedness incurred by the plaintiff was indebtedness in respect of money lent and not indebtedness in respect of unpaid purchase money. Mr. Meyer valiantly sought to argue that the handing of the cheque by the company to the plaintiff and the special endorsement of that cheque by the plaintiff in favour of the company's solicitors was merely a façade concealing the fact that there never was a loan at all, that there never was anything except an indebtedness for unpaid purchase money which, on the authority of the tax case that I have mentioned, is not a loan.

H

A   For my part, I consider that Mr. Meyer set himself an impossible task. The sale agreement required a loan to be made, and the purchase money to be paid. The memorandum of contract of loan recorded the existence of the loan. The legal charge acknowledged the payment of money lent and, although we have not seen a copy of the transfer, I have no doubt whatever that that contained an acknowledgment of receipt of the purchase money. The endorsement of the company's cheque in favour

B   of the company's solicitors by the plaintiff was an obvious method of completion because it avoided the trouble and expense of a banker's order, or, alternatively, the delay of having the purchaser's cheque cleared. To my mind the £8,000 indebtedness is not unpaid purchase money for the very simple reason that the purchase money was paid. I entirely agree with Vinelott J.'s conclusion on this point and with the way in which he expressed it.

C   I turn now to the question of estoppel. As I have indicated, in 1974 the plaintiff had asserted that the debt arose from a transaction of lending of money. In 1975, before the Court of Appeal, counsel accepted that the transaction was not a transaction of lending of money. The appeal was dismissed on that basis, so we are faced with this problem. Does that admission and the consent order so made give rise to estoppel

D   —more particularly to the brand of estoppel sometimes called issue estoppel? Or was the plaintiff at liberty, in 1977, once more to assert that the debt arose from a moneylending transaction because money was lent?

I will first read what the judge said:

E   "Next, Mr. Meyer said that the plaintiff is estopped from relying on the transaction as being or including a loan because, said Mr. Meyer, his counsel conceded in the Court of Appeal that the transaction was within the ratio decidendi of *Ramsden* v. *Inland Revenue Commissioners* 37 T.C. 619 and that the [company], therefore, throughout had a vendor's lien for the unpaid purchase price. The concession made by the then counsel for the plaintiff is, said Mr.

F   Meyer, only consistent with the view that the purchase price was not paid in full but was to be paid by instalments. The decision in *Ramsden* v. *Inland Revenue Commissioners* seems to me very remote indeed from the present case. There, moneys which in fact arose from the sale of shares were credited to a loan account of a director. Harman J. held that nonetheless repayment was not repayment of a loan within section 412 of the Income Tax Act 1952. I cannot see

G   how a mistaken view of the transaction, which apparently led counsel for the plaintiff to abandon his appeal, can by any intelligible process of reasoning found any form of estoppel."

The judge had been presented with an argument which was not based on issue estoppel at all. He was not referred to the cases which have been read to us in this court. The argument which proceeded before him

H   seems simply to have been that the plaintiff made a concession on the previous occasion as to the nature of the transaction, and he should not now be permitted to go behind it; in other words, estoppel by conduct. In this court we have been referred to a number of cases on issue estoppel which to my mind put a wholly different complexion on the company's case. I am not intending to refer to all the cases, but there are extracts from three which I would like to read. First, for the general

The Weekly Law Reports, December 5, 1980

1489

1 W.L.R.   Khan v. Golechha International (C.A.)   Brightman L.J.

A   principle, *Ord* v. *Ord* [1923] 2 K.B. 432.   I need not narrate the facts.
I will start where Lush J. said, on p. 439:

> " The words ' res judicata ' explain themselves.   If the res—the thing
> actually and directly in dispute—has been already adjudicated upon,
> of course by a competent court, it cannot be litigated again.   There
> is a wider principle, to which I will refer in a moment, often treated
B   > as covered by the plea of res judicata, that prevents a litigant from
> relying on a claim or defence which he had an opportunity of
> putting before the court in the earlier proceedings and which he
> chose not to put forward . . ."

I turn straight to the wider principle which is dealt with by Lush J.
at p. 443:

C   > " The maxim ' Nemo debet bis vexari ' prevents a litigant who has
> had an opportunity of proving a fact in support of his claim or
> defence and chosen not to rely on it from afterwards putting it
> before another tribunal.   To do that would be unduly to harass his
> opponent, and if he endeavoured to do so he would be met by the
> objection that the judgment in the former action precluded him
> from raising that contention.   It is not that it has been already
D   > decided, or that the record deals with it.   The new fact has not
> been decided; it has never been in fact submitted to the tribunal
> and it is not really dealt with by the record.   But it is, by reason
> of the principle I have stated, treated as if it had been."

The citation refers only to a question of fact, but issue estoppel has
E   a wider field: see *Hoystead* v. *Commissioner of Taxation* [1926] A.C.
155, an appeal to the Privy Council.   Lord Shaw said, at p. 165–166:

> " In the opinion of their Lordships, it is settled, first, that the
> admission of a fact fundamental to the decision arrived at cannot be
> withdrawn and a fresh litigation started, with a view of obtaining
> another judgment upon a different assumption of fact; secondly, the
F   > same principle applies not only to an erroneous admission of a funda-
> mental fact, but to an erroneous assumption as to the legal quality
> of that fact.   Parties are not permitted to begin fresh litigations
> because of new views they may entertain of the law of the case, or
> new versions which they present as to what should be a proper
> apprehension by the court of the legal result either of the con-
> struction of the documents or the weight of certain circumstances.
G   > If this were permitted litigation would have no end, except when
> legal ingenuity is exhausted.   It is a principle of law that this
> cannot be permitted, and there is abundant authority reiterating that
> principle.   Thirdly, the same principle—namely, that of setting to
> rest rights of litigants, applies to the case where a point, fundamental
> to the decision, taken or assumed by the plaintiff and traversable
> by the defendant, has not been traversed.   In that case also a defen-
H   > dant is bound by the judgment, although it may be true enough that
> subsequent light or ingenuity might suggest some traverse which had
> not been taken.   The same principle of setting parties' rights to rest
> applies and estoppel occurs."

The next citation indicates the inquiry which may be made to identify
the issue.   In *Carl Zeiss Stiftung* v. *Rayner & Keeler Ltd.* (No. 2) [1967]
1 A.C. 853, 964–965 Lord Wilberforce said:

" The doctrine of issue estoppel generally is not a new one. It   A
can certainly be found in the opinion of the judges delivered by
De Grey C.J. in *The Duchess of Kingston's Case* (1776) 20 St.Tr. 355,
538n., a passage from which has been quoted by my noble and
learned friend, Lord Reid, and an accepted re-statement of it was
given by Coleridge J. in *Reg.* v. *Inhabitants of the Township of
Hartington Middle Quarter* (1855) 4 E. & B. 780, 794, which is also
quoted by my noble and learned friend. Mr. Spencer-Bower, in his   B
work on res judicata states the principle as being ' that the judicial
decision *was, or involved,* a determination of the same question as that
sought to be controverted in the litigation in which the estoppel is
raised ' (*Res Judicata,* p. 9)—a formulation which invites the inquiry
how what is ' involved ' in a decision is to be ascertained. One way
of answering this is to say that any determination is involved in a   C
decision if it is a ' necessary step ' to the decision or a ' matter which
it was necessary to decide, and which was actually decided, as the
ground-work of the decision ' (*Reg.* v. *Inhabitants of Hartington
Middle Quarter Township*). And from this it follows that it is permissible to look not merely at the record of the judgment relied on,
but at the reasons for it, the pleadings, the evidence (*Brunsden* v.
Humphrey (1884) 14 Q.B.D. 141) and if necessary other material to   D
show what was the issue decided (*Flitters* v. *Allfrey* (1874) L.R. 10
C.P. 29). The fact that the pleadings and the evidence may be referred
to, suggests that the task of the court in the subsequent proceeding
must include that of satisfying itself that the party against whom the
estoppel is set up did actually raise the critical issue, or possibly,
though I do not think that this point has yet been decided, that he   E
had a fair opportunity, or that he ought, to have raised it."

Looking at the matter broadly, the issue of " lending of money " was
raised in the Queen's Bench action. The judge decided that there *was*
a lending of money within the meaning of the Act. The plaintiff
appealed. The Court of Appeal gave judgment dismissing the appeal.
The judgment was given by consent and the consent was given because   F
the company claimed, and the plaintiff accepted, that there was *no*
lending of money. In my view, that admission by the plaintiff, given
to the court and founding the judgment by consent, was just as efficacious
for the purpose of issue estoppel as a judicial decision by the court after
argument founding a similar judgment. The only sensible approach of
the law, in my view, is to treat an issue as laid at rest, not only if it is
embodied in the terms of the judgment, or implicit in the judgment   G
because it is embodied in the spoken decision, but also if it is embodied
in an admission made in the face of the court or implicit in a consent
order.

Mr. Cullen submitted that there is all the difference between an
order by consent at first instance founded on an admission made by
one party, which he conceded leads to res judicata, and an order by con-   H
sent on appeal, dismissing the appeal, founded on an admission made
by the appellant. The supposed distinction, as I understand the argument is based on the fact that an appellate court will not interfere with,
and without proper judicial consideration could not properly interfere
with, the decision of an inferior court. For that reason, it is said, the
dismissal of the appeal by consent cannot amount to res judicata. Mr.
Cullen supported his submission by reference to two passages from

The Weekly Law Reports, December 5, 1980

1491

1 W.L.R.   Khan v. Golechha International (C.A.)   Brightman L.J.

A   *Spencer Bower and Turner, Res Judicata,* 2nd ed. (1969). I read from
p. 39, para. 43:

> " Where a judgment or order which fulfils all the requisites of a
> good res judicata has once been pronounced, a subsequent order
> merely embodying a compromise by the parties, on appeal, of their
> rights and liabilities so adjudged, or merely purporting to rescind or
> B   set aside by consent the former judgment or order, without the court
> being called upon to exercise its functions of review, or having any
> judicial cognizance of the unofficial reversal, is not a decision at all,
> and has no effect whatever on the first judgment, which remains the
> only res judicata binding on the parties."

Page 58–59, para. 62:

C   > " When a judicial tribunal of competent original jurisdiction has
> granted, or refused, the relief claimed in an action or other pro-
> ceeding, and an appellate tribunal reverses the judgment or order
> of the court of first instance, and either refuses the relief granted
> below, or grants the relief refused below, as the case may be, the
> former decision, till then conclusive as such, disappears altogether,
> D   and is replaced by the appellate decision, which thenceforth holds
> the field, to the exclusion of any other, as the res judicata between
> the parties."

That, of course, is not this case. I go now to para. 64:

> " It should be noted here that, as has already been explained, where
> the so-called appellate ' decision ' is really nothing more than a mere
> E   registration and record by the appellate tribunal of an agreement or
> compromise between the parties, without the mind of the tribunal
> having been brought to bear on the questions so compromised, and
> without its having exercised any judicial function in the matter,
> there is nothing which can be deemed, or operate as, a res judicata."

Mr. Cullen also referred to *Jenkins* v. *Robertson* (1867) L.R. 1 Sc.
F   & Div. 117, which is the case on which those passages which I have read
from *Spencer Bower and Turner* seem to be based.

I do not think that the passages from that textbook or the case of
Jenkins v. *Robertson* are any foundation for the proposition sought to
be advanced by Mr. Cullen. They are dealing with res judicata strictly
so called and not with the wider principle of issue estoppel with which
G   we are here concerned. I refer back to what Lush J. said in *Ord* v. *Ord*
[1923] 2 K.B. 432, 443:

> " The maxim ' Nemo debet bis vexari ' prevents a litigant who has
> had an opportunity of proving a fact in support of his claim or
> defence and chosen not to rely on it from afterwards putting it before
> another tribunal."

H   In this case the plaintiff had his opportunity, in support of his appeal
on the previous occasion, of establishing that money was lent. He chose
not to establish that position. His counsel got up in court and deliberately abandoned it. So it seems to me that he loses his right of establishing that same position before another tribunal.

There is one other point. Mr. Cullen sought to persuade us that
when the matter came before the Court of Appeal on the previous
occasion there was no clear admission by counsel for the plaintiff that

1492

the transaction was not a lending of money. This is a matter of im- **A**
pression and is not susceptible of sustained argument. It is sufficient for
my purpose if I say that I regard the words which he spoke to the court
of appeal as a clear admission that there was no lending of money.

For my part, I would allow the appeal for the reasons I have stated.

CUMMING-BRUCE L.J.   I agree for the reasons stated by Brightman L.J.
The serious and interesting problem, and the only serious and interesting   **B**
problem, is the question of issue estoppel.   Brightman L.J. has stated the
law as it is now established on this topic and I do not repeat it.   I agree
with the final passage in Brightman L.J.'s judgment, but at the end of
the day the most difficult problem is the problem to determine the implication and effect of the words of Mr. Payne in the Court of Appeal
on appeal from the order of Thompson J.   As Brightman L.J. has said,   **C**
that is very much a matter of impression, difficult to elaborate by
sustained argument.   I agree with the view expressed in the first judgment on what were the implications of the concessions made.

BRIDGE L.J.   I also agree.   In the first round of litigation between
these parties, Thompson J. found at first instance that there had been a
loan of money by the company to the plaintiff.   After the plaintiff's con-   **D**
tention that there was no sufficient memorandum of that loan to satisfy
section 6 of the Moneylenders Act 1927 was rejected by the judge, the
plaintiff appealed against that decision.   The company entered a respondents' notice raising, inter alia, the issue as to whether there had in fact
been any loan.   In my judgment, when the matter came before the Court
of Appeal, the language used by counsel then appearing for the plain-   **E**
tiff was really quite definite although it was expressed by reference
to a case which he had had shown to him by counsel for the defence.
It amounted in effect to a categorical concession that he could not
contest the issue raised, inter alia, by the respondents' notice to the effect
that there had been no loan of money to his client.

The argument for the plaintiff in the present proceedings, ably
advanced by Mr. Cullen, is that no issue estoppel can be based on an   **F**
express concession in proceedings in the Court of Appeal in relation to an
issue raised by a respondents' notice which leads to the dismissal of the
appeal by consent.   It is common ground that in proceedings at first
instance a concession or admission on behalf of one party to the proceedings, or indeed a failure on behalf of one party to raise an issue which
it would be open to him to raise to defeat his opponent's claim, although   **G**
never a subject of judicial determination, can found what is known as an
issue estoppel since it leads to a judicial order.   The argument in this
court, and the kernel of the argument for the plaintiff, is that there is
a fundamental distinction between that situation and that which arises
where a similar concession or admission is made in proceedings before the
Court of Appeal.   The basis of the distinction is said to be that the
Court of Appeal will not, as a matter of practice, ever allow an appeal by   **H**
consent.   Accordingly it follows, so runs the argument, that, whatever
may have been said in the course of the Court of Appeal proceedings,
if the result is that an appeal is dismissed by consent, then the only
matters which can be the subject of issue estoppel are those matters which
have been decided by the court of first instance whose judgment has, by
the dismissal of the appeal, been affirmed.

That seems to me to be a highly artificial distinction if one bears in

A mind the basic principle on which the doctrine of issue estoppel is based.
I will not cite again the passages cited in the judgment of Brightman L.J.
from decided cases, which illustrate the application of the principle. The
basis of it is expressed in the Latin maxim " nemo debet bis vexari pro
una et eadem causa." Here the issue, loan or no loan, was in the first
round of litigation between the parties an issue raised in the Court of
Appeal which, if the appeal had run its course, would not necessarily have
B been determined by the court, but might well have been determined by
the court, as part of its reasoning in deciding whether or not the appeal
should be allowed. In the event what happened was that the plaintiff,
through his counsel, quite specifically and categorically chose to withdraw that issue from the consideration of the court on the basis that, in
relation to that issue, he was bound to accept defeat and acknowledge
C that the case against him was unanswerable. If the self-same issue were
now allowed to be raised and litigated in these proceedings, I ask myself,
would it not be a case of the company being vexed a second time in
relation to an issue which it was open to the plaintiff to have had determined in the previous proceedings? To that question, to my mind, there
really can only be one answer.

Of course it is quite immaterial that, as the judgment of Brightman
D L.J. establishes—and with this I entirely agree—the concession was in
fact quite wrongly made. On the facts I would have found, as Brightman L.J. has found, that there was a loan. The fact that the concession was wrongly made is neither here nor there. It was made. It
founds issue estoppel. It follows that the plaintiff in the present proceedings is estopped from contending that there was a loan to him to
E which the provisions of the Act can have any application.

For those reasons, in addition to those given by Brightman L.J., I
too would allow the appeal.

Appeal allowed with costs.

Solicitors: *Stuart Hunt & Co.; Syed A. Rafique.*

F   [Reported by MICHAEL HAWKINGS, ESQ., Barrister-at-Law]

[COURT OF APPEAL]

G   * WATSON *v.* LUCAS

1980 June 19, 20;   Stephenson and Oliver L.JJ.
      July 4   and Sir David Cairns

*Landlord and Tenant—Rent restriction—Death of tenant—Man
    living with tenant until her death — Man remaining at all
H   times legally married to wife — Whether " member of . . .
    tenant's family "—Rent Act 1977 (c. 42), s. 2 (1) (b), Sch. 1,
    para. 3*

The defendant was married in 1953 and there was one
child of the family. After about a year his wife left him,
taking the child with her. In 1958 he began to live with a
woman who was the protected tenant of a flat. They lived
together as man and wife, but continued to use their own
names. The defendant contributed to the housekeeping

A

expenses, but the tenant paid the rent and the bills, which were in her name. The defendant never sought to divorce his wife in order to marry the tenant, although he did refuse his wife's request for a reconciliation in about 1969. After the tenant's death, in 1977, the plaintiff, who had become the owner of the flat in 1962, brought an action for, inter alia, possession of the flat. The judge tried as a preliminary issue the question whether the defendant was a member of the tenant's family so as to be entitled to remain in the flat as statutory tenant by succession pursuant to section 2 (1) (b) of and paragraph 3 of Schedule 1 to the Rent Act 1977.[1] He held that since the defendant was at all times legally married to his wife he was not a member of the tenant's family.

B

On appeal by the defendant: —

Held, (1) that there was no rule of law that a man who remained married throughout the time that he had been living with a woman other than his wife might not become a member of the woman's family for the purpose of succeeding to a statutory tenancy under the provisions of section 2 (1) (b) of and paragraph 3 of Schedule 1 to the Rent Act 1977 (post, pp. 1499E–F, 1507A, G–H).

C

(2) Allowing the appeal (Oliver L.J. dissenting), that the facts that the defendant had remained married to his wife and that he and the tenant had continued to use their own names were of too little weight to contradict the evidence that there was a lasting relationship between them, and, accordingly, the defendant was entitled to a declaration that he was a member of the tenant's family (post, pp. 1500D, 1501E–H, 1508A).

D

Dyson Holdings Ltd. v. *Fox* [1976] Q.B. 503, C.A. applied.

Per Oliver L.J. The decision in *Dyson Holdings Ltd.* v. *Fox* rested on its own peculiar facts and stands at the very limit of any ordinarily accepted or acceptable definition of a family relationship. I would certainly not regard it as establishing a principle which is susceptible of further extension. The judge was not wrong to attribute weight to the factors which distinguish the instant case from *Dyson Holdings Ltd.* v. *Fox* (post, pp. 1506G–H, 1507c).

E

The following cases are referred to in the judgments:

F

Brock v. *Wollams* [1949] 2 K.B. 388; [1949] 1 All E.R. 715, C.A.
Dyson Holdings Ltd. v. *Fox* [1976] Q.B. 503; [1975] 3 W.L.R. 744; [1975] 3 All E.R. 1030, C.A.
Gammans v. *Ekins* [1950] 2 K.B. 328; [1950] 2 All E.R. 140, C.A.
Hawes v. *Evenden* [1953] 1 W.L.R. 1169; [1953] 2 All E.R. 737, C.A.
Helby v. *Rafferty* [1979] 1 W.L.R. 13; [1978] 3 All E.R. 1016, C.A.
Joram Developments Ltd. v. *Sharratt* sub nom. *Carega Properties S.A.* v. *Sharratt* [1979] 1 W.L.R. 928; [1979] 2 All E.R. 1084, H.L.(E.).
Ross v. *Collins* [1964] 1 W.L.R. 425; [1964] 1 All E.R. 861, C.A.
Salter v. *Lask* [1925] 1 K.B. 584, D.C.

G

The following additional case was cited in argument:

Joram Developments Ltd. v. *Sharratt* [1979] 1 W.L.R. 3; [1978] 2 All E.R. 948, C.A.

H

APPEAL from Judge Granville Slack sitting at Willesden County Court.

The defendant, Dennis Lucas, appealed from a declaration of Judge Granville Slack given in the Willesden County Court on February 29,

[1] Rent Act 1977, s. 2 (1) (b): see post, pp. 1495H—1496A.
Sch. 1, para. 3: see post, p. 1496c.

A 1980, that he was not a member of the family of Mrs. Christine Sullivan, deceased, within the meaning of the provisions of section 2 (1) (b) of and paragraph 3 of Schedule 1 to the Rent Act 1977 for the purpose of succeeding to her protected tenancy of a flat at 21, St. Julian's Road, London, N.W.6, owned by the plaintiff, Mrs. Edith Watson.

B The grounds of the appeal were that the judge had misdirected himself (1) in holding that the defendant could not become a member of the original tenant's family solely by reason of the fact that he had failed to divorce his wife; (2) in holding that the ordinary man would say that the defendant was not a member of the original tenant's family; and (3) in failing to hold that the defendant was the statutory tenant of the premises.

The facts are stated in the judgment of Stephenson L.J.

C

Mark George for the defendant.
Christopher Semken for the plaintiff.

Cur. adv. vult.

D July 4. The following judgments were read.

STEPHENSON L.J. On February 29, 1980, Judge Granville Slack declared in the Willesden County Court that Mr. Lucas, the defendant to proceedings brought against him by the plaintiff, Mrs. Watson, was not a member of the family of Mrs. Sullivan. Mrs. Sullivan had been the protected tenant of a basement flat in 21, St. Julian's Road, London, N.W.6 and was so when she died on June 21, 1977. Mr. Lucas

E had been residing with her there at the time of her death and, as the judge held, contrary to Mrs. Watson's evidence, for many years before her death. Mrs. Watson bought the freehold of the whole house, no. 21, in 1962, subject to Mrs. Sullivan's tenancy of the basement flat, and lived there on and off from 1962 to 1979. When Mrs. Watson gave him notice to quit, as she did in 1977 and again in 1979, he was there-

F fore entitled to remain in occupation of the flat as a statutory tenant by succession pursuant to section 2 (1) (b) of the Rent Act 1977 and paragraph 3 of Schedule 1 thereto, provided he was a member of Mrs. Sullivan's family. In his defence he raised that plea. The judge rejected it. He appeals against the judge's decision.

A good deal turns on this question and the outcome of this appeal

G because Mr. Lucas' continued occupation of the flat has prevented Mrs. Watson from completing work on the house which was required by the local authority; and that led Mrs. Watson to couple with her claim for possession a claim for damages limited to £2,000 and Mr. Lucas to counter-claim for an injunction and damages limited to £1,000. Those proceedings the judge has adjourned pending the hearing of this appeal.

H The statutory provisions on which Mr. Lucas relies are these. Section 2 of the Rent Act 1977 provides:

"(1) Subject to this Part of this Act—(a) after the termination of a protected tenancy of a dwelling-house the person who, immediately before that termination, was the protected tenant of the dwelling-house shall, if and so long as he occupies the dwelling-house as his residence, be the statutory tenant of it; and (b) Part I of Schedule 1 to this Act shall have effect for determining what person (if any)

is the statutory tenant of a dwelling-house at any time after the death   A
of a person who, immediately before his death, was either a
protected tenant of the dwelling-house or the statutory tenant of it
by virtue of paragraph (a) above. . . . (5) A person who becomes a
statutory tenant as mentioned in subsection 1 (b) above is, in this Act,
referred to as a statutory tenant by succession."

Schedule 1 contains these three paragraphs: B

"2. If the original tenant was a man who died leaving a widow
who was residing with him at his death then, after his death, the
widow shall be the statutory tenant if and so long as she occupies the
dwelling-house as her residence.

"3. Where paragraph 2 above does not apply, but a person who
was a member of the original tenant's family was residing with him   C
at the time of and for the period of 6 months immediately before his
death then, after his death, that person or if there is more than one
such person such one of them as may be decided by agreement, or
in default of agreement by the county court, shall be the statutory
tenant if and so long as he occupies the dwelling-house as his
residence.

"4. A person who becomes the statutory tenant of a dwelling-   D
house by virtue of paragraph 2 or 3 above is in this Part of this
Schedule referred to as 'the first successor'."

This protection was first conferred by section 12 (1) (g) of the
Increase of Rent and Mortgage Interest (Restrictions) Act 1920 by
defining the expression " tenant " to include a member of his (or her)
family residing with him at the time of his death. Section 13 of the   E
amending Act of 1933 introduced the qualification of residence for not
less than six months.

The facts are these. Mr. Lucas was born in 1933. He married at
20 and had one child, but after about a year his wife left him and went
to Ireland where later she had two more children. A few years later
he got to know Mrs. Sullivan. She was a widow with two children, who   F
had been living in this flat with her husband since 1943 and with his
children since his death in 1956. After about a year's acquaintance he
moved into the flat with her. That was in 1958 when he was 24 or
25 and she was 40, having been born in 1918. Her daughter had already
married and left home. Her son, Michael, who gave evidence for Mr.
Lucas, was then a schoolboy and continued to live in the flat with his
mother and Mr. Lucas until he married in 1964.   G

From 1958 until her death in 1977 Mr. Lucas and Mrs. Sullivan lived
together in the flat as husband and wife, and he lives there still with
another woman. The flat consists of two rooms used as bedrooms when
Michael was there, a kitchen and a hall, with its own front door and
an outside water-closet. They slept in the same bed and had sexual
intercourse, but no children. They both worked and he contributed out   H
of his earnings to the housekeeping expenses. She paid the rent and the
bills which were all in her name. They never married. He could have
divorced his wife but he never did. She was a Roman Catholic and did
not want a divorce. Indeed about 1969 she came over from Ireland and
asked for a reconciliation, but he refused: he would not leave Mrs.
Sullivan, and his wife went back to Ireland.

The judge, in the note which he based on notes of his judgment

A supplied by counsel appearing for the plaintiff and the defendant before
him and in this court, said:

> "For the most part they retained their own names, with one
> exception, regarding the ex-servicemen's club, of which Mr. Lucas
> was a member before he met Mrs. Sullivan. He could take her there
> as his wife, and she was regarded as his 'Missis.' When they went
B > on excursions, it was as Mr. and Mrs. Lucas. There is no evidence
> that he ever used her name until after her death. He used his own
> name, and usually she continued to use her own name."

This was the only respect in which they did not live as a married couple.
There was no evidence from other relations or friends as to how they
were regarded. Michael said, " It was as if they were married." Both
C the Sullivan children called Mr. Lucas " Dennis " and his mother referred
to him as " Dennis " when speaking to her son. So their relationship
was no different from that of step-father and step-son.

Was Mr. Lucas a member of Mrs. Sullivan's family? On the authority
of *Brock* v. *Wollams* [1949] 2 K.B. 388, 395, *per* Cohen L.J. the question
the judge in the county court should and did ask himself is: would an
ordinary man, addressing his mind to the question whether Mr. Lucas
D was a member of her family or not, have answered " Yes " or " No? "
We are bound by the decision of this court in *Dyson Holdings Ltd.* v. *Fox*
[1976] Q.B. 503 to place the ordinary man not in 1920 when Parliament
first used the phrase in this context, but in 1977 when Mrs. Sullivan died.
And we have also to place him in possession of the evidence which the
judge had before he gives his answer.

E *Gammans* v. *Ekins* [1950] 2 K.B. 328 would seem to have answered
the question for us, for in that case this court decided that an unmarried
man, who had lived with a tenant as man and wife for some 20 years
before her death (see [1950] 2 All E.R. 140, 141E) and taken her name, and
had no children, was not a member of her family because (as I read the
judgments) to hold that he was would be an abuse of language and would
presuppose an intention of Parliament to reward immorality with irremov-
F ability: the party to a union out of wedlock is out of the statutory
protection. But that decision was held in *Dyson Holdings Ltd.* v. *Fox*
[1976] Q.B. 503 to be no longer valid, either because it was wrongly
decided (*per* Lord Denning M.R.) or (*per* James and Bridge L.JJ.) because
it was outdated and no longer applied the popular meaning which would
guide the ordinary man's answer.

G These are only three of the reported cases in which the question who
is a member of a deceased tenant's family has been extensively canvassed
since the Act of 1920 first made an answer necessary. The hope expressed
in the most recent case in this court, *Helby* v. *Rafferty* [1979] 1 W.L.R.
13, that all these cases including *Dyson Holdings Ltd.* v. *Fox* [1976]
Q.B. 503 might be reviewed by the House of Lords, was disappointed by
the House in *Carega Properties S.A.* v. *Sharratt* [1979] 1 W.L.R. 928. It
H would, in my judgment and in Hamlet's words, be " weary, stale, flat and
unprofitable " to go through them all again. The judge went carefully
through them and Mr. George for the defendant has taken us through
them. I am satisfied that the decisive question for us is whether this
case is distinguishable from *Dyson Holdings Ltd.* v. *Fox* [1976] Q.B. 503.
It is submitted for the defendant that it is not and that the judge in the
county court was only able to distinguish it on a ground which is erroneous
in law or does not distinguish it in fact. In that case this court decided

that an unmarried woman, who lived with an unmarried man as man   A
and wife for 21 years before his death, but without children, and had
taken his name, was a member of his family residing with him at the
time of his death because, in the view of the majority, the union was
permanent and stable enough to make her a member of his family in the
eyes of the ordinary man and in the popular meaning of that phrase in
1975, or in 1961 when the man died.

That decision and its ratio have been doubted and distinguished by   B
this court in *Helby* v. *Rafferty* [1979] 1 W.L.R. 13. It was doubted
because it did not follow the earlier decision of this court in *Gammans* v.
Ekins [1950] 2 K.B. 328 on a ground which seemed inconsistent with
recognised principles of statutory construction. It was distinguished on
the facts there found by the judge; not because the deceased tenant was
(as in this case) a woman and the defendant, who claimed to be a member   C
of her family residing with her at the time of and for the period of six
months immediately before her death, was (as here) a man, but because
during their five years' cohabitation the parties never pretended to be
married and the tenant wished to remain independent, so that their
relationship lacked the permanence and stability necessary to create a
family unit. All three members of this court in *Helby* v. *Rafferty* [1979]   D
1 W.L.R. 13 regarded *Dyson Holdings Ltd.* v. *Fox* [1976] Q.B. 503 as
binding upon them, and we must do the same. To go back to *Gammans*
v. *Ekins* would be to introduce inpermanence and instability into our
own decision in this case. Only the House of Lords can reinstate
Gammans v. *Ekins* and that they have so far declined to do.

In *Carega Properties S.A.* v. *Sharratt* [1979] 1 W.L.R. 928 Lord
Diplock said, at p. 930:   E

" The facts of the instant case, if they are not unique, are certainly
most unusual, and for that reason they do not, in my opinion,
provide a suitable occasion for this House to undertake a general
consideration of what persons may be included in the expression
" a member of the original tenant's family " where at the time of
the tenant's death there did exist between him and the claimant to   F
a statutory tenancy by succession a relationship of one or other of
the various kinds to which I have referred above. In particular, the
difficult question posed by *Dyson Holdings Ltd.* v. *Fox* [1976] Q.B.
503 as to the extent, if any, to which changed social attitudes towards
cohabitation between unmarried couples and the offspring of such
liaisons may have enlarged the meaning of the expression " family " in
the Rent Act 1968 does not arise in the instant case and is best left for   G
consideration in the light of the actual facts of a case in which it
does arise."

But can it be distinguished? The judge thought it could. In his judgment
he said:

" One feature not present in any of those cases was that Mr. Lucas   H
was a married man, and so long as he was a married man he could
not become her husband in law, and I think that is a very important
factor. He deliberately chose to remain a married man. Each
remained independent of the other, each usually used his or her own
name, Lucas or Sullivan. The Lucases and Sullivans were Catholics,
and deliberately chose not to get a divorce after 1969. This is not
an easy case in which to apply the test, but I come to the conclusion

A that the defendant was not a member of Mrs. Sullivan's family, indeed could not become a member of her family so long as he remained a married man. If the ordinary man was aware of all the circumstances, he would say they were not members of the same family. Mr. Lucas never got himself in a position to marry Mrs. Sullivan. The facts have to be weighed. Mr. Lucas remained a married man, he was never a member of Mrs. Sullivan's family. The

B conclusion I reach is that Mr. Lucas was not a member of Mrs. Sullivan's family."

As I read his judgment he denied Mr. Lucas the protection of the statute because usually he and Mrs. Sullivan kept their own names and so remained independent of each other and because he deliberately chose not to get a divorce from his legal wife and so get into a position to marry

C Mrs. Sullivan. The judge seems to have regarded his married status as an absolute bar in law to his being in fact a member of her family. He was there accepting the argument of Mr. Semken for Mrs. Watson, plainly recorded in the judge's note of the evidence and argument and repeated in this court, that a man cannot have two families, Mr. Lucas had a family in Ireland and not having legally rid himself of wife and

D children in Ireland he could not be a member of another family here.

That is, in my view, a plain error of law. The ordinary man often has two families, one by his first wife and another by his second, and often has, or at any rate knows a man who has, one by his wife and another by his mistress. I can see no legal impossibility in a man being a member of both families, though he will have difficulty in fact in residing with more than one and it will be impossible in fact for him to reside with

E more than one, as required by the statute, if he is to succeed to a protected tenancy; and the question whether he is a member of his mistress' family cannot any longer be decided by any moral preference for the family to which his lawful wife belongs. There is no authority on the point, although it could have been taken in *Trowchurch Ltd.* v. *Pammer* decided on March 28, 1980, in the Bloomsbury and Marylebone County Court

F and may yet be taken on the appeal to this court which we were told is pending. But I agree with Mr. George's submission that there is no rule of law that a man who remains married throughout the time he has been living with an original tenant other than his wife may not become a member of the original tenant's family.

This error of law entitles us to reverse the judge's decision if it was wrong in treating Mr. Lucas's married status, and the retention of their

G own names by himself and Mrs. Sullivan with that one exception, as features of their relationship inconsistent with a family relationship between them in the eyes of an ordinary 1977 man.

I agree with the judge that Mr. Lucas's remaining married is an important factor, as may be the retention of the couple's own names. But not in this case. For both factors are of importance, in my judgment,

H only as indications of independence and instability. The retention of the woman's name may indicate both, as I think it did in *Helby* v. *Rafferty* [1979] 1 W.L.R. 13, but if it does not indicate either, it has little relevance to the right answer to the ordinary man's question. Without the guidance given in *Dyson Holdings Ltd.* v. *Fox* [1976] Q.B. 503, I might have thought that both factors might influence his answer, but I understand the ratio of the majority decision as holding that a union between a man and a woman, which in all the circumstances, known and unknown to

1500

the ordinary man, looks permanent and stable to him, creates a family A
unit and both parties are members of it, whether or not it consists of
more than those two. It was held long ago by the Divisional Court that
a husband could be a member of his wife's family (in fact there was a
young child, but the decision does not seem to have turned on that fact):
Salter v. *Lask* [1925] 1 K.B. 584. And we are prevented by *Dyson
Holdings Ltd.* v. *Fox* [1976] Q.B. 503 from regarding children as
necessary to constitute a family, although I think we are still permitted B
to regard their absence as a possible indication of impermanence. The
question " is there a family? " or " has he a family? " or " has he any
family? " is the wrong question, because there " a family " means or may
mean children. If this approach is right, and Mr. Lucas's decision to
remain married is not an absolute impediment to membership of another
woman's family, but a factor to be weighed with all others including their C
decision to keep their own names in every part of their life together but
one, I am of opinion that it was plainly outweighed by his refusal to give
Mrs. Sullivan up and return to his wife and by his continuing to live with
Mrs. Sullivan till she died some eight years later. The judge must have
given these two factors of names and marriage far too much weight or
this refusal to be reconciled far too little, or he could not have answered
the relevant question as he did. These two factors, in my judgment, D
are of far too little weight to contradict the evidence that this was a
lasting, indeed a lifelong association, more permanent and stable than
many marriages including Mr. Lucas's own; and I doubt if the judge could
have given them enough weight to justify his decision had he not fallen
into the error of regarding Mr. Lucas's membership of Mrs. Sullivan's
family as incompatible with his married status. E

Holding this man to be a member of this woman's family will not
promote the support of marriage or the reduction of illicit unions, which
were among avowed objects of divorce reform stated in the preamble to
Sir Alan Herbert's Matrimonial Causes Act 1937. But though those
objects might have influenced the judges who decided *Gammans* v. *Ekins*
[1950] 2 K.B. 328, they had lost their relevance to the interpretation of
this provision of the Rent Acts a quarter of a century later. Their irrele- F
vance in other fields has been recognised by Parliament; as demonstrated by
section 2 (2) of the Domestic Violence and Matrimonial Proceedings Act
1976, paragraph 3 (1) (*b*) of Part I of Schedule 1 to the Supplementary
Benefits Act 1976 and, I would add, more directly by the concept of a
family in section 1 (1) of the Family Income Supplements Act 1970, which
provides: G

" For the purposes of this Act a family shall consist of the following
members of a household—(*a*) one man or single woman engaged,
and normally engaged, in remunerative full-time work; and (*b*) if
the person mentioned in paragraph (*a*) above is a man and the
household includes a woman to whom he is married or who lives
with him as his wife, that woman; and (*c*) the child or children whose
requirements are provided for, in whole or in part, by the person H
or either of the persons mentioned in the preceding paragraphs."

The emphasis which in 1976 this court in *Dyson Holdings Ltd.* v. *Fox*
[1976] Q.B. 503 put on the permanence and stability of an extra-marital
relationship in constituting a family for the purpose of this provision, led
the court to regard the judge's answer, that Miss Fox was not a member
of Mr. Wright's family, as plainly wrong. I cannot find enough difference

A between her position and that of Mr. Lucas to allow of Judge Granville Slack's answer, that he was not a member of Mrs. Sullivan's family, being right.

I do not find it helpful to consider a couple's adoption of a common name to conceal the fact that the parties are not married to be a "masquerading" (Asquith L.J.'s word in *Gammans* v. *Ekins* [1950] 2 K.B. 328, 331) or a "charade" (Stamp L.J.'s word in *Helby* v. *Rafferty*

B [1979] 1 W.L.R. 13, 19A). Mr. Semken argued that it was essential to a family relationship that there should be a public assumption of the status of marriage by passing off or holding out; but though that may indicate an intention that the association shall last, its absence does not negative that intention and would be less likely to be thought to do so with every year that goes by.

C It was held in *Brock* v. *Wollams* [1949] 2 K.B. 388 that, where the parties could not have been granted a legal adoption, a de facto adoption might constitute a family for the purpose of succession to a statutory tenancy. So a married couple who keep their own names may constitute a family de facto when there was not and could not be a marriage de jure. If the de facto cohabitation is strong enough to repel an attempt by the

D other party to the legal marriage to put an end to the cohabitation, as in this case, I do not see why it should be prevented from being, as well as being treated as, a family relationship in its ordinary popular meaning because the couple do not pose as married persons. In spite of their separate names they would, by the time Mrs. Sullivan came to die, have come to be regarded as husband and wife, "as if they were married." That is how Mrs. Sullivan's son Michael told the judge that he regarded

E them when Mr. Lucas moved in; and that, I suspect, was Mrs. Watson's view of them which led her to pretend in the witness-box that, though she had been living in the house since 1962, she knew nothing of his living in her basement flat until a few months before Mrs. Sullivan's death.

The ordinary man has to consider whether a man or a woman is a member of a family in the light of the facts, and whatever may have been

F held before *Dyson Holdings Ltd.* v. *Fox* [1976] Q.B. 503 I do not think a judge, putting himself in the place of the ordinary man, can consider an association which has every outward appearance of marriage, except the false pretence of being married, as not constituting a family. If it looks like a marriage in the old and perhaps obsolete sense of a lifelong union, with nothing casual or temporary about it, it is a family until the House of Lords declares (as Mr. Semken reserves his right to ask them

G to declare) that *Dyson Holdings Ltd.* v. *Fox* was wrongly decided because the reasoning of the majority was wrong. The time has gone by when the courts can hold such a union not to be "familial" simply because the parties to it do not pretend to be married in due form of law.

I have no wish to extend *Dyson Holdings Ltd.* v. *Fox,* but we are bound to follow it; or to differ from an experienced circuit judge on the

H meaning and application of what ought to be plain English words, but we are bound to move with the times.

I would accordingly hold, not without reluctance, that the judge's decision was wrong. I would allow the appeal and declare that Mr. Lucas was a member of Mrs. Sullivan's family.

OLIVER L.J. The question raised on this appeal is a short and at first sight a simple one. It is whether, in the circumstances which have already

been stated in the judgment of Stephenson L.J., the defendant, who had A
lived on terms of intimacy for some 20 years with the tenant of the
basement flat at the plaintiff's premises at 21, St. Julian's Road, N.W. 6.
until the tenant's death in 1977, was a member of the tenant's family. If
he was then, under the provisions of the third paragraph of Part 1 of
Schedule 1 to the Rent Act 1977, he is entitled to continue to occupy the
flat as a statutory tenant in succession to her. If he was not, as the judge
held, then the plaintiff is entitled to possession of the flat and the appeal B
must be dismissed.

The particular provision under which the defendant claims to remain
in the premises as the successor to the original tenant is one which has
formed part of the Rent Act legislation in substantially, although not
exactly, the same form since 1920 and it has been the subject of judicial
construction in a number of cases. One of the curiosities of the statutory C
provisions is that whilst they cater expressly for the position of the widow
of the tenant residing with him at his death, there is no corresponding
reference to a widower, so that if he is given any protection at all it is
solely as a member of his late wife's " family." It was, however, held as
long ago as 1925 that the expression " family " was apt to include the
surviving husband of the tenant: see *Salter* v. *Lask* [1925] 1 K.B. 584.

The matter was taken a stage further in 1949 in *Brock* v. *Wollams* D
[1949] 2 K.B. 388 in which the expression " family " was held to include
an informally adopted child and in 1953 in *Hawes* v. *Evenden* [1953] 1
W.L.R. 1169, a unanimous Court of Appeal held that an unmarried lady
who had lived with the tenant for 12 years prior to his death and had
had two children by him, was entitled, in the circumstances that she and
the children were living together with him as one family unit, to be E
considered a member of his family. It is clear, however, that in that case
the conclusive features were the birth of the children and the establishment
and continuance of what the ordinary man would regard as a single
family unit.

The court there applied the test propounded by Cohen L.J. in *Brock*
v. *Wollams* [1949] 2 K.B. 388, namely, would the ordinary man answer F
" yes " or " no " to the question whether the person claiming the protection of the Act was a member of the tenant's " family." *Hawes* v.
Evenden [1953] 1 W.L.R. 1169 answered a question which had been left
unanswered in the earlier decision of *Gammans* v. *Ekins* [1950] 2 K.B.
328. In that case, in which the position was uncomplicated by the birth
of any children, the Court of Appeal firmly and unanimously rejected a
claim by a man who, although unmarried, had lived with the tenant for G
some years prior to her death as her husband to be a member of her
family.

Had the matter rested there, the instant case would have presented
no difficulty and, speaking for myself, I should, even unassisted by
authority, have required little argument to persuade me to the same
conclusion as that reached in *Gammans* v. *Ekins*. In 1976 however a very H
similar case came before the Court of Appeal again in *Dyson Holdings
Ltd.* v. *Fox* [1976] Q.B. 503. That was a very hard case of an elderly
lady of 74 who, although unmarried in fact, had lived with the tenant to
all outward appearances as his wife for 40 years until his death in 1961.
The 21 years immediately preceding his death were spent in the premises
of which possession was sought and she had continued to reside there
after his death up to the date of the hearing. She had taken the tenant's

A name and, as Lord Denning M.R. expressed it, at p. 507, "In every respect they were man and wife save that they had not gone through a ceremony of marriage." The court held unanimously that she was a member of the tenant's family and the majority decision (that of James and Bridge L.JJ.) was based upon two propositions, that is to say, first that the word "family" fell to be construed, not according to its accepted meaning at the time when the legislation was enacted, but (at any rate,

B as I read the majority judgments) according to its accepted meaning at the time of the hearing; and secondly that there had, since *Gammans* v. *Ekins* [1950] 2 K.B. 328 taken place such a change in social attitudes as to justify the conclusion that the ordinary man would, given a sufficient degree of apparent stability and permanence in an extra-marital relationship, say that the parties to it were members of one another's "family."

C In this way the court, whilst accepting that *Gammans* v. *Ekins* was binding upon it, felt able to distinguish that case from the case before it. One of the curious features of the case is that, although the tenant in that case had died in 1961 (which would have appeared, prima facie, to be the appropriate time for deciding whether the defendant was a member of his family) the court seems to have disregarded the fact that between

D 1961 and the hearing the Court of Appeal had, in 1964, considered *Gammans* v. *Ekins* in *Ross* v. *Collins* [1964] 1 W.L.R. 425 and had unanimously followed and applied it. *Ross* v. *Collins* was cited in *Dyson Holdings Ltd* v. *Fox* [1976] Q.B. 503 but does not appear to have been referred to in any of the judgments. So what the court actually did in 1975 was to apply to the word "family" in the context of the tenant's death in 1961 a meaning contrary to that which had subsequently been

E applied to it as the correct meaning by the Court of Appeal in 1964.

It is, I think, true to say that the ratio of *Dyson's* case has not met with universal approbation. In particular in *Helby* v. *Rafferty* [1979] 1 W.L.R. 13 the Court of Appeal expressed certain reservations about the approach to construction adopted by the court in *Dyson Holdings Ltd.* v. *Fox* [1976] Q.B. 503. However, it recognised that *Dyson's* case was

F binding upon it (although it distinguished the case before it on the facts).

Although I think that in the light of *Ross* v. *Collins* [1964] 1 W.L.R. 425 it is arguable (I put it no higher) that there are in fact two conflicting decisions of the Court of Appeal as to the meaning to be applied to the word, this was not argued before us and I am content to adopt the starting position in the instant case that *Dyson's* case is binding upon this court. The only question is whether the judge was right in distinguishing

G it. What he had to do was to ask himself the question, "In the circumstances of the instant case would the ordinary man, cognisant of the relevant facts, say that the defendant in *this* case was a member of the tenant's family?"; and in asking himself that question he had to bear in mind the way in which the matter was put by Bridge L.J. in *Dyson's* case when he said [1976] Q.B. 503, 513:

H "The ordinary man in 1975 would, in my opinion, certainly say that the parties to such a union, provided it had the appropriate degree of apparent permanence and stability, were members of a single family whether they had children or not."

The instant case is markedly similar in many respects to *Dyson's* case. The parties had shared the same dwelling for many years, each contributing to the household expenses and there was every outward indication that, had it not been for the tenant's death, they would have gone on

1504

living together indefinitely. It differs from *Dyson's* case, however, in   A
three respects. First it was the female partner who was the tenant and
the male who survived. Secondly, neither party sought, save on occasions
when they went together to, or on outings organised by, a club of which
the defendant was a member, to convey the impression that their
relationship was anything other than an extra-marital one. The tenant
was a widow and continued to be known by her married name of "Mrs.
Sullivan." The defendant continued to be known as "Mr. Lucas."   B
Thirdly, whereas the parties in *Dyson's* case were a bachelor and a spinster
respectively and thus able to marry if they wished, the defendant in the
instant case was, at all material times, a married man with a wife and
child living in Ireland. His evidence was that his wife had left him about
a year after his marriage (which had taken place some five years before
he went to live with Mrs. Sullivan) taking the child of the marriage with   C
her. She had two further children by another man in Ireland but in
about 1969 she came back to him seeking a reconciliation which he
declined. He continued to live with Mrs. Sullivan and his wife returned
to Ireland. She, apparently, was a Roman Catholic and did not want a
divorce, and he took no steps to obtain one although he was aware that
he could petition on the ground of five years' separation.

It was this last matter to which the judge attached particular   D
importance. I do not think that it was argued that the first ground of
distinction which I have mentioned carried any weight and the judge does
not mention it. That clearly, I think, must be right because the test
enunciated in *Dyson's* case clearly cannot depend for its application upon
whether the survivor is male or female. He does appear to have taken
some account of the fact that they normally and habitually used their   E
own names. But the matter to which he attached very great importance
was the fact that the defendant remained, at his own election, a married
man. He said:

"... so long as he was a married man he could not become her
husband in law, and I think that is a very important factor. He
deliberately chose to remain a married man. Each remained   F
independent of the other, each usually used his or her own name,
Lucas or Sullivan. The Lucases and Sullivans were Catholics, and
deliberately chose not to get a divorce after 1969."

The judge then continued—and this is the passage in his judgment
which is particularly criticised by the defendant:

"This is not an easy case in which to apply the test" (that is the   G
test of what the ordinary man would conclude) "but I come to the
conclusion that the defendant was not a member of Mrs. Sullivan's
family, indeed could not become a member of her family so long as
he remained a married man."

What is said about this is that this shows that the judge misdirected
himself because, instead of looking, as *Dyson's* case directs him to do, at   H
the question of whether as a matter of *fact* the relationship was one of
such stability and permanence as to justify the inference that the parties
were members of each other's "family," he considered only the legal
impediment to their actually marrying and treated that, as a matter of
law, as an insurmountable impediment. It is, I think, dangerous to seek
to construe a judgment—and, particularly, an ex tempore judgment—as
if it were a statute and I do not, for my part, put upon it the interpretation

A for which the defendant contends. The reference to the inability of the defendant to become a member of the tenant's family appears to have been something of an after-thought and I do not read it as more than a consideration which the judge treated as reinforcing the conclusion of fact at which he had arrived. One has to bear in mind that this passage came at the conclusion of two pages of notes of judgment in which the judge exhaustively reviewed the facts which had been proved, a review

B which would have been wholly unnecessary if the judge had really taken the view that a decision in the defendant's favour was precluded by what would, on this view, have been the only relevant fact, namely that he remained married to someone else. That it formed a very important factor in his decision, however, is beyond doubt, and the real question on this appeal is, as it seems to me, whether he was right to attribute any

C weight to it and, if so, whether he attached undue weight to it. Now the essential question was one of fact: was the relationship one which displayed the requisite qualities of *apparent* permanence and stability not simply to constitute what the ordinary man might categorise as a permanent relationship but to constitute what he would categorise as a de facto *family* relationship? In reaching the answer to that question I do not think that the judge was wrong to take into account both the

D manner in which the parties to the relationship treated themselves and their actual status. In the instant case the defendant and Mrs. Sullivan never appear (except for the purely temporary purpose of satisfying the social susceptibilities of the other members of the defendant's club) to have sought to convey to the world at large any impression that they were other than what they were in fact, that is to say, two people who were

E not husband and wife but had chosen to live together. As I read the judge's judgment he did attach some significance to this and I do not, for my part, think that he was wrong to do so. Whilst it may seem startling at first to attribute to persons who engage in a masquerade a higher status than that attributable to persons who do not seek to pose as other than what in fact they are, such a step is, to some extent, inherent in the very process of attributing the status of " family " to those who

F do not in fact possess it. Normally one expects members of a family to be related by blood or marriage and the application of the term to what are loosely called de facto relationships involves the artificial attribution to the persons concerned of a blood or de jure relationship which they do do not in fact possess. In reaching a decision, therefore, whether the case is a proper one in which to make such an attribution, having regard to what

G the ordinary man would conclude, it cannot I think be irrelevant to consider how the parties treated themselves and whether they themselves manifested any desire to be so treated vis-à-vis their friends and neighbours by publicly assuming the appearance and incidents of a family unit. If they themselves openly treated themselves as engaged only in a concubinage which each was free to continue or not and from which each

H was free to withdraw at will and without obligation, then this does appear to me to be at least a factor to be taken into account in considering whether (to apply the test propounded by Bridge L.J. in *Dyson's* case) the relationship had a sufficient degree of apparent permanence. That is not to say that pretence is a virtue but merely that one should not be too ready to accord to persons in the position of the defendant and Mrs. Sullivan in the instant case the incidents of a status which they never sought to claim for themselves. Equally, they did not seek to put

themselves in a position in which they could commit themselves A
de jure to a permanent relationship involving mutual obligations,
although they knew that they could do so and the judge inferred
from this that they had elected to preserve their independence. Of
course, the same could be said of the parties in *Dyson Holdings Ltd.* v.
Fox [1976] Q.B. 503 and thus it is argued that there is no valid distinction
between the two cases. In the ultimate analysis, however, the question
is, what would the ordinary man conclude in the circumstances of the B
particular case? Here the defendant had, at all material times, a de jure
wife who was alive and who, as a matter of law constituted, with the child
of his marriage, his family, so that the case raises directly for decision the
question which was postulated by counsel in the *Dyson's* case [1976] Q.B.
503, 507 and not specifically answered by the Court of Appeal. That
position he elected to continue and the ordinary man could, I think, be C
pardoned if he concluded that the defendant was intending, for whatever
reason, social, religious, economic, or merely idiosyncratic, to preserve the
familial status which the law and his Church had imposed upon him by
his marriage rather than to substitute a different and de facto familial
relationship to which he was not prepared to commit himself de jure or
even as a matter of outward semblance. Mr. George has drawn our D
attention to the provisions of the Supplementary Benefits Act 1976 and
the Domestic Violence and Matrimonial Proceedings Act 1976 to support
the submission that the legislature, in concurrence with current social
mores, now recognises extra-material relationships such as that with which
the instant case is concerned as deserving of the law's protection. But
I am not, speaking for myself, much impressed by that argument, because
the question is not whether the law will now countenance relationships E
which might previously have been disapproved, but whether the ordinary
man would regard the relationship between a man and his concubine of
many years as being a " family " relationship. Indeed the argument is a
double-edged one, for if we are to have reference to other statutes, it
can with equal force be pointed out that when the legislature in 1975
came to extend the ambit of the Inheritance (Family Provision) Act 1938 F
to persons in the position of, for instance, Mrs. Sullivan in the instant
case, it felt it necessary to alter the title to the Inheritance (Provision for
Family *and Dependants*) Act. I cannot help feeling that if the defendant
had, for instance, gone to a solicitor in 1976 in order to have a will
prepared and had been asked " Have you any family? " his answer would
have been, " Yes, I have a wife and child in Ireland but I have not seen
them for years and I want to leave my property to a lady with whom I G
am living."

Essentially every case of this kind turns upon its own facts and the
impression that these facts make upon the mind of the judge assuming for
the purpose the mantle of the ordinary man. Speaking for myself I would
regard the decision in *Dyson Holdings Ltd.* v. *Fox* [1976] Q.B. 503 as one
which rested on its own peculiar facts and as standing at the very limit H
of any ordinarily accepted or acceptable definition of a family relationship.
I would certainly not regard it as establishing a principle which is
susceptible of further extension or which ought to be extended. The
judge in the instant case had the difficult task of applying to the facts
before him a test which, though neither an easy one nor a certain one,
is certainly one which required him to consider all the available factors.
The decision was essentially one which depended on the inferences to be

A   drawn from all of the facts before him, which included the fact that the defendant was and remained by choice married to a lady who was living at the material time and who was the mother of his only child.

    If and so far as the judge was of opinion that the continued existence of the defendant's marriage was, in itself, and by itself, an absolute answer in law to his claim, I respectfully disagree. I think, however, that it was one factor, and a not unimportant factor, to be taken into account,

B   although I accept that a man may sometimes have two families. One possible inference to be drawn from it was that, however agreeable and convenient his relationship with Mrs. Sullivan may have been, he was not prepared to make himself responsible for her maintenance and support indefinitely or to put himself in a position in which he might have become susceptible to pressure to convert the relationship into a

C   permanent one by marrying her. I have to confess to more than one change of mind during the course of the very full arguments presented to us, but I have concluded, not without hesitation, that I am not prepared to say that the judge, who saw and heard the witnesses, in making his assessment as a whole and in reaching the conclusion which he did reach on all the facts, was wrong to attribute weight to the factors which I

D   have mentioned. They are, in my judgment, factors which do distinguish the instant case from *Dyson Holdings Ltd.* v. *Fox* [1976] Q.B. 503 and I would dismiss the appeal.

    SIR DAVID CAIRNS. I do not find Cohen L.J.'s test as helpful in this case as it was in *Brock* v. *Wollams* [1949] 2 K.B. 388. To the question " Was Mr. Lucas a member of Mrs. Sullivan's family," I have no idea

E   what " an ordinary man " would answer. Stephenson L.J. would answer " Yes " and Oliver L.J. would answer " No."

    I agree with both my brethren that we should proceed on the basis that *Dyson Holdings Ltd.* v. *Fox* [1976] Q.B. 503 was rightly decided, though I respectfully share the doubts that have been expressed about that decision and I recognise the force of the reasoning of Oliver L.J.

F   based on *Ross* v. *Collins* [1964] 1 W.L.R. 425.

    I have reached the conclusion that this case cannot sensibly be differentiated from *Dyson Holdings Ltd.* v. *Fox* [1976] Q.B. 503. I attach little or no importance to the continued use by Mr. Lucas and Mrs. Sullivan of different surnames. It is the relations between the man and the woman that are relevant rather than the appearance that they present to the public. In this case the permanence of the relationship is not in

G   doubt.

    That Mr. Lucas had a wife in Ireland is to my mind, having regard to the brevity of cohabitation, the long separation and the refusal by Mr. Lucas of reconciliation, neither an absolute bar to his being considered a member of Mrs. Sullivan's family nor a weighty reason for finding as a fact that he should not be so considered. Even if he could be regarded

H   as a member of his wife's family (which I doubt) I agree with Stephenson L.J. that it is perfectly possible for a man to be a member of more than one family.

    In my opinion the judge was wrong in law in holding that the very fact of Mr. Lucas's continuing state of marriage prevented him being a member of Mrs. Sullivan's family. If this part of his judgment cannot strictly be considered to be one of the rationes decidendi I think it

coloured his approach to the question of fact and led him to attach   **A**
excessive weight to that matter.

For these reasons I agree with Stephenson L.J. that the appeal should
be allowed.

                              Appeal allowed with costs.
                              Legal aid taxation of defendant's
                                 costs.   **B**
                              Declaration that defendant member
                                 of Mrs. Sullivan's family for
                                 purposes of Rent Act 1977.
                              Leave to appeal.

Solicitors: *Powell Magrath & Co.; Sylvester, Amiel & Co.*   **C**

                                               R. C. W.

                                      ———————   **D**

                        [QUEEN'S BENCH DIVISION]

         * G.U.S. MERCHANDISE CORPORATION LTD. *v.*
            CUSTOMS AND EXCISE COMMISSIONERS

1980   March 17, 18; 20   Woolf J.   **E**

       Revenue—Value added tax—Gift of goods under £10—Company
       operating special retail schemes—Associated mail order com-
       pany supplying goods without charge to agents under incentive
       scheme—Assessment by commissioners including tax on open
       market value of incentive supplies—Whether company account-
       able to tax on such supplies—Whether such supplies exempt
       as gifts—Finance Act 1972 (c. 41), Sch. 3, para. 6   **F**

         The appellant company G.U.S. was the nominated repre-
      sentative of a value added tax sub-division of a group of
      companies of which a retail mail order company, B.M.O.C.,
      was a member. G.U.S. operated special retail scheme 4 con-
      tained in Customs notice 707, and later special retail scheme
      H contained in Customs notice 727, issued pursuant to
      regulation 2 of the Value Added Tax (Supplies by Retailers)   **G**
      Regulations 1972 [1] and section 30 (3) of the Finance Act 1972.[2]
      Under the schemes a company's liability to output tax was
      calculated on the value of its gross receipts instead of on each
      taxable supply. B.M.O.C. encouraged the recruitment of new
      agents through an incentive scheme which included sending
      items valued at less than £10 free of charge to new agents who
      had placed a first order, worth at least £10, with the company.
      G.U.S. did not account for the inducements to agents as out-   **H**
      puts in its value added tax returns in reliance on the inducements
      being gifts not exceeding £10 and hence valued at nil for value
      added tax purposes by virtue of paragraph 6 of Schedule 3
      to the Act. G.U.S. further justified its failure to include the
      value of the inducements in its returns by the absence from the

    [1] Value Added Tax (Supplies by Retailers) Regulations 1972, reg. 2: see post,
p. 1515G–H.
    [2] Finance Act 1972, s. 30 (3): see post, p. 1515D–F.

The Weekly Law Reports, December 12, 1980

1509

1 W.L.R.   G.U.S. Merchandise Ltd. v. Customs & Excise (Q.B.D.)

A   special retail schemes of any express reference to such inducements and the absence of any requirement to record them
(although the schemes made special provision for certain other
activities). The Customs and Excise Commissioners made
two assessments to output tax on the open market value in
respect of the incentives in accordance with section 10 (3) of
the Finance Act 1972. G.U.S. appealed against the assessments
to a value added tax tribunal. The tribunal, dismissing the
B   appeal, found that the supplies were taxable supplies and not
gifts; that they did not come within the special retail schemes
as they did not form part of the retail stock of B.M.O.C.; and
that tax was chargeable on them in addition to the tax liability
in respect of the gross receipts of G.U.S.

      On appeal by G.U.S.: —

      Held, dismissing the appeal, (1) that the goods supplied
under the incentive scheme were not gifts, but were supplied in
C   consideration of the agents agreeing to act as such and placing
their orders; that the nature of the transactions was therefore
contractual and, accordingly, they were not gifts within the
meaning of paragraph 6 of Schedule 3 to the Finance Act 1972
(post, p. 1514D, G).

      Esso Petroleum Co. Ltd. v. *Customs and Excise Commis-
sioners* [1976] 1 W.L.R. 1, H.L.(E.) distinguished.

      (2) That, on their true construction, the Customs notices
D   were not exhaustive and were intended to deal with retail
sales; that the supply of goods as incentives was not a sale and
that therefore the supplies, as taxable supplies, had to be
assessed on their open market value in accordance with section
10 (3) of the Finance Act 1972 (post, pp. 1518F, 1519A).

    The following cases are referred to in the judgment:

E   *Chappell & Co. Ltd.* v. *Nestlé Co. Ltd.* [1960] A.C. 87; [1959] 3 W.L.R.
      168; [1959] 2 All E.R. 701, H.L.(E.).

Esso Petroleum Co. Ltd. v. *Customs and Excise Commissioners* [1976]
      1 W.L.R. 1; [1976] 1 All E.R. 117, H.L.(E.).

    No additional cases were cited in argument.

F   APPEAL from value added tax tribunal.

    G.U.S. Merchandise Corporation Ltd. (" G.U.S."), the nominated
representative of a value added tax subdivision of a group of companies
of which British Mail Order Corporation Ltd. (" B.M.O.C.") was a
member, appealed to the Manchester Value Added Tax Tribunal, against
two assessments to value added tax made by the Customs and Excise Commissioners in respect of items supplied free of charge by B.M.O.C. as
G   inducements to prospective mail order agents.

    The treatment for value added tax purposes of those inducements
had been discussed by the company secretary of G.U.S. and officers of the
commissioners before the relevant legislation came into operation. The
tribunal found that, at the meeting, the company secretary was told in
relation to inducement awards that goods costing less than £10 could be
H   treated as gifts, but that that was not the meaning which the officers
intended to convey.

    The tribunal held, inter alia, that except for certain items of negligible
value, goods supplied under the incentive scheme were supplied under
legally enforceable contracts and value added tax was chargeable on them;
that the incentive supplies were acquired by way of bulk purchase direct
from a manufacturer and that their administration was handled by a
separate department dealing with the appointment of agents, and that

they did not form part of the retail stock of B.M.O.C., and that therefore **A**
they did not fall to be included in special retail scheme 4 or H.

G.U.S. appealed on the grounds, inter alia, (i) that the tribunal erred in
law and misdirected itself in holding that the incentive supplies were not
gifts, the cost of which did not exceed £10, within paragraph 6 of Schedule
3 to the Finance Act 1972; (ii) that the tribunal erred in law and misdirected itself in holding that the inducements were not part of the retail
stock of B.M.O.C. within the terms of the special retail schemes contained **B**
originally in scheme 4 of Customs notice 707 and later in scheme H of
Customs notice 727, and that G.U.S. was liable to account for value added
tax outside the normal gross receipts basis of those schemes; and (iii) that
the tribunal misdirected itself in finding as a fact that the inducements
were not part of the retail stock of B.M.O.C. there being no evidence to
support such a finding. **C**

The facts are stated in the judgment.

Stewart Bates Q.C. and *Reginald Nock* for G.U.S.
Andrew Collins for the commissioners.

WOOLF J. This is an appeal under section 13 of the Tribunals and **D**
Inquiries Act 1971 against a decision of the Manchester Value Added
Tax Tribunal made on April 10, 1978.

There are two principal points raised on the appeal. The first is whether
or not the supply of certain goods, the cost of which did not exceed £10,
by the appellant company as inducements to people to become or to
remain agents of the appellant company's mail order business, were gifts
of goods to which paragraph 6 of Schedule 3 to the Finance Act 1972 **E**
applies, so that the value of the supply was to be treated as nil with the
result that no value added tax was chargeable in respect thereof.

The second is whether, assuming that the supply did not fall within
the provisions of paragraph 6 of Schedule 3 to the Act, the goods were
nonetheless supplied under the special schemes for retailers in consequence
of which the amounts of value added tax payable by the appellant company **F**
in respect of goods supplied without charge as inducements would not in
practice be increased.

The tribunal had before it both written and oral evidence and the facts
found by the tribunal can be summarised as follows. The appellant company is a subsidiary company of the Great Universal Stores Ltd. group
and is the nominated representative of a value added tax sub-division of
the group. The appeal arises in connection with the affairs of British Mail **G**
Order Corporation Ltd. (" B.M.O.C."), a subsidiary of Great Universal
Stores Ltd. and the largest member of the group. B.M.O.C. carries on a
mail order retail business using catalogues under a number of names, and
it has over one million agents acting in connection with its business.

As from April 1, 1973, the appellant company had been operating one
of the special schemes for retailers. Initially this was scheme 4 as contained **H**
in Customs notice 707, but in 1975 was re-categorised as scheme H with a
few alterations, by Customs notice 727.

Catalogues are issued twice yearly, normally in January and July.
The catalogues usually exceed 900 pages and are distributed to agents
who are normally housewives selling to their relatives and friends on a
part-time basis, but also purchasing goods on their own account. The
agents are remunerated by way of 10 per cent. commission upon their

The Weekly Law Reports, December 12, 1980

1511

1 W.L.R.   G.U.S. Merchandise Ltd. v. Customs & Excise (Q.B.D.)   Woolf J.

A sales, and purchases made by them on their own account are treated as being supplied at a 10 per cent. discount. Having persuaded relatives and friends to agree to purchase goods from the catalogue, the orders are posted to the agent by the mail order house. The vast majority of sales are on credit so the agent is substantially responsible for collection and remission of the instalments of the purchase price. Since dealings are so much on credit, the financial stability of a potential agent is of great importance and
B some degree of scrutiny is exercised over persons applying for appointments as agents in order to ensure their suitability. The credit-worthiness of agents' customers however, is not scrutinised and business is conducted on the assumption that if an agent is reliable, her friends and contracts from whom she finds her customers are likely to be equally reliable.

A major pre-occupation of the group is the recruitment and retention
C of good agents. The body of agents is not stable and there is a steady turnover of agencies. There is also a need to continue expanding and increasing the number of agents and not merely replacing those who cease to be active for whatever reason. There are five basic methods by which the group expands its body of agents. Nearly all of them include the provision by the group of inducements or incentives, which are normally
D described in the promotional literature as free gifts. These gifts, in fact, appear to have an incentive effect and promote the enthusiasm of existing or prospective agents. The five methods referred to above may be summarised as advertising for new agents; recommendation by existing agents; resuscitation of former or inactive agents; direct recruitment by the mail order house's own staff; and finally, chance. Each of the methods, apart from the direct recruitment method, involve the giving of inducements.

E It is not necessary to go into the detail of the procedure which is followed in the case of each of the first four methods adopted. The type of advertising material used is referred to in the decision of the tribunal and is among the papers before me on this appeal. It gives prominence to the fact that a person taking the steps referred to in the advertisements would be entitled to a free gift and describes that gift. The gifts fall into
F two categories; the first being items of negligible value such as free tea-spoons and those would be delivered with a catalogue on an application being received. The second category were items of greater value such as hair driers, tea sets, glasses and jugs. However, the value of these items did not exceed £10. Before this category of inducements was sent, in the case of the appointment of new agents, there had to be an application by someone whose personal particulars were considered satisfactory to be an
G agent and there had to be an order, which, at the time of the tribunal's decision, had to be for a minimum of £10. The personal particulars were considered in the context of the first order placed. A reason why B.M.O.C. required a first order to be placed was that while B.M.O.C. needed to get the applicant into the system, heavy administrative costs would be incurred in approving the appointment of agents who then placed no orders or who
H only placed orders after a period of time. If, for whatever reason, an applicant's application was not approved she was notified by letter and no gift would be sent. An existing agent or a person approached to become an agent, instead of agreeing to go on or become an agent herself, could obtain a gift by recommending a friend and on that friend becoming an agent and making the appropriate order, the goods would be sent to the person making the recommendation. Sometimes B.M.O.C. would run out of the advertised gifts and then substitution would have to be made.

Some of the advertising material, but by no means all, indicated that the   A
right was reserved to send a sum of money in lieu of a particular item
if stocks were exhausted. In addition to a gift being sent to the person
making the recommendation, a small inexpensive gift might be dispatched
to the new agent. An inactive agent could also obtain a gift in a similar
manner; there being again the requirement of the placing of an order.
The advertising material sometimes represented that a catalogue would be   B
sent " free and without obligation." In fact, the catalogue stated that it
remained the property of the company and if a person was not accepted
as an agent the company would request its return.

Items used as incentives were normally acquired by the marketing
department of B.M.O.C. by way of bulk purchase direct from manufacturers and the administration of the incentive scheme was handled by a
separate department which dealt with the appointment of agents.   C

The relevant part of the statutory provisions on which the first question
depends, namely, paragraph 6 of Schedule 3 to the Finance Act 1972
provides:

> " Where a supply is a gift of goods . . . the value of the supply shall
> be taken to be the cost of the goods to the person making the supply;
> except that if that cost does not exceed £10 and the supply is a gift   D
> its value shall be taken to be nil."

In relation to this provision, the only issue for the tribunal, and on the
appeal, for this court, was whether or not the supply of the inducements
was the supply of gifts. If they were, then they fall within the exception and
the value would be nil and no value added tax would be payable. With
regard to this, the view of the tribunal was that the advertising activities   E
fell into two stages. The tribunal said:

> " In our judgment the first stage taken by itself is to encourage a
> prospective agent to send for the catalogue with a view to making an
> application to be appointed as an agent. Even if sending for the
> catalogue and its despatch could be treated as an offer and an
> acceptance with the teaspoons as consideration relating thereto, which   F
> we consider to be doubtful, we do not think at this stage there was any
> intention to enter into any legal relationship. We therefore hold that
> the first stage does not constitute a binding contract, and that the
> three teaspoons, which are at any rate of negligible value, may pro-
> perly be treated as a free gift within paragraph 6 of Schedule 3. In
> relation to the second stage, which we think must be considered in
> conjunction with the first stage, we hold that the completion of the   G
> form of application to be appointed as an agent coupled with the
> placing of her first order constitutes an offer to become appointed as
> an agent on certain terms: namely, she will be remunerated on a
> continuing basis at the rate of 10 per cent. on all (or any) merchandise
> sold by her; and that she will receive the advertised tea set on the
> acceptance by the appellant company of her first order. This offer is   H
> accepted by the appellant company when she is appointed as an agent
> and when her first order is accepted (both of these are in fact
> simultaneous). In our view the tea set is part of the consideration
> moving from the appellant company for the contract constituted
> by the offer and acceptance . . . The effect of the conclusions which
> we have reached is that the teaspoons should be treated as a gift
> within paragraph 6 of Schedule 3 to the Finance Act 1972 and that

The Weekly Law Reports, December 12, 1980

1513

1 W.L.R.   G.U.S. Merchandise Ltd. v. Customs & Excise (Q.B.D.)   Woolf J.

A   no tax is chargeable in relation thereto. The tea set, on the other hand, is a taxable supply supplied pursuant to an enforceable contract and should not be treated as a gift."

That part of its decision in so far as the tribunal found that there was a taxable supply was limited to a tea set; however, the tribunal came to similar conclusions in respect of the other substantial gifts. The tribunal

B reached these decisions notwithstanding the fact that it was common ground that although an order was required before a substantial gift would be delivered, the gift could be kept, even though the goods ordered were returned by the purchaser and the price repaid.

No issue arose on the appeal to the tribunal as to the commission earned by the agents of 10 per cent. in respect of sales to third persons or

C the discount of 10 per cent. which agents were allowed in respect of their own purchases.

The Customs and Excise Commissioners have not appealed against the decision of the tribunal in relation to the teaspoons. The appellant company however, contend as its first ground of appeal:

> " That the tribunal erred in law and misdirected itself in holding that
D   the said supplies were not gifts (the cost of which did not exceed £10)
> within paragraph 6 of Schedule 3 to the Finance Act 1972."

In support of this ground of appeal, Mr. Bates contends that the articles which were provided as incentives were indeed supplied as gifts. They are described as such and they were intended to be such. The circumstances show that there was no intention to create legal relations and if there were

E no such intention, the proper categorisation of the transaction was as one of gift.

Both the appellant company and the commissioners relied upon the decision of the House of Lords in *Esso Petroleum Co. Ltd.* v. *Customs and Excise Commissioners* [1976] 1 W.L.R. 1. That was a case which con- cerned the provision in respect of every four gallons of petrol purchased of a coin bearing on one side the head of one of the 30 English footballers

F chosen for the World Cup competition in 1970. In that case it was the liability to purchase tax which was in question and it was the Customs and Excise Commissioners' contention that the coins were articles produced in quantity for general sale. The decision of the majority of the House of Lords (Lord Fraser of Tullybelton dissenting) was that the coins were not produced for sale. However, Viscount Dilhorne and Lord Russell

G of Killowen were of the view that on the facts there was no intention to create legal relations as to the supply of the coins and it is the views of their Lordships as to this which are relevant to the question now under consideration.

In deciding this question it is important to take into account what Lord Russell said about the fact that the scheme had been motivated for

H commercial reasons which is accepted by the appellant company to be also the case here. Lord Russell said, at p. 10:

> " It is to be borne in mind in this connection that the mere fact that Esso and the garage proprietors undoubtedly had a commercial aim in promoting the scheme does not deprive the delivery of a medal of the quality of a gift as distinct from a sale: for benevolence is not a necessary feature of a gift, which may well be motivated by self interest."

Woolf J.   G.U.S. Merchandise Ltd. v. Customs & Excise (Q.B.D.)   [1980]

However, it is also to be borne in mind what Lord Russell went on to say,   A
namely:

> " On the other hand it is trite law that if on analysis a transaction
> has in law one character, the fact that the parties either accidentally
> or deliberately frame the transaction in language appropriate to a
> transaction of a different character will not deny to it its true
> character."   B

Lord Russell and Viscount Dilhorne based their conclusion that there was
no intention to create legal relations on the fact that the value of the coins
in that case was like that of the teaspoons in this case, negligible, and
Viscount Dilhorne said at p. 4:

> " If what was described as being a gift, which would be given if
> something was purchased, was something of value to the purchaser,   C
> then it could readily be inferred that there was a common intention
> to enter into legal relations."

The conclusion of Viscount Dilhorne and Lord Russell in that case therefore, can be distinguished from this case on the facts because of the more
substantial value of the gifts which are in question on this appeal.

Lord Wilberforce, in a passage of his short speech which Mr. Bates   D
on behalf of the appellant company asked me to apply, regarded the *Esso*
case as being one of impression as to an essentially simple situation.
Approaching this case in that way and bearing in mind the passage which
I first quoted from Lord Russell, I have no doubt that the tribunal were
right in regarding these transactions, involving substantial gifts, as being
ones where a legal relationship was created.   E

I have come to this conclusion notwithstanding the fact that in this case,
unlike the *Esso* case, there is not the feature which Lord Fraser thought
important, namely, a co-relationship such as the one coin to every four
gallons which there was in the *Esso* case. Here the same article was given
irrespective of the value of the order and irrespective of whether that order
was returned. In the *Esso* case the direct aim was to sell petrol; in this case   F
the immediate aim of the advertising campaign was to recruit and keep
useful agents. The fact of receipt of an order even though the goods could
be returned must have been considered as justifying the expense of taking
on the applicant into the army of existing active agents.

In order to come to my conclusion, it is not necessary to analyse the
transactions and identify the precise stage of the transactions when
contracts were concluded, as long as contracts were concluded. The fact   G
is that there were contracts supported by consideration. The consideration
moving from the agent being her agreement to act as such and the placing
of the required order.

Mr. Bates contended that it was illogical of the tribunal to find that
there was no intention to create legal relations with regard to the teaspoons
but that there was with regard to the more substantial items. I can see the   H
force of this argument and were it not for the negligible value of the
teaspoons, I would have grave reservations concerning the tribunal's
decision in relation to the teaspoons and, indeed, I would probably have
come to a different conclusion to that of the tribunal on this point.

In support of his contention that there was no gift of the more valuable
items, Mr. Collins relied upon a passage in the speech of Lord Reid in
Chappell & Co. Ltd. v. *Nestlé Co. Ltd.* [1960] A.C. 87. Lord Reid

The Weekly Law Reports, December 12, 1980

1515

1 W.L.R.   G.U.S. Merchandise Ltd. v. Customs & Excise (Q.B.D.)   Woolf J.

A indicated that in activities involving a large number of transactions it was not desirable to consider isolated cases. That passage is consistent with my conclusion that the activities of B.M.O.C., in order to recruit and retain good agents, were commercial and that they in fact entered into legally enforceable obligations to supply what they categorised as gifts, in their advertising material.

B The second question, I am bound to say, has caused me much more difficulty than the first question. This depends upon the special scheme for retailers. In order to consider the issue it is first necessary to look at the relevant sections of the Finance Act 1972, which at the relevant time were unamended and read:

"1 (1) A tax, to be known as value added tax, shall be charged in accordance with the provisions of this Part of this Act on the
C supply of goods and services in the United Kingdom . . .
"2 (1) Except as otherwise provided by this Part of this Act the tax shall be charged and payable as follows. (2) Tax on the supply of goods or services shall be charged only where—(a) the supply is a taxable supply; and (b) the goods or services are supplied by a taxable person in the course of a business carried on by him; . . .
D "5 (2) Supply of goods includes all forms of supply and, in particular, the letting of goods on hire and the making of a gift . . .
"10 (3) If the supply is not for a consideration or is for a consideration not consisting or not wholly consisting of money, the value of the supply shall be taken to be its open market value. . . .
"30 (3) Regulations under this section may make special provi-
E sion for such taxable supplies by retailers of any goods or of any description of goods or of services or any description of services as may be determined by or under the regulations and, in particular,—(a) for permitting the value which is to be taken as the value of the supplies in any prescribed accounting period or part thereof to be determined, subject to any limitations or restrictions, by such method or one of such methods as may have been described in any notice published by
F the commissioners in pursuance of the regulations . . . "

Regulations were made pursuant to section 30 (3) and notices have been published in accordance with those regulations. But for those regulations and notices, value of articles provided by B.M.O.C. as inducements to agents would have to be ascertained by taking their open market value in accordance with section 10 (3).
G The regulations which were made pursuant to section 30 (3) are the Value Added Tax (Supplies by Retailers) Regulations 1972. Regulation 2 (1) provides:

"The commissioners may permit the value which is to be taken as the value, in any prescribed accounting period or part thereof, of supplies by a retailer which are taxable at other than the zero-rate to
H be determined . . . by any method described in a notice published by them for that purpose . . . "

Regulation 3 provides: "The commissioners may refuse to permit the value of taxable supplies to be determined in accordance with a scheme . . ." A series of notices has been issued pursuant to the Regulations. Those notices are notice 707 and notice 707 (revised March 1973) and notice 727 and the relevant supplement to that notice, namely,

the special scheme H supplement. In considering those notices it has to be **A**
borne in mind that they are far from being the normal form of delegated
legislation. Although they set out what is, in effect, a statutory scheme,
they also contain advice and recommendations which are of no statutory
effect.

There is no dispute that in relation to its selling to the public, B.M.O.C.
is permitted to calculate its liability to value added tax in accordance with **B**
the schemes set out in the notices. Clearly part of the activities of B.M.O.C.
are just the sort of activities which are intended to be covered by the
scheme. The advantages of the schemes are that whereas normally it is
necessary to calculate the value added tax payable on each supply, retailers
can instead use a less burdensome scheme for working out their liability
and in particular, in so far as the schemes relevant to this case are
concerned, in order to work out their output, calculate the tax on the **C**
value of their gross takings.

Notice 727 explains in paragraph 6 the purpose of the special retail
schemes as follows:

> " Normally a taxable person has to account for value added tax each
> time he supplies goods or services to a customer. This is called output
> tax. To account for output tax in the normal value added tax way, **D**
> the taxable person needs to have a record of every separate transac-
> tion, and more details about that are given in notice 700 (value added
> tax: General guide). But most retailers cannot keep a record of that
> kind for all their sales, because they do not usually issue invoices to
> their customers or make any written record at the time when a sale
> takes place. So the special schemes for retailers allow you, as a **E**
> retailer, to calculate your output tax (or most of it) in other ways,
> which vary according to the particular scheme."

Mr. Bates puts his argument in relation to the special schemes on
behalf of the appellant company very simply and clearly. He contends
that the appellants are a company to whom the special schemes apply. **F**
He pointed out that each notice describes a retailer for the purposes of the
scheme as anyone, not necessarily a shopkeeper, whose business consists
mainly of supplying goods or services directly to the public without tax
invoices. He stresses the word " mainly."

He adds that each of the schemes has special provisions dealing with
special activities. Either bringing them within or taking them out or
altering their treatment. He says there could have been like provisions made **G**
to deal with the supply of inducements of the sort made by his clients or
there could have been a refusal under regulation 2 (3) of the Value Added
Tax (Supplies by Retailers) Regulations 1972, which I have read; but as
there has not been and, as there is no express reference to such supplies,
they should be dealt with in accordance with the special scheme. The result
that would follow is that because the inducements were supplied without **H**
charge, the gross takings of the company would not be affected and
accordingly its liability to pay value added tax would be unchanged.
However, this does not mean that his clients have received what Mr.
Collins at one stage described in his argument as a windfall, because in
fixing its prices for articles which it sells, a company has to take into
account what can loosely be described as advertising expenditure and as
the money it receives for the goods sold, at such prices, will be taken

The Weekly Law Reports, December 12, 1980

1517

1 W.L.R.   G.U.S. Merchandise Ltd. v. Customs & Excise (Q.B.D.)   Woolf J.

A into account in assessing value added tax, there is no real loss to the revenue.

Initially I was very much persuaded by this argument of Mr. Bates and it is only under the careful guidance of Mr. Collins that I have come to the conclusion that it is wrong.

Mr. Collins's contention was that if you examine the schemes in detail
B the clear implication is that they do not normally cover supplies which are not sales to the public. He says that the schemes are not designed to, and do not, cater for the supplies which B.M.O.C. makes to its agents without charge. He points out that if this is right the result of Mr. Bates's argument is to put such supplies outside the charge for value added tax contrary to the express provision to which I have referred above. This he says cannot be correct.

C In considering Mr. Collins's contention it is necessary to look at the schemes in detail. For the purposes of this judgment I do not propose to set out the detailed provisions of the schemes, but merely draw attention to some of their features. The earlier scheme which the appellant company adopted was scheme 4 contained in notice 707 of August 1972. That indicated that the purpose of the scheme was the same as that in notice
D 727 to which I have already referred. I draw attention to the object of not having to account for each " sale." Paragraph 6 of notice 727 recognises that there may be situations where, notwithstanding the adoption of one of the special schemes, a retailer will still have to account in " the normal way " in respect of one department as well. In paragraph 13 dealing with scheme 4 it is stated:

E   " The retailer must split his gross takings for each tax period in
       proportion to the total amounts, including value added tax, payable
       by customers for standard rate and zero rated goods respectively."

The reference to customers and the amount payable has to be compared with the supply without charge to agents. Part V of the notice deals with records and tax returns. Paragraph 24 describes what are " gross takings "
F for the purpose of the special schemes. It is apparent from the description of the gross takings that there is no head in respect of which there can be any entry made in respect of the supply of inducements to the agents. The same point can be made with regard to the record requirements set out in the appendices to notice 707, scheme 4 being dealt with in Appendix 4. This refers in addition to records of the gross takings as defined in
G paragraph 24 for records of the retail selling price, that is the total amount including value added tax payable by customers, records for goods received for retailing, and supplies of goods under written hire purchase, credit sales or conditional sale agreements. There is no provision for a record which would be appropriate to deal with transactions relating to the supply of inducements for agents. Precisely the same points can be made with regard
H to the revised notice 707 of March 1973 and they are also generally applicable to the revised scheme contained in notice 727 and the notice dealing with special scheme H which was the special scheme applicable to the appellant company both of which were introduced in February 1975. In notice 727 it is specifically stated in paragraph 8:

    " You may find, however, on reading through this notice and the
      supplement about the special scheme you choose, that some of your
      output tax will need to be calculated outside the special scheme, in the

A

normal value added tax way. If so you should follow the rules in notice 700 for that part of your output tax."

Paragraph 13 is important because it provides:

B

" Most sections of notice 700 " which is the notice which deals with the normal method of accounting " apply to retailers in exactly the same way as they do to other taxable persons. But there are sections and paragraphs which do not apply to those parts of your business which you deal with under any of the special retail schemes. You will find it useful to have a general understanding of all the contents of notice 700, but you should read, especially:... "

and then it specifies various heads including section X which states:

C

" This section is very important, because it sets out the normal value added tax way of recording and accounting for every transaction. Paragraphs which do not apply to retailers operating a special scheme are clearly marked. But if you are going to use a special scheme you must read the paragraphs about: Information to be recorded. Supplies by retailers: less detailed tax invoices. Summary of tax records (value added tax account)."

D

Part VI of notice 727 deals with special kinds of transactions. Paragraph 47 provides:

E

" The main rules for special kinds of transaction are included in this section. Mostly, they explain what you must include or exclude from your gross takings or your scheme records, in making the calculations for your scheme, if you are concerned with a particular kind of transaction. Some of them also give advice about whether you should deal with particular kinds of transaction inside your special scheme— and if so, how—or whether they should be kept apart from your scheme altogether."

F

The passages from notice 727 to which I have just referred give some indication that the provisions of the notices dealing with special kinds of transactions are not exhaustive. I have stressed the fact that under each of those schemes the accounting system is inappropriate to record any reference to the transactions in respect of inducements for agents. It is true that the appellant company can rightly say that because it has no gross takings in respect of the supply of inducements it is not surprising that accounts which are related to gross takings should not be designed to include any reference to such transactions. However, the absence of any appropriate record is still, in my view, an important point in favour of the commissioners. The whole framework of the value added tax legislation, including the subordinate legislation and notices, is to require detailed records to be kept. Those records when made up, in due course provide the material to be entered into the value added tax return, which has to be submitted at the end of the appropriate accounting period, and which sets out the amount of value added tax payable. Unless an assessment is made by the Commissioners of Customs and Excise, the only amount which the commissioners can recover is that set out in the value added tax return and it is therefore most important for the working of the tax that all types of transactions should be recorded since otherwise it is difficult, if not impossible, to check that the tax returns disclose the value added tax payable.

G

H

A   Having examined the notices as a whole, I fully accept that it would have been desirable if the notices had more clearly stated the position. However, it is my view that the clear implication to be drawn from the notices is that they are intended to deal with retail sales to customers and are not designed or intended to deal with taxable supplies, which are special kinds of transactions not referred to in the notices, and which do not involve sale.

B   The transactions with the agents whereby they were supplied with inducements were not sales. Both parties to the appeal are agreed as to that and if authority were needed for that conclusion it is to be found in the speeches in *Esso Petroleum Co. Ltd.* v. *Customs and Excise Commissioners* [1976] 1 W.L.R. 1, apart from that of Lord Fraser of Tullybelton.

C   It follows that the second main point relied upon by the appellant must be rejected.

The appellant company took a further point about the manner in which the tribunal dealt with the application of the schemes. The tribunal said:

D   " We have found as a fact that the incentive ' gifts ' were acquired by way of bulk purchase direct from a manufacturer, and that their administration was handled by a separate department dealing with the appointment of agents, and they did not form part of the retail stock of B.M.O.C. In our judgment, therefore, they do not fall to be included in either special scheme 4 or H."

It is contended by the appellant company that there was no evidence
E   to support the finding in relation to stock. Mr. Collins pointed to one passage in the evidence which supported that finding and I would therefore have rejected this point as well. The point is, however, of no materiality on the approach that I have adopted as to the effect of the notices, which is different in emphasis from that adopted by the tribunal. The passage relied on by Mr. Collins is in the evidence of Mr. Stevens in the documents before me.

F   There were additional grounds raised by the appellant company in their notice of appeal based upon estoppel. They have been satisfactorily compromised by the parties and I need not deal with them.

It follows therefore that this appeal must be dismissed.

Appeal dismissed with costs.
G   *Leave to appeal.*

Solicitors: *Paisner & Co.*; *Solicitor, Customs and Excise.*

[Reported by MISS ISOBEL COLLINS, Barrister-at-Law]

H

A

[CHANCERY DIVISION]

* ARMOUR HICK NORTHERN LTD. AND OTHERS *v.*
WHITEHOUSE AND OTHERS

[1978 A. No. 2261]

B

1980 Feb. 14; 22

Judge Mervyn Davies sitting
as a High Court judge

*Company—Purchase of share capital—Payment to enable purchaser
to complete—Holding company owing money to majority shareholder—Agreement to transfer shares to company's directors* C
*on payment of debt—Subsidiary company discharging debt—
Whether constituting financial assistance in purchase of shares
—Companies Act* 1948 (11 & 12 *Geo.* 6, *c.* 38), *s.* 54 (1)

The first two plaintiffs were subsidiary companies of the
third plaintiff and the majority of that parent company's shares
were held by the defendant company. Two directors of the
three plaintiffs acquired the defendant company's shares in the D
parent company at par but it was alleged that the defendant
company only agreed to part with those shares if a debt of
£93,000 owed to it by the parent company was discharged.
The first plaintiff paid its parent company's debt direct to the
defendant company. The plaintiffs issued a writ seeking
various reliefs including the return of the £93,000. They
alleged by their statement of claim that the transaction was
in breach of section 54 of the Companies Act 1948 [1] in that E
the first plaintiff gave the directors financial assistance for
the purpose of or in connection with the purchase of the
shares in its parent company.
On the preliminary issue whether that transaction was
capable of constituting financial assistance within the meaning of the section: —
Held, that, although the discharge by a company of a
debt it owed could not be the giving of financial assistance F
for the purchase of its shares within the meaning of section
54 (1) of the Act, a payment by a subsidiary company of a
holding company's debt was not excluded from the ambit of
the section; that, since on the assumed facts the first plaintiff
would have known that the transaction between the directors
and the defendant company could only have been concluded
if its parent company's debt was paid, the payment of that
debt by the first plaintiff was capable in law of being the G
giving of financial assistance to the defendant company for
the purpose of or in connection with the purchase of shares
in its holding company (post, pp. 1525D—1526A).
Gradwell (Pty.) Ltd. v. *Rostra Printers Ltd.*, 1959 (4) S.A.
419 and *E.H. Dey Pty. Ltd.* v. *Dey* [1966] V.R. 464 considered.

The following cases are referred to in the judgment:

H

Belmont Finance Corporation Ltd. v. *Williams Furniture Ltd.* (un-
reported), May 25, 1979; Court of Appeal (Civil Division) Transcript
No. 343 of 1979, C.A.
Dey (E.H.) Pty. Ltd. v. *Dey* [1966] V.R. 464.
Gradwell (Pty.) Ltd. v. *Rostra Printers Ltd.*, 1959 (4) S.A. 419.
Wallersteiner v. *Moir* [1974] 1 W.L.R. 991; [1974] 3 All E.R. 217, C.A.

---

[1] Companies Act 1948, s. 54: see post, p. 1523G.

A   The following additional cases were cited in argument:
      Coleman v. *Myers* [1977] 2 N.Z.L.R. 225, Mahon J. and C.A.
      Spink (Bournemouth) Ltd. v. *Spink* [1936] Ch. 544; [1936] 1 All E.R.
          597.
      V.G.M. Holdings Ltd., In re [1942] Ch. 235; [1942] 1 All E.R. 224, C.A.
      Wellington Publishing Co. Ltd., In re [1973] 1 N.Z.L.R. 133.

B   PRELIMINARY ISSUE
      On July 27, 1978, the plaintiffs, Armour Hick Northern Ltd., Armour
Hick Parker Ltd. and Armour Hick & Partners Ltd., issued a writ making
certain money claims against the first and second defendants David Stuart
Whitehouse and Robert Michael Hick, who were directors of the first
and third plaintiffs; the third defendant, Armour Trust Ltd., and the
C   fourth and fifth defendants, E. C. Parker & Co. Ltd. and Valerie Diane
Whitehouse. The plaintiff companies were now in liquidation. By their
statement of claim, specially endorsed on the writ, the plaintiffs claimed,
inter alia, that prior to September 26, 1975, the third defendant owned
7,000 out of the 10,000 issued £1 shares in the third plaintiff which
owed the third defendant £93,000; that between September 26, 1975,
and March 31, 1976, the first two defendants procured the payment by
D   the first plaintiff of £93,000 to the third defendant in discharge of the
third plaintiff's indebtedness to the third defendant; that in consideration
for the payment of that sum the third defendant agreed to, and did,
transfer its shareholding in the third plaintiff to the first two defendants.
The statement of claim alleged that by that transaction the first plaintiff
gave to the first and second defendants financial assistance for the purpose
of and/or in connection with their purchase of the shares in the third
E   plaintiff and thereby acted unlawfully and in breach of section 54 of
the Companies Act 1948.
      The third defendant pleaded in defence that, as a matter of law, the
application by a company of its funds in the repayment of indebtedness
due from itself or its holding company to a vendor of shares of itself
or its holding company was not capable in law of constituting financial
F   assistance for the purpose of or in connection with the purchase of the
shares to be sold by that vendor within the meaning of section 54.
      On October 17, 1979, Master Gowers made an order on a summons
for directions that the issue raised by the pleadings should be tried as a
preliminary issue between the first and third plaintiffs on the one hand
and the first three defendants on the other hand.

G
      Richard Sykes for the third defendant.
      Alan G. Steinfeld for the first and third plaintiffs.
      The first and second defendants did not appear and were not
represented.
                                                        Cur. adv. vult.

H   February 22. JUDGE MERVYN DAVIES read the following judgment.
This is a preliminary issue. In the action the three plaintiffs sue the
five defendants alleging various money claims. The writ, with the statement of claim endorsed, is dated July 27, 1978. Defences have been
served, including the defence of the third defendant, Armour Trust Ltd.
      By an order of the master dated October 17, 1979, made on the
summons for directions, it was ordered that one of the questions raised
by the pleadings be tried as a preliminary issue between the first and third

plaintiffs on the one hand and the first, second and third defendants on the other hand, that is to say, between the plaintiffs Armour Hick Northern Ltd. and Armour Hick & Partners Ltd. and the defendants David Stuart Whitehouse, Robert Michael Hick and Armour Trust Ltd.

The issue to be tried as a preliminary issue is set out in the master's order as follows:

" Whether the payment by the plaintiffs Armour Hick Northern Ltd., a subsidiary of the plaintiffs Armour Hick & Partners Ltd., of sums totalling £93,000 to the defendants Armour Trust Ltd. in discharge of indebtedness due and payable by the plaintiffs Armour Hick & Partners Ltd. to the defendants Armour Trust Ltd. as alleged in paragraph 4 of the statement of claim was capable in law of constituting financial assistance within the meaning of section 54 of the Companies Act 1948 for the purpose of or in connection with the purchase of the 7,000 shares in the plaintiffs Armour Hick & Partners Ltd. purchased by the defendants David Stuart Whitehouse and Robert Michael Hick at par and being the sales mentioned in paragraph 5 of the statement of claim."

The order goes on with these words:

" For the purpose of this preliminary issue it is agreed that the defendants Armour Trust Ltd. were willing (and only willing) to sell their shares in the plaintiffs Armour Hick & Partners Ltd. if the indebtedness to them of the plaintiffs Armour Hick & Partners Ltd. were discharged in full."

Mr. Steinfeld appeared for the two plaintiffs mentioned in the preliminary issue, that is, the first and third plaintiffs, Armour Hick Northern Ltd. and Armour Hick & Partners Ltd. Mr. Sykes appeared for the third defendant, Armour Trust Ltd. The other defendants mentioned in the preliminary issue were notified of this hearing, but they did not attend.

I will now read paragraphs 1 to 6 of the statement of claim.

" 1. The first and second plaintiffs were at all material times subsidiary companies of the third plaintiff within the meaning of section 154 of the Companies Act 1948. Each of the plaintiffs is in liquidation. 2. At all material times the first and second defendants were directors of each of the plaintiffs, and employed by the third plaintiff (and/or the second plaintiff) as, respectively, deputy chairman/ financial director and chairman. At all material times prior to September 26, 1975, the third defendant owned the majority of the issued shares in the third plaintiff. The first defendant was also at the material times a director of the fourth defendant. 3. In the premises the first and second defendants and each of them were at all material times under a fiduciary duty or duties to the plaintiffs and each of them to act lawfully and bona fide in the interests of the plaintiffs and to discharge their duties as directors with reasonable skill and diligence. 4. Between about September 26, 1975, and March 31, 1976, the first and second defendants and each of them procured the payment by the first plaintiff of sums totalling £93,000 to the third defendant. The said sums were paid by the first plaintiff in discharge of the indebtedness of the third plaintiff to the third defendant. 5. In consideration for the payment of the said sums by the first plaintiff, the third defendant agreed to, and did, transfer its shareholding in the third plaintiff (7,000 out of the 10,000 issued £1 shares) to the first

The Weekly Law Reports, December 12, 1980

1523

1 W.L.R.   Armour Hick Ltd. v. Whitehouse (Ch.D.)   Mervyn Davies J.

A   and second defendants at par. As a result of the said transfers the first and second defendants (who already owned shares in the third plaintiff) held 3,750 and 6,250 of the said shares respectively. 6. In the premises, by the said transaction, the first plaintiff gave to the first and second defendants financial assistance for the purpose of and/or in connection with their purchase of the said shares in the third plaintiff, and thereby acted unlawfully and in breach of the provisions of section 54 of the Companies Act 1948."

B

I need read no further. I now read paragraph 8 of the defence of the third defendant:

"The third defendant denies each of the allegations in paragraph 6 of the amended statement of claim. The third defendant will contend that, as a matter of law, the application by a company of its funds in the repayment of indebtedness due from itself or its holding company to a vendor of shares of itself or its holding company is not capable in law of constituting financial assistance for the purpose of or in connection with the purchase of the shares to be sold by that vendor within the meaning of section 54 of the Companies Act 1948."

C

D   For the purpose of the preliminary issue I must assume the truth of the allegations in the statement of claim. It was accepted that it was for Mr. Sykes to begin before me. With the help of a most useful chart, Mr. Sykes summarised the material facts as at September 25, 1975. The third plaintiff was the holding company of the first plaintiff. The third plaintiff owed the third defendant £93,000. The third defendant owned 7,000 shares in the third plaintiff. The first and second defendants were directors of the first and the third plaintiffs. Mr. Sykes went on to explain the position reached by March 31, 1976. By that time the first and second defendants had acquired at par the 7,000 shares in the third plaintiff, previously owned by the third defendant, for £7,000 cash, paid to the third defendant. As well, the £93,000 owed by the third plaintiff to the third defendant had been paid off in full. The £93,000 was paid by the first plaintiff direct to the third defendant.

E

F

It is against those facts that one must consider the questions set out in the master's order, bearing in mind the agreement recorded in the order, which in effect was that the third defendant was willing to sell the 7,000 shares only if the £93,000 owing to it by the third plaintiff was discharged.

G   I now set out section 54 (1) of the Act of 1948, omitting the proviso:

"Subject as provided in this section, it shall not be lawful for a company to give, whether directly or indirectly, and whether by means of a loan, guarantee, the provision of security or otherwise, any financial assistance for the purpose of or in connection with a purchase or subscription made or to be made by any person of or for any shares in the company, or where the company is a subsidiary company, its holding company: . . . ."

H

Mr. Steinfeld conceded that if the events had been that the third plaintiff had itself paid its debt to the third defendant, then the third plaintiff would not have given financial assistance in connection with the share purchase. The third plaintiff would have been paying off its own debt. Mr. Sykes then went on to contend that if the repayment of a debt owed by a holding company is not financial assistance when made by itself, then a repayment of that debt is no more so when it is made by a subsidiary of the holding A company. I do not see that that proposition necessarily follows because it is one thing for a company to pay its own debt and another for a subsidiary company to pay the debt of its holding company. However, Mr. Sykes suggested that any financial assistance given by the first plaintiff in paying off the third defendant was given solely to the third plaintiff whose debt was discharged. Section 54 cannot, so the argument goes, be B intended to stop the giving of financial assistance to the company whose shares are being purchased, i.e. the third plaintiff, particularly since the penal provision in section 54 (2) indicates that the section is to be restrictively construed. He said that all would have been well if the first plaintiff had paid the third plaintiff and if the third plaintiff had then paid the third defendant. To short-circuit the matter by making the payment direct to the third defendant, he said, made no difference. C

Another approach to the argument that the transaction was outside section 54 was that any assistance which the first plaintiff gave was not financial assistance in connection with the purchase of shares. Rather was it assistance in connection with the repayment of the indebtedness of the third plaintiff to the third defendant. It was accepted that the first plaintiff's creditors might well have been, we do not know, prejudiced by the payment D made to the third defendant. That might have been a matter for misfeasance proceedings, but did not mean that the payment constituted conduct within section 54.

Finally, Mr. Sykes said that subsidiary companies are mentioned in section 54 to stop the doing by a subsidiary company of acts which if done by the holding company would be a breach of the section. In short, as I understand, he says that an act outside section 54 which is done by a E holding company is also outside section 54 if the act is done by the holding company's subsidiary. Mr. Steinfeld said—and I agree with him—there is nothing in the wording of section 54 to justify Mr. Sykes' final point.

Mr. Steinfeld's argument in summary was (1) that section 54 is to be construed widely and liberally. He referred to *Wallersteiner* v. *Moir* [1974] 1 W.L.R. 991; 1014, 1032; (2) the section prohibits the giving of F any financial assistance by a subsidiary in connection with the purchase of shares in a holding company; (3) for a subsidiary company to discharge its holding company's indebtedness to a shareholder, to enable the sale of that shareholder's shares in the holding company to a purchaser to go forward, plainly constitutes the giving of financial assistance not only to the vendor shareholder but also to the purchaser of the shares.

If the third plaintiff had paid its own debt with its own money, there G would have been no giving of financial assistance for the purpose of or in connection with the share purchase. In *Gradwell (Pty.) Ltd.* v. *Rostra Printers Ltd.,* 1959 (4) S.A. 419, Schreiner J.A. had under consideration section 86 *bis* (2) of the South African Companies Act (Act 46 of 1926 as amended). That section is for present purposes identical with section 54. Referring to the payment of a debt comparable with the third H plaintiff debt to the third defendant, he said, at p. 426:

"But whatever may be the position in such a case the paying off of an existing debt seems to be decidedly more difficult to bring within the notion of giving financial assistance. The payer's assets and liabilities are put into a different form but the balance is unchanged. And the same applies to the financial position of the payee. Here the company would have no more and no less after the completion of

The Weekly Law Reports, December 12, 1980

1525

1 W.L.R.   Armour Hick Ltd. v. Whitehouse (Ch.D.)   Mervyn Davies J.

A   the transaction than before. . . . Where there is an anticipation of the
date when a debt becomes due and payable the position may possibly
be different, but where the debt is presently due and payable and the
debtor can have no answer to the creditor's demand for payment, it
would be straining the language to hold that by paying his debt the
debtor gives the creditor financial assistance."

B   As I understand, those observations were noted without disapproval
by Buckley L.J. in *Belmont Finance Corporation* v. *Williams Furniture
Ltd.* (unreported) May 25, 1979, Court of Appeal (Civil Division),
Transcript No. 343 of 1979. Thus, if the third plaintiff had paid its
own debt to the third defendant, it would have given no financial
assistance within section 54, the reason being, as I understand, that
such a payment does not alter the financial position, save to the extent
C   that a debt due from the debtor is paid by the debtor, so that no
help or assistance is given. There is merely a due discharge of a debt.
But the first plaintiff paying the third plaintiff's debt is a horse of another
colour. The first plaintiff was not paying off its own debt. It may have
been making merely a voluntary payment. Accordingly, the payment may
have been financial assistance within section 54.

D   It follows that I must apply the words of section 54 (1) to the facts.
I do so reading the words neither widely nor restrictively, but in their
plain ordinary meaning. I see that it was not lawful for the first plaintiff,
a subsidiary of the third plaintiff, to give any financial assistance " for the
purpose of or in connection with " a purchase by any person of any shares
in the third plaintiff. The section does not say that the assistance is not
E   to be given to the purchaser. It simply says that assistance is not to be
given. In fact, no financial assistance, at any rate no direct financial
assistance, was given to the purchasers because the £93,000 was paid to the
vendors, and the purchasers themselves paid the £7,000 for the shares.

But is it the position that financial assistance is not to be given to the
vendor? In *E. H. Dey Pty. Ltd.* v. *Dey* [1966] V.R. 464, McInerney J.
had to deal with the Victorian equivalent of section 54. He said, at
F   p. 470:

"In my view, the prohibition is not confined to financial assistance to
the purchaser : it is directed to financial assistance to whomsoever
given, provided that it be for the purpose of a purchase of shares or
in connection with a purchase of shares."

G   I agree with those remarks. So the question here is, did the first
plaintiff, on the assumed facts, give financial assistance to the third defendant in connection with the first and second defendants' share purchase?
I have no doubt that the first plaintiff gave assistance, leaving aside for the
moment whether such assistance was financial assistance. The first plaintiff
paid the third defendant £93,000 and, with the first and second defendants
as directors of the first plaintiff, the first plaintiff must have known that
H   if the first plaintiff had not made that payment, then the share transaction between the third defendant and the first and second defendants
would not have gone forward. Thus, the first plaintiff gave help to the
third defendant in connection with the share purchase.

That leaves the question whether the assistance was financial assistance.
The answer is in the affirmative when one sees that the assistance was a
payment of £93,000. I do not see how the assistance can be described as
otherwise than financial. If the payment had not been made, the share

transfer would not have gone through. It appears to have been financial A
assistance within the phrase " or otherwise " in section 54 (1) and, as well,
financial assistance " for the purpose of or in connection with " a purchase
of shares.

Accordingly, in my opinion the payment referred to in the master's
order was capable in law of constituting financial assistance within section
54 for the purpose of or in connection with the purchase of the 7,000 shares.

I desire to add that at the trial it may, of course, emerge, when all the B
facts are examined, that the payment in question did not, in fact, breach
section 54.

> *Ruling accordingly.*
> *First and third plaintiff's costs*
> *in any event.*
> *Leave to appeal.*

Solicitors: *Clifford-Turner; Herbert Oppenheimer, Nathan & Vandyk.*

A. R.

[COURT OF APPEAL]

* REGINA *v.* SHAW (ELVIS)

1980 March 3; 11   Donaldson L.J., Kilner Brown and Wood JJ.

Crime—Practice—Defendant's presence at trial—Defendant abscon-
ding during trial—Defendant's counsel and solicitor wishing to
continue representation—Whether judge having power to rule
against continued representation

During his trial on a charge of robbery the defendant
absconded. The trial judge investigated the defendant's
absence and, deciding that it was voluntary, rejected an F
application to discharge the jury and order a new trial. The
defendant's counsel and solicitor wished to continue their
representation but the judge ruled that as the defendant was
absent intentionally, his instructions were deemed to be withdrawn and his counsel and solicitor could take no further part
in the trial. The defendant was convicted in his absence.

On appeal against conviction—

Held, allowing the appeal, that the question whether counsel G
and his instructing solicitors should continue to act for a client
who voluntarily absconded in the course of the trial was one
of professional conduct and etiquette and it was not within
the judge's province to dismiss counsel from the case in such
circumstances or to order him to remain if he was required
by the etiquette of the Bar to withdraw; that, accordingly, the
judge had wrongly prevented counsel and the solicitor from
continuing to represent the defendant, and since his ruling H
had prejudiced the fairness of the trial, as counsel would at
least have been able to call witnesses for the defence, the
verdict of guilty was unsafe and unsatisfactory and would be
quashed.

The following case is referred to in the judgment:

Reg. v. *Jones (Robert) (No. 2)* [1972] 1 W.L.R. 887; [1972] 2 All E.R.
731, C.A.

A   The following additional cases were cited in argument:

Hadkinson v. *Hadkinson* [1952] P. 285; [1952] 2 All E.R. 567, C.A.
Pett v. *Greyhound Racing Association Ltd. (No. 1)* [1969] 1 Q.B. 125;
   [1968] 2 W.L.R. 1471; [1968] 2 All E.R. 545, C.A.
Reg. v. *Jones (Robert)* [1971] 2 Q.B. 456; [1971] 2 W.L.R. 1485; [1971]
   2 All E.R. 731, C.A.
Rex v. *Lee Kun* [1916] 1 K.B. 337, C.C.A.

B
       APPEAL against conviction.
       On May 1, 1979, at Cambridge Crown Court (Judge Wild) the de-
fendant, Elvis Edward Shaw, pleaded not guilty to a charge of robbery.
At the conclusion of the prosecution case he was granted bail. The
following day his counsel applied for the discharge of the jury or an
adjournment on the ground that his client was absent. The judge
C refused the application and ruled that, as the defendant's absence was
intentional, his instructions were deemed to be withdrawn so that his
counsel and solicitors could no longer act in the trial on his behalf.
On May 4, 1979, the defendant was convicted in his absence. He
appealed on the grounds, inter alia, that there was a material irregularity
in that (1) the judge was wrong in law or in the exercise of his discretion
D to rule against the application for an adjournment or a discharge of the
jury, as there was nothing in the case which would have prejudiced the
prosecution in the event of a retrial; (2) the judge was wrong to rule that
the defendant had discharged his counsel; (3) the defendant was wrongly
deprived of his fundamental right to be represented by counsel throughout his trial; and (4) the defendant was wrongly deprived of his opportunity to give evidence himself, to call witnesses other than himself to the
E issue of alibi and to cross-examine co-defendants.

       John Farmer for the defendant.
       Michael McMullan for the Crown.
                                                 Cur. adv. vult.

F   March 11. KILNER BROWN J. read the following judgment of the
court. On May 4, 1979, at Cambridge Crown Court, before Judge Wild,
the defendant, who was present in the early stages of his trial, was
convicted in his absence of an offence of robbery and after arrest on
a bench warrant was sentenced, on May 8, to a term of three years'
imprisonment. He now appeals, by leave of the single judge, against
G that conviction, but there is no appeal against sentence, and the facts
of the case are of no relevance to the issue before this court. The
problem concerns the position and powers of a trial judge where a
defendant who is on bail absconds during the process of the trial.
Whereas in the past this was a question which rarely had to be considered, the court is aware that the application of the Bail Act 1976 is
leading to a regrettable increase in this state of affairs and the problem
H requires urgent further consideration by the Council of the Bar and
The Law Society.
       In the case before us counsel was properly instructed and his instruc-
tions were that the defendant would give evidence and that witnesses
were available to give evidence in accordance with proofs of evidence
which indicated support for the defendant in his defence. When the
defendant went absent the judge investigated the absence and concluded
that it was voluntary. He exercised his discretion properly and rejected

an application to discharge the jury and to order a new trial. Unfortu- A
nately as a second stage of his ruling and before deciding whether to
continue in the absence of the defendant he said:

> ". . . the next question is what is the position of counsel and solicitor
> here on his behalf. Again, I have no hesitation in saying that the
> absence being, in my judgment, intentional then his instructions are
> deemed to be withdrawn and they can take no further part in the   B
> trial on his behalf whether by way of cross-examination or calling
> other witnesses."

Although they wished to continue their representation, counsel and
solicitor were thus prevented from so doing by judicial order. It is on
this question that the appeal is argued.

At present the only judicial guidance on the matter is to be found   C
in *Archbold Criminal Pleading Evidence and Practice*, 40th ed. (1979),
p. 178, paras. 330 and 330a. Those paragraphs largely deal with the
trial judge's powers to reject a submission to discharge the jury and to
order the continuance of the trial in the absence of the defendant.
They also deal with the position of counsel and solicitor and the Court
of Appeal where an appeal purports to be lodged on behalf of an absconding convicted person. In *Reg.* v. *Jones* (*Robert*) (*No. 2*) [1972] 1   D
W.L.R. 887 it was recognised that it was for counsel to decide whether
to continue representation or not. On professional guidance a relevant
paragraph from the Annual Statement of the Council of the Bar 1978/79
is set out in the second supplement to the current edition of *Archbold*
under para. 350a. That paragraph in the main text begins with the
statement that a member of the Bar should not allow an accused client   E
to be unrepresented at any stage of the trial. The new rule of the
Council of the Bar under the heading, " Representation of an absconding
defendant—counsel's duty," reads as follows:

> " 1. If during the course of a criminal trial and prior to final
> sentence the defendant voluntarily absconds and defending counsel's
> instructing solicitor, in accordance with the ruling of The Law
> Society, withdraws from the case, then counsel too must withdraw.   F
> If counsel is instructed under a legal aid certificate he must apply
> to the court under section 31 (2) of the Legal Aid Act 1974.
> 2. If the trial judge requests counsel to continue in the case
> counsel has an absolute discretion whether he does so. If he does,
> he must act on the basis that his instructions are withdrawn and he
> will not be entitled to use any material contained in his brief save   G
> that part already established in evidence before the court. He
> should request the trial judge to instruct the jury that this is the
> basis on which he is prepared to assist the court."

That ruling and the authorities cited in paras. 330 and 330a of the main
text in *Archbold* provide little if any assistance in the circumstances of
the instant case. It is quite clear that the ruling of The Law Society and   H
the Council of the Bar stems from the application of the legal aid
regulations and it is plain common sense that public funds should no
longer be expended upon the defence of a person who has voluntarily
absented himself from the trial. In the course of argument before us
wider issues were canvassed. It does not follow that in every case
voluntary absence automatically terminates the relationship between
client and solicitor and between solicitor and counsel. What if, as in the

A　case before us, the solicitor feels constrained to continue the relationship albeit without further remuneration and counsel similarly feels himself under the same obligation?　It is not unknown that voluntary absence is due not so much to a recognition of the strength of the prosecution case but to a feeling, perhaps quite unjustified, that the trial is not proceeding fairly.　What if a solicitor has been sufficiently put in funds to cover his own entitlement and counsel's fees right up to the end of

B　trial?　These are all questions of professional conduct and etiquette in which a trial judge should not involve himself, and on which this court should not express an opinion.

It ought in the first place to be clearly recognised that a trial judge has to confine himself to matters within the judicial sphere.　In cases of absence, he has to investigate the absence and to conclude whether or not

C　it is voluntary.　In the instant case the judge did so.　He must consider any application which may be made to discharge the jury and order a new trial.　This also was properly done.　It is not however within his province to dismiss counsel from the case or to order him to remain if counsel is required by the etiquette of the Bar to withdraw.　In the latter event, the most that the judge can do is to invite counsel to assist the court in the

D　manner contemplated by the ruling of the Council of the Bar.

In the present case counsel and his instructing solicitor took the view that their retainer was not affected by the disappearance of their client. Whether they were right or wrong was a matter for them and their respective professional bodies and not for the judge.　He should have allowed counsel to continue to take part in the case.　What counsel could properly have done obviously gave rise to problems.　No doubt he

E　would have concluded that he could go no further than to act as he could have acted if, instead of absenting himself, his client had informed him that he did not intend to give evidence.　But counsel would, if he had thought it proper, have been able at least to call witnesses for the defence.　The judge's decision prevented counsel exercising his discretion and his ruling prejudiced the fairness of the trial.　The verdict of guilty in such circumstances was unsafe and unsatisfactory.　As it is

F　impossible to do more than speculate as to the verdict of the jury had they heard witnesses for the defence, it is not a proper case in which to apply the proviso.

Before parting with this matter, we should like to add that the sudden disappearance of the accused, for whatever reason, gives rise to very real problems concerning the professional duty of both solicitor and

G　counsel.　Each case will differ and the decision will in the end usually be a personal one.　But both branches of the profession need further guidance on the principles to be applied.　We hope that both the professional bodies concerned, after appropriate consultation with each other and with the judiciary, will feel able to give that further guidance and will do so as soon as possible.

H　The appeal is allowed and the conviction quashed.

Appeal allowed.
Conviction quashed.

Solicitors: *Pellys for Peter Masters & Co., Cambridge; David Beal, Cambridge.*

[Reported by MISS EIRA CARYL-THOMAS, Barrister-at-Law]

A

[QUEEN'S BENCH DIVISION]

*REGINA *v.* ENTRY CLEARANCE OFFICER, BOMBAY,
Ex parte AMIN

B

1980   April 30   Lord Lane C.J., Griffiths and Webster JJ.

*Commonwealth immigrant — Admission — Refusal of — Special
voucher—Refusal by entry clearance officer to entertain
application for special voucher—Whether applicant entitled
to appeal — Whether special voucher "entry clearance" —
Immigration Act 1971 (c. 77), ss. 13 (2), 33 (1)—Statement
of Immigration Rules for Control on Entry: Commonwealth
Citizens (1973) (H.C. 79), para. 38*

C

Section 13 (2) of the Immigration Act 1971 provides:
"Subject to the provisions of this Part of this Act, a
person who, on an application duly made, is refused
. . . an entry clearance may appeal to an adjudicator
against the refusal."
Section 33 (1) provides:
". . . 'entry clearance' means a visa, entry certificate
or other document which, in accordance with the immigration rules, is to be taken as evidence of a person's
eligibility, though not patrial, for entry into the United
Kingdom . . ."
Paragraph 38 of the Statement of Immigration Rules for
Control on Entry: Commonwealth Citizens (1973) provides:
"Where the passenger is a citizen of the United Kingdom
and Colonies holding a United Kingdom passport, and
presents a special voucher issued to him by a British
Government representative overseas (or an entry certificate
in lieu), he is to be admitted for settlement. . . ."
In 1976 the applicant, a United Kingdom passport holder
resident in Bombay, applied to an entry clearance officer for a
special voucher to enable her to settle in the United Kingdom.
The officer refused to entertain the application on the ground
that the applicant was not eligible to receive a special voucher.
The applicant was granted leave to apply to the Divisional
Court for judicial review of the officer's decision, and she
sought an order of mandamus requiring him to entertain her
application for a voucher.
On the question whether the applicant had a right of appeal
under section 13 (2) of the Immigration Act 1971 against the
officer's decision : —
Held, dismissing the application, that the applicant came
within the ambit of section 13 (2) of the Act of 1971 only if
the special voucher was an "entry clearance" as defined in
section 33 (1) of the Act; that on the true construction of
section 33 (1) a special voucher was not a document which,
in accordance with the immigration rules, was to be taken as
evidence of a person's eligibility for entry into the United
Kingdom, because it was itself the factual basis entitling a
person to enter; accordingly, since the refusal of a special
voucher was not the refusal of entry clearance, the applicant
had no right of appeal under section 13 (2) (post, pp. 1532E–G,
1534E–F).

D

E

F

G

H

The following case is referred to in the judgment:

Shah v. *Secretary of State for the Home Department* (1971) 1 Imm.A.R.
56.

No additional cases were cited in argument.

A   APPLICATION for judicial review.

Pursuant to leave given on January 13, 1978, the applicant, Bhadrabala Arvindbhai Amin, applied for judicial review by way of an order of mandamus directed to the entry clearance officer, Bombay, to entertain her application for an entry clearance document, namely a special quota voucher.

B   The grounds upon which the relief was sought were, inter alia: (1) that the entry clearance officer erred in law in holding that the applicant was not eligible to apply for a special quota voucher without having regard to section 33 (1) of the Immigration Act 1971, and paragraph 38 of the Statement of Immigration Rules for Control on Entry: Commonwealth Citizens (1973) (H.C. 79); and (2) that having taken a decision that the applicant was not entitled to a special voucher the entry clearance officer

C   should have given the applicant a statutory right of appeal under section 13 (2) of the Immigration Act 1971, by serving the appropriate notice under regulations 3 and 4 of the Immigration Appeals (Notices) Regulations 1972.

The facts are stated in the judgment.

D   *K. S. Nathan* for the applicant.
David Latham for the entry clearance officer.

LORD LANE C.J.   This is an application by Mrs. Bhadrabala Arvindbhai Amin for judicial review directed to the entry clearance officer at Bombay. The application is made pursuant to leave granted on January 13, 1978. This matter has already been before this court on one occasion, the court

E   then being composed of two judges. They were unhappily unable to agree and so now the matter has been listed before this three judge court.

The case is all about what is called the " special quota voucher " system and raises the question whether there is any right of appeal to the adjudicator against a decision to refuse such a voucher.

Briefly, the history of these vouchers is as follows. Up to 1968 people

F   with British passports by and large could come to this country freely, but the Commonwealth Immigrants Act 1968 imposed restrictions on such entry and raised the problem which the special voucher system sought to resolve. The problem was that a number of people holding British passports, particularly Asians in East Africa, found themselves in grave difficulties in not being able to come to this country when their circumstances in East Africa made it essential for them to leave. What happened

G   was that the Government set up a system of admitting some of those people holding British passports by giving them these special vouchers. It was an administrative act and it was subject to a maximum of 5,000 people a year. The limitation put upon the matter was this, that the special vouchers would only be granted to 5,000 heads of families. A quota of 5,000 heads of families might mean, of course, according to the size of

H   the family, a very much greater number of people coming in under the aegis of the system, though, as I understand it, the people coming in other than the head of the family would themselves have to have entry certificates.

In 1973 the applicant's father applied for one of these vouchers for himself and his dependent children. At that time the applicant herself was already married to an Indian national and therefore was no longer dependent upon the father, this father applying for the voucher. In due course vouchers were granted. The father and the family, apart from the applicant, duly entered this country, so I understand, sometime in the spring of 1975. Then on April 19, 1976 this applicant applied to the entry clearance officer at Bombay for one of these vouchers in order that she might be enabled to join her parents who were already here in the United Kingdom. That application was refused in May on the grounds that she was not the head of a family, which was a condition precedent which the Secretary of State had laid down as the basis for giving these vouchers. She was not the head of the family because she was married to an Indian national who himself was the head of the family and was not the holder of a British passport. There was correspondence between the applicant and the Home Office, and in due course the Secretary of State wrote a letter saying that he considered the entry clearance officer's view was correct.

The applicant contends that she has a right of appeal to the adjudicator against that refusal by the entry clearance officer to give her a special voucher.

The matter has been argued before us by Mr. Nathan with his usual skill and lucidity. He has referred us to the Immigration Appeals Act 1969, particularly section 2 (1) (c) which contains wording similar to but not identical with the Immigration Act 1971, which is the material Act for the purposes of this appeal. He has referred us likewise to the Commonwealth Immigrants Acts 1962 and 1968: Instructions to Immigration Officers (1970) (Cmnd. 4298) and various provisions which were contained in that, and also to a decision of the Immigration Appeal Tribunal in *Shah* v. *Secretary of State for the Home Department* (1971) 1 Imm.A.R. 56, decided under those rules, which supports the view put forward by the Secretary of State in this appeal, namely, that the method of the issue of special vouchers is outside the appeals system. But, speaking for myself, although they are interesting as a matter of history, it does not seem to me that those references are of particular importance or of particular help in determining the question that we have to decide here.

In order to determine that, one turns first of all to section 13 of the Immigration Act 1971, which deals with appeals to an adjudicator or tribunal in first instance. The material subsection is section 13 (2), which reads:

"Subject to the provisions of this Part of this Act, a person who, on an application duly made, is refused a certificate of patriality or an entry clearance may appeal to an adjudicator against the refusal."

One has next to determine whether the document in the present case—the special voucher—comes within the definition of "entry clearance," and that is the whole nub of the problem. It is easy to state but not quite so simple to solve. First, one turns to section 33 of the Act of 1971, which is the definition section, in order to find guidance as to the meaning of "entry clearance." Section 33 (1) provides:

". . . 'entry clearance' means a visa, entry certificate or other document which, in accordance with the immigration rules, is to be taken as evidence of a person's eligibility, though not patrial, for entry into the United Kingdom (but does not include a work permit); . . ."

That definition includes the expression "in accordance with the immigration rules," and one turns to a passage further down in the same section

The Weekly Law Reports, December 12, 1980

1533

1 W.L.R.   Reg. v. Entry Clearance Officer, Ex p. Amin (D.C.)   Lord Lane C.J.

A   to discover what is the definition of " immigration rules." One finds: ". . . ' immigration rules ' means the rules for the time being laid down as mentioned in section 3 (2) above; . . ."

Section 3 (2) reads:

" The Secretary of State shall from time to time (and as soon as may
B   be) lay before Parliament statements of the rules, or of any changes in the rules, laid down by him as to the practice to be followed in the administration of this Act for regulating the entry into and stay in the United Kingdom of persons required by this Act to have leave to enter, including any rules as to the period for which leave is to be given and the conditions to be attached in different circumstances; . . ."

C   The next publication to which one must pay regard is the Statement of Immigration Rules for Control on Entry: Commonwealth Citizens (1973) (H.C. 79) laid before Parliament on January 25, 1973 under section 3 (2) of the Immigration Act 1971. One turns there to paragraph 38, which is the material paragraph. It is under Part IV, which is headed " Passengers coming for settlement, United Kingdom passport holders."
D   Paragraph 38 reads:

" Where the passenger is a citizen of the United Kingdom and
Colonies holding a United Kingdom passport, and presents a special
voucher issued to him by a British Government representative
overseas (or an entry certificate in lieu), he is to be admitted for
settlement, as are his dependants if they have obtained entry
certificates for that purpose and satisfy the requirements of paragraph
E   39; but such a passenger who comes for settlement without a special
voucher or entry certificate is to be refused leave to enter."

We are told that the words in brackets, " or an entry certificate in lieu," were put there because in some cases what in fact was a special voucher was said on the face of it to be an entry certificate.

F   Mr. Nathan on behalf of the applicant submits simply that, taking the definition section, section 33, it is plain that the special voucher is a document which in accordance with the immigration rules is to be taken as evidence of a person's eligibility for entry. That is his argument, beginning and end, and a very powerful one it is too, because on the face of it it looks as though a person presenting this document is presenting it as evidence of his eligibility for entry into the United Kingdom.

G   The argument put forward by Mr. Latham on behalf of the Secretary of State is of necessity somewhat more complicated. He points out, first of all, that special vouchers are something out of the ordinary— extraordinary in the true sense of that word. They are designed to relieve hardship in particular parts of the world, and of course as hardship moves around different parts of the world, as it does, so the authorities may
H   desire to apply the system to different parts of the world. It has, he suggests (and one is inclined to agree with him), to be operated from the centre rather than from the periphery. What he submits is that on the broad view, before one gets down to particulars, the special voucher system is outside the appellate system because it is not properly subject to the ordinary idea of an appeal. For example, if the present case were to go to an adjudicator, how would he set about the difficult problem of substituting his own discretion for that of the people (a) operating the

scheme at the centre, and (b) distributing this scheme at the periphery? A
One can see that there would be very great difficulty indeed. In fact it is
hard to see in most cases how he would be able to substitute what he
thought was right for what those operating the scheme thought was right.

The part of the Immigration Act 1971 to which he particularly refers,
other than those which I have already mentioned, is section 19. Section
19 (1) reads:
B
"Subject to sections 13 (4) and 16 (4) above, and to any restriction
on the grounds of appeal, an adjudicator on an appeal to him under
this Part of this Act—(a) shall allow the appeal if he considers—
(i) that the decision or action against which the appeal is brought was
not in accordance with the law or with any immigration rules
applicable to the case; or (ii) where the decision or action involved
the exercise of a discretion by the Secretary of State or an officer, C
that the discretion should have been exercised differently; and (b) in
any other case, shall dismiss the appeal."

Those words, he submits, point to the difficulty which I have just
endeavoured to explain.

But the main point of his argument is this. On the strict wording of
the definition of "entry clearance" in section 33, this document, he D
suggests, is not a document which "is to be taken as evidence of a
person's eligibility." What it is, he says, is the factual basis which entitles
a person to entry into this country, which is a very different matter from
evidence of a person's eligibility. It is not evidence of eligibility, he
submits. It is a document which dispenses with the necessity of such
evidence because the person presenting it need do no more than present E
it, in distinction to the other members of the family coming, so to speak,
behind the gentleman holding the certificate who are subject to inquiry as
to whether they are members of his family and so on.

It is a very fine point, but, in my judgment, the way in which it is
put by Mr. Latham is the correct way. In my view, this is not a document
which is to be taken as evidence of a person's eligibility. It is a factual
basis entitling him to entry without further ado. For those reasons I would F
dismiss this application.

GRIFFITHS J.   I agree.

WEBSTER J.   I agree.
G
Application dismissed.
No order as to costs.

Solicitors: *Suchak & Co.*; *Treasury Solicitor.*

[Reported by MISS ISOBEL COLLINS, Barrister-at-Law]
H

A

[COURT OF APPEAL]

* ADEOSO *v.* ADEOSO

1980 July 14, 15

Ormrod L.J. and Dame
Elizabeth Lane

B

*Injunction—Domestic violence—County court jurisdiction—Man
and woman living as husband and wife—Joint tenancy of
two-room council flat—Relationship becoming strained—Each
occupying separate room and leading separate life but sharing
outgoings—Whether living in " same household "—Domestic
Violence and Matrimonial Proceedings Act 1976 (c. 50), s. 1 (2)*

C
The parties had been living together as husband and wife
for some time when, in May 1977, they were granted a joint
tenancy of a two-room council flat. The appellant alleged in
her evidence that because she had had no child the respondent
told her to leave; that since December 1978 there had been no
sexual intercourse between them and since July 1979 they had
been sleeping in separate rooms which were kept locked; that
she stopped cooking for him and washing his clothes. They
D
did not speak to each other but continued to share the outgoings on the flat. The appellant, alleging acts of violence,
applied to the county court under section 1 (2) of the Domestic
Violence and Matrimonial Proceedings Act 1976 [1] for, inter
alia, an order restraining the respondent from assaulting,
molesting or otherwise interfering with her and for an order
that he should leave the flat. The judge in the county court,
on the appellant's evidence without making any findings, dis-
E
missed the application on the ground that the parties were not
living together in the same household as husband and wife and,
thus, the court had no jurisdiction under section 1 (2).
On appeal : —
Held, allowing the appeal, that on its true construction
section 1 (2) of the Domestic Violence and Matrimonial Proceedings Act 1976 applied to a man and woman who were
F
living with each other in the same household as if they were
husband and wife and that, clearly, the parties were living in
the same household because, whatever might be the position
of a large household which could be divided into separate parts,
it would be artificial to say that two people living, even though
at arm's length, in a two-room flat, where all amenities were
shared, were living in two separate households; that, accordingly, the court had jurisdiction under the subsection and the
G
case should be remitted to the county court for consideration
on its merits (post, pp. 1538H—1539F).
Dicta of Lord Denning M.R. and Viscount Dilhorne in
Davis v. *Johnson* [1979] A.C. 264, 275, 334, C.A. and H.L.(E.)
applied.

The following cases are referred to in the judgment of Ormrod L.J. :

H
Davis v. *Johnson* [1979] A.C. 264; [1978] 2 W.L.R. 182; [1978] 1 All
E.R. 841, C.A.; [1979] A.C. 264; [1978] 2 W.L.R. 553; [1978] 1
All E.R. 1132, H.L.(E.).
McLean v. *Nugent,* June 22, 1979; Court of Appeal (Civil Division) Trans-
cript No. 490 of 1979, C.A.

No additional cases were cited in argument.

[1] Domestic Violence and Matrimonial Proceedings Act 1976, s. 1 (2): see post,
p. 1536G.

APPEAL from Judge Willis sitting at Shoreditch County Court.   A

On April 22, 1980, the appellant, Juliana Esive Adeoso (otherwise Ametepe), applied to the Shoreditch County Court under the Domestic Violence and Matrimonial Proceedings Act 1976 for orders, inter alia, (i) that the respondent, Ebenezer Olakunle Adeoso, should be restrained from assaulting, molesting or otherwise interfering with her and (ii) that he should leave the flat at 51, Southwold Road, London E., and should not return within such radius of the flat as the court might determine.   B

The parties were not married but had been living together as husband and wife for a few years. The appellant, in her affidavits, alleged that their relations had become strained and they were sleeping in separate rooms. She was not cooking for him or washing his clothes. They were not speaking to each other. She also alleged that there were acts of violence on Christmas Day and New Year's Eve 1979.   C

On May 16, 1980, Judge Willis dismissed the application holding that the parties were living separate and apart and were not within section 1 (2) of the Act of 1976. Thus the court had no jurisdiction to entertain the appellant's application.

By a notice of appeal dated June 19, 1980, the appellant appealed on the grounds that the judge was wrong in holding that he had no juris-   D
diction to entertain the application under section 1 (2) of the Act; and that by virtue of the fact that the parties lived together as man and wife in the same household until a date shortly prior to the application the judge did have jurisdiction to entertain the application and was, accordingly, wrong in law in dismissing it without full consideration of the relevant facts and merits.

E

R. P. Glancy for the appellant.
Peter Higginson for the respondent.

ORMROD L.J. This is an appeal by Miss or Mrs. Adeoso—perhaps we ought to call her Ms.—against a judgment by Judge Willis at Shoreditch County Court, on May 16, 1980, by which he dismissed an application   F
by her against Mr. Adeoso, the respondent, for an injunction turning him out of a council flat which they hold as joint tenants.

The case raises again the question of construction of section 1 (2) of the Domestic Violence and Matrimonial Proceedings Act 1976 which, just to remind ourselves, reads:

"(2) Subsection (1) above shall apply to a man and a woman who   G
are living with each other in the same household as husband and wife as it applies to the parties to a marriage and any reference to the matrimonial home shall be construed accordingly."

The point that is taken in this case by counsel on behalf of the respondent to this appeal is that the parties were not living as man and wife in the same household. It is necessary, therefore, to give a brief   H
summary of the facts. These parties have been living together on a sexual footing certainly since the middle of 1976, or probably earlier. According to the respondent's affidavit, he had a council flat in 77, Hendle House, London, E. and, at some time between 1974, when he met the appellant, and May 1977, when the Hackney Council moved them both from 77, Hendle House to 51, Southwold Road, they began living together as man and wife. They are and have been joint tenants of this council

A flat at 51, Southwold Road since May 1977. The flat consists of one bed-room, a sitting room, kitchen and bathroom.

The relationship has become more and more unhappy in recent years, and it culminated in the present appellant applying for an order turning the respondent out of the flat. The date of her application was April 22, 1980. She swore two affidavits in support of that application, alleging violence, saying that there had been no sexual intercourse between them
B since December 1978 and that they had been sleeping in separate rooms, he on the floor in the sitting room and she in the bedroom, since July 1979. There was an act of violence on Christmas Day and New Year's Eve 1979 which precipitated these proceedings. That is roughly the background.

In the course of her oral evidence the appellant took the matter a
C little further. She said that she had ceased to cook for him in January 1980 and stopped washing his clothes, but she added—and this, I cannot help thinking, is rather significant—that they had been living together for three years but, because there was no child, the respondent told her that she must go. That seems to throw a flood of light on the real relationship between the parties, and it turns out that she had been told,
D apparently, that she could not have children. They continued to share the electricity, gas and the rent between them. They have not been on speaking terms, at least, since some time last year, communicating by notes; and she or he keeps the door locked, whoever is in charge of the lock. So that is the state of the relationship. In other words, in ordinary human terms, the relationship is exactly comparable to a marriage which is in the last stages of break-up.

E It was submitted to Judge Willis below that they could not be said, in those circumstances, to be a man and woman who are living with each other in the same household as husband and wife; and the judge accepted that submission and ruled that he had no jurisdiction. He accepted, of course (as he must), that, if they had actually been married, there was no question about his jurisdiction. Section 1 (1) plainly provides for that;
F but it was said that, owing to the difficult drafting of section 1 (2), on the present facts there is no jurisdiction.

It would be plainly absurd, in the circumstances, to hold that there was no jurisdiction. These two have been living as man and wife to all intents and purposes for at least three years. She has taken his name and, to anyone looking at them from outside, there can be no doubt whatever that they were and are apparently living together as husband
G and wife. The judge, I think, attached, with respect, too much importance to the old cases about desertion and was thinking in terms of those old cases, which held that it was possible for a spouse to desert the other while living in closest possible contiguity in the same house, if they succeeded in severing the cooking and washing arrangements and so on. I do not, for my part, think that those cases have any application to the
H present situation. They were invented by a succession of judges to get over the impossible position where a couple had ceased to communicate altogether but neither could leave because they had no alternative accommodation; and so a certain amount of stretching of the law had to be done. I see no useful purpose in reviving those cases and that doctrine in this present situation.

Mr. Glancy has drawn attention to the relevant passages in the authorities which I will just briefly mention. The first is to be found in

Lord Denning M.R.'s judgment in *Davis* v. *Johnson* [1979] A.C. 264.   A
There Lord Denning M.R. was concerned with the words "are living"
in section 1 (3) and he said, at p. 275 :

> " The judges in *B*. v. *B*. [1978] Fam. 26 felt difficulty with the words
> ' are living with each other in the same household.' They felt that on
> the literal meaning of the words they must be living with each other
> at the time when the woman applies to the court. They realised that   B
> in most cases the woman would have already left the house at the
> time when she makes her application. So the literal meaning would
> deprive the subsection of much of its effect. To my mind these words
> do not present any difficulty. They are used to denote the relation-
> ship between the parties before the incident which gives rise to the
> application. If they were then living together in the same household
> as husband and wife, that is enough."   C

Mr. Glancy referred us also to a passage in Sir George Baker P.'s
judgment, which I do not think I need read; and then the other passage,
which is perhaps the more important one, is to be found in Viscount
Dilhorne's speech in the House of Lords in *Davis* v. *Johnson*, where
Viscount Dilhorne said, at p. 334:
                                                                         D
> " Our task is to give effect to the intention of Parliament if that
> can be seen from the language of the statute. Here the language is
> clear and unambiguous and Parliament's intention apparent. Un-
> married persons living together in the same household as husband
> and wife are for the purposes of section 1 (1) to be treated as if they
> were married. The unmarried woman to whom subsection (2) applies
> is to have the same rights as a married woman. A county court   E
> judge in the exercise of his discretion can grant an injunction
> excluding a husband from the home or requiring him to permit her
> to enter and remain there whether or not she has been subjected to
> or threatened with violence or molestation."

Then he continued on those lines.

In *McLean* v. *Nugent,* June 22, 1979; Court of Appeal (Civil Division)   F
Transcript No. 490 of 1979, dealing with this point, I said:

> " In my judgment the test, as it emerges from the passages I have
> cited, depends essentially on the existence at some time of a relation-
> ship which is that of ' a man and a woman living together as man
> and wife.' In other words, if the evidence shows that they have been
> living together as man and wife, they are, within limits which are   G
> not easy to define, to be treated as though they were married at that
> time. The question of fact which arises, of course, in such a situa-
> tion will be ' when has that relationship come to an end? How long
> after it comes to an end is a party entitled to take advantage of
> subsection (2)?' "

Then I went on to deal with the facts in that case, which were very   H
much more extreme than these, because the applicant in *McLean* v.
Nugent had been parted from the respondent for a long time.

I think, for my part, that we have to read section 1 (2) of the Act
of 1976 simply as if it read: " Subsection (1) shall apply to a man and
woman who are living with each other in the same household as if they
were husband and wife." That makes some sense of it because these two
people are clearly living in the same household as if they were husband

A and wife. For my part, I would deprecate any nice attempts to dissect households and ask the question and try to answer it: Are these two people living in the same household? In practical terms one cannot live in a two-room flat with another person without living in the same household. One has to share the lavatory, share the kitchen, share the bathroom and take great care not to fall over one another; and it would be quite artificial to suggest that two people living at arm's length in such

B a situation, from which they cannot escape by reason of the housing difficulties, are to be said to be living in two separate households. Of course, if this were a large household and they were middle class persons, no doubt one could live upstairs and the other could live downstairs; one of them could improvise some cooking facilities and one use the kitchen, and so on. There would, of course, then come a stage when one could

C say: "Well, they really have separated their households." But, on the facts of this case, it would be totally artificial, in my judgment, to say that they succeeded in separating themselves into two individual households. They obviously have not.

In those circumstances, it is plain that these two people have been living together as man and wife for a period of years and have deliberately arranged their lives so; and that they are now at the stage when the

D relationship is breaking down. Ultimately, somebody will have to deal with the joint tenancy. At the moment, both of them are completely boxed in. There is no way either of them can get out of this situation without an order of the court. It is only by getting an order of the court that they have any chance, as I understand it, of getting re-housed; so that it would be a great unkindness to both of them to decline juris-

E diction.

In my judgment, Judge Willis was wrong. He had jurisdiction to entertain this application. In those circumstances I would allow the appeal and send the case back to the county court for the application to be heard on its merits.

F DAME ELIZABETH LANE. I agree and I would add only this; and I add it, perhaps, for the comfort of the respondent. There was no determination by Judge Willis as to the facts which the appellant alleged as regards violence and so forth, and the judge, in rejecting her application for the order sought, was careful to look at the facts from her point of view. When the case is remitted for re-hearing, then both sides will be heard and, if the respondent is in a position to show that her allegations against

G him are false, doubtless she will fail to obtain her order.

Appeal allowed.
No order for costs.
Legal aid taxation for both parties.

H Solicitors: *M. Wernick & Co.; Peter Kingshill.*

A. R.

[1980]

A

[COURT OF APPEAL]

* YOUSIF v. SALAMA AND ANOTHER

[1980 Y. No. 572]

1980   May 7

Lord Denning M.R., Donaldson   B
and Brightman L.JJ.

*Practice—Discovery—Motion for—Ex parte application for order
to enter premises and remove documents—Plaintiff fearing
destruction of documents in defendant's custody—Whether
relief to be granted*

The plaintiff brought an action for sums which he alleged   C
were due to him arising out of an agreement between himself
and the first defendant whereby the plaintiff was to procure
the placing of certain business through the second defendant,
a company owned and controlled by the first defendant, and
the profits were to be shared between the plaintiff and the
second defendant. By an application made ex parte the plaintiff
sought an order requiring the defendants to permit his solicitor   D
to enter the defendants' premises and remove certain documents which the plaintiff claimed were essential to his case
and which he feared the first defendant might destroy. The
judge refused the application.

On appeal by the plaintiff : —

Held, allowing the appeal (Donaldson L.J. dissenting), that
the plaintiff had a legitimate fear that the documents might be
destroyed before the hearing of the action ; that the docu-   E
ments, though not the subject matter of the action, were the
best possible evidence to prove the plaintiff's case ; and that,
in those circumstances, the court ought to permit the plaintiff
to take such steps as were necessary to preserve them (post,
pp. 1542c–d, 1544f).

Per Donaldson L.J. In the limited class of case where there
is a very clear prima facie case leading the court to fear that
the defendant will conceal or destroy evidence in the grossest   F
possible contempt of court and where, should he do so, the
whole process of justice would be frustrated because the
plaintiff would be left without any evidence, the *Anton Piller*
order is absolutely right. But nothing in the present case
brings it within that category (post, p. 1543d–e).

Decision of Robert Goff J. reversed.

G

No cases are referred to in the judgments and no cases were cited in
argument.

APPEAL from Robert Goff J.

By writ dated April 16, 1980, the plaintiff, George Yousif, claimed
against the defendants, Bushra Ibrahim Salama and Selvex Marketing Ltd.,
sums totalling £15,245·98 which he contended were due to him pursuant   H
to an agreement made between the parties in September 1978, whereby
the plaintiff was to procure certain business to be placed with the second
defendant, a company owned and controlled by the first defendant, and
the commission due to the defendant company on such business was to
be shared between the plaintiff and the company. On May 6, 1980, the
plaintiff applied ex parte for an order that the defendants, or the persons
appearing to be in charge of the premises of the defendant company,

A   permit such persons not exceeding two as might be duly authorised by the
plaintiff provided that they be accompanied by the person serving the
order (being a solicitor) to enter the premises forthwith and such other
premises of the first defendant, at which documents comprising or relating to statements of account of the commission due or alleged to be due
to the plaintiff and any documents which were or at any time had been
contained in a file marked " George Yousif " or a file marked " Qitico "
B   and any documents relating to transactions carried out under the terms
of an alleged oral agreement made between the plaintiff and the first
defendant in or about September 1978 at which such documents or any
of them might be kept or stored by the defendants, for the purpose of
searching for the documents and removing the same into the plaintiff's
solicitor's custody; and that the plaintiff's solicitor be permitted to retain
C   the documents or any of them obtained as a result of the order until
after a date to be specified for the purpose of copying the same and that
he be permitted to retain any and all copies made until further order;
with liberty to the defendants to apply to vary or discharge the order on
24 hours notice. The judge refused the application but granted leave to
appeal. The plaintiff appealed.

D   The facts are stated in the judgment of Lord Denning M.R.

    Mary Vitoria for the plaintiff.

    LORD DENNING M.R.   This application raises an interesting new point.
The plaintiff, who was resident in the Middle East, says that he made
an agreement with the first defendant. Certain goods were to be pur-
E   chased in England and dispatched to the Middle East. They were then
to be re-sold there. In respect of those transactions, the profit was to be
divided between the plaintiff and the second defendant, a company controlled by the first defendant: 30 per cent. in some cases and 50 per cent.
in others. That was the agreement.
    Several transactions took place for a year or two. A statement of
F   account was rendered by the defendant company (giving the letter of
credit references) showing a sum due. Business continued thereafter.
Extra commission was accruing. The result was that in March 1980 the
plaintiff went with the first defendant to the defendant company's office
to go through the accounts. Two files were produced containing the
various accounts. They showed sums due to the plaintiff. Also a desk
G   diary.
    The plaintiff, being very anxious about the matter, brought proceed-
ings in the court for the sum due to him. On April 16, 1980, he issued
a writ for that purpose. The total sum claimed was £14,000-odd. The writ
was served. The solicitors for the defendants wrote to the plaintiff's
solicitors saying that they were going to defend the claim strenuously.
H   The plaintiff then became very anxious about the file and the desk
diary he had seen which contained details of the transactions. He became
fearful that the first defendant would destroy those documents before the
actual hearing of the case. On May 6, 1980, the plaintiff applied for an
Anton Piller order. He did not notify the defendant that he was making
that application: because he was afraid the defendant would destroy the
documents if he were notified. The plaintiff asked that he should be
granted an *Anton Piller* order to enable him to go to the defendant

1542

company's offices and inspect the documents before the first defendant A
had an opportunity to destroy them.

In many cases such an order would not be granted. But in this case
there is evidence (if it is accepted) which shows the first defendant to be
untrustworthy. The plaintiff has a legitimate fear that the documents will
be destroyed. In the circumstances, it seems to me that it would be
proper to make an *Anton Piller* order to the effect that the plaintiff's B
solicitor would be enabled to go and get the documents—take them into
his personal custody for a while—make copies of them—and then return
the originals to the defendants. The solicitor would have to keep them
personally himself and not let them out of his possession. It seems to me
that that would be an aid to justice. It would be preserving the evidence
in the case. Under R.S.C., Ord. 29, r. 2, there is a far-reaching power for
preserving documents which are the subject matter of the action. These C
files here are not the subject matter of the action. But they are the best
possible evidence to prove the plaintiff's case. There is a genuine fear
that, if the plaintiff waits till after the application is heard, the first
defendant may destroy the documents before the date of the hearing.
That is the sort of danger which the *Anton Piller* order is designed to
prevent.
D
In the particular circumstances of this case—subject to variations in
wording which we have discussed with counsel—it seems to me that an
Anton Piller order is available. But it should be limited to the documents
which were seen to be in the two files at the interview in March, and the
desk diary which was also seen at that time. So, with those variations
and an undertaking that the documents which are received in pursuance
of the *Anton Piller* order are kept in the solicitor's personal custody, it E
seems to me that the granting of the order can in no way harm the
defendants. It is an aid to justice as far as the plaintiff is concerned.
Instead of having to speculate or try and get evidence from elsewhere,
it should all be available in the files. It can do no harm to the first
defendant at all. If he is honest, he will produce the documents in any
case. If he is dishonest, that is all the more reason why the order should F
be made. Meanwhile, once the documents are handed to the plaintiff's
solicitor, copies can be made of them and the originals returned to the
defendants.

It is an exceptional case. Subject to the variations I have suggested,
I would therefore grant an *Anton Piller* order.

DONALDSON L.J. With great respect to all that has fallen from Lord G
Denning M.R., I have the misfortune to take a rather different view of
this case. The relationship between the parties seems to me to be a very
common one. The plaintiff is a procuring agent in the Middle East. The
terms of his agreement with the first defendant, who is an individual,
and the second defendant, which is a company, are both simple and
common. They are that he will try to procure business for the two H
defendants and that he will be paid a commission on any business which
he procures and passes to them for execution.

The parties of course have fallen out. Again a common situation.
It is true that judges only see the cases that go wrong, so perhaps it is
not as universal an ending as the judges might think. Perhaps some
agency transactions do reach a successful conclusion. But this is a not
uncommon situation again. As a matter of law the defendants are

A accounting parties if the situation is as set out in the plaintiff's affidavit. Again it is a very common situation that a defendant should be an accounting party, and that much of the information which the plaintiff needs should be in his possession. In those circumstances the ordinary order would be either for an account with all the usual inquiries, which would involve the defendants giving evidence on oath as to what was due and the facts on which that indebtedness was based, or perhaps an

B order for discovery.

Discovery can be ordered at any stage. It can be ordered even before statement of claim in an appropriate case. But the ordinary basis of litigation in the English courts is that the courts will make orders and that the parties will obey those orders. Thus it is that under an order for discovery one party gives discovery to the other—and I stress the

C word " gives." The party who is entitled to receive discovery has it given to him. He is not empowered to " take " discovery. What Miss Vitoria asks us to do in this case is to make an order that the plaintiff, on an ex parte application, should be entitled, armed with a warrant from this court, to enter the premises of the defendants and *take* discovery.

I regard that as a very serious invasion of the rights of the defendants. Of course there is precedent for doing it. It is in the *Anton Piller* line of

D cases. The essential feature of those cases, as I understand them, is that there is a very clear prima facie case leading the court to fear that the defendant will conceal or destroy essential evidence in the grossest possible contempt of the court and—and this is an important second limb— that should he do so the whole processes of justice will be frustrated because the plaintiff will be left without any evidence to enable him to

E put forward his claim. In that limited class of case I, for my part, think that the *Anton Piller* order is absolutely right. No court can stand by and see the processes of justice totally frustrated by a defendant in contempt of its order. But I cannot find anything in this case which brings it within that category. I regard the evidence of an intention to destroy the documentation as flimsy in the extreme. It is based upon an allega-

F tion of forgery in the indorsement of a cheque. This has nothing whatever to do with the destruction of documents which the plaintiff says that he fears.

The indorsement may not be that of the plaintiff, but if it was authorised there would be no forgery. If it is really said that there has been forgery here, why were the police not informed? It is a criminal offence, not quietly to be put on one side and then trotted out at a con-

G venient moment in support of an application for an *Anton Piller* order.

Apart from that, it is not irrelevant that the first defendant is a relation of the plaintiff. Family feelings are well-known to be very strong at times, and in a family environment suspicion can grow out of all reason. As I say, I regard the suspicions here as being flimsy in the extreme.

H Even if I am wrong about that, it is quite clear, as I see it, that if these documents are destroyed the plaintiff's case will be in no way weakened. In every agency case of this type the starting point of the calculation of commissions is orders placed through the plaintiff and money passing through the hands of the plaintiff or those with whom he could get in touch without any difficulty. The plaintiff can show quite easily how much money has been paid for goods and services which he has procured for the defendants. Starting from that point, it is the

1544

Donaldson L.J.   Yousif v. Salama (C.A.)   **[1980]**

A

defendants who will need the documents in order to prove that the
plaintiff is not entitled to a very large commission. And, if the defendants
cannot produce the documents, the court will rightly make every presumption in favour of the plaintiff.

Again, it is not a case where there are no documents relating to this
type of business so that the plaintiff, so to speak, starts from scratch.
The plaintiff has the documents for 1978 and can demonstrate the rate
of commission which was payable for that year. There is no suggestion
that the basis was altered for 1979. Given the cash flow for 1979, which
can be proved without difficulty, I can see no problem for him in proving
his prima facie entitlement to commission. The problems will be all for
the defendants.

As I say, I think this is a Draconian power which should be used
in only exceptional cases.

I have considered, of course, whether, as was suggested in argument,
it can rightly be said that no harm is done to an honest man by taking
discovery from him when eventually he would have been ordered to give
it. I think that great harm is done. The people of this country are
entitled not to have their privacy and their property invaded by a court
order except in very exceptional circumstances. That, in my judgment,
is not this case.

I would therefore dismiss the appeal.

B

C

D

BRIGHTMAN L.J. In my view, the order sought in this case is justified
if, but only if, there is prima facie evidence that essential documents are
at risk. If essential documents are at risk, then it seems to me that this
court ought to permit the plaintiff to take such steps as are necessary to
preserve them.

So there are two questions to be asked. First, are the documents
sought to be seized essential to the plaintiff's case? If so, are such documents at serious risk? Might they be dishonestly destroyed?

It is difficult to form any confident view on the merits of the application because inevitably the evidence is one-sided. The defendants have
had no opportunity to answer it. But I think on the plaintiff's evidence
that there are grounds for saying that the documents in question are
essential to the plaintiff's case. I also think that on balance there is
sufficient evidence to justify the court in concluding that the documents
are at risk. Therefore, I would myself favour the grant of an appropriate
order.

E

F

Appeal allowed.

G

Solicitors: *Bower Cotton & Bower.*

C. N.

H

A

[COMMISSARY COURT OF THE CITY AND DIOCESE OF CANTERBURY]

* *In re* ST. MARY THE VIRGIN, SELLING

1980 April 12   Newey Com. Gen.

B   *Ecclesiastical Law—Faculty—Crucifix—Petition to place crucifix behind pulpit—Crucifix gift in memory of former incumbent—Court's approach*

The priest-in-charge and the churchwardens of a country church petitioned for a faculty authorising the placing of a crucifix in the church on the wall by the pulpit. The crucifix, though bearing no words of memorial, was to be a gift in memory of a former incumbent. Three parishioners lodged
C   objections to the proposal on the grounds that it would provide a precedent for further memorials; that to cover the walls of the church with memorials would detract from its beauty; that the positioning of the crucifix would give an appearance of clutter, there already being a large notice board on the wall behind the pulpit; and that, the church not being a high Church, there was no special need for a crucifix.

On the petition:—
D   *Held,* that the crucifix was not a memorial, except to the crucified Christ, and would be of advantage to the church (post, p. 1548B); that the appearance of the church would not become more high Church because an additional crucifix was displayed within it (post, p. 1547C–D); that, aesthetically, it would be a mistake to have both crucifix and notice board and the notice board, though well made, was obtrusive (post, pp. 1547H—1548A); and that, accordingly, leave would be given
E   to place the crucifix in the position occupied by the notice board conditional on the latter being removed with liberty to apply in relation to the repositioning or removal of the notice board (post, p. 1548E).

No cases are referred to in the judgment.

F   PETITION

The priest-in-charge, the Reverend Jonathan Vincent Harman Russell, and the churchwardens, Mr. Eric Gunn and Mr. Sidney Thomas Sampson, petitioned, inter alia, for a faculty authorising the placing of a memorial crucifix in the church of St. Mary the Virgin, Selling, on the wall behind the pulpit. Objections, following advertisement equivalent to citation, were received from three parishioners.

G   The facts are stated in the judgment.

The petitioners in person.
The objectors in person.

NEWEY COM. GEN. In this case the Reverend Jonathan Vincent Harman Russell, priest-in-charge of Selling, and Mr. Eric Gunn and Mr.
H   Sidney Thomas Sampson, churchwardens of Selling, have presented a petition which was first of all for west porch gates and also incorporated a reference to a memorial crucifix. The petition is supported by the parochial church council of the parish.

On September 19, 1979, I directed that citation should issue in respect of the west porch gates and I said that if no objection be lodged the faculty should pass the seal in respect of that proposal. No objection was lodged and the faculty duly passed the seal.

At the same time as I directed citation in respect of the west porch A
gates I gave liberty to apply within 24 months in respect of a memorial
crucifix. In fact an application was made within the 24 months for the
memorial crucifix. That application, I directed on November 5, 1979,
should be the subject of advertisement equivalent to citation and that if
no objection be lodged then leave should be given in respect of the
memorial crucifix. The basis on which the application was made for the
memorial crucifix is really this, that the crucifix itself will be of value B
to the church and of importance to the congregation as providing a
reminder to all of Christ crucified, and that if it be placed in the position
which is proposed it will be visible to members of the congregation during
services and, of course, it will be visible to anybody entering the church.
It is further said in support of the application that the proposal has been
considered by the diocesan advisory committee, who recommended that C
the size originally contemplated for the crucifix should be reduced and
that the parochial church council accepts the reduction in size so that
what is suggested now is, in fact, a crucifix which would have, so far as
the cross is concerned, dimensions of 11 inches by 21 inches and 2¼
inches and that the figure of Our Lord be 9 inches. It is said further in
support of the application that the crucifix proposed would be a gift from
the widow of the late Reverend Ryder who was incumbent of this church D
and who during his period of ministry here wanted very much to place
a crucifix in the general position which is contemplated, and I think that
although it is not actually spelt out in terms but it is obviously the view,
or was initially the view, of the parochial church council that placing the
crucifix in the position suggested behind the pulpit would not detract
from the beauty of this ancient church. I am further told that this matter E
has been considered by the parochial church council on no less than
three occasions and that on the last occasion support for it was recorded
by 17 persons voting in favour and three against.

As a result of the advertisement taking place according to my direction, objections were received and, of course, it is primarily as a result
of those objections being received that this court has been convened here
today. The objections are from Mrs. Gaskain who has been a parishioner F
here for, I think, 47 years, from Mr. Hogben who was christened in this
church some 47 years or so ago, and from Mrs. Hilton who, although
strictly not a member of the Anglican Church, has obviously been a sup-
porter of it for many, many years. I have heard evidence from the
Reverend Russell, from Mr. Gunn and from each of the actual objectors.

The objectors' case can, I think, be summarised as follows. That this G
is a beautiful church; that it is a simple country church; that to cover
its walls with memorials would be to detract from its beauty; that to
permit a crucifix in the position proposed by way of memorial, although
it would not actually bear memorial words, would be a precedent for
further memorials to be introduced; that to place the proposed crucifix
in the position suggested would give an appearance of clutter since it
would be by the pulpit which is standing at the entrance to the choir H
leading to the sanctuary and the wall in that particular place is narrow
and there already is a large wooden notice board there, which is used to
display the name of the Sunday in the Church's year; and the final
objection, and this is one which has not been pressed to any great extent,
is one of tradition. This church is at the centre of the tradition of the
Anglican Church and is not a high church and there is no special need
for a crucifix. The bare Cross is to be seen in many places and there

A   is no particular requirement, therefore, for an actual crucifix. Now I have summarised the case in favour and the case against very briefly, without perhaps putting in all the detail which I could.

My conclusions are as follows. First of all as to the church itself, it is, of course, an ancient church; it is also an outstandingly beautiful church. We are fortunate in our diocese in having many beautiful churches and this is one which would certainly rank high if anyone were

B   to set out to try to provide a list in order of particular beauty and excellence. It is also a church which is obviously extremely well maintained. This is something which reflects great credit on those who look after it, and have looked after it over the years. One has only to see for example the state of the brasses set in the floor of the sanctuary to see how carefully somebody has performed what Mrs. Hilton described as the

C   " Martha " duties in this church. That is the position so far as the church is concerned.

It does not seem to me that the existence or absence of a crucifix, or two crucifixes, or possibly three, necessarily indicates high church, middle church or even low church. In many, many churches of the Church of England in the 20th century at any rate there are crucifixes and I would not have thought myself that anyone would be inclined to say that the

D   appearance of this church would in any way become more " high church " because of the fact that an additional crucifix was displayed within it. So I am not minded to attach much importance to that, nor do, I think, those who object to this proposal. It is obviously a pleasing and sympathetic idea that a crucifix should be placed in a position where the person in whose memory it has been given, although his name is not

E   being recorded upon it, wanted it placed.

Against that we all know that far too many churches are marred by an excessive number of memorials; that makes me, and I suspect also Mrs. Hilton, particularly alert in relation to memorials. I tried in the Diocesan Handbook, both in the last issue and in the previous issue, to give guidance as to where they should be placed and suggested that only persons of national fame who have a local association, or persons who

F   have performed particularly valuable services for the church can expect, or their relatives can expect, to have memorials to them placed in the church. I have also sought to obtain some uniformity in the use of materials for memorials, which certainly does not exist in this church. Basically it seems to me that this case comes down to a question of aesthetics primarily and not questions of churchmanship; nobody is going to fall out whatever the decision I make. There might be disappointment

G   on one side, there might be pleasure on another, but everybody is, I trust, going to be united as good Christians and members of our Anglican communion whatever conclusion I reach.

Actually I have formed a very firm view about this particularly after looking at the church and I will state it very simply and then try to put it in the form of a formal conclusion.

H   I think for my own part that it is a very great pity that the notice board which is behind the pulpit at the moment was placed there. It is a good idea obviously and an attractive idea to have a reminder to people each Sunday of what stage in the Church year we have reached, but that particular notice board, if I may say so before the original authors of it, is well made but obtrusive and I would have thought unnecessary and I am not sure that the choice of wood is particularly wise. At any rate I am pretty sure I would never have granted a faculty for it in its present

form and it was apparently introduced without a faculty. However, it is
there and it actually exists and at least the object behind it is a good one.
It is obvious that this is a narrow length of wall by the entrance to the
choir and it is one which is plainly visible from most parts of the nave
and the side aisles. I think myself it would be a mistake to have both
the crucifix and the notice board. On the other hand without the notice
board, the crucifix could be introduced. The crucifix is not a memorial,
except to the crucified Christ, and would be of advantage to the church
if in a position occupied by about the middle of the notice board. So my
view is crucifix yes, notice board no. But the notice board is there and
cannot be moved without a faculty. Obviously the placing of the crucifix
is important.

The judgment I give is this: that leave may issue for a crucifix of
the dimensions proposed or of lesser dimensions, but not of larger
dimensions, and of the materials which have been proposed, and that it
may be placed in the position which is at present occupied by the top
half of the notice board. That can only be done if the notice board is
removed and so, while I grant the application, its implementation is of
necessity conditional upon the notice board being removed either from
that position out of the church completely or possibly to a different
position in the church. I think that it must rest with the parochial
church council whether the notice board remains as it is at the moment,
or the crucifix be introduced. The council may affix the crucifix provided
it removes the board.

I am going to direct leave to issue in respect of the crucifix and I
am going to give a further liberty to apply to the petitioners as representing the parochial church council, to come back to me for leave to remove
the notice board and either to place it in another position or simply to
remove it altogether. I am also going to give liberty, if the petitioners,
the parochial church council, think fit to apply, to put a fresh, a different
notice board in another part of the church. So, my order is that there
will be leave to place the crucifix with the dimensions stated in the
position stated conditional upon the notice board being removed, and
liberty to apply in relation to the notice board.

Before I part with the case, may I say two other things. One, it has
occurred to me, though it is not my business but that of the parochial
church council, that as a temporary measure at least, one might conceivably put the name of the Sunday on one of the hymn boards while
using the other one for the numbers of hymns and so enable the notice
board to be removed quite speedily and the crucifix affixed as soon as is
convenient. This is only a suggestion. The other is that there is, if I may
say so, very clear evidence of affection for this church, which has been
shown not only by the incumbent but by all the objectors. This is just
as it should be and I hope that you will all unite together in Christian
fellowship and caring for this beautiful building.

Order accordingly.

C. N.

A

[COURT OF APPEAL]

* GASKIN v. LIVERPOOL CITY COUNCIL

[1979 G. No. 2754]

B
1980   June 27   Lord Denning M.R., Megaw and Dunn L.JJ.

Practice—Discovery—Privilege—Confidentiality—Child care records
—Personal injuries' claim for breach of duty while child in
local authority's care—Whether confidentiality of documents
to be preserved—Whether court to inspect documents—
Administration of Justice Act 1970 (c. 31), *s.* 31—R.S.C., Ord.
C   24, *r.* 7A (1)

The prospective plaintiff, who was nearly 21 years of age,
had been in the care of the defendant authority from the age
of six months until he was eighteen. He claimed to be suffering
from severe psychological injuries and anxiety neurosis which
he attributed to the negligence and, or alternatively, breach
of duty of the authority while he was in their care. He applied
D   for an order under section 31 of the Administration of Justice
Act 1970 [1] and R.S.C., Ord. 24, r. 7A,[2] for the disclosure and
production by the authority of " all case notes and/or records "
made upon him in respect of his period in the care of the
authority or their predecessors. Boreham J. held that it was
necessary for the proper functioning of the child care service
that the confidentiality of the documents should be preserved
and he dismissed the summons.

E   On appeal by the plaintiff:—
Held, dismissing the appeal,that the public interest in the
proper functioning of the child care service required that the
confidentiality of the child care documents in the possession
of the authority should be preserved, and that the judge had
been right not to inspect the documents.

D. v. *National Society for the Prevention of Cruelty to*
Children [1978] A.C. 171, H.L.(E.) and *In re D. (Infants)*
F   [1970] 1 W.L.R. 599, C.A. applied.

Burmah Oil Co. Ltd. v. *Governor and Company of the*
Bank of England [1979] 3 W.L.R. 722, H.L.(E.), considered.

Per Lord Denning M.R. Child care privilege and legal
professional privilege are analogous (post, p. 1553D). "Fishing
expeditions" to support claims for negligence should not be
allowed (post, p. 1553G).

G   *Per* Megaw L.J. Inspection of documents by the court
should be undertaken with caution (post, p. 1555c–D).

Decision of Boreham J. affirmed.

H

[1] Administration of Justice Act 1970, s. 31: "On the application, in accordance
with rules of court, of a person who appears to the High Court to be likely to be a
party to subsequent proceedings in that court in which a claim in respect of personal
injuries to a person or in respect of a person's death is likely to be made, the High
Court shall, in such circumstances as may be specified in the rules, have power to
order a person who appears to the court to be likely to be a party to the proceedings
and to be likely to have or to have had in his possession, custody or power any
documents which are relevant to an issue arising or likely to arise out of that claim—
(a) to disclose whether those documents are in his possession, custody or power;
and (b) to produce to the applicant such of those documents as are in his possession,
custody or power."

[2] R.S.C., Ord. 24, r. 7A: "(1) An application for an order under section 31 of the
Administration of Justice Act 1970 . . . shall be made by originating summons and
the person against whom the order is sought shall be made defendant to the
summons."

The following cases are referred to in the judgments:

A

Burmah Oil Co. Ltd. v. *Governor and Company of the Bank of England* [1979] 3 W.L.R. 722; [1979] 3 All E.R. 700, H.L.(E.).

D. (Infants), In re [1970] 1 W.L.R. 599; [1970] 1 All E.R. 1088, C.A.

D. v. *National Society for the Prevention of Cruelty to Children* [1978] A.C. 171; [1976] 3 W.L.R. 124; [1976] 2 All E.R. 993, C.A.; [1978] A.C. 171; [1977] 2 W.L.R. 201; [1977] 1 All E.R. 589, H.L.(E.).

Liverpool City Council, In re A Complaint Against [1977] 1 W.L.R. 995; B [1977] 2 All E.R. 650, D.C.

Reg. v. *Local Commissioner for the North and East Area of England, Ex parte Bradford Metropolitan City Council* [1979] Q.B. 287; [1979] 2 W.L.R. 1; [1979] 2 All E.R. 881, C.A.

The following additional cases were cited in argument:

Conway v. *Rimmer* [1968] A.C. 910; [1968] 2 W.L.R. 998; [1968] 1 All C E.R. 874, H.L.(E.).

Reg. v. *Greenwich Juvenile Court, Ex parte Greenwich London Borough Council* (1977) 76 L.G.R. 99, D.C.

Science Research Council v. *Nassé* [1979] 3 W.L.R. 762; [1979] I.C.R. 921; [1979] 3 All E.R. 673, H.L.(E.).

Shaw v. *Vauxhall Motors Ltd.* [1974] 1 W.L.R. 1035; [1974] 2 All E.R. D 1185, C.A.

INTERLOCUTORY APPEAL from Boreham J.

The prospective plaintiff, Graham Gaskin, applied by summons of July 18, 1979, against the defendants, Liverpool City Council, for an order pursuant to section 31 of the Administration of Justice Act 1970 and R.S.C., Ord. 24, r. 7A that (1) the defendants make an affidavit stating E whether any " case notes and/or records made upon the plaintiff in respect of his period in the care of the defendants or their predecessors [which had been under the provisions of section 1 of the Children's Act 1948] and/or made upon the plaintiff pursuant to the Boarding-Out of Children Regulations 1955 " were or at any time had been in their possession, custody or power and " if not now in their possession, custody F or power " when they parted with them and what had become of them; (2) in so far as the documents were in the defendants' possession, custody or power that they produce the same to the plaintiff.

On February 22, 1980, Boreham J. held that the question to be determined was whether it was " clearly demonstrated that in the particular case the public interest would . . . be better served by excluding evidence despite its relevance," that he was " left in no doubt " that it G was " necessary for the proper functioning of the child care service that the confidentiality of the relevant documents should be preserved " and he dismissed the summons and gave leave to appeal.

The defendants appealed on the grounds that the judge (1) was wrong in law to hold that the public interest demanded that the documents not be disclosed; (2) in balancing the conflicting public interests apparent H in the case failed to give sufficient weight to (a) the general public interest in the fair administration of justice which demanded that all evidence relevant to the determination of the issues in an action be disclosed and (b) the particular public interest in the welfare of children in the care of a local authority which demanded in an action by a plaintiff for damages for personal injuries based upon allegations of neglect and mismanagement of the plaintiff by the local authority its servants or agents while

A in the care of the local authority that all documents relevant to the
plaintiff's period in care be disclosed and (c) the doctrine that " there is
no confidence in iniquity "; (3) further or alternatively that the judge was
wrong not to inspect the documents before deciding whether the disclosure
of all or any of them would be contrary to the public interest.

The facts are stated in the judgment of Lord Denning M.R.

B
Gerard Wright Q.C. and *Timothy King* for the plaintiff.
Eric Somerset Jones Q.C. and *Ian Trigger* for the defendants.

Lord Denning M.R. Graham Gaskin, the prospective plaintiff, is
now nearly 21. His mother died when he was six months old. He was
taken into the care of the local authority—the Liverpool City Council—
C from the age of six months. He has a bad record. He was sent to various
approved schools. He was sent to Borstal. He was afterwards arrested on
a criminal charge, and was sent to prison for six months. Since he came
out of prison, he has been unable to find work. He is living on social
security. After this bad record, he blames it all on the Liverpool City
Council. He has got legal aid and has consulted solicitors, Messrs. E. Rex
D Makin & Co. Through them, he seeks to bring an action against the
Liverpool City Council. He says that they were guilty of negligence and
breach of duty whilst he was in their care. He attributes all his misfortunes
—and his present state of mind—to their want of care. He has not actually
started an action. He has made an application under section 31 of the
Administration of Justice Act 1970. That section enables the court, if it
thinks proper, to order a potential defendant to disclose any documents
E which are relevant to the case which the applicant wants to bring. So
here Graham Gaskin says : " I cannot prove a case of want of care unless
I can search through the records of the Liverpool City Council to see if
I can find a case of negligence and breach of duty against them." In
support of the application the solicitors produce the report of a Dr. Gould.
I think I should read a good deal of it :

F   " He tells me that when his mother died, when he was six months
old, he was put into care until he was 18 years old. His memories of
his early life are necessarily vague but unpleasant and disturbing so
far as he is concerned; he believes that he was moved on about 14
occasions, to various foster parents up to age 8 and afterwards to
various institutions. At one stage when he was about 13 years old,
G   he was put into the care of a single man, remained with him on and
off for a few weeks at a time, for an indefinite period and during
that time was subject to repeated sexual assaults.

" As a child he was unhappy and disturbed, never feeling any
identification with the people looking after him. When he was 9 years
old he was admitted to Mostyn Hospital and put into a men's
H   psychiatric ward for three months, this was frightening and upsetting,
he is unable to explain how he felt, has no real idea why he was
admitted. He was seeing a psychiatrist, Dr. Jarvis, from time to time
until he was about 15 years old, was attending a day clinic in West
Derby, from age 7 to 14, was for some reason given epanutin, but
does not recall ever having suffered any fits or blackouts, believes it
was in order to sedate him because he was overactive and difficult
to control, eventually he refused to take them anymore. When he

Lord Denning M.R.   **Gaskin v. Liverpool Council (C.A.)**   **[1980]**

was about 13 he underwent an EEG but of course he was never   A
informed of the results.

"He received the benefit of an apparently fragmented schooling,
from age 12 to 16 was in various approved schools, but he is able
to read, write, do sums, he passed three CSE examinations. Between
1976 and the end of 1977 he was in Borstal, he took his first job in
February 1978 for about three months, repairing cookers, was then   B
arrested on some criminal charge and sent away to prison for six
months where he saw an ordinary doctor but never a psychiatrist."

Those are his complaints. The doctor gives his opinion in these words:

"The history, as he gives it, is one of neglect and mismanagement.
. . . He has been left with still severe psychological problems, his
future must remain uncertain. . . . Certainly so far as I am concerned   C
there is prima facie evidence in support of his claim to warrant
production of his case notes."

It is obvious that the doctor had nothing to go by except the man's
statement. The history shows that this young man is a psychiatric case,
mentally-disturbed, and quite useless to society. His solicitors now want
to see all the reports so as to bolster up a claim for damages. Though   D
what good damages would do him, I do not know.

In answer the Liverpool City Council say that all the reports, files
and case notes were made confidentially by all those engaged in caring
for him—the social workers, the doctors, and those who arranged for
him to be boarded out. They say that those people would not make reports
frankly and freely unless they knew that they would be kept confidential.   E
They say that, if they are to carry out their obligations properly, they must
not disclose them.

On the other hand, it is said on behalf of Graham Gaskin that, if
things have gone wrong in the upbringing of a child like this, it is proper
that there should be a judicial investigation—on the basis of full discovery
of reports and records. It is said that it is very much in the public interest   F
that the court should see the reports to inquire whether things were done
wrongly or not.

Such is the contest. As always in these cases, it is a matter of balancing
the public interests. The judge did balance them in accordance with the
tests which have been laid down in the authorities. At the end of his
judgment he said:

"... I am left in no doubt that it is necessary for the proper function-   G
ing of the child care service that the confidentiality of the relevant
documents should be preserved. This is a very important service to
which the interests—also very important—of the individual must, in
my judgment, bow. I have no doubt that the public interest will be
better served by refusing discovery and this I do."
   H
The young man's advisers challenge that decision. They want to have
the files to see what they can find out.

The principle underlying this case was stated in this court in *In re D.*
(Infants) [1970] 1 W.L.R. 599. That was a wardship case. Counsel for
the mother wanted to see the records and cross-examine the witnesses
on them. This court held that—because of the regulations in that case—
the reports were to be kept confidential. I said, at p. 600:

The Weekly Law Reports, December 12, 1980

1553

1 W.L.R.   Gaskin v. Liverpool Council (C.A.)   Lord Denning M.R.

A   " . . . I think that these case records should be regarded as privileged:
just as are the records kept by a legal adviser. The child care officers
should not be compelled to produce them, any more than legal
advisers are compelled to produce their notes."

The principle of that case was accepted by this court and the House
of Lords in *D.* v. *National Society for the Prevention of Cruelty to*
B   *Children* [1978] A.C. 171. In the Court of Appeal I said, at p. 191:

" . . . where children's officers compile confidential reports about the
children in their cases, the courts will not compel the local authority
to produce them, even though they would assist in determining a
case: . . ."

Lord Hailsham of St. Marylebone said, at p. 227:

C   " Possibly *In re D. (Infants)* [1970] 1 W.L.R. 599 is another example,
for it decided, I think, for the first time, that local authority records
of child care investigations were immune from disclosure in wardship
proceedings to which they would otherwise be relevant. I believe that
traces of similar evolution, for instance in the field of legal professional privilege, can be found in the 19th century authorities."

D
So he drew a parallel—as I did—between child care privilege and legal
professional privilege. The other members of the House approved *In re
D. (Infants):* see Lord Simon of Glaisdale at p. 236 and Lord Edmund-
Davies at p. 245.

It seems to me that *In re D. (Infants)* [1970] 1 W.L.R. 599 should
now be regarded as of general application: not only in wardship or
E   custody proceedings: but also in actions such as the present—for personal
injury.

I would add that if there were anything in the complaints made on
behalf of this young man, the right way to ventilate them would be—not
by action at law—but by complaint to the local government ombudsman,
as in *Reg.* v. *Local Commissioner for Administration for the North and*
F   *East Area of England, Ex parte Bradford Metropolitan City Council*
[1979] Q.B. 287. On such grounds, the document would not be disclosed
unless the Minister so ordered: see *In re A Complaint Against Liverpool
City Council* [1977] 1 W.L.R. 995. Let us face it. This application is just
a preliminary to an action for damages. If it should be allowed, I wonder
how many more actions might follow by children who have been in care
G   up and down the country. How many of them would start blaming their
misfortunes upon the local authority in whose care they had been? I
regard this application as a " fishing expedition." In *Burmah Oil Co. Ltd.*
v. *Governor and Company of the Bank of England* [1979] 3 W.L.R. 722,
745, Lord Edmund-Davies indicated that " fishing expeditions " should
not be allowed.

The solicitors for the plaintiff ought not to be allowed to roam through
H   the whole of this young man's file to see if in some way or another they
can find a case to support his claim for damages for negligence. I think
that the judge was right, and I would dismiss the appeal.

MEGAW L.J. I agree that this appeal should be dismissed. In my
opinion the judgment of Boreham J. from which this appeal is brought
cannot be faulted. The judge approached the matter in the right way
and by the right route. He set out clearly and with precision the principles

which he was going to apply and the guide-rules by which he was going A
to decide the matter. Having applied the correct principle and given
proper attention to the proper guide-rules, he arrived at the clear conclusion that it was necessary for the proper functioning of the child care
service that the confidentiality of the relevant documents should be
preserved.

The principles or the guidelines on which Boreham J. acted were those B
set out in the speech of Lord Edmund-Davies in *D.* v. *National Society
for the Prevention of Cruelty to Children* [1978] A.C. 171, 242. Boreham
J. cited the first paragraph of that speech, which I need not repeat. Then
Boreham J. set out a summary of the statement by Lord Edmund-Davies
at pp. 245–246. The applicable principles are set out in the form of
propositions. The second proposition, so far as relevant, was:

> ". . . where . . . a confidential relationship exists . . . and . . .   C
> disclosure would be in breach of some ethical or social value involving
> the public interest, the court has a discretion to uphold a refusal
> to disclose relevant evidence provided it considers that, on balance,
> the public interest would be better served by excluding such
> evidence."

I need not read proposition (III), but I should mention that in stating that D
proposition (in the report at p. 245G) Lord Edmund-Davies referred,
obviously with approval, to the decision of this court in *In re D.* (*Infants*)
[1970] 1 W.L.R. 599.

Proposition (IV) reads:

> " The sole touchstone is the public interest, and not whether the
> party from whom disclosure is sought was acting under a ' duty '—   E
> as opposed to merely exercising ' powers '."

Proposition (V):

> " The mere fact that relevant information was communicated in
> confidence does not necessarily mean that it need not be disclosed.
> But where the subject matter is clearly of public interest, the
> *additional* fact (if such it be) that to break the seal of confidentiality   F
> would endanger that interest will in most (if not all) cases probably
> lead to the conclusion that disclosure should be withheld."

Finally, proposition (VI):

> " The disclosure of all evidence relevant to the trial of an issue being
> at all times a matter of considerable public interest, the question   G
> to be determined is whether it is clearly demonstrated that in the
> particular case the public interest would nevertheless be better served
> by excluding evidence despite its relevance. If, on balance, the matter
> is left in doubt, disclosure should be ordered."

As I say, Boreham J., applying those principles to what appeared on the
application before him, had no doubt in his mind that it was necessary H
for the proper functioning of the child care service that the confidentiality
of the relevant documents should be preserved.

The only criticism which I can see could be advanced against that
judgment—and it is a criticism which I think is not justified—would be
that the judge failed to say whether or not he had considered whether he
should himself look at the documents, the various reports and so forth,
of which discovery was sought. We are told—and I of course accept

A without hesitation—that the judge was invited on behalf of the applicant (now the appellant) to look at the documents himself. Therefore by implication, as he did not look at them, he declined so to do. It was vigorously contended on behalf of the applicant that the judge ought to have looked at them before he made up his mind.

In my judgment, the answer to that is to be found in the principle stated in one sentence of the speech of Lord Keith of Kinkel in *Burmah*
B *Oil Co. Ltd.* v. *Governor and Company of the Bank of England* [1979] 3 W.L.R. 722, 750:

"But there may be situations where grave doubt arises, and the court feels that it cannot properly decide upon which side the balance falls without privately inspecting the documents."

C In that case Lord Keith of Kinkel, as also the majority of their Lordships, thought that the doubt was such that the documents should be inspected. It is clear that in the present case Boreham J. did not feel that doubt. Therefore, if he was right about that, the necessity of inspecting the documents did not arise.

It is clear from the various authorities that inspection of a document is a course which it is proper for a court to take in certain cases. It does,
D however, appear to me that it is a course which, while it can be taken, should not be undertaken lightly or ill-advisedly. It may put upon the court a burden which it is extremely difficult, perhaps in some circumstances impossible, to discharge fairly and satisfactorily. It leaves open at any rate the possibility of a feeling on the part of one of the parties to the proceedings that the judge or the members of the court, who has
E or have looked at these documents in private, may have done so without the opportunity of proper guidance as to their possible relevance or their context. If, as might be the case here, the court's perusal were to involve a mass of documents—records which may go back over many years— there might well be, at the least, grave practical difficulties in arriving at fair and sensible decisions on the vital matter of public interest.

F However that may be, in the present case I am satisfied, as Boreham J. was satisfied, that this is not a case where the doubt arises which would make it proper for the court itself to inspect the documents.

DUNN L.J. I entirely agree with the reasoning of the judge. Having, as he said, been left in no doubt that it was necessary for the proper functioning of the child care service that the confidentiality of the relevant
G documents should be preserved, in my view he was right not to inspect the documents in question; and I too would dismiss this appeal.

Appeal dismissed.
No order for costs save legal aid
taxation of appellant's costs.
Leave to appeal refused.

H Solicitors: *Bulcraig & Davies* for *E. Rex Makin & Co., Liverpool;* K. M. Egan, Liverpool.

A. H. B.

A

[COURT OF APPEAL]

* CRESSWELL (VALUATION OFFICER) *v.* B.O.C. LTD.

1980   June 24   Megaw, Eveleigh and Watkins L.JJ.

B

*Rating—Valuation list—Alteration—Proposal by valuation officer
for increase in assessment of hereditament—Fish farm—Buildings and premises used for production of fish for human
consumption—Whether fish " livestock "—Whether fish farm
exempt from rating as agricultural buildings—General Rate Act
1967 (c. 9), s. 26—Rating Act 1971 (c. 39), ss. 1 (1) (3), 2 (1) (a)*

A company owned a site of 12½ acres on which were build-   C
ings and tanks where operations were carried on for the
production of fish, mainly rainbow trout, for food. Fish eggs
were imported from all parts of the world in season, hatched
out in tanks, prepared for sale and sold to hotels and shops.
The premises had a rateable value of £100 based on a previous
industrial user. In 1975 the valuation officer made a proposal
that the gross value and rateable value of the hereditament
should be £4,600 and £3,805 respectively. The company   D
objected on the ground that the buildings and premises were
" agricultural buildings " within the meaning of section 26 of
the General Rate Act 1967 [1] as extended by section 2 (1) (*a*)
of the Rating Act 1971 [2] and were therefore exempt from
rating. The local valuation court was of the opinion that fish
were " livestock " within the meaning of section 1 (3) of the
Act of 1971, found that the buildings and premises were
agricultural buildings, and dismissed the valuation officer's   E
appeal. He appealed to the Lands Tribunal but the President
upheld the decision of the local valuation court and dismissed
his appeal.

On appeal by the valuation officer: —

Held, allowing the appeal, that on the true construction of
section 2 (1) (*a*) of the Rating Act 1971, " livestock " had to
be given its ordinary meaning but used in an agricultural
context and was thus restricted to animals and birds usually   F
regarded as domestic; that section 1 (3) extended that interpretation to include animals or birds of an uncommon kind
used for the production of food or wool, but did not include
fish; and accordingly, the hereditament was not used for the
keeping of " livestock " and was not exempt from rating (post,
pp. 1560G—1561B, 1562F–H, 1563C–D, 1564C, E–F).

Wallace v. *Assessor for Perth and Kinross,* 1975 S.L.T. 118
applied.   G

The following cases are referred to in the judgments:

Belmont Farm Ltd. v. *Minister of Housing and Local Government* (1962)
13 P. & C.R. 417.

[1] General Rate Act 1967, s. 26: " (1) No agricultural land or agricultural   H
buildings shall be liable to be rated or be included in any valuation list or in any
rate."

[2] Rating Act 1971, s. 1: " (1) In section 26 of the General Rate Act 1967 . . . (*a*)
the expression " agricultural buildings " shall include any building which is an
agricultural building by virtue of section 2, 3 or 4 of this Act; . . . (3) In this Part
of this Act ' livestock ' includes any mammal or bird kept for the production of food
or wool or for the purpose of its use in the farming of land. "

S. 2: " (1) Subject to subsection (2) and (4) of this section, each of the following is
an agricultural building by virtue of this section—(*a*) any building used for the keeping
or breeding of livestock. . . . "

A   *Cozens* v. *Brutus* [1973] A.C. 854; [1972] 3 W.L.R. 521; [1972] 2 All
          E.R. 1297, H.L.(E.).
      Wallace v. *Assessor for Perth and Kinross* 1975 S.L.T. 118.

The following additional cases were cited in argument:

Assessor for Strathclyde Region v. *Isle of Jura Fish Farm* (unreported)
      October 9, 1979.

B   *Dilworth* v. *Commissioner for Stamps* [1899] A.C. 99, P.C.
      Eastwood (W. J. B.) Ltd. v. *Herrod* [1971] A.C. 160; [1970] 2 W.L.R.
          775; [1970] 1 All E.R. 774, H.L.(E.).
      Minister of Agriculture Fisheries and Food v. *Appleton* [1970] 1 Q.B.
          221; [1969] 3 W.L.R. 755; [1969] 3 All E.R. 1051, D.C.
      Normanton (Earl of) v. *Giles* [1980] 1 W.L.R. 28; [1980] 1 All E.R. 106,
          H.L.(E.).

C

APPEAL from the Lands Tribunal.

A valuation officer, Mr. G. D. Cresswell, appealed to the Lands
Tribunal (Sir Douglas Frank Q.C., President) from a decision of the local
valuation court for Cumbria given on November 2, 1976, deleting the
description and assessment of a hereditament described as Weighbridge and
Premises, Low Plains, Castlerigg, Cumbria, from the valuation list. On
D   February 26, 1979, the Lands Tribunal dismissed the valuation officer's
appeal. In the case stated by the Lands Tribunal at the request of the
valuation officer it was recorded that notice of appeal to the tribunal had
been given on the grounds (1) that the hereditament was not (and did
not include) " agricultural land " or " agricultural buildings " either within
the meaning of section 26 of the General Rate Act 1967 as originally
E   enacted or as extended by the Rating Act 1971 or at all; (2) that the
word " livestock " as used in the Rating Act 1971 did not include trout,
and the Rating Act 1971 had no application to the hereditament; (3) that
the decision of the local valuation court was incorrect and wrong in law;
and (4) that the hereditament should be included in the valuation list with
the description " Fish farm and Premises, Low Plains, Castlerigg, Cumbria "
at gross value £2,850, rateable value £2,347 (the figures agreed between the
F   parties, if the premises were held to be rateable).

The following facts are summarised from the agreed statement of facts
set out in the decision of the President of the Lands Tribunal annexed
to and forming part of the case. The fish farm and premises were
occupied by Shearwater Fish Farming Ltd. and owned by B.O.C. Ltd.
The current assessment was for a rateable value of £100 (the result of a
G   previous industrial user). The valuation officer made a proposal that the
gross value should be £4,600 and the rateable value £3,805. The ratepayers objected on the ground that a fish farm and premises was exempt
from rating as an agricultural hereditament. The local valuation court
accepted that contention being of the opinion that under section 1 (3) of
the Rating Act 1971 the word " livestock " could be interpreted to include
fish. The court accordingly dismissed the appeal of the valuation officer
H   and directed that the entry in the valuation list should be deleted. It was
agreed between the parties that if it should be held that the whole
hereditament was rateable the gross value should be £2,850 and the
rateable value £2,347.

The hereditament had an area of 12½ acres. It consisted of a number
of buildings and one large lake and three small lakes with a total capacity
of 18,278 cubic yards. Two header tanks and 20 growout tanks were
agreed not to be rateable. The purpose of the operations on the site was

the production of edible fish, mainly rainbow trout. Fish eggs were A imported from California and other parts of the world in rotation according to the season and when they were received at the hereditament they were placed in small tanks in a building known as the hatchery. The fish were hatched out after three to four weeks. After about two weeks the young fish (the alevins) were transferred to other tanks where they remained for about three months and developed into fry. When the fry were large enough they were transferred to the outside growout tanks B where they remained for about 12 months. When they weighed about eight ounces the fish were removed and prepared for sale. In March 1975 trout were being disposed of locally to hotels and shops in the area, but it was then anticipated that freezing plant would be installed on the site to enable fish to be sold in other parts of the country. The aim was to produce 100 tons of edible fish per annum. C

It was common ground that the question to be decided was whether trout were " livestock " within the meaning of section 1 of the Rating Act 1971. Mr. Alan Fletcher for the valuation officer pointed out that the relief was primarily given to land and no buildings were exempt unless they were occupied with agricultural land. Thus, relief would not be given to carp kept in a pond and so there was no logical reason for giving it to fish farms. He submitted that the meaning of " livestock " in section D 2 (1) of the Act of 1971 had to be ascertained by reading it with section 1 (3) and that section 1 (3) was both limiting and extending in that it limited the class to be exempt to mammals and birds and the class of mammals and birds to those kept for the production of food and wool. He conceded that the word " livestock " could include fish but did not in the context of the Act. E

The President said that it was common ground that the issue in the case was the same as that in *R. E. Jones (Valuation Officer)* v. *Bateman* [1974] R.A. 455 which he had decided in favour of the ratepayer and in which he held that in an agricultural context " livestock " meant all live creatures reared for the production of food. Since he gave that decision the Lands Valuation Appeal Court had reached the opposite view in *Wallace* v. F *Assessor for Perth and Kinross* 1975 S.L.T. 118. Their ratio decidendi seemed to have been that the breeding or keeping of trout would not amount to an agricultural use of land in the widest sense. Lord Fraser said that trout might become animals in the future and if so, it might be necessary for some ratepayer to prove the fact to a committee by leading evidence, but that situation was not before them. It seemed, therefore, G that the decision was based on one of fact. In that case the ratepayer appeared in person and the main arguments which were advanced in the instant case and in *R. E. Jones (Valuation Officer)* v. *Bateman* did not seem to have been fully explored. He did not feel compelled by the Scottish case to change the view he had formed in *R. E. Jones (Valuation Officer)* v. *Bateman.* Having regard to the speech of Lord Reid in *Cozens* v. *Brutus* [1973] A.C. 854, 861 it was open to doubt whether the meaning H of " livestock " was a question of law. If, then, the word " livestock " could reasonably include fish, and Mr. Fletcher had conceded that it could, then no question of law was involved. In the President's judgment the ordinary meaning of the word in an agricultural context was something which was alive and was stocked for the purpose of providing food. He confirmed the decision of the local valuation court and dismissed the appeal.

A   The valuation officer appealed claiming that the decision of the Lands Tribunal was erroneous on the grounds (1) that on a true construction of sections 1 (3) and 2 (1) of the Rating Act 1971, in the context of that Act and section 26 of the General Rate Act 1967, the word " livestock " did not include fish; (2) that the Lands Tribunal erred in law in holding that, as the word " livestock " could reasonably include fish, it was a question of fact whether " livestock " in section 1 (3) and 2 (1) included fish; and

B   (3) that the Lands Tribunal erred in law in disregarding the particular definition of " livestock " in section 1 (3).

Alan Fletcher for the valuation officer.
Guy Seward for the company.

C   EVELEIGH L.J., delivering the first judgment. This is an appeal from the decision of the Lands Tribunal, dated February 26, 1979, dismissing an appeal by the valuation officer from a decision of the local valuation court for Cumbria given on November 2, 1976, which ordered the deletion of the description and assessment of a hereditament Weighbridge and Premises, Low Plains, Castlerigg, Cumbria, from the valuation list. The point in dispute in the case is whether fish bred and kept in tanks for sale

D   as food are " livestock " within the meaning of section 2 of the Rating Act 1971.

Section 26 (1) of the General Rate Act 1967 provides: " No agricultural land or agricultural buildings shall be liable to be rated or be included in any valuation list or in any rate." " Agricultural land " is defined in subsection (3) of that section, and " agricultural buildings " in subsection

E   (4).

The Rating Act 1971 extended the definitions. The marginal note to section 1 of that Act reads: " Extension of definition of ' agricultural buildings ' and ' agricultural land ' for purposes of derating in England and Wales "; and subsection (1) of that section reads:

F   " In section 26 of the General Rate Act 1967 (in this Part of this Act referred to as ' the principal section ') the expression ' agricultural buildings ' shall include any building which is an agricultural building by virtue of section 2, 3 or 4 of this Act; . . . "

We are not concerned in this appeal with the expression " agricultural land," which is referred to in section 1 (1) (b). So one then turns to section 2 of the Rating Act 1971, and subsection (1) of that section reads:

G   " Subject to subsections (2) to (4) of this section, each of the following is an agricultural building by virtue of this section—(a) any building used for the keeping or breeding of livestock; . . . "

The word " livestock " is referred to again in section 1 (3) which reads: " In this Part of this Act ' livestock ' includes any mammal or bird kept for the production of food or wool or for the purpose of its use in the

H   farming of land."

The premises in question were situated in Low Plains, Castlerigg, Cumbria. At that site operations were carried on for the production of edible fish, mainly rainbow trout. Eggs were imported from California and other parts of the world. They were placed in small tanks on racks. Later, young fish were transferred to other circular tanks, where they developed into fry, and the fish were fed in those tanks. They were finally removed for sale as food.

1560

The President of the Lands Tribunal, who came to the conclusion that   A
the premises were exempt from rating, arriving at the conclusion that the
fish in question were "livestock." He said: " In my judgment the ordinary
meaning of the word in an agricultural context is something which is alive
and is stocked for the purposes of providing food."

Mr. Fletcher, on behalf of the valuation officer, has submitted that
section 1 (3) is restrictive of any possibly wide meaning that might be
given to " livestock " standing on its own in section 2. It is to be noted   B
that there is no specific definition of the word " livestock " in the Act of
1971. Therefore, says Mr. Fletcher, the livestock with which one is
concerned is mammal or bird for the purposes set out in section 1 (3). The
company, however, has said that in the first instance one should look at
section 2 and ask the question: is the fish " livestock " or not? and that
question should be approached in a general way, regarding the word   C
" livestock " as having a meaning of creatures that are not deadstock.
Counsel for the company says that section 1 (3) is extensive and not
restrictive but is for the purpose of this case irrelevant, because, applying
the natural meaning of the word " livestock," the fish in question already
come within the meaning of that word in section 2.

He also has submitted to this court that the decision of the Lands   D
Tribunal was in effect a decision of fact, applying a possible meaning and
reasonable meaning of the word " livestock," and he has submitted that
this court cannot go behind that decision. For that submission he has
relied on *Cozens* v. *Brutus* [1973] A.C. 854, and in particular upon the
words of Lord Reid at p. 861. It is not necessary to recite that well-known
passage, but counsel has summarised the case by saying that where a
statute uses an ordinary word and a judicial authority has the task of   E
deciding whether or not something comes within the meaning of that
word, then unless the decision is so unreasonable that the court can say
that no reasonable tribunal could arrive at that conclusion, we must not
interfere. To my mind, there is a short answer to that point, namely,
that the President in fact gave his definition of the word " livestock " in
the passage which I have already quoted; this court is in a position,   F
therefore, of seeing the meaning that he ascribed to that word, and if this
court itself ascribes a different meaning, then of course the court can
interfere, for it would then be a question of law as to whether or not the
Lands Tribunal applied the correct definition to the word in question. For
myself, I have come to the conclusion that the President did not apply
the correct definition, but employed a definition that was wider than that
justified by the wording in the Act of 1971.   G

For myself, I would be inclined, at a first look at section 2, to say
that " livestock " there contemplates domestic animals or birds which are
found on agricultural premises and which are supported by the land. In
my judgment, section 2 is the basic section granting relief, and the word
" livestock " is there used in its ordinary meaning, but in an agricultural
context. The agricultural context is, of course, made clear by the fact   H
that what is being extended by the Act of 1971 is the definition of
" agricultural buildings " and " agricultural land." Indeed, the heading
of Part I of the Act of 1971 reads " Agricultural derating in England and
Wales." So, consequently, it is livestock which one, in the ordinary sense
of the word, associates with agriculture; and, to my mind, that does refer
to domestic animals.

Taking that view, as I do, of section 2 of the Act I regard section 1 (3)

A as extensive. It will allow to be brought within the exemption provided
by the statute animals of an uncommon kind which may be kept for the
production of food or wool or for the purposes of use in the farming of
land, and could therefore include animals that are not usually regarded as
domestic. For the present case, I would first look at section 2 and having
decided, as I say, that the fish in this case do not come within the ordinary
meaning of the word " livestock " in an agricultural context, I would go
B no further. However, as an aid to construction of " livestock " in section
2, I think it is permissible to have regard to section 1 (3), and it seems to
me that Parliament there are revealing the kind of creature that it has
in mind in the use of the word " livestock " in section 2. By section 1 (3)
it is in effect saying that of the mammals and birds which one ordinarily
regards as being livestock, there may be some in addition to those and
C they shall be given special protection if kept for the purposes set out in
that subsection. But the use of the words " mammal " and " bird " to my
mind provides a clue to the kind of creature contemplated in the broad
use of the word " livestock " in section 2.

In *Wallace* v. *Assessor for Perth and Kinross* 1975 S.L.T. 118, the
court, in deciding a case the facts of which were very similar to those of
the present case (but, of course, there applying section 5 (2) (*a*) and
D section 6 of the Rating Act 1971, which applied to Scotland), came to the
conclusion that the fish were not livestock. Lord Fraser said, at p. 120:

"As I have already said, the solution of the problem is, in my
opinion, not to be found by reference to the Agricultural Holdings
(Scotland) Act 1949 but only by reference to the definition in section
5 (6) of the Rating Act 1971. In that subsection the word ' livestock '
E is said to ' include any mammal or bird kept for the production of
food. . . .' The fact that Parliament thought it necessary to make
express provision for including such mammals and birds shows, in my
opinion, that the word ' livestock ' cannot by itself have been intended
to include all kinds of living creatures; if that had been intended,
there would have been no need to make the special provision for
mammals and birds. That view is powerfully reinforced by considera-
F tion of section 6 of the 1971 Act which provides that a building
occupied and used solely in connection with the keeping of bees
shall be treated as agricultural lands and heritages. Again, if the
word ' livestock ' in section 5 (6) was enough by itself to cover all
kinds of living creatures, there would have been no need to make
special provision for bees. It follows, in my opinion, that the word
G ' livestock ' in section 5 (6) must have some more limited meaning.
That meaning may perhaps be found in earlier cases under the
Valuation Acts, dealing with the word ' livestock,' or, if that limitation
be too strict, it must at least be found by reference to the context,
which is that of agricultural buildings and agriculture."

The sections there quoted are, of course, the sections which apply to
H Scotland, but the wording used is the same as that to be found in Part I
of the Act applying to England and Wales. Furthermore, section 3 of
the Act makes similar provision as is found in the legislation relating to
Scotland in connection with beekeeping. The reasoning, therefore, of
Lord Fraser is equally applicable, in my view, in construing the sections
relating to England and Wales.

We have, in the course of argument, been referred to a number of
other Acts of Parliament in which the word " livestock " appears. For

myself, I do not find them very helpful. They appear in different settings; A
in the Town and Country Planning Act 1947, for example, in relation to
planning law. In each case, when construing a word which is in general
use, it is important to have regard to the context in which it is used. For
those reasons, I do not find references to decisions under those other
Acts helpful in coming to a decision on this Act.

I therefore would allow this appeal.
                                                                        B

WATKINS L.J. The President of the Lands Tribunal, whose decision
is appealed against to this court, found that the word " livestock " as used
in Part I of the Rating Act 1971 could reasonably and properly construed
include fish. The ordinary meaning of the word in an agricultural context,
he said, is something which is alive and is stocked for the purposes of
providing food. He appears to have thought that this decision did not C
arise out of a question of law. Construction of a word or phrase contained
in a section of an Act of Parliament, whether or not it is used in
conjunction with the provisions contained in other sections of the same
Act, involves inevitably in my opinion a question of law. What is the
proper construction to be put upon the word " livestock " as it is used
in the Rating Act 1971?
                                                                        D
In *Belmont Farm Ltd.* v. *Minister of Housing and Local Government*
(1962) 13 P.& C.R. 417, Lord Parker C.J., in dealing with the construction
of the identical word, said at p. 421:

"It may be that this is rather a matter of first impression, but I
confess that I approach it in this way: Of course, on one view
' livestock ' can be said to be used in contradiction to dead stock, and E
to include any animal whatsoever. In some contexts that might be
so, but it seems to me that in the context of agriculture, as here, it
has some less extensive meaning. What exact meaning should be
given to it if it stood alone in this agricultural context, I do not
propose to determine. I think that it is sufficient to say that there
must be a limitation in that context on what I may call the wide
dictionary meaning. I find it unnecessary to decide what it would F
mean if it stood alone because it does not stand alone, and the words
in brackets that follow assist in determining what is meant by
' livestock.' "

If it is permissible to have regard only to first impressions in deciding
what construction should be put upon the word " livestock " in the present
case, I should be driven to the view that by no stretch of the imagination G
could fish be said to be " livestock " in the agricultural context and more
especially when the word is regarded within the contexts in which it is
used in the Act. If it is impermissible to determine such a matter on that
basis, it becomes necessary to examine how this word has been interpreted
or construed in other Acts of Parliament. I begin with the Agriculture
Act of 1947, where in section 109 (3) " livestock " is interpreted as: H
" ' livestock ' includes any creature kept for the production of food, wool,
skins or fur, or for the purpose of its use in the farming of land."

The Town and Country Planning Act 1947, by section 119 (1) applied
a similar interpretation. Under the heading of the word " agriculture "
and, in brackets, following the word " livestock," it is provided: " including any creature kept for the production of food, wool, skins or fur, or
for the purpose of its use in the farming of land."

A   In the Agricultural Holdings Act 1948, the provisions of section 94 gave the word a somewhat wider interpretation. The provision reads:

> "'livestock' includes any creature kept for the production of food, wool, skins or fur or for the purpose of its use in the farming of land or the carrying on in relation to land of any agricultural activity."

B   More recently, the Selective Employment Payments Act 1966, by section 10 (1) thereof, provided:

> "'agriculture' includes . . . livestock breeding and keeping," and
> "'livestock' includes any creature kept for the production of food, wool, skins or fur, or for the purposes of its use in the farming of land," and so on.

C   It is noteworthy that in the Rating Act 1971 there is no reference whatsoever to "creatures," to "furs" or to "skins." All that appears in association with the word "livestock" are "mammal" and "bird," which seems to indicate an intention to give a more restricted meaning to the word than has been given in previous legislation. It can in my opinion properly be said that, so far as the Rating Act 1971 is concerned, "livestock" is restricted in its meaning so as to include only something D   which is either a mammal or a bird.

Accordingly, I see no reason for including fish within the category of the "livestock" referred to in the Act, whether they be bred or farmed in tanks, ponds, lakes or reservoirs.

I too would allow this appeal.

E   MEGAW L.J. I also agree that this appeal should succeed. Whether or not the contents of section 1 (3) of the Rating Act 1971 are strictly to be called a definition, having regard to the fact that the word used is "includes," I have no doubt that that section must have, at least, an important bearing on the construction of section 2 (1) (a) of the same Act, where that subsection refers to "any building used for the keeping or breeding of livestock." I am comforted to note that Lord Fraser, in F   his judgment in *Wallace* v. *Assessor of Perth and Kinross* 1975 S.L.T. 118 refers to the provisions of the Rating Act 1971 applicable to Scotland, which correspond identically with the provisions of section 1 (3) in relation to England, as "a definition." Lord Fraser says at p. 120:

> "As I have already said, the solution of the problem is, in my opinion, not to be found by reference to the Agricultural Holdings (Scotland)
G   Act 1949 but only by reference to the definition in section 5 (6) of the Rating Act 1971."

Section 5 (6), is the subsection corresponding to section 1 (3) in relation to England.

I agree respectfully and entirely with the way in which the issue was expressed and decided by Lord Robertson in his judgment in the same H   case. There Lord Robertson set out the terms of section 5 (6) of the Rating Act 1971, which he says "defines 'livestock' in the following terms." He then went on, at p. 121:

> "If 'livestock' *includes* any mammal or bird, it was argued, it must embrace other species, such as fish. This was the first time that 'livestock' had been defined in a Rating Act. The important question was the purpose for which the living creature was kept, and if, as in the present case, fish were kept for the production of food in

1564

the same way as cattle or sheep, then the definition was wide enough   A
to embrace fish." " This argument," Lord Robertson goes on, " is
attractive, but, in my opinion, it must fail.   The phrase ' includes any
mammal or bird kept for the production of food,' in my view, covers
some mammals or birds which otherwise might be excluded from
the word ' livestock ' for valuation and rating purposes.   It cannot be
read as covering species of living creatures other than mammals or
birds.   If Parliament had intended the word ' livestock ' to include   B
fish it would have been simple to say so.   This view is underlined by
section 6 of the 1971 Act "—I pause to say that corresponds to section
3 of the Act in relation to England—" which deals specially with
bees; if it had been intended that the definition of ' livestock ' in
section 5 (6) should cover all species of living creatures, section 6
would have been unnecessary."
                                                                                C
I pause there to say that I find that an unanswerable argument on the
question of construction.   Lord Robertson goes on:

    " In my opinion fish are excluded from the definition of ' livestock '
    in section 5 (6) of the 1971 Act, and the argument that the subjects
    of appeal are entitled to be treated as ' livestock buildings ' in terms
    of section 5 therefore fails."
                                                                                D
Lord Keith of Kinkel concurred in the judgments of Lord Fraser and
Lord Robertson.   As I understand it, therefore, Lord Keith was concurring in the ratio decidendi of Lord Robertson's judgment which is in
the passage which I have just read.

    If, contrary to my view, the provisions of section 1 (3) of the Act of
1971 were not to be treated as relevant for the question of the construction   E
of the meaning of " livestock " in section 2 (1) (a) I would nevertheless
arrive at the same result, agreeing—as I do—with the views which
Eveleigh L.J. has expressed as to the meaning to be given to " livestock "
in the absence of any assistance from the context of the Act or other
provisions of the Act.

    I agree, therefore, that the question of law stated by the President of   F
the Lands Tribunal falls to be answered " No," and the appeal should be
allowed.

                           Appeal allowed with costs to include
                           those of the hearing below, taxed
                           on the High Court scale.
                           Hereditament to be entered in valua-   G
                           tion list at the gross value of
                           £2,850, rateable value £2,347.

    Solicitors: *Solicitor of Inland Revenue; G. W. Beck.*

                                                  E. M. W.   H

A

[CHANCERY DIVISION]

In re SOUTH PLACE ETHICAL SOCIETY

BARRALET AND OTHERS *v.* ATTORNEY-GENERAL
AND OTHERS

B

[1978 S. No. 1769]

1980   June 3, 4, 5, 6, 9, 10, 11   Dillon J.

Charity—Charitable purposes—Ethical society—Society beginning as
congregation of Unitarian chapel—Subsequent change of name
and objects—Study and dissemination of ethical principles and
C
cultivation of rational religious sentiment—Whether objects for
advancement of religion or otherwise charitable—Imperfect
trust provisions—Whether provisions validated—Charitable
Trusts (Validation) Act 1954 (2 & 3 Eliz. 2, c. 58), s. 1

The society began in 1824 as the congregation of a Unitarian
chapel. By a deed dated February 1, 1825, its chapel was to
be held by trustees on trust to permit it to be used " for the
D
public worship of one God even the Father and for instruction
in the Christian religion," as professed by the society. The
deed contained a power to vary or rescind any of its provisions
" in relation to the mode of electing or removing trustees,
ministers or other officers or of charging or disposing of all
or any part of the . . . trust estate or of convening and
holding public meetings for the purposes of the . . . trust or
otherwise howsoever." In the event of dissolution of the
E
society so that the public worship of God was discontinued
for the space of two years successively, the trustees were
required, in a final proviso, to convey the trust estate " unto
such person or persons in such manner or for such purposes
either religious or civil " as the specified number of trustees
should direct. The society abandoned prayer in 1869, and in
1887 changed its name to the South Place Ethical Society.
Following legal advice to the effect that the deed of 1825
F
enabled the trustees to alter the trust's charitable purposes,
the trustees executed two deeds of variation, one in 1907 and
one in 1930, as a result of which the society's objects became
" the study and dissemination of ethical principles and the
cultivation of a rational religious sentiment." The chapel was
sold in 1927 and a site was bought on which the well-known
" Conway Hall " was erected, at which the society's activities
had been carried on since 1930. The members of the society
G
were agnostics but not atheists. The society held meetings on
Sundays open to the public, at which lectures were delivered,
followed by discussion. It also published a monthly magazine,
gave concerts of high quality, and indulged in certain social
activities.

On the trustees' summons for declarations, inter alia, as
to whether the society's present objects were for the advance-
H
ment of religion or otherwise charitable and whether it was
the trustees' duty or the trustees were able to convey the
trust assets cy-prés or otherwise: —

Held, (1) that the society's present objects, while possessing
the necessary element of benefit to the public in that they
were not devoted merely to self-improvement of the society's
members, were not for the advancement of religion, but that
they were for the advancement of education or, by analogy
with decided cases, were charitable as being for the public
benefit (post, pp. 1570B–D, 1572B–D, 1573H, 1577C–D).

In re Scowcroft [1898] 2 Ch. 638; *In re Hood* [1931] 1   **A**
Ch. 240, C.A. and *In re Price* [1943] Ch. 422, applied.

Income Tax Special Purposes Commissioners v. *Pemsel*
[1891] A.C. 531, H.L.(E.); *Williams' Trustees* v. *Inland
Revenue Commissioners* [1947] A.C. 447, H.L.(E.); *United
Grand Lodge of Ancient Free and Accepted Masons of
England* v. *Holborn Borough Council* [1957] 1 W.L.R. 1080,
D.C.; *United States* v. *Seeger* (1965) 38 U.S. 163; *Reg.* v.
Registrar General, Ex parte Segerdal [1970] 2 Q.B. 697, C.A.   **B**
and *Incorporated Council of Law Reporting for England and
Wales* v. *Attorney-General* [1972] Ch. 73, C.A. considered.

(2) That the power of variation contained in the deed of 1825,
on its true construction, extended only to matters of machinery
and administration, and that the deeds of 1907 and 1930 were
accordingly void and of no effect; but that the original society
of Protestant dissenters having ceased to exist, the provisions
of the final proviso to the deed of 1825 took effect, and that   **C**
those provisions, despite their initial invalidity, constituted an
imperfect trust provision, which had been validated by the
Charitable Trusts (Validation) Act 1954, and therefore the
trustees were bound to convey the estate " to such person or
persons in such manner and for such purposes, religious or
civil " being charitable as the requisite number of trustees
should direct (post, pp. 1578D–F, 1579F–H).

                                                                  D

The following cases are referred to in the judgment:

Attorney-General v. *Pearson* (1817) 3 Mer. 353.
Bowman v. *Secular Society Ltd.* [1917] A.C. 406, H.L.(E.).
Brisbane City Council v. *Attorney-General for Queensland* [1979] A.C.
    411; [1978] 3 W.L.R. 299; [1978] 3 All E.R. 30, P.C.
Friends' Free School, In re [1909] 2 Ch. 675.
Hood, In re [1931] 1 Ch. 240, C.A.   **E**
Hopkins' Will Trusts, In re [1965] Ch. 669; [1964] 3 W.L.R. 840; [1964]
    3 All E.R. 46.
Income Tax Special Purposes Commissioners v. *Pemsel* [1891] A.C. 531,
    H.L.(E.).
Incorporated Council of Law Reporting for England and Wales v.
    Attorney-General [1972] Ch. 73; [1971] 3 W.L.R. 853; [1971] 3
    All E.R. 1029, C.A.   **F**
Inland Revenue Commissioners v. *McMullen* [1980] 2 W.L.R. 416; [1980]
    1 All E.R. 884, H.L.(E.).
Inland Revenue Commissioners v. *Yorkshire Agricultural Society* [1928]
    1 K.B. 611, C.A.
Price, In re [1943] Ch. 422; [1943] 2 All E.R. 505.
Reg. v. *Registrar General, Ex parte Segerdal* [1970] 2 Q.B. 697; [1970]
    3 W.L.R. 479; [1970] 3 All E.R. 886, C.A.   **G**
Scottish Burial Reform and Cremation Society Ltd. v. *Glasgow Corpora-
    tion* [1968] A.C. 138; [1967] 3 W.L.R. 1132; [1967] 3 All E.R. 215,
    H.L.(Sc.).
Scowcroft, In re [1898] 2 Ch. 638.
United Grand Lodge of Ancient Free and Accepted Masons of England
    v. *Holborn Borough Council* [1957] 1 W.L.R. 1080; [1957] 3 All E.R.
    281, D.C.   **H**
United States v. *Seeger* (1965) 380 U.S. 163.
Washington Ethical Society v. *District of Columbia* (1957) 249 F. 2d 127.
Weir v. *Crum-Brown* [1908] A.C. 162, H.L.(Sc.).
Williams' Trustees v. *Inland Revenue Commissioners* [1947] A.C. 447;
    [1947] 1 All E.R. 513, H.L.(E.).

The following additional cases were cited in argument:

Astor's Settlement Trusts, In re [1952] Ch. 534; [1952] 1 All E.R. 1067.

A   *Atkinson's Will Trusts, In re* [1978] 1 W.L.R. 586; [1978] 1 All E.R. 1275.
    Attorney-General v. *Clapham* (1855) 4 De G.M. & G. 591.
    Bawden's Settlement, In re (Note) [1954] 1 W.L.R. 33; [1953] 2 All E.R. 1235.
    Berry v. *St Marylebone Borough Council* [1958] Ch. 406; [1957] 3 W.L.R. 1029; [1957] 3 All E.R. 677, C.A.

B   *Chartered Insurance Institute* v. *London Corporation* [1957] 1 W.L.R. 867; [1957] 2 All E.R. 638, D.C.
    Gilmour v. *Coats* [1949] A.C. 426; [1949] 1 All E.R. 848, H.L.(E.).
    Harpur's Will Trusts, In re [1962] Ch. 78; [1961] 3 W.L.R. 924; [1961] 3 All E.R. 588, C.A.
    Hummeltenberg, In re [1923] 1 Ch. 237.
    Inland Revenue Commissioners v. *Baddeley* [1955] A.C. 572; [1955] 2 W.L.R. 552; [1955] 1 All E.R. 525, H.L.(E.).

C   *Keren Kayemeth Le Jisroel Ltd.* v. *Inland Revenue Commissioners* [1931] 2 K.B. 465, C.A.
    Macaulay's Estate, In re (Note) [1943] Ch. 435, H.L.(E.).
    National Anti-Vivisection Society v. *Inland Revenue Commissioners* [1948] A.C. 31; [1947] 2 All E.R. 217, H.L.(E.).
    Neville Estates Ltd. v. *Madden* [1962] Ch. 832; [1961] 3 W.L.R. 999; [1961] 3 All E.R. 769.

D   *Oxford Group* v. *Inland Revenue Commissioners* [1949] 2 All E.R. 537, C.A.
    Pinion, decd., In re [1965] Ch. 85; [1964] 2 W.L.R. 919; [1964] 1 All E.R. 890, C.A.
    River Wear Commissioners v. *Adamson* (1877) 2 App.Cas. 743, H.L.(E.).
    Shaw's Will Trusts, In re [1952] Ch. 163; [1952] 1 All E.R. 49.
    Shore v. *Wilson* (1842) 9 Cl. & F. 355, H.L.(E.).

E   *Thackrah, In re* [1939] 2 All E.R. 4.
    Thornton v. *Howe* (1862) 31 Beav. 14.
    Watson, decd., In re [1973] 1 W.L.R. 1472; [1973] 3 All E.R. 678.
    Wedgwood, In re [1915] 1 Ch. 113, C.A.

ORIGINATING SUMMONS

By an originating summons dated April 17, 1978, Colin Eustace
F Barralet, Lily Louisa Booker and Benjamin Oliver Warwick, as trustees of the South Place Ethical Society, claimed (1) a declaration as to whether the property known as Conway Hall, 25, Red Lion Square, London, W.C.1 was held by them upon (a) the trusts of a deed of declaration of trusts dated February 1, 1825, (b) the trusts of that deed as modified by a deed dated July 4, 1907, or (c) as modified by the deed
G of 1907 and a deed dated November 5, 1930, or (d) upon some other and if so what trusts. (2) A declaration as to whether the trusts on which the property was held were (a) for the advancement of religion or otherwise charitable or (b) were not charitable. (3) A declaration as to whether the objects of the South Place Ethical Society were (a) for the advancement of religion or otherwise charitable or (b) were not charitable. (4) If the relief sought in either paragraph (2) or
H paragraph (3) were granted in sense (b) thereof, then a declaration that the trustees of the Conway Hall and the trustees of the other assets, if any, of the South Place Ethical Society were at liberty to convey and assign Conway Hall and such other assets to a company intended to be incorporated under the name of The South Place Ethical Society Ltd. or such other name as might be approved by the Registrar of Companies, with a memorandum and articles of association in the form of drafts annexed to the summons to be held for the purposes set out in

the draft memorandum. (5) A declaration that the objects in the draft **A**
memorandum were (a) for the advancement of religion or otherwise
charitable or (b) were not charitable. (6) Alternatively that, if
necessary, pursuant to sections 13 and 14 of the Charities Act 1960 or
otherwise a scheme might be ordered and settled for the administration
and management of the trusts affecting Conway Hall and such other
assets on the footing that the trusts now affecting the property had
become impracticable and that the property ought to be applied cy-près. **B**
The summons also asked for certain representation orders, execution
of the trusts, further or other relief and provision for the costs.

The facts are stated in the judgment.

Owen Swingland Q.C. and David Ritchie for the trustees.
John F. Mummery for the Attorney-General.   **C**
John L. Knox Q.C. and Robert Ham for the Treasury and Inland
Revenue Commissioners.

DILLON J. I have been asked to hear argument on question 3 raised
by this originating summons, and to give judgment on that question
before hearing argument on the other questions raised in the summons. **D**
Question 3 seeks a declaration as to whether the objects of the South
Place Ethical Society (a) are for the advancement of religion or otherwise charitable or (b) are not charitable.

The society started as the congregation of a chapel at South Place
in Finsbury, which was opened in 1824. It adopted the name " South
Place Religious Society " in the 1860s, and changed that name to
" South Place Ethical Society " in 1887. The name " South Place **E**
Ethical Society " has been retained ever since. The chapel was closed
in 1927 and sold, and a site in Red Lion Square was acquired, on which
the present and well-known Conway Hall was built. It is named after
Moncure Conway, who was minister at the chapel for a long time in
the last century, and has been the society's base ever since 1930.

The present objects of the society are stated in rule 2 of its rules: **F**
" The objects of the society are the study and dissemination of ethical
principles and the cultivation of a rational religious sentiment." These
objects have been among the objects of the society since around the
turn of the century, but before 1930 there was an additional and plainly
non-charitable object, namely, the promotion of human welfare in
harmony with advancing knowledge. The fact that there was at that
time this additional object, and that it was dropped without any **G**
apparent change in the substance of the actual activities of the society,
emphasises that the basic question in deciding whether or not the
society's objects are charitable is a question of construction of those
objects as set out in the society's rules, and then a question of assessing
the objects as so construed against the yardstick of what the law
regards as charitable.   **H**

The rules contain, in rule 22, reference to possible alteration of the
objects of the society, but it is common ground that any power to alter
the rules should be ignored until it is exercised. The question whether
the society is now a charity has to be decided on its objects as they
now are. This is in line with the observations of Atkin L.J. in *Inland
Revenue Commissioners* v. *Yorkshire Agricultural Society* [1928] 1
K.B. 611, 633.

The Weekly Law Reports, December 19, 1980

1569

1 W.L.R.   In re South Place Ethical Society (Ch.D.)   Dillon J.

A   There is no doubt at all that the members of the society are sincere
people of the highest integrity. Mr. Swingland, appearing for the
society, described it as being at the least a wholly learned society with
a deep and thoughtful philosophy. They are not atheists, opposed to
all belief in any god. They are agnostic about the existence of any
god.   The society is non-theistic, like all other ethical movements.
The existence of God is neither affirmed nor denied. In the objects,
B in the phrase "cultivation of a rational religious sentiment," the word
" religious " is used in a sense which eschews all supernatural belief.
I shall return to this later.

Ethical principles mean, in brief summary, the belief in the
excellence of truth, love and beauty, but not belief in anything supernatural.   The society's beliefs are an aspect of Humanism and in the
C tradition of Platonism, and its ideal really represents a philosophical
concept.   The society further believes that the great object of human
existence is the discovery of truth by, as I understand it, intellectual
appreciation or reason and not revelation.

The objects refer to the dissemination as well as the study of ethical
principles, and I should briefly mention the activities of the society.

It holds Sunday meetings, which are open to the public.   At these
D meetings lectures are given, often by visiting lecturers, who may be
persons of very considerable distinction, on subjects of serious and
mainly intellectual interest, and the lectures are followed by discussions.   There are other lectures on special occasions, such as the
Conway Memorial Lectures, in memory of Moncure Conway.   These
are also open to the public.   The society publishes a monthly magazine
E called the " Ethical Record," which is available to the public, and
others of its lectures are published and widely disseminated.   In addition, in pursuit of the ideal of beauty and the appreciation of it, since
the turn of the century, chamber music concerts have been given on
Sunday nights in winter, first at the South Place chapel, and, since
1930, in the Conway Hall.   These are open to the public.   Performers
F of high repute and quality take part, and the performances at these
concerts are regarded by music experts as of a very high standard
indeed.   There are also, and not unexpectedly, social activities, which
are broadly similar to the social activities of the congregation of a
parish church, but these social activities are, in my judgment, ancillary
to the other activities of the society.   At the highest it can be said
that they serve, as with the parish church, to further the esprit de corps
G of the congregation, and this in turn helps to further the cultivation
of the rational religious sentiment.

However high minded the members are, the question for decision is
whether the objects of the society are charitable.   It is well known that
the development of the English law as to what is or is not a charity has
been empirical, but Lord Macnaghten's division of charitable objects
H into four classes in his speech in Income Tax Special Purposes Commissioners v. Pemsel [1891] A.C. 531 has always been found
convenient and has been followed.

In the present case Mr. Swingland, for the members of the society,
contends primarily that the society is charitable because its objects
are for the advancement of religion, but he says, alternatively, that it
is charitable because its objects are for other purposes beneficial to the
community within the fourth of Lord Macnaghten's categories, or are

for the advancement of education. Mr. Mummery, for Her Majesty's A
Attorney-General, neither supports nor opposes the society in its claim
that its objects are for the advancement of religion, but he does support
the society in claiming to be charitable on the ground that its objects
are for the advancement of education or other purposes beneficial to
the community within the fourth category. The Inland Revenue Commissioners, for whom Mr. Knox appears, oppose the society's claims B
root and branch. They have been joined in these proceedings because
the solicitor for the affairs of Her Majesty's Treasury intimated that
there was no claim to the society's assets as bona vacantia, and there
was therefore no one else who opposed the arguments that the society
is a charity.

One of the requirements of a charity is that there should be some
element of public benefit in the sense that it must not be merely a C
members club or devoted to the self-improvement of its own members.
In the case of this society I have no doubt that it is not just a members
club and that it is not merely concerned with the self-improvement of
its members. In its objects there is reference to the cultivation of a
rational religious sentiment; that in my judgment means cultivation
wherever it can be cultivated and not merely cultivation among the
members themselves. D

I propose therefore to consider first the claim that the society is
charitable because its objects are for the advancement of religion. In
considering this, as in considering the other claims, I keep very much
in mind the observation of Lord Wilberforce in the *Scottish Burial
Reform and Cremation Society Ltd.* v. *Glasgow Corporation* [1968]
A.C. 138, 154G, that the law of charity is a moving subject, which may E
well have evolved even since 1891. Mr. Swingland's submissions seek
to establish that this is, indeed, so, having regard to current thinking
in the field of religion.

Of course it has long been established that a trust can be valid and
charitable as for the advancement of religion, although the religion
which is sought to be advanced is not the Christian religion. In F
Bowman v. *Secular Society Ltd.* [1917] A.C. 406, Lord Parker of
Waddington gave a very clear and valuable summary of the history
of the approach of the law to religious charitable trusts at pp. 448 to
450. He said, at p. 449: " It would seem to follow that a trust for the
purpose of any kind of monotheistic theism would be a good charitable
trust." Mr. Swingland accepts that so far as it goes, but he submits that
Lord Parker should have gone further, even in 1917 because the society's G
beliefs go back before that date and the court should go further now.
The society says that religion does not have to be theist or dependent
on a god; any sincere belief in ethical qualities is religious, because
such qualities as truth, love and beauty are sacred, and the advancement
of any such belief is the advancement of religion.

I have been referred to certain decisions in the United States of H
America, which suggest that Mr. Swingland's arguments on this point
would be likely to be accepted in the United States of America, and
that the society would there be regarded as a body established for the
advancement of religion. One decision is that of the Supreme Court
of the United States in *United States* v. *Seeger* (1965) 380 U.S. 163.
That was concerned with the exemption of a conscientious objector
from conscription on the ground of religion. The decision is not of

The Weekly Law Reports, December 19, 1980

1571

1 W.L.R.   In re South Place Ethical Society (Ch.D.)   Dillon J.

A course binding on me, but the reasoning merits serious consideration, not least because it really states the substance of much of the argument that Mr. Swingland is putting forward, and states it with great clarity. The judgment of the court really gives as the ratio in the opinion of the court, delivered by Clark J., at p. 176:

B "A sincere and meaningful belief, which occupies in the life of its possessor a place parallel to that filled by the God of those admittedly qualifying for the exemption [on the ground of religion] comes within the statutory definition."

In his separate opinion, concurring with the opinion of the court, Douglas J. said, at p. 192:

C "a sincere belief, which in his life fills the same place as a belief in God fills in the life of an orthodox religionist, is entitled to exemption."

There is also a decision of the United States Court of Appeals for the District of Columbia in *Washington Ethical Society* v. *District of Columbia* (1957) 249 F. 2d 127, in which it was held that the Washington Ethical Society was entitled to exemption from local taxes or

D rates in respect of its premises under an exemption accorded for buildings belonging to religious corporations or societies and used for religious worship. The report of the judgment of the court is brief. It seems, however, to have adopted a definition of the verb "to worship" as meaning to perform religious services, and to have adopted a dictionary definition of religion as "devotion to some principle; strict fidelity or faithfulness; conscientiousness, pious affecting or attachment,"

E see p. 129. In the *Washington Ethical Society* case the judgment is brief, and the context of the Act undoubtedly weighed with the court. In *United States* v. *Seeger*, 380 U.S. 163 the judgments and the reasoning are much more thorough, and a great deal of weight has been placed on the views of modern theologians, including Bishop John Robinson and the views that he expressed in his book "Honest to God."

F In a free country—and I have no reason to suppose that this country is less free than the United States of America—it is natural that the court should desire not to discriminate between beliefs deeply and sincerely held, whether they are beliefs in a god or in the excellence of man or in ethical principles or in Platonism or some other scheme of philosophy. But I do not see that that warrants extending the meaning of the word "religion" so as to embrace all other beliefs and philo-

G sophies. Religion, as I see it, is concerned with man's relations with God, and ethics are concerned with man's relations with man. The two are not the same, and are not made the same by sincere inquiry into the question: what is God? If reason leads people not to accept Christianity or any known religion, but they do believe in the excellence of qualities such as truth, beauty and love, or believe in the platonic

H concept of the ideal, their beliefs may be to them the equivalent of a religion, but viewed objectively they are not religion. The ground of the opinion of the court, in the United States Supreme Court, that any belief occupying in the life of its possessor a place parallel to that occupied by belief in God in the minds of theists prompts the comment that parallels, by definition, never meet.

In *Bowman* v. *Secular Society Ltd.* [1917] A.C. 406, 445 Lord Parker of Waddington in commenting on one of the objects of the society in that case, namely to promote the principle that human A conduct should be based upon natural knowledge and not upon supernatural belief, and that human welfare in this world is the proper end of all thought and action, said of that object, at p. 445:

" It is not a religious trust, for it relegates religion to a region in which it is to have no influence on human conduct."

That comment seems to me to be equally applicable to the objects of B the society in the present case, and it is not to be answered in my judgment by attempting to extend the meaning of religion. Lord Parker of Waddington has used the word " in its natural and accustomed sense."

Again, in *United Grand Lodge of Ancient Free and Accepted Masons of England* v. *Holborn Borough Council* [1957] 1 W.L.R. 1080, C Donovan J. in delivering the judgment of the Divisional Court, after commenting that freemasonary held out certain standards of truth and justice by which masons were urged to regulate their conduct, and commenting that, in particular, masons were urged to be reverent, honest, compassionate, loyal, temperate, benevolent and chaste, said, at p. 1090: " Admirable though these objects are it seems to us impossible to say that they add up to the advancement of religion." Therefore I D take the view that the objects of this society are not for the advancement of religion.

There is a further point. It seems to me that two of the essential attributes of religion are faith and worship; faith in a god and worship of that god. This is supported by the definitions of religion given in the *Oxford English Dictionary* (1914), although I appreciate that there are other definitions in other dictionaries and books. The *Oxford* E *English Dictionary* gives as one of the definitions of religion: " A particular system of faith and worship." Then:

" Recognition on the part of man of some higher unseen power as having control of his destiny, and as being entitled to obedience, reverence, and worship; "

In *Reg.* v. *Registrar General, Ex parte Segerdal* [1970] 2 Q.B. 697, F which was concerned with the so-called Church of Scientology, Buckley L.J. said, at p. 709:

" Worship I take to be something which must have some at least of the following characteristics: submission to the object worshipped, veneration of that object, praise, thanksgiving, prayer or intercession." G

He went on to say that, looking at the wedding ceremony of the scientologists, he could find nothing in the form of ceremony which would not be appropriate in a purely civil, non-religious ceremony such as is conducted in a register office, and that it contained none of the elements which he has suggested are necessary elements of worship. He then said: H

" I do not say that you would need to find every element in every act which could properly be described as worship, but when you find an act which contains none of those elements it cannot, in my judgment, answer to the description of an act of worship."

The society really accepts that worship by that definition, which in my view is the correct definition in considering whether a body is

The Weekly Law Reports, December 19, 1980

1573

1 W.L.R.   In re South Place Ethical Society (Ch.D.)   Dillon J.

A charitable for the advancement of religion, is not practised by the society, because, indeed, it is not possible to worship in that way a mere ethical or philosophical ideal. I have been referred, as setting out the views of the society, to a pamphlet issued in 1979 by Mr. Cadogan, the secretary of the society. It is headed " The Two Meanings of Worship." After referring to the fact that the society had abandoned prayer in 1869, that is to say, in Mr. Cadogan's words, that particular

B form of worship that is addressed to a personal god, a supreme being, a deity, Mr. Cadogan went on to say:

> " There are two kinds of worship, natural and supernatural. It is worship of the supernatural that we have transcended. For further guidance we should look to our appointed lecturers. The one who very specifically addressed himself to the subject of

C > worship was the late Lord Sorenson."

He then quotes from an article of Lord Sorenson's, published in the " Ethical Record " in 1971, where Lord Sorenson said:

> " Worship is not necessarily theological. The word is a contraction of ' worth-ship,' which means appreciation. Notwithstanding understandable prejudice, itself a feeling in any humanist, in fact

D > they too engage in worship. They do so when, like myself, they sit in their garden and do not argue with the flowers, but simply absorb their delight, and thus find benediction. They do so when for a while they allow music to nourish their hearts, when they have any kind of aesthetic experience, when in fellowship they possess a sense of profound kinship of hearts in communion, and

E > when they find emotional satisfaction in devoted service to an ideal or a great cause, or when they see an infant gazing into its mother's eyes. This appreciation others call worship. It is an emotional response to something or someone, beyond yet related to oneself."

It seems to me that that is not worship in the sense in which worship is an attribute of religion.

F One of the matters that has been pressed in argument and which weighed with Douglas J. in *United States* v. *Seeger*, 380 U.S. 163, is the position of Buddhism, which is accepted by everyone as being a religion. It is said that religion cannot be necessarily theist or dependent on belief in a god, a supernatural or supreme being, because Buddhism does not have any such belief. I do not think it is necessary to explore that further in this judgment, because I do not know enough about

G Buddhism. It may be that the answer in respect of Buddhism is to treat it as an exception, as Lord Denning M.R. did in his judgment in *Reg.* v. *Registrar General, Ex parte Segerdal* [1970] 2 Q.B. 697, 707. Alternatively, it may be that Buddhism is not an exception, because I have been supplied with an affidavit by Mr. Christmas Humphreys, an eminent English Buddhist, where he says that he does not accept the

H suggestion that " Buddhism denies a supreme being." I would not wish to suggest in any way that Buddhism is not a religion.

The society therefore fails in my judgment to make out its case to be charitable on the ground that its objects are for the advancement of religion. I turn therefore to the two other heads, the fourth category of other purposes beneficial to the community and the category of trusts for the advancement of education.

The fourth category developed from the matters specified in the

preamble to the Statute of Elizabeth, but it has long been recognised A
that it is not limited to those matters actually listed in the preamble
which do not fall within Lord Macnaghten's other three categories of
the relief of poverty, the advancement of education and the advancement of religion. It is also clear, as stated in *Tudor, Charities*, 6th
ed. (1967), p. 85 and also at p. 120, that the fourth category can include
trusts for certain purposes tending to promote the mental or moral
improvement of the community. It is on the basis of mental or moral B
improvement of the community that animal welfare trusts have been
supported. But it is plain that not all objects which tend to promote
the moral improvement of the community are charitable.

Again, as Wilberforce J. pointed out *In re Hopkins' Will Trusts*
[1965] Ch. 669, 680–681, " beneficial " in the fourth category is not
limited to the production of material benefit, but includes at least C
benefit in the intellectual or artistic fields.

In *Incorporated Council of Law Reporting for England and Wales*
v. *Attorney-General* [1972] Ch. 73, Russell L.J., at pp. 88–89, seems
to have taken the view that the court can hold that there are some
purposes " so beneficial or of such utility " to the community that they
ought prima facie to be accepted as charitable. With deference, I find
it difficult to adopt that approach, in view of the comments of Lord D
Simonds in *Williams' Trustees* v. *Inland Revenue Commissioners* [1947]
A.C. 447, 455, where, in holding that the promotion of the moral, social,
spiritual and educational welfare of the Welsh people was not charitable,
he pointed out that it was really turning the question upside down to
start with considering whether something was for the benefit of the
community. He said, at p. 455: E

" . . . there are, I think, two propositions which must ever be borne in
mind in any case in which the question is whether a trust is charitable. The first is that it is still the general law that a trust is not
charitable and entitled to the privileges which charity confers,
unless it is within the spirit and intendment of the preamble to the
Statute of Elizabeth, which is expressly preserved by section 13 (3) F
of the Mortmain and Charitable Uses Act 1888. The second is
that the classification of charity in its legal sense into four
principal divisions by Lord Macnaghten in *Income Tax Special
Purposes Commissioners* v. *Pemsel* must always be read subject to
the qualification appearing in the judgment of Lindley L.J. in
In re MacDuff [1896] 2 Ch. 451, 466: ' Now Sir Samuel Romilly
did not mean, and I am certain Lord Macnaghten did not mean, G
to say that every object of public general utility must necessarily
be a charity. Some may be, and some may not be.' This observation has been expanded by Lord Cave L.C. in this House in these
words: ' Lord Macnaghten did not mean that all trusts for
purposes beneficial to the community are charitable, but that there
were certain beneficial trusts which fell within that category; and H
accordingly to argue that because a trust is for a purpose beneficial
to the community it is therefore a charitable trust is to turn round
his sentence and to give it a different meaning. So here it is not
enough to say that the trust in question is for public purposes
beneficial to the community or for the public welfare; you must
also show it to be a charitable trust.' "

The Weekly Law Reports, December 19, 1980

1575

1 W.L.R.   In re South Place Ethical Society (Ch.D.)   Dillon J.

A Therefore it seems to me that the approach to be adopted in considering whether something is within the fourth category is the approach of analogy from what is stated in the preamble to the Statute of Elizabeth or from what has already been held to be charitable within the fourth category.

The question is whether the trust is within the spirit and intendment of the preamble, and the route that the courts have traditionally adopted
B is the route of precedent and analogy, as stated by Lord Wilberforce in *Brisbane City Council* v. *Attorney-General for Queensland* [1979] A.C. 411, 422. One of the difficulties of this approach is that it is often difficult to say which of Lord Macnaghten's categories has been held to cover some particular decided case. Many cases, such as *In re Hopkins' Will Trusts* [1965] Ch. 669 and, in the view of the majority
C of the court, the *Incorporated Council of Law Reporting* case [1972] Ch. 73 have been held to be charitable under two categories: advancement of education and the fourth category of other purposes beneficial to the community. The argument often puts the claim to charitable status, as in the present case, on two or three of the four headings, and the judgments have not differentiated.

D There are three cases which are put before me as analogies in the present case. The earliest is *In re Scowcroft* [1898] 2 Ch. 638. There, there was a devise of a village club and reading room to be maintained for the religious and mental improvement of people in the neighbourhood, and there was an additional reference that it was to be kept free from intoxicants and dancing and to be used for the further-ance of conservative principles. Stirling J. regarded this as being a
E valid charitable trust because it was for religious and mental improve-ment, and he held that the reference to conservative principles was ancillary and not a sufficient limitation to prevent it from being a perfectly good charitable gift, as he clearly thought it would be if it were for the furtherance of religious and mental improvement alone.

Then in *In re Hood* [1931] 1 Ch. 240 there was a trust for the
F application of Christian principles to all human relationships, and this was linked to the reduction and ultimate extinguishment of the drink traffic. It was held that the trust for the application of Christian principles to all human relationships was a good charitable trust. The trust was put forward in the lower court by Mr. Crossman for the Attorney-General as being charitable for three reasons: for the
G advancement of religion, for the advancement of education and for the benefit of the community as being calculated to promote public morality.

Then there is *In re Price* [1943] Ch. 422. There what Cohen J. said about the bequest being charitable was obiter because, even if it was not charitable, its was nonetheless a valid gift to a particular society,
H which the society was at liberty to spend. But Cohen J.'s views are expressed at some length in a considered judgment, and I find them helpful. Mr. Knox has reserved to a higher court, should this case go there, the submission that Cohen J. was not only obiter but wrong. The trust, there, was a trust of a fund to be used for carrying on the teachings of Dr. Rudolph Steiner, and the evidence set out at p. 431 said:

". . . The teachings of Steiner are directed to the extension of   A
knowledge of the spiritual in man and in the universe generally
and of the interaction of the spiritual and the physical."

The deponent went on to say that Rudolph Steiner sought to show both
how this knowledge could be acquired and how it could be applied for
the benefit of man in a wide range of activities. Cohen J. accepted
the submission that the teachings of Rudolph Steiner were directed   B
to the mental or moral improvement of man, and he would have held,
if he had not held the gift otherwise valid, that a trust carrying on those
teachings was a charitable trust. The submission had been that the
trust was charitable as being for mental, moral or religious improvement.   Those therefore are the available analogies.

On the question of trusts for the advancement of education the   C
authorities show that the term " education " is to be construed very
widely. In the *Incorporated Council of Law Reporting* case [1972]
Ch. 73 Buckley L.J. in his judgment at p. 102c said that this head should
be regarded as extending to the improvement of a useful branch of
human knowledge and its public dissemination. *In re Hopkins' Will
Trusts* [1965] Ch. 669, 680 Wilberforce J. said:

". . . that the word 'education'. . . must be used in a wide sense,   D
certainly extending beyond teaching, and that the requirement is
that, in order to be charitable, research must either be of
educational value to the researcher or must be so directed as to
lead to something which will pass into the store of educational
material, or so as to improve the sum of communicable knowledge
in an area which education may cover—education in this last   E
context extending to the formation of literary taste and
appreciation . . ."

The context indicates that literary taste and appreciation did not
exclude musical taste and appreciation.

I turn therefore to the objects of this society, as set out in its rules.
The first part of the objects is the study and dissemination of ethical   F
principles. Dissemination, I think, includes dissemination of the fruits
of the study, and I have no doubt that that part of the objects satisfies
the criterion of charity as being for the advancement of education.
The second part, the cultivation of a rational religious sentiment, is
considerably more difficult. As I have already said, I do not think
that the cultivation is limited to cultivation of the requisite sentiment   G
in the members of the society and in no one else. In the context the
society is outward looking, and the cultivation would extend to all
members of the public whom the society's teachings may reach. The
sentiment or state of mind is to be rational, that is to say founded in
reason. As I see it, a sentiment or attitude of mind founded in
reason can only be cultivated or encouraged to grow by educational
methods, including music, and the development of the appreciation of   H
music by performances of high quality. The difficulty in this part of
the society's objects lies in expressing a very lofty and possibly unattainable ideal in a very few words, and the difficulty is compounded by the
choice of the word " religious," which while giving the flavour of what is
in mind, is not in my view used in its correct sense. Despite this, however, I do not see that the court would have any difficulty in controlling
the administration of the society's assets.

The Weekly Law Reports, December 19, 1980

1577

1 W.L.R.   In re South Place Ethical Society (Ch.D.)   Dillon J.

A   It is well established that a trust cannot be charitable if its objects
are too vague to be carried into effect or controlled by the court.   In
Weir v. *Crum-Brown* [1908] A.C. 162, however, Lord Loreburn L.C.,
in discussing the kind and degree of certainty required, said, at p. 167:

> " All that can be required is that the description of the class to be
> benefited shall be sufficiently certain to enable men of common
> sense to carry out the expressed wishes of the testator."

B

He said that he was satisfied that the trustees, or, failing them, the
court, would find no difficulty in giving effect to the bequest.   Those
observations were approved and applied by Lord Hailsham of St.
Marylebone L.C. in *Inland Revenue Commissioners* v. *McMullen*
[1980] 2 W.L.R. 416, where he also referred to Lord Loreburn L.C.'s
C   doctrine of the benignant approach to charitable trusts.   It seems to
me that these objects are objects which the court could control and
the court could see that the purposes of the funds of the society were
not misapplied.   In my judgment the second part of the society's objects
is also charitable as being for the advancement of education.   Alternatively, by analogy to *In re Price* [1943] Ch. 422; *In re Hood* [1931]
1 Ch. 240 and *In re Scowcroft* [1898] 2 Ch. 638, the whole of the objects
D   of the society are charitable within the fourth class.   I propose therefore
to declare that the objects of the society are charitable, but not for
the advancement of religion.

[Counsel made submissions on question 4 in the originating summons.
His Lordship then delivered the following judgment.]

E   DILLON J.   The further questions which I am now asked to decide
arise in very exceptional circumstances.   When the South Place chapel
in Finsbury was established in 1824 a declaration of trust was made on
February 1, 1825, declaring the trusts of the chapel.   It is headed " A
declaration of trust of the Finsbury Unitarian Chapel in South Place."
The operative trust declared that the chapel should be held upon
F   trust, and the trustees would permit it:

> " . . . to be used and enjoyed by the society or Congregation of
> Protestant   Dissenters   now   assembling   therein   whereof   the
> Reverend William Johnson Fox is the present minister and by the
> future members for the time being of the said society as a place
> for the public religious worship of one God even the Father and
> G   for instruction in the Christian religion as professed by the said
> society. . ."

I am told that the expression " worship of one God even the Father "
was a common phrase used by Unitarians, that is to say, those who did
not believe in the doctrine of the Trinity, and therefore did not believe
in Jesus Christ and the Holy Spirit as God.   I think there is no doubt
H   at all that these trusts declared by the trust deed of 1825 were valid
charitable trusts for the advancement of religion.
    On p. 9 of the trust deed there is a power to vary certain provisions
of the trust deed, which is expressed in the following terms:

> " Provided nevertheless and it is hereby declared that upon or at
> any time or times after the date and execution of these presents it
> shall be lawful for two thirds of the members for the time being of
> the said society who shall be present at two distinct and successive

meetings to be duly convened for that purpose in manner here- A
inbefore expressed and which meetings shall be held at the distance
of one calendar month and not more than two calendar months
from each other to alter vary or rescind any of trusts powers
provisions regulations and restrictions hereby created or declared
or which shall for the time being subsist in relation to the mode
of electing or removing trustees ministers or other officers or of
charging or disposing of all or any part of the said trust estate or B
of convening and holding public meetings for the purposes of the
said trust or otherwise howsoever."

On the advice of eminent King's Counsel to the effect that this power
enabled the trustees to alter the charitable purposes of the trust, a deed
of variation was executed in 1907, substituting new objects, and a
further deed of variation was executed in 1930, further amending the C
objects, producing objects which, though as I have held in my judgment
delivered this morning, they are charitable, are not objects for the
advancement of religion. They are charitable under quite different
headings. In these circumstances I am asked to consider the validity
of the two deeds of variation.

The trouble, as it seems to me, is that if the words " or otherwise D
howsoever " in the proviso on p. 9 of the deed are to be construed
so widely as to enable the charitable objects to be altered, then there is
no limit constraining the new objects to be also charitable, and the
power of alteration would necessarily be void as perpetuitous. So I do
not see how the 1907 and 1930 deeds of variation can be of any effect
at all. I think the true view of the power of variation on p. 9 is that E
it merely enabled there to be an alteration of matters of machinery and
administration, and the power could not be exercised to convert the
charity which had been established by the deed and declared by the
primary trust into even a charity for a religion of a different description
or for teaching different doctrines than those imported by the terms
of the original trust: cf. the observations of Lord Eldon L.C. in *Attorney-
General* v. *Pearson* (1817) 3 Mer. 353, 411–412. F

The immediate effect of that is to leave the original trusts, which
are broadly the trusts of a Unitarian chapel, in operation. But there
is a further proviso at the end of the 1825 trust deed, which is very
unusual in its terms. It reads:

"Provided always and it is hereby lastly declared that ... in case
of [sic] the said Society of Protestant Dissenters shall at any time G
hereafter be totally dissolved or dispersed so that the public worship
of God in the said chapel shall be discontinued for the space of
two years successively then and in such case it shall be lawful for
the trustees for the time being thereof and they are entrusted and
required to convey and assure the said trust estate and the chapel
and other buildings thereon erected with the appurtenances unto H
such persons or persons in such manner or for such purposes either
religious or civil as two-thirds of such trustees for the time being if
exceeding eight in number, otherwise as the whole of such trustees
or any six or more of them shall jointly order direct or appoint
in that behalf. . . ."

That provision could not initially have been valid, because purposes
which are " either religious or civil " are not exclusively charitable, and

The Weekly Law Reports, December 19, 1980

1579

1 W.L.R.   In re South Place Ethical Society (Ch.D.)   Dillon J.

A therefore the power would have been perpetuitous: cf. the decision of Eve J. in *In re Friends' Free School* [1909] 2 Ch. 675.

In 1927 the chapel was closed and the site was sold, but the land in Red Lion Square on which the Conway Hall has since been erected was acquired with the proceeds and other moneys of the South Place Ethical Society, and it seems to me that the Conway Hall must be held on the trusts of the trust deed of 1825 so far as regards the moneys derived B from the proceeds of the South Place chapel.

The history has been set out in detail in the evidence which I have, and it shows the gradual change, particularly in the early and middle part of the last century, in the beliefs of the congregation of the South Place chapel. Prayer was discontinued in the early 1860s, and the congregation, which had adopted the name " South Place Religious C Society " in the 1860s, changed that name to " South Place Ethical Society " in 1887. There is evidence that, even in the time of Mr. Fox, who is named in the trust deed, and specifically in the 1830s, there was a movement of opinion on the part of Mr. Fox and his congregation away from the Unitarian position as it had been at the date of the trust deed, and there was some secession from the congregation, partly for that reason but partly also because of difficulties in Mr. Fox's D domestic life. The upshot is that for over 100 years the society meeting in the South Place chapel, and subsequently in the Conway Hall, has not been a " Society of Protestant Dissenters " at all. There has been, moreover, no public worship of God in the chapel or in the Conway Hall for over 100 years. This is plainly stated in the affidavit of an eminent Baptist minister, Dr. Payne, now deceased, and has been E accepted in cross-examination by Mr. Cadogan, the present secretary of the South Place Ethical Society.

There has been no violent dispersal of the Society of Protestant Dissenters. What has happened is that those who did not adhere to the views which came to be professed in the chapel, particularly when Dr. Moncure Conway was appointed minister, will have left. Others of course died. Those who remained no longer remained as members of F a Society of Protestant Dissenters. The consequence of discontinuance of public worship of God in the chapel for the space of two years and upwards therefore followed 100 years ago, possibly much earlier. I think the true view is that the Society of Protestant Dissenters, which was referred to in the trust deed, has effectively been totally dissolved and ceased to exist.

G Therefore, the events which bring the final proviso into operation have happened, but the invalidity of the final proviso has been cured by the Charitable Trusts (Validation) Act 1954, and I am satisfied, having had the authorities under that Act read to me, that this proviso is an imperfect trust provision within the meaning of that Act. Therefore the position is that the trustees are entitled and bound to convey and assure the trust estate, which will be the Conway Hall, " to H such person or persons in such manner and "—which I think must be the correct reading, rather than " or "—" for such purposes, religious or civil, being charitable " as the requisite number of the trustees appoint.

Declarations accordingly.

Solicitors: *Jacques & Co; Treasury solicitor; Solicitor to the Inland Revenue.*

T. C. C. B.

A

[QUEEN'S BENCH DIVISION]

* REGINA v. COMMISSION FOR RACIAL EQUALITY, Ex parte COTTRELL & ROTHON

1980 May 7

Lord Lane C.J. and Woolf J.

B

Discrimination, Race—Commission for Racial Equality—Functions —Formal investigation of complaint against estate agent— Investigation delegated to commissioners—Commissioners acting on reports of staff's investigations—Estate agent not having opportunity to cross-examine witnesses—Decision to issue non-discrimination notice—Whether investigation properly and fairly conducted—Race Relations Act 1976 (c. 74), ss. 48, 58 (5)

C

The Commission for Racial Equality, having received a complaint that the applicant firm was committing acts of unlawful discrimination in the course of its business as an estate agent, decided to conduct a formal investigation, under section 48 of the Race Relations Act 1976,[1] and nominated two commissioners to carry out their functions in relation to the investigation. Much of the investigation was carried out by the commission's staff, who reported to the commissioners. At the stage in the investigation when the commission were minded to issue a non-discrimination notice requiring the firm not to commit unlawful discriminatory acts, the commission in accordance with section 58 (5) of the Act notified the firm of their intention and gave the firm the opportunity to make written and oral representations to the nominated commissioners. The firm took advantage of the offer. At the hearing before the commissioners, no witnesses were available to give evidence to sustain the complaint or be cross-examined on behalf of the firm. The commission, accepting the commissioners' recommendation, decided to issue the notice.

D

E

On an application for a judicial review on the ground that the conduct of the hearing before the commissioners on which the commission's decision was based did not accord with the rules for a judicial hearing and the rules of natural justice: —

F

Held, dismissing the application, (1) that when the commission had reached the stage in the formal investigation when they were minded to issue a non-discrimination notice and, therefore, in accordance with section 58 (5) of the Act, they afforded the firm the opportunity to make representations, the nature of the resulting hearing was more administrative than judicial; that the strict rules of evidence did not apply to such proceedings and, since basically the commission were carrying out an investigation, fairness did not require that the firm should have the opportunity to cross-examine witnesses (post, p. 1587C–F).

G

Dictum of Diplock L.J. in *Reg.* v. *Deputy Industrial Injuries Commissioners, Ex parte Moore* [1965] 1 Q.B. 456, 458, C.A. applied.

(2) That in carrying out an investigation the commission were not only entitled but in practice were obliged to delegate to their staff the function of collecting information; that, since the commission could delegate that function, it followed that they could act on the information they received from their staff, which by its very nature was hearsay, and, accordingly,

H

---

[1] Race Relations Act 1976, s. 48 (3): post, p. 1583c.
S. 49 (2): see post, p. 1582E.
S. 58 (5): see post, p. 1584c–D.

A   the commissioners appointed to investigate the matter on
       behalf of the commission could not be criticised for not
       hearing evidence from witnesses (post, pp. 1588G—1589c).
            Reg. v. *Race Relations Board, Ex parte Selvarajan* [1975]
       1 W.L.R. 1686, C.A. followed.

       The following cases are referred to in the judgment:

B   *Reg.* v. *Board of Visitors of Hull Prison, Ex parte St. Germain* [1979]
            Q.B. 425; [1979] 2 W.L.R. 42; [1979] 1 All E.R. 701, C.A.
       Reg. v. *Deputy Industrial Injuries Commissioner, Ex parte Moore* [1965]
            1 Q.B. 456; [1965] 2 W.L.R. 89; [1965] 1 All E.R. 81, C.A.
       Reg. v. *Race Relations Board, Ex parte Selvarajan* [1975] 1 W.L.R. 1686;
            [1976] 1 All E.R. 12, C.A.

       The following additional cases were cited in argument:

C   *Blaise* v. *Blaise* [1969] P. 54; [1969] 2 W.L.R. 1047; [1969] 2 All E.R.
            1032, C.A.
       Board of Education v. *Rice* [1911] A.C. 179, H.L.(E.).
       Ridge v. *Baldwin* [1964] A.C. 40; [1963] 2 W.L.R. 935; [1963] 2 All E.R.
            66, H.L.(E.).
       W. L. W., In re [1972] Ch. 456; [1972] 2 W.L.R. 1207; [1972] 2 All E.R.
            433, Ct. of Protection.

D

       APPLICATION for judicial review.
            Pursuant to leave granted by the Divisional Court of the Queen's
       Bench Division on November 21, 1979, the applicant, Cottrell & Rothon,
       a firm of estate agents applied to the Divisional Court for a judicial
       review and relief by way of an order of certiorari to remove into the
E   court and quash a decision made by the respondent, the Commission
       for Racial Equality, on October 11, 1979, that a non-discrimination
       notice should be issued against the firm requiring it to comply with
       certain directions, under section 58 of the Race Relations Act 1976.
       The grounds of the application, inter alia, were that the conduct of the
       hearing before commissioners on which the decision of October 11 was
       based, did not accord with the rules for a judicial hearing and the rules
F   of natural justice in that (1) the firm was not permitted to cross-examine
       witnesses upon whose evidence the commission relied in reaching their
       decision, those witnesses not being produced at the hearing; and (2)
       evidence was heard and admitted which would not be admissible in a
       court of law, and upon which the commission relied in reaching its
       findings; that such witness evidence as was relied on was not produced
       in statement or affidavit form and that such evidence as was relied on
G   was inadmissible hearsay evidence.
            The facts are stated in the judgment.

       Lord Hooson Q.C. and *Jennie Horne* for the applicant.
       Desmond Browne for the respondent.

H   LORD LANE C.J. In this case a firm of estate agents called Messrs.
       Cottrell & Rothon applies for judicial review in the shape of an order of
       certiorari directed to the Commission for Racial Equality pursuant to
       leave given by this court on November 21, 1979.
            The case concerns an alleged infringement of the provisions of the
       Race Relations Act 1976, an Act which we are told has not previously
       been the subject of consideration by this court. It arises out of a situa-
       tion in which it was suggested that the applicant (to whom I shall refer

as the " the firm " hereafter) carried out a system of discrimination   A
against coloured people in the course of its business as estate agents.
One of the allegations, if not the primary allegation, was that vendors
of property who were coloured had their names entered upon cards which
were pink, whereas white people had their particulars entered on white
cards; and certain other discriminatory matters, it is said, were carried
on in the way of business by the firm so that, if a coloured purchaser
appeared on the scene, the likelihood would be that he would not   B
receive the same number, or possibly the same quality, of properties for
his consideration as would a white prospective purchaser.

The chronology of events is as follows, put as briefly as one may.
A Miss Prince was employed by the firm in some sort of clerical capacity
for a short time between December 5, 1977, and January 12, 1978. She
was, it seems, dismissed from her employment, and at the end of January   C
she was making allegations of racial discrimination against the firm.
She made those allegations to the commission. Certain tests were carried
out by the commission. I think they sent two white people and two
coloured people as pretended prospective clients, and the result of those
tests was that to that extent Miss Prince's allegations were substantiated.
On April 5, 1978, the commission, on the strength of those investigations
and tests, agreed the terms of reference for a possible formal investiga-   D
tion into these complaints made under the Race Relations Act 1976.

On April 21, the firm was informed and section 49 procedure was
instituted. Section 49 reads:

"(1) The commission shall not embark on a formal investigation
unless the requirements of this section have been complied with.
(2) Terms of reference for the investigation shall be drawn up by   E
the commission or, if the commission were required by the Secretary of State to conduct the investigation, by the Secretary of State
after consulting the commission. (3) It shall be the duty of the
commission to give general notice of the holding of the investigation
unless the terms of reference confine it to activities of persons
named in them, but in such a case the commission shall in the
prescribed manner give those persons notice of the holding of the   F
investigation. (4) Where the terms of reference of the investigation confine it to activities of persons named in them and the
commission in the course of it propose to investigate any act made
unlawful by this Act which they believe that a person so named
may have done, the commission shall—(a) inform that person of
their belief and of their proposal to investigate the act in question;   G
and (b) offer him an opportunity of making oral or written representations with regard to it (or both oral and written representations
if he thinks fit); and a person so named who avails himself of an
opportunity under this subsection of making oral representations
may be represented—(i) by counsel or a solicitor; or (ii) by some
other person of his choice, not being a person to whom the commission object on the ground that he is unsuitable."   H

This was an opportunity to make written representations, and those
representations were made. The representations contained an explanation of the pink and white card system which I have described, the
suggestion by the firm being that that distinction between card colour
was not based on any distinction between customer colour but was based
on the accent of the person applying or intending to become a customer.

The Weekly Law Reports, December 19, 1980

1583

1 W.L.R.   Reg. v. Commission for Racial Equality (D.C.)   Lord Lane C.J.

A   In other words, the pink cards indicated, according to this suggestion, that the person whose particulars were entered on that pink card spoke with a foreign accent. So much for that explanation.

On May 11 there was a letter from the firm explaining the system. On May 17 the commission's Equal Opportunities Committee altered the charges which had been drafted and deleted two of them, (c) and (d). It is not necessary to give any detail as to that. On June 5, 1978,

B   the commission decided to proceed with the formal investigation. On July 5, 1978, they nominated two persons to carry out that investigation—a Mr. Maan and a Mr. Campbell-Lee—under the provisions of section 48 (3) of the Act.

Section 48 has the sidenote " Power to conduct formal investigations." Subsection (3) reads:

C   " The commission may nominate one or more commissioners, with or without one or more additional commissioners, to conduct a formal investigation on their behalf, and may delegate any of their functions in relation to the investigation to the persons so nominated."

That is what happened in this case. There were minutes to that

D   effect which are before us, although the minutes are of a slightly later date owing to an administrative error. The nominated commissioners are clearly intended to be an extension of the personality of the whole commission. Their delegated functions are set out in a minute before us which there is no need for me to read.

Then came a slight hiccup in the proceedings because on May 18, 1979, the firm took steps to try and spike the guns of the commission.

E   It issued a writ claiming an injunction to prevent the commission from interviewing clients of the firm on whose cards were certain apparently discriminatory markings. On May 25, 1979, a week later, that matter was heard and the injunction was refused with costs. That was the end of that incident.

On July 4, 1979, the commission decided that the firm had contra-

F   vened certain sections of the Race Relations Act 1976, to wit, section 20 (1), which reads:

" It is unlawful for any person concerned with the provision (for payment or not) of goods, facilities or services to the public or a section of the public to discriminate against a person who seeks to obtain or use those goods, facilities or services—(a) by refusing or deliberately omitting to provide him with any of them; or (b) by

G   refusing or deliberately omitting to provide him with goods, facilities or services of the like quality, in the like manner and on the like terms as are normal in the first-mentioned person's case in relation to other members of the public or (where the person so seeking belongs to a section of the public) to other members of that section."

That has to be read in conjunction with section 1 (1) (a) of the Act. The

H   side-heading is " Racial discrimination " and it reads:

" (1) A person discriminates against another in any circumstances relevant for the purposes of any provision of this Act if—(a) on racial grounds he treats that other less favourably than he treats or would treat other persons; . . ."

The second infringement alleged was an infringement of section 30, which has the side-heading " Instructions to discriminate." It reads:

A

" It is unlawful for a person—(a) who has authority over another person; or (b) in accordance with whose wishes that other person is accustomed to act, to instruct him to do any act which is unlawful by virtue of Part II or III, or procure or attempt to procure the doing by him of any such act."

That is the instigation to act. That again has to be read in conjunction with section 1, the terms of which I have already set out.

B

Finally, a breach was alleged of section 33, which is " Aiding unlawful acts " and which reads:

" (1) A person who knowingly aids another person to do an act made unlawful by this Act shall be treated for the purposes of this Act as himself doing an unlawful act of the like description."

C

Those allegations were, as is necessary under the statute, communicated to the firm and the firm was told that the commission were minded to issue a notice and to act in accordance with section 58 (5). Again it is necessary to read that provision:

" The commission shall not serve a non-discrimination notice in respect of any person unless they have first—(a) given him notice that they are minded to issue a non-discrimination notice in his case, specifying the grounds on which they contemplate doing so; and (b) offered him an opportunity of making oral or written representations in the matter (or both oral and written representations if he thinks fit) within a period of not less than 28 days specified in the notice; and (c) taken account of any representations so made by him."

D

E

In order to set the matter in its true light, it is perhaps convenient at this stage to read the other provisions of section 58, namely, subsections (1) and (2). The side-heading to the section is headed " Issue of non-discrimination notice " and the subsections read:

" (1) This section applies to—(a) an unlawful discriminatory act; and (b) an act contravening section 28; and (c) an act contravening section 29, 30 or 31, and so applies whether or not proceedings have been brought in respect of the act. (2) If in the course of a formal investigation the commission become satisfied that a person is committing, or has committed, any such acts, the commission may in the prescribed manner serve on him a notice in the prescribed form (' a non-discrimination notice ') requiring him—(a) not to commit any such acts; and (b) where compliance with paragraph (a) involves changes in any of his practices or other arrangements— (i) to inform the commission that he has effected those changes and what those changes are; and (ii) to take such steps as may be reasonably required by the notice for the purpose of affording that information to other persons concerned."

F

G

On July 27, 1979, a Mr. Gribbin on behalf of the commission set out the grounds on which the commission had decided to proceed in a full letter. In that letter he sets out in minute detail those charges which have been laid, so to speak, against the firm, and the evidence upon which the commission are acting. The commission obviously (and one has only to read the letter to see this) went to great trouble and great pains in order to set out the basis of their allegations against the firm. In it there appears the following paragraph:

H

The Weekly Law Reports, December 19, 1980

1585

1 W.L.R.   Reg. v. Commission for Racial Equality (D.C.)   Lord Lane C.J.

A   " In the light of the above the commission is minded, subject to any representations the agency may make, to issue a non-discrimination notice requiring the agency, its servants and agents not to permit any such act as described in paragraphs (a), (b) and (c) above, or any other act which is an unlawful discriminatory act by virtue of sections 20, 30 and 33 of the Act."

B   Then the firm is reminded of its rights under section 58 (5) (b), which I have already read, and it is by that paragraph offered the opportunity of making representations, either oral or written or both, to Mr. Maan and Mr. Campbell-Lee, the two commissioners who have been designated to carry out the investigation.

On August 29, 1979, came a reply from the firm's solicitor's consisting of eight pages setting out in detail its answers to some of the allegations which are made against it. On September 24, 1979, oral

C   representations were made to the commissioners, solicitor and counsel appearing on behalf of the firm before the commissioners and the commissioners having the advantage of the submissions of Miss Horne of counsel who was instructed by the firm to put forward its case. It is plain, in fairness to her, that no one was au fait with procedure

D   which was likely to be adopted, and that, in the circumstances, is not altogether surprising because this type of procedure is at this stage at any rate by no means common.

It seems that she was expecting, or perhaps half-expecting in the back of her mind, that she might have the opportunity of cross-examining certain of the witnesses on whose evidence the commission were evidently relying. It seems that some such suggestion was made

E   by her at the outset, although it is true that no note of it appears in the very full note which was taken on behalf of the commission by two of their employees, a Miss Smith and a Mr. Deutsch. But there is no doubt that at paragraph 13 of the note of her submissions Miss Horne said there was no evidence other than hearsay evidence and she said that she expected the commission to operate on a judicial standard. She

F   reminded the commissioners that her clients had received no signed statement and had had no opportunity to cross-examine. She said that if the evidence was challenged in a higher court the failure to make witnesses available was a serious step.

It seems to me that what she was indicating there was that, although this was at the end of the day, she was making her submission and she was registering a complaint, and if the matter went further, she would

G   rely, so far as she was able, upon the fact that she had not been permitted to cross-examine any of the witnesses, as I say, on whose evidence the commission were relying.

That brings me to an examination of the nature of the grounds upon which this application for judicial review is based. The statement filed pursuant to the orders of the court reads:

H   " The grounds on which the said relief is sought are as follows: The conduct of the hearing before the commission on which this decision of the commission of October 11, 1979, was based, did not accord with the rules for a judicial hearing and the rules of natural justice in that; (1) the applicant was not permitted to cross-examine witnesses upon whose evidence the commission relied in reaching their decision, those witnesses not being produced at the hearing of the case; (2) evidence was heard and admitted which would not be

admissible in a court of law, and upon which the commission relied   A
in reaching its findings. That such witness evidence as was relied
on was not produced in statement or affidavit form and that such
evidence as was relied on was inadmissible hearsay evidence."

There is a third ground based upon the identity of the commissioners
who carried out the investigation and the fact that they were part of
the full commission which came to the ultimate determination. That   B
ground was very properly abandoned by Lord Hooson in the course
of argument as being untenable.

But there was a further ground adumbrated, although not expressly
set out, with which it will in due course be necessary to deal, and that is,
if I can paraphrase the more elegant words which Lord Hooson used,
that the two investigators appointed to determine—Mr. Maan and Mr.
Campbell-Lee—did not themselves carry out the investigation but left   C
it very largely to employees or servants or administrators of the commission and they passed on that information to the commission at
secondhand.

It is necessary now to deal with each of those three complaints in
turn. First of all, as regards the question that no cross-examination
was permitted, it is dealt with in the affidavit in reply by the commission   D
by a Dr. Sanders in this form:

"that as a matter of law those under formal investigation by the
commission have no right to cross-examine the witnesses seen by
the commission. (Furthermore, no application to cross-examine any
particular witness was ever made by Cottrell & Rothon's legal
advisers at or prior to the oral representation on September 24,
1979)."   E

As to the second point, I have said enough already to indicate that
Miss Horne could scarcely have been expected to do more than she did
to register her complaint about the matter. This point comes down to
decision as to whether in these circumstances the commission were in
the light of the rules of natural justice obliged to allow their witnesses
to be cross-examined.   F

Of course there is a wealth of authority upon what are and what
are not the rules of natural justice. The rules have been described in
various ways, as " an unruly horse," I think, in one decision, and there
is no doubt that what may be the rules of natural justice in one case
may very well not be the rules of natural justice in another. As has
frequently been said, and there is no harm in repeating it, all that the   G
rules of natural justice mean is that the proceedings must be conducted
in a way which is fair to the firm in this case, fair in all the circumstances.
All the circumstances include a number of different considerations:
first of all, the penalties, if any. There are no penalties under the Race
Relations Act 1976 in the form of fines or imprisonment or anything
like that, but what Lord Hooson has drawn to our attention quite
correctly is that, under the terms of the Estate Agents Act 1979 (and   H
no one has been able to discover whether that has come into operation
yet or not) there is no doubt that a person upon whom a non-discriminatory notice has been served may, if he is an estate agent, suffer, if certain
procedural steps are taken, grave disadvantages because it is open under
a number of safeguards into which I do not propose to go for the Director General of Fair Trading to take steps to see that a person against
whom this action has been taken under the Race Relations Act 1976

The Weekly Law Reports, December 19, 1980

1587

1 W.L.R.   Reg. v. Commission for Racial Equality (D.C.)   Lord Lane C.J.

A does not practice in business as an estate agent. Of course it is a very long call from saying that a person who has this non-discriminatory notice served upon him is necessarily going to suffer in his business by the action of the Director General of Fair Trading. Many procedures have to be gone through before that can take place, but there is that danger there, and that is one of the matters which is a circumstance to be taken into account.

B The next matter, and possibly the most important matter, is the nature of the provisions of the Race Relations Act 1976 itself. I have read sufficient of the contents of section 58 of that Act to indicate that there is no mention in that section, or indeed in any other section, of any right to cross-examine any of the witnesses. That perhaps is a surprising omission if it was the intention of Parliament to allow a person in the position of the firm in this case the full panoply of legal rights which would take place at a judicial hearing.

C It seems to me that there are degrees of judicial hearing, and those degrees run from the borders of pure administration to the borders of the full hearing of a criminal cause or matter in the Crown Court. It does not profit one to try to pigeon-hole the particular set of circumstances either into the administrative pigeon-hole or into the judicial D pigeon-hole. Each case will inevitably differ, and one must ask oneself what is the basic nature of the proceeding which was going on here. It seems to me that, basically, this was an investigation being carried out by the commission. It is true that in the course of the investigation the commission may form a view, but it does not seem to me that that is a proceeding which requires, in the name of fairness, any right in the firm in this case to be able to cross-examine witnesses whom the com- E mission have seen and from whom they have taken statements. I repeat the wording of section 58 (2) in emphasis of that point: " If in the course of a formal investigation the commission become satisfied that a person is committing, . . ." and so on. It seems to me that that is so near an administrative function as to make little difference and is the type of investigation or proceeding which does not require the formalities F of cross examination.

We have been referred to a number of cases, and in particular *Reg. v. Race Relations Board, Ex parte Selvarajan* [1975] 1 W.L.R. 1686. This was a decision under the earlier Race Relations Act 1968 and, as Lord Hooson has rightly pointed out, there are very sharp and material distinctions between the Act of 1968 and the Act of 1976. The Act of 1968 required the commission to act very largely as a purely investigating G and conciliating body, and any litigation or determination was left to the county court or the regular courts of the land to determine. But nevertheless there are passages which do cast some light on the attitude of the courts to this type of situation. Scarman L.J. says, at p. 1700:

" The Race Relations Board does not exercise judicial functions. Part II of the Act is absolutely clear. The board was created so H that in the sensitive field of race relations compliance with the law and the resolution of differences could first be sought without recourse to the courts with their necessarily open and formalised judicial process. The board is an administrative agency charged with a number of critically important functions in the administration of the law: but it is not a judicial institution—nor is it the apex of a hierarchy of judicial institutions. The procedures are not adversarial but conciliatory: settlement, not litigation, is the

business of the board; and it is left to the board to decide how best
to perform the functions which the statute requires it to perform,
namely, investigation, the formation of an opinion, conciliation, and,
if all else fails, the taking of legal proceedings in the county court."

Reg. v. *Deputy Industrial Injuries Commissioner, Ex parte Moore*
[1965] 1 Q.B. 456, was cited to us and a passage in the judgment of
Diplock L.J. seems to be appropriate, at p. 488:

"These technical rules of evidence, however, form no part of the
rules of natural justice. The requirement that a person exercising
quasi-judicial functions must base his decision on evidence means
no more than it must be based upon material which tends logically
to show the existence or non-existence of facts relevant to the issue
to be determined, or to show the likelihood or unlikelihood of the
occurrence of some future event the occurrence of which would be
relevant. It means that he must not spin a coin or consult an
astrologer, but he may take into account any material which, as a
matter of reason, has some probative value in the sense mentioned
above. If it is capable of having any probative value, the weight to
be attached to it is a matter for the person to whom Parliament
has entrusted the responsibiliy of deciding the issue. The supervisory jurisdiction of the High Court does not entitle it to usurp
this responsibility and to substantiate its own view for his."

Lord Hooson sought to derive assistance from some of the passages
of the decision of this court in *Reg.* v. *Board of Visitors of Hull Prison,
Ex parte St. Germain* [1979] Q.B. 425, but it seems to me that the
decision there was based upon facts widely differing from those in
the present case. That was truly a judicial proceeding carried out by the
prison visitors, and the complaint there was that there had been no
opportunity to cross-examine prison officers in hotly disputed questions
of identity. Speaking for myself, I derive little assistance from any
dicta in that case.

We are not here to substitute our view for the view of the commission.
They undoubtedly went to very great lengths to investigate and examine
all the voluminous evidence which was before them. There is now
before us, true at a late stage, the report of the formal investigation
which was carried out and a copy of which was sent to each member of
the commission (60 pages in all). No one can complain that this matter
was not thoroughly investigated. It seems to me for the reasons I have
endeavoured to set out that in this case there was no breach of the rules
of fairness in that cross-examination was not permitted and that the
witnessess did not attend.

The next point is the hearsay point, and that is dealt with succinctly
by what Lawton L.J. said in *Reg.* v. *Race Relations Board, Ex parte
Selvarajan* [1975] 1 W.L.R. 1686. His judgment reads, at p. 1698:

"For my part, I can see no reason at all why the board should not
delegate to its staff the function of collecting information. It would
be impractical for the members of the board themselves to make
investigations. How the board does what Parliament has entrusted
it to do is not a matter for the courts to decide as long as it acts
fairly and in good faith. It is for the board, not the courts, to
decide how much information each of its members should have
when considering a particular case. As long as the board, or one

A   of its constituent committees, has enough information to enable it
to make a fair assessment of the case, the courts will not interfere."

Similar passages are to be found in the other two judgments, and it is
plain that was the view of the court.

That answers both questions posed by Lord Hooson, namely, the
hearsay point and the delegation point, because once one reaches the
B stage of accepting that the commission are not only entitled to but as a
matter of practical politics are bound to delegate the investigation to their
underlings, or servants, it follows that the reports produced by those
servants were necessarily hearsay. But if it is proper to delegate in that
way, then equally it is proper to act upon the reports which the servants
or subordinates produce. I can see nothing wrong in the commission
acting as they did upon the evidence contained in these various reports.
C I can see nothing wrong in the fact that they delegated to those servants
the task of the investigation. In short, none of the three grounds relied
upon by the firm succeeds and I would accordingly dismiss this application.

WOOLF J.   I agree.

Application dismissed with costs, to
D   *include application to expedite*
hearing.

Solicitors: *Mohabir & Co; Bindman & Partners.*

[Reported by MISS ISOBEL COLLINS, Barrister-at-Law]

E

_____

[CHANCERY DIVISION]

F   * *In re* BERKELEY SECURITIES (PROPERTY) LTD.

[No. 001102 of 1975]

1980 March 31 ;   Vinelott J.
April 1 ;
May 16
G

Company—Winding up—Bankruptcy rules—Debts provable in
insolvency—Unliquidated claim for damages in tort—Applica-
tion for leave to institute such proceedings against company
in liquidation—Whether claim provable—Whether leave to be
granted—Companies Act 1948 (11 & 12 Geo. 6, c. 38), ss. 231,
316, 317 [1]*—Bankruptcy Act 1914 (4 & 5 Geo. 5, c. 59),*
s. 30 (1) [2]
H
On May 19, 1975, B Ltd., a property investment company,
was ordered to be wound up. Joint liquidators were appointed
later. As at June 27, 1974, B Ltd.'s property portfolio had
been valued at £631,130, and the property was then unincumbered. However, on December 31, 1974, B Ltd. executed a

[1] Companies Act 1948, s. 316: see post, p. 1602E–F.
S. 317: see post, p. 1603G–H.
[2] Bankruptcy Act 1914, s. 30 (1): see post, p. 1605F–H.

debenture in favour of A Ltd. over its property portfolio purportedly to secure repayment of a loan from A Ltd. of
£400,000, and on January 1, 1975, B Ltd. executed a debenture which purported to create a floating charge in favour of
C Ltd. to secure repayment of £57,215, with the result that at
the date of the winding up, since its assets were then valued
at substantially less than £400,000, there would be nothing
available for other creditors if the debenture in favour of A
Ltd. were valid. The joint liquidators therefore caused a full
investigation to be carried out to determine whether the debenture was valid. Following the investigation, proceedings were
instituted under section 37 of the Companies Act 1967 by the
Secretary of State for Trade, in the name of B Ltd. on its
behalf, to set aside the debenture and recover from A Ltd.
the moneys received by dealings with the debenture or with
B Ltd.'s property portfolio. In those proceedings, referred to
as the "main action," B Ltd. alleged, inter alia, that on June
28, 1974, the entire share capital of B Ltd. was sold by the
original shareholders to C Ltd. for £450,000, which sum was
lent to C Ltd. by A Ltd. and secured by a legal charge of that
date on B Ltd.'s property portfolio; that that legal charge was
not made for B Ltd.'s purposes or benefit, was a misapplication
of its property, ultra vires, and was made to enable C Ltd. to
purchase B Ltd.'s shares in contravention of section 54 of the
Companies Act 1948; that the charge was either ineffective to
create any interest in or security over B Ltd.'s property portfolio, or, if effective, that A Ltd. held any benefit received as
constructive trustee for B Ltd. It was further alleged that as
a result of negotiations begun in October 1974, C Ltd. agreed
to sell the shares in B Ltd. to D Ltd. for £513,000; that the
purchase price of £513,000 was obtained for D Ltd. indirectly
from moneys belonging to B Ltd.; that the £400,000 purportedly lent by A Ltd. to B Ltd. and secured by the debenture was
not in fact paid to B Ltd. but was used, in part, to discharge C
Ltd.'s debt to A Ltd. and, in part, for other purposes; that
accordingly the debenture was not made for the purposes or
benefit of B Ltd., but was a misapplication of B Ltd's property, ultra vires, and was made to assist D Ltd. to purchase
B Ltd.'s shares in contravention of section 54 of the Companies
Act 1948. Under an agreement of February 20, 1975, the
applicant, P Ltd. acquired the entire share capital of A Ltd.,
it being a term of the agreement that A Ltd.'s "loan portfolio" which included the loan of £400,000 purportedly made
to B Ltd. and secured by the debenture, should be sold to
another purchaser, W Ltd. In the course of the negotiations
leading up to that agreement a draft balance sheet and profit
and loss account of A Ltd. for the year ending December 31,
1974, was drawn up by A Ltd.'s auditors which included in
the "loan portfolio" the loan of £400,000 purportedly made
to B Ltd. By a notice of motion dated February 12, 1980,
P Ltd. sought leave, notwithstanding the winding up order
against B Ltd., to commence proceedings, pursuant to section
231 of the Companies Act 1948, to claim damages against
B Ltd. for negligent misrepresentation in having allegedly
represented and confirmed to A Ltd.'s auditors that B Ltd.
was indebted to A Ltd. in the sum of £400,000, the sum
secured by the debenture. The loss sought to be recovered in
the proposed action would be suffered if and only if B Ltd.
were to succeed in the main action.

On the application by P Ltd. for leave to bring
proceedings: —

Held, (1) that section 317 of the Companies Act 1948 did
not operate to exclude a claim for damages in tort which had
not been liquidated by judgment before the commencement of
the winding up, but only to exclude from proof a claim which
had not been liquidated by judgment at the time when the

A   claimant came in to prove his debt; that the claimant would not be entitled to disturb prior distributions to other creditors, although he would, as regards undistributed assets, be entitled to a dividend thereout equal to the dividends paid to those whose proofs had already been accepted; that on that interpretation, section 317 weighed heavily in favour of leave being given, pursuant to section 231 of the Companies Act 1948, to enable P Ltd. to institute its proposed action against B Ltd.,

B   since P Ltd.'s claim having been clearly formulated, it would be wrong to distribute any assets until the claim had been determined (post, pp. 1610G—1611A, C–E).

    In re McMurdo [1902] 2 Ch. 684, C.A. applied.

    Wyley v. *Exhall Coal Mining Co.* (1864) 33 Beav. 538; *In re Whitaker* [1901] 1 Ch. 9, C.A.; *In re Great Orme Tramways Co.* (1934) 50 T.L.R. 450 and *In re Fine Industrial Commodities Ltd.* [1956] Ch. 256 considered.

C   (2) That since the Secretary of State for Trade, who brought the main action, had no interest in and claimed to have no power to finance a defence to the proposed action by P Ltd. against B Ltd., which if successful would deprive B Ltd. of the fruits of its success in the main action, there was an insuperable objection to permitting the proposed action to proceed to trial before the main action had been heard; that in the very special circumstances fairness required, since

D   the two actions could not properly be heard together, that leave should be given for the issue of the writ, statement of claim, defence and any third party proceedings, but that no further step should be taken without further leave of the court (post, p. 1613A–B, F–H).

    In re Aro Co. Ltd. [1980] Ch. 196, C.A. applied.

The following cases are referred to in the judgment:

E   *Aro Co. Ltd., In re* [1980] Ch. 196; [1980] 2 W.L.R. 453; [1980] 1 All E.R. 1067, C.A.

Barned's Banking Co., In re (Kellock's Case) (1868) 3 Ch.App. 769.

Baum, Ex parte, In re Edwards (1874) 9 Ch.App. 673.

Brownsea Haven Properties Ltd. v. *Poole Corporation* [1958] Ch. 574; [1958] 2 W.L.R. 137; [1958] 1 All E.R. 205, C.A.

Fine Industrial Commodities Ltd., In re [1956] Ch. 256; [1955] 3 W.L.R.

F   940; [1955] 3 All E.R. 707.

Fryer v. *Ewart* [1902] A.C. 187, H.L.(E.).

Great Orme Tramways Co., In re (1934) 50 T.L.R. 450.

Grosvenor Metal Co., In re [1950] Ch. 63; sub nom. *Re Grosvenor Metal Co., Ex parte Bebb Industries* [1949] 2 All E.R. 848.

Hopkins, In re, Ex parte Stedingk (1902) 86 L.T. 676, C.A.

Leng, In re [1895] 1 Ch. 652, C.A.

G   *McMurdo, In re* [1902] 2 Ch. 684, C.A.

Mason v. *Bogg* (1837) 2 My. & Cr. 443.

Milan Tramways Co., In re, Ex parte Theys (1884) 25 Ch.D. 587, C.A.

Newman, In re, Ex parte Brooke (1876) 3 Ch.D. 494, C.A.

Whitaker, In re [1901] 1 Ch. 9, C.A.

Withernsea Brickworks, In re (1880) 16 Ch.D. 337, C.A.

Wyley v. *Exhall Coal Mining Co.* (1864) 33 Beav. 538.

H   The following additional case was cited in argument:

Post Office v. *Norwich Union Fire Insurance Society Ltd.* [1967] 2 Q.B. 363; [1967] 2 W.L.R. 709; [1967] 1 All E.R. 577, C.A.

MOTION

Berkeley Securities Property Ltd. (" Berkeley ") was incorporated on February 11, 1969, with a capital of £1,000. By the material time, its

1592

capital had been increased to £100,000, divided into 10,000,000 shares of   A
1p each, referred to in the report as " the Berkeley shares." On May 19,
1975, Berkeley was ordered to be wound up compulsorily, and on July
16, 1975, David Llewellyn Morgan and Malcolm Gee were appointed as
its joint liquidators. On February 14, 1978, certain proceedings, referred
to in the report as " the main action," were instituted, in Berkeley's
name, by the Secretary of State for Trade, pursuant to section 37 of the
Companies Act 1967, and with authority of the joint liquidators, against   B
the following defendants, viz. Robin Christopher Scott-Brown, Patrick
Robins, Timothy John Angus, Mrs. Susan Mary Thompson, Mrs. Anna
Christina Scott-Brown, Currency Index Deposit Co. Ltd. (" Cidco "),
Celoware Builders Ltd. (" Celoware "), Property Growth Pensions and
Annuities Ltd. (formerly Atlantic Assurance Co. Ltd., and referred to
herein as " Atlantic ") and Williams & Glyn's Bank Ltd.   Certain   C
declaratory and other relief was sought. In the main action in the state-
ment of claim it was alleged, inter alia, that on June 28, 1974, the
Berkeley shares were sold by the original shareholders for £450,000 to
Cidco, a company controlled by Robin Christopher Scott-Brown, Mrs.
Anna Christina Scott-Brown and other members of the Scott-Brown
family; that the necessary sum of £450,000 for the purchase, was lent to
Cidco by Atlantic, Robin Christopher Scott-Brown and Mrs. Anna   D
Christina Scott-Brown covenanting to repay the money on demand and
the loan being secured by a legal charge, dated June 28, 1974, on
Berkeley's property portfolio; that that legal charge was not made for
the purposes or benefit of Berkeley, which received no consideration, but
was a misapplication of Berkeley's property and was ultra vires; that the
real purpose of the loan was to enable Cidco to purchase the Berkeley   E
shares in contravention of section 54 of the Companies Act 1948. It was
further alleged that in certain negotiations in 1974, Celoware agreed to
buy the Berkeley shares from Cidco for £513,000; that by complex transactions involving a series of cheques of similar amount (described in an
affidavit as a circular cheque transaction), the sum of £513,000 was paid
out of Berkeley's moneys to Celoware; that a sum of £400,000 purportedly
paid by Atlantic to Berkeley, secured by a debenture dated December 31,   F
1974, (known as the " Atlantic debenture ") over Berkeley's property
portfolio was not in fact paid to Berkeley, but was used in part to
discharge the debt due from Cidco to Atlantic and in part for other
purposes; that the Atlantic debenture was therefore not made for the
purposes or benefit of Berkeley, was a misapplication of Berkeley's property, ultra vires, and was made in order to assist Celoware, which had
no assets, to purchase the Berkeley shares in contravention of section 54   G
of the Companies Act 1948. Accordingly the relief sought in the main
action included declarations that certain of the defendants were jointly
and severally liable to replace, with interest, the Berkeley property portfolio or the proceeds of sale thereof, and that the legal charge and the
Atlantic debenture were void or alternatively voidable.

   Towards the end of 1974, Property Growth Assurance Co. Ltd.,   H
(" P.G.A.") began negotiations for the purchase of the shares of
Atlantic, which was then in financial difficulties, and as a result of the
negotiations Atlantic became the wholly owned subsidiary of P.G.A.
under an agreement of February 20, 1975. It was a term of that agreement that Atlantic would sell to Williams & Glyn's Bank Ltd. Atlantic's
" loan portfolio," which included the loan of £400,000 purportedly made
by Atlantic to Berkeley. In the course of the negotiations for the purchase

A   by P.G.A. of the Atlantic shares, P.G.A. required the preparation of a balance sheet and profit and loss account for Atlantic for the year ended December 31, 1974, approved by Atlantic's directors and certified by Price Waterhouse & Co., who were Atlantic's auditors. On January 29, 1975, Price Waterhouse & Co. supplied P.G.A. with a report, as requested, into the financial affairs of Atlantic, and with a draft balance sheet and profit and loss account. By a letter dated January 3, 1975,

B   Atlantic's accounts department asked Berkeley for confirmation that as at December 31, 1974, Berkeley was indebted to Atlantic in the sum of £400,000.

By a notice of motion dated February 12, 1980, P.G.A. sought an order discharging an order of Mr. Registrar Bradburn, whereby he had refused P.G.A. leave, pursuant to section 231 of the Companies Act

C   1948, to commence proceedings against Berkeley for damages for negligent misrepresentation, and an order granting P.G.A. leave to commence such proceedings notwithstanding the making of the winding up order of May 19, 1975. In the proposed action, for which leave was sought, it was proposed to allege, inter alia, that Berkeley had duly confirmed that at the close of business on December 31, 1974, the balance of their loan account with Atlantic was £400,000; that in reliance on that confirmation

D   Price Waterhouse & Co. had included Berkeley as a debtor of Atlantic in preparing the accounts and that P.G.A. in reliance on those accounts had entered into the purchase agreement and had thereby suffered damage.

Further facts are stated in the judgment.

E   C. F. Dehn Q.C. and M. J. Brindle for the applicants, P.G.A.
R. A. Morritt Q.C. and Philip Heslop, for the company, Berkeley.

Cur. adv. vult.

May 16.   VINELOTT J. read the following judgment. This is an appeal by Property Growth Assurance Co. Ltd., which I will call " P.G.A.,"

F   against an order of Mr. Registrar Bradburn whereby he refused an application by P.G.A. made pursuant to section 231 of the Companies Act 1948 for leave to bring an action against Berkeley Securities (Property) Ltd., which I will call " Berkeley." Berkeley is in compulsory liquidation, a winding up order having been made on May 19, 1975, upon a creditors' petition which was presented on April 8, 1975. The

G   proposed action is an action for damages for negligent misrepresentation, and the loss which it is sought to recover will be suffered if, and only if, Berkeley succeeds in another action which has been commenced by the Secretary of State for Trade in the name and on behalf of Berkeley pursuant to the powers conferred on him by section 37 of the Companies Act 1967.

An explanation of the issue raised in that action—which I will call

H   " the main action "—is a necessary prologue to an analysis of the questions raised by P.G.A's application for leave to bring proceedings against Berkeley.

The main action

At all material times Berkeley carried on business as a property investment company, the acquisition of its portfolio being financed by moneys deposited with Berkeley by members of the public on interest-bearing deposit accounts. The accounts of Berkeley for the last accounting period before the making of the winding up order, that is, the year ended December 31, 1974, showed that at December 31, 1974, there were 337 depositors and that the aggregate amount owed to them at that date was approximately £410,000. Berkeley's records also reveal that at June 27, 1974, its portfolio of investment in property and ground rents was professionally valued at £631,130 and that that portfolio, which I will call " the property portfolio," was then unincumbered. At the commencement of the winding up the property portfolio appeared to be incumbered by, amongst other things, a debenture, which I will call " the Atlantic debenture," dated December 31, 1974 and purportedly securing the repayment of a sum of £400,000 to a company then known as Atlantic Assurance Co. Ltd., which has since changed its name to Property Growth Pensions and Annuities Ltd., which I will call " Atlantic." The repayment of the sum secured by the Atlantic debenture was guaranteed by a company, Celoware Builders Ltd., which I will call " Celoware," one Timothy John Angus, one Robin Christopher Scott-Brown, a company then known as Seven Oaks Financial Holdings Ltd., which is now known as Currency Index Deposit Co. Ltd., which I will call " Cidco," and by one Anna Christina Scott-Brown.

The property portfolio also appeared to be incumbered by a debenture dated January 1, 1975, and granted by Berkeley to Cidco, which purported to create a floating charge to secure payment to Cidco of the sum of £57,215, and a legal mortgage of that date also granted to Cidco by way of collateral security. Apart from the property portfolio, the assets of Berkeley available to its creditors amounted in value to a little over £8,000, a sum which will be absorbed by the costs and expenses of the winding up. The realisable value of the property portfolio was substantially less than £400,000 and, if the Atlantic debenture is valid, there will be nothing for Berkeley's other creditors, whatever may be the fate of the debenture and mortgage in favour of Cidco.

In those circumstances the joint liquidators of Berkeley caused a full investigation to be carried out to ascertain whether the Atlantic debenture and the debenture and mortgage in favour of Cidco were valid and binding on Berkeley. Following that investigation, the Secretary of State for Trade decided that it was in the public interest that proceedings be brought in the name and on behalf of Berkeley to set aside the Atlantic debenture and to recover from Atlantic any moneys received by it by dealings with the Atlantic debenture or the Berkeley property portfolio. I will return to the powers conferred by section 37 and the position of the Secretary of State in relation to costs later in this judgment. The main action is, of course, brought by the Secretary of State for Trade through the offices of the Treasury Solicitor.

The issues in the main action are very complex. A brief summary will suffice for the purposes of this judgment.

The main action relates primarily to two transactions which are as follows. (1) It is alleged that on June 28, 1974, the entire issued share capital of Berkeley, amounting to 10 million shares of 1p each, was sold by its then shareholders to Cidco at the price of £450,000; that the sum of £450,000 was lent by Atlantic to Cidco, a company controlled by the Scott-Browns, and was secured by a legal charge on the property portfolio; and that the legal charge (a) was not made for the purposes or

A benefit of Berkeley, which received no consideration, (b) was a misapplication of Berkeley's property and ultra vires and (c) was made to provide security for a loan made to enable Cidco to purchase the Berkeley shares in contravention of section 54 of the Companies Act 1948. It is further alleged that Atlantic knew or ought to have known the purposes for which the legal charge was made, and that the legal charge was either ineffective to create any interest in or security over the property portfolio,

B or, if it was effective for that purpose, that Atlantic held any benefit it obtained as a constructive trustee for Berkeley. The professional valuation of the property portfolio, to which I have referred, was made for the purposes of that transaction.

It is also alleged in the main action that in September 1974 Berkeley raised the sum of £184,750 by sale of part of the property portfolio, out

C of which the sum of £112,000 was paid to Atlantic as to £100,000 in part repayment of the loan to Cidco secured on the property portfolio by the mortgage of June 28, 1974, and as to £12,000 by way of penalty for early redemption. It is claimed against Atlantic that it is liable to account to Berkeley for that sum with interest.

(2) It is alleged that in or about October 1974 negotiations com-

D menced for the acquisition of the issued share capital of Berkeley by Celoware, which was controlled by Mr. Angus, the negotiations being conducted by Mr. Robin Scott-Brown on behalf of Cidco and Mr. Angus on behalf of Celoware; that as a result of those negotiations Celoware agreed to buy the Berkeley shares for £513,000, the purchase being conditional upon the repayment of the loan, then £350,000 plus interest, to Cidco from Atlantic, secured by the mortgage of June 28, 1974; that by

E a series of complex transactions, which it is unnecessary to describe in detail, the sum of £513,000 was paid out of Berkeley's moneys to Celoware; and that a sum of £400,000 purportedly paid to Berkeley and secured by the Atlantic debenture of December 31, 1974, was not paid to Berkeley but was used in part to discharge the debt due from Cidco and secured by the charge of June 28, 1974—which with interest amounted to £388,342—and in part to meet a commitment fee of £8,000 and

F interest payable in advance of January 1975 of £7,134.24, the balance of £3,476.24 being retained by Atlantic's solicitors to meet their charges.

It is accordingly alleged that the Atlantic debenture was not made for the purposes or for the benefit of Berkeley; that the creation of the charge was a misapplication of Berkeley's assets and ultra vires; and that it was made to give financial assistance to Celoware to assist in the

G purchase of Berkeley's shares in contravention of section 54.

It is claimed as against Atlantic that it knew or ought to have known the purposes for which the Atlantic debenture was created; that the Atlantic debenture constituted an application of Berkeley's property otherwise than for its benefit; and that accordingly (a) the Atlantic debenture was not effective to create any interest in or charge over Berkeley's assets in favour of Atlantic; or alternatively (b) that if it was effective

H to create any such interest or charge, Atlantic held any such interest or charge as a constructive trustee for Berkeley.

I should mention for completeness that it is also alleged that in January 1975 Berkeley raised approximately £19,000 by sale of part of the property portfolio and that part of the proceeds of sale was paid to Atlantic in partial discharge of the sums secured by the Atlantic debenture. Berkeley again claims repayment of any sums so paid with interest.

1596

Those are the main claims against Atlantic. They are, of course, coupled with claims against the Scott-Browns and Mr. Angus, and other directors and shareholders of Cidco and Celoware, and against Cidco and Celoware themselves. Other parties, in particular the solicitors acting for Atlantic, have been joined as third parties. If the action succeeds, there will be difficult and complex questions of contribution to be resolved. But a further claim is made against Atlantic which is coupled with a claim against Williams & Glyn's Bank Ltd., which I will call " Williams & Glyn's." That further claim is founded on events which took place between December 31, 1974, and the presentation of the petition for the winding up of Berkeley. To those events I now turn.

For many years before 1974 Atlantic carried on the business of life assurance. It was a wholly-owned subsidiary of Atlantic Assurance Holdings Co. Ltd., which I will call " Holdings," which in turn was owned as to 52 per cent. by or by companies controlled by a Mr. Pollard, and as to 48 per cent. by or by companies controlled by a company called Cornwallis Estates Ltd., which I will call " Cornwallis." Cornwallis was owned as to 75 per cent. by Kayrealm Ltd., and as to 25 per cent. by or by a company controlled by Williams & Glyn's. In 1974, Cornwallis and Kayrealm were in financial difficulties. An informal committee of creditors of Cornwallis had been appointed. Later, on February 11, 1975, Cornwallis went into a creditors' voluntary winding up. Williams & Glyn's had also appointed a receiver of Kayrealm Ltd. Atlantic in turn was in financial difficulties. Between December 6, 1973, and May 10, 1974, the Secretary of State for Trade issued notices pursuant to the Insurance Companies Amendment Act 1973 requiring Atlantic to maintain in the United Kingdom assets equivalent to a specified proportion of its net domestic liabilities and to vest them in a trustee approved by the Secretary of State. Williams & Glyn's, on appointing a receiver of Kayrealm, gave the Secretary of State an assurance, which was published, that it would take steps to safeguard the interests of Atlantic's policy-holders. Following that assurance, Williams & Glyn's looked for a reputable assurance company which would take over Atlantic or its life-assurance business and which could be relied on to meet Atlantic's liabilities to policy-holders. P.G.A. was approached. The assets of Atlantic available to meet claims of policy-holders included a portfolio of loans secured on land—which I will call " the loan portfolio "—of an aggregate face value of some £6.1 million. P.G.A. was unwilling to take over Atlantic, and so indirectly assume responsibility for ensuring that claims of its policy-holders were met, unless a purchaser could be found who would take over the loan portfolio, which comprised approximately half the assets available to meet the claims of policy-holders, at par. In these circumstances the following arrangement was entered into.

By an agreement dated February 20, 1975, which I will call " the Atlantic share agreement," to which, amongst others, P.G.A., Mr. Pollard, Williams & Glyn's, Holdings and Atlantic were parties, it was agreed, amongst other things, that P.G.A. would purchase from Holdings the entire issued share capital of Atlantic. Under the Atlantic share agreement, Holdings and Mr. Pollard entered into a series of warranties which included first, a warranty that information given to accountants and actuaries instructed by P.G.A. to make a full investigation into the affairs of Atlantic was, when given, true and was given after making all proper inquiries, and remained true at the date of the agreement; and secondly, a warranty that all information known or which should have

A   been known, or which pending completion should become or have become known to them and which was material to a purchaser of the shares of Atlantic, had been supplied to P.G.A. or its investigating accountants and actuaries acting in connection with the investigation to which I have referred.

It was also a term of the Atlantic share agreement that Atlantic and Williams & Glyn's would enter into a contemporaneous agreement in

B   the form of a draft annexed thereto. By that agreement, which was duly executed—and which I will call "the Atlantic loan portfolio agreement"—it was agreed that Atlantic would sell and Williams & Glyn's would purchase the loan portfolio, Williams & Glyn's paying therefor a sum equal to the face value of the loans as at December 31, 1974, subject to a provision for adjustment in respect of repayments or further advances

C   since December 31, 1974. Under the Atlantic loan portfolio agreement the consideration, £6,125,735, payable, subject to adjustment, by Williams & Glyn's, was to be paid into a deposit account in the name of Atlantic and withdrawn by instalments on March 1 and September 1, 1976, with interest. The loan portfolio, of course, included the loan purportedly made to Berkeley. Assignments were duly executed by Atlantic vesting the benefit of the loan portfolio and the securities therefor in Williams

D   & Glyn's. One of the assignments, which is dated March 25, 1975—and which was made in a form annexed to the agreement—was an assignment of the benefit of the debt apparently due from Berkeley and of the benefit of the Atlantic debenture. The debt is stated to be £400,000, although, as I have mentioned, some repayments may have been made in January 1975. By the assignment, Atlantic gave Williams & Glyn's the same covenants of title as would have been implied under section 76 (1)

E   of the Law of Property Act 1925 if Atlantic had transferred and had been expressed to transfer both as settlor and as mortgagor.

In the statement of claim in the main action, Berkeley claim delivery up and cancellation of the Atlantic debenture and an account of all moneys received by or on behalf of Williams & Glyn's in respect of assets purportedly charged by the Atlantic debenture. Berkeley claim, in the

F   alternative, that if the Atlantic debenture was effective to create any interest in or security over the property portfolio, Atlantic was a constructive trustee thereof and is liable to account for the sum of £400,000, the part of the total consideration paid by Williams & Glyn's for the Atlantic loan portfolio which is attributable to the Atlantic debenture. That sum has been retained on deposit with Williams & Glyn's in the name of Atlantic, and with accrued interest amounted on December 31

G   last to £702,857.29, since when further interest has accrued. Williams & Glyn's has, of course, refused to pay this sum to Atlantic pending the hearing of the main action, and indeed at an earlier stage Williams & Glyn's interpleaded, though the interpleader proceedings have been stayed since the commencement of the main action.

In third party proceedings Williams & Glyn's claims an indemnity

H   from Atlantic against any moneys for which Williams & Glyn's is liable to account to Berkeley in respect of its dealings with the properties charged by the Atlantic debenture under the first of the two heads of claim I have mentioned. Atlantic claim an indemnity from Williams & Glyn's in the event that Berkeley succeed in recovering the sum of £400,000 with accrued interest held by Williams & Glyn's on deposit in the name of Atlantic. There are other cross-claims and claims for indemnity or contribution against others concerned with the creation of the

legal charge of June 28, 1974, and the Atlantic debenture. Further, Wil- A
liams & Glyn's has commenced an action against the guarantors of the
Atlantic debenture, and Atlantic has commenced an action against
Holdings and Mr. Pollard under the warranties in the Atlantic share
agreement to which I have referred. This latter action has, I understand,
been ordered to be tried immediately after the trial of the main action.

There is, as Mr. Dehn on behalf of P.G.A. accepts—and indeed B
asserts—a possibility that the final outcome of this welter of claims and
cross-claims will be that Atlantic will either be held liable to indemnify
Williams & Glyn's against moneys recovered by Berkeley under the first
head of claim, or alternatively will be held liable as a constructive trustee
under the second head of claim and in either event will either fail to
make good a claim for indemnity or contribution, or in the case of persons other than Williams & Glyn's will make good a claim for indemnity C
or contribution but fail to recover. If that happens, P.G.A. will suffer in
that it bought the shares of Atlantic upon the footing that the assets of
Atlantic included the loan portfolio which would be taken over by Williams & Glyn's at the face value of the loans. To the extent of any loss
which falls on Atlantic and indirectly on P.G.A., as a result of recovery
from Atlantic of the sum of £112,000 paid to Atlantic in September 1974
in reduction of the debt due from Cidco and by way of penalty for early D
redemption, P.G.A. would appear to have no remedy against Berkeley or
Williams & Glyn's. But to the extent of any sums recovered from Atlantic
in respect of the loan of £400,000 and of any dealings with the Berkeley
property portfolio since December 31, 1974, P.G.A. asserts that it has a
claim for damages against Berkeley. That claim is the subject matter of
the proposed action.

E

The proposed action

The claim which P.G.A. wishes to bring against Berkeley is by comparison with the complex and interlocking claims in the main action a
straightforward one. The Atlantic share agreement was expressed to be
made subject to certain conditions being satisfied before the close of business on February 20, 1975, that is, the date of the Atlantic share agree- F
ment. One of the conditions was that before completion of the agreement
a balance sheet and a profit and loss account of Atlantic for the year
ended December 31, 1974, would be prepared upon an agreed basis and
approved by the directors of Atlantic and certified by Atlantic's auditors,
who were Price Waterhouse & Co., before completion of the agreement.
P.G.A. also instructed Price Waterhouse & Co. to carry out the investiga- G
tion into the financial affairs of Atlantic which I have already mentioned.
I have already referred to the warranty in the Atlantic share agreement
by Holdings and Mr. Pollard as to the accuracy and completeness of the
information to be supplied to P.G.A. and its investigating accountants.

Price Waterhouse & Co.'s report was, in fact, furnished to P.G.A.
before the date of the Atlantic share agreement, namely, on January 29,
1975. A draft balance sheet and profit and loss account were appended H
to the report. While Price Waterhouse & Co. were preparing the accounts
of Atlantic for the year ended December 31, 1974, a letter dated January
3, 1975, was sent by the accounts department of Atlantic to Berkeley
enclosing a statement of account as at close of business on December 31,
1974. The letter stated that " As part of their normal audit procedure,
our auditors, Price Waterhouse & Co., request direct confirmation of the

A amount outstanding at December 31, 1974." Berkeley were asked to complete an enclosed letter of confirmation and to return it in an enclosed stamped-addressed envelope to Price Waterhouse & Co. It is alleged in the draft statement of claim in the proposed action that Berkeley signed and sent this letter of confirmation to Price Waterhouse & Co.; that it was received by Price Waterhouse & Co. on or shortly before January 16, 1975, that is, before the date of Price Waterhouse & Co.'s report to

B P.G.A.; and that

"In reliance upon that letter of confirmation Price Waterhouse & Co.—as Berkeley knew or ought reasonably to have foreseen they would—included Berkeley as a debtor of Atlantic in the sum of £400,000—as at December 31, 1974—in the accounts of Atlantic which they were preparing and auditing."

C It is further alleged that Berkeley owed a duty to exercise reasonable care in and about dealings with the letter and inquiry of January 3, 1975, and sending that letter of confirmation to any person whom it knew or ought reasonably to have foreseen would or might rely on accounts prepared in reliance on the letter of confirmation, including any intending purchaser of shares of Atlantic; that in reliance on Atlantic's accounts

D P.G.A. entered into the Atlantic share agreement and that letter of confirmation was a breach of Berkeley's duty of care. It is said that if that letter of confirmation had not been sent P.G.A. would not have entered into the Atlantic share agreement without further safeguards, or alternatively would not have paid as large a sum as it in fact paid for the Atlantic shares.

E Those are the issues which it is sought to raise. It is said by Mr. Dehn on behalf of P.G.A., with I think considerable force, that although the claim is a contingent claim, in that it will only arise if the claims by Berkeley in relation to the Atlantic debenture ultimately fall to be borne by Atlantic, in addition to any liability in respect of properties sold in September 1976, none the less the main action and the proposed action by P.G.A. should, if possible, be consolidated and heard concurrently, or

F alternatively should be heard consecutively but by the same judge and in such a way that all parties to both actions are bound by findings of fact in the main action. Mr. Dehn points out that the letter of confirmation sent by Berkeley in reply to Atlantic's letter of January 3, 1975, is relied on by Williams & Glyn's in their defence, where the letter is said to have been signed by Mr. Angus, as founding an estoppel. Williams & Glyn's claim that they relied upon the accounts drawn up by Price Waterhouse

G & Co., which in turn were drawn up in reliance on that letter, when they agreed to pay £6,125,735 for the Atlantic loan portfolio. It is said by Mr. Dehn that the circumstances in which the letter of confirmation was sent, and the extent to which Price Waterhouse & Co. relied, and were intended to rely on it, are relied upon in Williams & Glyn's defence and are equally relevant to the proposed action, and that justice and con-

H venience require that the main action and the proposed action be heard either concurrently or consecutively by the same judge, so as to avoid the expense of having the same issues tried twice and the risk that there will be inconsistent findings of fact in the two actions. Mr. Dehn also points out that there is a danger that unless a writ is issued by P.G.A. before February 20, 1981, P.G.A.'s claim will be barred by limitation.

The situation in the main action, as I understand it, is that as between Berkeley and the defendants, pleadings are closed, subject to compliance

A with certain outstanding requests for particulars, but that the defences to certain third party statements of claim have yet to be delivered. Discovery is not yet complete. It is unlikely that an action of this complexity, and with matters of pleading and discovery as yet incomplete, will be ready for trial by February 20, 1981.

The objections to leave

B In an affidavit sworn by David Francis Campbell Evans, a partner in Wilde Sapte, the solicitors instructed by the liquidators to act for Berkeley, a number of objections are raised to the grant of leave to bring the proposed action. With one exception they appear to me to be without substance, and I can deal with them very briefly.

C First, it is said that section 54 is designed to protect a company and its creditors from the misuse of a company's assets in financing transactions involving its own share capital, and that as Mr. Angus, who signed the letter relied on in the proposed action, participated in the alleged breaches of section 54, it would be inequitable to allow an action to proceed founded on that letter, which will result, if successful, in a sum equal to any moneys recovered by Berkeley from Atlantic being in return recovered from Berkeley by P.G.A. That objection is, I think, wholly misconceived. There is no suggestion that P.G.A. or anyone connected with P.G.A. was in any way involved in the breaches of section 54 or had any knowledge or failed to make any reasonable inquiry that would have revealed those breaches. I can see nothing inequitable in allowing P.G.A. to rely upon a representation that Berkeley was indebted to Atlantic as founding a claim for damages if P.G.A. can show further that, because the loan infringed section 54, the statement was false, and secondly, that P.G.A. was entitled to rely, and did rely, on it in entering into the Atlantic share agreement.

D

E

Secondly, it is said that Berkeley has no assets available to defend the proposed action, and that if P.G.A. obtains judgment in default of appearance or defence and as a result P.G.A. is entitled to rank as an unsecured creditor, then the depositors on whose behalf the Secretary of State for Trade has intervened by bringing the main action will receive a much reduced dividend instead of the whole, or substantially the whole, of their deposits. It is said that in these circumstances the proposed action " if allowed to proceed at this stage will effectively frustrate the entire purpose of the main proceedings." In so far as this objection is founded upon Berkeley's inability to finance its defence to the proposed action, I will return to it later in this judgment. In so far as the objection is founded upon the more general proposition that no proceedings should be allowed which might diminish the fund available to meet the claims of Berkeley's depositors, it is in my judgment also misconceived. The fact that the transactions attacked in the main action have had the practical result of stripping Berkeley of assets derived originally from depositors leaving nothing to answer their claims, or even to finance litigation to remedy the wrong to Berkeley, and indirectly the depositors, no doubt founded the decision of the Secretary of State for Trade that it was in the public interest that the main action should be brought. But the main action is brought on behalf of Berkeley and not on behalf of the depositors, and any moneys recovered in the main action will, after payment of costs not recovered from the defendants, form part of the assets of Berkeley to be administered in the winding up. It would, I think, be quite wrong to refuse leave under section 231 in order to prefer one

F

G

H

A   class of creditor to a claimant innocent of participation in or of knowledge actual or constructive of any misuse of the company's moneys.
Nor, if it were relevant, do I see how the moral claims of depositors,
many of whom were no doubt attracted by the lure of very high rates of
interest, are to be weighed against the claims of P.G.A. which, on the
evidence before me, appears to have taken part in a rescue operation
designed to protect holders of policies issued by Atlantic.

B   Thirdly, it is said that in the absence of any allegation that Berkeley
knew or ought to have known that P.G.A. was contemplating the purchase of Atlantic or its assets—and there is no such specific allegation in
the draft statement of claim in the proposed action—the proposed action
is bound to fail. I do not think it would be right to refuse leave on that
ground. The claim in the proposed action is that Berkeley owed a duty
C   of care to anyone who might rely on accounts of Berkeley which had
been drawn on the basis that Berkeley owed Atlantic the sum of
£400,000 and that that duty extended to anyone who might purchase
the shares of Atlantic. The question whether Berkeley's duty of care
extended so far is not one which can be answered in the abstract. It can
only be answered in the full context of the circumstances as they existed
at the time and of the facts known to Mr. Angus and others concerned
D   with Berkeley's affairs who were aware of the inquiry and the answer
to it.

     Fourthly, it is said that there would be no advantage to the parties in
having the two actions tried together, in particular no substantial saving
of costs, and that, by contrast, if Atlantic were to succeed in its defence
or to recover against other defendants or third parties, costs incurred in
E   prosecuting the proposed action will have been thrown away. On the
material before me the advantages of having the two actions tried
together appear to me to be overwhelming. The factual background of
the two actions is the same and many of the issues overlap, in particular
the defence of estoppel raised in Williams & Glyn's defence. It appears
to me unlikely that there will be any further documentary evidence relevant to the proposed action which is not relevant to the main action, and
F   the attendance of most, if not all, the witnesses whose oral evidence will
be needed at the trial of the proposed action will also be required at the
trial of the main action. Of course, if Atlantic successfully defend the
main action or recover any moneys they are ordered to pay Berkeley
from other defendants or third parties, P.G.A. will fail to establish
damage and the proposed action will fail. That is a feature which the
proposed action shares with many of the third-party proceedings and
G   with P.G.A.'s action against Holdings and Mr. Pollard. To that extent
P.G.A. will be at risk as to costs. It is not in my judgment a reason for
refusing leave. I cannot on this application decide whether the main
action and the proposed action should be tried concurrently or consecutively before the same judge. That question will have to be decided in
applications for directions in the main action and the proposed action.
H   But in my opinion it would be wrong to preclude that course by refusing
leave to P.G.A. to commence and prosecute the proposed action.

     In my judgment, therefore, there is no substance in these objections.
However, in the course of argument two other objections were raised.
The first objection made is that the claim in the proposed action, being
a claim for unliquidated damages in tort, would not be capable, even if
liquidated by judgment, of being proved in the winding up so long as
Berkeley is insolvent. It is said, with some force, that there is no real

prospect that even if Berkeley succeeds in all the claims in the main   A
action and recovers the £112,000 realised and paid to Atlantic in September 1974, the £513,000 paid to Celoware in December 1974 and the
£19,000 realised and paid to Atlantic in January 1975—and that, apart
from interest, appears to be the maximum that Berkeley could recover—
Berkeley will be able to meet in full the costs and expenses of the
winding up and the claims of depositors, including interest, so far as
permissible under the bankruptcy rules.   Therefore, it is said it would be   B
futile and a waste of money to allow the proposed action to proceed.
That objection was raised for the first time in argument. It is inconsistent
with the first of the two objections I have already considered, which are
founded on the assumption that, in Mr. Evans's words, if P.G.A. recovers
judgment in the proposed action it " would be entitled to rank as an
unsecured creditor in Berkeley's liquidation and prove into the fund   C
recovered by the liquidator."

The second objection is that Berkeley has no moneys with which to
defend the proposed action. It is said that the Secretary of State for
Trade has power to bring the main action in the name of and on behalf
of Berkeley but no power to spend public money in defending proceedings against Berkeley. In those circumstances it is said that it would be
impractical for the main action and the proposed action to be heard   D
together or consecutively, and that if leave is granted, it should be limited
to the commencement of the proposed action. I will deal with these two
objections in turn.

The first objection

Section 316 of the Companies Act 1948 reads as follows: E

" In every winding up (subject, in the case of insolvent companies,
to the application in accordance with the provisions of this Act of
the law of bankruptcy) all debts payable on a contingency, and all
claims against the company, present or future, certain or contingent,
ascertained or sounding only in damages, shall be admissible to
proof against the company, a just estimate being made, so far as   F
possible, of the value of such debts or claims as may be subject to
any contingency or sound only in damages, or for some other reason
do not bear a certain value."

Save for the words in brackets at the beginning of that section, section
316 reproduces in substantially the same words section 158 of the Companies Act 1862. A similar section has appeared in every intermediate   G
Companies Act. It is clearly wide enough to admit to proof an unliquidated claim for damages for tort: see *Wyley* v. *Exhall Coal Mining
Co.* (1864) 33 Beav. 538, a case decided under the Act of 1862. Under
the Act of 1862 proof and adjudication of claims and liabilities were
governed by a general order made by the Lord Chancellor, the Master
of the Rolls and the Vice-Chancellor pursuant to powers conferred by
the Act of 1862. In the administration of the affairs of an insolvent com-   H
pany the court followed the practice of the Court of Chancery in administering an insolvent estate. The practice of the Court of Chancery in
administering an insolvent estate was altered by section 10 of the Supreme
Court of Judicature (1873) Amendment Act 1875, which amended and
re-enacted section 25 (1) of the Supreme Court of Judicature Act 1873
which had never come into operation. Section 10, so far as material,
reads as follows:

A　　". . . . Subsection 1 of clause 25 of the principal Act is hereby repealed, and instead thereof the following enactment shall take effect; (that is to say) in the administration by the court of the assets of any person who may die after the commencement of this Act, and whose estate may prove to be insufficient for the payment in full of his debts and liabilities, and in the winding up of any com-

B　pany under the Companies Acts, 1862 and 1867, whose assets may prove to be insufficient for the payment of its debts and liabilities and the costs of winding up, the same rules shall prevail and be observed as to the respective rights of secured and unsecured credi- tors, and as to debts and liabilities provable, and as to the valuation of annuities and future and contingent liabilities respectively, as may be in force for the time being under the law of bankruptcy with respect to the estates of persons adjudged bankrupt; and all

C　persons who in any such case would be entitled to prove for and receive dividends out of the estate of any such deceased person, or out of the assets of any such company, may come in under the decree or order for the administration of such estate, or under the winding up of such company, and make such claims against the same as they may respectively be entitled to by virtue of this

D　Act. . . ."

Section 10, so far as it related to companies, was repealed by the Com- panies (Consolidation) Act 1908 and reproduced in section 207 of that Act. Section 10 was finally repealed by the Administration of Estates Act 1925, so far as it related to the administration of insolvent estates and was replaced by section 34 (1) of that Act. Section 207 of the Act of

E　1908 was replaced by section 262 of the Act of 1929, save for omission of references to Ireland, and in turn by section 317 of the Act of 1948.

Section 206 of the Act of 1908 reproduced section 158 of the Com- panies Act 1862, except for the addition of the words " (subject in the case of insolvent companies to the application in accordance with the provisions of this Act of the law of bankruptcy)." Section 206 was in

F　turn replaced by section 261 of the Act of 1929 and is now section 316 of the Act of 1948 which I have already read and which is in the same terms as section 206 of the Act of 1908.

Section 317 which, as I have said, replaced or re-enacted sections of the Companies Act which replaced section 10, is not in precisely the same terms as section 10. It reads:

G　" In the winding up of an insolvent company registered in England the same rules shall prevail and be observed with regard to the respective rights of secured and unsecured creditors and to debts provable and to the valuation of annuities and future and contin- gent liabilities as are in force for the time being under the law of bankruptcy in England with respect to the estates of persons

H　adjudged bankrupt, and all persons who in any such case would be entitled to prove for and receive dividends out of the assets of the company may come in under the winding up and make such claims against the company as they respectively are entitled to by virtue of this section."

Section 10 of the Act of 1875 gave rise to many conflicting decisions. The problem was whether section 10 merely swept away the well-known

rule in Chancery known as the rule in *Mason* v. *Bogg* (1837) 2 My. & A
Cr. 443, that a secured creditor *could realise his security and prove
against the estate for the whole of his debt,* subject only to the limitation
that he could not recover more than 20s in the pound; he was not bound,
as is a secured creditor under the bankruptcy rules, to elect to abandon
his security and prove for the whole debt *or* to realise his security and
prove for the balance. The rule in *Mason* v. *Bogg* was applied to the
liquidation of an insolvent company under the Act of 1862: see the B
decision of the Court of Appeal in *In re Barned's Banking Co.* (*Kellock's
Case*) (1868) 3 Ch.App. 769. Initially the court gave a narrow interpretation to section 10 and held in a number of cases that section 10
reversed *Mason* v. *Bogg,* 2 My. & Cr. 443 and *Kellock's Case,* 3 Ch.App.
769 but did not introduce into the administration of insolvent estates
or into the winding up of insolvent companies the other rules applicable C
to the administration of the property of a bankrupt. Thus in *In re
Withernsea Brickworks* (1880) 16 Ch.D. 337, 341 James L.J. said:

> " The legislature, finding a well-known difference in the law as to
> proof by a secured creditor in administration by the Court of
> Chancery and in bankruptcy, intended to introduce the bankruptcy
> rule that a secured creditor could only prove for the balance of
> his debt after deducting the value of his security." D

Lush L.J. said at p. 343:

> " The whole object of section 10, as it appears to me, was to make
> this rule in bankruptcy applicable to administration of the assets of
> deceased persons, and to winding up."

E
But in later decisions the court gave a wider construction to section 10.
In *In re Whitaker* [1901] 1 Ch. 9, which is the watershed between the
old and the modern construction of section 10 and its successors, the
question was whether section 10 introduced into the administration of
an insolvent estate the old bankruptcy rule that voluntary creditors are
to be paid pari passu with creditors for value and not, as under the
Chancery practice, postponed to them. In explaining the effect of section F
10 Rigby L.J. said, at p. 12:

> " Section 10 provides (among other things) that the rules for the
> time being in force in bankruptcy as to debts provable shall apply in
> the administration by the High Court of the estate of a deceased
> insolvent. Upon the true construction of the words, I think they do
> not simply deal with the proof of debts. The same rules are to pre- G
> vail ' as to debts and liabilities provable.' I cannot read those words
> as meaning simply ' as to the proof of debts and liabilities.' I think
> they mean that whatever general rules are in force in the Court of
> Bankruptcy for the time being with regard to debts and liabilities
> provable shall apply in the administration of insolvent estates in
> Chancery. Now undoubtedly in bankruptcy (it does not matter how it
> came about) the rule as to debts and liabilities provable is that all H
> those debts and liabilities, whether contracted for value or not, shall
> rank pari passu. I think we should be cutting down unduly the plain
> words of section 10 if we were to allow the old rule of the Court of
> Chancery to override in the present case the existing rule in regard
> to bankruptcy."

Similarly, Vaughan Williams L.J. said at, pp. 12–13:

A   " One thing is quite clear, namely, that the section does not mean that in all respects the results of a bankruptcy, and the consequent administration of the estate, and the results of the death of an insolvent and the consequent administration of his estate, are to be absolutely identical. It was long ago decided that, notwithstanding section 10, you must still apply only in bankruptcy those bankruptcy rules, whether statutory or otherwise, which go to augment the

B   bankrupt's assets as against third persons. So far it is plain that there is intended to be a distinction between bankruptcy and the consequent administration and death followed by administration of the insolvent estate of the deceased. The section itself seems to me to point to an intention that the uniformity (if I may use the expression) shall be limited to some particular subjects, because it says

C   ' the same rules shall prevail and be observed as to the respective rights of secured and unsecured creditors, and as to debts and liabilities provable, and as to the valuation of annuities and future and contingent liabilities respectively.' The section specifies four heads as to which uniformity is for the future to prevail. And, in my view, we have in construing it to determine what are the limits of the four heads specified, and then to see whether this rule of administration

D   in Chancery, whereby voluntary creditors were postponed to creditors for value, is still to prevail."

That, of course, is not in any way a binding authority on the proposition before me, but applying the principle there stated, and indeed construing the language of section 10, unfettered by any presumption that it was intended only to reverse the rule in *Mason* v. *Bogg*, 2 My. & Cr. 443,

E   it is to my mind plain that section 10 and its successor sections, now section 317, restrict debts provable in the winding up of an insolvent company to those which are provable under the bankruptcy law and that only those persons who " would be entitled to prove for and receive dividends out of the assets " of a bankrupt are entitled to prove in the winding up.

F   I turn, therefore, to consider what debts and liabilities are capable of proof in bankruptcy.

Section 30 of the Bankruptcy Act 1914 reads as follows:

" (1) Demands in the nature of unliquidated damages arising otherwise than by reason of a contract, promise, or breach of trust shall not be provable in bankruptcy. (2) A person having notice of any

G   act of bankruptcy available against the debtor shall not prove under the order for any debt or liability contracted by the debtor subsequently to the date of his so having notice. (3) Save as aforesaid, all debts and liabilities, present or future, certain or contingent, to which the debtor is subject at the date of the receiving order, or to which he may become subject before his discharge by reason of any

H   obligation incurred before the date of the receiving order, shall be deemed to be debts provable in bankruptcy . . ."

Subsection (5) gives to any person aggrieved by any estimate by the trustee in bankruptcy a right to appeal to the court, and by subsection (6):

" If, in the opinion of the court, the value of the debt or liability is incapable of being fairly estimated, the court may make an order to that effect, and thereupon the debt or liability shall, for the pur-

poses of this Act, be deemed to be a debt not provable in bank- A
ruptcy."

Under subsection (7):

"If, in the opinion of the court, the value of the debt or liability is
capable of being fairly estimated, the court may direct the value
to be assessed before the court itself without the intervention of a
jury . . ."   B

This section is in substantially the same terms as section 31 of the
Bankruptcy Act 1869 which it replaced. The only material difference is
that the exception of claims for damages for breach of trust from the
general exclusion of demands in the nature of unliquidated damages does
not appear in the Act of 1869. As amended, subsection (1) appears to   C
exclude from proof only unliquidated claims for damages in tort. The
rule as to tort before the Act of 1869 was that damages in an action
for tort were not a provable debt unless judgment had actually been
signed before adjudication. Section 31 preserved that rule. It was a rule
which frequently operated to the benefit of a plaintiff who had not
obtained judgment and who wished to preserve his claim against the
defendant and to enforce it after discharge. Thus in *Ex parte Baum, In re*   D
Edwards (1874) 9 Ch.App. 673, an action was started by a firm of
bankers against two defendants who carried on business as commission
agents. The action was started on September 3, 1873. The plaintiffs
claimed first, damages for breach of contract in refusing to accept certain
bills, and secondly, damages for fraudulent misrepresentation. The defendants put in a defence, but before trial the defendants filed a petition   E
for liquidation by arrangement of the affairs of the firm under the procedure in section 125 of the Act of 1869, which had the same effect for
present purposes as a petition for adjudication. The defendants then
applied to the registrar to restrain the plaintiffs from proceeding with
the action. The registrar had power to make such an order if, and only
if, the claim in the action was one in respect of a liability provable in the
liquidation. It was held by the Court of Appeal that the claim, so far as   F
it was founded on a fraudulent misrepresentation, was not so provable,
and that accordingly the court had no power to restrain the plaintiffs
from bringing the action, though the plaintiffs were put to their election
between proceeding on the claim for damages in tort and proving for
damages in breach of contract.

Similarly, in *In re Newman, Ex parte Brooke* (1876) 3 Ch.D. 494, the   G
plaintiff, a Miss Brooke, commenced proceedings against an omnibus
proprietor, Newman, for damages for a tort committed by one of his
servants. The action was tried on January 14, 1876, when the plaintiff
obtained a verdict for £50. The defendant moved to have the verdict
entered for him. That motion was heard and refused on April 26. The
court ordered judgment to be entered for the plaintiff for £50 and costs.
On May 6, before judgment was signed, the defendant filed a liquidation   H
petition. An order was made by the bankruptcy registrar restraining
further proceedings by the plaintiff until after the first meeting of the
defendant's creditors. On June 3 the creditors resolved to accept a composition, and a second meeting was called for June 13 to confirm the
resolution. On June 9 the injunction against further proceedings by the
plaintiff was continued until after June 17, but with liberty for the
plaintiff to sign judgment in the action. On June 13 the resolution for

A a composition was confirmed. On June 17 the plaintiff signed judgment for £50 damages and £83 10s. 4d. for costs. Later the registrar made an order perpetually restraining the plaintiff from proceeding on the judgment. The effect of the order was to leave her without remedy. She could neither prove nor enforce her judgment. An appeal by the plaintiff was allowed. James L.J. said, at pp. 496–497:

B   " The first clause of section 31 contains clear negative words, and was, I think, meant to preserve the old law with regard to the proof in bankruptcy of damages for a tort. Certainly, under the old law damages in an action of tort were not a provable debt in bankruptcy until judgment had been signed. The old law as to that remains, in my opinion, now exactly as it was. Unless judgment has been signed damages for a tort are not included in the second clause of the C   section commencing with the words ' save as aforesaid; ' and when judgment for such damages is signed after the adjudication the amount of the judgment is not a debt or liability to which the bankrupt is subject at the date of the adjudication, or to which he has become subject afterwards by reason of any obligation incurred previously to the adjudication."

D Mellish L.J. added, at p. 497, that " . . . the costs, being a mere addition or appurtenance to the damages, must follow the same rule as that to which they are attached." That is still the law, though today judgment is entered and not signed.

       Mr. Morritt founded his argument upon this principle of bankruptcy law. The argument, shortly stated, is that a debt or liability is provable in the winding up of an insolvent company only if it would have been E provable if the company had been an individual and if a receiving order had been made. A claim for damages for tort is not so provable unless liquidated by judgment entered before the date of the receiving order. Similarly, it is said, the provisions of section 317

       " . . . must be treated as applicable to every company in liquidation unless and until it is shewn that its assets are in fact sufficient for F   the payment of its liabilities and the costs of winding up: "

see per Lord Macnaghten in Fryer v. Ewert [1902] A.C. 187, 192, a decision on section 10 of the Act of 1875 approving In re Milan Tramways Co. (1884) 25 Ch.D. 587. Therefore, it is said, until it is shown that the assets of a company which is being wound up by the court are sufficient for the payment of its debts and liabilities and the costs of winding G up, no claim for unliquidated damages for tort can be proved. By contrast, once it is shown that the company is solvent, the claim for unliquidated damages for tort becomes provable under section 316, though, unlike bankruptcy, the leave of the court is required under section 231 before the claim can be liquidated by judgment in proceedings whether commenced before or after the winding up.

H   In support of this argument Mr. Morritt relied on a statement in Gower, Modern Company Law, 4th ed. (1979) pp. 730–731, which reads as follows:

       " Prima facie, therefore, every sort of claim, whether in contract, tort or otherwise, can be proved. This is, however, subject to an important limitation in the case of insolvent companies, for there ' the same rules shall prevail . . . with regard to the respective rights of secured and unsecured creditors, and to debts provable, and to

valuation of . . . future and contingent liabilities' as are in force   A
under the law of bankruptcy. This does not have the effect of incorporating all the rules of bankruptcy law, but only those applying to
the three matters specifically mentioned. But it does mean that a
debt not provable in bankruptcy cannot be proved, and this excludes
claims for unliquidated damages arising otherwise than by reason
of contract or breach of trust, for example, unliquidated damages in
tort. It is therefore vital that a creditor whose sole claim is in tort,   B
should not delay in enforcing his rights against a company if its
financial stability is in doubt. Should it go into liquidation before his
claim has become liquidated by a judgment or agreement he will be
barred unless it proves to be solvent. His position is even worse than
in the case of bankruptcy, where his claim, not being provable, will
not be ended by the bankrupt's discharge so that he could sue him   C
thereafter. This, however, will not be open to him in the case of a
company's winding up, for the company will cease to exist."

The only other textbook which deals specifically with this point is
Pennington's Company Law, 4th ed. (1979), where the opposite view is
taken. The author says, at p. 763:

"The debts and liabilities which may be proved under the Bank-   D
ruptcy Act 1914, are as widely defined as those which may be proved
in the winding up of a solvent company, save that in bankruptcy
claims for unliquidated damages arising otherwise than by reason of
a contract, promise or breach of trust, are not provable. Consequently, claims for torts committed by an insolvent company cannot
be proved in its winding up, but, with leave of the court when   E
necessary, the claimant may sue the company, and then prove in the
winding up for the amount of his judgment debt."

No authority was cited by Mr. Morritt or is cited by Professor Gower
or Professor Pennington. However, the most recent edition of *Williams
and Muir Hunter on Bankruptcy*, 19th ed. (1979) refers in the notes on
section 30 at p. 161 to a decision of Eve J. in *In re Great Orme Tram-*   F
ways Co. (1934) 50 T.L.R. 450, where the appellant, a confectioner's
assistant on holiday in Llandudno, bought a return ticket on a tramway
to the top of the Great Orme. On the return journey the tramway got
out of control and she was seriously injured. An order for the compulsory winding up of the company was made and a proof of debt was
lodged claiming damages for tortious negligence on the part of the   G
defendant's servants. Later a proof was lodged claiming damages for
breach of a contract to carry her safely and securely. The liquidator
rejected both claims in reliance on section 262 of the Companies Act
1929, the immediate precursor of section 317 and on section 30 of the
Bankruptcy Act 1914. Eve J. is reported as having said, at pp. 450–451:

". . . that he must allow the appellant to substitute the proof based
on contract lodged in November for the proof of August in tort. It   H
seemed rather an extraordinary thing to have an inquiry in winding
up chambers as to the damages which Miss Beesley had sustained,
but there must be such an inquiry. All the claims arising out of the
accident and provable in the liquidation must be proved in order to
ascertain what was the total amount of them. There must be an
affidavit by the liquidator showing the total assets and the amount of

A   the claims, what was the possible dividend, and, therefore, for what amounts the claims should be admitted."

Eve J. thus assumed that in the winding up of an insolvent company an unliquidated claim for damages in tort could not be proved, but he did not decide the point. There was no argument to the contrary. The only point decided was that the appellant, if she abandoned the claim in tort,
B   could prove the co-extensive claim for breach of contract, a proposition which is, of course, well established in bankruptcy law: see *In re Hopkins* (1902) 86 L.T. 676, a case which was cited to Eve J. The decision is, therefore, not even of persuasive authority.

     The argument elaborated by Mr. Morritt is at first sight a formidable one, but it leads, as it seems to me, to absurd consequence. The following example will suffice as an illustration. Suppose that a three-fourths
C   majority of the members of a company, with assets of £100,000 and liquidated debts of £50,000 and no other liabilities except an unliquidated claim for damages in tort in respect of which proceedings have been commenced against the company, resolves by special resolution that the company be wound up by the court. The majority might, if Mr. Morritt's argument is right, pass such a resolution with a view to
D   stultifying the plaintiff's claim. The claim, let it be supposed, is one which the company has been advised is almost certain to succeed and is for the damages which are likely with costs to exceed £75,000. If the value of that claim is taken into account, the company is insolvent. If Mr. Morritt's argument is well founded, the consequence must be that the claim in tort being unliquidated at the commencement of the winding up cannot be proved. But it is still a liability of the company within section 316
E   and, as it seems to me, a liability, the existence of which would prevent a distribution of surplus assets to the contributories pursuant to section 302. Is the company then solvent or insolvent? The question appears to present a paradox worthy of Epimenides. Both an affirmative and a negative answer lead to a contradiction. If the company is treated as an insolvent company to which section 317 applies, the claim is excluded and
F   if the claim is excluded, the company is solvent. If the company is treated as a solvent company to which section 316 applies, the admission of the claim makes the company insolvent. Mr. Morritt's preferred answer, as I understand his argument, is that the claim in tort must be disregarded altogether and the surplus assets distributed amongst the contributories. If that is right then the effect of section 317 is not so much paradoxical as mischievous. It may be that, faced with such a situation, the plaintiff
G   in the action for unliquidated damages in tort could limit his claim to such a sum as with the costs and expenses of the winding up would not exceed the surplus assets of the company and then prove under section 316. But if Mr. Morritt's argument is well founded, there is no way in which he can prove and receive a dividend pari passu with other creditors.

H   The consequences which flow from a literal application of the bankruptcy rules in the winding up of an insolvent company are so absurd as to compel the conclusion that the bankruptcy rules must be modified in some way if they are to fit into the scheme of the winding up of an insolvent company. As Vaughan Williams L.J. said in *In re Whitaker* [1901] 1 Ch. 9, 12 in the passage I have already cited:

     ". . . the section does not mean that in all respects the results of a bankruptcy, and the consequent administration of the estate, and the

results of the death of an insolvent and the consequent administra- A
tion of his estate, are to be absolutely identical."

The fallacy in Mr. Morritt's construction lies, I think, in equating a
winding up order and a receiving order, and treating section 317 as excluding a claim in tort which has not been liquidated by judgment before the
commencement of the winding up. A receiving order operates both to
protect the debtor from claims in respect of debts provable in bankruptcy B
and to preserve his assets for distribution amongst creditors whose debts
are so provable. Once a receiving order has been made then, unless the
receiving order is stayed or rescinded, the bankrupt's assets must be
administered in accordance with the statutory scheme. If an order is
made for a company to be wound up by the court, it will be treated as
an insolvent company until it is shown that its assets are in fact sufficient
for the payment of its liabilities and the costs and expenses of the wind- C
ing up: see *Fryer* v. *Ewart* [1902] A.C. 187 and *In re Milan Tramways
Co.*, 25 Ch.D. 591. Those were decisions on section 10 of the Act of
1875, which applied to a case when the company's assets " may prove
to be insufficient for the payment of its debts and liabilities and the costs
of winding up," and that language is more susceptible of the construction adopted in those cases than section 317 and the predecessor sections D
in the Acts of 1908 and 1929 which refer simply to " the winding up of
an insolvent company." However, those cases have always been treated
as equally applicable to the sections of the Companies Acts which
replaced section 10. On the other hand, although a company which is
being wound up by the court is to be treated initially as insolvent, the
company may later be shown to be solvent: then " the court must be
deemed to be no longer winding up an insolvent company, but to be E
winding up a company which is solvent ": see *In re Fine Industrial
Commodities Ltd.* [1956] Ch. 256, 262 *per* Vaisey J. Similarly, a company which is shown in the course of the winding up to be solvent
may become again insolvent because the surplus of assets over liabilities
is insufficient to meet the costs and expenses of the winding up: see
In re Leng [1895] 1 Ch. 652, 658 *per* Lindley L.J. That was a case F
concerning the administration of an insolvent estate, but this principle
would be equally applicable to the winding up of an insolvent company.
A proof in respect of a claim for damages for tort which is unliquidated
at the commencement of the winding up cannot be first admissible and
then excluded and, perhaps, become again admissible according to the
vicissitudes of the company's apparent financial health.

The answer to Mr. Morritt's argument in my judgment is that section G
317 does not operate to exclude a claim for damages for tort which has
not been liquidated at the commencement of the winding up but only to
exclude from proof a claim for damages for tort which has not been
liquidated by judgment at the time when the claimant comes in to prove.
In the meantime, although the claim has not been liquidated by judgment, if the amount of the claim is such that if made good it will have H
the result that the company will be insolvent, the presumption that the
company is insolvent cannot be rebutted and no return can be made to
contributories. That produces a sensible and workable scheme. The
claimant will not be entitled to disturb prior distributions to other creditors although, as regards any undistributed assets, he will be entitled to a
dividend out of the undistributed assets equal to dividends distributed to
those whose proof has already been accepted. That has always been the

A rule in bankruptcy. Vaughan Williams L.J. said in *In re McMurdo* [1902] 2 Ch. 684, 699–700:

"Now, according to my experience of bankruptcy practice, there never has been any doubt as to the right of a creditor, whether he is a secured creditor or whether he is an unsecured creditor, to come in and prove at any time during the administration, provided only that he does not by his proof interfere with the prior distribution of
B the estate amongst the creditors, and subject always, in cases in which he has to come in and ask for leave to prove, to any terms which the court may think it just to impose; and, of course, in every case in which there has been a time limited for coming in to prove, although the lapse of that time without proof does not prevent the creditor from proving afterwards, subject to the conditions which I
C have mentioned, in every such case he can only come in and prove with the leave of the court. If that is so, leave must be granted upon such terms as the court may think just."

The rule is now embodied in section 65 of and paragraph 14 of Schedule 2 to the Act of 1914. In *In re McMurdo,* the bankruptcy rule was applied pursuant to section 10 of the Supreme Court of Judicature (1873) Amend-
D ment Act 1875 and to the administration of an insolvent estate. It must apply equally to the winding up of an insolvent company.

If that is the true effect of section 317, then consideration of section 317 must weigh heavily in favour of leave being given. P.G.A. will be unable to prove until its claim has been liquidated by a judgment. The claim having been clearly formulated, though not yet made in any action, it would be wrong if any distribution were to be made until it has been
E determined and it must be in the interests of the other creditors of Berkeley that it be determined at the earliest possible date.

There is one other matter which I should mention. It is not easy to see why an unliquidated claim for damages in tort should alone be excluded from proof in bankruptcy. It seems that historically the rule was that whenever damages were

F "... contingent and uncertain, as in some cases of demands founded in contract, and in all cases of torts, where both the right to any damages at all, and also the amount of them, depend upon circumstances of which a jury alone can properly judge, and which, therefore, it requires the intervention of a jury to ascertain, such damages are not capable of proof under a commission": see the passage in
G *Eden's Bankruptcy Law*, 1st ed. (1825), p. 129, cited in *Williams on Bankruptcy*, 16th ed. (1949), p. 155.

The rule was gradually relaxed by the courts in cases where the damages could be easily ascertained. The rule was further relaxed by section 153 of the Bankruptcy and Insolvency Act 1861, then, as regards all claims for damages for breach of contract, by section 30 (1) of the Bankruptcy
H Act 1869, and then, as regards claims for damages for breach of trust, by section 30 (1) of the Bankruptcy Act 1914. The continued exclusion of unliquidated claims in tort appears to me to be difficult to justify. As the editor of the 16th edition of *Williams on Bankruptcy* observed, at p. 156:

"In practice creditors seem to have found no difficulty in swearing to the amount of their claims. A creditor may swear to a certain amount ' and upwards.'"

Claims in contract may be no less difficult of ascertainment and evalua-　A
tion than claims in tort and, indeed, there are cases where the claim
can equally well be formulated for damages for tort or for breach of
contract: see *In re Great Orme Tramways Co.* (1934) 50 T.L.R. 450. It
is to the modern lawyer anomalous that the question whether a claim is
provable in bankruptcy should turn on the technical classification of the
form of action. I draw attention to this point because the reform of
bankruptcy law is currently being considered by the Cork committee. It　B
is a point which the Cork committee might wish to consider before it
reports.

The second objection

The effect of section 37 (3) of the Companies Act 1967, read together
with section 170 (1) and (3) of the Companies Act 1948, is to give the　C
Secretary of State for Trade a charge on any moneys or property
recovered in an action instituted by him under section 37 (1) for the
costs and expenses of the action; subject to that charge, the Secretary
of State is liable under section 37 (2) to indemnify the company in whose
name or on whose behalf the claim is brought against any costs or
expenses incurred by the Secretary of State and not recovered from other
parties. In the present case the Treasury Solicitor acts for the Secretary　D
of State in the main action. The second objection raised is that the Secretary of State has no power under section 37 or otherwise to defend the
proposed action. The Secretary of State will have no interest in any
moneys recovered which remain after meeting the charge for the costs
and expenses of the main action; and the Secretary of State can have
no interest in defending the proposed action in order to protect his　E
charge for the costs and expenses of the main action against any damages
or costs which may be recovered by P.G.A. in the proposed action, since
the statutory charge will have priority over them. In these circumstances,
it is said, the Crown has no such interest in the subject matter in dispute
in the proposed action as would justify the Treasury Solicitor in acting
on behalf of Berkeley in its role as defendant to the proposed action: see
Brownsea Haven Properties Ltd. v. *Poole Corporation* [1958] Ch. 574,　F
591–594 *per* Lord Evershed M.R. Berkeley has no money with which
it can instruct other solicitors to act on its behalf and instruct counsel
in relation to the proposed action. Although the opposition to P.G.A.'s
present application has, I understand, been financed by the Secretary
of State for Trade, Mr. Morritt made it clear that the Secretary of State,
despite his concern to protect depositors from what is represented in Mr.　G
Evans's affidavit as an inequitable claim by P.G.A., takes the view that
he has no power to make public money available for that purpose. It is
common ground that I would have no jurisdiction to order that Berkeley's costs of defending the proposed action be made a charge on the sum
held by Williams & Glyn's to the account of Atlantic. Further, even if
moneys could be made available to finance Berkeley's defence, the fact
that the Treasury Solicitor would be unable to act for Berkeley in rela-　H
tion to the proposed action and that other solicitors and counsel would
have to be employed, would largely, if not wholly, destroy any practical
benefit that might otherwise have been obtained by allowing the proposed action to proceed to trial in order that an application might be
made for the two actions to be tried together.

The situation is not a very satisfactory one. If the main action had
been brought by Berkeley on its own behalf, it would be no answer for

A Berkeley to say, in opposing P.G.A.'s application for leave to bring the proposed action, that it could not afford to defend it. But the main action is brought on behalf of Berkeley by someone who has no interest in and claims to have no power to finance a defence to an action which, if successful, will deprive Berkeley of the benefit of its success. This situation may, again, merit further consideration by the legislature. But as the law stands, it produces in my judgment an insuperable objection to per-
B mitting the proposed action to proceed to trial before the main action has been heard.

Conclusion

I was referred by Mr. Morritt to the judgment of Brightman L.J. in *In re Aro Co. Ltd.* [1980] Ch. 196, where Brightman L.J. giving the
C judgment of the Court of Appeal, at p. 209 approved the statement of Vaisey J. in *In re Grosvenor Metal Co. Ltd.* [1950] Ch. 63, 65, that section 325 (1) (c) of the Companies Act 1948 ". . . seems to give the court a free hand to do what is right and fair according to the circumstances of each case," and held that that statement of principle was equally applicable to the exercise of the court's discretion under section 321.
D In my judgment, unless there are very special circumstances, fairness requires that leave should be given to a litigant who seeks to bring or to continue an action for damages for tort against a company which is being wound up by the court and which is or may be insolvent. For the liability he seeks to enforce will be admissible for proof if, and only if, liquidated by a judgment before the assets of the company are distributed
E in the winding up. That principle must apply a fortiori where, as here, the action may be barred by limitation unless brought promptly and where, as here, it can conveniently be tried together with another related action brought by the company. If matters rested there, I would have no hesitation in granting P.G.A. leave to bring and prosecute the proposed action to judgment, leaving P.G.A. to apply in the main action for an order that the two actions be heard together. But I am satisfied that,
F having regard to the very special circumstances I have outlined, there is no way in which the main action and the proposed action can be heard together and that it would be unfair to allow any considerable expense to be incurred in relation to the proposed action until after the main action has been heard. In these circumstances, the only course I can take is to give leave to P.G.A. to issue the writ and serve its statement of
G claim in the proposed action and to give leave to Berkeley to serve its defence and to serve any third party proceedings it may be advised to bring. It may be that arrangements can be made without specific directions for lists of documents to be exchanged, if there are any documents which have not been already disclosed in the main action. But I must direct that no further step be taken in the proposed action without the further leave of the court.
H

Order accordingly.

Solicitors: *Linklaters & Paines; Wilde, Sapte.*

T. C. C. B.

A

[PRIVY COUNCIL]

*ROBINSON AND CO. LTD. AND ANOTHER . . APPELLANTS

AND

COLLECTOR OF LAND REVENUE, SINGAPORE . RESPONDENT

B

COLLECTOR OF LAND REVENUE, SINGAPORE . APPELLANT

AND

ROBINSON AND CO. LTD. AND ANOTHER . . RESPONDENTS

[APPEAL FROM THE COURT OF APPEAL OF THE REPUBLIC OF SINGAPORE]

C

1979 Dec. 11, 12, 13;   Lord Wilberforce, Lord Edmund-Davies,
1980 March 20   Lord Russell of Killowen, Lord Scarman
                                              and Lord Lane

*Singapore—Land—Compulsory acquisition—Assessment of com-
pensation — Land sub-let to trading company — Acquisition
following devastation by fire—Whether acquisition within six
months of devastation—Whether land subject to encumbrances
at time of devastation — Whether compensation to include
prospective earnings of trading company—Land Acquisition
Act (Statutes of Singapore, 1970 rev., c. 272), s. 33 (1)*

D

Section 33 (1) of the Land Acquisition Act [1] makes provision for determining the amount of compensation payable for
land acquired under the Act. By the first proviso to the section
where land is acquired after being devastated, inter alia, by   E
fire, the Land Acquisition Appeals Board:

" shall not, in the case of any such acquisition within a
period of six months of the land being devastated . . . take
into consideration the matters set out in paragraphs (a) and
(e) of this subsection, but shall instead consider the market
value of the land immediately before it was devastated . . .
having due regard to the fact that at the material time the   F
land could not have been conveyed with vacant possession
as it was subject to encumbrances, tenancies or occupation
by squatters, . . . "

The third proviso enacted that the market value of land
within the first proviso should not exceed one-third of the
value of such land if it had been vacant land.

The Crown leased land in Singapore to the head-lessee for
999 years from April 24, 1826. The head-lessee leased the land   G
to a company for 27 years from July 1, 1963, and the company
in its turn granted a lease of the remainder of its term less one
day to its subsidiary, the trading company. Both of the sub-
leases were registered on the Register of Deeds. The trading
company carried on its business in a building which had been
erected on the land. At no material time did any other person
occupy or have any interest in the land. On November 21,
1972, the building was destroyed by fire. On January 16, 1973,   H
the President of Singapore made a declaration under section
5 of the Land Acquisition Act that the land was required for
public purposes. More than six months after the fire, on
September 5, 1974, the Collector of Land Revenue took
possession of the land in accordance with section 16 of the
Act. In July 1976 the collector assessed the compensation

[1] Land Acquisition Act, s. 33 (1): see post, p. 1618A–H.

A   payable by the government in respect of the land. He applied the first and third provisos to section 33 (1) of the Land Acquisition Act and awarded compensation at one-third of the vacant land value which he apportioned between the head-lessee and the two companies. He disallowed a claim for loss of earnings made by the trading company under section 33 (1) (*d*) of the Act. The head-lessee and the two companies appealed to the Land Acquisition Appeals Board which, without making a determination, stated a case on three questions of law, to

B   the Court of Appeal. The Court of Appeal decided on question (1) that on the facts there had been an acquisition of the land within six months of the devastation; on question (2) that " encumbrances " used in the first proviso to section 33 (1) of the Land Acquisition Act included leases and that, accordingly, the collector had to consider the market value of the land immediately before its devastation on the basis that it could

C   not have been conveyed with vacant possession since it was subject to the sub-leases in favour of the companies; and on question (3) " actual earnings " in section 33 (1) (*d*) meant provable earnings and could include future earnings assessed on actualities.

    On the companies' appeal to the Judicial Committee on questions (1) and (2) and the collector's cross-appeal on question (3):—

D   *Held*, dismissing the appeal on the first question (1) that the purpose of the first proviso to section 33 (1) of the Land Acquisition Act was to ensure that the government should inform a landowner quickly of its intention to acquire compulsorily devastated land and that that purpose considered together with the scheme of the Act made it clear that the acquisition referred to in the first proviso meant the setting in motion of the compulsory acquisition proceedings by the

E   President's declaration that the land was required for public purposes; and that, therefore, the Court of Appeal had been right in deciding that there had been an acquisition of the land within six months of the devastation (post, pp. 1619G—1620C, E–G).

    (2) Allowing the companies' appeal on the second question, that on their true construction, the words " having . . . regard

F   to the fact " in the first proviso to section 33 (1) presupposed a state of facts which had to exist before the proviso became applicable, and therefore the decisive issue in determining the basis on which to assess compensation was whether immediately before the devastation, the land could not have been conveyed with vacant possession because it was subject to encumbrances and tenancies; that although it could be said that encumbrances could not include leases and that tenancies in the Act

G   meant tenancies by the month or at will, the proviso should be interpreted more broadly; and that since, if the head lessee had been the only person interested, the proviso would not have applied, it followed that where a lesser interest which had been created out of a greater was itself unencumbered, was of a kind unaffected by the devastation and was capable of compensation, the land could not be said to be subject to encumbrances in respect of either interest; alternatively, what-

H   ever the position of the head lessee since a sub-lessee whose unencumbered title appeared on the Register of Deeds was himself in a position to convey his interest in the land with vacant possession, the land could not be said to be subject to encumbrances; and that, accordingly, since, whichever approach the collector adopted, the land was not subject to encumbrances, the first and third provisos to section 33 (1) did not apply and the collector should have assessed the compensation on the basis of the full vacant possession value of the land (post, pp. 1621A–H, 1622E–F).

(3) Allowing the collector's cross-appeal, that the use of   A
the phrase " actual earnings " in paragraph (d) of section 33 (1)
of the Land Acquisition Act meant that in determining the
amount of compensation in respect of loss of earnings from
acquired land the collector could only take into account those
earnings which were being earned at the time of the acquisition and whose loss was the result of the acquisition itself
and that any future or speculative loss was not to be considered; and that, therefore, since on the facts the trading   B
company had not been carrying on business at the time of
the acquisition, it had lost no actual earnings as a result and,
accordingly, no compensation was payable in that regard
(post, p. 1622A–C, E–F).

Decision of the Court of Appeal of Singapore reversed in
part.

The following cases are referred to in the judgment: C

Attorney-General v. *Horner* (1884) 14 Q.B.D. 245, C.A.
David (J. E.) v. *S. P. A. De Silva* [1934] A.C. 106, P.C.

The following additional cases were cited in argument:

Guru Datta Sharma v. *State of Bihar* A.I.R. (48) 1961 Supreme Court
1684.
Joshi Jayantilal Laxmishankar v. *Gujarat State* A.I.R. (49) 1962 Gujarat   D
297.
Land Acquisition Officer v. *Jamnabai* A.I.R. (33) 1946 Bombay 142.
McEwing (D.) and Sons Ltd. v. *Renfrewshire County Council* (1959) 11
P. & C.R. 306.
Salubai Ramchandra v. *Chandu Saju* A.I.R. (53) 1966 Bombay 194.
Walsh v. *Secretary of State for India* (1863) 10 H.L.Cas. 367.
White v. *Works and Public Buildings Commissioner* (1870) 22 L.T. 591.   E

APPEAL (No. 2 of 1978) by leave of the Court of Appeal of Singapore
granted on November 14, 1977, by two companies, Robinson and Co. Ltd.
and Robinson and Co. (Singapore) Pte. Ltd. (the trading company), against
a decision of the Court of Appeal (Wee Chong Jin C.J., Chua and D'Cotta
JJ.) given on September 29, 1977, answering three questions of law put to   F
the court by a case stated on February 11, 1977, by the Land Acquisition
Appeals Board under section 30 of the Land Acquisition Act (c. 272) on an
appeal by the two companies and their head-lessee (the agent of the commission for the administration of the estate of the Portuguese Missions in
China at Singapore) against an award of compensation apportioned
between the head-lessee and the two companies, made by the respondent,
the Collector of Land Revenue, Singapore, on July 16, 1976, in respect of   G
land in Raffles Place, Singapore (Government resurvey map, lot 124, town
subdivision 1). At the material time the head-lessee held the land on
999 year leases from April 24, 1826 (Government leases Nos. 34, 35 and
36). The head-lessee granted a lease of the land to Robinson and Co. Ltd.
(Register of Deeds vol. 1740 No. 89) for 27 years from July 1, 1963. On
November 4, 1969, the company granted a lease to the trading company   H
(Register of Deeds vol. 1763 No. 76) for the unexpired residue of the 27
year term less one day.

The questions posed by the case stated by the Land Acquisition Appeals
Board were (1) whether there has been in the present case " an acquisition
for any purpose specified in subsection (1) of section 5 of this Act " of
the subject land within a period of six months of the land being devastated
or affected directly or indirectly by fire; (2) if, which was not admitted,

A   the acquisition was held to have taken place within the six months' period contemplated by the Act how was the board to interpret the requirement that it should " consider the market value of the land immediately before it was devastated or affected as aforesaid having due regard to the fact that at the material time the land could not have been conveyed with vacant possession as it was subject to encumbrances, tenancies or occupation by squatters, but without taking into account the

B   value of any buildings or structures, permanent or otherwise, on the land at the material time " in the context of the facts of the present case; (3) how was the Appeals Board to interpret section 33 (1) (d) (before its amendment by the Land Acquisition (Amendment) Act 1973) with particular reference as to whether in determining the amount of compensation the actual loss of earnings of the trading company ought to

C   be taken into consideration in the context of the facts of the present case.

    Peter Boydell Q.C. and *Richard Phillips* for the companies.
    William Glover Q.C. and *M. Karthigesu* (advocate and solicitor of the High Court of Singapore) for the Collector of Land Revenue, Singapore.

D   *Cur. adv. vult.*

    March 20, 1980. The judgment of their Lordships was delivered by LORD WILBERFORCE.
    This appeal is from a judgment dated September 29, 1977, of the Court of Appeal in Singapore in which answers were given to questions raised by case stated under the Land Acquisition Act (c. 272). The case was

E   stated by the Appeals Board constituted under section 19 of the Act.
    The questions relate to the compulsory acquisition of land situate at Raffles Place, Singapore. On the government resurvey map this land is marked as lot 124 of town subdivision I: it has an area of 24,123 square feet. It had on it a building occupied by the second appellant—Robinson and Co. (Singapore) Pte. Ltd. which will be referred to as the " trading

F   company." This building was destroyed by fire on November 21, 1972. At this date the land was held under a 999 year lease, commencing April 24, 1826, by the agent of the commission for the administration of the estate of the Portuguese Missions in China at Singapore (" the head-lessee "). The head-lessee granted a lease dated April 28, 1969, to the first appellant, Robinson and Co. Ltd. for 27 years commencing July 1, 1963. Robinson and Co. Ltd. in turn granted an underlease dated November 4, 1969, to the

G   trading company for the unexpired portion of their sub-lease, less one day.
    The following other dates are material. (1) On January 16, 1973, the President of the Republic of Singapore made a declaration under section 5 of the Land Acquisition Act that the subject land was needed for public purposes. (2) On January 17, 1973, the declaration was published in the government Gazette. (3) On February 7, 1973, the Collector of Land

H   Revenue, Singapore (" the collector ") issued and served a notice under section 8 of the Act. (4) On March 7, 1973, the collector held an inquiry under section 10 of the Act. (5) On May 21, 1973, the period of six months from the total destruction of the building expired. Various other steps then followed in the acquisition proceedings: claims were submitted and an award and a corrected award were made by the collector. Then (6) On September 5, 1974, the collector took possession of the subject land under section 16 of the Act. The relevance of the period of six

months referred to under (5) above arises from the terms of the first   A
proviso to section 33 (1) of the Land Acquisition Act. The subsection,
as it was at the relevant time, was as follows:

" (1) In determining the amount of compensation to be awarded for
land acquired under this Act, the [Appeals] Board shall take into
consideration the following matters and no others, namely: (a) the
market value at the date of the publication of the notification under   B
subsection (1) of section 3 of this Act, if the notification is within six
months from the date thereof followed by a declaration under section 5
of this Act in respect of the same land or part thereof, or in other
cases the market value at the date of the publication of the declaration
made under section 5 of this Act; (b) any increase in the value of the
other land of the person interested likely to accrue from the use to
which the land acquired will be put; (c) the damage, if any, sustained   C
by the person interested at the time of the collector's taking possession
of the land by reason of severing that land from his other land;
(d) the damage, if any, sustained by the person interested at the time
of the collector's taking possession of the land by reason of the
acquisition injuriously affecting his other property, whether movable
or immovable, in any other manner or his actual earnings; and (e) if, in   D
consequence of the acquisition, he is compelled to change his residence
or place of business, the reasonable expenses, if any, incidental to that
change:

" Provided that in the case of an acquisition for any purpose
specified in subsection (1) of section 5 of this Act of any land devastated or affected directly or indirectly by fire, explosion, thunderbolt,
earthquake, storm, tempest, flood or any act of God, or of any land   E
immediately adjoining such devastated or affected land as is required
for any such purpose, the Board shall not, in the case of any such
acquisition within a period of six months of the land being devastated
or affected as aforesaid, take into consideration the matters set out in
paragraphs (a) and (e) of this subsection, but shall instead consider
the market value of the land immediately before it was devastated or   F
affected as aforesaid having due regard to the fact that at the material
time the land could not have been conveyed with vacant possession
as it was subject to encumbrances, tenancies or occupation by squatters,
but without taking into account the value of any buildings or structures,
permanent or otherwise, on the land at the material time:

" And provided that such acquisition shall not affect the rights or
liabilities of any owner, lessee, tenant or occupier of such buildings   G
or structures in respect of any contract of insurance entered into by
such owner, lessee, tenant or occupier:

" And provided further that the market value of such land shall not
exceed one-third of the value of such land had it been vacant land
not subject to any such encumbrances, tenancies or occupation by
squatters unless the Minister in his discretion, by notification in the   H
Gazette, specifies otherwise."

It has been the contention of the collector that the land having been
devastated by fire and acquired under the Act within six months thereafter,
the provisos in the subsection apply with the result that the companies are
only entitled to one third of the vacant land market value, calculated under
the provisos as apportioned to them by the collector in respect of their